JONES & BARTLETT LEARNING
CDX Automotive

We support ASE
program certification
through

ASE NATEF
Improving Programs
Through Certification

FUNDAMENTALS OF
Automotive Technology
Principles and Practice

Kirk T. VanGelder

ASE Certified Master Automotive Technician & LI
NATEF Evaluation Team Leader
Certified Automotive Service Instructor
Vancouver, Washington

JONES & BARTLETT
LEARNING

World Headquarters

Jones & Bartlett Learning
5 Wall Street
Burlington, MA 01803
978-443-5000
info@jblearning.com
www.jblearning.com

Jones & Bartlett Learning books and products are available through most bookstores and online booksellers. To contact Jones & Bartlett Learning directly, call 800-832-0034, fax 978-443-8000, or visit our website, www.jblearning.com.

Substantial discounts on bulk quantities of Jones & Bartlett Learning publications are available to corporations, professional associations, and other qualified organizations. For details and specific discount information, contact the special sales department at Jones & Bartlett Learning via the above contact information or send an email to specialsales@jblearning.com.

Production Credits

Chief Executive Officer: Ty Field
President: James Homer
SVP, Editor-in-Chief: Michael Johnson
SVP, Chief Marketing Officer: Alison M. Pendergast
Executive Publisher: Kimberly Brophy
Acquisitions Editor—CDX: Ian Andrew
Managing Editor—CDX: Amanda J. Mitchell
Senior Editor: Jennifer Deforge-Kling
Associate Managing Editor: Janet Morris
Associate Editor: Olivia MacDonald
Production Editor: Jessica deMartin

Production Editor: Marcia Murray
Senior Marketing Manager: Brian Rooney
V.P., Manufacturing and Inventory Control: Therese Connell
Composition: diacriTech
Cover Design: Scott Moden
Cover Image: © Mark Evans/the Agency Collection/Getty Images
Rights & Photo Research Assistant: Gina Licata
Printing and Binding: LSC Communications
Cover Printing: LSC Communications

Fundamentals of Automotive Technology: Principles and Practice is an independent publication and has not been authorized, sponsored, or otherwise approved by the owners of the trademarks or service marks referenced in this product.

Some images in this book feature models. These models do not necessarily endorse, represent, or participate in the activities represented in the images.

The procedures and protocols in this book are based on the most current recommendations of responsible sources. The publisher, however, makes no guarantee as to, and assumes no responsibility for, the correctness, sufficiency, or completeness of such information or recommendations. Other or additional safety measures may be required under particular circumstances.

For every task, the following safety requirements must be strictly enforced: Comply with personal and environmental safety practices associated with clothing and eye protection; hand tools; power equipment; proper ventilation; and the handling, storage, and disposal of chemicals/materials in accordance with local, state, and federal safety and environmental regulations.

To order this product, use ISBN: 978-1-4496-7108-2

Library of Congress Cataloging-in-Publication Data
Fundamentals of automotive technology: principles and practice.
   p. cm.
Includes index.
ISBN 978-1-4496-2411-8
1. Motor vehicles—Design and construction. 2. Automobiles—Maintenance and repair. 3. Motor vehicles—Equipment and supplies. 4. Automobiles—Equipment and supplies. I. CDX Automotive.
   TL146.F86 2013
629.222—dc23
                                              2012015951

6048

Printed in the United States of America
20 19 18 17   10 9 8 7

CONTENTS

ACKNOWLEDGMENTS

CDX Automotive would like to thank the following individuals for their contributions to this textbook.

Editorial Board

Bob Rodriguez
Bob Rodriguez and Associates, LLC
Round Hill, Virginia

Keith Santini
Addison Trail High School
Addison, Illinois

Kevin Jesser
Lake MacDonald, Queensland
Australia

Merle Saunders
Nyssa, Oregon

Tim Dunn
Sydney, New South Wales
Australia

Contributors

Aims Community College
Greeley, Colorado

Addison Trail High School
Addison, Illinois

Larry Baker
Aims Community College
Greeley, Colorado

Ron Beaumont
Brisbane, Queensland
Australia

Roy Belding
King Limousine Service
King of Prussia, Pennsylvania

Michael Broud
Heritage High School
Palm Bay, Florida

Walter Brueggeman
Tidewater Community College
Chesapeake, Virginia

Casey's Independent Auto Repair
Vancouver, Washington

Kent Chambers
Northwest Technical Institute
Lowell, Arkansas

Sean Chesney
Vancouver, Washington

CJC Auto Parts
Lombard, Illinois

Clark College
Vancouver, Washington

Clark County Skills Center
Vancouver, Washington

Roger Duvall
Grayson County Technology Center
Leitchfield, Kentucky

John Frala
Rio Hondo Community College
Whittier, California

Fraser Automotive
Plainfield, Illinois

Brandon Fryman
Denver, Colorado

Tony Gumushian
Prairie State College
Chicago Heights, Illinois

Haggerty Automotive Group
Glen Ellyn, Illinois

Kaz Harris
Brisbane, Queensland
Australia

Ed Heim
Battleground High School
Yacolt, Washington

Kelly Herbert
WarrenTech
Arvada, Colorado

Nancy Hoffman
Dover, New Hampshire

Jim Hunnicutt
F. H. Peterson Academies of Technology
Jacksonville, Florida

Matthew Lamperd
Brisbane, Queensland
Australia

Les Schwab Tire Centers
Battle Ground, Washington
Orchards, Washington

McCord's Vancouver Toyota
Vancouver, Washington

Tom Millard
WarrenTech
Arvada, Colorado

Jennifer Miller
Port St. Lucie, Florida

Jesse Mitchell
Stark State College
North Canton, Ohio

Joe Moore
Southern Maine Community College
Portland, Maine

Kevin Murphy
Stark State College
North Canton, Ohio

Jeffrey Rehkhopf
Florida State College
Jacksonville, Florida

Ron's Automotive
Vancouver, Washington

David Sitchler
Burlington County Institute of Technology
Westampton, New Jersey

Emma Spencer
Brisbane, Queensland
Australia

Russ Strayline
Abington, Pennsylvania

Warren Tech
Lakewood, Colorado

 ## Reviewers

Michael A. Broud
Heritage High School
Palm Bay, Florida

Timothy Campbell
Wenatchee Valley Technical Center
Wenatchee, Washington

Matt Carpenter
Southern Alberta Institute of Technology
Calgary, Alberta
Canada

Frederick Cole
Tidewater Community College
Chesapeake, Virginia

Brett Colston
Oconee Fall Line Technical College
Dublin, Georgia

Al Cox
Metropolitan Community College
Omaha, Nebraska

Joe Cruz
Tennessee Department of Education/CTE
Nashville, Tennessee

Seth DeArmond
Indianapolis Public Schools Career Technology Magnet
Indianapolis, Indiana

Ken Dunn
Liverpool Community College
Everton, Liverpool
United Kingdom

Robert William Evans
Yankton Senior High School
Yankton, South Dakota

Hervey Forward
OCM BOCES, McEvoy Campus
Cortland, New York

Jerry Friesen
Brooks Composite High School
Brooks, Alberta
Canada

Joshua E. George
The Billings Career Center
Billings, Montana

Joe Glassford
Vested, LLC
Sunriver, Oregon

Curtis J. Goodwin
Northwest Kansas Technical College
Goodland, Kansas

Alan Grant
Westlake High School
Westlake Village, California

Allan Haberman
Blue Streak-Hygrade Motor Products
Winnipeg, Manitoba
Canada

Ben Haggeman
Southern Alberta Institute of Technology
Calgary, Alberta
Canada

Wade Hansma
West Central High School
Rocky Mountain House, Alberta
Canada

Kaz Harris
Brisbane, Queensland
Australia

Chance Henderson
Dauphin Regional Comprehensive Secondary School
Dauphin, Manitoba
Canada

Reginald Hildebrand
Assiniboine Community College
Brandon, Manitoba
Canada

Todd Hills
Northeast Iowa Community College
Calmar, Iowa

Robert Holm
Walla Walla University
College Place, Washington

David Howell
Tidewater Community College Regional
Chesapeake, Virginia

Kevin Human
Tennessee Technology Center at Harriman
Harriman, Tennessee

Tim Isaac
Foothills Composite High School
Okotoks, Alberta
Canada

Robert Jackson
Copper Mountain College
Joshua Tree, California

Shawn Klemm
Iowa Lakes Community College
Algona, Iowa
Algona High School
Algona, Iowa

Mark P. Lammers
Ivy Tech Community College
Evansville, Indiana

Harry Lewis
Niagara College
Niagara Falls, Ontario
Canada

Robbie Lindhorst
Southeastern Illinois College
Harrisburg, Illinois

Katherine Luhman
Montana State University
Billings College of Technology
Billings, Montana

David Macholz
Suffolk County Community College
Eastern Suffolk BOCES, Edward J. Milliken
    Technical Center

Oakdale, New York

Andy Murray
Motherwell College
Motherwell, United Kingdom

Michael Myrowich
Red River College
Winnipeg, Manitoba
Canada

Larry Nobles
Tidewater Community College
Portsmouth, Virginia

Raymond H. Oviyach
Consultant, Automotive Vocational &
    Technical Education
Kingwood, Texas

Joseph Palazzolo
GKN Driveline
Commerce Township, Michigan

Katherine Pfau
Montana State University
Billings, Montana

Jeffrey Rehkopf
Florida State College
Jacksonville, Florida

Mark Ridgeway
Gates Corporation
Denver, Colorado

Jon Severson
Sioux Falls Career and Technical Education Academy
Sioux Falls, South Dakota

Matthew Shanahan
College of DuPage
Bartlett, Illinois

Mark Spisak
Central Piedmont Community College
Joe Hendrick Center for Automotive Excellence
Charlotte, North Carolina

Jim Stafford
Tennessee Technology Center at Newbern
Newbern, Tennessee

Don Sykora
Morton College
Cicero, Illinois

Shane Taplin
Wellington Institute of Technology
Lower Hutt, Wellington
New Zealand

Donald Thompson
Florida State College
Jacksonville, Florida

Rob Thompson
South-Western Career Academy
Grove City, Ohio

Joe Wash
Clifton High School
Clifton, New Jersey
Lincoln Technical Institute
Union, New Jersey

Bill Weber
Seminole State College of Florida
Sanford, Florida

David W. Wharf
Thompson Rivers University
Kamloops, British Columbia
Canada

Kenneth Wurster
SUNY Canton
Canton, New York

Peter Zifovich
Campbelltown, New South Wales
Australia

Marty Zuzens
Assiniboine Community College
Brandon, Manitoba
Canada

SECTION I

Safety and Foundation

CHAPTER 1

NATEF Tasks

There are no NATEF tasks for this chapter.

Knowledge Objectives

After reading this chapter, you will be able to:
1. Outline the history of motor vehicles and their maintenance requirements. (pp 6–7)
2. Describe the roles and responsibilities of a:
   - lube technician (p 8)
   - light line technician (p 8)
   - heavy line technician (p 8)
   - chassis and brake technician (pp 8–10)
   - electrical technician (p 10)
   - drivability technician (p 11)
   - transmission specialist (p 11)
   - shop foreman (p 11)
   - service consultant (p 11)
   - service manager (p 11)
3. Describe the types of repair facilities. (p 12)
4. Describe ASE certification and NATEF accreditation. (pp 12–13)

Careers in Automotive Technology

Skills Objectives

There are no skills objectives for this chapter.

▶ Introduction

Early vehicles were very basic machines with engines that were started by manually operating a crank handle. The maintenance requirements of these early vehicles were vastly different from the highly technical requirements of modern vehicles. As vehicle technology has developed over time, the maintenance requirements have changed. Although the basic systems on the early vehicles and today's vehicles are the same—ignition, cooling, engine, drive train, suspension, and lubrication—the systems on modern vehicles are much more sophisticated and reliable. Modern vehicles travel much greater distances between maintenance appointments than their predecessors. For example, it is not unusual for a vehicle manufacturer to require maintenance at 7500- to 10,000-mile (12,000- to 16,000-km) intervals. And there is a push to extend maintenance intervals even further as new oils are being developed. In fact, some manufacturers are predicting maintenance intervals of 25,000 miles (40,000 km) in the near future; in comparison, some earlier vehicles required maintenance every 1000 miles (1600 km).

▶ TECHNICIAN TIP

Service or maintenance intervals will also be influenced by the severity of operating conditions; the more severe the conditions, the more frequent the required maintenance. Most service information gives both a normal-duty and a severe-duty maintenance schedule.

▶ A Brief History of the Automobile

In the late 1800s, several engineers were working on the concept and design of the automobile. Karl Benz is generally acknowledged to have invented the modern automobile around 1885 **FIGURE 1-1**. In those early days, the concept of the automobile continued to develop, with many inventors producing various models. The early versions of the automobile were little more than horse carriages converted into automobiles with engines. These early automobiles tended to be unreliable and expensive and were considered a novelty that only the wealthy could afford.

FIGURE 1-1 Karl Benz is generally acknowledged to have invented the modern automobile around 1885.

▶ You are the Automotive Technician

A customer brings her 2012 V6 Dodge Minivan to the dealership for its 15,000 mile oil change. After pulling the vehicle into the bay, you set the vehicle safely on the hydraulic hoist. Next, you reference the computer to check the service history and any technical service bulletins (TSBs) or recalls for the vehicle. All previous service has been performed according to the schedule and there are no TSBs or recalls for the vehicle. You then verify the manufacturer's scheduled maintenance recommendations for the mileage on the vehicle and find that the tires also need to be rotated and the air filter inspected. After you complete the tire rotation, you use the hydraulic hoist to raise the vehicle and then proceed to perform the oil and filter change. First, you drain and dispose of the old oil, remove and replace the filter, and then you add 4.5 quarts of new oil. When finished, you check all of the fluids, belts, hoses, and air filter and find them to be in good condition. You reset the oil life monitor on the vehicle, clean your area, return tools to the proper location, and process the customer's invoice with notes from your inspection, tire rotation, and oil change. You then review all work and the invoice with the customer. You thank the customer for her business and provide her with a reminder sticker to return at the next scheduled maintenance date and mileage.

1. If you had noticed a worn belt or hose during the oil change, which type of technician would you have asked to look at the vehicle?
2. In your shop, who is responsible for keeping track of the work that is performed on customer vehicles?

In the early 1900s, the advent of mass production made automobiles available to a wider community **FIGURE 1-2**. Henry Ford applied two concepts that helped make the Model T affordable for the masses. The first was the concept of "interchangeability," which meant parts did not have to be custom built to match a particular car. Each part was made to the same specification so it would fit properly with its related parts. Thus, parts did not have to be produced where the vehicle was being assembled; they could be stockpiled, ready for later use. The second concept was the assembly line. Instead of the workers moving to the car as it was being assembled, the assembly line brought the car to the worker. This approach made assembly much more efficient, increasing the number of vehicles that could be built in a shift and thereby lowering production costs. Developments over the ensuing years produced more powerful and reliable automobiles, and with the further development of larger, more reliable gasoline engines, they became the predominant mode of personal transportation.

Vehicle Manufacturing

Vehicle manufacturing developed from small independent makers in the late 1800s, which relied on large amounts of labor and limited automation, to the present methods, which use large-scale production lines and extensive automation. The globalization of the automotive industry has seen manufacturers sharing models and making vehicles that are sold across the world. Modern assembly lines require large-scale investments, so manufacturers must be sure that a new vehicle model will succeed in the market before they will invest billions of dollars in production line retooling **FIGURE 1-3**.

Today's vehicles are assembled on high-volume production lines, with robots used for many of the assembly processes, including welding seams. Assemblers continue to work up and down the assembly line doing tasks that are still far too complicated for robotic assembly. Often, various parts of the vehicle are made by large-scale parts manufacturers who supply the parts to the specific vehicle manufacturer's specifications. Vehicle manufacturing is a high-volume business, so everything needs to work in the correct timing and sequence, from the supply of parts required to build a vehicle, right down to the speed at which the production line runs. Modern vehicle plants use sophisticated technology to mass produce a product that is high quality and affordable.

Technology in Vehicles

Technology in vehicles continues to adapt and change as new research and development reach the production line. The automotive sector is very competitive and has been influenced over the years by competition between manufacturers, consumer expectations for increased technology, and, in more recent times, the need to reduce the impact on the environment. The modern vehicle contains complex electrical, electronic, and mechanical systems designed to improve efficiency, reduce emissions, and provide safety to vehicle passengers. The use of technology will continue to increase in the future as the automotive industry responds to the current pressures of climate change and the ever-decreasing availability and increasing cost of crude oil–based products like oil, gas, and diesel.

FIGURE 1-2 The assembly line was essential in the mass production of vehicles.

FIGURE 1-3 Modern assembly lines require large-scale investments in high-tech equipment.

▶ Careers in the Automotive Sector

The automotive sector provides for numerous career choices within the service, retail, and manufacturing industries. The automotive manufacturing sector provides a number of career choices, from factory workers and assemblers to design engineers and senior administrators **FIGURE 1-4**. In the service and retail sector, occupations range from maintenance/service technicians, light vehicle technicians, and heavy vehicle technicians to service advisors and service managers. As technical complexity has grown in modern vehicles, so has the need for more specialized job roles. For example, there is now a need for hybrid technicians, who service the systems on hybrid vehicles.

Lube Technician

Lube technicians carry out all aspects of manufacturer-scheduled maintenance activities on a range of vehicle components, such as the lubrication system **FIGURE 1-5**. Lube technicians change oil and filters and carry out lubrication, fluid inspection, fluid service, and tire rotations. While performing these duties, lube technicians also perform a visual inspection of the vehicle, looking for any other service needs such as worn belts, hoses, and suspension system parts. When servicing vehicles, lube technicians are required to raise vehicles using hydraulic hoists or jacks and to use hand tools.

In addition, lube technicians may have to complete time cards or scheduled maintenance paperwork. They may be required to assist other types of technicians with dismantling or removing engine assemblies, transmissions, steering mechanisms, and other components; repairing or replacing worn or defective parts; and reassembling mechanical components. Finally, lube technicians are responsible for keeping their workspace, tools, and equipment clean and organized.

Light Line Technician

Light line technicians diagnose and replace the mechanical and electrical components of motor vehicles, such as gaskets, belts, hoses, timing belts, water pumps, radiators, alternators, and starters. In doing their job, light line technicians may be required to discuss problems with vehicle owners, operate special test equipment, and test-drive vehicles to identify faults. They need to be able to research service information, interpret wiring diagrams, and use this information to diagnose and make repairs.

Sometimes they may be required to use oxyacetylene and electric welders to make repairs.

In addition, light line technicians reassemble, test, clean, and adjust repaired or replaced parts or assemblies using various instruments to make sure the parts are working properly. They also test and repair electrical systems such as lighting, instrumentation, vehicle sensors, and engine management systems. Finally, light line technicians inspect vehicles and may issue state safety certificates or list the work required before a certificate can be issued.

Heavy Line Technician

Heavy line technicians undertake major engine, transmission, and differential overhaul and repair. They may diagnose, overhaul, repair, or replace parts and assemblies. They must be able to research service information and use the information to help determine the cause of the problem and make the appropriate repairs. They also reassemble, test, clean, and adjust repaired or replaced parts or assemblies, using various test and measuring instruments and tools to make sure the parts are working properly. Some heavy line technicians are more generalized and work on a broad range of vehicles, while others specialize in particular areas by working on specific brand makes and models. Heavy line technicians may also specialize in particular vehicle systems, such as engines, transmissions, or final drives.

Chassis and Brake Technician

Chassis and brake technicians specialize and work only on the chassis and brakes of vehicles, which include steering and suspension. A chassis and brake technician may service the vehicle braking, steering, and suspension systems. A chassis and brake technician may also inspect and diagnose the steering, brakes, and suspension systems before performing repairs.

There are also separate brake technicians and chassis technicians. Chassis technicians diagnose, repair, and service steering system components and suspension systems on all types of vehicles. They diagnose faults in steering and suspension systems by speaking with the vehicle owner and test-driving the vehicle, noting its performance and comparing that to their knowledge of how the components and systems function. Chassis technicians also perform wheel alignments and wheel balancing, and they diagnose and replace faulty components. This work could include replacing bushings, servicing wheel bearings, or checking and replacing shock absorbers or steering joints and knuckles.

Automotive Sales and Service Career Ladders

Dealer Service / Sales	Dealer Technical Service	Dealer Parts	Dealer Finance	Dealer Management	Dealer Sales	Dealer Admin	Factory		Independent Repair	Independent Quick Lube	Independent Tires	Independent Retail Parts	Light / Medium / Heavy Duty Trucks	Training & Education	Future Research
															Auto Body
														Factory Trainer	RV's
							Regional Manager		Owner + Admin	Owner + Admin	Owner + Admin	Regional Manager	Owner / Manager	Independent Trainer	
Fixed Operations Manager	Shop Foreman / Dispatch	Parts & Service Director		General Manager		Controller / Business Mgr	Zone Sales Manager	Zone Service & Parts Mgr	Manager	Cashier / Admin	Shop Foreman	Branch Manager	Service Manager	Secondary / Post-Secondary Instructor	
Service Director	ASE Master Tech	Parts Manager		General Sales Manager		Office Manager	Marketing Manager	Sr. Area Service Mgr	Assistant Manager		ASE Master Tech	Store Manager	Sales		
Service Manager	Master Tech	Asst Parts Manager / Wholesale Counter		Sales Manager	Team Leader / Closer	Asst Office Manager	Financial Services Manager	Service Engineers	Master Tech	General Svc Tech	Master Tech	Sales: Back Counter	Master Tech		
Rental Car Manager	Line Tech	Outside Sales	F & I Manager		Internet Sales	Payroll / HR	Product Sales Trainer	Warranty Claim Auditor	Line Tech	Lube Tech	Line Tech	Sales: Front Counter	Tech 2		
Asst Svc Manager / Shop Foreman	Electrical / Alarms (Specialty Installations)	Back Counter	F & I Sales		Fleet Sales	Accounting	M.B.I. Sales Manager		Service Advisor			Parts Delivery	Lube Tech		
Electrical / Alarms (Specialty Installations)	Porter / Lube Tech / Training Tech / Entry Level Tech	Inventory Management	Sales Person		Delivery	Title Clerk / Car Biller	Vehicle Distribution Manager	Technical Trainer	General Service Tech	Lube Tech	Sales	Stocker	Tech 1		
Quick Service / New Car Prep		Front Counter			Sales Person	Cashier	Claims Auditor		Assistant Service Advisor	Asst Service Advisor	Lube Tech / Tire Changer		Parts		
Quick Lube Advisor / Service Advisor		Shipping & Receiving			CSI (Call Center)	Receptionist / Cashier	District Sales Manager	District Service Manager	Greeter / Scheduler		Greeter / Service Advisor		Service Porter		
Booker / Warranty Administrator		Driver					Contract Buyer	District Parts Manager	Lube Tech				Detail		
Cashier															
Service Greeter															
Lot Attendant / Auto Detailer															

This career ladder shows a series of jobs progressing from simpler to more complex duties and responsibilities in automotive sales and service. These pathways represent a sequence of defined job levels where the nature of work is similar throughout the pathway.

FIGURE 1-4 The opportunities for challenging and rewarding careers are endless in the automotive field.

Brake technicians diagnose and repair faults, replace or overhaul brake systems, and test the components of disc, drum, and power brake systems used on all types of vehicles **FIGURE 1-6**. They diagnose faults in brake systems by speaking with the vehicle's owner and driving the vehicle and noting its performance, or by reading data from the vehicle's computer control system. This information is used along with the technician's knowledge to properly diagnose and service the vehicle. Brake technicians also can visually inspect brake units for wear, damage, or possible failure, and repair or replace the components as required. Brake technicians can measure brake drums and disc rotors to the nearest 0.0005" (0.0127 mm) to determine if the wear or finished size meets specifications. Often, they will replace leaky brake cylinders, machine rotors, and drums when necessary and ensure that brake systems are filled with the correct brake fluid, are bled or flushed, and are functioning properly.

Electrical/Drivability Technician

The roles of the electrical and drivability technician may be performed by a single person or by technicians who specialize in more than one area. For example, in larger shops, roles could be assigned to separate electrical and drivability technicians, whereas in smaller shops, one technician could perform both roles. Often, roles cross over. For example, an electrical technician needs to understand drivability, and a drivability technician needs to understand electrical systems.

Electrical Technician

Electrical technicians diagnose, replace, maintain, identify faults with, and repair electrical wiring and computer-based equipment in vehicles **FIGURE 1-7**. They work with computer-controlled engine management systems to service, identify, and repair faults on electronically controlled vehicle systems such as fuel injection, ignition, anti-lock braking, cruise control, and automatic transmissions. They also install electrical components such as alternators and starter motors, accessories such as radios, air conditioners, driving lamps, and anti-theft systems.

Often, electrical technicians use meters, oscilloscopes, test instruments, and circuit wiring diagrams to diagnose electrical faults. They test and replace faulty charging system components, starter motors, and related items such as batteries. They also repair or replace faulty ignition components, electrical wiring, fuses, and lamps and switches, often using solder equipment when repairing electrical components.

FIGURE 1-5 Lube technicians are responsible for carrying out all aspects of the standard manufacturer's scheduled maintenance.

FIGURE 1-6 Brake technicians diagnose faults and repair those faults, replace or overhaul brake systems, and test the components of disc, drum, or power brake systems.

FIGURE 1-7 Electrical technicians install, maintain, identify faults with, and repair electrical wiring and computer-based equipment in vehicles.

Drivability Technician

Drivability technicians diagnose and identify mechanical and electrical faults that affect the performance and emissions of vehicles. They carry out maintenance activities, replace parts, and repair both electrical wiring and computer-based equipment in vehicles. They work with computer-controlled engine management systems to service, identify, and repair faults on electronically controlled vehicle systems such as fuel injection, ignition, and automatic transmissions.

Often, drivability technicians use electronic test equipment, scan tools, pressure transducers, exhaust gas analyzers, lab scopes, meters, and circuit wiring diagrams to locate electrical, fuel, and emission systems faults. They may be required to program or reprogram (reflash) engine control units using computerized equipment on a wide variety of vehicles; in doing so, they use updates supplied by the manufacturer to ensure that vehicles run at peak performance and within acceptable emissions limits.

Transmission Specialist

With the increasing complexity of modern transmissions and the requirement for even more specialized service equipment to repair them, comes the need for transmission specialists. Transmission specialists diagnose, overhaul, and repair transmission units. They work on various types of manual and automatic transmissions. Transmission specialists may work on both light vehicle and heavy vehicle transmissions or may specialize in either light vehicle or heavy truck transmissions, earth-moving transmissions, or automatic transmissions.

Transmission specialists may also work on the other components of the drivetrain, including the drive shafts and differentials. They test-drive vehicles and listen to customer concerns. They use many of the hand tools that heavy vehicle technicians use and also use specialized equipment to measure tolerances, check electrical circuits, and check hydraulic pressures.

Shop Foreman

A shop foreman is the supervisor in a shop. Shop foremen oversee the work of all types of technicians and staff, communicate with customers and external suppliers, and handle the various administrative duties involved with operating a business. Many shop foremen are responsible for hiring and training new workers and provide regular performance reviews. They oversee technicians' work to ensure that customers receive quality repair work. The shop foreman may own a small shop and provide services to the general public, work in a large commercial repair shop for light vehicles, or work in a shop that specializes in maintaining trucks. Finally, the shop foreman is responsible for enforcing safety procedures at all times to avoid accidental injuries to technicians or damage to vehicles.

Service Consultant

Service consultants (advisors) work with both customers and technicians FIGURE 1-8. They are the first point of contact for the customer and provide advice and assistance to customers concerning their vehicles. Service consultants will book customer work into the shop, fill out repair orders, price repairs, invoice, keep track of work being performed on customer vehicles, and build customer relations in order to provide a high level of customer support. They are the interface between the technician and the customer, so good communication and administration skills are essential. A service consultant can progress to become a service manager.

Service Manager

The role of a service manager is very demanding and challenging. Service managers are responsible for the functioning of the service department. This career requires well-established skills in communicating, motivating, and creating positive work environments. The service manager often supervises many people, has to deal with customer complaints, and is accountable for the overall performance of the shop.

This job requires a high level of personal commitment and focus, exceptional people skills, and excellent leadership qualities. Service managers may have worked their way up through the various roles within a shop. For example, the service manager may have once been a light vehicle technician on the floor, or a service consultant at the counter. Others may enter the field with backgrounds and college degrees in business management.

FIGURE 1-8 Service consultants work with both customers and technicians.

Types of Shops

There are many facilities that cater to specific customer needs. The types of repair facilities can generally be broken down into the following categories:

- Dealership
- Independent shop
- Specialty shop
- Franchise/retailer
- Fleet shop

Each type of shop caters to a particular segment of the industry. For example, dealerships are affiliated with a specific vehicle manufacturer. The dealership sells new and used vehicles. Dealership technicians perform maintenance, service, and warranty repairs on vehicles sold by that manufacturer **FIGURE 1-9**. In many cases, customers bring their new vehicles back to the dealership for maintenance and repair work while the vehicle is in warranty, and then seek out other shops after that.

Because dealership technicians are working on the latest vehicles, they are right at the cutting edge of technology. Most dealerships send their technicians to manufacturer training regularly so that they will know how to maintain, diagnose, and repair their vehicles. Because the dealership is affiliated with the manufacturer, dealership technicians generally have instant access to the manufacturer's service information as well as the manufacturer's service representatives when they encounter a difficult diagnostic situation.

Independent shops are not affiliated with vehicle manufacturers, making it harder for independent technicians to access training on new vehicle technology **FIGURE 1-10**. In many cases, they service a broad range of vehicles. Because vehicles are becoming more and more specialized and complex, it is common that they limit

their clientele to European, Asian, or domestic vehicles. Some independent shops may limit their work and specialize in a particular system of the vehicle, such as brakes and alignment. In many cases, independent technicians work on vehicles that are out of warranty and are not the latest technology.

Specialty shops are usually independent shops that focus on one type of service, such as transmission service, electrical system repair, or emission system diagnosis. Since these shops offer limited services, they usually work on a variety of vehicles from a variety of manufacturers. A shop that specializes in one area such as air-conditioning (AC) may experience a slow period during certain times of the year.

Franchises are similar to specialty shops, but they are connected to a larger parent organization that can help with marketing and provide a mechanism for warranty claims that are honored at related franchise shops across the country. Some examples include Goodyear Tire Company, AAMCO Transmissions, and Jiffy Lube.

A fleet shop is usually connected with either a business that runs multiple vehicles or with equipment that is maintained and repaired in house, or it could be a government agency such as a city or county would have for maintenance and repair of its vehicles and equipment. Since fleet shops maintain and repair vehicles for the company or agency, it is more likely that the vehicles will be serviced on a regular basis.

Automotive Industry Certification

The automotive service industry in the United States is generally not subject to licensure requirements. This means that a technician does not have to pass a licensure test in order to receive a license to work in the industry. At the same

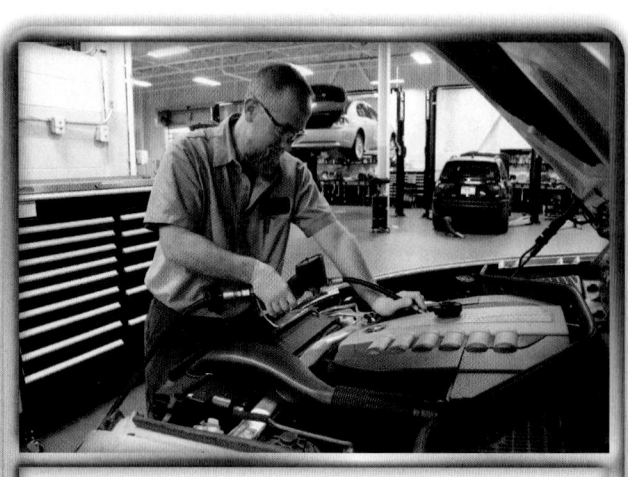

FIGURE 1-9 Dealership technicians perform maintenance, service, and warranty repairs on vehicles sold by a particular manufacturer.

FIGURE 1-10 Independent shops are not affiliated with vehicle manufacturers.

time, to promote professionalism and demonstrate a level of competence, many technicians become **Automotive Service Excellence (ASE)** certified **FIGURE 1-11**. ASE is an independent, nonprofit organization dedicated to the improvement of vehicle repair through the testing and certification of automotive professionals. A few localities require technicians to be ASE certified, and many shops require it of technicians they hire. But overall it is a voluntary certification.

To earn ASE certification, technicians are required to pass one or more ASE certification tests and have 2 years of qualifying work experience as a technician. ASE certification needs to be renewed every 5 years by taking and passing recertification tests. There are currently approximately 275,000 certified ASE technicians in the United States.

The **National Automotive Technicians Education Foundation (NATEF)** is an accrediting body for secondary and post-secondary automotive training programs **FIGURE 1-12**. NATEF is an independent, nonprofit organization under the umbrella of the ASE. In order for programs to be accredited by NATEF, they have to demonstrate their compliance to a rigorous list of standards developed by the automotive industry. Program instructors must also maintain ASE certification in the areas they teach, as well as receive a minimum of 20 hours of technical update training each year. NATEF accreditation is valid for 5 years, and then the program must go through a reaccreditation process.

The **Automotive Youth Educational Systems (AYES)** is an independent, nonprofit organization that is a partnership between automotive manufacturers, their dealerships, and affiliated secondary automotive programs **FIGURE 1-13**. Because of the partnership, AYES programs receive access to new vehicle technology as well as manufacturer service information to help prepare students for working on today's vehicles and technology. Students receive the opportunity to intern at participating dealerships working alongside a mentor technician. This is a great way for the students to put into practice what they are learning in the training program. The dealers and manufacturers benefit from gaining access to highly motivated students who are preparing to go to work for them. To become an AYES program, the school has to be NATEF certified and then be evaluated by AYES against another set of standards related to the commitments of carrying out the AYES training model.

Special Certification

The automotive industry has two special certification requirements for certain automotive technician specialists. To diagnose and repair emission failures on vehicles in some localities, technicians must be certified by the appropriate agency. In many cases, the technician must have ASE Advanced Engine Performance certification or have taken and passed a course specifically for emission specialists, as administered by the agency.

The second special certification required is for technicians who handle refrigerants or work on AC systems. They are required to be Environmental Protection Agency (EPA) Section 609 certified. This requires taking a training course and passing the 609 exam. Once certified, technicians are legally able to handle refrigerants and repair AC systems. It is advisable that all students obtain their 609 certification during their training program to show prospective employers when they graduate.

FIGURE 1-11 ASE logo.

FIGURE 1-12 NATEF logo.

FIGURE 1-13 AYES logo.

Wrap-up

Ready for Review

▶ Modern vehicles are more sophisticated with longer maintenance intervals than early vehicles.

▶ Karl Benz is considered the inventor of the modern automobile (in 1885).

▶ Application of interchangeability and the assembly line made cars more affordable for the masses.

▶ Today's production lines are high-volume, high-technology plants.

▶ Lube technicians carry out standard maintenance services.

▶ Light line technicians are responsible for maintenance and repair of mechanical and electrical components.

▶ Heavy line technicians diagnose and repair major engine or transmission problems and perform differential overhaul.

▶ Chassis and brake technicians repair the vehicle's chassis and brakes (respectively, or in combination), including steering and suspension.

▶ Electrical technicians diagnose and repair the vehicle's electrical wiring and computer-based equipment.

▶ Drivability technicians are responsible for inspecting the mechanical and electrical faults that can affect the performance and emissions of vehicles.

▶ Transmission specialists diagnose and repair transmission units (manual and automatic).

▶ The shop foreman is responsible for administrative duties, supervising technicians, and ensuring customer satisfaction.

▶ Service consultants work to ensure that customers are satisfied with their experience at the shop.

▶ Service managers run the service department and must create a positive work environment.

▶ Types of repair facilities are dealerships, independent shops, specialty shops, franchises/retailers, and fleet shops.

▶ Automotive technicians may become ASE certified; training programs may be NATEF accredited; school programs may be AYES authorized; and technicians may choose to receive certification in emission failures and/or air-conditioning systems.

Key Terms

Automotive Service Excellence (ASE) An independent, nonprofit organization dedicated to the improvement of vehicle repair through the testing and certification of automotive professionals.

Automotive Youth Educational Systems (AYES) An independent, nonprofit organization that is a partnership between automotive manufacturers, their dealerships, and affiliated secondary automotive programs.

brake technician A technician who specializes in working on vehicle brake systems.

chassis technician A technician who specializes in working on vehicle suspension and steering systems.

drivability technician A technician who diagnoses and identifies mechanical and electrical faults that affect vehicle performance and emissions.

electrical technician A technician who diagnoses, replaces, maintains, identifies fault with, and repairs electrical wiring and computer-based equipment in vehicles.

heavy line technician A technician who undertakes major engine, transmission, and differential overhaul and repair.

light line technician A technician who diagnoses and replaces the mechanical and electrical components of motor vehicles.

lube technician A technician who carries out scheduled maintenance activities on a range of mechanical and related vehicle components.

National Automotive Technicians Education Foundation (NATEF) An accrediting body for secondary and post-secondary automotive training programs; an independent, nonprofit organization under the umbrella of the ASE.

service consultant/advisor A service worker who works with both customers and technicians; the first point of contact for customers seeking vehicle repairs.

service manager The shop supervisor who is responsible for the management of the service department.

shop foreman The supervisor in a shop who oversees the work of technicians and staff and communicates with customers and external suppliers.

transmission specialist A technician who diagnoses, overhauls, and repairs transmissions.

ASE-Type Questions

1. Tech A says that newer vehicles require less maintenance compared to older vehicles. Tech B says that service intervals for an older vehicle can be extended if new oils are used. Who is correct?
   a. Tech A
   b. Tech B
   c. Both A and B
   d. Neither A nor B

2. Tech A says that Henry Ford is credited with the invention of the automobile. Tech B says that Carl Benz is credited with the invention of the automobile. Who is correct?
   a. Tech A
   b. Tech B
   c. Both A and B
   d. Neither A nor B

3. Tech A says that the production of vehicles today requires a mix of robotic and human assembly to be profitable. Tech B says that most parts on a car are preassembled before they reach the assembly line for higher assembly numbers per day. Who is correct?
   a. Tech A
   b. Tech B
   c. Both A and B
   d. Neither A nor B

4. Tech A says that the automotive industry is highly technical and only a certain few people will find jobs. Tech B says the automotive industry is wide open with job opportunities for almost every level of skill. Who is correct?
   a. Tech A
   b. Tech B
   c. Both A and B
   d. Neither A nor B

5. Tech A says that a technician can specialize in different areas based on his or her interest and ability. Tech B says that when a technician specializes in a certain area, he or she will only work on certain vehicle models. Who is correct?
   a. Tech A
   b. Tech B
   c. Both A and B
   d. Neither A nor B

6. Tech A says that the foreman is the frontline contact for customer relations. Tech B says that the service consultant is the frontline contact for customer relations. Who is correct?
   a. Tech A
   b. Tech B
   c. Both A and B
   d. Neither A nor B

7. Tech A says that dealership technicians generally have access to manufacturers training to help prepare them as technicians. Tech B says that an independent shop works on a wide variety of equipment that requires a broad skill level in technicians. Who is correct?
   a. Tech A
   b. Tech B
   c. Both A and B
   d. Neither A nor B

8. Tech A says that AYES certifies technicians. Tech B says that ASE certifications can help get you a job. Who is correct?
   a. Tech A
   b. Tech B
   c. Both A and B
   d. Neither A nor B

9. Tech A says that the maintenance requirements of a vehicle have not changed since the creation of the automobile. Tech B says that manufacturers are predicting 25,000-mile (40,000-km) intervals. Who is correct?
   a. Tech A
   b. Tech B
   c. Both A and B
   d. Neither A nor B

10. Tech A says that a technician can progress to different jobs within the industry. Tech B says that careers in the automotive industry include new car assembly lines. Who is correct?
    a. Tech A
    b. Tech B
    c. Both A and B
    d. Neither A nor B

CHAPTER 2

NATEF Tasks

There are no NATEF tasks for this chapter.

Knowledge Objectives

After reading this chapter, you will be able to:
1. Identify vehicle body types and their characteristics. (pp 18–21)
2. Describe vehicle chassis designs. (pp 21–22)
3. Describe how a vehicle operates in general terms. (pp 22–24)
4. Describe various drive train layouts. (pp 24–25)
5. Identify various engine configurations. (pp 25–27)
6. Describe live and dead axles. (pp 27–28)
7. Describe live axle locations. (p 28)
8. Describe two applications of torque in automotives. (pp 28–29)
9. Describe transmissions and final drives. (p 29)
10. Describe four-wheel drive and all-wheel drive systems. (p 30)

Introduction to Automotive Technology

Skills Objectives

There are no skills objectives for this chapter.

Introduction

As you prepare to work in the automotive repair industry, you will need to learn a whole new vocabulary. Terms like hygroscopic, asymmetrical, reciprocating motion, and volumetric efficiency are only a few examples of the new vocabulary you will need to master. Healthcare professionals need to know how each of the body's systems function, the organs that make up the system, and how to diagnose an issue. Automotive technicians need to have the same level of understanding about vehicles. The good news is that automotive names aren't in Latin; however, you will need to master the metric system.

Knowing the correct automotive terminology and concepts will help you fit into your new work environment as well as accurately communicate with customers, suppliers, and fellow employees. You will also be able to properly complete repair orders, parts requisitions, and warranty paperwork as you maintain, diagnose, and repair vehicles. This chapter will help you start the process of learning automotive terminology as it relates to vehicle types, drive train layouts, engine configurations, and axle arrangements.

Body Designs

Vehicle bodies come in a variety of designs primarily depending on the intended function of the vehicle. But they also are designed to accommodate style, aesthetics, and, most importantly, safety. Vehicle body design continues to evolve to accommodate the owners' lifestyles and personal tastes, such as the Scion XB or the M-Benz Smart Fortwo **FIGURE 2-1**. Vehicle body design is also used as a strong marketing tool by manufacturers to entice buyers to purchase their particular vehicles.

Common types of body design cater to both passenger and light commercial use. Terms to describe various body designs have become part of common automotive language, although names describing the same body design type can vary from country to country. For example, a vehicle described as a sedan in the United States is called a saloon in the United Kingdom. Other types of body designs include station wagons, hatchbacks, convertibles, coupes, vans, minivans, pick-ups, and sport utility vehicles (SUVs).

Sedan

A **sedan** has an enclosed body, with a maximum of four doors to allow access to the passenger compartment **FIGURE 2-2**. The sedan design also allows for storage of luggage or other items in a trunk located in the rear of the vehicle and accessible from a trunk lid. A sedan traditionally has a fixed roof; however, there are soft-top versions of sedans, which have only two doors.

Coupe

A **coupe** has only two doors. Reducing the number of doors to the passenger compartment makes the vehicle structure more rigid. Traditionally, a coupe has two

You are the Automotive Technician

The sales manager asks you to provide training for her new vehicle sales associates in your recently expanded dealership. The first training lesson takes place in the dealership showroom where several styles of vehicles are on display. You explain the concept of the unibody design and compare it to the full frame design. You also show examples of various drivetrain layouts and their pros and cons. The second lesson is in the shop area, designated for engine repair. You show them the various engine classifications and configurations.

1. What are the common vehicle body types and their characteristics?
2. What are the benefits of the unibody design? How does it differ from the full-frame vehicle?
3. What are the various engine configurations, and how do they differ?

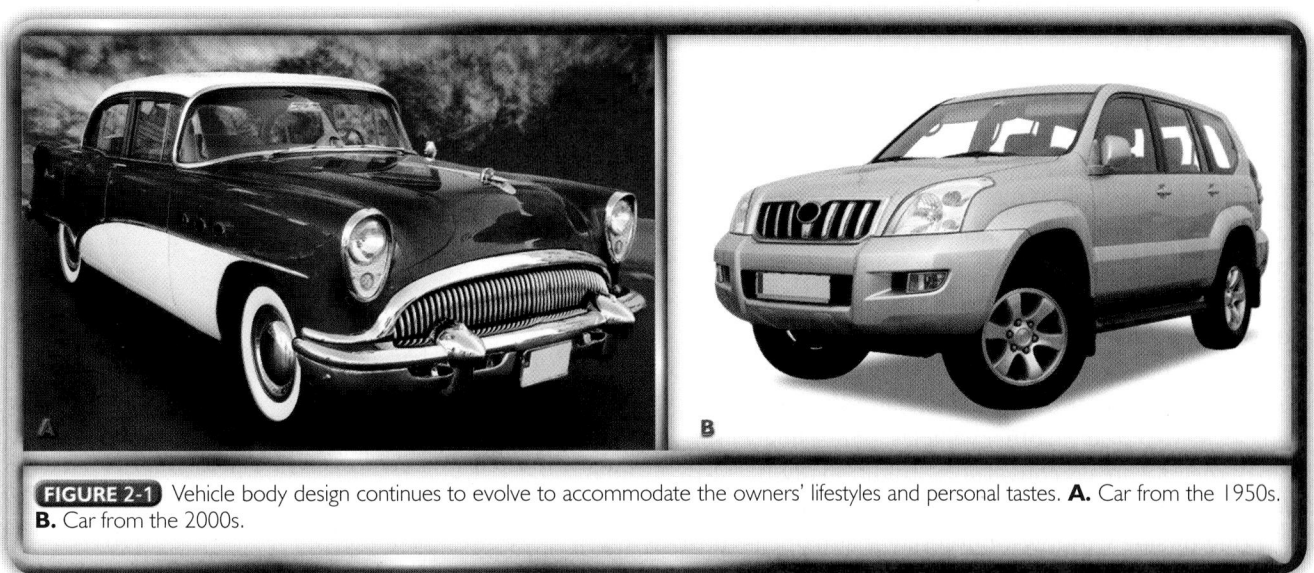

FIGURE 2-1 Vehicle body design continues to evolve to accommodate the owners' lifestyles and personal tastes. **A.** Car from the 1950s. **B.** Car from the 2000s.

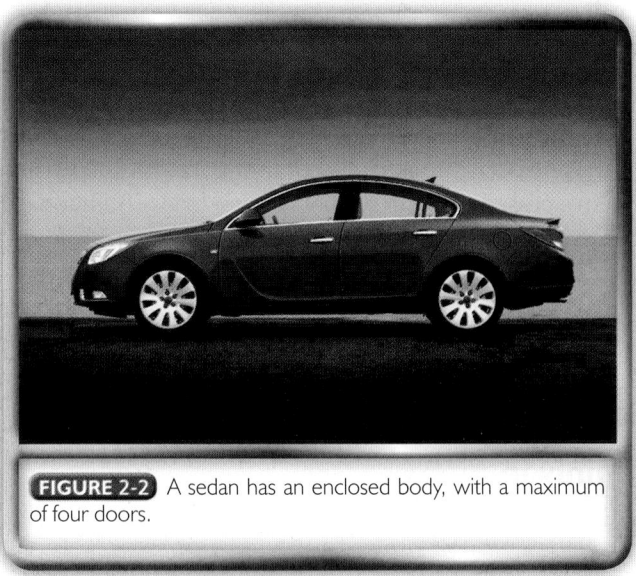

FIGURE 2-2 A sedan has an enclosed body, with a maximum of four doors.

FIGURE 2-3 Traditionally, the coupe has two standard-size seats in front with two smaller seats behind.

standard-size seats in front and possibly two smaller seats behind **FIGURE 2-3**. Coupes are available in both fixed-roof and convertible style. They also are equipped with a trunk for storage purposes, although they can sometimes be on the small side.

Hatchback

Hatchbacks are available in three-door and five-door designs, with the odd-numbered door being a hatch that lifts up at the rear of the vehicle. This gives access to the luggage area. The rear seats usually fold down to increase the luggage area **FIGURE 2-4**. Often the rear seat will be split, which provides more flexibility because only one side needs to be folded down if the other seat is required for a passenger. Hatchbacks are versatile vehicles, combining some of the benefits of both sedans and station wagons.

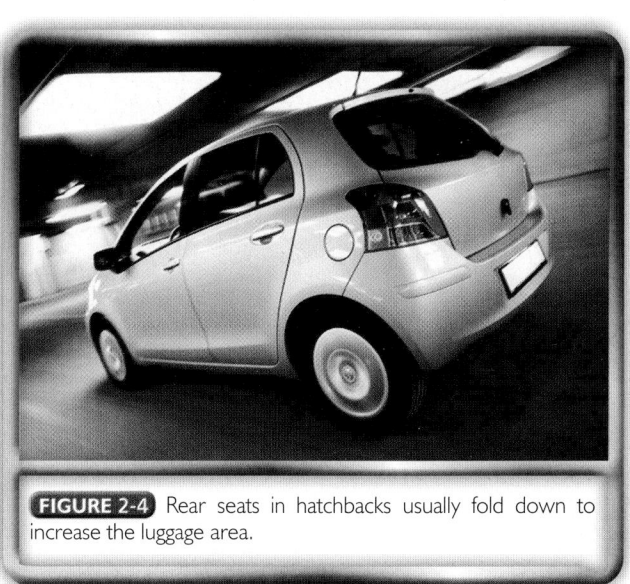

FIGURE 2-4 Rear seats in hatchbacks usually fold down to increase the luggage area.

Convertible

A **convertible** is an automobile that can convert from having an enclosed top to having an open top by means of a roof that can be removed, retracted, or folded away **FIGURE 2-5**. The roofing material is most often a flexible fabric such as canvas or vinyl, and most convertibles have a mechanism driven by electric motors that retracts or raises the roof cover. In some vehicles, known as hardtop convertibles, the roof can be a series of folding steel or fiberglass panels. When in place, the hard roof makes such vehicles look more like conventional fixed-roof coupe vehicles **FIGURE 2-6**. In other vehicles, only a smaller section of the roof area is convertible. Traditionally, the term roadster was applied to a vehicle with no permanent roof covering or side windows, but today that name is most often used to describe any convertible sports car.

FIGURE 2-5 A convertible is an automobile that can convert from having an enclosed top to having an open top by means of a roof that can be removed, retracted, or folded away.

FIGURE 2-6 Hardtop convertibles have a hard roof that makes the vehicle look more like a conventional fixed-roof vehicle.

> **TECHNICIAN TIP**
>
> A convertible is commonly known as a cabriolet in Europe.

Station Wagon

A **station wagon** has an extended roof that goes all the way to the rear of the vehicle. It is similar to a van but not as tall. The extra length in the roof increases the luggage capacity. In some cases, the passenger capacity is increased with extra seats in the very rear of the vehicle. Station wagons have a large rear door for easy access, and the rear seats can usually be folded to increase storage capacity even further **FIGURE 2-7**. Station wagons usually have fixed roofs.

Pick-up

The **pick-up**, or **truck**, carries and tows cargo. Usually it has heavier-duty chassis components and suspension than a passenger car to support greater loads. Traditionally, pick-ups had only a single cab with two doors, which limited the number of passengers they could carry. Today's pick-ups have options for extended cabs or four-door versions to carry more passengers **FIGURE 2-8**. In some cases, the four-door pick-up has a reduced cargo-carrying space to accommodate the extra seating in the passenger cab.

Minivan

Minivans are generally lighter-duty vehicles with suspension systems more like passenger cars than full-size vans, which use heavy-duty pick-up truck–type

FIGURE 2-7 A station wagon has increased luggage capacity and a large rear door for access.

suspension systems. Minivans can be configured to maximize the number of seats for passengers or redesigned so that maximum cargo space is available (FIGURE 2-9). Also, since they are lighter duty, the fuel economy of minivans is substantially better than that of full-size vans.

Sport Utility Vehicle

Sport utility vehicles (SUVs) are popular in the United States since they can easily be used to carry out functions that would otherwise require several different vehicles (FIGURE 2-10). They act like both a full-size van and a pick-up in that they have a heavier-duty chassis so they can carry heavier loads. This load can be in the form of passengers, luggage, or cargo. They can also tow moderately heavy loads, making them a great vehicle for family outings, since they can pull a trailer while still carrying a number of passengers and luggage.

FIGURE 2-10 Sport utility vehicles (SUVs) are designed for flexible use while being heavier duty than minivans.

FIGURE 2-8 More recent versions of pick-ups have options for extended cabs or four-door versions to carry more passengers.

Vehicle Chassis

A chassis is an underlying supporting structure for vehicles—similar to the skeleton of a human—on which additional components are mounted. In a vehicle, a traditional chassis gives the vehicle structural strength as well as a platform on which to mount the engine, the wheels, the transmission, and all the other mechanical components. Also bolted onto this frame is the body. Originally made of wood, vehicle chassis were soon changed to an open steel ladder-frame structure, which is easier to manufacture and is longer lasting (FIGURE 2-11).

Body-on-frame is the term used when a vehicle body is mounted on a rigid frame or chassis. It was the preferred way of building passenger vehicles because it allowed manufacturers to release new models of vehicles with different body styles without having to retool most of the

FIGURE 2-9 Minivans can be based on common interior sedan designs or redesigned so that maximum cargo space is available.

FIGURE 2-11 Steel ladder-frame chassis.

mechanical and structural components. However, by the 1960s, most manufacturers switched to vehicle designs that either partially or wholly integrated the bodywork into a single unit with the chassis so that the vehicle body became part of the vehicle structure rather than just an external skin. This is the **unibody design**, or single shell design **FIGURE 2-12**. The unibody design is constructed of a large number of steel sheet metal panels that are precisely formed in presses and spot-welded together into a structural unit.

The unibody design was first used in aircraft and then spread to automobiles. It became popular with vehicle manufacturers because with less of a chassis component, it was quicker to manufacture and lighter in weight. The lighter weight meant less cost in both material and labor. Another benefit of being lighter was that the vehicles became more fuel efficient.

> **TECHNICIAN TIP**
>
> Some high-performance racing cars today have no chassis at all. Their structural strength comes from their light, stiff, and stable body shells molded from newer lightweight materials such as carbon fiber–reinforced plastics.

Vehicle Closure Designs

A vehicle body contains many openings apart from the vehicle doors. They include the engine compartment hood, hatch and tailgate openings, the fuel door, and in some cases, a battery access cover. All of these openings have to be secured and may require a remote switch or lever to be activated. In some cases, the access door is opened mechanically by the driver pulling a lever, which moves a cable and releases a latch. Other doors may use electric- or vacuum-operated solenoids to release the latch. In this case, the driver pushes a switch that sends an electric or vacuum signal to the release mechanism, which releases the door. Some rear hatch doors have a hinged window incorporated; this window offers the owner easy access to the storage space without opening the entire back door.

Engine compartment hoods on today's vehicles usually have a remote release lever to prevent unauthorized access to the engine compartment for security reasons. The release lever is usually located inside the passenger compartment: under the dash, in the glove compartment, or on a doorjamb **FIGURE 2-13**. Once the hood is open, it is held in the open position by one of three methods: large springs on the hinges, pressurized gas strut assemblies, or a prop rod.

> **TECHNICIAN TIP**
>
> Some high-end sports car manufacturers are no longer fitting an engine compartment release to their vehicles. The hood can only be released by the manufacturer's scan tool or by a service key fitted into a secluded opening on the vehicle body (usually behind a manufacturer's badge).

FIGURE 2-12 The unibody design.

FIGURE 2-13 The engine compartment release may be located inside the passenger compartment under the dash, in the glove compartment, or on a doorjamb.

▶ Vehicle Operation Overview

For a vehicle to operate, it requires a means of converting stored energy into a form of energy that can turn the wheels. In the majority of vehicles, the stored energy is in the chemical form of gasoline or diesel fuel, but newer vehicles are using natural gas, alcohol, biodiesel, hydrogen, and battery acid as their stored chemical energy source. Chemical energy can be converted into mechanical energy in two primary ways: through the operation of an internal combustion engine or through the operation of an electric motor **FIGURE 2-14**. Both of

FIGURE 2-14 Stored chemical energy is converted to mechanical energy to propel the vehicle down the road. **A.** Internal combustion engine. **B.** Hybrid engine with internal combustion engine and electric motor.

these methods take energy in chemical form and convert it to mechanical energy by causing a shaft to rotate—the crankshaft in an internal combustion engine and the armature in an electric motor. The shaft then provides mechanical energy to move the vehicle as well as power all of the other accessories on the vehicle.

The vehicle's combustion engine converts the energy from the fuel supply by combining the fuel with the air to create a combustible mixture, which is compressed by the pistons and ignited by a spark plug in the engine cylinders. When the driver initiates the starting process by turning the ignition key to run (or using a smart key), power is supplied from the battery to various vehicle circuits and the fuel pump pressurizes the fuel system in preparation for the engine to start. When the key is moved to the crank position (or the start button is pressed), the starter motor is energized and cranks over the engine. As soon as the engine has started and is running, the ignition key is released from the start position and the engine continues to run while the ignition key is in the run position. Depressing the accelerator increases the amount of fuel and air entering the engine and increases the engine speed and power.

As the engine cranks, the engine management system monitors the engine sensors and makes decisions about such matters as the correct timing to fire the spark plugs and injecting and metering the proper amount of fuel. The fuel mixture is ignited by the ignition system, which causes the hot gases to expand. This expansion pushes each piston down into the cylinder, which in turn causes the crankshaft to rotate.

As the pistons continue moving up and down, they rotate the crankshaft, turning the **flywheel** or flex plate, which is bolted to the engine crankshaft. For a manual

> **TECHNICIAN TIP**

The unibody design is the predominant vehicle construction technology used today.

transmission, the flywheel transmits the engine output to the transmission through a clutch; for an automatic transmission, the flex plate transmits the engine output through a torque convertor.

The vehicle's transmission allows for a number of different gear ratios, which match the engine's speed and power output to the desired road speed. The transmission allows the vehicle to start at low speeds with high torque to the wheels to get the vehicle moving, and as gear ratios are changed, the vehicle attains higher road speed with lower engine speed. The vehicle's driveshaft connects the output from the transmission to the wheels via **axles** through a final drive assembly that divides up the drive to the powered wheels.

Vehicle brakes are fitted to the wheels to provide a means of slowing down or stopping the vehicle and operate on the principle of hydraulic pressure. They are fitted to each wheel and are operated by a brake pedal next to the accelerator pedal. The brake pedal is connected to a master brake cylinder fitted under the hood. The master brake cylinder has a power booster fitted to it that amplifies the hydraulic pressure to the wheel brake units. The wheel brake units apply brake friction pads to metal discs or drums connected to the wheels, creating friction, which slows the wheels' rotation. The harder the driver pushes on the brake pedal, the harder the brakes are applied.

The vehicle suspension system connects the wheels to the chassis or vehicle body through various linkages, shock absorbers, and springs. The suspension system evens out the road shocks caused by the irregular road surface. The suspension system provides the passengers with a comfortable ride and safely keeps the tires in contact with the road surfaces. The steering system makes the connection between the steering wheel and the road wheels so the driver can point the vehicle in the intended direction of travel. Power steering systems provide assistance to the driver to turn the vehicle's wheels and use either an engine-driven or an electric-driven pump to power the system.

The electrical system is interconnected to all of the other systems. It includes the battery, which stores a supply of electricity for the purpose of starting the vehicle and operating the electrical accessories such as lights, windshield wipers, and heater system when the engine is not operating. The battery is continually recharged, and the electrical accessories are operated by the charging system whenever the engine is running. The electrical system also includes the power train control system, the lighting system, accessory systems, safety systems, passenger comfort systems, and entertainment systems.

▶ Drive Train Layouts

The **drive train** encompasses the major assemblies that power the vehicle down the road, including the engine, transmission/transaxle, differential, axles, and wheels **FIGURE 2-15**. Drive trains are designed in different layouts based on the vehicle application and manufacturer's preferences. For example, the drive train layout is different

in a pick-up used for driving up muddy mountain roads than in a high-performance sports car that runs around a smooth asphalt track. Differences in configuration between each of the drive train's major assemblies define the drive train layout.

The drive train layout includes three main engine mounting positions: front, mid, and rear **FIGURE 2-16**. The front engine design is the most common in everyday vehicles and has the engine mounted between the front wheels. Mid-engine vehicles have the engine mounted in front of the rear wheels and provide a more equal weight distribution between the front and rear wheels. Rear-engine vehicles have the engine mounted between or behind the rear wheels. Mid- and rear-engine designs are usually reserved for performance-type vehicles, although there have been some exceptions, such as the Volkswagen

FIGURE 2-15 The drive train encompasses the engine, transmission, differential, axles, and wheels.

FIGURE 2-16 The three engine-mounting positions. **A**. Front. **B**. Mid. **C**. Rear.

Beetle. Manufacturers also mount engines in one of two orientations, **longitudinal** (front to back) and **transverse** (side to side), depending on which design best fits the vehicle and the rest of the drive train.

The engine does not necessarily drive all four wheels. Drive train layouts accommodate four common drive wheel arrangements. **Front-wheel drive (FWD)** is very common in modern vehicles; in this arrangement, only the front wheels are driven by the engine. **Rear-wheel drive (RWD)** is when the engine drives only the rear wheels. Both of these arrangements are called two-wheel drive vehicles. Becoming increasingly popular is **all-wheel drive (AWD)**, with all four wheels driven by the engine all the time. The final arrangement is **four-wheel drive (4WD)**, which is slightly different from all-wheel drive. In a 4WD vehicle, the driver can select between two-wheel drive and four-wheel drive.

The combination of engine position, engine orientation, and type of drive defines the drive train layout. For example, using the different variations can give the following drive train layouts:

- Front-engine, front-wheel drive
- Front-engine, rear-wheel drive
- Front-engine, all-wheel drive/4WD
- Rear-engine, rear-wheel drive
- Rear-engine, all-wheel drive
- Mid-engine, rear-wheel drive
- Mid-engine, all-wheel drive

▶ Classifying Engines

Engines are classified by type, cylinder arrangement, number of cylinders/rotors, and total engine displacement in cubic inches or liters. Two common types of engines are piston and rotary. The piston engine uses cylindrical pistons that move up and down in cylinder bores, while the rotary engine uses a triangular rotor that turns inside of an oval chamber. The vast majority of automotive engines are of the piston type rather than the less common rotary type because they have a longer life and produce fewer emissions.

Piston Engines

In a **piston engine**, the way engine cylinders are arranged is called the **engine configuration**. Multi-cylinder internal combustion automotive engines are produced in four common configurations:

- In-line: The pistons are all in one bank on one side of a common crankshaft.
- Horizontally opposed: The pistons are in two banks on both sides of a common crankshaft.

- V: The pistons are in two banks on opposite sides, forming a deep V with a common crankshaft at the base of the V.
- VR and W: In a VR engine, the pistons are in one bank but form a shallow V within the bank. The W engine consists of two VR banks in a deep V configuration with each other.

> ▶ **TECHNICIAN TIP**
>
> In-line, horizontally opposed, and V configurations are the most common engine configurations. Recent additions are the VR and W arrangements.

Engineers design engines with tilted cylinder banks to reduce engine height. This can reduce the height of the hood as well, which allows a more streamlined hood line **FIGURE 2-17**. Tilting can be carried to an extreme by designing the engine to lie completely on its side in the case of a horizontally opposed engine, also called a flat engine. This greatly reduces the engine height.

As the number of cylinders increases, the length of the engine block and the crankshaft can become a problem structurally and space-wise. One way to avoid this problem is by having more than one row of cylinders, as in a horizontally opposed, V, or W configuration. These designs make the engine block and the crankshaft shorter and more rigid. In vehicle applications, the number of cylinders can vary, usually up to 12. Some examples are:

- In-line 4: Compact, fairly inexpensive, easier to work on, and better fuel economy than other types.
- V8: Approximately twice as powerful as the in-line 4, but less than twice the space. Good power for its size and not overly complicated.
- Flat 6: Low-profile engine that fits well in vehicles with very low hood lines.
- W12: Most powerful compared to its overall dimensions, but more complicated and expensive than the other engines.

Common angles between the banks of cylinders are 180 degrees, 90 degrees, 60 degrees, and 15 degrees. Angles vary due to the number of cylinders and the manufacturer's design considerations.

In-line

Cylinders arranged side by side in a single row identify the **in-line engine** and can be found in 3-, 4-, 5-, and 6-cylinder configurations **FIGURE 2-18**. There have been in-line 8-cylinder engines, but they are too long to fit

FIGURE 2-17 Tilting cylinder banks can reduce both engine height and hood height, which allows a more streamlined hood line.

FIGURE 2-19 Horizontally opposed engines are commonly found in 4- and 6-cylinder configurations.

FIGURE 2-18 Cylinders arranged side by side in a single row identify the in-line engine.

into the engine bay of a conventional modern car. In-line engines can be mounted longitudinally (lengthwise) or transversely (sideways) in the engine bay. In-line engines are generally less complicated to design and manufacture since they do not have to share components with a second bank of cylinders. This lack of shared components can mean extra working room in the engine compartment when performing maintenance and repairs. As a general rule of thumb, in-line engines are easier to work on than the other cylinder arrangements.

Horizontally Opposed

<u>Horizontally opposed engines</u> are sometimes referred to as "flat" engines and are commonly found in 4- and 6-cylinder configurations **FIGURE 2-19**. They are shorter lengthwise than a comparable in-line engine but wider

than a V type. Horizontally opposed engines have two banks of cylinders, 180 degrees apart, on opposite sides of the crankshaft. It is a useful design when little vertical space is available. A horizontally opposed engine is only fitted longitudinally.

V

<u>V engines</u> have two banks of cylinders sitting side by side in a V arrangement sharing a common crankshaft **FIGURE 2-20**. This compact design allows for about twice the power output from a V engine as an in-line engine of the same length. In automotive applications, V engines can typically be found in 6-, 8-, 10-, and 12-cylinder configurations. A V6 will have two banks of 3 cylinders, a V8 two banks of 4 cylinders, etc. The angle of the V tends to vary according to the number of cylinders and can be found by dividing 720 degrees (two rotations of the crankshaft, which equals one complete cycle) by the number of cylinders. The natural angle for a V8 is 90 degrees. The natural angle for a V6 is 120 degrees, for a V10 is 72 degrees, and for a V12 is 60 degrees. Designing the engine around the natural angle means the engine can have a shorter length because each crankshaft throw can be shared between two cylinders. Some manufacturers vary their angles from those natural angles and use 90 degrees for a V6 and 15 degrees for a VR6 due to convenience or design requirements. Varying away from the natural angle means that the crankshaft must have one cylinder per crank throw, making the engine slightly longer.

VR and W

The <u>VR engine</u> uses a single bank of cylinders, but the cylinders are staggered at a shallow 15-degree V within the bank. This design not only allows the engine to be

FIGURE 2-20 V engines are shorter than in-line engines of equivalent capacity.

shorter than an in-line engine, but also makes it narrower than a typical V engine. The **W engine** consists of two VR cylinder banks in a deeper V arrangement to each other. This gives a very compact, yet powerful engine design.

Rotary Engines

Rotary engines are very powerful for their size, but they do not use conventional pistons that slide back and forth inside a straight cylinder. Instead, a rotary engine uses a triangular rotor that turns inside an oval-shaped housing. The rotary engine has three combustion events for each rotation of the rotor. As the rotor turns, it carries the air/fuel mixture around the chambers, which are created between the tips of the rotor and the chamber wall. The rotor compresses the air/fuel mixture, and spark plugs ignite the mixture just like a conventional engine.

The rotary engine does not have intake and exhaust valves like a traditional piston engine; instead it has exhaust and intake ports that are covered and uncovered by the rotating rotor in the chamber. This design reduces the number of parts and makes it less complicated than a piston engine. Rotary engines generally have more than one rotor, with two being most common. The design of the rotary engine provides a very compact power unit.

▶ Transmission and Axle Configurations

In most vehicles, the engine is bolted firmly to either a transmission or a transaxle **FIGURE 2-21**. A transmission transmits engine power to a drive shaft, final drive and differential gears, and driving axles. Transmissions are usually used in front-engine, rear-wheel drive vehicles. Alternatively, a transaxle is a self-contained unit with the transmission, final drive gears, and differential located in one casing. It is usually used on front-engine, front-wheel drive vehicles or rear-engine, rear-wheel drive vehicles. It can also be used on some sports cars with front-engine, rear-wheel drive, with the transaxle connected to the engine by a drive shaft.

Live and Dead Axles

Vehicles can be described by the number of axles and driven wheels. Each axle typically has one wheel on each end of the axle. Axles come in two configurations: live axle and dead axle. Live axles use the engine's torque to turn the wheels (drive the vehicle) and at the same time support the weight of the vehicle. The wheels and axles on a live axle are also called drive wheels and drive axles since they propel the vehicle. Dead axles support the weight of

FIGURE 2-21 **A.** Transmission. **B.** Transaxle.

FIGURE 2-22 Most light vehicles only have two axles. **A.** Live axle. **B.** Dead axle.

the vehicle only while allowing the wheels to rotate freely on the axle. The wheels on dead axles are not considered drive wheels since they support the vehicle's weight. Most light vehicles have only two axles: one live axle and one dead axle **FIGURE 2-22**. On commercial vehicles, the load carried on a single axle is limited by law, so vehicles with extra axles are common. A heavy vehicle may have six wheels (three axles) to support the vehicle, but only four wheels (two axles) actually drive it. The extra axle at the rear is used only to support the weight of the vehicle and is sometimes called a lazy axle. This vehicle is called a 6 × 2 (expressed as "6-by-2") vehicle. If the lazy axle is changed to a drive axle, this becomes a 6 × 4 vehicle. Some heavy transport vehicles have an extra steering axle, which allows even more weight to be carried.

Location of Live Axles

The location of the live axle determines whether the vehicle is classified as rear-wheel drive, front-wheel drive, four-wheel drive, or all-wheel drive. If the live axle is at the front of the vehicle, it is considered a front-wheel drive vehicle. Front-wheel drive vehicles use the front wheels to pull the vehicle along. In light passenger vehicles, a live front axle in the front of the vehicle gives it lighter body weight and increased interior room. The engine and transaxle are at the front and can be mounted transversely, with the engine parallel to the front axle, or longitudinally where the engine is in line with the centerline of the vehicle. This gives good traction on the front wheels but less traction on the rear wheels, especially when braking or making evasive maneuvers.

If the live axle is at the rear of the vehicle, it is considered a rear-wheel drive vehicle and pushes the vehicle along. With the engine in front, this spreads out the weight of the drive train assemblies throughout the vehicle, putting more of the weight on the rear wheels. Some rear-wheel drive vehicles have the engine at the rear, driving the wheels through a transaxle. Moving the engine to the rear allows a lower hood line, which may improve aerodynamics. The increase in weight over the rear wheels can improve their traction, but at the expense of less traction on the front wheels.

A vehicle in which the engine is located behind the driver but in front of the rear drive axle is called a mid-engine, rear-wheel drive vehicle. A mid-engine design locates the weight of the engine near the center of the vehicle. This allows for a low hood profile, balanced distribution of weight, and good handling. This layout is commonly used in sports cars.

The previous examples would be called two-wheel drive vehicles, or 4 × 2. This means that there are four wheels, but only two drive wheels. On all-wheel drive vehicles, both axles are live and all four wheels drive (4 × 4) the vehicle. Driving all four wheels requires additional components and complexity, which add weight and cost. Most 4 × 4 vehicles are more expensive and less fuel efficient than similar 4 × 2 vehicles.

Torque

Torque is the twisting force applied to a shaft. In a vehicle, torque is used to drive the vehicle down the road. Torque is developed in the engine when combustion of the air/fuel mixture causes high pressure to push the piston down the cylinder and apply a twisting force to the crankshaft. The torque in the crankshaft is then used to twist the gears in the transmission, which is then used to twist the gears in the final drive assembly, which is then used to twist the axles, which is then used to twist the wheels and tires, which drive the vehicle down the road.

Torque is also used by technicians when tightening bolts and nuts. Most of the bolts and nuts on the vehicle have a torque specified by the manufacturer that they must be tightened to. This is accomplished by using a special wrench that has the ability to measure torque. Thus, torque is an important concept for technicians to understand. Torque in the Imperial system is measured by the foot-pound (ft-lb) and inch-pound (in-lb), and in the metric system it is measured by the Newton meter (Nm). **TABLE 2-1** lists standard torque conversions.

TABLE 2-1: Torque Conversions	
12 in-lb	1 ft-lb
1 in-lb	0.08 ft-lb
1 Nm	0.74 ft-lb
1 Nm	8.8 in-lb

Torque Designations

The measure of torque is based on the equivalent twisting force exerted by an amount of weight (mass) applied to a perpendicular lever of a given length. The following designations are used in measuring torque:

- A foot-pound (ft-lb) is the twisting force applied to a shaft by a lever 1 foot long with a 1 pound mass on the end.
- An inch-pound (in-lb) is the twisting force applied to a shaft by a lever 1 inch long with a 1 pound mass on the end.
- A Newton meter (Nm) is the twisting force applied to a shaft by a lever 1 meter long with a force of 1 Newton applied to the end of the lever. (1 N is equivalent to the force applied by a mass of 102 grams, or .102 kg.)

Transmissions and Final Drives

A vehicle with a manual transmission uses a clutch to engage and disengage the engine from the transmission **FIGURE 2-23**. Engine torque is transmitted through the clutch to the transmission or transaxle. The transmission or transaxle contains sets of gears that increase or decrease the torque, which allows the vehicle to have more pulling power in low gears and higher road speed in higher gears. Drive from the transmission is then transmitted to the rest of the drive train. The lower the gear ratio selected, the higher the torque transmitted. A vehicle starting from rest needs a lot of torque, but once it is moving, it can maintain speed with only a relatively small amount of torque. A higher gear ratio can then be selected and engine speed reduced.

A conventional vehicle with the engine at the front and driving wheels at the rear uses a **drive shaft** to transmit torque from the transmission to the final drive. The **final drive** provides a final gear reduction to multiply the torque before applying it to the drive axles **FIGURE 2-24**. On front-engine, rear-wheel drive vehicles, the drive shaft is fitted down the centerline of the vehicle, and the final drive at the rear of the vehicle changes the direction of the drive by 90 degrees from the center of the vehicle out to the wheels via the axles. Inside the final drive, a **differential gear set** divides the torque to the axles and allows for the difference in speed of each wheel when cornering.

Axles transmit the torque to the driving wheels. In a rear-wheel drive vehicle, the axles can be solid or contain joints to allow for movement of the suspension. For a transaxle-equipped vehicle, each drive shaft has movable joints to allow for suspension and steering movement.

An automatic transmission or transaxle performs similar functions to a manual transmission or transaxle, except that gear selection is automatically controlled either hydraulically or electronically. The automatic transmission uses a **torque converter** (instead of a clutch), which acts as a hydraulic coupling to transfer the drive from the engine to the transmission. Automatic transmissions are covered in more depth in the Automatic Transmission section.

FIGURE 2-23 A vehicle with a manual transmission uses a clutch to engage and disengage the engine from the drive train.

FIGURE 2-24 Final drive assembly. Note: Differential gears and bearings removed from center of ring gear for illustration purposes.

Four-Wheel Drive

A four-wheel drive (4WD) vehicle can drive all four wheels so it has a drive shaft, a final drive and differential gears, and axles for both the front and rear axle assemblies. A transfer case is attached to the transmission. The transfer case controls the drive to the front and rear axles. It has a selector lever to select two- or four-wheel drive. Some transfer cases also allow for selection of high and low range, which changes the gear ratios to the wheels. This is helpful when driving in rough off-road conditions where vehicle speed is very slow.

Part-time 4WD means the vehicle is usually driven in two-wheel drive and switched to full-time when needed by engaging the transfer case. The transfer case locks the drive shafts together and directs torque through them to both axles. When disengaged, the vehicle transfer case is coupled to one drive shaft only. When 4WD is disengaged, most part-time 4WD vehicles drive the rear wheels. Constant 4WD, also called all-wheel drive, uses a third differential in the transfer case to allow for the difference in speed between the front and rear wheels during cornering.

All-Wheel Drive

All-wheel drive vehicles provide drive to all four wheels of the vehicle. All-wheel drive systems should not be confused with part-time four-wheel drive vehicles. The all-wheel drive cannot normally be disconnected or deselected. The all-wheel drive vehicle can be used on hard pavement with drive to all wheels because the transfer case employs a center differential unit that allows the front and rear axles to rotate at slightly different speeds. There are various methods of splitting the drive between the front and rear wheels. Some transfer cases use an electronically controlled multiplate clutch, while others use a **viscous coupling**. Both of these devices allow a small difference in speed between the front and rear axles when the vehicle is turning but do not allow any great difference in speed such as when one or more of the wheels lose traction. The driver can still temporarily lock the front and rear axles together by moving a separate lever as in a conventional 4WD or by moving the main gear selector. This is called a differential lock.

Some full-time 4WD sedans use a front engine and transaxle, with a drive shaft connected to drive the rear wheels. These cars are lighter and less rugged than conventional off-road types and usually operate at higher speeds. The drive to all four wheels provides better balanced handling and traction for cornering in slippery conditions.

Regardless of the type of system fitted, the aim is the same, to provide drive to all four wheels constantly while the vehicle is in motion. The power is not necessarily split 50/50 between the front and rear wheels; torque is usually split 60% to front wheels and 40% to rear wheels. Some vehicles incorporate sophisticated traction and torque control systems to the vehicle to maintain effective traction of the wheels to the road under all driving conditions. These systems vary the torque split between the front and rear wheels.

Wrap-up

Ready for Review

▶ Learning automotive terminology is essential to becoming an automotive technician.

▶ Vehicle body design types include sedan, station wagon, hatchback, convertible, coupe, van, minivan, pickup, and sport utility vehicle (SUV).

▶ Sedans have enclosed bodies with a maximum of four doors, while coupes only have two doors; either design can be fixed roof or convertible.

▶ The hatch of a hatchback lifts up at the rear of the vehicle to provide luggage area access.

▶ Convertibles can convert from enclosed top to open top via a retractable roof.

▶ Station wagons have increased luggage capacity due to an extended roof.

▶ Pickup trucks are designed to support greater loads than passenger cars.

▶ Minivans are lighter duty versions of full-size vans.

▶ SUVs can carry and/or tow moderately heavy loads.

▶ A vehicle chassis is the steel structure that supports the engine, wheels, and transmission.

▶ The unibody vehicle design replaced the body-on-frame design, allowing for lighter-weight cars that could be manufactured more quickly.

▶ Vehicle openings include: engine compartment hood, hatch and tailgate openings, fuel door, and battery access covers.

▶ Engine compartment hoods have remote release levers to prevent unauthorized access.

▶ Vehicles must convert stored chemical energy into active mechanical energy.

▶ Stored energy sources include: gasoline, diesel fuel, natural gas, alcohol, bio-diesel, hydrogen, and battery acid.

▶ Conversion of chemical energy occurs via an internal combustion engine or operation of an electric motor.

▶ The transmission changes gear ratios to match engine speed and output to desired road speed.

▶ The suspension system uses shock absorbers, linkages, and springs to connect the wheels to the chassis.

▶ The electrical system includes the battery, powertrain control system, lighting system, accessory systems, safety systems, passenger comfort systems, and entertainment systems.

▶ The drive train is comprised of the engine, transmission/transaxle, differential, axles, and wheels.

▶ Drive train layout can have a front-, mid-, or rear-mounted engine, which can be oriented longitudinally or transversely.

▶ The four common drive wheel arrangements are: front-wheel drive, rear-wheel drive, all-wheel drive, and four-wheel drive.

▶ Engines are classified according to type, cylinder arrangement, number of cylinders/rotors, and total engine displacement.

▶ The two types of engine are piston (most common) and rotary.

▶ Piston engines are configured in one of four ways: in-line, horizontally opposed, V, or VR/W.

▶ Multicylinder engines vary in the number of cylinders; examples include in-line 4, V8, Flat 6, W12.

▶ In-line engines have a single row of side-by-side cylinders.

▶ Horizontally opposed engines separate two banks of cylinders by 180 degrees, on either side of the crankshaft.

▶ V engines have two rows of side-by-side cylinders that share a crankshaft.

▶ VR/W engines are narrower and shorter than other engines.

▶ Rotary engines use one or more triangular rotors.

▶ Axles can be live and use engine torque to turn the wheels or dead and just support the weight of the vehicle.

▶ Axle location determines the drive wheel arrangement.

▶ Torque is a twisting force that is applied to the crankshaft by movement of the pistons or to nuts and bolts by a technician's wrench.

▶ Manual transmissions require a clutch to transmit torque and engage/disengage the engine from the transmission.

▶ A conventional vehicle uses a drive shaft to transmit torque from the transmission to the final drive.

▶ Automatic transmissions use a torque converter instead of a clutch.

▶ Four-wheel drive vehicles can switch from two-wheel to four-wheel drive by engaging the transfer case attached to the transmission.

▸ All-wheel drive vehicles cannot be switched to two-wheel drive.

▸ All-wheel drive vehicles provide constant drive to all four wheels, with only a small difference in speed between front and rear axles when the vehicle is turning.

Key Terms

all-wheel drive (AWD) A drive train arrangement in which all of the wheels drive the vehicle.

axle A shaft connected to wheels that transmits the driving torque to the wheels.

chassis The main support frame in a vehicle. It includes the running gear, such as suspension, the engine, and the drive train.

convertible A vehicle that converts from having an enclosed top to having an open top by a roof that can be removed, retracted, or folded away.

coupe A two-door vehicle that has seating for two people and may have a small rear seat.

differential gear set The arrangement of gears between two axles that allows each axle to spin at its own speed when the vehicle is going around a corner.

drive shaft The shaft or tube fitted with universal couplings that is connected between the transmission and other drive train components to transmit torque and rotation.

drive train A term used to identify the engine, transmission/transaxle, differential, axles, and wheels.

engine configuration The way engine cylinders are arranged—for example, V, flat, or in-line.

final drive A component that provides a final gear reduction and allows for the difference in speed of each wheel when cornering.

flywheel The heavy disc bolted to the rear of the crankshaft that smooths out the power pulses and stores energy from the power stroke for use in keeping the crankshaft rotating through the other three strokes.

four-wheel drive (4WD) A drive train layout in which the engine drive has either two wheels or four wheels depending on which mode is selected by the driver.

front-wheel drive (FWD) A drive train layout in which the engine drives the front wheels.

hatchback A vehicle that has a shared passenger and cargo area; it typically is available in three- and five-door arrangements.

horizontally opposed engine An engine with two banks of cylinders, 180 degrees apart, on opposite sides of the crankshaft. It is also called a flat engine or a boxer engine.

in-line engine An engine in which the cylinders are arranged side by side in a single row.

longitudinal A term used to describe the front-to-back engine orientation when mounted in the engine compartment.

minivan A lighter-duty van used for carrying six to eight occupants or light cargo.

pick-up A vehicle that carries cargo; it has stronger chassis components and suspension than a sedan.

piston engine An internal combustion engine that uses cylindrical pistons moving back and forth in a cylinder to extract mechanical energy from chemical energy.

rear-wheel drive (RWD) A drive train layout in which the engine drives the rear wheels.

rotary engine An engine that uses a triangular rotor turning in a housing instead of conventional pistons.

sedan A vehicle configuration that has an enclosed body, with a maximum of four doors to allow access to the passenger compartment.

sport utility vehicle (SUV) A passenger vehicle built on a light-truck chassis; it is usually equipped with four-wheel drive and capable of hauling heavier loads than typical passenger vehicles.

station wagon A vehicle configuration with four doors with a roof line that continues into the rear cargo area and a rear door for access.

torque Twisting force.

torque converter A device that is turned by the crankshaft and transmits torque to the input shaft of an automatic transmission.

transverse A term used to describe the side-to-side engine orientation when mounted in the engine compartment.

truck A large heavy vehicle for carrying cargo.

unibody design A vehicle design that does not use a rigid frame to support the body. The body panels are designed to provide the strength for the vehicle.

V engine A term used to describe an engine configuration that uses a single bank of cylinders staggered at a shallow 15-degree V.

viscous coupling A device that acts like a limited slip clutch.

W engine A term used to describe an engine configuration consisting of two VR cylinder banks in a deep V arrangement.

ASE-Type Questions

1. Tech A says that most vehicles today are built with a ladder frame. Tech B says that most vehicles today do not have a frame. Who is correct?
   a. Tech A
   b. Tech B
   c. Both A and B
   d. Neither A nor B

2. Tech A says that a roadster is a coupe. Tech B says that a station wagon and a hatchback are the same. Who is correct?
   a. Tech A
   b. Tech B
   c. Both A and B
   d. Neither A nor B

3. Tech A says that gasoline is energy in chemical form. Tech B says that chemical energy is converted to mechanical energy in the combustion process of an engine. Who is correct?
   a. Tech A
   b. Tech B
   c. Both A and B
   d. Neither A nor B

4. Tech A says that a live axle is an axle that can be steered. Tech B says that a dead axle supports the weight of the vehicle, but doesn't power it. Who is correct?
   a. Tech A
   b. Tech B
   c. Both A and B
   d. Neither A nor B

5. Tech A says that the gear ratio in the transmission helps the vehicle gain speed. Tech B says that the gear ratio of the final drive can be selected with a gearshift lever. Who is correct?
   a. Tech A
   b. Tech B
   c. Both A and B
   d. Neither A nor B

6. Tech A says that pushing on the brake pedal stops the vehicle by converting chemical energy into thermal energy. Tech B says that brake pedal pressure is transmitted to the brakes hydraulically. Who is correct?
   a. Tech A
   b. Tech B
   c. Both A and B
   d. Neither A nor B

7. Tech A says that one advantage of a mid-engine design is better weight distribution. Tech B says that the rear-engine design is commonly used in 4-wheel drive vehicles. Who is correct?
   a. Tech A
   b. Tech B
   c. Both A and B
   d. Neither A nor B

8. Tech A says that the purpose of the battery is to charge the vehicle. Tech B says that in-line engines are generally easier to work on than V engines. Who is correct?
   a. Tech A
   b. Tech B
   c. Both A and B
   d. Neither A nor B

9. Tech A says that the natural angle of a V6 is 90 degrees. Tech B says that the natural angle of a V10 is 60 degrees. Who is correct?
   a. Tech A
   b. Tech B
   c. Both A and B
   d. Neither A nor B

10. Tech A says that the definition of torque is how far the crankshaft twists. Tech B says that torque can relate to tightness of bolts. Who is correct?
   a. Tech A
   b. Tech B
   c. Both A and B
   d. Neither A nor B

CHAPTER 3

NATEF Tasks

Required Supplemental Tasks
Shop and Personal Safety

Knowledge Objectives

After reading this chapter, you will be able to:
1. Describe how to follow safe practices in the workplace. (pp 36–41)
2. Describe how the Occupational Safety and Health Administration (OSHA) and the Environmental Protection Agency (EPA) impact the workplace. (pp 38–39)
3. Describe the difference between a shop policy and a shop procedure. (pp 39–40)
4. Explain how shop policies, procedures, and safety inspections make the workplace safer. (pp 39–40, 58)
5. Describe how to identify hazardous environments and the safety precautions that should be undertaken in hazardous environments. (pp 40–41)
6. Identify workplace safety signs and their meanings. (pp 41–42)
7. Describe the standard safety equipment that should be in the workplace. (pp 42–43)
8. Describe how to maintain a safe level of air quality in the workplace. (pp 43–44)
9. Describe the safety precautions to be taken when working with electrical tools and equipment. (pp 44–45)
10. Explain how the shop layout contributes to efficiency and safety. (p 45)
11. Describe how to reduce the risk of fires in the shop. (pp 45–46)
12. Describe how to use firefighting equipment. (pp 46–48)
13. Explain how to use an MSDS. (pp 48–55)
14. Describe how to manage toxic dust. (pp 55–57)

Introduction to Automotive Safety

▶ Introduction

Occupational safety and health is very important to ensure that everyone can work without being injured. Governments will normally have legislation in place with significant penalties for those who do not follow safe practices in the workplace. Potential hazards are in most workplaces, especially automotive shops. It is important to learn about hazards so you can identify them and take action to protect yourself and your coworkers. Some hazards are obvious, such as vehicles falling from hoists or jacks or tires exploding during inflation. Other hazards are less obvious, such as the long-term effects of fumes from solvents. There are many things to learn about safety in the automotive shop, but it is impossible to cover every situation you will encounter. One of the most important skills to learn is the ability to recognize unsafe practices or equipment and put in place measures to prevent injuries from happening.

Occupational safety and health is everyone's responsibility. You have a responsibility to ensure that you work safely and take care not to put others at risk by acting in an unsafe manner. Your employer also has a responsibility to provide a safe working environment. To ensure the safety of yourself and others, make sure you are aware of the correct safety procedures at your workplace. This means listening very carefully to safety information provided by your employer and asking for clarification, help, or instructions if you are unsure how to perform a task safely. Always think about how you are performing shop tasks, be on the lookout for unsafe equipment and

FIGURE 3-1 Personal protective equipment (PPE) refers to items of safety equipment like safety footwear, gloves, clothing, protective eyewear, and hearing protection.

work practices, and wear the correct **personal protective equipment (PPE)**. PPE refers to items of safety equipment like safety footwear, gloves, clothing, protective eyewear, and hearing protection **FIGURE 3-1**.

▶ Safety Overview

Motor vehicle servicing is one of the most common vocations worldwide. Hundreds of thousands of shops service millions of vehicles every day. That means many people are conducting automotive servicing and there is a great potential for things to go wrong. It is up to

▶ You are the Automotive Technician

You are changing the oil on a new type of vehicle for the first time. The oil pan has the drain plug on the side of the oil pan, instead of the bottom of the pan. You place the drain pain directly under the drain plug like you normally do. Unfortunately, when the plug comes out, the oil shoots sideways right over the side of the drain pan. You reposition it quickly, but not before a large puddle is on the floor.

1. Why is it important to review the MSDS before cleaning up a spill?
2. What is the minimum PPE that should be worn to manage this spill?
3. What are some of the health hazards of coming into frequent or prolonged contact with used engine oil?

(continues)

Component	Material/Parts	Removal and Safety Information	Recommended Storage
Brake shoes and pads pre-2004	Asbestos	Fibers are dangerous if inhaled.	Put in a plastic bag in a sealed container for collection by contractor.
Coolant	Phosphoric acid, hydrazine ethylene glycol, alcohols	Radiator coolant can be toxic to the environment.	Store in sealed drums in a covered area for recycling or collection by a licensed operator.
Coverings for plastic parts, and plastic bags and containers for parts shipping	Plastic-made components	Plastic components that can be recycled will bear a recycling symbol: This symbol will have a number inside telling the recycling company what the product is made of.	If the plastic container has a recycle code on the product, then put it in the recycle bin. If it does not, then put in general waste. Plastic oil containers cannot be recycled.
Fuel	Unleaded, diesel	Avoid fumes. Fire hazard; keep well away from ignition sources. Siphon from tank to avoid spillage.	Store in a drum in a covered area.
Metal	Brake discs, housings made of metal (gearbox/engine case and components), metal cuttings	Some metal products can be heavy, so lift with care.	All metal components can be recycled; keep waste metal in a separate recycle bin for sale or disposal.
Oil	Engine, transmission, and differential oils	Fire hazard; keep well away from ignition sources.	Store in a drum/container in a covered area for collection by a licensed operator.
Oil filters	Steel paper fiber	—	Drain filter then crush and store in a leak-proof drum for collection.
Parts boxes and paperwork	Paper, cardboard	—	Store in a recycling bin to be taken away for recycling.
Tires	Rubber, steel, fabric	Keep away from ignition sources.	Store in a fenced area for collection by recycler.
Trim, plastic fittings, and seats	Plastic, metal, cloth	—	Store racked or binned for reuse, sale, or recycling.
Tubes and rubber components	Rubber hoses, mounts, etc.	Keep away from ignition sources.	Store in a collection bin, to be collected and recycled.
Undeployed airbags	Plastics, metals, igniters, explosives	Recommended specific training on airbags before attempting removal. Handle with care; accidental deployment can cause serious harm. If unit is to be scrapped, ensure that it is safely deployed first.	Store faceup in a secure area.

Shop Policies and Procedures

Shop policies and procedures are a set of documents that outline how tasks and activities in the shop are to be conducted and managed. They also ensure that the shop operates according to OSHA and EPA laws and regulations. A **policy** is a guiding principle that sets the shop direction, while a **procedure** is a list of the steps required to get the same result each time a task or activity is performed. An example of a policy would be an OSHA document for the shop that describes how the shop complies with legislation. A procedure would be a document that describes the steps required to safely use the vehicle hoist.

Each shop will have its own set of policies and procedures and a system in place to make sure the policies and procedures are regularly reviewed and updated. Regular reviews ensure that new policies and procedures are developed and old ones are modified in case something has changed. For example, if the shop moves to a new building, then a review of policies and procedures will ensure sure that they relate to the new shop, its layout, and equipment. In general, the policies and procedures are written to guide shop practice; help ensure compliance with laws, statutes, and regulations; and reduce the risk of injury. Always follow your shop policies and procedures to reduce the risk of injury to your coworkers and yourself and to prevent damage to property.

It is everyone's responsibility to know and follow the rules. Locate the general shop rules and procedures for your workplace. Look through the contents or index pages to familiarize yourself with the contents. Discuss the policy and the shop rules and procedures with your supervisor. Ask questions to ensure that you understand how the rules and procedures should be applied and your role in making sure they are followed.

Identifying Hazardous Environments

A **hazardous environment** is a place where hazards exist. A **hazard** is anything that could hurt you or someone else, and most workplaces have them. It is almost impossible to remove all hazards, but it is important to identify hazards and work to reduce their potential for causing harm by putting specific measures in place. For example, operating a bench grinder poses a number of hazards. While it is not possible to eliminate the hazards of using the bench grinder, by putting specific measures in place, the risk of those hazards can be reduced.

A risk analysis of a bench grinder would identify the following hazards and risks: a high-velocity particle that could damage your eyesight or that of someone working nearby; the grinding wheel breaking apart, damaging eyesight or causing cuts and abrasion; electrocution if electrical parts are faulty; a risk to your hands from heat or high-velocity particles; a risk to your hearing due to excessive noise; and a risk of entrapment of clothing or body parts through rotating machinery. To reduce the risk of these hazards, the following measures are taken: position the bench grinder in a safe area away from where others work; make sure electrical items are regularly checked for electrical and mechanical safety; when operating the equipment, wear PPE such as protective eyewear, gloves, hearing protection, hairnets, or caps; and do not wear loose clothing that can be caught in the bench grinder.

To identify hazardous environments, follow the steps in **SKILL DRILL 3-1**:

1. Familiarize yourself with the shop layout. There are special work areas that are defined by painted lines. These lines show the hazardous zone around certain machines and areas. If you are not working on the machines, you should stay outside the marked area.

2. Study the various warning signs around your shop. Understand the meaning of the signal word, the colors, the text, and the symbols or pictures on each sign. Ask your supervisor if you do not fully understand any part of the sign.

SKILL DRILL | 3-1 | Identifying Hazardous Environments

1. Familiarize yourself with the shop layout. Study and understand the various warning signs around your shop. Identify exits and plan your escape route.

2. Check for air quality. Locate the extractor fans or ventilation outlets and make sure they are not obstructed in any way. Locate and observe the operation of the exhaust extraction hose, pump, and outlet used on the vehicle's exhaust pipes.

3. Check the location, type, and operation of fire extinguishers in your shop.

SKILL DRILL | 3-1 | Identifying Hazardous Environments, continued

4 Find out where flammable materials are kept, and make sure they are stored properly.

5 Check the hoses and fittings on the air compressor and air guns for any damage or excessive wear.

6 Identify caustic chemicals and acids associated with activities in your shop. Ask your supervisor for information on any special hazards in your particular shop and any special avoidance procedures, which may apply to you and your working environment.

3 Identify exits. Find out where each door, window, and gate is, and whether it is usually open or locked. Plan your escape route, should you need to exit in a hurry. Also know the designated gathering point and go there in an emergency. **(Photo 1)**

4 Check for air quality. There should be good ventilation and very little chemical fumes or smell. Locate the extractor fans or ventilation outlets and make sure they are not obstructed in any way. Locate and observe the operation of the exhaust extraction hoses, pump, and outlets that are used on the vehicle's exhaust pipes. **(Photo 2)**

5 Check the location and types of fire extinguishers in your shop. Be sure you know when and how to use each type of fire extinguisher. **(Photo 3)**

6 Identify flammable hazards. Find out where flammable materials are kept, and make sure they are stored properly. **(Photo 4)**

7 Check the hoses and fittings on the air compressor and air guns for any damage or excessive wear. You must be particularly careful when troubleshooting

air guns. Never pull the trigger while inspecting it—severe eye damage can result. **(Photo 5)**

8 Identify caustic chemicals and acids associated with activities in your shop. Ask your supervisor for information on any special hazards in your particular shop and any special avoidance procedures, which may apply to you and your working environment. **(Photo 6)**

▶ Standard Safety Measures

Signs

Always remember that a shop is a hazardous environment. To make people more aware of specific shop hazards, legislative bodies have developed a series of safety signs. These signs are designed to give adequate warning of an unsafe situation. Each sign has four components:

- **Signal word:** There are three signal words— danger, warning, and caution. *Danger* indicates an immediately hazardous situation, which, if not avoided, will result in death or serious injury. Danger is usually indicated by white text with a red background. *Warning* indicates a potentially hazardous situation, which, if not avoided, could result in death or serious injury. The sign is usually in black text with a yellow background. *Caution* indicates a potentially hazardous situation, which, if not avoided, may result in minor or moderate injury. It may also be used to alert against unsafe practices. This sign is usually in black text with a yellow background **FIGURE 3-4**.

- **Background color:** The choice of background color also draws attention to potential hazards and is used to provide contrast so the letters or images stand out. For example, a red background is used to identify a definite hazard; yellow indicates caution for a potential hazard. A green background is used for emergency-type signs, such as for first aid, fire protection, and emergency equipment. A blue background is used for general information signs.
- **Text:** The sign will sometimes include explanatory text intended to provide additional safety information. Some signs are designed to convey a personal safety message.
- **Pictorial message:** In symbol signs, a pictorial message appears alone or is combined with explanatory text. This type of sign allows the safety message to be conveyed to people who are illiterate or who do not speak the local language.

Safety Equipment

Shop safety equipment includes items such as:

- **Handrails:** Handrails are used to separate walkways and pedestrian traffic from work areas. They provide a physical barrier that directs pedestrian traffic and also provide protection from vehicle movements.
- **Machinery guards:** Machinery guards and yellow lines prevent people from accidentally walking into the operating equipment or indicate that a safe distance should be kept from the equipment.
- **Painted lines:** Large, fixed machinery such as lathes and milling machines present a hazard to the operator and others working in the area. To prevent accidents, a machinery guard or a yellow painted line on the floor usually borders this equipment.

FIGURE 3-4 Signs. **A.** Danger is usually indicated by white text on a red background. **B.** Warning is usually in black text with an orange background. **C.** Caution is usually in black text with a yellow background.

- **Soundproof rooms:** Soundproof rooms are usually used when a lot of noise is made by operating equipment. An example is the use of a chassis dynamometer. A vehicle operating on a dynamometer produces a lot of noise from its tires, exhaust, and engine. To protect other shop users from the noise, the dynamometer is usually placed in a soundproof room, keeping shop noise to a minimum.

- **Adequate ventilation:** Exhaust gases in shops are a serious health hazard. Whenever a vehicle's engine is running, toxic gases are emitted from its exhaust. To prevent an excess of toxic gas buildup, a well-ventilated work area is needed as well as a method of directly venting the vehicle's exhaust to the outside.
- **Gas extraction hoses:** The best way to get rid of these gases is with a suction hose that fits over the vehicle's exhaust pipe. The hose is attached to an extraction pump that vents the gas to the outside.
- **Doors and gates:** Doors and gates are used for the same reason as machinery guards and painted lines. A doorway is a physical barrier that can be locked and sealed to separate a hazardous environment from the rest of the shop or a general work area from an office or specialist work area.
- **Temporary barriers:** In the day-to-day operation of a shop, there is often a reason to temporarily separate one work bay from others. If a welding machine or an oxyacetylene cutting torch is in use, it may be necessary to place a temporary screen or barrier around the work area to protect other shop users from welding flash or injury.

> **TECHNICIAN TIP**
>
> Stay alert for hazards or anything that might be dangerous. If you see, hear, or smell anything odd, take steps to fix it or tell your supervisor about the problem.

> **TECHNICIAN TIP**
>
> Whenever you perform a task in the shop, you must use personal protective clothing and equipment that are appropriate for the task and that conform to your local safety regulations and policies. Among other items, these may include:
>
> - Work clothing, such as coveralls and steel-capped footwear
> - Eye protection, such as safety glasses and face masks
> - Ear protection, such as earmuffs and earplugs
> - Hand protection, such as gloves and barrier cream
> - Respiratory equipment, such as face masks and valved respirators
>
> If you are not certain what is appropriate or required, ask your supervisor.

Air Quality

Managing air quality in shops helps protect you from potential harm and also protects the environment. There are many shop activities and stored liquids that can reduce the quality of air in shops. Some of these are dangerous fumes from running engines, welding (gas and electric), painting, liquid storage areas, air-conditioning servicing, and dust particles from brake servicing.

Running Engines

Running engines produce dangerous exhaust gases including carbon monoxide and carbon dioxide. Carbon monoxide in small concentrations can kill or cause serious injuries. Carbon dioxide is a greenhouse gas, and vehicles are a major source of carbon dioxide in the atmosphere. Exhaust gases also contain hydrocarbons and oxides of nitrogen. These gases can form smog and also cause breathing problems for some people.

Carbon monoxide in particular is extremely dangerous, as it is odorless and colorless and can build up to toxic levels very quickly in confined spaces. In fact, it doesn't take very much carbon monoxide to pose a danger. The maximum OSHA permissible exposure limit (PEL) is 50 parts per million (ppm) of air for an 8-hour period. The National Institute for Occupational Safety and Health has established a recommended exposure limit of 35 ppm for an 8-hour period. The reason the PEL is so low is because carbon monoxide attaches itself to red blood cells much more easily than oxygen does, and it never leaves the blood cell. This prevents the blood cells from carrying as much oxygen, and if enough carbon monoxide has been inhaled, it effectively asphyxiates the person. Always follow the correct safety precautions when running engines indoors or in a confined space, including over service pits since gases can accumulate there.

The best solution when running engines in an enclosed space is to directly couple the vehicle's exhaust pipe to an exhaust extraction system hose that will ventilate the fumes away from the enclosed space to the outside air. The extraction hose should be vented to where the fumes will not be drawn back indoors, to a place well away from other people and other premises **FIGURE 3-5**.

Do not assume that an engine fitted with a catalytic converter can be run safely indoors; it cannot. Catalytic converters are fitted into the exhaust system in a similar way as mufflers and have a ceramic core with a catalyst that when in operation controls exhaust emissions through chemical reaction. They require high temperatures to

FIGURE 3-5 Extraction hoses should be vented so that the fumes will not be drawn back indoors.

FIGURE 3-6 All electrical switches and fuses should be clearly labeled so that you know which circuits and functions they control.

operate efficiently and are less effective when the exhaust gases are relatively cool, such as when the engine is only idling or being run intermittently. A catalytic convertor can never substitute for adequate ventilation or exhaust extraction equipment. In fact, even if the catalytic converter were working at 100% efficiency, the exhaust would contain large amounts of carbon dioxide and very low amounts of oxygen, neither of which conditions can sustain life.

Electrical Safety

Many people are injured by electricity in shops. Poor electrical safety practices can cause shocks and burns, as well as fires and explosions. Make sure you know where the electrical panels for your shop are located. All circuit breakers and fuses should be clearly labeled so that you know which circuits and functions they control **FIGURE 3-6**. In the case of an emergency, you may need to know how to shut off the electricity supply to a work area or to your entire shop.

Keep the circuit breaker and/or electrical panel covers closed to keep them in good condition, prevent unauthorized access, and prevent accidental contact with the electricity supply. It is important that you do not block or obstruct access to this electrical panel; keep equipment and tools well away so emergency access is not hindered. In some localities, 3 feet (0.91 m) of unobstructed space must be maintained around the panel at all times.

There should be a sufficient number of electrical receptacles in your work area for all your needs. Do not connect multiple appliances to a single receptacle with a simple double adapter. If necessary, use a multi-outlet safety strip that has a built-in overload cutout feature. Electric receptacles should be at least 3 feet (0.91 m) above floor level to reduce the risk of igniting spilled fuel vapors or other flammable liquids.

Portable Electrical Equipment

If you need to use an extension cord, make sure it is made of flexible wiring—not the stiffer type of house wiring— and that it is fitted with a ground wire. The cord should be neoprene-covered, as this material resists oil damage **FIGURE 3-7**. Always check it for cuts, abrasions, or other damage. Be careful how you place the extension cord so it does not cause a tripping hazard. Also avoid rolling equipment or vehicles over it, as doing so can damage the cord. Never use an extension cord in wet conditions or around flammable liquids.

Portable electric tools that operate at 240 volts are often sources of serious shock and burn accidents. Be particularly careful when using these items. Always inspect the cord for damage and check the security of the attached plug before connecting the item to the power supply. Use 110-volt or lower voltage tools if they are available.

All electric tools must be equipped with a ground prong or double-insulated. If they are not, do *not* use them. Never use any high-voltage tool in a wet environment. Air-operated tools cannot give you an electric shock, because they operate on air pressure instead of electricity; so they are safer to use in a wet environment.

FIGURE 3-7 The extension cord should be neoprene-covered.

FIGURE 3-8 All droplights should be properly protected.

Portable Shop Lights

Portable shop lights/droplights can be very useful tools to add light to a particular area or spot on the vehicle you are working on. Always make sure you follow the safety directions when using shop lights. Shop lights should have protective covers fitted to them to prevent accidentally breaking the lamp. If a lamp breaks, it can be an electrical hazard, particularly if a metal object comes in contact with exposed live electricity. For this reason, often low-voltage lamps or lamps with safety switches fitted are used to prevent accidental electrocution. Some shop lights are now cordless, particularly those with LEDs fitted as the light source. Cordless lights are a very safe option because they isolate you from the high voltage.

Electric droplights are a common source of shocks, especially if they are the wrong type for the purpose or if they are poorly constructed or maintained. All droplights should be designed in such a way that the electrical parts can never come into contact with the outer casing of the device. Such lights are called **double-insulated**. The bulb should be completely enclosed in a transparent insulating case or protected within a robust insulating cage FIGURE 3-8.

The bulbs used in electric droplights are very vulnerable to impact and must not be used without insulating cage protection. Incandescent bulbs present an extreme fire hazard if broken in the presence of flammable vapors or liquids and should not be used in repair shops. LED and fluorescent bulbs, while still hazardous, are much safer.

> ## TECHNICIAN TIP
>
> Always inspect the wiring for damage and check the security of the attached plug before connecting a droplight to the power supply. Always switch off and unplug a droplight before changing the bulb.

Shop Layout

The shop should have a layout that is efficient and safe with clearly defined working areas and walkways. Customers should not be allowed to wander through work areas unescorted. A good shop layout can be achieved by thinking about how the work is to be done, how equipment is used, and what traffic movements, both pedestrian and vehicular, occur within the shop. A well-planned shop should have clearly defined areas for various activities, like parts cleaning, parts storage, tool storage, flammable liquid storage, jacking or lifting, tire fitting, and painting. All flammable items should be kept in an approved fireproof storage container or cabinet, with firefighting equipment close at hand.

> ## TECHNICIAN TIP
>
> The danger of a fire is always present in shops, particularly because of the amount of flammable liquids and materials used in shops and vehicles. Always be aware of the potential for a fire, and plan ahead by thinking through the task you are about to undertake. Know where firefighting equipment is kept and how it works.

Preventing Fires

The danger of a gasoline fire is always present in an automotive shop. Most automobiles carry a fuel tank, often with large quantities of fuel on board, which is more than sufficient to cause a large, very destructive, and potentially explosive fire. Take precautions to make sure you have the correct type and size of extinguishers on hand for a potential fuel fire. Make sure you clean up spills immediately and avoid ignition sources, like sparks, in the presence of flammable liquids or gases.

Fuel Vapor

Liquid fuel vaporizes rapidly, especially when spilled, and the vapor is extremely easy to ignite. Because fuel vapor is invisible and heavier than air, it can spread unseen across a wide area, and a source of ignition can be quite some distance from the original spill. Fuel can even vaporize from the cloths or rags used to wipe up liquid spills. These materials should be allowed to dry in the open air, not held in front of a heater element. Any spark or naked flame, even a lit cigarette, can start an explosive fire.

Spillage Risks

Spills frequently occur when technicians remove and replace fuel filters. They also occur during removal of a fuel tank sender unit, which can be located on the side of the fuel tank, without first emptying the tank safely. Spills also can occur when fuel lines are damaged and are being replaced, when fuel systems are being checked, or when fuel is being drained into unsuitable containers. Avoid spills by following the manufacturer's specified procedure when removing fuel system components. Also, keep a spill response kit nearby to deal with any spills quickly. Spill kits should contain absorbent material and barrier dams to contain moderate-sized spills.

Draining Fuel

If there is a possibility of fuel spillage while working on a vehicle, then you should first remove the fuel safely. Do this only in a well-ventilated, level space, preferably outside in the open air. Make sure all potential sources of ignition have been removed from the area, and disconnect the battery on the vehicle. Do not drain fuel from a vehicle over an inspection pit. Make sure the container you are draining into is an approved fuel storage container (fuel retriever) and that it is large enough to contain all of the fuel in the system being drained.

Using a Fuel Retriever

Always use a fuel retriever, preferably removing the fuel through the filler neck. A fuel retriever will minimize the chance of sudden large spills occurring **FIGURE 3-9**. You

Safety

> Never weld anywhere near a gas tank or any kind of fuel line. Welding work on a tank is a job for specialists. An empty fuel tank can still contain vapor and therefore can be even more dangerous than one full of liquid fuel. Do not attempt to repair a tank yourself.

FIGURE 3-9   Always use a fuel retriever; this tool will minimize the chance of sudden large spills occurring.

may need to use narrow-diameter hoses or adapters to drain fuel lines or to bypass anti-spillage devices. Check the service manual for details on how best to drain the fuel from the vehicle you are working on.

Extinguishing Fires

Three elements must be present at the same time for a fire to occur: fuel, oxygen, and heat. The secret of firefighting involves the removal of at least one of these elements, usually the oxygen or the heat, to extinguish the fire. For example, a fire blanket when applied correctly removes the oxygen, while a water extinguisher removes heat from the fire. In the shop, fire extinguishers are used to extinguish the majority of small fires. Never hesitate to call the fire department if you cannot extinguish a fire safely.

Fire Classifications

In the United States, there are five classes of fire:

- Class A fires involve ordinary combustibles such as wood, paper, or cloth.
- Class B fires involve flammable liquids or gaseous fuels.
- Class C fires involve electrical equipment.
- Class D fires involve combustible metals such as sodium, titanium, and magnesium.
- Class K fires involve cooking oil or fat.

Fire Extinguisher Types

Fire extinguishers are marked with pictograms depicting the types of fires that the extinguisher is approved to fight **FIGURE 3-10**:

- Class A: Green triangle
- Class B: Red square

- Class C: Blue circle
- Class D: Yellow pentagram
- Class K: Black hexagon

ORDINARY
A
COMBUSTIBLES

FLAMMABLE
B
LIQUIDS

ELECTRICAL
C
EQUIPMENT

COMBUSTIBLE
D
METALS

FIGURE 3-10 Traditional labels on fire extinguishers often incorporate a shape as well as a letter.

Fire Extinguisher Operation

Always sound the alarm before attempting to fight a fire. If you cannot fight the fire safely, leave the area while you wait for backup. You will need to size up the fire before you make the decision to fight it with a fire extinguisher by identifying what sort of material is burning, the extent of the fire, and the likelihood of it spreading.

To operate a fire extinguisher, follow the acronym for fire extinguisher use: PASS (Pull, Aim, Squeeze, Sweep). *Pull* out the pin that locks the handle at the top of the fire extinguisher to prevent accidental use. Carry the fire extinguisher in one hand, and use your other hand to *aim* the nozzle at the base of the fire. Stand about 8–12' (2.4–3.7 m) away from the fire and *squeeze* the handle to discharge the fire extinguisher. Remember that if you release the handle on the fire extinguisher, it will stop discharging. *Sweep* the nozzle from side to side at the base of the fire **FIGURE 3-11**. Continue to watch the fire. Although it may appear to be extinguished, it may suddenly reignite.

FIGURE 3-11 To operate a fire extinguisher, follow PASS. **A.** Pull. **B.** Aim. **C.** Squeeze. **D.** Sweep.

If the fire is indoors, you should be standing between the fire and the nearest safe exit. If the fire is outside, you should stand facing the fire with the wind on your back, so that the smoke and heat are being blown away from you. If possible, get an assistant to guide you and inform you of the fire's progress. Again, make sure you have a means of escape, should the fire get out of control. When you are certain that the fire is out, report it to your supervisor. Also report what actions you took to put out the fire. Once the circumstances of the fire have been investigated, and your supervisor or the fire department has given you the all clear, clean up the debris and submit the used fire extinguisher for inspection.

Fire Blankets

Fire blankets are designed to smother a small fire and are very useful in putting out a fire on a person. They are also used in situations where a fire extinguisher could cause damage. For example, if there is a small fire under the hood of a vehicle, a fire blanket might be able to smother the fire without running the risk of getting fire extinguisher powder down the intake system. Obtain a fire blanket and study the how-to-use instructions on the packaging. If instructions are not provided, research how to use a fire blanket or ask your supervisor. You may require instruction from an authorized person in using the fire blanket. If you do use a fire blanket, make sure you return the blanket for use or, if necessary, replace it with a new one.

Eyewash Stations and Emergency Showers

Hopefully you will never need to use an eye wash station or emergency shower. The best treatment is prevention, so make sure you wear all the PPE required for each specific task to avoid injury. Eye wash stations are used to flush the eye with clean water or sterile liquid in the event that you get foreign liquid or particles in your eye. There are different types of eye washers; the main ones are disposable eye wash packs and eye wash stations. Some emergency or deluge showers also have an eye wash station built in **FIGURE 3-12**.

When individuals get chemicals in their eyes, they typically need assistance in reaching the eye wash station. Take their arm and lead them to it. They may not want to open their eyes even in the water, so encourage them to use their fingers to pull their eyelids open. If a chemical splashed in their eyes, encourage them to rinse their eyes for 15 minutes. While they are rinsing their eyes, call for medical assistance.

FIGURE 3-12 The main types of eye washers include disposable eye wash packs and eye wash stations. Some emergency showers have an eye wash station built in.

▶ Hazardous Materials Safety

A **hazardous material** is any material that poses an unreasonable risk of damage or injury to persons, property, or the environment if it is not properly controlled during handling, storage, manufacture, processing, packaging, use and disposal, or transportation. These materials can be solids, liquids, or gases. Most shops use hazardous materials daily, such as cleaning solvents, gasket cement, brake fluid, and coolant. Hazardous materials must be properly handled, labeled, and stored in the shop.

Material Safety Data Sheets

Hazardous materials are used daily and may make you very sick if they are not used properly. **Material safety data sheets (MSDS)** contain detailed information about hazardous materials to help you understand how they should be safely used, any health effects relating to them, how to treat a person who has been exposed to them, and how to deal with them in a fire situation. MSDS can be obtained from the manufacturer of the material. The shop should have an MSDS for each hazardous substance or dangerous product. In the United States it is required that workplaces have an MSDS for every chemical that is on site.

Whenever you deal with a potentially hazardous product, you should consult the MSDS to learn how to use that product safely. If you are using more than one product, make sure you consult all the MSDS for those products. Be aware that certain combinations of products can be more dangerous than any of them separately.

MSDS are usually kept in a clearly marked binder and should be regularly updated as chemicals come into the workplace. Generally the MSDS must contain at least the following information **FIGURE 3-13**:

- Revision date
- Material and manufacturer ID
- Hazardous ingredients
- Health hazard data
- Fire and explosion data
- Details about the material mixing or reacting with other materials
- Special precautions

To identify information found on an MSDS, follow the steps in **SKILL DRILL 3-2**:

1 Once you have studied the information on the container label, find the MSDS for that particular material. Always check the revision date to ensure that you are reading the most recent update.

2 Note the chemical and trade names for the material, its manufacturer, and the emergency telephone number to call.

3 Find out why this material is potentially hazardous. It may be flammable, it may explode, or it may be poisonous if inhaled or touched with your bare skin. Check the **threshold limit values (TLVs)**. The concentration of this material in the air you breathe in your shop must not exceed these figures. There could be physical symptoms associated with breathing harmful chemicals. Find out what will happen to you if you suffer overexposure to the material, either through breathing it or by coming into physical contact with it. This will help you take safety precautions, such as eye, face, or skin protection, wearing a mask or respirator while using the material, or washing your skin afterwards.

4 Note the flash point for this material so that you know at what temperature it may catch fire. Also note what kind of fire extinguisher you would use to fight a fire involving this material. The wrong fire extinguisher could make the emergency even worse.

5 Study the reactivity for this material to identify the physical conditions or other materials that you should avoid when using this material. It could be heat, moisture, or some other chemical.

6 Find out what special precautions you should take when working with this material. This will include personal protection for your skin, eyes, or lungs and storage and use of the material.

7 Be sure to refresh your knowledge of your MSDS from time to time. Be confident that you know how to handle and use the material and what action to take in an emergency, should one occur.

MATERIAL SAFETY DATA SHEET

Section 1: Product & Company Identification

Product Name: **Brakleen® Brake Parts Cleaner** (aerosol)

Product Number (s):   **05089, 05089-6, 05089T, 75089, 85089, 85089AZ**

Product Use: Brake parts cleaner

Manufactured / Supplier Contact Information:

In United States:	In Canada:	In Mexico:
CRC Industries, Inc.	CRC Canada Co.	CRC Industries Mexico
885 Louis Drive	2-1246 Lorimar Drive	Av. Benito Juárez 4055 G
Warminster, PA 18974	Mississauga, Ontario L5S 1R2	Colonia Orquídea
www.crcindustries.com	www.crc-canada.ca	San Luís Potosí, SLP CP 78394
1-215-674-4300(General)	1-905-670-2291	www.crc-mexico.com
(800) 521-3168 (Technical)		52-444-824-1666
(800) 272-4620 (Customer Service)		

24-Hr Emergency – CHEMTREC: (800) 424-9300 or (703) 527-3887

FIGURE 3-13 An example of an MSDS.

(Continues)

Product Name: Brakleen® Brake Parts Cleaner (aerosol)
Product Number (s): 05089,05089-6, 05089T, 75089, 85089, 85089AZ

Section 2: Hazards Identification

Emergency Overview

DANGER: Vapor Harmful. Contents Under Pressure.
As defined by OSHA's Hazard Communication Standard, this product is hazardous.
Appearance & Odor: Colorless liquid, irritating odor at high concentrations

Potential Health Effects:

ACUTE EFFECTS:

EYE: May cause slight temporary eye irritation. Vapors may irritate the eyes at concentrations of 100 ppm.

SKIN: Short single exposures may cause skin irritation. Prolonged exposure may cause severe skin irritation, even a burn. A single prolonged exposure is not likely to result in the material being absorbed through skin in harmful amounts.

INHALATION: Dizziness may occur at concentrations of 200 ppm. Progressively higher levels may also cause nasal irritation, nausea, incoordination, and drunkenness. Very high levels or prolonged exposure could lead to unconsciousness and death.

INGESTION: Single dose oral toxicity is considered to be extremely low. Swallowing large amounts may cause injury if aspirated into the lungs. This may be rapidly absorbed through the lungs and result in injury to other body systems.

CHRONIC EFFECTS: Repeated contact with skin may cause drying or flaking of skin. Excessive or long term exposure to vapors may increase sensitivity to epinephrine and increase myocardial irritability.

TARGET ORGANS: Central nervous system. Possibly liver and kidney.

Medical Conditions Aggravated by Exposure: None known.

See Section 11 for toxicology and carcinogenicity information on product ingredients.

Section 3: Composition/Information on Ingredients

COMPONENT	CAS NUMBER	% by Wt.
Tetrachloroethylene (PERC)	127-18-4	> 95
Carbon Dioxide	124-38-9	< 5

Section 4: First Aid Measures

Eye Contact: Immediately flush with plenty of water for 15 minutes. Call a physician if irritation persists.

Skin Contact: Remove contaminated clothing and wash affected area with soap and water. Call a physician if irritation persists. Wash contaminated clothing prior to re-use.

Inhalation: Remove person to fresh air. Keep person calm. If not breathing, give artificial respiration. If breathing is difficult give oxygen. Call a physician.

Ingestion: Do NOT induce vomiting. Call a physician immediately.

Note to Physicians: Because rapid absorption may occur through lungs if aspirated and cause systemic effects, the decision of whether to induce vomiting or not should be made by a physician. If lavage is performed, suggest endotracheal and/or esophageal control. If burn is present, treat as any thermal burn, after decontamination. Exposure may increase myocardial irritability. Do not administer sympathomimetic drugs unless absolutely necessary. No specific antidote.

(Continues)

Product Name: Brakleen® Brake Parts Cleaner (aerosol)
Product Number (s): 05089,05089-6, 05089T, 75089, 85089, 85089AZ

Section 5: Fire-Fighting Measures

Flammable Properties: This product is nonflammable in accordance with aerosol flammability definitions. (See 16 CFR 1500.3(c)(6))

Flash Point: None (TCC)	Upper Explosive Limit: None
Autoignition Temperature: None	Lower Explosive Limit: None

Fire and Explosion Data:

Suitable Extinguishing Media: This material does not burn. Use extinguishing agent suitable for surrounding fire.

Products of Combustion: Hydrogen chloride, trace amounts of phosgene and chlorine

Explosion Hazards: Aerosol containers, when exposed to heat from fire, may build pressure and explode.

Protection of Fire-Fighters: Firefighters should wear self-contained, NIOSH-approved breathing apparatus for protection against suffocation and possible toxic decomposition products. Proper eye and skin protection should be provided. Use water spray to keep fire-exposed containers cool and to knock down vapors which may result from product decomposition.

Section 6: Accidental Release Measures

Personal Precautions: Use personal protection recommended in Section 8. Do not breathe vapors.

Environmental Precautions: Take precautions to prevent contamination of ground and surface waters. Do not flush into sewers or storm drains.

Methods for Containment & Clean-up: Dike area to contain spill. Ventilate the area with fresh air. If in confined space or limited air circulation area, clean-up workers should wear appropriate respiratory protection. Recover or absorb spilled material using an absorbent designed for chemical spills. Place used absorbents into proper waste containers.

Section 7: Handling and Storage

Handling Procedures: Vapors of this product are heavier than air and will collect in low areas. Make sure ventilation removes vapors from low areas. Do not eat, drink or smoke while using this product. Use caution around energized equipment. The metal container will conduct electricity if it contacts a live source. This may result in injury to the user from electrical shock and/or flash fire. For product use instructions, please see the product label.

Storage Procedures: Store in a cool dry area out of direct sunlight. Aerosol cans must be maintained below 120 F to prevent cans from rupturing.

Aerosol Storage Level: I

Section 8: Exposure Controls/Personal Protection

Exposure Guidelines:

COMPONENT	OSHA		ACGIH		OTHER		
	TWA	STEL	TWA	STEL	TWA	SOURCE	UNIT
Tetrachloroethylene	100	N.E.	25	100	N.E.		ppm
Carbon dioxide	5000	30000 v	5000	30,000	N.E.		ppm
N.E. – Not Established		(c) – ceiling	(s) – skin	(v) – vacated			

(Continues)

Product Name: Brakleen® Brake Parts Cleaner (aerosol)
Product Number (s): 05089,05089-6, 05089T, 75089, 85089, 85089AZ

<u>**Controls and Protection:**</u>

Engineering Controls: Area should have ventilation to provide fresh air. Local exhaust ventilation is generally preferred because it can control the emissions of the contaminant at the source, preventing dispersion into the general work area. Use mechanical means if necessary to maintain vapor levels below the exposure guidelines. If working in a confined space, follow applicable OSHA regulations.

Respiratory Protection: None required for normal work where adequate ventilation is provided. If engineering controls are not feasible or if exposure exceeds the applicable exposure limits, use a NIOSH-approved cartridge respirator with organic vapor cartridge. Air monitoring is needed to determine actual employee exposure levels. Use a self-contained breathing apparatus in confined spaces and for emergencies.

Eye/face Protection: For normal conditions, wear safety glasses. Where there is reasonable probability of liquid contact, wear splash-proof goggles.

Skin Protection: Use protective gloves such as PVA, Teflon, or Viton. Also, use full protective clothing if there is prolonged or repeated contact of liquid with skin.

Section 9: Physical and Chemical Properties

Physical State: liquid
Color: colorless
Odor: irritating odor
Odor Threshold: 50 ppm
Specific Gravity: 1.619
Initial Boiling Point: 250 F
Freezing Point: ND
Vapor Pressure: 13 mmHg @ 68 F
Vapor Density: 5.76   (air = 1)
Evaporation Rate: very fast
Solubility: 0.015 g/ 100 g @ 77 F in water
Coefficient of water/oil distribution (log P_{ow}):   2.88
pH: NA
Volatile Organic Compounds: <u>wt %</u>:   0   <u>g/L</u>:   0   <u>lbs./gal</u>:   0

Section 10: Stability and Reactivity

Stability: Stable

Conditions to Avoid: Avoid direct sunlight or ultraviolet sources. Avoid open flames, welding arcs, and other high temperature sources which induce thermal decomposition.

Incompatible Materials: Avoid contact with metals such as: aluminum powders, magnesium powders, potassium, sodium, and zinc powder. Avoid unintended contact with amines. Avoid contact with strong bases and strong oxidizers.

Hazardous Decomposition Products: Hydrogen chloride, trace amounts of chlorine and phosgene

Possibility of Hazardous Reactions: No

Section 11: Toxicological Information

Long-term toxicological studies have not been conducted for this product. The following information is available for components of this product.

(Continues)

Product Name: Brakleen® Brake Parts Cleaner (aerosol)
Product Number (s): 05089,05089-6, 05089T, 75089, 85089, 85089AZ

Acute Toxicity:

Component	Oral LD50 (rat)	Dermal LD50 (rabbit)	Inhalation LC50 (rat)
Tetrachloroethylene	2629 mg/kg	> 10 g/kg	5200 mg/kg/4H
Carbon dioxide	No data	No data	470,000 ppm/30M

Chronic Toxicity:

Component	OSHA Carcinogen	IARC Carcinogen	NTP Carcinogen	Irritant	Sensitizer
Tetrachloroethylene	No	Group 2A	Reasonably Anticipated to be a Carcinogen	E (mild) / S (severe)	No
Carbon dioxide	No	No	No	None	No

E – Eye	S – Skin	R - Respiratory

Reproductive Toxicity: No information available
Teratogenicity: No information available
Mutagenicity: Tetrachloroethylene: in vitro studies were negative
            animal studies were negative

Synergistic Effects: No information available

Section 12: Ecological Information

Ecological studies have not been conducted for this product. The following information is available for components of this product.

Ecotoxicity: Tetrachloroethylene -- 96 Hr LC50 Rainbow Trout: 5.28 mg/L (static)
          96 Hr LC50 Fathead minnow: 13.4 mg/L (flow-through)
Persistence / Degradability: Biodegradation under aerobic conditions is below detectable limits. Biodegradation may occur under anaerobic conditions. Biodegradation rate may increase in soil and/or water with acclimation.
Bioaccumulation / Accumulation: Bioconcentration potential is low (BCF less than 100).
Mobility in Environment: Potential for mobility in soil is medium.

Section 13: Disposal Considerations

Waste Classification: The dispensed liquid product is a RCRA hazardous waste for toxicity with the following potential waste codes: U210, F001, F002, D039. Pressurized containers are a D003 reactive waste. (See 40 CFR Part 261.20 – 261.33)
Empty aerosol containers may be recycled. Any liquid product should be managed as a hazardous waste.

All disposal activities must comply with federal, state, provincial and local regulations. Local regulations may be more stringent than state, provincial or national requirements.

Section 14: Transport Information

US DOT (ground): Consumer Commodity, ORM-D

ICAO/IATA (air): Consumer Commodity, ID8000, 9

IMO/IMDG (water): Aerosols, UN1950, 2.2, Limited Quantity

Special Provisions: None

(Continues)

Product Name: **Brakleen® Brake Parts Cleaner** (aerosol)
Product Number (s): 05089, 05089-6, 05089T, 75089, 85089, 85089AZ

Section 15: Regulatory Information

U.S. Federal Regulations:

Toxic Substances Control Act (TSCA):
   All ingredients are either listed on the TSCA inventory or are exempt.

Comprehensive Environmental Response, Compensation and Liability Act (CERCLA):
   Reportable Quantities (RQ's) exist for the following ingredients: Tetrachloroethylene (100 lbs)

   Spills or releases resulting in the loss of any ingredient at or above its RQ require immediate notification to the National Response Center (800-424-8802) and to your Local Emergency Planning Committee.

Superfund Amendments Reauthorization Act (SARA) Title III:
   Section 302 Extremely Hazardous Substances (EHS):   None

Section 311/312 Hazard Categories:	Fire Hazard	No
	Reactive Hazard	No
	Release of Pressure	Yes
	Acute Health Hazard	Yes
	Chronic Health Hazard	Yes

   Section 313 Toxic Chemicals: This product contains the following substances subject to the reporting requirements of Section 313 of Title III of the Superfund Amendments and Reauthorization Act of 1986 and 40 CFR Part 372:
                     Tetrachloroethylene (97.7%)

Clean Air Act:
   Section 112 Hazardous Air Pollutants (HAPs):   Tetrachloroethylene

U.S. State Regulations:

California Safe Drinking Water and Toxic Enforcement Act (Prop 65):
   This product may contain the following chemicals known to the state of
   California to cause cancer, birth defects or other reproductive harm: Tetrachloroethylene

Consumer Products VOC Regulations: This product cannot be sold for use in California and New Jersey. In other states with Consumer Products VOC regulations, this product is compliant as a Brake Cleaner.

State Right to Know:
New Jersey: 127-18-4, 124-38-9
Pennsylvania: 127-18-4, 124-38-9
Massachusetts: 127-18-4, 124-38-9
Rhode Island :   127-18-4, 124-38-9

Canadian Regulations:

Canadian DSL Inventory: All ingredients are either listed on the DSL Inventory or are exempt.

WHMIS Hazard Class: A, D1B, D2A, D2B

European Union Regulations:

RoHS Compliance: This product is compliant with Directive 2002/95/EC of the European Parliament and of the Council of 27 January 2003. This product does not contain any of the restricted substances as listed in Article 4(1) of the RoHS Directive.

Additional Regulatory Information: None

(Continues)

Product Name: Brakleen® Brake Parts Cleaner (aerosol)
Product Number (s): 05089,05089-6, 05089T, 75089, 85089, 85089AZ

Section 16: Other Information

HMIS® (II)	
Health:	2
Flammability:	0
Reactivity:	0
PPE:	B

NFPA

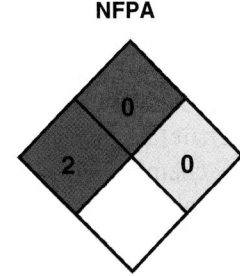

Ratings range from 0 (no hazard) to 4 (severe hazard)

Prepared By: Michelle Rudnick
CRC #: 491G
Revision Date: 01/25/2010

Changes since last revision: MSDS reformatted to meet the requirements of the Canadian Controlled Products Regulations.

The information contained in this document applies to this specific material as supplied. It may not be valid for this material if it is used in combination with any other materials. This information is accurate to the best of CRC Industries' knowledge or obtained from sources believed by CRC to be accurate. Before using any product, read all warnings and directions on the label. For further clarification of any information contained on this MSDS consult your supervisor, a health & safety professional, or CRC Industries.

ACGIH:	American Conference of Governmental Industrial Hygienists	NA:	Not Applicable
CAS:	Chemical Abstract Service	ND:	Not Determined
CFR:	Code of Federal Regulations	NIOSH:	National Institute of Occupational Safety & Health
DOT:	Department of Transportation	NFPA:	National Fire Protection Association
DSL:	Domestic Substance List	NTP:	National Toxicology Program
g/L:	grams per Liter	OSHA:	Occupational Safety and Health Administration
HMIS:	Hazardous Materials Identification System	PMCC:	Pensky-Martens Closed Cup
IARC:	International Agency for Research on Cancer	PPE:	Personal Protection Equipment
IATA:	International Air Transport Association	ppm:	Parts per Million
ICAO:	International Civil Aviation Organization	RoHS:	Restriction of Hazardous Substances
IMDG:	International Maritime Dangerous Goods	STEL:	Short Term Exposure Limit
IMO:	International Maritime Organization	TCC:	Tag Closed Cup
lbs./gal:	pounds per gallon	TWA:	Time Weighted Average
LC:	Lethal Concentration	WHMIS:	Workplace Hazardous Materials Information System
LD:	Lethal Dose		

Cleaning Toxic Dust Safely

<u>Toxic dust</u> is any dust that may contain fine particles that could be harmful to humans or the environment. If you are unsure as to the toxicity of dust, then you should always treat it as toxic and take the precautions identified in the MSDS or shop procedures. Brake and clutch dust are potential toxic dusts that automotive shops must manage. The dust is made up of very fine particles that can easily spread and contaminate an area. One of the more common sources of toxic dust is inside drum brakes and manual transmission bell housings.

It is a good idea to avoid all dust if possible, whether it is classified as toxic or not. If you do have to work with dust, never use compressed air to blow it from components or parts and always use PPE such as face masks, eye protection, and gloves. If you are cleaning up your area after a repair, do not dry sweep dust;

instead, use a low-pressure wet cleaning method. Such methods include a soap and water solution used in a dedicated portable wash station, a low-pressure aerosol brake cleaning solution, or a pump spray bottle filled with water. You may also use a HEPA vacuum cleaner to collect dust and clean equipment. HEPA stands for high-efficiency particulate absorbing. HEPA filters can trap very small particles and prevent them from being redistributed into the surrounding air.

After completing a servicing or repair task on a vehicle, there is often dirt left behind. The chemicals present in this dirt usually contain toxic chemicals that can build up and cause health problems. To keep the levels of dirt to a minimum, clean up dirt immediately after the task is complete. The vigorous action of sweeping causes the dirt to rise; therefore, when sweeping the floor, use a soft broom that pushes, rather than flicks, the dirt forward. Create smaller dirt piles and dispose of them frequently. Another successful way of cleaning shop dirt is to use a

water hose. The waste water must be caught in a settling pit and not run into a storm water drain.

Various tools have been developed to clean toxic dust from vehicle components. The most common one is the brake wash station. It uses an aqueous solution to wet down and wash the dust into a collection basin. The basin needs periodic maintenance to properly dispose of the accumulated sludge. This tool is probably the simplest way to effectively deal with hazardous dust because it is easy to set up, use, and store.

Another such tool uses a vacuum cleaner that has a large cone attachment at the nozzle end. The base of the cone is open so the brake assembly can fit into the cone. A compressed air nozzle, which is also attached to the inside of the cone, is used to loosen dirt particles. The particles are drawn into the cleaner via a very fine filter. Domestic vacuum cleaners are not suitable for this application because their filters are not fine enough to capture very small dust particles.

To safely clean brake dust, follow the steps in **SKILL DRILL 3-3**:

1. When performing any cleaning tasks on brake or clutch components, always wear a face mask, gloves, and eye protection. (**Photo 1**)

2. Position the brake wash station under the bottom of the backing plate. When cleaning drum brakes, remove the brake drum and check for the presence of dust and brake fluid. When cleaning a clutch, position the wash station underneath the bell housing. (**Photo 2**)

3. Turn on the wash station pump and paint the solution over the components to wet and clean the components and remove the dust. Any toxic dust will be washed down and caught in the wash station. (**Photo 3**)

4. Periodically dispose of the residue in an approved manner. (**Photo 4**)

Used Engine Oil and Fluids

Used engine oil and fluids are liquids that have been drained from the vehicle, usually during servicing operations. Used oil and fluids will often contain dangerous chemicals and impurities and need to be safely recycled or disposed of in an environmentally friendly way **FIGURE 3-14**. There are laws and regulations that control the way in which they are to be handled and disposed. The shop will have policies and procedures that describe how you should handle and dispose of used engine oil and fluids. Be careful not to mix incompatible fluids such as used engine oil and used coolant. Generally speaking,

> ## TECHNICIAN TIP
>
> - Some vehicle components, including brake and clutch linings, contain asbestos, which, despite having very good heat properties, is toxic. Asbestos dust causes lung cancer. Complications from breathing the dust may not show until decades after exposure.
> - Airborne dust in the shop can also cause breathing problems such as asthma and throat infections.
> - Never cause dust from vehicle components to be blown into the air. It can stay floating for many hours, meaning that other people will breathe the dust unknowingly.
> - Wear protective gloves whenever using solvents.
> - If you are unfamiliar with a solvent or a cleaner, refer to the MSDS for information about its correct use and applicable hazards.
> - Always wash your hands thoroughly with soap and water after performing repair tasks on brake and clutch components.
> - Always wash work clothes separately from other clothes so that toxic dust does not transfer from one garment to another.
> - Always wear protective clothing and the appropriate safety equipment.

> ## TECHNICIAN TIP
>
> Whenever using an atomizer with solvents and cleaners, make sure there is adequate exhaust ventilation. Wear appropriate breathing apparatus and eye protection.

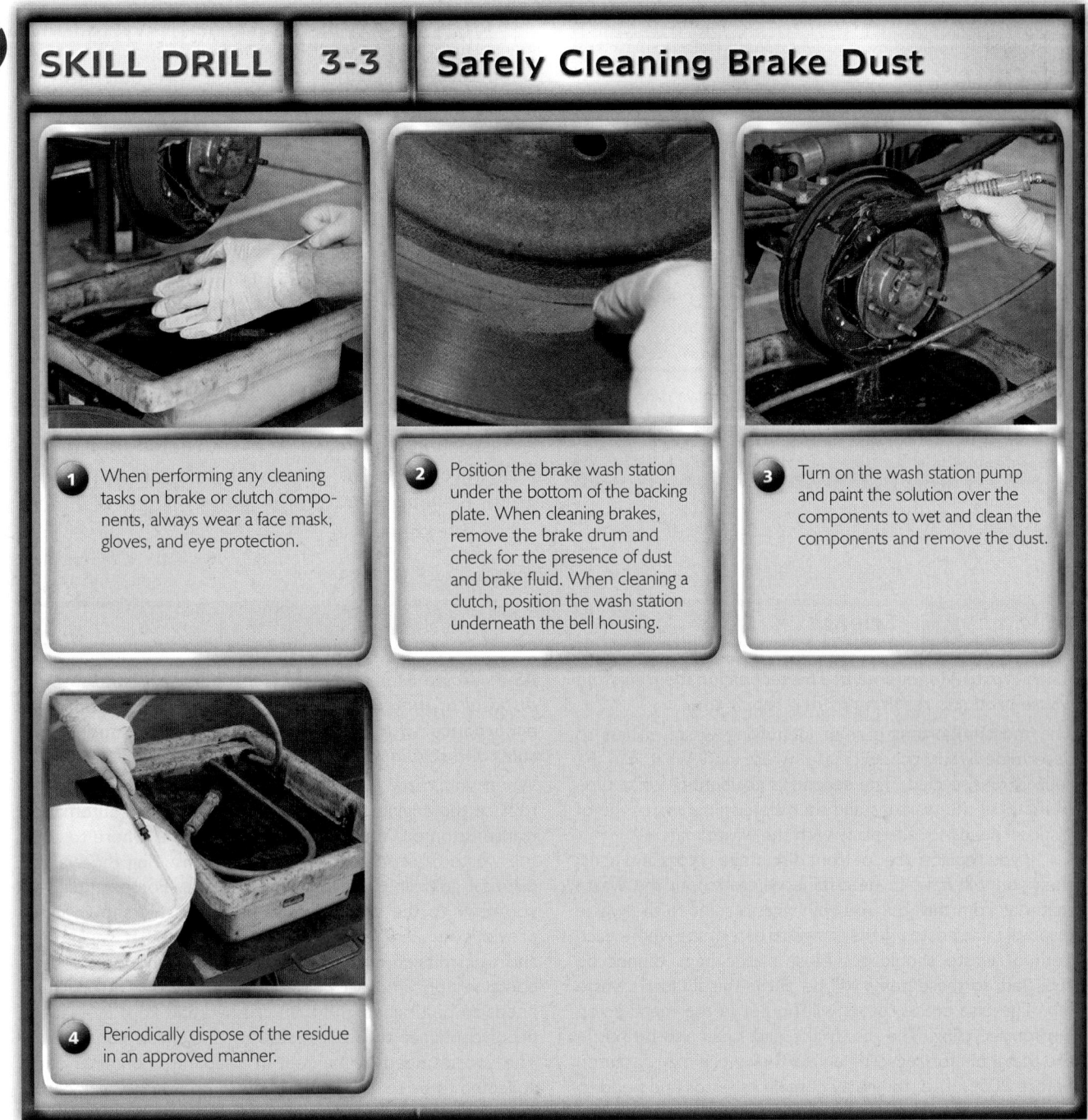

SKILL DRILL | 3-3 | Safely Cleaning Brake Dust

1. When performing any cleaning tasks on brake or clutch components, always wear a face mask, gloves, and eye protection.

2. Position the brake wash station under the bottom of the backing plate. When cleaning brakes, remove the brake drum and check for the presence of dust and brake fluid. When cleaning a clutch, position the wash station underneath the bell housing.

3. Turn on the wash station pump and paint the solution over the components to wet and clean the components and remove the dust.

4. Periodically dispose of the residue in an approved manner.

petroleum products can be mixed together. Follow your local, state, and federal regulations when disposing of waste fluids.

Used engine oil is a hazardous material containing many impurities that can damage your skin. Coming into frequent or prolonged contact with used engine oil can cause dermatitis and other skin disorders, including some forms of cancer. Avoid direct contact as much as possible by always using gloves and other protective clothing, which should be cleaned or replaced regularly. Using a

barrier-type hand lotion will also help protect your hands as well as make cleaning them much easier. Also follow safe work practices, which minimize the possibility of accidental spills. Keeping a high standard of personal hygiene and cleanliness is important so that you get into the habit of washing off harmful materials as soon as possible after contact. If you have been in contact with used engine oil, you should regularly inspect your skin for signs of damage or deterioration. If you have any concerns, see your doctor.

FIGURE 3-14 Used oil and fluids will often contain dangerous chemicals and need to be safely recycled or disposed of in an environmentally friendly way.

Shop Safety Inspections

Shop safety inspections are valuable ways of identifying unsafe equipment, materials, or activities so they can be corrected to prevent accidents or injuries. The inspection can be formalized by using inspection sheets to check specific items, or they can be general walk-arounds where you consciously look for problems that can be corrected. Some of the commons things to look for would be items blocking emergency exits or walkways, poor safety signage, unsafe storage of flammable goods, tripping hazards, faulty or unsafe equipment or tools, missing fire extinguishers, clutter, spills, unsafe shop practices, and people not wearing the correct PPE. Formal and informal safety inspections should be held regularly. For example, an inspection sheet might be used weekly or monthly to formally evaluate the shop, while informal inspections might be held daily to catch issues that are of a more immediate nature.

Applied   Science

AS-4: Waste Management: The technician identifies the waste products resulting from a repair task.

The most important part of identifying waste is first to determine what products are waste and what can be reused or recycled. The second is to identify what type of material the waste is and then determine what type of disposal needs to take place with the waste material.

If you replace a set of front disc brake rotors and pads, then you will have to determine where to put the waste material from this job. You will have to refer to the waste disposal table posted in the garage to determine where each item of waste should go. Most plastic bags cannot be recycled, so these items will be put in the standard waste bin. The disc brake rotors will be put in the metal scrap bin for recycling. The disc brake pads may also be put in the metal bin for recycling unless they were manufactured before 2004. If so, they may contain asbestos and need to be put in a plastic airtight bag for removal by a licensed contractor.

AS-5: Waste Management: The technician handles the disposal of materials such as automotive lubricants in accordance with applicable federal, state, and local rules and regulations.

When you carry out a major service, you may have to replace the engine oil and oil filter, coolant, and automatic transmission oil. You will have to determine where to put the waste material from this job by consulting the waste disposal guidelines posted in the garage. For example, if you refer to the sample waste disposal table shown in a previous Applied Science box, you can see that engine oil and transmission oil need to be collected and stored in a container for removal by a licensed contractor. The oil filter needs to be drained and then crushed and kept in a leak-proof container to be collected by a licensed contractor. The coolant needs to be kept in a separate container and collected to be recycled by a licensed operator. Cardboard boxes that oil or air filters may come in can be put in the recycling bin for recycling.

Wrap-up

Ready for Review

- Your employer is responsible for maintaining a safe work environment; you are responsible for working safely.
- Always wear the correct personal protective equipment, such as gloves or hearing protection.
- Accidents and injuries can be avoided by safe work practices.
- Every shop should mark evacuation routes; always know the evacuation route for your shop.
- OSHA is a federal agency that oversees safe workplace environments and practices.
- The EPA monitors and enforces issues related to environmental safety.
- Shop policies and procedures are designed to ensure compliance with laws and regulations, create a safe working environment, and guide shop practice.
- Identify hazards and hazardous materials in your work environment.
- Safety signs include a signal word, background color, text, and a pictorial message.
- Shop safety equipment includes handrails, machinery guards, painted lines, soundproof rooms, adequate ventilation, gas extraction hoses, doors and gates, and temporary barriers.
- Air quality is an important safety concern.
- Carbon monoxide and carbon dioxide from running engines can create a hazardous work environment.
- Electrical safety in a shop is important to prevent shocks, burns, fires, and explosions.
- Portable electrical equipment should be the proper voltage and should always be inspected for damage.
- Use caution when plugging in or using a portable shop light.
- Shop layouts should be well planned to maximize safety.
- Fuels and fuel vapors are potential fire hazards.
- Use fuel retrievers when draining fuel and have a spill response kit nearby.
- Fuel, oxygen, and heat must all be present for fire to occur.
- Types of fires are classified as A, B, C, D, or K, and fire extinguishers match them accordingly.
- Do not fight a fire unless you can do so safely.
- Operating a fire extinguisher involves the PASS method: pull, aim, squeeze, and sweep.
- Eyewash stations and emergency showers allow flushing of chemicals or other irritants.
- Material safety data sheets contain important information on each hazardous material in the shop.
- Vacuuming and using water are the safest methods of cleaning dust or dirt that may be toxic.
- Used engine oil and fluids must be handled and disposed of properly.
- Shop safety inspections ensure that safety policies and procedures are being followed.

Key Terms

double-insulated Tools or appliances that are designed in such a way that no single failure can result in a dangerous voltage coming into contact with the outer casing of the device.

Environmental Protection Agency (EPA) Federal government agency that deals with issues related to environmental safety.

hazard Anything that could hurt you or someone else.

hazardous environment A place where hazards exist.

hazardous material Any material that poses an unreasonable risk of damage or injury to persons, property, or the environment if it is not properly controlled during handling, storage, manufacture, processing, packaging, use and disposal, or transportation.

material safety data sheet (MSDS) A sheet that provides information about handling, use, and storage of a material that may be hazardous.

Occupational Safety and Health Administration (OSHA) Government agency created to provide national leadership in occupational safety and health.

personal protective equipment (PPE) Safety equipment designed to protect the technician, such as safety boots, gloves, clothing, protective eyewear, and hearing protection.

policy A guiding principle that sets the shop direction.

procedure A list of the steps required to get the same result each time a task or activity is performed.

threshold limit value (TLV) The maximum allowable concentration of a given material in the surrounding air.

toxic dust Any dust that may contain fine particles that could be harmful to humans or the environment.

ASE-Type Questions

1. Tech A says that exposure to solvents may have long-term effects. Tech B says that accidents are almost always avoidable. Who is correct?
   a. Tech A
   b. Tech B
   c. Both A and B
   d. Neither A nor B

2. Tech A says that after an accident you should take measures to avoid it in the future. Tech B says that it is OK to block an exit for a shop. Who is correct?
   a. Tech A
   b. Tech B
   c. Both A and B
   d. Neither A nor B

3. Tech A says that both OSHA and the EPA can inspect facilities for violations. Tech B says that a shop safety rule does not have to be reviewed once put in place. Who is correct?
   a. Tech A
   b. Tech B
   c. Both A and B
   d. Neither A nor B

4. Tech A says that all hazards can be removed from a shop. Tech B says that it is a good practice to disconnect an air gun when inspecting it. Who is correct?
   a. Tech A
   b. Tech B
   c. Both A and B
   d. Neither A nor B

5. Tech A says that both caution and danger indicate a potentially hazardous situation. Tech B says that an exhaust extraction hose is not needed if the vehicle is only going to run for a few minutes. Who is correct?
   a. Tech A
   b. Tech B
   c. Both A and B
   d. Neither A nor B

6. Tech A says that if you are unsure of what personal protective equipment (PPE) to use to perform a job, you should just use what is nearby. Tech B says that air tools are less likely to shock you than electrically powered tools. Who is correct?
   a. Tech A
   b. Tech B
   c. Both A and B
   d. Neither A nor B

7. Tech A says that firefighting equipment includes safety glasses. Tech B says that a class A fire extinguisher can be used to fight an electrical fire only. Who is correct?
   a. Tech A
   b. Tech B
   c. Both A and B
   d. Neither A nor B

8. Tech A says that a material safety data sheet (MSDS) contains information on procedures to repair a vehicle. Tech B says that you only need an MSDS if your safety may be in danger. Who is correct?
   a. Tech A
   b. Tech B
   c. Both A and B
   d. Neither A nor B

9. Tech A says that a good way to clean dust off brakes is with compressed air. Tech B says that asbestos may be in current auto parts. Who is correct?
   a. Tech A
   b. Tech B
   c. Both A and B
   d. Neither A nor B

10. Tech A says that when cleaning brake and clutch components, the wash station should be placed directly under the component. Tech B says that you should follow state and local regulations when disposing of used oil. Who is correct?
    a. Tech A
    b. Tech B
    c. Both A and B
    d. Neither A nor B

CHAPTER 4

NATEF Tasks

Required Supplemental Tasks
Shop and Personal Safety

Page

- Comply with the required use of safety glasses, ear protection, gloves and shoes during lab/shop activities.

64–7(

- Identify and wear appropriate clothing for lab/shop activities.

64–7(

- Secure hair and jewelry for lab/shop activities.

70

- Utilize proper ventilation procedures for working within the lab/shop area.

70–7

Knowledge Objectives

After reading this chapter, you will be able to:
1. Identify the standard items of personal protective equipment that should be worn in the shop. (pp 64–70)
2. Describe how to use personal protective equipment to reduce the risk of injury in the workplace. (pp 64–70)
3. Explain how to apply injury protection practices. (pp 70–71)
4. Explain the procedure for performing CPR. (p 72)
5. Explain the procedures for applying first aid. (pp 71–75)

Personal Safety

Skills Objectives

There are no skills objectives for this chapter.

Introduction

Personal protective equipment (PPE) is equipment used to block the entry of hazardous materials into the body or to protect the body from injury. PPE includes clothing, shoes, safety glasses, hearing protection, masks, and respirators **FIGURE 4-1**. Before you undertake any activity, think about all potential hazards and select the correct PPE based on the risk associated with the activity. For example, if you are going to change hydraulic brake fluid, put on some gloves to protect your skin from chemicals.

FIGURE 4-1 Personal protective equipment (PPE) includes clothing, shoes, safety glasses, hearing protection, masks, and respirators.

As you go through this chapter, you will learn how to identify the correct PPE for a given activity and how to wear it safely. It is important that the PPE you use fits correctly and is appropriate for the task you are undertaking. For example, if the task requires you to wear eye protection and specifies that you should use a full face shield, do not try to cut corners and only wear safety glasses. You also need to make sure the PPE you are using is worn correctly. For example, a hairnet that does not capture all of your hair is not protecting you adequately.

Personal Protective Equipment

Protective Clothing

Protective clothing includes items like shirts, pants, shoes, and gloves. These items are your first line of defense against injuries and accidents and must be worn when performing any work. Always make sure protective clothing is kept clean and in good condition. You should replace any clothing that is not in good condition, since it is no longer able to fully protect you.

> **TECHNICIAN TIP**
>
> Each shop activity will require specific clothing depending on its nature. Research and identify what specific type of clothing is required for every activity you undertake. Wear appropriate clothing for various activities according to the shop's policy and procedures.

You are the Automotive Technician

It's your first day on the job and you are asked to report to the main office where your new supervisor gives you your personal protective equipment (PPE). Before you can begin working on the shop floor, you are given training on the proper use of personal protective equipment.

1. Which type of gloves should be worn when handling solvents and cleaners?
2. Why must safety glasses be worn at all times in the shop?
3. Why should rings, watches and jewelry never be worn in the shop?
4. When should hearing protection be worn?
5. What types of tasks require that a face shield be worn?
6. Why must hair be tied up or restrained in the shop?
7. Which type of eye protection should be worn when using or assisting a person using an oxyacetylene welder?

Work Clothing

Always wear appropriate work clothing. Whether this is a one-piece coverall/overall or a separate shirt and pants, the clothes you work in should be comfortable enough to allow you to move, without being loose enough to catch on machinery. The material must be flame retardant and strong enough that it cannot be easily torn. A flap must cover buttons or snaps. If you wear a long sleeve shirt, the cuffs must be close fitting, without being tight. Pants should not have cuffs, so that hot debris cannot become trapped in the fabric.

Care of Clothing

Always wash your work clothes separately from your other clothes. Start a new working day with clean work clothes and change out of contaminated clothing as soon as possible. It is a good idea to keep a spare set of work clothes in the workshop in case a toxic or corrosive fluid is spilled on the clothes you are wearing.

Footwear

The proper footwear provides protection against items falling on your feet, chemicals, cuts, abrasions, and slips. The soles of your shoes must be acid and slip resistant, and the uppers must be made from a puncture-proof material such as leather. Some shops and technicians prefer safety shoes with a steel cap to protect the toes **FIGURE 4-2**. Always wear shoes that comply with your local shop standards.

Headgear

Headgear includes items like hairnets, caps, and hard hats. They help protect you from getting your hair caught in rotating machinery and protect your head from knocks or bumps. For example, your hard hat can protect you from bumping your head on a vehicle when the vehicle is raised on a hoist. It is also good practice to wear a cap to hold longer hair in place and to keep it clean when working under a vehicle. Some caps are designed specifically with additional padding on the top to provide extra protection against bumps.

Hand Protection

Hands are a very complex and sensitive part of the body with many nerves, tendons, and blood vessels. They are susceptible to injury and damage. Nearly every activity performed on vehicles requires the use of your hands, which provides many opportunities for injury. Whenever possible, wear gloves to protect your hands. There are many types of gloves available and their applications vary greatly. It is important to wear the correct type of glove for the various activities you perform.

Chemical Gloves

Heavy-duty and impenetrable chemical gloves should always be worn when using solvents and cleaners. They should also be worn when working on batteries. Chemical gloves should extend to the middle of your forearm to reduce the risk of chemicals splashing onto your skin **FIGURE 4-3**. Always inspect chemical gloves for holes or cracks before using them, and replace them when they become worn.

Some chemical gloves are also slightly heat resistant. This type of chemical glove is suitable for use when removing radiator caps and mixing coolant.

FIGURE 4-2 The proper footwear provides protection against items falling on your feet, chemicals, cuts, abrasions, and slips.

FIGURE 4-3 Chemical gloves should extend to the middle of your forearm to reduce the risk of chemical burns.

Leather Gloves

Leather gloves will protect your hands from burns when welding or handling hot components **FIGURE 4-4**. You should also use them when removing steel from a storage rack and when handling sharp objects. When using leather gloves for handling hot components, be aware of the potential for **heat buildup**. Heat buildup occurs when the leather glove can no longer absorb or reflect heat, and heat is transferred to the inside of the leather glove. At this point, the leather gloves' ability to protect you from the heat is reduced and you will need to stop work, remove the leather gloves, and allow them to cool down before continuing to work. Also, avoid picking up very hot metal with leather gloves because it causes the leather to harden, making it less flexible during use. If very hot metal must be moved, it would be better to use an appropriate pair of pliers.

Light-Duty Gloves

Light-duty gloves should be used to protect your hands from exposure to greases and oils **FIGURE 4-5**. Light-duty gloves are typically disposable and can be made from a few different materials, such as nitrile, latex, and even plastic. Some people have allergies to these materials. If you have an allergic reaction when wearing these gloves, try using a glove made from a different material.

General-Purpose Cloth Gloves

Cloth gloves are designed to be worn in cold temperatures, particularly during winter, so that cold tools do not stick to your skin **FIGURE 4-6**. Over time, cloth gloves will accumulate dirt and grime so you will need to wash them regularly. Regularly inspect cloth gloves for damage and wear, and replace them when required. Cloth gloves are not an effective barrier against chemicals or oils, so never use them for that purpose.

Barrier Cream

Barrier cream looks and feels like a moisturizing cream, but it has a specific formula to provide extra protection from chemicals and oils. Barrier cream prevents chemicals from being absorbed into your skin and should be applied to your hands before you begin work **FIGURE 4-7**. Even the slightest exposure to certain chemicals can lead to dermatitis, a painful skin irritation. Never use a standard moisturizer as a replacement for proper barrier cream. Barrier cream also makes it easier to clean your hands because it can prevent fine particles from adhering to your skin.

Cleaning Your Hands

When cleaning your hands, use only specialized hand cleaners, which protect your skin **FIGURE 4-8**. Your hands are porous and easily absorb liquids on contact. Never use solvents such as gasoline or kerosene to clean your hands,

FIGURE 4-5 Light-duty gloves should be used to protect your hands from exposure to greases and oils.

FIGURE 4-4 Leather gloves will protect your hands from burns when welding or handling hot components.

FIGURE 4-6 Cloth gloves work well in cold temperatures, particularly during winter, so that cold tools do not stick to your skin.

because they can be absorbed into the bloodstream and remove the skin's natural protective oils.

Ear Protection

Ear protection should be worn when sound levels exceed 85 decibels, when you are working around operating machinery for any period of time, or when the equipment you are using produces loud noise. If you have to raise your voice to be heard by a person who is 2' away from you, then the sound level is about 85 decibels or more. Ear protection comes in two forms: One type covers the entire outer ear, and the other is fitted into the ear canal **FIGURE 4-9**. Generally speaking, the in-the-ear style has higher noise-reduction ratings. If the noise is not excessively loud, either type of protection will work. If you are in an extremely loud environment, you will want to verify that the option you choose is rated high enough.

Breathing Devices

Dust and chemicals from your workspace can be absorbed into the body when you breathe. When working in an environment where dust is present or where the task you are performing will produce dust, you should always wear some form of breathing device. There are two types of breathing devices: disposable dust masks and respirators.

Disposable Dust Mask

A disposable dust mask is made from paper with a wire-reinforced edge that is held to your face with an elastic strip. It covers your mouth and nose and is disposed of at the completion of the task **FIGURE 4-10**. This type of mask should only be used as a dust mask and should not be used if chemicals, such as paint solvents, are present in the atmosphere.

FIGURE 4-7 Barrier cream helps prevent chemicals from being absorbed into your skin and should be applied to your hands before you begin work.

FIGURE 4-9 Ear protection comes in two forms: One type covers the entire outer ear, and the other is fitted into the ear canal.

FIGURE 4-8 When cleaning your hands, use only specialized hand cleaners, which protect your skin.

FIGURE 4-10 A disposable dust mask covers your mouth and nose and is disposed of at the completion of the task.

Respirator

The **respirator** has removable cartridges that can be changed according to the type of contaminant being filtered. Always make sure the cartridge is the correct type for the contaminant in the atmosphere. For example, when chemicals are present, use the appropriate chemical filter in your respirator. The cartridges should be replaced according to the manufacturer's recommendation to ensure their effectiveness. To be completely effective, the respirator mask must make a good seal onto your face **FIGURE 4-11**.

Eye Protection

Eyes are very sensitive organs and they need to be protected against damage and injury. There are many things in the workshop environment that can damage or injure eyes, such as high-velocity particles coming from a grinder or high-intensity light coming from a welder. In fact, the American National Standards Institute (ANSI) reports that 2000 workers per day suffer on-the-job eye injuries. Always select the appropriate eye protection for the work you are undertaking. Sometimes this may mean that more than one type of protection is required. For example, when grinding, you should wear a pair of safety glasses underneath your face shield for added protection.

Safety Glasses

The most common type of eye protection is a pair of safety glasses, which must be marked with "Z87" on the lens and frame. Safety glasses have built-in side shields to help protect your eyes from the side. Approved safety glasses should be worn whenever you are in a workshop. They are designed to help protect your eyes from direct impact or debris damage **FIGURE 4-12**. The only time they should be removed is when you are using other eye protection equipment. Prescription and tinted safety glasses are also available. Tinted safety glasses are designed to be worn outside in bright sunlight conditions. Never wear them indoors or in low light conditions because they reduce your ability to see.

Welding Helmet

Wear a **welding helmet** when using or assisting a person using an electric welder. The light from a welding arc is very bright and contains high levels of ultraviolet radiation. The lens on a welding helmet has heavily tinted glass to reduce the intensity of the light from the welding tip, allowing you to see the task you are performing more clearly **FIGURE 4-13**. Lenses come in a variety of ratings depending on the type of welding you are doing; always make sure you are using a properly rated lens.

FIGURE 4-11 To be completely effective, the respirator mask must make a good seal onto your face.

FIGURE 4-12 Safety glasses are designed to protect your eyes from direct impact or debris damage.

FIGURE 4-13 The lens on a welding helmet has heavily tinted glass to reduce the intensity of the light from the welding tip, allowing you to see what you are doing.

The remainder of the helmet is made from a durable material that blocks any other light from reaching your face. Welding helmets that tint automatically when an arc is struck are also available. Their big advantage is that you do not have to lift and lower the lens by hand.

Gas Welding Goggles

<u>Gas welding goggles</u> can be worn instead of a welding mask when using or assisting a person using an oxyacetylene welder **FIGURE 4-14**. The eyepieces are available in heavily tinted versions, but not as tinted as those used in an electric welding helmet. There is no ultraviolet radiation from an oxyacetylene flame, so the welding helmet is not required. However, the flame is bright enough to damage your eyes, so always use goggles of the correct rating.

Full Face Shield

It is necessary to use a full face shield when using solvents and cleaners, epoxies, and resins or when working on a battery **FIGURE 4-15**. The clear mask of the face shield allows you to see all that you are doing, but will protect your entire face from chemical burns should there be any splashes or battery explosions. It is also recommended that you use a full face shield combined with safety goggles when using a bench or angle grinder.

Safety Goggles

Safety goggles provide much the same eye protection as safety glasses but with added protection against harmful chemicals that may splash up behind the lenses of glasses **FIGURE 4-16**. Goggles also provide additional protection from foreign particles. Safety goggles must be worn when servicing air-conditioning systems or any other system that contains pressurized gas. Goggles can sometimes fog up when in use; if this occurs, use one of the special anti-fog cleaning fluids or cloths to clean them.

FIGURE 4-14 Gas welding goggles can be worn instead of a welding helmet when using or assisting a person using an oxyacetylene welder.

FIGURE 4-15 It is necessary to use a full face shield when using a grinder, solvents and cleaners, epoxies, and resins or when working on a battery.

FIGURE 4-16 Safety goggles provide much the same eye protection as safety glasses but with added protection against any harmful fluid that may find its way behind the lenses.

Hair Containment

It is easy to get hair caught in rotating machinery, such as drill presses or running engines, and it can happen very quickly. If your hair gets caught in the machinery, you can be pulled into the machinery and injured or killed. Hair should always be tied back and contained within a hairnet or cap.

Your workshop will have policies and procedures relating to appropriate hairstyles for shop activities. Research the policy and procedures to determine appropriate hairstyles for activities. Always wear your hair according to the policy and procedures. Use hairnets, caps, or elastic bands as required for each activity.

Watches and Jewelry

When in a workshop environment, watches, rings, and jewelry present a number of hazards. They can get caught in rotating machinery, and because they are mainly constructed from metal, they can conduct electricity. Imagine leaning over a running engine with a dangling necklace; it could get caught in the fan belt and be ripped from your neck; not only will it get destroyed, but it could seriously injure you. A ring or watch could inadvertently short out an electrical circuit, heat up quickly and severely burn you, or cause a spark that may make the battery explode. A ring can also get caught on moving

Applied Science

AS-1: Safety: The technician follows all safety regulations and applicable procedures while performing the task.

Using a bench grinder to grind down a steel component is a simple everyday activity in shops. In terms of its potential safety implications, it carries significant risk of injury. Before beginning the task, you must ensure that the machinery is safe and ready to use. Inspect and/or adjust the guards/shields, grinding wheels, electrical cord, etc. From a personal perspective, you must make sure your clothing is suitable and safe for the task. Clothing cannot be loose, as it may get caught in the grinder; it must be made of flame-retardant material, due to the risk of ignition from sparks. Long hair must be tied back or contained within a hairnet or cap due to the risk of it getting caught in rotating machinery.

Various items of PPE are required to safely carry out this task: safety goggles to protect against foreign objects entering the eyes, ear protection to guard against hearing damage due to excessive noise, steel-capped boots to prevent injury from falling heavy objects, and heavy-duty gloves to protect against skin contact with grinding wheels or burns due to heat buildup in the metal component.

parts, breaking the finger bone or even ripping the finger out of the hand. To be safe, always remove watches, rings, and jewelry before starting work. Not only is it safer to remove these items, but your valuables will not get damaged or lost.

▶ Injury Protection Practices
Safe Attitude

Develop a safe attitude toward your work. You should always think "safety first" and then act safely. Think ahead about what you are doing, and put in place specific measures to protect yourself and those around you. For example, you could ask yourself the following questions:

- What could go wrong?
- What measures can I take to ensure that nothing goes wrong?
- What PPE should I use?
- Have I been trained to use this piece of equipment?
- Is the equipment I'm using safe?

Answering these questions and taking appropriate action before you begin will help you work safely.

Proper Ventilation

Proper ventilation is required for working in the shop area. The key to proper ventilation is to ensure that any task or procedure that may produce dangerous or toxic fumes is recognized so that measures can be put in place to provide adequate ventilation. Ventilation can be provided by natural means, such as by opening doors and windows to provide air flow for low-exposure situations. However, in high-exposure situations, such as vehicles running in the shop, a mechanical means of ventilation is required; an example is an exhaust extraction system.

Parts cleaning areas or areas where solvents and chemicals are used should also have good general ventilation, and if required, additional exhaust hoods or fans should be installed to remove dangerous fumes. In some cases, such as when spraying paint, it may be necessary to use a personal respirator in addition to proper ventilation.

TECHNICIAN TIP

Before beginning a task, research the proper ventilation procedure for working within the shop area. Use the correct ventilation equipment and procedures for the activities you are working on within the shop area.

Lifting

Whenever you lift something, there is always the possibility of injury; however, by lifting correctly, you reduce the chance of something going wrong. Before lifting anything, you can reduce the risk of injury by breaking down the load into smaller quantities, asking for assistance if required, or possibly using a mechanical device to assist the lift. If you have to bend down to lift something, you should bend your knees to lower your body; do not bend over with straight legs because this can damage your back **FIGURE 4-17**. Place your feet about shoulder width apart and lift the item by straightening your legs while keeping your back as straight as possible.

Housekeeping and Orderliness

Good housekeeping is about always making sure the shop and your work surroundings are neat and kept in good order. Trash and liquid spills should be quickly cleaned up, tools need to be cleaned and put away after use, spare parts need to be stored correctly, and generally everything needs to have a safe place to be kept. You should carry out good housekeeping practices while working, not just after a job is completed. For example, get rid of trash as it accumulates, clean up spills when they happen, and put tools away when you are finished

Safety

Never lift anything that is too heavy for you to comfortably lift, and always seek assistance if you need help.

FIGURE 4-17 Prevent back injuries when lifting heavy objects by crouching with your legs slightly apart, standing close to the object, and positioning yourself so that the center of gravity is between your feet.

working with them. It is also good practice to periodically perform a deep clean of the shop so that any neglected areas are taken care of.

Slip, Trip, and Fall Hazards

Slip, trip, and fall hazards are ever present in the shop, and they can be caused by trash, tools and equipment, or liquid spills being left lying around. Always be on the lookout for hazards that can cause slips, trips, or falls. Floors and steps can become slippery so they should be kept clean and have anti-slip coatings applied to them. High-visibility strips with anti-slip coatings can be applied to the edge of step treads to reduce the hazard.

Clean up liquid spills immediately and mark the area with wet floor signs until the floor is dry. Make sure the workshop has good lighting so hazards are easy to spot, and keep walkways clear from obstruction. Think about what you are doing and make sure the work area is free of slip, trip, and fall hazards as you work.

▶ First Aid Principles

The following information is designed to provide you with an awareness of basic first aid principles and the importance of first aid training courses. You will find general information about how to take care of someone who is injured. However, this information is only a guide. It is not a substitute for training or professional medical assistance. Always seek professional advice when tending to an injured person.

First aid is the immediate care given to an injured or suddenly ill person. Learning first aid skills is valuable in the workplace in case an accident or medical emergency arises. First aid courses are available through many organizations, such as the Emergency Care and Safety Institute (ECSI). It is strongly advised that you seek out a certified first aid course and become certified in first aid. The following information highlights some of the principles of first aid.

In the event of an accident, the possibility of injury to the rescuer or further injury to the victim must be assessed. The first step is to survey the scene. While doing this, try to determine what happened, what dangers may still be present, and the best actions to take. Remove the injured person from a dangerous area only if it is safe for you to do so. When dealing with electrocution or electrical burns, make sure the electrical supply is switched off before attempting any assistance.

Always perform first aid techniques as quickly as is safely possible after an injury. When breathing or the heart has stopped, brain damage can occur within

4 to 6 minutes. The degree of brain damage will increase with each passing minute, so make sure you know what to do, and do it quickly.

> **TECHNICIAN TIP**
>
> Three important rules of first aid are:
> 1. Know what you must not do.
> 2. Know what you must do.
> 3. If you are not sure what procedures to follow, send for trained medical assistance.

First Aid Concepts

Prompt care and treatment prior to the arrival of emergency medical assistance can sometimes mean the difference between life and death. The goals of first aid are to make the immediate environment as safe as possible, preserve the life of the patient, prevent the injury from worsening, prevent additional injuries from occurring, protect the unconscious, promote recovery, comfort the injured, prevent any delay in treatment, and provide the best possible care for the injured person.

When attending to an injured victim, always send for assistance. Make sure the person who stays with the injured victim is more experienced in first aid than the messenger. If you are the only person available, request medical assistance as soon as reasonably possible. When you approach the scene of an accident or emergency, do the following:

1. **Danger:** Make sure there are no other dangers, and assist only if it is safe to do so.
2. **Response:** Check to see if the victim is responsive and breathing. If responsive, ask the victim if he or she needs help. If the victim does not respond, he or she is unresponsive.
3. Have a bystander call 9-1-1. If alone, call 9-1-1 yourself.
4. If unresponsive and not breathing, place your hands in the center of the victim's chest and provide 30 chest compressions hard and fast **FIGURE 4-18**.
5. Tilt the victim's head back and lift the chin to open the airway. Give one rescue breath lasting 1 second, take a normal breath for yourself, and then give the victim another breath lasting 1 second. Each rescue breath should make the victim's chest rise.

FIGURE 4-18 Chest compressions.

6. Repeat the compression and breath cycles until an AED is available or EMS personnel arrive.
7. Once an automated external defibrillator (AED) arrives, expose the victim's chest and turn on the AED. Attach the AED pads. Ensure that no one touches the victim. Follow the audio and visual prompts from the AED. If no shock is advised, resume CPR immediately (five sets of 30 compressions and two breaths). If a shock is advised, do not touch the victim and give one shock. Or, shock as advised by AED. Resume immediately 30 compressions and two breaths.

Bleeding

A wound that is severely bleeding is serious. If the bleeding is allowed to continue, the victim may collapse or die. Bleeding is divided into two categories: external and internal. **External bleeding** is the loss of blood from an external wound where blood can be seen escaping. **Internal bleeding** is the loss of blood into a body cavity from a wound with no obvious sign of blood.

Before providing first aid, make sure you are not exposed to blood. Wear latex gloves or an artificial barrier. Lay the victim down, then apply a gauze pad and direct pressure to the wound **FIGURE 4-19**. Apply a pressure bandage over the gauze. If blood soaks through the bandage, apply additional dressings and pressure bandage **FIGURE 4-20**. Call 9-1-1 if bleeding cannot be controlled. Give nothing by mouth and seek medical aid immediately.

FIGURE 4-19 Apply a gauze pad and direct pressure to the wound.

FIGURE 4-20 If blood soaks through the bandage, apply additional dressings and pressure bandage.

and becomes embedded in the eye, do not attempt to remove it. Lay the victim down, stabilize the object with a bulky dressing or clean cloths, ask the victim to close the other eye, and call 9-1-1 **FIGURE 4-21**.

If an object is loose on the surface of the eye, pull the upper lid over the lower lid. Hold the eyelid open and gently rinse with water. Examine the lower lid by pulling it down gently. If you can see the object, remove it with a moistened sterile gauze, a clean cloth, or a moistened cotton swab. Examine the underside of the upper lid by grasping the lashes of the upper lid and rolling the lid upward over a cotton swab. If you can see the object, remove it with a moistened sterile gauze or a clean cloth **FIGURE 4-22**.

FIGURE 4-21 If an object penetrates and becomes embedded in the eye, stabilize the object with a bulky dressing or clean cloths.

If an object punctures the victim's skin and becomes embedded in the victim's body, do not attempt to remove the object. Stabilize the object with a bulky dressing. Seek medical care immediately.

If the injured person has internal bleeding, it may not be immediately obvious. Symptoms of internal bleeding are bruising, a painful or tender area, coughing frothy blood, vomiting blood, stool that is black or contains bright red blood, and passing blood with urine. To assist an injured victim with internal bleeding, lay the victim down, loosen tight clothing, give nothing by mouth, and seek medical aid immediately.

Eye Injuries

Foreign objects can become embedded in the eye or chemicals can splash into the eye. If an object penetrates

FIGURE 4-22 Locate and remove a foreign object from the eye.

If a chemical splashes into the eyes, you may be able to flush it out using an eye wash station **FIGURE 4-23**. Hold the eye wide open and flush with warm water for at least 20 minutes, continuously and gently. Irrigate from the nose side of the eye toward the outside to avoid flushing material into the other eye. Loosely bandage the eyes with wet dressings. Call 9-1-1.

Fractures

A fracture is a broken or cracked bone. Always seek medical care for all fractures. There may be symptoms you are not aware of that may make the injury more complex than first thought. There are three types of bone fractures: A **simple fracture** involves no wound or internal or external bleeding, an **open fracture** involves bleeding or the protrusion of bone through the skin, and a **complicated fracture** involves penetration of a bone into a vital organ.

The symptoms of a fracture include hearing a snapping noise when the injury occurred, pain or tenderness at or near the injury, inability to move the limb, loss of strength in the limb, shortening of the limb or an abnormally shaped limb, swelling and/or bruising around the area, and a grinding noise if the limb is moved. Allow the victim to support the injured area in the most comfortable position. Stabilize the injured part with your hands or a splint to prevent movement. If the injury is an open fracture, do not push on any protruding bone. Cover the wound and exposed bone with a dressing. Apply ice or a cold pack if possible to help reduce swelling or pain. Call 9-1-1 for any open fractures or large bone fractures. Do not move the victim unless there is an immediate danger. Be aware of the onset of **shock**, which may present as the victim vomiting or fainting. Shock is when the body's tissues do not receive enough oxygenated blood.

FIGURE 4-23 Flush out the eye to prevent a chemical burn.

Sprains, Strains, and Dislocations

When a joint has been forced past its natural range of movement, or a muscle or ligament has been overstressed or torn, a sprain, strain, or dislocation may occur. A **sprain** occurs when a joint is forced beyond its natural movement limit. This causes stretching or tearing in the ligaments that hold the bones together. The symptoms of a sprain include pain and loss of limb function, with swelling and bruising present. When a sprain occurs, apply covered ice packs every 20 minutes, elevate the injured limb, and apply an elastic compression bandage to the area and beyond the affected area. You should always treat a sprain as a fracture until medical opinion says otherwise.

A **strain** is an injury caused by the overstretching of muscles and tendons. Symptoms of a strain are sharp pain in the area immediately after the injury occurs, increased pain when using the limb, or tenderness over the entire muscle. The muscle may also have an indentation at the strain location. When a strain occurs, have the victim rest, elevate the injured limb, apply covered ice packs every 20 minutes, and apply an elastic compression bandage.

A **dislocation** is the displacement of a joint from its normal position; it is caused by an external force stretching the ligaments beyond their elastic limit. Symptoms of a dislocation are pain or tenderness around the area, inability to move the joint, deformity of the joint, and swelling and discoloration over the joint. If a dislocation occurs, try to immobilize the limb and seek medical attention. Do not try to put the joint back in place.

Burns and Scalds

Burns are injuries to body tissues, including skin, that are caused by exposure to heat, chemicals, and radiation. Burns are classified as either superficial, partial thickness, or full thickness. Superficial burns, or **first-degree burns**, show reddening of the skin and damage to the outer layer of skin only **FIGURE 4-24**. Partial-thickness burns, or **second-degree burns**, involve blistering and damage to the outer layer of skin **FIGURE 4-25**. Full-thickness burns, or **third-degree burns**, involve white or blackened areas and include damage to all skin layers and underlying structures and tissues **FIGURE 4-26**.

Burns can be caused by excessive heat, such as from fire; friction, such as from a rope burn; radiation, such as from a welding flash or a sunburn; chemicals, including acids and bases; or electricity, such as from faulty appliances. Scalds are injuries to the skin caused by exposure to hot liquids and gases. The effects of burns and scalds can include permanent skin and tissue damage, blisters caused by damage to surface blood vessels, severe pain, and shock.

FIGURE 4-24 First-degree burn.

FIGURE 4-26 Third-degree burn.

FIGURE 4-25 Second-degree burn.

Remove the victim from any danger. If clothing is burning, have the victim roll on the ground using the "stop, drop, and roll" method. Smother the flames with a fire blanket or douse the victim with water. For minor burns, cool the burn with cool water until the body part is pain free. After the burn has cooled, apply antibiotic ointment. Do not apply lotions or aloe vera. Cover the burn loosely with a dry, nonstick, sterile or clean dressing. Do not break any blisters. Give an over-the-counter pain medication such as ibuprofen. Seek medical care. Any large or third-degree burn must be treated by a qualified medical practitioner. Serious burns include skin that is blackened, whitened, or charred; a burn that is larger than 2 cm (0.79") in diameter; or a burn that is in the airway or on the face, hands, or genitals. When presented with such burns, call 9-1-1 immediately.

Wrap-up

Ready for Review

▸ Personal protective equipment (PPE) protects the body from injury but must fit correctly and be task-appropriate.

▸ Work clothing should be clean, loose enough for movement, and flame-retardant.

▸ Footwear should be acid- and slip-resistant and made of puncture-proof material.

▸ Headgear can protect your head from bumps and should hold long hair in place.

▸ Hand protection includes chemical gloves, leather gloves, light-duty gloves, general-purpose cloth gloves, and barrier cream.

▸ Hazardous chemicals and oils can be absorbed into your skin.

▸ Wear ear protection if the sound level is 85 decibels or above.

▸ Breathing devices include disposable dust masks and respirators.

▸ Forms of eye protection are safety glasses, welding helmet, gas welding goggles, full face shield, and safety goggles.

▸ You may need two types of eye protection for some tasks.

▸ Before starting work, remove all jewelry and watches, and make sure your hair is contained.

▸ Thinking "safety first" will lead to acting safely.

▸ All shops require proper ventilation.

▸ Lifting correctly or seeking assistance will prevent back injuries.

▸ Safety includes keeping a clean shop with everything put where it belongs and all spills cleaned up.

▸ First aid involves providing immediate care to an ill or injured person.

▸ Do not perform first aid if it is unsafe to do so.

▸ Bleeding may be internal or external; do not remove embedded objects that cause bleeding.

▸ Flush eyes with warm water to remove chemicals or debris.

▸ Fractures can be simple, open, or complicated; all fractures require medical care.

▸ Sprains, dislocations, and strains are possible injuries to muscles and ligaments.

▸ Burns can be superficial, partial thickness, or full thickness.

▸ Burns are classified as first, second, or third degree; large or third-degree burns require immediate medical care.

Key Terms

barrier cream A cream that looks and feels like a moisturizing cream but has a specific formula to provide extra protection from chemicals and oils.

complicated fracture A fracture in which the bone has penetrated a vital organ.

dislocation The displacement of a joint from its normal position; it is caused by an external force stretching the ligaments beyond their elastic limit.

ear protection Protective gear worn when the sound levels exceed 85 decibels, when working around operating machinery for any period of time, or when the equipment you are using produces loud noise.

external bleeding The loss of blood from an external wound; blood can be seen escaping.

first aid The immediate care given to an injured or suddenly ill person.

first-degree burns Burns that show reddening of the skin and damage to the outer layer of skin only.

gas welding goggles Protective gear designed for gas welding; they provide protection against foreign particles entering the eye and are tinted to reduce the glare of the welding flame.

headgear Protective gear that includes items like hairnets, caps, or hard hats.

heat buildup A dangerous condition that occurs when the glove can no longer absorb or reflect heat and heat is transferred to the inside of the glove.

internal bleeding The loss of blood into the body cavity from a wound; there is no obvious sign of blood.

open fracture A fracture in which the bone is protruding through the skin or there is severe bleeding.

personal protective equipment (PPE) Equipment used to block the entry of hazardous materials into the body or to protect the body from injury.

respirator Protective gear used to protect the wearer from inhaling harmful dusts or gases. Respirators range from single-use disposable masks to types that have replaceable cartridges. The correct types of cartridge must be used for the type of contaminant encountered.

second-degree burns Burns that involve blistering and damage to the outer layer of skin.

simple fracture A fracture that involves no open wound or internal or external bleeding.

shock Inadequate tissue oxygenation resulting from serious injury or illness.

sprain An injury in which a joint is forced beyond its natural movement limit.

strain An injury caused by the overstretching of muscles and tendons.

third-degree burns Burns that involve white or blackened areas and damage to all skin layers and underlying structures and tissues.

welding helmet Protective gear designed for arc welding; it provides protection against foreign particles entering the eye, and the lens is tinted to reduce the glare of the welding arc.

ASE-Type Questions

1. Tech A says that personal protective equipment (PPE) does not include clothing. Tech B says that the PPE used should be based on the task you are performing. Who is correct?
   a. Tech A
   b. Tech B
   c. Both A and B
   d. Neither A nor B

2. Tech A says that protective clothing that is not in good condition should be replaced. Tech B says that safety glasses are adequate to protect your eyes regardless of the activity. Who is correct?
   a. Tech A
   b. Tech B
   c. Both A and B
   d. Neither A nor B

3. Tech A says that appropriate work clothes include loose-fitting clothing. Tech B says that you should always wear cuffed pants when working in a shop. Who is correct?
   a. Tech A
   b. Tech B
   c. Both A and B
   d. Neither A nor B

4. Tech A says that proper footwear may include both leather and steel-toed shoes. Tech B says that leather-soled shoes provide slip resistance. Who is correct?
   a. Tech A
   b. Tech B
   c. Both A and B
   d. Neither A nor B

5. Tech A says that a hat can help keep your hair clean when working on a vehicle. Tech B says that chemical gloves may be used when working with solvent. Who is correct?
   a. Tech A
   b. Tech B
   c. Both A and B
   d. Neither A nor B

6. Tech A says that you should only wear gloves when it is absolutely necessary. Tech B says that leather gloves are used to pick up very hot pieces of metal. Who is correct?
   a. Tech A
   b. Tech B
   c. Both A and B
   d. Neither A nor B

7. Tech A says that barrier creams are used to make cleaning your hands easier. Tech B says that hearing protection only needs to be worn by people operating loud equipment. Who is correct?
   a. Tech A
   b. Tech B
   c. Both A and B
   d. Neither A nor B

8. Tech A says that dust masks should be used when painting. Tech B says that a respirator should be used when the TLV for a chemical is exceeded. Who is correct?
   a. Tech A
   b. Tech B
   c. Both A and B
   d. Neither A nor B

9. Tech A says that tinted safety glasses can be worn when working outside. Tech B says that welding can cause a sunburn. Who is correct?
   a. Tech A
   b. Tech B
   c. Both A and B
   d. Neither A nor B

10. Tech A says that you should put tools away when done using them. Tech B says that a bystander can perform first aid. Who is correct?
    a. Tech A
    b. Tech B
    c. Both A and B
    d. Neither A nor B

CHAPTER 5

Knowledge Objectives

After reading this chapter, you will be able to:
1. Describe the purpose and use of owner's manuals and shop manuals/service information. (pp 80–85)
2. Explain how TSBs, service campaigns, and recall information are used. (pp 85–86)
3. Describe the purpose and use of labor guides. (pp 86–87)
4. Identify the purpose and use of a parts program. (pp 87–88)
5. Describe the information and its use within a repair/work order. (p 88)
6. Describe the purpose and use of service history. (pp 89–90)
7. Explain the purpose and application of VINs. (pp 90–92)
8. Explain how the 3 Cs are applied in repairing and servicing vehicles. (pp 93–94)

Vehicle, Customer, and Service Information

Skills Objectives

After reading this chapter, you will be able to:

1. Use an owner's manual to obtain vehicle information. (p 81)
2. Use a shop/repair manual while conducting a service or repair. (pp 82–83)
3. Use a service information program while conducting a service or repair. (pp 83–85)
4. Use a labor guide to estimate the cost or charge of conducting a service or repair. (pp 86–87)
5. Use a parts program to identify and order the correct replacement parts for a service or repair. (pp 87–88)
6. Use a repair/work order to identify the information needed and the service requested. (p 88)
7. Use service history in the repair and service of vehicles. (pp 89–90)
8. Use VINs when repairing and servicing vehicles. (pp 90–91)
9. Decode a North American VIN. (pp 91–92)
10. Apply the 3 Cs when repairing and servicing vehicles. (pp 93–94)

Introduction

Over the last 100 years, motor vehicles have become increasingly comfortable and reliable through the application of technology and improved manufacturing processes. For example, the modern motor vehicle has complex computer-controlled electrical systems where older vehicles had very basic wiring with no electronic components. The increased complexity and expanded range of makes and models have created a need for timely access to relevant, complete, and accurate information to perform maintenance and repair activities.

Vehicle and customer information from various sources provides the fundamental knowledge required to conduct repairs and servicing. Today, the ability to properly perform maintenance and repair activities is increasingly dependent on the technician's ability to research and apply technical information. Vehicle information can come from a number of sources, including vehicle identification plates, owner's manuals, shop manuals, repair orders, service and parts programs, and technical service bulletins. The various sources of information can be published in books or manuals or made available through software packages or the Internet. It is important that you know how to research and apply this information correctly so you can properly repair and service vehicles.

Owner's Manual

Manufacturers supply a vehicle owner's manual, which comes with every new vehicle purchased. The owner's manual is usually kept in the vehicle's glove compartment.

Secondhand vehicles may or may not have the owner's manual in the glove compartment. The **owner's manual** contains information about the vehicle and is a valuable source of information for both the owner and the technician.

The information contained in the owner's manual will vary for each manufacturer. In general, it contains basic information on the safe operation and specifications of the vehicle. A typical owner's manual includes an overview of the controls and features of the vehicle; the proper operation, care, and maintenance of the vehicle; owner service procedures; and specifications or technical data **FIGURE 5-1**. The owner's manual also details such elements

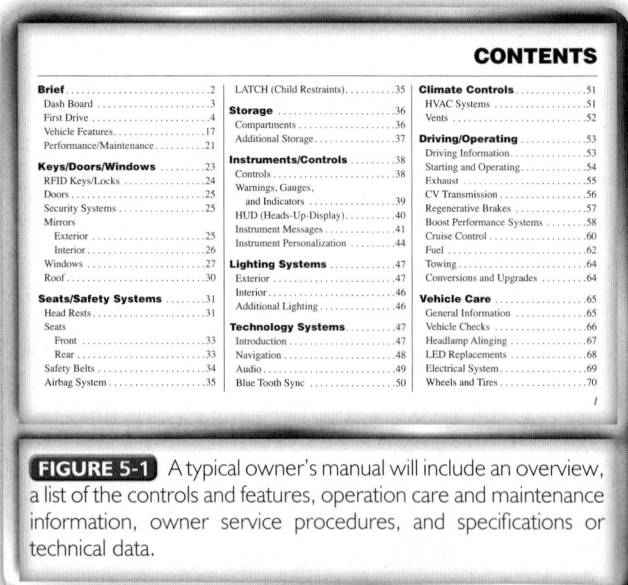

FIGURE 5-1 A typical owner's manual will include an overview, a list of the controls and features, operation care and maintenance information, owner service procedures, and specifications or technical data.

You are the Automotive Technician

A well-known foreign vehicle manufacturer has recalled over 400,000 of their vehicles for a brake issue. The issue can be repaired with a software update that will reprogram the vehicles PCM to overcome the problem. But not all of the suspect vehicles will need the software update. The technical service bulletin describes the steps needed to verify if the vehicle has the fault. The manufacturer has notified their customers of a product recall through both mail and email. The dealership that you work for has been receiving many calls from customers to set up recall appointments. Today, you are working on the first vehicle for this recall.

1. Where would you locate the Technical Service Bulletins (TSB), service campaigns, and recalls in the dealership?
2. Why is it important to verify if the TSB has been issued for that particular vehicle?
3. What sources would you use to look up the scheduled maintenance chart for the vehicle?

as vehicle security PIN codes; warranty and service information; fuel, lubricant, and coolant capacities; tire changing specifications; jacking and towing information; and a list of service facilities. The layout and amount of detail in an owner's manual will vary according to the manufacturer and age of the vehicle.

Using an Owner's Manual

To locate the specifications for servicing a vehicle, follow the steps in **SKILL DRILL 5-1**:

1. Decide what information you need to know about the job and about the vehicle. For example, if your job is to change the engine oil, make sure you know the make, model, and year of manufacture of the vehicle and the type and size of the engine. In order to change the oil, you need to know the engine oil specifications, how much oil to put in, and what grade of oil to use.

2. Locate the appropriate manual. This kind of information is most readily found in the vehicle's owner's manual, which is usually kept in the glove compartment. Open the owner's manual to the first page, which is usually a table of contents to help you quickly find the information you need. Find the correct page and turn to it.

3. Locate the vehicle specifications and identify the correct grade of motor oil for this vehicle. The table of contents lists a page number for the fuel and lubricant capacities and another page number for the refill capacities. First turn to the page listing all of the vehicle's lubricant specifications. Find the correct specifications for the engine crankcase oil and make a note. Next turn to the page listing the refill capacities **FIGURE 5-2**. You find that this

FIGURE 5-2 Locate the vehicle specifications.

FIGURE 5-3 Another way of finding information is to refer to the index at the back of the owner's manual.

eight-cylinder engine requires 5 quarts (4.7 liters) of oil.

4. Another way of finding information is to refer to the index at the back of the owner's manual **FIGURE 5-3**. For example, look under *E* for engine, and find "Engine Oil," or look under *L* for lubricants or *O* for oil. Each item should refer you to the same page.

5. Once you have the specific requirements of the vehicle, you are ready to begin servicing the vehicle.

▶ Shop Manual

Shop or service manuals are available for just about every make and model of every vehicle made. Service manuals come in two types—factory and after-market. Factory manuals are produced by vehicle manufacturers and specify the procedures to maintain, repair, and diagnose their vehicles. Usually a factory service manual is specific to one year and make of vehicle, such as a 2012 Ford Expedition.

After-market service manuals are published by independent companies for the same purpose. Usually, after-market manuals are not as detailed as factory manuals; they may not cover topics such as trim, entertainment systems, and so on. They are arranged in one of two ways: They either cover a range of years for a particular vehicle, such as 2005 to 2010 Ford Mustangs, or they cover a range of vehicles for a single year, such as 2011 General Motors vehicles.

Paper shop manuals have become less common over the years as less expensive electronic versions that can be installed on a computer have become available.

> **TECHNICIAN TIP**

While factory manuals are usually more complete, it can be very costly to maintain a library of individual manuals for each of the vehicles serviced by a shop. After-market manuals help make the cost of service information more affordable. The modern vehicle is becoming very complex with all the technology now fitted to it, and this means shop manuals have also grown in complexity and size, resulting in significant expense and storage requirements.

> **TECHNICIAN TIP**

Here is an example of how much more a technician of today needs to know versus 65 years ago. In 1947, MOTOR, an organization devoted to supplying automotive data, produced a repair manual that covered the repair procedures and specifications for all of the vehicles produced by more than 20 manufacturers from 1935 to 1946. This reference was only about 1100 pages long. Today it takes MOTOR two to three 1100-page books to cover the same information for one manufacturer for one year. Technicians rely on service information more now than ever before.

In addition, most manufacturers and providers of shop manuals have made the information available online. These services are usually provided through a daily, monthly, or yearly subscription. Electronic versions are becoming very popular because they allow shops to access the information they need without having to pay for and store large numbers of shop manuals. Also, it is easier for the publisher to update information as changes or corrections are needed, so the information is generally more accurate than printed materials, which require supplemental printed updates on a periodic basis.

Typical shop manuals will be broken into a number of sections that relate to systems within the vehicle—for example, engine, transmission, drivetrain, suspension, and electrical. The sections of the shop manuals will be further divided into topics or subject areas; for example, in the engine section, topics could be general description, engine diagnosis, and on-vehicle service. A typical shop manual page will have a task description broken into steps and diagrams or pictures to aid the technician **FIGURE 5-4**. It is important to know that all service manuals arrange the content in their own way, so using a variety of different manuals will help you become familiar with finding the information you are looking for.

FIGURE 5-4 A typical shop manual page will have a task description broken into steps and diagrams or pictures to aid the technician.

Using a Shop Manual

Shop manuals are developed by manufacturers or after-market publishers to provide you with correct information on performing all service and repair tasks on the vehicles produced. The information found in shop manuals provides a systematic procedure and identifies special tools, safety precautions, and specifications relevant to the task. Shop manuals are organized according to vehicle systems and have indexes for quick referencing. Knowing that a water pump is part of the cooling system and that the cooling system is part of the engine system (or in some cases the HVAC system) will help you locate the specific information you need.

To identify correct service procedures using a shop manual, follow the steps in **SKILL DRILL 5-2**:

1. Decide what information you need to know about the job and about the vehicle. Make sure you know the make, model, and year of manufacture of the vehicle, and the type and size of the engine. You should also have the vehicle identification number (VIN) handy.

2. Find the appropriate shop manual for the make, model, and year of the vehicle you are working on.

3. Locate the correct section that will contain the information you need. The first page of the shop manual is usually a table of contents.

4. Locate the service procedures in the proper section. For example, if you were performing brake repairs, you would turn to the "Brakes" section. The text and the pictures describe how to properly perform a procedure and tell you the tools to use and how to use them.

5. Locate the vehicle specifications by consulting the specifications page in the proper section. You may need to know the type of engine of the vehicle to

Applied | Science

AS-7: Maps/Charts/Tables/Graphs: The technician uses the information in service manual charts, tables, or graphs to determine the manufacturer's specifications for system(s) operation(s).

AS-8: Maps/Charts/Tables/Graphs: The technician uses the information in service manual charts, tables, or graphs to determine the appropriate repair/replacement procedure and/or part.

Most service manuals will have a chart that you will need to consult before performing preventative maintenance. The chart lists what needs to be performed according to the vehicle's mileage. As you can see, there is a big difference between a 43,000 mile (minor) service to a 52,000 mile (major) service. On the 52,000 mile service, far more items are inspected and or replaced. If the vehicle came into the workshop for a 43,000 mile service, you easily read from the service chart what needs to be done.

Mileage	43,000 Miles	52,000 Miles
Maintenance Items	I: Drive belts.	I: Drive belts
	R: Engine oil.	R: Engine oil
	R: Engine oil filter.	R: Engine oil filter
	I: Battery.	I: Cooling and heater system
	I: Engine air cleaner filter.	I: Engine Coolant
	I: Brake pedal and parking brake.	I: Exhaust pipe and mountings
	I: Brake pads and discs.	I: Battery
	I: Brake fluid.	R: Engine air cleaner filter
	I: Clutch fluid.	I: Brake pedal and parking brake
	I: Brake pipes and hose.	I: Parking brake linings and drums
	I: Power steering fluid.	I: Brake pads and discs
	I: Steering wheel.	R: Brake fluid
	I: Drive shaft boots.	I: Brake pipes and hoses
	I: Suspension ball joint and dust covers	I: Power steering fluid
	I: Tires and psi.	I: Steering wheel and linkage
	I: Rotate wheels.	I : Front and rear suspension
	I: Seatbelt, webbing condition, buckle and retractor mechanism operation	I: Lights, horns, wipers and washers
	C: Air conditioner filter	I: Seatbelt, webbing condition, buckle and retractor mechanism operation
	I: Refrigerant amount of air conditioner	C: Air conditioner filter
	I: Valve clearance	

Note: T = Tighten, R = Replace, I = Inspect, A= Adjust, L = Lubricate, and C= Clean.

find the correct specifications for the vehicle you are working on.

Using a Service Information Program

Service information programs are computer applications used to provide technical information for the repair and maintenance of vehicles **FIGURE 5-5**. The software can be installed on the computer, accessed via the Internet using a browser, or run from a CD or DVD.

To use a service information program, you need to have a basic understanding of how to start and use a computer. Usernames and passwords may be required to log in to the computer and the service information program, so make sure you have these available before you start. A printer is also helpful to print copies of the information so that you can use it when conducting service and repairs; alternatively, you may need to take notes.

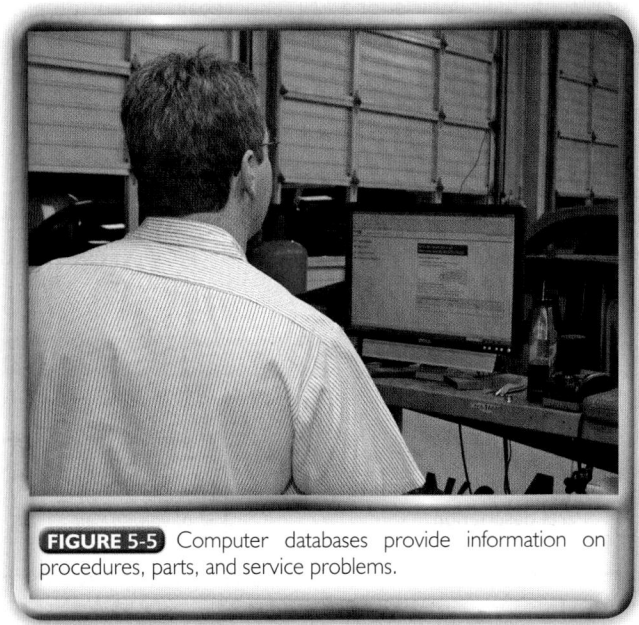

FIGURE 5-5 Computer databases provide information on procedures, parts, and service problems.

To obtain the correct information, you will need vehicle identification information, such as the date of manufacture, model, engine and VIN numbers, and an understanding of the type of repair or scheduled service that is being performed. The repair order may provide you with this information, or you may have to research vehicle identification information from the vehicle. You may need to perform some initial diagnosis of the fault to further continue the search for information.

Information can usually be obtained by searching for the vehicle and then selecting from the list of systems such as brakes or maintenance, followed by subsystems such as disc brakes or fluid capacities. A keyword search may also be available; for example, use the keyword "service interval" to obtain a list of scheduled service intervals. Using a generic word like "engine" may return a very large list. If this occurs, the search can be narrowed further by entering more specific criteria such as "engine oil," "water pump," or "camshaft."

The information will be displayed on pages that will have a mixture of text and diagrams with explanations. Some of the diagrams may have detailed views so you can see how parts fit together, while links may be provided to other relevant information such as a schematic diagram. Most systems will contain help menus or training guides with examples to assist you in using the software, if required.

To use a service information program, follow the steps in **SKILL DRILL 5-3**:

1 If necessary, start the computer and select the service information program.

2 Log in to the application using the appropriate username and password.

3 Enter the vehicle identification information into the system in the appropriate places: year, make, model, engine, and possibly VIN.

4 Search for the information you require to perform the service or repair.

5 The search engine will provide a list of possible matches for you to select from. If the initial search does not produce what you are looking for, try changing the search criteria. Keep searching until you find the information.

6 Finally, once the general details for the item are displayed, gather the specific information on the

---

Applied	Science

AS-11 Information Processing: The technician can use computer databases to input and retrieve customer information for billing, warranty work, and other record-keeping purposes.

Dealership service departments have access to databases run by manufacturers for the purposes of accessing warranty information, tracking vehicle servicing and warranty repair history, and logging warranty repair jobs for payment by the manufacturer. When a customer presents their vehicle for a warranty repair, the customer service department staff begin by consulting the database to confirm that the vehicle is within its warranty period, and that the warranty has not been invalidated for any reason. Once it is confirmed that the vehicle is still under valid warranty, the repair order will be passed to the workshop for diagnosis and repair. Any parts required for the warranty repair must be labeled by the technician and stored for possible recall by the manufacturer.

For example, a young man comes in complaining that his vehicle is "Running rough." The customer service staff will confirm that the vehicle is nine months old only has 14,500 miles, confirming that the vehicle is within the manufacturer's 3 year/100,000 mile warranty period. They check the manufacturer's database to confirm that the vehicle's warranty has not been invalidated before handing the repair order onto the workshop. Then a technician diagnoses the fault as a defective ignition coil and fills out a warranty parts form.

Once the repair has been completed and the parts labeled, the warranty parts form and any repair order papaerwork is passed back to administrative staff for processing. Processing will include billing the manufacturer for the correct, pre-approved amount of time, logging the repair on the database for payment, and ensuring that all documentation is correct for auditing purposes.

WARRANTY PARTS Form				
Customer complaint:	Vehicle running rough	VEHICLE INFORMATION.		
Cause:	# 6 ignition coil open circuit on primary winding.	VIN:	1G1123456789101111	
Correction:	Replaced #6 ignition coil	RO Number:	123456	
Parts description:	# 6 ignition coil	Date of repair:	10/04/2011	

specifications or repairs. You may need more than one piece of information.

7. Print out or write down the information needed. Put this on a clipboard and take it with you to perform the service or repair.

Technical Service Bulletins

Technical service bulletins (TSBs) are issued by manufacturers to provide information to technicians on unexpected problems, updated parts, or changes to repair procedures that may occur with a particular vehicle system, part, or component **FIGURE 5-6**. The typical TSB contains step-by-step procedures and diagrams on how to identify if there is a fault and perform an effective repair.

At the time of production, manufacturers prepare service and technical information and attempt to anticipate the information the technicians will require to undertake service and repairs. Once the vehicle is in use, situations can arise when particular components or repair procedures may need either additional information or changes. This is where TSBs are most useful. For example, a change to the procedure that bleeds air from the cooling system. In this situation, the manufacturer would issue a service bulletin explaining the problem and the changes to the current procedure performed to bleed air from the cooling system.

Using TSBs

To use a TSB, follow these guidelines. Locate where the TSBs are kept in your shop or look them up with your electronic service information system. Prior to performing

FIGURE 5-6 Technical service bulletin.

repairs, look through the TSBs and get to know the type of information contained in them. Before working on a vehicle, it is good practice to check if a TSB has been issued for that vehicle and type of fault or repair. This can save a lot of wasted time.

Compare the information contained in the TSB to that found in the shop manual. Note the differences, and if necessary, copy the TSB and take it with you to perform the repair. Perform the repair following the TSB where appropriate while also referring to the shop manual. If required in your shop policy, note the details of the service bulletin in the appropriate area on the repair order.

Service Campaigns and Recalls

Service campaigns and recalls are usually conducted by manufacturers when a safety issue is discovered with a particular vehicle. Recalls are costly to manufacturers because they can require the repair of an entire model or production run of vehicles. Potentially, this could involve many thousands of vehicles. Depending on the nature of the problem, recalls can be mandatory and enforced by law, or manufacturers may choose to voluntarily conduct a recall to ensure the safe operation of the vehicle or minimize damage to their business and product image.

Safety

Each country has specific laws regarding product recalls. Find out the laws in your jurisdiction.

An example of a mandatory recall is a fault within the airbag system of a vehicle that results in the airbag not deploying or deploying when it should not. In this case, the manufacturer would need to identify the problem, its cause, the vehicles affected, and the recertification requirements. A recall would then be issued and advertised in popular media. Letters would be sent from the manufacturer to known owners of the particular vehicle indicating that the vehicles should be returned for repair. Usually all costs associated with the recall are paid by the manufacturer.

Using Service Campaign Information

To utilize service campaigns or recall information, follow these guidelines. Locate where the special service messages, service campaigns/recalls, vehicle/service warranty applications, and service interval recommendations can be accessed in your shop. Look through the TSBs, service recalls, service warranty applications, and service interval recommendations, and get to know the type of information that is contained in them. Identify how they could be used in your daily tasks.

When working on vehicles, check to see if a TSB has been issued for that vehicle and type of repair. Perform service and repairs following the special service messages, service campaigns/recalls, vehicle/service warranty applications, and service interval recommendations. Fill in the required documentation as required in your shop policies. Note the details of the special service messages, service campaigns/recalls, vehicle/service warranty applications, and service interval recommendations in the appropriate area on the repair order.

> ### Caring for the Customer
>
> Customer satisfaction ratings are very important to dealerships and shops. One way to impress customers is to check for recalls on every vehicle that comes in for service and inform the customer if you find anything. Some manufacturers will flag a vehicle for any outstanding recalls when the VIN is entered into the dealership's computerized repair system when the vehicle is brought in for service.

▶ Labor Guide

Labor guides list how much time will be involved in performing a standard or warranty-related service or repair. They are regularly updated as new models are released into the market and provide a basis for making job estimates and standard charges for the customer. Flat rate servicing costs are usually derived from a labor guide. For example, if a customer wants to know how much it will cost to replace a leaking intake manifold gasket on a particular vehicle, then a technician can look up this procedure in a labor guide and find the information on the time and parts required for that particular repair on the specific vehicle.

With the advent of technology and the Internet, many providers of labor guides have started making them available online as well as in print. The online versions are paid for by subscription, which is usually a monthly or annual fee to access the information. Having access to online labor guides means the shop does not have to wait for a new version of the print publication to become available. Online versions of labor guides also can be updated as new models of vehicles are released or updates are made by the manufacturer.

Using a Labor Guide

The labor guide indicates how quickly an average technician can complete the task. Experienced technicians who have performed the task many times and who are working efficiently can usually perform the job quicker than the labor guide specifies. But since each task and vehicle has its small differences, the time is not always completely accurate. The information contained within a labor guide is referenced in a similar manner as a repair manual or online service information system.

To use a labor guide, follow the steps in **SKILL DRILL 5-4**:

1. Decide what specific labor operations you need to locate. Make sure you know the year, make, model, engine, and any other pertinent details of the vehicle.
2. Log in to the labor estimating system.
3. Enter the vehicle information into the system.
4. Find the labor operation either by working your way through the menu tree or by typing a keyword into the search bar.
5. Once you locate the labor operation, there are usually two columns that list the time. The first one is "warranty time." It is the amount of time the manufacturer would pay the shop for the operation under a customer warranty. The second time listed is the "customer pay" time. That is the amount of time a customer would be billed for and is usually 20–40% longer than warranty time. The length of time is usually listed in tenths of an hour. So 0.6 hours represents 36 minutes. Every tenth of an hour equals 6 minutes.
6. Check for any "combination" time that would need to be added to the base job when a related job is also being completed. Combination time recognizes that combined tasks in many cases save a lot of time over individual tasks because the customer is already being charged for part of the job in the first task. This could be time needed to flush the brakes while the main operation is to replace the brake pads.
7. Check for an "additional" time. This is extra time needed to deal with situations that occur on a relatively common basis, such as vehicle-installed options that are not common to all vehicles, like wheel locks. If you are replacing the brake pads on a vehicle with wheel locks, the customer should be charged for the extra time it takes to find the lock key and to remove and install the wheel locks (finding the lock key can add substantial time itself). Thus, "additional" time needs to be added to the base operation time if the vehicle meets the criteria for the particular "additional" situation.

8 Calculate the total time and multiply it by the shop's hourly labor rate. You now have the correct figure to estimate the charge for the particular service.

Parts Program

Parts programs are the modern-day version of parts manuals. They are essentially an electronic version of a parts manual. Parts programs may be available via a CD/DVD, a computer network, or the Internet. Technicians and parts specialists, the individuals working at the parts counter, use these programs to identify parts and find order numbers.

Parts manuals are produced for all makes and models of vehicles and are essentially a catalogue of all the parts that make up a vehicle. The parts are catalogued by systems—for example, brake, engine, and transmission. Diagrams of each part are shown along with a part number, which is a unique identifying number for that particular part.

TECHNICIAN TIP

Dealership technicians have one advantage over most independent technicians: They have an onsite parts department that stocks many of the parts needed for repairs. Many independent shops maintain a relatively small inventory of high-demand parts such as filters, belts, and light bulbs and use a local parts house to supply the less common parts. This can result in delays waiting for parts to arrive.

TECHNICIAN TIP

Follow these guidelines when using a technical service bulleting (TSB):

- Locate where the TSBs are kept in your shop or look them up with your electronic service information system.
- Prior to performing repairs, look through the TSBs and become familiar with the type of information contained in them.
- Before working on a vehicle, check whether a TSB has been issued for that vehicle and the type of fault or repair.
- Compare the information contained in the TSB to the shop manual information and note the differences. You may copy the TSB and take it with you to perform the repair.
- Perform the repair following the TSB where appropriate while also referring to the shop manual.
- If required by your shop policy, note the details of the service bulletin in the appropriate area on the repair order.

Using a Parts Program

A parts program is a computer application that is used to identify part numbers for vehicle components. Part numbers need to be identified so that correct replacement components can be ordered to replace faulty parts. The software can be installed on the computer, accessed via the Internet using a browser, or run from a CD or DVD.

To use a parts program, you need to have a basic understanding of how to start and use a computer. Usernames and passwords may be required to log in to the computer and the parts program, so make sure you have those available before you start. A printer is also helpful to print out copies of the information so that you can use it when ordering parts; alternatively, you may need to take notes.

To identify the correct part, you will need to know where on the vehicle the part is installed, what system or subsystem it comes from, and vehicle identification information, such as date of manufacture, model, and engine and VIN numbers. Make sure you have this information on hand before you use the system. Searches can be conducted by keywords. If the part is for the brake system, in the search criteria box, enter "brake." Using a generic word like "brake" may return a very large list. If this occurs, the search can be narrowed further by entering more specific criteria such as "disc brake."

The parts will be displayed in diagrams that are labeled and show individual parts in exploded view, making it easier to identify parts. The diagrams may number the parts and have a key on the page for reference to part numbers, or arrows may point to listed part numbers on the page. Most systems will contain help menus or training guides with examples to assist you in using the software, if required.

To locate parts information on the computer, follow the steps in **SKILL DRILL 5-5**:

1 Log in to the application using the appropriate username and password.

2 Enter the year, make, model, and engine and VIN number information into the system in the appropriate places.

3 Search for the parts you require to conduct the service or repair.

4 The search engine will provide a list of possible matches for you to select from. If the initial search does not produce what you are looking for, try changing the search criteria. Keep searching until you find the information.

5 Gather information on the identified parts, including part numbers, location, availability, and cost.

Print, write down, or directly place an order for the desired parts.

▶ Repair Order Information

A **repair order**, or work order, is a form used by shops to collect information regarding a vehicle coming in for repair **FIGURE 5-7** . Initial information for the repair order includes customer and vehicle details, along with a brief description of the customer's complaint(s). The repair order is used by the technician to guide him or her to the problem, and by the customer service staff to create the invoice when the work is completed.

Detailed information that will be on the repair order includes customer details such as name and address; the vehicle make, model, and year; the odometer reading; the date; customer concern information; the cause of the problem(s); the correction for the problem(s); the hours of labor; and the parts used for the repair. The repair order should always include all of the information pertaining to the customer, vehicle, and cost of repair. Repair orders are legal documents that can be used as evidence in the event of a lawsuit. Make sure the information is complete and accurate whenever filling out a repair order, and store it in an organized safe place, such as in a file cabinet or electronically on a secure computer network.

To identify the information needed and the service requested on a repair order, follow the steps in **SKILL DRILL 5-6** :

1 Locate a repair order used in your shop.

2 Familiarize yourself with the repair order, and identify the following information on the repair order:
   a. Date
   b. Customer details: name and address, daytime phone number
   c. Vehicle details: year, make, model, color, odometer reading, VIN
   d. Customer concern details
Note any additional information that is required on your shop's repair order.

3 Following the shop procedures, determine the workflow for the tasks that are listed.

4 Use the repair order to carry out the requested service or repair. Fill in the repair order with details of the cause of the customer concern(s) and the correction(s) conducted.

Accounting

The accounting section contains information about the methods of payment, which can be cash, credit card, or account. An account system can be set up to handle all payments related to a customer or to a company that uses your service for a number of vehicles. When a vehicle on an account system comes in, you need to record both the account number and the order number. To work out the total cost of the service, you need to know:

- The labor cost
- The cost of parts
- The tax amounts
- The cost of gas and consumables you used to service the vehicle

You also need to have the customer's authorization to carry out the service. Remember, before making any changes to this service invoice or work order after the authorization, you will need to receive the customer's approval.

> ### ▶ TECHNICIAN TIP
>
> Repair orders are used also to inform the customer of needed repairs or service. This usually results in the customer agreeing to the needed repair, in which case all is well. But if he or she does not agree to the repair and the vehicle is involved in an accident because of the faulty components, having the customer's initials on the repair order signifying that he or she understands the safety issues can help prevent the shop from being held liable for the accident.

FIGURE 5-7 A repair order.

AC-23: Repair Orders: The technician writes a repair order containing customer vehicle information, customer complaints, parts and materials used (including prices), services performed, labor hours, and suggested repairs/maintenance.

A repair order is a key document used to communicate with both your customers and co-workers. It is a legal contract between the service provider and the customer. It contains details of the services to be provided by you and the authorization from the customer. To make sure everyone understands clearly what is involved, a repair order should contain information about:

- Your company or service providers: The service provider section contains the company name, address, and contact details; the name of a service advisor who is overseeing the job; and the amount of time the service technician will have to service the vehicle.
- The customer: The customer section contains the customer's name, address, and contact phone numbers.
- The customer's vehicle: The vehicle section includes details about the vehicle to be serviced. Check the vehicle's license plate before starting work. The license plate numbers are usually unique within a country. You should also record information about the vehicle's make, model, and color. This information will make it easier for you to locate the vehicle on the parking lot. You need to know the manufacture date of the vehicle to be able to order the right parts. The odometer reading and the date will help keep track of how much distance the vehicle travels and the time period between each visit to the shop. The VIN is designed to be unique worldwide and contains

specific information about the vehicle. Many shops do a "walk-around" with the customer to note any previous damage to the vehicle and to look for any obvious faults such as worn tires, rusted-out exhaust pipes, or torn wiper blades.

- The service operations: This section contains the details of the service operations and parts.
  - The first part is the service operation details. For example, the vehicle is in for a 150,000-mile (240,000-km) service, which can be done in 3 hours resulting in approximately a $300 of labor cost. The information about the chargeable labor time to complete a specific task can be found in a labor guide manual. In some workplaces, this information is built into the computer system and will be automatically displayed.
  - The second part of this section is the details of parts used in the service including the descriptions, quantities, codes, and prices. The codes for each service and part are normally abbreviations that are used for easy reference in the shop. Some shops may have their own reference code system.
  - As you do the vehicle inspection, you may discover other things that need replaced or repaired. These additional services can be recorded in another section. It is essential that you check with your customers and obtain their approval before carrying out any additional services.
- The parts requirements: This section lists the parts required to perform the repair.

Some repair orders also contain accounting information so they can be used as invoices.

> **TECHNICIAN TIP**

Always obtain the customer's authorization before servicing his or her vehicle, and also make sure you have the customer's approval before making any changes to the service invoice or the work order.

> **TECHNICIAN TIP**

A vehicle's service history is valuable for several reasons:
- It can provide helpful information to the technician when performing repairs.
- It allows potential new owners of the vehicle to know how well the vehicle and its systems were maintained.
- Manufacturers use the history to evaluate warranty claims.

▶ Service History

Service history is a complete list of all the servicing and repairs that have been performed on a vehicle **FIGURE 5-8**. The scheduled service history is often recorded in a service booklet or owner's manual that is kept in the glove compartment. The service history can provide valuable information to technicians when conducting repairs. It also can provide potential new owners of used vehicles an indication of how well the vehicle was maintained. A vehicle with a regular service history is a good indication that all of the vehicle's systems have been well maintained and the vehicle will often be worth more during resale. Most manufacturers store all service history performed in their dealerships (based on the VIN) on a corporate server that is accessible from any of their dealerships. They will also use this vehicle service history when it comes to evaluating warranty claims. A vehicle that does not have a complete service history may not be

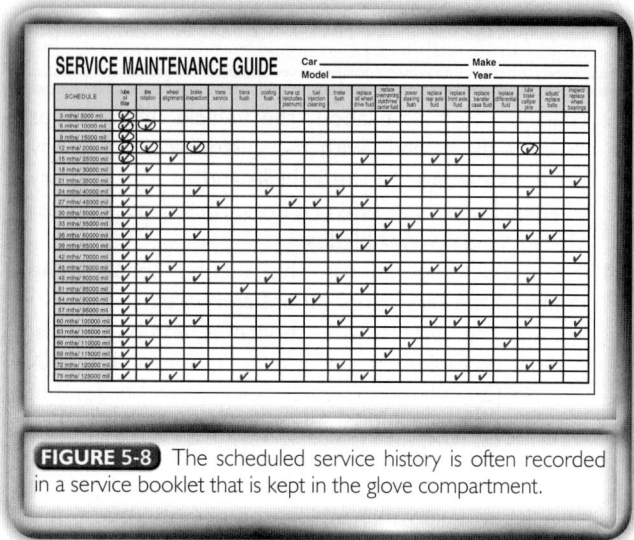

eligible for warranty claims. Independent shops generally keep records of the repairs they perform. However, if a vehicle is repaired at multiple shops, repair history is much more difficult to track and, again, may result in a denial of warranty claims.

To review the vehicle service history, follow the steps in **SKILL DRILL 5-7**:

1. Locate the service history for the vehicle. This may be in shop records or in the service history booklet within the vehicle glove compartment. Some shops may keep the vehicle's service history on a computer.

2. Familiarize yourself with the service history of the vehicle.
   a. On what date was the vehicle first serviced?
   b. On what date was the vehicle last serviced?
   c. What was the most major service performed?
   d. Was the vehicle ever serviced for the same problem more than once?

3. Compare the vehicle service history to the manufacturer's scheduled maintenance requirements and list any discrepancies.
   a. Have all the services been performed?
   b. Have all the items been checked?
   c. Are there any outstanding items?

▶ VIN and Production Date Code, and Vehicle Information Labels

Large numbers of vehicles with many variations of makes and models with different equipment levels are produced every day across the world. Vehicle information labels have become very important because they help to uniquely identify the vehicle.

VIN stands for vehicle identification number and is a unique serial number that is assigned to each vehicle produced. This means that no two vehicles have the same VIN **FIGURE 5-9**. Since 1981, the VIN has been made up of 17 characters. It is usually located on the front left corner of the windshield and is also inscribed on various vehicle parts. VINs can be used to check the service history of a vehicle and also are used to identify the vehicle for ordering components. Labeling the vehicle and vehicle parts with VINs also deters auto theft because it provides an easy way of uniquely identifying and tracing the vehicle and its major parts.

Production date codes and vehicle information labels also add to the identification information available on vehicles. The production date is the date of manufacture by year and month. Other information labels are fitted to the vehicle to provide ready access to information—for example, tire inflation pressures, vehicle weight, and load-carrying capacity. All of these information labels are used regularly by technicians to identify vehicles, order parts, and check service history.

Locating the VIN and Production Date Code

In order to locate a VIN and production date code, it is important to understand the principles of VINs and correctly identify the components that make up a vehicle identification number. The VIN is a 17-character identification composed of letters and digits. The VIN is designed to identify motor vehicles of all kinds: cars, trucks, buses, motorcycles, etc. It was originally defined in the International Standards Organization (ISO) Standard 3779 in 1977 and was revised in 1983.

FIGURE 5-9 A sample VIN.

The VIN is usually located on the front left corner of the windshield and is also inscribed on the engine, the transmission, both front guards, the hood, the doors, both bumpers, both rear quarter panels, and the trunk or hatchback. The VIN is unique worldwide, identifying the country of manufacture, manufacturer's name, division name, model, and other important information. Since 1981, all worldwide vehicle manufacturers use this numbering system. By learning to interpret the system, the identity of a vehicle or a component can be determined and verified.

Whenever a vehicle is registered or a registered vehicle is sold, a record of the VIN is kept. From this registry, information about the vehicle can be accessed, including the **title history**, which can tell you who has owned the vehicle. The registry may reveal a **salvage title**, which tells you that the vehicle has been wrecked and suffered irreparable damage. It also can tell you if a **lemon law buyback** has occurred. Lemon laws exist in some states to protect consumers from purchasing vehicles that have undergone several unsuccessful attempts to repair the same fault or from purchasing vehicles in which repair of the defects has caused the vehicle to be out of service for an extended time. The registry can also indicate if the vehicle has had an odometer rollback (mileage reduction), which is evidence of odometer tampering.

To locate the VIN and production date code, follow the steps in **SKILL DRILL 5-8**:

1 Locate the make of the vehicle from the body nameplate, which is usually found on the front or rear of the vehicle. Now locate the model from the body trim. The model may be a name, number, letter, or combination of these elements.

2 Next locate the VIN, usually found on a plate in the upper left dashboard and often visible through the windshield. In some instances, the plate may be mounted in a different location. If the plate is not visible through the windshield, check under the hood to see if it is mounted in the engine bay area. Note each letter and number exactly as it appears on the plate.

3 Decode the VIN and note the information. Each manufacturer provides a VIN decoding chart for its vehicles in its shop service information. This chart is normally found in the "general information" section of the manual or electronic service information system. Using the VIN decoding chart, write down the information or print it for later use when locating specifications or parts.

Decoding a VIN

There are two different, but essentially compatible, 17-character VIN standards: the North American VIN system and the ISO Standard 3779, which is used in most of the rest of the world. **FIGURE 5-10** shows how the numbers are structured.

To decode a North American VIN, follow the steps in **SKILL DRILL 5-9**:

1 The VIN is 1G1YN3DE-A5100001. The first character is the country of origin. This number or letter tells you where the vehicle was manufactured. For instance, a "1" means that the vehicle was made in the United States, a "2" is for Canada, a "J" means Japan, and so on.

2 The second character is usually a letter; it tells you the name of the manufacturer.

3 The third character tells you the division that made the vehicle. It could be a Pontiac, an Oldsmobile, or a GMC truck, for example.

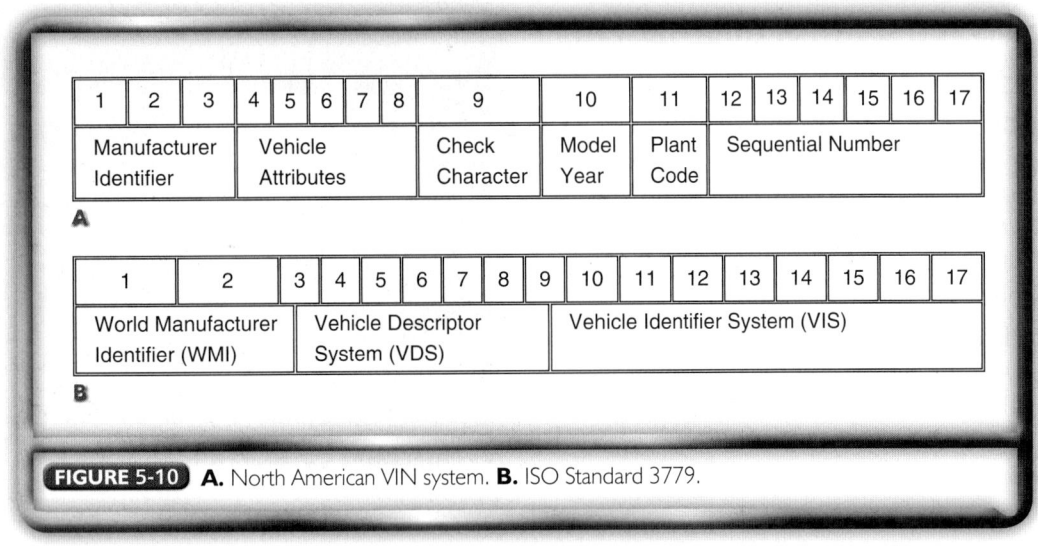

FIGURE 5-10 **A.** North American VIN system. **B.** ISO Standard 3779.

4 The fourth and fifth characters give you the model, or series, of the vehicle. You will need a decoding chart for the details. Here we have a Corvette ZR1 Custom 3ZR Manual.

5 The sixth character describes the body type: two-door, four-door, coupe, sedan, and so on. Here we have a two-door convertible.

6 The seventh character tells you the type of seat restraints fitted to the vehicle. In this case it is active manual seat belts, airbags front (driver and passenger) and front seat side.

7 The eighth character is the engine code, which provides details of the engine type, size, or displacement, and where the engine was made. Here we have a 7.0 L, LS&, gas, eight-cylinder, SFI, aluminum, GM.

8 The ninth character is the check character. It is used internally by the manufacturer.

9 The tenth character tells you the year of manufacture. You can decode this character according to a model year identification chart, which in this example shows us that the vehicle was assembled for the 2010 model year.

10 The eleventh character tells you the assembly plant or factory where the vehicle was put together.

11 The final six numbers make up the sequential number of the vehicle as it comes off the assembly line, starting at a base number, which is usually one hundred thousand (100000). So the first vehicle to be produced will usually, but not always, have the number 100001. In our example, the vehicle was the first to come off the assembly line in that year.

▶ Using Other Vehicle Information Labels

Vehicle Emission Control Information (VECI) Label

The <u>Vehicle Emission Control Information (VECI) label</u> is used by technicians to identify engine and emission control information for the vehicle **FIGURE 5-11**. It is usually located in the engine compartment on either the hood, strut tower, or radiator support. It typically includes the following information:

- Engine family and displacement
- Model year the vehicle conforms to
- Spark plug part number and gap
- Evaporative emission system family
- Emission control system schematic
- Certification application

Vehicle Safety Certification (VSC) Label

The <u>Vehicle Safety Certification (VSC) label</u> certifies that the vehicle meets the Federal Motor Vehicle Safety, Bumper, and Theft Prevention Standards in effect at the time of manufacture **FIGURE 5-12**. It is used by technicians to identify some basic types of information about the vehicle such as month and year of manufacture, Gross Vehicle Weight Rating (GVWR), and tire information. It is usually affixed to the driver's side door pillar or on the side of the door next to the pillar. It typically includes the following information:

- Month and year of manufacture
- GVWR and Gross Axle Weight Rating (GAWR)
- VIN
- Recommended tire sizes
- Recommended tire inflation pressures
- Paint and trim codes

FIGURE 5-11 VECI label.

FIGURE 5-12 VSC label.

FIGURE 5-13 Refrigerant label.

FIGURE 5-14 Coolant label.

FIGURE 5-15 Belt routing label.

Other Labels

Other labels include the refrigerant label, the coolant label, and the belt routing label. The **refrigerant label** lists the type and total capacity of refrigerant that is installed in the A/C system **FIGURE 5-13**. The **coolant label** lists the type of coolant installed in the cooling system **FIGURE 5-14**. The **belt routing label** lists a diagram of the serpentine belt routing for the engine accessories **FIGURE 5-15**.

▶ 3 Cs

The 3 Cs are an easy way to learn the fundamental steps in conducting repairs. They stand for **c**oncern, **c**ause, and **c**orrection. Concern stands for the customer's understanding of the vehicle problem. Customers experience an issue with their vehicle and attempt to communicate that to the service advisor, who helps the customer put the concern into words that make sense. For example, a customer has trouble starting his car. He may initially communicate that the engine won't crank over. With some questioning and answers, the service advisor helps the customer identify that the engine is cranking over, but not starting. So the actual concern is: "engine cranks, but won't start." That is a vastly different situation than "engine will not crank." By understanding the actual concern, you can plan your approach to diagnosing the vehicle by testing systems and components. This will require you to take the time to fully understand the concern, read the repair order, and talk to the customer to gather further information if needed. Think through the problem and develop a strategy to attack it. Then you will know what tests you need to conduct and the order in which to conduct them.

Cause stands for understanding the reason that there is a fault. Understanding the cause and effect of the fault enables the technician to conduct a repair that is effective. This step may require you to conduct tests or inspect various components to narrow down exactly where the fault lies, what is wrong, and what components may be faulty.

It is important that you determine the root cause of the fault. This means you must distinguish between the cause and the effect and determine the ultimate cause of the fault. For example, if the brake lights are not working, you might find the brake fuse blown. That is definitely the cause of the brake lights not working (effect). But what caused the brake fuse to blow? Maybe it was a chaffed wire in the trunk that intermittently short-circuits to ground (root cause). If you only replace the fuse, the problem will likely reoccur. The root cause in this case is an intermittent short circuit due to an improperly routed or protected brake light wire.

Correction stands for the procedure and parts that will be used to fix the problem. In the preceding situation, the correction would be: "Repair the brake light wire and reroute it so it doesn't chaff and short-circuit again." This step occurs once the problem and faults are fully understood and the damage assessed so the correct parts can be fitted to complete a successful repair. Don't forget that to ensure a successful repair, the system should be thoroughly checked to confirm that everything is working as it should before returning the vehicle to the customer.

To apply the 3 Cs, follow the steps in **SKILL DRILL 5-10**:

1. Using the 3 Cs, document the repair process required for a repair order.

2. Identify and document the concern. This should be on the repair order. Obtain as much information as possible, as this will help you to understand the problem. Identify what the problem is and what vehicle systems are involved. Gather information on any recent repairs or servicing. Ask questions like, How long has the problem been occurring? or, Does it occur at any particular time or temperature? All of this information will help to identify the problem.

3. Identify and document the root cause of the concern. Research shop manuals and conduct tests to identify the cause of the problem. This may require a number of tests across multiple systems.

4. Review the information you collect from the tests. To review effectively, you need to understand how the systems work and interact.

5. Always work safely and use the proper tools and correct personal protective equipment (PPE).

6. Identify and document the correction required, including work activities and parts required or used. Make repairs or replace parts to complete the repair.

7. Retest the vehicle to be sure the fault has been corrected.

8. Fill in the required repair order with details of the work conducted.

Wrap-up

Ready for Review

- The owner's manual, usually kept in the glove compartment, provides information on how to operate the vehicle and basic maintenance to be performed.
- Manufacturers provide shop (or service) manuals for each make and model of car; these manuals provide vehicle-specific instructions on service and repair.
- Service information programs allow users to access maintenance and repair information via computer.
- After-market repair manuals are not produced by manufacturers and provide less detailed information for specific makes and models.
- Manufacturers provide technical service bulletins (TSBs) as updates to shop manuals when new problems or maintenance concerns arise for certain vehicle makes or models.
- If a safety issue is discovered on a certain make of vehicle, the manufacturer may issue a service campaign or recall.
- Labor guides provide up-to-date information on service repair times and cost estimates.
- Parts programs are electronic catalogues of vehicle parts.
- Repair or work orders detail customer concern information to guide the service technician, as well as information on services as they are performed.
- Account systems track repair costs and customer methods of payment.
- A vehicle's service history consists of records of all maintenance and repairs performed on the vehicle.
- Vehicle information numbers (VINs) are unique identifiers for each vehicle produced.
- VINs are made up of 17 characters and are usually located on the front left corner of the windshield and on the engine, transmission, and other vehicle parts.
- VINs assist customers and technicians in tracking title history and reveal whether the vehicle has been wrecked or had repeated unsuccessful repairs for a particular fault.
- The two worldwide VIN systems are the North American VIN system and ISO Standard 3779.
- The VIN contains information on country of origin, manufacturer, make and model, body type, seat restraints, engine type, year of manufacture, assembly plant, and the order the vehicle came off the assembly line.
- Manufacturers also provide vehicle information labels to provide further specifications for each model of vehicle.
- The 3 Cs of vehicle repair are concern, cause, and correction.

Key Terms

belt routing label A label that lists a diagram of the serpentine belt routing for the engine accessories.

coolant label A label that lists the type of coolant installed in the cooling system.

labor guide A guide that provides information to make estimates for repairs.

lemon law buyback A consumer protection law used in some states to identify a new vehicle that has undergone several unsuccessful attempts to repair the same fault.

owner's manual An informational guide supplied by the manufacturer; it contains basic vehicle operating information.

parts program A computer software program for identifying and ordering replacement vehicle parts.

parts specialist The person who serves customers at the parts counters.

refrigerant label A label that lists the type and total capacity of refrigerant that is installed in the A/C system.

repair order A form used by shops to collect information regarding a vehicle coming in for repair, also referred to as a work order.

salvage title Also called a branded title; a record that a vehicle has been severely damaged or deemed a total loss by an insurance company.

service campaign and recall A corrective measure conducted by manufacturers when a safety issue is discovered with a particular vehicle.

service history A complete list of all the servicing and repairs that have been performed on a vehicle.

shop or service manual Manufacturer's or after-market information on the repair and service of vehicles.

technical service bulletin (TSB) Information issued by manufacturers to alert technicians of unexpected problems or changes to repair procedures.

vehicle emission control information (VECI) label A label used by technicians to identify engine and emission control information for the vehicle.

title history A detailed account of a vehicle's past.

vehicle identification number (VIN) A unique serial number that is assigned to each vehicle produced.

vehicle safety certification (VSC) label A label certifying that the vehicle meets the Federal Motor Vehicle Safety, Bumper, and Theft Prevention Standards in effect at the time of manufacture.

ASE-Type Questions

1. Tech A says that the owner's manual will have the oil pan drain plug torque information. Tech B says that oil pan capacity information for that specific vehicle will be in the owner's manual. Who is correct?
   a. Tech A
   b. Tech B
   c. Both A and B
   d. Neither A nor B

2. Tech A says that vehicle security PIN codes can be found in the service manual. Tech B says that vehicle security PIN codes can be found in the owner's manual. Who is correct?
   a. Tech A
   b. Tech B
   c. Both A and B
   d. Neither A nor B

3. Tech A says that paper service manuals are gone and electronic versions of the service manual are now available. Tech B says that online manuals are more current, as they can be updated periodically. Who is correct?
   a. Tech A
   b. Tech B
   c. Both A and B
   d. Neither A nor B

4. Tech A says that service information programs are extremely helpful, as the technician can use a laptop at the repair for quick access to the procedure to perform a repair. Tech B says that service information programs allow a technician to know the labor guide and, with the support of the program, perform the task in the time allowed. Who is correct?
   a. Tech A
   b. Tech B
   c. Both A and B
   d. Neither A nor B

5. Tech A says that TSBs are updates to the owner's manual. Tech B says that TSBs are generally updated information on model changes that do not affect the technician. Who is correct?
   a. Tech A
   b. Tech B
   c. Both A and B
   d. Neither A nor B

6. Tech A says that labor guides are necessary for the service writer to quote prices for a customer on the repair bill. Tech B says that labor guides are what the customer pays and that warranty pays more for labor using a different labor guide. Who is correct?
   a. Tech A
   b. Tech B
   c. Both A and B
   d. Neither A nor B

7. Tech A says that locating the part number the technician needs requires computer knowledge and mechanical knowledge. Tech B says that anybody can be a parts person. Who is correct?
   a. Tech A
   b. Tech B
   c. Both A and B
   d. Neither A nor B

8. Tech A says that the repair order is just a piece of paper telling the technician what to do. Tech B says that the repair order is a legal and binding contract between the customer and the repair facility. Who is correct?
   a. Tech A
   b. Tech B
   c. Both A and B
   d. Neither A nor B

9. Tech A says that customer authorization for a change in the repair order after initial authorization is the responsibility of the service writer or foreman. Tech B says that changes to the repair order can be dealt with after the repair is complete, as the customer will be satisfied if more repairs are completed. Who is correct?
   a. Tech A
   b. Tech B
   c. Both A and B
   d. Neither A nor B

10. Tech A says that the VIN number on a vehicle can help identify which engine is installed in the chassis. Tech B says that most digits in the VIN number can be an identifier for information pertinent to that vehicle. Who is correct?
    a. Tech A
    b. Tech B
    c. Both A and B
    d. Neither A nor B

CHAPTER 6

NATEF Tasks

Required Supplemental Tasks
Shop and Personal Safety

	Page
■ Utilize safe procedures for handling of tools and equipment.	101–105

Tools and Equipment

■ Identify tools and their usage in automotive applications.	101–179
■ Demonstrate safe handling and use of appropriate tools.	101–179
■ Identify standard and metric designation.	104–105
■ Demonstrate proper use of precision measuring tools (i.e., micrometer, dial-indicator, dial-caliper).	131–140
■ Demonstrate proper cleaning, storage, and maintenance of tools and equipment.	149–158

Engine Repair
General

■ Perform common fastener and thread repair, to include: remove broken bolt, restore internal and external threads, and repair internal threads with thread insert.	MLR AST MAST 158–160

Knowledge Objectives

After reading this chapter, you will be able to:
1. Describe the safety procedures to take when handling and using tools. (pp 101–105)
2. Describe the common air tools that a technician may use in the shop. (pp 105–106)
3. Describe the common fasteners used in the shop. (pp 107–111)
4. Describe how fasteners are used in the application of torque specifications. (pp 108–111)
5. Describe the common types of wrenches and when they are utilized in the shop. (pp 111–113)
6. Describe the common types of sockets and when they are utilized in the shop. (pp 113–114)
7. Describe the common types of pliers and when they are utilized in the shop. (pp 114–116)
8. Describe the common types of cutting tools and when they are utilized in the shop. (p 116)
9. Describe the common types of screwdrivers and when they are utilized in the shop. (pp 116–117)

Tools and Equipment

Skills Objectives, continued

20. Use a spray wash cabinet. (pp 152–153)
21. Use a solvent tank. (pp 154–155)
22. Use a brake washer. (pp 154–156)
23. Use a sand or bead blaster. (pp 157–158)
24. Perform thread repair. (pp 158–160)
25. Purge an oxyacetylene torch. (pp 161–162)
26. Set up an oxyacetylene torch. (pp 161–164)
27. Use an oxyacetylene torch for heating. (pp 164–165)
28. Use a welding tip for welding. (pp 165–166)
29. Use a welding tip for brazing. (p 167)
30. Use a cutting tip. (pp 168–169)
31. Use a plasma cutter. (pp 169–170)
32. Use a wire feed welder. (pp 171–172)
33. Charge a battery. (pp 174–176)
34. Jump-start a vehicle. (pp 176–177)
35. Clean tools and equipment. (pp 178–179)

Introduction

In this chapter, we will be exploring a variety of tool and equipment topics that are fundamental to your success as an automotive technician. Tools and equipment are very important to an efficient and effective shop operation. They provide the means for work to be undertaken on vehicles, from lifting to diagnosing, removing, installing, cleaning, and inspecting. Nearly all shop tasks involve the use of some sort of tool or piece of equipment. This makes their purchase, use, and maintenance very important to the overall performance of the shop. Always use tools and equipment in the way they are designed to be used. It is important to think about the task at hand, identify the most effective tools to do the task, inspect the tool before using it, use it correctly, clean and inspect it after you use it, and store it in the correct location.

General Guidelines

While it is important to be trained on the safe use of tools and equipment, it is even more critical to have a safe attitude. A safe attitude will help you avoid being involved in an accident. Students who think they will never be involved in an accident will not be as aware of unsafe situations as they should be. And that can lead to accidents. So while we are covering the various tools and equipment you will encounter in the shop, pay close attention to the safety and operation procedures. Tools are a technician's best friend, but if used improperly, they can injure or kill.

Work Safe and Stay Safe

Whenever using tools, always think safety first. There is nothing more important than your personal safety. If tools (both hand and power) are used incorrectly, you can potentially injure yourself and others. Always follow equipment and shop instructions, including the use of recommended personal protective equipment (PPE). Accidents only take a moment to occur but can take a lifetime to recover from. You are ultimately responsible for your safety, so remember to work safe and stay safe.

Safe Handling and Use of Tools

Tools must be safely handled and used to prevent injury and damage. Always inspect tools prior to use and never use damaged tools. Check the manufacturer and the shop procedures or ask your supervisor if you are uncertain about how to use tools. Inspect and clean tools when you are finished using them. Always return tools to their correct storage location.

To safely handle and use appropriate tools, follow the steps in **SKILL DRILL 6-1**:

1. Select the correct tool(s) to undertake tasks.
2. Inspect tools prior to use to ensure they are in good working order. If tools are faulty, remove them from service according to shop procedures. **(Photo 1)**
3. Clean tools prior to use if necessary. **(Photo 2)**
4. Use tools to complete the task while ensuring manufacturer and shop procedures are followed. Always use tools safely to prevent injury and damage.

You are the Automotive Technician

After finishing work on the last vehicle of the day, you are required to return your workstation back to order. You clean, inspect, and return tools and equipment to their designated place. You wipe up any spills according to the shop procedure and clear the floor of any debris to avoid slips and falls. During your workspace inspection, you determine that the insulation on the drop light cord is frayed, there are some tools that need to be cleaned, and air-powered tools to be put away.

1. What needs to happen with the drop light?
2. What should you do to air tools before using them each day?
3. What are the steps you take in cleaning electric power tools?

SKILL DRILL   6-1   Safe Handling and Use of Tools

1 Select the correct tool(s) to undertake tasks. Inspect tools prior to use to ensure they are in good working order. If tools are faulty, remove them from service according to shop procedures.

2 Clean tools prior to use if necessary.

3 Use tools to complete the task while ensuring manufacturer and shop procedures are followed. Always use tools safely to prevent injury and damage. Ensure tools are clean and in good working order after use. Report and tag damaged tools, and remove them from service following shop procedures.

4 Return tools to correct storage locations.

5 Ensure tools are clean and in good working order after use. Report and tag damaged tools, and remove them from service following shop procedures. **(Photo 3)**

6 Return tools to correct storage locations. **(Photo 4)**

Safe Procedures for Handling Tools and Equipment

Some tools are heavy or awkward to use, so seek assistance if required and use correct manual handling techniques when using tools. To utilize safe procedures

for handling tools and equipment, follow the steps in **SKILL DRILL 6-2**:

1 Seek assistance if tools and equipment are too heavy or too awkward to be managed by a single person.

2 Inspect tools and equipment for possible defects before starting work.

3 Report and/or tag faulty tools and equipment according to shop procedures. **(Photo 1)**

4 Select and wear appropriate PPE for the tools and equipment being used. **(Photo 2)**

SKILL DRILL | 6-2 | Safe Procedures for Handling Tools and Equipment

1 Seek assistance if tools and equipment are too heavy or too awkward to be managed by a single person. Inspect tools and equipment for possible defects before starting work. Report and/or tag faulty tools and equipment according to shop procedures.

2 Select and wear appropriate PPE for the tools and equipment being used.

3 Use tools and equipment safely. Check tools for faults after using them and report and/or tag faulty tools and equipment according to shop procedures. Clean and return tools and equipment to correct storage locations when tasks are completed.

5 Use tools and equipment safely.

6 Check tools for faults after using them and report and/or tag faulty tools and equipment according to shop procedures.

7 Clean and return tools and equipment to correct storage locations when tasks are completed. **(Photo 3)**

Tool Usage

Tools extend our abilities to perform many tasks; for example, jacks, stands, and hoists extend our ability to lift and hold heavy objects. Hand tools extend our ability to perform fundamental tasks like gripping, turning, tightening, measuring, and cutting. Electrical meters enable us to measure things we cannot see, feel, or hear, while power and air tools multiply our strength by performing tasks quickly and efficiently. As you are working, always think about what tool can make the job easier, safer, or more efficient. As you become familiar with more tools, your productivity, quality, and effectiveness will improve.

> ### TECHNICIAN TIP
>
> Using tools can make you much more efficient and effective in performing your job. Without tools, it would be very difficult to carry out vehicle repairs and servicing. It is also the reason that many technicians invest well over $20,000 in their personal tools. If purchased wisely, tools can help you perform more work in a shorter amount of time, thereby making you more money. So think of your tools as an investment that pays for itself over time.

Every tool is designed to be used in a certain way to do the job safely. It is critical to use a tool in the way it is designed to be used and to do so safely. For example, a screwdriver is designed to tighten and loosen screws, not to be used as a chisel. Ratchets are designed to turn sockets, not to be used as a hammer. Think about the task you are undertaking, select the correct tools for the task, and use each tool as it was designed.

Lockout/Tagout

<u>Lockout/tagout</u> is an umbrella term that describes a set of safety practices and procedures that are intended to reduce the risk of technicians inadvertently using tools, equipment, or materials that have been determined to be unsafe or potentially unsafe or that are in the process of being serviced. An example of lockout would be physically securing a broken, unsafe, or out-of-service tool so that it cannot be used by a technician. In many cases, the item is also tagged out so it is not inadvertently placed back into service or operated. An example of tagout would be affixing a clear and unavoidable label to a piece of equipment that describes the fault found, the name of the person who found the fault, the date that the fault was found, and that warns not to use the equipment **FIGURE 6-1**.

Safety

Standardized lockout/tagout procedures are a mandatory part of workplace safety regulations in most countries. Familiarize yourself with your local legislation and with the specific lockout/tagout practices that apply in your workplace.

Tool Location

The shop will usually have a selection of tools available for use, and these tools will be located in a number of areas. They include specialized manufacturer tools, high-cost tools, and tools that are not portable, such as hoists and compressors. Technicians will have a selection of their own tools, which will include various hand tools and electrical meters. Often they will add to their toolbox over time.

To identify tools and their usage in automotive application, follow these steps:

1. Create a list of tools in your tool chest and identify their application for automotive repair and service.
2. Look through the shop's tool storage areas and create a list of the tools found in each storage area; identify their application for automotive repair and service.

Standard and Metric Designations

Many tools, measuring instruments, and fasteners come in United States customary system (USCS) sizes, more commonly referred to as "standard," or in metric sizes. Tools and measuring instruments can be identified as standard or metric by markings identifying their size on tools or the increments on a measuring tool. Fasteners bought new will have their designation identified on the packaging. Other fasteners may have to be measured by a ruler or <u>vernier caliper</u> to identify their designation. Manufacturer's charts showing thread and fastener sizing will assist in identifying standard or metric sizing.

To identify standard and metric designation, follow these steps:

1. Examine the component, tool, or fastener to see if any marking identifies it as standard or metric.

FIGURE 6-1 **A.** An example of lockout would be physically locking out a tool or piece of equipment so that it cannot be accessed and used by someone who may be unaware of the potential danger of doing so. **B.** An example of tagout would be affixing a clear and unavoidable label to a piece of equipment that describes the fault found and that warns not to use it.

Manufacturer specifications and shop manuals can be referred to and may identify components as standard or metric.

2. If no markings are available, use measuring devices to gauge the size of the item and compare thread and fastener charts to identify the sizing. Inch-to-metric conversion charts will assist in identifying component designation.

▶ Air Tools

Compressed Air Equipment

The term **compressed air equipment** covers a wide range of tools and equipment required in a compressed air system. Tools that use compressed air include drills, grinders, pumps, grease guns, jacks, and impact wrenches **FIGURE 6-2**. The compressed air system is made up of a compressor, a pressure regulator, air hose or fixed piping, and the actual tool or item that is powered by the compressed air. The air compressor has a storage tank and is driven by an electric motor or, for more portability, a gasoline engine. In many shops, the air compressor is housed in a separate room to help isolate the noise.

Standard compressors have been, and still are, based on piston-type compressors, which operate similar to a piston engine where each piston compresses the air on the compression stroke. But in the case of a compressor, the piston forces the air out of the cylinder and into a storage tank under pressure. Many newer air

FIGURE 6-2 A wide variety of tools use compressed air, including drills, grinders, pumps, grease guns, jacks, and impact wrenches.

compressors are of the scroll compressor type, which uses a pair of rotating scrolls to compress the air and is much quieter and more efficient. With either type of compressor, a pressure regulator controls the air pressure being supplied to the distribution system while the air hose or lines transport the compressed air from the compressor to the tool.

Safety

Always respect compressed air: Wear appropriate PPE, and never use compressed air inappropriately.

Compressed Air Safety

Serious, sometimes fatal, injuries can be caused by compressed air being injected into the body through the skin or into a body opening, such as your mouth or ear. Do not play with air equipment, such as blowing air at another person or yourself. Internal human blood vessels and organs will rupture at much lower pressures than those found in compressed air lines. So always handle air equipment carefully and with respect. Be extra careful when working with air equipment in a confined or awkward space, such as under a vehicle, and when clearing or cleaning the equipment.

Safety

If air, grease, or any other substance is injected into someone's body, it is not always easy to tell how much damage has been done. Always provide initial first aid and then seek medical advice if any kind of penetration injury occurs.

Air Driers and Automatic Oilers

Air driers are fitted to compressed air systems to remove the moisture or water from the compressed air that is condensed as a result of compressing air from the atmosphere, which contains water in the form of humidity. If water gets into the air lines, it may damage air tools. Air driers can be a stand-alone device fitted to the compressed air system or incorporated into a filter/regulator system. The combination filter/regulator system removes water from the air, filters any debris that may come from the compressor tank, and regulates the line pressure from the tank.

An air drier can be a simple water trap that catches condensed water as hot air cools down slowly and the water condenses **FIGURE 6-3**. This type of air drier usually needs to be drained manually on a periodic basis. However, some devices drain automatically.

Another type of air drier is a chiller unit, which uses the principles of air conditioning to chill the hot compressed air and force condensation to occur at a higher rate. This system is much more expensive but does a good job of removing all traces of water. You may find this system in a body shop, where virtually all traces of water in the compressed air must be removed so that it cannot mix with the paint as it is being sprayed onto the surface of the vehicle.

Compressed air tools and equipment require a regular application of a lubricating oil to reduce wear and tear. **Automatic oilers** are designed to regularly oil an air tool or air equipment so it does not have to be done manually, before or during its use **FIGURE 6-4**. Automatic oilers are usually fitted near the air tool or equipment and regularly supply small amounts of

FIGURE 6-4 Compressed air automatic oiler.

oil into the stream of compressed air, which is then transported along with air to the tool or equipment. Automatic oilers need periodic inspection to make sure they deliver the correct amount of oil. The built-in oil reservoir also needs to be refilled with air tool oil on a regular schedule.

Chassis Dynamometers

A **chassis dynamometer** is a device that allows a vehicle to be run at road speed while safely contained within a shop bay. Chassis dynamometers are very useful for tuning engines, testing vehicle performance, and determining output in torque and horsepower. They are also used with sensors and test instruments to create simulated load conditions and diagnose any faults while in the shop. Chassis dynamometers are usually bolted down to the floor or built into the floor and have rollers that the wheels sit on. The vehicle is chained down so it cannot move forward or backward when the accelerator is pressed down. The chassis dynamometer has a control unit that displays the controls for the dynamometer and selected engine parameters such as engine revolutions per minute (rpm), drive wheel torque, and power.

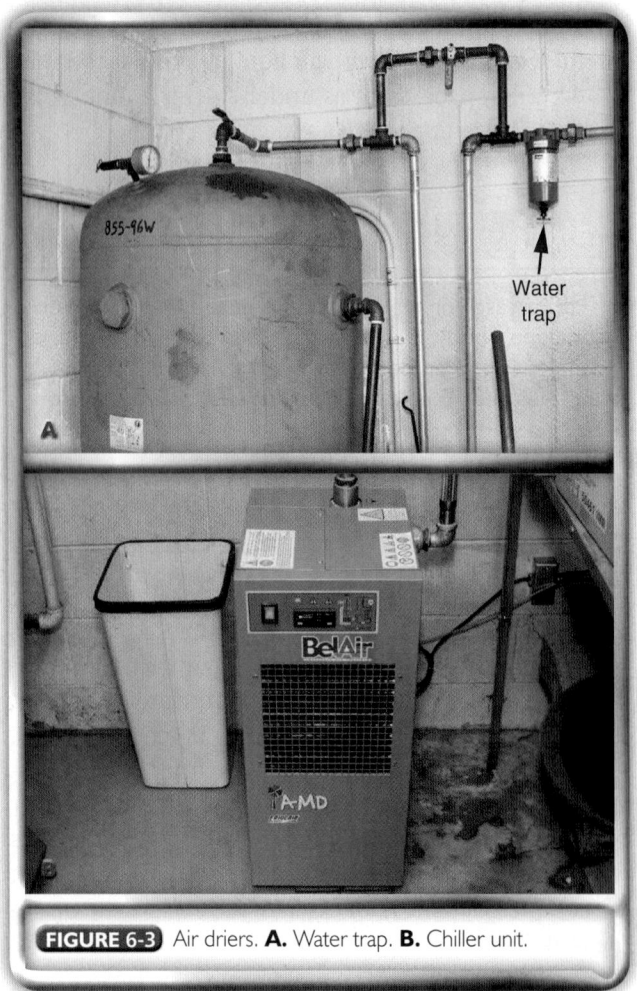

FIGURE 6-3 Air driers. **A.** Water trap. **B.** Chiller unit.

Safety

Always make sure the vehicle is secured effectively and the area is clear of tools, equipment, and people before using a chassis dynamometer. In many cases, the vehicle is being operated at full throttle and making maximum horsepower. If the vehicle were ever to break free, the resulting accident would be catastrophic.

Fasteners and Torque

Fasteners are designed to secure parts that are under various tension and sheer stresses. The nature of the stresses placed on parts and fasteners depends on their use and location. For example, head bolts withstand tension stresses by clamping the head gasket between the cylinder head and the block. The bolts must withstand the very high combustion pressures trying to push the head off of the engine block in order to leak past the head gasket. An example of fasteners withstanding sheer stresses is lug studs and lug nuts. They clamp the wheel assembly to the suspension system, and the weight of the vehicle tries to sheer the lug studs. If this were to happen, the wheel would fall off the vehicle, leading to an accident.

To accomplish their job, fasteners come in a variety of diameters and hardnesses, which are defined in grades. Fasteners with screw threads are designed to be tightened to a specific rating depending on the job at hand, the grade or hardness of the material they are made from, their size, and the thread type. If a fastener is overtightened, it could become damaged or could break. If it is undertightened, it could work loose over time. Torque is a way of defining how much a fastener should be tightened.

Bolts, Studs, and Nuts

Bolts, studs, and nuts are fasteners designed for heavier jobs than screws and tend to be made of metal or metal alloys **FIGURE 6-5**. Bolts are a cylindrical piece of metal with a hexagonal head on one end and a thread cut into the shaft at the other end. The thread acts as an inclined plane; as the bolt is turned, it is drawn into or out of the matching thread. Hexagonal nuts thread onto the bolt thread. The hexagonal heads for the bolt and nut are designed to fit tools such as combination wrenches and sockets.

A stud does not have a fixed hexagonal head; rather, it has a thread cut on each end. It is threaded into one part where it stays. The mating part is then slipped over it and a nut is threaded onto the end of the stud to secure the part. Studs are commonly used to attach a throttle body to the intake manifold. Studs can have different threads on each end. On one end, there is a thread that is best for gripping the hole in the intake manifold and to locate the throttle body, and on the other end, there is a thread for pulling everything together tightly with a steel nut.

Bolts, nuts, and studs can have either standard or metric threads. They are designated by their thread diameter, thread pitch, length, and grade. The diameter is measured across the outside of the threads; it is measured in fractions of an inch for standard-type fasteners, and millimeters for metric-type fasteners. So a $\frac{3}{8}$" (9.5 mm) bolt has a thread diameter of $\frac{3}{8}$" (9.5 mm), not the size of the bolt head.

The coarseness of any thread is called its **thread pitch** **FIGURE 6-6**. In the standard system, bolts, studs, and nuts are measured in threads per inch (tpi). To determine the

FIGURE 6-5 Bolts, studs, and nuts.

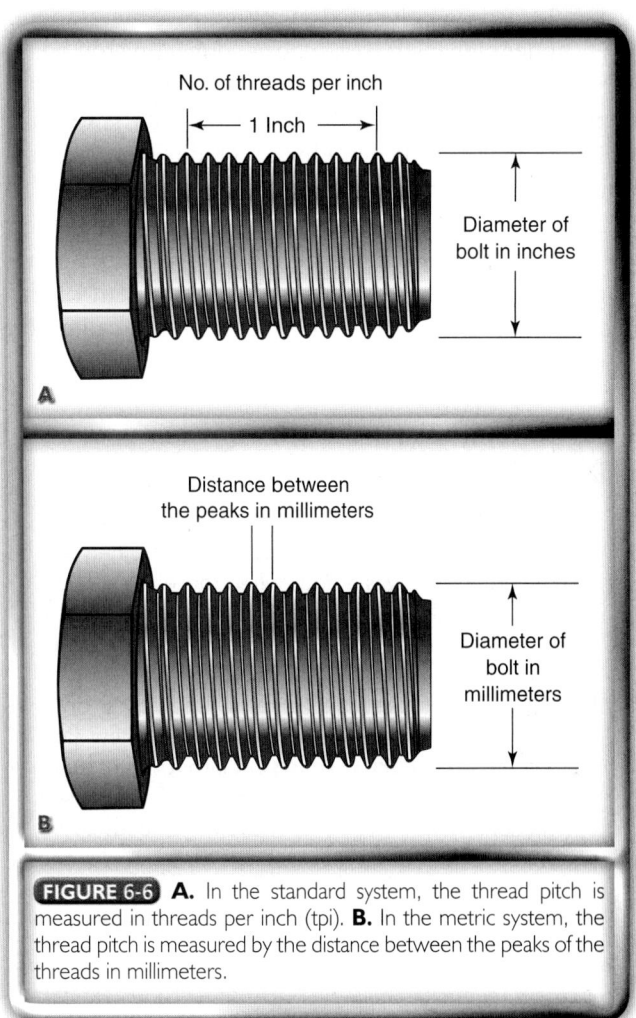

FIGURE 6-6 **A.** In the standard system, the thread pitch is measured in threads per inch (tpi). **B.** In the metric system, the thread pitch is measured by the distance between the peaks of the threads in millimeters.

tpi, simply count the number of threads there are in 1 inch. Each bolt diameter in the standard system can have one of two thread pitches, **coarse (UNC)** or **fine (UNF)**. For example, a ³⁄₈ – 16 is coarse, while a ³⁄₈ – 24 is fine. In the metric system, the thread pitch is measured by the distance between the peaks of the threads in millimeters. Each bolt diameter in the metric system can have up to four thread pitches. See a metric thread pitch chart since there is no clear pattern of thread pitches for metric fasteners. These charts can be found in tap and die sets or on the Internet.

The length of a bolt is fairly straightforward. It is measured from the end of the bolt to the bottom of the head and is listed in inches or millimeters. The grade of a fastener relates to its strength. The higher the grade number, the higher the **tensile strength**, which refers to how much tension it can withstand before it breaks. Tensile strength for fasteners is generally listed in pounds per square inch of bolt shaft area.

The Society of Automotive Engineers (SAE) is one certifying body that certifies fasteners. Their rating scale is from grade 1 to grade 8 for typical fasteners. Most general-purpose bolts used in automotive are grade 5. Bolts under higher stresses, such as connecting rod bolts, are a higher grade. In any critical component, you must replace an original bolt with a bolt of the same grade; use neither a lower grade nor a higher grade, as each could cause a failure if it is not designed for the task.

Many automotive bolts and nuts need to be tightened to a specified level—tight enough to hold components together but not so tight that the component or the fastener could fail. This level of tightness is called the **torque specification**. Bolts and nuts are often marked with grades to tell you their strength, which determines how much torque can be safely applied to them. For example, a grade 8 bolt is stronger and can be tightened to a higher torque than a grade 5 bolt. Once bolts are tightened, the challenge is to ensure they stay tight. There are several different ways for this to be accomplished. For example, a locking washer, a locking chemical compound, or a nylon locking device built into the nut may be used.

Torque Charts

Torque specifications for bolts and nuts in vehicles will usually be contained within shop manuals. Bolt, nut, and stud manufacturers also produce torque charts, which contain all the information you need to determine the maximum torque of bolts or nuts. For example, most charts include the bolt diameter, threads per inch, grade, and maximum torque setting for both dry and lubricated bolts and nuts. A lubricated bolt and nut will reach maximum torque value at a lower setting. In practice, most torque specifications call for the nuts and bolts to have dry threads prior to tightening. There are some exceptions, so close examination of the torque specification chart is critical.

Torque Wrenches

A **torque wrench** is also known as a tension wrench **FIGURE 6-7**. It is used to tighten fasteners to a predetermined torque. It is designed to tighten bolts and nuts using the drive on the end, which fits with any socket and accessory of the same drive size, found in an ordinary socket set. While manufacturers do not specify torque settings for every nut and bolt, when they do, it is important to follow the specifications. For example, manufacturers specify a torque for head bolts. The torque specified will ensure

> ### ► TECHNICIAN TIP
>
> Threads are cut on screws, bolts, nuts, and studs and inside holes to allow components to be attached and assembled. There was a time when there were many different thread designs used throughout the world. Modern vehicles still use a range of thread patterns, but due to standardization it is getting much simpler. Nearly all the nuts, bolts, screws, and studs on a vehicle have a V-thread cut into them. A screw jack or a clamp has **square threads** cut into it. The square thread is more difficult to machine and is mainly used in situations where rotational movement needs to be transferred into lateral movement—for example, the screw in a vice where the rotary movement of turning the handle is translated into the lateral movement of the jaws closing.

FIGURE 6-7 A torque wrench.

that the bolt provides the proper clamping pressure and will not come loose, but will not be so tight as to risk breaking the bolt or stripping the threads.

The torque value will be specified in foot-pounds (lb-ft), inch-pounds (in-lb), or newton meters (Nm). The torque value is the amount of twisting force applied to a fastener by the torque wrench. A foot-pound is described as the amount of twisting force applied to a shaft by a perpendicular lever 1 foot long with a weight of 1 pound placed on the outer end. A torque value of 100 lb-ft will be the same as a 100-lb weight placed at the end of a 1-foot-long lever. A torque value of an inch-pound will be 1 pound placed at the end of a 1-inch-long lever. Also note that 1 lb-ft equals 12 in-lb. A newton meter is described as the amount of twisting force applied to a shaft by a perpendicular lever 1 meter long with a force of 1 newton applied to the outer end. A torque value of 100 Nm will be the same as applying a 100-newton force to the end of a 1-meter-long lever. One lb-ft is equal to 1.35 Nm.

Torque wrenches come in various types: beam style, clicker, dial, and electronic. The simplest and least expensive is the beam-style torque wrench. It uses a spring steel beam that flexes under tension. A smaller fixed rod then indicates the amount of torque on a scale mounted to the bar. The amount of deflection of the bar coincides with the amount of torque on the scale. One drawback of this design is that you have to be positioned directly above the scale so you can read it accurately. That can be a problem when working under the hood of a vehicle.

The clicker-style torque wrench uses an adjustable clutch inside that slips (clicks) when the preset torque is reached. You can set it for a particular torque on the handle. As the bolt is tightened, once the preset torque is reached, the torque wrench will click. The higher the torque, the louder the click; the lower the torque, the quieter the click. Be careful when using this style of torque wrench, especially at lower torque settings. It is easy to miss the click and overtighten, break, or strip the bolt. Once the torque wrench clicks, stop turning it, as it will continue to tighten the fastener if you turn it past the click point.

The dial torque wrench turns a dial that indicates the torque based on the torque being applied. Like the beam-style torque wrench, you have to be able to see the dial to know how much torque is being applied. Many dial torque wrenches have a movable indicator that is moved by the dial and stays at the highest reading. That way you can double-check the torque achieved once the torque wrench is released. Once the proper torque is reached, the indicator can be moved back to zero for the next fastener being torqued.

The digital torque wrench usually uses a spring steel bar with an electronic strain gauge to measure the amount of torque being applied. The torque wrench can be preset to the desired torque. It will then display the torque as the fastener is being tightened. When it reaches the preset torque, it will usually give an audible signal, such as a beep. This makes it useful in situations where a scale or dial cannot be read.

Torque wrenches fall out of calibration over time or if they are not used properly, so they should be checked and calibrated on a periodic basis. This can be performed in the shop if the proper calibration equipment is available, or the torque wrench can be sent to a qualified service center. Most quality torque wrench manufacturers provide a recalibration service for their customers.

Using Torque Wrenches

The torque wrench is used to apply a specified amount of torque to a fastener. There are various methods used by torque wrenches to indicate that the correct torque has been reached. Some will give an audible signal such as a click or a beep, while others will give a visual signal such as a light or a pin moving or clicking out. Some must be observed while you are torquing the fastener. To help ensure that the proper amount of torque gets from the torque wrench to the bolt, support the head of the torque wrench with one hand. When using a torque wrench, it is best to not use extensions. Extensions make it harder to support the head, which can end up absorbing some of the torque. If possible, use a deep socket instead.

Torque-to-Yield and Torque Angle

Torque is not always the best method of ensuring that a bolt is tightened enough as to give the proper amount of clamping force. If the threads are rusty, rough, or damaged in any way, the amount of twisting force required to tighten the fastener increases. Tightening the rusty fastener to a particular torque will not provide as much clamping force as a smooth fastener torqued the same amount. All threads must be clean before tightening the fastener to a specified torque. This also brings up the question of whether threads should be lubricated. In most automotive cases, the torque values specified are for dry, non-lubricated threads. But always check the manufacturer's specifications.

When bolts are tightened, they are also stretched. As long as they are not tightened too much, they will return to their original length when loosened. This is called **elasticity**. If they continue to be tightened and stretch beyond their point of elasticity, they will not return to their original length when loosened. This is called the **yield point**. **Torque-to-yield** means that a fastener is torqued to, or just beyond, its yield point.

With the changes in engine metallurgy that manufacturers are using in today's vehicles, bolt technology had to change also. To help prevent bolts from loosening over time and to maintain an adequate clamping force when the engine is both cold and hot, manufacturers have adopted **torque-to-yield (TTY) bolts**. TTY bolts are designed to provide a consistent clamping force when torqued to their yield point or just beyond. The challenge is that the torque does not increase very much, or at all, once yield is reached. So using a torque wrench by itself will not indicate the point at which the manufacturer wants the bolt tightened. So TTY bolts generally require a new torquing procedure called torque angle. Also, it is important to note that in virtually all cases, TTY bolts cannot be reused because they have been stretched into their yield zone and would very likely fail if retorqued.

Torque angle is considered a more precise method to tighten TTY bolts and is essentially a multistep

process. Bolts are first torqued in the required pattern using a standard torque wrench to a required moderate torque setting. They are then further tightened an additional specified angle (torque angle) using an angle gauge, thus providing further tightening, which tightens the bolt to, or beyond, its yield point. In some cases, after torquing, the manufacturer first wants all of the bolts to be turned to an initial angle, and then turned an additional angle. And in other cases, the manufacturer wants all of the bolts torqued in a particular sequence, then detorqued in a particular sequence, then retorqued once again in a particular sequence, and finally tightened an additional specified angle. So always check the manufacturer's specifications and procedure before torquing TTY bolts.

To use a torque angle gauge in conjunction with a torque wrench, follow the steps in **SKILL DRILL 6-3**:

1. Check the specifications. Determine the correct torque value and sequence for the bolts or fasteners you are using. This will be in foot-pounds or newton meters. Also, check the torque angle specifications for the bolt or fastener, and whether it is one step or more than one step.

2. Tighten the bolt to the specified torque. If the component requires multiple bolts or fasteners, make

SKILL DRILL 6-3 | Using a Torque Wrench

1. Check the specifications for the bolt or fastener you are using. Tighten the bolt to the specified torque. If the component requires multiple bolts or fasteners, tighten them all to the same torque value in the sequence and steps that are specified by the manufacturer.

2. Install the torque angle gauge over the head of the bolt, and then put the torque wrench on top of the gauge and zero it, if necessary.

3. Turn the torque wrench the specified number of degrees as indicated on the angle gauge. If the component requires multiple bolts or fasteners, tighten them all to the same torque angle in the sequence that is specified by the manufacturer. Some torquing procedures could call for four or more steps to complete the torquing process properly.

sure to tighten them all to the same torque value in the sequence and steps that are specified by the manufacturer. **(Photo 1)**

3 Install the torque angle gauge over the head of the bolt, and then put the torque wrench on top of the gauge and zero it, if necessary. **(Photo 2)**

4 Turn the torque wrench the specified number of degrees as indicated on the angle gauge. If the component requires multiple bolts or fasteners, make sure to tighten them all to the same torque angle in the sequence that is specified by the manufacturer. Some torquing procedures could call for four or more steps to complete the torquing process properly. **(Photo 3)**

Safety

- Refer to the manufacturer's specifications when tightening fasteners.
- Return the torque wrench to its lowest setting when finished.
- If replacing a fastener, make sure it has the correct tensile value for the task it will perform.

▶ Basic Hand Tools

Like all tools, hand tools extend our ability to do work. Hand tools come in a variety of shapes, sizes, and functions. A large percentage of your personal tools will be hand tools. Over the years, manufacturers have introduced new fasteners, wire harness terminals, quick-connect fittings for fuel and other lines, and additional technologies that require their own different types of hand tools. This means that technicians need to add tools to their toolbox all of the time.

TECHNICIAN TIP

Invest in quality tools. Since tools extend your abilities, poor-quality tools will affect the quality and quantity of your work. Price is not always the best indicator of quality, but it plays a role. As you learn the purpose and function of the tools in this chapter, you should be able to identify high-quality tools versus poor-quality tools by looking at them, handling them, and putting them to work.

Wrenches

Wrenches are used to tighten and loosen nuts and bolts, which are two types of fasteners **FIGURE 6-8**. There are three commonly used wrenches: the **box-end wrench**, the **open-end wrench**, and the **combination wrench**. The box-end wrench fits fully around the head of the bolt or nut and grips each of the six points at the corners just like a socket. This is just the sort of grip needed if a nut or bolt is very tight and makes it less likely to round off the points on the head of the bolt than the open-end wrench. This grip gives you a better chance at loosening very tight fasteners. The ends of box-end wrenches are bent or offset so they are easier to grip and have different-sized heads at each end. One disadvantage of the box-end wrench is that it can be awkward to use once the nut or bolt has been loosened a bit because you have to lift it off the head of the fastener and move it to each new position.

The open-end wrench is open on the end and the two parallel flats only grip two points of the fastener. Open-end wrenches usually either have different-sized heads on each end of the wrench, or they have the same size, but with different angles. The head is at an angle to the handle and is not bent or offset, so it can be flipped over and used on both sides. This is a good wrench to use in very tight spaces as you can flip it over and get a new angle so the head can catch new points on the fastener. While an open-end wrench often gives the best access to a fastener, if the fastener is extremely tight, the open-end should not be used, as this type of wrench only grips two points. If the jaws flex slightly or the flats don't fit tightly around them, the wrench can suddenly slip when force is applied. This slippage can round off the points of

FIGURE 6-8 **A.** Box-end wrench. **B.** Open-end wrench. **C.** Combination wrench. **D.** Flare nut wrench. **E.** Ratcheting box-end wrench.

the fastener. The best way to approach the situation with a tight fastener is to use a box-end wrench to break the bolt or nut free, then use the open-end wrench to finish the job. The open-end wrench should only be used on fasteners that are no more than firmly tightened.

The combination wrench has an open-end head on one end and a box-end head on the other end. Both ends are usually of the same size. That way the box-end wrench can be used to break the bolt loose and the open end can be used for turning the bolt. Because of its versatility, this is probably the most popular wrench for technicians.

A variation on the open-end wrench is the **flare nut wrench**, also called a flare tubing wrench. It gives a better grip than the open-end wrench because it grabs all six points of the fastener, not two. However, since it is open on the end, it is not as strong as a box-end wrench. The partially open sixth side lets the wrench be placed over tubing or pipes so the wrench can be used to turn the tube fittings. Do not use the flare nut wrench on extremely tight fasteners as the jaws may spread, damaging the nut.

One other open-end wrench is the open-end adjustable wrench or crescent wrench. This wrench has a movable jaw that can be adjusted by turning an adjusting screw to fit any fastener within its range. It should only be used if other wrenches are not available because it is not as strong as a fixed wrench, so it can slip off of and damage the head of tight bolts or nuts. Still, it is a handy tool to have since it can be adjusted to fit most any fastener size.

A **ratcheting box-end wrench** is a useful tool in some applications because it does not require removal of the tool to reposition it. It has an inner piece that fits over and grabs the fastener points and is able to rotate within the outer housing. A ratcheting mechanism lets it rotate in one direction and lock in the other direction. In some cases, the wrench just needs to be flipped over to be used in the opposite direction. In other cases, it has a lever that changes the direction from clockwise to counterclockwise. Just be careful to not overstress this tool by using it to tighten or loosen very tight fasteners, as the outer housing is not very strong.

There is also a ratcheting open-end wrench, but it uses no moving parts. One of the sides is partially removed so that only the bottom one-third remains to catch a point on the bolt. When it is used, the normal side works just like a standard open-end wrench. The shorter side of the open-end wrench catches the point on the fastener so it can be turned. When moving the wrench to get a new bite, the wrench is pulled slightly outward, disengaging the short side while leaving the long side to slide along the faces of the bolt. The wrench is then rotated to the new position and pushed back in so the short side engages the next

point. This wrench, like other open-end wrenches, is not designed to tighten or loosen tight fasteners, but it does work well in blind places where a socket or ratcheting box-end wrench cannot be used.

Specialized wrenches such as the **pipe wrench**, grips pipes and can exert a lot of force to turn them **FIGURE 6-9**. Because the handle pivots slightly, the more pressure put on the handle to turn the wrench, the more the grip tightens. The jaws are hardened and serrated, and increasing the pressure also increases the risk of marking or even gouging metal from the pipe. The jaw is adjustable so it can be threaded in or out to fit different pipe sizes. Also, they come in different lengths, allowing you to increase the leverage applied to the pipe.

A specialized wrench called an **oil filter wrench** grabs the filter and gives you extra leverage to remove an oil filter when it is tight. They are available in various designs and sizes. Some oil filter wrenches are adjustable to fit many filter sizes. Also note that an oil filter wrench should be used *only* to remove an oil filter, never to install it. Almost all oil filters should be installed by hand.

FIGURE 6-9 **A.** Pipe wrench. **B.** Oil filter wrench.

Using Wrenches Correctly

Choosing the correct wrench for a job usually depends on two things: how tight the fastener is and how much room there is to get the wrench onto the fastener, and then to turn it. When being used, it is always possible that a wrench will slip. Before putting a lot of tension on the wrench, try to anticipate what will happen if it does slip. If possible, it is usually better to pull a wrench toward you than to push it away. If you have to push, use an open palm to push so your knuckles won't get crushed if the wrench slips.

Sockets

Sockets are very popular because of their adaptability and ease of use **FIGURE 6-10**. Sockets are a good choice where the top of the fastener is reasonably accessible. The **socket** fits onto the fastener snugly and grips it on all six corners, providing the type of grip needed on any nut or bolt that is extremely tight. They come in a variety of configurations, and technicians usually have a lot of sockets so they can get in a multitude of tight places. Individual sockets fit a particular size nut or bolt, so they are usually purchased in sets.

Sockets are classified by the following characteristics:

- Standard or metric
- Size of drive used to turn them: ½", ⅜", and ¼" are most common; 1" and ¾" are less common.
- Number of points: 6 and 12 are most common; 4 and 8 are less common.
- Depth of socket: Standard and deep are most common; shallow is less common.
- Thickness of wall: Standard and impact are most common; thin wall is less common.

Sockets are built with a recessed square drive that fits over the square drive of the ratchet or other driver **FIGURE 6-11**. The size of the drive determines how much twisting force can be applied to the socket. The larger the drive, the larger the twisting force. Small fasteners usually only need a small torque, so having too large of a drive may make it so the socket cannot gain access to the bolt. For fasteners that are really tight, an impact wrench exerts a lot more torque on a socket than turning it by hand. Impact sockets are usually thicker walled than standard wall sockets and have six points so they can withstand the forces generated by the impact wrench as well as grip the fastener securely.

Six- and 12-point sockets fit the heads of hexagonal-shaped fasteners. Four- and 8-point sockets fit the heads of square-shaped fasteners. Since 6-point and 4-point sockets fit the exact shape of the fastener, they have the strongest grip on the fastener, but they only can fit on the fastener in half as many positions as a 12-point or 8-point socket.

Another factor in accessing a fastener is the depth of the socket. If a nut is threaded quite a ways down a stud, then a standard length socket will not fit far enough over the stud to reach the nut. In this case, a deep socket will usually reach the nut.

> **TECHNICIAN TIP**
>
> Since sockets are usually purchased in sets, with each set providing a slightly different capability, you can see why technicians could easily have several hundred sockets in their toolbox.

FIGURE 6-10 The anatomy of a socket.

FIGURE 6-11 **A.** Deep socket. **B.** Ratchet. **C.** Breaker bar. **D.** T-handle. **E.** Square drive. **F.** An extension with a handle attached.

Turning a socket requires a handle. The most common socket handle, the **ratchet**, makes easy work of tightening or loosening a nut where not a lot of pressure is involved. It can be set to turn in either direction and does not need much room to swing. It is built to be convenient, not super strong, so too much pressure could damage it. For heavier tightening or loosening, a breaker bar gives the most leverage. When that is not available, a **sliding T-handle** may be more useful. With this tool, both hands can be used, and the position of the tee piece is adjustable to clear any obstructions when turning it.

The connection between the socket and the accessory is made by a square drive. The larger the drive, the heavier and bulkier the socket will be. The ¼" drive is for small work in difficult areas. The ¾" drive accessories handle a lot of general work where torque requirements are not too high. The ½" drive is required for all-around service. The ¾" and 1" drives are required for large work with high-torque settings. Many fasteners are located in positions where access can be difficult. There are many different lengths of extensions available to allow the socket to be on the fastener while extending the drive point out to where a handle can be attached **FIGURE 6-12**.

A **speed brace** or speeder handle is the fastest way to spin a fastener on or off a thread by hand, but it cannot apply much torque to the fastener; therefore, it is mainly used to remove a fastener that has already been loosened, or to run the fastener onto the thread until it begins to tighten. A universal joint can take the turning force that needs to be applied to the socket through an angle.

A **lug wrench** has special-sized lug nut sockets permanently attached to it. One common model, the lug wrench, has four different-sized sockets, one on each arm. Never hit or jump on a lug wrench when loosening lug nuts. If the lug wrench will not remove them, you should use an impact wrench. The impact wrench provides a hammering effect in conjunction with rotation to help loosen tight fasteners. *Never* use an impact tool to tighten lug fasteners. Torque all lug fasteners to the proper torque with a properly calibrated torque wrench.

Pliers

Pliers are a hand tool designed to hold, cut, or compress materials **FIGURE 6-13**. They are usually made out of two pieces of strong steel joined at a fulcrum point with jaws and cutting surfaces at one end and handles designed to provide leverage at the other. There are many types of pliers, including slip-joint, combination, arc joint, needle-nosed, and flat-nosed **FIGURE 6-14**.

Quality **combination pliers** are the most commonly used pliers in a shop. They are made from two pieces of high carbon or alloy steel. They pivot together so that any force applied to the handles is multiplied in the strong jaws. Some pliers provide a powerful grip on objects, while others are designed to cut. Combination pliers can do both, which is why they are the most common type of pliers.

Combination pliers offer two surfaces, one for gripping flat surfaces and one for gripping rounded objects, and two pairs of cutters. The cutters in the jaws should be used for softer materials that will not damage the blades. The cutters next to the pivot can shear through hard, thin materials, like steel wire or pins.

FIGURE 6-12 **A.** Speed brace. **B.** Universal joint. **C.** Lug wrench.

FIGURE 6-13 Pliers are used for grasping and cutting.

Most pliers are limited by their size in what they can grip. Beyond a certain point, the handles are spread too wide, or the jaws cannot open wide enough, but **arc joint pliers** overcome that limitation with a moveable pivot. Often, these are called Channellocks™ after the company that first made them. These pliers have parallel jaws that allow you to increase or decrease the size of the jaws by selecting a different set of channels. They are useful for a wider grip and a tighter squeeze on parts too big for conventional pliers.

There are a few specialized pliers in most shops. **Needle-nosed pliers**, which have long pointed jaws, can reach tight spots or hold small items that other pliers cannot. For example, they can pick up a small bolt that has fallen into a tight spot. **Flat-nosed pliers** have an end or nose that is flat and square; in contrast, combination pliers have a rounded end. A flat nose makes it possible to bend wire or even a thin piece of sheet steel accurately along a straight edge. **Diagonal cutting pliers** are used for cutting wire or cotter pins. Diagonal cutters are the most common cutters in the toolbox, but they should not be used on hard or heavy-gauge materials because the cutting surfaces will be damaged. End cutting pliers, also called **nippers**, have a cutting edge at right angles to their length. They are designed to cut through soft metal objects sticking out from a surface.

Snap ring pliers have metal pins that fit in the holes of a snap ring. Snap rings can be of the internal or external type. If internal, then internal snap ring pliers compress the snap ring so it can be removed from and installed in its internal groove. If external, then external snap ring pliers are used to remove and install the snap ring in its external groove. Always wear safety glasses when working with snap rings, as the rings can easily slip off the snap ring pliers and fly off at tremendous speeds, possibly causing severe eye injuries.

Safety

When applying pressure to pliers, make sure your hands are not greasy or they might slip. Select the right type and size of pliers for the job. As with most tools, if you have to exert almost all your strength to get something done, then you are using either the wrong tool or the wrong technique. If the pliers slip, you will get hurt. At the very least, you will damage the tool and what you are working on. Pliers get a lot of hard use in the shop, so they do get worn and damaged. If they are worn or damaged, they will be inefficient and can be dangerous. Always check the condition of all shop tools on a regular basis.

Locking pliers, also called vice grips, are general-purpose pliers used to clamp and hold one or more objects **FIGURE 6-15**. Locking pliers are helpful by freeing up one or more of your hands when working because they can clamp something and lock themselves in place to hold it. They are also adjustable so they can be used for a variety of tasks. To clamp an object with locking pliers, put the object between the jaws, turn the screw until the handles are almost closed, then squeeze them together to lock them shut. You can increase or decrease the gripping force with the adjustment screw. To release

FIGURE 6-14 **A.** Combination pliers. **B.** Needle-nosed pliers. **C.** Flat-nosed pliers. **D.** Diagonal cutting pliers. **E.** Nippers. **F.** Internal snap ring pliers. **G.** External snap ring pliers.

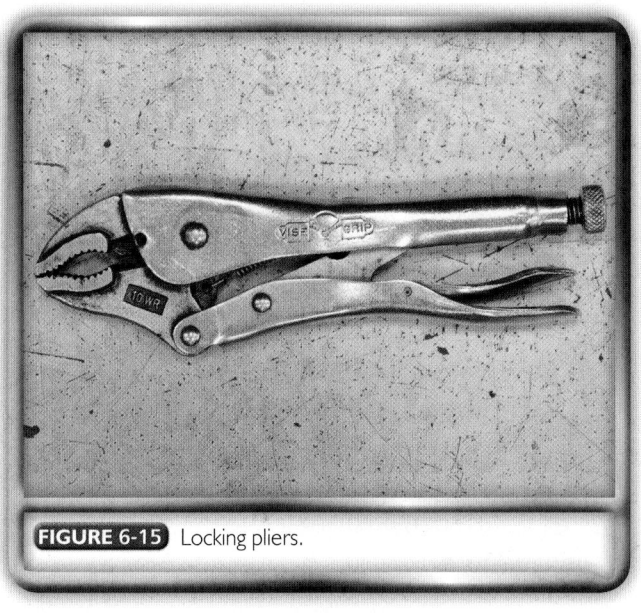

FIGURE 6-15 Locking pliers.

them, squeeze the release lever and they should open right up.

Cutting Tools

Bolt cutters cut heavy wire, non-hardened rods, and bolts **FIGURE 6-16**. Their compound joints and long handles give the leverage and cutting pressure that is needed for heavy gauge materials. **Tin snips** are the nearest thing in the toolbox to a pair of scissors. They can cut thin sheet metal, and lighter versions make it easy to follow the outline of gaskets. Most snips come with straight blades but if there is an unusual shape to cut, there is a pair with left or right hand curved blades. **Aviation snips** are designed to cut soft metals. They are easy to use because the handles are spring loaded open and double pivoted for extra leverage.

Allen Wrenches

Allen wrenches, sometimes called Allen or hex keys, are tools designed to tighten and loosen fasteners with Allen heads **FIGURE 6-17**. The Allen head has an internal hexagonal recess that the Allen wrench fits in. Allen wrenches come in sets, and there is a correct wrench size for every Allen head. They give the best grip on a screw or bolt of all the drivers, and their shape makes them good at getting into tight spots. Care must be utilized to make sure the correct size of Allen key is used or the key and/or socket head will be rounded off. The traditional Allen wrench is a hexagonal bar with a right angle bend at one end. They are made in various sizes in both metric and standard. As their popularity has increased, so too has the number of tool variations. Now Allen sockets are available, as are T-handle Allen keys.

Screwdrivers

The correct screwdriver to use depends on the type of slot or recess in the head of the screw or bolt, and how accessible it is **FIGURE 6-18**. Most screwdrivers cannot grip as securely as wrenches, so it is very important to match the tip of the screwdriver exactly with the slot or recess in the head of a fastener. Otherwise the tool might slip, damaging the fastener or the tool and possibly injuring you. When using a screwdriver, always check where the screwdriver blade can end up if it slips off the head of the screw. Many technicians who have not taken this precaution have stabbed a screwdriver into or through their hand.

The most common screwdriver has a flat tip, or blade, which gives it the name **flat blade screwdriver**. The blade should be almost as wide and thick as the slot in the fastener so that twisting force applied to the screwdriver is transferred right out to the edges of the head where it has most effect. The blade should be a snug fit in the slot of the screw head. Then the twisting force is applied evenly along the sides of the slot. This will guard against the screwdriver suddenly chewing a piece out of the slot and slipping just when the most force is being exerted. Flat blade screwdrivers come in a variety of sizes and lengths, so find the right one for the job.

If viewed from the side, the blade should taper slightly until the very end where the tip fits into the slot. If the tip of the blade is not clean and square, it should be reshaped or replaced.

When you use a flat blade screwdriver, support the shaft with your free hand as you turn it (but keep it behind the tip). This helps keep the blade square on the

FIGURE 6-16 **A.** Bolt cutters. **B.** Tin snips. **C.** Aviation snips.

FIGURE 6-17 Allen wrench.

slot and centered. Screwdrivers that slip are a common source of damage and injury in shops.

A screw or bolt with a cross-shaped recess requires a **Phillips head screwdriver** or a Pozidriv screwdriver. The cross-shaped slot holds the tip of the screwdriver securely on the head. The Phillips tip fits a tapered recess while the Pozidriv fits into slots with parallel sides in the head of the screw. Both a Phillips and a Pozidriv screwdriver are less likely to slip sideways because the point is centered in the screw, but again the screwdriver must be the right size. The fitting process is simplified with these two types of screwdrivers because four sizes are enough to fit almost all fasteners with this sort of screw head.

The **offset screwdriver** fits into spaces where a straight screwdriver cannot and is useful where there is not much room to turn it **FIGURE 6-19**. The two tips look identical, but one is set at 90 degrees to the other. This is because sometimes there is only room to make a quarter turn of the driver. Thus the driver has two blades on opposite ends so that offset ends of the screwdriver can be used alternately.

The **ratcheting screwdriver** is a popular screwdriver handle that usually comes with a selection of flat and Phillips tips. It has a ratchet inside the handle that turns the blade in only one direction depending on how the slider is set. When set for loosening, a screw can be undone without removing the tip of the blade from the head of the screw. When set for tightening, a screw can be inserted just as easily.

An **impact driver** is used when a screw or a bolt is rusted/corroded in place or overtightened and needs a tool that can apply more force than the other members of this family. Screw slots can easily be stripped with the use of a standard screwdriver. The force of the hammer pushing the bit into the screw and at the same time turning it makes it more likely the screw will break loose. The impact driver accepts a variety of special, impact tips. Choose the right one for the screw head, fit the tip in place, and then tension it in the direction it has to turn. A sharp blow with the hammer breaks the screw free, and then it can be unscrewed.

Magnetic Pickup Tools and Mechanical Fingers

Magnetic pickup tools and **mechanical fingers** are very useful for grabbing items in tight spaces **FIGURE 6-20**. A magnetic pickup tool typically is a telescoping stick that has a magnet attached to the end on a swivel joint.

FIGURE 6-18 **A.** Flat blade screwdriver. **B.** Phillips screwdriver. **C.** Pozidriv screwdriver.

FIGURE 6-19 **A.** Offset screwdriver. **B.** Ratcheting screwdriver. **C.** Impact driver.

FIGURE 6-20 **A.** Magnetic pickup tools. **B.** Mechanical fingers.

The magnet is strong enough to pick up screws, bolts, and sockets. For example, if a screw is dropped into a tight crevice where your fingers cannot reach, a magnetic pickup tool can be used to extract it.

> ### ▶ TECHNICIAN TIP
>
> It may be challenging getting the magnet down inside some areas because the magnet wants to keep sticking to other objects. One trick in this situation is to roll up a piece of paper so that a tube is created. Stick that down into the area of the dropped part, then slide the magnet down the tube, which will help it get past magnetic objects. Once the magnet is down, you may want to remove the roll of paper. Just remember two things: First, patience is important when using this tool, and second, don't drop anything in the first place!

Mechanical fingers are also designed to extract or insert objects in tight spaces. Because they actually grab the object, they can pick up non-magnetic objects, which makes them handy for picking up rubber or plastic parts. They use a flexible body and come in different lengths but typically are about 12–18" (305–457 mm) long. They have expanding grappling fingers on one end to grab items while the other end has a push mechanism to expand the fingers and a retracting spring to contract the fingers.

Hammers

Hammers are a vital part of the shop tool collection, and a variety are commonly used **FIGURE 6-21**. The most common hammer in an automotive shop is the **ball-peen (engineer's) hammer**. Like most hammers, its head is hardened steel. A punch or a chisel can be driven with the flat face. Its name comes from the ball peen or rounded face. It is usually used for flattening or **peening** a rivet. The hammer should always match the

> ### Safety
>
> The hammer you use depends on the part you are striking. Hammers with a metal face should almost always be harder than the part you are hammering. Never strike two hardened tools together, as this can cause the hardened parts to shatter.

size of the job, and it is usually better to use one that is too big than too small.

Hitting chisels with a **steel hammer** is fine, but sometimes you only need to tap a component to position it. A steel hammer might mark or damage the part, especially if it is made of a softer metal, such as aluminum. In such cases, a soft-faced hammer should normally be used for the job. Soft-faced hammers range from very soft with rubber or plastic heads to slightly harder with brass or copper.

When a large chisel needs a really strong blow, it is time to use a **sledge hammer**. The sledge hammer is like a small mallet, with two square faces made of high carbon steel. It is the heaviest type of hammer that can be used one-handed. The sledge hammer would be used in conjunction with a chisel to cut off a bolt where corrosion has made it impossible to remove the nut.

The most common mallet in the shop has a head made of hard rubber. A **hard rubber mallet** is a special-purpose tool and is often used for moving things into place where it is important not to damage the item being moved. For example, it can be used to tap a crankshaft, to measure end play, or to break a gasket seal on an aluminum casing.

A **dead blow hammer** is designed not to bounce back when it hits something. A rebounding hammer can be dangerous or destructive. A dead blow hammer can be made with a lead head or more commonly a hollow polyurethane head filled with lead shot or sand. The head absorbs the blow when the hammer makes contact, reducing any bounce-back or rebounding. This hammer can be used when working on the vehicle chassis or when dislodging stuck parts.

FIGURE 6-21 **A.** Sledge hammer. **B.** Ball-peen hammer. **C.** Dead blow hammer. **D.** Hard rubber mallet.

When using hammers and chisels, safety goggles must always be worn.

Chisels

The most common kind of chisel is a **cold chisel** **FIGURE 6-22**. It gets its name from the fact it is used to cut cold metals, rather than heated metals. It has a flat blade made of high-quality steel and a cutting angle of approximately 70 degrees. The cutting end is tempered and hardened because it has to be harder than the metals that need to be cut. The head of the chisel needs to be softer so it will not chip when it is hit with a hammer. Technicians sometimes use a cold chisel to remove bolts whose heads have rounded off.

Chisels and punches are designed with a softer striking end than hammers. Over time, this softer metal "mushrooms" and small fragments are prone to breaking off when hammered. These fragments can cause eye or other penetrative injuries to people in the area. Always inspect chisels and punches for mushrooming and dress them on a grinder when necessary.

A **cross-cut chisel** is so named because the sharpened edge is across the blade width. This chisel narrows down along the stock, so it is good for getting in grooves. It is used for cleaning out or even making key ways. The flying chips of metal should always be directed away from the user.

Punches

Punches are used when the head of the hammer is too large to strike the object being hit without causing damage to adjacent parts **FIGURE 6-23**. A punch transmits the hammer's striking power from the soft upper end down to the tip that is made of hardened high carbon steel. A punch transmits an accurate blow from the hammer at exactly one point, something that cannot be guaranteed using a hammer on its own.

When marks need to be drawn on an object like a steel plate to help locate a hole to be drilled, a **prick punch** can be used to mark the points so they will not rub off. They can also be used to scribe intersecting lines between given points. The prick punch's point is very sharp, so a gentle tap leaves a clear indentation. The **center punch** is not as sharp as a prick punch and is usually bigger. It makes a bigger indentation that centers a drill bit at the point where a hole is required to be drilled.

A **drift punch** is also named a starter punch because you should always use it first to get a pin moving. It has a tapered shank and the tip is slightly hollow so it does not spread the end of a pin and make it an even tighter fit. Once the starter drift has gotten the pin moving, a suitable pin punch will drive the pin out or in. A drift punch also works well for aligning holes on two mating objects, such as a valve cover and cylinder head. Forcing the drift punch in the hole will align both components for easier installation of the remaining bolts.

Pin punches are available in various diameters. A pin punch has a long slender shaft that has straight

FIGURE 6-22 **A.** Cold chisel. **B.** Cross-cut chisel.

FIGURE 6-23 **A.** Prick punch. **B.** Center punch. **C.** Drift punch.

sides. It is used to drive out rivets or pins **FIGURE 6-24**. A lot of components are either held together or accurately located by pins. Pins can be pretty tight and a group of pin punches is specially designed to deal with them.

Special punches with hollow ends are called **wad punches** or **hollow punches**. They are the most efficient tool to make a hole in soft sheet material like shim steel, plastic, and leather, or, most commonly, in a gasket. When being used, there should always be a soft surface under the work, ideally the end grain of a wooden block. If a hollow punch loses its sharpness or has nicks around its edge, it will make a mess instead of a hole.

Numbers and letters, like the engine numbers on some cylinder blocks, are usually made with number and letter punches that come in boxed sets. The rules for using a number or letter punch set are the same as for all punches. The punch must be square with the surface being worked on, not on an angle, and the hammer must hit the top squarely.

Pry Bars

Pry bars are tools composed of a strong metal that are used as a lever to move, adjust, or pry **FIGURE 6-25**. Pry bars come in a variety of shapes and sizes. Many have a tapered end that is slightly bent, with a plastic handle on the other end. This design works well for applying force to tension belts or for moving parts into alignment. Another type of pry bar is the **roll bar**. One end is sharply curved and tapered, which is used for prying. The other end is tapered to a dull point and is used to align larger holes such as transmission bell housings or engine motor mounts. Because pry bars are made of hardened steel, care should be taken when using them on softer materials to avoid any damage.

Gasket Scrapers

A **gasket scraper** has a hardened, sharpened blade. It is designed to remove a gasket without damaging the sealing face of the component when used properly **FIGURE 6-26**. On one end, it has a comfortable handle to grip like a screwdriver handle; on the other end, a blade is fitted with a sharp edge to assist in the removal of gaskets. The gasket scraper should be kept sharp to make it easy to remove all traces of the old gasket and sealing compound. The blades come in different sizes, with a typical size being 1" (25 mm) wide. Whenever you use a gasket scraper, be very careful not to nick or damage the surface being cleaned.

Safety

Hands should always be kept away from the surface of the file and the metal that is being worked on. Filing can produce small slivers of metal that can be difficult to remove from a finger or hand. Clean hands will help avoid slipping and lessen the corrosion caused by acids and moisture from the skin.

FIGURE 6-25 **A.** Pry bar. **B.** Roll bar.

FIGURE 6-26 A gasket scraper.

FIGURE 6-24 **A.** Pin punch. **B.** Wad punch. **C.** Number punch set.

Files

Files are hand tools designed to remove small amounts of material from the surface of a workpiece. Files come in a variety of shapes, sizes, and coarseness depending on the material being worked and the size of the job. Files have a pointed tang on one end that is fitted to a handle. Files are often sold without handles, but they should not be used until a handle of the right size has been fitted. A correctly sized handle will fit snugly without working loose while using the file. Always check the handle before using the file. If the handle is loose, give it a sharp rap to tighten it up, or if it is the threaded type, screw it on tighter. If it fails to fit snugly, you must use a different size handle.

> ### ▶ TECHNICIAN TIP
>
> Many engine components are made of aluminum. Since aluminum is quite soft, it is critical that you use the gasket scraper very carefully so as not to damage the surface. This can be accomplished by keeping the gasket scraper at a fairly flat angle to the surface. Also, the gasket scraper should only be used by hand, not with a hammer. Some manufacturers specify using plastic gasket scrapers only on certain aluminum components such as cylinder heads and blocks.

What makes one file different from another is not just the shape but how much material it is designed to remove with each stroke. The teeth on the file determine how much material will be removed **FIGURE 6-27**. Since the teeth face one direction only, the file cuts in one direction only. Dragging the file backward over the surface of the metal only dulls the teeth and wears them out quickly.

Teeth on a coarse-grade file are longer, with a greater space between them. A coarse-grade file working on a piece of mild steel will remove a lot of material with each stroke, but it leaves a rough finish. A smooth-grade file has shorter teeth cut more closely together. It removes much less material on each stroke, and the finish is much smoother. On a job, the coarse file is used first to remove material quickly, then a smoother file gently removes the last of it and leaves a clean finish to the work.

The full list of grades in flat files, from rough to smooth, follows:

- Rough files have the coarsest teeth, with approximately 20 teeth per inch. They are used when a lot of material must be removed quickly. They leave a very rough finish and will have to be followed by the use of finer files to produce a smooth final finish.
- Coarse bastard files are still a coarse file, with approximately 30 teeth per inch, but they are not as course as the rough file. They are also used to rough out or remove material quickly from the job.
- Second cut files have approximately 40 teeth per inch and provide a smoother finish than the rough or coarse bastard file. They are good all-round intermediary files and leave a reasonably smooth finish.
- Smooth files have approximately 60 teeth per inch and are a finishing file used to provide a smooth final finish.
- Dead smooth files have 100 teeth per inch or more and are used where a very fine finish is required.

Some flat files are available with one smooth edge, called safe edge files. They allow filing up to an edge without damaging it. Flat files are fine on straightforward jobs, but files must be able to work in some awkward spots as well. A **warding file** is thinner than other files and comes to a point; it is used for working in narrow slots **FIGURE 6-28**. A **square file** has teeth on all four sides, so you can use it in a square or rectangular hole. A square file can make the right shape for a squared

FIGURE 6-27 The teeth on a file determine how much material will be removed from the object being filed.

FIGURE 6-28 **A.** Warding file. **B.** Square file. **C.** Triangular file.

metal key to fit in a slot. A **triangular file** has three sides. It is triangular, so it can get into internal corners. It is able to cut right into a corner without removing material from the sides.

Curved files are either half-round or round. A half-round file has a shallow convex surface that can file in a concave hollow or in an acute internal corner **FIGURE 6-29**. The fully round file, sometimes called a rat-tail file, can make holes bigger. It can also file inside a concave surface with a tight radius.

The **thread file** cleans clogged or distorted threads on bolts and studs. Thread files come in either standard or metric configurations, so make sure you use the correct file. Each file has eight different surfaces that match different thread dimensions, so the right face must be used.

Files should be cleaned after each use. If they are clogged, they can be cleaned by using a file card, or file brush. This tool has short steel bristles that clean out the small particles that clog the teeth of the file. Rubbing a piece of chalk over the surface of the file prior to filing will make it easier to clean.

Clamps

There are many types of vices or clamps available **FIGURE 6-30**. The **bench vice** is a useful tool for holding anything that can fit into its jaws. Some common uses include sawing, filing, or chiseling. The jaws are serrated to give extra grip. They are also very hard, which means that when the vice is tightened, the jaws can mar whatever they are gripping. To prevent this, a pair of soft jaws can be fitted whenever the danger of damage arises. They are usually made of aluminum or some other soft metal or can have a rubber-type surface applied to them.

When materials are too awkward to grip vertically in a plain vice, it may be easier to use an **offset vice**.

The offset vice has its jaws set to one side to allow long components to be held vertically. For example, a long threaded bar can be held vertically in an offset vice to cut a thread with a die.

A **drill vice** is designed to hold material on a drill worktable. The drill worktable has slots cut into to it to allow the vice to bolted down on the table to hold material securely. To hold something firmly and drill it accurately, the object must be secured in the jaws of the vice. The vice can be moved on the bed until the precise drilling point is located and then tightened down by bolts to hold the drill vice in place during drilling.

FIGURE 6-29 **A.** Curved file. **B.** Thread file. **C.** File card.

FIGURE 6-30 **A.** Bench vice. **B.** Drill vice. **C.** C-clamp.

The name for the <u>C-clamp</u> comes from its shape. It can hold parts together while they are being assembled, drilled, or welded. It can reach around awkwardly shaped pieces that will not fit in a vice. It is also commonly used to retract disc brake caliper pistons. This clamp is portable, so it can be taken to the work.

Taps and Dies

<u>Taps</u> cut threads inside holes or nuts **FIGURE 6-31**. They normally come in three different types. The first is known as a <u>taper tap</u>. It narrows at the tip to give it a good start in the hole where the thread is to be cut. The diameter of the hole is determined by a tap drill chart, which can be obtained from engineering suppliers. This chart shows what hole size has to be drilled and what tap size is needed to cut the right thread for any given bolt size. Just remember that if you are drilling a .250" (6 mm) or larger hole, use a smaller pilot drill first. Once the properly sized hole has been drilled, the taper tap can tap a thread right through a piece of steel to enable a bolt to be screwed into it.

The second type of tap is an <u>intermediate tap</u>, also known as a plug tap, and the third is a <u>bottoming tap</u>. They are used to tap a thread into a hole that does not come out the other side of the material, called a blind hole. A taper tap is used to start the thread in the hole and then the intermediate tap is used, followed by a bottoming tap to take the thread right to the bottom of the blind hole.

A <u>tap handle</u> has a right-angled jaw that matches the squared end that all taps have. The jaws are designed to hold the tap securely, while the handles provide the leverage for the operator to comfortably rotate the tap to cut the thread. To cut a thread in an awkward space, a T-shaped tap handle is very convenient. Its handles are not as long, so it fits into tighter spaces; however, it is harder to turn and to guide accurately.

To cut a brand new thread on a blank rod or shaft, a die held in a <u>die stock</u> is used. The die may be split so that it can be adjusted more tightly onto the work with each pass of the die as the thread is cut deeper and deeper, until the nut fits properly. The die nut is also common in the shop. It is hexagonal shaped to fit a wrench, and it is commonly used to clean up threads that are rusty or have been damaged.

<u>Screw extractors</u> are devices designed to remove screws, studs, or bolts that have broken off in threaded holes. A common type of extractor uses a course left-hand tapered thread formed on its hardened body. Normally, a hole is drilled in the center of the broken screw and then the extractor is screwed into the hole. The left-hand thread grips the broken part of the bolt and unscrews it. The extractor is marked with the sizes of the screw it is designed to remove and the hole that needs to be drilled. It is important to carefully drill the hole in the center of the bolt or stud in the case you end up having to drill the bolt out. If you drill the hole off center, you will not be able to drill it out all the way to the inside diameter of the threads and removal will be nearly impossible.

Pullers

<u>Pullers</u> are a very common universal tool that can be used for removing bearings, bushings, pulleys, and gears **FIGURE 6-32**. Specialized pullers are also available for

FIGURE 6-32 **A.** Puller. **B.** Gear puller.

FIGURE 6-31 **A.** Taps. **B.** Tap handle. **C.** Die and die stock. **D.** Die nut.

specific tasks where a standard puller is not as effective. The most common pullers have two or three legs that grip the part to be removed. A center bolt, called a forcing screw or jacking bolt, is then screwed in, producing a jacking or pulling action, which extracts the part.

<u>Gear pullers</u> come in a range of sizes and shapes, all designed for particular applications. They consist of three main parts: jaws, a cross-arm, and a forcing screw. There are normally two or three jaws on a puller. They are designed to work either externally around a pulley or internally. The <u>forcing screw</u> is a long, fine-threaded bolt that is applied to the center of the cross-arm. When the forcing screw is turned, it applies many tons of force through the component you are removing. The cross-arm attaches the jaws to the forcing screw. There may be two, three, or four arms. If the <u>cross-arm</u> has four arms, three of the arms will be spaced 120 degrees apart. The fourth arm will be positioned 180 degrees apart from one arm. This allows the cross-arm to be used as either a two- or a three-arm puller.

Using Gear Pullers

Gear and bearing pullers are designed for hundreds of applications. Their main purpose is to remove a component, such as a gear, pulley, or bearing from a shaft, or to remove a shaft from inside a hole. Normally these components will have been pressed onto that shaft or into the hole, so removing them will require considerable force.

To select, install, and use a gear puller to remove a pulley, follow the steps in **SKILL DRILL 6-4**:

1. Examine the gear puller you have selected for the job. Identify the jaws; there may be two or three of them, and they must fit the part you want to remove. The cross-arm enables you to adjust the diameter of the jaws. The forcing screw should fit snugly onto the part you are removing. Finally, select the right wrench size to fit the nut on the end of the forcing screw.

2. Adjust and fit the puller. Adjust the jaws and cross-arms of the puller so that it fits tightly around the part to be removed. The arms of the jaws should be pulling against the component at close to right angles. **(Photo 1)**

3. Position the forcing screw. Use the appropriate wrench to run the forcing screw down to touch the shaft. Check that the point of the forcing screw is centered on the shaft. If not, adjust the jaws and cross-arms until the point is in the center of the shaft. Also be careful to use the correct foot on the end of the puller. A tapered cone style of foot does a good job of centering the puller, but it

SKILL DRILL | 6-4 | Using Gear Pullers

1. Examine the gear puller and ensure the jaws will fit the part you want to remove. Select the right size wrench to fit the nut on the end of the forcing screw. Adjust and fit the puller so that it fits tightly around the part to be removed. The arms of the jaws should be pulling against the component at close to right angles.

2. Position the forcing screw. Use the appropriate wrench to run the forcing screw down to touch the shaft. Check that the point of the forcing screw is centered on the shaft. If it is not, adjust the jaws and cross-arms until the point is in the center of the shaft.

3. Tighten the forcing screw slowly and carefully onto the shaft. Check that the puller is not going to slip off center or off the pulley. If the forcing screw and puller jaws remain in the correct position, tighten the forcing screw and pull the part off the shaft.

also creates a very large amount of wedging effect, which can distort the end of the shaft. In the same way, the wrong foot size can push on the internal threads of the shaft, damaging them. (**Photo 2**)

4 Tighten the forcing screw slowly and carefully onto the shaft. Check that the puller is not going to slip off center or off the pulley. Readjust the puller if necessary.

5 If the forcing screw and puller jaws remain in the correct position, tighten the forcing screw and pull the part off the shaft. You may sometimes have to use a hammer to hit directly on the end of the forcing screw to help break the part loose. (**Photo 3**)

Safety

- Always wear eye protection when using a gear puller.
- Make sure the puller is located correctly on the workpiece. If the jaws cannot be fitted correctly on the part, then select a more appropriate puller. Do not use a puller that does not fit the job.

Flaring Tools

A **tube flaring tool** is used to flare the end of a tube so it can be connected to another tube or component. One example of this is where the brake line screws into a wheel cylinder. The flared end is compressed between two threaded parts such that it will seal the joint and withstand high pressures. The three most common shapes of flares are the **single flare**, for tubing carrying low pressures like a fuel line; the **double flare**, for higher pressures such as in a brake system; and the ISO flare (sometimes called a bubble flare), which is the metric version used in brake systems **FIGURE 6-33**.

Flaring tools have two parts, a set of bars with holes that match the diameter of the tube end that is being shaped, and a yoke that drives a cone into the mouth of the tube. To make a single flare, the end of the tube is placed level with the surface of the top of the flaring bars. With the clamp screw firmly tightened, the feed screw flares the end of the tube.

Making a double flare is similar, but an extra step is added and more of the tube is exposed to allow for the folding over into a double flare. A double flaring button is placed into the end of the tube, and when it is removed after tightening, the pipe looks like a bubble. Placing the cone and yoke over the bubble allows you to turn the feed screw and force the bubble to fold in on itself, forming the double flare.

FIGURE 6-33 **A.** Single flare, double flare, and ISO flare. **B.** Components of a flare tool. **C.** Tubing cutter.

An ISO flare uses a flaring tool made specifically for that type of flare. It is similar to the double-flare process but stops with the use of the button. It does not get doubled back on itself. It should resemble a bubble shape when you are finished.

A <u>tubing cutter</u> is more convenient and neater than a saw when cutting pipes and metal tubing. The sharpened wheel does the cutting. As the tool turns around the pipe, the screw increases the pressure, driving the wheel deeper and deeper through the pipe until it finally cuts through. There is a larger version that is used for cutting exhaust pipes.

Safety

A flaring tool is used to produce a pressure seal for sealing brake lines and fuel system tubing. Make sure you test the flared joint for leaks before completing the repair; otherwise the brakes could fail or the fuel could catch on fire.

Using Flaring Tools

To make a successful flare, it is important to have the correct amount of tube protruding through the tool before clamping. Otherwise, too much of the end will fold over too far and leave too small of a hole for fluid to pass through. Too little and there won't be enough tube to fold over properly and the joint won't have full surface contact. If you are making a double flare or ISO flare, make sure you use the correctly sized button for the tubing size. The button is also used to measure the amount of tube required to protrude from the tool prior to forming it. To prevent the tool from slipping on the tube and ruining the flare, make sure the tool is sufficiently tight around the tube before starting to create the flare.

To use a flaring tool to make a flare in a piece of tubing, follow the steps in **SKILL DRILL 6-5**:

1. Choose the tube you will use to make the flare, and put the flare nut on the tube before creating the flare. **(Photo 1)**

2. Match the size of the tube to the correct hole in the tubing clamp. **(Photo 2)**

3. Holding the flaring tool, put the tube into the clamp. Position the tube so the correct amount is showing through the tool. If you are conducting a double flare, use the correctly sized button to ensure the proper amount of the tube is sticking up above the top of the clamp. Tighten the two

SKILL DRILL   6-5   Using Flaring Tools

1. Choose the tube you will use to make the flare, and put the flare nut on the tube before creating the flare.

2. Match the size of the tube to the correct hole in the tubing clamp.

3. Holding the flaring tool, put the tube into the clamp. Position the tube so the correct amount is showing through the tool. If you are conducting a double flare, use the correctly sized button to ensure the proper amount of the tube is sticking up above the top of the clamp. Tighten the two halves of the clamp together using the wing nuts.

SKILL DRILL | 6-5 | Using Flaring Tools, continued

4 Put the cone and forming tool over the clamp and turn the handle to make the flare. If you are doing a double flare or ISO flare, place the button in the end of the tube, install the cone and forming tool, and turn the handle to make the bubble. Remove the button from the tube. If this is an ISO flare, inspect it to see if it is properly formed.

5 If it is a double flare, put the cone and forming tool back on and reclamp the tube to produce the double flare.

6 Remove the clamp. Remove the tube from the clamp and check the flare to ensure it is free of burrs and is correctly formed.

halves of the clamp together using the wing nuts. Make sure the tool is tight enough to clamp the tube so it will not slip. **(Photo 3)**

4 Put the cone and forming tool over the clamp and turn the handle to make the flare. If you are doing a double flare or ISO flare, place the button in the end of the tube, install the cone and forming tool, and turn the handle to make the bubble. Remove the button from the tube. **(Photo 4)**

5 If this is an ISO flare, inspect it to see if it is properly formed. If it is a double flare, put the cone and forming tool back on and reclamp the tube to produce the double flare.**(Photo 5)**

6 Remove the clamp.

7 Remove the tube from the clamp and check the flare to ensure it is free of burrs and is correctly formed. **(Photo 6)**

Safety

Always wear eye protection when using a flaring tool. Make sure the tool is clean and in good condition and is suitable for the type of material you are going to flare.

Riveting Tools

There are many applications for blind rivets, and various rivet types and tools may be used to do the riveting. **Pop rivet guns** are convenient for occasional riveting of light materials **FIGURE 6-34**. A typical pop or **blind rivet** has a body, which will form the **finished rivet**, and a mandrel,

FIGURE 6-34 Pop rivet guns.

which is discarded when the riveting is completed **FIGURE 6-35**. It is called a blind rivet because there is no need to see or reach the other side of the hole in which the rivet goes to do the work. In some types, the rivet is plugged shut so that it is waterproof or pressure-proof.

The rivet is inserted into the riveting tool, which, when squeezed, pulls the end of the **mandrel** back through the body of the rivet. Because the **mandrel head** is bigger than the hole through the body, it swells out as it comes through the body. Finally, the mandrel head will snap off under the pressure and fall out, leaving the rivet body gripping the two sheets of material together.

Using Riveting Tools

Rivet tools are used to join two pieces of metal together— for example, when sheet metal needs to be attached to a frame. To perform a riveting operation, you will need a rivet gun, rivets, a drill, the properly sized drill bit, and the materials to be riveted.

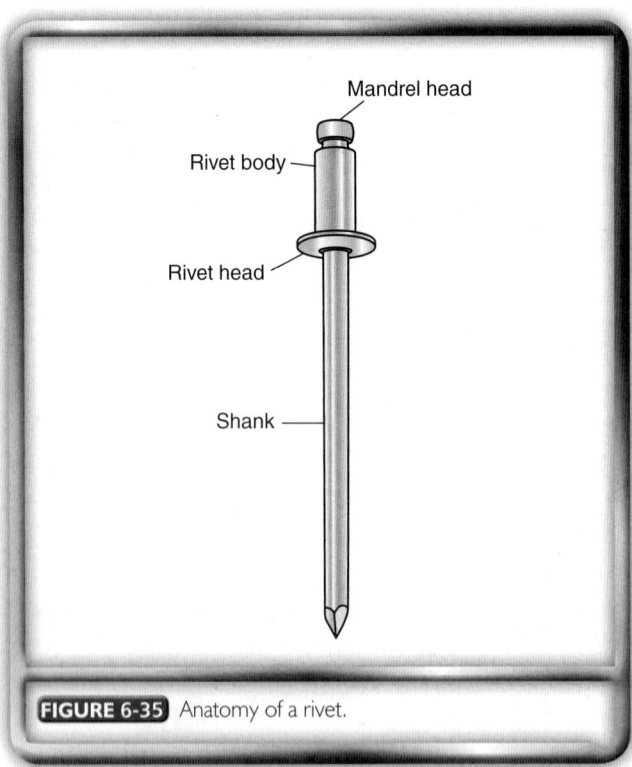

FIGURE 6-35 Anatomy of a rivet.

TECHNICIAN TIP

A rivet is a one-time use fastener. Unlike a nut and bolt, which can normally be disassembled and reused, a rivet cannot. The metal shell that makes up a pop rivet is crushed into place so that it holds the parts firmly together. If it ever needs to be removed, it must be drilled out.

Rivets come in various diameters and lengths for different sizes of jobs and are made of various types of metals to suit the job at hand. When selecting rivets to suit the job, consider the diameter, length, and rivet material. Wider diameter rivets should be used for jobs that require more strength. The rivet length should be sufficient to protrude past the thickness of the materials being riveted by about 1.6 times the diameter of the rivet stem. Always select rivets that are made from the same material as that being riveted. For example, stainless steel rivets should be used for riveting stainless steel, and aluminum rivets should be used to rivet aluminum.

Pilot holes will need to be drilled through the metal to be riveted. Ensure that the hole is just large enough for the rivet to comfortably pass through it, but do not make it too large. If the hole is too large, the rivet will be loose and will not hold the materials securely together. When drilling holes for rivets, provide clearance from the material's edge to ensure that the rivets do not break through the edge of the materials being riveted. A good rule of thumb is to allow at least twice the diameter of the rivet stem as clearance from any edge.

The rivet tool is capable of riveting various sizes of rivets and has a number of nosepiece sizes to work with different sizes of rivets. Make sure you select the correct nosepiece size for the rivet you are using.

Safety

When compressing the rivet handles, be careful not to place your fingers in the mechanism.

To use a riveting tool to rivet two pieces of material together, follow the steps in **SKILL DRILL 6-6**:

1 Select the correct rivet for the material you are riveting.

2 Make sure the rivet is the correct length.

3 Drill pilot holes in the material to be riveted. Remove any burrs. Ensure that the pilot hole is the correct size, not too large or too small. **(Photo 1)**

4 Make sure the correctly sized nosepiece is fitted to the rivet tool for the rivet size. **(Photo 2)**

5 Insert the rivet into the gun and push the rivet through the materials to be riveted. Hold firm pressure while pushing the rivet into the work.

6 Squeeze and release the rivet tool handle to compress the rivet. Continue this process until the rivet stem or shank breaks away from the rivet head. **(Photo 3)**

7 Check the rivet joint to ensure the pieces are firmly held together. **(Photo 4)**

SKILL DRILL | 6-6 | Using Riveting Tools

1 Select the correct rivet and correct size of rivet. Drill pilot holes in the material to be riveted and remove any burrs.

2 Check that the rivet tool has the correctly sized nosepiece to match the size rivet you are using. Change the nosepiece if necessary to match the rivet.

3 Insert the rivet into the gun and push the rivet through the materials to be riveted. Squeeze and release the rivet tool handle to compress the rivet. Continue this process until the rivet stem or shank breaks away from the rivet head.

4 Check the rivet joint to ensure the pieces are firmly held together.

Soldering Tools

Solder is a mixture of metals with low melting points and is used to join metals together. Tin/lead solder has been used for soldering wires and other metals together for decades. Tin/lead solder for automotive applications consists of approximately 60% tin and 40% lead, and melts at approximately 370°F (188°C). With the environmental hazards of lead becoming an issue over the past 30 years, lead-free solder was introduced in the past decade. Lead-free solder is made up of tin and copper, or of tin, copper, and silver, and usually has a melting point about 20–30°F higher than tin/lead solder. Because solder is a relatively soft compound, it is not used to make joints in situations where high stresses are involved.

In automotive applications, solder generally comes in the form of a wire. It can be solid, requiring an external **flux** cleaning agent of **rosin** if soldering electrical connections or acid if soldering non-electrical connections. The solder can also be hollow, with the rosin or acid in the core. In this case, it would be referred to as rosin-core solder or acid-core solder. Make sure you use rosin with electrical connections and acid with all other connections.

The process of soldering involves heating the metals (wires) hot enough so that the solder melts and fills the spaces between the metals. When the solder cools, the solder holds the parts together and transmits electricity, if used in electrical circuits. The temperature of the soldering operation is critical. If it is not hot enough, the solder does not flow very well and does not make good contact with the metal surfaces and tends to glob up. This makes for a weak joint and poor electrical conductivity. If it is too hot, the solder tends to run off the joint and overheat the components being soldered. In the case of electronic components, overheating can make them inoperative. Only heat the components enough to melt the solder and cause it to flow.

The heat is provided by a <u>**soldering iron**</u> or gun. The heat in soldering irons is usually generated from electricity or gas. A typical soldering iron has a handle that is thermally insulated. The soldering tip is heated and the heat is transferred by metal-to-metal contact from the tip into the metal to be soldered.

Basic soldering irons are heated manually by a gas flame while more sophisticated soldering irons are electrically operated and have thermal tips that are controlled by thermostats to maintain more accurate tip temperatures. Soldering irons can either have fixed tip sizes or tips can be interchanged with different sizes for different sizes of jobs.

Using Soldering Tools

Apply flux to the joint if <u>**cored solder**</u> is not used. Always remove any excess flux when finished. Ensure that the joint is held steady during and after the solder is applied. A dull solder surface indicates a cold and high-resistance joint and should be resoldered. Select the correct tip size to heat the joint and solder within a few seconds. Overheating a joint or using too small of a tip will produce a poor solder joint.

To use a soldering iron to solder two pieces of wire or metal together, follow the steps in **SKILL DRILL 6-7**:

1. Prepare the materials to be soldered. Strip wires or clean metal parts before soldering. **(Photo 1)**
2. Prepare the soldering iron by ensuring the correctly sized tip is fitted and is clean (you may have to use a file to reshape and clean it). Tin the soldering

SKILL DRILL 6-7 Using Soldering Tools

1. Prepare the materials to be soldered. Strip wires or clean metal parts before soldering.

2. Prepare the soldering iron by ensuring the correctly sized tip is fitted and is clean. Tin the soldering iron tip by melting some solder to it and wiping any excess from the tip.

3. Apply flux to the wires or metal to be soldered. This may not be necessary if you are using cored solder.

4. Apply the hot solder iron tip to heat the joint, then apply solder to the joint (not the iron). If the solder does not melt within a few seconds, remove it and allow the joint to heat further before reapplying.

5. Once the solder has been applied, ensure the joint does not move until the solder has cooled sufficiently to set. Once cooled, inspect the joint; it should be shiny and firm.

6. Clean any excess flux from the joint.

iron tip by melting some solder to it and wiping any excess from the tip with a rag.(**Photo 2**)

3. Apply flux to the wires or metal to be soldered. This may not be necessary if you are using cored solder. (**Photo 3**)

4. Apply the hot solder iron tip to heat the joint, then apply solder to the joint (not the soldering iron). If the solder does not melt within a few seconds, remove it and allow the joint to heat further before reapplying.(**Photo 4**)

5. Once the solder has been applied, ensure the joint does not move until the solder has cooled sufficiently to set.

6. Once cooled, inspect the joint; it should be shiny and firm. (**Photo 5**)

7. Clean any excess flux from the joint. (**Photo 6**)

Safety

- Always wear eye and hand protection when soldering.
- Always wipe excess solder from the iron; never flick the iron to remove excess solder.
- Make sure the tool is clean and in good condition and is suitable for the type of material you are going to solder.
- Check electrical leads and plugs for damage prior to use.

Precision Measuring Tools

Technicians are required to perform a variety of measurements while carrying out their job. This requires knowledge of what tools are available and how to use them. Measuring tools can generally be classified according to what type of measurements they can make **FIGURE 6-36**. A measuring tape is useful

FIGURE 6-36 **A.** Measuring tape. **B.** Steel rule.

for measuring longer distances and is accurate to a millimeter or fraction of an inch. A steel rule is capable of accurate measurements on shorter lengths, down to a millimeter or a fraction of an inch. Precision measuring tools are accurate to much smaller dimensions, such as a micrometer, which in some cases can accurately measure down to $1/10,000$ of an inch (0.0001"), or $1/1000$ of a millimeter (0.001 mm).

Measuring Tapes

Measuring tapes are a flexible type of ruler and are a common measuring tool. The most common type found in shops is a thin metal strip about 0.5" to 1" (13 to 25 mm) wide that is rolled up inside a housing with a spring return mechanism. Measuring tapes can be of various lengths, with 16' or 25' (5 or 8 m) being very common. The measuring tape is pulled from the housing to measure items, and a spring return winds it back into the housing. The housing will usually have a built-in locking mechanism to hold the extended measuring tape against the spring return mechanism.

TECHNICIAN TIP

The United States customary system (USCS), also called the standard system, and the metric system are two sets of standards for quantifying weights and measurements. Each system has defined units. For example, the standard system uses inches, feet, and yards while the metric system uses millimeters, centimeters, and meters. Conversions can be undertaken from one system to the other. For example, 1 inch is equal to 25.4 millimeters, while 1 foot is equal to 304.8 millimeters.

Tools that make use of a measuring system, such as wrenches, sockets, drill bits, micrometers, rulers, and many others, come in both standard and metric measurements. To work on modern vehicles, an understanding of both systems and their conversion is required. Conversion tables can be used to convert from one system to the other. The more you work with both systems, the easier it will be to understand how they relate to each other.

Steel Rulers

As the name suggests, a **steel rule** is a ruler that is made from steel. Steel rules commonly come in 12", 24", and 36" lengths. They are used like any ruler to measure and mark out items. They are a very strong ruler, have precise markings, and resist damage. When using a steel rule, you can rest it on its edge so the markings are closer to the material being measured, which helps to mark the work precisely. Always protect the steel rule from damage by storing it carefully; a damaged ruler will not give an accurate measurement. Never take measurements from the very end of a damaged steel rule, as damaged ends may affect the accuracy of your measurements.

> **TECHNICIAN TIP**
>
> If the end of a rule is damaged, you may be able to measure from the I" mark and subtract an inch from the measurement.

Outside, Inside, and Depth Micrometers

Micrometers are precise measuring tools designed to measure small distances and are available in both inch and millimeter (mm) calibrations. Typically they can measure down to a resolution of $\frac{1}{1000}$ of an inch (0.001") for a standard micrometer or $\frac{1}{100}$ of a millimeter (0.01 mm) for a metric micrometer. Vernier micrometers equipped with the addition of a vernier scale can measure down to $\frac{1}{10,000}$ of an inch (0.0001") or $\frac{1}{1000}$ of a millimeter (0.001 mm).

The most common types of micrometers are the outside, inside, and depth micrometers **FIGURE 6-37**. As the name suggests, an **outside micrometer** measures the outside dimensions of an item. For example, it could measure the diameter of a valve stem. The **inside micrometer** measures inside dimensions. For example, the inside micrometer could measure an engine cylinder bore. **Depth micrometers** measure the depth of an item such as how far a piston is below the surface of the block.

The most common micrometer is an outside micrometer. The horseshoe-shaped part is the frame. It is built to make sure the micrometer holds its shape. Some frames have plastic finger pads so that body heat is not transferred to the metal frame as easily, as heat can cause the metal to expand slightly and affect the reading. On one end of the frame is the anvil, which contacts one

> **TECHNICIAN TIP**
>
> Micrometers are precision measuring instruments and must be handled and stored with care. They should always be stored with a gap between the spindle and anvil so metal expansion does not interfere with their calibration.

FIGURE 6-37 **A.** Outside micrometer. **B.** Inside micrometer. **C.** Depth micrometer.

side of the part being measured. The other contact point is the spindle. The micrometer measures the distance between the anvil and spindle, so that is where the part being measured fits.

The measurement is read on the sleeve/barrel and thimble. The sleeve/barrel is stationary and has the linear markings on it. The thimble fits over the sleeve and has the graduated marking on it. The thimble is connected directly to the spindle, and both turn as a unit. Since the spindle and sleeve/barrel have matching threads, the thimble rotates the spindle inside of the sleeve/barrel and the thread moves the spindle inward and outward. The thimble usually incorporates either a ratchet or a clutch mechanism, which prevents overtightening of the micrometer thimble when taking a reading. A lock nut, lock ring, or lock screw is used on most micrometers and locks the thimble in place while you read the micrometer.

Standard micrometers use a specific thread of 40 tpi on the spindle and sleeve. This means that the thimble will rotate exactly 40 turns in 1 inch. Every complete rotation moves the spindle a 40th of an inch, or 0.025" (1 ÷ 40 = 0.025). In four rotations, the spindle moves 0.100" (0.025 × 4 = 0.100). The linear markings on the sleeve show each of the 0.100" marks between 0 and 1 inch as well as each of the 0.025" marks. Since the thimble has graduated marks from 0 to 24 (each mark representing 0.001"), every complete turn of the thimble will uncover another one of the 0.025" marks on the sleeve. If the thimble stops short of any complete turn, it will indicate the exact number of 0.001" marks past the zero line on the sleeve.

FIGURE 6-38 **A.** Read how many 0.100" marks the thimble has uncovered. **B.** Read the number on the thimble that lines up with the zero line on the sleeve.

> **TECHNICIAN TIP**
>
> All micrometers need to be checked for calibration (also called "zeroing") before each use. A 0–1" or 0–25 mm outside micrometer can be lightly closed all of the way. If the anvil and spindle are clean, the micrometer should read 0.000, indicating the micrometer is calibrated correctly. If the micrometer is bigger than 1" or 25 mm, then a "standard" is used to verify the calibration. A standard is a hardened machined rod of a precise length, such as 2" or 50 mm. When inserted in the same-sized micrometer, the reading should be exactly the same as listed on the standard. If a micrometer is not properly calibrated, it should not be used until it is recalibrated. See the tool's instruction manual for the calibration procedure.

To read a standard micrometer, perform the following steps **FIGURE 6-38**:
1. Verify that the micrometer is properly calibrated.
2. Verify what size of micrometer you are using. If it is a 0–1" micrometer, start with 0.000. If it is a 1–2" micrometer, start with 1.000". A 2–3" micrometer would start with 2.000", and so on. (To give an example, let's say it is 2.000".)
3. Read how many 0.100" marks the thimble has uncovered. (example: 0.300")
4. Read how many 0.025" marks the thimble has uncovered past the 0.100" mark in step 3. (example: 2 × 0.025 = 0.050")
5. Read the number on the thimble that lines up with the zero line on the sleeve. (example: 13 × 0.001 = 0.013")
6. Lastly, total all of the individual readings. (example: 2.000 + 0.300 + 0.050 + 0.013 = 2.363")

A metric micrometer uses the same components as the standard micrometer. However, it uses a different thread pitch on the spindle and sleeve. It uses a 0.5-mm thread pitch (2.0 threads per millimeter) and opens up approximately 25 mm. Each rotation of the thimble moves the spindle 0.5 mm, and it therefore takes 50 rotations of the thimble to move the full 25-mm distance. The sleeve/barrel is labeled with individual millimeter marks and half-millimeter marks from the starting millimeter to the ending millimeter, 25 mm away. The thimble has graduated marks from 0 to 49.

Reading a metric micrometer involves the following steps:
1. Read the number of full millimeters the thimble has passed. (To give an example, let's say it is 23.00 mm.)
2. Check to see if it passed the 0.5-mm mark. (example: 0.50 mm)
3. Check to see which mark on the thimble lines up with or is just passed. (example: 37 × 0.01 mm = 0.37 mm)
4. Total all of the numbers (example: 23.00 mm + 0.50 mm + 0.37 mm = 23.87 mm)

If the micrometer is equipped with a vernier gauge, meaning it can read down to $\frac{1}{10,000}$ of an inch (0.0001") or $\frac{1}{1000}$ of a millimeter (0.001 mm), you need to complete one more step. Identify which of the vernier lines is closest to one of the lines on the thimble. Sometimes it is hard to determine which is the closest, so decide which three are the closest and then use the center line. At the frame side of the sleeve will be a number that corresponds to the vernier line. It will be numbered 1-0. Take the vernier number and add it to the end of your reading. For example: 2.363 + 0.0007 = 2.3637", and 23.77 + 0.007 = 23.777 mm.

For inside measurements, the inside micrometer works on the same principles as the outside micrometer and so does the depth micrometer. The only difference is that the scale on the sleeve of the depth micrometer is backward, so be careful when reading it.

Using Micrometers

To maintain accuracy of measurements, it is important that both the micrometer and the items to be measured are clean and free of any dirt or debris. Also make sure the micrometer is zeroed before taking any measurements. Never overtighten a micrometer or store it with its measuring surfaces touching, as this may damage the tool and affect its accuracy. When measuring, make sure the item can pass through the micrometer surfaces snugly and squarely. This is best accomplished by using the ratchet to tighten the micrometer. Always take the measurement a number of times and compare results to ensure you have measured accurately.

To correctly measure using an outside micrometer, follow the steps in **SKILL DRILL 6-8**:

1 Select the correct size of micrometer. Verify that the anvil and spindle are clean and that it is calibrated properly.

2 Clean the surface of the part you are measuring. **(Photo 1)**

3 In your right hand, hold the frame of the micrometer between your pinky, ring finger, and palm of your hand with the thimble between your thumb and forefinger. **(Photo 2)**

4 With your left hand, hold the part you are measuring and place the micrometer over it. **(Photo 3)**

5 Using your thumb and forefinger, lightly tighten the ratchet. It is important that the correct amount of force is applied to the spindle when taking a measurement. The spindle and anvil should just touch the component with a slight amount of drag when the micrometer is removed from the measured piece. Be careful that the part is square in the micrometer so the reading is correct. Try rocking the micrometer in all directions to make sure it is square. **(Photo 4)**

6 Once the micrometer is properly snug, tighten the lock mechanism so the spindle will not turn.

7 Read the micrometer and record your reading. **(Photo 5)**

8 When all readings are finished, clean the micrometer, position the spindle so it is backed off from the anvil, and return it to its protective case. **(Photo 6)**

SKILL DRILL   6-8   Using Micrometers

1 Select the correct size of micrometer. Verify that the anvil and spindle are clean and that it is calibrated properly. Clean the surface of the part you are measuring.

2 In your right hand, hold the frame of the micrometer between your pinky, ring finger, and palm of your hand with the thimble between your thumb and forefinger.

3 With your left hand, hold the part you are measuring and place the micrometer over it.

SKILL DRILL | 6-8 | Using Micrometers, continued

4 Using your thumb and forefinger, lightly tighten the ratchet so there is a slight amount of drag.

5 Once the micrometer is properly snug, tighten the lock mechanism so the spindle will not turn. Read the micrometer and record your reading.

6 When all readings are finished, clean the micrometer, position the spindle so it is backed off from the anvil, and return it to its protective case.

Telescoping Gauges

For measuring distances in awkward spots like the bottom of a deep cylinder, the **telescoping gauge** has spring-loaded plungers that can be unlocked with a screw on the handle so they slide out and touch the walls of the cylinder **FIGURE 6-39**. The screw then locks them in that position, the gauge can be withdrawn, and the distance across the plungers can be measured with an outside micrometer or calipers to convey the diameter of the cylinder at that point. Telescoping gauges come in a variety of sizes to fit various sizes of holes and bores.

Split Ball Gauges

A **split ball gauge** or small hole gauge **FIGURE 6-40** is good for measuring small holes where telescoping gauges cannot fit. They use a similar principle to the telescoping gauge, but the measuring head uses a split ball mechanism that allows it to fit into very small holes. Split ball gauges are ideal for measuring valve guides on a cylinder head for wear. A split ball gauge can be fitted in the bore and expanded until there is a slight drag. Then it can be retracted and measured with an outside micrometer. Like some of the other measuring instruments discussed, the split ball gauge may have a dial or digital measurement scale fitted for direct reading purposes.

FIGURE 6-39 Telescoping gauge.

FIGURE 6-40 Split ball gauge.

Dial Bore Gauges

A **dial bore gauge** is used to measure the inside diameter of bores with a high degree of accuracy and speed **FIGURE 6-41**. The dial bore gauge can measure a bore directly by using telescoping pistons on a T-handle with a dial mounted on the handle. The dial bore gauge combines a telescoping gauge and dial indicator in one instrument. A dial bore gauge determines if the diameter is worn, tapered, or out-of-round according to the manufacturer's specifications. The resolution of a dial bore gauge is typically accurate to $5/10,000$ of an inch (0.0005") or $1/100$ of a millimeter (0.01 mm).

Using Dial Bore Gauges

To use a dial bore gauge, select an appropriate-sized adapter to fit the internal diameter of the bore, and install it to the measuring head. Many dial bore gauges also have a fixture to calibrate the tool to the size you desire. The fixture is set to the size desired, and the dial bore gauge is placed in it. The dial bore gauge is then adjusted to the proper reading. Once it is calibrated, the dial bore gauge can be inserted inside the bore to be measured. Hold the gauge in line with the bore and slightly rock it to ensure it is centered. Read the dial when it is fully centered and square to the bore to determine the correct measurement.

Store a bore gauge carefully in its storage box and ensure the locking mechanism is released while in storage. Bore gauges are available in different ranges of size. It is important to select a gauge with the correct range for the bore you are measuring. When measuring, make sure the gauge is at a 90-degree angle to the bore and read the dial. Always take the measurement a number of times and compare results to ensure you have measured accurately.

FIGURE 6-41 A dial bore gauge set.

To correctly measure using a dial bore gauge, follow the steps in **SKILL DRILL 6-9**:

1. Select the correct size of the dial bore gauge you will use and fit any adapters to it.
2. Check the calibration and adjust it as necessary.
3. Insert the dial bore gauge into the bore. The accurate measurement will be at exactly 90 degrees to the bore. To find the accurate measurement, rock the dial bore gauge handle slightly back and forth until you find the centered position. **(Photo 1)**
4. Read the dial to determine the bore measurement. **(Photo 2)**
5. Always clean the dial bore gauge and return it to its protective case when you have finished using it. **(Photo 3)**

Vernier Calipers

Vernier calipers are a precision instrument used for measuring outside dimensions, inside dimensions, and depth measurements, all in one tool. They have a graduated bar with markings like a ruler. On the bar, a sliding sleeve with jaws is mounted for taking inside or outside measurements. Measurements on older versions of vernier calipers are taken by reading the graduated bar scales, while fractional measurements are read by comparing the scales between the sliding sleeve and the graduated bar. Technicians will often use vernier calipers to measure length and diameters of bolts and pins or the depth of blind holes in housings.

Newer versions of vernier calipers have dial and digital scales. The dial vernier has the main scale on the graduated bar, while fractional measurements are taken from a dial with a rotating needle. These tend to be easier to read than the older versions. More recently, digital scales on vernier calipers have become commonplace. The principle of their use is the same as any vernier caliper; however, they have a digital scale that reads the measurement directly.

Using Vernier Calipers

Always store vernier calipers in a storage box to protect them and ensure the measuring surfaces are kept clean for accurate measurement. If making an internal or external measurement, make sure the caliper is at right angles to the surfaces to be measured. You should always repeat the measurement a number of times and compare results to ensure you have measured accurately.

To correctly measure using vernier calipers, follow the steps in **SKILL DRILL 6-10**:

1. Verify that the vernier caliper is calibrated (zeroed) before using it. **(Photo 1)**

2 Position the caliper correctly for the measurement you are making. Internal and external readings are normally made with the vernier caliper positioned at 90 degrees to the face of the component to be measured. Length and depth measurements are usually made parallel to or in line with the object being measured. Use your thumb to press or withdraw the sliding jaw to measure the outside or inside of the part. **(Photo 2)**

SKILL DRILL | 6-9 | Using Dial Bore Gauges

1 Select the correct size of the dial bore gauge you will use and fit any adapters to it. Check the calibration and adjust it as necessary. Insert the dial bore gauge into the bore. The accurate measurement will be at exactly 90 degrees to the bore. To find the accurate measurement, rock the dial bore gauge handle slightly back and forth until you find the centered position.

2 Read the dial to determine the bore measurement.

3 Clean the dial bore gauge and return it to its protective case when you have finished using it.

SKILL DRILL | 6-10 | Using Vernier Calipers

1 Verify that the vernier caliper is calibrated (zeroed) before using it.

2 Position the caliper correctly for the measurement you are making. Use your thumb to press or withdraw the sliding jaw to measure outside or inside of the part.

3 Read the vernier caliper, being careful not to change the position of the moveable jaw. If using a non-digital caliper, always read the dial or face straight on to avoid parallax.

3 Read the scale of the vernier caliper, being careful not to change the position of the moveable jaw. If using a non-digital caliper, always read the dial or face straight on. A view from the side can give a considerable **parallax error**. Parallax error is a visual error caused by viewing measurement markers at an incorrect angle. **(Photo 3)**

Dial Indicators

Dial indicators can also be known as dial gauges, and as the name suggests, they have a dial and needle where measurements are read. They have a measuring plunger with a pointed contact end that is spring-loaded and connected via the housing to the dial needle. The dial accurately measures movement of its plunger in and out as it rests against an object. For example, they can be used to measure the trueness of a rotating disc brake rotor.

A dial indicator can also measure how round something is. A **crankshaft** can be rotated in a set of **V blocks**. If the crankshaft is bent, it will show as movement on the dial indicator as the crankshaft is rotated. The dial indicator senses slight movement at its tip and magnifies it into a measurable swing on the dial.

Dial indicators normally have either one or two indicator needles. The large needle indicates the fine reading of thousandths of an inch. If it has a second needle, it will be smaller and indicates the coarse reading of tenths of an inch. The large needle is able to move numerous times around the outer scale. One full turn may represent 0.100" or 1 mm. The small inner scale indicates how many times the outer needle has moved around its scale. In this way, the dial indicator is able to read movement of up to 1" or 2 cm.

Dial indicators can measure with an accuracy of 0.001" or 0.01 mm. The type of dial indicator you use will be determined by the amount of movement you expect from the component you are measuring. The indicator must be set up so that there is no gap between the dial indicator and the component to be measured. Most dial indicator sets contain various attachments and support arms so they can be configured specifically for the measuring task.

Using Dial Indicators

Dial indicators are used in many types of service jobs. They are particularly useful in determining runout on rotating shafts and surfaces. Runout is the side-to-side variation of movement when a component is turned.

When attaching a dial indicator, keep support arms as short as possible. Make sure all attachments are tightened to prevent unnecessary movement between the indicator and the component. Make sure the dial

indicator plunger is positioned at 90 degrees to the face of the component to be measured. Always read the dial face straight on, as a view from the side can give a considerable parallax error. The outer face of the dial indicator is designed so it can be rotated so that the zero mark can be positioned directly over the pointer. This is how a dial indicator is zeroed.

To correctly measure using a dial indicator, follow the steps in **SKILL DRILL 6-11**:

1 Select the gauge type, size, attachment, and bracket that fit the part you are measuring. Mount the dial indicator firmly to keep it stationary. **(Photo 1)**

2 Adjust the indicator so that the plunger is at 90 degrees to the part you are measuring and lock it in place. **(Photo 2)**

3 Rotate the part one complete turn and locate the low spot. Zero the indicator. **(Photo 3)**

4 Find the point of maximum height and note the reading. This will indicate the runout value. **(Photo 4)**

5 Continue the rotation and make sure the needle does not go below zero. If it does, rezero the indicator and remeasure the point of maximum variation.

6 Check your readings against the manufacturer's specifications. If the deviation is greater than the specifications allow, consult your supervisor. **(Photo 5)**

Straight Edges

Straight edges are usually made from hardened steel and are machined so that the edge is perfectly straight. A straight edge is used to check the flatness of a surface. It is placed on its edge against the surface to be checked. The gap between the straight edge and the surface can be measured by using feeler gauges. Sometimes the gap can be seen easily if light is shone from behind the surface being checked. Straight edges are often used to measure the amount of warpage the surface of a cylinder head has.

Feeler Gauges

Feeler gauges (also called feeler blades) are used to measure the width of gaps, such as the clearance between valves and rocker arms. Feeler gauges are flat metal strips of varying thicknesses. The thickness of each feeler gauge is clearly marked on each one. They are sized from fractions of an inch or fractions of a millimeter. They usually come in sets with different sizes and are available in standard and metric measurements. Some sets contain feeler gauges made of brass. These are used

SKILL DRILL | 6-11 | Using Dial Indicators

1 Select the gauge type, size, attachment, and bracket that fit the part you are measuring. Mount the dial indicator firmly to keep it stationary.

2 Adjust the indicator so that the plunger is at 90 degrees to the part you are measuring and lock it in place.

3 Rotate the part one complete turn and locate the low spot. Zero the indicator.

4 Find the point of maximum height and note the reading. This will indicate the runout value.

5 Continue the rotation and make sure the needle does not go below zero. If it does, rezero the indicator and remeasure the point of maximum variation. Check your readings against the manufacturer's specifications. If the deviation is greater than the specifications allow, consult your supervisor.

to take measurements between components that are magnetic. If steel gauges were used, the drag caused by the magnetism would mimic the drag of a proper clearance. Brass gauges are not subject to magnetism, so they work well in that situation.

Some feeler gauges come in a bent arrangement to be more easily inserted in cramped spaces. Others come in a stepped version. For example, the end might be 0.010" thick while the rest of the gauges is 0.012" thick. This works well for adjusting valve clearance. If the specification is 0.010", then the 0.010 section can be placed in the gap. If the 0.012 section slides into the gap, then the valve needs to be readjusted. If it stops at the lip of the 0.012" section, then the gap is correct.

Two or more feeler gauges can be stacked together to make up a desired thickness. For example, to measure a thickness of 0.029 of an inch, a 0.017 and a 0.012 feeler gauge could be used together to make up the size. Alternatively, if you want to measure an unknown gap, you can interchange feeler gauges until you find the one or more that fits snugly into the gap and total their thickness to measure the gap. In conjunction with a straight edge, they can be used to measure surface irregularities in a cylinder head.

Using Feeler Gauges

If the feeler gauge feels too loose when measuring a gap, select the next size larger and measure the gap again. Repeat this procedure until the feeler gauge has a slight drag between both parts. If the feeler gauge is too tight, select a smaller size until the feeler gauge fits properly. When measuring a spark plug gap, feeler gauges should not be used because the surfaces are not perfectly parallel, so it is preferable to use wire feeler gauges. Wire feeler gauges use accurately machined pieces of wire instead of metal strips.

To select and use feeler gauge sets, follow the steps in **SKILL DRILL 6-12**:

1 Select the appropriate type and size feeler gauge set for the job you are working on.

2 Inspect the feeler gauges to make sure they are clean, rust-free, and undamaged, but slightly oiled for ease of movement.

3 Choose one of the smaller wires or blades, and try to insert it in the gap on the part. If it slips in and out easily, choose the next size up. When you find one that touches both sides of the gap and slides with only gentle pressure, then you have found the exact width of that gap. **(Photo 1)**

4 Read the markings on the wire or blade, and check these against the manufacturer's specifications for this component. If gap width is outside the tolerances specified, inform your supervisor.

5 Clean the feeler gauge set with an oily cloth before storage to prevent rust. **(Photo 2)**

▶ Power Tools

Power tools are typically powered by an electricity or compressed air. They can also be powered by burning of propellant, such as in a nail gun, or by a gasoline engine, such as in a portable compressor. A power tool can be stationary, such as a bench grinder, or portable, such as a portable electric drill. There are many different power tools designed to perform specific tasks. Some are corded and have to be plugged in, while others are cordless and have batteries. Power tools make many tasks quicker and easier to perform, and they can save many hours of work when used and maintained correctly.

Safety

Never use feeler gauges on operating machinery.

SKILL DRILL 6-12   Using Feeler Gauges

1 Select the appropriate type and size feeler gauge set for the job you are working on. Inspect the gauges to make sure they are clean, rust-free, and undamaged, but slightly oiled for ease of movement. Choose one of the smaller wires or blades, and try to insert it in the gap on the part. When you find one that touches both sides of the gap and slides with only gentle pressure, then you have found the exact width of that gap.

2 Read the markings on the wire or blade, and check these against the manufacturer's specifications for this component. If gap width is outside the tolerances specified, inform your supervisor. Clean the feeler gauge set with an oily cloth to prevent rust when you store the set.

Safety

Feeler gauges are strips of hardened metal that have been ground or rolled to a precise thickness. They can be very thin and will cut through skin if not handled correctly.

Drills and Drill Bits

Many components make up a drill set **FIGURE 6-42**. A portable drill can be corded or cordless. A corded drill has a cord that you have to plug into an electrical supply. The operating voltage of a drill will depend on the country's supply. Corded drills are a good choice when moderate power is needed or if extended drilling is required. Cordless drills use their own internal batteries. When you cannot bring the work to the drill, you can take the drill to the work. But don't expect a cordless drill to be able to drill large holes through hard metal. Although they are very versatile, they are limited to the amount of work they can do by their power rating. The biggest drill bit that will fit into the chuck of these drills is usually marked on the body of the drill or chuck, along with the speeds at which it will turn. Some portable drills have two operating speeds, but most portable drills have a variable speed rating that is determined by how much pressure is placed on the trigger and can be set to any speed within the drill's range.

Drill bits come in many closely spaced sizes and types. The most common is the **twist drill** bit. It has a point with cutting flutes that form a common angle of 118 degrees. Its body, which usually has two spiral grooves, and its shank are gripped in the jaws of the **drill chuck**. A drill chuck is a device for securely gripping drill bits

in a drill. The twist drill bit is a good all-purpose bit for drilling metals.

A **drill press** allows for accurate drilling with more control than is offered by a portable drill, which although convenient, can be difficult to guide accurately. A mounted drill can feed the drill bit at a controlled rate, and the worktable on the drill typically has a vice to secure the job at a constant angle to the drill bit. Also, this drill can be set to run at different drilling speeds. Most drill presses have a drill chuck that takes bits up to 0.5" (13 mm) or more in diameter.

Morse taper is a system for securing drill bits to drills. The Morse taper size changes according to drill size. The shank of the drill bit is tapered and looks like the tang of a file. It fits snugly into the drill spindle, which has a similar taper on its inside. The tang on the drill bit is located in the spindle, and it drives the drill. It is a quick way to change drills without constantly adjusting the chuck.

When there is already a hole drilled in sheet metal that needs enlarging, a multi-fluted tapered hole drill will do the job in practically the same time it takes to say the name of this tool. A drilling speed chart is usually supplied with the drill press and should be kept nearby for handy reference. It compares drill sizes and metals to show the proper speed. For example, to drill a 0.375" (10-mm) hole through a piece of aluminum, the drill speed should be 1800 rpm. Drilling metals is also best performed with the aid of a lubricant. The lubricant helps cool the cutting edges of the drill bit as well as lubricate it. Each metal requires its own type of lubricant, so check a drilling guide for the metal you are working on.

Bench and Angle Grinders

Power grinders come in different ranges of sizes and speeds **FIGURE 6-43**. The size of a power grinder is normally determined by the diameter of the largest grinding wheel or disc that can be fitted to it. Some grinders are fixed to a bench or pedestal and the work is brought to the grinder; others are portable devices that can be taken to the work. Bench or pedestal grinders tend to be powered by electricity, while portable ones can be electric or air powered.

FIGURE 6-42 **A.** Portable drill. **B.** Cordless drill. **C.** Drill bits. **D.** Drill press.

FIGURE 6-43 **A.** Bench grinder. **B.** Angle grinder.

<u>Grinding wheels and discs</u> usually have a maximum safe operating speed printed on them. This maximum speed must never be exceeded or the wheel or disc could disintegrate. Every well-equipped shop has a solidly mounted grinder, either on a pedestal bolted to the shop floor or securely attached to the workbench. Appropriate eye protection must be worn when grinders are being used, and the wheel guards and shields must be correctly and firmly in place.

A **bench grinder (pedestal grinder)** normally has a rating with the size of the grinding wheel it can take. Do not try to attempt to install a grinding wheel larger or smaller than it is rated for. Grinding wheels come in grades from coarse to very fine, depending on the size of the abrasive grains that are bonded together to make the wheel. They also range in hardness, depending on the abrasive used and the material that bonds the particles together. If a particular grinding application is required, a check should be done to find out the most suitable grinding wheel for it.

An **angle grinder** is usually needed when the bench grinder is not appropriate. The angle grinder uses discs rather than wheels. During grinding, the face of the disc is used instead of the edge. An angle grinder can throw sparks many feet, so direct the sparks in a safe direction or set up a guard to catch them. Also use hearing protection whenever grinding, as it is very noisy and can damage your ears.

While not as common in an automotive shop, the **straight grinder** takes conventional grinding wheels, just like the stationery grinders. However, the grinding wheel diameter is limited to about 4.75" (126 mm). In many cases, the grinder has a long shaft that moves the grinding wheel away from the motor. This makes it handy to get into recessed areas.

Hand-held cut-off wheels can be powered by electricity or air. They use a special thin grinding disk to enable them to cut. They use the edge of the wheel for cutting and are useful for jobs that cannot be reached with a hacksaw.

Using Bench Grinders

When grinding metal, it must not be allowed to overheat, because this will adversely affect its hardness. If the metal becomes too hot and is allowed to cool slowly, it may become soft. If it is cooled quickly (quenched), it may become brittle. As you grind the metal, stop and dip it regularly into the water pot attached to the base of the grinder, which will prevent the metal from getting too hot. Some bench grinders are not supplied with a water pot. If this is the case, you will need to have a water can located near the grinder so that you can cool the piece you are grinding.

To set up, adjust, and use a bench grinder, follow the steps in **SKILL DRILL 6-13**:

1. Before you start using the bench grinder, inspect the wheels and check to see if the tool rest, safety shield, and shatter guard are adjusted properly. There should also be water in the pot. **(Photo 1)**

2. If needed, adjust the tool rest (maximum of 0.125" [3.2-mm] gap) and the shatter guard (maximum of 0.0625" [1.6-mm] gap) between the wheel. The tool rest should be slightly below the center of the wheel. To adjust the tool rest, locate the adjusting bolt and loosen it with a box-end wrench. Set the tool rest at the right height and distance from the wheel and then tighten the adjusting bolt. If you are unsure of how to do this, ask your supervisor.

3. Connect the grinder to the power supply. Adjust your face protector, stand to the side of the wheel, and switch the grinder on. **(Photo 2)**

SKILL DRILL | 6-13 | Using Bench Grinders

1 Inspect the wheels of the bench grinder and check to see if the tool rest, safety shield, and shatter guard are adjusted properly. There should also be water in the pot.

2 If needed, adjust the tool rest (maximum of 0.125" [3.2-mm] gap) and the shatter guard (maximum of 0.0625" [1.6-mm] gap) between the wheel. The tool rest should be slightly below the center of the wheel. Tighten the adjusting bolt. Connect the grinder to the power supply. Adjust your face protector, stand to the side of the wheel, and switch the grinder on.

3 After the grinder is fully up to speed, move to the front of the wheel, hold the part you are going to grind firmly onto the tool rest, and move it slowly and gently forward until it comes into contact with the wheel. Use the full face of the grinding wheel to prevent wearing one area of the wheel.

4 Occasionally dip the part into the water to keep it cool. When you have finished, turn off the power and unplug the grinder.

4 After the grinder is fully up to speed, move to the front of the wheel, hold the part you are going to grind firmly onto the tool rest, and move it slowly and gently forward until it comes into contact with the wheel. The grinding wheel removes the metal it contacts. Use the full face of the grinding wheel to prevent wearing one area of the wheel. **(Photo 3)**

5 Occasionally dip the part into the water to keep it cool.

6 When you have finished, turn off the power and unplug the grinder. **(Photo 4)**

Safety

Ask your supervisor to demonstrate the differences between grinding wheels for soft and hard materials and wire brush wheels. As the abrasive wheel wears down, the gap between the wheel and the tool rest will increase. This creates a dangerous situation because if the gap enlarges toward the thickness of the metal you are grinding, the metal could be pulled into the gap, which could cause the metal to be thrown with much force.

Be very careful when grinding thin metal pieces, as they are more easily grabbed by the wheel.

Using Angle Grinders

The angle grinder uses an electric motor to drive an abrasive disc at a high speed **FIGURE 6-44**. The grinder disc is turned at speeds that range from 5000 to 12,000 rpm. The turning disc is used to grind or cut metal. The grinder size relates to the diameter of the cutting disc, which can range from 4" to 9" (102 mm to 229 mm). The size of grinder you use depends on the type of job you are doing. The smaller the grinder, the higher the speed it turns. Sanding discs and wire wheels can be fitted on the grinder, making it a versatile electric tool. An extra handle is provided that can be attached to the grinder head. This handle can be fitted to either the left, right, or top of the head to make it easy to use for left-handed as well as right-handed people.

- Make all adjustments with the grinder stopped and unplugged.
- Stand to the side of the grinder when starting the electric motor.
- Never use a cracked or gouged grinding wheel.
- Do not operate a grinder unless it is securely mounted to the bench or floor.
- Do not grind on the side of the wheel because it may cause the wheel to shatter.
- Maintain a 2" (0.6-m) perimeter around the grinder free of flammables, clutter, and people.

When using a bench grinder, the face of the abrasive wheel must be kept square. This is done with a dressing tool, which removes some of the abrasive compound. If the abrasive wheel is not square, use a dressing tool. Then readjust the tool rest to the proper clearance.

The **abrasive disc**, or cutting wheel, is attached to the grinder by a flange and nut. The nut is specially designed to fit in a recess in the center of the pad or wheel. It is tightened by a tool that is provided with the grinder when purchased. Do not lose this wrench because it is the only tool that can tighten the nut properly. When using the grinder with cutting discs, you should always use the edge of the disc rather than the face.

Do not confuse a grinder with a **sander/polisher**. The sander/polisher turns at lower speeds, typically 600 to 3000 rpm. It is commonly used to sand and polish paint. The pads these tools use cannot be turned at a high speed. If the polish pad were attached to an angle grinder, the higher rotational speed would cause the polishing pad to burn the paint and cause the polish pad to fly apart.

To correctly use an angle grinder, follow the steps in **SKILL DRILL 6-14**:

1. Inspect the grinding disc for any cracks or damage. **(Photo 1)**

FIGURE 6-44 **A.** The angle grinder uses an electric motor to drive an abrasive disc at a high speed. **B.** An extra handle is provided that can be attached to the grinder head.

SKILL DRILL │ 6-14 │ Using Angle Grinders

1 Inspect the grinding disc for any cracks or damage.

2 Check the area for any flammables and to determine where the sparks will fly. Take any precautions necessary.

3 Hold the grinder firmly with the face of the disc, not the edge, against the work. Be careful that the motor's torque does not cause the grinder to slip out of your hand. Do not press too hard. Let the grinder do the work.

4 If using the grinder with a cutting disc, use the edge of the disc, not the face.

2 Check the area for any flammables and to determine where the sparks will fly. Take any precautions necessary. **(Photo 2)**

3 Hold the grinder firmly with the face of the disc, not the edge, against the work.

4 Be careful that the motor's torque does not cause the grinder to slip out of your hand. Do not press too hard. Let the grinder do the work. **(Photo 3)**

5 If using the grinder with a cutting disc, use the edge of the disc, not the face. **(Photo 4)**

Air Tools

Air tools use compressed air at high pressure to operate **FIGURE 6-45**. Air compressors in automotive shops typically run at greater than 90 psi (621 kPa), so caution

FIGURE 6-45 **A.** Air impact wrench. **B.** Air ratchet. **C.** Air hammer. **D.** Air drill. **E.** Blowgun or air nozzle.

Safety

- Always wear impact-resistant protective glasses, ear protection, and a full-face shield when using an angle grinder.
- Wear safety shoes, leather gloves, and an apron to protect your body from flying metal chips. Make sure the blade guard is firmly secured.
- Use the correct type of disc.
- Make sure the guard handles are secure.
- Use the correct flange or spindle nut for the type of disc being used. If you do not, the disc can shatter at high speeds and injure you.
- Angle grinders, like all portable grinding tools, need to be equipped with safety guards to protect you from flying fragments in case the disc breaks apart.
- Always follow the manufacturer's recommendations to make sure the spindle wheel does not exceed the abrasive wheel specifications.
- Make sure there are no obvious defects or damage to the disc before you install it.

needs to be exercised around them. Compressed air is transported through pipes and hoses. Air tools have quick-connect fittings so that various air tools can be used on the same air hose. There are several styles of quick-connect fittings, and a shop will usually use one style throughout the entire shop.

The most common air tool in an automotive shop is the **air impact wrench**. It is sometimes called an impact gun or **rattle gun**, and it is easy to understand why when you hear one. Taking the wheels off a car to replace the tires is a typical application for this air tool. Removing lug nuts often requires a lot of torque to twist the nuts free, and air impact wrenches work well for that.

The air impact wrench can be set to spin in either direction, and a valve roughly controls how much torque it applies. It should never be used for final tightening of wheel nuts. There is a danger in overtightening the wheel nuts, as it can cause the bolts to fail and the wheel to separate from the vehicle while it is moving. Another rule with the air impact wrench is that you have to use special hardened impact sockets, extensions, and joints. The sockets are special heavy-duty, six-point types, and the flats can withstand the hammering force that the impact wrench subjects them to.

An **air ratchet** uses the force of compressed air to turn a ratchet drive. It is used on smaller nuts and bolts. Once the nut is loosened, the air ratchet spins it off in a fraction of the time it would take by hand. It also works well where there isn't much room to swing a ratchet handle.

An **air hammer**, sometimes called an air chisel, is useful for driving and cutting. The extra force that is generated by the compressed air makes it more efficient than a hand chisel and hammer. Just as there are many chisels, there are many bits that fit into the air hammer, depending on the job at hand.

An **air drill** has some important advantages over the more common electric power drill. With the right attachment, it can drill holes, grind, polish, and clean parts. Unlike the electric drill, it does not run the risk of producing sparks, which is important around flammable liquids or gasoline tanks. An air drill does not trail a live electric cable behind it that could be cut, possibly causing shock and burns. It also does not get hot with heavy use.

A blowgun, or **air nozzle**, is probably the simplest air tool. It controls the flow of compressed air. It is controlled by a lever or valve that is used to blast debris and dirt out of confined spaces. Blasting debris and dirt can be dangerous, so eye protection must be worn whenever this tool is used. Noise levels are usually high, so ear protection should also be worn. It is dangerous to use an air nozzle to clean yourself off. Its blast should always be directed away from the user and anyone else working nearby. Also note that OSHA-approved nozzles lower the tip pressure by venting some of the air for safety reasons. Only use OSHA-approved nozzles for general blowing purposes.

Using Air Nozzles

An air nozzle can be a handy tool for blowing dirt and debris out of holes such as around spark plugs prior to removing them. It is helpful to activate the air nozzle away from the area you intend to blow off before doing it; this way you can get a feel for how the valve operates. To operate an air nozzle, pull the trigger gently and modulate the flow of air through the nozzle. If too much air is allowed through, you may blow dirt particles back at you, so always wear your safety glasses. Also keep your mouth closed, as it helps prevent eating a bunch of dirt!

To correctly operate an air nozzle, follow the steps in **SKILL DRILL 6-15**:

1. Fit an OSHA-approved air nozzle to the end of the air hose. Make sure there are no air leaks. **(Photo 1)**

2. The air nozzle is used to blast dirt and debris out of confined spaces. To avoid injury, be sure to wear eye and ear protection whenever you use the air nozzle.

3. Do NOT use the air nozzle to dust yourself off because you risk injury. Be sure to direct the air jet away from yourself and away from anyone else who may be working nearby. **(Photo 2)**

SKILL DRILL | 6-15 | Using Air Nozzles

1 Fit an OSHA-approved air nozzle to the end of the air hose. Make sure there are no air leaks.

2 Apply eye and ear protection. Be sure to direct the air jet away from yourself and away from anyone else who may be working nearby.

Safety

- Do not use the air nozzle to clean brake dust from brake components. It will disperse the hazardous dust.
- Do not use a high-pressure air nozzle to disperse liquid solvents or fuels. A low-pressure blowing action can help these volatile materials to evaporate more quickly, but a high-pressure air jet could atomize the liquid, allowing it to form a flammable mixture.
- Do not point the air nozzle at other people.
- Never use the air nozzle to blow air over yourself or other people.
- Always wear eye protection when using air tools.
- Do not drive over the air hoses.
- Make sure the hoses are in good condition before using.

Using Air Impact Wrenches

The amount of torque an air impact wrench can produce will be determined by the tool and the pressure in the air system feeding it. Because this pressure will vary, there is no way of determining how much torque an impact wrench is applying to a fastener, so it is easy to over- or undertighten fasteners. An air impact wrench can generally be used to take up the looseness in a nut or stud, but the final tightening must be performed by using a torque wrench set to the manufacturer's specifications.

Every impact wrench will have a control mechanism that allows it to be driven in either direction. Always use six-point impact sockets when using an air impact wrench;

these sockets are manufactured from a different blend of materials and have thicker walls than a standard socket.

To correctly operate an air impact wrench, follow the steps in **SKILL DRILL 6-16**:

1 Select the properly sized impact gun and socket, inspect them for damage, and lubricate the gun if an automatic oiler is not installed in the system. (**Photo 1**)

2 Adjust the direction of spin—forward or backward—with the selector. (**Photo 2**)

3 Turn the valve to increase or reduce the torque to match the needs of the fastener. If removing lug nuts, adjust it toward the upper middle torque setting. If running a nut back on a stud, adjust it toward the lowest torque setting. You can always readjust it if you end up needing more torque. (**Photo 3**)

4 Place the impact wrench fully over the bolt or nut and give the trigger a quick squeeze to verify that the impact wrench is turning the correct direction.

5 Continue to remove or install the fastener by squeezing the trigger only long enough to get the job done. Release the trigger before getting to the, end as it takes time for the impact wrench to slow down; otherwise the nut could fly off the end of the stud, or if tightening, you could end up overtightening. (**Photo 4**)

Safety

- Air tools generally produce more noise than electric tools, so wear ear protection when using air tools.
- Always use impact sockets with impact guns.

SKILL DRILL | 6-16 | Using Air Impact Wrenches

1 Select the properly sized impact gun and socket, inspect them for damage, and lubricate the gun if an automatic oiler is not installed in the system.

2 Adjust the direction of spin—forward or backward—with the selector.

3 Turn the valve to increase or reduce the torque to match the needs of the fastener. If removing lug nuts, adjust it toward the upper middle torque setting. If running a nut back on a stud, adjust it toward the lowest torque setting.

4 Place the impact wrench fully over the bolt or nut and give the trigger a quick squeeze to verify that the impact wrench is turning the correct direction. Continue to remove or install the fastener by squeezing the trigger only long enough to get the job done. Release the trigger before getting to the end, as it takes time for the impact wrench to slow down.

Using Air Drills

Air drills are another tool operated by compressed air. Since they are powered by air and not electricity, they are safer to use in an environment where flammable materials are present. The amount of torque an air drill can produce will be determined by the pressure in the air system feeding it. Air drills are smaller and turn at slower speeds than electric drills. Air drills operate similarly to their electric counterparts and are equipped with the same type of drill chuck, which clamps onto the drill bit using a special key. Most air drills are of the 90-degree angle style and fit in places a typical electric drill might not.

To correctly operate an air drill, follow the steps in **SKILL DRILL 6-17**:

1 Select the properly sized air drill and drill bit, inspect them for damage, and lubricate the gun if an automatic oiler is not installed in the system.

2 Adjust the direction of spin—forward or backward—with the selector.

SKILL DRILL | 6-17 | Using Air Drills

1 Select the properly sized air drill and drill bit, inspect them for damage, and lubricate the gun if an automatic oiler is not installed in the system. Adjust the direction of spin—forward or backward—with the selector. Turn the valve to increase or reduce the torque to match the needs of the job.

2 Place the air drill into position and hold it firmly. Give the trigger a quick squeeze to verify that the air drill is turning the correct direction and does not slip. Continue to operate the air drill by squeezing the trigger only long enough to get the job done.

3 Turn the valve to increase or reduce the torque to match the needs of the job. (**Photo 1**)

4 Place the air drill into position and hold it firmly. Give the trigger a quick squeeze to verify that the air drill is turning the correct direction and does not slip.

5 Continue to operate the air drill by squeezing the trigger only long enough to get the job done. (**Photo 2**)

Using Air Hammers

Air hammers act in a manner similar to a jackhammer; however, their size makes their cycling rate faster. There are a variety of attachments, so use the correct attachment for the task you are performing. This could be a chisel for cutting a bolt or a punch for driving out a broken lug stud. The attachment is held in place by a coil spring that tends to break over time, so inspect it and never use the air hammer if it is broken. Place the tool bit against the workpiece and hold it firmly before you pull the trigger, as it is likely to want to jump around.

To use an air hammer, follow the steps in **SKILL DRILL 6-18**:

1 Select the properly sized air hammer and attachment, inspect them for damage, and lubricate the gun if an automatic oiler is not installed in the system.

2 Fit the appropriate bit into the nose of the air hammer and ensure the spring is installed correctly. (**Photo 1**)

3 Place the air hammer into position and hold it firmly. Give the trigger a quick squeeze to see how the air hammer will react.

4 Continue to operate the air hammer by squeezing the trigger and watching the progress carefully. Allow the air hammer to do the work, and work slowly around the item. (**Photo 2**)

Safety

An air hammer's operation produces a noise level that exceeds the maximum exposure level for human ears. Always wear ear protection when using an air hammer.

Cleaning Tools

Pressure Washers and Cleaners

Pressure washers and cleaners are valuable tools for cleaning vehicles, engine compartments, and components. They can be powered by an electric motor or a gasoline engine fitted to a high-pressure pump.

SKILL DRILL | 6-18 | Using Air Hammers

1. Select the properly sized air hammer and attachment, inspect them for damage, and lubricate the gun if an automatic oiler is not installed in the system. Fit the appropriate bit into the nose of the air hammer and ensure the spring is installed correctly.

2. Place the air hammer into position and hold it firmly. Give the trigger a quick squeeze to see how the air hammer will react. Continue to operate the air hammer by squeezing the trigger and watching the progress carefully. Allow the air hammer to do the work, and work slowly around the item.

The pressure washer takes water at normal pressure and boosts it through the high-pressure pump to exit through a cleaning gun, which has a control trigger. The **cleaning gun** has a high-pressure nozzle that focuses high-pressure water (possibly over 2000 psi [13790 kPa]) to quickly clean accumulated dirt and grease from components. Some pressure washers have a provision for detergent to be injected into the high-pressure output to more effectively clean. Others have the ability to heat the water, in some cases hot enough to turn it to steam. Hot water and steam help loosen oil and grease buildup.

Pressure washers are dangerous because of their high pressure and possibly high temperature. Always wear appropriate PPE when working with pressure cleaners—for example, goggles or face shield, protective gloves, close-fitting clothes with long sleeves and full-length pants, and leather-type boots or shoes.

Using Pressure Washers

Pressure washers and cleaners used in automotive applications are available in a range of makes and types depending on the application. There are fixed washers for cleaning components and mobile pressure washers that can be used to wash vehicle systems and engine compartments. Familiarize yourself with the equipment prior to use; incorrect handling can result in damage to the washer or to the vehicle or components you are cleaning, in addition to health risks to yourself and your coworkers.

The biggest advantage of using fluid to clean vehicles, components, and spaces is that it wets the dirt or contaminants, so no dust is created. However, the waste products must be caught and disposed of properly in either a catch basin or a waste water settling system. The waste materials must not be released into a storm water drain.

It is imperative that you read the instructions beforehand and be familiar with the operation of the pressure washer. When cleaning exterior paintwork, extreme care must be taken to ensure that the pressure does not damage or remove paint. If in doubt, clean the area manually using a clean sponge and clean water. It is very important to note the type of solvent being used in a pressure washer, as some vehicle components can be damaged by some solvents and should only be cleaned in wash tanks containing the correct cleaning fluid.

When using high-pressure washers, it is always important not to spray in areas where water and water-based solvents can have a detrimental effect on electrical equipment such as fuse boxes, relays, and control units. If you are required to use a pressure washer in those areas of the vehicle, take precautionary measures to protect the units from high-pressure water damage by covering them with sturdy plastic bags. The damage may not become apparent for some time after the cleaning process, but it can have a catastrophic effect on the vehicle, causing system failures, which are difficult to diagnose.

If the washer results in the wheel brake units getting wet, ensure that the vehicle is driven for a short distance with the brakes slightly applied. This will remove any residual water from the brake shoes or pads through heat transfer and subsequent evaporation of the water.

Depending on the outside temperature, it usually only takes several seconds to return the brakes to their proper operation.

On completion of the job, the correct disposal of contaminated materials is a top priority. Operators of cleaning equipment may be subject to prosecution for the incorrect disposal of waste materials. So always know the regulations and follow all policies and guidelines for the jurisdiction you are in.

To safely use pressure washers, follow the steps in **SKILL DRILL 6-19**:

1. Before using the pressure washer, locate the position of safety switches and don a face shield,

SKILL DRILL | 6-19 | Using Pressure Washers

1. Locate the position of safety switches and put on a face shield, work apron, and gloves. Note the location of the eyewash and first aid stations. If not permanently connected, follow the manufacturer's instructions and connect the pressure washer hose to the water supply, and the electrical plug to a power outlet protected by a ground fault circuit interrupter (GFCI). Protect adjacent areas from water spray.

2. If necessary, apply a degreasing agent with a spray bottle and hand brush to penetrate and soften excess dirt.

3. Turn on the water supply but not the power switch. Water should flow freely but not at high pressure. Turn the power on and you will hear the motor engage. Point the wand toward the ground and test that the water is flowing at high pressure.

4. Pull the trigger and using either a circular or a sweeping motion, direct the high-pressure water onto the area to be cleaned.

5. When the contaminants have been removed, release the trigger and remove the wand from the cleaning area. Turn the electrical power off, then turn the water supply off.

6. Use an air nozzle to disperse any residual water from electrical components that have come into contact with the cleaning fluids. Start the vehicle and let it run for a few moments to dry, and then remove any residual water in the engine compartment area. Clean up any residual material and place it in a bin or an environmental waste container.

work apron, and gloves. Note the location of the eyewash and first aid stations.

2 If not permanently connected, follow the manufacturer's instructions and connect the pressure washer hose to the water supply, and the electrical plug to power outlet protected by a ground fault circuit interrupter (GFCI). Make sure electrical connections and adjacent areas are protected from water spray by using appropriate protective shields. **(Photo 1)**

3 It may be necessary to apply a degreasing agent with a spray bottle and hand brush to penetrate and soften excess dirt before you operate the pressure washer. **(Photo 2)**

4 Turn on the water supply but not the power switch. Make sure water is flowing through the washer unit by testing the flow through the pressure wand before turning the power on. It should flow freely but not at high pressure.

5 Turn the power on and you will hear the motor engage. Point the wand toward the ground and test that the water now flows at high pressure. **(Photo 3)**

6 Pull the trigger and using either a circular or a sweeping motion, direct the high-pressure water

onto the area to be cleaned to remove the contaminants. Avoid getting the high-pressure spray on the exterior paintwork of the vehicle by placing the wand close to the area to be cleaned. **(Photo 4)**

7 When the contaminants have been removed, release the trigger and remove the wand from the cleaning area. Turn the electrical power off, then turn the water supply off. If it is a hot water or steam cleaner, let the water run until it cools off so that you do not overheat the water in the heating coils. **(Photo 5)**

8 Use an air nozzle to disperse any residual water from electrical components that have come into contact with the cleaning fluids.

9 Start the vehicle and let it run for a few moments to dry, and then remove any residual water in the engine compartment area.

10 Clean up any residual material and place it in a bin or an environmental waste container. **(Photo 6)**

Spray Wash Cabinets

Spray wash cabinets spray high-temperature, high-pressure cleaning solutions onto parts inside a sealed cabinet. They are automated and act like a dishwasher for parts. This significantly reduces the labor required to clean parts because once the door is closed and the unit is turned on, the technician is free to move onto other tasks. They are available in a variety of sizes to cater to different-sized parts and provide a high level of cleaning performance. The cleaning solution is designed to effectively clean without leaving residue on the parts, and most spray cabinets are fitted with a filtering system to reduce the frequency of cleaning solution changes.

Using Spray Wash Cabinets

Spray wash cabinets used in automotive applications are available in a range of makes and types depending on the application. It is imperative that you read the instructions beforehand and be familiar with the operation of the spray wash cabinet. Incorrect handling can result in damage to the components that you are cleaning in addition to health risks to yourself and your coworkers.

Spray wash cabinets must either incorporate a built-in waste recovery system or be used only where the contaminated washer fluids can be captured to enable disposal in an environmentally friendly manner. Always follow recommended safety procedures. Spray wash cabinets use potentially dangerous chemicals at very high pressure to clean away the contaminants.

Safety

- Always wear a face shield and gloves when using cleaning and washing equipment.
- Always wear safety shoes when using any washing equipment to prevent slips on slippery surfaces.
- Always be aware of the location of safety switches located on equipment and of eyewash and first aid stations should an accident occur.
- Do not place your hand or any other part of your body in the stream of water from the high-pressure wand. Many pressure washers generate enough pressure to instantly cut skin and muscle to the bone.
- Do not aim the high-pressure wand at another person.
- Always test the temperature of the wand and the hose before you pick it up. The handle of the pressure wand is insulated to protect the user from heat, but the wand extension and the hose are not.
- If the pressure cleaner uses a heating element, turn the heater off and allow water to flow through the wand until is has cooled before you turn the unit off.
- If you are unfamiliar with a solvent or a cleaning agent, refer to the material safety data sheet (MSDS) for information about its correct use and applicable hazards.

It is very important to note the type of cleaning agent being used, as some vehicle components can be damaged by some agents. On completion of the job, the correct disposal of any contaminated materials is a top priority. Operators of this equipment may be subject to prosecution for the incorrect disposal of waste materials.

To use a spray wash cabinet to clean components, follow the steps in **SKILL DRILL 6-20**:

1. Always refer to the manufacturer's manual for specific operating instructions. Before using the equipment, locate the position of safety switches and put on a face shield and gloves. Note the location of the eyewash and first aid stations.

2. Check the spray wash cabinet to ensure it is operating correctly with enough cleaning fluid.

3. Open the spray wash cabinet. Place the components to be cleaned into the wash tray. Seek assistance if parts are too heavy to be handled by one person. Distribute them so each part will be cleaned effectively. **(Photo 1)**

4. Close the spray wash cabinet and start the cleaning cycle.

5. Make sure the cleaning cycle has finished before you open the spray wash cabinet door. Ensure you are wearing appropriate eye and hand protection.

When opening the door, be careful because parts will be hot to the touch. Examine the parts to ensure they have been completely cleaned. In some models, you need to rinse the components after removing them from the washer. Follow the directions for the model you are using. **(Photo 2)**

Safety

- Do not operate the spray wash cabinet without the door securely closed.
- The spray wash cabinet uses high-pressure, high-temperature cleaning fluid, and parts will be hot after being in the spray cabinet.

Solvent Tanks

A **solvent tank** is a cleaning tank that is filled with a suitable solvent to clean parts by removing oil, grease, dirt, and grime. Solvent tanks are available in different sizes. Many solvent tanks have a pump that pushes solvent out a nozzle into a sink where it can be directed to the parts being cleaned. A brush either on the nozzle or separate from it can be used to loosen the grease and grime. The solvent falls back into the bottom of the solvent tank

SKILL DRILL 6-20 Using Spray Wash Cabinets

1. Check the spray wash cabinet to ensure it is operating correctly with enough cleaning fluid. Open the spray wash cabinet. Place the components to be cleaned into the wash tray. Seek assistance if parts are too heavy to be handled by one person. Distribute them so each part will be cleaned effectively.

2. Close the spray wash cabinet and start the cleaning cycle. Make sure the cleaning cycle has finished before you open the spray wash cabinet door. Ensure you are wearing eye and hand protection.

where the heavier residue can settle to the bottom. Other solvent tanks are designed so that parts can be immersed into the tank on racks or suspended on pieces of wire, and slowly lowered and soaked in the tank for a period of time. Some solvent tanks may have an agitation system or use a heated cleaning fluid to speed up the process. They may also have a circulation system and filters to remove debris and residue in the solvent to extend its life between changes.

Using Solvent Tanks

Familiarize yourself with the equipment prior to use; incorrect handling can result in damage to components that you are cleaning in addition to health risks to yourself and your coworkers. Solvent tanks may use potentially poisonous and/or flammable chemicals to clean parts. It is very important to note the type of solvent being used and to take all necessary precautions as listed on the MSDS. Also, some vehicle components can be damaged by some solvents, so ask your supervisor about what can be safely washed and what cannot. On completion of the job, the correct disposal of contaminated materials is a top priority. Operators of this equipment may be subject to prosecution for the incorrect disposal of waste materials.

To use a solvent tank to clean components, follow the steps in **SKILL DRILL 6-21**:

1. Always refer to the manufacturer's manual for specific operating instructions. Before using the equipment, locate the position of safety switches and put on a face shield and gloves. Note the location of the eyewash and first aid stations.

2. Do a pre-operating check of the solvent tank to ensure it is operating correctly with enough cleaning fluid. (**Photo 1**)

3. Lift the components to be cleaned into the wash tray or lower them into the solvent tank. Seek assistance if parts are too heavy to be handled by one person. Distribute them so each part will be cleaned effectively. (**Photo 2**)

4. Start the circulating or agitating pump if equipped.

5. Soak or run the solvent onto the components in the solvent tank for the appropriate amount of time. You may need to use a brush to help clean the

parts. Be careful not to cause excessive splashing of cleaning fluid. (**Photo 3**)

6. Examine the parts to ensure they have been completely cleaned.

7. Remove parts carefully from the solvent tank, allowing excess cleaning solvent to drip back into the tank. Ensure contaminated cleaning fluids can be captured to enable disposal in an environmentally friendly manner. (**Photo 4**)

Brake Washers

Brake washers are used to wash brake dust from wheel brake units and their components. Since it is possible that the brake dust may contain asbestos, which is a cancer-causing agent, and dust in general is a lung irritant, brake washers are designed to capture the brake dust before it enters the shop environment. It does so by wetting down the dust on the brake parts and then washing it into the cleaning tray. Brake washers incorporate a built-in waste recovery system where the contaminated washer fluids can be captured to enable disposal in an environmentally friendly manner.

Brake washers are normally designed to operate at low pressure and use a range of cleaning agents. The most popular agent is an aqueous solution made up of water and a water-soluble detergent. A low-pressure air blower may be provided to remove the fluid from the component into the tray area and then back to the tank by gravity.

Avoid using solvent when cleaning brake components, as it contaminates friction materials and may cause seals to swell. Never use kerosene as a general cleaning agent to clean brake components, as it does not clean away brake fluid, can be absorbed into lining materials, and can cause seals to swell. Soapy water is a good cleaning agent for brake components.

Using Brake Washers

Brake washers are a handy piece of shop equipment to deal with hazardous dust in a quick and relatively easy manner, especially if the washer uses an aqueous (water

SKILL DRILL | 6-21 | Using Solvent Tanks

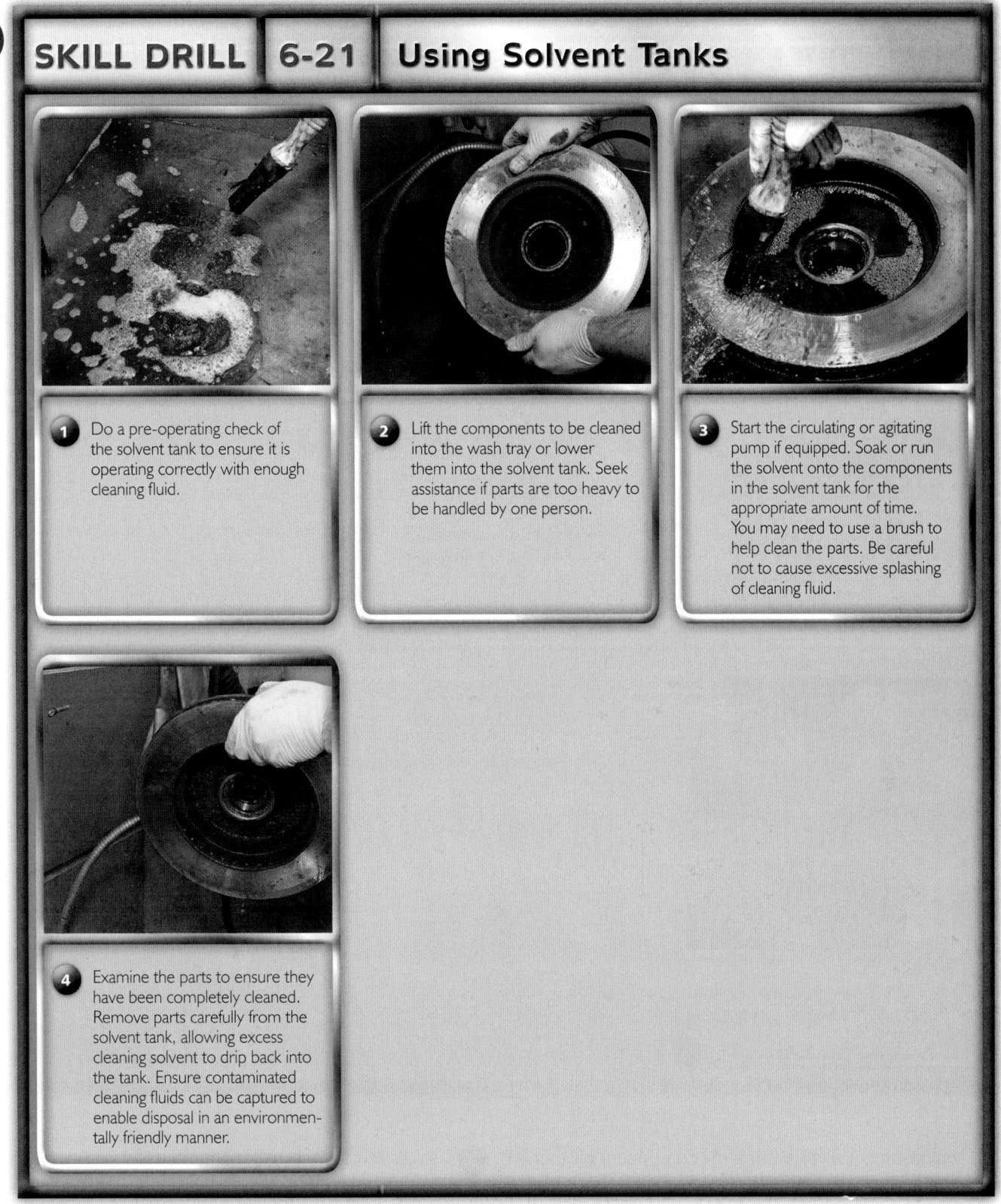

1. Do a pre-operating check of the solvent tank to ensure it is operating correctly with enough cleaning fluid.

2. Lift the components to be cleaned into the wash tray or lower them into the solvent tank. Seek assistance if parts are too heavy to be handled by one person.

3. Start the circulating or agitating pump if equipped. Soak or run the solvent onto the components in the solvent tank for the appropriate amount of time. You may need to use a brush to help clean the parts. Be careful not to cause excessive splashing of cleaning fluid.

4. Examine the parts to ensure they have been completely cleaned. Remove parts carefully from the solvent tank, allowing excess cleaning solvent to drip back into the tank. Ensure contaminated cleaning fluids can be captured to enable disposal in an environmentally friendly manner.

and detergent) cleaning solution. The one thing that this solution is not suited for is cleaning greasy residue. If you need to remove grease, you might be able to first use a paper towel or grease rag to wipe it off, and then clean the brake dust with the brake washer.

To use a brake washer to clean components, follow the steps in SKILL DRILL 6-22:

1. Make sure all the washing solution is contained within the cleaning tray and returns to the reservoir. Washing solution must not enter the

SKILL DRILL | 6-22 | Using Brake Washers

1 Make sure all the washing fluid is contained within the cleaning tray and returns to the reservoir. Washing solution must not enter the environment. Make sure the solution is compatible with the component to be cleaned. An aqueous detergent solution is an environmentally friendly solution.

2 Put on gloves and safety glasses or a face shield and move the brake washer under the wheel brake unit to be cleaned. Make sure the waste drain is not blocked and the low-pressure air nozzle, if equipped, is operational.

3 Using a semi-stiff brush, paint the solution over the components both to wet and clean the components and to remove contaminants. Continue to do so until the components are clean.

4 Use the low-pressure air nozzle to dry any excess solution from the component.

environment. Before using the component cleaner, make sure the solution is compatible with the component to be cleaned. An aqueous solution is an environmentally friendly solution. (**Photo 1**)

2 Put on gloves and safety glasses or a face shield and move the brake washer under the wheel brake unit to be cleaned. Make sure the waste drain is not blocked and the low-pressure air nozzle, if equipped, is operational. (**Photo 2**)

3 Using a semi-stiff brush, paint the solution over the components both to wet and clean the components and to remove contaminants. Continue to do so until the components are clean. (**Photo 3**)

4 Use the low-pressure air nozzle to dry any excess solution from the component, and make sure the waste materials are caught in the cleaning tray and strained back into the tank below. (**Photo 4**)

Sand or Bead Blasters

<u>Sand or bead blasters</u> use high pressure to blast small abrasive particles to clean the surface of parts. The most common method of propelling the sand or glass beads is with compressed air. Sand or bead blasting can occur in a specially designed cabinet or there are portable models that are available for use in open-air situations. The cabinets contain the blasting operation in a controlled safe environment and are best for smaller parts that can fit into the cabinet. Portable systems that do not operate within a cabinet can blast larger parts but do require more protection for the operator and surrounding environment.

The sand or bead blaster cabinet is fitted with a hand-operated blasting nozzle, a viewing port, and an on/off switch (often this may be a foot-operated switch), and it has openings with tough rubber gloves sealed into them to allow a technician's hands to be inside the cabinet while being protected from the abrasive sand or beads. Wet sand or bead blasters are also available and have the added advantage of reducing the amount of dust and providing additional cleaning to the part being cleaned.

Using Sand or Bead Blasters

Technicians use sand or bead blasters to clean paint, corrosion, or dirt from metal parts. Since the sand or beads are abrasive, they can remove metal from the surface of the components, so be careful what you use it on. Sand or bead blasters used in automotive applications are available in a range of makes and models, depending on application.

To use a sand or bead blaster to clean components, follow the steps in **SKILL DRILL 6-23**:

1. Always refer to the manufacturer's manual for specific operating instructions. Before using the equipment, locate the position of safety switches. If not using a cabinet, then a face shield, dust mask, and gloves are required. Note the location of the eyewash and first aid stations.

2. Check the sand or bead blaster to ensure it is operating correctly with enough cleaning sand/beads. **(Photo 1)**

3. Open the sand or bead blaster. Lift the components to be blasted into the cabinet. Seek assistance if parts are too heavy to be handled by one person. **(Photo 2)**

4. Close the sand or bead blaster and start sand or bead blasting. Direct the blaster nozzle toward the parts to be cleaned. Avoid accidentally blasting the viewing port, as doing so will reduce the transparency of the port.

SKILL DRILL | 6-23 | Using Sand or Bead Blasters

1. Check the sand or bead blaster to ensure it is operating correctly with enough cleaning sand/beads.

2. Open the sand or bead blaster. Lift the components to be blasted into the cabinet. Seek assistance if parts are too heavy to be handled by one person.

3. Close the sand or bead blaster and start sand or bead blasting. Direct the blaster nozzle toward the parts to be cleaned. Avoid accidentally blasting the viewing port, as doing so will reduce the transparency of the port. Make sure the sand or bead blasting has finished before opening the door.

5 Make sure the sand or bead blasting has finished before you open the cabinet door. **(Photo 3)**

6 Open the door and examine the parts to ensure they have been completely cleaned. If parts are not sufficiently cleaned, continue blasting.

7 Remove parts and clean, preferably with a liquid cleaning solution or water, to ensure all abrasive materials are removed.

Safety

Familiarize yourself with the equipment prior to use; incorrect handling can result in damage to components that you are cleaning in addition to health risks to yourself and your coworkers. The waste products must be caught and disposed of properly.

Safety

Sand or bead blasters use potentially very fine particles at high pressure to clean away the contaminants. Also, silica from the sand particles should not be inhaled; it can cause lung damage, called silicosis, over a long period of time.

Safety

- Do not operate the sand/bead blaster without the door securely closed.
- Wear appropriate breathing apparatus or a dust mask.
- Always wear eye protection to prevent injury from flying particles or escaping compressed air.
- On completion of the job, the correct disposal of contaminated materials is a top priority.

▶ Thread Repair

<u>Thread repair</u> is used in situations where it is not possible to replace a damaged component. This may be because the thread is located in a large expensive component, such as the engine block or cylinder head of a vehicle, or because parts are not available. The aim of thread repair is to restore the thread to a condition that restores the fastening integrity. It can be performed on internal threads, such as in a housing, engine block, or cylinder head, or on external threads, such as on a bolt.

Types of Thread Repair

Many different tools and methods can be used to repair a thread. The least invasive method is to reshape the

threads. If the threads are not too badly damaged, such as the outer thread is slightly damaged from being started crooked (cross-threaded), then a thread file can be used to clean them up or a restoring tool can be used to reshape them. Each thread file has eight different sets of file teeth that match various thread pitches. Select the set that matches the bolt you are working on and file the bolt in line with the threads. The file will remove any distorted metal from the threads. Only file until the bad spot is reshaped. The thread-restoring tool looks like an ordinary tap and die set, but instead of cutting the threads, it reshapes the damaged portion of the thread.

Threads that have substantial damage require other methods of repair. A common method for repairing damaged internal threads is a thread insert. A number of manufacturers make thread inserts, and they all work in a similar fashion. The thread insert is a sleeve that has both internal and external threads. The internal thread on the insert matches the original damaged thread size. The hole with the damaged thread is made larger and a fresh larger-diameter thread is cut. This thread matches the external thread on the insert. The thread insert can then be screwed and secured into the prepared hole. The insert provides a brand new internal thread that matches the original size.

You should always make sure the tools are clean and in good condition and are suitable for the thread repair. Determine the type and size of the thread to be repaired. Thread pitch gauges and vernier calipers may be used to measure the thread. Thread repair can include removal of a broken bolt, restoration of internal and external threads, and the use of a thread insert to repair an internal thread.

To remove a broken bolt, inspect the site. If enough of the bolt is sticking out of the surface, then a pair of pliers or locking pliers may be enough to turn and remove the bolt. If the bolt is broken off flush with the surface, then a screw or bolt extraction tool will be needed. Select the correct size of extractor, and drill the designated hole size in the center of the broken bolt to accommodate the extractor. Use a center punch to mark the bolt to assist in centering the hole to drill. Once the hole is drilled, insert the extractor and turn it counterclockwise. The flutes on the extractor should grab the inside of the bolt and hopefully back out. Be careful not to exert too much force on the extractor if the bolt is extremely stuck in place. If the extractor breaks, it is almost impossible to remove it since it is made of hardened metal that cannot be cut by most drill bits. Once the broken bolt is removed, run a lubricated tap or thread-restoring tool of the correct size and thread pitch through the hole to clean up any rust or damage.

To conduct thread repair, follow the steps in **SKILL DRILL 6-24**:

1 Always refer to the manufacturer's manual for specific operating instructions.

SKILL DRILL 6-24 Thread Repair

1 Inspect the condition of the threads and determine the repair method.

2 Determine the type and size of the thread to be repaired. Thread pitch gauges and vernier calipers may be used to measure the thread.

3 Prepare materials for conducting the repair: dies and taps or a drill bit and drill, cutting oil, if required, and inserts. Select the correctly sized tap or die if conducting a minor repair. Run the die or tap through or over the thread; be sure to use cutting lubricant.

4 If using inserts, select the correctly sized insert. Drill the damaged hole, ensuring the drill is in perfect alignment with the hole.

5 Cut the new thread to hold the insert using the appropriate tap. Make sure you use cutting lubricant if required.

6 Using the insert-installing tool, install the insert by screwing it into the newly cut threads. Make sure the insert is secure or locked into the hole using the method specified by the manufacturer.

7 Test the insert to ensure it is secure and the bolt will screw all the way in.

2 Inspect the condition of the threads and determine the repair method. (**Photo 1**)

3 Determine the type and size of the thread to be repaired. Thread pitch gauges and vernier calipers may be used to measure the thread. (**Photo 2**)

4 Prepare materials for conducting the repair: dies and taps or a drill bit and drill, cutting oil, if required, and inserts.

5 Select the correctly sized tap or die if conducting a minor repair. Run the die or tap through or over the thread; be sure to use cutting lubricant. (**Photo 3**)

6 If using inserts, select the correctly sized insert based on the original bolt size. Drill the damaged hole, ensuring the drill is in perfect alignment with the hole. (**Photo 4**)

7 Cut the new thread using the proper size tap. Make sure you use cutting lubricant if required. (**Photo 5**)

8 Using the insert-installing tool, install the insert by screwing it into the newly cut threads. Make sure the insert is secure or locked into the hole using the method specified by the manufacturer. Some inserts use a locking tab, while others use a liquid thread locker that hardens and holds the insert in place. (**Photo 6**)

9 Test the insert to ensure it is secure and the bolt will screw all the way in. (**Photo 7**)

▶ Welding and Cutting Equipment

Oxyacetylene

Oxyacetylene torches are occasionally used by technicians to heat, braze, weld, and cut metal. Acetylene is a highly combustible gas, and when combined with oxygen, it produces a very hot temperature of 6300°F to 6800°F (3480°C to 3760°C). Heating is used to loosen rusted fasteners to help remove them. Brazing uses brass filler rod, which is melted by the torch to join or patch metals. Welding is the process of joining metals by melting the metals together, usually along with a filler rod, which provides extra material to fill any gaps. Cutting involves heating metals until they are so hot that when given an extra shot of oxygen, the metal burns.

The torch consists of an acetylene cylinder, an oxygen cylinder, a pressure regulator for each cylinder, hoses, a flashback arrestor for each hose, the torch handle, and the tip. The cylinders hold the gases. Each pressure regulator has two pressure gauges. One gauge shows how much pressure is in the cylinder, and the other gauge shows how much pressure is in the line. The line

(hose) pressure is adjusted on the pressure regulator by the operator. The hoses run from each regulator to the flashback arrestors on the torch handle. The acetylene hose is red, and the oxygen hose is green. The **flashback arrestors** are spring-loaded check valves that allow flow through the hoses in one direction only—from the cylinders to the torch handle. They prevent flame from traveling back up the hose in the case of a flashback, which is when the oxygen and acetylene ignite inside the torch handle. Flashback happens if the torch valves are set lower than they should be for a particular tip, which produces low gas flow out of the tip; if a welding spark jumps up into the tip; or if the torch is set with too much oxygen flowing. The torch handle may have the flashback arrestors screwed into it or they may be built directly into the handle. The gas flow valves are near the base of the handle. The top of the handle is threaded so that different tips can be installed.

Different tip sizes are available depending on the size and thickness of the metal to be heated, welded, or cut **FIGURE 6-46**. Larger tips allow more gas (oxygen and acetylene) mixture to flow out of the hole in the tip, which produces a larger flame. Welding tips usually have a single hole in the tip—a small hole for thin metals or a larger hole for thicker metals. Larger heating tips, usually called "rose buds," have multiple holes, typically five or more in a circle toward the outside tip face. The multiple holes allow the rose bud to create the same amount of heat as a much larger single-hole tip but with a lower chance of flashback. The cutting torch tip uses multiple holes in a circle similar to a rose bud, but it also has a central hole for pure oxygen inside the circle of holes.

FIGURE 6-46 **A.** Rose bud tip. **B.** Cutting torch tip. **C.** Welding tip.

When oxyacetylene is used to cut steel, a cutting torch is fitted in place of the welding tip. The outer circle of holes provides the oxygen and acetylene for heating the metal. The center hole injects a stream of pure oxygen into the red-hot metal and causes it to burn, thereby cutting the metal. The oxygen flow is controlled by a spring-loaded lever and activated by the technician.

Oxyacetylene Torch Safety

Safety needs to be first and foremost when working with an oxyacetylene torch. Oxyacetylene cylinders carry very high pressures. The acetylene pressure in a full cylinder is approximately 250 psi (1724 kPa), and the oxygen cylinder is approximately 2200 psi (15,168 kPa). If an oxygen cylinder falls over and breaks the main valve off, the cylinder will become a missile and can even go through concrete block walls, so always secure the cylinders properly to the wall or an approved welding cart.

Wear a leather apron or similar protective clothing and welding gloves when using an oxyacetylene torch. T-shirts, nylon, and polyester blend clothing will not provide enough protection because ultraviolet light and sparks of hot metal will pass through them. Always use proper welding goggles. Do not use sunglasses because they do not filter the extreme ultraviolet light as effectively and the plastic used in the lenses of sunglasses will not protect your eyes from sparks.

Never point the lighted flame toward another person or any flammable material. Always light the oxyacetylene torch with the striker. A cigarette lighter could explode, and a match would put your hand too close to the igniting tip. Wherever possible, use a heat shield behind the component you are heating. This will prevent nearby objects from becoming hot. After heating a piece of metal, label it as "HOT" with a piece of chalk so that others will not attempt to pick it up.

Purging Oxyacetylene Torches

Purging the oxyacetylene system is the process of venting all of the gas in the system from the cylinder valve to the torch handle tip and setting the valves so nothing can enter the system. Purging the system is required when you are finished with the torch for the day, if you are not sure if the torch was shut down properly the last time it was used, or if you are making repairs to the system.

To properly purge an oxyacetylene system, follow the steps in **SKILL DRILL 6-25**:

1 Verify that the valves are firmly closed on both cylinders. The valves normally turn off in a clockwise direction.

2 Verify that both valves on the torch handle are closed only finger tight, and no more. The seals in the torch handle valves are relatively soft and seal very easily. In contrast, the seals in the cylinder valves are solid tapered metal and need to be firmly tightened when being shut off. (**Photo 1**)

3 Turn the T-handle on each pressure regulator clockwise until drag is felt, and then another half turn. This may cause the pressure to rise on the line pressure gauge. (**Photo 2**)

4 Open the acetylene valve on the torch handle slightly. Any acetylene in the line should purge. (**Photo 3**)

5 When both acetylene gauges read zero, close the valve on the torch handle finger tight only. (**Photo 4**)

6 Back off the T-handle counterclockwise on the acetylene pressure regulator until it turns freely. If it falls out, thread it back in a few turns.

7 Perform steps 3 through 5 on the oxygen side of the system. (**Photo 5**)

Setting up Oxyacetylene Torches

Setting up an oxyacetylene torch means getting it ready to use. There are precise steps that need to be followed for the sake of safety. Each of these steps are used no matter what kind of torch work you are performing. If in doubt, always refer the torch manufacturer's instructions.

To set up an oxyacetylene torch for heating, follow the steps in **SKILL DRILL 6-26**:

1 First, verify that the two cylinders are secured in an upright position.

2 Verify that the valves on each of the cylinders are completely and firmly turned off. Look at the hose pressure and cylinder pressure gauges on top of each cylinder. Both gauges on each cylinder should read zero. If both gauges do not read zero, you must purge the system of any gas following the steps in Skill Drill 6-25, Purging Oxyacetylene Torches.

3 Verify that the T-handles on the pressure regulators are backed off and turn freely. (**Photo 1**)

4 Select the tip you will be using and thread it onto the torch handle by hand. Position the tip so that it faces away from you. Tighten it only moderately hand tight, as it normally uses O-rings to seal the joint. (**Photo 2**)

5 Standing off to the side of the pressure gauges (in case they explode), very slowly open the valve on the top of the oxygen cylinder. When pressure stabilizes, continue to open it all the way until it stops. This seats a solid tapered valve at the top of the cylinder and helps protect the softer shaft seal.

6 While still standing off to the side of the pressure gauges, slowly open the valve on the top of the acetylene cylinder ¼ to ½ turn only. This will allow for quick closing of the valve in the case of a fire or other emergency requiring quick shutoff. **(Photo 3)**

7 Open the acetylene valve on the torch handle about ⅛ turn and then turn the T-handle on the acetylene pressure regulator (clockwise) until the low-pressure gauge reads 5 psi. (Never exceed 15 psi line pressure on the acetylene side.) Lightly turn off the valve on the torch handle.

8 Open the oxygen valve on the torch handle about ⅛ turn and then turn the T-handle on the oxygen pressure regulator (clockwise) until the low-pressure gauge reads 10 psi (if welding or heating) or 20–25 psi (if cutting). Lightly turn off the valve on the torch handle. **(Photo 4)**

9 Before you light the torch, check the area you are working in to make sure there are no flammable materials or fluids nearby. Coworkers should also be clear of the area. The welding flame is not only extremely hot, it also produces dangerous ultraviolet rays, which will damage your eyes. It is absolutely vital that you wear the right safety gear: gloves and tinted gas welding goggles or gas welding helmet. Put them on and adjust them comfortably. Also make sure that there is plenty of

SKILL DRILL | **6-25** | **Purging Oxyacetylene Torches**

1 Verify that the valves are firmly closed on both cylinders. The valves normally turn off in a clockwise direction. Verify that both valves on the torch handle are closed only finger tight, and no more.

2 Turn the T-handle on each pressure regulator clockwise until drag is felt. This may cause the pressure to rise on the line pressure gauge.

3 Open the acetylene valve on the torch handle slightly. Any acetylene in the line should purge.

4 When both acetylene gauges read zero, close the valve on the torch handle finger tight only.

5 Back off the T-handle counterclockwise on the acetylene pressure regulator until it turns freely. If it falls out, thread it back in a few turns. Perform steps 3, 4, and 5 on the oxygen side of the system.

slack in the welding hoses and that they are out of the way of the torch area.

10 Now you are ready to ignite the torch with the striker. The tip of the torch must be pointing downward away from your body and away from the gas cylinders. Turn the acetylene valve on the torch handle slightly counterclockwise. You should hear the gas hissing. Hold the striker against the tip of the torch with the lighter cup pointing away from you. Flick the striker to create the spark that will ignite the gas at the tip of the torch. Open the acetylene valve until the sooty smoke produced by the torch disappears. Then slowly open the oxygen valve on the torch handle. **(Photo 5)**

11 As you open the oxygen valve, you will see the color of the flame change. The pure acetylene flame is yellow, and it will change to blue as you add the oxygen. Continue to open the oxygen valve slowly until you can observe a single small, sharp blue cone in the center of the torch flame. Do not open the oxygen valve beyond where the two flames become a single blue cone. This is the neutral flame you need for general heating and welding. If you turn the oxygen down slightly, a yellow and blue cone will result, which is called a carburizing flame. It is used for brazing. If you turn the oxygen up a bit more just past where the two cones turn into one cone, an "oxidizing" flame will result; this flame tends to burn metal.

12 You can change the heat of the torch a fair amount by increasing or decreasing the flow of oxygen and acetylene. If you want more heat, open the acetylene valve a bit further, then open the oxygen valve to bring the flame back to neutral. To create less heat, close the oxygen valve slightly, then close the acetylene valve until a neutral flame is obtained.

13 When you are ready to shut down the torch, quickly close the oxygen valve finger tight on the torch handle, followed by closing the acetylene valve finger tight on the handle. **(Photo 6)**

14 When you are finished with the torch for the day, go through the process of purging the system. (See Skill Drill 6-25, Purging Oxyacetylene Torches.)

SKILL DRILL 6-26 Setting up Oxyacetylene Torches

1 Verify that the two cylinders are secured in an upright position. Verify that the valves on each of the cylinders are completely and firmly turned off. If both gauges on each cylinder do not read zero, you must purge the system of any gas on each cylinder following the steps in the previous skill drill. Verify that the T-handles on the pressure regulators are backed off and turn freely.

2 Select the tip you will be using and thread it onto the torch handle by hand. Position the tip so that it faces away from you. Tighten it only moderately hand tight.

3 Standing off to the side of the pressure gauges, very slowly open the valve on the top of the oxygen cylinder. When pressure stabilizes, continue to open it all the way until it stops. While still standing off to the side of the pressure gauges, slowly open the valve on the top of the acetylene cylinder $1/4$ to $1/2$ turn only so it can be quickly shut off if needed.

SKILL DRILL 6-26 Setting up Oxyacetylene Torches, continued

4 Open the acetylene valve on the torch handle about ⅛ turn and then turn the T-handle on the acetylene pressure regulator (clockwise) until the low-pressure gauge reads 5 psi. (Never exceed 15 psi line pressure on acetylene.) Lightly turn off the valve on the torch handle. Open the oxygen valve on the torch handle about ⅛ turn and then turn the T-handle on the oxygen pressure regulator (clockwise) until the low-pressure gauge reads 10 psi (if welding or heating) or 20–25 psi (if cutting). Lightly turn off the valve on the torch handle.

5 Before you light the torch, check the area you are working in to make sure there are no flammable materials, fluids, or people nearby. Wear the right safety gear: gloves and tinted goggles or welding helmet. Turn the acetylene valve on the torch handle slightly counterclockwise. You should hear the gas hissing. Hold the striker against the tip of the torch with the lighter cup pointing away from you. Flick the striker to create the spark that will ignite the gas at the tip of the torch. Open the acetylene valve slowly until the sooty smoke produced by the torch disappears. Then slowly open the oxygen valve on the torch handle.

6 As you open the oxygen valve, you will see the color of the flame change. Continue to open the oxygen valve slowly until you can observe a single small, sharp blue cone in the center of the torch flame. This is the neutral flame you need for general heating and welding. If you want more heat, open the acetylene valve a bit further, then open the oxygen valve to bring the flame back to neutral. To create less heat, close the oxygen valve slightly, then close the acetylene valve until a neutral flame is obtained. When you are ready to shut down the torch, quickly close the oxygen valve finger tight on the torch handle, followed by closing the acetylene valve finger tight on the handle. Purge the system.

Using Oxyacetylene Torches for Heating

Technicians use an oxyacetylene torch to heat a variety of objects such as rusted bolts or brake drums that will not break loose. A torch might also be used to heat a container of water to test a thermostat in. Being able to safely use a torch is a valuable skill in a shop.

To use an oxyacetylene torch for heating, follow the steps in **SKILL DRILL 6-27**:

1 Select the proper tip for the amount of heating you need to perform.

2 Place a flywheel and ring gear assembly on a set of insulating spacers to elevate it from the working surface. **(Photo 1)**

3 Light the torch and adjust the gas flow so that you have a neutral flame. **(Photo 2)**

4 Direct the flame onto the ring gear and apply the heat until smoke starts to appear. Stop applying the heat. At this stage, the ring gear is hot enough to remove by gently tapping with a hammer and drift.

DO NOT TOUCH the metal with your hands. Use welding gloves and tools that are designed for use in a hot environment. **(Photo 3)**

5 When you have finished the job, you will need to shut down the equipment. Put the tip away and return the oxyacetylene cart to its proper storage area. **(Photo 4)**

Using Welding Tips for Welding

Welding is a handy skill for technicians to have. Sometimes tools need to be modified so they will work in particular situations, or a bracket breaks and needs to be welded back together. Being able to weld gives you another option in your quest to fix and repair vehicles.

To use an oxyacetylene torch for welding, follow the steps in **SKILL DRILL 6-28**:

1 Select and fit the correct size tip for the weld you are about to undertake. **(Photo 1)**

2 Before starting, make sure you have assembled all the materials you need to undertake the weld, including safety equipment, a fire extinguisher close at hand, welding filler rod, and the items to be welded.

3 Position the items to be welded and secure them with clamps if necessary. **(Photo 2)**

SKILL DRILL | 6-27 | Using Oxyacetylene Torches for Heating

1 Select the proper tip for the amount of heating you need to perform. Place a flywheel and ring gear assembly on a set of insulating spacers to elevate it from the working surface.

2 Light the torch and adjust the gas flow so that you have a neutral flame.

3 Direct the flame onto the ring gear and apply the heat until smoke starts to appear. Stop applying the heat and remove the ring gear by gently tapping with a hammer and drift. DO NOT TOUCH the metal with your hands. Use welding gloves and tools that are designed for use in a hot environment.

4 When you have finished the job, shut down the equipment. Put the tip away and return the oxyacetylene cart to its proper storage area.

4 Light the torch and adjust the gas flow so that you have a neutral flame. (**Photo 3**)

5 Direct the flame into the area to be welded and apply the heat until the metal just starts to melt a small pool of metal. Be careful to not overheat the metals. Slowly add the welding rod into the molten pool of metal. This will cause some of the welding rod to melt and fill the gap and slightly build up the weld. If the welding rod sticks to the metal, twist it with your thumb and finger to break it loose. (**Photo 4**)

6 Move the torch along the weld joint, continuously adding filler rod until the weld is complete. Avoid overheating the joint and try to confine the heated area just to the spot you are welding. (**Photo 5**)

7 When the weld is complete, stop applying the heat. DO NOT TOUCH the metal with your hands. Use welding gloves and tools that are designed for use in a hot environment.

8 When you have finished the job, you will need to properly shut down the equipment. (**Photo 6**)

SKILL DRILL 6-28 Using Welding Tips for Welding

1 Select and fit the correct size of tip for the weld you are about to undertake.

2 Make sure you have assembled all the materials you need to undertake the weld, including safety equipment, a fire extinguisher close at hand, welding filler rod, and the items to be welded. Position the items to be welded and secure them with clamps if necessary.

3 Light the torch and adjust the gas flow so that you have a neutral flame.

4 Direct the flame into the area to be welded and apply the heat until the metal just starts to melt a small pool of metal. Be careful to not overheat the metals. Slowly add the welding rod into the molten pool of metal.

5 Move the torch along the weld joint, continuously adding filler rod until the weld is complete.

6 When the weld is complete, stop applying the heat. DO NOT TOUCH the metal with your hands. Use welding gloves and tools that are designed for use in a hot environment. When you have finished the job, properly shut down the equipment.

Using Welding Tips for Brazing

Brazing allows a technician to join metals in a similar manner to soldering, but at higher temperatures of about 850°F (454°C), but not as hot as welding. Brazing typically uses brass filler rod, which melts at higher temperatures and is stronger than solder. Brazing works well when joining a heavier metal part to a thinner metal part such as a brass fitting to a thin sheet metal oil pan. It also bonds tighter to the metals, so it is more permanent than soldering.

To use an oxyacetylene torch for brazing, follow the steps in **SKILL DRILL 6-29**:

1 Select and fit the correct size tip for the braze you are about to undertake.

2 Before starting, make sure you have assembled all the materials you need to undertake the braze, including safety equipment, a fire extinguisher close at hand, brazing filler rod, appropriate flux, and the items to be brazed.

3 Position the items to be brazed and secure them with clamps if necessary.

4 Light the torch and adjust the gas flow so that you have a slightly carburizing flame (not quite to neutral flame status). **(Photo 1)**

5 Direct the flame into the area to be brazed and apply the heat until the metal is cherry red. Be careful to not overheat the metals. Slowly add the brazing rod with flux into the space to be brazed. Some filler rods come with a coating of flux attached; others require the addition of flux. This is achieved by slightly heating the brazing rod with the welding torch and dipping the heated brazing rod into the flux. **(Photo 2)**

6 Move the torch along the weld joint, continuously adding filler rod until the braze is complete. Avoid overheating the joint and try to confine the heated area to only the spot you are brazing. This will reduce the spread of the filler into unwanted areas.

7 When the braze is complete, stop applying the heat. DO NOT TOUCH the metal with your hands. Use welding gloves and tools that are designed for use in a hot environment.

8 When you have finished the job, you will need to properly shut down the equipment. **(Photo 3)**

SKILL DRILL | 6-29 | Using Welding Tips for Brazing

1 Select and fit the correct size tip for the braze you are about to undertake. Make sure you have assembled all the materials you need to undertake the braze, including safety equipment, a fire extinguisher close at hand, brazing filler rod, appropriate flux, and the items to be brazed. Position the items to be brazed and secure them with clamps if necessary. Light the torch and adjust the gas flow so that you have a slightly carburizing flame.

2 Direct the flame into the area to be brazed and apply the heat until the metal is cherry red. Be careful to not overheat the metals. Slowly add the brazing rod with flux into the space to be brazed. Some filler rods come with a flux coating attached; others require the addition of flux. This is achieved by slightly heating the filler rod with the welding torch and dipping the heated brazing rod into the flux.

3 Move the torch along the weld joint, continuously adding filler rod until the braze is complete. Avoid overheating the joint and try to confine the heated area to only the spot you are brazing. When the braze is complete, stop applying the heat. DO NOT TOUCH the metal with your hands. Use welding gloves and tools that are designed for use in a hot environment. When you have finished the job, you will need to properly shut down the equipment.

Using Cutting Torches

Technicians use a cutting torch for various reasons. They may need to cut fasteners that cannot be disassembled due to rust and corrosion, such as exhaust pipe clamps that are frozen in place. Or they may need to cut a wrench to shorten it so it will fit into a tight space. Technicians who are very skilled with a torch can even cut out a broken-off bolt from its threaded hole. However, don't try this unless you are *very* skilled with a cutting torch.

To use an oxyacetylene torch for cutting, follow the steps in **SKILL DRILL 6-30**:

1. Select and fit the correct size cutting tip for the cut you are about to undertake. Attach any cutting accessories, such as a cutting guide, to the torch.

SKILL DRILL | 6-30 | Using Cutting Tips

1. Select and fit the correct size cutting tip for the cut you are about to undertake. Attach any cutting accessories, such as a cutting guide, to the torch. Make sure you have assembled all the materials you need to undertake the cut, including safety equipment, a fire extinguisher close at hand, and the item(s) to be cut. Also clear the area of all flammable objects. Position the items to be cut and secure them with clamps if necessary.

2. Light the torch and adjust the gas flow so that you have a neutral flame. Press the oxygen cutting lever and make sure additional oxygen is injected through the center nozzle. Further refine the gas and oxygen settings if required.

3. Direct the flame into the area to be cut and apply the heat until the metal is cherry red. Press the oxygen cutting lever; if the metal is hot enough, doing so should instantly cause the metal under the flame to blow away.

4. Slowly draw the torch along the cut line, checking to make sure the cut is being made. When the cut is complete, stop applying the heat. DO NOT TOUCH the metal with your hands. When you have finished the job, you will need to properly shut down the equipment.

2 Before starting, make sure you have assembled all the materials you need to undertake the cut, including safety equipment, a fire extinguisher close at hand, and the item(s) to be cut. Also clear the area of all flammable objects.

3 Position the items to be cut and secure them with clamps if necessary. **(Photo 1)**

4 Light the torch and adjust the gas flow so that you have a neutral flame. Press the oxygen cutting lever and make sure additional oxygen is injected through the center nozzle. Further refine the gas and oxygen settings if required. **(Photo 2)**

5 Direct the flame into the area to be cut and apply the heat until the metal is cherry red. Press the oxygen cutting lever; if the metal is hot enough, doing so should instantly cause the metal under the flame to blow away. **(Photo 3)**

6 Slowly draw the torch along the cut line, checking to make sure the cut is being made.

7 When the cut is complete, stop applying the heat. DO NOT TOUCH the metal with your hands.

8 When you have finished the job, you will need to properly shut down the equipment. **(Photo 4)**

Plasma Cutters

A **plasma cutter** is a tool for cutting various thicknesses of metal. Plasma cutters work by applying a pressurized gas such as air, oxygen, nitrogen, or argon through a nozzle located in the center of a hand piece with an electrode. When power is applied to the electrode and a return electrical path is established through the metal that needs to be cut, a powerful spark is created. The spark heats the gas, changing it to plasma, a fourth state of matter. The plasma is very hot—approximately 30,000°F (16,600°C)—and moving very fast. The plasma heats the metal very quickly and blows the molten metal out to produce a clean cut through the metal.

Plasma cutters have been around for quite a long time, but in the past they have been expensive, large machines reserved for large-scale manufacturing. More recently, shop-sized machines have been developed and are relatively inexpensive. This has made them very accessible and an alternative to using oxyacetylene as a cutting tool for metal.

Using Plasma Cutters

If using the plasma cutter on a vehicle, make sure the battery is disconnected.

Wherever possible, use a heat shield behind the component you are heating. This will prevent nearby objects

from becoming hot. After cutting a piece of metal, label it as "HOT" with a piece of chalk so that others will not attempt to pick it up.

To use a plasma cutter for cutting, follow the steps in **SKILL DRILL 6-31**:

1 Always refer to the manufacturer's manual for specific operating instructions. Before using the equipment, locate the position of safety switches and put on a welding helmet and gloves. Note the location of the eyewash and first aid stations.

2 Ensure the cut line is free of rust and dirt. Make sure there are no flammable materials in close vicinity. **(Photo 1)**

3 Connect the air hose or gas, plug the unit in, and adjust the power setting to suit the thickness of the material being cut.

4 Before starting, make sure you have assembled all the materials you need to undertake the cut, including safety equipment, a fire extinguisher close at hand, and the item(s) to be cut. **(Photo 2)**

5 Connect the ground lead to a clean part of the metal to be cut, away from the cut line. **(Photo 3)**

6 Turn on the plasma cutter. Put the welding helmet down and position the hand piece to cut, then press the trigger. Check that the metal is cut all the way through. Stop and adjust the control settings if required. **(Photo 4)**

7 Slowly draw the hand piece along the cut line, checking to make sure the cut is being made.

8 When the cut is complete, release the trigger. DO NOT TOUCH the metal with your hands. Use welding gloves and tools that are designed for use in a hot environment.

9 When you have finished the job, shut down the equipment. Turn off the power and disconnect the ground lead. Put the hand piece away, and return the cutter to its proper storage area. **(Photo 5)**

Safety

- Plasma cutters require high amperage. Make sure you plug the cutter into an appropriately sized outlet.
- A plasma cutter can produce a large amount of heat. Be aware that any objects you cut will become hot.
- Always have a suitable fire extinguisher near your work area.
- Do not use a plasma cutter near any flammable materials.

SKILL DRILL | 6-31 | Using Plasma Cutters

1. Put on a welding helmet and gloves. Ensure the cut line is free of rust and dirt. Make sure there are no flammable materials in close vicinity.

2. Connect the air hose or gas, plug the unit in, and adjust the power setting to suit the thickness of the material being cut. Make sure you have assembled all the materials you need to undertake the cut, including safety equipment, a fire extinguisher close at hand, and the item(s) to be cut.

3. Connect the ground lead to a clean part of the metal to be cut, away from the cut line.

4. Turn on the plasma cutter. Put the welding helmet down and position the hand piece to cut, then press the trigger. Check that the metal is cut all the way through. Stop and adjust the control settings if required.

5. Slowly draw the hand piece along the cut line, checking to make sure the cut is being made. When the cut is complete, release the trigger. DO NOT TOUCH the metal with your hands. Use welding gloves and tools that are designed for use in a hot environment. When you have finished the job, shut down the equipment. Turn off the power and disconnect the ground lead. Put the hand piece away, and return the cutter to its proper storage area.

Wire Feed Welders

<u>Wire feed welders</u> are a type of welder that has the filler rod automatically feeding into the welding joint via the hand piece. They are becoming commonplace in shops. The wire feed is controlled by a trigger on the hand piece, and its rate of feed can be adjusted on the welder to accommodate the size of weld being conducted. The welder has controls for amperage, like on a traditional arc

welder, and this is adjusted depending on the thickness of metal to be welded.

Like any electric welder, the weld requires a flux or inert gas shield to prevent the oxidization of the weld. In a standard arc welder, this is provided by a coating on the filler stick. For wire feed welders, this can be provided either by an inert gas that is supplied through a nozzle to the welding tip or by a flux core in the center of the filler wire that evaporates as it is heated by the arc. This method shields the weld from oxidization. Wire feed welders are usually classified as gas or gasless. The gas wire feed welder has a provision for an inert gas bottle to be fitted to the welder to supply the shield gas to the welding tip. Gasless welders rely on the flux being in the core of the filler wire. Many wire feed welders can accommodate both gas and gasless operation.

Using Wire Feed Welders

Wear a leather apron or similar protective clothing and welding gloves when using a plasma cutter. T-shirts, nylon, and polyester blend clothing will not provide enough protection. Ultraviolet light and sparks of hot metal will pass through them. Always use appropriate eye protection and a welding helmet. Do not use sunglasses because they do not filter the extreme ultraviolet light as effectively. The plastic used in the lenses of sunglasses will not protect your eyes from sparks.

If using the wire feed welder on a vehicle, make sure the battery is disconnected. Wherever possible, use a heat shield behind the component you are welding. This will prevent nearby objects from becoming hot. After welding a piece of metal, label it as "HOT" with a piece of chalk so that others will not attempt to pick it up.

To use a wire feed welder, follow the steps in **SKILL DRILL 6-32**:

1. Always refer to the manufacturer's manual for specific operating instructions. Before using the equipment, locate the position of safety switches and put on a welding helmet and gloves. Note the location of the eyewash and first aid stations.

SKILL DRILL | 6-32 | Using Wire Feed Welders

1. Prepare the area to be welded. Ensure the material is free of rust and dirt. Make sure there are no flammable materials in close vicinity. Prepare the wire feed welder. Ensure enough wire is in the reel, set up the gas if using gas operation, plug the unit in and adjust the power setting and wire feed speed to suit the material thickness being welded. Make sure you have assembled all the materials you need to undertake the weld, including safety equipment, a fire extinguisher close at hand, and the item(s) to be welded.

2. Connect the ground lead to a clean part of the metal to be welded, as close as possible to the weld but away from the welding line.

3. Position the items to be welded and secure them with clamps if necessary.

SKILL DRILL | 6-32 | Using Wire Feed Welders, continued

4 Turn on the welder. Put on the welding helmet, position the hand piece to weld, and press the trigger. Direct the weld into the joint at about a 15-degree angle. Don't let the welding wire protrude more than about half an inch from the gun. Check that the weld is satisfactory. Stop and adjust the control settings if required.

5 Slowly draw the hand piece along the line to be welded, checking to make sure the weld is being made. When the weld is complete, release the trigger. DO NOT TOUCH the metal with your hands. When you have finished the job, you will need to shut down the equipment. Turn off the power and disconnect the ground lead. Put the hand piece away, and return the welder to its proper storage area.

2 Prepare the area to be welded. Ensure the material is free of rust and dirt. Make sure there are no flammable materials in close vicinity.

3 Prepare the wire feed welder. Ensure enough wire is in the reel, set up the gas if using gas operation, plug the unit in, and adjust the power setting and wire feed speed to suit the thickness of the material being welded.

4 Before starting, make sure you have assembled all the materials you need to undertake the weld, including safety equipment, a fire extinguisher close at hand, and the item(s) to be welded. **(Photo 1)**

5 Connect the ground lead to a clean part of the metal to be welded, as close as possible to the weld but away from the welding line. **(Photo 2)**

6 Position the items to be welded and secure them with clamps if necessary. **(Photo 3)**

7 Turn on the welder. Put on the welding helmet, position the hand piece to weld, and press the trigger. Direct the weld into the joint at about a 15-degree angle. Don't let the welding wire protrude more than about half an inch from the gun. Check that the weld is satisfactory. Stop and adjust the control settings if required. **(Photo 4)**

8 Slowly draw the hand piece along the line to be welded, checking to make sure the weld is being made.

9 When the weld is complete, release the trigger. DO NOT TOUCH the metal with your hands. Use welding gloves and tools that are designed for use in a hot environment.

10 When you have finished the job, you will need to shut down the equipment. Turn off the power and disconnect the ground lead. Put the hand piece away, and return the welder to its proper storage area. **(Photo 5)**

Safety

- Wire feed welders require high amperage. Make sure you plug the welder into an appropriately sized outlet.
- A wire feed welder can produce a large amount of heat. Be aware that any objects you weld will become hot.
- Always have a suitable fire extinguisher near your work area.
- Do not use a wire feed welder near any flammable materials.

Batteries and Chargers

<u>Batteries</u> are common in shops and are used in vehicles and rechargeable tools. Extreme caution should be taken when working around or with batteries, whether or not they are being charged. Batteries can produce dangerous and explosive hydrogen gases, so sparks and short circuits across the battery terminals should be avoided. Always wear appropriate PPE such as goggles, gloves, and protective clothing when working around or with batteries. Also, some regulatory agencies require that an eyewash station be located near a battery charging station in the case of a battery explosion. Check with your local authorities to determine any distance requirements.

> ▶ TECHNICIAN TIP
>
> Vehicle batteries are usually lead acid types, often in a 12-volt configuration. If a vehicle requires 24 volts, then either one 24-volt battery or two 12-volt batteries can be connected in series (by connecting the positive of one battery to the negative of the other battery) to provide 24 volts.
>
> Technology changes in vehicles have increased the need for more electrical power, and in the future this will drive the need for higher-voltage battery systems. Hybrid vehicles are an example of this. Their operating voltages are typically 200–600 volts. Generally, the higher the system voltage, the more efficient the system is because the electrical current can be lower for a given amount of power. And since wire size is determined by current, the wires can be smaller. However, higher voltages also create a greater shock hazard, so bear this in mind when working around and with batteries.

There are many different types of <u>battery chargers</u>, and each is designed for a particular purpose and application. Battery chargers can be <u>fast chargers</u>, with high current output to charge a battery quickly. <u>Slow chargers</u> take longer to charge a battery and have lower current outputs; they put less stress on the battery, which is ideal if time is not a consideration. <u>Smart chargers</u> incorporate microprocessors to monitor and control the charge rate so the battery receives the correct amount of charge depending on its state of charge. These types of chargers are becoming more popular and ensure that the battery receives the optimal charge, promoting longer battery life.

Even though typically a motor vehicle battery is 12 volts, it stores a lot of energy. The high current supply from a battery can be very dangerous. Remember, they have to deliver enough power to crank over a cold engine.

They also produce enough power to melt a metal rod resting across the terminals. High-voltage battery packs, like those fitted to hybrid vehicles, are even more dangerous because of the potential for high voltage and current, so special precautions for dealing with high-voltage systems must be taken **FIGURE 6-47**. Always treat batteries with care and respect.

> Safety
>
> High voltages used in a hybrid vehicle are extremely dangerous. The voltage and current flow is several times greater than that needed to kill a person. Most hybrid manufacturers require technicians to undergo special factory training before they will allow them to service a hybrid vehicle. Also, they usually allow only very experienced technicians to undergo the training, not novices. In fact, one of the tools that Toyota requires of their shops for working on a hybrid vehicle is a nonconductive shepherd's hook. This can be used to drag a technician away from high voltage if the technician is electrocuted while working on the vehicle.

FIGURE 6-47 High-voltage battery packs, like those fitted to hybrid vehicles, are extremely dangerous because of the potential for high voltage and current. Take special precautions for dealing with high-voltage systems.

> Safety
>
> Always remove your hand, wrist, and neck jewelry before working with batteries and electrical systems. If it comes into contact with the battery terminals or power wire, it can cause a short circuit. You will receive painful skin burns from the very rapid heating of the metal you are wearing, or even flash burns from an arcing current. A wristwatch or ring is much harder to take off when it is red- or white-hot and burned onto your skin!

Safety

Batteries give off hydrogen gas while they are being charged and for some time afterward. Hydrogen is a light and highly explosive gas that is easily ignited by a simple spark. Batteries are filled with **sulphuric acid**, so if the hydrogen does explode, the battery case can then rupture and spray everything and everyone nearby with this dangerous and corrosive liquid.

Be very careful not to create a spark when you are connecting or disconnecting battery cables or hooking up a charger to the battery terminals. Switch off the charger before connecting and disconnecting them from the battery **FIGURE 6-48**.

Do not try to charge a battery faster than the battery manufacturer recommends, and never use a battery load tester immediately after charging a battery. This is because both charging and rapidly discharging a battery generate heat and hydrogen. If you load-test a battery after charging it without waiting for it to cool down, you will increase the risk of distorting the plates inside the battery, as well as increase the risk of explosion.

How to Charge Batteries

Batteries go dead for a variety of reasons. A common cause is the driver forgetting to turn off the headlights when exiting the vehicle. Or maybe the owner went on vacation for a month and the battery discharged slowly over that time. Since the battery only stores electricity, anything that stays on when the vehicle is not running drains the battery.

Slow charging a battery is less stressful on a battery than fast charging, so if possible, slow charge a battery instead of fast charging it. Removing the negative battery terminal while changing a battery reduces the risk of burning up any electronic devices on the vehicle, especially with today's electronically intensive cars. However, disconnecting the

vehicle's battery risks losing information such as radio presets and other learned data. Use a **memory saver (memory minder)**, which provides backup power to retain electronic memory settings in the vehicle's computer systems.

Manufacturers install multiple batteries in some vehicles to provide additional battery power when needed, such as in diesel pick-up trucks and SUVs. Knowing how the batteries are connected together will determine how you connect a battery charger properly. Batteries can be connected in series (connected in line with each other, with the positive of one connected to the negative of the other) or parallel (connected side by side, with positive connected to positive and negative to negative). Two 12-volt batteries connected in series will have the positive terminal of one battery connected to the negative terminal of the second battery. The output voltage will be equal to the sum of the voltages of the individual batteries and is taken from the negative terminal of one battery and the positive terminal of the other battery. For example, two 12-volt batteries connected in series will have a nominal output voltage of 24 volts across the most negative and most positive battery terminals. If you have a 24-volt battery charger, you can charge both batteries at once by connecting the battery charger to these same terminals. If you only have a 12-volt charger, you will have to either charge one battery at a time, or reconnect them so they are connected in parallel. Just make sure you charge both batteries fully, which could take more than 12 hours each, if slow charging.

Batteries connected in parallel have the negative terminals of both batteries connected to each other and the positive terminals of each battery connected to each other. The output voltage will be equal to the voltage of one battery and is taken from the positive and negative posts of either battery. For example, two 12-volt batteries connected in parallel have an output voltage of 12 volts. In this situation, a 12-volt charger can be used to charge both batteries at the same time while the batteries are connected together. But it is likely to take about twice as long as it would if only charging one battery.

After charging and reinstalling the battery, it is good practice to clean the battery terminals and posts. To correctly charge a battery using battery charging equipment, follow the steps in **SKILL DRILL 6-33**:

1. Determine the voltage of the system that needs charging. If you are charging a 12-volt battery, use the 12-volt setting on the charger. If you are charging a 24-volt battery, or two 12-volt batteries connected in series, use the 24-volt setting on the charger, if it has one.

2. Identify the positive and negative terminals. Never simply use the color of the cables to determine the positive or negative terminals; use the + and − or the Pos and Neg marks.

FIGURE 6-48 Switch off the charger before connecting it to or disconnecting it from the battery.

SKILL DRILL | 6-33 | Charging Batteries

1 Determine the voltage of the system that needs charging. If you are charging a 12-volt battery, use the 12-volt setting on the charger. If you are charging a 24-volt battery, or two 12-volt batteries connected in series, use the 24-volt setting on the charger, if it has one. Identify the positive and negative terminals. Inspect the battery to ensure there are no cracks, holes, or damage to the casing.

2 Verify that the charger is unplugged from the wall and turned off. Connect the red lead from the charger to the positive battery terminal. Connect the black lead from the charger to the negative battery terminal.

3 Check the settings on the charger and verify that they are correct for what you are charging. Turn the charger on and select the automatic setting, if equipped. Select the rate of charge. Verify that the voltage and amperage the charger is putting out is proper.

4 Once the battery is charged, turn the charger off. Disconnect the black lead from the negative battery terminal and the red lead from the positive battery terminal.

5 Allow the battery to stand for at least 5 minutes before testing the battery. Using a capacitance tester, load tester, or hydrometer, test the charged state of the battery.

3 Inspect the battery by carrying out a visual inspection of the battery to ensure there are no cracks, holes, or damage to the casing. **(Photo 1)**

4 Verify that the charger is unplugged from the wall and turned off. Connect the red lead from the charger to the positive battery terminal. Connect the black lead from the charger to the negative battery terminal. **(Photo 2)**

5 Check the settings on the charger and verify that they are correct for what you are charging.

6 Turn the charger on and select the automatic setting, if equipped. Select the rate of charge. A slow charger usually charges at a rate of less than 5 amperes. A fast charger charges at a much higher ampere rate depending on the original battery state of charge; a fast charge should be carried out only under constant supervision.

7 Verify that the voltage and amperage the charger is putting out is proper. **(Photo 3)**

8 Once the battery is charged, turn the charger off. Disconnect the black lead from the negative battery terminal and the red lead from the positive battery terminal. **(Photo 4)**

9 Allow the battery to stand for at least 5 minutes before testing the battery. Using a load tester or hydrometer, test the charged state of the battery. **(Photo 5)**

Jump-Starting Vehicles

Jump-starting a vehicle is the process of using one vehicle with a charged battery to provide electrical energy to start another vehicle that has a discharged or dead battery. Since starting a vehicle requires a high amount of electrical energy, jump-starting a vehicle can put stresses on both vehicles. When the discharged vehicle is being cranked, the battery voltage tends to fall very low because the battery is already discharged. This causes the alternator on the running vehicle to put out its maximum current, putting it under heavy load. But as soon as the jumped vehicle stops cranking, the voltage shoots up quickly, potentially high enough to damage electronic components in either vehicle. The same voltage spike can happen when the battery cables are being disconnected.

Some vehicle manufacturers are now recommending that their vehicles should not be jump-started and that instead the battery be charged or replaced. In the same way, some towing companies have policies stating that they will not jump-start certain vehicles and that they will only replace the battery or tow the vehicle to a shop to be recharged. If you do decide to jump-start a vehicle, *always* read the owner's manual for both vehicles and follow their jump-starting guidelines. And never attempt to jump-start a frozen battery.

It is usually best to let the running vehicle charge the battery on the other vehicle for 5 to 10 minutes before trying to start the vehicle. Once the dead vehicle's engine has started, let both vehicles come to an idle for a moment. Do not turn off the vehicle with the discharged battery; it needs an extended amount of time to recharge. Before you disconnect the service battery from the discharged battery, it is good practice to place a load on the charged battery by turning on an accessory. Turning on the headlights will help absorb any sudden rise in voltage that may occur as the load on the alternator is suddenly decreased. In most modern vehicles there are many sensitive electronic devices. These devices are very susceptible to voltage surges. One method of reducing the risk of damage to such devices is by using jumper leads that have a built-in or auxiliary **surge protector**.

To start a vehicle with a discharged battery using jumper leads and a second vehicle or battery, follow the steps in **SKILL DRILL 6-34**:

1 Position the charged battery close enough to the discharged battery that it is within comfortable range of your jumper cables. If the charged battery is in another vehicle, make sure the two vehicles are not touching.

2 Always connect the leads in this order: First, connect the red jumper lead to the positive terminal of the discharged battery in the vehicle you are trying to start. The positive terminal is the one with the plus sign. Next, connect the other end of this lead to the positive terminal of the charged battery. Then connect the black jumper lead to the negative terminal of the charged battery. The negative terminal is the one with the minus sign. Connect the other end of the negative lead to a good ground on the engine block of the vehicle with the discharged battery, and as far away as possible from the battery. Do not connect the lead to the negative terminal of the discharged battery itself; doing so may cause a dangerous spark. Also, do not connect the negative lead to the body or chassis as the ground wire from the body back to the negative battery terminal is usually too small to carry current needed for jump-starting the vehicle. **(Photo 1)**

3 Try to start the vehicle with the discharged battery. If the booster battery does not have enough charge or the jumper cables are too small of diameter to do this, start the engine in the booster vehicle and allow it to partially charge the discharged battery for several minutes. Try starting the first vehicle again with the booster vehicle's engine running. Turn on the head lights on the booster vehicle to reduce the possibility of a voltage spike damaging electronic equipment. **(Photo 2)**

4 Disconnect the leads in the reverse order of connecting them. Remove the negative lead from the ground away from the battery. Then disconnect the negative from the booster battery. Next remove the positive lead from the booster battery, and lastly, disconnect the other positive end from the battery in the vehicle you have just started. If the charging system is working correctly and the battery is in good condition, the battery will be recharged while the engine is running, although it could end up overheating and damaging the alternator. **(Photo 3)**

SKILL DRILL | 6-34 | Jump-Starting Vehicles

1 Position the charged battery close enough to the discharged battery that it is within comfortable range of your jumper cables. If the charged battery is in another vehicle, make sure the two vehicles are not touching. Always connect the leads in this order: First, connect the red jumper lead to the positive terminal (+) of the discharged battery. Next, connect the other end of this lead to the positive terminal of the charged battery. Connect the black jumper lead to the negative terminal (–) of the charged battery. Connect the other end of the negative lead to a good ground on the engine block of the vehicle with the discharged battery, and as far away as possible from the battery. Do NOT connect the lead to the negative terminal of the discharged battery itself; doing so may cause a dangerous spark. Also, do not connect the negative lead to the body or chassis, as the ground wire from the body back to the negative battery terminal is usually too small to carry current needed for jump-starting the vehicle.

2 Try to start the vehicle with the discharged battery. If the booster battery does not have enough charge or the jumper cables are too small of diameter to do this, start the engine in the booster vehicle and allow it to partially charge the discharged battery for several minutes. Try starting the first vehicle again with the booster vehicle's engine running. Turn on the head lights on the booster vehicle to reduce the possibility of a voltage spike damaging electronic equipment.

3 Disconnect the leads in the reverse order of connecting them. Remove the negative lead from the ground away from the battery. Then disconnect the negative from the booster battery. Next remove the positive lead from the booster battery, and lastly, disconnect the other positive end from the battery in the vehicle you have just started. If the charging system is working correctly and the battery is in good condition, the battery will be recharged while the engine is running, although it could end up overheating and damaging the alternator.

TECHNICIAN TIP

Alternators are not generally designed to charge a dead battery while running several accessories. If a battery must be jump-started, it is always best to recharge the battery using a battery charger. That way, the alternator will not have to work so hard. Some technicians say it takes only 15 minutes to burn up an alternator when charging a dead battery.

Safety

When connecting jumper cables, a spark will almost always occur on the last connection you make. That is why it is critical that you make the last connection on the engine block away from the battery and any other flammables. A spark also occurs when you disconnect the first jumper cable connection, so that also needs to be the connection at the engine block.

Make sure the hood is secured with a hood prop before going under it; otherwise it could fall and injure someone or short out the jumper cables causing a spark, which could result in the battery blowing up.

- Keep your face and body as far back as you can while connecting jumper leads.
- Do not connect the negative cable to the discharged battery because the spark may blow up the battery.
- Use only specially designed heavy-duty jumper cables to start a vehicle with a dead battery. Do not try to connect the batteries with any other type of cable.
- Always make sure you wear the appropriate PPE before starting the job. Remember, batteries contain sulfuric acid and it is very easy to injure yourself.
- Always follow any manufacturer's personal safety instructions to prevent damage to the vehicle you are servicing.

► Cleaning Tools and Equipment

Clean tools and equipment work more safely and efficiently. At the end of each working day, clean the tools and equipment you used and check them for any damage. If you note any damage, tag the tool as faulty and organize a repair or replacement. Electrical current can travel over oily or greasy surfaces. Be sure to keep electrical power tools clean.

All shop equipment should have a maintenance schedule. Always complete the tasks described on the schedule at the required time. This will help to keep the equipment in safe working order.

Store commonly used tools in an easy-to-reach location. If a tool or piece of equipment is too difficult to return, then it will likely be left on a workbench or on the floor where it will become a safety hazard. Keep your work area tidy. This will help you work more efficiently and safely.

Keep a trash can close to your work area and place any waste in it as soon as possible. Dispose of liquid and solid waste, such as oils, coolant, and worn components, in the correct manner. Local authorities provide guidelines for waste disposal with fines for noncompliance. When cleaning products lose their effectiveness, they will need to be replaced. Refer to the supplier's recommendations

for collection or disposal. Do not pour solvents or other chemicals into the sewage system. This is both environmentally damaging and illegal.

Always use chemical gloves when using any cleaning material because excessive exposure to cleaning materials can damage skin. Also, absorbing some chemicals through the skin over time can cause permanent harm to your body. Some solvents are flammable; never use cleaning materials near an open flame or cigarette. The fumes from cleaning chemicals can be toxic, so wear appropriate respirator and eye protection wherever you are using these products.

To keep work areas and equipment clean and operational, follow the steps in **SKILL DRILL 6-35**:

1. Clean hand tools. Keep your hand tools in good, clean condition with two types of rags. One rag should be lint-free to clean or handle precision instruments or components. The other should be oily to prevent rust and corrosion. **(Photo 1)**
2. Clean floor jacks. Wipe off any oil or grease on the floor jack and check for fluid leaks. If you find any, remove the jack from use and have it repaired or replaced. Occasionally, apply a few drops of lubricating oil to the wheels and a few drops to the posts of threaded jack stands. **(Photo 2)**
3. Clean electrical power tools. Keep power tools clean by brushing off any dust and wiping off excess oil or grease with a clean rag. Inspect any electrical cables for dirt, oil, or grease, and for any chafing or exposed wires. With drills, inspect the chuck and lubricate it occasionally with machine oil. **(Photo 3)**
4. Clean air-powered tools. Apply a few drops of oil into the inlet of your air tools every day. Although these tools have no electrical motor, they do need regular lubrication of the internal parts to prevent wear. **(Photo 4)**
5. Clean hoists and heavy machinery. Locate the checklist or maintenance record for each hoist or other major piece of equipment before carrying out cleaning activities.
6. You should clean equipment operating mechanisms and attachments of excess oil or grease. **(Photo 5)**

Do not use flammable cleaners or water on electrical equipment.

SKILL DRILL | 6-35 | Cleaning Tools and Equipment

1 Clean hand tools. Keep your hand tools in good, clean condition with two sets of rags. One rag should be lint-free to clean or handle precision instruments or components. The other should be oily to prevent rust and corrosion.

2 Clean floor jacks. Wipe off any oil or grease on the floor jack and check for fluid leaks. If you find any, remove the jack from use and have it repaired or replaced. Occasionally, apply a few drops of lubricating oil to the wheels and a few drops to the posts of threaded jack stands.

3 Clean electrical power tools. Brush off any dust and wipe off excess oil or grease with a clean rag. Inspect any electrical cables for dirt, oil, or grease, and for any chafing or exposed wires. With drills, inspect the chuck and lubricate it occasionally with machine oil.

4 Clean air-powered tools. Apply a few drops of oil into the inlet of your air tools every day. Although these tools have no electrical motor, they do need regular lubrication of the internal parts to prevent wear.

5 Clean hoists and heavy machinery. Locate the checklist or maintenance record for each hoist or other major piece of equipment before carrying out cleaning activities. You should clean equipment operating mechanisms and attachments of excess oil or grease.

Wrap-up

Ready for Review

- Tools and equipment should be used only for the task they were designed to do.
- Always have a safe attitude when using tools and equipment.
- Do not use damaged tools; inspect before using, then clean and inspect again before putting them away.
- Lockouts and tagouts are meant to prevent technicians from using tools and equipment that are potentially unsafe.
- Many tools and measuring instruments have USCS or metric system markings to identify their size.
- Compressed air systems are comprised of a compressor, a pressure regulator, an air hose or fixed piping, and the tool to be powered.
- Standard compressors use a piston to force air into a storage tank, while scroll compressors use rotating scrolls to compress air.
- Always use caution: Compressed air injuries can be fatal.
- Many compressed air systems use air driers to remove all traces of moisture from the compressed air.
- Automatic oilers provide a regular application of lubricating oil to the stream of compressed air which then lubricates air tools and equipment.
- Chassis dynamometers allow technicians to run vehicles at road speed without leaving the shop.
- Threaded fasteners include bolts, studs, and nuts, and are designed to secure vehicle parts under stress.
- Torque defines how much a fastener should be tightened.
- Bolts, nuts, and studs use threads to secure each part; these threads can be in standard or metric measures.
- Thread pitch refers to the coarseness of the thread; USCS bolts, nuts, and studs are measured in threads per inch (tpi), classified as coarse (UNC) or fine (UNF).
- Fasteners are graded by tensile strength (how much tension can be withstood before breakage).
- The SAE rates fasteners from grade 1 to grade 8; always replace a nut or bolt with one of the same grade.
- Torque specification indicates the level of tightness each bolt or nut should be tightened to; torque charts list torque specifications for nuts and bolts.
- Torque (or tension) wrenches tighten fasteners to the correct torque specification.
- Torque value—the amount of twisting force applied to a fastener by the torque wrench—is specified in foot-pounds, inch-pounds, or newton meters.
- Torque wrench styles are beam (simplest and least expensive), clicker, dial, and electronic. Each gives an indication of when proper torque is achieved.
- Bolts that are tightened beyond their yield point do not return to their original length when loosened.
- Torque-to-yield (TTY) bolts can be torqued just beyond their yield point, but should not be reused.
- Torque angle can be used to tighten TTY bolts and requires both a torque wrench and an angle gauge.
- Common wrenches include box end, open end, combination (most popular), flare nut (or flare tubing), open-end adjustable, and ratcheting box end.
- Box-end wrenches can loosen very tight fasteners, but open-end wrenches usually work better once the fastner has been broken loose.
- Use the correct wrench for the situation, so as not to damage the bolt or nut.
- Sockets grip fasteners tightly on all six corners and are purchased in sets.
- Sockets are classified as follows: standard or metric, size of drive used to turn them, number of points, depth of socket, and thickness of wall.
- The most common socket handle is a ratchet; a breaker bar gives more leverage, or a sliding T-handle may be used.
- Fasteners can be spun off or on (but not tightened) by a speed brace or speeder handle.
- Pliers hold, cut, or compress materials; types include slip-joint, combination, arc joint, needle nose, flat, diagonal cutting, snap ring, and locking.
- Always use the correct type of pliers for the job.
- Cutting tools include bolt cutters, tin snips, and aviation snips.
- Allen wrenches are designed to fit into fasteners with recessed hexagonal heads.
- Screwdriver types include flat blade (most common), Phillips, Pozidriv, offset, ratcheting, and impact.
- The tip of the screwdriver must be matched exactly to the slot or recess on the head of a fastener.
- Magnetic pickup tools and mechanical fingers allow for the extraction and insertion of objects in tight places.

▸ Types of hammers include ball peen (most common), sledge, mallet, and dead blow.

▸ Chisels are used to cut metals when hit with a hammer.

▸ Punches are used to mark metals when hit with a hammer and come in different diameters and different points for different tasks; types of punches include prick, center, drift, pin, ward, and hollow.

▸ Pry bars can be used to move, adjust, or pry parts.

▸ Gasket scrapers are designed to remove gaskets without damaging surrounding materials.

▸ Files are used to remove material from the surface of an automotive part.

▸ Flat files come in different grades to indicate how rough they are; grades are rough, coarse bastard, second cut, smooth, and dead smooth.

▸ Types of files include flat, warding, square, triangular, curved, and thread.

▸ Bench vices, offset vices, drill vices, and C-clamps all hold materials in place while they are worked on.

▸ Taps are designed to cut threads in holes or nuts; types include taper, intermediate, and bottoming.

▸ A die is used to cut a new thread on a blank rod or shaft.

▸ Gear and bearing pullers are designed to remove components from a shaft when considerable force is needed.

▸ Flaring tools create flares at the end of tubes to connect them to other components; types include single, double, and ISO.

▸ Rivet tools join together two pieces of metal; each rivet can be used only once.

▸ Solder is a mixture of metals, often in the form of a wire, that is melted with a soldering gun or iron to join metals together.

▸ Measuring tapes and steel rules are commonly used measuring tools; more precise measuring tools include micrometers, gauges, calipers, dial indicators, and straight edges.

▸ Micrometers can be outside, inside, or depth.

▸ Learn to read micrometer measurements on the sleeve/barrel and thimble; always verify the micrometer is properly calibrated before use.

▸ Gauges are used to measure distances and diameters; types include telescoping, split ball, and dial bore.

▸ Vernier calipers measure outside, inside, and depth dimensions; newer versions have dial and digital scales.

▸ Dial indicators are used to measure movement.

▸ A straight edge is designed to assess the flatness of a surface.

▸ Feeler blades are flat metal strips that are used to measure the width of gaps.

▸ Power tools can be stationary or portable, corded or cordless, and are powered by electricity, batteries, compressed air, a propellant, or a gasoline engine.

▸ Drills are designed to drive a drill bit into metal (or other material) to create a hole; check drilling speed charts for proper drilling speed.

▸ Portable grinders are designed to grind down metals, but can also be fitted with a cutting disc to cut sheets of metal.

▸ Air tools use compressed, pressurized air for power; types include the air impact wrench, air ratchet, air hammer, air drill, and blowgun/air nozzle.

▸ Always wear eye and ear protection when using air tools; never use air nozzles on yourself or other people.

▸ Pressure washers/cleaners use focused, pressurized water to clean accumulated dirt and grease from vehicle components; water must be directed properly so as not to damage other parts.

▸ Familiarize yourself with pressure washer operating instructions and waste water disposal regulations.

▸ Spray wash cabinets are designed to clean automotive parts in a sealed cabinet, much like a dishwasher.

▸ Solvent tanks are designed for immersion of vehicle parts to remove oil, dirt, grease, and grime; always note the type of solvent being used and take necessary precautions.

▸ Brake washers are designed to remove brake dust from wheel brake units and their components.

▸ Sand or bead blasters are designed to clean paint, corrosion, or dirt from metal parts by blasting small abrasive particles onto the surface.

▸ Thread repair is performed to restore fastening integrity to a damaged fastener.

▸ Threads can be reshaped with a file, or a thread insert may be used.

▸ Oxyacetylene torches are designed to heat, braze, weld, and cut metal by combining acetylene with oxygen at a high temperature.

▸ Flashback arrestors prevent flames from traveling back up the hose in the event the oxygen and acetylene ignite inside the torch handle (flashback).

▸ Wear protective clothing and gear when using an oxyacetylene torch and follow all related safety precautions.

▸ Plasma cutters are designed to cut various thicknesses of metal and are an alternative to oxyacetylene torches.

▸ A wire feed welder has a filler rod automatically feeding into the welding joint at an adjustable rate.

▸ Battery chargers can be fast or slow, depending on current output; smart chargers calculate and provide the correct amount of charge needed for the battery.

▸ Vehicle batteries can be dangerous due to their high voltage; hybrid vehicle batteries have extremely high voltage and current flows.

▸ Batteries should be charged slowly, if possible.

▸ Jump-starting a vehicle places a stress on both vehicles; the current can damage electrical components in both vehicles.

▸ Keep work area, tools, and equipment clean and organized.

Key Terms

abrasive discs (cutting wheels) Abrasive wheels or flat discs fitted to bench, pedestal, and portable grinders.

air drier A device fitted to compressed air lines to remove moisture.

air drill A compressed air–powered drill.

air hammer A tool powered by compressed air with various hammer, cutting, punching, or chisel attachments. Also called an air chisel.

air impact wrench An impact tool powered by compressed air designed to undo tight fasteners.

air nozzle A compressed air device that emits a fine stream of compressed air for drying or cleaning parts.

air ratchet A ratchet tool for use with sockets powered by compressed air.

Allen wrench A type of hexagonal drive mechanism for fasteners.

angle grinder A portable grinder for grinding or cutting metal.

arc joint pliers Pliers with parallel slip jaws that can increase in size. Also called Channellocks.

automatic oiler A device fitted to compressed air systems to oil air tools.

aviation snips A scissor-like tool for cutting sheet metal.

ball-peen (engineer's) hammer A hammer that has a head that is rounded on one end and flat on the other; designed to work with metal items.

battery A device that converts and stores electrical energy through chemical reactions.

battery charger A device that charges a battery, reversing the discharge process.

bench grinder (pedestal grinder) A grinder that is fixed to a bench or pedestal.

bench vice A device that securely holds material in jaws while it is being worked on.

blind rivet A rivet that can be installed from its insertion side.

bolt A type of threaded fastener with a thread on one end and a hexagonal head on the other.

bolt cutters Strong cutters available in different sizes, designed to cut through non-hardened bolts and other small-stock material.

bottoming tap A thread-cutting tap designed to cut threads to the bottom of a blind hole.

box-end wrench A wrench or spanner with a closed or ring end to grip bolts and nuts.

C-clamp A clamp shaped like the letter C; it comes in various sizes and can clamp various items.

center punch Less sharp than a prick punch, the center punch makes a bigger indentation that centers a drill bit at the point where a hole is required to be drilled.

chassis dynamometer A machine with rollers that allows a vehicle to attain road speed and load while sitting still in the shop.

cleaning gun A device with a nozzle controlled by a trigger fitted to the outlet of pressure cleaners.

coarse (UNC) Used to describe thread pitch; stands for Unified National Coarse.

cold chisel The most common type of chisel, used to cut cold metals. The cutting end is tempered and hardened so that it is harder than the metals that need to be cut.

combination pliers A type of pliers for cutting, gripping, and bending.

combination wrench A type of wrench that has an open end on one end and a box-end wrench on the other.

compressed air equipment Tool or machinery that operates on compressed air.

cored solder Solder that is in the form of a hollow wire. The center is filled with flux, which is used as a cleaning agent while the solder is being applied to the metal surfaces.

crankshaft A vehicle engine component that transfers the reciprocating movement of pistons into rotary motion.

cross-arm A description for an arm that is set at right angles or 90 degrees to another component.

cross-cut chisel A type of chisel for metal work that cleans out or cuts key ways.

curved file A type of file that has a curved surface for filing holes.

dead blow hammer A type of hammer that has a cushioned head to reduce the amount of head bounce.

depth micrometer A measuring device that accurately measures the depth of a hole.

dial bore gauge An accurate measuring device for inside bores, usually made with a dial indicator attached to it.

dial indicator An accurate measuring device where measurements are read from a dial and needle.

diagonal cutting pliers Cutting pliers for small wire or cable.

die stock A handle for securely holding dies to cut threads.

double flare A seal that is made at the end of metal tubing or pipe.

drift punch A type of punch used to start pushing roll pins to prevent them from spreading.

drill chuck A device for securely gripping drill bits in a drill.

drill press A device that incorporates a fixed drill with multiple speeds and an adjustable worktable. It can be free-standing or fixed to a bench.

drill vice A tool with jaws that can be attached to a drill press table for holding material that is to be drilled.

elasticity The amount of stretch or give a material has.

fast chargers A type of battery charger that charges batteries quickly.

fasteners Devices that securely hold items together, such as screws, cotter pins, rivets, and bolts.

feeler gauge A thin blade device for measuring space between two objects.

finished rivet A rivet after the completion of the riveting process.

fine (UNF) Used to describe thread pitch; it stands for Unified National Fine.

flare nut wrench A type of box-end wrench that has a slot in the box section to allow the wrench to slip through a tube or pipe. Also called a flare tubing wrench.

flashback arrestor A spring-loaded valve installed on oxyacetylene torches as a safety device to prevent flame from entering the torch hoses.

flat blade screwdriver A type of screwdriver that fits a straight slot in screws.

flat-nosed pliers Pliers that are flat and square at the end of the nose.

flux A liquid or paste that protects a soldering or welding joint from oxidization.

forcing screw The center screw on a gear, bearing, or pulley puller. Also called a jacking screw.

gasket scraper A broad sharp flat blade to assist in removing gaskets and glue.

gear pullers A tool with two or more legs and a cross bar with a center forcing screw to remove gears.

grinding wheels and discs Abrasive wheels or flat discs fitted to bench, pedestal, and portable grinders.

hard rubber mallet A special-purpose tool with a head made of hard rubber; often used for moving things into place where it is important not to damage the item being moved.

hollow punch A punch with a center hollow for cutting circles in thin materials such as gaskets.

impact driver A tool that is struck with a hammer to provide an impact turning force to remove tight fasteners.

inside micrometer A micrometer designed to measure internal diameters.

intermediate tap One of a series of taps designed to cut an internal thread. Also called a plug tap.

locking pliers A type of plier where the jaws can be set and locked into position.

lockout/tagout A safety tag system to ensure that faulty equipment or equipment in the middle of repair is not used.

lug wrench A tool designed to remove wheel lugs nuts and commonly shaped like a cross.

magnetic pickup tools An extending shaft, often flexible, with a magnet fitted to the end for picking up metal objects.

mandrel The shaft of a pop rivet.

mandrel head The head of the pop rivet that connects to the shaft and causes the rivet body to flare.

measuring tape A thin measuring blade that rolls up and is contained in a spring-loaded dispenser.

mechanical fingers Spring-loaded fingers at the end of a flexible shaft that pick up items in tight spaces.

memory saver (memory minder) Battery backup device for vehicle computer systems.

micrometer An accurate measuring device for internal and external dimensions. Commonly abbreviated mic.

Morse taper A tapered mounting shaft for drill bits and chucks in larger drills and lathes.

needle-nosed pliers Pliers with long tapered jaws for gripping small items and getting into tight spaces.

nippers (pincer pliers) Pliers designed to cut protruding items level with the surface.

nut A fastener with a hexagonal head and internal threads for screwing on bolts.

offset screwdriver A screwdriver with a 90-degree bend in the shaft for working in tight spaces.

offset vice A vice that allows long objects to be gripped vertically.

oil filter wrench A specialized wrench that allows extra leverage to remove an oil filter when it is tight.

open-end wrench A wrench with open jaws to allow side entry to a nut or bolt.

outside micrometer A micrometer designed to measure the external dimensions of items.

oxyacetylene torch A gas welding system that combines oxygen and acetylene.

parallax error A visual error caused by viewing measurement markers at an incorrect angle.

peening A term used to describe the action of flattening a rivet through a hammering action.

Phillips head screwdriver A type of screwdriver that fits a head shaped like a cross in screws.

pin punch A type of punch in various sizes with a straight or parallel shaft.

pipe wrench A wrench that grips pipes and can exert a lot of force to turn them. Because the handle pivots slightly, the more pressure put on the handle to turn the wrench, the more the grip tightens.

plasma cutter A tool that uses electricity and compressed gas to produce a stream of high-temperature gas to cut metal.

pliers A hand tool with gripping jaws.

pop rivet gun A hand tool for installing pop rivets.

power tools Tools powered by electricity or compressed air.

pressure washer/cleaner A cleaning machine that boosts low-pressure tap water to a high-pressure output.

prick punch A pinch with a sharp point for accurately marking a point on metal.

pry bar A high-strength carbon steel rod with offsets for levering and prying.

pullers A generic term to describe hand tools that mechanically assist the removal of bearings, gears, pulleys, and other parts.

punches A generic term to describe a high-strength carbon steel shaft with a blunt point for driving. Center and prick punches are exceptions and have a sharp point for marking or making an indentation.

ratchet A generic term to describe a handle for sockets that allows the user to select direction of rotation. It can turn sockets in restricted areas without the user having to remove the socket from the fastener.

ratcheting box-end wrench A wrench with an inner piece that is able to rotate within the outer housing, allowing it to be repositioned without being removed.

ratcheting screwdriver A screwdriver with a selectable ratchet mechanism built into the handle that allows the screwdriver tip to ratchet as it is being used.

rattle gun A term used describe an air impact wrench based on the noise it makes.

roll bar Another type of pry bar, with one end used for prying and the other end for aligning larger holes, such as engine motor mounts.

rosin A type of liquid or paste (flux) used to prevent oxidization that is in solid form contained within the solder.

sand or bead blasters A cleaning system that uses high-pressure fine particles of glass bead or sand.

sander/polisher A power tool with a rotating disc or head to which polishing or sanding discs can be attached.

screw extractor A tool for removing broken screws or bolts.

single flare A sealing system made on the end of metal tubing.

sledge hammer A heavy hammer, usually with two flat faces, that provides a strong blow.

sliding T-handle A handle fitted at 90 degrees to the main body that can be slid from side to side.

slow charger A battery charger that charges at low current.

smart charger A battery charger with microprocessor-controlled charging rates and times.

snap ring pliers A pair of pliers for installing and removing snap rings or circlips.

socket An enclosed metal tube commonly with 6 or 12 points to remove and install bolts and nuts.

solder A mixture of lead and tin with a low melting point for connecting wires.

soldering irons A heating tool to heat solder and wires to produce a low-resistance joint.

solvent tank A tank containing solvents to clean vehicle parts.

speed brace A U-shaped socket wrench that allows high-speed operation. Also called a speeder handle.

split ball gauge A measuring device used to accurately measure small holes.

spray wash cabinet A cleaning cabinet that sprays cleaning solution under pressure to clean vehicle parts.

square file A type of file with a square cross section.

square thread A thread type with square shoulders used to translate rotational to lateral movement.

steel hammer A hammer with a head made of hardened steel.

steel rule An accurate measuring ruler made of steel.

straight edge A measuring device generally made of steel to check how flat a surface is.

straight grinder A powered grinder with the wheel set at 90 degrees to the shaft.

stud A type of threaded fastener with a thread cut on each end rather than having a bolt head on one end.

sulphuric acid A type of acid that when mixed with pure water forms the basis of battery acid or electrolyte.

surge protector An electrical protection device for preventing electrical surges.

tap A term used to generically describe an internal thread-cutting tool.

taper tap A tap with a tapper; it is usually the first of three taps used when cutting internal threads.

tap handle A tool designed to securely hold taps for cutting internal threads.

telescoping gauge A gauge that expands and locks to the internal diameter of bores; a caliper or outside micrometer is used to measure its size.

tensile strength In reference to fasteners, the amount of force it takes before a fastener breaks.

thread file A type of file that cleans clogged or distorted threads on bolts and studs.

thread pitch The coarseness or fineness of a thread as measured by either the threads per inch or the distance from the peak of one thread to the next. Metric fasteners are measured in millimeters.

thread repair A generic term to describe a number of processes that can be used to repair threads.

tin snips Cutting device for sheet metal, works in a similar fashion to scissors.

torque Twisting force applied to a shaft that may or may not result in motion.

torque angle A method of tightening bolts or nuts based on angles of rotation.

torque specifications Supplied by manufacturers and describes the amount of twisting force allowable for a fastener or a specification showing the twisting force from an engine crankshaft.

torque-to-yield A method of tightening bolts close to their yield point or the point at which they will not return to their original length.

torque-to-yield (TTY) bolts Bolts that are tightened using the torque-to-yield method.

torque wrench A tool used to measure the rotational or twisting force applied to fasteners.

triangular file A type of file with three sides so it can get into internal corners.

tubing cutter A hand tool for cutting pipe or tubing squarely.

tube flaring tool A tool that makes a sealing flare on the end of metal tubing.

twist drill A hardened steel drill bit for making holes in metals, plastics, and wood.

V blocks Metal blocks with a V-shaped cutout for holding shafts while working on them. Also referred to as vee blocks.

vernier calipers An accurate measuring device for internal, external, and depth measurements that incorporates fixed and adjustable jaws.

wad punch A type of punch that is hollow for cutting circular shapes in soft materials such as gaskets.

warding file A type of thin, flat file with a tapered end.

wire feed welder A welding machine that automatically feeds the filler wire by operating a trigger mechanism on a welding gun.

wrenches A generic term to describe tools that tighten and loosen fasteners with hexagonal heads.

yield point The point at which a bolt is stretched so hard that it will not return to its original length when loosened; it is measured in pounds per square inch of bolt cross section.

ASE-Type Questions

1. Tech A says that knowing how to use tools correctly creates a safe working environment. Tech B says that a flare nut wrench is used to loosen very tight bolts and nuts. Who is correct?
   a. Tech A
   b. Tech B
   c. Both A and B
   d. Neither A nor B

2. Tech A says that lockout/tagout is a safety procedure for a safe working environment. Tech B says that a soldering iron is used to weld, cut, and braze steel components. Who is correct?
   a. Tech A
   b. Tech B
   c. Both A and B
   d. Neither A nor B

3. Tech A says that torque wrenches need to be calibrated periodically to ensure proper torque values. Tech B says that when a bolt is torqued the bolt stretches beyond its yield point and the bolt has to be replaced when removed. Who is correct?
   a. Tech A
   b. Tech B
   c. Both A and B
   d. Neither A nor B

4. Tech A says that head bolts are tightened past their yield point. Tech B says that head bolts are torqued then tightened to their yield point. Who is correct?
   a. Tech A
   b. Tech B
   c. Both A and B
   d. Neither A nor B

5. Tech A says that a box-end wrench is more likely to round the head of a bolt than an open-end wrench. Tech B says that 6-point sockets and wrenches have more surface area on the bolt and will hold more firmly when removing and tightening. Who is correct?
   a. Tech A
   b. Tech B
   c. Both A and B
   d. Neither A nor B

6. Tech A says that it is usually better to pull a wrench to tighten or loosen a bolt. Tech B says that pushing a wrench will protect your knuckles if the wrench slips. Who is correct?
   a. Tech A
   b. Tech B
   c. Both A and B
   d. Neither A nor B

7. Tech A says that when jump starting a vehicle, a spark typically occurs when making the last jumper cable connection. Tech B says that all four of the jumper cable connections should be made at the battery terminals. Who is correct?
   a. Tech A
   b. Tech B
   c. Both A and B
   d. Neither A nor B

8. Tech A says that a dead blow hammer reduces rebound of the hammer. Tech B says that a dead blow hammer should be used to cut the head of a bolt off with a chisel. Who is correct?
   a. Tech A
   b. Tech B
   c. Both A and B
   d. Neither A nor B

9. Tech A says that gaskets can be removed quickly and safely with a portable grinder as long as the grinding wheel isn't too coarse. Tech B says that extreme care must be used when removing a gasket on an aluminum surface. Who is correct?
   a. Tech A
   b. Tech B
   c. Both A and B
   d. Neither A nor B

10. Tech A says that when using a file, apply pressure to file in the direction of the cut and no pressure when pulling the file back. Tech B says that file cards are used to file uneven surfaces. Who is correct?
    a. Tech A
    b. Tech B
    c. Both A and B
    d. Neither A nor B

CHAPTER 7

NATEF Tasks

Knowledge Objectives

After reading this chapter, you will be able to:
1. Explain the precautions and procedures to prevent vehicle damage while conducting repairs. (pp 190–194)
2. Describe the application and purpose of lifting equipment. (pp 194–195)
3. Describe the safe use of lifting equipment. (pp 194–208)
4. Explain how to prepare a vehicle for customer pickup. (p 208)

Vehicle Protection and Jack and Lift Safety

Introduction

Whenever a shop conducts repairs, its professionalism is on display. Customers expect their vehicle to be repaired and returned clean and free of any additional damage. A professional shop always takes precautions to guarantee that the customer's vehicle is treated with respect by ensuring that all work is conducted safely and efficiently. Before you undertake a task, pause for a moment to identify good work practices that will help prevent accidental damage to a customer's vehicle. For example, before starting work, install protective covers to ensure that interiors, steering wheels, and fenders are protected from accidental spills and scratches.

For your personal safety, it is important that lifting equipment such as vehicle lifts, jacks, jack stands, engine hoists, slings, and chains are inspected before each use and are well maintained. Some states require annual certification inspections of vehicle lifts and hydraulic jacks to help ensure their safety.

Preventing Vehicle Damage

Customers expect their vehicles to be treated with care and respect while in your shop. To accomplish this, you need to protect the vehicle from damage, keep it clean, and ensure that all property is returned in satisfactory condition to its owner. This can be achieved by taking the appropriate actions to protect the vehicle from further damage while conducting repairs. For example, you should use vehicle protective covers as a barrier for the fender, floor, seat, and steering wheel.

Customer Property

To avoid customer dissatisfaction, it is good practice for the service advisor to perform a vehicle walk-around with the customer. During this time, any existing

Caring for the Customer

The preservice vehicle walk-around with the customer can be very valuable. Occasionally, a customer will be unaware of damage to his or her vehicle that was sustained before dropping the vehicle off at the shop for service. For example, maybe the customer stopped by the store to pick up a couple of things before dropping the vehicle off at the shop. While in the store, another car sideswiped the passenger side of the vehicle. Since it was on the passenger side, the driver never saw it. However, when the customer picks up the car from the shop and looks it over to make sure nothing is damaged, she sees that the passenger side has been sideswiped. The customer immediately blames the shop, saying, "My car wasn't that way when I dropped it off." A good preservice walk-around can prevent this kind of misunderstanding.

You are the Automotive Technician

A customer brings her 2009 BMW 325i into the auto dealership for routine service. During the vehicle walk-around, you determine that the rear tires are worn and need replacement. Using a tread-depth indicator, you demonstrate to the customer that the tires are worn below the legal amount. After determining the best tires for the customer, you escort her to customer service to purchase new tires and wait for her vehicle. Before moving the vehicle for service, you install seat covers, a steering wheel cover, and floor mats.

1. What type of hoist is best for rotating and changing vehicle tires?
2. Why is it important to check safe working load (SWL) of the lifting equipment before using it?
3. A vehicle is about to be removed from the vehicle inspection pit; what are some safety precautions you must perform before it can be removed?
4. What are some steps you need to take before returning the vehicle to the customer?

damage or missing components on the vehicle should be noted on the check-in sheet or repair order and discussed with the customer. This helps prevent the customer from coming back to the shop and complaining that his or her vehicle was damaged in the shop. You should also check the customer's vehicle before starting to work on it. If there are any valuables in the vehicle or if it has damage, note this on your repair order and notify your supervisor.

Always use seat and steering wheel covers, floor mats, and fender covers when working on a vehicle to protect it from grease or corrosive materials. Clean any oil and grease off the vehicle when you have completed the job. If a vehicle has been damaged in the course of its repair, immediately notify your supervisor.

Fender, Seat, Carpet, and Steering Wheel Covers

Working on vehicles requires the use of tools, equipment, and chemicals and the physical process of testing and replacing parts. All of these activities have the potential to damage the vehicle if the proper precautions are not taken. For example, a dropped screwdriver or wrench may scratch the paint if fender covers are not used.

The vehicle and its components tend to be more prone to accidental damage in areas that have higher levels of service activity such as the engine bay and passenger compartment. The engine bay is the center of activity where many tools are used, batteries serviced, and oil changed. The chance of an accident in the engine bay is high if caution and care are not applied.

Protective equipment for vehicles is used to prevent damage to sensitive areas while conducting repairs and servicing FIGURE 7-1 . Fender covers are a protective layer used to cover the fenders when work is conducted around the engine bay. They are usually made from either a durable fabric blanket or a flexible energy-absorbing foam compound about a quarter of an inch thick. They are designed to fit across the top and down the side of the

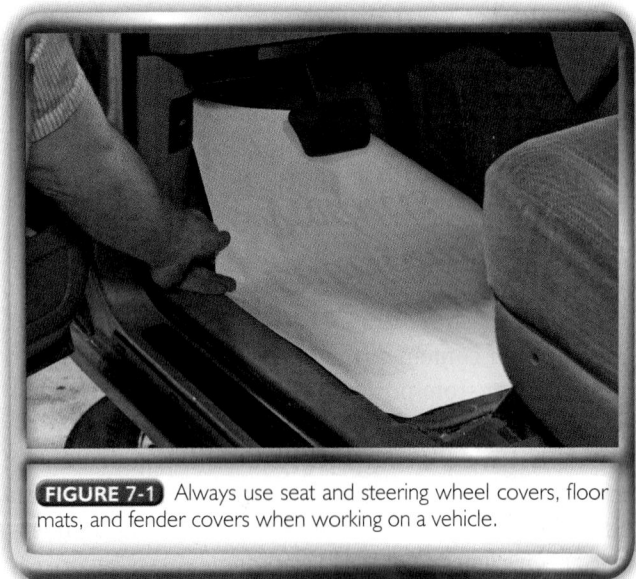

FIGURE 7-1 Always use seat and steering wheel covers, floor mats, and fender covers when working on a vehicle.

fender, providing protection to those areas vulnerable to accidental damage.

Seats, carpets, and steering wheels are made from materials that are sensitive to marks and damage from grease, oil, and dirt. Protectors for these areas are made from materials that provide a barrier to oil, grease, and dirt and are designed to prevent accidental damage to the delicate materials. For example, waxed or plastic laminated carpet protectors, plastic or fabric seat protectors, and plastic steering wheel covers can be used to prevent damage and stains.

Caring for the Customer

Always use the appropriate protection to prevent accidental damage to vehicles. Fender, carpet, seat, and steering wheels covers should be the first thing on and the last thing removed when working on vehicles.

TECHNICIAN TIP

Many of today's vehicles use very thin sheet metal in their fenders, making them easily dented if you lean against them or put your body weight against them. Fender covers *cannot* protect the vehicle from this kind of damage.

TECHNICIAN TIP

Never place tools in your back pocket. If you were to put a screwdriver in your back pocket and then sit in the driver's seat, the screwdriver would likely poke a hole in the seat upholstery, even if you used a seat cover.

Corrosives and Greases

Corrosives, such as battery acids and greases, such as wheel bearing grease, have the potential to cause damage. Use proper precautions when handling these substances. Special containers are designed to hold specific substances; for example, corrosives are stored in a special type of plastic container **FIGURE 7-2**. Greases are stored in a container designed to hold grease, often made from plastic or tin. Incorrectly storing materials in the improper containers may lead to a spill. Do not reuse containers or store products in them that the container was not designed to handle.

If spills do occur, be sure to clean them up thoroughly using appropriate methods, which can usually be found in the material safety data sheets (MSDS) for each material. Damage caused by corrosive agents may not be immediately visible and may lead to other problems, such as rust or corrosion, if the corrosive agents are not cleaned up and neutralized immediately. If you are handling corrosive materials and believe they have spilled, take precautions, clean the area immediately, and use a neutralizer. For example, a battery electrolyte contains acid. This material can be cleaned up by neutralizing it with an alkaline such as common baking soda and flushing the area with fresh water. Special absorbent materials in granular form can also be used to absorb some liquid spills such as engine oil **FIGURE 7-3**. Once the engine oil is absorbed, the granules can be swept up for disposal in an environmentally safe way.

Greases and liquids can cause stains at any time, so be sure to work as cleanly as possible and use protective covers to prevent damage. If a liquid spill does occur, clean up any excess with an absorbent material. Then use a cleaner suitable for the type of spill and the material being cleaned. For example, use upholstery cleaner for spills on vehicle seats or carpet cleaner for carpets.

Mechanical Damage

The possibility for accidental mechanical damage is always present when a vehicle is in the shop. It can occur easily; for example, an incorrectly jacked vehicle may damage the suspension or body. The best way to minimize accidental mechanical damage is to think carefully about the task or work you are performing, plan what you intend to do, follow shop and manufacturer

FIGURE 7-2 Corrosives are stored in a special type of plastic container.

FIGURE 7-3 Special absorbent materials in granular form can be used to absorb some liquid spills, such as engine oil.

procedures, use tools and equipment correctly, and seek advice if you are not sure. For example, if you have to rotate a vehicle's tires, you would use the proper jacking or hoisting equipment to ensure easy and safe access to the wheels and tires.

Moving and Road Testing Vehicles

Vehicles often need to be road tested or simply moved from one place to another in the shop. Accidents can occur at this time, especially if the driver involved is inexperienced or unqualified. Only authorized, fully trained, and licensed drivers should be given the responsibility to move vehicles. Only the most skilled and experienced drivers available should be allowed to test-drive higher performance vehicles.

Have someone outside the vehicle supervise and guide any vehicle movement inside the shop, especially in restricted spaces, when reversing, and when nearing blind corners. Often hand signals will be used by someone directing you to maneuver the vehicle. Make sure you understand what the hand signals mean by discussing them before moving the vehicle. If you are the person guiding the driver, use large hand signals and make sure you stand where the driver can clearly see you, but not directly in front of or behind the vehicle **FIGURE 7-4**.

FIGURE 7-4 If you are the person guiding the driver, use large hand signals and make sure you stand where the driver can clearly see you.

Safety

Vehicles do not always run properly when they are brought in for service, which can lead to an accident. For example, a car with a hesitation problem will not move until the throttle is pressed down farther than normal. When the car does move, it lurches forward. In the tight spaces of a shop, this could cause the vehicle to run into something or someone. You have two options in this situation. The safest option is to push the vehicle instead of driving it. The second is a bit controversial—two-footing the pedals. Two-footing means that you put your left foot on the brake pedal, ready to apply the brakes, and your right foot on the gas pedal. Thus, as you are driving, you can use the brakes to keep the speed of the vehicle very slow. This method takes practice and goes against most driver's training. But when the engine is not running properly, the standard method puts the vehicle at risk of an accident.

► Using Protective Covers

Proper Use of Fender Covers and Floor Mats

Since the purpose of fender covers and floor mats is to protect the vehicle, you should always inspect them for damage prior to use. Ensure that fender covers and floor mats are clean on both sides and do not have any metal or hard objects stuck to them. Ensure that they fit securely and provide adequate protection.

To properly apply fender covers and floor mats, follow the steps in **SKILL DRILL 7-1**:

1. Prepare the fender covers and floor mats by checking that they are clean and in good condition.
2. Select appropriate fender covers and floor mats for the vehicle and type of repair. Inspect the fender cover backs for rocks, metal, or fluids that would damage the vehicle. (**Photo 1**)
3. Position the fender covers and floor mats so they provide adequate protection.
4. Ensure that fender covers and floor mats stay in position, providing protection while the vehicle is in the shop. (**Photo 2**)
5. Remove fender covers and floor mats prior to customer pickup. (**Photo 3**)

SKILL DRILL 7-1 Applying Fender Covers and Floor Mats

1. Prepare the fender covers and floor mats by checking that they are clean and in good condition. Select appropriate fender covers and floor mats for the vehicle and type of repair. Inspect the fender cover backs for rocks, metal, or fluids that would damage the vehicle.

2. Position the fender covers and floor mats so they provide adequate protection. Ensure that fender covers and floor mats stay in position, providing protection while the vehicle is in the shop.

3. Remove fender covers and floor mats prior to customer pickup.

TECHNICIAN TIP

Some fender covers are made with a magnetic strip in them, which is designed to help hold the fender cover in place. Unfortunately, the magnet attracts metal particles, which can be held between the cover and the fender and scratch the paint. Always check these types of covers very thoroughly for metal particles.

FIGURE 7-5 Some examples of lifting equipment are vehicle hoists, floor jacks, jack stands, engine and component hoists, chains, slings, and shackles.

Lifting Equipment

Many different types of lifting equipment may be used in a shop. Some examples include vehicle hoists, floor jacks, jack stands, engine and component hoists, chains, slings, and shackles **FIGURE 7-5**. Lifting equipment is designed to lift and securely hold loads. Each piece of lifting equipment is designed for a specific purpose and has an operating capacity. The operating capacity is usually expressed as the **safe working load (SWL)**. For example, if the SWL is 1 ton, the equipment can safely lift up to 1 ton, or 2,000 lb (907 kg). When using lifting equipment, never exceed its capacity and always maintain some reserve capacity as an extra safety margin.

Each piece of lifting equipment should only be used for the purpose for which it is designed. For example,

TECHNICIAN TIP

When multiple pieces of lifting equipment are used, the SWL is limited to the lowest rated piece of equipment. For example, if a chain with an SWL of 2 tons is used with a 5-ton SWL shackle and a 3-ton SWL engine hoist, then the maximum amount of weight that can be lifted is 2 tons.

a vehicle hoist should only be used to lift vehicles within its capacity. Using lifting equipment incorrectly may lead to equipment failure that can cause serious injury and damage.

Testing of Lifting Equipment

Lifting equipment should be periodically checked and tested to make sure it is safe. The testing should be recorded for each piece of lifting equipment in accordance with local legislation or shop procedures and the equipment tagged with its inspection date and SWL. Inspections should identify any damage, such as cracks, dents, marks, cuts, and abrasions, that may prevent the lifting equipment from performing as it is designed. Refer to the manufacturer's manual to find out how often they recommend maintenance inspections. The time frame is usually every 12 months in the case of hoists and lifts, but may be longer for items of lifting equipment such as chains and slings. Always check local regulations to determine the requirements for periodic testing of lifting equipment.

Check the Test Certificate

In some countries, lifting equipment is subject to statutory testing and certification. If this is the case where you work, the **test certificate** should be attached to or displayed near the lifting equipment. Before using a piece of lifting equipment, make sure the most recent inspection recorded on the test certificate is within the prescribed time limit. If it is not, the test certificate has expired and you should notify your supervisor.

Jacks and Jack Stands

Jacks

A **vehicle jack** is a lifting tool used to raise part of a vehicle from the ground prior to removing or replacing components or to raise heavy components into position. The vehicle's emergency jack can be used to raise and support the vehicle while changing a wheel on the side of the road. Vehicle jacks must not be used to support the weight of the vehicle during any task that requires you to get underneath any part of the vehicle. For those shop tasks, a vehicle jack should be used only to raise

FIGURE 7-6 A vehicle jack should be used only to raise the vehicle so that it can then be lowered onto suitably rated and carefully positioned stable jack stands.

the vehicle so that it can then be lowered onto suitably rated and carefully positioned stable jack stands **FIGURE 7-6**.

There are three main types of mechanisms that provide the lifting action for vehicle jacks: **hydraulic jacks**, **pneumatic jacks**, and **mechanical jacks**. Hydraulic and pneumatic jacks are the most common types of vehicle jacks. They can be mounted on slides or on a wheeled trolley. In hydraulic jacks, pressurized oil acts on a piston to provide the lifting action; in pneumatic jacks, compressed air lifts the vehicle. In mechanical jacks, a screw or gears provide the mechanical leverage required for lifting.

Different jacks are available for different purposes, including **FIGURE 7-7**:

- Floor jacks are a common type of hydraulic jack that is mounted on four wheels, two of which swivel to provide a steering mechanism. The floor jack has a long handle that is used both to operate the jacking mechanism and to move and position the jack. Floor jacks have a low profile, making them suitable to position under vehicles.
- High-lift (or farm) jacks are a versatile type of jack designed to lift, winch, clamp, pull, and push. They have a mechanical mechanism and are designed to provide high lift capability—for example, 36 inches (0.91 m) or more. Because of their high lift capability, they are often used on farms or on four-wheel drive vehicles.
- Bottle jacks are a portable jack that usually has either a mechanical screw or a hydraulic ram mechanism that rises vertically from the center of the jack as the handle is operated. They are

FIGURE 7-7 Jacks. **A.** Floor jacks. **B.** High-lift (or farm) jacks. **C.** Transmission jack.

jacks are usually used in the shop and not for mobile operations.

- Scissor jacks are one of the most common types of jacks provided as part of the vehicle tool kit. They are used to jack a vehicle one wheel at a time. They employ a scissor action that is controlled by turning a long horizontal screw that acts on levers to raise or lower the scissor jack.

- Sliding bridge jacks are usually fitted in pairs to four-post hoists as an accessory to allow the vehicle to be lifted off the drive-on hoist runways. Operated by a hydraulic mechanism or compressed air, they use a platform mounted to a scissor-action jack to lift the vehicle along the length of the runway, thus making it more convenient to work on wheels and brakes.

- Transmission jacks are specialized jacks for lifting and lowering transmissions during removal and installation. Transmission jacks are usually mounted on a trolley with wheels and have a large flat plate area on which the transmission rests securely. They are usually operated by a hydraulic mechanism but can also be powered by compressed air.

Safety

All vehicle jacks must always be used in accordance with the manufacturer's instructions and should be inspected on a regular basis to ensure that they are in safe working order.

▶ TECHNICIAN TIP

Make sure you always use the correct type of jack with the correct load capacity for your task.

relatively inexpensive and may be provided with vehicles for the purpose of changing flat tires.

- Air jacks use compressed air to either operate a large ram or inflate an expandable air bag to lift the vehicle. Often the air jack is fitted to a moveable platform with a long handle. Air jacks are used to lift vehicles as an alternative to floor jacks. Because a compressed air supply is required, air

Jack Stands

Jack stands (axle stands) are adjustable supports that are used with vehicle jacks and are designed to support the weight of the vehicle after the vehicle has been raised by a vehicle jack. Jack stands are mechanical devices, meaning they mechanically lock in place at the height selected. This makes them very dependable if they are rated strong enough for the load they are holding and if they are used properly.

Always grip jack stands by the sides to move them. Never grip them by the top or the bottom to move them, as they can slip and pinch or injure you. Check that the base of the stand is flat on the ground before lowering the vehicle onto it; otherwise the stand might tip over, causing the vehicle to slip off. When positioned correctly, the vehicle can be lowered onto the jack stands and the vehicle jack can be moved out of the way.

Jack stands provide a stable support for a raised vehicle that is safer than the jack because the vehicle cannot be accidentally lowered while the jack stands are in place. To lower a vehicle that is on jack stands, it first has to be raised again so that the jack stands can be removed.

Lifting devices are also lowering devices, so it is unsafe to work underneath a vehicle that is supported only by a vehicle jack because it could give way or be accidentally lowered. Jack stands should never be used for a job for which they are not recommended. They normally come in matched pairs and should always be used as a pair FIGURE 7-8 . Jack stands are load rated and should only be used for loads less than the rating indicated on the jack stand.

Some shops have tall jack stands that are used along with a vehicle hoist; they are much taller than standard jack stands. Tall jack stands are used to stabilize a vehicle up on a hoist that is having a heavy component, such as a transaxle, removed or installed. Do not try to lower the vehicle with the tall jack stands still in place; doing so can cause the vehicle to slip off of the hoist.

Vehicle Hoists

Vehicle hoists raise whole vehicles off the ground so that a technician can easily work on the underside of the vehicle. The vehicle hoist is also useful for raising the vehicle to a height that removes the need for the technician to bend down. For example, when changing tires the vehicle can be raised to waist height to avoid excessive bending.

There are a number of different designs of vehicle hoists, and they come in a range of sizes and configurations to meet the particular needs of the shop. For instance, there are vehicle hoists that are mobile and vehicle hoists that are designed for use where the ceiling height is limited. Some vehicle hoists can be linked together electronically so they can be used on longer vehicles such as trucks and buses.

The most common types of vehicle hoists in general use are single-post, two-post, and four-post hoists. Other types of hoists include: scissor lifts, parallelogram lifts, and mobile or specialty lifts. A **single-post hoist** raises the vehicle on a platform supported by a single solid shaft located centrally under the vehicle. This type of hoist is very compact in the workshop and leaves the perimeter of the vehicle easily accessible, but the central post obscures part of the underside of the vehicle, making jobs such as transmission removal difficult or impossible.

Four-Post Hoist

A **four-post hoist** is very easy to use with most vehicles. The vehicle is driven between the four posts so that the wheels rest on two long, narrow platforms, one on each side of the vehicle FIGURE 7-9 . The platforms are then raised, taking the vehicle with them. The underside of the vehicle is accessible to the technician. Since the vehicle rests on its wheels on the four-post hoist, the wheels cannot be removed, unless the hoist is fitted with sliding bridge jacks.

FIGURE 7-8 Jack stands normally come in matched pairs and should always be used as a pair.

FIGURE 7-9 A four-post hoist.

Two-Post Hoist

<u>Two-post hoists</u> come in two configurations—symmetrical and asymmetrical. Symmetrical two-post hoists have arms that are of approximately equal length so that the vehicle is roughly centered lengthwise between the posts. This positioning creates a challenge because the posts of the hoist are usually right in the way of the vehicle's front doors, making it harder to get into and out of the vehicle. Asymmetrical hoists have shorter arms in front of the posts than in the rear of the posts. This allows the vehicle to be positioned farther back on the hoist, allowing better access to the doors on the vehicle. Both types of two-post hoists leave the underside of the vehicle easily accessible and also allow a technician to remove the wheels while the vehicle is raised.

Two-post hoists and single-post hoists require careful positioning of the hoist arms so that they are under the appropriate lifting points, two on each side of the vehicle **FIGURE 7-10**. The service information for the vehicle will detail where those lifting points are so that the vehicle can be raised without causing structural damage.

> ▶ **TECHNICIAN TIP**
>
> Some vehicles are equipped with an automatic leveling system, which must be disabled before lifting the vehicle. Always check the service information to see if this applies to the vehicle you are lifting.

FIGURE 7-10 A two-post hoist requires careful positioning of the lift arms so that they are under appropriate lifting points, two on each side of the vehicle.

Safety Locks

Every vehicle hoist in the shop must have a built-in mechanical locking device so that the vehicle hoist can be secured at the chosen height after the vehicle is raised. This locking device prevents the vehicle from being accidentally lowered and holds the vehicle in place, even if the lifting mechanism fails. You should never physically go under a raised vehicle for any reason unless the safety locking mechanism has been activated.

Ratings and Inspections

All vehicle hoists are rated for a particular weight and/or type of vehicle and should never be used for any task other than that recommended by the manufacturer. In particular, a vehicle hoist should never be used to lift a vehicle that is heavier than its rated limit. In most countries, there are regulations that require hoists to be periodically inspected, typically annually, and certified as fit for use. Before you use a vehicle hoist, check the identification plate for its rating, and make sure it has a current registration or certification label.

Engine Hoists and Stands

<u>Engine hoists</u>, or mobile floor cranes, are capable of lifting very heavy objects, such as engines, while they are being removed from a vehicle or refitted. The lifting arm of the engine hoist is moved by a hydraulic cylinder and is adjustable for length. However, extending the lifting arm reduces its lifting capacity because it moves the load farther away from the supporting frame. The supporting legs can be extended for stability, but the more the arm and the legs are extended, the lower the lifting capacity of the engine hoist. The safe lifting capacity at various extensions is normally marked on the lifting arm.

The engine or component to be lifted is attached to the lifting arm by a sling or a lifting chain. The sling and lifting chain must be rated as capable of lifting weights in excess of the engine or component being lifted and must be firmly attached before the engine hoist is raised. When the engine or other component has been lifted and slowly and carefully moved away from the vehicle, it should be lowered onto an engine stand or onto the floor **FIGURE 7-11**. The farther off the

> **Safety**
>
> Never use a hoist to lift any weight greater than the lifting capacity of the hoist, sling, chains, or bolts.

FIGURE 7-11 When the engine or other component has been lifted and slowly and carefully moved away from the vehicle, it should be lowered onto an engine stand or onto the floor.

ground an engine is lifted, the less stable the engine hoist becomes.

Engine stands are a convenient device to support an engine when it is out of the vehicle and being worked on. Engine stands come in a variety of ratings, some of which are very light duty and should not be used with any but the smallest engines. When mounting an engine on the stand, use bolts of the proper strength and ensure that they thread into the hole at least six to eight complete turns. You should also mount the arms of the stand so that the weight of the engine is centered on the mounting head pivot. Otherwise the engine could be top-heavy and rotate quickly, injuring you.

Vehicle Inspection Pits

__Vehicle inspection pits__ are usually built into the floor area of a vehicle repair bay. The vehicle inspection pit allows the technician to access the underside of the vehicle without the need for a hoist or jacks to raise the vehicle. Vehicle inspection pits have a center pit that is wide enough to allow a technician to move along but narrow enough to fit between the wheels of a vehicle. Stairs or steps are usually positioned at each end of the vehicle inspection pit to allow access for the technician. Lighting is fitted in the vehicle inspection pit area for greater visibility. The depth of the vehicle inspection pit is fixed and is set so as to afford a general working height to the underside of the vehicle.

Many people have been injured falling into vehicle inspection pits, even if they have been working in or near the vehicle inspection pit for a long time. When there is no vehicle over the vehicle inspection pit, you

should fence it or place boards over the top to stop people from accidentally stumbling into it. If you have to leave a vehicle inspection pit unattended, do so for the shortest possible time and leave the vehicle inspection pit lights on so that it is more likely to be noticed. You should also restrict general access to that work area.

> ### TECHNICIAN TIP
>
> Even low-voltage shop lights can set off an explosion. Whenever possible, use an explosion-proof lamp that will not break, even if it is dropped 6' (1.8 m). Lighting units in a vehicle inspection pit should be sealed behind toughened glass or polycarbonate and set into the vehicle inspection pit walls so that falling objects will not damage them.

> ### Safety
>
> Fuel, paints, and solvents can all give off flammable vapors that are heavier than air. Like water, these vapors tend to flow down and accumulate in places like vehicle inspection pits, increasing the risk of explosion and polluting the breathable air. Unless bulkier and more expensive explosion-protected power tools are available in your shop, the only safe power tools to use in a vehicle inspection pit are air-powered, which are less likely to cause sparks that could ignite flammable gases.

▶ Using Lifting Equipment
Using Vehicle Jacks and Stands

The size of vehicle jack you use will be determined by the weight of the vehicle you want to lift. Most workshops will have a vehicle jack that has a lifting capacity of about 2.5 tons. If the end of the vehicle is heavier than that, or if the vehicle is loaded, you will need to use a vehicle jack with a larger lifting capacity.

Make sure the jack stands are in good condition before you use them to support the vehicle. If they are cracked or bent, they will not support the vehicle safely. Always use matched pairs of jack stands.

Never support a vehicle on anything other than jack stands. Do not use wood or steel blocks to support the vehicle; they may slide or split under the weight of the vehicle. Do not use bricks or concrete blocks to support the vehicle; they will crumble under the weight of the vehicle.

To lift and secure a vehicle with a floor jack and jack stands, follow the steps in **SKILL DRILL 7-2**:

1. Position the vehicle on a flat, solid surface.
2. Put the vehicle into neutral or park and set the parking brake.
3. Place wheel chocks in front of and behind the wheels that are not going to be raised off the ground. **(Photo 1)**
4. Before you try to use the jack, check for leaks in the hydraulic system. Check the pad, or saddle, and the wheels of the jack. They should rotate freely and show no signs of damage.
5. Check the manufacturer's label on the vehicle jack. The specifications will tell you the maximum load (weight) it will bear; it must suit the vehicle you want to raise.
6. Refer to the owner's manual to find out where you can safely place the vehicle jack. This is usually a major point on the chassis, a cross member, or an axle unit.
7. Before operating the vehicle jack, select two jack stands of the same type, suitable for the weight of the vehicle. Check the jack stands for any cracks. If the jack stands are the type with threaded adjusting posts, lubricate the threads with a few drops of engine oil.
8. Place one jack stand on each side of the vehicle at the same point. Adjust them so that they are both the same height and high enough to slip under the vehicle once you have raised it. **(Photo 2)**
9. Roll the vehicle jack under the vehicle, and make sure the pad, or saddle, is positioned correctly under the frame or cross member.
10. Turn the jack handle clockwise to close the release valve on the jack, and begin pumping the handle up and down until the jack pad touches and begins to lift the vehicle. Make sure the wheels of the jack are not blocked or in a crack in the floor so the jack can roll toward the vehicle as it is being lifted; otherwise the jack can slip or tip over. **(Photo 3)**
11. Once the wheels lift off the floor, stop and check the placement of the jack lifting pad under the vehicle to make sure there is no danger of slipping.
12. Double-check the position of the wheel chocks to make sure they have not moved. If the vehicle is stable, continue lifting it until it is at the height at which you can safely work under it; remember that the vehicle will be slightly lower after you lower it onto the jack stands. **(Photo 4)**
13. Gripping the jack stands by their sides, slide each jack stand under the vehicle. Make sure they are positioned at a point that can support the weight of

SKILL DRILL | **7-2** | **Lifting and Securing a Vehicle with a Vehicle Jack and Jack Stands**

1. Position the vehicle on a flat, solid surface. Put the vehicle into neutral or park and set the parking brake. Place wheel chocks in front of and behind the wheels that are not going to be raised off the ground.

2. Select two jack stands of the same type, suitable for the weight of the vehicle. Place one jack stand on each side of the vehicle at the same point, and adjust them so that they are both the same height.

3. Roll the vehicle jack under the vehicle, and position the lifting pad correctly under the frame or cross member. Turn the jack handle clockwise, and begin pumping the handle up and down until the lifting pad touches and begins to lift the vehicle.

SKILL DRILL	7-2	Lifting and Securing a Vehicle with a Vehicle Jack and Jack Stands, continued

4 Once the wheels lift off the floor, stop and check the placement of the lifting pad under the vehicle to make sure there is no danger of slipping. Double-check the position of the wheel chocks to make sure they have not moved. If the vehicle is stable, continue lifting it until it is at the height at which you can safely work under it.

5 Slide the two jack stands underneath the vehicle and position them to support the vehicle's weight. Slowly turn the jack handle counterclockwise to open the release valve and gently lower the vehicle onto the jack stands. When the vehicle has settled onto the jack stands, lower the vehicle jack completely and remove it from under the vehicle. Gently push the vehicle sideways to make sure it is secure. Repeat this process to lift the other end of the vehicle.

6 When the repairs are complete, use the jack to raise the vehicle off the jack stands. Slide the jack stands from under the vehicle. Make sure no one goes under the vehicle or puts any body parts under the vehicle since the jack could fail or slip.

7 Slowly turn the jack handle counterclockwise to gently lower the vehicle to the ground. Return the jack, jack stands, and wheel chocks to their storage area before you continue working on the vehicle.

the vehicle. Both jack stands should be adjusted to the same height and placed as far apart as practical.

14 Slowly turn the handle on the jack counterclockwise to open the release valve and gently lower the vehicle onto the jack stands.

15 When the vehicle has settled onto the jack stands, lower the jack completely and remove it from under the vehicle. Check that the bases of the jack stands are in full contact with the ground and vehicle. With all body parts out from under the vehicle, give the vehicle a couple of gentle sideways pushes to see if it is really safe. Repeat this process to lift the other end of the vehicle. Be aware that the vehicle is now supported on jack stands and will not be as stable as if the wheels were on the ground. **(Photo 5)**

16 When you have finished working under the vehicle, make sure you have removed all tools and equipment before you attempt to lower it.

17 After completing the repair, use the vehicle jack to raise the vehicle off the jack stands. The end of the vehicle you raised *last* is the end you will lower *first*.

18 Slide the jack stands from under the vehicle. **(Photo 6)**

19 Slowly turn the handle on the jack counterclockwise to gently lower the vehicle to the ground. Do not allow the vehicle to drop quickly, which could cause serious damage.

20 Clean the vehicle jack, jack stands, and wheel chocks and then return them to their storage area before you continue working on the vehicle. **(Photo 7)**

Safety

> Some independent suspension components are not strong enough to support the weight of the vehicle. Make sure you always use the specified lift points to lift the vehicle.

Using Two-Post Hoists

Before lifting any vehicle, make sure the frame is structurally sound. If you see rust or signs of major repair, lifting the vehicle with a vehicle hoist may cause damage to the vehicle or may be dangerous to you. Make sure you know exactly how to operate the vehicle hoist. Take particular care that you know exactly where the stop control is so that you can use it quickly in an emergency. Refer to the operations manual for the correct procedure.

Check the amount of clearance under the vehicle. If any of the lifting mechanism is designed so that the vehicle is driven over it, verify that the vehicle has enough clearance. Driving a low-slung vehicle over the lifting mechanism may result in damage to the underside of the vehicle. These vehicles may require shallow ramps that raise the vehicle's wheels so it can go onto the hoist.

The lifting points on a vehicle are typically located at the same place as the jacking points. Check the vehicle's

service manual if you are not sure where the lift points are. The lifting arms must be positioned under the center of the lift points so that the weight of the vehicle is distributed evenly. Check whether the vehicle requires rubber pads to protect the undercoating. If the vehicle is equipped with running boards, verify that the hoist arms will not contact the running boards before contacting the lift points. You may be able to set the hoist pads to a higher setting so that the running boards clear the hoist arms.

Make sure there will be adequate headroom above the vehicle once it is raised. Taller vehicles, especially those fitted with roof racks, may need more headroom than you think. Ask your supervisor if there is the least bit of doubt!

The vehicle hoist should be raised so you can comfortably work under it. Lock the lift in place before moving underneath or working on the vehicle. To lift a vehicle using a two-post hoist, follow the steps in **SKILL DRILL 7-3**:

1 Read and follow the safety instructions that are provided with the two-post hoist. They should be displayed near the lift operating controls.

2 Check the hydraulic system for leaks. Make sure there are no oil spills around or under the two-post hoist.

3 Prepare the two-post hoist. The two-post hoist should be completely down before you attempt to drive the vehicle into place. You should also check the arms and pads for any signs of damage, including any damaged stops. Then position them as far as possible toward the outside to allow vehicle access in the center of the hoist.

4 Check under the vehicle to make sure there are no parts that will interfere with the two-post hoist operation and that the vehicle is structurally sound and not badly corroded.

5 Check the vehicle's service manual or your shop service information and locate the correct contact points for the lifting pads.

6 Carefully drive the vehicle so that it is centered between the two posts, left and right. Also ensure that it is positioned properly, front to back, for the type of hoist and vehicle you are using. Leave the vehicle in neutral with the emergency brake applied. You may need to move the vehicle forward or backward to allow the arms to swing under the vehicle. **(Photo 1)**

7 Position the lifting pads under the vehicle lifting points. Make sure the lifting pads are adjusted to the same height for both sides of the vehicle.

8 Move to the operating controls and raise the two-post hoist just far enough to come into contact with the vehicle. Make sure the lifting pads are centered under the contact points. **(Photo 2)**

9 Make sure no one is near the vehicle and then raise the hoist just until the wheels are a couple

of inches off the floor. Check the position of the lifting pads to make sure they have not moved, and push the vehicle's front and back gently up and down to confirm that it is stable on the hoist. It should wiggle a few inches but should make no noise! Noise indicates the vehicle is moving into

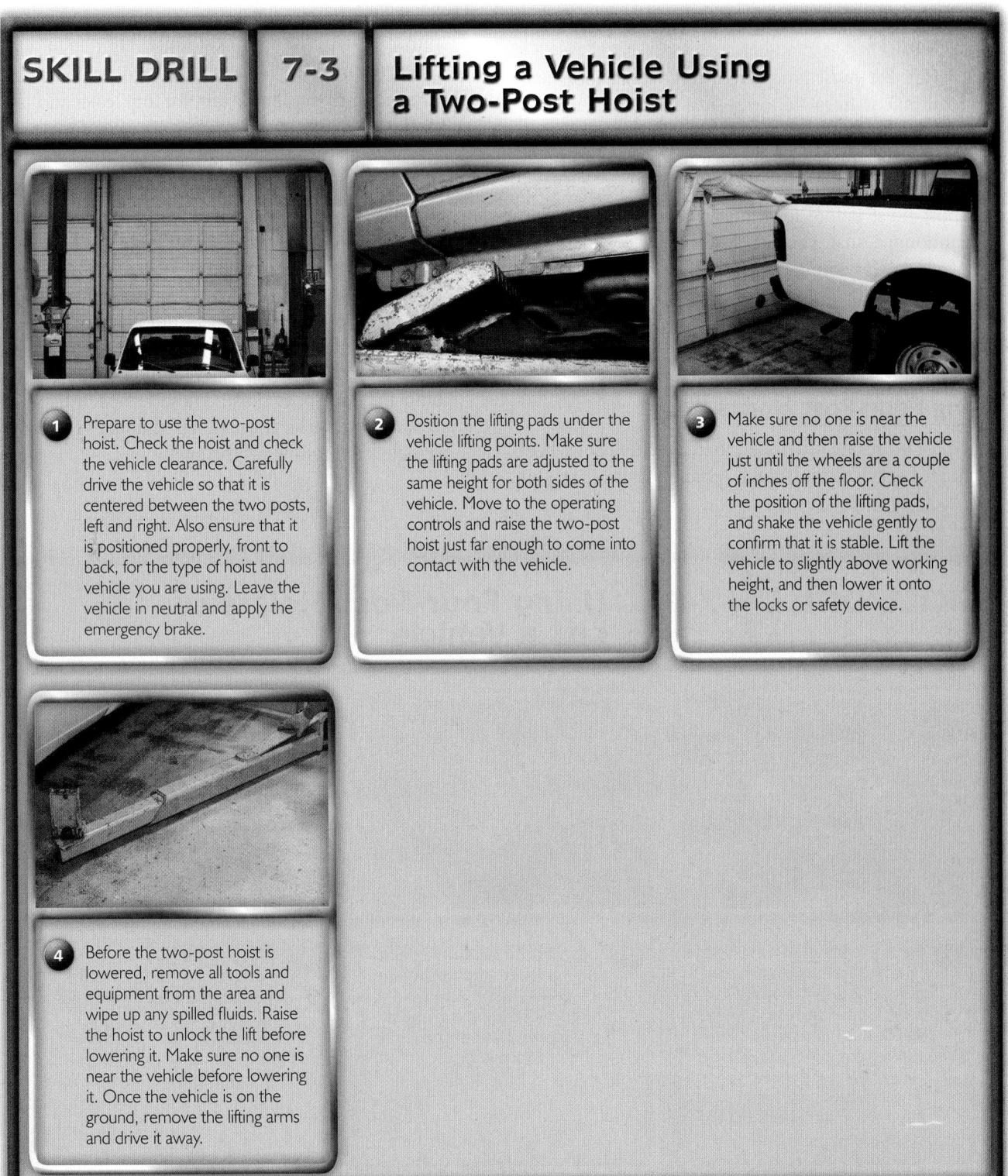

SKILL DRILL 7-3 Lifting a Vehicle Using a Two-Post Hoist

1 Prepare to use the two-post hoist. Check the hoist and check the vehicle clearance. Carefully drive the vehicle so that it is centered between the two posts, left and right. Also ensure that it is positioned properly, front to back, for the type of hoist and vehicle you are using. Leave the vehicle in neutral and apply the emergency brake.

2 Position the lifting pads under the vehicle lifting points. Make sure the lifting pads are adjusted to the same height for both sides of the vehicle. Move to the operating controls and raise the two-post hoist just far enough to come into contact with the vehicle.

3 Make sure no one is near the vehicle and then raise the vehicle just until the wheels are a couple of inches off the floor. Check the position of the lifting pads, and shake the vehicle gently to confirm that it is stable. Lift the vehicle to slightly above working height, and then lower it onto the locks or safety device.

4 Before the two-post hoist is lowered, remove all tools and equipment from the area and wipe up any spilled fluids. Raise the hoist to unlock the lift before lowering it. Make sure no one is near the vehicle before lowering it. Once the vehicle is on the ground, remove the lifting arms and drive it away.

and out of contact with the lift pads, which means it is *not* on the hoist.

10 Once you are sure the vehicle is safely positioned on the hoist, lift the hoist to slightly above the working height.

11 Lower the vehicle and hoist onto the safety locks. Some safety locks engage automatically, but some on older hoists have to be set by the operator. **(Photo 3)**

12 Before the hoist is lowered, remove all tools and equipment from the hoist area and clean up any spilled fluids. Raise the vehicle slightly to unlock or release the safety locks before lowering it.

13 Make sure no one is near the vehicle on the two-post hoist before lowering it. With a loud voice, announce that you are lowering the vehicle by saying, "Car coming down."

14 Once the vehicle is on the ground, you can use a grappling hook to remove the lifting arms before driving the vehicle away from the hoist. **(Photo 4)**

Using Four-Post Hoists

Four-post hoists are often used to lift a vehicle for wheel alignment services and brake repairs. Make sure you know how to operate the four-post hoist, taking particular care to know where the stop control is so that you can use it quickly in an emergency. Always refer to the operations manual for the correct procedure for stopping the four-post hoist.

To lift a vehicle using a four-post hoist, follow the steps in **SKILL DRILL 7-4**:

1 Read and follow the safety instructions that are provided with the four-post hoist. They should be displayed near the lift operating controls.

2 Check the hydraulic system for any leaks and the steel cables for any sign of damage. Make sure there are no oil spills around or under the hoist.

3 The four-post hoist should be completely down before you attempt to drive the vehicle onto it. The platform may have built-in wheel restraints or attachments for wheel alignment equipment. A set of bars is normally mounted at the front of each ramp to prevent the vehicle from being driven off the front of the four-post hoist. At the back there will be ramps that allow the vehicle to be driven onto the four-post hoist. These ramps will pivot upward when the hoist is raised and prevent the vehicle from rolling off the back.

SKILL DRILL 7-4 Using Four-Post Hoists to Lift a Vehicle

1 Prepare to safely use the vehicle hoist. With the aid of an assistant guiding the driver, or a large mirror in front of the hoist, drive the vehicle slowly and carefully onto the four-post hoist and position it centrally. If the vehicle has front wheel restraints, drive the vehicle forward until the wheels lock into the brackets.

2 Get out of the vehicle and check that it is correctly positioned on the platform. If it is, apply the emergency brake and select first gear for a manual transmission or park for an automatic.

3 Make sure the four-post hoist area is clear. Move to the controls and lift the vehicle until it reaches the appropriate work height. If the four-post hoist has a manual safety mechanism, lock it in place to engage whatever safety device is used.

SKILL DRILL | **7-4** | **Using Four-Post Hoists to Lift a Vehicle, continued**

4 Before the four-post hoist is lowered, remove all tools and equipment from the area and wipe up any spilled fluids. Remove the safety device or unlock the lift before lowering it. Make sure no one is near the area. Once the four-post hoist is fully lowered, with the help of a guide, you can carefully back the vehicle off the hoist.

4 With the aid of an assistant guiding the driver, or a large mirror in front of the hoist, drive the vehicle slowly and carefully onto the four-post hoist and position it centrally. If the vehicle has front wheel restraints, drive the vehicle forward until the wheels lock into the brackets. **(Photo 1)**

5 Get out of the vehicle and confirm that it is correctly positioned on the platform. If it is, apply the emergency brake and select first gear with a manual transmission or park with an automatic transmission. **(Photo 2)**

6 Make sure the four-post hoist area is clear. Move to the controls and lift the vehicle until it has reached the appropriate work height.

7 Most four-post hoists will have an automatic locking mechanism. If the hoist has a manual safety mechanism, you should lock it in place to engage whatever safety device is used. **(Photo 3)**

8 Before the four-post hoist is lowered, remove all tools and equipment from the area and wipe up any spilled fluids. Remove the safety device or unlock the lift before lowering it. Make sure no one is near the vehicle or the four-post hoist. Announce that you are going to lower the hoist by saying, "Car coming down," and then lower the vehicle.

9 Once the four-post hoist is fully lowered, with the help of a guide, you can carefully back the vehicle off the hoist. **(Photo 4)**

Using Engine Hoists and Stands

Engine hoists are capable of lifting very heavy objects, which make them suitable for lifting engines. Make sure the lifting attachment at the end of the lifting arm is strong enough to lift the engine and is not damaged or cracked. When attaching the lifting chain or sling to an engine, make sure it is firmly attached and that the engine hoist is configured to lift that weight. Make sure the fasteners attaching the lifting chain, or sling, have a tensile strength that is in excess of the weight of the engine. To keep from overstressing the sling, leave enough length in the sling so that when the engine is hanging, the angle at the top of the sling is close to 45 degrees and not exceeding 90 degrees.

If removing an engine from an engine bay, lower the engine so that it is close to the ground after removal. If the engine is lifted high in the air, the engine hoist will be unstable. When moving a suspended engine, move the engine hoist slowly. Do not change direction quickly because the engine will swing and may cause the whole apparatus to tumble.

To use an engine hoist and choose the correct attachments to lift an engine, follow the steps in **SKILL DRILL 7-5**:

1. Make sure the weight rating of the engine hoist is greater than the weight of the object you are lifting. Lower the lifting arm and position the lifting end and chain over the center of the engine. **(Photo 1)**

2. Inspect the chain, steel cable or sling, and bolts to make sure they are in good condition. They must be strong enough to support the weight of the engine. The sling should be long enough so that when you lift the engine the angle at the top of the sling is about 45 degrees.

3. Look carefully around the engine to determine if it has lifting eyes or other anchor points. **(Photo 2)**

4. If the engine has lifting eyes, attach the sling with "D" shackles or chain hooks. If you need to screw in bolts and spacer washers to lift the engine, make

SKILL DRILL | 7-5 | Using Engine Hoists and Stands

1. Prepare to use the engine hoist. Lower the lifting arm and position the lifting end and chain over the center of the engine.

2. Inspect the chain, steel cable or sling, and bolts to make sure they are in good condition. Look carefully around the engine to determine if it has lifting eyes or other anchor points.

3. If the engine has lifting eyes, attach the sling with "D" shackles or chain hooks. If you need to screw in bolts and spacer washers to lift the engine, make sure you use the correct bolt and spacer size for the chain or cable. Screw the bolts until the sling is held tight against the engine.

4. Attach the hook of the hoist under the center of the sling and raise the engine hoist just enough to lift the engine an inch or two. Double-check the sling and attachment points for safety. The center of gravity of the engine should be directly under the hook of the engine hoist, and there should be no twists or kinks in the chain or sling.

5. Raise the engine hoist until the engine is clear of the ground and any obstacles. Slowly and gently move the engine hoist and engine to the new location.

6. Make sure the engine is positioned correctly. You may need to place blocks under the engine to stabilize it. Once you are sure the engine is stable, lower the engine hoist and remove the sling and any securing fasteners. Finally, return the equipment to its storage area.

sure you use the correct bolt and spacer size for the chain or cable. Screw the bolts until the sling is held tight against the engine. **(Photo 3)**

5 Attach the hook of the hoist under the center of the sling and raise the hoist just enough to lift the engine an inch or two.

6 For safety, double-check that the sling is not catching on any parts and that the attachment points are secure. The center of gravity of the engine should be directly under the hook of the engine hoist, and there should be no twists or kinks in the chain or sling. **(Photo 4)**

7 Raise the engine hoist until the engine is clear of the ground and any obstacles. Slowly and gently move the engine hoist and engine to the new location. **(Photo 5)**

8 Make sure the engine is positioned correctly. You may need to place blocks under the engine to stabilize it. Once you are sure the engine is stable, lower the engine hoist and remove the sling and any securing fasteners. Finally, clean the equipment and return it to its storage area. **(Photo 6)**

Using Vehicle Inspection Pits

When using a vehicle inspection pit, you should get someone to assist in guiding you as you drive over the vehicle inspection pit. Make sure you understand each other's hand signals. Before using the vehicle inspection pit, check its lighting. Ensure that there are no obstacles in the vehicle inspection pit or its surrounding area. Do not drive or move the vehicle over a vehicle inspection pit if someone is in the vehicle inspection pit.

> **TECHNICIAN TIP**
>
> - The load rating of the engine hoist must be greater than the weight of the object to be lifted.
> - Never leave an unsupported engine hanging on an engine hoist. Secure the engine on an engine stand, or on the ground, before starting to work on it.
> - If using an engine stand, make sure it is designed to support the weight of the engine and that you have the correct number of bolts to hold the engine to the stand.
> - Always extend the legs of the engine hoist in relation to the lifting arm to ensure adequate stability.

To use a vehicle inspection pit, follow the steps in **SKILL DRILL 7-6**:

1 Ensure that the vehicle inspection pit and surrounding area are clear of obstructions and that

SKILL DRILL 7-6 Using Vehicle Inspection Pits

1 Ensure that the vehicle inspection pit and surrounding area are clear of obstructions and you have a clear pathway to drive the vehicle over the vehicle inspection pit.

2 Turn the lights on in the vehicle inspection pit. Get someone to help guide you as you drive the vehicle over the vehicle inspection pit. Drive the vehicle slowly and carefully and position it centrally.

3 Get out of the vehicle and check that it is correctly positioned on the platform. If it is, apply the emergency brake and select first gear or park depending on the transmission. Before driving the vehicle off the vehicle inspection pit, remove all tools and equipment from the vehicle inspection pit area and wipe up any spilled fluids. Make sure no one is near the vehicle or in the vehicle inspection pit. Have someone guide you off the pit area.

you have a clear pathway to drive the vehicle over the vehicle inspection pit. **(Photo 1)**

2 Turn the lights on in the vehicle inspection pit.

3 Get someone to help guide you as you drive the vehicle over the vehicle inspection pit.

4 Drive the vehicle slowly and carefully over the vehicle inspection pit and position it centrally. **(Photo 2)**

5 Get out of the vehicle and check that it is correctly positioned on the platform. If it is, apply the emergency brake and select first gear on a manual transmission or park with an automatic transmission.

6 Before driving the vehicle off the vehicle inspection pit, remove all tools and equipment from the vehicle inspection pit area and clean up any spilled fluids. Make sure no one is near the vehicle or in the vehicle inspection pit.

7 Have someone guide you off the pit area. **(Photo 3)**

Preparation for Customer Pickup

Make sure all vehicle protection is removed prior to releasing the vehicle to the customer. After removing the vehicle protection, such as fender covers, floor mats, and steering and seat covers, ensure that no damage to the vehicle has been sustained during repair. Check the vehicle for cleanliness by ensuring that all trash has been removed and no oil or grease marks are on the vehicle prior to returning it to the customer. Check that all of the windows are crystal clear, that the dashboard, knobs, steering wheel, and center console are spotless and clean, that floor mats have no dirt, and that there are no

FIGURE 7-12 Preparing a vehicle for a customer.

fingerprints on the door latches, fenders, or the backs of the mirrors **FIGURE 7-12**. Now go back through the vehicle and look for tools. Wear appropriate personal protective gear such as safety glasses and gloves when working with cleaning materials.

To ensure that the vehicle is prepared to return to the customer per school/company policy, follow the steps in **SKILL DRILL 7-7**:

1 Identify shop policy or procedures for returning a customer's vehicle.

2 Check the vehicle for cleanliness.

3 Clean the vehicle according to shop policy.

4 Remove all vehicle protection prior to customer pickup.

5 Dispose of any waste products in an environmentally safe manner, and clean and return fender covers, seat covers, and floor mats to the appropriate storage area.

Wrap-up

Ready for Review

- Vehicles under repair must be protected from further damage occurring while in the shop.
- A preservice vehicle walk-around will ensure that the shop and customer are in agreement about existing damage to the car.
- Use protective equipment, such as seat covers, floor mats, and fender covers, to prevent damage and to protect vehicles against grease, oil, and dirt.
- Use specified containers for corrosives and grease; clean up spills thoroughly.
- Carefully use tools and jacking or hoisting equipment to prevent mechanical damage to a customer's car.
- Only experienced, licensed drivers should test-drive high-performance vehicles.
- Moving cars in and out of the shop is another opportunity for damage to occur.
- Inspect protective covers (fender covers and floor mats) for existing damage prior to use.
- The safe working load indicates the operating capacity for lifting equipment.
- Lifting equipment includes vehicle hoists, floor jacks, jack stands, engine and component hoists, chains, slings, and shackles.
- Periodically check and test lifting equipment; consult the test certificate if available.
- Vehicle jacks can be classified by the type of lifting mechanism they use: hydraulic, pneumatic, or mechanical.
- Jack types include floor jacks, high-lift (farm) jacks, bottle jacks, air jacks, scissor jacks, sliding bridge jacks, and transmission jacks.
- Jack stands support a vehicle's weight when it has been raised; always use jack stands in pairs.
- Vehicle hoists raise the vehicle to allow technicians underside access.
- Vehicle hoists are most commonly single-post, four-post, or two-post.
- Never use a vehicle hoist without activating the safety lock or for lifting a vehicle heavier than the rated limit.
- Engine hoists can lift heavy objects out of a vehicle and onto an engine stand.
- Vehicle inspection pits allow access to the vehicle's underside without using a hoist or jack.
- Cover or fence inspection pits when not in use to prevent others from falling in.
- Choose vehicle jacks according to size and lifting capacity.
- Do not use a vehicle hoist if the vehicle's frame is not structurally sound.
- Make sure a vehicle has enough clearance over the lifting mechanism.
- Check for damage before using an engine hoist, and make sure all components have the lifting capacity needed for the task.
- Clean the vehicle and remove tools and vehicle protection before returning it to the customer.

Key Terms

engine hoist A small crane used to lift engines.

four-post hoist A type of hoist that the vehicle is driven onto that uses two long, narrow platforms to lift the vehicle.

hydraulic jack A type of vehicle jack that uses oil under pressure to lift vehicles.

jack stands Metal stands with adjustable height to hold a vehicle once it has been jacked up.

mechanical jack A type of vehicle jack that uses mechanical leverage to lift a vehicle.

pneumatic jack A type of vehicle jack that uses compressed gas or air to lift a vehicle.

safe working load (SWL) The maximum safe lifting load for lifting equipment.

single-post hoist A type of vehicle hoist that uses a single central platform to lift a vehicle.

test certificate A certificate issued when lifting equipment has been checked and deemed safe.

two-post hoist A type of vehicle hoist that uses two parts (one on each side of vehicle) and four arms to lift the vehicle.

vehicle hoist A type of vehicle lifting tool designed to lift the entire vehicle.

vehicle inspection pit A trench permanently fitted into the floor of the shop to allow easy work access to the vehicle's underside.

vehicle jack A tool for lifting a vehicle.

ASE-Type Questions

1. Tech A says that you should always deal with the customer's valuables according to company policy. Tech B says that you should protect a customer's vehicle by washing it when you are finished with it. Who is correct?
   a. Tech A
   b. Tech B
   c. Both A and B
   d. Neither A nor B

2. Tech A says that it is a good practice to perform a walk-around inspection of the vehicle with the customer. Tech B says that fender covers will protect the fenders from dents when working on the engine. Who is correct?
   a. Tech A
   b. Tech B
   c. Both A and B
   d. Neither A nor B

3. Tech A says that a vehicle jack can be used to support the vehicle while working under it. Tech B says that a jack stand automatically adjusts to the vehicle's height. Who is correct?
   a. Tech A
   b. Tech B
   c. Both A and B
   d. Neither A nor B

4. Tech A says that hoists should be inspected and certified perodically. Tech B says that safety locks do not need to be applied before working under the vehicle, unless you will be working for more than 10 minutes. Who is correct?
   a. Tech A
   b. Tech B
   c. Both A and B
   d. Neither A nor B

5. Tech A says that an engine hoist can lift more weight when the legs and arm are extended. Tech B says that the bolts used to mount an engine to a stand should complete at least six turns. Who is correct?
   a. Tech A
   b. Tech B
   c. Both A and B
   d. Neither A nor B

6. Tech A says that gasoline vapors are lighter than air, so inspection pits do not have a fire hazard like above ground hoists. Tech B says that you should never lift a fully loaded vehicle off the ground. Who is correct?
   a. Tech A
   b. Tech B
   c. Both A and B
   d. Neither A nor B

7. Tech A says that you should always ensure that the vehicle has enough ground clearance before driving on a lift. Tech B says that you should center the vehicle on the lift before raising it. Who is correct?
   a. Tech A
   b. Tech B
   c. Both A and B
   d. Neither A nor B

8. Tech A says that you should always inspect a lifting device for leaks and operation before using it. Tech B says that all mechanical safety locks on a hoist should be in place before getting under the vehicle. Who is correct?
   a. Tech A
   b. Tech B
   c. Both A and B
   d. Neither A nor B

9. Tech A says that an engine sling should have an angle greater than 90 degrees. Tech B says that all slings and lifting chains should be inspected for damage prior to use. Who is correct?
   a. Tech A
   b. Tech B
   c. Both A and B
   d. Neither A nor B

10. Tech A says that you should have a coworker help guide you onto an inspection pit. Tech B says that all lights should be on in the pit before driving over it. Who is correct?
    a. Tech A
    b. Tech B
    c. Both A and B
    d. Neither A nor B

CHAPTER 8

▶ Knowledge Objectives

After reading this chapter, you will be able to:
1. Describe what fluids are used in the typical modern automobile. (pp 214–219)
2. Explain the systems to be inspected when performing an underhood inspection. (pp 214–223)
3. Describe possible faults found on engine drive belts. (pp 219–220)
4. Explain why the belts and hoses need to be inspected on a regular basis. (pp 219–221)
5. Explain how to tell whether the vehicle air filter needs replacement. (pp 221–223)
6. Describe what to check when performing a vehicle exterior inspection. (pp 223–228)
7. Explain the procedure for checking interior and exterior lighting. (pp 226–227)
8. Describe what is checked during an in-vehicle inspection. (pp 228–230)
9. List the areas that are to be inspected during an under-vehicle inspection. (pp 230–234)
10. Describe the characteristics of different types of leaking fluids. (pp 232–234)

Vehicle Maintenance Inspection

Skills Objectives

After reading this chapter, you will be able to:

1. Check and refill windshield washer fluid. (pp 218–219)
2. Change the air filter. (pp 221–223)
3. Perform a visual inspection. (pp 223–224)
4. Check and replace the windshield wiper blades. (pp 224–225)
5. Inspect the windshield. (pp 225–226)
6. Inspect the interior lights.(pp 226–227)
7. Inspect the exterior lights. (pp 227–228)
8. Check instrument panel warning lamps. (pp 229–230)
9. Perform a horn check. (pp 229–231)
10. Perform an under-vehicle components inspection. (pp 230–234)

Introduction

A regular inspection of the many systems and components of a vehicle helps to ensure the safe and reliable operation of the vehicle. These inspections include an underhood inspection, an exterior inspection, certain in-vehicle inspections, and an under-vehicle inspection. Vehicle fluid levels, lighting systems, tires, suspension, belts, and hoses will all be checked. Any faults or concerns should be noted for service or repair. This chapter will explain what to look for and how to perform these important services.

Underhood Inspection

A check under the hood is important to the life and operation of the vehicle **FIGURE 8-1**. The inspection should be performed at the manufacturer's recommended intervals and also prior to any long driving trip. Component damage or failure is often caused by a lack of service or low fluid level in the related system. For example, low oil level in the engine can cause major damage to the engine bearings and crankshaft. Future problems also can be prevented by a thorough inspection of the underhood systems, where the discovery of a torn belt or a low fluid level may help to avoid a breakdown on the highway.

Fluids

Some of the fluids used in a vehicle, such as engine oil, are needed to keep the mechanical systems lubricated and functioning correctly. Other fluids may be safety related, such as windshield washer fluid and brake fluid. Always use the manufacturer's recommended type and amount of fluid when checking these items.

FIGURE 8-1 A check under the hood is vital to the life and operation of the vehicle.

For the engine, the lubrication oil and engine coolant levels must be checked. The brake, hydraulic clutch, and anti-lock brake systems all depend on the proper level of brake fluid. Power steering fluid and transmission fluid need to be at the recommended level for these systems to operate properly. The windshield washer is an important safety feature and the fluid level should be checked as needed.

Just as the level of the fluid is important, so too is the quality of the fluid. Nearly all of the fluids in a vehicle, except some automatic transmission/transaxle fluids, get old and wear out, requiring replacement; therefore, whenever you check the level of any fluid, check the quality of the fluid, too. You might notice a change in color, a change in consistency, a mix of fluids, or a change

You are the Automotive Technician

You work for a car rental company that maintains their vehicles in house. Your main task today is to perform preventive maintenance on a vehicle in the fleet that is scheduled for its next service. To perform a routine maintenance check, you follow a procedural checklist that includes changing the oil and filter; rotating the tires and inspecting brake, steering, and suspension systems; and checking/inspecting other important parts. During the inspection, you notice that the brake fluid level is low, the wiper blades smear badly, and the left rear brake light isn't working, which requires a bulb replacement.

1. What two conditions can low brake fluid level indicate?
2. How do you determine what engine oil to use?
3. What must be done after an oil change to remind the customer of the next change?
4. What is used to check the oil level after it has been changed?

in smell, such as burnt transmission/transaxle fluid. Each fluid shows its age differently, so become familiar with how to identify both good and bad fluids.

Engine Oil

The level of the oil in the engine's lubrication system is critical to the engine's operation **FIGURE 8-2**. The engine oil is picked up by the oil pump, filtered through the oil filter, and then sent under pressure to the crankshaft and camshaft bearings. If the level is too low, the oil pump will starve for oil. If the level is too high, the oil will be struck by the crankshaft, churning it into foam. The bearings require a steady flow of oil for lubrication, not air. If the oil is too low or too high, the engine bearings can be damaged.

The engine oil level should be checked periodically, usually at every fuel stop or two, as part of a preventive maintenance plan. Always check the oil level when the vehicle is on a level surface, not on a hill or slope. The oil can be checked with the dipstick, which is usually marked "oil" or brightly colored. Always check engine oil with the engine off. Wipe off the dipstick, identify the marks on the dipstick, and reinsert it fully in the tube. Then pull it out and hold it horizontally to read it. The marks on the oil dipstick usually have lines that indicate "full" and "add," or "min" and "max." The difference in quantity between the add and full marks on an engine oil dipstick is typically 1 quart (0.9 liters), but can be as much as 2 quarts (1.9 liters). Refer to the manufacturer's recommendations as noted in the vehicle owner's manual or the manufacturer's published service information.

When checking the oil level, also consider checking whether it is time for an oil change. The manufacturer will specify that the vehicle's oil-life monitoring (OLM) system be referenced to determine the amount of oil life remaining, or the manufacturer will specify when the oil should be changed depending on the miles traveled or period of time since the last oil change. If the vehicle is due for an oil change, the level should still be checked first. A low reading on the dipstick could indicate that a seal or gasket is leaking or that the engine is using oil. Either of these situations requires further investigation.

> ▶ **LINK**
> Refer to the Engine Lubrication chapter for information on selecting the correct oil for the vehicle being serviced and for skill drills on how to change the oil in the engine lubrication system.

Engine Coolant

The engine <u>coolant</u> level and condition should be checked whenever the oil level is checked. The engine cooling system depends on the coolant to transfer excessive heat from the engine to the radiator. The engine temperature must be controlled to prevent overheating and to maintain proper exhaust emission levels. Some vehicles will have a transparent reservoir or surge tank marked with "hot" and "cold," which allows checking the coolant without removing the cap **FIGURE 8-3**. Some also may have an overflow tank with a tube leading from the radiator cap filler neck to a transparent overflow tank. The level can usually be seen through the side of the tank and compared to the marks. Older vehicles, which do not have an overflow tank, usually have a radiator cap located on top of the radiator that

Safety

Do not remove the pressure cap (radiator cap) when the engine is warm or hot. The system is under pressure, and removing the cap could allow the coolant to immediately boil and spray out, causing severe burns. Always allow the system to cool before removing the cap.

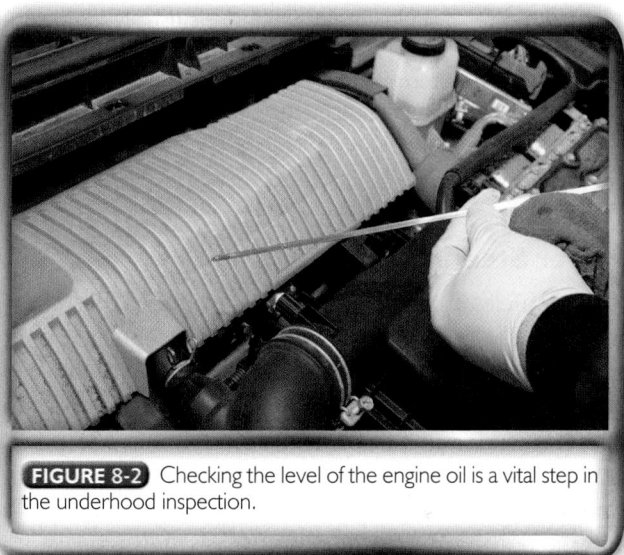

FIGURE 8-2 Checking the level of the engine oil is a vital step in the underhood inspection.

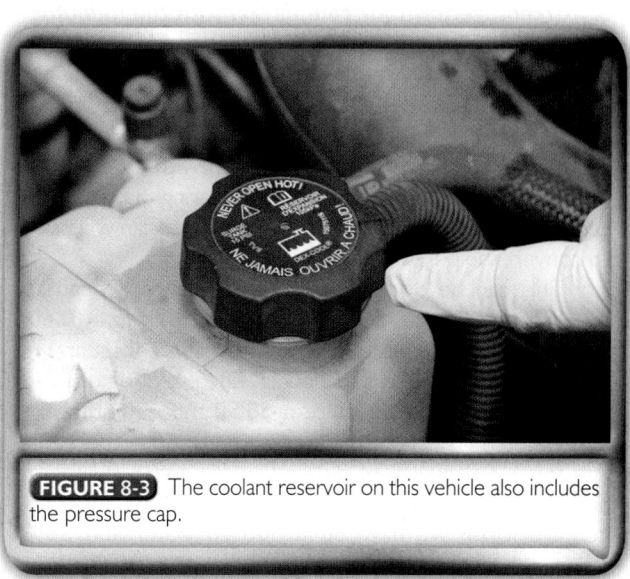

FIGURE 8-3 The coolant reservoir on this vehicle also includes the pressure cap.

must be removed when checking the coolant level. If there is no overflow tank, then the coolant level in the radiator should be about 1.5" (38 mm) below the filler neck.

Low coolant levels can cause engine overheating, which will lead to damaged cylinder head gaskets or piston rings. The technician should note at each maintenance inspection if any coolant needs to be added and if so, how much. Coolant levels that are consistently low indicate a coolant leak that will need to be diagnosed and repaired.

Since the coolant also provides freeze protection, the coolant freezing point also should be checked during the underhood inspection. An insufficient amount of anti-freeze could allow the coolant to freeze during temperatures below freezing. Since water expands when frozen, freezing of the coolant could crack the engine block, cylinder head, radiator, or other engine components. The anti-freeze protection level can be checked with an anti-freeze **hydrometer**. Select a hydrometer that is designed to be used with the type of anti-freeze being tested. Draw enough coolant into the hydrometer to bring it up to the "fill" line. Hold the hydrometer vertically and read the freeze protection level.

A refractometer also can be used to measure the freeze protection level of coolant. A drop or two of coolant is placed on a sample plate. A cover plate is then lowered onto the sample and the reading is taken. If held roughly level with a light source directly above the refractometer, you can look into the eyepiece and see a sharp line between a dark section and a light section. The sharp line indicates the reading. In many cases, there will be several scales that you can check, such as battery acid, ethylene glycol, and propylene glycol. Make sure you are reading the proper scale.

Applied | Math

AM-36: Ratios/Percentages: The technician can convert test readings in decimal or fractional form to a ratio or percentage form for comparison with the manufacturer's specifications and vice versa.
A technician is servicing the cooling system of a vehicle with a 12-quart capacity per service information. Because of the cold climate of the location, the shop supervisor informed the technician to fill the cooling system with a 60/40 mix of antifreeze and distilled water. Considering that the total capacity of the system is 12 quarts, the technician will need to convert the percentages to a fractional form.

This can be done by multiplying the total quantity by each percentage. So 12 quarts × 60% is 12 × 0.60, which equals 7.2 quarts of antifreeze. And, 2 quarts × 40% is 12 × 0.40, which equals 4.8 quarts of distilled water. Most climates require a 50/50 mix of antifreeze and water. This can be converted to a ratio or percentage form. Six quarts of distilled water and 6 quarts of antifreeze would be a 1:1 ratio. Concerning the percentage form, we have 50% distilled water and 50% antifreeze. This is often referred to as a 50/50 mix.

> ▸ **LINK**
> Refer to the Engine Cooling chapter for a detailed discussion on the proper type and amount of coolant for the vehicle and how to check and fill the engine cooling system.

Brake and Clutch Fluid

A hydraulic braking system depends on a special fluid called brake fluid. The brake fluid is stored in a reservoir attached to or near to the brake system master cylinder **FIGURE 8-4**. If the brake fluid level gets too low, air can be pulled into the hydraulic system, which will cause the brake pedal to be soft or too low. This will cause the brakes to work poorly or not at all. The brake fluid should be checked whenever the oil level is checked or at least monthly. Also check the color of the brake fluid. Most brake fluid is very clear. If it is getting dark, it is most likely becoming oxidized or contaminated and will need to be changed. Most brake fluids are **hygroscopic**, meaning they absorb water from the atmosphere. Because of this, most manufacturers recommend changing brake fluid every 2 to 4 years. However, the best process is to check the condition of the brake fluid with either a brake fluid tester or brake fluid test strips. Check service information or the vehicle owner's manual for specific recommendations.

Vehicles with a manual transmission may have a hydraulic clutch system that uses both a master cylinder and brake fluid. Depending on the vehicle, the brake fluid reservoir also may supply the clutch master cylinder, or the clutch may have a separate fluid reservoir **FIGURE 8-5**. Be sure to check both of these reservoirs for the proper fluid level.

> ▸ **TECHNICIAN TIP**
>
> Low master cylinder brake fluid levels usually indicate an issue with the system. Either there is a brake fluid leak in the system or, on vehicles equipped with disc brakes, the brake pads are worn. If the brake fluid level is low, inform your supervisor; a brake lining inspection may be necessary.

Power Steering Fluid

Most vehicles are equipped with power-assisted steering systems. The power for the system usually comes from an engine-driven hydraulic pump. Some vehicles, typically hybrid-electric vehicles, use an electrically driven pump. The pump delivers fluid under pressure to the power unit at the steering box, or rack-and-pinion, through connecting hoses and pipes. The fluid reservoir can be mounted as part of the engine-driven hydraulic pump, or it can be a separate container **FIGURE 8-6**. The power

FIGURE 8-4 The brake fluid is stored in a reservoir attached to or near to the brake system master cylinder.

FIGURE 8-6 The power steering fluid reservoir. **A.** Mounted on the engine-driven hydraulic pump. **B.** Mounted separately.

FIGURE 8-5 Check both the brake fluid reservoir and the clutch fluid reservoir in vehicles with manual transmissions.

FIGURE 8-7 A few automatic transmissions are checked using a fill plug or level plug on the side of the transmission.

> **▶ LINK**
> Refer to the Hydraulics and Power Brakes chapter for an explanation of the different types of brake fluid.

> **▶ LINK**
> Refer to the Servicing Steering Systems chapter for more information on power steering fluid types and how to check them.

steering fluid level must be at the proper level to avoid drawing air into the hydraulic system and to prevent fluid overflow when the engine is hot.

In most cases, the power steering fluid level can be checked with a dipstick connected to the filler cap. The engine should be idling and the fluid hot. In many cases, the dipstick lists both a "cold" and a "hot" level, or a "safe" level. When checking the level, you also should check the appearance of the fluid. Dark or black fluid usually means the fluid is old and needs to be changed. The power steering fluid level should be checked as a normal part of the underhood inspection.

Automatic Transmission/Transaxle Fluid

The correct automatic transmission/transaxle fluid level (referred to as automatic transmission fluid from here

on) is critical to the effective and efficient operation of the transmission. If the level is too low, slipping and shift timing faults can result. Since reverse gear usually requires a larger volume of fluid, a shift into reverse could be delayed. If the fluid level is too high, the transmission fluid will churn and aerate, which can lead to low pressures, resulting in slipping clutches. Always make sure the transmission fluid level is correct.

Automatic transmission fluid level is usually checked with a dipstick located under the hood, usually toward the back of the engine compartment. Some automatic transmissions do not have a dipstick; they are checked using a fill plug or level plug on the side of the transmission **FIGURE 8-7**. If the transmission does use a dipstick, the fluid level is usually checked with the engine running, the transmission warmed up fully, and the gear selector in park or neutral, depending on the vehicle. When checking transmission fluid, wipe off the dipstick, observe the markings, and reinsert the dipstick into the tube briefly. Remove the dipstick and hold it horizontally to read it.

If adding transmission fluid, make sure you select the correct fluid, as there are a number of different transmission fluids specified for various vehicles. Fluid is added through the dipstick tube, so use a funnel. The lines between "full" and "add" are usually only about 1 pint (0.5 liters), so add only a small amount of fluid and then recheck the fluid level.

> ### ▶ TECHNICIAN TIP
>
> Many newer vehicles—typically European models and some Asian imports—do not have a specified method of checking the transmission fluid level. The transmissions are considered sealed and lubricated for the life of the vehicle. The manufacturers have determined that the transmission fluid will not be low as long as there are no leaks; any leak will require that the transmission be repaired.

In a manual transmission/transaxle, fluid splashing up from the lower gear sets lubricates the bearings. Early bearing failure is the result of driving with the transmission fluid level too low. In most cases, transmission fluid level on manual transmissions/transaxles can only be checked from under the vehicle. The vehicle must be level. The level is usually accessed through a fill plug on the side of the transmission/transaxle. If fluid comes out of the fill hole when the plug is removed, allow any extra to drain out, then reinsert the fill plug. If no fluid comes out of the fill hole, carefully stick a finger in the hole and bend your finger down to feel the level of the fluid.

> ### Safety
>
> Do not rotate the wheels or engine with your finger in the hole, as transmission parts could pinch or sever your finger.

If the level is within a quarter inch of the bottom of the fill hole, the level is OK and the fill plug can be reinserted. If the fluid level is lower than that, the proper fluid will need to be added until the level is even with the bottom of the fill hole. Always check the manufacturer's specifications to identify the proper fluid for the vehicle you are working on.

> ### ▶ LINK
>
> Refer to the Servicing the Automatic Transmission chapter for more details about fluid types and checking fluid levels.

Diesel Exhaust Fluid

Some late-model diesel-powered vehicles use a fluid called **diesel exhaust fluid (DEF)**, or AdBlue™ DEF is injected into the exhaust stream to reduce oxides of Nitrogen during certain driving conditions. Since the DEF is consumed over time, it needs to be replenished periodically, ideally during oil changes. The DEF fluid filler cap is often located under the hood and may be colored blue. *Do not* make the expensive mistake of putting washer fluid (or any other fluid) in the DEF tank.

Windshield Washer Fluid

The windshield washer system on any vehicle is an important safety feature. Driving in muddy conditions, light mist, fog, or any other condition that causes the windshield to be obstructed requires that the washer system be ready to work when needed. The washer fluid reservoir is normally located under the hood of the vehicle **FIGURE 8-8**. Some vehicles also may have a separate washer reservoir for the rear wiper, located somewhere in the rear hatch or trunk area. Refer to the owner's manual or service information to locate the filler cap.

The windshield washer fluid should be checked whenever the oil is changed or at each vehicle service. Driving in dusty or wet conditions may require that the windshield washer fluid be checked more often. It is important to use properly formulated and mixed washer fluid, especially in freezing weather. The fluid is normally purchased premixed in the proper ratio that protects against freezing.

FIGURE 8-8 The washer reservoir is usually located under the hood.

To check and add to the windshield washer fluid, follow the steps in **SKILL DRILL 8-1**:

1. Locate the windshield wiper fluid container. It is normally found under the hood and is usually a plastic bottle. Note that there may be a separate reservoir for the rear wiper and/or headlight washer. **(Photo 1)**

2. Check the windshield washer fluid level. Some vehicles have electrical sensors incorporated into the reservoir, and an indicator lamp on the inside of the vehicle will show the driver when the system needs to be filled. In most vehicles, the windshield washer fluid level is visible, and a marker on the reservoir indicates the correct fluid level.

3. If the windshield washer fluid level is low, refill the reservoir with an appropriate windshield washer fluid. Most fluids are premixed and do not need to be mixed with water. Take care not to spill the fluid, and fill the reservoir to the maximum or full mark. **(Photo 2)**

> **TECHNICIAN TIP**
>
> Never use laundry or dishwashing detergent to top off the reservoir, as the chemicals in the detergent can damage the vehicle's paint.

Belts and Hoses

The engine drive belts and coolant hoses are maintenance items that should be inspected and replaced according to the manufacturer's service schedule. They do not last the life of the vehicle. Whenever the vehicle is being serviced, the belts and hoses should be checked. On most vehicles, the failure of a belt or hose when driving will result in overheating of the engine, causing extensive damage to the engine.

Engine Drive Belts

Engine drive belts are used to operate the various accessories on the engine, such as the water pump, power steering pump, air conditioner compressor, and alternator. As the vehicle ages, these belts will wear, along with their associated idler and tensioner pulleys. Some manufacturers recommend that the belts be replaced at about 5 years of age, as part of a preventive maintenance program.

There are two types of drive belts: the V-type and the serpentine type. A V-type belt sits inside a deep V-shaped groove in the pulley. The sides of the V-belt contact and wedge in the sides of the V in the pulley. Serpentine-type belts have a flat profile with a number of grooves running lengthwise along the belt. These grooves are the exact reverse of the grooves in the outer diameter of the pulleys; they increase the contact surface area and

SKILL DRILL 8-1 Checking and Refilling Windshield Washer Fluid

1. Locate the windshield wiper fluid container.

2. Check the windshield washer fluid level. If the level is low, refill the reservoir with the appropriate washer fluid.

prevent the belt from slipping off the drive pulley as it rotates **FIGURE 8-9**.

Check the drive belts whenever the hood is opened for service. The water pump is the most important component driven by the belt, and the engine will quickly overheat if the belt breaks or comes off. If the belts are more than 5 to 6 years old, check the manufacturer's replacement schedule in the service information. Most vehicles using a serpentine belt also have a spring-operated tensioner and pulley. This tensioner may have a built-in damper that reduces noise and vibration. Some manufacturers recommend that the tensioner be replaced along with the belt. Some belts, called stretchy belts or Stretch Fit™ belts, do not use a method for tensioning the belt. Their stretchiness applies an appropriate amount of tension to the belt over its useful life, which some vehicle manufacturers claim can be up to 150,000 miles.

The belts should be checked for the following:

- Cracks: Cracks that exceed a certain number per inch in a belt indicate that the belt may soon fail and should be replaced **FIGURE 8-10**.

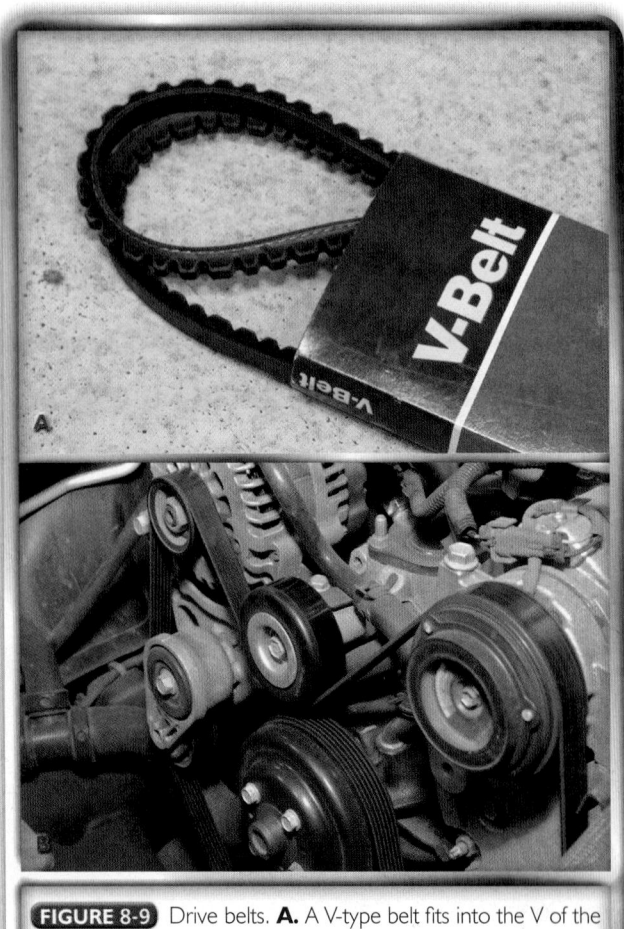

FIGURE 8-10 A serpentine belt with many cracks should be replaced.

FIGURE 8-9 Drive belts. **A.** A V-type belt fits into the V of the drive pulley. **B.** Serpentine-type belts have a flat profile with a number of grooves running lengthwise along the belt.

- Oil soaking: A belt that has been soaked in oil will not grip properly on the pulleys and will slip. If the oil contamination is severe enough for this to happen, replace the belt.
- Glazing: Glazing is shininess on the surface of the belt, which comes in contact with the pulley. If the belt is very worn, the glazing could be due to the belt bottoming out, and it should be replaced. If it is not old and worn, glazing could indicate that the belt is not tight enough. Tightening the belt may be all that is necessary, depending on how bad the glazing is.
- Tears: Torn or split belts are unserviceable and should be replaced.
- Bottoming out: When a V-type belt or serpentine belt becomes very worn, the bottom of the V may contact the bottom of the groove in the pulley, preventing the sides of the belt from making good contact with the sides of the pulley grooves. This reduced friction causes slippage. A belt worn enough to bottom out should be replaced **FIGURE 8-11**.

Hoses

The vehicle will usually have at least two large radiator hoses and some smaller heater hoses. At the radiator, there will be a large upper radiator hose (near the top of the radiator) and a large lower radiator hose (near the bottom of the radiator). The smaller heater hoses (usually two) run from the engine block, manifold, or water pump to connections at the heater assembly (near the firewall). The engine should be cool when inspecting the hoses. A hot engine will have pressure in the cooling system that may make a soft hose feel stiff, when it really

FIGURE 8-11 A V-type belt worn enough to bottom out should be replaced.

Applied | Math

AM-50: Deductive Reasoning: The technician can identify the specific cause of the problem by generating conclusions based on known symptoms related to the problem.
Drive belt squeal is typically a high-pitched squealing noise caused by the V or serpentine belt slipping against the pulleys. This frequently occurs only when a load is applied to the belt, so may be noticed only when turning with power steering or when air conditioning is turned on. Common causes include worn or age-hardened belts, incorrect belt adjustment, incorrect length or pitch belt fitted, oil contamination of the belt, or the belt pulleys being worn or incorrectly aligned.

A practical example may be a car that emits a loud squealing noise occurring only when the steering wheel is turned. A technician can easily reproduce the noise in the shop and can hear that the noise is coming from the drive belt area. A visual inspection will determine the condition and adjustment of the belt. If the belt is replaced with a new, correct part, and the noise returns, the technician can reason that the fault is related to the belt tensioner or pulley, and can inspect them for condition and alignment.

may need to be replaced. If the engine is hot, look for bulging in the hoses.

If you find one defective hose, chances are that the other hose(s) may be deteriorating in the same way and will soon need to be replaced. For this reason, most technicians will generally recommend replacing all of the coolant hoses at once as a sensible precaution. This will include the upper and lower radiator hoses and both heater hoses. Also check for any small hoses that may connect components, such as between the water pump and the engine block.

> **TECHNICIAN TIP**
>
> In most cases, hoses need to be felt to determine their condition. They should be neither too hard nor too soft. Also, the relative stiffness should be consistent over the length of the hose. If you feel differences in stiffness, the hose should be replaced.

Changing the Air Filter

The engine needs a free flow of clean air in order to operate correctly and with low emissions. Dust and grit in the air can be very abrasive and will shorten the life of the engine if not filtered out. If the filter element is not fitted correctly and does not seal properly, air can bypass the filter and enter the engine without being filtered.

The location of the air filter will vary, depending on the type of fuel system on the vehicle, so check the vehicle service information or owner's manual for the exact procedure. Some air filters are mounted to the top of the engine, usually found on older vehicles using a carburetor or throttle body fuel injection. The air cleaner on a multiport fuel-injected vehicle is typically located in a rectangular box within the air induction system. While inspecting the air filter, take a look at the air cleaner housing and duct work for cracks or holes, which would allow unfiltered air to enter the engine.

> **TECHNICIAN TIP**
>
> The paper filter element actually becomes more efficient at filtering dirt particles as it is used. This is because the passageways become smaller as dirt is caught in them, so smaller and smaller dirt particles are caught over time. However, if the filter becomes too clogged, it will restrict air, which reduces engine power output. If it is left too long, the filter can become deformed from the excess vacuum caused by the restricted air filter.

To change the air filter, follow the steps in **SKILL DRILL 8-2**:

1. On fuel-injected engines, unlatch or unscrew the filter housing fasteners to remove the air filter. It may be necessary to loosen the clamps and hoses on the induction tubing to remove the filter housing cover. Note the position of the clamps so they can be reinstalled correctly. **(Photo 1)**

SKILL DRILL | 8-2 | Changing the Air Filter

1 On fuel-injected engines, unlatch or unscrew the filter housing fasteners to remove the air filter. It may be necessary to loosen the clamps and hoses on the induction tubing to remove the filter housing cover.

2 On carbureted or throttle body injected engines, remove the top of the air filter by unscrewing the wing nut, and remove the air filter.

3 Inspect the air cleaner element by holding the filter element up to light and looking through it. If it is bright with no tears or cracks, it can be reused. If it is dark or damaged in any way, it will need to be replaced.

4 Clean the inside of the air filter housing, and inspect it and any ducts for cracks. If the air filter is being replaced, obtain a new air filter and compare it with the old one to ensure that they are exactly the same.

5 Place the new air filter inside the filter housing, making sure it is aligned properly on both sides. Replace the cover of the air filter housing and tighten the latches, screws, or wing nut until completely closed. Reinstall any induction tubing or clamps.

2 Engines with carburetors or throttle body injection usually have a large round air filter mounted on top of the throttle body. Remove the top by unscrewing the wing nut, and remove the air filter. **(Photo 2)**

3 Inspect the air cleaner element. A good way to do this is to hold the filter element up to light and look through it. If it is bright with no tears or cracks, it can be reused. If it is dark or damaged in any way, it will need to be replaced. Do not blow it out with air or bang it on the ground to dislodge the dirt. Doing so will damage the filter matrix so that dirt will pass through it if it is reused. **(Photo 3)**

4 Clean the inside of the air filter housing to make sure the new air filter will seal properly when fitted. Also inspect the housing and any ducts for cracks or holes.

5 Obtain the correct replacement air filter. If the air filter is being replaced, obtain a new air filter and compare it with the old one, making sure they are exactly the same. (**Photo 4**)

6 Place the new air filter inside the filter housing. Make sure it is aligned properly on both sides. Replace the cover of the air filter housing and tighten the latches, screws, or wing nut until completely closed. Reinstall and tighten any induction tubing or clamps. (**Photo 5**)

► Exterior Vehicle Inspections

A periodic inspection of the vehicle's exterior can prevent troubles that may cause safety or operational concerns. It is much better to discover a worn tire or broken taillight lens during an inspection than when broken down on the side of the road or pulled over by the police. A small percentage of owners check their own vehicle for problems, but most depend on the service technician to do it for them. Any maintenance procedure should include this inspection.

► Caring for the Customer

The customer or owner of the vehicle can perform an inspection while washing the vehicle. Bad wiper blades, loose trim, and other items may be noticed that are otherwise not seen.

Performing a Visual Inspection

Once a month or prior to any long trip, a vehicle should be checked for overall roadworthiness. Although the vehicle owner may perform this inspection, the service technician more often does it during periodic maintenance of the vehicle. The inspection also should be made any time the vehicle is serviced at the dealer or repair shop. While doing this inspection, the technician should be sure to work in a systematic manner. Using an inspection sheet and inspecting each vehicle the same way will ensure that a faulty bulb or other component is not missed.

To perform a visual inspection, follow the steps in **SKILL DRILL 8-3**:

1 Prepare the vehicle. Park the vehicle in a well-lit area. Turn the engine off and unlock the doors and trunk or rear hatch. (**Photo 1**)

2 Begin your inspection by walking around the vehicle, observing any obvious items that need attention. Look for broken or missing lighting lenses. Do not forget to check the license plate lights, which may be located in a hard-to-see part of the rear bumper or hatch. (**Photo 2**)

3 Check exterior component and system operation. Check the body condition to make sure all the body components are secure. Look for front spoilers and plastic underbody trim that may be damaged or loose. (**Photo 3**)

SKILL DRILL 8-3   Performing a Visual Inspection

1 Prepare the vehicle. Park the vehicle in a well-lit area. Turn the engine off and unlock the doors and trunk or rear hatch.

2 Walk around the vehicle, observing any obvious items that need attention.

3 Check exterior component and system operation. Check the body condition to make sure all the body components are secure. Look for loose plastic trim.

SKILL DRILL   8-3   Performing a Visual Inspection, continued

4 Open and close doors to check that they are operating correctly.

5 Push and pull on the bumpers or fenders to ensure that they are secure.

6 Inspect the external mirrors to ensure that they are secure and not broken.

4 Open and close doors to check that they are operating correctly. **(Photo 4)**

5 Push and pull on the bumpers or fenders to ensure that they are secure. **(Photo 5)**

6 Inspect the external mirrors to ensure that they are secure and not broken. **(Photo 6)**

Checking the Wiper Blades

The windshield wiper blades and arms are an important safety system on every vehicle. Many states with a vehicle inspection program will fail a vehicle if the wiper blades are missing, torn, or worn out. The blades, along with the washer system, help the driver to see clearly under all driving conditions.

The wiper blades should be checked as part of the exterior inspection. Usually any wiper blade that is more than a year old will be ready for replacement, especially if the vehicle is parked outside. Both the blade and the wiper arm should be checked. The wiper blade should be flexible and not torn. The wiper arm should flex at the hinge and be held firmly against the windshield by the wiper arm spring. The rear wiper blade and arm are checked in the same way.

Never operate the wipers when they are dry because this may damage the blades or scratch the surface of the windshield. Never bend the arms to make better contact with the windshield. The arms are pre-tensioned by the manufacturer, and damage could result. If the arms

seem to have lost their spring tension, obtain a suitable replacement.

To check and replace windshield wiper blades, follow the steps in **SKILL DRILL 8-4**:

1 Check the windshield wiper blades. Lift the wiper arm away from the windshield and inspect the condition of the blades. Look for damage or loss of resilience in the material. Note whether the arm hinge and spring move freely, with firm tension on the spring. **(Photo 1)**

2 Wet the windshield with a hose or with the washers and switch the wipers on. If the windshield is being wiped cleanly, do not replace the wiper blades. If

▶ TECHNICIAN TIP

Many a windshield has been broken while inspecting or replacing windshield wiper blades. The spring holds the wiper arm firmly against the windshield. If you drop the wiper arm while holding it away from the windshield, the spring will snap it against the windshield with enough force to potentially break the windshield, especially if the wiper blade is removed from the arm. You can prevent a broken windshield by making sure the arm is never allowed to slip or by placing a fender cover on the windshield where the wiper blade would hit.

the wiper blades are not wiping the glass evenly or are smearing the windshield, you will need to replace the wiper blades. **(Photo 2)**

3 Remove the blade assembly. Depending on the vehicle, you may need to remove the wiper arm from its mounting, or you may be able to just undo a spring clip and remove the blade insert. **(Photo 3)**

4 Obtain a replacement blade. Check the vehicle service information or the application guide at the parts counter to obtain the correct replacement size. If measuring the blade with a ruler, measure the wiping rubber part of the blade, not the metal

blade housing. Due to new developments in blade design, the profile of the new blade may not be identical to the original.

5 After installing the new wiper blades, test them. Wet the windshield again, and operate the wipers to check their performance, making sure they remove the water evenly. **(Photo 4)**

Inspecting the Windshield

The windshield should be inspected during the wiper blade inspection process. Scratched, scored, or pitted glass will not wipe clean, even with new blades.

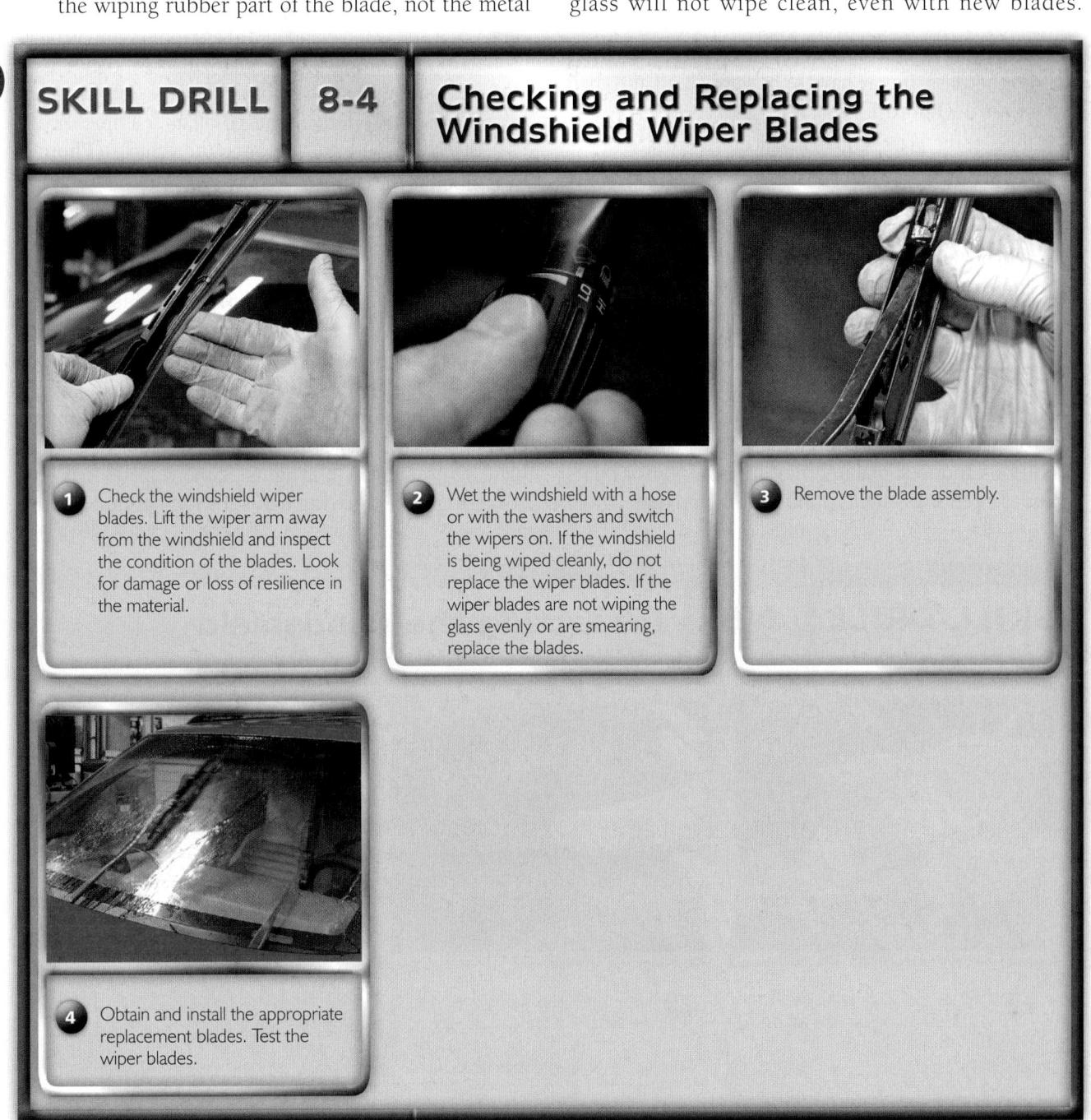

SKILL DRILL | **8-4** | **Checking and Replacing the Windshield Wiper Blades**

1 Check the windshield wiper blades. Lift the wiper arm away from the windshield and inspect the condition of the blades. Look for damage or loss of resilience in the material.

2 Wet the windshield with a hose or with the washers and switch the wipers on. If the windshield is being wiped cleanly, do not replace the wiper blades. If the wiper blades are not wiping the glass evenly or are smearing, replace the blades.

3 Remove the blade assembly.

4 Obtain and install the appropriate replacement blades. Test the wiper blades.

Windshields may become etched or pitted, causing the wipers to function poorly. This is a safety hazard and should be repaired. The glass in some cases may be polished to repair the condition or it may have to be replaced. Some small chips or cracks can be repaired with special resins and tools. These services can be performed by an automotive glass repair service or at some collision repair shops. Large chips or cracks longer than 3" (76 mm) may be reasons to replace the windshield.

To inspect the windshield, follow the steps in **SKILL DRILL 8-5**:

1. Prepare the windshield. First, use glass cleaner to clean the windshield thoroughly. If the vehicle has been in the paint shop, look for fine paint particles on the glass. It may have to be scraped off and then cleaned. **(Photo 1)**

2. Inspect the glass. Look closely at the surface of the glass. Look for chips, scratches, or etching that does not wash off. Look at the edges and corners of the windshield for cracks or signs of delamination. It may help to use a flashlight or trouble light at an angle while inspecting. **(Photo 2)**

Inspecting the Interior and Exterior Lights

The lighting system allows the driver to see the road and sides of the road when driving at night or in poor-visibility conditions and to signal to other drivers. Interior lights include the courtesy lights, dome lights, and map lights.

To inspect the interior lights, follow the steps in **SKILL DRILL 8-6**:

1. Park the vehicle inside or in a shaded area to make the lights easier to see. Begin with the doors shut and locked, if using a remote door lock system.

2. Using the remote key fob or the door key, unlock the doors. On most vehicles, unlocking the doors will cause the interior lights to come on. Check that each light that is supposed to come on actually does come on. This could include as many as six lights. On some vehicles, the lights will not come on until the door is actually opened. Check each door on the vehicle. **(Photo 1)**

3. Enter the vehicle and close the door. Many vehicles have a dimming feature that will cause the lights to stay on for 10 to 15 seconds after the door is closed. Wait to see that the lights go off after a time. Repeat this check with each door on the vehicle. **(Photo 2)**

4. Operate the courtesy lights from any other switches, which may be found on the lights themselves or on the dash.

5. Check the map lights. Some vehicles have map lights in addition to the courtesy lights. Usually a manual switch is pushed to turn them on and off. Check the owner's manual if you are not sure how to operate them. **(Photo 3)**

The exterior lighting system includes the headlights, taillights, turn signals, side markers, brake lights, license plate lights, and backing lights. Some vehicles may have cornering lights, driving lights, or fog lights. Note that

SKILL DRILL | **8-5** | **Inspecting the Windshield**

1. Prepare the windshield. First, use glass cleaner to clean the windshield thoroughly.

2. Inspect the glass. Look closely at the surface of the glass. It may help to use a flashlight or trouble light at an angle while inspecting.

SKILL DRILL | 8-6 | Inspecting the Interior Lights

1 Park the vehicle inside or in a shaded area. Using the remote key fob or door key, unlock the doors. On most vehicles, unlocking the doors will cause the interior lights to come on. Check that each light works as intended. On some vehicles, the lights will not come on until the door is actually opened. Check each door on the vehicle.

2 Enter the vehicle and close the door. Wait to see that the lights go off after a time. Repeat this check with each door on the vehicle.

3 Operate the courtesy lights from any other switches. Check the map lights, if they exist.

the rear lights may have three or more bulbs per side; be sure to check that they all are working.

To inspect the exterior lights, follow the steps in **SKILL DRILL 8-7**:

1 Park the vehicle inside or in a shaded area so that the lights are easier to see.

2 Check the rear lights. Have someone stand behind the vehicle to report any problems while you turn the ignition on. Switch the lighting switch to the park light position. Check that the taillights and any side markers come on and are equal in brightness. **(Photo 1)**

3 Check the rear license plate lights to be sure they are operating.

4 Put the turn signal switch in the left and then right turn position, and check that the signals flash equally on each side. **(Photo 2)**

5 Depress the brake pedal to make sure the brake lights work. Check that the third (center) brake light works. **(Photo 3)**

6 Check the front lights. With someone in front of the vehicle, make sure the high and low headlight beams, park lights, side markers, and turn indicators are all working properly. **(Photo 4)**

Inspecting the Tires

Tires should be inspected as part of the vehicle inspection process. They are checked for pressure, wear patterns, cuts, and tread depth **FIGURE 8-12**. The tires and their condition are one of the most important safety considerations on the vehicle. A tire worn to a minimum tread depth may work fine on dry pavement

FIGURE 8-12 Tires are checked for pressure, wear patterns, cuts, and tread depth.

SKILL DRILL | 8-7 | Inspecting the Exterior Lights

1 Park the vehicle inside or in a shaded area. Have someone stand behind the vehicle to report any problems while you turn the ignition on. Switch the lighting switch to the park light position. Check that the taillights and any side markers come on and are equal in brightness.

2 Check the rear license plate lights to be sure they are operating. Put the turn signal switch in the left and then right turn position, and check that the signals flash equally on each side.

3 Depress the brake pedal to make sure the brake lights work. Check that the third (center) brake light works.

4 Make sure the high and low headlight beams, park lights, side markers, and turn indicators are all working properly.

but be dangerous in wet weather. Keep this in mind as you inspect the tires.

Tires are inflated using pressurized air or nitrogen to support the weight of the vehicle. Normal tire pressures will vary from vehicle to vehicle, according to the vehicle's use and driver preference. Recommended tire pressures for the vehicle are located on the vehicle manufacturer's tire placard, typically placed on the driver's side door pillar. The maximum tire pressure, located on the tire sidewall, is the maximum pressure for that tire, not the pressure for the vehicle. Never inflate the tire above the recommended maximum pressure, as the tire may explode.

> ▶ **LINK**
> Refer to the Servicing Wheels chapter for more information on tires, checking the tire pressure, and inspecting the tire tread.

▶ In-Vehicle Inspections

Certain in-vehicle inspections and checks should be made as the vehicle is driven into the service bay. Pay attention to the instrument cluster and warning lights. Note how the pedals feel and how the vehicle sounds when first started. Report anything unusual to the shop foreman or supervisor. These checks can be done quickly when the vehicle is first started and then completed as the vehicle is positioned in the stall.

> ## ▶ Caring for the Customer
>
> There may be concerns with the brake pedal feel or instrument panel warning lights that the customer is unaware of. The customer is used to the way the vehicle drives and feels; the technician can detect a fault when the customer may think the fault is a normal condition.

Checking the Brake Pedal

The brake pedal acts as a lever to increase the force applied to the brake assemblies by the driver. Changes to how far the pedal travels or to its resistance—if it feels harder or softer than normal—can be an indicator of problems such as low fluid levels or even a leak in the hydraulic system. You should always check the brake pedal feel and travel before driving a vehicle into or out of the shop. Also listen for unusual brake noises when driving the vehicle into the shop. High-pitched scraping noises or heavy grinding noises could indicate a worn brake lining. The owner of the vehicle may be used to the feel of a low pedal or the sound of noisy brakes, while you will recognize it as an indication of a problem.

> ### ▶ LINK
> See the Hydraulics and Power Brakes chapter for more information on checking the brake pedal.

Checking the Parking Brake

All vehicles must be manufactured with a foot brake (service brake) system and a parking brake system. Most light vehicles use a foot brake that operates through a hydraulic system on all wheels, and a hand-operated parking brake that acts mechanically on the rear wheels only. The parking brake is used to hold the vehicle in position when parked. The parking brake should be checked as part of a routine safety or vehicle inspection. On vehicles with automatic transmissions, the parking brake may not work at all and the owner would not know until it is needed. In climates with below-freezing temperatures, the parking brake cable can freeze in the applied position, making it so the parking brake will not release. In this situation, it is probably best not to test the parking brake operation.

> ### ▶ TECHNICIAN TIP
>
> If the vehicle does not have a hand- or foot-operated parking brake, check for a "P" button on the console or dash. The vehicle may be equipped with an electronically controlled parking brake.

> ### ▶ LINK
> See the Disc Brake System chapter for more information on checking the parking brake.

Checking the Instrument Panel Warning Lamps

The many instrument panel warning lamps can indicate faults with various systems on the vehicle. They also can indicate proper operation of the system. The warning lamps perform a self-check each time the ignition is switched on or the engine cranked. You should observe the action of the lights when operating the vehicle to determine whether any additional service may be required. For example, the amber anti-lock brake system (ABS) warning lamp will come on, then stay on for a few seconds, and then go off, indicating that the ABS control module has successfully completed a preliminary self-check.

To check instrument panel warning lamps, follow the steps in SKILL DRILL 8-8:

1. Perform an instrument panel self-test. When the key is switched on (before starting the engine), most of the dash warning lamps will light up as a bulb check. Note any that do not light up as expected. A warning lamp that does not come on at all may indicate a problem in that system, so check the service information. **(Photo 1)**

2. Perform an engine running check. Start the engine and observe the warning lamps. All should go off after a few seconds as the related control module runs a self-check and then commands the lamp to go off. Any lamp that goes off and then comes back on indicates a problem. **(Photo 2)**

Checking the Horn

The vehicle horn is usually operated by a relay or by the vehicle **body control module (BCM)**. There may be a single horn or a pair of horns, depending on the vehicle. With two horns, one will sound at a lower pitch than the other. The horns are located at the front of the vehicle, behind the grill or bumper. The horn can easily be checked before driving the vehicle into the shop.

SKILL DRILL   8-8   Checking Instrument Panel Warning Lamps

1. Perform an instrument panel self-test. When the key is switched on (before starting the engine) most of the dash warning lamps will light up as a bulb check. Note any that do not light up as expected.

2. Perform an engine running check. Start the engine and observe the warning lamps. All should go off after a few seconds as the related control module runs a self-check and then commands the lamp to go off.

To perform a horn check, follow the steps in **SKILL DRILL 8-9**:

1. Check the vehicle horn. On some vehicles the horn will work only with the key turned on. Turn on the ignition and press the horn button. The horn should sound. Do this outside the shop to keep from irritating the other technicians. **(Photo 1)**

2. Evaluate the results. If the horn is not working, locate it under the hood with the help of the manufacturer's service information. Check the wiring to make sure it is connected securely. **(Photo 2)**

Under-Vehicle Inspection

The under-vehicle inspection is a systematic visual inspection of all major vehicle systems. Be prepared to write down any faults to discuss later with your supervisor. With the vehicle safely lifted on a hoist, an under-body inspection is a good way to get a feel for the overall condition of the vehicle. Additional areas of concern will often be found during the inspection, saving the customer an extra trip to the shop for repairs.

The under-vehicle inspection includes:

- The steering area: The steering area inspection includes the tie-rods and tie-rod ends, idler and pitman arm, steering rack, wheel bearings, and tires and wheels. Suspension bushings, shock absorbers, and brake hoses and lines are also inspected.
- The front-wheel drive axles: This inspection includes the constant velocity joints (**CV joints**) and dust boots. Look for cracked, torn, or leaking boots.
- The engine area: Check for coolant, oil, and fuel leaks. Look for torn or cracked motor mounts, coolant hoses, and belts.
- The transmission area: This inspection includes the transmission case, clutch housing, external linkages, and wiring connectors. In the transmission area, check for fluid leaks, loose mounting bolts, and faults or looseness in the clutch mechanism or shift linkage.
- The exhaust system: Clamps and bolts may need tightening on the exhaust system or on the exhaust system-to-manifold bolts or gaskets. Check for signs of exhaust leaks, corrosion, or deterioration, including the exhaust hanger hardware. Check the condition of any heat shields.
- The parking brake cables: The cables are encased in a housing that attaches the parking brake lever or pedal to the rear brakes. Check for rusted, frozen, broken, or crushed cables.
- The driveshaft: The driveshaft transmits power from the transmission to the rear axle on rear-wheel

SKILL DRILL | 8-9 | Performing a Horn Check

1. Check the vehicle horn. Turn on the ignition and press the horn button. The horn should sound.

2. If the horn is not working, locate it under the hood with the help of the manufacturer's service information. Check the wiring to make sure it is connected securely.

drive vehicles. Check for any excess movement in driveshaft universal joints. Look for any dents or bending of the shaft.

- The differential, rear axle, and rear suspension area: The rear axle includes the differential and axle shafts. Look for leaks around the differential, and check the rear shock absorbers, leaf springs, brake hoses, and lines.
- The fuel tank: The fuel tank is metal or plastic, depending on the vehicle. Inspection should include the filler tube and hose, the vent and fuel delivery lines, and the fuel tank straps and protective shields. The fuel tank must be secure and fuel lines inspected for damage or abrasion.

To perform an under-vehicle components inspection, follow the steps in **SKILL DRILL 8-10**:

1. Safely raise the vehicle to a comfortable working height. Be ready to record any faults found, and begin the inspection at either end of the vehicle. Whichever end you choose, work systematically in one direction. Note any problems you find and discuss them with your supervisor. Pay particular attention to any fluid leaks, which will probably be the easiest problems to spot. **(Photo 1)**

2. Check the steering area. Locate the tie-rods and twist, push, and pull on them. The action should be smooth without binding. Grasp the front and rear of the tire and wheel assembly and pivot it in and out to detect lateral movement in the tie-rod end. Grasp the tire at the top and bottom and

pivot it in and out to detect movement in the wheel bearings or ball joint. Look carefully for missing or torn rubber boots around the tie-rod ends and steering rack. At the same time, check the security of the steering box or rack mountings. Inspect any rubber suspension bushings for swelling or damage, and check shock absorbers for signs of damage or leaks. Inspect any wiring harness that is accessible for any obvious damage. Check the brake hoses and lines, looking for signs of cracking or abrasions. **(Photo 2)**

3. Check the front-wheel drive axles. On vehicles with front-wheel drive, check the drive axles for up-and-down looseness. Excessive movement indicates a bad inner or outer CV joint. Examine the inner and outer boots for cracks or tears. **(Photo 3)**

4. Check the transmission area. Look for loose mounting or cover bolts. Trace and record the source of fluid leaks if you find any. With a manual transmission, check the clutch operating mechanism for any damage. For an automatic transmission, check the shift linkage for any damage. If the transmission is electronically controlled, check any wiring for obvious damage. **(Photo 4)**

5. Check the exhaust system. Check the tightness of the flange bolts on the engine manifold pipe. It is also important to make sure all the clamps on the exhaust system are tight. If there is an exhaust leak, it is usually identified by a blackish soot deposit

at the source of the leak. Examine the catalytic converter, muffler, and resonator for any signs of corrosion or deterioration. Inspect any heat shields for looseness or damage. Check the tailpipe for any corrosion, and check for looseness in the mounting brackets or hangers. **(Photo 5)**

6 Check the parking brake cables. Inspect the hand brake cable to make sure it is not frayed, damaged, or binding. Look for rusted or swollen cable housings. Pull on the cables and check that the parking brake actually applies. **(Photo 6)**

7 Check the drive shaft. On any rear-wheel drive vehicles, inspect the drive shaft universal joints for signs of excess movement or rust. Rusty powder marks near the front and rear universal joints could indicate a rusted and/or seized universal joint. To check for wear, rotate the shaft and flange in opposite directions. There should be no movement in the joint. On four-wheel drive vehicles, repeat this procedure on the front drive shaft universals. **(Photo 7)**

8 Check the differential and rear suspension area. On rear-wheel drive vehicles, the rear axle housing supports the differential unit. Inspect the **pinion shaft** oil seal for any obvious signs of leakage. Next, check the rear shock absorbers for any signs of physical damage or fluid leaks. Tighten all the suspension mounting bolts, noting any bolt that was loose. Inspect the suspension mounting bushings for any signs of deterioration or damage. This will include any control arms or struts. If the vehicle is fitted with leaf springs, inspect the leafs for any cracks or misalignment. On a vehicle with independent suspension, inspect the rear strut assemblies for any physical damage or signs of fluid leaks. Inspect the brake hoses and lines for any obvious signs of cracking or abrasion. **(Photo 8)**

9 Check the fuel tank area. Tighten the fuel tank mounting bolts or retaining strap bolts, noting any bolt that was loose. Carefully check all the fuel lines and brake lines for any signs of damage, abrasions, or rust that may cause a leak. Check the fuel delivery lines and the vent lines for leaks. **(Photo 9)**

> ### ▶ TECHNICIAN TIP
>
> When checking the fuel tank, any odor of gasoline indicates a leak. Keep checking until you find it. It is not normal for today's vehicles to have any odor of gasoline.

Checking for Fluid Leaks

The service bay should be clean and dry before driving the vehicle into the shop. This will help you to locate any fluid leaks that may be present on the vehicle. Active leaks will leave telltale drips or puddles on the clean floor, making it easier to identify what may be leaking. Fluids that may be leaking include brake fluid, transmission fluid, power steering fluid, coolant, fuel, and engine oil. Some fluids come in a variety of colors, such as red, which can be used for automatic transmission fluid or anti-freeze. Become familiar with each fluid's distinctive colors, feel, or smell:

- Brake fluid: May be clear or light amber looking for DOT 3 and DOT 4, while DOT 5 is usually purple; slightly slippery; has an unpleasant, slightly acid-type smell.
- Automatic transmission fluid and some manual transmission fluid: Normally reddish in color, although some manufacturers may use a clear or amber color; very slippery and oily; has an oily smell.
- Power steering fluid: Has similar characteristics as automatic transmission fluid.
- Coolant: Normally green, orange, or yellow in color; some manufacturers (e.g., General Motors) use a coolant that is red or light red; slippery; has a sweet smell, like syrup.
- Engine oil: Brown or black in color; very slippery and a bit thick; has an oily smell.
- Manual transmission fluid: Light brown in color; very slippery and thick, like syrup; has an oily smell.
- Gasoline: Clear in color; evaporates easily; has a distinctive gas odor.
- Diesel: Dirty clear in color; thin; has an oily smell.

Checking for leaks can be done as part of the under-vehicle inspection or with a light on a clean floor. The leaks will normally be more visible on a warmed-up vehicle, although some coolant leaks only appear when the engine is cold. Discuss with the customer whether there are any unusual smells in the morning when the vehicle is first started.

To check for leaks, drive the vehicle into a clean, well-lit work stall. Ideally, the stall will also have a lift so that the vehicle can be further inspected if a leak is suspected. Use a flashlight or trouble light to inspect the underside of the vehicle for any drips or wet areas. With the engine running, wait a few minutes to see if any leaks appear. Turn the engine off and wait for a time to see if anything drips on the floor. Try to identify the type of fluid that is leaking and the area from which it is leaking. Remember that gravity will tend to pull any leaking fluids down, so

SKILL DRILL | 8-10 | Performing an Under-Vehicle Components Inspection

1 Safely raise the vehicle to a comfortable working height. Work systematically in one direction. Pay particular attention to any fluid leaks.

2 Check the steering area. Locate the tie-rods and twist, push, and pull on them. Grasp the front and rear of the tire and wheel assembly and pivot it to detect lateral movement in the tie-rod end. Grasp the tire at the top and bottom and pivot it to detect movement in the wheel bearings or ball joint. Look for missing or torn rubber boots around the tie-rod ends and steering rack. Check the security of the steering box or rack mountings. Inspect rubber suspension bushings, and check shock absorbers for signs of damage or leaks. Inspect any wiring harness that is accessible for damage. Check the brake hoses and lines for signs of cracking or abrasions.

3 Check the front-wheel drive axles. On vehicles with front-wheel drive, check the drive axles for up-and-down looseness. Examine the inner and outer boots for cracks or tears.

4 Check the transmission area. Look for loose mounting or cover bolts. Trace and record the source of fluid leaks. With a manual transmission, check the clutch operating mechanism for damage. For an automatic transmission, check the shift linkage for any damage. If the transmission is electronically controlled, check the wiring for damage.

5 Check the exhaust system. Check the tightness of the flange bolts on the engine manifold pipe. Examine the catalytic converter, muffler, and resonator for signs of corrosion or deterioration. Inspect the heat shields. Check the tailpipe for corrosion, and check for looseness in the mounting brackets or hangers.

6 Check the parking brake cables. Inspect the hand brake cable to make sure it is not frayed, damaged, or binding. Look for rusted or swollen cable housings. Pull on the cables and check that the parking brake applies.

SKILL DRILL | **8-10** | **Performing an Under-Vehicle Components Inspection, continued**

7 Check the drive shaft. On rear-wheel drive vehicles, inspect the drive shaft universal joints for signs of excess movement or rust. To check for wear, rotate the shaft and flange in opposite directions (there should be no movement). On four-wheel drive vehicles, repeat this procedure on the front drive shaft universals.

8 Check the differential and rear suspension area. Inspect the pinion shaft oil seal for any signs of leakage. Check the rear shock absorbers for signs of damage or leaks. Tighten the suspension mounting bolts. Inspect the suspension mounting bushings for signs of deterioration or damage. If the vehicle is fitted with leaf springs, inspect the leafs for any cracks or misalignment. On a vehicle with independent suspension, inspect the rear strut assemblies for physical damage or signs of fluid leaks. Inspect the brake hoses for signs of cracking or abrasion.

9 Check the fuel tank area. Tighten the fuel tank mounting bolts or retaining strap bolts. Check all the fuel lines and brake lines for signs of damage, abrasions, leaks, or rust.

always look toward the top of the wet area to help determine the source of the leak. If fluid leaks onto a moving part, it can be thrown a good distance, so check for a common source. Lastly, a leak under pressure such as coolant can be sprayed a good distance from a small hole, so always use a good light to help identify the location of the leak. Finding the leak's source will tell you which component on the vehicle to inspect more closely.

Safety

If a fuel leak is discovered or suspected, the vehicle is unsafe to drive. Inform your supervisor if a fuel leak is found.

Wrap-up

Ready for Review

▶ A check under the hood is important to the life and operation of the vehicle.

▶ The correct type and amount of fluid is important for reliable and safe operation of the vehicle.

▶ The engine drive belts and coolant hoses are maintenance items that should be inspected and replaced according to the manufacturer's service schedule.

▶ The engine needs a free flow of clean air from the air filter in order to operate correctly.

▶ A periodic inspection of the vehicle's exterior can prevent troubles that may cause safety or operational concerns.

▶ Once a month or prior to any long trip, a vehicle should be visually checked for overall roadworthiness.

▶ The windshield wiper blades and arms are an important safety system on every vehicle.

▶ The windshield should be inspected during the wiper blade inspection process.

▶ The lighting system allows the driver to see when driving at night or in poor-visibility conditions and to signal to other drivers.

▶ The tires and their condition are one of the most important safety considerations on the vehicle.

▶ Certain in-vehicle inspections and checks should be made as the vehicle is driven into the service bay.

▶ The technician should always check the brake pedal feel and travel before driving a vehicle into or out of the shop.

▶ The parking brake should be checked as part of a routine safety or vehicle inspection.

▶ The many instrument panel warning lamps can indicate faults with various systems on the vehicle.

▶ The horn can easily be checked before driving the vehicle into the shop.

▶ With the vehicle safely lifted on a hoist, an underbody inspection is a good way to get a feel for the overall condition of the vehicle.

Key Terms

body control module (BCM) An onboard computer that controls many vehicle functions including the vehicle interior and exterior lighting, horn, door locks, power seats, and windows.

coolant When anti-freeze concentrate is mixed with water, the resulting mixture is called engine coolant. Most manufacturers recommend a 50/50 mixture.

CV joint CV is an abbreviation for constant velocity, a type of universal joint used on the drive axles or half-shafts of a vehicle. Usually refers to front-wheel drive vehicles.

diesel exhaust fluid (DEF) A mixture of urea and water that is injected into the exhaust system of a late-model diesel-powered vehicle to reduce exhaust nitrogen oxide emissions.

hydrometer A tool that measures the specific gravity of a liquid.

hygroscopic A property of a substance or liquid that causes it to absorb moisture (water), as a sponge absorbs water. Brake fluid will absorb water out of the air; thus it is hygroscopic.

pinion shaft On a drive axle using a ring-and-pinion gear assembly, the input component that drives the ring gear.

ASE-Type Questions

1. Tech A says that during an exterior inspection of a vehicle you should open and close doors to check that they are operating correctly. Tech B says you should never pull on bumpers or fenders. Who is correct?
   a. Tech A
   b. Tech B
   c. Both A and B
   d. Neither A nor B

2. Tech A says wiper blade condition cannot cause a vehicle to fail a safety inspection in some states. Tech B says check wiper blades for wear and tear. Who is correct?
   a. Tech A
   b. Tech B
   c. Both A and B
   d. Neither A nor B

3. Tech A says that a low oil level is bad for the engine but that it is OK for the level to be too high. Tech B says that overfilling the engine oil is bad for the engine. Who is correct?
   a. Tech A
   b. Tech B
   c. Both A and B
   d. Neither A nor B

4. Tech A says that improper handling of a windshield wiper can lead to a broken windshield. Tech B says you should place a fender cover on the windshield to prevent damage while working on windshield wipers. Who is correct?
   a. Tech A
   b. Tech B
   c. Both A and B
   d. Neither A nor B

5. While servicing an automatic transaxle–equipped vehicle, the transaxle dipstick cannot be found. Tech A says that some of these vehicles do not have a transaxle dipstick. Tech B says that the dipstick may have fallen off, since all vehicles have a transaxle dipstick. Who is correct?
   a. Tech A
   b. Tech B
   c. Both A and B
   d. Neither A nor B

6. Tech A says to test new wiper blades against a dry windshield to ensure they seat properly. Tech B says to wet the windshield and operate the wipers to check their performance. Who is correct?
   a. Tech A
   b. Tech B
   c. Both Tech A and Tech B
   d. Neither Tech A nor Tech B

7. An engine serpentine belt has broken and come off of the pulleys. Tech A says that it is OK to drive the vehicle without the belt. Tech B says that the belt only runs the charging system, so it is OK to drive a short distance without the belt. Who is correct?
   a. Tech A
   b. Tech B
   c. Both A and B
   d. Neither A nor B

8. Tech A says to clean a windshield first, and then inspect the windshield for chips, scratches, or etching. Tech B says to always clean a windshield first and then inspect the windshield for cracks or signs of delamination. Who is correct?
   a. Tech A
   b. Tech B
   c. Both A and B
   d. Neither A nor B

9. Tech A says that unlocking doors on most vehicles turns on the interior lights. Tech B says on some vehicles the interior light will not turn on until a door is actually opened. Who is correct?
   a. Tech A
   b. Tech B
   c. Both A and B
   d. Neither A nor B

10. Tech A says you should test the rear lights with the help of an assistant. Tech B says some shops have a mirror mounted in the service bay so the technician can check rear lights. Who is correct?
    a. Tech A
    b. Tech B
    c. Both A and B
    d. Neither A nor B

CHAPTER 9

NATEF Tasks

There are no NATEF tasks for this chapter.

Knowledge Objectives

After reading this chapter, you will be able to:
1. Describe the barriers to effective listening. (pp 240–241)
2. Describe the components of active listening. (pp 240–242)
3. Explain the elements of effective speaking, including asking constructive questions and proper phone etiquette. (pp 242–245)
4. Explain the purpose of people skills and self-presentation, including appearance, body language, and tone of voice. (p 246)
5. Describe the elements of good customer service. (p 247)
6. Explain effective reading and researching techniques. (pp 248–251)
7. Describe effective writing or documentation techniques. (pp 251–255)

Communication

▶ Introduction

Although we've been communicating all of our lives, most of us aren't aware of the listening, reading, writing, and speaking skills needed to be a good communicator. It doesn't require any extra effort to communicate well, once you know the principles behind each communication skill. Learning and applying good communication skills will save you time and help you avoid or get through tricky situations. These skills will build over time, and you will find that you learn something new every day when you encounter new situations or meet new people. It's a lifelong learning process to perfect your communication skills.

Since communication is an essential workplace skill needed to function successfully in the automotive service facility, this entire chapter is dedicated to communication. This chapter describes the steps to becoming an effective communicator, offers tips on how to be a good listener—the first step in good communication—and explains how to speak to both customers and your coworkers. Along the way, we will discuss the requirement for writing and preparing documentation used in the workplace.

Note: The majority of NATEF's Applied Academic Skills for Communication are covered in the context of this chapter. While the applied science and math boxes found in other chapters provide examples of how to apply concepts to everyday activities in the shop, this chapter provides examples of how to apply the concepts of good communication in everyday life.

▶ Active Listening

Applied | **Communication**

AC-15: Listening/Reading/Speaking/Writing: The technician identifies and uses effective strategies for listening, reading, speaking, and writing when dealing with customers, coworkers, and supervisors.
AC-34: Listening: The technician adapts a listening strategy that will obtain the information required for solving the problem.

Active listening is an essential skill. We may hear what someone is saying, but are we truly understanding what the person is trying to communicate? The listening process can be difficult to perfect but is one of the most important skills to possess when gathering information from a customer or any other person. The active listener focuses all of his or her attention on the speaker, including verbal and nonverbal messages. When appropriate, the active listener encourages the speaker to further communicate details that may have otherwise been left out.

The Listening Process

To be a good listener, we need to be aware of barriers that can disrupt the listening process. These barriers can be mental and physical.

Mental barriers are thoughts and feelings that interfere with our listening, such as our own assumptions,

You are the Automotive Technician

During your second week on the job, your supervisor has pulled you off the shop floor and into the service department office. You will be shadowing the service manager, Bob, to gain firsthand experience communicating effectively with customers in person. The first customer has an appointment with the service department for a safety recall issue. Bob asks questions to gather all the necessary information from the customer while making eye contact with him. As a new service technician, you will practice writing up your own work orders for Bob to critique after the customer has been taken care of. After the customer has answered all the questions, Bob reviews and reiterates to the customer his understanding of the concern to be sure it is accurate. Bob writes up a work order, reviews the concern and agreed upon course of action with the customer, and then guides the customer to the service department lounge to wait for his vehicle.

1. What are the three types of "right questions" to ask when gathering information?
2. What are the three Cs all work orders should contain?
3. Explain why empathy is an important skill to have when dealing with upset customers.

emotions, and prejudices. To fully absorb what someone is telling us, we need to learn to set these feelings aside. It takes effort and isn't always easy, but it is important to keep an open mind throughout the listening process. For example, when listening to a customer who is describing his or her vehicle concern, it is good practice to allow the customer to fully complete what he or she is saying, even if you believe you have all the information you need. Keeping an open mind is also an important first step in practicing empathy, discussed later.

As a listener and active participant, we can encourage the flow of communication by welcoming the speaker, letting him or her know that we care enough to want to understand the message, and acknowledging the speaker's feelings and concerns. To accomplish that, give the speaker your undivided attention by focusing on him or her. This means removing as many distractions as possible. Stop what you are doing, clear your mind of distractions, and look the speaker in the eye.

As the person is speaking, you will also need to provide listening feedback, which indicates to the speaker that you are engaged in what he or she is saying. Feedback can be nonverbal (e.g., facial expressions, body posture) and verbal. Nonverbal language, such as nodding while listening and gesturing while speaking, is used to reinforce or add emphasis. If, while speaking, you send a conflicting message, such as looking annoyed while stating that you value the customer's opinion, the person may tend to believe the nonverbal message over the verbal one, even though it is only half of the total message. For example, a customer has his car, which will not start, towed in to your shop. He tells you that the cause is a bad headlight. You may be tempted to roll your eyes at this assertion, but regardless of your personal opinion, you must, as a professional, maintain a sincere and attentive attitude toward the customer. Because nonverbal communication is perceived to be more spontaneous and less conscious, most people tend to believe the nonverbal message more than the actual words expressed. In this case, rolling your eyes would likely override any amount of "correct" words that you might say.

▶ Caring for the Customer

In many situations, nonverbal communication can be more important than the verbal message itself.

Empathy

Empathy can help us to avoid selective hearing. To empathize with someone is to attempt to see the situation from his or her point of view. It requires good listening skills, which include an effective use of verbal and nonverbal listening feedback, in order to take in and consider the message without applying our own biases. True empathy means breaking down or putting aside existing mental barriers. For example, when a customer brings a vehicle in with a fault requiring an expensive repair that is not in his or her budget, we can come across as uncaring with a take it or leave it attitude. Expressing your understanding of the customer's situation and seeking to explore valid options to resolve the issue will go a long way in building trust with the customer. Remember, we can empathize with people even if we do not agree with them. Also, we don't have to take responsibility for their problem. But we can at least attempt to help them find the best possible solution that will work for them. You will know that you have demonstrated empathy when no valid options were found but the customer thanks you deeply for your assistance.

Empathy not only helps you understand the message better, but also helps you to be less reactive in a negative way as you realize you could feel the same way in that person's position. It may also help to motivate you to find a better resolution of the situation, knowing that it could be you in the very same situation.

Nonverbal Feedback

Applied Communication

AC-35: Nonverbal and Verbal Cues: The technician uses verbal and nonverbal cues in discussion to help identify, verify, and solve problems.

Nonverbal feedback can be a very useful tool when listening. Your body position, eye contact, and facial expression can all set the direction of a conversation.

We use body language to help emphasize our message, and when listening, we can use it to provide listening feedback. When listening to a speaker, try to sit or stand upright, while making eye contact. Try to avoid folding your arms, as this can be perceived as either an aggressive stance or defensive. At the same time, do not act too casual, such as standing with your hands in your pockets. It may seem harmless, but a customer or supervisor would likely see such a posture as a sign of disrespect or disinterest. Imagine that you are talking to a service manager during a job interview and the manager leans back and puts his or her feet up on the desk. That one gesture would send you a message about the manager's level of professionalism and his or her respect for you and overall interest in the conversation, and in turn would have an effect on the way you viewed the meeting.

Maintaining some eye contact during the conversation, and not looking down at something or someone else, will also let your speaker know you are paying attention. If you are taking notes, be sure to look up periodically and make eye contact with the person.

Just as our own facial expressions are being noted by the speaker, remember to pay attention to the speaker's facial expressions to get a clearer sense of his or her message. If, for example, a customer scrunches up her face while talking about the squealing noise the brakes are making, you can probably assume the customer would be happy if you could make that noise go away.

Verbal Feedback

Verbal feedback includes very simple signals that can enhance the conversation and let the person know you comprehend. Some examples are the use of validating statements and supporting statements.

A **validating statement** shows common interest in the topic being discussed. A phrase such as "I see" or "Tell me more" indicates that you are paying attention. A validating statement also helps show empathy for the person speaking and can be a simple "I understand" or "That must be frustrating for you."

A **supporting statement** can urge the speaker to elaborate on a particular topic. Statements like "Go on" and "Give me an example" let the speaker know you would like more detail because you are genuinely interested in finding a solution. This is a necessary part of communication when you are gathering information from the customer—by asking for more details, you are likely to obtain more thorough information, giving you a better starting point for solving the problem. For example, imagine you are talking with a customer about a noise his car made while going over a bump. If you were to say "Tell me more," the customer would know that you understood but wanted a little more information.

As an example, a customer brings in a car as a "no start," meaning it will not crank over. Technician A speaks with this customer and gets enough information to fill out the work order, but does not ask any clarifying questions, so doesn't gather any further details. Technician B gathers the same information as technician A, but also uses supporting statements to gather further details that will assist in diagnosis. What is the end result for the two technicians? Technician B was able to find out that the customer had recently gotten a new key cut for the vehicle. This led the technician to check to see if the key had been programed to the security system, causing the no start, which is exactly what was wrong. Technician A and technician B were both able to diagnose the fault, but technician B was able to come to a conclusion much quicker than technician A because of the extra information acquired using supporting statements.

The Art of Speaking

Applied | Communication

AC-28: Speaking: The technician employs communication strategies for customers, supervisors, and coworkers that will yield high-quality information for use in problem solving.
AC-29: Information–Oral: The technician evaluates the usefulness of oral information provided by customers and coworkers when analyzing a problem.
AC-30: Information–Oral: The technician makes logical inferences and recommends solutions to problems based on discussions with customers, coworkers, and supervisors.
AC-31: Information–Oral: The technician comprehends information gathered during discussions with customers, supervisors, and coworkers regarding problem symptoms and possible solutions.
AC-32: Information–Oral/Written: The technician analyzes information based on discussions, notes, observations, personal experiences, and data searches that will assist in solving the problem.
AC-33: Information Supplying: The technician clarifies information to customers, associates, parts suppliers, and supervisors.

Speaking is often referred to as an art. That is because there are so many facets to effectively communicate and/or information gather. Whether you are asking a customer about a vehicle or your boss for a raise, knowing how to "artfully speak" will benefit you.

Speaking is a three-step process:

1. *Think* about the message.
2. Accurately *present* the message.
3. *Check* whether the message is correctly understood. If it's not, we have to respond by rethinking and re-presenting the message and rechecking with our listener. This process continues until we are satisfied that the listener correctly understands our message.

Think before you speak is easier said than done, but it's not impossible. In some situations, we have time to think and plan beforehand. Others require us to think on our feet. Thinking on your feet simply means you may be called upon to answer or handle a difficult situation quickly. Having to get things right in a fast-paced setting can result in rash decisions, but there are a few tactics you can use to make these situations easier:

1. *Relax.* It is not easy to do in an urgent situation, but attempting to remain calm is extremely beneficial,

keeping your mind clear and helping you to embody the confidence needed in such a situation.

2. *Listen*: If the situation requires you to answer a tough question, make sure you fully understand the question before answering. You can always ask the questioner to repeat or, better yet, rephrase the question. This gives you more time to think about your answer and also another chance to read into the intent of the question. Remember that if someone is asking a question of you, then he or she is showing interest. Interest is a good thing!

3. *Pause*. Silence is golden—when used properly. Most people are uncomfortable with silence, but it is perfectly acceptable to take slight pauses before speaking to organize your thoughts. This will also give you the advantage of controlling the pace of the conversation. If a situation that you have been put in charge of is slipping out of control, regain control with slight pauses and thoughtful answers. It may be beneficial to say something like, "Let me think about that for a second." Or you may take a few seconds to restate your understanding of the problem and the person's question. Doing so can help the other person understand that you are devoting effort to the question while giving you a bit of time to decide on an answer.

Before speaking, take a moment to consider that your tone of voice reveals a lot about your feelings and adds significant meaning to your message. The tone of voice includes how high or low the pitch of our voice is, how fast or slow we speak, how soft or loud, and most importantly, what our voice characteristics or emotional indications are.

Even if you disagree with what is being asserted, try to first use empathizing statements, such as "I understand" or "I can imagine how frustrating that would be" before offering a solution. For example, a regular customer had brought his vehicle in last week for a malfunction indicator lamp (MIL). The vehicle was fixed and the codes were erased. Now the same customer is back with the MIL on again and furious that he had to return. Regardless if the MIL is on for the same cause or not, you still have an upset customer to deal with. Most times, people who are angry will respond well to a statement like, "I can imagine how frustrating it is for you to have to return." When you say this, remember to keep a calm and steady tone of voice. Ultimately, the goal is to de-escalate the customer's anger. Try not to argue with the customer but rather support the customer and offer a solution that will work for both of you. In the same situation, you could say, "I can imagine how frustrating that is for you. Let's bring it in and see if it is the same problem as before or something different. If it is

the same problem, our one-year warranty will cover it. Can I get you a cup of coffee in our waiting room while we look into it?" So, when encountering an upset customer, the goal is to de-escalate the anger, guide the situation back to rational communication, and come to an agreement about how the problem will be resolved. Always empathize, de-escalate, do not argue, and focus the discussion on finding a mutually agreeable solution, if possible.

After thinking about what we want to say, and how to say it, we can then use the second step of the process by presenting a message using verbal and nonverbal language. Remember that when we say verbal language, we mean the actual words that are being spoken. Nonverbal language includes how we speak those words—our tone of voice, body language, and appearance—and takes into consideration the environment. Imagine you are with a friend in a quiet café, drinking coffee, and she is telling you how much she values your opinion. Now imagine that she is clenching her fists, scowling, and screaming those same words to you. It would change the message a little, wouldn't it?

The last step of the speaking process is to make sure our message is correctly understood by the listener. Look to see that the listener is making eye contact with you. If you perceive a lack of understanding or confusion, be prepared to repeat yourself while trying to explain it in another way or by using an example. Make sure you suppress any outward irritation you may feel at needing to do so. In stressful situations, the parties involved are often not as open minded as in calmer moments and are therefore not as receptive to your words. This can also end with misunderstandings and expectations that go unmet. So take the extra step and ask clarifying questions or summarize the message.

Caring for the Customer

A calm and happy customer or coworker is normally easy to communicate with. Most people struggle with how to handle the angry one. In almost all cases, keeping a calm and steady tone of voice and overall demeanor is the best bet. Never lose your temper; doing so will only escalate the situation and lead to an unwanted outcome.

Asking Questions

Questioning is an important speaking skill that helps keep us out of a lot of trouble. We speak to deliver a message, but many times we need more information or we need to confirm the details of an agreement. Asking questions to gather more information can provide us with enough information to make good decisions. Or once we come to an agreement with another person, we can use questions to confirm those details. In either of these situations, we have avoided trouble. In the first case, we gathered enough information to avoid a bad decision. And in the second, we confirmed the expectations that each person had regarding the agreement, helping to avoid disappointment and loss of trust.

To use questions effectively, we need to know how to ask the right questions. We can ask three types of questions:

- Open questions
- Closed questions
- Yes or no questions

Each type of question is beneficial when used appropriately. Good communicators know when and how to use the appropriate type. If you have mastered each of these types of questions, you can keep a conversation going while speaking very little. These questions can be used in all types of situations, from casual conversations with new acquaintances to detailed conversations with customers. In dealing with customers, we usually start with open questions to gather general information about the issue. Then we use closed questions to find out specific details. We use yes/no questions to further check or confirm the listener's responses or to gain the customer's agreement to authorize a repair or diagnostic procedure.

Open Questions

An open question encourages people to speak freely so we can gather facts, insights, and opinions from them. It's a good way to start a conversation with a new acquaintance or even a customer. Open questions usually begin with the words:

- What
- How
- Why
- Could you tell me

For example, if you were questioning a customer about her visit to a repair facility, you could ask, "What type of service did you receive from XYZ Automotive?" This question opens the topic up for discussion and allows the customer to give details about her visit.

Closed Questions

If we want to know more information, we can use closed questions to establish facts and details. Closed questions usually begin with the words:

- When
- Where

- Which
- Who
- How many
- How much

This type of question requires a specific answer, and there is usually only one answer. For example, you could ask a customer, "How many times have you visited XYZ Automotive?" or, "When did you start going to them?" These closed questions allow for only one answer, without much room for discussion. These questions help you to narrow the topic and guide the discussion in the direction you would like it to go, which is helpful when talking with a customer.

Yes/No Questions

Yes/no questions allow individuals to answer with a simple yes or no. This type of question is useful for checking or confirming a person's responses. For example, "Would you recommend them?" gets to the point and helps clarify information. We should generally not start out with yes/no questions because they discourage further explanation or discussion. However, ending with yes/no questions is a good way to get confirmation. For example, after explaining the need for replacing the customer's water pump and answering the customer's questions about the job, it would be very appropriate to ask, "Can we go ahead and replace that leaky water pump for you?"

Telephone Skills

We've learned about the important aspects of the speaking process. A phone conversation presents some different challenges. Since we can't see each other, we can rely only upon verbal messages and some nonverbal cues, such as the tone of voice. Other nonverbal cues that we miss are body language, appearance, and the environment.

On the phone, we are limited in how we present our messages, so we need to think about our words and tone more carefully perhaps than in person. It is a good idea to plan and even write down each of the points you want to say before even picking up the phone.

Phone communication consists of three parts: greeting, exchanging messages, and finishing the call.

We should always answer a phone call by first saying hello, identifying ourselves, and identifying our place of business, succinctly and clearly. An example could be, "Hello, this is John with XYZ Automotive. How may I help you?" Try to keep your greeting friendly and short.

The second part of the phone conversation is exchanging messages. This requires concise, clear communication followed by clarifying questions and summarizing any main points. At all times, we should be polite and considerate, and remember that the most important nonverbal clue we send out over the phone is our tone of voice, since it reveals a lot about our feelings. Here are a few tips to create a good impression:

- Do not sound bored. Try to keep some inflection in your voice; do not speak in a monotone.
- Sound calm and in control, even if you were caught at a busy moment.
- No matter what, never lose your temper or patience.
- If there is a need to keep someone on hold for an extended time, offer to call him or her back, and do it.

Finish a call by confirming actions both you and the caller will take to ensure that the messages on both sides were accurately received, and end with a pleasant and friendly goodbye **FIGURE 9-1**. Remember to thank all customers for their business, and invite them to come back. When taking a phone message for someone else, make sure you have the caller's name and organization, contact details, the date and time of the call, and a summary of the caller's message.

When making a phone call, use these same skills and always have necessary information available to give to the person you are calling. For example, if you need to order parts, relevant vehicle information should be shared with your parts supplier. You usually need to have vehicle make, model, year, engine size, and transmission type, and many times you will need the vehicle identification number (VIN).

FIGURE 9-1 Always end calls with a friendly goodbye.

Giving and Receiving Instructions

Applied   Communication

AC-14: Directions/Task: The technician follows all written and oral directions that relate to the applicable task or system.

A critical aspect of an efficient and well-run workshop is the ability to give clear, logical instructions and to receive instructions. Usually, instructions should contain information about who, what, when, where, and why, and direction on how a task should be completed. What is the job that needs to be done? Who should do it? When should the job be done? Apart from knowing what information we should include in our instructions, we should also know how to present them.

When receiving instructions, we should make sure we can understand and follow the instructions successfully. For example, the instruction "Use the tire machine to mount a set of four tires" indicates what to do. Asking follow-up questions such as, "White lettering or sidewalls out?" "Install new valve stems?" or "Install them back on the vehicle once mounted?" helps ensure we understood correctly. Such questions may not be needed every time an instruction is given, but by clarifying, the quality of work will be closer to the person's expectations and will save time in the long run.

Communication in a Team

Being part of a team can make working an enjoyable experience or a horrible experience, depending on the team. In large part, the ability of each team member to communicate effectively will determine the success of the team. A high-performing team can accomplish much. As the saying goes, the sum is greater than its parts. We can achieve more when we effectively work together. Being part of a team allows us to:

- Learn new things from other team members
- Share ideas, knowledge, and resources
- Complement each other's strengths and weaknesses
- Feel a sense of belonging

A poorly functioning team spends a lot of time and energy bickering and blaming, and not enough time and energy being productive. Transitioning from a poorly functioning team to a high-performing team requires commitment to the team along with self-discipline. When all team members are committed to a set of common goals, they can contribute in positive ways to the success of the team.

Developing such a team requires good leadership skills as well as good followership skills. Good leadership skills involve setting a clear vision of the goals, empowering each team member to contribute his or her best efforts, and recognizing each team member's strengths and weaknesses. Good leadership also provides training or mentoring to address any weaknesses in the team. Followership is just as important as leadership. Not much would get done if everyone were a leader. Good followership skills involve being fully engaged in the team and its goals, stepping in and performing the work that needs to be done, participating fully in all decision making, and giving honest feedback.

We need to be committed to the team and team goals to make teamwork successful. Each team member should have a defined role and responsibilities that go with that role. Each member is then able to rely on the others to do their part. Think of a team as a chain; one broken link can break the whole chain. A good team player is someone who commits to being a part of that team and contributes to its success by fulfilling his or her role.

> **TECHNICIAN TIP**
>
> To be able to fulfill the team commitment, we need to know what our roles and responsibilities are and what is expected of us. Leaders help facilitate that. Good communication is then required for the team to come together and work efficiently.

Appearance and Environment

Our appearance is the image we present of ourselves to the public. All aspects of our physical appearance, including our clothes, jewelry, hairstyle, posture, and outward demeanor, culminate to create the first impression made in any encounter. That first impression often informs the judgment others make about us, which in turn affects the level of respect and trust you achieve. It is much harder to convey your message effectively if your audience is distracted by some aspect of your appearance or does not take you seriously. When working in a professional environment, always do your best to look professional. Remember that while you are at work, you embody the image of your company. Shorts, improper footwear, or untucked or filthy clothes can all send negative signals to a customer. A customer will be much more willing to have his or her vehicle serviced by someone who looks well put together than someone who does not **FIGURE 9-2**.

FIGURE 9-2 When working in a professional environment, always do your best to look professional.

The surrounding environment is also worth consideration, as it can affect the outcome of our communication. A disorganized, cluttered, and dirty area leaves a negative impression with most customers, leading them to believe that you don't care about appearances or quality. Look around you and evaluate the housekeeping. Is it clean, organized, and inviting? Or is it neglected, dirty, and gross? A little housekeeping goes a long way toward making customers feel comfortable. You will also want to avoid distractions such as excessive background noise, a blaring radio, or inappropriate coworker conversations. Interruptions by both coworkers and phone calls can hinder communication. Whenever it is in your power to do so, work to keep these distractions at a minimum.

Be aware of dangers around you as well. While most insurance policies prohibit customers in the work area, there may be occasional times when they need to see a particular issue. If you have to take customers into the shop, always escort them, and be sure to keep them safe. Do they need safety glasses on? Escort them back out of the shop as soon as possible and continue the conversation in the customer write-up area.

Time and Space

We know that in the work environment, time is money. This is especially true in most repair shop environments, where every minute is costing somebody something—the customer, the shop owner, and/or the technician. Punctuality is an important nonverbal message in a business environment. When you are punctual, you demonstrate a good work attitude and professionalism. Punctual means showing up on time (typically 5–10 minutes early to get ready to start work at the appointed time). If you have an unexpected delay, such as finding a flat tire when you get into your car to go to work, make sure you call your supervisor and let him or her know what happened and when you will be in. The same applies if you need to call in sick; do so as soon as you can so that other arrangements can be made.

Punctuality also means you will complete the job when you say you will. If you tell a customer his vehicle will be finished at 3:00, you should plan on finishing it prior to that just in case something goes wrong. Occasionally there will be unforeseen events that keep you from completing a job on time, but those should be rare exceptions. If there is a delay, then you need to communicate that to your customers as quickly as possible so that they can make other arrangements.

Lastly, you should be giving a full measure of work for the time you are being paid. Routinely texting your friends or taking personal calls during work hours is stealing from your employer. Use your work time efficiently, just as you would want your own employees to do.

When we say that space is a part of nonverbal language, we are referring to the physical space between ourselves and the people with whom we are communicating, commonly known as "personal space" (generally 3 feet). How we use personal space depends on how we feel about others; it is also a consideration for another person's comfort level. Familiarity, gender, status, and culture will determine the use of our personal space. Be aware of space as a nonverbal message and adjust accordingly.

▶ Customer Service

Good customer service is vital in today's competitive business environment. The quality of our customer service influences people to choose us over our competitors; good service makes people feel good about continuing to buy our products or services, which is how the business gets the money to pay your wages. So customer service has a direct impact on the ability of employers to hire employees, provide wages, and offer promotions. In fact, vehicle manufacturers place great importance on the customer satisfaction index (CSI) rating at their dealerships. The CSI rating is gathered from virtually all of the customers who have service work completed. The CSI rating is reported each month and used to evaluate individual technicians and the entire service facility. If the CSI rating is high, bonuses can be paid to everyone who contributed to that success. If the CSI rating slips, bonuses can be withheld, and new processes can be implemented to help restore the CSI rating.

To be able to provide good customer service, we must first understand who our customers are and then identify their needs. Internal customers, such as parts suppliers, are as important as external customers. By helping our coworkers with their jobs, it will ultimately help our external customers and our organization. It is helpful to remember that it is almost always external customers who bring resources into your organization when they trade their money for your service or product.

Being focused on customer service means you are fully engaged in providing the highest level of service that you can. This includes clear, friendly communication to help prevent misunderstandings and helping to establish achievable expectations **FIGURE 9-3**. It also means simple things like not getting grease on the vehicle's steering wheel, upholstery, or paint. And it means taking extra steps such as washing the vehicle when the work is completed or vacuuming it out so it is cleaner than when you started working on it. Keep in mind, one of the most important parts of customer service is repairing the vehicle correctly the first time. This goes a long way toward maintaining customer satisfaction.

Identifying Our Customers' Needs

Applied | **Communication**

AC-25: Notes: The technician makes notes regarding symptoms, possible causes, and other data that will aid in diagnosing and solving the problem.
AC-36: Information Requests: The technician requests specific symptom information from the customer and discusses solutions with supervisors and associates.

Different customers have different needs. The same customer may have different needs at different times.

FIGURE 9-3 Focus on customer service and communicate clearly.

In most cases, we can divide our customers into three categories: those who are more concerned about getting things right; those who want to get things done; and those who just want to get along with people. Each of these customers is motivated by different factors. The person who wants the job done right will usually not be interested in lesser quality parts and will want you to take the time to make sure the job isn't rushed. If the diagnosis was rushed and was incorrect, this person will likely not be happy. People who are most interested getting things done will probably be very keen to have the repairs finished on schedule. If the vehicle is not finished on schedule, this person will likely not be happy. For the person who just wants to get along with people, it will be important that a level of trust is maintained. If trust is broken, it will be hard to regain. We have to identify what our customers' needs are, so we can serve them properly.

If you are the one in charge of questioning the customer about symptoms, be sure to get specific information from the customer about what happens, when it happens, and how often it happens. Take notes that will help to diagnose the problem. Then be sure that when relaying this information to someone else, the other person understands the symptoms with the same detail in which you do. For example, a customer is concerned about a particular noise in his vehicle. If the noise doesn't happen all the time, then we would ask when the noise happens or under what conditions the noise happens. We may need to prompt the customer with follow-up questions like, "Does it happen when it is cold or hot, or when going around a corner or over bumps, or when braking or accelerating?" We may need to ask where he thinks the noise is coming from. Of course, if the noise can be reproduced, we may need to drive or ride with the customer so that he can identify the noise for us.

▶ Effective Reading

Every day we are faced with interpreting service information, emails, voicemails, and work orders with customer concerns. Understanding these messages without the verbal and nonverbal clues that come with face-to-face communication can be more difficult.

Reading Comprehension

Technicians are required to read a lot of information, including repair orders, service information, technical service bulletins (TSBs), and training materials. Many of these reading materials can be written at high grade levels. For example, many service manuals and TSBs are written at grade level 14 and higher. Technicians need

---

Applied	Communication

AC-1: Reading: The technician adapts a reading strategy for all written materials (e.g., customer's notes, service information, and computer/data readouts) to help identify the solution to the problem.

AC-3: Abbreviations/Acronyms: The technician identifies and uses written abbreviations and acronyms in diagnosing and solving problems.

AC-6: Charts/Tables/Graphs: The technician consults charts, tables, and graphs to determine the manufacturer's specifications to identify out-of-tolerance system components.

AC-7: Sequence: The technician consults service information to determine the appropriate sequence of procedures required for solving a specific problem.

AC-13: Skimming/Scanning: The technician reviews service information to identify problems and applies that information to appropriate repair procedures.

---

to be proficient readers to be able to comprehend this information. Before we start reading, we need to know the purpose of the particular material and what we intend to do with the information once we understand it. In reading, the objective may be to:

- Access information quickly, such as a particular specification
- Understand the information, such as how to perform a particular series of tests on a system you are diagnosing
- Remember the information, such as learning about new technology that a manufacturer is introducing to its vehicles, how it works, and what kind of tests are used during diagnosis

Once we know our reading purpose, we can choose the suitable reading method, which can be selective, comprehending, or absorbing. *Selective* reading is reading only the parts we need to know. This method is useful when looking for a particular piece of information. The quickest way to use selective reading is to read through the table of contents, introduction, conclusion, headings, and index until we find what we are looking for. When we use *comprehending* reading, we need to interpret and understand the information. Understanding what is being communicated requires careful attention to the structure of the sentences and paragraphs. To use an *absorbing* reading method, we need to:

- Interpret and understand the information
- Absorb it into our memory
- Review the information regularly

When we talk about reading, we are not concerned only about how fast we can read but also how well we understand and retain what we have read. Unfortunately, the faster we try to read, the less we are likely to concentrate on the meaning, so these two objectives (speed and comprehension) work against each other. Reading is about practice, and the more we practice, the faster, more efficiently, and more accurately we can read.

All of these reading strategies can be used when researching a particular problem with a vehicle. For example, if you have a vehicle that is hard to start only when it is cold outside, you might first check the service information to see if there are any related TSBs. A TSB is released when there are many of the same vehicles having the same symptoms and causes, so you can quickly skim through hundreds of TSBs looking for specific symptoms. When one is found, read it and interpret the information. Then if the TSB addressing the fault is found, absorb the information presented, including the symptoms, cause, test procedures, and corrective actions, into your memory.

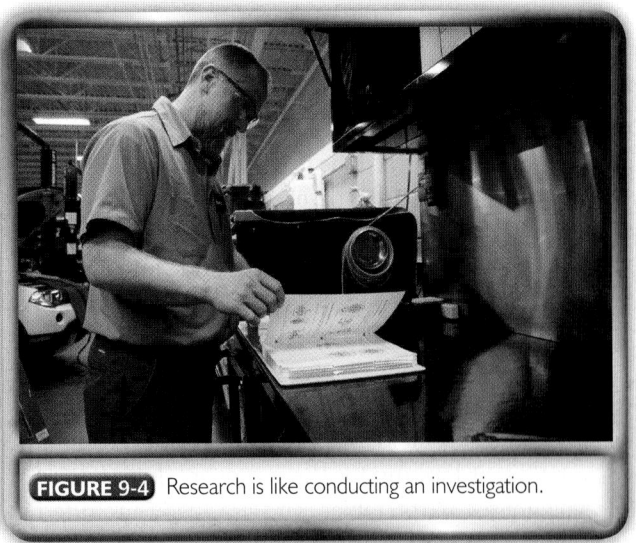

FIGURE 9-4 Research is like conducting an investigation.

> ### TECHNICIAN TIP
>
> Charts, tables, and graphs help you to find information in a timely manner. An example would be torque specifications listed in an easy-to-use format. This information is usually presented as a chart showing the component and the required torque, usually listed in newton-meters (Nm) as well as foot-pounds (ft-lb).

> ### TECHNICIAN TIP
>
> The Society of Automotive Engineers (SAE) has a well-known list of J1930 terms, which are abbreviations used by the automotive manufacturers. In addition, each manufacturer may have additional abbreviations that differ from the SAE terms. For example, the term GEN (generator) is used by the SAE, and the term ALT (alternator) is used by several automotive manufacturers.

Researching and Using Information Sources

Technicians spend a lot of time researching information **FIGURE 9-4**. This could be looking for a specification needed to perform a specific step in a task, or it could be researching how a manufacturer designed the system to operate in order to determine if it is operating correctly or not. In some cases, research is needed to see what work has been performed on the vehicle in previous shop visits so you will know what has and hasn't been performed previously.

Applied | Communication

AC-8: Dictionary: The technician refers to a dictionary to check spelling and define unfamiliar terms.

AC-9: Text Resources: The technician uses glossaries, indexes, database menus, and tables of contents to gather the information needed for diagnosis and repair.

AC-10: Database: The technician uses databases to obtain service information.

AC-11: Operator's Manual: The technician comprehends and applies information from accompanying manuals in order to use and maintain automotive tools and equipment.

AC-12: Service (Shop) Manual: The technician uses service information in both database and print formats to identify potential malfunctions.

AC-16: Study Habits/Methods: The technician uses proven research methods when consulting the manufacturer's service information (e.g., shop manuals, service bulletins, and computer databases).

AC-17: Prior Knowledge: The technician uses prior knowledge of similar problems to determine the specific cause(s) of problems.

AC-18: Cause/Effect Relationships: The technician comprehends and uses cause-and-effect relationships presented in service information problem-solving trees.

AC-19: Definitions: The technician applies industry definitions to solve problems in automotive components and systems.

Researching is like conducting an investigation. It can be done in three steps. When we first come across a problem, we have to define what the real issue is; that requires us to know how the system or part is meant to work. Then, we look for information or clues that can help us solve the problem. Finally, we put the pieces together to determine the best solution.

If using a book for reference, start at the table of contents to help find the section you are looking for. If you come across a word you do not understand, look up the definition. Most books will have a dictionary or glossary of terms toward the rear of the text. When using an online resource or database, try to familiarize yourself with the site's/database's navigation first. Take note of all drop-down menus, shortcut options, and search features.

While using these types of resources, you can use the skimming technique discussed earlier to find information quickly. Try skimming for key words. For example, if you are looking for information on oil specifications for a particular vehicle, you could just skim through the resource's text looking for the words *oil*, *lubrication*, or *specifications*. Charts, tables, and graphs, if included in the reference material, are usually easy to scan.

Most automotive resources will include diagnostic trouble charts. These provide a great way to narrow down faults without missing any steps in the procedure. Trouble trees also use the cause-and-effect approach to diagnosis. For example, if a fuse is blown, you can use the trouble tree to help you, step by step, find the cause of what made the fuse blow, rather than simply replace the fuse. As you gather symptoms and perform the diagnostic tests, you should take notes on your results to aid you in diagnosing and solving the problem as well as to complete the repair order when finished.

Always save the manuals for shop equipment and tools, and organize them in one place for future reference. Refer to these documents to maintain the equipment and tools. For example, most air tools require a drop or two of hydraulic oil every day, along with the use of a water separator in the air line.

When encountering problems with a new or unique system, it is often helpful to look up a definition or description of that system. This information can typically be found in either the front or the back of a book, or you may be able to search for it on computer-based information systems.

As you gain experience in the automotive industry, you will find that many vehicles have similar faults. Don't hesitate to use your prior knowledge to assist you in a new diagnostic situation. Just don't assume that all similar problems are caused by the same fault. You will want to test and verify your assumptions before suggesting a course of action to the customer.

Defining the Problem

Before you spend much time researching information, it is important that you define the problem. As you are defining the problem, make sure you narrow it down as accurately as possible. For example, if the car won't start, does it not crank over at all, or does it crank over but not start? Narrowing the problem down in this way will help you to filter out irrelevant information. If the problem is very broad, it is better to break it into smaller chunks and conduct a separate research activity on each one. Once the research is complete, you will have a better idea of how to proceed with determining the cause of the problem.

The next step is to look for the information that may help solve the problem. There is plenty of information readily available, but to determine how useful and reliable the information is, we need to know the sources of that information. We can obtain information from two sources: primary and secondary. The primary sources of information are people who have direct experience with the same or a similar problem. We can obtain information by interviewing those primary sources directly. However, information from primary sources can be subjective. Therefore, it is not always reliable. Information from secondary sources, or secondhand information, is compiled from a variety of sources. It is usually more reliable since it is more generic and objective.

This secondhand information is available in various formats, including print, audiovisual, and computerized **FIGURE 9-5**. We can divide this information into different content categories, including:

- Vehicle service information
- Automotive educational sources
- Troubleshooting

Vehicle Information

The first place to look for information about a vehicle is in the shop. Computer databases, shop manuals, aftermarket

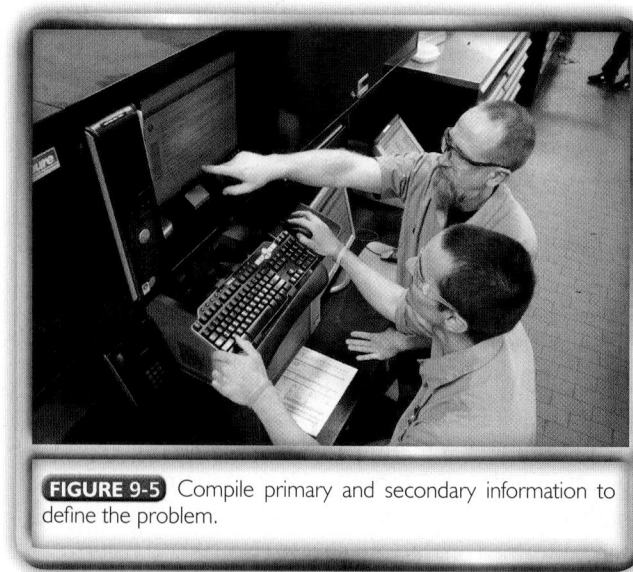

FIGURE 9-5 Compile primary and secondary information to define the problem.

manuals, and owner manuals are good resources for basic service information, including vehicle systems and how to operate them, the locations of major components and lifting points, and vehicle care and maintenance information.

Manufacturers usually provide training videos covering specific information about a vehicle of a particular make and model. Similarly, aftermarket and components suppliers will provide specific information about their products. This information is also available from their DVDs and websites.

The manufacturer's service information will guide the technician in the correct sequence of procedures to correct a given problem. The basic idea is to check the simple things first. In most cases, this will involve a visual inspection for obvious issues such as a vacuum line or electrical connector that is loose or disconnected. If no problem is found, then the technician will go to the next step in the service procedure, which will likely involve test equipment. The service information will continue to guide the technician in other steps as necessary.

Educational Sources

Publishers provide extensive materials covering the basic theory of operation of automotive systems and components. These materials come in a variety of forms. Textbooks and workbooks come as paper-based materials. Then there are computer-based materials, which provide more options for interactivity and visual engagement of the student. While there is free information available, most of these sources require a subscription to enroll in their courses.

Technical Assistance Services

For troubleshooting, there is help available on the phone and on the Internet. To use either resource, you must subscribe as a member, which normally involves paying a fee. Technical assistance hotlines put you in contact with professionals who can assist you in diagnosing a particularly difficult problem over the phone. The technical assistant has access to a variety of technical service information. Some of this information is gathered while helping other technicians with their issues. Thus, a large database of information can be accumulated, which can save a technician a lot of time.

For free information, there are chat rooms and bulletin boards where questions can be posted to other technicians online, although there is no guarantee of the accuracy and availability of the resources. The websites of automotive hobbyists, enthusiasts, and car clubs are often good resources as well.

One very good online reference that is available only to professional automotive technicians is the International Automotive Technicians Network (www.iatn.net). This organization consists of over 75,000 active members, with more than 1.7 million years of combined experience, who share their knowledge with each other on over a dozen forums. They recently have begun granting free student accounts to students of member instructors. These free student accounts allow students to monitor the forums and learn from them, while not allowing the students to interact with the technicians.

TECHNICIAN TIP

If you are ever working on a vehicle and seem to have hit a dead end in diagnosis, don't be afraid to discuss the symptoms with other technicians or supervisors around you. Sometimes others have seen the same issue or have a bit more experience and will be able to help. Or maybe they will look at the problem from a slightly different perspective, which can give you something new to try.

▶ Effective Writing

Technicians need to document their findings, conclusions, and any repairs on the repair order. This requires an accurate, short, but complete summary of the work you completed. In fact, the shop and ultimately the technicians get paid based on the quality of the write-up of the repair order. If there is ever a problem in the future, such as a customer filing a lawsuit against the shop over the repair, the repair order becomes a legal document that will be used by the court to determine if the shop has any liability in the situation. Thus, if the repair order is poorly written, incomplete, or inaccurate, the shop will be much more likely to lose the court case, putting it at risk of having to pay thousands of dollars—or more in the case of an injury accident. So writing is one of the most important tasks a technician does on a daily basis.

Writing Business Correspondence

Writing for technicians generally involves completing a write-up of diagnosis and repair conclusions on repair orders and filling out parts requests. However, they may sometimes need to undertake a more formal business correspondence using complete paragraphs. As with any type of writing, first think about what you want to say and draft your message, then refine and finalize your message. Just as it is important to think before we speak, we also

AC-2: Information–Written: The technician can comprehend and apply the available written information needed to diagnose, analyze, and solve a problem.
AC-4: Information–Written: The technician evaluates the usefulness of available written information clearly and thoroughly when analyzing a problem.
AC-5: Information–Written: The technician makes logical inferences and recommendations based on information provided on the repair order.
AC-20: Summaries: The technician uses appropriate grammar and sentence structures when summarizing problems in reports.
AC-21: Sentences: The technician uses conventional sentence structure, spelling, capitalization, and punctuation when composing sentences for warranty reports.
AC-22: Writing: The technician adapts a writing strategy that is most appropriate for the intended audience (e.g., customers, supervisor, and fellow employees) when documenting repairs.
AC-24: Purpose: The technician adapts speaking and/or writing styles that are consistent with the purpose of the communication.
AC-26: Paragraphs: The technician composes complete paragraphs, with appropriate details, presenting accurate information regarding symptoms, diagnosis, and results when preparing warranty claims and work orders.
AC-27: Diction/Structure: The technician adapts diction and structure to the context of all verbal and written communication based on the audience, purpose, and specific situation.

need to think about what we want to say, and what we want to achieve, before we compose our written message. Using your notes, sketch out a short outline of major topics; this is a great place to start when writing. Then use the outline to assist you in the writing. Use complete sentences. Remember to carefully proofread your writing so that you catch and fix any spelling or grammatical errors. You should use spell-check, but don't rely on it to catch everything; spell-checkers can't tell you when you have used "two" and "to" incorrectly, or "there" and "their," or when you meant to use "they" and only typed "the"—to mention a few examples. Once you have completed the draft, it may be necessary to create a final version of the write-up.

When writing a business letter, after creating an outline of the main points, you must then organize and put them together. Here are a few tips:

- Structure your letter logically so readers can follow your flow of thoughts; check the content by reading it out loud.

- Use plain English when addressing a customer, avoiding complicated words or technical jargon. On the other hand, when addressing a manufacturer or warranty clerk, be very specific.
- Check your spelling and punctuation. This is easily done using spell-check or by looking up the term(s). Be aware that spell-check can misinterpret your words, so you need to double-check spelling corrections.
- Be courteous and empathize with the readers, especially when writing a complaint letter or delivering bad news.
- Be precise, direct, and to the point. Repetition or unnecessary words waste time and can confuse readers.

There is a simple but necessary format to follow when creating a business letter. The letter should have your company name and address at the top. Most business letterheads have these details preprinted. Next include the date, followed by the recipient's name and address. Usually, you should start a letter with a greeting like "Dear Sir or Madam," or when we know the receiver's name, "Dear Mr. Mortenson." "Re:" or "Reference" is followed by the subject or purpose of the letter. The next part is the content that you composed in your outline. A business letter usually concludes with a complimentary closing, such as "Sincerely." Finally, a letter needs to be signed and followed by the sender's typewritten name and position.

Completing a Repair Order

If you are writing up your findings, conclusions, and repairs performed on a repair order, one thing to remember is that the information needs to be concise, yet complete. This is a difficult skill to develop, but will improve with practice.

A work order should contain:

- The customer's concern: Describe the concern and how you verified the concern and any related issues found.
- The cause of the concern: Describe what specifically is the root cause of the concern.
- The action taken, or needed to be taken, to correct the concern: Describe specifically how the concern was, or could be, resolved.

These elements constitute what is called the three "Cs": Concern, Cause, and Correction. Remember that each of these sections needs to be written up as concisely yet completely as possible. For example:

Concern: The vehicle overheats within about 10 minutes of vehicle operation from a cold start, no matter whether it is hot or cold outside. Coolant is full and protected to –30°F. Started vehicle, monitored engine temperature with temp gun. Temperature exceeded specified 195°F thermostat opening temperature, and still not open at 205°F.

Cause: Thermostat faulty, not opening at specified temperature. Removed, no external damage noted.

Correction: Replaced thermostat with new OE thermostat. Retested, thermostat starts to open at 193°F, which is within specifications.

While in school, you will document tasks performed in the shop on forms referred to as job sheets or tasksheets. You can use these forms to develop your ability to accurately complete the 3 Cs. Doing so will prepare you for the repair orders you will complete when working out in the industry.

A repair order should also contain the customer's contact information, vehicle information (e.g., make/model/VIN), parts, prices, labor time, taxes, and any recommended service that is found while repairing the vehicle.

Completing a Shop Safety Inspection Form

Most shops should have a safety inspection form that needs to be completed on a regular basis, typically weekly or monthly, although some tasks may need to be performed daily. This form will guide you to visually inspect critical items in the shop such as automotive lifts, overhead doors, hydraulic equipment, pneumatic equipment, hoses and cords, fire extinguishers, and emergency exits. The importance of these inspections should not be taken lightly, as neglect of these items can cause safety issues and cause premature product failure. These pieces of equipment are used often and will require frequent inspection.

Safety inspection forms are also a way of keeping up on routine maintenance tasks, such as changing the oil or replacing the belt of an air compressor, refilling the tire machine automatic oiler, and draining any water traps in the compressed air system. If you are the person completing the inspection, make sure you are trained to evaluate the safety and condition of the items you are inspecting. Inspect the items carefully and thoroughly so you don't miss any issues.

Completing a Defective Equipment Report

One way to help ensure safety in the workshop is to inspect equipment regularly and arrange for repair or replacement whenever it does not meet safety standards.

Keeping equipment well maintained will help avoid equipment downtime to provide a safer work environment.

Whenever you come across any defective equipment, you should do the following:

- Tag the defective items and either place them in a secured area or secure them so no one else can use them by mistake.
- Complete a defective equipment report.
- Notify your supervisor.

Your immediate actions can help protect coworkers from accidents and injuries. If there is an accident resulting from defective equipment, you will need to complete both an accident report and a defective equipment report.

On the report, you will record the date when the defect was detected, the location of the defective equipment, the name of the equipment, the serial number (if possible), and a description of the defect and the action you have taken. Then sign your name as the reporter. Finally, notify your supervisor.

Completing an Accident Report

Safety is the most important issue in the workplace. We must make a conscious decision to work safely and act responsibly to protect others and ourselves. Unfortunately, accidents do happen. When one occurs, an accident report should be completed by those involved, both the victim and witnesses, if possible. The information in the report is used to protect both employees and employers. It protects the employer and employee against false claims. And it protects future employees by calling attention to a situation that caused an accident, so hopefully measures can be taken to prevent it in the future. To ensure that the information is accurate, the accident report should be completed as soon as practically possible while the facts of the accident are still fresh in everyone's memory.

A typical accident report includes the date and time when the accident happened, the location where the accident happened, the name of the person who was injured, the name of any witnesses, the details of the accident, any first aid treatment provided, and any medical assistance rendered. It is also important to note if the accident will be subject to, or covered by, any insurance claims. Finally, the form needs to be signed by the person reporting the accident and turned in to the supervisor.

Completing a Vehicle Inspection Form

We provide customers with a very beneficial service when we perform a thorough inspection of their vehicles. When performing an inspection, we need to check that all major components and systems are operational, secured, and safe in accordance with the vehicle manufacturer's recommendations. This means testing the operation of the electrical and mechanical systems, such as lights and brakes, and visual inspections of the components such as tires and glass.

An inspection form is a useful guide when conducting a vehicle inspection. By following the checklist, a technician can test all the components in a systematic way and ensure that they are operational or serviceable. It also becomes a record for the shop to bring a customer's attention to needed service, or in the event that a customer declines repairs, shows that the shop made the customer aware of them. Many shops use their own inspection form that lists every item tested, which are known as points. Depending on the number of points covered, the inspection may be called a 30-point inspection, a 72-point inspection, and so forth.

To complete the inspection form, you must inspect all the components and systems on the checklist, including:

- Fluids, belts, and hoses
- Steering and suspension system
- Brakes
- Drive line
- Fuel system
- Exhaust system
- Tires
- Lighting system
- Electrical system
- Visibility
- Seat belts
- General components

Once the inspection is completed, the results should be presented to the customer so he or she can decide if any repairs are to be made. This is where verbal communication comes back into play, as it is important to accurately communicate with the customer so he or she has a good understanding of what the vehicle needs, why it is important to have it repaired, and the consequences of not repairing it. All of this conversation should be based on trust and the relationship you have built with the customer during his or her experience with you and the shop. And as you can see, successful communication includes good verbal, nonverbal, listening, clarifying, writing, and presentation skills.

Lockout/Tagout

There are many dangers in the automotive repair facility that may need to be properly documented and tagged. One example could be a defective automotive lift. If a problem is noticed with a piece of equipment, the lockout/tagout procedure should be followed. Lockout/tagout

procedures have been developed to prevent avoidable and unnecessary workshop accidents. These procedures have many functions:

- The tag notifies other users that the tool or component is dangerous to use. Any equipment that is found to be faulty needs to be identified so that other users are not put at risk. Write the fault, the date, and your name on the tag. Attach the tag to the tool. Smaller equipment should also be tagged and placed in a location where it is not forgotten. Notify your supervisor so that repairs or a replacement can be arranged.
- If a machine is faulty, the lockout procedure is used. Most large workshop equipment is permanently wired to the electrical supply and usually will have an isolation switch that will disconnect the electrical power. A lockout tag should be placed on the isolation switch as well as the equipment. Turn the machine off at the power and master switches, attaching the lockout tag in a manner that prevents the switches from being turned on. Once again, notify your supervisor so repairs can be arranged.
- The lockout/tagout procedure is also used to notify other technicians that a vehicle is not drivable.

Your workshop will have a procedure for vehicle lockout/tagout. It may involve the technician filling out a "defective vehicle" label listing the nature of the defect, name of the technician, and date and time of the defect.

If you remove the vehicle keys, do not keep them in your pocket or on your workbench. Attach a label or tag to the keys that identify the vehicle they belong to and store them in a secure key organizer.

If a vehicle is going through a relearn process (i.e., the vehicle's computer communicating with another computer), it may be necessary to leave the ignition on for many hours. In this case, tag the vehicle with instructions to leave the ignition on; otherwise a passing technician may turn it off in an effort to be helpful. If a vital component has been removed for service, it may not be obvious to a casual observer, so it is necessary to tag the vehicle. The best place to tag the vehicle is in on the steering wheel or driver's window where others trying to operate the vehicle will see it. Also, remove the ignition key and store it in a safe place.

Ask your supervisor to demonstrate the lockout/tagout process used in your workshop and to show you the location of the key organizer.

To properly identify faulty equipment, follow the steps in **SKILL DRILL 9-1**:

1. Basic workshop tools that are broken or worn should be replaced. Make sure you tag the tool as

faulty or broken and do not use it until you buy a replacement. Then discard the tool.

2 Power tools that have been identified as faulty, due to failure of parts, should also be tagged and set aside. The tool can only be used again after an authorized agent has made the repair.

3 Isolation tags are also used on disabled vehicles or vehicles undergoing a repair. In this case, you will have to locate and complete the "Disabled Vehicle" warning notice. Write the license number of the vehicle and the nature of the defect. Write your name and then the date and time you completed the notice. Attach the notice to the steering wheel or driver's window.

4 Remove the keys and lock the vehicle, if appropriate. Attach a tag to the keys that identifies the vehicle they belong to. Store the keys in the key organizer and notify your supervisor.

In conclusion, communication is a critical component of a successful business and an efficient workplace. Often overlooked in our current digital world, where face-to-face contact is getting less and less common, it is increasingly important to familiarize yourself with a wide variety of communication skills. From listening to simply filling out an inspection report, using and practicing these skills can be a big determining factor in how far you can go and how much money you make in the automotive industry. And the good news is that it doesn't even require expensive tools!

Wrap-up

Ready for Review

▸ Communication includes listening, reading, writing, and speaking skills—soft skills that every good automotive technician needs to master over time.

▸ To empathize with someone is to attempt to see the situation from his or her point of view.

▸ Nonverbal feedback helps to emphasize our message. When listening, we can use it to provide listening feedback.

▸ Verbal feedback includes very simple signals that can enhance the conversation and let the person know you comprehend.

▸ A supporting statement can urge the speaker to elaborate on a particular topic.

▸ Speaking is often referred to as an art because there are so many facets involved in effectively communicating and/or information gathering.

▸ Speaking is a three-step process: think about the message, present it, and check that it was understood.

▸ When encountering an upset customer, empathize, de-escalate, do not argue, and stay calm.

▸ There are three types of questions: open, closed, and yes/no.

▸ A critical aspect of an efficient and well-run workshop is the ability to give clear, logical instruction and to receive instruction.

▸ Your appearance makes the first impression and informs others' judgment of who you are.

▸ In the work environment, time is money. Always strive to be on time, ready to do your part by being present, both physically and mentally.

▸ Good customer service is vital in today's competitive business environment.

▸ Every day we are faced with interpreting service information, emails, voicemails, and work orders with customer concerns.

▸ Researching is an important part of troubleshooting a vehicle. First define the problem, then gather clues, and then put all the pieces together to get the conclusion.

▸ When a technician is writing a repair order, the three Cs need to be included: concern, cause, and correction. The customer and vehicle information should also be included.

Key Terms

supporting statement A statement that urges the speaker to elaborate on a particular topic.

validating statement A statement that shows common interest in the topic being discussed.

ASE-Type Questions

1. Tech A says that repair orders are legal documents so they need to be filled out accurately and carefully. Tech B says that ensuring the repair order is well written, clear, and concise promotes a professional reputation. Who is correct?
   a. Tech A
   b. Tech B
   c. Both A and B
   d. Neither A nor B

2. Tech A says that you shouldn't waste time inspecting a vehicle in for a repair unless the customer requests it. Tech B says that performing an inspection in addition to a repair can lead to discovery of additional concerns. Who is correct?
   a. Tech A
   b. Tech B
   c. Both A and B
   d. Neither A nor B

3. Tech A says that the proper way to listen to a customer is to maintain eye contact with the customer in between taking notes. Tech B says that eye contact distracts you from taking good notes. Who is correct?
   a. Tech A
   b. Tech B
   c. Both A and B
   d. Neither A nor B

4. Tech A says it is best to quietly listen to the customer and refrain from asking questions as much as possible. Tech B says it is constructive to ask questions throughout the conversation to obtain more details. Who is correct?
   a. Tech A
   b. Tech B
   c. Both A and B
   d. Neither A nor B

5. Tech A says that maintaining an appearance of neatness is important as it conveys to the customer the idea of careful, professional technicians. Tech B says that a dirty and cluttered shop indicates that the shop gets a lot of quality work done. Who is correct?
   a. Tech A
   b. Tech B
   c. Both A and B
   d. Neither A nor B

6. Tech A says researching the service information is a waste of time. Tech B says that researching the service information saves time. Who is correct?
   a. Tech A
   b. Tech B
   c. Both A and B
   d. Neither A nor B

7. Tech A says that an example of an open question is: "What are the conditions like when your A/C is not working?" Tech B says that an example of an open question is: "Does your A/C work at all?" Who is correct?
   a. Tech A
   b. Tech B
   c. Both A and B
   d. Neither A nor B

8. Tech A says that one customer who has a bad experience stemming from miscommunication and a misdiagnosed repair due to a technician's failure to listen has more of an effect on the repair shop than several good and happy customers. Tech B says that it is only one customer, and since the happy ones paid their bills, all is well. Who is correct?
   a. Tech A
   b. Tech B
   c. Both A and B
   d. Neither A nor B

9. Tech A says that it is primarily the job of the service writer to be customer-oriented and learn listening skills. Tech B says that customer service is the responsibility of all service employees to achieve the goal of customer satisfaction. Who is correct?
   a. Tech A
   b. Tech B
   c. Both A and B
   d. Neither A nor B

10. Tech A says that the 3 Cs are the "customer, complaint, and concern." Tech B says that the 3 Cs are "concern, cause, and correction." Who is correct?
   a. Tech A
   b. Tech B
   c. Both A and B
   d. Neither A nor B

SECTION II

Engine Repair

CHAPTER 10

Engine Mechanical Testing

Knowledge Objectives

After reading this chapter, you will be able to:
1. Explain the basic principles of engine mechanical testing. (pp 262–264)
2. List the tools required for engine testing. (pp 262–264)
3. Describe the various types and causes of fluid leaks in engines. (pp 264–265)
4. List the factors involved in a cranking sound diagnosis. (p 267)
5. Explain how vacuum testing can be used to determine the engine's general condition. (pp 268–269)
6. Describe a cylinder power balance test. (pp 270–271)
7. List the factors involved in cranking and running compression tests. (p 272)
8. Describe the principles of the cranking compression test. (p 272)
9. Describe the principles of the running compression test. (p 272)
10. Explain the factors involved in a cylinder leakage test. (p 276)
11. Describe the variety of noises and vibrations that a running engine creates. (p 278)
12. Describe how consumption of oil or coolant not located due to visual leaks may be determined by the color of the exhaust. (p 278)

Skills Objectives

After reading this chapter, you will be able to:
1. Perform a fluid leak inspection by looking under the hood. (pp 265–266)
2. Perform a fluid leak inspection by looking under the vehicle. (pp 266–267)
3. Perform a cranking sound diagnosis. (p 268)
4. Test engine vacuum using a vacuum gauge. (p 269)
5. Test engine vacuum using a pressure transducer and lab scope. (pp 269–270)
6. Perform a cylinder power balance test. (pp 271–272)
7. Perform a cranking compression test. (pp 272–274)
8. Perform a running compression test. (pp 274–275)
9. Perform a cylinder leakage test. (pp 276–278)

Introduction

For an engine to operate efficiently and effectively, the mechanical condition of the engine must be in good working order. The pistons, piston rings, cylinder walls, head gasket, and valves must seal properly. If they do not, then the engine will not operate correctly and all of the tuning in the world will not be able to fix it. So assessing the condition of the engine is a critical step in the diagnostic process before tune-up parts are replaced. There are few things more dreaded than having to tell a customer that the $300 tune-up you just performed did not resolve the vehicle's misfiring problem caused by a burned valve and that the vehicle really needs a $1500 valve job, or a $4000 engine replacement. First, the customer will not be happy that the vehicle is not fixed. Second, the repair will now cost substantially more money than the customer expected. Third, the customer now has very good reason to doubt your competence and wonder if you are correct now, when you were wrong earlier. This is a no-win situation, but it can be avoided by always diagnosing the problem instead of throwing parts at it.

Engine mechanical testing is also performed to diagnose more accurately what major engine work is needed, such as replacing a head gasket, rebuilding of the cylinder heads, or performing a full engine replacement. Understanding exactly what is wrong will allow you to better advise the customer on the appropriate repairs. It will also help you build credibility with your customers by fully understanding the situation and clearly communicating it to the customers in a professional manner. This chapter will help you learn the skills and procedures for performing engine mechanical tests.

Engine Mechanical Testing

Engine mechanical testing uses a series of tests to assess the mechanical condition of the engine. The tests start off broad and narrow down as each test is performed. This process will first help you to identify the location of the fault and then the cause of the fault. Having a good understanding of engine theory will help you evaluate the results of each test and provide you the information needed to know what path to follow after each step.

Mechanical testing starts with a good visual inspection. A visual inspection of the engine assembly for leaks will affirm the ability of the seals and gaskets to contain each of the engine's fluids. Starting the engine and listening to its operation can indicate a host of problems, from loose belts to worn main bearings. It can also reveal if the engine is misfiring and how steady the misfire is. After a good inspection, it is time to pull out the tools and equipment to take a deeper look at the mechanical condition of the engine.

Testing Tools

Although some seasoned mechanics have been known to use bubble gum and a bubble gum wrapper to diagnose a burned valve (see the Technician Tip on page 264), a

You are the Automotive Technician

A customer comes into the dealership complaining that her vehicle is not running as smoothly as before and the check engine light is flashing, which indicates a potentially catalyst damaging fault. As an experienced, certified technician, you explain to the customer that she did the right thing by bringing in the vehicle for diagnosis. First, you locate the customer's vehicle history and write up a repair order including the customers concerns. Second, you use a scan tool to retrieve the DTCs and find a P0304-cylinder 4 misfire detected code. Third, you hold the throttle to the floor with the ignition switch in the off position; and then crank the engine over. The engine exhibits an uneven cranking sound indicating a compression related fault. Next, you research the technical service bulletins (TSBs) and find one that relates to this code and low compression condition. The TSB indicates possible soft camshaft lobes, which can wear down and not open the valve/s fully. To verify whether this is the case, the TSB directs you to perform a cranking compression test along with a running compression test on any misfiring cylinders. The TSB then lists the acceptable minimum pressures for each test.

1. Why did the engine have an uneven cranking sound?
2. What does the running compression test indicate?
3. How would you determine which cylinder is misfiring if the engine computer doesn't have that capability?

variety of tools and equipment are available today that allow technicians to fully assess the mechanical condition of modern engines. Each of the tools introduced here has a specific function and will be further described in the Skill Drills later in this chapter:

- Compression tester: A **compression tester** is used when a technician suspects a cylinder may have low compression. The compression tester measures the amount of compression pressure a cylinder can generate (**FIGURE 10-1**).
- Vacuum gauge: The **vacuum gauge** measures the amount of vacuum an engine can generate during various operating conditions (**FIGURE 10-2**).
- Pressure transducer and lab scope: The **pressure transducer** measures engine vacuum or pressure and displays it graphically on a lab scope. Because

it is very accurate, it creates a detailed trace on the lab scope, which can be compared to a known good trace and used to determine mechanical issues in the engine (**FIGURE 10-3**).

- Cylinder leakage tester: A **cylinder leakage tester** pumps air into the cylinder and measures the percentage of air that is leaking from the cylinder. The technician can determine where the pressurized air is leaking from the cylinder by looking, listening, or feeling (**FIGURE 10-4**).
- Scan tool: The scan tool communicates to the vehicle's computers through the **data link connector (DLC)**. It displays the readings from the various sensors; retrieves trouble codes, freeze-frame data, and system monitor data; and on some vehicles performs output tests such as a cylinder

FIGURE 10-1 A compression tester.

FIGURE 10-3 A pressure transducer and lab scope.

FIGURE 10-2 A vacuum gauge.

FIGURE 10-4 A cylinder leakage tester.

power balance test, or commands other output devices to operate **FIGURE 10-5**.

- Stethoscope—standard and electronic: A stethoscope is used by technicians to listen to unusual noises in the vehicle. Stethoscopes come in both standard and electronic **FIGURE 10-6**.

FIGURE 10-5 A scan tool.

FIGURE 10-6 A standard stethoscope and an electronic stethoscope.

So how is it that a mechanic could diagnose a burned valve with just a piece of bubble gum and its wrapper? Knowing that each power pulse pushes exhaust gases out of the exhaust pipe, there should be steady pressure pulses if all of the cylinders are operating correctly. Besides listening to the engine and hearing a misfire, the technician used the gum to attach the wrapper to the end of the exhaust pipe. Each pulse pushed the wrapper away from the opening of the pipe, and each misfire tended to pull it back. If the engine had a burnt exhaust valve, the negative pressure pulse was stronger than just a misfire because some of the exhaust gases were pulled back into the cylinder through the burned exhaust valve, creating more of a vacuum in the exhaust pipe. The wrapper was pulled into the exhaust pipe during the misfire in this case and blown back out during the next power pulse, resulting in a wrapper that was slapping the exhaust pipe.

Suspecting that the exhaust valve was burned, the mechanic would shut off the engine, disable the ignition system, crank the engine over, and hear the telltale uneven cranking sound of a cylinder with low compression. Taking the results of both tests, the mechanic would conclude that the engine had a burnt exhaust valve. Pulling the spark plug wires off one at a time with the engine running resulted in one cylinder not contributing to the engine idle revolutions per minute (rpm), so the mechanic knew the burnt valve was located in this cylinder.

The process is similar today but involves tools and equipment that measure the results and display them numerically or graphically to more accurately assess the mechanical condition of the engine.

Fluid Leaks

Inspecting the engine assembly for fluid leaks is a common task that technicians perform during any kind of routine maintenance or service. It is also common to inspect the vehicle for leaks when the customer complains about fluid spots left on his or her driveway or if the fluid levels need to be topped off more frequently than is considered normal. It is a good practice to inspect the engine assembly for leaks before performing any engine repairs so that leaks can be taken care of at the same time.

The color of the leaking fluid can give you a clue as to the source. Black fluid could be engine oil or gear lube, reddish-orange or green fluid could be anti-freeze, and red could be transmission or power steering fluid. The smell of the fluid can also provide a clue; fuel and brake fluid have very different scents. Remember that gravity will cause fluid to be pulled downward, so be sure to inspect all the way up to a place where there is no more fluid present. Also, be aware that air from the fan or wind created by the speed of the vehicle can push the fluid in the direction of the airflow.

There are several processes you may need to undertake to discover the origin of the fluid leak. The vehicle might need to be pressure washed or cleaned and reinspected for leaks. Sometimes adding a special fluorescent dye to the fluid will help locate the leak; the fluid becomes fluorescent when using a black light and can then be more easily located. If a coolant leak is suspected, it will be easier to locate the leak if you pressure test the cooling system using a cooling system pressure tester.

Inspecting the Engine Assembly for Fuel, Oil, Coolant, and Other Leaks

Most leaks can be identified and located by means of a thorough visual inspection. Use of a good light and mirror will help you pinpoint the source of the leak. Sometimes, leaks can be seen from the top of the engine under the hood; others can be seen only from under the vehicle. And in some cases, covers or heat shields will need to be removed so that you can see the area that needs inspection. If you identify the source of the leak with the engine off, you may need to start the vehicle and perform the visual inspection with the engine running. If you do so, be extremely careful around the moving parts. Sometimes seals leak only when the engine is running. Sometimes seals leak only when the engine is off. You may have to try it both ways.

If you cannot locate the source of the leak visually, you may need to use a fluorescent dye. If this is the case, add a compatible dye to the fluid you suspect is leaking, then operate the vehicle for the time recommended by the dye manufacturer to circulate the dye through the system. If it is a small leak, you may need to have the customer drive the vehicle for a few days to help make the leak show up. Once the dye has had a chance to circulate, inspect the engine assembly for leaks using the recommended light for the dye you are using. In some cases, you are required to wear special glasses to enhance the fluorescence of the dye.

To perform a fluid leak inspection by looking under the hood, follow the steps in **SKILL DRILL 10-1**:

1. Raise the hood and make sure it is secure.
2. Check for any coolant leaks or seepage, starting at the radiator. Check the radiator hoses, heater hoses, water pump, heater control valve, and any coolant lines. (**Photo 1**)

Applied Science

AS-34: Ultraviolet: The technician can demonstrate an understanding of why dyes are added to lubricants fluoresce in ultraviolet light.

An ultraviolet dye leak detection kit can be one of the technician's most valuable tools for locating the source of a fluid leak. In the case of an engine oil leak, a special dye will be added to the engine oil. The engine will be started in order to circulate the dye. An ultraviolet light will be used to search for the source of the leak as evidenced by a fluorescent yellow dye. In some cases, the detection kit may contain a special pair of glasses to assist the operator in finding the leak.

The basic scientific principle of how this works is based upon the electromagnetic spectrum. Light travels in waves called electromagnetic waves. The electromagnetic spectrum covers a wide range of components such as gamma rays, X-rays, visible light, ultraviolet light, infrared rays and radio waves. Visible light is generally considered to be in the middle of the electromagnetic spectrum. There are many different types of electromagnetic waves that cannot be seen with the human eye. By the use of an ultraviolet light, we are able to see another part of the electromagnetic spectrum. The use of special dyes enhances our ability to find fluid leaks under the ultraviolet light source. The ultraviolet dye leak detection kit is an excellent tool for troubleshooting difficult to find leaks.

Applied Science

AS-35: Ultraviolet: The technician can demonstrate a process for determining the source of leakage using ultraviolet light.

A vehicle is in the shop due to an engine oil leak. This is the third repair attempt to solve the customer's concern. On two previous occasions, a technician had replaced the oil pan gasket. The technician was convinced that the engine oil pan gasket was the source of the leak; however, after a short period of time, the owner brought the vehicle back to the shop.

On this third repair attempt, the service manager suggested the use of an ultraviolet dye leak detection kit be used. A special dye was added to the engine lubricating oil. After running the engine for 10 minutes, the technician used an ultraviolet light to search for the leak.

After checking the engine over carefully with the ultraviolet light, the technician discovered that a slight crack in the oil pressure sending unit was the actual source of the leak. The oil was running down the block and collecting on the lip of the oil pan. The exact source of the leak was easily found as the dye showed up with a fluorescent yellow color under the ultraviolet light.

SKILL DRILL | 10-1 | Performing a Fluid Leak Inspection by Looking Under the Hood

1 Raise the hood and make sure it is secure. Check for any coolant leaks. Check the radiator, radiator hoses, heater hoses, water pump, heater control valve, and any coolant lines.

2 Check for engine oil leaks or seepage at the valve covers, intake manifold, cam seal, and so on.

3 Check for power steering leaks at the power steering pump, lines, and steering box or rack and pinion.

4 Check the master cylinder brake lines. Check the rear seal of the brake master cylinder, looking for signs of seepage between the master cylinder and the vacuum booster.

3 Check for any engine oil leaks or seepage at the valve covers, intake manifold, cam seal, and so on. **(Photo 2)**

4 Check for power steering leaks at the power steering pump, lines, and steering box or rack and pinion. **(Photo 3)**

5 Check the master cylinder brake lines. Check the rear seal of the brake master cylinder, looking for signs of seepage between the master cylinder and the vacuum booster. **(Photo 4)**

To perform a fluid leak inspection by looking under the vehicle, follow the steps in **SKILL DRILL 10-2** :

1 Raise the vehicle using a hoist, making sure the vehicle is being lifted on the proper lift points.

Raise it a few inches off the ground and make sure it is stable.

2 Check for any coolant seepage or leakage on each side of the block around the soft plugs. **(Photo 1)**

3 Inspect for engine oil leaks around the front main seal, oil pan, oil filter, oil pressure switch, and rear main seal. **(Photo 2)**

4 Inspect the sector shaft on the steering box if so equipped, and inspect the steering rack if equipped.

5 Inspect for transmission and transaxle leaks. **(Photo 3)**

6 Inspect the front and rear differentials if equipped. Determine any necessary actions. **(Photo 4)**

SKILL DRILL | 10-2 | Performing a Fluid Leak Inspection by Looking Under the Vehicle

1. Raise the vehicle using a hoist, making sure the vehicle is being lifted on the proper lift points. Check for any coolant seepage or leakage on each side of the block around the soft plugs.

2. Inspect for engine oil leaks around the front main seal, oil pan, oil filter, oil pressure switch, and rear main seal.

3. Inspect for transmission and transaxle leaks.

4. Inspect the front and rear differentials if equipped.

▶ Cranking Sound Diagnosis Overview

Engine noises can give a technician valuable insight into the condition of the engine. As you have learned, compression is one of the five critical requirements for each cylinder to operate properly. If the compression in one or more cylinders is too low, then the affected cylinders will not create as much power as cylinders with the proper amount of compression. If one or more cylinders have low compression, the engine will run rough, in many cases misleading the customer to request a "tune-up." Yet, performing a tune-up by replacing spark plugs and any other related tune-up items will not fix the low compression issue, causing the engine to still run poorly after the tune-up. This results in an unhappy customer as well as technician. To help avoid that situation, a cranking

sound diagnosis can identify whether the compression is similar across all of the cylinders. If compression is not similar across all cylinders, a tune-up will not fix the problem. If compression is similar across all cylinders, then compression is not likely causing the engine to run rough.

When you perform a cranking sound diagnosis, you should disable the engine so that it will not start. Then crank the engine over using the key and listen to the cranking sounds. It might take a few times to isolate any noises. The noise could be from a misaligned starter, the clunk of a spun crankshaft bearing noise, an uneven cranking sound that a low-compression cylinder gives, or a fast cranking sound from a no-compression condition that is due to bent valves caused by a broken timing belt. Each of these noises can give you a clue as to where the problem may lie.

AS-6: Operational: The technician can relate scientific terms to automotive system diagnosis, service, and repair.

The use of pressure gauges is a common procedure in most automotive repair facilities. When assigned to perform engine mechanical testing, the technician will work with pounds per square inch (psi) as related to engine compression gauge readings and cylinder leakage tests. A vehicle with low compression will produce a number of drivability problems including a rough idle condition. For a smooth running engine, cylinder compression should be as uniform as possible between cylinders. Psi refers to the primary units of measure for pressure in the United States. The metric unit is the Kilopascal or kPa. 10 psi is equal to approximately 68.95 kPa. Most manufacturers will supply both units as technical information. If necessary, the technician can consult conversion charts to obtain the U.S. standard or metric unit that is needed.

Diagnosing Cranking Sound

During engine cranking, the engine will make a rhythmic cranking sound if the compression is similar across the cylinders. As each piston comes up on compression, it loads down the starter motor and slows the cranking speed. If the compression of the engine is not the same at each cylinder, the engine will make an uneven sound. To train your ear to pick up the different compression sounds, take a vehicle with known good compression and disable the engine so that it will not start. To disable the engine, disable the fuel pump by pulling the fuel pump fuse or relay. You can also disable the ignition system (see service manual for proper procedure) so that it will crank but not start. You can then crank the engine and listen to the sounds it makes. Next perform the same task on a vehicle with known bad compression and listen to the difference in cranking sounds.

> **TECHNICIAN TIP**
>
> Many newer vehicles are programmed with a "clear flood" capability. This effectively shuts off the fuel injectors as long as the throttle is held to the floor before the ignition key is turned to the run or crank position. When the key is turned to crank (with the throttle still held down), the vehicle's power train control module (PCM) will shut off the fuel injectors. This allows the engine to crank without starting. If the engine starts, it means either that the vehicle is not equipped with clear flood mode or that fuel has leaked into the intake manifold and will need to be diagnosed. Using the clear flood mode is a quick way of performing a cranking sound diagnosis on these vehicles.

To perform a cranking sound diagnosis, follow the steps in **SKILL DRILL 10-3**:

1. Raise the hood and make sure it is secure.
2. Disable the engine by disabling the fuel pump or the ignition system. Refer to the service manual for proper procedures, or use the "clear flood" mode described above.
3. Crank the engine over using the key, and listen to the sound the engine makes while cranking. Determine any necessary actions.

Vacuum Testing

A vacuum gauge is used to determine the engine's general condition. The vacuum gauge reading shows the difference between outside atmospheric pressure and the amount of vacuum (manifold pressure) in the engine. The vacuum gauge is installed in a vacuum port on the intake manifold. Always select the largest and most centrally located vacuum port. This may require using a vacuum tee so that the vacuum gauge can be connected and, at the same time, vacuum can still be supplied to the existing component. The typical vacuum reading for a properly running engine at idle is a steady 17" to 21" of vacuum (57.6 to 71.1 kPa) **TABLE 10-1**. A low reading could relate to a problem with ignition or valve timing. A sharp oscillation back and forth in the needle or a dip in the gauge reading could relate to a problem such as a bad valve. A low reading at a constant 2500 rpm could indicate a restricted exhaust system.

TABLE 10-1: Chart of Vacuum Readings—Vacuum Gauge

Reading	Indication
17" to 21", steady needle at idle.	Good reading
Needle oscillates back and forth about 4" to 8".	Burned or constantly leaking valve
A low and steady reading.	Possible late valve timing or late ignition timing
Snap acceleration needle drops to zero and then only reads 20" to 23" of vacuum; should be much higher, around 27".	Possible worn rings
Good reading at idle. As engine speeds up to a steady 2500 rpm, the needle slowly goes down and may continue to drop.	Possible restricted exhaust system

FIGURE 10-7 Vacuum trace.

With the advent of lab scope diagnostics, many technicians are using a pressure transducer to measure the engine's manifold pressure and display it graphically on a lab scope. The pressure transducer is a very accurate measuring tool; when attached to a vacuum port and hooked up to a lab scope, it gives a pressure trace that shows the low pressure created by each piston's intake stroke **FIGURE 10-7**. If the ignition pattern for cylinder 1 is monitored on a separate trace, the vacuum pulses can be tied to specific cylinders. Technicians can view these traces and see how well each cylinder is functioning at producing and maintaining a vacuum.

> ## TECHNICIAN TIP
>
> A pressure transducer can be adapted to fit in the spark plug hole to create a pressure trace of running and cranking compression. It can also be used in the exhaust system to measure the exhaust pulses. Pressure transducers are used more and more commonly when diagnosing engine problems.

Testing Engine Vacuum Using a Vacuum Gauge

During an engine vacuum test, all vacuum gauges are calibrated at sea level and all instructions and readings are referenced to sea level. When testing above sea level, you will need to compensate. For instance, if the gauge reads 18" of vacuum at sea level, it would drop to 17" at 1000' above sea level.

The vacuum gauge reading shows the difference between outside atmospheric pressure and the amount of vacuum in the engine in a non-turbo or non-supercharged engine. The average inches of vacuum for a good running engine at idle is a steady 17" to 21" of vacuum. The average inches of vacuum at idle for a performance camshaft with a high lift and large overlap duration is around 15". The amount of vacuum an engine creates relies on the piston rings, valves, ignition timing, and fuel.

To test engine vacuum using a vacuum gauge, follow the steps in **SKILL DRILL 10-4**:

1. Connect the vacuum gauge to the intake manifold. You might have to use a vacuum tee.
2. Make sure the engine is at operating temperature. Start the engine, take a reading at idle, and record the reading.
3. Snap accelerate the engine by quickly opening and closing the throttle; record the highest vacuum reading attained.
4. Hold the throttle steady at 2500 rpm and record your reading.

Testing Engine Vacuum Using a Pressure Transducer

Using a pressure transducer and lab scope is a similar process to using a vacuum gauge, except it is much more accurate and allows you to look at the vacuum graphically. When paired with a second trace consisting of the ignition pattern for cylinder 1, any issues with the vacuum trace can be tied to a specific cylinder. By using a pressure transducer on a variety of vehicles with various issues, you will become familiar with the patterns of common faults.

To use a pressure transducer and lab scope for testing engine vacuum, follow the steps in **SKILL DRILL 10-5**:

1. Connect the pressure transducer to the intake manifold and the lab scope. You might have to use a vacuum tee. **(Photo 1)**
2. Connect the second channel of the lab scope to the ignition system so it can identify cylinder 1. **(Photo 2)**
3. Start the engine and let it idle. Adjust the lab scope so that the screen captures the vacuum pulses for all of the cylinders.
4. Observe the vacuum trace and compare it to known good readings. **(Photo 3)**
5. Snap accelerate the engine by opening and closing the throttle, and compare the trace to known good readings. **(Photo 4)**
6. Hold the throttle steady at 1200–1500 rpm and compare the trace to known good readings.
7. Hold the throttle steady at 2500 rpm and compare the trace to known good readings. **(Photo 5)**

SKILL DRILL | 10-5 | Testing Engine Vacuum Using a Pressure Transducer

1. Connect the pressure transducer to the intake manifold and the lab scope.

2. Connect the second channel of the lab scope to the ignition system so it can identify cylinder 1.

3. Start the engine and let it idle. Adjust the lab scope so that the screen captures the vacuum pulses for all of the cylinders. Observe the vacuum trace and compare it to known good readings.

4. Snap accelerate the engine by opening and closing the throttle, and compare the trace to known good readings.

5. Hold the throttle steady at (1200–1500 rpm) and compare the trace to known good readings. Then hold the throttle steady at 2500 rpm and compare the trace to known good readings.

▶ Cylinder Power Balance Test Overview

A cylinder power balance test (also called a power balance test for short) is used for two purposes. First, it identifies which cylinder(s) are not operating properly when the vacuum test indicates a mechanical issue or when the engine is not running smoothly. Second, it is used as a general indication of each cylinder's overall health. Every cylinder in the engine should contribute equally to the engine's power output. When a mechanical, electrical, or fuel problem occurs within an engine, the affected cylinders will not produce as much, if any, power when compared to the other cylinders. We can test to see how much each cylinder is contributing to the engine's output by disabling one cylinder at a time and measuring the rpm drop. Disabling a cylinder that is not operating correctly will not produce much, if any, rpm drop. Disabling a cylinder that is working properly, however, will produce a much larger rpm drop. The greater the difference in rpm drop, the greater the difference between each cylinder's ability to produce its share of the engine's power.

Many newer vehicles control the idle speed electronically through the PCM. In these vehicles if something loads the engine down, such as the air-conditioning compressor turning on, the PCM will allow more air and fuel into the engine so that the idle speed stays relatively the same. In the case of a manual power balance test, disabling one of the cylinders will not produce a drop in rpm because the PCM will compensate for it. In these cases, use the PCM's built-in power balance feature, if equipped. Alternatively, in some vehicles you can disconnect the electrical connector on the idle speed control system to prevent the PCM from changing the idle speed. Unfortunately, in some vehicles if you disconnect the connector on the idle speed control system, the engine will die. On these vehicles, you can usually perform the power balance test slightly above idle, since the PCM only controls engine speed at idle. Raising the rpm can be accomplished by wedging an appropriate tool between the throttle body and the throttle linkage or by having an assistant hold the throttle steady while you perform the test.

The purpose of the power balance test is to see whether the cylinders are creating equal amounts of power and, if not, to isolate the problem to a particular cylinder or cylinders. Once the problem is isolated, we can take the next step, which is to determine whether it is a mechanical issue related to compression or an ignition- or fuel-related issue.

Performing a Cylinder Power Balance Test

There are several ways that a power balance test can be performed. Knowing each of the options will allow you to choose the easiest one for the vehicle you are diagnosing. Which is easiest is determined by the capabilities of the PCM, the ease of accessing the required components, and the tools available. For many OBDII vehicles, you can identify which cylinders are misfiring by using a scan tool to access stored diagnostic trouble codes (DTCs) in the PCM. Or you can access mode 6 data, which will give you information on how prevalent misfires are on each cylinder. In some cases, you can also use the scan tool to command the PCM to perform an automatic power balance test and report the results right on the scan tool. On most newer vehicles, using the scan tool is by far the best method of performing a power balance test.

If the system is not set up to perform the test automatically, you will have to do it manually. You will need to determine whether to disable the ignition or the fuel to each individual cylinder. If the engine has port fuel injectors that are accessible, disconnecting the electrical connector from each injector one at a time will shut off the fuel to the cylinder. Shutting off the fuel to the cylinder is the preferred method since it stops injecting fuel in the cylinder. If the ignition system is disabled for a cylinder, the fuel will still be delivered but will not be burned in the cylinder. However, it will burn in the catalytic converter, which can cause it to overheat and possibly be damaged. Therefore, shutting down the fuel is preferable if it is an option on the engine you are working on.

If the engine has individual ignition coils on each spark plug, you can disconnect the primary electrical connector, which will shut off the spark to the spark plug. If the vehicle has coils that share cylinders (waste spark system), then you can place a 1" (25-mm) section of vacuum hose between each coil tower and spark plug wire. Then connect the alligator clip from a nonpowered test light to a good engine ground and touch the tip of the test light to each length of vacuum hose to short out each spark plug one at a time. If the vehicle is equipped with a distributor, disconnect one spark plug at a time from the distributor cap (it is good to use a test lead to ground the spark at the distributor cap terminal to prevent the spark from damaging the ignition module in the distributor), which shuts down the spark for the cylinder being tested.

To perform a cylinder power balance test, follow the steps in **SKILL DRILL 10-6**:

1. Visually inspect the engine to determine the best method to disable the cylinders. If this involves connecting a scan tool, installing vacuum lines on each coil, or removing spark plug wires, prepare the engine accordingly. If necessary, disable the idle control system.

2. Start the engine and allow it to idle. Record the idle rpm. **(Photo 1)**

3. Using the method chosen to disable cylinders, disable the first cylinder and record the rpm. (Do not leave the cylinder disabled for more than a few seconds.) **(Photo 2)**

4. Reactivate the cylinder and allow the engine to run for approximately 10 seconds to stabilize.

5. Repeat the steps on each of the cylinders and record your readings. Determine any necessary actions. **(Photo 3)**

SKILL DRILL | 10-6 | Performing a Cylinder Power Balance Test

1. Visually inspect the engine to determine the best method to disable the cylinders. If necessary, disable the idle control system. Start the engine and allow it to idle. Record the idle rpm.

2. Using the method chosen to disable cylinders, disable the first cylinder and record the rpm. (Do not leave the cylinder disabled for more than a few seconds.)

3. Reactivate the cylinder and allow the engine to run for 10 seconds to stabilize. Repeat the steps on each of the cylinders and record your readings. Determine any necessary action.

▶ Cranking and Running Compression Tests

In a cranking or a running compression test, a high-pressure hose is hand-threaded in the spark plug hole of the cylinder to be tested and then connected to the compression gauge. The engine needs to be cranked over or started, depending on the test that is being performed. The compression gauge reads the amount of pressure that the piston is producing by compressing the air in the cylinder. You should always check factory specifications before performing the test so that you know what the results should be.

Performing a Cranking Compression Test

During a cranking compression test, the engine is cranked over but is not started by the starter. As the piston moves up, it compresses the air in the cylinder. The engine should crank until at least five compression pulses are observed on the compression gauge to get an accurate reading. If the final reading is low, there could be a problem with the valves, rings, pistons, or head gasket.

The cranking compression test is performed when indications show a misfiring or dead cylinder that is not caused by an ignition or fuel problem. A compression test measures the air pressure as it is compressed in the cylinder. The cylinders should all measure within 10% to 15% of each other.

Applied | Math

AM-16: Charts/Tables/Graphs: The technician can construct a chart, table, or graph that depicts and compares a range of performance characteristics of various system operational conditions.

A typical diagnostic test would be checking the compression of an engine. In this scenario, we have a four cylinder engine that has the customer's concern of running rough at idle. A visual inspection did not reveal any problems that could easily be identified. A compression gauge will be used to measure the compression on each cylinder. The technician will record the information as the readings are taken from each cylinder and the results could be recorded on the following chart. By consulting the manufacturer's specifications, the technician will be able to determine if the compression is satisfactory or not.

Cylinder	Cranking Compression in PSI	Running Compression in PSI
Cylinder 1		
Cylinder 2		
Cylinder 3		
Cylinder 4		

For the compression test to be completely accurate, it is recommended that the engine be at operating temperature, all of the spark plugs be removed, the battery be fully charged, the throttle be held wide open, and at least five compression pulses be made on each cylinder (the same number of pulses for each cylinder). All of these conditions will help the engine create maximum compression and accurate readings. At the same time, if a technician suspects that only one or two cylinders have excessively low compression (due to failing the power balance test), then only the suspect spark plugs will be removed and a compression test made. If the compression is substantially low on that cylinder, then the engine has a compression problem and further testing of the cylinder will be required. If the compression is reasonably close to the specifications, then the compression is not causing the issue and there is likely a fuel or ignition fault causing the problem.

To perform a cranking compression test, follow the steps in **SKILL DRILL 10-7**:

1. Remove any spark plug wires or ignition coils connected directly to the spark plugs. **(Photo 1)**
2. Disable the ignition system by grounding the coil wire(s) or disconnecting the coil primary circuit(s). **(Photo 2)**
3. Disable the fuel injectors or remove the fuel pump fuse or relay. **(Photo 3)**
4. Remove all spark plugs. **(Photo 4)**

> ### TECHNICIAN TIP
>
> Another way to measure compression is with a relative compression test. This test uses an inductive ammeter connected to a lab scope to measure the current flow for the starter as the engine is being cranked. As each cylinder comes up on the compression stroke, the engine is harder to turn, so the starter works harder and the current flow is higher. If every cylinder has the same relative compression, then the current spikes will be similar. If a cylinder has low compression, then that current spike will be lower than the rest. This is a quick way of checking to see if there is a compression-related problem.

> ### TECHNICIAN TIP
>
> When performing a compression test, the final reading is not the only thing to observe. If the piston rings are sealing well, then the first compression pulse on the gauge should be at least half as much pressure as the final reading.
>
> When a low-compression cylinder is found, you should put a couple squirts of oil (about a tablespoon) into the spark plug hole, crank the engine a few turns, and recheck the compression. If the compression rises significantly, the problem is typically worn piston rings in that cylinder, as indicated by the higher compression due to the short-term sealing ability of the added oil. Worn piston rings are a substantial problem that typically requires rebuilding or replacement of the engine. If the oil did not make the compression rise, then the problem is likely to be either a leaky valve or head gasket or a hole in the piston. A cylinder leakage test can determine which.

SKILL DRILL   10-7   Performing a Cranking Compression Test

1. Remove any spark plug wires or ignition coils connected directly to the spark plugs.
2. Disable the ignition system by grounding the coil wire(s) or disconnecting the coil primary circuit(s).
3. Disable the injectors or remove the fuel pump fuse or relay.

SKILL DRILL | **10-7** | **Performing a Cranking Compression Test, continued**

4 Remove all spark plugs.

5 Connect the compression tester to the spark plug hole to be tested.

6 Hold the throttle down and crank the engine over so that the compression tester needle jumps at least five times. Record the first and last needle readings. Repeat this procedure on the other cylinders.

7 Perform a wet test on any cylinders with low compression. Determine any necessary action.

5 Screw in the proper fitting and hose from the compression tester (check the thread length and diameter for the proper fitting). If separate, connect the hose to the compression tester. (**Photo 5**)

6 Hold the throttle down and crank the engine over, making sure the compression tester needle jumps at least five compression pulses. Watch the first needle bump. Record the first and the final reading. Repeat the process with the same number of compression pulses for each cylinder. (**Photo 6**)

7 If any of the cylinders have low compression, perform a wet test by placing a couple of squirts of clean engine oil in the low cylinder, and retest the compression. If the compression pressure increases substantially, the piston rings are worn. If the compression doesn't change much, a valve, the head gasket, or top of the piston have a leak. Determine any necessary action. (**Photo 7**)

Performing a Running Compression Test

In a running compression test, the engine is running during the compression test. Unlike the cranking compression test, which checks the sealing capability of the cylinder, the running compression test checks the engine's ability to move air into and out of the cylinder.

This is referred to as the engine's ability to breathe. For example, if a camshaft lobe is badly worn, less air will be entering or exiting the cylinder, depending on which valve is affected. The running compression test helps a technician to evaluate this process.

The test is performed in two parts, idle and snap throttle. During idle, since the engine is running and the throttle is relatively closed, the compression pressure will be approximately half of the cranking compression pressure. The second part of the test is a snap throttle test. With the engine idling, the throttle is snapped open and then closed fairly quickly, which allows a big rush of air into the intake manifold. The idea is to not make the rpm change very much during the test. If the intake and exhaust system are operating correctly, then the compression tester needle will jump to about 80% of the cranking compression pressure. If the intake side of the system is restricted, then the reading will be lower than the 80% threshold. If there is a restriction on the exhaust side of the system, then the pressure will be substantially higher than the 80% threshold.

The running compression test is performed by leaving all of the spark plugs in the engine except for the one in the cylinder that you are testing. Most technicians leave the Schrader valve in the compression tester to hold pressure in the tester while performing the running compression test, although it can be hard

on the Schrader valves. Always have a couple of spares handy. Also know that compression tester Schrader valves use lighter-weight springs than tire Schrader valves, so do not interchange them. The compression tester needs to be installed in the cylinder to be tested and then the engine can be started. This test can detect flat cam lobes, broken valve springs or rocker arms, carboned-up valves, or restricted intake and exhaust passageways in general. To confirm your diagnosis, do a visual inspection of the suspect components.

To perform a running compression test, follow the steps in **SKILL DRILL 10-8** :

1. Remove the spark plug on the cylinder that you are testing, and ground the spark plug wire with a test lead. **(Photo 1)**

2. Install the proper hose and compression tester into the spark plug hole.

3. Start the engine, allow it to idle, press and release the bleed valve, and record the reading once the pressure stabilizes. **(Photo 2)**

4. Have your partner quickly snap the throttle open for about 1 second and then close it quickly. (Make sure the key can be turned off quickly if the throttle sticks.) Record the reading.

5. Repeat the process on the other cylinders. Determine any necessary action. **(Photo 3)**

SKILL DRILL | **10-8** | **Performing a Running Compression Test**

1. Remove the spark plug on the cylinder that you are testing and ground the spark plug wire.

2. Install the proper hose and compression tester into the spark plug hole. Start the engine, allow it to idle, press and release the bleed valve, and record the reading.

3. Have your partner quickly snap the throttle open for about 1 second and then quickly close it. (Make sure the key can be turned off quickly if the throttle sticks.) Record the reading. Repeat the process on the other cylinders. Determine any necessary action.

▶ Cylinder Leakage Test Overview

The cylinder leakage test is performed on a cylinder with low compression to determine the severity of the compression leak and where the leak is located. Compressed air is applied to the cylinder through a tester that is calibrated to show the amount of cylinder leakage as a percent of air entering the cylinder. An ideal reading is close to 0%. But since piston rings have a small gap between their ends to allow for expansion as the engine heats up, a cylinder will not be sealed 100%. There will almost always be at least a small amount of leakage past the piston ring gaps. Typically manufacturers will consider up to 20% cylinder leakage past the piston rings acceptable, but the smaller the leakage, the better. Although it is OK to have a small amount of leakage past the piston rings, it is not OK to have *any* leakage past one of the valves or the head gasket. Leaks at these places mean the engine likely has a major mechanical engine issue.

The point of this test is to measure how much air is leaking as well as to determine where it is leaking from. The gauge tells you the percentage of air leaking from the cylinder, so that is straightforward. Determining where the air is leaking from is a bit more challenging. Because there is always some air leaking past the piston rings, you will be able to hear some air leaking out of the oil fill hole when the oil fill cap is removed. If that is the only leak that you end up diagnosing, then the gauge will indicate if the leakage past the piston rings is excessive.

If an exhaust valve is burnt or warped, then you will hear leakage out of the exhaust pipe. If the intake valve is burnt or warped, then you will hear leakage out the air intake system. There should be no leakage past either of the valves, so any leak in the exhaust or intake is a bad leak. If the head gasket is blown, then you will either hear air coming out of an adjacent spark plug hole or see bubbles in the coolant when the radiator cap is removed.

Performing a Cylinder Leakage Test

There are a couple of critical steps needed to make sure the cylinder leakage test is accurate. First, the engine should be near operating temperature, which will ensure that oil has been circulated to the piston rings to help them seal. Next, it is helpful to loosen each of the spark plugs about one turn for the cylinders you will be testing and then run the engine at 1500 rpm for 10 to 15 seconds. This process helps blow out any chunks of carbon that were straddling the spark plug to cylinder head gap that break off when the spark plugs are removed. If you do not do this, it is possible for one of these chunks of carbon to get stuck between a valve and valve seat, holding the valve open slightly and producing a false reading.

Since the cylinder leakage test is usually only performed on a cylinder with low compression, you must remove only the spark plug for the cylinder you are testing and the spark plug for each of the cylinders next to that one. If the suspect cylinder is in the middle of the bank, then you will need to remove the spark plug on either side. If the suspect cylinder is at the end of the bank, then you will need to remove only the nearest spark plug. It also helps to remove the air cleaner assembly and radiator cap for listening purposes during the test.

Cylinder leakage is measured when the piston is on top dead center on the compression stroke. This means that you will have to turn the crankshaft to position each piston in this position before pressurizing the system. The challenge is that the piston, connecting rod, and crankshaft throw must be in near perfect alignment; otherwise the pressure on the piston from the cylinder leakage tester will push the piston down, which turns the crankshaft. If this happens, then the intake or exhaust valve will open, depending on which way the piston ends up turning the crankshaft.

The hardest part is getting the piston exactly on top dead center. There are two primary ways to do so. One is to screw the cylinder leakage tester into the spark plug hole and then slowly turn the engine over by hand while lightly floating your thumb over the end of the hose to feel pressure and vacuum. When you feel the transition from pressure to vacuum, turn the engine in the opposite

▶ TECHNICIAN TIP

There are a couple of ways that a technician can get in trouble when interpreting the results of a cylinder leakage test. First, if a valve is being held open due to a piece of carbon, or not enough valve lash, then the problem could be misdiagnosed. To verify a leaky valve, remove the valve cover and verify that the valve has the proper valve lash. Also try tapping the valve open with a soft hammer while watching the cylinder leakage gauge. If tapping on the valve stops the leakage, there was likely some carbon holding the valve slightly open. If the valve is being held open by the valve train, try adjusting the valve and retest the valve for leakage. You should know that a valve that had too little valve lash is likely to be burnt. The longer it was operated with too little clearance, the more likely it is burnt.

direction slightly and stop right as the pressure stops and before the vacuum begins. It takes experience to get the feel for this. The second way is to use a plastic straw that fits down the spark plug hole and that can be pushed up by the piston without damaging the cylinder or piston. Rotate the engine by hand until the piston is as high as it will go, as indicated by the plastic straw. While the piston is on top dead center, you will not know if it is on the top of the compression stroke or the exhaust stroke until you pressurize the cylinder (unless the engine is equipped with a distributor and you can see where the rotor is pointing). If it is wrong, turn the engine one complete revolution and try it again.

To perform a cylinder leakage test, follow the steps in **SKILL DRILL 10-9**:

1. Remove the spark plug of the low-compression cylinder and any adjacent spark plugs. Install the cylinder leakage tester adapter hose into the spark plug hole. **(Photo 1)**
2. Position the piston for the cylinder being tested at top dead center on the compression stroke. You can do this by making sure you feel air escaping the cylinder leakage hose when you are turning the crankshaft by hand. **(Photo 2)**
3. Connect the compressed air hose to the tester and adjust the tester so it reads zero. **(Photo 3)**

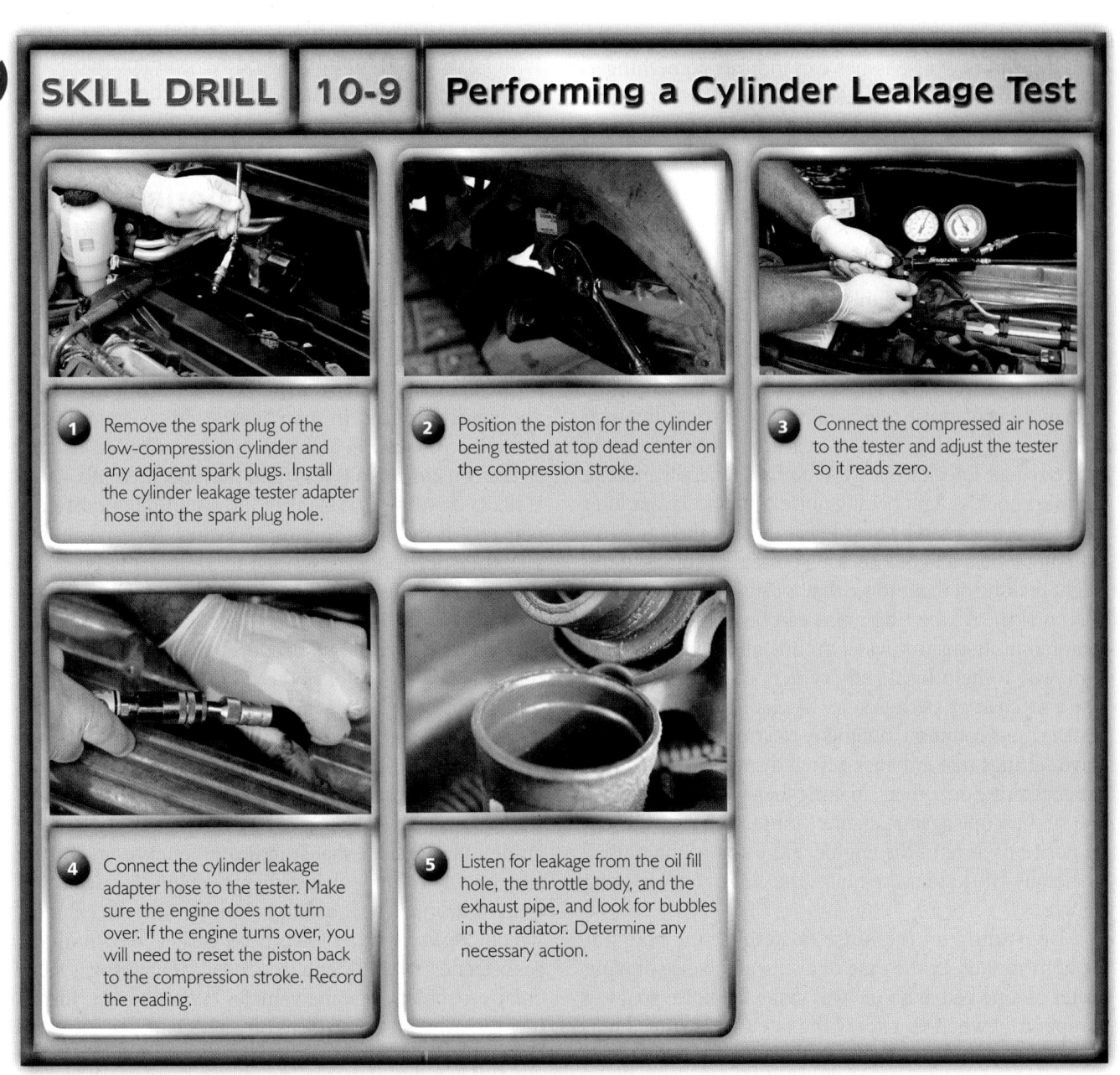

SKILL DRILL | 10-9 | Performing a Cylinder Leakage Test

1. Remove the spark plug of the low-compression cylinder and any adjacent spark plugs. Install the cylinder leakage tester adapter hose into the spark plug hole.

2. Position the piston for the cylinder being tested at top dead center on the compression stroke.

3. Connect the compressed air hose to the tester and adjust the tester so it reads zero.

4. Connect the cylinder leakage adapter hose to the tester. Make sure the engine does not turn over. If the engine turns over, you will need to reset the piston back to the compression stroke. Record the reading.

5. Listen for leakage from the oil fill hole, the throttle body, and the exhaust pipe, and look for bubbles in the radiator. Determine any necessary action.

4. Connect the cylinder leakage adapter hose to the tester.

5. Make sure the engine does not turn over. If the engine turns over, you will need to reset the piston back to the compression stroke. Record the reading. **(Photo 4)**

6. Listen for leakage from the oil fill hole, the throttle body, and the exhaust pipe, and look for bubbles in the radiator. Determine any necessary actions. **(Photo 5)**

▶ Diagnosing Engine Noise and Vibrations

Running engines are fairly quiet considering all of the mechanical activity that happens within them. But if something starts to go wrong, noises can be one of the first indicators. Noise issues can indicate something as simple to fix as a worn accessory belt or as complicated as a spun connecting rod bearing, which would generally require rebuilding the entire engine. Understanding the engine's theory of operation and how the individual components of an engine work will give you a good foundation to start from.

Many sounds can be pinpointed through an experienced technician's previous knowledge, so investigate unusual noises and build your experience. A loud knocking noise could be from a bad main bearing or connecting rod bearing due to a worn or spun bearing. A main bearing noise is generally deeper sounding than a rod bearing. Also, a main bearing makes an evenly spaced single knock while a rod bearing generally makes a double knock. A light ticking noise could be a valve lifter problem, which can be heard near the camshaft area. Or you might hear a light knocking noise that comes under slight rocking of the throttle that is caused by a collapsed piston skirt. A whirring noise can be caused by worn bearings in alternators, water pumps, and belt tensioners. One way to help locate any type of engine noise is to use a mechanic's stethoscope. Mechanical stethoscopes are the most common, but many electronic stethoscopes have settings that enhance selected sound frequencies, while filtering out others, making them very handy. Place the stethoscope against engine components in a variety of positions around the engine and listen to the noises. Generally, the louder the noise, the closer you are to its source.

Depending on the noise, a stethoscope may not be appropriate. In the case of a squeaky belt, spraying water on one belt at a time will make the noise go away temporarily when you spray the one that is squeaking. Squeaks and creaks that come from linkage and joints can sometimes be sprayed one at a time with a lubricant and operated until the offending joint is found.

Vibrations can be difficult to pinpoint. Vibrations can come from the engine or the drive train. The best clue is to determine if the vibration occurs only when the vehicle is being driven or if it occurs with the engine running irrespective of vehicle movement. If the vibration occurs only when the vehicle is moving, suspect a component within the drive train or drive line, the U-joints, or even the tire balance. A good way to isolate the drive train is to drive the vehicle up to the speed at which the vibration is noticeable. Then place the transmission in neutral and allow the engine to idle. If the vibration is still there, then the issue is probably associated with the wheels, tires, or axles. If the vibration goes away, then raise the engine rpm while still in neutral. If the vibration reoccurs, then the issue is most likely with the engine. If there is no vibration, reengage the appropriate drive gear and accelerate moderately. If the vibration reappears, then the issue is likely with the driveshaft, U-joints, or CV joints.

▶ Diagnosing Oil Consumption, Coolant Consumption, and Exhaust Color

While coolant should have no consumption if the cooling system is working properly, engine oil can have a small amount of consumption and still be considered normal. Most manufacturers will specify the maximum allowable consumption. In many cases, this is stated as no more than 1 quart in a certain number of miles. As long as the consumption is less than that specified, no action is necessary, unless it is related to a particular customer concern. If the consumption is greater than specified, a visual inspection as described in Skill Drills 10-1 and 10-2 at the beginning of this chapter is the first order of business. Consumption of oil or coolant that cannot be located with a visual inspection may in some cases be diagnosed by the color of the exhaust. If the color has a bluish tint, it indicates that engine oil is burning. If the blue color is constant while the engine is running, it is likely that the rings are not sealing due to worn rings or cylinder walls. If the blue color is present only when you start the engine, it is likely to be a valve stem seal or valve guide issue. Black exhaust indicates an excessively rich fuel mixture. White exhaust after the engine is warmed up is an indication that coolant is leaking into the exhaust, which could mean a blown head gasket, blown intake gasket, cracked cylinder head, or leaky exhaust gas recirculation cooler on some vehicles. When coolant leaks into the exhaust, it also gives off a sweet anti-freeze odor. This is the same smell as when the heater core is leaking.

Wrap-up

Ready for Review

▶ Appropriate service information is needed to make an accurate diagnosis.

▶ The best source for vehicle service information is the vehicle manufacturer.

▶ Major vehicle components often have identification numbers.

▶ A systematic mechanical testing and verification process is needed to diagnose and repair an engine problem.

▶ Engine mechanical testing tools include a compression gauge, vacuum gauge, cylinder leakage tester, and scan tool.

▶ The color of a leaking fluid can assist in identifying the source of a leak.

▶ During engine cranking, the engine will make an even cranking sound if the compression is even between the cylinders.

▶ A vacuum gauge is used to determine the general condition of an engine.

▶ A cylinder power balance test is used to determine whether all of the engine cylinders are working properly.

▶ A cranking compression test measures the compressed air pressure in the cylinder.

▶ A running compression test checks the engine's breathing ability.

▶ A cylinder leakage test is performed on a cylinder with low compression.

▶ A stethoscope can be used to isolate an engine noise.

▶ Exhaust smoke can indicate the source of an engine problem.

▶ An odor can help diagnose an engine problem.

▶ Engine tests must be properly interpreted to correct an engine problem.

Key Terms

<u>**compression tester**</u> A device used to measure the amount of compression pressure a cylinder can generate.

<u>**cylinder leakage tester**</u> A device that pumps air into the cylinder and measures the percentage of air that is leaking out of the cylinder.

<u>**data link connector (DLC)**</u> The connector through which the scan tool communicates to the vehicle's computers; it will display the readings from the various sensors and can retrieve trouble codes, freeze-frame data, and system monitor data.

<u>**pressure transducer**</u> A device used to measure engine vacuum and display it graphically on a lab scope.

<u>**vacuum gauge**</u> A device used to measure the amount of vacuum an engine can generate during various operating conditions.

ASE-Type Questions

1. Tech A says that a cranking sound diagnosis can be used to diagnose problems in the ignition system. Tech B says that a cranking sound diagnosis can indicate differences in compression. Who is correct?
   a. Tech A
   b. Tech B
   c. Both A and B
   d. Neither A nor B

2. Tech A says that a power balance test is a good way to narrow a misfire down to a particular cylinder or cylinders. Tech B says that a cylinder power balance test measures the volumetric efficiency of the cylinder being tested. Who is correct?
   a. Tech A
   b. Tech B
   c. Both A and B
   d. Neither A nor B

3. Tech A says that a cranking compression wet test can indicate if the cylinder has worn piston rings. Tech B says that the throttle should be held wide open during a cranking compression check. Who is correct?
   a. Tech A
   b. Tech B
   c. Both A and B
   d. Neither A nor B

4. Tech A says that low compression on a single cylinder will cause an engine not to start. Tech B says that low compression on a single cylinder will affect the engine's cranking sound. Who is correct?
   a. Tech A
   b. Tech B
   c. Both A and B
   d. Neither A nor B

5. Tech A says that a cylinder leakage test is performed on a cylinder with low compression to determine the severity of the leak and where it is located. Tech B says that manufacturers will consider up to 50% cylinder leakage past the piston rings acceptable. Who is correct?
   a. Tech A
   b. Tech B
   c. Both A and B
   d. Neither A nor B

6. Tech A says that a scan tool connected to the data link connector (DLC) will perform a cylinder power balance test and report cylinder pressures. Tech B says that a scan tool will perform a cylinder power balance test and report whether the rings or valves have failed. Who is correct?
   a. Tech A
   b. Tech B
   c. Both A and B
   d. Neither A nor B

7. Tech A says that researching related service information for a vehicle repair will assist the technician. Tech B says that research should be done only when the technician needs direction. Who is correct?
   a. Tech A
   b. Tech B
   c. Both A and B
   d. Neither A nor B

8. Tech A says that a vacuum gauge needle that dips 4–8 inches rhythmically can indicate a burned valve. Tech B says that a stethoscope can be used to determine the source of unusual engine noises. Who is correct?
   a. Tech A
   b. Tech B
   c. Both A and B
   d. Neither A nor B

9. Tech A says that a vacuum test can determine exhaust restriction. Tech B says that when performing a cylinder power balance test, results should be 5% or less. Who is correct?
   a. Tech A
   b. Tech B
   c. Both A and B
   d. Neither A nor B

10. Tech A says that a bad cam lobe or broken valve spring will show up during a running compression test. Tech B says that when performing a cylinder leakage test the engine must be running to get proper results. Who is correct?
    a. Tech A
    b. Tech B
    c. Both A and B
    d. Neither A nor B

CHAPTER 11

Knowledge Objectives

After reading this chapter, you will be able to:
1. Describe the tools used to remove an engine. (pp 284–285)
2. Explain the steps involved in safely preparing to remove and reinstall an engine. (p 285)
3. Describe the engine removal process from the top side of the engine. (pp 286–287)
4. Describe the components involved in front accessories disconnection. (pp 287–289)
5. Describe the components involved in underside disconnection. (pp 289–291)

Engine Removal and Replacement

Skills Objectives

After reading this chapter, you will be able to:
1. Remove an engine. (pp 291–292)
2. Reinstall an engine. (pp 292–293)
3. Perform prestart engine checks. (pp 293–294)
4. Restore the vehicle to running condition. (p 294)

Introduction

Once a major engine failure has been diagnosed, the engine will often need to be removed for repair or replacement. Typically, if well maintained, an engine will last many years and 200,000 miles (322,000 kilometers [km]) or more; however, abuse or defective components can severely shorten the life of an engine. If an engine has failed, the customer needs to get the vehicle to a clean, professional, and well-equipped shop for repair or replacement.

Generally, an engine will let you know if there is a serious mechanical problem. It will produce excessive noise or may not even crank over. Usually, before the engine fails, there have been warning signs such as dash lights indicating low oil pressure, high operating temperature, or a malfunctioning emission control system. A **malfunction indicator light (MIL)** is a dash light that indicates the presence of a diagnostic trouble code or a malfunction such as dead engine cylinders.

A major mistake made by technicians when removing and replacing an engine is rushing to get the job done. To perform this task well, technicians must be organized, careful, and methodical in their work. The very first step in the performance of this task is to reference the appropriate service information, preferably the manufacturer's service information. It is important to follow the steps listed in the service information in order and step by step. Keep in mind the cost of replacing damaged components caused by sloppy or hasty workmanship. Some of the electronically controlled components in today's vehicles can cost several thousands of dollars.

Engine Removal Tools

The tools you will need to remove and replace an engine include special service tools, a vehicle lift, an engine hoist, an engine stand, jacks, and general shop hand tools. Additionally, a scan tool is important on all but vintage vehicles to check and clear trouble codes, relieve pressure from fuel systems, and monitor engine and transmission systems after starting the replacement engine.

An engine hoist is necessary if the engine will be pulled from the top of the engine compartment **FIGURE 11-1**. Make sure the engine hoist is rated for

FIGURE 11-1 Removing the engine.

You are the Automotive Technician

Today you will be removing and replacing the engine of a 2004 Ford Taurus. Before you begin the job, you look at the customer work order. The customer has complained of dash warning lights illuminating and noises coming from under the hood. You confirm the customer complaints and diagnose the engine as having low oil pressure due to worn main bearings. The engine also exhibits a worn or spun connecting rod bearing as evidenced by the "rod knock" noise the customer was hearing. These conditions verify the need to replace the engine. You gather the tools needed to remove and reinstall an engine, including special service tools, a vehicle lift, an engine hoist, jacks, and general shop hand tools.

1. What are the considerations prior to disconnecting the battery?
2. Why is it important to be organized, careful, and methodical when removing or repairing an engine?
3. What are the important checks to make before starting the engine after installation?

the capacity you will be lifting. A strong chain is also required. Make sure the chain can exceed the weight capacity that it will be supporting. Some engines have pulling brackets that allow the chains to be attached by hooks when pulling the engine. The hooks, too, must exceed the weight capacity of the engine being pulled. If a vehicle hoist is not being used, a floor jack and jack stands are required to support the vehicle, or the vehicle components **FIGURE 11-2**.

If the engine is being removed by lowering it from underneath of the vehicle, as is recommended for many front-wheel drive vehicles, a scissor jack is required, along with a vehicle two-post hoist. Once the engine has been removed from the vehicle, an engine stand will make the procedure of taking the engine apart much easier **FIGURE 11-3**.

FIGURE 11-2 A floor jack and jack stands.

FIGURE 11-3 An engine stand.

Preparation and Safety

There are many engine installation configurations, including front-wheel drive, rear-wheel drive, and all-wheel drive designs. Although it is impossible to go into detail for every vehicle ever made, they all have similar engine removal procedures. In this chapter, a typical rear-wheel drive and a typical front-wheel drive vehicle will be used. Always refer to the service information for the specific vehicle for step-by-step disassembly procedures.

Most engines in rear-wheel drive vehicles are best removed from the top of the engine compartment, while many engines in front-wheel drive vehicles can be removed from the top or the bottom of the engine compartment. If removing from the top of the engine compartment, the engine can be separated from the transmission and removed by itself, or in some cases, the engine and transmission are removed as a unit. If the engine is removed from the bottom of the engine compartment, the engine and transaxle are usually removed as a unit attached to the engine cradle, which bolts the engine and transmission to the vehicle.

Engine removal and installation can be dangerous; therefore, it is important to put safety first in each step of the process. Vehicles and engines are heavy. During the removal and installation procedure, one of those heavy items will be lifted high enough to clear the other. If the engine slips, it can crush or pinch fingers, hands, and feet. Many parts have sharp edges that can cut through skin and tendons, which gloves can help protect. Fluids and chemicals can spray into your eyes and mouth, or they can be absorbed through your skin, so always use personal protective equipment. Fluids on the floor can cause slips and falls, so clean up messes quickly. It is important to follow the vehicle manufacturer's guidelines to the letter. Always respect and implement shop safety standards and regulations.

Safety

Always put safety first in each step of the engine removal and installation process. Vehicles and engines are heavy. During the removal and installation procedure, one of those heavy items will be lifted high enough to clear the other. If the engine slips, it can crush or pinch fingers, hands, and feet.

▶ Topside Disconnection

The first step in the engine removal process is to remove the hood. With the hood removed, you have greater access to the engine compartment and greater visibility because more light can get in. If the vehicle is front-wheel drive and the engine is coming out from underneath the vehicle, or if the hood opens at least 90 degrees, you may not need to remove the hood. Before removing the hood, scribe or otherwise mark the hood bracket **FIGURE 11-4** where the bolts attach the hood to the hinge. By doing this, you will have a reference mark showing the exact place to reinstall the hood.

After referencing the appropriate service information, you will begin the engine removal process from the top side of the engine. You will disconnect everything necessary for engine removal that is within reach from the top of the engine. One of the first things you will do is disable the electrical system by disconnecting the battery. Doing so reduces the risk of fire or explosion due to an inadvertent spark near exposed gases during the engine removal process. It also protects the electrical/electronic circuits from short circuiting. Before the fluids are properly drained, you will need to avoid removing anything that would cause a fluid leak.

Fuel and Fuel Lines

Most vehicles are fuel injected. Typically, a fuel injection supply line stays under pressure even when the engine is not running; therefore, you will need to relieve the pressure on the fuel system before disconnecting the lines. Check the service information for proper procedures to release the fuel system pressure.

If the vehicle is in running condition, one example of relieving the pressure would be to remove the fuel pump fuse while the engine is running and wait until the engine runs out of fuel. If the fuel-injected vehicle is not running, install a fuel pressure gauge and relieve the pressure **FIGURE 11-5** by venting the extra fuel into a plastic bottle. Once the fuel pressure has been relieved, you can disconnect the fuel line. For most fuel-injected vehicles, you will need a fuel disconnect tool **FIGURE 11-6**. Be sure to block off and seal the fuel supply line from the fuel tank. This can be accomplished by wedging a tapered punch inside the line, or taping over the end of the line with duct tape.

Battery

Most modern vehicles have 10 or more computers monitoring and controlling nearly every operational system of the vehicle. In fact, an automobile could have 50 separate microprocessors onboard. Considering the sophistication of the onboard electronics, it is easy

FIGURE 11-5 A fuel gauge used to relieve fuel pressure.

FIGURE 11-4 Scribing the hood bracket.

FIGURE 11-6 A fuel injection disconnect tool being used.

to understand why the vehicle's electrical/electronic system is vulnerable to damage from short-circuiting or grounding during the removal and installation process. Disconnecting the battery before disconnecting any other component from the engine will help prevent damage. Some electronic components, such as radios and navigation devices, have an anti-theft system built into them. If power is removed from the component, it will not work until the proper unlock code is keyed into it. Therefore, before disconnecting the battery, make sure you have the unlock codes available. These codes usually come with the owner's manual.

When disconnecting the battery, remove the negative terminal of the battery first **FIGURE 11-7**. The negative side is always disconnected first because it is already grounded and is considered safe. After disconnecting the negative side of the battery, disconnect the positive terminal at the battery. As a note of caution, do not lay tools or anything else on the battery because an accidental connection could be made between the positive and the negative posts of the battery, which could cause the battery to explode.

Electrical Components

Before removing the engine from the vehicle, there are many electrical wires and connectors to disconnect from the engine, bearing in mind that they must be reconnected after installation. This can be time consuming and tedious work. Take your time; be methodical and careful during this process. If your work is rushed and sloppy, this job could become your worst nightmare.

To begin, look closely at the electrical wire harnesses to evaluate the best area to disconnect them. Often, it is easier to disconnect main harnesses at their central connector instead of at the end of each branch, so you will want to investigate this option. Before disconnecting

FIGURE 11-7 A technician disconnecting the negative terminal of the battery.

FIGURE 11-8 Wires and connectors labeled and ready to be disconnected.

the electrical wire harness plug ends, it is a good idea to take pictures. If you take pictures for later identification, examine the pictures before disconnecting anything. You want to be sure you can identify connector and wire locations based on the pictures. For vehicles built in the 1980s and earlier, you might want to label the plug-in connectors **FIGURE 11-8**. For late-model vehicles, the electrical plug ends are not interchangeable. However, pictures will work to help you remember the general locations. When in doubt, label them and save yourself time and aggravation later.

▶ Front Accessories Disconnection

Continuing through the steps of engine removal, you will next remove the radiator and accessories. The air-conditioning compressor, power steering pump, and related mounting brackets and components are included in the accessory section. After checking the appropriate service information, you can determine if the air-conditioning or power steering systems will need to be opened for the engine to be removed. If the air-conditioning system needs to be opened, the refrigerant will need to be removed and stored by a properly trained technician using the appropriate recycling machine. If the power steering circuit needs to be opened, the fluid must be drained first.

Radiator

The boiling point of engine coolant is increased by the coolant properties and the cooling system pressure maintained by the pressure cap. The boiling point of plain water is 212°F (100°C); however, a typical boiling point for automotive anti-freeze or coolant is 223°F (106°C), and for each pound of pressure maintained by the radiator cap, the boiling point increases about 3°F (1.67°C). With a typical 13- to 15-psi radiator cap, the boiling point can rise about another 39°F to 45°F (21.7°C to 25.05°C). If a technician removes a cooling system pressure cap from a hot engine, the sudden reduction in the coolant boiling point can violently turn the water to superheated steam. Unfortunately, this often results in a scalded technician. Always make sure the engine is cool before removing the radiator cap.

At the bottom of the radiator, there should be a drain valve or plug **FIGURE 11-9**, but if not, you will need to disconnect the lower radiator hose, place the drain pan underneath the valve, and open the valve. If there is no valve, place the pan under the lower radiator hose. Next, disconnect the lower radiator hose until all the coolant has been drained, and then disconnect the upper radiator hose. For rear-wheel drive vehicles, disconnect the fan shroud, unbolt the radiator, and remove. For most front-wheel drive vehicles, disconnect the electric fan, determine whether there is enough room to remove the radiator without removing the electric fans, and, if not, remove the electric fans **FIGURE 11-10**, unbolt the radiator, and remove the radiator **FIGURE 11-11**.

Brackets

Air-conditioning compressors and power steering pumps are examples of accessory components that are mounted to the engine. They are mounted with brackets. Often, these brackets have several pieces because they are not only used to mount, but also to adjust the mounted components. Therefore, if the brackets must be removed, keep

as many of the components and attachment bolts together as possible to make reassembly easier.

Take off only the brackets that are necessary to remove the engine. Again, pictures are helpful in reminding you of the locations and positioning of the brackets. When removing the air-conditioning system, it is best to keep the system sealed, using mechanics' wire to secure the compressor and hoses up and out of the way **FIGURE 11-12**. If you are removing the air-conditioning pump and you have to disconnect the air conditioning, use the proper air-conditioning recovering equipment. It is best to leave all the air-conditioning lines intact and use mechanics' wire to hold the air-conditioning components off to the side of the engine. Remove the power steering pump, take it off the bracket, and wire it out of the way. It is usually not necessary to disconnect the hydraulic lines.

FIGURE 11-10 Removing the electric fans.

FIGURE 11-9 Draining the radiator.

FIGURE 11-11 Removing the radiator.

FIGURE 11-12 Wiring the air-conditioning compressor and hoses out of the way.

TECHNICIAN TIP

Only technicians who are EPA 609 certified are allowed to handle refrigerants, including breaking open any air-conditioning components. In order to be certified, you need to study a booklet, take a test, and pay the test fee. If you pass, you will be certified for life. This is a very cost-effective certification to obtain.

▶ Underside Disconnection

When preparing to raise the vehicle and make the necessary disconnections for removing the engine, start by reviewing the manufacturer's information. By following the steps for the specific vehicle you are working on, you can avoid missing components, bolts, hoses, and wires that must be disconnected before the engine can be removed. When the engine is loose, hanging from the engine hoist and unsupported by the vehicle, it is not the time to discover that you missed removing something under the vehicle. Remember to take your time and work carefully and methodically as you make the underside disconnections.

Draining Remaining Fluids

Since most fluid drain points are located under the vehicle, now is the time to drain fluids not previously drained. Drain the engine oil. If the transmission or transaxle will be coming out with the engine, you will need to drain the transmission/transaxle fluid as well. If not already drained, drain the cooling system. Look for related units that may need to be drained, such as the power steering fluid if the pump is being removed from the lines.

Exhaust System

Exhaust systems are not quite as simple as they once were. Currently produced vehicles could have three or four oxygen sensors, a catalytic converter, and a turbocharger driven by the exhaust gases **FIGURE 11-13**. Light-duty diesel-powered vehicles are now equipped with particulate filters. It is important to understand the exhaust system and related components on the vehicle before removing the exhaust system.

To begin the exhaust removal process, identify the oxygen sensors that need to be removed or disconnected. Disconnect the sensors. Check the exhaust pipe and component routing to determine the best places to disconnect the system, and be certain that the exhaust pipes will not restrict engine removal. Disconnect the exhaust pipe from the exhaust header, or manifold **FIGURE 11-14**. On most vehicles, there usually is enough room to remove the engine with the stock exhaust header

FIGURE 11-13 Exhaust assembly with oxygen sensors.

FIGURE 11-14 Removing the exhaust pipe from the vehicle.

in place. Nonetheless, always follow the exhaust removal guidelines in the manufacturer's information, or other reliable service information.

Starter

The starter motor is normally located where the engine and the transmission/transaxle are mounted together. That mounting point is called the bell housing, and the starter is usually bolted to it **FIGURE 11-15**. The starter needs to be removed before the engine is removed. It is important to understand that the positive battery cable connects to a terminal on the starter; therefore, it is imperative that the battery be disconnected before removing the cable and wires from the starter. To remove the starter motor, disconnect the starter electrical wires and mark where they go **FIGURE 11-16**. Then, while holding the starter firmly (it is heavy), remove the starter bolts and lower the starter from the engine or bell housing **FIGURE 11-17**.

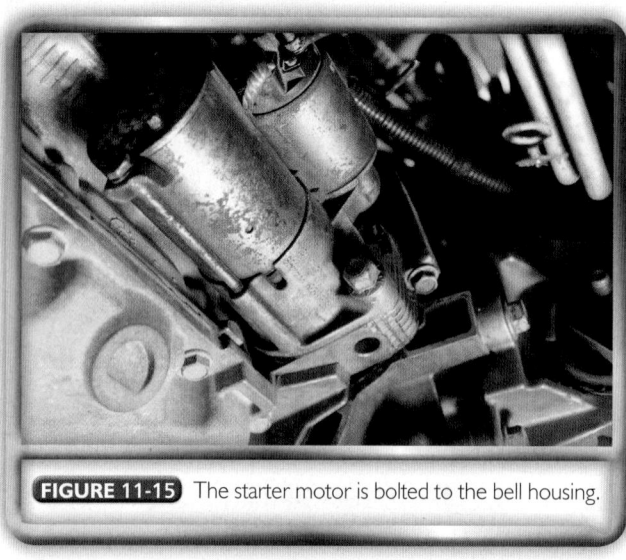
FIGURE 11-15 The starter motor is bolted to the bell housing.

FIGURE 11-16 Removing the starter wires.

FIGURE 11-17 Removing the starter bolts.

Automatic Transmissions Torque Converter

Remove the inspection cover on the bell housing to access the torque converter bolts on rear-wheel drive and front-wheel drive vehicles, if the engine is being removed from the top. For front-wheel drive vehicles in which the engine is being removed from the bottom, the engine and **subframe**, also called a cradle, will need to be removed together. A subframe is a mount used to support the engine and transaxle assembly and is attached to the vehicle. Disconnecting the torque converter is not needed at this time, because the engine, transaxle, axles, and subframe are removed at the same time.

After the inspection cover is removed, turn the flex plate so that one of the torque converter bolts is accessible. If the bell housing does not have an inspection cover, then you may have to access the flex plate by going through the starter mounting hole. Turn the flex plate by hand to align the flex plate bolts or nuts for easy access, and unbolt the torque converter bolts or nuts. If there is no inspection cover, you may have to turn the flex plate by turning the harmonic balancer in the front of the engine. Once the bolts or nuts have been removed, push the torque converter back into the bell housing so it will not fall out during engine removal.

Note: For the purposes of this text, the term "transmission" may include "transaxle" and vice versa, but not always. We will leave it up to the reader to determine its use, based on the vehicle being worked on.

Transmissions/Transaxles, Automatic and Manual

If the engine is being removed from the bottom of the vehicle using a subframe scissor jack, do not disconnect the transaxle at this time. If the engine is being removed from the top of the vehicle without the transmission/transaxle, you ultimately will need to unbolt the transmission/transaxle, but do not try to separate the transmission/transaxle from the engine until the transmission is supported and the engine is on the hoist.

If you are working on a manual transmission on a rear-wheel drive vehicle, determine if it can be separated from the bell housing or if the bell housing is integral with the transmission case. Determine if the bell housing should be unbolted from the engine or transmission. Support the transmission and then unbolt it or the bell housing at this time, but do not yet separate the two.

Engine Removal

When removing an engine, it is always helpful to have two other people assisting you . Most importantly, it is much safer to have someone readily available to assist in an emergency or to get the appropriate assistance, if needed. Also, it is good to have one person operating the hoist while two others guide the engine as it is being lifted or lowered from the vehicle. Before removing the engine, it is a good work practice to do a final check for anything that needs to be disconnected that was missed earlier.

Engine Hoist/Boom Lift—Rear-Wheel Drive

Using a chain, connect it to the proper lifting points, making sure the chain and attaching bolts are rated for the engine weight. Use at least grade 5 bolts, and make sure they screw in at least five full turns. Connect the chain to the engine hoist and center it on the chain as well as you can. Start by taking up the chain's slack; do not try lifting the engine because the engine mounts are still connected. Unbolt the engine motor mounts and begin lifting the engine out of the vehicle. A floor jack may be required to support the transmission. Once you have the engine out of the vehicle, set the engine on the floor, leaving tension on the chain.

Engine Subframe Jack—Front-Wheel Drive

On a front-wheel drive engine, position the subframe scissor jack under the engine and subframe, according to the service information. After the scissor jack is positioned in place, strap the engine and transaxle to the scissor jack FIGURE 11-18 . Unbolt and remove the upper motor mounts FIGURE 11-19 . Remove the front brake calipers and secure them to the vehicle, or remove the front brake lines to the calipers. Remove the cradle bolts FIGURE 11-20 and lower

FIGURE 11-18 The engine of a front-wheel drive vehicle strapped to a scissor jack.

FIGURE 11-19 Unbolt the motor mounts.

FIGURE 11-20 Remove the cradle bolts.

the subframe scissor jack very carefully **FIGURE 11-21**. After the engine and transaxle have been lowered, you can begin disassembly. Remove the engine from the transaxle by disconnecting the torque converter bolts or nuts first. Make sure the transaxle and subframe are secured to the subframe jack. Secure the chain of the engine hoist/ boom lift to the engine following the vehicle's service information. Take out the chain's slack; do not try to lift the engine yet, because the transaxle and engine mounts are still attached to the engine. Remove the transaxle bolts, and remove the engine motor mounts. Raise the engine about an inch and start to separate the engine from the transaxle while starting to raise the engine. After the engine has been separated from the transaxle, lower the engine to the floor. Once the rear-wheel drive or front-wheel drive engine is on the floor, remove the flex plate and the exhaust if they are in the way. The engine is ready for the engine stand; make sure the engine stand is rated

FIGURE 11-21 Lower the scissor jack.

FIGURE 11-22 Bolt the engine to an engine stand.

for the proper weight of the engine and accessories, and use a minimum of grade 5 bolts threaded at least five complete turns into their holes. Mount the engine to the engine stand, making sure the engine's center of gravity is balanced on the engine stand **FIGURE 11-22**. Finally, drain any remaining oil and remove the coolant soft plugs.

Engine Installation

Just as in the engine removal process, have assistants help you install the engine. First, organize the work site. Begin by making sure the area is clean and clear of obstructions. To be prepared, conveniently arrange the bolts and engine mounts needed to secure the engine. Additionally, lay out tools that will be needed for the initial installation of the engine. Time spent organizing the work site will ensure a safe and smooth engine installation.

To reinstall the engine, basically, reverse the process used to remove it. However, there are some additional procedures. For vehicles equipped with automatic transmissions, it is a good idea to consider changing the front transmission seal while the torque converter is removed. It only takes a few minutes and will avoid having to remove the transmission again if it were to leak. Also be sure to fill the torque converter with the proper transmission fluid. Lay the torque converter down facing up and pour enough transmission fluid into the torque converter to fill it about halfway **FIGURE 11-23**. When reinstalling the torque converter, push in and turn the torque converter, making sure it engages into the front pump . You should feel three distinct clunks. If the torque converter is not being replaced, make sure it is engaged into the front pump. When mating the engine up to the transmission, make sure the torque converter does not bind against the

FIGURE 11-23 Fill the torque converter about halfway with the proper transmission fluid.

flex plate. If it does, remove the engine and reengage the torque converter into the transmission. Some converters have studs that protrude out and are connected with nuts. The converter will have to be rotated to match the holes in the flex plate for the two to mate up.

FIGURE 11-24 Installation of engine mounts.

> ### TECHNICIAN TIP
>
> You can make alignment pins by taking two bolts that are longer than the bell housing bolts, cutting off their heads, and chamfering the cut ends. Screw these by finger into two of the bell housing holes in the block. The pointed ends will guide the bell housing into alignment against the block. Once a couple of bell housing bolts are threaded into the block, remove the guide pins and replace them with the proper bolts (either automatic or manual).

For vehicles equipped with manual transmissions, the clutch disc needs to be aligned with the clutch pilot hole using a clutch alignment tool. First verify that the correct pilot bearing or bushing is installed in the rear of the crankshaft. Once you know the correct pilot bearing is in place, you can use an alignment tool that has the same splines as the clutch disc and fits snugly in the pilot bearing. Align the clutch disc and install the pressure plate.

> ### ▶ LINK
> Refer to the Clutch System chapter for more information on the clutch disc and pressure plate.

When installing a manual transmission to the engine, you will sometimes need to turn the splined input shaft to align it with the clutch disc splines. A good way to do this is to leave the transmission in fourth gear and then turn the output shaft. Also, the front of the input shaft needs to align with the flywheel pilot bearing or bushing. Make sure the bell housing holes are aligned with the engine's dowel pins, and tighten all of the bell housing bolts evenly.

Engine Motor Mounts

After the transmission is bolted to the engine, the engine needs to be mounted to the vehicle frame or cradle. To do so, attach the motor mounts that connect the engine to the frame or mounting platform **FIGURE 11-24**. To mount the engine, lower the engine carefully, aligning the motor mounts. On some vehicles, the exhaust header must be aligned to the exhaust pipe at this time. Tighten

the motor mounts when the engine and mounts are in place. Reinstall all parts and components in reverse order of disassembly.

▶ Engine Start-up

Engine start-up after installation is a critical time for engine operation and longevity. It is important to make sure all fluid levels are checked and at the correct level. Keep your eyes and ears open, listening for unusual noises and looking for fluid leaks. Monitor the temperature and oil pressure gauges, and shut the engine down immediately if the gauges indicate overheating or low oil pressure. If the engine is not starting, do not crank the engine excessively because the starter might be damaged from excessive heat. Also, the lack of proper lubrication from the slow-turning oil pump can cause premature engine damage. Crank the engine for 10 seconds or less at a time. Some new camshaft break-in procedures require the engine to start immediately and to run at 1200 to 2000 revolutions per minute (rpm) for 20 or 30 minutes to provide proper lubrication and break-in.

Prestart Engine Checks

Before starting the engine after installation, you will need to make several checks, including the following:

1. Check all fluid levels, especially the engine oil and coolant levels. If a vacuum fill method of filling the cooling system was used, the cooling system will be full. If this method was not used, the system will look full but likely will have air pockets in the system. If there is a vacuum pocket at the thermostat, the air pocket may prevent the thermostat from getting up to temperature and opening, potentially causing the brand new engine to overheat.

2. Check that the battery terminals are connected firmly and the battery is charged.

3. Make sure the fuel is supplied to the injection system by turning the key to the run position, and check that there are no fuel leaks at the connections and fittings.

4. If the ignition timing is adjustable, make sure it is set close enough to start and then hook up a timing light to make an adjustment when the engine first starts **FIGURE 11-25**.

5. Check all of the auxiliary components, such as the air conditioner and the power steering pump, for proper installation and hose routing.

6. Check the serpentine belt and/or other belts and pulleys for proper installation.

7. Determine that electrical connectors and vacuum hoses are properly connected.

8. Connect the exhaust removal hose to the exhaust pipe.

9. Verify that the brake pedal is not spongy.

Initial Break-in

To ensure that the piston rings are seated properly and that the camshaft and other internal components are not damaged, it is important to follow the manufacturer's break-in procedures. If required during the initial engine break-in period, run the engine at high idle (1200–2000 rpm). Observe the temperature and oil pressure gauges. If the engine begins to run hot or the oil pressure drops, shut

FIGURE 11-25 If the ignition timing is adjustable, make sure it is set close enough to start and then hook up a timing light to make an adjustment when the engine first starts.

the engine off immediately. Also, monitor the engine for external leaks. If any are found, shut the engine down and repair the leak.

Run the engine at fast idle until it reaches and holds normal operating temperature or for the prescribed break-in time, then shut down the engine. Check the engine oil and oil level to ensure that there is no evidence of coolant in the oil. If the oil looks milky or if the oil level has risen above the full line, there may be an internal coolant leak.

Engine Timing Adjustment and Diagnostic Trouble Code Inspection

After starting the engine, you will need to determine whether the engine ignition timing is set correctly if it is adjustable. There are almost as many methods of setting the timing as there are vehicle models. Again, you need to consult the appropriate service literature to determine the correct method.

You will notice that there are significant differences in timing methods from one decade to another. On vehicles from the 1970s and earlier, the primary method for setting the timing is to adjust the distributor while using a timing light. For 1980s models, you might need to disconnect a computer spark control wire or ground a particular wire or disconnect a sensor, and then set the timing by adjusting the distributor while using a timing light. On most vehicles made since the mid to late 1980s, the computer controls the timing, and you do not need to manually set it.

Another important task to complete after you have started the engine is connecting a diagnostic scan tool to the **data link connector (DLC)** and checking for **diagnostic trouble codes (DTCs)**. If you find that a DTC was set during the engine break-in period, diagnose the condition. Once corrected, run the engine until it is fully warm again and check for any DTCs.

Once the engine is timed properly and the engine runs without turning on the MIL, and the engine has reached operating temperature and there are no sign of leaks or other problems, take the vehicle for a test-drive. Drive it for 30 minutes without exceeding 50 mph (80 kph) and 2000 rpm. This will allow the piston rings to seat and ensure good seating of other internal components such as cam lobes. Once back at the shop, recheck all of the fluid levels, and look for any leaks. Also check for any loose or missing components. If everything is in working order, clean the vehicle and return it to the customer.

Wrap-up

Ready for Review

▸ Before the engine fails, there are usually warning signs such as dash warning lights indicating low oil pressure, high operating temperature, or a malfunctioning emission control system.

▸ The first step in performing an engine removal and installation task is to reference the appropriate service information.

▸ The tools needed to remove and replace an engine include special service tools, a vehicle lift, an engine hoist, jacks, and general shop hand tools.

▸ Make sure the engine hoist is rated for the weight capacity you will be lifting.

▸ Once the engine has been removed from the vehicle, use an engine stand to support the engine while taking it apart.

▸ There are many engine installation configurations. They include front-wheel drive, rear-wheel drive, and all-wheel drive designs.

▸ Engine removal and installation can be dangerous; therefore, it is important to put safety first in each step of the process.

▸ Modern vehicles typically have 10 or more computers monitoring and controlling virtually every operational system of the vehicle.

▸ Disconnect the battery before disconnecting any other component from the engine.

▸ When disconnecting the battery, remove the negative terminal from the battery first.

▸ Typically, a fuel injection supply line stays under pressure even when the engine is not running. Therefore, you will need to relieve the pressure on the fuel system before disconnecting the fuel line.

▸ If an air-conditioning system needs to be opened, the refrigerant will need to be removed and stored using the appropriate recycling machine.

▸ The boiling point of engine coolant is increased by the coolant properties, and the cooling system pressure is maintained by the pressure cap.

▸ Make sure the engine is cool before draining the radiator.

▸ Air-conditioning compressors and power steering pumps are examples of accessory components that are mounted to the engine.

▸ Currently-produced vehicles could have three or four oxygen sensors, a catalytic converter, and a turbocharger driven by the exhaust.

▸ The starter motor is normally located where the engine and the transmission are mounted together.

▸ When removing an engine, it is always helpful to have two other people assisting you.

▸ Time spent organizing the work site will ensure a safe and smooth engine installation.

▸ When reinstalling the torque converter, push in and turn the torque converter, making sure three distinct clunks are felt.

▸ Engine start-up after installation is a critical time for engine operation and longevity.

▸ To ensure that the piston rings are seated properly and that the camshaft and other internal components are not damaged, it is important to follow appropriate break-in procedures.

▸ An important task after you have started the engine is to connect a diagnostic scanner to the data link connector (DLC) and check for diagnostic trouble codes (DTCs).

Key Terms

data link connector (DLC) An underdash connector for connecting a diagnostic scanner.

diagnostic trouble code (DTC) A code set by the computer indicating system or component malfunction.

malfunction indicator light (MIL) A dash light usually indicating the presence of a diagnostic trouble code or malfunction.

subframe A mount attached to the vehicle that is used to support the engine and transaxle assembly.

ASE-Type Questions

1. Tech A says that the first step in performing an engine removal and installation procedure is to research the appropriate service information. Tech B says that looking up service information is a waste of time for an experienced technician. Who is right?
   a. Tech A
   b. Tech B
   c. Both A and B
   d. Neither A nor B

2. Tech A says that front-wheel drive, rear-wheel drive, and all-wheel drive are examples of drive train configurations. Tech B says that before an engine fails, there are usually warning signs such as dash warning lights indicating low oil pressure, high operating temperature, or abnormal engine noises. Who is right?
   a. Tech A
   b. Tech B
   c. Both A and B
   d. Neither A nor B

3. Tech A says that when disconnecting the battery, remove the positive terminal from the battery first. Tech B says that you should disconnect the negative terminal first when preparing to disconnect the battery. Who is right?
   a. Tech A
   b. Tech B
   c. Both A and B
   d. Neither A nor B

4. Tech A says that a fuel injection system automatically relieves pressure when the engine is turned off. Tech B says that you will need to relieve fuel pressure from most fuel-injected vehicles before disconnecting the lines. Who is right?
   a. Tech A
   b. Tech B
   c. Both A and B
   d. Neither A nor B

5. Tech A says that if refrigerant removal is necessary, air-conditioning refrigerant must be removed with an approved recycling machine. Tech B says that if refrigerant removal is needed, it is much better to release it into the atmosphere because modern refrigerants are safe. Who is right?
   a. Tech A
   b. Tech B
   c. Both A and B
   d. Neither A nor B

6. Tech A says that the boiling point of engine coolant is increased by the coolant properties, and the cooling system pressure is maintained by the pressure cap. Tech B says that if a technician were to remove a cooling system pressure cap from a hot engine, the sudden reduction in the coolant boiling point could boil the water violently and scald the technician. Who is right?
   a. Tech A
   b. Tech B
   c. Both A and B
   d. Neither A nor B

7. Tech A says that after starting the engine, it should be revved higher than 4000 rpm for a few minutes to break in the rings. Tech B says that after starting the engine, connect a diagnostic scan tool to the DLC and check for DTCs. Who is right?
   a. Tech A
   b. Tech B
   c. Both A and B
   d. Neither A nor B

8. Tech A says that a technician needs to make sure an engine hoist is rated for the lifting capacity needed for the engine being removed. Tech B says that when installing a manual transmission, a clutch alignment tool is needed. Who is right?
   a. Tech A
   b. Tech B
   c. Both A and B
   d. Neither A nor B

9. Tech A says to check all fluid levels before starting a newly installed engine, especially the engine oil and coolant levels. Tech B says that to ensure that the piston rings are seated properly and that the camshaft and other internal components are not damaged, it is important to follow appropriate engine break-in procedures. Who is right?
   a. Tech A
   b. Tech B
   c. Both A and B
   d. Neither A nor B

10. Tech A says that a torque converter should engage at three different levels as it is being installed in a transmission. Tech B says that the torque converter requires an alignment tool when installing it in the transmission. Who is right?
    a. Tech A
    b. Tech B
    c. Both A and B
    d. Neither A nor B

CHAPTER 12

Knowledge Objectives

After reading this chapter, you will be able to:
1. Describe the functions of a cylinder head. (pp 300–301)
2. Describe the purpose of a head gasket. (pp 300–301)
3. Describe the advantages and disadvantages of cast iron and aluminum heads. (p 301)
4. Describe the differences between overhead valve, overhead camshaft, and dual overhead camshaft engines. (pp 301–302)
5. Describe the components that make up a cylinder head. (p 302)
6. Identify the different combustion chamber designs. (pp 302–304)
7. Identify different valve train designs. (pp 305–306)
8. Describe the parts of a poppet valve. (pp 306–307)
9. Describe how integral and non-integral valves differ. (p 308)
10. Describe valve stem seals and valve seats. (pp 308–310)
11. Describe the three types of valve trains. (p 310)
12. Describe the role of the camshaft in valve operation. (pp 310–311)
13. Describe valve lifters and followers. (pp 311–312)
14. Describe the role of pushrods and rocker arms. (pp 312–313)
15. Describe valve springs, retainers, and keepers. (pp 313–314)
16. Describe different gasket materials and types. (pp 314–315)
17. Describe room temperature vulcanizing (RTV) sealer and its use. (p 316)
18. Describe the process of diagnosing cylinder head issues. (p 317)

Cylinder Head Components

Skills Objectives

After reading this chapter, you will be able to:

1. Remove a cylinder head. (pp 318–319)
2. Clean and inspect a cylinder head. (pp 320–321)
3. Inspect valves and valve seats. (pp 322–323)
4. Inspect valve guides for wear and check valve stem-to-guide clearance. (p 323)
5. Inspect valve springs. (pp 323–324)
6. Reassemble a cylinder head. (pp 324–325)
7. Inspect pushrods, rocker arms, and rocker arm pivots and shafts for wear, bending, cracks, looseness, and blocked oil passages (orifices). (pp 326–327)
8. Inspect and/or measure the camshaft for runout, journal wear, and lobe wear. (pp 327–329)
9. Inspect camshaft bearing surface for wear, damage, out-of-round, and alignment. (pp 329–330)
10. Install the camshaft in heads with bucket-style lifters. (pp 331–332)
11. Assemble cam follower/rocker arm–style heads. (pp 332–333)

▶ Introduction

The modern internal combustion engine consists of many parts that were present in the original engines of a century ago. Over time, the form and efficiency of these parts have changed significantly, though their basic function has not. The cylinder head, in particular, is an example of what many years of improvement on a solid design can yield. Today's cylinder heads are more durable and efficient than any of their past counterparts. In this chapter, the modern cylinder head will be explored, including the theory behind its many designs and its role in the combustion process.

The cylinder head relates to the entire engine assembly by providing the "end cap" for the combustion chamber. It provides a means for admitting air and fuel to the combustion chamber and exhausting gases after combustion. The cylinder head is also an integral part of the engine cooling system; it allows coolant to flow around the top of the combustion chamber, removing excess heat and preventing overheating of the engine.

The camshaft works with the cylinder head and **valves** to regulate the flow of the air/fuel mixture into, and the exhaust gases out of, the combustion chamber by opening and closing the valves at the proper times. The camshaft may be located either in the cylinder head or adjacent to it in the cylinder block. Each location has its own pros and cons. Engines with a camshaft located in the block have been around for decades and therefore, are inexpensive to continue manufacturing. But they do not allow for varying of the valve timing, which is used to reduce emissions and increase engine efficiency. Engines with camshafts in the cylinder head are usually bulkier

and require a more complicated drive system, so they are usually more expensive. Nonetheless, overhead camshafts make the engine more efficient and powerful, so they are used in more and more engines.

▶ Cylinder Heads (Gasoline Engines)

There are five events in the operation of any internal combustion engine: intake of the air/fuel mixture, compression of the air/fuel mixture, ignition of the air/fuel mixture, a power stroke triggered by combustion of the air/fuel mixture, and the exhaust of burned gases from the combustion chamber. The **cylinder head** is integral to each of these steps. It controls the entry of the air/fuel mixture through the intake valve, allows compression of the air/fuel mixture by capping the top of the cylinder, contains a spark plug that ignites the air/fuel mixture, forces the pistons down the cylinder in a power stroke by not allowing the expanding gases to escape, and contains an exhaust valve to release the burned gases from the cylinder once the piston reaches the bottom of the cylinder. Because of the vital roles that the cylinder head plays, cylinder head design has a prime influence on the engine's efficiency and power output.

The cylinder head forms the top of the **combustion chamber**, the area of the engine in which the air/fuel mixture is ignited and combustion occurs. To withstand the very high combustion pressures, the cylinder head must be firmly clamped to the engine block with head bolts or studs. The **head gasket** is a thin metal sheet, often made of layers of different materials, with holes cut to

You are the Automotive Technician

You have diagnosed a blown head gasket on a customer's 2010 Shelby GT500, which is run regularly on the local road race track. Because of the stresses from racing and because the vehicle is nearing 75,000 miles, she would like you to disassemble, clean, and inspect the cylinder heads while you have them off to see if they need to be rebuilt. She agrees with your suggestion to have them checked for flatness and cracks. She is considering a high performance camshaft, which she has been told would create more power. But she is confused by the terms "duration," "lift," and "lobe separation," and asks if you could explain them to her so she can decide which camshaft to use.

1. What do the terms "duration," "lift," and "lobe separation" mean?
2. How are heads checked for cracks?
3. What two locations are checked for flatness on heads equipped with overhead cams?

accommodate the piston openings and passageways for oil and coolant. It is installed between the head surface and the block surface to seal the cylinder head assembly to the engine block **FIGURE 12-1**. The head gasket keeps combustion pressure, coolant, and oil inside their proper areas. The cylinder head also distributes air and fuel into the engine's cylinders.

Cylinder heads can be made of cast iron or aluminum alloy **FIGURE 12-2**. In today's vehicles, you will find most cylinder heads are made of aluminum alloy because of its light weight. The lighter cylinder heads help reduce the vehicle's overall weight, which helps increase fuel economy. Aluminum also conducts heat away from the combustion chamber more rapidly than cast iron. Thus, with an aluminum-alloy head, the heat of combustion can be conducted to the coolant faster, reducing the chance of localized hot spots. At the same time, engine efficiency is reduced when heat is removed too quickly from the combustion chamber, so aluminum cylinder heads may be designed with smaller water jackets to prevent them from overcooling the engine.

Overhead Valve Engine

In an __overhead valve (OHV) engine__, the valves are positioned in the cylinder head assembly, directly over the top of the piston **FIGURE 12-3**. The valves are operated by a camshaft that is located in the cylinder block. They transmit valve lifting force through lifters, pushrods, and rocker arms. This is a relatively simple design that is inexpensive to build.

Overhead Cam Engine

In the __overhead cam (OHC) engine__, the camshaft is housed inside the cylinder head and directly actuates the valves, using either cam followers or rocker arms **FIGURE 12-4**. This system is more complicated than the OHV engine due to the need for a more extensive cam drive as well as the need for enhanced oiling at the top of the engine for the camshaft, lifters, and followers.

FIGURE 12-2 Cylinder heads. **A.** Aluminum. **B.** Cast iron.

> ### ▶ TECHNICIAN TIP
>
> Soft plugs (or core plugs) have been used to plug the holes left over from the casting process. For years the term *freeze plugs* has also been used; however, the term *freeze plugs* is inaccurate. The cylinder head was never designed to withstand freezing with water in the cooling passages, and the soft plugs were never designed to prevent damage by popping out during a freeze. If the engine freezes and the soft plugs do pop out, more than likely the cylinder heads are cracked. The crack will typically be found in the thin portions of the water jacket.

FIGURE 12-1 A cylinder head with head gasket and head bolts.

FIGURE 12-3 Overhead valve (OHV) engine.

FIGURE 12-4 Overhead cam (OHC) engine.

FIGURE 12-5 Dual overhead cam (DOHC) engine.

Dual Overhead Cam Engine

The **dual overhead cam (DOHC) engine** contains two camshafts per cylinder head **FIGURE 12-5**. Typically, one camshaft operates the **intake valves** and the other operates the **exhaust valves**. In most cases, the camshaft sits right on top of the valves and operates the valves directly through a bucket lifter, with no rocker arms or cam followers. This design makes adjusting and servicing the valves more difficult because the camshaft usually needs to be removed to gain access. Offsetting the camshaft and using rocker arms or followers allow easier access.

Cylinder Head Components

The cylinder head is composed of many distinct parts. At its core is the bare cylinder head casting, the name given to the base onto which all other parts are attached. Other parts of the cylinder head include:

- Intake valves: The air/fuel mixture enters the combustion chamber through these valves.
- Exhaust valves: The exhaust gases exit the combustion chamber through these valves.
- Valve keepers: These devices keep a valve spring's retainer attached to the valve while in the cylinder head.
- Valve retainer: This thick washer-shaped piece of metal with a tapered center hole is fitted over the top of the valve stem and holds the top of the valve spring to keep pressure on the valves.
- Valve springs: These coil springs return valves to their fully closed positions, and hold them closed, after being opened.

- Oil seals: These seals keep oil from leaking past a rotating camshaft.
- Valve stem seals: These seals allow only enough oil past them to lubricate the valve guide.
- Rocker arm: This lever actuates a valve by pivoting near the center and pushing on the tip of the valve stem to open it.
- Plugs (e.g., galley, coolant): Much like seals, plugs are used to block off passages where oil and coolant flow and are primarily used to block holes used in the original casting and machining of the head.
- Camshaft (only fitted in the cylinder heads of OHC and DOHC engines): This device provides the force to open the valves.

Cylinder Head Design

The combustion chamber is located inside the engine where fuel and air are compressed by the piston and then ignited by the spark plug. The combustion chamber is generally formed into the cylinder head during the casting process. The movable floor of the combustion chamber is formed by the top of the piston. The overall efficiency of the combustion chamber is determined by its design, including the shape of the combustion chamber, the positioning of the valves, the location of the spark plug, the placement of the water jackets near the combustion chambers, and the shape of the top of the piston. Some engines use two spark plugs per combustion chamber, but this is not very common.

Today's cylinder heads are designed to help improve the swirl and turbulence of the air/fuel mixture. This prevents fuel droplets from settling on the surfaces of the combustion chamber and cylinder walls, as well as reducing emissions. In the cylinder head, swirl is initially created by the shape and angle of the **intake port**, which allows entry of the air/fuel mixture from the intake manifold and throttle body into the combustion chamber. Turbulence is increased in the **quench or squish area**, which is the area between the piston head at top dead center and the cylinder head. Its name comes from the squishing of the air/fuel mixture into a small "charge." The piston squeezes the air/fuel mixture and forces it with great speed out of the squish area. This creates turbulence, which helps to thoroughly mix the heavier fuel and lighter air.

Hemispherical Combustion Chamber

The **hemispherical cylinder head** has been around since approximately 1901. Several early designs were by a Belgian car maker by the name of Pipe in 1905. In the early 1960s, Chrysler Corporation trademarked the name Hemi, which is perhaps the most widely known hemispherical combustion chamber engine created.

A hemispherical or pent-roof combustion chamber has the intake valve on one side of the chamber and the exhaust valve on the other **FIGURE 12-6**. This design provides good cross-flow of the gases and is known as a cross-flow cylinder head. The air/fuel mixture enters on one side, and exhaust gases exit out the other side. Positioning the valves with the spark plug just off center of the combustion chamber leaves more room for relatively large valves and ports, which helps the engine breathe.

With the spark plug located near the center of the chamber, the air/fuel mixture starts to burn at the plug and then continues burning outward in all directions. This moving **flame front** is called **flame propagation**. With the hemispherical design, the flame front, or front edge of the burning air/fuel mixture, has less distance to travel than in some other designs, which gives rapid and effective combustion.

One of the drawbacks of the original hemispherical combustion chamber engine was that it required a complex valve train design that included two rocker arm shafts per head, with uneven rocker arm lengths. In later engines, manufacturers overcame this complex valve train design by using either the OHC design or the DOHC design. Thus, the benefits of the hemispherical combustion chamber were combined with the benefits of the OHC and DOHC cylinder heads. In today's DOHC engines it is very common to see multivalve, hemispherical cylinder heads. The addition of multiple intake and/or exhaust valves on the cylinder increases engine efficiency. The faster air and fuel can be moved into the combustion chamber and exhaust gases can be moved out of the combustion chamber, the more air and fuel the engine can burn. This concept is similar to having a room full of people and trying to evacuate them with just one door versus multiple doors: The more doors, the faster the flow. This increased flow increases engine power output.

Cylinder Head Shapes

Oval Combustion Chamber (Bathtub)

The bathtub combustion chamber is oval shaped, like an inverted antique bathtub **FIGURE 12-7**. The valves are mounted vertically and are side by side, making the

FIGURE 12-6 A hemispherical cylinder head and combustion chamber.

FIGURE 12-7 Oval (bathtub) combustion chambers.

valve train simple in its design. On some of the newer designs, the surface of the head overlaps the piston and forms two squish areas: a large area near the spark plug and a smaller one on the opposite side.

Wedge Combustion Chamber

The <u>wedge combustion chamber</u> tapers away from the spark plug, which is at the thick end of the wedge. The valves are typically arranged in a straight line positioned along the tapered angle, which puts them at an angle to the top of the piston **FIGURE 12-8**. The wedge design has a smaller combustion chamber surface area than the other types of cylinder heads, and that means less of a boundary area where fuel cannot burn as easily, which lowers hydrocarbon (unburned fuel) emissions.

Since the flame is directed toward the small end of the wedge, damage caused by detonation is reduced. This wedge design speeds up the velocity of the flame front. If the velocity of the flame front is not fast enough, the pressure building up in the combustion chamber causes the remaining gases to spontaneously ignite, which is called detonation. Detonation creates a second flame front that collides with the first flame front. A very intense pressure wave and audible detonation or pinging sound can be heard. Extreme detonation can damage the engine by concentrating high temperatures and pressures, which can melt a hole in the top of the piston.

Gas Direct Injection Cylinder Head

The latest cylinder head design is the <u>gas direct injection (GDI) cylinder head</u>. GDI refers to gasoline injected directly into the combustion chamber just above the piston **FIGURE 12-9**. Instead of mixing the fuel/air in the intake manifold, it mixes in the combustion chamber. Some GDI systems spray fuel into the combustion chamber during the intake stroke and use the fuel to

FIGURE 12-9 Gas direct injections.

actually cool the incoming air, which increases its density and resistance to detonation. Other GDI systems have the ability to spray fuel not only on the intake stroke but also near the top of the compression stroke, thus preventing detonation and allowing a lean air/fuel mixture to be burned by concentrating the sprayed fuel very close to the spark plug. The computer has control of the amount and timing of the injection sequence. It varies based on a variety of engine conditions, such as engine load, speed, and temperature. With the GDI cylinder head design, some manufacturers have been able to remove the throttle plate and control engine speed and power by controlling the fuel by itself. This reduces the engine's pumping losses of trying to pull air past the throttle plate. Overall, GDI can improve fuel economy up to about 35% and reduce emissions, especially carbon dioxide.

Intake and Exhaust Ports

The size of intake and exhaust ports in the cylinder head can affect engine output by affecting the speed of the air flowing through them. It takes a certain amount of speed to maintain good turbulence and air/fuel mixing. If airflow is too slow, fuel will fall out of the air. If airflow is too fast, the air will be restricted, which reduces the total amount of air/fuel mixture that can enter the combustion chamber.

The use of smaller intake and exhaust ports allows the engine to develop more torque at low engine speeds. By comparison, larger intake and exhaust ports allow greater airflow during the engine's high-speed operation, giving the engine more torque at higher engine speeds. Engines with smaller ported heads, meaning a cylinder head with smaller ports, work well in applications such as four-wheel drive vehicles, which are typically operated at lower engine speeds on trails. Larger port heads work well in engines that operate at high speeds and loads such as in circle-track racing.

FIGURE 12-8 Modern wedge combustion chamber.

▶ Valves and Valve Trains

The valve train is responsible for moving air and fuel through the engine. This means that all of the valve train components must be opened and closed at precise times. In fact, the optimum points in the cycle that the valves open and close change with engine revolutions per minute (rpm) and load. Newer engines have valve trains that are computer controlled and can adjust valve timing while the engine is operated.

The term valve train incorporates all of the parts between the drive of the camshaft and the valves. Valve train configuration is determined by the manufacturer, so valve trains come in a variety of configurations. The following sections will familiarize you with each of the components and layout.

Valve Sizes and Components

Valves come in different sizes depending on the engine. Valves experience enormous stress even in normal conditions. In a vehicle that is driven at 2500 rpm, each valve opens and closes approximately 21 times per second, and at 6000 rpm, each valve opens and closes 50 times per second. The opening and closing is controlled by the **camshaft lobe** and valve spring. The **valve train** includes all of the components that are driven from the camshaft drive, including the lifters, pushrods, rocker arms or cam followers, valves, valve springs, valve keepers, and valve retainers **FIGURE 12-10**.

The valve spring is compressed when the cam lobe pushes the valve open. The valve spring pushes the valve to its fully closed position as the cam lobe returns to its base circle. Valve keepers, also called valve retaining devices, are usually half-circle, wedge-shaped pieces that lock onto a groove, or grooves, near the top of the valve stem to keep the valve spring retainer and spring retained on the valve while in the head. The valve retainer is similar to a thick washer with a tapered center hole that mates with the wedge-shaped valve keepers. The retainer is placed near the top of the valve stem and keeps the valve spring compressed between it and the surface of the cylinder head. The retainer works in conjunction with the valve keeper to retain the valve in the cylinder head. There are different types of valve trains, depending on how many camshafts there are and where they are located.

The components of the valve include the following **FIGURE 12-11**:

- **Valve tip**: The portion of the valve stem that comes in direct contact with the rocker arm, cam follower, or bucket lifter, which opens the valve.

FIGURE 12-10 Valve train.

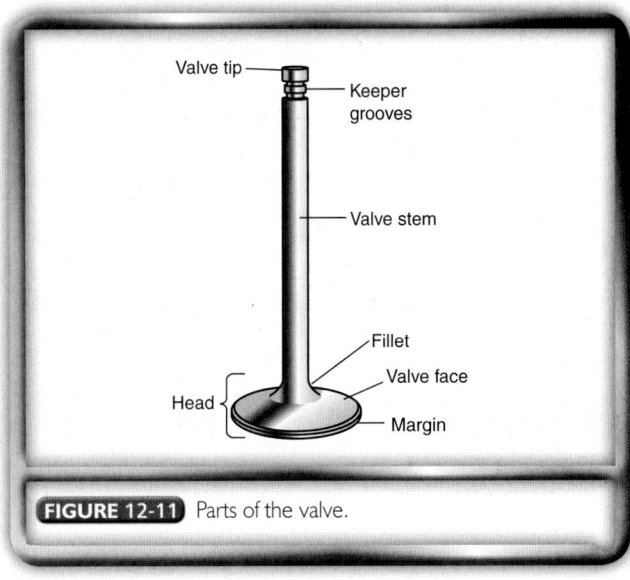

FIGURE 12-11 Parts of the valve.

- **Keeper groove**: The specific notch in the valve stem into which the keeper fits securely.
- **Valve stem**: A long shaftlike portion of the valve assembly that allows the valve to move freely inside a valve guide and contains the valve groove(s) into which the keeper is inserted.
- **Valve face**: The portion of the valve that does the actual closing and sealing off of the port. It is commonly ground to a 45-degree angle to provide a positive seal during the combustion process.
- **Valve head**: The mushroomed portion of the valve, which contains the face and margin.
- **Valve margin**: The portion of the valve between the valve face and the valve head.

> **TECHNICIAN TIP**
>
> The valve margin gets thinner as the valve face is cut or surfaced during a valve job. If it is too thin, the valve will burn in a short time. Always measure the margin and compare it to specifications before reusing it.

Valve Arrangement

In early engine designs, the valves were positioned with the valve head facing up; they were located in the engine block off to one side of the cylinder. This design was called the **L-head** (flat head). In today's engines, the valves are located in the cylinder head above the pistons (OHV).

In OHV engines, there are several different valve arrangements, ranging from one intake valve and one exhaust valve to a five-valve arrangement. A three-valve arrangement usually has two intake valves and one exhaust valve. A four-valve arrangement usually has two intake and two exhaust valves **FIGURE 12-12**. A five-valve

arrangement usually has three intake and two exhaust valves. By adding more than one intake or exhaust valve, volumetric efficiency can be increased while keeping the speed of the air/fuel mixture high, leading to greater power output.

> **TECHNICIAN TIP**
>
> It has always been said that the intake valve is larger than the exhaust valve. When we had only one intake valve and one exhaust valve per cylinder, that was an accurate statement. Now, with multivalve heads, that is not always the case. In many three-valve and five-valve engines, the extra valve is an intake valve. In these situations, since there are more intake valves than exhaust valves, the intake valves might be smaller. Therefore, be careful when identifying the valves; these newer multivalve designs might trip you up.

Types of Valves

Valves control the flow of air and fuel into and out of the cylinder. There are many different valve designs with variations to suit the unique features of the engine into which it is installed. Some engines, like those in heavy construction vehicles, need valves with strength and longevity to handle long, grueling work. Other engines, such as those in a race car, require valves that are lightweight and capable of withstanding high stress situations usually for shorter longevity.

The vast majority of automotive engines use a **poppet, or mushroom, valve**. It is called this because it "pops" up and down to open and seal its port. It also resembles a mushroom with a narrow stem and larger head. It fits into a port in the cylinder head. Its valve face makes a gas-tight seal against the valve seat **FIGURE 12-13**. The

FIGURE 12-12 Four-valve arrangement.

FIGURE 12-13 A poppet, or mushroom, valve, which makes a gas-tight seal against the valve seat.

intake valve opens and closes the intake port to allow air and fuel to enter the combustion chamber and to seal it during the compression, power, and exhaust strokes. The exhaust valve covers the exhaust port during the intake, compression, and power strokes.

Because the poppet valve is exposed to both the high-combustion temperatures and the hot exhaust gases, it can become red-hot under high-power conditions, so it needs to withstand high temperatures. At the same time, it must be able to stand up to both the **spring pressure** trying to pull the valve apart and the **combustion pressure** trying to force it into the valve seat. Valve tensile failure is when the valve is stretched or pulled apart by the action of the valve spring. Tensile failure of a valve generally results in a cylinder misfire due to loss of compression from the valve being stretched. In an extreme case, it could cause the head to separate from the stem and drop into the combustion chamber, causing catastrophic engine damage. Exhaust valves are made of nickel-based alloys to help withstand the extreme heat. The majority of the valve cooling happens when the hot valve face sits in the cooler valve seat in the head, although some of the cooling takes place through the stem and across into the valve guide. Some exhaust valves are manufactured to have hollow stems that are half filled with sodium during the manufacturing process to help transfer heat away from the head of the valve. Generally, sodium-filled valves cannot be repaired and must be replaced when problems occur.

Various surface treatments are used to help the valve resist wear, burning, and corrosion. Intake valves are made of steel mixed with chromium or silicon, to make them more resistant to corrosion, and manganese and nickel, to improve their strength **FIGURE 12-14**. Intake valves must also withstand spring pressure and combustion pressure,

just as the exhaust valves do. However, the intake valve does not get as hot as the exhaust valve does for two reasons. First, it is closed when exhaust gases are expelled from the exhaust so hot gases do not flow around it. Second, the cool intake charge flows around it on the intake stroke, which helps to cool it. In high-performance applications, the intake and exhaust valves can be made of stainless steel or titanium, which are suited to extreme conditions.

Valve Guides

Valve guides are the hollow metal passageways in the cylinder head in which the stem of the valve rides. The valve guide allows the valve to only move up and down, while holding it in the same position side to side. To give long life, the valve guide must be able to retain lubrication for the valve stem. The valve moves back and forth inside the guide approximately 21 times a second at 2500 rpm, so lubrication is critical to reduce wear on the guide and stem. Clearance between the valve stem and the valve guide must be within the manufacturer's specifications. When insufficient valve stem clearance occurs, the valve stem will not be able to be lubricated properly and can gall or stick **FIGURE 12-15**. When excessive valve stem clearance occurs, the engine suffers from premature wear on the valve stem, valve face, and valve seat. If the stem wear is bad enough, it can cause an intermittent loss of compression. Also, oil will be drawn down the intake valve guide, causing oil to enter the intake airstream. Oil will also seep down the exhaust port when the engine is off, or be drawn past the exhaust valve stem during engine deceleration. Any oil burned in the combustion chamber or exhaust system will result in excessive oil consumption and exhaust smoke (the engine is consuming oil).

FIGURE 12-14 Intake valves are made of steel mixed with chromium or silicon, to make them more resistant to corrosion, and manganese and nickel, to improve their strength.

FIGURE 12-15 Insufficient valve stem clearance leads to improper lubrication, which can gall or stick the valve.

Integral Valve Guide

The <u>integral valve guide</u> (non-replaceable valve guide) is cast into the cylinder head when the cylinder head is formed and is machined into the casting. Because it is constructed as part of the cylinder head, it cannot be removed and replaced. Instead, an integral guide can be repaired by machining it oversize and installing a thin wall bronze liner. A machinist can also repair the integral guide by using a head shop to machine the valve guide (boring out) then installing a thick wall guide, which can be made of iron or bronze, and then machining it to the proper size. Integral guides need to be repaired when the valve guide has worn past its service limits. For example, if a valve guide's size is stated in the service information as 0.250" (6.35 mm) plus or minus 0.0005" (0.0127 mm) and the guide is worn to 0.252" (6.4008 mm), then the guide is 0.0015" (0.0381 mm) too big to be put into service.

Non-integral Valve Guide

The <u>non-integral valve guide</u> (replaceable valve guide) is manufactured separately from the cylinder head and press-fit into a specially machined hole in the cylinder head that was formed as the head was cast. Non-integral guides can be removed and replaced as needed for repairs. They are typically made of cast iron or bronze—robust materials that can withstand the process of being pressed or driven into the cylinder head as well as provide a durable surface for the valve stem **FIGURE 12-16**. The non-integral valve guide has an interference fit to the cylinder head and is usually driven into place by using a valve guide driver and air hammer or small sledge hammer.

Valve Stem Seals

Since valve stems require a small amount of running clearance as well as a small amount of lubrication, it is possible for an excessive amount of oil to leak past the valve stems into the intake and exhaust ports. The intake valve is more likely to pass oil through its guide than the exhaust valve because the intake port has low manifold pressure (vacuum) due to the intake stroke, especially during deceleration, such as coasting downhill. However, the exhaust port typically is lightly pressurized while the engine is operating under load, so oil cannot be pulled in as easily. In fact, some older engines do not have exhaust valve stem seals. Still, oil can be pulled past the exhaust valve stem during deceleration just like an intake valve.

Worn exhaust valve seals and/or guides can also allow oil to seep down the stems and puddle in the port or exhaust manifold, causing a puff of blue smoke during start-up. In an engine with the proper valve guide clearance, this oil leakage is reduced but not eliminated. To control the amount of oil that lubricates the valve stems, valve stem seals are used on both the intake and the exhaust valves. These seals fit around the valve stem and usually seal to the top of the valve guide. Valve stem seals are designed to allow just enough oil to get past them to lubricate the valve stems and guides. If valve stem clearance is excessive or if the valve seals wear out or become damaged, excessive oil will pass through the guide, resulting in high oil consumption, excessive smoke emitted from the exhaust pipe, and possibly fouling of the spark plugs.

Cylinder heads can have one of three basic types of valve seals:

- **Umbrella-style valve stem seals** fit tightly around the top of the valve stems and ride up and down with the valves **FIGURE 12-17**. The umbrella is a larger diameter than the valve guide, so oil drips off the umbrella outside of the guide. Umbrella-type seals are generally found on older (1980s and earlier) American-built V8 engines. They are not typically found in modern engines.

FIGURE 12-16 Non-integral valve guides are typically made of cast iron or bronze, providing a durable surface for the valve stem.

FIGURE 12-17 An umbrella-style valve stem seal.

- <u>O-ring valve stem seals</u> fit on top of the valve in a groove just below the valve spring keepers **FIGURE 12-18**. The O-ring seals the oil from leaking between the valve stem and the valve retainer. These seals were used primarily on General Motors V8 engines from the 1980s and earlier. O-ring seals are not typically found in modern engines.
- <u>Positive valve stem seals</u> are used in today's engines **FIGURE 12-19**. The positive seal fits tightly on the valve guide as the valve stem moves up and down inside of the seal. This type of seal is the most effective because it forms a positive seal between the guide and the valve stem. Positive valve stem seals have a small groove cut into the top of the seal that rides on the stem. This design keeps a small amount of oil against the valve stem and only allows a very small film of oil past it to lubricate the valve guide.

FIGURE 12-18 An O-ring valve stem seal.

FIGURE 12-19 A positive valve stem seal.

Valve Seats

The <u>valve seat</u> is the part of the cylinder head that mates with the face of the valve when it is fully closed. It is typically made of hardened steel in order to withstand the extreme temperatures and pressures encountered during engine operation. Valve seats must be compatible with today's gasoline. Use of today's unleaded gasoline in an engine with non-hardened valve seats will cause the seats to slowly wear away and sink deeper into the head, a condition known as valve seat recession.

Valve seat inserts are made of metal rings that match the shape of the valve face in order to form a strong and complete seal. They are usually made of an iron alloy because the alloy is stronger than iron itself and provides a more durable surface. Most late-model, or "newer," vehicles require hardened seats in both the intake and the exhaust ports due to the extreme temperatures and pressures that newer engines must handle. With government air quality standards constantly rising, achieving a cleaner burn for an internal combustion engine means a hotter burn and higher pressure and thus, a more intense combustion process. Valves, valve seats, pistons, and cylinders all need to be able to meet these increased demands.

> ### ▶ TECHNICIAN TIP
>
> Up until the early 1970s, gasoline contained tetraethyl lead, which was used to inexpensively boost the octane. Lead also lubricated the valve seats by providing a cushioning effect, which allowed the valve seats to be machined into the base cast iron material and still give good life. However, when the installation of catalytic converters was mandated for emission control purposes in the mid-70s, lead could not be used in fuel anymore, as lead would contaminate and kill the converter. This situation required the use of hardened valve seats to resist wearing out quickly.

Valve seats are either ground or cut (machined) into the proper shape and <u>concentricity</u> so that the valve face and seat seal tightly. Valve seat grinding is when the seat is ground to the proper angle with a special grinding stone. Valve seat machining uses a special hardened cutter to cut the proper angles into the seat.

Some engines use valves that have a 30-degree valve face angle. Others have a 45-degree valve face angle. In some cases, the intake valve angles are different than the exhaust valve angles. The differences in angles simply represent the manufacturer's engine design; the exact angle has minimal affect on the cylinder head function as long as the valve and seat fit tightly enough to seal the force of combustion in the combustion chamber. In many cases, the valve and seat are machined about 1 degree different than each other for sealing purposes. For instance, the valve is cut to a 45-degree angle, and the seat is cut to a 46-degree angle. This is done so that the angles will meet at a "point" toward the outside of the valve face and seat. This difference is called an **interference angle** `FIGURE 12-20`. An interference angle allows for a quick **bedding-in** of the valve face to the valve seat on new engines. Bedding-in is the process of the valve face wearing into the valve seat during the initial breaking-in of the engine. This provides a long-lasting, leak-proof seal.

Valve Trains

As discussed earlier, valve train is the name given to all parts contributing to the opening or closing of intake and exhaust valves. The valve train as a whole controls the opening and closing of each valve. There are different types of valve trains, depending on how many camshafts there are and where they are located. There is the OHV valve train, OHC valve train, and the DOHC valve train.

In an OHV engine, the valves are in the cylinder head and the camshaft is in a block near the crankshaft. A valve lifter (tappet) rides on the camshaft lobe and transmits the movement of the lobe to the pushrod. Valve lifters can be solid, which require periodic adjustment, or hydraulic, which are self-adjusting. One valve lifter is located on each lobe of the camshaft. As the camshaft rotates, the lifter rises and transfers the motion to the pushrod. The pushrod is a metal, usually hollow, rod that transfers the motion from a lifter to the rocker arm. The pushrod then moves a rocker arm, which pivots near the center and pushes the valve open.

In a single OHC engine, the valve train works by having one camshaft mounted between the rows of intake and exhaust valves. Rocker arms, which pivot near the center, or cam followers, which pivot on one end, ride on each cam lobe and directly operate each valve. Some systems incorporate hydraulic lash adjusters right in the rocker arms or in the cam follower pivot so that the valve train will be self-adjusting.

In a DOHC engine, there is a camshaft for the intake valves and a separate camshaft for the exhaust valves. In most cases, the camshaft sits right on top of the corresponding valves and operates the valve through a bucket lifter, which may also have a built-in lash adjuster. This design makes for a very compact valve train. It also allows intake and exhaust valve timing to be controlled separately from each other, which can reduce emissions, increase power, and increase engine efficiency or mileage.

Camshaft

The camshaft provides the motion to open and close each of the valves. The camshaft is a shaft with offset eccentrics, called cam lobes `FIGURE 12-21`. The cam lobe determines when each valve opens, how far it opens, and how long it stays open. The profile of the cam lobe determines these functions. The base circle takes up about half of the entire profile. When the lifter is on the base circle, the valve is closed. The nose is the highest point of the cam lobe and determines how far the valve opens. The difference between the base circle is called lobe lift. The opening ramp is what opens the valve. The opening ramp starts at the base circle and ends at the nose. The closing ramp is the opposite of the opening ramp and allows the valve to close. It starts at the nose and ends at the base circle.

Camshafts are ground for specific applications and may or may not be symmetrical, meaning that the opening and closing ramps may or may not be identical. Also, different camshaft profiles create different engine operating

FIGURE 12-20 Valve-to-valve seat interference angle.

FIGURE 12-21 Typical camshaft.

characteristics. Two terms that you need to understand are *lift* and *duration*. Lift refers to how far the cam lobe will *lift* the lifter, cam follower, or bucket lifter. The greater the lift, the further the valve opens and the easier it is for air to enter the cylinder. However, the greater the lift, the faster the valve has to move from closed to open and the harder the valve springs have to work at closing the valve. *Duration* refers to how long the valve is held open. The longer it is held open, the more time there is for air to enter the cylinder. Higher-duration camshafts are usually used in engines that operate at higher rpm. One other important term is *lobe separation angle*, which refers to how far the intake lobe is offset from the exhaust lobe. The wider the separation, the better the camshaft is for building power at higher rpm. Narrowing the separation builds power at lower rpm.

Types of Lifters

There are two types of lifters: solid and hydraulic. <u>Hydraulic valve lifters</u> are constructed as a centrally located plunger inside a hollow cylindrical body. Engine oil fills the inside of the lifter body, pushing the plunger up until all the play in the valve train is removed. Because they are self-adjusting, these lifters can automatically accommodate changes caused by part wear or temperature fluctuations. Hydraulic lifters are more frequently used in today's engines because they are quieter and require no periodic maintenance.

    <u>Solid valve lifters</u> are constructed as a hollow cast iron cylinder, capped on both ends. They function by simply transferring the action of the cam lobe to the pushrod. Because there is no means for changing the length of the solid lifter, as seen in the oil-filled plunger action of the hydraulic lifter, they are not able to self-adjust to changes caused by wear or thermal conditions. As a result, all adjustments must be performed manually. These types of lifters require frequent valve adjustments and are typically noisier than their hydraulic counterparts. An advantage of the solid lifter is that it can be made lighter than a hydraulic lifter, so it can be used at higher engine rpm without contributing to valve float.

    The valve lifters can be located in four different places: on the engine block, on the cylinder head, on the rocker arms, and between the cam and the valve tip (bucket style) **FIGURE 12-22**. Both solid and hydraulic lifters can be of either the <u>flat tappet</u> or the roller tip design. The flat tappet style has a nearly flat surface that rides directly on the camshaft lobe. The lifter face-to-camshaft lobe contact is one of the highest load areas in the engine. Using a roller tip lifter reduces the friction on the camshaft lobe. Instead of sliding on the camshaft lobe as a flat tappet does, the roller rolls along the lobe with less

friction. Because the roller must remain in rolling contact with the cam lobe, the lifter must incorporate a method of preventing it from rotating in the lifter bore. This can be accomplished by connecting two adjacent lifters together with a pivoting link, or it could use a pin on the side of the lifter that rides in a groove in the lifter bore.

FIGURE 12-22 **A.** Engine lifter in the engine block. **B.** Engine lifter in the cylinder head. **C.** Engine lifter in between the cam and the valve tip (bucket style).

In most OHC engines, you will find no rocker arms. Instead, these engines use **camshaft followers** **FIGURE 12-23**. A camshaft follower performs the same basic function as a rocker arm: It opens a valve. The camshaft follower has a pivot on one end and a slider or roller near the center that directly contacts the camshaft lobe. As the camshaft turns, the roller rolls over the surface of the camshaft. The lobes push the followers away, transmitting the movement to the valve and pushing it down (open).

If the camshaft is located on top of and centered over the valves, the engine will use **bucket-style lifters** **FIGURE 12-24**. These lifters have a lifter assembly that is mounted on top of the valve and are hollowed out, like a bucket. The hollow portion is placed upside down over the top of the valve stem and provides a wear surface between the camshaft and the valve stem. They perform the same job as all lifters: They transmit movement from the cam lobe to the tip of the valve. Bucket-style lifters may be hydraulic or mechanical. To adjust the valve clearance in the mechanical lifter, you must change the wafer installed on the top of the bucket. Some technicians refer to wafers as spacers or pucks. These wafers are replaced to obtain the proper valve clearance between the camshaft and the valve stem. They come in different thicknesses to achieve the correct valve clearance. Hydraulic bucket lifters are self-adjusting in the same manner as a standard hydraulic lifter and therefore do not require periodic maintenance.

FIGURE 12-23 Camshaft follower.

FIGURE 12-24 Bucket-style lifter.

Lockring
Metering disc
Plunger cap
Plunger
Valve seat
Valve spring
Valve
Valve retainer
Valve lifter
Plunger return spring

Applied Science

AS-14: Distance/Length: The technician can use precision measuring devices to determine if wear and adjustments are within the manufacturer's tolerances. The use of precision measuring devices is common within shops and takes place in some form in the maintenance of almost all mechanical systems on a vehicle. Looking only at engines, two common examples are the use of an inside micrometer to measure the inside diameter of camshaft bores in alloy cylinder heads to determine wear from the manufacturer's specification, and the use of feeler gauges to measure valve clearances when carrying out adjustments during servicing.

Pushrods

OHV engines incorporate **pushrods**. The pushrod transfers the motion from the valve lifter to the rocker arm. Pushrods vary in design, depending on the engine. Some pushrods are hollow inside and transfer oil to the rocker arms. Some engines have different lengths of pushrods; the exhaust is a different length than the intake. Pushrod ends come in several different styles: ball to ball, ball to cup, and ball to adjustable tip **FIGURE 12-25**. A ball-to-ball pushrod is smooth and rounded at each end. One end fits into a "cup" or dished-out piece in the valve lifter, and the other fits into a cup in the rocker arm assembly. A ball-to-cup pushrod has a smooth, rounded ball at one end that sits in a cup on the valve lifter and a cup at the other end into which a smooth, round end of the rocker arm assembly fits. The ball-to-adjustable screw pushrod is the same as the ball-to-ball pushrod, except that there is a screw thread and lock nut near the end closest to the rocker arm that, when turned, lengthens or shortens the pushrod.

FIGURE 12-25 Two types of pushrod ends.

Rocker Arms

The **rocker arm** pivots inward near the middle, which results in a change of the direction of movement. The camshaft lobe pushes up, and as the rocker arm is pushed up on one end, the other end pushes the valve down to open. Rocker arms can be used on OHV or OHC engines. In OHV engines, each valve has one lifter, one pushrod, one rocker arm, and one lobe on the camshaft dedicated to its opening and closing. In OHC engines, each valve has one rocker arm and one lobe on the camshaft. The rocker arm comes in different rocker arm ratios depending on the engine design. The ratio refers to the amount of movement on the valve side of the rocker arm in comparison with that on the opposite side. For example, a 1.5:1 rocker arm will move a valve 1.5 times the lift and speed of the camshaft lobe. The most common ratios are 1.5:1, 1.6:1, and 1.7:1.

Rocker arm ratios allow manufacturers to use smaller lift camshafts. That is, a camshaft with smaller lobes than needed to generate a specified amount of lift can be used because the rocker arm ratio magnifies the camshaft's lift. There are different styles of rocker arms, including stamped, cast, or forged. Stamped rocker arms are "stamped" from a piece of metal. They are not a high-strength or high-horsepower rocker arm and are intended for regular passenger vehicles. Cast rocker arms are cast in a die with molten metal. Metal alloys can be used, making cast, forged, or billet rocker arms that are more durable than their non-alloy counterparts. These rocker arms are generally used in sports cars and other high-performance vehicles. Forged rocker arms use localized pressing forces to form a rocker arm from steel or a steel alloy. The forging process enables the metal to withstand extreme pressure, heat, and wear. These rocker arms are used in high-torque, high-horsepower applications such as race cars and hot rods.

In many pushrod engines, the valves are positioned in a line on one side of the cylinder head and the pushrods on the other side of the head, with the rocker arms positioned between them. To aid in mounting and aligning all the rocker arms, the rocker arms may be mounted on a common rocker shaft **FIGURE 12-26**. Or in the case of **canted valves** used in hemispherical-shaped and some wedge-shaped combustion chambers, the rocker arms may be individually mounted to the cylinder head. In OHC engines, typically the intake valves are on one side of the cylinder head and the exhaust valves are on the other side of the head, with the camshaft sitting between them. Rocker arms would then be positioned between the camshaft and the valves on each side of the camshaft.

With the push for increased fuel efficiency, many manufacturers use roller rocker arms on their engines. Roller rocker arms use rolling pivots at both ends and the center of the rocker arm. The rolling action at the pivot points reduces friction as well as wear on the rocker arm. The reduced friction gives a small increase in fuel efficiency and performance.

Valve Springs

The **valve spring** closes the valve and holds the valve firmly against the valve seat. Valve springs in automotive applications are almost always of the coil spring variety. Valve springs have several specifications they must meet. One is the *valve spring closed pressure*, which is a measure of the amount of pressure the spring exerts on the valve to close it tightly against the valve seat. Another specification is *valve spring open pressure*, which is a measure of the amount of pressure the valve spring is exerting to overcome the inertia of the valve train as the valve reaches its fully opened position. Both of these specifications are dependent on the type of valve train used in the engine and are measured in pounds. The *spring installed*

FIGURE 12-26 Rocker arm assembly.

height is another important specification that must be met. It indicates how tall the spring is when everything is assembled in the cylinder head. This measurement is important because spring length affects the amount of pressure the spring exerts on the valve train.

The valve could have one spring or multiple springs per valve **FIGURE 12-27**. Usually in engines that operate at high rpm, the manufacturer uses multiple springs to close the valve. This is done to increase spring pressure and prevent **valve float**, a condition that occurs when the valves cannot be closed (sealed) by the valve springs as fast as is needed before the next stroke. Two springs can close a valve faster than one spring can.

It is important to not have overly strong valve springs (too much pressure), as excessive pressure could cause premature wear on the other valve train components. This is especially true for the cam lobes and lifters as well as the pushrods and rocker arms. Insufficient spring pressure is also problematic, as it causes valve float, which can allow the piston to hit an open valve on some engines.

Valve Spring Retainer

The **valve spring retainer** is used along with valve keepers to hold the valve spring in place, centered around the valve stem **FIGURE 12-28**. The valve spring retainer has a tapered center hole that provides a mating surface for the valve keepers. Valve retainers are usually made from steel; however, aluminum and titanium are used in some high-performance engines.

Some exhaust valve spring retainers have a built-in device called a valve rotator. Just like regular valve spring retainers, the exhaust valve spring retainers are used as an end cap to help trap the valve spring under pressure on the end of the valve stem. These retainers also have a rotation function driven by a built-in valve rotator to keep the exhaust valve turning in one direction or the other, thus preventing hot spots and carbon buildup and

FIGURE 12-28 Valve spring retainers.

FIGURE 12-29 Valve keepers lock the valve stem to the retainer.

evening out the wear on the valve face and valve seat. They are found only on exhaust valves, as the intake valve is cooled by incoming fuel and air.

Valve Keepers

Valve keepers (also called valve locks) lock the valve stem to the retainer **FIGURE 12-29**. The valve keepers are usually a split taper design that matches the valve retainer taper with a protruding ridge or rings that fit into a groove on the valve stem. The valve keepers are hardened to withstand the pounding action of the opening and closing of the valves.

Gaskets

Gaskets form a seal by being compressed between stationary parts where liquid or gases could pass. Gaskets are generally designed to be single use and therefore cannot be reused. They can be made of soft materials such as cork, rubber, and paper. They can also be made of soft

FIGURE 12-27 Single- and dual-valve springs.

alloys and metals such as brass, copper, aluminum, and stainless steel. Such materials may be used individually or in some cases as blends to produce the required functional material.

With the increasingly hostile environment that gaskets are required to seal, and with the reduction in the use of asbestos, enhanced gasket materials have been developed. One of the few ways to make engines run cleaner is to raise the temperature at which they operate. Today's cleaner engines typically run 30–40°F hotter than their counterparts of 30 years ago. Thus, the gaskets used in modern engines need to be made of more robust materials, such as vulcanized rubber or EPDM (ethylene propylene diene monomer [M-class] rubber).

Modern gasket manufacturers are producing improved material combinations such as nitrile–cork blends to deal with the extreme demands placed on modern engines, such as higher temperatures, higher compression, longer engine service life, and longer manufacturer warranties. Such combinations can better deal with these issues while maintaining compressibility and minimizing wicking.

Some gasket materials are designed to swell once they are put into service and increase sealing ability. For instance, when oil inside a valve cover penetrates the edge of the gasket material, it may be designed to swell by approximately 30%. This swelling effect increases the sealing pressure between the head and the valve cover sealing surfaces and helps to seal potential leaks.

Choosing which material and design to use depends on the substance to be sealed (i.e., oil, fuel, exhaust gases), the pressures and temperatures involved (i.e., combustion gases, coolant), and the materials the mating surfaces to be sealed are made of (i.e., what materials the gasket will seal against—aluminum, plastic, cast iron, etc.). The best way to determine which gasket material is appropriate for an engine is to refer to the manufacturer's service information.

Head Gaskets

The head gaskets seal and contain the pressures of combustion within the engine, between the cylinder head and the engine block. They also seal oil passages between the engine block and the cylinder head. Finally, head gaskets control the flow of coolant between the engine block and the cylinder head.

Some high-temperature head gaskets are called **anisotropic** in nature. Anisotropic means that the gasket is designed to conduct heat laterally to transfer heat from the combustion chamber to the coolant faster. These gaskets are normally constructed with a steel core. Special facing materials are added to both sides of the gasket core to provide a comprehensive seal under varying expansion conditions.

On some engines, the head gasket provides or adjusts the proper clearances between the piston and the cylinder head by the thickness of the gasket. The service information (or repair information) for a vehicle will specify how to select the proper thickness of gasket and why that thickness is needed. Sometimes, it is as simple as looking for a mark denoting the thickness of the old gasket and using that to order the new gasket.

Other head gaskets incorporate stainless steel **fire rings** to help contain heat and pressure within the cylinder. Fire rings are steel rings built into the cylinder head gasket. The rings provide extra sealing on the top of the cylinder to help seal in the high-combustion pressures (hence the name "fire ring"). For high-performance use, such as in race cars, some engine builders use soft metal O-rings, which fit in shallow grooves cut in the head around the cylinders and passageways to seal the compression and fluids. The O-rings are crushed in place when the head bolts are torqued into place. This is a very effective but expensive way to seal the heads.

For many late-model vehicles, the preferred head gasket is a **multilayer steel (MLS) head gasket FIGURE 12-30**. These gaskets offer a wide range of benefits, such as strategically placed sealing beads that help eliminate leak paths, extra strong layers that provide superior combustion sealing, and a stainless steel material that maintains its shape despite thermal expansion and scrubbing between the engine block and the cylinder head. Many MLS and other head gaskets have an added silicone-based outer coating on both sides of the side material layers to provide additional cold sealing ability during start-up and warm-up.

Seals

Gaskets cannot be used around a rotating part, such as where the camshaft protrudes through the front of the cylinder head, because they would quickly wear out and

Top sheet
Stopper layer
Bottom sheet

FIGURE 12-30 Multilayer steel (MLS) head gasket.

leak. To seal the rotating parts of an engine, **oil seals** are needed. Oil seals are round seals made of rubber or a rubber-type compound of silicone, EPDM, or another durable, flexible material, placed in a metal housing. These seals are typically driven into a machined bore around a rotating part. A metal spring, called a **garter spring**, is wrapped circularly around the inside of the seal and applies a small, constant pressure to keep the lip in contact with the rotating part it is sealing. The most widely used seal for rotating parts is the **lip-type dynamic oil seal**. This seal is a precisely shaped, dynamic rubber lip. Like other oil seals, the lip-type dynamic oil seal also uses a garter spring to help keep the lip of the seal in contact with the shaft.

> ### TECHNICIAN TIP
>
> As a general rule, oil seals must be replaced with new ones when they are removed or when a component is overhauled or replaced.

A similar sealing principle is used to seal the valve stem to prevent oil from entering the engine combustion chamber. Like the oil seals, the valve stem seal is pressed onto the valve guide. It allows the valve to be wiped almost clean of oil on its opening trip, keeping a minimum amount of oil pulled down between the valve stem and the guide for lubrication purposes.

Stationary and slowly rotating or sliding shafts can also be sealed by using O-rings, a simple sealing device consisting of a rounded ring of rubber or plastic. O-rings are typically used to seal a joint against high pressure or the circumference of a rotating shaft from high- or low-pressure fluid leakage. The O-ring is inserted around the part to be sealed and held in place by an external housing. The O-ring seals the two surfaces. In many cases, the housing supplies the force to keep the ring in direct contact with the shaft. O-rings are generally effective at sealing high pressures where the differential speed between the opposing surfaces is minimal. In contrast, a lip seal is effective at sealing low pressures, but the differential speed between of the opposing surfaces can be substantial. As the lip-type seal wears, the garter spring holds tension on the seal, keeping it against the part it is sealing. The O-ring seal has no mechanism for self-adjustment. Once worn, its sealing ability is compromised.

Applied Science

> **AS-13: Pulleys: The technician can explain how pulleys can be used to increase an applied force over distance.** To increase applied force over distance, a multiple or moveable pulley system must be used. This theory relies on the concept of mechanical advantage, which is the multiplication of applied force through the use of a mechanical device.
>
> For a workshop example, imagine that you are trying to lift an engine block from the workshop floor using a rope and a single pulley attached to the ceiling. To lift the engine block off the floor, you must pull down on the rope with a force greater than the weight of the engine block. To keep the block suspended in the air, your exerted force must equal the weight of the block. The mechanical advantage of this system is 1. If you were to add a second pulley attached to the engine block, the weight of the block is now supported by both you and the section of rope between the upper and the lower pulleys, providing an increased mechanical advantage. The force you apply to the rope is now multiplied by the factor of mechanical advantage to exert more force to lift the block.

Sealants

Sealants are used to seal two surfaces that are in stationary contact with each other, such as between a gasket and the sealing surface of the part being sealed. Or it could be between two mating surfaces without a gasket between them. There are different sealants for various applications. And there are applications in which sealants are not to be used. For example, sealants are almost never applied to head gaskets.

To aid in gasket sealing, there are many different brands and types of sealants. One of the most popular types is **room temperature vulcanizing (RTV) silicone**. This adhesive is able to set or "vulcanize" at room temperature **FIGURE 12-31**. When RTV is applied, it has the consistency of a gel, and as it sets, it becomes rubbery. RTV should only be applied thick enough to fill the gaps with a small amount of squeeze out. If too much is used, it will squeeze out from between the surfaces and form large globs of material on the inside of the engine that can break off and plug up the oil pump screen, starving the engine of oil. Another caution when using RTV silicone is to make sure you use oxygen sensor–safe RTV on engines equipped with oxygen sensors. Regular RTV gases will be drawn through the PCV system and burned in the combustion chamber. The resulting burned silicone gases will then coat the surface of the oxygen sensor, rendering it inoperative.

FIGURE 12-31 Room temperature vulcanizing (RTV) silicone material being applied.

Some technicians prefer a nonhardening gasket sealant so that the sealant will "give" when the metal parts expand and contract under normal heating and cooling cycles. Additionally, this type of sealant is very forgiving with gasket surfaces that are less than perfect (e.g., scratched, nickel pitted). Gasoline-proof hardening sealants are also available, but they have little to no give once dry and are only used in extreme situations such as to help hold a cracked component together when a new component is not available. Always follow the manufacturer's recommendations for application.

A variety of different chemicals are available to hold gaskets in place and to aid in sealing. The most popular adhesive to hold a gasket in place is a form of contact cement that comes in an aerosol can. Contact cement is capable of adhering to many different surfaces, including felt, cork, metal, paper, rubber, and asbestos gaskets. In an automotive application, contact cement has been used on **valve cover gaskets**, fuel pump gaskets, and intake and exhaust manifold gaskets. However, adhesive sealants are not typically used on most newer-model vehicles. Before using any sealant, check the vehicle manufacturer's service information to be sure the product can be used with your application.

Cylinder Head Diagnosis

The cylinder head is subject to a variety of problems that can affect engine function. Cylinder head gaskets wear over time, cracking and creating holes through which coolant and compression can leak. Cracks in the cylinder block or head also may leak compression gases into the cooling system. The continual exposure to heat and cold (thermal cycles) over time may warp the cylinder

head, causing secondary problems such as compression, coolant, and oil leaks. Other relatively common cylinder head problems include burnt or warped valves and stripped spark plug hole threads.

Diagnosis of cylinder head problems begins with confirming the customer's observation about the vehicle, such as checking to see if the vehicle is actually misfiring or overheating. If it is misfiring, then a scan tool, scope, or power balance test can be used to identify which cylinders are misfiring. If the cause of the misfire is determined to be compression related, then compression and cylinder leakage tests should be performed.

If the engine is overheating due to a cylinder head or head gasket problem, then a cylinder leakage test or combustion gas detection test should be performed on the suspect cylinders. If the cylinder leakage test or combustion gas detection test indicates a combustion gas leak into the cooling system, the head will need to be removed so the head gasket and head can be inspected for leaks. Refer to the service information to identify the applicable procedures for these tests.

Cylinder Head Repair

Cracks in the cylinder head are a serious problem that is relatively common because of its lightweight construction. The main cause of cylinder head cracks is thermal stress. When metal is heated, it expands. While cylinder heads are designed to withstand a certain amount of expansion and their retaining bolts or studs a certain amount of stretch, the elevation in engine operating temperatures due to faults in the cooling system can push a cylinder head and retainers beyond their design limits. Over time, expansion and contraction can cause the metal to deform, causing cracks to form. Depending on the location of the crack, coolant, oil, or combustion gases may leak out of the cylinder head into the surrounding engine parts. Pressure testing the cylinder block and heads is a reliable method for identifying hard-to-see cracks.

The presence of a crack does not automatically condemn the cylinder head to the scrap bin. In some cases, repair methods have proven successful and less costly than replacement. Small cracks can be fixed by pinning (also known as cold repair), a process of drilling holes in a crack and installing overlapping pins to fill it that are then peened over to seal and blend the surface. While pinning sounds simple enough, it should only be performed by a highly trained machinist, preferably an ASE-certified master machinist. Furnace welding can also be used to repair cylinder head cracks. This process involves heating the cylinder head to extreme temperatures (about 1300°F [704°C]) and welding iron into the crack with an acetylene torch. This process requires even more skill than pinning and should not be attempted by anyone who is not an expert.

Heat stress and pressure stress can also cause the head to warp so that the sealing surface is no longer perfectly flat. Resurfacing the cylinder head restores a perfectly flat and specified surface finish to the head for placement of a new gasket. Resurfacing is best performed by milling the surface but can also be performed by grinding with the proper head-surfacing machine. The resurfacing process must be precise, with no more material removed than is necessary to clean up the surface, and is best left to a skilled machinist.

If you are dealing with an OHC head, then there are two surfaces that must be in alignment—the head surface and the camshaft journal bores. If the head surface is warped, it is likely that the camshaft bore is also warped. Since the camshaft is straight, if camshaft bore is warped, the camshaft will bind in the journal bearings. This means that a warped OHC head should be straightened so that the journal bore is aligned before the head surface is machined. Straightening a head is usually performed by bolting a head down to a straightening plate with shims placed between the head and the plate so that the head will be under tension. Then the head is heated up not more than 500°F and allowed to cool slowly. The head is again checked for flatness, and if it is flat, the head surface and camshaft journals can then be machined.

Damaged valves and valve seats can sometimes be reconditioned and reused rather than replaced. However, the price of new valves has dropped significantly over the years, making replacement the more common option for newer vehicles. For older vehicles for which replacement parts are not readily available, reconditioning is necessary. Reconditioning involves cleaning, fault detection, and machining. The process requires special equipment and a skilled and knowledgeable machinist.

Removing Cylinder Heads

Removing a cylinder head is considered a major task and is usually time intensive; therefore, cylinder head removal is done only after extensive testing and with a certainty that the problem lies in the cylinder head itself, its associated parts, or a part requiring removal of the cylinder head to access it (such as a piston). Once the diagnosis has been made, you will need to follow the steps as listed in the service information for the vehicle you are working on, since every engine is different. In fact, some manufacturers require that their head bolts be loosened in a specified pattern in specified steps and at certain temperatures. Failure to follow the manufacturer's instructions can lead to damage to the head.

Applied | **Science**

AS-93: Metallurgy: The technician can explain the critical need for metals of different hardnesses in automotive parts.
A typical automotive application of metals with different hardnesses is the relationship between crankshaft journals and crankshaft bearings in engines. Crankshafts are typically manufactured from cast iron or steel and are frequently surface-hardened to provide a hard surface for bearing contact, providing resistance to wear. Crankshaft bearings are surfaced with soft materials, typically babbitt, copper–lead, or aluminum alloys.

In normal running, a pressurized film of oil is maintained between the crankshaft and the bearing. Two essential properties are achieved through the use of soft surface materials—embeddability and conformability. Embeddability refers to the ability of the soft surface to absorb foreign materials forced between the crankshaft and the bearing, helping to prevent crankshaft wear. Conformability allows the bearing surface to move or shift to conform to a worn or damaged crankshaft journal.

To remove a cylinder head, follow the steps in **SKILL DRILL 12-1**:

1 Research the procedure for removing the cylinder head(s) in the appropriate service information. Determine whether the head bolts are torque-to-yield (TTY) bolts. If so, you will need to discard them and replace them with new TTY bolts upon reassembly. Determine if the head bolts need to be loosened in a specified sequence.

2 Before the heads come off, make sure you put an identifying mark on at least one of the heads so you know which head goes on which side of the block. Follow the specified procedure to remove all of the head bolts and set them aside. **(Photo 1)**

3 If dealing with a head gasket that is stuck to the head and block surface, reinstall two corner head bolts three or four turns in their respective holes. When you break the seal of the head gasket, these bolts will stop the head from falling off. **(Photo 2)**

4 If the engine is mounted on an engine stand, double-check that the safety pin is in your engine stand so the weight of the engine does not shift when you try to loosen the heads. Insert a pry bar or a long breaker bar handle into one of the intake port openings of the head and give it a firm push. You don't want to damage the inside of the intake port, so don't push too hard. **(Photo 3)**

5 Remove the safety bolts from the head. Put a few fingers in one of the intake ports and your other hand in an exhaust port to get a good grip before carefully lifting it. Cast iron cylinder heads are very heavy, especially if you have a big engine, so get some help lifting if you need it.

6 Inspect the cylinder head visually for any unusual conditions. Crusty flakes inside the combustion chamber are burned oil, which is a good indication of worn valve guides or piston rings. Engine symptoms can often be diagnosed by looking at the sealing surfaces of the head, block, and old gaskets, which sometimes stick to the head or block. **(Photo 4)**

Safety

When lifting heavy cylinder heads, you are probably leaning over the fender or front of the vehicle. This puts a large amount of strain on your lower back. Always get help when lifting cylinder heads and other heavy components.

SKILL DRILL | 12-1 | Removing Cylinder Heads

1 Before the heads come off, put an identifying mark on at least one of the heads. Follow the specified procedure to remove all of the head bolts and set them aside.

2 If dealing with a head gasket that is stuck to the head and block surface, reinstall two corner head bolts three or four turns in their respective holes.

3 If the engine is mounted on an engine stand, check that the safety pin is in your engine stand. Insert a pry bar or a long breaker bar handle into one of the intake port openings of the head and give it a firm push.

4 Remove the safety bolts from the head and carefully lift it. Inspect the cylinder head visually for any unusual conditions.

Cleaning, Disassembling, and Inspecting a Cylinder Head

The cylinder head must be cleaned after removal to make the inspection and repair process more efficient. You cannot have a good repair on a cylinder head if there are chunks of sludge and grime concealing damage or constantly falling into the area where you are working. Cleaning the cylinder head usually involves mechanically cleaning it with a scraping device such as a gasket scraper. If so, most aluminum heads must be scraped with a nonmetallic tool such as a plastic or nylon scraper made for the job. In most cases, the head will also need to be chemically cleaned in a spray tank, hot tank, cold tank, ultrasonic cleaner, or specially designed oven once it has been disassembled.

> ▶ **TECHNICIAN TIP**
>
> It is always a good idea to measure and record the installed valve height for at least one exhaust valve and one intake valve. This specification can be hard to locate for some vehicles. Since hydraulic lifters can only compensate approximately 0.060" to 0.080", knowing the installed height will be invaluable.

Follow the equipment manufacturer's recommendations when using a particular type of cleaner.

To clean and inspect a cylinder head, follow the steps in **SKILL DRILL 12-2**:

1. Place your cylinder head in a cylinder head holding fixture. These fixtures are usually designed to hold the cylinder head off of the work bench, allowing you to gain access for valve removal.

2. Tap the valve retainers lightly with a hammer and socket to break the valve keepers loose from the retainers. **(Photo 1)**

3. Use a valve spring compressor to compress the valve spring on each valve (one at a time), and remove the valve keepers.

4. After the keepers are removed, the valve can be removed and all parts kept in order of the way they came off. That way, if they are going to be reused, their wear patterns will match.

5. All parts you take off of the cylinder head need to go into a cylinder head disassembly board or small labeled bins. These will help you keep track of what valve and spring goes where for later installation. When in doubt, write it down and label it! **(Photo 2)**

6. Clean the gasket mating surfaces. On a cast iron head, cleaning is usually done with a flexible abrasive pad or by hand with a gasket scraper. If it is an

SKILL DRILL | **12-2** | **Cleaning and Inspecting a Cylinder Head**

1. Place your cylinder head in a cylinder head holding fixture. Tap the valve retainers lightly with a hammer and socket to break the valve keepers loose from the retainers.

2. Use a valve spring compressor to compress the valve spring on each valve (one at a time), and remove the valve keepers, then remove the valve. Place all parts you take off into a cylinder head disassembly board or small labeled bins.

3. Clean the gasket mating surfaces. On a cast iron head, cleaning is usually done with a flexible abrasive pad or by hand with a gasket scraper. If it is an aluminum head, use only plastic or nylon gasket scrapers.

SKILL DRILL | 12-2 | Cleaning and Inspecting a Cylinder Head, continued

4 Using a straightedge, measure the cylinder head warpage by setting the straightedge against the surface you are checking and seeing what size feeler blade will fit between the straightedge and the head surface.

5 Clean the cylinder head. Be aware that aluminum heads cannot generally be cleaned in a hot tank or high-temperature oven.

6 If the head is made of cast iron, you can locate small cracks with a Magnaflux tool. If there is a crack present, the powder will adhere to the crack.

aluminum head, use only plastic or nylon gasket scrapers. Refer to the service information to ensure the proper procedure is being used to clean all gasket mating surfaces. **(Photo 3)**

7 Using a straightedge, measure the cylinder head warpage by setting the straightedge on the surface you are checking. See if you can slide a 0.001" (0.0254 mm) feeler gauge under the straightedge. If you *can't*, then keep checking the surface in various places to ensure the same reading across the cylinder head. If you *can* slide a 0.001" feeler gauge underneath it, then you need to find out how big the deformation (warpage) is. Keep going up in value—0.002" (0.051 mm), 0.003" (0.0762 mm)—until the feeler will no longer fit underneath it. The last feeler blade that will go under the straightedge is the reading. Compare the reading to the service information warpage limit. Typical allowed warpage is 0.003" or less. **(Photo 4)**

8 Clean the cylinder head in an approved manner. This could be with a spray wash cabinet, hot tank, cold tank, ultrasonic cleaner, or high-temperature oven. Be aware that aluminum heads cannot generally be cleaned in a hot tank or high-temperature oven. Follow the manufacturer's recommended procedure for thoroughly cleaning the head. **(Photo 5)**

9 If the head is made of cast iron, you can locate small cracks with a Magnaflux tool. The Magnaflux

process involves placing a strong electromagnet across each part of the head surface at 90-degree offsets and lightly dusting the head with a magnetic powder. If there is a crack present, the powder will adhere to the crack because the crack creates a north and south magnetic field at that point, and the powder sticks to it. **(Photo 6)**

10 If the head is made of aluminum, the Magnaflux process cannot be used because the metal is nonferrous. Spray or wipe a penetrating die over the surface to be checked, followed by a light coat of developer. Once the developer dries, any cracks should show up as colored lines.

11 Pressure checking can be used on both cast iron and aluminum heads, but is usually available only at well-equipped machine shops. The cooling system passages are blocked off and filled with compressed air. They are then either immersed in water and inspected for leaks or sprayed with a soapy solution and inspected for bubbles.

Safety

When cleaning and scraping a cylinder head, be very careful: Many of the surfaces are sharp and can cut you severely.

Inspecting Valves and Valve Seats

Valves and valve seats must operate in very hostile conditions, so they need to be inspected closely whenever the cylinder head is removed from the engine. Valves can burn or warp, which leads to misfire issues. The valve tip can also become worn from lack of lubrication, leading to a ticking sound, and the valve stems can wear in the area that moves inside the valve stem, leading to burning of engine oil. When valves are removed from the cylinder head, the valves and seats should be inspected visually for cracks, burn marks, signs of leaks, and damage to the valve face, stem, and tip. If any of these issues are found, the valve will need to be replaced and the seat will need to be either replaced or repaired, depending on the damage. If there are no apparent issues, then the valves and seats should be measured and compared to specifications.

The valve stem diameter should be measured in the area that rides in the valve guide with a micrometer and compared to specifications. Some valves come with a tapered valve stem where the stem closest to the head end of the valve is slightly narrower to allow for expansion of the stem on today's hotter-running engines. The margin of the valve will need to be measured with a machinist's rule to make sure it is within specifications. The valve seat width will also need to be measured and compared to specifications.

To inspect valves and valve seats and determine any necessary actions, follow the steps in **SKILL DRILL 12-3**:

1. Visually inspect each valve for signs of burning, warpage, and excessive face, stem, and tip wear. If found, replace the valves with new ones. **(Photo 1)**

SKILL DRILL 12-3 | Inspecting Valves and Valve Seats

1. Inspect each valve for signs of burning, warpage, and excessive face, stem, and tip wear. If found, replace the valves with new ones.

2. Inspect each valve seat for signs of burning, leakage, or excessive wear. If found, the seat must be machined or replaced.

3. Using a micrometer, measure each valve stem diameter in three places where the valve rides in the valve guide, and average your answers.

4. Measure the valve margin with a machinist's rule and record your readings.

5. Measure the width of the valve seats and record your readings. Compare readings to the specifications and determine needed actions.

2 Visually inspect each valve seat for signs of burning, leakage, or excessive wear. If found, the seat must be machined or replaced. **(Photo 2)**

3 Using a micrometer, measure each valve stem diameter in three places where the valve rides in the valve guide, and average your answers. **(Photo 3)**

4 Measure the valve margin with a machinist's rule and record your readings. **(Photo 4)**

5 Measure the width of the valve seats and record your readings.

6 Compare all readings to the specifications and determine any needed actions. **(Photo 5)**

Inspecting Valve Guides and Valve Stem-to-Guide Clearance

Valves and valve guides are subject to high temperatures and pressures that tend to wear their sides. If they wear much at all, oil can be pulled down the valve stem and burned in the combustion chamber of exhaust. If the wear continues, the valve can move around in the guide so far that the head of the valve does not close properly and catches on the top of the valve seat. This causes the valve to leak and leads to intermittent misfires in that cylinder.

Valves and guides can be measured in two ways: with a micrometer or with a dial indicator. If using a micrometer, a ball gauge is used to measure the top, center, and bottom of the valve guide. The ball gauge is placed in the valve guide in each of those positions and expanded until both sides of the gauge touch the inside of the guide. It is then removed from the guide, measured with a micrometer, and recorded. The center reading is then subtracted from the ends to determine how much the guide is tapered. The smallest reading (usually the center reading) is used to determine the overall size of the guide. The valve stem is also measured and recorded. If the valve stem is within specifications, then the difference between the valve guide and the valve stem is the valve-to-guide clearance and all of the readings can be compared to the manufacturer's specifications.

A dial indicator is used with the valve installed in the valve guide. The dial indicator is mounted on the head and placed against the side of the valve stem near the top of the valve. With the valve at its normally open height, rock the head of the valve stem back and forth, observing the movement on the dial indicator, and compare to specifications.

To inspect valve guides for wear, check valve stem-to-guide clearance, and determine any necessary actions using a micrometer, follow the steps in **SKILL DRILL 12-4**:

1 Clean the guide with solvent and a valve guide brush if not already cleaned.

2 Insert the ball gauge into the top of the guide and expand it until it touches both sides with a slight amount of drag.

3 Carefully pull the ball gauge out of the guide without disturbing the setting and measure it with a micrometer. Record your reading.

4 Repeat this procedure on the center portion of the valve guide and record your reading.

5 Repeat this procedure on the bottom portion of the valve guide and record your reading.

6 Measure the valve stem diameter at the top, center, and bottom of the wear area and record your readings.

7 Calculate the taper and valve clearance; compare all of the readings to specifications and determine any necessary actions.

To inspect valve guides for wear using a dial indicator, follow the steps in **SKILL DRILL 12-5**:

1 Verify that the valve guide is clean. Reinstall the valve in the guide at the fully open length.

2 Set the dial indicator so it can measure the side-to-side movement of the head of the valve.

3 Move the valve side to side and measure the movement with the dial indicator. Record your reading. Compare to specifications and determine any necessary actions.

Inspecting Valve Springs

Using the correct size and strength of valve spring is critical to engine operation. Valve springs must be able to quickly and firmly force the valves closed. It is important to always measure the valve springs and confirm that they meet the specifications before installing them. The three key steps in testing a valve spring are (1) checking for squareness, (2) measuring spring height, and (3) measuring the installed pressure. Checking for squareness is a test to ensure that the spring is not damaged and can compress and load the valve evenly. Measuring spring height is simply checking that the spring is indeed the correct height and has not fatigued. A valve with uneven pressure or the incorrect installed pressure will cause the valve to wear the valve stem and guide due to the side-to-side pulling force exerted by the "bent" spring.

Measuring the valve spring's installed pressure involves determining how much pressure the spring can produce when it is at its installed height and making sure it meets specifications. This pressure is measured by compressing the spring to its installed height with a valve spring tester. The tester will show the pressure exerted by the spring. This tester looks like a drill press without the drill and is typically a freestanding or bench-mounted unit.

To inspect valve springs, follow the steps in **SKILL DRILL 12-6**:

1. Check the valve springs for squareness by setting each spring on a perfectly flat surface such as calibrated blocks made for this purpose. Place a combination square against the spring and rotate the spring as you check for any gaps around it. Measure any gap with a feeler gauge. If any gap is above 0.0625" (1.6 mm), replace the spring. Check the rest of the valve springs in the exact same manner. Replace all suspect springs. **(Photo 1)**

2. Using a vernier caliper, measure the spring free height and compare your measurement with the specifications provided in the service information. If the spring is out of specifications or close to being out of specifications, replace the spring. Repeat this process for all other springs. **(Photo 2)**

3. To measure the spring's installed pressure (the pressure the spring is capable of producing when it is at its installed height), install the valve spring on the valve spring tester. Pull the side handle and compress the spring to the installed height specified in the service information (or measured during disassembly if no specifications are available) while reading the tester. Record the force that the spring produced and compare that to the specifications. Any spring that is out of specifications or close to being out of specifications should not be used! **(Photo 3)**

Reassembling a Cylinder Head

Once all work on the valves, springs, and head is completed, the cylinder head will need to be cleaned again and then reassembled. The following is a generic version of cylinder head reassembly and is not meant to supersede any manufacturer's cylinder head reassembly instructions. You should always check for the most current information on the vehicle you are working on through the manufacturer's recommended service information.

To reassemble a cylinder head, follow the steps in **SKILL DRILL 12-7**:

1. Ensure that all parts and passageways have been cleaned, checked for defects, and replaced if necessary. If any defects are found, correct them before continuing. **(Photo 1)**

2. Dip the valve stem that is about to be installed in clean engine oil or use the appropriate assembly lubrication. This provides initial start-up lubrication. **(Photo 2)**

SKILL DRILL | 12-6 | Inspecting the Valve Springs

1. Set the spring on a perfectly flat surface. Place a combination square against the spring and rotate the spring as you measure any gaps around it using a feeler gauge. Gaps should not exceed 0.0625" (1.6 mm). Replace all suspect springs. Repeat this process for all springs.

2. Using a vernier caliper, measure the spring free height and compare your measurements with the specifications provided in the service information. Replace the spring if it is out of specification. Repeat this process for all springs.

3. To measure the spring's installed pressure, install the valve spring on the valve spring tester. Pull the side handle and compress the spring to the installed height specified in the service information while reading the tester. Record the force that the spring produced and compare that to the specifications. Do not use springs out of specification.

SKILL DRILL | 12-7 | Reassembling a Cylinder Head

1 Ensure that all parts and passageways have been cleaned, checked for defects, and replaced if necessary. If any defects are found, correct them now.

2 Dip the valve stem that is about to be installed in clean engine oil or use the appropriate assembly lubrication.

3 Insert the corresponding valve into the valve guide and place the protective sleeve over the grooves near the end of the valve stem.

4 Dip the valve seal in clean engine oil and install it down over the exposed top of the valve guide assembly, using an installer if necessary.

5 Remove the protective sleeve and place the valve spring and retainer over the installed valve.

6 Compress the valve spring and retainer with the valve spring compressor and install the valve keepers. Be sure the keepers are locked into their groove before releasing pressure on the valve spring compressor. Repeat this process for the remaining valves.

3 Insert the corresponding valve into the valve guide and place the protective sleeve over the grooves near the end of the valve stem. The sleeve will protect the seal from being cut by the keeper grooves as it passes over them. **(Photo 3)**

4 Dip the valve seal in clean engine oil and install it down over the exposed top of the valve guide assembly, using an installer if necessary. Be careful! Valve seals can differ in size from intake to exhaust, so be sure you are putting the valve seal on the correct valve. (Note: O-ring valve seals are put on after the spring and retainer are compressed, but before the keepers are installed.) **(Photo 4)**

5 Remove the protective sleeve and place the valve spring and retainer down over the installed valve. **(Photo 5)**

6 Compress the valve spring and retainer with the valve spring compressor and install the valve keepers. Be sure the keepers are locked into their groove before releasing pressure on the valve spring compressor!

7 Repeat this process for the installation of the remaining valves. **(Photo 6)**

Inspecting Pushrods and Rocker Arms

Since pushrods and rocker arms operate under large sliding forces, they tend to experience wear over time and need to be inspected at each point of contact. On pushrods, that means each end. The balls or sockets typically lose their roundedness and become slightly pointy. Also, there is typically a small flat spot on the top of the pushrod. If the pushrod is worn, the flat spot will be smaller than it should be or worn off altogether. Pushrods also need to be perfectly straight; otherwise they are subject to bending, which would render them inoperative. Rolling them on a piece of glass or perfectly flat surface plate will indicate if they are bent.

Rocker arms have three potential wear surfaces to inspect: the pushrod end, the valve end, and the pivot. The pushrod end of the rocker arm mates with the end of the pushrod, so they usually wear similarly. The valve end of the rocker arm can also wear, creating a groove in the face. The pivot can mate to a ball-shaped pivot, a T-shaped pivot, or a pivot shaft. Look at both the pivot and the mating surface on the rocker arm to see if there is excessive wear. If any of the three surfaces of the rocker arm are excessively worn, the rocker arm and pivot will need to be replaced.

To inspect pushrods, rocker arms, and rocker arm pivots and shafts for wear, bending, cracks, looseness, and blocked oil passages (orifices) and determine any necessary actions, follow the steps in **SKILL DRILL 12-8**:

1. Visually inspect the ends of the pushrods for excessive wear. If the pushrod is hollow, blow compressed air through it to verify it is not plugged. **(Photo 1)**
2. Roll each pushrod on a piece of glass or surface plate to check if it is bent. If the pushrods are hollow, check that they are clear by blowing compressed air through them. **(Photo 2)**
3. Visually inspect the valve end of the rocker arms for excessive wear or damage. **(Photo 3)**
4. Visually inspect the pushrod end of the rocker arms for excessive wear or damage. If they are equipped with an oil passage, blow compressed air through them to check that they are not plugged. **(Photo 4)**
5. Visually inspect the center pivot surface of the rocker arms for wear or damage. **(Photo 5)**
6. Visually inspect the pivots or rocker arm shafts for wear or damage. If the rocker arm shafts are equipped with oil passages, blow compressed air through them to check that they are not plugged. **(Photo 6)**

SKILL DRILL | **12-8** | **Inspecting Pushrods, Rocker Arms, and Rocker Arm Pivots and Shafts**

1. Inspect the ends of the pushrods for excessive wear. If the pushrod is hollow, blow compressed air through it to verify it is not plugged.

2. Roll each pushrod on a piece of glass or surface plate to check if it is bent. If the pushrods are hollow, blow compressed air through them.

3. Inspect the valve end of the rocker arms for excessive wear or damage.

SKILL DRILL	**12-8**

Inspecting Pushrods, Rocker Arms, and Rocker Arm Pivots and Shafts, continued

4 Inspect the pushrod end of the rocker arms for excessive wear or damage. If they are equipped with oil passages, blow compressed air through them.

5 Inspect the center pivot surface of the rocker arms for wear or damage.

6 Inspect the pivots or rocker arm shafts for wear or damage. If the rocker arm shafts are equipped with oil passages, blow compressed air through them.

Inspecting and Measuring Camshaft

The camshaft experiences heavy loads on the cam lobes and journals, which need to be inspected and measured if the camshaft is being reused. A good inspection will reveal whether the cam needs to be measured. Look for obvious indicators of excessive wear such as heavy scoring on cam lobes or a bluish color indicating overheating. If there is not obvious wear, take a closer look at the cam lobes. Can you see worn layers, similar to tree rings, in the surface? If so, the hardened surface of the cam lobe is worn through and needs to be replaced.

Camshafts can also warp, which can put extra wear on the camshaft journals as well as on the camshaft bearings. The cam journals first should be measured for diameter and out-of-round with a micrometer and compared to specifications. If the journals do not meet the specifications, the camshaft will need to be replaced and the other measurements can be skipped.

The camshaft warpage and camshaft lobes are best measured with a dial indicator and set of "V"-blocks. The camshaft is placed on the V-blocks so that two of the camshaft journals are each sitting in a V. Some manufacturers specify the two center journals, while others specify the outer two journals. The dial indicator is used first to check for warpage; it is placed on either the center journal or the outer journal, whichever is not sitting in a V. The dial indicator must be at 90 degrees to the journal. Once set properly, the camshaft is carefully rotated and the dial indicator watched, noting the maximum variation. This process is repeated on each of the other journals and compared to specifications. If the cam is not warped, then use the dial indicator to measure the maximum lift on each cam lobe and compare to specifications.

To inspect and/or measure the camshaft for runout, journal wear, and lobe wear, follow the steps in **SKILL DRILL 12-9**:

1 Visually inspect the camshaft journals and lobes for obvious damage such as heavy wear, wear through the hardened layers on the lobes, or rough friction surfaces. If found, replace the camshaft.

2 Install the camshaft on a set of V-blocks so that two specified cam journals are resting in the Vs. **(Photo 1)**

3 Set the dial indicator so it is engaged on one of the other cam journals perpendicularly. **(Photo 2)**

4 Rotate the camshaft until the dial indicator reads the lowest point and zero the dial. **(Photo 3)**

5 Rotate the camshaft until the dial indicator reads the highest point and record the reading.

6 Continue rotating the camshaft to verify that the needle does not go below zero. If it does, zero it again and remeasure the runout. Perform this process on all of the remaining journals and compare to the runout specifications. **(Photo 4)**

7 Using a micrometer, measure each journal in two places 90 degrees apart to determine any out-of-round condition. Record your readings, and compare to the specifications. **(Photo 5)**

8 Reset the dial indicator so it is engaged on one of the cam lobes perpendicularly.

9 Rotate the camshaft until the dial indicator reads the lowest point and zero the dial. **(Photo 6)**

SKILL DRILL | 12-9 | Inspecting and/or Measuring the Camshaft

1 Inspect the camshaft journals and lobes for obvious damage or wear. If found, replace the camshaft. Install the camshaft on a set of V-blocks so that two specified cam journals are resting in the Vs.

2 Set the dial indicator so it is engaged on one of the other cam journals perpendicularly.

3 Rotate the camshaft until the dial indicator reads the lowest point and zero the dial.

4 Rotate the camshaft until the dial indicator reads the highest point and record the reading. Continue rotating the camshaft to verify that the needle does not go below zero. If it does, zero it again and remeasure the runout. Perform this process on all of the remaining journals and compare to the runout specifications.

5 Using a micrometer, measure each journal in two places 90 degrees apart to determine any out-of-round condition. Record your readings, and compare to the specifications.

6 Reset the dial indicator so it is engaged on one of the cam lobes perpendicularly. Rotate the camshaft until the dial indicator reads the lowest point and zero the dial.

SKILL DRILL | 12-9 | Inspecting and/or Measuring the Camshaft, continued

7 Rotate the camshaft until the dial indicator reads the highest point and record the reading. Continue to rotate the camshaft to verify that the needle does not go below zero. If it does, zero it again and remeasure the lobe. Measure each of the remaining cam lobes and compare your readings to specifications.

---

10 Rotate the camshaft until the dial indicator reads the highest point and record the reading. Continue to rotate the camshaft to verify that the needle does not go below zero. If it does, zero it again and remeasure the lobe.

11 Measure each of the remaining cam lobes and compare your readings to specifications. **(Photo 7)**

Inspecting Camshaft Bearings

Camshaft bearings support the camshaft; therefore, their alignment and size are critical to the operation of the camshaft and engine oil pressure. In cast iron heads, the cast iron is too hard of a surface for the camshaft journals to ride on, so bearing inserts are used in the camshaft towers. Most aluminum heads allow the camshaft journal to ride directly on the aluminum because it is a softer material and provides a reasonable bearing surface. The bearing diameter will need to be measured with a dial bore gauge or inside micrometer and compared to specifications. If the diameter is oversized and the head uses replaceable bearings, then the bearing will need to be replaced with new ones. If the head uses a bolt-on aluminum cap as a bearing, then a machinist can remachine the bore to its original size, but the camshaft will sit just a bit lower in the head, which can affect valve timing. If the head uses solid cam towers as

camshaft bearings and the bores are oversized or damaged, in many cases the head will need to be replaced; however, in some cases, oversized camshafts or bushings are available.

The last thing to check is for camshaft bore alignment. This can be checked by laying a straightedge along the bottom of the camshaft bearings and using a feeler blade to measure any space between the straightedge and the camshaft bearing surface. Or, if the camshaft is straight and not undersized, it can be installed and checked for binding. If there is no binding, the cam bearing alignment is OK.

To inspect the camshaft bearing surface for wear, damage, out-of-round, and alignment and determine necessary actions, see **SKILL DRILL 12-10**:

1 Visually inspect the camshaft bearing surfaces for obvious wear or damage. If observed, the bearing surfaces will have to be replaced or, if possible, machined.

2 If the cam bearings bolt onto the head, bolt them on and torque them to specifications. **(Photo 1)**

3 Place the dial bore gauge vertically in each camshaft bearing and measure the diameter. Record your reading. **(Photo 2)**

4 Place the dial bore gauge horizontally in each camshaft bearing and measure the diameter. Record

your reading. Also calculate any out-of-round by subtracting the horizontal reading from the vertical reading. Record that calculation. **(Photo 3)**

5 Lay a straightedge within the camshaft bearings, and measure any clearance between the straight-edge and the bearing with a feeler blade. **(Photo 4)**

6 Another way to check for bearing alignment, if you have already verified that the camshaft is straight and the journals are the specified size, is to slide the camshaft into the bearing bores and check for any binding. If there is no binding, the bearing alignment is OK. **(Photo 5)**

Installing the OHC and DOHC Camshaft

Now that the valves are installed, it may or may not be time to install the camshaft(s) and valve actuators. In some engine designs, the camshaft(s) prevent access to tighten the head bolts; therefore, the camshaft(s) need to be installed after the head has been properly torqued into place on the block. In other engines, the camshaft and valve actuators can be installed while the head is off the engine without interfering with torquing the head bolts. Always check the manufacturer's procedure to know when to install the camshaft(s).

SKILL DRILL   12-10   Inspecting Camshaft Bearings

1 Inspect the camshaft bearing surfaces for obvious wear or damage. If observed, the bearing surfaces will have to be machined or replaced. If the cam bearings bolt onto the head, bolt them on and torque them to specifications.

2 Place the dial bore gauge vertically in each camshaft bearing and measure the diameter. Record your reading.

3 Place the dial bore gauge horizontally in each camshaft bearing and measure the diameter. Record your reading and calculate any out-of-round.

4 Lay a straightedge within the camshaft bearings, and measure any clearance between the straightedge and the bearings with a feeler blade.

5 If you have already verified that the camshaft is straight and the journals are the specified size, slide the camshaft into the bearing bores and check for any binding. If there is no binding, the bearing alignment is OK.

Bucket-Style Lifter Heads

Assembling the camshaft and valve actuators is fairly straightforward on a head that uses bucket-style lifters, but mistakes can be made. Some engines use the same bucket lifters for intake and exhaust, while other engines use separate ones. Verify that the proper bucket lifter is installed in the correct hole. Some bucket lifters use an integrated hydraulic lifter, and no adjustment is necessary if the valve installed height is correct. Other engines use solid bucket lifters, which typically use shims to adjust the valve clearance. The clearance is usually adjusted after the camshaft is installed and torqued into place.

When installing the camshafts on a bucket lifter head, you must be careful to install the intake camshaft on the intake valves and the exhaust camshaft on the exhaust valves; otherwise the engine is likely to not run or to run improperly since the valve timing will be way off. Another challenge is to get the timing marks of the timing gears aligned to the manufacturer's specifications. In many cases with dual cams, once the cams and valve actuators are in place and any valve adjustments are made, a special tool is used to hold the cam gears in the proper position while waiting for installation of the head on the block.

To install the camshaft in heads with bucket-style lifters, follow the steps in SKILL DRILL 12-11:

1. Lubricate the top of the valve stem and the bucket lifters with clean engine oil or assembly lube.
2. Install the bucket lifters on top of the valve in the same hole they were removed from originally if they are being reused. Remember that in some engines, the intake and exhaust lifters are different from each other. Also, if the lifters and camshaft are being reused, they have worn together and must be reinstalled in their original orientation. (Photo 1)
3. Lubricate the cam bearings, journals, and lobes with clean oil or assembly lube. Doing so will provide initial lubrication during start-up.
4. Install the camshaft in the bearings, and place the bearing caps in their original position, since they are mated to the bottom half of the bearing.
5. Tighten all of the cam bearing bolts finger tight. (Photo 2)
6. Tighten each cam bearing bolt about one turn at a time following the specified bolt tightening sequence. This usually means starting with the center bearing cap and working outward.

SKILL DRILL 12-11 Installing the Camshaft in Heads with Bucket-Style Lifters

1. Lubricate the top of the valve stem and the bucket lifters with clean engine oil or assembly lube. Install the bucket lifters on top of the valve in the same hole they were removed from originally if they are being reused.
2. Lubricate the cam bearings, journals, and lobes with clean oil or assembly lube. Install the camshaft in the bearings, and place the bearing caps in their original position. Tighten cam bearing bolts finger tight.
3. Tighten each cam bearing bolt about one turn at a time following the specified sequence. Once all of the bolts have the caps against the cylinder head, torque the bolts to the specified torque. If the camshaft is driven by a timing belt, lubricate the camshaft seal(s) and install them around each camshaft.

7 Once all of the bolts have the caps against the cylinder head, torque the bolts in the specified sequence to the proper torque. This may require a multistep torquing procedure, or a TTY process.

8 If the camshaft is driven by a timing belt, lubricate the camshaft seal(s) and install them around each camshaft, being careful to not cut the seal or damage the seal housing. (**Photo 3**)

Cam Follower/Rocker Arm–Style Heads

Assembling a head that uses cam followers or rocker arms may begin with the installation of the camshaft, or the rocker arms may need to be installed first depending on the design. If the assembly is to begin with the camshaft according to manufacturer, lubricate the camshaft journals and slide the camshaft into place in the bearings, making sure the cam can be turned freely. If it binds, you either have a warped camshaft, or one or more bearings are too tight and will need to be scraped with a bearing scraper. Once the camshaft is free to turn, install any lifters into their bores, preferably not pumped up. You should then be able to slide the camshaft into place on the tips of the valves and lifters.

If the head uses a rocker arm shaft instead of cam followers, position the rocker arm shaft onto the engine with the rocker arms sitting on top of each valve and up against each cam lobe. Once everything is in place, you should be able to bolt the rocker arm shaft down slowly. Only turn each bolt about one turn at a time, to help draw it down evenly. Once all of the bolts are seated, torque each one following the specified order to the specified torque. This could take multiple passes, torquing each bolt in order.

To assemble cam follower/rocker arm–style heads, follow the steps in **SKILL DRILL 12-12**:

1 Temporarily install the camshaft into the cam bearings and install the bearing caps.

2 Make sure the camshaft turns freely in the bearings. If not, you may need to lightly scrape the cam bearings or replace the camshaft if it is warped.

3 Lubricate the rocker arm pivot points and the valve tips using engine assembly lube or clean engine oil. (**Photo 1**)

4 Install the rocker arms into the pivot points and over the tip of the valve. (**Photo 2**)

5 Lubricate the rocker arm where the camshaft lobe will ride using engine assembly lube or clean engine oil.

6 Lubricate the camshaft bearings, journals, and cam lobes with engine assembly lube or clean engine

SKILL DRILL 12-12 Assembling Cam Follower/Rocker Arm–Style Heads

1 Lubricate the rocker arm pivot points and the valve tips using engine assembly lube or clean engine oil.

2 Install the rocker arms into the pivot points and over the tip of the valve.

3 Lubricate the rocker arm where the camshaft lobe will ride using engine assembly lube or clean engine oil. Lubricate the camshaft bearings, journals, and cam lobes with engine assembly lube or clean engine oil. Install the camshaft into the camshaft bearings.

SKILL DRILL | 12-12 | Assembling Cam Follower/Rocker Arm–Style Heads, continued

4 Install the camshaft support caps. Tighten the support cap bolts finger tight and torque the bolts to the manufacturer's specification.

5 Use a feeler gauge to measure the valve clearance following the manufacturer's recommended procedure.

6 Adjust the valve clearance to the manufacturer's specifications. Be sure to retighten the adjustment jam nut to prevent the clearance from changing.

oil. Doing so will protect the camshaft during initial start-up.

7 Install the camshaft into the camshaft bearings. (**Photo 3**)

8 Install the camshaft support caps. Tighten the support cap bolts finger tight and then torque the bolts to the manufacturer's specification. (**Photo 4**)

9 Use a feeler gauge to measure the valve clearance following the manufacturer's recommended procedure. (**Photo 5**)

10 Adjust the valve clearance to the manufacturer's specifications. Be sure to retighten the adjustment jam nut to prevent the clearance from changing. (**Photo 6**)

Wrap-up

Ready for Review

- Functions of the cylinder head include: admit air and fuel to combustion chamber, release exhaust after combustion, and allow coolant to flow around the top of the combustion chamber.
- The cylinder head forms the top of the combustion chamber and is securely fastened with a head gasket between the head and block.
- Cylinder heads may be aluminum alloy (lighter weight, boosts fuel economy) or cast iron (heavier, but lower engine operating temperatures).
- Engines may be overhead valve, overhead cam, or dual overhead cam.
- Cylinder head parts include: base cylinder head casting, intake valves, exhaust valves, valve keepers, valve retainers, valve springs, oil seals, coolant seals, rocker arms, plugs, and camshaft.
- Cylinder heads are designed to improve the swirl and turbulence of the air/fuel mixture moving into the combustion chamber.
- A hemispherical (HEMI) combustion chamber has intake and exhaust valves located on opposite sides to create cross flow of gasses.
- The amount of air an engine can take in and remove is referred to as "breathing."
- The greater the air/fuel mixture, the more heat is generated, and thus more engine power.
- Dual overhead cam engines often have multivalve cylinder heads to create quicker, more efficient air/fuel movement.
- Cylinder head shapes can be oval (bathtub), wedge, hemispherical, or gas direct injection (GDI).
- Smaller intake and exhaust ports are generally better for engines that operate at low speeds (4-wheel drive), while larger intake and exhaust ports are ideal for engines operating at high speeds.
- Components of the valve train are driven from the camshaft and include: lifters, push rods, rocker arms or cam followers, valves, valve springs, keepers, and retainers.
- Components of the valve are: valve tip, keeper grooves, valve stem, valve face, and valve margin.
- Valves are located in the cylinder head and are configured in two-, three-, four-, and five-valve arrangements.
- Most engines are fitted with poppet (mushroom) valves.
- Exhaust valves are designed to withstand higher temperatures than intake valves.
- Valve guides are integral (non-replaceable) or non-integral (replaceable) and are designed to limit a valve's movement to up-and-down and retain lubrication for the valve stem.
- Valve stem seals are designed to prevent oil leakage; the three basic types are umbrella style, O-ring, and positive.
- Valve seats form a strong seal with the valve face and must withstand high temperatures and extreme pressure.
- Valve train refers to all the parts that contribute to the opening or closing of the intake and exhaust valves.
- Types of valve trains correspond to engine types: overhead valve, overhead cam, or dual overhead cam.
- Rocker arms are categorized by the ratio of movement on the valve side to movement on the push rod side.
- Push rods, found in overhead valve engines, transfer the motion from the valve lifter to the rocker arm; push rod types are: ball-to-ball, ball-to-cup, and ball-to-adjustable tip.
- Lifters can be solid (manually adjusted) or hydraulic (self-adjusting) and are located in the engine block, cylinder head, rocker arms, and between the cam and valve tip.
- Camshaft followers are used in overhead camshaft engines in place of rocker arms.
- Bucket-style lifters transmit movement from the cam lobe to the tip of the valve.
- The valve spring is designed to close the valve and exert pressure to hold it firmly against the valve seat.
- Valve-spring retainers and valve locks (keepers) hold the valve spring in place.
- Gaskets are designed to create a seal when compressed between two stationary parts.
- Gaskets are single use only and must withstand engine heat.
- Functions of a head gasket are to seal and contain combustion pressure, seal oil passages, and control coolant flow.
- Anisotropic head gaskets conduct heat laterally.
- Oil seals can seal the rotating parts of an engine and are made of rubber or a rubber-type compound

comprised of silicone, EPDM, or other flexible material.

▸ The lip-type dynamic oil seal is the most commonly used type.

▸ O-rings are used to seal stationary or slowly rotating shafts.

▸ Sealants are designed to seal together two surfaces in stationary contact with one another.

▸ Always check manufacturer recommendations for the proper type of sealant.

▸ Common cylinder head problems include: wear, cracks, leaking coolant or compression gasses, warped cylinder head, burnt or warped valves, and stripped spark plug hole threads.

▸ Thermal stress is the main cause of cylinder head cracks.

▸ Many cylinder head repairs require the skill of a certified machinist.

▸ Only remove the cylinder head after extensive testing and certainty that removal is required.

▸ Always clean the cylinder head after removal.

▸ Test valve springs for squareness and measure both spring height and installed pressure.

Key Terms

anisotropic An object that has unequal physical properties, along its various axes. Used in head gaskets to pull heat laterally from the edge surrounding the combustion chamber to the water jacket.

bedding-in The process of a valve wearing into the valve seat and creating a positive seal around the whole diameter.

bucket-style lifter A bucket-shaped lifter assembly that sits on top of the valves and is operated directly by the camshaft. It can be hydraulic or mechanical.

camshaft follower A slider or roller placed in direct contact with the lobes of the OHC camshaft that pushes on the tip of the valve to open it.

camshaft lobe The eccentric "egg-shaped" portion of the camshaft that pushes on the valve lifter or camshaft follower.

canted valves A valve arrangement in the cylinder head where the valves are at an angle to the cylinder bore. Canting the valves can make for a straighter path for air to flow into and out of the intake and exhaust ports.

combustion chamber The area of an engine in which the air/fuel mixture is burnt. It consists of the bottom of the cylinder head and the top of the piston.

combustion pressure The force exerted by the expanding gases during the burning process. It is what causes the internal combustion engine to operate.

concentricity A term used to describe a valve seat where the valve seat and valve stem share a common center. In this design, the valve can seal against the seat no matter how it is rotated.

cylinder head The part of the engine that is bolted to the engine block and caps off the top of the combustion chamber.

dual overhead cam (DOHC) engine An engine design that is like the overhead cam engine but with two camshafts used per cylinder head; one operates the intake valves and the other operates the exhaust valves.

exhaust valve The valve through which exhaust gases are forced out of the combustion chamber.

fire rings Steel rings integrated into the cylinder head gasket nearest the combustion chambers that provide extra sealing to seal in the high combustion pressures.

flame front The front edge of the burning air/fuel mixture in the combustion chamber.

flame propagation The movement of the flame through the combustion chamber during the combustion process.

flat tappet A camshaft specifically designed to push on flat bottom lifters (nonroller types). It typically has a higher rolling resistance than the roller-style camshafts.

garter spring A metal spring wrapped circularly around the inside of a lip seal to keep it in constant contact with the moving shaft.

gas direct injection (GDI) cylinder head A cylinder head designed to accept a gasoline injector directly in the combustion chamber instead of in the intake manifold.

gasket Any material used on an engine to seal a fluid or gas into a particular area.

head gasket A thin piece of material, often a multi-layered, bimetallic sheet used to seal the cylinder head assembly to the engine block.

hemispherical cylinder head A combustion chamber that is hemispherical in shape with the valves in a crossflow arrangement and the spark plug near the center of the cylinder head directly over the top of the piston.

hydraulic valve lifter A small mechanical cylinder with a hydraulically operated internal piston used to automatically take up the slack (valve clearance) in the valve train.

intake port The port through which the air or air/fuel mixture travels from the throttle body area to the combustion chamber.

intake valve The valve through which air and fuel enter the combustion chamber.

integral valve guide A valve guide machined into the cylinder head during cylinder head construction.

interference angle The built-in differences in the angles between the valve seat and the valve face for the purpose of providing quick wearing-in of the surfaces; there usually must be between ½ and 1 degree of difference.

keeper groove A groove machined into the top of the valve stem near the tip of the valve that is used to "lock in" the valve keepers to help retain the valve spring onto the valve assembly.

L-head A type of four-stroke internal combustion engine having both intake and exhaust valves located in one side of the engine block, which are operated by lifters actuated by a single camshaft. It is sometimes called a flat head because there are no valves in the head.

lip-type dynamic oil seal A seal with a precisely shaped dynamic rubber lip that is held in contact with a moving shaft by a garter spring. An example would be a valve seal or camshaft seal.

multilayer steel (MLS) head gasket A gasket composed of multiple layers of steel and coated with a rubberlike substance that adheres to metal surfaces. They are typically used between the cylinder head and the cylinder block.

non-integral valve guide Also called a replaceable valve guide, a valve guide that is pressed into the cylinder head after the head has been constructed. These guides can be removed and replaced.

oil seal Any seal used to seal oil in and dirt, moisture, and debris out.

O-ring valve stem seal A seal used where the valve spring retainer attaches to the valve stem to seal the juncture and prevent excessive oil from leaking into the valve stem.

overhead cam (OHC) engine Any engine in which the camshaft is housed inside the cylinder head and directly actuates the valves through rocker arms or cam followers or by pushing directly above the valve stem on a bucket.

overhead valve (OHV) engine An engine in which the valves are positioned in the cylinder head assembly, directly over the top of the piston.

poppet (mushroom) valve A cam-operated, spring-loaded mushroom-type valve used to control intake into, and exhaust out of, the combustion chamber.

positive valve stem seal A valve seal located at the top of the valve guide that is a more positive seal than an umbrella or O-ring seal.

pushrod A long, often hollow, metal tube that transfers the force from the valve lifter to the rocker arm assembly.

quench or squish area The narrow area between the top of the piston at top dead center and the cylinder head. It derives its name from the squishing of the air/fuel mixture into a small "charge."

rocker arm A lever that actuates a valve by pivoting near the center and pushing on the tip of the valve to open it.

room temperature vulcanizing (RTV) silicone A silicone adhesive that sets up or "vulcanizes" at room temperature.

solid valve lifter A non-hydraulic valve lifter.

spring pressure Pressure exerted by a metal coil usually measured in pounds.

umbrella-style valve stem seal A seal that surrounds the top of the valve stem to prevent excessive oil from leaking into the valve stem.

valve A device used to control the flow of air and fuel into the combustion chamber and exhaust gases out of the combustion chamber.

valve cover gasket A gasket used to seal the valve cover (also called a rocker arm cover or cylinder head cover) to the cylinder head assembly.

valve face The portion of the valve that does the actual sealing to the valve seat.

valve float A condition that occurs when the valves are moving so fast that the spring tension is not great enough to fully seat the valves as designed.

valve guide A hole machined into the cylinder head or a hollow metal tube pressed into the cylinder head in which the valve stem rides, holding the stem in the proper position within the cylinder head.

valve head The portion of the valve that is exposed to the combustion chamber and contains the valve face and margin.

valve keeper A device used to keep the valve spring retainers attached to the valve while in the cylinder head.

valve margin The portion of the valve between the valve face and the valve head.

valve seat An integral part of the head, or circular metal rings that are pressed into the cylinder head, that makes up the mating surface where the valve face sits when it is closed.

valve spring A metal coil spring that returns valves to their fully closed positions after being opened.

valve spring retainer A washer-shaped piece of metal positioned near the top of the valve stem that holds the top of the valve spring to keep pressure on the valve while in the cylinder head.

valve stem The long shaftlike portion of the valve.

valve tip The end of the valve stem against which the rocker arm, cam follower, or hydraulic bucket-style lifter directly presses to open the valve.

valve train A system encompassing all of the parts used in the opening and closing of the valves.

wedge combustion chamber A combustion chamber design where the valves are often directly lined up beside each other in a row and positioned at an angle over the pistons, forming a wedge-shaped combustion chamber.

ASE-Type Questions

1. Tech A says that variable valve timing allows better control. Tech B says that in-block cams usually include variable valve timing. Who is correct?
   a. Tech A
   b. Tech B
   c. Both A and B
   d. Neither A nor B

2. Tech A says that the cylinder head design determines the output power of the engine. Tech B says that some engines use 3 valves: 1 intake and 2 exhaust. Who is correct?
   a. Tech A
   b. Tech B
   c. Both A and B
   d. Neither A nor B

3. Tech A says that the head gasket is designed to seal between the head and the block. Tech B says that most head gaskets require that you coat them with special sealers before installation. Who is correct?
   a. Tech A
   b. Tech B
   c. Both A and B
   d. Neither A nor B

4. Tech A says that some head bolts can be reused. Tech B says that some head bolts are torqued to their yield point. Who is correct?
   a. Tech A
   b. Tech B
   c. Both A and B
   d. Neither A nor B

5. Tech A says that an interference angle is the difference in angle between the valve face and valve seat. Tech B says an interference angle is when a piston hits a valve. Who is correct?
   a. Tech A
   b. Tech B
   c. Both A and B
   d. Neither A nor B

6. Tech A says that soft plugs allow the block to expand and contract without cracking. Tech B says that soft plugs will prevent damage to the head or block if coolant freezes. Who is correct?
   a. Tech A
   b. Tech B
   c. Both A and B
   d. Neither A nor B

7. Tech A says that valve seals are designed to stop combustion gases from entering the valve train area. Tech B says that valve retainers hold the valve in the spring. Who is correct?
   a. Tech A
   b. Tech B
   c. Both A and B
   d. Neither A nor B

8. Tech A says that gas-direct injection engines have injectors mounted in the cylinder heads. Tech B says that turbulence in the combustion area creates a better burn of the air/fuel mixture. Who is correct?
   a. Tech A
   b. Tech B
   c. Both A and B
   d. Neither A nor B

9. Tech A says that when the lifter is on the base circle of the cam lobe, the valve is closed. Tech B says that the valve has a small amount of clearance when the valve is fully open. Who is correct?
   a. Tech A
   b. Tech B
   c. Both A and B
   d. Neither A nor B

10. Tech A says that smaller ports and valves in a cylinder head will create more power and torque at high rpm. Tech B says that smaller ports and valves in a cylinder head will create more power and torque at low rpm. Who is correct?
    a. Tech A
    b. Tech B
    c. Both A and B
    d. Neither A nor B

CHAPTER 13

NATEF Tasks

Engine Repair
Engine Block Assembly

Page

■ Remove, inspect, or replace crankshaft vibration damper (harmonic balancer). **AST** **MAST** 359

Knowledge Objectives

After reading this chapter, you will be able to:
1. List and describe the components of the engine block. (pp 342–343)
2. Describe the general processes behind engine block manufacturing. (pp 343–344)
3. Describe the construction of the engine block. (pp 344–345)
4. Explain the components and function of pistons. (pp 346–348)
5. Explain the two processes in manufacturing pistons. (pp 348–349)
6. Describe the types of piston rings. (p 350)
7. Describe the purpose and types of connecting rods. (pp 350–352)
8. Describe the assembly of the crankshaft and its related parts. (pp 353–360)
9. Explain the primary role of the crankshaft. (p 353)

Engine Block Components

Skills Objectives

After reading this chapter, you will be able to:

1. Inspect the engine block for visible cracks, passage condition, core and gallery plug condition, and surface warpage. (pp 368–369)
2. Inspect the crankshaft for straightness, journal damage, keyway damage, thrust flange and sealing surface condition, and visual surface cracks; check the oil passage condition; measure end play and journal wear; and check the crankshaft position sensor reluctor ring. (pp 369–371)
3. Inspect main and connecting rod bearings for damage and wear. (pp 371–372)
4. Identify piston and bearing wear patterns that indicate connecting rod alignment and main bearing bore problems. (p 372)
5. Remove and replace the piston pin. (pp 372–374)
6. Inspect and measure the cylinder walls/sleeves for damage and wear. (pp 374–375)
7. Inspect and measure piston skirts. (pp 374–375)
8. Deglaze and clean a cylinder wall. (p 376)

Introduction

The engine block (also called the cylinder block, or simply the block) is the main structural member of the internal combustion engine. Although many different engine designs are available, in all configurations the engine block acts as the framework for the entire engine and provides for the mounting of all the components. In the early days of the automobile, the distinct parts of the engine, such as the cylinders, intake and exhaust passages, and crankcase, were constructed as separate pieces that were then bolted or welded together. Today, engine blocks are cast in one piece with machined surfaces and holes added for the placement and attachment of the engine components. The process of constructing a single block into which all parts fit is more efficient from a manufacturing standpoint. It also gives the block more strength and rigidity.

This chapter discusses the engine block as a whole, describes each component of the engine block and the procedures for inspecting it, and explains how all the components work together to generate the power that drives the vehicle.

Engine Block

The engine block is the largest part of the engine; it is the main supporting structure for all of the engine parts **FIGURE 13-1**. The block is also the main aligning structure for all parts of the engine. Within the engine block are the cylinders and pistons; the top of the piston and the matching cylinder head form the combustion chamber. When fuel and air are brought together in the combustion chamber, along with the presence of an ignition source, combustion occurs.

Combustion is carefully timed to occur when the piston is near the top of its travel on the compression stroke. The rapidly expanding gases produced by combustion pressurize the combustion chamber and push down on the piston during the power stroke, forcing it through the cylinder until it reaches the bottom of its travel. This movement causes the crankshaft to spin, which pushes the piston back up the cylinder in preparation for the

FIGURE 13-1 The engine block of an overhead cam engine.

next combustion event. The crankshaft also powers the rest of the drive train through the flywheel or flex plate and the accessories from the crankshaft pulley.

For optimum performance and engine life, the engine block must be designed, cast, and machined within precise tolerances, meaning that the components must be designed and connected together within narrow specifications. These precise specifications are critical to prevent leakage of air and fuel, withstand the thermal stresses of combustion, and accommodate shocks and vibration applied to the engine during the power pulses.

The upper section of the engine block contains the cylinders and pistons. The lower section of the engine block forms the crankcase, which supports the main bearings, crankshaft, camshaft (some engines), and balance shafts (some engines). A few engine designs, like the various Subaru models, have a **horizontally opposed engine**, sometimes called a boxer engine. In these engines, the cylinders are positioned side to side, rather than up and down, and the crankcase is located between the cylinders **FIGURE 13-2**.

Engine Block Manufacturing

In the metal casting foundry process, different types of materials and techniques are used to create steel or cast iron and aluminum engine blocks. The most common methods are the green sand, shell, and **lost foam** processes. In all three processes, hot molten metal is poured into a mold. The engine block can be cast in one piece from gray iron, or it can be alloyed with other metals such as nickel or chromium. The specific type of metals or metal used depends on many factors, including the intended use of the engine block, the type of environment it will be run in, and the cost.

The casting process begins by making the shapes for what will become **water jackets** and cylinders as sand cores or foam shapes, which are then fitted into molds. The term water jacket is used to describe the area created by the sand, shell, or foam shapes during the casting process. The water jackets create passageways around the cylinders and throughout the engine block that hold coolant to keep engine temperature in functional ranges. Molten metal is poured into the casting mold from a tub or ladle without the use of pressure, a process known as **gravity pouring**. Different engine block molds are used depending on the specific engine type desired, such as V8, V6, or four-cylinder in-line.

Core sand is used in the casting process to create cavities. It is a mix of fine-grit sand and oil that is highly moldable, yet holds its shape, making it great for sculpturing. During the casting process, molten metal is poured around the molded core sand and allowed to harden. Once the metal cools, the core sand is removed through holes in the sides and ends of the engine block casting, leaving cavities for the cooling and lubricating passages.

These holes are sealed with **core plugs**, which may also be called **Welch plugs** or **soft plugs**. The plugs are rounded discs or cups that are used to seal the openings created in the casting process for removal of core sand. The discs can be flat, concaved, or threaded to fit the particular opening. For years, the term *freeze plugs* has also been used; however, the term is inaccurate. The engine block was never designed to withstand freezing of the water in the cooling passages. Water expands approximately 10% as it freezes into ice. If the engine temperature drops below freezing, the pressure of the expanding ice may cause the block to crack even if the core plugs pop out.

Once the engine block casting is inspected and cleaned, it goes through a series of machining processes to bore, flatten, and thread the various surfaces and holes **FIGURE 13-3**. Parts of the engine block that typically

FIGURE 13-2 A horizontally opposed engine.

FIGURE 13-3 Engine block being machined.

require machining include the top of the engine block (also called the **deck**), cylinders, front of the block, rear of the block, bottom of the block including the crankshaft main bearing and thrust areas, and any other area to which another engine part is attached such as the cam bearing or balancer shaft journals. Other finishing processes include honing the cylinders, drilling holes, and cutting threads.

As more manufacturers try to make vehicles lighter and more fuel efficient, more engine blocks are being cast from aluminum. An engine block made of aluminum alloy is lighter than one made of cast iron. The lighter aluminum engine provides a higher power to weight ratio and also provides the vehicle with greater fuel efficiency.

Engine Block Construction and Crankshaft Support

The engine block assembly, or lower end as it is sometimes called, consists of the following: oil galleries and plugs (oil passage plugs), water jacket and plugs, pistons and rings, piston pins, connecting rods and caps, rod bearing inserts, main bearing caps, main bearing inserts, the thrust bearing, the crankshaft, rear seals (lip or rope seal), the camshaft (for overhead cam engines), and a vibration balancer. The engine block also has smooth surfaces in certain areas to which the mating parts, such as the cylinder heads, oil pan, timing cover, water pump, and transmission, are attached with a precise and tight fit.

The engine lubrication system also begins in the engine block assembly, with a system of oil passages that feed oil to the main and rod bearings, cam bearings, and cylinder heads. Oil pressure is developed by an attached oil pump and the resistance to flow of the oil is provided by the tight spaces the oil is pumped into. The oil pump may be attached on either the front or the bottom of the block, generally near the crankshaft. The oil pump may be driven by the crankshaft or by a gear off of the camshaft. Usually adjacent to the oil pump is a mounting surface for attachment of the oil filter.

In casting the engine block, **ribs**, **webs**, and **fillets** are used to provide rigidity to the casting while reducing overall engine weight **FIGURE 13-4**. These structures are made of the same materials as the engine block but are constructed into the shape of a rib, web, or fillet. They are placed near areas that encounter high levels of stress and vibration, reinforcing and adding strength to the engine block without bulk.

The crankshaft is supported in the engine block's main bearing bores by **main bearing caps**. The main

FIGURE 13-4 Ribs, webs, and fillets.

FIGURE 13-5 Integrated main cap girdle.

bearing bores and caps provide support for the crankshaft. The caps can be fastened using a two- or four-bolt design. The shape is the same for each design; only the number of bolts—two or four—varies. The main bearing caps can be inset within the block. The bolts can be fastened through the top of the main cap or they can be fastened with two bolts on top and two bolts on the side of the main bearing cap.

Some engines use an integrated **main cap girdle** **FIGURE 13-5** that has all the main caps cast in a single supporting structure. Others use a main cap girdle that is separate from the main caps. It acts as a cover to the main bearing caps and links the caps together by connecting each individual cap to all of the others in order to reinforce their strength. The girdle also helps position the main bearings in the engine block assembly, supplies engine block rigidity and structure, and prevents lateral or vertical movement.

Cylinders

Cylinders are the large holes in the block in which the pistons move up and down. Cylinders can be machined directly into the cylinder block as in the case with most cast iron blocks, or they can be made of a separate steel or cast iron sleeve in the case of some aluminum blocks. In the case of a cast iron block, the cast iron provides a relatively hard wear surface for the pistons and piston rings. In blocks made from softer materials such as aluminum, cylinder sleeves are used to provide a durable surface for pistons and piston rings to ride against.

Hardened materials can better withstand the continuous scuffing forces of the piston and piston rings, especially under extreme temperatures. Most aluminum engine blocks use cast iron cylinder sleeves that are cast into the engine block and cannot be removed or replaced. The sleeves have grooves on the outside that form ridges; once the cylinder heads are bolted on, these ridges lock the cylinder to the engine block and prevent the cylinder from shifting during engine operation. They also increase the surface area of the sleeve, which assists in the transfer of heat away from the sleeve to the cylinder block and ultimately the water jacket. The movement of combustion heat away from the engine block is critical in preventing damage from overheating such as when a piston seizes to the cylinder wall.

There are three main types of cylinder sleeves: dry, dry flanged, and wet **FIGURE 13-6**. The **dry sleeve** gets its name because it is not in direct contact with the water jacket. Dry sleeves are held in place by an **interference fit** with the cylinder walls. An interference fit is a fastening between two parts that is activated by friction after the two parts are pushed together. In this type of fit,

one part slightly interferes with the space that the other occupies, such as a slightly oversized piece being pushed into a slightly undersized hole. The wall of the dry sleeve is usually between $\frac{3}{32}$" and $\frac{1}{8}$" thick (2.4–3.2 mm)—just thick enough to create the necessary friction for a strong interference fit within the engine cylinder block. When pressed into the engine block, the cylinder sleeve is smooth at the top and has full surface contact through the engine cylinder. The top of the cylinder is flush with the top of the engine block and is difficult to see. Once in place, dry sleeves become a permanent part of the cylinder block.

A **dry flanged sleeve** is similar to a normal dry sleeve in that it too is not in direct contact with the water jacket; however, it differs from the traditional cylinder sleeve in its installation. The dry flange sleeve is not held in place by an interference fit, but has a flange at the top of the cylinder that is used to lock the sleeve into the engine block. The flange fits in a matching recessed area at the top of the engine cylinder block. The cylinder head then clamps the flange in place so it cannot move. However, this type of sleeve must be thicker than a normal dry sleeve since it is not an interference fit.

FIGURE 13-6 Cylinder sleeves. **A.** Dry. **B.** Dry Flanged. **C.** Wet.

'O' Ring grooves
(located either in the sleeve *or* in the block)

Applied | Math

AM-31: Length/Volume/Weight: The technician can determine the degree of conformance to the manufacturer's specifications for length, volume, weight, and other appropriate measurements in the standard and metric systems.

An automotive engine is being overhauled in a repair facility. Various measurements are being taken to determine the degree of conformance to the manufacturer's specifications. The technician uses an inside micrometer to measure the diameter of the cylinders. The measurement was 3.8 inches (which is 96.5 mm). This information verified to the technician that the engine matched the specifications in the service information.

In order to measure the cylinders with a more exact procedure, a dial bore gauge was used. This gauge is a special tool used to measure cylinder bore for taper and out of round conditions. The dial bore gauge is able to measure cylinders to within one ten thousandth of an inch. Service information for this engine allows a maximum out-of-round of 0.0004 inch. The maximum allowable taper is 0.0005 inch. The metric units would be a maximum out-of-round of 0.010 mm and a maximum taper of 0.013 mm. If a cylinder is worn beyond these limits, the piston rings would not seal properly. When an engine is found to have excessive out-of-round and taper, the likely solution would be to bore the cylinders oversize. In some cases, this could be .030 inch or .060 inch oversize and larger pistons would be installed. By comparing the measurements to manufacturer's specifications, the technician is able to determine the degree of conformance.

In a <u>wet sleeve</u>, the outer surface is in direct contact with coolant in the water jacket that surrounds the cylinder. It is called a wet sleeve because coolant from the cooling system circulates against the wet sleeve's outer surface. This design helps speed up heat transfer between the wet sleeve and the coolant because there is direct contact between the wet sleeve and the water jacket. The wet sleeve is sealed at the top and bottom to prevent coolant leaks. The recessed fit of the sleeve forms the top seal. At the bottom, one or two neoprene seals fit tightly between the outside of the sleeve and the block. Proper sealing of the wet sleeve is important to prevent coolant from leaking into the combustion chamber at the top and the crankcase at the bottom. Since the sleeve is in direct contact with the water jacket, corrosion can be a problem. Corrosion can insulate the wet sleeve from the coolant, creating a layer that slows down heat transfer to the water jacket.

▶ Pistons

The <u>piston</u> fits in the cylinder like a close-fitting, movable plug. The clearance between the piston and the cylinder wall is typically within a few thousandths of an inch, and on some current model engines, it can be less than a thousandth of an inch. A good way to think of the piston is as the "movable floor of the combustion chamber." When the air/fuel mixture burns in the combustion chamber, it creates pressure that pushes the piston down on the power stroke. The job of the piston is to extract the thermal energy from the burning fuel and convert it into mechanical energy, which can be used to power the vehicle. Accordingly, it is critical that the piston fit the cylinder with close tolerance so that the pressurized gases cannot easily leak past it. The piston, with its connecting rod and bearing, transfers the force of the <u>power stroke</u> to the crankshaft.

The piston comprises many parts, together referred to as the <u>piston assembly</u> **FIGURE 13-7**. The top of the piston is referred to as the head or crown. It comes in different designs, depending on the specific function or engine type into which it will be placed. The piston skirt is the area around the side of the piston that slides against the engine cylinder walls and helps keep the piston straight in the cylinder. The skirt has two thrust faces 90 degrees to the piston pin. These skirt thrust faces are usually longer than the piston pin sides of the skirt so there is more surface area for the piston and cylinder wall to spread the load over. Also, the curved cutouts of the skirt prevent the crankshaft counterweight from hitting the piston skirt when the piston moves down the cylinder. Some skirt designs also include a small groove called the expansion slot that allows piston expansion.

The <u>piston pin (wrist pin)</u> is a tubular structure that connects the piston to the top of the connecting rod. The pin passes through the piston skirt into an area called the piston boss, a heavily reinforced area designed to help the pin withstand the pressures exerted on it, and is joined to the top of the connecting rod. Because of this extra material in the piston boss, the piston is not perfectly round. It is slightly oval in shape to allow for the extra expansion of the metal in the piston boss area as the piston heats up from the heat of combustion as the engine is operating. When the engine is at operating temperature, the piston becomes round. When it is cold, the piston is narrower across the wrist pin diameter than the thrust surfaces of the piston.

<u>Piston rings</u> are thin, metallic, C-shaped rings set into grooves located around the piston skirt that fill the space between the piston and the cylinder wall. Generally, three to four rings are used per piston. The first two rings are called <u>compression rings</u> and are designed to seal and create a close fit between the piston and the cylinder wall **FIGURE 13-8**. The other rings are specially designed to hold a small amount of lubrication oil to lubricate the piston and cylinder walls. They also scrape excessive oil from the walls and release it back to the crankcase as needed. The compression rings are typically splash lubricated by the oil released onto the cylinder wall from the oil leaking out of the connecting rod bearing. Rings can be square, tapered, flat, or slanted on the ring surface. The different ring designs are available so that the best possible fit can be created between pistons and cylinder walls of different manufacturers.

The most common piston arrangement has two thin <u>compression ring grooves</u> and one larger <u>oil ring groove</u>; they are known collectively as <u>piston ring grooves</u>. The sides of the grooves, called <u>ring lands</u>, support the piston rings. The piston ring grooves are located between the top

FIGURE 13-7 Piston assembly.

FIGURE 13-8 Compression rings.

FIGURE 13-9 Oil rings. **A.** One-piece design. **B.** Three-piece design.

FIGURE 13-10 Piston pin (wrist pin) installed in the connecting rod.

of the piston and the piston pin. The width and depth of the piston ring groove dictate the width and depth of the piston rings that should be used.

Oil rings have two rails separated by a groove around the outer surface of the ring, giving them a U-shaped cross section. The groove holds a small amount of oil and directs excess oil back to the crankcase. Because of this U-shaped cross section, oil rings can be of a one-piece design or of a three-piece design with two side rails and an expander. Both styles perform the same job; they just look different **FIGURE 13-9**.

The piston pin (wrist pin) is made of steel and is hollow in the center to reduce weight, thereby reducing the engine's reciprocating mass **FIGURE 13-10**. The wrist pin design can be a **floating pin** or a **press-fit pin**. In both cases, the pin is slightly smaller than the pin bore in the piston and the piston is free to move on the pin. With the floating pin design, the piston pin floats in both the piston and the rod, with the piston pin being held in place by snap rings on each side of the piston.

With the press-fit pin design, the piston is held in place by a wrist pin that is pressed into the connecting rod. The small end of the connecting rod uses an interference fit with the wrist pin to lock the pin firmly in place. The wrist pin is installed into the connecting rod by pressing it in or by heating the end of the rod with a rod heater. The rod heater heats up the small end of the connecting rod, expanding the size of the hole just enough for the pin to slide into the connecting rod. When it cools, the pin is firmly locked into the rod.

Each piston has a major thrust face and a minor thrust face. The side of the piston that is forced into the cylinder wall on the power stroke is the major thrust face. The side of the piston that is forced into the cylinder wall on the compression stroke is the minor thrust face. Most

piston pin bores are not centered in the piston. They are set slightly off center of the piston. Having the pin offset preloads the piston toward the minor thrust side of the piston. The piston pin is offset because the connecting rod changes its angle as the piston transitions between the compression and power strokes and the piston moves from the minor thrust face to the major thrust face. If the clearances between the piston and the cylinder wall become too great, the transfer from one piston skirt to the other can cause a condition known as **piston slap**. Piston slap causes an audible noise that is most noticeable when the pistons are cold and at their smallest diameter and also increases piston/cylinder wear. Piston slap occurs as the piston pivots on the pin near **top dead center (TDC)**, when the piston is forced to the thrust side of the cylinder at the top of the power stroke. Offsetting the wrist pin in the piston helps reduce piston slap.

Control of Heat in Pistons

The piston must stand up to great heat and pressure. All pistons expand as they heat up. Because there is more metal near the wrist pin, this area tends to expand more. To allow for this, many pistons are machined into a slightly oval shape. This process of machining pistons into an oval shape is called cam grinding, and the piston is called a cam-ground piston. As an oval piston heats up to operating temperature, it expands and becomes round.

Other methods that allow, and help to control, piston expansion involve using steel struts or ribs, expansion slots in the skirt of the piston, or slots called heat dams that restrict movement of the heat. In the first method, steel struts or ribs are built into the piston assembly. Their sole purpose is to control expansion by slowing heat flow and stiffening the piston. However, they cause more piston weight. In the second method, expansion slots are cut vertically into the piston skirt. As the piston expands, the slots are slowly closed. The third method uses a horizontal slot cut directly beneath the piston head. The "T" slot acts like a dam or retardant, preventing heat from traveling down from the top of the piston.

> ### ▶ TECHNICIAN TIP
>
> A piston becomes round once it is up to operating temperature. But what if it overheats? Then the piston boss areas will continue to expand and grow faster than the rest of the piston. This makes the piston wider at the piston bosses, which can cause it to expand larger than the cylinder bore. If this happens, then the piston will be forced against the cylinder walls and quickly seize in the cylinder, requiring rebuilding or replacement. Low-mileage engines have smaller clearances and are therefore more prone to this problem. The best prevention is ensuring proper piston clearance and maintaining the cooling system.

Piston Head Shape

The shape of the top of the piston depends on the shape of its combustion chamber and its compression ratio. Combustion chambers vary in shape depending on the manufacturer and type of engine for which it is intended. The top of the piston forms the bottom of the engine's combustion chamber. The **compression ratio** is the difference between the volume in the combustion chamber above the piston when the piston is at **bottom dead center (BDC)** and the volume of the combustion chamber above the piston when the piston is at TDC. The compression ratio can be changed by using a piston with a different head design or a cylinder head with a different chamber size. This is because the sizes of the piston head and chamber affect the ratio between the volume at BDC and the volume at TDC within the combustion chamber. A taller piston head takes up some of the available volume in the combustion chamber as compared to a shallower piston head. The automotive engineer or manufacturer will select the correct piston head shape for the performance level desired.

In designing an engine, the automotive engineer will create the design with a particular piston head in mind. The piston head must be able to work in accordance with the rest of the piston assembly, as well as with the structure of the combustion chamber and the valve train assembly because they all work together in obtaining the engineer's goals for engine output and performance. Different piston heads are used to accommodate variations in combustion chamber and valve train designs. Variations in piston head shapes can also be used to change the compression ratio. The top of the piston may be flat, concave, dome shaped, or recessed **FIGURE 13-11**, and it can have one to five valve relief areas. Valve relief areas are used to prevent pistons from hitting the valves, or vice versa. Depending on the needs and shape of the engine, valve relief areas may be used on just one side of the piston head or on both.

There are two processes in manufacturing pistons: forging and casting. The forged piston is the stronger and more costly of the two. In forging a piston, metal molecules are compressed into a denser area. This makes the piston stronger and more desirable for diesel engines and racing applications. With the stronger forged piston, the higher compression ratios that create hotter exhaust gases and higher pressures can be used without piston damage.

There are two versions of the cast piston: (1) cast aluminum with steel struts and (2) cast aluminum with 16% to 19% silicon, which is called a **hypereutectic piston**. Steel struts are used to help control the flow of heat from the combustion process and can be embedded

FIGURE 13-11 Piston shapes. **A.** Flat. **B.** Concave. **C.** Dome. **D.** Recessed.

into the piston assembly to help control piston expansion. Hypereutectic pistons are stronger than 100% aluminum pistons and are used in many applications. While the cost of hypereutectic pistons is considerably less than forged pistons, the trade-off is that forged pistons are stronger than hypereutectic pistons. Another advantage of hypereutectic pistons is that the clearance between the piston and the engine block cylinder is extremely small, which allows for a tighter fit of the piston assembly inside the cylinder as compared to all other piston types. The smaller clearance allows (requires) the use of lower viscosity oils that can provide lubrication between the closer running components.

Piston Coatings

It is not uncommon today to see pistons with a coating on them. The most popular is a black <u>moly</u>, which is a molybdenum disulfide, coating on the piston skirt, which helps reduce friction between the piston skirt area and the cylinder wall. Ceramic coating is also available.

Some manufacturers and aftermarket companies coat the top of the piston with a ceramic coating, which creates a thermal barrier. The ceramic coating prevents the piston metal from absorbing heat as quickly, which allows the piston to operate at a lower temperature and withstand greater combustion temperatures without deforming. It also increases the efficiency of the engine by retaining more heat in the combustion chamber rather than transferring it through the piston to the cooling system. Designing the exhaust system to take advantage of the faster exhausting of gases due to the increase in exhaust gas temperature can aid in the scavenging effect and help the engine breathe more efficiently.

Types of Piston Rings

Compression Rings

Compression rings must seal against compression loss during the compression and power strokes. Compression loss results in low compression pressures and excessive amounts of blow-by gases into the crankcase, leading to reduced combustion efficiency, less engine power, more emissions, and poor fuel economy. The compression ring is typically made of cast iron. It is subject to wear due to its movement against the cylinder wall. To enhance the longevity of the compression rings, the rings may have a coating on the sealing surface. The ring coating could be made of chromium, nitride, plasma, molybdenum, or a ceramic material.

Piston rings are not a complete circle; they are split and must have a specified piston ring end gap. This **ring gap** allows the piston rings to be expanded so they can fit over the ring lands when the rings are being installed on the piston. The gap also allows the piston rings to expand when they heat up as the engine is operating. The small gap should almost close when the engine is up to full operating temperature, but should not close entirely. Insufficient end gap results in the compression ring binding, breaking, twisting, or scoring the cylinder walls when the compression ring expands as the engine warms up. Conversely, if the gap is too large, then compression pressure will be lost through the gap, which leads to excessive blow-by and lost efficiency. Thus, technicians measure the piston ring end gap to make sure the gap is within the specified tolerances.

The piston ring end gaps should be staggered around the piston when the piston rings are installed. Staggering prevents a straight path for the compression or gases to escape. If the path is too straight and smooth, the speed of gas escape is far too rapid, increasing the blow-by gases. There must also be side clearance between the compression rings and the ring lands. The clearance prevents the piston ring from becoming stuck in the groove when it expands due to combustion heat. The ring must also have **back clearance** inside the piston groove to accommodate heat expansion of the piston.

The compression ring is built to have static pressure, with its diameter larger than the piston, thus creating **ring tension** so that the piston ring is forced against the cylinder wall to help provide a good seal. It must not have too much tension or it will wear out prematurely, but it needs to have enough tension to maintain an adequate seal. The compression rings must be able to seal under all conditions found in the combustion chamber—vacuum during the intake stroke and high pressure during the compression and power strokes. Some compression rings and pistons are designed so that combustion pressure can get behind the compression ring and force it out against the cylinder wall during the power stroke, increasing its sealing effectiveness **FIGURE 13-12**. This design also allows the compression rings to have a smaller amount of static pressure, which reduces piston ring drag and improves fuel efficiency. It also means that most compression rings have a top and bottom and will not function correctly if installed improperly.

FIGURE 13-12 Combustion pressure forcing the top compression ring against the cylinder.

Oil Rings

Oil control rings prevent excessive oil from working up into the combustion chambers. The oil control ring is designed to leave a film of lubricating oil less than a thousandth of an inch thick on the cylinder wall. It can be a one-piece ring that depends on its own tension to hold it against the cylinder walls, or it can be a three-piece ring with two side rails and an **expander**, which provide the tension for the side rails. Both styles have slots or holes in the oil ring and the piston ring groove. These holes allow oil return to the crankcase, and in some pistons they also direct oil to the wrist pin. This movement of oil helps with the cooling process. On modern engines, most oil rings are made of steel. The expander is made of thin steel with a series of **crimps** or folds in the metal that give it an outward spring force. The expander has a top and a bottom groove that hold the solid **side rails** and together make up the oil control ring. The side rails depend on the expander to hold them against the cylinder walls.

Connecting Rods

The **connecting rod** connects the piston to the crankshaft. It has a small end that houses the piston pin and connects it to the piston assembly. The middle of the rod, called the beam area, transmits the power flow to the bottom of the rod. At the bottom, or big end, the connecting rod houses the bearing inserts and attaches firmly around the crankshaft **FIGURE 13-13**.

In order for the connecting rod to fit over the crankshaft rod journal, the big end is split in half; the bottom half is removable and is called the **rod cap**. The connecting rod's big end is connected to the crankshaft **rod journal**; the rod cap bolts or nuts are then torqued (using manufacturer specifications) in place using a

FIGURE 13-13 Connecting rod.

torque wrench. The crankshaft rod journal is an area machined to the highest quality. It contains an oil hole for lubrication of the rod bearings. A thin layer of oil coats the surface, and a bearing insert rides on top of the film of oil.

The crankshaft rod throw (distance from the center of the crankshaft main journals to the center of the rod journals) determines the stroke of the piston. As the crankshaft rotates, the **crankshaft journal** rotates on bearing inserts inside the connecting rod's big end and is part of the **rotating assembly**. The connecting rod transfers the **reciprocating** motion and force of the piston to the rotating crankshaft.

Most stock connecting rods are shaped like an I beam down the length of the connecting rod, while some aftermarket performance connecting rods have an H shape down the length of the connecting rod. The H-shaped rod is the stronger of the two. Most connecting rods have extra metal on each end (balance pads) for balancing.

There are four types of connecting rods: cast, forged, aluminum, and powdered metal. Regardless of how the connecting rod is manufactured, when the rod cap is taken off, it must go back on the same connecting rod; it is not interchangeable. It must also be reinstalled in the exact orientation. The best process to make sure the caps and connecting rods do not get mixed up is to mark them close to the parting line.

The big end of the rod is where the **rod bearings** are inserted. There is a notch in the connecting rod and a notch in the rod cap. The rod bearings have **tangs** on the end; these tangs are inserted in the notch of the rod and the rod cap. The tang in the bearing shell of the rod cap butts up against the parting surface of the rod. The tang in the rod butts up against the rod cap. When the rod cap is torqued into place, the tangs are able to prevent

the rod bearing halves from spinning inside the big end of the rod. Some connecting rods and rod bearings have a hole that sprays oil out to lubricate the cylinder wall, wrist pin, and camshaft when the hole lines up with the lubricating hole in the rod journal. When installing the rod bearings, the lubricating hole in the connecting rod must line up to the hole in the bearing shell.

> **TECHNICIAN TIP**
>
> Although most bearings are held in place by tangs, some bearings are held in place by a hole in the bearing, which fits over a short pin in the rod or cap. Failure to line up the hole and pin will result in a locked up crankshaft that won't turn.

In the manufacturing of connecting rods, most are made using a metal casting process wherein molten metal is poured into a mold. Down the center of the connecting rod mold, there is an imperfection in the shape of a line separating one half of the rod from the other. This mold line is referred to as a **casting line** and can be used to identify whether a rod was created by the metal casting process. The **cast rod** is the most common connecting rod style. Rods manufactured by this process are inexpensive yet strong enough to meet the requirements for most small truck, passenger car, and small engine applications.

The other method for manufacturing connecting rods is through a forging process. In this process, metal is hammered by large presses into the rod shape. The hammering squeezes the molecular structure of the metal tightly, creating an extremely strong, durable rod. These rods are referred to as **forged connecting rods**. Forged rods are much stronger than cast rods and are usually used in high-performance applications. However, because the process is more labor intensive, forged rods are more costly to manufacture, resulting in a higher price for the buyer. To identify this type of rod, look on the side of the **rod beam** for a wide flat line where the rod was forged.

The **aluminum rod** is used in some drag race cars. It is lighter and wider than cast or forged rods. The extra width strengthens the rod, enabling it to withstand the pressures and forces applied to the connecting rod and crankshaft assembly during the short, intense duration of a drag race. Frequent replacement of aluminum connecting rods is necessary because of their lack of durability. They are not appropriate for endurance race cars, aircraft, or general-purpose vehicles.

The **powdered metal rod** is the most recent technology. The rod starts with a precise amount of powdered metal, which includes iron, copper, carbon, and other agents. The powder is placed in a die and forged (pressed) under great pressure and then put through a **sintering process**, where the rod is heated up until it almost melts. Sintering is a process used in metal fabrication. It uses high temperatures, ranging from about 2000°F to 2500°F (1093°C to 1371°C), to melt several powdered metals into one high-quality, **metallurgically bonded** metal alloy. It is an old process that provides excellent surface finish and allows for the creation of hard-to-make parts. Additionally, the end alloy is stronger than the original individual metals. Some of the benefits are that the rod is lighter than the typical cast and forged rod and that approximately 40% less metal is used, compared to a standard forged rod. The powdered metal rod meets or exceeds the tensile and yield strength of forged rods, and the cost is considerably less.

The powdered metal rod is then fracture split at the big end, giving more adhesion at the parting line of the two halves of the connecting rod assembly **FIGURE 13-14** than the machined cap and rod. This is also a time saver, eliminating the machining involved on the parting line between the rod and the rod cap. With the fracture split design, the rod cap is a precision fit on the rod, and the rod bolt is not relied upon to align the cap to the rod. The powdered metal rod is used on most newer engines.

> ### ▶ TECHNICIAN TIP
>
> Do not use a punch or stamping die to mark powdered metal rods and caps. They are easily damaged. Use paint or permanent marker instead.

FIGURE 13-14 Mating surfaces of a powdered metal fracture split rod.

▶ Crankshaft Assembly and Related Parts

The crankshaft assembly and related parts are responsible for transferring the power created inside the cylinder and combustion chamber to the external drives of the engine. The piston and connecting rod assembly inside the cylinder are connected to the crankshaft. The movement of the piston and connecting rod assembly driven by the force of combustion turns the crankshaft. Rotation of the crankshaft drives the flywheel/flex plate, and then the drive train, which rotates the wheels. The crankshaft also transmits power to the front of the crankshaft assembly, which drives the valve train assembly through a series of belts, chains, and gears. The power to the front of the crankshaft assembly also drives the pulley configuration that connects to the power steering pump, air-conditioning compressor, water pump, and alternator.

Crankshaft

The main role of the **crankshaft** is to transfer the up-and-down strokes of the pistons into rotary motion. It is situated in the **crankcase**, which is the lower part or bottom of the engine block. Connecting rods are attached to offset journals called **throws**. This is where the reciprocating motion of the piston is changed into a rotary motion. The rotary motion is then used to power the vehicle.

Applied | Math

AM-20: Place Value: The technician can interpret standard or metric units when conducting precision measurements.

A technician and his helper are rebuilding an automotive engine. It has been disassembled and the task is to measure the components with micrometers. The helper is familiar with use of a micrometer, which can measure parts to within one thousandth of an inch. The micrometer set that is being used is capable of measuring parts to within one ten thousandth of an inch.

To assist the helper, the technician mentions the term "place value". Place value is the value of the position of a digit in a number. For example, in the number 2.4137 inch, the "3" represents thousandths of an inch. Most automotive engine specifications will be listed with four numbers to the right of the decimal. This will indicate the ten thousandths position. In our example, the "7" is four numbers to the right of the decimal, which is the ten thousandths position.

Concerning the metric system, the unit of linear measurement is the millimeter or centimeter. Understanding place value of this system is essential. A typical specification in the metric system would be 45.428 mm, which is equal to 1.7885 inches. In metric units, engine specifications would extend three numbers to the right of the decimal for linear measurement in millimeters.

The crankshaft now also plays a role in creating the spark for the combustion process. In newer engine models, the crankshaft houses the reluctor for the crankshaft positioning sensor, which is a device that lets the engine computer know the position of the crankshaft in order to help produce high-voltage sparks at the right times for ignition. The crankshaft may also have teeth and notches embedded in it or have shields and windows to help create the Hall-effect signal that the computer uses to know the position of the crankshaft.

The back end of the crankshaft serves as the mounting area for the flywheel or flex plate, and the front end serves as the drive for the camshaft and accessories. Many current engines also drive the oil pump off of the front of the crankshaft.

Crankshafts are a one-piece casting or forging, or they can be machined out of a **billet**, which is a solid piece of metal. The raw crankshaft is then machined into the desired shape for the particular engine into which it will be installed. If the crankshaft journals are worn or damaged, they can generally be refinished to a smaller size and reused with undersized bearings—that is, bearings that are thicker.

▶ LINK
Refer to the Engine Machining chapter for more information on crankshafts.

Main Journals and Connecting Rod Journals

Main bearing journals are the part of the crankshaft assembly that mate to the main bearings found at the bottom of the engine block. Main bearing journals are very smooth and perfectly round so that they can rotate inside of the softer main bearings. The main bearing journals are positioned in a straight line down the center of the crankshaft and are used to position the crankshaft assembly into the lower part of the engine block. The **main journals** are ground to manufacturer specifications from the **crank core** (the rough, unfinished crankshaft assembly that has just left the foundry or forging area) or billet. The center of the main journals is referred to as the centerline of the crankshaft.

The crankshaft is held in the block by main bearing caps, which can be separate from one another or attached to each other by an assembly called a **girdle**. Main bearing caps mate to **journal saddles**, which are smooth, curved, machined areas located at the bottom of the engine block. The main bearing cap and the journal saddle create a perfectly round bore that clamps bearing inserts in place to support the crankshaft journals. The main bearing inserts are secured by main bearing caps and bolts.

As discussed earlier, the number of journal saddles in an engine is generally dependent on the length of the engine block. A common V8 has five main journals on the crankshaft, while many straight in-line six-cylinder engines have seven main journals, and a V6 typically has only four main journals.

The crankshaft main journals rotate in bearing inserts called **main bearings**. Cross-drilled passages in the crankshaft carry lubricant under pressure from the main bearings to the adjacent crank throws (rod throws). Rod throws, also called rod journals, are located in the **offset area** of the crankshaft assembly, as opposed to the main journals that sit in a straight line with the centerline of the crankshaft assembly. The crank throws are offset from the centerline of the crankshaft; the amount of offset determines the **piston stroke** (the distance the piston travels from TDC to BDC). The crankshaft design in some 90-degree V6 engines differs significantly from that of 60-degree V6 engines. In order for a 90-degree V6 to have evenly spaced power pulses, the crankshaft must have connecting rod journals that are splayed **FIGURE 13-15**. A splayed journal is designed with two connecting rod journals, each one offset from the other. The crank pin,

FIGURE 13-15 Splayed crankshaft from a 90-degree V6 engine.

or journal, appears split, but both journals are actually located between the crankshaft throws or counterweights. This arrangement creates a 90-degree V6 engine with evenly spaced power pulses and is called an even fire V6. It is smoother running than an odd fire V6, which has uneven power pulses because it does not use splayed connecting rod journals.

Counterweights are formed on the crankshaft to balance the components of the rotating assembly that are mounted inside and attached to the engine block, including the rod journals, rod bearings, connecting rods, pistons, piston pin, and rings. The balancing of the rotating assembly is done by drilling out weight or by adding weight to the counterweights. A heavy metal called **Mallory metal** is added to the counterweights during manufacturing to balance the counterweights. Mallory is approximately 117% heavier (more than twice as heavy) than steel.

Some crankshafts are internally balanced, which means the crankshaft is balanced solely from the counterweights of the crankshaft. No external counterweights are needed. Other crankshafts are externally balanced, which means the crankshaft counterweights are not heavy enough so counterweights need to be positioned on the flywheel or flex plate at the rear of the crankshaft and the harmonic balancer at the front. On an externally balanced engine, it is critical to use the proper externally balanced flywheel or flex plate and harmonic balancer for the engine, and they need to be installed in the proper orientation. Check the service information carefully.

Most crankshafts use **induction-hardened** journal surfaces to give good wear qualities. Induction hardening is a process for hardening the outer surface of a metal structure by rapid heating and cooling. Using the induction hardening process allows the crankshaft to be reground on the main and rod bearing surfaces without

grinding through the hardened layer. Regrinding is used to smooth and polish the main and rod journals so they can be reused when the engine is being rebuilt. It is used as an alternative to replacing the entire crankshaft assembly.

Some heavy-duty and performance crankshafts use a **nitridization process**, which takes longer and is more costly but results in an extremely hard surface. **Nitriding** is a surface hardening heat treatment that introduces nitrogen into the surface of steel at a temperature range of approximately 930°F to 1020°F (499°C to 549°C). Nitriding creates a surface that is harder than that produced by the induction hardening process, but the hardened layer is not as thick. The crankshaft will have to be re-nitrided if the main journals or connecting rod journals need to be reground due to wear.

Applied | Math

AM-37: Mentally: When comparing the observed measurement with the manufacturer's specifications, the technician can mentally compute whether the observed measurement meets specifications.

A technician is assigned to overhaul a V8 engine. He is currently measuring the crankshaft, which has been removed from the block and cleaned. The manufacturer's service information lists the minimum diameter for the main bearing journals as 2.6576", maximum taper of 0.0002", and maximum out-of-round of 0.0003'. While measuring each journal in four places with an outside micrometer, the technician will compare each reading to the minimum diameter specification and mentally compute whether they meet it or not. Also, the technician will compare the two readings used to measure the amount of taper, and mentally compute the difference between them to come up with the amount of taper, which again is compared to specifications. The same process is performed with the out-of-round measurement. The two measurements are taken, the difference is calculated mentally, and that difference is compared to specifications. These measurements are then performed on each of the other crankshaft journals.

Crankshaft Bearings

Bearings are used to help support the crankshaft in the block as well as the connecting rods on the crankshaft journals. Crankshaft bearings are of the friction bearing type as compared to the antifriction type. This means that the surfaces are in sliding contact with each other rather than rolling contact, such as in a wheel bearing. Connecting rod bearings and the crankshaft main bearings are of the split-sleeve type, which means they are in two halves, called **bearing inserts** or half-shell bearings **FIGURE 13-16**.

FIGURE 13-16 Bearing inserts. **A.** Main bearings. **B.** Rod bearings.

Bearing inserts are made from Babbitt metal bonded to a steel shell. The shell gives rigidity to the bearing, and the Babbitt metal is relatively soft and provides the bearing wear surface. Bearings, along with lubricant, are used in engines to support and protect rotating parts and allow them to turn freely. Between the bearing insert and the journal is a very thin layer of oil that separates the bearing material from the surface of the crankshaft journals. The oil acts as a shock absorber and is designed to keep the journal from making contact with the surface of the bearing.

Crankshaft bearings are split into two halves so that they can be assembled over the corresponding journal. The bearing shells each have a tang built into them that fits into a matching machined notch in the bearing saddle and cap. The tang prevents the bearing from spinning inside of the saddle and cap by butting up against the machined faces of the saddle and cap. In a main bearing, the upper half of the bearing fits into a machined section of the cylinder block called the main bearing saddle. The main bearing saddle has a notch for the bearing tang to fit within and a drilled oil passage for supplying oil to the bearing and journal.

It is important to pick the proper bearing half with the matching oil hole, as it must align to the oil passage in the main saddle. The lower half is carried in the main bearing cap. The bearing cap also has a notch for the bearing tang to fit into. The main cap is held in place on the main saddle by main bearing cap bolts. It is important that the bearing tang fits into the bearing slot; otherwise the bearing will be pinched and cause excessive drag on the crankshaft journal, damaging both the bearing and the journal. Refer to the manufacturer's specifications for torque procedures.

In a connecting rod bearing, the bearing's upper half is carried in the big end of the connecting rod, which has a notch for the bearing tang. The lower half is carried in the connecting rod cap, which also contains a notch for the bearing tang. The cap is bolted to the connecting rod and torqued to specifications. Refer to the manufacturer's specifications for torque procedures.

The crankshaft requires a thrust bearing, which limits the end play movement of the crankshaft. These bearings can be in the form of bearing flanges that are part of one of the main bearings, giving each main bearing insert a U shape. This U-shaped bearing insert fits over a precisely machined main bearing saddle and cap **FIGURE 13-17**. The thrust bearing will only fit on the specified bearing support. Alternatively, a separate two-piece **thrust bearing** can be fitted into a machined recess in each side of the bearing support and cap and act as the thrust bearing for the crankshaft. In the same way that the bearing-to-journal clearance is important, so is the clearance between the bearing flange (or thrust bearing) and the mating surface on the crankshaft. The thrust bearing clearance prevents excessive end play (forward or backward movement) of the crankshaft, especially in a vehicle equipped with a manual transmission/transaxle and clutch since the crankshaft thrust surfaces bear all of the force of compressing the pressure plate springs when the operator pushes down on the clutch pedal.

FIGURE 13-17 Thrust bearing.

Oil flows through an oil gallery in the cylinder block. Each main bearing receives its own oil under pressure from the oil hole in the main bearing saddle, which connects directly to the oil gallery. Some top bearing inserts have a groove around the middle. The groove provides a space for oil to flow around the journal, which helps provide more lubrication for the bearing. The grooved bearing also helps extend the time that the rod bearing receives pressurized oil, since the oil hole in the crankshaft lines up to the bearing groove for half of the rotation of the crankshaft. Passageways drilled in the crankshaft carry oil from the main bearing journals to the rod journals **FIGURE 13-18**.

Oil flow maintains an oil cushion between the crankshaft and the bearing as the engine is operating. But when the engine is first started up, especially when it is cold, it takes a few seconds to pump oil to the bearings, which can result in the crankshaft touching the bearing surface for a short time. The oil flow also carries away heat and particles that could cause wear. If the cushion of oil did not exist, the bearing would overheat and fail. Engine manufacturers specify the clearance required between the bearing material and the crankshaft. This clearance specification helps maintain the balance between adequate oil pressure and adequate oil flow.

All **main bearings** and rod bearings are held in place by what is called **bearing crush** **FIGURE 13-19**. Bearing crush is a term meaning that the bearing inserts are slightly larger than the bore they fit into and are therefore slightly crushed into position when tightened into place. The proper bearing crush is designed into the bearing when they are made by allowing the bearing insert to slightly protrude from the parting line of the bearing support and cap. When the cap is tightened properly, the bearing inserts are forced very tightly into the bore, which helps hold them in place.

FIGURE 13-19 Bearing crush.

Main bearings and rod bearings come in various sizes. The most common bearing size is a standard size (std), which means that it fits the same size journal as originally manufactured. Undersized bearings can be purchased for many engines in the following sizes: 0.001" (0.025 mm), 0.010" (0.25 mm), 0.020" (0.51 mm), and 0.030" (0.76 mm). If you are replacing the crankshaft, it is important to measure the crankshaft journals and check to make sure they are within the specifications set out by the crankshaft supplier. The clearance between the crankshaft journal and the bearings is crucial and must be within the manufacturer's specifications. If there is too little clearance, the oil will not be able to flow through the clearance in the bearing, which can cause the bearing material to overheat and possibly seize to the journal. If the clearance is too large, the oil pressure will be lowered and the oil will be squished out of the clearance in the bearing, which will allow the journal to come into direct contact with the bearing, creating a knocking noise and extreme wear.

FIGURE 13-18 Oil passageway drilled in the crankshaft.

Bearing Materials

Bearings require a difficult mix of properties; they must be hard enough to resist wear, but soft enough not to damage the crankshaft. One bearing material, called Babbitt metal, is an alloy that can include metals such as tin, lead, aluminum, and copper. This mix of metals creates a unique combination of hardness and softness.

The two most popular **engine bearings** in use are the **trimetal** and the **bimetal** types. Both bearings have their distinct advantages. Most trimetal bearings are made of a lead, tin, and copper overlay that rides next to the crankshaft, followed by a nickel barrier, and next a high-fatigue strength copper and lead lining, which is bonded to a steel backing. The biggest advantage of the trimetal bearing is that it has a higher load capacity; thus, it is ideal for high-performance and racing engines. Most bimetal bearings are made of an aluminum, tin, and silicon alloy that is bonded on a steel backing. There are also some aluminum bearings that are made of an aluminum alloy that contain tin and copper, which is bonded to a steel backing. Some of the advantages of the aluminum bearings are that they are less expensive and they contain no lead (which is an environmental concern).

Bearing Wear

Bearing wear can be caused by many sources, but the four most common causes seen by the automotive technician are dirt, insufficient oil, improper assembly, and operational faults. Dirt can enter the engine through the oil system or air intake system or from engine rebuilding. Particles of dirt can become sandwiched between the bearing and the bore, appearing as a distortion on the bearing. Conditions of insufficient oil arise from low engine oil levels, clogged oil passageways, or a bad oil pump. Without proper lubrication, the parts will grind against each other creating extreme wear in the bearing and journal. Improper assembly can arise from reversed caps on the journals, insufficient clearance allowance, misalignments, or bearing inserts placed in the wrong position. The wear patterns on the bearing will differ depending on the exact assembly error. Operational faults that lead to bearing wear include engine lugging at low rpm, too much spark advance, and abnormal combustion. As with improper assembly, the exact pattern of wear will vary by issue **FIGURE 13-20**.

FIGURE 13-20 Bearing wear patterns.

Flywheel

The <u>flywheel</u> is a heavy metal disc that bolts to the rear of the crankshaft of all engines equipped with a manual transmission/transaxle. The flywheel is very heavy, and its momentum helps smooth out engine operation. It maintains crankshaft momentum during the nonpower strokes of the piston. Essentially, it stores up rotational energy, which ensures less fluctuation in crankshaft speed between the engine's power strokes. The flywheel is bolted to the rear of the crankshaft **FIGURE 13-21**. It links the crankshaft to the manual transmission/transaxle, through the clutch assembly. The size of the flywheel varies based on the manufacturer's priorities. Heavier flywheels do a better job of smoothing out the power pulses but do not allow the engine to accelerate as quickly. Lighter flywheels allow much quicker engine acceleration, but they do not smooth out the power pulses as well.

The flywheel rim carries the <u>ring gear</u>. The teeth on the ring gear mesh with the <u>starter teeth</u> and are used to crank over the engine. The ring gear is typically attached to the flywheel by an interference fit, so no bolts or welds are used to hold it on. The ring gear is installed by heating it up until it has expanded enough to fit over the edge of the flywheel. Once it cools, it shrinks enough to firmly lock it in place. The face of the flywheel is machined smooth and flat and acts as one of the friction surfaces for the clutch.

> ▶ **LINK**
> Refer to the Clutch System chapter for information on dual-mass flywheels.

Flex Plate

In automatic transmission engines, a <u>flex plate</u> is used instead of a flywheel **FIGURE 13-22**. Unlike the flywheel, the flex plate has a torque converter bolted to it. Like the flywheel, the flex plate is constructed as a round disc and mounted to the end of the crankshaft. The flex plate is lighter than a conventional flywheel because the weight of the torque converter performs the function of the flywheel. Since the torque converter is quite heavy, the flex plate can be constructed to be much lighter and thinner than a flywheel. The torque converter is bolted to the flex plate. The flex plate often has a ring gear welded to its edge because of the flex plate's light weight. If an interference fit were used, the flex plate would warp under the pressure created by the fit. Some manufacturers weld the ring gear to the outside of the torque converter and use a smaller flex plate.

Harmonic Balancer

The <u>harmonic balancer</u> is also known as the crankshaft damper. It is located on the front of the crankshaft assembly, and its function is to reduce vibration from the crankshaft and piston assembly. When the crankshaft deflects or twists slightly (vibrates) from the power pulses, the harmonic balancer absorbs the vibrations and reduces their severity. Minimizing vibration is critical in preventing damage to the crankshaft. Excessive torsional vibration can cause a crankshaft to break in two.

A harmonic balancer is composed of two elements—a mass and an energy dissipating system, mounted to a central hub. The mass is a heavy circular steel disc that absorbs and releases the energy from the twisting of the crankshaft. A rubber or <u>fluid dissipater</u> is fitted between the circular mass and the hub **FIGURE 13-23**. The dissipater allows the mass to rotate at a more constant speed than the crankshaft. This helps to even out the

FIGURE 13-21 Flywheel, with ring gear, installed on the crankshaft.

FIGURE 13-22 Flex plate with ring gear.

torsional vibrations of the crankshaft. Over time, the rubber material can get brittle and hard, letting the mass of the harmonic balancer slip. When the mass slips on the rubber, or if the rubber is brittle and cracked, the harmonic balancer cannot provide the needed dampening effect and needs to be replaced with a new or remanufactured one.

The harmonic balancer is attached to the crankshaft using a **Woodruff key** or a square key and **center bolt**. The Woodruff key is a metal half-moon–shaped piece that protrudes from a slot near the end of the crankshaft. It fits into a slot in the harmonic balancer center hub and prevents the harmonic balancer from spinning on the end of the crankshaft. Some manufacturers use a square-cut key instead of the Woodruff key. The center bolt is threaded so that it will clamp the front side of the harmonic balancer to the front of the crankshaft.

The **accessory drive pulleys** are bolted to the front hub of the harmonic balancer. In modern vehicles, there typically is one pulley and one serpentine drive belt attached to the balancer to operate the various accessories. The pulley and belt transfer the power output needed for various systems in the vehicle. Older vehicles generally contained multiple pulleys and belts to operate systems that are now powered electronically or through other means.

> **TECHNICIAN TIP**
>
> The harmonic balancer may have counterweights for an externally balanced engine. Be sure to replace it with the correct harmonic balancer or the engine will be out of balance and have a bad vibration.

Crankshaft Seals

Crankshaft seals are located at each end of the crankshaft assembly where it projects through the crankcase. The seals help contain the lubricating oils inside the lower part of the crankcase and prevent them from leaking out. A rear main seal is located just after the rear main bearing **FIGURE 13-24**. In engines that use a **timing chain** or **timing gears**, the front main seal is located in the front timing cover. In engines equipped with a timing belt, the front main seal is located in a housing bolted to the front of the engine block **FIGURE 13-25** and sits between the block and the timing belt. Most crankshaft seals today are a circular one-piece style with a sealing lip. Some seals use a small spring, called a **garter spring**, around the inside of the sealing lip to tension the lip against the sealing surface of the crankshaft or harmonic balancer.

FIGURE 13-24 Rear main seal.

FIGURE 13-23 Harmonic balancer.

FIGURE 13-25 Front main seal.

Balance Shaft

Some in-line four-cylinder and 90-degree V6 engines use one or two <u>balance shafts</u> to reduce vibrations from engine operation. Their asymmetrical design, or lack of symmetry in cylinder configuration, causes these engines to have an inherent <u>second-order vibration</u>. The second-order vibration is at twice the engine rpm. It cannot be eliminated no matter how well the internal parts are balanced. This vibration is produced because of the even firing of the four-cylinder and the uneven firing of some 90-degree V6 engines. The descending and ascending pistons are not always completely opposed in their acceleration.

To address this problem, engine manufacturers have developed a balance shaft with counterweights spaced so as to cancel out the inherent vibrations. The balance shafts are mounted in the engine block, either below the crankshaft, next to the crankshaft, or above the crankshaft, depending on design. The shafts are typically driven at twice the engine rpm, usually by a chain, gear, or belt from the crankshaft. The weights on the shaft are timed to cancel the second-order vibrations in the engine.

Compression Ratio

Compression ratio relates to how tightly the air/fuel mixture is compressed in the combustion chamber. The tighter the air/fuel mixture, the more power that can be extracted from a given amount of air and fuel. Unfortunately, increased compression ratios can cause engine damage. Increased compression ratios increase compression pressures, thereby increasing the temperature of the mixture within the combustion chamber as it is being compressed. If the mixture gets too hot, it will ignite by itself before it should, which is known as preignition or detonation. This is very hazardous to the engine, so compression ratios must not be raised too high. Typical compression ratios for stock gasoline engines run between 8:1 and 10.5:1. High-performance vehicles can be around 12:1. Diesel engines run around 20:1.

To calculate the compression ratio, divide the volume of the combustion chamber above the piston at BDC by the volume of the combustion chamber above the piston at TDC. For example, a cylinder that has a total combustion chamber volume of 50 cubic inches at BDC and 5 cubic inches at TDC, has a compression ratio of 50 to 5, or 10 to 1, which is written 10:1. In other words, the piston is compressing 50 units of volume into 5 units of volume **FIGURE 13-26**.

Compression ratio can be raised in several ways. First, a taller piston or one with a dome will reduce the volume of the combustion chamber at both TDC and BDC, thus

FIGURE 13-26 Compression ratio.

raising the ratio. Another option is to use cylinder heads with smaller chambers so that the mixture is squeezed into a smaller space. Likewise, machining the cylinder head surface or using a thinner head gasket will increase the compression ratios slightly. Also, using a crankshaft with longer throws increases the engine's stroke, which increases how high and low the piston travels in the cylinder, raising the compression ratio but also changing engine size. Finally, boring out the cylinders and using larger pistons will make the cylinder volume larger so the compression ratio will be increased, but this method also changes engine size.

What we have just discussed is theoretical compression ratio, which does not take into consideration valve timing. We have assumed that the intake valve closed at BDC, which would mean that compression could start at BDC. In reality, intake valves close after BDC, so compression cannot start until the intake valve is fully closed. Complete closure could be substantially after BDC in the case of a high-performance camshaft, and the piston has already moved partially up the cylinder, lowering the effective compression ratio. So the effective compression ratio is the volume above the piston when the intake valve just closes, compared to the volume above the piston at TDC.

▶ Disassembly of Engine Block Components

Engine disassembly is usually performed only when major repairs or rebuilding is needed. In many cases a new or rebuilt engine is used rather than rebuilding the existing engine so that the vehicle can be returned to the customer more quickly. Usually if the decision is made to repair or rebuild the engine, the engine will be removed from the vehicle and disassembled once it is out, although some tasks, such as replacing head gaskets, are usually performed with the engine still installed. Disassembling the engine is a very large task, so make sure it is the proper course of action before proceeding.

If the engine is being rebuilt, then the cylinder head(s) and, if it is an overhead cam engine, the timing belt or chain(s) have already been removed following the steps in the Cylinder Head Components chapter. Now the engine should be disassembled down to the short block. The exact process for disassembling an engine block varies from engine to engine because each manufacturer's engines are assembled differently. Therefore, only an overview of the process is presented here. Always refer to the manufacturer's service information and follow the steps exactly.

Removing the Oil Pan

To gain access to the rotating assembly of the engine, the oil pan has to be removed. If the engine has a lot of miles on it, was poorly maintained, or had extensive damage, there will probably be a layer of oil sludge and possibly metal particles or other foreign objects in the bottom of the oil pan. In order to keep this evidence intact, do not rotate the engine block upside down yet.

To remove the oil pan, you will need to remove the bolts holding the oil pan, or sump, onto the block and store them in a bin or bag. If you are removing the oil pan with the engine side up, leave two bolts in opposite corners threaded in about halfway. Insert a putty knife or gasket scraper between the engine block and the oil pan, and start to pry the pan loose **FIGURE 13-27**. Use care to avoid bending the pan while prying. When you separate the oil pan enough to rest on the catch bolts, support the

oil pan from the bottom and remove those remaining two bolts. Pull the oil pan away carefully, working around any obstructions such as the oil pump or baffles.

Draining the Engine Block

The first step in disassembling the engine is to remove any remaining fluids, such as the oil and the coolant, from the engine block. It is not uncommon to find some leftover oil and coolant inside the engine block once the heads have been removed. The coolant often becomes trapped inside the water jacket passages, especially if you were unable to remove one of the drains plugs earlier in the disassembly process. Leftover oil is also frequently found in trapped oil passageways. It is a good idea to always place a catch tray underneath the engine when it is rolled over to catch these fluids as they drain out of the engine **FIGURE 13-28**.

Disassembling the Block Underside

The block underside refers to the area located in the oil pan and timing chain part of the engine cylinder block assembly. These areas are fully covered by the timing chain cover and the oil pan cover, which are stamped sheet metal assemblies or cast aluminum assemblies.

Removing the Oil Pump and Tray

Some oil pumps are located inside the crankcase and need to be removed before the pistons, while others are located on the front of the block and need to be removed along with any timing components. On a crankcase-mounted oil pump, you may be able to unscrew one bolt and simply pull off the oil pump. Other oil pumps have two bolts and may also have a few other bolts that hold the pickup

FIGURE 13-27 Break the oil pan loose.

FIGURE 13-28 Catch any remaining fluids in a catch tray.

tube and screen in place **FIGURE 13-29**. As the oil pump is removed, you may see the plastic collar that holds the oil pump drive rod onto the oil pump. If the collar is broken, you will need to replace it.

If the engine has a windage tray (to prevent oil from splashing onto the crankshaft), remove it now, along with any dipstick tube or extension that might be inside the oil pan area. With the oil pan removed, it is easier to check for evidence of engine problems. If there were knocking noises heard coming from deep inside the engine, then it may be visible or apparent that one of the rod bearings has disintegrated and/or spun.

Labeling the Connecting Rods and Caps

The connecting rod caps must be replaced in the same orientation as they are removed. If they are not already labeled, label them in two places: above and below the parting line of the cap and rod body. It is a good idea to also label the main caps of the block in the same way. One way to label these components is with a number punch set, but you could use a regular center punch. *Note*: Do *not* stamp or center punch powdered metal rods; doing so could destroy them. Clean the side of a powdered metal rod with a solvent and use paint to mark it instead **FIGURE 13-30**.

You will need to rotate the crankshaft over during disassembly, so you may want to use a crankshaft turning tool that will allow you to turn the crankshaft assembly. Or you can also reinstall the harmonic balancer and turn the engine over by grabbing the harmonic balancer and turning the engine over by hand. Do not use pliers or vice grips because they will damage the crankshaft and/or Woodruff key.

Removing the Pistons

Removing the pistons is a multistep process that requires making some decisions before starting the process. The two most basic decisions are deciding if the pistons are going to be reused or replaced and if the ridge at the top of the cylinder needs to be reamed off. The answer to those questions will determine the order at which you perform the steps and the amount of care you use to remove the pistons.

It may be obvious that the pistons will need to be replaced, such as when the cylinders are worn enough that they will need to be bored oversize or when the engine exhibits enough wear requiring piston replacement. When a motor is running, the piston rings slowly wear away the cylinder wall where they ride and create what is called a ridge at the top of the cylinder. Higher mileage and harder worked engines develop more severe ridges than other engines. Carbon buildup also adds thickness to the ridge of a cylinder, but this can be removed with a razor blade. A thick ridge will make it more difficult to push the piston out.

The ridge at the top of the cylinder is too big if after the carbon has been scraped off it catches a fingernail. If the ridge is significant, and you are planning on reusing the pistons, you will need to remove the ridge with a tool called a **ridge reamer** **FIGURE 13-31**. The ridge reamer is a cutting tool that will cut into the metal ridge and carbon buildup at the top of the cylinder and remove the lip. If the ridge is not removed, the piston rings could break as they move across the ridge. The piston itself could be damaged if it is forced over the ridge when removing the piston.

FIGURE 13-29 Unbolt and remove the oil pump and pickup tube.

FIGURE 13-30 Number both halves of the connecting rods.

FIGURE 13-31 Remove the ridge with a ridge reamer if the ridge is significant.

FIGURE 13-32 Position a piston at BDC and remove the connecting rod nuts.

If the pistons are going to be reused, any excessive ridge will need to be removed first, and then the pistons can be tapped out carefully. Also, care needs to be taken to not damage the connecting rod journal on the crankshaft when removing the piston. Using rod bolt covers will help protect the connecting rod journal.

Removing the Rod Caps

To remove the rod caps, start by positioning the number 1 piston at BDC. Then remove the nuts or bolts for the connecting rod cap on the number 1 piston **FIGURE 13-32**. Next, remove the rod cap. You can do this by tapping the end of the connecting rod on the parting line or by tapping the bolts that are pressed into the rod body with a brass hammer **FIGURE 13-33**. When the cap separates, pull it off by maneuvering it back and forth **FIGURE 13-34**. Inside the cap, there should be a bearing insert. If the bearing insert is not in the cap, it will be stuck to the rod journal of the crankshaft, so remove it from there.

Preparing to Remove the Pistons

Before you remove the pistons, it is important to put some protecting sleeves onto the rod bolts so they cannot

FIGURE 13-33 Loosen the rod cap by tapping on the side of the rod at the parting line, or on the bolts.

FIGURE 13-34 Remove the rod cap.

> ▷ **TECHNICIAN TIP**
>
> It is easy for the ridge reamer to remove more than the ridge, which could damage the cylinder wall. If you know the pistons will be replaced with new ones, it may be less hazardous to risk breaking the old, useless pistons than to risk damaging the cylinder with the ridge reamer.

scratch the rod journal or cylinder walls as the pistons are pushed out (**FIGURE 13-35**). To prevent the piston from falling out of the engine block and onto the ground when you push it out of the cylinders, thread two long bolts partially into the block on either side of the cylinder, and then stretch some rubber bands or twist a piece of wire between them to catch the piston (**FIGURE 13-36**).

Removing the Pistons

Make sure the rod journal of the crank is at the centerline of the cylinder bore. Place a wood or plastic dowel of about ½" (13 mm) in diameter and 2' (0.6 m) in length inside the bottom of the piston. Several hits to the dowel in the right spot should cause the piston to slide out (**FIGURE 13-37**). In extreme cases where the piston might be frozen in its bore by corrosion, a wooden dowel might not be strong enough. In that case, it may be necessary to switch to a metal rod of some sort and then apply more force with the hammer. Be careful not to scratch the cylinder walls with the edges of the connecting rod as you slide the piston out. Also be careful to avoid damaging the rod journal.

Remove the other pistons in the same way. Line up the rod journal with the bore centerline again and hit the dowel until the piston pops out. You may have to hit the piston with enough force that it breaks the rings to get it past the ridge. In that case, have someone there to catch it so you do not cause more damage than necessary.

> ### TECHNICIAN TIP
>
> It is not uncommon for a piston ring or even a piston skirt to break when worn pistons are being forced out. Piston assemblies need to be replaced if the technician determines that the cylinder needs to be repaired or that the piston itself has been damaged while inside the engine cylinder block. The cylinders should be inspected for a smooth surface and measured for out-of-round and taper. If these measurements are not within specifications, then the cylinder will have to be remachined and new pistons will be needed to fit the newly sized cylinders.

Removing the Crankshaft and Bearings

Before removing the main bearing caps, make sure they are marked for reinstallation. To do so, use a number punch or marking paint. To remove the crankshaft

FIGURE 13-35 Place protective covers on the rod bolts to protect the rod journal.

FIGURE 13-36 Use bolts and rubber bands to catch a piston.

FIGURE 13-37 Use a long dowel or hammer handle to tap a piston out of the cylinder.

bearing caps, you may need some additional leverage to loosen the bolts that hold the crankshaft caps. Some engine blocks have two bolts per cap. Others have four. Remove the bolts **FIGURE 13-38**. The cap may not come away easily, especially if it has long alignment dowels. Make sure the bolts are not threaded in at this point. Hold them up halfway out of their bolt holes and tap lightly side to side on the bolt heads. You will need to alternate sides until the cap is clear to be removed. The lower half of the main bearing inserts may come away with the cap as you remove it, or they may stick to the crankshaft journal **FIGURE 13-39**.

To remove the crankshaft on an application with a one-piece rear main seal, you first need to remove the rear main seal and housing **FIGURE 13-40**. This may require removing the engine from the engine stand to gain access to the rear of the block. Depending on the maker of engine

stand, and the engine block, sometimes the engine stand adapter will prevent the ease of removing the crankshaft assembly due to the end part of the crankshaft sticking out past the engine block and the adapter covering it. Crankshafts are both heavy and awkwardly shaped, so be very careful lifting it out of the engine block, or ask for assistance **FIGURE 13-41**.

When the crankshaft is removed from the engine cylinder block, sometimes the oil has become sticky and the crankshaft bearings may get stuck to the crankshaft assembly. In this case, you must examine the crankshaft thoroughly and remove the sticky bearings. Also examine the engine cylinder block saddles, where the crankshaft lies inside the block, to see if there are any bearings left inside the engine block. Next, remove any bearing inserts left in the engine cylinder block. Push each half-shell to the side from the center with your fingers opposite the

FIGURE 13-38 Remove the main bearing cap bolts.

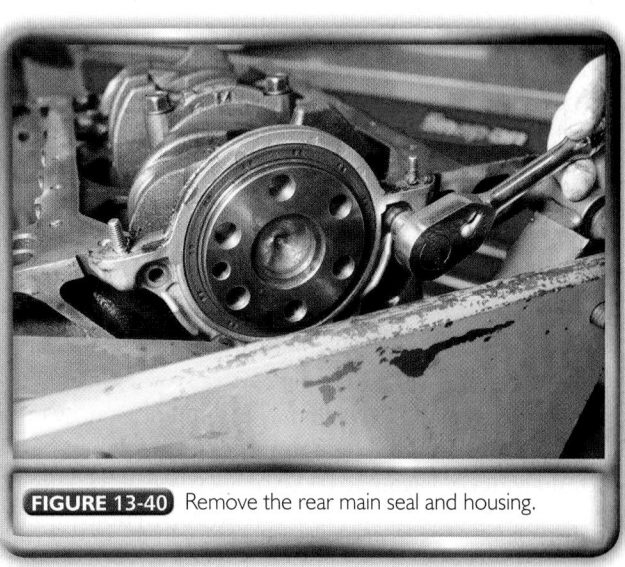

FIGURE 13-40 Remove the rear main seal and housing.

FIGURE 13-39 Remove the main bearing caps.

FIGURE 13-41 Lift out the crankshaft.

bearing tang **FIGURE 13-42**. If necessary, use a wooden hammer handle to help remove the bearing. The thrust bearing is a special bearing for the crankshaft assembly. It is the largest bearing insert, and its purpose is to prevent the crankshaft from moving forward or backward during engine operation. This crankshaft movement is also known as lateral movement. In addition to being the largest bearing, the thrust bearing can be identified by the sides it has on it. These sides are to cover the engine cylinder block saddles and prevent bearing movement.

Bearings with visible wear patterns, especially if the copper core is showing through in some areas, are not reusable and should be replaced. If you are not sure of their reusability, take them to a machine shop specialist for advice. If the engine has a rope seal or a two-piece rear main seal, pull out both halves with needle-nose pliers, a scratch awl, or a flat-blade screwdriver.

Removing Passage Plugs

Remove the water jacket core plugs. The water jacket core plugs cannot be easily pulled out, but they can usually be tilted so that channel lock pliers can grab them and pry them out. Use a punch to carefully drive one side of the core plug toward the water jacket. This should tilt them **FIGURE 13-43**. If not, keep tapping one side in, but be careful to hang on to it because some core plugs can fall into the water jackets and drop down out of sight. Grip one side of the plug with channel lock pliers, and pry it back out **FIGURE 13-44**.

If you have a stuck water jacket drain plug, now is the time to remove it. Drill right through the plug, then heat it up and let it cool again to try to break some of the threads loose. Insert an extractor tool into the open hole and use a wrench to break it free and unthread it. Next, take the

engine block off the stand. Lower the engine block carefully onto a bench and remove the engine stand adapter **FIGURE 13-45**. Remove the oil gallery plugs **FIGURE 13-46**. If they are square-type plugs, only use the proper hardened steel tool to remove them. Do not use the square part of a socket wrench. If they are stuck, do not force them to the point of stripping them. Use an oxyacetylene torch to heat up frozen plugs. Get them very hot, then let them cool, after which they may be loose enough to undo. If not, or if they strip, a machining specialist may have to remove them for you.

With the rear plugs out, you can pass a metal rod through the oil gallery and hammer out the front plugs from the rear, if they are the hammer-in type **FIGURE 13-47**. Hammer-in types do not have any threads showing, but rather a smooth surface on the sides and top of the plug.

FIGURE 13-43 Carefully hammer one side of the core plug until it tilts or pushes into the water jacket.

FIGURE 13-42 Remove the bearing inserts from the bearing saddles in the block.

FIGURE 13-44 Grip the core plug with channel lock pliers and pry it out.

FIGURE 13-45 Remove the block from the engine stand and remove the adapter.

FIGURE 13-46 Remove the oil gallery plugs.

FIGURE 13-47 Remove the front oil plugs.

A threaded plug has visible threads on the side and a square recessed area on top where a drive from a ratchet would be placed during installation or removal.

Each engine block has its own particular engine block plugs. Plug type is decided by the manufacturer of the engine cylinder block based on the engine cylinder block application. Check the service information to locate all of the plugs. Go around the engine block taking notes as you remove any plug, adapter, or fitting that might hinder the cleaning process.

Cleaning the Components

Before the parts are examined beyond a quick visual inspection, they need to be cleaned. The cleaning process of the engine cylinder block can vary depending on what is available to the technician. Most shops use a spray wash cabinet, which operates much like a dishwasher and usually uses environmentally friendly degreasers and hot water **FIGURE 13-48**. Some machine shops dip the major engine parts for several hours in a hot or cold caustic solution. The strong corrosive chemicals remove mineral deposits in the water jackets, carbon deposits, oil, greases, and paints.

Depending on the condition of the components, everything from the engine block and disassembled heads to the crankshaft and all the covers may need to be put into the spray wash for degreasing. After that, the heads and engine block will need to be hot tanked, blasted, or baked until they are perfectly clean, and any of the external covers will need to be bead blasted to be ready for paint later on. It is much easier to inspect and properly assess the condition of the parts when everything is clean. *Note:* It is of utmost importance to remember that,

FIGURE 13-48 Place the components in a spray wash cabinet to be cleaned.

after beading, all of the beads will have to be thoroughly cleaned out and off of the parts. Beads will get stuck in parts with baffles and myriad other places, and will quickly destroy a newly rebuilt engine when they become dislodged and circulate inside the engine.

Engine Block Component Inspections

Now that the engine has been disassembled and cleaned, all of the components need a thorough inspection to assess their condition. A quick visual inspection should have been made as each part was removed from the engine and any obvious damage noted. With the parts clean, inspect each part more thoroughly for any obvious damage that you missed before. If found, determine if the part needs to be replaced or if it can be repaired. If there are no obvious issues, perform any measurements or structural tests to verify that the parts are in useable or repairable condition. To do so, you need to know how to use the various tools involved, including measuring tools, crack detection tools, and various testers.

Inspecting the Engine Block

The engine block should be inspected for cracks after the cleaning process is finished and the block is thoroughly dried. You want to determine if the block is cracked before performing any machining work so that the crack can be repaired or the block replaced;

otherwise, time and materials will likely be wasted. Cracks can occur anywhere in the block, inside or outside, so you will need to thoroughly test all of the surfaces of the block. This includes applying compressed air or a strong vacuum to the engine block water jackets and oil galleries to check for any internal leaks. Cracks in cast iron parts can be detected by a process called magnetic particle inspection, more commonly referred to as **magnafluxing**. In this process, an electromagnet is attached to the part, which is then sprayed with a special magnetic powder or liquid that will stick to the magnetic field created at any cracks, thereby making them visible.

Another option is to use a leak detection dye. The product used could be a fluorescent dye such as **Zyglo™**, which is sprayed on the surface being checked, soaks into cracks, and is wiped off. A special black light is then shone on the surface and the dye appears in any cracks. Another type of dye detection system uses a two-part process. First the dye is applied and wiped off. Then a white developer is sprayed onto the surface. If the dye has soaked into any cracks, it will bleed out of the crack and stain the white developer. Leak detection dyes can be used on nonferrous metals such as aluminum. The purpose of the inspection is to make sure the engine block is still useable and can be rebuilt into an operating automotive engine.

To inspect the engine block for visible cracks, follow the steps in **SKILL DRILL 13-1**:

1. Visually inspect the engine block for any damage, excessive wear, or cracks. If none are visible, it

SKILL DRILL | 13-1 | Inspecting the Engine Block

1. Perform a visual check for cracks. If more detection is needed, magnaflux or use dye. Check all plug areas for obstruction or blockage.

2. Clean the deck surface using an appropriate gasket scraper, wire brush or bristle discs for cast iron. Use nonmetallic and nonabrasive scrapers on aluminum sealing surfaces.

3. Check the deck surface for warpage using a straightedge and a feeler gauge.

should be checked for hard-to-see hairline fractures or cracks by magnafluxing or a dye check method.

2 Check all core plug and galley plug areas for obstruction or blockage. You should also check the sealing surface of the plug holes for cleanliness and to make sure there are not any nicks or burrs. **(Photo 1)**

3 Clean the deck surface using a gasket scraper, wire brush, or bristle discs for cast iron. Use only non-metallic and nonabrasive scrapers on aluminum sealing surfaces. **(Photo 2)**

4 Using a straightedge and feeler gauge, check the deck surface for **warpage** across the top in several different angles. Most machine shops will resurface an engine block with more than 0.0025" (0.064 mm) warpage. Check the manufacturer's specifications for maximum warpage. **(Photo 3)**

Inspecting the Crankshaft

A crankshaft can be faulty in several ways. First, it could be warped, which would cause the journals to be forced against the bearings wearing them out prematurely. Second, the main and rod journals could be excessively worn, leading to too much bearing clearance, which would cause low engine oil pressure. Third, the bolt holes, keyways, and sealing surfaces could be damaged, causing their own set of issues. These situations mean that a thorough inspection along with precise measurements must be made to ensure the crankshaft can be put back in service.

To inspect the crankshaft, follow the steps in **SKILL DRILL 13-2**:

1 Check the crankshaft for straightness. There are two methods you can use to check the crankshaft for straightness.

SKILL DRILL | 13-2 | Inspecting the Crankshaft

1 Check the crankshaft for straightness with a dial indicator.

2 Measure the rod and journals using a micrometer and record your findings.

3 Visually inspect the square-cut or Woodruff key and keyway for damage.

4 Visually inspect the thrust flange, bolt holes, and rear seal surface for nicks or scratches.

5 Visually inspect the crankshaft for cracks; magnaflux, if necessary.

6 Make sure the oil passages are clear. Check the crankshaft position sensor reluctor ring to make sure there is no damage.

a. Crankshaft in block: With the pistons and rods removed, make sure all main caps are numbered; the main caps must not be mixed up because they must go back in the exact order in which they were removed. Pull the number 1 main cap, and clean the main journal on the crankshaft. Using a dial indicator with a 0.001" (0.025 mm) scale and a magnetic base, attach the dial indicator on the pan rail and center the dial indicator over the number 1 main journal. Preload the dial indicator on the main journal and move the face on the dial indicator to zero. Rotate the crankshaft one full rotation, watching the dial indicator, and record your findings. Repeat the process to check the center main and record your findings. Determine any necessary actions based on your findings.

b. Crankshaft out of block: With the crankshaft removed, make sure the main journals are clean. Position the crankshaft on two V-blocks, using the first main journal and the last main journal. Using a dial indicator with a 0.001" (0.025 mm) scale, attach the dial indicator on the bench with a magnetic base or clamp. Position the dial indicator over the number 1 journal. Preload the dial indicator on the main journal and set the face on the dial indicator to zero. Rotate the crankshaft one full rotation, watching the dial indicator. Record your findings. Repeat the process on the center main and record your findings. Determine any necessary actions based on your findings. **(Photo 1)**

2 Visually inspect the journals for grooves. The journals should be smooth to the touch. Use an outside micrometer to measure the rod and main journals. Both rod and main journals should have measurements taken 90 degrees apart. Also, rod journals should be measured across the face of the journal to check for taper. Compare your findings to factory specifications and determine the necessary action. **(Photo 2)**

3 Visually inspect the square-cut or Woodruff key and keyway. If the square key or Woodruff key is out, make sure the keyway is straight with sharp edges. The square-cut or Woodruff key must fit snugly. **(Photo 3)**

4 Visually inspect the thrust flange, bolt holes, and rear seal surface to make sure there are no nicks or scratches. **(Photo 4)**

5 Visually inspect the crankshaft for cracks. If you need a more detailed inspection, the crankshaft

should be checked by magnafluxing. Determine any necessary actions. **(Photo 5)**

6 Probe the oil passages with a small plastic tube (a spray can nozzle extension works well), making sure the oil passages from the mains into the rod journals are clear. Determine any necessary actions.

7 Check the crankshaft position sensor reluctor ring, when applicable. Visually inspect the reluctor ring to make sure there is no damage. **(Photo 6)**

Inspecting Main and Connecting Rod Bearings

The main and connecting rod bearings must be inspected to determine whether they are in good condition or need replacing. Both normal wear and traumatic events can damage the bearings, resulting in a knocking noise and/or low oil pressure. Typically a visual inspection is all that is needed to determine that they need to be replaced, since excessive wear will be apparent. If the bearings look to be in good shape, then the bearing clearance should be measured to determine if it meets the manufacturer's specifications. This will be covered in a later skill drill.

To inspect main and connecting rod bearings, follow the steps in **SKILL DRILL 13-3**:

1 If you are considering reusing the main and rod bearing inserts, be sure to keep them together and mark them once they are removed. The main caps and connecting rods should have already been marked with numbers to avoid mixing them up.

2 Remove each main bearing insert from the main cap and main housing support, one at a time. If the bearing insert will not come out using your fingers, take a wooden hammer handle and push the bearing on the opposite side of the tang at the parting line. The bearing should slip out. **(Photo 1)**

3 Clean each main bearing and mark the back of each half-shell with a permanent marker with the correlating bearing support number. It is important to know what journal the bearings were located on to identify any unusual wear patterns. **(Photo 2)**

4 Visually check that there are no grooves or imbedded foreign matter. Check with the bearing wear chart to see if the bearings are wearing normally or if the wear pattern indicates that the bearings need replacement. Repeat the process for the connecting rod bearings.

5 Before you inspect the thrust bearing, go back to your crankshaft end play findings. If it was excessive, you should be able to determine why by

SKILL DRILL | 13-3 | Inspecting Main and Connecting Rod Bearings

1 Take each main bearing insert out of the main cap and main bearing support, one at a time.

2 Clean each main bearing and mark the back of each half-shell with a permanent marker with the correlating bearing support number.

3 Check that there are no grooves or imbedded foreign matter. Check with the bearing wear chart to see whether the wear pattern indicates that the bearings need replacement. Repeat the process for the connecting rod bearings. Before you inspect the thrust bearing, go back to your crankshaft end play findings. If it was excessive, you should be able to see why by checking for damage or wear on either side of the thrust surface.

checking for damage or wear on either the front or the rear thrust bearing surface. **(Photo 3)**

6 If the rear surface of the thrust bearing is worn and the vehicle is equipped with an automatic transmission, the wear is usually caused by a torque converter ballooning, which causes pressure on the thrust bearing. If it is a manual transmission, the wear could be caused by someone holding the clutch pedal down excessively or by a pressure plate with too much pressure.

Identifying Piston and Bearing Wear Patterns

Examining the piston and bearing wear patterns is useful because the patterns serve as a diagnostic tool for determining whether the parts are operating normally or if there are possible alignment issues or engine operating problems with the engine block and its internal components. The technician must compare the wear patterns with those provided in the manufacturer's wear chart. The wear chart will correlate the wear pattern with the

contributing problem, such as a component failure or a damaged crankshaft assembly, lubrication system, or cooling system.

To identify piston and bearing wear patterns that indicate connecting rod alignment and main bearing bore problems, follow the steps in **SKILL DRILL 13-4**:

1 Visually inspect the rod bearings. There should be an even wear pattern across the full face of the bearing. Greater wear on one side than the other is an indication of a bent connecting rod. A bent rod will also typically show an increased wear pattern on one side of the piston skirt. If uneven wear is observed, have a machine shop check the rod for straightness. **(Photo 1)**

2 Inspect the main bearings. There should be an even wear pattern across the full face of the bearing. Greater wear on one side than the other is an indication that the main line that supports the crankshaft is no longer straight. If uneven wear is observed, inspect the crankshaft for straightness and determine if it needs to be straightened or replaced. **(Photo 2)**

SKILL DRILL | 13-4 | Checking Piston and Bearing Wear Patterns

1. Inspect the rod bearings. There should be an even wear pattern across the full face of the bearing.

2. Inspect the main bearings. There should be an even wear pattern across the full face of the bearing.

Removing and Replacing the Piston Pin

Removing and replacing the piston pin is typically performed when new pistons are being used or if the rods are being rebuilt/replaced. Removing and inspecting the pins is important to see if the piston or the piston pins have developed any abnormal wear patterns during the operation of the engine. Full floating pins can be removed by hand once the snap rings have been removed. Semi-floating pins must be pressed apart with a hydraulic press.

To remove and replace the floating piston pin, follow the steps in **SKILL DRILL 13-5** :

1. In the floating pin style, using the proper snap ring pliers that fit the holes in the snap ring, remove both snap rings. (**Photo 1**)

2. Push on the wrist pin to separate the wrist pin from the piston and connecting rod; you might need a wrist pin driver. If you do not have a wrist pin driver, you can use a deep-well socket that is smaller in diameter than the outer diameter of the piston pin to push out the piston pin. (**Photo 2**)

3. Using an outside micrometer, measure the piston pin outside diameter and record your findings. (**Photo 3**)

4. Using a bore gauge or inside micrometer, measure the inside of the small end of the connecting rod. If you used a small bore gauge, you used the setting fixture for the bore gauge to check for proper settings; be sure to recheck the bore gauge with the outside micrometer.

5. Record the clearance. The typical clearance for a floating pin is 0.0004" to 0.0008" (0.01 to 0.02 mm). Check the manufacturer's recommended clearance for the engine you are working on. Note that the floating pin clearance is much closer than the clearance of the rod and main bearings. Determine any necessary actions. (**Photo 4**)

6. Install the floating pin design. Lubricate the wrist pin hole on the piston and the small end of the connecting rod along with the wrist pin, with an oil or assembly lube. The additive has an anti-galling agent that will help lubricate the piston pin during the engine start. Using snap ring pliers, install one snap ring in the groove in the piston. Be aware that some snap rings are directional and if installed backward, can come out and allow the snap ring and pin to score the cylinder wall. (**Photo 5**)

7. Position the piston so it is in the proper relationship to the connecting rod (see service information). Make sure the piston notch or arrow on top of the piston, if so equipped, is pointing toward the front of the engine and the bearing tangs are facing the proper direction. (**Photo 6**)

8. Place the small end of the connecting rod between the piston pin bosses. Using your fingers or a wrist pin driver, push the wrist pin through the piston and small end of the rod until it stops against the snap ring. (**Photo 7**)

SKILL DRILL | 13-5 | Removing and Replacing the Piston Pin

1 Using the proper snap ring pliers that fit the holes in the snap ring, remove both snap rings.

2 Push on the wrist pin to separate the wrist pin from the piston and connecting rod.

3 Using an outside micrometer, measure the piston pin outside diameter and record your findings.

4 Using a bore gauge or inside micrometer, measure the inside of the small end of the connecting rod. Record the clearance.

5 Install the floating pin design. Lubricate the wrist pin hole on the piston and the small end of the connecting rod along with the wrist pin. Using your snap ring pliers, install one snap ring on the piston.

6 Position the piston so it is in the proper relationship to the connecting rod (see service information).

7 Place the small end of the connecting rod between the piston pin bosses. Using your fingers or a wrist pin driver, push the wrist pin through the piston and small end of the rod until it stops against the snap ring.

8 Install the second snap ring, and move the piston and connecting rod, rocking the rod back and forth to ensure that it moves freely and smoothly.

9 Install the second snap ring, and move the piston and connecting rod, rocking the rod back and forth to ensure that it moves freely and smoothly. **(Photo 8)**

Inspecting and Measuring the Cylinder Walls/Sleeves

The surfaces of the cylinder bores wear over time as the pistons travel up and down the cylinders millions of times over their life. The cylinder bore in both sleeved and nonsleeved engine blocks must be perfectly round and of a uniform diameter from top to bottom. Careful measurement is required to determine if the cylinders can be reused or if they will need to be replaced (sleeves) or bored oversize. The tool that most quickly measures the cylinder bores is a dial bore gauge. It uses a dial indicator gauge connected to a handle. Once it is calibrated to a certain size, it can be inserted into the cylinder and a quick measurement made. Another tool that is just as accurate, but not as easy and quick, is the inside micrometer.

To inspect and measure cylinder walls/sleeves for damage and wear, follow the steps in **SKILL DRILL 13-6**:

1 If the visual inspection showed obvious scoring or damage to the cylinder walls in the block, then the pistons cannot be reused and the block will need to be machined. **(Photo 1)**

2 If there are no cracks or scratches, then you can use a dial bore gauge or inside micrometer to measure the cylinders.

3 If using the dial bore gauge, set it to the original size of the cylinder. This way, you will be able to see if the cylinders are oversize or out of round or if there is a taper from the bottom to the top of the cylinder. If using an inside micrometer, assemble the proper adapters to measure the bore.

4 Measure each cylinder at the top, center, and bottom, 90 degrees across the thrust side and pin side at each level. Compare the readings to specifications. **(Photo 2)**

Inspecting and Measuring Piston Skirts

Pistons, like cylinder walls, wear over time. If they are to be reused, they must be carefully inspected, measured, and compared to specifications first. It does no good to put new piston rings on a piston that has too much wear at the ring lands, as the rings will leak oil and compression. If the piston skirt is worn, the piston may make a knocking noise due to too much clearance between the skirt and the cylinder wall.

To inspect and measure piston skirts, follow the steps in **SKILL DRILL 13-7**:

1 With the piston inverted, measure the skirt just above the pin bore with a micrometer. **(Photo 1)**

2 Measure the diameter of the bottom of the piston skirt. It should never be smaller than the measurement taken at the pin measurement area.

SKILL DRILL | **13-6** | **Inspecting and Measuring the Cylinder Walls/Sleeves**

1 If there is obvious scoring or damage, then the block will need to be machined. If there is no obvious damage, set a dial bore gauge or inside micrometer to measure the cylinders.

2 Measure each cylinder at the top, center, and bottom, 90 degrees across the thrust side and pin side at each level. Compare the readings to specifications.

SKILL DRILL | 13-7 | Inspecting and Measuring Piston Skirts

1 With the piston inverted, measure the diameter of the skirt just above the pin bore with a micrometer.

2 With the piston inverted, measure the diameter of the bottom of the piston skirt. This reading should never be smaller than the previous reading.

3 With the piston inverted, measure the diameter of the piston skirt just below the oil ring groove and compare to specifications. Replace the pistons if necessary.

If the measurement is smaller, then the piston has a collapsed skirt and the piston will need to be replaced. **(Photo 2)**

3 Measure the diameter of the piston skirt just below the oil ring groove and compare the reading to the specifications. If it is found to be worn or there is too much clearance between the piston and the cylinder wall, the piston will need to be replaced. **(Photo 3)**

Deglazing and Cleaning Cylinder Walls

If the cylinder measures within specifications, it will need to be prepared for the new piston rings. The cylinder wall will probably have a polished "glaze" on its surface that must be removed. Removing the glazed surface with an abrasive stone of the proper grit will give the cylinder walls a nice crosshatch pattern, which allows a small amount of oil to be retained in the fine scratches. This oil helps to lubricate the piston rings during engine operation, and the fine crosshatched scratches allow the new piston rings to seat against the surface of the freshly honed cylinder wall. The recommended crosshatch for a cylinder wall is approximately 45 degrees.

A cylinder hone can be rigid, flexible, or ball style. A rigid hone uses fixed rectangular abrasive stones and is used on a cylinder after it has been bored to give a perfectly cylindrical shape with the proper finish. A flexible hone uses spring-loaded rectangular stones that can more easily follow the contours of a minimally used cylinder; thus, it is used to deglaze a cylinder that will be reused. A ball hone uses round abrasive stones on the ends of flexible metal spokes. A ball hone also works well on a minimally worn cylinder that will be put back into service.

To deglaze and clean a cylinder wall, follow the steps in **SKILL DRILL 13-8**:

1 Using a drill, attach the proper-sized **flex hone**.

2 Apply honing oil to the cylinder walls. **(Photo 1)**

3 Using the drill with the attached flex hone, stroke up and down in the cylinder that you are honing for approximately 10 to 15 seconds, at a speed at which you get a good crosshatch. Be sure to pull the flex hone (ball hone) out of the bore before stopping the drill.

4 Use a rag to wipe the cylinder out so you can inspect the cylinder walls. Repeat as necessary to get a good crosshatch pattern. **(Photo 2)**

5 For final cleaning, use a pressure wash cabinet.

6 After removing the block from the wash cabinet, clean the cylinders with soap and water using a cylinder block brush; rinse and blow-dry the cylinders. Ensure that the cylinders are completely clean. There should be no color when you wipe them with a white cloth. Wipe down the cylinders with an antirusting spray to prevent rust. **(Photo 3)**

SKILL DRILL | 13-8 | Deglazing and Cleaning a Cylinder Wall

1 Using a drill, attach the proper-sized flex hone. Apply honing oil to the cylinder walls.

2 Using the drill with the attached flex hone, stroke up and down in the cylinder that you are honing for approximately 10 to 15 seconds, at a speed at which you get a good crosshatch. Pull the flex hone (ball hone) out of the bore before stopping the drill. Use a rag to wipe the cylinder out so you can inspect the cylinder walls. Repeat until a good crosshatch pattern is achieved.

3 For final cleaning, use a pressure wash cabinet for the block. Clean the cylinders with soap and water using a cylinder block brush; rinse and blow-dry. Wipe down the cylinders with an anti-rusting spray.

Wrap-up

Ready for Review

- The engine block is the main structure of the internal combustion engine; it provides the engine's framework and a mounting surface for all components.
- The engine block is machined in one piece, with precise specifications that help to prevent air and fuel leakage, withstand the thermal stresses of combustion, and accommodate any resulting shocks and vibration from power pulses.
- Engine block casting must accommodate cylinders and water jackets (passageways around the cylinders); this can be done with core sand or foam shapes.
- Manufacturers are increasingly making aluminum alloy engine blocks, as they are lighter weight and increase fuel efficiency.
- The engine block assembly (lower end) includes: oil galleries and plugs, water jacket and plugs, pistons and rings, piston pins, connecting rods and caps, rod bearing inserts, main bearing caps, main bearing inserts, the thrust bearing, crankshaft, rear seals, camshaft (in block cam), a vibration balancer, and smooth surfaces to accommodate mating parts.
- Ribs, webs, and fillets provide reinforcement and strength to high-stress areas of the engine block.
- The main bearing caps, which provide crankshaft support, are sometimes supported by a main bearing cap girdle (some of which are integrated).
- Cylinders are either machined into the cylinder block or are made of a cast iron sleeve.
- Cylinder sleeves are dry (not in contact with a water jacket; held by an interference fit), dry flange (also not in contact with a water jacket; locked into engine block with a flange), or wet (direct contact with water jacket coolant).
- The piston fits into the cylinder and is responsible for transferring power stroke force to the crankshaft.
- The piston assembly includes a head, skirt, pin, connecting rod, piston boss, compression rings, oil rings, piston ring grooves, ring lands, and wrist pin.
- Piston slap occurs when there is too great a clearance between the piston and the cylinder wall.
- Cam-ground pistons are slightly oval shaped to accommodate heat expansion.
- Compression ratio refers to the difference between the volume in the combustion chamber above the piston when the piston is at bottom dead center and the volume of the combustion chamber above the piston when the piston is at top dead center.
- The compression ratio can be changed by altering the shape of the piston head (e.g., flat, concave, dome-shaped, recessed, machined reliefs).
- Pistons can be manufactured via forging (more expensive, but stronger) or casting (cast aluminum or hypereutectic).
- Piston skirts may be coated with ceramic or molybdenum disulfide to reduce friction with the cylinder wall.
- Piston compression rings must have proper end gap, back clearance, and ring tension.
- Connecting rods are H- or I-beam shaped and types include cast, forged, aluminum, and powdered metal (most recent technology); rod caps are not interchangeable among the different types.
- The crankshaft is designed to transform piston stroke power into rotary motion.
- The crankshaft assembly contains main bearing journals that help to center the crankshaft at the bottom of the engine block, where they mate with main bearings.
- Crankshafts may be internally or externally balanced, using counterweights.
- Crankshaft bearings are split in two parts, each with a tang that fits into the bearing saddle and cap.
- A thrust bearing is used to limit end play movement of the crankshaft.
- An oil hole in the main bearing saddle allows oil from the oil gallery to lubricate the main bearings.
- Bearings can be undersized or standard and are generally either trimetal or bimetal.
- An engine will have either a flywheel (manual transmission) or flex plate and torque converter (automatic transmission) to store rotational energy.
- The harmonic balancer (crankshaft damper) reduces vibration from the piston and crankshaft assembly.
- Crankshaft seals are designed to contain lubricating oil.
- Balance shafts reduce engine vibrations and may use counterweights to reduce second-order vibrations.
- Stock compression ratios typically run between 8:1 and 10.5:1 and can be intentionally increased if necessary.
- When disassembling the engine, refer to manufacturer's service information.

Key Terms

accessory drive pulley A round circular metal disc attached to the front of the engine crankshaft with a rubber/fiber belt that helps operate automotive accessories.

aluminum rod A lightweight, strong, either cast or forged metal shaft that connects the piston assembly to the crankshaft assembly.

back clearance The area or space behind the piston rings when the rings are in the piston ring grooves.

balance shaft A metal shaft attached and located inside the engine cylinder block assembly to counteract crankshaft vibrations.

bearing crush The force created to seat the bearing by the extra bearing material when the ends of the bearing inserts touch each other and are forced against each other.

bearing inserts Components made out of soft metal materials that are replaceable and come in pairs; also called half-shell bearings.

billet The roughly shaped steel piece that has been cast or forged but has not undergone its final machining.

bimetal Aluminum, tin, and silicon alloy metals placed together with steel to form one piece of material and used for bearing materials.

bottom dead center (BDC) A piston's lowest point of travel inside the engine block cylinder.

casting line A by-product of the metal casting process that forms a line found on parts that are cast in metal.

cast rod A connecting rod that is created by the metal casting process.

center bolt A fastener or bolt found in the middle of the harmonic balancer or cam sprocket that attaches it to the crankshaft or the camshaft.

compression ratio A numerical representation of the volume of the cylinder when the piston is at the top of its travel divided by the volume in the cylinder when the piston is at the bottom of its travel.

compression ring A metal ring found inside the grooves on the side of the engine piston.

compression ring groove A square groove found on the outside of the piston skirt in which the piston ring fits.

connecting rod A cast or forged metal rod that connects the engine pistons to the engine crankshaft.

core plug A metal cap for the holes that are used to remove core sand used during the casting process.

crankcase The bottom area of the engine cylinder block where the crankshaft is located.

crank core The rough, unfinished crankshaft assembly that has just left the foundry or forging area.

crankshaft A part mounted in the lower side of the engine block that has offset journals that rotate to change the up-and-down motion of the pistons into rotary motion at the crankshaft.

crankshaft journal A metal part of the crankshaft that is positioned offset to the main bearing journal on the crankshaft.

crimp The bent shape of the oil ring expander that allows it to provide outward force on the oil rings.

deck The surface area at the top of the engine block against which the cylinder head seals.

dry flanged sleeve A metal cylinder with a flange embedded into the block pressed into an engine cylinder to give it a new wear surface. The flanged sleeve is held in by the cylinder head.

dry sleeve A metal cylinder that is pressed into an engine cylinder block that does not come in direct contact with coolant. It is held in place with an interference fit.

engine bearing A specially designed metal piece that supports circular moving parts.

expander The part of an oil control ring that holds the ring against the cylinder wall.

fillet The radius portion of an inside corner that reduces stress at the corner.

flex hone A machine tool with abrasive stones that is used to refinish the inside of the cylinder walls.

flex plate A metal part attached to the rear of the crankshaft that connects to the torque converter in a vehicle with an automatic transmission.

floating pin A round metal pin that has a very small clearance but is free to float in the piston and connecting rod.

fluid dissipater A silicone fluid component that allows the mass of a fluid type harmonic balancer to rotate at a more constant speed than the crankshaft to help even out the torsional vibrations of the crankshaft.

flywheel A heavy round metal disc attached to the end of the crankshaft to smooth out vibrations from the crankshaft assembly and provide one of the friction surfaces for a clutch disc used on manual transmission/ transaxle applications.

forged connecting rod A strong metal connecting rod hammered into shape by large presses used to connect the piston to the crankshaft.

garter spring A round circular spring used in seals to provide tension on oil seal lips.

girdle A metal device connected to the bottom of the engine cylinder block to create strength for the main bearing caps.

gravity pouring The casting process used for creating metal parts.

harmonic balancer A round metal disc connected to the front of the crankshaft that smoothes out torsional vibrations created by the crankshaft.

horizontally opposed engine An engine cylinder block where all the cylinders are placed in a horizontal position across from each other, often referred to as a boxer engine.

hypereutectic piston An aluminum piston that is cast with a 16% to 19% silicon content and that has minimal expansion rates.

induction hardening A metal hardening process that uses an electromagnetic field to quickly heat up the surface of a metal part so it can be quenched to provide an appropriate amount of hardness.

interference fit A fastening between two parts that is activated by friction after the two parts are pushed together.

journal saddle A semicircular cut located at the bottom of the engine block that is used to support the engine crankshaft.

lost foam A metal casting process that uses a foaming process to create the pattern of the part being cast in metal.

magnafluxing An electromagnetic process used to locate cracks in ferrous engine blocks and cylinder heads and other ferrous metal parts.

main bearing Metal bearing insert located in the main saddles that support the main journals.

main bearing caps Sturdy caps placed over the main journals of the crankshaft assembly and fastened with either two or four bolts.

main cap girdle A metal attachment that strengthens and connects all the main bearing caps together. It can be integral from the main bearing caps, or separate.

main journal The smooth machined area of the crankshaft assembly that allows the crankshaft to rotate within the main bearings.

mains The specific round smooth journals of the crankshaft that rotate in main bearings.

Mallory metal A tungsten alloy of copper and nickel that is used as a metal substitute added to the crankshaft counterweight for balancing purposes.

metallurgical bonding A process of sintering metals until they are fused together as one metal.

moly The abbreviation for the lubricant called molybdenum disulfide.

nitriding A metal surfacing process that uses nitrogen ammonia gas to create a very thin, highly hardened surface.

nitridization process The nitriding metal surfacing process in which nitrogen ammonia gas is used inside a furnace and heated up and then cooled.

offset area An area on the crankshaft that is offset from the crankshaft centerline and that becomes a counterweight.

oil control ring The widest of the metal rings on the piston head assembly that controls oil flow to and from the cylinder walls.

oil ring groove A metal groove cut into the piston head assembly designed to hold the oil control ring, which lubricates the cylinder wall and pistons.

piston The round metal plug found inside the engine cylinder that moves up and down inside the cylinder.

piston assembly All of the parts of the piston including the piston, piston rings, and piston pin.

piston pin (wrist pin) A round circular metal manufactured part that attaches the piston assembly to the connecting rod assembly.

piston ring A metal ring that is placed in a square groove around a piston for sealing purposes.

piston ring groove A square-cut groove located on the piston designed to hold a metal piston ring.

piston slap An engine noise caused by excessive clearance between the piston skirt area and the cylinder wall.

piston stroke The distance the piston travels through the engine cylinder from top dead center to bottom dead center.

powdered metal rod A connecting rod manufactured through the process of heat, compression, and forging of powdered metals into a connecting rod.

power stroke The travel of the piston following ignition of the air/fuel mixture as the expanding gases of combustion push the piston down the cylinder.

press-fit pin A description of how a piston pin is placed inside a connecting rod by pressing the pin into the connecting rod.

reciprocation The back-and-forth movement of the piston assembly inside the cylinder.

rib A design feature created in the metal casting/forging process that places extra metal area on a part for strength and durability, yet keeps the weight of the engine block low.

ridge reamer A tool used to remove the metal lip on top of the cylinder walls caused by engine wear.

ring gap The distance between the ends of the piston rings when the rings are seated against the inside of the engine cylinder.

ring gear A large circular gear that is typically mounted on the flywheel or flex plate and mates to the starter gear, for the purpose of cranking the engine over.

ring land The area between the piston ring grooves found on the piston head assembly.

ring tension The built-in force created inside the piston rings due to the fact that the piston rings are made bigger than the cylinder walls to generate a scraping action against the cylinder walls.

rod beam The area of connecting rod between the big and small ends.

rod bearing A bearing insert located in the big end of the connecting rod.

rod cap The very bottom part of the connecting rod that retains the rod bearing inserts.

rod journal Also called the crankshaft rod throw, an area machined to a very smooth finish that contains an oil hole to provide oil to lubricate the surfaces of the crankshaft and rod bearing inserts.

rotating assembly The assembly of the crankshaft, connecting rod, and piston that are found inside the engine cylinder block.

second-order vibration Vibration that occurs at twice the engine rpm.

side rail The thin portion of the oil control ring that is used to scrape oil off of the cylinder walls.

sintering process A metal hardening process in which the metal is fused together without melting.

soft plug A thin-walled, metal, cup-shaped disc designed to be pressed into a machined passageway in the block for the purpose of plugging it.

starter teeth Machined teeth located on the ring gear for meshing with the starter drive teeth located in the starter motor.

tang A part of the bearing insert that helps to lock the bearing insert into the bearing saddles and caps.

throw The part of the crankshaft that is offset for the connecting rods to mate with; also called connecting rod journal.

thrust bearing A main bearing insert that either has integrated flanges or separate flanges that provide bearing surfaces that prevent forward or lateral movement of the crankshaft assembly.

timing chain A steel chain connecting the crankshaft assembly to the camshaft assembly.

timing gear A sprocket attached to the crankshaft assembly and the camshaft assembly.

top dead center (TDC) The position of the piston in the cylinder farthest from the crankshaft.

trimetal The use of three different types of metals to build up a bearing insert to give it long-lasting wear characteristics.

warpage The bending of flat materials primarily due to extreme hot and cold temperature changes.

water jacket A passageway for coolant to flow inside the engine block that is formed when the block is cast.

web A reinforced area of a metal part formed during the casting process to create strength and durability.

Welch plug A soft, round, metal disc pressed into the engine block to plug a water jacket or oil passageway.

wet sleeve A replaceable steel cylinder installed into the block that provides a wear surface for the piston and rings. It is in direct contact with coolant on its outside surface.

Woodruff key A half-round, rectangular key that is placed into a half-round, rectangular opening in the nose of the crankshaft or other round shafts found on the engine.

Zyglo™ A crack detection method used on engine blocks and cylinder heads that uses magnetism and a fluorescent light to find cracks in ferrous metal.

ASE-Type Questions

1. Tech A says that soft plugs or freeze plugs are designed to prevent the coolant from freezing. Tech B says that soft plugs or freeze plugs were designed to plug holes or galleys. Who is correct?
   a. Tech A
   b. Tech B
   c. Both A and B
   d. Neither A nor B

2. Tech A says that most pistons use one compression ring and one oil control ring. Tech B says that most pistons use two compression rings and one oil control ring. Who is correct?
   a. Tech A
   b. Tech B
   c. Both A and B
   d. Neither A nor B

3. Tech A says that the thrust bearing should be aligned by tapping the crankshaft forward and backward before tightening the main bearing cap. Tech B says that the thrust bearing is located on the flywheel. Who is correct?
   a. Tech A
   b. Tech B
   c. Both A and B
   d. Neither A nor B

4. Tech A says that using a thicker head gasket would lower the compression ratio. Tech B says that the effective compression ratio is affected by valve timing. Who is correct?
   a. Tech A
   b. Tech B
   c. Both A and B
   d. Neither A nor B

5. Tech A says that when removing the pistons, you must first remove the piston rings. Tech B says that cracks in a cylinder can be measured with a dial indicator, and are ok as long as they are less than 0.003" wide. Who is correct?
   a. Tech A
   b. Tech B
   c. Both A and B
   d. Neither A nor B

6. Tech A says that a piston is manufactured slightly oval in shape. Tech B says that the piston pin is slightly oval in shape to allow for heat expansion and lubrication. Who is correct?
   a. Tech A
   b. Tech B
   c. Both A and B
   d. Neither A nor B

7. Tech A says that cylinder walls are manufactured with a slight taper so that the piston rings will seal tighter at TDC. Tech B says that piston coatings assist in the control of piston temperature, which allows for tighter bore clearances and greater engine efficiency. Who is correct?
   a. Tech A
   b. Tech B
   c. Both A and B
   d. Neither A nor B

8. Tech A says that fractured rods have a unique mating surface and that only the cap that was fractured is the one that will fit that rod. Technician B says that a powdered metal rod is less expensive, lighter, and as strong as a forged rod. Who is correct?
   a. Tech A
   b. Tech B
   c. Both A and B
   d. Neither A nor B

9. Tech A says that when grinding main journals, an undersized main bearing will be required. Technician B says that the main bearing journals should be measured for minimum diameter, out-of-round, and taper. Who is correct?
   a. Tech A
   b. Tech B
   c. Both A and B
   d. Neither A nor B

10. Tech A says that a failed harmonic balancer can cause a crankshaft to break. Tech B says that the crankshaft rod journals are typically measured using a dial indicator. Who is correct?
    a. Tech A
    b. Tech B
    c. Both A and B
    d. Neither A nor B

11. Tech A says that main and rod bearings are glued in place with special bearing cement. Tech B says that main and rod bearings are held in place by a precise amount of "bearing crush." Who is correct?
    a. Technician A
    b. Technician B
    c. Both A and B
    d. Neither A nor B

CHAPTER 14

NATEF Tasks

There are no NATEF tasks for this chapter.

Knowledge Objectives

After reading this chapter, you will be able to:
1. Explain the aspects of engine machining. (pp 384–385)
2. Describe the composition of the engine cylinder block and cylinder head mating surface. (pp 385–386)
3. Explain the process of crankshaft grinding and polishing. (pp 391–393)
4. Explain the purpose of cylinder head machining and what is involved in the process. (pp 393–398)
5. Describe cylinder head resurfacing and why it is necessary. (p 398)
6. Explain the aspects involved in engine balancing. (pp 399–401)

Engine Machining

Skills Objectives

There are no skills objectives for this chapter.

Introduction

In the past 20 years, the field of automotive technology has changed dramatically. More often than not, the vehicle manufacturer takes failed parts back for analysis and sends the technician brand new parts. For example, if a connecting rod failed and caused catastrophic engine damage, the manufacturer would ask for the engine back for a complete analysis of why it failed. The technician's responsibility would be to replace the broken engine with a newly supplied unit.

If the vehicle is not under warranty, it is still usually less expensive to replace most engine assemblies than to tear down and repair them. Typically, once the engine is replaced, the broken engine is sent to the parts store from which the new engine was purchased for a "core return." The parts store sends the broken engine back to the manufacturer to have it professionally rebuilt and all worn parts replaced or remachined. The automotive technician of today does not necessarily need to know how to proficiently perform each of the procedures listed in this chapter, but he or she does need to know that these processes exist and understand what is possible to repair and what is not. The ability to recognize failures of engines that are beyond repair will help the technician to know whether it is more cost effective for the customer to replace rather than repair.

Engine Machining

Engine machining is done any time the tolerances of an engine component must be adjusted by adding or removing material. Typically, this process is performed by taking precise measurements and comparing those measurements to a set of factory specifications that are found in service information for that particular vehicle. Engine machining is performed when an engine exhibits a problem and the technician determines that problem is coming from a component of the engine that is not operating within specifications. For example, a customer complains of a noise when the engine is started up cold. Due to the tone and frequency of the noise and the fact that the volume of the noise goes away as the engine warms up, the technician diagnoses the noise as excessive piston-to-cylinder wall clearance, which is called piston slap. The technician disassembles the engine, checks the piston-to-cylinder wall clearance, and finds that the pistons have excessive clearance. The pistons are replaced and the block is bored oversize to accommodate the larger pistons. The engine is reassembled and the technician verifies the repair by testing the vehicle on a cold start-up.

Most technicians and shop owners in today's competitive market have chosen to sublet, or send out,

> **TECHNICIAN TIP**
>
> Replacing the pistons can change the engine's balance. Take engine balance into consideration when selecting new pistons, or consider having the engine rebalanced during the machining process. See the Engine Balancing section later in this chapter.

You are the Automotive Technician

You are an ASE-certified Engine Machinist at the local machine shop. A customer wants to know about the machining processes your shop can handle. The Boss 429 spun a main bearing and wore a few thousandths of an inch off of the #3 crankshaft main bearing journal as well as the main bearing saddle in the block. He wants to know what the options are for repairing those issues. He also said the cylinder bores are worn 0.015–0.016 inch oversize and would like to know how much larger you would have to bore it.

1. How can the crankshaft be saved, even though it is worn badly?
2. What process would you use to repair the worn main bearing saddle in the block?
3. How much would you most likely bore the cylinders out to? What also then needs to be replaced?

all of their machining work to a machine shop. The main task of machine shops is to restore engine parts to factory specifications. The amount of money it takes to purchase the equipment necessary to perform these machining functions makes it financially unwise for most automotive shop owners to purchase these tools and train their employees on them, when they will use them only once in a while. It is best to leave machining to the Automotive Service Excellence (ASE) Master Certified Machinist professionals.

▶ Engine Cylinder Block and Cylinder Head Mating Surface Composition

Surface roughness refers to the irregularities found in the surface texture. These irregularities are the result of the machining process employed to refinish the surface. **Surface roughness average (Ra)** is a measure of how rough a surface is at the microscopic level. It is rated as the arithmetic average of the surface valleys and peaks. For precise and consistent results, surface finish should be a specified range or maximum level of Ra. The Ra is the measurement used to classify how rough a certain mating surface is **FIGURE 14-1**. A 30-Ra finish is smoother than a 60-Ra finish. Today's cylinder heads are much lighter and less rigid and use a multilayered steel (MLS) gasket; as a result, the surface needs to be smoother than in the past. A cast iron head must be no rougher than 60 to 100 Ra, while an aluminum cylinder must be approximately 30 Ra. The surface must be smooth

enough for initial cold seal when starting the engine, and the gasket requires a certain amount of support so the gases from the combustion chamber cannot distort the head gasket. If the surface is too rough (too much bite) and the cylinder head is aluminum and the block cast iron, then sideways shearing from the aluminum cylinder head during expansion and contraction will occur, causing the gasket to fail.

The engine block can be resurfaced by a surface grinder using a stone wheel or a broach-style surfacer, applying a **cubic boron nitride (CBN) cutter** for cast iron and a **polycrystalline diamond (PCD) cutter** for aluminum. This procedure is performed because the cylinder head and the engine cylinder block need to be perfectly flat at the mating surface where they are bolted together. If they are not perfectly flat, leaks or ruptures will quickly occur. The desired surface finish for today's engines that use MLS gaskets can be lower than a 30-Ra finish. Always check the manufacturer's specifications.

The desired procedure in surfacing the **engine block's deck** (the portion of the engine cylinder block on which the head gasket lies and to which the cylinder head is bolted) is to surface the engine block parallel to the **mainline** where the crankshaft is installed. Surfacing the engine block this way makes the deck height on each cylinder the same. It is important that the deck height be the same at each cylinder to ensure that all pistons have the exact same amount of space between the cylinder head and the cylinder block to maintain equal compression values. There are several different types of

FIGURE 14-1 Surface roughness. **A.** 60 Ra. **B.** 30 Ra.

equipment available for resurfacing the engine block, differing mainly in the cutting bit type. For aluminum cylinder heads or blocks, a PCD cutting bit is needed. In refinishing cast iron cylinder heads or blocks, a CBN cutting surface is needed. Each metal has different characteristics, and thus requires different tooling and cutting speeds.

To check the engine block, measure the distance from where the bearing insert is installed on the mainline to the top of the engine block on each end of the deck surface. Some surface machines use a precision bar that runs through the mainline, and the measurements and settings are taken from the precision bar **FIGURE 14-2**. The computer numerical control (CNC) machine is a tool that uses computer programs to automatically execute a series of machining operations. These programs are usually completely computer automated, requiring little input from the operator. With some of the newer CNC-style machines, the measurements are taken from the top of the **engine block dowel pinhole**. The engine block dowel pinhole is where the engine block dowel pins are fixed. These pins are guides that allow exact alignment of the cylinder head and cylinder head gasket when reassembling the engine assembly. During the machining process, the engine block dowel pins are removed and the dowel pinholes (which are precision-drilled holes) are used as depth markers. There are usually two or more of these holes in an engine block deck surface. The machinist will measure the depth of each hole to determine exactly how much metal to take off to get the holes to the exact same depth. In this process, the engine block surface will be resurfaced to be completely flat and true.

FIGURE 14-2 Measuring the deck height from the setting fixture.

Applied Math

AM-38: Estimate/Exact Value: The technician can distinguish the need to use a specified value versus an estimated value, depending upon the system malfunction.

In the case of certain mechanical failures, it may be possible to determine whether or not a component requires replacement based on estimation, rather than measurement and comparison to specified values. One example is lobe wear on camshafts. Worn cam lobes can cause different symptoms depending on the extent of the wear.

Mildly worn lobes result in a loss of valve lift but still open and close the valve at the correct time with correct lash adjustment. Engine running at low speed is normal but higher RPM performance is lost due to insufficient valve opening restricting air flow. Excessive valve train noise may be evident, particularly at low speed. Mild lobe wear may not be visible and may require measurement to confirm.

More severe wear can result in the lobe wearing to nearly circular and results in late valve opening, early closure, and dramatically reduced lift. The engine may exhibit only a slight loss of idle quality but will misfire on the affected cylinder at speeds much above idle. Severe wear is generally noticeable to the eye when comparing against other lobes. Cams are generally case hardened, resulting in only a thin hard layer on their surface. Once the hardened surface is worn through, the tappet will run on the softer base metal, causing rapidly accelerated wear.

Boring the Cylinder Block

If the cylinders are damaged, have too much **taper** (meaning they are smaller in diameter at one end), or are out of round, then they should be rebored and honed to fit oversized pistons. Oversized pistons need to be used following boring because the boring process enlarges the cylinder walls, leaving the regular piston too small to be effectively reused. In some cases, the cylinder **bore** might be damaged beyond boring, worn beyond the limits for an oversized piston, or cracked. To repair the cylinder, it must be **bored out** (machined) and a cylinder sleeve installed to fill the extra space created in the boring process. Dry cylinder sleeves require the cylinder to be bored out and the sleeve to have an **interference fit** of approximately 0.002" to 0.0025" (0.05 to 0.06 mm). Dry cylinder sleeves are pressed into the existing bore and *do not* come into contact with an engine coolant passage **FIGURE 14-3**. Wet cylinder sleeves are installed and *do* come into contact with engine coolant. Using sleeves allows the original size of pistons to be used, restoring the factory bore dimensions.

Dry sleeve not touching water jackets — Water jacket

A

Wet sleeve touching water jackets — Water jacket

B

FIGURE 14-3 Cylinder sleeves. **A.** Dry sleeve. **B.** Wet sleeve.

AM-11: Decimals: The technician can multiply decimal numbers to determine conformance with the manufacturer's specifications.

During the overhaul of a V-6 engine, it is discovered that the cylinders are worn beyond manufacturer's specifications. The technician determines that the cylinders must be bored 0.060 inch (1.52 mm) oversize. The current displacement of the engine is 231 cubic inches (3.79 liters). Our task is to use a formula to determine the new cubic inch displacement of the engine.

The bore of the engine is 3.860 inches (98.04 mm) after it was enlarged and the stroke is 3.4 inches (86.36 mm). For the first step, we will calculate the cubic inch displacement of one cylinder, and then multiply times 6 cylinders. The volume of a cylinder is determined by multiplication of p (3.14) x radius squared x length of stroke. In our scenario, this is 3.14 x 3.725 inches (2403 mm) = 11.69 square inches (7542 square mm) x 3.4 inches (86.36 mm) = 39.768 cubic inches (0.651 liters)

This is the volume or cubic inch displacement of one cylinder. When multiplied by 6 cylinders, we have a "new" displacement of 239 cubic inches (3.9 liters). This new displacement is the result of boring the cylinders and installing new pistons which are 0.060 inch (1.52 mm) oversize. Now each cylinder will meet manufacturer's specifications because excessive cylinder taper and out of round conditions have been resolved. This engine should give many miles of satisfactory service regarding the pistons and block assembly.

TECHNICIAN TIP

Boring an engine increases its displacement slightly. To calculate an engine's displacement, you must find the swept volume of the cylinder, based on the bore and **stroke** dimensions. The formula is bore squared, times stroke, times 0.785, times number of cylinders.

Boring of the engine cylinders to a larger size requires the use of a boring machine. The boring machine typically used by engine machine shops is semiautomated. The semiautomatic machine cuts the engine block cylinders to their new oversized dimensions. To start, the engine block must be correctly mounted underneath the cutting bit. The machinist tells the boring machine what engine is being bored and performs preliminary adjustments to the machine, such as inserting the correct cutting bit for the application to be serviced. After all preliminary setup

steps are completed, the machine centers itself in the first bore and begins the cutting process. After the first bore is finished, the machine automatically moves to the next cylinder bore, centers itself, and begins the boring process all over again.

When boring the cylinder for a dry sleeve with no top lip, the cylinder wall must be bored to have a lip on the bottom of the cylinder wall. This is done by not running the boring bar all the way through the cylinder, so the cylinder sleeve cannot slip in the cylinder bore.

If the cylinder can be bored oversize, usually the cylinder is bored for the first oversized piston available that will fit in the now slightly enlarged cylinder space. For example, if the cylinder is supposed to be 4.000" and the cylinder measures 4.016" at the top and 4.009" at the bottom, the machinist will bore out the cylinder to 4.030" because oversized pistons only come in a few assorted sizes. The most common sizes of oversized pistons available are 0.02" (0.51 mm), 0.03" (0.76 mm), 0.04" (1.0 mm), and 0.06" (1.5 mm). Before boring begins, the exact diameter of the new pistons must be determined to know how much material to leave in the cylinders to hone out for final clearance. Be sure to refer to the manufacturer's specifications to see how large a particular engine can be bored oversize.

A **boring bar** is a long bar used to position and align a single-point tool, such as an engine block boring machine, for boring operations. There are three styles of boring bars: the portable boring bar, which can be mounted to the top of the engine cylinder block or to a boring machine stand, the semiautomated boring bar machine, and the CNC-style boring machine **FIGURE 14-4**.

All boring bars fracture the surface as they cut the material away from the cylinder walls, so there must be enough material left to hone and get past these fractures in the metal. The boring machine simply cuts away metal with a sharp bit, leaving microscopic hills and valleys that must be ground down to prevent premature cylinder wear. This grinding is done with a cylinder hone. Typically, the portable boring bar needs to leave more material to hone out, approximately 0.005" (0.13 mm), while the more rigid machines with the optional cutters and spindle speeds need only 0.0015" to 0.002" (0.04 to 0.05 mm) to hone out to get past the fractured metal. The portable boring bar should not be used on modern thinner-walled engine blocks, since cylinder distortion can take place from the weight of the boring bar bolted to the engine block. The weight of the boring bar is enough to flex the cylinders and change the cylinder dimensions, resulting in incorrect dimensions when the boring job is finished.

The boring process leaves a corkscrew pattern on the walls of the cylinder. If left like this, the cylinder rings would catch and tear on the lands of the corkscrew. Hone stones are used to sand down and file away the cylinder walls, leaving a unidirectional finish also known as a **crosshatch** pattern. This pattern appears as a series of

FIGURE 14-4 Semiautomated boring bar.

big Xs etched into the walls and is much smoother than the corkscrew left by the boring process. Most hones are self-tensioning, which alleviates the need for the technician to determine the amount of tension needed. The crosshatch pattern is made at either a standard 45- or 60-degree angle. Refer to the manufacturer's specifications for the engine you are working on.

A good crosshatch helps to trap the oil and retain it in the cylinder bores where it is needed. Achieving the desired crosshatch is a matter of adjusting the speed for stroking the cylinder hone. As the cylinder hone is moved up and down inside the cylinder, it is also moving in a circle. This up-and-down circular motion allows the hone stones to make slanted streaks on the cylinder walls. These slanted streaks make the crosshatched pattern after a number of up-and-down cycles. For a 45-degree pattern, move the stones at a normal pace, which is (depending on cylinder size and depth) about half of a second in the down direction and half of a second in the up direction. If a more aggressive or steeper-angled X pattern is needed, the process must be sped up. It is not an exact science except when an actual cylinder hone machine is doing the work.

The faster or more rapid the hone is stroked in the cylinder, the higher the angle of the crosshatch becomes. If the angle gets too high, then the cylinder wall will allow oil to run down the wall and not provide enough lubricant to the rings and pistons, causing scoring and leading to low compression. If the angle gets too steep, then too much oil will be held on the cylinder walls and the oil will be burned.

Torque Plate

A **torque plate** is approximately 2" (51 mm) thick and bolted in place where the cylinder head is fastened on the engine block. When the cylinder head is torqued, it exerts force around the cylinder wall and can change the machined dimensions, especially on lighter-weight engine blocks. To eliminate this problem, a torque plate is installed that simulates the cylinder head torqued in place. Now, when the cylinder is honed, it stays true to the dimensions. The torque plate is used in performance machine shops and is also being used more often on the new style of engines that have lightweight cores made of thinner aluminum, which are more prone to cylinder shifting. Some cylinders can distort as much as 0.0015" (0.04 mm) when the cylinder head is bolted down. One high-performance industry, NASCAR, has even gone to the trouble of not only using a torque plate but also using hot water through the block to ensure that the cylinder bores are the size they will be at full temperature. This process is known as hot honing. The use of hot honing is not cost effective for the typical engine, as the machine is very expensive to purchase and operate.

Honing Cylinders

There are several options to consider before **honing**. If there are no imperfections or grooves, and the cylinder walls need only to be deglazed, a **ball hone** will be used. If the cylinder was bored oversize, then the cylinders will need to be honed to final size with a rigid hone. A ball hone consists of a metal center rod with various other metal rods branching out from it, similar to branches on a tree. Stone balls are attached to the ends of these metal rods. When this assembly is inserted into the cylinder and spun with a hand drill and moved back and forth, the abrasive stones wear the "glazing" off the cylinder walls and give the cylinder walls a neat new crosshatched pattern **FIGURE 14-5**. Glazing refers to the finish produced when the crosshatch scratches have been worn away, leaving the cylinder smooth and shiny and unable to retain oil. This condition reduces compression, since oil helps the rings to seal, and can also result in oil moving past the rings and burning in the combustion chamber. The honing process with a ball hone is done only if the cylinder does not need to be bored and is in good shape in regard to taper and wear. The ball hone does not restore cylinder size; it simply reapplies the crosshatching. Producing the

correct pattern takes practice to get just the right speed of the stone moving up and down in the cylinder in relation to the spinning speed.

After the boring process, a rigid hone is used for the smoothing-out process of the cylinder walls and is performed as the final step in refinishing the cylinder. A crosshatched pattern allows the proper amount of oil to stay on the cylinder walls, which allows the piston rings to seat into the cylinder walls and ensures a proper seal so as to not lose compression or burn oil **FIGURE 14-6**.

Honing is typically performed by a honing machine. This machine consists of three or more elongated smooth stones attached to an arbor. This assembly is inserted inside a finished/bored cylinder and is spun (either by

FIGURE 14-5 The ball hone is used by hand with a drill motor to restore the crosshatch pattern in the engine cylinder.

Typical crosshatch pattern

FIGURE 14-6 The proper crosshatching pattern ensures that the piston rings will seat properly and not result in oil burning.

a computer-controlled honing machine or by a machine operated by a machinist) until the proper surface texture and final bore size of the cylinder are reached. Honing is always performed by the engine rebuilder or machinist.

Once the cylinders are at the proper dimension and have the correct crosshatch pattern, it is time to clean and lubricate them. First, clean the cylinder walls with solvent; then scrub them with warm, soapy water and a stiff brush to remove any metal and stone particles. Next, take a clean lint-free rag and pour some clean oil on it. Rub the oil into the cylinder walls. If any discoloration appears, rewash the cylinders and recheck them with a clean, oiled rag. When no dirt or discoloration occurs, the cylinders are ready for the next step in the rebuilding process.

Main Bearing Bores

Premature bearing failure and crankshaft failure can occur with an out-of-line main bearing bore. Proper bore alignment must be ensured between all the main bearing bores. The bore alignment can be checked for straightness by using a straightedge with a feeler gauge. The engine main bearing bores can become misaligned due to the stresses released over time from the initial casting process. Over time, engine blocks can distort with temperature changes, and the bearing bores can become misaligned. Engine bearings will be excessively worn, particularly the center bearing because of the bore shift. Checking that the main crankshaft bores are concentric and perfectly circular ensures that they are not out of round or egg shaped. Just like engine block cylinders, these bores can wear into an oblong or egg-shaped hole, which can damage the crankshaft. Out of round is checked with a bore gauge tool.

To correct a bore alignment issue, the engine block has to be **line bored** or **line honed**. In this process, the main journals must be made smaller. This is done by removing the main caps and cutting the mating surface down **FIGURE 14-7**. The amount of metal to be removed from the main cap is usually 0.003" to 0.005" (0.076 to 0.13 mm). After all of the main caps are cut, the engine block mating surface is cleaned to remove dust or debris. The main caps are torqued back into place, the line hone or line bore machine is set up, and the original main bearing bore size is cut. Cutting the main bearing bores ensures that the bores line up properly and stop the bearing wear problem **FIGURE 14-8**.

The manufacturer's specifications for the main bearing bore must be followed when line honing to ensure that the proper oil clearance is established between the bearing and the crankshaft main journal when main bearings are

> **TECHNICIAN TIP**
>
> Whenever the crankshaft centerline is refinished, the centerline of the crankshaft moves slightly upward. If the centerline moves too far, then cam timing issues can occur. It can also cause the compression ratio to be increased slightly. So always make sure that only a minimal amount of material is removed during line boring.

installed. Main bearing oil clearance can be found by measuring the crankshaft main journal size and subtracting this measurement from the inside diameter of the main bearing inserts with the bearings installed and the main bearing caps torqued. If the crankshaft measurements are near the large size of the specifications, then the main bearing bores should be resized to the large size of the

FIGURE 14-7 Cutting main caps.

FIGURE 14-8 Line honing a mainline.

FIGURE 14-9 Using Plastigauge to check oil clearance. If the width of the Plastigauge doesn't match the band on the chart, move to the next band.

factory specifications. If the crankshaft measurements are closer to the small size of the factory specifications, then the main bearing bores should be resized to the small size of the factory specifications.

The proper oil clearance must be maintained to ensure proper oil pressure of the engine and to ensure that the proper amount of lubricant can reach all the engine bearings. Oil clearance can also be quickly checked before engine assembly through the use of Plastigauge. Plastigauge is a thin calibrated piece of soft plastic string that is laid on the main bearing journal of the crankshaft and squished between the journal and the bearing. The main bearing cap is torqued down so that the Plastigauge is squished, and the Plastigauge is then removed. The width of the squeezed Plastigauge is compared to a chart to determine the amount of bearing clearance **FIGURE 14-9**. The wider the Plastigauge, the smaller the bearing clearance.

▶ Crankshaft Grinding and Polishing

The **crankshaft journals** need to be inspected for scratches, pits, cracks, and grooves when rebuilding the engine. The bearings need a true, clean surface to run on or they will be torn up on the very first running of the engine. When imperfections cannot be polished out to 0.0005" (0.013 mm) or less, the crankshaft needs to be reground. Regrinding involves placing the crankshaft in a lathe set for metal cutting. The lathe spins the crankshaft while a special bit shaves or grinds the metal away.

Most crankshafts are **induction hardened**. This process hardens the metal by raising the temperature of the part with heat or magnetic fields and then suddenly cooling it in water, oil, or another chemical. Using the induction hardening method allows the crankshaft to be reground on the mains and rod bearing journals without having to redo the hardening process, which is important since the hardening will be as deep as 0.08" (2.03 mm). Some heavy-duty and performance cranks use **nitriding**. Nitriding is the process of slowly heating the crankshaft in a sealed container with the oxygen removed. Nitrogen is introduced and penetrates the surface. Nitriding produces a harder, more durable surface than induction hardening but only penetrates approximately 0.02" (0.51 mm). The crankshaft will have to be rehardened if the mains or rod journals need to be reground. Heating and hardening cause the crankshaft to grow, which the machinist must take into account when performing the initial metal removal before hardening.

Crankshafts are usually ground to 0.01" (0.25 mm), 0.02" (0.51 mm), or 0.03" (0.76 mm) undersize, meaning they are ground slightly smaller than their original size. When choosing a crankshaft main or rod journal bearing, it must match the amount of material that was removed during grinding. For example, a crankshaft ground to 0.01" undersize must match up to a 0.010" undersize bearing, usually marked ".010 US" on the back of the bearing shell. The undersize bearing is actually thicker to make up for the smaller crankshaft bearing. The crankshaft main and rod journals can be ground to different sizes, but all rod journals must be cut to the same size. Likewise, all the main journals must be the same size as each other. For example, the crankshaft could be a 0.010/0.020, which equals 0.01" rods and 0.02" mains. During the grinding process of the crankshaft, the **fillet area** of the crankshaft (the area where the rod bearing journal or main bearing journal meets the crankshaft) should be radial or tapered, radiating from the crankshaft and fanning outward, up along the crankshaft counterweight. The **radius** is important because it helps strengthen the crankshaft. The whole "fillet" process gets rid of sharp edges, which are stress points inside the engine. If a crankshaft is going to break, it will usually break on a sharp edge or corner. These fillet areas help to alleviate those stressed areas.

When a crankshaft cannot be restored because the grooves are too deep, or a bearing has spun on the journal, then it is a common practice to use spray welding or submerged arc welding. Spray welding adds materials to the journal by melting and spraying molten metal onto the crankshaft journal surface so that there is material that can be ground. Submerged arc welding uses a steady stream of flux to protect the molten metal from oxygen as the filler material melts and binds to the crank surface. Crankshafts are usually ground the opposite direction of the crank's rotation and then polished the same direction of the crank's rotation to counteract the corkscrew effect of grinding.

The oil passage holes in the crankshaft need to be chamfered before polishing the journals. **Chamfering** is cutting into the top of the oil passage hole (which is usually right in the center of the bearing's operating surface on the crankshaft journals) with a chamfering tool or drill bit. This process takes that sharp edge at the top of the oil hole and makes it more like a 45-degree angle, which will allow the edge to not dig into the bearing the way a 90-degree edge would. It also alleviates the 90-degree edge stress point on the crankshaft. Crankshaft polishing must be performed by a specialist called a crankshaft polisher. The crankshaft polishing machine rotates the crankshaft slowly, and a polishing belt slides over the journals to clean up the surface. The polishing belt is usually 320 grit or finer.

Connecting Rods

Before any machining of connecting rods can be performed, the pistons must be removed. If the rods are of the full-floating style, then the snap rings can be removed from the piston and the pins can be worked out of the piston and rod. If the rods are of the semi-floating style, then the piston pins will have to be pressed out of the piston and rod with a small hydraulic press. When pressing piston pins, be sure to use the proper piston support tool to cradle the piston to avoid damaging it during removal and installation **FIGURE 14-10**.

Rod—Big End

The big end of the connecting rod is made up of two halves. Each mating half can have either machined surfaces or, in the case of powdered metal connecting rods, **fracture split**

surfaces, which are identified by the ragged finish of the parting surfaces on the big end **FIGURE 14-11**. The ragged fracture line ensures better rod cap alignment on assembly because the fractured surfaces fit together in perfect alignment. The connecting rod's big end needs to be checked for roundness. This measurement is just as important as measuring the roundness of the crankshaft main bearing journals and main bearing bores. Any time the old rod bolts are removed and new bolts are installed, the size of the "big end bore" may become distorted due to the press-fit of the bolts. Accordingly, the size of the big end of the connecting rod should be rechecked and adjusted if necessary.

To resize the connecting rod's big end, the bolts are removed **FIGURE 14-12** and the cap and rod mating surfaces are ground approximately 0.0015" to 0.0025" (0.038 to 0.14 mm). Then the rod cap is bolted back onto the rod and the bore machined back to the proper size. The challenge with powdered metal rods is that since the fractured surface is critical to their alignment, they cannot tolerate having those surfaces ground smooth. Thus, they cannot be resized, unless bearing

FIGURE 14-11 Big end connecting rods. **A.** Standard connecting rod with machined faces. **B.** Powdered metal with fracture split faces.

FIGURE 14-10 Installing a piston pin in a rod that has been heated in a rod heater.

FIGURE 14-12 Removing the connecting rod bolts.

inserts of a larger diameter are available for that particular engine.

Once the rod mating surfaces have been machined lightly and bolted back together, either a rod honing machine or a rod boring machine can be used for resizing. A rod honing machine removes metal by honing the big end of a connecting rod. This is accomplished by attaching various hone stones to an arbor and spinning inside the big end of the connecting rod bore. A machinist will frequently measure the size of the connecting rod to ensure that it is not oversized during this process. A rod boring machine cuts material away with a cutting bit and resizes the big end portion of the connecting rod assembly. The big end of the connecting rod must be resized to factory specifications to achieve the proper amount of bearing crush. Bearing crush is the additional height that is purposely manufactured into each bearing half to ensure complete contact of the bearing back with the housing bore when the engine is assembled and the main and rod bearing caps are torqued. This torque process actually "squeezes" the bearings, causing them to maintain just the right amount of oil clearance for the engine crankshaft to spin smoothly within them.

Rod—Small End

Connecting rods may have pressed-in wrist pins or, in some engines, a floating wrist pin. The pressed-in wrist pin can be either press-fit into the piston pin boss or press-fit into the small end of the connecting rod. With the floating type of wrist pin, the pin can turn in both the piston pin bosses and the small end of the connecting rod. The wrist pin is typically held in place with a snap ring on each side of the piston pin boss. Some floating wrist pin designs use a bushing or bearing on the small end of the connecting rod. A small hydraulic press is used to press the bushing out of the rod and install a new one.

When removing and installing pressed-in pins, be sure to use the proper piston support tool or piston damage will result. Some manufacturers require the bushing to be burnished (rubbed until smooth or glossy) when installed. A rod honing machine or rod boring machine can be used for this procedure.

▶ Cylinder Head Machining

Cylinder head machining is fairly time intensive, so make sure you are fully prepared before beginning. When disassembling a nonadjustable valve-type cylinder head, it is recommended that before removing the valves from the cylinder head, the valve installation height be measured and recorded for future reference. This information is needed during the machining and assembly process. Also, before any machining can begin after the disassembly and cleaning of the cylinder head, the cylinder head should be **magnafluxed** or dye checked to locate any external cracks. To check for internal cracks, pressure testing is performed.

Crack Detection

If a cylinder head is made of cast iron, then the **ferrous metal**—which includes any metal that has an iron compound in its makeup or that is magnetic—in the cylinder head can be tested using a dry or wet method. The dry method consists of using an iron dusting powder that is available in different colors. After applying the powder, a permanent magnet or electromagnet creates a magnetic field that causes a high concentration of magnetic flux at the surface cracks, which attract the iron powder when applied **FIGURE 14-13**. The machinist will notice a nice solid line of powder sticking to the cracked area since a north and south magnetic pole will be created along the crack. The wet method uses a liquid iron and fluorescent dye mixture. It is used along with an electromagnet to

FIGURE 14-13 Magnafluxing a cast iron cylinder head with cracks.

pull the dye into any cracks and then a black light to illuminate it.

A dye check works by soaking the metal surfaces with a special dye that wicks down into any surface cracks. The surface is then wiped dry and either a black light is used to illuminate any cracks or a white chemical developer is sprayed onto the surface and the dye bleeds into the developer, making the crack visible. Dye checking works on both ferrous and nonferrous metals, including aluminum.

Pressure Testing

Pressure testing is normally used on aluminum cylinder heads since the magnaflux process cannot be used. There are two different styles of pressure testers. In the first, a plate is cut out for the combustion chamber areas and used to seal off the water jackets, except for one where air pressure is injected. The cylinder head is checked for leaks by submerging the cylinder head in water or by using a soapy water formula that is sprayed all over the cylinder head with a squirt bottle. The technician looks for bubbles, which result from an air leak. In the other type of pressure tester, the cylinder head is placed on a pressure-testing bench. The bench is usually made of softer rubber, which acts as the seal around the bottom of the cylinder head. Pressure is then introduced into the combustion chamber via the spark plug hole, and the machinist notes if any pressure is lost or if a "hissing" or leaking noise is heard coming from around the valves or any part of the casting.

Overhead Cam Bearings

Overhead cam engines have camshafts that typically ride directly in bores in the cylinder head. There are no removable bearings. The cam rides right on the machined aluminum and is lubricated by a thin coating of oil that is fed to the surface through an oil galley or hole. Oil pressure must make its way up from the bottom of the engine to the top of the cylinder head to lubricate the camshaft. If oil pressure falls, then the camshaft lacks lubrication and can score the camshaft bores in the cylinder head. This is a problem because if the surface is damaged, there are no bearings to replace.

Another potential problem occurs if the engine has overheated and the cylinder head is warped; in this case, the cam bores can become misaligned, just as the main bearing bores for the crankshaft can become misaligned. If the cam bores are misaligned enough, it can cause the camshaft to bind up and possibly break.

When machining a head surface for a warpage concern, do not forget to check the cam bore alignment. To do so, use a straightedge designed for this purpose, or use a straight camshaft and make sure it turns freely in the bores. If the cam bores are misaligned, then the head most likely will need to be straightened. A machine shop can do this using heat and pressure to pull the head back into line. Once the head is straight, the cam bores can be rechecked. If the head has removable cam bearing caps **FIGURE 14-14**, then the bore can be machined in a process similar to line boring of the main bearing journals. Simply cut a small amount of metal off of the bottoms of the cam bore caps and remachine the bore back to its original specification. If the bore has one-piece cam towers, then the machinist may have to see if a camshaft with oversized cam journals can be purchased for the engine. Oversized cam journals can sometimes be found for an engine in 0.015" or 0.03" (0.38- or 0.76-mm) sizes. This means that the original bore size will have to be machined 0.015" to 0.03" larger. Another possible option is to find replacement bearing shells or inserts

FIGURE 14-14 **A.** Cam bores using removable bearing caps. **B.** Cam bearing with one-piece cam towers.

made by some aftermarket companies to repair the cam bore. These bearing inserts work similar to a standard camshaft bearing. The last repair option would be to either spray weld the cam journals to a larger size, or weld the cam bores and remachine to the proper size. This process is very costly and would be done only when a replacement head is not easily found.

Valve Grinding

If the valves are in reusable condition, both the valve face and the valve tip will need to be ground. If the engine uses adjustable valves, then both surfaces can be ground at this time. If the engine uses non-adjustable valves, then the tips will need to be ground after the valve face and valve seat have been ground so that the installed valve height can be adjusted by grinding the valve tip to the proper length.

The valve stem must be within factory specifications, which is why the valve stems and margins should have been checked previously. There are multiple styles of valve grinding benches or valve refacing benches; follow the manufacturer's specific procedures. The valve stem end is first chamfered so that when inserted in the **collet** that holds the valve **FIGURE 14-15** it is held centered. The valve grinding machine can be set up to grind the valves at any angle, typically specified by the manufacturer. Always check the specifications and set the machine to the proper valve face angle. When the machine is turned on, the valve rotates in one direction and the grinding stone rotates in the other. The valve is slowly fed into the grinding stone, not taking too much off at a time, while making sure the face of the valve moves across the face of the grinding stone from side to side until the valve face is refinished and true **FIGURE 14-16**. When grinding the valves, make sure not to remove any more metal

FIGURE 14-15 Installing the valve in a collet.

FIGURE 14-16 Grinding the valve.

than necessary to avoid making the margin thinner. This margin, if allowed to become too thin, can cause the edge of the valve to burn or melt because the thinner metal cannot dissipate the heat as well. The smaller the valve margin, the hotter the edge of the valve becomes and the harder it is to dissipate the heat to other parts of the cylinder head. That is why the thickness of the valve margin is important.

Valve Guides

Before grinding the valve seats, the valve guides must be checked and repaired to ensure they are within factory specifications. The valves and valve stems must also be checked to verify that they are reusable. If the valves are worn beyond specifications, they need to be replaced. If the valve guides are worn, they need to be repaired. There are different procedures to repair valve guides in an integral cylinder head (non-replaceable guide) or a non-integral cylinder head (replaceable guides). Each procedure will be described next.

For the integral cylinder head (non-replaceable guide), there are four methods of repairing the valve guides:

1. **Knurling** the cylinder head using a diamond knurl, a tool offered by Sunnen Products. Knurling is when a bit with a spiral groove (unique to the cylinder head that is being worked on due to its specific diameter) is threaded through or run through the valve guide. This tool leaves behind raised ridges on either side of the groove and effectively shrinks the size of the valve guide due to these raised ridges. This process takes the current material and squeezes it out, closer to the area where the valve stem rides. The knurled

guide is then reamed so that it is back within specifications. Reaming removes a small amount of the material displaced by the knurling tool. The knurling process is not used by most reputable machine shops anymore because it is typically considered a "quick fix" and would typically only last for 20,000 to 40,000 miles. Knurled guides do not stand up to the same abuse and wear and tear that an insert or liner would typically stand up to.

2. Reaming the guide oversize and using a valve with an oversized valve stem. Valves with oversized stems are usually very expensive and may not be available for all engines.

3. Installing a thin-walled bronze liner. The valve guide is reamed out on a piece of equipment called a head shop, and an oversized thin-walled bronze liner is installed and is burnished to size.

4. Installing a thick-walled guide that is made of bronze or heat-treated cast iron. Thick-walled guides can usually be driven out with an air hammer, but in some cases, they may need to be machined out by a head shop. Thick-walled valve guides are generally installed with an air hammer.

Hardened Seat Inserts

Hardened seats are valve seats that have been heat treated to make them more robust and capable of withstanding the severe demands of today's engines and fuels. Hardened valve seats are used to prevent valve seat regression. Regression refers to the valve actually sitting farther up inside the cylinder head due to the missing material that has been worn away from the valve seat over the life of the vehicle. Hardened seats are also necessary in aluminum heads, since the aluminum is relatively soft.

Installing hardened seats is also a common practice on early cast iron heads that have seats that were not induction hardened from the factory. Lead was added to gasoline starting in the 1920s as an anti-knock additive. It also proved to be an anti-wear additive for valve seats. The lead acts as a chemical buffer keeping the hot valves from "microwelding" themselves to the seat. After lead was taken out of gas, if the exhaust valve seat was not induction hardened or a hardened seat insert was not installed, the valve seat would deteriorate and fail. This would result in the valve being sunk into the head, quickly causing valve seat failure.

Valve seats can be of the integral type or the replaceable type. Integral valve seats are used in some cast iron heads by induction hardening the valve seat area. Replaceable valve seats can come in many different materials—nickel alloy, chrome alloy, cobalt alloy, stainless steel, or even cast iron. Valve seats intended for compressed natural gas

(CNG) or propane engines may be made of tungsten steel with additives blended for lubricating qualities. Check with the manufacturer to determine which hardened seat they recommend. Depending on which fuels are being used, different seats will be recommended.

To install a hardened seat, a head shop is needed and the proper cutter must be used. If the head uses replaceable valve seats, the seats will have to be removed by either prying, heating the head in a cylinder head oven, or even welding the seat, which will cause the seat to contract when the weld cools. Integral valve seats must be machined out of the head with the head shop so that new seats with an interference fit can be pressed into their place.

Grinding/Cutting Valve Seats

Valve seats must be newly refinished to create a near-perfect sealing area for the valves when they are installed into the cylinder head. Refacing removes minor pits and wear that appear over time. There are two basic ways to refurbish the **valve seats**. The first way is to grind the valve seat with stones **FIGURE 14-17**. When using grinding stones, a **three-angle grind** is typically used to properly form the valve seat. The three-angle grind provides three different angles—one to create the surface of the valve seat, one to narrow the valve seat from the top, and one to narrow the valve seat from the bottom. Using the top- and bottom-narrowing stones allows the width and height of the valve seat to be properly created and positioned **FIGURE 14-18**. The second way to refurbish valve seats is with a cutter. Valve seat cutters are available in different forms. One style uses individual cutters with a particular size and angle, similar to how the grinding stones work. The other type of cutter is a single cutter made to cut all three angles at once.

Valve seat contact is critical to the operation of the valve since much of the valve's cooling occurs where the

FIGURE 14-17 Grinding a valve seat.

valve face contacts the valve seat. Usually, this is near the center of the valve face. This contact area is what seals the valve to the cylinder head and makes a completely sealed combustion chamber. Valve seat contact needs to be checked to ensure that the valves are sealing at the proper location on the valve and also to ensure that the valves are actually sealing. A good way to check the valve seat contact on the valve is to use Prussian blue or a dry-erase marker. Put Prussion blue or a dry-erase marking on the face of the valve. Install the valve in the cylinder head and open and close the valve rapidly against the valve seat. Remove the valve and inspect the valve face. There should be a small area of no contact on the top of the face and a small area of no contact on the bottom of the face.

Valve seat runout is how much the valve seat is out of round, called valve seat concentricity. Valve seat runout should be checked with a special runout gauge. The seat runout gauge uses a pilot shaft to slide tightly into the valve guide. The tool is able to spin on the pilot shaft, and the top has a dial indicator. As you spin the dial indicator against the seat contact surface, runout can be determined. The ideal runout is zero; however, most engines will function well with less than 0.002" (0.05 mm). For an idea of how much that is, the thickness of a sheet of notebook paper is typically about 0.004" (0.1 mm). Runout shows how round the valve seat is and is very important to ensure proper sealing of the valve as well as proper seating so it can adequately cool.

Valve guide-to-valve stem clearance should typically be less than 0.0025" (0.064 mm), depending on the engine specifications. Any more than this will affect valve sealing. Excessive valve guide clearance will also cause valve stem seals to leak, since the valve stem will move and wear the seal quickly. If the clearance is too small, the valve could seize or be hung up in the cylinder head assembly causing a cylinder misfire and possibly

catastrophic damage if the piston hits the open valve at top dead center. The valve stem can be sitting cocked in the guide, causing a reduction in clearance at the top of the guide on one side and the bottom of the guide at the opposite side. This will cause valve stem galling, wherein the two metals rub together in such a manner that localized welding of the two metals occurs, which may not hold the valve open but will cause guide failure in a very short time. Also, if the valve hangs open on pushrod engines, the pushrod can be dislodged from the rocker and lifter, and on some applications, the lifter may come out of its bore, resulting in a loss of oil pressure.

When the valve and seat are first machined, their surfaces need to wear together to create an effective seal. To help the valves and seats initially wear together, the valves are ground or cut at a half or one degree less than the valve face angle. This allows the valve face and seat to meet at a very narrow ring near the top of the valve face and creates what is called an **interference angle**. An interference angle is the angle that is formed between the valve face and the valve seat. For instance, if the valve face is cut to a 44-degree slope, then the seat will be cut to a 45-degree slope, thus allowing the two metal pieces to meet at a point. The valve face and seat would then wear in to create a tight seal across the complete seat width.

Another consideration for the engine machinist to remember is that as material is cut from the valve seat and the valve face, the valve will move higher up in the head. This change in position can result in a valve that is held open when the valve train is installed. A critical measurement is valve stem height after the machining of the valve and valve seat **FIGURE 14-19**. Refer to the manufacturer's specifications or ensure an initial reading was taken before valve work was done if no specifications are published. Valve stem height is measured with the valve in the head and seated fully. The machinist then measures

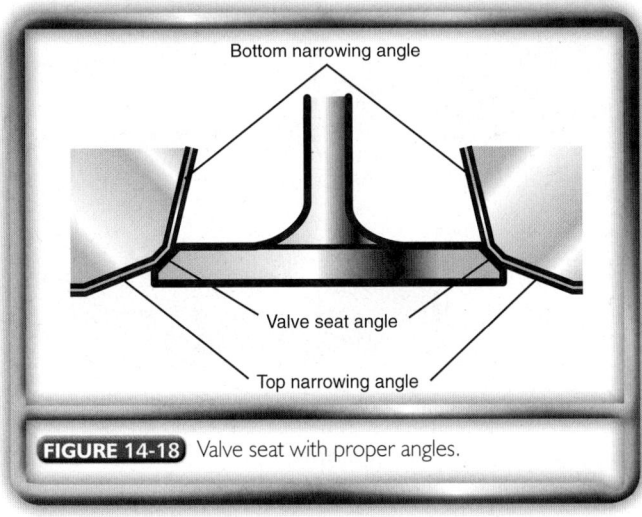

FIGURE 14-18 Valve seat with proper angles.

FIGURE 14-19 Valve stem height. The machinist in these photos is measuring valve stem.

from the tip of the valve stem to the bottom of the valve spring pocket. If the valve stem height is not correct, then the machinist will use the valve grinding machine to remove the required amount of material from the tip of the valve stem. Care must be taken to not remove too much material, as doing so could cause excessive valve clearance leading to valve train noise. The machinist also must be sure not to machine the valve stem of sodium-filled exhaust valves; if these types of valves are used, then replacement of the seat and valve may be required to restore original engine specifications. Sodium reacts violently with water, so be aware of what you are working with.

Also remember that when the valve stem moves up in the head, so does the retainer groove on the valve stem. This movement affects valve spring installed height, which affects spring pressure. If the spring installed height is too high, then pressure will not be as high and the valve could hang open at high rpm and create lots of problems, such as being contacted by a piston. Valve spring installed height is restored by using shims under the valve spring to bring the bottom of the spring up. Measurement of the valve spring height is from the bottom coil of the spring to the top coil of the spring. Be sure to shim correctly because if the spring installed height is too small, coil spring binding could occur when the valve reaches full lift, and this will result in valve spring breakage or valve train damage. There should be about 0.06" (1.52 mm) of clearance between coils of a valve spring when fully compressed, but like all rule-of-thumb specifications, be sure to follow the manufacturer's specifications if available.

▶ Cylinder Head Surface

It is necessary to resurface the cylinder head when the cylinder head surface either is warped (not perfectly flat) or has pitting or some type of corrosive metal displacement that would compromise the sealing capability of the cylinder head to cylinder head gasket and engine block. Cylinder head resurfacing is typically performed when the cylinder head has been removed for some type of service. The repair technician measures the straightness of the cylinder head deck surface with a calibrated straightedge and finds it to be warped beyond the manufacturer's allowable specifications or the technician notices that there is excessive pitting (typically found around coolant passages).

The cylinder head surface is critical because of the combustion pressures, water passages, and, sometimes, oil passages. The cylinder head must be flat and surfaced to the proper Ra. A surface roughness Ra is rated as the arithmetic average of the surface valleys and peaks. The cylinder head will warp much more easily than the engine block because of its design; it does not have the same supporting structure. A precision ground straightedge and feeler gauge are used to determine flatness.

When checking the cylinder head for flatness, lay the calibrated straightedge parallel with the combustion chambers across the already-cleaned cylinder head deck surface. Starting at the top of the cylinder head, try to fit a 0.001" (0.025-mm) feeler gauge under any part of the mating surface between the calibrated straightedge and the cylinder head. This process is repeated 5 to 10 times at various places—5 or so times with the straightedge parallel to the combustion chambers and another 5 or so times with the straightedge running at a 90-degree angle to the combustion chambers. Also be sure to cross the straightedge from one side to the other, making an X across the head with the two measurements. This approach will show any twisting of the head from end to end. Before surfacing the cylinder head, check the manufacturer's cylinder head thickness specifications to make sure the cylinder head has enough material to be surfaced. If the cylinder head is warped more than 0.003" (0.076 mm), it is recommended the cylinder head be surfaced; always check the manufacturer's specifications. The cylinder head can be surfaced by a surface grinder using a stone wheel or a **broach-style surfacer** using a CBN cutter for cast iron or a PCD for aluminum **FIGURE 14-20**. A cylinder head with overhead cams usually cannot be machined as much as an adjustable pushrod engine, since the timing chain or timing belt tension will be affected. Again, refer to specifications before machining.

FIGURE 14-20 Surfacing a cylinder head.

If an overhead cam head is warped, the cam bearing bores should be checked for straightness before surfacing the head. If the cam bores are not straight, then surfacing the head will leave the cam journals out of line when the head is bolted onto the block. This will cause binding of the cam in the bearings. If the cam journals are not in line, then the head will have to be straightened before resurfacing.

Engine Balancing

Almost all production engines on the road today, as well as 99.9% of all vehicles that a technician encounters on a daily basis, have been "prebalanced" at the factory. Because of manufacturing tolerances, that balancing is relatively close, but not perfect. In a standard engine rebuild, no further balancing should normally be necessary. Still, if you are rebuilding a performance engine, or you just want the extra comfort of knowing that the engine is within much tighter tolerances, consider having the engine balanced. This process is usually only done in a machine shop. Engine balancing is performed to ensure that all weight imbalances in the engine are neutralized by taking away or adding the proper amount of weight in the proper places.

Some engines are internally balanced, while others are externally balanced. An internally balanced engine is balanced completely from the inside. This means the piston assemblies, rods, and crankshaft are balanced so that their rotating forces cancel out. In some in-line four-cylinder engines and 90-degree V6 engines, manu-facturers may use an extra counterbalance shaft to smooth out engine vibrations **FIGURE 14-21**. Counterbalance shafts are only added at the factory or by the original equipment manufacturer, and they must be timed with the crankshaft.

An externally balanced engine has external weights added on the harmonic balancer and on the flex plate or flywheel **FIGURE 14-22**. These weights work in conjunction with the internal counterweights to balance the rotating mass of the engine. The challenge of externally balanced engines is that if the harmonic balancer or flywheel ever needs to be replaced, the new component will not match the rotating assembly and the engine will not be as balanced.

If an engine has a balance issue during initial creation and testing, the factory will calculate the necessary amount of counterforce needed and exactly where it

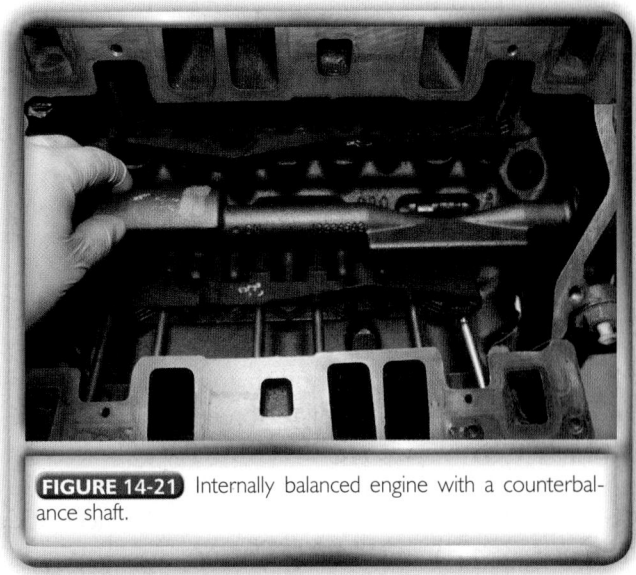

FIGURE 14-21 Internally balanced engine with a counterbalance shaft.

FIGURE 14-22 Engine balancing. **A.** Externally balanced harmonic balancer. **B.** Externally balanced flywheel.

should be applied. This process has worked very well for manufacturers over the years and helps explain why our vehicles are as smooth and quiet as they are even though the engine parts are moving very fast in various directions within the engine.

With the production advancements of the past years, engine parts are being manufactured with much closer tolerances and weights. The closer weights of pistons and connecting rods make it much easier and faster to balance engines. Thus, manufacturers can produce a crankshaft that is "relatively balanced" because the company is assuming that every connecting rod and piston will weigh a given amount. For example, a piston for a new Lexus on a parts counter in Pennsylvania will weigh virtually the same amount as a piston for a new Lexus on a parts counter in Alaska. This consistency makes the balancing process much easier, as the parts are all held within the factory tolerance.

For engine balancing purposes, the parts of the crankshaft assembly are divided into two categories: **rotating weight** and **reciprocating weight**. Rotating weight is the amount of weight that is moving in a circular motion. It includes everything from the center of the connecting rod down to the connecting rod cap and all components of the crankshaft. Reciprocating weight is the amount of weight that is moving up and down. It is everything from the middle of the connecting rod upward, including the piston, wrist pin, and rings. Even the estimated weight of the oil that will be on the piston and rings is added to the reciprocating weight. The crankshaft spins, so it is part of the rotating mass, and so are the components that spin with it, such as the rod bearings, the crank gear, the flex plate or flywheel, and the harmonic balancer. The pistons, rings, and wrist pins, move up and down, so they are part of the reciprocating weight. With the connecting rods, the small end reciprocates while the big end rotates.

To balance an engine, you need an **engine balancer**, a connecting rod balance fixture, a gram scale, gram calibration weights, **bob weights**, lead shot, and a disc sander with 80-grit disc paper. Equipment that makes the job easier includes a lathe, a milling machine, and a drill press. Modern computerized engine balancers are expensive bench units complete with computer controls, a lathe and drill press for machining metal for the balancing procedure, and all necessary adapters for most applications of crankshaft assemblies. Bob weights are weights used during the balancing process that are used to mimic the exact weight of the piston and connecting rod weights for that particular rod bearing journal. It is impossible to put the pistons and connecting rods on the crankshaft when it is mounted on the engine balancer and spin it, as there is nothing to hold the assemblies steady. These bolt-on weights are the next-best thing.

The first step in balancing is ensuring that all pistons and connecting rods weigh the same amount. All pistons are weighed and compared, the lightest piston is identified and some of the aluminum from the heavier pistons is removed so that all pistons are made equal in weight. The weight is then recorded. The same procedure is performed on the wrist pins. If there are wrist pin retainers, one is weighed and recorded.

The rotating rod (the big end) is weighed on the connecting rod balance fixture. All of them must weigh the same, so weight is removed as needed on the balance pad on the big end to match the weight of the lightest rod. The weight is recorded. The reciprocating end of the rod (the small end) is weighed using the connecting rod balance fixture. All small ends must weigh the same. Some of the material on the balance pad is ground away as needed on the small end so all the rods match the lightest rod, and then the weight is recorded.

Applied | **Science**

AS-16: Balance: The technician can measure and balance rotating systems.

The bottom-end components of an engine function as a unit, balancing them as an assembly ensures reliable and vibration-free operation. Bottom-end balancing occurs in two stages: the static balancing of reciprocating components and the dynamic balancing of the crankshaft.

The first stages of the balancing operation address the weight of the connecting rods, pistons, and associated components. Connecting rods are mounted in a balancing fixture and their ends are weighed. First, all big ends are weighed, the lightest is determined, and metal is machined from the heavier rods until within close specification of the lightest. This procedure is repeated for the small ends. Next, the pistons and their associated wrist pins, clips, and rings are weighed and lightest identified. Again, machining is carried out to remove metal from the heavier pistons until within close tolerance of the lightest.

The weights of the balanced connecting rods and piston assemblies are used to calculate the rotating and reciprocating weights. Bob weights are used to simulate the weight of the reciprocating components and are fitted to the crank journals. The crankshaft is mounted in a specialized balancing machine and spun at optimum speed. A computer indicates the amount of imbalance present and at which points on the crankshaft weight needs to be added or removed. Weight may be removed by machining metal from existing counterweights or adding heavy metal. In some situations, flywheels, clutch pressure plates, and harmonic balancers may be fitted to the crankshaft during dynamic balancing.

Once the pistons and connecting rods are balanced and weighed, the bob weights are bolted to the rod journals on the crank to mimic this weight. The reciprocating weight is balanced first, using a bob weight card (a generic card for recording specific weights as they are added and removed) to record the weights.

The bob weight card will say "x2" on the rod's big end since there are two rods sitting on one journal in a V8 application. We must multiply the weight of the big end by two to come up with the weight of the bob weight we will bolt to the journal. An estimate of the oil in the crank is added to the bob weight card. The rotating weight (the big end of connecting rod, the main bearings, and a bit of oil) is added to 50% of the reciprocating weight (wrist pin, small end of the connecting rod, and piston). This calculation will give the total weight needed for the bob weight.

For example, say that the total calculated bob weight is 1260 grams, which includes the lead shot (adapters). The bob weights will be adjusted to weigh 1260 grams and bolted onto the rod journals. The Woodruff key (a piece of metal used to position the harmonic balancer on the crankshaft), the timing chain crankshaft gear, the harmonic balancer, and the flywheel or flex plate are installed. The crankshaft is spun, and using a strobe light, the engine balancer will show the operator the heavy spot on the crankshaft and how much weight to remove. The balancer works very similar to a wheel and tire spin balancer.

The crankshaft is balanced by either adding weight in a certain area or removing weight from a certain area. Weight is removed by selectively drilling the already-present counterweights on the crankshaft assembly. Weight is added by drilling holes and inserting Malloy metal plugs. Malloy is about twice as heavy or dense as regular steel; for example, for every 10 ounces of steel you drill out, you can fit 20 ounces of Malloy metal into the resulting hole. All weights should be recorded in grams because it is the unit of weight used by manufacturers and in most shops.

Wrap-up

Ready for Review

- Most automotive shops and technicians send their engine machining work to a specialty machining shop where components are restored to factory specifications.
- The measure of surface roughness is based on surface valleys and peaks and is specified as surface roughness area (Ra).
- The deck height of an engine block must be identical at each cylinder in order to maintain equal compression values.
- The engine cylinder block dowel pinholes are used as alignment guides for the cylinder head and cylinder head gasket.
- Damaged cylinders must be rebored to fit oversized pistons.
- Boring bars, which position and align a single-point tool, can be portable, semiautomated, or CNC style.
- After boring, the cylinder walls must be honed to the proper surface texture.
- A ball hone may be used to reapply the cylinder's crosshatch pattern.
- Most hones are self-tensioning but must be adjusted to the correct speed to achieve the desired angle of crosshatch.
- A torque plate may be used to keep the cylinder true to the machined dimensions when honed.
- Main bearing bores must be properly aligned to prevent premature bearing failure and crankshaft failure.
- The engine block must be line bored or line honed to correct a bore alignment issue.
- Oil clearance can be checked quickly with Plastigauge or by subtracting the size of the main bearing journal from the size of the main bearing bore with bearings installed.
- Crankshaft journals must have clean surfaces, with imperfections polished out.
- Crankshaft rods must all be cut to the same size, as must all main journals.
- A crankshaft can be spray welded to add enough surface material for grinding.
- Crankshaft oil passage holes must be chamfered before journal polishing begins.
- The big end of a connecting rod must be resized to ensure proper rod cap alignment; this can be done with a rod honing machine or a rod boring machine.
- Before disassembling a non-adjustable valve-type cylinder head, measure and record the valve installation height.
- Cylinder heads should be magnafluxed, using the wet or dry method, to check for cracks.
- Aluminum cylinder heads cannot be magnafluxed; therefore, they must be pressure tested via water or a pressure testing bench.
- Overhead cam engines may have camshafts that lose lubrication if oil pressure drops or misaligned cam bores if the engine overheats.
- Cam bores must always be aligned, typically within 0.004" (0.1 mm) of each other.
- The four methods of repairing valve guides are knurling, reaming the guide oversize and using a valve with an oversized valve stem, installing a thin-walled bronze liner, or installing a thick-walled guide (bronze or cast iron).
- When grinding valve faces, be careful not to grind away too much valve margin.
- Hardened valve seats are installed to prevent the valve from sinking into the head.
- Valve seats may be made of nickel alloy, chrome alloy, cobalt alloy, stainless steel, cast iron, or tungsten steel (for CNG or propane engines).
- Valve seats can be refurbished with stones or cutters.
- Check valve seat contact, valve seat runout, and valve guide-to-valve stem clearance.
- It is critical to measure valve stem height after machining to ensure that the valve will close once the valve train is installed.
- Measure valve spring height and adjust to correct height with shims.
- Cylinder head resurfacing may be performed if the head deck surface is found to be warped or if there is excessive pitting.
- The majority of production engines are "prebalanced" before leaving the factory.
- Engines can be internally or externally balanced.
- Crankshaft assembly parts are divided into rotating (moving in a circular motion) and reciprocating (moving up and down) weight categories.
- Equipment needed to simulate balance of a V8 engine includes an engine balancer, a connecting rod balance fixture, a gram scale, gram calibration weights, bob weights, lead shot, a disc sander, and an equipment lathe or milling machine.

Key Terms

ball hone An assembly of metal rods, with abrasive stones attached, that is inserted into the cylinder and spun to break the glazing off the cylinder walls and make a new crosshatched pattern.

bob weights Weights used during the balancing process that are used to mimic the exact weight of the piston and connecting rod weights for that particular rod bearing journal.

bore A tool used to make a hole in or through an object.

bored out An object that has been bored.

boring bar A long bar used to position and align a single-point tool, such as an engine cylinder block boring machine, for boring operations.

broach-style surfacer A tool used in resurfacing the engine block.

chamfering The process of cutting into the top of the oil passage hole with a specialized chamfering tool or regular drill bit to make the top of the oil hole more like a 45-degree angle, to keep the edge from digging into the bearing the way a 90-degree edge would.

collet A cone-shaped tool that encloses and grips a rod or shaft when inserted into the sleeve of a lathe or other machine.

crankshaft journals Smooth, curved, machined areas where other parts fit to the crankshaft.

crosshatch A pattern of lines placed at angles to each other, appearing as a series of Xs across a surface.

cubic boron nitride (CBN) cutter An engine block resurfacing tool used on cast iron parts.

engine balancer An expansive bench unit complete with computer controls, a lathe and drill press for machining metal for the balancing procedure, and all necessary adapters for most applications of crankshaft assemblies.

engine block deck The portion of the engine cylinder block on which the head gasket lies on and to which the cylinder head is bolted.

engine block dowel pinhole The hole where the engine cylinder block dowel pins are fixed.

ferrous metals Metals that have an iron compound in their makeup or that are magnetic.

fillet area The area of the crankshaft that meets up with the rod bearing journal or main bearing journal.

fracture split A method used on powdered metal connecting rods where the big end of the connecting rod is broken in half and can be identified by a ragged finish of the big end's parting surfaces.

hardened seat A valve seat that has undergone a heat-treating process to become more robust and capable of withstanding the severe demands of today's vehicles and drivers.

honing The smoothing-out process of the cylinder walls performed after the boring process. This is the final step in refinishing the cylinder; it creates the proper crosshatched pattern necessary for the piston rings to seal and seat into to give the combustion chamber the proper seal.

induction hardening A process for hardening metal by touching it to a device that raises the temperature of the part with heat or magnets and then suddenly cooling it in water, oil, or another chemical.

interference angle The angle formed between the valve face and the valve seat; usually it is ½ to 1 degree.

interference fit A process used for holding parts in place where the inside diameter of the outer piece is slightly smaller than the outside diameter of the inner piece.

knurled A process in which a drill bit with a spiral groove is threaded through or run through the valve guide to create raised ridges on either side of the groove, effectively shrinking the size of the valve guide.

line bored/line honed A process for correcting a mainline that is out of line.

magnafluxing A process for checking the cylinder head for cracks that uses a magnetic powder.

mainline The imaginary centerline down the engine cylinder block.

nitriding A metal surface-hardening process using nitrogen and high temperatures.

polycrystalline diamond (PCD) cutter An engine block resurfacing tool used on aluminum parts.

pressure testing A process for checking the aluminum cylinder heads for cracks using air pressure.

radius A straight line extending from the center of a circle to its edge or from the center of a sphere to its surface.

reciprocating weight The amount of weight that is moving up and down. It is everything from the middle of the connecting rod upward, including the piston, wrist pin, and rings.

rotating weight The amount of weight that is moving in a circular motion, including everything from the center of the connecting rod down to the connecting rod cap and all components of the crankshaft.

stroke The movement of the piston up and down.

surface roughness average (Ra) A measurement used to classify how rough a particular mating surface is at the microscopic level.

taper An object that is smaller in diameter at one end.

three-angle grind A process of grinding the valve openings on the cylinder head so that air can pass through them more smoothly and quickly.

torque plate A 2" (51 mm) thick plate that is bolted where the cylinder head is fastened on the engine block.

valve seat The surface against which a valve rests during the portion of the engine operating cycle when that valve is closed.

ASE-Type Questions

1. Tech A says that failure analysis will assist the technician in making an estimate of repairs. Tech B says that failure analysis will help prevent reoccurence of the problem. Who is correct?
   a. Tech A
   b. Tech B
   c. Both A and B
   d. Neither A nor B

2. Tech A says that Ra is critical in the machining process to ensure gasket sealing. Tech B says that a Ra rating of 0-1 is the best sealing surface. Who is correct?
   a. Tech A
   b. Tech B
   c. Both A and B
   d. Neither A nor B

3. Tech A says that full floating pistons use keepers to retain the piston pin. Tech B says that some piston pins are press fit in the rod. Who is correct?
   a. Tech A
   b. Tech B
   c. Both A and B
   d. Neither A nor B

4. Tech A says that when measurement of the cylinder bore is out of specifications, just install an oversized piston. Tech B says that cylinders can typically be bored out to only a few specific sizes. Who is correct?
   a. Tech A
   b. Tech B
   c. Both A and B
   d. Neither A nor B

5. Tech A says that after using a portable boring bar, the cylinder bore will need to be honed by 0.0015" to 0.002". Tech B says that the portable boring bar is the best way to go as it can be used on all current engines. Who is correct?
   a. Tech A
   b. Tech B
   c. Both A and B
   d. Neither A nor B

6. Tech A says that when boring a cylinder, it should be bored to the final cylinder size. Tech B says that it should be bored smaller than the final size to allow for honing of the cylinder. Who is correct?
   a. Tech A
   b. Tech B
   c. Both A and B
   d. Neither A nor B

7. Tech A says that a torque plate bolts to the bottom of the block to strengthen the block when boring. Tech B says that the use of a torque plate compensates for the cylinder head being torqued in place. Who is correct?
   a. Tech A
   b. Tech B
   c. Both A and B
   d. Neither A nor B

8. Tech A says the proper crosshatch pattern is critical for proper lubrication of the pistons and rings. Tech B says that the smoother the cylinder walls, the better the rings will seal. Who is correct?
   a. Tech A
   b. Tech B
   c. Both A and B
   d. Neither A nor B

9. Tech A says that main bearing clearance can be calculated by knowing the inner diameter of the main bearing and the outer diameter of the main journal. Tech B says that rod bearing and main bearing clearance can be measured with Plastigauge. Who is correct?
   a. Tech A
   b. Tech B
   c. Both A and B
   d. Neither A nor B

10. Tech A says that bearing crush is when the main caps are torqued and the bearing is crushed against the crankshaft. Tech B says that crankshaft journals can be machined undersized and undersize bearings can be used. Who is correct?
    a. Tech A
    b. Tech B
    c. Both A and B
    d. Neither A nor B

CHAPTER 15

Knowledge Objectives

After reading this chapter, you will be able to:
1. Describe the steps in crankshaft and block preparation. (p 408)
2. Perform piston, ring, and block clearance checks. (pp 408–409)
3. Explain the importance of a temporary test buildup. (p 411)
4. Describe the different approaches used to check the main bearing clearance. (pp 411–413)

Engine Assembly

Skills Objectives

After reading this chapter, you will be able to:

1. Test install the crankshaft and the pistons. (pp 413–417)
2. Check piston-to-valve clearance. (pp 418–420)
3. Paint the engine and covers. (pp 420–421)
4. Fit engine plugs. (pp 421–422)
5. Install the crankshaft. (pp 422–423)
6. Fit piston rings and install the pistons. (pp 424–427)
7. Install the heads onto the block. (pp 427–430)
8. Install the timing cover and oil pan. (pp 433–434)
9. Pre-oil the engine. (pp 434–435)
10. Install the intake manifold and the external engine components. (pp 435–437)
11. Assemble the accessories to the engine. (p 438)
12. Inspect and replace the camshaft and drive belt/chain. (pp 439–441)
13. Establish camshaft position sensor indexing. (p 441)
14. Replace valve stem seals on an assembled engine; inspect valve spring retainers, locks/keepers, and valve lock/keeper grooves. (pp 441–443)

▶ Introduction

Engine assembly is a process that must be carried out in a very clean environment and with the utmost attention to detail. Failure to heed this advice or carelessness during this process will result in an engine that may not live for more than a few minutes after being started up. In this chapter, we will first perform a test buildup of the engine to measure all of the critical clearances and to make sure all of the parts work together properly. Next, if everything is within specifications, the engine will be carefully disassembled, cleaned once more, and painted so it is ready for final assembly.

> ▶ **LINK**
> Refer to the *CDX Engine Repair Tasksheet Manual* for NATEF proficiency for an "Engine Build SpecSheet," which you can use for recording all of the measurements and specifications so that you will have a reference of all the critical measurements on one page.

Following the procedures laid out in this chapter, along with the service manual's procedures for the engine you are rebuilding, will result in a long-lasting, good-running engine.

▶ Engine Preassembly

Prior to final assembly of the engine, some preparatory work is necessary. It is recommended to examine all clearances and surface finishes prior to assembly, especially if the engine has been machined. In most cases,

measurements will be taken, but keep your eyes open for any defects that would affect the engine operation. We will also show you how to measure piston-to-valve clearance in case you are using a nonstock camshaft. All of this will help avoid issues once the engine is reassembled and running.

Crankshaft and Block Preparation

The engine block should have been cleaned and sprayed with rust inhibiter at the machine shop. It is good practice to reclean the block and crankshaft passages. Using a small brush or other similar tool, ensure that all oil galleries and passages are clean. You may need to run a matching thread chaser down all of the holes in the block to make sure they are clean. Spray the block with a rust inhibiter and wrap the engine with a plastic bag until you are ready to assemble the engine.

Prepare the crankshaft by cleaning it, drying it, and spraying a rust inhibitor over it. Clean the crankshaft using an industrial parts cleaner. After the crankshaft has been washed, take a small wire brush and make sure all oil passages are clean. Next, flush the passages with hot water. After the entire crankshaft has been cleaned and rinsed with hot water, blow it dry and spray an antirust inhibitor over the crankshaft.

Piston, Ring, and Block Clearance Checks

Measuring the piston-to-cylinder wall clearance and the piston ring end gap ensures that the machining was performed properly and that the parts you have are fitted properly to the cylinders. Be sure to check the piston-

▶ You are the Automotive Technician

You have successfully disassembled, cleaned, and machined the engine parts and checked all necessary clearances. Prior to the final reassembly of the engine, you performed a temporary test buildup to verify that no additional machining was needed. After assembling the block and heads, you will need to install the timing belt and set the timing for all four camshafts.

1. Why is it important to perform a temporary test buildup of the rotating assembly prior to final assembly?
2. What damage is possible if you install the timing belt/chain with the wrong camshaft timing?
3. How are rod and main bearing clearances measured?

to-cylinder wall clearance and the piston ring end gap before installing the soft plugs and oil gallery plugs. This step could prevent you from having to remove and reinstall the gallery plugs and soft plugs if clearances are not within specifications. If the block were to need further machining, the plugs would have to be removed again.

Piston-to-Cylinder Wall Clearance

Using an outside micrometer, measure the piston skirt just below the wrist pin centerline, and record the piston size. Repeat this process for all the pistons and record your findings **FIGURE 15-1**. Set the cylinder bore gauge indicator dial to the piston size using the bore gauge setting fixture. Recheck the bore gauge with the outside micrometer, and make sure the dial is set to zero. With the bore gauge set to the exact piston size, the dial will indicate the cylinder size with a plus or minus reading, as compared to the piston. This reading will indicate the amount of oil clearance for that piston and cylinder. For example, if the cylinder bore is larger than the piston

by 0.002" (0.051 mm), the dial will indicate a reading of + 0.002 **FIGURE 15-2**. Check each cylinder wall with the bore gauge, adjusting the bore gauge if the pistons differ in size, and record your findings. Make sure your findings are within the manufacturer's specifications. If the clearance is not correct, contact the machine shop to explore the options for correcting the issue.

Measuring Piston Ring End Gap

Before installing piston rings on the piston, you need to check the ring end gap. Carefully slide the top compression ring into the cylinder bore about an inch down into the cylinder bore. Turn a piston upside down and use the head of the piston to square up the ring in the cylinder bore **FIGURE 15-3**. Using a feeler gauge, measure the width of the ring end gap **FIGURE 15-4**. Repeat this process with the other compression ring and oil control ring. If the oil ring is the three-piece version, then only the end gap of the side rails are measured. Record each reading and compare to the manufacturer's ring gap specifications.

FIGURE 15-1 Measuring a piston.

FIGURE 15-3 Squaring up piston rings.

FIGURE 15-2 Measuring the piston-to-cylinder clearance using a bore gauge.

FIGURE 15-4 Checking compression ring end gap.

Installing the Piston on the Connecting Rod

Refer to the manufacturer's specifications to determine which direction the piston is installed on the connecting rod. This is important, since many engines use a slightly offset pin on the piston. In addition, the rod may have an oil "spit" hole that helps to lubricate the bottom of the cylinder walls; if the oil hole is on the wrong side, the oil will not be sprayed at the right time or place. The two most popular types of piston pins are the full-floating and the semi-floating pins, also called wrist pins.

Floating Pin Design

The full-floating pin is a slide-fit in both the piston and the connecting rod bore. The pin is retained by a pair of snap rings. Note that some snap rings are directional, which means they must be installed with the correct side facing the wrist pin. Otherwise the snap ring can work its way out of its groove and score the cylinder wall, destroying the engine. Install one snap ring on one side of the piston **FIGURE 15-5**, then lubricate the pin area of the piston, the connecting rod, and the pin. Next, slide the piston pin in place and secure the pin with the other snap ring **FIGURE 15-6**.

Semi-floating Pin Design (Interference Fit)

Most engines have semi-floating or wrist pins, in which case the machine shop will have already attached the pistons to the rods. The semi-floating pin moves freely in the piston bore but is press-fit in the connecting rod bore. The preferred method for installing the wrist pin is to use a rod heater. Adjust the setting fixture where the piston pin needs to stop **FIGURE 15-7**. When installed correctly, the wrist pin will be centered in the connecting rod **FIGURE 15-8**. Make sure the rod heater is hot;

lubricate the piston pin bore with a thin film of automatic transmission fluid (ATF). The small end of the connecting rod will have a slight glow from heat; slide the piston pin in using a mandrel or pin press and let cool.

FIGURE 15-6 Sliding the piston pin into the piston and rod.

FIGURE 15-7 Adjusting the pin stop on the rod heater.

FIGURE 15-5 Installing the snap ring.

Connecting rod needs to be centered on wrist pin when the wrist pin is centered in the piston.

FIGURE 15-8 Wrist pin centered in the connecting rod.

Temporary Test Buildup

It is very important to perform a temporary test buildup of the rotating assembly. This buildup does not need to include the piston rings or a rear main seal for the crankshaft, but you should install the cylinder heads and the valve train. Do not skip this section of the rebuild. It will determine if additional machining or exchange of any parts will be necessary.

All of your components should now be refurbished, new, or thoroughly cleaned. The decks, cylinders, and main bores of the block should all be refurbished to specifications. The pistons should be clean or new and the rods refurbished on both the big and the small ends. All of the crankshaft journals should have been inspected and reground if necessary. The camshaft and lifters, as well as the timing set, should have passed inspection or been replaced with new parts. The cylinder heads and all related valve train components should also be clean, refurbished, or new. For this preassembly, have the head and intake gaskets as well as the oil pan and valve cover gaskets nearby. Also have the main and rod bearings ready for when you install their related components.

Installing Main Bearings

Before installing the main bearings, you will need to make sure the bearings are the proper size. The crankshaft could have been turned undersize by 0.010" (0.25 mm), 0.020" (0.51 mm), or 0.030" (0.76 mm). Make sure the bearings match the crank size. You can do this ahead of time by checking the stamp on the back of the bearings or by looking at the mark on the bearing box. The back of the bearing insert and the bearing cap and saddle should be clean and dry.

> ### TECHNICIAN TIP
>
> The back of the bearing insert and the bearing cap and saddle should all be clean and dry when installing the bearings. Do not apply grease or oil to the back side of the bearing shell. Even the smallest bit of dirt on the bearing back can cause a raised spot on the bearing, which will lead to scoring of the crankshaft.

To insert the bearing, start the **tang** of the bearing into the main journal slot. Make sure the bearing with the oil hole is inserted in the block and not the main bearing cap. Use your fingers to push the bearing insert into place **FIGURE 15-9**. Check to make sure the oil hole is aligned with the main oil hole when inserted **FIGURE 15-10**. The oil hole provides the supply of oil for that main journal and one or more rod journals.

FIGURE 15-9 Installing main bearing insert.

FIGURE 15-10 Oil hole lined up.

The thrust bearing can be installed only in its proper journal. This location can be in the center of the block or at the rear main journal of the block. You will need to look for the cut-out area for the thrust bearing flange to fit. Repeat this process until all the main bearings are installed in the block, including all of the main caps. Make sure the thrust bearing is installed. If the thrust bearing is not a flange thrust bearing, grease will need to be applied to the back side of the bearing to hold the bearing in place until the crankshaft is installed or the main cap is installed.

Checking Main Bearing Clearance

It is critical that the main bearing clearances be within the manufacturer's tolerances. The specifications usually have a range of approximately plus or minus 0.0005", so careful measurement is required. There are several methods used to check clearance. If you want to check the clearance prior to installing the crankshaft, you can use an inside and outside micrometer or a bore gauge **FIGURE 15-11**. If you want to check the bearing clearance with the crankshaft installed, then you can use a plastic gauging material (**Plastigauge**®).

Using a Micrometer

Before using a micrometer to measure the crankshaft, it is important to make sure the crankshaft is clean and free of oil and grease. Use the **outside micrometer** to measure each main bearing journal, and record your findings **FIGURE 15-12**. With all the main caps and bearings installed and torqued (crankshaft is *not* installed at this time), use an inside micrometer or snap gauge to measure the inside diameter of the main bearing bore **FIGURE 15-13**. Take care to not damage the bearing surface. This procedure does take some experience, but when performed correctly, it is very accurate.

Once the inside micrometer or snap gauge is set to the correct size, read the inside micrometer or use the

outside micrometer to measure the outside of the snap gauge, and record your findings. Subtract the crankshaft main journal readings from the main bearing bore readings, and record your findings. The difference will be in thousandths and ten-thousandths of an inch, giving you the bearing clearance. Check this with the manufacturer's specifications.

Using a Bore Gauge

When using a bore gauge, it is important to make sure the crankshaft is clean and free from oil or grease. You will need to measure the main journals with an outside micrometer and record your findings. Next, use a bore gauge setting fixture to set the bore gauge according to the crankshaft main journals measurements and zero the dial. With all the main bearings in place and the main caps torqued to the proper torque setting, use the bore gauge and check your clearance **FIGURE 15-14**.

FIGURE 15-11 Using a bore gauge to measure a cylinder.

FIGURE 15-13 Measuring the inside of a main bearing.

FIGURE 15-12 Measuring crankshaft journals with an outside micrometer.

FIGURE 15-14 Checking bearing clearance with a bore gauge.

The reading on the bore gauge is the bearing clearance. Record the clearance, and check the reading against the manufacturer's specifications.

Using Plastigauge

Plastigauge is an extruded plastic thread that comes in different sizes, depending on the expected clearances to be checked. For main bearings, choose the gauge that is sized for 0.0005" to 0.003" (0.013 to 0.076 mm); it should be green in color. Put a drop of oil on each bearing and wipe it so that there is a very thin, even layer. It is not a good idea to lay a crankshaft on totally dry bearings. Install the crankshaft into the main journals, making sure you do not turn the crankshaft.

Cut a piece of plastic gauge just short of the width of the bearing, and lay it across the width of the crankshaft main journal. Using the proper main cap, torque the main cap bolts to manufacturer's specifications, making sure the crankshaft does not turn. If the crankshaft turns during this measurement, the gauge strip will smear, giving an inaccurate reading.

After the main cap has been torqued into place, loosen the bolts and take the cap off. The plastic gauge strip will be stuck to the crankshaft journal or the bearing insert. Check the paper that the plastic gauge came in to see which width matches the plastic gauge, and read the chart for the proper bearing clearance. Check your findings against the manufacturer's specifications.

Repeat this process for all the main journals and record your findings.

Test Installing the Crankshaft

Testing crankshaft bearing clearances is done to ensure that all clearances are correct. Any problems can be noted and corrected before the rest of the engine is assembled. After the main bearing inserts are installed, the crankshaft is installed, and then the clearance between the crankshaft journals and the main bearings is measured. This skill drill uses the Plastigauge method to check clearances.

To test install a crankshaft, follow the steps in **SKILL DRILL 15-1**:

1. If the main journals of the crankshaft were cut undersize, make sure the new main bearing inserts match the undersized journals. Before you open the sealed bearing insert package, double-check the labels to make sure they are the correct type and size.

2. Wipe out the saddles of the block and the cap-to-block mating surfaces, being sure there is no debris or lint left behind. Then press the bearings (which have an oil hole) into place by hand. Make sure the tang in the bearing fits into the groove in the bearing saddle. Check that the oil holes in the block line up with the holes in the bearings. **(Photo 1)**

SKILL DRILL | 15-1 | Test Installing the Crankshaft

1. Wipe out the saddles of the block and the cap-to-block mating surfaces. Press the bearings into place by hand. The bearing insert with the oil hole fits in the saddle.

2. Clean the main bearing caps and install the bearing inserts in the same manner. Wipe a small amount of oil on each bearing insert and on the thrust surface of the thrust bearing.

3. Lift the crankshaft and set it into place. Ask for lifting help if it is needed, and then gently set the crank into the block.

SKILL DRILL | 15-1 | Test Installing the Crankshaft, continued

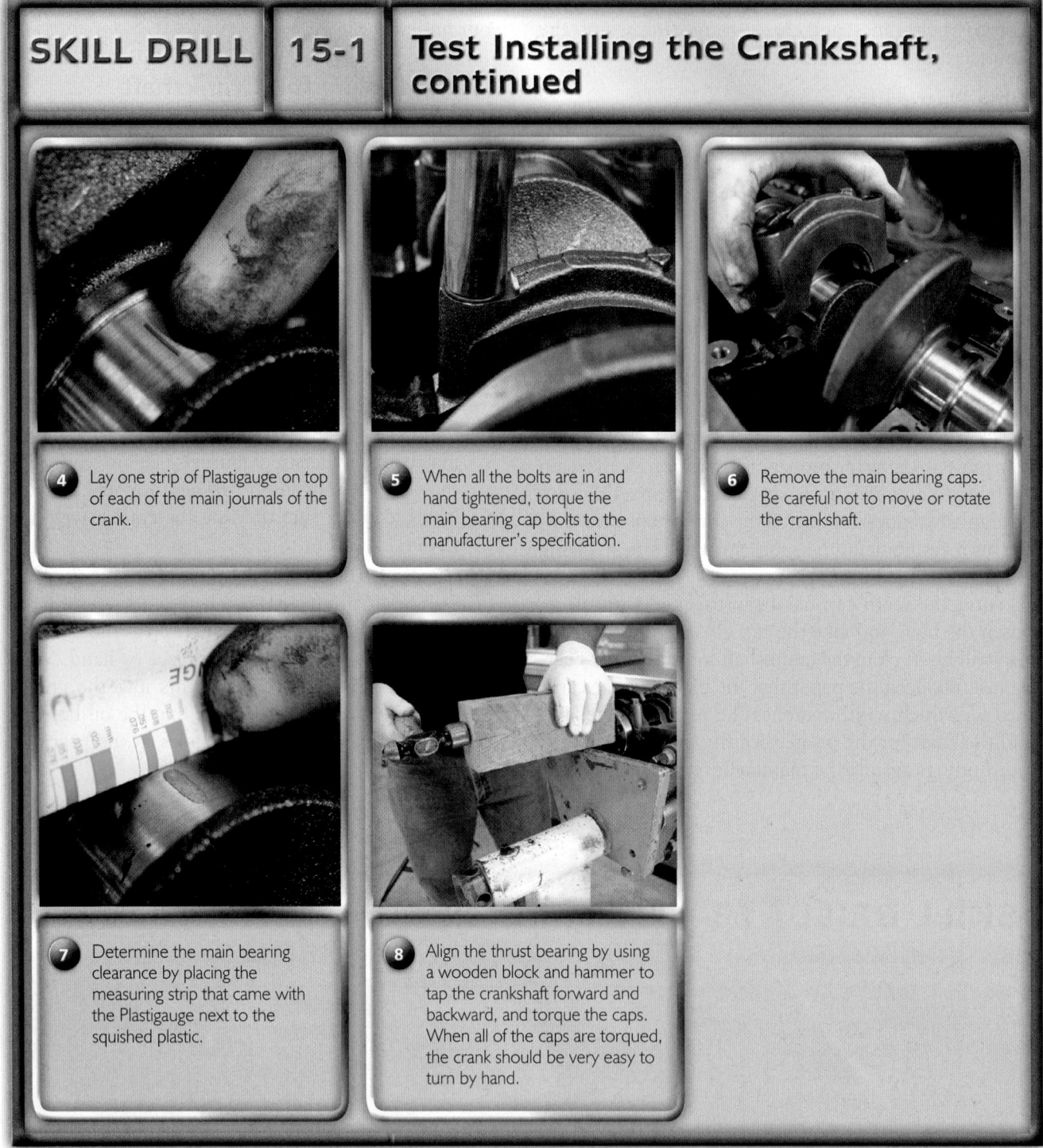

4 Lay one strip of Plastigauge on top of each of the main journals of the crank.

5 When all the bolts are in and hand tightened, torque the main bearing cap bolts to the manufacturer's specification.

6 Remove the main bearing caps. Be careful not to move or rotate the crankshaft.

7 Determine the main bearing clearance by placing the measuring strip that came with the Plastigauge next to the squished plastic.

8 Align the thrust bearing by using a wooden block and hammer to tap the crankshaft forward and backward, and torque the caps. When all of the caps are torqued, the crank should be very easy to turn by hand.

3 Install the bearings in the bearing caps, being careful to line up the bearing tang with the groove in the cap.

4 Put a drop of oil on each bearing insert and wipe it so that there is a thin, even layer. Make sure to wipe some oil on the thrust surface of the thrust bearing as well. (**Photo 2**)

5 Ask for some lifting help if it is needed, and then gently set the crank into the block. (**Photo 3**)

6 Lay a strip of the Plastigauge on top of each of the main journals of the crank. (**Photo 4**)

7 Place the main caps in their proper places, following any stampings or markings you made during disassembly.

8 When all the main bearing cap bolts are in and hand tightened, torque them to the manufacturer's specification. It is good practice to tighten the bolts in steps and following the manufacturer's sequence, if given. **(Photo 5)**

9 Once the bolts are tightened to the correct torque, unscrew them, but again, be very careful not to move the crankshaft accidentally. When the bolts are fully unscrewed, lift them up and tap on them gently to loosen the cap. **(Photo 6)**

10 The squashed piece of plastic gauge material should be stuck to the main journal or to the bearing insert in the cap. Hold the measuring strip that came with the gauge next to the squashed plastic. Make sure you are looking at the correct side of the measure; there is usually an inch scale and a metric scale. The number next to the strip that is the closest match to the compressed Plastigauge strip will be the size of the main bearing clearance. **(Photo 7)**

11 Put some oil on the bearing inserts in the caps. Refer to the marks that you stamped on the caps to make sure the correct ones go in the correct place. Torque all of the regular main caps first, and leave the cap that has the thrust bearings as the last one.

12 You need to seat the thrust bearing before you torque it. Put a block of wood against the crankshaft and tap it forward and backward with a hammer. Doing so will ensure that the upper and lower thrust bearing shells are lined up with each other. Now you can torque the cap that has the thrust bearings in it. When all of the caps are torqued, the crank should be very easy to turn by hand. You should not feel any binding or tight spots. **(Photo 8)**

Thrust Bearing and Crankshaft End Play

Crankshaft end play is controlled with the thrust bearings. Checking the thrust bearing end play can be done with a feeler gauge after the crankshaft is installed. Push the crankshaft forward and slide a feeler gauge on the back side of the thrust bearing **FIGURE 15-15**. Check the manufacturer's specifications; an average for the thrust bearing end play is 0.003" to 0.004" (0.076 to 0.1 mm). If checking using a dial indicator, set up the indicator and zero the dial indicator with the crankshaft pushed all the way back against the rear thrust. Next, carefully push the crankshaft forward and read the amount of end play on the dial indicator **FIGURE 15-16**.

FIGURE 15-15 Checking thrust bearing clearance using a feeler gauge.

FIGURE 15-16 Checking the crankshaft end play using a dial indicator.

Test Installing the Piston and Rod Assemblies

The same method used to check main bearing clearances can be used to check the rod bearing clearance. If a micrometer or bore gauge is used, these checks can be done before the pistons are assembled on the connecting rods. A rod vise will be needed to hold the connecting rod while it is being torqued. Be sure to record all of the connecting rod clearances, and check your findings against the manufacturer's specifications.

Checking Rod Bearing Clearance

It is easier to check the bearing clearance when using the Plastigauge method if the connecting rod is installed on the piston. After the piston has been installed on the connecting rod, you can check rod clearance by test installing the pistons without the piston rings installed. Be careful, however, because the piston could fall out of the cylinder bore and become damaged. Once the piston and rod are in place, you will need to use the same process that was followed previously for checking main bearing clearance. Cut the Plastigauge the same length as the bearing insert width and set the Plastigauge on the rod journal. Torque the connecting rod nuts or bolts to the manufacturer's specifications. Take the rod cap off and compare to the paper graph for your clearance measurement **FIGURE 15-17**.

Test-Installing Pistons

The piston and rod assemblies are test fitted next. This allows you to check rod bearing clearances and internal clearances to ensure there are no problems. The piston and rods should already have been assembled.

To test install pistons, follow the steps in **SKILL DRILL 15-2**:

1 A preassembly check of the piston bearing clearance can be done more quickly if you leave the piston rings off during the test install. Leaving them off will also make it easier to rotate the crank for the rest of the checks. Make sure everything is clean. Wipe any dust off the rod journals, then wipe out the cylinder bores with a clean, dry paper towel. Do not use a shop rag; they tend to leave cloth fibers on the cylinder walls. When the bores are clean, wipe an even coat of fresh engine oil over the insides of the cylinder bores. Turn the crankshaft so that the rod journals farthest forward are facing up (engine upside down), and lock the crankshaft.

FIGURE 15-17 Rod bearing clearance using Plastigauge.

2 With the caps separated from the rods, install the new rod bearings. First verify the part numbers to be sure they match the sizes on your crankshaft. If the crankshaft was cut undersize on the rod journals, the bearings should have an indicator in the part number to tell you that the bearings are a similar amount oversized. **(Photo 1)**

3 Place the Plastigauge strip on the bearing in the connecting rod, not the bearing in the rod cap. It is placed on the bearing in the connecting rod so that it will not get squished further when the rod cap is being removed from the rod. Thus, placing the Plastigauge strip on the bearing in the connecting rod gives you the most accurate reading. Some technicians use a very thin layer of petroleum jelly to keep it from falling off, but that can take up a small amount of the clearance, so take that into consideration. Bolt protectors slipped over the rod studs make it easier to line up the rod bearing to the journal of the crank and help prevent scratching the cylinder wall or nicking the crank journal. Do not let go of the piston; because there are no rings to hold it in place, it will fall right out. Keep your hand on the rod, and have the cap and bolts nearby so that your other hand can install the cap. Do not forget to line up the tangs in the rod and the cap on the same side as each other. When you have at least one nut threaded on, you can let go and make the nuts hand tight. **(Photo 2)**

4 Set the wrench to one-third of the final torque setting for the rod nuts. Next, torque the nuts to the two-thirds measurement, and then finish tightening them all at full torque. Immediately afterwards, loosen the rod nuts. The most important thing is to make sure not to rotate the crank at all while you are tightening and removing the caps. **(Photo 3)**

5 Remove the pistons and check bearing clearance. Sometimes the caps can be worked off by hand. Usually, you have to hit the bolts to break the caps loose. That is why you put the gauge in the rod and not the cap. If the gauge strip were in the cap, it would be distorted when the cap is tapped for removal. Keep a hand on the piston or the rod; because there are rings to hold the piston in place, it will want to fall right out of the cylinder when it breaks loose. Install the protector boots and remove the piston. If the clearance is correct, clean the plastic off the bearing or the crank. Now lubricate the bearing, slip the

SKILL DRILL | 15-2 | Test Installing Pistons

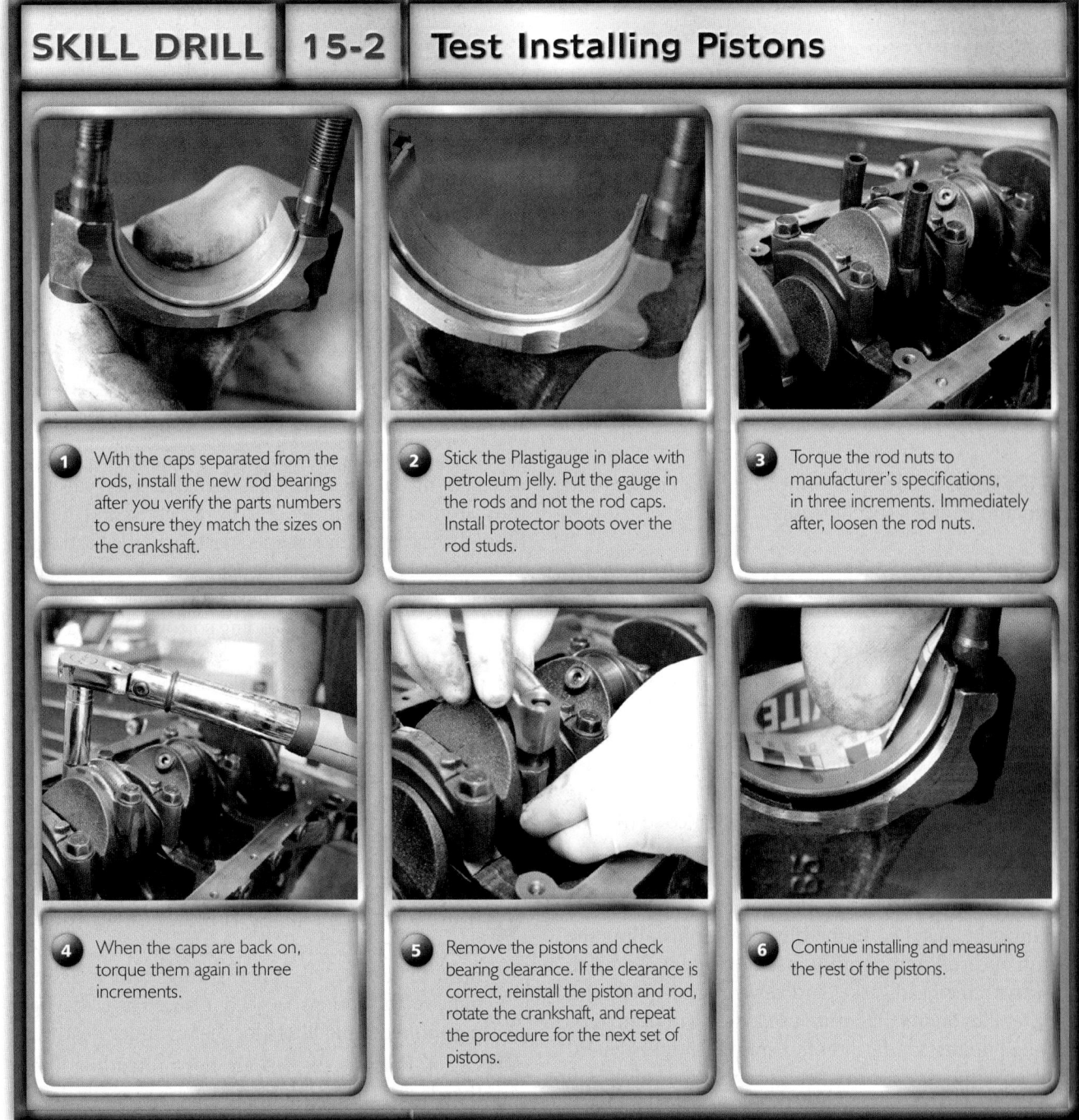

1. With the caps separated from the rods, install the new rod bearings after you verify the parts numbers to ensure they match the sizes on the crankshaft.

2. Stick the Plastigauge in place with petroleum jelly. Put the gauge in the rods and not the rod caps. Install protector boots over the rod studs.

3. Torque the rod nuts to manufacturer's specifications, in three increments. Immediately after, loosen the rod nuts.

4. When the caps are back on, torque them again in three increments.

5. Remove the pistons and check bearing clearance. If the clearance is correct, reinstall the piston and rod, rotate the crankshaft, and repeat the procedure for the next set of pistons.

6. Continue installing and measuring the rest of the pistons.

piston back into its cylinder, and snug the rod nuts.

6. When the caps are back on, torque them again in three even increments. **(Photo 4)**

7. Now rotate the crank at least twice, slowly. If everything is clear, rotate the crankshaft so that the next set of rod journals are facing up. **(Photo 5)**

8. Continue installing and measuring the rest of the pistons. When all of the pistons are installed, check to make sure they rotate smoothly. **(Photo 6)**

Checking Piston-to-Deck Height

Most engines have a specification for piston height as compared to the cylinder block deck. It is important to check this dimension, especially if the deck of the block has been machined or if new, nonstock pistons are being installed. Improper height will affect the engine's compression ratio and could cause interference issues if the piston rises above the deck. Using a depth gauge micrometer, you can measure the piston height at top dead center (TDC), referenced to the block's deck

FIGURE 15-18 Checking piston-to-deck height.

FIGURE 15-19 Valve impression in clay on top of piston.

FIGURE 15-18. Record your findings, and compare to the manufacturer's specifications.

Checking Piston-to-Valve Clearance of a Performance Camshaft

If a performance camshaft is used and there is a higher lift and more duration in the cam profile than in a stock camshaft, it is recommended to check piston-to-valve clearance. At the end of the exhaust stroke, as the piston travels to the top of the cylinder (TDC), the exhaust valve will be just closing and the intake valve just beginning to open. There needs to be enough clearance so that the pistons do not hit the valves, resulting in bent valves and damaged pistons.

To check this clearance, the crankshaft, piston, and rod must be installed in the block. After installing the piston and rod, temporarily install the cylinder head, along with the head gasket and valve train. Just remember that if hydraulic lifters are used, they will need to be pumped up first, and lighter test springs should be used in place of the stock valve springs so that the valves will open fully. The clearance can be checked by using one of two methods: the clay method or the dial indicator method. Both methods show you the minimum amount of clearance between the piston and the valve. The clay method gives an imprint of where the valve and piston have an interference issue, so that you will be better able to determine how to fly cut the pistons if necessary. The dial indicator method allows you to check the clearance at various positions of the piston.

Clay Method

Checking clearance with the clay method is performed by putting clay on top of the piston where the valves will open. As the valves open, they will leave an imprint in the clay. Cutting the clay after it has been deformed will allow the piston-to-valve clearance to be measured and the profile of the valve to be assessed in relation to the head of the piston. Slowly rotate the crankshaft. You will feel resistance when the piston compresses the clay against the valves. Do not force the crankshaft, as doing so could bend a valve. Remove the valve train and cylinder head. Cut the clay in half to get a cross section of the imprint **FIGURE 15-19**. Measure the thickness of clay left after the valve has made its impression to get the piston-to-valve clearance.

To perform a piston-to-valve clearance check using the clay method, follow the steps in **SKILL DRILL 15-3**:

1. Determine the use of solid or hydraulic lifters. If solid lifters, obtain a pair of solid lifters from a parts store. **(Photo 1)**

2. If using hydraulic lifters, prepare using hydraulic lifters. If your heads are preassembled, you will need to remove the stock springs and install the lightweight springs in their place. Have the right pair of hydraulic lifters for that cylinder nearby.

3. Check that the pistons are not protruding above the deck. They should be set fractionally below the deck. Measure the clearance by sliding a feeler gauge under a straightedge laid across the cylinder. **(Photo 2)**

4. Make two balls using modeling clay, one for each valve. Stick them to the piston in the upper valve reliefs (if present) that are cut into the top of the piston. Cover them with a little oil to keep the valves from sticking to the clay when they make an imprint in it. **(Photo 3)**

5. Make sure the pistons are positioned somewhere in midstroke. Lay the head in place without the head gasket, install a few bolts in the number 1 cylinder area, and tighten them by hand. If using a wrench,

SKILL DRILL | 15-3 | Checking Piston-to-Valve Clearance (Clay Method)

1. Assemble the valve train for the number 1 cylinder.

2. Install lightweight test springs. Put a little piece of wood, or something similar, under the valve to keep it in the closed position while you install the lightweight springs.

3. Make balls using modeling clay, one for each valve. Stick them to the piston in the valve reliefs that are cut into the top of the piston, and coat the clay with clean engine oil.

4. Place the cylinder head on the block. Tighten the head bolts by hand.

5. Install the valve train and adjust the valves to the specified lash, or if using hydraulic lifters, zero lash.

6. Carefully rotate the crank until you see the exhaust and intake valves open and close two times each.

7. Remove the valve train and head. Cut each piece of clay and remove half. Measure the distance from the piston to the top of the valve imprint with a ruler or the depth end of a dial caliper.

do not tighten the bolts very much—no more than 15 foot-pounds (ft-lb). Most head gaskets must be replaced once they have been torqued even once. **(Photo 4)**

6 Install the valve train and adjust the valves to the specified lash, if applicable. If the engine uses hydraulic lifters, set the clearance to zero lash. **(Photo 5)**

7 Carefully rotate the crank until you see the exhaust and intake valves open and close two times each. If you feel solid resistance, STOP; the piston may be contacting the valve. **(Photo 6)**

8 Now remove the valve train and head. When you remove the head, the two balls of clay now have valve imprints pressed into them. Cut each piece of clay and remove half. Measure the distance from the piston to the top of the valve imprint with a ruler or the depth end of a dial caliper. Compare this measurement with the specification in the service information. If it is greater than the minimum allowed, there is very little danger of your valves contacting the piston once the engine is heated up and running, unless the valves float at high engine revolutions per minute (rpm). If the clearance is smaller than specified, the pistons will need to be fly cut by a machine shop, or a smaller camshaft must be installed. Clean any leftover clay off the piston. **(Photo 7)**

Dial Indicator Method

Using a dial indicator involves test assembling one cylinder of the engine and using a dial indicator to measure the amount of clearance between the piston and the valves when the piston is near TDC. Since the dial indicator will be mounted so it can measure valve movement, and the valve will need to be compressed by hand, the stock valve springs cannot be used. Lighter-duty test springs will need to be used in their place. It is also helpful to know where the piston is in relation to TDC, so the use of a **degree wheel** or the harmonic balancer and timing cover with timing marks will help identify the crankshaft position.

Once the test piston and valve train are assembled for the test, and the dial indicator is set perpendicularly on the spring retainer, you are ready for the test. The crankshaft is turned until the piston is about 20 degrees before TDC of the exhaust stroke (between the end of the exhaust stroke and the beginning of the intake stroke). At that point, the dial indicator is zeroed and the valve is carefully pushed down at least 0.250" (6.4 mm), if possible. If the valve contacts the piston, the distance measured by the dial indicator is the valve-to-piston clearance. Write down the measurement and recheck in 5-degree increments until about 20 degrees after TDC. If the valve does not

contact the piston, turn the crankshaft 5 degrees and recheck the clearance. Continue doing this until about 20 degrees after top dead center (ATDC). Once you are finished with the first valve, repeat this process for the exhaust valve. Note that many rebuilders recommend a minimum piston-to-valve clearance of at least 0.080" (2.0 mm).

▶ Final Assembly of the Engine Rotating Components (Short Block)

Now that the test fitting of the components is done, and assuming that all measurements are within the manufacturer's specifications, the block is ready for final assembly. If everything fits, completely disassemble the engine again, making sure the valve train parts all go back to their places in the organizer tray and the gaskets go back into their packages to stay clean. The pistons should go back in their tray, and any bolts you remove should go back to the correct storage bins or bags.

When the crankshaft is out of the block again, wipe off the main bearings and the rod bearings, and put them in bins away from any dust that could collect on them. Use extreme caution while you remove the camshaft, as it is very easy to gouge new bearings.

> ### ▶ TECHNICIAN TIP
>
> The engine block, including the assembled crankshaft, rods, pistons, camshaft, and timing gear set (in overhead valve [OHV] engines), is referred to as a **short block**. A short block has all of the rotating parts of the engine installed—everything except the heads, covers, manifolds, accessories, or oil pan. A rebuilt engine that includes the heads, covers, timing components (in overhead cam [OHC] engines), oil pan, and sometimes the flywheel is referred to as a **long block**.

Painting the Engine

The engine needs to be painted to protect from rust and corrosion. It also gives the whole rebuilding job a professional, finished look. Painting is especially necessary if the cast iron castings have been cleaned such that all of the original paint is removed. The various stamped or cast metal covers should also be painted. The engine can be painted before or after installing the oil gallery and soft plugs (see Skill Drill 15-5).

To paint the engine and covers, follow the steps in **SKILL DRILL 15-4**:

1 Prepare the engine parts for painting by building an empty shell of the long block, and then paint everything. Install all the bolts you want to have painted, but make sure you tighten at least four bolts for the heads and the intake. You do not need any gaskets or internal parts. The covers will mask off all the big openings, but for all the other holes, use some masking tape and cut around the edges with a razor blade.

2 When the masking is done, wipe all the surfaces to be painted with a degreaser or lacquer thinner to prepare the surface and remove any oil residue. Put some old spark plugs in the heads.

3 *In a well-ventilated area* and wearing a painter's mask, spray the engine with your chosen color of engine paint. You can also spray a coat or two on any accessories that you want to protect and brighten up with some color.

Installing the Soft Plugs and Oil Gallery Plugs

To help ensure that the engine has no leaks when started up, all the oil gallery plugs and soft plugs need to be installed. Make sure all oil galleries are clean and clear of debris. You can check this visually with a flashlight, or blow air through the passageways. Next, apply a small amount of appropriate sealer on the gallery plug's threads and thread them into the block and head. The soft plugs will need an appropriate sealer applied to the soft plug and the block's sealing edge. Soft plugs are hammered into place in the block and in some heads.

To install the engine plugs, follow the steps in **SKILL DRILL 15-5**:

1 Start with the bare block sitting on the floor with the rear area facing up. The rebuild kit should come

SKILL DRILL 15-5 Installing Engine Plugs

1 Start with the bare block sitting on the floor with the rear area facing up. Apply a small amount of sealer to the threaded oil gallery plugs and screw them in.

2 Clean the edges of the rear water jacket holes before you install the soft plugs.

3 Coat the soft plug with a nonhardening sealer. Wipe it thin and even, being careful not to leave any bare spots.

4 Carefully tap in each soft plug using an impact socket and hammer.

5 Turn the block over so that the front is facing up, and select a punch that is smaller than the inner diameter of the front oil gallery plugs. Wipe sealer evenly around each plug and tap it in until it is 1/16" (1.6 mm) below the rim.

6 Turn the block on its side. Clean, apply sealer, and install the soft plugs in the side of the block, making sure not to miss any.

with all of the oil gallery and soft plugs included. Any threaded plugs such as the rear oil gallery plugs should be coated with a sealer, preferably a liquid Teflon or a similar nonhardening sealer. Do not use Teflon tape; pieces can break off inside and cause an oil system clog. These plugs are usually a tapered pipe thread, so do not overtighten them. **(Photo 1)**

2 Clean the edges of the water jacket holes before you install the soft plugs. **(Photo 2)**

3 Next, coat the soft plug with a nonhardening sealer. Wipe it thin and even, being careful not to leave any bare spots. **(Photo 3)**

4 Select a large impact socket that is slightly smaller than the inside diameter of the soft plug. Tap each soft plug in until it is just below the beveled edge of the water jacket opening. **(Photo 4)**

5 Turn the block over so that the front is facing up and select a punch that is smaller than the inner diameter of the front oil gallery plugs. Wipe a small dab of sealer evenly around each plug and tap it in until it is 1/16" (1.6 mm) below the surface of the block. **(Photo 5)**

6 When the oil gallery plugs are installed, use a chisel to indent the surface of the block around each opening in at least two places. This will keep the plugs from backing out when the oil pressure builds.

7 Turn the block so the soft plug holes are facing up. This way it will be easier to clean and seal the side water jacket holes. Be careful as you tap the plugs in; sometimes they start to go crooked. If one does start to go in at an angle, tap it on the high side and the plug will straighten out as it goes in. To finish off the water jacket, install the drain plugs while the block is upside down, also with some thread sealer. Put the block back on the engine stand. **(Photo 6)**

8 Check for miscellaneous plugs. Almost every engine has some hidden plug, like an oil gallery plug, in an odd place. Carefully review your disassembly notes and the service information to make sure you do not miss any plugs.

Installing the Crankshaft

With the main caps off the block, make sure the main bearings are clean; denatured alcohol works great for cleaning the bearings. Most bearing manufacturers sell assembly lubricant. Using this, lubricate both the main journals of the crankshaft and the main bearings with the bearing assembly oil. If the rear main seal is a split type (two pieces), install the top half into the block and the bottom half into the cap. It is important during this installation to make sure the lip on the seal is facing toward the inside of the engine.

Install the crankshaft in the main saddles, and make sure it spins freely. Next, install the main caps. Make sure the bearing tangs are installed in their grooves. Start one side of the cap and then tap the other side in with a light tap, making sure the caps are in the correct position. When installing a girdle-style main cap design, all the caps are anchored together and installed at once. If called for by the manufacturer, apply a light coat of oil on the main cap bolt threads and the head of the bolt where it makes contact with the main cap. Torque the main caps to the manufacturer's specifications in three steps, as explained during the test fitting procedure.

To install a crankshaft, follow the steps in **SKILL DRILL 15-6**:

1 Clean the saddles of the block, both sides of all the bearings, and the crankshaft to make sure there is no dust or remains from any previous lubricant.

2 Install the main bearing inserts and double-check that the oil holes line up with the ones in the block. At the same time, clean the caps and install the bearings for them as well. Spread assembly lubricant or clean engine oil on the crankshaft journals and the main bearings. Make sure to wipe some on the faces of the thrust bearing, as well.

3 If the engine has a two-piece main seal, install the upper half before lowering the crankshaft into place. Offset the ends of the seal so that one end sits slightly higher than the block surface and the other end slightly lower than the block surface. That way the parting seam on the seal is not exactly lined up with the block surface, which will help prevent leaks. On a neoprene rubber seal, the pointy lip must point toward the inside of the engine. When you press it into place, use the plastic protector shim between the seal and the block to keep the rubber back of the seal from being damaged by the sharp edge of the block. For engines with an older type of rope seal, work the rope into the groove of the block and then use a large socket to tap it deeper into the groove. Cut off the excess flush with the block using a razor knife. Put a little oil or assembly lube on the lip of the rope so the seal will not burn out on start-up. For all types of engines, it is very important to put a dab of silicone sealer on each side of the seal where the rear cap meets the metal of the block. If you do not apply this sealer, oil will leak from the rear of the block. Spread a little silicone sealer on the ends of neoprene or rope seals as well. **(Photo 1)**

4 Install the crankshaft and caps. Be gentle as you lay the crankshaft in place. Next, lubricate the bearings with assembly lube on each of the caps and put them in place. Make sure the main cap bolts are threaded in a few turns, then tap on the caps to seat them. If you have rubber rear main seals, remember to use the protector shim on the seal when you put it in the rear main cap; of course, rubber or rope seals require a small amount of oil on the seal itself. Before the main cap bolts can be torqued, some oil should be applied to the cap where the head of the bolt will contact it. **(Photo 2)**

5 Carry out the final torquing of the main caps following the manufacturer's procedure. Torquing is usually done in three increments. Whatever the torque specification, tighten the bolts first to one-third that amount, then two-thirds, then again to the final specification. If you have four bolt main caps, start with the inner bolts. Leave the cap that has the thrust bearing in it for last. When the other caps are correctly tightened, hit the back of the crank with a rubber mallet or wood block and hammer to line up and seat the thrust bearings.

Now go through the three increments to torque the cap with the thrust bearings, starting with the inner bolts, if it is a four-bolt cap. **(Photo 3)**

6 For a one-piece rear main seal, you will need access to the rear of the block. Many engines use an adapter housing that bolts to the back of the block. The rear main seal is fitted in, after the adapter is sealed and bolted into place. To install the seal, you will probably have to take the block out of the stand so that you can access the rear area of the block. You will then need to lift the engine back onto the stand, after installing the seal. You may be able to install the adapter while it is on the block if you can get it past the engine stand adapter. Alternatively, you can leave the main seal out and install it later, just before installing the flywheel or flex plate—just don't forget it. **(Photo 4)**

SKILL DRILL 15-6 Installing the Crankshaft

1 Install the main bearing inserts and double-check that the oil holes line up with the ones in the block. If the engine has a two-piece seal, install the upper half before lowering the crankshaft into place. For engines with an older type of rope seal, work the rope into the groove of the block and then use a large socket to tap it deeper into the groove.

2 Carefully lay the crankshaft in place. Get someone to help you if the crankshaft is heavy. Next, lubricate each of the caps and put them in place.

3 Place the main cap bolts into their respective holes. Carry out the final torquing of the main caps in three increments.

4 Mount the adapter plate and install the one-piece main seal.

Installing Piston Rings

Most engines use an oil control ring set made up of an expander ring and a pair of thin scraper rails. Some vehicles use a one-piece oil control ring. Install the oil ring expander, if so equipped. Position the parting line of the expander to the center of the piston pin. Install the first of the oil scraper rails, which go above and below the oil expander ring. Start it about 45 degrees to one side of the expander gap, and slide it in between the roof of the groove and the top of the expander ring. Start the other scraper rail about 45 degrees to the other side of the expander gap and slide it into the bottom slot. Make sure the **pip marks** are facing up on the compression rings. If there are no pip marks, refer to the installation instructions that came with the rings. Install the bottom compression ring using a ring expander. Do not twist the compression rings, as doing so will cause them to break. Position the compression ring gap between the 3 o'clock and the 4 o'clock positions. Use a ring expander to install the top compression ring; position the ring gap between the 8 o'clock and the 9 o'clock positions.

To fit the piston rings, follow the steps in **SKILL DRILL 15-7**:

1. Install the expander ring and scraper rails. Check that your piston rings are in order and hold the rod and piston assembly in a vice. The ring kit should have a label that says what each ring in the package is. The first ring to go on is the oil expander ring, which slips into the bottom groove. Make sure the ends of the expander ring do not overlap. Now install the first of the oil scraper rails, which go above and below the oil expander ring. Start it about 45 degrees to one side of the expander gap, and slide it in between the roof of the groove and the top of the expander ring. When the edge of the ring is in, slowly work it clockwise around the piston. Slow down when you get to the other side of the piston. The edge of the ring could scratch the side of the piston, so grasp it firmly and carefully pull it slightly away from the piston, then drop the end of it in place above the expander ring. Start the other scraper rail about 45 degrees to the other side of the expander gap and slide it into the bottom slot. Work this ring around in the opposite direction, guiding it past the top scraper and into the bottom groove as you go. Pull it away slightly at the end, and drop into its groove. Double-check that the expander ring gap is not overlapped. If it is, use two paper clips or picks to pull them apart until they click into alignment with the rails. It is important to rotate the rings now and make sure nothing is stuck or crooked. **(Photo 1)**

2. Install the piston rings. The packaging or instruction sheet should tell you which compression rings

SKILL DRILL | **15-7** | **Fitting the Piston Rings**

1. Install the oil control rings. The first ring to go on is the oil expander ring, which slips into the bottom groove. Make sure the ends of the expander ring do not overlap. Install the scraper rails positioned 45 degrees to each side of the expander gap.

2. Locate the new compression rings. Find the ring for the lower groove first. Look closely at the ring. There is usually a label on one side of the ring, such as a dot, a pip mark, a "T," or some other marking. The ring has a 2F marking to identify the ring and its piston.

3. Use a ring expander to install the rings, and position the gaps at the 3 o'clock and the 9 o'clock positions.

are which. Find the ring for the lower groove first. Look closely at the ring. There is usually a label on one side of the ring, such as a dot, a pip mark, a "T," or some other marking. The marked side of the ring needs to face up. Hold the ring expander with one hand, and steady the ring with the other. Expand it only enough to get the ring to slip down past the first ring groove and into its place in the second groove at the 3 o'clock position. It should rotate freely. Using the same technique as earlier, expand the top compression ring just enough with the top mark facing up and lower the ring into its place at the 9 o'clock position. Lubricate the upper bearing halves with oil or assembly lube. Repeat the process for the rest of the pistons in the tray. **(Photo 2)**

Installing Pistons in the Block

Installing the pistons requires a few special steps. First, the piston rings must be aligned in their proper positions to minimize blow-by gases. All of the pistons, rings, and cylinder walls must be lubricated with assembly lube or clean engine oil. Once the piston rings are aligned and lubricated, they need to be compressed with a ring compressor so they will fit into the cylinder. Make sure the rings collapse into the ring lands. If any ring overlaps onto the surface of the piston, it will be broken as the piston is inserted. It is also important to use bolt protectors on the rod bolts so that the rod bolts do not nick the rod journals on the crankshaft. Also, a liberal amount of bearing assembly lube should be placed on both halves of the connecting rod bearing inserts and the rod journal on the crankshaft. When the piston is being installed, the crankshaft should be positioned so its journal is at bottom dead center (BDC), and the front of the piston should be facing the front of the engine.

The piston will most likely need to be tapped into the cylinder with the handle end of a hammer or other soft tool. It is important to make sure the connecting rod is aligned to the crank journal so it slides over without gouging the surface. When you install the rod cap, the bearing tangs should line up on the same side of the connecting rod and rod cap, and the numbers you marked on the connecting rod and cap during disassembly should match.

To install the pistons, follow the steps in **SKILL DRILL 15-8**:

1. Install the rod bearing inserts into the clean rods and caps. Use the appropriate assembly lubricant to protect the bearings during start-up, until the oil pressure stabilizes. Install the rod bolt protectors all the way to the rod body. Also, double-check that the bearing shell is fully seated in the rod. **(Photo 1)**

2. Position the ring gaps as explained in Skill Drill 15-7, and dip the head of the piston in clean engine oil. **(Photo 2)**

3. Fit the piston into the ring compressor and tighten it until it is just holding the rings. Square up the compressor and look down inside. As you slowly tighten the compressor, make sure the ring gap positions stay where you want them, and make sure the rings are not caught on the edges of their grooves. When the compressor is snug against the side of the piston, it is ready to go into its bore. **(Photo 3)**

SKILL DRILL 15-8 Installing the Pistons

1. Install and lubricate the rod bearing inserts in the rod and cap. Also install the rod bolt protectors.
2. Set the positions of the ring gaps in the piston and dip the head of the piston in clean engine oil.
3. Fit the piston into the ring compressor and tighten it until it is firmly against the piston.

SKILL DRILL | 15-8 | Installing the Pistons, continued

4 Check to make sure the crankshaft rod journal is at BDC and the forward mark on the piston is facing the front of the engine. Tighten the compressor. Tap the compressor down until it is square against the block. Slide the connecting rod over.

5 Use the handle of a hammer to tap the piston in place. Hit it just hard enough to make it slide past the grip of the ring compressor into the cylinder. If you feel even the slightest resistance, stop and check the compressor.

6 Guide the connecting rod onto the rod journal. Lubricate the cap that goes with the rod, and line up the marks you stamped on the sides of the rod and cap. Torque the rod nuts to one-third the final torque.

7 If the rod bearings are binding, the crank will be hard to turn. If a ring broke while you were putting in the pistons, you should notice some scratching on the walls. If you see a scratch, pull the piston out and check the rings.

8 Rotate the next rod journal to its bottom position. When the ring compressor is tight, tap on it again to make sure it is square with the block. Then tap the piston into the cylinder.

9 Using a crank turning tool, rotate the first rod journal up. Torque the rod bolts the last two steps. After all the bolts are torqued, rotate the crankshaft to verify that the bearings are not dragging.

4 Check to make sure the crankshaft rod journal is at BDC and the forward mark on the piston is facing the front of the engine. Now tighten the compressor until it pinches tight on the piston. With the compressor against the deck of the block, tap on the compressor's edges so that it sits square to the block on all sides. Look up into the cylinder from below, and slide the connecting rod over so that there is some clearance between it and the crank journal. **(Photo 4)**

5 Using the handle of a hammer, tap the piston solidly enough to make it slide past the grip of the ring com-

pressor; however, if you feel even the slightest resistance, stop and check the compressor. If you see any of the oil scraper rings or compression rings popping out, stop and immediately pull the compressor off. If you are tapping very slowly, and a ring keeps popping out, try hitting a little harder in the beginning so that the piston will move quickly past the entrance at the block deck. Once the piston is in, remove the compressor and tap lightly to move the rod down while guiding it over the rod journal. **(Photo 5)**

6 The protector boots will help guide the rod into place on the crank, and the rod will seat nicely on the rod journal, as long as the bearing is still in place. Lubricate the cap that goes with the rod, and line up the marks you stamped on the sides of the rod and cap to fit the cap on the right way. When the cap is in place, thread the nuts on hand tight, and tighten to one-third of the final torque. (**Photo 6**)

7 Rotate the crank a few times to make sure the rod bearings are not binding and the rings are not scarring the walls of the cylinder. If a ring broke while you were putting in the pistons, you should notice some scratching on the walls. If you see a scratch, run your fingernail against it. If you are concerned that the scratch might be from a broken ring, pull out the piston and check the rings. (**Photo 7**)

8 Rotate the next rod journal to its bottom position. When the ring compressor is tight, tap on it again to make sure it is square with the block. You should start to get a feel for how much force is required to get the rings to slide out of the compressor and past the block deck. With each piston that goes in, you will feel the rotation of the crank getting a bit harder to turn. There should be a steady increase in resistance as each piston is added. (**Photo 8**)

9 Rotate the block upside down. Using a crank turning tool, rotate the first rod journal up. Set the torque wrench to the second of the three increments, and torque all of the rod bolts. Next, set the wrench to the third and final setting and torque all of the bolts. After you have torqued all of the rod journals, leave the wrench on the final setting and go through every bolt once more. Lastly, turn the crankshaft to make sure the rod bearings are not dragging. (**Photo 9**)

Connecting Rod Side Clearance

After all of the pistons and rods are installed, use a feeler gauge to check the rod side clearance **FIGURE 15-20**. Refer to the manufacturer's specifications. If there is not enough side-to-side clearance, make sure the large radius of the connecting rod is toward the rod fillet area on the crankshaft. If the radius of the rod is not facing the fillet area, either the connecting rod was installed on the piston wrong, or the piston is in the cylinder backward. If you check and everything is installed correctly, then the crankshaft was machined wrong. If there is too much clearance, either the crankshaft was machined wrong or the connecting rod's big end is too narrow and should be replaced.

FIGURE 15-20 Checking rod side clearance.

Cylinder Head Installation

With the pistons and rods installed, the short block is complete. The next step is to install the cylinder head or heads (V-type engines). Clean the block deck surface and the decks of the heads with the appropriate cleaner (spray brake cleaner), making sure to leave no fuzz on the surface. The head and block need to be clean and dry, with no particles or lint that may cause the gasket to leak.

If the head bolts are of the torque-to-yield design, then they will need to be replaced with new head bolts. Never reuse torque-to-yield bolts, as they will likely fail in use. If the head bolts are reusable, retrieve them from their storage bin and make sure the threads are clean. If any of the head bolts go into holes that extend into the **water jacket**, it is essential to put some non-hardening sealer on the threads of the bolts to keep the coolant from leaking past the threads. Some oil or assembly lubricant will also be needed on the underside of the bolt heads.

Installing Head Gaskets

Before installing a head gasket, look for "this side up" or "front" labels on the head gaskets. If there are no labels, it should not matter which side goes up. Double-check that for every hole in the block or heads there is a corresponding hole in the gasket.

Most engines use a composition-type gasket that does not require sealant on either side. Some older engines use a metal shim gasket that requires an even coat of a high-tack gasket sealer to be sprayed on both sides or high-heat aluminum paint to be sprayed lightly on both sides. This type of gasket coating should dry before the gasket is installed.

AS-102: Adhesives/Sealants: *The technician can demonstrate an understanding of how surface processes and cohesive/adhesive forces determine the effectiveness of glues, tapes, and sealants.*

When working in an automotive repair facility, the technician will use adhesives and sealants on a regular basis. In the area of engine assembly, there are many applications of parts that require sealing. Every part that requires a gasket or sealant must be installed correctly to avoid a costly mistake resulting in an additional teardown to correct.

Sealant chemistry often uses the terms *cohesive* and *adhesive*. Cohesive comes from a Latin word that means to cling together. An adhesive is a material designed to hold two surfaces together. The adhesion/cohesion theory is part of the Science of Adhesion. Adhesion is the force that holds substrates together in opposition to stresses exerted to pull the substrates apart. Cohesion is the attraction of particles within the adhesive that holds the mass together. The combination of adhesion and cohesive strength determines sealing effectiveness. In most cases, surface preparation determines how well and for how long a bond will hold. The surface cannot be a layer of grease, dirt, oil, or some other contaminant. All surfaces should be properly prepared per instructions of the product being used.

Installing the Head

If you have not done so already, install the safety pin in the stand to keep the engine from spinning upside down. Gently lay the head on the head gasket that is on the block using the alignment dowels to guide the head into place **FIGURE 15-21**. Make sure to lay it down flat and to not slide it on the gasket. Thread in the head bolts by hand. If you have a few different sizes of head bolts, make sure the right bolts go in the right places. Also, remember to use a nonhardening sealer on any bolts that thread into the water jackets.

Torquing Head Bolts

Go through each bolt on both heads, running the bolts down with a ratchet and socket until they are just snug. If the bolts are standard bolts, torque in increments recommended by the manufacturer. The manufacturer will also specify the sequence that the bolts must be torqued. Many engines use either a **torque angle** or a **torque-to-yield** method when tightening the head bolts. The torque angle method is a more precise way of torquing a standard fastener to a predetermined tension. When using this method, the bolts are torqued to a minimal

FIGURE 15-21 Align cylinder head on dowel pins.

specification, say 20 ft-lb, and then tightened a further specified number of degrees, say 90 degrees. This process tends to cause each fastener to create an equal clamping pressure, regardless of any imperfections on the threads that would affect torque readings. The torque-to-yield method uses the same process, except that the fastener is stretched to, or near, its yield point, which means it is at the point where it will not return to its original length when loosened. Thus, the fastener will provide the best overall clamping pressure over a wide range of conditions, such as thermal expansion of the cylinder head and head gasket relaxation. Torque-to-yield bolts cannot be reused; they must be replaced with new fasteners each time they are disassembled.

Sometimes it is hard to keep track of which bolts have been torqued and which have not. Make a note of how many total bolts you have, and count as you go. If you get to what you think is the last bolt in the sequence and your count is one short, then you will know that you missed one. You should double-check regardless, especially when you get to the final torque specification.

To install the heads, follow the steps in **SKILL DRILL 15-9**:

1. Ensure the bolt holes and bolt threads are clean. Use new bolts if they are of the torque-to-yield type. If the head bolts go into holes that have solid bottoms, blow out any debris with compressed air. If specified, oil the threads and the undersides of the heads of the head bolts themselves. Apply some nonhardening sealer to the threads of any bolts that extend into the water jacket. **(Photo 1)**

2. Clean the block deck surface and the decks of the heads with the appropriate cleaner. Install head

gaskets. Look for any "this side up" or "front" labels on the head gaskets. Composition gaskets do not require any sealant. **(Photo 2)**

3 On OHC cam engines, make sure the crankshaft is set to the specified position before installing the head. **(Photo 3)**

4 On OHC engines, make sure the camshaft is set to the specified position before installing the head.

Failure to do so could lead to damaged or bent valves. **(Photo 4)**

5 Carefully lay the head over the alignment dowels of the block and start threading in the bolts. If you have a few different sizes of head bolts, make sure the right bolts go in the right places. One general indicator that they are in the correct holes is that each bolt sticks up from its hole the same amount when set in place.

SKILL DRILL 15-9 | Installing the Heads

1 Clean all the head bolt threads and bores. Use sealer on any bolts that extend into the water jacket. Lubricate the threads and under the heads on other bolts, if specified.

2 Clean the deck surface of the block and head, and install the head gaskets. Look for any "this side up" or "front" labels on the head gaskets.

3 On OHC cam engines, make sure the crankshaft is set to the specified position before installing the head.

4 On OHC engines, make sure the camshaft is set to the specified position before installing the head. Failure to do so could lead to damaged or bent valves.

5 Gently lay the head over the alignment dowels of the block and start threading in the bolts. If torque-to-yield head bolts are used, tighten each bolt in the specified sequence to the specified torque. Torquing may need to be performed in several stages.

6 Install the torque angle gauge and tighten each bolt in the specified sequence to the specified angle. If torquing standard head bolts, torque them in the specified sequence in three increments, resetting the torque wrench and increasing by one-third each time.

6 Run each bolt down finger tight. If using torque-to-yield head bolts, follow the specified sequence and torque the bolts to the proper torque. Achieving proper torque may require two or more passes at specified torques. It may also require loosening and retorquing the bolts a second or third time. **(Photo 5)**

7 Install the torque angle gauge and set it to zero, or set the torque angle wrench to the specified torque angle. Tighten the bolts in sequence to the specified angle. Repeat if a second torque angle is specified.

8 If torquing standard head bolts, torque the bolts to specification in three increments, resetting the wrench and increasing by one-third each time. Cylinder heads require that you torque the bolts in a certain sequence. Typically, you start from the center and tighten in a spiral pattern toward the outer bolts. If your engine has its own particular pattern, follow the instructions in the repair information. **(Photo 6)**

Installing Timing Chain and Gears or Timing Belt—OHC Engines

On OHC engines, the timing chains or belts are installed after the cylinder head is installed. They also use a tensioner to keep the belt or chain properly tensioned. This design can make it harder to get the timing correct, since the tensioner pulls all of the slack to one side of the belt or chain, which causes the cam to rotate slightly. Thus, the cam timing can be out of specifications. There are many different timing set configurations for these engines. It is essential that the correct service information be used when setting the cam-to-crankshaft timing on these types of engines.

Chain Drive

OHC chain drives typically are of the roller chain style, which looks a lot like a bicycle chain. Roller chain has a long life, usually lasting the life of the engine as long as the engine oil is maintained properly. Chains need lubrication to operate, so engine oil is usually sprayed onto the chain from the front of the block. The timing chain area of the engine is sealed from the outside. OHC engines using timing chains have guides and chain tensioners to keep the chain in place, in addition to two or more sprockets. Refer to the service information for timing mark locations and the specific instructions for installing these.

Chain tensioners are installed with the tensioner in the collapsed position **FIGURE 15-22**. When installing the chain, you might be directed to count the chain links

between the mark on the crank sprocket and the mark on the cam sprocket to get the right timing. Usually the timing links are a different color to make alignment easier. Align the links to the chain gear pip marks on both the crank and the cam sprockets **FIGURE 15-23**. Install any chain guides and then release the chain tensioner to take up the slack in the chain. Before rotating the engine, recheck the timing marks to be sure they are still lined up after the tensioner is released. Always refer to the manufacturer's installation procedures and diagrams.

Belt-Driven Timing Sets

Belt-driven timing sets use a flexible belt to transmit drive from the crankshaft to the camshaft. The belt runs more quietly than a chain and does not require lubrication. But timing belts do wear out and need to be changed periodically, typically between 50,000 and 100,000 miles

FIGURE 15-22 Chain tensioner in collapsed position.

FIGURE 15-23 Chain links in position on the timing sprocket marks.

(80,000 to 160,000 km), depending on the vehicle manufacturer. Since they do not need to be lubricated, they are generally behind a timing belt cover that is not sealed to the front of the engine. The cover acts more as a belt guard and to protect it from dirt and debris.

As with the timing chain type of engine, always refer to current service information for timing mark locations. Install the cogged gears onto the camshaft if not already installed, being sure not to forget the keys, if equipped. They should have already been aligned when the cylinder head was on the bench, but it is best to double-check for the proper alignment of the timing marks. Be careful not to move the camshaft very much, as the valves could have an interference fit to the pistons. If the camshaft does need to move substantially, turn the crankshaft so it is approximately 20 to 30 degrees before or after TDC. This will pull all of the pistons down from the top of the cylinder so that the valves will not hit the pistons when the cam is turned. With the timing marks aligned **FIGURE 15-24**, install the timing belt with as much of the slack as possible on the tensioner side of the belt, and then install the belt tensioner **FIGURE 15-25**. Verify that all timing marks are aligned. Always refer to the manufacturer's installation procedures on timing belts and belt tension.

TECHNICIAN TIP

On dual overhead cam (DOHC) engines, it is important to install the correct cam gear on each camshaft. Failure to do so will cause the cam timing to be off, which could lead to valve and piston damage, as well as an engine that will not run. The same thing can happen if the camshafts are installed in the wrong place.

Installing the Oil Pickup Tube and Oil Pump

The oil pump may be located in the oil pan, on the side of the block, or in the timing cover. It is typically driven by the crankshaft or camshaft. It is recommended that you pack the oil pump with assembly lube. Doing so helps to provide the suction that is needed when the engine is started in order to get the oil moving through the pickup tube and into the oil pump. Be sure to install it to the manufacturer's specifications and torque.

The pickup tube generally includes a strainer that prevents chunks of debris from entering the oil pump. It also is designed to pull oil from the bottom of the oil pan. In many cases, the oil pickup tube is not part of the oil pump. The tube is installed as a separate component. Oil pickup tubes come in three different versions—a screw-in style that screws into the oil pump or engine block, a bolt-on type **FIGURE 15-26**, and a press-in style

FIGURE 15-25 Timing belt tensioner installed.

FIGURE 15-26 Bolt-on style oil pickup tube.

FIGURE 15-24 Timing marks aligned.

Timing mark lined up with head surface

FIGURE 15-27. The screw-in style has a pipe thread and requires a nonhardening sealer to ensure that the oil pump does not pull air around the threads. The bolt-on type is bolted onto the pump or block and usually uses a gasket for sealing purposes. The press-in style pickup tube is held in place with an interference fit, but the oil pump needs to be installed first. Be sure to install the oil pump drive gear or shaft before installing the pump, since it cannot be installed later **FIGURE 15-28**. Once the oil pump is mounted, the pickup tube can be installed.

It is usually good practice to adjust the strainer so it is at the proper height inside the bottom of the oil pan. This can be done by installing the pickup tube in the pump just enough so that it is fairly solid but can still twist. Rotate the strainer so that it is obviously going to touch the bottom of the oil pan. Then set the oil pan in place, which will rotate the strainer until the pan contacts both block rails fully. Lift off the oil pan and measure the height of the strainer from the block. Adjust the strainer until it has between 1/4" and 3/8" (6.4–9.5 mm) of clearance from the bottom of the pan. Then tap the pickup tube into the oil pump or block until it is firmly in place. Some engine builders tack-weld the pickup assembly to the oil pump to prevent the pickup tube from falling out or loosening up. If you do weld it in place, make sure the pump is removed from the engine when you weld it and the pump cover is removed from the pump so that there is no chance the welding process will hurt the gears.

Adhesives and Sealers

When installing engine covers, manifolds, and oil pans, sealers are often used to ensure there are no leaks. There are many different engine applications and engine designs, which require various sealers. Refer to the service information for your specific engine. There are also many types of adhesives and brands of room temperature vulcanizing (RTV) oxygen-safe silicone produced. Always follow the manufacturer's instructions when deciding which adhesive or sealer to use.

Adhesives

To help hold the gaskets in place, you can use a product by 3M called trim adhesive, which is contact cement in a liquid or spray form. It does a good job of holding a gasket to a smooth metal surface while the parts are being assembled. The spray type has a spray nozzle that can be controlled and directed in a specific fan direction. However, use caution when you apply it around areas that you do not want any spray adhesive to get inside or on. Use a piece of light cardboard or paper shop rags to catch any overspray.

Silicone Sealers

There are many different silicone sealers, which are based on the temperature range the silicone can withstand or the type of fluid it is designed to seal. RTV is used to help seal fiber gaskets and gasket joints and sometimes on surfaces designed to be assembled with no gasket. Make sure the RTV is labeled oxygen sensor safe. Otherwise, it could harm the oxygen sensors on the engine by coating them with a silicone film, which, after a short time of engine operation, would negatively affect the operation of the oxygen sensor. Be sure to use the appropriate product and follow its instructions.

Applying Gaskets with Adhesive

For cork, felt, or neoprene gaskets, a light coat of adhesive spray is used on each surface of the block and the gasket. Avoid getting overspray into the engine, which can

FIGURE 15-27 Press-in style oil pickup tube.

FIGURE 15-28 Oil pump installed.

be done in two different ways: One way is to spray the gasket only with a heavy coat and then put the sprayed side of the gasket on the block surface and slide it around to smear the adhesive on the block surface. Then pull the gasket off, making sure there is adhesive on both surfaces. Let both the gasket and the block area dry. Position the gasket and make sure it is aligned, because you will not be able to move the gasket after you set it in place. The other way is to spray the gasket and then spray the block carefully, not allowing any overspray to get into the engine. You might have to use thin cardboard or paper towels to block any overspray. Let the adhesive dry and position the gasket, making sure all holes are aligned. Once in place, the gasket will not move.

Applying RTV Silicone

Using silicone RTV on gaskets is debatable. Most technicians agree that RTV can be used on paper gaskets. Some technicians say that cork and cork/rubber gaskets should be installed dry. Other technicians say that neoprene gaskets should use an adhesive rather than RTV, since RTV can make the neoprene slippery causing the gasket to slip out of place during assembly. Do not use RTV on neoprene gaskets with multi-sealing edges. These gaskets are designed so that when one edge fails another edge will seal. If you use RTV on this style of gasket, the RTV fills up the multi-sealing edges and leaves only one sealing edge. Also, RTV should be used in appropriate amounts. Using too much RTV will cause excess RTV to be squeezed out from between the surfaces and form ribbons inside the engine. This excess RTV can then tear away and be carried by oil or coolant throughout the system and clog up the oil pickup screen or passages in the lubrication or cooling system.

Applying RTV Where the Manufacturer Specifies No Gaskets

On some engines, the manufacturer has designed some sealing surfaces that do not require a gasket, only RTV. When using only RTV and no gasket, a moderately larger bead of RTV is required to seal between the two surfaces. An example of this application is an oil pan; the manufacturer may have designed the engine to use no gasket. This is another reason that checking the manufacturer's procedures is so important.

Installing the Oil Pan and Timing Cover

There is a sequence that must be followed during installation of oil pans and timing covers since the parts can overlap one another. For example, in some engines, the timing cover also forms part of the mating surface for the oil pan, so the timing cover must be installed first.

In other arrangements, the bottom of the timing cover has a half-moon shape with a deep groove that holds a neoprene gasket in place, against which the oil pan fits. In this case, the parts are easier assembled if the timing cover is installed first. If the wrong sequence is used, the parts may not line up properly, which could lead to a fluid leak. Refer to the manufacturer's installation specifications for the particular engine you are working on.

To install the timing cover and oil pan, follow the steps in **SKILL DRILL 15-10**:

1. On engines equipped with timing chains, install the timing cover to the front of the engine. Refer to service information to determine the proper sequence of assembly.

2. Make sure the rod bolts are tight, then check your notes and the manual to make sure you have not forgotten to reinstall other parts such as a windage tray. Clean the block rail and the edge of the oil pan with some solvent. Dab some gasket sealant at a few points along the block rail to help the gasket stay lined up over the bolt holes. Dab some silicone sealer at the four points where the rear main seal and the front timing cover seal arch up, away from the block rail. Lay the block rail gaskets in place. If they do not fit perfectly in the corners, you may need to cut a few small pieces with some scissors. You should always follow the manufacturer's instructions, but in most cases you will not need any sealant for rubber or cork gaskets. Gasket sets can come with a few choices for the oil pan front and rear seals. Make sure to pick the right size gasket from the kit that will match your timing cover seal and oil pan. The same thing applies to the rear cap seal. Once you have the right seal, press it firmly into place.

   If you have a cork rear cap gasket, it is a good idea to coil up the gasket and hold its shape together with a rubber band. Doing so will give a pre-curl to the gasket, making it easier to install in the curved slot on the rear cap. With all types of engines, after the front and rear oil pan seals are in place, you should put another four dabs of silicone sealer in each of the corners where the oil pan will curve from the block rail to the arch of the front or rear seal.

3. Lower the oil pan carefully into place. Start with the four corner bolts, which will make it easier to line up all of the others. Thread in the rest of the bolts a few turns by hand. You may need to tap on the pan a little to get some of the bolts to start in their holes, but make sure you do not dislodge the gasket or push it inside the block. When the

bolts are all seated hand tight, switch to a torque wrench. These bolts will have a low torque rating, so make sure your wrench is accurate at low settings. These fasteners are usually torqued in inch-pounds. Work around the pan from the center bolts in a spiral outward to the front and rear bolts.

With almost all oil pan gaskets, it is a good idea to let the pan sit for a minute after you torque the final setting. Then go back through all the bolts again. You will probably find they need a third torquing to achieve the torque specification. If your engine has a thin gap between the oil pan and the timing cover, it is a good idea to lay a thin bead of silicone sealer along this lip. Spread the silicone evenly with a finger.

▶ Oil Priming (Pre-oiling) the Engine

Priming the engine is very important; you want to make sure all moving parts receive oil as soon as the engine is started. There are a couple ways to prime the engine. One way is to spin the oil pump with a drill attached to the pump drive. To do this, you will need a mechanical oil gauge installed in an oil gallery, the correct amount of oil installed in the engine, and a heavy-duty reversible drill. Make sure you spin the oil pump in the correct rotation. Leave the valve cover or covers off so that you can make sure all the oil is getting to the upper valve train. While priming the engine, watch the oil pressure gauge to make sure it reads within the normal measurement.

Another way is to use a pressure bleeder tapped into the engine oil galleries. You will need to release all pressure in the bleeder and empty any oil in the engine, and then fill the bleeder with the correct amount and proper rating of oil you will be using. Close the valve on the hose and pressurize the bleeder. Install the bleeder hose in an oil gallery, install a mechanical oil gauge, and make sure the valve cover is off. Open the valve and make sure the oil reaches all of the valve train. Watch the oil pressure gauge on the engine; it should have a reading close to the pressure bleeder's setting.

To pre-oil the engine, follow the steps in **SKILL DRILL 15-11**:

1. Install the rear camshaft plug, if it has not already been done. Cam plugs are usually narrower than water jacket freeze plugs. Spread a thin layer of nonhardening sealant on the edge of the plug itself. Be careful not to use silicone, and do not put the sealant directly onto the block, as sealant may get into the oil galleries and plug them up. Hammer the plug flush with the opening of the cam bore. The best way to do this is to use a bearing race driver or a similar oversized flat metal object. Tap on the plug until it is flush with the back of the camshaft bore. Then use a large socket to tap the plug in slightly so that it is just inside the sealing lip of the camshaft bore. **(Photo 1)**

2. Install the oil filter. Lubricate the rubber seal of the oil filter with a little engine oil, and thread it on hand tight. **(Photo 2)**

3. Install an oil pressure gauge into one of the ports that lead to the oil gallery.

4. If you have not done so already, install the one-piece rear main seal to finish closing off the oil system.

5. Fill up the crankcase with the type and quantity of engine oil recommended in the repair manual.

6. If the oil pump is driven by the distributor, put an oil pump primer rod into the distributor hole. The primer rod will engage onto the oil pump drive rod so you can spin the oil pump with a drill from the outside of the engine. The drill should be spinning in the same direction that the distributor rotates when the engine is running. Check the repair information for this information. If you spin it the wrong way, the pump will not show any oil pressure on the gauge. Even at normal drill speeds, the oil gauge should read that it has plenty of pressure. Now run the drill and spin the oil pump for about 30 seconds to a minute. **(Photo 3)**

7. When oil pressure builds inside the engine, oil will make it through the galleries and into the crankshaft and the lifters. After oil goes through the lifters, it will move up the pushrods and will start to drip out of the holes in the rocker arms. Make sure this happens for each of the rockers. If you run the drill for a minute or two and a few of the rockers do not produce oil, have a helper rotate the crankshaft two full turns while operating the drill. This will change the positions of the lifters and should make it easier for the remaining lifters to produce oil. Since there are no valve covers installed, be aware that oil might spill out of the head when the rockers get full. **(Photo 4)**

8. If the oil pump is driven by the crankshaft, use a pressurized pre-oiler to pressurize the system and verify that oil is getting to all valves.

9. Once the engine has been pre-oiled, install the valve covers. Rubber-style gaskets should not require any sealant, but may require a gasket adhesive. If you have cork gaskets and want to use some

SKILL DRILL | 15-11 | Pre-oiling the Engine

1. Install the rear camshaft plug, if it has not already been done. Spread a thin layer of nonhardening sealant on the edge of the plug itself and hammer it in place.

2. Install the oil filter. Lubricate the rubber seal of the oil filter with a little engine oil, and thread it on hand tight.

3. Fill the crankcase with the type and quantity of engine oil recommended in the repair information. If the oil pump is driven by the distributor, use a drill to spin the oil pump.

4. Check that oil is reaching the valve train. You may need to rotate the engine two turns to get oil to flow to each valve.

5. If the oil pump is driven by the crankshaft, use a pressurized pre-oiler to pressurize the lubrication system. Once the engine has been pre-oiled, install the valve covers.

kind of sealer, spray one side of the gasket with a high-tack aerosol gasket sealant. Stick the sealed side to the valve cover so that the gasket stays with the cover. When you place the gaskets, make sure the gaskets contact the edges of the heads on all sides so that you do not have any oil leaks once the engine starts. The valve cover bolts do not have a very high torque rating, so be careful not to torque them beyond specifications. **(Photo 5)**

External Engine Components and Accessories

The engine is now ready for installation of the external components, such as the manifolds, sensors, water pump, thermostat, alternator, power steering pump, air-conditioning compressor, or any other component removed during disassembly. Make sure all components are installed in the proper order, as many parts fit behind or over other parts. Also be careful to install and properly tighten all fasteners. You should not have any parts left over that were not replaced with new parts. If you do have leftover parts, determine where they came from.

Installing the Intake Manifold

With the heads installed, the intake manifold is the next component to be installed. New gaskets will be required, which may or may not require additional sealants. Also, the intake manifold bolts must be torqued to the proper specifications, in the proper sequence. It is usually a good idea to tighten the bolts in three steps, one-third of the torque at a time. Refer to service information for the proper torque values and sequence for the manifold bolts. An error here could result in a coolant, oil, or vacuum leak that may be difficult to diagnose and repair after the engine is in the vehicle.

To install the intake manifold, follow the steps in **SKILL DRILL 15-12**:

1. Clean the surfaces of the manifold and head with a solvent, such as brake cleaner. **(Photo 1)**

2. On V-type engines, put some RTV sealant in the four corners where the heads meet the block. Put a thin layer of gasket sealer around the water jacket ports and their mating surfaces on the intake gaskets, if equipped. When the sealer on the gaskets is tacky, line up the bolt holes and stick the gaskets in place. Then spread some more gasket sealer on the tops of the gaskets, around the water jacket ports. On any engine, if the decks of the heads or the block, or both, were machined, the heads will sit a little bit lower and the gap between the intake manifold and the block rail will be smaller. Some gasket sets have rubber or cork gaskets that will be too thick to allow the intake to seat properly. Such gaskets are not recommended. Instead, to seal the block rail to the intake, run a solid bead of silicone sealer along the front and rear upper rails of the block. Run the bead evenly from gasket to gasket. This is a good idea for many engines, whether the decks have been machined or not, because it usually provides a much better seal.

3. When the block is ready, double-check that everything is in place (including the oil splash guard on the bottom of the intake), and then set the intake manifold in place. Get some help if you think you may need it; cast iron manifolds are very heavy, and it is important to lower it as close to its final position as you can. The aim is to need very little adjustment to align the bolt holes. **(Photo 2)**

4. On most V-type engines, the intake manifold bolts lead directly into the oil-soaked area under the valve covers. Treat the threads of these bolts with nonhardening sealer to avoid oil leaks. It is sometimes hard to get to the bolts near the plenum of the intake with a socket. In such cases, use the box end of a wrench. The intake bolts usually have a tightening sequence and specified torque similar to the heads, but the sequence usually starts with the middle bolts near the plenum.

SKILL DRILL | 15-12 | Installing the Intake Manifold

1. Clean the manifold and head sealing surfaces with a solvent cleaner.

2. Make sure the manifold is ready to install, and then set the intake manifold in place.

3. Torque the manifold bolts to specifications.

If you cannot get to all of the bolts with a torque wrench, tighten one of the bolts to the first torque increment, then put a box-end wrench on the same bolt and feel with your hand how tight it is. Now you can tighten the first few inaccessible bolts for each of the three increments, and you should end up with all of the bolts torqued to a similar rating. **(Photo 3)**

Installing the Remaining External Components

The remaining external components may include the balancer, exhaust manifolds, sensors, water pump (on some engines), thermostat, alternator, or any number of other components that will complete the engine assembly. The fasteners of these components are often different from one another, so it is easy to get them confused, which can lead to stripped bolt holes or damaged fasteners. This is where organization during disassembly pays off.

To install the engine externals, follow the steps in **SKILL DRILL 15-13**:

1. Fit the balancer onto the nose of the crank and line it up with its key and keyway. For a press-on balancer, do not hammer it onto the crank. Use a quality harmonic balancer installing tool and

thread it into the same threads as the center bolt of the crank. Draw up the installer nut and start turning. If it seems to bind as it is going in, check it or pull it off and start again. If it starts to go crooked and you do not adjust it, you could end up snapping off the nose of the tool in the end of the crankshaft. When it gets close or is all the way in, the crank will start to spin. If it is not fully seated, install the flex plate, and disable the rotation of the crank to draw it on the last little bit. **(Photo 1)**

2. Make sure your thermostat is installed facing the correct direction before you install the housing. Put gasket sealer on both sides of the thermostat housing gasket and install the housing. O-ring seals typically do not require sealer. **(Photo 2)**

3. Prepare the threads of the exhaust manifold bolts by cleaning them with a wire brush or thread chaser. Apply plenty of anti-seize lubricant. It is messy but absolutely necessary to keep these bolts from seizing up, given the constant amount of heat stress they have to endure. Exhaust gaskets usually do not require any sealant. If the gasket has a metallic finish on one side, that side will typically face toward the manifolds. Some engines do not use exhaust gaskets. Torque all bolts to the proper specifications. **(Photo 3)**

SKILL DRILL 15-13 Installing the Engine Externals

1. Thread a harmonic balancer installing tool into the same threads as the center bolt of the crank. Use the bolt to pull the balancer onto the crankshaft.

2. Install the thermostat in the correct direction. Put gasket sealer on both sides of the thermostat gasket and install the housing. O-ring seals typically do not require sealer.

3. Prepare the threads of the exhaust manifold bolts by cleaning them with a wire brush or thread chaser. Coat the threads with plenty of anti-seize lubricant. Torque bolts to the proper specifications.

Assembling the Accessories

As a last step, there are various accessories that need to be installed on the engine. Depending on the vehicle, these may be installed before or after the engine is installed in the vehicle. Refer to service information for the correct procedure.

To assemble the accessories, follow the steps in **SKILL DRILL 15-14**:

1 Install the miscellaneous accessories. Once again, check your notes from the disassembly. The engine must be brought back to the same state it was in prior to coming out of the chassis. Replace any sensors, plugs, or brackets. You might even go as far as reinstalling the fuel injection system or the carburetor. **(Photo 1)**

2 Install the flex plate. All engines will need the flex plate or flywheel torqued back into place. Many engines require that new bolts be used each time the flywheel is installed; check service information for the engine you are working on. Use a flywheel wrench to keep the crank from moving while you tighten the bolts. Automatic transmission engines will only need the flex plate installed for now.

3 For engines with a flywheel and clutch assembly, the clutch pressure plate and disc should be installed.

After the flywheel is torqued into place, set the friction disc into a centered position. A clutch alignment tool will center this disc where it needs to be, while you fit the pressure plate on and tighten its screws. When the pressure plate is torqued onto the flywheel, the disc will be pinched into its proper position and will not move. Now pull out the alignment tool and put it away. **(Photo 2)**

4 For most engines, the torque rating for the crankshaft front center bolt is the highest in the entire engine. Make sure you have the crank held still with a flywheel wrench while you tighten this bolt. **(Photo 3)**

5 Decide what else you need to bolt to the engine. Keep in mind that you might still need to roll the engine through a doorway or past some other obstacle to get it to the hoisting location, but the aim is to be close to the completed assembly, ready for reinstallation in the vehicle.

Inspecting and Replacing Camshaft and Drive Belt/Chain

The camshaft and drive belt/chain assembly make up an important system for the internal combustion engine. They link the valve train system to the crankshaft and determine the right time in the engine cycle for the valves

SKILL DRILL 15-14 Assembling the Accessories

1 Install the miscellaneous accessories, checking your notes from the disassembly.

2 Install the flex plate and torque it into place. Use a flywheel wrench to hold the flex plate. For engines with a flywheel and clutch assembly, the clutch pressure plate and disc should be installed using a clutch alignment tool to align the clutch disc.

3 Torque the front crankshaft center bolt. Make sure you have the crank held still with a flywheel wrench while you tighten this bolt.

to open and close. Due to operational wear, these areas need to be serviced to make sure the engine continues to operate correctly. The system is first inspected through a visual inspection of the parts to check for wear or worn parts that can be seen. Through visual inspection, it can be determined which parts are in need of replacement by following the manufacturer's recommendations in the service information.

To inspect and replace the camshaft and drive belt/chain, follow the steps in **SKILL DRILL 15-15**:

① Determine all specifications for timing chain or belt tension assembly according to the manufacturer of the engine assembly being serviced. Many manufacturers use the standards that steel timing chains be changed if they have 1/2" (13 mm) of deflection between gears and that timing belts be changed

SKILL DRILL | 15-15 | Inspecting and Replacing the Camshaft and Drive Belt/Chain

1 Determine all specifications for timing chain or belt tension assembly according to the manufacturer of the engine assembly being serviced. Remove all fluids. Remove all components that cover the timing chain/belt assembly, such as the harmonic balancer, water pump, alternators, and power steering pump.

2 Remove the camshaft timing chain/belt cover. Inspect the cover for wear marks, and replace if worn. Look for causes for the worn cover.

Timing mark lined up with head surface

3 With the timing chain/belt cover off and the timing gears and belts/chains in full view, turn the engine over manually to line up the timing marks of the crankshaft and camshaft sprockets with the appropriate marks on the block and head.

4 Inspect the belt/chain and measure for wear, and replace if not within specifications. Measure the clearance between tensioners, if applicable, and replace if not within specifications.

5 Remove the chain or belt following the specified procedure. Use the proper cam holding tool, if specified, to prevent damage to valves.

6 If the tensioner is oil operated, check the oil passages to the tensioner for clogs or buildup of dirt sludge, and clean or replace according to recommendations.

SKILL DRILL | 15-15 | Inspecting and Replacing the Camshaft and Drive Belt/Chain, continued

7 Inspect any guide pulleys for smooth rotation on their bearings, and replace if damaged. With the chain/belt removed, inspect the cam sprockets visually for wear, cracking, and damage. Inspect sprockets for backlash and end play, if applicable, on the vehicle.

8 On engines with any type of variable valve timing, check components for worn and damaged parts on the gears, inspect any oil control devices for leaks, and perform other tests on components according to the manufacturer's recommendations.

9 Reinstall new parts according to the manufacturer's recommendations. Reassemble the timing chain/belt assembly. Turn the crankshaft two complete revolutions by hand, and recheck the timing marks and belt/chain tension. Reassemble components following the specified procedure.

---

after approximately 60,000 miles (100,00 km) of use. If the manufacturer says to disconnect the battery, keep in mind that memory will be lost in many electrical devices and that they will have to be reset.

2 Remove all fluids from systems that require to be removed during timing chain/belt inspection according to the manufacturer's service procedures.

3 Remove all systems that cover the timing chain/belt assembly, such as the harmonic balancer, water pump, alternators, and power steering pump. For internal inspection and replacement of the timing chain/belt assembly, follow the manufacturer's service procedures. **(Photo 1)**

4 Note: In some operations, the manufacturer will want to replace the water pump or other devices that are operated by the chain/belt assembly.

5 Remove the camshaft timing chain/belt cover. Inspect the metal or nonmetal cover for any wear marks. Replace if worn according to the manufacturer's specifications. Look for possible causes for the worn cover. **(Photo 2)**

6 With the timing chain/belt cover off and the timing gears and belts/chains in full view, turn the engine over manually to align the timing marks of the crankshaft and camshaft sprockets with the appropriate marks on the block and head. **(Photo 3)**

7 Inspect the chain and measure for wear. Replace if not within the manufacturer's specifications.

8 Measure the clearance between tensioners, if applicable, and replace if not within specifications or according to the manufacturer's recommendation. **(Photo 4)**

9 Remove the chain or belt following the specified procedure. Use the proper cam holding tool, if specified, to prevent damage to valves. **(Photo 5)**

10 If the tensioner is oil operated, check the oil passages to the tensioner for clogs or buildup of dirt sludge, and clean or replace according to the manufacturer's recommendations. **(Photo 6)**

11 Inspect any guide pulleys for smooth rotation on their bearings, and replace if damaged or according to the manufacturer's recommendations.

12 With the chain/belt removed, inspect the cam sprockets visually for wear, cracking, and damage.

13 Inspect sprockets for backlash and end play, if applicable, on the vehicle being inspected according to the manufacturer's recommendations. (**Photo 7**)

14 On engines with any type of variable valve timing, check components visually for worn and damaged parts on the gears, inspect any oil control devices for leaks, and perform other tests on components according to the manufacturer's recommendations. (**Photo 8**)

15 Reinstall new parts according to the manufacturer's recommendations and specifications. Reassemble the timing chain/belt assembly and adjust if needed according to specifications. (**Photo 9**)

16 Turn the crankshaft two complete revolutions by hand, and recheck the timing marks and belt/chain tension.

17 Reassemble all components following the specified procedure.

Establishing Camshaft Position Sensor Indexing

Camshaft position sensors must be positioned correctly so that they accurately signal the position of the camshaft to the power train control module and the ignition module. Any misadjustment of the sensor will cause the fuel system timing to be off. Most newer engines do not have an adjustable camshaft position sensor, so indexing is usually needed only on sensors that can be manually adjusted. The adjustment can typically be made in one of two ways: A special tool can be used to properly align the sensor or a lab scope can be used to compare the camshaft position sensor adjustment to the crankshaft position sensor. If one channel of the lab scope is connected to the camshaft position sensor signal wire and another channel is connected to the crankshaft position sensor signal wire, then when the engine is running, the camshaft position sensor can be adjusted so they align. This is also a great way to measure timing chain or belt stretch on a vehicle with nonadjustable camshaft sensors. The greater the two signals are out of line, the more stretch in the belt or chain.

To establish camshaft position sensor indexing, follow the steps in **SKILL DRILL 15-16**:

1 Attach a lab scope to the crankshaft position sensor signal wire and the camshaft position sensor signal wire.

2 Start the engine and observe the lab scope. The readings should line up. Adjust the camshaft position

sensor, if adjustable, to bring it in line with the crankshaft position sensor.

Inspecting and Replacing Valve Stem Seals on an Assembled Engine

It is sometimes necessary to replace the valve stem seals on an assembled engine. This is performed when the engine is in relatively good condition but the valve seals are causing the engine to burn oil that is getting past the valve seal and valve guides. The seals can be changed once the engine is disassembled far enough to remove the valve springs. Removing the valve springs presents a problem. With the valve springs off, there is nothing to hold the valves from falling down into the cylinders. Thus, compressed air, typically from a cylinder leakage tester, is used to hold the valves closed while the valve spring is off. Careful work is required around the valve so the pressure seal is not broken and the valve dropped into the cylinder. Once the valve springs are off, the seal can be replaced with a new one. When you do so, use a special sleeve that fits over the valve keeper grooves and protects the seal as it is installed.

To replace valve stem seals on an assembled engine and to inspect valve spring retainers, locks/keepers, and valve lock/keeper grooves, follow the steps in **SKILL DRILL 15-17**:

1 Remove any engine components that are in the way of removing the valve cover(s), then remove the valve cover(s). (**Photo 1**)

2 Remove the rocker arms or cam followers. (**Photo 2**)

3 Rotate the engine so the cylinder you are working on is at TDC on the compression stroke, and pressurize the cylinder. If the engine rotates, reset it in the proper position. (**Photo 3**)

4 Use a socket and hammer to tap on the valve retainers. This will help break the keepers loose from the retainer. (**Photo 4**)

5 Use a spring compressor to compress the valve spring, and remove the keepers and valve spring assembly. Using a magnet may help to remove the keepers. Do not allow them to fall into the engine, as they may become lost and pose a hazard to the engine.

6 Remove the old valve seal by carefully pulling it off of the valve stem. Remove any broken pieces that may be lying in the head. (**Photo 5**)

7 Install the protective sleeve over the valve stem. Lubricate the valve stem with clean engine oil, and install the valve seal into position. The valve stem

SKILL DRILL   15-17   Replacing Valve Stem Seals and Inspecting Valve Spring Retainers, Locks/Keepers, and Valve Lock/Keeper Grooves

1 Remove any engine components that are in the way of removing the valve cover(s). Remove the valve cover(s).

2 Remove the rocker arms or cam followers.

3 Rotate the engine so the cylinder you are working on is at TDC on the compression stroke, and pressurize the cylinder. If the engine rotates, reset it in the proper position.

4 Use a socket and hammer to tap on the valve retainers.

5 Use a spring compressor to compress the valve spring, and remove the keepers and valve spring assembly. Remove the old valve seal.

6 Install the protective sleeve over the valve stem. Lubricate the valve stem, and install the valve seal into position. The valve stem may need to be pushed onto the valve stem boss.

SKILL DRILL	15-17	Replacing Valve Stem Seals and Inspecting Valve Spring Retainers, Locks/Keepers, and Valve Lock/Keeper Grooves, continued

7 Reinstall the valve spring and keepers. Repeat the process on the other valve(s) on that cylinder, then repeat the process for the valve seals on the other cylinders. Reassemble the engine and check for proper operation.

may need to be pushed onto the valve stem boss. (**Photo 6**)

8 Reinstall the valve spring and keepers, making sure everything is seated properly.

9 Repeat the process on the other valve(s) on that cylinder. And then repeat the process for the valve seals on the other cylinders. Reassemble the engine and check for proper operation. (**Photo 7**)

Wrap-up

Ready for Review

▶ Preparation work necessary prior to engine assembly includes recleaning the engine block and crankshaft passages; ensuring piston, ring, and block clearances are within specifications; and determining the correct direction for piston installation on the connecting rod.

▶ Engine assembly includes:

- Check piston-to-cylinder wall clearance by using an outside micrometer.
- Check piston ring end gaps prior to installing piston rings.
- Piston pins are full-floating or semi-floating pins (wrist pins).
- It is a good idea to always perform a temporary test buildup of the rotating assembly (including cylinder heads and valve train).
- Ensure that main bearings are properly sized to the crank and that the bearing cap and saddle are clean and dry.
- Main bearing clearance must meet the manufacturer's specifications and can be measured using an inside micrometer, outside micrometer, bore gauge, or Plastigauge.
- Check thrust bearing end play, as this controls crankshaft end play.
- Check rod bearing, internal, and piston-to-valve clearances.
- Two methods for checking piston-to-valve clearance are clay and dial indicator.
- The clay method clearance check uses a valve impression in clay to indicate where the valve and piston may have interference.
- The dial indicator method checks clearance at various piston positions.
- Paint the engine to protect it from rust and corrosion.
- Install new soft plugs and cleaned oil gallery plugs.

- Install the crankshaft, first ensuring that main bearings are clean and properly lubricated.
- Carefully install piston rings with any marks facing the correct way.
- Pistons can be installed after all piston prep work is finished, including properly positioning piston rings; lubricating pistons, rings, and cylinder walls; compressing piston rings; and lubricating connecting rod bearing inserts and rod journal.
- Check rod side clearance with a feeler gauge following piston and rod installation.
- Check the height of the piston to the cylinder block deck using a depth micrometer.
- Install the cylinder head(s) after ensuring the head and block are clean and dry.
- Use new torque-to-yield head bolts or ensure reusable bolts have clean threads.
- Ensure the head gasket is properly positioned and apply sealant if necessary.
- Torque head bolts to the manufacturer's specifications.
- Install the timing belt (or chains) following cylinder head installation; ensure it is properly tensioned.
- Ensure timing marks on chains and belts are aligned according to the manufacturer's specifications.
- Install the oil pump and oil pickup tube.
- Oil pickup tubes may be one of three types: screw in, bolt on, or press in.
- Only use adhesives and sealers that meet service requirements for the specific engine you are working on.
- Room temperature vulcanizing (RTV) silicone should not be used on neoprene gaskets with multi-sealing edges, but is safe for paper gaskets.
- Priming the engine will ensure all moving parts receive oil once the engine is started.

- The engine can be primed by spinning the oil pump with a drill attached to the pump drive or by using a pressure bleeder tapped into the engine oil galleries.
- The following external engine components should be installed in the proper order: manifolds, sensors, water pump, thermostat, alternator, balancer, power-steering pump, and air-conditioning compressor.

- The first external component to install is the intake manifold.
- Install engine accessories after installation of the external components.
- The final step is to visually inspect the camshaft and drive belt/chain assembly and to replace parts as necessary.

Key Terms

degree wheel A disc with 360 one-degree markings near its outer edge; it bolts to the front of the crankshaft and is used to check valve and cam timing.

long block An engine assembly that includes the short block and adds the valve train cylinder heads, timing cover, oil pan, and, in some cases, manifolds.

outside micrometer A precision measuring instrument meant to measure the outside of components. It is usually accurate to 0.0001" (0.0025 mm).

pip mark A small indent or dimple on the piston ring that indicates which side of the ring is installed upward. It is also used on some timing sprockets.

Plastigauge® The trademarked name for a plastic gauging material used to check the clearances between two surfaces.

short block An engine assembly that includes the engine block, camshaft, timing set, pistons, rods, and crankshaft installed.

tang A raised or slightly bent corner on an engine bearing shell that fits into a matching recess in the bearing mounting surface to keep the bearing from rotating in the bore.

torque angle A tightening procedure in which a bolt is torqued to a set torque value and then tightened using a measured angle instead of a torque value. Example: A bolt is torqued to 40 ft-lb and then tightened another 90 degrees.

torque-to-yield A tightening procedure in which a bolt is designed to be slightly elastic when tightened; the elastic bolt retains an even pressure on the head gasket.

water jacket That area of the engine block casting that holds the engine coolant; cylinder head bolt holes are sometimes drilled through to the water jacket, requiring the bolt threads to be sealed.

ASE-Type Questions

1. Tech A says that measuring piston ring end gap in the cylinder bore will verify that the rings are properly sized for the bore. Tech B says that measuring piston-to-cylinder bore clearance determines the compression ratio of the cylinder. Who is correct?
   a. Tech A
   b. Tech B
   c. Both A and B
   d. Neither A nor B

2. Tech A says that semi-floating wrist pins can be pressed into the rods. Tech B says that a rod heater can be used to install semi-floating wrist pins. Who is correct?
   a. Tech A
   b. Tech B
   c. Both A and B
   d. Neither A nor B

3. Tech A says that the bearing tang's purpose is to be used as a balance pad that can be ground, if needed, to lighten the bearing. Tech B says that bearing tangs are designed to prevent the bearing from spinning in its bore. Who is correct?
   a. Tech A
   b. Tech B
   c. Both A and B
   d. Neither A nor B

4. Tech A says that the wider the Plastigauge is squished out, the smaller the bearing clearance. Tech B says that the narrower the Plastigauge is squished out, the smaller the bearing clearance. Who is correct?
   a. Tech A
   b. Tech B
   c. Both A and B
   d. Neither A nor B

5. Tech A says that when checking rod bearing clearance, it is best to install Plastigauge on the bearing in the rod. Tech B says that when checking rod bearing clearance, it is best to install Plastigauge on the cap bearing. Who is correct?
   a. Tech A
   b. Tech B
   c. Both A and B
   d. Neither A nor B

6. Tech A says that rod bearings are held in place by the torque of the rod bolts crushing the bearing into the bore. Tech B says that piston rings are installed so that all ring gaps are not lined up with each other. Who is correct?
   a. Tech A
   b. Tech B
   c. Both A and B
   d. Neither A nor B

7. Tech A says that when installing a performance camshaft, the cam-to-lifter clearance should be measured and recorded. Tech B says that when installing a performance camshaft, piston-to-valve clearance should be checked. Who is correct?
   a. Tech A
   b. Tech B
   c. Both A and B
   d. Neither A nor B

8. Tech A says that when installing rod caps on a rod, the bearing tangs should be installed on the same side of the rod. Tech B says that when installing rod caps on a rod, the bearing tangs should be installed on opposite sides of the rod. Who is correct?
   a. Tech A
   b. Tech B
   c. Both A and B
   d. Neither A nor B

9. Tech A says that torque-to-yield head bolts are special bolts that are reusable. Tech B says that head bolts should be torqued in only one step to provide the proper bolt stretch. Who is correct?
   a. Tech A
   b. Tech B
   c. Both A and B
   d. Neither A nor B

10. Tech A says that the use of some RTV sealants to seal components on an engine can damage the oxygen sensor. Tech B says that prelubing an engine is very important. Who is correct?
    a. Tech A
    b. Tech B
    c. Both A and B
    d. Neither A nor B

SECTION III

Automatic Transmission

CHAPTER 16

NATEF Tasks

Automatic Transmission and Transaxle
General   Page

■ Research applicable vehicle and service information, fluid type,
  vehicle service history, service precautions, and technical service bulletins.   **MLR** **AST** **MAST**   463

Knowledge Objectives

After reading this chapter, you will be able to:
1. Describe the principles of operation of the automatic transmission. (pp 452–454)
2. Explain the principles of a torque converter. (pp 454–459)
3. Explain the basic operation of planetary gear sets. (pp 459–463)
4. Identify the different common components of the automatic transmission. (pp 463–471)
5. Describe band and clutches, servos, and multidisc clutches as they relate to an automatic transmission.
   (pp 471–474)

Automatic Transmission Fundamentals

Skills Objectives

There are no skills objectives for this chapter.

Introduction

Automatic transmissions were once considered an expensive option on automobiles. Today, the majority of vehicles sold in the United States are equipped with automatic transmissions as standard equipment. Given the number of automatic transmission vehicles being produced, it is necessary for every technician to have a working knowledge of automatic transmission fundamentals even if they may never rebuild a transmission while working in the field. Technicians will come across problems that will mask themselves as transmission problems only to be correctly diagnosed later, after transmission replacement, as a problem relating to an entirely different system, or vice versa. For example, a plugged catalytic converter can make a transmission shift erratically, or a bad vehicle speed sensor can make a transmission not shift at all. In this section, we will cover the types of automatic transmissions, theory of operation, service and repair procedures, and diagnosis of hydraulically and electronically controlled transmissions.

Function of an Automatic Transmission

An automatic transmission has two major functions that separate it from a manual transmission. First, the transmission can select and shift gears without input from the driver. This function is accomplished within the gear train of the transmission along with the aid of the hydraulic system. Second, the transmission can automatically couple and uncouple from the engine when needed, much like a clutch on a manual transmission vehicle but without any work by the driver. This is the function of the torque converter. Without the ability to automatically connect and disconnect the transmission from the engine, a vehicle would stall when it came to a stop, much like a manual transmission vehicle will do if the driver forgets to depress the clutch pedal. These two functions separate automatic transmissions from manual transmissions and will be discussed in depth over the next several chapters.

Types of Automatic Transmissions

There are several types or classifications of automatic transmissions: conventional transmissions, transaxles, dual clutch, continuously variable, a Honda/Saturn type of transmission, and hybrid transmissions. Each of these types of automatic transmissions has elements common to the conventional transmission, but we will explain only the major differences here.

A conventional automatic transmission uses one or more planetary gear sets to create several gear ratios needed to drive the vehicle. Conventional automatic transmissions are typically connected to the engine through a torque converter. The torque converter will be covered in detail later in the chapter. The gears inside a conventional transmission are constantly meshed to each other. Holding devices, such as clutches or bands, will stop the rotation of gears or drive the gears in a planetary gear set in order to create the needed gear ratio.

In the 1970s most manufacturers developed front-wheel drive vehicles for several reasons: improved traction over rear-wheel drive vehicles, less overall

You are the Automotive Technician

It is your second day as a new technician and you are asked to report to the main office. Your supervisor informs you that your first oil change of the day will include checking and possibly replacing the automatic transmission fluid (ATF). Before you can begin working on the shop floor, your supervisor asks you to review the shop manual for directions on handling and disposing of hazardous fluids. After completing your first oil change, you take a sample of transmission fluid and put it on a piece of white paper towel. Contaminants are left on the towel, indicating that the transmission fluid is dirty. Your recommendation to the customer is to drain and replace the transmission fluid. The customer is adamant about wanting only an oil change at this time.

1. How do you convince the customer that his transmission fluid needs to be replaced?
2. Why is it necessary to check the manufacturer's recommendation and technical service bulletins when replacing any fluid in vehicles?
3. What are some of the additives in automatic transmission fluid and what is their purpose?

weight, and increased passenger compartment space. On front-wheel drive vehicles, a **transaxle** is often used, rather than a typical transmission. A transaxle is a conventional transmission that has a built-in differential and final drive gear **FIGURE 16-1**. The differential allows for the vehicle to make turns. When a vehicle turns, the wheels on the outside of the turning circle must spin faster than the ones on the inside of the turning circle. Each wheel will follow a circle with a different radius. Without a differential, the wheels would not be able to spin at different speeds, resulting in scuffing of tires, binding in the drive train, and probable broken drive train parts. On most rear-wheel drive vehicles, the differential and final drive gear are located in the rear axle assembly. Some rear-wheel drive vehicles, such as late-model Chevy Corvettes, will also use a transaxle assembly located in the rear of the vehicle while the engine is located in the front of the vehicle. The Corvette uses this transaxle arrangement to better distribute weight between the front and rear wheels to improve handling.

Dual-clutch transmissions are a newer type of automatic transmission that uses two, typically wet, clutches in place of a **standard torque converter** to connect the engine to the transmission **FIGURE 16-2**. A wet clutch is one that is immersed in hydraulic oil or transmission fluid rather than being dry like a conventional manual transmission clutch. Each clutch is connected to different driving gears. Clutch 1 would be connected to gears 1, 3, and 5, while clutch 2 would power gears 2, 4, and 6. The transmission operates by locking the individual driving gears to the output shaft in order to change the speed of the output shaft. Their operation is similar in some ways to that of a manual transmission, but the changing of gears is controlled by the vehicle computer, not the driver.

Continuously variable transmissions (CVTs) are transmissions that do not use typical gears as in other transmissions. Rather, CVTs commonly use two pulleys that change diameter in response to vehicle load and speed. There is a large, heavy metal belt connecting the two pulleys **FIGURE 16-3**. When the vehicle is starting from a stop, the input pulley, which is coupled to the engine, has a small

FIGURE 16-2 An example of a dual-clutch transmission.

FIGURE 16-3 The pulleys and metal belt of a CVT transmission.

FIGURE 16-1 A typical front-wheel drive vehicle transaxle. Note the differential components inside the case.

diameter while the output pulley, which is coupled to the drive wheels, has a large diameter. This size difference creates a large amount of torque multiplication as the smaller pulley will turn approximately three times for every one turn of the output pulley. When the vehicle reaches cruising speed, the input pulley will have compressed, causing the diameter of the pulley to increase, while the output pulley will reduce in diameter. At this point the output pulley will spin up to three times for every revolution of the input pulley. Using this system, the transmission does not have fixed gear ratios like a conventional transmission; instead it is able to vary the gear ratio infinitely within the changing diameters of the pulleys. This variability allows the engine to operate in its most efficient revolutions per minute (rpm) range to save fuel.

Many Honda and Saturn vehicles use an automatic transmission that more closely resembles a manual transmission, as they do not use planetary gear sets. These transmissions are sometimes called dual-shaft transmissions because they have a main shaft and a countershaft, like in a manual transmission **FIGURE 16-4**. In these transmissions, the synchronizer assemblies that would be in a manual transmission are replaced with multidisc clutch packs to engage the individual gears onto the main shaft.

Hybrid vehicles use drive trains that can be categorized as series or parallel hybrid drive trains. In a series drive train, the power going into the transmission from the engine is supplemented with power from an electric motor. In a **series hybrid drive train**, the electric motor is not typically able to propel the vehicle on its own. This electric motor is often placed between the engine and the transmission.

A **parallel hybrid drive train** has two or more methods for the power to flow through the transmission. The engine can mechanically send power through the transmission to the wheels, or one or more electric motors can send power through the transmission to the wheels. Either the electric motors or the gasoline engine can propel the vehicle along, individually or in combination.

A **series-parallel hybrid drive train** is designed so that it can function as both a series hybrid and a parallel hybrid. It uses what is called a **power-splitting transmission (PST) FIGURE 16-5**. This transmission is sometimes referred to as a type of CVT transmission. It uses a planetary gear set to obtain an infinitely adjustable transmission. It allows power to be applied to the planetary gear set (epicyclic gearing) through three sources: the internal combustion engine (ICE) and two motors/generators. This design is an ingenious application of the planetary gear set, as in its normal use one member is held and another is driven. But in the case of a hybrid vehicle, where you have more than one power source, two components

FIGURE 16-4 A Honda automatic transmission with a main shaft and countershaft.

FIGURE 16-5 A power splitting transmission (PST) uses a planetary gear set to obtain an infinitely adjustable transmission.

can be driven. Moreover, they can be driven at different speeds, and in the case of the electric motors, they can be driven in reverse. This ability to drive more than one member at various speeds allows the planetary gear to act like a CVT. In this configuration, the planetary gear set acts as a power divider and uses all three power sources or two generators to balance the overall needs of the system, including vehicle speed, traction motor battery charge, and ICE efficiency. This system is operated by sophisticated computer controls. Hybrids and CVT transmissions are covered in greater detail in the chapter on that topic.

▶ Torque Converters
Torque Converter Principles

The purpose of a vehicle transmission is to transmit engine torque to the driving wheels. The transmission needs to be able to adapt the engine torque to meet the speed and power demands of the vehicle. In a manual transmission, engine torque is controlled by the driver manually selecting the proper gear. In an automatic transmission, torque is also controlled by selecting the proper gear, but in this case, gear selection is automatic. The transmission also works in concert with the torque converter to modify the engine's torque **FIGURE 16-6**.

The torque converter is mounted between the engine and the transmission, in the same place as a manual transmission clutch **FIGURE 16-7**. The torque converter effectively connects the engine flywheel to the input shaft of the transmission. The torque converter does the same job as a manual clutch, transmitting engine torque to the input shaft of the transmission. But it can do one thing a manual transmission clutch cannot do—multiply torque from the engine to the input shaft

of the transmission when required by driving conditions. This is one reason that vehicles equipped with automatic transmissions make good tow vehicles. The torque converter can multiply the engine torque when starting from a standstill, which is just what is needed when pulling a boat trailer out of the water on a steep boat ramp. How can it do that, you ask? Well, keep reading and we will explain how each of the torque converter components work together to multiply torque under certain conditions.

Fluid Couplers

Early automatic transmissions used a **fluid coupler** rather than a torque converter. A fluid coupler is basically two fans facing each other **FIGURE 16-8**. One fan is the driving fan, and it is driven by the engine. The second fan is attached to the input shaft of the transmission. When the fluid is thrown off of the driving fan, it hits the driven fan, causing the second fan to begin to spin. When the second fan spins, the input shaft of the transmission also begins to spin.

The device is called a fluid coupler because none of the converter components are physically connected to the others; rather, the force of the fluid flow causes the transfer of power. This fluid coupler acts as an automatic clutch. At engine idle speeds, it allows the engine to operate while the vehicle is stationary and the transmission is in a drive range, without the driver having to shift the transmission to neutral or step on a clutch pedal.

Modern transmissions no longer use fluid couplers, but the principle of the torque converter operation is still similar to the fluid coupler. In its simplest form, a single-stage torque converter has three elements: the impeller,

FIGURE 16-6 A typical torque converter that has been removed from a vehicle.

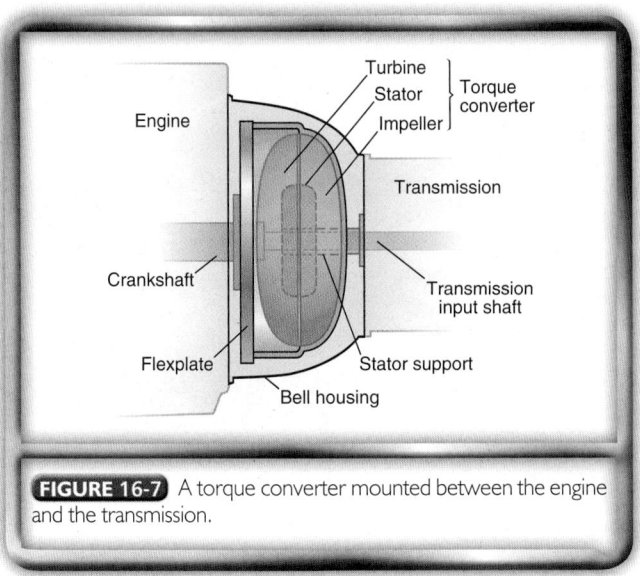

FIGURE 16-7 A torque converter mounted between the engine and the transmission.

FIGURE 16-8 One fan driving a second fan functions much like a fluid coupler, with air as the medium rather than transmission fluid.

the turbine, and the stator **FIGURE 16-9**. All three have angled or curved vanes and are contained in a single housing. They are separated from each other by thrust bearings, but maintain a close relationship for efficient torque transmission.

The impeller has a large number of vanes attached to the converter housing to form the driving member (like the fan that is plugged in for the fluid coupler) **FIGURE 16-10**. The vanes rotate with the housing as the engine runs. Each vane has a slight curvature and is set radially in the case.

The turbine is similar in construction to the impeller, but with more vanes and a greater curvature. The direction of curvature of the turbine vanes is opposite to that of the impeller vanes. The turbine is free to rotate in the housing, and the center hub has splines that mate with splines on the input shaft of the transmission **FIGURE 16-11**.

When the fluid coming from the impeller rotates the turbine, the transmission input shaft also rotates.

Both the impeller and the turbine are fitted with a guide ring. This ring helps to secure the vanes in position. It also reduces turbulence as fluid is flowing in a circle from the impeller to the turbine, and back to the impeller again. It also improves torque converter efficiency.

The stator has a small set of curved blades attached to a central hub and is positioned between the impeller and the turbine. The center hub is mounted on a one-way clutch splined to a stator support shaft **FIGURE 16-12**. The stator support shaft is attached to the transmission case and does not spin. The one-way clutch allows the stator to rotate only in the same direction as the impeller. Trying to rotate the stator in the opposite direction locks the stator on the support shaft and holds it stationary.

FIGURE 16-9 A torque converter that has been cut open to reveal the impeller, turbine, and stator.

FIGURE 16-11 A turbine mounted inside the converter case. Note that the turbine is free to spin inside the housing on bearings.

FIGURE 16-10 An impeller brazed to the housing of the torque converter.

FIGURE 16-12 A stator removed from a torque converter.

Converter Operation

When the engine starts, the transmission pump rapidly fills and pressurizes the converter. The impeller is driven by the engine and turns at crankshaft speed. The turbine is splined to the transmission input shaft. When a gear is selected by the driver, the input shaft becomes locked to the output shaft of the transmission through the various gears, bands, and clutches in the transmission. Centrifugal force throws fluid between the impeller vanes outward, around the back of the guide ring in a forward direction. This is because of the shape of the housing and the curvature of the vanes. With the engine idling, little torque is transferred from the impeller to the turbine, as the fluid flow is too slow. When the engine accelerates, higher impeller speed discharges the fluid across and against the turbine vanes with greater force, causing the turbine to begin to spin and transferring torque to the input shaft of the transmission.

The fluid, still at high velocity, now flows between the turbine vanes. The fluid leaves the turbine in a direction opposite to impeller rotation due to the curvature of the turbine vanes. In a fluid coupler, this fluid flow would then strike the impeller in the opposite direction of impeller rotation, reducing efficiency and torque. In a torque converter, the stator redirects the fluid so that it reenters the impeller in the same direction as impeller rotation **FIGURE 16-13**. The energy that was left in the fluid after turning the turbine is recycled and helps to spin the impeller, which allows the engine to turn faster. This process creates torque multiplication. During torque multiplication, the stator remains stationary while the turbine and impeller spin.

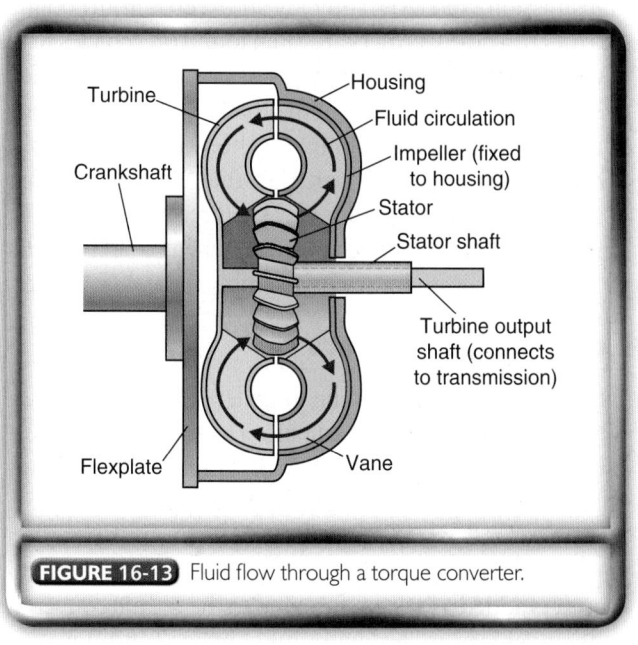

FIGURE 16-13 Fluid flow through a torque converter.

Torque Multiplication

Torque multiplication exists only when there is a difference in speed between the impeller and the turbine. The amount of torque multiplication depends on load. When the turbine is stalled, it has a maximum torque multiplication of about 2.5:1 for most passenger vehicles.

<u>Stall</u> is an operating condition where the turbine is stationary and the engine throttle is wide open, making the rotational speed of the impeller as high as possible. Stall can be approximated when a vehicle moves from rest, up an incline, towing a heavy trailer. Instantaneously, as the vehicle begins to move, maximum torque multiplication occurs because there is a large difference between the speed of the impeller and the turbine. At a stall speed of 2100 rpm, if the torque at that speed is 200 ft-lbs (271.16 Nm), the torque input to the transmission could be as high as 2.5 times that value, which is 500 ft-lbs (677.91 Nm). This torque enters the transmission, where it is multiplied further by the planetary gears, and again at the final drive assembly, before being applied to the vehicle's wheels.

Safety

Stall speed can be tested by performing a stall test (brake torque) in the shop. To perform this test, place the transmission in low gear, apply the brake pedal fully, and then carefully push the throttle open all the way. The maximum rpm the engine achieves is the stall speed. This can be a dangerous test and should only be performed under your supervisor's direct guidance.

This multiplication tapers off as the turbine speed begins to match the speed of the impeller. When turbine speed reaches around 90% of impeller speed, torque multiplication falls to zero. Torque multiplication is then about 1:1. This is known as the coupling point. At the coupling point, fluid flow from the turbine vanes is relatively low, but it is at high speed, following the direction of the torque converter rotation. The rapidly turning turbine discharges its fluid against the back of the stator blades. This force unlocks the stator's one-way clutch, allowing the stator to rotate with the fluid. The stator, turbine, and impeller all rotate as one unit at this time. Unlocking the stator prevents turbulence in the fluid and improves efficiency by preventing the stator from being in the way of the fluid flow.

Fluid Flow

The rotating impeller carries the fluid with it inside the converter housing. The fluid is rotating around with each of the three converter components. This is known as **rotary flow**. At the same time, centrifugal force moves the fluid outward, away from the converter axis. During torque multiplication, the shape of the converter case makes the fluid flow in a circular motion, through the impeller, turbine, and stator. This is known as **vortex flow**. Combining these two fluid flows produces a progressive circular, or spiraling, motion. This is known as the spiral flow **FIGURE 16-14**.

In a stalled converter, fluid flows at high velocity from the revolving impeller through the stationary turbine and stator. This condition results in a fast-moving vortex flow and high torque multiplication. When the turbine starts to rotate and increases in speed, the centrifugal force on the fluid in the turbine opposes the high-velocity flow from the impeller, reducing vortex flow and torque multiplication. At coupling point, the vortex flow of fluid is slight and there is no torque multiplication. The converter now acts as a fluid coupler.

During acceleration or hill climbing, the torque needed by the driveshaft can exceed the engine output torque. As a result, the turbine slows, causing an increase in vortex flow. This again causes torque multiplication, although at a slower output rpm. The converter automatically adjusts its output, within design limits, to meet driveshaft requirements.

Heat Exchanger

Torque converter slip and loss of power through the transmission produce heat, which must be dissipated. At stall, a lot of engine output is converted into heat, bringing the oil operating temperature closer to its boiling point. Excessive temperature can produce cavitation bubbles in the fluid, which reduce converter efficiency. It can also shorten the life of the transmission fluid greatly. Too hot and it oxidizes; too cold and it does not lubricate as well. Most automatic transmission vehicles use a heat exchanger, sometimes called a transmission cooler, in one tank of the radiator. In this way, the transmission fluid can be cooled, but the engine coolant at the outlet side of the radiator will prevent it from overcooling the transmission fluid.

Fluid flows from the pump to the converter. Since the converter creates a lot of heat, the fluid then flows through the heat exchanger before returning to the transmission where it is used to lubricate the planetary gears and operate the transmission. Heavy-duty vehicles or those with towing packages installed have an extra external transmission cooler installed in front of the radiator to help cool the fluid. When using an external transmission fluid cooler, it is generally agreed that it is best to run the transmission fluid through the external cooler first and then through the cooler in the radiator. Doing so prevents overcooling of the transmission fluid.

> ### ▶ TECHNICIAN TIP
>
> If installing an additional transmission cooler onto a vehicle, the lines should be set up so the fluid flows from the converter to the add-on transmission cooler in front of the radiator. From the add-on cooler, it should flow to the factory heat exchanger in the radiator before returning to the transmission. This arrangement allows the fluid to warm up in cold operating conditions to prevent excessive transmission wear and harsh shifting.

Some manufacturers incorporate a transmission fluid warmer that uses engine coolant to warm up the automatic transmission fluid (ATF) quickly and keep it from cooling too much. These warmers are often found on vehicles with CVTs. They help reduce the viscosity of the ATF, which reduces the friction losses of the thicker ATF. At least one manufacturer routes coolant to the warmer assembly, which provides heat to warm up the ATF. The warmer assembly uses a thermostatic valve to direct the flow of ATF through the heated warmer assembly when the ATF is cold, or bypass the heated warmer assembly if the ATF is hot.

Lock-up Converters

Under a drive condition, the impeller and turbine generally never achieve a 1:1 speed ratio. The turbine will almost always spin slightly slower than the impeller. This means that the converter is typically slipping approximately 5% to 10% when comparing engine speed to transmission input speed. During the late 1970s and early 1980s, manufacturers added a lock-up function to the torque converter in their vehicles to deal with this slippage condition.

FIGURE 16-14 Rotary fluid flow, vortex flow, and spiral flow.

Vortex flow

Rotary flow

Spiral flow is the combination of rotary and vortex flows

FIGURE 16-15 A lock-up torque converter piston with friction material bonded to the back of the piston.

In a lock-up converter, the impeller and turbine are locked together, when conditions are suitable, to provide a 1:1 drive from the engine to the transmission input shaft. Lock-up normally occurs at higher road speeds and when the vehicle is under light load. Inside the torque converter, there is a large piston that has friction material bonded to its surface near its outside diameter **FIGURE 16-15**. When the piston is applied with hydraulic fluid from the transmission, the piston and friction material are pressed against the front housing of the torque converter, locking the turbine to the housing. This provides a 1:1 connection from the engine to transmission, with no slippage between components. The lock-up torque converter also helps to reduce transmission fluid temperatures, which in some cases requires an ATF warmer system.

Torsional damper springs are built into the piston assembly. When the clutch is engaged, these springs dampen engine and drive line torsional vibrations. Without these damper springs, every power pulse of the pistons would be felt by the driver as excessive engine vibration.

▶ Gear Train—Principles of Operation

Most automatic transmissions use hydraulic pressure to apply individual clutches and bands in order to hold components of one or more planetary gear sets, called the gear train. A planetary gear set is a device with several gears assembled in a compact design. The planetary gear set has a **sun gear** in the center with smaller **planetary gears** revolving around the sun gear **FIGURE 16-16**. These planetary gears are held together in a **planet carrier**. The planetary gears revolve inside a larger **ring gear** that wraps around the outside of the whole planetary gear set. When an individual component of a planetary gear set is prevented from turning, one of three gear ratios results: forward

torque reduction with a speed increase (overdrive), forward speed reduction with a torque increase, or reverse. Combining two or more planetary gear sets (compound planetary gear sets) creates the needed gear ratios, or speeds, for the modern transmission.

Gear Ratio/Torque Multiplication

<u>Gear ratio</u> refers to the difference in diameter between the driving (input) gear and the driven (output) gear. When you loosen a bolt, what tool do you use? Do you use a socket alone? No, that would not give you much leverage. Instead, you place a long ratchet or breaker bar onto the end of the socket to increase the amount of leverage. This increase in leverage is the same as torque multiplication in a gear ratio.

FIGURE 16-17 shows a gear with 8 teeth driving a gear with 24 teeth. The smaller drive gear will be able to turn

FIGURE 16-16 Simple planetary gear set.

FIGURE 16-17 Having a smaller input gear with 8 teeth driving a larger output gear with 24 teeth results in a 3:1 gear reduction.

three times before the large driven gear turns once. In this scenario, we have created a gear ratio of three to one (3:1). This gear ratio will create three times more torque, but the driven gear will turn at three times less speed and distance, otherwise known as gear reduction. If we were to put 100 foot-pounds (ft-lb; 136 Nm) of torque into this gear system, we would get 300 ft-lb (407 Nm) of torque out, but at one-third the speed and distance.

If we have a gear with 15 teeth driving a gear with only 10 teeth, we will have a gear ratio of 0.67:1. This is an **overdrive** ratio. It will result in less torque being transmitted to the wheels, but will increase wheel speed. Any ratio of less than 1:1 is considered an overdrive ratio. Overdrive ratios are typically used to increase fuel economy while traveling at highway speeds by slowing the engine speed.

A typical automatic transmission will have four or more forward gear ratios and one reverse. Transmission gear ratios vary by transmission and manufacturer but are often approximately 3:1 for first gear, resulting in a large increase in torque, but a major decrease in speed. Second gear is a ratio of approximately 1.75:1, still resulting in a torque increase with a smaller speed decrease. In most transmissions, third gear is a 1:1, or direct, ratio. A direct ratio means that power is sent directly through the transmission with no torque increase or speed increase. Fourth gear is commonly an overdrive ratio of approximately 0.80:1. This ratio means that the engine is turning more slowly than the output shaft of the transmission in order to increase fuel economy. Reverse is often a ratio of approximately 2:1, resulting in a torque increase with a speed reduction.

Early transmissions were simple two-speed automatics with a low gear and a direct gear. As engine size in vehicles decreased, the two gear ratios were no longer adequate to propel the vehicles being produced. Three-speed automatic transmissions became the norm through the early 1980s, when four-speed automatics were installed in vehicles to improve fuel economy. Now with an even greater need to increase fuel economy, manufacturers have turned to adding more gear ratios to their transmissions. Many vehicles are leaving the factory today with five- and six-speed transmissions, with one manufacturer even using an eight-speed automatic. Even with all of these gears, the basic principle of gear reduction and overdrive remains the same.

Gear Set Styles

Individual gears in automatic transmissions are typically one of three types: helical cut, spur (also known as straight-cut gears), or hypoid gears **FIGURE 16-18**.

Spur gears were used in early transmissions due to ease of manufacturing and lower cost. Spur gears also tend to be much louder and do not offer as much strength as the other types of gears; for this reason, manufacturers usually use helical gears for passenger vehicles.

Helical-cut gears (or simply "helical gears") are cut on a spiral around the axis of the shaft. Helical gears offer the benefit of always having more than one gear tooth in contact with the driving gear, thus increasing the strength. Helical gears are quieter than spur gears but have more thrust motion due to the spiral cut of the gear teeth. Because of this increased thrust, helical gears in an automatic transmission must have a method to control the amount of thrust movement, such as **thrust washers** or **thrust bearings**.

Hypoid gears are often used in the final drive of front-wheel drive transaxles and also in conventional final drives on rear-wheel drive vehicles. Hypoid gears are often used to change the direction of power flow by 90 degrees. They are a type of helical gear in which the axes of the two gears are not aligned **FIGURE 16-19**. These gears therefore have the thrust action of helical gears along with a scraping action between the teeth. Due to this scraping action and very high pressure on the gear teeth, hypoid gears require a special lubricant to prevent damage.

FIGURE 16-18 Spur, helical, and hypoid gears.

FIGURE 16-19 A hypoid gear arrangement.

Planetary Gear Sets

A simple planetary gear set is the backbone of most modern automatic transmissions. One of their biggest benefits is that they are in constant mesh. And since they involve multiple gears, a variety of speeds can be obtained without having to take them out of mesh or put them back in mesh. As described earlier, planetary gear sets use either helical gears or straight-cut gears. A simple planetary gear set contains a sun gear in the center with multiple revolving planetary gears around it. The planetary gears are held in place by the planet carrier. On the outside edge of the planetary gears is the ring gear. By holding one of the components (planet carrier, sun, or ring) and driving one of the other components, we can create up to six separate gear ratios—four in the forward direction (two reduction and two overdrive) and two in the reverse direction (one reduction and one overdrive). If any two components are locked together, we end up with another speed—1:1, called direct drive.

Just because a planetary gear can obtain four forward gears and two reverse gears does not mean the manufacturer designs the transmission to use each of those ratios. In reality, vehicle manufacturers can obtain only three ratios from any particular planetary gear set due to constraints on transmission design. Manufacturers have to design the planetary gear sets to get the required number of gear ratios as well as gear ratio splits to work with the particular application. The benefit of designing transmissions with planetary gears is that if you need more gear ratios than you have, you can combine multiple planetary gear sets to create the needed ratios. We will cover these compound planetary gear sets later in the chapter.

Holding/Driving Gears

As we stated earlier, to create a gear ratio we need to hold one member of a planetary gear set and drive another. There are three basic holding devices used in transmissions today: bands, multidisc clutches, and one-way clutches. These holding devices will either lock two turning members of the transmission together or lock a member to the transmission housing to prevent it from spinning.

The **band** is a friction-lined steel belt that wraps around the outside of a drum inside the automatic transmission **FIGURE 16-20**. When a servo applies pressure to one end of the band, it closes the diameter of the band, squeezing the drum and preventing it from turning. The drum is then locked to one member of a planetary gear set.

Multidisc clutches are unique in that they not only can be used to hold a member of the planetary gear set, but they are the only type of component that can be used to drive a member of the planetary gear set. In a multidisc clutch, individual friction discs, often called frictions, are stacked between smooth steel plates, often called steels. Both the frictions and the steels have a hollow center allowing them to wrap around the outside of a hub or drum connected to a member of the planetary gear set. The steels typically have splines, or teeth, on the outside edge to hold them in place inside a drum, while the frictions have splines or teeth on the inside edge to hold them to a member of the planetary gear set. When the steels and frictions are forced together by a hydraulic

---

Applied | **Math**

AM-43: Direct/Inverse Variation: The technician can solve problems requiring the use of fractions, decimals, ratios, and percentages.

When working out gear combinations, it may be necessary to calculate gear ratios based on counting the number of gear teeth. This is simple in the case of differentials and manual transmissions, but the planetary gear sets used in automatic transmissions require more involved calculations.

In the case of a four-speed automatic transmission with an overdrive top gear obtained by driving the planet carrier, the sun gear (30 teeth) held, and the ring gear (72 teeth) driven, the formula to calculate the gear ratio would be:

$$1 / (1 + Sun/Ring).$$

The effective ratio is therefore calculated as:

$$1 / (1 + 30/72), \text{ or } 0.71:1.$$

Different combinations of driving, driven, and held gears require different formulae to calculate ratios.

FIGURE 16-20 A typical transmission band.

piston, the separately revolving steels and frictions match speed and lock the drum or hub to the member of the planetary gear set.

<u>One-way clutches</u> can be either one-way rollers or sprags. Both the one-way roller and the sprag operate on the same principle, but sprags have a greater torque-holding capacity. On both the one-way roller and the sprag, an inside hub is allowed to spin freely in one direction, but spinning the hub in the opposite direction will cause the rollers or sprags to become wedged in place **FIGURE 16-21**. This wedging action prevents rotation of the hub. In the one-way roller clutch, each roller has a waved compression spring that pushes the roller toward the narrow end of the wedge. Rotating the hub in the opposite direction locks the outer race onto the rollers wedged between the two races. Thus, a one-way clutch allows rotation in one direction but prevents rotation in the opposite direction.

Automatic Transmission Fluids

ATF is a specialized fluid that has been designed for a specific job. The ATF must be able to transfer heat from the internal components of the transmission to the transmission cooler in order to prevent damaging the internal seals of the transmission. The fluid must also lubricate the internal gears, bearings, and bushings of the transmission, yet have a large enough **coefficient of friction** to allow the clutches to grab and not slip. Coefficient of friction is the force required to move two sliding surfaces over each other. ATF fluids are typically dyed red for easy identification and contain many additives such as:

- *Rust and corrosion inhibitors:* These additives prevent the internal parts of the transmission from developing rust and corrosion on metal components. Rust and corrosion can affect the shift quality and longevity of the transmission. As rust particles break off, they become an abrasive in the fluid, causing increased wear.
- *Friction modifiers:* Manufacturers add friction modifiers to the fluid to ensure that the fluid has the proper coefficient of friction in order to produce the desired shift quality. A fluid with a lower coefficient of friction will produce softer, longer shifts, causing an increase in clutch slippage. A fluid with a higher coefficient of friction will cause shorter, harsher shifts, reducing clutch slippage but increasing drive line shock.
- *Seal conditioners:* These additives are designed to help protect the seals inside a transmission and cause the seals to swell slightly to help prevent leaks and clutch slippage.
- *Detergents:* ATF has a large amount of detergent to prevent dirt and other foreign particles from

FIGURE 16-21 One-way clutches. **A.** A one-way roller in the locked position and in the freewheeling position. **B.** A sprag in its locked position and in its freewheeling position.

becoming trapped inside the transmission. The detergent causes the dirt and other particles to be attracted to the fluid so they transfer with the fluid. When the fluid passes through the filter, the large particles become trapped in the filter; the small particles are removed during the next transmission fluid change.

- *Antifoam:* These additives help to prevent foaming of the transmission fluid. When moving parts spin through a fluid, they tend to produce air bubbles. These air bubbles can quickly multiply and become foam. Foam is compressible and can cause a transmission to slip because insufficient pressure is applied to the clutches.
- *Viscosity modifiers:* These additives are similar to the engine oil additives that allow us to have multiviscosity engine oils such as 5W-30. These additives allow the fluid to remain thin when the temperature is cold and prevent the fluid from becoming too thin as the transmission fluid warms up.

ATFs can be mineral oil based or a synthetic lubricant. Many late-model vehicles recommend a specific synthetic ATF. Originally, most manufacturers used and recommended General Motors and Ford Motor Company fluids. In the past few decades, most auto manufacturers have developed their own fluids for use in their transmissions. This practice has required repair facilities and quick lube shops to carry many different types of fluids. Some shops carry a few major types of fluids and use those in every vehicle, but that is not recommended as it may cause undesirable transmission operation and may void the transmission warranty. Several vehicle manufacturers have published technical service bulletins (TSBs) related to incorrect fluid use and the negative effects on the transmission. Research all applicable information, including service history and precautions.

ATF needs to be changed periodically to remove dirt and contaminants from the transmission. Technicians used to tell if the transmission fluid needed to be changed by looking at and smelling the fluid. If the fluid was dark or smelled burnt, it needed to be changed. You cannot determine the condition of modern ATF by looks and smell. Some newer synthetic fluids will have a burnt smell when they are brand new and are often darker than mineral-based ATF. To check ATF for contaminants, drop a few drops of transmission fluid onto a white paper towel. The fluid will spread out on the paper towel, but the contaminants will remain where the fluid was dropped.

Automatic Transmission Components

Front Pump

The hydraulic system of an automatic transmission requires a continuous supply of fluid under pressure. This is accomplished by the **front hydraulic pump**. The pump is driven by the torque converter when the engine is running. The pump driving member is engaged by tangs, machined flats, or slots on the converter hub or snout **FIGURE 16-22**.

Pump output always exceeds normal operating demands. Pressures are controlled by a pressure relief valve on older vehicles or a computer-controlled pressure control solenoid on late-model vehicles. Excess fluid returns to the pump inlet or is dumped into the oil pan, where it can be reused **FIGURE 16-23**.

There are four types of pumps used in automatic transmissions: the gear, or "crescent," pump; the rotor pump; the vane pump; and a variable displacement pump. All of these begin pumping as soon as the engine is cranked, no matter which position the gear selector is in.

Gear pumps have been used in automatic transmissions for a long time and are classified as a positive displacement pump. This means that the pump produces the same amount of flow each time the pump turns. Gear pumps are extremely reliable and rarely fail during operation. A gear pump has an outer driven gear and an inner driving gear **FIGURE 16-24**. The inner gear is driven by the torque converter. The outer gear is meshed with the inner gear and is turned by the movement of the inner gear. A crescent is placed on one side of the pump between the two gears. As the gears turn toward the crescent, they are pushed away from each other. This creates a low-pressure area at the front

Pump tangs

FIGURE 16-22 A front pump showing the converter drive engaged in the pump.

FIGURE 16-23 A pressure relief valve on a TH200 front pump. The relief valve will send pressure back to the oil pan at approximately 175 psi (1207 kPa).

FIGURE 16-25 A rotor pump.

FIGURE 16-24 A typical gear pump.

> **TECHNICIAN TIP**
>
> Automatic transmissions since the 1960s have been equipped with only a front pump. This means that the vehicle cannot be push-started because there is no way to turn the pump without the engine running. If the pump is not turning, then the bands and clutches cannot be applied to drive the torque converter, meaning the engine will not turn. Some older transmissions were equipped with an additional pump located in the rear of the transmission and turned by the output shaft. This design allowed the transmission to create pressurized fluid to apply the bands and clutches if the vehicle was rolling, making it possible to push-start the vehicle.

of the crescent and draws fluid in between the gear teeth. As the gears continue to turn past the crescent, they remesh together. When the two gears remesh, the space between the gear teeth becomes smaller, forcing the fluid out. Since it is a positive displacement pump, restricting the fluid flow after the pump can create very high pressure. This pressure is used to apply bands and clutches. Most gear pump housings and gears are made of cast iron, which resists wear. Often during a transmission overhaul the gear pump will not need any service other than replacing the pump bushing and seal.

A **rotor pump** is another type of positive displacement pump. Rotor pumps have two rotors, an inner rotor and an outer rotor **FIGURE 16-25**. The inner rotor is driven by the torque converter. The outer rotor is driven by the inner rotor. Each rotor has multiple lobes on it. There is no crescent in a rotor pump, but the principle of operation

is similar to that of a gear pump. When the two rotors move away from each other, they create a low-pressure area that draws fluid in. When the rotors move closer together, the fluid is forced out under pressure.

A **vane pump** has a center rotor that is driven by the torque converter. The rotor has vanes located around its outside circumference **FIGURE 16-26**. The vanes are free to move in and out of the rotor. Centrifugal force causes the vanes to be pressed against the pump housing, creating a seal. The pump housing is slightly larger than the rotor, with the rotor mounted off-center in the pump housing. On the pump inlet side, the space between the pump vanes and the pump housing increases in volume as the pump turns. This creates a low-pressure area and draws the fluid into the pump. As the rotor spins past its midpoint, the volume between the vanes and the housing starts to decrease. This causes an increase in pressure, forcing the fluid out of the pump outlet.

In recent years, the vane pump has become popular due to the invention of a variable displacement version of the vane pump **FIGURE 16-27**. A **variable displacement vane pump** reduces the pumping load on the engine when the transmission requires less fluid to be pumped.

FIGURE 16-26 A vane pump.

In the variable displacement pump, the pump housing can pivot in relation to the rotor. As the housing moves in one direction, the volume change between the inlet side of the pump and the outlet side decreases. This decreased volume change results in less fluid being pumped and at a lower pressure. When the pump housing moves in the opposite direction, the amount of volume change increases, resulting in more fluid flow and higher pressure. Usually, transmissions do not require maximum pressure and volume of fluid. By reducing the pump load, manufacturers are able to improve fuel efficiency.

Front pumps should be inspected when catastrophic engine damage occurs, such as a thrown connecting rod. The sudden stopping of the engine, and the connected front pump, can damage the pump. It would be wise to remove and inspect the pump while the engine is out of the vehicle. Technicians have been known to replace an engine only to find that the front pump makes knocking noises after the new engine is installed and started.

Flex Plate and Ring Gear

On an automatic transmission there is no flywheel; rather, there is a thin lightweight steel **flex plate**. The flex plate bolts to the rear crankshaft flange in the same manner as a flywheel would. The torque converter is bolted to the flex plate with three or more bolts. Because there is no thrust force of a clutch as in a manual transmission, the flex plate can be significantly lighter than a traditional flywheel **FIGURE 16-28**. Also, the large mass of the torque converter dampens the engine pulses in a similar manner to a flywheel.

Wrapped around the outside edge of the flex plate is a ring gear that is used when starting the vehicle.

FIGURE 16-27 A variable displacement vane pump from a General Motors 4L60E transmission. Note the moveable housing and the large spring.

FIGURE 16-28 **A.** An automatic transmission flex plate and ring gear. Note the ring gear around the outside edge of the flex plate that is used when starting the vehicle. **B.** A manual transmission flywheel and ring gear.

When a faulty engine or transmission is suspected because of knocking noises, double-check that the flex plate bolts are tight. Loose bolts on the flex plate can sound like a knocking engine. Also, a cracked flex plate can cause a knocking noise that can sound like a defective rod bearing. In some cases, the entire center of the flex plate can break free of the rest of the flex plate, preventing the engine from cranking over when the starter is engaged. It is easy for a technician to think that the engine has a broken crankshaft because the front pulley does not turn when the engine is cranked, when in reality, the outer portion of the flex plate is spinning on the broken center piece.

FIGURE 16-29 A front pump bushing properly installed. Note the front pump seal in front of the bushing.

The starter pinion gear moves out to contact the ring gear, and the starter motor cranks the engine over when the driver turns the ignition switch to the crank position. This ring gear is not typically a serviceable, separate part of the flex plate. If the ring gear wears out, the entire flex plate will typically need to be replaced. Ring gears on flywheels are often available as separate parts from the flywheel and can be serviced. In some applications, manufacturers weld the ring gear to the torque converter instead of the flex plate.

Front Pump Seal, Bushing, and Pump Drive

On the front pump, there is a seal between the pump and the torque converter. This seal is similar in appearance to an axle seal you would find on a wheel bearing. This seal is designed to keep dirt out of the inside of the transmission and keep low-pressure transmission fluid from leaking out of the front of the transmission.

Behind the seal is the front pump bushing. The bushing is a friction-type bearing similar to a camshaft bearing. This bushing supports the torque converter hub and should always be replaced when overhauling a transmission, replacing a failed torque converter, or replacing a leaking front pump seal. A special bushing installation tool is needed to correctly install the front pump bushing without damaging it **FIGURE 16-29**.

Inside the front pump opening where the torque converter enters the pump, there are two tangs, or flats, that drive the pump. The end of the torque converter hub or snout has matching tangs, flats, or slots that engage into the front pump. These components drive the pump when the engine is spinning. It is critical that the torque converter drive tangs or slots engage the pump tangs or flats properly when installing the torque converter. If the tangs or flats are not engaged properly and the transmission is reinstalled into the vehicle, the front pump will be destroyed when the engine is first started. Keep in mind that more than one student has failed to install the torque converter properly, which has earned the student the additional experience of removing the transmission again, replacing a front pump, and cleaning the filings out of the cooler and transmission pan.

Case, Extension Housing, and Pan

Modern automatic transmission cases are made of lightweight aluminum and alloys. Early transmission cases were sometimes made of cast iron. When a transmission is new, the manufacturer typically leaves the transmission case uncoated. When the transmission is rebuilt, the rebuilders often paint the transmission a particular color. This serves two purposes: (1) It helps identify a transmission that was previously rebuilt, and (2) it helps seal the transmission after it has been cleaned. Aluminum can become porous after excessive cleaning of the case with detergents and solvents. The paint helps to fill in any case porosity.

On the rear or output side of the transmission, there is an aluminum housing called the **extension housing**. The extension housing is usually bolted to the transmission case with a **gasket** between the housing and the case. The extension housing may contain the vehicle speed sensor drive gear or speedometer drive gear and/or a governor assembly to measure vehicle speed **FIGURE 16-30**.

Inside the end of the extension housing is the extension housing bushing that supports the driveshaft. The extension housing on most four-wheel drive pick-ups and SUVs has a surface that bolts the transmission up to the transfer case.

On the bottom of most transmissions is a sheet metal or aluminum pan. Inside this pan, the transmission filter and possibly the transmission valve body are located. Most front-wheel drive transaxles have a second pan called the side pan, which houses the valve body **FIGURE 16-31**. The bottom transmission pan is often removed during routine transmission fluid service to change the filter and clean a magnet, if equipped, located inside the pan that catches small particles of steel and iron that are floating in the fluid. The transmission pan holds about half of the transmission fluid when the vehicle is off. When the vehicle

is running, the pump draws fluid from the transmission pan to supply lubrication and pressure to the different parts of the transmission.

Gaskets and Seals

Gaskets are used throughout the automatic transmission. Some gaskets are made from paper, fiber, or cork material that must be replaced every time a component is removed. Other gaskets are a reuseable type with neoprene inserted into a plastic housing. Reuseable gaskets are fairly common for transmission pan gaskets where the part is frequently removed for routine service. Some reusable gaskets have built-in torque limiters. These torque limiters are metal sleeves built in the gasket around the bolt holes to help prevent overtorquing of the gasket.

There are many types of internal seals for an automatic transmission **FIGURE 16-32**. These internal seals are often the root cause of a transmission slipping and eventually failing. All seals need to be properly lubricated when assembling the transmission to prevent premature failure and to help with installation. Seals are lubricated with ATF, petroleum jelly, or automatic transmission assembly lubricant. Do not use grease to lubricate the seals, as grease can clog up the internal passages of the transmission when the vehicle is put back into service. A description of seals used in a transmission system follows:

- *Square-cut seals:* Square-cut seals can be made from neoprene rubber or Teflon. Teflon seals require special handling and will be discussed separately. Square-cut seals are similar to the seal found inside a brake caliper. They are sometimes located on the piston of a multiple disc clutch.

FIGURE 16-30 A typical extension housing with the speedometer cable connected.

FIGURE 16-31 A common front-wheel drive transaxle showing the bottom oil pan and side pan.

FIGURE 16-32 Typical seals used in an automatic transmission.

- *Lip seals:* Lip seals are made from neoprene. Lip seals have a greater sealing ability than a square-cut seal because when pressure is applied to the back of the seal, it forces the seal out against the inside of the clutch drum. These seals are similar to the cup seals located inside a drum brake wheel cylinder. Lip seals can be easily damaged by careless installation and infrequent fluid and filter changes. Lip seals are typically used inside multi-disc clutch assemblies on the piston.
- *Locking seal:* The locking seal is made from cast iron and is similar to a piston compression ring except that the ends overlap and lock together. Locking seals are typically used between the front pump and the rotating clutch drums.
- *O-rings:* O-rings are made from neoprene rubber and are often found sealing external parts of the transmission such as a speedometer cable assembly or governor cover. O-rings can also be used on accumulators and servo covers.
- *Teflon seals:* Teflon seals come in several styles—continuous, butt cut, scarf cut, and step joint. The continuous seal provides the best sealing action and should be used whenever possible, but it does require special tools for proper installation. Teflon seals have replaced the locking seals on most modern transmissions and are found sealing the front pump to input shafts and clutch drums.

Parking Pawl Assembly

Most automatic transmissions for passenger vehicles include an internal parking mechanism. When the driver shifts the transmission into park, a lever, called a parking pawl, is forced into notches cut into a hardened steel drum on the output shaft of the transmission **FIGURE 16-33**. This parking pawl prevents rotation of the output shaft when it is engaged. The parking pawl is often operated through a spring in case the driver accidentally places the vehicle into park while it is still moving. In this scenario, the vehicle will make a loud ratcheting noise as the parking pawl bounces against the rotating notches of the output

TECHNICIAN TIP

Often, Teflon seals are placed in boiling water prior to assembly to help expand the seal, while the component the seal is being installed on may be placed in the freezer to contract the part.

FIGURE 16-33 A parking pawl assembly on a late-model CVT transmission.

shaft drum. The spring is designed to help minimize damage to the parking pawl and the output shaft. The spring also allows the driver to place the vehicle shift selector into park even when the parking paw does not quite align with the notches in the drum. If this occurs, the gear shift is placed in park but the vehicle may need to roll an inch or two for the parking pawl to engage.

Planetary Gears

As mentioned earlier, most automatic transmissions use planetary gears. They are constantly in mesh with each other. A basic planetary gear set has a sun gear, which meshes with planetary gears, also called planet **pinions**. The planet pinions, in sets of three or more, rotate on bearings in a planet carrier. The planet carrier equally spaces the planets around the sun gear. It also locates them so they can mesh with an internally toothed ring gear. This design means the planet pinions are always in mesh with the sun gear and the ring gear.

The planetary gears' motion is described as either "walking" or "**idling**." Walking means that if either the sun gear or the ring gear is held stationary, the opposite driving member rotates the planetary gears in the carrier. This rotating motion turns the planet carrier in the same direction as the driving member. Planetary gears always turn in the same direction on their pins as the planet carrier while they walk around a stationary sun gear. They always turn in the opposite direction on their pins while walking inside a stationary ring gear **FIGURE 16-34**.

Idling refers to the rotation of the planetary gears on their pins whenever the planet carrier is stationary **FIGURE 16-35**. Torque is transmitted from the sun gear to the ring gear or from the ring gear to the sun gear via the planetary gears and the stationary carrier.

In both cases, the driven member is turned in the opposite direction from the driving member. To provide the ratios available from the gear set, one or more of the components must be held or released. This is normally done by a band, by a multidisc clutch, or by one-way clutches. In practice, a combination of these devices is normally used to hold individual members of the planetary gear set.

In Figure 16-36, the planet carrier is attached to the output shaft. The sun gear is attached to the input

shaft from the turbine. The ring gear is not held. When the input shaft rotates the sun gear, the planetary gears idle in the carrier and turn the ring gear in the opposite direction to engine rotation. This free rotation of the gears provides a neutral state. No torque is transmitted to the output shaft.

For low gear, we use a holding device to hold the ring gear stationary. Now when the sun gear rotates, the planetary gears can no longer idle. They must walk around the inside of the stationary ring gear. The planet carrier must move with them in the same direction as engine rotation, but at a slower speed and with an increase in torque.

A direct drive, or 1:1 ratio, is obtained by locking together any two members of the gear set. A multidisc clutch is used for this purpose. The outer drum and steels are attached to the ring gear. The frictions and inner drum are attached to the planet carrier. When fluid under pressure is directed onto the clutch piston, the frictions and steels are locked together, thus locking the planet carrier to the ring gear. Now when the sun gear is rotated, the planetary gears can neither idle nor walk. The whole gear set turns as one unit to give direct drive.

For reverse, the ring gear is attached to the output shaft and the planet carrier is held stationary. Rotating the sun gear causes the planetary gears to idle in the planet carrier. This turns the ring gear, and the output shaft, in the opposite direction to engine rotation at a reduced speed but increased torque, resulting in reverse **FIGURE 16-36**.

FIGURE 16-34 A planetary set with the ring gear held so the planet gears are "walking" around the sun gear.

FIGURE 16-35 A planetary set with the planet carrier held. The planet gears idle in place.

FIGURE 16-36 A simple planetary gear set with the planet carrier held to create reverse.

Compound Planetary Gear Sets

The simple gear set illustrates basic principles, but it cannot obtain all the ratios required in a modern vehicle. In practice, **compound planetary gear sets** are used. One type of compound planetary gear set is the **Simpson gear set**. A Simpson gear set has two planetary gear sets that share a common sun gear FIGURE 16-37. The sun gear is free to rotate on the output shaft. It is constantly meshed with the planets of both sets. They in turn mesh with their individual ring gears. Both sets are also connected by each having a part splined to the output shaft—the ring gear of the rear set and the planet carrier of the front set. The input shaft is isolated from the gear set by one or more clutches, depending on the gear and range engaged. The Simpson gear set is capable of producing three forward gears along with a reverse. Simpson gear sets are common in domestic vehicles.

A second compound planetary gear set is the **Ravigneaux gear set**. Ravigneaux gear sets use two different-sized sun gears connected to long and short pinion gears (planets) and one ring gear. All gears are always in mesh, just as in a simple gear set. The primary sun gear meshes with short primary pinions. The secondary sun gear meshes with long secondary pinions FIGURE 16-38. Both sets of planet pinions are mounted in a common planet carrier, and they mesh in pairs. The outer secondary pinions mesh with the ring gear, which is attached to the output shaft. The Ravigneaux gear set is capable of producing four forward gears—two with gear reduction, a direct, and an overdrive—along with reverse. Ravigneaux gear sets are common in import vehicles.

Thrust Washers and Thrust Bearings

Forward and backward motion of components inside a transmission must be controlled. Typically, when there are two parts spinning next to each other, a thrust washer or thrust bearing is used.

Thrust washers are a friction type of bearing similar to engine main bearings. They can be made of plastic or steel coated with a bronze bearing material. Thrust bearings must have a small amount of clearance for proper oil flow. A typical manufacturer specification for a thrust bearing clearance is 0.005" (0.13 mm). Thrust washers need to be checked during a rebuild and are sometimes replaced if they are worn FIGURE 16-39.

FIGURE 16-38 A Ravigneaux gear set showing the two sun gears, with the long and short pinions.

FIGURE 16-37 A Simpson gear set. Note the single sun gear driving two sets of planets.

FIGURE 16-39 **A.** A typical thrust bearing (bearing has been opened to show individual rollers). **B.** A plastic thrust washer. **C.** A typical thrust washer. Note the copper color, as the outer coating of the washer has been worn away.

Thrust bearings are a type of flat needle roller bearing with the rollers placed radially around the center of the bearing. These bearings are typically called Torrington bearings. Thrust bearings must have less clearance than thrust washers. If a thrust bearing has excessive clearance, it will suffer impact damage.

Bushings

Most automatic transmissions use bushings around spinning components, rather than a roller bearing. These bushings are a friction-type bearing, similar to an overhead valve camshaft bearing. One of the most critical bushings to be replaced during an overhaul of an automatic transmission is the front pump bushing. The front pump bushing is used to support the torque converter and sees the largest amount of wear in the transmission because it is in use anytime the engine is running **FIGURE 16-40** .

Another bushing that is prone to wear is the output shaft bushing. It supports the driveshaft on a rear-wheel drive vehicle and is located in the extension housing. The output shaft bushing is subject to higher amounts of wear both from the spinning of the driveshaft and from the in-and-out action of the driveshaft as the suspension moves up and down. This movement can also allow small particles of dust and dirt to move past the extension housing seal and cause more wear to this bushing. The remaining bushings inside the transmission should be checked, but not necessarily replaced, during an overhaul of the transmission.

▶ Bands and Clutches

Bands and clutches perform very specific roles within a transmission. A band is specifically used to hold one member of the planetary gear set stationary. In other words, it locks the member to the transmission case. There are two types of clutches: multidisc and one way. Multidisc clutches are used for three purposes. The first is like the band; the clutch holds one member of the planetary gear set stationary. The second is to drive a member of the planetary gear set. In other words, the clutch transmits twisting force from one component to another. The last purpose of a clutch is to hold one rotating member to another rotating member. For example, the clutch can lock two members of the planetary gear set together to create direct drive. One-way clutches hold a component when it is trying to turn in one direction and allow it to freewheel when turning the other direction.

Automatic Transmission Brake Bands

All bands inside an automatic transmission are externally contracting types. They have a thin layer of friction material bonded onto spring steel or cast steel backing. One end of the band rests against a stop, or strut, in the transmission case. The other end is operated by linkage from a hydraulically operated servo. When the servo pushes on the linkage, the band is squeezed tightly around the drum, stopping the drum from spinning and holding whichever planetary gear component the drum is attached to. Bands come in a variety of configurations. The most common is the one-piece band, which is one solid band with friction lining on it. Other bands come in a multi-wrap configuration, which use a band made up of three parallel straps that give increased gripping power as well as allow fluid to be squeezed out of the slots for quicker band application.

Servos

__Servos__ are used in automatic transmissions to convert the hydraulic pressure acting on a piston to a mechanical force that is then applied to a brake band. The simplest servo consists of a cylinder containing a piston, a piston

FIGURE 16-40 A front pump bushing removed from the transmission.

return spring, and a pushrod. Servos are designed for the particular application, so they come in a variety of configurations.

Fluid under pressure is directed onto one side of the piston in the closed cylinder, moving it to apply the band. When this fluid is "dumped," or exhausted from the supply line, the spring returns the piston and flexible band to their released position. Some servos are of the "pressure release" type. This means that the servo is applied in the normal way by fluid pressure acting on one side of the servo piston. Release is obtained by applying fluid at the same pressure to the opposite side of the servo piston. Once pressure equalizes, the return spring pushes the piston to its release position. This method of releasing a servo allows the speed of release to be carefully controlled.

Sometimes servos can be accessed from the outside of the transmission, which means they can be serviced without removing the transmission from the vehicle **FIGURE 16-41**. Some servos have multiple pistons to stage the application of the band for different gears. A common example of this is the General Motors 4L60 and 4L60E transmissions. These transmissions are used in rear-wheel drive vehicles and have a second and fourth gear band. The servo is a selective apply servo based on the gear required.

Servo Springs, Seals, and Linkage

To aid in the release of a servo, a large spring is typically located behind the servo piston. The servo piston typically has either a neoprene-type seal or a Teflon seal to prevent fluid pressure leaks.

The linkage connected to the servo needs to be checked for proper length. If the linkage is too short when the servo applies, the band will slip. If the linkage is too long, the band will drag when the servo is released. On older vehicles, the band and servo linkage was adjustable, and adjustment was required when the transmission fluid was serviced. Often the technician would adjust the band adjustment bolt to a specified torque, loosen the bolt a specified number of turns, then lock it in place with a jam nut **FIGURE 16-42**.

Multidisc Clutches

Multidisc clutches can be used to hold members of the planetary gear set to the case instead of using bands, but in most transmissions, they couple planetary gear members to input and output shafts.

FIGURE 16-41 A servo being removed from the transmission.

FIGURE 16-42 A band with an adjustment bolt inside the transmission pan.

A servo-operated band can only hold a member stationary, but multidisc clutches can hold or drive individual members of the planetary set. Multidisc clutches have a set of driving plates and a set of driven plates, collectively called a clutch pack. Both types of plates are made from steel, with one having friction material bonded to both sides. The plates without friction materials are called steels, while the ones with friction material are called frictions. Since they both operate in the transmission fluid, they are called wet clutches.

The friction material may be plain or grooved. Grooving allows the fluid to escape from between the plates when the clutch engages and creates a firmer, quicker shift. Using a plain or smooth friction material will result in a softer, delayed shift. Over time, as the clutch engages and disengages, the friction material slowly wears away **FIGURE 16-43**. If the clutch slips due to low transmission fluid level, or a faulty clutch seal, the friction material will be destroyed very quickly.

Three to five frictions and steels are commonly used in a multidisc clutch. The frictions and steels are pressed together for engagement by a hydraulically operated piston. It moves in a short cylinder inside a clutch drum, or in a cylinder machined in the transmission housing. The steels are flat and have external splines or teeth that sit in matching grooves in the clutch drum.

The inner driven plates are the frictions and their splines, or teeth, mate with splines on the outside of a hub located in the center of the clutch pack. The hub is splined to the primary sun gear. The frictions and steels are placed alternately to make up the pack and are loaded into the clutch drum against the relatively thick pressure plate **FIGURE 16-44**.

The number of plates installed determines the torque capacity of the clutch. Installing more plates increases the torque capacity, but in all cases the clutch must maintain its specified clearance so that the plates can separate from one another while in the released position. Thinner frictions and steels can be installed to increase the total number of clutch plates and increase the torque capacity.

Releasing of the clutch can be helped by one large coil spring, a pack containing many small springs, or a diaphragm spring. When a diaphragm spring is used, it gives extra leverage to increase the applied force on the clutch pack and to provide the release force. The outer circumference of the diaphragm spring rests against a step in the clutch drum. The piston pushes against the inner circumference of the spring to apply the clutch. The force exerted on the clutch pack is multiplied by leverage from the diaphragm as it pivots against the pressure plate.

Trapped fluid can accumulate at the outer portion of the clutch cylinder. Due to centrifugal force, at high speed the trapped fluid can produce enough pressure to cause partial application of the clutch. A centrifugal relief valve in the clutch piston or clutch drum releases fluid trapped in the cylinder when the clutch is released. This prevents partial application of the clutch during high-speed operation when the particular clutch should be disengaged, thus preventing unwanted wear of the clutch discs.

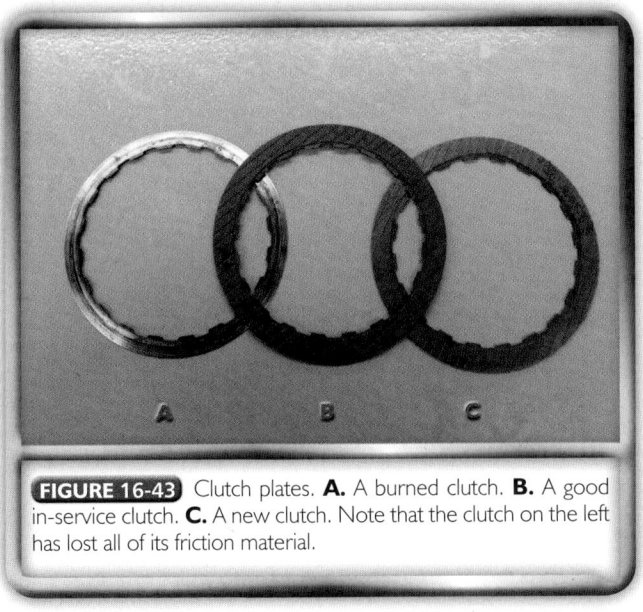

FIGURE 16-43 Clutch plates. **A.** A burned clutch. **B.** A good in-service clutch. **C.** A new clutch. Note that the clutch on the left has lost all of its friction material.

FIGURE 16-44 A piston removed from a drum on a multidisc clutch pack.

Plate Clearance

In the released position, the plates must retain a set clearance. This clearance allows them to separate from one another to allow oil to flow between the clutches and the steels and avoid excessive or premature wear. Clutch pack clearance must be checked when rebuilding an automatic transmission **FIGURE 16-45**. Most transmissions give a range for clutch pack clearance. As mentioned previously, greater clearance results in harsher shifts, while less clearance produces slow, smooth shifts. When the clutch pack has more clearance, the piston will develop more speed as it is applied, creating a harsh engagement with very little clutch pack slippage. This could be compared to hitting a window with a hammer, or placing a hammer against the window and pushing on it. The hammer will obviously hit the window harder if it is swung (and will break the window!). If a clutch pack has less clearance, the piston will have a slower apply speed and squeeze the oil out of the clutches, resulting in a smoother shift as the clutches slowly apply.

> **TECHNICIAN TIP**
>
> Always check TSBs, Automatic Transmission Rebuilders Association (ATRA) publications, or Automatic Transmission Service Group (ATSG) manuals for revised clutch pack clearances. Some transmission specifications are revised after the transmission is put into service. The revised specifications are important for the longevity of the transmission rebuild.

FIGURE 16-45 A technician checking clutch pack clearance with a set of feeler gauges.

Wrap-up

Ready for Review

▸ Automatic transmissions are now standard equipment in vehicles.

▸ Automatic transmissions contain planetary gear sets.

▸ Automatic transmissions have four or more forward gear ratios and one reverse ratio.

▸ Typical forward gear ratios are as follows: first gear, 3:1; second gear, 1.75:1; third gear, 1:1; and fourth gear, 0.80:1.

▸ Adding more gear ratios to the transmission boosts fuel economy.

▸ Automatic transmissions select and shift gears without driver input and can couple or uncouple from the engine as necessary.

▸ Types of automatic transmissions include conventional, transaxle, dual clutch, continuously variable, dual shaft, and hybrid (series or parallel).

▸ Conventional automatic transmissions have planetary gear sets, connect to the engine via torque converter, and use holding devices to stop one or more parts of the planetary gear.

▸ Transaxle transmissions add a differential and final drive gear to a standard transmission.

▸ Dual-clutch transmissions use two wet clutches instead of a standard torque converter.

▸ Continuously variable transmissions use two moveable pulleys rather than typical gears.

▸ Honda and Saturn vehicles use dual-shaft transmissions that have a main shaft and a countershaft, as well as multidisc clutch packs.

▸ Hybrid vehicles often use series transmissions, in which an electric motor supplements power to the transmission.

▸ A hybrid vehicle may use a parallel hybrid transmission, in which either the engine or an electric motor can power the transmission.

▸ Automatic transmission gears are typically helical (most commonly used), spur (straight cut), or hypoid.

▸ Planetary gear sets use either helical- or straight-cut gears and are comprised of three components: planet carrier, sun gear, and ring gear.

▸ Bands, multidisc clutches, and one-way clutches are the three basic holding devices used in transmissions.

▸ Automatic transmission fluid (ATF) transfers heat from the internal transmission components to the transmission cooler.

▸ ATFs are oil-based or synthetic and may contain these additives: rust and corrosion inhibitors, friction modifiers, seal conditioners, detergents, antifoam, and viscosity modifiers.

▸ Components of an automatic transmission include the front pump; flex plate and ring gear; front pump seal, bushings, and pump drive; case, extension housing, and pan; gaskets and seals; and parking pawl assembly.

▸ The front hydraulic pump ensures a continuous pressurized supply of fluid to the transmission.

▸ The four types of automatic transmission front pumps are gear/crescent, rotor, vane, and variable displacement.

▸ On automatic transmissions, the flywheel is replaced with a flex plate, with a ring gear wrapped around the outside edge.

▸ Gaskets may be made of paper, fiber, cork, or neoprene (which may be reusable).

▸ Types of internal seals include square cut, lip, locking, O-ring, and Teflon.

▸ Compound planetary gear sets are used to create all the ratios needed for modern vehicle travel.

▸ Two types of compound planetary gear sets are Simpson and Ravigneaux.

▸ Thrust washers and thrust bearings are used to control forward and backward motion of transmission components.

▸ Bushings should be checked during transmission overhaul; the front pump bushing or the output shaft bushing will likely need replacing.

▸ Automatic transmission brake bands use friction material and servo pressure to stop the drum from spinning.

▸ Multidisc clutches are used to couple planetary gear members to input shaft, output shaft, or the case.

▸ Clutch release may be assisted via a large coil spring, a pack of small springs, or a diaphragm spring.

▸ Check clutch pack clearance when rebuilding an automatic transmission.

▸ A torque convertor works with the transmission to select the proper gear to meet the speed and power demands of the vehicle.

▸ A single-stage torque converter contains an impeller, a turbine, and a stator.

▸ Torque multiplication is a state that occurs when the impeller is turning substantially faster than the turbine. The greater the difference in speed the greater the torque multiplication.

▸ A torque converter clutch is used to lock the turbine to the impeller when the vehicle is operating under light loads, to improve fuel economy.

Key Terms

band A metal band with friction material bonded to one side. The band is contracted around a drum to stop the drum from spinning.

coefficient of friction A value assigned to materials to describe the amount of friction when two objects slide against each other.

compound planetary gear set Two or more simple planetary gear sets connected together.

continuously variable transmission (CVT) A transmission that does not have conventional set gear ratios, but is instead infinitely variable between the transmission's lowest gear ratio and highest gear ratio.

dual-clutch transmission A type of automatically shifting manual transmission in which two separate input shafts are connected to their own clutch. Shifting of the gears alternates between the two input shafts.

extension housing A component of the automatic transmission housing that covers the output shaft of the transmission. The extension housing also supports the end of the driveshaft and may hold components such as the vehicle speed sensor, speedometer drive assembly, and governor assembly.

flex plate Typically a circular steel plate that is bolted to the rear of the crankshaft. The torque converter is bolted to this flex plate. The outside of the flex plate will often have a ring gear that the starter motor engages with to crank the engine over.

fluid coupler A type of hydraulic coupling used on vintage vehicles to connect and transfer power from the engine to the transmission.

front hydraulic pump A hydraulic pump used to supply lubrication oil and hydraulic pressure to the different components inside the automatic transmission.

gasket A rubber, cork, or paper spacer that goes between two parts to seal the gap between the parts.

gear pump A type of front pump used on some vehicles that uses two rotating gears to force fluid out of the pump.

gear ratio The ratio of the size or teeth of one gear compared to the size or teeth of a mating gear.

helical-cut gear A type of gear in which the teeth are cut in a spiral down the axis of the gear.

hypoid gear A type of helical gear used to change the direction of motion 90 degrees. The axis of the input gear does not line up on the centerline of the output gear

idling A condition in which a gear is spinning but not moving.

multidisc clutch A type of holding device used by an automatic transmission to stop the movement of one component of a planetary gear set. It uses several thin friction discs and thin steel plates that are squeezed together when hydraulic pressure is applied to a piston in the clutch.

one-way clutch A type of holding device used by an automatic transmission to stop the movement of one component of a planetary gear set. It allows free spinning in one direction but will lock up when the part attempts to spin in the opposite direction.

overdrive Any gear ratio that results in a torque reduction with a speed increase. Overdrive is used on vehicles to reduce the engine speed when traveling at highway speed in order to save fuel.

parallel hybrid drive train A type of hybrid transmission in which power can flow from either a gasoline engine or an electric motor and any combination of the two.

pinions The small gears in a planetary gear set that revolve around the sun gear, also known as planetary gears.

planet carrier The device that holds the planet gears in place, keeping them equally spaced.

planetary gears The small gears in a planetary gear set that revolve around the sun gear; also known as pinion gears.

power-splitting transmission (PST) A type of hybrid transmission that splits the power flow going to the wheels from one or more electric motors and an internal combustion engine.

Ravigneaux gear set A type of compound planetary gear set that uses two different sun gears and two different-diameter planets while only using one ring gear.

ring gear The outer gear of a planetary gear set. The ring gear wraps around the outside of the planetary gears.

rotary flow A type of fluid flow in a torque converter in which fluid flows around the centerline of the torque converter in a circle.

rotor pump A type of front pump found in automatic transmissions. The rotor pump has two different-sized rotors that mesh together to force fluid out of the pump.

series hybrid drive train A type of hybrid transmission in which power flows from the engine through an electric motor. The electric motor supplements the power from the engine to the wheels.

series-parallel hybrid drive train A type of hybrid drive train that can function as both a series hybrid and parallel hybrid. That means the gasoline engine can turn a generator that can be used to power an electric motor. The gasoline engine can also drive the vehicle directly through the transmission. And the electric motor can work in parallel with the gasoline engine to drive the vehicle.

servo A hydraulic device consisting of a piston inside a cylinder that is used to apply a band. The servo also has a spring that releases the servo when it is no longer needed.

Simpson gear set A type of gear set with two planetary gear sets that share a common sun gear.

spur gear A type of gear in which the teeth of the gear are cut in a straight line down the axis of the gear.

stall Often referred to as stall speed, the maximum rpm difference between the turbine and the impeller in the torque converter.

standard torque converter A hydraulic coupling device consisting of an impeller, turbine, stator, and housing; located between the engine and the transmission.

sun gear The center gear of a planetary gear set around which the other gears rotate.

thrust bearing Also called a Torrington bearing, a small roller bearing assembly with the rollers laid flat axially around the centerline of the bearing. The bearing is used to control forward and backward movement of a part in an automatic transmission.

thrust washer A small steel washer coated with bearing material. The thrust washer is used to control forward and backward movement of a part in an automatic transmission.

transaxle A type of transmission typically used in front-wheel drive vehicles in which the transmission also includes the differential and final drive gear.

vane pump A type of front pump in an automatic transmission that uses small vanes placed radially around a center hub. The vanes may be forced out against the housing of the pump by centrifugal force. The volume between the vanes varies as the pump turns, resulting in fluid being forced out of the pump.

variable displacement vane pump A type of front pump that uses a vane-style pump that can pivot so that its displacement can be varied.

vortex flow State in which the fluid in the torque converter is traveling between the turbine, stator, and impeller.

ASE-Type Questions

1. Tech A says that the higher the numerical gear ratio (4:1), the more torque that will be applied to the wheels. Tech B says that the lower the numerical gear ratio (2:1), the more torque that will be applied to the wheels. Who is correct?
   a. Tech A
   b. Tech B
   c. Both A and B
   d. Neither A nor B

2. Tech A says that helical cut gears are stronger than straight cut gears. Technician B says that helical cut gears are noisier than straight cut gears. Who is correct?
   a. Tech A
   b. Tech B
   c. Both A and B
   d. Neither A nor B

3. Tech A says that a transaxle must have a type of differential assembly to allow the front wheels to turn at different speeds while driving around a curve. Tech B says that a conventional rear wheel drive vehicle will typically use a differential assembly that is located in the rear axle assembly. Who is correct?
   a. Tech A
   b. Tech B
   c. Both A and B
   d. Neither A nor B

4. Tech A says that a parallel hybrid transmission has two or more different devices to propel the vehicle. Tech B says that hybrid power splitting transmissions use 2 adjustable pulleys and a heavy metal belt. Who is correct?
   a. Tech A
   b. Tech B
   c. Both A and B
   d. Neither A nor B

5. Tech A says that planetary gear sets are used in all automatic transmissions. Tech B says that planetary gear sets are often combined together to create the needed gear ratios for a transmission. Who is correct?
   a. Tech A
   b. Tech B
   c. Both A and B
   d. Neither A nor B

6. Tech A says that the torque converter hub drives the front pump in an automatic transmission. Tech B says that the turbine shaft drives the front pump. Who is correct?
   a. Tech A
   b. Tech B
   c. Both A and B
   d. Neither A nor B

7. Tech A says that most automatic transmissions have a ring gear for the starter as part of the flex plate. Tech B says that the ring gear is typically replaceable (interference fit) on a flex plate. Who is correct?
   a. Tech A
   b. Tech B
   c. Both A and B
   d. Neither A nor B

8. Tech A says that a knocking noise in the engine/transmission area is typically a bad front pump in the transmission. Tech B says that a knocking noise in the engine/transmission area is more likely to be loose flex plate bolts. Who is correct?
   a. Tech A
   b. Tech B
   c. Both A and B
   d. Neither A nor B

9. Tech A says that painting a rebuilt transmission helps to identify it as being a rebuilt transmission. Tech B says that painting a rebuilt transmission prevents the housing from leaking due to case porosity. Who is correct?
   a. Tech A
   b. Tech B
   c. Both A and B
   d. Neither A nor B

10. Tech A says that the torque converters multiply the amount of torque transmitted from the engine to the transmission. Tech B says that the torque converter couples and uncouples the engine and transmission as the vehicle stops and starts in traffic. Who is correct?
    a. Tech A
    b. Tech B
    c. Both A and B
    d. Neither A nor B

CHAPTER 17

NATEF Tasks

Automatic Transmission and Transaxle
General   Page

- Diagnose transmission/transaxle gear reduction/multiplication
  concerns using driving, driven, and held member (power flow)   **AST** **MAST**   493–494
  principles.

Knowledge Objectives

After reading this chapter, you will be able to:
1. Explain the purpose of the hydraulic system. (p 482)
2. Explain the principle of Pascal's law and how it relates to the operation of an automatic transmission.
   (pp 482–483)
3. Describe the components of the hydraulic system and their operation. (pp 483–489)
4. Describe the different valve types and functions of each. (pp 489–494)

Hydraulic Fundamentals

Skills Objectives

There are no skills objectives for this chapter.

Introduction

Automatic transmissions function using the principles of hydraulic operation to apply and release different clutches and bands. This system achieves the different gear ratios needed for vehicle operation. Using hydraulics to apply clutches and bands is a good choice since fluids are non-compressible and therefore transmit force effectively. Another benefit of hydraulics is that fluids, having no shape of their own, take the shape of the container. This allows force to easily be applied in a variety of directions. A good understanding of how the hydraulic system operates is necessary to properly diagnose and repair modern automatic transmissions. The basic hydraulic principles and components covered in this chapter are common to most automatic transmissions, whether they are modern computer-controlled transmissions or older hydraulically controlled transmissions.

Pascal's Law

<u>Pascal's law</u> is one of the fundamental physics principles behind the operation of an automatic transmission. Simply put, Pascal's law states that if we place fluid in a confined space, such as a transmission hydraulic system, pressure will be transferred equally in all directions inside the space. For example, in the brake system, if the master cylinder produces 100 pounds per square inch (psi) of hydraulic pressure, that pressure is transmitted everywhere in the system. There will be 100 psi (689 kilopascals [kPa])in the brake lines and 100 psi (689 kPa)in the calipers and wheel cylinders.

We are also able to multiply force using Pascal's law. For example, if we have 100 psi (689 kPa)and apply that pressure to a piston, whose surface area is 3 square inches (in²), the resulting force will be equivalent to 300 lb (100 psi × 3 in² = 300 lb) **FIGURE 17-1**.

Another example: Suppose we apply 200 psi (1379 kPa)to a piston that has an area of 4 in². The resulting force will be 800 lb (200 psi × 4 in² = 800 lb). Before we can calculate the amount of force created by a piston, we must calculate the area of the piston. A piston is

FIGURE 17-1 Hydraulic pressure of 100 psi applied to a 3-square inch piston will result in 300 lb of output force.

You are the Automotive Technician

A customer recently purchased a 2006 Ford Taurus with an automatic transmission and stops by your shop to ask about her car. She informs you that the car hasn't been running smoothly lately and she has seen dark red fluid from the car on the garage floor. Also, she isn't sure if the transmission fluid has ever been checked or serviced. First, you see there is no vehicle service history in the shop's computer. Next, you check the transmission fluid level and find it looks dirty, but not burnt, and is a bit below the safe mark. You notify the customer that you will need to complete a thorough inspection of the vehicle to diagnose the car's problem. The customer agrees to leave the vehicle with you for further inspection.

1. What different areas of the transmission would you check for external fluid leaks?
2. What are the roles that automatic transmission fluid plays in an automatic transmission?
3. What type of transmission fluid should be used in this vehicle? How would you locate that information?

FIGURE 17-2 A piston with a radius of 3" under a pressure of 175 psi will create 4900 lb of output force.

classified as a circle. To calculate the area of a circle, we need to use the formula $\pi \times r^2$. Recall that $\pi = 3.14$, and r = the radius of the circle (in other words, the center of our piston to the outside edge). For example, a piston that has a radius of 1.5" (3" diameter) would have an area of 7.065 in² ($\pi \times 1.5^2 = 7.065$ in²).

The principles of Pascal's law allow us to apply an enormous amount of force to our hydraulic application devices inside our transmission. In one typical transmission, the hydraulic system is regulated to approximately 175 psi (1207 kPa) of pressure. That 175 psi (1207 kPa) is applied to a piston with a radius of 3" (6" diameter). Now we can calculate the total force output of the piston. First, we need to calculate the area of the piston: $\pi \times 3^2$ = 28.26 in². Our piston has a surface area of roughly 28 in². Apply the 175 psi to 28 in² and we have a total force of 4900 lb (2223 kg) **FIGURE 17-2**!

Hydraulic System Components

The hydraulic system of an automatic transmission includes a filter, a hydraulic pump (front pump), a pressure regulation device, hydraulic application devices for clutches and bands, and several types of control valves and accumulators. Each of the components works with the others to direct fluid under the proper pressure to the appropriate places in the transmission. Learning the function and purposes of each of these hydraulic components will help you to diagnose transmission-related problems as well as inspect and test the components when replacing them.

Filter

The pump (and the rest of the transmission) must be provided with a steady stream of clean transmission fluid. Any dirt or particles in the fluid can cause excessive wear to the inside components of the transmission. This dirt can also cause any of the precision valves inside the transmission to become stuck. Vehicle transmissions can use either internal or external filters **FIGURE 17-3**. Some vehicles have both an internal and an external filter, such as the Allison series of transmissions found in General Motors heavy-duty pick-up trucks.

An external filter looks very similar (or almost identical) to an engine oil filter. The filter can be changed without removing the transmission oil pan. A vehicle that used an external filter was the (now discontinued) Saturn S series, as well as many Subaru models.

> **TECHNICIAN TIP**
>
> Many beginning technicians or students have accidentally removed an external transmission filter instead of the oil filter when performing an oil change. Always double-check that the filter you are removing is the correct one.

Internal filters are much more common than external filters. Replacement of an internal filter requires removing the transmission pan. Internal filters can be one of two types: a **surface filter** or a **depth filter**. A surface filter is often a simple fine-mesh screen made out of metal or a plastic such as polyester. The screen catches particles of dirt as the fluid is drawn through the filter. Surface

FIGURE 17-3 Transmission filters. **A.** A typical internal transmission filter. **B.** A typical external filter.

filters do not have the ability to trap a large amount of material. Most surface filters can stop particles between the size of 50 and 100 microns. One micron is 0.000039" (0.0001 mm), so the smallest particle a surface filter would be able to stop is 0.00195" (0.05 mm)—approximately the thickness of an average human hair.

Depth filters have a thick filter medium that the fluid must pass through. As the fluid passes through the filter, particles become trapped throughout the medium. They use felt or other filter media to trap dirt. Depth filters are able to hold a much larger volume of dirt and particles. This allows them to be effective for a longer period of time. They can also filter out much smaller particles than a surface filter. High-quality depth filters can filter out particles as small as 10 microns, or 0.00039" (0.001 mm).

Inside the transmission, there is often a magnet stuck to the transmission pan. This magnet is designed to help catch ferrous (iron-containing) particles that could cause severe damage to the internal surfaces of the pump as well as the seals, bearings, and bushings within the transmission. This magnet needs to be cleaned off when the transmission fluid and filter are serviced.

Transmission filters should be changed according to the manufacturer's recommended service interval, using high-quality parts and the correct fluid. Changing the filter and fluid on a regular schedule can greatly increase the life of a transmission. This task will be covered later in the chapter.

Front Pump

Modern automatic transmissions have a hydraulic pump referred to as a front pump. They are called front pumps because they are located at the front of the transmission (closest to the engine). In some antique vehicles, transmissions had a front pump and a rear pump—hence how the specific term front pump came to be. The front pump is turned by the torque converter hub, which is directly turned by the flex plate and crankshaft. Thus, the pump is turning whenever the engine is turning, and hydraulic pressure is available inside the transmission when the engine is operating.

Front pumps can be one of four types of pumps, as discussed in the Automatic Transmission Fundamentals chapter. This pump is like the heart of the transmission. Without the pump, the transmission cannot function. The types of pumps used in an automatic transmission are gear, rotor, vane, and a variable displacement style of the vane pump. Each of these pumps has a different design, but all serve the same purpose: They provide hydraulic pressure to all of the hydraulically operated components, supply lubrication oil to internal

transmission components, and circulate fluid to help cool the transmission.

Pump housings can be made from cast iron or aluminum. Cast iron housings tend to resist wear very well and require replacement less often than aluminum pump housings; however, cast iron is much heavier than aluminum and most manufacturers have switched to aluminum to reduce vehicle weight and improve fuel economy.

The gear pump is a very simply designed pump. Often during a transmission overhaul, the gear pump will not require any service other than replacing any seals and the front pump bushing. However, it is still important to check the pump for wear to prevent any problems when the transmission is put back into service. Most manufacturers will specify a clearance measurement between the outer pump gear and the pump housing. This clearance can be measured with a small feeler gauge **FIGURE 17-4**.

Manufacturers will also usually specify a clearance measurement between the teeth of the driving gear and the crescent. One more clearance measurement is required to complete the front pump inspection. This last measurement is completed by placing a precision straightedge across the pump halves with the two pump gears installed. The clearance between the pump gears and the straightedge is then measured with a feeler gauge. Some manufacturers will also specify an inner gear tooth to outer gear tooth clearance that must be checked with a feeler gauge **FIGURE 17-5**.

A generic method for quickly checking a gear pump on a high-mileage vehicle is to run your hand across the face of the pump gears. If you feel a sharp edge on the gear, it is worn out and will require replacement. When the gears for a gear pump are machined at the factory, a bevel is machined into the edge of the gears. As the gear wears, this bevel will wear away, leaving a sharp edge.

FIGURE 17-4 Pump gear-to-housing clearance being measured with a feeler gauge.

FIGURE 17-5 Pump gears-to-housing clearance being checked with a straightedge and feeler gauge.

FIGURE 17-6 A vane pump's rotor thickness being measured to check for wear.

The housing of the pump also needs to be checked for wear. This can be accomplished with a straightedge and a feeler gauge. Often, a pump on a transmission that has suffered from infrequent fluid changes will wind up with a small piece of dirt trapped between the gear and the housing, causing a groove to be ground into the pump housing. These grooves can be felt by running your fingernail across the surface of the pump housing. If you can feel your fingernail catch on a groove, the groove is at least 0.001" (0.0254 mm) deep. Light scratches and grooves can be removed on some pumps by rubbing a whet stone across the pump housing while running solvent over the pump in the solvent tank. A whet stone is a type of flat stone used to sharpen knives and other cutting tools.

The rotor pump has two rotors that mesh together, one inside the other. As with the gear pump, most manufacturers will specify rotor-to-pump housing clearance, along with rotor lobe-to-rotor lobe clearance. The same methods for quickly checking a gear pump can be used on the rotor pump.

The vane pump and the variable displacement vane pump are quite a bit different from the gear pump and rotor pump. The center section of the vane pump is the rotor. The rotor has vanes that stick out from grooves radially spaced around the rotor. The vanes seal against the housing, which is offset to the rotor. Vehicle manufacturers typically recommend measuring the thickness of the rotor and comparing it to specifications **FIGURE 17-6**.

The housing of the vane pump, like that of the gear pump and rotor pump, must be checked for wear, grooves, or scoring. The vanes need to be inspected for excessive wear. The vanes must be reinstalled in the same direction that they were removed. If the vanes are flipped, rapid wear will result when the transmission is placed back into service. The vane pump typically has sealing

rings on the rotor that will need to be replaced during service. The sealing rings are usually made from cast iron or Teflon.

A variable displacement vane pump uses a rotor and vanes just like the standard vane pump. However, the variable displacement vane pump uses a spring-loaded movable pump housing that pivots in such a way that the volume of the pumping chambers can be increased or decreased based on fluid pressure. This design allows the pump chambers to have a large volume during low engine speeds, and smaller chambers during higher engine speeds. This results in less pumping losses and reduces fluid foaming in a pressure regulator.

Pressure Regulation

Fluid pressure in an automatic transmission needs to be regulated to help control the quality of the shift. Without regulation, fluid pressure coming out of the front pump will vary greatly as engine speed increases and decreases while the customer drives the vehicle. When the engine speed is low, the pump output is low, resulting in low pressure. When engine speed increases, the volume of fluid and the pressure coming out of the front pump increase. Front pumps are designed with the capacity to provide more than enough fluid volume and pressure at low speeds to ensure proper transmission operation; therefore, we need to reduce the pressure to the correct amount. The fluid pressure or line pressure can be controlled either by using a mechanical pressure control regulator valve or by using an electronic pressure control solenoid.

A **mechanical pressure control regulator valve** is a simple mechanism that uses a spring and a **spool valve** to dump excess fluid back to the transmission pan **FIGURE 17-7**. A spool valve is a type of valve commonly used in automatic transmissions. The spool valve got its name because of its resemblance to the spool that thread or fishing line comes on. The spool valve operates back and forth inside of a bore in the valve body or the front pump. The larger ends of the spool, called lands, fit inside the bore with a very small amount of clearance, typically less than 0.001" (0.0254 mm) **FIGURE 17-8**. Such a limited clearance means that even the smallest dirt or debris in a valve body can cause a valve to stick in its bore. All internal transmission work must be performed in a clean environment.

This tight fit will prevent most fluid from slipping past the land. The clearance between the land and the bore must be just great enough to prevent the valve from sticking as it moves back and forth. This clearance will allow a very small amount of fluid to leak past the spool valve, but it should be insignificant if the valve-to-bore clearance is correct.

FIGURE 17-7 A typical mechanical pressure control regulator valve.

Labels in figure: Regulator spring · Regulator valve · Exhaust to oil pan · Regulated line pressure out · Pump input

FIGURE 17-8 A typical spool valve installed in its bore.

Fluid coming out from the front pump is forced against one side of the spool valve. The other side of the spool valve has a spring that pushes back against the fluid. The spring pressure is set at the factory to a predetermined value. This value determines the regulated fluid pressure. When the pump pressure acting on the spool valve becomes greater than the spring pressure, the spool valve moves slightly, opening an exhaust port, and excess fluid pressure is exhausted back to the transmission pan. As the fluid pressure drops, the spring forces the spool valve back into position to block the exhaust port in the bore, thereby raising the fluid pressure. This process happens continuously as the vehicle is driven.

One way to think of a pressure regulator valve is to picture a garden hose turned on all the way. If the end of the hose is open, the water flows out of the hose easily and the pressure in the hose is very small. But when you place your thumb over the end of the hose and block the flow of water, pressure in the hose increases. You can vary the pressure in the hose by increasing or decreasing your thumb pressure, thus controlling the flow of water out of the hose. This is the same way a standard pressure regulator valve works, except the valve is controlled by spring pressure, which can be assisted by applying hydraulic pressure or by using linkage to increase the spring pressure.

On a vehicle with a variable displacement pump, some of the output fluid is sent to the moveable housing of the pump. This pressure causes the housing to move to the right, as shown in **FIGURE 17-9**. When the housing moves, the pump's volume is reduced. The balance between pump pressure and spring pressure causes the pump's displacement to be controlled so that the specified fluid pressure is maintained under all operating conditions.

On computerized transmissions, an __electronic pressure control (EPC) solenoid__ is used to regulate line pressure. Most EPC solenoids are a pulse-width modulated valve **FIGURE 17-10**. Pulse-width modulated means that they are pulsed on and off continuously. A 50% pulse width modulation means that the valve is open 50% of the time and closed 50% of the time.

EPC solenoids are usually designed so that they reduce pressure when they are operating. The solenoid is normally closed, resulting in no fluid being returned to the transmission pan **FIGURE 17-11**. If the solenoid is pulsed on 25% of the time, line pressure is reduced by approximately 25%. The higher the pulse width, the lower our line pressure is. If the solenoid fails, the transmission will have maximum line pressure to prevent transmission damage.

Application Devices

In an automatic transmission, there are three basic types of holding devices used to hold a member of the planetary gear set, as discussed in the Automatic Transmission Fundamentals chapter. These holding devices are a multidisc clutch, a band, and a one-way roller or sprag.

FIGURE 17-10 An electronic pressure control (EPC) solenoid mounted on a valve body from a General Motors 4L60E transmission.

FIGURE 17-9 Pressure regulation with a variable displacement pump.

FIGURE 17-11 A typical EPC solenoid and the fluid passages going to and from the valve.

Both multidisc clutches and bands are hydraulically operated, so we will go into more detail about them now.

As discussed earlier, the multidisc clutch is often located inside of a drum. It may also be mounted inside the case using the case as the drum (housing). At the bottom of the drum, after you have removed the clutches and steels, you will find a snap ring and one or more piston return springs. By properly compressing the return spring(s) to remove the snap ring, you can see a large piston that fits snugly inside the drum. This piston typically has a lip seal around the outside edge to seal the piston to the drum and prevent fluid and pressure leakage. There is another lip seal around the center of the piston. Often, transmission failure can be traced back to failed lip seals that have been leaking and preventing the piston from applying the full pressure needed to lock up the multidisc clutch **FIGURE 17-12**.

When the transmission sends fluid pressure to the multidisc clutch piston, the piston is forced out by the fluid. The average piston has an approximate surface area of 12 in² (197 mm²). If the pump applies 150 psi (1034 kPa) of pressure to the piston, the piston will apply a force of 1800 lb (816 kg) to squeeze the friction discs and steels together. If there is a leak in the system, the amount of force exerted will be greatly reduced and can result in clutch slippage.

When rebuilding a clutch pack, the piston needs to be carefully inspected for cracks **FIGURE 17-13**. Cracks in the piston will cause a pressure loss resulting in a clutch pack that will fail. New lip seals should always be installed before the piston is reinstalled in the drum. Seals should be properly lubricated with transmission assembly lube or petroleum jelly to prevent damaging the seals. Reinstalling the piston into the drum will take some patience and practice to prevent ripping the lips of the seals. After rebuilding a multidisc clutch, always check the operation of the clutch using the shop's compressed air to actuate the piston.

When the transmission stops sending fluid pressure to the clutch pack piston, the piston return spring(s) pushes the piston back into its seat in the drum. Once the

> **TECHNICIAN TIP**
>
> Operating the clutch with compressed air to check it for leaks is called "air checking." If a seal was damaged during installation, there will be a large air leak from inside the clutch requiring disassembly and replacement of the damaged seal. A word of warning: Only air check a clutch with all of the clutch plates and snap rings installed; this approach will prevent the piston from traveling too far and coming out of its bore, leaking, and then cutting the lips of the seals between the piston and the edge of the bore.

pressure is relieved, typically a check ball in the piston or drum opens and allows the fluid to be thrown out of the drum as it is rotating. The fluid then is returned to the transmission pan.

Bands are applied by applying fluid pressure to a servo. The servo is a piston inside a bore. The edge of the piston is sealed to the bore using a square-cut seal. As the fluid pressure pushes on the piston, the piston pushes a linkage to contract the band. An average servo piston is approximately 2" (51 mm) in diameter, with a surface area of approximately 3 in² (49 mm²). This means if we apply the 150-psi (1034 kPa) pump pressure to the servo piston, the piston will exert a force of 450 lb (204 kg) on the band. A large spring around the linkage returns the piston to its seat in the bore when the pressure is released. Some transmissions use a staged or dual-piston servo to apply a band. This dual piston allows for greater force to be applied to the band

FIGURE 17-12 A piston removed from a multidisc clutch.

FIGURE 17-13 A piston from a multidisc clutch that has cracked, leading to a failed transmission.

by increasing the effective surface area of the pistons. Some servos operate a lever with an offset fulcrum that multiplies the force from the piston to the band.

> **TECHNICIAN TIP**
>
> When building performance transmissions, some standard servos can be swapped out for high-performance servos, which increase the surface area of the piston. An example of this is the General Motors 4L60E transmission, where the servo can be replaced with a servo from the Corvette version of the transmission.

▶ Valve Types and Functions

The majority of automatic transmission control valves are located inside the **valve body**. The valve body is a housing made of aluminum or cast iron that holds many different spool valves, check valves, springs, and orifices to make the transmission operate properly. The valve body may be located in the transmission oil pan, or in a side pan, as on many front-wheel drive transaxles **FIGURE 17-14**.

FIGURE 17-14 **A.** Transmission valve body location. **B.** Transaxle valve body location.

Spool Valves

Spool valves are used quite often in automatic transmissions. As we discussed earlier, spool valves resemble the "spool" that thread or fishing line comes on. The spool valve has larger lands located on the valve that fit tightly inside a bore in the valve body. A spool valve may have several lands placed in different spots on the valve. Smaller-diameter sections called valleys are located between the lands. The face of each land is machined square and sharp to the land diameter, and some valves have a stem or extension on one end to locate a regulating or return spring or to limit valve travel **FIGURE 17-15**. The sharp corners on the lands prevent the entry of dirt particles and also give the valve a self-cleaning action as it moves back and forth in the bore.

Fluid is able to flow around the valleys easily. As the land of the spool valve is pushed, either by a spring or by hydraulic pressure, the land moves to block the flow of hydraulic oil from a passage in the valve body. Spool valves can also work in the opposite direction, so that when spring pressure or hydraulic pressure is applied to the land, the valve may move, exposing a passage in the valve body. This design allows fluid to flow past the valley of the spool valve. Spool valves must be handled with care when servicing a transmission because they have very tight clearances and any damage will make them unusable. Because the clearances are so small, always use lint-free towels when working around automatic transmissions. A small piece of lint can cause a valve to stick in position and not operate, affecting the operation of the transmission.

Spool valves can be positioned manually, by springs, or by pressure, and many applications have lands

FIGURE 17-15 A spool valve and return spring that have been removed from the transmission valve body.

of different diameters. In **FIGURE 17-16**, the different diameters result in a larger face area on land 1 than on land 2. This is known as a differential area. When fluid under pressure enters at port B, this differential area creates a differential force. This force moves the valve to the left because the force acting on land 1 is greater than the force on land 2. Alternatively, the valve could be actuated by admitting fluid at port C. In both cases, the valve movement allows previously blocked fluid at port D to flow between lands 3 and 4 and either exhaust at port E or pass to some other part of the system. If fluid pressure is removed from port C, the valve will remain stationary. Even if fluid is admitted at port A, no movement can occur because the surface areas of lands 2 and 3 are equal and both generate an equal force. The valve can be moved back to its original position only by introducing spring pressure or fluid pressure on the left side of land 1.

The manual valve is a type of spool valve directly connected to the gearshift mechanism in the vehicle. When the driver selects a drive gear, the manual valve is positioned in the valve body to allow line pressure to push fluid to the proper valves and components inside the transmission. The manual valve is often connected to the gearshift through a metal linkage inside the transmission that is connected to a cable on the outside of the transmission **FIGURE 17-17**. Some older models used complicated linkages from the gearshift lever to the transmission that were prone to wear and often needed adjustment.

Shift valves are spool valves that direct the flow of hydraulic oil to a clutch or band upon upshift when they are moved by a pressure called governor pressure, or, on a modern transmission, when the computer commands

Applied Science

AS-49: Pressure: The technician can demonstrate an understanding of the concept of pressure in relation to the concept of force.

Pressure and force are two terms that share some similarities and whose meanings are often confused. Force can be simply defined as a push or a pull (or both) that tends to make an object change its state of motion. Pressure is a physical quality, defined as the amount of force per unit of area applied to the surface of an object.

Let's say that we have a hydraulic circuit in an automatic transmission which activates a clutch piston. The piston has an area of 10 sq/in (64.5cm²) and when the circuit is activated, a pressure of 75 psi (517 kPa) is applied to the piston. The force generated by the piston to apply the clutch is determined by multiplying the piston area by the pressure applied, in this case, 75 psi (517 kPa) of pressure results in 750 lb (3.3 kN) of force holding the clutches together.

FIGURE 17-17 A manual valve installed in an automatic transmission.

fluid pressure to the shift valve. Governor pressure is a type of hydraulic pressure that increases in a nearly linear manner as vehicle speed increases. Shift valves are labeled in a manner such as 2-3 upshift or 3-2 downshift to distinguish their function.

Pressure-regulating valves are similar to the line pressure regulation valve except these valves reduce line pressure even further for specific components.

FIGURE 17-16 A typical spool valve with different-sized lands.

> ▸ **LINK**
> Refer to the Hydraulically Controlled Transmission chapter for more detail on governors.

Some typical places where manufacturers use additional pressure regulation valves to lower line pressure are the transmission cooler and the torque converter. These pressure regulators are often located in the transmission valve body, but they can also be located inside the front pump.

Solenoid Valves

On modern computer-controlled transmissions, shifting is accomplished by one of two methods. In the first method, the computer commands a solenoid valve to open, allowing line pressure to push fluid past the solenoid valve and move a spool-type shift valve **FIGURE 17-18**. A solenoid valve is an electromagnetic valve. When electrical current is passed through the solenoid, a plunger is pulled up, allowing fluid to flow past the solenoid. In the second method, the computer commands a solenoid valve to allow line pressure to be directly sent to the correct application device to complete the shift.

Check Valves

Check valves can be one of two types in an automatic transmission: one-way check valves or two-way check valves (also known as shuttle valves). Fluid flow in one direction causes the valve to unseat and allows hydraulic oil to flow freely. Fluid flow in the opposite direction causes the valve to close, blocking the passage of hydraulic oil. Check valves can have springs inside to help with the closing of the valve, or they can be a simple check ball design, which uses gravity to close the valve **FIGURE 17-19**.

One-way check valves are often used in the release circuit for application devices. For example, some

Applied | Science

AS-86: Action/Reaction: The technician can demonstrate an understanding of the action/reaction of fluids involving valves or pistons.
According to Newton's third law of motion, for every acting force there is an equal (in strength) and opposite (in direction) reacting force. This principle is applied in several areas within automatic transmission hydraulic circuits.

For gear changes to occur at optimum times the transmission must balance engine load and road speed. In hydraulically controlled transmissions, engine load may be sensed by means of a throttle valve connected directly to the accelerator pedal. When changes occur in engine load, the throttle valve raises or lowers its output pressure correspondingly. Road speed is monitored via a governor valve, which is sensitive to centrifugal force and is mounted on the transmission's output shaft. The governor valve increases or decreases its output pressure in proportion to output shaft speed.

Shift valves are exposed to both throttle pressure and governor pressure on opposite sides of a piston. The position of the shift valve is dependent on their relationship. If governor pressure overcomes throttle pressure (+spring pressure), an upshift will result. If throttle pressure (+spring pressure) overcomes governor pressure, a downshift occurs.

transmissions have one small passage that supplies oil to an application device, but have two passages that allow oil to release from the application device **FIGURE 17-20**. If we did not have a check ball or check valve in the second passage, the fluid pressure would simply dump out the exhaust port rather than applying the clutch or band. By having a second larger passage for the release of oil from

FIGURE 17-18 A shift solenoid that sends line pressure to a secondary shift valve.

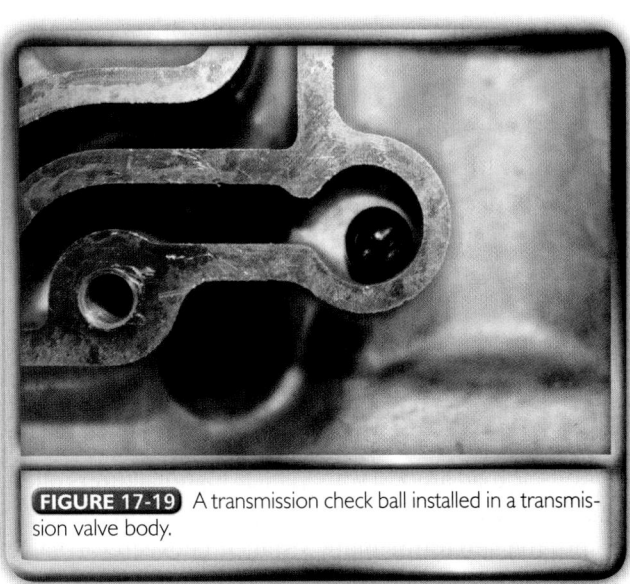

FIGURE 17-19 A transmission check ball installed in a transmission valve body.

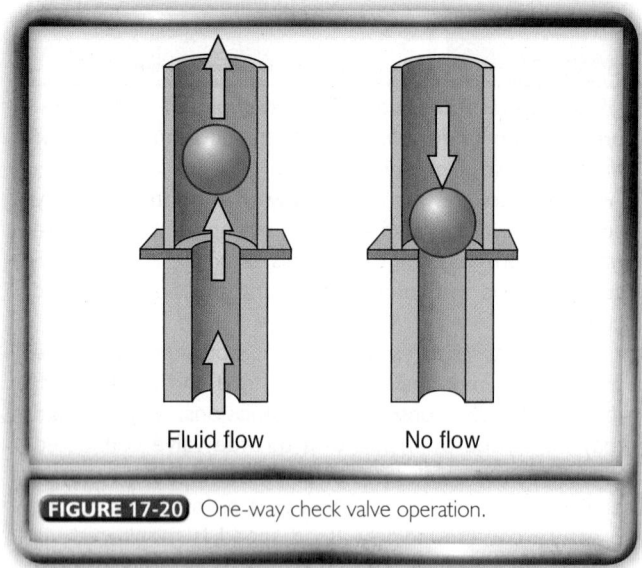

FIGURE 17-20 One-way check valve operation.

FIGURE 17-21 A two-way check valve.

the clutch or band, we can exhaust the oil pressure more quickly to prevent clutch dragging.

Two-way check valves also commonly use a check ball **FIGURE 17-21**. In the two-way check valve, there are two fluid inlet ports and one fluid outlet port. Thus, two different control devices can share the outlet passage. An example of this system would be a transmission that has a band applied in all gears when the gear selector is placed in second. This allows line pressure to pass from the manual valve to the servo controlling the band, but this transmission only uses the band for first gear when the gear selector is placed in D. Without the two-way check valve, when the gear selector is placed in second, fluid would flow from the manual valve and bypass the band servo, which would then dump out the first gearshift valve.

Orifices

Orifices are often used in conjunction with spool valves to restrict fluid flow for timing purposes or to prevent valve fluctuations. An orifice is a precision hole. The orifice is smaller in diameter than the passage or line feeding the orifice. It is designed to prevent sudden or undue movement of a valve. It is much like a section of highway where a few lanes must merge together. We have all been stuck in a construction zone waiting for our turn to merge with another lane because our lane has ended. This reduction in the size of the passage (or the highway) causes the fluid to be delayed and reduces pressure after the orifice. After the construction zone on the highway, is there much traffic, or does it seem to have reduced the number of cars on the road around you? Vehicle manufacturers often build orifices into automatic transmission valve bodies, or into the **separator plate** installed between the valve

body halves or between the valve body and the transmission case. The orifices control the flow of hydraulic fluid between the valve body and the transmission.

Orifices are often used in the passage feeding oil pressure to a clutch or band. The narrow section or orifice slows the application of the reverse gear to prevent the transmission from having a harsh reverse application.

> ### ▶ TECHNICIAN TIP
>
> If you purchase a high-performance rebuild kit for a transmission, often the kit will come with a different valve body separator plate with larger holes. These larger holes are actually larger orifices that will result in less of a delay in clutch application. Some high-performance kits specify that you use a specific drill bit size to enlarge the hole in the spacer plate. These modifications affect the operation of the transmission, so only experienced transmission specialists should perform this work.

Accumulators are another hydraulic device found in automatic transmissions **FIGURE 17-22**. Accumulators are used to dampen the application of clutches and bands **FIGURE 17-23**. Without an accumulator in an application device circuit, the transmission might apply the clutch or band harshly enough to cause the customer to complain about the shift quality. Or, the transmission might shift harshly enough to break the tires loose from the pavement during each transmission shift. Harsh shifting increases wear to the rest of the drive train and puts more extreme forces on pistons, drums, planetary gears, and linkages. Accumulators contain a piston installed in

FIGURE 17-22 An automatic transmission accumulator being removed from a transmission case.

FIGURE 17-23 Accumulator operation in a servo circuit.

> ▷ **TECHNICIAN TIP**
>
> Often when building high-performance transmissions, specific accumulator springs are removed to improve the shift quality of a transmission that is installed behind a high-performance, high-horsepower engine. Without the spring installed in the accumulator, the piston will remain in the bottom of the bore so that the piston cannot move. Without the piston movement, the clutch or band will apply much more quickly, but will result in a harsh shift.

a bore. The piston has rubber or Teflon seals around the outside edge to seal the piston to the bore. There is a large spring behind the accumulator piston. When the shift valve moves to send line pressure to the clutch or band,

fluid is sent to the side of the accumulator piston opposite of the spring and the clutch or band at the same time. The clutch or band begins to apply progressively as the accumulator spring is completely compressed by the piston.

Clutch and Band Application Charts

When diagnosing an automatic transmission problem, it is important to first verify the customer complaint by taking the vehicle on a road test, if possible. If the vehicle transmission will not function at all, this is not possible. After you have verified the customer complaint, pay attention and document when the problem occurs. For example, if you place the gearshift into 2 rather than D, does the problem still occur? Does the problem only occur during hard acceleration, or during light acceleration as well? Use this information when you look at the manufacturer's clutch and band application chart, sometimes referred to as a truth chart. The chart lists specifically which clutches, bands, and other components are used for the different functions of the transmission.

TABLE 17-1 is a sample of an application chart for a transmission. Using this chart, we can start our diagnosis of a failed transmission *before* we pull the transmission. By having this information before beginning the repair, we can give a better estimate of the repair costs to the customer. We may also determine that it is not even necessary to remove the transmission from the vehicle in order to fix the problem.

Using the table, what are the possible problems if the transmission operates only in third gear, no matter which forward range the gear selector is in? If you said that it must be a problem with the shift solenoids, you are correct. By looking at the table, we can determine that neither shift solenoid is used in third gear. What if the vehicle has no reverse but moves forward? When you look at the table, you will see that there are several components of the transmission in use. If the transmission seems to drive forward fine, could the problem be a bad 1-2 shift solenoid, or a 2-3 shift solenoid? If you answered no, you are correct. If it were one of the shift solenoids, other gears would also show a problem. Now you have reduced the number of possible components to two: the low reverse clutch and the reverse input clutch. If you were to put the vehicle into first, you would be able to diagnose further. When in first, the transmission is supposed to hold onto the engine and not freewheel or coast when you decelerate. If the transmission holds on deceleration in first, you can eliminate all of the possible choices except the reverse input clutch. You now have a very good idea of what has failed inside the transmission before you have even turned a wrench.

TABLE 17-1: Sample Application Chart for a Transmission

Gear Range (Selector Lever Position)	1-2 Shift Solenoid	2-3 Shift Solenoid	Forward Clutch	Forward Sprag	Low Roller Clutch	2-4 Band	3-4 Clutch	Overrun Clutch	Low Reverse Clutch	Reverse Input Clutch
Park	x	x							x	
Neutral	x	x								
Reverse	x	x							x	x
D (Overdrive), First gear	x	x	x	x	x					
D (Overdrive), Second Gear		x	x	x		x				
D (Overdrive), Third Gear			x	x			x			
D (Overdrive) Overdrive	x		x			x	x			
D (Drive), First Gear	x	x	x	x	x					
D (Drive), Second Gear		x	x	x		x				
D (Drive), Third Gear			x	x		x	x			
2, First Gear	x	x	x	x	x			x		
2, Second Gear		X	x	x		x		x		
1, Low Gear	x	x	x	x	x			x	x	

Wrap-up

Ready for Review

- Hydraulic operation is used to apply and release different clutches and bands in automatic transmissions.
- Pascal's law states that if fluid is placed in a confined space, then pressure will be equally transferred in all directions within that space.
- Force can be multiplied using Pascal's law.
- Vehicle transmissions use filters (internal, external, or both) to ensure clean transmission fluid.
- Internal filters (most common) can be surface or depth filters.
- Surface filters have a fine-mesh screen, but cannot trap a large amount of material.
- Depth filters use thicker filter media, trap a larger volume of material, and are effective longer than surface filters.
- A magnet stuck to the transmission pan is designed to catch iron-containing particles.
- Components of a hydraulic system are the hydraulic pump (front pump), the pressure regulation device, hydraulic application devices, control valves, and accumulators.
- Types of front pumps are gear, rotor, vane, and the variable displacement style of the vane pump.
- Purposes of the hydraulic/front pump are to provide hydraulic pressure to all hydraulically operated components, supply lubrication oil to internal transmission components, and circulate fluid to cool the transmission.
- Pump housings can be cast iron (wear resistant, require less frequent replacement) or aluminum (lighter weight).
- A feeler gauge is used to measure pump gear-to-pump housing clearance, driving gear teeth-to-crescent clearance, and pump gear-to-straightedge on pump halves clearance.
- Gear pumps can be checked for wear by hand, while the pump housing should be checked with a straightedge and feeler gauge.

- Rotor pumps are checked in a similar fashion to gear pumps.
- Vane pumps are checked for wear by comparing rotor thickness to specifications.
- Check vane pump housing and vanes for wear; reinstall vanes in the same direction they were removed.
- Automatic transmission fluid pressure is controlled via either a mechanical pressure control regulator valve or an electronic pressure control (EPC) solenoid.
- A mechanical pressure control regulator valve uses a spring and a spool valve to ensure that excess fluid spills into the transmission pan.
- Variable displacement pumps rely on movement of the housing to reduce volume and regulate pressure.
- Computerized transmissions use EPC solenoids to regulate line pressure.
- EPC solenoids are generally pulse-width–modulated valves that are continuously pulsed on and off and reduce pressure during their "on" cycle.
- The multidisc clutches and bands used to stop a member of the planetary gear set are hydraulically operated.
- The transmission sends fluid pressure to the multidisc clutch piston, forcing the piston to transfer that force into squeezing friction discs and steels together; any leaks will reduce the amount of force.
- When fluid pressure is applied to a servo piston, it will in turn exert force on a band.
- Types of automatic transmission valves are spool, solenoid, and check.
- Spool valves have lands and valleys that are used to block or allow flow of transmission fluid.
- Differential diameters of the spool valve's lands create differential force when receiving pressurized fluid.
- Types of spool valves include manual and shift valves.

▶ On computer-controlled transmissions, the computer can direct a shift solenoid to send line pressure to a secondary shift valve.

▶ Check valves can be one-way or two-way valves (shuttle valves).

▶ Check valves can allow fluid to flow past them, but fluid flowing in the opposite direction will close the valve, blocking the fluid.

▶ Check valves may contain a spring or a check ball (common in two-way check valves).

▶ Orifices are precision holes that work with spool valves to restrict fluid flow for timing purposes or to prevent valve fluctuations.

▶ Accumulators are designed to dampen the application of clutches and bands.

▶ Automatic transmission problem diagnosis should start with a road test. Verify the customer's complaint and document the circumstances under which the problem occurs.

▶ Use a manufacturer-provided clutch and band application chart to assist in diagnosis and estimate repair costs.

Key Terms

accumulator A device used to reduce the speed of clutch or band application to help prevent harsh shifting.

check valve Also known as a shuttle valve, a valve that allows the flow of hydraulic oil in one direction only. It is typically used to allow oil to escape quickly from an application device when shifting gears.

depth filter A hydraulic filter that has thick filter media to trap dirt and other particles of various sizes as they pass through the filter.

electronic pressure control (EPC) solenoid A solenoid used to regulate line pressure on a computerized transmission.

mechanical pressure control regulator valve A spool valve and spring assembly that are used to control the amount of line pressure in a transmission.

orifice A precisely sized hole used to reduce the speed and pressure of hydraulic oil flowing to a clutch or band.

Pascal's law One of the fundamental physics principles behind the operation of an automatic transmission, this law states that if fluid is placed in a confined space, pressure will be transferred equally in all directions inside the space.

separator plate Sometimes called a spacer plate, a thin sheet metal plate installed between the valve body and the transmission case. Orifices can be installed in the separator plate, and check valves can work with holes in the plate.

shift valve A spool valve used to control oil flow to a clutch or band for a particular gear.

spool valve A type of valve commonly used in automatic transmissions that resembles the spool that thread or fishing line comes on.

surface filter A filter that is a simple screen mechanism to catch dirt and other particles in the hydraulic oil as it passes through.

valve body An aluminum or cast iron housing inside the transmission that houses the majority of the valves that control transmission operation.

ASE-Type Questions

1. Tech A says that band and clutch application charts can help to diagnose faults in a transmission. Tech B says that 100 psi of pressure on a 2-square-inch piston results in 50 lb of force. Who is correct?
   a. Tech A
   b. Tech B
   c. Both A and B
   d. Neither A nor B

2. Tech A says that hydraulic pressure is the same in all directions within a closed container. Tech B says that one benefit of using hydraulic pressure is that it is not affected by leaks in the system. Who is correct?
   a. Tech A
   b. Tech B
   c. Both A and B
   d. Neither A nor B

3. Tech A says that when performing a routine change of the transmission fluid and filter, the cooler should also be flushed. Tech B says that if the transmission pan is removed, the magnet must be replaced. Who is correct?
   a. Tech A
   b. Tech B
   c. Both A and B
   d. Neither A nor B

4. Tech A says that the greater the clearance between the gear pump housing and the gear, the more fluid can be pumped through the circuit. Tech B says that the front pump is turned by the torque converter hub. Who is correct?
   a. Tech A
   b. Tech B
   c. Both A and B
   d. Neither A nor B

5. Tech A says that spring tension against a spool valve regulates system pressure. Tech B says that a 50% pulse width modulation means the valve is closed 50% of the time. Who is correct?
   a. Tech A
   b. Tech B
   c. Both A and B
   d. Neither A nor B

6. Tech A says that transmission failures are often caused by failed lip seals preventing full pressure from being applied to the clutches. Tech B says that fluid leaks are the greatest cause of clutch slippage. Who is correct?
   a. Tech A
   b. Tech B
   c. Both A and B
   d. Neither A nor B

7. Tech A says that spool valves tend to be self-cleaning. Tech B says that park is obtained by mechanically locking one band and one clutch together. Who is correct?
   a. Tech A
   b. Tech B
   c. Both A and B
   d. Neither A nor B

8. Tech A says that multi-plate clutches must have a specified amount of clearance when they are installed. Tech B says that there should be no clearance when they are installed because the clutch would slip. Who is correct?
   a. Tech A
   b. Tech B
   c. Both A and B
   d. Neither A nor B

9. Tech A says that an orifice is a restriction. Tech B says that orifices are used to slow down clutch engagement. Who is correct?
   a. Tech A
   b. Tech B
   c. Both A and B
   d. Neither A nor B

10. Tech A says that accumulators are used to filter contaminates. Tech B says that accumulators are used to soften clutch engagement. Who is correct?
    a. Tech A
    b. Tech B
    c. Both A and B
    d. Neither A nor B

CHAPTER 18

NATEF Tasks

There are no NATEF tasks for this chapter.

Knowledge Objectives

After reading this chapter, you will be able to:
1. Describe the operation of a governor valve. (pp 500–503)
2. Identify the components of a hydraulically controlled transmission. (pp 500–506)
3. Describe the operation of a vacuum modulator and throttle valve. (pp 503–505)
4. Describe how the pressure regulator controls line pressure. (pp 506–508)
5. Understand and explain the operation of a hydraulically controlled transmission. (pp 508–510)

Hydraulically Controlled Transmission

Skills Objectives

There are no skills objectives for this chapter.

Introduction

In fully hydraulically controlled transmissions, the timing and speed of shifts are completely controlled by hydraulic and/or mechanical devices. Although none of the automobile manufacturers in the United States is still producing fully hydraulically controlled transmissions, it is nonetheless important for students and technicians to understand how these transmissions operate. This is because on a modern computer-controlled transmission, the electronic sensors and actuators that replaced the hydraulic and mechanical control devices perform the exact same function: controlling the flow of hydraulic fluid to and from the transmission components. In fact, both hydraulic and electronic transmissions with multiplate clutches and bands use hydraulic pressure to apply the bands and clutches. The only difference between the two types is how the fluid is controlled. We will go into detail about each of the parts used to control the hydraulically controlled transmission in this chapter. Electronically controlled transmissions are covered in the Electronically Controlled Transmission chapter.

Hydraulically Controlled Transmission Components

The hydraulic controls in a hydraulically controlled transmission work together to cause upshifts and downshifts at the proper times. For the controls to work properly, a supply of pressurized automatic transmission fluid is required. This pressurized fluid is supplied by the pump and is maintained at the proper pressure by the pressure regulator valve. The pressure controlled by the pressure regulator valve is called line pressure and is what applies the bands and clutches as well as supplies fluid to the governor and throttle valves. Line pressure is varied based on engine load and the selection of certain gears to maintain firm application of the clutches and bands. We will explore each of the valves, the job it performs, and its operation.

Governor

The **governor** is a hydro-mechanical valve that produces a variable pressure, based on vehicle speed, otherwise known as ground speed. This variable pressure is called **governor pressure**. Governors can be installed in the transmission in one of two places—mounted in the transmission case or mounted on the output shaft of the transmission **FIGURE 18-1**. Both types are driven by the output shaft so that the governor pressure that they create is proportional to output shaft speed or ground speed.

The governor is supplied with line pressure and then uses centrifugal force to vary the line pressure in proportion to ground speed. Visualize what happens when you place some water in a bucket and quickly swing the bucket in a circle from your side up over your head and back down repeatedly. The water stays inside the bucket, even when the bucket is upside down, as long as the bucket continues moving in a circle. The force acting on the water is centrifugal force. The centrifugal force causes the water to be pushed to the bottom of the bucket, no matter which direction the bucket is facing. If you swing

You are the Automotive Technician

A customer has come into your shop requesting a custom transmission rebuild for his modified high performance Corvette. You will be working alongside your co-worker who has extensive experience in transmission rebuilds. Before you begin the rebuild, your coworker asks you to prepare the workspace and make sure you have the two most essential tools ready: a transmission jack and a vehicle lift. Your coworker explains to you that this will be a longer process due to the nature of a performance rebuild than a traditional transmission rebuild. This is in part due to the fact that adjustments to the valve body and governor will have to be done slowly and road tested after each adjustment. The valve body is one part you will need to carefully disassemble so that you can clean and inspect each of the valves and valve bores. The repair order states that the transmission had some performance modifications when it was rebuilt six years ago and the vehicle has several high performance aftermarket components installed on it.

1. What are some of the modifications to the governor that can change performance?
2. Why would high performance components change how you perform a rebuild on a transmission?
3. What modifications can be made to accumulators, and how would shift feel be changed?

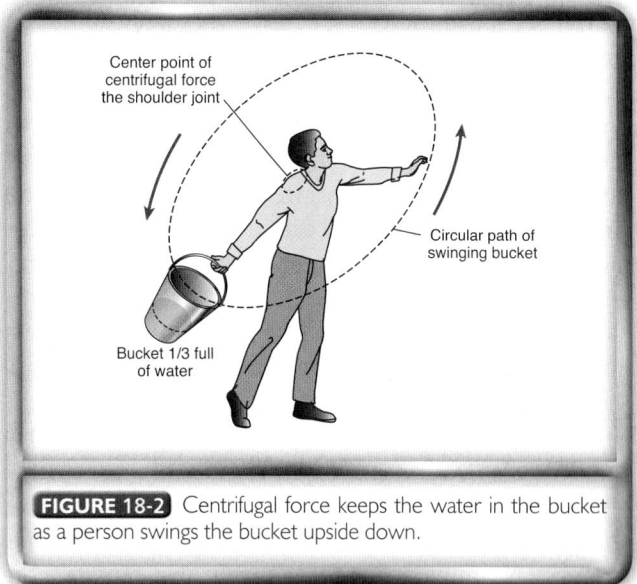

FIGURE 18-2 Centrifugal force keeps the water in the bucket as a person swings the bucket upside down.

the bucket more slowly, the water will fall out of the bucket. If you increase the speed at which you swing the bucket, the amount of force on the bucket will increase **FIGURE 18-2**. The governor uses the same principle to convert line pressure to governor pressure.

As stated previously, the governor is mounted either on the output shaft or in the transmission case. We will address the transmission case-mounted governor first. The case-mounted governor is mounted perpendicular, or at 90 degrees, to the output shaft.

The governor is free to spin inside a precision bore that is lubricated with transmission fluid. At the inboard end of the governor, there is a gear that engages with another gear that is pressed onto the output shaft. These gears are often made of plastic and can have issues with wear on high-mileage vehicles. They are replaceable on most transmissions. On the opposite end of the governor, the outboard end, there is a pair of weights that are free to pivot **FIGURE 18-3**. At low speed, these weights are tucked in next to the governor shaft by either spring pressure or hydraulic pressure. As the vehicle speed increases, centrifugal force causes these weights to move outward on their pivots against the spring or hydraulic pressure in proportion to the vehicle speed. As these weights move outward, they move the governor valve within its housing, causing governor pressure to increase.

The governor valve inside the governor shaft moves back and forth in its bore in response to the movement of the weights on the outboard side of the governor. Line pressure is supplied to the valley of the valve from port B in **FIGURE 18-4**. When the vehicle is stopped, the governor valve is seated in the bore all the way to the left. With the valve seated, the line pressure is exhausted out port A, where the fluid will be returned to the transmission pan.

FIGURE 18-3 A governor that has been removed from a transmission.

FIGURE 18-4 A hydraulic diagram of a governor valve.

As vehicle speed increases, centrifugal force causes the weights to fly out on their pivots, moving the governor valve to the right, pushing against spring or hydraulic pressure. As vehicle speed increases, this valve is moved to the right by spring or hydraulic pressure, which exposes fluid port C. The fluid pressure leaving this port is the governor pressure discussed earlier. The farther the valve moves to the right, the greater the governor pressure, and the less pressure that is exhausted back to the pan.

Springs behind the weights help to calibrate the governor to the particular engine that is installed in the vehicle. Increasing the strength of the springs causes an increase in governor pressure, which causes the vehicle to shift earlier.

When rebuilding a transmission, the governor assembly needs to be cleaned thoroughly. If the valve has dirt and old clutch material stuck in it, the valve may become jammed. A jammed valve will prevent the transmission from shifting properly. Some governors have a screen or filter installed in line to help prevent debris from becoming trapped in the valve. This screen needs to be cleaned or replaced during transmission overhaul.

FIGURE 18-5 An output shaft-mounted governor valve.

FIGURE 18-6 A hydraulic diagram of an output shaft-mounted governor.

> **TECHNICIAN TIP**
>
> When rebuilding a transmission for a high-performance vehicle, an experienced transmission rebuilder often modifies or replaces the governor with a different governor. If manual shifting is desired, it may be removed entirely. Placing weaker springs in the governor will cause a delay in the transmission shift. Also, drilling small holes in the governor weights will reduce their weight, and in turn the centrifugal force, thereby delaying the shift. Any modifications should be made carefully and slowly; it is very easy to remove too much material. Removing too much material can cause the transmission's shift point to be beyond the engine's red line.

The second type of governor is mounted directly on the output shaft. This type of governor can have one or two valves that are moved by centrifugal force. Springs hold these valves against the bottom of their bore near the centerline of the output shaft. As the output shaft spins, the valves begin to move outward and compress the springs because of the centrifugal force **FIGURE 18-5**.

Line pressure is applied to the governor valve through port B **FIGURE 18-6**. When the vehicle is stopped, the valve is fully seated to the left in its bore. The spring helps ensure that the valve is fully seated. When the valve is pushed to the left, line pressure is exhausted out port A and returned to the transmission pan. As vehicle speed increases, centrifugal force causes the governor valve to

move to the right. Moving the valve to the right exposes fluid port C. Fluid flowing out of port C is governor pressure. The farther the valve moves to the right, the more port C is exposed and the higher the governor pressure.

Typically, governors have trouble accurately measuring ground speed when the vehicle is moving slowly. To reduce this problem, manufacturers can install larger springs in the governor, but this affects the high-speed operation of the governor. Some manufacturers fix this problem by using a **staged governor**. A staged governor is one in which the assembly uses two valves: a primary valve and a secondary valve **FIGURE 18-7**. The primary valve begins moving as soon as the vehicle begins moving, creating a small amount of governor pressure. The secondary valve begins moving at a higher speed, creating additional governor pressure. This two-stage governor enables more precise control of governor pressure and, therefore, the transmission shift.

As we consider the operation of each valve, it is interesting to note that if a transmission has only a governor valve and no throttle valve or modulator valve, the transmission will shift at the same speeds regardless of the engine load. In other words, the transmission will shift at the same speed if the throttle is held wide open or just barely open. Once governor pressure exceeds spring pressure (assisted by throttle pressure) on the shift valves, the shift occurs **FIGURE 18-8**.

Vacuum Modulator

An automatic transmission can vary its shift points based on engine load. When a vehicle is under heavy load, such as when towing a trailer or going up a hill, the transmission delays the shift to allow the engine to operate at higher revolutions per minute (rpm), creating more power. In gasoline engines, as the piston moves downward in the cylinder bore on the intake stroke, it creates suction in the intake manifold. This suction is called manifold vacuum, sometimes referred to as engine vacuum or manifold pressure. Manifold vacuum can be used to determine the amount of engine load. When an engine is operating under a light load, the engine manifold vacuum is high (manifold pressure is low). When the engine is operating under a heavy load, the engine manifold vacuum is low or even zero (manifold pressure is high, near 14.7 pounds per square inch [psi], or 101 kilopascals [kPa]). On many hydraulically controlled transmissions, this vacuum is sent to a **vacuum modulator** **FIGURE 18-9**. The vacuum modulator converts this engine vacuum signal into a hydraulic pressure called **modulator pressure**. When engine vacuum is high, the modulator produces a low modulator pressure, and when engine vacuum is low, the modulator produces a high modulator pressure.

FIGURE 18-10 shows a vacuum modulator assembly. You can see that the modulator has a rubber diaphragm that is compressed to the bottom of the housing by a large

FIGURE 18-7 A cutaway of a staged governor that contains a primary valve piston and a secondary valve piston. Note the size difference of the two valves.

FIGURE 18-9 A vacuum modulator installed in a General Motors TH400 transmission.

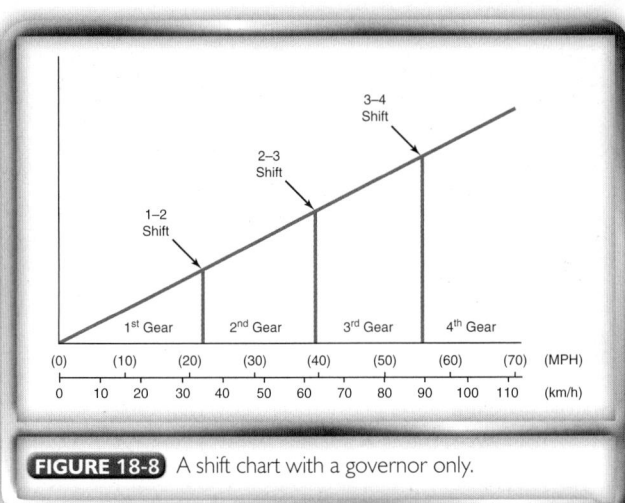

FIGURE 18-8 A shift chart with a governor only.

FIGURE 18-10 A cross-sectional view of a vacuum modulator.

spring when there is no engine vacuum. As engine vacuum is applied to the vacuum port on the modulator, the diaphragm is drawn to the left, compressing the spring. The diaphragm is attached to a plunger that moves the valve on the right side of the figure. Line pressure is applied to port A on the vacuum modulator valve. When there is no vacuum applied to the modulator, the diaphragm, and in turn the modulator valve, is pushed to the right by spring pressure. When the modulator valve is moved to the right, the exhaust port (port C) is blocked, preventing any pressure from being sent back to the transmission pan. All pressure is sent out port B as modulator pressure.

As engine vacuum increases, the modulator valve moves to the left, exposing the exhaust port and reducing the amount of modulator pressure. The modulator pressure is proportional to engine load, or inversely proportional to engine vacuum.

Vacuum modulators should be replaced when rebuilding a transmission. They can often be replaced without pulling the transmission from the vehicle and can be a simple, low-cost transmission repair. The rubber diaphragm can become ripped or torn in service. If the diaphragm becomes ripped, the customer may report that the vehicle shift is extremely delayed and harsh, often shifting only at the engine red line, regardless of the driving condition or throttle position. The customer may also report white smoke coming from the vehicle's exhaust pipe. This white smoke is from automatic transmission fluid being sucked up from the modulator and burned inside the engine.

The vacuum line leading from the engine to the vacuum modulator on the transmission is also susceptible to damage. The steel section of the line can become rusted, causing a vacuum leak and a delayed shift, and the rubber connectors on the ends of the steel line can deteriorate over time.

Replacement vacuum modulators are often adjustable to fine-tune the shift timing **FIGURE 18-11**. If you remove the vacuum hose from the modulator, you will see a small screw inside if the modulator is adjustable. Turning the screw puts more or less spring pressure on the diaphragm and, depending on the direction the screw is turned, advances or delays the shift. When adjusting the modulator, adjustments should be made in small increments to prevent shifting problems.

Throttle Valve

Some hydraulically controlled transmissions use a **throttle valve** in place of a vacuum modulator, or in addition to a vacuum modulator. Throttle valves, along with many of the other valves, are located inside the transmission valve body. The throttle valve is connected to the engine throttle linkage by a cable or, in older vehicles, a system of mechanical linkages **FIGURE 18-12**. As the throttle opening increases, **throttle valve pressure** increases. Increased throttle pressure delays the upshift, while decreased throttle pressure allows upshifts at lower vehicle speeds **FIGURE 18-13**.

When the throttle is closed, throttle valve pressure is reduced in the following way. As shown in **FIGURE 18-14**, line pressure is supplied to port A. When the throttle is closed, the spring causes the throttle valve to remain pushed all the way to the right in its bore. This allows all of the fluid pressure to be exhausted out port B and returned to the transmission pan. As the throttle is opened, the throttle valve moves to the left, blocking part of the exhaust port and opening part of the throttle valve pressure port, port C.

The pressure exiting the throttle valve pressure port is proportional to the amount of valve movement and

FIGURE 18-11 A replacement adjustable vacuum modulator.

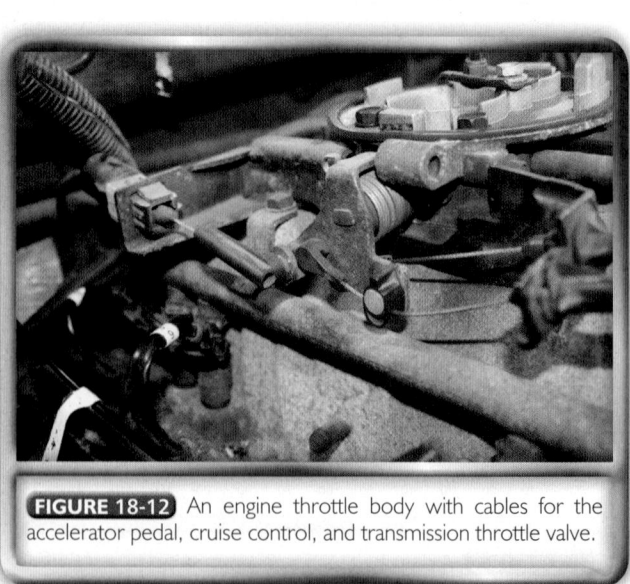

FIGURE 18-12 An engine throttle body with cables for the accelerator pedal, cruise control, and transmission throttle valve.

FIGURE 18-13 A shift chart with a governor and throttle valve or modulator.

FIGURE 18-14 A hydraulic diagram of a throttle valve.

throttle position. Throttle valve cables and linkages are a critical adjustment on a hydraulically controlled transmission. A common generic adjustment specification is that the cable should have no slack when the throttle is fully opened. If the cable is adjusted with too much slack, the throttle valve pressure is too low, resulting in early shifts and poor downshifts. If the cable is adjusted so that there is no slack before the throttle reaches wide open throttle (WOT), the throttle valve in the transmission could become damaged. The vehicle will also not have the capability to operate at WOT because the throttle will not be able to be opened fully. Follow the manufacturer's procedure for adjusting the throttle valve cable or linkage.

Kickdown Valve

With most transmissions, if you apply the accelerator pedal all the way to the floor, the transmission will downshift to accelerate faster. On older hydraulically controlled transmissions, this downshift was often accomplished through a **kickdown valve**. In some transmissions, the kickdown valve is called a **detent valve**. The kickdown valve can be operated by a cable **FIGURE 18-15**), linkage, or electric solenoid that moves a valve inside the transmission when the accelerator is pressed all the way down (i.e., WOT). This kickdown valve opens a passage, allowing full line pressure to pass the kickdown valve.

On vehicles with a kickdown solenoid, a switch is either installed under the accelerator pedal or attached to the throttle linkage on the engine. When the throttle is opened all the way, the electric switch closes, allowing current to flow to the kickdown electric solenoid inside the transmission.

Some transmissions combine a kickdown valve with a throttle valve. The throttle valve is moved back to the left by the pressure created by the spring. The kickdown valve is moved by the throttle linkage, in turn moving the spring to the left as the throttle is opened. When the accelerator pedal is depressed all the way, the throttle valve is forced to the bottom of the bore by the kickdown valve, compressing the spring until the kickdown valve is bottomed out against the throttle valve. When this occurs, line pressure is free to flow in through port A and directly out port B.

Flow Control Orifices

Hydraulic circuits are also controlled by precisely sized orifices. An orifice provides a restriction in line with the device being applied. The restriction delays, or slows, the application of the device. This delay enables the engineers to control the amount of time it takes to apply the device.

FIGURE 18-15 A kickdown valve connection inside the transmission.

In many cases, the orifice is drilled to a specific size within the separator plate in the valve body **FIGURE 18-16**. However, some manufacturers place a restriction within the passage feeding the device, or even in the device itself.

Accumulators

Accumulators are devices that cushion and absorb application pressures within the transmission. For example, when line pressure is sent to a clutch or band without an accumulator, the device is applied harshly, causing very firm shifts that most drivers do not like. Accumulators are composed of a spring-loaded piston within a bore. Fluid under pressure enters the cylinder opposite the spring, compressing the spring **FIGURE 18-17**. As the accumulator spring is compressed, fluid moves into the cylinder and builds pressure relatively slowly. Since this is the application pressure for the clutch or band, the clutch or band is applied much more progressively.

> ### ▶ TECHNICIAN TIP
>
> Experienced transmission rebuilders will sometimes increase the size of the clutch and band application orifices to cause quicker shifts. They may also install heavier accumulator springs or longer accumulator pistons to produce a firmer, quicker shift. These modifications should only be attempted by an experienced transmission rebuilder, as they will affect the operation of the transmission as well as increase the stresses on the various internal components.

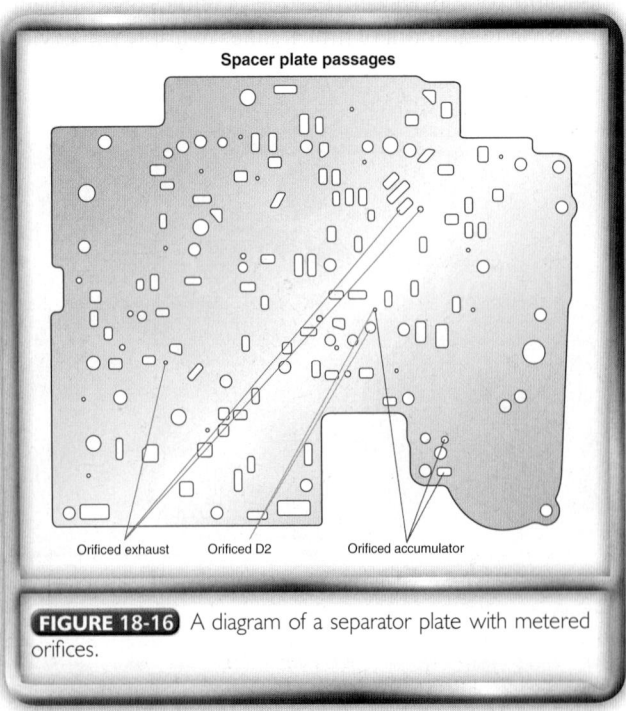

Spacer plate passages

Orificed exhaust   Orificed D2   Orificed accumulator

FIGURE 18-16 A diagram of a separator plate with metered orifices.

Chamber

Apply fluid

Accumulator piston

Vent

Spring

FIGURE 18-17 Accumulator action.

▶ Line Pressure

In a hydraulically controlled transmission, clutches and bands are applied using a pressure called **line pressure**. Line pressure is created by regulating hydraulic pressure that is created in the front pump. A pressure regulator valve regulates that pressure before it can be used by the clutches and bands. However, since the line pressure must vary according to engine load, other valves are used to act on the pressure regulator valve. We will now look at these in greater depth.

Controlling Line Pressure

The Hydraulic Fundamentals chapter describes the operation of the front pump and pressure regulator. For the purposes of that chapter, the operation of the pressure regulator is simplified to help you build your understanding of the way an automatic transmission operates. Now we need to go into greater detail as to how the pressure regulator controls line pressure. In a transmission, line pressure cannot remain constant through all driving ranges and vehicle demands. The line pressure must increase when needed to help create greater holding power in the clutches and bands, and decrease when the additional pressure is not needed so that fuel economy can be improved. Also, if the line pressure is too high during normal cruising speeds, the customer may complain about a harsh-shifting transmission.

FIGURE 18-18 shows the standard pressure regulator discussed in the Hydraulic Fundamentals chapter but with a few more hydraulic passages added to it. As explained in that chapter, the pump supplies pressure to port A. Line pressure flows out of port B. When the pump pressure exceeds the spring pressure, the valve moves to the left, exposing the exhaust port (port C) and allowing excess fluid pressure to be returned to the transmission pan.

FIGURE 18-18 A diagram of a common pressure regulator valve in a hydraulically controlled transmission.

As the throttle is opened further, line pressure must be increased to help hold the clutches and bands with the additional engine force being produced. To increase the line pressure, throttle valve pressure is allowed to flow into port F, thus pushing the throttle valve. By boosting valve pressure to the right and adding additional pressure to the spring force keeping the pressure regulator valve closed, the line pressure is increased.

Transmission pressures vary greatly between manufacturers and different transmissions, but line pressure with the throttle closed is as low as 75 psi (517 kPa) and could be almost 200 psi (1379 kPa) when the throttle is wide open. To test the operation of the throttle valve boost valve, you must install a pressure gauge to the transmission line pressure test port. Disconnect the throttle valve cable or linkage and start the vehicle. With the vehicle idling in gear, measure the line pressure with the throttle valve closed and again with the throttle valve all the way open. Compare your results with the manufacturer's specifications. The same test can be performed on a transmission equipped with a vacuum modulator. A vacuum pump is applied to the vacuum modulator. As the vacuum changes, so should line pressure. As vacuum increases, line pressure should decrease. Check the manufacturer's specifications.

Applied   Science

AS-94: Dynamics: The technician can explain the forces and motions involved in a hydraulic system.
Hydraulic systems operate on a very simple principle: Force that is applied to one point in the system is transferred to all other points by means of an incompressible fluid. In a simple hydraulic system consisting of two pistons connected by a hydraulic line, force applied to one piston is transferred via the fluid to the other piston. The amount of force applied and the amount of piston movement are governed by the relative sizes of the pistons.

Often line pressure needs to be increased in the reverse and L1 gear positions, or "1" range. The torque multiplication from the torque converter is greatest when starting from a stop, especially when in reverse. The combination of starting from a stop along with the reverse gear's lower ratio means the clutches and bands need to be held tighter to prevent slippage. In Figure 18-19, you can see that there is another valve called the L1 and **reverse boost valve**. When the transmission is placed in reverse, the manual valve allows hydraulic pressure to flow to port E. This pressure is added to the spring pressure acting against the pressure regulator valve, which increases the line pressure. Often line pressure at WOT in the reverse gear is near the pump's maximum pressure. It is not uncommon to see line pressures approach 300 psi (2068 kPa) in reverse at WOT. If the transmission is placed in the L1 gear position again, the manual valve will allow line pressure to flow to port E. This additional pressure is added to the pressure-regulating spring as was done in reverse, thus increasing line pressure to approximately the same pressure that we had in reverse.

Shift Valves

A **shift valve** typically refers to a spool valve with multiple lands on it. Remember that the lands are the larger part of a spool valve that fits with minimal clearance into the bore to prevent fluid from flowing around the valve. The spool valve is located inside of the transmission valve body. The shift valve will either block or allow the passage of line pressure to a particular clutch or band in order to apply the gear. A typical shift valve is shown in **FIGURE 18-19**. In the figure, notice the calibrated spring on the left side of the valve. The spring keeps the shift valve against the right side of the bore until the valve needs to move. Line pressure enters the spool valve at port A and is free to flow

FIGURE 18-19 A hydraulic diagram of a simple shift valve.

out of port B to the clutch or band. Governor pressure is applied to port C of the spool valve. The governor pressure pushes against the calibrated spring at the left side of the valve. Modulator pressure or throttle valve pressure is applied to port D of the valve. When the valve moves far enough to the left, port B is covered, causing the clutch or band to be released. Port E becomes exposed and line pressure is allowed to flow to the clutch or band for the next gear range.

Operation of the Hydraulically Controlled Transmission

Park

When the driver starts the vehicle, the front pump draws fluid up from the transmission pan, through the filter, and into the pump, as shown in. The pump then sends fluid out under pressure to the pressure regulator valve, the throttle valve or vacuum modulator valve, the governor, and the manual valve. This release of fluid creates line pressure. The pressure regulator valve keeps the pressure at a regulated level by exhausting excess pressure back to the transmission pan. With the manual valve in the park position, line pressure is not able to flow past the valve to any other components of the transmission **FIGURE 18-20**. Line pressure that is sent to the governor is allowed to be exhausted back to the transmission pan when the vehicle is not moving and the governor is not creating any pressure. Line pressure sent to the throttle valve, or vacuum modulator, is mostly exhausted to the transmission pan when the throttle is closed and the vehicle is under no load.

Drive: First Gear

When the driver shifts the vehicle into drive, the manual valve moves **FIGURE 18-21**, allowing line pressure to flow to port A of the 1-2 shift valve. The 1-2 shift valve is held to the right (downshift) side of its bore by the spring. This allows the line pressure from port A to flow freely from port B. Port B is connected to the clutch or band that applies first gear. As the vehicle accelerates, the governor sends fluid pressure to port D. This fluid pressure compresses the shift spring and moves the shift valve to the left. The vacuum modulator or throttle valve applies fluid pressure to port C. This pressure adds force to the spring in order to resist the pressure from the governor. Remember that the vacuum modulator and the throttle valve create fluid pressure that varies with engine load or throttle opening. The higher the engine load, or the more the throttle is opened, the greater the pressure that develops. Governor pressure increases linearly as vehicle speed increases. When the governor pressure exceeds the spring pressure plus the vacuum modulator or throttle valve pressure, the shift valve moves to the left (upshift position), resulting in fluid flow being cut off from port B. When the fluid pressure stops flowing from port B, the clutch or band for first gear is disengaged.

Drive: Second Gear

As the driver proceeds, fluid pressure is still flowing into port A. The governor pressure has exceeded the spring pressure and vacuum modulator, or throttle valve, pressure, and the shift valve moves to the left (upshift positon), compressing the shift spring. Port B becomes

FIGURE 18-20 A simplified hydraulic diagram of a transmission in park.

FIGURE 18-21 A simplified hydraulic diagram of a transmission in first gear.

blocked, cutting off fluid flow to the clutch or band that is used for first gear. As the valve moves, port E becomes exposed and now line pressure is allowed to flow from port A to port E. Port E sends line pressure to the 2-3 shift valve, as shown in **FIGURE 18-22**. The 2-3 shift valve allows line pressure to flow from port A of the 2-3 shift valve to port B of the 2-3 shift valve. If the vehicle speed decreases, governor pressure is reduced, resulting in the shift valve moving back to the right, blocking port E of the 1-2 shift valve and re-exposing port B of the 1-2 shift valve. This causes the vehicle to downshift back into first gear. The same downshift would happen if the vehicle were cruising down the road and the driver applied the accelerator pedal far enough to overcome the governor pressure, resulting in a downshift. The shifting of the hydraulically controlled transmission is caused by the constant push-pull between the pressure of the governor and pressure of the shift spring and vacuum modulator or throttle valve pressure.

Drive: Third Gear

As the driver continues to accelerate, governor pressure continues to increase. This increased fluid pressure moves our 2-3 shift valve farther to the left, blocking port B of the 2-3 shift valve. This prevents line pressure from going to the clutch or band for second gear as shown in **FIGURE 18-23**. The spring at the left of the 2-3 shift valve is stiffer than the spring found in the 1-2 shift valve. Line pressure has been supplied to port A of the 2-3 shift valve since the transmission shifted into second gear. Governor pressure is applied to port D of the 2-3 shift valve. (Note that some transmissions use a combined 1-2, 2-3 shift valve.) The vacuum modulator or throttle valve applies pressure to

FIGURE 18-23 A simplified hydraulic diagram for a transmission in third gear.

port C. When the governor pressure becomes great enough to overcome the spring pressure and the modulator/throttle valve pressure in the 2-3 shift valve, line pressure is allowed to flow to port E. Port E sends line pressure to the clutch for third gear. If the vehicle slows down, governor pressure is reduced, causing the valve to move back to the right and a downshift to second gear. The same will happen if the driver applies pressure to the accelerator pedal, as modulator or throttle valve pressure adds additional force to the shift spring. This will push the shift valve back to the right and return the vehicle to second gear. This process, as mentioned previously, is called kickdown. Transmissions are designed to prevent a downshift if it exceeds the maximum rpm that an engine is designed for. If the vehicle speed is not too high in third gear, and the driver steps on the accelerator hard enough, the transmission can downshift from third to second to first in one shift.

Reverse

In reverse, line pressure is allowed to flow from the manual valve directly to the clutches and/or bands that are used for reverse **FIGURE 18-24**. Governor pressure and modulator pressure/throttle valve pressure are not used in reverse because there is only one speed available. These pressures are instead exhausted directly to the transmission pan while in reverse. Reverse does often require greater line pressure, so the manual valve will direct additional fluid under pressure to port D of the pressure regulator valve. This results in additional force added to the spring pressure in the regulating valve, which causes a much higher line pressure for reverse.

FIGURE 18-22 A simplified hydraulic diagram of a transmission in second gear.

FIGURE 18-24 A simplified hydraulic diagram for a transmission in reverse.

FIGURE 18-25 A secondary pressure regulator valve showing a hydraulic circuit.

Secondary Regulator Valve

Many hydraulically controlled transmissions regulate the pressure to the torque converter, cooler, and lubrication circuit lower than line pressure; therefore, they use a secondary regulator valve. Typically, the regulator valve uses a simple spring-loaded valve that dumps fluid above the intended pressure back to the oil pan **FIGURE 18-25**. This pressure is used to fill the torque converter, thereby circulating fluid through and out of the converter. Transmission fluid leaving the torque converter can be extremely hot, so it goes next to the transmission cooler. After leaving the cooler, it is ready to enter the transmission and lubricate the planetary gears and bushings. In some designs, the throttle pressure or modulator pressure acts on the secondary regulator valve to increase the converter pressure so that the converter clutch can be applied more firmly under moderate load conditions.

Wrap-up

Ready for Review

- Hydraulically controlled transmissions are no longer produced in the United States.
- Governors are hydro-mechanical valves that produce governor pressure proportional to ground speed.
- A governor can be located on the output shaft or in the transmission case.
- A staged governor uses a primary valve at lower speeds and a secondary valve at higher speeds.
- Manifold vacuum is the suction created at the intake manifold by the piston's intake stroke.
- Vacuum modulators convert manifold vacuum into modulator pressure.
- Modulator pressure and engine vacuum have an inverse relationship.
- A throttle valve may be used in place of, or in addition to, a vacuum modulator.
- Kickdown valves (detent valves) respond when the accelerator is completely depressed to downshift the transmission and increase acceleration.
- Line pressure is the hydraulic pressure used to apply clutches and bands.
- Line pressure is controlled by the pressure regulator.
- More line pressure is needed as engine load is increased, and in reverse.
- A shift valve is a spool valve with multiple lands that is designed to block or allow line pressure to pass to a band or clutch in order to apply the gear.
- When the manual valve is in the park position, line pressure cannot flow past the manual valve.
- Shifting the vehicle into first gear moves the manual valve and allows line pressure to flow.
- As vehicle speed increases, governor pressure increases linearly.
- Governor pressure is reduced as vehicle speed decreases.
- Shifting of a hydraulically controlled transmission is due to the push–pull between the governor pressure on one side and the shift spring and throttle pressure on the other.
- Transmissions can prevent a downshift that would exceed the engine's maximum rpm.
- Reverse only uses one speed; therefore, governor pressure and modulator/throttle valve pressure are not required.

Key Terms

detent valve See *kickdown valve*.

governor A mechanical device that creates a pressure using centrifugal force. The pressure is proportional to vehicle speed.

governor pressure The pressure created by the governor, which is used to make the shift valves upshift and is proportional to vehicle speed.

kickdown valve A type of spool valve that is connected to the throttle on the vehicle. The valve is used to force a downshift when the throttle is opened all the way, assuming the governor pressure is below a specified point. Kickdown valves are also called detent valves.

line pressure A hydraulic pressure that is used to apply bands and clutches, and is regulated by the pressure regulator valve.

modulator pressure A pressure created by the vacuum modulator that is proportional to engine load. Modulator pressure is used to delay transmission upshifting based upon engine load. It may also be used to raise line pressure to more firmly apply bands and clutches under higher engine loads.

reverse boost valve A component of the pressure regulator valve that increases line pressure when the vehicle is in reverse.

shift valve A type of spool valve that has multiple fluid inputs and a spring; it is used to direct hydraulic pressure to a clutch or band needed for a shift.

staged governor A governor in which the assembly uses two valves: a primary valve and a secondary valve.

throttle valve A type of spool valve that is connected to the throttle on a vehicle. The throttle valve creates a pressure proportional to throttle opening and is used to delay upshifting based on throttle opening.

throttle valve pressure The pressure created by the throttle valve that is proportional to throttle opening.

vacuum modulator A device on a hydraulically controlled transmission that converts engine manifold vacuum into an engine load signal called modulator pressure.

ASE-Type Questions

1. Tech A says that measuring line pressure and comparing it to specifications is a good diagnostic procedure. Tech B says that the manual valve is moved by governor pressure to force a shift. Who is correct?
   a. Tech A
   b. Tech B
   c. Both A and B
   d. Neither A nor B

2. Tech A says that governor pressure is controlled by torque converter rpm. Tech B says that governor pressure is controlled by output shaft speed. Who is correct?
   a. Tech A
   b. Tech B
   c. Both A and B
   d. Neither A nor B

3. Tech A says that reciprocating force controls governor pressure. Tech B says that centrifugal force controls governor pressure. Who is correct?
   a. Tech A
   b. Tech B
   c. Both A and B
   d. Neither A nor B

4. Tech A says that modifying governor weights will alter transmission shifting. Tech B says that excessive modification of the governor weights may cause the transmission to not shift. Who is correct?
   a. Tech A
   b. Tech B
   c. Both A and B
   d. Neither A nor B

5. Tech A says that converter and cooler operate at line pressure. Tech B says that line pressure causes the manual valve to move during upshifts and downshifts. Who is correct?
   a. Tech A
   b. Tech B
   c. Both A and B
   d. Neither A nor B

6. Tech A says that the throttle valve is controlled by a cable or linkage hooked to the engine throttle linkage. Tech B says that a misadjusted throttle valve cable can prevent wide open throttle (WOT) on an engine. Who is correct?
   a. Tech A
   b. Tech B
   c. Both A and B
   d. Neither A nor B

7. Tech A says that line pressure is reduced during light throttle conditions to improve fuel economy. Tech B says that as the engine speeds up in rpm, the transmission line pressure gradually reduces to maintain clutch pack pressure. Who is correct?
   a. Tech A
   b. Tech B
   c. Both A and B
   d. Neither A nor B

8. Tech A says that when governor pressure on one side of a shift valve overcomes spring pressure and throttle pressure on the other side, an upshift occurs. Tech B says when reverse boost pressure on one side of the reverse valve overcomes governor pressure on the other side, shift into reverse occurs. Who is correct?
   a. Tech A
   b. Tech B
   c. Both A and B
   d. Neither A nor B

9. Tech A says that fluid pressure in an automatic transmission is controlled by engine rpm. Tech B says that modulator pressure changes with engine vacuum. Who is correct?
   a. Tech A
   b. Tech B
   c. Both A and B
   d. Neither A nor B

10. Tech A says that in reverse, governor pressure regulates line pressure. Tech B says that in reverse, modulator pressure regulates line pressure. Who is correct?
    a. Tech A
    b. Tech B
    c. Both A and B
    d. Neither A nor B

CHAPTER 19

NATEF Tasks

There are no NATEF tasks for this chapter.

Knowledge Objectives

After reading this chapter, you will be able to:
1. Describe the operation of an electronically controlled transmission. (p 516)
2. Describe and understand the sensors required for the power train control module (PCM) to shift the transmission. (pp 517–523)
3. Describe the operation of an electronic pressure control system. (pp 523–525)
4. Describe and understand the operation of electronic shift solenoids. (pp 525–528)
5. Perform preliminary diagnosis related to a computer-controlled transmission. (pp 528–530)

Electronically Controlled Transmission

Introduction

Transmissions began changing from hydraulically controlled to electronically controlled during the late 1980s and early 1990s. Currently, there are no auto manufacturers in the United States still producing hydraulically controlled transmissions for use in new vehicles. This shift is partially because of the increased need for greater fuel economy and the additional gears required to achieve it. More accurate control of vehicles' emissions is another reason why manufacturers have gone to electronically controlled transmissions. The computer can better predict engine load changes when the vehicle computer is in charge of the shift timing, keeping emissions under better control by preparing for the shift. On a conventional hydraulically controlled transmission, the computer can react to the increased load only *after* the transmission shifts. Fully computer-controlled transmissions have also allowed the manufacturers to install smaller transmissions into vehicles because the computer controls can be used to reduce the amount of torque flowing through a transmission as it shifts. Note that computer controlled means that the computer is controlling hydraulic valves in most cases, thereby directing hydraulic pressure to activate the various clutches and bands within the transmission.

Electronically Controlled Transmission Components

Electronic Control

As discussed in the Hydraulically Controlled Transmission chapter, in a fully hydraulically controlled transmission, the shift points are controlled by hydraulic and mechanical devices such as springs and valves. In the fully electronically controlled transmission, the shift points are controlled by the vehicle's **power train control module (PCM)** or a **transmission control module (TCM)**. Most vehicle manufacturers have integrated the TCM into the construction of the PCM, so we will use the abbreviation PCM for this chapter. The PCM receives various inputs from the engine and transmission to determine the shift timing and the firmness of the shift. We will come back to the PCM after we learn about some of the inputs and outputs that the PCM uses **FIGURE 19-1**.

FIGURE 19-1 A typical vehicle PCM that has been removed from a vehicle.

You are the Automotive Technician

A customer brings her vehicle into the transmission shop complaining that it has not been shifting properly for the last few days. The customer is concerned that she may need to have the transmission replaced, which can be a very expensive repair. After gathering all of the customer's information, you review the service history and technical service bulletins for this vehicle. You then tell the customer that you need to verify the fluid level and condition and then perform a test drive to verify the problem and gather information. The fluid level is within the safe zone but is a bit dirty. During the test drive, you notice that the speedometer is erratic, during which the transmission shifts erratically. You also verify that there is no apparent slippage in any of the gears. After the test drive, you explain to the customer that the erratic speedometer could be causing the transmission to shift erratically. She agrees to allow you to continue to diagnose the issue, and says that if the speedometer is causing the shifting problem, she would like it fixed, along with changing the fluid and filter based on your recommendation.

1. How could a malfunctioning speedometer cause the transmission to shift incorrectly?
2. While the technician didn't feel any slippage, how is slippage monitored in some electronically controlled transmissions?
3. What is limp-in mode? And how does it operate?

Vehicle Speed Sensor

In a hydraulically controlled transmission, vehicle speed, or ground speed, is measured by the governor. The governor produces a hydraulic pressure that moves shift valves inside of the transmission. In a computerized transmission, the governor is replaced by a **vehicle speed sensor (VSS)**. This VSS is sometimes called an output shaft speed sensor **FIGURE 19-2**.

The VSS is often also responsible for sending the vehicle speed information to the vehicle speedometer. Sometimes this information is sent to the PCM and the PCM relays the information, or they may both receive the same signal. On early electronically controlled transmissions, sometimes the manufacturer would use an electronic VSS *and* a mechanical speedometer cable because the vehicle was still using a mechanical speedometer in the instrument panel.

> ## TECHNICIAN TIP
>
> When a customer states that the automatic transmission will not shift, perform some basic diagnostic tests before replacing a transmission. A simple diagnostic test is to observe whether the speedometer is working. If the speedometer is not working, there is probably a problem with the VSS or its wiring.

Most VSSs are a type of sensor called a magnetic pickup, or magnetic reluctance, sensor. The sensor assembly consists of an iron core wrapped with fine copper wiring. There is also a reluctor wheel, which has raised "teeth" located around the circumference of the wheel. **FIGURE 19-3** shows the parts of the magnetic pickup sensor. The reluctor wheel is attached to the output shaft of the transmission and spins with the output shaft. As the teeth of the reluctor wheel get closer to the iron core, a positive voltage is produced. As the tooth moves away, the voltage becomes negative. This process repeats over and over again as the reluctor wheel spins, creating an AC voltage. This signal is sent to the PCM where the vehicle speed can be determined from the signal frequency. The magnetic pickup sensor produces its own voltage while the reluctor wheel is spun. These sensors do not need a separate wire to supply them with a reference voltage.

> ## TECHNICIAN TIP
>
> Magnetic pickup sensors can be bench tested in the transmission or when the transmission is installed in the vehicle. If you place a multimeter or lab scope set to AC volts on the leads of a magnetic pickup sensor and spin the output shaft of a transmission, you should get an AC voltage reading. To a certain point, the faster the shaft is spun, the higher the voltage.

FIGURE 19-2 A vehicle speed sensor (VSS) installed in a transmission. The case on the transmission has been disassembled to show the sensor through the case and the reluctor wheel.

FIGURE 19-3 A typical VSS magnetic pickup sensor diagram.

Another type of VSS is called a <u>reed switch</u>. There is a thin movable blade switch inside the sensor and a magnet installed in a rotating part, called the rotor, on the output shaft. As the output shaft spins, the rotor spins. When the magnet comes near the reed switch, the switch closes, allowing current to flow through the switch. When the magnet moves away from the switch, the switch opens, breaking the current flow. This opening and closing of the switch creates a DC square wave pattern that the PCM can use to determine vehicle speed. Reed switches need to be supplied with electricity to operate. The amount of voltage that the sensor is supplied with varies among vehicle manufacturers. Some of these switches apply a ground to a wire coming from the PCM; others simply allow a voltage to pass from a voltage source, through the reed switch, to the PCM.

Input Shaft Speed Sensor

Many transmissions also incorporate an **input shaft speed sensor**, also called a turbine speed sensor because the input shaft is splined to the turbine of the torque converter. The input shaft speed sensor is very similar to a VSS. These sensors can also be a magnetic pickup type or a reed switch type. Both types send their signal as an input to the PCM.

Some PCMs compare the input shaft speed sensor to the output shaft speed sensor to determine gear ratios. For example, if the input shaft is spinning at 3000 revolutions per minute (rpm) and the output shaft is spinning at 1000 rpm, the PCM knows that the transmission has a 3:1 gear ratio. The PCM can also use this information to determine if a clutch or band is slipping. For example, the PCM knows that the transmission should have a 3:1 first gear ratio. When the PCM looks at the input shaft speed sensor and sees 3000 rpm while the output shaft speed sensor is only reading 900 rpm, the PCM knows that first gear is slipping **FIGURE 19-4** and will trigger a diagnostic trouble code (DTC) such as a P0731—gear ratio error in first gear.

Some manufacturers compare the input shaft speed sensor to the output shaft speed sensor to measure the amount of time required to complete the shift from one gear to another. Chrysler vehicles often use this information and list it as the clutch volume index (CVI). This CVI number can be used by the PCM to determine how worn the clutch or band is and to adjust shift timing and pressures accordingly.

Transmission Oil Temperature

Another input the PCM uses when controlling the shifting of an electronically controlled transmission is the **transmission oil temperature (TOT) sensor**. Most TOT sensors are a type of resistor called a thermistor. A thermistor

changes its resistance based upon its temperature. The PCM will supply a reference voltage to the sensor and measure the amount of voltage returned to the PCM through the TOT sensor **FIGURE 19-5**.

The PCM varies shift timing and pressures based upon the TOT sensor because cold transmission oil is thicker than hot transmission oil and does not flow as easily through small orifices and passages in the transmission. So, if the transmission oil is cooler, the PCM will allow higher engine rpm before shifting the transmission and allow more time for the transmission to complete the shift. If the transmission oil is hot, the PCM may increase line pressure to compensate for internal leaks, as thinner oil flows past valves and seals more easily. The TOT sensor's temperature can typically be viewed using a scan tool. If the vehicle has completely cooled down overnight, the TOT should be fairly close to ambient temperature, engine coolant temperature, and intake air temperature. This means

FIGURE 19-4 Input shaft speed sensor versus output shaft speed sensor.

FIGURE 19-5 A General Motors transmission oil temperature (TOT) sensor and pressure switch assembly.

that if the temperature of the air around the vehicle was 60°F (16°C) for most of the night, the TOT, and other temperature sensors, should be reading close to 60°F.

Transmission Pressure Switches

Inside many transmissions, there are small pressure switches. The switches are a simple open or closed type. When there is no pressure in a hydraulic circuit, the switch is open, and when pressure is applied, it closes. The PCM uses this information to determine if a particular hydraulic circuit of the transmission has pressure, such as the circuit for the **torque converter clutch (TCC)** lock-up system. The pressure switches can also be used to determine what gear range the transmission is operating in. Figure 19-6 shows a common General Motors pressure switch used to verify which gear the transmission is operating in.

Line Pressure Sensor

The PCM receives voltage signals on some transmissions from a **line pressure sensor**. The line pressure sensor is a pressure transducer, which is a type of resistor that changes its resistance based upon pressure. The sensor is supplied with reference voltage from the PCM. The sensor varies the voltage based upon the line pressure and sends the signal back to the PCM. The PCM can then interpret the signal and vary the line pressure inside the transmission and adapt the shift timing based upon line pressure.

Throttle Position Sensor

The **throttle position sensor (TPS)** is a critical sensor for an electronically controlled transmission **FIGURE 19-6**. The TPS is a type of variable resistor called a **potentiometer**. The potentiometer varies its resistance based on its position. A volume knob on a stereo is another example of a potentiometer.

The TPS is mounted on the side of an engine throttle body assembly, and the inside of the TPS moves with the position of the throttle valve. The PCM supplies the TPS with a steady reference voltage and monitors the voltage returned through the potentiometer. Most TPSs have a relatively high resistance at closed throttle, dropping the reference voltage, which results in a low-voltage signal being returned to the PCM through the signal return wire. Usually this voltage is around 0.5 volts at closed throttle. The sensor's resistance steadily drops as the throttle valve is opened. This drop causes the voltage signal returned to the PCM to increase to approximately 4.5 volts at wide open throttle.

Although TPS voltage can be monitored using a scan tool, it is recommended to verify the operation of the sensor using a digital storage oscilloscope (DSO), as the scan tool's data rate is relatively slow and cannot display the TPS voltage quickly enough to find flaws in the sensor.

To test a TPS sensor, measure the voltage on the signal return wire with the vehicle in key on, engine off (KOEO) mode. Using the throttle pedal, slowly open the throttle all the way and release it. The voltage should rise steadily and return to the closed-throttle level. **FIGURE 19-7** shows

FIGURE 19-6 A throttle position sensor (TPS) mounted on the side of a throttle body assembly.

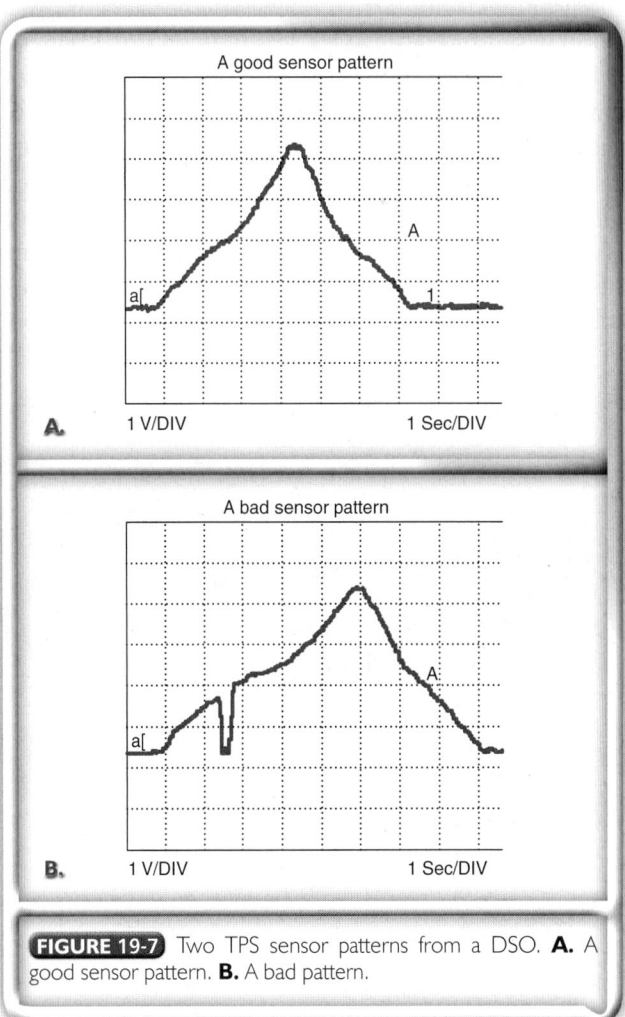

FIGURE 19-7 Two TPS sensor patterns from a DSO. **A.** A good sensor pattern. **B.** A bad pattern.

a good sensor pattern measured with a DSO on the left, and a bad pattern on the right. The sensor on the right is from a vehicle that exhibited a severe hesitation and erratic shifting. The sensor on the left is from the same vehicle after the sensor was replaced, fixing the problem.

> ### TECHNICIAN TIP
>
> If a customer brings a vehicle in complaining about erratic shifting and a vehicle hesitation problem, it is a good idea to check the TPS first. It is difficult for the PCM to determine whether there is a problem with the TPS because the sensor is directly tied to human reaction. Often, if the PCM sees the voltage drop out on a TPS signal, it believes the driver released the accelerator. This makes it difficult to determine sensor failure unless the sensor fails completely, resulting in either 0 volts or reference voltage being returned to the PCM.

Accelerator Pedal Position Sensor

A sensor that is similar to the TPS is the accelerator pedal position sensor **FIGURE 19-8**. It is used on drive-by-wire vehicles to determine the driver's intent as related to acceleration/deceleration. Beyond indicating the position of the accelerator pedal, the signal can also be used to determine how quickly or slowly the pedal is being pressed or released. Quick application of the pedal can indicate the need for more engine power, and the corresponding need for a downshift and a delay of the upshifts. Quick release of the pedal can indicate the start of a panic stop.

So the PCM can start to anticipate taking actions that would help avoid an accident, such as downshifting and applying the brakes.

Engine Coolant Temperature Sensor

The PCM will look at the **engine coolant temperature (ECT) sensor** not only for starting the engine, but also for transmission operation. An ECT sensor is another thermistor, a resistor that varies its resistance based upon temperature, like the TOT sensor. The ECT sensor is installed in an engine coolant passage, often near the thermostat housing on an engine **FIGURE 19-9**. The PCM sends out reference voltage to the ECT. The sensor varies the voltage returned to the PCM through the thermistor, allowing the PCM to determine the temperature of the engine from the voltage.

The PCM varies shift timing and pressures based upon engine temperature. When the engine is cold, the PCM delays transmission shifts to allow the engine to warm up faster and allows for more consistent engine and transmission operation.

ECT can be seen using a scan tool. If the temperature seems extremely low, around −40°F (−40°C), or extremely high, exceeding 280°F (138°C), you may have a bad sensor, or possibly faulty wiring. A quick test to determine if you have a bad sensor or bad wiring is to turn the vehicle off and unplug the sensor. Turn the vehicle back on (KOEO) and look at the scan tool data. Did the data change? Next turn the vehicle off again. Insert a paper clip into the ECT connector to short across the two terminals going back to the PCM (just be sure you are on the proper connector!). Turn the vehicle back on (KOEO). Did the value change? The reading should have gone from the lowest possible

FIGURE 19-8 Accelerator pedal position sensor.

FIGURE 19-9 An ECT sensor installed near the thermostat housing.

reading to the highest possible reading (or the other way around, depending on the vehicle). If there was no change in the reading, you have a wiring problem on the vehicle. If it did change, your problem may lie with the ECT sensor. Note that vehicles may have more than one sensor to read coolant temperature. Some vehicles use separate sensors for the temperature gauge on the instrument cluster, and possibly another one to control the radiator fan. Make sure you are testing the correct sensor. Also, the current flow through the ECT sensor is very small. If the sensor terminals are corroded, dirty, or loose, it is possible that by disconnecting the ECT sensor and reconnecting it, it will start reading properly again. If so, this is not likely to be a permanent fix. You may have to clean or repair the terminals, or replace the sensor to repair it permanently.

FIGURE 19-10 A common manifold absolute pressure (MAP) sensor installed on an intake manifold.

> ### TECHNICIAN TIP
>
> An ECT sensor cannot accurately read engine temperature when the coolant level is low. Before condemning the ECT sensor, make sure the coolant level is up to the proper level and the thermostat is operating properly on the vehicle.

Some engines use a cylinder head temperature (CHT) sensor instead of an ECT sensor. The CHT sensor is a thermistor that measures the cylinder head temperature to accomplish the same thing but can always accurately measure temperature because it does not rely on the level of coolant to touch the sensor. Thus, its readings are not affected by low coolant. Check the vehicle's service information to determine which type of sensor is used on the vehicle.

Manifold Absolute Pressure Sensor

The PCM needs to know how much load the engine and transmission are under. One method of determining engine load is through the use of a **manifold absolute pressure (MAP) sensor**. The MAP sensor can be either directly bolted to the intake manifold or connected through a vacuum hose **FIGURE 19-10**. Most modern MAP sensors use a type of flexible silicon chip within a sealed chamber; the chip changes resistance when manifold pressure flexes the chip. The varying resistance then changes the output signal based on the manifold pressure. When the engine has more vacuum, the chip is pulled down, changing its resistance. The PCM supplies a reference voltage to the sensor, which is reduced as it travels through the potentiometer and is then returned to the PCM. Since manifold pressure is an indication

of engine load, the PCM can use this voltage signal to monitor engine load.

Manifold pressure is a good indicator of engine load and was used by the vacuum modulator on our hydraulically controlled transmission. When an engine is operating under light load, engine manifold pressure is low. When the engine is operating under heavy load, engine manifold pressure is high. As the manifold pressure changes, so does the shift points. When the engine is under heavy load, the shifts are delayed, and vice versa. The engine load is also used to determine when the TCC should be applied and released. The TCC cannot transmit very much torque without slipping, which would burn it up quickly. Thus, when the engine is under more load than the TCC is designed for, the PCM turns the TCC off.

Although many vehicles still have a MAP sensor on the intake manifold, most of these sensors on vehicles built after 1996 are not the primary sensor used for determining engine load as you will see in the next section. MAP sensors are now used to test if certain emissions-related components are functioning properly, as they will cause changes in manifold pressure if they are.

> ### TECHNICIAN TIP
>
> MAP sensors were originally connected to the intake manifold through a vacuum hose. Over time these hoses deteriorate and can develop small holes and cracks in the lines, or they get soft and collapse. Vacuum hoses should be replaced periodically as they start to show signs of deterioration. A vacuum hose that has deteriorated will affect fuel economy and result in a late, harder shift, as the PCM thinks the vehicle is under greater load than it really is.

Mass Airflow Sensor

To meet more stringent emission standards, most vehicles come equipped with a **mass airflow (MAF) sensor**, rather than a MAP sensor, to measure engine load. MAF sensors are a much more accurate and faster means of measuring engine load. The MAF sensor actually measures the mass of the air coming into the engine, so the PCM can accurately inject the proper amount of fuel. MAF sensors measure airflow in grams per second (gps). The more airflow, the harder the engine is working. As engine speed increases, so does airflow. The MAF sensor is typically installed in the air intake hose leading to the throttle body assembly. Some MAF sensors are built into the throttle body assembly, while others are mounted on the air cleaner assembly **FIGURE 19-11**.

There are many different types of MAF sensors currently being installed on vehicles, and you need to check the specific vehicle's service information for testing methods. It is important to check that all of the air intake hoses are tightly secured to the engine so that the MAF sensor will measure all of the air entering the engine. Any air leaks *after* the sensor will result in an inaccurate reading by the MAF sensor, resulting in early shifting and poor vehicle drivability. Some MAF sensors require periodic cleaning, as dirt and contaminants can build up on the sensing surface inside the sensor. Clean these components carefully using a cleaner recommended for MAF sensor cleaning. Note some manufacturers specifically say not to clean their MAF sensors and to instead replace them if they are not reading correctly. Be careful to check the manufacturer's recommendation regarding whether the MAF sensor can be cleaned. And if it can, follow the manufacturer's directions precisely.

Crankshaft Position Sensor

The PCM uses the **crankshaft position (CKP) sensor** to determine engine speed **FIGURE 19-12**. CKP sensors can be a magnetic pickup-style sensor, a Hall-effect sensor, or an optical-style sensor. All three types of sensors serve the same function: to send a pulsed signal to the vehicle PCM to determine engine speed.

The PCM compares the CKP sensor signal to the input shaft speed sensor in the transmission to determine torque converter slippage between the impeller and the turbine. It is also used as the PCM operates the TCC to monitor the engagement and slippage of the TCC. Most TCCs are pulsed on slowly to prevent a harsh engagement that drivers might complain about. By observing the difference in speed, the PCM can precisely control how long it takes for the TCC to become fully locked.

Brake On/Off Switch

Another input the PCM looks at is the brake on/off switch **FIGURE 19-13**. The brake switch is used to control the brake lights on the vehicle when the driver applies the brakes, but the PCM also uses this information for transmission control. The brake on/off switch is a normally open switch that closes when the driver applies the brake pedal, allowing current to flow to the stop lamps and to the PCM. In some vehicles, the brake on/off switch is separate from the brake light switch, so always check the service information to make sure you are testing the correct switch.

The PCM uses the brake switch input to disengage the TCC. As soon as the driver applies any pressure to the brake pedal, the TCC must be released to prevent excessive

FIGURE 19-11 A MAF sensor installed in the air intake tube on a vehicle. It is important to make sure all of the clamps are securely fastened.

FIGURE 19-12 A crankshaft position (CKP) sensor installed on the front of a crankshaft.

FIGURE 19-13 A common brake on/off switch wiring diagram.

FIGURE 19-14 A manual lever position (MLP) switch mounted on the outside of the transmission. Note the manual lever linkage passing through the middle of the switch.

drag on the engine and a possible stall. On some newer vehicles, the brake switch is also used to put the transmission into neutral while idling at a stop light. As long as the driver has the brake pedal applied, the vehicle will remain in neutral to save fuel. As soon as the driver releases the brake pedal, the transmission reengages into gear.

Manual Lever Position

The **manual lever position (MLP) switch** is sometimes called a transmission range switch or a neutral safety switch. It is a simple multiposition switch that sends a signal to the PCM regarding which gear the manual lever is in. This information is used to prevent the vehicle from starting in any gear except park or neutral. The PCM also uses this information to turn on the reverse lights and to control the selection of gears and automatic shifting.

The MLP is often mounted directly on the transmission case where the shift linkage connects to the transmission **FIGURE 19-14**. On some vehicles, this switch is adjustable and will need to be adjusted after replacing the transmission, the shift cable, or the switch.

TECHNICIAN TIP

Make sure the MLP switch is adjusted correctly *before* starting the vehicle after replacing a transmission. If the switch has not been adjusted properly, when the technician continues to add hydraulic oil to top off the transmission, the vehicle may suddenly have enough transmission fluid to engage the clutches and begin moving.

Overdrive Switch

The overdrive switch is operated by the driver to manually select or deselect overdrive. Many manufacturers recommend not using overdrive when pulling a trailer or heavy loads because doing so can overload the transmission. Therefore, the driver can activate the overdrive switch (sometimes labeled as "Tow/Haul"), which sends a simple on/off signal to the PCM indicating that the driver wants to disable overdrive. The PCM then modifies the shifting pattern accordingly, locking out overdrive. The driver activates the overdrive switch again when overdrive is desired. The PCM then allows shifting into overdrive when appropriate. Some vehicles automatically reset the overdrive switch to allow overdrive when the vehicle is restarted.

▶ Power Train Control Module Outputs

Electronic Pressure Control Solenoid

On electronically controlled transmissions, line pressure is controlled using an **electronic pressure control (EPC) solenoid**. Most EPC solenoids are a pulse-width–modulated type of solenoid. Pulse-width modulation means that the solenoid is not on all of the time; instead it pulses rapidly on and off to control pressure. A pulse width of 50% means the solenoid is on 50% of the time and off the other 50% of the time. If we were to look at the voltage to the EPC solenoid using a DSO, we would see a square wave pattern like that shown in **FIGURE 19-15**.

EPC solenoids are installed in the line pressure circuit and exhaust some of the line pressure back to the transmission pan. If the line pressure is 200 pounds per square inch (psi) and we have an EPC pulse width of 50%, the line pressure will be approximately 100 psi. Roughly 50% of the line pressure will be exhausted back to the pan. If higher line pressure is required, the PCM will reduce the pulse width. At a 25% pulse width, the line pressure would be approximately 150 psi, or 75% of the available line pressure in this example.

Most EPC solenoids are designed so that if there is a problem with the PCM, the wiring, or the EPC solenoid, the vehicle will have only maximum line pressure.

FIGURE 19-16 An electronic pressure control (EPC) solenoid hydraulic diagram.

The EPC solenoid will be forced closed by an internal spring, and no line pressure will be exhausted to the pan. In using a scan tool, you will notice that some manufacturers give you the amount of amperage being used by the EPC solenoid, rather than the pulse width. This amperage will change as the pulse width of the solenoid is changed. **FIGURE 19-16** shows an EPC solenoid hydraulic diagram.

Shift Solenoids

Shift solenoids are typically an electromagnetic type of valve that is either open or closed. These solenoids can directly control line pressure to an application device, such as a clutch or band, or they may control a shift valve, which in turn directs fluid to the clutch or band. Many four-speed automatic transmissions use two shift solenoids to control the transmission. **TABLE 19-1** lists the shift solenoid operation on a typical four-speed automatic transmission. By turning the different solenoids on and off, all of the gears needed can be hydraulically applied.

Based on the information in Table 19-1, what gear would the vehicle start in if both solenoids failed? Notice that only third gear does not use either shift solenoid. If the vehicle has a problem with the PCM, the shift solenoids, or the wiring, the customer may complain about a very poor-performing vehicle that will only start in third gear. This is often called limp-in mode, as the vehicle would still be drivable with a shift solenoid failure.

FIGURE 19-17 is a simplified diagram for a common Chrysler 41TE transmission, found in many of the Chrysler minivans. In this transmission, the solenoids directly operate the clutches to control the shifting of gears. This particular transmission has four solenoids. They are labeled 1, 2, 3, and 4 on the diagram. Solenoid 1 controls the underdrive clutch, solenoid 2 controls the overdrive clutch, solenoid 3 controls the low reverse clutch, and solenoid 4 controls the 2–4 clutch. Looking at Figure 19-18, you can see that solenoids 1 and 3 are being used. Line pressure is being routed through the solenoids to the underdrive clutch and the low reverse clutch to engage first gear.

In **FIGURE 19-18**, you can see the transmission in second gear. For this transmission to operate in second gear, the PCM commands solenoids 1 and 4 on. This allows line pressure to flow to the underdrive clutch through solenoid 1. Line pressure is allowed to flow through solenoid 4 to the 2–4 clutch. With both the underdrive clutch and the 2–4 clutch engaged, the vehicle is in second gear.

FIGURE 19-19 shows the same transmission in third gear. In third gear on this vehicle, the PCM commands solenoids 1 and 2 on. Solenoid 1 again supplies line pressure to the underdrive clutch, and solenoid 2 supplies line pressure to the overdrive clutch. With both the

FIGURE 19-17 A simplified diagram of a Chrysler 41TE transmission in first gear.

FIGURE 19-18 A simplified diagram of a Chrysler 41TE transmission in second gear.

TABLE 19-1: Shift Solenoid Operation on a Typical Four-Speed Automatic Transmission		
PCM Commanded Gear	**1–2 Shift Solenoid**	**2–3 Shift Solenoid**
Park, Neutral, Reverse	On	On
First	On	On
Second	Off	On
Third	Off	Off
Fourth	On	Off

FIGURE 19-19 A simplified diagram of a Chrysler 41TE transmission in third gear.

FIGURE 19-20 A simplified diagram of a Chrysler 41TE transmission in fourth gear.

FIGURE 19-21 A simplified hydraulic diagram for a transmission in which the shift solenoids indirectly operate the clutches or bands in first gear.

underdrive clutch and the overdrive clutch engaged, the vehicle is in third gear.

FIGURE 19-20 shows fourth gear operation. For fourth gear in this transmission, solenoids 2 and 4 need to be engaged by the PCM. Solenoid 2 allows line pressure to flow to the overdrive clutch, and solenoid 4 allows line pressure to flow to the 2–4 clutch. When both the 2–4 clutch and the overdrive clutch are engaged, the vehicle is in fourth gear.

In many transmissions, the solenoids do not directly operate the clutches and bands. Rather, the solenoid allows hydraulic oil to flow to a spool valve. The spool valve then moves, allowing line pressure to flow past and engage the clutch or band. **FIGURE 19-21** is a simplified

hydraulic diagram for a transmission. In the figure, the transmission is in first gear. The manual valve allows line pressure to flow to all four of the pressure control valves, and to the four shift solenoids. The PCM has energized solenoids 1 and 3. Solenoid 1 is now able to flow line pressure to pressure control valve 1, causing the spool valve to move to the left. When the spool valve moves to the left, line pressure is allowed to flow to the low reverse band. Solenoid 3 allows line pressure to flow to shift valve 3, causing the spool valve to move to the left. As this valve moves to the left, line pressure is allowed to flow to the underdrive clutch. When the low/reverse band and the underdrive clutch are engaged, the vehicle is in first gear.

FIGURE 19-22 shows the same transmission in second gear. For second gear, the PCM energizes solenoids 2 and 3. The manual valve allows line pressure to flow to all four shift valves and all four solenoids. Opening solenoid 2 allows line pressure to be applied to shift valve 2, causing the spool valve to move to the left. This movement

FIGURE 19-22 A simplified hydraulic diagram of a transmission in second gear that uses indirect solenoids to control the shifts.

FIGURE 19-23 A simplified hydraulic diagram of a transmission in third gear that uses indirect solenoids to control the shifts.

allows line pressure to flow past shift valve 2 and to the second band. Opening solenoid 3 allows line pressure to be applied to the right side of shift valve 3, causing the valve to move to the left. As the spool valve moves to the left, line pressure is allowed to flow through the shift valve to the underdrive clutch. When the underdrive clutch and the second band are applied, the vehicle is in second gear.

The same generic transmission, this time in third gear, is shown in **FIGURE 19-23**. Looking at the diagram, we can see that the PCM has energized solenoids 3 and 4. Again, line pressure has been supplied to all four shift solenoids and the four shift valves. Opening solenoid 3 allows line pressure to flow to the right side of shift valve 3, causing the spool valve to move to the left. When the valve moves to the left, line pressure is allowed to flow through the spool valve to the underdrive clutch. When solenoid 4 is engaged by the PCM, line pressure flows to the right side of shift valve 4, again moving the spool valve to the left. Line pressure is then allowed to flow to the overdrive clutch.

When both the underdrive clutch and the overdrive clutch are engaged, this transmission is in third gear.

In **FIGURE 19-24**, we have the same transmission once more. This time the PCM has commanded operation of fourth gear. The PCM has energized solenoids 2 and 4. Each of these solenoids then allows line pressure to its respective shift valve. The line pressure causes the spool valve to move to the left, allowing line pressure to flow from shift valve 2 to the second band and from shift valve 4 to the overdrive clutch. When both the second band and the overdrive clutch are engaged, this transmission is in fourth gear.

In the hydraulic diagrams for these examples, the direct solenoid shift type and the indirect solenoid shift type have been simplified to ease understanding. Having grasped the basic concept of how these systems control the transmission, you can follow a more complicated hydraulic diagram. On many transmissions, the manufacturers will use multiple valves to ensure proper operation

FIGURE 19-24 A simplified hydraulic diagram of a transmission in fourth gear that uses indirect solenoids to control the shifts.

FIGURE 19-25 A lock-up torque converter solenoid being removed from a General Motors 4L60E transmission.

of the clutches and bands, and to prevent the transmission from being in two gears at once. If a transmission were allowed to be in two gears at once, the results would be disastrous for the transmission, as it would tend to lock up and the weakest part would burn out or break.

Torque Converter Clutch

The PCM controls the TCC (torque converter clutch) lock-up solenoid **FIGURE 19-25**. Early torque converters always had some slippage, so in the late 1970s and early 1980s manufacturers added a lock-up clutch to the torque converter. When the PCM determines that the torque converter should be locked up (i.e., the vehicle is operating under an appropriate load, at an appropriate speed, in the appropriate gear, and at the proper engine temperature, etc.), it engages the TCC lock-up solenoid. The solenoid allows line pressure to be applied to the TCC and locks up the turbine to the impeller, providing direct drive through the torque converter.

Some TCC solenoids are a pulse-width–modulated solenoid. Remember that pulse-width modulation means that the solenoid is only on for a percentage of the time. For a solenoid with a 25% pulse-width modulation, the solenoid is on 25% of the time and off 75% of the time. Manufacturers slowly pulse the TCC on to prevent a harsh engagement that a customer might complain about. The PCM monitors the CKP sensor and the input shaft speed sensor to determine the amount of torque converter slippage and control the lock-up of the TCC.

> ### TECHNICIAN TIP
>
> Always test-drive a vehicle to verify the reported problem. One customer brought in a turbocharged vehicle he had recently purchased, complaining that the turbocharger was not functioning correctly. After a quick test-drive, it was determined that the turbocharger was not the cause of the poor performance; rather, the transmission solenoids had failed and the vehicle only had third gear. Replacing the solenoids fixed the problem and the customer was happy. If the technician had listened to the customer and replaced the turbo unit, the vehicle would still have had very poor performance.

▶ Power Train Control Module/Transmission Control Module

The PCM or the TCM is the brain in the system. In basic terms, it comprises a storage memory section, a data processor section, an input sensor control and processing section, and a section for output drivers. The storage memory contains the software for the computer, as well as a place to retain DTCs, freeze-frame data, and learned data. Software is loaded into the memory, which is the basis for processing data. The software contains all of the information needed for the processor to interpret the sensor information and make decisions based on the programmed information. It also contains the instructions for performing diagnostic tests on the circuits and PCM itself. In many cases, the software can be updated by uploading software updates, called a relearn process. With software that can be updated, manufacturers can design fixes for many of the issues that may arise once their vehicles go into operation. This makes it easier, quicker, and less expensive to resolve some common customer or drivability issues rather than replacing the PCM with an updated part.

The processor and drivers are hardware related, so they make up the physical portion of the PCM. The input sensor section is responsible for sending the proper reference voltage to many of the sensors. It also receives the sensor signals and processes them into information that the main computer processor can use. The processor processes the data and compares them to data maps in the memory. Once the sensor data have been analyzed, the processor looks up the appropriate data map and determines the necessary actions. The processor then sends the appropriate commands to each of the drivers, which are electronic switching or control devices that control each of the actuators in the transmission. The processor also commands the diagnostic tests on the system and evaluates the results compared to the information stored in memory. The output drivers typically send either simple on/off signals or pulse-width–modulated signals to the actuators, depending on the actuator being controlled.

> ▶ **LINK**
> Refer to the chapters on Servicing Steering and Suspension Systems for more detailed information on the PCM.

Electronic Shift Programs

Most vehicles can identify and adapt to a driver's individual style and to environmental conditions. In time, the PCM learns how a particular driver uses the vehicle. For example, does the driver always accelerate hard, or is the driver more casual?

The PCM monitors the TPS sensor along with the VSS to determine a driver's driving pattern. For a driver who has a more aggressive driving pattern, the PCM will delay

the shift points to allow the engine to operate closer to its peak rpm range. The PCM will also increase the line pressure to give firmer, quicker shifts. During deceleration, the transmission will downshift at a higher rpm so the engine will be at an ideal rpm for maximum performance after the downshift.

For a more conservative driver, the PCM will allow the transmission to shift earlier to keep the engine's rpm lower and help improve fuel economy. The PCM will also reduce the line pressure to soften the shifts and allow for a more comfortable drive.

Some vehicles have a mode selection switch on, or near, the gear shift lever to change the shift characteristics. The mode selector might have modes such as sport or normal, or sport or economy. On some hybrid vehicles, a brake mode, or regenerative braking mode, is available. This mode is used when going down steeper hills and increases the amount of regeneration that is commanded. It provides greater braking power than in the normal mode.

Since a driver's driving responses can vary considerably within a short time, depending on traffic and road conditions, response patterns are analyzed continuously. If a driver's requirements change suddenly after a stop, the driving style identification circuits within the control unit must be able to adapt.

> ▶ **TECHNICIAN TIP**
>
> If the adaptive memory is lost due to clearing of the memory, or disconnection of the battery on some vehicles, the customer may come back and complain, "What did you do to my transmission? It doesn't work the same as before!" To prevent this, you can either use a memory minder while the battery is disconnected, or you can test-drive the vehicle to help it relearn a driving style. The other alternative is to educate drivers and tell them that they will have to drive the vehicle for a few days for it to relearn their driving style.

Environment Identification

Identification of environment means identifying unusual ambient conditions in which the vehicle is operating. Slippery conditions require a gear ratio that enhances traction and the stability of motion of the vehicle. On vehicles equipped with traction control, one method of providing improved traction is to change the gear ratio of the transmission. Wheel slip monitoring via the anti-lock braking sensors may confirm poor tire grip, and a winter shift program can be initiated by the PCM on a vehicle with traction control. When traction control is activated, if a tire starts to spin, the PCM will command the brake for that wheel to apply to slow down the wheel so power can be given to the other wheel. The PCM typically commands a higher transmission gear, and reduced engine torque, when the vehicle is just starting from a stop. This helps to prevent the tires from losing traction.

Electronic Transmission Fault Detection

On electronically controlled transmissions, the PCM must be able to monitor the transmission for proper operation. One of the first methods of fault detection is a basic circuit test. On solenoids and switches, the PCM can test the continuity of those circuits and tell if they are open, shorted to ground, or shorted to power. If the test value is out of range, the PCM will set a DTC and turn the malfunction indicator lamp (MIL) on.

A more sophisticated type of fault detection is when the PCM monitors the input shaft speed sensor and compares it to the VSS to determine gear ratios. If the ratio is not correct, the PCM will set a DTC for a ratio error and turn the MIL on.

Newer PCMs also have logic programmed into them. No longer will the PCM only look for opens, shorts, and ratio errors. It will now also apply logic to the operating conditions it sees. For example, suppose the PCM is sent a signal from the CKP sensor of 650 rpm, an MLP signal of neutral, and a TPS signal of 75% throttle. The PCM has the logic built into its programming to realize that it is not possible to have the vehicle in neutral, an engine speed of only 650 rpm, and the throttle at 75% open. The PCM would trigger a code for the TPS. Before PCMs were programmed with this type of logic, the PCM could not make these kinds of determinations.

Torque Management

On many modern electronically controlled transmissions, the PCM can manage the torque output of the engine and vary the amount of torque being sent to the transmission. By having a completely electronically controlled transmission and engine, the PCM is able to reduce the amount of torque being produced by the engine right before the transmission shifts. Much of the wear and tear

in an automatic transmission occurs during the relatively short time that the transmission is shifting between gears. By reducing the amount of torque being transmitted to the transmission during this time, transmission wear is greatly reduced and smoother shifting is experienced. Manufacturers have also found that by using torque management to reduce the amount of torque during shifting, they can install a smaller transmission in the vehicle. For example, a manufacturer might be able to install a transmission that was designed to handle less torque than otherwise would be necessary without affecting the transmission's longevity.

To manage the engine torque, the PCM might be programmed to cut back on the ignition timing of the engine right before the transmission shifts. As soon as the transmission has completed the shift, the PCM returns the ignition timing to normal. During normal operation, the spark plug is fired anywhere between about 10 degrees and 45 degrees of crankshaft revolution *before* the piston reaches top dead center. By retarding the ignition timing, the engine torque is dramatically decreased, reducing the strain on the transmission. All of this happens in less than 1 second, so the driver rarely feels any loss of power. If anything, the driver might notice that the transmission shifts more smoothly than a vehicle without torque management.

Limp-in Mode

Most electronically controlled transmissions have a fail-safe or **limp-in mode**. Limp-in mode means that even if the computer for the transmission or the part of the PCM that controls the transmission fails, the vehicle will still be drivable. The transmission will have only one forward gear. Whichever gear does not require any shift solenoids will be the limp-in gear. On many transmissions, third gear is designed to be the limp-in gear.

Also, on most transmissions, if the PCM fails, the EPC solenoid will mechanically default to maximum line pressure to prevent clutch and band slippage, which would severely damage the transmission. This will result in additional holding power for the clutches and bands. Failure of the transmission in any of these ways should turn on the MIL, notifying the driver of the failure and allowing him or her to safely drive the vehicle to a repair facility.

Wrap-up

Ready for Review

- U.S. auto manufacturers switched to electronically controlled transmissions by the late 1980s.
- Shift points in an electronically controlled transmission are controlled by the power train control module (PCM) or transmission control module (TCM).
- A vehicle speed sensor (VSS) relays vehicle speed information to the speedometer.
- Types of VSS are magnetic pickup and reed switch.
- An input shaft speed sensor is similar to a VSS and relays its signal to the PCM.
- Shift timing and pressure are regulated based on input from the transmission oil temperature (TOT) sensor.
- Transmission pressure switches are used to determine when pressure is in a particular circuit.
- Transmission line pressure is adjusted based on feedback from the line pressure sensor.
- The throttle position sensor (TPS) is a variable resistor (potentiometer) that moves with the position of the throttle.
- The engine coolant temperature (ECT) sensor relays information to the PCM, enabling the PCM to vary shift timing and pressures based on engine temperature.
- The manifold absolute pressure (MAP) sensor allows the PCM to monitor how much load the engine and transmission are under.
- Modern MAP sensors (installed after 1996) are primarily used to determine functionality of emissions-related components.
- Mass airflow (MAF) sensors measure the mass of air (in grams per second) entering the engine, enabling the PCM to inject the correct amount of fuel.

- Types of crankshaft position (CKP) sensors are magnetic pickup, Hall effect, and optical.
- The PCM relies on the CKP sensor to determine engine speed.
- The PCM reads signals from the brake on/off switch to know when the driver has applied the brake pedal.
- The manual lever position (MLP) switch may be referred to as the transmission range switch or a neutral safety switch.
- The PCM reads the manual lever position to prevent the vehicle from starting unless it is in park or neutral.
- An electronic pressure control (EPC) solenoid is used to control line pressure.
- Shift solenoids are used to direct line pressure directly to an application device or via a shift valve.
- Shift solenoids may allow hydraulic oil to flow to a spool valve rather than directly operate clutches and bands.
- A torque converter clutch (TCC) lock-up solenoid is engaged once vehicle speed has stabilized.
- The PCM is designed to adapt to a driver's individual driving pattern.
- The PCM can also identify and adapt to environmental conditions.
- The first step in a PCM's fault detection system is a basic circuit test.
- The PCM monitors gear ratios as a method of fault detection.
- The PCM can reduce transmission wear by torque reduction during gear shifting.
- The PCM manages engine torque via retarding engine ignition timing prior to transmission shifts.
- Limp-in mode refers to the vehicle still functioning in the event of a failure of the transmission computer or part of the PCM that controls the transmission.

Key Terms

crankshaft position (CKP) sensor A sensor used by the PCM to monitor engine speed. It can be one of three types of sensors—Hall effect, magnetic pickup, or optical.

electronic pressure control (EPC) solenoid A pulse-width–modulated solenoid used to control transmission line pressure in an automatic transmission.

engine coolant temperature (ECT) sensor A sensor that changes resistance based upon coolant temperature; also known as a thermistor.

input shaft speed sensor A sensor inside the transmission that measures the rpm of the input shaft. Also called a turbine shaft sensor.

limp-in mode A transmission operating mode in which limited computer controls are needed to operate for the purpose of getting the vehicle to a shop.

line pressure sensor A variable resistor sensor used to monitor line pressure. It sends a signal back to the PCM where it can be translated into a psi reading.

manifold absolute pressure (MAP) sensor A vacuum sensor that is attached to the intake manifold by a passageway or vacuum hose. The sensor measures engine intake manifold pressure to determine engine load and sends a corresponding signal to the PCM.

manual lever position (MLP) switch A switch that is used by the PCM to tell which gear range the driver has selected with the shift lever.

mass airflow (MAF) sensor A sensor located in the air intake system that is used to measure the mass of the air flowing into the engine.

potentiometer A type of variable resistor that increases or decreases its resistance as it is turned, which creates a varying voltage signal.

power train control module (PCM) A computer module that controls the engine and possibly the transmission on a computer-controlled vehicle.

reed switch A type of speed sensor that uses a magnetic field to open and close a movable set of contacts. It is used with a rotating magnet to measure rpm of a shaft and send the signal to the PCM.

shift solenoid An electromechanical device used to control oil flow to bands and clutches in an automatic transmission to help shift the transmission.

throttle position sensor (TPS) A type of potentiometer used by the PCM to measure throttle angle.

torque converter clutch (TCC) A hydraulically operated clutch located inside the torque converter that applies at predetermined conditions and stops torque converter slippage.

transmission control module (TCM) A computer module that controls the transmission operation. It may be integrated into the PCM.

transmission oil temperature (TOT) sensor A type of variable resistor used inside the transmission to monitor oil temperature.

vehicle speed sensor (VSS) A sensor used by the PCM to measure vehicle speed. It is often located in the transmission extension housing.

ASE-Type Questions

1. Tech A says that manufacturers developed the electronically controlled automatic transmission to improve fuel economy. Tech B says that manufacturers have added more gears to their electronically controlled transmission to improve fuel economy. Who is correct?
   a. Tech A
   b. Tech B
   c. Both A and B
   d. Neither A nor B

2. A vehicle comes in only operating in 3rd gear. Tech A says the transmission will need to be replaced. Tech B says that the transmission can be operating in limp-in mode. Who is correct?
   a. Tech A
   b. Tech B
   c. Both A and B
   d. Neither A nor B

3. Tech A says that reed switches produce an AC signal. Tech B says that a magnetic VSS can be diagnosed by observing the pattern on a lab scope and comparing it to a known good pattern. Who is correct?
   a. Tech A
   b. Tech B
   c. Both A and B
   d. Neither A nor B

4. Tech A says that transmissions with an input shaft speed sensor and a vehicle speed sensor (VSS) can use this information to determine shift solenoid failure. Tech B says the input shaft speed sensor is also called a turbine speed sensor. Who is correct?
   a. Tech A
   b. Tech B
   c. Both A and B
   d. Neither A nor B

5. Tech A says that delayed shifts could be caused by a malfunctioning TPS. Tech B says that this information can be used to determine clutch slippage. Who is correct?
   a. Tech A
   b. Tech B
   c. Both A and B
   d. Neither A nor B

6. Tech A says that the ECT and the TOT will delay transmission shifting. Tech B says that the ECT and the TOT could cause the transmission to shift sluggishly. Who is correct?
   a. Tech A
   b. Tech B
   c. Both A and B
   d. Neither A nor B

7. Tech A says that on most vehicles if the EPC solenoid fails the vehicle will have high line pressure. Tech B says that if an EPC fails it will cause a delayed shift in most vehicles. Who is correct?
   a. Tech A
   b. Tech B
   c. Both A and B
   d. Neither A nor B

8. A vehicle stalls when coming to a stop. After test driving the vehicle it is found that the TCC solenoid is remaining engaged as the vehicle slows down. Tech A says that the vehicle probably needs a new torque convertor. Tech B says that the TCC solenoid may be sticking and needs to be replaced. Who is correct?
   a. Tech A
   b. Tech B
   c. Both A and B
   d. Neither A nor B

9. A vehicle comes in with the check engine light on. The vehicle is scanned and has transmission ratio error codes for 1st, 2nd, 3rd, and 4th gears. Tech A says that the problem could be a faulty output shaft speed sensor. Tech B says that the problem could be a faulty transmission front pump. Who is correct?
   a. Tech A
   b. Tech B
   c. Both A and B
   d. Neither A nor B

10. Tech A says that automatic transmissions will change gear ratios based upon winter weather conditions. Tech B says that on a vehicle with traction control, the transmission will change shift programming to assist. Who is correct?
    a. Tech A
    b. Tech B
    c. Both A and B
    d. Neither A nor B

CHAPTER 20

NATEF Tasks

Automatic Transmission and Transaxle
General

Servicing the Automatic Transmission/ Transaxle

Knowledge Objectives

After reading this chapter, you will be able to:
1. Describe the various methods of tests used in diagnosing an automatic transmission. (pp 542–544)
2. Explain the process involved in servicing the automatic transmission, including:
   a. Inspecting, replacing, and aligning power train mounts. (pp 510–553)
   b. Diagnosing fluid loss and condition concerns. (pp 537–539)
   c. Replacing the fluid and internal filter. (pp 539–542)
   d. Diagnosing electronic transmission control systems. (pp 544–545)
   e. Performing pressure tests. (pp 547–548)

Knowledge Objectives, continued

f. Inspecting for leakage and replacing external seals, gaskets, and bushings. (pp 549–550)
g. Performing lock-up converter system tests. (pp 553–555)
h. Removing and reinstalling the transmission and torque converter. (pp 555–559)

Skills Objectives

After reading this chapter, you will be able to:
1. Diagnose fluid loss and condition concerns, and check fluid level in transmissions with and without a dipstick. (pp 537–539)
2. Replace the fluid and internal filter. (pp 539–542)
3. Diagnose electronic transmission control systems using appropriate test equipment and service information. (pp 544–545)
4. Perform a stall test. (pp 545–547)
5. Perform pressure tests (including on transmissions/transaxles equipped with electronic pressure control). (pp 547–548)
6. Inspect for leakage and replace external seals, gaskets, and bushings. (pp 549–550)
7. Inspect, replace, and align power train mounts. (pp 550–553)
8. Perform lock-up converter system tests and determine necessary action on electronically controlled transmissions. (pp 553–554)
9. Remove and reinstall the transmission and torque converter. (pp 555–556)
10. Inspect, adjust, and replace the manual valve shift linkage, transmission range sensor/switch, and park/neutral position switch. (pp 555–558)
11. Inspect the torque converter and flex plate. (pp 558–559)
12. Inspect, leak test, and flush or replace transmission cooler lines and fittings. (pp 559–561)
13. Check bearings for preload and end play. (pp 561–562)
14. Disassemble, clean, and inspect the transmission. (pp 562–565)
15. Inspect, measure, and reseal a removed pump assembly and components. (pp 565–569)
16. Inspect and measure removed planetary gear assembly components. (p 569)
17. Inspect bushings on a disassembled transmission. (pp 569–570)
18. Inspect, measure, and replace thrust washers and bearings on a disassembled transmission. (pp 570–571)
19. Inspect the one-way roller or sprag and related components in a disassembled transmission. (pp 571–572)
20. Inspect fluid delivery circuits. (pp 572–574)
21. Inspect case bores, passages, bushings, vents, mating surfaces, servo, accumulator bores, pistons, seals, pins, springs, and retainers in a disassembled transmission. (pp 574–576)
22. Inspect bands and drums in a disassembled transmission. (pp 574–576)
23. Inspect clutch drum, piston, check-balls, springs, retainers, seals, and friction and pressure plates on a disassembled transmission. (pp 576–579)
24. Measure clutch pack clearance. (p 579)
25. Air test operation of clutch and servo assemblies. (p 580)
26. Inspect, measure, clean, and replace the removed valve body. (pp 580–581)
27. Inspect the transaxle drive, link chains, sprockets, gears, bearings, and bushings. (pp 582–583)
28. Inspect, measure, and repair or replace transaxle final drive components. (pp 583–584)
29. Assemble the transmission. (pp 584–587)
30. Install and seat the torque converter to engage drive/splines. (pp 587–588)

Introduction

Most automotive technicians will not perform complete rebuilding of automatic transmissions and transaxles in their shops, but it is very important for technicians to have a good understanding of how the transmission operates and the correct testing and service procedures. A technician who does not have the ability to diagnose a transmission failure may be doomed to transmission replacement. Or worse, this technician may replace the transmission only to find that the existing problem is still there. If a customer brings a vehicle to a shop for a transmission problem and is told that the vehicle needs a new transmission for $3500, that customer may then take the vehicle to another shop for a second opinion. What if that other shop actually does some diagnostic work and finds that the transmission is only leaking from a gasket and is low on fluid? The total bill may be less than $100 and the customer has now found a new, reliable shop. Not only that, but the customer may tell other potential customers not to take their vehicles to the original shop—all because of that one critical experience.

Note, when we say *transmission*, we use the term generically to include transaxles also. When we use transaxle, we generally only mean transaxle. Readers should use their understanding of transmission and transaxle theory to understand the intended meaning. For example, if we are discussing ring and pinion backlash, that can only apply to a transaxle.

General Transmission Maintenance

Most automatic transmissions require some periodic preventive maintenance. This maintenance is designed to reduce transmission failure and save the customer money in the long run. It should include a visual inspection for leaks and a check of the transmission for proper fluid level. Periodic maintenance often also includes transmission fluid and filter replacement, which allows for the inspection of debris or contaminants in the bottom of the transmission pan.

Checking Transmission Fluid

Checking transmission fluid should be done at least at every oil change. Checking the fluid level in an automatic transmission is one of the first steps in diagnosing a transmission problem. Without the proper fluid level, the transmission will not shift properly and may suffer internal damage when the fluid level is too low or too high. If the fluid level is low, it is important to properly identify the source of fluid loss, which we will cover in more depth as we discuss the individual components.

For most, but not all, automatic transmissions, the fluid level is checked with the vehicle idling in park or neutral. Check the service information for the vehicle you are working on. It is important that the vehicle be on level ground to accurately measure the fluid level.

You are the Automotive Technician

Today a customer visits your shop with a transmission concern in a 2009 Chevy Impala. He tells you that it takes about 5 seconds for it to go into gear the first thing in the morning, and sometimes the engine revolutions per minute (rpm) flare on an upshift. You start by checking the fluid level and find it well below the safe mark. It leaves a dark center when placed on a white paper towel. You top it off with about 1.5 quarts of the proper transmission fluid to get it ready for a test-drive. During the test-drive, you notice that the malfunction indicator light (MIL) is illuminated and the torque converter clutch doesn't engage, but the customer says the flaring on upshifts is gone. Everything else appears normal.

1. What might a visual inspection reveal on this vehicle?
2. What test(s) should be performed based on the results of the test-drive?
3. Assuming the tests reveal that the transmission does not need to be rebuilt, what service(s) should be recommended to the customer?

When reading a transmission dipstick, it is important to realize that on most transmission dipsticks it only takes a pint of fluid to raise the level from the bottom of the crosshatched area or add mark to the full mark, unlike on the engine oil dipstick, which typically requires 1 quart **FIGURE 20-1**. In recent years, vehicle manufacturers have been eliminating the transmission dipstick on some of their vehicles. One of the reasons for this is to prevent the vehicle owner from installing the incorrect transmission fluid into a vehicle or overfilling the transmission. Another reason is that by eliminating the transmission dipstick there is one less entry point for dirt and contaminants to enter the transmission.

On transmissions without a dipstick, it is critical to check the service information for the proper procedure for checking the fluid level. Many late-model Ford and Toyota vehicles have what looks like a drain plug installed in the transmission pan. With the vehicle running, this plug is removed and fluid is forced up into the transmission through this hole. The hole has a tube attached to it inside the transmission. If the fluid level is too high, the fluid will simply drain back out. Allow any excess fluid to drain out of the hole, then reinstall the plug.

General Motors vehicles often have a threaded plug located on the transmission case that you remove while the vehicle is running to check the fluid level. Again, fluid is added until transmission fluid flows out of the hole. Allow the fluid to stop flowing, then reinstall the plug.

Locating Leaks

When fluids leak, they travel downward due to gravity and typically toward the back of the vehicle because of air movement during driving. This fluid travel can make

FIGURE 20-1 A typical transmission dipstick. This transmission typically requires 1 pint to bring the fluid level from the bottom of the crosshatched area to the full mark.

finding a leak more challenging, especially if the vehicle has been leaking for a while. If the transmission has a large amount of oil and dirt on it, locating the leak might require cleaning the transmission case with an engine degreaser or pressure washer. Another option if the leak is hard to locate is to place a leak detection dye in the transmission fluid. After running the transmission for a few minutes, any leaking dye will be visible with a black light.

To diagnose fluid loss and condition concerns and to check fluid level in transmissions with and without a dipstick, follow the steps in **SKILL DRILL 20-1**:

1. Look up the procedure for checking the transmission fluid level in the appropriate service information.

2. Locate the transmission dipstick (if equipped). Most, but not all, transmissions are checked with the engine at operating temperature, idling, and the transmission in park. If the transmission has a dipstick, wipe it off and reinsert it into the transmission before checking the level of fluid on the dipstick. Check both sides of the dipstick; the side that is the lowest is the accurate fluid level. On some transmissions, the fluid returning to the transmission pan will splash up on one side of the dipstick resulting in a high reading on that side. **(Photo 1)**

3. If the transmission fluid level is low, add the recommended type and amount of transmission fluid. Be careful not to overfill the transmission.

4. Inspect the transmission for signs of leakage. Some places to check are the transmission pan, area around the entrance of the filler tube to the transmission, extension housing gasket, output shaft seals, selector shaft seal, area around the electrical connectors that go into the transmission case, front pump seals, fluid cooler lines, and fittings. Also, if the vehicle has a vacuum modulator, remove the vacuum hose from the modulator and see if there is any transmission fluid in the hose. If there is, the modulator is bad. Be sure to remove the radiator cap (with vehicle cold) and check for any transmission fluid in the radiator. **(Photo 2)**

5. If the transmission has a large amount of transmission fluid or engine oil covering it, you may need to clean it with a pressure washer or some engine degreaser or use a leak detection dye in the transmission fluid.

6. Restart the vehicle and allow it to run for a while. The leak detection dye will be easy to spot using a black light, or look for fresh transmission fluid leaking. **(Photo 3)**

7 Record the location of the leak and inform the customer to obtain approval for repairs.

Replacing Fluid and Filters

The most common transmission work that the average technician will perform is a visual inspection along with fluid and filter replacement. At the minimum, transmission fluid should be changed according to the manufacturer's maintenance schedule. If the vehicle is used for towing or operates in dusty environments, the fluid should be changed more often. Some manufacturers recommend fluid and filter changes every 25,000 miles (40,000 km), while others advise against changing the fluid for the life of the vehicle because the transmission is sealed—and you will find recommendations everywhere in between.

As discussed in the Automatic Transmission Fundamentals chapter, it used to be possible to check the quality of transmission fluid by looking at its color and smelling it. If the fluid was a darkish red or had a burnt smell to, it was time for fluid replacement. Some modern transmission fluids are a darker red when they are brand new and even have a slightly burnt smell to them. For this reason, it is important to check the fluid in a new way. Take a few drops of transmission fluid and place them on a clean paper towel. The fluid will disperse on the paper towel, but any contaminants will remain where the fluid was placed. If the fluid spot on the paper towel has a darker center, it is a sign that there are contaminants in the transmission fluid and it should be changed **FIGURE 20-2**.

FIGURE 20-2 Place a drop of transmission fluid on a clean paper towel. If the fluid is dirty, the center of the drop will appear darker.

SKILL DRILL | 20-1 | Checking Fluid Level and Inspecting Fluid Loss

1 Look up the procedure to check the transmission fluid level. If appropriate, start the engine and allow to idle in park. Locate the transmission dipstick (if equipped). Wipe off the dipstick and reinsert it into the transmission before checking the level of fluid on both sides of the dipstick.

2 If the transmission fluid is low, add the recommended amount of the proper fluid. Do not overfill the transmission. Inspect transmission for signs of leakage.

3 If the transmission has a large amount of transmission fluid or engine oil covering it, you may need to clean it or use a leak detection dye in the fluid. Restart the vehicle and allow it to run for a while. The leak detection dye will be easy to spot using a black light or look for fresh transmission fluid leaking.

Some manufacturers install an in-line filter in the cooler line that is replaceable. Be aware of that when you research the replacement procedure for the transmission filter. Also, some transmissions have external filters that look like a typical engine oil filter.

To replace the fluid and internal filter, follow the steps in **SKILL DRILL 20-2**:

1. Look up the proper transmission fluid and filter service procedure, including the correct type of transmission fluid and capacity (which is approximated for a filter change) for a fluid and filter change.

2. Run the vehicle to bring the engine and transmission up to operating temperature.

3. Shut off the engine and raise the vehicle on the hoist.

4. Place a drain pan with a large transmission drain funnel under the transmission pan.

5. If the transmission has a drain plug, remove it and place it to the side to prevent losing it. *Be careful: The transmission fluid will be hot.*

6. If the transmission does not have a drain plug, loosen and remove all of the bolts except for two or three that are next to each other in a corner. **(Photo 1)**

7. Hold the pan against the transmission with one hand while loosening the remaining bolts a few turns.

8. Slowly allow the transmission pan to tilt downward and allow transmission fluid to flow into the drain pan.

9. Once most of the fluid has been drained, push the pan up against the transmission again and remove the remaining bolts the rest of the way. **(Photo 2)**

10. Lower the pan and inspect it inside for debris. Check for nonferrous metal and old clutch

SKILL DRILL 20-2 Draining and Replacing Fluid and Filter

1. Identify the correct type of transmission fluid and capacity. Run the vehicle to bring the engine and transmission up to operating temperature. Shut off the engine and raise the vehicle on the hoist. Place a drain pan with a large funnel under the transmission pan. If the transmission has a drain plug, remove it. *The transmission fluid will be hot.* If the transmission does not have a drain plug, loosen and remove all of the bolts except for three that are at a corner and next to each other.

2. Hold the pan against the transmission with one hand and loosen the remaining bolts a few turns. Allow the transmission pan to tilt downward and the transmission fluid to flow into the drain pan. Once most of the fluid has been drained, push the pan up against the transmission again and remove the remaining bolts.

3. Lower the pan and inspect the inside of the pan for debris. Check for nonferrous metal and old clutch material. Inspect the magnet in the pan (if equipped) for the amount of ferrous metal present.

SKILL DRILL | 20-2 | Draining and Replacing Fluid and Filter, continued

4 Remove any bolts or clips holding the transmission filter in place and lower the filter.

5 Clean the pan and the magnet thoroughly in a parts washer. Dry the pan with a lint-free shop towel or compressed air.

6 Compare the new filter and transmission gasket to the old one to make sure they are correct. If the filter kit came with a new filter gasket or grommet, install the new one. Install the new filter and torque any retaining bolts to specifications.

7 Put the new gasket on the transmission pan, clean the transmission sealing surface, and place the pan onto the transmission. Start all of the bolts before tightening.

8 Torque the bolts to specifications. Lower the vehicle and install 75% of the new fluid. Start the vehicle and check the fluid level. Add enough fluid to bring it to the bottom of the safe or add mark. With your foot firmly depressing the brake pedal, place the gear selector in each of the gear ranges. Check the fluid level with the engine at operating temperature, and top off as necessary. Raise the vehicle and check for any leaks.

material. Metal will be sparkly and clutch material will be a dark residue in the bottom of the pan. The presence of some clutch material is normal. Also, inspect the magnet in the pan (if equipped) for the amount of ferrous metal present. A small amount of metal is normal. **(Photo 3)**

11 If equipped, remove any bolts or clips holding the transmission filter in place and lower the filter. **(Photo 4)**

12 Clean the pan and the magnet thoroughly in a parts washer. Dry the pan with a lint-free shop towel or compressed air. There can be no residue left on the pan when it is reinstalled on the vehicle. Check that the sealing surface of the pan is flat. See your supervisor if it is not. **(Photo 5)**

13 Compare the new filter and transmission gasket to the old one to make sure they are correct. Note: Some transmissions have a reusable transmission pan gasket, so the filter kit may not come with a new gasket.

14 If the filter kit came with a new filter gasket or grommet, install the new one to prevent air leaks and possible transmission damage.

15 Install the new filter and torque any retaining bolts to the manufacturer's specifications. **(Photo 6)**

16 Put the new gasket on the transmission pan, clean the transmission sealing surface, and place the pan onto the transmission. Start all of the bolts before tightening any of them. Make sure the gasket remains in the correct place. **(Photo 7)**

17 Torque all of the bolts to specifications.

18 Lower the vehicle and install about 75% of the correct new fluid.

19 Start the vehicle and check the fluid level. Add fluid as necessary to bring it to the bottom of the safe or add mark. **(Photo 8)**

20 While your foot is firmly depressing the brake pedal, place the gear selector in each of the gear ranges. This will ensure that all of the hydraulic circuits are filled with fluid.

21 Check the fluid level and top off as necessary once the transmission is up to temperature. Raise the vehicle and check for any leaks.

▶ Transmission In-Vehicle Diagnosis

In-vehicle diagnosis enables you to test the transmission in a variety of ways and with a variety of tests that are impossible to reproduce once the transmission is removed from the vehicle. To properly diagnose a transmission (and not simply replace it), you need to do a thorough inspection of the transmission and perform several diagnostic tests. These inspections and tests are done both during a test-drive and in the shop. You will need to use your knowledge of transmissions to determine which tests are necessary based on the customer complaint. Scan tools and pressure gauges are often required to perform those tests. The goal is twofold: (1) diagnose whether the fault is inside or outside of the transmission, and (2) if it is inside of the transmission, then diagnose the faulty components before removing the transmission and tearing it down.

Safety and Precautions

Most of the testing on an automatic transmission requires that the vehicle be running, or even running in a drive gear. Use extreme caution around moving parts of the vehicle to prevent injury. Often, transmissions are located right next to hot exhaust components, such as the catalytic converter and exhaust pipes. Wearing insulated gloves and arm sleeves can help prevent a technician from being severely burned by these components.

Some tests require the vehicle to be "driven" while in the air on a hoist. Vehicle speed should never be allowed to exceed 45 mph (72 kph) on the speedometer, since one wheel's speed may be double that due to the operation of the differential assembly. That means that even though the speedometer reads 45 mph (72 kph), if one drive wheel is stopped, the other wheel is spinning at 90 mph (145 kph). At high speeds, tires can fly apart and send pieces of tire across the shop. Tires that are not in perfect balance can cause the vehicle to shake, which puts it in danger of falling off the hoist.

Often, a road test will need to be completed to properly diagnose the transmission. You may need to use a scan tool to monitor electronic components inside and outside of the transmission during a road test. Distracted driving can lead to an accident; always use the "movie" feature of a scan tool or a data logger to record the information while you test-drive a vehicle, or have another person drive the vehicle while you monitor the scan tool data. Also, you should never drive with a scan tool in front of an airbag in case of an airbag deployment.

Methods of Testing

When diagnosing an automatic transmission, whether it is a hydraulically controlled transmission or an electronically controlled transmission, there are several tests that a technician will perform. Not all of these tests are done on every transmission or for every problem; nor are they always done in the same order. The order and appropriateness of the test depends on the customer complaint, the service procedure listed in the service information, your understanding of how the system operates, and the results of any previous test:

- *Fluid check:* Although we have already discussed how to check transmission fluid, having the proper level of transmission fluid is critical to the proper operation of the transmission and should be double-checked any time there is a possible transmission problem. The fluid in the transmission needs to be at the proper level and in good condition and must be the fluid specified by the manufacturer. It cannot be stressed enough that the wrong fluid or low fluid can cause many issues with an automatic transmission.

- *Road test:* A road test is typically required when the transmission is not so bad that the vehicle cannot easily be driven. In some cases, just driving the vehicle enough to get it in the shop is enough to start the diagnostic process. If the vehicle is brought in on a tow truck, then a test-drive is not an option. If the vehicle can be driven, then a test-drive will give you lots of information and help to verify the customer complaint. What a customer describes as a slipping transmission may not actually be a slipping transmission. The best way to accurately verify the customer complaint is usually by performing a road test.

- *Visual inspection:* A quick check under the hood or under the vehicle often identifies problems that can be causing undesirable transmission operation. For example, on a hydraulically controlled transmission, is the throttle valve cable attached to the throttle body? Did a vacuum hose fall off that leads to a vacuum modulator? On an electronically controlled transmission, an air intake hose after the mass airflow sensor can cause the transmission to shift erratically. After an oil change, this hose may be left disconnected. Or maybe the customer backed into a curb and kinked the exhaust pipe, causing a restriction that affects the operation of both the engine and the transmission. A quick visual inspection of the entire vehicle can point out issues that relate to the customer concern.

- *Scan of computer for codes (on electronically controlled transmissions):* Scanning the power train control module (PCM) will not necessarily find the exact problem, but it may give the technician a general direction of focus. All codes, not just transmission codes, should be documented and evaluated. Often, a code for the engine may be affecting the transmission operation or vice versa. Once codes are obtained, the diagnostic procedure can be researched in the service information to determine the best way to continue with the diagnosis.

- *Stall test:* A **stall test** checks the torque converter operation and also checks the transmission for slippage by operating the engine at full throttle with the transmission in gear and the brakes applied. It heavily stresses the torque converter and transmission, so any weaknesses that are present will be reflected in the results of the stall test. Because the stall test stresses the drive train so

much, many manufacturers do not recommend performing a stall test anymore. It is important to check the service information for the particular vehicle.

- *Hydraulic pressure test:* The **hydraulic pressure test** checks the pump operation, the pressure regulator, and the seals and gaskets inside the transmission. Some transmissions provide a test port for line pressure only, while others provide ports for each individual gear, line pressure, modulator pressure, and so on. The results can be compared against the manufacturer's specifications. Some electronically controlled vehicles have a PID, which can show pressure(s) on a scan tool. Just remember that this information is coming from a pressure sensor and is interpreted by the PCM before being transmitted to the scan tool. Thus, you may have to verify hydraulic pressure manually with a pressure tester.

- *Leak check:* Leak checking the transmission is often done during many other routine services, as mentioned earlier. If a transmission problem is suspected or a low fluid level is found, the transmission should be inspected for leaks. This check can be a visual inspection, or it can be aided by a special fluorescent dye that is added to the transmission fluid.

- *Pan inspection:* **Pan inspection** was discussed as part of the general service of the transmission, under fluid and filter replacement, but removing the transmission pan to check for debris in the pan can be a good indicator of transmission failure and of what part of the components failed. Check the pan for excessive clutch material or metal particles. A small amount of clutch material and metal particles in the pan is due to normal wear and tear over time.

- *Air checking:* **Air checking** or testing uses compressed air to check the different circuits and components in the hydraulic system. Air checking can indicate if a clutch or band is holding pressure and moving. It can also identify a leak in the circuit or unusual application of a band or clutch.

- *Cooler flow test:* A **cooler flow test** uses a flowmeter on the cooler circuit of the hydraulic system of the transmission to help identify poor pump performance, restriction in the cooler, converter clutch problems, and worn spool valves in the valve body.

- *Noise, vibration, and harshness test:* The **noise, vibration, and harshness (NVH) test** describes a process that technicians have always done—listening for noise and feeling for vibrations and harshness. Now there are test tools than can help pinpoint noises in a vehicle while the vehicle is driven, called NVH analyzers.

A technician will use all of the tests just described in conjunction with the service information to make a comprehensive diagnosis of the transmission. By comparing the transmission operation during a test-drive to the correct clutch and band application charts in the service information, the technician can pinpoint the best method for further testing, including applying scan tools, checking on noises heard during the test-drive, pressure testing, air checking, and so on. Another critical step in diagnosis is checking for technical service bulletins (TSBs). In many cases, the manufacturer has identified common problems that occur with a particular vehicle and has provided updated programming, parts, or test procedures to verify the problem. This assistance from the manufacturer can save a technician a lot of time and the customer a lot of money. If a technician knows how the system works and has access to the right service information, knowledge of the proper tests, and the correct tools, he or she should be able to form a correct diagnosis.

Test-Driving

Test-driving, or performing a road test, is a critical part of the diagnostic procedure. Transmissions operate much differently when they are placed under a load, such as driving up a hill, than they do sitting in a shop on a hoist. A transmission might operate perfectly fine when operated on the hoist, but have a major amount of clutch slippage when taken on a road test. Very few repair shops have access to a chassis dynamometer that would allow them to "test-drive" the vehicle in the shop, so a road test is a great option. Test-driving the vehicle must be done in a safe manner to prevent an accident. If you need to monitor test equipment such as a scan tool or pressure tester, then request the assistance of another technician to operate the vehicle safely.

During the test-drive, it is critical to place the transmission in the same operating conditions as the customer stated the problem occurred in. Did the customer state that the problem occurred during hard acceleration? Or maybe the problem only occurs when the transmission is cold or during shifts.

When test-driving, it is important to test the transmission in many different operating conditions and record the results for further analysis. Test the transmission during light, medium, and hard acceleration. Place the

transmission in different gear ranges. For example, does the problem occur only in the overdrive range, or does it still occur in the L2 range? While test-driving, listen for noises that the customer may interpret as a transmission problem but that in fact indicate a problem with another component, such as a U-joint or transmission mount.

Applied | Math

AM-53: Word Problem: The technician can evaluate symptoms of problems with a customer or associate technician and identify any relevant missing data required to solve the problem.
Perhaps the most important element of automotive diagnostics is to obtain all of the important information about the problem from the customer. Most customers do not understand the technical operation of their vehicles; they can only describe the symptoms of a problem that they can feel, see, or hear. They may have additional relevant information but not think to include it. It is up to the technician to ask questions that will guide the customer to provide all the information that could help with the diagnosis.

An example might be a complaint of, "The car sometimes seems to rev too hard and then bang into gear." As technicians, we may think this "sounds" like an automatic transmission problem, but to guide our diagnostic process, we need more information from the customer. Clarifying questions in this scenario may include:

- Does the reported problem occur when the vehicle is cold or after driving for a long time?
- Has the transmission been serviced recently?
- How long has the reported problem been occurring?
- Is the vehicle used to carry or tow heavy loads?

Answers to these questions guide us in different directions when looking at a problem and may help us reproduce the required conditions to get a fault to occur during testing. Sometimes it can be useful to take the customer along during a road test to provide further clarification or have him or her reproduce the fault.

Scanning the Transmission Control Module/PCM

A high-quality or factory scan tool can be an invaluable asset while diagnosing an electronically controlled transmission. A code reader can read codes, but a high quality aftermarket scan tool and a factory scan tool can also view live data from sensors and actuators inside the transmission. Further, many high quality scan tools and factory scan tools give the technician **bidirectional control** of the transmission. Bidirectional control means the technician will be able to command different solenoids

SKILL DRILL 20-12 Inspecting and Flushing Cooler Lines, continued

4 Start the flush machine or aerosol can, and allow it to run the recommended time. If necessary, switch directions on the lines so they can be flushed in the other direction.

5 Remove the flush machine and blow out the lines again so no residue remains inside the lines.

6 Reinstall the lines onto the transmission, or cap them if the transmission is removed from the vehicle. After properly filling the transmission with fluid, start the vehicle and inspect the lines and fittings for any signs of leakage. Check inside the radiator for signs of the transmission cooler leaking into the radiator.

5 If necessary, switch directions on the lines so they can be flushed in the other direction. **(Photo 4)**

6 Remove the flush machine and blow out the lines again so no residue remains inside the lines. **(Photo 5)**

7 Reinstall the lines onto the transmission, or cap them if the transmission is removed from the vehicle.

8 After properly filling the transmission with fluid, start the vehicle and inspect the lines and fittings for any signs of leakage.

9 Check inside the radiator for signs of the transmission cooler leaking into the radiator. **(Photo 6)**

Checking Bearings for Preload and End Play

When working with bearings, there are two terms you need to become familiar with: **preload** and **free play**. Preload refers to the amount of force placed on a bearing *before* any load is on the bearing. It is the overtightening of a bearing to the point that it becomes difficult to spin. In most scenarios, we do not want much preload on a bearing, as it will cause bearing failure. The opposite of preload is free play. Free play refers to the amount that a bearing is able to move before hitting the bearing race.

If a bearing has too much free play, it will suffer from impact damage as the bearings move back and forth against the bearing race.

A critical measurement of a transmission is its end play. End play is similar to free play, except that it measures the amount of free play not only in the bearing but also in the gear train inside the transmission. The end play is checked by placing the transmission so that the input shaft is vertical. A dial indicator is placed on the end of the input shaft. Depending on the transmission, either the input shaft will need to be pulled up, which will allow the amount of end play to be measured on the dial indicator, or the output shaft will need to be pushed up, which moves the dial indicator. For some transmissions, there is a special fixture that can be used to pull on the input shaft to check for end play.

If the end play on a transmission is insufficient, there will be preload on the bearings inside the transmission, which may cause dragging of the clutch packs, resulting in premature wear. If the end play is excessive, the inside of the transmission may suffer from impact damage and possible harsh shifting. Transmissions with incorrect end play may have been reassembled incorrectly. Many transmissions have a variety of select fit thrust washers of different thicknesses available that can be installed in the transmission to correct the end play.

To measure transmission end play or preload, follow the steps in **SKILL DRILL 20-13**:

1. Look up the proper service information, and note any special tools required to perform the measurement. With the transmission mounted in a transmission fixture, place the input shaft in the vertical direction.

2. Install a dial indicator onto the top edge of the input shaft. Zero the needle on the face of the dial indicator. **(Photo 1)**

3. Pull up on the input shaft or push up on the output shaft, depending on the transmission.

4. Record how far the dial indicator moves. This measurement is the input shaft end play. Compare to the manufacturer's specifications. **(Photo 2)**

5. Release the input shaft. The dial indicator should return to zero. If it does not return to zero, reset and measure again. Your measurement should be repeatable. **(Photo 3)**

▶ Disassembly and Inspection

A transmission that will be repaired or rebuilt needs to be carefully disassembled. Many students quickly tear apart a transmission and begin cleaning the parts, which is not the best method because they miss clues.

While disassembling the transmission, you can discover clues as to why a transmission failed in the first place, enabling you to correct the problems. Without finding and correcting these problems, the rebuilt transmission is doomed to fail again from the same cause.

When disassembling a transmission, it is good to disassemble it into its unit pieces, such as front pump, clutch assemblies, planetary gear sets, valve body, or shafts. Once the transmission is disassembled to this level, you can work on each unit one at a time. This methodical approach helps to prevent missed steps and to locate any faults. And it makes it easier to remember how the parts go back together since you are only working on one unit at a time.

Safety and Precautions

Transmissions can have many sharp parts and edges on castings that may cut you. Be careful when handling these parts. Also, many parts have large return springs that must be compressed with specialty tools. Always follow the manufacturer's recommended disassembly and service procedures to prevent injury.

Small parts can be easily lost if the technician is not careful. Place small parts in trays or plastic bags and label them for easy identification later. Also, many parts are round and can roll off a work bench easily, so always place them flat. If that is not possible, place them in a

SKILL DRILL | **20-13** | **Measuring Transmission End Play or Preload**

1. Look up the proper service information, and note any special tools required. With the transmission mounted in a transmission fixture, place the input shaft in the vertical direction. Install a dial indicator onto the top edge of the input shaft of the transmission. Set the indicator needle to zero.

2. Pull up on the input shaft or push up on the output shaft, depending on the transmission, and record the dial indicator movement. This measurement is the input shaft end play.

3. Release the input shaft. The dial indicator should return to zero. If it does not, reset and measure again.

tray with sides that will prevent them from rolling off the edge. Hitting the shop floor can cause damage that will require replacement of the part.

To disassemble, clean, and inspect the transmission, follow the steps in **SKILL DRILL 20-14**:

1 First look up the proper disassembly procedure and follow the procedure step by step. Mount the transmission properly in a transmission fixture.

2 Remove the transmission pan and reinstall the bolts into their proper holes or place them in trays or a labeled plastic bag. Inspect the pan for debris and record your findings.

3 Remove all external components such as speed sensors, governors, modulators, and switches. Keep all seals and gaskets as you remove them to compare to the new ones.

4 If the transmission has a removable bell housing, remove it now. If the transmission is a transaxle, remove the side transmission pan (if equipped). **(Photo 1)**

5 If equipped, disconnect electrical connectors from the solenoids and sensors inside the transmission, and inspect the connectors for damage and corrosion.

SKILL DRILL | **20-14** | **Disassembling, Cleaning, and Inspecting the Transmission**

1 Follow the disassembly procedure after mounting the transmission in a transmission fixture. Remove the transmission pan and all external components. If the transmission has a removable bell housing, remove it now. If the transmission is a transaxle, remove the side transmission pan (if equipped).

2 If equipped, disconnect electrical connectors from the solenoids and sensors inside the transmission, and inspect the connectors. If equipped, remove the wiring harness from inside the transmission.

3 If equipped, remove the shift solenoids, EPC solenoid, and TCC solenoid from the transmission.

4 Unbolt and remove the valve body assembly. Remove the manual valve from the valve body to prevent damaging it. Place the valve body on a flat surface to prevent it from becoming warped.

5 Remove the bolts holding the front pump, and use the recommended puller to remove the pump.

6 Remove the front clutch and the band, drum, and input shaft assembly.

SKILL DRILL	**20-14**

Disassembling, Cleaning, and Inspecting the Transmission, continued

7 Remove the planetary sets. Note: There may be a snap ring holding the planetary set to the output shaft.

8 Remove the extension housing assembly. Remove the governor assembly, if equipped.

9 Remove the output shaft and any clutches, bands, and one-way rollers that are with it.

10 Remove any servos from the transmission case.

11 Remove any remaining clutch pack pistons. After all electrical components are removed from the transmission, clean the transmission case. Inspect all threaded holes, bores, and splines for damage. Fluid passages should be blown out using compressed air to check for blockages.

6 If equipped, remove the wiring harness from inside the transmission. **(Photo 2)**

7 If equipped, remove the shift solenoids, EPC solenoid, and TCC solenoid from the transmission. Note: Some transmissions require removal of the valve body before you can remove the solenoids. Keep track of where the solenoids came from. **(Photo 3)**

8 Unbolt and remove the valve body assembly. Be careful not to lose any check balls, and pay

attention to their location. Place check balls into a labeled plastic bag or tray.

9 Remove the manual valve from the valve body to prevent damaging it. Place the valve body on a flat surface to prevent it from becoming warped. **(Photo 4)**

10 Remove the bolts holding the front pump, and use the recommended puller to remove the pump. **(Photo 5)**

11 Remove the front clutch.

12 Remove the band, drum, and input shaft assembly. (**Photo 6**)

13 Remove the planetary sets. Note: There may be a snap ring holding the planetary set to the output shaft. (**Photo 7**)

14 Remove the extension housing assembly. Remove the governor assembly, if equipped. (**Photo 8**)

15 Remove the output shaft and any clutches, bands, and one-way rollers that are with it. Note: This may require removing large snap rings using a large flat-blade screwdriver. (**Photo 9**)

16 Remove any servos from the transmission case. (**Photo 10**)

17 Remove any remaining clutch pack pistons using the manufacturer's service procedure.

18 Make sure all electrical components are removed from the transmission and then clean the transmission case. Inspect all threaded holes, bores, and splines for damage. Fluid passages should be blown out using compressed air to check for blockages. (**Photo 11**)

Servicing the Front Pump

The front pump is the heart of the transmission. Without the front pump, the transmission cannot function. The pump needs to be disassembled and checked for wear separately. Often, if a pump is severely worn, a technician will purchase a new or rebuilt pump for the transmission.

To inspect, measure, and reseal a removed pump assembly and components for a gear/crescent pump (a rotor pump is similar) and for a vane pump, follow the steps in **SKILL DRILL 20-15**:

Gear Pump

1 First look up the proper service procedure in the appropriate service information. Remove the front pump thrust washer or bearing, gaskets, sealing rings, and converter seal. (**Photo 1**)

2 Unbolt the two halves of the pump and disassemble.

3 Mark the gears (without damaging them) so they can be reassembled in the proper position. Remove the gears and any remaining valves from the pump. (**Photo 2**)

4 Use a bushing driver to remove the front pump bushing. (**Photo 3**)

5 Clean the pump thoroughly in a solvent tank, then blow-dry.

6 Inspect the sealing ring grooves for damage and wear.

7 Install the gears into the pump housing in their original orientation.

8 Using a feeler gauge, measure the clearance between the outer gear and the housing. Compare to specifications. (**Photo 4**)

9 Using a feeler gauge, measure the clearance between the inner gear teeth and the crescent, and compare to specifications.

10 Using a feeler gauge, measure the clearance between the outer gear teeth and the crescent, and compare to specifications. (**Photo 5**)

11 Use a straightedge and feeler gauges to check for clearance between the pump cover and the gears. Compare to specifications. If any of the measurements are out of specifications, the pump will need to be replaced and you can stop at this step. (**Photo 6**)

12 Remove the gears again.

13 Using a bushing driver, carefully install the new front pump bushing. (**Photo 7**)

14 Using a seal driver, install a new converter seal.

15 Lightly lubricate the gears with transmission fluid or transmission assembly lube, and reinstall in the proper position.

16 Place two halves of the pump together and start the pump housing bolts, but do not tighten. Follow the manufacturer's instructions to line up pump halves, and torque the bolts to specifications. (**Photo 8**)

17 Install new sealing rings on the front pump. If ready to install the pump, place a new gasket onto the pump. (**Photo 9**)

Vane Pump

1 First look up the proper procedure in the appropriate service information. Remove the front pump thrust washer or bearing, gaskets, sealing rings, and converter seal.(**Photo 1**)

2 Unbolt the two halves of the pump and disassemble. (**Photo 2**)

3 Remove the vanes from the rotor, keeping them organized. The vanes must go back into the rotor in the same direction or they will rapidly wear out when the transmission is placed back into service. (**Photo 3**)

4 Remove the rotor, pressure spring, slide, pivot, and sealing rings. (**Photo 4**)

5 Use a bushing driver to remove the front pump bushing. Clean the pump thoroughly in a solvent tank, then blow-dry. (**Photo 5**)

SKILL DRILL | 20-15A | Inspecting, Measuring, and Resealing the Pump (Gear Pump)

1 After looking up the proper service procedure, remove the front pump thrust washer or bearing, gaskets, sealing rings, and converter seal.

2 Unbolt the two halves of the pump and disassemble. Mark the gears so they can be reassembled in the proper position, and remove the gears and any remaining valves from the pump.

3 Use a bushing driver to remove the front pump bushing.

4 Clean and blow-dry the pump. Inspect the sealing ring grooves for damage and wear. Install the gears into the pump housing in their original orientation.

5 Using a feeler gauge, measure the clearance between the outer gear and the housing. Compare to specifications. Measure the clearance between the inner gear teeth and the crescent. Compare to specifications. Using a feeler gauge, measure the clearance between the outer gear teeth and the crescent, and compare to specifications.

6 Use a straightedge and feeler gauges to check for clearance between the pump cover and the gears. Compare to specifications.

7 Remove the gears again. Using a bushing driver, carefully install the new front pump bushing and a new converter seal.

8 Lightly lubricate the gears with transmission fluid or transmission assembly lube, and reinstall in the proper position. Place the two halves of the pump together, and use the appropriate tool to line up pump halves. Install pump housing bolts and torque to specifications.

9 Install new sealing rings and a new pump gasket onto the pump.

SKILL DRILL 20-15B Inspecting, Measuring, and Resealing the Pump (Vane Pump)

1 First look up the proper procedure in the appropriate service information, then remove the front pump thrust washer or bearing, gaskets, sealing rings, and converter seal.

2 Unbolt the two halves of the pump and disassemble.

3 Remove the vanes from the rotor.

4 Remove the rotor, pressure spring, slide, pivot, and sealing rings.

5 Use a bushing driver to remove the front pump bushing. Clean the pump thoroughly in a solvent tank, then blow-dry.

6 Inspect the sealing ring grooves for damage and wear. Inspect the housing and the slide where the rotor and vanes ride for deep scratches and wear.

7 Measure the thickness of the rotor, and compare to specifications.

8 Using a bushing driver, carefully install the new front pump bushing.

9 Using a seal driver, install a new converter seal.

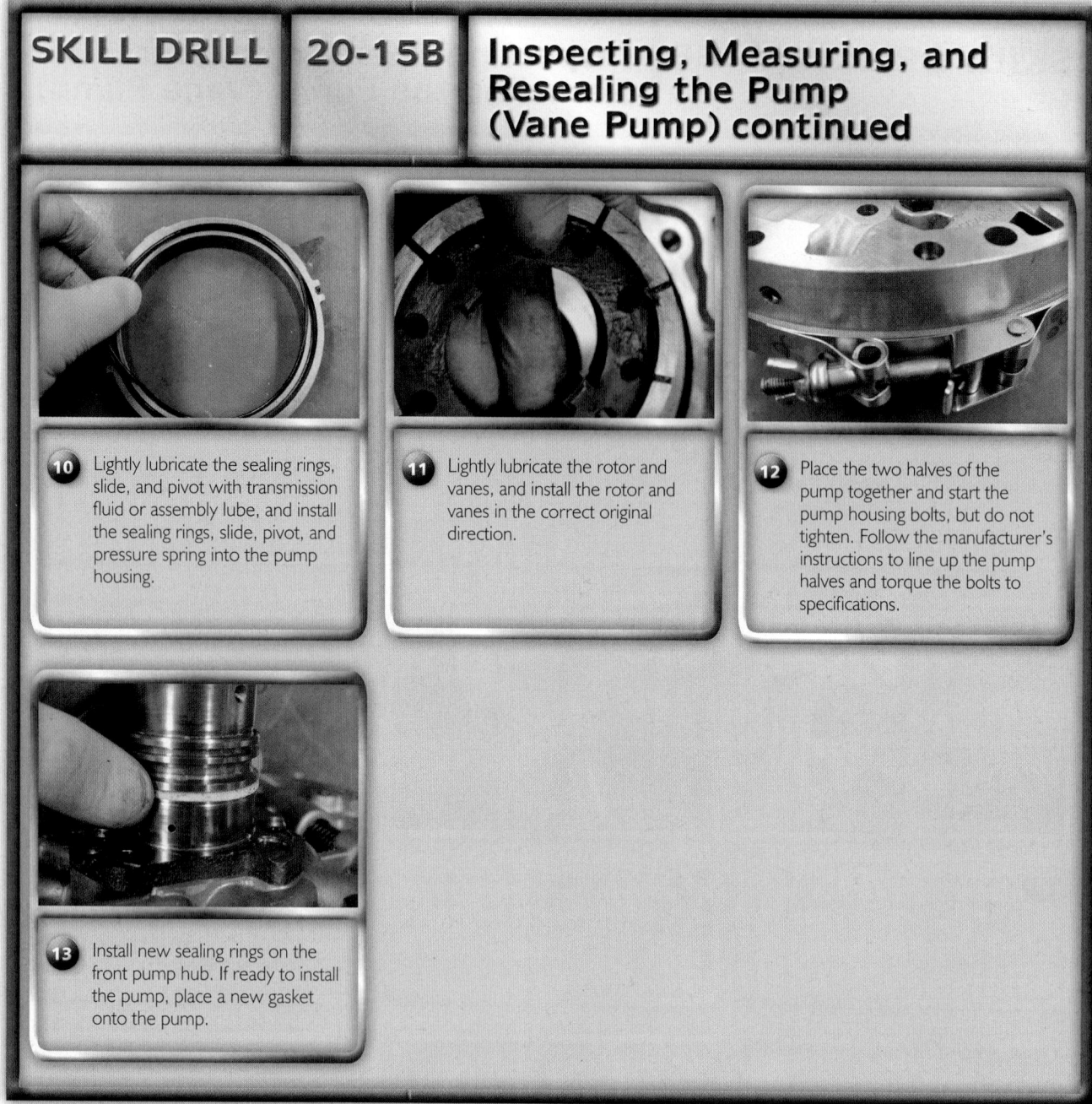

SKILL DRILL | **20-15B** | Inspecting, Measuring, and Resealing the Pump (Vane Pump) continued

10 Lightly lubricate the sealing rings, slide, and pivot with transmission fluid or assembly lube, and install the sealing rings, slide, pivot, and pressure spring into the pump housing.

11 Lightly lubricate the rotor and vanes, and install the rotor and vanes in the correct original direction.

12 Place the two halves of the pump together and start the pump housing bolts, but do not tighten. Follow the manufacturer's instructions to line up the pump halves and torque the bolts to specifications.

13 Install new sealing rings on the front pump hub. If ready to install the pump, place a new gasket onto the pump.

6 Inspect the sealing ring grooves for damage and wear.

7 Inspect the housing and the slide where the rotor and vanes ride for deep scratches and wear. **(Photo 6)**

8 Measure the thickness of the rotor, and compare to specifications. **(Photo 7)**

9 Using a bushing driver, carefully install the new front pump bushing. **(Photo 8)**

10 Using a seal driver, install a new converter seal. **(Photo 9)**

11 Lightly lubricate the sealing rings, slide, and pivot with transmission fluid or assembly lube, and install the sealing rings, slide, pivot, and pressure spring into the pump housing. **(Photo 10)**

12 Lightly lubricate the rotor and vanes, and install the rotor and vanes in the correct original direction. **(Photo 11)**

13 Place the two halves of the pump together and start the pump housing bolts, but do not tighten. Follow the manufacturer's instructions to line up the pump halves and torque the bolts to specifications. **(Photo 12)**

14 Install new sealing rings on the front pump hub. If ready to install the pump, place a new gasket onto the pump. **(Photo 13)**

Inspecting and Measuring Planetary Gear Sets

Planetary gear sets are generally very durable and do not require service when rebuilding a transmission, but they must be checked properly to prevent a second visit from the customer relating to the transmission. When checking planetary gear sets, there are several considerations.

The first check is for discoloration of the planetary gears or the planet carrier. Discoloration can be a sign of a failed lubrication circuit in the transmission and must be repaired before the discolored gears are replaced and the transmission is placed back into service.

The next inspection is of each gear in the planetary set for cracked or worn teeth. If any gear is found to be damaged, the companion gears must also be replaced to prevent noisy gears after the rebuild.

Check each planetary pinion gear by spinning it. The gear should spin freely without binding. Check that the gear is not loose on its shaft. The end play of each of the planetary pinion gears must be checked with a feeler gauge. If the clearance is not correct, the planetary set will need to be disassembled, if it is a serviceable type,

and thrust bearings of a different thickness will need to be installed.

To inspect and measure removed planetary gear assembly components, follow the steps in **SKILL DRILL 20-16**:

1 Look up the proper service procedure for the planetary gear set you are working on in the appropriate service information.

2 Carefully inspect the planetary gears, carrier, sun gear, and ring gear for discoloration due to lack of lubrication. **(Photo 1)**

3 Carefully inspect the teeth of each gear in the planetary gear set for wear and damage.

4 Check the operation of the pinion gears on their shafts. Check for binding and looseness. **(Photo 2)**

5 Measure the end play of the planetary pinions using a feeler gauge, and compare to the manufacturer's specifications. **(Photo 3)**

Inspecting Bushings

Bushings inside the transmission do not necessarily require replacement, except for the front pump bushing and the extension housing bushing. All of the bushings inside a transmission do, however, require inspection to prevent later problems. On high-mileage transmissions, it may be necessary to purchase a complete bushing replacement kit and replace every bushing inside the transmission.

SKILL DRILL   20-16   Inspecting and Measuring Planetary Gear Assemblies

1 Look up the proper service procedure for the planetary gear set you are working on. Inspect the planetary gears, carrier, sun gear, and ring gear for discoloration due to lack of lubrication.

2 Inspect the teeth of each gear in the planetary gear set for wear and damage. Check the operation of the pinion gears on their shafts. Check for binding and looseness.

3 Measure the end play of the planetary pinions using a feeler gauge and compare to the manufacturer's specifications.

Each bushing inside the transmission should be inspected for scratches, scoring, and large pits. Place the shaft that rides on the bushing into the bushing. Wiggle the shaft back and forth. More than about 0.003" (0.076 mm) of clearance will require replacement of most bushings. You can also check the amount of clearance with a wire-style feeler gauge.

Always use a bushing driver to install new bushings into a transmission. Make sure any lubrication holes are correctly lined up or severe transmission damage could result. Many bushings are a split ring bushing that must be installed carefully to prevent splitting the new bearing apart. More than one student or beginning technician has had to purchase a second bushing to replace the first one that split on installation.

To inspect bushings on a disassembled transmission, follow the steps in **SKILL DRILL 20-17**:

1. Look up the proper procedure and specifications for checking bushings in the appropriate service information. Wipe the bushing dry with a lint-free shop towel. (**Photo 1**)
2. Inspect each bushing in the transmission for pitting, scoring, or scratches. (**Photo 2**)
3. Measure the clearance between the bushing and the corresponding shaft with a wire-style feeler gauge, and compare to the manufacturer's specifications.
4. Replace any bushings that are not within specifications and/or that show signs of wear. (**Photo 3**)

Inspecting Thrust Bearings and Washers

Thrust bearings and washers need to be inspected during a transmission rebuild. If the thrust bearings or washers are worn, lateral movement of components inside the transmission will be allowed, affecting their operation.

Thrust bearings should be cleaned, and the races and rollers inspected carefully for pitting, scoring, and scratches. If any damage or wear is found, the entire bearing assembly should be replaced.

A micrometer should be used to check the thickness of a thrust washer, and the thickness should be compared to the manufacturer's specifications. A small degree of scratching on the face of a thrust washer is acceptable. When reinstalling thrust bearings or washers in a transmission, apply a small amount of transmission assembly lube. This will help hold the bearing or washer in place while related parts are assembled.

To inspect, measure, and replace thrust washers and bearings on a disassembled transmission, follow the steps in **SKILL DRILL 20-18**:

1. Look up the proper procedure and specifications for inspecting the thrust bearings and washers in the appropriate service information.
2. Inspect each thrust bearing race and roller for pitting, scoring, and scratches. Replace any bearings that show signs of wear. (**Photo 1**)

SKILL DRILL   20-17   Inspecting Bushings

1. First look up the proper procedure and specifications for checking bushings. Wipe the bushing dry with a lint-free shop towel.

2. Inspect each bushing in the transmission for pitting, scoring, or scratches.

3. Measure the clearance between the bushing and the corresponding shaft with a wire-style feeler gauge, and compare to the manufacturer's specifications. Replace any bushings that are not within specifications and/or that show signs of wear.

SKILL DRILL 20-18 Inspecting, Measuring, and Replacing Thrust Washers and Bearings

1 Look up the proper procedure and specifications for inspecting the thrust bearings and washers. Inspect each thrust bearing race and roller for pitting, scoring, and scratches. Replace any bearings that show signs of wear.

2 Measure the thickness of each thrust washer using a micrometer, and compare to the manufacturer's specifications. Replace any washers that are not within specifications.

3 Measure the thickness of each thrust washer using a micrometer, and compare to the manufacturer's specifications. Replace any washers that are not within specifications. (**Photo 2**)

Inspecting One-Way Rollers and Sprags

Both one-way rollers and sprags must be able to stop the rotation of an object in one direction, but allow the object to spin freely in the opposite direction. One-way rollers are easy to disassemble, but sprags cannot easily be completely disassembled.

On a one-way roller, the unit should be disassembled to inspect each individual roller. The roller should be checked for pitting, scoring, and brinelling, such as in a wheel bearing. Brinelling is damage found in the race from high bearing load **FIGURE 20-3**. The race of the one-way roller should be checked to make sure it is smooth and has no nicks or pits in it. Rollers or races that show any signs of damage must be replaced, and the lubrication circuit for the one-way roller should be carefully inspected for blockage. The folded springs should be checked for cracks. Often the ends of the springs will crack off, leaving a shorter spring. The springs should all look about the same. A one-way roller will not work if assembled in the wrong direction, so be careful to assemble it in the correct direction.

Sprags can be only partially disassembled. Check the faces of the sprags and the races for any damage. Sprags also must be assembled in the correct direction. Sprags must be serviced as a complete unit if any damage is found.

After visually inspecting one-way rollers and sprags, they should be reassembled. The one-way roller or sprag should spin freely in one direction and lock up in the opposite direction. To inspect the one-way roller or sprag

Brinelling Marks

FIGURE 20-3 A bearing race showing brinelling.

and related components in a disassembled transmission, follow the steps in **SKILL DRILL 20-19**:

1. Look up the proper service procedure for the one-way roller or sprag in the appropriate service information. Disassemble the one-way roller or sprag. **(Photo 1)**

2. Inspect each roller and race for signs of pitting, scoring, or brinelling. **(Photo 2)**

3. Inspect the folded springs on the one-way roller for cracks or broken springs. **(Photo 3)**

4. Inspect the faces of the sprags and the race for signs of scoring or damage.

5. If any damage is found, replace the one-way roller or sprag. **(Photo 4)**

6. Reassemble the one-way roller or sprag, and lubricate with transmission fluid.

7. Test the operation of the one-way roller or sprag. The one-way roller or sprag should spin freely in one direction and lock up in the other direction. **(Photo 5)**

Inspecting Fluid Delivery Circuits

Fluid flow in an automatic transmission is critical to the operation of the transmission. Any debris from a transmission failure can become trapped in a fluid passage, preventing the flow of fluid for lubrication or clutch/band application. It could also dislodge and move into the bearings and bushings where it could cause damage. All fluid passages should be checked during a rebuild of the transmission.

The proper service information is critical for checking the operation of the fluid delivery circuits. A technician

SKILL DRILL | **20-19** | **Inspecting One-Way Roller and Sprag Clutch Assemblies**

1. Look up the proper service procedure for the one-way roller or sprag, and disassemble the one-way roller or sprag.

2. Inspect each roller and race for signs of pitting, scoring, or brinelling.

3. Inspect the folded springs on the one-way roller for cracks or broken springs.

4. Inspect the faces of the sprags and the race for signs of scoring or damage. If any damage is found, replace the one-way roller or sprag.

5. Reassemble the one-way roller or sprag, lubricate with transmission fluid, and test the operation of the one-way roller or sprag.

will need to use a transmission case diagram to identify the fluid passages through the case. Compressed air should be blown through each fluid passage in the transmission case, the valve body, the input and output shafts, and the front pump.

Feed pipes should be checked for cracks and damaged ends. Sealing rings should be replaced or inspected for damage, along with their corresponding sealing surface. Often on high-mileage vehicles, a groove may become worn in the sealing surface, requiring replacement of the part for proper sealing.

Check valves and/or check balls should be inspected for proper operation. Plastic check balls tend to wear and are often replaced during a rebuild. Metal check balls can

cause wear to the valve body or separator plate. Check the area around the check ball for damage or enlargement of the hole in the separator plate.

To inspect fluid delivery circuits, including sealing rings, ring grooves, sealing surface areas, feed pipes, orifices, and check valves/balls in a disassembled transmission, follow the steps in **SKILL DRILL 20-20**:

1. First look up the proper service procedure for the fluid delivery circuit in the appropriate service information. Use compressed air to blow through each of the fluid delivery circuits to check for blockages. **(Photo 1)**

2. Inspect each sealing ring and corresponding sealing surface for damage and wear. **(Photo 2)**

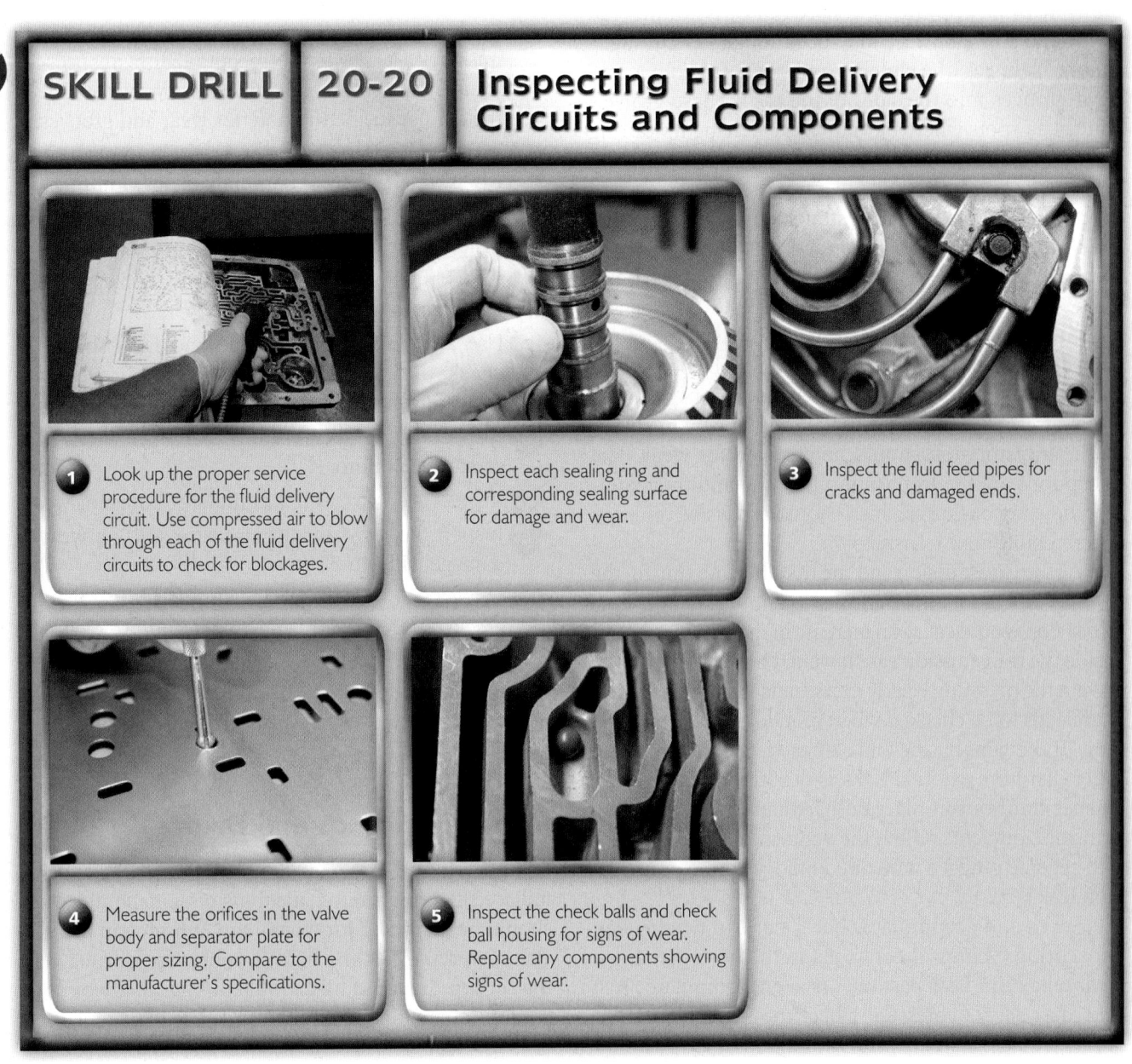

SKILL DRILL | 20-20 | Inspecting Fluid Delivery Circuits and Components

1. Look up the proper service procedure for the fluid delivery circuit. Use compressed air to blow through each of the fluid delivery circuits to check for blockages.

2. Inspect each sealing ring and corresponding sealing surface for damage and wear.

3. Inspect the fluid feed pipes for cracks and damaged ends.

4. Measure the orifices in the valve body and separator plate for proper sizing. Compare to the manufacturer's specifications.

5. Inspect the check balls and check ball housing for signs of wear. Replace any components showing signs of wear.

3 Inspect the fluid feed pipes for cracks and damaged ends. **(Photo 3)**

4 Measure the orifices in the valve body and separator plate for proper sizing. Compare to the manufacturer's specifications. **(Photo 4)**

5 Inspect the check balls for wear. Inspect the check ball housing for signs of wear.

6 Replace any components showing signs of wear. **(Photo 5)**

Servicing the Transmission Case, Servo, and Accumulator

After thorough cleaning of the transmission case and all components, an inspection of the transmission case is necessary. Inspect the inside bore of the transmission along with any splines. If any damage is found, the entire transmission case may need replaced. On high-mileage vehicles, the clutches and steels can sometimes wear grooves into the sides of the case. These grooves can create spots where the clutches can hang up during their application and release.

The sealing surfaces of the transmission case need to be checked with a precision straightedge to ensure that the surface has not become warped. A gasket is designed to fill in small imperfections in the sealing surface, but if the surface has deep gouges or scratches, the gasket will be unable to do its job. If the sealing surface of the transmission has become damaged, it may be possible to machine it back to within an acceptable limit.

As was covered earlier in the chapter, any bushings in the transmission should be checked for wear. The exceptions are the front pump bushing and the extension housing bushing, which should always be replaced when rebuilding a transmission.

As the transmission and the fluid heat up during the vehicle's operation, the transmission fluid expands. This expansion would cause an increase in the pressure found inside the transmission case if we did not have a method to vent the pressure. Nearly every transmission has a vent that needs to be checked when rebuilding the transmission. If the vent has become clogged, the transmission will suffer from external leaks as the buildup of pressure pushes fluid out in places other than the appropriate transmission vents. Often the vents in off-road vehicles will become plugged with dried mud, creating transmission leaks.

Servo and accumulator bores need to be checked for scoring. Scores or scratches in the bore will allow hydraulic fluid flow past the servo or accumulator seal and cause a loss of pressure. Check the piston on both an accumulator and a servo for cracks. Aluminum pistons are more prone to cracking. Look closely; sometimes the top of the piston is stuck in the housing after it has completely separated from the rest of the piston. Check that the piston fits tightly on its pin. If the center hole of the piston is worn, the piston will be allowed to rock in the bore as it is applied, resulting in binding. Check the bore for the pin. The pin should not be allowed to wobble in the bore. Check the spring because often springs in accumulators can become cracked, requiring replacement. Also check the spring seat to make sure a groove has not been worn.

To inspect case bores, passages, bushings, vents, and mating surfaces and determine any necessary actions, and to inspect servo and accumulator bores, pistons, seals, pins, springs, and retainers in a disassembled transmission, follow the steps in **SKILL DRILL 20-21**:

1 Look up the proper service procedure for the transmission case, servos, and accumulators. Inspect the transmission case bore for excessive wear. Check the splines inside the bore for wear and grooves.

2 Inspect all hydraulic passages in the transmission case with the help of compressed air. **(Photo 1)**

3 Inspect and measure the clearance on all bushings inside the transmission case. **(Photo 2)**

4 Check the operation of the transmission vent using compressed air. **(Photo 3)**

5 Use a precision straightedge and feeler blade to check the pan gasket surfaces and valve body mounting surface for flatness.

6 Inspect the gasket sealing areas for nicks and scratches. **(Photo 4)**

7 Inspect the servo and accumulator bores for wear.

8 Inspect the servo and accumulator seals for wear or damage. **(Photo 5)**

9 Inspect the servo and accumulator pistons for cracks and loose-fitting pins and/or retainers. **(Photo 6)**

10 Inspect the servo and accumulator springs for cracks and wear grooves in the spring seats. **(Photo 7)**

11 Replace any components as necessary.

Inspecting Bands and Drums

Bands should be inspected for wear if they are not being replaced during an automatic transmission rebuild. They should be inspected for cracks and chipping in the friction material. Also, the band can become burned during service or glazed like a brake lining. If any of these conditions are identified, the band should be replaced.

SKILL DRILL | 20-21 | Inspecting the Transmission Case and Servo/Accumulator Bores and Components

1. First look up the proper service procedure for the transmission case, servos, and accumulators. Inspect the transmission case bore for excessive wear. Check the splines inside the bore for wear and grooves. Inspect all hydraulic passages in the transmission case using compressed air.

2. Inspect and measure the clearance on all bushings inside the transmission case.

3. Check the operation of the transmission vent using compressed air.

4. Use a precision straightedge and feeler blades to check the pan gasket surfaces and valve body mounting surface for flatness. Inspect gasket sealing areas for nicks and scratches.

5. Inspect the servo and accumulator bores and seals for wear or damage.

6. Inspect the servo and accumulator pistons for cracks and loose-fitting pins and/or retainers.

7. Inspect the servo and accumulator springs for cracks and wear grooves in the spring seats.

The drum should also be checked for wear. Place a straightedge across the drum where the band rides, and check that the drum is straight. Use a feeler gauge to measure the amount of warpage on the drum, and compare your measurement to the manufacturer's specifications. Inspect the drum for any discoloration due to band slippage. A drum that is not badly scored can be refinished by running emery cloth across the drum while it is spun on a machinist lathe.

To inspect bands and drums in a disassembled transmission, follow the steps in **SKILL DRILL 20-22** :

1 Look up the proper service procedure and specifications for the band in the appropriate service information. Inspect the band friction material for cracks, chips, flaking, glazing, and burn marks. **(Photo 1)**

2 Inspect the band's strut (if equipped) for wear.

3 Inspect the drum for discoloration and scoring where the band rides. **(Photo 2)**

4 Use a straightedge and feeler gauge to check the drum for straightness. Compare your measurements with the manufacturer's specifications. **(Photo 3)**

Rebuilding and Testing the Clutch Assembly

When rebuilding an automatic transmission, all clutch assemblies should be rebuilt. Part of the rebuilding process is a thorough inspection of all of the components in the assembly. Since most transmissions have multiple

clutches, it is good practice to rebuild only one at a time, so that parts do not get interchanged.

The clutch drum should be checked for cracks and broken or worn splines. The splines should be straight with no worn edges. On high-mileage transmissions, you may find that the clutch discs become stuck as they move up and down on splines. If the drum has a check ball, make sure the check ball is free to move. The sealing ability of the check ball also needs to be checked. Place some solvent in the bore of the drum and check the sealing operation of the check ball. If the solvent leaks out, the drum will need to be replaced.

The spring retainer and springs should all be checked for straightness, and each spring's height should be checked. Any springs that are bent should be replaced to prevent the clutch from becoming stuck when it is disengaged.

Check the friction discs for loose or flaking friction material. Friction material that is discolored was overheated and should be replaced. The friction discs must be flat. Warpage is a sign of overheating or improper installation. The steels should be checked for flatness, and their thickness should be measured. Compare your measurements against the manufacturer's specifications. The pressure plate should also be checked for warpage and replaced if necessary.

Inspect the clutch piston for cracks and warpage. Replace all of the seals on the clutch piston. If the piston has a check ball, verify that the ball is free to move. If the ball will not move, use solvent and a small wire to free up the check ball.

SKILL DRILL | **20-22** | **Inspecting Bands and Drums**

1 Look up the proper service procedure and specifications for the band. Inspect the band friction material for cracks, chips, flaking, glazing, and burn marks.

2 Inspect the band's strut (if equipped) for wear. Inspect the drum for discoloration and scoring where the band rides.

3 Use a straightedge and feeler gauge to check the drum for straightness. Compare your measurements with the manufacturer's specifications.

To inspect the clutch drum, piston, check balls, springs, retainers, seals, and friction and pressure plates on a disassembled transmission, follow the steps in **SKILL DRILL 20-23**:

1 First look up the manufacturer's procedure and specifications for rebuilding the clutch pack. Disassemble and clean the clutch pack assembly. Do not put the frictions in a solvent tank. Thoroughly dry the clutch assembly. **(Photo 1)**

2 Inspect the clutch drum for spline damage. Inspect the check ball(s). **(Photo 2)**

3 Inspect the clutch piston for warpage and cracks. Check operation of the check ball (if equipped). **(Photo 3)**

4 Inspect the springs for length and squareness. Inspect the spring retainer for warpage. **(Photo 4)**

5 Inspect the friction discs for damaged or deteriorating friction material. **(Photo 5)**

6 Inspect the steels for warpage. Measure the thickness and compare to the manufacturer's specifications.

7 Inspect the pressure plate for warpage and cracks. **(Photo 6)**

8 Replace all seals and lubricate with transmission assembly lube. **(Photo 7)**

9 Using the proper seal tools, carefully reinstall the clutch piston. **(Photo 8)**

10 Install the clutch return spring assembly. **(Photo 9)**

11 Use the correct clutch spring compression tool to slowly compress the spring assembly and install the snap ring. **(Photo 10)**

SKILL DRILL 20-23 Inspecting Clutch Assemblies

1 Look up the manufacturer's procedure and specifications for rebuilding the clutch pack. Disassemble and clean the clutch pack assembly.

2 Inspect the clutch drum for spline damage, and inspect the check balls for proper operation.

3 Inspect the clutch piston for warpage and cracks. Check operation of the piston check ball (if equipped).

4 Inspect the springs for length and squareness. Check the spring retainer for warpage.

5 Inspect the friction discs for damaged or deteriorating friction material.

6 Inspect the steels for warpage. Measure the thickness and compare to the manufacturer's specifications. Inspect the pressure plate for warpage and cracks.

SKILL DRILL	20-23	Inspecting Clutch Assemblies, continued

7 Replace all seals and lubricate with transmission assembly lube.

8 Using the proper seal tools, carefully reinstall the clutch piston.

9 Install the clutch return spring assembly.

10 Use the correct clutch spring compression tool to slowly compress the spring assembly and install the snap ring.

11 Slowly release the clutch spring tool and remove.

12 Install the friction discs and steels back into the clutch pack in the correct order according to the service manual.

13 Install the wave washer or Belleville spring (if equipped) into the clutch pack.

14 Install the pressure plate into the clutch pack. Make sure the pressure plate is facing the correct direction, and reinstall the large snap ring.

12 Slowly release the clutch spring tool and remove. (**Photo 11**)

13 Install the friction discs and steels back into the clutch pack in the correct order according to the service manual. (**Photo 12**)

14 Install the wave washer or Belleville spring (if equipped) into the clutch pack. (**Photo 13**)

15 Install the pressure plate into the clutch pack. Make sure the pressure plate is facing the correct direction, and reinstall the large snap ring. (**Photo 14**)

> ► **TECHNICIAN TIP**
>
> Some transmissions come with multiple variations of different clutches. Always carefully check that you have the correct parts for the job. For example, one particular transmission has a variation of a clutch with one less spline. The difference is very difficult to see until you attempt to put the transmission back together and the parts will not go together.

After rebuilding and reassembling a clutch pack, it is necessary to measure the amount of clearance. If the clutch pack has too little clearance, the clutch will drag when it is disengaged, causing the frictions to be burned up. If the clutch pack has too much clearance, the clutch may slip or have a very harsh engagement. If the clutch pack clearance is not correct, there are several methods manufacturers use to change the amount of clearance. One method is to change the thickness of the steels in the clutch pack. Another method is to change the pressure plate to one of a different thickness. And a final method is to change the thickness of the snap ring holding the frictions and steels into the clutch pack. It is necessary to check which method the manufacturer specifies for that particular clutch pack.

To measure clutch pack clearance, follow the steps in **SKILL DRILL 20-24**:

1 Look up the manufacturer's procedure and specifications for clutch pack clearance. The assembled clutch assembly needs to be lightly slammed down on a bench to make sure the plates are seated. Locate the feeler gauge that fits between the pressure plate and the first friction. The feeler gauge should have some drag as it is removed from the clutch pack. (**Photo 1**)

2 Compare your measurement to the manufacturer's specifications. Adjust the clutch pack clearance to specifications, if necessary, by measuring the selective fit component and determining the correct replacement. (**Photo 2**)

3 Install the correct selective fit component and remeasure the clutch pack clearance. (**Photo 3**)

SKILL DRILL | 20-24 | Measuring Clutch Pack Clearance

1 Look up the manufacturer's procedure and specifications for clutch pack clearance. Locate the feeler gauge that fits between the pressure plate and the first friction. It should have some drag as it is removed from the clutch pack.

2 Compare your measurement to the manufacturer's specifications, and adjust, if necessary, by measuring the selective fit component and determining the correct replacement.

3 Install the selective fit component and remeasure the clearance.

Air Checking

After a clutch or servo has been completely rebuilt, it should be tested before installing the transmission back into the vehicle. Using compressed air is a good method of determining if the clutches and servos will function properly. However, never air check a clutch without the clutch pack assembled and the snap ring fully engaged. Doing so will cause the piston to travel too far, and the sealing lips will pop out of their bore. Once that happens, the seals cannot seal and the return springs will pinch the seal between the piston and the bore, damaging it.

To air test the operation of clutch and servo assemblies, follow the steps in **SKILL DRILL 20-25**:

1 First look up the manufacturer's recommended procedure to air check the clutch or servo in the appropriate service information. Apply compressed air to the fluid inlet hole for the clutch or servo. **(Photo 1)**

2 Ensure that the clutch or servo is holding properly with the air pressure applied, with limited air leakage. **(Photo 2)**

3 Release the air pressure and ensure that the clutch or servo releases properly. **(Photo 3)**

Servicing the Valve Body

To properly rebuild an automatic transmission, the valve body must be completely disassembled. There are commercially made fixtures to keep all of the different valves and springs in order. Disassemble the valve body and clean all of the components in the solvent tank or parts washer. Be careful not to lose any parts, and remember how, and where, each valve goes so that you can reassemble it properly.

Each valve in the valve body must be checked for wear. On modern electronically controlled transmissions, many of the valves pulse back and forth slightly during vehicle operation. This motion results in more wear on the valves than was seen on hydraulically controlled transmissions. Also, modern transmissions often use aluminum valves, which wear faster than the older steel valves. The valve bore should be measured to check for valve clearance. Use a telescoping gauge and micrometer to measure the clearance of the valve to the bore. Compare the clearance to the manufacturer's specifications. If the clearance is too great, the valve body will need to be replaced or a service kit will be needed. Many common transmissions have repair kits for the valve body assemblies that involve reboring the valve body bore and installing a sleeve or larger valve. Many transmission rebuild shops will replace every valve body on transmissions that have common valve body problems.

The valve body to transmission case surface should be checked for warpage using a precision straightedge and feeler blades. If the valve body is warped, it is recommended that it be replaced with a reconditioned unit.

Each valve should be reinstalled and checked to make sure it moves freely in its bore. If the valve hangs up, the bore can be lightly sanded using a small roll of crocus cloth. Steel valves can be rotated on a wet sharpening stone to remove any small burrs.

SKILL DRILL | **20-25** | **Air Testing Clutch and Servo Assemblies**

1 Look up the manufacturer's recommended procedure to air check the clutch or servo. Apply compressed air to the fluid inlet hole for the clutch or servo.

2 Ensure that the clutch or servo is holding properly with the air pressure applied with limited air leakage.

3 Release the air pressure and observe that the clutch or servo releases properly.

To inspect, measure, clean, and replace the removed valve body, follow the steps in **SKILL DRILL 20-26**:

1 First look up the proper service procedure for the valve body. Disassemble the valve body completely, keeping valves, springs, sleeves, and other components in order.

2 Clean the valve body, valves, sleeves, and springs in a solvent tank or parts washer. **(Photo 1)**

3 Inspect the valves and valve bores for wear. Measure valve bores for clearance, and compare to the manufacturer's specifications. **(Photo 2)**

4 Inspect springs for damaged or distorted coils. **(Photo 3)**

5 Check the valve body to transmission case surface for warpage. **(Photo 4)**

6 Check that all check balls and screens are functioning and are in the correct place.

7 Reinstall valves, springs, and sleeves in the valve body, and check that they move freely. **(Photo 5)**

SKILL DRILL | **20-26** | **Inspecting, Measuring, Cleaning, and Replacing the Valve Body**

1 Look up the proper service procedure for the valve body. Disassemble the valve body completely, keeping valves, springs, sleeves, and other components in order. Clean the valve body, valves, sleeves, and springs in a solvent tank.

2 Inspect valves and valve bores for wear. Measure valve bores for clearance and compare to manufacturer's specifications.

3 Inspect springs for damaged or distorted coils.

4 Check valve body to transmission case surface for warpage.

5 Check that all check balls and screens are functioning and are in the correct place. Reinstall valves, springs, and sleeves in the valve body, and check that they move freely.

▶ Transaxle Types and Components

Transaxles are a transmission with an integrated final drive unit such as that found in the differential of a rear-wheel drive vehicle. These transaxles have a few more components than a traditional transmission and have a few more tests involved with their diagnosis. In transaxles, the power from the transmission portion of the transaxle needs to be transferred to the final drive portion of the transaxle. This power transfer can occur in one of two methods—a gear style or a chain style **FIGURE 20-4**.

Gear Style

In the gear-style transaxle assembly, power is transferred from the transmission planetary gears to the differential through a set of helically cut gears. One of the helical gears is splined to the output shaft of the transmission, and the other is splined to a transfer shaft. The transfer shaft transmits the power to the ring gear of the differential case. These gears need to be checked for wear when servicing the transmission. If excessive wear is found on

FIGURE 20-4 Power transfer. **A.** Gear style. **B.** Chain style.

either gear, both gears in the set will require replacement, as they are a matched set.

Chain Style

Many transaxles use a large **Morse-style chain** and sprockets to connect the output shaft of the transmission to the differential assembly. Some transaxles use a chain to connect from the torque converter to the input shaft of the transmission, as in many General Motors transaxles. When rebuilding the transmission, the chain and sprockets need to be checked for wear. Many manufacturers specify a limit for the amount of chain deflection allowed. If the chain is replaced, both sprockets should also be replaced.

To inspect the transaxle drive, link chains, sprockets, gears, bearings, and bushings, follow the steps in **SKILL DRILL 20-27**:

1. First look up the manufacturer's recommended procedure and specifications for checking the transaxle drive components. Measure the amount of chain slack and compare to the manufacturer's specifications (if equipped). **(Photo 1)**

2. Inspect the sprockets for tooth wear (if equipped). **(Photo 2)**

3. Inspect the transfer gears for excessive wear (if equipped). **(Photo 3)**

4. Inspect the bearings for damage and wear to the needle bearings and their races. **(Photo 4)**

5. Inspect the bushings for scoring, pitting, or wear.

6. Replace any components worn beyond the manufacturer's specifications. **(Photo 5)**

Final Drive Assembly

The transaxle final drive assembly needs to be inspected for wear during a rebuild. The measurements and adjustments are similar to those that would be completed during a differential overhaul. Each gear in the final drive unit should be inspected for worn, chipped, or broken teeth. The bearings should be inspected for scoring or overheating. If the unit is a planetary gear set style, the pinion gears need to be checked for proper operation in the same manner as they were when checking the planetary gear sets in the transmission.

Output shaft end play and side gear backlash must be checked in order to prevent seizing of the gears or excessive noise. When assembling the final drive unit, bearing preload must be measured following the manufacturer's procedure. Changing the preload and backlash often involves changing selective thickness shims.

SKILL DRILL | 20-27 | Inspecting Transaxle Drive Assembly

1. First look up the manufacturer's recommended procedure and specifications for checking the transaxle components. Measure the amount of chain slack and compare to the specification (if equipped).

2. Inspect the sprockets for tooth wear (if equipped).

3. Inspect transfer gears for excessive wear (if equipped).

4. Inspect bearings for damage and wear to the needle bearings and their races.

5. Inspect the bushings for scoring, pitting, or wear. Replace any components worn beyond the manufacturer's specifications.

To inspect, measure, repair, adjust, or replace transaxle final drive components, follow the steps in **SKILL DRILL 20-28**:

1. Look up the manufacturer's recommended procedure and specifications for the final drive unit. Inspect all gears in the final drive unit for worn, chipped, or broken teeth.

2. Inspect the planetary gear assembly (if equipped). **(Photo 1)**

3. Use a dial indicator to check the side gear backlash, and compare the backlash to the manufacturer's specifications. **(Photo 2)**

4. If the backlash is too great, install a thicker shim behind the side gear. If the backlash is too little, install a thinner shim behind the side gear. **(Photo 3)**

5. Install the final drive assembly into the transaxle.

6. Torque the retaining bolts to the proper specifications.

7. Set up a dial indicator to measure end play on the differential assembly. If the end play is not correct, change the selective shim behind the bearings to change the end play. **(Photo 4)**

8. Reinstall the final drive and recheck end play.

9. Measure the rotating torque of the final drive unit. **(Photo 5)**

10. If the torque is above the amount recommended by the manufacturer, replace the shim with a slightly thinner shim.

SKILL DRILL	20-28	Inspecting, Measuring, and Repairing the Transaxle Final Drive Components

1 First look up the manufacturer's recommended procedure and specifications for the final drive unit. Inspect all gears in the final drive unit for chipped or broken teeth. Inspect the planetary gear assembly (if equipped).

2 Use a dial indicator to check the side gear backlash, and compare the backlash to the manufacturer's specifications.

3 If the backlash is too great, install a thicker shim behind the side gear. If the backlash is too little, install a thinner shim behind the side gear.

4 Install the final drive assembly into the transaxle and torque the retaining bolts. Use a dial indicator to measure end play on the differential assembly, and compare to specifications. If the end play is not correct, change the selective shim behind the bearings to change the end play.

5 Reinstall the final drive and check end play. Measure the rotating torque of the final drive unit, and compare to specifications.

6 If the torque is above the recommended amount, replace the shim with a slightly thinner shim. If it is lower than the amount recommended by the manufacturer, replace the shim with a slightly thicker one.

11 If the torque is lower than the amount recommended by the manufacturer, replace the shim with a slightly thicker shim. **(Photo 6)**

12 Recheck the rotating torque.

Assembling the Transmission

After taking the time to rebuild each of the individual transmission components, the transmission needs to be carefully assembled. Check the service information for the correct procedure before beginning assembly. All components should be lubricated with the correct automatic transmission fluid, or transmission assembly lube, as they are installed in the transmission. Transmission parts should not need to be forced together. They may require lots of wiggling and turning, but if you try to force them together, you will succeed only in damaging the parts. All gaskets and seals should be replaced at this time, if they have not already been replaced.

Take the time to look up torque specifications and torque sequences. The manufacturer published them for a reason. Failure to torque parts correctly can result in an early failure of the transmission and a second visit from an unhappy customer. Many bolts also have a specific location and need to be installed only where they belong.

A misplaced valve body bolt can cause catastrophic damage when the vehicle is started if the bolt protrudes into any of the rotating parts of the transmission from the valve body.

To assemble the transmission, follow the steps in **SKILL DRILL 20-29**:

1. Look up the proper assembly procedure and specifications in the appropriate service information. Install the rear clutch piston and return springs. **(Photo 1)**
2. Install the rear thrust bearing and output shaft into the transmission. **(Photo 2)**
3. Install any rear clutch or band assembly into the transmission. **(Photo 3)**

SKILL DRILL | 20-29 | Assembling the Transmission

1. First look up the proper assembly procedure and specifications. Install the rear clutch piston and return springs.

2. Install the rear thrust bearing and output shaft into the transmission.

3. Install any rear clutch or band assembly into the transmission.

4. Install the planetary sets and any snap rings into the transmission.

5. Install the clutches, drums, and bands with the input shaft. Make sure all components are fully engaged; otherwise there will be no end play and components will be damaged.

6. Install the front pump. Make sure the pump lines up correctly and that there is a small amount of end play. Torque the bolts to specifications.

SKILL DRILL	20-29	Assembling the Transmission, continued

7 Check the transmission end play (refer to Skill Drill 20-13). Adjust any bands if adjustable with the proper torque wrench.

8 Install any check valves and the valve body spacer plate.

9 Install the valve body and torque the bolts following the manufacturer's specified sequence.

10 Install the manual valve and manual valve linkage.

11 Install the shift solenoids, EPC solenoid, and sensors into the valve body. Install the wiring harness.

12 Install the extension housing.

13 Install the transmission filter and transmission pan. Install the bell housing, if removed.

14 Install all external sensors, plugs, and covers, and remove the transmission from the transmission vise. Prepare to install it in the vehicle.

4 Install the planetary sets and any snap rings into the transmission. **(Photo 4)**

5 Install the clutches, drums, and bands with the input shaft. Make sure all components are fully engaged; otherwise there will be no end play and components will be damaged. **(Photo 5)**

6 Install the front pump. Make sure the pump lines up correctly. Usually a couple of studs screwed into the bolt holes will help with alignment. Verify that the parts are fully seated, meaning that there should be a small amount of end play and the input shaft can be turned by hand. If so, torque the bolts to specifications. **(Photo 6)**

7 Check the transmission end play (refer to Skill Drill 20-13). **(Photo 7)**

8 If the end play is not correct, disassemble the transmission and fix the problem before continuing.

9 Adjust the bands, if adjustable, using the proper torque wrench. **(Photo 8)**

10 Install any check valves and the valve body spacer plate. **(Photo 9)**

11 Install the valve body and torque the bolts to specifications following the manufacturer's specified sequence.

12 Install the manual valve and manual valve linkage. (Sometimes this must be performed before bolting the valve body down.) **(Photo 10)**

13 Install the shift solenoids, EPC solenoid, and sensors into the valve body. **(Photo 11)**

14 Install the wiring harness, making sure the harness is installed in all of the correct retainers, to prevent damage. **(Photo 12)**

15 Install the extension housing. **(Photo 13)**

16 Install the transmission filter.

17 Install the transmission pan and torque properly.

18 Install the bell housing if it was removed.

19 Install all external sensors, plugs, and covers.

20 Remove the transmission from the transmission holding devise, and prepare to install it in the vehicle. **(Photo 14)**

Installing a Torque Converter

Installing the torque converter properly is often where beginning students and technicians have a problem. Sometimes it is difficult to get the torque converter fully seated when installing it into the transmission. It takes practice to feel when each of the three separate components engage with their mating parts. The first engagement is the pump drive. Aligning the pump gears with the slots or flats on the torque converter will get them close. The second and third engagements are the stator support to the stator and the input shaft to the turbine. A torque converter that is not properly installed will cause catastrophic damage to the front pump when the vehicle is first started. If the transmission was rebuilt by a transmission shop, this damage will not be covered under the warranty.

To install and seat the torque converter to engage drive/splines, follow the steps in **SKILL DRILL 20-30**:

1 Look up the manufacturer's recommended procedure for installing the torque converter.

2 Prefill the new or rebuilt torque converter about halfway with clean automatic transmission fluid. Make sure the fluid is correct for the transmission. **(Photo 1)**

3 Install the torque converter onto the input shaft of the transmission.

4 Spin and wiggle the torque converter to install it fully. You should feel the torque converter catch and go in three times as the converter engages the pump gear, the stator, and the turbine. **(Photo 2)**

5 Some manufacturers specify a measurement to check that a torque converter is installed properly. Install the transmission into the vehicle. If the torque converter will not spin, or is bound against the flex plate as the transmission is being bolted up, STOP. Remove the transmission. The torque converter is not installed properly. On torque converters that have studs and that are bolted to the flex plate using nuts, you will have to properly align the studs so that the studs fit through the holes in the flex plate during installation. If the studs are sticking through the holes, the converter will not spin. Make sure the converter has to be pulled slightly toward the flex plate to install and tighten the nuts. **(Photo 3)**

Transmission Final Checks

After the transmission is installed properly into the vehicle, add about 75% of the total transmission fluid to the transmission. Firmly apply the brakes and start the engine, and check the fluid level. Add fluid as necessary to bring it to the bottom of the safe or add mark on the dipstick. Make sure you clear any transmission codes that are in the PCM, if equipped. Double-check that all

SKILL DRILL | **20-30** | **Installing and Seating the Torque Converter**

1. Look up the manufacturer's recommended procedure for installing the torque converter. Prefill the new or rebuilt torque converter about halfway with clean automatic transmission fluid.

2. Install the torque converter onto the input shaft of the transmission. Spin and wiggle the torque converter to install it properly. You should feel the torque converter catch three times.

3. Install the transmission into the vehicle. If the torque converter will not spin, or is bound up against the flex plate, STOP. Remove the transmission. The torque converter is not installed properly.

of the adjustments are correct, and then test-drive the vehicle. If required, make sure to look up any procedures for resetting the adaptive memory after a rebuild so the PCM will reprogram its shift timing and pressures for the rebuilt transmission.

After the test-drive, double-check the fluid level. Make sure there are no leaks and all of the mounting bolts are properly torqued.

Wrap-up

Ready for Review

- Automatic transmissions require periodic maintenance, which includes checking transmission fluid and replacing fluid and filters.
- If transmission fluid levels are low, identify the source of fluid loss.
- Visually inspect transmission fluid and replace as necessary.
- Diagnosis of transmission problems requires a thorough transmission inspection.
- Use extreme caution and wear proper protective clothing and equipment when diagnosing a transmission in a running vehicle.
- Diagnostic transmission tests include the fluid check, road test, visual inspection, scan of the computer for codes, stall test, hydraulic pressure test, leak check, pan inspection, air check, cooler flow test, and noise, vibration, and harshness test.
- Always perform a diagnostic test-drive under a range of operating conditions.
- Using a factory scan tool allows technicians bidirectional transmission control.
- Stall testing involves determining whether the engine can achieve manufacturer-specified rpm in each gear.
- Hydraulic system pressure testing should be performed via manufacturer-supplied test ports.
- In-vehicle transmission repairs include replacement of the vehicle speed sensor, extension housing bushing, and power train mount; repair of the valve body and the external gaskets and seals; and adjustments of the servo and bands.
- Leaks from gaskets or seals may require bushing replacement to properly repair the leak.
- Repair of power train mounts is critical for keeping the engine and transmission in proper position.
- Hydraulically controlled transmission vehicles will likely require a test-drive to determine functionality of the torque converter clutch.
- Adjust the shift linkage and transmission range sensor as part of automatic transmission servicing.
- Always follow safety precautions and wear personal protective clothing and equipment when removing the transmission for repair.
- Thoroughly inspect the flex plate, even though it is unlikely to need repair.
- If not replacing the torque converter, be sure to inspect the bolts, pump drive, pump drive tangs, pump drive lugs, and converter snout, and to check the end play.
- Always clean and inspect the transmission oil cooler and lines prior to installing a new or repaired transmission.
- Check bearings to ensure preload and end play are at optimum levels.
- Disassemble a transmission in a stepwise fashion to avoid missing transmission failure clues.
- Take care during transmission disassembly to not lose or damage any parts.
- Check planetary gear sets for discoloration, cracked or worn teeth, and end play.
- Inspect the smaller transmission parts, including bushings, thrust bearings, and washers.
- Disassemble and inspect one-way rollers for signs of damage.
- Visually inspect sprags, as they cannot be completely disassembled.
- All components of the oil delivery circuits must be inspected for debris, damage, and proper operation.
- Inspect the transmission case for damage or warping, and ensure the vent is unclogged.
- Inspect bands for damage, wear, or burns; inspect the drum for wear and warpage.
- Always rebuild clutch assemblies during transmission rebuilding, and thoroughly inspect all components for damage and wear.
- Measure clutch pack clearance after reassembly.
- Disassemble the transmission valve body, and inspect each valve for wear.
- Both gear-style and chain-style transaxle assemblies must be inspected for wear.
- Carefully reassemble the transmission in the correct sequence, with all components properly lubricated.
- Install the torque converter and ensure that all three components (oil pump drive, stator support, and turbine input shaft) engage with their mating parts.
- When finished, test-drive the vehicle and double-check the fluid level to ensure there are no leaks.

Key Terms

<u>air checking</u> The use of compressed air to check clutch and servo operation on transmissions during and after assembly.

<u>bidirectional control</u> The ability to command different solenoids and actuators "on" and "off" to check their operation.

<u>cooler flow test</u> The placement of a specialty measuring device into the transmission cooler line to measure fluid flow to the cooler. Low cooler flow can be a sign of other issues with the pump and lubrication system.

<u>free play</u> The amount of movement between two mating parts.

<u>hydraulic pressure test</u> The use of a hydraulic pressure gauge to measure the amount of hydraulic pressure produced in each gear range.

<u>Morse-style chain</u> A heavy-duty chain constructed of many links and held together with pins. It is used in some transaxles and transfer cases to transmit torque from one component to another.

<u>noise, vibration, and harshness (NVH) test</u> A test to measure for any audible noises, vibrations, and harsh operation. It can be completed by the technician with or without the aid of an NVH tester. The tester is used to pinpoint the exact frequencies of the noise and vibrations.

<u>pan inspection</u> The process of removing the transmission pan to check for clutch material, metal, and other debris or contaminants.

<u>power train mount</u> A rubber or metal bracket used to secure the engine and transmission into the vehicle. Some vehicles use hydraulic or electrohydraulic power train mounts.

<u>preload</u> Further pressure applied to bearing-supported parts after all the free play is taken up.

<u>stall test</u> A test that involves raising the engine rpm to wide-open throttle while the brake is firmly applied and the transmission is in gear. The test is used to check torque convertor and transmission operation on some vehicles.

ASE-Type Questions

1. Tech A says that you should check fluid level in many automatic transmissions with the engine idling and the transmission in park. Tech B says that most manufacturers use selectively fit thrust washers to adjust transmission end play. Who is correct?
   a. Tech A
   b. Tech B
   c. Both A and B
   d. Neither A nor B

2. Tech A says that increasing the transmission fluid level from the add mark to the full mark will require a quart of fluid, just like with engine oil. Tech B says that transmission solenoids should be tested electrically and mechanically. Who is correct?
   a. Tech A
   b. Tech B
   c. Both A and B
   d. Neither A nor B

3. Tech A says that when checking the fluid level on the dipstick, always read the highest level on either side. Tech B says that when air checking a clutch, the clutch plates should be removed so you can see if the clutch seals are leaking. Who is correct?
   a. Tech A
   b. Tech B
   c. Both A and B
   d. Neither A nor B

4. Tech A says that transmission pan gaskets are always replaced. Tech B says that some newer transmissions have reusable pan gaskets. Who is correct?
   a. Tech A
   b. Tech B
   c. Both A and B
   d. Neither A nor B

5. Tech A says that the cooler and cooler lines should be flushed as part of a transmission rebuild. Tech B says that the torque converter can be fully seated in the transmission by tightening the bell housing bolts to the engine. Who is correct?
   a. Tech A
   b. Tech B
   c. Both A and B
   d. Neither A nor B

6. Tech A says that performing a stall test can reveal slippage within the torque converter or transmission. Tech B says that a stall test can damage some transmissions and should not be performed on all transmissions. Who is correct?
   a. Tech A
   b. Tech B
   c. Both A and B
   d. Neither A nor B

7. Tech A says that using a scan tool to activate the TCC with the engine idling in drive and the brakes applied is a typical troubleshooting task. Tech B says that diagnosis is a waste of time on a faulty transmission since it will be rebuilt anyway. Who is correct?
   a. Tech A
   b. Tech B
   c. Both A and B
   d. Neither A nor B

8. Tech A says that when checking line pressure, the engine should be off. Tech B says that when checking line pressure, the engine should be running. Who is correct?
   a. Tech A
   b. Tech B
   c. Both A and B
   d. Neither A nor B

9. Tech A says that low line pressure can be caused by a plugged transmission vent. Tech B says that high line pressure is caused by a restricted filter. Who is correct?
   a. Tech A
   b. Tech B
   c. Both A and B
   d. Neither A nor B

10. Tech A says that some transmissions are made without dipsticks. Tech B says that transmission end play should be measured after the front pump is installed. Who is correct?
    a. Tech A
    b. Tech B
    c. Both A and B
    d. Neither A nor B

CHAPTER 21

Automatic Transmission and Transaxle
Off-Vehicle Transmission and Transaxle

Page

- Describe the operational characteristics of a hybrid vehicle drive train. **MLR** **AST** **MAST** 594–596

- Describe the operational characteristics of a continuously variable transmission (CVT). **MLR** **AST** **MAST** 599–602

Knowledge Objectives

After reading this chapter, you will be able to:
1. Explain how the hybrid drive system works. (pp 594–596)
2. Discuss and compare hybrid and hybrid electric vehicle models. (pp 596–599)
3. Explain how a continuously variable transmission (CVT) works. (pp 599–602)
4. Explain the operation of electronic continuously variable transmission (ECVT), variable-diameter pulley CVT, and toroidal CVT. (pp 600–602)

Hybrid and Continuously Variable Transmissions

Introduction

With the need for increased fuel economy, lower carbon dioxide emissions, and a smaller global footprint, manufacturers have been working to create more efficient new power train systems. Automobile manufacturers have had hybrid vehicles and vehicles with **continuously variable transmissions (CVT)** in mass production for more than 20 years. These vehicles are showing up in non-dealer repair facilities in greater numbers every day; therefore, it is important that technicians become familiar with both their operation and repair techniques.

Hybrid Drive Systems

A **hybrid drive system** is defined as a system that uses two or more power sources, such as an internal combustion engine (ICE) and an electric motor, to propel the vehicle. There are many different styles and systems of hybrid vehicles being sold today. We will cover several of the more common hybrid vehicles on the market at the time of this writing—primarily gasoline–electric hybrids—and how they operate. Also expect various other hybrid arrangements, such as diesel–electric hybrids and fuel cell–electric hybrids, in the near future.

Before exploring how a hybrid operates, it is important to first discuss the purpose of a hybrid drive system. Hybrid vehicles have several different functions that separate them from conventional vehicles, such as idle stop and regenerative braking. Not all hybrids have every one of these functions, but often they will have most of them. Hybrids may be considered mild hybrids or full hybrids based on the number of hybrid functions they use. Knowing what functions a hybrid vehicle is equipped with and how the vehicle operates is necessary for two reasons: first, so you will know whether it is operating correctly, and second, so you will know what precautions you need to take in order to work on it safely.

Idle Stop

Idle stop is one of the most common functions of a hybrid vehicle and when used with an integrated starter/generator qualifies the vehicle for mild hybrid status. When the driver stops the vehicle, such as at a stoplight, the power train control module (PCM) shuts off the engine. Shutting off the engine reduces fuel consumption and carbon dioxide emissions. By using high-voltage electric motors, the PCM is able to crank the vehicle over very quickly and smoothly, creating an almost instant start as soon as the driver presses down on the accelerator. This cranking speed can be as high as 1000 revolutions per minute (rpm).

Stopping the engine at stoplights or when idling creates several problems that need to be addressed, such as the operation of the heating and cooling systems when the engine is stopped. In a conventional vehicle, the water pump and air-conditioning compressor are driven by an engine belt. This is not possible on a vehicle with the idle stop function **FIGURE 21-1**.

Many hybrid vehicles that use idle stop have a small, electric transmission hydraulic pump. This hydraulic

> ▶ **LINK**
> Refer to the Principles of Heating and Air-Conditioning Systems chapter for more information on the heating and cooling system in hybrid vehicles.

You are the Automotive Technician

Recently the Express Delivery Company you work for has converted its fleet from diesel to hybrid vehicles. Hybrid vehicles have lower carbon dioxide emissions, increased fuel economy, and a smaller global footprint. These vehicles often use very high-voltage batteries that present a severe shock hazard, which can easily lead to death if handled improperly. Your supervisor has asked you to complete a scheduled maintenance service on one of the hybrid vehicles.

1. Why is it important to fully understand the hybrid system and its operation before attempting any repairs on a hybrid vehicle?
2. What processes do most hybrid vehicles go through as they are braking and coming to a stop?
3. What are the most common types of CVTs being used in vehicles today?

FIGURE 21-1 A picture of the driver information center on a Toyota Prius showing the vehicle in an idle stop situation. The engine is not running in this mode.

FIGURE 21-2 The driver information screen from a Toyota Prius showing power flow from the electric motor to the battery.

pump is used to prevent a delay in the engagement of the transmission when the vehicle is restarted.

Torque Smoothing

Torque smoothing refers to the ability of the hybrid vehicle to use an electric motor to help smooth out the power pulses of the ICE and create a flatter torque output curve. This feature is especially helpful on small three- and four-cylinder engines, which tend to produce more engine pulsations at lower engine speeds. When the ICE is on a compression pulse, the electric motor can be used to increase the amount of torque during compression. As the ICE is on a power stroke, the electric motor creates less torque. As the ICE's rpm increases, the torque pulses are needed less and less.

Regenerative Braking

Accelerating a vehicle from a stoplight requires a large amount of energy. When a conventional vehicle is being stopped, most of the kinetic energy of the vehicle's movement is converted into heat by the friction of the brake pads against the brake rotors; therefore, all of this energy is lost on a conventional vehicle. Most hybrid vehicles use regenerative braking to ensure that not all of the energy that was used to accelerate the vehicle is lost during braking.

On a hybrid vehicle, when the driver initiates a stop, the electric motor becomes a generator. The kinetic energy of the vehicle's movement is used to turn the generator and create electricity to charge the high-voltage battery. The harder the driver steps on the brake pedal, the more electricity is generated. It is important to remember that the more electricity that a generator is required to produce, the harder it is to turn the generator. This action causes the vehicle to slow down and eventually stop with the help of a conventional braking system **FIGURE 21-2**.

Regenerative brakes can only develop a certain amount of stopping power. If the driver needs more braking power than the regenerative brakes can supply, mechanical brakes are available as backup. However, they cannot recapture any of the kinetic energy. Judicious use of the brakes on a hybrid vehicle, such that the mechanical brakes are not activated, results in the best fuel economy.

Continuous driving, such as on the interstate, does not offer the regenerative braking system an opportunity to energize the battery. It is during stop-and-go driving that hybrids benefit most from this system, often resulting in a significantly higher gas mileage (MPG) rating during city driving than on the highway. The regenerative braking system also makes hybrids ideal for delivery vehicles and city transit buses that operate in stop-and-go conditions all day long.

Torque Assist

An electric motor is capable of creating its maximum torque as soon as it begins spinning. This torque can be used to help propel the vehicle from a stop, creating torque assist for the ICE, which creates its maximum torque much higher in the rpm range. By using an electric motor with an ICE, the overall displacement of the ICE can be reduced. For example, a vehicle that might have needed a 2.0-liter engine to operate might only need a 1.4-liter engine to perform the same way when it is combined with the hybrid electric motor. This reduction in size of the ICE results in a fuel savings, not only during city driving but also on the highway **FIGURE 21-3**.

Electric-Only Propulsion

On many full hybrids, the vehicle can operate at low speeds using the electric motor only. When a driver presses on the accelerator pedal, the PCM commands the high-voltage battery pack to apply electricity to the

FIGURE 21-3 A picture of the driver information center from a Toyota Prius showing the ICE and the electric motor being used to propel the vehicle.

electric motor until the vehicle reaches speeds up to approximately 40 miles per hour (64 kilometers per hour) (depending on the model), at which point the PCM starts the ICE to continue accelerating the vehicle **FIGURE 21-4**.

Safety

Extreme caution should be exercised when working around hybrid vehicles. These vehicles often use very high voltages that can cause serious harm or death. Only begin working on a hybrid vehicle after you have had the proper safety training and thoroughly understand the system and its operation, and have the proper safety equipment. Always check with the appropriate service information before attempting any repairs on a hybrid vehicle. In addition to the high voltages, many systems have very strong permanent magnets that will attract any ferrous metal that gets close to them and can pinch your fingers or hand between the part and the magnet. The magnets often cannot be removed without a special tool.

Hybrid Electric Vehicle Models

Currently, hybrid vehicles are available from almost every vehicle manufacturer, with new models being added every month as the demand for more fuel-efficient vehicles increases. In this section, we will cover some of the more common hybrid vehicle systems used by the different manufacturers.

Belt Alternator Starter

Belt alternator starter (BAS) vehicles have been produced primarily by the General Motors Corporation **FIGURE 21-5**. The BAS unit is a belt-driven alternator and starter motor. Conventional starter motors and alternators operate on nominal 12 volts, while the BAS system uses a 42-volt battery.

When the engine is running, the belt spins the BAS motor, which in turn produces electricity, like a conventional alternator, to charge the high-voltage battery. When the engine is stopped, the BAS motor can crank the vehicle over very quickly through the belt drive. This design allows the vehicle to use the fuel savings of the idle stop function.

As the vehicle is slowing down, the BAS motor is used to produce a large amount of current to charge the battery, while also slowing the vehicle down due to the extra drag of the alternator. This allows the vehicle to capture some of the fuel savings of the regenerative braking.

The transaxle used in vehicles with the BAS systems is relatively the same as that used in non-hybrid counterparts. The only major difference, other than PCM programming, is the addition of an electrically operated transaxle hydraulic pump. This pump allows a smooth acceleration as the engine restarts after an idle stop. Without this

FIGURE 21-4 A driver information center on a Toyota Prius showing the electric motor alone propelling the vehicle.

FIGURE 21-5 A BAS system installed on a Chevrolet Malibu.

electric pump, there would be a momentary lag as the transaxle reengaged after the engine was restarted.

Honda Integrated Motor Assist

Honda hybrids use a system called the **integrated motor assist (IMA)**. The IMA system uses a thin electric motor in place of a conventional flywheel or flex plate. This electric motor is used to supplement the gasoline engine's power when accelerating. The Honda IMA system is classified as a parallel hybrid because the electric motor is operating at the same time as the gasoline engine. The Honda IMA system uses between 144 volts and 158 volts, depending on the year of the vehicle and the specific model of hybrid. Currently, Honda IMA hybrids cannot drive using the electric motor only because the IMA is not able to disconnect from the gasoline engine. Therefore, in order for electricity to be produced, the gasoline engine must be spinning. (It does not have to be using gasoline, though; it can be coasting.)

The electric motor is used to charge the high-voltage battery pack when the vehicle is decelerating, converting some of the kinetic energy of the vehicle motion into electrical energy, rather than wasting some of the energy in heat during braking. The electric motor is also used to rapidly restart the engine after the driver releases the brake pedal.

The Honda IMA system does also use a conventional 12-volt starter to initially start the vehicle when it is cold out or when the high-voltage battery is not charged. The transaxle used in combination with the IMA system can be a conventional automatic transmission, a manual transmission, or, more typically, a CVT. CVTs will be covered later in this chapter. All three types of transmissions have been modified to be smaller so they can fit with the IMA assembly between the engine and the transmission. Both conventional transmissions and CVTs use an auxiliary electric transaxle hydraulic pump to keep the clutches engaged when the vehicle is stopped at a light. Other transaxle modifications include a stronger lock-up torque converter, which allows the drive wheels to run the IMA assembly during deceleration in order to charge the high-voltage battery pack. Gear ratios are different in the transaxles used in conjunction with IMA assembly than in conventional vehicles to maximize the fuel savings and performance of the hybrid functions **FIGURE 21-6**.

Two-Mode Hybrid

The **two-mode hybrid** was a joint venture by the General Motors, Chrysler, and BMW companies to create a hybrid system that could be used on trucks and larger luxury vehicles. The system is mostly housed

FIGURE 21-6 An electric motor from a Honda IMA system.

in what looks like a conventional truck transmission housing. It uses a system voltage of 300 volts to power the two electric motor/generators housed inside the transmission case. The transmission uses three or four planetary gear sets, depending on the application.

The first mode is used at low speeds and light engine load. During mode 1, the vehicle can be propelled by the ICE, the electric motor/generator, or any combination of the ICE and electric motor/generator. When operating in mode 1, one of the electric motor/generators is used to keep the high-voltage battery charged, while the second motor/generator is used to assist in propelling the vehicle. The vehicle can be driven by the electric motor only if the PCM determines that the high-voltage battery has enough charge to operate the vehicle. If at any time the PCM determines that the battery voltage is too low, or if the driver demands more power, the ICE will be restarted automatically, using the one motor/generator to crank the engine.

In mode 1, the electric motor/generators in combination with the planetary gear sets allow the transmission to operate as a type of CVT, keeping the engine operating in its most efficient rpm range. During deceleration, both electric motor/generators are switched to generator mode to recharge the battery.

The second mode is used for higher vehicle speed and/or load. During the second mode, the gasoline engine is running to propel the vehicle. When maximum power is needed, both electric motor/generators are used to help propel the vehicle. When less power is needed or the PCM determines that the battery voltage is low, one of the motor/generators is switched over to generate power to recharge the battery. The PCM will phase in and out each of the planetary gear sets to create four distinct gear ratios. This also keeps the electric motor/generators operating in their efficient rpm range.

During the second mode, the PCM employs different fuel-saving techniques, such as shutting down cylinders and using variable cam timing, to achieve the highest fuel economy without sacrificing power when it is needed. When the vehicle's ICE is operating and cylinders are shut down to save fuel, the electric motor/generators are used to smooth out the power demands and compensate for the reduced power from the ICE **FIGURE 21-7**.

Toyota and Lexus Hybrids

Toyota and Lexus hybrids use a power-splitting device that could be considered a type of CVT. These hybrids use voltages from 200 to 650 volts, depending on the application. The Toyota and Lexus hybrids can be classified as a series-parallel hybrid because either the gasoline ICE or the electric motor/generator can propel the vehicle, or both can be used together.

Safety

Because the vehicle can be driven by the electric motor only, and the ICE can be started by the PCM at any time that the key is turned on or the system is powered up by the start button, it is very important that you follow the manufacturer's procedure for testing the vehicle. This imperative could be illustrated by a simple turn signal bulb inspection. You would normally turn the ignition switch to the run position, turn on the turn signal, and then go look at the front and rear turn signal bulbs. Unfortunately, with a hybrid system, the vehicle could start on its own and travel across the shop, putting others and the vehicle in danger. Follow the manufacturer's procedures exactly when working on a hybrid vehicle.

The transaxle contains two electric motor/generators, a final drive gear set, a differential, and a planetary gear set. Each of the electric motor/generators and the ICE are connected to a separate part of the planetary gear set, as shown in **FIGURE 21-8**.

The ring gear of the planetary gear set is connected to the final drive through a drive chain as in many front-wheel drive (FWD) transaxles. The ring gear is also directly connected to motor/generator 2 (M/G2). The sun gear of the planetary gear set is attached to the motor/generator 1 (M/G1). M/G1 is used as a generator to charge the high-voltage battery pack and to crank the engine over. The planet carrier of the planetary gear set is attached to the ICE.

When starting the gasoline engine, M/G1 spins the planetary carrier, which is attached to the ICE, in order to crank the engine. With the vehicle stopped, M/G2 is basically locked and prevented from turning.

When the engine starts, M/G1 begins spinning. M/G1 switches to generator mode and begins charging the high-voltage battery pack. M/G2 then begins to spin and the power from the ICE is added to M/G2 to spin the ring gear and propel the vehicle **FIGURE 21-9**.

Toyota and Lexus hybrids are able to propel the vehicle in electric-only mode at low speeds. During electric-only mode, the ICE is shut down, effectively holding the planet carrier from spinning. High voltage is supplied to M/G2, which spins the ring gear and drives the wheels. M/G1 is allowed to spin freely **FIGURE 21-10**. In reverse, the current flow to M/G2 is reversed and causes the motor to spin in the opposite direction. In reverse, the ICE is not used to propel the vehicle.

During deceleration at low speeds, the engine is shut off to hold the carrier. M/G1 is allowed to freewheel while

FIGURE 21-7 A chart showing the operation of the two modes of a two-mode hybrid.

FIGURE 21-8 The planetary operation as the engine is started.

FIGURE 21-9 The planetary operation as the vehicle is moving and M/G2 and the ICE are moving the vehicle.

FIGURE 21-11 The planetary gear operation during deceleration.

FIGURE 21-10 The planetary operation as M/G1 is propelling the vehicle without the aid of the ICE.

FIGURE 21-12 A cutaway of a Ford hybrid transmission. Notice M/G1 and M/G2.

M/G2 is driven by the wheels. M/G2 is switched to generator mode and the power generated is used to recharge the high-voltage battery pack **FIGURE 21-11**.

The vehicle's PCM controls the amount of current produced from M/G2 during deceleration to prevent wheel lock-up and skidding. During electric-only operation, the PCM continuously monitors the battery voltage and restarts the ICE as needed. There is no torque converter or clutch mechanism. There is, however, a damper assembly that is used to cushion the power pulses from the engine and reduce the drive line shock.

Ford Motor Company Hybrids

The Ford Escape and Fusion hybrids (along with the Lincoln and Mercury versions) are very similar in operation to the Toyota system. The Ford transaxle also uses two electric motor/generators that in conjunction with an ICE split power through a planetary gear set. The only major difference between the Ford and the Toyota is that rather than having the two electric motor/generators directly connected to the ring gear and the sun gear, they are attached through a set of transfer gears **FIGURE 21-12**.

▶ Continuously Variable Transmission (CVT)

A CVT has no fixed gear ratios; the transmission can infinitely change the gear ratio within its operational design. Changes to the gear ratio occur in a smooth stepless progression to suit speed and load conditions. This design allows the engine to operate in its most efficient operating rpm range for fuel economy or performance, depending on the driver's demands.

Types of CVTs

There are three basic types of CVTs commonly used in production vehicles. The first type is often referred to as an **electronic continuously variable transmission (ECVT)** and is found in hybrid vehicles. The second type is the most common CVT, called a variable-diameter pulley or Reeves drive CVT. The last type of CVT found in automobiles is a toroidal or roller-based CVT.

We have already covered the ECVT because it is the transmission/transaxle found in Toyota and Ford hybrid vehicles. By using the combination of two electric motor/generators and an ICE driven through a specially designed planetary gear set, the manufacturer is able to create an infinite number of gear ratios.

Variable-Diameter Pulley CVT

The **variable-diameter pulley (VDP)** CVT is one of the most common types of CVTs being used in vehicles today. The VDP system operates using two variable diameter pulleys with either a steel or a rubber belt between them. Some of the early CVTs in Europe used a stiff rubber belt, as do many snowmobiles and all-terrain vehicles (ATVs). The rubber belt has a limited service life in an automobile, so most manufacturers use a steel drive belt. Each of the pulleys has two movable drive faces called sheaves. These sheaves can be moved inward or outward, relative to each other, to change the effective diameter of the pulley **FIGURE 21-13**.

When the vehicle starts from a stop, the input pulley has a small diameter while the output pulley has large diameter. This size difference creates a high torque multiplication (low speed) gear ratio to start the vehicle from a stop. The drive ratio from a stop is approximately 3:1 through the pulleys. As the vehicle gains speed, the input pulley diameter increases, while the output pulley diameter decreases (high speed).

The input pulley diameter is changed by applying hydraulic oil to one of the pulley sheaves to push the two sheaves closer together. The belt is forced to ride higher on the faces of the pulley, changing the effective diameter of the pulley, as shown in figure 21-14. When the two pulleys have the same diameter, the gear ratio of the pulleys is 1:1. As vehicle speed increases, the input pulley continues to increase in diameter, and the output pulley decreases in diameter, to create an overdrive ratio of 1:2, or even greater on some transmissions. Remember that this ratio does not include any final drive gearing, which will reduce the actual gear ratio of the CVT.

Belt tension is maintained by large springs in the output shaft pulley. The springs cause the sheaves of the output pulley to be close together, creating a large-diameter pulley. As the input pulley diameter increases, the springs in the output pulley are compressed, decreasing the diameter of the output pulley. The diameter of the pulleys is controlled to keep the engine operating in its most efficient rpm range **FIGURE 21-14**. The PCM monitors the speed of the two pulleys to maintain the correct gear ratio. Some CVTs also incorporate a sensor to measure the position of one of the input pulley sheaves. This allows for greater control and monitoring of the CVT.

FIGURE 21-13 A VDP CVT. Note the small-diameter input pulley on the left and the large-diameter output pulley on right. The two sheaves that are moveable are labeled. The other two sheaves remain stationary.

FIGURE 21-14 An illustration of the changing sizes of the input and output pulleys.

Some manufacturers have programmed into the PCM regular shift points, at which the pulley sheaves will move to predetermined positions to create the feel of separate conventional shifts. Some manufacturers also allow the driver to manually shift through these predetermined pulley diameters while driving the vehicle.

Currently, most manufacturers do not recommend repairing internal components of a CVT. Instead, they recommend the transmission be replaced as a complete unit with a new or rebuilt transmission. CVTs can be rebuilt, but many parts are difficult and costly to obtain. Specialty tools are required to compress the output pulley and reinstall the belt.

The steel belt is made up of hundreds of transversely mounted steel plates that are held in place with several steel bands running longitudinally around the edge of the plates. The transverse steel plates grab the sides of the pulley and in turn are pushed by the pulleys. The longitudinal steel bands are used to hold the belt together and keep the steel plates lined up. These bands hold the plates closely together in a very strong and flexible ring. The plates are guided by the bands but not attached to them. Drive is transmitted by compressing the plate elements rather than relying on tension in the band. Each block leaving the primary pulley pushes the blocks ahead of it to the secondary pulley, where the bands keep the blocks in contact with the pulley faces. The blocks are compressed on the drive side and float loosely along the bands on the return side.

The large number of plates that are in contact with the pulleys keeps the surface pressures low on the belt, allowing high torque to be transmitted. The belt is lubricated by transmission fluid sprayed directly onto it at high pressure. A typical steel belt is shown in **FIGURE 21-15**.

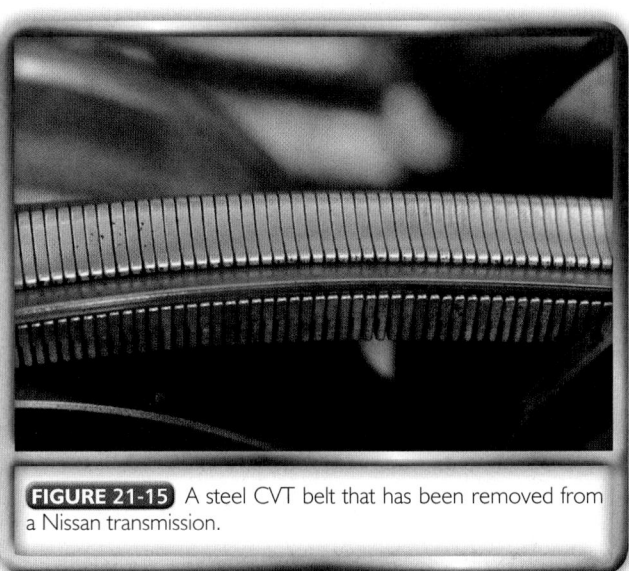

FIGURE 21-15 A steel CVT belt that has been removed from a Nissan transmission.

CVTs require special transmission fluid, and many CVTs have a special transmission oil heater built into them. This heater is used to warm up the transmission oil so the transmission can operate properly during cold weather operation. Filter and fluid change intervals must be adhered to in order to prevent damage to the transmission.

Applied Science

AS-98: Simple Machines: The technician can demonstrate an understanding of how cams, pulleys, and levers are used to multiply forces or change the direction of force in a mechanical system.

Simple machines, such as cams, pulleys, and levers, have become much improved and refined over the years. Looking back into history, we can understand that these three mechanical units have transformed the way that we perform many tasks.

Cams have the ability to change rotary motion to linear motion; for example, a camshaft in an engine. Cams have also been used in printing presses, textile machinery, and machine shop equipment of various types.

Pulleys can be used to change the direction of a force or provide a mechanical advantage with a multiple part line. As an example, raising a flag on a flagpole requires the use of a pulley.

Levers are one of the basic tools that may have been used in prehistoric times. The Greek mathematician, Archimedes, described the use of levers in 260 BC. Examples of levers include pry bars, pliers, claw hammers, and tongs.

As described in our text, the Variable- Diameter Pulley (VDP) continuously variable transmission is one of the most common types of CVT being used in vehicles today. The VDP system operates using two variable diameter pulleys with either a steel or rubber belt between them. The rubber belt has a limited service life in an automobile, so most manufacturers use a steel drive belt. Each of the pulleys has two movable drive faces called sheaves. These sheaves can be moved inward or outward, relative to each other, to change the effective diameter of the pulley.

A CVT is a transmission that can change through an infinite number of gear ratios. This infinite number is limited only between the minimum and maximum capabilities of the particular unit. This contrasts with other mechanical transmissions that offer a fixed number of gear ratios. Fuel economy is enhanced by the engine being allowed to run at its most efficient rpm for a range of vehicle speeds.

Toroidal CVT

The <u>toroidal CVT</u> design currently is limited in production because of high manufacturing costs. The toroidal, or roller, design uses two curved discs—an input disc and an output disc. Power is transferred from the input disc to the output disc through a set of variable-angle rollers **FIGURE 21-16**. When the rollers are tilted down toward the center axis of the input disc, the opposite side of the roller moves up toward the outer edge of the output disc. This positioning creates a high gear ratio of approximately 4:1 to begin accelerating the vehicle. As the vehicle accelerates, the roller angle changes. When the rollers are perpendicular to the input and output discs, the gear ratio is 1:1. As the vehicle continues to accelerate, the rollers angle in the opposite direction, toward the center axis of the output disc. When the roller is near the center axis of the output disc, its opposite side is near the outer edge of the input disc, creating a gear ratio of approximately 1:4. Remember that these ratios do not include any final drive gearing in their calculations.

The toroidal CVT is currently more costly to manufacture than a belt-style CVT, but it can handle larger amounts of torque. A special transmission fluid is needed for these transmissions to prevent wear to the rollers and discs while providing the correct coefficient of friction for the rollers to operate.

FIGURE 21-16 An illustration of a toroidal CVT. The transmission on the left is in a high torque multiplication ratio, and the transmission on the right is in an overdrive ratio.

Low and Reverse

Most manufacturers use a limited number of multidisc clutch packs and a set of planetary gears to allow the transmission to operate in reverse. These clutch packs are typically located on the input pulley shaft to change the direction of rotation of the pulleys and belt.

Ford Motor Company also uses these planetary gear sets to create a low ratio when it is requested by the driver. Ford advertises their CVTs as two-speed CVTs. When the driver selects low, the planetary gear set is used to create a greater torque multiplication for higher pulling power and greater traction with limited vehicle speed.

Wrap-up

Ready for Review

▸ Vehicles with continuously variable transmissions (CVTs) are becoming more prevalent.

▸ A system that uses two or more power sources is a hybrid drive system.

▸ A hybrid vehicle may have the following functions: idle stop, torque smoothing, regenerative braking, torque assist, and electric-only propulsion.

▸ Idle stop refers to engine shutoff when the driver stops (but does not turn off) the vehicle.

▸ A hybrid vehicle that uses an electric motor to smooth out internal combustion engine (ICE) power pulses is using torque smoothing.

▸ Most hybrid vehicles use braking power to generate electricity to charge the battery (regenerative braking).

▸ Torque assist refers to using torque to help propel the vehicle when additional torque is needed.

▸ Common hybrid vehicle systems include belt alternator starter (BAS), Honda integrated motor assist (IMA), two-mode hybrid, Toyota and Lexus hybrids, and Ford hybrids.

▸ A BAS system uses a 42-volt battery and relies on the belt drive to help quickly crank the vehicle over following an idle stop.

▸ The IMA system replaces the conventional flywheel with a thin electric motor to supplement the engine's torque during acceleration.

▸ The two-mode hybrid system uses approximately 300 volts to power the two generators inside the transmission case.

▸ The Toyota, Lexus, and Ford hybrid systems are series-parallel systems because the ICE and the electric generator can propel the vehicle, either individually or together.

▸ In Toyota, Lexus, and Ford hybrid systems, the PCM monitors battery voltage; if voltage is low, the ICE is engaged.

▸ Ford hybrid systems have two electric motors attached through a set of transfer gears.

▸ A CVT is able to change gear ratios to suit vehicle speed and load conditions for optimum fuel economy and performance.

▸ Types of CVTs are the electronic continuously variable transmission (ECVT), variable-diameter pulley (VDP) CVT, and toroidal (or roller-based) CVT.

▸ The most common CVT in vehicles today is the VDP.

▸ A VDP has two pulleys (input and output) with movable drive faces that can be adjusted to change the pulleys' effective diameter.

▸ The output pulley of a VDP utilizes large springs to maintain belt tension.

▸ Manufacturers recommend replacing CVTs as a whole, rather than repairing internal components.

▸ Change CVT fluid and filters on a regular basis to maintain transmission functionality.

▸ Toroidal CVTs use curved discs (input and output) with a set of variable-angle rollers instead of pulleys.

▸ Toroidal CVTs are costly to manufacture, and production is limited.

▸ In some VDP CVTs, multidisc clutch packs and planetary gear sets are designed to allow transmission operation in reverse and to create a low gear ratio.

Key Terms

belt alternator starter (BAS) A type of hybrid drive system that uses a belt-driven alternator/starter that operates on 42 volts.

continuously variable transmission (CVT) A type of transmission that has no fixed gears, as in a conventional transmission, but rather can adjust gear ratios infinitely within the design of the transmission.

electronic continuously variable transmission (ECVT) A type of hybrid transmission that often uses two electric motors in combination with an ICE. The two electric motors and the ICE transfer power through a planetary gear set, allowing an infinite amount of gear ratios.

hybrid drive system A drive system that uses two or more propulsion systems such as electric motors and an ICE.

integrated motor assist (IMA) A Honda hybrid drive system that uses a moderate-sized electric motor installed between the engine and the transmission.

regenerative braking A type of braking in which the kinetic energy of the vehicle's motion is captured rather than being lost to heat in a conventional braking system.

toroidal CVT A type of CVT that uses moveable rollers in contact with input and output drive discs. The rollers transfer power from one drive disc to the other. Their position determines the effective gear ratio.

torque assist Use of an electric motor to supplement the engine's torque whenever additional torque is needed, allowing for a smaller ICE to be used.

torque smoothing A process that uses an electric motor to smooth out engine power pulses when an ICE is operating at low rpm or when the vehicle is using fuel management techniques such as cylinder deactivation.

two-mode hybrid A type of hybrid drive system in which there are two distinct modes of operation. In one mode, the electric motor can propel the vehicle and be used for regenerative braking; in the second mode, the electric motors can be used to assist the engine while the engine uses fuel management techniques such as cylinder deactivation.

variable-diameter pulley (VDP) A type of CVT that uses two pulleys with moveable sheaves, allowing the effective diameter of the pulleys to change, resulting in variable gear ratios.

ASE-Type Questions

1. Tech A says that hybrid vehicles have an internal combustions engine and an electric motor. Tech B says that most hybrid vehicles utilize regenerative braking to help improve fuel economy. Who is correct?
   a. Tech A
   b. Tech B
   c. Both A and B
   d. Neither A nor B

2. Tech A says that it is critical to have the proper safety equipment before working on a hybrid. Tech B says that hybrid vehicles use safety interlocks to prevent technician injury so it is not necessary to use protective gloves. Who is correct?
   a. Tech A
   b. Tech B
   c. Both A and B
   d. Neither A nor B

3. Tech A says that hybrid vehicles will typically use the same transmission as a non-hybrid vehicle. Tech B says that some hybrid transmissions have a small electric fluid pump for when the transmission is in idle/stop mode. Who is correct?
   a. Tech A
   b. Tech B
   c. Both A and B
   d. Neither A nor B

4. Tech A says that BAS vehicles use an alternator to help slow the vehicle and act as a starter. Tech B says that the BAS alternator can be used to propel the vehicle without the ICE. Who is correct?
   a. Tech A
   b. Tech B
   c. Both A and B
   d. Neither A nor B

5. Tech A says that the transmission in a Toyota hybrid has a separate gear to provide reverse. Tech B says that Toyota hybrids use a VDP CVT transmission. Who is correct?
   a. Tech A
   b. Tech B
   c. Both A and B
   d. Neither A nor B

6. Tech A says that VDP CVTs are commonly rebuilt. Tech B says that VDP CVTs require more frequent fluid changes than a conventional automatic transmission. Who is correct?
   a. Tech A
   b. Tech B
   c. Both A and B
   d. Neither A nor B

7. Tech A says that some CVTs require a heating system to warm the transmission fluid during cold weather operation. Tech B says that CVTs use conventional automatic transmission fluid. Who is correct?
   a. Tech A
   b. Tech B
   c. Both A and B
   d. Neither A nor B

8. Tech A says that VDP CVTs will often have a planetary gear set to produce reverse. Tech B says that many CVTs in vehicles use a rubber drive belt between two pulleys to transfer power. Who is correct?
   a. Tech A
   b. Tech B
   c. Both A and B
   d. Neither A nor B

9. Tech A says that two-mode hybrid transmissions use two electric motors to propel the vehicle. Tech B says that the two-mode hybrid transmission can use one motor to propel the vehicle and one to charge the battery. Who is correct?
   a. Tech A
   b. Tech B
   c. Both A and B
   d. Neither A nor B

10. Tech A says that the Honda IMA system uses a thin electric motor between the engine and the CVT transmission. Tech B says that the Honda IMA system uses voltages between 144 and 158 volts. Who is correct?
    a. Tech A
    b. Tech B
    c. Both A and B
    d. Neither A nor B

SECTION IV

Manual Transmissions

CHAPTER 22

NATEF Tasks

There are no NATEF tasks for this chapter.

Knowledge Objectives

After reading this chapter, you will be able to:
1. Describe the principle of mechanical advantage. (p 612)
2. Describe the meaning of gear ratio. (pp 612–613)
3. Describe the trade-off between mechanical advantage and the rotational speed of gears. (pp 612–613)
4. Calculate the gear ratio of given sets of gears. (pp 612–613)
5. Describe the principle of power flow. (pp 613–614)
6. Describe the purpose of the drive train, its operation, and components. (pp 614–615)
7. Identify spur and helical gears. (pp 615–617)
8. Describe radial and axial loads. (pp 615–617)
9. Describe the purpose of the clutch. (p 617)
10. Describe the purpose of the transfer case. (pp 619–620)
11. Describe the purpose of the final drive and differential assembly. (pp 619–620)
12. Describe the difference between a live axle and a dead axle. (p 620)
13. Describe preventive maintenance and the importance of lubrication. (pp 620–621)

Manual Transmission/ Transaxle Principles

Skills Objectives

There are no skills objectives for this chapter.

Introduction

In this chapter, we will explore the history and principles of the modern manual transmission **drive train** system. Some of those principles involve certain aspects of physics, such as mechanical advantage and gear ratios. Other principles require an understanding of the nomenclature and theory of operation of the major drive train assemblies. Having a good understanding of these principles will give you a framework on which to hang the higher-level theory and concepts covered in later chapters.

A good starting place is to understand what is meant by "drive train." The drive train consists of the component assemblies that transmit power from the engine all the way to the drive wheels. The manual transmission is at the heart of the drive train and receives power from the engine by way of the clutch assembly. The clutch can be operated by the driver to disconnect and connect the transmission from the engine. The transmission provides the driver with a range of shiftable gears from which to select as he or she is operating the vehicle. In a front-engine, rear-wheel drive vehicle, the transmission sends power to the final drive assembly, which then changes the direction of the twisting force 90 degrees so it can be sent out the axles to the wheels and tires. In a front-engine, front-wheel drive vehicle, the transaxle contains both the transmission and the final drive assembly in a common unit and sends the power out the axles to the front wheels and tires. In four-wheel drive vehicles, the transmission or transaxle sends power to all four wheels and tires.

History of Manual Transmissions

In 1877, a patent for a front-wheel drive carriage with a one-cylinder engine was obtained by George Selden. The "claim to fame" of that vehicle was the transmission **FIGURE 22-1**. The power from the engine drove a set of bevel gears, which in turn drove a shaft and a pulley. Leather belts were used on a pulley and a geared wheel on the axle to make it move. One small wheel on the engine got the car going by meshing with the ring gear

FIGURE 22-1 The engine and transmission, which were on the front axle, drove this early vehicle.

You are the Automotive Technician

A customer brings his Buick into the dealership for its 60,000-mile preventive maintenance service appointment. He has faithfully followed the manufacturer's preventive maintenance schedule since he bought the vehicle and would like to have his manual transmission/transaxle and drive train components serviced today. He believes that if you follow the specific manufacturer's schedule, the vehicle will last forever.

1. Why is preventive maintenance so important for the service life of the transmission/transaxle and drive train components?
2. What rationale would you give a customer to have regular maintenance on these parts rather than rebuilding?
3. Why does understanding how the power flows help you to diagnose manual transmission concerns more easily?

on one of the drive wheels. The big wheel on the axle then made the car move along at a staggering, at the time, 20 miles per hour.

This early engine had one belt-driven high gear for speed and one belt-driven low gear for increased torque. If the car needed to climb a hill, the driver had to stop, get out, and change the belt to the lower gear. This setup was similar to a 10-speed bicycle, where the bike has a shifting mechanism to physically move a chain from one gear to another.

In 1894, a couple of Frenchmen, Louis René Panhard and Émile Levassor, designed a front-wheel drive multi-gear manual transmission **FIGURE 22-2**. When they tried to put on a demonstration of their new transmission, the engine in their demo vehicle encountered problems and they were unable to make it move under its own power. One year later, Panhard and Levassor successfully demonstrated their new multi-gear transmission. Their transmission and clutch arrangement is the prototype for most manual transmissions today in that it used a clutch-driven, three-speed, sliding gear transmission. When the driver wanted to shift gears, he or she would push the clutch pedal to disengage the engine. Then the driver would move the shifter lever, which slid the previous gears out of mesh and the newly selected gears into mesh. This process allowed the vehicle to move at higher and lower speeds. This sliding gear arrangement became the basis for nearly all manual transmissions since then, with manufacturers developing enhancements to the design.

Prior to 1898, vehicles were either belt or chain driven. Since the chain or belt was exposed to the elements, this design required frequent maintenance. It could also be dangerous if someone got too close to it.

In 1898, Louis Renault connected an engine to a transmission and created a live rear axle by using a metal axle shaft supported by bushings. Renault then adapted a differential-type rear axle that was based on an idea that American C. E. Duryea had back in 1893. The differential assembly had a number of gears set in such a way as to allow each wheel to turn at its own speed when going around a corner. This alleviated the problems of loss of traction and rapid tire wear due to scuffing of tires when making turns with a solid axle.

By 1904, most of the car makers had adopted the sliding gear manual transmission design in one form or another. Many improvements have been made since then, including the invention of the **gear synchronizer** (syncromesh), which applies a friction device between the gear and the shaft to match the gear speed to the shaft speed. As a result, the gear and shaft spin at the same speed, which allows gear selection to be made without "grinding" of the gears. In 1928, Cadillac introduced the first **synchromesh transmission**. Porsche improved the design in 1952 by using moly-coated steel rings, which were more efficient and reliable and were licensed by many of the manufacturers of the time. In the early 1960s, BorgWarner introduced the modern cone-style synchronizer, which is still widely used today.

> ### TECHNICIAN TIP
>
> In the time span between the sliding gear transmission and the synchromesh transmission, there were other attempts to make it easier for the driver to change gears. In 1907, the Ford Model T was equipped with a transmission that used constantly meshed planetary gear sets. These sets consist of a central gear—called a Sun Gear—that is meshed with multiple planetary pinion gears, which are meshed inside of a ring gear. Although this gear arrangement is not common in manual transmissions, it is widely used in automatic transmissions today.

FIGURE 22-2 Panhard and Levassor's attempt at a front drive axle.

> ### TECHNICIAN TIP
>
> All designs of transmissions since Panhard and Levassor have always had one goal in mind: to make shifting easier for the driver. The easiest transmission to shift is the automatic transmission, which is strictly an American innovation.

▶ Principles of Manual Transmissions

Mechanical Advantage

Mechanical advantage is defined as the amplification of the input force by trading distance moved for greater output force. For example, imagine using a 10' lever to move a large rock. If you place a short section of log (the pivot point) 2' from the end of the lever nearest the rock, you would have a mechanical advantage of 8 to 2 **FIGURE 22-3**. Ratios are normally expressed as the equivalent of the first number to 1; thus, 8 to 2 would be expressed as 4 to 1, which is written as 4:1. Assuming no frictional loss, a lever with this mechanical advantage would exert four times as much force against the rock as the amount of force being applied by the person to the other end of the lever. So we could say the lever gives a mechanical advantage of 4:1.

Given this 4:1 mechanical advantage, if a person pushes the lever down with a force of 100 pounds (lb), the force the lever generates against the rock is 400 lb. By using a lever, the person achieves more output force than he or she puts in. However, the person also is moving the long side of the lever four times as far as the rock side of the lever. So although the output force is four times greater than the input force, the input distance moved is four times greater than the output distance. Also, the input speed is four times faster than the output speed. Thus, the total amount of work on each end of the lever is the same (work = force × distance); it is simply rearranged to give an increase of the output force. The lesson here is that mechanical advantage can be used to generate a larger output force, but it requires an increase in the input distance and speed.

This concept applies directly to manual transmissions. Each set of gears, called a **gear set**, in the transmission provides a certain amount of mechanical advantage and has a specific speed differential associated with it. For example, in low gear, where the smallest gear in the transmission turns the largest gear in the transmission, one complete turn of the small gear will turn the larger gear only a small portion of a full turn. This provides mechanical advantage and is called gear reduction. At the same time, because the small gear is turning much faster than the output gear, the output speed is slow compared to the input speed. The driver can select the transmission gear set that best matches the operating conditions under which he or she is driving. If driving on rough and hilly off-road terrain, then a lower gear will work well. If driving on a smooth, straight, and level freeway, a higher gear will be best.

Gear Ratios

How do gear sets create mechanical advantage? They do so by having different ratios. Gears with the same number of teeth have a ratio of 1:1, meaning that this set of gears has no mechanical advantage. At the same time, there is no difference of speed between the gears; they each turn at the same speed because they have the same number of teeth. A gear set in which the input gear has half as many teeth as the output gear has a ratio of 2:1. **Gear ratios** can be found by comparing the number of teeth each gear has **FIGURE 22-4**. If the drive gear

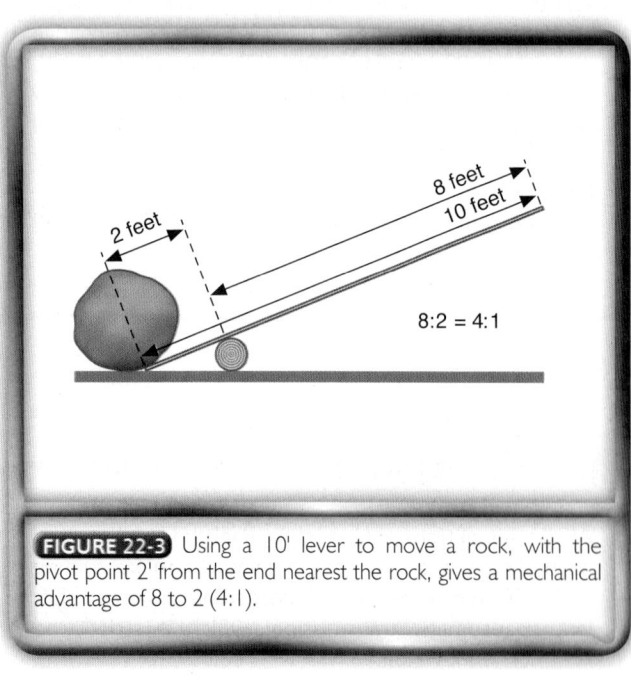

FIGURE 22-3 Using a 10' lever to move a rock, with the pivot point 2' from the end nearest the rock, gives a mechanical advantage of 8 to 2 (4:1).

FIGURE 22-4 The mechanical advantage of two gears with a different ratio, which provides torque to get moving.

(the input gear) has fewer teeth than the driven gear (the output gear), then the gear set will have mechanical advantage because the smaller drive gear has to rotate faster than the larger driven gear, giving an increase in output force.

All gear ratios are calculated by the formula:

$$\frac{\text{Driven}}{\text{Drive}}$$

or the number of driven gear teeth divided by the number of drive gear teeth. For example, if the drive gear has 10 teeth and the driven gear has 30 teeth, then the mechanical advantage is 3:1. In this case, the driven gear has three times the output force (torque), but only one-third of the <u>rotational speed</u>. In other words, if the drive gear is turning at 100 revolutions per minute (rpm), the driven gear is turning at 33.3 rpm, but with three times the torque. If you were to make the drive gear larger by increasing it to 15 teeth and connect it to a driven gear with 30 teeth, the gear ratio would drop to 2:1, but the speed of the driven gear would increase to one-half as fast as the drive gear. In other words, if the drive gear is turning at 100 rpm, the driven gear is now turning 50 rpm, but with only two times the torque.

As the gear ratio decreases, the output speed increases. This is what happens inside of a transmission each time the driver selects a different gear ratio. The output torque and speed can be varied as necessary based on the speed and load of the vehicle. When the vehicle speed is low, the driver selects a lower gear (which has a high gear ratio) so that the engine can be used to accelerate the vehicle. As the engine speed increases, the driver selects the next gear so that the vehicle can be accelerated further. This continues to happen until the vehicle reaches the speed desired by the driver.

Speed and torque output is the result of which gear ratio is selected and gives the driver a wider range of vehicle speeds to choose from, depending on the road conditions. Controlling an automobile over different terrains and weather conditions is accomplished by using the various gear ratios that are appropriate for those conditions. The ultimate task of the manual transmission is to allow the vehicle to move away from a stop by multiplying the torque through use of low gear, which has a high ratio,

> ▸ **LINK**
> Refer to the Manual Transmissions/Transaxles Diagnosis and Maintenance chapter for more information on gear ratio.

> ▸ **Caring for the Customer**
> Following manufacturer-recommended shifting speed guidelines will ensure good fuel economy. In fact, many vehicles have an indicator on the dash that signals the driver when an upshift or downshift would provide better fuel economy.

and, once moving, to allow the driver to sequentially select higher gears as vehicle speed increases.

Power Flow

<u>Power flow</u> is defined as the path in which power is transmitted through a series of components. There is a power flow for the entire drive train. The engine in the vehicle is the main source of all mechanical power for the vehicle. The power that the engine creates flows from the flywheel, which is bolted to the engine crankshaft, to the clutch assembly, which is bolted to the flywheel. When the clutch is released or the pedal is in the up position, the clutch transmits power from the flywheel to the transmission/transaxle. Power leaves the transmission/transaxle and flows to the final drive assembly, where it changes directions and flows through the axles and out to the wheels. This is a very simple and generic explanation of the path for power to flow from the engine to the tires.

When it comes to the manual transmission, power flows into the transmission through the input shaft, where a gear is used to transfer power to a meshed gear on the countershaft. The countershaft has a number of gears that mesh with gears on the output shaft **FIGURE 22-5** . The gear the driver selects will determine the power flow from the countershaft to the output shaft.

FIGURE 22-5 Power flow in a transmission.

Because of the various gear sets and driver selection, the transmission/transaxle has multiple paths for the power to flow along.

▶ Manual Transmission Drive Train Overview

The manual transmission drive train consists of all of the assemblies that transfer power from the engine all the way to the wheels. The **clutch system** is the medium by which the driver can connect and disconnect the engine from the transmission, resulting in the vehicle's forward or rearward movement. On the driver's side, there are usually three pedals on the floor, which, from the driver's right to left, are as follows: the **accelerator pedal**, used for acceleration or deceleration of the engine; the brake pedal, used to stop the vehicle's motion; and the **clutch pedal**, which operates the clutch system. Pushing down on the clutch pedal disconnects the clutch components and allows the selection of the forward or reverse gears within the transmission. Letting the clutch pedal back up reconnects the clutch components and allows the vehicle to move.

The transmission/transaxle is the medium by which the driver selects transitions through the various gear sets to control the speed and power of the vehicle for various types of driving conditions. The term **transmission** relates to layouts where the transmission sends power externally to the final drive assembly and is usually used in rear-wheel drive. The term **transaxle** relates to layouts where the transmission and final drive are integrated into a common assembly and is usually used on front-wheel drive vehicles.

The **final drive assembly** gives the final gear reduction to the drive train and powers the drive wheels through axles **FIGURE 22-6**. The final drive gear ratio takes the torque from the transmission and increases it further by means of mechanical advantage. This has an effect on the torque applied by the wheels to the ground, the speed of the engine, and the fuel economy. If the final drive has a high gear ratio (higher numerical number), then the vehicle will have more pulling power but the engine will operate at a higher rpm at any vehicle speed, thereby decreasing the fuel economy. Manufacturers match the

final drive gear ratio to the vehicle based on the engine, vehicle weight, and expected use of the vehicle.

When a vehicle travels around a corner, the outside wheel travels a greater distance and thus, turns at a faster rate than the inside wheel. If both wheels were connected to a solid axle, the tires would scuff on the road surface. In modern automobiles, the final drive assembly sits between the ends of two separate axles. The final drive assembly incorporates a set of **differential gears** arranged so that they sit between the two axles. This connects them in such a way that they allow each axle to rotate at its own speed while going around a corner. At the same time, the final drive assembly powers both axles through the differential gear assembly.

On rear-wheel drive vehicles, the **drive shaft** transmits power from the transmission to the final drive assembly **FIGURE 22-7**. The drive shaft uses **universal joints**, which allow the drive shaft to change angles due to the

Pinion gear

Spider gears

Ring gear

FIGURE 22-6 Typical final drive assembly.

Transmission

Final drive assembly

Rear tire

Drive shaft

Universal joint

Universal joint

FIGURE 22-7 A typical drive shaft.

FIGURE 22-8 Drive axles. **A.** Solid drive axle. **B.** Half-shaft drive axle.

movement of the suspension relative to the body. Since front-wheel drive vehicles incorporate the final drive in the transaxle, no external drive shaft is needed. Both front-wheel drive and rear-wheel drive vehicles use **drive axles** to power the wheels. The axles can be solid, as is the case with many rear-wheel drive vehicles, or flexible **half-shafts**, which use **constant velocity (CV) joints**, as is the case with front-wheel drive vehicles **FIGURE 22-8**. Front-wheel drive axles must be able to change length as the vehicle goes over bumps and dips and allow for the wheels to be steered. This is provided by different types of CV joints.

Operation

The driver steps on the clutch pedal, which releases the clutch and disconnects the engine from the transmission. Depressing the clutch pedal also closes the contacts of the **clutch safety switch**. The closed clutch safety switch allows the starter motor to crank the engine over when the driver turns the key to the "crank" position. The engine then starts and idles. With the clutch pedal fully depressed, the driver moves the gear shift lever to select first gear or reverse gear. Once in gear, the driver can slowly release the clutch pedal and progressively connect the engine to the transmission.

With the transmission in first gear, the transmission is in the lowest gear; in this gear, the vehicle cannot travel very fast, but it provides the best pulling power. Torque is then sent to the final drive, where its speed undergoes a further gear reduction, which increases the torque again before it is sent to the axles. The axles turn the wheels, which are connected to the ground and cause the vehicle to move. When the driver wants to change gears, he or she pushes the clutch pedal and moves the gear shift lever to the next gear position. Once the gear is selected, the driver again slowly releases the clutch pedal to reconnect the engine and transmission and continues driving the vehicle.

▶ Manual Transmission Components

Today's manual transmissions/transaxles are precisely machined, mechanical wonders packed into a relatively small package. Each of the components plays a critical role in allowing the driver to easily operate the transmission. Understanding the main components will give you a good overview of the transmission, which will help you understand how the individual components fit into the overall function of the transmission. Also, understanding the internal workings provides you with a foundation to draw upon when diagnosing transmission problems. We will now cover some of the main components of the manual transmission.

Shafts, Gears, and Bearings

Inside of a manual transmission is a series of shafts, gears, and bearings that make it possible for the driver to select the preferred gear for the road conditions. The availability of several different gear ratios within the transmission allows the vehicle to accelerate from a dead stop almost effortlessly, as well as travel at a variety of speeds without over-revving the engine.

Shafts are used to support gears and are machined precisely to accommodate bearings and individual gears. The surfaces are smooth, allowing the bearings and gears to rotate on a thin film of oil **FIGURE 22-9** in order to reduce metal-to-metal friction and prevent catastrophic failure from overheating. Some surfaces on the shaft are <u>splined</u> (parallel grooves in a shaft that mate with a component with matching grooves) to allow other parts of the transmission such as synchronizers to be held stationary on the shaft. Other machining may create raised areas on the shafts such as shoulders, which provide a firm support for gears and bearings to butt up against. Alternately, grooves may be cut into the shafts to accommodate <u>snap rings</u> and <u>thrust washers</u>, which are used for holding the gears in the proper position on the shaft once the gears are installed. The ends of the shafts have machined surfaces to allow for bearings. Bearings are used to center and hold the shafts in alignment so the gears rotate smoothly when in mesh with their mating gears. Friction bearings provide sliding metal-to-metal contact between components and are usually made of brass or bronze. Non-friction bearings provide rolling metal-to-metal contact between components and usually use ball or roller-type bearings.

<u>Gears</u> are round parts with teeth cut on the outside perimeter in order to mate with one or more other gears to achieve a specific gear ratio. The mated gears are called a gear set. Each set is cut on the same angle or pitch to allow for proper contact of the gears with each other. Manual transmission gear teeth are usually of two configurations: spur or helical. <u>Spur gears</u> have straight teeth that are parallel to the shaft the gear turns on **FIGURE 22-10**. They can be noisy during operation. However, they are stronger than helical gears, so they are used in heavy-duty vehicles such as off-road equipment. <u>Helical gears</u> have angled teeth that are cut on an angle to the shaft **FIGURE 22-11**. They operate more quietly and are more commonly used in passenger vehicles.

Bearings are necessary to maintain the position and alignment of the shafts and gears while under two types of loads: radial and axial. <u>Radial loads</u> are perpendicular to the shaft and occur because the gears have a tendency to push each other apart as torque is transmitted between them while driving **FIGURE 22-12**. <u>Axial loads</u> are in line

FIGURE 22-9 Shafts are used to support gears and are machined precisely to accommodate bearings and individual gears.

FIGURE 22-11 Helical gears are cut on an angle for better coverage. They operate quietly.

FIGURE 22-10 Spur gears have straight teeth. They can be noisy during operation.

FIGURE 22-12 Radial-loaded bearing.

with the shaft and occur in transmissions because the cut of the helical gear teeth, which are at an angle to each other, causes a fore and aft load **FIGURE 22-13**. Bearings also allow shafts and gears to have greater rotational speeds, while at the same time minimizing metal-to-metal friction, which contributes to increased fuel economy and longer transmission life. Bearings can be of the friction type or non-friction type. Both are used in transmissions to resist overheating and keep shafts aligned.

> ## TECHNICIAN TIP
>
> Manual transmission failures occur, which is why a proper preventive maintenance program is critical to the life of all parts inside the transmission. Proper oil levels, types, and viscosities contribute to longevity of these units.

Clutch System

In a manual transmission vehicle, the component that locks the engine and transmission together is the clutch system. The engine is connected to the clutch, and the clutch is connected to the transmission. The clutch is designed so it can connect and disconnect. Imagine a wall-mounted dimmer switch for a ceiling light in a house. When the dimmer switch is in the off position, no electrical power is transmitted to the light, resulting in no illumination of the room. When the clutch pedal is in the depressed or down position, no power is transmitted to the transmission, resulting in no forward movement of the vehicle. When the dimmer switch is in the full on position, electrical power is transmitted to the light bulb, resulting in illumination. Similarly, when the clutch pedal is in the released or

up position, power is transmitted to the transmission and forward or rearward movement of the vehicle can be achieved.

Much like the dimmer switch, the clutch pedal requires movement to connect and disconnect power to the transmission many times repeatedly **FIGURE 22-14**. This movement can cause the clutch components to wear (just as wear can be present in the dimmer switch over time). When the dimmer switch is turned on, there is a drag of amperage on the power source as the light draws power to illuminate a room. This is also what happens when the clutch is released—a drag on the engine is required to get the vehicle to move from the stationary position. This transition from no power to power creates heat, which is detrimental to both the dimmer switch and the clutch system. If the clutch is only partially released, there will be only a partial transmission of the power through the clutch, just like power being reduced by the dimmer switch when it is left in a partially on position. The difference is that the dimmer switch is designed to handle the resulting heat, but the clutch is not.

> ## ▶ Caring for the Customer
>
> The clutch system must be inspected and maintained at regular intervals depending on the driver's habits. Customers who tend to slip the clutch, rest their foot on the clutch pedal, or drive aggressively put more wear on the clutch components. It is always a good practice to follow the preventive maintenance schedule to catch a problem before it becomes serious.

FIGURE 22-13 Axial-loaded thrust washer.

FIGURE 22-14 Clutch components are designed to connect and disconnect the power to the transmission.

Transmission/Transaxle

Since the invention of the automobile, the need for a device to control engine power and torque for various applications has been satisfied by the transmission. As vehicle design has evolved over the decades, the transaxle was developed **FIGURE 22-15**. The only difference between the transmission and the transaxle is that the transaxle incorporates the final drive assembly in its construction, making the transmission and final drive a single unit. In a vehicle with a transmission, the final drive is a separate unit.

While an automatic transmission shifts by itself, a manual transmission/transaxle requires input from the driver to determine which gear to select. A manual transmission/transaxle uses a series of shafts, gears, and bearings and the driver's input to select the right gear ratio for the situation. Once a gear ratio is selected, the manual transmission takes the power from the engine and modifies the torque and speed based on the driver-selected gear and sends power to the axles, wheels, and tires. A shifting mechanism is also a part of the transmission/

FIGURE 22-15 Transmissions/transaxles. **A.** Typical rear-wheel drive transmission. **B.** Typical front-wheel drive transaxle.

> **TECHNICIAN TIP**
>
> Most manual transmissions/transaxles are manually shifted, but some are electronically controlled. This type of transmission will be discussed in detail in the Manual Transmissions/Transaxles Basic Diagnosis and Maintenance chapter. In these systems, a computer plays a part in how and when the shift will occur. These new electronic systems require the use of a scan tool to diagnose faults in the transmission as well as to program all parameters for transmission shifting.

> **TECHNICIAN TIP**
>
> The manufacturer determines the gear ratios in the transmission/transaxle based on the power-to-weight ratio, the vehicle size, the application, and the intended use. This concept will be discussed in depth in the Manual Transmissions/Transaxles Basic Diagnosis and Maintenance chapter.

transaxle and is used by the driver to select the appropriate gear for the driving conditions during upshifts and downshifts.

Transmissions/transaxles are rated by the manufacturers for how much twisting force (torque), measured in foot-pounds (ft-lb), they can handle. This rating system ensures that the transmission/transaxle is strong enough for the engine it is used with. Automobile manufacturers design transmissions to be used with their various vehicles—be it a passenger vehicle, pick-up truck, or sport utility vehicle (SUV)—and to meet customer expectations. In some cases, customers have a choice between a five-speed and a six-speed transmission, or between a six-speed and a seven-speed.

Transfer Case

The **transfer case** is typically mounted to the rear of the transmission. Its purpose is to transfer power to both the front and rear axles, providing four-wheel drive so the vehicle can move with more stability in inclement weather and compromised road conditions. Steering ability is also increased, making the vehicle track better in slippery conditions.

The transfer case takes the power from the transmission and directs it to one or both axles, depending on the mode selected **FIGURE 22-16**. This system requires that the front wheels be powered; thus, a front differential and two front axles were added. A second drive shaft is necessary to provide power to the front axle assembly.

FIGURE 22-16 A typical transfer case used for four-wheel drive.

The transfer case and the manual transmission are similar in operation in that they both have a series of shafts, gears, and bearings and include shift mechanisms. The transfer case can be made of cast iron to provide strength or magnesium or aluminum to lessen the weight. It also is filled with lubricant to reduce friction, increase life span, and maintain quiet operation of the gears by providing a thin film of oil between them.

Transfer cases can be operated manually or electronically. Mechanically shifted transfer cases have a shift lever that is usually next to the transmission gear shift. The transfer case shift lever is also usually shorter, since it is not used as frequently as the transmission gear shift. Electronically shifted transfer cases use either an electronically controlled vacuum actuator or an electric motor to shift the transfer case. Sensors may be used to operate a light that informs the driver which mode is selected.

> **TECHNICIAN TIP**
>
> There are two types of four-wheel drive systems—full-time four-wheel drive and part-time four-wheel drive. These will be explained in greater depth in the Drive Train Components chapter. Most manufacturers of SUVs incorporate some form of four-wheel drive or all-wheel drive as a selling/safety feature to the public. Early four-wheel drive vehicles were not very fuel efficient due to heavy and bulky designs. Over time, manufacturers have made fuel efficiency and safety priorities.

Differential and Final Drive

The term *differential* is used in two different ways. The first is the most technically accurate and refers to the components inside of the differential housing that allow the axles to turn at different speeds when the vehicle is cornering or turning. This is called the differential assembly. Since the outside tire must travel farther when cornering than the inside tire, it must turn at a faster speed. The differential assembly allows this to happen; otherwise, the tires would bind, skip, hop, and slide when going around a corner, which causes them to wear out quickly and could easily cause a loss of vehicle control.

The second way technicians use the term *differential* is as another name for the complete final drive assembly. The final drive assembly provides the final gear reduction necessary for drive train operation. The gear reduction happens because the drive gear (called a pinion gear) is much smaller than the driven gear (called the ring gear). This difference in size results in an increase in mechanical advantage. In addition, the final drive assembly takes the power from the transmission, turns it 90 degrees, and sends it out the axles to the tires. Then the differential assembly allows the tires to travel around corners without binding while the final drive is powering them. Since the differential assembly is housed within the final drive assembly, many technicians simply call the entire final drive assembly the differential. Any time you hear the term *differential*, you need to ask whether the speaker means the final drive assembly or the differential assembly.

There are two types of rear axle assemblies used in modern vehicles: the solid rear axle and the independent rear axle. The **solid rear axle** uses a solid axle housing, which means movement of one wheel affects the other wheel. As the wheel on one side of the vehicle hits a bump, the wheel on the other side pivots, affecting the ride of the vehicle. An **independent rear axle** allows each wheel to move independently of the other wheel, which results in a more comfortable ride and better handling.

Differential assemblies also come in two varieties. First, there is the **open differential assembly**. With the open differential assembly, power is supplied to both

> **TECHNICIAN TIP**
>
> If the vehicle is equipped with traction control, the traction control system can help overcome the loss of traction by applying the brakes to the wheel that is slipping. This results in more power being sent to the wheel that is not slipping.

> **TECHNICIAN TIP**
>
> Preventive maintenance is important because the axles are filled with special lubricants and additives that promote long life and maintain quiet operation of the gears. Maintenance schedules help technicians know when each component requires maintenance and when visual and physical inspection are due, thus preventing premature failure.

wheels equally only when each tire maintains traction, which is not likely on ice and snow. If one wheel is stuck in the snow or ice, the other wheel cannot supply power because of the nature of the open differential assembly. The second type is the **limited slip differential assembly**, which allows both of the rear wheels to supply power to the ground in order to continue forward motion.

Drive Axle

The drive axle is the component that supplies the power from the final drive to the wheels. It is part of the **drive axle assembly**. There are two types of axles—live and dead. A **live axle** powers the wheels attached to it. **Dead axles** allow the wheels to freely rotate on the axle assembly and do not drive the wheels.

There are two types of live axles. The first type is the **independent suspension drive axle**. It uses one half-shaft axle for each of the two wheels. These axles must flex to allow suspension movement, so they incorporate what are called constant velocity (CV) joints. CV joints connect the transaxle final drive to the wheels. CV joints are known for their flexibility in allowing greater operating angles; they are used to allow for steering of the front wheels while at the same time supplying them with power. Rubber boots are on each end to contain the lubricant that lubricates each CV joint to maintain its integrity.

The second type of live axle in use today is the **solid axle**. These axles are fitted within a strong housing. The outer ends of the axles have flanges with studs and nuts that are used to secure matching-sized wheels and tires. The other end of the axle has splines that slide into the differential side gears inside the differential housing. This is where the solid axle gets its power from. There are three types of solid live axles used today in rear-wheel drive vehicles: the semi-floating axle, the three-quarter floating axle, and the full floating axle. All three types will be discussed in detail in the Drive Train Components chapter.

Preventive Maintenance

Preventive maintenance is designed to extend the service life of the transmission/transaxle and drive train components. It usually consists of checking and replacing lubricants on a regular basis, lubricating linkage pivot points, performing adjustments such as the clutch adjustment, and inspecting all drive train components for damage or wear. Maintenance also improves the reliability of the vehicle and helps prevent vehicle breakdowns that could leave the occupants stranded. Although most vehicle owners understand this, not all of them choose to have professional preventive maintenance performed on a regular basis. Many owners do not know the extent of the maintenance needed or how it is performed. This is where you come in. By learning how the components operate, what maintenance is needed, and how to perform it, you can help the customer get the maximum reliability and life span out of the vehicle.

> **Caring for the Customer**
>
> Most of the problems that occur in transmissions/transaxles occur because much of the public is unaware that periodic maintenance of the drive train is needed on a regular basis. As a technician, you need to help the customer understand that in almost all cases, maintenance is much less expensive than rebuilding the drive train units.

Lubrication

When it comes to lubrication, every component in the manual transmission requires lubrication according to manufacturer specifications even after the warranty runs out. Clutches, the transmission, the final drive, drive shafts, and drive axles need to be checked or lubricated to maintain their integrity on a regular basis. Proper lubricants will ensure that all manual transmission components last a long time. Manufacturers have used a variety of lubricants for their particular transmissions over the years. The most common lubricant is gear lube. However, some manufacturers have used a specific weight of engine oil. Some manufacturers even specify automatic transmission fluid for their manual transmission. Considering the amount of stress put on the manual transmission, it is important to maintain all lubricants on a regular basis.

The transmission/transaxle and differential lubricant/oil levels keep all rotating parts cool by removing heat and transferring it to the case, which can dissipate the heat to the atmosphere. The lubricant also supplies a thin film of oil between close tolerances of gears, shafts, and bearings to reduce metal-to-metal contact. This oil film prolongs the life of these parts. Improper lubricant/oil levels could cause leaks and unwanted failures to occur.

Components such as CV joints require different types of semisolid lubricants or grease. Considering the amount of torque that CV joints must endure, special lead-based grease is used in most applications. Grease possesses a property called **thixotropy**. This term refers to its ability to be a solid but while under stress to flow or become thin in order to lubricate properly. Many types of semisolid lubricants are in use today. Always remember to consult the manufacturer's service information for correct usage.

TECHNICIAN TIP

A good preventive maintenance program will keep on top of all leaks and fluid losses. Always consult manufacturer specifications for correct fluid types.

Wrap-up

Ready for Review

- The drive train comprises component assemblies that transmit power from the engine to the wheels.
- Early engines had belt-driven gears that required drivers to manually change the belt.
- Some form of the multigear transmission, with clutch operation, has been used since its invention in 1894.
- A gear synchronizer matches the gear speed and the shaft speed to allow gear selection without "grinding" the gears.
- Mechanical advantage refers to gaining greater output force by increasing input distance, such that the total work on either end is equal (work = force × distance).
- Each gear set creates mechanical advantage by the ratio of teeth of the input gears to that of the output gears.
- Gear ratios are calculated by the number of driven gear teeth divided by the number of drive gear teeth; as the gear ratio decreases, the output increases.
- Power flow refers to the path by which power is transmitted from one component to another.
- The manual transmission drive train consists of the clutch system, transmission/transaxle, and final drive assembly.
- When depressed, the clutch pedal disconnects the engine from the transmission and allows the driver to change gears.
- Releasing the clutch pedal reconnects the engine to the transmission.

- The main components of a manual transmission are shafts, gears, bearings, and the clutch assembly.
- Shafts support the gears, and bearings maintain the position and alignment of shafts.
- Helical gears have angled teeth; spur gears have straight teeth and are stronger than helical gears.
- Transaxles have final drive assemblies incorporated into their construction.
- Transmissions/transaxles are rated as to how much torque they can handle.
- The transfer case transfers power to both axles to provide four-wheel drive.
- Differential refers to the components that allow the axles to turn at different speeds when a vehicle is cornering.
- The final drive assembly houses the differential and provides the final gear reduction necessary for drive train operation.
- Differentials can be open or limited slip.
- Drive axles supply power from the final drive to the wheels.
- An axle can be live (powers the wheels attached to it) or dead (allows the wheels to rotate freely).
- The two types of live axles are independent suspension and solid (which can be semi-floating, three-quarter floating, or full floating).
- Preventive maintenance extends the service life of the transmission/transaxle and drive train components.
- All components of the manual transmission require lubrication.

Key Terms

accelerator pedal The foot-operated pedal used by the driver to increase and decrease the amount of power the engine develops.

axial load The load applied in line with a shaft. It can be controlled with thrust bearings.

clutch pedal The foot-operated pedal used by the driver to engage and disengage the clutch.

clutch safety switch An electrical switch that is operated by the clutch pedal and keeps the starter motor from cranking the engine over until the clutch is fully depressed.

clutch system A mechanically operated assembly that connects and disconnects the engine from the transmission.

constant velocity (CV) joints Joints commonly used in front-wheel drive vehicles to allow flexibility of the axle while turning.

dead axle An axle that supplies no power to the wheels.

differential gears Gears situated in the final drive assembly that are meshed together and with both axles, allowing the wheels to rotate at different speeds when turning a corner.

drive axle assembly The components that make up the drive axle including the axles, final drive assembly, bearings, and axle housing.

drive axle An axle that provides power to a wheel.

drive shaft The hollow tube with flexible joints on each end that transmits power from the transmission to the final drive unit.

drive train The component assemblies that transmit power from the engine all the way to the drive wheels.

final drive assembly An assembly used to power the drive wheels and allow the wheels to rotate at different speeds as the vehicle turns.

gear ratio The description of the difference in speed between gears in mesh, determined by comparing the number of teeth on each gear (driven/drive). For example, a gear set that has a drive gear with 5 teeth in mesh with a driven gear of 25 teeth has a gear ratio of 5:1.

gear set Two or more gears that are in mesh with each other.

gear synchronizer An assembly in the transmission that is used to bring two unequally spinning shafts or gears to the same speed when upshifting or downshifting.

gear A relatively round, rotating part with internal or external teeth that are designed to mesh with another gear for the purpose of transmitting torque.

half-shaft An axle that has CV joints on each end and that fits between the transaxle and wheel. Typically, one is used on each side of a vehicle.

helical gears Gears that have teeth set on an angle to the gear face; they operate more quietly than spur gears.

independent rear axle A type of rear suspension system that allows each wheel on the axle to move independently of the other.

independent suspension drive axle A type of suspension that allows each wheel on a drive axle to move independently of the other.

limited slip differential assembly A differential assembly that uses a clutch assembly or gear assembly to allow a limited amount of slip between the two axles. It is used to increase drive wheel traction in slippery conditions.

live axle An axle that provides power to the wheels.

mechanical advantage The process of using a device to get more output force than the amount of input force, with the trade-off being that the input distance is proportionately longer than the output distance.

open differential assembly A differential assembly that allows both axles to turn at their own speed when turning a corner, but is dependent on the traction of the tires to deliver torque to the ground. If one wheel has no traction, all of the engine's torque will be used at that wheel, causing it to simply spin.

power flow The path that power takes from the beginning of an assembly to the end. In a transmission, power flow changes as different gears are selected by the driver.

radial load The load that is perpendicular to a shaft, usually controlled by bearings or bushings.

rotational speed The speed at which an object rotates, measured in revolutions per minute (rpm).

shaft The long, narrow component that carries one or more gears or has gears machined into it.

snap ring The spring-steel C-shaped ring that is fitted in a groove and holds gears, bearings, and shafts in place.

solid rear axle A type of axle that has a one-piece axle housing, so that the action of hitting a bump with one wheel affects the other wheel.

solid axle A type of axle that is not flexible, with splines on one end to fit the final drive unit and a flange on the other end to power the wheel.

splined Typically, a shaft and gear that have parallel grooves machined in them so they mate with each other and lock together rotationally.

spur gears Gears with straight-cut gear teeth.

synchromesh transmission A modern transmission that uses gear synchronizers to match the speeds of gears and shafts during upshifts and downshifts.

thixotropy The ability of a semisolid grease to flow when agitated or stressed.

thrust washers Flat, washer-shaped bearings that provide a wear surface between two rotating components that are loaded axially.

transaxle A drive train layout in which the transmission and final drive are integrated into a common assembly; used most often on front-wheel drive vehicles.

transfer case An assembly used in four-wheel drive vehicles to transmit power to either two wheels only or all four wheels.

transmission An assembly that houses a variety of gear sets that allow the vehicle to be driven at a wider range of speeds and terrain conditions than would be possible without a transmission.

universal joint A cross-shaped joint with bearings on each leg where one set of parallel legs is connected to the end of one shaft and the other set of parallel legs is connected to the end of a second shaft. This arrangement allows the shafts to operate at shallow angles to each other.

ASE-Type Questions

1. Tech A says that friction bearings are made up of balls and rollers. Tech B says that non-friction bearings are in sliding contact between moving surfaces. Who is correct?
   a. Tech A
   b. Tech B
   c. Both A and B
   d. Neither A nor B

2. Tech A says that gear ratios are all the same in any five-speed transmission. Tech B says that gear ratios vary from transmission to transmission. Who is correct?
   a. Tech A
   b. Tech B
   c. Both A and B
   d. Neither A nor B

3. Tech A says that a road test is helpful in diagnosing transmission issues. Tech B says that having a thorough understanding of the customer concern is important when diagnosing transmission issues. Who is correct?
   a. Tech A
   b. Tech B
   c. Both A and B
   d. Neither A nor B

4. Tech A says that gear lube can be used in all manual transmissions. Tech B says that some manual transmissions use engine oil as a lubricant. Who is correct?
   a. Tech A
   b. Tech B
   c. Both A and B
   d. Neither A nor B

5. Tech A says that the final drive is used to provide an increase in the rotational speed of the axles. Tech B says that the final drive is used to provide an increase of twisting force to the axles. Who is correct?
   a. Tech A
   b. Tech B
   c. Both A and B
   d. Neither A nor B

6. Tech A says that a gear set that has a drive gear with 9 teeth and a driven gear with 27 teeth has a gear ratio of 3:1. Tech B says that the drive gear is also called the output gear. Who is correct?
   a. Tech A
   b. Tech B
   c. Both A and B
   d. Neither A nor B

7. Tech A says that transmission fluid levels are critical to the life of the transmission. Tech B says that transmission oil should be changed when changing the engine oil. Who is correct?
   a. Tech A
   b. Tech B
   c. Both A and B
   d. Neither A nor B

8. Tech A says that a road test is part of a good process for diagnosing a customer drive train complaint. Tech B says that the ring gear and pinion gear are part of the final drive assembly. Who is correct?
   a. Tech A
   b. Tech B
   c. Both A and B
   d. Neither A nor B

9. Tech A says that the clutch uses a cone-style synchronizer to match the speed of the engine to the manual transmission. Tech B says that the fill plug hole is where to check the fluid level in most manual transmissions. Who is correct?
   a. Tech A
   b. Tech B
   c. Both A and B
   d. Neither A nor B

10. Tech A says that the differential assembly provides a means for the inside and outside wheels to turn at different speeds when going around a corner. Tech B says that the differential assembly provides smooth shifts and reduces gear "grinding" by matching gear speeds. Who is correct?
    a. Tech A
    b. Tech B
    c. Both A and B
    d. Neither A nor B

CHAPTER 23

The Clutch System

Introduction

The clutch is a mechanical device located in the bell housing, which sits between the engine and the transmission **FIGURE 23-1**. The clutch allows the driver to engage and disengage the engine from the transmission while operating the vehicle. The driver controls the operation of the clutch with his or her foot through the clutch pedal. The clutch has a series of components that help to make driving an interactive experience, allowing the driver to control the shifting of gears in the vehicle. An automatic transmission does not use a manual clutch, giving the driver very little control over transmission operation other than to put it in or out of gear.

FIGURE 23-1 The clutch, engages and disengages the engine from the transmission.

Clutch Principles

The purpose of the clutch is to allow the driver to disconnect and progressively connect the engine to the transmission. It progressively transmits torque from the engine to the transmission. It also allows the driver to disconnect the transmission from the engine for the purpose of shifting between gears while accelerating or decelerating the vehicle.

Automotive manual transmission clutches are dry clutches, as opposed to wet clutches in automatic transmissions, which run in a lubricating fluid. Dry clutches use the friction between the clutch surfaces to transmit torque from the engine to the transmission. The amount of torque a clutch can transmit depends on the amount of friction between the clutch disc and the mating surfaces of the flywheel and pressure plate. This friction is dependent on four variables: the **coefficient of friction** of the clutch disc facings, the diameter of the clutch, the number of clutch discs in the clutch assembly, and the total spring force clamping the parts together.

Increasing the friction of the clutch disc increases the torque-carrying ability, but makes the clutch grab, which makes it more difficult to start from a stop. Increasing the diameter of the clutch gives it more leverage, which increases its torque capacity, but takes up more area. Increasing the number of clutch discs increases torque capacity, but is more complicated due to the extra parts. Increasing the spring force clamping the parts together increases torque capacity, but takes more foot pressure to operate the clutch pedal. Manufacturers balance all of these factors when designing a clutch for a particular application.

You are the Automotive Technician

A customer brings her 2000 Ford Mustang into the shop for a clutch inspection. She has noticed the clutch slipping when she is in 4th gear, driving on the highway. You inform the customer that it would be beneficial to perform a road test to properly diagnose this problem. She is reluctant, and decides that she is not comfortable giving you the keys to her Mustang. As an experienced auto technician, you suggest performing a test in the shop to determine the necessary repair.

1. What is the first step in determining the necessary repairs on the clutch?
2. Why is a test drive important to help diagnose clutch system issues?
3. What are the main components to the clutch assembly?
4. What is the difference between single-plate and multi-plate clutches?

Input and Output Shaft Speed

Because vehicles are dependent on shifting between various gears to be able to drive down the road at a variety of speeds, it is important to understand how the transmission input and output shaft speeds play a critical role in shifting. First, you need to understand that output shaft torque and speed can each be increased, but not at the same time. In low gear, the input shaft speed is relatively high, while the output shaft speed is relatively low. This results in an increase of torque from the output shaft. However, the speed of the output shaft (and the speed of the vehicle) is relatively low. This setup makes for good acceleration from a stop or slow speeds. As higher transmission gears are selected, the output shaft speed increases with each higher gear. However, the torque of the output shaft is lessened with each higher gear, allowing the vehicle to travel at higher speeds without over-revving the engine, but with decreased torque.

The second role that the input and output shaft speeds play is during the actual shift. When transitioning from one gear to another, the relative speeds of the shafts must change to allow the gears to shift from one set to another. In order for a gear to be selected, at least one of the shafts must be able to turn freely for this speed change to happen. The input shaft is able to connect to and disconnect from the engine's flywheel through the operation of the clutch, thus allowing the input shaft's speed to change during a shifting of the gears. Since the output shaft is connected directly to the wheels through the drive train components, it cannot be disconnected. This means that any time the vehicle is moving, the output shaft is turning. The faster the vehicle speed, the faster the rotation of the output shaft. This has an impact on shifting because the speeds of both shafts must be such that the individual gears can be selected. The clutch plays the role of engaging and disengaging the input shaft, so the input shaft speed can be changed as needed.

▶ Clutch Components

The main components of a clutch assembly are the **flywheel**, **clutch disc**, **pressure plate**, **throw-out bearing**, **clutch fork**, and **pilot bearing** **FIGURE 23-2**.

The flywheel bolts onto the rear of the crankshaft, and the pressure plate bolts onto the flywheel. Most light vehicles use a single-plate, clutch disc with two friction facings attached to a central hub and splined to engage the **transmission input shaft**. The friction facings on the clutch disc are clamped between the flat surfaces of the engine flywheel and the spring-loaded pressure plate. With engine rotation, the flywheel and pressure plate rotate together with the clutch disc. The flywheel and pressure plate are the drive unit, and the clutch disc is the driven unit. Engine torque is transferred from the flywheel and pressure plate through the friction facings of the driven clutch disc to the splines of the input shaft and into the transmission.

Pushing the clutch pedal operates the **release mechanism**, which controls the flow of torque between the engine and the transmission. Depressing the clutch pedal retracts the pressure plate against the force of its springs and frees the friction disc from its clamping action **FIGURE 23-3**. Releasing the clutch pedal

FIGURE 23-2 A standard light vehicle clutch.

FIGURE 23-3 Depressing the clutch pedal retracts the pressure plate against the force of its springs or diaphragm and frees the friction disc from its clamping action.

reapplies the clamping force and reconnects the engine and transmission by firmly clamping the clutch disc between the pressure plate and the flywheel, allowing them to rotate as a unit **FIGURE 23-4**.

Flywheel

The main purpose of the flywheel is to smooth out the power pulses from the pistons during the power strokes. It also provides a friction surface for the clutch disc and a mounting surface for the pressure plate **FIGURE 23-5**. The flywheel is quite heavy. It is usually made of cast iron so that it can store energy from each power pulse from the engine; it uses that energy to keep the crankshaft turning through the intake, compression, and exhaust strokes. However, a heavy flywheel means that it slows the engine's acceleration. A lighter flywheel does not smooth out the power pulses as effectively, but it works

well on a drag-racing car, for example, because it allows the engine to accelerate faster.

The flywheel is bolted to the rear of the crankshaft and allows the crankshaft to mate with the transmission via the clutch system. It also incorporates the __flywheel ring gear__, which enables the starter motor drive gear to crank the engine over. In most cases, the ring gear is made of hardened steel and is press-fitted onto the outer edge of the flywheel.

Types of Flywheels

There are two main types of flywheels: the single one-piece flywheel and the dual mass flywheel. The single one-piece flywheel is by far the most common on light vehicles and is what most people think of when they think of a flywheel. Its one-piece construction makes it simple, inexpensive, and reliable. It usually has a starter ring gear pressed onto its outer edge and a machined mating surface for the clutch disc. The center of the flywheel has machined holes for bolts to mount it firmly to the flywheel. In some cases, the bolt pattern is equal so it can be mounted in any position. In other cases, where the flywheel is used as the primary method of balancing the engine, it may have offset bolt holes so it can be mounted in only one position on the crankshaft. It is generally designed for a particular application, so do not try to use a flywheel from one type of engine on another type.

Some flywheels are of the stepped style. In this design, the friction surface of the flywheel is recessed, while the outer diameter, against which the pressure plate is bolted, is raised. The depth of the step is critical for proper operation of the clutch assembly. If it is too deep, the clutch will slip or not engage. If it is too shallow, the clutch will be stiff and may not disengage. Both stepped and flat flywheels can be resurfaced if the wear or defects are minor.

FIGURE 23-4 Releasing the clutch pedal reapplies the clamping force and reconnects the engine and transmission, firmly clamping them together to continue rotating as a unit.

FIGURE 23-5 The flywheel.

TECHNICIAN TIP

Refinishing the flywheel moves the pressure plate toward the engine and away from the throw-out bearing, increasing <u>free-play</u>. If too much material is removed from the flywheel surface, some release mechanisms will not be able to compensate for the loss and the clutch will not fully release. Also, as the flywheel is machined thinner, the clutch center hub may contact the flywheel bolts. So even though most manufacturers do not list a minimum thickness for the flywheel, know that it can cause problems if it becomes too thin.

The dual mass flywheel improves the engine's fuel economy by smoothing out the power pulses and focusing them in the direction of engine rotation. Its inner workings help absorb engine vibrations, thus minimizing gear rattle and putting less strain on the drive train components. This also makes for smoother shifting. There are two basic types of dual mass flywheels. The first is composed of a primary and a secondary flywheel with a series of torsion springs and cushions. The second uses a planetary gear and torsional springs **FIGURE 23-6**.

In the first type of dual mass flywheel, a friction ring is located between the inner and the outer flywheel that allows the inner and the outer flywheel to slip. This

feature is designed to alleviate any damage to the transmission when torque loads exceed the vehicle rating of the transmission. The friction ring is the weak spot in the system and can wear out if excessive engine torque loads are applied. This type of dual mass flywheel also has a center support bearing that carries the load between the inner and the outer flywheel and is fitted with damper springs to absorb shocks.

The second type of dual mass flywheel incorporates planetary gearing along with torsion springs. It is designed for engines with stronger vibrations at lower engine speeds. Some manufacturers use this style for their high-performance vehicles to gain greater driving and shifting comfort. Because of the increased dampening effect at lower engine speeds, the engine can be idled at fewer revolutions per minute (rpm), which reduces fuel consumption slightly.

Dual mass flywheels are most often fitted to light-duty diesel trucks with standard manual transmissions and to higher performance luxury vehicles. However, dual mass flywheels are now being used in economy-type vehicles to dampen vibrations in the drive train. The function of the dual mass flywheel is to absorb torsional crankshaft vibrations, which are twisting forces created in opposite directions. A twisting force happens in one direction when a piston is on the compression stroke and the opposite direction on the power stroke. This vibration is magnified in diesel engines, which have higher compression ratios than gasoline engines. By minimizing the

FIGURE 23-6 There are two types of dual mass flywheels. **A.** The first is composed of a primary and a secondary flywheel with a series of torsion springs and cushions. **B.** The second uses a planetary gear and torsional springs.

torsional vibration, the dual mass flywheel eliminates any potential damage to the transmission gear teeth. If the dual mass flywheel were not used, the torsional vibration could cause increased wear or even chipping of the transmission gears.

The dual mass flywheel construction relocates the light-duty torsional damper from the clutch disc in a one-piece flywheel to the engine flywheel on the dual mass flywheel style. This repositioning and heavy-duty torsional damper dampens engine torsional vibrations much more effectively than is possible with standard clutch disc dampening technology.

> **TECHNICIAN TIP**
>
> Dual mass flywheels are designed to provide maximum isolation of the frequency below the engine's operating rpm, usually between 200 and 400 rpm. They are also most effective during engine startup and shutdown.

Pressure Plates

The pressure plate provides the clamping force to clamp the clutch disc between the pressure plate and the flywheel so that torque can be transmitted between those parts. The force is generated by one or more very strong springs. When the driver pushes on the clutch pedal, the spring(s) in the pressure plate are what the driver is pushing against. Pushing the clutch pedal compresses the spring(s) and removes the clamping force from the clutch disc. Releasing the clutch pedal allows the spring(s) to apply their clamping force to the clutch disc again. Most

automotive pressure plates are of either the diaphragm spring style or the coil spring style.

Diaphragm Pressure Plate

In light vehicles, the pressure plate is normally a diaphragm type and is serviced as an assembly, which means it is not designed to be disassembled and repaired **FIGURE 23-7**. A **diaphragm pressure plate** consists of a pressed steel cover, a pressure plate with a machined flat surface, a number of spring steel drive straps, and the diaphragm spring. This diaphragm is located inside the clutch cover on two **fulcrum rings**, held in place by a number of rivets passing through the diaphragm. The pressure plate is connected to the cover by the spring steel drive straps, which are riveted to the cover at one end, and two or more projecting lugs on the plate at the other. Retraction clips hold the pressure plate in contact with the outer edge of the diaphragm. During clutch operation, the throw-out bearing pushes on the diaphragm levers. The diaphragm pivots on the fulcrum rings and pulls the outer edge of the diaphragm away from the flywheel. The retraction clips pull the pressure plate away from the clutch disc.

Coil Spring Pressure Plate

The **coil spring pressure plate** uses coil springs to create the clamping pressure and uses release levers to release the clutch disc **FIGURE 23-8**. Typically, three or four release levers are used, depending on if the application is in a car or a truck. The release levers control the movement of the friction portion of the pressure plate. They pivot on the pedestals that are part of the pressure plate housing. When the release bearing pushes

FIGURE 23-7 A diaphragm pressure plate consists of a pressed steel cover, a pressure plate with a machined flat surface, a number of spring steel drive straps, and the diaphragm spring.

the levers toward the flywheel, they pivot and pull the friction portion of the pressure plate back toward the driver, which then relinquishes its clamping pressure on the clutch disc. When the clutch pedal is released, the levers return to their rest position, the clamping force is restored to the clutch disc, torque is transmitted, and the vehicle moves forward.

An advantage of the coil spring pressure plate is that the more coil springs there are, the tighter the clamping force and torque capacity. A disadvantage is that if the clutch disc overheats, the springs can become weak and the clamping force is compromised. This slippage causes more heat, which weakens the coil springs even further. Once a clutch starts slipping, it likely will need to be replaced very soon. Additional disadvantages are that the spring pressure is less evenly spaced on many coil spring pressure plates and there are fewer release levers, which can cause uneven wear on the friction surface over time.

> ## ▶ TECHNICIAN TIP
>
> The coil spring–type pressure plate generally requires more pedal pressure to operate and may be less comfortable to drive. This is why diaphragm pressure plate clutches, which require less pedal effort to operate, are more desirable for light-duty passenger vehicles.

Clutch Disc

The clutch disc is also called a **driven center plate** or a friction disc FIGURE 23-9. The clutch disc provides the friction material needed to transmit engine torque from the flywheel and pressure plate to the input shaft of the transmission. On the clutch disc, the friction facings are riveted to waved spring steel segments, which are themselves riveted to a steel disc. The central alloy-steel–splined hub is separate from the steel disc. Drive is transmitted from the steel disc to the hub through heavy torsional coil springs or rubber blocks. This spring hub arrangement dampens torsional vibrations from the engine. It also absorbs shock loads imposed on the drive line by sudden or violent clutch engagement. A molded friction washer between the hub and the spring retaining plate also acts as a damper.

FIGURE 23-8 The coil spring pressure plate uses coil springs to create the clamping pressure and uses release levers to release the clutch disc.

FIGURE 23-9 The clutch disc components.

Waved spring steel segments located between the friction facings cause the facings to spread apart slightly when the clutch is disengaged and to compress as it is engaged **FIGURE 23-10**. This gives a cushioning effect during clamping of the clutch disc in the pressure plate. These waved springs allow a progressive application of the pressure plate clamping force as the waved springs are being compressed when the pedal is being released. The result is smoother engagement of the clutch when starting from a stop.

Throw-out Bearing and Clutch Fork

The clutch throw-out bearing and clutch fork work together (along with the clutch linkage) to compress the pressure plate springs when the clutch pedal is pressed. Since the pressure plate rotates with the engine flywheel when the engine is running, the throw-out bearing must be able to rotate with the pressure plate while the clutch fork remains stationary. Thus, the throw-out bearing must include a thrust bearing as part of its assembly. Throw-out bearings are usually **thrust-type angular-contact ball bearings** that are pressed onto a **carrier**. The carrier slides on the sleeve of the **front bearing retainer** that extends from the front of the transmission. This is considered a **push-type clutch** design, as the throw-out bearing pushes on the levers of the pressure plate. However, there are pull-type designs used on heavy truck applications. The bearing carrier is located on the clutch release bearing fork **FIGURE 23-11**.

Moving the clutch release fork (clutch fork) brings the bearing thrust face into contact with the pressure plate levers. This causes the bearing thrust face to rotate against the linear motion of the clutch fork and absorb the rotary motion of the levers. The thrust-type angular contact ball bearing is packed with lubricant during manufacture and requires no periodic maintenance during its service life as long as it is not abused and the clutch free-play is maintained.

The clutch fork is usually made of stamped steel or cast iron. It pivots either in the center or at the end inside the bell housing. The pivot is generally screwed into the bell housing and is usually replaceable. The pivot should be inspected for wear and lubricated whenever the clutch is replaced. The release bearing engages in tabs in the clutch fork and is usually held in place by clips.

Not all release bearings are operated by a clutch fork. Some are operated directly by collar-style slave cylinders. These are sometimes called central or concentric slave cylinders because they are donut shaped and fit around the input shaft. This style uses hydraulic pressure to directly push the release bearing against the pressure plate fingers without the use of a clutch fork.

Pilot Bearing

The pilot bearing is essentially an alignment support bearing for the snout of the input shaft to ride on **FIGURE 23-12**. It takes two bearings to support a rotating shaft. The pilot bearing is the front bearing, and at the other end of the

FIGURE 23-10 Waved springs allow progressive application of the clutch.

FIGURE 23-11 A clutch release bearing fork.

FIGURE 23-12 Pilot bearing and input shaft.

input shaft is the transmission input bearing. The pilot bearing can be a brass or bronze bushing, a needle-type bearing, or a roller-type bearing FIGURE 23-13. Larger vehicles, such as trucks, may use a ball bearing type. Some of these bearings are installed in the cavity on the end of the crankshaft, or they may be placed or pressed into the center of the flywheel. To access the pilot bearing, should it fail in any way, the transmission and clutch assembly must be removed. Some vehicles do not require a pilot bearing because of the construction of the input shaft. On this type of shaft, the input shaft is long enough (typically front-wheel drive) so it is supported on the front and back of the transaxle case by support bearings.

▶ Clutch Operation

When initially placing the transmission into gear, the transmission input shaft must be disconnected from the engine to prevent gear grinding. In doing so, the transmission input shaft is stopped to allow the shifting of gears on the stopped transmission output shaft. Because both shafts are stopped, the gears can be engaged without grinding. When moving the vehicle from rest, releasing the clutch pedal gradually engages the clutch. As the **friction facings** on the clutch disc initially allow slippage, the torque is applied progressively until the pressure plate and clutch disc are solidly clamped. If the driver releases the clutch pedal properly, the vehicle will move smoothly away from a stop.

While the vehicle is in motion, the transmission of engine torque must be interrupted for shifting of the gears. The input shaft speed must be able to allow the selected gear to match the output shaft speed. Depressing the clutch pedal disconnects the input shaft from the engine so the input shaft speed can allow the desired

FIGURE 23-13 **A.** Brass or bronze bushing. **B.** Needle-type bearing. **C.** Roller-type bearing.

gear to be engaged. When bringing the vehicle to a stop, the transmission is disengaged by depressing the clutch, which allows the engine to idle while waiting to start moving again.

Clutch Operating Mechanisms

Movement of the clutch pedal is transferred through an operating mechanism to the clutch assembly on the rear of the flywheel. This mechanism may be one of two types of mechanical systems or a hydraulically operated system. The two types of mechanical systems are the linkage style and the cable style. Linkage-style systems use a system of links, rods, and levers between the clutch pedal and the clutch fork. Cable-operated linkage uses a strong cable in a flexible housing. This style offers more flexibility and is easier to install in the factory. Hydraulic systems use a series of steel, plastic, or reinforced rubber lines along with fluid to accomplish movement for engagement and disengagement of the clutch system.

Caring for the Customer

Regardless of the operating mechanism, it is always a good idea for the driver to make sure when shifting gears to completely remove his or her foot from the clutch pedal to preserve the life of the throw-out bearing and friction facings.

Cable Mechanisms

Cable-operated clutch control systems are easily installed in the vehicle during manufacture and take up less overall engine compartment room. The outer cable housing is fixed to the pedal support inside the vehicle and to the transmission bell housing in the engine compartment. The inner cable connects between the upper end of the clutch pedal and an external lever on the end of the clutch fork **FIGURE 23-14**. This lever is part of the clutch fork, which operates the throw-out bearing. Depressing the clutch pedal transfers the movement through the cable, and the throw-out bearing thrusts against the levers on the pressure plate, pushing the clutch pressure plate into the released position.

An adjustment on the clutch cable provides for the specified amount of free-play to be maintained between the throw-out bearing and the pressure plate levers when the clutch pedal is in the released position. This free-play prevents constant contact of the bearing with the pressure plate levers and subsequent rotation of the bearing when the engine is running, which would cause it to wear prematurely as well as produce a rotating sound. Some cable-operated clutches are adjusted manually by turning a threaded nut or collar to obtain the proper free-play. Some vehicles use a **quadrant ratchet**, which automatically adjusts the clutch pedal free-play as needed when the pedal is lifted by the driver's toe.

Hydraulic Clutch Mechanisms

In hydraulic clutch release mechanisms, the clutch pedal acts on a master cylinder connected by a hydraulic tube and flexible hose to a slave cylinder mounted on (external type) or in (internal type) the transmission bell housing **FIGURE 23-15**. The **slave cylinder** operates the clutch fork (external type) or directly on the throw-out bearing (internal type) on some vehicles. With the clutch pedal in the released position, the center valve in the master cylinder is clear of the inlet port and fluid is free to flow to or from the reservoir into the cylinder. This allows for expansion and contraction of the fluid as it heats and cools.

When the clutch pedal is initially depressed, the master cylinder piston moves forward, taking the valve assembly with it. The center valve closes off the inlet port from the reservoir, trapping fluid in the cylinder bore. Further piston movement displaces fluid through the outlet port and into the connecting lines to act on the slave cylinder piston. The movement of the slave cylinder piston is commonly transferred through a pushrod to

FIGURE 23-14 A cable-operated clutch.

FIGURE 23-15 A hydraulic clutch control.

the clutch release fork to operate the clutch. In other configurations, the slave cylinder is located directly behind the throw-out bearing and pushes directly on it (collar style). When the clutch pedal is released, displaced fluid returns to the master cylinder and the center valve returns to being slightly clear of the inlet port, allowing excess fluid to return to the reservoir. Most hydraulic clutches are self-adjusting since the clutch fork causes the slave cylinder piston to return as far as necessary, venting any excess hydraulic fluid to the master cylinder reservoir. This system automatically compensates for any clutch disc wear and makes it so the clutch, in most cases, does not have to be adjusted.

Lever-Operated Systems

Older technology systems used a series of levers with an equalizing mechanism called a bell crank (equalizer bar) that rotated and was attached to the engine and the vehicle frame **FIGURE 23-16**. The bell crank pivoted

in plastic or nylon bushings and wore out over time. Adjustments were made at the end of the lever connected to the clutch fork using a threaded rod and lock nuts. As the clutch plate wore, adjustments were necessary to maintain proper clutch pedal free-play so the clutch would operate correctly.

▶ Types of Clutches

Vehicles use different types of clutches depending on the amount of torque they are designed to transmit. Most ordinary light vehicles use a single-plate clutch; it is simple and can carry moderate amounts of torque. Heavier duty or high-performance vehicles may use a multiplate clutch assembly due to the higher torque-carrying ability multiple clutch plates provide.

Single-Plate Clutches

The **single-plate clutch** is the most common type of clutch used on light vehicles. It consists of a friction-type disc and a pressure plate assembly. The friction-type disc has two friction facings and a **splined torsional dampening center hub** that attaches the clutch disc to the transmission input shaft. The pressure plate assembly consists of a pressed steel cover, a pressure plate with a machined flat face, and a segmented diaphragm spring or multiple coil spring assembly **FIGURE 23-17**.

The friction disc is sandwiched between the machined surfaces of the flywheel and the pressure plate when the pressure plate is bolted to the outer edge of the flywheel face. The clamping force on the friction facings is provided by the diaphragm spring or multiple coil springs. When the clutch pedal is depressed, the clamping pressure is released and the flat facings on the pressure plate and

> ### ▶ TECHNICIAN TIP
>
> You might think that because a clutch plate wears over time, the clutch free-play would increase. In fact, it decreases. As the lining wears, the pressure plate levers move backward toward the throw-out bearing, reducing clutch pedal free-play. If the clutch disc wears enough, all of the free-play can be lost, meaning that even with the driver's foot off of the clutch pedal, the linkage is holding some pressure on the lining. This reduces the pressure plate clamping force and, if bad enough, can cause the clutch to slip, leading to a burnt clutch requiring replacement.

FIGURE 23-16 A lever-operated system.

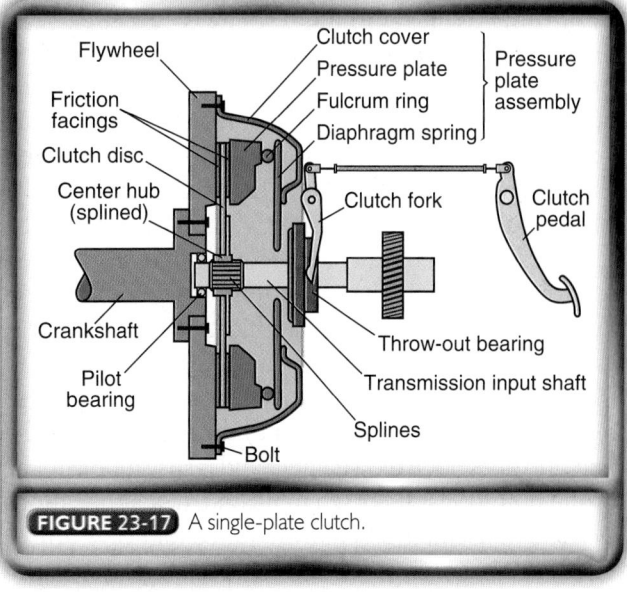

FIGURE 23-17 A single-plate clutch.

flywheel allow the clutch disc to spin free, interrupting the flow of torque. As the clutch pedal is released, the springs in the pressure plate cover exert a clamping force on the clutch disc facing.

The transmission input shaft passes through the center of the pressure plate and into the pilot bearing in the back of the crankshaft or flywheel. The input shaft has parallel splines that engage with the internal splines of the central hub on the friction disc. With engine rotation, the torque can now be transmitted and interrupted by releasing and depressing the clutch pedal. This allows torque to be transmitted from the flywheel and pressure plate, through the friction disc, to the central hub, and to the input shaft of the transmission.

When the clutch pedal is depressed, the movement is transferred through the operating mechanism to the clutch fork and the throw-out bearing. The throw-out bearing moves forward and pushes the center of the diaphragm spring or levers toward the flywheel. This causes the diaphragm spring to pivot on its fulcrum ring. The outer edge of the diaphragm spring moves in the opposite direction and pulls on the pressure plate's retraction clips. This pulling draws the pressure plate away from the clutch disc, and torque is no longer transmitted through the clutch plate. Releasing the clutch pedal allows the diaphragm spring to reapply its clamping force to the clutch disc, which once again transfers torque to the input shaft of the transmission.

Multiplate Clutches

Vehicles that have high-torque engines, such as heavy-duty diesel pick-ups and high-performance vehicles, may use multiplate clutches to handle the torque. Adding plates to a clutch unit to form a **multiplate clutch** increases its torque capacity without increasing the spring strength or clutch diameter **FIGURE 23-18**. The increased torque capacity is due to the increased surface area of the friction materials, which spreads the torque load over a larger surface. A typical multiplate clutch assembly has two friction discs with friction material riveted to both sides of each disc. An internally splined hub on each disc mates with the splines on the transmission input shaft. These hubs can be dampened in normal automotive applications or rigid on heavy-duty and high-performance applications. A damper is a separate part of the hub. It has a series of springs to dampen the twisting pulsations of the engine and helps to prevent damage to the center of the friction disc. The rigid hub does not have a damper and is susceptible to the torque pulsations. It is used in heavy truck applications such as a dual clutch assembly required for heavy torque requirements.

FIGURE 23-18 A multiplate clutch assembly.

A cast-iron separator plate fits between each disc. The separator plate is located on driving pins on the flywheel. These pins drive the separator plate with the flywheel and pressure plate and provide a friction surface that mates to each of the two friction discs. The drive pins must be aligned properly for the separator plate to operate correctly. If these pins are misaligned, the operation of the clutch will result in severe component damage.

The friction discs and separator plate fit between the flywheel and the pressure plate when the pressure plate assembly is bolted to the flywheel. The pressure plate spring then provides a frictional clamping force on each of the mating surfaces.

Torque is transmitted from the flywheel, separator plate, and pressure plate through the friction facings to the transmission input shaft. When the clutch pedal is depressed, the release bearing acts on the pressure plate levers and moves the pressure plate away from the flywheel. This releases the clamping force on the facings and separator plate and allows each clutch driving member to rotate freely without turning the transmission input shaft. When the clutch pedal is released, the spring tension forces the pressure plate, discs, and separator plate against the flywheel, clamping all components together.

▶ Diagnosis

Clutch diagnosis is usually only performed when the driver complains about abnormal sounds or operation of the clutch. Clutch diagnosis generally starts with a test-drive to gather information about the fault. Depending on the condition present, you may be able to determine what is causing the condition based on the test-drive alone. In some cases, further inspection needs to happen to pinpoint the cause. This could include inspecting the linkage or could require the removal of the transmission for further inspection of the clutch components.

To diagnose a clutch issue, obtain the customer concern. If appropriate, test-drive the vehicle to verify the concern. List your observations on the repair order or tasksheet. If the clutch pedal is spongy, you may need to do some preliminary checks, such as checking the level of fluid in the hydraulic clutch master cylinder, before test-driving the vehicle.

Research the concern in the appropriate service information and determine the possible causes of the concern. Next, research the steps to diagnose the concern in the vehicle's service manual. Following the specified procedure, diagnose the cause of the customer concern. Be sure you identify the "root cause" of the concern. For example, if the clutch disc is badly worn, it could be caused by weak pressure plate springs or misadjusted clutch freeplay. Determine any necessary actions to correct the fault.

Common Issues

The more familiar you are with clutch fundamentals and the manufacturer's diagnostic procedure, the more likely you are to successfully diagnose the cause of the customer complaint. Some common clutch-related complaints include noises, pedal pulsations, slippage, clutch binding or drag, clutch vibration, and clutch chatter. These issues will be explored individually.

Noises

Clutch-related noises come from three general places: the pilot bearing, the release bearing, and the transmission input shaft bearing. A worn pilot bearing can make a howling or squeaking sound. The noise generally can be heard by fully depressing the clutch pedal with the engine idling and the transmission in first gear. This causes the pilot bearing to rotate on the input shaft, which will cause noise if the bearing is faulty.

A typical throw-out bearing noise may be more pronounced when the clutch pedal is partially or fully depressed and may disappear when the clutch pedal is released. A growling noise or whirring noise is prevalent when the throw-out bearing is going bad. Thus, forcing the throw-out bearing into the pressure plate levers by slightly depressing the clutch pedal will reveal the difference between a worn pilot bearing and a worn throw-out bearing. A worn throw-out bearing generally will make noise starting with contact of the throw-out bearing with the pressure plate levers, while a pilot bearing will not start making noise until the clutch disengages. A worn throw-out bearing could be caused by a clutch

adjustment that has not been properly maintained or holding the clutch down at stoplights. Noise that occurs when the engine is idling in neutral and the clutch pedal is in the released position may indicate a worn transmission input shaft bearing due to misalignment of the transmission, low transmission fluid level, or abuse by the operator.

Pedal Pulsations

Pedal pulsations are continual up-and-down pulsations due to release bearing contact from diaphragm lever misalignment and coil spring pressure plates that have lever misalignment. Pedal pulsations also may be due to abuse of the clutch, such as heavy slippage while trying to pull a heavy boat and trailer up a steep boat ramp. As a result of the clutch abuse, the flywheel and/or pressure plate may overheat and acquire hot spots.

Excessive slippage from a misadjusted clutch can contribute to overheating of the clutch components and pedal pulsations. To check for this, place your foot on the clutch pedal and lightly push down. Usually the pedal pulsations can be felt as soon as the release bearing starts to contact the pressure plate levers. Further diagnosis will require removal of the clutch assembly and replacement of worn and damaged parts.

Applied | Math

AM-49: Conditionals: The technician understands that if the described problem has certain conditions (symptoms), then there are a limited number of probable solutions.

In all automotive systems, effective diagnosis requires an operational understanding of the system in which the problem has occurred. A typical workshop scenario would be a customer concern regarding a slipping clutch. The presence of the fault would generally be confirmed by a road test before starting work on the vehicle.

As outlined in the chapter, a typical clutch system is made up of only a limited number of components, so the slipping condition can be attributed to only a limited number of causes. Potential causes could include worn clutch plate friction material, over-adjustment causing the release bearing to ride on the pressure plate springs preventing full engagement, weak pressure plate springs creating insufficient clamping force, or oil-soaked clutch plate friction material reducing friction (although this generally results in a clutch chatter condition first).

The diagnostic process should start with the less labor-intensive checks first. For example, you should check the clutch adjustment and check for oil leaks around the bellhousing area before removing the transmission from the vehicle to physically inspect the clutch assembly.

Slippage

A <u>slippage</u> condition can usually be identified while driving the vehicle in fourth gear while accelerating. Observe both the engine speed and the vehicle speed. They should both increase proportionately. If there is slippage, the engine rpm will increase much faster than the vehicle speed. In this case, the clutch is unable to transmit full engine torque so it slips, which is indicated by the increased engine speed.

As the clutch disc starts to wear, it becomes thinner. This results in less clamping pressure from the pressure plate and less clutch pedal free-play. This will then result in an engine rpm increase as slippage starts to occur, which will decrease the amount of torque being transferred to the transmission. To properly diagnosis this problem, a road test is required. You also may be able to feel the slippage as each gear is being shifted and the throttle is being depressed.

Another way to diagnose this condition can be performed while the vehicle is at rest. Engage the emergency brake and shift the transmission into fourth gear. Slowly let the clutch pedal release. If the clutch disc and pressure plate are still working properly, the engine should stall. If the engine continues to run, check the clutch adjustment and then repeat the same procedure. If it fails to stall and continues to run, the assembly must be replaced and the flywheel should be checked for warpage and hot spots. This condition may require flywheel resurfacing or replacement.

Clutch Binding

<u>Clutch binding</u> occurs when the clutch does not quite disengage when the clutch pedal is depressed, causing a dragging of the clutch assembly. Clutch binding causes a grinding noise when shifting into and between gears because the clutch does not fully disengage. Trying to shift into a gear while the gears are being powered by the binding clutch is very difficult and results in the grinding noise. It also can make it difficult to put the transmission into neutral.

If clutch binding is present, it will be evident when trying to engage a gear with the engine running. Clutch binding may result from a damaged clutch disc, a warped clutch disc, or rusted input shaft splines and clutch hub. A bad input shaft bearing or pilot bearing also may cause clutch dragging. Loose transmission bolts cause misalignment of the input shaft, and clutch dragging will occur. A twisted input shaft will affect the engagement and disengagement of the clutch disc. This condition may result from driver abuse or possibly from the driver's foot slipping off the clutch pedal due to rain, snow, or ice.

Other possible causes of clutch binding include a clutch linkage that is bent or binding due to excessive wear, or a damaged or rusted firewall that flexes and does not allow the clutch to be released fully. The firewall can sometimes be reinforced by bolting a metal plate to it.

Clutch Vibration

Clutch vibration can be very annoying to drivers so you need to be familiar with how to diagnose it. First, isolate the type of vibration that is present. <u>Torsional vibrations</u> may be the result of engine parts that are starting to go bad. A vibration damper, flywheel, or clutch disc that is out of balance can cause torsional vibrations. If this is the case, the vibration will be felt throughout the rpm ranges of the engine. <u>Driveline vibrations</u> may come from a loose pressure plate along with motor mounts that are worn and are allowing the engine to contact the frame or cross member. A thorough inspection and diagnosis of all of these conditions should be performed before removal of the clutch assembly parts for inspection.

Clutch Chatter

Clutch chatter should not be taken lightly, as the result may be clutch failure. <u>Clutch chatter</u> is a shuddering feeling as

Caring for the Customer

When diagnosing vehicle problems, it is sometimes helpful to let the owner drive the vehicle while you observe the way he or she operates the vehicle. All too often we take for granted that people drive the way we expect them to. Some problems can be solved only by observing the owner's driving habits, and then educating him or her. A technician tells a story of an elderly lady who had recently purchased a new vehicle. She brought it back several times complaining of a vibration. The technician test-drove and inspected the vehicle each time and found nothing wrong. Finally, he had the customer drive the vehicle while he rode along. He was quite surprised when she put it in gear, pushed down the throttle pedal and spun the tires a good distance, making the wheels hop and creating the vibration she was describing. The technician took her back to the sales department and had her exchange the high-performance version of the vehicle for a less powerful version that fit her needs better. Don't forget—our job is to diagnose almost any problem and find appropriate solutions, and as long as we have all the data available, this can be accomplished.

the clutch pedal is being released. If there is uneven wear of the friction disc or friction surfaces of the pressure plate and flywheel, you may feel chatter as the pressure plate starts to contact the friction disc. Oil on the friction disc from either a leaking rear main seal or front transmission seal can also contribute to this condition.

Too much crankshaft end play from a severely worn crankshaft thrust bearing may also create clutch chatter. As the engine is running, the crankshaft can move back and forth, and a shuttering may be felt. Verification of this may require the removal of the engine oil pan to inspect the thrust bearing. Clutch chatter can also be caused by binding clutch linkage, worn or broken motor mounts, misalignment of the bell housing, a bent or warped friction disc, the friction disc hub binding on the input shaft, or loose friction disc facings. A thorough inspection of each component is required to determine the cause of the chatter.

> ## TECHNICIAN TIP
>
> As with all test-drives, obey all speed laws and treat the customer's car better than your own.

Maintenance and Repair
Clutch Safety and Hazards

Clutch maintenance and repair can be hazardous if the proper safety precautions are not taken. Wear appropriate clothing and eye protection while servicing all clutch components . Gaining access to work on clutches generally requires a lift or jack stands. Always make sure the vehicle is properly secured on jack stands or lifts before performing any type of service. Since transmissions are heavy and awkward to remove and install, use an approved transmission jack along with the appropriate tie-down adapters. In many cases, it is best to get the assistance of another technician when removing or installing a transmission. This will give you an additional set of hands to aid in preventing an injury. Always be mindful of spills and clean the area as necessary to avoid any slips or falls.

Asbestos is a carcinogen. In fine particles, it can be breathed into the lungs, making it a health hazard. It was commonly present in older clutch disc linings. Modern technology has generally replaced asbestos by using organic compound resins with imbedded copper filings and some ceramic materials. Use equipment approved by the Occupational Safety and Health Administration

FIGURE 23-19 Protect yourself by wearing appropriate clothing and eye protection while servicing clutch components.

Safety

Removing a heavy component such as a transmission from a vehicle while it is supported by a hoist can cause the vehicle to shift and possibly fall. It is good practice to always consider how the vehicle's center of gravity will shift with the removal of the component and to set the hoist appropriately. It also is prudent to use support stands to stabilize the vehicle while it is on the hoist. Just remember to not lower the vehicle while the stands are in place.

(OSHA) to remove clutch dust and debris, and follow all local, state, and federal regulations for particulate disposal.

Never use compressed air to blow off clutch parts such as the flywheel, pressure plate, clutch plate, transmission, or engine bell housings. Although it is possible that the dust does not contain asbestos, even non-asbestos dust is hazardous and can damage lungs. Blowing the dust off of parts puts it up in the air where it can be inhaled. OSHA-approved methods entail using either a soap and water solution brushed onto the component to loosen and remove the dust or a vacuum with a high-efficiency particulate air (HEPA) filter that is able to trap very fine particles of asbestos or other dust.

Above all, work in a clean and orderly manner whenever servicing a clutch. Keeping things clean will help prevent grease and dirt stains, and keeping things organized will help ensure nothing is forgotten during reassembly. The end result will show the customer what kind of technician you are. Remember that your main objective is to keep the customer satisfied!

Tools

The following are the main tools used to maintain and repair the clutch system FIGURE 23-20 :

- **Transmission jack**—A tool used to support a transmission during removal and installation.
- **Dial indicator**—A tool used to measure runout or end play in clutch service.
- **Clutch alignment tool**—A tool used to center the clutch plate between the flywheel and the pressure plate during the installation of the pressure plate.
- **Flywheel wrench**—A lever-type tool that grabs onto the ring gear teeth and holds the flywheel while the flywheel bolts are being torqued.
- **Clutch wash station**—Typically an air-operated soap and water cleaning station that is portable and used to clean potential asbestos debris from bell housings and clutch parts.

Preventive Maintenance

Regular preventive maintenance should be performed on the clutch per manufacturer-specified intervals. Clutch pedal free-play should be checked and compared to specifications. Maintaining the specified clutch pedal free-play is critical to maintaining clutch life. This can be accomplished by following the specified adjustment procedures for the clutch system you are maintaining.

The operation of the clutch pedal and return springs should be checked for binding and excessive movement. If a clutch switch is used on the clutch pedal, check that it is functional to prevent cranking the engine while the clutch pedal is released. Mechanical linkage should be inspected for damage and lubricated with specified lubricants at all pivot points.

Hydraulic lines should be checked for leaks at the master cylinder and the slave cylinder. If accessible, pull the boot back on the slave cylinder and inspect it for signs of leakage. Check that all hydraulic lines are not kinked or leaking at their connections. Make sure all hydraulic components are secure in their mountings.

Checking and Adjusting a Mechanical Clutch

As the clutch wears, the friction disc becomes thinner. This results in the pressure plate release levers moving closer to the release bearing and the clutch linkage losing its operational clearance. Some clutches are self-compensating for wear, while others require checking and adjusting. You must refer to the manufacturer's shop information to find out exactly where any adjustment should be made.

FIGURE 23-20 **A.** Transmission jack. **B.** Dial indicator. **C.** Clutch alignment tools. **D.** Flywheel wrench. **E.** Clutch wash station.

It is important to check the clutch linkage mechanism for proper operation and correct the adjustment (free-play) periodically. It is common to do so during every routine maintenance service. If the clutch pedal has too little free-play, the throw-out bearing could remain in contact with the pressure plate levers. As a result, the pressure plate may be unable to apply full pressure, which would result in an incomplete clamping of the disc, leading to premature wear or failure of the clutch assembly and requiring removal and replacement. Also, the pedal will have to be released a long way before the clutch starts to engage. If the adjustment has too much free-play, the clutch pedal may not have enough travel to fully release the pressure plate, causing the gears to clash (grind) when shifting and resulting in heavy synchronizer wear. With this condition, the clutch will start to engage right from the floor when releasing the pedal.

To check and adjust a mechanical clutch, follow the steps in **SKILL DRILL 23-1**:

1 Research the procedure and specifications for inspecting and adjusting the clutch linkage in the appropriate service information. You are looking specifically for the proper clutch pedal height, the proper clutch pedal free-play, and the procedure for making adjustments.

2 Following the specified procedure, inspect the clutch linkage parts for damage, wear, or bent or missing components. Look for signs of binding, looseness, and excessive wear.

3 Start with the clutch pedal assembly and inspect all components under the dash. It is good practice to operate the clutch pedal while you are inspecting the components to observe any looseness or binding. **(Photo 1)**

4 Check the clutch linkage components under the hood for the same signs as the components under the dash. **(Photo 2)**

5 Measure the clutch pedal height. Clutch pedal height is normally measured from the floor pan to the top of the clutch pedal pad with the clutch pedal released. Make sure there are no floor mats or other obstructions that will affect the operation of the pedal. Compare your reading to the specifications and determine any necessary actions to correct any fault. **(Photo 3)**

6 Measure the clutch pedal free-play. Pedal free-play is normally measured from the top of the pedal at rest to where all play is taken up between the pedal and the pressure plate. This can be felt by hand

SKILL DRILL | 23-1 | Checking and Adjusting a Mechanical Clutch

1 Following the specified procedure, inspect the clutch linkage parts for damaged, worn, bent, or missing components. Look for signs of binding, looseness, and excessive wear. Start with the clutch pedal assembly and inspect all components under the dash. Operate the clutch pedal while you are inspecting the components to observe looseness or binding.

2 Check the clutch linkage components under the hood for the same signs of wear or damage as the components under the dash.

3 Measure the clutch pedal height. Compare your reading to the specifications and determine any necessary actions to correct any fault.

SKILL DRILL | **23-1** | **Checking and Adjusting a Mechanical Clutch, continued**

4 Measure the clutch pedal free-play. Perform any adjustments as necessary, following the manufacturer's procedure.

or foot. Perform any adjustments as necessary, following the manufacturer's procedure. **(Photo 4)**

7 Start the vehicle and depress the clutch. The clutch should engage at the proper height and have the proper free-play. Make a gear selection to ensure the gears do not clash going into mesh. While in gear, slowly release the clutch and see how far the clutch pedal must travel before the clutch starts to engage in forward motion. If it is not within the manufacturer's specifications, discuss this with your supervisor.

Checking and Adjusting a Hydraulic Clutch

It is important to check the clutch hydraulic system and components for proper operation and correct adjustment. It is common to do so during periodic routine maintenance service. If the hydraulic clutch system is improperly maintained, clutch operation could be compromised in a similar manner as the operation of a mechanical linkage clutch, resulting in pressure plate, friction disc, and transmission synchronizer failure. Also, improper or old fluid in the hydraulic system can cause master cylinder and slave cylinder damage.

To check and adjust a hydraulic clutch, follow the steps in **SKILL DRILL 23-2** :

1 Research the procedure and specifications for inspecting and adjusting the hydraulic clutch components in the appropriate service information.

2 Inspect the clutch master cylinder for correct fluid level and test the quality of the fluid (see the Hydraulics and Power Brakes chapter).

3 Inspect all line connections to the master cylinder. If a leak at the rear of the master cylinder is suspected, it may be necessary to remove the master cylinder from the firewall to inspect behind it for leaks if no other visible external leaks are present. **(Photo 1)**

4 Check that all hydraulic lines are not kinked or leaking at their connections. This will require that the system be repaired and bled of any air.

5 Check all rubber hoses for dry rot, bulges, or leaks.

6 Make sure all hydraulic components are secure in their mountings. **(Photo 2)**

7 Check the boot on the slave cylinder for seepage, which may indicate a leaking slave cylinder piston seal. **(Photo 3)**

8 Check clutch pedal height. Clutch pedal height is normally measured from the floor pan to the top of the clutch pedal pad with the clutch pedal released. Compare your reading to the specifications and determine any necessary actions to correct any fault.

9 Measure clutch pedal free-play using a tape measure. Pedal free-play is normally measured from the top of the pedal at rest to where all play is taken up between the pedal and the pressure plate. Compare your reading with the factory

SKILL DRILL | 23-2 | Checking and Adjusting a Hydraulic Clutch

1. Inspect the clutch master cylinder for correct fluid level and test the quality of the fluid. Inspect all line connections to the master cylinder.

2. Check that all hydraulic lines are not kinked or leaking at their connections. This will require that the system be repaired and bled of any air. Check all rubber hoses for dry rot, bulges, or leaks. Make sure all hydraulic components are secure in their mountings.

3. Check the boot on the slave cylinder for seepage, which may indicate a leaking slave cylinder piston seal.

4. Check clutch pedal height. Measure clutch pedal free-play using a tape measure. Compare your readings to the specifications and determine any necessary actions to correct any fault.

specifications and determine any necessary actions to correct. (Photo 4)

> **TECHNICIAN TIP**
>
> Make sure there are no floor mats or other obstructions that will affect the operation of the clutch pedal.

Bleeding a Hydraulic Clutch System

In the case of a hydraulic clutch system failure, it may be necessary to bleed the air from the system. Bleeding is also needed whenever any hydraulic component is replaced or the hydraulic fluid becomes unfit for use due to age or contamination. Not all systems are fitted with a bleeder screw due to how the system is constructed. It may be necessary to bleed the system from the line entering the slave cylinder.

Research the procedure and specifications for bleeding the hydraulic clutch system. There are three types of bleeding: gravity bleeding, manual bleeding, and pressure bleeding. Determine the proper method of bleeding to use by consulting the manufacturer's specifications.

Gravity bleeding uses gravity to push fluid and air from the master cylinder and lines out through the slave cylinder bleeder screw. In most vehicles, the clutch master cylinder is quite a bit higher than the slave cylinder. The weight of the fluid can therefore be used to supply the pressure to push fluid and air out of the system.

To bleed/flush a hydraulic clutch system using the gravity method, follow the steps in **SKILL DRILL 23-3**:

1. If the fluid needs to be flushed, use a suction gun or old anti-freeze tester to suck the fluid out of the clutch master cylinder reservoir. Fill it with the specified fluid. **(Photo 1)**
2. Open the bleeder screw on the slave cylinder.
3. Allow air and fluid to drain from the system into a container. **(Photo 2)**
4. Keep the master cylinder filled.
5. Once all air and old fluid are removed, close the bleeder screw and operate the clutch pedal to check for normal operation.

6. After bleeding the hydraulic clutch system, fill the master cylinder to the correct level with the specified type of brake fluid. **(Photo 3)**

The manual bleeding method uses the master cylinder to push fluid and air from the system. The procedure usually requires an assistant to hold the clutch pedal down while the other person opens the bleeder valve on the slave cylinder. Pumping of the pedal will result in a single air bubble breaking up into smaller bubbles or foam, which will require more time to bleed the system properly.

To bleed/flush a hydraulic clutch system using the manual method, follow the steps in **SKILL DRILL 23-4**:

1. If the fluid needs to be flushed, use a suction gun or old anti-freeze tester to suck the fluid out of the clutch master cylinder reservoir. Fill it with the specified fluid.
2. Have an assistant depress the clutch pedal slowly. **(Photo 1)**
3. Open the bleeder valve on the slave cylinder and let fluid run out into a container.
4. When all of the fluid stops flowing, close the bleeder valve and slowly release the pedal.
5. Repeat this process until all air and old fluid are removed from the system. **(Photo 2)**

SKILL DRILL | 23-3 | Bleeding/Flushing Hydraulic Clutch System Using the Gravity Method

1. If the fluid needs to be flushed, use a suction gun or old anti-freeze tester to suck the fluid out of the clutch master cylinder reservoir. Fill it with the specified fluid.

2. Open the bleeder screw on the slave cylinder. Allow air and fluid to drain from the system into a container.

3. Keep the master cylinder filled. Once all air and old fluid are removed, close the bleeder screw and operate the clutch pedal to check for normal operation. After bleeding the clutch hydraulic system, fill the master cylinder to the correct level with the specified type of brake fluid.

SKILL DRILL | 23-4 | Bleeding/Flushing Hydraulic Clutch System Using the Manual Method

1 Remove all old fluid from the reservoir. Fill it with the specified fluid. Have an assistant depress the clutch pedal slowly.

2 Open the bleeder valve on the slave cylinder and let fluid run out into a container. When all of the fluid stops flowing, close the bleeder valve and slowly release the pedal. Repeat this process until all air and old fluid are removed from the system.

3 After bleeding the clutch hydraulic system, check for correct pedal feel, and fill the master cylinder to the correct level with the specified type of brake fluid.

6 After bleeding the clutch hydraulic system, check for correct pedal feel, and fill the master cylinder to the correct level with the specified type of brake fluid. **(Photo 3)**

The pressure or vacuum bleeding method uses pressure or vacuum to push or pull fluid and air from the system. This method works well for systems that tend to trap air in the hydraulic system that cannot be bled manually. It does require special bleeding tools or equipment.

To bleed a hydraulic clutch system using the pressure method, follow the steps in **SKILL DRILL 23-5**:

1 Hook up the pressure or vacuum bleeding tool to the vehicle with the correct adapters. **(Photo 1)**

2 Apply pressure or vacuum to the system. **(Photo 2)**

3 Open the bleeder screw and allow the fluid and air to be purged from the system. Capture the fluid in the bleeder or use a hose to direct it into a plastic container. Repeat this process as necessary.

4 After bleeding the hydraulic clutch system, check for correct pedal feel, and fill the master cylinder to the correct level with the specified type of brake fluid. **(Photo 3)**

TECHNICIAN TIP

Be careful of the pressure that comes out of the slave cylinder, as it may splash or spray into your eyes. Also, brake fluid will eat paint, so when handling brake fluid, cover fenders and clean up any spilled fluid with generous amounts of water.

Removing a Transmission/Transaxle

Removal of the transmission is usually required only when the clutch is not operating correctly, the flywheel ring gear is damaged, there is a major concern with the transmission, or access to the rear of the engine is needed for leaks involving core plugs, oil gallery plugs, or the crankshaft rear main seal. This job can be time consuming and requires the ability to remember how components and parts go back together again. Depending on the vehicle, it can be difficult to gain access to the fasteners and other components necessary to remove and reinstall the transmission. Since the transmission is heavy and awkward, use a transmission jack with a solid support system during removal and installation.

SKILL DRILL | 23-5 | Bleeding Hydraulic Clutch System Using the Pressure Method

1. Hook up the pressure or vacuum bleeding tool to the vehicle with the correct adapters.

2. Apply pressure or vacuum to the system.

3. Open the bleeder screw and allow the fluid and air to be purged from the system. Repeat this process as necessary. After bleeding, check for correct pedal feel, and fill the clutch master cylinder to the correct level with the specified type of brake fluid.

▶ TECHNICIAN TIP

In some applications, such as four-wheel drive and all-wheel drive vehicles, it may be quicker to remove the engine than it is to remove the transmission to gain access to the clutch assembly. Look up the flat rate time for removing the engine and compare that time to the transmission removal time.

To remove and reinstall a transmission/transaxle, follow the steps in **SKILL DRILL 23-6**:

1. Research the procedures and specifications for removing and installing the transmission/transaxle in the appropriate service information.

2. Make sure all bolts, clips, and fasteners are kept in containers to prevent losing them. Make sure the vehicle is secure on the lift to avoid it falling off. If necessary, drain the transmission fluid to avoid a spill on the floor that may cause a safety hazard. **(Photo 1)**

3. Disconnect the drive shaft or axles and secure them from hanging.

4. Disconnect all wires, tubes, and hoses that may be present and inspect for damage.

5. Disconnect the clutch and shifter linkage and inspect for wear or damage.

6. Secure the transmission with a transmission jack and remove any transmission mounts. **(Photo 2)**

7. Following the specified procedure for the specific type of transmission/transaxle, remove the transmission/transaxle from the vehicle. At this time, you may want to overhaul the transmission/transaxle or perform other tasks such as inspecting and replacing the clutch assembly or replacing the rear crankshaft main seal. **(Photo 3)**

8. Prepare the transmission to be reinstalled. Ensure that the release (throw-out) bearing and clutch fork are properly installed and the clutch disc is centered in the pressure plate. If specified, lubricate the pilot bushing/bearing. **(Photo 4)**

9. Lightly lubricate the input shaft splines to make sure there is no binding upon entering the clutch disc hub. Position all wires, hoses, and tubes out of the way and in their specified positions. Secure them temporarily if necessary. **(Photo 5)** It is easy for wires and hoses to fall down and get pinched between the engine and the bell housing. Pinched wires and hoses will cause electrical issues in the vehicle as well as alignment issues with the transmission.

10. Following the specified procedure for the specific type of transmission/transaxle, reinstall the transmission/transaxle. Be sure to tighten all fasteners to the proper torque. Do not hang the transmission from the engine without bolts, as the clutch disc may incur damage. Always use a quality transmission jack and secure adapters.

11 If the vehicle is equipped with a cable- or linkage-style clutch release system, reinstall and adjust it for the proper free-play. **(Photo 6)**

12 If the vehicle is equipped with a hydraulic clutch, reinstall the slave cylinder and bleed and/or adjust if necessary. **(Photo 7)**

13 Refill the transmission/transaxle to the proper level with the specified fluid. **(Photo 8)**

SKILL DRILL 23-6 Removing and Reinstalling a Transmission/Transaxle

1 Research the procedures and specifications.
Ensure that bolts, clips, and fasteners are kept in containers. Make sure the vehicle is secure on the lift. If necessary, drain the transmission fluid to avoid a spill on the floor that may cause a safety hazard.

2 Disconnect the drive shaft or axles and secure them from hanging. Disconnect all wires, tubes, and hoses that may be present and inspect for damage. Disconnect the clutch and shifter linkage and inspect for wear or damage. Secure the transmission with a transmission jack and remove any transmission mounts.

3 Following the specified procedure for the specific type of transmission/transaxle, remove the transmission/transaxle from the vehicle. At this time, you may want to overhaul the transmission/transaxle or perform other tasks such as inspecting and replacing the clutch assembly or replacing the rear crankshaft main seal.

4 Prepare the transmission to be reinstalled. Ensure that the release (throw-out) bearing and clutch fork are properly installed and the clutch disc is centered in the pressure plate. If specified, lubricate the pilot bushing/bearing.

5 Lightly lubricate input shaft splines to ensure that there is no binding upon entering the clutch disc hub. Position all wires, hoses, and tubes out of the way and in their specified positions. Secure them temporarily if necessary.

6 Following the specified procedure for the specific type of transmission/transaxle, reinstall the transmission/transaxle. Tighten all fasteners to the proper torque. If the vehicle is equipped with a cable- or linkage-style clutch release system, reinstall and adjust it for the proper free-play.

SKILL DRILL 23-6 Removing and Reinstalling a Transmission/Transaxle, continued

7. If the vehicle is equipped with a hydraulic clutch, reinstall the slave cylinder and bleed and/or adjust if necessary.

8. Refill the transmission/transaxle to the proper level with the specified fluid.

9. Check that all electrical wires, connectors, linkages, and other removed components are properly installed and adjusted. Place exhaust hose(s) over the exhaust pipe(s) and set the parking brake.

14. Check that all electrical wires, terminals, linkages, and other removed components are properly installed and adjusted.

15. Place exhaust hose(s) over the exhaust pipe(s) and set the parking brake. **(Photo 9)**

16. Make sure no one is standing in front of or behind the vehicle. Start the vehicle and check the action of the clutch and gear shift linkage. If the clutch engages at the correct height and everything is working properly, obtain your supervisor's permission to take the vehicle for a test-drive to confirm proper operation of the clutch and transmission.

17. After the test-drive, raise the vehicle on a hoist and double-check your work. Verify that there are no leaks, loose fasteners, or misrouted components. Verify proper clutch adjustment. It is always wise to place the vehicle on the lift one more time to make sure all parts are secure in their mountings and there are no leaks.

Safety

Due to designs of the manufacturer, it may be necessary to maneuver the transmission in awkward positions. Make sure the transmission is secured to the transmission jack to avoid injuring yourself.

Inspecting the Flywheel and Ring Gear

Any time the clutch assembly has been removed, it is a good idea to conduct a thorough visual inspection of the flywheel and ring gear. Poor driving habits or slippery weather conditions have a tendency to put a strain on the clutch system. When a clutch is being replaced, also inspect the flywheel for bluing, hot spots, and cracks. These conditions can result from possible driver abuse or maladjustment of the clutch, causing the clutch disc to overheat. Also inspect the flywheel friction surface for cupping with a straightedge and feeler blades. Cupping can happen because the pressure plate exerts a pulling effort on the outside diameter of the flywheel, which then allows the outer portion to cup over time; in addition, the outer edge of the friction surface wears more quickly than the inner edge. A straightedge can help you identify this situation quickly.

Some flywheels are designed with a step, meaning that the friction surface is lower than the outer surface against which the pressure plate is bolted. The depth of the step is critical to the operation of the pressure plate. If it is too deep, the pressure plate will not develop enough clamping force to keep the clutch from slipping. If it is not deep enough, the clutch might not be able to be released. In any case, the depth of the step must be within the manufacturer's specifications. This becomes more important to check if the flywheel has been resurfaced. The machinist should have made sure the depth is correct, but you need to double-check it.

In regard to resurfacing flywheels, most vehicle manufacturers as well as clutch suppliers suggest that the flywheel be resurfaced whenever the clutch is replaced. This gives a new, flat, and consistent friction surface that helps prevent clutch chatter. It is good practice to check flywheel runout once a resurfaced flywheel is reinstalled on the crankshaft so you can identify any machining errors.

Ring gears must be inspected for missing teeth and excessive wear on the teeth. If any of these conditions are present, the ring gear should be replaced. Many ring gears are press-fitt onto the flywheel; others are a permanent part of the flywheel. If a ring gear is press-fitted onto the flywheel, it can be removed by heating it up carefully with an acetylene torch to a few hundred degrees Fahrenheit and using a hammer and punch to quickly drive it off of the flywheel. To reinstall it, a good method is to cool the flywheel in a freezer for 30 minutes and to place the ring gear in an oven at about 300°F. Then, using welding gloves, quickly take them out, set the flywheel on a solid surface and slide the ring gear over the flywheel. Use a hammer and flat punch to seat the ring gear against the flange on the flywheel.

TECHNICIAN TIP

If replacement of the starter was performed due to failure, the teeth on the ring gear should be inspected thoroughly as well. If the teeth on the ring gear are damaged, they will likely destroy the matching teeth on the starter motor.

To inspect the flywheel and ring gear (with the transmission removed), follow the steps in **SKILL DRILL 23-7**:

1. Research the procedure for inspecting the flywheel and ring gear in the appropriate service information. Following the specified procedure, remove the pressure plate and clutch disc. It is good practice to remove the pressure plate bolts evenly. This requires backing each bolt out one turn at a time to avoid warping the pressure plate. Also, have an assistant hold the pressure plate and clutch disc when they get close to becoming loose to avoid dropping them on the floor and damaging them or injuring yourself. **(Photo 1)**

SKILL DRILL 23-7 Inspecting the Flywheel and Ring Gear

1. Follow the specified procedure to remove the pressure plate and clutch disc. Remove the pressure plate bolts evenly, backing each bolt out one turn at a time to avoid warping the pressure plate. Have an assistant hold the pressure plate and clutch disc when they get close to becoming loose.

2. Clean up any debris using an approved method for disposing of hazardous dust. Use approved equipment and methods for the removal and disposal of clutch dust.

3. Inspect the flywheel for wear, hot spots, bluing, and cracks. Use of a straightedge can give a preliminary check for flatness.

SKILL DRILL 23-7 | Inspecting the Flywheel and Ring Gear, continued

4 Inspect the ring gear for wear, chipped teeth, and cracks. If teeth are worn in one area, it may also be necessary to replace the starter drive.

5 Check that the ring gear is secure on the flywheel.

6 Inspect the starter drive, as it may have been damaged from a faulty ring gear.

2 Clean up any debris using an approved method for disposing of hazardous dust. Asbestos is a human hazard and must be avoided and disposed of properly. Use approved equipment and methods for removal and disposal of clutch dust. (**Photo 2**)

3 Inspect the flywheel for wear, hot spots, bluing, and cracks. Use of a straightedge can give a preliminary check for flatness. (**Photo 3**)

4 Inspect the ring gear for wear, chipped teeth, and cracks. It is common for the ring gear teeth to be worn in a pattern. For example, a four-cylinder engine will have greater wear every 180 degrees, a six-cylinder engine every 120 degrees, and an eight-cylinder engine every 90 degrees. Therefore, be sure to inspect all of the teeth, not just a few of them. If teeth are worn in one area, it may also be necessary to replace the starter drive. (**Photo 4**)

5 Check that the ring gear is secure on the flywheel. (**Photo 5**)

6 Inspect the starter drive, as it may have been damaged from a faulty ring gear. (**Photo 6**)

Measuring the Flywheel Runout and Crankshaft End Play

The flywheel must rotate true. This means that the surface of the flywheel must not wobble, which would indicate excessive runout. It is always a good idea to check and measure the flywheel runout in the case of catastrophic clutch failure or routine clutch replacement any time the transmission is removed. Flywheel runout can be measured with a dial indicator, which is firmly held in position against the flywheel friction surface. When the flywheel is turned, the runout should be within specifications, near zero. If the runout is excessive, you will need to use the dial indicator to measure the crankshaft runout to see if that is causing the flywheel runout.

Crankshaft end play is the amount of forward and rearward movement of the crankshaft and must be within the specifications for the vehicle you are working on. Crankshaft end play must be checked if any irregular clutch noises have been detected. Too much crankshaft end play could be a result in an engine's crankshaft thrust bearing becoming worn past its specified tolerance. Crankshaft end play can also result in clutch chatter when the clutch pedal is being released.

Use a dial indicator to measure crankshaft end play at the end of the crankshaft. If the engine oil pan has been removed, you also can measure the thrust bearing clearance with a feeler gauge. Check runout of the pilot bearing cavity, as this could indicate that the pilot bearing may not be held in position as is required for proper operation; if so, damage to the clutch assembly may result.

To measure flywheel runout and crankshaft end play, follow the steps in **SKILL DRILL 23-8**:

① Research the specifications and procedure for measuring flywheel runout and crankshaft end play in the appropriate service information. Following the specified procedure, measure flywheel runout.

Flywheel runout should be checked with a dial indicator for proper flatness of the flywheel surface to ensure that the clutch will operate smoothly. Mount the dial indicator base on the engine block and place the dial on the flywheel friction surface. **(Photo 1)**

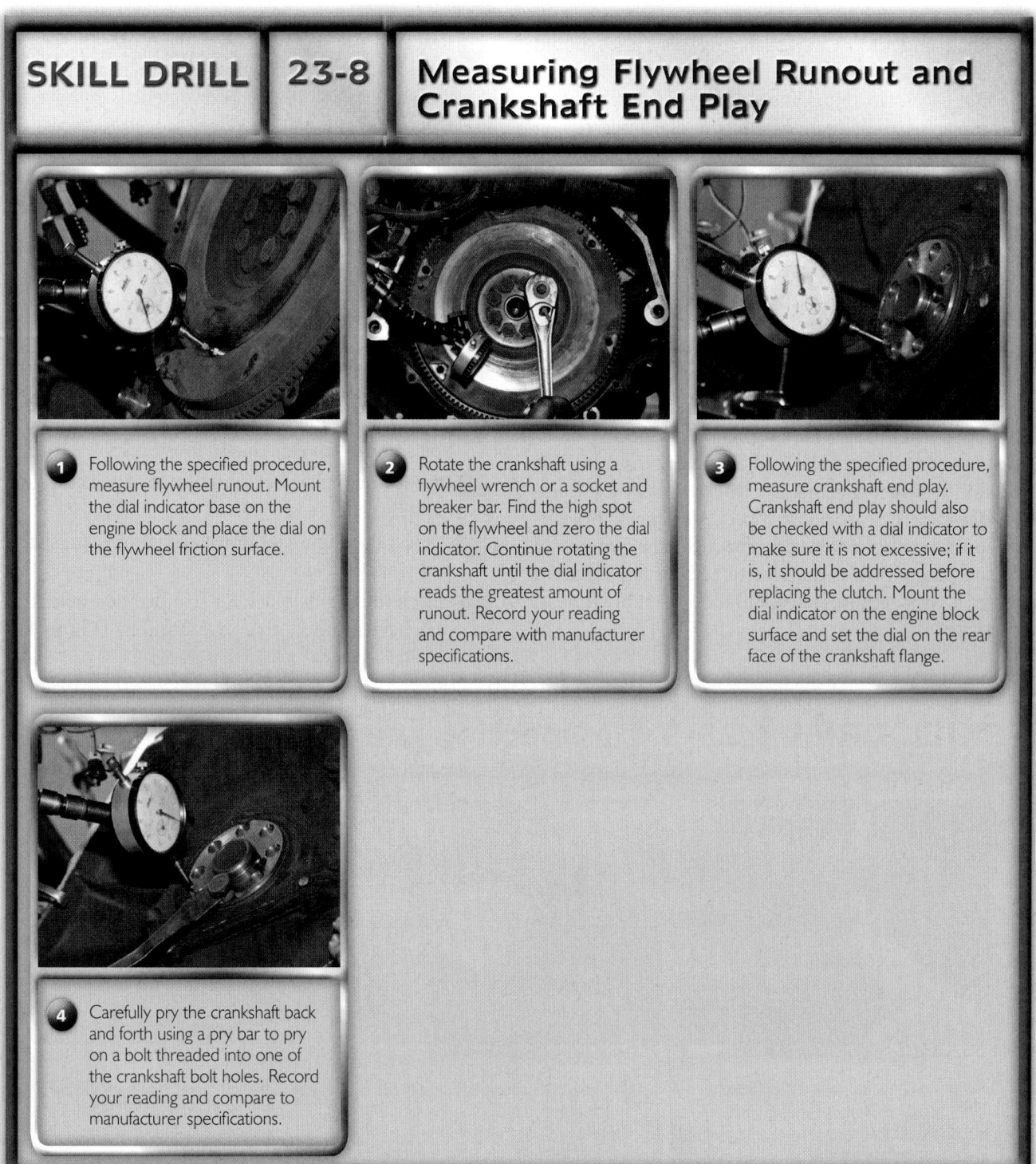

SKILL DRILL 23-8 Measuring Flywheel Runout and Crankshaft End Play

1. Following the specified procedure, measure flywheel runout. Mount the dial indicator base on the engine block and place the dial on the flywheel friction surface.

2. Rotate the crankshaft using a flywheel wrench or a socket and breaker bar. Find the high spot on the flywheel and zero the dial indicator. Continue rotating the crankshaft until the dial indicator reads the greatest amount of runout. Record your reading and compare with manufacturer specifications.

3. Following the specified procedure, measure crankshaft end play. Crankshaft end play should also be checked with a dial indicator to make sure it is not excessive; if it is, it should be addressed before replacing the clutch. Mount the dial indicator on the engine block surface and set the dial on the rear face of the crankshaft flange.

4. Carefully pry the crankshaft back and forth using a pry bar to pry on a bolt threaded into one of the crankshaft bolt holes. Record your reading and compare to manufacturer specifications.

2 Rotate the crankshaft using a flywheel wrench or a socket and breaker bar. Find the high spot on the flywheel and zero the dial indicator. Continue rotating the crankshaft until the dial indicator reads the greatest amount of runout. Record your reading and compare with manufacturer specifications. **(Photo 2)**

3 Following the specified procedure, measure crankshaft end play. Crankshaft end play also should be checked with a dial indicator to make sure it is not excessive; if it is, it should be addressed before replacing the clutch. Mount the dial indicator on the engine block surface and set the dial on the rear face of the crankshaft flange. **(Photo 3)**

4 Carefully pry the crankshaft back and forth using a pry bar to pry on a bolt threaded into one of the crankshaft bolt holes. Record your reading and compare to manufacturer specifications. **(Photo 4)**

Inspecting the Engine Block

While the flywheel is removed, it is a good practice to inspect the rear of the engine block for any damage to the mating surfaces and alignment dowels. This should include inspecting the threads of all bolt holes to make sure they are not stripped. Also check for leaking coolant and/or engine oil, and check the integrity of the soft plugs. Now is the time to address any issues in this area, as it requires substantial disassembly time to access it.

Many newer engines use a full-circle rear main seal around the crankshaft flange at the rear of the block. This can be replaced only by removing the transmission and flywheel. If the clutch and flywheel have been removed, now would be an ideal time to inspect and change the full-circle rear main seal.

To inspect the engine block, follow the steps in **SKILL DRILL 23-9** :

1 Research the procedure for inspecting the engine block. Mark the flywheel-to-crankshaft position with a center punch or grease pencil. Remove the flywheel if it is not already removed to access the rear of the engine.

2 Inspect the engine block for any obvious defects such as cracks and porosity. **(Photo 1)**

3 Inspect the core plugs. Test their integrity by tapping on them lightly with a punch.

4 Replace the core plugs if they are leaking or show signs of deterioration. **(Photo 2)**

5 Check the rear crankshaft oil seal for seepage, since this could leak on to the clutch assembly. **(Photo 3)**

6 Inspect the clutch (bell) housing for elongated holes or broken ears due to loose bolts.

7 Inspect the transmission/transaxle case mating surfaces for flatness.

8 Inspect the alignment dowels for proper fit, sizing, and wear.

9 Check the engine block for stripped bolt holes that may have resulted from overtorquing. **(Photo 4)**

SKILL DRILL   23-9   Inspecting the Engine Block

1 Mark the flywheel-to-crankshaft position. Remove the flywheel to access the rear of the engine. Inspect the engine block for obvious defects.

2 Inspect the core plugs. Test their integrity by tapping on them lightly with a punch. Replace the core plugs if they are leaking or show signs of deterioration.

3 Check the rear crankshaft oil seal for seepage, since this could leak onto the clutch assembly.

SKILL DRILL | 23-9 | Inspecting the Engine Block, continued

4. Inspect the clutch (bell) housing for elongated holes or broken ears due to loose bolts. Inspect the transmission/transaxle case mating surfaces for flatness. Inspect the alignment dowels for proper fit, sizing, and wear. Check the engine block for stripped bolt holes that may have resulted from overtorquing.

▶ TECHNICIAN TIP

Core plugs seal the holes in the block as part of the casting process and are located around the outside of the cylinder block and head(s), including behind the flywheel. Core plugs can rust from either side. They may look good on the outside, but they may be almost rusted through from the inside. A variety of core plugs are available if replacement is required. Be aware of hot coolant that may be leaking from the core plugs if the engine has recently been running.

▶ TECHNICIAN TIP

The alignment dowels ensure that the transmission and engine line up correctly. They can be easily damaged when removing or installing the transmission, so inspect them for damage whenever the transmission has been removed.

Installing a Clutch Assembly

Whether you are replacing a clutch because of a failure or removing the clutch and reinstalling it after replacing an engine, thorough inspection of all components is critical to ensure that the clutch will last a long time. Installing the clutch assembly requires a few precautions. First, the clutch disc is directional, meaning that it must be installed with the correct face toward the flywheel. New clutch discs usually are marked with a sticker or paint indicating the "flywheel side" or "engine side." This marking cannot be read on used discs, so always mark the clutch disc when you remove it if you will possibly be reinstalling it. Second, alignment of the clutch disc is required prior to bolting down the pressure plate so that the input shaft can align with the clutch disc hub and pilot bearing. Use of a pilot shaft or clutch alignment tool will help ensure proper clutch disc alignment. With the clutch disc inserted, under *no circumstances* should you remove the pilot shaft until after the clutch pressure plate has been installed and torqued to specification. If it is removed prematurely, misalignment of the clutch disc will occur and installation of the transmission will be extremely difficult or impossible.

Upon installation of the pressure plate, insert bolts and tighten in a multistep, crisscross pattern, which will allow the pressure plate to be seated slowly and without distortion. Double-check all torque values to assure proper installation.

To install a clutch assembly, follow the steps in **SKILL DRILL 23-10**:

1. Research the procedure and any specifications for inspecting the clutch assembly. Inspect the pressure plate assembly for worn springs or diaphragm and also for irregularities associated with any kind of failure, including hot spots.

2. Inspect the clutch disc for loose dampening springs or rubber blocks, and check the condition of the rivets. **(Photo 1)**

3. Check the release (throw-out) bearing and linkage for damage or binding.

4. Check the pilot bearing/bushing for damage and its cavity.

5. Determine any necessary action(s) for correcting failures, or replace any worn parts with new/remanufactured components. **(Photo 2)**

6. Following the specified procedure, install the pilot bushing/bearing, if removed. Lubricate it with the specified lubricant, if applicable. **(Photo 3)**

7. Following the specified procedure, install the flywheel. Be sure to torque the flywheel bolts in the proper sequence. **(Photo 4)**

8. Following the specified procedure, install the clutch disc and pressure plate. Use an appropriate clutch alignment tool to ensure proper positioning of the clutch disc. **(Photo 5)**

9. The pressure plate bolts should be tightened down evenly. This is usually done by tightening each bolt a turn or two, one at a time, until the pressure plate is evenly seated on the flywheel surface.

10. Torque each pressure plate bolt according to the specified torque and sequence.

11. Install the release (throw-out) bearing and linkage in the bell housing. **(Photo 6)**

SKILL DRILL 23-10 Installing a Clutch Assembly

1. Research the procedure. Inspect the pressure plate assembly for worn springs or diaphragm and also for irregularities associated with any kind of failure, including hot spots. Inspect the clutch disc for loose dampening springs or rubber blocks, and check the condition of the rivets.

2. Check the release (throw-out) bearing and linkage for damage or binding. Check the pilot bearing/bushing for damage and its cavity. Determine any necessary action(s) for correcting failures, or replace any worn parts with new/remanufactured components.

3. Following the specified procedure, install the pilot bushing/bearing, if removed. Lubricate it with the specified lubricant, if applicable.

SKILL DRILL | 23-10 | Installing a Clutch Assembly, continued

4 Following the specified procedure, install the flywheel. Be sure to torque the flywheel bolts in the proper sequence.

5 Following the specified procedure, install the clutch disc and pressure plate. Use an appropriate clutch alignment tool to ensure proper positioning of the clutch disc.

6 Tighten the pressure plate bolts down evenly by tightening each bolt a turn or two, one at a time, until the pressure plate is evenly seated on the flywheel surface. Torque each pressure plate bolt according to the specified torque and sequence. Install the release (throw-out) bearing and linkage in the bell housing.

Wrap-up

Ready for Review

▸ The clutch is designed to engage and disengage the engine from the vehicle's transmission.

▸ The driver controls the shifting of gears via the clutch while the vehicle is in operation.

▸ Dry (automotive) clutches rely on friction to transmit torque from the engine to the transmission.

▸ There are four variables affecting the clutch torque transmission: amount of friction between the clutch disc and mating surfaces of the flywheel and pressure plate; diameter of the clutch; number of clutch discs in the clutch assembly; and total spring force clamping the parts together.

▸ Speed and output shaft torque have an inverse relationship: when one is increased, the other is decreased.

▸ The clutch disengages the input shaft from the engine flywheel in order to switch gears.

▸ The output shaft cannot be disengaged because it is directly connected to the wheels.

▸ The clutch assembly is composed of: flywheel, clutch disc, pressure plate, throw-out bearing, clutch fork, and pilot bearing.

▸ Flywheels are designed to provide a friction surface for the clutch disc and dampen the power pulses from pistons during power strokes.

▸ Types of flywheels are: single one-piece flywheel (light duty vehicles) and dual mass flywheel (diesel trucks and luxury vehicles).

▸ A dual mass flywheel can be made of a primary and secondary flywheel with a series of torsion springs and cushions or can use a planetary gear and torsional springs.

▸ The pressure plate uses springs to clamp the clutch disc between the pressure plate and flywheel, allowing it to transmit torque.

▸ Pressure plates use diaphragm spring pressure (light-duty vehicles) or coil spring pressure.

▸ A clutch disc (also known as a driven center plate or friction disc) allows engine torque to transmit from the flywheel and pressure plate to the transmission input shaft by providing necessary friction material.

▸ The clutch throw-out bearing and clutch fork compress the pressure plate springs.

▸ Pilot bearings can be brass or bronze bushing, needle type, or roller type and provide alignment support for the input shaft.

▸ Clutch operating mechanism styles can be linkage, cable, or hydraulic.

▸ Cable-operated clutch control systems must be adjusted to ensure adequate free-play between the throw-out bearing and pressure plate levers.

▸ Hydraulic clutch control systems rely on a slave cylinder to operate the clutch fork.

▸ Clutches can be single plate (light duty vehicles) or multiple plate (heavy duty vehicles).

▸ Common clutch-related problems are: noises, pedal pulsations, slippage, clutch binding or drag, clutch vibration, and clutch chatter.

▸ Clutch vibrations may be torsional or driveline.

▸ Proper clutch diagnosis will likely require a test-drive.

▸ Take proper safety precautions during clutch maintenance and repair; older clutch disc linings may contain asbestos.

▸ Tools needed to maintain and repair a clutch system include: transmission jack, dial indicator, clutch alignment tool, flywheel wrench, and clutch was station.

▸ Perform regular preventive clutch maintenance per the manufacturer's guidelines.

▸ Check and adjust the clutch linkage mechanism (mechanical or hydraulic) during routine maintenance service.

▸ Hydraulic clutch systems may need bleeding: if the system fails, when a component is replaced, or if the hydraulic fluid becomes unfit for use.

▸ Hydraulic clutch systems may be bled via gravity, manually, or via the pressure/vacuum method.

▸ Removing a transmission and transaxle is difficult; remember how components go back together again.

▸ Inspect the flywheel, ring gear, and engine block whenever the clutch assembly has been removed.

▸ Measure the flywheel run out and crankshaft end play anytime the transmission is removed.

▸ Be sure to properly align the clutch disc when installing a clutch assembly.

Key Terms

carrier The part of the throw-out bearing assembly that holds the bearing.

clutch binding A condition in which the clutch disc is dragging, leading to grinding gears during gear shifts and possibly clutch chatter.

clutch chatter A condition in which the clutch shudders when the clutch pedal is released and the vehicle starts to move forward.

clutch disc The center component of the clutch assembly, with friction material riveted on each side. Also called a clutch plate or friction disc.

clutch fork The part of the clutch linkage that operates the throw-out bearing.

coefficient of friction The amount of resistance to movement between any two surfaces that are in contact with each other.

coil spring pressure plate A type of pressure plate that uses coil springs to provide the clamping force.

crankshaft end play The amount of forward and rearward movement of the crankshaft in the main bearings. Crankshaft end play is controlled by the engine main bearing thrust bearing.

diaphragm pressure plate A slightly conical, spring steel plate used to provide the clamping force for the clutch assembly.

driveline vibrations Rotational fluctuations caused by out-of-balance, misaligned, worn, or bent driveline components.

driven center plate The friction disc that is held firmly against the flywheel by a pressure plate and transfers power from the flywheel to the transmission input shaft.

flywheel A heavy metal disc bolted to the crankshaft that is used to smooth out the engine's power pulses and keep the engine moving through the non-power strokes. Also provides the mating surface for the clutch disc and pressure plate.

flywheel ring gear Large, round, externally toothed gear that is usually press-fit to the outer diameter of the flywheel and used along with the starter to crank the engine over.

free-play The amount of clearance in the clutch release mechanism as measured at the clutch pedal. The proper amount of free-play is critical to clutch operation and longevity.

friction facing The material riveted to each side of the clutch disc that mates to the flywheel and pressure plate. Used to provide friction and a wear surface for the clutch assembly.

front bearing retainer The housing that bolts the input shaft bearing in place on the front of the transmission.

fulcrum ring A steel ring that is used as a pivot point for the diaphragm spring in the pressure plate.

multiplate clutch A clutch assembly that is comprised of two or more clutch plates and used to increase the torque-carrying capacity of the clutch.

pilot bearing The bearing or bushing that supports the front of the transmission input shaft.

push-type clutch A typical clutch system used in modern vehicles where the clutch fork pushes the release bearing forward to release the friction facing from the pressure plate.

pressure plate The assembly that applies and removes the clamping force on the clutch disc.

quadrant ratchet The device used in some cable-operated clutches to provide self-adjustment as the clutch disc wears. Some quadrant ratchets adjust if you lift up on the clutch pedal.

release mechanisms Components that operate the clutch. Usually included are the throw-out bearing and the clutch fork. Some manufacturers include the operating system.

single-plate clutch A clutch assembly that uses only one plate to transfer torque from the engine to the transmission. This is the most common type of light vehicle clutch.

slave cylinder The component in a hydraulically operated clutch that converts hydraulic pressure to mechanical movement at the clutch fork.

slippage A condition in which two surfaces in firm contact with each other slide.

splined torsional dampening center hub The center portion of a clutch disc that splines to the input shaft. It also incorporates a spring-loaded damper that absorbs engine pulsations for a smoother ride.

throw-out bearing The part of the clutch release mechanism that imparts clutch pedal force to the rotating pressure plate levers.

thrust-type angular-contact ball bearing A type of bearing that uses a deep groove in the bearing races where the ball bearings ride; this design is for thrust conditions.

torsional vibrations The speeding up and slowing down of a shaft, which happen at a relatively high frequency. Crankshafts have torsional vibrations due to the power pulses of the pistons.

transmission input shaft The shaft that brings engine torque into the transmission.

ASE-Type Questions

1. Tech A says that the pressure plate friction surface rides on the flywheel friction surface to transmit torque. Tech B says that the flywheel can either be flat or stepped. Who is correct?
   a. Tech A
   b. Tech B
   c. Both A and B
   d. Neither A nor B

2. Tech A says that insufficient clutch pedal clearance (free-play) can cause gear clashing when shifting. Tech B says that when the engine is idling and the clutch pedal is released, the friction disc should stop rotating. Who is correct?
   a. Tech A
   b. Tech B
   c. Both A and B
   d. Neither A nor B

3. Tech A says that hot spots on the flywheel are a result of excessive heat. Tech B says that a pulsation in a clutch pedal could be due to uneven clutch pressure plate levers. Who is correct?
   a. Tech A
   b. Tech B
   c. Both A and B
   d. Neither A nor B

4. Tech A says that a leaking rear main seal can cause clutch damage. Tech B says that clutch chatter is a result of a bad throw-out bearing. Who is correct?
   a. Tech A
   b. Tech B
   c. Both A and B
   d. Neither A nor B

5. Tech A says that the flywheel runout can be checked with a dial indicator. Tech B says that when checking flywheel runout, it is good practice to also check crankshaft end play. Who is correct?
   a. Tech A
   b. Tech B
   c. Both A and B
   d. Neither A nor B

6. Tech A says that clutch slippage can be a result of excessively strong pressure plate spring(s). Tech B says that when replacing the friction disc, it is good practice to also replace the pressure plate. Who is correct?
   a. Tech A
   b. Tech B
   c. Both A and B
   d. Neither A nor B

7. Tech A says that the pilot bearing can be a needle-style bearing. Tech B says that the pilot bearing can be a brass bushing style. Who is correct?
   a. Tech A
   b. Tech B
   c. Both A and B
   d. Neither A nor B

8. Tech A says that a bad pilot bearing can cause a whirring noise. Tech B says that a clutch fork can cause a whining noise. Who is correct?
   a. Tech A
   b. Tech B
   c. Both A and B
   d. Neither A nor B

9. Tech A says that most friction discs are made of asbestos. Tech B says that new friction discs can be made from ceramic materials. Who is correct?
   a. Tech A
   b. Tech B
   c. Both A and B
   d. Neither A nor B

10. Two technicians are discussing pressure plates. Tech A says that diaphragm pressure plates require more pedal effort than coil spring pressure plates. Tech B says that the two types require different free pedal adjustment procedures. Who is correct?
    a. Tech A
    b. Tech B
    c. Both A and B
    d. Neither A nor B

CHAPTER 24

NATEF Tasks

Manual Drive Train and Axles
General

Manual Transmissions/ Transaxles Basic Diagnosis and Maintenance

Knowledge Objectives

After reading this chapter, you will be able to:

1. Explain the theory behind gear ratios. (pp 664–666)
2. Explain how compound gear trains are used. (pp 666–667)
3. Explain how gear selection is accomplished. (pp 667–669)
4. Describe the purpose of bearings and thrust washers. (pp 669–671)
5. Describe the purpose of seals and gaskets. (pp 671–672)
6. Describe the different gearbox layouts and how a gearbox operates. (pp 672–676)
7. Describe transaxle designs. (p 674)
8. Describe the purpose and types of synchronizer assemblies. (pp 676–678)
9. Describe the operation of a dual-clutch manual transmission/transaxle. (pp 678–679)

Skills Objectives

After reading this chapter, you will be able to:

1. Check and adjust the gearbox fluid level. (pp 684–685)
2. Check and adjust the differential/transfer case fluid level. (pp 685–686)
3. Change the gearbox fluid. (pp 686–687)
4. Identify the cause of fluid loss in a transmission/transaxle. (pp 687–688)

Introduction

Manual transmissions have been around since the invention of the automobile. The ability of the technician to drive, service, repair, and maintain the manual transmission/transaxle is a critical skill. The manual transmission/transaxle is not the most common transmission used in automobiles but there are enough used to create a need for technicians that can service these devices. Transmissions have made improvements in gear ratios, weight reduction, and fuel saving features such as closer gear ratios and more gear selections. Proper diagnosis of the manual transmission/transaxle will be a required skill of the service technician.

Note, when we say *transmission*, we use the term generically to include transaxles also. When we use transaxle, we generally only mean transaxle. Readers should use their understanding of transmission and transaxle theory to understand the intended meaning.

Manual Transmission Layout and Operation

Gear Ratios

In light vehicle applications, the engine operates over a wide range of speeds, or revolutions per minute (rpm), but it produces maximum torque only within a relatively narrow rpm range (approximately 1200 rpm to 3000 rpm). A relatively large twisting force must be applied to the wheels to accelerate the vehicle from a stop. Once the vehicle is up to speed, the required twisting force is generally much less, although this force must vary to overcome wind resistance along with **gradient resistance** while going up hills and **rolling resistance** while driving down the road. Gradient resistance is the resistance caused by inclines, and rolling resistance is the resistance caused by the tires scrubbing on the road surface due to front end alignment defects or road crown. Because of the rpm and torque limitations of the engine, a multigear transmission is used to provide adequate acceleration at slow speeds while not over-revving the engine at cruising speeds.

A manual transmission allows the driver to directly vary the gear ratio between the engine and the driving road wheels. The **gear ratio** is the number of times the input gear must turn to achieve one turn of the output gear. The gear ratio varies the speed differential and torque multiplication to suit load and speed requirements for an actual driving condition. Having several gears with varying ratios gives the driver options that best match a variety of driving conditions. Manual transmissions typically have three to six forward gears along with a reverse gear and a neutral position, which disconnects the engine from the driving wheels, allowing the engine to idle at a stoplight.

When two gears are in mesh, one is a driven (output) gear. The other, providing the turning action, is the drive (input) gear. If the gears have the same number of teeth, they will create a one-to-one gear ratio, commonly known as direct drive **FIGURE 24-1**. In **direct drive** rotation, both the output and the input gears turn at the same speed, and the turning effort of the output gear equals the effort applied by the input gear.

You are the Automotive Technician

A customer brings her 2005 Acura RSX 6-speed into the shop for a manual transmission inspection. She informs you that when she is shifting into 3rd gear she sometimes hears a loud grinding noise. You carefully document the issue, review her vehicle service history, check for technical service bulletins, and then take her vehicle for a test drive. You notice that 3rd gear does grind, mostly on downshifts, but also a bit on upshifts. There are no other unusual gear or bearing noises. You bring the vehicle into the shop and inspect the lubricant level and condition. Both are OK. You also check the shift linkage for worn bushings or pivots. All are in good shape. You notify the customer that the blocker ring on the 3rd gear synchronizer is worn and needs to be replaced. You also recommend that the transmission should be rebuilt at the same time, since the entire transmission has to be disassembled to get to the blocker ring. She has several questions for you:

1. What is a blocker ring and what does it do?
2. How do you know it isn't worn gears that are making the grinding noise?
3. Why doesn't it grind when shifting into other gears?

Calculating the Gear Ratio

Gear ratios of different gear sizes can be calculated by dividing the number of teeth on the driven gear by the number of teeth on the drive gear **FIGURE 24-2** . For example, if the driven gear has 30 teeth and the drive gear has 10 teeth, the gear ratio is 30:10, which reduces to 3:1. In this case, the drive gear has to turn three times to turn the driven gear once. In continuous rotation, the driven gear turns three times slower than the drive gear.

Driving a large gear with a smaller gear results in a **gear reduction**, just as a bicycle with a large gear in the back and a small gear in the front gives you a very low gear ratio. If we think of the radius of the gear as a lever, then a large gear being turned by a small gear results in more leverage and, therefore, more torque. We turn the input gear quickly but the output gear speed is very low, resulting in higher torque. For example, with a gear ratio of 3:1, if input torque is 100 foot-pounds (ft-lb), then output torque is three times that, or 300 ft-lb. Different gear ratios are used inside the transmission to achieve varied torque to accelerate the vehicle. The increase of torque is referred to as **torque multiplication**.

In reverse, three gears are in mesh and the input and output gears are meshed with an idler or intermediate gear commonly used in reverse. When two gears are in mesh, the output gear turns in the opposite direction of the input gear. When an idler gear is used between the input and output gears, the output gear turns in the same direction as the input gear. This means the output gear in a three-gear arrangement will rotate in the reverse direction as compared to the output gear on a two-gear arrangement. The **idler gear** simply transfers motion and does not have an effect on the gear ratio of the input to output gears, which is why it is called an idler gear **FIGURE 24-3** .

FIGURE 24-1 Gears with the same number of teeth rotate at the same rate of speed, resulting in direct drive.

8 teeth
(100 ft lbs torque input)

24 teeth
(300 ft lbs torque output)

3:1 gear reduction

FIGURE 24-2 Gear ratios are determined by the size difference of each gear or the number of teeth on each gear.

Applied | **Math**

AM-35: Standards: The technician can demonstrate conformance to standards defined by the industry and/or manufacturer for the system being analyzed.
A vehicle requires a remanufactured transmission. The owner of the vehicle has indicated to the automotive repair shop service advisor that he would like to inspect the transmission before it is installed. As the owner compares the original five speed transmission with the remanufactured unit he has some concerns. The part numbers on the housing are not exactly the same and the customer has some doubts about the remanufactured unit being correct.

Using service information for the customer's vehicle, the technician asks the customer to verify the correct gear ratios for the remanufactured transmission. With the transmission on a work bench, the technician places the shifter into first gear. The service information states that the gear ratio should be 3.5:1 for first gear. This means that the engine would rotate 3.5 times as compared to the output shaft of the transmission rotates 1 time. Using a marker, the technician places reference marks on the input and output shafts of the transmission. The technician rotates the input shaft exactly three and one half turns as the customer observes the output shaft turning exactly one turn. This action demonstrates conformance to the standards of the manufacturer's service information. The same procedure was conducted to indicate a ratio of 2:1 for second gear, 1.4:1 for third gear, 1:1 for fourth gear and 0.76:1 for fifth gear. After verifying that all gear ratios were correct, the owner was convinced that the remanufactured transmission was correct for his vehicle.

FIGURE 24-3 The idler gear is a gear used to change the direction of the rotation of shafts and is used to provide reverse.

FIGURE 24-4 Compound gear trains have two or more gear sets in constant mesh at all times.

The terms input gear and drive gear have the same meaning. The same goes for output gear and driven gear. For the sake of simplicity, we will generally refer to the gears as input and output. Note that other textbooks or service information may use the alternate terms.

> ### TECHNICIAN TIP
>
> Gear ratio theory will help you to understand how power is distributed and how power and speed vary as the vehicle travels.

Compound Gear Trains

In keeping with the gear ratio theory, compound gear trains have two or more pairs of gears in constant mesh so that they rotate together **FIGURE 24-4**. They are found inside the transmission. Compound gear trains enable a variety of gear ratios, also accounting for torque output and speed requirements.

On a simple compound gear train, the gear on the input shaft meshes with a larger gear on a countershaft or cluster gear, which is usually the bottom shaft in the manual transmission. The countershaft has a smaller gear on it, in mesh with the output shaft gear. The rotation of the input shaft is transferred through the large gear on the countershaft, then along the countershaft to the smaller gear, then to the output shaft gear. The output gear turns in the same direction as the input gear, but at a reduced ratio, depending on the relative sizes and ratios of the gears. Since two pairs of gears are involved, their ratios are compounded, or multiplied together. This is how the overall gear train ratio is calculated.

The input shaft gear, with 12 teeth, drives its mating gear on the countershaft, which has 24 teeth. This creates a gear ratio of 2:1. This ratio of output over input at the input (2:1) is then multiplied by the output ratio, which has an output-to-input ratio of 3:1. Multiplying these two calculations together results in a gear ratio of 6:1 between the input and the output, resulting in a speed reduction and a corresponding increase in torque.

For example, the ratio of the input gear to the countershaft is multiplied by the ratio of the countershaft to the output shaft, yielding the total reduction ratio.

> ### TECHNICIAN TIP
>
> Gear reductions in the lower gears of manual transmissions can be provided by compound gear trains. The typical ratios are first gear = 4.41:1, second gear = 2.63:1, third gear = 1.61:1, fourth gear = 1:1, and fifth gear = 0.87:1.

Fourth gear is normally a gear ratio of 1:1, or direct drive. The input and output shafts turn at the same rate of speed. There is no torque multiplication, but there is an increase of vehicle speed from third gear as the vehicle has reached a point where torque output is no longer needed, and speed is the final result. A fifth gear is normally an **overdrive** ratio, typically with a value of 0.87:1. The output shaft of the transmission turns faster than the input, but the output torque is reduced. Now output speed is again increased over fourth gear, and fuel mileage is usually increased as the engine is turning at a slower speed. Another way to describe overdrive is to say the output speed of the transmission is faster than its input speed. Many vehicles employ a sixth gear, which can be an additional gear overdrive to reduce the engine speed even further, increasing fuel mileage. A sixth gear may have an overdrive ratio of approximately 0.75:1.

A further gear reduction is always provided by the final drive assembly. The final drive ratio needs to be included when calculating overall gear reduction. It can be calculated by using the preceding compound gear ratio math to find the overall gear ratio. The overall gear ratio is the gearbox ratio multiplied by the final drive ratio. For example, a gearbox ratio of 3:1 with a final drive ratio of 4:1 results in an overall ratio of 12:1. This means 12 revolutions of the crankshaft result in 1 turn of the road wheels. Assuming 100% efficiency, the torque applied is 12 times the engine torque.

▶ Gear Selection

A **gear shift lever** allows the driver to manually select gears via a gear shift mechanism.

The gear shift lever can be mounted separate from the gearbox on the floor or center console or on the steering column, and is connected to the gearbox by a rod-style linkage or cables. It can also be mounted in the top of the gearbox (called a top loader transmission), where it acts through a ball pivot in the top of the extension housing **FIGURE 24-5**. In this design, the lower end of the gear shift lever fits into a socket in a control shaft inside the transmission extension housing and is used to move the shift rails. Typically, on the bottom of the shift lever, below the ball portion, is a flattened end that fits into U-shaped cutouts in several shafts.

Shifting Mechanisms and Components

The flattened portion at the bottom of the shifter fits into U-shaped cutouts in several shafts called selector shift rails. The **selector shift rail** is the set of shafts that are connected to pieces called shift forks. **Shift forks** are the parts that actually move the components that change the gears selected inside the transmission. There is typically a shift fork for each two gear selections; thus, for a five-speed transmission, there are three shift rails. When we move one shift rail forward or backward, we engage one of two gear possibilities. We must have a way to then

move between the other two shift rails. This is where the U-shaped cutouts come in. The U-shaped cutouts that are located on the selector shift rails are referred to as the **selector gate** **FIGURE 24-6**. To select one of the other two shift rails, the shift lever must be moved to the side to engage the U-shaped cutout in one of the other shift rails and then pulled back or pushed forward. To select the opposite shift rail, the lever is moved to the other side and pulled back or pushed forward.

The selector shift rails are supported in the casing and are moved backward or forward by the gear shift lever. One selector shift rail moves to engage first and second gear, another operates third and fourth, and the other operates fifth and reverse. Note that some five-speed transmissions use four shift rails, which means fifth gear uses a shift rail separate from the reverse shift rail. A shift fork is attached to each selector shift rail. It sits in a square section groove on the outside of the **synchronizer sleeve** **FIGURE 24-7**. A synchronizer sleeve is part of the

FIGURE 24-6 The selector gate.

FIGURE 24-5 This type of gear shift lever is mounted in the top of the transmission and is sometimes called a top loader.

FIGURE 24-7 The shift fork is the part that fits into the square groove in the synchronizer sleeve.

synchronizer assembly and is what engages the dog teeth on the selected gear and transmits torque from the gear to the output shaft. The **synchronizer** will be discussed in greater detail later in this chapter.

The fifth gear/**reverse shift fork** engages in a groove in the synchronizer sleeve of the reverse gear synchronizer. The operation is no different from the other gear selections. The shift lever engages the correct shift selector rail and moves the attached shift fork, which moves the correct synchronizer sleeve forward or backward. For the example we have used in this material, you have a total of three shift forks—one for first and second gear, one for third and fourth, and one for fifth and reverse.

Each selector shift rail has a **detent mechanism**, usually in the form of a spring-loaded steel ball held in the casing **FIGURE 24-8**. The ball engages in a groove in the rail when the gear lever is in neutral and in a similar groove when a gear is selected. This helps hold the gear in the selected position along with the synchronizer **spring-loaded keys** that hold the synchronizer collar in the neutral position **FIGURE 24-9**. The detents also give the driver a feel of when the shift is complete. When a gear is changed or selected, an **interlock mechanism** prevents more than one gear from being engaged at the same time **FIGURE 24-10**. Some manufacturers have combined the interlock and detent mechanisms into one unit.

The interlock mechanism's function in ensuring that two gears cannot be selected at the same time is vital; if two gears could be selected, then the transmission main shaft or countershaft would break due to the binding condition created. In Figure 24-10, the interlock mechanism is made up of two steel balls that are located in the casing, between the center and the outside shift rails, and in alignment with grooves machined in the selector shift rails. A small plunger is captive in a hole drilled in the center rail. In the neutral position, the balls and plunger can move laterally. But when an outside rail is moved, the ball is pushed sideways to contact the plunger and move the opposite ball into the groove of the other outside rail. The two balls held in the casing prevent movement of the interlocked rails and hold them in the neutral position. When the center rail is moved, the balls move into the grooves of the outside rails and hold them in a similar manner.

> ### ▶ TECHNICIAN TIP
>
> All gearboxes are fitted with interlock and detent mechanisms, although designs vary according to manufacturer. Some manufacturers combine the two.

FIGURE 24-8 The transmission detent mechanism helps to hold the transmission in the gear.

FIGURE 24-9 Spring-loaded keys aid in holding the sleeve in the neutral position.

FIGURE 24-10 The interlock mechanism keeps two gears from being selected at the same time.

Paddle Shifters

The ability to shift gears and operate the clutch electronically or by **hydraulic actuators** such as a clutch slave cylinder is now facilitated by buttons or **paddles** on the steering wheel **FIGURE 24-11** . Some of these paddle units can be operated in a fully automatic mode. Most paddle shifters are installed by the manufacturers to control an automatic transmission, but there are some manufacturers using them to control a manual transmission. The shifter discussed here is strictly for manual transmissions. The paddles control switches that send signals to the power train control module/transmission control module (PCM/TCM) indicating the driver's desire to either upshift or downshift to the next gear. Paddle-shifted transmissions typically can only be shifted sequentially. In other words, you cannot skip gears like you can do with a typical manual transmission. These transmissions will be further explored later in the chapter.

Many newer manual transmissions are equipped with **electronic reverse lockout** systems, which use an electronic solenoid to prevent the transmission from being shifted into reverse while the vehicle is in forward motion. When the vehicle is moving, a signal from the **power train control module (PCM)** energizes the reverse **lockout solenoid** at a speed of around 5 to 10 mph (8 to 16 kph) and above. Once the cam and lock pin is operated by the electronic solenoid, it is impossible for the manual transmission to be shifted into reverse gear. However, at very low speeds, the solenoid is not energized and the return spring keeps the lock pin away from the interlock, enabling the transmission to be shifted into reverse.

Bearings and Thrust Washers

In a manual transmission, the gears and shafts are supported on bearings or bearing surfaces to reduce rolling friction. This design allows for smooth rotation and also maintains the alignment of the components due to rotational forces that work against each shaft due to the cut of the teeth on each gear. The type of bearing used at each locating point depends on the load that must be sustained. Radial loads try to force the gears and shafts apart. The bearing therefore carries the load along its radius. Thrust loads are applied along the length of the components, so the bearing must cater to side thrusts. In many cases, these loads are combined, and some bearings designed for radial loads will also accept light thrust loads. This description applies to most ball bearings.

Single-row, deep-groove ball bearings normally support the input shaft and main shaft in conventional rear-wheel drive transmissions **FIGURE 24-12** . They can also be used at each end of the countershaft. The helical gearing creates radial and thrust loads as the gears try to force each other apart and move endwise. A circlip or snap ring, in a groove on the outside of the bearing, can locate each bearing and shaft in the casing, which maintains the alignment of the gears and engagement hubs.

FIGURE 24-11 Steering wheel-mounted paddles are being used to shift manual transmissions electronically.

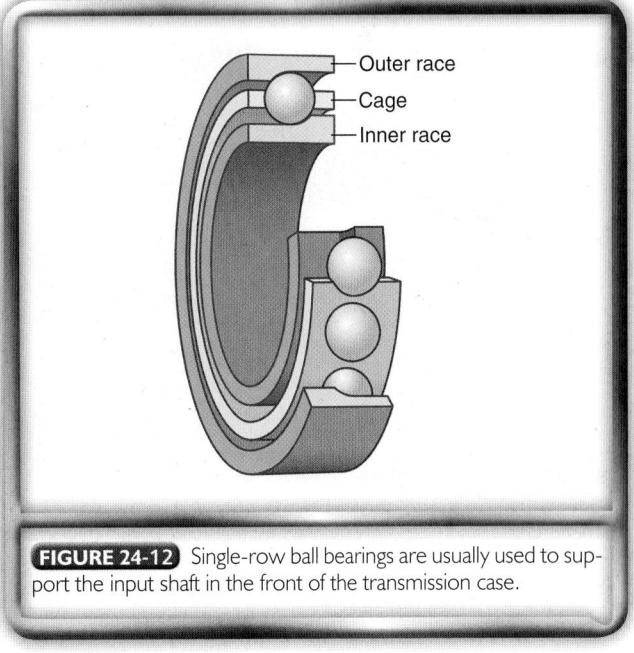

FIGURE 24-12 Single-row ball bearings are usually used to support the input shaft in the front of the transmission case.

Pocket bearings are used in transmissions and are roller bearings that sit in the pocket of the input shaft FIGURE 24-13. The input shaft is separated from the main shaft in order to transmit power to the countershaft. The main shaft is supported by the output bearing in the rear of the housing, and the front of the shaft is supported by the pocket bearing, which is held in place in the rear of the input shaft. The two shafts must be able to turn at differing speeds, so the pocket bearing reduces friction between the two shafts. This style of bearing is used only in rear-wheel drive transmissions.

Roller bearings are common where loads are purely radial FIGURE 24-14. Needle roller bearings can be caged, or can be a loose number assembled to operate directly on a hardened gear or shaft FIGURE 24-15. Typical applications are pilot bearings, pocket bearings, and flat thrust bearings. Some caged-style roller bearings are also used inside of the freely rotating gears on the main shaft.

Thrust washers are designed to fit between parts that rotate against each other. They protect against thrust loads and act as a wear surface, reducing friction between the rotating parts FIGURE 24-16. They are often of a selective thickness to allow for end play adjustments. Thrust washers are plain bearings, meaning they have no rollers. They are usually bronze, but can be steel, with a bronze facing on one side. They can be dimpled or grooved to allow for improved lubrication when under constant rotation.

A plain copper bushing is also used as a bearing wear surface in the extension housing to support the front of the yoke on the driveshaft. Machined and hardened surfaces on the main shaft can provide a bearing surface

FIGURE 24-14 Roller bearings are used to support radial loads.

FIGURE 24-15 Caged roller bearings can be used to support gears rotating on an output shaft.

FIGURE 24-13 The pocket bearing is located in the end of the input shaft and supports the front of the main shaft.

FIGURE 24-16 Thrust washers act as wear surfaces and can be used to adjust end play.

for the freely rotating gears. Flanges and snap rings on the main shaft locate the gears and hold them in place against any end thrust forces. A plain copper or bronze bearing is also used for the inside of the reverse idler gear to rotate on the idler shaft.

Tapered roller bearings are normally used in pairs and can sustain heavy radial and thrust loads in either direction (**FIGURE 24-17**). They are commonly used in transaxles, where they support the front and rear of the primary and secondary shafts, and the final drive assembly. **Selective thickness shims** are washers that can be used to provide for adjustment of end play or preload (**FIGURE 24-18**).

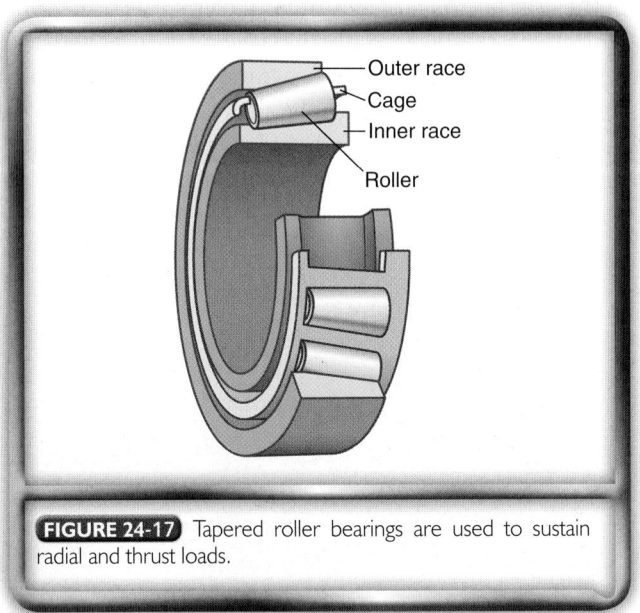

FIGURE 24-17 Tapered roller bearings are used to sustain radial and thrust loads.

FIGURE 24-18 Shims are used for correcting preload adjustments.

Oil Seals and Gaskets

The bearings are lubricated by being submerged in gear fluid. Gear fluid is splashed inside the casing while the transmission shafts rotate. Lubrication is extremely important for long gearbox life. Where the input and output shafts extend from the casing, oil seals prevent fluid leakage and the entrance of dirt and moisture into the transmission. Oil seals are an important part of the lubrication of the transmission because they ensure the proper level of gear fluid. If fluid levels are too high, pressure can build up and damage the seals. Low fluid levels cause heating up of all parts and may cause major damage to the wear surfaces of all of the internal components within a transmission.

Garter spring lip seals are normally used (**FIGURE 24-19**). They can be single or double lipped, depending on the application. They can also be **hydrodynamic seals**, with helical flutes molded into the sealing lip. The flutes or swirls create a pumping action as the input or output shaft rotates, causing any fluid at the sealing edge to be drawn back inside the casing. Since the flutes are molded in one direction during manufacture, care must be taken to ensure they are installed with the correct direction of shaft rotation.

O-ring seals are typically used for static locations such as the speedometer drive gear housing, while gaskets are used to seal the mating surfaces between the casing and the retaining plates or housings (**FIGURE 24-20**). In some cases, the gaskets that seal flat surfaces may be used by the manufacturer as selective thickness shims or spacers, in addition to their sealing function.

FIGURE 24-19 Seals prevent fluid leakage and keep dirt from entering the transmission.

FIGURE 24-20 O-ring seals are typically used for static locations.

Cork gaskets are cut out of a large sheet of cork and rubber mixture. They compress and provide a sealing action for case covers on the transmission. Because cork gaskets tend to absorb oil and will leak over time, they are not commonly used. Most gaskets used on manual transmissions are made of fiber material or a rubber material. Rubber or fiber gaskets tend to leak less and last longer. Some transmissions use a bead of room temperature vulcanizing (RTV) sealant to form the gasket. Room temperature vulcanizing means the liquid gasket material will cure at room temperature. This type of gasket costs less to manufacture since gaskets do not have to be produced for each transmission.

> ▶ TECHNICIAN TIP
>
> Some manufacturers use reusable silicone gaskets in some applications that can be used more than once.

▶ Gearbox Layouts

In a manual transmission for a rear-wheel drive vehicle, the gear train is built on three shafts—the input shaft, the countershaft, and the main shaft (sometimes referred to as the output shaft) FIGURE 24-21. The input shaft extends from the rear of the crankshaft through the front of the transmission and engages with the front of the main shaft. An external parallel-splined section engages with internal splines on the driven friction plate. A main drive gear on the input shaft is an integral part of the shaft. It meshes constantly with a mating gear on the countershaft that has a number of gears formed and/or pressed onto it. These gears are in constant mesh with mating gears on the main shaft, or output shaft. This main shaft is supported by

bearings on either end of the shaft—the pocket bearing on the front and the rear main shaft bearing on the rear. The gears can freely rotate on the main shaft until they are locked to the main shaft when a particular gear is selected. Each freewheeling main shaft gear has an external toothed section (commonly called dog teeth) on one side. The teeth face an internally toothed engagement sleeve and **blocking ring**, located on a central hub. This is part of the synchronizer and is splined to the main shaft FIGURE 24-22.

The engagement sleeve or sliding collar can slide in either direction to engage the dog teeth on the appropriate gear. Engagement of the dog teeth locks the gear through the sleeve and hub to the main shaft. Before engagement of the gear occurs, a synchromesh device called the synchronizer assembly matches the speed of the gear with the sleeve so that the sleeve can engage the dog teeth, transmitting power from the gear to the sleeve, and ultimately to the main shaft. For more on how the synchronizer works, see the synchronizer section later in this chapter.

FIGURE 24-21 Input shaft.

FIGURE 24-22 The synchronizer sleeve engages the dog teeth on the mating gear.

The gears constantly in mesh have their teeth cut on a <u>helix</u> at an angle to the gear centerline. This design reduces gear noise and distributes the load more evenly, as several teeth are in contact at any time **FIGURE 24-23**.

TECHNICIAN TIP

In the early days of automotives, gear designs were all spur-type gears and did not have synchronizers to enable a smooth shift. These gear arrangements required special clutch operation called double-clutching when shifting from one gear to another. <u>Double-clutching</u> refers to depressing the clutch pedal twice for each gear change—once to enter neutral and again to select the next gear. The clutch pedal is then released a second time and the vehicle can be accelerated. The reason for double-clutching was to match the engine speed with the gear speed to ensure a relatively smooth engagement of the gears, thereby avoiding gear clashing and transmission damage. Double-clutching a transmission was not an easy task, as the clutch pedal pressure was usually very high in an older vehicle to ensure the disc did not slip (spring technology was not the same as it is today). In today's transmissions with synchronizers, there is no need to double-clutch to change gears; the synchronizer automatically matches the gear speed to the shaft speed as the gear shift is being performed.

Teeth on the reverse idler gear are normally straight-cut, or spur, gears, which are cut parallel to the gear centerline and in most cases are very noisy when rotating in mesh **FIGURE 24-24**. Spur gears provide a strong contact for the gear teeth and are used in heavy-duty applications and in some high-performance applications. The noise made by spur-cut gears is demonstrated by the whining of the transmission when a car is backed up rapidly.

When the reverse gear is selected, one of two things occurs. In one design, the reverse idler gear connects and slides into its two mating gears on the countershaft

FIGURE 24-23 Helical gears have teeth that are cut on a helix for quieter operation.

and main shaft. This results in an opposite rotation of the output shaft as compared to the forward direction, propelling the vehicle in the reverse direction. The reverse idler rotates on a shaft fixed in the casing. It transfers the drive from the countershaft to the main shaft. In the second design, reverse is engaged by a constant-mesh reverse gear that uses a synchronizer sleeve to lock the reverse gear to the main shaft **FIGURE 24-25**.

FIGURE 24-24 Spur gears use straight-cut teeth for more coverage and heavy-duty operation.

Sliding reverse idler

FIGURE 24-25 **A.** Sliding reverse idler. **B.** Constant-mesh reverse gear. Both cause the output shaft to rotate in the reverse direction.

Transaxle Designs

In transaxle designs, the drive is transferred through the clutch unit to a primary or input shaft. In this design, the primary shaft carries gears of different sizes, meshed with gears on the secondary shaft. Each pair of gears typically has one gear fixed to the primary shaft and one free to rotate on bearings on the secondary or output shaft.

An engagement sleeve and hub assembly, with a synchromesh unit facing each gear, is on the secondary shaft between first and second, and similarly between third and fourth.

The engagement sleeve moves to engage with the dog teeth of the relevant gear when a gear is selected. This locks the gear to the shaft so that drive can be transmitted.

A drive pinion gear fixed to the end of the secondary shaft is constantly in mesh with a final drive ring gear **FIGURE 24-26**. The drive is transferred through these gears to the differential unit.

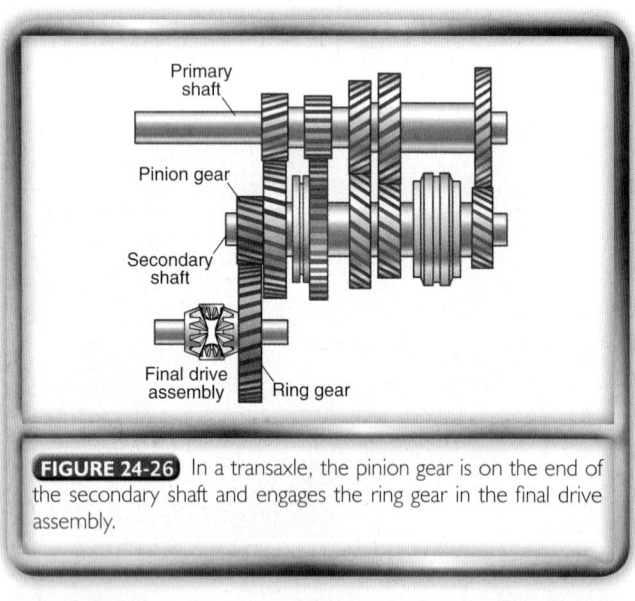

FIGURE 24-26 In a transaxle, the pinion gear is on the end of the secondary shaft and engages the ring gear in the final drive assembly.

FIGURE 24-27 The fifth gear is attached to the output shaft to provide higher vehicle speeds at lower engine rpm, which increases fuel economy.

A reverse idler transmits the drive from the primary to the secondary shaft when reverse is selected. One design of a five-speed transaxle has an extra fixed gear on the primary shaft, meshed with a mating free gear on the secondary shaft **FIGURE 24-27**. The free gear has its own engagement sleeve and synchromesh unit beside it. Selecting fifth gear locks the gear to the shaft. The gear on the primary shaft is larger than the gear on the secondary, so an overdrive ratio is provided. The secondary shaft will then rotate faster than the primary shaft.

> **TECHNICIAN TIP**
>
> Having the gearbox and final drive gears in one casing provides a compact and relatively quiet unit and fits well into front-wheel drive vehicles.

Gearbox Operation

In a rear-wheel drive manual transmission, the splines on the front of the input shaft engage with the splines of the clutch-driven plate. With engine rotation and the clutch engaged, the input shaft transfers its motion through the countershaft to rotate the gears on the main shaft. In neutral condition, the engagement sleeves and hubs splined to the main shaft are stationary. No drive is transmitted to the main/output shaft.

Depressing the clutch pedal disconnects the engine from the input shaft, allowing an engagement sleeve to be moved into engagement with the external dog teeth on the gear selected. Engaging the dog teeth locks the gear to the main shaft. When the clutch is released, the drive is transmitted to the input gear, along the countershaft to the gear selected. Since this gear is now locked to the main shaft, the main shaft rotates and transfers the drive to the final drive unit.

The speed ratio and the torque transferred depend on which gear is selected. In a four- or five-speed transmission, the first gear, the smallest on the countershaft, meshes with the largest gear on the main shaft, producing first gear **FIGURE 24-28**. First gear is always the lowest of the gear ratios in forward. Remember, reverse often has a lower gear ratio since the vehicle needs high torque, more than fast speeds, when moving in reverse. The greatest number of turns of the input shaft is required to achieve one turn of the output shaft when we are in the lowest gear ratio, in this case first or reverse. A low gear ratio also gives the greatest amount of torque multiplication.

In second gear, power flow is through the next adjacent gear **FIGURE 24-29**. The difference in speed between input and output shafts is reduced. Fewer turns of the input shaft are required to give one turn of the output shaft, but there is less torque multiplication.

FIGURE 24-28 Power flow for first gear in a transmission.

FIGURE 24-30 Power flow for third gear in a transmission.

FIGURE 24-29 Power flow for second gear in a transmission.

FIGURE 24-31 Power flow for fourth gear in a transmission.

▶ **LINK**
Refer to the Manual Transmission/Transaxle Principles chapter to learn more about power flow.

When the engagement sleeve for third gear moves into place, drive is transmitted through the meshing gears at an even higher gear ratio **FIGURE 24-30**. In fourth gear, the input and output shafts are directly locked together **FIGURE 24-31**. This provides a direct drive with a 1:1 ratio, with no reduction through the countershaft gears. The input and output shafts turn at the same speed, and there is therefore no torque multiplication.

The countershaft gears and their corresponding gears on the main shaft continue to rotate, as the countershaft is constantly in mesh with the input gear. They do not transmit any drive, but the countershaft still provides lubrication by its movement, which picks up and flings transmission fluid within the housing. With the vehicle in motion, these gears turn at different speeds in relation to the main shaft

and to the engagement sleeves, which are locked to the main shaft by the mating splines on the sleeve and synchronizer hub. A transaxle operates in a similar manner, transferring drive through gears on the primary and secondary shafts, which then transfer drive to the final drive assembly.

Role of Electronics

For the most part, historically, manual transmissions have not required the use of electronics. But as with all vehicle systems, electronics are starting to play more of a roll. **Vehicle speed sensors** are mounted in the transmission case and are used to generate a signal based on the vehicle's speed that is sent to the PCM and/or speedometer. A sensor may also be used to tell the PCM/TCM what gear is selected. The PCM uses that information along with data from other sensors to control various aspects of the vehicle, including the speedometer reading (on some vehicles) as well as some electronic shift routines, which are covered in the Manual Transmission/Transaxle

Principles chapter. Another innovation in technology is the dual-clutch, six-speed or seven-speed transmission designed by several manufacturers that makes shifting easy and effortless by incorporating electronics into the mix. See the Dual-Clutch Manual Transmissions section later in this chapter for more information.

▶ Baulk-Ring Synchromesh Unit

A **baulk-ring synchromesh unit**, commonly called a blocker ring synchromesh unit, is used to synchronize the speeds of gear and shaft before engagement **FIGURE 24-32**. Once the speeds of the gear and shaft are matched, the engagement sleeve slides on its splines on the hub and engages with the dog teeth on the gear, effectively locking them together. The synchronizer assembly makes this possible. Three metal inserts, with a center ridge, fit into slots in the hub. A radial spring at each end holds them out so that the ridge on each insert sits in a groove inside the sleeve and holds each one centered on the hub. When the synchronizer is assembled, the hub is splined to the main shaft, and the engagement sleeve is splined to the hub. A bronze blocker ring with recesses to accommodate the ends of the inserts is located in each end of the hub, and a conical inner surface faces a matching steel cone on the gear.

Fine grooves are machined on the conical surface of the blocker ring and help with cutting through the oil film on the cone-shaped surface on the gear **FIGURE 24-33**. The teeth on the outer edge of the blocker ring are the same size as the dog teeth on the gear and the splines on the sleeve. The recesses in the blocker ring are wider than the inserts to allow the blocker ring to move radially. Then the teeth on the blocker ring can be rotated so they are out of alignment with the teeth on the sleeve.

When the sleeve is moved to select a gear, the spring-loaded inserts move the blocker ring into contact with the conical face of the gear. The grooves in the face of the blocker ring start to cut through the oil film. The difference in speed between the two components causes the blocker ring to be dragged around with the gear to the limit of the recesses, where it is held by the inserts.

Since the teeth of the blocker ring are now out of alignment with the teeth of the sleeve, the sleeve is blocked from moving over the ring into engagement **FIGURE 24-34**. The force exerted by the driver on the gear lever, shift rails, and shift fork now presses the sleeve against the teeth of the blocker ring and increases the force of the conical face of the blocker ring against the cone of the selected gear until the friction causes the two components to rotate at the same speed. The blocker ring teeth can now come into alignment,

FIGURE 24-33 Fine grooves on a blocker ring.

FIGURE 24-32 Blocker ring teeth line up with the dog teeth to allow smooth engagement of the sleeve.

FIGURE 24-34 Blocker ring teeth out of alignment, which allows the blocker ring to bring the gear to the same speed.

and the sleeve slides over them and into engagement without grinding. This step is assisted by a **chamfer** (a tapered cut) on the teeth of the gear, blocker ring, and sleeve, which helps to guide the sleeve into position over each of those parts. Smooth and rapid gear changes are thus ensured.

▶ Transaxle Synchromesh Unit

In transaxles, the synchromesh unit plays a similar role. It is located between the end of each engagement sleeve and the gear. In this arrangement, the engagement hub and sleeve assembly for first and second gears is typically on the secondary shaft, as is the third and fourth speed hub. The fifth gear engagement hub is at the end of the secondary shaft, farthest from the main drive pinion. When first gear is selected, the engagement sleeve locks the first gear to the secondary shaft. When the clutch is released, the drive is transferred through the fixed first gear on the primary shaft to the locked gear on the secondary shaft. The secondary shaft rotation transfers the drive through the main drive pinion to the final drive ring gear and the differential case.

In first gear, the smallest gear on the primary shaft drives the largest gear on the secondary shaft, resulting in the lowest gear ratio—in this case, approximately 3.4:1 **FIGURE 24-35**. In second gear, a higher gear ratio is obtained, as the fixed second gear on the primary shaft is larger. Fewer turns of the primary shaft are required to obtain one turn of the secondary—in this case, resulting in an approximate ratio of 1.95:1 **FIGURE 24-36**.

In third gear, the engagement sleeve locks the freely rotating third gear to the secondary shaft **FIGURE 24-37**. Drive is transferred from the fixed gear on the primary shaft to the locked gear on the secondary shaft, and

then to the final drive. The drive transfer is similar for fourth gear, but the gears are the same size **FIGURE 24-38**.

FIGURE 24-36 Power flow for second gear.

FIGURE 24-37 Power flow for third gear.

FIGURE 24-35 Power flow for first gear.

FIGURE 24-38 Power flow for fourth gear.

The fifth gear ratio is provided by transferring the drive through the fixed fifth gear on the primary shaft to the engaged fifth gear on the secondary shaft. This is often an overdrive ratio, with the driving gear larger than the driven gear, making the driven gear rotate at a higher speed **FIGURE 24-39**.

For reverse, the reverse idler moves to mesh with a reverse gear on the primary shaft, and the matching gear teeth on the outside of the first and second gear engagement sleeve **FIGURE 24-40**. Drive transfers through the idler to the splined secondary shaft sleeve. The idler between the shafts makes the secondary shaft rotate in the reverse direction. This reverses the direction of the final drive ring gear and, thus, the road wheels.

FIGURE 24-39 Power flow for fifth gear.

FIGURE 24-40 Power flow for reverse gear.

Dual-Clutch Manual Transmissions

A dual-clutch transmission is sometimes referred to as a semiautomatic or automated manual transmission since it uses a gear train more similar to a manual transmission than an automatic transmission. Still, dual clutches are controlled by the PCM/TCM, so there is no clutch pedal. The dual-clutch arrangement also requires two input shafts. Each clutch powers one of the input shafts **FIGURE 24-41**. The dual-clutch transaxle uses electric solenoid valves to hydraulically engage and disengage each clutch. This transaxle has dual input shafts that are connected by gears to two main shafts containing the synchronizers. One shaft has gears two, four, and six, and the other shaft has gears one, three, and five. The transaxle control module is able to move the shift forks by electric actuators to select each gear. Only one gear on one input shaft transmits power at a time. While one gear is engaged on one input shaft, the control module commands an actuator on the other input shaft to engage the next sequential gear. Since the clutch on the second input shaft is disengaged, the gear can be selected, ready and waiting to be applied, for either an upshift or downshift. This type of transaxle provides a very quick shift since all it takes to upshift is releasing one clutch and activating the other. This makes for extremely fast and accurate shifts.

The dual clutches are typically hydraulically operated wet clutches, similar to clutches in an automatic transmission, but dry clutches are coming into more use. The PCM/TCM controls their application and release by sending hydraulic pressure to each clutch to apply it,

FIGURE 24-41 Dual-clutch transmission layout.

and venting hydraulic pressure to release it. Hydraulic pressure is controlled by solenoid valves that react to the signals sent from the PCM/TCM. The PCM/TCM monitors data such as engine rpm, rpm of each input shaft, gear selected, vehicle speed, throttle position, brake pedal position, and other sensor information. Based on this information, the PCM/TCM sends the appropriate signals to the solenoid valves.

▶ Diagnosis

Diagnosing Common Noise Concerns

In many cases, manual transmissions will start making noises as they begin to fail. Listening to, and evaluating, noises is an important part of transmission diagnosis. It is usually a good practice to take the vehicle out on a road test to verify the customer's complaint and listen to any unusual noises. Some noises may be a normal characteristic of that vehicle, such as the whining noise that is produced in reverse due to the spur-cut gears. Obviously, most noises are a valid concern, so it is always worth looking into.

When listening to noises, listen for when they occur along with the type of noise. For example, is the noise only evident or worse while the transmission is in neutral, when in a particular gear, or only when driving down the road? The key is to be sure the customer has given you all the information about when the noise is happening. Be aware that some noises may not emanate from the manual transmission but may be coming from other sources such as the engine, transfer case, and/or differential. In fact, even bad motor mounts can cause noises that can be mistaken for noises coming from the transmission area.

Most transmission noises will stop or become much quieter when the vehicle is brought to a standstill; therefore, test-driving the vehicle will help you determine the source of the noise. Transmissions can create many different types of noises. The following paragraphs will help you to diagnose the common noises associated with the manual transmission.

Grinding or clashing noises during upshifts and downshifts are fairly common on manual transmissions. In some cases, it could be as simple as the driver not fully disengaging the clutch between shifts and may be solved by training the customer to push the clutch pedal all the way to the floor. A related cause could be the clutch having too much free play and needing an adjustment or replacement of worn parts. Or if it is a hydraulic clutch, the fluid may have air in the system, preventing the clutch from fully releasing.

Grinding noises could also be caused by a component such as a worn synchronizer blocker ring that cannot grip the gear and match the gear speed to the shaft speed. The synchronizer blocker rings have ridges on them that grab the gear cone. If the ridges are worn, the synchronizer cannot grip the gear as well and will slip. Another cause could be that a shift rail is binding, causing two gears to try to engage at the same time, which will create grinding noises.

A less common cause of grinding noises relates to the alignment of the bell housing. If the bell housing of the transmission is misaligned, the clutch disc will be out of alignment with the flywheel and pressure plate, which can cause the clutch disc to drag, making it harder for the synchronizers to match the speed for shifting into gear. This results in grinding noises.

Another noise that can come from the transmission is a rough growling noise while driving down the road. This type of noise can be caused by a couple of faults— worn bearings or worn gears. If the bearings on the input shaft, countershaft, or main shaft are worn, either front or rear, a growling noise will result when driving. It may be necessary to drive the vehicle on a lift to pinpoint the exact location of the noise. Teardown of the transmission may be necessary to diagnose the exact bearing issue.

Clicking noises in any gear selection are typically related to a tooth of a gear that is damaged on the main shaft, input shaft, or countershaft. The clicking will increase with speed, or may change with gear shifts. Pinpointing the exact gear that is chipped will require a teardown of the transmission.

If there is a rough growling noise in neutral, you will need to know if the clutch is engaged or disengaged. Think about what you know is spinning when the engine is running and the transmission is in neutral. The flywheel is spinning, and if the clutch is disengaged, then the input shaft is not spinning; thus the pilot bearing is operating between the turning flywheel and the stationary input shaft. In this case, the growling noise is likely caused by a worn pilot bearing. If the clutch is engaged, then the input shaft and countershaft are spinning but the output shaft will be stationary, as no gears are locked to the main shaft and they are freewheeling. By thinking through and visualizing what is moving inside the transmission, you can figure out that the noise must be related to the input shaft front bearing or one of the countershaft bearings.

If the customer concern is that there is a growling noise in all gears except direct drive, then focus on the parts that are under load such as the input bearing, countershaft bearings, pocket bearing in the back of the input shaft, and the individual gears themselves. If the noise gets much quieter when the shafts are turning at the same speed (fourth gear), then it is related to the power flow through the countershaft, which could be any of the bearings on all three shafts. Noises in transaxle vehicles would be diagnosed in the same manner, first knowing how the transaxle operates, then applying that logic to when and what is causing the noise.

These concerns are not necessarily all the possible customer concerns related to manual transmissions and transaxles. Be sure to refer to the manufacturer's service information for all transmission-related problems. Do not forget to check technical service bulletins (TSBs) for any information related to the concern you are diagnosing. Many concerns could have been solved quickly and efficiently if TSBs had been checked before beginning service work on a transmission and not finding anything wrong inside.

> ### ▶ Caring for the Customer
>
> Sometimes it is a good idea to let the customer drive during a test-drive. This may allow the technician to observe any bad driving practices that may contribute to the customer concern.

Diagnosing Hard Shifting

During the life of the vehicle, components wear and **hard shifting** can occur. Hard shifting is when the shifter will not move smoothly into the desired gear and requires excessive force by the driver to force it into gear. The hard shifting may also be accompanied by grinding gears. Hard shifting concerns can be the result of an incorrectly adjusted clutch or most other clutch problems. If the clutch does not disengage fully, then the input shaft will still spin, preventing the synchronizers from matching the speed between the gear and the output shaft. A grinding noise and hard shifting will result. The easiest way to diagnose this issue is to lift the drive wheels of the vehicle and place the transmission in first gear with the clutch pushed in. If the wheels spin when the clutch is pushed in, then the input shaft is still spinning. Check the clutch adjustment at this point or check for travel issues in the hydraulic clutch due to air in the system or incorrect slave cylinder or master cylinder installation. Another reason for hard shifting is the clutch pedal binding. If the clutch does not move freely, it can result in a clutch that stays partially engaged. Remember, anything keeping the clutch from fully disengaging can result in hard shifting, so if the bell housing to transmission is misaligned or loose, then hard shifting can result.

Shift rails can be another reason that the transmission shifts hard. If the shift rails will not move freely, then hard shifting will result and more force will have to be placed on the shifter by the driver. With this in mind, it is easy to see that if the synchronizers or shift forks are binding, this will also result in hard shifting. One test to see if the synchronizers are able to do their job is to try shifting the transmission into gear with the engine running, and compare that to how hard it is to shift into the same gear with the engine not running. Any difference means the synchronizers cannot adequately do their job. At the same time, the synchronizers may be overworked by a dragging clutch.

A simple issue that can cause hard shifting is created by maintenance work that is performed improperly on a manual transmission. Let's say that a customer changes transmission fluid as part of the preventive maintenance, but is used to a different vehicle that uses an 80W-90 gear oil in the transmission. The customer drains the fluid and installs 80W-90 in the transmission, which requires 10W-30 motor oil. The thick gear oil will result in shift linkage that is sluggish and hard to move. The fix for this is simple, remove the thick oil and change with the required fluid. If the transmission will not shift into one or more gears, then check the square portion of the shift lever for wear or check for worn shift linkages. Check for the detent system sticking. The detent ball must move up out of the way as the shift rail moves forward. If the detent ball is stuck down and will not move up, then the transmission may not be able to shift into that related gear(s). If we go inside the transmission, there may be an issue with the dog teeth on the front of the gear being worn to the point that they will not accept the synchronizer sleeve as the driver moves it into mesh with the worn teeth.

If the transmission is stuck in one gear, the technician will need to check for a stuck detent mechanism. A detent that is stuck could keep the shifter from moving to select the next gear. Another cause of this concern would be a binding synchronizer that will not allow movement of the shifter. If a gear has broken dog teeth, it is possible that the synchronizer has become jammed and will not allow changing gears. The technician's first step would be to disconnect the linkage to the transmission, if equipped, and verify that the shifter will now move freely. The issue could simply be a cable that is frozen or a linkage that is binding. It would be very bad for the technician to tear down a transmission only to find that a stuck shift cable was the cause of the customer's concern.

If the transmission is jumping out of gear, then the technician should first check for shift linkage, shift cable, or shifter boot binding. A shifter boot has been known to cause popping out of gear concerns as the engine is accelerated or decelerated. Remember, the engine and transmission twist with torque; if the boot is pulled tight, it could push the shifter out of gear. Be sure to check TSBs for any issues of redesigned shifter boots. Popping out of gear can also be caused by issues inside the transmission. Be sure to eliminate all causes outside the transmission before pulling the transmission down for inspection.

The synchronizer is used to ensure proper engagement of the gear without grinding. The blocking ring of the synchronizer grips the cone of the gear to slow or speed the gear to shaft speed, and it helps the synchronizer sleeve move over and lock into the gear dog teeth. If the blocking ring is worn, it is possible that the synchronizer sleeve will not move fully over the dog teeth and with torque applied will pull back off the dog teeth. This leads to another possible cause—worn dog teeth. The dog teeth have a back cut that ensures that the synchronizer sleeve locks into mesh with the teeth. If the dog teeth are worn, the synchronizer sleeve will not lock into place and can pull back off with torque from the engine. If the transmission has too much shaft end play, the moving of the shafts can cause the shift fork to walk the synchronizer sleeve out of mesh with the gear dog teeth. Worn or broken power train mounts can also pull the transmission out of gear if it uses an external shifter as the engine moves when applying a load.

Diagnosing Transaxle Noises and Vibrations

Transaxles can exhibit similar noises as a transmission when the issue is related to the bearings or gears, so diagnose them in a similar manner, realizing that the gear train and power flow are slightly different. Since the transaxle includes a final drive assembly, which transmits power out of the transaxle to the half-shaft drive axles, it can have noises that are different from a regular transmission. The transaxle's secondary shaft drives the final drive ring gear. The ring gear then transfers torque and engine power to the differential case. The transaxle case houses the ring gear with its counterpart the pinion gear. The differential axle side gears drive the half shaft axles that are splined to the front axle hubs. The main difference between the differential in a rear-wheel drive vehicle and the differential in a front-wheel drive transaxle is the direction of power flow. The rear-wheel drive differential power flow changes 90 degrees between the drive pinion gear and the ring gear. This 90-degree change in direction is not necessary with most front-wheel drive vehicles. Noise and vibration can be a concern in the front-wheel drive differential, as this usually can be felt in the steering wheel assembly.

Transaxle final drive assembly noise and vibrations can be caused by multiple things. Be sure to check for TSBs and service information for the vehicle you are working on. Differential noise can be related to ring gear bearings, which could have been damaged by low transaxle fluid levels or fluids of the wrong viscosity type. Bearings can be damaged by bent half-shafts and can create vibrations while driving. If the transaxle ring and pinion assembly has too little clearance, then a whining noise can result. This clearance is referred to as backlash and is typically set with selective thickness shims. Backlash is a critical inspection item upon assembly, and care should be taken to ensure it is set to the manufacturer's specifications. If backlash is excessive, then a clunking noise can result as the vehicle accelerates or decelerates.

Other issues related to transaxles include noises from damaged teeth on the ring and pinion gears. Typically, a clicking noise will result from chipped teeth. A customer who races his or her front-wheel drive vehicle may chip teeth due to the excessive shock placed on gear teeth. Constant-velocity (CV) joints can create vibration if the engine cradle assembly is shifted or bent. This will result in CV joints running at incorrect angles and therefore binding, which creates vibration. If either of the outer CV joints is damaged, then clicking will result when the steering wheel is turned completely to one side, especially while accelerating. If you notice the CV boot is torn and a clicking is coming from one side, check noise while on a lift to pinpoint to the CV axle.

Diagnosing Drive Train Concerns

Customer concerns related to the drive train will typically be evident while the vehicle is moving. The first step in diagnosis is to verify the customer concern. If the concern cannot be verified at the shop, then a test-drive with the customer may be necessary.

A customer interview is critical to the diagnosis to obtain all of the information concerning the symptoms and to ensure a proper and lasting repair. Service consultants may use a check sheet to help the customer express all of the conditions related to the concern. The check sheet will ask the customer a series of questions to help determine when the noise is occurring, if the noise is louder on acceleration or on deceleration, or if the noise is in a particular gear. If a check sheet is not available, then the consultant will need to ask similar questions to ensure the technician has as many details as possible to aid in diagnosis. If the service consultant has failed to obtain the proper information, it may be necessary for the technician to interview the customer personally or go on a test-drive with the customer.

Depending on the depth of the problem, researching for TSBs or recalls may play a critical role in the proper diagnosis and repair. Perform any necessary diagnostic tests according to the manufacturer's specifications to identify the cause of the problem. The troubleshooting procedure in the service information will help the technician to diagnose the issue. For example, let's say a noise is found only in third gear on a pick-up truck. The technician verifies that the noise is in third gear. The service information states that the technician should note the rpm range in which the noise occurs. The technician notes that the rpm is 3000 when the concern is occurring. The service information tells the technician to ensure that the noise is not occurring when the transmission is in neutral at that rpm. The technician finds that the noise does occur at 3000 rpm in neutral. This finding tells the technician that the concern is not in the transmission, but in the engine. Further diagnosis of the engine is needed at this point.

A visual inspection should always be performed when diagnosing the manual transmission. Manufacturers have designed prescribed tests to aid in finding a solution to the complaint. Once all data have been collected and analyzed, determine the correct action to make the repair.

Diagnosing an Electronically Controlled Manual Transmission

Manual transmissions are now being equipped with shift mechanisms using new electronic technologies. These shift mechanisms are fully electronic and are controlled by a series of modules that provide better control of gear engagement while monitoring optimum shift force at time of the shift. By controlling this shift force, which relies on engine, transmission, and vehicle operation, they are able to vary shift forces to complete a gear shift. These forces include synchronizer clearances and shift rail end forces for shifting into gear smoothly. Special electronic shift routines assure that shift rails operate at maximum efficiency and shifts are made at the right times. Transmission gear selection is done by shift solenoids, actuators, and modules, which are controlled by the PCM/TCM according to the vehicle data, programmed software, and driver commands. The PCM/TCM then provides an output signal to operate the appropriate shift solenoid or actuator for the shift to occur. Clutch operation can be mechanical or solenoid operation. The shift lever itself is not connected to any linkage; rather, it is a shift-by-wire or electronic connection to the transmission and information comes from the control module. When shifts are made, the computer determines the correct time to allow the transmission to shift. This type of transmission also has fail-safes built in to the computers in case the computer sees a problem in the system.

To diagnose an electronically controlled manual transmission, consult the manufacturer's service information to identify all possible problems that might result from a fault in the system. Start by locating the description and operation section to define operational characteristics of the electronic manual transmission. Understanding how the system works will help you avoid misdiagnosing the fault, as well as point you in the right direction for diagnosing it. Once you know how the transmission should be acting, verify that it is not acting properly. Use a scan tool to read any codes that may be present. You can also look at any freeze-frame and data-stream information while operating the vehicle. Doing so will give you further clues as to the cause of the fault. If the vehicle has codes, follow the troubleshooting chart for the code found. Be sure to check for codes that are related to the customer concern. Do not chase codes that are unrelated to the customer concern. For example, if the customer disconnected the battery with the ignition key on, multiple codes might be set. None of these codes is likely to be related to a noise issue.

▶ Maintenance and Repair

While some newer vehicles have fewer requirements for transmission maintenance due to self-adjusting clutches and fill-for-life lubricants, those that do require maintenance must be serviced according to the manufacturer's schedule to ensure long life. Research all applicable vehicle and service information. Failure to perform required maintenance of transmissions can result in severe damage to the internal components, which are expensive to repair. For example, operating the transmission with substantially low lubricating fluid because it had a small leak and never got checked during engine oil changes can ruin the transmission way before its time. Don't overlook the maintenance; your customer expects it to be performed properly and at the specified time.

Tools

When performing service and repair operations on a manual transmission, you will need to be familiar with several tools **FIGURE 24-42**:

- Dial indicator: The dial indicator is used to check input or output shaft end play. The end play of the shafts is set by selective thickness shims. The selective thickness shims are measured with an outside micrometer.
- Hydraulic press: The press may be used to tear down and reassemble the transmission for service.
- Bearing splitter: A bearing splitter is used to press bearings from the transmission shafts or to remove synchronizer sleeves.

FIGURE 24-42 Properly servicing manual transmissions requires a variety of tools. **A.** Hydraulic press. **B.** Bearing splitter. **C.** Snap ring pliers. **D.** Bearing puller or gear puller. **E.** Seal installer.

- Various gear pullers and bearing pullers: These tools are manually operated.
- Snap ring pliers: These pliers are needed to remove snap rings that may be used to retain gears or synchronizers.

- Seal installer: The seal installer is used to ensure that seals are not damaged when being installed into transmission housings.

Preventive Maintenance

Preventive maintenance is designed to extend the service life of the transmission. It also improves the reliability of the vehicle, and helps to prevent vehicle breakdowns that could leave the driver and passengers stranded. While most vehicle owners understand this, not all of them do. And of those who do, many do not know the extent of the preventive maintenance needed or how it is performed. This is where you come in. By learning what maintenance the manufacturer requires, and how to perform it, you can help the customer get the maximum reliability and life out of the vehicle.

Fluid level and condition should be checked as part of a thorough visual inspection anytime a transmission fault is suspected. Condition and level of the transmission fluid can tell a technician a lot about what is going on inside. For example, if metal is found floating inside the transmission fluid, then the technician knows that

the transmission will need to be pulled apart or replaced. Make it a habit to visually inspect the transmission every time it is in for an oil change or other service so you can catch issues before they become severe.

Checking Gearbox Fluid

As a preventive maintenance task, fluid level of the manual transmission should be checked when other tasks are performed, such as engine oil and filter change or lubrication of steering parts, according to the manufacturer's periodic intervals. In the event of a suspected leak, the transmission fluid level should be checked to prevent catastrophic failure.

To check and adjust the fluid level, follow the steps in **SKILL DRILL 24-1**:

1. Safely raise the vehicle on an approved lift, making sure it is secure.
2. Perform a visual inspection of the transmission before checking the gearbox fluid level. Obtain a clean drain pan before removing the filler plug, as fluid may spill out.
3. Remove the filler plug using the proper wrench to make sure the filler plug does not become damaged. Perform a visual inspection of the filler plug for thread damage, and replace if necessary. Inspect the threads in the transmission fill hole for damage also. (**Photo 1**)
4. If the gearbox fluid begins to run out as the filler plug is removed, let the gearbox fluid seek its own

> ### Caring for the Customer
>
> It is always a good idea to keep up with preventive maintenance on a regular basis. Remind the customer that preventive maintenance is the road to long life for the vehicle and can help save thousands of dollars in repairs.

SKILL DRILL | 24-1 | Checking the Fluid Level of a Manual Transmission

1. Raise the vehicle on the lift. Inspect the transmission for leaks. Remove the filler plug using the proper wrench. Inspect the filler plug and fill hole for thread damage, and replace/repair if necessary.

2. If the gearbox fluid begins to run out as the filler plug is removed, let the gearbox fluid seek its own level before reinstalling the filler plug. The gearbox fluid level should be at the bottom of the filler plug hole.

3. If the fluid level is low, refill with the specified fluid, reinstall the filler plug, and wipe the area around the filler plug hole with a clean shop towel. Tighten the filler plug to the specified torque.

level before reinstalling the filler plug. The gearbox fluid level should be at the bottom of the filler plug hole. If the level is left over full, aeration of the gearbox fluid could result, as well as buildup of pressure in the transmission and damage to the seals that keep the gearbox fluid at the proper level. **(Photo 2)**

5 If the fluid level is low, refill with the manufacturer's specified fluid, reinstall the filler plug, and wipe the area around the filler plug hole with a clean shop towel. Tighten the filler plug to the specified torque. **(Photo 3)**

Checking and Adjusting Differential/ Transfer Case Fluid

Checking and adjusting the differential/transfer case fluid level is very similar to the process for checking the transmission fluid level, but there are some differences. First, some differential/final drive assemblies, such as limited-slip and posi-traction assemblies, require specially designed additives or fluid. Transfer cases may also require special lubricants as specified by the manufacturer.

Always check the service information for the vehicle you are working on. Differentials and transfer cases generally have fill plugs that can be used when checking the fluid level in the same way a transmission does. However, they often do not have a drain plug. In these cases, either a specific bolt may need to be removed or a cover may need to be unbolted and removed. Follow the service information.

To check and adjust the differential/transfer case fluid level, follow the steps in **SKILL DRILL 24-2**:

1 Safely raise the vehicle on an approved lift, making sure it is secure.

2 Perform a visual inspection of the differential and transfer case before checking the fluid level. Obtain a clean drain pan before removal of the filler plug, as fluid may spill out.

3 Remove the filler plug using the proper wrench to make sure the filler plug does not become damaged. Perform a visual inspection of the filler plug for thread damage, and replace if necessary. Inspect the threads in the differential and transfer case fill holes for damage also. **(Photo 1)**

SKILL DRILL | 24-2 | Checking and Adjusting the Differential/Transfer Case Fluid Level

1 Raise the vehicle on an approved lift. Inspect the differential and transfer case before checking the fluid level. Obtain a clean drain pan before removal of the filler plug, as fluid may spill out. Remove the filler plug using the proper wrench. Inspect the filler plug for thread damage, and replace if necessary. Inspect the threads in the differential and transfer case fill holes for damage also.

2 If the fluid begins to run out as the filler plug is removed, let the fluid seek its own level before reinstalling the filler plug. The fluid level should be at the bottom of the filler plug hole.

3 If the fluid level is low, refill with the specified fluid, reinstall the filler plug, and wipe the area around the filler plug hole with a clean shop towel. Tighten the filler plug to the specified torque.

4 If the fluid begins to run out as the filler plug is removed, let the fluid seek its own level before reinstalling the filler plug. The fluid level should be at the bottom of the filler plug hole. (**Photo 2**)

5 If the fluid level is low, refill with the manufacturer's specified fluid, reinstall the filler plug, and wipe the area around the filler plug hole with a clean shop towel. Tighten the filler plug to the specified torque. (**Photo 3**)

Changing Manual Gearbox and Final Drive Fluid

At the manufacturer's specified intervals, the gearbox fluid must be changed in those vehicles in which manufacturers require it. Gearbox fluid left unchanged will break down from heat and lose its capacity to lubricate all rotating parts, causing premature bearing and gear failure. This potential damage also makes it critical to maintain proper gearbox fluid levels. If the level becomes too low, bearings and gears will starve for lubrication; if levels are too high, aeration of the gearbox fluid will be present and cause premature damage. Regular change intervals help to ensure that none of these conditions occur.

Manual transmissions use fluids specified by the manufacturer. Do not assume that all transmissions use the same fluid. They don't. Some use gear lube of differing viscosities. Some use engine oil of a specified viscosity. And some even specify automatic transmission fluid in the transmission. Therefore, always verify that you are using the specified fluid in a particular vehicle. One other thing to keep in mind, some transaxles use a separate reservoir for the final drive, which is separate from the transaxle reservoir. And in some cases, they use different types of fluid. Always check the manufacturer's specifications before changing out the fluids.

To prepare for a gearbox fluid change, it is a good idea to have the gearbox fluid warm. When it is warm, it will flow better to ensure proper draining. If possible, drive the vehicle until the engine is at operating temperature and then change the gearbox fluid. Do not touch the gearbox fluid. It will be hot and could cause burns.

To change the gearbox fluid, follow the steps in **SKILL DRILL 24-3**:

1 Raise the vehicle using an approved lift, and make sure it is secure. Check all lift specifications and operating mechanisms, including adapters, before the vehicle is elevated. Obtain a clean drain pan to put the used fluid in. (**Photo 1**)

2 Inspect the transmission for any leaks. (**Photo 2**)

3 Remove the drain plug from the bottom of the transmission, being careful of the hot gearbox fluid. Let gearbox fluid drain until it has stopped running. If necessary, remove the drain plug for the final drive and drain the fluid. (**Photo 3**)

SKILL DRILL | **24-3** | **Changing the Gearbox Fluid**

1 Raise the vehicle using an approved lift. Obtain a clean drain pan to put the used fluid in.

2 Inspect the transmission for leaks.

3 Remove the drain plug from the bottom of the transmission, being careful of the hot gearbox fluid. Let gearbox fluid drain until it has stopped running. If necessary, drain the final drive assembly in the same manner.

SKILL DRILL | 24-3 | **Changing the Gearbox Fluid, continued**

4 Replace the drain plug(s) and tighten to specification, and remove the fill plug(s).

5 Refill the transmission and final drive to the proper level using manufacturer-approved gearbox fluid. Replace the fill plug(s) and tighten. Use a shop towel to wipe away any spillage. Road test the vehicle. If necessary, put the vehicle back on the lift and check for any leaks that may have resulted from the service.

---

4 Replace the drain plug(s) and tighten to the manufacturer's specification, and remove the fill plug(s). **(Photo 4)**

5 Refill the transmission and final drive to the proper level using manufacturer-approved gearbox fluid. Replace the fill plug and tighten to the manufacturer's specification. Use a shop towel to wipe away any spillage.

6 Road test the vehicle. If necessary, put the vehicle back on the lift and check for any leaks that may have resulted from the service. Always double-check your work before returning the vehicle to the customer. **(Photo 5)**

Identifying the Cause of Fluid Loss

Performing preventive maintenance on a regular basis helps ensure that fluid leaks and concerns are addressed before they can become a major problem. In some cases, repairing fluid leaks and loss requires removal of the transmission. Diagnosing leaks and concerns will require that you put the vehicle on a hoist or jack stands. Noises and shifting concerns can be signs of fluid leaks or problems.

Fluid leaks may be a result of the following conditions:

- Too much fluid in the transmission
- Leaking seals, including:
  - Half-shaft axle seals
  - Input shaft retainer O-rings or lip seals
  - Speed sensor seals or O-ring
  - Backup light switch O-ring
  - Shifting lever shaft seals
  - Transmission rear seal
  - Side covers or access plates
- Improper fluid type
- Transmission case porosity or cracks
- Missing, loose, or stripped case bolts
- Damaged gaskets for case halves
- Loose drain or fill plugs

To identify the cause of fluid loss in a transmission, follow the steps in **SKILL DRILL 24-4**:

1 Safely raise the vehicle on a hoist or jack stands. Look for leaks in the transmission bell housing to the engine block (front seal). **(Photo 1)**

2 Look for leaks in the transmission breather outlet. Look for leaks in all case gasket areas. **(Photo 2)**

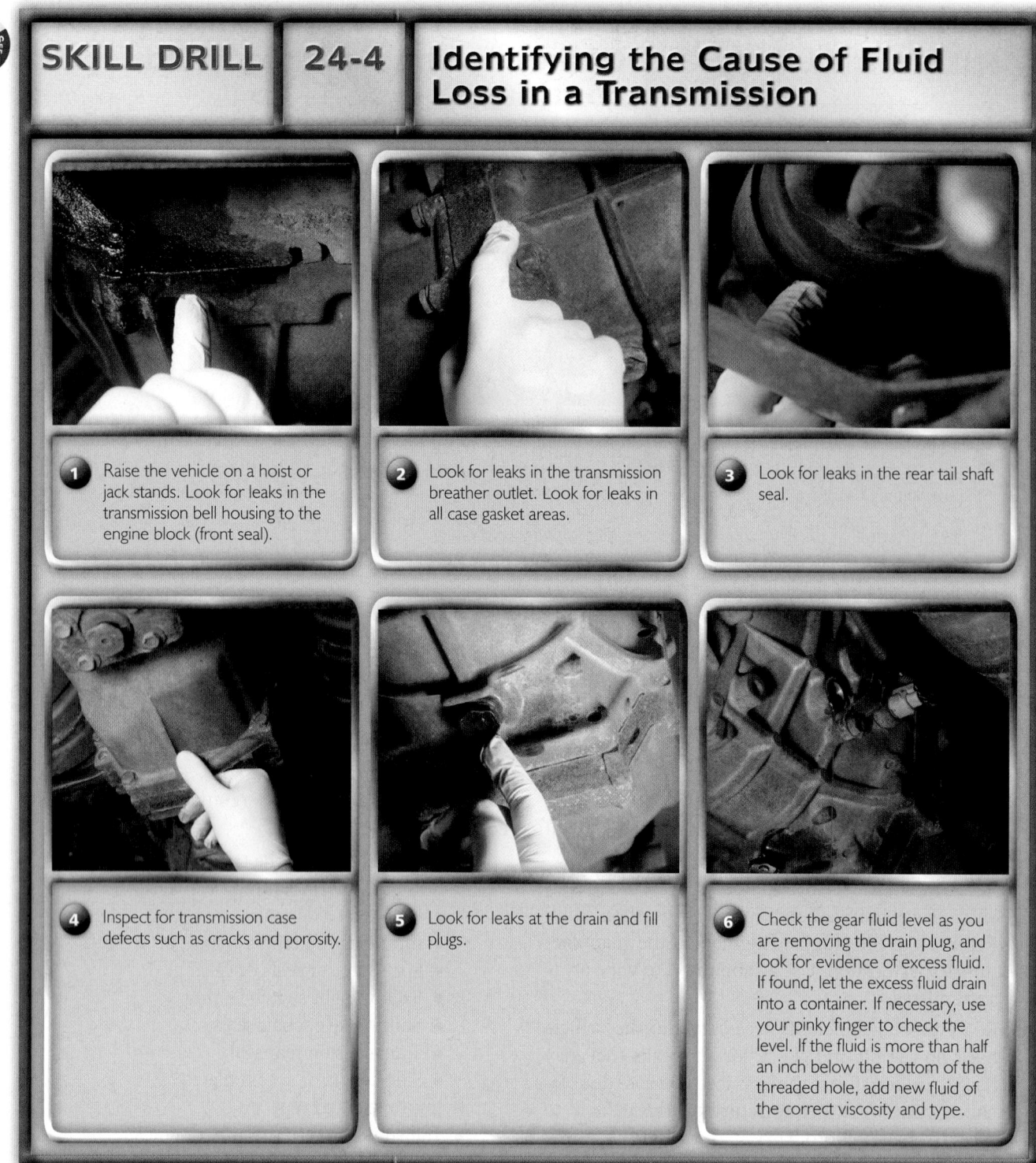

SKILL DRILL | **24-4** | **Identifying the Cause of Fluid Loss in a Transmission**

1. Raise the vehicle on a hoist or jack stands. Look for leaks in the transmission bell housing to the engine block (front seal).

2. Look for leaks in the transmission breather outlet. Look for leaks in all case gasket areas.

3. Look for leaks in the rear tail shaft seal.

4. Inspect for transmission case defects such as cracks and porosity.

5. Look for leaks at the drain and fill plugs.

6. Check the gear fluid level as you are removing the drain plug, and look for evidence of excess fluid. If found, let the excess fluid drain into a container. If necessary, use your pinky finger to check the level. If the fluid is more than half an inch below the bottom of the threaded hole, add new fluid of the correct viscosity and type.

3. Look for leaks in the rear tail shaft seal. Tail shaft seals can be damaged by excessive play in the tail shaft bushing. (**Photo 3**)

4. Inspect for transmission case defects such as cracks and porosity. (**Photo 4**)

5. Look for leaks at the drain and fill plugs. (**Photo 5**)

6. Check the gear fluid level as you are removing the drain plug, and look for evidence of excess fluid. If found, let the excess fluid drain into a container. If necessary, use your pinky finger to check the level. If the fluid is more than half an inch below the bottom of the threaded hole, you must add new fluid of the correct viscosity and type. (**Photo 6**)

Wrap-Up

Ready for Review

▸ The manual transmission allows a driver to manually vary engine torque and output to the drive train.

▸ The ability of the technician to drive, service, repair, and maintain the manual transmission/transaxle is a critical skill.

▸ A manual transmission/transaxle allows the driver to directly vary the gear ratio by manual selection, between the engine and the driving road wheels.

▸ The components of a manual transmission can vary depending on the use and size of the transmission.

▸ The gear ratio is the number of turns of the input gear, necessary to achieve one turn of the output gear.

▸ Gear ratio theory will help you to understand how power is distributed and how power and speed varies as the vehicle travels.

▸ In keeping with the gear ratio theory, compound gear trains have two or more pairs of gears in constant mesh, so that they rotate together and are found inside the transmission/transaxle.

▸ In direct drive rotation, both the output and input gears turn at the same speed, and the turning effort of the output gear will equal the effort applied by the input gear.

▸ All gear boxes have shift rails and shift forks. The gear shift lever/mechanism can be located on the top, on the side or on the column.

▸ The interlock mechanism is the device that ensures two gears cannot be selected at the same time.

▸ Many newer manual transmissions are equipped with Electronic Reverse Lockout systems, which use an electronic solenoid to prevent the transmission/transaxle from being shifted into reverse while the vehicle is in forward motion.

▸ In a manual transmission/transaxle, the gears and shafts are supported on bearings or bearing surfaces to reduce rolling friction.

▸ Roller bearings are used to support radial loads.

▸ Caged roller bearings can be used to support gear rotating on an output shaft.

▸ Thrust washers act as wear surfaces and can be used to adjust end-play.

▸ Tapered roller bearings are used to sustain radial and thrust loads.

▸ Transmission problems include nose, hard shifting, jumping out of gear, no gear selection, and fluid leaks.

▸ Lubrication type and condition are critical factors in transmission performance and reliability.

▸ Having the gearbox and final drive gears in one casing provides a compact and relatively quiet unit and fits well into front wheel drive vehicles.

▸ Historically, manual transmissions have not required the use of electronics, but as with all vehicle systems, electronics are starting to play a more common role.

▸ Manual transaxles problems can be diagnosed with the guidance of the manufacturer's diagnostic tables.

▸ A simple issue that can cause hard shifting is created by maintenance work that is performed improperly on a manual transmission/transaxle.

▸ Always adjust shift linkage following the manufacturer's methods.

▸ Always refer to the manufacturer's prescribed maintenance schedules and fluid changes to ensure the unit lasts the life of the vehicle.

Key Terms

baulk-ring synchromesh unit A synchronizer used in all current transmissions. It uses a blocking ring. Also called a blocker ring synchromesh unit.

blocking ring A synchronizer part that increases or decreases a gear's speed to match shaft speed so that the synchronizer sleeve can lock the gear to the shaft. Also called baulk ring.

chamfer A rounded or angled edge located on the blocking ring, with ridges machined into it to help grab the cone surface of the gear.

detent mechanism The mechanism that holds or helps hold the shift rail into position to ensure that the gear does not pop out when selected and to let the driver feel when a shift is completed.

direct drive A condition in which the engine and transmission output are turning at the same rate of speed.

double-clutching A technique used to shift gears when a nonsynchronized transmission is used. The driver must push the clutch in multiple times to change gears.

electronic reverse lockout An electronic solenoid used to prevent accidental engagement into reverse gear while the vehicle is moving forward.

garter spring lip seal A seal that has a spring to maintain pressure on the seal's surface to prevent leakage.

gear ratio The ratio of the number of turns that a drive gear must complete to turn the driven gear one turn.

Typically this is a calculation of the driven gear to the drive gear. Ratios are listed, for example, as 2:1 or 4.3:1.

gear reduction The use of a small gear to drive a large gear. The result is in an increase in torque but a decrease in speed.

gear shift lever The lever that the driver uses to shift the transmission.

gradient resistance Resistance encountered when a vehicle travels up a hill, requiring torque to be applied to overcome it.

hard shifting A shifting problem in which the shifter will not move smoothly into the desired gear, requiring excessive force by the driver to set it into gear.

helix The curve created by a smooth spiral and used in the angle of gear teeth and coil springs.

hydraulic actuator A hydraulically controlled cylinder that engages or disengages the clutch pedal.

hydrodynamic seal Oil seal flutes or swirls that are part of the oil seal and that create a pumping action to return oil to the transmission as the shaft rotates, enabling lubrication.

idler gear A gear used in between two gears to change the direction of the rotation of the driveshaft or drive axles in the transmission.

interlock mechanism A mechanical device that prevents engagement of two different gears at the same time.

lockout solenoid The cam and lock pin operated by an electronic solenoid that keeps the reverse gear in lockout until it is selected.

needle roller bearing Typically a small-diameter pin rolling bearing that can be held in a cage or placed into the inside diameter of a hole.

O-ring seal A seal that is a complete circle. If a cutaway is done, it will also be a complete circle. These seals are usually set into a groove that is machined into the housing or part that does not move and is intended to be sealed.

overdrive A gear in which the output speed is faster than the engine speed.

paddle A shifting mechanism or electronic control usually attached to the steering wheel.

pocket bearing A roller in the rear of the input shaft that supports the front of the main shaft.

power train control module (PCM) A module used to control engine and/or transmission shifting.

reverse shift fork A shift fork used to engage the reverse gear.

roller bearing A long cylindrical roller held in position by a cage.

rolling resistance Resistance that is present from tires contacting the road and wind resistance against the vehicle while rolling down the highway.

selective thickness shim A shim of a prescribed thickness that is used to control shaft clearances in a transmission.

selector gate The U-shaped cutaway in shift shafts that the shifter lever fits into.

selector shift rail A rod that is attached to the shift fork. These rails move when the shifter lever is moved against them.

shift fork A mechanism that moves the synchronizer sleeve to lock the gear to the main shaft.

spring-loaded key A part of the synchronizer that helps hold the synchronizer collar in position.

synchronizer An assembly that allows for the selection of gears without grinding by matching the speed of the two assemblies.

synchronizer sleeve The sleeve that slides to lock the selected gear to the main shaft. The synchronizer sleeve is part of the synchronizer assembly.

thrust washer A copper or brass washer that controls clearances on all transmission shafts.

torque multiplication The increase of torque.

vehicle speed sensor An electronic sensor that reads the driveshaft speed and sends either an analog or a digital signal to the computer that corresponds to the road speed of the vehicle.

ASE-Type Questions

1. Tech A says that in a conventional transmission, the gears freewheel around the main shaft until they are locked to it by the synchronizer. Tech B says that when not engaged, main shaft gears slide away from the counter gears until they are no longer in mesh. Who is correct?
   a. Tech A
   b. Tech B
   c. Both A and B
   d. Neither A nor B

2. Tech A says that the countershaft assembly can be made up of several gears machined out of a single piece of steel. Tech B says that the countershaft assembly is driven by the gear on the input shaft, and drives the gears on the main shaft. Who is correct?
   a. Tech A
   b. Tech B
   c. Both A and B
   d. Neither A nor B

3. Tech A says that the speeds at which two meshed gears turn depend on the number of teeth on each gear. Tech B says that if the driving gear has fewer teeth than the driven gear, the speed of the driven gear increases. Who is correct?
   a. Tech A
   b. Tech B
   c. Both A and B
   d. Neither A nor B

4. Tech A says that an overdrive gear ratio means the input gear turns faster than the output gear. Tech B says that overdrive ratios provide less torque output than underdrive ratios. Who is correct?
   a. Tech A
   b. Tech B
   c. Both A and B
   d. Neither A nor B

5. Tech A says that a benefit of helical gears is that they do *not* create radial or thrust loads. Tech B says that spur gears run quieter than helical gears. Who is correct?
   a. Tech A
   b. Tech B
   c. Both A and B
   d. Neither A nor B

6. Tech A says that some manual transmissions use two input shafts and two clutches. Tech B says that many manual transmissions now use planetary gear sets. Who is correct?
   a. Tech A
   b. Tech B
   c. Both A and B
   d. Neither A nor B

7. Tech A says that blocker rings prevent the vehicle from rolling when parked. Tech B says that engine torque is transferred from the dog teeth through the synchronizer sleeves. Who is correct?
   a. Tech A
   b. Tech B
   c. Both A and B
   d. Neither A nor B

8. Tech A says that shift forks slide the gears into mesh with each other when a shift occurs. Tech B says that blocker rings have fine grooves that cut through the oil on the tapered cone of the matching gear. Who is correct?
   a. Tech A
   b. Tech B
   c. Both A and B
   d. Neither A nor B

9. Tech A says that a broken detent spring can cause the transmission to pop out of gear. Tech B says that a broken interlock pin can cause the transmission to go into two gears at the same time? Who is correct?
   a. Tech A
   b. Tech B
   c. Both A and B
   d. Neither A nor B

10. Tech A says that some manufacturers specify automatic transmission fluid to be used in their manual transmissions. Tech B says that some manufacturers specify engine oil to be used in their manual transmissions. Who is correct?
    a. Tech A
    b. Tech B
    c. Both A and B
    d. Neither A nor B

CHAPTER 25

Manual Drive Train and Axles
Transmission/Transaxle

Page

■ Inspect, adjust, and reinstall shift linkages, brackets, bushings, cables, pivots, and levers.

AST **MAST** 696–72

Knowledge Objectives

After reading this chapter, you will be able to:
1. Explain the causes of transmission failure. (p 694)
2. Describe the tools associated with transmission service. (pp 694–695)
3. Describe proper transmission service and sealing. (p 696)

Drive Train Components

Skills Objectives

After reading this chapter, you will be able to:
1. Disassemble a manual transmission. (pp 698–701)
2. Clean the parts of the manual transmission and inspect a transmission case. (pp 701–704)
3. Inspect the manual transmission. (pp 704–706)
4. Perform a gasket inspection. (pp 706–707)
5. Inspect and reinstall a synchronizer hub. (pp 707–709)
6. Inspect and service an oil pump and related lubrication devices. (p 709)
7. Inspect and service a shift cover and shift linkages. (pp 709–712)
8. Remove the transaxle final drive. (pp 712–714)
9. Remove and service the transaxle final drive pinion gears. (pp 714–716)
10. Reassemble the major components of a manual transmission. (pp 716–720)
11. Measure and adjust end play/preload. (pp 720–721)

Introduction

Occasionally, it may be necessary to service and/or perform a complete overhaul of a transmission/transaxle. For example, if the transmission is grinding when going into gear, it may need to be disassembled and the parts inspected and replaced. The manual transmission must be diagnosed properly to verify that the concern is indeed a fault inside the transmission and not something external that could be easily fixed, such as a bound-up shift boot that is causing the transmission to pop out of gear. You should be positive that the issue requires the teardown and inspection of the internals of the manual transmission before removing the transmission. This chapter will help guide you through the teardown and replacement of faulty components after a proper diagnosis has been performed.

Note, when we say *transmission*, we use the term generically to include transaxles also. When we use transaxle, we generally only mean transaxle. Readers should use their understanding of transmission and transaxle theory to understand the intended meaning. For example, if we are discussing ring and pinion backlash, that can apply only to a transaxle.

Rebuilding the Transmission

As with anything mechanical, a transmission will wear with use and time. As the transmission wears, it will develop behaviors that are of concern to the customer, such as popping out of gear, making growling noises, or becoming difficult to shift. A transmission that has been operating with insufficient gear oil will wear extremely quickly and will require rebuilding or replacement.

Rebuilding a transmission can be a large undertaking considering all of the makes and models produced for the automotive market. Rebuilding a transmission often requires specialty tools that are specific to each transmission. The cost of these tools is usually quite high. The differences between each transmission will also require you to have access to transmission repair manuals for specifications and instructions. The most important part of any rebuild/overhaul is paying attention to detail and making sure you locate the cause(s) of a transmission failure, such as worn synchronizer rings, a broken detent spring, or a worn bearing. Gear oil can be sent to a local laboratory to be analyzed for contamination or chemical breakdown. This analysis can help determine the origin of a transmission failure; for example, the wrong type of oil may have been used in the transmission or some type of incorrect additive may have been added to the oil. Locating the cause of transmission failure is critical to making an accurate and lasting repair.

Tools and Equipment

When performing a rebuild of a transmission, proper tool usage is vital. Manufacturer specifications require that certain tools and equipment be used to rebuild these units. Some special tools and equipment may be required to disassemble and reassemble modern manual transmissions, such as special pullers or electronic devices. Remember, the proper tool for the proper job makes the

You are the Automotive Technician

Today you are working alongside Dave, a senior technician, to rebuild a manual transmission. Dave has several years of experience doing this complicated repair and you are assisting him. Dave has informed you that Mrs. Marston's Jeep makes grinding noises when shifting gears. The fluid level is fine but the gold flakes in the fluid indicate worn synchronizer assemblies, requiring a transmission rebuild. Dave carefully checks the service information prior to transmission disassembly and explains the importance of patience, organization, and cleanliness during the rebuilding process. As Dave has the transmission disassembled into its subassemblies, he disassembles the main shaft and shows you the worn blocker rings and how the fine grooves are mostly worn away. The dog teeth on the gears and collars on first and second gear are worn due to repeated grinding and will require replacement.

1. Why is it important to be organized during a transmission replacement?
2. Why are gold flakes in the fluid an indicator of worn synchronizers?
3. Why are manual transmissions disassembled by subassemblies?

job go smoothly and easily. Wherever possible consult the manufacturer's publications. Some of the tools that may be needed for rebuilding the transmission include FIGURE 25-1:

- Dial indicator
- Outside micrometer
- Bearing press tools
- Seal driver tools
- Bearing preload tools to assist in finding correct free play
- Engine support tool
- Bushing driver kit
- Slide hammer and adapters
- Bearing splitter
- Gear pullers

- Depth micrometer
- Snap ring pliers of the proper size for the transmission
- Transmission holding fixture

Some of these tools will be necessary for one transmission but not for another. Refer to the manufacturer's unit repair manual for the necessary tools to repair the unit you are working on.

Failures inside the transmission may simply indicate replacement of wear items, such as seals, gaskets, bearings, and synchronizer blocker rings, or may indicate the failure of hard parts, such as gears, synchronizer assemblies, and input, output, or countershafts. Rebuild kits can be purchased in various levels. The most basic kits may include only gaskets and seals. Other kits may

FIGURE 25-1 Depending on the transmission being serviced, specialty tools may be necessary. Some of the basic tools needed are pictured here.

include only bearings. Higher level kits may include gaskets, seals, and synchronizer rings. Top-level kits include gaskets, seals, synchronizer rings, bearings, and possibly even shafts. It is possible that the kit you need will not be available and that you will have to order individual parts as needed.

▶ Transmission Disassembly

The disassembly of a transmission is not something to be performed by a novice technician without any training. Many clearances must be checked as the transmission is torn down and again as it is reassembled. Specialty tools must be used to ensure that damage is not done to the parts that do not need to be replaced. The goal of the rebuild is to restore the transmission to like-new condition for the customer at the agreed-upon price. Damaging components because of lack of knowledge and skill is not keeping the customer's or shop owner's interests in mind. Use of a unit repair manual will be necessary to perform this task properly.

Among the first tasks when doing any kind of service to a manual transmission is obtaining and reading all manufacturer publications and service information. The manufacturer's information should provide the technician with a good idea of how the transmission is disassembled before the technician actually tears the unit down. It is wise to take some time to look over the procedures in the manual, ensure that the proper tools are available, and check for any technical service bulletins related to the customer concern you are addressing.

Diagnosis

If it is necessary to disassemble a manual transmission because of an internal problem, a complete and thorough diagnosis is warranted to complete an error-free repair. This diagnosis involves a thorough understanding of the customer complaint, which may require an interview with the customer to determine the events that led to the failure and bring to light any symptoms that were present before the failure occurred. Once the concern is fully understood, the technician needs to verify the concern, usually by test-driving the vehicle, and diagnose the possible causes. A troubleshooting chart should help you track the customer concern to the specific fault inside the transmission. For example, if you find that the customer does not fully depress the clutch to shift between gears, then the popping out of gear concern may be related to the dog teeth on the gear being worn due to the grinding that would happen as the driver forces the synchronizer sleeve into mesh. The following are some additional areas of diagnosis that you should consider before tearing a transmission down. Once all the information is obtained, you may begin

the disassembly process knowing that you have a good understanding of what may have happened and what you expect to find.

Inspecting, Replacing, and Aligning Power Train Mounts

The power train mounts should be inspected when a customer is complaining of gear shifting issues or clunking sounds when accelerating or decelerating. The power train mounts can also create issues with constant-velocity (CV) axles as a result of axles running at incorrect angles. This can result in vibrations when driving or possible early failure of the CV axles.

Applied | **Math**

AM 23: Angles: The technician can visually formulate an angle (e.g. in a suspension system or driveline) and verify its conformance to the manufacturer's specified angle.

A vehicle has been traded in at a dealership and a technician is assigned to perform a major inspection to determine whether it could qualify as a certified used vehicle. The vehicle has been raised on a lift and the technician is conducting a visual inspection of the power train on this rear wheel drive automobile. The technician examines the driveshaft and the universal joints on each end of the shaft. The driveshaft is a long, hollow metal tube that connects the transmission to the final assembly. The manufacturer's service information for this vehicle states two requirements regarding the universal joint angles: 1) The operating angle at any individual joint must be between 0.1 degrees and 2 degrees, and 2) The operating angles at either end of a shaft should be within 1 degree of each other.

As the technician visually formulates the angles, he believes that the components do not meet the manufacturer's specified angle. An angle indictor, sometimes called a universal protractor, is used to measure the angles. The angles do not meet the specifications. A further examination of the rear transmission mount shows deterioration and causes the rear of the transmission to sag, changing the driveling angle. Replacing the mount will restore the proper angles. This relates to one of our skills objectives in this chapter to inspect and service power train mounts.

Inspecting and Servicing Power Train Mounts

The purpose of the power train mounts (motor mounts) is to support the engine and transmission as it is placed in the vehicle. They also isolate **torsional vibrations** created by the running engine and vibrations from the transmission, and allow for flexing as torque is achieved in various gear selections. Power train mounts are subject to the elements and are known to break, crack, chunk (broken pieces), and become oil soaked. They can also cause hard shifting and other shift-related symptoms. To inspect and service power train mounts, refer to the Servicing the Automatic Transmission/Transaxle chapter.

> **TECHNICIAN TIP**
>
> It is always a good practice to inspect power train mounts whenever the vehicle is on the lift or if the customer complains of unusual shifting or noises.

Inspecting and Servicing Sensors and Switches

Although a manual transmission is being shifted manually, electronics are used to a small degree in the process of selecting gears on some transmissions. A backup light switch is used to let people know that the driver will be reversing the vehicle. A speed sensor is used to tell the computer how fast the driver is traveling down the highway.

With electronic shifting mechanisms, some electronic switches and solenoids are involved. Some vehicles use a hydraulic fluid pressure sensor or a gear selecting sensor. Some of these transmission shifting systems require the use of a scan tool when troubleshooting. Use a scan tool that can communicate with the vehicle's transmission control module.

To inspect and service sensors and switches, follow the steps in **SKILL DRILL 25-1**:

1. Hook up a scan tool to the diagnostic link connector, which is located under the steering column, and read information or any codes that may be present. Go to the transmission section on the scan tool screen. **(Photo 1)**

2. Perform the manufacturer's recommended tests using the scan tool and wait for the information to be displayed.

3. If there are any codes, go to the diagnostic code section to read and identify the code. Consult the manufacturer's publications for code listings. Codes will be present if the diagnostic light is illuminated on the dashboard.

4. If necessary, remove the switch or solenoid and use an ohmmeter to check the resistance specification, if available, and replace the switch or solenoid as necessary. Also check for burnt or corroded connections in all wiring harnesses. **(Photo 2)**

5. It is always a good idea to check all wiring and connectors, as high resistance can cause failures as well. Voltage drop checks are a way to find faulty wiring and connectors.

6. Once all repairs are made, verify the repair has been successful by road testing or bench shifting. **(Photo 3)**

SKILL DRILL 25-1 Inspecting and Servicing Sensors and Switches

1. Hook up a scan tool to the diagnostic link connector to read information or any codes that may be present. Go to the transmission section on the scan tool screen.

2. Perform recommended tests with the scan tool. If necessary, remove the switch or solenoid, and use an ohmmeter to check the resistance specification if available; replace as necessary.

3. Check for voltage to the switch or solenoid. Check all wiring and connectors for excessive voltage drops as high resistance can cause failures as well. Once all repairs are made, verify that the repair is successful.

Disassembly Procedures

For example purposes, this disassembly procedure is based on the Borg-Warner T-5 transmission. First, remove the manual transmission according to the manufacturer's guidelines. Once the manual transmission is removed, place it on a clean and organized bench. If not already performed, drain the transmission fluid by removing the drain plug as required. Remove any electronic sensors or wiring that may be attached to the transmission case. Perform a thorough inspection of the outside of the transmission, looking for any obvious signs of the failure or any other damage.

In most cases, manual transmissions come apart in main assemblies, such as the shift cover, extension housing, input shaft, output shaft, and countershaft. But the parts can be close fitting, requiring patience in determining how they will come apart. Some parts may be held together only by the positioning of the assemblies, and when you start to remove them, these loose parts will fall off. Take your time as each assembly is removed. Have a number of parts trays available to store parts during the disassembly. Labeling unknown parts is a good idea to ensure that they are reassembled correctly. Pay close attention to detail here, as organization during disassembly is a critical part of any repair.

> ▶ **TECHNICIAN TIP**
>
> There may be a check ball under the speedometer gear. Make sure to secure it as the gear is removed.

To disassemble a manual transmission, follow the steps in **SKILL DRILL 25-2** :

1 Start by removing the shift lever in the top of the transmission. Remove the retaining bolts and remove the lever from its seat. On some manual transmissions, it is best to place the gear shift in neutral prior to removing the shift lever. **(Photo 1)**

2 Remove the bolts that retain the tail shaft housing to the manual transmission case, then remove the housing. **(Photo 2)**

3 Remove the speedometer gear and retainer and slide it off of the output shaft. Some gears are pressed on, so you may have to use a gear puller to remove it. **(Photo 3)**

4 Remove the shift mechanism housing bolts, and remove the shift mechanism housing from the top of the manual transmission. **(Photo 4)**

5 Remove the input shaft bearing retainer bolts, and remove the retainer from the transmission case. **(Photo 5)**

6 Rotate the input shaft so the dog teeth cutout is lined up with the gear on the cluster shaft for easy removal. Pay attention to the roller bearings in the end of the input shaft, as they are likely to fall out during removal.

7 Remove the input shaft. To do so simply pull the shaft from the transmission case; the bearing retainer has been unbolted and the bearing should slip fit into the case. If the bearing does stick, try wiggling the input shaft while pulling to get the input shaft to come out of the case. **(Photo 6)**

8 Remove the fifth gear driven gear from the countershaft by removing the synchronizer and snap ring for access. Be sure the correct-sized snap ring pliers are used. Snap rings typically have holes in the ends for the pliers to fit into. Using pliers that are too small will result in damage to the tips and damage to the snap ring or possible injury to the technician when the pliers slip. **(Photo 7)**

9 Remove the rear bearing race from the transmission case using a brass drift and hammer. Be sure to drive on the outer race to ensure that damage is not done to the bearing. Driving the bearing on the cage or the inner race will damage the bearing. **(Photo 8)**

10 Tilt the output shaft on an upward angle to allow removal of the shaft from the transmission case. Before removal, make sure the third gear synchronizer is engaged to make clearance for removal of the output shaft.

11 Remove the output shaft from the transmission case. **(Photo 9)**

12 Remove the reverse idler gear shaft retaining roll pin from the idler shaft. Remove the idler shaft and gear from the transmission case. **(Photo 10)**

13 To remove the countershaft from the transmission case, it may be necessary to put the transmission case in a press to remove the rear countershaft bearing. Press out the bearing and then remove the countershaft from the transmission. The front pocket bearing (which is a caged roller-type bearing in a pocket-type cylinder) will also have to be removed in order to be replaced upon overhaul. The pocket bearing may be used in other locations as well. (**Photos 11 and 12**)

14 To disassemble the main shaft/output shaft:
- Position the main shaft/output shaft in a soft-jaw vice.
- Remove the first snap ring that holds third and fourth gears in place.
- Remove the third and fourth gear sets and roller bearing cages.

- Remove the second snap ring and remove the second gear.
- Remove the first and second/reverse synchronizer sliding collar paying attention to the inserts that will be exposed upon removal. (**Photo 13**)

15 Mount the main shaft/output shaft in the press to remove fifth gear, which is pressed on to the shaft. This will also remove first gear and the rear output shaft bearing. (**Photo 14**)

SKILL DRILL | **25-2** | **Disassembling a Manual Transmission**

1 Remove the retaining bolts and remove the shift lever from its seat. On some manual transmissions, it is best to place the gear shift in neutral prior to removing the shift lever.

2 Remove the bolts that retain the tail shaft housing, then remove the housing.

3 Remove the speedometer gear and retainer, and slide it off of the output shaft. Some gears are pressed on, so you may have to use a gear puller to remove it.

4 Remove the shift mechanism housing bolts, and remove the shift mechanism housing from the top of the manual transmission.

5 Remove the input shaft bearing retainer bolts, and remove the retainer from the transmission case.

6 Rotate the input shaft so the dog teeth cutout is lined up with the gear on the cluster shaft for easy removal. Pay attention to the roller bearings in the end of the input shaft. Now pull the input shaft from the transmission case.

SKILL DRILL | 25-2 | Disassembling a Manual Transmission, continued

7 Remove the fifth gear driven gear from the countershaft by removing the synchronizer and snap ring for access.

8 Remove the rear bearing race from the transmission case with a brass drift and hammer.

9 Tilt the output shaft on an upward angle to enable removal of the shaft from the transmission case. Before removal, make sure the third gear synchronizer is engaged to make clearance for removal of the output shaft. Remove the output shaft from the case.

10 Remove the reverse idler gear shaft retaining roll pin from the idler shaft. Remove the idler shaft and gear from the transmission case.

11 To remove the countershaft from the transmission case, it may be necessary to put the transmission case in a press to remove the rear countershaft bearing. Press out the bearing and then remove the countershaft from the transmission.

12 The front pocket bearing (which is a caged roller-type bearing) will also have to be removed in order to be replaced upon overhaul.

16 To disassemble the countershaft:
- Place the countershaft in the press and press all gears off that are not part of the shaft.
- Pay attention to any snap rings that may be present.

17 To disassemble the input shaft:
- Remove the output shaft pocket bearings from the inside of the input shaft.
- Place the input shaft in the press and press off the front bearing using the appropriate adapters. **(Photo 15)**

SKILL DRILL | 25-2 | Disassembling a Manual Transmission, continued

13 To disassemble the main shaft/output shaft:
- Position the shaft in a soft-jaw vice. Remove the first snap ring that holds third and fourth gears in place.
- Remove the third and fourth gear sets and roller bearing cages.
- Remove the second snap ring and remove the second gear.
- Remove the first and second/reverse synchronizer sliding collar.

14 Disassemble the output shaft:
- Mount the output shaft in the press to remove fifth gear, which is pressed on to the shaft. This will also remove first gear and the rear output shaft bearing.

15 Remove the output shaft pocket bearings from the inside of the input shaft. Place the input shaft in the press and press off the front bearing.

> **TECHNICIAN TIP**
>
> Pay close attention to the magnet in the bottom of the transmission case. It will indicate gear and bearing wear by the amount of filings found on it.

Transmission Case and Components Inspection

When <u>overhauling</u> a transmission, all transmission case components should be cleaned and inspected to make sure they can be reused. A close inspection of all vital parts is necessary to complete a manual transmission. If there is any doubt as to whether a case component is reusable, then it should be replaced. You have an important cost analysis job to perform for the customer. If the transmission rebuild will cost more than a remanufactured unit from a parts supplier, then the customer should be informed of the option of using a remanufactured unit. Remanufactured transmissions come with a warranty from the remanufacturer and will ensure that the customer is covered against any warranted defects for the term of the warranty, typically up to 1 year. This may present a significant savings to the customer and ensure that the repair facility performing the repair is providing the best value for the customer.

Next, clean the parts of the manual transmission by following the steps in **SKILL DRILL 25-3**:

1. Clean all parts in an approved cleaning solvent machine, typically containing mineral spirits or a soap and water solution. It may be necessary to clean the transmission case parts with an approved pressure washer or steam cleaner.

2. Thoroughly dry all parts with an air gun or blower rated to 30 pounds per square inch (psi, or 207 kilopascals [kPa]) that is approved by the Occupational Safety and Health Administration

(OSHA). Be careful not to spin the bearings with the compressed air, as the bearings can fly apart causing personal injury.

To inspect a transmission case, follow the steps in **SKILL DRILL 25-4**:

1 To inspect the main transmission case:
- Check all flat mating surfaces for <u>warpage</u> using a straightedge and a feeler gauge to ensure straight surfaces. **(Photo 1A)**
- Check all bores for <u>concentricity</u> or roundness and any specific defects. Concentricity is checked with a dial bore gauge or a telescoping gauge. This test is performed the same as testing an engine cylinder for out of round.
- Check that all plug hole threads are in good shape and are able to accommodate the plug without stripping. Plugs are used for draining the transmission or sometimes to seal off holes that contain roll pins. **(Photo 1B)**
- Check the transmission case for cracks and porosity.
- Check that all attaching ears are in good shape and are not elongated. **(Photo 1C)**
- Check the condition of the magnet in the bottom of the transmission case and replace as necessary.

- Make sure all old gasket material has been removed so it does not cause a leak. **(Photo 1D)**

2 To inspect the output or tail shaft housing:
- Inspect the mating surface for flatness using a straightedge and feeler gauge. **(Photo 2A)**
- Inspect the output shaft bushing and replace as necessary. Replacement of the output shaft bushing will require the use of a bushing driver

FIGURE 25-2 Scoring on the retaining collar.

SKILL DRILL | 25-4 | Inspecting a Transmission Case

1A To inspect the main transmission case:
- Check flat mating surfaces for warpage using a straightedge and a feeler gauge to ensure straight surfaces.

1B
- Check bores for concentricity or roundness and any specific defects. Check that all plug hole threads are in good shape and are able to accommodate the plug without stripping.

1C
- Check the transmission case for cracks and porosity. Check that all attaching ears are in good shape and are not elongated.

SKILL DRILL | 25-4 | Inspecting a Transmission Case, continued

1D • Check the condition of the magnet in the bottom of the transmission case and replace as necessary. Make sure old gasket material has been removed.

2A To inspect the output or tail shaft housing:
• Inspect the mating surface for flatness using a straightedge and feeler gauge.

2B • Inspect the output shaft bushing and replace as necessary.

2C • Check the speedometer opening for any damage, and install a new O-ring when assembling the transmission.

2D • Inspect the tail shaft housing for cracking and/or porosity problems.

2E • Inspect the tail shaft seal surface, and replace the seal when reinstalling it on the transmission case. Inspect the housing vent to make sure it is not clogged.

3A To inspect the input shaft retainer:
• Inspect the retaining collar that the release bearing rides on for imperfections.

3B • Inspect the bearing cone surface for galling or cracking, or out-of-round conditions.

3C • Inspect the front seal surface, and replace the front seal as necessary.

SKILL DRILL | 25-4 | **Inspecting a Transmission Case, continued**

3D • Check to make sure the bolt holes are not elongated or damaged from bolts that were loose.

to push the bushing from the transmission case. A bushing driver is used with a hammer to push the bearing free from the case without damaging the case. **(Photo 2B)**

■ Check the speedometer opening for any damage, and install a new O-ring when assembling the transmission. **(Photo 2C)**

■ Inspect the tail shaft housing for cracking and/or porosity problems. **(Photo 2D)**

■ Inspect the tail shaft seal surface, and replace the seal when reinstalling it on the transmission case.

■ Inspect the housing vent to make sure it is not clogged. **(Photo 2E)**

3 To inspect the input shaft retainer:

■ Inspect the retaining collar that the release bearing rides on for any imperfections such as scratches or galling. **(Photo 3A)**

■ Inspect the bearing cone surface for any galling or cracking, or out-of-round conditions. **(Photo 3B)**

■ Inspect the front seal surface, and replace the front seal as necessary. **(Photo 3C)**

■ Check to make sure the bolt holes are not elongated or damaged from bolts that were loose. **(Photo 3D)**

Next, inspect the manual transmission by following the steps in **SKILL DRILL 25-5** :

1 Inspect the front seal surface on the input shaft for damage. **(Photo 1)**

2 Inspect the input shaft:

■ Inspect the input shaft gear for excessive wear on the gear teeth.

■ Inspect the teeth for any broken, cracked, or unusual distortions. The dog teeth are pointed to assure complete synchronous hub engagement.

■ Inspect the input shaft splines for wear and twisting to prevent the clutch friction plate from sliding abnormally.

■ Inspect the synchronizer smooth surface for any brinelling or unusual wear.

■ Inspect the pilot bearing surface of the input shaft for any wear. **(Photo 2)**

3 Inspect the output shaft gear and components:

■ Start by inspecting all necessary gears for tooth wear and broken or cracked dog teeth; also check the **blocking ring** surface and ensure that it is smooth.

■ Inspect all caged needle bearings that are used inside the rotating output shaft gears.

■ Check all washers and snap rings for tension and possible distortion.

■ Inspect all smooth surfaces that gears rotate on for out of round and brinelling from poorly lubricated bearings.

- Inspect all splines that gears slide over for any wear that would inhibit proper installation of the gears.
- Inspect the output shaft hub for any imperfections that will hinder synchronizer collar operation.
- Inspect the output shaft pilot surface for any brinelling from the input pocket bearing. **(Photo 3)**

4 To inspect the countershaft gears and shaft:

- Inspect the bearing ends of the countershaft for imperfections.

- Inspect all gears for wear and any cracking or chipping.
- Inspect all gears that are not part of the shaft for wear, cracks, and chipping. **(Photo 4)**

5 To inspect the reverse idler gear:

- Inspect the reverse gear brass bushing for excessive wear.
- Inspect the idler shaft for any brinelling or wear. **(Photo 5)**

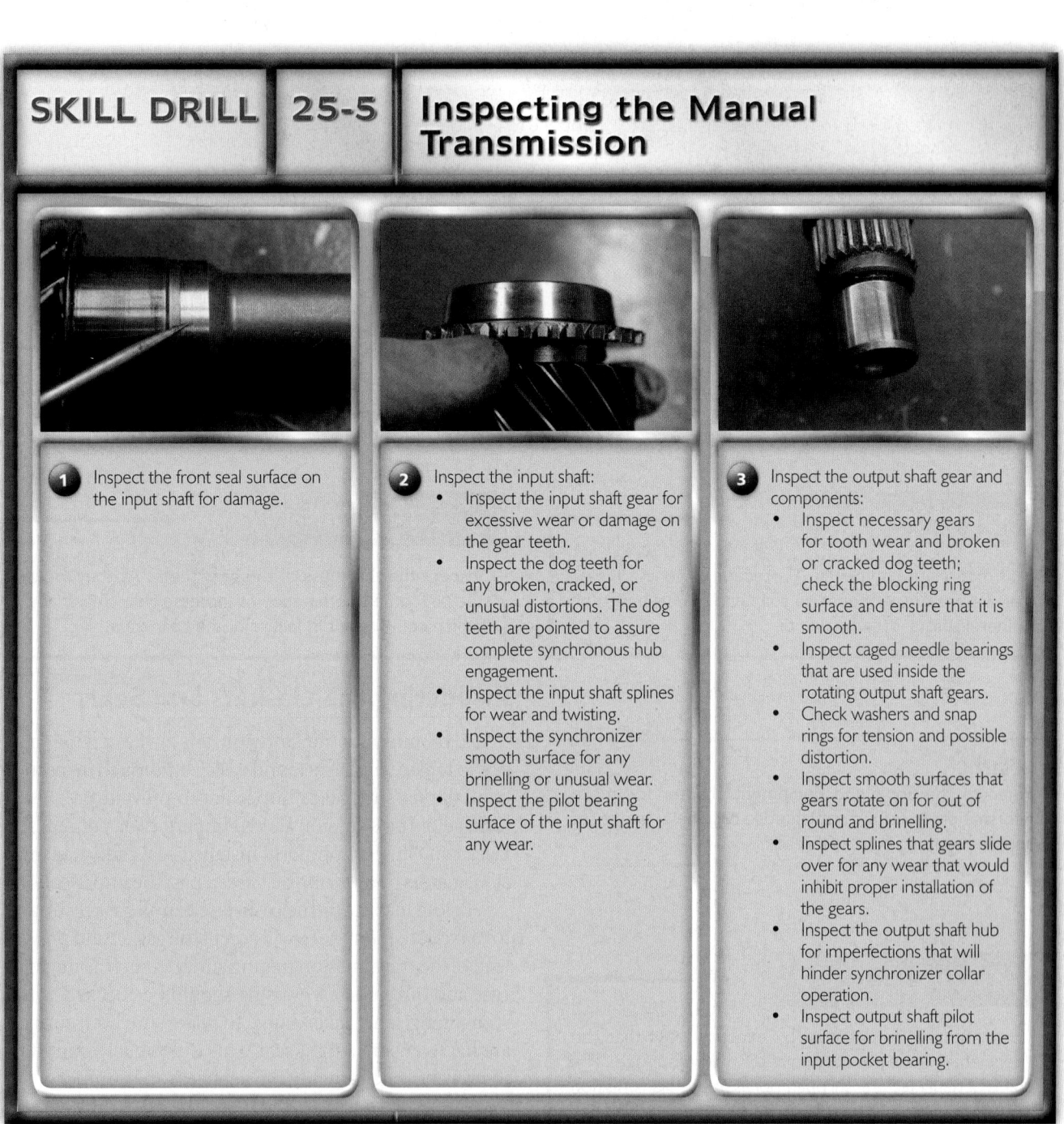

SKILL DRILL | 25-5 | Inspecting the Manual Transmission

1 Inspect the front seal surface on the input shaft for damage.

2 Inspect the input shaft:
- Inspect the input shaft gear for excessive wear or damage on the gear teeth.
- Inspect the dog teeth for any broken, cracked, or unusual distortions. The dog teeth are pointed to assure complete synchronous hub engagement.
- Inspect the input shaft splines for wear and twisting.
- Inspect the synchronizer smooth surface for any brinelling or unusual wear.
- Inspect the pilot bearing surface of the input shaft for any wear.

3 Inspect the output shaft gear and components:
- Inspect necessary gears for tooth wear and broken or cracked dog teeth; check the blocking ring surface and ensure that it is smooth.
- Inspect caged needle bearings that are used inside the rotating output shaft gears.
- Check washers and snap rings for tension and possible distortion.
- Inspect smooth surfaces that gears rotate on for out of round and brinelling.
- Inspect splines that gears slide over for any wear that would inhibit proper installation of the gears.
- Inspect the output shaft hub for imperfections that will hinder synchronizer collar operation.
- Inspect output shaft pilot surface for brinelling from the input pocket bearing.

SKILL DRILL | 25-5 | Inspecting the Manual Transmission, continued

4 To inspect the countershaft gears and shaft:
- Inspect the bearing ends of the countershaft for imperfections.
- Inspect gears for wear, cracking, or chipping.
- Inspect gears that are not part of the shaft for wear, cracks, and chipping.

5 To inspect the reverse idler gear:
- Inspect the reverse gear brass bushing for excessive wear.
- Inspect the idler shaft for brinelling or wear.

▶ TECHNICIAN TIP

To meet Environmental Protection Agency (EPA) regulations, most shops use soap and water–based or mineral spirits–based solvents.

▶ LINK

Refer to the Tools and Equipment chapter for more information on using a straightedge or a feeler gauge set and on repairing broken threads.

▶ TECHNICIAN TIP

Porosity may be detected by external leaks that can be seen in areas not near a gasket mating surface. The oil is actually leaking through pores in the transmission case.

▶ TECHNICIAN TIP

Inspect the thickness of the gear teeth. As they wear, they become thinner and will increase gear clearances, which could result in failure of the gear train.

Inspecting the Gaskets and Seals

When rebuilding a transmission, it is always a good practice to replace the gaskets and seals. A thorough inspection of all gasket surfaces is important to prevent premature leakage of transmission fluids. Imperfections of seal surfaces can cause improperly installed seals and transmission failures by allowing oil to seep past the imperfections.

Before inspecting the gaskets, clean all gasket surfaces to make sure the surface will accept the gasket and prevent leaks. The transmission mating surfaces such as the main case and output shaft housing should be checked with a straightedge and feeler gauge to make sure both surfaces are flat to ensure a tight seal. This is especially important to prevent leakage while the vehicle is in operation.

The front bearing retainer and the main transmission case should also be checked with a straightedge and feeler gauge. If this area starts to leak, it could contaminate the clutch friction disc surface and cause a catastrophic failure of the clutch system. In addition, consider checking the shift tower surface for flatness with a straightedge and feeler gauge, as a leakage of fluid can occur in this area.

All seal surface openings should be checked for concentricity with a dial caliper or bore gauge. If you are using a dial caliper, then expand the dial caliper to touch the surfaces of the bore and get a size reading. Now move the dial caliper to a position 90 degrees from the original and ensure that the reading is the same or very close. Refer to the manufacturer's information for concentricity of the case bores. If no specifications are given, inspect for scoring or cracks, and replace if present. Sealants should be applied where necessary and according to the manufacturer's specifications.

To perform a gasket and seals inspection, follow the steps in **SKILL DRILL 25-6**:

1 Clean all gasket surfaces to prepare the case for a new gasket. Be sure that no gasket material is left on the case or the cover you removed, as this will result in leaks when reassembled.

2 Check the main case and output shaft housing by laying a straightedge across the flat surface and trying to insert a feeler gauge to check for flatness or warpage. Follow the manufacturer's specifications. A warped case or cover plate will result in gasket leaks.

3 Use a straightedge and feeler gauge to check the front bearing retainer and main case and the shift tower surface on the main case, again looking for warped parts. **(Photo 1)**

4 Measure seal surface openings with a dial caliper.

5 When appropriate, apply all necessary sealants. Some manufacturers use a fiber, rubber, or cork gasket. Other manufacturers use a liquid-type sealant. Follow the manufacturer's service information for the correct gasket service. **(Photo 2)**

Inspecting and Reinstalling the Synchronizer Hub

Synchronizer assemblies allow for the smooth shifting of the transmission. When overhauling a manual transmission, it is important to inspect for damage if you are reusing the synchronizer assembly. If the synchronizer assembly is damaged, replace all parts or the entire component as necessary.

A good place to start when inspecting for synchronizer wear and damage is when you drain the transmission fluid from the transmission. Any gold-colored particles may indicate that the blocking rings are excessively worn and may need to be serviced. Sloppy or loose shifting, or jumping out of gear can indicate damaged synchronizer units as well as other shift mechanism problems. A thorough inspection of all synchronizer parts is critical to make sure the transmission gear selections will be smooth, quick, and easy.

To inspect and reinstall a synchronizer hub, follow the steps in **SKILL DRILL 25-7**:

SKILL DRILL | **25-6** | **Inspecting Gaskets and Seals**

1 Clean all gasket surfaces as required. Use a straightedge and feeler gauge to check the main case and output shaft housing, the front bearing retainer and main case, and the shift tower surface on the main case.

2 Measure seal surface openings with a dial caliper. When appropriate, apply all necessary sealants as required.

SKILL DRILL 25-7 Inspecting and Reinstalling a Synchronizer Hub

1 Inspect the synchronizer hub for any malformations such as chipping, cracking, or broken parts. Such damage may require replacement of the output shaft in some cases.

2 Inspect the synchronizer sleeve for any visible defects such as chipping or cracking.

3 Check the inserts for any defects. If bent or cracked, replace the synchronizer inserts by sliding the synchronizer sleeve off the synchronizer hub. The keys and springs will fall out. It is necessary to disassemble the synchronizer for inspection.

4 Inspect the blocking rings for wear, which can be seen on the friction side of the ring. There are usually serrations or friction material that are visible, but if missing or worn, replace the blocking rings as a pair. On transmissions that give blocking ring clearance specifications, measure the clearance with a feeler blade.

5 Inspect the insert springs for tension and replace as necessary.

6 To assemble the synchronizer hub:
- Lubricate the synchronizer hub.
- Install the insert springs, paying attention to orientation.
- Lubricate the inserts and install in slots in the synchronizer hub.
- Insert the blocking rings into the hub and align the slots in them so as to accommodate the inserts.
- Align the synchronizer sleeve, paying attention to grooves that may line up with the inserts, and slide into position.
- Reinstall the synchronizer on the output shaft, or if already a part of the output shaft, check for proper operation.
- Check synchronizer clearance using a feeler gauge.

1. Inspect the synchronizer hub for any malformations such as chipping, cracking, or broken parts. Such damage will require replacement of the output shaft in some cases. **(Photo 1)**

2. Inspect the synchronizer sleeve for any visible defects such as chipping or cracking. **(Photo 2)**

3. Check the inserts for any defects. If bent or cracked, replace the synchronizer inserts by sliding the synchronizer sleeve off the synchronizer hub. The keys and springs will fall out. It is necessary to disassemble the synchronizer for inspection. **(Photo 3)**

4. Inspect the blocking rings for wear, which can be seen on the friction side of the ring. There are usually serrations or friction material that are visible, but if missing or worn, replace the blocking rings as a pair. Some manufacturers give a minimum clearance specification between the blocker ring and the face of the gear to indicate if a blocker ring is excessively worn. This clearance can be measured with a feeler blade. **(Photo 4)**

5. Inspect the insert springs for tension, and replace as necessary. **(Photo 5)**

6. To assemble the synchronizer hub:

   - Use transmission gel or Vaseline to lubricate the synchronizer hub.
   - Install the insert springs, paying attention to orientation following the manufacturer's guidelines.
   - Lubricate the inserts and install in slots in the synchronizer hub.
   - Insert the blocking rings into the hub and align the slots in them so as to accommodate the inserts. If misaligned, the synchronizer sleeve will not be able to slide into position properly.
   - Carefully align the synchronizer sleeve, paying attention to any grooves that may line up with the inserts, and slide into position.
   - Reinstall the synchronizer on the output shaft, or if already a part of the output shaft, check for proper operation.
   - Check synchronizer clearance using a feeler gauge. **(Photo 6)**

Inspecting and Servicing Lubrication Devices

Some manual transmissions use an **oil slinger** behind the input shaft. The oil slinger ensures that oil is directed toward the front bearing and oil is returned to the transmission case. The oil slinger should be inspected for any defects or damage such as scratches or bending of the slinger that might have occurred during the transmission failure.

Sometimes it is necessary to use an oil pump to lubricate a transmission in order to maintain a safe temperature inside the case. Some manufacturers such as Ford Motor Company use the ZF six-speed transmission. This manual transmission has an oil pump with an external oil cooler used to carry heat out of the transmission, similar to an automatic transmission during heavy-duty usage of the vehicle. During a rebuild, it is always good practice to inspect or replace the oil pump parts when necessary. Loss of oil pressure could result in transmission damage.

To inspect and service an oil pump and related lubrication devices, follow the steps in **SKILL DRILL 25-8**:

1. Start by removing the oil pump from the transmission case following the specified procedure.

2. Inspect all gears for excessive wear and clearances, and replace as necessary.

3. Inspect the regulator piston for wear and etching in the bore.

4. Replace any parts that have wear or etching.

5. Reassemble the oil pump in the transmission case and check clearances if they are specified. If any oil slingers are used, they should be replaced as necessary with the gaskets and seals.

Inspecting and Servicing the Shift Cover

The shifting mechanism of a manual transmission takes a lot of abuse from the driver. Shift lever bushings, shafts, pivot points, and seals wear over time and may require service. To prevent failure in the future, it is always a good practice to inspect and service the shift mechanism when rebuilding a transmission. Upon disassembly of the transmission, the shift cover and associated parts should be inspected along with the rest of the transmission parts. Shift mechanisms may also be part of the reason the manual transmission needs to be rebuilt. Disassembly and cleaning should be the first priority before inspection.

When removing the shift cover and mechanism, make sure the manual transmission is in neutral. This will make it easier to install the shift cover when the reassembly is complete.

To inspect and service the shift cover, follow the steps in **SKILL DRILL 25-9**:

1. If an O-ring is present that is used to seal the cover to the output shaft housing, the O-ring should be replaced by removing it from its groove; during assembly, a new one should be installed. **(Photo 1)**

2 Check all shifter forks for wear in the gear selector slots.

3 If the gear shift fork inserts are worn or cracked, they should be replaced before the installation of the shift cover. Most of these inserts are made of plastic. **(Photo 2)**

4 Check the gear selector interlock sleeve for excessive wear, and, if necessary, replace. The gear selector interlock sleeve should allow the plunger to move freely when the shift rails are moved front and back. If the shift interlock is sticking, it will be necessary to clean or replace the shift rails and interlock assembly. **(Photo 3)**

5 Lubricate all main shift control shafts with petroleum jelly before installation. **(Photo 4)**

6 As the shift rails are being installed, check all detent springs and balls for damage, and replace as necessary. The detent springs should not be stretched or

SKILL DRILL | **25-9** | **Inspecting and Servicing the Shift Cover**

1 If an O-ring is present that is used to seal the cover to the output shaft housing, it should be replaced.

2 Check all shifter forks for wear in the gear selector slots. If the gear shift fork inserts are worn or cracked, they should be replaced before the installation of the shift cover.

3 Check the gear selector interlock sleeve for excessive wear and binding. If necessary, clean or replace.

4 Lubricate all main shift control shafts with petroleum jelly before installation.

5 As the shift rails are being installed, check all detent springs and balls for damage, and replace as necessary.

6 If roll pins are used to secure shift forks or sleeves, inspect for tightness and replace as necessary by driving the pin out and replacing with a new one. If the new pin fits loosely in the case, the case may be damaged and need to be replaced or repaired.

SKILL DRILL 25-9 Inspecting and Servicing the Shift Cover, continued

7 Secure a new shift cover gasket usually by using a dab of RTV sealer, and install the shift cover. Some transmissions will use RTV without an additional gasket, as does the transmission in the picture. Follow the manufacturer's directions to ensure a leak-free repair. Make sure the shift forks line up with the corresponding gears.

8 Install the shift lever and check that all gears can be shifted without binding.

broken. Check for a length specification in the service information; if none is given, compare springs to each other. Check the detent balls for flat spots due to wear. **(Photo 5)**

7 If roll pins are used to secure shift forks or sleeves, inspect for tightness and replace as necessary by driving the pin out and replacing with a new one. If the new pin fits loosely in the case, the case may be damaged and need to be replaced or repaired. **(Photo 6)**

8 Secure a new shift cover gasket usually by using a dab of room temperature vulcanizing (RTV) sealer and install the shift cover. Be sure to follow the manufacturer's directions to ensure a leak-free repair. Make sure the shift forks line up with the corresponding gears. **(Photo 7)**

9 Install the shift lever and check that all gears can be shifted without binding. **(Photo 8)**

Inspecting and Servicing Shift Linkages

Upon removal of the transmission, it is necessary to remove the shift linkage and associated parts. Any adjustments that were present will have to be performed again

since the shifter cables or linkages will have to be loosened. It is always a good practice to check all components of the shifting mechanism and replace any parts that are damaged or broken. Upon inspection, it may be possible to find out what caused the failure of the transmission to begin with; for example, if the transmission shift linkage is keeping one gear partially engaged, the dog teeth of the transmission can be damaged.

To inspect and service shift linkages, follow the steps in **SKILL DRILL 25-10**:

1 Start by laying all shifting components and the associated parts out on a bench to get a clear picture for inspection. **(Photo 1)**

2 Inspect the cable linkage for fraying and stretching. **(Photo 2)**

3 Inspect the mechanical linkage for worn or elongated holes where the bushings ride. **(Photo 3)**

4 Inspect all plastic or brass bushings for excessive wear, and replace as necessary. **(Photo 4)**

5 Inspect all linkage rod ends for excessive wear from abuse.

6 Inspect all linkage rods for abnormal shape, which can occur due to abuse by the driver. **(Photo 5)**

SKILL DRILL | **25-10** | **Inspecting and Servicing Shift Linkages**

1. Lay all the associated parts out on a bench to get a clear picture for inspection if possible. Clean off the dirt and grease in order to properly inspect.

2. Inspect the cable linkage for fraying and stretching.

3. Inspect the mechanical linkage for worn or elongated holes where the bushings ride.

4. If the vehicle has plastic or brass bushings, inspect them for excessive wear and replace as necessary.

5. Inspect linkage rod ends for excessive wear from abuse. Inspect the rods for abnormal shape, which can occur as a result of driver abuse.

6. Inspect mounting brackets for excessive wear and looseness, and replace as necessary. Check all sensors and solenoids.

7. Inspect all mounting brackets for excessive wear and looseness, and replace as necessary.

8. Check all sensors and solenoids using a scan tool or scope. See Skill Drill 25-1, Inspecting and Servicing Sensors and Switches, for more information. (**Photo 6**)

Removing and Replacing the Transaxle Final Drive

Sometimes it is necessary to remove the transaxle final drive, whether because of a failure or because of a noise problem emanating from that area, such as gear or bearing noise. The procedure for this task is specific to each vehicle. Because bearing preload and gear contact patterns are crucial to the longevity of the transaxle, be sure to carefully follow the specified procedure in the service information.

SKILL DRILL 25-11 is based on a Ford MTX transaxle and is used solely as an example of the process:

1. Following the manufacturer's specifications, disassemble the transaxle case and shafts as necessary to gain access to the final drive assembly. Parts of the final drive include the output shaft that has the pinion gear molded on to it and the differential case. (**Photo 1**)

SKILL DRILL | 25-11 | Removing and Replacing the Transaxle Final Drive

1 Following the manufacturer's specifications, disassemble the transaxle case and shafts as necessary to gain access to the final drive assembly. Parts of the final drive include the output shaft that has the pinion gear molded on to it and the differential case.

2 Remove the output shaft from the transaxle case and inspect. See Skill Drill 25-4 for more information. Remove the differential case from the transaxle housing. Be careful of the spider gear orientation, and do not let them fall out of the differential case. In some cases, there is no retaining pin to hold them in place.

3 After performing any needed service, reinstall the differential case in the transaxle housing, seating the bearing in its race.

4 Reinstall the output shaft in the transaxle case and mate with all other shafts.

5 Measure the preload and correct by using shims under the case bearings of the differential by using a dial indicator following the manufacturer's procedure. Reassemble the transaxle's major components.

2 Remove the output shaft from the transaxle case and inspect. See Skill Drill 25-4, Inspecting a Transmission Case, for more information.

3 Remove the differential case from the transaxle housing. Be careful of the spider gear orientation, and do not let them fall out of the differential case. In some cases, there is no retaining pin to hold them in place. **(Photo 2)**

4 After performing any needed service, reinstall the differential case in the transaxle housing, seating the bearing in its race. **(Photo 3)**

5 Reinstall the output shaft in the transaxle case and mate with all other shafts. **(Photo 4)**

6 Measure the preload and correct by using shims under the case bearings of the differential by using a dial indicator following the manufacturer's procedure.

7 Reassemble the transaxle's major components. **(Photo 5)**

Removing and Servicing Transaxle Final Drive Pinion Gears

After transaxle disassembly, the transaxle final drive is exposed for service. The pinion gear is part of the output shaft of the transaxle. The pinion gear is what drives the differential ring gear, which is located inside the transaxle assembly. If it needs to be replaced, it will also be necessary to replace the ring gear as well. These are, as in a rear-wheel drive vehicle, a matched set. Remove the differential case following the manufacturer's procedures.

To remove and service the transaxle final drive pinion gears, follow the steps in **SKILL DRILL 25-12**:

1 Remove the ring gear from the differential case. If inspection shows that it should be replaced,

SKILL DRILL | 25-12 | Removing and Servicing Transaxle Final Drive Pinion Gears

1 Remove the ring gear from the differential case. If inspection shows that it should be replaced, remove by drilling the rivets out of the ring gear itself for replacement.

2 Start disassembly of the differential case by removing the roll pin from the pinion shaft lock pin.

3 Remove the differential lock pin by sliding it out of the housing.

4 Remove the differential pinion side gears and differential pinion thrust washers.

5 Remove the differential spider gears and differential spider gear thrust washers.

6 Use a push-type bearing puller and a step plate to remove the differential case bearings.

SKILL DRILL | 25-12 | Removing and Servicing Transaxle Final Drive Pinion Gears, continued

7 Remove the speedometer drive gear.

8 Inspect the transaxle final drive pinion gears:
- Inspect the ring gear for abnormal wear or cracking.
- Inspect differential spider gear sets as well as the side gears for abnormal wear and cracks or scratches or galling in the thrust washer area.
- Inspect thrust washers; if unusable, replace as necessary.
- Inspect locking pins for wear and distortion.
- Inspect the thrust surfaces in the differential case for damage in the thrust washer areas.
- Inspect the differential case for any damage, and replace as necessary.
- Check bearing surfaces on the differential case for any problems.

9 Reassemble the differential case following the manufacturer's procedures. Install a new ring gear with either bolts or new rivets.

10 Reinstall the differential case in the transaxle case. Measure any necessary clearances.

remove by drilling the rivets out of the ring gear itself for replacement. (**Photo 1**)

2 Start disassembly of the differential case by removing the roll pin from the pinion shaft lock pin. (**Photo 2**)

3 Remove the differential lock pin by sliding it out of the housing. (**Photo 3**)

4 Remove the differential pinion side gears and differential pinion thrust washers. (**Photo 4**)

5 Remove the differential spider gears and differential spider gear thrust washers. (**Photo 5**)

6 Use a push-type bearing puller and a step plate to remove the differential case bearings. (**Photo 6**)

7 Remove the speedometer drive gear. (**Photo 7**)

8 Inspect the transaxle final drive pinion gears:

- Inspect the ring gear for abnormal wear or cracking.
- Inspect all differential spider gear sets as well as the side gears for abnormal wear and cracks or scratches or galling in the thrust washer area. Galling can occur from a lack of lubrication in the thrust washer area.
- Inspect all thrust washers; if unusable, replace as necessary.
- Inspect all locking pins for wear and distortion, as it may be necessary to replace them as well.
- Inspect the thrust surfaces in the differential case for damage in the thrust washer areas. If these areas are bad or unusable, it will be necessary to obtain a new differential case.
- Inspect the differential case for any damage, and replace as necessary.
- Check all bearing surfaces on the differential case for any problems such as a bearing that may have spun on the bearing mounting surface. (**Photo 8**)

9 Reassemble the differential case following the manufacturer's procedures.

10 Install a new ring gear with either blots or new rivets. (**Photo 9**)

11 Reinstall the differential case in the transaxle case being careful to align the ring gear with the pinion gear on the output shaft. Measure any necessary clearances.(**Photo 10**)

Reassembling the Transmission

After inspection and replacement of faulty components, the transmission is now ready for reassembly.

If it was found to be cheaper to use a replacement transmission, then the transmission may need to be reassembled for a core return to the manufacturer. The core is the faulty part that will be sent to a rebuilder for refurbishing and then resold as a remanufactured transmission. In most cases, rebuilders require you to either give them your old transmission or pay a core charge, which allows the rebuilder to purchase another core for rebuilding purposes. You may need to use some of the special tools previously mentioned to reassemble the transmission. Take extreme care to ensure the transmission is assembled correctly and the proper clearances and bearing end play/preloads have been set.

To reassemble the major components of a manual transmission, follow the steps in **SKILL DRILL 25-13**:

1 To reassemble the input shaft assembly:

- Install a new input shaft bearing using a hydraulic press by pushing the bearing down on to the shaft.
- Pack and install the pocket bearings.
- Install the spacer on top of the pocket bearing. (**Photo 1**)

2 To reassemble the output shaft assembly:

- Install the output shaft in a hydraulic press.
- Install the first gear and blocking ring and the rear bearing and fifth gear.
- Press all items into their proper position.
- Install the fifth gear snap ring.
- Install the speedometer check ball and speedometer gear according to the manufacturer's specifications.
- Remove the output shaft from the press. Install the output shaft in a vice.
- Assemble the first and second gear synchronizer assembly.
- Install the second gear with a spacer and snap ring.
- Install the third gear along with the fourth gear synchronizer.
- Install the third gear retaining snap ring. (**Photo 2**)

3 To reassemble the countershaft:

- Press all gears back onto the countershaft shaft.
- Press all bearings back onto the ends of the countershaft shaft. (**Photo 3**)

4 To reassemble the reverse idler shaft, see Skill Drill 25-14, Reassembling a Manual Transmission.

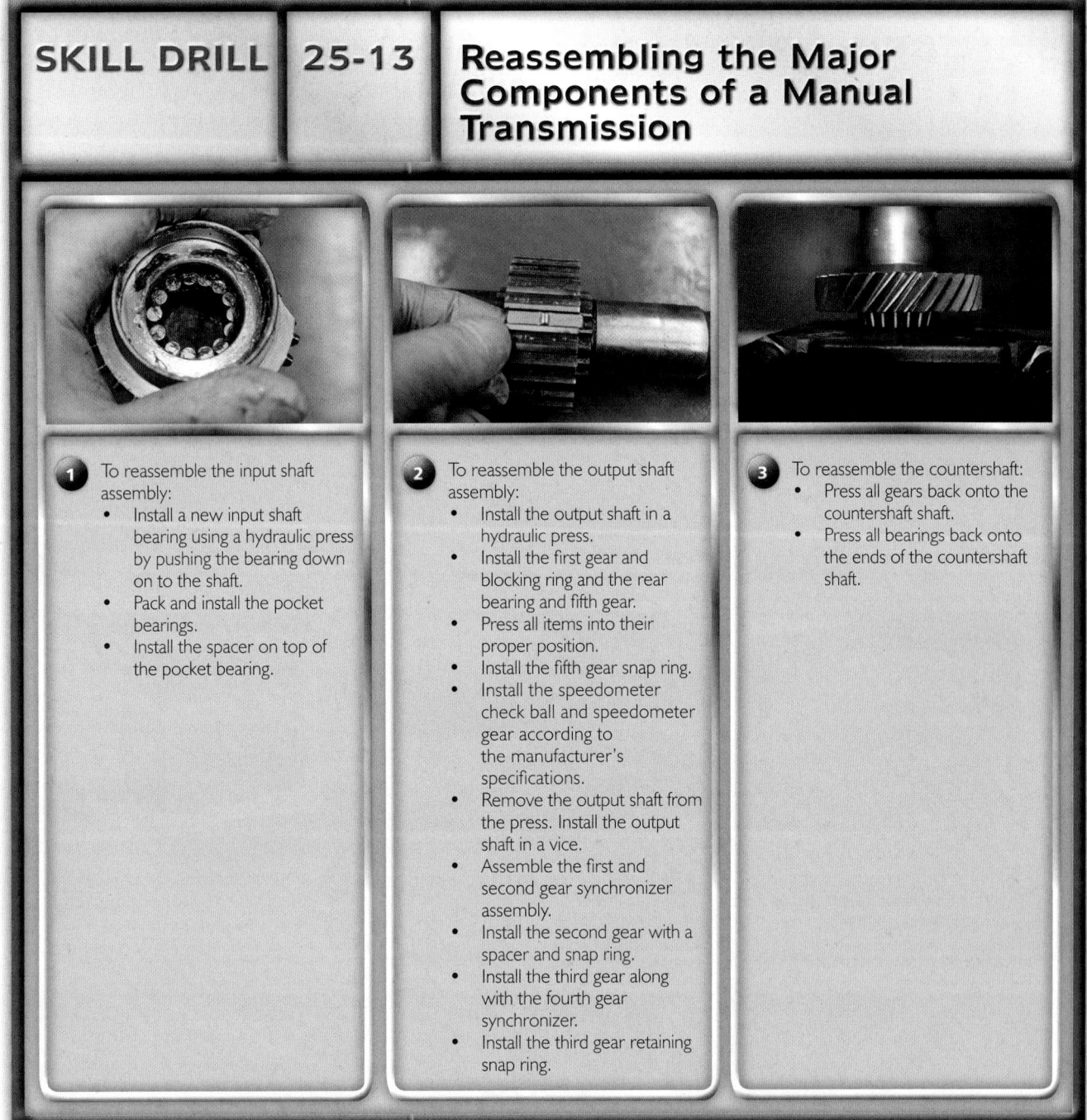

SKILL DRILL | 25-13 | Reassembling the Major Components of a Manual Transmission

1 To reassemble the input shaft assembly:
- Install a new input shaft bearing using a hydraulic press by pushing the bearing down on to the shaft.
- Pack and install the pocket bearings.
- Install the spacer on top of the pocket bearing.

2 To reassemble the output shaft assembly:
- Install the output shaft in a hydraulic press.
- Install the first gear and blocking ring and the rear bearing and fifth gear.
- Press all items into their proper position.
- Install the fifth gear snap ring.
- Install the speedometer check ball and speedometer gear according to the manufacturer's specifications.
- Remove the output shaft from the press. Install the output shaft in a vice.
- Assemble the first and second gear synchronizer assembly.
- Install the second gear with a spacer and snap ring.
- Install the third gear along with the fourth gear synchronizer.
- Install the third gear retaining snap ring.

3 To reassemble the countershaft:
- Press all gears back onto the countershaft shaft.
- Press all bearings back onto the ends of the countershaft shaft.

To reassemble the manual transmission, follow the steps in **SKILL DRILL 25-14**:

1 Start by installing a new countershaft pocket bearing flush in the transmission case. This will require a bearing driver made for this purpose. Drive the bearing until it is flush in the case. Check for free turning effort of the bearing after driving it into place. If the bearing binds, then it has been damaged and will need to be replaced.

Be careful not to crush the needle bearing cage; this is why a special tool is used in this step. **(Photo 1)**

> ## TECHNICIAN TIP
>
> When reassembling all components, it is a good practice to lubricate parts as they are being installed.

SKILL DRILL   25-14   Reassembling a Manual Transmission

1 Start by installing a new countershaft pocket bearing flush in the transmission case. Be careful not to crush the needle bearing cage; this is why a special tool is used in this step.

2 Install the countershaft into the transmission case by slowly lowering it into the bottom of the case and slipping it into the front pocket bearing.

3 Install the rear countershaft bearing race by aligning and tapping it gently with a hammer into the case.

4 Install the idler shaft and gear in the transmission case by sliding the shaft through the case holes.

5 Install the idler shaft roll pin with a hammer.

6 Install the output shaft in the transmission case, being careful to align all gears as necessary.

7 Install the rear bearing race. Install the input shaft in the transmission case, paying attention to align the cutout on the dog teeth portion of the shaft so the input shaft will mate with the output shaft.

8 Install the front bearing retainer with a new gasket and seal, and torque the bolts to the manufacturer's specifications.

9 Install the fifth driven gear and the washer and retaining snap ring.

SKILL DRILL | 25-14 | Reassembling a Manual Transmission, continued

10 Install the fifth gear synchronizer assembly and shift fork.

11 Install the shifter housing and new gasket, paying attention to the neutral position, and align all shift forks with the appropriate gears.

12 Install shifter housing bolts and torque to specifications.

13 Install the rear transmission housing with a new seal and gasket, and align the shift mechanism to be able to install the retaining roll pin.

14 Install the shift lever and the bolts, and torque to specifications. Operate the shift lever to make sure all gears can be selected without binding.

15 Install the speed sensor and any other wiring or component that was removed during disassembly.

16 Reinstall the manual transmission into the vehicle.

17 Fill the manual transmission system with the proper type and level of lubricant according to the manufacturer's specifications.

18 Perform a thorough road test. Raise the vehicle on the lift and check for any leaks before returning it to the customer.

2 Install the countershaft into the transmission case by slowly lowering it into the bottom of the case and slipping it into the front pocket bearing. Be sure to lubricate the bearing surfaces before you install the countershaft. **(Photo 2)**

3 Install the rear countershaft bearing race by aligning and tapping it with a hammer into the case. This is a gentle procedure; do not drive the bearing with excessive force; doing so will damage the bearing surface and create noise when driving down the road. **(Photo 3)**

4 Install the idler shaft and gear in the transmission case by sliding it through the case holes. **(Photo 4)**

5 Install the idler shaft roll pin with a hammer. **(Photo 5)**

6 Install the output shaft in the transmission case, being careful to align all gears as necessary. **(Photo 6)**

7 Install the rear bearing race.

8 Install the input shaft in the transmission case, paying attention to align the cutout on the dog teeth portion of the shaft so the input shaft will mate with the output shaft. **(Photo 7)**

9 Install the front bearing retainer with a new gasket and seal, and torque the bolts to the manufacturer's specifications. **(Photo 8)**

10 Install the fifth driven gear and the washer and retaining snap ring. **(Photo 9)**

11 Install the fifth gear synchronizer assembly and shift fork. **(Photo 10)**

12 Install the shifter housing and new gasket, paying attention to the neutral position, and align all shift forks with appropriate gears. **(Photo 11)**

13 Install shifter housing bolts and torque to specifications. **(Photo 12)**

14 Install the rear transmission housing with a new seal and gasket, and align the shift mechanism to be able to install the retaining roll pin. **(Photo 13)**

15 Install the shift lever and install the bolts, and torque to specifications.

16 Operate the shift lever to make sure all gears can be selected without binding. **(Photo 14)**

17 Install the **speed sensor** and any other wiring or components that were removed during disassembly. **(Photo 15)**

18 Reinstall the manual transmission into the vehicle. **(Photo 16)**

19 Fill the manual transmission system with the proper type and level of lubricant according to the manufacturer's specifications. **(Photo 17)**

20 Perform a thorough road test.

21 Raise the vehicle on the lift and check for any leaks before returning it to the customer. **(Photo 18)**

Measuring and Adjusting End Play/Preload

End play and **preload** adjustments are a necessary part of the disassembly and assembly of the transmission. End play is the movement back and forth of the input or output shaft. It is typically set by using preselected spacers or washers to ensure the correct clearance is present. The need for end play and preload adjustments can be an indicator of washer wear or bearing failure, which causes the shaft to walk back and forth in the case. This movement leads to misalignment of shift forks, making shifting difficult or popping the transmission out of gear. Axial or radial clearances (i.e., end play and preload adjustments) can be used to determine whether gears and shafts are to be replaced or reused.

Most manufacturers require that certain end play and preload adjustments be done upon assembly of transmissions. Preload ensures that enough pressure is placed on the bearing to keep the shaft from moving around, but not so much that the bearing will run hot and begin to fail. Most of these adjustments require the use of a dial indicator or feeler gauge to obtain proper clearances. Follow all manufacturer specifications and procedures upon disassembly and assembly to ensure a proper and lasting repair.

If one of the transmission shafts is found to have too much free play, then a thorough inspection will need to be performed to ensure that there is not wear on a component, such as a thrust bearing, causing the fault. If there is no issue with components, then check for thrust washer or shim and install a proper-sized thrust washer, if needed.

Measuring end play is critical to ensure that the transmission stays in service for a long time. Incorrect end play and bearing preload will result in failure of the transmission.

To measure and adjust end play/preload, follow the steps in **SKILL DRILL 25-15**:

1 Once the transmission assembly is together, turn the transmission case on its end and mount a dial indicator on the end of the output shaft.

2 Rotate the dial indicator to zero. **(Photo 1)**

SKILL DRILL | **25-15** | **Measuring and Adjusting End Play/Preload**

1 Once the transmission assembly is together, turn the transmission case on its end and mount a dial indicator on the end of the output shaft. Rotate the dial indicator to zero.

2 Grab the output shaft and raise it upward until the end play is totally removed; doing so will give you an accurate reading. Record the measurement and compare with the manufacturer's specifications. Most are usually around 0.005" to 0.025" (0.127 to 0.635 mm).

3 If an adjustment is necessary, remove the front bearing retaining cover. Remove the front bearing race, which may expose any existing shims.

4 Install the correct shims to bring the end play into specifications. Reinstall the front bearing retainer and gasket. Torque the bolts to the manufacturer's specifications.

3 Grab the output shaft and raise it upward until the end play is totally removed; doing so will give you an accurate reading.

4 Record the measurement and compare with the manufacturer's specifications. Most are usually around 0.005" to 0.025" (0.127 to 0.635 mm). **(Photo 2)**

5 If an adjustment is necessary, remove the front bearing retaining cover.

6 Remove the front bearing race, which may expose any existing shims. **(Photo 3)**

7 Install the correct shims to bring the end play into specifications. Reinstall the front bearing retainer and gasket. Torque the bolts to the manufacturer's specifications. **(Photo 4)**

Wrap-up

Ready for Review

▸ As the transmission wears, it may begin to develop concerns for the customer such as popping out of gear, making growling noises, or becoming difficult to shift.

▸ A transmission that has been run low on gear oil will wear extremely quickly and will result in the need for rebuilding or replacement.

▸ Rebuilding a transmission/transaxle can be a large undertaking considering its complexity and all of the makes and models produced for the automotive market.

▸ The most important part in any rebuild/overhaul is to pay attention to detail and make sure you locate the cause/s of a transmission/transaxle failure, such as worn synchronizer rings, broken detent spring, worn bearing.

▸ Some special tools and equipment may be required to disassemble and reassemble today's modern manual transmissions, such as special pullers or electronic devices.

▸ Failures inside the transmission can simply indicate replacement of wear items such as seals, gaskets, bearings and synchronizer blocker rings or the failure of hard parts, such as input, output, or counter shafts, gears, and synchronizer assemblies.

▸ The rebuilding of a transmission/transaxle is not something to be performed by a novice technician without any training.

▸ Among the first things to consider when doing any kind of service to a manual transmission/transaxle is obtaining and reading all manufacturer publications and service information.

▸ If it is necessary to disassemble a manual transmission because of an internal problem, a complete and thorough diagnosis is warranted in order to affect a complete and error free repair.

▸ Once the concern is fully understood, the technician needs to verify the concern, usually by test driving the vehicle, and diagnose the possible causes.

▸ The purpose of the power train mounts (motor mounts), is to support the engine and transmission/transaxle as it is placed in the car.

▸ It is always a good practice to inspect power train mounts whenever the vehicle is on the lift or if the customer complains of unusual shifting or noises present.

▸ Although a manual transmission/transaxle is being shifted manually, there is a bit of electronics used in the process of selecting gears on some transmissions.

▸ When overhauling a transmission/transaxle, all transmission case components should be cleaned and inspected to make sure that they can be reused.

▸ You have an important cost analysis job to perform for the customer.

▸ When rebuilding a transmission/transaxle, it is always a good practice to replace the gaskets and seals.

▸ Before replacing the gaskets, clean all gasket surfaces to make sure that the surface will accept the gasket and prevent leaks.

▸ The transmission/transaxle mating surfaces such as the main case and output shaft housing should be checked with a straight edge and feeler gauge to make sure that both surfaces are flat to ensure a tight seal.

▸ The front bearing retainer and the main transmission/transaxle case is another area that should be checked with a straight edge and feeler gauge.

▸ The shift tower surface is also an area to consider and check for flatness with a straight edge and feeler gauge as this may cause a leakage of fluid.

▸ When overhauling a manual transmission, it is important to inspect the synchronizer assemblies for damage before reusing them.

▸ A good place to start when inspecting for synchronizer wear and damage is when you drain the transmission fluid from the transmission/transaxle.

▸ Any gold colored particles may indicate that the blocking rings are excessively worn and may need to be serviced.

▸ The oil slinger should be inspected for any defects or damage such as scratches or bending of the slinger that might have occurred during the transmission failure.

- During a rebuild, it is always good practice to inspect or replace the oil pump parts if equipped.
- To prevent failure in the future, it is always a good practice to inspect and service the shift mechanism when rebuilding a transmission.
- Shift linkage adjustments that were present, will have to be performed again since the shifter cables or linkages will have to be loosened.
- Sometimes it is necessary to remove the transaxle final drive, whether there was a failure or for service because of a noise problem emanating from that particular area, such as gear or bearing noise.
- If it was found to be cheaper to use a replacement transmission, then the transmission may need to be reassembled for a core return to the manufacturer.

- When reassembling all components it is a good practice to lubricate parts as they are being installed.
- Endplay and preload adjustments are a necessary part of the disassembly and assembly of the transmission/transaxle.
- Endplay and preload adjustments can be an indicator of washer wear or bearing failure, which causes the shaft to walk back and forth in the case.
- Measuring endplay is critical to ensure that the transmission stays in service for a long time.
- It is highly important that the technician always follow the manufacture's service and maintenance procedures, as well as safety precautions.

Key Terms

blocking ring The ring on the synchronizer assembly that slows or speeds up the gear to match the main shaft speed, which allows smooth shifts.

concentricity The roundness of a hole. If the hole is not round it can also be referred to as out of round.

end play Referring to the input or output shaft, fore-and-aft movement in the transmission.

oil slinger A device that rides partially in the transmission fluid; as it spins, it flings oil to lubricate the internal workings of the transmission.

overhauling The process of refurbishing the transmission to like-new condition.

preload The level of pressure placed on bearings that ensures the bearings will be held together.

speed sensor A sensor responsible for measuring the speed of the vehicle that is read by the speedometer.

torsional vibrations Pulsations in the crankshaft rotation caused by the power pulses on the crankshaft and felt as a vibration.

warpage A change in the shape of a surface due to distortion or wear.

ASE-Type Questions

1. Tech A says that broken or worn power train mounts can cause a transaxle to have shifting problems. Tech B says that poor shift boot alignment cannot cause a transaxle to jump out of gear. Who is correct?
   a. Tech A
   b. Tech B
   c. Both A and B
   d. Neither A nor B

2. Tech A says that a leaky transmission output shaft seal is likely to cause clutch plate contamination. Tech B says that a worn transmission rear bushing may contribute to output shaft seal leakage. Who is correct?
   a. Tech A
   b. Tech B
   c. Both A and B
   d. Neither A nor B

3. A car jumps out of gear into neutral when decelerating or going down hills. Tech A that the shift lever and internal gearshift linkage should be checked. Tech B says that a detent spring could be broken. Who is correct?
   a. Tech A
   b. Tech B
   c. Both A and B
   d. Neither A nor B

4. Tech A says that as long as the dog (clutch) teeth of the synchronizer are rounded, the synchronizer can be reused. Tech B says that the synchronizer sleeve should slide smoothly on its splines. Who is correct?
   a. Tech A
   b. Tech B
   c. Both A and B
   d. Neither A nor B

5. A transmission is being assembled, but the input shaft does not slide all the way in. Tech A says this is normal and to use the bolts to pull the front bearing retainer into place. Tech B says that you should use a hammer to tap the bearing retainer into place. Who is correct?
   a. Tech A
   b. Tech B
   c. Both A and B
   d. Neither A nor B

6. A rough growling noise occurs when the vehicle is moving and the transmission is in the forward or reverse gear. The noise is not heard when the transmission is in neutral. Tech A says that the output shaft (main shaft) bearings may be faulty. Tech B that says the pilot bearing may be faulty. Who is correct?
   a. Tech A
   b. Tech B
   c. Both A and B
   d. Neither A nor B

7. Tech A says that the input shaft normally needs to be installed before the main shaft. Tech B says that most manual transmissions are first disassembled into subassemblies before further disassembling. Who is correct?
   a. Tech A
   b. Tech B
   c. Both A and B
   d. Neither A nor B

8. Tech A says that the condition of blocking rings should be checked by measuring the clearance between the blocking ring and the face of the gear. Tech B says that the blocking ring should be visually inspected for worn clutch teeth and smooth internal surfaces. Who is correct?
   a. Tech A
   b. Tech B
   c. Both A and B
   d. Neither A nor B

9. Transaxle inspection is being discussed. Tech A says that in some cases, a magnet is installed in the case to catch any ferrous metal particles, and it should be inspected. Tech B says that tapping on the gears with a ball-peen hammer and listening for a ringing sound is a good way to determine if a gear is reusable. Who is correct?
   a. Tech A
   b. Tech B
   c. Both A and B
   d. Neither A nor B

10. Transmission end play is being discussed. Tech A says that a dial indicator should be used to measure the inward and outward movement of the output shaft. Tech B says that an angle gauge should be used to measure output shaft rotation. Who is correct?
    a. Tech A
    b. Tech B
    c. Both A and B
    d. Neither A nor B

CHAPTER 26

NATEF Tasks

Basic Drive Layouts

NATEF Tasks, continued

- Drain and refill differential housing. **MLR** **AST** **MAST** 766–767

- Clean and inspect differential housing; check for leaks; inspect housing vent (refill with correct lubricant and/or additive) **MLR** **AST** **MAST** 766–767

- Check and adjust differential housing fluid level. **MLR** **AST** **MAST** 766–767

Four-Wheel Drive/All-Wheel Drive

- Diagnose noise, vibration, and unusual steering concerns; determine necessary action. **MAST** 745

- Identify concerns related to variations in tire circumference and/or final drive ratios. **AST** **MAST** 745

- Diagnose, test, adjust, and replace electrical/electronic components of four-wheel drive systems. **MAST** 746

- Check for leaks at drive assembly seals; check vents; check lube level. **MLR** **AST** **MAST** 755–756

- Inspect, adjust, and repair shifting controls (mechanical, electrical, and vacuum), bushings, mounts, levers, and brackets. **AST** **MAST** 768

- Inspect front wheel bearings and locking hubs. **MLR** 772

- Inspect front wheel bearings and locking hubs; perform necessary actions. **AST** **MAST** 772

Knowledge Objectives

After reading this chapter you will be able to:
1. Describe rear-wheel drive layout. (pp 729–730)
2. Describe front-wheel drive layout. (p 730)
3. Describe four-wheel drive layout. (pp 730–731)
4. Describe all-wheel drive layout. (p 731)

Knowledge Objectives, continued

5. List the three types of shafts that make up the drive line subassemblies. (pp 731–732)
6. Explain the three varieties of drive axles and how each functions. (pp 732–734)
7. Describe universal joints and constant-velocity joints and how they function. (pp 735–736)
8. Explain the terms *final drive* and *differential*. (p 737)
9. Explain the purpose of transfer cases. (pp 741–743)

Skills Objectives

After reading this chapter, you will be able to:
1. Identify concerns related to variations in tire circumference and/or final drive ratios. (p 745)
2. Diagnose CV joint issues. (pp 745–746)
3. Check driveshaft joints, phasing, angles, balance, and runout. (pp 746–748)
4. Inspect and service center support bearings. (pp 748–749)
5. Measure drive axle flange runout and shaft end play. (p 749)
6. Remove the integral-type differential axles. (pp 749–751)
7. Remove the removable carrier-type differential axles. (pp 751–752)
8. Perform integral axle housing seal and bearing replacement. (pp 752–753)
9. Perform removable carrier seal and bearing replacement. (pp 752–754)
10. Inspect half-shaft components. (pp 754–755)
11. Inspect fluid leakage. (pp 755–756)
12. Inspect and replace the companion flange and pinion seal. (pp 756–757)
13. Inspect the ring gear and measure runout. (pp 757–758)
14. Remove, inspect, and reinstall the drive pinion and ring gear. (pp 758–759)
15. Disassemble, inspect, measure, and adjust the differential pinion gear assembly. (pp 759–761)
16. Adjust pinion depth. (pp 761–762)
17. Measure and adjust drive pinion preload. (pp 762–763)
18. Reassemble and reinstall the differential case assembly, and measure runout. (p 763)
19. Adjust backlash of an integral differential. (pp 763–764)
20. Adjust backlash of a removable carrier differential. (pp 764–765)
21. Check contact patterns. (pp 764–766)
22. Clean and inspect the differential housing, and refill it with lubricant. (pp 766–767)
23. Inspect and reinstall limited slip differential components. (pp 767–768)
24. Measure rotating torque. (p 768)
25. Inspect, adjust, and repair shifting controls. (p 768)
26. Remove and reinstall the transfer case. (pp 768–769)
27. Disassemble and reassemble a transfer case and related components. (pp 769–771)
28. Inspect front wheel bearings and locking hubs. (p 772)
29. Remove and replace a four-wheel drive front wheel bearing. (p 772)

Introduction

In previous chapters we have covered how the engine's torque is modified and delivered through the transmission, whether it is a manual or an automatic type. Now the torque must get delivered to the appropriate wheels. That job is performed by the remainder of the drive train components, such as driveshafts, transfer cases, final drives, differentials, and drive axles. All of these assemblies are made up of subcomponents that allow them to perform their task. Depending on the vehicle, the arrangement of these assemblies can vary. For example, most passenger vehicles are driven by two wheels, while most off-road vehicles are driven by all four wheels. This chapter discusses these various assemblies and components of the drive train, their layout, how they operate, what can go wrong with them, how to diagnose them, and ultimately how to maintain and repair them.

FIGURE 26-1 A typical rear-wheel drive solid axle assembly with the final drive assembly enclosed in one housing.

Rear-Wheel Drive Layout

In a conventional rear-wheel drive vehicle, the engine and transmission are mounted longitudinally at the front. Drive from the engine is transmitted to a rear axle assembly by a drive (propeller) shaft. **Beam-type** or solid rear axle assemblies enclose the final drive gears, differential gears, and axle shafts into one housing **FIGURE 26-1**. In vehicles with an independent rear suspension, the final drive unit is mounted on the chassis frame, and drive is transferred to each road wheel through external driveshafts (half-shafts), which have flexible joints on each end. Vehicles with rear- or mid-mounted engines normally use a transaxle in the rear of the vehicle and transfer the drive to the road wheels by external drive half-shafts.

In beam axle or solid rear axle applications, suspension action makes the final drive assembly rise and fall relative to the vehicle frame. This happens as a vehicle goes over bumps and various types of terrain. This movement produces continuous change in the distance from the transmission output shaft to the final drive pinion, and in the angle between the driveshaft and its connections. In addition, the pinion nose is forced up on acceleration by torque and down when the brakes are applied on deceleration.

You are the Automotive Technician

After a long, icy-cold Michigan winter, Mrs. Simpson visits her local repair shop because she has started to notice an unusual noise that sometimes comes from the front of the vehicle. She drives her vehicle to and from work on Highway 94, which has multiple potholes as a result of the heavy trucking industry and harsh winter weather. You complete an interview with Mrs. Simpson and take her 2006 Toyota Camry for a test-drive, during which you notice that the vehicle makes a popping noise when turning corners. Your preliminary diagnosis is a worn constant-velocity (CV) joint, but you will need to further inspect the vehicle in the service bay. The visual inspection of the underside of the vehicle confirms your preliminary diagnosis: the right front CV joint boot is torn and dripping water. There is also dirt mixed with the little bit of grease still inside the boot.

1. What is likely causing the customer's concern? And what will you recommend to correct it?
2. What are the three different drive axle arrangements used with a rear-wheel drive solid axle? Which drive axle is most commonly used on medium to heavy trucks?
3. What is the difference between a final drive unit and the differential assembly?

FIGURE 26-2 The ring and pinion gear set allows power to be transferred ninety degrees from the power source.

Despite these movements, the driveshaft must transfer the drive smoothly. Change in length is accommodated by a sliding coupling built into the driveshaft or through the use of a **slip yoke** on the front of the driveshaft. The slip yoke has splines that mate to the splines on the transmission output shaft. The slip yoke slides in and out on the output shaft, allowing the length changes needed as the suspension moves up and down. If the vehicle uses a **sliding spline driveshaft**, a two-piece driveshaft is joined in the middle with splines. The driveshaft can slide on itself to increase and decrease in length. Universal joints (or simply "U-joints") are fitted at the front and rear ends of the driveshafts to allow for up-and-down suspension movement. The engine crankshaft and driveshaft rotate in line on this arrangement.

As shown in Figure 26-1, the centerline of the rear-wheel drive vehicle is not in line with the axle lines; this means the power needs to be turned 90 degrees to get it to the rear wheels. A ring gear and pinion assembly is commonly used for this purpose. The ring and pinion gear set allows the transfer of power 90 degrees **FIGURE 26-2**. It also reduces the rotational speed of the axles relative to the driveshaft, which increases the torque applied to the wheels.

Front-Wheel Drive Layout

Front-wheel drive vehicle engines may be mounted transversely or longitudinally. **Longitudinally** means the front of the engine is facing the front of the vehicle, while **transverse** mounting means the front of the engine is facing the side of the vehicle; that is, the engine is facing one of the fenders. Most front-engine front-wheel drive vehicles use a transverse-mounted engine coupled to a transaxle. Power is transmitted in a straight line

from the engine through the transmission and final drive (differential) gearing and out to the front axles (half-shafts). This design eliminates the need to transfer power 90 degrees as with a rear-wheel drive arrangement.

Front-wheel drive power reaches the front wheels through the transaxle. In transverse applications, the transaxle is normally mounted at the rear of the engine and a primary shaft engages with the splines of the clutch center plate. When a gear is selected, the drive is transferred to a secondary shaft, and through a secondary shaft pinion, to a helical ring gear attached to the differential case. Drive is then transferred through the differential gears to each driveshaft and into each front wheel.

Four-Wheel Drive Layout

Vehicles with part-time four-wheel drive are designed for optional off-road use. Four-wheel drive can be selected as needed for abnormal surfaces (mud, snow, ice, etc.) and can be disconnected for normal road surfaces. Selection is made by a manual lever or by electronic control via a push button. In such applications, the engine and transmission are normally mounted longitudinally at the front. A transfer case is mounted to the rear of the transmission. The transfer case is a device designed to split the power from the transmission to both the front and the rear drive axles when four-wheel drive is selected. Driveshafts are used to move power from the transfer case to the front and rear drive axles. The transfer case gives the driver control of four possible power transfer options:

1. The selection most often used is two-wheel drive, since most driving is done on clear non-slippery roads. Two-wheel drive sends power to the rear wheels only; the front axle is not being supplied with any power.
2. The next selection is typically neutral, which allows the vehicle to be towed if it is stuck in mud or snow, or towed down the highway with the engine off, such as behind a motor home; no power is being transmitted to either axle in this selection.
3. Another selection is four-wheel drive *high range*, which transmits power to the front and rear drive axles at normal drive speed.
4. The last selection is four-wheel drive *low range*. This position provides a gear reduction inside the transfer case and results in higher torque to the front and rear drive axles. This position causes the vehicle to move slowly while the engine turns at a higher rpm. Thus, to avoid over-revving the engine, the low range should be selected only when driving at slow vehicle speeds.

The beam-type or solid axle housings enclose the ring gear and pinion and differential gears, and driveshafts supply power from the transfer case. The front drive axle must allow for steering, and to do this, front wheel hubs are mounted to upper and lower ball joints, or pins and bearings. To transfer power to the movable hubs, U-joints must be used in the axle shafts that are splined to the hubs. Newer designs in pick-up trucks and SUVs use **constant-velocity (CV) joint**–type front axles. CV joints allow for smoother transfer of power and allow for the vehicle to turn more tightly without the joint binding. CV joints also allow for differences in working angles, a condition that would have caused vibrations from standard U-joint setups.

All-Wheel Drive Layout

All-wheel drive vehicles are widely used today because they offer both the convenience of not having to select four-wheel drive when needed and the necessary traction when on-road (or occasionally off-road) conditions warrant it. Such vehicles are intended for lighter duty and are sometimes referred to as "boulevard SUVs."

In some all-wheel drive vehicles, only two of the wheels are normally powered, typically the front wheels. In this case, the rear-wheel drive is applied automatically when needed to maintain traction. The driver is not normally aware of when this takes place, but has the peace of mind that it happens when needed. In other all-wheel drive vehicles, all four wheels are powered all of the time, but the torque may be split unevenly when driving under normal conditions.

Drive Line Subassemblies and Components

The drive line subassemblies are made up of driveshafts, axle shafts, and half-shafts. Each shaft transfers torque from one component to the next. Terminology of the components varies depending on the type of drive train. For example, on most rear-wheel drive vehicles, there is one driveshaft from the transmission to the final drive assembly and two axle shafts—one from each side of the final drive to one of the rear wheels. On front-wheel drive vehicles, there are two half-shafts (axles)—one on each side of the transaxle to each of the front wheels. Four-wheel drive and all-wheel drive vehicles use combinations of driveshafts and half-shafts depending on if the axle shafts are independent or non-independent. We will explore each of these types of shafts and the joints that allow them to transfer torque.

Driveshafts—Rear-Wheel Drive

The driveshaft is a device that transfers torque from one component to another, such as from the transmission output shaft to the final drive assembly **FIGURE 26-3**. The driveshaft is typically made from metal tubing material. The driveshaft can be constructed from steel or aluminum and can come in various sizes and lengths depending upon the application. The driveshaft can be a short one-piece assembly with a U-joint at each end, or in some vehicles with a long wheel base, such as a school bus, the driveshaft can be made up of as many as four separate segments. The driveshaft typically requires the use of joints (described later in this chapter) to allow power to transfer smoothly as the driveshaft follows the movement of the suspension system.

U-joint yokes are typically welded to each end of the tube. The front U-joint connects to the driveshaft's internally splined slip yoke, which engages with splines on the transmission output shaft. The front slip yoke on the driveshaft slides over the output shaft in the transmission and is supported on the outside by a bushing located inside the rear transmission housing. This design enables the slip yoke to move longitudinally and vary the shaft length with suspension movement. The rear U-joint mates with a **companion flange** on the differential pinion shaft. The companion flange is a splined flange that transmits power to the pinion gear as discussed in the differential section.

FIGURE 26-3 Rear-wheel driveshaft.

Some applications use a two-piece driveshaft that is able to flex in the middle. The front section of the driveshaft is supported at its rear end by a center bearing, called the carrier bearing. The carrier bearing is bolted to a mounting bracket on the vehicle frame that supports the center of the driveshaft. Since the maximum length of a single section of driveshaft tubing is approximately 72" (183 cm) to prevent twisting of the tube from the torque output, two or more sections may be used. The other reason to use the two-piece driveshaft is because the angle of the U-joint may be too great if the driveshaft were just a single piece. The use of three, or more, U-joints breaks up the excessive angle between the transmission to the rear axle. The U-joint is capable of working at a maximum angle of 3 degrees; beyond this, vibration and additional wear will occur. Be sure to check the drive line angles when diagnosing this concern. Provision is normally made for adjusting the alignment of the two shafts using shims under the carrier bearing.

When working with a two-piece driveshaft or a splined driveshaft, it is critical that the yokes on both halves of the driveshaft be phased correctly, which means the pivot points of the U-joints are lined up in the same exact orientation from one shaft to the other. If the driveshaft halves are not assembled correctly, then vibration will result. With a one-piece driveshaft, the yokes are welded to the tube and cannot be moved. When working on a two-piece driveshaft, be sure to mark the location of each driveshaft half with a marker or white paint mark to ensure the yokes line up **FIGURE 26-4** .

Driveshafts—Four-Wheel Drive

In four-wheel drive applications, driveshafts transfer the drive from the transfer case (torque splitter) to the final drive units at the front and rear axle assemblies. Each

drive shaft has a U-joint at each end to transmit the drive through varying angles, and a sliding joint (slip joint) incorporated into the shaft to accommodate changes in driveshaft length by allowing the driveshaft to slide on the splines of its counterpart.

Axles and Half-Shafts

There are two types of axles used today—the **dead axle** and the **live axle** (**drive axle**). The dead axle does not provide any drive capabilities and is used on the rear of front-wheel drive vehicles, and the front of rear-wheel drive vehicles. It works the same as a trailer axle, allowing the wheels to spin freely and follow the drive axle. The purpose of the drive axle is to transfer the torque that comes from the engine, transmission, driveshaft, and differential to the wheels and tires, propelling the vehicle forward or backward.

Rear-Wheel Drive Solid Axles

Drive axles used with a rear-wheel drive solid axle assembly come in three varieties:

1. **Semi-floating axle**: On the semi-floating axle, the axle shafts are splined to the differential side gears, and the outer bearing is between the outer end of the axle shaft and the inside of the axle housing **FIGURE 26-5** . Wheel studs are pressed into the axle flange at the end of this type of axle. The axles support the weight of the vehicle and are also subject to bending forces as the vehicle corners. If the vehicle with a semi-floating axle were to hit a curb and break or snap the axle shaft, the wheel would come off of the vehicle.

2. **Three-quarter floating axle**: On this type of axle, there is a single roller bearing between the hub and

FIGURE 26-4 The driveshaft yoke alignment is critical for smooth operation.

FIGURE 26-5 Semi-floating axle—bearing located between the axle and housing.

the outside of the axle housing **FIGURE 26-6**. The axle flange is bolted to the housing and stabilizes the wheel vertically, while the vehicle's weight is supported by the hub and the bearing. Three-quarter floating axles were used on older vehicles, such as Chrysler vehicles and pick-up trucks.

3. **Full floating axle**: On the full floating axle, there are two tapered roller bearings between the hub and the outside of the axle housing **FIGURE 26-7**. This arrangement helps to isolate the weight of the vehicle on the hub and bearings, not on the axle itself. Since full floating axles can carry more weight, they are commonly used on medium- to heavy-duty pick-up trucks. This type of axle floats between the axle side gears and the wheel hub. Torque is delivered to the wheel hub by the flange on the end of the axle that is bolted to the hub. Heavy-duty applications sometimes use conical

FIGURE 26-6 Three-quarter floating axle—one bearing between the outside of the axle housing and the hub.

FIGURE 26-7 Full floating axle—two bearings between the axle housing and hub.

wedges to keep the full floating axle centered on the hub. The flange requires a gasket or room temperature vulcanizing (RTV) sealer to seal the oil in the axle housing from leaking out while driving down the highway. The inner axle seal is part of the hub and can be serviced only by the removing the wheel and hub assembly.

> **TECHNICIAN TIP**
>
> Because of their design, full floating axles can be removed without removing the wheels; thus, the vehicle may not even need to be lifted off the ground.

Whether a vehicle is two-wheel drive, four-wheel drive, or all-wheel drive, axles deliver torque from the differential(s) to the drive wheels. In some four-wheel drive vehicles, the front axle driveshafts are enclosed within an axle housing. They are splined at their inner end to the differential side gears, and to the front wheel hubs at their outer end. A CV joint in each driveshaft allows for greater steering angle movement on turns while continuing to transmit drive to the front wheels.

> **TECHNICIAN TIP**
>
> On full floating axles, the two tapered roller wheel bearings that support the hub on the axle housing require adjustment to maintain the proper bearing play as specified by the manufacturer.

Axle Flanges

In most cases, the flange on the end of the axle in either the semi-floating or the full floating axle is a molded part of the axle, whereas the three-quarter floating axle may or may not have a built-in flange as part of it. It is always good practice to check runout on the flange in case of any vibration complaints. If flange damage is diagnosed, replacement of the entire axle shaft will often be required. Also, lug studs are pressed into the axle flange and used to secure the wheel onto the vehicle. It is good practice to inspect the studs for damaged threads, stretching, or even breaking off. Lug studs that are damaged can usually be replaced.

> ▶ **LINK**
> Refer to the Disc Brake Systems chapter for the process of replacing lug studs.

Axle Seals

Axle seals can be of the single-lip or double-lip design depending on the application **FIGURE 26-8**. The purpose of axle seals is to contain the lubricating fluid in the final drive assembly, to maintain quiet operation, and to seal contaminants out of the sealed cavity. Too much oil inside the axle housing can cause the oil to be forced against the axle seal, which can lead to seepage past the axle seals. Failure of any of the axle shaft bearings or differential bearings can cause leaking of the axle seals as well. Worn bearings allow the axle shafts to move, and the shaft movement will wear the seals quickly and create gaps that the fluid can leak out of.

Sometimes the seal surface on the axle becomes worn or nicked. An aftermarket repair kit called a **speedy sleeve** is available for the seal surface on some axles **FIGURE 26-9**. The speedy sleeve is a thin metal sleeve that fits tightly over the seal surface of the axle, providing a new, undamaged surface for the seal to ride against. The

FIGURE 26-9 The speedy sleeve restores a damaged surface so that the seal has a clean smooth surface to ride against.

seal is designed slightly oversize to maintain lubrication integrity.

Front-Wheel Drive/All-Wheel Drive Axles/Half-Shafts

In front-wheel drive vehicles and all-wheel drive vehicles, the driveshafts transfer the drive directly from the final drive inside the transaxle to the front wheels. Front-wheel drive vehicles typically use axles called half-shafts, which have an inner and an outer CV joint.

A front-wheel drive transaxle typically does not place the final drive directly in the center of the vehicle; because the final drive is bolted to the end of the transversely mounted engine, it is offset to one side. Thus, the half-shafts are usually different lengths. The use of different-sized axle shafts can cause a problem known as torque steer. **Torque steer** is when the vehicle pulls to one side during hard acceleration. When half-shafts are not equal lengths, more torque is applied to the side with the short half-shaft, creating the pulling condition. In addition to the unequal axle length, the angles at the CV joints are different, which also results in the pulling concern and can create vibration. To combat this condition, many manufacturers use an intermediate shaft **FIGURE 26-10**. The intermediate shaft is a short section of shaft that typically has a bearing pressed onto it (similar to a carrier bearing). The intermediate shaft makes it so that both half-shafts are the same length from left to right. In some cases the manufacturer uses a longer half-shaft on one side, and a rubber dynamic damper may be fitted to help absorb vibrations, although this does not reduce torque steer issues.

> ▶ TECHNICIAN TIP
>
> A common issue you might find is the leaking of the axle grease onto the rear drum brakes. Typically, this will be found as part of a state inspection or during a routine brake system inspection. A customer may complain of the rear brakes grabbing. The sticking could be the result of axle gear oil creating a thin, sticky layer on the surface of the brake lining. This in turn makes the brake material grab the drum brake surface and can create a lock-up of the brake, especially at slow speeds.

FIGURE 26-8 Single-lip and double-lip seals.

FIGURE 26-10 Intermediate shaft.

FIGURE 26-11 Cross-and-roller U-joint.

▶ Joints and Couplings

The driveshaft and half-shafts require a flexible joint at either end to allow for angular changes as the suspension travels up and down. There are two common types of joints used in this way—the U-joint and the CV joint. Both types of joints allow the shaft to transmit torque through a change of drive angle. The U-joint does so with an increase and decrease in velocity as the joint rotates every 90 degrees. A CV joint maintains the same velocity as it goes through its rotation. While both can transfer torque through an angle, the CV joint can do so at a much greater angle than the U-joint, which is why it is used on front half-shafts to accommodate large steering angles. U-joints are typically used on driveshafts because they generally need to accommodate only small angles, although some manufacturers use CV joints to provide a smoother ride, or on off-road vehicles that have been lifted and experience a greater amount of suspension travel. A large amount of torque is transmitted through the driveshaft and half-shafts, so joints can wear over time, making inspection and diagnosis important.

Universal Joints

A **universal joint (U-joint)** is a cross-shaped flexible joint. There are caps that fit over the ends of the cross. Needle bearings fit between the ends of the cross and the caps, allowing the caps to rotate smoothly. The U-joint is considered a non-CV joint. The most common type is a **Hooke's joint** (cross-and-roller joint) **FIGURE 26-11**. The Hooke's joint consists of a steel cross with four hardened bearing journals, mounted on needle rollers in hardened caps, which locate the cross in the eyes of the yokes. The cross swivels in the yokes as the drive is transferred across the joint. However, the swiveling conflicts with the rotation,

and in each revolution the velocity of the yoke changes every 90 degrees due to the angles that the driveshafts are operating on. This change in the angular velocity increases as the angle that the joint operates on increases.

There are two planes of stop/start as the joint flexes due to the cross shape of the joint. As the shaft rotates, it changes the velocity of the shaft up and down and then side to side, creating a speeding up and slowing down of the joint. The sharper the angle of the joint, the more pronounced the velocity change becomes, which may cause a vibration complaint from customers. The effect of the changing velocity can be minimized by having identical non-CV joints at each end of the propeller shaft in phase (in alignment). This is done by having the yokes of the driveshaft in line with each other. An increase in the velocity of the front yoke is canceled out by a similar decrease in the velocity of the rear yoke in each revolution. In some designs, engineers fit a CV joint to the front end of the driveshaft, which allows for an increase of angles of the shafts without creating vibration.

A **double Cardan joint** greatly reduces the change in velocity of a single Cardan joint by using the second joint to cancel out the changes in velocity of the first joint. A double Cardan joint is considered by most technicians to be a CV joint under normal drive line angles. The double Cardan joint uses two Cardan joints housed in a short carrier. Each cross has either a centering ball or a socket that is connected to its back side and joins with its mating component on the other cross. The ball-and-socket assembly keeps each Cardan joint at an equal angle, thereby canceling the change in velocity.

Constant-Velocity Joints

For independent suspension vehicles, the external drive axle shafts (half-shafts) to each road wheel most likely use CV joints at their connecting points. CV joints allow for more torque transfer than U-joints due to their larger bearing surfaces. Also, because of their construction, CV joints can operate at greater angles than U-joints.

Often, a sliding spline or a **plunge-type joint** is used as the inner half-shaft joint to accommodate for changes in shaft length when traveling on different types of terrain. Plunge-type joints allow smooth power flow while allowing the joint to slide in and out, effectively increasing and decreasing the length of the axle shaft during up and down suspension travel. One type of plunge CV joint is the tulip tripod joint. The **tulip/tripod joint** has three equally spaced fingers shaped like a star. On the ends of the star are three round bearing surfaces that sit on needle bearings on each finger. The round bearing surfaces move on the fingers by needle bearings. The outer race has three straight grooves that run from side to side. This configuration allows in-and-out movement of the shaft while allowing flexing **FIGURE 26-12**.

The **fixed-type joint** does not slide to allow for shaft lengthening or shortening; it simply allows for angle changes as the suspension moves. The fixed joint is typically used on the outboard side of the half-shaft.

One type of fixed joint that you will service as a technician is the **Rzeppa joint**. The Rzeppa joint has an inner race, six steel ball bearings, a bearing cage, and an outer race. The ball bearings, retained by a spherical cage, are carried in angular grooves in each race. These balls transfer the drive from one race to the other. The inner race is splined to the axle shaft while the outer race is splined to the wheel hub. The Rzeppa joint has been modified so that it will allow a limited amount of plunge capability.

CV Joint Lubrication and Inspection

Each CV joint must be lubricated. Special bearing grease is used to keep the bearing surfaces moving freely. To keep the grease inside the joint, and to keep dirt and debris out, an accordion-type synthetic rubber boot, called a CV boot, is attached to the outside of the joint **FIGURE 26-13**. The CV boot should be inspected during routine maintenance, such as during an oil change, for cracks or splits. If a boot is leaking, traces of lubricant thrown on nearby components will be noted. In some cases, split-type boots can be used as replacements. Otherwise, the half-shaft will need to be removed to replace the defective boot. If any leakage is noted, the boot should be replaced since dirt and water can enter the joint, causing the joint to ultimately fail.

Although CV joints are larger than U-joints, they are still subject to wear. The indication of excessive wear is typically a clicking or popping noise when the vehicle is driven with the wheels fully turned in one direction or the other. The noise is caused by the drive balls being forced into and out of the wear grooves. Severe cases are indicated by noise at lesser steering angles.

FIGURE 26-12 The CV joint comes in several forms. The Rzeppa joint **(A)** and the tulip tripod joint **(B)** are two types that are commonly found on half-shafts.

FIGURE 26-13 CV boot.

Final Drives/Differentials

The terms final drive and differential are confused by technicians. Specifically, the term differential gets used in two different ways. The first is the most technically accurate and refers to the components inside of the differential housing that allow the axles to turn at different speeds when the vehicle is cornering or turning. These components make up what is called the differential assembly. Since the outside tire must travel farther around a corner than the inside tire, it must turn at a faster speed. The differential assembly allows this to happen; otherwise the tires would bind, skip, hop, and slide when going around a corner, which would then cause them to wear out quickly.

The second way technicians use the term "differential" is as another name for the complete final drive assembly. The final drive assembly provides the final gear reduction necessary for drive train operation, and it houses the "differential assembly." The final drive takes the power from the transmission and sends it to the wheels. And the differential assembly within it allows the tires to travel around corners without binding while the final drive is powering them. Since the differential assembly is housed within the final drive assembly, many technicians improperly call the entire final drive assembly the differential. Thus, any time you hear the term "differential," you need to ask whether the person means the final drive assembly or only the differential assembly.

Final drives can be found in axles either at the front or rear of the vehicle or can be found in the transaxle of a front-wheel drive vehicle. The speed reduction gears in the final drive are called the ring and pinion gears. Various "rear axle" ratios are available to suit the demands of the vehicle use. Lower ratios are used to increase low-speed pulling power, while higher ratios are used to improve high-speed fuel economy, such as on the freeway. Some "rear axles" allow for final drive ratios to be quickly changed, such as for racing on different track surfaces (dirt, paved, etc.) or track sizes. If the vehicle uses a front or rear axle, the driveshaft attaches to the final drive. (In the case of a front-wheel drive transaxle, half-shafts attach to the final drive.)

On some of the final drive assemblies manufactured today, the anti-lock brake system (ABS) wheel speed sensor is incorporated in them. Speed sensors read wheel speed and are part of the final drive gear set. If the vehicle is equipped with traction control, the traction control system can overcome the loss of traction by applying more power to the wheel that is not slipping by applying the brake on the wheel that is slipping.

Differential assemblies come in two varieties. First there is the open differential, which means power is supplied to both wheels equally only when each tire maintains traction, which on ice and snow is nearly impossible. If one wheel is stuck in the snow or ice, the other wheel can supply virtually no power due to the nature of the open differential assembly. The second type is the limited slip differential, which allows, under the same conditions, power to be delivered to both of the rear wheels to supply power to the ground to drive the vehicle.

Preventive maintenance of the final drive assembly, regardless of its design, is important, as these axles are filled with special lubricants that promote long life and maintain quiet operation of the gears. Maintenance schedules tell technicians when each component requires maintenance or inspection and thereby help prevent premature failure. More information on final drive assemblies will be provided in subsequent sections in this chapter.

Rear-Wheel Final Drive

In a conventional rear-wheel drive vehicle, such as a pickup truck, a solid axle assembly incorporates and encloses the final drive gears, differential, and axle shafts in one housing. A ring gear and a pinion gear transfer power through 90 degrees and provide a final gear reduction to the driving road wheels. **Hypoid bevel gears** are normally used for this purpose. Hypoid gears are a special design of spiral bevel gears, with the centerline of the pinion below the centerline of the ring gear **FIGURE 26-14**.

FIGURE 26-14 A hypoid gear arrangement.

This design reduces the height of the driveshaft tunnel, allowing for a flatter vehicle floor pan. The tooth shape also provides a greater area of tooth contact, and therefore greater strength.

In a rear-wheel drive vehicle, the ring gear is bolted to the differential carrier, which is supported in the axle housing or case by tapered roller side bearings, retained by bearing caps and bolts. In some axle designs, threaded adjusting rings engage with threads in the housing and will push against the side bearings of the carrier. These threaded rings are used to set the carrier bearing preload and a **backlash clearance** between the ring and pinion. Backlash is the amount of movement between the pinion teeth versus the ring teeth. If you hold the ring gear and turn the pinion, you will have a slight clearance back and forth. On other axle designs, shims are used to push against the side bearings to adjust bearing preload and backlash.

The two smaller bevel gears, or pinions, are mounted on a driving pin that passes through the carrier. Two **side gears** mesh with the pinions and are in recesses in the differential carrier. The drive axles are splined to these side gears. With the ring gear bolted to the carrier, the splines on the axle shafts are engaged with the splines in the differential side gears, and drive is transferred through the ring gear to the differential carrier pins, which carry the pinion gears with the carrier. The pinion gears carry the side gears with them, turning the axles and wheels. The pinion and side gears are also called "spider gears."

When the vehicle travels in a straight line, the ring gear rotates the case. The driving pin and pinion gears rotate end over end, carrying the side gears with them. The side gears, which are splined to the axles, then turn the drive axles. There is no relative motion between the pinion gears and the side gears; each side gear turns at the same speed.

As soon as the vehicle turns from a straight-ahead position, the inner wheel slows down and its side gear turns more slowly than the differential case. The turning effort applied to the driving pin allows the pinion gears to rotate slowly on their pin. They walk around the inner side gear while still being turned end over end.

This rotation of the pinion gears makes the outer side gear and its road wheel speed up while the inner side gear and its road wheel slow done in rotation by an equivalent amount. The outer side gear then turns faster than the case. This provides an equal torque to each drive axle while allowing for their rotational speed difference.

Limited Slip Differentials

Limited slip differentials allow normal differential action under normal driving conditions, but when road conditions are not normal, the limited slip differential reduces or prevents differential action so that a wheel cannot spin freely. Drive is maintained to both wheels. There are two main types of limited slip differentials— clutch style and gear style. The clutch-style limited slip differential uses a multiplate clutch pack between each side gear and the differential case. Each clutch pack has two different types of flat steel plates, placed alternately in the pack. One type has internal splines that mate with splines on the side gear pressure ring. The other has driving lugs that locate in slots in the differential carrier.

The outside plate is dished, or cup shaped, to provide initial tension on the clutch pack when the two halves of the carrier are assembled. Four differential pinions are mounted on two driving pins, at right angles to each other, so that they mesh with the side gears. The pinion shafts are relieved, so as not to make contact at their intersection. The ends of the shafts have two flat surfaces forming wedge shapes, which fit into similar wedges in the carrier.

In straight-ahead driving, the driving force through the ring gear to the differential carrier causes the pinion shafts to rotate end over end. This transfers the drive through the pinion gears and the side gears to the axles. There is no relative motion between the gears; however, the resistance at the road wheels forces the pinion shafts up the incline formed by the wedges in the case. As a result, the piston shafts are forced apart and the pinion gears exert a greater force on the side gears and on the clutch packs. The force locks the side gears to the carrier, preventing any sudden spinning of either wheel. Under normal operating conditions, the driving torque is transmitted equally to each axle shaft and wheel, but when patches of loose gravel or mud are encountered, the ratio of torque delivered depends on the traction available at each road wheel.

The greatest amount of torque will be transmitted to the wheel with the most traction. When turning a corner, the limited slip differential gives normal differential action and permits the outer wheel to turn faster than the inner wheel. At the same time, the differential applies the major driving force to the inner wheel, improving stability and cornering.

Torsen Style

Some manufacturers use a gear-style limited slip differential design rather than the usual clutch-type design **FIGURE 26-15**. This design was used to improve vehicle stability and tire traction. Some use gear-based, or torque-biased or torque-sensing (Torsen), units. The heart of these limited slip differentials is the parallel-axis helical gear set. The idea behind the Torsen differential is to

FIGURE 26-15 A Torsen helical gear limited slip differential.

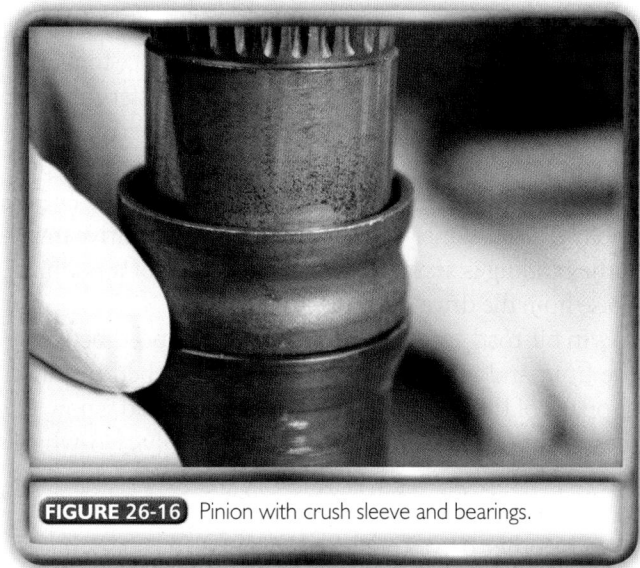

FIGURE 26-16 Pinion with crush sleeve and bearings.

multiply the torque available from the wheel that is losing traction and turn it over to the slower turning wheel with better traction. Torque application to the wheel with better traction begins because of the resistance between the sets of gears in mesh.

Helical-geared limited slip differentials respond very quickly to changes in traction. They also do not bind from friction in turns and do not lose their effectiveness since there are no clutches, like a clutch-style unit. The unit described here is the Torsen differential, which is a very popular limited slip differential. Another manufacturer, Eaton, uses a similar design. The side gears of the differential are cut in a worm gear configuration. The pinion gears are also cut with a worm gear cut, and they are splined to each other. When one wheel begins to slip under torque, the worm gears create a locking situation that transfers power to the wheel with greater traction.

> ▶ TECHNICIAN TIP
>
> Oil changes are required less frequently with gear-style units because there are no clutch discs to wear as the vehicle makes turns, which contaminates the gear oil.

Differential Adjustments

The tapered roller bearings support the pinion in the carrier. The companion flange splines engage with the pinion splines to transfer the drive torque from the driveshaft. A collapsible spacer, called a **crush sleeve**, between the bearings allows a specified preload to be set FIGURE 26-16. The crush sleeve provides a means of maintaining a preset torque on the pinion nut, which holds the companion flange while keeping the proper amount of bearing

preload so that the pinion gear bearings are not running too tight or too loose. The depth that the pinion sits at in the axle housing is controlled by shims. The depth of the pinion determines how the pinion gear teeth will mesh with the ring gear.

The ring gear is bolted to the differential carrier, which is supported in the axle housing or case by tapered roller side bearings, retained by bearing caps and bolts. In some axle designs, threaded adjusting rings engage with threads in the housing and will push against the side bearings of the carrier. These threaded rings are used to set the bearing preload and a backlash clearance between the ring and pinion gears. Backlash is the amount of movement between the pinion teeth versus the ring teeth. If you hold the ring gear and turn the pinion, you should feel a slight clearance back and forth. On other axle designs, shims are used to push against the side bearings to adjust bearing preload and backlash.

Four-Wheel Drive Differentials

In part-time four-wheel drive vehicles, differentials are fitted to both front and rear axle assemblies. When a two-wheel drive range is selected, the drive is transferred through the rear final drive and the differential gears to the rear axle shafts and road wheels, but not to the front wheels. The differential gears allow the rear wheels to rotate at different speeds when the vehicle is turning, while continuing to transmit an equal turning effort to each wheel. When four-wheel drive is engaged, the drive is transmitted through both front and rear final drive assemblies, and differential action occurs in both.

However, when making a turn, the front wheels travel a greater distance than the rear wheels. This causes a difference in the rotational speeds of the front and rear wheels due to the changing arcs that each wheel is tracing. Since front and rear driveshafts are locked together at the transfer case, the difference in speed cannot be absorbed in the transmission, and the drive lines can be subjected to torsional binding due to the driveshafts being forced to rotate at the same rate of speed. The customer will notice binding of the drive train. If the binding is severe, the tires may chirp, or a popping noise from the drive train may occur.

In off-road conditions, differences in speed between the front and rear driveshafts can be absorbed through slippage of the tires on the ground—be it mud, snow, or ice conditions. On firm road surfaces, only two-wheel drive should be engaged. Using two-wheel drive prevents excessive tire wear and possible damage to the drive lines or other drive train components. It also increases performance and fuel economy.

> ### ▶ Caring for the Customer
>
> Differences in wheel speed can also arise from any condition that will cause uneven tire circumferences, such as unmatched tires, unevenly inflated tires, or uneven wear. Whenever excessive binding is experienced in a four-wheel drive vehicle, it is a good idea to check for these issues. Once you have determined that all the tires match and are inflated properly, use a tape measure to measure the circumference of each tire. Manufacturers' recommendations for the maximum difference in tire circumferences typically vary from 0.125" to 0.5" (3.2 to 12.7 mm). This difference can easily occur when one tire is damaged enough that it has to be replaced, but the other tires are partially worn. Replacing just one tire may not be a viable option, unless the new tire is shaved to match the wear of the other tires.

Four-Wheel Drive Locking Hubs

On part-time four-wheel drives, the front wheels and axle driveshafts are splined together through the differential side gears. When the vehicle is operating in two-wheel drive range, the front axle driveshafts, final drive assembly, and front driveshaft all turn with the road wheels, but do not transmit any drive. The drag from turning all of these components with the wheels while driving down the highway causes reduced fuel economy and vehicle performance. Freewheeling hubs or manually **locking hubs** can be installed on the front hubs to disconnect the hubs from the axle shafts and prevent rotation of the front axle components. This reduces wear and noise and

improves performance and fuel economy when driving in a two-wheel drive range.

When "lock" is selected on a manually locking hub, it acts on a sleeve. The sleeve has external splines that engage matching splines on the freewheel hub body, and internal splines to engage splines on the axle shaft. The sleeve slides in and out to lock the two splined components together. In a four-wheel drive range, the drive is transmitted from the axle shaft, through the sleeve, to the hub and road wheel. Unfortunately, in inclement weather conditions, the driver must get out of the vehicle and turn the locking hub knobs located on the front wheels to lock in the front drive axles.

When "free" mode is selected, the compressed spring pushes the sleeve out of engagement, leaving the wheel free to rotate without turning the axle shaft. Most vehicles require slightly reversing the vehicle in order to disengage the sleeve since binding can happen. Reversing the motion of the axle shafts will unbind the sleeve.

Another type of hub is the automatic hub. The automatic hub is factory installed on many newer vehicles. The automatic hub has a spring-loaded sleeve that moves out to engage the hub when power is applied to the front axle. So if four-wheel drive is selected and the vehicle is driven forward, the sleeve will lock the hub to the axle. When four-wheel drive is deactivated, the front axle is not transmitting power, so the spring automatically pushes the sleeve out of engagement and the hub freewheels.

Front-Wheel Drive Differentials

The differential action is the same for front-wheel drive vehicles as it is for rear-wheel and four-wheel drive differentials **FIGURE 26-17**. The only real difference with a front-wheel drive vehicle is that the differential is located inside

Final Drive and Differential Assembly

FIGURE 26-17 A typical front-wheel drive differential.

the transaxle and is driven by the secondary shaft, which is connected to the pinion drive gear. Some automatic transaxles use a chain to drive the differential assembly.

Transfer Cases

Transfer cases are used in four-wheel drive and all-wheel drive vehicles to split power to the front and rear drive axles. The transfer case, or in some cases a power take-off (PTO), performs this task. A transfer case is used on vehicles that are primarily rear-wheel drive; a PTO (also called a power transfer unit [PTU]) is used on vehicles that are primarily front-wheel drive. The transfer case is typically bolted to the rear of the transmission, while the PTO is bolted to the side of the transaxle. In either situation, transfer cases and PTOs perform the same task, splitting power between the front and rear axles.

Four-Wheel Drive Transfer Case

There is a variety of styles of transfer cases used in four-wheel drive vehicles, depending on the manufacturer. If the vehicle uses a front-wheel drive transaxle, then a component similar to a transfer case called the PTO is used. In a typical four-wheel drive vehicle, the transfer case is bolted to the rear of the transmission. The output shaft of the transmission is splined to the input shaft of the transfer case. Power comes into the transfer case through the input shaft and moves to the rear output shaft and, if four-wheel drive is selected, also to the front output shaft. Some transfer cases use a large chain to allow power to move to the front output shaft. The chain rides on bearings on the input shaft and will typically freewheel unless four-wheel drive is selected. When four-wheel drive is selected, the mode fork, which is similar to a shift fork found in a manual transmission, moves a synchronizer sleeve to the input shaft chain sprocket. This locks the chain sprocket to the input shaft and transfers power to the front output shaft. Power then moves out of the transfer case front output shaft to the front driveshaft and to the front axle. In this style of transfer case, the function of four-wheel drive low and neutral is possible through the use of a range fork and a planetary gear set. When the planetary gear carrier is held stationary, a lower gear ratio results than when the sun gear is held.

Another style of transfer case uses a gear drive. The transfer case described here was used by Toyota in their Land Cruiser model. Gear drive transfer cases tend to be noisier than chain drives and are not used as much as they once were. Drive is transmitted from the transmission to the transfer case through the input shaft. The input shaft has a gear that mates to an idler gear that mates to a drive gear on the output shaft. In two-wheel drive, power

comes into the transfer case by the input shaft through the idler gear to the output shaft and to the rear driveshaft. The idler shaft contains two gears: a high-speed gear and a low-speed gear. The low-speed gear is free to rotate on bearings and is only locked to the shaft when the shift fork moves to engage the low-speed gear. When in four-wheel high range, power is transferred from the input gear to the idler to the output shafts, which are locked together by the high and low shift fork. This transfer case uses a differential assembly on the output shaft to allow for slowing of the front axle when turning in tight corners. Some vehicles use an electronic center lock to lock this differential in the event that the driver is stuck and needs full lock of front and rear axles.

All-Wheel Drive Transfer Case

Many vehicles today are using transverse front-mounted engines with all-wheel drive. In an all-wheel drive vehicle, both the front drive axle and the rear drive axle propel the vehicle. Depending on the system, the majority of engine drive torque is normally delivered to just one set of wheels, but upon demand, all four wheels receive drive torque and share the load. The transfer case powers both the front and the rear driveshafts, which power both final drive assemblies. Axles may be either solid or half-shafts, depending on whether the vehicle uses an independent suspension.

The all-wheel drive transfer case is bolted to the output of the transaxle **FIGURE 26-18**. Drive is transferred from the transmission output shaft to an internally splined helical gear on the transfer case input shaft. The internally splined helical gear is constantly meshed with the larger of two idler gear pinions. They are constantly meshed with the high- and low-output pinions on the transfer case output shaft. The low-range output pinion is bolted to a

FIGURE 26-18 The all-wheel drive transfer case is bolted to the output of the transaxle.

differential case that contains the third set of differential gears. The high range pinion can rotate on needle roller bearings on one side of the differential case.

The idler gear pinions are also separated, with the smaller low-speed gear free to rotate on needle rollers on the idler shaft formed with the high-speed gear. A common selector fork links a splined engagement sleeve on the idler, and a similar sleeve on the output moves the fork to engage the high range and locks the high-output pinion to the differential case.

Drive is transmitted at a one-to-one ratio, through the larger pinion of the idler gear and the locked output pinion, to the differential case. It is then transmitted through the differential gears to the front and rear output shafts, which drive the front and rear driveshafts. Engaging low range moves the selector fork in the opposite direction. This locks the low idler gear pinion to the idler shaft.

From the transmission output, drive is transmitted to the large idler pinion, and through the smaller locked pinion to the low-range output pinion, bolted to the differential case. This double reduction provides a low-output speed ratio of about 2.48 to 1 to both front and rear shafts, which can be used to gain traction in snow and ice or even mud. In addition, in some vehicles, when low range is selected, a geared electric motor automatically operates an engagement sleeve splined to the front output shaft. It engages mating splines on the differential case. This locks out all differential action between the front and rear output shafts; thus, it should only be used in off-road situations so that both the front and rear shafts rotate at the same rate of speed.

In high range, the differential lock is disengaged. Differential action is provided for by the differential gears located in the output case and splined to the output shafts. This design allows for a difference in speed between front and rear wheels when the vehicle is on firm road surfaces.

Transfer Case Differential Action

On all-wheel drive vehicles, when high range is engaged for driving on firm road surfaces, differences in speed between the front and rear wheels while turning and driving into curves must be provided. This can be accomplished by use of a third set of differential gears in the transfer case output assembly. However, the third differential operation means that if a front wheel spins on a slippery surface, virtually no drive is transmitted to the rear wheels.

There are several ways manufacturers have addressed this slipping condition. One of the easiest is to use the traction control system to apply the brake unit at the wheel that is slipping, which increases the amount of torque to the other wheels that have more traction. Other manufacturers use a **viscous coupling** unit between the front and rear driveshafts to act as a limited slip differential and drive both axles if one is slipping **FIGURE 26-19**. A viscous coupler uses two sets of clutch plates that are alternated front to back. One set of plates is splined to the outer housing (one driveshaft), and the other set of plates is splined to the inner housing (other driveshaft).

In normal driving conditions, the third differential operates to provide the small degree of differential action necessary. In this condition there is only a minor speed difference between the viscous coupling plates, so the viscous coupling allows them to move without much resistance. However, when a wheel spins, there is a higher level of third differential action and a greater speed difference between the front and rear drive shafts. This speed difference also applies to the viscous coupling plates. Fluid in the unit is sheared by the relative motion between them. This shearing action causes the silicone to heat up and become much thicker (higher viscosity), transferring torque to the wheels that are not slipping.

The degree of locking achieved depends on the severity of the wheel slippage occurring. Only under severe conditions is 100% locking achieved. When the plates are fully locked, the fluid starts to cool, and the cycle of shearing and locking starts all over again.

Some manufacturers control the differential action electronically through the use of an electromagnetic clutch to lock the driveshafts together **FIGURE 26-20**. This device squeezes the clutches together by applying a magnetic force on the clutch discs. In some models, the clutch can be pulse-width modulated, which controls

FIGURE 26-19 This viscous coupling allows slippage to keep the rotational speeds of the front and rear axles separate.

FIGURE 26-20 Some manufacturers control the differential action electronically through the use of an electromagnetic clutch to lock the driveshafts together.

FIGURE 26-21 The electronically controlled transfer case shown here uses a control module to lock the front and rear axles automatically, as needed, and monitors wheel speed to determine the torque needed.

the amount of torque that is being transferred. The use of a control module is necessary to operate this clutch.

Another type of differential used in transfer cases is the Torsen style, which uses gears similar to the version used in final drives. This style is good for splitting torque to each axle as long as the tires maintain traction, but it is not as effective in low-traction conditions.

The last type of coupling device is the mechanical differential lock. This type locks the driveshafts together using a mechanical sleeve that slides over the splines on both shafts. The differential lock is generally activated by a switch on the dash that operates either an electric or a vacuum motor, which engages or disengages the locking sleeve. This type of locking mechanism does not allow for slippage in the transfer case, so it should be used only on slippery surfaces, and disengaged before driving on high-traction surfaces.

Electrical Components— Four-Wheel Drive/All- Wheel Drive

Today's vehicles almost exclusively use computer-controlled transmissions with solenoids and actuators built in. The transmission control module (TCM) manages line pressures, shift functions, etc., and even incorporates a "self-healing" adjustment capability, along with the ability to memorize driver preferences/behaviors. Pulse-width modulated shift patterns are used to save transmission component wear. The TCM knows when to switch from two-wheel drive to four-wheel drive along with many other functions; all of these are managed by the TCM FIGURE 26-21.

Noise/Vibration/Harshness and Other Issues

Drive train noises and vibrations can occur at any point in the life of the vehicle. As a vehicle starts to age, things begin to wear out. Differential gears and bearings can wear, putting adjustments out of specifications. U-joints or bent rear axles can contribute to noise or vibration conditions. Proper diagnosis is a priority if a reliable repair is to be performed. A thorough customer interview and road testing is essential.

Road testing the vehicle for vibrations will reveal the type of vibration that is present. First eliminate any torsional vibrations by starting the engine and running it at various revolutions per minute (rpm). If a vibration is felt, it may be engine noises or vibrations causing the problem rather than the drive train.

Once the engine is eliminated as an issue, road test the vehicle at different speed ranges. Axle and wheel bearing noises will tend to change in severity when steering side to side. Pinion bearing noises will remain constant as the vehicle drives straight down the highway. Differential gears (spider gears) can make a whining or popping noise as the vehicle makes turns or travels around curves in the road. A clunking noise on acceleration and deceleration can be caused by worn ring and pinion gears and also tends to make a variable whirring noise when decelerating from 40 mph (64 kph) to a complete stop.

Knocking noises may indicate excessive clearance between gears such as the spider gears or axle side gears. Limited slip differentials may also contribute to noises in the differential. Rapid clicking or chattering noises may be coming from the clutch packs or cones that are part of the limited slip configuration. A fluid change may be required to eliminate these noises, or a friction modifier may need to be added.

Vibrations may result from a bent axle, bent driveshaft, or bent tire and rim combination. A thorough interview of the customer is important when diagnosing the complaint, since he or she can generally give you clues to what is causing the fault. The problem may be a result of damage from hitting a curb or an extremely large pothole. A thorough road test of the vehicle by operating the vehicle at different speeds and conditions will verify the driver's complaint.

Diagnosing Axle Shafts, Bearings, and Seals

Axle shafts and bearings are subject to radial and axial forces that under the right conditions can cause damage to these components. Conditions such as accidents can cause axles to bend or break, and bearings to fail. Seals can develop leaks, which can cause bearings to become dry, overheat from a lack of lubrication, and become damaged. When bearings fail, they generally will cause a whirring or growling noise that can increase and disappear as the vehicle turns from side to side. Lack of lubrication will also result in failure of all the differential bearings, requiring a complete overhaul if not addressed.

Fluid leaks can be caused by a plugged breather in the housing, which causes a pressure buildup within the housing. They can also be caused by overfilling the final drive assembly, which will exert additional pressure on the seals. The weakest points on the final drive assembly are the seals. Seals are in constant contact with a rotating shaft. If pressure is allowed to build in the system, this pressure will force the seal onto the shaft harder, increasing the wear. Also, if the seal does start to leak, the pressure will force the fluid past it much more quickly than it otherwise would. Leaks can also be a result of dragging brakes, which create heat and destroy the seal. Sometimes vintage vehicles sit for long periods without being driven, and the seals dry out or shrink as a result of disuse.

Diagnosing Noise, Slippage, and Chatter in Limited Slip Differentials

Noise diagnosis requires a thorough road testing under all conditions necessary to recreate the problem. The type of noise will in most cases tell the technician where the noise is coming from. Whining noises while swerving or cornering usually come from the differential pinion gears and pinion shaft. Damage to these components or scoring of the pinion shaft can cause this noise to occur. This problem can happen when the one of the wheels is turning faster than the other for an extended period of time—usually the result of mismatched tire sizes on the same axle or too much wheel spinning on one wheel. A "hmm, hmm" noise or chuckle noise can be the result of too much clearance between the ring gear and pinion gears that occurs during deceleration at around 40 mph (64 kph) or less. Harsh acceleration or driver abuse can contribute to this condition.

A knocking or clunking noise is usually the result of parts that are broken inside the final drive. Chipped or broken ring and pinion gears, broken spider or axle side gears, or damaged bearings can be the problem. Driver abuse or potholes will contribute to this issue by making one wheel leave the ground for a split second and then grab quickly to take up clearances suddenly. The result is chipped or cracked gear teeth. Limited slip differential growling or chattering can result from clutch parts that are worn; in some cases, changing the limited slip lubricating oil will fix the problem. Slippage can result from worn clutches in the limited slip differential.

Applied | Math

AM-42: Everyday Occurrences: *The technician compares the performance outcome of a normally operating system with the anticipated outcome of an everyday occurrence, such as comparing system tolerances to the manufacturer's specifications.*

When an all-wheel drive vehicle with properly inflated tires goes around a corner, the process is very different than when that same vehicle has a substantially low tire. Low tire pressure reduces the rolling circumference of the tire. It is like having a smaller tire on one side. The difference in wheel speeds must be absorbed in the transfer case. If a viscous coupling or an electric clutch is used, it will be subjected to extreme torsional stress due to the uneven rotational speeds. The customer will notice binding or chirping of the tires, or there may be a banging or popping noise from the drive train. This condition will result in a damaged viscous coupling or electric clutch after a short time of driving in this situation.

The solution for this problem is to maintain all tires at the manufacturer's specified tire pressure. The tire pressure specification will usually be found on the driver's side door jamb. Another source of information for correct tire pressure is the owner's manual.

Starting in 2008, a tire pressure monitoring system, or TPMS, was required by law on all passenger cars and light trucks. The TPMS monitors the air pressure in the tires, and the driver is alerted of low tire pressure by a dashboard warning. This system is not meant to be a substitute for checking the pressures on a regular basis, since the TPMS warning may not come on until the air pressure drops by 25% or more below the correct pressure.

To perform a diagnosis, thoroughly interview the customer to gain information on when or how the condition first started. Thoroughly road test the vehicle under all conditions necessary to recreate the condition being diagnosed. Consult the service information, including technical service bulletins (TSBs), to help with diagnosis. Follow all manufacturer guidelines when performing the repair. Once the repair is complete, road test the vehicle to make sure the condition no longer exists.

Diagnosing Noise and Unusual Steering Concerns

In four-wheel drive vehicles, steering concerns can be present due to the arrangement of the axles and steering linkage. Most pick-ups and SUVs use a parallelogram-type steering, and any stresses caused by the four-wheel drive system will be applied to the linkage. This can cause vibrations and shimmying problems. Stress may come in the form of driving in four-wheel drive mode with the hubs in the locked position on a dry road. Front axles and U-joints will experience stress from the same practice.

Wheel bearings and hubs are also subject to wheel rim offsets that will throw off the wheel's scrub radius and cause premature failure of the bearings and hubs. Tire types and profiles as well as tire pressure will also be a cause of unwanted noise or vibrations. Periodic inspection of the front steering/driving axle is always a good practice.

Caring for the Customer

The use of oversized tires puts additional strain on the front axle and associated components. Many truck enthusiasts like to install larger tires on their four-wheel drive pick-ups and must be careful to compensate for things like wheel speed sensor and vehicle speed sensor calibration, since the tires will be turning slower than normal. With these larger tires, it may also be necessary to install a steering damper on the steering linkage to prevent wheel shimmy.

Identifying Concerns Related to Tire Circumference and/or Final Drive Ratios

When it comes to vehicle computer systems, everything hinges on the computer monitoring the vehicle for proper operation. Sensors such as those for the ABS rely on accurate information while the vehicle is traveling down the highway. Any deviation from the programmed

routines in the electronic control module (ECM) may cause a malfunction indicator lamp (MIL) or other system warning light to illuminate, alerting the driver of a system malfunction. Tire sizes and final drive gear ratios must be maintained at the manufacturer's specifications. Tire wear can also have an effect on the ECM routines to report a malfunction. Wheel speed is monitored and if out of specifications might cause an MIL to illuminate. Installing a spare tire of a different size on the same axle could cause the light to come on. Installing the wrong gear ratios in the final drive will cause the drive train to bind when four-wheel drive is called for. Final drive gear ratios in a four-wheel drive unit are almost always the same in the front as in the rear. The only exception is in vehicles that use a slightly different ratio front to rear, so as to apply more torque to one set of wheels than the other. In this instance, a viscous coupler is used to provide the needed slippage and prevent binding.

To identify concerns related to variations in tire circumference and/or final drive ratios, follow the steps in **SKILL DRILL 26-1**:

1. Check all tires for mismatches or unusual wear, and set the tire pressures to specifications.
2. If the vehicle is equipped with ABS and you can access the data stream, connect the appropriate scan tool and test-drive the vehicle. Compare each wheel speed sensor reading to the others. They should be within 0.2 mph (0.3 kph) of each other.
3. If necessary, measure the circumference of the tires and compare to each other. They should be within 0.25" (6.4 mm) of each other.
4. Check the differentials for correct ratios, which may require removal of the inspection plates. The number of teeth of the pinion and ring gear is often written on the ring gear's outer perimeter so the ratio can be calculated.
5. Consult the manufacturer's service information for any necessary procedures to further diagnose the fault.

Diagnosing CV Joint Issues

CV joints have to withstand and transmit tremendous amounts of force when the vehicle is being driven. Grease helps to lubricate and cool the joint, which prevents or reduces wear. CV joints use rubber boots to contain the grease in the joint, while still allowing the joint to pivot. Sometimes the CV joint boots crack or become torn. The grease then runs out and contaminants can get in. This combination of problems causes the joint to overheat and wear out, resulting in a failed CV joint that must be replaced. This is one reason that periodic inspection of the CV boots are important. If caught soon enough, the boot and grease can be replaced before the joint is damaged. One indicator of CV joint wear is clicking or popping noises when cornering. The ball bearings roll into and out of the worn spot in the bearing races, making the popping noise. CV joints that make this noise need to be replaced; they cannot be repaired. A thorough road test along with a visual inspection on a lift may be warranted in order to diagnose CV joint problems.

To diagnose a potential issue with a CV joint, talk to the customer to fully understand his or her concern. Verify the concern with a test-drive or visual inspection, depending on the concern. You should then have enough information to make a diagnosis of the fault.

To diagnose CV joint issues, follow the steps in **SKILL DRILL 26-2**:

1. Thoroughly road test the vehicle to verify the customer complaint. Safely raise the vehicle on an approved lift, and make sure it is secure.

2. Visually inspect all four CV joints.

3. Look for broken or ruptured boots. Look for cracked or dry-rotted boots, as they are subject to all types of weather.

4. Manually move the axle shaft up and down, looking for unnecessary play or bad bearings. These conditions can cause a vibration coming from the side that is bad. They will also cause a clicking sound emanating from the side that is affected.

5. Look for any type of axle damage, such as a bent axle from a recent accident. Axle damage will cause a vibration from the affected shaft as well.

▶ Diagnosis and Maintenance

Diagnosing, Testing, Adjusting, and Replacing Electrical Components of Four-Wheel Drive Systems

In older, mechanically controlled four-wheel drive vehicles, visual inspection of all mechanical components is the best way to diagnose customer concerns. This includes the transfer case linkage and the locking hubs. If the fault cannot be identified by an external inspection, you may have to isolate the fault to a particular area or unit and then disassemble it to inspect the internal components. Today, diagnosis of the electrical aspects of four-wheel drive and all-wheel drive vehicles is done with a digital volt-ohmmeter (DVOM) and a scan tool. With the inception of the second generation of on-board diagnostic standards (OBDII), many of the older mechanical components have been replaced by the electronic and electrical components common on today's vehicles. Typical

electrical components are ECMs, sensors, and solenoids (also known as electronic actuators).

Sensors provide input signals to control modules or computers. Modules are preprogrammed with instructions on what to do under certain conditions, and, if possible, they compensate for any unwanted conditions and/or store a code and alert the driver by illuminating an MIL of a fault. Computers can send output signals to actuators. Actuators and solenoids then cause the desired actions to be performed.

If the four-wheel drive system is electronically controlled, typical diagnosis might start with connecting a scan tool and reading any current codes or real-time data to make an accurate assessment of the customer's concern. A quick visual inspection of each of the exposed connectors on the circuit should be performed, as a corroded, dirty, or loose connection can cause a component not to operate correctly. From there, a DVOM is used to measure the voltage at the component. If the voltage is not correct, then the voltage drop on each side of the affected circuit will be measured to determine which side of the circuit has the voltage drop. Generally, each side of a control circuit should have less than a 0.5-volt drop. Signal circuits should have less than a 0.1-volt drop. If all voltage readings are within specifications, you will need to inspect and test the electrical component's resistance to see if it has failed.

Resistance checks look for high resistance within the component that would not allow enough current to flow to allow the component to operate. This type of problem is common in today's electronic age. Resistance testing requires the component to be disconnected from the circuit and tested for its specified resistance. If the resistance is outside of specifications, the part is faulty and will need to be replaced. Make sure you have determined the cause of the fault so that it does not occur again. Upon replacement of any electrical component, there may be some necessary adjustments, such as to servo length or linkage or to the part's orientation. Always follow all manufacturer recommended procedures for correct installation and adjustments.

Checking Driveshaft Joints, Phasing, Angles, Balance, and Runout

Vehicles today are put through a tremendous variety of driving styles and scenarios and terrains. Delivering torque to a driveshaft is a violent action due to different engine sizes and torque. Driver abuse can also play an important role in driveshaft diagnosis. Each component of the drive train can develop a small amount of play as components wear. One of the most common places for wear is in the U-joint. As the U-joints wear, vibrations can occur and major damage can happen if the joint were to break. Regular inspection of the drive line should be performed when any vehicle service is performed.

U-joint phasing is important when multiple shafts are involved. If you are going to disassemble a multipiece driveshaft, then it is critical to mark the parts in relation to each other. If the parts are not marked during disassembly, then an out-of-phase condition could result, and vibration will occur even if the shaft is in balance. Along with balance and phasing, runout and concentricity should be checked. If any damage has occurred, then the damaged parts will need to be replaced.

Drive line angularity is critical to making sure U-joints are working at their proper angle. Drive line angularity is the relationship of the driveshaft to the component that the driveshaft attaches to, as measured in degrees. For example, the angle of the rear axle assembly companion flange should be perpendicular to the transmission output shaft. If any deviation is present, the U-joints will bind, which will cause both a vibration and additional wear on the joints. An angle gauge or a protractor should be used to measure these angles **FIGURE 26-22**. If the angles are out of specifications, follow the manufacturer's procedure to bring the components into alignment.

To check drive shaft joints, phasing, angles, balance, and runout, follow the steps in **SKILL DRILL 26-3**:

1. Safely raise the vehicle on an approved lift, and make sure it is secure. Do a proper under-vehicle inspection of the entire drive line by physically

FIGURE 26-22 **A.** An angle gauge. **B.** A protractor.

SKILL DRILL | **26-3** | **Checking Driveshaft Joints, Phasing, Angles, Balance, and Runout**

1. Raise the vehicle on a lift, making sure it is secure. Inspect the entire drive line by grasping the driveshaft and checking for abnormal play

2. Move the shaft fore and aft and radially. Play indicates worn U-joints.

3. Start the vehicle and safely allow it to run in drive at slow speed on the lift. Watch and listen to the joints. Any noise or off-centeredness indicates damaged U-joints. Check that the joints are in phase by checking the U-joint yoke on each end of the driveshaft with a level.

SKILL DRILL	**26-3**	**Checking Driveshaft Joints, Phasing, Angles, Balance, and Runout, continued**

4 Slowly raise the speed and watch for balance issues on the driveshaft. If any balance issues are present, slow the speed so the vehicle does not slip on the hoist. If all is well, stop the engine and measure the runout with a dial indicator, and check the driveshaft for concentricity.

5 Check the angularity using a protractor, and make all necessary adjustments. Shims may be required.

6 Check the driveshaft for any missing weights that are used to balance the shaft. Usually missing weights will be evident by the welds that are made when the driveshaft is balanced.

grasping the driveshaft and checking for abnormal play. **(Photo 1)**

2 Move the shaft fore and aft and radially. Any play indicates worn U-joints. **(Photo 2)**

3 Start the vehicle and safely allow it to run in drive on the lift. Watch and listen to the joints at slow speed. Any noise or off-centeredness indicates damaged U-joints.

4 Check that the joints are phased properly by placing your angle gauge 90 degrees to the length of the drive line mounted across one U-joint yoke. Turn the shaft to level your gauge, then measure the angle on the other end of the shaft. Both U-joint yokes should be level; if not, the joints are not in phase. **(Photo 3)**

5 Slowly raise the speed and watch for balance issues on the driveshaft. If any balance issues are present, slow the speed so the vehicle does not slip on the hoist.

6 If all is well, stop the engine and measure the runout with a dial indicator, and check the driveshaft for concentricity. **(Photo 4)**

7 Check the angularity using a protractor, and make all necessary adjustments. If adjustment is necessary, this will require changing transmission position and angle or possibly the angle of the axle assembly. Shims may be required. **(Photo 5)**

8 Also check the driveshaft for any missing weights that are used to balance the shaft. Usually missing weights will be evident by the welds that are made when the driveshaft is balanced. **(Photo 6)**

Inspecting and Servicing Center Support Bearings

The center bearing is an important part of the drive line. The center bearing is subject to weather and the same abuses as a U-joint. Whenever an under-vehicle service is performed, the center bearing should be inspected for any type of damage that can happen along the way. If this bearing is equipped with a grease zerk, it should be lubricated whenever an oil change and filter and chassis lubrication is performed. Without lubrication, it could cause a major vibration and a catastrophic failure to occur.

To inspect and service center support bearings, follow the steps in **SKILL DRILL 26-4**:

1 Safely raise the vehicle on an approved lift. Inspect the center bearing components for any major defects, such as looseness or noises.

2 Inspect the center bearing for proper mounting.

3 Inspect the bearing mount rubber insert for dry rotting and cracking.

4 If the bearing must be replaced, follow the manufacturer's specifications and procedures for proper installation of a new bearing. Typical bearing replacement may go as follows: mount the drive-shaft in an approved vise.

5. Mark the shafts so they may be properly phased when put back together. Separate the two driveshafts.

6. Remove the U-shaped metal mounting bracket. Remove the rubber mount from around the center bearing.

7. Remove any snap rings or circlips that may be holding the bearing in place.

8. Use an appropriate puller or press to remove the bearing from the driveshaft.

9. Check the splines for the slip yoke for any defects. Check the slip yoke on the mating shaft for wear and defects.

10. Press on a new bearing. Reinstall any necessary snap rings or circlips.

11. Install a new rubber mount around the new bearing. Reinstall the mounting bracket.

12. Put the two shafts back together, paying attention to driveshaft phasing.

13. Remove the driveshaft from the vise, and reinstall it into vehicle.

Measuring Drive Axle Flange Runout and Shaft End Play

Once axles have been serviced or replaced, it is a good practice to measure axle flange runout and axle end play. Runout is important to make sure the brake drum or rotor and the tire and wheel assembly will rotate properly and not cause any kind of vibrations. If all repairs have been done properly, runout and end play should be in specifications. Some procedures may differ due to the manufacturer's protocol. Always consult the manufacturer's guidelines and service information to ensure proper procedures for runout and end play.

To measure drive axle flange runout and shaft end play, follow the steps in **SKILL DRILL 26-5**:

1. Measure axle flange runout with the tires, wheels, and brake drum or rotor removed. Start by mounting a dial indicator on the backing plate, and set the dial gauge on the flange of the axle; zero out the indicator to obtain a correct reading.

2. Slowly rotate the axle and observe the runout as it is turning.

3. Compare with the manufacturer's specifications. If it does not match, replace the axle.

4. Once runout has been completed, mount the dial on the rim perch of the axle and zero out the indicator.

5. Pry the axle in and out, and obtain an end play reading.

6. Compare to the manufacturer's specifications. If it does not match, the axle may need to be removed and the axle groove should be inspected (integral axle type), or the bearings in the housing should be inspected or replaced (removable carrier type).

Inspecting and Replacing Wheel Studs and Lug Nuts

Lug nuts and studs are what hold the drive wheels in place and have been known to come loose or go bad over time. In some states, the law requires an inspection of the brakes that involves removal of the tires to gain access to the brake system. Lug nuts must be removed to do this. Inspection of the studs should be done in order to look for stretching or thread defects of these studs. If any defects or thread damage is present, the stud should be replaced. Sometimes improper torquing of the lug nuts can cause the studs to fail or lose a wheel when driving. Under- or overtorquing can result in these conditions. Uneven torquing can cause warping, which can cause problems with the brakes.

> ▶ **LINK**
> Refer to the Disc Brake Systems chapter for the procedure to replace lug studs.

> **TECHNICIAN TIP**
> Never use an air gun to torque lug nuts without using a torque stick followed by a torque wrench that is set to the manufacturer's torque specifications; otherwise, lug and stud damage can be present and result in loss of a wheel and tire assembly while driving down the highway.

Removing and Replacing Drive Axle Shafts

Sometimes it may be necessary to remove the drive axles due to seal leakage or differential damage or possibly a bent or damaged axle. Depending on the type of differential (integral or removable carrier), the removal process differs between the two. If it becomes necessary to remove the axles, make sure to follow all manufacturer guidelines and procedures explicitly.

To remove the integral-type differential axles, follow the steps in **SKILL DRILL 26-6**:

1. Put the vehicle on an approved lift, and make sure it is secure. Remove the wheels and tires and the brake drum or rotor.

SKILL DRILL   26-6   Removing the Integral-Type Differential Axles

1 Put the vehicle on a lift. Remove the wheels and tires. Drain the differential fluid in a clean pan if reusing; otherwise, refill with fresh fluid.

2 Remove the rear differential cover bolts. Clean and remove the old gasket material to allow for the new gaskets.

3 Remove the lock pin from the differential lock pin, and remove the pin.

4 Slide one axle inward to remove the circlip from the end of axle. Then remove the other clip from the opposite axle. Slide the old axles out of the differential housing.

5 Replace the axle seals to avoid any leaks along with new outer axle bearings. Slide the new axles into the housing, paying attention to the axle side gear splines. Make sure they align properly.

6 Reinstall the circlips in the grooves on the new axles.

7 Slide the lock pin back into place and reinstall the lock pin retainer. Tighten it to specifications.

8 Reinstall the differential cover with a new gasket, and torque the bolts to specifications.

9 Refill the axle housing with appropriate type fluid recommended by the manufacturer. After a road test, put the car back on the lift and inspect for any leaks.

2 Drain the differential fluid in a clean pan if reusing; otherwise, it can be drained into any used oil container. **(Photo 1)**

3 Remove the rear differential cover bolts.

4 Clean and remove the old gasket material to allow for the new gaskets. **(Photo 2)**

5 Remove the lock pin from the differential pinion shaft, and remove the shaft. **(Photo 3)**

6 Slide one axle inward to remove the circlip from the end of axle. Then remove the other clip from the opposite axle.

7 Slide the old axles out of the differential housing. **(Photo 4)**

8 Replace the axle seals to avoid any leaks along with new outer axle bearings if required.

9 Lubricate the seals and carefully slide the new axles into the housing, paying attention not to damage the seals that are in the end of the housing and making sure the axle side gear splines align properly with the side gears. **(Photo 5)**

10 Reinstall the circlips in the grooves on the new axles, and lightly pull back out on each axle to hold the clips in place. **(Photo 6)**

11 Slide the lock pin back into place and reinstall the lock pin retainer. Tighten it to specifications. **(Photo 7)**

12 Reinstall the differential cover with a new gasket or RTV and torque the bolts to specifications. **(Photo 8)**

13 Reinstall the brakes, bleed if necessary, and torque the wheels in place.

14 Refill the axle housing with the fluid recommended by the manufacturer.

15 Road test the vehicle.

16 Put the vehicle back on the lift and inspect for any leaks. **(Photo 9)**

To remove the removable carrier-type differential axles, follow the steps in **SKILL DRILL 26-7**:

1 Put the vehicle on an approved lift and secure it. Remove the tires and wheels and the brake drum or rotor.

2 Remove the axle flange retaining bolts by rotating the axle and aligning the hole in the flange with the bolt to be loosened. **(Photo 1)**

3 Pull the axles from the differential housing, using a puller if necessary. **(Photo 2)**

4 Replace the axle seals and bearings as required. **(Photo 3)**

Note: Some axles may have the seals and bearings already on the axle, and other models may have the bearings and seals in the housing. Consult the manufacturer's publications for proper procedures for replacement of these items.

5 Install the new axles, and turn until the splines are aligned and you feel they have fallen into place. **(Photo 4)**

6 Reinstall the bolts and torque to the manufacturer's specifications.

SKILL DRILL 26-7 Removing the Carrier-Type Differential Axles

1 Put the vehicle on an approved lift and secure it. Remove the tires and wheels. Remove the axle flange retaining bolts by rotating the axle and aligning the hole in the flange with the bolt to be loosened.

2 Pull the axles from the differential housing, using a puller if necessary.

3 Replace the axle seals and bearings (see Skill Drill 26-8).

SKILL DRILL | **26-7** | **Removing the Carrier-Type Differential Axles, continued**

4 Install the new axles, and turn until splines are aligned and felt to have fallen into place.

5 Replace the axle retaining bolts and torque to the manufacturer's specifications. Reinstall the tires and wheels. Refill or top off the fluid level. After a road test, put the vehicle on the lift and inspect for any leaks.

7 Reinstall the brake drums or rotors and calipers, and tires and wheels.

8 Refill or top off the fluid (some models do not require a full draining of the fluid).

9 Road test the vehicle.

10 Put the vehicle on the lift and inspect for any leaks. **(Photo 5)**

Inspecting and Replacing Drive Axle Shaft Seals, Bearings, and Retainers

While the axle is out, depending on the type of final drive, seals, bearings, and retainers can be serviced. Follow the manufacturer's procedures for the removal of the drive axles. If axles will be replaced, it is a good practice to replace the bearings and seals. Some retainers can be reused if clearances are still within specifications on integral-type final drives. Clearances on the end of the axle shafts for snap rings should be checked, as the axle has a tendency to move axially and cause the end of the axle shaft groove to become wide enough to drop the snap ring into the housing, which will cause the axle to walk out of the housing while the vehicle is traveling down the highway. Check the manufacturer's specification for axial clearances between the clip and the axle groove.

To replace the integral axle housing seal and bearing, follow the steps in **SKILL DRILL 26-8**:

1 Remove the axle according to the manufacturer's specific procedures, if any. **(Photo 1)**

2 On some models, you will remove the bearings and seal by putting the axle in a press and pressing them both off at the same time.

3 On some models, you will pull the bearing out of the housing using a manufacturer-specific puller. **(Photo 2)**

4 Replace all seals to make sure there will be no leakage from that area.

5 If reusing the axle, inspect the seal surface of the axle for damage such as grooving or pitting from bearing failure. **(Photo 3)**

To replace the removable carrier seal and bearing, follow the steps in **SKILL DRILL 26-9**:

1 With the tire and wheel removed, remove the bolts of the axle retainer.

2 Remove the axle by using the manufacturer-specific puller. **(Photo 1)**

3 Press the bearing and seal off the axle shaft. **(Photo 2)**

4 Remove the seal and bearing from the bearing housing. **(Photo 3)**

5 Install new bearing and seal into the housing using the appropriate driver tool. **(Photo 4)**

6 Inspect the axle for any damage.

7 Press the bearing assembly back onto the axle using a hydraulic press. **(Photo 5)**

8 Align the splines of the axle side gears and push the axle back in the housing, being careful not to damage the seal.

SKILL DRILL | 26-8 | Replacing the Integral Axle Housing Seal and Bearing

1 Remove the axle.

2 On some models, remove the bearings and seal by putting the axle in a press. On some models, pull the bearing out of the housing.

3 Replace all seals and inspect the seal surface of the axle.

SKILL DRILL | 26-9 | Replacing the Removable Carrier Differential Seal and Bearing

1 Remove the bolts of the axle retainer, then remove the axle.

2 Press the bearing and seal off.

3 Remove the seal and bearing from the bearing housing.

4 Install new bearing and seal into the bearing housing.

5 Inspect the axle for any damage. Press the bearing assembly back onto the axle.

6 Push the axle back in the housing. Reinstall the flange bolts and torque.

9 Reinstall the bolts and torque to the manufacturer's specifications. (**Photo 6**)

Inspecting Half-Shaft Components

It is important to make the proper diagnosis before entering into any type of repair. If a repair of the CV joints is necessary, follow all manufacturer guidelines and procedures.

Service of CV joints depends on the type of failure that has occurred. For example, if the axle is clicking when turning sharply, then the joint or the entire half-shaft will need to be replaced. If the CV boot is torn, it can be replaced without replacing the entire joint or shaft. Some can be easy and some can be extremely hard, but a thorough inspection is a good practice to diagnose whether to replace the half-shaft in its entirety or to replace and service one CV joint or boot.

To inspect half-shaft components, follow the steps in **SKILL DRILL 26-10**:

SKILL DRILL | 26-10 | Inspecting Half-Shaft Components

1 Clamp the entire half-shaft into a soft-jawed vice, and make sure it is secure. Remove the retaining clamps from the CV boot. Slide the boot down the shaft, paying attention to the condition of the boot.

2 Wipe out as much grease as possible to be able to access the retaining ring from the CV joint itself. If there is a retaining ring present, remove the retaining ring with the appropriate tool. When the retaining ring is removed, remove the CV joint from the half-shaft and inspect the splines on the end of the half-shaft. This also applies to the other end of the half-shaft.

3 Inspect the old joint to gain an accurate assessment of the failure to prevent a reoccurrence of this failure. Reinstall the new CV joint onto the shaft splines as required.

4 Apply the lubrication grease that comes with the new CV joint. Tighten the boot clamp to ensure that grease will not be lost. This applies to both sides of the half-shaft. Reinstall the half-shaft following the manufacturer's guidelines.

1. Clamp the entire half-shaft into a soft-jawed vice, and make sure it is secure. Start by removing the retaining clamps from the CV boot.

2. Remove the retaining clamps from the CV boot. Slide the boot down the shaft, paying attention to the condition of the boot. **(Photo 1)**

3. Wipe out as much grease as possible to be able to access the retaining ring from the CV joint itself.

4. If there is a retaining ring present, remove it with the tool recommended by the manufacturer.

5. When the retaining ring is removed, remove the CV joint from the half-shaft and inspect the splines on the end of the half-shaft. This will apply to the other end of the half-shaft as well. **(Photo 2)**

6. Inspect the old joint to gain an accurate assessment of the failure to prevent a reoccurrence of this failure.

7. Reinstall the new CV joint onto the shaft splines as required. **(Photo 3)**

8. Apply the lubrication grease that comes with the new CV joint. Do not apply any more than that. Doing so could result in a premature failure of the boot by forcing a hydraulic lock situation and force the grease past the new boot seal.

9. Tighten the boot clamp using the appropriate tool to ensure that grease will not be lost. This procedure will apply to both sides of the half-shaft.

> ### ▶ TECHNICIAN TIP
>
> Some CV joints do not require a retaining ring and just need to be driven off with a soft metal hammer, preferably a brass one.

10. Reinstall the half-shaft following the manufacturer's guidelines. **(Photo 4)**

Inspecting Fluid Leakage

Fluid loss and leaks are a part of the aging process of a vehicle. Fluid leakage concerns are important and should be checked for on a regular basis. Axle seals and pinion seals are usually the likely places to investigate. Seals are subject to expansion and contraction through heat and cold changes that take place on a regular basis. Overfilling of the differential will create a pressure buildup in the differential from foaming of the liquid that the breather cannot handle, so the weakest place to vent pressure will be through the axle seal itself.

A lack of lubrication will cause the axle bearing to heat up and damage the seal. Brake heat that comes from a dragging brake can also cause an axle seal to leak. A bent axle or axle bearing failure will add to the cause of a failure of the seal. Preventive maintenance can identify some of these concerns and should be practiced on a regular basis.

To inspect fluid leakage, follow the steps in **SKILL DRILL 26-11**:

1. Put the vehicle on an approved lift, and make sure it is secure. Visually inspect around the housing where the axle seats for any seepage. **(Photo 1)**

2. Inspect the pinion flange for any seepage. **(Photo 2)**

3. If necessary, remove the rear wheels and install a dial indicator on the axle flange to check for any distortion. **(Photo 3)**

4. Check and clean the breather or vent for any obstructions that may cause a pressure buildup to occur. **(Photo 4)**

SKILL DRILL | 26-11 | Inspecting Fluid Leakage

1. Put the vehicle on a lift and make sure it is secure. Inspect around the housing where the axle seats for any seepage.

2. Inspect the pinion flange for possible seepage.

3. If necessary, remove the rear wheels and install a dial indicator on the axle flange to check for any distortion.

SKILL DRILL 26-11 Inspecting Fluid Leakage, continued

4 Check and clean the breather or vent for any obstructions that may cause a pressure buildup to occur.

5 Check the differential cover for a leaking gasket, if so equipped, and tighten if loose or replace as necessary.

6 Check the fluid level for lack of fluid or overfilling of the differential, as either one can indicate that a leak is present.

5 Check the differential rear cover for a leaking gasket, if so equipped, and tighten if loose or replace as necessary. (**Photo 5**)

6 Check the fluid level for lack of fluid or overfilling of the differential, as either one can indicate that a leak is present. (**Photo 6**)

Inspecting and Replacing the Companion Flange and Pinion Seal

The pinion companion flange is what the driveshaft bolts up to and connects the transmission to the differential. Inspection from time to time may reveal any problems that may be present. Customer concerns can also warrant an inspection of the pinion companion flange. It is held on by a large nut that also sets the preload for the pinion gear on crush sleeve types. If replacement is necessary, consult the service information for complete replacement procedures.

To inspect and replace the companion flange and pinion seal, follow the steps in **SKILL DRILL 26-12**:

1 Safely raise the vehicle on an approved lift, and make sure it is secure. Inspect the pinion companion flange for any visible defects.

2 Inspect the pinion seal for leakage and replace as necessary. (**Photo 1**)

3 Remove the driveshaft to expose the retaining nut.

4 If replacement is necessary:
   a. Remove the large retaining nut
   b. Slide the flange off of the pinion gear spline using a soft hammer or puller, and inspect the splines

and sealing surface for any damage. Replace as necessary. (**Photo 2**)
   c. Remove the companion flange seal with the proper removal tool. Inspect the seal surface for any damage.
   d. Replace the seal with the proper part using the proper driver to install it. Lubricate the seal lip with the gear oil. (**Photo 3**)
   e. Reinstall the companion flange, paying attention to the spline alignment if necessary.
   f. Install the retaining nut and torque it to the proper specifications. (**Photo 4**)

5 Using a dial indicator, check the runout of the companion flange, and compare it to the manufacturer's specifications. (**Photo 5**)

6 Reinstall the driveshaft, paying attention to the alignment of the slip yoke.

7 Check and refill the differential fluid to the manufacturer's specified level.

8 Thoroughly road test the vehicle. If necessary, put it back on the lift and double-check your work. (**Photo 6**)

> **TECHNICIAN TIP**
>
> When installing any type of seal, it is a good practice to lubricate the seal and spring with grease to prevent the spring from popping off upon installation. Failure to do so may result in seal leakage and flange damage.

SKILL DRILL | 26-12 | Inspecting and Replacing the Companion Flange and Pinion Seal

1. Raise the vehicle on an approved lift. Inspect the pinion companion flange for any visible defects. Inspect the pinion seal for leakage and replace as necessary.

2. Remove the driveshaft to expose the retaining nut. Remove the large retaining nut. Slide the flange off of the pinion gear spline using a soft hammer or puller, and inspect the splines for any damage.

3. Remove the companion flange seal with the proper removal tool. Inspect seal surface for any damage. Replace the seal using the appropriate driver.

4. Reinstall the companion flange, paying attention to the spline alignment if necessary. Install the retaining nut and torque it to the proper specifications.

5. Using a dial indicator, check the runout of the companion flange, and compare it to the manufacturer's specifications.

6. Reinstall the drive shaft, paying attention to the alignment of the slip yoke. Check and refill the differential fluid. Road test the vehicle, and put it back on the lift to double-check your work.

Inspecting the Ring Gear and Measuring Runout

When disassembling a differential case, it is good practice to measure ring gear runout before disassembly and after reassembly. This will indicate if there is a problem with the differential case or the ring gear itself, which can be an indicator of reuse or replacement. Any excessive runout could be the result of debris caught between the ring gear and the differential case upon assembly of the unit or possibly bad bearings on the differential case housing.

To inspect the ring gear and measure runout, follow the steps in **SKILL DRILL 26-13**:

1. Clean off the flat side of the ring gear to remove any excess oil.

2. Attach a dial indicator to the differential housing near the area of the ring gear.

3. Zero out the indicator so an accurate reading can be taken. **(Photo 1)**

4. Rotate the ring gear by installing a socket and a ratchet to the pinion companion flange nut.

SKILL DRILL | 26-13 | Inspecting the Ring Gear and Measuring Runout

1 Clean off the flat side of the ring gear to remove any excess oil. Attach a dial indicator to the differential housing near the area of the ring gear. Zero out the indicator so an accurate reading can be taken.

2 Rotate the ring gear by installing a socket and a ratchet to the pinion companion flange nut. Load the ring gear up by wedging a screwdriver or equivalent in order to get an accurate reading.

3 Rotate the ring gear slowly, paying attention to the dial, and compare the reading with specifications. Determine any necessary actions.

---

5 Load the ring gear up by wedging a screwdriver or equivalent to get an accurate reading. **(Photo 2)**

6 Rotate the ring gear slowly, paying attention to the dial, and compare the reading with the manufacturer's specifications. Determine any necessary actions. **(Photo 3)**

Removing, Inspecting, and Reinstalling the Drive Pinion and Ring Gear

The overhaul process for a set of differential gears, including the ring gear and pinion gear, will require an overhaul kit. In the kit are new bearings and gaskets along with spacers and washers. A new crush sleeve may need to be purchased as these are not reusable. If shims are underneath the bearing race cups or pinion gear, they will need to be added to or subtracted from in order to make any necessary adjustments. All bearings should be replaced along with the bearing races that they mate with.

To remove, inspect, and reinstall the drive pinion and ring gear, follow these step in **SKILL DRILL 26-14** :

1 Remove the pinion bearing by installing it in a press with a bearing splitter.

2 Pump the handle and watch the bearing start to move and come off. **(Photo 1)**

3 Install any pinion depth shims and the new pinion bearing by pressing only on the inner race by using the proper-sized adapters or pipe. (You will either need to transfer the old shim to between the bearing and pinion or on some sets, compare the markings on the old pinion to the new pinion and use the manufacturer's chart to determine to add a thicker or thinner shim and by how much). **(Photo 2)**

4 Install the bearing splitter on the differential case bearings and press these off using a press. **(Photo 3)**

5 Install the new bearings and any necessary shims using the press, and make sure they are seated correctly again by pressing on the inner race only. **(Photo 4)**

> ### TECHNICIAN TIP
>
> Lubricate the new bearings in the appropriate type of fluid used by the manufacturer.

SKILL DRILL | 26-14 | Removing, Inspecting, and Reinstalling the Drive Pinion

1. Remove the pinion bearing by installing it in a press with a bearing splitter. Pump the handle and watch the bearing start to move and come off.

2. Install the new pinion bearing (and any proper shims) by pressing the new bearing back on in the same fashion.

3. Install the bearing splitter on the differential case bearings, and press these off using a press.

4. Install the new bearings (and any necessary shims) using the press, and make sure they are seated correctly.

Disassembling, Inspecting, Measuring, and Adjusting the Differential Pinion Gear Assembly

In the case of a catastrophic failure or just an upgrade of parts for performance purposes, it is extremely import to follow the correct procedures to replace or adjust the ring and pinion gears. The pinion to ring gear backlash should be measured and recorded for future reference. It will be helpful should it be necessary to reinstall the same gear set back in the housing. Once the final drive assembly is removed from the housing, the differential assembly can be disassembled,

inspected and measured. Removal of some carriers will require that the axle housing be spread using the proper housing spreader tool recommended by the manufacturer. Remove the ring gear and differential case to access the differential side gears and pinion (or spider) gears for service.

To disassemble, inspect, measure, and adjust the differential pinion gear assembly, follow the steps in **SKILL DRILL 26-15**:

1. Disassemble the differential case by removing the ring gear bolts and separating the ring gear from the case.

SKILL DRILL | 26-15 | Disassembling, Inspecting, Measuring, and Adjusting the Differential Pinion Gear Assembly

1 Disassemble the differential case by removing the ring gear bolts and separating the ring gear from the case. Then remove the spider gears and axle side gears and thrust washers from the case.

2 Inspect all gears for chipping and discoloration; this will determine if the gears should be renewed.

3 Inspect all thrust washers for chipping or galling and discoloration to determine whether they should be replaced.

4 Inspect the differential case for any defects that would cause a problem for new or used gears and washers, especially the thrust washer surfaces.

5 Inspect the ring gear surface for trueness using a straightedge, and inspect the ring gear mounting holes for elongation.

6 Reassemble the differential case using new or used gears and thrust washers, and check the clearances between the gear sets.

7 Using a feeler gauge, check the clearances between the axle side gears and the spider gears. Check the clearances between the axle side gears and the differential case. Reinstall the ring gear and torque the bolts to manufacturer specifications.

2 Once the case is separated, remove the spider gears, side gears, and thrust washers from the case. **(Photo 1)**

3 Inspect all gears for chipping and discoloration, as this will determine if the gears should be renewed. **(Photo 2)**

4 Inspect the pinion shaft and all thrust washers for wear, chipping, or galling and for discoloration to determine if they should be replaced as well. **(Photo 3)**

5 Inspect the differential case for any defects that would cause a problem for new or used gears and washers, especially the thrust washer surfaces. **(Photo 4)**

6 Inspect the ring gear surface for trueness using a straightedge, and inspect the ring gear mounting holes for elongation. **(Photo 5)**

7 Reassemble the differential case using new or used gears and thrust washers, and check the clearances between the gear sets. **(Photo 6)**

8 Using a feeler gauge, check the clearances between the side gears and the spider gears.

9 Using a feeler gauge, check the clearances between the side gears and the differential case. Consult all manufacturer service information for the correct specifications.

10 Reinstall the ring gear, and torque the bolts to the manufacturer's specifications. **(Photo 7)**

Measuring and Adjusting Drive Pinion Depth

The purpose of measuring pinion depth is to ensure that the pinion gear teeth are making correct contact with the ring gear teeth. The depth must be correct in order for the ring to be driven properly or there could be a catastrophic failure. When these spiral bevel gears rotate, they try to separate each other by a twisting motion, which makes the gears want to walk away from each other. The bearings keep them in check as they rotate, but the separation effect is always present. Correct depth and gear contact will keep separation at a minimum.

To adjust pinion depth, follow the steps in **SKILL DRILL 26-16**:

1 Install the pinion gear bearing race and any shims that were present on its removal. These shims control the depth of the gear in the housing. **(Photo 1)**

2 Use the factory-designated tool to set the depth of the pinion gear in the housing.

3 After the measurement is made, the proper shims can be installed to meet the required height. Reassembly of the pinion can be performed for

SKILL DRILL | **26-16** | **Measuring and Adjusting Drive Pinion Depth**

1 Install the pinion gear bearing race and any shims that were present upon its removal.

2 Use the factory-designated tool to set the depth of the pinion gear in the housing. After the measurement is made, install the proper shims to meet the required height. Reassembly of the pinion can be performed for the next adjustment, called pinion bearing preload.

the next adjustment, called drive pinion preload (see Skill Drill 26-17). **(Photo 2)**

Measuring and Adjusting Drive Pinion Preload

Adjusting pinion bearing preload is necessary to make sure the conical bearings that support it are seated and positioned correctly. The pinion rotates and drives the ring gear. The forces on the pinion gear are tremendous in that the driveshaft, which is connected to it, transmits the power to the pinion gear then to the ring gear and then to the axles and tires. Pinion bearing preload positions the bearings such that the pinion gear is held firmly in place, but still allows smooth rotation of the gear.

To measure and adjust drive pinion preload, follow the steps in **SKILL DRILL 26-17**:

1. Reinstall the pinion into the housing with a new bearing, making sure to install the crush sleeve, if equipped. On types that use shims to control preload, ensure they are positioned correctly. **(Photo 1)**

2. Install the front bearing over the splined end of the gear. **(Photo 2)**

3. Reinstall the pinion seal using the manufacturer-recommended tool. **(Photo 3)**

4. Reinstall the companion flange, lining up the splines. **(Photo 4)**

5. Reinstall the nut and washer. Torque the nut to the manufacturer's specifications. **(Photo 5)**

SKILL DRILL | 26-17 | Measuring and Adjusting Drive Pinion Preload

1. Reinstall the pinion into the housing with a new bearing, making sure to install the crush sleeve, or shims.

2. Install the front bearing over the splined end of the gear.

3. Reinstall the pinion seal.

4. Reinstall the companion flange, lining up the splines.

5. Reinstall the nut and washer. Torque the nut to the manufacturer's specifications.

6. Check the preload using an inch-pound torque wrench or pull scale, looking for the correct specification.

6. Check the preload using a deflecting beam inch-pound torque wrench or pull scale, looking for the correct specification. (Photo 6)

Reassembling and Reinstalling the Differential Case, and Measuring Runout

Now that the differential case has been serviced, the assembly can be reinstalled. This should be done carefully, with attention given to the installation specifications. Upon installation, put the new differential case bearing races on the bearings and any spacers that were removed. These spacers will determine backlash, which will be addressed in Skill Drill 26-19 and 20.

To reassemble and reinstall the differential case assembly and measure runout, follow the steps in **SKILL DRILL 26-18**:

1. Use a factory-recommended housing spreader so as to be able to reinstall the differential case as a unit.

2. Insert the differential case back in the housing, paying attention to the spacers that were present. (Photo 1)

3. Reinstall the bearing caps on the housing, paying attention to the marks made as they were removed. Torque to specifications. *Note:* If the caps are installed backward, binding of the ring gear may be present. (Photo 2)

4. Attach a dial indicator to the housing, set the dial on the ring gear, and check the runout.

5. Set the dial to zero and rotate the ring gear using the companion flange nut and a socket and ratchet.

6. Check the manufacturer's specifications for proper runout. (Photo 3)

Measuring and Adjusting Side Bearing Preload and Ring and Pinion Gear Backlash

Setting backlash on a set of differential gears is critical in that if it is too loose or tight, a catastrophic failure will happen for sure. Carrier bearing preload should be adjusted at the same time as a backlash setting. Side bearing preload limits the amount of lateral movement that the ring gear can travel, whereas backlash sets the closeness of the ring gear into the pinion gear. If this is an

SKILL DRILL 26-18 Reassembling and Reinstalling the Differential Case Assembly, and Measuring Runout

1. Use a factory-recommended housing spreader to reinstall the differential case as a unit. Insert the differential case back in the housing, paying attention to the spacers that were present.

2. Reinstall the bearing caps on the housing, paying attention to the marks made as they were removed. Torque to specifications.

3. Attach a dial indicator to the housing, set the dial on the ring gear, and check the runout. Set the dial to zero and rotate the ring using the companion flange nut and a socket and ratchet. Check specifications for proper runout.

integral differential setup, backlash and bearing preload are usually set using shims. Removable center section carriers usually have bearing cone adjusters that are turned to set preload and backlash.

To adjust backlash of an integral differential, follow the steps in SKILL DRILL 26-19:

1. Make sure the bearing preload is set and attach a dial indicator to the housing. Set the dial indicator on the teeth of the ring gear, and zero the gauge out. **(Photo 1)**

2. Rock the ring gear back and forth without letting the pinion move, and take a reading. Compare to the manufacturer's specifications.

3. If adjustment is required, the case will have to be removed and spacers of the required thickness will have to be installed. **(Photo 2)**

4. Repeat the measurement process by following steps 1 through 4. **(Photo 3)**

To adjust backlash of a removable carrier differential, follow the steps in SKILL DRILL 26-20:

1. Install the ring gear/differential assembly and bearing cones and caps. **(Photo 1)**

2. Snug the bolts on the bearing caps. **(Photo 2)**

3. Thread the bearing adjusting nuts into the cap and housing threads, being careful not to cross-thread the adjusters (adjust so there is slight bearing preload for this test). **(Photo 3)**

4. Attach a dial indicator to the housing. Set the dial indicator on the ring gear teeth, and zero out the dial indicator.

5. Rock the ring gear back and forth, and take a measurement. **(Photo 4)**

6. Set the backlash to the manufacturer's specifications by alternately turning the adjuster nuts until the reading falls into the manufacturer's reading.

7. Torque the bearing cap bolts to specifications. **(Photo 5)**

Checking Ring and Pinion Tooth Contact Patterns

Once a differential gear set has been replaced, checking the gear tooth contact pattern is a good practice to make sure there is proper contact between the ring and pinion. On the ring gear tooth, there are several parts that need to be identified. The first thing to identify is the coast side of the ring gear tooth and the drive side of the ring gear tooth. The drive side of the ring gear tooth is the convex side that torque is applied to when the power is being transferred through the gear teeth. Coast is when the vehicle is coasting and contact is being made on the concave side of the ring gear teeth. The pinion drive gear is now the driven gear in coast mode. The ends of the tooth are the toe and the heel, with the heel being the

SKILL DRILL   26-19   Adjusting Backlash of an Integral Differential

1. Make sure the bearing preload is set and attach a dial indicator to the housing. Set the dial indicator on the teeth of the ring gear, and zero out the gauge.

2. Rock the ring back and forth, and take a reading. Compare to the specifications. If adjustment is required, the ring gear will have to be removed and spacers of the required thickness will have to be installed.

3. Repeat the measurement process.

SKILL DRILL | 26-20 | Adjusting Backlash of a Removable Carrier Differential

1 Install the ring gear/differential assembly and bearing cones and caps.

2 Snug the bolts on the bearing caps.

3 Thread the bearing adjusting nuts into the cap and housing threads, being careful not to cross-thread the adjusters (slight bearing preload for test).

4 Attach a dial indicator to the housing. Set the dial indicator on the ring gear teeth, and zero out the dial indicator. Rock the ring gear back and forth, and take a measurement.

5 Set the backlash to the manufacturer's specifications by alternately turning the adjuster nuts until the reading falls into the manufacturer's reading. Torque the bearing cap bolts to specifications.

wider part of the tooth farther from the gear centerline. Looking at the tooth where the contact is made, the top of the tooth surface is called the face, the middle of the tooth is the flank, and the bottom is called the under-cut. These parts must be understood, as the gear contact pattern needs to be in the center or the flank of the gear tooth. It is a good idea to check the tooth contact pattern before disassembly, as this will create a comparison between the old and the new tooth pattern and will allow the technician to see if the pinion depth is set correctly **FIGURE 26-23**.

This pattern represents the distance between the ring and pinion gears and ensures quiet operation while they are in mesh. Any necessary adjustments should be made in the event that the contact pattern is not acceptable.

FIGURE 26-23 Understanding the tooth pattern is important in ensuring that setup of the ring and pinion has been correctly performed.

A contact pattern is made by using some type of grease or Prussian blue marking compound to make the pattern stand out. Paint several teeth and turn the companion flange nut while holding back on the ring gear to prevent the ring gear backlash from affecting the tooth contact pattern.

To check contact patterns, follow the steps in **SKILL DRILL 26-21**:

1 Paint several teeth with a suitable compound to make the pattern stand out in order to read it for any corrective actions that may be necessary. **(Photo 1)**

2 Rotate the ring gear a full 360 degrees with a ratchet and a socket using the companion flange nut. **(Photo 2)**

3 Wedge the ring gear with a screwdriver to hold back on the ring gear in order to limit the backlash from affecting the pattern.

4 Read the pattern and compare to the manufacturer's specifications, and determine the necessary course of action if it is not satisfactory.

5 Adjust the pattern as necessary and clean the components thoroughly before reassembling. After reassembly, recheck the pattern and confirm the correct contact pattern. **(Photo 3)**

Cleaning, Inspecting, and Lubricating the Differential Housing

If a catastrophic failure has occurred, then it will be necessary to clean the differential housing. Start by disassembling all major parts to expose the bare housing. Use an approved parts cleaner or pressure washer to clean the housing. The entire tubes must be flushed of all debris and particles that are present. Doing so will ensure that the new parts being used will not be contaminated and cause a premature failure. Inspect the housing for any major defects that may be present from any type of failure that may have occurred. Reassemble all major parts and components as described in previous skill drills.

SKILL DRILL   26-21   Checking Ring and Pinion Tooth Contact Patterns

1 Paint several teeth with a suitable compound to make the pattern stand out in order to read it for any corrective actions that may be necessary.

2 Rotate the ring gear a full 360 degrees with a ratchet and a socket using the companion flange nut.

3 Wedge the ring gear with a screwdriver in order to limit the backlash from affecting the pattern. Read the pattern and compare to the specifications, and determine the necessary course of action if it is not satisfactory. Adjust the pattern as necessary and clean the components thoroughly before reassembling.

To clean and inspect the differential housing and to refill it with lubricant, follow the steps in **SKILL DRILL 26-22**:

1. Disassemble all major parts and components to expose the bare housing. **(Photo 1)**
2. Flush and clean with manufacturer-approved solvents using proper procedures and equipment. **(Photo 2)**
3. Inspect the housing for any defects that may warrant replacement of the housing. **(Photo 3)**
4. Reassemble all parts and components into the housing using the manufacturer's specifications.
5. Refill with manufacturer-specific differential fluids or additives.

Inspecting and Reinstalling Limited Slip Differential Components

If the differential clutches must be replaced because of a catastrophic failure, then all components should be thoroughly inspected to ensure a lasting repair. Inspection of the housing is described in Skill Drill 26-22. Inspect the differential casing for any damage that may require replacement of the housing. Inspect all axle side gears and differential pinion gears and shafts for damage, and replace as necessary.

Start by placing the new clutch facings in the differential lubricant, and soak them thoroughly. If they are put into the housing dry, a growling noise on turns will be present and damage to the clutches can occur prematurely. Once they have been soaked, install them in proper order by putting in a steel plate first, then a clutch facing, and then alternating them. Install the side gears; then install the pinion gears into the housing with all pinion shafts in proper order. Once this process is completed, the assembly may be reinstalled into the axle housing. Make sure the differential is filled with the proper oils and additives to ensure quiet operation. Not all limited slip assemblies are assembled the same way; always consult the manufacturer's guidelines and procedures.

To inspect and reinstall limited slip differential components, follow the steps in **SKILL DRILL 26-23**:

1. Inspect all components to be reused for damage that may require replacement of the parts.
2. Soak all of the clutch friction facings prior to assembly to ensure quiet operation of the differential.
3. Insert the clutches into the housing, paying attention to the orientation of the steel plates and the friction facings.

SKILL DRILL | **26-22** | **Cleaning and Inspecting the Differential Housing, and Refilling with the Correct Lubricant**

1. Disassemble all major parts and components.

2. Flush and clean using proper procedures and equipment.

3. Inspect the housing for any defects. Reassemble all parts and components. Refill with manufacturer-specific differential fluids or additives.

4 Install the side gears against the clutches with the flat side facing the clutch friction facings.

5 Install the pinion gears and pinion shafts in the order they were removed, paying attention to any roll pins or retaining pins that were present at the time of disassembly.

6 Install the unit into the housing along, and perform any necessary measurements.

7 Fill the differential with the manufacturer-recommended oils and additives.

8 Road test the vehicle to ensure a proper repair.

Measuring Rotating Torque

Measuring rotation torque on a limited slip differential tests the condition and adjustment of the clutch pack. If the clutch disks are worn, rotating torque will be lower than specifications. If rotating torque is above specifications, the vehicle may try to go straight when steered on slightly slippery surfaces, or chirp the tires on dry surfaces. Rotating torque is measure with one drive wheel off the ground and the other on the ground. Rotating torque is the amount of torque it takes to rotate the wheel which is off the ground. It is easiest to use a beam style torque wrench when measuring rotating torque.

To measure rotating torque, follow the steps in **SKILL DRILL 26-24**:

1 Raise one drive wheel a few inches off the ground and secure it with a jack stand.

2 Bolt the torque wrench adapter to the raised wheel.

3 Use the torque wrench to turn the wheel. Rotating torque is the torque required to keep the wheel turning, not the break-away torque. Compare to specifications

Inspecting, Adjusting, and Repairing Shifting Controls

There are various types of transfer case shifting controls in use today, ranging from the older mechanical and vacuum controls to the newer electronically motorized control systems. Periodic inspection of all of these components is always a good practice. Mechanical shifting controls can wear out over time, and electrical problems may develop due to corrosion or looseness. Furthermore, vacuum controls have rubber diaphragms in them and can start to deteriorate over time due to heat and moisture.

Mounting bushings and grommets wear out as they are used over and over again. Inspection of these parts is critical to prevent problems along the way. Mounting brackets are used to hold components in place. They are subject to weather and will rust, wear, or bend under constant usage. These problems usually show up over time and should be inspected under normal preventive maintenance practices.

To inspect, adjust, and repair shifting controls, follow the steps in **SKILL DRILL 26-25**:

1 Raise the vehicle with an approved vehicle hoist, and make sure it is secure. Check the manufacturer's publications for proper procedures for inspection of any special parts.

2 Check for any codes that may be present by using a scan tool on the vehicle.

3 Perform a visual inspection of all mechanical linkages or mounting brackets for any damage or excessive wear of bushings or grommets.

4 Make any necessary adjustments to linkages or cables if they are loose or have been replaced.

5 Inspect any hoses that are dry rotted or cracked on any vacuum-operated components.

6 Refer to the service information for proper diagnosis of any electrical components that are in question.

7 After all repairs have been made, road test the vehicle to ensure that it was repaired properly.

Removing and Reinstalling Transfer Case

In some cases it may be necessary to remove the transfer case, such as when there has been a failure of the transfer case or of the transmission in a four-wheel drive vehicle. Four-wheel drive vehicles can be used for various purposes and must endure a variety of stress situations depending on the type of weather, climate, or terrain they are subjected to. For example, snowplowing can put stress on the transfer case, as can off-roading.

To remove and reinstall the transfer case, follow the steps in **SKILL DRILL 26-26**:

1 Remove the driveshafts and attaching bolts.

2 Remove all electronic wiring and shift linkage. *Note: It may be necessary to remove any skid plates or protective plates from the frame and transfer case.*

3 Remove the attaching bolts for the transmission and store them in a safe place.

4 Using a transmission jack, slowly back the transfer case away from the transmission.

5 Perform all necessary operations or repairs according to the manufacturer's specifications and operations.

6 Refill the oil to its proper level if it was drained.

7 Lubricate the splines of the transfer case input shaft. Align it with the transmission output shaft splines and slide it into position.

8 Reattach the transfer case bolts and torque them to specifications.

9 Attach all wiring and connections as required.

10 Reinstall all linkage that was removed and adjust as necessary.

11 Align and reinstall the front and rear driveshafts.

12 Road test the vehicle to ensure proper operation.

Disassembling, Servicing, and Reassembling the Transfer Case and Components

Most transfer cases are fairly durable, so they don't usually need more than routine maintenance. If there are any unusual bearing or gear noises coming from inside the transfer case, it will most likely need to be disassembled and inspected to determine the cause. As always, check the manufacturer's service information for all necessary procedures when servicing the transfer case.

When removing the transfer case, always support the unit with an approved transmission jack, as serious personal injury may result. See Skill Drill 26-26 for information on removing the transfer case. Once it has been removed, inspect the outer casing for any cracks or oil leaks or other signs of damage, as this will dictate the proper overhaul process. This task is based on a typical Ford transfer case, which we will use for teardown procedures.

To disassemble a transfer case and related components, follow the steps in **SKILL DRILL 26-27**:

1 If the transfer case has not been drained, it is a good idea to remove the drain plug and drain all oil before starting the disassembly process. **(Photo 1)**

2 Remove the output flange yokes and any nuts, seals, or washers upon removal. **(Photo 2)**

3 Remove the four-wheel drive dash light switch from the transfer case.

4 Unplug the shift harness connector and check for corrosion or any other signs of electrical resistance problems.

5 Remove the speed sensor from the side of the case. **(Photo 3)**

6 Remove the electric shift motor and attaching bolts from the case, paying attention to any specific orientation that the motor may need to be set for upon installation.

7 Remove the front case retaining bolts and put them in a secure location.

8 Separate the halves of the transfer case using a pry bar in the pry bosses embedded in the case. **(Photo 4)**

9 Remove any snap rings holding the speed sensor reluctor wheel and remove the reluctor wheel. **(Photo 5)**

SKILL DRILL | 26-27 | Disassembling the Transfer Case and Components

1 Remove the drain plug, and drain all oil before the disassembly.

2 Remove the output flange yokes.

3 Remove the four-wheel drive dash light switch. Unplug the shift harness connector. Remove the speed sensor.

SKILL DRILL | 26-27 | Disassembling the Transfer Case and Components, continued

4 Remove the front case retaining bolts. Separate the halves of the transfer case.

5 Remove snap rings. Remove the reluctor wheel.

6 Remove the oil pump assembly.

7 Remove the driven and drive sprockets with the chain.

8 Remove the output shaft assembly.

9 Remove the four-wheel drive shift fork and collar.

10 Remove the high/low shift fork and collar.

11 Remove the planetary gear set.

12 Clean and inspect all components for wear or damage. Replace any defective parts.

10 Remove the oil pump assembly on the main shaft while still together. (**Photo 6**)

11 Remove the driven and drive sprockets with the chain as a unit. (**Photo 7**)

12 Remove the output shaft assembly. (**Photo 8**)

13 Remove the two- or four-wheel drive shift fork and lock-up assembly from the main shaft. (**Photo 9**)

14 From the inside track of the shift cam, remove the high/low shift fork and collar. (**Photo 10**)

15 Remove the planetary gear mounting from the case.

16 Remove the planetary gear set from its mountings in the mounting plate. (**Photo 11**)

17 Clean and carefully inspect all parts for damage and wear as recommended by the unit's manufacturer, paying attention to any upgrades or TSBs that may be recommended for repair. **(Photo 12)**

18 Check the drive chain slack according to the manufacturer's procedure. If it becomes necessary, replace any defective parts.

19 Measure the shaft assembly end play according to the manufacturer's procedures, and if it proves to

be excessive, acquire new snap rings and shims in order to correct the problems.

To reassemble the transfer case and related components, follow the steps in **SKILL DRILL 26-28**:

1 Reinstall the planetary gear set into the case. Reinstall any snap rings holding the planetary gear set. **(Photo 1)**

SKILL DRILL 26-28 Reassembling the Transfer Case and Components

1 Reinstall the planetary gear set into the case. Reinstall any snap rings holding the planetary gear set.

2 Reinstall the high/low shift fork and collar into the case.

3 Reinstall the four-wheel drive shift fork and collar into the case. Make sure the shift rod is installed in the correct position in the case.

4 Reinstall the output shaft into the case. Make sure the shift collars line up properly on the shaft.

5 Reinstall the chain and driven sprocket.

6 Reassemble the oil pump assembly and pickup tube.

7 Apply a thin bead of RTV to one case half. Reassemble the two halves of the case and torque.

8 Reinstall all electrical sensors and switches.

9 Reinstall output flange yokes and torque to specification.

2 Reinstall the high/low shift fork and collar into the case. (**Photo 2**)

3 Reinstall the 4wd shift fork and collar into the case. Make sure the shift rod is installed in the correct position in the case. (**Photo 3**)

4 Reinstall the output shaft into the case. Make sure the shift collars line up properly on the shaft. (**Photo 4**)

5 Reinstall the chain and the driven sprocket. (**Photo 5**)

6 Reinstall the oil pump assembly and pickup tube. (**Photo 6**)

7 Apply a thin bead of RTV to one case half. Reassemble the two halves of the case and torque. (**Photo 7**)

8 Reinstall all electrical sensors and switches. (**Photo 8**)

9 Reinstall output flange yokes and torque to specification. (**Photo 9**)

Inspecting Front Wheel Bearings and Locking Hubs

To connect the front wheels with the front drive axles on a four-wheel drive vehicle, some sort of hub locking mechanism must be used. These vehicles have either automatic locking hubs or manual locking hubs. All of these systems require periodic service and inspection to maintain functionality and prevent early failure of these parts.

To inspect front wheel bearings and locking hubs, follow the steps in **SKILL DRILL 26-29**:

1 Raise the front axle off the ground and secure it with jack stands. Loosen the lug nuts, and remove the tire and wheel assembly.

2 Remove the screws from the manual locking hub and pull the hub from the axle.

3 Inspect the O-ring on the back side of the cover, and if necessary replace it.

4 Remove the wire ring from the hub, and pull the retaining plate out of the hub.

5 Remove the snap ring from the axle.

6 Remove the locking sleeve from the hub.

7 Remove the bearing retaining nut(s) from the hub assembly to expose the bearings, and remove the hub and rotor assembly for inspection.

8 Knock out the seal and rear bearing for inspection. Replace the seal with a new one when reassembling.

9 Clean and inspect the bearings closely for brinelling and bluing due to heat concerns, and replace as necessary.

10 Pack and install new bearings and races using the proper bearing race driver.

11 Install the new seal assembly. *Note:* When replacing the seal, be sure to put some grease on the spring inside the seal to prevent it from coming off when the seal is driven into the hub.

12 Reinstall the hub and rotor on the axle, and place the outer wheel bearing in the hub.

13 Thread the bearing adjusting nut on by hand.

14 Set the wheel bearing preload following the manufacturer's specifications using the proper tool.

15 Install the locking washer over the adjusting nut.

16 Thread the lock nut up against the locking washer and tighten to the specified torque. If necessary, bend the lock tang up against the locking nut.

17 Install the locking sleeve.

18 Install the retaining plate and wire clip.

19 Install a new O-ring on the hub cover, and reinstall the hub cover on the axle.

20 Tighten the hub cover screws to the manufacturer's specifications.

21 Road test the vehicle to ensure that it was repaired properly.

Inspecting, Removing, and Replacing Front-Wheel Drive Front Wheel Bearings

Wheel bearings on a four-wheel drive vehicle operate in severe conditions such as puddles, dust and dirt, as well as jarring terrain, all of which can cause wheel bearings to go bad and need replacement. Most manufacturers suggest periodic inspection of the bearings and in some cases, preventive maintenance consisting of disassembly, cleaning, inspecting and repacking. When the scheduled maintenance chart or if looseness is present in the bearings, they must be removed and inspected to determine whether they need to be replaced, or just cleaned and repacked with grease.

Wrap-up

Ready for Review

▶ Without a set of gears, flexible joints, and shafts to transfer the power from the engine and transmission, the vehicle would not be able to propel itself up hills, handle turns, or hold itself back as it goes down hills.

▶ In a conventional rear-wheel drive vehicle, the engine and transmission are mounted longitudinally at the front.

▶ Vehicles with rear- or mid-mounted engines normally use a transaxle and transfer the drive to the road wheels by independent half-shafts.

▶ The front-engine front-wheel drive vehicle typically, but not always, uses a crosswise-mounted (transverse) engine coupled to a transaxle.

▶ CV joints allow for smoother transfer of power and allow for the vehicle to turn more tightly without the joint binding.

▶ CV joints are most often used on the half-shafts of front-wheel drive vehicles and may be mounted at the end of the drive axles in some rear-wheel drive vehicles.

▶ The most common type of joint is the universal joint or simply "U-Joint" (the correct term for it is a Hooke's joint).

▶ The driveshaft itself allows power transfer from one component to another such as from the transmission output shaft to the differential and drive axles.

▶ The rear-wheel driveshaft transfers the power from the transmission to the final drive at the rear of the vehicle.

▶ Since the maximum length of a driveshaft is approximately 72" (183 cm), to prevent twisting from the torque output, two or more sections may be used.

▶ The front section of the two-piece driveshaft is supported at its rear end by a center bearing, called the carrier bearing.

▶ The U-joint is capable of working at a maximum angle of 3 degrees; beyond this, vibration and damage will result from U-joint binding.

▶ When working with a two-piece driveshaft or a splined driveshaft, it is critical that the yokes of the driveshaft (the portion of the shaft that has the holes in it for the U-joint end caps to fit into) line up with each other from one end of the driveshaft to the other.

▶ In front-wheel drive vehicles, the driveshafts transfer the drive directly from the differential inside the transaxle to the front wheels.

▶ A front-wheel drive transaxle typically does not place the differential directly in the center of the vehicle; instead it is offset to one side since it is bolted to the end of the transversely mounted engine.

▶ Torque steer is caused by the flexing of the longer half-shaft, resulting in lower torque to one side than the other, creating the pulling condition. To combat this condition, many manufacturers use an intermediate shaft.

▶ The differential provides the means of transferring power from the driveshaft (propeller) to the drive wheels, while allowing the vehicle to turn smoothly.

▶ Final drives can be found in axles either at the front or rear of the vehicle or can be found in the transaxle of a front-wheel drive vehicle.

▶ A ring gear and pinion gear located in the final drive transfer power through 90 degrees and provide a final gear reduction to the driving road wheels.

▶ The transfer case or power take-off (PTO) allows the transfer of power to the front and rear axles.

▶ Limited slip differentials allow normal differential action under normal driving conditions, but when road conditions are not normal, the limited slip differential reduces or prevents differential action so that a wheel cannot spin freely.

▶ Helical-geared limited slip differentials respond very quickly to changes in traction. They also do not bind from friction in turns and do not lose their effectiveness as wear develops in the clutch-style units.

▸ There are different final drive setups. Some are semi-floating and others are full floating axle assemblies. The difference is how they are attached to the final drive.

▸ The purpose of axle seals is to maintain the required amount of oil in the differential to maintain quiet operation of the differential and related parts and to ensure lubrication for the bearings and gears.

▸ The transmission control module (TCM) manages line pressures, shift functions, etc., and even incorporates a "self-healing" adjustment capability, along with the ability to memorize driver preferences/behaviors.

▸ Proper diagnosis of vibration, noise, and other problems can keep a vehicle running and lasting longer. Always ask clarifying questions when a customer complains of noises or vibrations.

Key Terms

backlash clearance The amount of movement between the pinion teeth versus the ring teeth.

beam-type axle A rear-wheel drive axle assembly that has a solid tube incorporating the differential gears

brinelling Damage done to the surface of a bearing caused by excessive load, which exceeds the limit of the bearing material, typically from shock loads.

companion flange A splined flange that transmits power from the drive shaft to the pinion gear.

constant-velocity (CV) joint A joint used to transmit torque through wider angles and without the change of velocity that occurs in u-joints..

crush sleeve A collapsible spacer between the bearings that provides a means of maintaining a preset torque on the pinion nut.

dead axle An axle that does not have the capability to drive the vehicle. It is usually found on the rear of front-wheel drive vehicles.

double Cardan joint A type of joint that uses two Cardan joints housed in a short carrier and that reduces the change in velocity of a single Cardan joint by using the second joint to cancel out the changes in velocity of the first joint.

drive axle See *live axle*.

drive line angularity The relationship of the drive-shaft to the component that the driveshaft attaches, measured in degrees of angle.

fixed-type joint A joint that does not slide to allow for shaft lengthening or shortening; it simply allows for angle changes as the suspension moves.

full floating axle An axle that does not support any weight; if removed, the vehicle will still roll on its wheels.

helical-geared limited slip differential A type of differential that responds very quickly to changes in traction and that does not bind from friction in turns or lose its effectiveness since there are no clutches.

Hooke's joint A joint that consists of a steel cross with four hardened bearing journals, mounted on needle rollers in hardened caps, which locate the cross in the eyes of the yokes. The cross swivels in the yokes as the drive is transferred across the joint.

hypoid bevel gear A special design of spiral bevel gear, with the centerline of the pinion below the centerline of the ring gear.

limited slip differential A differential assembly that transmits power to both wheels when one is on a slippery surface, but will still allow slippage on cornering and turns.

live axle An axle that is powered and can move the vehicle. It is usually found on the rear of rear-wheel drive vehicles.

locking hub four-wheel drive front axle hubs that are manually locked or unlocked by turning the knob on the hub.

longitudinal The orientation of the engine in which the front of the engine is facing the front of the vehicle. It is most commonly found in rear-wheel drive vehicles.

plunge-type joint The inner joint on the half shaft that allows for changes in shaft length.

power take-off (PTO) A device attached to the transmission that is gear driven and can be used to run accessories such as winches and towing equipment. It can also refer to the gears that send power to the rear axle in a predominantly front wheel drive vehicle.

Rzeppa joint A type of fixed constant velocity joint that has an inner race, six steel ball bearings, a bearing cage, and an outer race.

semi-floating axle An axle that carries the weight of the vehicle; if removed, there is no way to connect the wheel to the vehicle.

side gear A gear that is splined to the axle shaft and meshes with the spider gears and allows the axles to rotate at their own speeds when cornering and turning.

sliding spline driveshaft A two-piece driveshaft that is joined in the middle with splines. The driveshaft can slide on itself to increase or decrease in length.

slip yoke Part of a two-piece driveshaft that is splined and allows for a change in length of the shaft as the suspension compresses and rebounds.

speedy sleeve An aftermarket repair kit that consists of a thin metal sleeve that fits tightly over the seal surface of the axle, providing a new, undamaged surface for the seal to ride against.

three-quarter floating axle An axle on which there is only one wheel bearing which bears the weight of the vehicle, but the axle prevents the wheel from tipping inward or outward.

torque steer A condition in which the vehicle pulls to one side during hard acceleration.

transfer case A component that is bolted to the back of the transmission and connects the front and rear axles via the driveshafts.

transverse The orientation of the engine in which the front of the engine is facing the side of the vehicle.

tulip/tripod joint A constant velocity joint that has three equally spaced fingers shaped like a star. This configuration allows in-and-out movement of the shaft while allowing flexing.

universal joint (U-joint) A cross-shaped flexible joint on which caps fit over the ends of the cross. Needle bearings fit between the ends of the cross and the caps, allowing the caps to rotate smoothly.

viscous coupling An silicone clutch assembly used in all-wheel drive differentials to provide a slight amount of differential action for control of axle rotational speeds.

ASE-Type Questions

1. Tech A says that viscous clutch oil should generally be changed at regular intervals. Tech B says that if a viscous clutch fails, it should be replaced. Who is correct?
   a. Tech A
   b. Tech B
   c. Both A and B
   d. Neither A nor B

2. Tech A says that all-wheel drive vehicles have a differential in the middle of the drive train. Tech B says that many all-wheel drive vehicles incorporate a viscous clutch in the center differential. Who is correct?
   a. Tech A
   b. Tech B
   c. Both A and B
   d. Neither A nor B

3. Tech A says that all front wheel hubs lock automatically. Tech B says that all front wheel hubs lock manually. Who is correct?
   a. Tech A
   b. Tech B
   c. Both A and B
   d. Neither A nor B

4. Tech A says that some front differentials are operated by a vacuum motor. Tech B says that some front differentials are operated by electric motors. Who is correct?
   a. Tech A
   b. Tech B
   c. Both A and B
   d. Neither A nor B

5. Tech A says that part-time four-wheel drive does not use a transfer case. Tech B says that a viscous clutch is located in the rear axle. Who is correct?
   a. Tech A
   b. Tech B
   c. Both A and B
   d. Neither A nor B

6. Tech A says that constant-velocity joints are used on some four-wheel drive vehicles. Tech B says that a slip joint is part of a driveshaft. Who is correct?
   a. Tech A
   b. Tech B
   c. Both A and B
   d. Neither A nor B

7. Tech A says that a limited slip differential causes spring loaded clutch plates to provide torque to both wheels. Tech B says that wrong tire sizes can affect the transfer case operation. Who is correct?
   a. Tech A
   b. Tech B
   c. Both A and B
   d. Neither A nor B

8. Tech A says that some transfer cases have a chain inside them to transfer torque to the wheels. Tech B says that the fluid level in a transfer case should be within ¼ inch of the bottom of the fill hole. Who is correct?
   a. Tech A
   b. Tech B
   c. Both A and B
   d. Neither A nor B

9. Tech A says that the drive train in some all-wheel drive vehicles are controlled by the PCM/TCM. Tech B says that some all-wheel drive vehicles can activate the wheel brake unit on a wheel that is spinning because it lost traction. Who is correct?
   a. Tech A
   b. Tech B
   c. Both A and B
   d. Neither A nor B

10. Tech A says that u-joints can make a chirping or squeaking nose when they are going bad. Tech B says that u-joints are typically used on front wheel drive axles to provide torque through all angles of steering. Who is correct?
    a. Tech A
    b. Tech B
    c. Both A and B
    d. Neither A nor B

SECTION V

Steering and Suspension

CHAPTER 27

Servicing Wheels

Knowledge Objectives

After reading this chapter, you will be able to:
1. Explain the principles of tire distortion, center of gravity, and wheel offset. (pp 782–784, 786)
2. Describe the components that compose a vehicle's wheel. (pp 784–789)
3. Describe the components of a vehicle's tire. (pp 784–789)
4. Describe the types of tire construction. (p 789)
5. Explain how to decipher the tire markings on the sidewall of each tire. (pp 791–792)
6. Describe the common safety features found on today's tires. (pp 793–796)
7. Describe the components of a standard preventive tire service program. (pp 796–801)
8. Describe the common tire and wheel issues that a driver may experience. (pp 801–802)

Skills Objectives

After reading this chapter, you will be able to:
1. Use a tire pressure gauge. (pp 802–804)
2. Adjust the tire pressure. (pp 804–805)
3. Check for tire wear patterns. (pp 805–806)
4. Rotate the tires. (pp 807–808)
5. Dismount a tire. (pp 808–811)
6. Replace a rubber press-fit valve stem. (pp 811–812)
7. Replace a screw-in valve stem. (pp 812–813)
8. Mount a tire. (pp 813–816)
9. Dismount, inspect, and remount a tire and wheel with a tire pressure monitoring system (TPMS). (pp 816–819)
10. Balance a tire. (pp 819–821)
11. Use the spray bottle method to determine the location of air loss. (pp 822–823)
12. Use the dunk method to determine the location of air loss. (p 823)
13. Patch a tire. (pp 823–825)
14. Measure tire runout. (pp 826–827)
15. Measure wheel runout. (pp 827–828)
16. Measure axle flange or hub runout. (pp 828–830)
17. Inspect, diagnose, and calibrate the TPMS. (pp 830–831)

Introduction

The wheel and tire assembly is the only point of contact between the vehicle and the road surface. The entire vehicle literally rests on the wheel and tire assembly. The contact between the tire and the road surface plays a large role in determining how a vehicle handles and rides. Today's newer, lightweight vehicles are more sensitive than ever to minor tire or wheel issues. Poorly maintained wheels and tires will decrease effective handling, fuel economy, and ride quality and increase the potential for accidents or breakdowns.

Paying attention to the wheels and tires can also assist in identifying problems with other vehicle systems, particularly in steering and suspension systems. The wear patterns on a tire correlate with damage to particular vehicle components. Overlooking the wheel and tire assembly may result in missed faults, leading to larger issues and associated costs. It is critical that you be familiar with each part of the wheel and tire assembly and possess the skills necessary to identify and correct problems associated with them.

Principles

Tires and wheels work together to allow the vehicle to roll smoothly down the road. Tires by themselves have very little rigidity; they flex and deform whenever a force is put against them. On the other hand, wheels are very rigid and have no way of absorbing the unevenness of the road surface, so driving would be annoying were they used by themselves. Also, since wheels have a low coefficient of friction, traction would be almost nonexistent. But when you pair a tire with a wheel, you get the rigidity needed to provide directional control (from the wheel), and you get flexibility and traction to grip the road surface while smoothing out the bumps in the surface of the road (from the tire).

Tires on most passenger vehicles are called pneumatic tires because they are filled with pressurized air, which gives them support. Some vehicles, such as forklifts, may use solid rubber tires. These tires are not susceptible to punctures, so they are used where tire hazards are present such as garbage dumps or construction sites. Early pneumatic tires were called tube-type tires because they used an inner tube inside the tire to seal the air in the tire/wheel assembly. Recent vehicles use tubeless tires; these tires are designed to seal tightly to the wheel in such a way that the pressurized air does not leak out.

The air pressure gives the tire its shape when the weight of the vehicle is sitting on it. Air pushes on the entire inside surface of the tire, pushing it outward. Tires on many vehicles are inflated to about 32 pounds per square inch (psi). This means that the air pressure is pushing against every square inch of the inside of the tire. It would not be unreasonable to say there is approximately 1600 square inches of surface area inside a typical passenger car tire. So 32 psi multiplied by 1600 square inches equals 51,200 pounds (lb) of force trying to expand the tire. So why doesn't the tire expand like a balloon? It has lots of strong reinforcing strands molded into it, which gives it strength while still allowing it to be flexible. So the air inside the tire pushes outward on the tire, stretching the strands tightly, which prevents the tire from ballooning. The relatively high pressure in the

You are the Automotive Technician

A customer brings her 2010 Dodge Caravan to the dealership with the tire pressure light on. The customer tells you that the tires are filled with nitrogen, and on the drive to the dealership, the van pulled to the right. You bring the vehicle into the shop and notice that the right front tire looks low, and the pressure reads 22 psi. You inspect the tire and notice a small screw embedded near the center of the half-worn tread. You mark a big "X" across the tire (centered on the screw) to mark the hole. Air leaks out as you pull the screw out of the tire. You remove the wheel from the vehicle in preparation for repairing the tire.

1. How can you identify if tires have been inflated with nitrogen?
2. What is the proper method of repairing a tire?
3. What are some conditions when a tire should not be repaired?
4. What happens if you repair a high performance speed rated tire?
5. What must be done once the tire is repaired and back on the vehicle?

tire stiffens the tire so that it will support the weight of the vehicle. This design also explains the appearance of a tire that is substantially low on air pressure: The bottom will appear flat, and the sidewall relatively soft. The air pressure is not fully stretching the cords in the tire.

Tire Distortion

During cornering, centrifugal force acts on a vehicle to produce a **side force**. The side force is the pressure on the wheel that pushes it toward the outside or inside of the rim as the vehicle makes a turn. In most instances, the contact of the tire with the surface of the road produces enough friction to prevent this force from actually pushing the wheel and tire sideways across the road surface. However, when the roads are icy, the tire is unable to grip the road surface adequately to generate enough friction to overcome the side force, resulting in the wheels and vehicle skidding sideways during a turn. Without the resistance created by friction, side force will cause the vehicle to continue in a straight line.

The tire provides this opposing force by being able to distort while still gripping the road **FIGURE 27-1**. Since the tire's construction makes it elastic, it exerts a force, called **cornering force**, that acts between the tread and the road surface. It pulls the distorted rubber back to its normal position. The tire's sideways distortion makes the vehicle follow a path at an angle to the direction the road wheel is pointing. This is called the **slip angle**. As the cornering force increases, so does slip angle.

When a vehicle is being driven into a turn with a decreasing radius, both slip angle and cornering force increase, until a point is reached where the tire slides. At this point, the only resistance comes from sliding kinetic friction across the road surface. The tire grips again only when the vehicle has slowed or the wheels are not turned so sharply—that is, when the side force is reduced to a level the tire can withstand without skidding.

Since both front and rear tires develop a slip angle in a turn, the vehicle's path is determined by the steering of the front tires and the slip angles of both the front and the rear tires. These slip angles depend on the weight distribution within the vehicle, the wheelbase, the tire track, and the overall length of the vehicle. The weight distribution is affected by whether the engine is front, mid, or rear mounted. Another factor is if the vehicle is front- or rear-wheel drive.

During cornering, centrifugal force puts more weight on the outside wheels. Acceleration puts more weight on the rear wheels. Deceleration or braking puts more weight on the front wheels. In a turn, centrifugal force tries to push the vehicle away from the corner. This is resisted by the cornering force of the tires. The tires' slip angles may not be equal, due to the cornering, deceleration, or acceleration forces acting on them. When the front slip angles are larger than the rear slip angles, the vehicle is said to be in an **understeer** condition, which is referred to as the vehicle "pushing" in the corners. Understeer results in the front of the vehicle being pushed toward the outside of the corner. At its worst, it causes the vehicle's front wheels to slide toward the outside of the corner and into the curb or off the track. **Oversteer** is when the rear slip angle is larger than the front slip angle; it is referred to as the vehicle being "loose" in the corners. Oversteer tends to cause the rear of the vehicle to slide toward the outside of the corner. In this situation, the rear wheels lose traction, typically resulting in the vehicle spinning out. When both the front and the rear tires have equal amounts of slip angle, the vehicle is said to have **neutral steer**, in which case the vehicle tends to go in the direction that the front tires are pointing.

Center of Gravity

The center of gravity is the balance point of the entire vehicle. Its actual position depends on location of the engine and transmission **FIGURE 27-2**. It is always located above

FIGURE 27-1 Tires distort during cornering, providing an opposing force that allows a vehicle to make a turn.

FIGURE 27-2 The vehicle's center of gravity.

the road surface and between the tires. When a vehicle is cornering, this is the point through which all centrifugal force is assumed to act. Its position is determined by the load carried by the front and rear wheels—that is, by how weight is distributed. In a typical rear-wheel drive vehicle, the weight distribution is approximately 60% fore and 40% aft; 60% of the weight is carried on the front wheels, 40% on the rear, and the center of gravity is closer to the rear than the front. On a typical front-wheel drive vehicle, the weight distribution is approximately 75% fore and 25% aft. Lateral, or side-to-side, weight distribution can be expressed in the same way and is affected by things like the location of the fuel tank and battery.

Every vehicle has static weight distribution, whether it is at rest or traveling in a straight line at a steady speed. This distribution is changed laterally by centrifugal force when the vehicle is turning and in a fore-and-aft direction during acceleration or braking.

Wheels and Tires

Wheels are usually made from pressed steel or cast aluminum alloy. They are lightweight, yet strong enough to withstand normal operational forces. Alloy wheels are popular because of their appearance and because they are lighter than steel wheels. Aluminum is a better conductor of heat, so alloy wheels can dissipate heat from the brakes and tires more effectively than steel. Alloy wheels are often called mag or magnesium wheels, but wheels made of magnesium are rarely used on vehicles.

The terms wheel and rim are often used synonymously. Technically, the **rim** of a wheel is the outer circular lip of the metal on which the inside edge of the tire is mounted **FIGURE 27-3**. The purpose of the rim is to hold and seal the tire to the wheel.

Rim width is the distance across the **rim flanges** at the **bead seat**. The bead seat is the edge of the rim that creates a seal between the tire bead and the wheel. The rim flange is the exterior lip that holds the tire in place. The rim diameter is the distance across the center of the rim from bead seat to bead seat. The width of the rim and the diameter are traditionally stated in inches, although some are stated in millimeters.

Most passenger vehicle **wheel rims** are of the **drop-center** design. In drop-center rims, the inner section sits

FIGURE 27-3 Rim of the wheel.

lower than the sides **FIGURE 27-4**. This design allows for tire removal and fitting. The drop-center rim is made in one piece and is permanently fastened to the wheel disc. The drop center is used for mounting and demounting the tire onto the rim. When inflated, the tire is locked to the rim by tapering the bead seat toward the flange, or more commonly by safety ridges or humps, close to the flange.

An important feature in a rim is the location of the drop center in the rim. The drop center can be closer to the front of the wheel or the rear of the wheel, depending on the desired position of the wheel relative to the axle flange. In most stock wheels, the drop center is closer to the front side of the wheel. In **deep dish wheels**, the drop center is closer to the rear of the wheel **FIGURE 27-5**. Since the drop center is crucial to removing the tire from the wheel, the side of the wheel that is closest to the drop center is the side the tire should be removed from. In fact, it is virtually impossible to remove the tire from the side of the wheel farthest from the drop center.

FIGURE 27-4 Drop-center rim.

FIGURE 27-5 Deep dish wheel.

With safety in mind, manufacturers and legislators are insisting that passenger cars and light trucks be equipped with safety-type drop-center rims. **Safety-type drop-center rims** have a slight ridge, or hump, at the inside edge of the bead ledges. This ridge helps to hold the tire beads in place when the tire goes flat. In the event of sudden deflation, or blowout, safety ridges prevent the tire from moving down into the well. This helps maintain control of the vehicle while the driver is braking.

Rims can be made from two sections of pressed steel—a flange or disc that is drilled for the wheel fasteners and the rim. The rims for passenger vehicles are usually the **steel-disc type**. The disc may be solid, but the major manufacturers place holes in them to reduce the disc's weight and to provide ventilation for cooling the brakes. The disc is either welded or riveted to the rim and bolted to the axle or axle flange. Additional types of rims can be found in TABLE 27-1.

> ### TECHNICIAN TIP
>
> The tire must be an exact fit on the rim to fulfill a number of functions:
>
> - To ensure that the narrow contact area between the beads of the tire and the rim will seal the air in a tubeless tire.
> - To transfer all the forces between the tire and the wheel, without slipping or chafing.
> - To ensure that the friction between the tire and the rim prevents the tire from turning on the rim.

TABLE 27-1: Types of Rims

Type	Purpose
Steel rims	Rims that can be painted or chromed. Generally used on bottom-of-the-line vehicles.
One-piece alloy rims	Rims that are constructed in one piece including the well to facilitate the mounting and dismounting of the tire.
One-piece alloy billet rims	Rims that are machined out of a solid piece of alloy.
Two-piece alloy rims	Rims that are constructed as two separate pieces of aluminum, one being the center piece and the other a mounting flange, that are welded together.
Multipiece alloy rims	Rims that are constructed by welding together several separately molded pieces.
Custom rims	Rims that are built to suit the specific, unique needs and requirements of the customer.
Spinning rims (spinners)	Rims that are constructed with a piece that rotates independent from the wheel. High-speed roller bearings placed within the rim create the piece's movement.
Split rims	Rims that are constructed of a single long piece of metal formed into a circle, but the ends are not welded together (a "split" ring). The split allows removal of the outside flange so the tire can be demounted. This type of rim is common on tractor trailers and other big-wheeled trucks.
Semi-drop well rims	Rims constructed of a solid rim to allow removal of the outside flange, as in the split rim.
Drop well rims	Rims constructed with a trough in the center of the rim that is smaller in diameter than the edge by the lip where the bead of the tire seals. The trough allows the tire to be mounted on the rim.
Safety rims	Rims designed to hold the tire bead in place on the rim in the event of inadequate tire pressure.

Safety

The rim width and diameter can also be stated in millimeters. Metric rims are not interchangeable with imperial rims; nor can you fit a metric tire to an imperial rim. Conversely, you cannot fit an imperial tire to a metric rim. Doing so could result in personal injury or a vehicle accident.

Applied Math

AM-27: Distance: The technician can measure distance using a variety of devices to determine conformance to the manufacturer's specifications and tolerances.
A technician may be called upon to measure distances with a variety of devices to determine conformance of components to manufacturer's tolerances and specifications. Some examples may include measuring tire tread with a depth gauge, measuring brake pad thickness with a ruler, measuring vehicle ride height with a tape measure, measuring brake disc thickness with a vernier caliper, measuring engine valve clearance with feeler gauges, measuring crankshaft journal thickness with a micrometer, or measuring wheel runout with a dial gauge.

Wheel Offset

The offset of a wheel is the distance from its hub mounting surface to the centerline of the wheel. Offset is important because it is typically used to bring the tire centerline into close alignment with the larger inner wheel bearing, and it reduces load on the stub axle. This requires the inside of the wheel assembly to be shaped so that there is space for the brake assembly, especially disc brakes, which are typically larger in diameter than drum brakes.

The offset can be either zero, positive, or negative:

- **Zero offset**: The plane of the hub mounting surface is even with the centerline of the wheel. Vehicles manufactured in the mid-70s through the 80s were typically built with zero offset wheels.
- **Positive offset**: The plane of the hub mounting surface is shifted from the centerline toward the outside or front side of the wheel. Positive offset wheels are generally found on front-wheel drive vehicles and the newer rear-wheel drive vehicles.
- **Negative offset**: The hub mounting surface is toward the brake side or back of the wheel's centerline. Older model vehicles and specialized high-performance vehicles with deep dish wheels typically have wheels with negative offset.

Wheel Studs and Lug Nuts

Wheels are fastened to the rims by **wheel studs** and **lug nuts**. Wheel studs and lug nuts are highly stressed by loads from the weight of the vehicle and the forces generated by its motion. Wheel studs and nuts are made from heat-treated, high-grade alloy steel. The threads between the studs and the nuts are close fitting and accurately sized. All wheel nuts must be tightened to the correct torque with the proper sequence; otherwise the wheel could break free from the hub.

You must use the correct type of wheel retaining stud or nut—which include **tapered seat**, **flat seat with washer**, or **flat seat without washer** **FIGURE 27-6**—for the wheel. Tapered seat lug nuts have a tapered end that

FIGURE 27-6 **A.** Tapered seat lug nut and wheel. **B.** Flat seat with integrated washer and wheel. **C.** Flat seat with separate washer and wheel.

is placed toward the rim and fit into a matching taper in the rim to help center the wheel on the lug studs. Flat seat studs are flat at the point where it contacts the wheel. Those with washers have a washer affixed to the lug nut enabling it to turn independent from the hex part of the lug nut. When a wheel assembly is changed, it is imperative that the mating surfaces of the wheel inner hub and the axle flange mounting face are clean and free of dirt and mud. After the wheel assembly has been fitted, the **wheel retaining nuts** that hold the wheel onto the vehicle are torqued to the manufacturer's specifications. Many shops request that the customer return and have the lug nut torque rechecked within a few days or about 100 miles. If the nut/stud is overtightened, then there is a good chance that the stud can break due to overstressing, and fatigue fractures can occur.

Most lug nuts and studs are right-hand threaded, which means they tighten when turned clockwise. However, some manufacturers use lug nuts and studs with left-hand threads on the right side (passenger side) of the vehicle and right-hand lug nuts and studs on the left side (driver side) of the vehicle. The manufacturers claim that left-hand lug nuts are less likely to back off when used on the right side of the vehicle. This may or may not be true, but properly torqued lug nuts do not generally loosen up, no matter if they are left-hand or right-hand. Left-hand lug nuts can usually be identified by an "L" stamped on the end of the lug stud. When you place the socket or lug wrench over the lug nut, make sure you check for the "L." If there is one, then you will need to turn the lug nut clockwise to loosen it.

> ### TECHNICIAN TIP
>
> Don't be like the apprentice technician who was trying to get a vehicle ready for a brake job for the journeyman technician. When the journeyman came into work, the apprentice was just taking off the last wheel and the journeyman could hear the impact wrench hammering away and then the impact wrench zing to full speed. By the time he got to the apprentice, he was on the next to last lug nut. The journeyman stopped him. The apprentice said that all of the lug nuts were rusted on the studs on the right side of the car and every one broke off when he tried to loosen them. The journeyman took the impact wrench, switched directions on it, and proceeded to easily remove the lug nuts. The apprentice was quite embarrassed, especially when the other technicians in the shop started calling him "Lefty."
>
> If a lug nut does not start to loosen quickly when you are trying to remove it, always stop and try to turn it the other direction. It could be a left-hand lug nut, which you will need to turn clockwise to remove. And even if it is a right-hand lug nut, sometimes tightening it just a bit will help break loose any rust so that it will come off easier.

The **wheel center** is the part of the wheel containing the holes for the lug studs. It usually has a machined hole in the center, which accurately centers the wheel rim on the axle. In some cases, the fit of the centering hole is snug enough that it can rust in place and stick to the axle. This can require penetrating oil, a hammer, or even heat from a torch to break it loose. Always seek the assistance of your supervisor if you encounter a wheel rusted to the axle flange. The wheel center also provides the required offset from the centerline of the wheel to the face of the mounting flange.

Bolt Pattern

The bolt pattern refers to the number and spacing of the lug nuts or wheel studs on the wheel hub on the wheel rim **FIGURE 27-7**. As the studs are most often evenly spaced, the number of studs determines the pattern. For example, some smaller cars have three studs, some may have four studs, but most passenger cars have five. Pick-up trucks and large SUVs can have as many as 6, 8, or 10 studs. The exact number and pattern of studs vary depending on the vehicle type and manufacturer design.

> ### TECHNICIAN TIP
>
> Along with the bolt pattern configuration is **pitch circle diameter (PCD)**. PCD is the diameter of a circle drawn through the center of the wheel's bolt holes. It is a fixed measure set during manufacture that cannot be altered. PCD is measured in both inches and millimeters, and it also indicates the number of studs or bolts the wheel will have. One of the most common configurations has four studs and a PCD of 100 mm, hence the size 4 × 100 designation.

FIGURE 27-7 The bolt pattern refers to the number and spacing of lug nuts or wheel studs on the wheel hub on the wheel rim.

Tires

Tires are hollow, donut-shaped structures designed to provide traction to the wheel assembly and act as a cushion to absorb shock from road surfaces **FIGURE 27-8**. The air in the tire supports the vehicle's mass, and the tire tread provides frictional contact with the road surface, so the vehicle can maneuver safely. The tire itself is generally composed of the tread, plies or cords, sidewalls, inner liner, and bead. The tread is the exterior rubber portion of the tire that comes in contact with the road. It is configured in a variety of patterns based on the application of the tire, such as for driving in mud and snow. The plies or cords are the reinforcing material that gives the tread and sidewall their ability to hold their shape. The sidewalls are the lightly reinforced sides of the tire that provide lateral strength to the tire and prevent it from ballooning. They do not come into direct contact with the road. The inner liner is a covering of the casing material and seals the air in the tire. Beads are bands of steel wire coated in rubber that give the bead area the stiffness to hold the bead against the bead seat and to seal to the wheel rim. Tires can be inflated through a valve assembly located in the wheel.

Modern tires are made from a range of materials. The rubber used is mostly synthetic, with carbon black added to increase strength and toughness. When used in the tread, this combination gives the tire a long life. Natural rubber is weaker than the synthetic version, so it is used mainly in sidewalls.

Cords of synthetic strands or fabric have high **tensile strength**. Tensile strength is a measure of the innate strength of a material. Because of their high strength, the cords resist stretching but are flexible under load. The cords are placed in parallel and impregnated with rubber to form sheets called plies or belts. Plies have high strength in one direction and are flexible in other directions. When cotton was used as a cord, the number of plies or layers in a tire was a measure of the tire's strength. Newer cord materials use fewer plies. A modern steel-belted radial tire with a six-**ply rating** may have six plies in the tread but just two plies in its sidewall. Having fewer plies makes the tire more flexible. Higher numbers of plies make a tire's response to bumps harsher, but the tire can withstand punctures much better.

The bead of the tire is made of a cord of high-tensile steel coated with rubber. The end of the plies is wrapped around the bead, which is then wrapped in rubber to stop chafing of the plies and also to seal the bead against the rim. The length of the wire used for the bead determines the rim diameter of the tire. Belts that reinforce the tread area of the tire are typically made of braided, high-tensile steel wire, but they can also be made of rayon or polyester. The inner liner of a tubeless tire is made of soft rubber. The inner liner must be flexible and airtight.

Applied | **Math**

AM-28: Distance: The technician can use standard and metric measurement instruments to determine correct sizes and distances.
In practice, both standard and metric measurement instruments must be used to determine correct sizes and distances because specifications may be published in either scale. Some common examples may include, measuring the diameter of wheel rims, which are almost universally measured in inches, and measuring the pitch circle diameter (PCD) of wheel studs, which are usually quoted in millimeters.

Tire Valve Stems, Cores, and Caps

The **tire valve** is a specially designed opening that allows a tire to be inflated and then automatically closes to prevent air from escaping. It consists of a **valve stem**, into which a **valve core** is threaded, and it is used on virtually all automobile tires. The valve stem is a rubber or steel piece that attaches the valve to the rim of the tire. The valve core is a **Schrader valve** (a spring-loaded, one-way valve) **FIGURE 27-9**. The primary function of the **valve stem cap** is to assist in keeping debris out of the valve stem, which could cause the valve stem core to fail. The valve stem cap is removed to check air pressure and to inflate or deflate the tire. Some valve stem caps come with a built-in tool for tightening or loosening the valve core. In wet climates, the valve stem cap keeps mud, water, and ice from entering the valve stem. The valve stem cap can also slow a leak from a valve core, but will not stop a leak completely. In newer vehicles, a green valve stem cap indicates that the tire is filled with nitrogen and, to prevent contamination, should only be topped off with nitrogen.

FIGURE 27-8 The tire itself is generally composed of the tread, sidewalls, inner liner, and bead.

FIGURE 27-9 Components of a tire valve.

Types of Tire Construction

Although there are two types of tire construction—**bias-ply** and **radial**—radial tires are by far the most common. In fact, one tire retailer estimates that 98% of the tires sold today for passenger vehicles are radial tires.

Bias-Ply Tires

The bias-ply tire is the older form of tire and is still in use on some trailers and off-road vehicles, primarily because of a slightly lower cost and their more durable construction. Bias tire construction uses body ply cords extended diagonally from bead to bead at 30- to 40-degree angles with successive plies laid at opposing angles, resulting in a crisscross pattern onto which tread is applied. This design provides a strong, stable casing, but with relatively stiff sidewalls. However, during cornering, stiff sidewalls can distort the tread and partially lift it off the road surface, which reduces the friction between the road and the tire.

Radial Tires

Radial tire construction uses the same body ply cords, but they are laid across the tread extending from bead to bead, so the cords end up parallel to each other at approximately 90 degrees to the centerline of the tread. Radial tires are extremely durable and maintain good traction with the road, providing better steering control. Most passenger cars now use radial tires, as do most four-wheel drive vehicles and heavy transport vehicles.

> **TECHNICIAN TIP**
>
> The bias-ply tire's stiff sidewalls can make tires run at a higher temperature. This is because, as the tire rotates, the body ply cords in the plies flex over each other, causing friction and heat. A bias-ply tire that overheats can wear prematurely. At the same time, stiffer sidewalls can resist punctures from sharp rocks or other objects better than a radial tire.

Radial ply tires have much more flexible sidewalls because of their construction **FIGURE 27-10**. They use two or more layers of **casing plies**, the cords that give the tire shape and strength, with the cord loops, which are loops of high-strength material (typically polyester) inlaid with rubber, running radially from bead to bead. The sidewalls are more flexible because the casing plies do not cross over each other; however, a bracing layer of two or more steel belts running horizontally must be placed under the tread to strengthen and stabilize the tire. The cords of the bracing layers may be of fabric or steel and are placed at 12 to 15 degrees to the circumference line. This design forms triangles where the belt cords cross over the radial cords. The stiff bracing layer links the cord loops together to give stability when accelerating or braking, and it prevents any movement of the cords during cornering. The cord plies flex and deform only in the area above the road contact patch. There are no heavy plies to distort, and flexing of the thin casing generates little heat, which is easily dispersed. A properly inflated radial tire runs cooler than a comparable bias-ply tire, increasing tread life. Also, a radial tire has less rolling resistance as it moves over the road surface, increasing fuel economy.

FIGURE 27-10 Radial tires.

> **TECHNICIAN TIP**
>
> The sidewalls of radial tires bulge where the tire meets the road, making it difficult to estimate the inflation pressure visually. Tire pressure needs to be checked with an accurate tire gauge. Using the correct inflation pressures extends the life of the tire and is vital for safety. Sidewalls of an underinflated tire flex too far, which causes the center section of the tread to be pushed up and away from the road surface. This causes wear at the shoulders of the tire. In an overinflated tire, the sidewalls are straightened, which pulls the edges of the tread away from the road and causes wear at the center of the tread.

Tread Designs

Differing tread patterns give manufacturers the ability to design tires for special applications, such as rainy, snowy, muddy, highway, or high-performance driving. Manufacturers spend a lot of money trying to design better tread patterns than their competitors. And when they discover a good design, it can be very profitable. Tire tread patterns can be classified with these general characteristics **FIGURE 27-11**:

- **Directional tread patterns** are designed to provide a range of attributes during particular driving conditions, such as driving in wet weather where there is a possibility of hydroplaning (sliding across water). The predominate tread pattern is mounted in such a manner as to provide maximum moisture dissipation, thereby creating a drier surface for the tire to adhere to. Specifically, these tread patterns actually pump water out from under the tire, bringing it in direct contact with the surface of the road. This type of tire can only be mounted to the wheel so that it revolves in a particular direction to correspond with the tread pattern. An arrow on the tire sidewall indicates the designed direction of forward travel.

FIGURE 27-11 Tread designs. **A.** Directional tread pattern. **B.** Nondirectional tread pattern. **C.** Symmetric tread pattern. **D.** Asymmetric tread pattern. **E.** Directional and asymmetric tread pattern.

- **Non-directional tread patterns** are designed in such a way that the tire can be mounted on the wheel for any direction of rotation. This allows the tire to be installed on either the left or the right side of the vehicle and to be mounted in multiple directions. These tires are used for general applications when the customer may not be looking for a high-performance tire. They are usually cheaper to manufacture than the specialized tires, and they allow tire stores to stock less tires.
- **Symmetric tread patterns** have the same tread pattern on both sides of the tire and are usually nondirectional tires. As the name indicates, they tend to feature treads that are similar in continuous designs across both sides of the tire tread as well as around the tire. A main feature of most symmetric tires is that they are nondirectional and thus can be fitted in either direction.
- **Asymmetric tread patterns** have a tread pattern that is different from one side of the tire to the other. They are designed to provide good grip when traveling straight and in turns. Asymmetric tires are labeled "outside" on the side of the tire that faces outward from the vehicle.
- **Directional and asymmetric tread patterns** are both directional and asymmetric, which means the tire is designed to rotate in only one direction and has one side that must face outward to ensure that the tire performs as designed under operating conditions.

Tire Markings

Tires come in a variety of sizes and ratings to accommodate the wide range of vehicles and driving situations. To help select the most appropriate tire for a particular application, tires use common sizing and rating systems. All tires meeting legislative codes must have the following information clearly marked on the sidewall:

- Manufacturer or brand name.
- International Organization for Standardization (ISO) tire class:
  - P—passenger
  - LT—light truck
  - C—commercial
  - T—temporary use as a spare wheel
  - No letter designation before the section width—either a European metric tire or an off-road tire
- Section width: Measured in millimeters from sidewall to sidewall.
- Aspect ratio: The height of the sidewall expressed as a percentage of the section width.

- Type of tire construction: R for radial; blank for bias-ply.
- Wheel diameter: Diameter of wheel from bead seat to bead seat, usually measured in inches.
- Speed rating designation: The maximum speed for which a particular tire is rated. Vehicles should not be driven in excess of their speed ratings with the exception of Z-rated tires, which are rated for speeds above 149 miles per hour (mph; 240 kilometers per hour [kph]). Note: Virtually all tires are rated for higher speeds than legal speed limits. Tire speed ratings do NOT give you legal cover for speeding! Speed ratings are as follows:
  - Q—Up to 100 mph (161 kph)
  - R—Up to 106 mph (171 kph)
  - S—Up to 112 mph (180 kph)
  - T—Up to 118 mph (190 kph)
  - U—Up to 124 mph (200 kph)
  - H—Up to 139 mph (224 kph)
  - V—Up to 149 mph (240 kph)
  - W—Up to 168 mph (270 kph)
  - Y—Up to 186 mph (299 kph)
  - Z—149 mph (240 kph) and over
- Maximum air pressure: The maximum pressure that the tire can be inflated to. This does not indicate the vehicle manufacturer's recommended inflation pressure. Always refer to the **tire placard** on the vehicle to determine proper inflation pressures.
- Load index: The maximum amount of weight that a tire can safely carry at the maximum rated tire pressure. When replacing tires, verify that the load index meets the vehicle manufacturer's specifications.
- Uniform Tire Quality Grading (UTQG) system:
  - Tread wear grade: An approximation of how long a tire will last when compared to another tire from the same manufacturer. For example, a tire rated at 450 will last approximately three times as long as one rated 150.
  - Traction grade: A representation of a tire's wet traction characteristics. From highest to lowest: AA, A, B, and C.
  - Temperature grade: A representation of a tire's ability to resist and dissipate heat. From highest to lowest: A, B, and C.
- Department of Transportation compliance symbols and serial numbers, including date of manufacture code:
  - First two letters following the letters "DOT" identify the tire manufacturer and manufacturing plant.

- The third and fourth letters are codes that indicate the tire's size.
- The final three or four letters are codes indicating manufacturer-specified characteristics.
- Week of manufacture: The first pair of digits represent the week of the year in which the tire was manufactured, starting in January.
- Year of manufacture: The last two digits represent the year of manufacture; for example, a 12 indicates a tire manufactured in 2012.

> **TECHNICIAN TIP**
>
> Radial tires are marked with the section width in millimeters, but with the rim diameter in inches.

Tire Sizes and Designations

The size of a tire must be appropriate for the vehicle application and intended use. The vehicle manufacturer designates the recommended size and load rating of the tires to be used on each particular vehicle. The bead diameter must match the rim diameter. The section width must be suitable for use on the rim and large enough to have a suitable load-carrying capacity for the vehicle. The overall tire size must allow sufficient clearance between the tire and the chassis and body components.

The section width of the tire is measured in millimeters by the tire manufacturer from sidewall to sidewall when installed on a standard wheel, inflated to its recommended pressure and without any load on it. Section width will vary from manufacturer to manufacturer, so do not assume tires with the same section width are all the same.

The **aspect ratio** of a tire is the ratio of its height to its width. It is usually given as a percentage. Information on tire aspect ratio is now included in the sidewall marking, along with the type of construction and the speed rating. The lower a tire's aspect ratio, the wider the tire is in relation to its height. An aspect ratio of 75 means the height of the sidewall is 75% as much as the section width. Generally, the higher the aspect ratio, the smoother the ride will be, but there will be more flex during corning.

Low-profile tires have very short sidewalls and can be difficult to remove and install **FIGURE 27-12**. They have an aspect ratio as low as 25. The low-profile tire improves corning performance but sacrifices a smooth ride, and there is a greater danger of wheel and suspension damage when hitting potholes. Often, low-profile tires will have a higher speed rating, as there is less centrifugal force trying to throw the tire apart.

FIGURE 27-12 Tire profile. **A.** Standard-profile tire. **B.** Low-profile tire.

Tire Ratings for Tread Wear, Traction, and Temperature

One of the markings on the sidewall of a tire is a **Uniform Tire Quality Grading (UTQG)** rating. As discussed previously, the tire's UTQG rating provides information on three aspects of the tire's durability and operational characteristics: tread wear, traction, and temperature.

The **tread wear grade** comes from testing the tire in controlled conditions. The higher the number, the longer the life expectancy of the tread as compared to another tire from the same manufacturer. Since no one vehicle will be subjected to exactly the same surfaces and at the same speeds as the controlled conditions, the number can only be an indicator of expected tread life in normal conditions. The rating is based on a percentage of the projected wear life. For instance, when looking at two tires from the same manufacturer, one tire rated at 400 has a projected life of four times that of a tire rated at 100.

> **TECHNICIAN TIP**
>
> There are many factors that influence wear, such as vehicle speed, road surface, climate, vehicle wheel alignment, and the driving characteristics of the driver. The rating can only be an indication of the anticipated wear characteristics of the tire in controlled conditions.

A **traction grade** is a letter-based indicator system. The rating is based on the tire's ability to stop a vehicle on wet concrete and asphalt in a straight-line situation. It does not indicate the tire's cornering ability. The tire traction indicators are rated from highest to lowest as AA, A, B, or C. It is important to note that the relevant rating does not indicate hydroplaning resistance, dry or snow traction capacity, or cornering capability in wet, dry, or snow conditions.

The **temperature grade** of a tire is a letter based on a test performed by the tire manufacturer and overseen by the US government. The goal of the test is to determine how well a tire stands up to heat and measures how well the tire dissipates heat. The US government uses the UTQG criteria for tire temperature ratings. The tires are graded from C (least tolerant of heat dissipation) to A (most tolerant of heat dissipation). While a C-graded tire runs hotter, it is not necessarily unsafe.

It is important to remember that these ratings are based on standardized test conditions, and the tests do not reflect tires that are operated in overloaded, under-inflated, and/or misaligned conditions. It should also be noted that one tire might be rated a low A and another a high B, so the actual operating performance differences might be relatively small.

It is not uncommon for there to be differences in UTQG ratings within a given tire design. Sometimes a particular vehicle manufacturer will require certain properties for the tires supplied to their vehicles, which can affect the ratings, both positively and negatively. Sometimes there are differences between small sizes and large sizes of tires in a given design. All of these aspects can affect the actual rating that is put on the sidewall.

Tire Date of Manufacture Coding

The **US Department of Transportation (DOT)** inspects everything and anything pertaining to transportation—

FIGURE 27-13 The DOT tire date manufacturing code is a four-digit code.

including tires. As part of DOT regulations, there must be a tire manufacture date code stamped on the sidewall of every tire. In fact, it is illegal to sell a tire intended for use on a public road within the United States without a DOT stamp. Some manufacturers mold this code on only one sidewall, so you might need to get under the vehicle and look at the inward-facing side of the tire. You will find a three- or four-digit code. This code denotes when the tire was manufactured. For safety concerns and as a rule of thumb, you should never use tires more than 6 years old. The rubber in tires degrades over time, irrespective of whether the tire is being used or not.

Reading the DOT code is relatively simple. A three-digit DOT code was used for tires manufactured before 2000. For example, 176 means that the tire was manufactured in the 17th week of the 6th year of the decade, or 1986.

For tires manufactured in the 1990s, there may be a little triangle after the DOT code. For example, a tire manufactured in the 17th week of 1996 might have the code 176Δ. After 2000, the code was switched to a four-digit code. For example, 30 11 means the tire was manufactured in the 30th week of 2011 **FIGURE 27-13**.

▶ Tire Safety Features

Flat tires are one of the leading causes of vehicle breakdowns. Generally speaking, vehicles cannot be driven with one or more flat tires. Attempting to do so will ruin a potentially reparable tire very quickly. Manufacturers address this situation in various ways. The most common is through the use of tire pressure monitoring systems to monitor the air pressure in each tire and warn the driver if one or more tires is low. Another tactic that manufacturers use is run-flat tires. These tires are designed so that they can still be driven for a reasonable amount of time when the tire pressure is low or empty. Similar to the run-flat tires, manufacturers can use self-sealing tires, which resist leaks and help maintain air pressure. The last safety feature involves the use of a spare tire, which is usually of the space-saving type, also called a temporary tire. It is designed to be used for reduced speeds and distances so that a driver can get the vehicle to a service facility. Each of these safety features will be discussed further in the following sections.

Tire Pressure Monitoring Systems

Maintaining proper tire pressure is essential for the safety and performance of a vehicle. It also plays a significant role in decreasing fuel consumption, reducing CO_2 emissions, and extending tire life. All tires lose inflation over time and, as many modern vehicles have extended service intervals, tires can become dangerously underinflated without regular checking by the vehicle driver.

In addition to increased fuel consumption and tire wear, long periods of driving with low tire pressures can cause additional stress on the tire sidewalls. This results in increased operating temperatures that can lead to premature tire failure. Tires operating with low pressures can also affect the vehicle's handling and performance. In a worst-case scenario, underinflation can lead to a tire blowout or tread separation. Because of these situations, the Transportation Recall Enhancement, Accountability, and Documentation (or TREAD) Act called for all new passenger vehicles under 10,000 lb (4536 kg) to be equipped with a TPMS by October 1, 2007.

The automated **tire pressure monitoring system (TPMS)** provides a means of reliable and continuous monitoring of the vehicle tire pressure and is designed to increase safety, decrease fuel consumption, and improve vehicle performance. A TPMS monitors the tires for low air pressure and alerts the driver when one or more tires are lower than (or in some cases, higher than) the designated thresholds. This alert can be an illuminated warning lamp or a chime. A TPMS can be fitted to all vehicles using conventional and run-flat tires. With some TPMS systems, drivers can monitor the tire pressures and temperatures from the driver's seat to ensure that their tires are properly inflated under all operating conditions. The TPMS is designed to ignore normal pressure variations caused by changes in ambient temperature.

There are two basic configurations used to monitor the vehicle's tire pressures: direct and indirect. A **direct TPMS** directly measures the tire pressure via a sensor that is installed inside each wheel, which helps protect

FIGURE 27-14 The tire pressure monitoring system (TPMS).

it from damage. There is a sensor with an antenna in each wheel that wirelessly relays the information it senses to receivers located within the vehicle **FIGURE 27-14**. The receivers send the signal to the control unit. The sensor is able to respond to a drop in pressure of as little as 2 psi (14 kilopascals [kPA]). The control unit sends an appropriate signal to the driver's information circuit or, in some vehicles, the on-board computer, which in turn illuminates a display in the vehicle's multifunction screen to warn the driver of low tire pressure in a certain wheel. An audible and visual warning instantly alerts the driver, allowing time for the vehicle to stop or be driven to a service station.

The sensors are powered by an internal battery that is designed to last between 5 and 10 years. The use of a **centrifugal switch** in the sensor allows the sensor to go to sleep when the vehicle stops, which extends battery life. When the battery goes dead, it will need to be replaced, which usually means that the entire sensor must be replaced because the battery is typically sealed inside the sensor.

> **TECHNICIAN TIP**
>
> In vehicles with a direct TPMS, the dashboard may show:
>
> - The required tire pressure
> - The actual tire pressure
> - The tire pressure status
> - The temperature of the tire
>
> In some vehicles, the driver can use the display control buttons to check the status of each tire.

A direct TPMS can be of two types: one-way communication or two-way communication. In one-way communication, the TPMS sensor can only transmit to the receiver; it cannot receive any information. In this type of system, the sensors usually use a centrifugal switch to turn them on and off to conserve the battery energy. In a two-way communication TPMS, the sensor can receive signals as well as transmit signals. This allows the control unit to send signals to wake up or cause the sensor to sleep, thus extending the sensor's battery life. The two-way communication system is more complex and expensive than the one-way system.

The wheel sensors are located inside the tire and fastened in some manner to the wheel. Many wheel sensors are integrated into a one-piece design along with the valve stem, while others are a separate unit screwed into the valve stem. The latter style uses a band or strap that fastens around the wheel in the drop center and holds the sensor in place. In a band-style wheel sensor, the sensor is typically located opposite of the valve stem **FIGURE 27-15**. When removing and replacing a tire on a wheel, you must be aware of the sensor's location and take steps to avoid damaging it.

An **indirect TPMS** indirectly monitors tire air pressure. The most prevalent indirect tire pressure monitoring systems in use today utilize the wheel speed anti-lock braking systems (ABS) to measure the difference in the rotational speed of the four wheels. A wheel that is rotating faster than the others indicates that the tire has lower pressure than the other tires. For example, if a tire loses pressure, then its rolling radius is reduced, which increases the speed of rotation. Since it is rolling faster than the other tires, the wheel speed sensor will send a slightly faster wheel speed signal for that wheel to the ABS control unit. The control unit monitors the changes in wheel speed, and when a low tire pressure failure is detected, it sends a signal to the low tire pressure light and/or chime on the dashboard.

Run-Flat Tires

The major safety benefit of **run-flat technology** is that it enables a driver to maintain vehicle control if a tire suffers a rapid pressure loss when in motion. In addition, run-flat tires enable the driver to continue the journey within specified speed and distance limits (about 50 mph [80 kph] and at least 50 miles 80 [km]). This alleviates the need to replace the wheel on the side of the road or in an unsafe area. But as with any tire, the run-flat tire cannot continue to be driven if the sidewall has been compromised or blown out. In these instances, the tire needs to be changed. A TPMS is normally mandatory for all run-flat technology applications to monitor the driveability of the vehicle's run-flat tires.

Tire manufacturers also maintain that run-flat technology usually saves weight and space by eliminating the need to carry a spare tire. However, because of their construction, they are generally between two to three times heavier than their conventional counterparts. This adds unsprung weight (weight not held up by the vehicle's springs) to the vehicle, affects the suspension, and can increase fuel consumption.

Because of the extra materials used in the construction of run-flat tires, they are also more expensive to purchase. In addition, run-flat tires are usually harsher riding and noisier in operation, which can be a disadvantage in some applications, such as in luxury cars that are expected to have a quiet, smooth ride. From a manufacturing perspective, the free space created by eliminating a standard spare wheel gives the vehicle manufacturer a range of additional design opportunities, such as providing more storage space in the trunk.

The design features of run-flat technology generally focus on two aspects of operational use: rigidity and heat resistance. The objective is for the tire to support the vehicle's weight when it is rotating with a total air loss. The sidewall is constructed with reinforced rubber and

> **TECHNICIAN TIP**
>
> Most wheels with TPMS sensors use an aluminum valve stem, which requires a nickel-plated valve core to prevent corrosion. Also, the valve stem acts as the antennae for the TPMS sensor on some applications.

FIGURE 27-15 Band type TPMS sensor.

is thicker than in conventional tires, enabling it to carry the vehicle's weight at zero pressure **FIGURE 27-16**.

The bead shape configuration of the run-flat tire is largely unchanged from conventional tires to enable compatibility with conventional rims. However, the bead wire is normally wider and reinforced to ensure a secure fit on the specialized rim, even at zero pressure. A special bead filler with low heat generation is used as part of the run-flat technology construction to help prevent excess heat buildup that can be generated with zero pressure.

The rim used with some run-flat technology tires is referred to as an **EH2 rim**. EH2 is an abbreviation for double extended hump. These rims have a wider, or more extended, safety hump than a standard safety rim to accommodate the wider and more square-shaped tire bead. The run-flat technology tire bead also has a larger diameter than the standard safety bead of a conventional radial ply tire.

Self-Sealing Tires

<u>Self-sealing tires</u> were introduced recently to commercial passenger cars. One self-sealing tire manufacturer states that its self-sealing tire is designed to repair most small tread-area punctures instantly and permanently. Self-sealing tires feature standard tire construction with the addition of a flexible and malleable lining inside the tire in the tread area. This lining serves as a puncture sealant that can permanently seal most punctures from nails, bolts, or screws up to 3/16" (or 5 mm) in diameter. Self-sealing tires first provide a seal around the object when the tire is punctured and then fill in the hole in the tread if the object is removed. Most drivers will never even know that they just had a puncture. Because these tires can still leak air from between the bead and the rim or the valve stem and the valve core, they still require a TPMS to detect any low-pressure conditions on 2008 and newer vehicles.

Space-Saver Spare Tires

Space-saver spare tires are designed for emergency use only. They are designed to get the driver to a service center to have the regular tire fixed or purchase a new one. When provided with the vehicle as part of the original manufacturer's equipment, most manufacturers warn not to exceed 50 mph (80 kph) and not to go farther than 50 miles (80 km) on the space-saver spare tire. Some vehicles have miniature or collapsible space-saver spare tires as spares. These normally require a specially charged canister for inflation when being installed. Other vehicles have small, temporary spare tires that have been inflated normally with a compressed air supply but, because of their small size, to a much higher pressure than normal road tires.

▶ Tire Service

A periodic inspection of the tires is necessary to ensure a long life. The tire pressure should be checked and adjusted on vehicles that do not have a TPMS. The tread area is inspected for cuts, flat spotting, or irregular wear patterns. The tread depth is inspected to ensure that it is above the built-in wear indicators, which indicate that the tire is at the end of its legal life and should be replaced. The sidewalls are inspected for cuts or gashes and any signs of damage from impacting solid objects such as curbs. At the same time, vehicle and tire manufacturers recommend that the tires be rotated during each oil change. Tire balance is performed when the tires are new and any time

---

> **TECHNICIAN TIP**
>
> Tire manufacturers will call their run-flat safety tire by various terminologies, but all have the same characteristics. Some run-flat tires are known as:
>
> - Run-Flat Technology (RFT) tires
> - <u>Extended Mobility Technology (EMT)</u> tires
> - Continuous Mobility Technology (CMT) tires
> - Zero-pressure (ZP) tires
>
> EMT tire sidewalls can be six times thicker than the sidewalls of traditional tires. As a result, the manufacturers claim that run-flat tires can be driven at speeds of about 50 mph (80 kph) for at least 50 miles (80 km) in a deflated condition before being damaged. These tires are not indestructible. Major damage that slices the tire casing can still result in complete tire failure.

FIGURE 27-16 Run-flat tire construction.

Specialized compound supports the side wall if the tire loses air pressure there is a customer concern regarding vibrations that are diagnosed to be caused by tire balance faults, or if tire wear indicates an out-of-balance condition.

Wheel alignment is another service that is performed on occasion. The alignment is normally checked and adjusted in cases such as when there is abnormal tire wear, when steering/suspension parts are replaced, when the vehicle does not handle/drive correctly, and after an accident that could affect the alignment. Most tire stores will try to sell an alignment when new tires are purchased, but if the old tires were wearing normally, then the new tires will wear normally also. Still, some customers like the peace of mind of knowing that the alignment was checked when they get new tires.

▶ LINK
Refer to the Servicing Suspension Systems chapter for more detailed information on wheel alignment.

Proper Tire Inflation

Tire inflation pressure is the amount of air pressure in the tire that provides it with load-carrying capacity and affects the overall performance of the vehicle. Vehicle manufacturers determine the tire inflation pressure based on the vehicle's designed load limit, which is the greatest amount of weight a vehicle can safely carry, and the vehicle's tire size. The proper tire pressure for the vehicle is referred to as the recommended cold inflation pressure. It is measured in psi or kPa. You will find this information on the tire placard expressed in psi or kPa **FIGURE 27-17**. The tire placard can be located on the A- or B-pillar door frame, in the glove compartment, or on the fuel filler flap.

Because tires are designed to be used on more than one type of vehicle, tire manufacturers list the maximum safe inflation pressure on the tire sidewall. This number is the highest amount of air pressure that should ever be put in the tire. The maximum tire pressure should never be exceeded, even when the vehicle's tire placard indicates a higher pressure. As explained earlier, 32 psi of air pressure can generate over 50,000 lb of force on a tire. If the maximum tire pressure is exceeded, the force from the air pressure generates even greater forces and can cause the tire to explode violently. Too many young technicians have lost their life when they overinflated a tire and it blew up in their face. This is one of the more dangerous situations for inexperienced technicians. It is also why it is good to use a tire cage when inflating a tire. If the tire blows up, the explosion will affect your hearing, but the cage is likely to contain most of the tire debris.

To get an accurate pressure reading, the tires must be checked when cold. The term *cold* does not relate to the outside temperature. Rather, a cold tire is one that has not been driven on for at least 3 hours or less than 1 mile (1.6 km). While driving, tires get warmer due to the heat of friction created as the tire materials flex against each other. As tires rotate and the sidewalls flex due to variations in the road surfaces, they generate heat as the layers of plies are forced to accommodate the sidewall flexing. Flexing results in heat. The heated tire materials, in turn, heat the air within the tire. As the air within the tire warms, it expands, causing the air pressure within the tire to increase. To obtain an accurate tire pressure reading, then, you must measure tire pressure when the tires are cold or compensate for the extra pressure in warm tires. Some manufacturers supply this information, while others do not.

FIGURE 27-17 Typical tire placard.

▷ TECHNICIAN TIP

According to the US Department of Energy, underinflated tires can lower gas mileage by 0.3% for every 1 psi drop in pressure in all four tires. So running them 10 psi low reduces gas mileage approximately 3%. Underinflation wastes approximately 2 billion gallons of fuel each year in the United States alone.

Nitrogen Fill

Oxygen is harmful to rubber and other tire materials. The oxygen reacts with the rubber through oxidation and causes the rubber to lose its flexibility and sealing ability. This allows oxygen to permeate the rubber and degrade it further over time. Also, as the inner liner oxidizes, more air molecules can pass through it, causing an increased rate of pressure loss. In addition, potential problems can occur from the rust and dust the corrosion of rubber produces, which clog the valve stems, causing them to leak. In recent years, some manufacturers have been filling their tires with pure or nearly pure nitrogen in hopes that the problems associated with oxygen-filled tires can be avoided. Nitrogen is an inert gas that does not react with the rubber compounds in the tire. Nitrogen generators also remove any moisture from the nitrogen gas so corrosion effects are reduced on TPMS sensors and other metal components of the wheels and tires.

Advantages for Nitrogen Fills

While both nitrogen and oxygen can permeate rubber, nitrogen does so at a much slower rate. It might take 6 months to lose 2 psi (14 kPa) with nitrogen, compared to just a month with normal air. In addition, nitrogen is far less reactive. It does not cause rust and corrosion on steel or aluminum, and it does not degrade rubber. Wheel surfaces stay smooth and clean, and rubber remains supple and resilient.

Since tires operate most efficiently when they are at the correct pressure, nitrogen filling can better maintain a tire's performance over time. It will also increase the vehicle's fuel efficiency and tire life by reducing the effects of pressure loss due to permeation. Proper tire inflation also helps prevent accidents by reducing the possibility of blowouts and maintaining maximum tire traction with the road surface.

The air that we breathe and that is typically used to inflate tires chemically consists of 78% nitrogen, 21% oxygen, and 1% other. When using pure nitrogen as an inflation gas, the composition of nitrogen increases from 78% to near 100%. To meet the standards for proper nitrogen fill means that the nitrogen level in the tire must be at 95% or higher. This typically requires two or three inflations and deflations to remove the oxygen. Nitrogen-filled tires can be identified by the green valve stem caps that are placed on the valve stem when the tire is inflated. Although tire manufacturers generally support the use of nitrogen, they do not generally mandate its use based on its ability to better retain a consistent tire pressure over a period of time.

Tire Rotation Pattern

Tire rotation service is the removal and relocation of each tire/wheel assembly on the vehicle. Each tire on the vehicle can wear differently. Regular tire rotation pro-

motes uniform tread wear, extending the life of the set of tires. Uniform tread wear can also boost the vehicle's fuel economy and increase the vehicle's performance. Each manufacturer designates the proper rotation sequence depending on whether the vehicle is front-wheel drive, rear-wheel drive, or all-wheel drive; the type of tires (e.g., directional); and whether a spare tire is involved in the rotation **FIGURE 27-18**. In general, a four-tire rotation with nondirectional tires can have one of three rotation patterns: forward-cross, rearward-cross, and X pattern. Directional tires require keeping the tires on the same side of the vehicle and generally use a front-to-rear pattern. If the directional tires are differently sized front to rear, then the tires will have to be dismounted and remounted on the wheels from the other side of the vehicle. If the vehicle uses a full-sized spare tire, then the pattern will be one of two five-tire rotations, which are variations of the four-tire forward-cross or rearward-cross pattern. Generally, it is recommended to rotate the tires on vehicles approximately every 5000 miles (8000 km) or with every oil change.

Wheel Balance

Wheels and tires are mass produced so many times that there are small (or sometimes big) imbalances manufactured into them. Also, they are not always perfectly round (concentric), but can still be sold as long as they are within the tolerances specified by the manufacturer. To complicate matters, tolerance stacking can happen. For example, the wheel hub may have an out-of-round tolerance of 0.005" (0.13 mm), the wheel may have a tolerance of 0.005" (0.13 mm), and the tire may have a tolerance of 0.025" (0.64 mm). If all of the tolerances stack up (one on top of another), then the wheel will experience balance and runout issues. Wheels and tires that are not balanced or that are out of balance generally produce an uncomfortable vibration and result in premature wearing of suspension and steering components, as well as uneven tire wear. An out-of-balance tire will cause the vehicle to vibrate at certain speeds, usually between 50 and 70 mph (80 to 113 kph). A tire is out of balance when one section of the tire is heavier or stiffer than the others. One ounce of imbalance on a front tire is enough to cause a noticeable vibration in the steering wheel at highway speeds.

There are two ways wheels can be balanced: off-car and on-car. Although most shops use off-car balancers, if the brake rotor, drum, or hub is out of balance, then a balanced wheel cannot compensate for that, so on-car balancers are used to balance the entire rotating assembly. The only problem with on-car balancing is that the wheel will need to be rebalanced when it is rotated to another

FIGURE 27-18 **A.** Forward-cross pattern. **B.** Rearward-cross pattern. **C.** X pattern. **D.** Front-to-rear pattern. **E.** Side-to-side pattern from the other side of the vehicle. **F.** Five-tire forward-cross pattern. **G.** Five-tire rearward-cross pattern.

position on the vehicle. This is one reason that most shops use off-car balancers **FIGURE 27-19**.

Tires and wheels can be balanced in three ways: static, dynamic, and road force. With static balancing, the tire's imbalance is measured when the tire is stationary. Static balancing does not take into consideration that the tire has width; thus, static balancing can address the imbalance only as it relates to how much weight is needed to counterbalance the imbalance X inches away from the center of the axle. Static balancing assumes the imbalance is centered across the width of the tire. Therefore, it can be effective only when dealing with an imbalance condition that is centered within the width of the tire. <u>Static imbalance</u> tends to cause the tire to move purely up and down. Static balancing is no longer an acceptable method of balancing tires on today's vehicles.

Dynamic balancing is performed when the tire is rotating. It takes into consideration that the tire has width; therefore the imbalance is not only a certain weight and distance from the centerline of the axle, but it can also be anywhere within the width of the tire. **Dynamic imbalance** can cause the tire to move side to side as well as up and down. Dynamic balancing is performed by placing specific amounts of weight on each side of the rim to provide the exact counterbalance needed. It can effectively account for an imbalance located anywhere within the volume of the tire/wheel assembly. Dynamic balancing is used in most shops today.

It is possible that the tire and wheel can be perfectly in balance statically and dynamically, yet the vehicle still experiences a shimmy or shake that feels just like an out-of-balance tire. This problem is caused by road force imbalance. Road force imbalance occurs when the wheel or tire is not concentric or when the tire's sidewall has uneven stiffness. As the tire rotates and contacts the surface of the road, any issues with concentricity or sidewall stiffness

will push up and down on the vehicle and simulate a tire that is out of balance. Road force balancing a tire gives the best ride quality to owners as it takes into consideration all balance factors related to the wheel and tires.

When dynamically balancing a tire using an off-car balancer, the wheel and tire assembly is mounted on the balancer. It is then spun up to speed so that the precise location and amount of the imbalance can be identified. The balancer then shows the technician where and how much weight to add on each side of the wheel. The wheel is spun up again to ensure that the weights have been affixed in the correct location and there is no more imbalance. If a road force balancer is used, then the tire is run up against a roller and any uneven forces are measured. If an uneven force is encountered, the machine will usually direct you to rotate the tire on the wheel and spin it again to see if there are any concentricity issues with the wheel. It can also tell you where the best location is for the tire on the rim to reduce road force fluctuations. After this process is completed, the wheel is reinstalled on the vehicle and the wheel nuts are torqued to the manufacturer's specification.

Applied Science

AS-47: Force, Balance/Unbalanced: The technician can demonstrate an understanding of the role of balanced and unbalanced forces on linear or rotating vehicle assemblies.

When a tire is fitted to a wheel, two imperfectly weighted components are assembled together to form a heavy, large-diameter rotational component. The chances of this assembly having perfect weight distribution are extremely small, hence the importance of adding weight in specific areas to balance the assembly.

A car wheel rotates on a central axis, supported by bearings. When a wheel turning at high speed is out-of-balance, either statically or dynamically, forces are created perpendicular to the rotational axis. These forces are typically experienced as a vibration through the steering wheel if the front wheels are out-of-balance, although in extreme cases a vibration may also be felt through the vehicle's body if the rear wheels are out-of-balance. When a wheel is in perfect balance no forces exist to interrupt the smooth rotation around the central axis.

TECHNICIAN TIP

Not all shimmies and shakes are caused by tire balance issues. Sometimes belts inside the tire carcass break, creating a lump in the tire. Every time the lump hits the road, the tire pushes back. This really is just an extreme case of road force imbalance.

FIGURE 27-19 Off-car balancer.

The majority of top-quality tires will hold their balance reasonably well, as long as the vehicle is not driven over potholes. If the driver should notice a vibration that was not there the day before, it is possible that one of the balancing weights fell off. If the driver feels the vibration mostly in the steering wheel, the problem is most likely in a front wheel. If the vibration is mostly in the seat, the problem is probably in one of the rear tires.

Wheel weights come in a variety of styles to fit different rim configurations, so you will need to verify the type of weight needed for a particular wheel. Weights come in 0.25-ounce (7-gram) increments. Although wheel weights have been primarily made of lead for decades, several states have outlawed them because of the potential environmental hazards of lead. In those states, steel weights coated with zinc or another protective layer are being used instead of lead weights. It is good practice to always use new wheel weights when balancing a tire. Do not reuse the old wheel weights, since they are likely to be thrown from the wheel when driven at freeway speeds.

TPMS Service

TPMS sensors need to be treated carefully when tires are being removed and reinstalled. Sometimes normal corrosion can damage the TPMS sensors, but more likely, a careless technician can damage the TPMS sensors by not removing the tire properly. If a sensor is damaged during a tire change, then the entire TPMS sensor unit will generally need to be replaced.

The TPMS sensor unit is a sealed component. Some models are powered by a small sealed disposable battery. These batteries are designed to last for 5 to 10 years without replacement. When the battery does expire, the sensor will need to be removed from the rim and checked. In most instances, the sensor will need to be replaced as a unit. The cost of replacing a battery compared to the sensor may not be economically viable, and new TMPS sensors may need to be installed.

Many TPMS sensors use nickel-plated valve cores in an aluminum valve stem. Never use brass valve cores or unplated brass caps; doing so can cause galvanic corrosion between the two different metals. Many TPMS sensors must be torqued into place. This torque is a very small amount measured in inch-pounds. Be careful as they are easily stripped or broken. Always use new sealing washers with TPMS sensors when removing them from a rim.

▶ Maintenance and Repair

Tires are one of the most maintenance-intensive parts of a vehicle. They require regular visual inspections, pressure inspections, and rotations. Visual inspections of the tires and wheels should be made whenever a vehicle comes into a shop for any work. It is common to check for any unusual wear patterns and for any embedded objects or other signs of damage. If the vehicle is not equipped with a TPMS, then the operator should be encouraged to check the pressure at least monthly. Another task is rotating the tires. Most manufacturers recommend that the tires be rotated at each oil change to even out the wear and extend the life of the tires. Research the vehicle and service information for more information.

Tools

To service tires in an efficient manner, you must have the appropriate tools and equipment. The basic equipment list should consist of:

- Tire pressure gauge: Used to check the air pressure in tires.
- Tread depth gauge: Used to measure the tire's tread depth.
- Valve stem tool: Used to remove and install tubeless valve stems in rims.
- Valve core tool: Used to remove and install valve cores in valve stems.
- Tire-changing machine capable of handling the range of tires that the shop stocks: If the shop handles run-flat tires, then the tire-changing machine must be designed to handle the more robust bead and sidewalls.
- Tire dunk tank: Used to locate leaks in tires and rims.
- Tire spreader: Used to spread the sidewalls of a tire for easier access during tire patching.
- Air tire buffer: Used to lightly buff the inside surface of the tire as preparation for tire patching.
- Patch stitching tool: Used to apply pressure to the patch when positioning it.
- Tire inflation cage: Used to contain the tire and rim during tire inflation in the event of a tire explosion.
- Wheel balancing machine capable of handling the range of tires that the shop stocks.
- Variety of wheel weight styles to cover the various styles of wheels.
- Wheel weight hammer: Used to remove and install wheel weights onto rims.
- TPMS reset tool: Used to reset the TPMS (not required on all TPMS-equipped vehicles).

Common Issues

Common tire and wheel issues include:

- Air loss: The most common issue with tires is air loss. Tires normally lose a small amount of air over time and require periodic refilling. Punctures occur that cause leaks of various sizes. Valve stems and tire beads can also allow air to leak from the tire.

- An out-of-balance tire or wheel: The wheel and tires must be balanced, with the weight equally distributed throughout. When a tire rotates, any points of unequal weight will cause the tire to wobble, placing stress on the shocks, bearings, and wheel assembly. Additionally, the vehicle will vibrate at speeds of about 35 mph (56 kph) and above, it will have a rough ride, and the steering wheel may vibrate. A wheel balancer is used to identify and correct wheel imbalances.
- Excessive loaded radial runout on the tire, wheel, and hub assembly: With radial runout, the tire tread moves up and down. It is caused by incorrect manufacture or by damage to the tire, such as a broken belt. Correction involves replacing the tire.
- Excessive lateral runout on the tire, wheel, and hub assembly: Runout occurs when a part of the wheel assembly becomes bent or was manufactured improperly. The result is a wobble. When lateral runout occurs, the only method for fixing it is to replace the bent or improperly manufactured component.
- Wheel trim imbalance (if fitted): The term "wheel trim" refers to any pieces attached to a wheel that are not necessary for actual wheel function, such as a hubcap or trim ring. Imbalance or wear in trim pieces is corrected by removing or replacing the part.
- Heavy pulling of a vehicle to either the left or the right while the customer is driving is an indication of these possible problems:
  - Mismatched front tire sizes or pressures
  - Tire with broken or misaligned belts
  - Out-of-alignment wheels
  - Worn suspension or steering components
  - A dragging front brake assembly

Using a Tire Pressure Gauge

There are two main types of **tire pressure gauges**: fixed workshop gauges and portable pocket-size gauges **FIGURE 27-20**. The three most popular types of pocket tire pressure gauges are the pencil type, the dial type, and the digital type. The pencil type looks similar to a pencil and contains a graduated sliding extension that is forced out of the sleeve by air pressure when it is attached to the tire valve. The dial type has a similar chuck to the pencil type but includes a graduated gauge and needle. The digital type can look like any of the others, but it gives a digital reading of the pressure and is generally the most accurate. Some digital pressure gauges can also read the temperature.

Each tire pressure gauge measures pressures in pounds per square inch (psi), kilopascals (kPa), or **bars**.

One bar is equivalent to 14.5 psi or 100 kPa. One psi is equivalent to approximately 7 kPa. Some tire pressure gauges have scales for both units of measurement.

The tire pressure will vary from vehicle to vehicle, its use, and driver preference. Recommended tire pressures are located on the vehicle's tire placard, usually on the driver door pillar. The maximum tire pressure is located on the tire sidewall. Never inflate the tire above the maximum pressure listed on the sidewall. The tire may explode or the wheel rim may give way and cause a blowout, which can easily be fatal.

FIGURE 27-20 Tire pressure gauges. **A.** Fixed workshop gauge. **B.** Portable pocket-size gauge.

> **TECHNICIAN TIP**
>
> A common mistake when inflating tires is to use the pressure listed on the sidewall instead of the tire placard. The pressure listed on the sidewall is the maximum pressure that the tire is designed to withstand and should *never* be exceeded, even when the placard lists a higher pressure! So you should always first check the placard and then verify that it is not higher than the maximum pressure listed on the sidewall. If it is, someone installed underrated tires on the vehicle.

To use a tire pressure gauge, follow the steps in **SKILL DRILL 27-1**:

1 First, remove the valve cap from the valve stem. Be sure to place it where you can find it later.

2 Fit the pencil tire pressure gauge to the valve. Make sure the graduated sleeve is seated into the gauge body, and then push the tire gauge chuck firmly onto the head of the valve. If air escapes, adjust the angle and your hand pressure until no more air leaks out.

3 When the graduated sleeve slides out, remove the gauge from the valve without moving the sleeve and examine the scale.

4 Read the bottom number, then count the marks and determine the value of each mark. Add them up to obtain the tire pressure. **(Photo 1)**

5 When using a dial gauge, check the graduations on the dial. They may be in psi, or if it is a metric gauge they will be in kPa or bar. Many gauges have

SKILL DRILL 27-1   **Checking the Tire Pressure with a Tire Pressure Gauge**

1 Remove the valve cap from the tire valve. Fit the pencil gauge to the valve. Make sure the graduated sleeve is seated into the gauge body, and then push the tire gauge chuck firmly onto the head of the valve. Read the scale and add up the numbers.

2 Attach the dial pressure gauge to the top of the valve. Adjust your hand pressure and angle so that no air escapes from the valve. When the needle has jumped, remove the dial pressure gauge from the valve and read the dial.

3 Reset the dial pressure gauge to zero by pressing the button on the neck of the dial.

4 Repeat the procedure for all wheels. Remember to replace the valve cap on each wheel as you go.

all three graduations. Once again, remove the valve cap and put it in a safe place.

6 Attach the dial pressure gauge to the top of the valve. Adjust your hand pressure and angle so that no air escapes from the valve.

7 When the needle has jumped, remove the dial pressure gauge from the valve and read the dial. Determine the value of each mark to obtain an accurate reading. **(Photo 2)**

8 Reset the dial pressure gauge to zero by pressing the button on the neck of the dial. **(Photo 3)**

9 Repeat the procedure for all wheels. Remember to replace the valve cap on each wheel as you go. **(Photo 4)**

10 For a digital pressure gauge, apply the gauge to the valve stem in the same way as the others.

Caring for the Customer

Pocket-type tire pressure gauges are inexpensive and generally more accurate than the gauges provided by service stations. Service station gauges are often damaged by weather, misuse, or being run over. There may also be a significant difference in readings between the tire pressure gauge of one service station and the gauge from another service station. If the same pocket-type tire pressure gauge is always used to check tire pressures, then there will be no variation of readings.

TECHNICIAN TIP

If you check the tire pressures after the vehicle has been driven and the tires are warm or hot, *do not* release this excess pressure. If you bleed the tire pressure down to the manufacturer's recommendation, it will be underinflated when the tire is cold or at normal operating temperature. This could cause premature wear on the tires and handling issues with the vehicle. Most tire manufacturers recommend checking tire pressures before the vehicle has been driven more than 1 mile (1.6 km).

TECHNICIAN TIP

The tire pressures should be checked when the tires are cold (around 70°F [21°C]). On average, the pressure in a tire will increase or decrease by about 1 psi for each 10°F (or 12.5 kPa for each 2°C) the tire is above or below its normal operating temperature.

11 Remove the gauge and read the digital display. On some gauges, you may have to read the pressure while the gauge is hooked up to the valve stem. No calculations are necessary.

12 Check your tire pressure readings against the specifications on the tire placard. This is usually located on the driver's door, driver's door pillar, or glove compartment lid.

Adjusting Tire Pressure

Even brand new high-quality tires lose air over time, so tire pressure needs to be adjusted periodically. It is good practice to check tire pressure at least monthly to catch a leaking tire. Vehicles that are 2008 model year and newer are required to be equipped with a TPMS, designed to monitor the pressures in each individual tire and alert the driver of a problem if a tire pressure is outside of the specified limits. These vehicles may have a specific tire inflation and TPMS reset procedure required by the manufacturer, so make sure you investigate that before inflating the tire.

Many tires are filled with nitrogen instead of regular air to reduce the amount of air that is lost over time as well as reduce oxidation of the rubber on the inside of the tire. It is best to fill these tires only with nitrogen to avoid introducing oxygen into the tire, but regular compressed air can be used in an emergency. Nitrogen-filled tires can usually be identified by a green cap on the valve stem. Nitrogen-filled tires are best topped off at the manufacturer's dealership or a tire store.

To adjust the tire pressure using a tire pressure gauge, follow the steps in **SKILL DRILL 27-2**:

1 Park the vehicle so you can reach all four tires with the air hose.

2 Check the recommended tire size and pressures on the tire placard, usually located on the driver's side door pillar or surrounding location.

3 Check the sidewall markings on the tire for the maximum operating pressure. At the same time, check the tire size and maximum load-carrying capacity of each tire, as customers sometimes install mismatched tires. If the tire markings do not meet the specifications of the vehicle, ask your supervisor for direction. Never allow a vehicle to be operated with tires that do not meet the vehicle manufacturer's specifications. Doing so can have serious safety repercussions. **(Photo 1)**

4 Check the pressure when the tires are cold. Remove the cap from the valve stem on the first tire. Use a reliable tire gauge to check the air pressure in the tire. A pocket-type pencil gauge is ideal for this purpose. A gauge attached to the tire inflator is

SKILL DRILL | 27-2 | Adjusting the Tire Pressure

1. Park the vehicle so you can reach all four tires with the air hose. Check the tire sidewall markings. At the same time, check the tire specifications and maximum load-carrying capacity.

2. Remove the cap from the tire valve on the first tire. Use a reliable tire pressure gauge to check the air pressure in the tire.

3. If you need to add air, use short bursts with the air hose so you do not overinflate the tire. Recheck the tire pressure after filling it and replace the cap on the tire valve. Repeat the process for the other tires.

less likely to be accurate as it is more vulnerable to damage. (**Photo 2**)

5. If you need to add air or nitrogen, use short bursts so you do not overinflate the tire. Recheck the tire pressure after filling it and replace the cap on the valve stem. Repeat the process for the other tires. Check the pressure in the spare tire. It may require a different amount of air pressure than the road tires. (**Photo 3**)

Checking for Tire Wear Patterns

Tires come in a wide variety of tread patterns. Patterns differ based on the manufacturer and the tire's intended purpose. For example, tires designed to wick water away from the road surface will have deep grooves angled back toward the side of the road. Racing tires will have no grooves, as the smooth tire surface grips dry road surfaces tightly, increasing friction. Regardless of the exact pattern, all four tires should be inspected regularly to ensure they are wearing evenly. Irregular wear patterns are indicative of a problem. Common irregular wear patterns encountered include feathering, one-sided wear, cupping, center wear, and edge wear.

Feathering is observed as a rib with a slightly rounded edge on one side and a sharp edge on the other. This condition can be difficult to identify visually, so the technician should run a hand across the tire in both directions, feeling for the sharp edges. Feathering is most commonly a result of the tires set with excessive toe-in or toe-out. If the tire's sharp edge is toward the outside of the treads, then the tire is toed out. If there are sharp edges toward the inside of the treads, then the tire is toed in. One-sided wear refers to ribs on one side of the tire wearing out faster than those on the other side. This type of wear indicates that the wheels are not properly aligned. Cupping is the appearance of dips around the edge of the tread, usually on just one side of the tire. It occurs when one or more suspension parts are worn or bent. Center wear is when the ribs in the middle of the tire wear faster than those on each side. It results from driving on overinflated tires. Edge wear occurs when the ribs on the outer edges of the tire wear out faster than those in the middle of the tire (the reverse of center wear). It indicates that the vehicle has been driven with the tires consistently underinflated, or the driver regularly corners the vehicle at excessive speeds.

To check for tire wear patterns, follow the steps in **SKILL DRILL 27-3**:

1. Inspect the tires for embedded objects in treads and remove them. If any object penetrates the tread, mark the hole with a tire crayon. (**Photo 1**)

2. Look for signs of wear on all tires, including the spare.

3. Check the air pressure in the tires. (**Photo 2**)

4. Check the tread depth. Most tires have wear indicator bars incorporated into the tread pattern.

SKILL DRILL | 27-3 | Checking Tire Wear Patterns

1. Inspect the tires for embedded objects in treads and remove them. If anything penetrates the tread, mark the hole with a tire crayon.

2. Look for signs of wear on all tires, including the spare. Check the air pressure in the tires (see Skill Drill 27-2).

3. Check the tread wear depth. Inspect the wear indicator bars. Tires should have at least 1/16" (2 mm) of tread remaining. If the tread is worn down to that level or below, the tires are unserviceable and must be replaced.

4. Check the tread wear patterns with the vehicle's service information to indicate the types of wear that have occurred.

5. Inspect the sidewalls of the tires for signs of weather cracking and gouges from impacts with blunt objects. Carefully examine the tread area for separation. This is usually identified as bubbles under the tread area.

6. Spin the wheel and see if it is running true. If it is wobbling as it rotates, report it to your supervisor.

Inspect the wear indicator bars. Tires should have at least 1/16" (2 mm) of tread remaining. The wear indicator bars are normally set at this depth. If the tread is worn down to that level or below, the tires are unserviceable and must be replaced. (**Photo 3**)

5. Check the tread wear patterns with the vehicle's service information to indicate the types of wear that have occurred. Causes of uneven wear can include faulty shock absorbers, incorrect front alignment angles, and out-of-balance wheels. Uneven tread and bald spots can indicate over- or underinflated tires and poor alignment. (**Photo 4**)

6. Inspect the sidewalls of the tires for signs of weather cracking and gouges from blunt objects.

7. Carefully examine the tread area for separation. This is usually identified as bubbles under the tread area. (**Photo 5**)

8. Spin the wheel and see if it is running true. If it is wobbling as it rotates, report it to your supervisor. (**Photo 6**)

Rotating the Tires

Rotating the tires to new positions on the vehicle helps to even out the tire wear, which extends their useful life. Manufacturers recommend certain tire rotation patterns for their vehicles, so always research this information for the vehicle you are working on. Many manufacturers recommend tire rotations at every oil change. This means that the tires generally should be rotated at intervals of approximately 5000 to 10,000 miles (8000 to 16,000 km). When the tires are removed, it is a good time to measure brake lining thickness and look for any leaks or damage to the brake assembly.

To rotate the tires, follow the steps in **SKILL DRILL 27-4**:

1. Consult the owner's manual for the recommended rotation sequence, and check and compare the type of tire fitted with the original specification. If the original wheels and tires have been replaced with aftermarket replacements, locate the recommendations for wheel rotation according to the aftermarket manufacturer.

SKILL DRILL | 27-4 | Rotating the Tires

1. Prepare the vehicle by removing any hubcaps or lug nut covers. If using hand tools, break loose the lug or wheel nuts while some of the weight is still on the ground, then raise the vehicle to a comfortable working position.

2. Remove the lug nuts and place them in a convenient place such as the arm of the hoist.

3. Remove the tire and wheel from the vehicle. Rotate the tires to the new specified position.

4. Reinstall the lug nuts by hand at least two full turns, making sure the correct side of the lug nut is facing the wheel. Do *not* put the nut or stud into the socket of an impact wrench and power them on directly. Tighten the lug nuts to the correct torque in the proper tightening sequence as specified in the service information.

2 Prepare the vehicle by removing any hubcaps or lug nut covers. If you are using hand tools, break loose the lug or wheel nuts while some of the weight is still on the ground, then raise the vehicle to a comfortable working position. **(Photo 1)**

3 Remove the lug nuts and place them in a convenient place such as the arm of the hoist. **(Photo 2)**

4 Remove the tire and wheel from the vehicle. Rotate the tires to the new specified position. **(Photo 3)**

5 Reinstall the lug nuts by hand at least two full turns. Make sure the correct side of the lug nut is facing the wheel; this is usually the tapered side that matches the taper in the wheel. Do *not* put the nut or stud into the socket of an impact wrench and power them on directly. This practice can lead to the lug nuts or studs going on cross-threaded. Once the lug nuts are started onto the studs, an impact wrench can be used to run the lug nuts down lightly. Do *not* tighten them with the impact wrench.

6 Tighten the lug nuts to the correct torque in the proper tightening sequence, as specified in the service information. Typically, the lug nuts are tightened in a crisscross sequence on four stud wheels and in a star arrangement for five stud wheels until all of the nuts are torqued, but there are exceptions, so refer to the manufacturer's recommendations. Normally, the lug nuts should be tightened to 50% of the recommended torque for the first stage and then to 100% of the specification at the second stage, using the same tightening sequence for the particular wheel. **(Photo 4)**

> **TECHNICIAN TIP**
>
> Lug nuts and lug bolts are designed with a specific grade (i.e., strength or amount of holding force) indicating a certain amount of stretch. Why do they stretch? Through proper torque, which stretches the bolt, stretching is what allows the threads of the stud/bolt to tightly mate to prevent them from working loose. Also, the torque listed for lug nuts is a dry torque, meaning that no lubricant should be used. Using a lubricant will cause the lug nuts to be overtorqued, which will likely result in failure.
>
> As with all types of wheels, retorquing lug nuts per the manufacturer's specifications is typically recommended between 25 and 100 miles (40 to 160 km) after the initial tightening. Always refer to the owner's manual for proper factory specifications, which take precedence over any listed recommendations.

Dismounting a Tire

Tires generally need to be removed from a rim for only a few reasons: replacing old tires with new tires, patching a leaky tire, and possibly switching between snow tires and regular tires. Since the tire is held in place by the air pressure forcing the bead of the tire into the wheel flange, repeatedly removing a tire from its wheels risks damaging the sealing surface of the bead. So it is best to remove the tire only when absolutely necessary.

Dismounting a tire is usually performed on a tire machine, which is very powerful, so use extreme care and closely follow the manufacturer's procedure. Tire machines are strong enough to break the bead loose from the rim as well as hold the rim while the bead is forced over the flange during removal and installation. This means the tire machine has several operations that you must become familiar with. Since different machines have different operating parameters, make sure you understand the manufacturer's specified operating procedure.

The turntable jaws on the tire changer can hold the rim by grasping it from the outside or the inside. When mounting an alloy rim, it is normal that the rim be clamped from the outside, whereas steel rims are clamped from the inside. Always check the instruction manual for the tire changer you are using for the correct method of clamping a rim.

To dismount a tire, follow the steps in **SKILL DRILL 27-5**:

1 Before removing the tire, check to see whether the wheel is equipped with a TPMS sensor. If it is, there will be special procedures to follow during the tire replacement process. Follow the vehicle manufacturer's guidelines to avoid damaging the TPMS sensor.

2 Inspect the tread and sidewalls for barbs or pieces of steel belt that may injure you. Also inspect the tire for any obvious signs of damage. If there is any damage, the tire should be discarded. **(Photo 1)**

3 Check the wheel for any balance weights, and pry them off with the wheel weight tool. **(Photo 2)**

4 Locate the valve stem, unscrew the dust cap, and store it for later use.

5 Using the valve core tool, unscrew the valve core. Remember that compressed air inside the tire can cause the core to be shot like a bottle rocket if you do not hold onto it firmly, so make sure the valve stem is pointing away from your face. Also, since the air in the tire is undergoing a pressure drop as it leaves the valve stem, moisture in the airstream can form ice in the valve stem, which can become a projectile. **(Photo 3)**

SKILL DRILL | 27-5 | Dismounting a Tire

1. Before removing the tire, check to see if the wheel is equipped with a TPMS sensor. If it is, follow the manufacturer's procedures. Inspect the tread and sidewalls for any sharp cords sticking out that could injure you. If there is any damage, the tire should be discarded.

2. Check the wheel for any balance weights, and pry them off with the wheel weight tool.

3. Locate the valve stem, unscrew the dust cap, and store it for later use. Using the valve core tool, unscrew the valve core carefully.

4. Once all the air has been removed from the tire, locate the wheel in the bead breaker with the outside of the rim facing toward the blade. Locate the blade close to the edge of the rim while keeping your hands at a safe distance. Activate the bead breaker, which will force the tire bead away from the edge of the rim and over the safety ridge.

5. Release the blade, turn the wheel one-third to one-half of a turn, reposition the blade, and release this section of the tire as well. Release the blade. Roll the tire away from the machine, and reposition it with the inside of the rim facing toward the blade. Repeat the bead-breaking procedure on all four tires.

6. Set the wheel on the turntable with the shallow dish side of the wheel facing up. Position the wheel and tire assembly on the turntable and activate the jaws so the wheel is centered in the jaws. Activate the turntable to verify that the wheel is centered and securely held.

6. Once all the air has been removed from the tire, locate the wheel in the bead breaker with the outside of the rim facing toward the blade. Locate the blade close to the edge of the rim while keeping your hands at a safe distance.

7. Activate the bead breaker, which will force the tire bead away from the edge of the rim and over the safety ridge. (Photo 4)

8. Release the blade, turn the wheel one-third to one-half of a turn, reposition the blade, and release this section of the tire as well.

9. Release the blade, roll the tire away from the machine, and reposition it with the inside of the rim facing toward the blade. Repeat the bead-breaking procedure on all four tires. (Photo 5)

SKILL DRILL | 27-5 | Dismounting a Tire, continued

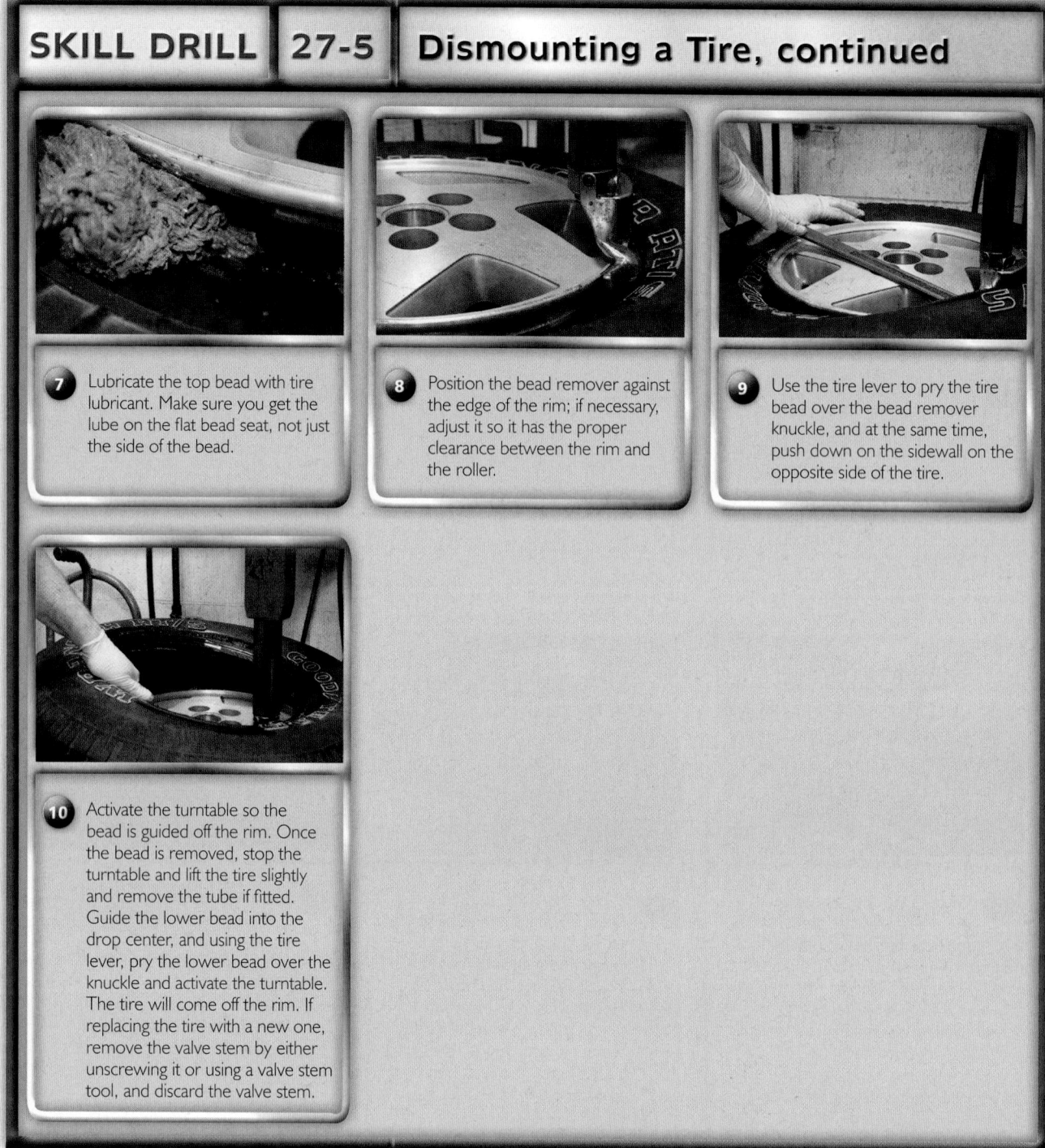

7 Lubricate the top bead with tire lubricant. Make sure you get the lube on the flat bead seat, not just the side of the bead.

8 Position the bead remover against the edge of the rim; if necessary, adjust it so it has the proper clearance between the rim and the roller.

9 Use the tire lever to pry the tire bead over the bead remover knuckle, and at the same time, push down on the sidewall on the opposite side of the tire.

10 Activate the turntable so the bead is guided off the rim. Once the bead is removed, stop the turntable and lift the tire slightly and remove the tube if fitted. Guide the lower bead into the drop center, and using the tire lever, pry the lower bead over the knuckle and activate the turntable. The tire will come off the rim. If replacing the tire with a new one, remove the valve stem by either unscrewing it or using a valve stem tool, and discard the valve stem.

10 Set the wheel on the turntable with the shallow dish side of the wheel facing up. This will allow the drop center to be as high as possible, which will make it much easier to remove the tire. Failure to position the rim so the drop center is as high as possible will make it unlikely that you will be able to remove the tire, and will likely damage the bead of the tire permanently.

11 Position the wheel and tire assembly on the turntable and activate the jaws so the wheel is held firmly and centered in the jaws. Activate the turntable to verify that the wheel is centered and securely held. **(Photo 6)**

12 Lubricate the top bead with tire lubricant. Make sure you get the lube on the flat bead seat, not just the side of the bead. **(Photo 7)**

13 Position the bead remover against the edge of the rim; if necessary, adjust it so it has the proper clearance between the rim and the roller. **(Photo 8)**

14 Use the tire lever to pry the tire bead over the bead remover knuckle, and at the same time, push down on the sidewall on the opposite side of the tire. **(Photo 9)**

15 Activate the turntable so the bead is guided off the rim.

16 Once the bead is removed, stop the turntable and lift the tire slightly and remove the tube if fitted.

17 Guide the lower bead into the drop center, and using the tire lever, pry the lower bead over the knuckle and activate the turntable. The tire will come off the rim. If replacing the tire with a new one, remove the valve stem by either unscrewing it or using a valve stem tool, and discard the valve stem. **(Photo 10)**

Safety

For your safety, follow these tips:

- An inflated tire is a pressure vessel that must be treated with care and respect. Always fully deflate the tire before performing any repair tasks.
- Keep your hands clear of the bead breaker when it is operating. It applies great force to the tire that will cause you a severe injury if your hand is trapped.
- Always use correct lifting techniques when lifting a tire on and off the tire changer and vehicle.
- The tire tread comes in contact with many unknown substances that are transferred directly to your hands. For this reason, it is recommended that you wear protective gloves when handling tires. If you do not wear gloves, wash your hands after the tire change is complete and before eating.

TECHNICIAN TIP

Always remove any balance weights from both sides of the rim before mounting it on the tire changer. If they are not removed, the bead remover could drag the weights around the rim, causing damage to the rim face. This is particularly important with alloy rims. The damage done by the balance weights is not repairable and usually requires the rim to be replaced, costing the shop a lot of money.

Replacing a Valve Stem

Valve stems come in a few styles: rubber press-fit valve stems, screw-in valve stems, and TPMS sensor–integrated valve stems. Rubber press-fit stems are normally replaced when new tires are mounted on the rims. Screw-in valve stems normally are not replaced, but may have rubber washers or O-rings that may require replacement when new tires are installed. TPMS-integrated valve stems may be made as part of the valve stem or may screw onto, or snap into, the valve stem, which is replaceable. It is important to know if the TPMS sensor is connected to the valve stem or not so you do not damage it during service and repair. Many TPMS valve stems have valve cores with coated threads and should not be replaced with noncoated threads. They should always be torqued with a valve core torque wrench.

Valve stems can also be damaged by trauma from loose objects on the road, from scraping into curbs or other low structures, or through improper tire changes. Luckily, valve stems are generally inexpensive and relatively easy to replace. To change the valve stem, the wheel must be removed from the vehicle. The tire is then deflated and the top bead broken. On some tires, the sidewall can be pushed down by hand to gain access to the valve stem. In other instances, the tire must be removed from the rim.

After removing the old rubber valve stem, a new one is put into place with some lubricant around the base of the stem. The stem is then pulled into place using the proper installing tool. The tire is reassembled and inflated to the recommended pressure. Spray some soapy water around the valve stem and core to detect air leaks.

For the valve stems that have a threaded shank with a locking nut and sealing washers, the process is similar. The wheel is removed from the vehicle, deflated, and the top bead is broken. The nut on the valve stem is then unscrewed and the stem is removed from the inside of the rim. The old sealing washers can be replaced with new ones. Then the valve stem can be reinstalled in the rim. In some cases only the valve stem core requires replacement. In this case, the old core is screwed out and the new core is installed and the tire pressure re-adjusted to vehicle specifications.

To replace a rubber press-fit valve stem, follow the steps in **SKILL DRILL 27-6**:

1 If the tire is already removed from the wheel, skip to the next step. If not, remove the wheel from the vehicle, deflate the tire, and break the top bead using the tire machine. **(Photo 1)**

2 On rubber press-fit valve stems, screw the valve stem tool onto the old valve stem. **(Photo 2)**

SKILL DRILL | 27-6 | Replacing a Rubber Press-Fit Valve Stem

1 Remove the wheel from the vehicle, deflate the tire, and break the top bead using the tire machine.

2 Screw the valve stem tool onto the old rubber press-fit stem.

3 Pry the rubber press-fit valve stem from the rim. Use one hand to hold onto the portion of the valve stem in case it breaks off.

4 Clean and inspect the hole in the rim. Clean any rust or corrosion with some sandpaper or other appropriate tool. Lubricate the new valve stem with tire lube.

5 Insert the valve stem into the hole in the rim from the inside, remove the cap, and screw the valve stem tool onto the threaded end of the stem.

6 Use the handle of the valve stem tool as a lever to pull the retaining ridge through the hole in the rim, and verify that the valve stem is properly installed.

3 Using the handle of the valve stem tool as a lever, pry the valve stem from the rim. Use one hand to hold onto the portion of the valve stem, which is inside the rim, in case it breaks off, so you can keep it from falling inside the tire. If the stem will not pry out easily, carefully cut off the inside portion of the stem. **(Photo 3)**

4 Clean and inspect the hole in the rim. Clean any rust or corrosion with some sandpaper or other appropriate tool, and lubricate the new valve stem with tire lube. **(Photo 4)**

5 Insert the valve stem into the hole in the rim from the inside, remove the valve stem cap, and screw the valve stem tool onto the threaded end of the stem. **(Photo 5)**

6 Use the handle of the valve stem tool as a lever to pull the retaining ridge through the hole in the rim, and verify that the valve stem is properly installed. **(Photo 6)**

To replace a screw-in valve stem, follow the steps in **SKILL DRILL 27-7** :

1 If the valve stem is a screw-in valve stem, remove the wheel from the vehicle, deflate the tire, break the top bead using the tire machine, and mount the wheel on the tire machine. **(Photo 1)**

2 Unscrew the nut that holds the valve stem to the rim. Remove the valve stem from the inside of the rim. **(Photo 2)**

3 Discard the old sealing washers and replace them with new ones. Place the valve stem with one new sealing washer through the hole on the inside of the rim. (**Photo 3**)

④ Place a new sealing washer over the valve stem and thread the nut on by hand. Tighten the nut to the specified torque. (**Photo 4**)

Mounting a Tire

In today's vehicles, mounting a tire means more than just installing a properly sized tire onto the rim. Since tires do not come perfectly round and balanced, most tire manufacturers indicate the tire's highest point with a red dot and the tire's lightest point with a yellow dot. The red dot should be lined up with the rim's lowest point, which is called **match mounting**. The yellow dot should be matched up with the rim's heaviest point, which is called **weight matching**. These points occur innately as part of the manufacturing process because it is impossible

to create an absolutely perfect, even, round tire. Slight variations in density and shape of the tire are unavoidable. Matching up the tire and rim using one of these methods will help avoid "tolerance stacking," which is when tolerances in mating parts are aligned in such a way that the tolerances are added together, rather than canceling each other out. In the case of wheels and tires, it would occur when the tire's heavy or high points are aligned with the rim's heavy or high points.

In addition, the type of tread—directional, symmetric, and asymmetric—affects the direction in which tires are mounted on the rims and which side of the vehicle they are installed on. Directional tires are designed to operate better in one direction, requiring that they be mounted accordingly. Symmetric tires can be operated in either direction, so they can be mounted in either direction. Asymmetric tires are generally side specific, but they may also be directional, in which case specific tires must

SKILL DRILL | 27-7 | Replacing a Screw-in Valve Stem

① Remove the wheel from the vehicle, deflate the tire, break the top bead using the tire machine, and mount the wheel on the machine.

② Unscrew the nut that holds the valve stem to the rim. Remove the valve stem from the inside of the rim.

③ Discard the old sealing washers and replace them with new ones. Place the screw-in valve stem with one new sealing washer through the hole on the inside of the rim.

④ Place a new sealing washer over the valve stem and thread the nut on by hand. Tighten the nut to the specified torque.

be mounted on certain rims. Do not fit a tire that is too wide or too narrow for the rim. Check the tire manufacturer's recommendation for the correct range of rim sizes for a particular tire.

The turntable jaws on the tire machine can hold the rim by grasping it from the outside or the inside. When mounting an alloy rim, it is normal that they be clamped from the outside, whereas steel rims are usually clamped from the inside. If the tire is clamped from the outside on the tire machine, it is necessary to release the clamps before fully inflating the tire. Always check the instruction manual for the tire machine you are using for the correct method of clamping a rim.

Inflating a tire for the first time is always dangerous. Some types of tires, such as split rims, must be inflated inside of a tire cage. Doing so contains any pieces if the tire blows up while being inflated. Always follow the manufacturer's guidelines and shop policies when inflating a newly installed tire.

To mount a tire, follow the steps in **SKILL DRILL 27-8**:

1. If you have not already done so, mount the wheel on the tire machine. Depending on the type of rim, you will need to grab it from either the inside or the outside. Examine the wheel. Check for and remove any rust or dirt from the rim bead seat. (**Photo 1**)

SKILL DRILL | **27-8** | **Mounting a Tire**

1. Mount the wheel to the tire machine. Examine the wheel and remove any rust or dirt from the rim bead seat.

2. Select the correct type of tubeless valve stem, lube it with tire lube, and insert it through the hole in the rim from the inside. Using the valve stem tool, pull the stem through until its groove locates in the hole. Use the valve core tool to unscrew the valve core from the valve stem.

3. Apply some lubricant to the tire bead and rim ridges.

4. Position the tire on top of the rim so that a portion of the lower bead is positioned in the drop center while keeping the lower bead in the tire machine guide.

5. Activate the turntable and guide the lower tire bead onto the rim.

6. Once the lower bead is fitted, position the upper bead into the guide while holding the other side of the upper bead in the drop center.

SKILL DRILL | 27-8 | Mounting a Tire, continued

7 Activate the turntable and guide the tire onto the rim. As the turntable rotates, push the sidewall down, keeping your fingers clear of the rim, so that the tire bead is guided below the safety ridge into the drop center.

8 Attach the tire inflator chuck to the valve stem. Stand clear of the tire and inflate it, being careful to not exceed 30 psi (207 kPa) if both beads have not seated against the rim. If they have not seated by 30 psi, deflate the tire and inspect the rim and tire for damage. If they are OK, relube the tire and rim and reattempt to inflate the tire. If it still will not seat the beads by 30 psi, inform your supervisor.

9 Check the location of the bead indicator ridge to make sure the bead is fully seated. If the rim is clamped from the outside, it will be necessary to release the clamps so the tire can inflate fully.

10 When the beads are properly seated, remove the tire inflator chuck, keeping your hands and face clear of the valve stem opening. Once the tire has completely deflated, screw the valve core into the valve stem using the valve core tool.

11 Reattach the inflator, stand clear, and inflate the tire to the correct pressure as listed on the vehicle's tire placard or in the owner's manual. Be careful to *never* exceed the maximum tire pressure listed on the tire sidewall.

12 Use a soft brush and apply a small amount of soapy water to the bead. If there are any air leaks, they will be indicated by bubbles.

2 Select the correct type of tubeless valve stem, lube it with tire lube, and insert it through the hole in the rim from the inside. Using the valve stem tool, pull the stem through until its groove locates in the hole. Use a valve core tool to unscrew the valve core from the valve stem. **(Photo 2)**

3 Apply some lubricant to the tire bead and rim ridges. **(Photo 3)**

4 Position the tire on top of the rim so that a portion of the bead is positioned in the drop center while keeping the lower bead in the tire machine guide. **(Photo 4)**

5 Activate the turntable and guide the lower tire bead onto the rim. **(Photo 5)**

6 Once the lower bead is fitted, position the upper bead into the guide while holding the other side of the upper bead in the drop center. **(Photo 6)**

7 Activate the turntable and guide the tire onto the rim. As the turntable rotates, push the sidewall down, keeping your fingers clear of the rim, so that the tire bead is guided below the safety ridge into the drop center. This approach will prevent tearing of the tire bead, which would cause an air leak. **(Photo 7)**

8 Attach the tire inflator chuck to the valve stem, stand clear of the tire, and inflate it, being careful to not exceed 30 psi (207 kPa) if both beads have not seated against the rim. If they have not seated by 30 psi, deflate the tire and inspect the rim and tire for damage. If they are OK, relube the tire and rim and reattempt to inflate the tire. If it still will not seat the beads by 30 psi, inform your supervisor. **(Photo 8)**

9 Check the location of the bead indicator ridge to make sure the bead is fully seated. If the rim is clamped from the outside, it will be necessary to release the clamps so the tire can inflate fully. **(Photo 9)**

10 When the beads are properly seated, remove the tire inflator chuck. Remember that compressed air will escape with some force, so keep your hands and face clear of the valve stem opening.

11 Once the tire has completely deflated, screw the valve core into the valve stem using the valve core tool. **(Photo 10)**

12 Reattach the inflator, stand clear, and inflate the tire to the correct pressure as listed on the vehicle's tire placard or in the owner's manual. Be careful to *never* exceed the maximum tire pressure listed on the tire sidewall. **(Photo 11)**

13 Use a soft brush and apply a small amount of soapy water to the bead, valve stem, and valve core. If there are any air leaks, they will be indicated by bubbles. **(Photo 12)**

> **▶ TECHNICIAN TIP**
>
> Most tire changers dismount and mount the tire by turning the turntable clockwise. This is especially helpful to know so you position the tire on the turntable correctly to mount and dismount tires equipped with a TPMS.

Safety

> Overinflated tires can explode. Do not inflate the tire to a pressure greater than what is listed on the sidewall. The possibility of an explosion is why tire inflators have a spring-loaded (dead man's) trigger that does not lock into position. When the tire is being inflated, use a tire cage if required, or an inflator that allows you to stand clear of the tire. Keep hands and body well away from the tire. When a tire explodes, the tire, rim, or components from the tire changer may cause serious injury or death to any person nearby.

Dismounting, Inspecting, and Remounting a Tire on a Wheel Equipped with a TPMS Sensor

Dismounting and mounting tires equipped with a TPMS requires special care to avoid damaging the expensive sensors mounted inside the wheels. There are two general ways that TPMS sensors are mounted in the wheel. The first way involves either attaching it to the valve stem or making it integral to the valve stem, so care must be exercised around the valve stem area. If the TPMS sensor is integrated into the valve stem with a threaded locknut on the valve stem, some manufacturers recommend unscrewing the locknut and pushing the valve stem and TPMS sensor into the tire for safekeeping during disassembly. The second way is by using a band that fits all the way around the drop center of the rim to hold the TPMS sensor to the inside of the wheel. In many cases, the band-style TPMS sensor is positioned 180 degrees away from the valve stem, so care must be exercised on the side opposite of the valve stem. Always check the service information to verify the manufacturer's specified tire dismounting and mounting procedure.

To dismount, inspect, and remount a tire on a wheel equipped with a TPMS sensor, follow the steps in **SKILL DRILL 27-9**:

1 After you research the tire dismounting and remounting procedure in the service information, remove the wheel from the vehicle and deflate the tire by removing the valve core. If the sensor is mounted to a threaded valve stem, unscrew the locknut and push the valve stem into the tire.

2 Break the tire beads in the positions specified. **(Photo 1)**

3 Position the tire assembly on the turntable with the shallow side of the wheel up, and engage the jaws to lock the wheel in place. **(Photo 2)**

SKILL DRILL | **27-9** | **Dismounting, Inspecting, and Remounting a Tire on a Wheel Equipped with a TPMS sensor**

1. Following the specified procedure, remove the wheel from the vehicle and deflate the tire by removing the valve core. Break the tire beads in the positions specified.

2. Position the tire assembly on the turntable with the shallow side of the wheel up, and engage the jaws to lock the wheel in place.

3. Activate the turntable to verify that the wheel is centered and securely held. Stop it in the specified position for removing the top bead.

4. Lubricate both beads with tire lubricant. Make sure you get the lube on the flat bead seat, not just the side of the bead.

5. Position the bead remover against the edge of the rim; if necessary, adjust it so it has the proper clearance between the rim and the roller. Use the tire lever to pry the tire bead over the bead remover knuckle, and at the same time, push down on the sidewall on the opposite side of the tire.

6. Activate the turntable while lifting up on the tire directly behind the remover knuckle to help work the top bead over the flange of the rim.

4. Activate the turntable to verify that the wheel is centered and securely held. Stop it in the specified position for removing the top bead. **(Photo 3)**

5. Lubricate the top bead with tire lubricant. Make sure you get the lube on the flat bead seat, not just the side of the bead. **(Photo 4)**

6. Position the bead remover against the edge of the rim; if necessary, adjust it so it has the proper clearance between the rim and the roller.

7. Use the tire lever to pry the tire bead over the bead remover knuckle, and at the same time, push down on the sidewall on the opposite side of the tire. **(Photo 5)**

8. Activate the turntable while lifting up on the tire directly behind the remover knuckle to help work the top bead over the flange of the rim. **(Photo 6)**

SKILL DRILL | 27-9 | Dismounting, Inspecting, and Remounting a Tire on a Wheel Equipped with a TPMS sensor, continued

7 Rotate the turntable to the position specified for removing the lower bead.

8 Carefully pry the lower bead over the knuckle while holding the other side of the tire up in the drop center.

9 Activate the turntable while lifting up on the tire directly behind the remover knuckle to help work the bottom bead over the flange of the rim. Inspect the tire, rim, and TPMS sensor according to the manufacturer's procedure.

10 To install the tire, adequately lube both bead seats of the tire with tire lube. Activate the turntable to position the valve stem in the specified position for installing the lower bead.

11 Position the lower bead into the drop center while holding the lower bead in the tire machine shoe.

12 Activate the turntable while helping keep the lower bead in the drop center.

9 Rotate the turntable to the position specified for removing the lower bead. (**Photo 7**)

10 Carefully pry the lower bead over the knuckle while holding the other side of the tire up in the drop center. (**Photo 8**)

11 Activate the turntable while lifting up on the tire directly behind the remover knuckle to help work the bottom bead over the flange of the rim.

12 Inspect the tire, rim, and TPMS sensor according to the manufacturer's procedure. (**Photo 9**)

13 To install the tire, adequately lube both bead seats of the tire with tire lube.

14 Activate the turntable to position the valve stem in the specified position for installing the lower bead. (**Photo 10**)

SKILL DRILL | 27-9 | Dismounting, Inspecting, and Remounting a Tire on a Wheel Equipped with a TPMS sensor, continued

13 Activate the turntable to position the valve stem in the specified position for installing the upper bead.

14 Place the upper bead into the drop center while holding the lower bead in the tire machine shoe.

15 Activate the turntable while pushing the top bead into the drop center.

16 Inflate the tire as a non-TPMS wheel and check for leaks.

15 Position the lower bead into the drop center while holding the lower bead in the tire machine shoe. (**Photo 11**)

16 Activate the turntable while helping keep the lower bead in the drop center. (**Photo 12**)

17 Activate the turntable to position the valve stem in the specified position for installing the upper bead. (**Photo 13**)

18 Place the upper bead into the drop center while holding the lower bead in the tire machine shoe. (**Photo 14**)

19 Activate the turntable while pushing the top bead into the drop center. (**Photo 15**)

20 Inflate the tire as a non-TPMS wheel and check for leaks. (**Photo 16**)

Dynamic Balancing a Tire

A tire that is dynamically in balance is in balance when it is spinning as opposed to when it is stationary. Dynamic imbalance occurs when a spot on either the inside or the outside of the tire's centerline is heavy. This induces a side-to-side imbalance in the tire as it rotates, which can cause a vibration as well as the steering wheel to shimmy. Dynamic imbalance is usually a result of manufacturing variations, but it can be caused by a damaged tire or wheel. Obviously, dynamic imbalance reduces ride quality and tends to increase wear on the tires and on steering and suspension system components. Dynamic balancing of the tires should be performed when new tires are installed on the vehicle as well as any time that tire imbalance is suspected.

Dynamic balancing is performed on a tire balancer that is capable of spinning the tire and then measuring the location of any dynamic imbalance. Some balancers are spun at low speed, but others are driven by the balancer at higher speeds. If the tire is spun by the balancer, embedded objects may fly off the tire, so it is important to wear safety glasses. If the wheel balancer is fitted with a safety hood, ensure that it is in place when the wheel is being rotated to further protect against flying objects.

All wheels require one of several specific designs of wheel weights. If the weights fitted to the wheel are not the correct type, they can fly off when the vehicle is driven down the road, causing possible injury or damage. It is good practice to use new wheel weights when balancing a wheel for the same reason. If the vehicle has directional tires, ensure that the wheels are reinstalled in their correct position when balancing is complete.

To balance a tire, follow the steps in **SKILL DRILL 27-10**:

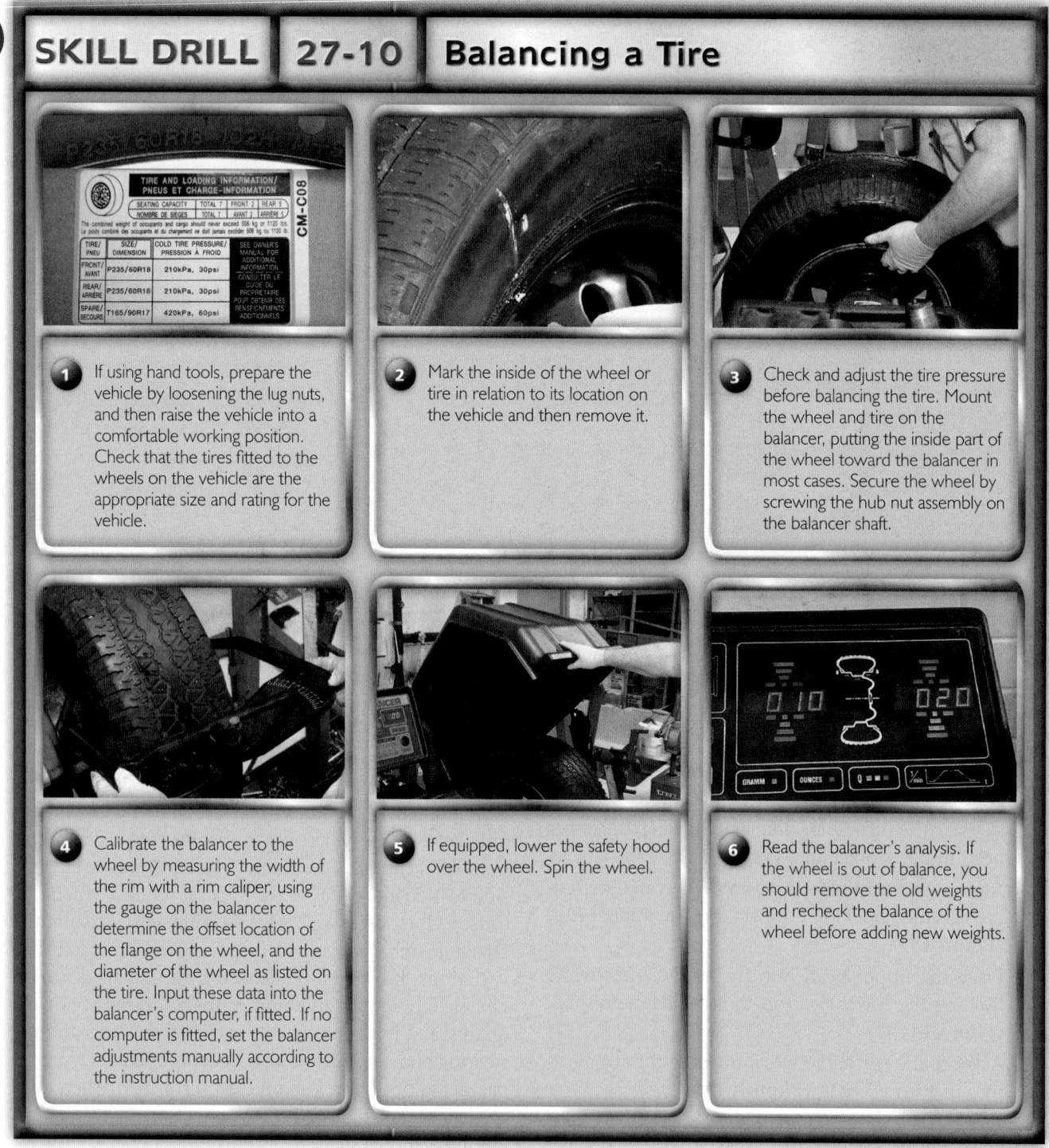

SKILL DRILL 27-10 Balancing a Tire

1. If using hand tools, prepare the vehicle by loosening the lug nuts, and then raise the vehicle into a comfortable working position. Check that the tires fitted to the wheels on the vehicle are the appropriate size and rating for the vehicle.

2. Mark the inside of the wheel or tire in relation to its location on the vehicle and then remove it.

3. Check and adjust the tire pressure before balancing the tire. Mount the wheel and tire on the balancer, putting the inside part of the wheel toward the balancer in most cases. Secure the wheel by screwing the hub nut assembly on the balancer shaft.

4. Calibrate the balancer to the wheel by measuring the width of the rim with a rim caliper, using the gauge on the balancer to determine the offset location of the flange on the wheel, and the diameter of the wheel as listed on the tire. Input these data into the balancer's computer, if fitted. If no computer is fitted, set the balancer adjustments manually according to the instruction manual.

5. If equipped, lower the safety hood over the wheel. Spin the wheel.

6. Read the balancer's analysis. If the wheel is out of balance, you should remove the old weights and recheck the balance of the wheel before adding new weights.

SKILL DRILL | 27-10 | Balancing a Tire, continued

7 Install new weights as recommended by the machine's display.

8 Respin the wheel to check for accuracy of the balancing job and to confirm that balance has been achieved. Repeat the process for the rest of the wheels and tires. Reinstall the wheels and tires to the vehicle.

1 If using hand tools, prepare the vehicle by loosening the lug nuts, and then raise the vehicle into a comfortable working position.

2 Check that the tires fitted to the wheels on the vehicle are the appropriate size and rating for the vehicle, as listed on the tire placard. In most cases, the vehicle should have four completely matched tires. As a minimum, the front tires should match each other and the rear tires should match each other. **(Photo 1)**

3 Mark the inside of the wheel or tire in relation to its location on the vehicle and then remove it. This is so that it can be reinstalled in the same position on the vehicle. **(Photo 2)**

4 Check and adjust the tire pressure before balancing the tire.

5 Mount the wheel and tire on the balancer, putting the inside part of the wheel toward the balancer in most cases. Secure the wheel by screwing the hub nut assembly on the balancer shaft. **(Photo 3)**

6 Calibrate the balancer to the wheel by measuring the width of the rim with a rim caliper, using the gauge on the balancer to determine the location of the flange on the wheel (offset), and the diameter of the wheel as listed on the tire. **(Photo 4)**

7 Input this data into the balancer's computer, if fitted, according to the manufacturer's instruction manual.

If no computer is fitted, set the balancer adjustments manually according to the instruction manual.

8 If equipped, lower the safety hood over the wheel. **(Photo 5)**

9 Spin the wheel. Read the balancer's analysis, which is normally displayed visually on the machine. It tells you whether the wheel is out of balance and, if so, how much weight to use and where to put it to balance the wheel. If the wheel is out of balance, you should remove the old weights and recheck the balance of the wheel before adding new weights. **(Photo 6)**

10 Install new weights recommended by the machine's display, usually by hammering them onto the edge of the rim where indicated, although some are held in place by tape on the back side of the weight. **(Photo 7)**

11 Now respin the wheel to check for accuracy of the balancing job and to confirm that balance has been achieved. A reading of zero on both sides of the wheel means the wheel is ready to reinstall on the vehicle. Repeat the process for the rest of the wheels and tires.

12 Reinstall the wheels and tires to the vehicle, remembering to lower the vehicle just enough so the tires will be held in place while torquing the lug nuts to the correct specification and in the correct sequence. **(Photo 8)**

Inspecting the Wheel Assembly for Air Loss

One of the most frustrating complaints from drivers is that they constantly have to pump their tires up as the result of an air loss somewhere. To efficiently check the suspect tire, it must be removed from the vehicle and aired up to its recommended pressure. A preliminary check can be carried out with a spray bottle of soapy water. You need to spray the soapy water around the valve stem and core. In addition, spray around the bead area. Also spray the entire tread area. If there is any air leakage, soapy air bubbles will indicate where the problem is. Mark the tire where the air bubbles are coming from so that the repairs can be carried out.

Another good method for checking where the air loss is coming from is to immerse the wheel assembly in a container of water. The container must be large enough to immerse the tire either on its side, with the tire completely underwater, or upright, with approximately half the wheel assembly underwater. If there is a leak, it will be obvious by the discharge of air bubbles in the water **FIGURE 27-21**. Mark the source of the air bubbles. Remove the wheel from the water tank and carry out the appropriate repairs.

To inspect the wheel assembly for air loss using the spray bottle method, perform the steps in **SKILL DRILL 27-11**:

1. Remove the tire from the vehicle and inflate it to its proper pressure.

2. Using a spray bottle of soapy water, spray the valve stem and core, tire tread, and tire bead area.

FIGURE 27-21 A good method for identifying the location of an air leak is to immerse the tire assembly in water and watch for air bubbles.

SKILL DRILL | **27-11** | **Inspecting the Wheel Assembly for Air Loss Using the Spray Bottle Method**

1. Remove the tire from the vehicle and inflate it to its proper pressure. Using a spray bottle of soapy water, spray the valve stem and core, tire tread, and tire bead area. Inspect the tire, valve stem, and wheel assembly for bubbles.

2. Mark any leaks in the tire with a tire crayon.

3 Inspect the tire, valve stem, and wheel assembly for bubbles, which would indicate a leak. **(Photo 1)**

4 Mark any leaks in the tire with a tire crayon. **(Photo 2)**

To inspect the wheel assembly for air loss using the dunk tank method, follow the steps in **SKILL DRILL 27-12**:

1 Place the tire into the dunk tank and hold it still.

2 Inspect the tire and wheel for any escaping bubbles, including the valve stem and core. If necessary, rotate the wheel assembly so that more of it can be held underwater to inspect for leaks.

3 Mark any leaks in the tire with a tire crayon.

▶ Diagnosis

Tire Repair

Driving a short distance on a tire while it is severely underinflated will cause the tire to overheat as well as weaken the sidewall belts, creating a dangerous, nonrepairable condition. The damage is not visible from the outside, so every tire needing repairs must be removed from the wheel for inspection and to assess its repairability. The tire needs to be inspected externally first, then internally for any signs of serious damage, such as chaffing of the sidewalls or cords sticking through the inner liner. If the inspection shows no signs of nonrepairable failure, then the tire can be repaired in accordance with the procedures recommended by the tire associations, including the Rubber Manufacturers Association.

Repairs from any nail or similar object should be limited to the actual tread area. Among the criteria to perform a proper repair are:

- Repairs are limited to the tread area only.
- Puncture injury cannot be greater than 1/4" (6 mm) in diameter.
- Repairs must be performed by removing the tire from the rim/wheel assembly to perform a complete inspection to assess all damage that may be present.
- Repairs cannot overlap. This means that if there are two or more repairs required to fix the tire, then each repair patch must not overlap.
- A rubber stem, or plug, must be applied to fill the puncture injury, and a patch must be applied to seal the inner liner. A common repair unit is a one-piece unit with a stem and patch portion. A plug by itself is an unacceptable repair.

To patch a tire, you will need a tire machine to remove the tire from the wheel, a buffer to clean the inside of the tire, glue for attaching the patch, and a tire plug patch. The tire plug patch is a superior product to the old-fashioned tire plug, and in many states, it is the only legal way to repair a hole in a tire. It is more expensive but is a much safer alternative for repairing a tire because it patches the inside of the tire in addition to filling the hole in the tire.

To patch a tire, follow the steps in **SKILL DRILL 27-13**:

1 After marking the location of the air leak on the tread of the tire, and the position of the tire and weights on the rim, remove the tire from the rim assembly so that an internal patch can be used to rectify the problem. **(Photo 1)**

2 Mount the tire in a tire spreader so that the hole can be accessed from both the inside and the outside of the tire. **(Photo 2)**

3 Use an air die grinder with a pointy bit that matches the plug patch, and drill into the tire where the leak was located. This will roughen up the sides and make a cleaner hole for where the patch will be installed. **(Photo 3)**

4 Use a tire buffer to smooth the area inside the tire around the hole. Smooth the area approximately 1/2" (13 mm) beyond the expected patch area. **(Photo 4)**

5 After completing the buffing process, clean out all the accumulated debris. A vacuum works well for this. **(Photo 5)**

6 Liberally apply the liquid buffing solution to a clean rag and scrub the area just buffed. Some patching systems use a liquid cleaner that is applied to the tire and scraped off with a scraper. Repeat this step once or twice, as needed. **(Photo 6)**

7 Apply vulcanizing cement evenly to the inner buffed surface of the tire, and work it down into the hole. Doing so will prevent water from entering the hole and moving its way into the tire's tread. As with most contact-type cements, it needs to stand until the cement is relatively dry and is only tacky to touch. **(Photo 7)**

8 After selecting the appropriate tire patch, remove the plastic protective cover that is on the sticky side of the tire patch without getting your fingerprints on the sticky side. **(Photo 8)**

9 Take the pointed part of the patch and push it through the inner side of the tire's hole that was roughed previously, pushing it through to the outside of the tire. **(Photo 9)**

SKILL DRILL | 27-13 | Patching a Tire

1 After marking the location of the air leak on the tread of the tire and the position of the tire and weights on the rim, remove the tire from the rim assembly.

2 Mount the tire in a tire spreader so that the hole can be accessed from both the inside and the outside of the tire.

3 Use an air die grinder with the properly sized pointy bit that matches the plug patch, and drill into the tire where the leak was located.

4 Use a tire buffer to smooth the area inside the tire around the hole. Smooth the area approximately 1/2" (13 mm) beyond the expected patch area.

5 After completing the buffing process, clean out all the accumulated debris with a vacuum.

6 Liberally apply the liquid buffing solution to a clean rag and scrub the area just buffed. Or use cleaner and a scraper to clean the area. Repeat this step once or twice, as needed.

7 Apply vulcanizing cement evenly to the inner buffed surface of the tire. The cement needs to stand until the cement is relatively dry and is only tacky to touch.

8 After selecting the appropriate tire patch, remove the plastic protective cover that is on the sticky side of the tire patch without getting your fingerprints on the sticky side.

9 Take the pointed part of the patch and push it through the inner side of the tire's hole that was roughed previously, pushing it through to the outside of the tire.

SKILL DRILL 27-13 Patching a Tire, continued

10 Using a pair of pliers, grip the stem of the patch and pull it out so that the disc portion of the patch comes into contact with the cemented area. Pull this pointy part of the patch away from the tire's tread. The sticky side of the patch has now been tightly pressed onto the buffed surface.

11 Use a stitching tool and roll the inner side of the tire patch tight onto the inner surface of the tire. Start at the center of the patch and work outward. Cover the buffed area and newly applied patch with a rubber patch sealant. Trim the plug material even with or just above the tread using a utility knife or other appropriate cutting tool.

12 After the rubber patch sealant has dried, the tire can be reassembled onto the rim in its original position and inflated to the recommended pressure. Check the wheel assembly for balance before it is reinstalled on the vehicle.

10 Using a pair of pliers, grip the stem of the patch and pull it out so that the disc portion of the patch comes into contact with the cemented area. Pull this pointy part of the patch away from the tire's tread. The sticky side of the patch has now been tightly pressed onto the buffed surface. **(Photo 10)**

11 Use a stitching tool and roll the inner side of the tire patch tight onto the inner surface of the tire. Start at the center of the patch and work outward. This will remove any air bubbles from between the sticky side of the patch and the buffed surface. The patch is now installed properly onto the tire. It is a good practice to cover the buffed area and newly applied patch with a rubber patch sealant. Doing so will ensure a long-term, airtight repair. Trim the plug material even using a utility knife or other appropriate cutting tool. **(Photo 11)**

12 After the rubber patch sealant has dried, the tire can be reassembled onto the rim in its original position and inflated to the recommended pressure. Check the wheel assembly for balance before it is reinstalled on the vehicle. **(Photo 12)**

Measuring Wheel, Tire, Axle Flange, and Hub Runout

Runout is the side-to-side or up-and-down variation in a part in the wheel assembly. In many cases, runout issues cannot be observed when the vehicle is stationary on the ground. Instead, runout problems can be felt as a vibration while the vehicle is being driven, usually getting more noticeable as speed is increased. If the vibration is primarily observed in the steering column or hood, the runout is most likely in one or both of the front wheel assemblies. Vibration felt throughout the entire vehicle suggests that the problem is with one or both of the back wheels.

Runout can be defined as radial or lateral. Radial runout occurs when the component is out of round or off center and is felt more as a vertical vibration. Lateral runout occurs when the component is bent or improperly manufactured and causes the wheels to jiggle side to side, creating a horizontal vibration that feels like a shimmy. Lateral runout is felt in the steering wheel even at slower speeds. Runout of the wheel, tire, axle, and hub are all measured in the same way using a special runout gauge inserted onto the surface of the component being measured.

To measure tire runout, follow the steps in **SKILL DRILL 27-14**:

1. Research the procedure and specifications for measuring tire runout in the service information. Raise the vehicle on a hoist or place a jack under the vehicle at a suitable lifting point and raise the vehicle. If using a jack, be sure to place safety stands under the frame of the vehicle and slowly lower the vehicle onto the stand. **(Photo 1)**

2. Select the runout gauge or dial indicator, attachment, and bracket that fit the tire.

3. Mount the dial indicator on a firm surface to keep it still. **(Photo 2)**

4. Adjust the dial indicator so the plunger is 90 degrees to the tread of the tire.

5. Press the dial indicator gently against the tire and rotate the tire one full turn. Keep pressing until the

SKILL DRILL | 27-14 | Measuring Tire Runout

1. Research the proper procedure and specifications. Raise the vehicle on a hoist or place a jack under the vehicle at a suitable lifting point and raise the vehicle.

2. Select the runout gauge or dial indicator, attachment, and bracket that fit the tire. Mount the dial indicator on a firm surface to keep it still.

3. Adjust the dial indicator so the plunger is 90 degrees to the tread of the tire. Press the dial indicator gently against the tire and rotate the tire one full turn. Keep pressing until the plunger settles about halfway into the indicator.

4. Verify that the plunger is still 90 degrees to the tire and lock the indicator assembly into position. Carefully rotate the tire a couple of times while observing the dial readings. If the pointer hovers around a single graduation on the dial, the part has minimal runout or surface distortion and the test is complete. If the pointer moves significantly left and right, note the variations.

5. Find the point of maximum movement to the left and move the dial so that zero is over this point.

6. Continue to rotate the tire. Find the point of maximum movement to the right and note the reading. Confirm this value by rotating the tire several more times to verify the zero point and high point. Compare these values to the manufacturer's specifications. If the deviation is greater than the specifications, the wheel and/or hub runout must be measured.

SKILL DRILL | 27-14 | Measuring Tire Runout, continued

7 Reposition the dial indicator or runout gauge so it is 90 degrees to the sidewall of the tire. Perform steps 3 through 6 to obtain the lateral runout measurement for the tire, and compare to the vehicle's specifications.

plunger settles about halfway into the indicator. **(Photo 3)**

6 Verify that the plunger is still 90 degrees to the tire and lock the indicator assembly into position.

7 Carefully rotate the tire a couple of times while observing the dial readings. If the pointer hovers around a single graduation on the dial, the part has minimal runout or surface distortion and the test is complete. If the pointer moves significantly left and right, note the variations. **(Photo 4)**

8 Find the point of maximum movement to the left and move the dial so that zero is over this point. **(Photo 5)**

9 Continue to rotate the tire. Find the point of maximum movement to the right and note the reading. This measure indicates the runout value. Confirm this value by rotating the tire several more times to verify the zero point and high point. The result will be the radial runout measurement for the tire.

10 Compare these values to the manufacturer's specifications. If the deviation is greater than the specifications, the wheel and/or hub runout must be measured. **(Photo 6)**

11 Reposition the dial indicator or runout gauge so it is 90 degrees to the sidewall of the tire. **(Photo 7)**

12 Perform steps 6 through 11 to obtain the lateral runout measurement for the tire, and compare to the vehicle's specifications.

To measure wheel runout, follow the steps in **SKILL DRILL 27-15**:

1 If equipped, remove the hubcap, mark the position of any wheel weights, and use a wheel weight tool to remove any wheel weights. **(Photo 1)**

2 Select the runout gauge or dial indicator, attachment, and bracket that fit the wheel. Mount the dial indicator on a firm surface to keep it still. Adjust the dial indicator so the plunger is 90 degrees to the flat portion of the wheel where the wheel weights are installed. **(Photo 2)**

3 Press the dial indicator gently against the wheel and rotate the wheel one full turn. Keep pressing until the plunger settles about halfway into the indicator. Verify that the plunger is still 90 degrees to the wheel and lock the indicator assembly into position. **(Photo 3)**

4 Carefully rotate the wheel a couple of times while observing the dial readings. If the pointer hovers around a single graduation on the dial, the wheel has minimal runout or surface distortion and the test is complete. If the pointer moves significantly left and right, note the variations. **(Photo 4)**

5 Find the point of maximum movement to the left and move the dial so that zero is over this point. **(Photo 5)**

6 Continue to rotate the wheel. Find the point of maximum movement to the right and note the

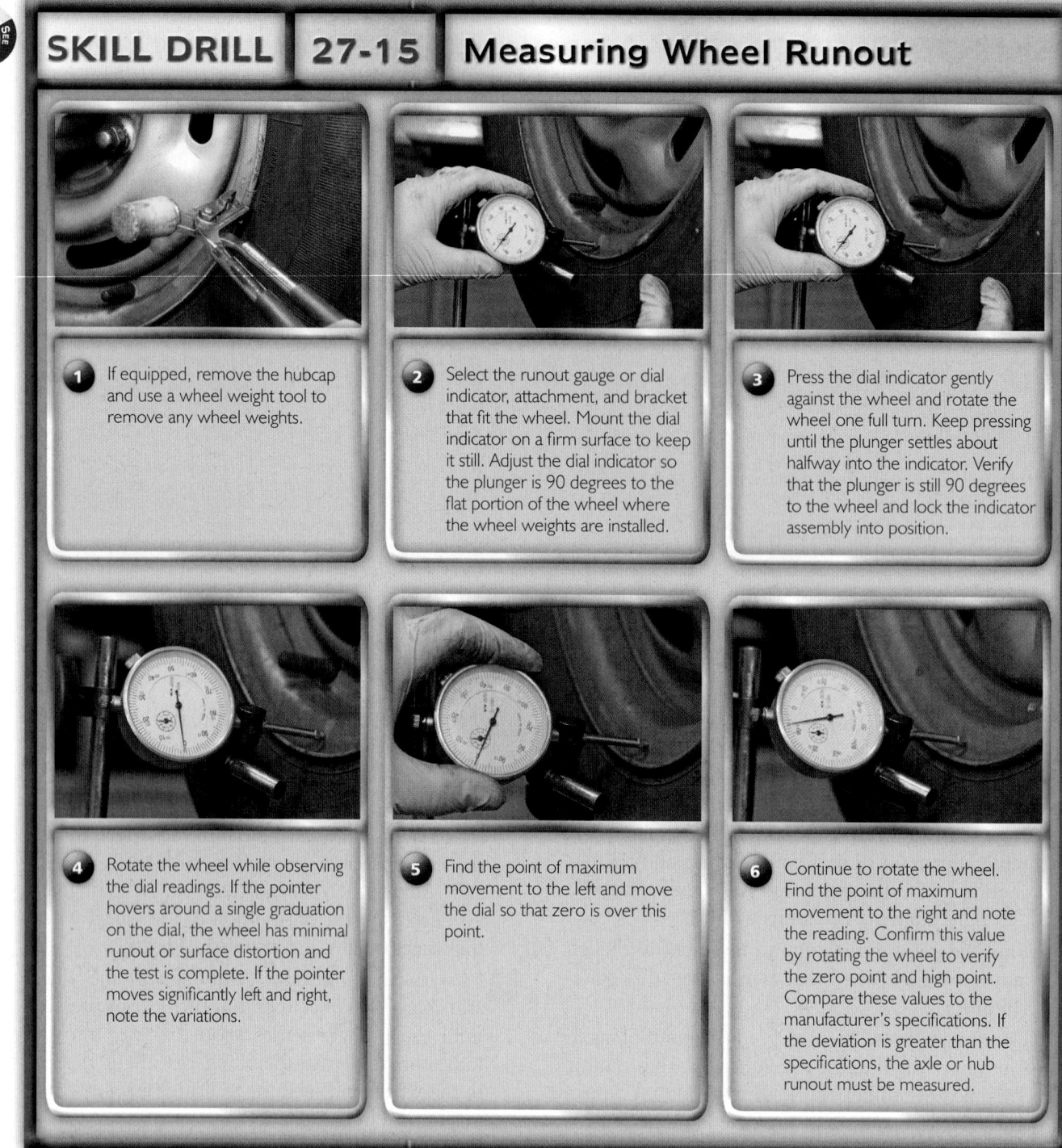

SKILL DRILL | **27-15** | **Measuring Wheel Runout**

1 If equipped, remove the hubcap and use a wheel weight tool to remove any wheel weights.

2 Select the runout gauge or dial indicator, attachment, and bracket that fit the wheel. Mount the dial indicator on a firm surface to keep it still. Adjust the dial indicator so the plunger is 90 degrees to the flat portion of the wheel where the wheel weights are installed.

3 Press the dial indicator gently against the wheel and rotate the wheel one full turn. Keep pressing until the plunger settles about halfway into the indicator. Verify that the plunger is still 90 degrees to the wheel and lock the indicator assembly into position.

4 Rotate the wheel while observing the dial readings. If the pointer hovers around a single graduation on the dial, the wheel has minimal runout or surface distortion and the test is complete. If the pointer moves significantly left and right, note the variations.

5 Find the point of maximum movement to the left and move the dial so that zero is over this point.

6 Continue to rotate the wheel. Find the point of maximum movement to the right and note the reading. Confirm this value by rotating the wheel to verify the zero point and high point. Compare these values to the manufacturer's specifications. If the deviation is greater than the specifications, the axle or hub runout must be measured.

reading. This measure indicates the runout value. Confirm this value by rotating the wheel several more times to verify the zero point and high point. The result will be the lateral runout measurement for the wheel.

7 Compare these values to the manufacturer's specifications. If the deviation is greater than the

specifications, the axle or hub runout must be measured. **(Photo 6)**

To measure axle flange or hub runout, follow the steps in **SKILL DRILL 27-16**:

1 Research the procedure and specifications for measuring runout in the service information. Prepare the vehicle by removing any hubcaps or lug nut covers.

2 With the vehicle on the ground, loosen the lug or wheel nuts. Raise the vehicle on a hoist or place a jack under the vehicle at a suitable lifting point and raise the vehicle. If using a jack, be sure to place safety stands under the frame of the vehicle and slowly lower the vehicle onto the stand.

3 Remove the lug nuts and wheel. **(Photo 1)**

4 Select the runout gauge or dial indicator, attachment, and bracket that fit the axle flange or hub. Mount the dial indicator on a firm surface to keep it still. **(Photo 2)**

5 Adjust the plunger so it is 90 degrees to the axle flange or hub.

6 Press the dial indicator gently against the flat surface of the axle flange or hub and rotate it one full turn. Keep pressing until the plunger settles about halfway into the indicator.

7 Verify that the plunger is still 90 degrees to the tire and lock the indicator assembly into position. Carefully rotate the axle flange or hub a couple of times while observing the dial readings. **(Photo 3)**

8 If the pointer hovers around a single graduation on the dial, the axle flange or hub has minimal runout or surface distortion and the test is complete. If the pointer moves significantly left and right, note the variations.

9 Find the point of maximum movement to the left and move the dial so that zero is over this point. **(Photo 4)**

10 Continue to rotate the axle flange or hub. Find the point of maximum movement to the right and note the reading. This measure indicates the runout value. Confirm this value by rotating the axle several more times to verify the zero point and high point. The result will be the lateral runout measurement for the axle flange or hub.

SKILL DRILL | **27-16** | **Measuring Axle Flange or Hub Runout**

1 Prepare the vehicle by removing any hubcaps or lug nut covers. With the vehicle on the ground, loosen the lug or wheel nuts. Raise the vehicle and remove the lug nuts and tire.

2 Select the runout gauge or dial indicator, attachment, and bracket that fit the axle flange or hub. Mount the dial indicator on a firm surface to keep it still.

3 Adjust the plunger so it is 90 degrees to the axle flange or hub. Press the dial indicator gently against the flat surface of the axle flange or hub and rotate it one full turn. Keep pressing until the plunger settles about halfway into the indicator. Verify that the plunger is still 90 degrees to the tire and lock the indicator assembly into position. Rotate the axle flange or hub while observing the dial readings.

SKILL DRILL | 27-16 | Measuring Axle Flange or Hub Runout, continued

4 If the pointer hovers around a single graduation on the dial, the axle flange or hub has minimal runout or surface distortion and the test is complete. If the pointer moves significantly left and right, note the variations. Find the point of maximum movement to the left and move the dial so that zero is over this point.

5 Continue to rotate the axle flange or hub. Find the point of maximum movement to the right and note the reading. Confirm this value by rotating the axle several more times to verify the zero point and high point. Compare these values to the manufacturer's specifications. If the deviation is greater than the specifications, the axle or hub must be discarded. Reinstall the wheels and torque the lug nuts following the specified procedure and torque specifications.

11 Compare these values to the manufacturer's specifications. If the deviation is greater than the specifications, the axle or hub must be discarded.

12 Reinstall the wheels and torque the lug nuts following the specified procedure and torque specifications. **(Photo 5)**

Inspecting, Diagnosing, and Calibrating the TPMS

Inspection, diagnosis, and calibration of the TPMS is required in several general situations. Inspection is needed whenever the tires have been dismounted from the wheels. In some cases the TPMS sensor batteries need to be replaced and the sensor mounts need to be inspected. Diagnosis of system faults is required when the system detects a fault and turns on the warning light. This could be caused by one or more tires that are not at the proper pressure, requiring an inspection for leaks or incorrect pressures, or it could be a system fault requiring a scan tool capable of communicating with

the TPMS. Calibration of the system is needed on some systems whenever a tire rotation is performed or a sensor is replaced so that the TPMS knows on which wheel each sensor is located.

To inspect, diagnose, and calibrate the TPMS, follow the steps in **SKILL DRILL 27-17**:

1 Turn the ignition key to the run position and observe the TPMS warning light. If the light indicates low tire pressure at any wheel, check the pressure of that wheel with an accurate tire pressure gauge. If incorrect, adjust the pressure using compressed air (or compressed nitrogen if indicated). You may have to refer to a pressure chart if the tire is not approximately 70°F (21°C). **(Photo 1)**

2 If the light indicates a system fault, connect an appropriate scan tool to the system and read any diagnostic trouble codes (DTCs). Since TPMS systems are not standardized, research DTCs in the appropriate service information, and follow the diagnostic steps listed to identify the cause of the fault. **(Photo 2)**

SKILL DRILL | 27-17 | Inspecting, Diagnosing, and Calibrating the TPMS

1. Turn the ignition key to the run position and observe the TPMS warning light. If the light indicates low tire pressure at any wheel, check the pressure of that wheel with an accurate tire pressure gauge. If incorrect, adjust the pressure using compressed air.

2. If the light indicates a system fault, connect an appropriate scan tool to the system and read any DTCs. Research DTCs in the appropriate service information, and follow the diagnostic steps listed to identify the cause of the fault.

Wrap-up

Ready for Review

- Poorly maintained wheels and tires decrease effective handling and may lead to steering and suspension problems.
- The main principles of understanding service of tires and wheels are: tire distortion, center of gravity, and wheel offset.
- Tire distortion refers to the tire's cornering force countering the side force that occurs when a vehicle corners, to create a slip angle.
- Center of gravity refers to the balance point of the vehicle, which is determined by location of the engine and transmission.
- Wheel offset refers to the distance from the hub mounting surface to the centerline of the wheel.
- Wheel offset can be zero, positive, or negative.
- Tire and wheel assemblies must be balanced to prevent both static and dynamic imbalance.
- Tire and wheel components include the wheel or rim, wheel studs and nuts, wheel center, and tires.
- Rims usually have a deep well—a widened area on one side of the wheel.
- The design of passenger vehicle wheels is generally either well based or drop center.
- Types of rims include: steel, one-piece alloy, two-piece alloy, multipiece alloy, custom, spinning, split, semi-drop well, drop well, and safety.
- Wheel studs and lug nuts fasten the wheels to the rims.
- Wheel retaining studs or nuts can be tapered seat, flat seat with washer, or flat seat without a washer.
- Tires provide the wheel with coverage and protection and absorb shock from road surfaces.
- Tires are composed of treads, sidewalls, inner liners, and beads.
- Synthetic fabric cords are used to create plies, giving the tire strength and flexibility.
- Tires are most commonly either cross-ply or radial (used by most passenger vehicles).

Key Terms

aspect ratio The ratio of sidewall height to section width of a tire.

asymmetric tread pattern A tread pattern that differs on each side and, therefore, is usually directional.

bar A metric unit of measure for pressure.

bead seat The part of the wheel that the tire seals against.

bias-ply A tire constructed in a latticed, crisscrossing structure, with alternate plies crossing over each other and laid with the cord angles in opposite directions.

casing plies A network of cords that give the tire shape and strength; also known as casing cords.

centrifugal switch A switch that is only activated when centrifugal forces are placed on a vehicle.

cornering force The force between the tread and the road surface as a vehicle turns.

deep dish wheel A wheel with negative offset, which gives the outside of the wheel a deep dish appearance. Deep dish refers to the side of the wheel that is farthest from the drop center.

direct TPMS A type of automated tire pressure monitoring system that measures tire pressure and possibly temperature via a sensor installed inside each wheel.

directional and asymmetric tread pattern A tread pattern that is both directional and asymmetric, which means the tire is designed to rotate in only one direction and has one side that must face outward to ensure that the tire performs as designed under operating conditions.

directional tread pattern A tread pattern designed to pump water out from under the tire; each tire must be placed in a particular spot on the vehicle.

drop center A wheel design with part of the center section of the wheel a smaller diameter than the rest. It is used for mounting and demounting the tire.

dynamic imbalance A tire imbalance that causes the wheel assembly to turn inward and outward with each half revolution.

EH2 rim The specialized rim design that is used with some run-flat tires.

Extended Mobility Technology (EMT) Tires with thick sidewalls that allow the tire to be driven on even when it has no air pressure.

flat seat with washer A type of lug nut that is flat where it bolts to the wheel and has a washer affixed that allows it to turn independent of the hex part of the lug nut.

flat seat without washer A type of lug nut that is flat where it bolts to the wheel.

indirect TPMS A type of automated tire pressure monitoring system that uses the anti-lock braking system of a vehicle to measure the difference in the rotational speed of the four wheels to determine tire pressure.

lug nuts Nuts that secure the wheel onto the wheel studs.

match mounting The process of matching up the tire's highest point with the rim's lowest point for the purpose of reducing the tire's radial runout.

negative offset A condition in which the plane of the hub mounting surface is positioned toward the brake side or back of the wheel centerline.

neutral steer A condition in which both the front and the rear tires of a vehicle are experiencing the same slip angle.

nondirectional tread pattern A tread pattern that is nonspecific, allowing the tire to be placed on any wheel of a vehicle.

oversteer A condition in which a vehicle's front slip angles are larger than the rear slip angles. This vehicle is said to be "pushing" in the corners.

pitch circle diameter (PCD) The diameter of the imaginary circle drawn through the center of the wheel bolt holes.

ply rating A rating system that denotes the number of belt layers or plies that make up the tire carcass. In radial tires, ply rating denotes the relative strength of the plies, not the actual number of plies.

positive offset A condition in which the plane of the hub mounting surface is positioned toward the outside or front of the wheel centerline.

radial tire A tire with two or more layers of casing plies and cord loops running radially from bead to bead.

rim the outer circular lip of the metal on which the inside edge of the tire is mounted.

rim flanges The outside edge of the wheel that helps keep the tire from popping off the wheel.

rim width The distance across the rim from one rim flange to the other.

run-flat technology A tire design that allows the vehicle to keep moving under driver control following a puncture or rapid loss of pressure.

safety-type drop-center rim A rim designed with a slight hump at the inside edge of the bead ledges to hold the tire beads in place during a flat tire.

Schrader valve A one-way valve used in a valve stem.

self-sealing tire A tire constructed with a flexible and malleable lining inside the tire around the inner tubeless membrane. The lining can seal small tread-area punctures instantly and permanently.

side force The pressure on the wheel that pushes it toward the outside or inside of the rim as the vehicle makes a turn.

slip angle A tire's sideways distortion that makes the vehicle follow a path at an angle to the direction the road wheel is pointing.

static imbalance A tire imbalance resulting from a heavy spot on a tire; it will vibrate vertically with the heavy area slapping the road surface with each turn of the wheel.

steel-disc–type rim A plain steel wheel that is typically covered by a hubcap.

symmetric tread pattern A tread pattern with the same tread pattern on both sides of the tire; typically nondirectional.

tapered seat A type of lug nut with a tapered end toward the rim that helps center the wheel on the wheel studs.

temperature grade A standardized grading system that indicates the extent to which heat is generated or dissipated by a tire.

tensile strength A measure of how strong a material is as it is being pulled apart.

tire inflation pressure The level of air in the tire that provides it with load-carrying capacity and affects overall vehicle performance.

tire placard A metal, vinyl, or paper tag permanently affixed to a vehicle that indicates the appropriate tire size and inflation pressure for the vehicle.

tire pressure gauge A gauge used to measure the air pressure within a tire.

tire pressure monitoring system (TPMS) An automatic sensor system in most modern vehicles that alerts drivers of tire pressure problems.

tire valve The valve through which air is inserted into a tire to inflate it.

traction grade A standardized grading system that indicates how well a tire will maintain contact with the road surface when wet.

tread wear grade The number imprinted on the sidewall of a tire by the manufacturer as required by the National Highway Traffic Safety Administration (NHTSA) that indicates the tread life of a tire's tread.

understeer A condition in which a vehicle's front wheels turn sharper than the vehicle's direction when the vehicle is steered around a corner. This vehicle is said to be "loose" in the corners.

Uniform Tire Quality Grading (UTQG) A standardized grading system established by the National Highway Traffic Safety Administration (NHTSA) designed to provide tire buyers with a comparative measure of a tire's tread life, traction, and temperature characteristics.

US Department of Transportation (DOT) A federal agency that regulates transportation safety in the United States, including vehicles' wheels and tires. The DOT requires a code—a series of letters and numbers—to be stamped into the sidewall of every tire made for public use in the United States. These codes contain information such as the date of manufacture and the plant where the tire was manufactured.

valve core The one-way spring-loaded valve that screws into the valve stem that allows air to be pumped into a tire and prevents it from flowing out.

valve stem A rubber or steel piece that attaches the tire valve to the rim.

valve stem cap A cap that fits tightly onto the valve stem to prevent debris from clogging it and acts as a secondary seal.

weight matching The process of matching the tire's lightest point with the rim's heaviest point (generally at the valve stem) for the purpose of reducing the tire's radial imbalance.

wheel center The part of the wheel containing the holes for the lug studs.

wheel retaining nuts Lug nuts used to hold the wheel on the hub.

wheel rim The part on which the tire is mounted. Also called a "wheel" or "rim."

wheel studs The threaded fasteners that attach the wheel to the vehicle.

zero offset A condition in which the plane of the hub mounting surface is even with the centerline of the wheel.

ASE-Type Questions

1. Tech A says that when turning a corner, both wheels being steered remain parallel to each other as the wheels are steered. Tech B says that on some vehicles, the rear wheels also can be steered. Who is correct?
   a. Tech A
   b. Tech B
   c. Both A and B
   d. Neither A nor B

2. Tech A says that most wheels have a drop center or deep well that is used in installing a tire on the wheel. Tech B says that the drop center or deep well is used to prevent the tire from coming off the wheel in the case of low tire pressure. Who is correct?
   a. Tech A
   b. Tech B
   c. Both A and B
   d. Neither A nor B

3. Tech A says that all wheels must be torqued to prevent wheels from loosening up and falling off. Tech B says that all wheels must be torqued to prevent overtightening, which can weaken lug studs and warp brake rotors. Who is correct?
   a. Tech A
   b. Tech B
   c. Both A and B
   d. Neither A nor B

4. Tech A says that underinflated tires reduce fuel economy. Tech B says that underinflated tires are unsafe and cause accelerated tire wear. Who is correct?
   a. Tech A
   b. Tech B
   c. Both A and B
   d. Neither A nor B

5. Tech A says that incorrect toe settings will cause feathered wear across the tire tread. Tech B says that underinflated tires have more wear in the center of the tread. Who is correct?
   a. Tech A
   b. Tech B
   c. Both A and B
   d. Neither A nor B

6. Tech A says that tires are marked with a date code indicating the date the tires should be discarded. Tech B says that any tires with a three-digit date code should be discarded. Who is correct?
   a. Tech A
   b. Tech B
   c. Both A and B
   d. Neither A nor B

7. Tech A says that a TPMS system can save fuel over time. Tech B says that a TPMS will help prevent blowouts. Who is correct?
   a. Tech A
   b. Tech B
   c. Both A and B
   d. Neither A nor B

8. Tech A says that the use of nitrogen to fill a tire will prevent the tire from blowing out. Tech B says that when mounting or dismounting a tire on a wheel with a TPMS sensor, you need to position the wheel/tire properly on the tire machine or the TPMS sensor can be easily broken. Who is correct?
   a. Tech A
   b. Tech B
   c. Both A and B
   d. Neither A nor B

9. Tech A says that using a tire plug to repair a hole in a tire is the best and fastest way to fix a tire. Tech B says that using a tire plug patch is the only approved method of repairing a tire in many states. Who is correct?
   a. Tech A
   b. Tech B
   c. Both A and B
   d. Neither A nor B

10. Tech A says that directional tires cannot be rotated. Tech B says that all old wheel weights should be removed before balancing a tire. Who is correct?
    a. Tech A
    b. Tech B
    c. Both A and B
    d. Neither A nor B

CHAPTER 28

NATEF Tasks

Suspension and Steering
Steering Systems

Servicing the Steering System

NATEF Tasks, continued

- Inspect pitman arm, relay (center link/intermediate) rod, idler arm and mountings, and steering linkage damper. **MLR** 877–880

- Inspect and replace pitman arm, relay (center link/intermediate) rod, idler arm and mountings, and steering linkage damper. **AST** **MAST** 877–880

- Inspect tie-rod ends (sockets), tie-rod sleeves, and clamps. **MLR** 881

- Inspect, replace, and adjust tie rod ends (sockets), tie-rod sleeves, and clamps. **AST** **MAST** 881

- Test and diagnose components of electronically controlled steering systems using a scan tool; determine necessary action. **MAST** 883

- Identify hybrid vehicle power steering system electrical circuits and service and safety precautions. **MLR** **AST** **MAST** 883

- Disable and enable supplemental restraint system (SRS). **MLR** **AST** **MAST** 883–885

- Remove and replace steering wheel; center/time SRS coil (clock spring). **AST** **MAST** 885–888

- Inspect steering shaft universal joint(s), flexible coupling(s), collapsible column, lock cylinder mechanism, and steering wheel; determine necessary action. **AST** **MAST** 888–890

Suspension Systems

- Inspect electric power assist steering. **MLR** **AST** **MAST** 882–883

Related Suspension and Steering Service

- Describe the function of the power steering pressure switch. **MLR** **AST** **MAST** 855

Knowledge Objectives

After you have read this chapter, you will be able to:
1. Identify the components of the basic steering system. (pp 839–846)
2. Describe the types of steering boxes, including the rack-and-pinion gearbox and the worm gearbox, and how they function. (pp 846–851)
3. Describe the purpose and types of power steering. (pp 851–857)
4. Explain the various tools and their uses in proper diagnostics of steering systems. (pp 857–860)
5. Describe the maintenance and repair of a steering system. (pp 860–890)

Skills Objectives

After reading this chapter, you will be able to:
1. Check and adjust power steering fluid. (p 861)
2. Replace the power steering pump filter(s). (pp 861–862)
3. Flush and pressure test a power steering system. (pp 862–866)
4. Remove and reinstall a power steering pump and a press-fit power steering pump pulley. (pp 866–869)
5. Inspect and replace power steering hoses and fittings. (pp 869–871)
6. Inspect mounting bushings and brackets. (pp 871–872)
7. Remove and replace a rack-and-pinion steering gear. (pp 871–875)
8. Inspect and replace rack-and-pinion steering gear inner tie-rod ends and bellows boots. (pp 875–877)
9. Inspect and replace the idler arm and the pitman arm. (pp 877–879)
10. Inspect and replace the center link (relay rod/intermediate rod). (pp 879–880)
11. Inspect and replace the steering linkage damper. (pp 879–880)
12. Inspect and replace preloaded tie-rod ends. (p 881)
13. Adjust non–rack-and-pinion worm bearing preload and sector lash. (p 882)
14. Disable and enable the supplemental restraint system (SRS). (pp 883–885)
15. Remove and replace the steering wheel, and center-time the SRS coil. (pp 885–888)
16. Inspect the steering shaft universal joint(s), flexible coupling(s), and collapsible column. (pp 886, 888–890)

Introduction

Every driver knows that turning the steering wheel steers the wheels, which steer the vehicle. What is not readily apparent are the many components that are installed between the steering wheel and the wheels that relay the signal and make the wheels steer. This chapter discusses the different steering systems, how they operate, and the purpose and function of each part within them. It also discusses the steps and tools needed to inspect and service steering systems. Maintaining a well-functioning steering system is necessary for the safety of the driver, passengers, and others sharing the road.

Steering System Overview

The **steering system** provides control over the vehicle's direction of travel, good maneuverability for parking the vehicle, smooth recovery from turns as the driver releases the steering wheel, and minimal transmission of road shocks from the road surface through the steering wheel. As vehicle technology has progressed, steering systems have gone through a number of refinements to enhance vehicle safety, performance, and even fuel economy.

A basic steering system has four main parts: a steering column, a steering box, a steering linkage, and a steering knuckle **FIGURE 28-1**. Added to the basic steering system is a power assist system that makes it easier for the driver to steer the vehicle. The power steering system can be either a hydraulic type or electric type. In the case of electric power steering, in addition to providing power assist, the system can be integrated with the electronic

FIGURE 28-1 The components of a basic steering system.

stability control system, such that the power train control module (PCM) can take command of the steering, if needed, to prevent loss of control of the vehicle. Electric power steering also makes four-wheel steering more of a feasible option.

The **steering column** transmits the driver's steering effort from the steering wheel down to the steering box. The **steering box** converts the rotary motion of the steering wheel to the **linear motion** needed to pivot the wheels. The steering box also uses principles of gear reduction to give the driver mechanical advantage over the wheels, making it easier to steer them. The **steering linkage** transfers the linear steering effort to the wheels by connecting the steering box to the **steering arm** on each

You are the Automotive Technician

A customer is driving on the highway and notices a burning oil smell and smoke coming from the front of his 6-year-old vehicle with power rack-and-pinion steering. He is able to pull into a visitor's center and check under the vehicle's hood. He identifies a large amount of power steering fluid sprayed all over the engine compartment, and the power steering reservoir is nearly empty. He calls you for advice and wants to know if he can drive it to your shop 35 miles away.

1. What would you advise he do, and why?
2. What are the most likely leak points?
3. While you are working on the vehicle, what other steering-related inspections would you perform?

of the steering knuckles, which pivot on the ball joints, allowing the wheels to steer the vehicle.

There are two main types of steering systems used on vehicles today: rack and pinion and parallelogram. Each one has its strengths and weaknesses, but rack-and-pinion systems are the most commonly used. The rack-and-pinion system gets its name because a rotating pinion gear is used to move a flat, toothed rack **FIGURE 28-2**. The rack is connected through pivoting socket ends and a **tie-rod** directly to the steering arms. It is a simple, compact system with only a few moving and pivoting parts. It fits well into most engine compartments and takes up less space than other systems, which means it is less likely to get in the way of other components. And because of the fewer parts and the orientation of the pinion gear to the rack, it gives a more precise steering feel, making it more sporty.

The **parallelogram steering system** gets its name because the center link and axle, along with the pitman arm and idler arm, always move parallel to each other **FIGURE 28-3**. Pivoting tie-rods connect the parallelogram to the steering arms. Parallelogram steering uses a **worm** gearbox, which changes the direction of steering wheel rotation 90 degrees, and a pitman arm and center link to turn the rotary motion into lateral motion. The worm gear design reduces the road shock that is transmitted to the steering wheel, so a parallelogram design provides an advantage especially in off-road four-wheel drive vehicles or non-sporty vehicles.

The **steering knuckles** are stout components that firmly connect the wheels to the suspension and steering systems. They provide a stub axle upon which the wheel bearings ride, or a hub-style wheel bearing assembly that is pressed or bolted onto the steering knuckle.

The steering knuckle pivots on one or two ball joints, depending on the type of suspension, which is covered in the Servicing Suspension Systems chapter. The steering arm either is integrated into the casting of the steering knuckle or is bolted on. Either way, it transmits the steering force from the steering linkage to the wheel and tire assembly.

Steering Geometry

The relationships between the steering system, the wheel positions, and the suspension system form what is called the steering geometry. Steering geometry is a geometric arrangement of linkages in the steering of a vehicle designed to solve the problem of keeping the wheels properly oriented through various positions of the steering and suspension systems. As the wheels move up and down relative to the body, the steering linkage swings vertically through an arc. The wheel would thus turn in and out as the vehicle goes over bumps if it were not for steering geometry. In this case, the pivots for the suspension components cause the wheel to go through a similar arc as the steering components, allowing the wheel to track straight ahead, or in a consistent direction if it is in a turn.

Also, when rounding a corner, the inner and outer wheels must trace circles of different radii; otherwise the tires would scrub. This is a challenge because no matter which way the vehicle turns, the inside wheel must always turn more sharply than the outside wheel, which is called toe-out on turns. The Ackermann principle, named after the man who patented it in 1818, provides the needed geometry. The Ackermann principle angles the steering arms toward the center of the vehicle such that imaginary lines drawn from the center of the steering knuckle pivot points, through the center of the outer tie-rod ends,

FIGURE 28-2 Rack-and-pinion steering system.

FIGURE 28-3 Parallelogram steering system.

intersect at the center of the rear axle **FIGURE 28-4**. This angle is what allows the wheels to navigate a corner without scrubbing. Steering geometry and suspension geometry must be within the manufacturer's specifications for the vehicle to operate correctly. If it is not correct, it is usually due to worn or bent components that the technician will have to diagnose and ultimately repair to restore proper operation.

Rack-and-Pinion Steering Gear and Linkage

The <u>rack-and-pinion steering system</u> is used on the majority of front-wheel drive vehicles due to the restriction of space under the hood. Rack-and-pinion steering gears are used because their construction makes them compact and lightweight **FIGURE 28-5**. Their steering response is very sharp because the rack operates directly on the steering knuckle and there is very little sliding and rotational resistance, which gives lighter operation.

The primary components of the rack-and-pinion steering system are:

- <u>Pinion</u>: A toothed gear that meshes with the rack. The pinion is connected to the steering column. As the driver turns the steering wheel, the forces are transferred to the pinion, causing the rack to move in either direction. This is achieved by having the pinion in <u>constant mesh</u> (constant contact) with the rack.
- <u>Rack</u>: A toothed, straight piece of metal that meshes with the pinion in the middle of the rack and has tie-rods on each end that fasten to the knuckle. The rack slides in the housing and is moved by the action of the <u>meshed pinion</u> (the

pinion it is in contact with). It normally has an <u>adjustable bushing</u> positioned opposite the pinion to control the components' meshing, and it has a nylon bushing at the other end. This adjustable bushing allows the technician to adjust play out of the rack and pinion. The function of the rack is to transfer motion to the tie-rod.

- <u>Inner tie-rod or socket</u>: The inner tie-rod is attached to the end of the rack and allows for suspension movement and slight changes in steering angles.

FIGURE 28-5 The rack-and-pinion steering system. **A.** Pinion and rack. **B.** Inner ball joint or socket. **C.** Tie-rod.

FIGURE 28-4 The inner wheel will have to turn more sharply than the outer wheel and by angling the steering arms inward.

- **Outer tie-rod**: An outer tie-rod end is attached between the tie-rod shaft and the steering arm. It transfers the movement of the rack. The outer tie-rod pivots as the rack is extended or retracted when the vehicle is negotiating turns. Some tie-rods and tie-rod ends are left- or right-hand threaded. This allows toe-in or toe-out to be adjusted to the manufacturer's specifications. Toe-in is a condition where the fronts of the wheels, as seen from above, are closer together than the rears of the wheels. Toe-out is the opposite condition, where the rears of the wheels are closer together than the fronts. A tie-rod end connects the center link to the steering knuckle on vehicles with parallelogram steering systems.

- **Rubber bellows**: The rubber bellows protects the inner joints from dirt and contaminants. In addition, it retains the grease lubricant inside the rack-and-pinion housing. There are two ends of the rack. Each side contains an identical bellows.

Parallelogram Steering Gear and Linkage

The parallelogram steering system is used on larger vehicles where ride comfort is more important than sporty handling. Parallelogram steering linkage is more complicated than the rack-and-pinion linkage, so there are more wear points to know about and inspect. The primary components of the parallelogram steering system, from the gearbox on, are:

- Pitman arm: The pitman arm transfers movement from the steering box to the center link. It is attached to the steering box by a **spline** and nut. Splines are ridges or teeth on a driveshaft that mesh with grooves in a mating piece and transfer torque to it and maintain the angular correspondence between the components. As the driver turns the steering wheel, the steering box mechanism moves the steering linkages via the pitman arm either left or right, depending on the direction in which the steering wheel is turned. The steering box provides the change of angle at 90 degrees to the steering linkage and also provides a steering ratio (the number of turns of the steering wheel compared to the number of turns of the sector shaft) to assist in the ease of turning the steering wheel and linkages.

- Idler arm: The idler arm is attached to the **chassis** (the frame of the vehicle) and is positioned parallel to the pitman arm. The idler arm assembly is the pivoting support for the steering linkage. It consists of a rod that pivots on a bracket bolted to the frame of the vehicle on one end and supports a ball socket on the other end. Generally, an idler arm is attached between the opposite side of the center link from the pitman arm and the vehicle's frame to hold the center link at the proper height so it can accurately relay the pitman arm's movement. Idler arms are generally more vulnerable to wear than pitman arms because of the pivot function built into them.

- Center link: The center link connects the pitman arm to the idler arm. In this way, any movement in the pitman arm is directly applied to the idler arm.

- Tie-rod: The tie-rods connect the center link to the steering arms that are located on the steering knuckles. All movement from the pitman arm is relayed directly to the front wheels, which steer the vehicle.

- Tie-rod end: Tie-rod ends are attached to the tie-rod shaft. They pivot as the rack is extended or retracted when the vehicle is negotiating turns. Tie-rods and tie-rod ends are left- or right-hand threaded. The inner tie-rod ends are attached to either end of the center link and serve as pivot points for the steering gear.

- **Adjustment sleeve**: The adjustment sleeve connects the tie-rod to the tie-rod end. It provides the adjustment point for toe-in or toe-out, depending on the manufacturer's specifications. It is considered a turnbuckle, usually with one end having left-hand threads and the other having right-hand threads. When turning the sleeve, the tie-rods thread apart or together to set the vehicle toe.

> ### ▶ TECHNICIAN TIP
>
> Each type of steering system makes provision for adjustment of the linkage to achieve the manufacturer's recommended **toe-setting**. The toe-setting is the symmetric angle that each wheel makes with the longitudinal axis of the vehicle. The track rods or tie-rod ends are threaded to provide for their lengthening or shortening.

A tie-rod on each side of the vehicle connects each **wheel assembly** to the center link. Each connection point in the linkage system has a pivoting joint, which is a ball-and-socket construction **FIGURE 28-6**.

Flexible joints on the center link and on the ends of the tie-rods allow for steering and suspension movement. The tie-rods have ball sockets that allow steering movement and movement of the suspension. The tie-rod end

FIGURE 28-6 The flexible joints of the steering linkage are a ball-and-socket construction, which allows movement of the linkage with no play in the joint.

FIGURE 28-7 Steering linkage layout on a solid-axle four-wheel drive vehicle.

FIGURE 28-8 Collapsible steering column.

swivel joints are at equal heights and pivot so that movement in the suspension does not affect steering operation. Movement of the suspension that does affect steering is called bump steer. **Bump steer** is the undesired condition produced when, upon hitting a bump, the vehicle darts to one side as the steering linkage is pushed or pulled as a result of the travel of the suspension. Typically, bump steer is due to a bent tie-rod end or another bent component that would cause unequal heights of the tie-rod ends. The tie-rod end swivel joints allow the suspension to move up and down without affecting vehicle steering.

In four-wheel drive vehicles with a **beam axle**, a single tie-rod connects the steering arms on each wheel assembly. In this design, the drag link is connected to an arm on the front of the left-hand wheel assembly. Movement of the pitman arm is transferred through the drag link to the left-hand wheel, and through the single tie-rod to the right-hand wheel **FIGURE 28-7**. The steering box is offset from the steering column, so two universal joints and an intermediate steering shaft are used. Four-wheel drive vehicles of this type often use a **steering damper** on the single tie-rod. It resembles a shock absorber and operates on a similar principle. Specifically, it keeps the steering wheel from shaking when the driver hits a pothole or other road irregularity. The steering damper is mounted between the tie-rod and either the rigid axle or the vehicle frame. When the vehicle is driven over rough terrain, its purpose is to prevent shock forces being transmitted through the steering linkage and back to the steering wheel.

Steering Columns

Effort applied to the steering wheel is transferred down the steering column, or shaft, to a steering box. In early

vehicles, the steering column was a straight shaft, running inside a hollow tube. The steering wheel was attached to one end, and the steering box to the other. In many frontal collisions, however, this design caused serious injury to the driver, partly because the steering wheel was forced back toward the driver's head and chest and partly because the sudden stop forced the driver onto the wheel. To reduce this hazard, all steering columns are now fitted with collapsible sections that help protect the driver. During a collision, two forces are applied to the steering column. The first is the force of the steering box being forced toward the steering column and toward the driver. Plastic shear pins allow the lower shaft to move over the upper shaft. The second force is the mass of the driver striking the steering wheel. This force breaks the brackets on the upper part of the column, driving the upper column into the lower column **FIGURE 28-8**. Most vehicles also integrate a driver's side airbag into the steering wheel for collision protection. This system will be discussed in greater detail in a later section.

The steering column is connected to the input shaft of the steering gear by a flexible joint. This flexible joint

FIGURE 28-9 Steering column with an intermediate shaft for enhanced protection in an accident.

allows for smooth turning of the steering wheel since the steering column sits at a different angle than the steering box. It also reduces the transmission of road shocks to the driver. Some steering columns have an **intermediate shaft**, which runs at an angle, from the column to the steering gear. In a collision, the universal joints on the intermediate shaft allow it to fold under, preventing the impact force from being transferred directly to the column **FIGURE 28-9**.

Some manufacturers fit sensors and an electric motor to the steering column. The sensors in the steering column provide information to a steering control module for electric power steering assist or for the electronic stability control system. The sensors are able to sense rotational direction and speed exerted by the driver and control both the speed and the direction of the electric motor, which is used to provide the electric power steering assist. This system will be discussed further in a later section.

The steering column generally accommodates for an ignition switch and lock assembly, although more new vehicles are coming with a push-button start switch located in the dash. The steering column also incorporates a multifunction switch (or separate switches) that may include switches for lights, turn signal indicators, wipers, and cruise control. The steering wheel itself may have integrated control switches for the entertainment system, a cell phone, and instrument panel display options **FIGURE 28-10**.

Tilt/Telescoping Mechanism

To compensate for variations in driving positions, many manufacturers have included a steering column tilting and/or telescoping mechanism to their vehicles. These features allow drivers to control the steering wheel position so that it best suits their preferences. The tilting mechanism allows drivers to raise or lower the steering column position, while the telescoping mechanism allows

FIGURE 28-10 **A.** Multifunction switch. **B.** Steering wheel entertainment controls.

the driver to move the steering wheel closer or farther away. However, the amount of movement in any direction does have its limitations.

The tilt mechanism uses a heavy spring, a pivoting joint, and a ratchet mechanism to operate. These added components make the steering column more complicated to repair. The telescoping mechanism includes a slip joint and locking mechanism. Both of these features can also put the wires in the steering column under additional stress due to more frequent movement, so remember that when diagnosing wiring faults.

Driver's Side Airbag

The driver's side airbag is designed to provide a collapsing cushion that decelerates a driver's head and chest during an accident. One of the leading causes of fatalities in accidents is the rapid deceleration forces that occur within a body during the accident. The body's internal organs cannot handle the force of sudden deceleration, so engineers devise ways to slow the deceleration during an accident. They do this through the use of crumple zones in the vehicle, which fold and crush accordionlike to provide some deceleration. Restraint systems such as tear-away seat belts also are designed to slow the deceleration. Airbags also decelerate the driver and prevent the head from contacting the steering wheel or dash. Side curtain airbags ensure that the driver does not hit the side rail of the roof when involved in a side collision. Next to the seat belt, airbags are the biggest lifesaver in accidents. In most countries, government regulation requires that a vehicle equipped with airbags be capable of having the airbags replaced as part of the repair process of a crashed vehicle. If the airbag has been deployed in an accident, a new airbag and cover must be installed to meet legislative requirements in most states.

When a technician needs to carry out a servicing procedure on the steering column, it is good practice to disarm the triggering system for the driver's side airbag, which is located in the top cover of the steering wheel. If not properly disarmed, the airbag could trigger accidentally, injuring or killing the technician due to the large deployment force created by the ignited propellant, which is rocket fuel. Unintended deployment also creates the need to replace the airbag assembly, which is expensive. Generally, to disarm a driver's side airbag, the correct supplemental restraint system (SRS) fuse must be located and removed, and then verified by turning the ignition switch to run and observing the SRS light, which should remain on. Once the fuse is removed, the negative battery terminal is disconnected and the vehicle is allowed to sit for about 15 minutes to discharge the capacitors. Note that a memory minder SHOULD NOT be used when working on, or around, the SRS system.

Some manufacturers will have you disconnect the airbag connector located under the dash near the steering column. Disconnecting this connector will generally activate a shorting bar in the airbag side of the connector, which will make it much harder for the airbag to accidentally deploy. With the airbag disarmed, you can carry out any needed diagnosis or repair on the steering column. Just remember to rearm the airbag once service is completed. Follow the service information to properly deactivate the airbag prior to steering column diagnosis and repair and to reactivate it when finished.

Safety

Never lean over or in front of an armed airbag when working on the dash, instrument panel, or airbag system. Doing so can cause serious injury or death if it accidentally deploys. Always follow the manufacturer's procedure when disarming and arming the airbag.

Because of the critical nature of the airbag, it is imperative that it is always connected electrically to its control module, so it can be deployed when needed. Since the airbag is mounted in the steering wheel, a method of maintaining the electrical connection to the airbag is not as easy. This is overcome by incorporating a clock spring into the steering column. The **clock spring** is a special rotary electrical connector located between the steering wheel and the steering column that maintains a constant electrical connection with the wiring while the vehicle's steering wheel is being turned. The wires from the airbag and its electrical system connect through the clock spring, which coils and uncoils as the wheel is turned, and maintains constant electrical contact. When removing the airbag assembly from the steering wheel, inspect the wiring and connector of the airbag to clock spring to ensure there is no damage. When the steering wheel is removed and the clock spring is easily visible, inspect it to ensure that it and the clock spring wire is not damaged. Typically, if the electrical wiring inside the clock spring is damaged, an SRS system code will set and the SRS light will be turned on. If it has been damaged in any way, it must be replaced it cannot be repaired.

TECHNICIAN TIP

When removing the rack-and-pinion or steering gear, make sure the wheels are pointing straight ahead before disassembly. Also, either lock the steering column with the ignition key or wrap a seat belt around the steering wheel to prevent the clock spring from being moved off center. Make sure to also reassemble the parts in the straight-ahead position.

Steering Boxes

There are a number of variations for steering boxes. They are either manual steering or power-assisted steering. Manual steering has no power source to help make the wheel easier for the driver of the vehicle to turn, whereas power-assisted steering uses a hydraulic pump or electric motor that aids the driver in turning the wheel. Older vehicles were available with manual steering, and power steering was an expensive option. This is not the case now, as any vehicle purchased will come standard with a form of power steering. The function of all steering boxes is the same, whether manual or power—to transfer the rotary motion of the steering wheel into the side-to-side motion needed to make the wheels pivot left and right.

Steering Box Types

There are two basic types of steering boxes: those with rack-and-pinion gearing and those with worm gearing and a sector shaft. In both cases, the gearing in the steering box makes it easier for the driver to turn the steering wheel and, hence, the wheels. The variations of steering boxes include:

- The rack-and-pinion gearbox
- The worm gearbox, consisting of:
  - Worm and sector
  - Worm and roller
  - Worm and nut (commonly referred to as the recirculating ball)

Rack-and-Pinion Gearbox

The rack-and-pinion gearbox has a pinion connected to the bottom of the steering column. This pinion runs in mesh with a rack that is connected to the steering tie-rods. This connection gives more direct operation, which enables the driver to feel the road better. Turning the steering wheel rotates the pinion and moves the rack from side to side. On end take-off racks, ball sockets at the end of the rack locate the tie-rods and allow movement in the steering and suspension. On center take-off racks, the tie-rods connect to the center of the rack and pinion. The center of the rack is what moves on this style of rack and pinion.

Both the pinion and the rack teeth are helical gears. If an inclined plane is wrapped around a cylinder, the edge of the plane forms a shape called a **helix**. Rotation of the cylinder causes a point on the helix to move along the surface of the cylinder. The distance the point moves in one revolution of the cylinder is called the **pitch**. The helix shape is commonly used as a thread on nuts and bolts, and also for teeth in steering gears and transmissions.

The particular shape and positioning of the teeth in a helical gearing enable smoother and quieter operation for the driver.

Mechanical advantage is gained by the **reduction ratio**, the ratio between the turns of the steering wheel and the angle turned of the wheel (both measured in degrees). The value of this ratio depends on the size of the pinion. A small pinion gives easy steering, but it requires many turns of the steering wheel to travel from lock to lock, which is as far as the steering wheel can be turned from one side to the other. So, instead of a single hard turn of the steering wheel, the driver turns the wheel several times with less force behind each turn. A large pinion means the number of turns of the steering wheel is reduced, but the steering is harder to turn.

Reduction ratios vary depending on the type of vehicle, such as a passenger vehicle versus a tractor trailer. But in each case, in fixed-ratio rack-and-pinion systems, the ratio is the same for all positions of the wheels. It is a fixed ratio, meaning that within a single vehicle, the ratio is the same no matter where the steering wheel is positioned. The rack-and-pinion system produces a ratio between the degrees of steering wheel movement and the degrees of wheel movement. The ratio is called steering ratio and is typically calculated by turning the steering wheel one time and checking the number of degrees that the wheel assembly moves. For example, if one turn of the steering wheel produces 20 degrees of movement at the wheel, then dividing 360 degrees of steering wheel rotation by 20 degrees of wheel movement results in an 18:1 ratio. Steering ratio is not the same on all vehicles and is designed by engineers to provide the best steering response for the vehicle.

In some applications a variable-ratio gear is used, which allows a slow turn rate when the steering wheel is centered and a quicker rate when turned toward the steering lock. This feature provides easier and quicker turning, but keeps the vehicle very stable when traveling straight at high speeds. The variable-ratio rack-and-pinion system uses a specially designed pinion gear tooth, which is more rounded. The rack has teeth that are narrowly spaced in the center and further apart toward the end. Closer teeth provide slower movement of the rack in relation to the turns of the pinion. On other vehicles, it is preferable that the steering be more responsive near the center point, which is ideal for maneuvering at slower speeds. This is accomplished by having widely spaced teeth in the center of the rack and closer spaced teeth near the ends. When designed this way, the steering wheel moves the rack further for each rotation of the pinion when in the center position than at the ends. This also helps prevent stiffer steering toward the full lock positions, since the steering arm leverage is reduced when the wheels are turned sharply.

The rack-and-pinion steering system has the advantages of a large degree of feedback and direct steering feel, meaning the driver can feel the road well. A disadvantage of the rack-and-pinion steering system is that it typically is not manually adjustable. Over time it does wear and develop lash between the pinion teeth and the rack teeth, which is felt as play, or movement, in the steering wheel that does not move the wheels. In many cases, replacement of the rack and pinion is the only cure for excessive lash in the gear teeth.

In the rack-and-pinion steering system, the steering rack is supported at the pinion end by being sandwiched between the pinion and a **spring-loaded rack guide yoke**, sometimes called the rack bearing. Spring-loaded rack guide yokes are made of metal, nylon, or other durable material and have a spring that pushes on the back side of the rack to help reduce the play between the rack and the pinion, while still allowing for relative movement. There may be an adjuster plug that screws into the body of the rack to put pressure on the rack guide yoke. This adjustment produces the correct mesh of the rack teeth to the pinion teeth. It also affects the amount of torque required to turn the pinion. If the setting is incorrect, such as if you are trying to eliminate play in the rack and pinion, turning force of the pinion will become greater and may result in a steering wheel that will not return properly, a condition sometimes referred to as memory steer. Do not adjust the mesh of the rack-and-pinion gears unless directed by service information.

The rack is typically supported at both ends of the **rack housing** or tube by a bushing, a nylon piece that keeps the rack from wearing on the metal housing **FIGURE 28-11**. Nylon is used because it has a low coefficient of friction and low wear rates. The bushings are an integral part of any steering and suspension system. The bushings enable the flexibility needed to accommodate slight radial or lateral movement to assist in **antibinding**, or release when something gets stuck. However, when the bushings wear beyond the limits, they become a liability because they no longer are effective at eliminating play in the steering rack. Regular maintenance and inspection of the steering system is necessary to ensure the safety of the vehicle and its occupants.

The pinion is supported by two bearings in the rack housing. The bearings must be **preloaded** (already compressed from pressure) to ensure the pinion is in the correct position, relative to the rack, and to eliminate free play.

A rack-and-pinion steering box is normally lubricated by grease. Each end of the rack is protected from dirt and

FIGURE 28-11 Rack housing bushings and pinion bearings.

water by a flexible synthetic rubber bellows attached to the rack housing and to the tie-rod. The rubber bellows extends and collapses as the tie-rods move away from and toward the rack housing as the rack moves. On some vehicles, the rubber bellows are interconnected by a tube so that as the steering wheel is moved from side to side, air is transferred from the collapsing bellows side to the expanding bellows side. This process keeps the rubber bellows from collapsing.

With rack-and-pinion steering, the rack is directly connected to the **tie-rod assembly**, which is attached to the steering knuckle. The tie-rod assembly consists of an inner and an outer tie-rod end that are threaded together.

Applied | Math

AM-52: Probability: The technician can relate problem symptoms to the probability of the malfunction of a specific part or system.
A common problem with steering systems, particularly in older vehicles, is excessive free play. Typically, the customer will describe the problem as the steering feeling "loose" or "sloppy." A road test will quickly verify the concern; there will be excessive movement of the steering wheel in the straight-ahead position, before the wheels even begin to turn.

With a pick-up truck that has a basic steering system, the excessive free play could be caused by wear in a number of points within the system. There is a higher probability of the fault being caused within the steering linkage than within the steering gearbox, so components such as tie-rod ends, idler arms and bushings, and pitman arms and bushings should be checked and eliminated first, before inspecting the steering gearbox.

FIGURE 28-12 Two-piece steering knuckle and steering arm.

The inner tie-rod is threaded onto the rack and has a ball-and-socket swivel joint to allow movement in any direction. The other end of the inner tie-rod is threaded to allow attachment of the outer tie-rod end, which provides the method used to adjust the toe angle.

The steering arm, the **stub axle** knuckle, and the **stub-axle carrier** (the body of the stub axle knuckle) can be forged as one piece, and can be referred to as a steering **knuckle** **FIGURE 28-12**. They can also be made as separate units and assembled to form one piece.

Worm Gearbox

Worm gear steering boxes made the process of turning the front wheels an easier task for drivers of the early automobile. The worm gearbox uses two gears: a worm and a worm gear (also called a worm wheel). The worm has teeth cut in a helical (spiral) shape and operates the same as a screw. In this case, the helix on the worm moves the worm wheel one tooth for each revolution of the worm. The helix provides smooth and quiet steering operation for the driver. It converts the rotary motion of the steering wheel to the linear motion needed to control the wheels. This system also produces a large **gear reduction**. The **gear ratio** of the gear train within the gearbox is a comparison of the angles of movement between the steering wheel and the wheel assembly and is expressed as a ratio; for example, 18:1. The gear ratio of a worm gearbox increases output torque and reduces the effort the driver has to apply. Within the steering system, gear reduction transforms a large turn of the steering wheel into a smaller turn of the road wheels. Use of gear reduction makes steering easier for the driver. Wheels require a large force to be steered due to the weight of the vehicle pushing the tire into contact with the road. If there were no gear reduction in the steering gear, the driver would not be able to force the tires to pivot on the road's surface.

Worm gears have another benefit: they do not transmit nearly as much road shock as a rack-and-pinion gear assembly. When the worm is driven (by the steering wheel), the output gear moves easily since each turn of the worm advances the worm wheel one tooth. But if the worm wheel is driven (such as by road shock), the worm wheel teeth butt up against the teeth on the worm, preventing most of the force from being transmitted as rotary motion to the worm. This occurs because most of the force from the output gear is nearly perpendicular to the rotation of the worm gear.

Several forms of the worm gearbox have been used throughout the history of the automobile, although they all use the same component—the worm gear arrangement. Three popular styles have included the worm-and-sector, worm-and-roller, and recirculating ball gearboxes.

Worm-and-Sector Gearbox

The first worm gearbox was of the worm-and-sector style. The worm is meshed with a sector, or portion of a gear, mounted on its own shaft (called a sector shaft), at right angles to the worm. The outer end of the sector shaft has a tapered or straight spline that mates with an internal spline on the pitman arm. As the steering wheel rotates, the worm causes the sector to move through an arc and transfer the motion, through the pitman arm, to the steering linkage. This style of gearbox produced more friction between the gears as the driver turned the steering wheel than later worm gearboxes, which made steering difficult. Variations include the worm-and-roller and the recirculating ball worm gear.

Worm-and-Roller Gearbox

The **worm shaft** in a worm-and-roller steering box has an hourglass shape, and it meshes with a double-track roller, mounted on bearings, on a pin attached to the pitman shaft **FIGURE 28-13**. This gearbox was an improvement to the worm-and-sector style and reduced the friction due to the roller, which reduced the friction between the two gears. This design makes turning the steering wheel easier. As the driver turns the steering wheel, the worm rotates and the roller rolls against the worm, moving in an arc, following the hourglass shape, and transferring the motion to the pitman shaft. The hourglass shape changes the steering ratio slightly as the steering wheel is turned from the central position toward each lock.

Recirculating Ball Gearbox

The worm-and-nut steering gear is also known as a recirculating ball steering gear. The **recirculating ball**

FIGURE 28-13 The worm-and-roller steering gearbox.

FIGURE 28-14 The recirculating ball steering system uses a worm gear that moves a ball nut by turning against ball bearings, reducing the force needed to turn the wheels.

steering box contains a worm gear inside a block (nut) with a threaded hole in it and gear teeth cut into its outside that engage the sector shaft to move the pitman arm. It was developed in 1940 and is an improved version of the worm-and-sector and worm-and-nut types of worm gear. In the recirculating ball gearbox, both ends of the worm shaft are supported in the housing by angular bearings, which are preloaded to reduce lateral movements known as **end play** and side-thrust movements of the worm gear when it is under load. A ball nut rides on the worm gear, supported on the spiral grooves of the worm and the inside of the nut by many balls **FIGURE 28-14**. The balls form a low-friction internal thread, which causes the nut to thread up or down on the worm as it rotates. With rotation, the balls are rolled along the grooves, partly in the worm and partly in the nut. When they get to the end of the groove, they circulate by passing through **ball-return guides** to the other end of the nut. Ball-return guides are simply special passages through which the balls move. External teeth on one side of the nut mesh with the teeth of the sector gear formed on the sector shaft, and these transfer the motion through the pitman arm to the steering linkage to produce the left and right motion at the front wheels.

The sector gear and nut teeth are designed so that when the teeth are in the straight-ahead position, they have minimum clearance. This is called the high point. This design reduces free play when the steering wheel is straight. The pitman shaft is supported by two caged needle roller bearings in the steering box housing. The sector teeth are angled, and an adjustment screw on the steering housing cover allows for adjustment of the sector gear height, which provides proper engagement of the sector gear and nut teeth.

> **TECHNICIAN TIP**
>
> On passenger vehicles with independent suspension and a recirculating ball-type steering box, the steering box may be mounted so that the steering linkage is in front of (front steer) or behind (rear steer) the suspension cross member. When the steering linkage is behind the suspension cross member, it is protected by the cross member from possible damage, and the position of the steering box reduces the length of the steering column. This protects the steering box from damage by road debris.

> **TECHNICIAN TIP**
>
> In forward-control vehicles, the steering system is mounted in front of the engine and wheels. The steering box is mounted on the frame, with the pitman arm vertical. A **drag link** is a steel rod that transfers movement of the pitman arm to a **relay lever**. The relay lever is another steel rod that is used to transfer the movement from the drag link to an idler arm. The relay lever has two arms, one connected to the drag link and the other to the idler arm by the track rod. The longitudinal movement of the drag link pivots the relay lever. As a result of these connections, motion is transferred through the track rod to the idler arm and through the tie-rods to the wheels.

Four-Wheel Steering Systems

Some vehicles have <u>four-wheel steering</u>, meaning the rear wheels can be steered independently of or in conjunction with the front wheels. The ability to steer the rear wheels improves high-speed handling and increases maneuverability during driving tasks such as U-turns and parallel parking. There are two types of four-wheel steering systems—active and passive. Passive systems use compliant rubber bushings that allow a limited amount of rear-wheel steering, typically toward the inside of the corner, under cornering maneuvers. The passive system operates independently of the steering wheel and driver input, which is why it is called a passive system.

In active four-wheel steering systems, the front wheels are controlled normally, and the rear wheels are typically steered through use of a computer and electric motors. In past designs, rear-wheel steering systems could be controlled mechanically through a direct connection between the front and the rear steering boxes. In modern computer-controlled four-wheel steering, an actuator similar to a front rack-and-pinion assembly attaches to the rear steering knuckles with tie-rod ends. The actuator turns the wheels when commanded by the steering control module. Originally, some actuators were powered hydraulically by the power steering pump and electronic control valves. Most systems still in use today use a rack-and-pinion assembly driven by an electric motor. Some manufacturers have adopted the standard that at low speeds the rear wheels will turn in the opposite direction to the front wheels, providing a substantially reduced turning radius, while at higher speeds the rear wheels will turn in the same direction as the front wheels, producing smaller yaw forces during turning maneuvers. This standard provides better control of a vehicle at high speeds and better handling at low speeds, which is useful for functions like parallel parking. Other manufacturers use systems that disable rear steering at higher speeds and only allow rear steering at slow speeds to allow tighter cornering, such as when backing up a trailer.

Power Steering

As vehicles became heavier in the front end due to the increased use of front-wheel drive and wider low-profile tires, more steering effort became necessary. As a result, <u>power steering</u> was introduced. One type has an <u>engine-driven hydraulic pump</u> that delivers hydraulic fluid to the power unit at the steering box or rack-and-pinion assembly through connecting hoses and pipes. When the driver moves the wheel, the hydraulic pressure is sent to the rack or steering box. The power steering system is designed so that the vehicle can still be controlled even if the engine or the power steering system were to fail—though greater effort would be required.

There are three types of power steering:

1. Hydraulically assisted power steering
2. Electrically powered hydraulic steering
3. Fully electric power steering

Hydraulically Assisted Power Steering

Hydraulically assisted power steering uses hydraulic fluid under pressure to assist the driver in steering the wheels. This design is especially helpful at slower vehicle speeds when steering wheel turning effort is much higher. An engine-driven hydraulic pump delivers hydraulic fluid to the power unit at the steering gearbox, or rack-and-pinion assembly, through the control valve and connecting hoses and tubes. The fluid reservoir can be mounted on the pump, or it can be remotely mounted. With the engine running, fluid flows continuously from the <u>power steering pump</u> to the steering gear control valve and back to the power steering pump. With the steering wheel in the neutral position, minimal pressure is needed to maintain fluid flow, and minimal engine power is needed to operate the system.

Some manufacturers task the power steering system with double duty. The pressure from power steering pumps has been used to power hydraulic brake boosters on hydroboost vehicles. It has also been used to turn the radiator fan on a number of vehicles. Be aware that the power steering system is integrated into those systems on some vehicles.

Power Steering Fluid and Hoses

The hydraulic fluid in a power steering system transmits the pressure from the power steering pump to the working chambers in the power steering gear or rack. The fluid must withstand high temperatures and pressures, and at the same time lubricate the pump and steering gear, while preserving the system seals and pressure hoses. The fluid must also flow freely at very cold temperatures. Many manufacturers have specified certain types of automatic transmission fluid for their power steering systems over the years, while others call for specific formulations of a separate power steering fluid. Since there is typically only a quart or two of power steering fluid in the system, it gets worked pretty hard. The harder it is worked, the hotter it gets. The hotter it gets, the shorter its life. For this reason, some vehicles are equipped with a power steering fluid cooler. This is usually built into the high-pressure line and helps cool the fluid before it gets to the steering gear.

Power steering fluid also gets contaminated with rubber and metallic particles from internal wear in the system. Because of this, some manufacturers install a replaceable filter in the power steering system. While many manufacturers do not specify a power steering fluid change interval, the fluid does degrade over time and becomes contaminated. Many technicians recommend flushing power steering fluid every 50,000 to 100,000 miles, depending on the vehicle and how it is driven.

Power steering hoses are used to carry power steering fluid from the pump to the steering gear. This is the high-pressure hose and is usually made of flexible, high-pressure hose material. The return hose runs from the steering gear back to the pump reservoir and carries fluid under much lower pressure. These hoses must also allow movement between the engine and chassis, so they can't be too stiff. Over time, power steering hoses can become weak or damaged. If they leak, they can quickly cause the system to run dry. And since the pressure is very high, if the high-pressure hose leaks, it can spray hot power steering fluid all over the engine and exhaust. Power steering fluid is flammable, so leaks can cause extreme fire hazards. Because of this, they should be inspected for seepage or wear during each oil change. Also, most power steering hoses use an O-ring to seal the end of each hose to the pump and steering gear. These seals can wear or leak, requiring replacement of the O-ring.

Steering Process

The hydraulic pressure is controlled by a rotary valve located on the input shaft of the steering gear. When the steering wheel is turned, the rotary valve directs fluid to one side or the other of a piston attached to the steering gear. Pressure then increases as required to provide steering assistance.

In a rack-and-pinion steering gear, the piston is formed centrally on the steering rack, and the rack housing provides the working cylinder **FIGURE 28-15**. Pressure seals at each end of the cylinder isolate the **power section** from the rest of the rack and pinion. Seals in the rotary valve section at the pinion input prevent internal and external fluid leakage.

In a recirculating ball steering box, the power piston and seals slide in a cylinder in the housing **FIGURE 28-16**. The power piston has an extension formed on one side,

FIGURE 28-15 Power-assisted rack-and-pinion system.

FIGURE 28-16 Power-assisted recirculating ball gearbox.

with teeth that engage teeth on the sector shaft. Pressure applied to either side of the power piston produces a force, which is transferred through the teeth, to help turn the sector shaft.

Connecting pipes transfer fluid from the rotary valve housing to one side of the piston or the other to provide assistance, which acts directly on the steering gear. The rotary valve is located between the steering gear input shaft and the pinion gear, or worm. It consists of an inner member, which forms part of the input shaft, and a surrounding sleeve member, fixed to the pinion gear or worm. It appears as a shaft within a shaft.

Turning the steering wheel makes both members rotate in the steering gear housing, but it is the slight rotary displacement of the inner member and the sleeve member that controls and directs the power steering fluid flow. This slight rotary displacement is allowed by a **torsion bar**, which is a spring-loaded piece of steel connected to the pinion gear or worm at its bottom end and the input shaft at its top end **FIGURE 28-17**.

When the steering wheel is turned, there is resistance from the front wheels at the road surface. This resistance is transmitted through the steering gear so that the input shaft twists slightly on the torsion bar. Since the inner member is also attached to the input shaft, this twisting provides a relative rotary displacement of the inner and outer members. It is this displacement that lets fluid flow through the valve to act on the piston at the steering gear. The input shaft can twist through only a small angle before it contacts a stop on the pinion gear or worm. This is needed as a fail-safe to provide manual steering when power assistance is not available.

With the engine running and the steering in the neutral position, fluid flow is directed into the valve assembly through drilled holes in the outer sleeve **FIGURE 28-18**. As soon as the steering is turned to the left or right, the slight relative movement occurs between the inner and the outer members. In the neutral position, the inner member lets fluid pass equally to both sides of the rack piston and return to the fluid reservoir. Equal, but low, pressure is applied to both sides of the power piston. No power assistance is needed.

When the steering wheel is turned, fluid is restricted from making a free return to the reservoir. It is now directed to the side that matches the turning action. At the same time, fluid on the opposite side is directed to the return circuit, back to the reservoir. Slight rotation of the valve gives a small amount of assistance, which becomes progressively greater as the torsion bar flexes and more assistance is needed. The grooves of the inner member are precisely shaped to meter the flow of fluid between the apply and release passageways.

Flow-Control Valve

All power steering pumps have a **flow-control valve** to vary fluid flow and power steering system pressures. A pressure relief valve prevents excessive pressures from developing when the steering is on full lock (turned all the way to one side) and is held against its stops in that position. The flow-control valve is located at the outlet fitting of the power steering pump and regulates pressures to as high as 1200 to 1500 pounds per square inch (psi), or 8274 to 10,342 kilopascals (kPa). When the flow-control valve is forced open at a steering stop, there is usually an audible whine from this very high pressure.

During slow cornering or when parking, power steering pump speeds are normally low. There is less demand for fluid flow at this time because the engine speed is low, but high pressure is still needed to provide the required assistance. Discharge ports direct fluid to the pressure side outlet and then to the steering gear. The outlet fluid pressure is slightly lower than the internal high pressure coming from the power steering pump. This drop in pressure occurs as the fluid flow passes the needle and orifice in the outlet fitting. This lower pressure is transmitted through a bypass fluid passage to the spring end of the control valve. The pressure difference on the valve causes it to move away from the outlet fitting, but

FIGURE 28-17 Power steering rotary valve and torsion bar.

FIGURE 28-18 Drilled passageways through the outer sleeve over the rotary valve.

the force of the spring prevents it moving far enough to uncover a return port back to the pump inlet. Movement of the control valve controls the position of the needle valve in the outlet fitting. This controls the fluid flow to the steering gear **FIGURE 28-19**.

At higher speeds with no steering maneuvers, fluid flow is increased. This reduces pressure at the outlet. The lower pressure is transmitted to the spring end of the control valve. The valve moves and opens the return port back to the pump inlet. Movement of the control valve also controls the movement of the flow control needle in the outlet fitting. The needle closes in the orifice, and fluid flow to the steering gear reduces.

With the steering wheel held at full lock, the steering rack power piston chamber becomes fully pressurized and fluid flow through the steering gear stops.

Safety

When replacing or topping off power steering fluid, you must ensure that the correct type and brand of fluid is used. If the wrong type or brand is used, serious damage to the power steering pump and lines can develop, creating a potentially dangerous situation. Different fluids react differently to pressure and temperature changes. Using the incorrect fluid may result in the creation of excessive pressure within the system, bursting the high-pressure lines and potentially spraying fluid at high pressure all over the engine, creating a severe fire hazard. It would also cause a loss of steering assist, which could result in an accident.

This high pressure is transmitted back to the spring end of the control valve, opening the pressure relief valve. A small amount of fluid passes through the pressure relief orifice, providing a pressure drop. The valve moves and uncovers the return port to the pump inlet **FIGURE 28-20**. A predetermined relief pressure is thus maintained.

Idle Speed Strategy

When maneuvering a vehicle at slow speeds, the power steering demand will be high and the engine speed will be low. If the idle speed is not maintained during this condition, the engine could possibly stall. To prevent stalling, engineers program a strategy into the PCM that raises or maintains the idle speed under these conditions. A power steering switch or sensor inputs power steering pressure information to the engine control module, and based on this input and the actual engine idle revolutions per minute (rpm), the PCM is able to determine when additional airflow is needed to raise or maintain the desired engine rpm.

Electric Power Steering

The use of electronics in automotive steering systems enables much more sophisticated control to be achieved. Electric steering is more economical to run and easier to package and install than conventional hydraulic power steering systems and reacts faster to quick steering changes from the driver. Typically, electric and electrohydraulic power steering systems are also lighter and more compact than conventional hydraulic power steering systems. Both the electric power steering system and the electrohydraulic power steering systems are

FIGURE 28-19 Movement of the control valve controls the position of the needle valve in the outlet fitting; this controls the fluid flow to the steering gear.

FIGURE 28-20 Flow-control valve—steering wheel at full lock.

now considered as viable alternatives to conventional hydraulic power steering systems because of their energy efficiency and size.

Electrically powered hydraulic steering (EPHS) replaces the customary drive belts and pulleys that drive a power steering pump in a conventional rack-and-pinion steering system with a brushless motor. This system still uses a pump, but it is driven by an electric motor to reduce power drawn from the engine. Pump speed is regulated by an electronic controller to vary pump pressure and flow. This provides steering efforts tailored for different driving situations. The pump can be run at low speed or shut off to provide energy savings during straight-ahead driving. An EPHS system is said to use only 20% of the engine power used by a standard belt-driven pump and improves fuel mileage by approximately 10%. The engine still contributes power to the steering system through electrical demand on the alternator of the vehicle, but it is greatly reduced from that of hydraulic power steering systems.

Electrically assisted steering (EAS) is a completely electrically powered power-assist system that eliminates all hydraulic components and fluid. An electric motor replaces the hydraulic pump. EAS or direct electric power steering completely eliminates hydraulic fluid and the accompanying hardware from the power steering system, creating a fully **electric power steering (EPS) system**. The reduction of components saves weight and reduces drag on the engine, vastly improving fuel mileage. The EPS system is said to require only 2% of the engine power that a standard belt-driven power steering pump uses. There is still a small amount of power required from the engine, which supplies the electrical demand, but as you can see, it is greatly reduced.

An EPS steering system uses an electric motor attached either to the steering rack or to the steering column via a gear mechanism and torque sensor. A microprocessor or electronic control unit and diagnostic software control the steering dynamics and driver effort. Inputs include vehicle speed, steering wheel torque, angular position, and turning rate.

There are four primary types of electric power assist steering systems:

- Column-assist type: In this system, the **power assist unit**, controller, and **torque sensor** are attached to the steering column. The power assist unit is the electric motor, the controller is the electronic control unit, and the torque sensor measures the load on the steering wheel.
- Pinion-assist type: In this system, the power assist unit is attached to the steering gear pinion shaft. The power assist unit sits outside the vehicle

passenger compartment, allowing assist torque to be increased greatly without raising interior compartment noise.

- Rack-assist type: In this system, the power assist unit is attached to the steering gear rack. It is located on the rack to allow for greater flexibility in the layout design **FIGURE 28-21**.
- Direct-drive type: In this system, the steering gear rack and power assist unit form a single unit. The steering system is compact and fits easily into the engine compartment layout. Direct assistance to the rack enables low friction and **inertia** (resistance to a change in motion), which in turn gives an ideal steering feel.

In these systems, **active control** provides constant feedback from sensors in the vehicle to the **control unit**, which calculates sophisticated computer algorithms. These features allow the steering system to react to the road, the weather, and even the type of driver, and provide assistance to the front or rear road wheels independent of direct driver input. For example, if the electronic stability control system detects the start of an oversteer condition, the control unit can actually steer the wheels in the opposite direction, trying to prevent loss of control of the vehicle. Thus, an EPS system might steer the vehicle opposite of the driver's input, if that input would lessen the control of the vehicle.

Basic EPS Operation

A steering sensor is located on the input shaft, where it is bolted to the gearbox housing.

The **steering sensor** performs two functions. First, as a torque sensor, it converts steering torque input and direction into voltage signals for the engine control unit (ECU) to monitor. Second, as a rotation sensor, it converts the

FIGURE 28-21 Rack assist steering system.

rotation speed and direction into voltage signals for the ECU to monitor. An interfaced ECU circuit converts the voltage signals from the torque and rotation sensor into signals that the PCM can process, and ultimately provides the proper output signal to the EPS assembly.

The microprocessor control unit also analyzes inputs from the vehicle's speed and wheel speed sensors. The sensor inputs are then compared to determine how much power assistance is required according to the **forces capability map data** stored in the ECU's memory. These map data are preprogrammed by the manufacturer. The ECU sends the appropriate command to the **power unit**, which supplies the electric motor with the necessary current to operate as commanded. The electric motor then pushes the rack to either the right or the left. The direction of rack movement depends on which way the current flows; reversing the current flow reverses directional rotation of the electric motor. Increasing current to the electric motor increases the amount of power assist.

The EPS system has three operating modes:

- Normal control mode: Provides left or right power assist in response to input from the torque and rotation sensor's inputs
- Return control mode: Assists steering return after completing a turn
- Damper control mode: Adjusts the amount of assist according to the vehicle speed to improve road feel and dampen kickback

If the steering wheel is turned and held in the full-lock position—which is as far as the wheel can turn in one direction—and steering assist reaches maximum, the power unit reduces current to the electric motor to prevent an overload situation that might damage the electric motor. The power unit is also designed to protect the electric motor against voltage surges from a faulty alternator or charging system problem.

The electronic steering control unit is capable of self-diagnosing faults by monitoring the system's inputs and outputs and the driving current of the electric motor. If a problem occurs, the electronic steering control unit turns the system off by **actuating** (turning on) a fail-safe relay in the power unit. This eliminates all power assist, causing the system to revert to manual steering. An in-dash EPS warning light is also illuminated to alert the driver.

Higher Voltage Electrically Assisted Power Steering

Higher voltage electrically assisted power steering systems were developed for modern hybrid vehicles. In hybrid vehicles, the engine is typically off during idling, deceleration, and braking; thus, an EPS system was needed. The higher voltage battery system of the hybrid vehicle provides all the power, with no reliance on engine or hydraulic power. The parts are similar to an electrically assisted power steering system. The electric steering system does not use the full battery voltage from the high-voltage battery pack; instead, it is reduced to a lower voltage through a DC-to-DC converter, which basically just steps the voltage down. Some early hybrids simply used the 12-volt system that was used on gasoline vehicles, but newer models are using voltage as high as 46 volts. One thing to remember is that when voltage goes up, amperage can come down to produce the same wattage. Because of this principle of electricity, smaller gauge wires can be used in the electric steering system.

Diagnosis

Many of the problems associated with steering systems are mechanical, but as more EPS systems are produced, electrical faults are becoming more common. Mechanical joints and bushings, as well as motors, pumps, and switches, wear over time, decreasing in functionality and eventually failing. Sensors also are subject to wear, resulting in inaccurate readings and faulty reactions. The wires are subject to damage and breaks from other mechanical parts, as well as loose connections and wear. When confronted with a steering system problem, it is important to consider both the mechanical and the electrical components before finalizing a diagnosis. Also, since the suspension system is directly related to the steering system and helps to hold the wheels in the proper geometry, you will need to have an understanding of the suspension system. That way you will be able to determine exactly what is causing the customer's concern. Suspension systems are discussed fully in the Servicing Suspension Systems chapter.

Tools and Equipment

Some of the tools used in diagnosing and repairing steering system problems can be broken into two categories: tools for mechanical diagnosis and tools for electrical diagnosis. Tools for electrical diagnosis include the factory scanner and the digital volt-ohmmeter (DVOM). The factory scan tool is recommended by most manufacturers because it can perform tests and identify faults with the electrical portion of steering systems. The scan tool can read almost every system on a vehicle and provides valuable data to assist the technician in identifying problems. It is particularly useful in assessing electronic steering systems for wiring and sensor malfunctions. Typically, electronic steering system faults set a diagnostic trouble code that can be retrieved by the scan tool. Use of the service information to diagnose the fault is necessary as well as a DVOM. The DVOM is used to measure voltage and to check the continuity of the electronic circuit. Breaks in the wiring of an EPS system are not uncommon. When this occurs, the system opens or shorts out. The continuity test can pick up on any opens or shorts and help determine where the problem is located.

Tools and equipment used on the mechanical portion of the steering system include a power steering system pressure tester and various measuring devices, such as dial indicators and belt tension gauges. The mechanical components need to be removed and replaced, requiring tools such as a tie-rod puller, pickle forks, a pitman arm puller, tie-rod sleeve adjusting tools, inner tie-rod socket tools, inch-pound and foot-pound torque wrenches, hammers, air hammers, and pry bars **FIGURE 28-22**.

FIGURE 28-22 Steering system specialty tools. **A.** Pitman arm puller. **B.** Tie-rod end puller. **C.** Tie-rod sleeve tool. **D.** Pickle fork. **E.** Power steering system analyzer. **F.** Inner tie-rod tool.

The following tools and parts are used in servicing the power steering system:

- **Floor jacks and safety stands:** Jacks are used to lift a vehicle, and the safety stands provide stability while working on a raised vehicle.
- **Pry bar:** The pry bar is a lever used to apply pressure for testing purposes or to move various components.
- **Dial indicators:** Dial indicators are used to measure the runout or movement on different parts of the steering system, such as play in tie-rod ends.
- **Pitman arm puller:** This heavy-duty puller is made specially for removing the pressed-on pitman arm from the sector shaft.
- **Tie-rod end puller:** This tool is used to pull the tapered shaft on a tie-rod end from its mating steering component.
- **Tie-rod sleeve adjusting tool:** This tool has a tab designed to grab the slot in the sleeve and is used to turn the sleeve when adjusting the toe setting.
- **Pickle fork:** This U-shaped wedge is used for separating tie-rod ends and is operated by hammer or air hammer. This tool will usually destroy the dust boot during the process, so it is not the best tool to use on tie-rods that will be reused.
- **Inner tie-rod end tool:** This tool is used to loosen and tighten inner tie-rod ends.
- **Manufacturer-specific checking tools:** The following tools are made specifically for auto dealerships. There is a wide variety of these tools designed for many different purposes:
  - **Power steering system analyzer:** This tool includes a pressure and flow gauge set with various fittings to attach in line with the power steering pump. It is used to check volume of fluid flow, maximum pressure, and leaks internal to the steering gear.
  - **Scan tool:** This tool is used to read codes and data from the vehicle's PCM when diagnosing the vehicle's computer-controlled systems.
  - **DVOM:** The DVOM, which stands for digital volt-ohmmeter, is used to measure voltage and ohms in a vehicle's electrical systems.
  - **Various jumper leads:** These are small wires with clips on the ends used to diagnose electrical problems.
  - **Circuit tester:** This is a test light used to diagnose electrical problems.
  - **Belt tension gauge:** This tool is designed to measure the amount of flex in a drive belt. Some manufacturers require the use of this tool to adjust proper belt tension.
  - **Black light and dye kit:** This tool is used to pinpoint fluid leaks. Dye is added to the fluid of the leaking system, and the black light makes the dye glow fluorescent.

Diagnosing Steering Systems

The main problems that arise in the steering system are play and hard steering. The common culprit for these problems is wear or poor lubrication. Play is the wiggling or increased movement of parts that results from wear in the connections between parts. In the steering system, play generally results from worn ball sockets and/or idler arms or too much clearance in the steering gearbox. Hard steering is difficulty in steering the vehicle. There are many faults that can cause hard steering, from low tire pressure to overly tight adjustments in the steering gearbox, to power steering that is not working properly. It is important to thoroughly check the entire steering system to identify all problems when hard steering is the issue. The best way to do this is by physically inspecting each of the components, checking or measuring play, looking for bent or damaged linkage, and testing the operation of the power steering system.

Diagnosing Power Steering Fluid Leakage

Power steering fluid is critical to the proper functioning of the entire steering system. Any power steering fluid leak, no matter how small, is cause for repair. Because a leak can occur anywhere throughout the system, it is necessary to thoroughly inspect it all. One method for checking for leaks is to clean all power steering fluid off the vehicle and then run it for a little while. Turn off the vehicle and reexamine for new leaks. Any drops of fluid are indicative of a leak. Another method uses standard fluorescent dyes. Following the dye manufacturer's instructions, add the appropriate amount of dye to the power steering system. After waiting the recommended amount of time, inspect the vehicle with a black light, which will illuminate the fluorescent dye and make it easy to spot leaks.

Diagnosing Power Steering Gear Issues (Non–Rack and Pinion)

Steering gear issues in a non–rack-and-pinion system can be one of the following: uneven effort needed for turning, looseness of steering, hard steering, unusual noises when steering, or leaks. If the issue is related to the power steering system, such as leaks, noise, or hard steering, you will need to perform a visual inspection of the drive belt and the fluid level and condition, as well as pressure testing of the power steering system if necessary.

If the issue is related to the steering linkage, you will need to perform a visual inspection of the linkage, joints, and steering gear. With the vehicle jacked up and placed on safety stands, have someone turn the steering wheel as you visually inspect the steering linkage. Check for binding, wear or loose connections, and other abnormal conditions. To check for binding issues, it may be necessary to separate the steering linkage to verify that binding is in the steering gearbox, linkage, ball joints, or steering column. For looseness concerns, do not forget to check the universal joint or coupler between the intermediate shaft and the steering gearbox. These components are prone to wear, which creates play. Refer to the manufacturer's service information for diagnostic information and tests for the concern you are working on.

Diagnosing Power Steering Gear Issues (Rack and Pinion)

Diagnosing steering gear issues in a rack-and-pinion system is similar to a non–rack-and-pinion system and includes the same common complaints, such as uneven effort needed for turning, looseness of steering, hard steering, and unusual noises when steering. If the issue is related to the power steering system, perform the inspection and tests associated with the power steering. If the issue is related to the steering linkage, perform a visual and hands-on inspection of the linkage, joints, and steering gear. With the vehicle raised on a hoist or jacked up and placed on safety stands, have someone turn the steering wheel as you visually inspect the steering linkage. Check for binding, wear or loose connections, debris, or any other anomaly.

Diagnosing Steering Column Issues

Common steering column issues include unusual noises, looseness, and binding. These problems generally arise from wear or debris lodged in the steering column. The process of diagnosing each of these problems is the same: The vehicle is raised on a hoist or jacked up and placed on safety stands, and one person turns the steering wheel as the technician watches for looseness or binding and listens for noises. Once diagnosed, the best repair plan can be created based on the service information.

Because of the amount of electrical components, such as radio control switches and cruise control switches mounted to the steering wheel of modern vehicles, a device called a clock spring must be used in the steering column. The clock spring is a flexible ribbon that is coiled inside of a plastic holder. It carries all the electrical signals that flow to the components on the steering wheel and allows the steering wheel to rotate. The clock spring must be centered when steering column work has been done. Refer to service information to be sure that the clock spring is centered correctly, as the position may vary by manufacturer. The typical clock spring will have four or so turns of movement before it runs out of travel (turn very gently or you will break the wires). The clock spring is normally marked to show the center position or where the clock spring should be positioned when the wheels are straight ahead. If you do not know where the center point of the clock spring is, you can carefully turn the clock spring in the correct direction, counting the number of total turns until it reaches the end, then move back half that number of turns. The clock spring should now be centered. Also, be careful to not wind the clock spring in the opposite direction it was designed to be wound since that will greatly shorten its life.

The steering column of a vehicle with EPS or stability control will be equipped with a torque sensor and steering angle sensor. If the steering column is being serviced, a steering angle sensor calibration will typically be required. Refer to the service information for the correct method of recalibrating the angle sensor. Typically, a scan tool is required to perform this function.

> **TECHNICIAN TIP**
>
> When the technician has removed the steering wheel and is removing the steering shaft, he or she must be extremely careful not to damage or impair the operation of any multifunction switch or the clock spring.

▶ Maintenance and Repair

The steering system, while being very critical to the safe operation of the vehicle, does not normally require a lot of maintenance. In older vehicles, each of the steering and suspension joints needed to be lubricated with grease during each oil change. Most, but not all, of these joints have been replaced with greased-for-life joints, so most vehicles do not have grease zerks to lubricate the joints. However, always be on the lookout, since many replacement joints use zerk fittings to keep them lubricated. Another area of scheduled maintenance on the steering system is replacement of the power steering belt and also possibly the power steering fluid.

To maintain a safe-operating vehicle, regular inspection of the steering components is essential. This can be performed both by visually inspecting the components and joints for damage, looseness, or leakage and by operating the steering system and looking or feeling for play in the components. Also, listening and feeling the steering components can help identify any needed maintenance or repair. Manufacturers will list the most appropriate method of inspecting and testing their systems. Always refer to the manufacturer's workshop information for these methods and wear specifications.

Checking and Adjusting Power Steering Fluid

The power steering fluid transmits pressure throughout a vehicle's power steering system. It also provides lubrication to the moving parts. It must be able to perform these functions in any weather conditions, maintaining its chemical integrity in the face of subfreezing temperatures or scorching heat. Given its importance, it is critical that the power steering fluid be inspected regularly for both purity (no contamination with debris) and level. The power steering fluid usually has both a hot and a cold indicator on the dipstick to ensure an accurate reading of the fluid level in both conditions. Always refer to the service information for the recommended type of power steering fluid.

To check and adjust power steering fluid, follow the steps in **SKILL DRILL 28-1**:

1 Locate the power steering reservoir. Clean around the cap if dirt is present. Unscrew the cap on top of the reservoir and wipe the dipstick clean. **(Photo 1)**

2 Reinstall the cap for a few seconds, then remove it again and check the fluid level on the dipstick. If the vehicle has not been driven recently, the level should be at the cold mark. If the engine is fully warm, the level should be at the hot mark. **(Photo 2)**

3 If the level is low, check the owner's manual or service information to see what kind of fluid the power steering system requires, and fill it to the proper level. If the vehicle has a plastic reservoir, check the marks to see if any fluid needs to be added. Remember that using the wrong type of fluid can result in damage to the pump, gearbox, and various seals in the system. **(Photo 3)**

Replacing Power Steering Pump Filter(s)

Some, but not all, vehicles use a replaceable power steering pump filter. It can be located in the fluid reservoir or in the return line. If it is in the reservoir, it may be a separate filter that sits in the bottom of the reservoir and can be carefully fished out of the reservoir and replaced. Other manufacturers build the filter into the reservoir such that the reservoir and filter are one unit and changed together. If it is an inline filter, it is usually installed in the return line due to the lower pressure. It may be spliced into the hose between the steering

SKILL DRILL 28-1 Checking and Adjusting Power Steering Fluid

1 Locate the power steering reservoir. Clean around the cap if dirt is present. Unscrew the cap on top of the reservoir and wipe the dipstick clean.

2 Reinstall the cap for a few seconds, then remove it again and check the fluid level on the dipstick. Verify that the level matches the temperature of the system—hot or cold.

3 If the level is low, top it off with the specified fluid. If the vehicle has a plastic reservoir, check the marks to see if any fluid needs to be added.

gear and the pump, or it could fit inside the return hose where the return hose connects onto the pump. When changing the filter, you may want to consider flushing the power steering system first to remove as much of the old fluid as possible before installing the new filter. Always check the service information to determine the scheduled service interval and the location of the filter.

To replace the power steering pump filter(s), follow the steps in **SKILL DRILL 28-2** :

1 Research the vehicle you are working on to determine if it has a power steering pump filter, its change interval, and its location.

2 Following the specified procedure, remove the filter.

3 Inspect any hoses or fittings for cracks and damage.

4 Install the new filter, top off the reservoir with the correct fluid, and check for proper operation and leaks.

Flushing a Power Steering System

Flushing the power steering system is the process of removing all the old power steering fluid and replacing it with new. It is performed whenever the manufacturer specifies a fluid change, the fluid appears contaminated or dirty, a major part of the hydraulic steering system is replaced, or there is a serious mechanical problem involving the power steering pump or steering gear that could cause metal shavings to be circulated through the system.

Only use the manufacturer's specified power steering fluid when flushing the system. When the service is complete, inspect for leaks after turning the steering wheel to the full-lock position in both directions and back to the center. Also ensure that none of the power steering hoses makes contact with any of the components. Typically a power steering system flush is performed with a flushing machine that is connected in line with the power steering system pump to remove all old dirty fluid and install new clean fluid without introduction of air. Note that air introduced into the power steering pump can be harmful to the pump since the pump is lubricated by the power steering fluid, and scoring of the pump can result if the pump is run dry. There are several types of flushing machines; if one is not available, flushing will have to be performed as shown in the following skill drill. Be sure to follow the manufacturer's procedure for flushing power steering fluid.

To flush a power steering system, follow the steps in **SKILL DRILL 28-3** :

1 Safely raise the vehicle, making sure the front wheels are off the ground.

2 Using a suction gun, remove as much power steering fluid from the reservoir as possible. **(Photo 1)**

3 Disconnect the power steering return hose from the reservoir, and stick the end in a suitable container of between 2 quarts and 1 gallon (1.9–3.8 liters). (If the hose is not long enough, use a length of hose to extend it so it will reach the container.) **(Photo 2)**

SKILL DRILL | **28-3** | **Flushing a Power Steering System**

1 Raise the vehicle, making sure the front wheels are off the ground. Using a suction gun, remove as much power steering fluid from the reservoir as possible.

2 Disconnect the power steering return hose from the reservoir, and stick the end in a suitable container.

3 Temporarily plug the return fitting on the reservoir with a snug-fitting rubber cap.

SKILL DRILL | 28-3 | Flushing a Power Steering System, continued

4 Add the recommended fluid into the reservoir until it is at the correct level.

5 Start the engine and have an assistant turn the steering wheel from lock to lock while keeping the reservoir at or near the full mark. When the fluid coming out of the return hose is clear, stop adding fluid and keep running the engine until the level in the reservoir is just below the return line inlet. Turn off the engine.

6 Reinstall the return hose on the reservoir, top off the fluid level, and start the engine. Turn the steering wheel lock to lock a few more times, turn off the engine, and check the fluid level. Top off if necessary.

7 Lower the vehicle, start the engine, and turn the steering wheel from lock to lock to check if the system is working correctly with the vehicle weight on the tires. Dispose of the waste power steering fluid in an environmentally approved manner.

---

4 Temporarily plug the return fitting on the reservoir with a snug-fitting rubber cap. (**Photo 3**)

5 Add the recommended fluid into the reservoir until it is at the correct level. (**Photo 4**)

6 Start the engine and have an assistant turn the steering wheel from lock to lock while keeping the reservoir at or near the full mark.

7 When the fluid coming out of the return hose is clear, stop adding fluid and keep running the engine until the level in the reservoir is just below the return line inlet. Turn off the engine. (**Photo 5**)

8 Reinstall the return hose on the reservoir, top off the fluid level, and start the engine. Turn the steering wheel lock to lock a few more times, turn off the engine, and check the fluid level. Top off if necessary. (**Photo 6**)

9 Lower the vehicle, start the engine, and turn the steering wheel from lock to lock to check that the system is working correctly with the vehicle weight on the tires. Dispose of the waste power steering fluid in an environmentally approved manner. (**Photo 7**)

Pressure Testing a Power Steering System

Pressure testing of the power steering system is performed when the driver complains of hard steering or when there are repeated hose failures. The test checks the operation of the power steering pump, pressure relief valve, control valve, power piston, and hoses. Dispose of discarded fluid properly in accordance with the relevant Environmental Protection Agency and government legislation. Use only the manufacturer's specified power steering fluid for the vehicle. When the service is complete, check for leaks, check operation by turning the steering wheel to full lock in both directions and back to the center, and check the fluid level. Ensure that none of the power steering hoses makes contact with any linkage or other obstructions.

To pressure test a power steering system, follow the steps in **SKILL DRILL 28-4**:

1 Prepare the vehicle. Safely raise the vehicle, making sure the front wheels are off the ground, and position a drain pan under the power steering system.

2 Following the manufacturer's instructions for the pressure gauge/analyzer you are using, disconnect the high-pressure hose from the power steering pump. (**Photo 1**)

3 Connect the inlet hose from the gauge to the high-pressure connection on the power steering pump using the appropriate adapter. Be careful not to cross the threads. (**Photo 2**)

4 Connect the high-pressure hose to the outlet valve on the pressure gauge using the appropriate adapter. (**Photo 3**)

5 With the pressure gauge control valve open, start the engine and run it at idle until fluid circulates through the tester and hoses, and the air is purged from the fluid. Turn the engine off. Check the power steering fluid level, and add the specified fluid as necessary. (**Photo 4**)

6 Start the engine again. Record the initial pressure and flow readings on the pressure gauge.

7 Close and open the pressure gauge control valve, making sure the valve is not left closed for more

SKILL DRILL   28-4   Pressure Testing a Power Steering System

1 Raise the vehicle and position a drain pan under the power steering system. Following the manufacturer's instructions for the pressure gauge/analyzer you are using, disconnect the high-pressure hose from the power steering pump.

2 Connect the inlet hose from the gauge to the high-pressure connection on the power steering pump using the appropriate adapter.

3 Connect the high-pressure hose to the outlet valve on the pressure gauge using the appropriate adapter.

SKILL DRILL | 28-4 | Pressure Testing a Power Steering System, continued

4 With the pressure gauge control valve open, start the engine and run it at idle until fluid circulates through the tester and hoses, and the air is purged from the fluid. Turn the engine off. Check the power steering fluid level, and add the specified fluid as necessary.

5 Start the engine again. Record the initial pressure and flow readings on the pressure gauge. Close and open the pressure gauge control valve two or three times, making sure the valve is not left closed for more than 5 seconds. Record the highest pressure indicated.

6 With the pressure tester control valve open, turn the steering wheel to the extreme left and to the extreme right. Record the highest indicated pressure at lock. Turn off the engine. Compare these readings to the specifications, and take the results to your supervisor.

7 Be careful when disconnecting the analyzer hose from the high-pressure connection point on the power steering pump, as the fluid will be extremely hot. Replace any O-rings and reconnect the vehicle's power steering system high-pressure hose to the power steering pump outlet.

8 Top off the power steering reservoir and follow the manufacturer's procedure to bleed any air from the system. Some systems require the use of an adapter on the reservoir and a vacuum pump to remove all of the air.

than 5 seconds. Record the highest pressure indicated. Close and open the valve two more times, noting the high-pressure readings each time. **(Photo 5)**

8 With the pressure tester control valve open, turn the steering wheel to the extreme left. Record the highest indicated pressure at lock. Turn the steering

wheel to the extreme right and record the pressure again. Turn off the engine. Compare these readings to the specifications in the vehicle service information, and take your findings to your supervisor. **(Photo 6)**

9 Be careful when disconnecting the analyzer hose from the high-pressure connection point on the power steering pump, as the fluid will be extremely hot. Replace any O-rings and reconnect the vehicle's power steering system high-pressure hose to the power steering pump outlet. **(Photo 7)**

10 Top off the power steering reservoir. Follow the manufacturer's procedure to bleed any air from the system. Usually the procedures will include lowering the vehicle. Start the engine and turn the steering wheel from lock to lock to check that the system is working correctly with the vehicle weight on the tires. Dispose of the waste power steering fluid in an environmentally approved manner. Some systems require the use of an adapter on the reservoir and a vacuum pump to remove all of the air. **(Photo 8)**

Applied Science

AS-49: Pressure: The technician can demonstrate an understanding of pressure in reaction to the concept of force.
A vehicle is in the shop with a customer concern of extremely hard steering. The technician confirms the concern as lack of power steering assist. After doing a visual inspection for the fluid level, leaks, and belt tension, the technician connects a pressure gauge. Using the manufacturer's service information, the technician conducts the pressure test to discover a reading of only 200 psi (1380 kPa). The specifications for this test are 1500 psi (10,343 kPa).

The technician understands that the lack of steering pressure is resulting in the lack of steering assist, which results in the extremely hard steering of the vehicle.

Pascal's law states that force is equal to pressure multiplied times area. The area in the formula is the size of the piston in square inches or square millimeters. After a new power steering pump is installed, the result will be a greater amount of force needed to steer the vehicle properly.

This is a basic hydraulic application of Pascal's law, which applies to many systems on the automobile. In our example, we are considering the power steering but the same principles apply to the hydraulic lift that raises the vehicle for service.

Removing and Reinstalling the Power Steering Pump

The power steering pump drives the flow of power steering fluid throughout the steering system. As with any mechanical device, it can fail. Failure is usually described by the driver as difficult or noisy steering, which will need to be fully diagnosed before condemning the power steering pump. For example, excessive noise can occur when the power steering fluid level is low, which can allow air into the system. In this case, replacing the power steering pump is not the correct repair.

Safety

- Be aware of moving drive belts and accessories when the engine is running.
- Power steering fluid can become very hot in operation. Take precautions to avoid burns.
- Power steering systems can reach a working pressure of over 1400 psi, or 9650 kPa, during operation. Always follow the vehicle or equipment manufacturer's procedure when working on the system.
- Power steering fluid is flammable. Always keep it away from hot exhaust manifolds, pipes, or catalytic converters.
- Clean up any spills immediately.
- Wear appropriate heat-proof chemical gloves when working on hot systems.

Assuming that proper pressure testing and noise diagnosis have confirmed a faulty pump, the pump will need to be replaced. Because there are so many ways that power steering pumps can be installed in different vehicles, always refer to the manufacturer's service information before beginning this operation.

To remove and reinstall a power steering pump, follow the steps in **SKILL DRILL 28-5** :

1 Research the specified procedure for removing the power steering pump. Raise the vehicle on a lift or support it on safety stands.

2 Drain the power steering system's fluid by disconnecting the power steering return line, and dispose of fluid in accordance with environmental legislation. **(Photo 1)**

3 Disconnect the power steering hoses from the pump and check for damage or leaks. Replace hoses if needed. New O-rings should be used on hose ends on reassembly, if equipped. **(Photo 2)**

4 Disconnect the drive belt(s) and inspect for cracking or groove depth with a belt groove depth gauge. Replace any belt that is cracked or worn beyond specifications. **(Photo 3)**

5 Remove the pump retaining bolts, and remove the power steering pump. If replacing the pump with a new one, follow Skill Drill 28-6 to remove and replace the pulley. **(Photo 4)**

6 To reinstall the new or overhauled power steering pump, reinstall in the reverse order. Fill and bleed the system with the specified power steering fluid. **(Photo 5)**

SKILL DRILL | 28-5 | Removing and Reinstalling the Power Steering Pump

1. After researching the procedure for removing the power steering pump, raise the vehicle on a lift or support it on safety stands. Drain the power steering system's fluid by disconnecting the power steering return line, and dispose of fluid in accordance with environmental legislation.

2. Disconnect the power steering hoses from the pump and check for damage or leaks. Replace hoses if needed. New O-rings should be used on hose ends on reassembly, if equipped.

3. Disconnect the drive belt(s) and inspect for cracking or groove depth with a belt groove depth gauge. Replace any belt that is cracked or worn beyond specifications.

4. Remove the pump retaining bolts, and remove the power steering pump. If replacing the pump with a new one, follow Skill Drill 28-6 to remove and replace the pulley.

5. To reinstall the new or overhauled power steering pump, reinstall in the reverse order. Fill and bleed the system with the specified power steering fluid.

Removing and Reinstalling the Press-Fit Power Steering Pump Pulley

Power steering pumps pressurize and pump the power steering fluid throughout the power steering system by a belt-driven pulley. Whenever the power steering pump is removed or replaced, the pulley typically must also be removed from the old pump and installed on the new pump. Power steering pump pulleys are installed differently than most other pulleys; they are typically held in place by a press fit. As such, the pulley will need to be pulled off of the power steering pump shaft with a special puller and pressed onto the new pump. Some pulleys are now being made of plastic and pose an additional challenge, especially if they have become brittle. On some vehicles, the pulley needs to be removed before the pump can be removed. On others, the pump can be removed before the pulley. Because there are many pump and pulley systems available today, always refer to the manufacturer's service information before beginning this operation.

To remove and reinstall a press-fit power steering pump pulley, follow the steps in **SKILL DRILL 28-6** :

1 Assuming the pump is removed from the vehicle, install the correct power steering pulley puller on the pulley, making sure the puller is installed in the correct direction. **(Photo 1)**

2 Tighten the center bolt (while holding the outer nut) to press off the old drive pulley. If replacing the pump, remove the old one and install the new one. **(Photo 2)**

3 Place the pulley onto the power steering pump shaft with the removal flange facing forward. Using the install portion of the pulley puller tool kit, thread the bolt portion of the tool all the way into the shaft of the new power steering pump. **(Photo 3)**

4 Thread the outer nut down so that the bearing or washer is against the pulley. **(Photo 4)**

SKILL DRILL | **28-6** | **Removing and Reinstalling Press Fit Power Steering Pump Pulley**

1 Assuming the pump is removed from the vehicle, install the correct power steering pulley puller on the pulley, making sure the puller is installed in the correct direction.

2 Tighten the center bolt (while holding the outer nut) to press off the old drive pulley. If replacing the pump, remove the old one and install the new one.

3 Place the pulley onto the power steering pump shaft with the removal flange facing forward. Using the install portion of the pulley puller tool kit, thread the bolt portion of the tool all the way into the shaft of the power steering pump.

4 Thread the outer nut down so that the bearing or washer is against the pulley.

5 Tighten the outer nut (while holding the center bolt) until the pulley bottoms on the shaft. Remove the puller.

6 Reinstall the drive belt or replace it with a new one if needed. Refill and bleed the power steering system with the specified fluid.

5 Tighten the outer nut (while holding the center bolt) until the pulley bottoms on the shaft. Remove the puller. **(Photo 5)**

6 Reinstall the drive belt or replace it with a new one if needed. Refill and bleed the power steering system with the specified fluid. **(Photo 6)**

Inspecting and Replacing Power Steering Hoses and Fittings

Any leakage of power steering fluid out of a power steering pressure hose can be catastrophic. Because it is being actively pumped, the fluid could spray out of the hose at high speed and spray all over the hot engine and exhaust system. The heat of the engine parts will cause the power steering fluid to smoke and billow out from under the hood and even catch on fire. Small leaks or leaks in the return line will result in low fluid level in the power steering reservoir and will leave spots on the floor or parking space. If the fluid level gets low enough, it can cause a buzzing noise when driving. This noise is louder when steering the vehicle. The level of power assist may also fluctuate. If any of these symptoms are present, or to catch issues before they become this severe, it is important that the power steering hoses be inspected regularly and replaced at any sign of wear. Always refer to the manufacturer's workshop information before beginning this operation.

To inspect and replace power steering hoses and fittings, follow the steps in **SKILL DRILL 28-7**:

1 Safely raise the vehicle on a lift or support it on safety stands.

2 Inspect each of the hoses and fittings for leaks and damage. If a fitting is leaking, it may be because of a worn O-ring that will need to be replaced by disconnecting the fitting. **(Photo 1)**

3 Place a drain pan under the fitting to be disconnected. Use a flare nut wrench to loosen the fitting while you are holding the nut on the pump or steering gear with a wrench. **(Photo 2)**

4 If replacing the O-ring, inspect the mating surfaces of the fitting for damage. If no damage is found, replace the O-ring and reinstall the fitting, being careful not to cross-thread or overtighten. **(Photo 3)**

5 If replacing the hose, disconnect the fitting on the other end of the hose.

6 Compare the old and new hoses to verify the correct replacement part. **(Photo 4)**

7 Carefully start the fitting on each end of the hose by hand, making sure they are not cross-threaded. **(Photo 5)**

8 Check the routing of the new hoses, ensuring that they do not make contact with any components that could cause a failure; then tighten the fittings to the proper torque. **(Photo 6)**

SKILL DRILL | **28-7** | **Inspecting and Replacing Power Steering Hoses and Fittings**

1 Raise the vehicle on a lift or support it on safety stands. Inspect each of the power steering hoses and fittings for leaks and damage.

2 Place a drain pan under the fitting to be disconnected. Use a flare nut wrench to loosen the fitting while you are holding the nut on the pump or steering gear with a wrench.

3 If replacing the O-ring, inspect the mating surfaces of the fitting for damage. If no damage is found, replace the O-ring and reinstall the fitting, being careful not to cross-thread or overtighten.

SKILL DRILL | 28-7 | Inspecting and Replacing Power Steering Hoses and Fittings, continued

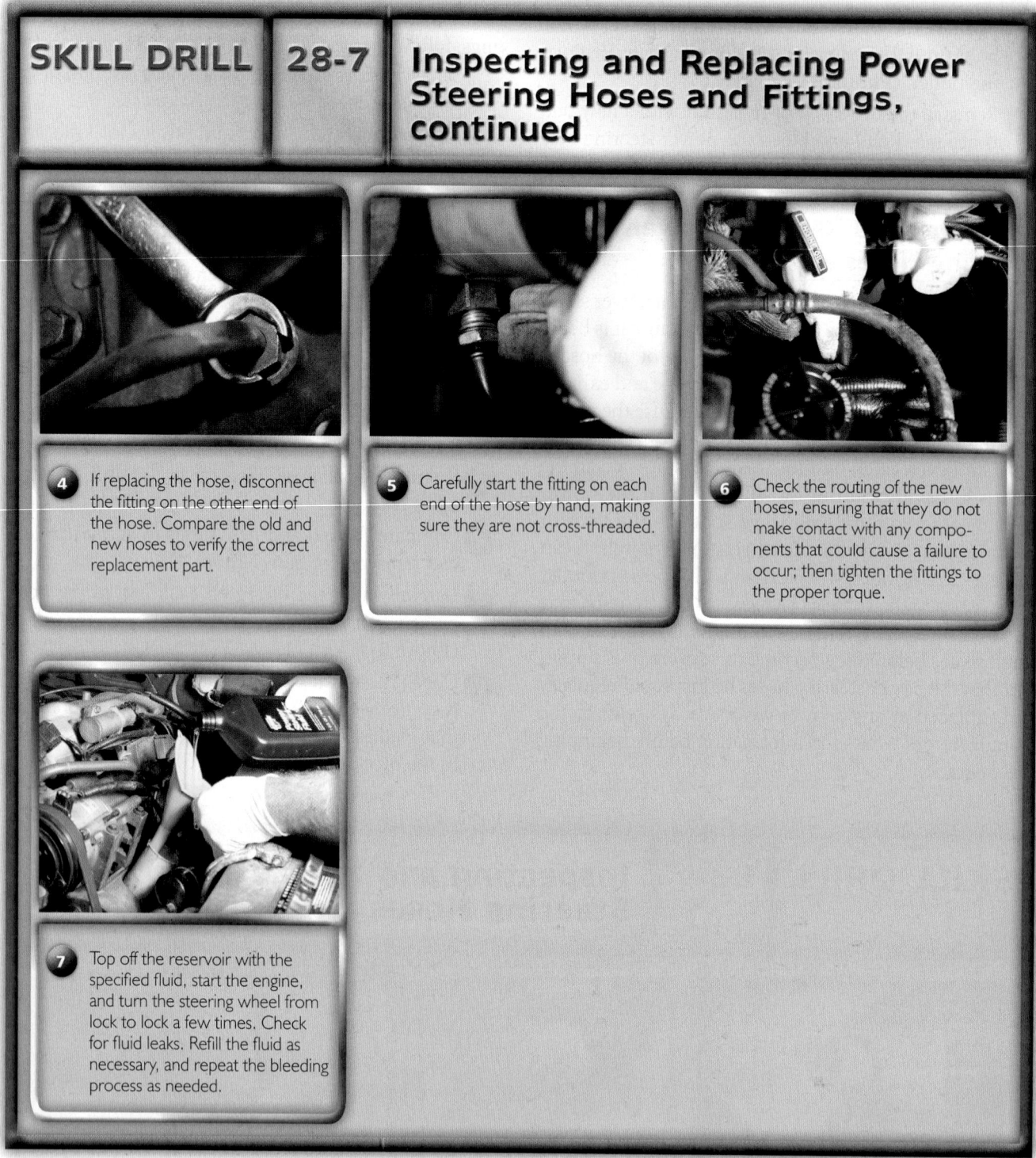

4 If replacing the hose, disconnect the fitting on the other end of the hose. Compare the old and new hoses to verify the correct replacement part.

5 Carefully start the fitting on each end of the hose by hand, making sure they are not cross-threaded.

6 Check the routing of the new hoses, ensuring that they do not make contact with any components that could cause a failure to occur; then tighten the fittings to the proper torque.

7 Top off the reservoir with the specified fluid, start the engine, and turn the steering wheel from lock to lock a few times. Check for fluid leaks. Refill the fluid as necessary, and repeat the bleeding process as needed.

9 Top off the reservoir with the specified fluid, start the engine, and turn the steering wheel from lock to lock a few times. Check for fluid leaks. Refill the fluid as necessary, and repeat the bleeding process as needed. **(Photo 7)**

Inspecting Mounting Bushings and Brackets

During the normal wear and tear of vehicle use, the rack-and-pinion mounting bushings become compressed, brittle, or torn, and brackets may be damaged or lost. If the vehicle has an oil or power steering fluid leak, the fluid may leak onto the mounting bushings. The oil tends to soften and degrade the bushings. When this happens, the driver typically complains of either loose steering or noises when driving or turning. In either scenario, a quick inspection of these parts is warranted.

To inspect mounting bushings and brackets, follow the steps in **SKILL DRILL 28-8**:

1 Safely raise the vehicle on a lift, keeping the weight of the vehicle on the wheels, if possible.

SKILL DRILL | 28-8 | Inspecting Mounting Bushings and Brackets

1. Raise the vehicle on a lift, keeping the weight of the vehicle on the wheels, if possible. Inspect the bushings and brackets for any faults.

2. Try moving the rack-and-pinion assembly up and down by hand.

3. Have an assistant rock the steering wheel back and forth while you look for movement in the rack-and-pinion bushings. If the rack moves significantly, place a torque wrench on the mounting bolts and tighten them to specifications. If the rack still moves, then bushing replacement will be necessary.

4. Remove the bracket bolts.

5. Remove the bushings from the rack.

6. Install new bushings in reverse order of removal.

2. Visually inspect the bushings and brackets for any faults. **(Photo 1)**

3. Try moving the rack-and-pinion assembly up and down by hand. **(Photo 2)**

4. Have an assistant rock the steering wheel back and forth while you look for movement in the rack-and-pinion bushings.

5. If the rack moves significantly, place a torque wrench on the mounting bolts and tighten them to the manufacturer's specifications.

6. If the rack still moves, then bushing replacement will be necessary. **(Photo 3)**

7. Remove the bracket bolts. **(Photo 4)**

8. Remove the bushings from the rack. **(Photo 5)**

9. Install new bushings in reverse order of removal. **(Photo 6)**

Removing and Replacing the Rack-and-Pinion Steering Gear

Removing and replacing the rack-and-pinion steering gear is not to be undertaken lightly. It should be considered only after carefully examining all parts of the steering system and performing a full diagnosis to ensure the problem is not a result of some other fault. Many symptoms can point to a worn rack-and-pinion assembly, such as tire wear, wandering, and hard or uneven steering. But those symptoms can result from other faults as well. Regardless of the symptoms, all other steering problems should be considered and eliminated before undertaking the removal or replacement of the rack-and-pinion steering gear. Because these systems vary across vehicle types and manufacturer designs, there is no single set procedure for removal and replacement; therefore, the steps that follow are nonspecific. Consult the service information for the specific steps for the vehicle you are working on.

To remove and replace a rack-and-pinion steering gear, follow the steps in **SKILL DRILL 28-9** :

1. Research the procedures and specifications in the appropriate service information.

2. Start the engine and straighten the wheels. Turn the engine off and lock the steering column. You may also want to wrap a seat belt around the steer-

SKILL DRILL | **28-9** | **Removing and Replacing the Rack-and-Pinion Steering Gear**

1. After researching the service information, start the engine and straighten the wheels. Turn the engine off and lock the steering column. This will keep the clock spring centered. Remove the front tires.

2. Locate the universal joint coupler from the intermediate shaft to the pinion shaft of the rack-and-pinion assembly. Remove the bolt from this coupler. Place a paint line on the coupler and the pinion shaft if reinstalling the same rack.

3. Pry the universal joint coupler off the pinion shaft.

4. Place an oil catch container under the power steering lines. Use flare nut wrenches to disconnect the power steering lines from the rack, and plug them to keep fluid from leaking.

5. Remove cotter pins and nuts from the outer tie-rod ends, and separate tie-rod ends with an approved tie-rod end puller, hammer method, or pickle fork.

6. Remove bolts from the rack-and-pinion bushing brackets, and remove brackets, if equipped.

SKILL DRILL | 28-9 | Removing and Replacing the Rack-and-Pinion Steering Gear, continued

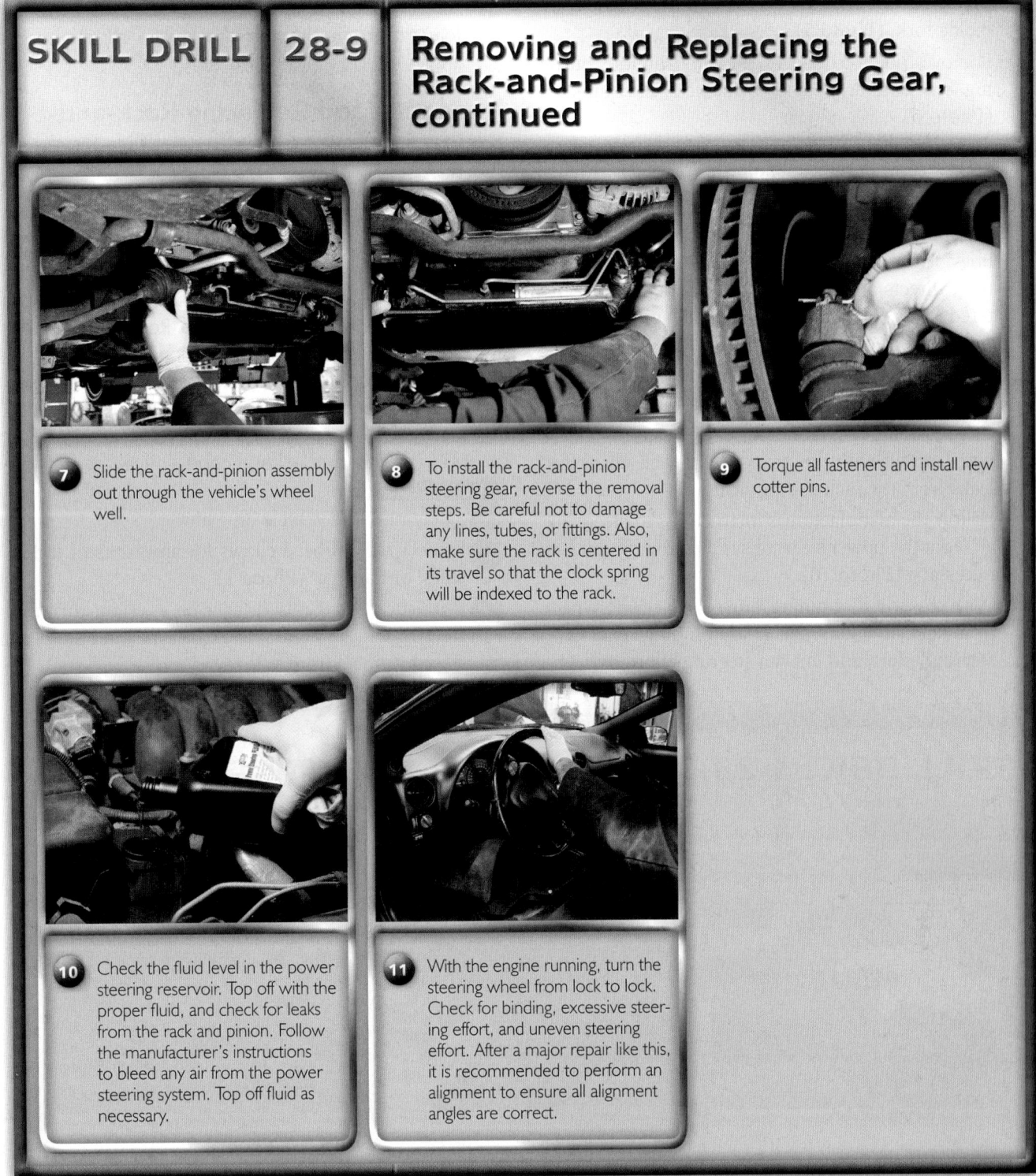

7 Slide the rack-and-pinion assembly out through the vehicle's wheel well.

8 To install the rack-and-pinion steering gear, reverse the removal steps. Be careful not to damage any lines, tubes, or fittings. Also, make sure the rack is centered in its travel so that the clock spring will be indexed to the rack.

9 Torque all fasteners and install new cotter pins.

10 Check the fluid level in the power steering reservoir. Top off with the proper fluid, and check for leaks from the rack and pinion. Follow the manufacturer's instructions to bleed any air from the power steering system. Top off fluid as necessary.

11 With the engine running, turn the steering wheel from lock to lock. Check for binding, excessive steering effort, and uneven steering effort. After a major repair like this, it is recommended to perform an alignment to ensure all alignment angles are correct.

ing wheel to make sure no one moves it. This will keep the clock spring centered.

3 Remove the front tires. **(Photo 1)**

4 Locate the universal joint coupler from the intermediate shaft to the pinion shaft of the rack-and-pinion assembly. Remove the bolt from this coupler. Place a paint line on the coupler and the pinion shaft if reinstalling the same rack. **(Photo 2)**

5 Pry the universal joint coupler off the pinion shaft. **(Photo 3)**

6 Place an oil catch container under the power steering lines. Use flare nut wrenches to disconnect the power steering lines from the rack, and plug them to keep fluid from leaking. **(Photo 4)**

7 Remove the cotter pins and nuts from the outer tie-rod ends, and separate the tie-rod ends with an

8 Remove bolts from the rack-and-pinion bushing brackets, and remove brackets, if equipped. **(Photo 6)**

9 Slide the rack-and-pinion assembly out through the vehicle's wheel well. **(Photo 7)**

10 To install the rack-and-pinion steering gear, reverse the removal steps. Be careful not to damage any lines, tubes, or fittings. Also, unless the manufacturer directs otherwise, make sure the rack is centered in its travel so that the clock spring will be indexed to the rack. **(Photo 8)**

11 Torque all fasteners, and install new cotter pins. **(Photo 9)**

12 Check the fluid level in the power steering reservoir. Top off with the proper fluid, and check for leaks from the rack and pinion.

13 Follow the manufacturer's instructions to bleed any air from the power steering system. Top off fluid as necessary. **(Photo 10)**

14 With the engine running, turn the steering wheel from lock to lock. Check for binding, excessive steering effort, and uneven steering effort.

approved tie-rod end puller, hammer method, or pickle fork. **(Photo 5)**

15 After a major repair like this, it is recommended to perform an alignment to ensure all alignment angles are correct. **(Photo 11)**

Inspecting and Replacing Rack-and-Pinion Steering Gear Inner Tie-Rod Ends and Bellows Boots

Over time, the inner tie-rod ends wear and can cause excessive play in the steering linkage. Also, bellows boots may become torn or dislodged from their seat. When bellows boots are torn, dirt or abrasives may enter the unit, accelerating wear of rack-and-pinion seals and bushings. Routine inspection can identify damage early, before additional problems arise. Refer to the appropriate service information when replacing the inner tie-rod ends and bellows boots.

To inspect and replace rack-and-pinion steering gear inner tie-rod ends and bellows boots, follow the steps in **SKILL DRILL 28-10**:

1 Safely raise the vehicle on a lift.

2 Inspect the rubber bellows for any signs of leaks, tears, or damage. **(Photo 1)**

3 With the vehicle raised, have an assistant turn the steering wheel to one side or the other and rock the steering wheel from side to side.

| SKILL DRILL | 28-10 | Inspecting and Replacing Rack-and-Pinion Steering Gear Inner Tie-Rod Ends and Bellows Boots |

1 Raise the vehicle on a lift. Inspect the rubber bellows for any signs of leaks, tears, or damage.

2 With the vehicle raised, have an assistant turn the steering wheel to one side or the other and rock the steering wheel from side to side. On the side farthest out, squeeze the bellows until you make contact with the inner ball joint, and feel for play in the inner tie-rod joint. Repeat this procedure for the other side. If play is found, replacement of the inner tie-rod ends will be necessary.

3 Remove the front wheel for the side being replaced, and loosen the locknut on the tie-rod end.

SKILL DRILL	28-10	Inspecting and Replacing Rack-and-Pinion Steering Gear Inner Tie-Rod Ends and Bellows Boots, continued

4 Remove the cotter pin and nut holding the outer tie-rod end to the steering arm, and separate the tie-rod end from the knuckle using a tie-rod removal tool, the double-hammer method, or a pickle fork.

5 Count the number of turns to remove the outer tie-rod end from the threaded sleeve.

6 Remove the spring clamp from the bellows boot end to the inner tie-rod shaft, and remove the crimp clamp from the bellows boot to the rack-and-pinion housing. A new crimp clamp will have to be used on replacement of the boot.

7 Remove the bellows boot.

8 Using an inner tie-rod tool and the specified wrench to hold the rack, loosen the inner tie-rod from the rack, and remove the inner tie-rod end.

9 Install the new inner tie-rod in reverse order of removal, and verify that the play is gone. Perform alignment to reset toe after replacement is performed.

4 On the side farthest out, squeeze the bellows until you make contact with the inner ball joint, and feel for any play in the inner tie-rod joint.

5 Repeat this procedure for the other side.

6 If play is found, replacement of the inner tie-rod ends will be necessary. (**Photo 2**)

7 Remove the front wheel for the side being replaced and loosen the locknut on the tie-rod end. (**Photo 3**)

8 Remove the cotter pin and nut holding the outer tie-rod end to the steering arm, and separate the tie-rod end from the knuckle using a tie-rod removal tool, the double-hammer method, or a pickle fork. (**Photo 4**)

9 Count the number of turns to remove the outer tie-rod end from the threaded sleeve. (**Photo 5**)

10 Remove the spring clamp from the bellows boot end to the inner tie-rod shaft, and remove the crimp clamp from the bellows boot to the rack-and-pinion housing. A new crimp clamp will have to be used on replacement of the boot. (**Photo 6**)

11 Remove the bellows boot. **(Photo 7)**

12 Using an inner tie-rod tool and the specified wrench to hold the rack, loosen the inner tie-rod from the rack, and remove the inner tie-rod end. **(Photo 8)**

13 Install the new inner tie-rod in reverse order of removal, and verify that the play is gone.

14 Perform alignment to reset toe after replacement is performed. **(Photo 9)**

15 Test-drive to verify repair.

Inspecting and Replacing the Pitman Arm, Relay (Center Link/Intermediate) Rod, Idler Arm and Mountings, and Steering Linkage Damper

With any steering complaints, it is necessary to check the components of the steering linkage for wear and damage. Slight problems in any of these components may result in significant steering problems and tire wear. Looseness in the idler arm may cause excessive toe change on rough road surfaces, leading to a wandering condition. Looseness in and of the tie-rod ends may be felt as loose steering and is frequently mistaken as a steering gearbox problem. Because of these issues, each of the steering system joints needs to be inspected for excessive wear or damage. If the vehicle is equipped with a steering damper, it can cause a shimmy in the steering wheel after hitting a bump in the road. Refer to the manufacturer's service information for the procedure and specifications for inspecting and replacing these components.

To inspect and replace the idler arm, follow the steps in **SKILL DRILL 28-11**:

1 Safely raise the vehicle with the lift set at the manufacturer's suggested lifting points.

2 Push the center link at the idler arm up and down, and watch the idler arm for excessive movement. **(Photo 1)**

3 If the movement is out of specifications, the idler arm will need to be replaced.

4 Remove the cotter pin and loosen the nut connecting the idler arm taper stud to the center link. **(Photo 2)**

5 Separate the idler arm taper stud using the double-hammer method, a pickle fork, or the appropriate puller. **(Photo 3)**

6 Remove the bolts holding the idler arm to the frame. **(Photo 4)**

7 Install the new idler arm in reverse order of removal. Note that some idler arms must be installed with the steering centered to avoid inducing a twisting force on the steering linkage, causing the vehicle to pull to one side. **(Photo 5)**

To inspect and replace the pitman arm, follow the steps in **SKILL DRILL 28-12**:

SKILL DRILL   28-11   Inspecting and Replacing the Idler Arm

1 Raise the vehicle with the lift set at the manufacturer's suggested lifting points. Push the center link at the idler arm up and down, and watch the idler arm for excessive movement.

2 If the movement is out of specifications, the idler arm will need to be replaced. Remove the cotter pin and loosen the nut connecting the idler arm taper stud to the center link.

3 Separate the idler arm taper stud using the double-hammer method, a pickle fork, or the appropriate puller.

SKILL DRILL | **28-11** | **Inspecting and Replacing the Idler Arm, continued**

4 Remove the bolts holding the idler arm to the frame.

5 Install the new idler arm in reverse order of removal. Note that some idler arms must be installed with the steering centered to prevent inducing a twisting force on the steering linkage, causing the vehicle to pull to one side.

SKILL DRILL | **28-12** | **Inspecting and Replacing the Pitman Arm**

1 Push and pull side to side on the front driver's side tire while watching for looseness in the pitman arm joint. If the movement is out of specifications, the joint will need to be replaced. This joint can be located on the pitman arm or the center link.

2 If the center link needs to be replaced, remove the cotter pin and nut holding the pitman arm taper stud to the center link.

3 If the pitman arm needs to be replaced, place an alignment mark on the pitman arm to the sector shaft with white paint or a punch to ensure correct positioning on reassembly.

SKILL DRILL   28-12   Inspecting and Replacing the Pitman Arm, continued

4 Remove the pitman arm nut holding the arm to the sector shaft of the steering gear.

5 Using a pitman arm puller, pull the pitman arm free from the sector shaft.

6 Install the new pitman arm and center link in reverse order of removal.

1 Push and pull side to side on the front driver's side tire while watching for looseness in the pitman arm joint.

2 If the movement is out of specifications, the joint will need to be replaced. This joint can be located on the pitman arm or the center link. **(Photo 1)**

3 If the center link needs to be replaced, remove the cotter pin and nut holding the pitman arm taper stud to the center link. **(Photo 2)**

4 If the pitman arm needs to be replaced, place an alignment mark on the pitman arm to sector shaft with white paint or a punch to ensure correct positioning on reassembly. **(Photo 3)**

5 Remove the pitman arm nut holding the arm to the sector shaft of the steering gear. **(Photo 4)**

6 Using a pitman arm puller, pull the pitman arm free from the sector shaft. **(Photo 5)**

7 Install the new pitman arm in reverse order of removal. **(Photo 6)**

To inspect and replace the center link (relay rod/intermediate rod), follow the steps in **SKILL DRILL 28-13**:

1 Push and pull the tire/wheel assembly from side to side, checking each of the center link joints for excess movement.

2 If the movement is out of specifications, the joint(s) will need to be replaced.

3 Remove the cotter pin and nuts from the tapered studs of the pitman arm, idler arm, and inner tie-rod ends. **(Photo 1)**

4 Separate the tapered studs using the double-hammer method, a pickle fork, or the approved puller. Remove the center link. **(Photo 2)**

5 Install the new center link in reverse order of removal. **(Photo 3)**

To inspect and replace the steering linkage damper, follow the steps in **SKILL DRILL 28-14**:

1 Safely raise the vehicle with the lift set at the manufacturer's suggested lifting points.

2 Look for fluid leaking out of the damper or a bent rod in the damper, and check that the bushings are tight in the damper. **(Photo 1)**

3 Grab the wheels and turn them right and left. If the damper is working properly, there should be a fair amount of resistance when trying to turn the wheels quickly.

4 If any of these conditions are found, replacement will be necessary. Remove the cotter pin and nut from the center link and frame attaching point, and remove the steering damper. **(Photo 2)**

5 Install the new damper in reverse order of disassembly. **(Photo 3)**

Inspecting and Replacing Tie-Rod Ends, Tie-Rod Sleeves, and Clamps

Tie-rods make the final connection between the steering linkage and the steering arms. The point of connection with the steering linkage is considered the inner tie-rod

SEE

SKILL DRILL | 28-13 | Inspecting and Replacing the Center Link (Relay Rod/Intermediate Rod)

1. Push and pull the tire/wheel assembly from side to side, checking each of the center link joints for excess movement. If the movement is out of specifications, the joint(s) will need to be replaced. Remove the cotter pin and nuts from the taper studs of the pitman arm, idler arm, and inner tie-rod ends.

2. Separate the taper studs with the double-hammer method, a pickle fork, or the approved puller. Remove the center link.

3. Install the new center link in reverse order of removal.

SEE

SKILL DRILL | 28-14 | Inspecting and Replacing the Steering Linkage Damper

1. Safely raise the vehicle with the lift set at the manufacturer's suggested lifting points. Look for fluid leaking out of the damper or a bent rod in the damper, and check that the bushings are tight in the damper.

2. Grab the wheels and turn them right and left. If the damper is working properly, there should be a fair amount of resistance when trying to turn the wheels quickly. If any of these conditions are found, replacement will be necessary. Remove the cotter pin and nut from the center link and frame attaching point, and remove the steering damper.

3. Install the new damper in reverse order of disassembly.

end, and the end that connects to the steering arm is considered the outer tie-rod end. Checking tie-rods is important in identifying steering problems because the ends are frequently damaged or worn. There are two basic types of tie-rod ends: spring-loaded and preloaded. Each type has its own procedure for inspection and replacement of the ends. Replacement of tie-rod ends requires an alignment to be performed or rapid tire wear will occur. Note: If removing a tie-rod from an aluminum steering knuckle, do not use a pickle fork, as it will damage the soft aluminum. Use the approved tie-rod end puller to separate the end from an aluminum knuckle or steering arm. Be sure to follow the manufacturer's service information for testing and replacement of tie-rod ends.

To inspect and replace preloaded tie-rod ends, follow the steps in **SKILL DRILL 28-15**:

1. Preloaded tie-rods have only enough internal clearance for the socket to pivot in the joint. The joint does not have a spring and clearance, so it cannot be compressed. With the vehicle's weight on the tires, have an assistant gently rock the steering wheel between the 10 o'clock and the 1 o'clock positions. As the steering wheel is rocked, note any side-to-side or up-and-down movement in the tie-rod ends. Sometimes it is easier to feel the play by placing your hand around the joint while an assistant wiggles the tires.

2. If the ball and socket is worn, replacement will be necessary.

3. Loosen the tie-rod locknut found where the inner tie-rod end threads to the outer tie-rod end. (**Photo 1**)

4. Remove the cotter pin and nut from the tapered stud of the tie-rod end, and separate it from the steering knuckle with the double-hammer method, a pickle fork, or the approved puller. Count the number of turns the tie-rod end rotates until it is backed out of the sleeve. (**Photo 2**)

5. Install the new tie-rod end using the number of turns counted in the previous step; this will get the toe angle close to the correct position.

6. Reinstall the new tie-rod end in reverse order of removal. Perform a test-drive to verify repair. (**Photo 3**)

Adjusting Non–Rack-and-Pinion Worm Bearing Preload and Sector Lash

The gearbox in non–rack-and-pinion steering systems may require adjustment over time, particularly if the driver complains of loose steering. The two adjustments

SKILL DRILL   28-15   Inspecting and Replacing Tie-Rod Ends

1. With the vehicle's weight on the tires, have an assistant gently rock the steering wheel between the 10 o'clock and the 1 o'clock positions. Note any side-to-side or up-and-down movement in the tie-rod ends. If the ball and socket is worn, replacement will be necessary. Loosen the tie-rod locknut found where the inner tie-rod end threads to the outer tie-rod end.

2. Remove the cotter pin and nut from the tapered stud of the tie-rod end, and separate it from the steering knuckle with the double-hammer method, a pickle fork, or the approved puller. Count the number of turns the tie-rod end rotates until it is backed out of the sleeve.

3. Install the new tie-rod end using the number of turns counted in the previous step; this will get the toe angle close. Reinstall the new tie-rod end in reverse order of removal. Perform a test-drive to verify repair.

that should be checked are the worm bearing preload and the sector lash. The goal for the worm bearing preload adjustment is to remove play at the worm bearings while maintaining a low resistance to worm shaft movement. The goal for the sector lash adjustment is to remove play from between the worm-and-sector gear teeth in the centered position, while not binding up at any point in the travel. For the adjustments to be accurate, the steering shaft and the pitman arm should be disconnected so that turning effort can be measured with an inch-pound torque wrench. Thus, it is easier to perform this task when the steering gear has been removed from the vehicle, although it is possible to do it with the steering gear on the vehicle on some vehicles. The adjustment process should be performed according to the manufacturer's service information and specifications.

To adjust non–rack-and-pinion worm bearing preload and sector lash, follow the steps in **SKILL DRILL 28-16**:

① Research the specified procedure and specifications for the adjustments. With the steering gear removed from the vehicle and mounted in a vise, loosen the locknut and back off the sector shaft adjustment screw so it is not loading the worm gear. **(Photo 1)**

② Fit a socket onto the input shaft and use an inch-pound torque wrench to measure the rotating torque from lock to lock. If the rotating torque is too low, loosen the locknut on the worm bearing adjusting plug. **(Photo 2)**

③ Tighten the adjusting plug slightly tighter and retest the rotating torque. Make adjustments until the rotating torque is within specifications. Tighten the locknut without allowing the adjusting plug to move. Verify that the rotating torque has not changed. **(Photo 3)**

Inspecting and Testing Electric Power Assist Steering

On vehicles equipped with EPS, the electric power assist system should be tested any time a driver complains of steering difficulties, either hard or loose. The first step is to verify the concern by starting the vehicle and operating the steering wheel while observing the EPS warning lamp. If the lamp goes out as it should and the power steering feels normal, you may need to perform a test-drive and check the operation of the steering system under driving conditions. The test-drive should confirm the customer's concern and give you valuable information regarding the fault.

If the EPS lamp is off, you will want to perform a visual inspection of the mechanical components such as tire pressure, tires, tie-rod ends, rack bushings, and steering column for excessive play or damage. If the EPS lamp indicates a fault, a scan tool will need to be hooked up

SKILL DRILL   28-16   Adjusting Non–Rack-and-Pinion Worm Bearing Preload and Sector Lash

① Research the specified procedure and specifications for the adjustments. With the steering gear removed from the vehicle and mounted in a vise, loosen the locknut and back off the sector shaft adjustment screw.

② Fit a socket onto the input shaft and use an inch-pound torque wrench to measure the rotating torque from lock to lock. If the rotating torque is too low, loosen the locknut on the worm bearing adjusting plug.

③ Tighten the adjusting plug slightly and retest the rotating torque. Make adjustments until the rotating torque is within specifications. Tighten the locknut without allowing the adjusting plug to move. Verify that the rotating torque has not changed.

to the vehicle's data link connector. The scanner accesses and retrieves data from the vehicle's onboard computer and identifies the diagnostic trouble codes (DTCs). The DTCs are used with the manufacturer's flowchart for that code (found in the service information) to identify the exact problem. Consult the service information for the exact steps for repair or replacement.

Testing and Diagnosing Components of Electronically Controlled Steering Systems with a Scan Tool

Once a problem in an electronically controlled steering system has been confirmed and codes have been pulled, it is time to research the codes, technical service bulletins (TSBs), and diagnostic procedure in the appropriate service information. With the proper diagnostic procedure decided, a scan tool updated to the latest calibrations, and a DVOM, you are ready to start tracking down the fault. Depending on the system and the fault, the service information or TSB will lead you through the diagnosis one step at a time. Just be careful that you understand how the particular system is designed to operate, and read through the procedure carefully so that you don't become confused or start down the wrong diagnostic path.

Adjusting, Repairing, or Replacing Components of Electronically Controlled Steering Systems

Electronically controlled steering systems are complicated, with little allowance for adjustment or repair in the face of problems. Generally, the only course of action available is a complete replacement with a new unit or a wiring repair on the system's harness. Each electronic system, including how it fits into the various makes and models of vehicles, is unique. The technician must look up the specific instructions supplied by the manufacturer and follow them step by step. Once repairs or replacement is complete, the PCM will generally need to be accessed with a scan tool to perform the process for recentering the steering wheel position sensor.

Identifying Hybrid Vehicle Power Steering System Electrical Circuits

A technician may be called upon to identify the electrical circuits within the power steering system of a hybrid vehicle, particularly when an electrical problem is suspected. Because the technology in hybrid vehicles varies and is continuously evolving, and because some of these vehicles run on high voltage, the best procedure is to refer to the manufacturer's service information. This

information will include a section devoted to diagnosis, along with the wiring diagrams for the various systems. The technician should examine the diagrams and compare them to the systems in the vehicle. Most manufacturers identify their high-voltage wires with specific colors, but there is not a uniform color designation across all manufacturers. Currently, orange, yellow, and blue are used by manufacturers for circuit voltages higher than 12 volts. Always research the color of high-voltage wiring in the service information for any hybrid or electric vehicles prior to working on them.

Safety

On vehicles with high-voltage systems (50 volts or higher), you may be required to wear insulated gloves appropriate for the system voltage you are working on. Always make sure the gloves have been tested for electrical leaks within the required time frame. And always test the gloves before using them by rolling up the sleeve, trapping air inside, and verifying that there are no air leaks. If there are any air leaks, do NOT use them, as electricity could travel through the hole.

Disabling and Enabling the SRS

The SRS system must be disabled and enabled while working on or around the steering column, any of the airbags or other pyrotechnic devices, and any of the sensors. Failure to disable the SRS system could cause one or more of the SRS devices to deploy, which can cause serious injury or death, along with an expensive repair. It is important to know that most airbags are inflated by igniting a solid fuel similar to rocket fuel.

Every manufacturer has its own procedures for disabling and enabling the SRS system on its vehicles, and those procedures can be different for each of the vehicle models they sell. Always follow the manufacturer's specified procedure for the model of vehicle you are working on. Also, this is one time that you DO NOT use a memory minder or auxiliary power supply on the vehicle. Doing so could supply power to the SRS system after it has been disabled.

To disable and enable the SRS, follow the steps in **SKILL DRILL 28-17**:

1. Find and remove the SRS fuse. Verify correct fuse removal by turning the key on and observing that the SRS light remains lit for at least 30 seconds and does not go out. If it goes out, you did not remove the correct fuse or all of the required fuses.

2. Make sure the wheels are steered straight ahead. Turn the key off. **(Photo 1)**

3 Remove the negative battery cable and allow a minimum of 15 minutes to pass to let the SRS system's capacitors discharge. Note any radio presets or other memory features of the vehicle that will be erased when the battery is disconnected. DO NOT USE A MEMORY MINDER OR AUXILIARY POWER SOURCE. Doing so could cause an accidental deployment! **(Photo 2)**

4 To enable the SRS system, verify that all SRS modules, components, and connectors are installed and connected properly. **(Photo 3)**

5 Reinstall the SRS fuse. **(Photo 4)**

6 Reconnect the negative battery terminal and tighten properly. **(Photo 5)**

Safety

Many airbags are now of the two-stage variety so they can deploy with the proper amount of force depending on the severity of the accident, approximate weight of the occupant, etc. This means that even a deployed airbag is still potentially dangerous and needs to be treated with caution during removal. It should be deployed soon after removal, following the manufacturer's specified procedure, which will render it safe for disposal.

7 Without being in front of or reaching across the driver's side airbag, turn on the ignition switch and observe the SRS light. It should illuminate briefly and then go out, and stay out. If so, the SRS system should be ready to be placed back into service. **(Photo 6)**

Removing and Replacing the Steering Wheel and Center/Time the SRS Coil (Clock Spring)

The clock spring assists in supplying a constant electrical connection to a vehicle's SRS and horn, and in some vehicles, the cruise control, message center controls, and entertainment controls. The clock spring coils and uncoils as needed during turning of the steering wheel to ensure that the airbag is always ready to be deployed in the event of a collision. Because of this winding and unwinding, the wires in the clock spring can break over time, illuminating the SRS light and disabling the SRS system. Since it is considered an important safety feature, it must be replaced if it is damaged in any way. Be sure to follow the manufacturer's service information to replace a clock spring. Failure to properly disable the airbag could result in serious injury or death. This skill drill uses an example vehicle only. ALWAYS follow the service information for the vehicle you are working on.

SKILL DRILL | **28-17** | **Disabling and Enabling the SRS**

1 Find and remove the SRS fuse. Verify by turning the key on and observing that the SRS light remains lit for at least 30 seconds. If it goes out, you did not remove the correct fuse or all of the required fuses. Make sure the wheels are steered straight ahead. Turn the key off.

2 Remove the negative battery cable and allow a minimum of 15 minutes to pass to let the SRS system capacitors discharge. Note any radio presets or other memory features of the vehicle that will be erased when the battery is disconnected. *Do not use a memory minder or auxiliary power source!*

3 To enable the SRS system, verify that all SRS modules, components, and connectors are installed and connected properly.

SKILL DRILL 28-17 | Disabling and Enabling the SRS, continued

4 Reinstall the SRS fuse.

5 Reconnect the negative battery terminal and tighten properly.

6 Without being in front of or reaching across the driver's side airbag, turn on the ignition switch and observe the SRS light. It should illuminate briefly and then go out, and stay out. If so, the SRS system should be ready to be placed back into service.

To remove and replace the steering wheel and center-time the SRS coil, follow the steps in **SKILL DRILL 28-18**:

1 Find the SRS fuse and remove. Verify correct fuse removal by turning the key on and observing that the SRS light remains lit for at least 30 seconds and does not go out. Make sure the wheels are straight ahead. Turn the key off. (**Photo 1**)

2 Remove the negative battery cable and allow a minimum of 5 minutes to pass to let the SRS system's capacitors discharge. Note any radio presets or other memory features of the vehicle that will be erased when the battery is disconnected. DO NOT USE A MEMORY MINDER OR AUXILIARY POWER SOURCE! (**Photo 2**)

3 Locate the SRS connector at the bottom of the steering column and disconnect. Remove upper and lower trim panels. (**Photo 3**)

4 Locate the bolts or spring clips on the back of the steering wheel that hold the airbag to the steering wheel, and remove or release them. (**Photo 4**)

5 Lift the airbag from the steering wheel, and disconnect the airbag connector to the steering wheel harness. (**Photo 5**)

6 Sit the airbag on a bench face up in a safe place. (**Photo 6**)

7 Remove the fasteners that hold the steering wheel on. (**Photo 7**)

8 Remove the steering wheel with the manufacturer's recommended puller (this information can be found in the service information). (**Photo 8**)

9 Remove the clock spring screws or snap ring, and lift the clock spring from steering column shaft. Attach a thin wire to the clock spring connector (airbag connector was disconnected earlier) at the base of the steering column, and pull the clock spring and connector up through the steering column. The wire will allow you to pull the new connector back down through the steering column. (**Photo 9**)

10 Gently pull the clock spring harness down through the steering column. (**Photo 10**)

11 If the antirotation key is still installed, skip to step 13. If the antirotation key is not installed, center the clock spring following the manufacturer's procedure. In this case, we will gently rotate the inner rotor counterclockwise until it stops. (**Photo 11**)

12 Rotate the inner rotor clockwise the required number of turns—in this case four full turns. Verify that all of the marks are aligned in their specified positions. (**Photo 12**)

13 Reinstall the clock spring assembly in the proper orientation, and secure it with the screws or snap ring. Reinstall components in the reverse order of removal, ensuring that torque specifications are

SKILL DRILL | 28-18 | Removing and Replacing Steering Wheel and Center/Time the SRS Coil

1. Find and remove the SRS fuse. Verify by turning the key on and observing that the SRS light remains lit for at least 30 seconds and does not go out. Make sure the wheels are straight ahead. Turn the key off.

2. Remove the negative battery cable and allow a minimum of 5 minutes to pass to let the SRS system's capacitors discharge. *Do not use a memory minder or auxiliary power source!*

3. Locate the SRS connector at the bottom of the steering column and disconnect. Remove upper and lower trim panels.

4. Locate the bolts or spring clip on the back of the steering wheel that hold the airbag to the steering wheel, and remove or release them.

5. Lift the airbag from the steering wheel, and disconnect the airbag connector to the steering wheel harness.

6. Sit the airbag on bench face up in a safe place.

followed. Also remove the antirotation key at the appropriate step. **(Photo 13)**

Inspecting the Steering Shaft Universal Joint(s), Flexible Coupling(s), Collapsible Column, Lock Cylinder Mechanism, and Steering Wheel

The steering wheel and column are responsible for transferring the driver's steering input to the steering gear and on to the wheels, dictating the direction in which the vehicle travels. Any damage or failures of the steering column and steering wheel can cause the vehicle to move in unexpected directions, putting the lives of the driver and those around him or her at risk. Regular inspection of the steering column and its components can identify problems before they become dangerous.

To inspect the steering shaft universal joint (U-joint) or flexible coupler for play, visually inspect the steering shaft U-joint or coupler as another person turns the steering wheel from side to side. The coupler or U-joint should have zero play. If play is noted, replacement will be necessary. Follow service information for replacement of the coupler or U-joint.

Steering columns are designed to collapse in the event of an accident so the steering main shaft in the

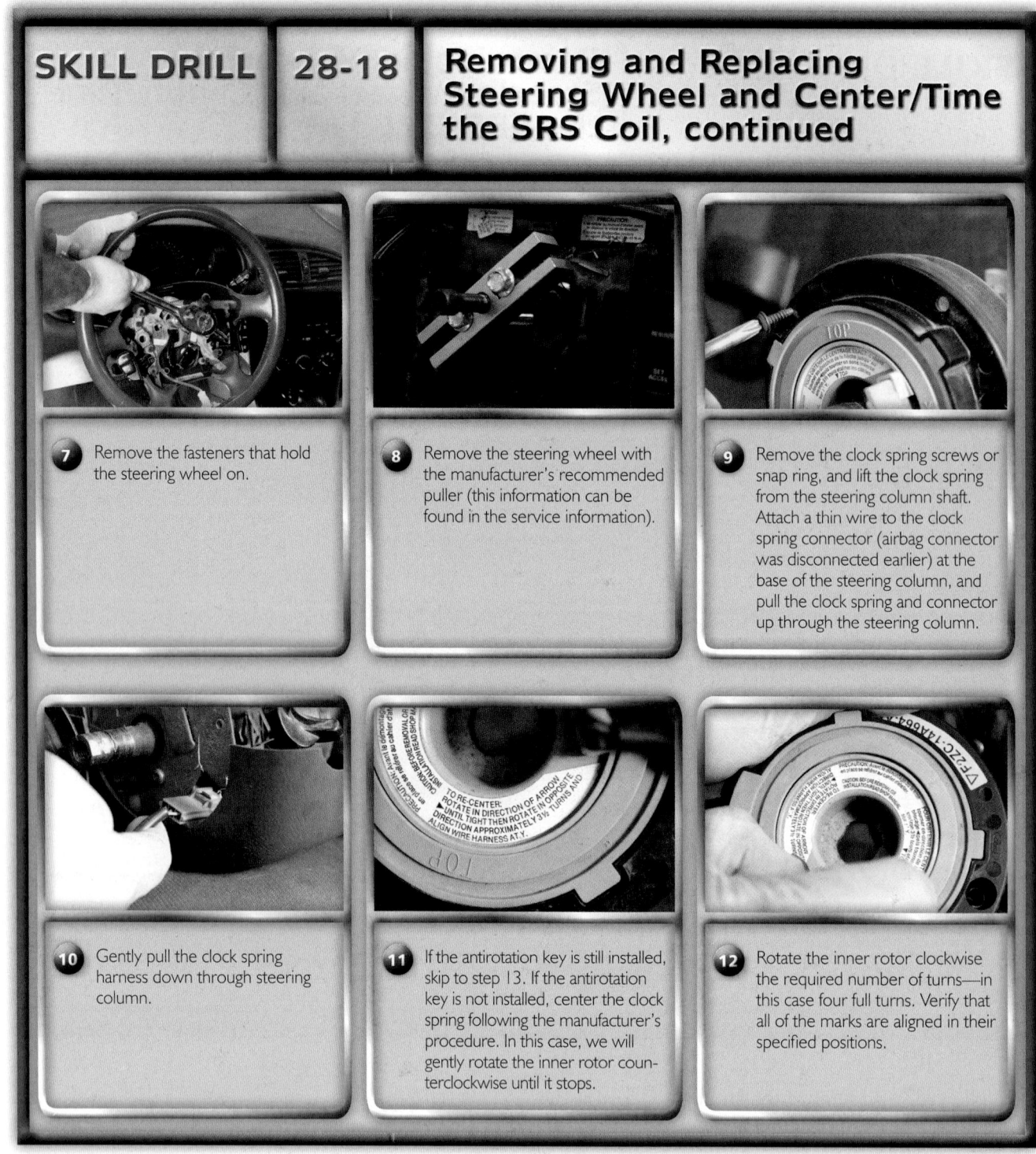

7 Remove the fasteners that hold the steering wheel on.

8 Remove the steering wheel with the manufacturer's recommended puller (this information can be found in the service information).

9 Remove the clock spring screws or snap ring, and lift the clock spring from the steering column shaft. Attach a thin wire to the clock spring connector (airbag connector was disconnected earlier) at the base of the steering column, and pull the clock spring and connector up through the steering column.

10 Gently pull the clock spring harness down through steering column.

11 If the antirotation key is still installed, skip to step 13. If the antirotation key is not installed, center the clock spring following the manufacturer's procedure. In this case, we will gently rotate the inner rotor counterclockwise until it stops.

12 Rotate the inner rotor clockwise the required number of turns—in this case four full turns. Verify that all of the marks are aligned in their specified positions.

column does not injure or kill the driver. The column has a sliding shaft that will slide into itself in the event of an accident, and the column housing mounting points are designed to allow the column to slip downward as the driver makes contact with the steering wheel. An inspection of the collapsible steering column normally takes place if the vehicle has been in an accident and the column is suspected to have moved. To inspect the collapsible column for play, position yourself inside the vehicle on the driver's side looking under the dashboard while an assistant pulls and pushes on the column. Movement of the column at the mounting

SKILL DRILL | 28-18 | Removing and Replacing Steering Wheel and Center/Time the SRS Coil, continued

13 Reinstall the clock spring assembly in the proper orientation, and secure it with the screws or snap ring. Reinstall components in the reverse order of removal, ensuring that torque specifications are followed. Also remove the antirotation key at the appropriate step.

locations will be visible if the mounting points have collapsed.

To inspect the lock cylinder, insert the key and ensure that the lock cylinder rotates freely without binding and locks the steering wheel in the lock position. Binding of the lock cylinder may require the cylinder to be removed and replaced or further teardown of the steering column to find the binding concern. Follow the manufacturer's service information for this concern. To inspect the steering wheel, pull and push on the steering wheel, checking for looseness or play. If play is found in the steering wheel, it may be due to wear in the tilt mechanism or play in the steering column upper bearing. Always check for any TSBs on diagnostic concerns, as there may be a known condition and revised parts. Teardown of the steering column or replacement may be necessary to correct play in the steering column assembly.

To inspect the steering shaft U-joint(s), flexible coupling(s), collapsible column, lock cylinder mechanism, and steering wheel follow the steps in **SKILL DRILL 28-19**:

1 Visually inspect the steering shaft flexible couplings for obvious damage or wear.

2 Have an assistant wiggle the steering wheel back and forth as you watch for play or improper move-

ment. If any is noted, the joint will need to be replaced. **(Photo 1)**

3 To inspect the collapsible column, push and pull on the steering wheel to check for any looseness of the steering shaft or column assembly. **(Photo 2)**

4 Look under the dashboard at the steering column, and inspect the mounting bolts. Any broken bolts indicate a collapsed steering column. **(Photo 3)**

5 Look on the column for the plastic inserts that are typically used to connect the upper and lower halves of the steering shaft. Any damage indicates a collapsed steering column. **(Photo 4)**

6 To inspect the lock cylinder mechanism, insert and remove the key from the lock cylinder, checking for any resistance or difficulties. **(Photo 5)**

7 Place the key inside the lock cylinder, and turn the key to each position, checking for smooth and proper operation. **(Photo 6)**

8 Place the key in the lock position, and check that the steering wheel is locked. If any faults are found, follow the service information for the repair procedures. **(Photo 7)**

SKILL DRILL | **28-19** | **Inspecting the Steering Shaft U-Joint(s), Flexible Coupling(s), Collapsible Column, Lock Cylinder Mechanism, and Steering Wheel**

1 Inspect the steering shaft flexible couplings for obvious damage or wear. Have an assistant wiggle the steering wheel back and forth as you watch for play or improper movement. If any is noted, the joint will need to be replaced.

2 To inspect the collapsible column, push and pull on the steering wheel to check for any looseness of the steering shaft or column assembly.

3 Look under the dashboard at the steering column, and inspect the mounting bolts. Any broken bolts indicate a collapsed steering column.

4 Look on the column for the plastic inserts that are typically used to connect the upper and lower halves of the steering shaft. Any damage indicates a collapsed steering column.

5 To inspect the lock cylinder mechanism, insert and remove the key from the lock cylinder, checking for any resistance or difficulties.

6 Place the key inside the lock cylinder, and turn the key to each position, checking for smooth and proper operation.

| SKILL DRILL | 28-19 | Inspecting the Steering Shaft U-Joint(s), Flexible Coupling(s), Collapsible Column, Lock Cylinder Mechanism, and Steering Wheel, continued |

7. Place the key in the lock position, and check that the steering wheel is locked. If any faults are found, follow the service information for the repair procedures.

Wrap-up

Ready for Review

▸ The power steering system can be either a hydraulic or electric type.

▸ A basic steering system has four main parts: a steering column, a steering box, a steering linkage, and a steering knuckle.

▸ Steering geometry is a geometric arrangement of linkages in the steering of a vehicle, designed to keep the wheels properly oriented through various positions of the steering and suspension systems.

▸ The rack-and-pinion steering system is used on the majority of front-wheel drive vehicles because of the space restriction under the hood.

▸ The parallelogram steering system is used on larger vehicles where ride comfort is more important than sporty handling.

▸ When servicing the steering column, it is good practice to disarm the triggering system for the drigver's side airbag. If not properly disarmed, it could trigger accidentally.

▸ Because of the critical nature of the airbag, it is imperative that it is always connected electrically to its control module, so it can be deployed when needed.

▸ The function of all steering boxes, whether manual or power, is the same: to transfer the rotary motion of the steering wheel into the side-to-side motion needed to make the wheels pivot left and right.

▸ There are two basic types of steering boxes: those with rack-and-pinion gearing and those with worm gearing and a sector shaft. In both types, the gearing in the steering box makes it easier for the driver to turn the steering wheel and, hence, the wheels.

▸ Four-wheel steering means the rear wheels can be steered independently of or in conjunction with the front wheels. There are two types: active and passive.

▸ There are three types of power steering: hydraulically assisted power steering, electrically powered hydraulic steering, and fully electric power steering.

▸ Electrically powered hydraulic steering replaces the customary drive belts and pulleys that drive a power steering pump in a conventional rack-and-pinion steering system with a brushless motor.

▸ The steering sensor performs two functions: First, as a torque sensor, it converts steering torque input and direction into voltage signals for the ECU to monitor. Second, as a rotation sensor, it converts the rotation speed and direction into voltage signals for the ECU to monitor.

▸ Higher voltage electrically assisted power-steering systems were developed for modern hybrid vehicles. The higher voltage battery system of the hybrid vehicle provides all the power, with no reliance on engine or hydraulic power.

▸ Many of the problems associated with steering system are mechanical, but as more EPS systems are produced, electrical faults are becoming more common. The main problems that arise in the steering system are play and hard steering; common causes are wear and poor lubrication.

▸ Power steering fluid is critical to the proper functioning of the entire steering system. Any leak, no matter how small, is cause for repair.

▸ To maintain a safe-operating vehicle, regular inspection of the steering components is essential.

▸ Pressure testing the power steering system is performed when the driver complains of hard steering or when there are repeated hose failures.

▸ Removing and replacing the rack-and-pinion steering gear should be considered only after examining all parts of the steering system and performing a full diagnosis to ensure the problem is not the result of some other fault.

▸ Checking tie-rod ends is important in identifying steering problems because the ends are frequently damaged or worn.

▸ On vehicles equipped with EPS, the electric power assist system should be tested any time the driver complains of steering difficulties, either hard or loose.

Key Terms

active control A system of providing constant feedback from sensors in the vehicle to the control unit.

actuating The act of making something move or work.

adjustable bushing A brace or nylon part that pushes against the rack to adjust the mesh of the rack teeth to the pinion teeth.

adjustment sleeve A component that connects the tie-rods together and to the center link on some applications, providing the adjustment point for toe-in or toe-out, depending on the manufacturer's specifications.

antibinding The release of something when it gets stuck.

ball-return guide A special passage or metal tube through which the balls move in recirculating ball steering boxes.

beam axle A suspension system in which one set of wheels is connected laterally by a single beam or shaft.

bump steer The undesired condition produced when hitting a bump where the vehicle darts to one side as the steering linkage is pushed or pulled as a result of the travel of the suspension.

chassis The frame of a vehicle, to which the suspension pieces attach.

clock spring A special rotary electrical connector located between the steering wheel and the steering column that maintains a constant electrical connection with the wiring system while the vehicle's steering wheel is being turned.

constant mesh A term used to describe two or more parts, such as gears, that are in constant contact with each other.

control unit Any device that controls another object such as a computer.

drag link A steel or iron rod that transfers movement of the pitman arm to a relay lever.

end play Unwanted lateral movements of the worm shaft.

electric power steering system (EPS) A steering system that uses an electric motor and sensors to provide feedback to the vehicle's computer systems to decrease steering effort.

electrically assisted steering (EAS) A power-assist system that uses an electric motor to replace the hydraulic pump to decrease steering effort.

electrically powered hydraulic steering (EPHS) A steering system that uses an electric motor to produce hydraulic assist for steering.

engine-driven hydraulic pump A power steering pump driven by a belt or gear off of the crankshaft.

flow-control valve A valve used in power steering pumps to control the amount of flow out of the power steering pump.

forces capability map data Data preprogrammed into the electronic control unit's memory by the manufacturer and used to determine how much power assistance is needed based on input from the vehicle's speed sensor and steering sensor.

four-wheel steering system A steering system in which the front wheels are controlled normally and the rear wheels use a computer and electric motors to turn the rear linkage.

gear ratio A comparison of the number of turns or speed of the input (first) gear in the train to the number of turns or speed of the output (last) gear in the train.

gear reduction A gear ratio used to make large turns of the steering wheel into smaller turns of the tire to ease steering for the driver.

helix A spiral or coil shape.

inertia The resistance to a change in motion.

inner tie-rod or socket The inner tie-rod is attached to the end of the rack and allows for suspension movement and slight changes in steering angles.

intermediate shaft A steel rod positioned at an angle from the steering column to the steering gear that functions in transferring movement from one to the other.

knuckle The part that contains the wheel hub or spindle and attaches to the suspension components.

linear motion Movement in a straight line.

meshed pinion A pinion when it is mated with the rack.

outer tie-rod The tie-rod attached between the tie-rod and the steering arm. It transfers the movement of the rack, pivoting as the rack is extended or retracted when the vehicle is negotiating turns.

parallelogram steering system A non–rack-and-pinion system that uses a series of parts consisting of the pitman arm, idler arm, center link, and tie-rod assemblies that relays movement from the steering gearbox to the wheel assembly.

pinion A gear located at the end of the steering shaft connected to the rack. It moves the rack from side to side as the pinion rotates, controlling the direction of the wheels.

pitch On a helix, the distance moved in one full revolution of the cylinder.

power assist unit The electric motor in electric power assist steering systems.

power section A chamber in the rack where pressurized fluid acts upon pistons that assist in steering.

power steering An option on a vehicle that allows movement of the steering wheel with decreased driver effort.

power steering pump A small hydraulic pump that provides assistance to the driver when turning the steering wheel.

power unit A belt- or gear-driven pump that produces hydraulic pressure for use in the steering box or rack.

preloaded A part that is already compressed from pressure.

rack A steel rod driven by the pinion with tie-rods on each end or tie-rods connected to the center of the rack.

rack housing The outer shell of the rack-and-pinion steering system that is mounted to the chassis.

rack-and-pinion steering system A steering system composed of a steering wheel, a main shaft, universal joints, and an intermediate shaft. When the steering wheel is turned, movement is transferred by the main shaft and intermediate shaft to the pinion.

recirculating ball steering box A steering box that has worm gear inside a block with a threaded hole in it and gear teeth cut into its outside that engage the sector shaft to move the pitman arm; generally used on trucks and heavy vehicles.

reduction ratio The ratio between the turn of the steering wheel and the turn of the wheel, both measured in degrees.

relay lever A steel rod that transfers movement from the drag link to an idler arm.

rubber bellows Rubber pieces positioned on each end of the rack to protect the inner joints from dirt and contaminants and retain the grease lubricant inside the rack-and-pinion housing.

spline A ridge or tooth on a driveshaft that meshes with grooves in a mating piece and transfers torque to it, maintaining the angular correspondence between them.

spring-loaded rack guide yoke A spring-containing part that pushes on the back side of the rack to help reduce the play between the rack and the pinion while still allowing for relative movement.

steering arm An arm that extends from the steering knuckle. The tie-rods connect to these arms in order to steer the wheels.

steering box A device that converts the rotary motion of the steering wheel to the linear motion needed to steer the vehicle.

steering column A column affixed between the steering wheel and the steering box, usually made to collapse during a crash.

steering damper A device used to prevent shocks from irregular roads from being transmitted through the steering linkage and back to the steering wheel.

steering knuckle The knuckle located between the lower control arm and MacPherson strut or upper control arm, which has a spindle made or bolted onto it to which the wheel hub is attached.

steering linkage Steel rods that connect the steering box to the steering arms on the steering knuckle.

steering sensor A sensor that can read both torque and rotation from the steering wheel.

steering system A term used to describe all of the components and parts involved in steering a vehicle.

stub axle An axle used for one wheel.

stub-axle carrier The body of the stub-axle knuckle.

tie-rod A steering component that transfers linear motion from the steering box to the steering arms at the front wheels.

tie-rod assembly The part that fits between the rack and the steering arms and transfers the movement of the rack.

toe-setting Setting of the toe-in or toe-out of the tires to the centerline of the vehicle.

torque sensor A device used to measure the load on the steering wheel.

torsion bar A spring-loaded piece of steel connected to the pinion gear at its bottom end and the input shaft at its top. Also, a torsion bar is a type of spring that some vehicles use to hold up a corner of the vehicle.

wheel assembly A term used to encompass all components of the wheel and tire.

worm A gear with a helical, threaded shaft that is attached to the steering column and meshes with a worm wheel that transfers motion from the steering wheel to the steering linkage.

worm gear steering A robust steering system frequently used on heavier vehicles that uses a worm to turn a meshed worm wheel to provide gear reduction, making steering easier for the driver.

worm shaft The protrusion of the worm gear that serves as the point of attachment to the steering column.

ASE-Type Questions

1. Tech A says that the steering column uses one or more flexible joints to connect to the steering gearbox. Tech B says that the pitman arm is bolted to the frame and relays the steering linkage movement to the opposite wheel from the steering gearbox. Who is correct?
   a. Tech A
   b. Tech B
   c. Both A and B
   d. Neither A nor B

2. Tech A says that the clock spring assists the turning of the steering wheel on vehicles with EPS. Tech B says that the clock spring is used to transmit an electrical signal to the driver's side airbag. Who is correct?
   a. Tech A
   b. Tech B
   c. Both A and B
   d. Neither A nor B

3. Tech A says that power steering fluid is universal and can be used in virtually any vehicle's power steering system. Tech B says that in a power steering system, the force needed to turn the wheels is created by the hydraulic pump or electric motor. Who is correct?
   a. Tech A
   b. Tech B
   c. Both A and B
   d. Neither A nor B

4. Tech A says that rack-and-pinion steering systems generally do not use power steering due to their lighter duty construction. Tech B says that rack-and-pinion steering systems use a worm gear arrangement to move the rack. Who is correct?
   a. Tech A
   b. Tech B
   c. Both A and B
   d. Neither A nor B

5. Tech A says that to properly check a tie-rod end, the technician should twist the tie-rod end, and any rotational movement means the joint is bad. Tech B says that to properly check tie-rod ends, the vehicle's weight should be on the wheels, and as an assistant wiggles the steering wheel, you can check for movement in the tie-rod ends. Who is correct?
   a. Tech A
   b. Tech B
   c. Both A and B
   d. Neither A nor B

6. Tech A says that worn rack-and-pinion mount bushings can cause excessive play in the steering system. Tech B says that a worn idler arm can cause excessive play in the steering system. Who is correct?
   a. Tech A
   b. Tech B
   c. Both A and B
   d. Neither A nor B

7. Tech A says that when the vehicle is being driven straight ahead, a belt-driven power steering pump will pump fluid continuously, placing a minimal load on the engine. Tech B says that a belt-driven power steering pump is activated by an electro-magnetic clutch, so it only pumps fluid when the wheels are being steered. Who is correct?
   a. Tech A
   b. Tech B
   c. Both A and B
   d. Neither A nor B

8. Tech A says that the pressure relief valve maintains a preset minimum pressure in the system. Tech B says that the pressure relief valve prevents excessive pressure. Who is correct?
   a. Tech A
   b. Tech B
   c. Both A and B
   d. Neither A nor B

9. Tech A says that worn tie-rod ends can cause a steering wandering complaint. Tech B says that a hard steering complaint could be caused by a worn power steering pump. Who is correct?
   a. Tech A
   b. Tech B
   c. Both A and B
   d. Neither A nor B

10. Tech A says that a pickle fork is used to hold a tie-rod while it is being tightened. Tech B says that power steering pump pulleys are typically bolted onto the pump shaft. Who is correct?
    a. Tech A
    b. Tech B
    c. Both A and B
    d. Neither A nor B

CHAPTER 29

NATEF Tasks

Servicing the Suspension System

NATEF Tasks, continued

- Check steering axis inclination (SAI) and included angle; determine necessary action. **AST** **MAST** 963–96•

- Check rear wheel thrust angle; determine necessary action. **AST** **MAST** 964–96!

- Check front and/or rear cradle (subframe) alignment; determine necessary action. **AST** **MAST** 965–96•

Knowledge Objectives

After reading this chapter, you will be able to:
1. Explain the principles of the suspension system. (pp 895–898)
2. Describe the principle of suspension force and how it affects the suspension system. (pp 896–897)
3. Explain the principles of unsprung weight and dampening. (p 897)
4. Discuss wheel unit location as it relates to the suspension system. (p 897)
5. Describe yaw, pitch, and roll as they relate to the vehicle. (pp 897–898)
6. Discuss the construction and purpose of the different automotive frames. (pp 898–899)
7. Describe the construction of a unibody frame and a body and chassis frame. (pp 898–899)
8. Describe the purpose and the components of the suspension system. (pp 899–911)
9. Explain the solid axle type of suspension and how it functions. (pp 911–912)
10. Explain the dead axle/live axle types of suspension and how they function. (p 912)
11. Explain how independent suspension works. (p 912)
12. Explain how rear suspension works. (pp 914–917)
13. Explain the fundamentals and the four basic types of wheel alignment. (pp 919–930)
14. Discuss the various common issues with the suspension system, including vehicle wander, pull, bump steer, and torque steer. (pp 930–931)

Skills Objectives

After reading this chapter, you will be able to:
1. Diagnose a suspension system. (pp 931–932)
2. Measure play in the suspension system. (pp 932–934)
3. Perform ride height diagnosis. (pp 935–936)
4. Check shock absorbers. (pp 935–937)
5. Remove and inspect the stabilizer bar bushings and mount brackets. (pp 937–938)
6. Remove and inspect the sway bar end links. (pp 938–939)
7. Replace a shock absorber. (pp 939–940)
8. Remove and inspect short-/long-arm (SLA) suspension system coil springs and spring insulators. (pp 940–941)
9. Remove and inspect a steering knuckle assembly. (pp 941–942)
10. Remove, inspect, and install upper and lower control arms and components. (pp 942–944)
11. Remove, inspect, and install upper and lower ball joints. (pp 944–948)
12. Lubricate a suspension system and a steering system. (pp 948–950)
13. Remove, inspect, and install the strut assembly, the strut coil spring, and the insulators. (pp 950–951)
14. Remove, inspect, and install a strut coil. (pp 951–953)
15. Remove, inspect, and install leaf springs. (pp 953–954)
16. Remove, inspect, and install strut rods and bushings. (pp 953, 955–956)
17. Remove, inspect, install, and adjust the torsion bar. (pp 956–959)
18. Perform a pre-alignment inspection. (pp 959–961)
19. Perform a four-wheel alignment. (pp 961–963)
20. Check steering axis inclination (SAI). (pp 963–964)
21. Check the rear wheel thrust angle. (pp 964–965)
22. Check cradle alignment. (pp 965–966)

Introduction

The suspension system of a vehicle is designed to follow the road surface for the purpose of maintaining traction and control of the vehicle, while at the same time providing a smooth ride for the passengers. It is composed of a network of springs, arms, struts, and shocks that work together to achieve these purposes **FIGURE 29-1**. Wear from extended use is the main cause of suspension problems, though impact from potholes and accidents may cause bent or broken components in the suspension and steering systems. Driver complaints of a bouncy ride, a reduction in steering control, or unusual noises when going over bumps indicate problems in the suspension system. Regular inspection of each component in the suspension system is helpful in identifying wear before it causes severe problems for the owner. Also know that the suspension system interacts very closely with the steering system. Thus, part of the challenge in accurately diagnosing the vehicle is knowing how both systems operate.

Even if all of the suspension and steering system components are in good working condition, they also need to be aligned correctly with each other and with the vehicle's centerline for the vehicle to operate properly and safely. For this reason, the wheels must be in proper alignment from the factory. Technicians need to verify proper alignment typically when the tires are replaced, when parts are replaced, or if a suspension related concern is being diagnosed. This chapter will help you become familiar with the various types of suspension systems, their components, how they operate, and how to inspect and service them.

FIGURE 29-1 The suspension system.

Labels: Top cap (strut insulator); Coil spring; McPherson Strut assembly (shock absorber); Subframe; Lower control arm; Steering knuckle; Ball joint; Wheel hub; Wheel rim; Tire

Suspension System Principles

The **suspension system** isolates the vehicle body from road shocks and vibrations that would otherwise be transferred to the driver and passengers. It also must keep the tires in contact with the road. A suspension system must be strong enough to withstand loads imposed by the vehicle's mass during cornering, accelerating, braking, and uneven road surfaces.

You are the Automotive Technician

You work for County Fleet Services in the vehicle service department. One of the drivers wrote up a complaint sheet on a relatively new Dodge full-size delivery van with short/long arm suspension on front and leaf-spring suspension on the rear. The truck has a little more than 100,000 miles (160,000 km) on it. The complaint sheet lists several complaints. First, the operator admitted to hitting a curb with the right front wheel. Second, the vehicle pulls hard to the right when driven. Third, it makes an audible clunking noise in the front when going over bumps at around 10 mph (17 kph).

1. What are the potentially damaged components from when the vehicle hit the curb?
2. What will you do to diagnose the pulling condition?
3. What are the possible causes of the clunking noise when hitting a bump?

When a tire hits an obstruction, there is a **reaction force**, meaning the tire will move in response to the force applied by the obstruction. The size of this reaction force depends on the **unsprung mass**, or **unsprung weight**, of each wheel assembly. The sprung mass is that part of the vehicle supported by the springs, such as the body, the frame, the engine, and associated parts. The *unsprung* mass is all the parts of the vehicle that are *not* supported by springs, including the components that follow the road contours, such as wheels, tires, axles, and outboard brake assemblies.

Vehicle ride and handling can be improved by keeping the unsprung mass as low as possible. The heavier the unsprung mass, the harder the vehicle is to control. Think of trying to control a beach ball versus a bowling ball. When large and heavy wheel assemblies encounter a bump or pothole, they experience a larger reaction force, sometimes large enough to make the tire lose contact with the road surface. If the tires are not in contact with the road, they have lost all traction and cannot control the vehicle's direction of travel, a potentially dangerous situation. Some suspension systems are designed to combat that situation, and others are designed to be less costly and complicated.

Suspension Force

Suspension systems must tolerate a huge amount of forces when the vehicle is being driven down the road. Think about all of the weight of the vehicle being supported by the suspension system, and then subjecting the parts in that system to the normal cornering, accelerating, and braking forces, and then adding in the abnormal forces from potholes and speed bumps **FIGURE 29-2**. Applying a force to an object deforms it. Removing the force allows it to return to its original shape. This characteristic is called **elasticity**. Automotive suspension systems generally use the elastic properties of special metals to provide the springing medium that a suspension system requires.

Springs are located between the frame and the axle assemblies and are shaped to suit specific applications. **Leaf springs** are normally semi-elliptical. They absorb the **applied force** (pressure of the load) by flattening out under load. They are often used at the rear end of a car or truck to help the vehicle carry larger loads. **Coil springs** are formed in a spiral from a single steel rod. They absorb the force of impact by twisting and compressing. They are generally used on smaller vehicles to smooth the ride and improve handling. **Torsion bars** are held rigid at one end and twist around their center as the **control arm** is deflected. Control arms, also known as A-arms or wishbones, attach to the chassis with rubber bushings and allow for the movement of the tire and wheel assembly. Torsion bars all return to their original shape when the **deflecting force** (a force that moves an object in a different direction or into a different shape) is removed. They are typically used in the front of most pick-up trucks because they handle better than leaf springs.

Nonmetallic materials, such as rubber, can provide the main springing action but would not perform as well as a steel spring. Rubber is more commonly used as **stops** to limit extreme suspension movement. Stops, called jounce stops, bump stops, bumper stops, or rebound stops, are rubber parts used to control the movement of suspension components so they do not bang against each other or the frame of the vehicle, damaging the components over time **FIGURE 29-3**. These stops are typically shaped in a triangle or a cone to provide a collapsible cushion.

FIGURE 29-2 Suspension system subjected to a speed bump.

FIGURE 29-3 Rubber stops.

In light vehicle applications, air is used primarily for ride height control. Rubber bags filled with air are placed at the rear of some vehicles to help support additional weight. This is predominately a function of SUVs for when they are driven off-road, where ground clearance can be a problem.

When a vehicle strikes an uneven surface, the springs are deformed from their original shape. They return to their original position but tend to **overshoot**, or spring back, past their original length following compression, producing oscillations in the spring. **Oscillations** refer to the fluctuating of an object between two states, basically meaning the spring compresses and rebounds over and over again. As a result, the vehicle bounces up and down, making the ride unstable. It can also produce forces that make the tires bounce off the ground and lose their grip on the road.

Unsprung Weight

Most of a vehicle's weight is supported by its suspension system. It suspends the body and associated parts so that they are insulated from road shocks and vibrations that would otherwise be transmitted to the passengers and the vehicle itself. However, other parts of a vehicle are not supported by the suspension system, including the wheels, tires, brakes, axles, and steering and suspension parts not supported by springs **FIGURE 29-4**. These parts determine a vehicle's unsprung weight. Unsprung weight exerts momentum to the vehicle body whenever the unsprung weight is moved. For example, when a tire hits a speed bump, it moves upward. The heavier it and everything directly connected to it is, the greater the upward force it will generate. In fact, it can have enough force that it keeps on moving upward at the top

FIGURE 29-4 Unsprung weight versus sprung weight.

of the bump. This may cause it to lose traction with the road surface. It also transfers a lot of momentum to the vehicle body, causing it to move upward as it absorbs the energy from the wheel assembly. Conversely, if the wheel and tire are very light, they will not generate as much upward force, so it is easier for the spring to push them back down, maintaining contact with the road. As a general rule, unsprung mass should be kept as low as possible while maintaining enough strength to handle the stresses of the vehicle being driven in rough conditions.

Dampening

Different materials have different levels of elasticity. Up to a certain point, they can be deformed and released, and they will try to return to their original condition. Beyond that point, they stay deformed. With some materials, returning to their original state too quickly can produce a bouncing effect (oscillation). Preventing or reducing oscillations is called dampening. It can occur in many different ways. The dampening material absorbs the energy from the oscillation. In a vehicle suspension, a hydraulic shock absorber dampens oscillation in the spring. And rubber bushings dampen road shock. These concepts will be explored in more depth later in this chapter.

Wheel Unit Location

When a vehicle is in motion, certain forces exert pressure against the wheel units: driving thrust, braking torque, and cornering force. **Driving thrust** is the force transferred from the tire contact patch through the axle housing. It places a twisting pressure on the suspension members that push the vehicle along the road. **Braking torque** places a twisting pressure on the axle housing in the opposite direction around its center during braking. **Cornering force** refers to the lateral movement of the axle housing during turning.

These forces are transferred to the frame of the vehicle, but while they act, the wheel units must stay aligned with each other and with the frame. The wheels must be securely located longitudinally, laterally, and vertically while still having the freedom to move vertically to allow for suspension travel and pivot to allow for steering. When a vehicle drives over a bump, the tires are forcibly moved. The suspension system must absorb these forces while maintaining precise control of the wheels. Each of the suspension components contributes to keeping the wheel units in proper alignment.

Yaw, Pitch, and Roll

The terms yaw, pitch, and roll describe the movement of a vehicle around three axes **FIGURE 29-5**. The x-axis is

FIGURE 29-5 Yaw, pitch, and roll.

FIGURE 29-6 Unibody construction is the most common chassis design for passenger vehicles today.

the imaginary line drawn down the center of the vehicle from front to back. The y-axis is the imaginary line across the vehicle from left to right. The z-axis is the vertical line that runs through the center of the vehicle from top to bottom. **Roll** is vehicular movement along its x-axis. It is the rolling motion you feel when making a sharp corner and is generally what causes rollovers. **Pitch** is movement around the vehicle's y-axis, commonly felt during hard braking or fast acceleration, when the front of the vehicle noses down or rises up slightly. **Yaw** is movement around the z-axis, felt when the vehicle deviates from its straight path, as when the rear wheels slide out during drifting. Movement around each of these axes must be controlled during all of the maneuvers of the vehicle for it to be safe. Many safety systems, such as electronic stability control, are designed to keep vehicles within the safe limits of these axes.

FIGURE 29-7 Crumple zones in the unibody construction.

 Types of Body Construction

There are two principle types of auto body construction: full-frame and unibody construction. In either type, the basic purpose is to provide a mounting location for components such as the power train and suspension while allowing for the carrying of occupants and any loads the vehicle was designed to carry. The differences and benefits of each construction will be discussed next.

Unibody Construction

Unibody construction is the most common chassis design for passenger vehicles today. In fact, all front-wheel drive vehicles are of the unibody design. Rather than a separate frame, unibody construction uses the body sheet metal to give the structure support and rigidity. The integral floor pan that forms the underside of the vehicle is used along with the roof and pillars as the main structural element to which the other parts of the vehicle are attached **FIGURE 29-6**. Subframes of heavier boxed metal are used in the front and rear of the vehicle as connection points for the drive train and suspension system. Elimination of a complete heavy metal frame under the entire vehicle makes for a lighter, more fuel-efficient vehicle. Another benefit of unibody construction is the ability to build crumple zones into the structure **FIGURE 29-7**. Crumple zones are designed to fold in upon themselves in a collision, thus providing a lengthened time of deceleration and absorbing the energy of the collision. The more crumpling that the vehicle can do without crushing the occupants, the less force the occupants sustain.

FIGURE 29-8 Ladder type frame.

Full-Frame Construction

In **full-frame construction**, the frame and vehicle body are separately constructed pieces. A solid heavy steel channel iron or boxed steel frame runs the entire length of the vehicle. The body sits on rubber bushings and is bolted to the frame, which can be made of lightweight or heavy-duty materials as needed to suit the intended purpose of the vehicle. The frame is typically of the ladder type **FIGURE 29-8**. This means there are two main side rails and then a number of cross members that fit perpendicularly across the rail. Most of the vehicle's mechanical components are also attached to the frame or cross members. This design is most frequently used in trucks and heavy-duty vehicles. The strong frame can support heavy loads and handle driving on rough terrain.

▶ Suspension System Components

A basic suspension system consists of the following parts:

- **Springs**: The spring is the flexible component of the suspension. Basic types are leaf springs, coil springs, and torsion bars. Modern passenger vehicles usually use light coil springs. Light commercial vehicles have heavier springs than passenger vehicles. They can have coil springs at the front and leaf springs at the rear. Heavy commercial vehicles usually use leaf springs, or air suspension.
- **Axles**: Axles are used to drive and/or support the wheels.
- **Shock absorbers**: Shock absorbers dampen spring oscillations by forcing oil through small holes in a piston. The oil heats up as it absorbs the

energy of the motion. This heat is then transferred through the body of the shock absorber to the atmosphere.

- **Arms**: Arms are the primary load-bearing elements of a vehicle's suspension system and are commonly known as control arms. They are isolated from the chassis with rubber bushings that allow the up-and-down movement of the tire and wheel assembly.
- **Rods**: Rods are straight pieces of steel used to control motion within the vehicle's suspension system. They typically have pivoting or flexible mounts on each end.
- **Ball joints**: Ball joints are swivel connections mounted in the outer ends of the control arms.

FIGURE 29-9 shows the components of the suspension system.

Springs

Springs suspend the weight of the vehicle on the axles in such a manner that allows the wheels to follow unevenness in the road surface; therefore, springs must be elastic. Most springs are made out of spring steel and sag over time, requiring replacement. Some manufacturers have used composite materials for their leaf springs, which are said to resist sagging better than spring steel, as well as substantially reduce weight. The most common spring configurations are coil springs, leaf springs, and torsion bars.

Coil Springs

Coil springs, also known as helical springs, are used on the front suspension of most modern light vehicles, and

FIGURE 29-9 The components of a suspension system.

in many cases, they have replaced leaf springs in the rear suspension **FIGURE 29-10** . A coil spring is made from a single length of special wire, which is heated and wound on a former to produce the required shape. The load-carrying ability of the spring depends on the diameter of the wire, the overall diameter of the spring, its shape, and the spacing of the coils. On a small passenger car, they are lighter and more flexible than springs on a light commercial vehicle, which are more robust and stiff. The stiffer springs are designed to withstand heavier loads, but also make the ride much rougher. Smaller vehicles that do not need to haul heavy loads are built with lighter, flexible springs so they have a smoother ride.

The pitch of a spring is the distance from the center of one coil to the center of the adjacent coil. The coils may be evenly spaced, called **uniform pitch**, or unevenly spaced. The wire can be the same thickness throughout, or it may taper toward the end of the spring. The spring itself may be cylindrical, barrel shaped, or conical. Generally, a cylindrical spring with uniform wire diameter and uniform pitch has a constant rate of deflection, meaning it takes the same amount of force to compress each coil. Its length reduces in direct proportion to the load applied. When the pitch is varied, the deflection rate varies too **FIGURE 29-11** . The spring is then said to have a **progressive rate of deflection**, meaning it deflects easily under a light load, but its resistance increases as the load increases. This provides a softer ride when the vehicle is lightly loaded than if the vehicle has heavier constant-rate springs. Coil springs can look alike but give very different load ratings, which are often color coded for identification. They also normally use rubber pads at their seats to prevent the transmission of noise and vibration.

As conical and barrel-shaped springs compress, they have the ability to collapse into themselves **FIGURE 29-12** . This creates a longer suspension travel for a given length of the spring than for a cylindrical spring. The result is a softer ride for light loads and a stiffer ride for heavy loads, which makes them useful in the rear of some pick-up trucks that are also intended as passenger vehicles. As a cylindrical coil compresses, it can become coil-bound, which limits its travel. This can be observed in heavily loaded trucks.

Leaf Springs

The leaf spring is one of the oldest forms of spring. It is usually used on rear-wheel drive vehicles and is mounted longitudinally. Leaf springs consist of one or more flat

FIGURE 29-11 Constant rate versus a progressive rate spring.

FIGURE 29-12 As conical and barrel-shaped springs compress, they have the ability to collapse into themselves.

FIGURE 29-10 Coil springs, also known as helical springs, are used on the front suspension of most modern light vehicles.

springs, commonly made of tempered steel **FIGURE 29-13**. A number of leaves of different length are used to form a multileaf spring. Multileaf springs are used in vehicles that haul heavy loads, such as dump trucks and large pick-up trucks.

The multileaves are held together by a center bolt that passes through a hole in the center of each leaf. The center bolt is also used to locate the spring on the axle. The axle is then clamped to the multileaf spring by U-bolts that wrap around the axle housing and through a spring plate underneath the spring. **Rebound clips** are metal straps wrapped at intervals around the leaf spring to prevent excessive flexing of the main leaf during rebound, and also keep the end of the leaves in alignment.

The longest leaf, called the main leaf, is rolled at both ends to form **spring eyes**. These eyes are used to mount the spring to the frame of the vehicle. Some multileaf springs have the ends of the second leaf rolled around the eyes of the main leaf as reinforcement. This leaf is called the **wrap leaf**.

The front of the multileaf spring is attached to a **rigid spring hanger** on the vehicle frame. This rigid hanger holds the spring and ultimately the axle in position with the frame. The rear of the multileaf is connected to the frame by a **swinging shackle**, which provides a link between the spring eye and a bracket on the frame. This swinging link is needed because the front of the spring is held rigidly to the frame, and as the spring flexes and flattens out under load, the distance between the spring eyes increases. The swinging shackle allows for this lengthening and shortening.

Some multileaf springs have inserts between the leaves of plastic, nylon, or rubber. They act as insulators to reduce noise transfer and friction as the leaves move across each other under load. Some older vehicles completely enclose the leaf springs in grease for this same reason. The spring eyes are fitted with replaceable bushings, usually with a rubber, flexible section, but nylon and urethane bushings are also used, and sometimes bronze for heavy-duty applications. Rubber insulating pads between the spring mounting pad and the spring also act as insulators and, similarly, between the spring plate and the spring. Most springs are arched upward at the ends, but reverse-arch springs are used occasionally, most often when lowering a vehicle. No matter what, leaf springs support the weight of the vehicle while holding the rear axle in line with the frame, as well as the front tires.

Torsion Bars

A torsion bar is a long, alloy-steel bar that is fixed rigidly to the chassis or subframe at one end and to a control arm at the other end **FIGURE 29-14**. The torsion bar is connected to the control arm in the unloaded condition (no pressure on the bar), and as the suspension control arm is raised, the torsion bar twists around its center, which places it under a **torsional load**. Torsional load is a twisting force that is applied by anchoring one end of an object and then applying a twisting force to the other end.

When the vehicle is placed on the road, with the control arm connected to the suspension assembly, the torsion bar supports the vehicle load and twists around its center to provide the springing action. Spring rate depends on the length of the torsion bar and its diameter. The shorter and thicker the torsion bar, the stiffer its spring rate. This is useful in heavier vehicles or vehicles that regularly haul loads.

FIGURE 29-13 Leaf springs and components.

FIGURE 29-14 A torsion bar is a long, alloy-steel bar that is attached rigidly to the chassis or subframe at one end and to a control arm at the other.

Torsion bars can be used across the chassis frame in a **trailing arm suspension**, or as part of the connecting link between two axle assemblies on a semirigid axle beam. After a lot of use, all springs can sag, including the torsion bar, meaning the ride height on one or both sides of the vehicle will be lower than specified. On many vehicles, it can be adjusted back to the proper ride height by tightening the bolt on the torsion bar adjuster.

Sway Bars

A bar similar to the torsion bar is the **sway bar**, or antiroll bar. The sway bar is used in light vehicles as a stabilizer, or antiroll bar. It is connected to the chassis in the center, and each end is connected to one side of the suspension system **FIGURE 29-15**. Sway bars are most common on the front suspension since it is most prone to sway, but are also installed on the rear suspension in some vehicles. When the vehicle is turning, centrifugal force acts on the body and tends to make it lean outward (roll). The sway bar uses its connections to each side of the suspension to resist this roll tendency. In this way, the spring on the inside of the corner can assist the spring on the outside of the corner to bear the additional load on the outside wheels. This tends to make the vehicle corner flatter. But because the sway bar can pivot in bushings on the frame, the sway bar just pivots when both wheels go over a speed bump. Also, stiffer roll bars can be installed in a vehicle to enhance its cornering ability.

Rubber Stops

Rubber is used in most suspension systems as stops. If the suspension reaches its limit of travel, stops prevent direct metal-to-metal contact, thereby reducing jarring of the suspension components **FIGURE 29-16**. The rubber stops protect the suspension parts as when they bottom out. The stops also reduce the shock to the driver as the suspension bottoms out. Stops can be shaped to provide an auxiliary springing function, increasing their resistance progressively with suspension contact. Rubber spring stops can be found on most vehicles. For vehicles with MacPherson **struts**, there is a cone-shaped rubber stop located on the strut below the strut bearing surface. In other applications, these stops are found on the frame of the vehicle where the suspension components will make contact.

> ### ▶ TECHNICIAN TIP
>
> Rubber has a number of advantages. It doesn't need to be lubricated, it can be made into any shape, as required, and it is silent during use.

FIGURE 29-15 A sway bar reduces body roll when cornering.

FIGURE 29-16 Variety of rubber stops.

Axles

Axles are shafts to which the wheel assembly is attached. In vehicles, the axle is usually fixed to the wheels, rotating with them. Axles perform many functions. Some are load-bearing elements of the suspension system, helping support the weight of the vehicle. Others are used only to drive the wheels, not support it. They help maintain the position of the wheels relative to each other and the vehicle body.

Many different types of axles are available on the market today to suit the needs of vehicle designers. The straight axle or solid axle is a single shaft that connects the front wheels together or the rear wheels together **FIGURE 29-17**. These axles provide extra support and rigidity to keep the wheels positioned even under heavy loads. Because they are able to withstand extreme stress, straight axles are typically found on many rear-wheel drive vehicles, off-road vehicles, and commercial trucks.

FIGURE 29-17 Solid axle.

FIGURE 29-18 Full-floating axle.

The dead axle is one that does not transmit drive to the wheel, acting only to support it. These axles are used on the rear of some front-wheel drive vehicles and other vehicles that have more than two rear wheel sets to provide added support for carrying heavy loads. Axles use bearings in different arrangements to support the axle or wheel, depending on the type.

In full-floating axles, the axle bearing is placed on the outside of the axle housing. This places all the vehicle weight on the housing and none on the axle itself **FIGURE 29-18**. The axle in this arrangement functions only in transmitting the rotational torque out to the wheel. In the semi-floating axle, the axle bearing is placed between the axle and the axle housing; therefore, it participates in carrying the load of the vehicle **FIGURE 29-19**.

Shock Absorbers

A shock absorber is a device on a vehicle designed to absorb shock loads caused from driving on irregular surfaces. During compression (jounce), which happens when the tire travels over a bump in the road, the rod and its piston move into the shock absorber. In extension (rebound), which is when the tire travels over a dip in the road, the rod and piston move out of the shock absorber. For dampening to be effective, resistance is needed in both directions, although not in the same proportions. This resistance is provided by the piston forcing oil past disc valves in the piston and the base of the inner tube of the shock absorber **FIGURE 29-20**. Oil fills the inner tube and surrounds its outer surface to a level that allows a free space or reservoir to exist above it, between the inner and the outer tubes.

FIGURE 29-19 Semi-floating axle.

FIGURE 29-20 A shock absorber is a device on a vehicle designed to absorb shock loads caused from driving on irregular surfaces.

A way to think about the basic function of a shock absorber is to think of a rod with a washer fastened to it through the center hole. If a small hole is drilled on the flat of the washer, this will let oil move from one side of the washer to the other. Add some oil to a capped tube and insert the rod and washer into the tube. Add oil to the top, and cap the tube with a sealed cap that will allow the rod to move in and out of the tube but not leak oil. Moving the rod in the oil will produce resistance since oil will be forced through the small hole in the washer. Resistance will be felt in both directions. If the size of the hole in the washer is increased, there will be less resistance. This is the basic operation of the shock absorber, except in a shock absorber, valves can be used to allow different rates of flow on compression and rebound. Thus, the resistance on compression will vary as compared to rebound so that manufacturers can design the desired ride characteristics into the shock absorber.

The valves in the shock absorber provide control over the amount of force required to pass fluid through them at any given piston velocity. They can be made to open in stages, according to fluid pressure **FIGURE 29-21**. This allows light resistance to motion when the piston moves slowly, and heavy resistance when piston velocity is high.

The rapid movement of the piston, continually forcing the oil backward and forward through the valves, causes the oil to heat up as it absorbs the energy of motion of the springs. The heat is transferred through the outer tube to the outside air. However, the hotter the oil becomes, the greater its tendency to aerate. Aeration occurs because of the high velocity of the oil as it passes through the small passages in the valves. If the velocity is high enough, air dissolved in the oil comes out of the solution as small bubbles and forms foam. As we know from Pascal's law, fluid cannot be compressed, but air can. Air in the shock absorber results in a lack of dampening, which creates a soft, bouncy ride; if the suspension members contact the stops, this creates a harsh ride.

The twin-tube type of shock absorber is the most common. The outer tube is normally attached to the suspension member at its base, and the inner tube provides a working cylinder for a piston that is attached to a piston rod. The piston rod is connected to the vehicle's frame at its outer end, and a bushing in the top of the outer tube keeps the rod in alignment as it moves in and out of the shock absorber, with **suspension action** (or movement of the chassis up and down). A seal above the bushing prevents oil leakage and keeps out dirt and moisture. A **shroud** is a steel, plastic cover, or rubber boot that is typically placed over the shock rod to protect it from damage.

Strut-type Shock Absorbers

The most widely used hydraulic shock absorber is the **direct-acting telescopic type**. It can be fitted to the suspension as a self-contained unit that is designed to control only spin oscillations, or it can be combined with a **suspension strut**, which is used to support the top of the steering knuckle as well as dampen spring oscillations. A suspension strut functions exactly like a shock except it is much stronger since it functions as a structural part of the suspension when it is integrated into MacPherson strut suspensions. On a MacPherson strut suspension system, the top of the hydraulic strut supports the top of the steering knuckle, so it must be much stronger than an ordinary shock absorber. The hydraulic shock absorber and the hydraulic strut provide their dampening action by transferring oil under

FIGURE 29-21 Shock absorber valves.

> ### TECHNICIAN TIP
>
> Aerated oil has a certain amount of compressibility, so it is unable to provide the dampening force previously achieved in the nonaerated condition, just as a brake pedal will feel spongy when air is present in the brake's hydraulic system. The performance of the shock absorber is thus considerably reduced. This effect is called shock absorber dissolve.

pressure through valves in the piston, which restrict the oil flow.

Gas-Pressurized Shock Absorbers

Fluid fills the chambers above and below the piston of the hydraulic shock absorber. As the piston moves in the cylinder, valves control the movement of oil from one chamber to the other. In a gas shock, pressure on the oil is provided by nitrogen gas at the base of the cylinder, acting on a free-floating separation piston that separates the gas from the oil **FIGURE 29-22**. On jounce, the piston moves downward, and the penetration of the piston rod displaces a quantity of oil equal to its volume. The separation piston is displaced accordingly, and gas pressure increases. On rebound, the piston and rod move upward, and gas pressure reduces as the separation piston follows the movement. Pressure on the oil is maintained, even when the piston and rod are at the top of their stroke. The pressure applied to the oil keeps air bubbles (or aeration) from forming as easily and thus provides a better job of dampening.

Adjustable Shock Absorbers

In the search for a comfortable ride, while maintaining some level of sporty handling or the ability to handle occasional heavy loads, manufacturers have developed a variety of shock absorbers with enhanced capabilities. As you recall, having a few smaller passageways in a shock absorber causes it to provide a high amount of resistance to jounce and rebound, creating a sporty feel. And larger passageways provide less resistance, creating a smoother ride. Manufacturers have machined more passageways into their shock absorber pistons but then provide either manual, electric, or automatic selection and blockage of certain passageways with valves, depending on the desired ride characteristics. As far as extra loads, some shocks incorporate an expandable air bladder that can be used to support some of the load.

Load-Adjustable Shock Absorbers

When vehicles carry heavy loads, their suspension is compressed, causing the rear of the vehicle to be lower than normal. As a result, steering can become lighter (less responsive), the alignment of the headlights becomes too high, and the compression length of travel of the suspension over bumps is reduced, causing the suspension to bottom out more easily, which is uncomfortable for passengers. To reduce these effects, a **manually adjustable air spring** can be incorporated into each rear shock absorber. This type of shock absorber is commonly referred to as an air shock **FIGURE 29-23**. The **air spring** consists of a flexible rubber bladder, which seals the outside of the upper and lower halves of the shock absorber. When inflated, the bladder pushes the halves apart.

The shock absorber is a standard hydraulic type, providing normal dampening action, but when a heavy load is placed on the rear of the vehicle, the rubber air bladder can be gas-pressurized to assist the vehicle's springs. By changing the air pressure in the bladder, the ride height can be adjusted, as well as the stiffness of the suspension. Compressed air in the bladder can absorb smaller road shocks and provide better ride characteristics than stiff springs alone.

FIGURE 29-22 Gas pressurized shock absorber.

FIGURE 29-23 Air shock.

The rubber air cylinder is connected to a filling valve, similar looking to a tire valve stem, by a flexible plastic hose. Air from a tire pump or air compressor forces more air into the rubber cylinder, allowing the suspension to support more weight. The maximum air pressure setting must not be exceeded, as excessive air pressure can damage the shock absorber's air spring. When the load is removed, the extra air can be released through the filling valve, which allows the suspension to return to its original settings, just as you would release air from a tire. A minimum air pressure must be maintained in the cylinder to prevent chafing of the rubber as it collapses internally with shock absorber action. Refer to the manufacturer's specifications for the air shock's minimum and maximum air pressure.

Another type of load-adjustable shock absorber uses a coil spring around the outside of the shock. The spring is installed from the factory under tension and connects to both the upper half and the lower half. This tends to push the halves apart, assisting the regular springs in supporting the load.

FIGURE 29-24 On some models, the position of the valve is adjusted by turning a spindle located on the shock plunger rod. On other models, when the shock absorber is extended to its maximum length, a pin is depressed, locking in an adjusting slide on the piston assembly.

Manual Adjustable-Rate Shock Absorbers

A **manual adjustable-rate shock absorber** has a manual, external damper rate adjustment. The number of valves and size of the passageways in the piston can then be selected to vary the amount of restriction on the flow of oil through the piston and to vary the force needed to open the valves. Just like in our hole in the washer example from earlier, making the hole larger lets the rod move more freely; whereas, making the hole smaller provides more resistance.

When all of the orifices are open, a small dampening effect is applied to the oil. The spring force applied to the valve can also be reduced to allow the valve to open more easily. This means the oil can flow through the valves more easily, which gives a softer ride, but can also allow more rolling and pitching of the body of the vehicle. Closing some of the orifices, and increasing the spring force applied to the valves, makes it harder for fluid to flow through the piston. This increases the dampening effect of the shock absorber.

The method of changing the position of the valve varies. On some models, it is adjusted by turning a spindle located on the shock plunger rod. Turning the spindle moves the valves and changes the size of the orifices in the valve. On other models, when the shock absorber is extended to its maximum length, a pin is depressed, locking in an adjusting slide on the piston assembly **FIGURE 29-24**. Twisting the two halves of the shock absorber changes the number of orifices and the spring force on the valves. The first type of adjustable shock absorber can be adjusted with

the shock on the vehicle, while the second type must be removed to change the dampening.

Electronic Adjustable-Rate Shock Absorbers

Some vehicles equipped with electronic ride control systems provide driver-selected control of the ride quality. Typically, a switch is located inside the passenger compartment that allows the driver to select sport, touring, or automatic. For example, if the driver selects sport, the ride will become firmer by adjusting the shock dampening. Electronic ride control can also be automatic with no provision for driver control. In automatic ride control, the vehicle's electronic module chooses a softer or firmer ride, sometimes based on the speed of the vehicle or the driving that is being done.

In order to change dampening of the shocks, the shock must be adjustable. Some vehicles use a rotary stepper motor called an actuator to change the dampening. The shock works very similar to the manual adjustment shock that has the spindle that is turned. In the manual adjustable shock, you turn this spindle with an allen wrench or other tool to make dampening changes. In the electronic-controlled shock, the actuator is mounted to the top of the shock and turns the spindle as needed. The actuator changes the number of restrictions or orifices that the oil must pass through. When all orifices are open, oil can flow more easily through the passageways in the piston. Only a small dampening effect is applied to the oil. This provides a dampening force that emphasizes ride comfort when traveling at low speeds. Closing some orifices makes it harder for fluid to flow through the piston. This increases the dampening effect of the shock absorber, providing a firmer ride that is more suitable for higher speeds and faster cornering. The need to increase dampening at high speeds becomes evident when we think about hitting a bump at high speeds, which could cause the wheels to come off the ground, disrupting our ability to steer the vehicle.

Another type of electronic adjustable shock is the solenoid-controlled shock. The solenoid is located in the side of the shock absorber or strut and opens a passageway internal to the shock to allow more fluid to bypass the piston. If the solenoid is commanded closed, the fluid will not be able to bypass, which will result in more dampening. This type of shock is still controlled by the electronic control unit (ECU).

The newest style of electronic adjustable shock uses a special type of fluid called **magneto-rheological fluid**. This fluid has the unique characteristic of changing viscosity when exposed to a magnetic field. General Motors has been using this fluid in vehicles equipped with MagneRide suspension systems. The fluid is mixed with very small ferrous particles that react to magnetic fields. As the fluid is subjected to a magnetic field, the ferrous particles bind together, effectively increasing the viscosity of the fluid. The stronger the magnetic field, the thicker the fluid. The ability to increase and decrease the viscosity of the fluid eliminates the need to change orifice sizes since it is harder to pass a thicker fluid through a hole than a thinner one. Simply varying the magnetic field at the shock absorber causes varied dampening of the suspension **FIGURE 29-25**.

In fact, the viscosity can be changed in a millisecond or less, allowing active dampening of each individual shock absorber as the vehicle is being driven. This means that the power train control module (PCM) can stiffen the appropriate shocks in a continuously active manner as the steering wheel is being turned or the brakes are being applied. On the other hand, a particular shock can be softened as a wheel goes over a bump to prevent the shock from being transmitted as fully to the vehicle. Other manufacturers are beginning to use this technology since it is a faster-acting electronic dampening suspension. This technology is also used in some motor mounts and other applications.

Automatic Load-Adjustable Shock Absorbers

Automatic load-adjustable shock absorbers are also called **self-leveling**, meaning they have a sensor that measures the ride height and uses that information to adjust the load, leveling shocks automatically. An automatic load-adjustable suspension system controls the vehicle ride height automatically, according to the load placed over the rear axle. It consists of air-adjustable shock absorbers fitted to the rear suspension, an electrically driven compressor and air-dryer assembly, a ride height sensor, a control unit, and associated wiring and tubing **FIGURE 29-26**.

The ride height sensor is mounted to the cross member over the rear axle, and a moveable link connects it to a rear suspension member. As the vehicle is loaded, the normal suspension springs are compressed, which lowers

FIGURE 29-25 Electromagnetic shock absorber.

FIGURE 29-26 An automatic load-adjustable suspension system controls the vehicle ride height automatically, according to the load placed over the rear axle.

the height of the vehicle. When the ignition is switched on, the control unit senses the lowered ride height and switches on the air compressor. Air is directed to the shock absorbers, causing the airbag around them to expand and raise the suspension to the normal **trim height**. If the load is removed, the suspension springs expand, raising the height of the vehicle. The control unit senses the raised ride height, and air is exhausted from the shock absorbers, causing the airbag to deflate and thereby lowering the suspension to the normal ride height.

During normal suspension operation, continual adjustment of vehicle ride height is prevented by a time delay in the control unit. This delay allows the trim height to be adjusted only when the ECU reads an out-of-trim signal for a short period of time—for example, 5 to 15 seconds. Thus, the system does not try to compensate for bumps in the road or weight transfer during braking. The compressor run time or exhaust time is limited to a few minutes. Limiting the operational time prevents it from continuing to operate if the system develops an air leak or if an exhaust vent remains open. If a fault like this develops, most self-leveling systems will set a diagnostic code.

Arms

Arms, commonly known as control arms, are components that serve as a primary load-bearing element of a vehicle's suspension system.

Control arms can be formed in different ways. In the A-arm style, sometimes referred to as a **wishbone control arm**, the arm is a relatively flat triangular part that mounts to the frame or subframe at each leg of the A **FIGURE 29-27**. These widely spaced mounting points

prevent forward or backward movement of the steering knuckle. The mounting points typically use rubber bushings that allow the arm to pivot up and down while dampening or isolating the road shock and vibrations from the rest of the vehicle. The other end of the control arm has a ball joint that connects the control arm to the steering knuckle assembly. This arrangement provides a smooth yet stable ride for the vehicle.

Another type of control arm uses only one contact point at the frame or body **FIGURE 29-28**. With this style of control arm, another supporting piece called a strut rod or radius rod must be used to keep the control arm from pivoting forward and backward with changes in braking or acceleration. Other types of control arms are made from round tube material and can be used in independent suspensions. These control arms may be called transverse and trailing arms.

Rods

Rods are typically straight pieces of steel used to either transfer motion or prevent motion within a vehicle's suspension system. More specific names are given to rods based on their location or attachments. For example, a suspension system may use tie-rods, lateral rods, tension rods, control rods, panhard rods (track bars), steering track rods, or strut rods. Many of the rods use either a bushing or a joint on one or both ends of the rod. Each of these components is discussed elsewhere in this chapter, but it is important to remember that the exact number and types of rods within a vehicle vary greatly, depending on the make and model of vehicle, as well as its intended use.

FIGURE 29-27 Wishbone control arm.

FIGURE 29-28 Single-point control arm.

Steering Knuckle

The steering knuckle, also known as a stub axle or spindle assembly, can be found in many variations. One type uses a forged piece containing the wheel hub or spindle and attaches to the suspension components. Other knuckles may provide a hole for the axle to pass through and the wheel hub to mount to **FIGURE 29-29**. Some knuckles will be cast iron while newer vehicles may have a cast aluminum steering knuckle to reduce unsprung weight as well as total vehicle weight. Typically, the steering knuckle also has a steering arm, which either is cast as part of the knuckle or is a separate piece bolted to the knuckle. The steering arm connects to the steering system and in either form serves to transmit the steering force to the steering knuckle when the driver turns the steering wheel. The steering knuckle pivots on a ball joint on the bottom and either a ball joint or a strut bearing on the top.

Ball Joints

Ball joints are swivel connections mounted in the outer ends of the control arms **FIGURE 29-30**. Ball joints are typically constructed of a ball and socket. And while ball-and-socket joints are used in most tie-rod ends, the term *ball joints* is typically reserved for the primary joints that the steering knuckle pivots on, and *tie-rod ends* is the term used for the ball-and-socket joints on the steering linkage.

Suspension ball joints allow the control arms to move up and down with suspension deflection, and also let the wheel and knuckle assembly rotate for steering. The ball joint in most modern vehicles is a sealed, self-contained unit that is replaced as a unit when it is worn out. The ball joint can be fastened to the control arm in several ways. In the past, a ball joint housing was threaded and then screwed into the control arm. This type of ball joint is no longer used and will only be found on classic cars. The ball joint on modern vehicles will either be press-fit into the control arm or held by rivets or bolts. If the ball joint is pressed into the control arm, a special tool called a ball joint press tool will be used to remove and install the joint.

A ball joint is made up of a pressed-steel housing, fitted with **<u>sintered</u>** (bonded using pressure and heat) iron seats and a hardened ball stud. Some ball joints use a Belleville spring to hold tension on the joint, which will need to be compressed when tested. Typically, a taper on the stud locates in a mating taper on the steering knuckle, although some use a straight stud that has a crescent-shaped relief that allows a clamping bolt to orient the stud and clamp it securely. A rubber seal retains grease and keeps out dirt and water. Some ball joints have grease fittings (grease zerks) installed, which allow for periodic lubrication of the moving ball and stationary socket inside the ball joint **FIGURE 29-31**. Grease fittings can sometimes be found on other suspension components and need to be lubricated as part of a preventive maintenance program provided by the manufacturer. Most light-duty vehicles manufactured today have maintenance-free suspension components that do not provide access for lubrication. Be sure to check the manufacturer's service information when performing maintenance to see if provisions are provided, or check

FIGURE 29-29 A type of knuckle that has a hole for the axle to pass through and the wheel hub to mount to.

FIGURE 29-30 Ball joint.

FIGURE 29-31 Some ball joints have grease fittings (grease zerks) installed, which allow for periodic lubrication of the moving ball and stationary socket inside the ball joint.

Follower ball joint

Loaded ball joint

FIGURE 29-32 Loaded vs follower ball joints.

to see if grease fittings are present on the suspension, steering, and drive line components.

Ball joints can be referred to as loaded or unloaded. A loaded ball joint supports the weight of the vehicle. An unloaded ball joint does not support any weight; it just holds the steering knuckle in position and is referred to as a follower ball joint. For example, in a short/long-arm (SLA) suspension system with an upper and lower control arm, and the coil spring located between the frame and the lower control arm, the lower ball joint is the loaded ball joint **FIGURE 29-32**. This is because the force of the spring is placed against the lower control arm and ball joint. In this situation, the upper ball joint is the follower joint. If the spring is located between the frame and the upper control arm, then the upper ball joint is the loaded joint and the lower ball joint is the follower joint. This distinction becomes important when testing the ball joints for play, as the technician will need to unload the joint to accurately test for play.

Also, the ball joints can be designed to primarily carry either compression loads or tension loads. Compression forces tend to push the ball into the socket, so those types of joints have most of their bearing surface and socket strength near the base of the ball. Tension ball joints are being pulled apart, so they have most their bearing surface and socket strength near the stud end of the ball. Never mix up the positioning of ball joints; doing so will cause them to wear out quickly and fail.

Bushings

Bushings act as pivot points and cushions at suspension fulcrum points such as control arm bushings and strut rod bushings, to allow for limited movement of the component, while maintaining its alignment **FIGURE 29-33**. They can be metallic or made of rubber, nylon, or urethane. Many rubber bushings have a metal inner and outer housing to allow for wear surfaces or for being pressed into place. Rubber bushings isolate noise and harshness and dampen unwanted vibrations. The rubber absorbs small impacts from the suspension action, without transmitting them directly to the driver. Rubber requires no lubrication. Rubber bushings can also be used on strut rods. Rubber-bonded bushings can be used to mount the steering rack to the vehicle frame.

Spring shackle bushings can be molded to form two halves, to fit into each side of the spring eye on the swinging shackle, which is located on the vehicle frame. With the spring loaded, and the shackle plates tightened, the rubber is compressed in the eye and at the face of the plates. As the spring deflects, the rubber deflects without tearing.

Rubber-bonded bushings are normally used for the front eye of the spring at the fixed shackle point, and also in control arm applications. The rubber-bonded bushing has a steel outer housing and inner sleeve. The rubber medium is bonded between both to provide flexibility between them. The outer casing is normally pressed into place in the component. Relative movement between the casing and the inner sleeve causes the rubber to flex without tearing.

In control arm applications, particularly at the rear of a vehicle, the rubber bushing may be molded with a voided section **FIGURE 29-34**. This is known as a **compliance bushing** because it allows the unit or component to comply with a controlled amount of movement in the direction of the void. This movement relative to the vehicle frame may be designed to allow compliance or deflection steer of the road wheels when cornering. Since this influences the steering behavior of the vehicle, it is very important that the voided section is in its correct relative position. It is easy to forget how a bushing was positioned after it is removed. Marking the position with a paint mark is a good way to ensure that the bushing is replaced correctly.

Types of Suspension Systems

Manufacturers use various types of suspension systems, depending on the intended use of the vehicle, cost of manufacturing, and layout of the drive train. One of the simplest designs is the nonindependent, solid axle system, which is fairly inexpensive and not very complicated. Then there are the independent suspension types, such as the MacPherson strut and the SLA suspension systems. Each system comes in various configurations, which we will examine in this chapter. Each design has pros and cons that you need to be aware of when diagnosing and servicing suspension systems. For example, an independent drive axle uses flexible joints in the axle while a solid axle does not; they will create different types of noises when parts are going bad.

Solid Axle

The **solid axle** (beam axle) provides a simple means of mounting the hub and wheel units. Together with leaf springs, it forms an effective, nonindependent suspension system. It is used in the rear suspension of many front-engine, rear-wheel drive vehicles and light commercial vehicles and as the front suspension on many heavy commercial vehicles.

A solid axle is a nonindependent suspension because the wheels on both sides of the axle are connected together. This means when one wheel goes over a bump, the other wheel tilts **FIGURE 29-35**. This tilting reduces

FIGURE 29-33 Bushings. **A.** Control arm bushing. **B.** Strut rod bushing.

FIGURE 29-34 Compliance bushing.

FIGURE 29-35 A solid axle is a nonindependent suspension because the wheels on both sides of the axle are connected together.

the tire-to-road contact patch, reducing friction. Thus, vehicles with solid axles are said to not handle as well as vehicles with independent suspensions. But they are inexpensive and good for hauling heavy loads.

Dead Axle/Live Axle

The terms <u>dead axle</u> and <u>live axle</u> refer to whether the axle is a driving axle or not **FIGURE 29-36**. A dead axle simply holds the wheels in their proper orientation. A good example of a dead axle is a boat trailer. It does not power the wheels at all, just holds them in place. A live axle not only holds the wheels in position, it also drives them. Live axles are connected to the drive train in such a way that power can be transferred through the components in the live axle. Live axles can be part of either a nonindependent or an independent suspension system.

On front-wheel drive vehicles, a simple dead axle is used on the rear wheels. On a rear-wheel drive vehicle, the front axle is a dead axle. And on four-wheel drive or all-wheel drive vehicles, both the front and rear axles are live. Again, they can be of the independent or nonindependent styles.

Independent Suspension

An independent suspension allows the wheel on each side of the axle to move up and down independently of each other. In this arrangement, if a wheel on one side hits a road irregularity, it will not upset the wheel on the other side on the same axle. One of the main benefits claimed for <u>independent suspension</u> is that unsprung mass can be kept low since a heavy center axle housing is eliminated. One of the simplest, and most common, independent suspension systems is the <u>MacPherson strut</u> **FIGURE 29-37**. It can be used on either the front or

the rear of the vehicle. It consists of a spring and heavy-duty shock absorber unit called a strut. The lower end of the strut is connected to the knuckle and located by a ball joint, fitted to the end of the control arm. Its upper end is located in a strut tower formed in the unibody. It sits in a molded rubber mounting. If the strut is on the front, the upper mounting includes a bearing to allow the complete strut assembly to rotate with the steering.

A slightly more complicated, yet common type of independent suspension system is the SLA suspension system **FIGURE 29-38**. It uses upper and lower control arms to control the movement of the knuckle. It typically uses either a coil spring or torsion bar connected to one of the control arms to support the weight of the vehicle. This system will be discussed further in a following section.

Front Suspension

The front wheels of a vehicle can have a different type of suspension system than the rear wheels. The exact type of system used in the front can vary depending on the vehicle type, such as whether it is front-wheel or rear-wheel drive. The two main types of front suspension systems are the independent and the solid axle systems. In the independent

FIGURE 29-36 The terms dead axle and live axle refer to whether the axle is a driving axle or not.

FIGURE 29-37 The MacPherson strut suspension system.

FIGURE 29-38 The SLA suspension system.

FIGURE 29-39 Strut suspension.

system, the two front wheels can move independently. In the solid axle system, the two wheels are fixed by a rigid axle that binds their movement together. Regardless of design, the primary function of the front suspension system is to keep the tires in constant contact with the road.

Strut Suspension

In strut suspension, the shock absorber is contained inside the strut **FIGURE 29-39**. It is a direct-acting telescopic-type shock absorber and is a type of hydraulic shock absorber. A coil spring is mounted over the strut, inside the suspension tower of the front wheel housing. The strut has an upper mounting point in the suspension tower.

When used on the front suspension, the strut's upper mounting is bearing-mounted, to allow for the steering movement. The lower control arm is mounted (or held in place) to the frame or subframe by control arm bushings. The outer end of the control arm contains a ball joint and connects the steering knuckle to the control arm. The steering knuckle can then pivot on the ball joint on the bottom of the knuckle and the strut bearing on the top.

SLA Suspension

The **short-/long-arm (SLA) suspension** gets its name from using two different-length control arms, one short and one long. The primary reason that the SLA suspension system was designed was to ensure correct wheel alignment as the vehicle corners. If the arms were the same length, then the wheel would stay perfectly straight as the suspension moved up and down over bumps. This is OK for straight ahead driving, but not OK when cornering. Having arms of the same length would result in incorrect positioning of the tire in relation to the road surface since the body tends to roll. The body roll would tilt the wheel outward (toward positive camber) at the top, reducing the tire-to-road contact patch, which reduces

FIGURE 29-40 The coil spring can be mounted two ways. **A.** Between the frame and the lower control arm (type 1). **B.** Between the shock tower and the upper control arm (type 2).

traction. The SLA system, with the short arm on top, tends to pull the tire toward negative camber, keeping the tire-to-road contact patch as large as possible.

The shock absorber is located inside the coil spring and is a direct-acting telescopic-type shock absorber. The coil spring can be mounted either between the frame and the lower control arm (type 1) or between the shock tower and the upper control arm (type 2) **FIGURE 29-40**. Both control arms pivot on control arm bushings. These bushings twist on the control arm pins, which are bolted to the cross member or subframe of the vehicle. Rubber jounce and rebound stops are used to prevent direct metal-to-metal contact between the control arms and the frame if the suspension should reach its maximum limit of travel.

The steering knuckle is mounted at the ends of the control arms by ball joints and allows both up-and-down and steering movement of the tire. The ball joints can be designed to be mounted so they are under compression or tension forces. Compression forces tend to push the ball into the socket, while on tension pulls the ball away from the socket.

There are two arrangements of steering knuckles used on SLA suspensions—short knuckle and long knuckle **FIGURE 29-41**. The short knuckle design locates the upper ball joint inside of the wheel. The long knuckle design moves the upper ball joint above the tire, meaning the knuckle may even partially wrap around the tire. The long knuckle design affords the manufacturer a more ideal kingpin geometry, as well as better leverage against braking and cornering forces.

Twin I-Beam Suspension

The twin I-beam suspension is a type of independent suspension. It uses separate I-beams for each front wheel that pivot from the opposite side of the vehicle's frame or cross member **FIGURE 29-42**. This system gives a wide radius that the wheel assembly swings through as the suspension compresses and rebounds. Most twin I-beam systems use a coil spring to support the weight of the vehicle. This means each I-beam must be supported longitudinally, which is accomplished by use of a radius rod. The radius rod connects to the I-beam from the rear and is attached to the vehicle's frame with bushings, which allow the radius rod to pivot slightly as the suspension operates.

Rear Suspension

The main function of the rear suspension system is to keep the rear tires in contact with the road and aligned with the front tires **FIGURE 29-43**. However, rear-wheel drive or all-wheel drive rear suspension systems are a bit more complicated. In these vehicles, the rear suspension system must not only keep the rear tires in contact with the road and aligned with the front tires, but must also be engineered to transfer engine torque to the rear wheels. And in vehicles with four-wheel steering, the rear suspension must allow the rear wheels to be steered in a similar manner as the front wheels.

Rear-wheel suspension systems can be of the independent or nonindependent design. It is purely up to the preference of the designer. Many, but not all, rear-wheel drive vehicles use a solid axle, nonindependent suspension system. On front-wheel drive vehicles, the type of rear suspension system leans toward a higher percentage of independent systems, but nonindependent systems are also common.

FIGURE 29-41 Steering knuckles. **A.** Long knuckle SLA. **B.** Short knuckle SLA.

FIGURE 29-42 Twin I-beam suspension system.

FIGURE 29-43 In front-wheel drive vehicles, the rear suspension system serves to keep the rear tires in contact with the road and aligned with the front tires.

FIGURE 29-44 A rigid-axle leaf-spring suspension.

Rigid-Axle Leaf-Spring Suspension

A rigid-axle leaf-spring suspension can be used in both dead axles and live axles. The front of the leaf spring is attached to the chassis at the rigid spring hanger **FIGURE 29-44**. The spring eyes typically use rubber bushings to connect with the vehicle's frame. The axle housing is rigid between each road wheel. Thus, any deflection to one side is transmitted to the other side. The rear of the leaf spring is attached to the swinging shackle, which allows for suspension movement by allowing the spring to extend or reduce in length, as the vehicle moves over uneven ground.

The top of the direct-acting shock absorber is attached to the chassis and to the spring pad at the bottom. The U-bolts attach the axle housing to the leaf spring. They have a clamping force that helps to keep the leaf spring together. Leaf springs are usually made of tempered steel. They hold the axle in position, both laterally and longitudinally. The leaf spring is usually made up of a number of leaves of different length. The top, or longest leaf, is normally referred to as the main leaf. Most leaf-spring suspensions rely only on the sideways stiffness of the leaf spring to keep the axle in position when turning a corner, while some suspension systems use a rod called a panhard rod to help keep the axle from shifting sideways through turns.

Rigid-Axle Coil-Spring Suspension

In **rigid-axle coil-spring suspensions**, the coil spring is mounted between the axle housing and the vehicle body **FIGURE 29-45**. One drawback of a coil spring is that it cannot provide any side-to-side or front-to-back stability to the axle. All it can do is suspend the body above the axle. Therefore, unlike the with leaf-spring suspension, control rods must be used to control this potential axle movement during braking, acceleration, and cornering.

FIGURE 29-45 Rigid-axle coil-spring suspension.

Manufacturers use a variety of configurations to address this concern.

The first style uses lower control arms near each coil spring that are parallel with the **centerline** of the vehicle and connect between the frame and the axle. They maintain the longitudinal position of the axle. The upper control arms are angled toward the center of the vehicle to counteract any lateral forces as well as twisting forces. Another style uses upper and lower control arms that all are parallel with the centerline of the vehicle. They control the twisting force of the axle but cannot control any lateral forces during cornering. One of two methods is used to control the lateral forces—a panhard rod or a Watt's linkage.

A **panhard rod**, also referred to as a track bar, sits parallel with the axle. One end connects to the frame of the vehicle, and the other end connects to the axle **FIGURE 29-46**. The panhard rod uses bushings on each end so the joints can pivot as the suspension compresses and rebounds. The position of the axle is maintained laterally by the rod. A **Watt's linkage** is a bit more complex but functions in a similar way **FIGURE 29-47**. A lever that is able to pivot in the middle is mounted vertically to the rear axle near its center. The top of the lever is connected to a rod that is parallel to the axle and mounted high on one side of the frame. The bottom of the lever is connected to a similar rod, which is also parallel to the axle but mounted low on the other side of the frame. These two rods allow up-and-down movement of the axle but prevent lateral movement.

Rigid Nondrive Axle Suspension

A rigid nondrive axle is sometimes referred to as a beam axle. It can come in a variety of configurations. With **rigid nondrive axle suspension**, the longitudinal and lateral position of the axle must be maintained as in all axles, but since it is a dead axle, it typically has to withstand only braking forces. One common rigid nondrive axle suspension uses lower trailing arms connecting the vehicle frame and axle and a strut assembly on top. These trailing arms maintain the longitudinal position of the axle **FIGURE 29-48**, while the springs and strut support the weight of the vehicle and assist in controlling any braking forces. The struts have an upper mounting point in the suspension tower. They are nonsteerable and therefore do not require an upper strut bearing. This type of suspension typically uses a panhard rod to control lateral forces.

Another style of dead axle uses a U-shaped axle beam with a torsion bar mounted inside it. A trailing arm holds the axle longitudinally, a panhard rod holds it laterally, the strut and spring support the weight of the vehicle, and the torsion bar provides a measure of resistance to twisting forces as one wheel goes over a bump.

Other types of dead axles are tube style, using the axle stub shafts as mounting points for the wheel hub. These axles typically use trailing arms with a coil-over-shock arrangement, and a stabilizing bar such as a panhard rod.

Rear Independent Suspension (Nondrive)

The kind of nondrive independent suspension used on the rear of a vehicle can be fairly simple since the wheels typically do not steer or drive the vehicle. In this case, the suspension system only needs to hold the wheels in the proper orientation while the vehicle is being driven. Since it is an independent type of system, each wheel is

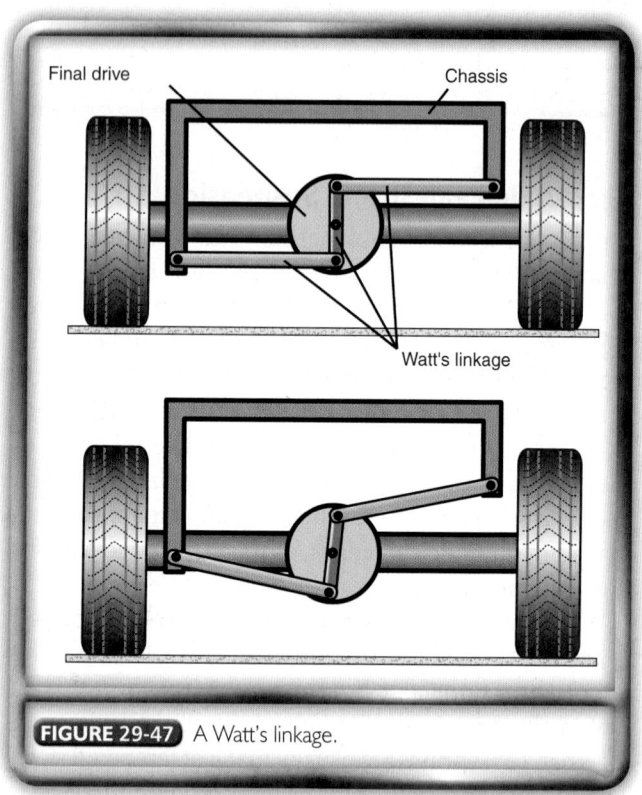

FIGURE 29-47 A Watt's linkage.

FIGURE 29-46 A panhard rod sits parallel with the axle.

FIGURE 29-48 A rigid nondrive axle suspension.

not connected to the other, so they can move separately. A MacPherson strut system is commonly used at the rear, which can be similar to the front suspension system, using either a wishbone-shaped lower control arm or two control arms, along with a strut assembly. It can also use a trailing arm with a strut assembly and a panhard rod to control all three axes.

Rear-Wheel Drive Independent Suspension

On rear-wheel drive vehicles with independent rear suspension, the final drive unit is fixed to the vehicle frame **FIGURE 29-49**. Drive is transmitted to each wheel by **external drive shafts**, shafts that transfer power from the final drive to the live axle. Suspension is normally provided by coil springs, and each wheel unit is located by a combination of lateral and longitudinal control arms, or by trailing arms to the frame. The final drive assembly is normally bolted to the chassis, and since it must absorb the torque reaction, it must be securely fastened. Drive shafts, with either conventional universal joints or constant-velocity joints, rotate and transmit the drive to the wheels. **Universal joints** are placed on the end of a drive shaft to compensate for the up-and-down movement of the rear wheels. When conventional universal joints are used, each drive shaft may have a **splined section**, a special section of the shaft that can move in or out to vary the shaft's length due to changes in the suspension action **FIGURE 29-50**.

On some vehicles equipped with an independent rear suspension, the drive shafts or half-shafts themselves can be used as the upper link of the suspension, providing the upper pivot point **FIGURE 29-51**. In this case, the half-shafts are fixed, meaning they do not extend or collapse. This makes the splined section unnecessary, and the shaft can be made as a one-piece unit. The outer wheel bearing hub is held in position laterally and longitudinally at the

bottom by a pivot on the end of the lower control arm, and the half-shaft holds the top of the hub in position vertically. Since the hub pivots on both the lower control arm and the half-shaft, the wheel can move up and down. The lower control arm has widely spaced pivots to provide stability. It is longer than the half-shaft, which allows the camber to move slightly positive during cornering, just like an SLA suspension.

> ## TECHNICIAN TIP
>
> External forces, such as curb impact or a collision, can damage control arms or linkages and move the wheel units from their correct position. This can make a vehicle pull to one side, cause abnormal tire wear, and make the vehicle difficult to control.

FIGURE 29-50 The independent rear suspension may have upper and lower control arms.

FIGURE 29-49 Live independent rear suspension.

FIGURE 29-51 On some vehicles equipped with an independent rear suspension, the drive shafts or half-shafts themselves can be used as the upper link of the suspension, providing the upper pivot point.

Adaptive Air Suspension

Adaptive air suspension is an electronically controlled air suspension system at all four wheels with a continuously adaptive dampening system, meaning it is able to automatically change the dampening power of the shocks when the road conditions change to give the driver a smoother ride. It combines sporty handling with a high level of ride comfort. Additionally, the air suspension allows the speed-dependent lowering of the body; this change in ride height means a low center of gravity, resulting in significantly increased directional stability, as well as increased aerodynamic efficiency. On a bumpy road, it makes the shocks softer so the vehicle rides better. The vehicle's handling characteristics are improved at the same time by the addition or removal of air from the system.

The information obtained from sensors on the axles for ride height, and acceleration sensors on the body for vehicle pitch, is evaluated in the adaptive air suspension's central control unit. This computer can control the adjustment of the individual shock absorbers within milliseconds, depending on driving situations. As long as no higher dampening forces are required—for instance, when driving straight ahead on good roads—the damper settings remain comfortably soft.

Specific adjustments to the dampening force at individual wheels eliminate body movement, which could affect occupant comfort and vehicle control. In some cases, when cornering, braking, or accelerating, adaptive dampening can automatically reduce rolling or pitching movements. Adaptive air suspension also offers the following advantages:

- The vehicle's suspension height remains constant regardless of the load it is carrying.
- Adjustable dampening characteristics and ride height are maintained by a single process, via the manufacturer's "Vehicle Performance" menu, which can be found on the dash or console switch.
- The driver can influence the suspension characteristics, and thus the operating dynamics, as individually preferred. This enables drivers to set the suspension to a sport or performance setting when desired, so that the vehicle will handle better.

Adaptive Air Suspension Operation

On some vehicles, when the ignition is switched on, or when the vehicle's door is opened before ignition, the control system is activated. The height sensor uses the induction principle to constantly monitor the distance between the vehicle's axle and its chassis. If the control system determines that the ride height is too low, it will command that air be added to the appropriate adaptive shock absorbers. When the vehicle is being loaded, unloaded, or lowered due to driver command or vehicle speed, the height sensor monitors the changes and reports them to the control unit. The ECU compares this information to the stored reference values.

The ECU activates either the electric motor of the compressor or the exhaust solenoid valve, which is located on the top of each adaptive shock absorber **FIGURE 29-52**. This also requires the solenoid valve to be actuated or moved to maintain the required level once reached. The adaptive shock absorber solenoid valves are subject to stringent leakage requirements to maintain the vehicle's height even when the system is not being operated.

When the vehicle is being loaded, the compressor delivers air into the four air suspension bellows through fill solenoids or gate solenoids, until the normal level has once again been reached. For additional air delivery or rapid response, the reservoir solenoid valve is opened and air flows directly from the reservoir. When the vehicle is being unloaded, the exhaust solenoid valve is activated. Activation of this valve results in airflow from the air suspension bellows being removed via the air dryer solenoid valve in the compressor, then via the relay valve. The air is then exhausted into the atmosphere through a computer-controlled vent valve. Any dynamic air spring movement while the vehicle is in motion is ignored and does not cause the control system to respond. However, the system can adjust the air pressure based on other parameters such as vehicle speed, driver selection of a different mode, or any automatic adjustments that the control system determines are necessary.

FIGURE 29-52 Adaptive shock absorber.

Computer-Controlled Suspension

Just like many other functions on a modern vehicle, the suspension system has been computerized. Computer-controlled suspension systems, often referred to as active or adaptive suspension, use computers to constantly monitor all aspects of the suspension system and ride features to improve vehicle handling and generate a smoother ride. For example, the computer system can set the suspension for sporty handling during situations where precise steering control, fast braking, and high-speed driving are needed. It can then almost instantly shift the suspension system in response to normal driving to provide a smooth ride. Advanced systems are also available that monitor and respond to changes in cargo load and vehicle height. Computer-controlled suspension systems are available on front and rear suspensions. Examples of some computerized suspension systems are:

- Active: Makes adjustments without any driver input
- Hydraulic actuated: Uses fluid to implement changes to the suspension system
- Electromagnetic rheological: Uses an electromagnetic response to make changes to the viscosity of the hydraulic fluid, thereby adjusting the stiffness of the suspension system
- Semi-active: Requires some driver input to change the suspension system
- Solenoid valve actuated: Uses a solenoid valve to change the dampening of the shocks
- Stepper motor actuated: Uses an electric stepper motor to adjust the valving in the shock absorber to change the rate of dampening

▶ Wheel Alignment Fundamentals

All wheels of a vehicle must be correctly positioned in relation to the vehicle and to each other for the vehicle to drive and steer properly. A driver should not need to keep manipulating the steering wheel to maintain the vehicle in a straight-ahead position on straight, level roads. Similarly, little effort should be needed to turn the vehicle into curves or to let it return to the straight-ahead position once the curve has been negotiated. Wheels are positioned on the suspension at certain angles to provide for easy driving of the vehicle. These angles, taken together, determine the vehicle's **wheel alignment**. The alignment is set using the control arms, strut rods, tie-rods, knuckles, and vehicle frame to obtain the proper angles. Alignments should be performed for several reasons, including when handling issues related to alignment

angles are found, when tire wear shows any tire wearing angle issue, and when components are replaced that have alignment angle adjustment capabilities. It is also good practice to check vehicles for alignment whenever new tires are being installed. But before you can check alignment, you need to know what the alignment angles are and how they affect driving.

Camber

Camber is the side-to-side vertical tilt of the wheel. It is viewed from the front of the vehicle and is measured in degrees **FIGURE 29-53**. A wheel that leans away from the center of the vehicle at the top is said to have **positive camber**. A wheel that leans toward the center of the vehicle is said to have **negative camber**. A vehicle with camber pull will pull in the direction of the greatest positive camber. To picture why it pulls in this direction, think of a paper cup lying on its side. When it is rolled, it turns in the direction of the narrower end of the cup. Tires do the same thing in regard to their camber. Camber is affected by ride height and can be seen by looking at the tilt of the wheel in vehicles that are lowered incorrectly. Camber used to be a heavy tire wearing angle when tires were of the bias ply type and had stiff sidewalls. Camber wear is now debatable, given the much more pliable sidewalls in radial tires. It is safe to say that tires can tolerate moderate amounts of improper camber much better than before. There are also studies that say most of what technicians diagnose as camber wear is really toe wear. Pay attention to this debate as it plays out.

On earlier vehicles with narrow, large-diameter tires, large camber angles were used to bring the centerline of road contact closer to the steering axis. They also ensured

FIGURE 29-53 Camber.

the vehicle weight was carried by the large inner bearing. On modern vehicles, however, tires are much wider and generally smaller in diameter, and large camber angles would cause the tire to ride on the outer edges of the tires. The amount of camber is now reduced so that most vehicles when in forward motion have what is called **zero camber**, or no tilt, to provide maximum tire patch contact with the road, as well as long tire life.

> ### ▶ TECHNICIAN TIP
>
> Changes in running camber can be caused by driving over road irregularities, load variations, and worn suspension components.

Caster

Caster is the forward or backward tilt of the steering axis from vertical when viewed from the side of the vehicle **FIGURE 29-54**. The steering axis is an imaginary line passing through the center of the ball joints on SLA suspensions or passing through the center of the upper strut bearing and lower ball joint on MacPherson strut suspensions. So caster is the tilt of the steering axis from vertical, measured in degrees. Backward tilt from the vertical is **positive caster**. Forward tilt is **negative caster**. When a vehicle has positive caster, a line drawn through the steering axis centerline meets the road surface ahead of the vertical centerline of the wheel. The center of the tire contact point is behind the steering axis.

When the wheel is turned to the right, the tire contact point is moved to the left of the direction of travel. Conversely, when the wheel is turned to the left, the contact point is moved to the right of the direction of travel. In forward motion, this generates a self-centering force that helps return the wheels to the neutral position when the steering wheel is released.

Most vehicles have positive caster, because it causes the tires to travel in a straight line with minimal driver action. However, as positive caster increases, more and more effort is needed to turn the steering wheel to overcome the increased self-straightening force. Also, positive caster causes the spindle to tilt as the wheel is steered, and this places more weight on the inside tire because of the body lifting that occurs with the inside tire. This lift can be seen by turning the steering from lock to lock while the vehicle is stationary.

> ### ▶ TECHNICIAN TIP
>
> Some vehicles have by design an amount of negative caster, which makes the steering light. Negative caster is created by placing the suspension system pivots so that they are tilted forward from the vertical line. Generally, such vehicles would operate only at low speeds; vehicles with negative caster can become unstable as speed increases. Steering will pull toward the side of the vehicle with the most negative caster. Caster is affected by ride height and on most modern vehicles is a nonadjustable angle without aftermarket components.

> ### Applied | Math
>
> *AM-21: Parallel/Perpendicular: The technician can use measurement devices to determine the parallelism or perpendicularity of chassis, suspension, and other vehicle systems requiring the application of geometric alignment principles.*
>
> A vehicle was purchased at an auction and has been taken to an automotive repair shop for evaluation. When the vehicle was set up on the alignment machine and alignment readings taken, several of the angles were substantially out of specification, including front-wheel setback, rear thrust angle, and SAI. These angles being out of specification indicate the potential of a bent frame or chassis. Upon further examination, the technician observes cracked undercoat and paint on the subframe components, as well as shifting of the engine cradle bolts. This verifies what the alignment angles are telling him; that the chassis is not parallel and perpendicular. The technician knows that the wheels cannot be brought back into proper alignment with the chassis out of alignment.

FIGURE 29-54 Caster.

Steering Axis Inclination

The axis around which the wheel assembly swivels as it turns to the right or left is called the steering axis. It is formed by drawing a line through the center of the upper and lower pivot points of the suspension assembly **FIGURE 29-55**. Seen from the front of the vehicle, it is tilted inward at the top. The angle formed between this line and the vertical provides the **steering axis inclination (SAI)** angle. Since the SAI is not adjustable, if the camber angle is correct, then the SAI should also be correct; that is, it should match the manufacturer's specifications.

SAI acts with caster to provide a self-centering of the front wheels. When the wheels are in the straight-ahead position, the ends of the stub axles are almost horizontal. When the wheels turn to either side, the effect of SAI is to make the ends of the stub axle tend to move downward, but this tendency is prevented by the wheel and tire on the ground. The stub axle carrier then must move up, which raises the corner of the vehicle. When the steering wheel is released, the weight of the vehicle forces the stub carrier back down, which pushes the wheels back to a central position. When the wheels are turned the other way, the same thing happens. With a perfectly vertical steering axis, no self-centering would occur. The wheel would pivot on a radius, not under the center of the tire patch, but off to the inside of the tire. This would introduce a turning movement on the wheel whenever

the tire hit a bump, transmitting road shocks back to the steering wheel, and steering would be difficult to control.

SAI also brings the pivot point close to the center of the tire contact patch at the road surface. For steering purposes, ideally SAI intersects with the camber line (drawn through the center of the tire and the wheel) at the road surface. Any difference in distance between these two lines produces another suspension angle called the scrub radius, which will be discussed further in a later section.

Included Angle

The angle formed between the SAI and the camber line is called the **included angle**, or diagnostic angle. It is found by adding the SAI angle and the camber angle together. If the camber angle is specified as negative, then it is subtracted from the SAI angle. When an angle is referred to as a diagnostic angle, it means the angle cannot be changed but is measured to determine if any parts are bent, such as a spindle, control arm, or steering arm.

Scrub Radius

Scrub radius is also known as steering offset and scrub geometry. It is the distance between two imaginary points on the road surface. One point is the centerline of the tire using the camber line, and the other point is where the SAI centerline contacts the road surface **FIGURE 29-56**. If these two lines intersect at the center of the tire, at the

FIGURE 29-55 The axis around which the wheel assembly swivels as it turns to the right or left is called the steering axis. It is formed by drawing a line through the upper and lower pivot points of the suspension assembly.

FIGURE 29-56 The scrub radius is the distance between two imaginary points on the road surface: the point of center contact between the road surface and the tire and the point where the steering axis centerline contacts the road surface.

road surface, then the vehicle is said to have zero offset, or <u>zero scrub radius</u>. If the camber line is outside of the SAI line, then it has positive offset or <u>positive scrub radius</u>. If the camber line is inside of the SAI line, then it has negative offset or <u>negative scrub radius</u>. Scrub radius can be changed accidentally a number of ways. Changing the diameter of wheels and tires affects scrub radius, as does the distance that the center of the wheel and tire sits relative to the vehicle body, which is called wheel offset. SAI and camber also affect scrub radius since we are changing the angles that determine scrub radius.

Incorrect scrub radius can produce undesirable effects. Too much positive scrub radius (the camber line is outside of the SAI line) will cause the vehicle to dart when the brakes are applied. Too much negative scrub radius (the camber line is inside of the SAI line) will cause the vehicle to be unstable while driving (not braking) and will result in less driver feedback. Driver feedback is the feel of the road through the steering wheel. Most front-wheel drive vehicles use a negative scrub radius to provide a measure of safety in the event that one brake circuit fails since they use a diagonal split brake system.

On a rear-wheel drive vehicle with positive scrub radius, the vehicle's forward motion and the friction between the tire and the road cause a force that tends to move the front wheels back. This causes the wheels to toe-out. If it has negative scrub radius, the front wheels again tend to move back and the wheels now toe-in. On front-wheel drive vehicles, the opposite occurs. Positive scrub radius causes toe-in, and negative causes toe-out. During braking, if braking effort is greater on one side of the vehicle than the other, positive scrub radius will cause the vehicle to veer toward the side with the greater braking effort. Negative scrub radius will cause the vehicle to veer away from the side of greatest effort. How much it veers depends on the size of the scrub radius. This is why vehicles with a diagonal-split brake system have negative

scrub radius built into the steering geometry. If one half of the brake system fails, then the vehicle will tend to pull up in a straight line.

Toe-in and Toe-out

Toe is the angle of the tires relative to each other when viewed from above. The condition in which the fronts of the wheels are closer together than the rears of the wheels is called <u>toe-in</u>. The condition in which the fronts of the wheels are farther apart than the rears is called <u>toe-out</u>. Some manufacturers use the terms *positive toe* for toe-in and *negative toe* for toe-out. Toe can be measure in inches or degrees. The <u>static toe</u> setting is designed to compensate for slight wear in steering joints and components, which may cause the wheels to splay outward or inward while the vehicle is being driven. This effect is designed into the vehicle based on several factors, such as front-wheel drive versus rear-wheel drive, front/rear brake system split versus diagonal brake system split, and specific desired handling characteristics. Manufacturers specify the proper static toe for the design of the vehicle such that the wheels will be parallel when the vehicle is in forward motion, which avoids scrubbing of the tires.

Toe-out on Turns

<u>Toe-out on turns</u> is the relative toe setting of the front wheels as the vehicle turns **FIGURE 29-57**. When a vehicle makes a turn, each wheel should rotate with true rolling motion that is free from tire scrub. True rolling motion is obtained only when each wheel is at 90 degrees to a line drawn between the steering axis and the center point of the turn. The steering axis is the point where the tire turns at the knuckle. Because the rear wheels

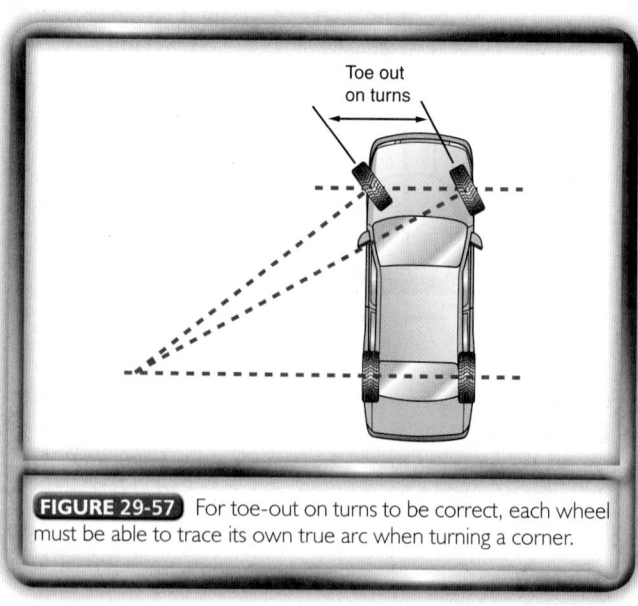

FIGURE 29-57 For toe-out on turns to be correct, each wheel must be able to trace its own true arc when turning a corner.

are fixed, the center of the turn will lie somewhere along the centerline of the rear axle, depending on how far the steering wheel is turned from the straight-ahead position.

To provide true rolling motion, the inner wheel must be turned through a greater angle than the outer wheel. This allows the inner wheel to turn through a smaller turning radius than the outer wheel. This correct positioning of the wheels when steering around a corner is obtained by use of the **Ackermann principle** and layout. The Ackermann principle is a geometric alignment of linkages in a vehicle's steering such that the wheels on the inside of a turn are able to move in a different circle radius than the wheels on the outside. The inner wheels must move on a circle with a smaller radius, and the outer wheels move on a circle with a

Applied   Science

AS-15: Force: The technician can use a tension gauge such as a torque wrench to measure the force or tension required to tighten connections to manufacturer's specifications.

A good quality torque wrench is one of the technician's most valuable tools. Proper torque applied to fasteners is critical for the repair job to successful. This is true for chassis work as well as for engines.

A torque wrench measures the amount of twisting force or "torque" applied to the fastener. In physics, torque is sometimes called a rotational force. The formula to calculate the torque applied to a bolt is torque = force x distance. In the study of physics, the distance is known as the moment arm. It takes twice the force at half the distance (or moment arm) to equal a certain torque value. It takes half of the force at twice the distance (or moment arm) to equal the same torque value.

When using a torque wrench, the following precautions should be observed:

1. Use manufacturer's service information to obtain the torque specifications.
2. Verify that you have the correct torque wrench for the job that you are doing. The 80/20 rule states that the torque wrench should be used only in the approved range. This would be from 20 to 80 ft.-lb., when using a 0 to 100 ft.-lb. wrench, or 40 to 160 ft.-lb. on a 0 to 200 ft.-lb. wrench.
3. Support the head of the torque wrench with one hand and pull the wrench handle in a steady motion.
4. Use a general crisscross pattern for tightening fasteners unless a manufacturer's torque pattern is available.
5. Tighten nuts and bolts in at least three stages: one-third recommended torque, two-thirds torque, full torque, and full torque to double check, once again.

Applied   Science

AS-52: Circular: The technician can demonstrate an understanding of circular motion as it relates to toe and camber on turns.

When you steer a vehicle through a turn, the outside front wheel has to travel a wider arc than the inside wheel; therefore, the inside front wheel must steer at a sharper angle than the outside wheel. To provide true rolling motion, the inner wheel must be turned through a greater angle than the outer wheel. This allows the inner wheel to turn through a smaller turning radius than the outer wheel. With the tires on the turntable, toe-out on turns is measured by the turning angle gauges (turn plates) on the wheel alignment machine. The readings are measured electronically and displayed on the screen. Camber is the vertical angle of the wheels relative to the vehicle. This is best viewed from the front of the car. If the vehicle has negative camber, the tops of the wheels will be closer together than the bottom. During cornering, camber compensates for vehicle weight transfer and body roll.

larger radius. The **Ackermann angle** is the angle the steering arms make with the steering axis, projected toward the center of the rear axle **FIGURE 29-58**. The angling of the steering arms forces the inner wheels to turn through a smaller angle when the steering wheel is turned to that side. When the steering wheel is turned the opposite direction, the wheels that were on the outside are now on the inside of the turn and will turn more sharply than the wheels that are now on the outside of the turn. Toe-out on turns is a nonadjustable angle. If it is not correct according to the manufacturer's specifications, then you know that a steering linkage is bent, typically the steering arm. This will also cause the tires to scrub when turning corners.

FIGURE 29-58 Ackermann angle.

Turning Radius

Turning radius is a measure of how small a circle the vehicle can turn in when the steering wheel is turned to the limit (**FIGURE 29-59**). All vehicles have stops to limit how far the front wheels can turn. In some designs, these stops can be adjusted as part of a wheel alignment. If the stops are incorrectly adjusted, they could allow too sharp of a turning angle and the steering box could bottom out and be damaged.

Applied | Math

AM-26: Visual Perception: The technician can visually perceive the geometric relationships of systems and subsystems requiring alignment.

Bill is an automotive technician trainee who is working with an experienced technician. Bill has an interest in front-end alignment and has performed several alignments with the assistance of his mentor. A vehicle has just come into the shop for an alignment, and Bill has been given permission to do this job on his own. The experienced technician will do a final check to be sure that everything has been done properly. The shop has the latest type of laser-controlled alignment equipment, which makes the job a lot easier for the technician.

Bill drives the vehicle onto the alignment rack, but before attaching the wheel sensors, he looks the car over. He positions himself at the front of the vehicle, sighting from the front tires toward the rear. Bill wants to see the relationship of the front tires to the rear. He observes that there is a small amount of the rear tread showing on each side and that it appears to be an equal amount of tread on each side. He begins the alignment procedure by attaching the sensors on each wheel. The VIN is scanned into the computerized system and the alignment system calculates the thrust angle and geometric centerline. The final result is that a slight toe adjustment is needed but everything else is within specifications. Bill's visual perception of the relationship of the components helped him to predict this reading before the alignment machine verified it.

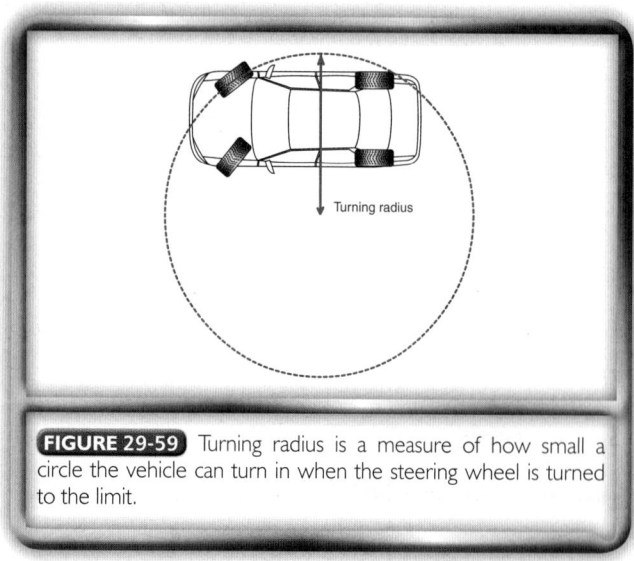

FIGURE 29-59 Turning radius is a measure of how small a circle the vehicle can turn in when the steering wheel is turned to the limit.

Applied | Math

AM-51: Trial and Error: The technician is able to solve problems by trying a suggested solution and observing the results.

A vehicle with a MacPherson strut design is in the shop for repairs. The technician who is assigned to this project has done similar jobs in the past. The repair order calls for two new front struts plus an alignment. In the past, the technician has done very little regarding marking of the position of the old strut. In this case, the technician is going to try a new method that was suggested by another technician. The new strategy is to employ careful marking of the old start's position. This will include the upper and lower positions of the original strut using a sharp scribe. The technician wants to observe the results of his procedure when the alignment is completed. The strategy is to produce a less involved alignment or perhaps eliminate the need for alignment adjustments to be necessary. The technician understands that this is only a trial and error procedure to be tested and could vary from one type of vehicle to another type. He was pleasantly surprised that the alignment was much closer to the specifications than previous vehicles he hadn't used this process on.

Thrust Angle, Centerlines, and Setback (Tracking)

On a vehicle with independent rear suspension, undertaking a front-wheel-only alignment is considered an inadequate procedure. The rear tires also need to be aligned or they will experience accelerated tire wear and the vehicle will not drive properly. The thrust angle refers to the relationship between the centerline of the vehicle and the angle of the rear tires. The term thrust line refers to the direction in which the rear wheels are pointing (**FIGURE 29-60**). The thrust angle can be adjusted on vehicles with adjustable rear suspensions. On vehicles that do not have adjustable rear suspensions, a small amount of thrust angle can be compensated for by aligning the front wheels to the rear wheels. Referencing the front steering geometry to the rear is very important.

Ideally, the thrust line and the vehicle's geometric centerline should line up closely. The centerline is drawn through points midway between each pair of wheels; however, the thrust line is not always as straightforward to determine. It is normally perpendicular to the rear axle on solid-axle vehicles. In vehicles with an independent rear suspension, it is derived by splitting the toe angle of each of the rear wheels on the vehicle. For instance, if the right rear wheel is toed-in 6°, and the left rear wheel is at 0°, the thrust line will veer off 3° to the left of the vehicle's centerline when the vehicle is moving forward.

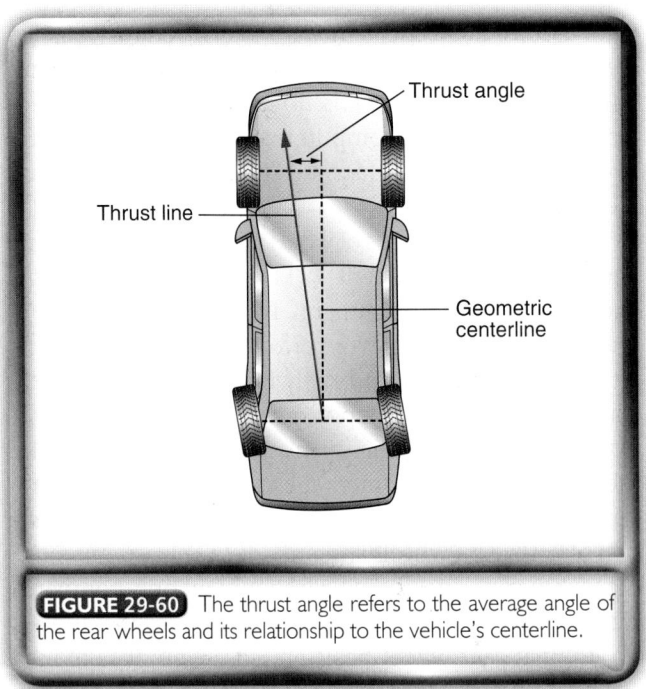

FIGURE 29-60 The thrust angle refers to the average angle of the rear wheels and its relationship to the vehicle's centerline.

FIGURE 29-61 Setback refers to the distance one wheel is set back from the wheel on the opposite side of the axle, relative to lines running through the center of each wheel and perpendicular to the vehicle's centerline.

Ideally, the thrust and centerlines coincide; however, given the size of a vehicle, the tolerances during manufacture, operational stresses, and component wear, it is rare that they do. If the deviation is very small, then remedial action is normally unnecessary. However, a large deviation can cause considerable concern when the vehicle is being driven, and the cause of this condition needs to be identified and corrected. Under such conditions the rear wheels are steering the vehicle away from its centerline and the driver has to turn the steering wheel to one side to keep the vehicle going in a straight line. Thrust angle issues may be caused by a leaf-spring suspension that has a broken center bolt, a bent axle, a bent frame or unibody, or simply misadjusted rear toe.

Setback is another alignment angle that is not adjustable but that allows the technician to diagnose the vehicle. Setback is the distance one wheel is set back from the wheel on the opposite side of the axle, relative to imaginary lines running through the center of each wheel and perpendicular to the vehicle's centerline **FIGURE 29-61**. Setback is best measured on an alignment machine so it can be measured correctly from the centerline of the vehicle. But an indication of setback can be made by measuring the distance of the wheel base on one side of the vehicle and comparing it to the wheelbase on the other side. If the vehicle has setback, then one wheel base measurement will typically (but not always) be shorter than the other.

Setback can be incorrect due to damage from a collision or due to a cradle that has been installed incorrectly or has shifted. Setback in the front wheels will create a pull condition for the driver to the side with the most setback or the wheel that is farther toward the rear of the car; a setback issue in the rear will pull toward the side

with the least setback. Setback due to a cradle shift may also affect the camber from side to side. On a vehicle that has no adjustment for camber, check for a cradle shift by looking for witness marks around the head of the bolt that holds the cradle to the body. If a partial shiny metal ring surrounds the bolt head, then the cradle has shifted. Loosen the cradle bolts and reposition to achieve proper alignment specifications. Usually, setback should be no more than a quarter of an inch from side to side.

> ### TECHNICIAN TIP
>
> In extreme conditions of setback or thrust angle, the tracks the rear tires make are beside those of the front. This condition is known as dog-tracking or crabbing and can cause diagonal tire pattern wear on the rear tires as well as vehicle instability in some driving conditions. A vehicle that is dog-tracking will appear to be driving slightly sideways down the road.

Ride Height

Ride height, sometimes referred to as trim height, is the amount of distance between the ground and a specified part of the vehicle such as the fender well, upper control arm, or rocker panel. Ride height is measured with standard vehicle weight. For cars, it is usually given with no cargo or passengers. Changes in ride height alter the position of the control arms, which can have a detrimental effect on wheel alignment. Ride height that is not within specifications can be caused by improper tires or tire pressure; weak, sagging springs; or bent components such as a control arm or axle, or even a frame or unibody.

Ride height should typically not vary by more than half an inch from side to side.

Ground clearance is similar to ride height, but is the distance from the ground to the lowest part of the chassis, typically a cross member, final drive, or oil pan. Ground clearance is especially important for off-road vehicles. Ground clearance can be increased by replacing stock components with aftermarket performance parts, but increasing ground clearance also increases the vehicle's center of gravity, making it more prone to rollover. It also affects scrub radius and potentially other wheel alignment angles. Thus, increasing ground clearance increases the risk of an accident in several ways; consider that carefully before modifying a vehicle in this way.

Applied | Science

AS-88: Pneumatics: The technician can demonstrate an understanding of the forces and motions in pneumatic systems.

A vehicle is in the shop due to an inoperative automatic leveling control, which is part of an air suspension system. This vehicle has an (ALC) automatic level system that maintains the correct rear suspension trip height. This height will be maintained even if a heavy weight is placed in the trunk.

Pneumatics is a system operated by compressed air. In the case of the automatic level system, a battery powered air compressor is used to power the system. Nylon air lines connect from the compressor to the rear air shocks to lift the rear of the vehicle to the correct height. The forces involved are linear as the weight of the rear of the vehicle is applied to the air shocks. The vehicle height sensor triggers the air compressor to control the amount of run time needed. When weight is removed from the trunk, the rear of the vehicle will rise. At this point, the vehicle height sensor will give the appropriate signal to the pressure release solenoid valve to release air from the shocks. The body of the vehicle will return to the correct height. This type of system is usually found on luxury vehicles.

The technician inspects the vehicle and discovers a broken airline. After replacing the line, the vehicle is tested by the addition of some heavy items in the trunk. The air compressor starts and the rear of the vehicle rises to the correct trim height. When the weight is removed, the vehicle lowers to the proper height.

Types of Wheel Alignment

Performing a wheel alignment will require the use of an alignment machine. In the past, simpler devices (such as using a measuring tape or a piece of string to set wheel toe)

were used to align the vehicle's wheels. Today's vehicles are more sensitive to the position of the wheels, so using a tape measure to set toe is no longer acceptable. The technician will use a computerized alignment machine to ensure all the angles discussed in the previous sections are correct.

The three basic types of wheel alignment are (1) front-end, two-wheel alignment, (2) thrust-angle alignment, and (3) four-wheel alignment. Two-wheel alignment is outdated and almost never performed on modern vehicles, but we will cover it briefly here so you will understand why it would be inappropriate for most vehicles. In front-end, two-wheel alignment, the technician positions the vehicle on the alignment rack and attaches the wheel sensors to the two front wheels. The sensors read the position of both front wheels and provide the measurement to the technician. The two-wheel alignment only compares the front wheel angles to the vehicle's centerline; it does not look at rear wheel position, so it cannot take into account any thrust angle. The technician compares the measurements to the alignment specifications provided by the manufacturer. If they are different, the technician adjusts the angles of the wheels until they match the specifications.

In a thrust-angle alignment, the technician attaches wheel sensors to all four wheels. The front wheels are compared to the angles of the rear wheels and adjusted to them. This technique is typically done on a vehicle with a solid rear axle where no adjustment is possible in the rear. If the thrust is out of specifications, the technician will need to diagnose what is causing the issue, such as a shifted axle or collision damage. If the thrust angle is within specifications, the front wheels are adjusted to compensate for any slight thrust angle of the rear wheels.

In a four-wheel alignment, the technician positions the vehicle on the alignment rack and attaches the wheel sensors to all four wheels. The rear angles are adjusted first so they conform to the vehicle's centerline; then the front wheels are adjusted to conform to the vehicle's centerline and the position of the rear wheels. The four-wheel alignment provides the most accurate alignment of the wheels, if adjustment of the rear suspension is possible.

Remember that anytime a part that has adjustment for alignment angles is removed, an alignment will have to be performed. For example, if the front struts have adjustment slots and are being replaced, an alignment will need to be performed to ensure the correct wheel alignment angles are restored. If unsure of what parts replacements require an alignment, refer to the manufacturer's service information.

Applied | Math

AM-22: Angles: The technician can use angle measurement equipment and techniques to determine any vehicle angle measurement variance from the manufacturer's specifications.

A front-wheel drive vehicle is in the shop for a routine tire rotation. The technician notices that one of the front tires is slightly worn on one side. He reports his findings to the service advisor, who contacts the vehicle owner and obtains authorization for a four-wheel alignment. The technician starts with a pre-alignment inspection including a check for any loose suspension components. No unusual problems are found, and the technician is now ready to use angle measurement equipment and techniques to determine variance from the manufacturer's specifications.

An electronic sensor is attached to each of the four wheels. The technician scans the VIN, and the alignment system automatically goes to the correct specifications for the vehicle. In addition, the video screen of the alignment system gives a step-by-step approach to the procedure. Since there are many different ways to make alignment corrections, the technician is shown the exact procedure for the vehicle being aligned. A color-coded system—red for out of specifications and green for within specifications—is also helpful.

Computer printouts with before and after adjustments will be available to the customer. In this scenario, the alignment equipment indicates that a toe adjustment is needed for the front of the vehicle. As the technician makes the adjustment, the display shows the results on the video screen. When the exact manufacturer's specifications are obtained, the technician locks down the jam nuts to secure the setting.

Performing Wheel Alignment

Performing an alignment can be done for maintenance purposes, or it can be done when tires or other steering and suspension components have been replaced. It can also be a helpful diagnostic step when a driver is complaining of uneven tire wear, pulling, hard steering, or wandering conditions. The use of the alignment machine will help you identify problems that might not be identifiable by a visual inspection, such as bent suspension components, worn parts, or improper repairs that have been performed to the steering or suspension system.

While four-wheel alignments are the norm for current vehicles, many technicians jokingly refer to a proper alignment as a five-wheel alignment. This is because the steering wheel also needs to be centered at the completion of a wheel alignment or the customer will be returning for the concern of a crooked steering wheel while driving.

Most modern vehicles now use a steering angle sensor that tells the vehicle's stability control module where the steering wheel is pointed. These vehicles may need to have the steering angle sensor recalibrated if changes are made to the alignment or if components are replaced. Typically this process is performed with a scan tool.

To perform the wheel alignment, you will need to first perform a pre-alignment inspection to ensure that the vehicle can be aligned. If any suspension or steering components are found to be loose or damaged, replacement of these components will be necessary before aligning the wheels. The technician will be checking the following primary angles: caster (which is not adjustable on all vehicles and must be checked by turning the wheels of the vehicle in a process called the caster sweep), camber, and toe. The secondary angles that the technician will look at are the SAI, included angle, wheel setback, thrust angle, and toe-out on turns.

The secondary angles are typically not adjustable and, if out of specifications, normally mean that a suspension component or the vehicle frame is bent. When the vehicle has an adjustable rear independent suspension, thrust angle can typically be adjusted by turning tie-rods or turning eccentric bolts to toe the tires in or out to correct the thrust angle. Typically, thrust angle is adjusted as close to the vehicle's centerline as possible.

Adjusting wheel alignment angles must be done in a specific order of caster, camber, and toe. To begin with caster adjustment, locate the method of adjustment for the vehicle you are working on. Most modern alignment machines will include a video to demonstrate how the adjustment process works, but if not, refer to the manufacturer's service information. Not all vehicles have adjustment for caster; if they do not, an aftermarket kit will need to be installed to adjust caster, or the vehicle may need to go to a body shop for frame straightening

For vehicles equipped from the factory with provisions for adjustment, four common types of adjustment systems are used. Shim adjustment for the front wheels was used typically on older rear-wheel drive vehicles and was a bit challenging when adjusting caster **FIGURE 29-62**. In this method, shims are added together or removed from a pack and slipped between the control arm pivot shaft and the vehicle frame at the attachment bolts. This changes the position of the pivot shaft and ultimately the control arm and ball joint, affecting the alignment angles as desired. The attaching bolts fit through the frame of the vehicle and into holes in the cross bar where they are held with nuts. There are two shim packs used—one at the front attaching bolt and one at the rear attaching bolt. Shims are added or removed to shift the ball joint in or out, or back or forward, or a combination of the two.

FIGURE 29-62 A shim-type adjustment is probably the most time-consuming alignment adjustment. Moving shims from one attaching bolt to the other will affect the caster setting, while changing shim pack size in both packs will affect camber.

Applied | **MATH**

AM-24: Geometric Figures: The technician can distinguish whether or not the angles between related parts (e.g., suspension components) are within the manufacturer's specifications.

A 3/4 ton pickup truck is in the shop with a driveshaft vibration problem. The owner of the vehicle is requesting an inspection of the rear driveshaft including the measurement of the operating angles.

A driveshaft is a component that connects the transmission (or transfer case) to the axles, transmitting torque from the engine to the driving wheels. This component is also known as a propeller shaft. The cardan style universal joint is sometimes known as the "cross and caps" type. When the driveline has an operating angle of zero, the universal joint is operating under the best possible conditions for long service life. This "perfect" situation is not realistic for a number of reasons. The suspension system will allow the rear axle to move up and down, which will change the operating angle of the driveline. Worn components such as transmission mounts or worn bushings in the spring hangers can change the operating angle.

The technician assigned to the job has a good working knowledge of suspension components and driveline angles. Manufacturer's service information has been accessed and the technician is aware of the 3° maximum operating angle. A special tool called an inclinometer or angle finder will be placed on the driveline to determine the angles at the front and rear of the driveshaft. The operating angles on each end of the driveshaft should be equal to or within 1° of each other. The technician finds that the driveshaft angles are correct, but the rear universal joint is worn, causing the shaft to be out of alignment and balance and creating the vibration. Replacement of the rear universal joint corrects the problem.

Applied | **MATH**

AM-25: Relationships: The technician verifies that the relationship of parallel lines and angles is in conformance with the manufacturer's specifications.

An experienced technician is assigned to assist a technician trainee with an alignment. The shop has recently purchased a state-of-the-art, computerized, laser-operated alignment system. After showing the trainee the basics of a pre-alignment inspection, the vehicle is pulled onto the alignment rack. The technician shows the trainee how to attach a target to each of the four wheels. The target is another name for an electronic device that is attached to each wheel. The VIN number of the vehicle is scanned onto the alignment system. Manufacturer's data will be selected and available for alignment purposes. The experienced technician explained that the alignment system is set up to guide the operator in a step-by-step procedure. On a video screen are instructions that are specific to the exact make and model of the vehicle. There are clear illustrations of all of the adjustments that are needed for each phase of the operation. Concerning the specifications for the vehicle being aligned, caster has a preferred setting of 3.33° with a range of 2.33° to 4.33°. Camber is 0° preferred with a range of -1° to 1°. Toe-in for front is .16" preferred with a range of .11" minimum and .21" maximum. The technician and trainee then compare the alignment readings with the specifications to determine any needed adjustments.

Shim adjustment can affect both caster and camber. If the same amount of shims are taken out of, or added to, each pack, the camber will be changed. If shims are taken from one pack and placed in the other, only the caster will be changed. Shims are available in various thicknesses and typically come in 1/64" (0.015") up to 1/4" (0.250"). Typically, a shim change of 1/32" will move caster by 0.5 degrees, and camber will move around 0.3 degrees with the same shim change.

Shims are still used on some vehicles to adjust rear camber and toe. They are placed behind the backing plate of the brake assembly or behind the hub of the wheel assembly to move the camber or toe to the correct position. These are aftermarket fixes and typically not used from the factory.

Another type of alignment adjustment for caster and camber is the eccentric bolt **FIGURE 29-63**. The eccentric bolt is slightly egg shaped or has a slightly egg-shaped washer attached to one side of the bolt. This egg shape pushes against ridges in the control arm to change caster and camber. The same strategy applies as with the shim-style adjustment; turning both attaching bolts will move

FIGURE 29-63 Eccentric bolt adjustment.

FIGURE 29-64 The strut rod on some vehicles is the adjustment point for caster.

the camber angle. Turning one bolt in one direction and the other bolt in the opposite direction will change caster.

If the vehicle has only one attachment point for the control arm to the body or frame, then it will use a strut rod to support the control arm. Some strut rods have an adjustment nut on the front and the rear of the attachment point to the control arm **FIGURE 29-64**. If both nuts are moved, then the control arm will be pushed forward or pulled backward, which will affect the caster setting.

The last method of adjusting caster and camber involves the ball joint adjusting sleeve **FIGURE 29-65**. The adjusting sleeve is used on several four-wheel drive vehicles and mounts into a solid axle or a dual I-beam axle. The ball joint tapered stud fits into the sleeve. This sleeve can be turned to change caster and camber slightly. The sleeve has a slightly offset hole so the ball joint tapered stud can fit into it. When turning the adjusting sleeve, the ball joint stud is pushed either forward or backward, or in or out, changing caster or camber. The factory adjusting sleeve typically only gives a half degree of alignment change, so an aftermarket adjusting sleeve is often installed if more adjustment is needed.

Adjustment of toe is typically accomplished by lengthening or shortening the tie-rod assembly. Lengthening the tie-rod pushes the steering arm and changes the toe setting; shortening moves the steering arm the opposite direction and changes the toe in the other direction. On a vehicle with an adjusting sleeve, the technician must loosen the two clamp bolts that hold the adjusting sleeve tight and turn the sleeve in the proper direction for toe setting **FIGURE 29-66**. Don't forget to tighten the clamp bolts when the toe is adjusted properly. On a vehicle with a rack-and-pinion steering system, typically the inner

FIGURE 29-65 The adjustable ball joint sleeve gives limited adjustment for caster and camber and is often replaced with an aftermarket part with more adjustment potential.

FIGURE 29-66 The tie-rod assembly comes in two forms and is adjusted by threading the assembly to lengthen or shorten.

tie-rod threads into the outer tie-rod and no adjusting sleeve is used. To lengthen the tie-rod assembly on this vehicle, loosen the lock nut on the outer tie-rod and turn the inner tie-rod in or out to lengthen or shorten the tie-rod assembly. Tighten the lock nut when adjustment is finalized.

Diagnosis

Problems in the suspension system generally result in driver complaints of a poor ride, poor handling, or noises. While these may seem to be trivial complaints, they may indicate a serious and costly suspension problem that, if left untreated, could lead to additional issues or safety hazards.

> **Safety**
>
> Remember that steering and suspension concerns can result in injury or death to the driver and occupants, so extreme attention to safety must be given while diagnosing suspension and steering concerns.

Diagnosis of a problem must always start with a good interview of the driver to fully understand the concerns he or she is having. This is typically performed by the service advisor and then written on the repair order. In some cases, you may need to speak with the customer directly or perform a road test with the customer to verify the concern. Once you have gathered information from the customer and performed a road test, you should have a good idea of what the next step should be based on your understanding of steering and suspension systems. Many times this will be a visual inspection of the tires, wheels, steering system, and suspension system, and a general vehicle inspection. If these initial inspections do not uncover the cause of the concern, the vehicle's wheel alignment should be checked.

Common Issues

There are many types of driver complaints relating to the steering and suspension system. Some of the most common are listed here with their typical cause and the diagnostic method:

- Vehicle wander: This complaint means the vehicle is not driving in exactly the direction the driver is steering it. It tends to happen when the caster angle is off or there is looseness in the steering/suspension components. A front-end alignment machine is the best tool for diagnosing caster angle problems, and a pre-alignment inspection would find wear problems on joints, bushings, and components.

- Drift: Drift occurs when the driver is holding the steering wheel steady and straight, but the vehicle slowly begins to move to either the right or left. This condition requires correction from the driver to keep the vehicle straight. It generally results from loose or worn steering components, low tire pressure, insufficient caster, and incorrect toe settings. The front-end alignment machine is used to measure toe settings, and a pre-alignment inspection would find wear problems on joints, bushings, and components.

- Pull: Pull is felt when the driver feels the steering wheel wanting to go to one side. It can mean the air pressure in one or more of the front tires is low. A simple tire pressure gauge is used to check the tire pressures. Be sure to check the simple things before spending the customer's money on a four-wheel alignment.

  Pull can occur from a bad tire. Try switching the tires side to side. If the pull is now gone or has moved to the opposite side, then a tire is at fault. Pull can also happen when the camber or caster is out of adjustment from one side to the other by as little as half a degree. A vehicle will pull to the side with the most positive camber. If the caster is off by as little as half a degree from side to side, the vehicle will pull to the side with the most negative caster. A four-wheel alignment will be needed to verify the alignment angles. Pulls can also result from power steering problems. Power steering problems can be diagnosed by lifting the front tires off the ground and starting the engine while watching for steering wheel movement. If the vehicle pulls only while braking, looseness in steering/suspension components will need to be found, and/or problems in the braking system will need to be diagnosed.

- Hard steering: When the act of steering is difficult for the driver, there may be a problem in the power steering system, too much positive caster, or binding in the steering system. A pressure gauge is used to check the power steering system and a front-end alignment machine to check the caster. Hard steering could also be caused by something as simple as underinflated tires. A tire pressure gauge would be used to diagnose this. Check for binding in the steering system components by disconnecting components to verify the location of the binding.

- Bump steer: Bump steer is when the vehicle turns itself upon hitting a bump. This is caused by incorrect angles in the steering linkage due to a component being bent or an incorrectly positioned steering gear or rack and pinion. The steering linkage must follow the same arc as the suspension. Start with a visual inspection of the steering parts, and if necessary, check the alignment.

- Torque steer: Torque steer is a pull that occurs during heavy acceleration. It can be the result of unequal axle lengths as designed, which cannot be repaired by the technician. Compare this vehicle to a known good vehicle to ensure it is a design issue. Abnormal torque steer can result from inner or outer tie-rod ends that are worn. Loose, worn, or broken engine or transmission mounts or control arm bushings can also create this issue. Installing a compliance bushing incorrectly with the void facing the wrong way can also create torque steer. Be sure to look for shifting components under load.

- Steering return concerns: This condition is commonly referred to as memory steer. Memory steer can result from binding conditions in any pivot points in the steering or suspension system, including the ball joints, tie-rods, strut bearings, idler arm, binding steering gear, or rack and pinion. Or it can result from unbalanced power steering assist. It can also be caused by insufficient positive caster on the front wheels. Raise the vehicle wheels and turn the steering while observing components. Disconnecting components one by one may be necessary to find binding in swivel points such as ball joints, strut bearings, or tie-rod ends. If these methods do not uncover the issue, check the caster with an alignment machine.

- Noises: Noises can be tracked down through the use of a specialty tool called chassis ears. This tool involves microphones that can be placed at various locations on the vehicle and a set of earphones worn by the technician. The microphones can be selected one by one by the technician to pinpoint the noise. *Operation of this tool during a road test should be performed by another person and not the driver because using the tool can be distracting to the driver.* Some noises can be identified and located while steering the vehicle when it is raised on a lift. Listen and feel for any noises and vibrations. Just be very careful around moving and hot components.

Tools

The tools commonly used in diagnosing suspension or wheel alignment issues include:

- Wheel alignment machine: Used to measure and view alignment angles on a vehicle.
- Four-post alignment rack: Used to raise and level the vehicle off of the ground so you can align it.
- Turntables: Used on alignment racks so you can turn the front wheels to check caster angle.
- Wheel clamps and extensions: Used to hold alignment targets to the wheels.
- Specification charts: Used to ensure manufacturer-specified angles and measurements for vehicles.
- Workshop manuals or electronic information systems: Used to look up specifications and instructions for replacing parts on the vehicle.
- Specialty alignment tools: Used to align steering angles on a vehicle.
- Steering wheel holder: Used to keep steering wheel from turning when centering steering wheel during an alignment.
- Brake pedal depressor tool: Used to lock the brakes during caster sweep so wheels of vehicle cannot move.
- Steering angle sensor calibration tool or scan tool.
- Dial indicators: Used to measure play in ball joints.
- Pry bars: Used to pry parts to check for play.
- Measuring tapes and tools: The measuring tape is used to check ride height; other tools used as needed.
- Steering system pullers, such as pitman arm puller, tie-rod end puller, idler arm puller. Always use a puller on aluminum steering arms.
- Steering system tools, such as tie-rod splitter (commonly referred to as pickle fork).
- Various lift devices (e.g., jack): Used to raise vehicle off of the ground and safety stands to hold it there. These devices include the air jacks found on the alignment lift.
- Wheel chocks: Used to keep the vehicle from rolling on the rack.
- Electronic stethoscope: Used to locate unusual noises.

Diagnosing a Suspension System

The most common problem in the suspension system is play or looseness of the parts. Although many of the parts are designed with special connections that allow for movement to accommodate movement of the wheels, excessive play is actually a bad thing. Excessive play magnifies the feel of road imperfections and makes the steering less responsive to steering wheel input. Excessive play is potentially very damaging, as it causes wear on the connecting parts and tires. Naturally, any amount of play in a fixed part is problematic and is frequently a result of part failure. Remember, unwanted looseness in the suspension system can be extremely dangerous and should be corrected as soon as possible. In some cases, driving the vehicle should not be allowed until the repair is performed. Repair of excessive play typically means replacement of the loose part or parts. To perform diagnosis of loose components, refer to the manufacturer's service information for proper testing and follow the steps in the upcoming skill drills.

Testing Components of Electronically Controlled Suspension Systems Using a Scan Tool

Electronically controlled suspension systems are tested whenever a driver complains of a suspension problem or the warning light is on. Because it is computerized, diagnosis also requires the use of a scan tool. A diagnostic scan tool is the only way to see inside this type of suspension system and determine what problems exist. The scan tool can retrieve any diagnostic trouble codes (DTCs), as well as provide access to sensor data. In some cases, the scan tool can command the PCM to operate various components in the system so that you can check their operation and any circuit issues. Every manufacturer uses its own system, so it is best to use the service information from that manufacturer to diagnose any related customer concerns.

Unloading a Suspension for Measuring Play

Play in the suspension system can be damaging to other components or can be a major safety hazard on the road. Testing for play requires the proper technique for the results to be accurate. For play to be measured, the joint must be unloaded. This means the joint cannot be under compression or tension forces. In the case of suspension ball joints, the joint cannot be supporting the weight of the vehicle or the force from the vehicle spring when measuring the play.

The method of unloading the ball joints depends on the layout of the suspension. On a type 1 suspension where the coil spring or torsion bar is pushing against the lower control arm, a floor jack must be placed under the lower control arm and the wheel raised off the ground. The weight of the vehicle is thus supported through the spring to the control arm and then the jack, leaving the

ball joint only supporting the wheel, tire, spindle, and upper control arm. In this case, a pry bar can then be used to pry the wheel up and down while measuring the ball joint play. The upper ball joint can be tested by pushing in and out on the top of the tire and measuring any play in the joint.

Some manufacturers specify that their type 1 suspensions be tested with the suspension system left hanging. The vehicle would be supported by the frame in this case. Manufacturers may also specify that only hand pressure be applied when checking for play in the joints. Check the service information before testing a particular vehicle.

On a type 2 suspension where the spring is on the top control arm, it is best to fit a wooden block between the upper control arm and the frame, so that the control arm and spring will be held in a position as close to normal ride height as possible. This method allows measurement of the play in the joint where maximum wear occurs. The top of the tire can again be pushed in and out, and measurement of play in the joint can be taken.

In a MacPherson strut suspension with only a lower control arm, testing is performed by raising the vehicle by the frame and allowing the suspension to hang free. This approach tests the point in a position that it does not normally operate in, but if there is play, it will likely still be evident. Since it is a follower joint, most manufacturers say if it has any noticeable play, the joint will need to be replaced.

Be sure to test the ball joint correctly. Refer to the manufacturer's instructions and specifications on how to test these joints, as they are not all tested the same way and may require different tools.

To measure play in the suspension system, follow the steps in **SKILL DRILL 29-1**:

1. Jack up the vehicle and place safety stands under the control arms.

2. Place a dial indicator on the lower control arm and vertically against the steering knuckle. **(Photo 1)**

3. Place a pry bar under the tire and pry it upward, watching the dial indicator reading as you pry and release. Record the total amount of movement in the joint and compare to the manufacturer's specifications. **(Photo 2)**

4. Rock the top of the tire in and out, watching for any play in the upper ball joint and compare to specifications. **(Photo 3)**

To measure play in the suspension system, follow the steps in **SKILL DRILL 29-2**:

1. Obtain a properly sized block of wood to fit between the upper control arm and the frame.

2 Place the block of wood between the upper control arm and frame, so it is secure. (**Photo 1**)

3 Raise the vehicle by lifting the body using the specified lift points so that the tire is a few inches off the ground. Support the body with a jack stand.

4 Place a dial indicator on the upper control arm and vertically against the steering knuckle. (**Photo 2**)

5 Place a pry bar under the tire and pry it upward, watching the dial indicator reading as you pry and release. Record the total amount of movement in the joint and compare to the manufacturer's specifications. (**Photo 3**)

6 Rock the bottom of the tire in and out, watching for play in the lower ball joint and compare to specifications. (**Photo 4**)

SKILL DRILL | 29-1 | Loaded Lower Ball Joint

1 Place a dial indicator on the lower control arm and vertically against the steering knuckle.

2 Place a pry bar under the tire and pry it upward, watching the dial indicator reading as you pry and release. Record the total amount of movement in the joint and compare to the manufacturer's specifications.

3 Rock the tire in and out at the top, watching for any play in the upper ball joint and compare to specifications.

SKILL DRILL | 29-2 | Loaded Upper Ball Joint

1 Obtain a properly sized block of wood to fit between the upper control arm and the frame. Place the block of wood between the upper control arm and frame, so it is secure.

2 Place a dial indicator on the upper control arm and vertically against the steering knuckle.

3 Place a pry bar under the tire and pry it upward, watching the dial indicator reading as you pry and release. Record the total amount of movement in the joint and compare to specifications.

SKILL DRILL **29-2** **Loaded Upper Ball Joint, continued**

4 Rock the bottom of the tire in and out, watching for any play in the lower ball joint and compare to specifications.

Diagnosing Suspension Noise

A noise that is heard coming from the front end whenever a vehicle hits a bump could indicate a problem with a component of the suspension system. Testing the vehicle while turning and hitting bumps may be necessary to pinpoint the source of the noise. Be sure you have complete information on the customer's concern, such as if the vehicle only makes the noise when cold while going over bumps. In this case, test-driving over bumps while the vehicle is hot will probably not reveal the noise. Suspension system noise can be related to bushings that are worn or broken, ball joints that are worn, spring isolators that have broken or fallen out of place, loose bolts, faulty strut mount or bearing, bushing or joint that has lost its lubrication, or dirt that has gotten into a pivoting point. To diagnose this concern, the use of an assistant to drive the vehicle may be necessary as you listen from different points inside the vehicle to pinpoint if it is a front suspension or rear suspension issue. The use of chassis ears can provide a quick solution to where the noise is originating. Using an assistant allows one person to focus on finding the problem while the other focuses on safe driving.

To diagnose a suspension noise that can be duplicated while not driving, bounce the vehicle up and down while listening for noise. If there are noises, confirm where the noise is coming from. Have an assistant bounce the vehicle while you check for the noise under the vehicle. You can listen by ear or with a stethoscope, or you can feel by hand for vibrations

or clunks. Listen around sway bar bushings, control arm bushings, springs, shock absorbers, component bolts, body panels, steering gear, the MacPherson strut mount, and ball joints. Inspect the component making the noise for damage and replace if necessary. If the noise is found at a component bolt, check the bolt to see if it is loose and retighten to the manufacturer's specifications.

Body Sway

To diagnose body sway, first test-drive the vehicle to verify the customer's concern. Because you will have to swerve from side to side to perform the test, drive the vehicle in a safe area with little to no traffic, such as in a large empty parking lot. While driving the vehicle, move the steering wheel back and forth to make the vehicle swerve slightly, this will shift the vehicle weight from side to side. Observe how much body sway occurs. It may be necessary to compare the sway of the vehicle to a like vehicle to ensure that the condition is not normal. If there is excessive sway, and the suspension is not electronically controlled, then check the vehicle's front and rear (if equipped) sway bar system. Inspect the sway bar bushings, brackets, and link bushings. Bushings should not be cracked and should have little give when pried against. Replacement of faulty components will be necessary.

If the vehicle is equipped with an electronically controlled suspension, it is possible that the system is not providing the active control needed to dampen body sway. In this case, the electronically controlled system will need to be checked for DTCs and diagnosed according to the manufacturer's specified procedure. This can be found in the service information.

Ride Height

The ride height of a vehicle can only be measured if it has matching tires, which are properly inflated, and no additional weight in the vehicle. Once these issues are taken care of, the ride height can be measured as specified by the service information. Most ride height specifications require the measurement to be within half of an inch side to side. If the measured ride height is greater or less than specified, the vehicle is not in correct alignment and may be causing, or contributing to the customer's concern. Check for bent or sagging vehicle springs, bent spring mounting points, a leaking gas pressurized shock absorber, a faulty electronically controlled suspension system, or a bent frame or axle. The use of a measuring tape from a fixed point on the frame or body of the vehicle to the component in question can help determine the cause of improper ride height. If the ride height issue is related to the coil or leaf spring, then replacement of the spring(s) may be necessary. If the ride height issue is on a vehicle equipped with a torsion bar system, then you may be able to adjust the torsion bar so that ride height is returned to specifications.

To perform ride height diagnosis, follow the steps in **SKILL DRILL 29-3**:

1. Refer to the manufacturer's service information for correct measurement points and specifications. **(Photo 1)**

2. Check for properly sized, matching, and inflated tires. Correct any issues found. **(Photo 2)**

3. Check the vehicle for any nonstandard loads in the trunk or luggage area. Remove them temporarily while measuring ride height. **(Photo 3)**

4. Measure from the specified points, such as from frame to ground on all four corners of the vehicle, and compare measurements to the specifications. **(Photo 4)**

5. Inspect for bent components or a weak or broken spring if any measurements are not correct. If working with a torsion bar suspension, adjustment of ride height may need to be performed to correct the condition. **(Photo 5)**

6. Refer to the manufacturer's service information for proper adjustment of ride height. Remember that any time ride height is changed, a wheel alignment will need to be performed also.

Inspecting the Shock Absorbers

Shock absorbers and struts are located near each wheel and dampen body movement from bumps. Common reasons for testing the shock absorbers are unusual tire wear, such as having a cupped appearance. Also, the driver may complain of a soft or bouncy ride. In some cases, a shock absorber can bind up, creating a very stiff ride.

If a vehicle has adjustable shock absorbers, make sure the shock absorber adjustments are the same for the left- and right-hand side. Some shock absorbers contain

SKILL DRILL 29-3 Ride Height

1. Refer to the manufacturer's service information for correct measurement points and specifications.
2. Check for properly sized, matching, and inflated tires. Correct any issues found.
3. Check the vehicle for any nonstandard loads in the trunk or luggage area. Remove them temporarily while measuring ride height.

SKILL DRILL   29-3   Ride Height, continued

4. Measure from points specified, such as from frame to ground on all four corners of the vehicle, and compare measurements to specifications.

5. Inspect for bent components or a weak or broken spring if any measurements are not correct. If working with a torsion bar suspension, adjustment of ride height may need to be performed to correct the condition.

---

pressurized gas, which can leak out, causing uneven ride height and shock absorber performance issues. Many of today's vehicles are equipped with a strut-type suspension instead of conventional shock absorbers, but testing either type of system involves the same procedure. Basically, while the vehicle is stationary, push up and down on a strong point at each corner of the vehicle (not the fenders as they can be dented) several times, and watch how the vehicle responds after you release it. Typically, if you let go at the bottom, a good shock will allow the corner of the vehicle to rise and then settle back into position on most vehicles. On some with softer suspensions, it may allow the corner of the vehicle to rise, fall, and rise back into position. Any more oscillations than that indicate worn shock absorbers.

To check shock absorbers, follow the steps in **SKILL DRILL 29-4**:

1. The simplest form of suspension test is known as a bounce test. Carefully bounce the corner of the vehicle. Place your weight on a bumper and begin to bounce the vehicle until it reaches its maximum amount of travel produced by your weight. Stop bouncing at the bottom of the bounce and watch what happens. If the vehicle rebounds and compresses more than twice, you will need to replace

the shock absorbers. If the shock absorbers are performing well, the vehicle will rebound once or one and a half times, then slowly return to its original position. (**Photo 1**)

2. Pay particular attention to the top strut mounting during the bounce test. Place your hand on top of the mounting during the bounce test. Any noise or movement in the mounting could indicate the need to replace the strut mount. If you do feel movement, hear noise, or see signs of leakage, report it to your supervisor.

3. While driving, the same test can be performed by stopping the vehicle suddenly from a very low speed. If the vehicle "bounces" up and down a couple of times when coming to rest, you need to replace the shock absorbers. (**Photo 2**)

4. Visually inspect the shock absorber mounting points for security and corrosion, and note any wet-looking patches on the sides of the shock absorbers. This is a common indicator that the strut or shock absorber needs replacing because of a fluid leak. Slight dampness on the shock is typically normal, but a drip on the shock is not normal and indicates leaking. (**Photo 3**)

SKILL DRILL | 29-4 | Inspecting the Shock Absorbers

1. Place your weight on a bumper and begin to bounce the vehicle until it reaches its maximum amount of travel produced by your weight. Stop bouncing at the bottom of the bounce. If the vehicle rebounds and compresses more than twice, replace the shock absorbers. If the shock absorbers are performing well, the vehicle will rebound once or one and a half times, then return to its original position.

2. Pay particular attention to the top strut mounting during the bounce test. Place your hand on top of the mounting during the bounce test. Any noise or looseness in the mounting could indicate the need to replace the mount. While driving, the same test can be performed by stopping the vehicle suddenly from a very low speed. If the vehicle "bounces" up and down when coming to rest, you need to replace the shock absorbers.

3. Visually inspect the shock absorber mounting points for security and corrosion, and note any wet-looking patches on the sides of the shock absorbers. Slight dampness on the shock is typically normal, but a drip on the shock is not normal and indicates leaking.

Safety

> To prevent personal injury, do not puncture or incinerate gas-charged shock absorbers.

▶ Maintenance and Repair

Tools

Many of the tools applied in servicing the suspension system were listed previously with the tools used for diagnosing suspension complaints. In addition, the following tools may be used in maintenance and repair procedures:

- Coil spring compressor: Used to compress coil springs during removal and installation.
- Scan tool: Used to check for codes in the vehicle's computer.
- Spring compressor/tools: Used for changing coil springs.
- Ball joint press tool: Used to remove and replace press-fit ball joints.

- Pickle forks: Used to separate ball joints, but ruins the grease seal.
- Air chisel: Air-operated hammer that can accept a variety of bits including chisels and punches.
- Strut compressor: Used to compress MacPherson struts to remove the coil spring.
- Strut servicing kit: Used for changing coil springs on struts.
- Universal strut nut wrench kit: Used to remove a strut.
- 24-mm strut rod socket: Used to remove a strut.

Removing, Inspecting, and Installing Stabilizer Components

The stabilizer components (sway bar) help prevent body roll when cornering. While the stabilizer bar itself rarely gives any trouble, the rubber bushings on the bar and links wear out. This usually results in increased body roll, as well as a clunking noise in the suspension. The stabilizer components should be checked whenever a vehicle is brought into the shop because of handling concerns or suspension-related noises. Before beginning the procedure, research the manufacturer's procedure and specifications for removing and inspecting the stabilizer components.

Note: We will be using the same vehicle to perform most of the SLA-related tasks. Also, we will address each task as a sequence, as if you were doing the entire series of tasks, one after the other. So the disassembly of each component will assume the previously removed components have already been removed. And reassembly will be held off until all of the related tasks are completed.

To remove and inspect the stabilizer bar bushings and mount brackets, follow the steps in SKILL DRILL 29-5:

1. Safely raise the vehicle on a hoist, or use a jack and place safety stands under the frame.
2. Remove the bolts holding the stabilizer bar bushing mount brackets; inspect for cracks in the brackets. **(Photo 1)**
3. Remove the bushings by hand.
4. Visually inspect the rubber bushings for cracks, brittleness, softness, or wear. **(Photo 2)**

To remove and inspect the sway bar end links, follow the steps in SKILL DRILL 29-6:

1. Safely raise the vehicle on a hoist, or use a jack and place safety stands under the frame.
2. Remove the nut holding the stabilizer bar link. **(Photo 1)**
3. Remove the link by hand. **(Photo 2)**
4. Visually inspect the rubber link grommets for cracks, softness, brittleness, or wear. Repeat on the other link. **(Photo 3)**

Removing and Replacing Shock Absorbers

Worn shock absorbers will cause the vehicle to ride poorly, especially on rough roads. When the tires encounter a bump in the road, a faulty shock absorber cannot dampen the spring oscillations to promote a smoother ride. The suspension will continue to rebound and bounce. This action is then transferred to the vehicle frame and ultimately to the driver and passengers. Loose or damaged shock absorbers can be distinguished by abnormal, and in some case, loud and unusual noises.

SKILL DRILL 29-5 Removing and Inspecting the Stabilizer Bar Bushings and Mount Brackets

1. Raise the vehicle on a hoist, or use a jack and place safety stands under the frame. Remove the bolts holding the stabilizer bar bushing mount brackets and inspect the brackets for cracks.

2. Remove the bushings by hand. Inspect the rubber in the bushings for cracks, brittleness, softness, or wear.

SKILL DRILL | 29-6 | Removing and Inspecting Sway Bar Links

1. Raise the vehicle on a hoist, or use a jack and place safety stands under the frame. Remove the nut holding the stabilizer bar link.

2. Remove the link by hand.

3. Inspect the rubber link grommets for cracks, softness, brittleness, or wear. Repeat on the other link.

Visually inspect the shock absorbers for any signs of deterioration, such as oil leaking from the shock absorber shaft seal or damaged body. A slight oil film on the shock is considered normal. The mounting bushings must also be carefully inspected for splits and deteriorated or missing rubber mountings. The mounting supports must be checked for good security and tightness.

Many shock absorbers come from the factory pressurized with gas to reduce aeration of the fluid when operating. This pressure tends to expand the shock absorber, making it difficult to install. For this reason, pressurized shocks come compressed with a band holding them together. It is usually easiest to install one end, or in some cases, both ends of the shock before cutting the band.

On some suspension systems (typically nonindependent suspensions), the shocks provide the limit for full extension. This means the shocks may be holding the axle up when the shock is fully extended. In this case, removing the shock could cause the axle to slip, pinching fingers or causing the vehicle to shift on the hoist. It is always good practice to place stands under the axle to support it while the shocks are being removed and installed.

> ### TECHNICIAN TIP
>
> Shock absorbers use rubber bushings to isolate them from the vehicle body. Always replace these bushings when replacing the shock absorbers.

> ### TECHNICIAN TIP
>
> Always replace shock absorbers in pairs so the suspension has the same characteristics for the left and right sides. Shock absorbers are rated for "bump" or "jounce," the rate at which they compress, and "rebound," the rate at which they expand.

If a shock absorber must be replaced, it is industry practice to replace them as pairs, thus ensuring the ride equilibrium of the vehicle. To replace a shock absorber, follow the steps in **SKILL DRILL 29-7**:

1. Safely raise the vehicle on a lift, or raise it with a jack and support it with safety stands under the frame.

2. Remove the upper bolts or stud holding the shocks in place with a socket and box-end wrench. If the top end uses a stud mount, you may have to use a wrench to hold the top of the stud while you unthread the nut. **(Photo 1)**

SKILL DRILL | 29-7 | Replacing a Shock Absorber

1 Raise the vehicle on a lift, or raise it with a jack and support it with safety stands under the frame. Remove the upper bolts holding the shocks in place with a socket and box-end wrench.

2 Remove the lower bolts holding the shock in place.

3 Pull the shock out by hand. Repeat on the other side.

3 Remove the lower bolts holding the shocks in place. (**Photo 2**)

4 Pull the shock out by hand. Repeat on the other side. (**Photo 3**)

Removing, Inspecting, and Installing SLA Suspension System Coil Springs and Spring Insulators

Coil springs absorb the road force by twisting, which compresses them. Whenever a driver complains of the way the vehicle sits or an issue related to the ride quality, the coil springs should be inspected for wear and the vehicle's ride height measured.

Coil springs used in vehicles store very large amounts of energy; thus, extreme caution is required when removing and installing them. Always use an adequately rated spring compressor that is in good working condition when working on a spring. Also, never stand in the direction the spring can fly, should something slip, which is generally in a position near where the tire sits, and beyond. Since the spring can be mounted on either the lower control arm or the upper control arm, you will need to unload it in the same manner as the same type of ball joint. Failure to follow service information can result in serious injury

or death. In this skill drill, we will work with the spring located on the lower control arm.

To remove and inspect SLA suspension system coil springs and spring insulators, follow the steps in **SKILL DRILL 29-8**:

1 Following the previous skill drills, remove the shock absorber and the stabilizer bar end links.

2 Place a spring compressor on the inside or outside of the coil spring to keep the pressure of the spring contained. (**Photo 1**)

3 Place a jacking device under the lower control arm that is being dismantled; maintain pressure on the lower control arm. (**Photo 2**)

4 Remove the cotter pin and loosen the nut from the upper ball joint. (**Photo 3**)

5 Using a ball joint separator or pickle fork, break loose the ball joint stud taper from the steering knuckle, and remove the nut. This is the step where spring pressure is being contained only by the compressor. Extreme caution must be used at this point. (**Photo 4**)

6 Slowly and carefully lower the hydraulic jack supporting the lower control arm to allow the coil spring to be removed. Remember,

SKILL DRILL | 29-8 | Removing and Inspecting SLA Suspension System Coil Springs and Spring Insulators

1. Following the previous skill drills, remove the shock absorber and the stabilizer bar end links. Place a spring compressor on the inside or outside of the coil spring to keep the pressure of the spring contained.

2. Place a jacking device under the lower control arm that is being dismantled; maintain pressure on the lower control arm.

3. Remove the cotter pin and loosen the nut from the upper ball joint.

4. Using a ball joint separator or pickle fork, break loose the ball joint stud taper from the steering knuckle, and remove the nut.

5. Slowly and carefully lower the hydraulic jack supporting the lower control arm to allow the coil spring to be removed. (Extreme caution must be used here so the spring compressor does not slip and injure you.)

6. Release the spring compressor slowly. Clean and inspect the ball joint stud hole in the steering knuckle boss.

the coil spring contains high pressure in its compressed state. Extreme care must be taken at this point so the spring compressor does not slip and allow the spring to fly out and hurt you. **(Photo 5)**

7. Release the spring compressor slowly.

8. Clean and inspect the ball joint stud hole in the steering knuckle boss. **(Photo 6)**

9. Inspect the spring insulator for distortion or cracking. If noted, replacement is necessary. Repeat on the other side of the vehicle.

Removing, Inspecting, and Installing the Steering Knuckle Assembly

The steering knuckle serves as the pivot point for the wheels. Since they rotate on ball joints or tie-rod ends, they are not subject to much wear, but they can be damaged in an accident, requiring replacement. It is more likely that you will remove one in order to access other pieces of the steering assembly. This skill drill will assume a steering knuckle removal on the vehicle in the previous skill drill. Remember, coil springs are under extreme pressure! Follow the service information to correctly remove any steering knuckle.

To remove and inspect a steering knuckle assembly, follow the steps in **SKILL DRILL 29-9**:

1. Disconnect the lower ball joint, and remove the spring as in the previous skill drills.
2. Disconnect the upper ball joint in the same manner as the lower ball joint. **(Photo 1)**
3. Remove the steering knuckle from the ball joint stud. **(Photo 2)**
4. Inspect the tapered portion of the stud for any bright, worn metal, which would indicate a worn steering knuckle boss.
5. Inspect the steering knuckle for any signs of wear or visible signs of bending or twisting. **(Photo 3)**

Removing and Inspecting Upper and Lower Control Arms and Components

Control arms themselves do not generally wear out, but the control arm bushings and ball joints do, so you will likely need to remove them to service those components. However, some manufacturers do not sell bushings and ball joints separately, so you may have to purchase the entire control arm and replace it as a unit. Also, control arms can become bent or damaged as the result of a collision or driving through a deep pothole, so control arms do need to be inspected for damage. Lastly, some customers request that the height of their vehicles be lifted or lowered, which can involve modifying suspension components such as springs and control arms with new upgraded ones. Obviously this will change the ride height, alignment, and handling of the vehicle. Only very experienced and highly trained technicians should diagnose and repair these vehicles.

The vehicle used in this skill drill has a coil spring on the lower control arm. Not all vehicles are the same. Refer to the manufacturer's service information to correctly service the vehicle.

To remove, inspect, and install upper and lower control arms and components, follow the steps in **SKILL DRILL 29-10**:

1. Remove the coil spring and steering knuckle by following the steps in previous skill drills.
2. Loosen the bolts holding the upper control arm in place. Note that there might be shim packs held in by the bolts. If so, tape them together in their packs and label their positions. **(Photo 1)**
3. Remove the lower control arm by removing the bolts holding the control arm in place. As you

SKILL DRILL | **29-9** | **Removing and Inspecting the Steering Knuckle Assembly**

1. Disconnect the lower ball joint, and remove the spring as in the previous skill drills. Disconnect the upper ball joint in the same manner as the lower ball joint.

2. Remove the steering knuckle from the ball joint stud. Inspect the tapered portion of the stud for any bright, worn metal, which would indicate a worn steering knuckle boss.

3. Inspect the steering knuckle for any signs of wear or visible signs of bending or twisting.

dismantle the system components, carry out a constant inspection of the parts being removed. Doing so will aid you when you need to order replacement parts. **(Photo 2)**

4 Inspect the upper and lower control arm for wear or damage. If the control arm bushings show signs of excessive wear or deterioration of the bushing material, they will need to be replaced.

5 Replace the worn bushings in the upper and/or lower control arm. Replacement of control arm bushings can be performed two ways—with a hydraulic press with correctly sized press tools or with an air chisel. Be careful using an air chisel; damage to the control arm can result, such as gouging the mounting surface of the bushing if you slip with the chisel. **(Photo 3)**

SKILL DRILL | **29-10** | **Removing, Inspecting, and Installing Upper and Lower Control Arms and Components**

1 Remove the coil spring and steering knuckle by following the steps in previous skill drills. Loosen the bolts holding the upper control arm in place.

2 Remove the lower control arm by removing the bolts holding the control arm in place. As you dismantle the system components, inspect the parts being removed to help you when you need to order replacement parts.

3 Inspect the upper and lower control arm for wear or damage. If the control arm bushings show signs of excessive wear or deterioration of the bushing material, they will need to be replaced. Replace the worn bushings in the upper and/or lower control arm with a hydraulic press or with an air chisel.

4 *Press method:* Place the control arm in a hydraulic press supported so the bushing is level to the press head. Using the correct-sized adapter, press the bushing out.

5 Using the press, install the new bushing into the control arm. Be careful to start the bushing in straight or you could bend the control arm. Press it in until the flange bottoms out.

6 *Air chisel method:* Install the control arm in a vise. Use an air chisel to work the bushing out. Be careful to not gouge the mating surface of the control arm.

SKILL DRILL 29-10 — Removing, Inspecting, and Installing Upper and Lower Control Arms and Components, continued

7. Using the air hammer, drive the new bushing into place, making sure it is fully seated.

6. *Press method:* Place the control arm in a hydraulic press supported so the bushing is level to the press head. Using the correct-sized adapter, press the bushing out. **(Photo 4)**

7. Using the press, install the new bushing into the control arm. Be careful to start the bushing in straight or you could bend the control arm. Press it in until the flange bottoms out. **(Photo 5)**

8. *Air chisel method:* Install the control arm in a vise. Use an air chisel to work the bushing out. Be careful to not gouge the mating surface of the control arm. **(Photo 6)**

9. Using the air hammer, drive the new bushing into place, making sure it is fully seated. **(Photo 7)**

TECHNICIAN TIP

Remember that modifying a vehicle by raising or lowering the vehicle may be illegal in some states and will affect alignment angles.

Removing, Inspecting, and Installing Upper and Lower Ball Joints

The ball joint connects the upper and lower control arms to the steering gear. Over time, these parts will wear and

must be replaced. Removal of ball joints varies from vehicle to vehicle. Refer to the manufacturer's service information for the correct procedures. This skill drill uses the coil-spring suspension with two control arms and is the more dangerous type that a technician will service.

To remove, inspect, and install upper and lower ball joints, follow the steps in **SKILL DRILL 29-11**:

1. Remove the control arms following the previous skill drills. Ball joints are held into the control arm either by a press fit or by rivets or bolts.

2. *Press-fit style:* Support the control arm with the correct adapter so there is room for the ball joint to be pressed out of it. **(Photo 1)**

3. Press the joint out of the control arm. **(Photo 2)**

4. Inspect the bore in the control arm to make sure it isn't cracked or damaged. **(Photo 3)**

5. Turn the control arm over, and support it so the ball joint has room to be installed. **(Photo 4)**

6. Press the ball joint into the control arm until it bottoms out. **(Photo 5)**

7. *Riveted style:* Mount the control arm in a vise with the rivet heads facing up or outward. **(Photo 6)**

8. Use an air chisel to chisel off the rivet heads, or use a drill to drill approximately three-quarters the diameter of the rivet head to carefully drill the head of the rivet off.

| SKILL DRILL | 29-11 | Removing, Inspecting, and Installing Upper and Lower Ball Joints |

1 Remove the control arms as in the previous skill drills. Ball joints are held into the control arm either by a press fit or by rivets or bolts. *Press-fit style:* Support the control arm with the correct adapter so there is room for the ball joint to be pressed out of it.

2 Press the joint out of the control arm.

3 Inspect the bore in the control arm to make sure it isn't cracked or damaged.

4 Turn the control arm over, and support it so the ball joint has room to be installed.

5 Press the ball joint into the control arm until it bottoms out.

6 *Riveted style:* Mount the control arm in a vise with the rivet heads facing up or outward.

7 Use an air chisel to chisel off the rivet heads, or use a drill to drill approximately three-quarters the diameter of the rivet head to carefully drill the head of the rivet off. Use a hammer and a punch to tap the rest of the rivet out of the ball joint and control arm.

8 Inspect the holes, and remove any burrs with a file. Install the new ball joint with nuts and bolts, and tighten to the proper torque.

9 Install the lower control arm in position, and torque the bolts to specification.

SKILL DRILL | **29-11** | **Removing, Inspecting, and Installing Upper and Lower Ball Joints, continued**

10 Install the upper control arm in position, and screw in the bolts finger tight. Insert shim packs, if equipped. Torque the bolts to specifications.

11 Place the steering knuckle in place on the lower ball joint stud. Finger-tighten the ball joint nut.

12 Install the spring compressor on the spring so that it can be installed in the vehicle between the lower control arm and the frame.

13 Position the spring on the lower control arm, and use a jack to hold it in place.

14 Continue to raise it while guiding the steering knuckle over the upper ball joint stud. Install the nut on the upper ball joint stud finger tight.

15 Use a cotter pin tool to turn the ball joint stud to align the cotter pin hole lengthwise to the vehicle so the cotter pin will be easy to install.

16 Torque both ball joints to specifications, and install the cotter pins.

17 Remove the spring compressor.

18 Install the new washers and bushings onto the new shock, if not already installed. Place the shock in the proper position by hand, and install the other bushings, if needed.

19 Install and properly torque the bolts or nuts to hold the shock in place using a torque wrench. Install the tie-rod end into the steering knuckle, torque the nut, and secure with a cotter pin.

20 Install new stabilizer bar bushings, placing the bushing around the bar.

21 Install bolts in the mounting bracket and tighten to specifications.

22 Install the stabilizer link to the control arm by assembling it onto the stabilizer bar and control arms with the spacer, washers, and rubber grommets installed in their proper places.

23 Install the nut on the threaded end of the link, then tighten to the manufacturer's specifications.

24 Reinstall the rotor assembly if removed.

25 Reinstall the brake caliper by placing the caliper over the rotor and tightening to the proper torque.

26 Jack up the lower control arm so the spring is compressed to its normal height, and properly torque the control arm bolts to specifications.

27 Install the wheel and snugly tighten the lug nuts. Lower the vehicle and torque the wheel nuts to specifications.

9 Use a hammer and a punch to tap the rest of the rivet out of the ball joint and control arm. **(Photo 7)**

10 Inspect the holes, and remove any burrs with a file.

11 Install the new ball joint with nuts and bolts, and tighten to the proper torque. **(Photo 8)**

12 Install the lower control arm in position, and torque the bolts to specifications. **(Photo 9)**

13 Install the upper control arm in position, and screw in the bolts finger tight. Remember to insert any shim packs, if equipped. Torque the bolts to specifications. **(Photo 10)**

14 Place the steering knuckle in place on the lower ball joint stud. Finger-tighten the ball joint nut. **(Photo 11)**

15 Install the spring compressor on the spring so that it can be installed in the vehicle between the lower control arm and the frame. Be careful to position the compressor so that it will not be in the way when the spring is being installed, and so that you can remove it once installed. **(Photo 12)**

16 Position the spring on the lower control arm, and use a jack to hold it in place. **(Photo 13)**

17 Continue to raise it while guiding the steering knuckle over the upper ball joint stud. Install the nut on the upper ball joint stud finger tight. **(Photo 14)**

18 Use a cotter pin tool to turn the ball joint stud to align the cotter pin hole lengthwise to the vehicle so the cotter pin will be easy to install. **(Photo 15)**

19 Torque both ball joints to specifications and install the cotter pins. If a self-locking nut is used, it is sometimes difficult to tighten the nut because the stud tends to rotate, so you may have to put more pressure on the ball joint by raising the jack a little further. **(Photo 16)**

20 Remove the spring compressor. **(Photo 17)**

21 Install the new washers and bushings onto the new shock, if not already installed. Place the shock in the proper position by hand, and install the other bushings, if needed. **(Photo 18)**

22 Install and properly torque the bolts or nuts to hold the shock absorber in place using a torque wrench.

23 Install the tie-rod end into the steering knuckle, torque in place, and secure with a new cotter pin. **(Photo 19)**

24 Install new stabilizer bar bushings, placing the bushing around the bar. **(Photo 20)**

25 Install bolts in the mounting bracket, and tighten to the manufacturer's specifications. **(Photo 21)**

26 Install the stabilizer link to the control arm by assembling it onto the stabilizer bar and control arms with the spacer, washers, and rubber grommets installed in their proper places. **(Photo 22)**

27 Install the nut on the threaded end of the link, then tighten to the manufacturer's specifications. **(Photo 23)**

28 Reinstall the rotor assembly if removed. **(Photo 24)**

29 Reinstall the brake caliper by placing the caliper over the rotor and tightening to the proper torque. **(Photo 25)**

30 Jack up the lower control arm so the spring is compressed to its normal height, and properly torque the control arm bolts to the manufacturer's specifications. **(Photo 26)**

31 Install the wheel and snugly tighten the lug nuts. Lower the vehicle and torque the wheel nuts to the manufacturer's specification. **(Photo 27)**

Lubricating Suspension and Steering Systems

To function properly, the suspension and steering system must be lubricated. On most modern vehicles, the joints are sealed and lubricated for life, so there are no grease fittings present. However, some vehicles do have grease fittings installed on them, either from the factory or on aftermarket parts. If grease fittings are present, then lubrication must be performed. Lubrication keeps the parts from rubbing and wearing on each other, which extends their life.

To lubricate a suspension system and a steering system, follow the steps in **SKILL DRILL 29-12**:

1 Determine the location of lubricating points. Check the shop service information to determine where the grease points are and the type of grease required. The service information will also indicate which components have a lube fitting or if an auxiliary lube fitting has to be temporarily fitted for the function. The factory parts may have been replaced with aftermarket parts, so always be on the lookout for grease zerks. **(Photo 1)**

2 To start the lubrication job, clean each of the lubrication fittings and the grease gun nozzle by wiping them with a clean rag. This should be done before you attach the nozzle to any of the fittings. In some instances, you may need to remove a component's plug and temporarily install a lubrication fitting. After the component has been lubricated, you must reinstall the original plug. Cleaning the fitting ensures that you do not push any external dirt into the joint. **(Photo 2)**

SKILL DRILL | 29-12 | Lubricating Suspension and Steering Systems

1. Determine the location of lubricating points. Check the shop service manual to determine where the grease points are and the type of grease required. Also look to see if any aftermarket grease fittings are installed. If so, grease them.

2. Clean each of the lubrication fittings and the grease gun nozzle by wiping them with a clean rag. You may need to remove a component's plugs and temporarily install a lubrication fitting. After the component has been lubricated, reinstall the original plug.

3. Push the grease gun nozzle fully over the fitting. It should snap into place. Add enough grease to see the seal or rubber boot rise slightly. Do not overfill a lubricated joint with grease.

4. If the fitting is clean and will not take grease, remove the grease zerk and check for blockage. If found, the fitting must be replaced with a new fitting of the same size and angle, and the joint relubricated.

5. Remove the nozzle from the fitting and wipe away any excess grease from it. Repeat the procedure until all the appropriate joints have been lubricated.

6. After you have completed lubricating all the appropriate joints and cleaned off any excess grease, attach a static cling sticker to the windshield, or reset the maintenance reminder system. Lower the vehicle and remove it from the lifting device.

3. Push the grease gun nozzle over the fitting. The nozzle must completely cover the fitting to ensure that the pressure of the gun forces the grease through the fitting into the joint. Add enough grease to see the seal or rubber boot rise slightly. Under no circumstances should you overfill a lubricated joint with grease. Doing so can rupture the seal or rubber boot or bellows. Make sure the grease does not leak out from around the nozzle end. If it does, check that the fitting has been properly cleaned, so as to allow the nozzle to go all the way onto the fitting. **(Photo 3)**

4. If the fitting is clean and will not take grease, remove the grease nipple and check for blockage. If a blockage is found, the fitting must be replaced with a new fitting of the same size and angle, and the joint relubricated. Remove the nozzle from the fitting and wipe away any excess grease from

it. Repeat the procedure until all the appropriate joints have been lubricated. (**Photos 4 and 5**)

5 After you have completed lubricating all the appropriate joints and cleaned off any excess grease, it may be appropriate to attach a static cling window sticker to the windshield, or reset the maintenance reminder system. This will tell the owner when the service was carried out and when the vehicle could be due for future service. Lower the vehicle and remove it from the lifting device. (**Photo 6**)

> **TECHNICIAN TIP**
>
> Clean lubricating equipment very carefully. If you don't thoroughly clean the fitting or nozzle before pumping the grease into the fitting, dirt could be forced into the component. Any dirt entering a component will cause premature failure.

Removing, Inspecting, and Installing the Strut Cartridge or Assembly

When a vehicle arrives in the shop with chopped tire wear or if the driver complains of ride comfort problems, the parts of the strut assembly should be checked. Some vehicles have a strut housing that has a replaceable strut insert cartridge, while others are one piece and the entire housing is replaced. In a strut with a strut insert, some manufacturers fill the housing with a lightweight oil to allow heat from dampening to be transferred to the outer housing more efficiently. Follow the manufacturer's instructions regarding oil type and the amount to use when replacing inserts. Be sure to follow manufacturer's service information to replace struts on the vehicle you are working on. This skill drill uses a vehicle with a replaceable strut cartridge insert.

To remove the strut assembly, follow the steps in **SKILL DRILL 29-13**:

SKILL DRILL | 29-13 | Removing the Strut Assembly, the Strut Coil Spring, the Insulators, or the Upper Strut Bearing Mount

1 Using your hand, push down on one corner of the front bumper continuously until the front of the vehicle is bouncing. When at the bottom, remove your hand and stop pushing. In most vehicles, the corner of the vehicle will rise and the settle into place. A vehicle with softer suspension may rise, fall, and rise to its settling point. If the vehicle bounces more than that, the strut needs to be replaced.

2 Loosen the lug nuts one turn if removing by hand.

3 Safely raise and support the vehicle on a hoist or on jack stands.

SKILL DRILL | 29-13 | Removing the Strut Assembly, the Strut Coil Spring, the Insulators, or the Upper Strut Bearing Mount, continued

4 Remove the lug nuts and then take off the wheels.

5 Remove the disc brake caliper, and wire it so it does not hang by its brake hose.

6 Remove the bolts holding the top of the strut to the strut tower (not the center strut bolt).

> **TECHNICIAN TIP**
>
> If you are to remove the shock absorbers, make sure the vehicle suspension is supported by suitable means. Strut assemblies contain a coil spring that is held under compression. Always use a spring compressor to release the spring pressure before disassembly.

1 Using your hand, push down on one corner of the front bumper continuously until the front of the vehicle is bouncing. When at the bottom, remove your hand and stop pushing. In most vehicles, the corner of the vehicle will rise and the settle into place. A vehicle with softer suspension may rise, fall, and rise to its settling point. If the vehicle bounces more than that, the strut needs to be replaced. **(Photo 1)**

2 Loosen the lug nuts one turn if removing by hand. **(Photo 2)**

3 Safely raise and support the vehicle on a hoist or on jack stands. **(Photo 3)**

4 Remove the lug nuts and then take off the wheels. **(Photo 4)**

5 Remove the disc brake caliper, and wire it so it does not hang by its brake hose. **(Photo 5)**

6 Remove the bolts holding the top of the strut to the strut tower (not the center strut bolt). **(Photo 6)**

7 Remove the strut from the vehicle.

To remove, inspect, and install a strut coil spring, insulators, and the upper strut bearing mount, follow the steps in **SKILL DRILL 29-14**:

1 Remove the strut from the vehicle following the previous skill drill. **(Photo 1)**

2 To remove the springs, place the strut assembly in the spring compressor and slightly tighten the compressor to relieve some of the spring pressure. **(Photo 2)**

3 Carefully remove the large nut holding the strut rod in place while using your other hand to let the strut assembly drop out of the spring. Place the strut assembly on the work bench. **(Photo 3)**

4 Loosen the pressure on the compressor so the spring is free. Remove the spring from the compressor. **(Photo 4)**

5 To install a new spring, place the new spring in the spring compressor and set the compressor to apply pressure to the spring. **(Photo 5)**

6 Place the strut assembly through the spring, and put the spring insulators and upper strut bearing mount on top of the rod install nut. Tighten to the manufacturer's specifications. **(Photo 6)**

7 Release the compressor for the spring and remove it from the spring compressor. **(Photo 7)**

SKILL DRILL | **29-14** | **Removing, Inspecting, and Installing a Strut Coil Spring, Insulators, and the Upper Strut Bearing Mount**

1 Remove the strut from the vehicle following the previous skill drill.

2 Place the strut into the strut compressor. Adjust the lower arms of the strut compressor so the spring is supported properly.

3 Properly place the upper arms of the strut compressor onto the spring.

4 Slowly turn the handle of the strut compressor and compress the spring. Ensure that the strut compressor arms are properly placed and are not sliding.

5 Once the spring is compressed enough that the strut is free from spring pressure, loosen and remove the center strut nut.

6 Remove the old strut from the spring.

SKILL DRILL 29-14 Removing, Inspecting, and Installing a Strut Coil Spring, Insulators, and the Upper Strut Bearing Mount, continued

7 Remove any strut bellows, bumpers, spring seats from the old strut that need to be transferred to the new strut. Install them on the new strut.

8 Install the new strut into the spring. Reinstall the upper strut mount in the correct position.

9 Install the upper washer and nut. Torque to the manufacturer's specification. Slowly release the spring compressor and reinstall the strut into the vehicle.

Removing, Inspecting, and Replacing Leaf Springs

The leaf springs of a vehicle need to be inspected whenever the ride height does not match the manufacturer's specifications. If found to be sagging, bent, or broken, they will need to be replaced. Removal and inspection is also necessary if noise is found to be coming from the leaf spring or bushings in the leaf spring. Follow the manufacturer's service information to remove and replace a leaf spring. If new leaf spring bushings will be needed, the use of proper press tools will ensure proper bushing replacement. Remember that when the leaf springs are removed, the axle will not be supported; the use of screw jacks to support the axle during removal will be necessary.

To remove, inspect, and install leaf springs, follow the steps in **SKILL DRILL 29-15**:

1 Safely raise the vehicle on a hoist, and support the axle with tall screw jack stands.

2 Check to see if any of the leaves are cracked or broken and that the noise-deadening inserts are positioned correctly between the leaves. (**Photo 1**)

3 Test the security of the spring center bolt, and make sure the U-bolts are tight. (**Photo 2**)

4 Check the condition of the bushings or mountings and the spring shackles by placing a lever between the frame and the eye of the spring and levering against the spring. (**Photo 3**)

5 Remove the bolts holding the leaf spring to the shackle and hanger. (**Photo 4**)

6 Having an assistant help remove the U-bolts, holding the leaf spring to the axle. (**Photo 5**)

7 To install a new leaf spring, hang the new leaf spring into position by inserting bolts into the hanger and the shackle. Be sure to use new fasteners whenever specified by the service information. (**Photo 6**)

8 Reinstall the U-bolts that hold the leaf spring to the axle, tightening them a little at a time so they are evenly tensioned.

9 Tighten all bolts to the manufacturer's specifications. (**Photo 7**)

Removing, Inspecting, and Installing Strut Rods and Bushings

The strut rods and bushings hold the control arm and therefore the wheel in position longitudinally. The strut

SKILL DRILL 29-15 Removing, Inspecting, and Replacing Leaf Springs

1 Raise the vehicle on a lift and support the rear axle with tall screw jack stands. Check to see if any of the leaves are cracked or broken and that the noise deadening inserts are positioned correctly between the leaves.

2 Test the security of the spring center bolt, and make sure the U-bolts are tight.

3 Check the condition of the bushings or mountings and the spring shackles by placing a lever between the frame and the eye of the spring and levering against the spring.

4 Remove the bolts holding the leaf spring to the shackle and hanger.

5 Have an assistant help hold the spring while removing the U-bolts, holding the leaf spring to the axle.

6 To install a new leaf spring, hang the new leaf spring into position by inserting bolts into the hanger and shackle. Use new fasteners whenever specified by service information.

7 Reinstall U-bolts to the axle and snug them down a little at a time. Tighten all bolts to the manufacturer's specifications.

rod bushings wear and degrade over time, requiring replacement whenever they are loose. On some vehicles the strut rod is the adjustment point for caster. An alignment may have to be performed after performing this task. Refer to the manufacturer's service information for the vehicle you are working on.

To remove, inspect, and install strut rods and bushings, follow the steps in **SKILL DRILL 29-16** :

1 Safely raise the vehicle on a lift and inspect the strut rods and bushings visually. Pry the rod side to side and front to back to check for looseness. **(Photo 1)**

2 Remove the bolts and/or nuts holding the strut rod to the frame.

3 Remove the bolts and/or nuts holding the strut rod to the lower control arm.

4 Remove the strut rod by hand. The bushings may fall out, or may need to be pried out, when the strut rod is removed. **(Photo 2)**

5 To install new strut rod bushings, place half of the bushing onto the rod. **(Photo 3)**

6 Slide the rod through the hole in the frame. **(Photo 4)**

SKILL DRILL | 29-16 | Removing, Inspecting, and Installing Strut Rods and Bushings

1 Raise the vehicle on the hoist and inspect the strut rods and bushings. Pry the strut rod side to side and front to back to check for looseness.

2 Remove the bolts and nuts holding the strut rod to the lower control arm and frame. Remove the rod by hand. The bushing may fall out, or need to be pried out, when the strut rod is removed.

3 To install new strut rod bushings, place half of the bushing onto the strut rod.

4 Slide the rod through the hole in the frame.

5 Place the other half of the bushing onto the rod sticking out of the frame and start the nut.

7 Place the other half of the bushing onto the rod sticking out of the frame and thread the nut onto the strut rod. (**Photo 5**)

8 Place bolts through the lower control arm and outer end of the strut rod, and torque all fasteners to the manufacturer's specifications.

Removing, Inspecting, Installing, and Adjusting Torsion Bar Suspension

The torsion bar provides the spring action in a torsion bar front-end suspension system. In many cases, it is adjustable to allow for corrections in ride height. It has a large bolt in the torque arm that, when adjusted, changes the amount of pressure it places on the control arm to raise or lower the suspension. The torsion bar should be checked whenever the driver complains of suspension problems. Torsion bars are typically stamped or marked with a left or right and must be installed in the proper side. If it has marks for left or right, then it is preset for twisting in that specific direction and will not have the same spring force if twisted the opposite way. If the torsion bars are not marked, then be sure to place a paint mark on them to identify left and right; they have been subjected to torsion

in one direction for the life of the vehicle, and installing them backward can result in breakage or incorrect spring rate. The torsion bar may be found on either the lower or upper control arm on certain vehicles. The following skill drill will not be the same for all vehicles. Follow service information for proper operation of this task.

To remove, inspect, install, and adjust the torsion bar, follow the steps in **SKILL DRILL 29-17**:

1 Loosen the lug nuts one turn if removing by hand. Safely raise and support the vehicle on a hoist, or on jack stands. Remove the wheels. Place a supporting jack under the lower control arm. (**Photo 1**)

2 If equipped, remove the torsion bar dust cover by removing its bolts. (**Photo 2**)

3 To aid in reinstallation, paint matching marks on the torsion bar spring and its corresponding arm. (Under NO circumstances should you use a scribe to scratch these marks on the torsion bar and corresponding arm; doing so can seriously damage the bar, leading to catastrophic failure.) (**Photo 3**)

4 If the torsion bar system has an anchor bolt protrusion, measure the distance from the washer to the end of the stud with a tape measure and record the value. This will help during reassembly

SKILL DRILL | 29-17 | Removing, Inspecting, Installing, and Adjusting Torsion Bar Suspension

1 Loosen the wheel studs. Safely raise and support the vehicle on a hoist, or on jack stands. Remove the wheels.

2 Install the correct torsion bar compression tool and compress the torsion bar.

3 To aid in reinstallation, paint matching marks on the torsion bar spring and its corresponding arm. (Under NO circumstances should you scribe these marks on the torsion bar and corresponding arm; doing so can seriously damage the bar in the long term leading to catastrophic failure.)

SKILL DRILL | 29-17 | Removing, Inspecting, Installing, and Adjusting Torsion Bar Suspension, continued

4 If the torsion bar system has an anchor bolt protrusion, measure the distance from the washer to the end of the stud with a tape measure and record the value.

5 Remove the adjustment bolt and anchor plate. Before removing these nuts or bolts, ensure that the torsion bar force has been released.

6 Slowly loosen and remove the torsion bar compression tool.

7 Remove all the remaining securing bolts using a socket or wrench as required, and remove the torsion bar spring. Release the pressure on the supporting jack and slowly lower the lower control arm.

8 Ensure that the torsion bar springs were fitted in the correct location by identifying the location marks on the end of the spring (R for right side; L of left side).

9 Inspect the torsion bar spring for any signs of fretting or cracking, twisting, bends, or wear. Check the serrations of each part for any cracking, twisting, or signs of wear.

10 Lubricate the ends of the torsion bar with a high-quality, multipurpose grease.

11 Inspect the anchor plate and adjustment bolt for damage or excesseive rust.

12 Reinstall the torsion bar spring by sliding it onto the hole with your hands. At this point it is vital that you have ensured that the correct spring (L or R) has been located in its correct side.

SKILL DRILL | 29-17 | Removing, Inspecting, Installing, and Adjusting Torsion Bar Suspension, continued

13 Reinstall the torsion bar support or vehicle crossmember.

14 Use the correct torsion bar compression tool to compress the bar and install the anchor plate.

15 Install the adjustment bolt and tighten to the correct distance as measured in step 4.

16 Carry out recommended inspection procedures to ensure the torsion bar settings are within specifications. Compare the final measurements to the manufacturer's specifications. If needed, adjust the torsion bar height as required by turning the bolt with a socket.

to get you close on restoring the correct ride height adjustment. **(Photo 4)**

5 Loosen the lock nut and back off the adjusting bolt to relieve tension on the torsion bar. Remove the lock nut and adjusting nut with a wrench or socket. Before removing these nuts, ensure that any twisting force has been eliminated from the torsion bar spring(s). **(Photo 5)**

6 Remove the snap ring (circlip) from the anchor arm if equipped. To do this, place snap ring pliers in the hole of the snap ring and compress the pliers while pulling on the ring. (**Photo 6**)

7 Remove all the remaining securing bolts using a socket or wrench as required, and remove the torsion bar spring. Release the pressure on the supporting jack and slowly lower the control arm. (**Photo 7**)

8 Ensure that the torsion bar springs were fitted in the correct location by identifying the location marks on the end of the spring (R for right side; L of left side). (**Photo 8**)

9 Inspect the torsion bar spring for any signs of fretting or cracking, twisting, bends, or wear. In addition, check the splines or flats of each part for any cracking, twisting, or signs of wear and tear. (**Photo 9**)

10 If equipped, inspect the torsion bar dust cover(s) for cracks or poor fit.

11 Install the torque arm to the lower control arm, and lubricate the torsion bar ends with a high-quality multipurpose grease, if lubrication is called for. The best way to do this is to place the grease on your hand and rub it onto the splines. (**Photo 10**)

12 Place the lower control arm in its position where the torsion bar tension is zero.(**Photo 11**)

13 Reinstall the torsion bar spring by sliding it onto the hole with your hands. At this point it is vital that you have ensured that the correct spring (L or R) has been located in its correct side. If the springs are installed in the improper locations, then ride height and spring durability will suffer. (**Photo 12**)

14 While aligning the anchor arm with the matching mark, install the anchor arm to the torsion bar. Install the snap ring (circlip) to the anchor arm and dust cover. Ensure that this ring/circlip is correctly installed. Place the snap ring pliers in the hole of the snap ring, and compress the pliers while pushing on the ring. Visually inspect the ring to see that it is in the groove. Snap rings do not always seat in their groove when installed and can pop out as the vehicle is driven, creating a very dangerous situation. (**Photo 13**)

15 Tighten the adjusting nut to the recorded measurement list for the original torsion bar spring when disassembling the unit; or if a new torsion bar is being installed, then refer to the workshop information for the correct specifications. (**Photo 14**)

16 Tighten the lock nut. Install and properly torque the wheel. (**Photo 15**)

17 Carry out recommended inspection procedures as outlined in the workshop information to ensure that the torsion bar settings are within specifications. Typically, this involves measuring the ride height before you remove the torsion bar and then rechecking it after installation of the new torsion bar. Compare the final measurements to the manufacturer's specifications.

18 If they are not within specifications, adjust the torsion bar height as required by turning the adjustment bolt with a socket while making sure to jounce the vehicle before rechecking your measurements. (**Photo 16**)

Performing a Pre-alignment Inspection

Incorrect wheel alignment results in a vehicle that may pull or be hard to steer and causes rapid or improper wearing of the tires. A pre-alignment inspection is performed to ensure that the vehicle is an appropriate candidate for alignment. Worn and loose suspension or steering components, low tire pressure, and heavy objects in the trunk make it impossible to perform an accurate alignment. As with any diagnosis, verifying the customer's concern is the first step. Be sure to test-drive the vehicle prior to the pre-alignment inspection, listening carefully for any unusual noises and noting any improper driving control issues related to the suspension and steering systems.

To perform a pre-alignment inspection, follow the steps in **SKILL DRILL 29-18**:

1 Remove any heavy items from the trunk and passenger compartments. Do not remove any item or equipment that is supplied with the vehicle and normally kept in the vehicle. (**Photo 1**)

2 Check all four tires for proper tire size, and adjust tire pressure to specifications. (**Photo 2**)

3 Check the vehicle's ride height. Carrying out a successful wheel alignment with the vehicle's ride height incorrect is impossible. (**Photo 3**)

4 Check the play of the steering wheel. Excess play must be corrected before undertaking the wheel alignment. (**Photo 4**)

5 Bounce each corner of the vehicle to check the correct functioning of the shock absorbers. (**Photo 5**)

6 With the vehicle raised on a hoist or jack, inspect all suspension and steering components according to service information, including the wheel bearings. Repair or replace all damaged or worn suspension components prior to aligning the vehicle. (**Photo 6**)

SKILL DRILL   29-18   Preparing a Vehicle for a Wheel Alignment

1 Remove any heavy items from the trunk and passenger compartments.

2 Check the size and condition of all four tires. Adjust the air pressure to specifications.

3 Measure the vehicle's ride height.

4 Check the play of the steering wheel. Correct any excess play before undertaking the wheel alignment.

5 Bounce each corner of the vehicle to check the correct functioning of the shock absorbers.

6 With the vehicle raised, inspect all suspension and steering components, including the wheel bearings. Repair or replace all damaged or worn suspension components.

7 Position the vehicle on the wheel alignment ramp, making sure the front tires are positioned correctly on the turntables.

8 Position the rear wheels on the slip plates or rear turntables.

9 Attach the wheel units of the wheel alignment machine.

7. Position the vehicle on the wheel alignment rack, making sure the front tires are positioned correctly on the turntables. **(Photo 7)**

8. Position the rear wheels on the slip plates or rear turntables. **(Photo 8)**

9. Attach the wheel units of the wheel alignment machine. **(Photo 9)**

Performing Four-Wheel Alignment

Improper wheel alignment results in a vehicle that may be difficult to steer, pulls to one side or the other, wanders, or wears the tires. The alignment machine measures the angles the wheels are at compared to each other and the centerline of the vehicle. Since the alignment machine wheel adapters do not attach to the wheels perfectly straight, the alignment machine has the ability to compensate for any runout in the wheel assemblies so that the alignment machine can ensure it is reading the angle of the wheels accurately, no matter where each tire is positioned.

Alignments always follow a specific order of adjustments. The rear wheels should be adjusted before the front wheels so that the vehicle can be made to track straight down the road. The order is (1) rear caster, (2) camber, and (3) toe; then move to the front to adjust (4) caster, (5) camber, and (6) toe. This sequence is for vehicles with fully adjustable caster, camber, and toe on the front and rear of the vehicle. Performing the alignment adjustment in this way will prevent having to go back and readjust previous settings, which saves you time. Not all vehicles have adjustable caster and camber, so only toe can be set, unless aftermarket components are installed that allow caster and camber adjustment. This skill drill is for a vehicle equipped with two eccentric bolts attaching the lower control arm to the frame, allowing caster and camber adjustment. Perform the alignment as the service information instructs or the alignment machine guides you. This skill drill is not designed to be an accurate example for all vehicles.

To perform a four-wheel alignment, follow the steps in **SKILL DRILL 29-19**:

1. Position the vehicle on the alignment rack.

2. Raise the vehicle to a comfortable working height, and set the rack on its mechanical locks to ensure a level surface. **(Photo 1)**

3. Raise the vehicle with the air jacks on the alignment rack. **(Photo 2)**

4. Attach the wheel sensors to the wheels at the locations recommended by the sensor manufacturer and compensate the alignment machine sensors. In most cases, this will require you to lift the vehicle and rotate the tire through a certain number of degrees of rotation while telling the machine what position you are in. This procedure allows the machine to measure the runout in the wheel assemblies and make the necessary compensation. **(Photo 3)**

5. Pull the lock pins from the slip plates and turntables. **(Photo 4)**

SKILL DRILL 29-19 Performing Four-Wheel Alignment

1. Position the vehicle on the front-end rack. Raise the vehicle to a comfortable working level, and set the rack on its mechanical locks to provide a level surface.

2. Raise the vehicle with the air jacks on the alignment rack.

3. Attach sensors and compensate each one.

SKILL DRILL | 29-19 | Performing Four-Wheel Alignment, continued

4 Pull the lock pins from the slip plates and turntables.

5 Lower the vehicle as instructed by the machine. Install a brake pedal depressor.

6 Perform a caster sweep by selecting caster sweep on the machine and turning the wheel the number of degrees on the turntables as designnated by the machine.

7 Take the alignment readings and compare them to the vehicle manufacturer's specifications.

8 Prepare to adjust rear caster, camber, and toe, if possible, by loosening the eccentric bolts.

9 Adjust front caster and camber by turning the eccentric bolts attaching the control arm until alignment is within specifications.

10 Install a steering wheel holder to center the steering wheel.

11 Adjust front toe by lengthening or shortening the tie-rod assemblies until toe is within specifications. Tighten the lock nuts on the tie-rod assemblies. Test-drive the vehicle to make sure the repair was successful.

6 Lower the vehicle as instructed by the machine.

7 Install a brake pedal depressor to hold the front wheels from turning during the caster sweep, if required. **(Photo 5)**

8 Perform a caster sweep by selecting caster sweep on the machine and turning the wheel the number of degrees on the turntables as designated by the machine. Typically, you will turn the wheel and tire assembly to the 20° position in both directions and then to the 10° position in both directions. The final step will be to return the wheels to the zero position. **(Photo 6)**

9 Read the alignment specification on the machine and compare to the vehicle manufacturer's specifications. (photo7)

10 Prepare to adjust rear caster, camber, and toe, if adjustable, by finding and loosening the adjustment points. **(Photo 8)**

11 Adjust the front caster by turning both eccentric bolts in opposite directions until the caster is at the specified setting. Adjust front camber by turning the eccentric bolts in the same direction until the camber is in the proper position. Remember that moving the eccentrics will affect both caster and camber, so adjust carefully. Tighten the nuts on the bolts when adjustment is finalized. **(Photo 9)**

12 Adjust toe as the last step. Ensure that the machine is on the toe adjustment screen. Center the steering wheel and lock it in place with a steering wheel holder. **(Photo 10)**

13 Loosen the tie-rod lock nut, and turn the inner tie-rod to lengthen or shorten the tie-rod assembly until toe setting is correct for one wheel. Tighten the lock nut and perform the same operation on the other side. **(Photo 11)**

14 Test-drive the vehicle to ensure that the repair has corrected the customer's concern.

Checking Toe-Out on Turns

When you steer a vehicle through a turn, the outside front wheel has to travel a wider arc than the inside wheel. For this reason, the inside front wheel must steer at a sharper angle than the outside wheel to prevent the inside tire from dragging along or sliding through a turn. To provide true rolling motion, the inner wheel must be turned through a sharper angle than the outer wheel. This allows the inner wheel to turn through a smaller turning radius than the outer wheel. Toe-out on turns is sometimes referred to as TOOT, the Ackermann angle, or the track

differential angle. Refer to service information to find the correct name and specifications for toe-out on turns.

With the tires on the turntable, toe-out on turns is measured by the turning angle gauges (turn plates) on the wheel alignment machine. Depending on the wheel alignment equipment being used, the readings either are displayed directly on the turn plate or are measured electronically and displayed on the screen. Refer to the manufacturer's specifications in the service information for the correct toe-out on turns angles. Typically, a vehicle will have an angle of 20° on the inside tire and 18° on the outside tire. This is not the same for every vehicle, so be sure to check specifications. Make sure the readings are at zero on each side when the wheels are straight ahead. Turn the steering wheel so that the inside wheel is at the inside specification and then check the outside wheel measurement.

If differences from specifications are found, then typically one or both steering arms are bent, but ensure that the tie-rod ends are not bent or the individual toe misadjusted. Be sure that caster, camber, and toe settings are within specifications before checking this angle, as incorrect angles will affect toe-out on turns. Compare the maximum turning angle of each wheel as well. If there are differences from specifications, then check for bent or shifted components such as a rack that is shifted or a steering wheel that was not properly centered during a repair, causing the wheels to not turn as sharply in one direction as the other.

Checking SAI and Included Angle

The SAI is the angle formed by an imaginary line running through the upper and lower steering pivots relative to a plumb line—the vertical line created when a weight is hung from a string. It cannot be adjusted, though a technician will on occasion be asked to check the SAI to ensure it is within the manufacturer's specifications after an accident or body repair. Generally, SAI should not vary more than half a degree, plus or minus. If SAI is incorrect, check for a bent strut, bent control arms, or a bent spindle or steering knuckle. If incorrect, SAI will create an issue with the steering wheel not returning to center after cornering.

To check SAI, follow the steps in **SKILL DRILL 29-20**:

1 Position the vehicle on the alignment rack.

2 Attach the wheel sensors on the vehicle to the locations specified by the sensor manufacturer, and compensate. **(Photo 1)**

3 Follow the alignment machine instructions for taking the SAI measurements, and compare them to

SKILL DRILL | **29-20** | **Checking SAI and Included Angle**

1 Position the vehicle on the alignment rack. Attach the wheel sensors on the vehicle to the locations specified by the sensor manufacturer, and compensate.

2 Follow the alignment machine instructions for taking the SAI measurements, and compare them to the vehicle manufacturer's specifications. Typically, the SAI reading will require a caster sweep to be performed. SAI is a nonadjustable angle. No changes can be made; the angle will help the technician to verify that suspension components are bent.

3 Calculate the included angle, if the alignment machine doesn't, by adding the camber reading of each wheel to the SAI of each wheel, and compare to specifications. Remember that if camber is a negative number, you will need to subtract the camber from the SAI to get the included angle.

the vehicle manufacturer's specifications. Typically, the SAI reading will require a caster sweep to be performed.

4 SAI is a nonadjustable angle. No changes can be made; the angle will help the technician to verify that suspension components are bent. **(Photo 2)**

5 Calculate the included angle, if the alignment machine doesn't, by adding the camber reading of each wheel to the SAI of each wheel, and compare to specifications. Remember that if camber is a negative number, you will need to subtract the camber from the SAI to get the included angle. **(Photo 3)**

Checking Rear Wheel Thrust Angle

The rear thrust angle refers to the relationship between the rear wheels and an imaginary centerline down the center of the vehicle. Rear thrust angle problems often result from an accident or other impact that bends the rear axle or axle mounting points. Incorrect rear thrust

angle can also be caused by wear on independent rear suspension components or incorrectly set rear toe. Incorrect thrust angle will try to steer the vehicle in the direction the wheels are pointing. Think of a monster truck with rear steering that becomes stuck, as you might have seen on TV. The rear of the vehicle will turn in the direction the rear wheels are pointing and the driver will have to turn the front wheels to make the vehicle crab walk in a straight line. As this vehicle moves in a straight line, it will look like the body is sitting sideways. Typically, the steering wheel will be off-center while driving since the driver will have to turn the front wheels to compensate for the rear. The ideal thrust angle will be close to zero, but refer to the manufacturer's specifications for correct thrust angle for the vehicle you are working on.

To check the rear wheel thrust angle, follow the steps in **SKILL DRILL 29-21**:

1 Position the vehicle on the alignment rack.

2 Attach the wheel sensors on the vehicle to the locations specified by the sensor manufacturer, and compensate. **(Photo 1)**

SKILL DRILL | 29-21 | Checking Rear Wheel Thrust Angle

1 Position the vehicle on the alignment rack. Attach the wheel sensors on the vehicle to the locations specified by the sensor manufacturer, and compensate.

2 Thrust angle can be indicated on most alignment machines, although you may have to go to a special screen. Take the thrust angle reading, and compare it to the vehicle manufacturer's specifications.

3 Thrust angle can be indicated on most alignment machines, although you may have to go to a special screen. Take the thrust angle reading, and compare it to the vehicle manufacturer's specifications. **(Photo 2)**

Checking Front and/or Rear Cradle Alignment

Damage to the cradle of a vehicle can force the wheels out of alignment, possibly changing caster, camber, and toe and creating pull and tire wear issues. The cradle should always be perpendicular to the centerline of the chassis. It is possible that after an accident the cradle mounting points have moved (bent), and the vehicle will have to be sent to a frame shop to straighten the body before the alignment can be performed.

It is also important to ensure that the cradle is centered when removing and replacing this major component during service, such as when replacing the transmission. It is recommended on some vehicles that an alignment be performed after cradle removal and reinstallation. Refer to the manufacturer's service information on cradle adjustment.

To check cradle alignment, follow the steps in **SKILL DRILL 29-22**:

1 Position the vehicle on the alignment rack.

2 Attach the wheel sensors on the vehicle, and compensate.

3 Take the alignment readings. Compare the readings to the manufacturer's specifications. If camber and caster are incorrect and not adjustable, check for bent parts. **(Photo 1)**

4 If the parts are not bent, check the positioning of the cradle. Loosen cradle bolts and shift in the necessary direction to correct alignment angles. **(Photo 2)**

5 If adjustment is still not possible, check for a bent cradle or cradle mounting points by measuring from fixed points on one side compared to the same points on the other side. If they are different, the cradle needs adjusting. **(Photo 3)**

SKILL DRILL | 29-22 | Checking Front and/or Rear Cradle Alignment

1 Position the vehicle on the alignment rack. Attach the wheel sensors on the vehicle, and compensate. Take the alignment readings and compare to the specifications. If camber and caster are incorrect and not adjustable, check for bent parts.

2 If the parts are not bent, check the positioning of the cradle. Loosen cradle bolts and shift in the necessary direction to correct alignment angles.

3 If adjustment is still not possible, check for a bent cradle or cradle mounting points by measuring from fixed points on one side, compared to the same points on the other side. If they are different, the cradle needs adjusting.

Wrap-up

Ready for Review

▸ The suspension system is designed to absorb road shock and vibrations.

▸ Unsprung weight refers to the vehicle parts not supported by springs (wheels, tires, brake and steering assemblies); this weight should be kept as low as possible.

▸ Metal springs, rubber, and air all work to provide suspension system support by absorbing some amount of force.

▸ Springs react to road shock by not immediately returning to their original state. They may oscillate—that is, fluctuate in length, until the energy from the road shock is dissipated.

▸ Vehicle movement may be due to yaw, pitch, or roll.

▸ Suspension system components include the springs, axles, shock absorbers, arms, rods, sway bars, steering knuckle, bushings, and ball joints.

▸ Types of springs include coil springs, leaf springs, and torsion bars.

▸ Coil springs can be cylindrical, barrel shaped, or conical and are used on the front suspension of most modern light vehicles.

▸ Leaf springs are primarily used on rear-wheel drive vehicles and consist of multiple flat springs made of tempered steel.

▸ Functions of axles include helping support vehicle weight, maintaining wheel position, providing forward propulsion of the vehicle, and transmitting torque to the wheel.

▸ Axle types include straight, dead, full-floating, or semi-floating.

▸ Types of shock absorbers are hydraulic, gas pressurized, and adjustable (which can be load adjustable, annual adjustable rate, electronic adjustable rate, and automatic load adjustable).

▸ Shock absorbers use the resistance of a rod and piston, and oil and disc valves, to provide a dampening effect on the force created by the bumps and jolts of driving.

▸ Manually adjustable air springs can be incorporated into rear shock absorbers for vehicles designed to carry heavy loads.

▸ The dampening rate of electronic adjustable rate shock absorbers can be manually or automatically altered.

▸ The primary load-bearing elements of a SLA suspension system are known as control arms, which attach to the wheel assembly on one end and the chassis on the other.

▸ The primary load-bearing elements on a MacPherson strut suspension system is the strut itself.

▸ Bushings act as bearings at suspension fulcrum points, allowing movement of the component without losing its alignment.

▸ The two types of auto body construction are unibody (most common) and full frame.

▸ Types of suspension systems are solid (beam) axles, independent, rear, front, adaptive air, and computer controlled.

▸ A live axle transfers power from the engine to the wheels; a dead axle does not transmit any drive.

▸ Independent suspension allows for lower unsprung mass.

▸ Independent suspension systems adjust wheel camber individually.

▸ Struts are commonly used in independent suspension systems; the most common type is the MacPherson strut.

▸ Types of rear suspension systems are rear independent, rear-wheel drive independent, rigid-axle leaf spring, rigid-axle coil spring, and rigid nondrive.

▸ Rear suspension systems in front-wheel drive vehicles are designed to keep the rear tires in contact with the road, and aligned with front tires.

▸ The rear suspension system on a rear-wheel drive vehicle must allow for swiveling of the front wheels during steering; on four-wheel steering vehicles, the system must allow for swiveling of rear wheels as well.

▸ Front suspensions are generally either independent (front wheels move independently) or solid (an axle forces the front wheels to move together).

▸ Front suspension system types include MacPherson strut, short/long arm (SLA), and torsion bar.

▸ Adaptive air suspension systems electronically control the height of all four wheels based on vehicle speed and load.

▸ Types of computer-controlled suspension systems are active, hydraulic actuated, electromagnetic rheological, semi-active, and solenoid/valve actuated.

▸ Wheel alignment is set using the vehicle's control arms, knuckles, and frame.

▸ Factors affecting wheel alignment include camber, caster, steering axis inclination, toe-in and toe-out, scrub radius, toe-out on turns, turning radius, thrust angle, and ride height.

▶ Positive camber refers to the top of tires tilting away from the vehicle; negative camber refers to the top of tires tilting toward the vehicle; zero average camber refers to no tire tilt.

▶ Caster refers to the angle formed between the centerline of steering axis and true vertical, or the forward/backward tilt of the ball joints.

▶ Steering axis inclination (SAI) provides the front wheels with a self-centering function; it is formed by drawing a line through the upper and lower pivot points of the suspension assembly.

▶ Scrub radius (steering offset) is the distance between the center point of the tire contact patch at the road surface and the point of steering axis centerline contact with the road.

▶ The Ackermann principle ensures that the inner wheels turn at a sharper angle than the outer wheels when turning.

▶ Thrust angle refers to the relationship of the rear wheels to the vehicle's imaginary centerline.

▶ When performing a wheel alignment, be sure to check front and rear cradle, thrust angle, wheel setback, wheel camber, caster, toe, SAI, and toe-out on turns.

▶ There are three basic types of wheel alignment: two-wheel alignment, thrust-angle, and four-wheel alignment.

▶ Common issues related to the suspension system are vehicle wander, drift, pull, hard steering, bump steer, torque steer, and steering return concerns.

▶ Tools commonly needed to diagnose suspension or wheel alignment issues are the wheel aligner, ramp, turntable, wheel clamps, specification charts, workshop manuals, specialty alignment tools, dial indicators, measuring tapes, scan tools, general hand tools, various lift devices, air ratchets, and wheel braces.

▶ A common suspension system problem is excessive play in the parts, usually from wear in the joints and bushings.

▶ Common tools for maintenance and repair of suspension systems include those used in diagnosis as well as the following: component compression devices, levers, spring compressor tools, a strut-servicing tool kit, a universal strut nut wrench kit, and a 24-mm strut rod socket.

▶ Wheel alignment servicing equipment is used to measure the steering and suspension alignment angles.

Key Terms

Ackermann angle The angle the steering arms make with the steering axis, projected toward the center of the rear axle.

Ackermann principle The geometric alignment of linkages in a vehicle's steering such that the wheels on the inside of a turn are able to move in a different circle radius than the wheels on the outside.

adaptive air suspension A suspension system that uses rubber bags or bladders filled with air to support the weight of the vehicle.

air spring A part that provides the springing action or auxiliary spring. It is typically used in air suspension systems or heavy truck applications.

applied force Pressure placed on something.

arm The primary load-bearing element of a vehicle's suspension system, commonly known as control arm. Can also mean the steering arm, which applies the driver's turning effort to the steering knuckle.

automatic load-adjustable shock absorber Typically, an air shock absorber used in an automatic load-sensing system that adjusts ride height (ground clearance) automatically such as when additional weight is added to the vehicle.

automatic ride control actuator An electric stepper motor mounted on top of the shock that changes orifice size inside the shock.

axle The shaft of the suspension system to which the tires and wheels are attached; they are used to drive or support the wheels.

ball joint A swivel connection mounted in the outer end of the front control arm. These swivels are typically constructed with a ball and socket to allow pivoting.

braking torque The torque acting to twist the axle housing around its center during braking.

bushing A rubber, nylon, or urethane part that allows for movement while maintaining alignment.

camber The side-to-side vertical tilt of the wheel. It is viewed from the front of the vehicle and measured in degrees. Negative camber is when the top of the tire is closer to the center of the vehicle than the bottom of the tire.

caster The angle formed through the wheel pivot points when viewed from the side in comparison to a vertical line through the wheel.

centerline The imaginary line drawn down the exact center of the vehicle from front to back.

coil spring Spring steel wire that is heated and wound into a coil that is used to support the weight of a vehicle.

compliance bushing A rubber bushing with a voided section molded in it that allows component movement under torque application. It is typically used in control arms on front-wheel drive vehicles to minimize torque steer issues.

control arm The primary load-bearing element of a vehicle's suspension system, commonly referred to as an A-arm or wishbone. These arms may be used as an upper and lower pivot point for the wheel assembly. They attach to the chassis with rubber bushings that allow up-and-down movement of the tire and wheel assembly.

cornering force The force applied to an axle that shifts the axle in relation to the position of the body when turning.

dead axle An axle, used on a rear- or front-wheel drive vehicle that does not drive the vehicle.

deflecting force A force that moves an object in a different direction or into a different shape.

direct-acting telescopic shock absorber A shock absorber designed to reduce spring oscillations.

driving thrust The force transferred from the tire contact patch through the axle housing and front half of the spring to the fixed shackle point that pushes the vehicle along the road.

elasticity The ability to deform and reform into the same shape.

external drive shaft A shaft used to transfer power from the transmission to the live axle.

full frame construction Construction of the frame using a heavy steel channel iron or boxed steel. The frame runs from the front of the vehicle to the rear as one solid piece, and the body of the vehicle attaches to this part by bolts and rubber body mounts.

included angle The angle of camber added or subtracted to the SAI angle. This is the angle of the pivot points in relation to the camber angle of the wheel. Also referred to as the diagnostic angle.

independent suspension A system for allowing the up-and-down movement of one tire without affecting the other tire on that axle.

leaf spring A spring made of one or more flat, tempered steel springs bracketed together that is used in the suspension system to support the weight of the vehicle.

<u>live axle</u> An axle with a final drive unit made into it that transfers the power from the engine to the wheels so the vehicle can move.

<u>MacPherson strut</u> A strut used on an independent suspension where the spring and shock are joined together. Used on most front-wheel drive vehicles.

<u>magneto-rheological fluid</u> A fluid that has the unique characteristic of changing viscosity when exposed to a magnetic field.

<u>manual adjustable-rate shock absorber</u> A shock absorber that allows manual adjustment of the dampening rate.

<u>manually adjustable-air spring</u> A rubber air bag placed inside coil springs to increase the spring's load-carrying ability. It is filled manually through a valve similar to a tire valve stem.

<u>negative camber</u> Tilt of the top of the tire toward the centerline of the vehicle.

<u>negative caster</u> Forward tilt of the wheel pivot points from the vertical line.

<u>negative scrub radius</u> A condition in which the point of center contact between the road surface and the tire and the point where the steering axis centerline contacts the road surface intersect above the road surface.

<u>oscillation</u> The fluctuation of an object between two states. With regard to suspension springs, it refers to the uncontrolled compression and decompression of the spring following overshoot.

<u>overshoot</u> The amount a spring extends (springs back) past its original length following compression.

<u>panhard rod</u> A metal rod used to hold the dead axle and keep it from moving from side to side through corners. It is mounted on the body or frame of the vehicle and the axle. Also referred to as a track bar.

<u>pitch</u> Movement of a vehicle around its y-axis (the imaginary line across the center of the vehicle from left to right) that causes the vehicle to lower or rise on the front end during quick braking or acceleration.

<u>positive camber</u> Tilt of the top of the tire out from the centerline of the vehicle.

<u>positive caster</u> Backward tilt of the wheel pivot points from the vertical line.

<u>positive scrub radius</u> A condition in which the point of center contact between the road surface and the tire and the point where the steering axis centerline contacts the road surface intersect below the road surface.

<u>progressive rate of deflection</u> The change in deflection rate that occurs as the weight of the vehicle changes. The greater the weight, the lower the rate of deflection due to increased resistance.

<u>reaction force</u> A force that acts in the opposite direction to another force.

<u>rebound clip</u> A metal strap that is warped around the leaf spring to prevent excessive flexing of the main leaf during rebound.

<u>rigid-axle coil-spring suspension</u> A dead axle that uses a coil spring.

<u>rigid nondrive axle suspension</u> A type of dead axle suspension system that is non-independent and uses a beam or solid axle.

<u>rigid spring hanger</u> The rigid part typically welded to the body or frame of the vehicle to which the front of the leaf spring is attached.

<u>rod</u> A straight piece of steel used to transfer motion within the vehicle's suspension system. It typically has treads cut on one or both ends.

<u>roll</u> Movement of a vehicle around its x-axis (the imaginary line down the center of the vehicle from front to back). It is commonly referred to as body roll or lean; when cornering, the body will try to move to the outside of the corner against the suspension.

<u>rubber-bonded bushing</u> A bushing that has a steel outer housing and inner sleeve with rubber inside; also known as a metalastic bushing.

<u>scrub radius</u> The distance between two imaginary points on the road surface—the point of center contact between the road surface and the tire, and the intersecting point where the steering axis centerline and the tire centerline contact the road surface.

<u>self-leveling</u> A vehicle with automatic load-adjustable shock absorbers.

<u>setback</u> The distance one wheel is set back from the wheel on the opposite side of the axle.

<u>shock absorber</u> A device on a vehicle designed to absorb bumps and jolts caused from driving on irregular surfaces and to dampen body movement.

<u>short-/long-arm (SLA) suspension</u> A type of control arm suspension system that uses a short control arm on the top and a long control arm on the bottom. This design ensures correct alignment angles when moving through bumps.

<u>shroud</u> A steel or plastic cover placed over the shock rod.

sintering The process of using pressure and heat to bond metal particles.

solid axle A single piece of steel that provides a simple means of mounting the hub and wheel units. Also called beam axle or straight axle.

splined section A flat key made into a shaft to accommodate changes in shaft length due to movement in wheel camber with suspension action.

spring A resilient steel part that stores energy when compressed and releases energy when released to its original state; available as a leaf spring, coil spring, or torsion bar.

spring eyes Rolled ends of some springs used to mount springs to the chassis.

spring shackle bushing A bushing that is positioned in the shackle that the leaf spring mounts to. Bushings allow the spring shackle to move as the leaf spring dimensions change over bumps.

static toe A setting designed to compensate for slight wear in steering components that may cause the wheels to turn outward or inward while the vehicle is in motion.

steering axis inclination (SAI) The angle formed by an imaginary line running through the upper and lower steering pivots relative to vertical as viewed from the front.

stop A rubber part used to control the movement of control arms (suspension arms).

strut A shock absorber used on a MacPherson strut–type suspension.

suspension action Movement of the chassis up and down.

suspension strut A shock absorber designed to reduce spring oscillations.

suspension system A system within a vehicle designed to isolate the vehicle body from road bumps and vibrations.

sway bar A part used in vehicles as a stabilizer, or antiroll bar. It is connected to the chassis in the center, and each end is connected to one side of the suspension system. It is typically installed on the front, and sometimes the rear suspension.

swinging shackle A shackle connected to the rear of the multileaf spring that allows the leaf spring to move downward when a load is placed on the rear of the vehicle.

thrust angle The angle formed between the centerline of the rear axle in comparison to the centerline of the vehicle.

thrust line The imaginary line drawn through the center of the rear axle.

toe-in When the front of the wheels, as seen from above, are closer together than the rear of the wheels.

toe-out When the rear of the wheels, as seen from above, are closer together than the front of the wheels.

toe-out on turns The difference in turning angle of the inside tire in comparison to the outside tire. This angle difference allows the tires to roll through the corner rather than the inside tire dragging. Also referred to as Ackermann angle.

torsion bar A bar made of a steel alloy that is fixed rigidly to the chassis at one end and the suspension control arm at the other to support the weight of a vehicle.

torsional load A force that is applied by clamping one end of an object to another object that is then twisted.

trailing arm suspension A type of suspension system that uses upper and lower control arms.

trim height The amount of ground clearance a vehicle has, measured from a point on the body or frame depending on the manufacturer. Also known as ride height.

turning radius A measure of how small a circle the vehicle can turn around when the steering wheel is turned to the limit.

unibody construction A construction style that uses the body sheet metal as the frame of the vehicle. Typically this type of construction uses small frame sections called subframes.

uniform pitch A spring whose pitch (the distance from the center of one coil to the center of the adjacent coil) is the same distance throughout.

universal joints Joints placed on each end of a driveshaft that help compensate for movement of the rear end housing up and down.

unsprung mass Any part of the steering and suspension system that is not supported by springs. A large amount of unsprung weight will cause the tire to hop off the ground when hitting bumps, as the weight will overcome dampening of the shock absorbers.

unsprung weight *See* unsprung mass.

Watt's linkage Another name for a rigid-axle coil-spring suspension that uses two bars similar to a panhard rod and a pivot point on the axle to keep the axle from moving in turns.

wheel alignment The practice of aligning the wheels of the vehicle to the centerline of the vehicle and to each other. It ensures that the vehicle will handle correctly and gives best tire wear.

wishbone control arm Another term for an A-arm.

wrap leaf A spring containing spring eyes.

yaw Movement of a vehicle around its z-axis (vertical axis) felt when the vehicle deviates from its straight path, as when skidding sideways and the rear comes around.

zero camber A tire with no tilt or zero camber angle.

zero scrub radius A condition in which the point of center contact between the road surface and the tire and the point where the steering axis centerline contacts the road surface intersect at the road surface.

ASE-Type Questions

1. Tech A says that the wheel and tire are examples of unsprung weight. Tech B says that the exhaust system is an example of sprung weight. Who is correct?
   a. Tech A
   b. Tech B
   c. Both A and B
   d. Neither A nor B

2. Tech A says that thrust angle refers to the direction the front wheels are pointing. Tech B says that scrub radius refers to the vertical centerline of the tire in relation to an imaginary line through the steering knuckle pivots. Who is correct?
   a. Tech A
   b. Tech B
   c. Both A and B
   d. Neither A nor B

3. Tech A says that yaw is when a vehicle deviates from its straight path. Tech B says that roll is felt during hard braking. Who is correct?
   a. Tech A
   b. Tech B
   c. Both A and B
   d. Neither A nor B

4. Tech A says that a vehicle will tend to pull toward the side with the most positive camber. Tech B says that a progressive-rate spring offers a soft ride but can also carry a heavier load. Who is correct?
   a. Tech A
   b. Tech B
   c. Both A and B
   d. Neither A nor B

5. Tech A says that a shock dampens movement of the suspension in both upward and downward movement. Tech B says that a shock only dampens upward movement. Who is correct?
   a. Tech A
   b. Tech B
   c. Both A and B
   d. Neither A nor B

6. Tech A says that ball joints must be unloaded when checking them for wear. Tech B says that ball joints must be loaded when checking them for wear. Who is correct?
   a. Tech A
   b. Tech B
   c. Both A and B
   d. Neither A nor B

7. Tech A says that positive toe is when the front of the tires are farther apart than the rear of the tires. Tech B says that a ball joint in a MacPherson strut suspension is a follower joint (not loaded). Who is correct?
   a. Tech A
   b. Tech B
   c. Both A and B
   d. Neither A nor B

8. Tech A says that a dead axle is designed to carry the weight of the vehicle with no drive capability. Tech B says that checking toe-out on turns is a pre-alignment check. Who is correct?
   a. Tech A
   b. Tech B
   c. Both A and B
   d. Neither A nor B

9. Tech A says that loose ball joints can cause the vehicle to wander. Tech B says that loose control arm bushings can affect alignment angles. Who is correct?
   a. Tech A
   b. Tech B
   c. Both A and B
   d. Neither A nor B

10. Tech A says that the front wheels should be aligned before the rear wheels. Tech B says that front wheel toe should be adjusted after front wheel camber and caster. Who is correct?
    a. Tech A
    b. Tech B
    c. Both A and B
    d. Neither A nor B

SECTION VI

Brakes

CHAPTER 30

NATEF Tasks

Brakes
General Brake Systems   Page

- Research applicable vehicle and service information, vehicle service   (MLR) (AST) (MAST)   988
  history, service precautions, and technical service bulletins.

Electronic Brakes, Traction and Stability Control Systems

- Describe the operation of a regenerative braking system.   (MLR) (AST) (MAST)   980, 993–99

Knowledge Objectives

After reading this chapter, you will be able to:
1. Describe the evolution of braking systems from scrub brakes to brake-by-wire systems. (pp 978–980)
2. List the factors that can influence vehicle braking. (pp 980–981)
3. Identify the two types of brake systems on all vehicles. (pp 981–982)
4. Describe how the principles of kinetic energy, Newton's first law of motion, conservation of energy, and friction apply to the brake system. (pp 978–984)
5. Describe how brake design must account for heat transfer. (p 985)
6. Describe the three causes of brake fade. (p 985)
7. Describe rotational force and weight transfer. (pp 985–986)
8. Describe how the principles of levers and fulcrum apply to the brake system. (pp 986–988)
9. Describe the adjustable brake pedal system. (p 988)
10. Describe the principles of braking. (p 988)
11. Describe the legal standards that apply to brake repair and the range of potential liability of the technician. (pp 988–989)
12. List the types of brake systems and describe how they operate. (pp 988–991)
13. List the types of parking brake systems and describe how they operate. (pp 991–993)
14. Describe the brake systems for hybrid vehicles. (pp 993–994)

Principles of Braking

Skills Objectives

There are no skills objectives for this chapter.

▶ Introduction

The brake system is one of the most critical systems on a vehicle. It allows the driver to slow or stop the vehicle as needed. In ideal situations, the driver will have enough time to anticipate the need to slow down well in advance of an event, allowing the vehicle to slow down gradually. However, many situations require the quick use of a very efficient braking system to avoid an accident. In this chapter, we will explore the history, theory, and operation of modern braking systems.

▶ The History of Brakes

Early automobiles evolved from horse-drawn buggies and used a similar scrub braking system. **Scrub brakes** are a simple mechanical system that uses leverage to force a friction block against one or more wheels. In a buggy, for example, the friction between the two surfaces transformed the energy of the moving buggy into heat energy. As heat was created in the friction materials, the buggy slowed down. The scrub braking system was used for more than 2000 years with virtually no change. It worked reasonably well on dry wheel surfaces made of wood or steel but became quickly outdated once rubber tires were developed around 1900, since the scrubbing action on the softer tires significantly decreased tire life.

Faced with the need to replace the scrub braking system with a system that did not apply friction materials directly to the new rubber tires, designers had to consider other options. One option was the **band brake**. It used a metal band lined with friction material that was operated mechanically to clamp around the outside of a small-diameter wheel or was drum-mounted to the axle or wheel. This system worked well in the forward direction, but the band would try to unwind in the reverse direction; the system was therefore impractical and was abandoned after just a few short years.

The next major development was the **drum brake**, which is similar to the drum brakes that are used today. The drum brake consisted of two brake shoes that would push against the inside of the brake drum. Early drum brake systems were mechanically operated by rods, links, and levers **FIGURE 30-1**. This worked fine for applying a single brake unit, but as vehicle

FIGURE 30-1 An early drum brake system.

▶ You are the Automotive Technician

A customer comes into the shop with a brake concern on her 2009 Ford Taurus. She recently drove down a long mountain pass, using her brakes to stay within the speed limit. As she neared the bottom of the pass, the brakes felt like they weren't working, even though the engine was running and she was pushing very hard on the pedal. You recognize the smell of overheated brakes coming from the car. She asks you why her brakes didn't work correctly.

1. How will you explain what happened to the brakes?
2. What would you advise her to do if she is in that situation again?
3. Which type of brakes are more susceptible to this condition?

FIGURE 30-2 Disc brakes force the brake pads against the outside of the brake rotor.

▶ LINK
For more information on ABS brake systems, see the chapter Electronic Brake Control.

operating speeds increased, greater braking demands required brake units to be mounted to each wheel. With this mechanically operated system of rods, links, and levers, it was difficult to maintain equal braking forces at each wheel. The old drum braking systems caused the vehicle to veer dangerously to one side when braking. This system also required frequent adjustment of the brakes. Over time, the mechanical drum brake system gave way to the modern hydraulic drum brake system due to its ability to automatically equalize braking forces at each wheel.

Disc brakes were originally developed in the early 1900s but didn't find common use until the 1960s. Because the effectiveness of friction brakes depends on the braking components' ability to dissipate heat quickly into the atmosphere, drum brakes—with their friction materials on the inside—were at a disadvantage. This led to the greater use of **disc brakes** on most vehicles **FIGURE 30-2**. Disc brakes force brake pads against the outside of the brake rotor and create heat where atmospheric air can quickly remove the heat at its source, making them more efficient under prolonged use.

Advanced Brake Systems

Electronic Brake Control

You might think, "If some brake force is good, then more would be better." But this is not the case. Applying too much brake force can cause the tire to lose traction and skid. If this happens, the driver can lose control of the vehicle. This problem led to the design of electronic brake control (EBC) systems. The first versions of EBC systems were the **anti-lock brake systems (ABS)**. ABS systems

have helped to reduce the number of vehicle accidents each year. They use a computer to monitor each wheel's speed and either hold, decrease, or apply the hydraulic pressure to each wheel to prevent wheel lock-up and maintain the maximum amount of braking power just short of brake lock-up. Additional safety demands led to the development of traction control systems (TCS) and electronic stability control (ESC). TCS systems help to prevent tires from slipping during acceleration by reducing engine torque and, if necessary, applying brake pressure to the slipping wheels. ESC adds additional functionality to ABS and TCS to help prevent the tires from losing traction when the vehicle is being steered aggressively or evasive maneuvers are being undertaken. In both TCS and ESC, the control unit can independently apply individual brake units even though the driver is not stepping down on the brake pedal.

Brake Assist and Brake-by-Wire Systems

Electronic brake control systems have been further enhanced with additional programmed features such as **brake assist (BA)**. BA gives greater control of the braking system to the computer, which can react more quickly and more deliberately than a driver, especially in a panic situation. An example of BA is the **brake-by-wire system**. A full brake-by-wire system does away with the hydraulic portion of the brake system and replaces it with sensors, wires, an electronic control unit, and electrically actuated motors to apply individual brake units at each wheel. The driver applies foot pressure to a **brake pedal emulator**. This tells the computer how firmly the driver intends to brake. The control unit then sends control signals to the appropriate brake actuators, which generate the commanded clamping force and slow the vehicle. All of this is being monitored by sensors reporting data to the control unit, so the desired braking occurs.

Giving greater control of the braking system to the computer increases driving safety. For example, it takes a certain amount of time and stopping distance for the driver to lift his or her foot from the accelerator pedal, step on the brake pedal, and apply the wheel brake units. In a brake-by-wire system, that time and distance can be reduced. The computer can determine that the driver is quickly releasing the accelerator, which indicates a potential panic stop. As the pedal is being released, the control system immediately applies the brakes lightly,

Caring for the Customer

Many auto insurance companies give their customers a discount when the vehicle is equipped with brake safety features, such as ABS systems, as they help avoid or minimize accidents.

which dries any moisture from the braking surfaces and takes up any clearance in the brake system. This prepares the brakes to be fully applied by the control system if the driver steps on the brake pedal or if the computer detects that a collision is about to happen.

Regenerative Brake Systems

With the pressure to improve fuel economy, some manufacturers have equipped their hybrid vehicles with regenerative braking. Regenerative braking takes brake-by-wire technology to the next level. Instead of applying friction brakes and losing energy as heat, the brake-by-wire system uses the electric motor as a generator, which slows the vehicle by converting the vehicle's kinetic energy into electrical energy. The amount of stopping power is controlled by how much electricity is being generated. The more stopping power needed, the more electrical output is demanded of the generator (up to its maximum rated output) by the control system. The electricity is stored in the vehicle's high-voltage battery and can then be used later by the electric motor to drive the vehicle. This regeneration process makes the vehicle more fuel efficient, especially in stop-and-go traffic.

Brake Fundamentals

Several factors can influence vehicle braking. An effective braking system takes all of the following factors into account:

- Road surface: Generally asphalt and concrete road surfaces allow for good braking while gravel surfaces or dirt roads do not.
- Road conditions: Roads that are wet, icy, or covered with loose gravel reduce the tire's traction and result in longer stopping distances. Extremely hot temperatures on asphalt roads can soften the asphalt, making it slippery.
- Weight of the vehicle: Heavier vehicles require more braking force to stop than lighter vehicles and therefore usually have larger wheel brake units. Also, loading down a vehicle increases its stopping distance due to the vehicle's extra mass.
- Load on the wheel during stopping: Heavier loads increase the downward force on the wheels, thereby increasing tire traction **FIGURE 30-3**.
- Height of the vehicle: Stopping power is exerted at the point where the tire and the road connect. The centerline of the vehicle's weight is above this tire-to-road contact point. The taller the vehicle, the greater the leverage on the contact point. This increases the load on some tires, while decreasing the load on other tires. Thus, controlling the vehicle in a panic situation becomes much more difficult.

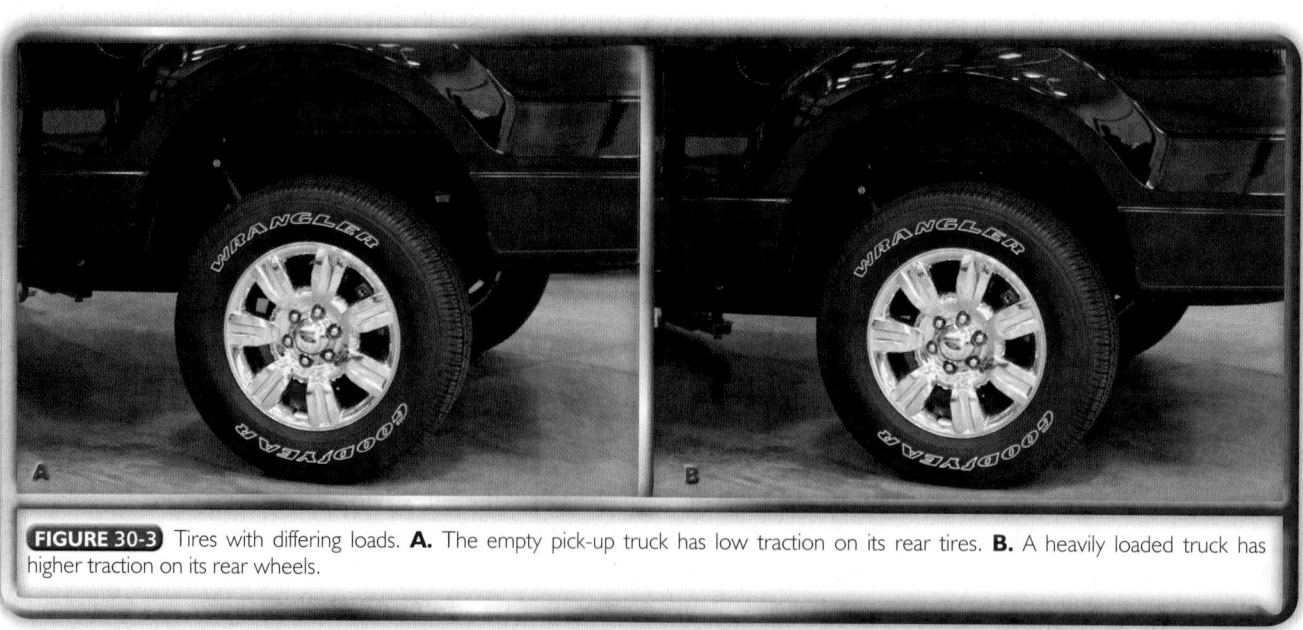

FIGURE 30-3 Tires with differing loads. **A.** The empty pick-up truck has low traction on its rear tires. **B.** A heavily loaded truck has higher traction on its rear wheels.

- How the vehicle is being driven: Aggressive driving causes the tires to become hot and possibly overheated, thus reducing the tire's ability to obtain maximum traction. Also, increased speed and aggressive handling force the brakes to work under extreme conditions.
- The tires on the vehicle: A tire's composition, tread style, tread condition, and inflation pressure all affect its traction **FIGURE 30-4**. Manufacturers design tires with different qualities based on vehicle need. Tires are rated for their traction ability. Using the wrong tire will affect the vehicle's stopping power. For example, a tire with tread designed to channel water away from the tire-to-road contact point will have greater traction when the road surface is wet than the tires used on drag race cars, which have a slick tread.

Brake Systems

There are two brake systems on all vehicles—a service brake and a parking brake. The **service brake** is used for slowing or stopping the vehicle when it is in motion and is operated by a foot pedal **FIGURE 30-5**. Service brakes consist of drum and/or disc brakes. Some have disc brakes on the front wheels and drum brakes on the rear wheels, while others have disc brakes on all four wheels. The **parking brake** is used for holding the vehicle in place when it is stationary. The parking brake is usually operated by hand, but some vehicles use a foot-activated pedal **FIGURE 30-6**.

Modern braking systems are hydraulically operated and have two main sections: the brake assemblies at the wheels and the hydraulic system that applies them. The driver pushes the brake pedal, which applies mechanical force to the pistons in the master cylinder. The pistons

FIGURE 30-4 The condition of the tires will affect braking performance. **A.** Tire in excellent condition. **B.** Worn-out tire.

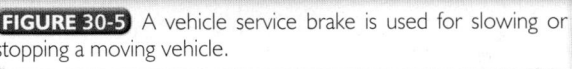

FIGURE 30-5 A vehicle service brake is used for slowing or stopping a moving vehicle.

FIGURE 30-6 A vehicle parking brake is used to hold the vehicle in place when it is stationary.

apply hydraulic pressure to the fluid in the cylinders. The lines transfer the pressure—which is applied equally in all directions within the confines of the brake lines—to the hydraulic cylinders. The hydraulic cylinders at the wheel assemblies apply the brakes **FIGURE 30-7**.

Force is transmitted hydraulically through the fluid. For cylinders of the same size, the force transmitted from one is the same value as the force applied to the other. By using cylinders of different sizes, forces can be increased or reduced, allowing designers to obtain the desired braking force for each wheel **FIGURE 30-8**. The cylinders force friction linings into contact with the braking surfaces. The resulting friction between the surfaces generates heat energy and slows the vehicle.

In drum brakes, the wheel cylinders force brake linings against the inside of the brake drum **FIGURE 30-9**.

In disc brakes, pads are forced against the outside of a brake disc **FIGURE 30-10**. In both systems, heat spreads into other parts and the atmosphere, so brake linings and drums, pads and discs, and brake fluid must withstand high temperatures and high pressures. On modern vehicles, the basic brake system has some refinements such as a power booster and EBC systems. These help the driver apply the brakes, prevent skidding, and maintain directional control of the vehicle under various driving situations **FIGURE 30-11**.

Kinetic Energy

Kinetic energy is the energy of an object in motion. All moving objects have kinetic energy. Heavier objects have more kinetic energy than lighter objects moving

FIGURE 30-7 A braking system in a typical modern vehicle.

FIGURE 30-9 In drum brakes, the wheel cylinders force brake linings against the inside of the brake drum.

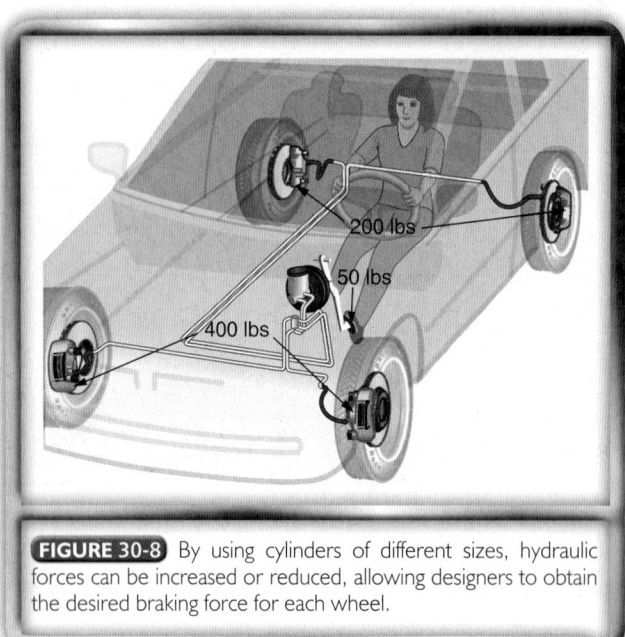

FIGURE 30-8 By using cylinders of different sizes, hydraulic forces can be increased or reduced, allowing designers to obtain the desired braking force for each wheel.

FIGURE 30-10 In disc brakes, pads are forced against the outside of a brake disc.

FIGURE 30-11 ABS brakes help to prevent skidding and maintain directional control of the vehicle.

Applied | **Science**

AS-51: Acceleration/Deceleration: The technician can demonstrate an understanding of a vehicle's acceleration and deceleration as a function of vehicle weight and power.

Kinetic energy is the energy of an object in motion. All moving objects have kinetic energy. Heavier objects have more kinetic energy than lighter objects moving at the same speed. If the weight doubles, the kinetic energy doubles. Energy is needed to start a vehicle. Heat energy is generated in the engine via chemical energy (fuel); it is then converted via mechanical energy to kinetic energy, putting the vehicle in motion. Kinetic energy is converted to heat energy once again through the operation of the brakes. This heat energy is then dissipated in the surrounding air through the brake system, bringing the vehicle to rest.

Newton's first law of motion states that the greater the weight, the more energy is needed to accelerate and maintain speed. For example, it is easier for three people to push a two-door hatchback than an SUV. Also, the more the vehicle weighs, the more energy it takes to decelerate.

at the same speed. If the weight doubles, the kinetic energy doubles. Faster-moving objects have more kinetic energy than slower-moving objects of the same weight. Kinetic energy increases by the square of the speed. This means that if we double the speed of an object, the kinetic energy will increase by four times. If we triple the speed, the kinetic energy will increase by nine times. Thus, the heavier and faster an object is, the greater its kinetic energy. During braking, all of the kinetic energy in the moving vehicle must be converted to another form of energy (in most cases heat) for the vehicle to stop moving; this is the function of the braking system.

Acceleration and Deceleration

Newton's first law of motion states that "an object will stay at rest or uniform speed unless it is acted upon by an outside force." **Acceleration** refers to an increase in an object's speed. In an automobile, acceleration, or an increase in kinetic energy, is caused by the power from the engine. When the driver steps down on the throttle pedal, the engine's power output is increased and the vehicle accelerates. This acceleration requires a certain amount of energy. The heavier the vehicle, the more energy required to accelerate it to a given speed. A lighter vehicle requires less energy to accelerate; this is why race cars are stripped of all unnecessary weight.

Deceleration refers to a decrease in an object's speed. Remember that an outside force is needed for the speed of an object to change. So we need an outside force to act upon the vehicle to cause it to decelerate. That force comes from the mass of the Earth. If you thought it came from the brakes, you would only be partially correct. Imagine traveling at a high speed in a four-wheel drive

vehicle and hitting a bit of a jump. Stepping on the brakes in midair to slow the vehicle wouldn't do you much good, would it? So the brakes only function when they connect the vehicle to the ground or roadway. In fact, that is what they do; they connect the vehicle to the ground through the rolling wheel and tire assembly. In doing so, they apply a varying amount of force from the ground to the vehicle, thereby causing the vehicle to decelerate. The force of the brakes absorbs the kinetic energy of the vehicle. The heavier the vehicle and the faster it is going, the more kinetic energy must be dissipated and the harder the brakes must work.

Energy Transformation

The law of **conservation of energy** states that energy cannot be created or destroyed. This means that the energy used to cause a vehicle to accelerate and decelerate must be transformed from one form of energy to another. Let's follow the cycle of energy transformation in a typical vehicle.

Gasoline or diesel fuels are potential energy in chemical form. A portion of the fuel's chemical energy is transformed within the engine, first into heat energy and then into mechanical energy. Engines are not very efficient, only transforming about 25% to 35% of the chemical energy into mechanical energy. The rest of the chemical energy is wasted as heat energy, mostly through the exhaust and cooling systems. The mechanical energy is used to accelerate the vehicle, thus converting the mechanical energy to kinetic energy. Once the vehicle is up to speed, the engine only needs to transform enough chemical energy into kinetic energy to overcome wind resistance, climb hills, and power the vehicle's accessories. This is why most vehicles get better fuel economy while operating at steady speeds than in stop-and-go traffic—it takes a lot more energy to accelerate a vehicle than it does to maintain a particular speed.

Does deceleration require an energy transformation? Yes, it does. The kinetic energy has to be removed for the vehicle to decelerate. In other words, the kinetic energy must be transformed into another form of energy for the vehicle to slow down. In a standard vehicle, the braking system transforms the kinetic energy into heat energy **FIGURE 30-12**. In essence, it takes the same amount of energy to slow a vehicle as it does to accelerate it. For safety's sake, we expect a vehicle to stop from a given speed faster than the time it took to accelerate to that speed. For this reason, the braking system can transform energy faster than the engine.

Friction and Friction Brakes

__Brakes__ transform kinetic energy to another form of energy. Standard brakes do this through the principle of friction. __Friction__ is the resistance created by surfaces in contact. Static friction is resistance between nonmoving surfaces and is present in parking brakes. Kinetic friction is resistance between moving surfaces and is present in standard brakes. Just as rubbing sandpaper over a block of wood produces heat, operating the brakes causes the moving friction surfaces to come into contact with each other and generate heat. This transformation of energy converts kinetic energy into heat energy and slows the vehicle. If you have seen an old go-kart, you may have noticed the scrub brake. The metal pad scrubbing against the tire causes friction, which slows the go-kart—while also wearing down the tires. As discussed previously,

modern vehicles use a more sophisticated braking system with separate braking components that operate more efficiently.

The amount of friction between two moving surfaces in contact with each other is expressed as a ratio and is called the __coefficient of friction__. It can be found by comparing the amount of force pushing the two surfaces together to the amount of resistive force generated between the two surfaces sliding against each other. For example, a stationary steel surface pushed against a moving steel surface with 100 lb (45.36 kg) of force might generate 20 lb (9.07 kg) of resistive force. This is expressed as $^{20}/_{100}$ ($^{9.07}/_{45.36}$), which equals a coefficient of friction of 0.20. A stationary block of rubber that is pushed against a moving steel surface with 100 lb of force might generate 125 lb (56.7 kg) of friction. This would be $^{125}/_{100}$ ($^{56.7}/_{45.36}$), which equals a coefficient of friction of 1.25.

> **TECHNICIAN TIP**
>
> A higher coefficient of friction usually results in a faster wearing of the softer material, such as rubber. This is one reason why the brake lining is designed to be made of softer materials than the drum or rotor, which leads to the wearing out of the brake lining instead of the drum or rotor.

> **Applied | Science**
>
> **AS-90: Friction: The technician can demonstrate an understanding of friction and its effects on linear and rotational motion.**
> When adjusting drum brakes, the common method is to adjust the brake and turn the wheel at the same time in order to feel how hard it is to turn the wheel while adjusting the brake. As the brake becomes tighter, the friction between the brake drum and the brake shoe increases; therefore the rotational motion requires more torque or force to produce the same speed of movement.
>
> Linear friction is demonstrated when a heavy object is pulled across a flat surface. The more surface area that is in contact with the object, the harder it is to pull. The larger the surface area that the object is covering, then the greater the force required to move it. For example, try to pull a tool box across a bench. Now lift one end of the toolbox and pull. It is far easier to pull the toolbox with one end lifted because the lifted tool box is in contact with less surface area, reducing the force required to move the box.

FIGURE 30-12 During deceleration, kinetic energy is transformed into heat energy.

Potential Energy ⊏⎯⎯⎯⎯➤ Kinetic Energy⊏⎯⎯➤ Heat Energy

Brake Heat

Heat Transfer

Heat transfers from a hot area to a cool area. Since there is a lot of kinetic energy converted to heat during the braking process, the brakes must be able to dissipate that heat to the atmosphere effectively. Heat transfer is critical to this process. Heat must continually be transferred away from the friction materials so that the brakes can perform their job of transforming the kinetic energy into heat energy.

Ultimately, most of the heat generated by the braking process radiates into the atmosphere. How it radiates into the atmosphere depends on the type of braking system. In drum brakes, the heat is created inside of the drum and transfers through the drum to the outside surface where it radiates into the atmosphere. In disc brakes, the heat is created on the outer surfaces of the rotors, which are in contact with the atmosphere. Disc brakes also may have internal ventilation to help dissipate the heat transferred from the outer surface even faster.

Brake Fade

In automobiles, **brake fade** is the reduction in stopping power caused by a change in the brake system. Brake fade can be caused by three factors. The first and most common is **heat fade**. Heat fade is caused by the buildup of heat in the braking surfaces, which get so hot they cannot create any additional heat, leading to a loss of friction. Remember, the brakes must transform kinetic energy into heat energy to decelerate the vehicle. If heat energy cannot be generated, then the kinetic energy cannot be reduced and the vehicle will not decelerate. Heat transfer is used to move heat away from the friction surfaces and allow them to continue generating heat. Once the temperature

of the friction materials become so hot that they cannot generate any additional heat, the coefficient of friction drops and the brakes cannot generate stopping power until some of the heat dissipates.

A driver will experience heat fade after using the brakes too much, such as during high-performance driving or when going down a long, steep hill, particularly when towing. The brake pedal will be hard, but the braking effect "fades" away and the vehicle's rate of deceleration decreases. This is a dangerous condition and is why many long hills on freeways have truck escape ramps made of sand or some other soft material to slow a vehicle by absorbing the truck's kinetic energy in the soft material.

The second type of brake fade is called **water fade** and is caused by water-soaked brake linings. The water acts like a lubricant and lessens the coefficient of friction between the braking surfaces. This leads to a hard brake pedal but very little braking power. Once the water is removed from the friction surfaces through evaporation, the normal coefficient of friction will be restored.

The third kind of brake fade is called **hydraulic fade** and is caused by the brake fluid becoming so hot that it boils. Once it boils, it is no longer only a liquid, converting in part to a vapor, which can be compressed. The brake fluid can no longer transfer force effectively to the wheel brake units and apply them firmly enough to create friction. Since the boiling fluid can be compressed, hydraulic fade can be recognized by the brake pedal becoming soft and having increased pedal travel during heavy brake usage.

Rotational Force

When brakes are operated on a moving vehicle, a **rotational force** is generated. As the wheel rotates, the friction between the brake components tends to twist the brake support in the direction of wheel rotation **FIGURE 30-13**. Since the brake support is ultimately connected to the body of the vehicle, the body too tends to rotate in the same direction. A good example of rotational force is when a motorcycle rider applies the front brake hard enough that the rear wheel is lifted completely off the ground. Rotational forces are usually controlled by the suspension components, but they can become worn and allow movement, which can be felt as a clunk or pop during brake application.

Another result of rotational force is **weight transfer**. The rotational force tends to push the nose of the vehicle down and lift the rear of the vehicle, transferring weight to the front wheels. Rotational force and weight transfer also happen because the centerline of the vehicle is higher than the centerline of the axles; thus, the center of gravity tends to move forward when the brakes are applied firmly **FIGURE 30-14**.

Weight transfer causes the front wheels to have increased traction, allowing them to bear more of the stop-ping load, and causes the rear wheels to have less traction, reducing the amount of load they can bear. Engineers take this into account when designing the brakes; otherwise the front wheels will not get enough stopping power and the rear will have too much, resulting in rear wheel lock-up and loss of control of the vehicle. Lock-up is avoided by engineering the system with the proper-sized master and wheel cylinders and valving that modifies the hydraulic pressure to the rear wheels under hard braking. This is covered in greater detail in the Hydraulic Components section in the Hydraulics and Power Brakes chapter.

Levers and Mechanical Advantage

Brake systems use levers and mechanical advantage to apply service and parking brakes. A simple example of a **lever** is a bar. The point around which a lever rotates and that supports the lever and the load is called the **fulcrum**. A lever allows the user to lift a large load over a small distance at one end by applying a small force over a greater distance from the other end. The effort distance is from the fulcrum to the point effort is applied. The load distance is from the fulcrum to the point the load is applied.

The effort required to move a load depends on the relative distance of the load and the effort from the fulcrum. The ratio of load and effort is called **mechanical advantage**. If the effort distance from the fulcrum is greater than the load distance, then the effort required will be less than the load being moved. If the load distance is greater than the effort distance, then the effort required is greater than the load being moved. This is known as a negative mechanical advantage or **mechanical disadvantage**.

▶ Caring for the Customer

Some owners raise their vehicles for better off-road clearance by installing a lift kit and/or large-diameter tires. Doing so raises the vehicle's center of gravity and increases the amount of weight transfer the vehicle experiences, making it more prone to rear-wheel lock-up and vehicle rollovers. It is important to only use lift kits engineered for the particular vehicle. After installing such a kit, inform the driver of the effect that a higher center of gravity will have on vehicle operation.

FIGURE 30-13 Braking rotational force occurs when the friction between the brake components twists the brake support in the direction of the wheel rotation.

FIGURE 30-14 Weight transfer during braking.

Using the right kind of lever in the right way allows a user to move larger loads with less effort. There are three basic types of levers:

1. Lever of the first order: The fulcrum is in the middle, between the load and the effort **FIGURE 30-15**. Examples are a pry bar or a seesaw. The force applied in this situation is in the opposite direction of the load.

2. Lever of the second order: The load is in the middle, between the effort and the fulcrum **FIGURE 30-16**. An example is a wheelbarrow. The force applied in this situation is in the direction of the load. Brake pedals are usually of the second order. They pivot at the top end (fulcrum). The foot pressure (effort) is applied to the bottom end. And the master cylinder (load) is applied between the two. Mechanical advantage is engineered into the brake pedal to provide the proper brake pedal application and feel **FIGURE 30-17**.

3. Lever of the third order: The effort is in the middle, between the load and the fulcrum **FIGURE 30-18**.

Applied Science

AS-12: Levers: The technician can explain how levers can be used to increase an applied force over distance. The lever action is applied many times on a daily basis. The simplest example is the use of a wrench. If a bolt or nut is tight, then instead of using a wrench with a short handle, you can use a wrench with a longer handle. The longer handle improves the lever's mechanical advantage by increasing the ratio of the effort distance to the load distance, thus providing more torque to undo the nut or bolt.

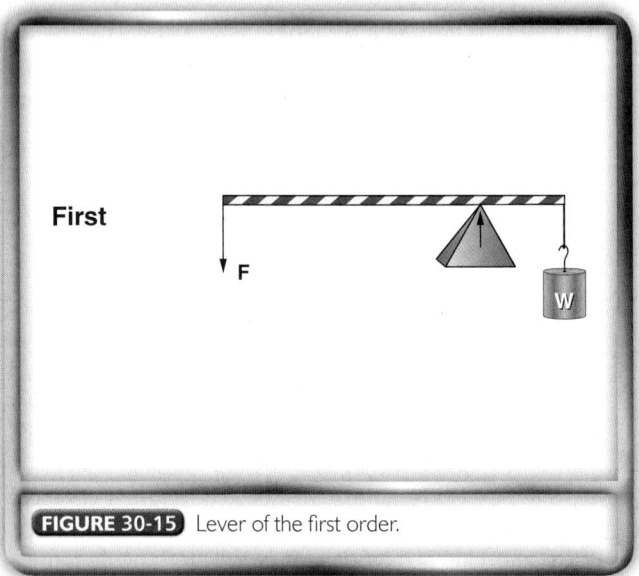

FIGURE 30-15 Lever of the first order.

FIGURE 30-17 The brake pedal uses leverage to multiply the force applied to the master cylinder.

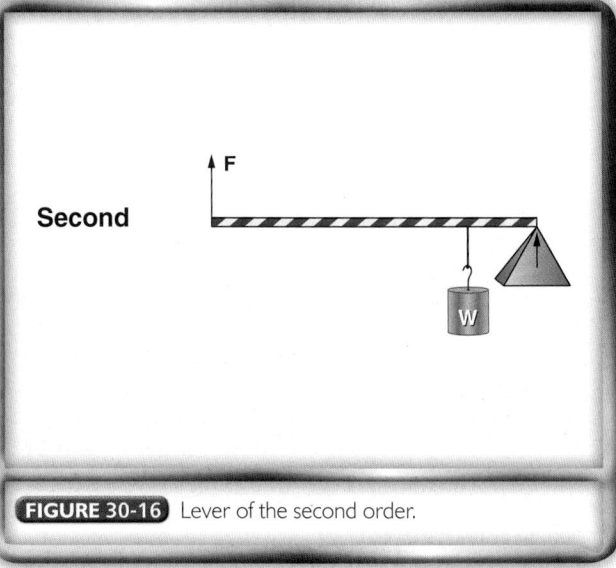

FIGURE 30-16 Lever of the second order.

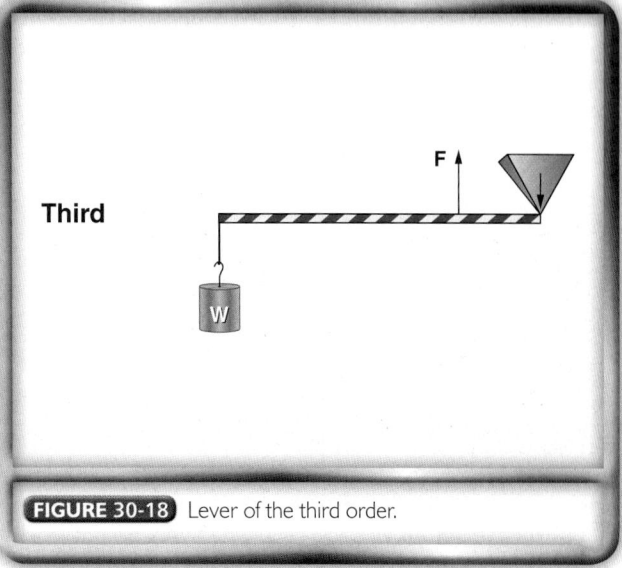

FIGURE 30-18 Lever of the third order.

An example is an oar when paddling a canoe, where the hand holding the top of the oar is the fulcrum, the other hand holding the middle of the oar is providing the effort, and the water is the load. The force in this situation is in the direction of the load.

Adjustable Brake Pedal System

Some vehicles come equipped with adjustable pedal assemblies. Such assemblies allow the driver to raise or lower the brake and throttle pedal assembly for personal comfort. These are usually adjusted by electrically driven motors that are operated by a switch on the steering column or dash (FIGURE 30-19).

Principles of Engine Braking

When a vehicle is in gear, the crankshaft of the engine and the wheels are mechanically connected. When turning force is applied to the crankshaft by the engine, the transmission applies that force to the wheels. Alternatively, if force is applied to the wheels, the transmission applies that force to the engine through the crankshaft. This is the principle behind push-starting a vehicle equipped with a manual transmission. Force is applied to the wheels by pushing the vehicle; when the vehicle has some momentum, engaging a gear turns over the engine, enabling it to start without the assistance of a starter motor.

Engine braking uses this same principle. If you take your foot off the accelerator, so that the engine ceases to apply force to the wheels, the engine begins to act as a brake on the vehicle. As the engine slows down, the momentum of the wheels will keep it turning over. The compression stroke of the engine will soak up some of this kinetic energy, slowing the vehicle. Engaging a lower gear will slow the vehicle more quickly, as the engine will be turned over more rapidly by the movement of the wheels.

Slowing a vehicle while traveling down a steep or very long decline using normal wheel brakes alone can lead to heat buildup and potentially dangerous brake fade. It is good practice to slow the vehicle initially with the brakes, then to shift the transmission into lower gears and let the inertia of the engine assist in slowing the vehicle, and prevent it from accelerating again. This approach is safer because engine braking can be sustained for longer periods of time without reducing braking effectiveness. It also reduces the wear and tear on the brake assemblies.

▶ Brake Repair Legal Standards and Technician Liability

Brake repair is right up with steering and suspension repair on the liability scale. Improperly repaired brakes can function reasonably well under normal driving situations but can fail during a panic situation when they are needed the most. The likelihood of accidents, injury, or death goes up drastically in those situations. Shops and technicians have been successfully sued for improper brake repairs resulting in large cash settlements. Technicians also risk being found criminally negligent if they are determined to have acted maliciously. Always follow the manufacturer's procedures when servicing brake systems. Research service information, precautions, and technical service bulletins. Never take shortcuts, which could cause the vehicle to be unsafe. Remember, safety first!

Safety

Asbestos is a naturally occurring mineral mined from the earth. Asbestos is a long, very thin fibrous crystal. When asbestos is disturbed, small needle-like fibers can break off and remain airborne, where they are inhaled by people. Since these fibers are so small, they embed themselves deep within lung tissue, causing scarring. Repeated exposure can lead to asbestosis and lung cancer.

While asbestos has been removed from most brake and clutch materials, it is still present in some replacement and old components. Therefore, you must treat all brake and clutch dust as if it contains asbestos. This is accomplished by using an aqueous brake wash station, a HEPA brake dust vacuum system, or, in some states, an aerosol can of brake cleaning solution to carefully wash down the brake components.

FIGURE 30-19 An adjustable pedal system. **A.** Low position. **B.** High position. **C.** Activating switch.

Types of Brakes

Now it is time to explore the different types of brakes used on various vehicles. Each vehicle application lends itself to a particular type of brake system. For example, consider trailers. Since they must be able to be hooked up to multiple tow vehicles, connecting a hydraulic brake system becomes difficult due to the leaking of hydraulic fluid as well as air entering the lines. Thus, some heavy trucks use air-operated brakes. That way, when connecting and disconnecting the brake air line, only air will leak, not brake fluid. On passenger-type tow vehicles, electric brakes are often used.

Drum and Disc Brakes

Friction brakes use two kinds of wheel brake units. Drum brakes have a drum attached to the wheel hub and rotate with the tire. Braking occurs by means of stationary brake shoes expanding against the inside of the drum, which creates friction and slows the vehicle. Disc brakes have a disc brake rotor attached to the wheel hub and rotate with the tire. The braking occurs by means of stationary pads clamping against the outside of the rotor, creating friction to slow the vehicle. On light vehicles, both of these systems are hydraulically operated, meaning they use hydraulic fluid to transfer the force from the driver. The brake pedal operates a **master cylinder**. Hydraulic lines and hoses connect the master cylinder to the wheel brake units **FIGURE 30-20**.

Most modern light vehicles have either disc brakes on the front wheels and drum brakes on the rear or disc brakes on all four wheels. Disc brakes require greater force to operate than drum brakes and usually include a power brake booster to assist the driver by increasing the force applied to the master cylinder when the brake is operated **FIGURE 30-21**.

Modern drum and disc brake systems are regularly fitted with an ABS that monitors the speed of each wheel and prevents wheel lock-up or skidding, no matter how hard brakes are applied or how slippery the road surface. This allows the driver to better maintain directional control of the vehicle. ABS also generally reduces stopping distances. The system consists of a brake pedal, power booster, master cylinder, wheel speed sensors, the electronic control unit (ECU), and the hydraulic control unit, also called a hydraulic modulator.

> ▶ **LINK**
> For more information on air-operated braking systems, see the chapter Hydraulics and Power Brakes.

Air Brakes

Air-operated braking systems are used on heavy vehicles and are commonly called air brakes **FIGURE 30-22**.

FIGURE 30-21 A power brake booster.

FIGURE 30-20 The hydraulic brake system.

FIGURE 30-22 The air brake system.

Compressed air, operating on large-diameter diaphragms, provides the large forces at the brake assembly that are needed to apply the brakes and slow the vehicle. The wheel brake units can be either drum or disc style.

Some brake canisters incorporate a separate air chamber and large spring assembly **FIGURE 30-23** and are referred to as spring brakes. The spring applies the brakes when air pressure is released from the separate chamber. Air pressure applied to this chamber compresses the spring and releases the brakes. This system acts as a parking brake when the vehicle or trailer is parked and as a safety measure by applying the brakes in the case of an inadvertent loss of air pressure in the brake system. A vehicle or trailer with this type of air-operated brakes must have a minimum amount of air pressure in the system to compress the spring and release the brakes.

The air pressure for air brake systems comes from an engine-driven air compressor that pumps air into storage tanks. The tanks provide a reservoir of pressurized air to operate the system. Driver-controlled valves then direct the compressed air to different wheel units to operate the wheel brake units. When the driver releases the brakes, the control valve releases the air in the system and the brakes retract.

On articulated vehicles, such as tractor/trailers, any delays in applying the trailer brakes should be minimized. This is achieved by using a relay valve and a separate air tank on the trailer **FIGURE 30-24**. This arrangement also applies the brakes if the trailer becomes disconnected from the tractor.

Exhaust Brakes

Heavy-duty vehicles often require increased braking in situations where friction brakes overheat and fail. This can be achieved by using an exhaust brake. An **exhaust brake** works by restricting the flow of exhaust gases through the engine by closing a butterfly valve located in the exhaust manifold. Restricting the exhaust flow results in high pressure in the exhaust manifold and the engine's cylinders. Since the engine acts as an air compressor, restricting the exhaust flow causes the engine speed to slow down, which in turn slows the road wheels through the transmission or power train **FIGURE 30-25**.

FIGURE 30-24 The relay valve and separate air reservoir.

FIGURE 30-23 An air brake canister.

FIGURE 30-25 Exhaust brakes.

Jake Brakes

In heavy diesel vehicles, engine braking is less effective because more of the compression energy in the cylinders is returned to the crankshaft after the piston reaches top dead center. This results in an engine that wants to free-wheel and does not create much force to slow the vehicle. A jake brake (or compression brake) uses an extra lobe on the camshaft to control an auxiliary exhaust valve at the top of each cylinder. When engaged, the jake brake releases the compression stroke pressure before it can be transmitted back to the power stroke of the piston. This causes a substantial amount of energy to be used on the compression stroke, which slows the crankshaft and increases the braking effectiveness of the engine. The disadvantage with this form of braking is that it is very noisy, producing a chattering, machine-gun sound, usually requiring additional muffling. It is loud enough that some municipalities ban the use of compression brakes in residential or other sensitive areas.

Electric Brakes

Trailers towed by light vehicles must have a braking system if their gross weight exceeds a certain value. An **electric braking system** is commonly used to activate drum-type friction brakes on the trailer **FIGURE 30-26**. The braking effect can be increased or reduced by the driver by adjusting a control unit to suit the load on the trailer. This manual override can be used in certain driving conditions to dampen a trailer's tendency to sway.

When the brakes in the towing vehicle are applied, the brake light circuit sends the signal to the control unit.

The control unit then sends an appropriate current to the trailer brake actuators to operate the trailer brakes at the braking level selected. The electric current is supplied to the brake units at the wheels. The brake assembly uses lever-operated brake shoes. The lever incorporates an electromagnet on the end. The electric current flows through the electromagnet, creating magnetism that draws the magnet toward the spinning brake drum. The magnet contacts the drum and is pulled around, applying the brake shoes. If the driver steps harder on the brake pedal, the trailer controller sends a stronger electric current to the electromagnet, causing it to be held tighter to the spinning drum, which increases the braking force.

In some places, trailers above a specified weight must also have an auxiliary battery-powered braking system that automatically applies the brakes and keeps them applied if the trailer ever breaks away from its towing vehicle.

▶ Parking Brakes

As mentioned previously, all vehicles must be fitted with a service brake and a parking brake. The service brake is usually hydraulically operated and is used while the vehicle is being driven. It applies brake units at all four wheels. The parking brake is mechanically operated to hold the vehicle in place when it is parked. It applies the brake units on two wheels only.

There are several types of parking brakes. Some vehicles equipped with disc brakes incorporate a mechanically operated drum-style parking brake in the center of the rear disc brake rotors, commonly called a **top hat parking brake** design **FIGURE 30-27**. Other vehicles

FIGURE 30-26 An electric braking system.

FIGURE 30-27 A top hat design parking brake.

use a mechanical linkage to directly operate a disc-style service brake **FIGURE 30-28** .

On drum brakes, a **drum-style parking brake** mechanically applies the brake shoes against the drum. The parking brake cable pulls on an actuating lever inside the brake drum assembly **FIGURE 30-29** . The actuating lever is connected to the secondary brake shoe by a pin or tang and to the primary shoe by a strut. Movement of the lever forces both shoes against the drum.

Less common, older arrangements of parking brakes include a front wheel–mounted parking brake, which activates each front brake caliper, and a **transmission-mounted parking brake**, which uses a small drum brake to prevent the drive shaft from turning **FIGURE 30-30** . This latter brake is sometimes called a transmission brake.

Parking Brake Cables

Parking brake cables transmit force from the parking brake actuating lever to the brake unit. Part of the cable is inside a wound steel housing **FIGURE 30-31** , which allows it to be somewhat flexible, yet non-compressible to guide the cable and hold everything in place. Other sections of the cable are exposed, which can make them susceptible to damage by being caught on road hazards, especially on off-road vehicles. Also, since the cables are steel, they can rust and stick to the inside of the wound housing. This is especially true where de-icing chemicals are used on roads. Periodic lubrication of the parking brake cables with the lubricant specified by the vehicle manufacturer helps reduce this problem.

Parking brake strut

Parking brake pivot

Parking brake cable   Parking brake lever

FIGURE 30-29 A drum-style parking brake.

Transmission

Parking brake drum (brake shoes inside)

FIGURE 30-30 Parking brake—transmission style.

FIGURE 30-28 A disc brake system with an integral parking brake.

FIGURE 30-31 A parking brake cable.

Parking Brake Apply Mechanisms

Parking brakes are commonly applied in two ways. The first is a hand-operated lever, usually mounted between the front seats. The lever has its fulcrum on the bottom end, and the cable is attached a few inches from the fulcrum. The driver grasps the handle on the end opposite of the fulcrum, which gives the driver substantial mechanical advantage and ensures that the parking brake can be firmly applied. The handle contains a ratcheting

FIGURE 30-32 Methods of adjustment. **A.** Parking brake adjustment—under the car. **B.** Parking brake adjustment—brake lever. **C.** Parking brake adjustment—disc brake caliper.

mechanism that engages automatically when the driver pulls up on the parking brake lever. This mechanism holds the handle in the applied position and maintains tension on the parking brake cables and assembly. The driver can release the mechanism by lifting slightly up on the handle and pushing the release button, which retracts the ratcheting tab and allows the driver to lower the parking brake handle.

The second type of operating mechanism works similarly, but is foot operated. It uses mechanical advantage to firmly apply the parking brake, as well as a ratcheting mechanism to hold it once applied. It is usually mounted under the dash near the kick panel toward the outside of the car. Some foot-mounted parking brake levers can be released by pulling a release handle, which retracts the ratcheting tang and allows the pedal to return to its rest position. Other pedals can be released by simply pushing the pedal a bit farther down, which automatically retracts the ratchet and allows the pedal to return. The last method uses vacuum or electric power to release the parking brake when the gear selector is moved out of the park position.

Parking Brake Adjustment

Parking brake systems incorporate some method of adjustment, although it is not the same for all vehicles. The method of adjustment could be accomplished by an adjustment nut on the cable under the vehicle, an adjustment on the brake lever assembly, or an adjustment at the rear calipers **FIGURE 30-32**. When adjusting parking brakes, the order of adjustment is as follows: (1) the parking brake cable, which should have slack in it, (2) the service brakes, which are adjusted according to the manufacturer's procedure, and (3) the parking brake. This sequence will ensure that both brake systems are adjusted properly.

▶ Hybrid Vehicles

Regenerative Braking

Friction brakes convert the kinetic energy of the moving vehicle into heat, which is dissipated to the atmosphere. This is a waste of good energy. **Regenerative braking** is technology that allows a vehicle to recapture and store part of that kinetic energy in a reusable form when braking. Regenerative braking is accomplished by causing the hybrid vehicle's electric motor to act as a generator (commonly called a motor/generator) that converts kinetic energy into electrical energy that is stored in the form of chemical energy within the vehicle's high-voltage battery for future use **FIGURE 30-33**. The amount of braking force applied by the regeneration system is controlled by a computer. This system still requires traditional friction-based brakes to be used when quick, heavy braking is required. The interaction between the regenerative braking system and the friction braking system must be carefully designed and serviced so that each operates seamlessly with each other.

Brake-by-Wire

Brake-by-wire means there is no mechanical or hydraulic connection between the brake pedal and the wheel brake units. There are two types of brake-by-wire systems: electric and electric/hydraulic **FIGURE 30-34**. The electric type uses wheel brake units with an integrated motor system that applies clamping force to the disc brake pads. The electric/hydraulic type uses a hydraulic controller to apply hydraulic pressure to standard wheel brake units. The brakes, in either case, are computer controlled. They use the brake pedal position and pedal application speed as indicators of what the driver wants to do. The computer evaluates that information in light of other data such as vehicle speed and traction conditions. It then compares that data to preloaded information in memory. The computer then commands the brake controller to create a specific amount of brake pressure at the appropriate wheel brake units. The driver can modify the programmed braking effort by depressing or releasing the brake pedal an additional amount.

Many vehicles use this same principle to control the engine's throttle (drive-by-wire), meaning there is no mechanical connection between the throttle pedal and the throttle plate. On a throttle, it is easy to replicate throttle pedal feel, as the pedal only works against spring tension. Integrating a spring with similar characteristics will result in a similar-feeling throttle pedal. The feel of a brake pedal is not as easily replicated because in addition to spring pressure, the driver is also pushing against hydraulic pressure, giving the pedal a much firmer feel. This problem can be overcome by using a brake pedal emulator, which is a sealed cylinder that builds pressure similar to a master cylinder. It also incorporates the sensors that send brake pedal data to the ECU.

There are several benefits to brake-by-wire, including the following: weight is reduced and space is saved; drivers do not feel ABS brake pulsations, making them less likely to remove their foot from the brake pedal during a panic stop; and the brakes are applied more quickly in an emergency situation. There are also several

drawbacks, such as the risk of a system failure and the initial cost. Some current hybrid vehicles use brake-by-wire technology during regeneration but with a hydraulic backup brake system. In this case, the brake-by-wire system initiates braking first by applying a load to the vehicle from the generator, and once that is at its maximum output, it can also apply the hydraulic brakes to get additional stopping power, if needed.

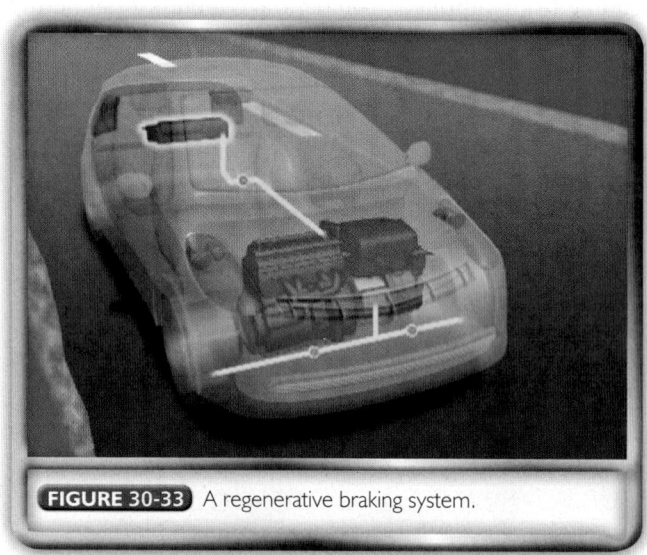

FIGURE 30-33 A regenerative braking system.

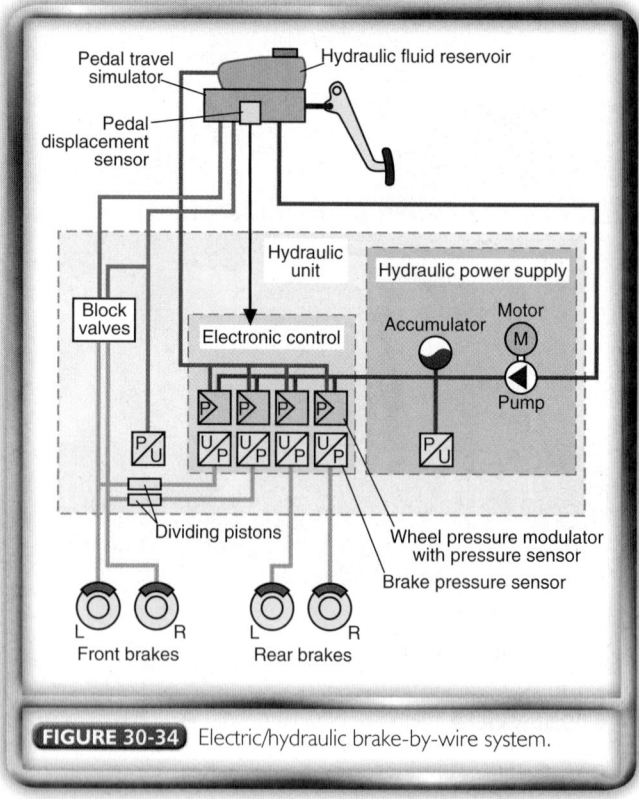

FIGURE 30-34 Electric/hydraulic brake-by-wire system.

Wrap-up

Ready for Review

▶ Braking systems evolved from scrub brakes to band brakes to the drum and disc brakes that are used today.

▶ Electronic brake systems use computer technology to assist with braking by determining speed and needed force to stop.

▶ The development of electronic brake systems has led to improvements in consumer safety and fuel economy.

▶ Brake-by-wire systems use computer technology in place of the mechanical or hydraulic connection between the brake pedal and wheel brake units.

▶ Regenerative brake systems (used in hybrid vehicles) convert a vehicle's energy into electrical energy, which is stored in the battery for later use.

▶ Factors affecting the effectiveness of braking systems include road surface, road conditions, vehicle weight and height, load on wheels, type of tire, and aggressive vs. defensive driving.

▶ Every vehicle has two brake systems: service brake (for stopping the vehicle in motion) and parking brake (for holding the vehicle when stationary).

▶ Hydraulically operated braking systems use a system of cylinders to transfer pressure from the brake pedal to the wheel.

▶ The braking system converts a vehicle's kinetic energy (the energy of an object in motion) into an alternate form of energy (e.g., heat).

▶ Acceleration and deceleration determine whether the vehicle's speed is increasing or decreasing. Both require an outside force for action, such as the vehicle's engine (acceleration) or braking system (deceleration).

▶ The law of conservation of energy requires that energy must be transformed from one form to another; it cannot be created or destroyed.

▶ Standard brakes use friction to create resistance, thus transforming kinetic energy into heat energy.

▶ The amount of force pushing two surfaces together compared to the amount of resistive force generated between the two surfaces sliding against each other is called the coefficient of friction.

▶ Heat energy created by the braking process gets dissipated into the atmosphere.

▶ Reduction in a vehicle's stopping power (brake fade) can be caused by heat fade, water fade, or hydraulic fade.

▶ Braking systems create rotational force on the vehicle's suspension, resulting in weight transfer to the front wheels.

▶ There are three types of levers: lever of the first order (fulcrum in the middle), lever of the second order (load in the middle), and lever of the third order (effort in the middle).

▶ Engine braking allows the engine to act as a brake by absorbing energy during deceleration.

▶ Technicians can be held liable for improperly repaired brakes.

▶ Disc brakes and drum brakes are two types of friction brakes that are used on lighter vehicles; both can be equipped with antilock braking systems.

▶ Air-operated braking systems, used on heavier vehicles, use air pressure to apply the brakes (drum or disc style).

▶ An exhaust brake may be used in addition to friction brakes in heavy vehicles and creates engine pressure by restricting the exhaust flow.

▶ Jake brakes are used in heavier diesel vehicles and rely on compression to slow the crankshaft and increase braking effectiveness.

▶ Trailers over a certain weight often use an electric braking system to give the driver braking control.

▶ Parking brake styles include: top hat parking brake, drum-style parking brake, and transmission-mounted parking brake.

▶ Parking brakes use a ratcheting mechanism to maintain tension on the parking brake cables and assembly when applied.

Key Terms

<u>acceleration</u> An increase in a vehicle's speed.

<u>air-operated braking system</u> A braking system that uses compressed air operating on large-diameter diaphragms to provide force to the braking assembly; also called air brakes.

<u>anti-lock brake system (ABS)</u> A safety measure for the braking system that uses a computer to monitor the speed of each wheel and control the hydraulic pressure to each wheel to prevent wheel lock-up.

<u>asbestos</u> A mineral with needle-like fibers that can become embedded in lung tissue and cause cancer.

<u>band brake</u> A braking system that uses a metal band lined with friction material to clamp around the outside of a wheel or drum.

brake assist (BA) An enhanced safety system built in to some ABS systems that anticipates a panic stop and applies maximum braking force to slow the vehicle as quickly as possible.

brake-by-wire system A braking system that uses no mechanical connection between the brake pedal and each brake unit. The system uses electrically actuated motors to apply brake force.

brake fade The reduction in stopping power caused by a change in the brake system such as overheating, water, or overheated brake fluid.

brake pedal emulator A brake pedal assembly used in electronically controlled braking systems to send the driver's braking intention to the computer; it mimics the feel of a standard brake pedal.

brakes A system made up of hydraulic and mechanical components designed to slow or stop a vehicle.

coefficient of friction The amount of friction between two moving surfaces in contact with each other.

conservation of energy A physical law that states that energy cannot be created or destroyed.

deceleration A decrease in a vehicle's speed.

disc brakes A type of brake system that forces stationary brake pads against the outside of a rotating brake rotor.

drum brakes A type of brake system that forces brake shoes against the inside of a brake drum.

drum-style parking brake A mechanically operated drum brake that can be set while the vehicle is not moving to serve as a parking brake.

electric braking system A braking system used to provide braking to trailers; the drum brakes are electrically activated in the trailer when the driver applies the brakes on the towing vehicle.

exhaust brake A brake system that restricts the flow of exhaust gases through the engine by closing a butterfly valve located in the exhaust manifold. Restricting the exhaust flow causes the engine speed to slow down, slowing the vehicle.

friction The resistance created by surfaces in contact. Kinetic friction is resistance to motion when one surface moves over another. Static friction is resistance to motion between two surfaces that are not moving.

fulcrum The point around which a lever rotates and that supports the lever and the load.

heat fade Brake fade caused by the buildup of heat in braking surfaces, which get so hot they cannot create any additional heat, leading to a loss of friction.

hydraulic fade Brake fade caused by boiling brake fluid.

jake brake A brake system that consists of an extra exhaust valve on a diesel engine, which releases compressed gases from the combustion chamber at the top of the compression stroke; also called a compression brake.

kinetic energy The energy of an object in motion; it increases by the square of the speed.

lever A tool that allows the user to move a large load over a small distance at one end by applying a small force over a greater distance from the other end.

master cylinder Converts the brake pedal force into hydraulic pressure, which is then transmitted via brake lines and hoses to one or more pistons at each wheel brake unit.

mechanical advantage The ratio of load and effort for any simple machine such as a lever.

mechanical disadvantage When the load distance on a lever is greater than the effort distance, which means the effort required to move the load is greater than the load itself.

Newton's first law of motion A physical law that states that "an object will stay at rest or uniform speed unless it is acted upon by an outside force."

parking brake A brake system used for holding the vehicle when it is stationary.

parking brake cable A mechanism used to transmit force from the parking brake actuating lever to the brake unit.

regenerative braking Technology used in vehicles that allows the vehicle to recapture and store part of the vehicle's kinetic energy in a reusable form when braking. Primarily used in hybrid and electric vehicles.

rotational force The force created by the rotating wheel when the brakes are applied; it causes the brake components to twist the brake support and ultimately the vehicle in the direction of wheel rotation.

scrub brakes A brake system that uses leverage to force a friction block against one or more wheels.

service brake A brake system that is operated while the vehicle is moving to slow or stop the vehicle.

top hat parking brake A drum brake that is located inside a disc brake rotor in order to act as a parking brake.

transmission-mounted parking brake A drum brake that is mounted on the drive shaft just after the transmission to serve as a parking brake.

water fade Brake fade caused by water-soaked brake linings.

weight transfer Weight moving from one set of wheels to the other set of wheels during braking, acceleration, or cornering.

ASE-Type Questions

1. Tech A says that regenerative braking converts brake heat into electricity. Tech B says that regenerative braking converts electrical energy into braking energy. Who is correct?
   a. Tech A
   b. Tech B
   c. Both A and B
   d. Neither A nor B

2. Tech A says that an anti-lock brake system (ABS) allows the front wheels to be steered during a panic stop. Tech B says that ABS sensor inputs control wheel speed during brake events. Who is correct?
   a. Tech A
   b. Tech B
   c. Both A and B
   d. Neither A nor B

3. Tech A says that water soaked brake shoes will cause brake fade. Tech B says that disc brakes dissipate heat faster than drum brakes. Who is correct?
   a. Tech A
   b. Tech B
   c. Both A and B
   d. Neither A nor B

4. Tech A says that a brake-by-wire system can start to apply brakes before the driver can step on the brake pedal. Tech B says that brake-by-wire systems use heavy cables to transmit the brake pedal force to the wheel brake units. Who is correct?
   a. Tech A
   b. Tech B
   c. Both A and B
   d. Neither A nor B

5. Tech A says that tire pressure does not affect braking. Tech B says that heavy vehicle loads increase stopping distance. Who is correct?
   a. Tech A
   b. Tech B
   c. Both A and B
   d. Neither A nor B

6. Tech A says that light-duty service brakes are applied hydraulically. Tech B says that light-duty parking brakes are applied hydraulically. Who is correct?
   a. Tech A
   b. Tech B
   c. Both A and B
   d. Neither A nor B

7. Tech A says that the heavier the vehicle, the more stopping power is needed. Tech B says that the faster a vehicle is moving, the more braking power is needed. Who is correct?
   a. Tech A
   b. Tech B
   c. Both A and B
   d. Neither A nor B

8. Tech A says that kinetic energy is created during braking to stop the vehicle. Tech B says that kinetic energy is converted to heat energy during braking. Who is correct?
   a. Tech A
   b. Tech B
   c. Both A and B
   d. Neither A nor B

9. Tech A says that the brake pedal uses leverage to multiply foot pressure. Tech B says that when braking hard while moving forward, the vehicle's weight transfers to the rear wheels, increasing their traction. Who is correct?
   a. Tech A
   b. Tech B
   c. Both A and B
   d. Neither A nor B

10. Tech A says that friction brakes can fade due to overheating of the brake lining. Tech B says that friction brakes can fade due to overheating of the brake fluid. Who is correct?
    a. Tech A
    b. Tech B
    c. Both A and B
    d. Neither A nor B

CHAPTER 31

Hydraulics and Power Brakes

NATEF Tasks, continued

Power Assist Units

- Measure and adjust master cylinder pushrod length. **AST** **MAST** 1031–1032

- Check brake pedal travel with, and without, engine running to verify proper power booster operation. **MLR** **AST** **MAST** 1033–1034

- Check vacuum supply (manifold or auxiliary pump) to vacuum-type power booster. **MLR** **AST** **MAST** 1035

- Inspect vacuum-type power booster unit for leaks; inspect the check-valve for proper operation; determine necessary action. **AST** **MAST** 1036–1037

- Inspect and test hydraulically-assisted power brake system for leaks and proper operation; determine necessary action. **AST** **MAST** 1037–1038

Miscellaneous

- Check parking brake operation and parking brake indicator light system operation; determine necessary action. **MLR** **AST** **MAST** 1045

- Check parking brake cables and components for wear, binding, and corrosion; clean, lubricate, adjust or replace as needed. **MLR** **AST** **MAST** 1045–1046

- Check operation of brake stop light system. **MLR** **AST** **MAST** 1046

Knowledge Objectives

After reading this chapter, you will be able to:

1. Describe the principles behind the hydraulic braking system. (pp 1023–1024)
2. Describe the principles of hydraulic pressure and force, and discuss how the principles apply to the hydraulic braking system. (pp 1023–1024)
3. Describe the principles of working pressures, input force, and output force, and discuss how the principles apply to the hydraulic braking system. (p 1024)
4. Define Pascal's law and discuss how it applies to the hydraulic braking system. (pp 1024–1025)
5. Describe the role of brake fluid in a hydraulic braking system. (pp 1025–1026)
6. Describe the purpose of a master cylinder. (pp 1026–1030)
7. Describe how master cylinders operate within the hydraulic braking system. (pp 1026–1030)

Knowledge Objectives, continued

8. Describe the purpose of a brake pedal. (pp 1030–1031)
9. Describe how brake pedals operate within the hydraulic braking system. (pp 1030–1031)
10. Describe the purpose and standard materials of brake lines. (pp 1031–1032)
11. Describe how to inspect and replace brake lines and brake hoses. (pp 1031–1034)
12. List the types of brake line flares. (pp 1032–1033)
13. Describe the purpose and standard materials of brake hoses. (pp 1033–1034)
14. List the common issues in brake hoses. (p 1034)
15. Describe how a proportioning valve operates. (pp 1035–1036)
16. Describe the purpose of a metering valve and how it operates. (pp 1036–1037)
17. Describe the purpose of a pressure differential valve and how it operates. (p 1037)
18. Describe how brake warning lights and stop lights operate. (p 1038)
19. Discuss how to diagnose common issues with brake warning lights and stop lights. (p 1038)
20. Describe the types of power brakes. (pp 1039–1040)
21. Describe how a vacuum booster operates. (pp 1039–1040)
22. Discuss how to diagnose common issues with power brake systems. (pp 1039–1040)
23. Describe how a dual-diaphragm booster operates. (p 1040)
24. Describe the purpose and operation of a hydraulic brake booster. (pp 1040–1041)
25. Describe the purpose and operation of electrohydraulic braking. (p 1041)
26. Discuss the common questions to ask the customer during diagnosis of a fault in the hydraulic braking system. (p 1055)

Skills Objectives

After reading this chapter, you will be able to:
1. Select, handle, store, and fill brake fluid. (pp 1020–1021)
2. Perform a DVOM–galvanic reaction test. (p 1022)
3. Test brake fluid with a brake fluid tester. (pp 1022–1023)
4. Test brake fluid with brake fluid test strips. (p 1023)
5. Perform the manual bleeding method. (pp 1023–1024)
6. Perform the pressure bleeding method. (pp 1024–1025)
7. Perform the vacuum bleeding method. (pp 1025–1026)
8. Measure the brake pedal height. (pp 1027–1028)
9. Measure the brake pedal free play. (p 1028)
10. Measure brake pedal travel. (p 1028)
11. Perform a master cylinder inspection. (pp 1028–1029)
12. Perform master cylinder service and bench bleed. (pp 1030–1031)
13. Adjust the master cylinder pushrod length. (p 1032)
14. Test the brake pedal free travel and check the power assist operation. (p 1034)
15. Check the vacuum supply to a vacuum-type power booster. (p 1035)
16. Check a vacuum-type power booster unit for leaks and inspect the check valve. (pp 1036–1037)
17. Inspect and test a hydraulically assisted power brake system. (p 1038)
18. Inspect the brake lines, brake hoses, and associated hardware. (pp 1038–1039)
19. Replace the brake lines, hoses, fittings, and supports. (pp 1038–1040)
20. Perform the ISO flare method on a brake line. (pp 1040–1041)
21. Perform the double flare method on a brake line. (p 1041)
22. Check the brake light warning system. (pp 1042–1044)
23. Check the parking brake and indicator light system. (p 1045)
24. Inspect and maintain parking brakes. (p 1045)
25. Check operation of a stop light system. (p 1046)
26. Perform proportioning valve testing. (p 1046)
27. Perform metering valve testing. (p 1046)
28. Perform pressure differential valve testing. (p 1048)

oduction

...odern vehicles, the wheel brake units are ...sing the principles of hydraulics. This means ...s are operated by the force transferred by non-...sible brake fluid flowing through the brake lines ...es. Pressing down on the brake pedal creates ... in the brake fluid, which transmits that pres-...the brake units, which apply force to the fric-...terials, which transform the kinetic energy of the ...g vehicle into heat energy and cause the vehicle to ...rate.

...o make it easier for the driver to apply the brakes, ...ver booster is fitted to the brake system to increase ...driver's brake pedal force to the master cylinder. ...s power booster can be operated by engine vac-...m or through hydraulic pressure, which is usually ...erated by the power steering pump or an electric-...iven pump.

Principles of Hydraulics

Pascal's Law(s)

In the 1600s, Blaise Pascal observed the effects of pressure applied to a fluid in a closed system. **Pascal's law** states that "pressure applied to a fluid in one part of a closed system will be transmitted without loss to all other areas of the system." This law is the principle behind hydraulic brakes. Pressure created in the master cylinder

is transmitted through the hydraulic braking system as long as the system remains closed and has no leaks. In a closed system, hydraulic pressure is transmitted equally in all directions throughout the system. What happens to the pressure levels if there is a leak in the system? According to Pascal's law, a substantial leak will prevent the pressure from building up and therefore the pressure within the system will be equally low. This means that the vehicle may lose some or all of its braking ability if a leak develops.

Pascal's law helps in diagnosing problems with the hydraulic braking system. For example, if the brake pedal is squishy (soft or spongy), there is a good chance that the hydraulic braking system has air in it and needs to be bled. If the brake pedal slowly sinks to the floor, there is likely a small leak in the system that needs to be found. If the vehicle pulls to one side, it could be that a brake hose is plugged up and is not transmitting pressure to one of the brake units.

Hydraulic Pressure and Force

Varying amounts of mechanical force can be extracted from a single amount of hydraulic pressure. Since pressure is force per unit area (e.g., 50 pounds per square inch [psi], or 344.7 kPa), the same pressure applied over different-sized surface areas will produce different levels of force **FIGURE 31-1**. This principle allows engineers to design brakes to have a precise amount of braking force at each wheel. For example, the front wheels

You are the Automotive Technician

A customer brings his 2007 Chevrolet Tahoe with 96,000 miles to the shop to have a brake concern addressed. The vehicle is regularly driven on the beach and has been pulling to the left, especially after braking. It has gotten worse over the last few weeks. You check the service history and see that the front brake pads were replaced, the rotors refinished, and the brake fluid flushed three years ago at 54,000 miles. Before road testing the vehicle, you ask yourself these questions.

1. What faults in the brakes system could cause the vehicle to pull to the left?
2. How can Pascal's Law be used to help you to diagnose this problem?
3. What are some tests you can perform to help diagnose the fault?

FIGURE 31-1 Engineers apply hydraulic principles to create varying amounts of mechanical force in hydraulic braking systems.

on some front-wheel drive vehicles can produce up to 80% of the vehicle's stopping power due to the weight distribution and weight transfer. For these vehicles to brake smoothly, more pressure must be applied to the front brake units than the rear brake units. This is accomplished through the front and rear brake pistons. The larger brake pistons on the front wheels give greater mechanical force and braking power to the front wheels.

Figure 31-1 illustrates a hydraulic system that has cylinders of different sizes. When the brake pedal is pressed, the force against the piston in the master cylinder applies pressure to the brake fluid. This same pressure is transmitted equally throughout the fluid, but each output piston develops a certain amount of force depending on its diameter (surface area). The top cylinder is smaller than the master cylinder, so the amount of force it exerts will be less than the force applied to the master cylinder. The middle cylinder is the same size as the master cylinder, so the force will be the same. The bottom cylinder is larger than the master cylinder, and so its force will be greater.

There are three variables to consider when talking about pressure and force in hydraulic systems:

- **Input force**: The force applied to the input piston is measured in pounds (lb), newtons, or kilograms (kg). For example, if 100 lb (45.36 kg) of force were applied to the input piston, this force would be labeled as 100 lb (45.36 kg).

- **Working pressure**: The working pressure of the hydraulic fluid is expressed as the amount

of force per spec...
of force per squar...
It could also be expr...
(kPa). Note, 1 pascal = ...
meter, or 1 N/m². To find tr...
take the input force and div...
of the input piston. The exam...
(45.36 kg) of force applied to a...
piston creates 100 psi of working...
same 100 lb of force applied to...
inch piston creates 200 psi of work...
(100/0.5 = 200 psi). Conversely, th...
force applied to a 2-square inch pis...
50 psi of working pressure.

- **Output force**: Output force is exerte...
output piston and is expressed as ...
newtons, or kilograms. Finding this m...
ment is fairly simple: Take the working pr...
and multiply it by the surface area of the o...
piston. For example, 200 psi of working ...
sure pushing on a 1-square inch piston ex...
200 lb of force. The same 200 psi of worki...
pressure acting on a 0.5-square inch outpu...
piston will create 100 lb of output force. And...
if 200 psi of working pressure is applied to a...
2-square inch output piston, 400 lb of force will be created.

► TECHNICIAN TIP

There are very few adjustable components in the hydraulic brake system. One notable exception is the load-sensitive proportioning valve, which is used on some pickup trucks and other load-carrying vehicles. Load-sensing proportioning valves operate so that as load weight increases, more brake pressure is applied to the rear wheels as required.

In the case of a rear-wheel lock-up on one of these vehicles, excessive pressure to the rear brakes may be suspected. To check the operation and adjustment of load-sensing proportioning valves, pressure gauges are fitted in-line to the front and rear brakes. After the hydraulic brake system is opened to install the gauges, air is bled out before accurate readings can be obtained.

The weight on the rear axle must be set according to charts or graphs published by the manufacturer to determine the correct relationship between front and rear pressure at a given load. For example, according to a graph in the service information, if a rear axle is loaded to 1984 lb (900 kg), and front brake pressure is raised to 1138 psi (7846 kPa), then rear brake pressure should fall within the range of 569 to 711 psi (3923 to 4902 kPa). The rear axle is then loaded to 3700 lb (1678 kg). If the rear pressure is outside the specified range, adjustment of the linkage between the proportioning valve and the rear suspension may be required.

Rear Axle Load lb (kg)	Front Brake Pressure psi (kPa)	Rear Brake Pressure psi (kPa)
1984 (900)	1138 (7846)	569–711 (3923–4902)
3699 (1678)	1707 (11769)	1323–1493 (9122–10294)

► Hydraulic Components

The hydraulic system is made up of a number of components that work together to transmit the driver's effort to the brake pads or shoes. These components must be able to withstand the force, pressure, and temperatures generated in the hydraulic system. They must also be protected from the elements, as they are generally exposed to weather and road hazards. In this section we will explore each of the basic components of the hydraulic braking system.

Brake Fluid

Types and Characteristics

Brake fluid is hydraulic fluid that has specific properties designed for mobile applications. It is used to transfer force while under pressure through hydraulic lines to the wheel braking units. Braking applications produce heat, so the brake fluid used must have a high boiling point to remain effective under extreme temperatures. If brake fluid boils, it turns from a liquid to a vapor, which is compressible. This will cause a spongy brake pedal and loss of braking ability. Brake fluid must also have a low freezing point so it will not freeze or thicken in cold conditions. If this were to happen, the force from the brake pedal would not be transferred to the wheel brake units.

Standard brake fluid is harmful to painted surfaces because it tends to soften paint; it must therefore be kept off all painted surfaces. Standard brake fluid is also hygroscopic, which means it absorbs water. It can absorb water from the atmosphere when it comes into contact with the air in the master cylinder reservoir. Over time, it can even absorb moisture through the flexible brake hoses. Since water boils at a lower temperature than brake fluid, this will gradually reduce the brake fluid's boiling point, making the fluid more likely to boil and cause a hydraulic braking failure. Brake fluid must be flushed periodically to replace old contaminated fluid with new brake fluid to ensure the continued effectiveness of the hydraulic braking system.

► TECHNICIAN TIP

Even if they have similar base composition, brake fluids with different Department of Transportation (DOT) ratings should not be mixed.

► Safety

Because silicone-based fluid tends to aerate (tendency to create air bubbles) when forced at high pressure through small passages, it is *not* to be used in any vehicle equipped with anti-lock brakes (ABS). The control valves in ABS brakes would cause DOT 5 brake fluid to aerate under an active ABS stop. This would lead to a spongy pedal and poor brake application.

> **TECHNICIAN TIP**

If the brake system needs to be bled, then the brake fluid should be tested to see if it needs to be flushed out with and replaced with new brake fluid.

Brake fluids are graded against compliance standards set by the United States Department of Transportation (DOT) **TABLE 31-1**. Brake fluids that meet these standards qualify for the DOT rating and are considered to be quality brake fluids. Brake fluids are tested to ensure they meet the standards for:

- pH value
- Viscosity
- Resistance to oxidation
- Stability
- Boiling point

Master Cylinder

The master cylinder converts the brake pedal force into hydraulic pressure that is transferred to the wheel brake units. Its mounting ears allow it to be mounted to a power booster or the firewall. The cylinder itself has threaded passageways to which the brake lines firmly connect, and a brake fluid reservoir supplies the brake system with an adequate amount of brake fluid. The master cylinder piston is operated by a pushrod from the power booster or the brake pedal.

While all vehicles manufactured for sale in the United States are required to use tandem master cylinders for safety purposes, we will start our discussion with the less-complicated single-piston master cylinder.

Single-Piston Master Cylinder

Single-piston master cylinders have one piston with two cups: a primary cup and a secondary cup **FIGURE 31-2**. These cups are also known as seals because they keep the brake fluid from leaking past the piston. When force is

FIGURE 31-2 A single-piston master cylinder with primary and secondary cups.

TABLE 31-1: DOT Ratings for Brake Fluid

Type	Materials	Minimum Dry Boiling Point	Minimum Wet Boiling Point	Additional Specifications
DOT 2	Castor oil-based	Not specified	Not specified	• Outdated type of brake fluid that should not be used in any modern vehicles
DOT 3	Various glycol esters and ethers	401°F (205°C)	284°F (140°C)	
DOT 4	Various glycol esters and ethers	446°F (230°C)	311°F (155°C)	
DOT 5	Silicone-based	500°F (260°C)	356°F (180°C)	• Not hygroscopic, will not absorb water • Less harmful to painted surfaces than glycol-based brake fluids • Provides better protection against corrosion • More suitable for use in wet driving conditions • NOT to be used in any vehicle equipped with anti-lock brakes (ABS)
DOT 5.1	Contains polyalkylene glycol ether	Not specified	375°F (190.6°C)	• Suitable for ABS-equipped vehicles due to high boiling point • More expensive than other brake fluids

Source: United States Department of Transportation, Federal Motor Carrier Safety Administration: S5.1.2 Wet ERBP.

applied to the piston by the pushrod, the **primary cup** seals the pressure in the cylinder, while the **secondary cup** prevents loss of fluid past the rear end of the piston. An **outlet port** links the cylinder to the brake lines. An **inlet port** connects the reservoir with the space around the piston and between the piston cups. A **compensating port** connects the reservoir to the cylinder, just barely ahead of the primary cup.

With the brake pedal in the released position, the compensating port connects the brake system with the reservoir. The compensating port adjusts for changes in the volume of the brake fluid ahead of the piston. This occurs due to the expansion or contraction of the brake fluid as it heats up or cools down. It can also compensate for brake fluid that does not return to the master cylinder due to worn disc brake pads moving the caliper pistons outward, increasing the brake fluid volume in the caliper. In this way, brake fluid can move as needed between the reservoir and the master cylinder bore.

As the pushrod from the brake pedal or power booster moves the piston forward, the compensating port is closed off, trapping brake fluid ahead of the primary cup. Fluid can no longer return to the reservoir. Fluid trapped in the cylinder is then forced from the master cylinder outlet port into the brake lines.

When the brakes are released, the master cylinder piston returns to its original position by action of the spring. When the piston fully returns against its stop, the primary cup uncovers the compensating port. Fluid ahead of the primary cup can now return to the reservoir as needed.

When the brake pedal is released quickly, a spring in the brake pedal pushes the piston back quickly. However, because of the restrictions in the hydraulic system, the brake fluid cannot return as quickly to the cylinder, creating a low-pressure area ahead of the primary cup. As a result, air can be drawn into the system at the wheel cylinders on a drum brake system. To prevent this, small holes are drilled in the piston so that brake fluid from the reservoir can pass through the inlet port and past the edge of the primary cup, thus preventing a vacuum from being created. This is called **recuperation** **FIGURE 31-3**.

On a drum brake system, when the brake fluid in the lines returns to the master cylinder, brake fluid pressure is held slightly above atmospheric pressure by a valve called the **residual pressure valve**. The residual pressure helps to stop air from entering at the wheel cylinder cups when the brakes are not being applied. The residual pressure valve is located at the outlet end of the master cylinder on single-piston master cylinders, or under the tube seats on tandem master cylinders. Residual pressure valves are not used on disc brake circuits, as the caliper piston seal seals tightly between the piston and bore so air cannot

be easily drawn past it into the hydraulic system. Also, the small residual pressure would keep the brake pads slightly applied to the brake rotors causing brake drag, premature wear, and reduced fuel mileage.

Tandem Master Cylinder

With a single-piston master cylinder in the braking system, any fluid leak could mean the whole braking system fails. To reduce this risk, modern vehicles must have at least two separate hydraulic braking systems, hence the development of the tandem master cylinder. If one system fails, the other system can still provide a measure of braking ability, although it will not be as effective. For example, the pressure can be 0 psi (0 kPa) in one circuit and normal in the other circuit. **Tandem master cylinders** combine two master cylinders within a common housing that share a common cylinder bore **FIGURE 31-4**.

FIGURE 31-3 A single-piston master cylinder with small holes in the piston to allow for recuperation.

FIGURE 31-4 A tandem master cylinder showing common cylinder.

The two systems can be **split front to rear** so that the front brakes operate from one circuit and the rear brakes from the other. They also can be **split diagonally** so that one front wheel is paired with the rear wheel on the opposite side of the vehicle in one brake circuit, and vice versa in the other circuit.

Like two single-piston cylinders built end to end, a tandem cylinder has a primary piston and a secondary piston. The **primary piston** is in the rear of the cylinder. It is called primary since it is pushed directly by the push-rod. The **secondary piston** is in the front of the cylinder. The secondary piston has a rear-facing seal that seals fluid in the primary chamber and is what ultimately pushes the secondary piston during normal operation. Each half of the cylinder has an inlet port, an outlet port, and a compensating port. There can be two separate reservoirs feeding each half of the cylinder, or just one reservoir divided into separate sections. In the event of a hydraulic leak, a single reservoir with undivided sections would allow brake fluid to become so low in the reservoir that the working side of the system would draw in air and cause the brakes to fail completely.

When the brakes are applied, the primary piston moves forward and closes its compensating port. Continued movement of the piston causes fluid pressure in front of the primary piston to rise, which acts upon the secondary piston, moving it forward and closing its compensating port. Pressure now builds up equally in both circuits of the master cylinder. Both pistons continue moving forward, displace fluid into their separate circuits, and apply the brake units on each wheel.

Just like the single-piston master cylinder, the tandem master cylinder can have problems with a low-pressure area developing when the piston returns quickly but the brake fluid lags. The tandem master cylinder overcomes this by using holes in the piston and grooves in the side of the primary cup. These primary cup grooves allow brake fluid to flow from the inlet port into the low-pressure area, preventing air from entering the system.

If there is a failure in the secondary circuit, the primary system pushes the secondary piston until it contacts the end of the cylinder bore. Once that happens, the primary circuit can start building pressure and operate its brake units. In this situation, it operates but with increased pedal travel. If the primary circuit fails, no pressure is generated to move the secondary piston; thus a rod attached to the front of the primary piston will push the secondary piston directly so that it is still able to generate pressure to operate its brake units. This also results in a lower than normal brake pedal. A differential pressure switch in the master cylinder or hydraulic system can illuminate the brake warning light on the instrument panel, alerting the driver of loss of pressure between the two hydraulic circuits.

Quick Take-up Master Cylinders

Quick take-up master cylinders are used on disc brake systems that are equipped with low-drag brake calipers. These calipers are designed to maintain a larger running clearance between the disc brake pads and rotor. If a standard master cylinder were used, the brake pedal would have to be pushed much farther down before the running clearance would be overcome and the pads would contact the rotor. Hence, a quick take-up master cylinder was designed. It uses a relatively large-diameter piston in the rear of the cylinder to push a large volume of fluid into the hydraulic system at low pressure. This moves the brake pads into contact with the rotor. Once the pressure rises above a predetermined point, a **quick take-up valve** opens and bleeds off any extra pressure created by the large piston. At this point a smaller-diameter piston takes over and builds pressure within the hydraulic system to apply the brakes normally.

ABS Master Cylinders

The ABS master cylinder is a tandem master cylinder used in divided systems. It has a primary piston and a secondary piston. It may also incorporate the quick take-up principles of operation. In some applications, the compensating port in the secondary chamber is removed, so there is only an inlet port on the secondary piston. The primary chamber still uses a compensating port and an inlet port. The secondary piston incorporates a center valve that controls the opening and closing of a supply port drilled into the piston. At rest, the supply port is open and connects the reservoir with the front brake circuits. This supply port replaces the compensating port in a normal master cylinder **FIGURE 31-5**. The primary piston still has an inlet port and a compensating port.

When the brake pedal is applied, the primary piston moves and closes its compensating port. Brake fluid pressure in the primary circuit rises and acts with the primary piston spring to move the secondary piston forward, closing the center valve. The pressure builds in the secondary circuit. Pressure keeps building in both circuits and applies force in both circuits. If there is a leak in either circuit, the master cylinder acts like a standard master cylinder and builds pressure in the working circuit.

When the brake pedal is released, the springs in the master cylinder push both pistons back more quickly than the brake fluid can return from the wheel brake units. This creates a low-pressure area in front of each piston and could cause air to be drawn into the system. To prevent this, there are recuperating grooves in the

FIGURE 31-5 An ABS master cylinder.

Caring for the Customer

The ABS pedal pulsation has been blamed for actually causing some accidents. Since the ABS system is normally only activated in a panic stop situation, drivers who are unfamiliar with the pedal pulsation have been known to lift their foot off the brake pedal, causing an accident. It is good for drivers to familiarize themselves with the feel of the ABS pedal pulsation by activating the ABS in a safe location, such as an abandoned parking lot. To address this issue, manufacturers have started to move toward electronic braking (brake-by-wire), which prevents hydraulic pulsations from being transmitted to the brake pedal.

primary piston and the seal. Brake fluid at atmospheric pressure flows through the inlet port and past these grooves. When the primary piston is returned fully, any extra brake fluid returning from the wheel brake units displaces brake fluid into the reservoir, through the compensating port. In the secondary circuit, brake fluid at atmospheric pressure is forced back into the inlet port. The inlet port connects with the supply port drilling in the piston. Any difference in pressure lifts the center valve from its seat and lets the brake fluid enter the chamber ahead of the secondary seal, thus preventing low pressures from developing. When the piston has returned to the "rest" position, the seal is pulled off its seat by the action of the link and spring. This lets the brake fluid still returning from the wheel brake units displace the brake fluid back to the reservoir.

If braking conditions are such that the hydraulic modulator must return brake fluid to the master cylinder, then for the front brake circuits, brake fluid is returned to the front section. This forces the secondary piston back against the force of the primary piston spring and the rear brake pressure and pushes both pistons rearward. If enough brake fluid returns, the center valve opens and allows brake fluid to return to the reservoir.

If brake fluid is returned from the rear brake circuit, the secondary and primary pistons tend to be forced apart, causing the primary piston to be driven rearward. If enough brake fluid returns, the compensating port is uncovered and allows brake fluid to return to the reservoir. The amount of brake fluid that returns to the master cylinder is determined by the degree of ABS control. The driver may be aware of a rising brake pedal during this time.

Reservoirs and Float Switches

Master cylinder reservoirs can be built into the master cylinder housing or can be a separate unit. Built-in reservoirs are made of the same material as the master cylinder, which is usually aluminum or cast iron, and are formed on top of the master cylinder. The reservoir cover on these master cylinders must be removed to inspect the brake fluid level. The cover uses a rubber diaphragm to isolate the brake fluid from the air. These covers are usually held on by bail clips or tabs molded into the cover.

On two-piece master cylinders, the reservoirs are usually made of a see-through plastic material and use grommets or O-rings to seal them to the master cylinder. Because they are see-through, it is usually unnecessary to remove the cover to check the brake fluid level. The covers can be screw-on caps or clip-on covers. The caps usually incorporate a device to minimize contact of the brake fluid with air. Some systems use a disc that floats on the brake fluid to minimize the surface area of the brake fluid in contact with the air.

To ensure that a leak in one brake circuit will not affect the other circuit, master cylinder reservoirs have two separate chambers. These reservoirs can be two totally separate chambers, or they can use a divider in a common reservoir, which keeps the brake fluid level from falling below a minimum amount.

TECHNICIAN TIP

Master cylinder reservoirs should always have air space at the top of the reservoir to allow for the expansion of brake fluid as it heats up. Never fill master cylinder reservoirs all the way to the top.

Most modern master cylinder reservoirs are equipped with a low brake fluid level float switch that turns on the red brake warning light on the instrument panel and/or sets a notification on the driver information system. The warning system can be activated by the float directly or a float with an embedded magnet may activate a switch when the float falls to a certain level. The brake fluid level could be low due to worn brake pad linings or a leak in the system; both situations require further investigation. Adding brake fluid without further investigation into what is causing the low fluid condition could lead to a brake failure, putting the driver and occupants in danger.

Brake Pedals

The brake pedal uses leverage to multiply the effort from the driver's foot to the master cylinder. Different lever designs can be engineered to alter the brake pedal effort required of the driver by using different levels of mechanical advantage. Brake pedals should be mounted securely, free from any excessive sideways movement, and at a height and angle that will allow the driver to quickly move from pressing the accelerator (throttle pedal) to applying the brakes. Brake pedals are covered with a rubber nonslip cover to maintain sure footing. These covers can become worn and lead to slippage, so they need to be inspected periodically.

The brake pedal is usually suspended from a bracket between the dash panel and the firewall **FIGURE 31-6**. It works as a force-multiplying lever. The pushrod transmits the brake pedal force either directly to the master cylinder or to the power booster. If the power assist

FIGURE 31-6 Brake pedal assembly.

> **TECHNICIAN TIP**
>
> Changes to how far the pedal travels or to its resistance—if it feels harder or softer than normal—can indicate problems such as a faulty power booster or air in the hydraulic system due to a leak.

> **TECHNICIAN TIP**
>
> When ABS brakes are activated during heavy braking, the pulsations of the system can be felt by the driver through the pedal. This is normal. However, a pulsating pedal during normal or light braking can indicate potential braking system problems, such as a rotor that has thickness variation beyond the manufacturer's specifications or that is possibly warped.

fails, the brake pedal's leverage is designed to allow the driver to still generate a reasonable braking force at each wheel brake unit but with substantially increased foot pressure.

Brake pedals must be free to return to their starting position when pressure is removed. This allows the master cylinder piston and pushrod to return to their undepressed position. The pedal is enabled to return to its starting position by a return spring. The spring action also causes the brake pedal to push the brake light switch open and stop current flow to the brake lights. When the brake pedal is applied, a lighter spring in the brake light switch causes the brake light switch contacts to close and activate the brake lights. Brake light switches are adjustable on some vehicles. Misadjusted brake light switches can cause the brake lights to stay on when they should be off, or not come on when they are supposed to. Both situations can be corrected by adjusting the switch to the proper position. If the switch is nonadjustable, it will likely need to be replaced if it is not operating correctly.

Types of Divided Hydraulic Systems

A wheel's braking ability depends on the load it is carrying; therefore, the type of vehicle is a major factor in determining how its system should be divided. A front-engine rear-wheel drive car has around 40% of its load on its rear wheels and 60% on its front wheels. Its braking system can therefore be divided in a vertical, or front–rear, split. This design puts the front wheels on a different system than the rear wheels. If one half of the system fails—the front or the rear—there is still enough separate braking capability left in the other half to stop the vehicle.

On a front-wheel drive vehicle, a load of about 20% on the rear wheels cannot provide enough braking force to stop the vehicle. Therefore, front-engine, front-wheel drive vehicles use a braking system split in a diagonal, or X, pattern. The left-hand front brake unit is connected to the right-hand rear unit, and the left-hand rear unit is connected to the right-hand front unit. If one system fails, a 50% braking capability is available in the other system.

An alternative arrangement for front-engine, front-wheel drive vehicles is an L split **FIGURE 31-7**. The front disc brake units have four piston calipers. One inner and one outer piston on each front caliper connect to the right-hand rear brake unit, and the other two pistons of each front caliper connect to the left-hand rear brake unit. As with the diagonal split system, if there is a failure of either half of the system, it still leaves 50% of the braking capability.

> ### TECHNICIAN TIP
>
> When diagnosing and servicing brakes, it is helpful to know how the hydraulic system is divided. If the vehicle is pulling to one side due to a leak in one half of the system, it will generally pull toward the side that is working in the front. Diagnosis and inspection of the other diagonal half will usually lead to the leak. In the same way, if air is trapped in one half of the hydraulic braking system, then bleeding the corresponding diagonal half will make it easier to remove the air.

▶ Brake Lines and Hoses

Brake Lines

Brake lines and hoses carry brake fluid from the master cylinder to the brake units. They are basically the same on all brake systems and passenger vehicles. For most of their length, they are double-walled steel, coated to resist corrosion, and attached to the body with clips or brackets to minimize damage from vibration **FIGURE 31-8**. In some vehicles, the brake lines are inside the vehicle to better protect them from corrosion and physical damage. Where the lines must move, flexible brake

FIGURE 31-7 Divided hydraulic systems. **A.** Vertical, or front–rear, split hydraulic system. **B.** Diagonal, or X, pattern hydraulic system. **C.** L-split hydraulic system.

FIGURE 31-8 Steel brake line.

FIGURE 31-9 Flexible brake hose.

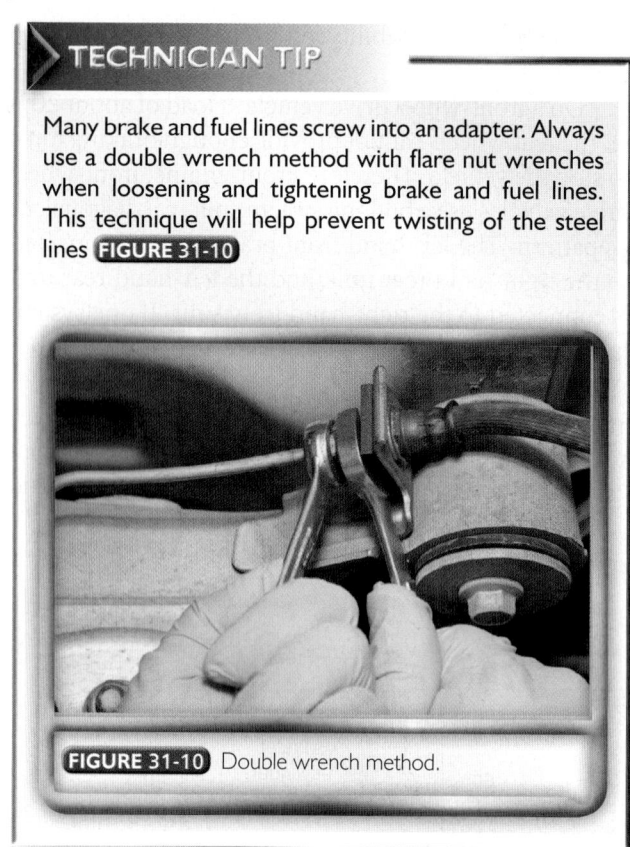
hoses allow for steering and suspension movement **FIGURE 31-9**.

Brake Line Materials

The **brake lines** must be able to transmit considerable hydraulic pressure, 1500 psi (10342 kPa) or more during panic stops. They are made of seamless, double-walled steel, rather than a softer but less corrosive, and easier-to-form, material such as copper. They also must conform to applicable standards such as the Society of Automotive Engineers. Only brake lines that meet those standards can be used on vehicles.

If a brake line is damaged, it is common practice to replace the entire brake line with a factory replacement rather than repair it. Also, universal brake lines are available in a variety of lengths that are already factory flared with the correct fitting installed. They just need to be formed with the proper tubing bender to the specified shape following the original brake line routing. Avoid kinks by only using the correct tubing bender. Kinked lines cannot be used or repaired.

Types of Brake Line Flares

Since brake lines connect all of the various hydraulic braking system components, their ends must make leak-proof connections. This is accomplished by

using the following types of flared lines and matching fittings:

- **Inverted double flare**: This type of flare is created by first flaring the end of the tube outward in a Y shape. Then about half of the flared end is folded inside of itself (inverted), leaving a double-thick section of brake line on the flared portion of the Y **FIGURE 31-11**. The flared portion of the tube is clamped between the mating surfaces of the two fittings to provide a secure, leak-proof connection when performed properly.

- **International Standards Organization (ISO) flare**: This type of flare is sometimes called a "bubble flare." The brake line is flared slightly out and then back in, leaving the brake line "bubbled" near the end **FIGURE 31-12**. The bubble is then clamped between two matching fittings.

Brake Line Flaring

While it is common practice to replace the entire brake line if it is damaged, sometimes a technician has to fabricate a new one from a section of new universal brake line. Only attempt this when a new factory replacement line is unavailable. Also, ensure that the proper flaring tools are used and the required procedures are followed

FIGURE 31-11 An inverted double flared line and matching fitting.

FIGURE 31-12 An ISO flared line and matching fitting.

exactly. Never use compression fittings to splice a section of brake line.

Brake Hoses

A flexible section of the brake lines must be included between the body and suspension to allow for steering and suspension movement. This is accomplished by using flexible hoses made of tough, reinforced tubing. These flexible **brake hoses** transmit the brake system hydraulic pressures to the wheel units. They also must be tough so as not to be damaged easily by objects thrown by the tires or other hazards. When replacing brake hoses, always make sure they are of the proper length. If they are too short, they can be damaged by being stretched. If they are too long, they can contact moving components such as tires or a suspension member, which could weaken or wear a hole in the hose. This is especially common when a vehicle has a lift kit installed.

Brake Hose Materials

Brake hoses are made of several layers of alternating materials. The inside is a liner that helps seal the brake fluid in and any moisture out. The liner is wrapped with two or more layers of flexible webbing, which are usually embedded in a synthetic rubber material and provide reinforcement for the hose. These layers are covered with a tough flexible outer housing jacket designed to resist abrasion and damage **FIGURE 31-13**.

While brake hoses are designed to be flexible, they should *never* be pinched, kinked, or bent tighter than a specified radius. Doing so will reduce their life and can cause failure of the brake hose. Some technicians mistakenly use vice grip pliers to crimp a brake hose while disconnected from the caliper or wheel cylinder to prevent brake fluid from leaking out. This practice can damage the brake hose and should be avoided.

Teflon inner core
Kevlar braid
Protective layer
Stainless steel braid
Protective layer
1 pc Crimp design

FIGURE 31-13 Flexible brake hose construction.

Sealing Washers and Fittings

Many brake hoses use banjo fittings to connect the hose to the wheel unit. These fittings are comprised of the banjo fitting, banjo bolt, and two copper or aluminum sealing washers **FIGURE 31-14**. The banjo bolt, banjo fitting, and wheel unit usually have sealing ridges machined in them. These ridges dig into the softer sealing washers to ensure a leak-proof connection. The banjo bolt is hollow and allows the brake fluid through the middle to continue on to the wheel unit. It fits in the banjo fitting and clamps it to the wheel unit. The sealing washers fit on both sides of the banjo fitting. One sealing washer is between the head of the banjo bolt and the banjo fitting, while the other sealing washer is between the banjo fitting

and the wheel unit. Always use the proper torque when tightening banjo bolts so they are not twisted off or left loose to leak.

Brake hoses need to be inspected periodically for damage or defects. Some possible issues are **FIGURE 31-15**:

- **Cracks**: The outer layers become brittle and crack over time. Replacement is required.

> **TECHNICIAN TIP**
>
> Because the sealing washers are made of soft metal, they become crushed after use. It is good practice to replace them each time the banjo fittings are removed; otherwise leaks could occur.

- **Bulges**: The reinforcing layers become weak and break over time resulting in bulges in the outer cover. Replacement is required.
- **Abrasion or wear**: This usually happens because the brake hose was routed incorrectly or was too long or short for the application and the brake hose rubbed on a component, resulting, over time, in the abrasion. Replacement and rerouting are required.
- **Kinks**: Kinking usually happens when the brake hose has been pinched with vice grips or twisted on installation. Replacement is required.
- **Internal deterioration causing blockage of the passageway**: Replacement is required.

FIGURE 31-14 Banjo bolt assembly.

FIGURE 31-15 Possible brake hose issues. **A.** Brake hose with abrasion/wear. **B.** Brake hose with kinks.

Hydraulic Braking System Control

The hydraulic braking system must be controlled accurately to maintain adequate control of the vehicle during braking. As we learned earlier, hydraulic working pressure is equally applied throughout a sealed hydraulic braking system. We also learned that the hydraulic braking system can be designed to optimize the output force at each of the wheel brake units. In a perfect scenario, that would work just fine. But since machines are not perfect, you need to be able to modify the hydraulic pressure to accommodate different scenarios. Components such as proportioning valves, metering valves, pressure differential valves, or anti-lock hydraulic control units are used to modify the pressures within the hydraulic braking system.

Proportioning Valves

Proportioning valves reduce brake pressure to the rear wheels when their load is reduced during moderate to severe braking. Proportioning valves can be pressure-sensitive or load-sensitive. The pressure-sensitive valve is in the master cylinder or in a separate unit in the rear brake circuit, while the load-sensitive type is mounted on the body or on the axle, where it can respond to load changes.

The effectiveness of braking force is determined by tire-to-road friction. The greater the load on the tire, the greater the friction; the greater the friction, the greater the stopping ability. When a vehicle stops abruptly, a portion of the weight on the rear wheels transfers to the front wheels, resulting in greater tire-to-road friction on the front tires and less on the rear. This is called load transfer—weight is being transferred from the rear wheels to the front wheels.

If equal braking force is applied to the front and rear wheels during this load transfer condition, the smaller load in the rear can result in the rear wheels locking up. Skidding tires on the surface of the road (kinetic friction) do not have as much friction as rolling tires, and therefore the stopping distance is increased, which can lead to an accident. A pressure-sensitive proportioning valve reduces the pressure applied to the rear brakes under heavy braking to prevent rear wheel lock-up and to help maintain traction.

The load-sensitive proportioning valve reduces rear brake pressure when the vehicle is lightly loaded and allows higher pressure when it is heavily loaded. The load-sensitive proportioning valve is usually located on the chassis and has a lever that is connected to the rear axle. As the vehicle is loaded, the chassis squats on the rear suspension and the lever is moved, applying more force on the load-sensitive proportioning valve. The lever increases or decreases the point at which pressure is limited by the load-sensitive proportioning valve. Heavier loads allow more pressure through the load-sensitive proportioning valve to the rear brakes, and lighter loads restrict pressure through the load-sensitive proportioning valve. A diagonally split system may have two load-sensitive proportioning valves, one for each rear brake unit. Each load-sensitive proportioning valve is mounted on the chassis, around the rear suspension. If the vehicle is equipped with ABS, it may not be equipped with a proportioning valve, as the ABS system can make up for wheel slippage due to the changes in load transfer. This will be covered in detail in the Electronic Brake Control chapter.

Pressure-Sensitive Proportioning Valve Operation

The pressure-sensitive proportioning valve adjusts the braking force to allow for load transfer or variations in loads. During normal braking, the pressure-sensitive proportioning valve's poppet piston is held in a relaxed position by a large pressure spring. The poppet valve is held against its retainer by a light return spring, and brake fluid passes freely through the pressure-sensitive proportioning valve to the rear brakes. In this condition, the rear brakes operate normally without any modification to the pressure.

During heavy braking, master cylinder pressure can reach the poppet valve's crack point. The pressure applied to the two different areas of the poppet piston creates unequal forces, which act on the pressure-sensitive proportioning valve. The higher hydraulic pressure moves the poppet piston against the large pressure spring to close the pressure-sensitive proportioning valve. At a specified inlet pressure, the conical section of the pressure-sensitive proportioning valve is held against the seat, which holds the pressure steady to the rear brakes until there is a further change in inlet pressure.

As greater pedal force increases pressure in the master cylinder, brake fluid pressure rises on the smaller end of the poppet piston. This combines with the force of the pressure spring to overcome the lower pressure now on the larger (output) end. As a result, the piston is forced back, opening the poppet valve and allowing pressure to rise to the rear brakes.

The increased pressure now acts on the larger end of the poppet piston and again forces the piston forward to close the poppet valve and hold pressure steady. This repeated action causes a lowering of outlet pressure versus inlet pressure. When the brake pedal is released, the pressure of the rear brake fluid unseats the poppet valve, letting the brake fluid return to the master cylinder. The pressure spring now returns the poppet piston to its relaxed position.

Should the front brake system fail, the warning lamp spool moves forward, taking the poppet valve with it. Pressure in the rear brakes rises and the piston moves forward; however, it cannot close the poppet valve, so full system pressure remains available for the rear brakes in this situation. Should the rear brake system fail, the warning lamp spool will move backward to activate the warning light. The pressure-sensitive proportioning valve cannot operate in this situation.

A diagonally divided system requires one pressure-sensitive proportioning valve for each rear wheel, so they are usually located away from the master cylinder. Each pressure-sensitive proportioning valve operates in a similar way to the pressure-sensitive proportioning valve in the master cylinder, but without the pressure differential warning light circuit.

Adjustable Proportioning Valves

After-market adjustable proportioning valves are available for performance applications. They have a method of adjusting the proportioning valve's crack point and can be customized to the specific vehicle. Adjustable proportioning valves are popular with kit car builders who use components from a variety of vehicles that were not originally designed to work together. Adjustable proportioning valves are not recommended for most applications due to the amount of trial and error necessary to set them properly.

Metering Valves

Metering valves are used to hold off the application of the front brakes on vehicles with disc brakes on the front wheels and drum brakes on the rear wheels **FIGURE 31-16**. Drum brakes use springs to return the brake shoes to their rest position. This means that it takes a certain amount of hydraulic pressure to overcome the tension of the return springs and move the shoes to contact the drums. Disc brakes use the much smaller force of the square-cut O-ring to return the caliper piston to its rest position.

FIGURE 31-16 A metering valve.

Thus, very little hydraulic pressure is needed to move the brake pads into contact with the rotor.

Vehicles handle better when the rear brakes engage before the front brakes. This helps keep the vehicle tracking straight while the brakes are initially applied. The metering valve keeps the front disc brakes from being applied until the rear drum brakes have had a chance to overcome the tension of the return springs.

Metering Valve Operation

The metering valve operates like a radiator cap. It has a relatively heavy spring that holds the metering valve closed until a specified pressure is reached. Pressure rises in the hydraulic braking system, overcomes the rear brake return spring tension, and starts to apply the rear brakes. As pressure continues to rise above the metering valve's crack point, brake fluid flows to the front disc brake calipers and starts to apply the front brakes. Since the metering valve only has hydraulic pressure on the inlet side, any pressure above its crack point will hold it open.

When the brake pedal is released, the metering valve is pushed closed by the spring and a fluid return valve opens up, allowing brake fluid to flow freely back to the master cylinder. During bleeding, if there is air in the lines, it may be difficult to raise the brake fluid pressure enough to open the metering valve. This makes it almost impossible to bleed any air out of the front part of the hydraulic braking system. Most metering valves are designed so that they can be manually held in the open position to allow bleeding to take place. Also, many pressure bleeders operate at an insufficient pressure to open the metering valve, and the valve will have to be held open manually.

Vehicles equipped with a diagonally split system are generally front-wheel drive. They usually do not use metering valves for two reasons. First, the torque of the spinning engine during braking compensates for the earlier application of the front brake pads and offsets not having a metering valve. Second, since up to 80% of the braking occurs at the front wheels, they need to be applied as quickly as possible to start braking the vehicle effectively.

Pressure Differential Valve

A **pressure differential valve** monitors any pressure difference between the two separate hydraulic brake circuits. If there is a moderate leak anywhere in the system, it will illuminate the brake warning light on the instrument panel. Sometimes the light will only flicker, or come on when the brake pedal is pushed, indicating a small leak. The valve can be located in the master cylinder or in the combination valve.

Safety

After bleeding the hydraulic braking system, always remember to remove the tool that is holding open the metering valve. Failure to do so could cause the vehicle to brake improperly.

TECHNICIAN TIP

On a front–rear split system, there can also be a pressure difference if the rear drum brake shoes are grossly underadjusted. When the brake pedal is pushed, the shoes do not make contact. The primary piston moves so far that it contacts the secondary piston, which starts to apply the front brakes. This raises the pressure in the secondary circuit higher than in the primary circuit, moving the pressure differential valve toward the primary circuit and thus illuminating the brake warning light.

Pressure Differential Valve Operation

The pressure differential valve is connected between the two halves of the hydraulic braking system so pressure is applied to each end of the pressure differential valve. As long as the pressure stays the same in both circuits, the pressure differential valve remains in the

same position and the light stays off. A moderate leak in the hydraulic brake system will lower the pressure on that side of the circuit. This system will allow the higher pressure in the nonleaking side to push the pressure differential valve off-center toward the side with the leak. The pressure differential switch will then close and illuminate the brake warning light on the instrument panel, telling the driver that there is a serious leak in the hydraulic brake system that needs to be diagnosed **FIGURE 31-17**.

During hydraulic braking system bleeding, the pressure differential valve may need to be centered. Most pressure differential valves have springs that help center them. Applying the brakes firmly will cause the pressure to equalize, and the spring returns the pressure differential valve to center. On vehicles without this feature, once the hydraulic braking system has been bled, you must bleed a small amount of brake fluid out of the opposite hydraulic circuit to allow the pressure differential valve to move back to center. Follow the manufacturer's procedure.

FIGURE 31-17 A pressure differential valve with a leak in the hydraulic braking system.

IN
Front
circuit

OUT
Front
circuit

Warning lamp switch

IN
Rear
circuit

Proportioning
valve

OUT
Rear
circuit

OUT
Front
circuit

Metering
valve

Pressure
differential
valve

FIGURE 31-18 A combination valve.

Combination Valve

The combination valve can combine the pressure differential valve, metering valve, and proportioning valve(s) in one unit **FIGURE 31-18**. Some combination valves combine just the pressure differential valve and proportioning valve(s). On others, just the pressure differential valve and metering valve are combined. Each valve operates individually as it was designed and is collected in one unit. Combination valves are not serviceable. If they become faulty, they must be replaced.

Electronic Brake Proportioning

Many ABS-equipped vehicles integrate an electronic brake proportioning function within the hydraulic control unit on vehicles that require it. This function reduces hydraulic pressure to the rear wheels under heavy braking, similar to the proportioning valve. However, in these vehicles the pressure reduction is handled electronically and can compensate for differences in traction by monitoring wheel slip.

▶ Brake Warning Light and Stop Lights

Red lights are used on vehicles as warning devices to warn drivers and others of specific conditions. When a red light comes on, the driver should take notice and respond appropriately. There are two general categories—the brake warning light and stop lights. The brake warning light is a single light located in the instrument panel, while the stop lights are made up of at least three lights at the rear of the vehicle.

Brake Warning Light

The brake warning light is designed to warn the driver of a condition in the braking system that needs attention. Usually the light can be illuminated by four causes. The first is if the parking brake is engaged. The light is turned on by the parking brake lever or pedal when the parking brake is applied. This is to alert the driver that it is on so the driver will release it before driving. The second reason the brake warning light comes on is because the brake fluid level is too low in the master cylinder reservoir. This could be caused by a leak in the hydraulic braking system or worn brake pads on the disc brakes. On vehicles without ABS, the third cause of the brake warning light coming on is unequal pressure in the hydraulic brake system, which causes the pressure differential valve to activate the brake warning light switch. The fourth cause of the brake warning light illuminating is called a "prove out" or "proffing" circuit. On most vehicles designed without controller area network bus (CAN-bus), turning the ignition switch to the "crank" position causes the warning light to illuminate so the driver knows the bulb is good.

Stop Lights

Stop lights are designed to warn others that the vehicle is braking. This information is critical to help avoid accidents. The regular stop lights are mounted on the rear of the vehicle and must conform to federal laws for brightness and location. They are activated by a normally closed stop light switch located on the brake pedal assembly. When the driver applies the brake, the brake pedal moves away from the stop light switch. A spring in the switch closes the contacts, allowing current to flow and illuminate the stop lights. Releasing the brakes causes the brake pedal to force the stop light switch open, turning the stop lights off.

In 1986, North America mandated that all new passenger vehicles be equipped with a center high mount stop lamp (CHMSL). Light trucks and vans were added in 1994. This lamp is located higher than the regular brake lights, near the centerline of the vehicle. It is designed to be more in the driver's line of sight while he or she is looking down the road to anticipate traffic hazards. This higher-mounted lamp helps reduce rear-end collisions by being more visible to drivers, giving them more warning time for stopping.

Power Brakes

Types and Purpose

A power booster or power brake unit uses an external source of force to multiply the driver's pedal effort and apply that to the master cylinder pistons, thus increasing the hydraulic pressure available from the master cylinder. There are two main types of power brake units: vacuum-assist and hydraulic-assist. The vacuum-assist power booster is the most common.

Units on gasoline engines use the vacuum produced in the intake manifold to power the brake booster. This supplies approximately 20″ of vacuum to the booster. Vehicles with diesel engines do not have manifold vacuum, so they are fitted with an engine-driven vacuum pump.

The vacuum-assisted power booster operates between the brake pedal and the master cylinder. It uses the difference between engine vacuum and atmospheric pressure to increase the force that acts on the master cylinder pistons. The level of assistance this power booster gives depends on the pressure applied to the brake pedal and the pressure difference between the vacuum side of the booster and the atmospheric pressure side.

The hydraulic-assisted power booster operates between the brake pedal and the master cylinder. It usually uses hydraulic pressure from the power steering pump to increase the force that acts on the master cylinder. The level of assistance this power booster gives depends on the pressure applied to the brake pedal and the hydraulic pressure in the system.

Vacuum Booster

The most common types of vacuum boosters are the single diaphragm and the dual diaphragm. Just as the names imply, they have either one or two diaphragms that are used to extract power from atmospheric pressure. Using two diaphragms allows the diameter of the booster to be smaller, although it is a bit longer than a single-diaphragm unit.

Vacuum boosters consist of the following:

- A housing, which encases all of the other parts
- One or two sealed diaphragms, which transmit the force to the master cylinder
- A diaphragm return spring, which pushes the diaphragm back when the brake pedal is released
- A control valve, which controls vacuum and atmospheric pressure to each chamber

- A one-way check valve, which holds vacuum in the booster when it is higher than intake manifold vacuum
- Seals, which prevent air leaks

How much force can a vacuum booster create? Let's do the math using a panic stop situation. The booster receives approximately 20″ (51 cm) of vacuum from the intake manifold. That is equal to about 10 psi (69 kPa) of pressure since 2″ (5.1 cm) of vacuum equals 1 psi (6.9 kPa). So the booster diaphragm can generate approximately 10 psi (69 kPa). If the diaphragm has a circumference of 12″ (31 cm), then it has an area of approximately 113 square inches (729 cm²). Therefore, 10 psi (69 kPa) × 113 square inches (729 cm²) = 1130 lb (513 kg). That means that a 12″ (31-cm) booster can add 1130 lb (513 kg) of force to whatever the driver's foot effort is after being multiplied through the leverage of the brake pedal. That force is magnified further by the hydraulic system. This is why a vehicle weighing thousands of pounds can be stopped with minimal foot pressure.

Vacuum Booster Operation

When the driver steps on the brake pedal, it moves the brake pedal pushrod forward, which transmits movement through the power unit to the master cylinder piston to apply the brakes. It also operates a control valve that controls the flow of vacuum and atmospheric pressure to each side of the diaphragm. How it works depends on the position of the control valve.

A hose connects the intake manifold to a vacuum check valve on the power brake unit. With the engine running, the check valve allows air to be evacuated from the booster, but not to return. Vacuum in the intake manifold is used to evacuate the power unit. The valve stays open until vacuum in the unit is as high as or higher than manifold vacuum. It then seals the booster off from the intake system. It also holds vacuum in the booster in the case of an engine failure where it will allow at least one full boosted brake application.

The booster chambers are separated by a flexible rubber diaphragm attached to the diaphragm plate. It is held in the off position by a large-diaphragm return spring. The master cylinder pushrod and the control valve assembly are centrally located on each side of the plate. The master cylinder pushrod normally incorporates a system to provide an adjustment for pushrod length. The adjustable length provides the proper clearance between the master cylinder pushrod and the master cylinder piston. The length normally does not need to be adjusted, but if adjustment is required, use the proper tools and follow the service information completely.

As the brakes are applied, the pedal pushrod and plunger move forward in the diaphragm plate, which brings the vacuum valve into contact with the vacuum port seat. This closes the vacuum port, sealing off the passage connecting the two chambers and holding the pressure and vacuum steady in each chamber. This is called the hold position.

Further movement of the pushrod and plunger moves the atmospheric valve away from the atmospheric port seat. Air at atmospheric pressure comes in through the air filter in the rear of the unit and enters the chamber behind the diaphragm. The difference in pressure now on both sides of the diaphragm moves the diaphragm plate forward, and it takes the master cylinder pushrod with it, applying greater force to the master cylinder. In this position, called the apply position, the vacuum valve is closed and the atmospheric valve is open.

Once the brake pedal stops moving, the atmospheric pressure continues to build up in the rear chamber. As hydraulic pressure rises, a counterforce acts through the master cylinder pushrod and the reaction disc. This counterforce allows the diaphragm plate and control valve to continue moving forward a little bit until the movement causes the atmospheric valve to close off the atmospheric port. Closing off the atmospheric port stops the atmospheric pressure from entering the booster, which causes it to hold in that position, ready for increased or decreased pedal pressure from the driver.

During application, the reaction force against the valve plunger works against the driver to close the atmospheric port. With both the atmospheric and the vacuum ports closed, the power unit is in a hold position. It stays this way until increased pedal force reopens the atmospheric port, causing more boost; or a drop in pedal force reopens the vacuum port, reducing boost. When the force on the pedal is held constant, and both the vacuum valve and the atmospheric valve are closed, the valve always returns to the hold position.

When the brake pedal is released, the atmospheric valve is closed and the vacuum valve opens. As a result, any atmospheric pressure is evacuated from the rear chamber, through the front chamber, out the booster, through the check valve, and into the intake manifold. This reduces the atmospheric pressure pushing on the diaphragm plate. The return spring then pushes the diaphragm plate back to its off position. With the driver's foot off of the brake pedal, the vacuum valve remains open, ensuring that there is equal vacuum on both sides of the diaphragm plate ready for the next application.

When the engine is switched off or stops for any reason, no manifold vacuum is available to supply the booster. The vacuum remaining in the booster, held by the one-way check valve, will provide for at least one power-boosted brake application. After this, the brakes will still operate, but without power assistance, they require more brake pedal effort from the driver.

Dual-Diaphragm Boosters

Dual-diaphragm power boosters work on the same principle of operation as the single-diaphragm power booster and are smaller in diameter to better fit in the limited space under the hood of some vehicles. However, to keep the surface area of the diaphragm plate large enough to provide the needed boost, two smaller diaphragms in tandem are used, one behind the other. There are separate vacuum and atmospheric chambers for each diaphragm plate. They use the same control valve concepts and therefore apply, hold, and release in the same manner as a single-diaphragm booster.

▶ Hydraulic Brake Booster
Purpose and Operation

Although not as common as a conventional brake system fitted with a vacuum booster, many vehicles are now equipped with hydraulically assisted brake boosters. The hydraulic booster system uses hydraulic pressure generated by the power steering pump rather than engine vacuum to provide the required power **FIGURE 31-19**. This application is particularly suitable

FIGURE 31-19 Hydraulic power brake booster.

SKILL DRILL | 31-1 | Selecting, Handling, Storing, and Filling Brake Fluid

1 Research the specified type of brake fluid in the appropriate service information. Wipe around the master cylinder reservoir cover to prevent any dirt from entering the system. Remove the reservoir cover.

2 Check the fluid level in the reservoir. The fluid should be near the full mark on the side of the cylinder or within half an inch of the top of each chamber if there are no marks.

3 Once you are sure there are no unresolved issues, add the manufacturer's recommended brake fluid to bring the level to the full mark. Replace the cover and check that it is properly seated. Check for any leaks around the master cylinder. Dilute any brake fluid that may have been spilled with fresh clean water.

usually require one or two bail clips to be pried off. **(Photo 1)**

4 Check the brake fluid level in the reservoir. The fluid should be near the full mark on the side of the cylinder or within half an inch of the top of each chamber if there are no marks. If the brake fluid level is not near the full mark, you will need to identify why it is low. A low level could be caused by worn brake linings/pads or a slow leak in the hydraulic braking system. Investigate these possibilities fully and inform your supervisor of your findings. **(Photo 2)**

5 Once you are sure there are no unresolved issues, add the manufacturer's recommended brake fluid to bring the level to the full mark, if needed.

6 Inspect the cover and refold the rubber diaphragm, if equipped.

7 Replace the cover and check that it is properly seated.

8 Check for any leaks or problems around the master cylinder.

9 Dilute any brake fluid that may have been spilled with fresh clean water. Do not rub the brake fluid with a cloth, as this could damage any softened paint. **(Photo 3)**

Brake Fluid Testing

Brake fluid replacement is a maintenance item for virtually all vehicles. Consult the vehicle's service information to determine the correct intervals for brake fluid flushing. Some manufacturers neglect to specify this time frame, so you will need to determine the proper interval based on the type of environment the vehicle is driven in. In humid or wet climates, the brake fluid may need to be flushed every 2 years. In dry climates, every 4 years might be appropriate.

There are several ways of determining if the brake fluid should be flushed:

- Time/mileage: The manufacturer may specify a time/mileage interval for flushing the brake fluid.

- DVOM–galvanic reaction test: The majority of today's braking systems use a combination of dissimilar metals. Manufacturers use aluminum in pistons and housings, and steel in brake lines and some wheel cylinders. When moisture mixes with brake fluid, a galvanic reaction (corrosion) can occur. The higher the moisture content in brake fluid, the higher the galvanic reaction and the greater the erosion/corrosion it causes. The DVOM–galvanic reaction test uses a DVOM to measure the voltage created by the galvanic reaction due to the level of moisture in the fluid **FIGURE 31-22**.

- Boiling point test: Measuring the boiling point of the brake fluid using a special tool can determine the moisture content of the brake fluid **FIGURE 31-23**.

- Test strip: Measuring specific chemicals/metals in the brake fluid can indicate whether there is a chemical breakdown of the brake fluid. Brake fluid test strips contain special color-changing pads that react in the presence of moisture or specific chemicals that have built up in the fluid and that indicate the need for flushing the brake fluid **FIGURE 31-24**.

To test the brake fluid for contamination, you can use the DVOM–galvanic reaction test, the brake fluid tester, or brake fluid test strips. For all three tests, follow these steps first: Brake fluid condition and level should be inspected at every oil change and the fluid replaced according to the manufacturer's recommended service schedule, or when it fails the following tests. Clean around the master cylinder cap to prevent contaminants from entering the reservoir. Remove the master cylinder reservoir cap.

To perform a DVOM–galvanic reaction test, follow the steps in **SKILL DRILL 31-2**:

1. Set the DVOM to DC volts. Insert the red lead in the "v/Ω" slot and the black lead in the "common" slot.

2. Place the red voltmeter probe in the reservoir brake fluid, and place the black lead on the metal housing of the master cylinder. Make sure to use an unpainted surface of the housing.

3. Compare the voltage reading you obtained to specifications. Less than 0.3V is OK. More than 0.3V means the fluid needs to be flushed.

To test brake fluid with a brake fluid tester, follow the steps in **SKILL DRILL 31-3**:

1. Follow the directions for the tester you are using.

2. Test the brake fluid. This is usually accomplished by placing an amount of brake fluid from the

FIGURE 31-22 A DVOM will measure the voltage created by the galvanic reaction due to the level of moisture in the fluid.

FIGURE 31-23 A brake fluid safety meter boils brake fluid to test for moisture.

FIGURE 31-24 Brake fluid test strips react to moisture or chemicals in the brake fluid.

master cylinder into the tester. Some testers are designed to be placed directly into the brake fluid.

3 Compare the results you obtained to specifications. Most testers will tell you the boiling point of the fluid or the percent of moisture in the fluid.

To test brake fluid with a brake fluid test strip, follow the steps in **SKILL DRILL 31-4**:

1 Follow the directions for the brake fluid test strips you are using.

2 Test the brake fluid. Most test strips need to be dipped into the brake fluid for a specified amount of time (usually about 1 or 2 seconds).

3 Shake off excess fluid. An additional amount of specified time is allowed to pass before comparing the colored pad with the color chart to determine the level of contaminates or pH level.

4 Compare the results you obtained to specifications.

Maintenance and Repair

Bleeding

When pressure is applied to brake fluid in a hydraulic braking system, the brake fluid can not be compressed into a smaller volume, and therefore the pressure rises within the hydraulic braking system. Pressure is transmitted throughout the hydraulic braking system without loss. If air enters the hydraulic braking system, it can be dangerous. Unlike fluids, gases are compressible; when pressure is applied to air (a gas), the air decreases its volume and the pressure does not build up as quickly throughout the hydraulic braking system. The brakes will feel spongy and will not be fully functional. **Bleeding** the brakes means removing air from the hydraulic braking system so that only the brake fluid is left in the system.

There are a number of different brake bleeding methods. The three most common are:

- **Manual bleeding**: Using a helper to manually operate the brake pedal while you open and close the bleeder screws on the wheel units to allow the air and old brake fluid to be pushed out of the hydraulic braking system.
- **Pressure bleeding**: Using clean brake fluid under pressure from an auxiliary tool or piece of equipment to force the air and old brake fluid from the hydraulic braking system.
- **Vacuum bleeding**: Using a vacuum bleeder to pull the air and old brake fluid from the hydraulic braking system.

For all three methods, follow these general steps first: Remove as much of the old brake fluid from the reservoir as possible using a suction gun, old antifreeze tester, or turkey baster. Refill the master cylinder reservoir using the specified fluid type. Then determine which method of bleeding you will use. Also research the service information to obtain the bleeding sequence for the vehicle.

The manual bleeding method requires the least amount of equipment and tools. It requires more time if a large percentage of the brake fluid needs changed. It also is less effective at removing trapped air in systems that have high spots in the brake lines or in vehicles that have a large vertical drop between the master cylinder and the wheel brake units, such as a truck that has been lifted. This method is best when only a small amount of brake fluid needs to be bled, such as after replacing front brake calipers, or when more expensive equipment is not available.

To perform the manual bleeding method, follow the steps in **SKILL DRILL 31-5**:

1 Ask an assistant to slowly push the brake pedal down. (If it is an old/neglected master cylinder, make sure the assistant does not depress the pedal beyond its normal range of travel. Have the assistant place his or her left foot under the brake pedal to avoid pushing the pedal to the floor). Clear communication between you and the assistant is required for successful bleeding. **(Photo 1)**

2 Start with the bleeder screw that is the farthest from the master cylinder. With a clear bleeder hose connected to the bleeder screw and inserted into a clear plastic container, open the bleeder screw one-quarter to one-half turn. Observe any old brake fluid and air bubbles coming out of the bleeder screw.

3 When the brake fluid stream stops, close the bleeder screw lightly and have the assistant slowly release the pedal. This allows the master cylinder to pull a fresh charge of brake fluid from the reservoir, ready to be bled again.

4 Repeat the previous three steps until there are no more air bubbles coming out of the brake unit. Close off the bleeder screw and tighten it to the manufacturer's specifications. Be sure that you DO NOT bleed the system so much that the reservoir runs dry and admits air into the hydraulic braking system. If this happens, it will be much harder to bleed the hydraulic braking system since air is compressible, making it harder to build pressure within the hydraulic braking system.

SKILL DRILL | 31-5 | Performing Manual Bleeding

1 Ask an assistant to slowly push the brake pedal down, keeping his or her left foot underneath the pedal to limit full pedal travel.

2 Install a clear hose on the farthest bleeder screw. Open the bleeder screw one-quarter to one-half turn. Observe any old brake fluid and air bubbles coming out. When the brake fluid stops, close the bleeder screw lightly, and then have the assistant slowly release the brake pedal. Repeat these steps until there are no more air bubbles or old fluid coming out of the hose. Close off the bleeder screw and tighten it to the manufacturer's specifications. Check the level in the master cylinder reservoir, top it off, and reinstall the reservoir cap. Repeat this bleeding procedure for each of the brake units, moving closer to the master cylinder, one wheel at a time.

5 Check the level in the master cylinder reservoir, top it off, and reinstall the reservoir cap.

6 Repeat this procedure for each of the wheel brake units, moving closer to the master cylinder, one wheel at a time until all of the air has been removed and the brake pedal is not spongy.

7 You may have to start the engine to make sure the brake pedal is still firm with the power brake booster in operation. **(Photo 2)**

The pressure bleeding method uses equipment that can provide a continuous supply of brake fluid under pressure to the master cylinder reservoir. It may also include small-diameter hoses that attach to the bleeder screws and recover all of the old brake fluid. Since this method takes a bit of work to connect the equipment to the vehicle, it is best used when the hydraulic system needs a full flush or on systems that have a tendency to trap air, making manual bleeding much more difficult. To perform the pressure bleeding method, follow the steps in **SKILL DRILL 31-6**:

1 Prepare the pressure bleeder and connect it to the vehicle according to the manufacturer's procedure. Make sure it has enough fresh, clean brake fluid for the job you are performing. **(Photo 1)**

2 Start with the bleeder screw that is the farthest from the master cylinder. Connect the bleeder hose (or a clear tube inserted in a clear plastic container) to the bleeder screw and open it one-quarter to one-half turn.

SKILL DRILL 31-6 | Performing Pressure Bleeding

1 Prepare the pressure bleeder and install it on the vehicle.

2 Install a clear hose on the farthest bleeder screw, and open it one-quarter to one-half turn. Observe any old brake fluid and air bubbles coming out.

3 Close off the bleeder screw when the brake fluid is clear and has no bubbles. Tighten it to the manufacturer's specifications. Repeat this procedure for each of the wheel brake units, moving closer to the master cylinder, one wheel at a time.

3 Observe any old brake fluid and air bubbles coming out of the bleeder screw. **(Photo 2)**

4 Close the bleeder screw when the brake fluid is clear and has no bubbles.

5 Repeat this procedure for each of the wheel brake units, moving closer to the master cylinder, one wheel at a time. You may have to start the engine to make sure the brake pedal is still firm with the power brake booster in operation. **(Photo 3)**

To perform the vacuum bleeding method, follow the steps in **SKILL DRILL 31-7**:

1 Prepare the vacuum bleeder for use.

2 Start with the bleeder screw that is the farthest from the master cylinder. Connect the bleeder hose from the vacuum bleeder to the bleeder screw and open it one-quarter to one-half turn. **(Photo 1)**

3 Operate the vacuum bleeder to pull brake fluid from the bleeder screw. Observe any old brake fluid and air bubbles coming out. Note that air can be drawn around the threads of the bleeder screw, so those can fool you into thinking there is still air in the system.

4 Close the bleeder screw when the brake fluid is clear and has no bubbles.

5 Check the level in the master cylinder reservoir and top it off.

6 Repeat this procedure for each of the wheel brake units, moving closer to the master cylinder, one wheel at a time. **(Photo 2)**.

TECHNICIAN TIP

One other method that you need to know about is gravity bleeding. This method relies on the master cylinder being mounted higher than the wheel brake units. Because gravity tries to pull the brake fluid down, gravity bleeding can occur just by opening one or more bleeder screws. If the height difference is great enough, the brake fluid will slowly drain out of the system. A technician can use this method to start the bleeding process while working on other wheel brake units. However, gravity bleeding can be a disadvantage. If a technician inadvertently leaves a hose disconnected or a bleeder screw open, *all* of the brake fluid can drain out of the system, leaving it full of air and harder to bleed. Be very careful and do not leave the hydraulic braking system open for too long.

SKILL DRILL | 31-7 | Performing Vacuum Bleeding

1 Prepare the vacuum bleeder for use. Install the vacuum bleeder on the farthest bleeder screw, and open it one-quarter to one-half turn.

2 Operate the vacuum bleeder to pull brake fluid from the bleeder screw. Observe any old brake fluid and air bubbles coming out. Close off the bleeder screw and tighten it to the manufacturer's specifications. Check the level in the master cylinder reservoir and top it off. Repeat this procedure for each of the brake units, moving closer to the master cylinder, one wheel at a time.

After performing one of these three methods, follow these steps:

1. Double-check that all bleeder screws are properly tightened.
2. Replace all bleeder screw dust caps when finished.
3. Refill the master cylinder to the proper level and reinstall the master cylinder reservoir cap.
4. Start the vehicle and check for proper brake pedal feel (it should be firm and high).
5. Verify that there are no leaks at each bleeder screw.
6. Dispose of any old brake fluid in an environmentally approved method.

> **TECHNICIAN TIP**
>
> Never run the master cylinder dry during bleeding; doing so will make it much more difficult to bleed!

> **TECHNICIAN TIP**
>
> Many manufacturers recommend that brake fluid be changed every 2 to 4 years. Consult the vehicle's owner manual for the specified intervals for the model you are working on and the type of replacement brake fluid recommended.

> **TECHNICIAN TIP**
>
> When bleeding the brakes, top off the brake fluid after bleeding each wheel brake unit.

Flushing Process

Flushing brake fluid is similar to brake bleeding except that it is designed to not only remove any trapped air, but to also replace all of the old brake fluid with new brake fluid. A flush using clean brake fluid can be performed to remove any remaining residue and all air. Usually clean brake fluid of the proper type for the vehicle is used for flushing a hydraulic braking system. However, if the hydraulic braking system has been contaminated with petroleum products or other improper fluids, some manufacturers specify flushing it with clean alcohol. The alcohol will help dissolve any oil in addition to flushing the system. Once the alcohol flush is complete, dry compressed air can be used to blow out the majority of the alcohol.

Inspecting Brake Pedal

Brake pedal height, free play, and travel are critical for proper brake operation. Having the proper brake pedal height helps to ensure that the brake pedal has enough starting height to fully apply force to the brakes even if one half of the hydraulic system is rendered useless by a leak. In other words, there needs to be a specified distance the brake pedal can travel before it contacts the floor or anything else. **Free play** is the amount of clearance between the brake pedal linkage and the master cylinder piston. To measure it, you can apply very light hand pressure to the brake pedal, measuring how far the pedal travels before you start to feel resistance **FIGURE 31-25**.

Brake pedal travel is sometimes called reserve pedal. Travel is the distance the brake pedal travels, from its rest position to its applied height. Travel is measured by reading brake pedal height and subtracting the height from the floor **FIGURE 31-26**. For example, if the brake pedal height is 8″ (203.2 mm) and the travel takes it down to 5″ (127 mm) off the floor, then the travel is 3″ (76.2 mm). Reserve pedal is the measurement from the floor to the applied brake pedal and represents how much reserve is left for the brake pedal to travel if needed **FIGURE 31-27**.

To measure brake pedal height, follow the steps in **SKILL DRILL 31-8**:

1. Research the procedure and specifications for measuring brake pedal height, travel, and free play for the vehicle you are working on. Some manufacturers specify how much travel the brake pedal should have while others specify how much reserve pedal should remain when the brake pedal is fully applied. Know which process applies to the vehicle you are working on.

2. Remove any removable floor mats or anything lying on the floor near the brake pedal.

3. With the engine off, measure the brake pedal height between the two specified points using a measuring stick.

FIGURE 31-26 Travel is measured by reading brake petal height and subtracting the height from the floor.

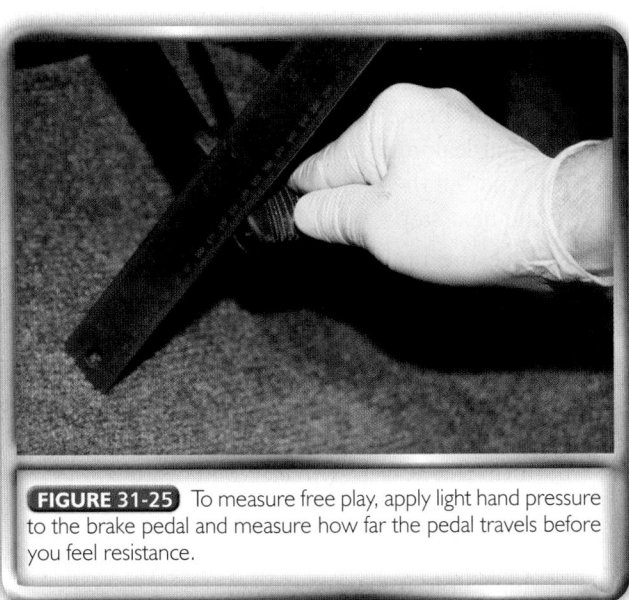

FIGURE 31-25 To measure free play, apply light hand pressure to the brake pedal and measure how far the pedal travels before you feel resistance.

FIGURE 31-27 Reserve pedal is the measurement from the floor to the applied brake pedal.

AS-96: Contamination: The technician can demonstrate an understanding of how a contaminated liquid can cause a chemical reaction that results in the deterioration of performance.

As moisture levels increase in brake fluid, the boiling point of the brake fluid decreases. This chemical reaction results in the deterioration of the brake fluid's performance. In any liquid, when boiling occurs, the liquid turns to vapor. Brakes work on the principle of liquid being incompressible; however, vapor is compressible. The result of brake fluid boiling in brake systems is a spongy pedal and a loss of braking effort at the wheels, including potential for complete brake failure. SAE field tests have documented that the average 1-year-old car has approximately 2% moisture in the brake fluid, making regular brake fluid changes necessary to ensure safety.

Safety

Never use any petroleum- or mineral-based products, such as gasoline or kerosene, to clean a hydraulic braking system or its components. They are not compatible with the seals used in the braking system and will result in a failure of the hydraulic braking system and its components. This failure may result in injury to the passengers or damage to the vehicle.

TECHNICIAN TIP

Make sure you understand and observe all legislative and personal safety procedures when carrying out tasks. If you are unsure of what these procedures are, ask your supervisor.

4 Compare this reading to the specifications and determine any necessary actions.

To measure brake pedal free play, follow the steps in **SKILL DRILL 31-9**:

1 Research the specified procedure to measure the pedal free play.

2 Use light hand pressure to apply the brake pedal until all clearances are taken up, while measuring the distance the brake pedal moved.

3 Compare this reading to the specifications and determine any necessary actions.

To measure brake pedal travel, follow the steps in **SKILL DRILL 31-10**:

1 Research the specified procedure to measure the brake pedal travel or reserve pedal height.

2 Start the engine. This will allow the booster to operate normally.

3 Apply the brake pedal with the specified force.

4 Measure the brake pedal travel or reserve height.

5 Compare this reading to the specifications and determine any necessary actions.

Inspecting Master Cylinder

Inspecting the master cylinder for internal and external leaks is usually performed under the following conditions: the brake pedal sinks when the brakes are applied, the brake fluid is low in the reservoir, the brake warning light is on, or the brake pedal reserve height is too low. To check the master cylinder for internal or external leaks and proper operation, follow the steps in **SKILL DRILL 31-11**:

1 Check the brake fluid level in the reservoir to see if it is low. Reinstall the reservoir cap.

2 Inspect the master cylinder for obvious signs of leakage. Be sure to check all brake line fittings, sensor connections, reservoir seals, and the areas at the rear of the master cylinder near the power booster.

3 Check the inside of the vacuum hose to the power booster for signs of brake fluid, which would mean brake fluid is leaking past the primary piston in the master cylinder and the front seal on the power booster.

4 Start the vehicle and apply the brake pedal beginning with a very light pressure. The brake pedal should hold its position without sinking for at least 1 minute. If it continues to sink, the hydraulic brake system may have an external or internal leak and further inspection of the system is needed. If the brake pedal holds steady, continue to the next step.

5 Release the brake pedal and apply it a bit more firmly. Hold that pressure and see if the brake pedal holds steady. If it does, repeat this step, increasing the brake pedal pressure until firm pressure is applied. **(Photo 1)**

6 Inspect the master cylinder for internal leaks. Only perform this test if the brake pedal sinks.

- Remove the master cylinder reservoir cap.
- Have an assistant apply the brake pedal firmly and hold it.

SKILL DRILL | 31-11 | Inspecting Master Cylinder

1   Check the brake fluid level in the reservoir to see if it is low. Reinstall the reservoir cap. Inspect the master cylinder for obvious signs of leakage. Check the inside of the vacuum hose to the power booster for signs of brake fluid. Start the vehicle and apply the brake pedal beginning with a very light pressure. The brake pedal should hold its position without sinking for at least 1 minute. Release the brake pedal and apply it a bit more firmly. Hold that pressure and see if the brake pedal holds steady. If it does, repeat this step with increasing pedal pressure until firm pressure is applied.

2   Inspect the master cylinder for internal leaks using the visual method. Only perform this test if the brake pedal sinks.
- Remove the master cylinder reservoir cap.
- Have an assistant apply the brake pedal slowly and hold it firmly.
- Watch the brake fluid in the reservoir; there should be an initial spurt of brake fluid from each of the two compensating ports as the brake pedal is first moved. If the brake fluid level rises while holding the brake pedal down, then the master cylinder has an internal leak.

- Watch the brake fluid in the reservoir; there should be an initial spurt of brake fluid from each of the two compensating ports as the brake pedal is first moved. If the brake fluid level rises while holding the brake pedal down, then the master cylinder has an internal leak. **(Photo 2)**

7 Inspect the master cylinder for internal leaks using the blocked-off method. Only perform this test if the brake pedal sinks and the preceding inspection is not conclusive.

- Unscrew the brake line fittings from the master cylinder and carefully move them out of the way.
- Install block-off fittings into the master cylinder.
- Bleed any air from each master cylinder port and tighten the block-off fittings properly.

- Have an assistant apply the brake pedal slowly and hold it firmly.
- Verify that the fittings do not leak. If the brake pedal sinks, then the master cylinder has an internal leak.

Master Cylinder Service and Bench Bleeding

Removing and bench bleeding the master cylinder are usually only performed when the master cylinder is being replaced. Bench bleeding makes bleeding the hydraulic system much easier by removing all of the air from the master cylinder. Failure to bench bleed the master cylinder prior to installing it into the hydraulic brake system will prevent the master cylinder from building much brake fluid pressure. As a result, very little brake fluid will be bled out of each wheel cylinder or caliper, increasing the time it takes to bleed the hydraulic brake system.

To remove, bench bleed, and reinstall the master cylinder, follow the steps in **SKILL DRILL 31-12**:

1 If the master cylinder is being replaced with a new or rebuilt unit, compare the new unit to the old one to verify that it is the correct replacement. If it is not, inform your supervisor/instructor.

2 Remove all of the old brake fluid from the master cylinder reservoir with a suction gun, old antifreeze tester, or turkey baster.

3 Remove the master cylinder brake lines, being sure to use flare nut or line wrenches on the brake line fittings. Use the double wrench method of loosening the fittings if fitted with an adapter. **(Photo 1)**

4 Remove the nuts holding the master cylinder to the power brake booster.

5 Remove the master cylinder. Now would be a good time to perform the next task, measuring and adjusting the master cylinder pushrod length, since it requires removal of the master cylinder.

6 Mount the master cylinder in a vise with the reservoir facing up, by the mounting ears, or carefully by the cylinder housing. **(Photo 2)**

7 Install the bleeder lines into the master cylinder outlet ports with the ends of the lines deep within the master cylinder reservoir below the normal fluid level.

8 Fill the reservoir about half full with clean brake fluid.

9 With an appropriate tool, slowly push the master cylinder piston into the bore. This should push any air and old brake fluid out of the cylinder and bleeder lines.

10 Allow the piston to return to its rest position.

11 Repeat the last two steps until all air bubbles have been removed from the master cylinder. **(Photo 3)**

12 Place the master cylinder on the power booster and install the nuts just far enough to hold it from falling off. This will allow for slight movement of the master cylinder to aid in lining up the brake lines. **(Photo 4)**

SKILL DRILL **31-12** **Performing Master Cylinder Service and Bench Bleeding**

1 Compare the new unit to the old one to verify that it is the correct replacement. Remove all of the old brake fluid from the master cylinder reservoir. Remove the master cylinder brake lines using a flare wrench and, if necessary, the double wrench method.

2 Remove the nuts holding the master cylinder to the power brake booster. Remove the master cylinder. Mount the master cylinder in a vise with the reservoir facing up.

3 Install the bleeder lines into the master cylinder outlet ports with the ends of the lines deep within the master cylinder reservoir below the normal fluid level. Fill the reservoir about half full with clean brake fluid. With an appropriate tool, slowly push the master cylinder piston into the bore. Allow the piston to return to its rest position. Repeat the last two steps until all air bubbles and old fluid have been removed from the master cylinder.

SKILL DRILL | 31-12 | Performing Master Cylinder Service and Bench Bleeding, continued

4 Place the master cylinder on the power booster and install the nuts just far enough to hold it from falling off.

5 Carefully line up the brake lines and start them by using your fingers to thread them into the master cylinder outlet ports at least four or five threads from when they first catch.

6 Tighten the bolts connecting the master cylinder to the power booster to their proper torque. Tighten the brake line fittings using a flare nut or line wrench. Use the double wrench method if the master cylinder is fitted with an adapter. Top off the master cylinder and bleed all wheel brake units to remove any remaining air. Start the engine and check brake pedal feel to verify proper height and firmness and that there is no sinking condition. Visually inspect all fittings and bleeder screws to make sure they are not leaking.

13 Carefully line up the brake lines and start them by using your fingers to thread them into the master cylinder outlet ports. The brake line fittings should thread in by using your fingers only at least four or five threads from when they first catch. To prevent cross-threading, do *not* use a wrench to start the threads. **(Photo 5)**

14 Tighten the bolts connecting the master cylinder to the power booster to their proper torque.

15 Tighten the brake line fittings using a flare nut or line wrench. Use the double wrench method if the master cylinder is fitted with adapters.

16 Top off the master cylinder and bleed all wheel brake units to remove any remaining air.

17 Start the engine and check the brake pedal feel to verify proper height and firmness and that there is no sinking condition.

18 Visually inspect all fittings and bleeder screws to make sure they are not leaking. **(Photo 6)**

Measuring and Adjusting Master Cylinder Pushrod Length

The master cylinder pushrod length is critical for proper brake operation. If it is too short, the driver will usually have to depress the brake pedal further than specified to operate the brakes. This reduces the amount of reserve pedal available in the case of a hydraulic leak. If the pushrod length is too long, it could prevent the master cylinder piston from returning far enough to uncover the compensating ports, trapping brake fluid pressure in front of the pistons and holding the brakes in the applied position. As important as pushrod length is, normally it does not need to be adjusted since it is locked in place. The situations that would call for adjusting it are as follows: someone changed the adjustment setting, the brake pedal linkage has been repaired or adjusted, or the power booster is being replaced. Just changing the master cylinder does not normally require pushrod length adjustment.

To measure and adjust master cylinder pushrod length, follow the steps in **SKILL DRILL 31-13**:

1 Remove the master cylinder following the specified procedure if still installed on the power booster.

2 Make sure the brake pedal is fully released, not bound up, and adjusted properly.

3 Using the specified tool, measure the master cylinder pushrod length. (**Photo 1**)

4 If the length is incorrect, loosen the locknut. (**Photo 2**)

5 Adjust the pushrod to the proper length. (**Photo 3**)

6 Retighten the locknut and recheck the pushrod length.

7 Reinstall the master cylinder. (**Photo 4**)

SKILL DRILL **31-13** **Measuring and Adjusting Master Cylinder Pushrod Length**

1 Remove the master cylinder following the specified procedure if still installed on the power booster. Make sure the brake pedal is fully released and not bound up. Using the specified tool, measure the master cylinder pushrod length.

2 If the length is incorrect, loosen the locknut.

3 Adjust the pushrod to the proper length.

4 Retighten the locknut and recheck the pushrod length. Reinstall the master cylinder.

Diagnosis

Overview

Diagnosis of hydraulic braking system faults begins with an understanding of the system being worked on and familiarity with Pascal's law. Add to that the customer's description of the concern and you will have enough to start investigating the cause of the customer concern. It is good practice to gather as much related information as possible about the concern from the customer. The more information you obtain, the better chance you will have in diagnosing the issue. Ask the customer questions such as:

- Does the brake pedal sink under hard pressure? Or light pressure?
- Does the vehicle pull to the left when braking? Or the right?
- Does the wheel lock up under hard brake pressure? Or light pressure?

Once you have an understanding of how the vehicle is acting, try to determine what conditions are present with the concern by asking questions such as:

- Does it happen when it is wet? Dry? Or always?
- Does it happen when it is hot? Cold? Or always?
- Does it happen when you are driving at highway speeds? At stop-and-go speeds? Or always?
- Does it happen when you are carrying a heavy load? Light load? Or always?

If the vehicle is safe to drive, it is common practice to test-drive the vehicle to verify the customer concern. If it is an intermittent problem or if it is hard to reproduce, you may need to take the customer along on the test-drive to point out what she or he is experiencing. While on the test-drive, reproduce the conditions that the customer identified and observe the concern. Do your best to determine where the fault is located by safely operating the vehicle in a variety of manners.

As you are gathering information, compare what is happening in the vehicle with your knowledge of the hydraulic braking system and Pascal's law to identify possible causes of the fault. If the fault is fairly substantial, the cause may be easy to identify. If this situation is not easily identified, then determine whether further test-driving will be useful.

Once the test-drive has accomplished as much as possible, it is time to identify the cause of the concern. Doing so may involve further testing in the shop or it could require disassembly and inspection of the suspected component or system. If you have been thorough in your diagnostic process, this should lead you to the cause of the fault. If not, take what you learned on the further diagnosis and/or inspection, determine what the next best step is, and perform it. Continue this process until you have identified the cause of the fault.

Once the cause of fault is identified, consider if it is the root cause. For example, if the customer concern is that the brake pedal is spongy, you cannot stop your diagnosis when you find low brake fluid level in the master cylinder reservoir. Adding brake fluid and bleeding the brakes might restore proper function to the brake pedal, but you have to ask, "Why was the brake fluid low?" It is likely that there is a leak in the hydraulic braking system that will cause the customer concern to return. In this case, the root cause might be a leaky wheel cylinder. Because the brake fluid was low, you should perform a visual inspection of the hydraulic braking system to verify there are no leaks.

Diagnosing Power Brake Systems

All power brake systems should be inspected and tested whenever the customer complains that the brakes are dragging, the brake pedal is harder to push than normal, the pedal height has changed, or if the engine operation changes more than a minimal amount when the brake pedal is applied. Vacuum boosters should also be tested if you determine that the vehicle has an unlocated vacuum leak. Single-diaphragm and dual-diaphragm vacuum brake boosters are diagnosed in the same manner. The following tests can be performed on single-diaphragm and dual-diaphragm boosters:

- Brake pedal free travel: Tests to see if there is the proper brake pedal linkage clearance
- Performance/operation test: Tests to see if the booster is operational
- External leak test: Tests for leaks to the atmosphere
- Internal leak test: Tests for leaks between the booster chambers

Testing Power Booster

Power booster testing starts with a brake pedal free travel test and then follows up with a performance test to see if the booster is operating properly. The brake pedal free travel is critical for proper brake operation. The proper amount of free travel ensures that the brake pedal linkage allows the master cylinder piston to return to its proper rest position and uncover the compensating ports. Insufficient free travel can cause the brakes to drag due to trapped fluid pressure in front of the piston not being able to return to the reservoir through the blocked compensating ports. Excessive free travel is not good either, as it reduces the amount of reserve pedal for braking in the event of a hydraulic brake system leak.

As important as brake pedal free travel is, it normally does not need to be adjusted since the components are locked in place. The situations that would call for adjusting it include the following: someone has changed the adjustment setting, the brake pedal linkage has been repaired or adjusted, the linkage has worn over time leading to increased free travel, or the power booster is being replaced. Just changing the master cylinder does not normally require brake pedal free travel adjustment; however, it is good practice to verify that it is within specifications. If adjustment is needed, the manufacturer usually incorporates a locking adjustment rod between the power booster and the brake pedal.

After verifying that the free travel is correct, it is time to performance test the power booster. To do so, operate the booster to test its ability to provide boost to the master cylinder. To test pedal free travel and check power assist operation, follow the steps in **SKILL DRILL 31-14**:

1. To test brake pedal free travel, with the engine off, depress the brake pedal several times to remove any vacuum or hydraulic pressure from the power booster.

2. Measure the distance of the brake pedal free travel by depressing the brake pedal by hand until you just feel all of the slack taken up. **(Photo 1)**

3. Measure the distance the brake pedal travels from the highest reading to the point that all slack is taken up; compare the findings to the specifications.

4. Check power assist operation (performance test) by beginning with the vehicle engine off.

5. Apply and release the brake pedal five or six times to bleed off any vacuum or hydraulic pressure in the power booster. **(Photo 2)**

6. Hold the brake pedal down with moderately firm pressure (20–30 lb [9.1–13.6 kg]).

7. Start the engine and observe the brake pedal. **On vacuum-assisted vehicles**, if the pedal drops an inch or two, the booster is providing boost. If it does not drop, the booster is not providing boost and the following tests will need to be performed to determine the cause of the fault. **On some hydraulic-assisted vehicles**, when starting the engine with your foot on the brake pedal, the

SKILL DRILL | 31-14 | Testing Pedal Free Travel and Checking Power Assist Operation

1. To test brake pedal free travel, with the engine off, depress the brake pedal several times to remove any vacuum or hydraulic pressure from the power booster. Measure the distance of the brake pedal free travel by depressing the brake pedal by hand until you just feel all of the slack taken up.

2. Measure the distance the brake pedal travels from the highest reading to the point that all slack is taken up; compare the findings to the specifications. Check power assist operation by beginning with the vehicle engine off. Apply and release the brake pedal five or six times to bleed off any vacuum or hydraulic pressure in the power booster.

3. Hold the brake pedal down with moderately firm pressure (20–30 lb [9.1–13.6 kg]). Start the engine and observe the brake pedal. On vacuum-assisted vehicles, if the pedal drops an inch or two, the booster is providing boost. If it does not drop, the booster is not providing boost and the following tests will need to be performed to determine the cause of the fault. On some hydraulic-assisted vehicles, when starting the engine with your foot on the brake pedal, the pedal should rise or fall an inch or so (depending on the vehicle you are working on) if the booster is providing assist.

brake pedal will rise an inch or so if the booster is providing assist. On other vehicles, the pedal will drop an inch or two in the same way that a vacuum booster drops. Consult the service information to verify the specific testing procedure and results for the vehicle you are working on. **(Photo 3)**

Checking Vacuum Supply to Vacuum-Type Power Booster

The brake booster must have an adequate amount of vacuum to operate correctly. Insufficient vacuum will require the driver to increase foot pressure to activate the brakes. Excessive vacuum is not usually a problem because the booster is designed to work using maximum engine vacuum. Many manufacturers specify a minimum

of 16 inches of mercury (in. Hg; 406 mm Hg) of intake manifold vacuum. To check vacuum supply to a vacuum-type power booster, follow the steps in **SKILL DRILL 31-15**:

1. With the engine off, remove the inlet hose from the vacuum-type booster. **(Photo 1)**
2. Connect a vacuum gauge to the vacuum supply end of the hose. **(Photo 2)**
3. Start the engine and read the vacuum supply available to the vacuum-type booster.
4. The vacuum should be greater than 16 in. Hg (406 mm Hg) on most vehicles.
5. If the reading is insufficient, check for vacuum leaks or restrictions in the supply hose or for an improperly tuned engine. **(Photo 3)**

SKILL DRILL 31-15 Checking Vacuum Supply to Vacuum-type Power Booster

1. With the engine off, remove the inlet hose from the vacuum-type booster.
2. Connect a vacuum gauge to the vacuum supply end of the hose.
3. Start the engine and read the vacuum supply available to the vacuum-type booster. Vacuum should be greater than 16 in. Hg (406 mm Hg) on most vehicles. If the reading is insufficient, check for vacuum leaks or restrictions in the supply hose or for an improperly tuned engine.

Checking Vacuum-Type Power Booster Unit for Leaks and Inspecting the Check Valve

Vacuum leaks in the power booster require increased driver foot pressure to activate the brakes. Since the vacuum normally comes from the intake manifold, a leaky power booster can affect the operation of the engine by changing the air/fuel mixture. Power boosters can leak internally or externally. Perform the external leak test before the internal leak test to avoid confusion in identifying the cause of the leak. To inspect the vacuum-type power booster unit for leaks and inspect the check valve for proper operation, follow the steps in **SKILL DRILL 31-16**:

1 The first step is to perform an external leak test. Start the engine and allow it to run for at least 10 seconds. With your foot *off* of the brake pedal, turn the engine off.

2 Wait at least 10 minutes, then apply the brake pedal with moderately firm pressure (20–30 lb [9.1–13.6 kg]). Note the feel and pedal reserve height.

3 Apply the brake pedal a couple more times with the same moderately firm pressure. Each application should result in a higher and firmer brake pedal as the vacuum is released from the booster. If it does, then there are no substantial external leaks in the system. If it does not hold vacuum, you will need to inspect the booster for external vacuum leaks. The cause could be:

- The vacuum check valve and/or grommet
- The front or rear seals of the unit
- The atmospheric valve at the rear of the booster
- The case where the halves are crimped together
- A hole worn or rusted through the case **(Photo 1)**

4 The second step is to perform an internal leak test. Begin by starting the engine and letting it idle. Apply the brake pedal with firm pressure (30–50 lb [13.6–22.7 kg]).

SKILL DRILL | **31-16** | **Checking Vacuum-Type Power Booster Unit for Leaks and Inspecting the Check Valve**

1 The first step is to perform an external leak test. Start the engine and allow it to run for at least 10 seconds. With your foot *off* of the brake pedal, turn the engine off. Wait at least 10 minutes, then apply the brake pedal with moderately firm pressure (20–30 lb [9.1–13.6 kg]). Note the feel and pedal reserve height. Apply the brake pedal a couple more times with the same moderately firm pressure. Each application should result in a higher brake pedal as the vacuum is released from the booster.

2 The second step is to perform an internal leak test. Begin by starting the engine and letting it idle. Apply the brake pedal with firm pressure (30–50 lb [13.6–22.7 kg]). Without moving your foot, shut off the engine and observe the brake pedal for approximately 1 minute. If it stays steady, there are no internal leaks. If the brake pedal rises, there is an internal leak.

3 The third step is to perform a check valve operation test. Start the engine and allow it to run for 30 seconds to evacuate the booster.

SKILL DRILL | 31-16 | Checking Vacuum-Type Power Booster Unit for Leaks and Inspecting the Check Valve, continued

4. Turn off the engine, wait at least 10 minutes, and then remove the check valve from the booster. There should be a large rush of air into the booster if the check valve is holding a vacuum properly. If there is not, test the check valve by blowing through it.

5. Without moving your foot, shut off the engine and observe the brake pedal for approximately 1 minute. If it stays steady, there are no internal leaks. If the brake pedal rises, there is an internal leak in either the diaphragm, the control valve, or the check valve. (Photo 2)

6. The third step is to perform a check valve operation test. Start the engine and allow it to run for 30 seconds to evacuate the booster. (Photo 3)

7. Turn off the engine, wait at least 10 minutes, and then remove the check valve from the booster. There should be a large rush of air into the booster. If there is, the check valve is holding a vacuum and is OK. If there is not, test the check valve by blowing through it. Air should flow from the booster side of the check valve to the engine side only. (Photo 4)

Inspecting and Testing a Hydraulically Assisted Power Brake System

Operation problems can be caused by a number of things such as leaks inside the booster unit, a worn power steering pump, a slipping or broken pump drive belt, badly contaminated power steering fluid, or leaky hose connections. Most of these issues can be verified with a visual inspection. To inspect and test a hydraulically assisted power brake system for leaks and proper operation, follow the steps in SKILL DRILL 31-17:

1. First, perform the performance test. Begin with the vehicle engine off. Apply and release the brake pedal five or six times to discharge the accumulator.

2. Hold the brake pedal down with moderately firm pressure (20–30 lb [9.1–13.6 kg]).

3. Start the engine and observe the brake pedal. Depending on the vehicle, the brake pedal will either drop an inch or two or rise an inch or so if the booster is providing boost. If it does not drop or rise, check the power steering pump belt and power steering pump system. If they are in good condition, consult the service information for further diagnosis. (Photo 1)

4. Second, perform the accumulator leak test. Start the engine, apply the brake pedal, and note the pedal feel and applied height.

5. Release the brake pedal, turn off the engine, and wait at least 10 minutes. (Photo 2)

SKILL DRILL | **31-17** | **Inspecting and Testing a Hydraulically Assisted Power Brake System**

1. First, perform the performance test. Begin with the vehicle engine off. Apply and release the brake pedal five or six times. Hold the brake pedal down with moderately firm pressure (20–30 lb [9.1–13.6 kg]). Start the engine and observe the brake pedal. It should drop or rise an inch or so if the booster is providing boost.

2. Second, perform the accumulator leak test. Start the engine, apply the brake pedal, and note the pedal feel and applied height. Release the brake pedal, turn off the engine, and wait at least 10 minutes.

3. Apply the brake pedal with moderately firm pressure (20–30 lb [9.1–13.6 kg]). Note the feel and brake pedal height. Apply the brake pedal a couple more times with the same moderately firm pressure. Each application should result in a higher brake pedal as the accumulator pressure is released from the booster.

6. Apply the brake pedal with moderately firm pressure (20–30 lb [9.1–13.6 kg]). Note the feel and brake pedal height.

7. Apply the brake pedal a couple more times with the same moderately firm pressure. Each application should result in a higher brake pedal as the accumulator pressure is released from the booster. If it does hold pressure, there are no substantial leaks in the system. If it does not hold pressure, you will need to perform manufacturer-specified tests to determine what is causing the loss in pressure. **(Photo 3)**

Inspecting Brake Lines and Hoses

Inspecting brake lines and brake hoses can show where maintenance is needed to prevent vehicle breakdowns and unsafe vehicle operation. Regular inspection of these components is recommended by all manufacturers. Be sure to take into account regional differences, such as regions that are highly susceptible to corrosion from de-icing chemicals or high humidity. Also, off-road vehicles may be more prone to dents, kinks, and cuts. Inspect all vehicles carefully.

To inspect brake lines, brake hoses, and associated hardware, follow the steps in **SKILL DRILL 31-18**:

1. Safely raise the vehicle on a hoist.

2. Trace all brake lines from the master cylinder to each wheel's brake assembly. Inspect the steel brake lines for leaks, dents, kinks, rust, and cracks. Pay special attention to any low spots in steel lines, as they can collect water inside them and rust from the inside out. **(Photo 1)**

3. Inspect all flexible brake hoses for cracks, bulging, and wear. **(Photo 2)**

4. Tighten any loose fittings and supports. **(Photo 3)**

Replacing Brake Lines, Brake Hoses, Fittings, and Supports

To replace brake lines, brake hoses, fittings, and supports, follow the steps in **SKILL DRILL 31-19**:

1. To prevent an excessive amount of brake fluid from leaking out of the hydraulic brake system while the brake line or brake hose is removed from the vehicle, depress the brake pedal with a brake pedal depressor. This will push the master cylinder piston past the compensating ports and prevent brake fluid from leaving the reservoir. **(Photo 1)**

2. Remove the stop light fuse to avoid draining the battery. Don't forget to replace it when you are finished.

3. Safely raise the vehicle on a hoist.

SKILL DRILL | 31-18 | Inspecting Brake Lines, Brake Hoses, and Associated Hardware

1. Safely raise the vehicle on a hoist. Trace all brake lines from the master cylinder to each wheel's brake assembly. Inspect the steel brake lines for leaks, dents, kinks, rust and cracks.

2. Inspect all flexible brake hoses for cracks, bulging, and wear.

3. Tighten any loose fittings and supports.

SKILL DRILL | 31-19 | Replacing Brake Lines, Hoses, Fittings, and Supports

1. Depress the brake pedal with a brake pedal depressor.

2. Remove the stop light fuse to avoid draining the battery. Safely raise the vehicle on a hoist. Using flare nut wrenches and the double wrench method, carefully remove any brake lines, hoses, fittings, and supports that are to be replaced. Inspect all components for damage and wear.

3. Carefully reassemble the removed components, but until everything is assembled, tighten any fittings or supports by using your fingers only. Once everything is assembled, tighten each fitting and support using flare nut wrenches and the double wrench method wherever two fittings connect. Bleed the hydraulic braking system to remove any trapped air. Start the vehicle to verify proper brake pedal height, firmness, and feel. Reinstall the brake light fuse if removed.

4 Using flare nut wrenches and the double wrench method, carefully remove any brake lines, brake hoses, fittings, and supports that are to be replaced.

5 Inspect all components for damage and wear. **(Photo 2)**

6 Carefully reassemble the removed components, but until everything is assembled, tighten any

AS-87: Hydraulics: The technician can explain how fluid pressure transmits force from one location to another.

Pascal's law states that incompressible liquids transmit pressure in all directions. This is the basic principle underpinning the operation of hydraulic braking systems on motor vehicles. When braking, brake pedal pressure is applied, via the master cylinder, to the brake fluid. The hydraulic fluid under pressure pushes against the caliper or wheel cylinder pistons, forcing friction material against the brake discs or drums to stop the movement of the vehicle.

For the sake of simplicity, let's think of a hydraulic brake system like a tube of toothpaste. Start with a full tube (no air). If you punch a hole in the tube and squeeze, toothpaste (a thick liquid) will be displaced from the hole. If you punch three holes through various parts of the tube and squeeze in only one place, toothpaste will be displaced from all three holes. This illustrates that force applied to a liquid in one area is transferred to all areas within a container.

fittings or supports by using your fingers only. Doing so will help to avoid cross-threading of the fittings and fasteners.

7 Once everything is assembled, tighten each fitting and support using flare nut wrenches and the double wrench method wherever two fittings connect.

8 Bleed the hydraulic brake system to remove any trapped air.

9 Start the vehicle to verify proper brake pedal height, firmness, and feel.

10 Reinstall the brake light fuse if removed. **(Photo 3)**

Brake Line Flaring

To fabricate brake lines, decide whether you will be using the double flare or ISO method. First select new, double-walled brake line of the specified diameter. Make sure the end you are flaring is cut smooth and square, without dings or gouges. Clean up with a file or recut the end with a tubing cutter. Obtain the flaring tool for the type of flare you are fabricating: double flare or ISO.

To perform the double flare method, follow the steps in **SKILL DRILL 31-20**:

1 Install the proper fitting onto the brake line. You may want to tape it out of the way temporarily.

2 Use a bench vise to hold the brake line clamping tool.

SKILL DRILL | 31-20 | Fabricating Brake Lines Using the Double Flare Method

1 Install the proper fitting onto the brake line. Use a bench vise to hold the brake line clamping tool. Select the proper adapter to match the tubing size. Use it to set the height of the tube in the clamp. Tighten down the clamp securely.

2 Insert the adapter into the tubing, and install the flaring tool onto the clamp and over the adapter.

3 Tighten down the flaring tool until the adapter touches the clamp.

SKILL DRILL | 31-20 | Fabricating Brake Lines Using the Double Flare Method, continued

4 Remove the adapter and reinstall the flaring tool. Tighten down the flaring tool to fold over the flare. Stop when the tool starts to tighten.

5 Remove the flaring tool and inspect the flare to see if it has been formed correctly. Remove the flared line from the clamp and inspect it.

3 Select the proper adapter to match the tubing size and use it to set the height of the tube in the clamp. Tighten down the clamp securely. **(Photo 1)**

4 Insert the adapter into the tubing, and install the flaring tool onto the clamp and over the adapter. **(Photo 2)**

5 Tighten down the flaring tool until the adapter touches the clamp. **(Photo 3)**

6 Remove the adapter and reinstall the flaring tool. Tighten down the flaring tool to fold over the flare. Stop when the tool starts to tighten. **(Photo 4)**

7 Remove the flaring tool and inspect the flare to see if it has been formed correctly.

8 Remove the flared line from the clamp and inspect it. **(Photo 5)**

To perform the ISO flare method, follow the steps in **SKILL DRILL 31-21**:

1 Install the proper fitting onto the brake line. You may want to tape it out of the way temporarily.

2 Use a bench vise to hold the brake line clamping tool.

3 Select the proper adapter to match the tubing size. Use it to set the height of the tube in the clamp. Tighten down the clamp securely.

4 Insert the adapter into the tubing, and install the flaring tool onto the clamp and over the adapter.

5 Tighten down the flaring tool until the adapter touches the clamp.

6 Remove the flared line from the clamp and inspect it.

Diagnosing Brake Warning Lamp

A mechanical brake warning lamp system (non-CAN-bus) circuit is a simple light bulb in series with as many as four switches that are connected in parallel with each other **FIGURE 31-28**. Each switch can illuminate the warning lamp under the right conditions. The warning lamp should be off when the ignition key is in the "run" position if the parking brake is released and there are no faults in the hydraulic system. When the ignition

FIGURE 31-28 Brake warning light circuit.

is turned to the "crank" position, the warning lamp should illuminate. In the "run" position, the warning lamp can be illuminated only when one of the switches is closed. One switch is on the parking brake assembly and illuminates the warning lamp when the parking brake is applied. This alerts the driver that the parking brake should be released before driving the vehicle. The second switch is located on the pressure differential assembly and illuminates the warning lamp if there is a moderate-sized hydraulic system leak. The third switch, if equipped, is located on the master cylinder reservoir and illuminates the warning lamp if the fluid level falls below a certain point. The last switch, if equipped, is located on the ignition switch and acts as a bulb check feature, which illuminates the warning lamp when the ignition switch is in the "crank" position.

When diagnosing the brake warning lamp, it is good to start by verifying that the bulb is operational using the circuit's bulb check feature if equipped. To do so, turn the ignition key to the "crank" position. The brake warning lamp on the dash should illuminate on most vehicles. If the bulb illuminates, then you know the bulb is good, it has power, and the ground circuit through the ignition switch is operating as it should. If it does not illuminate, first check the fuse with a test light FIGURE 31-29. If the fuse is OK, remove the bulb and verify that it is not burned out by measuring its resistance with an ohmmeter and comparing it to specifications or the resistance of a known good bulb.

If the brake warning lamp illuminated in the "crank" position, turn the ignition key to the "run" position. The brake warning lamp should be off. If it is, apply the parking brake. The warning lamp should illuminate. If it does not illuminate, you will need to

refer to the vehicle's wiring diagram to determine the best strategy to diagnose the system. If it is similar to the one in Figure 31-25, then locate the parking brake switch, disconnect the wire harness connector from the switch, and jump it to ground with a jumper wire. With the ignition switch on, the brake warning light should now be illuminated. If it is, then the switch either needs adjustment or replacement. If it is not, then there is a problem between the switch and the bulb. Use the same process for the low brake fluid switch, the pressure differential switch, and the ignition switch.

If the brake warning lamp always stays on in the "run" position, you will need to disconnect each of the four switches one at a time, checking to see if the warning lamp goes off. If it does, then you will need to test each switch and determine whether it is adjusted properly, or whether it is shorted. If the switches test OK, then there is likely a short circuit in one of the wires leading to the switches. This is the hardest part of testing the circuit; thankfully, it doesn't happen very often.

In a **CAN-bus circuit**, the parking brake sensor and the low brake fluid sensors send signals over the CAN-bus network regarding their status FIGURE 31-30. The appropriate module will then signal the instrument panel module to illuminate the brake warning light. Diagnosis involves using a scan tool capable of interrogating the system, a wiring diagram, and a digital volt-ohmmeter (DVOM) to perform specific tests.

> ▶ **LINK**
> Refer to the Disc Brake System chapter for more information on parking brakes.

Checking the Brake Warning Light System

To check a brake warning light system on a non-CAN-bus system, follow the steps in SKILL DRILL 31-22:

1. Perform a bulb check by turning the ignition key to the "crank" position and observing the brake warning light. If it is on, go to step 2. If it is off, check the fuse with a test light. If it is OK, check the warning lamp bulb with an ohmmeter. **(Photo 1)**

2. Make sure the parking brake is released and turn the ignition key to the "run" position. The brake warning lamp should be off. If not, go to step 6. **(Photo 2)**

3. If the warning lamp is off, apply the parking brake. The lamp should illuminate. If it does, check the

FIGURE 31-29 Checking a brake fuse with a test light.

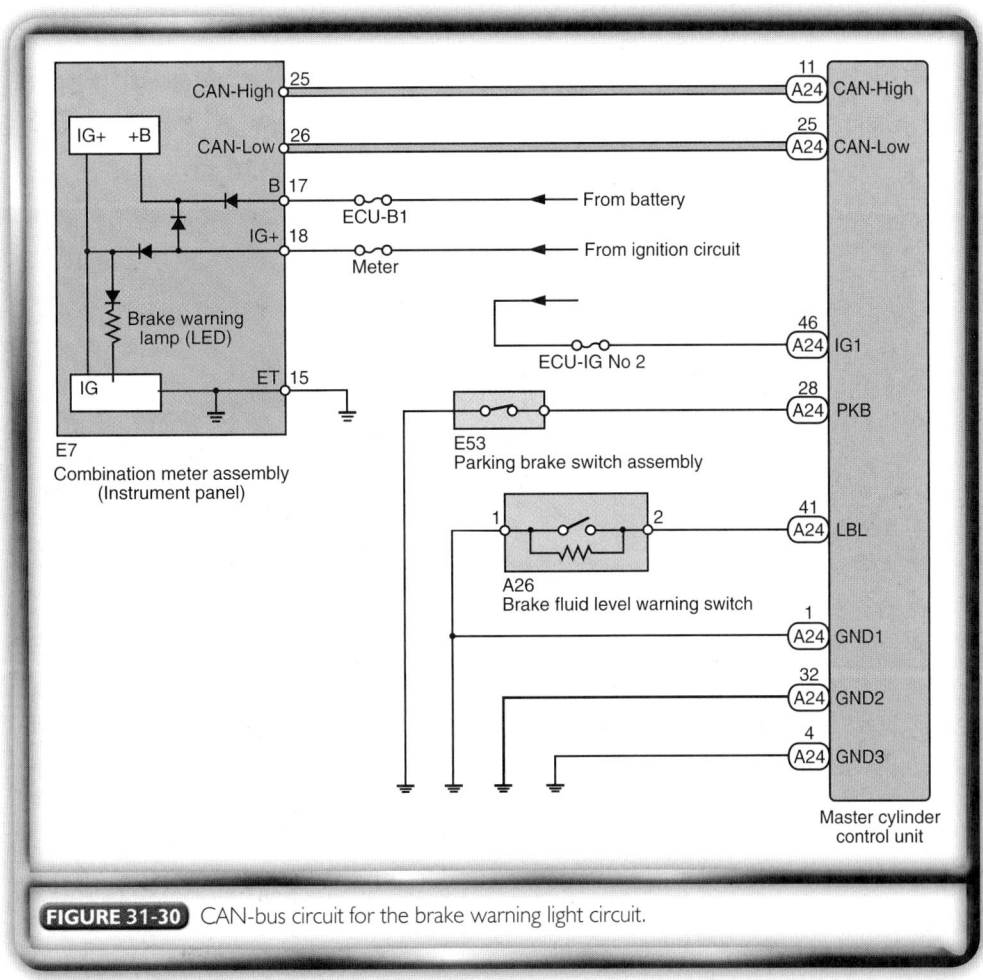

FIGURE 31-30 CAN-bus circuit for the brake warning light circuit.

SKILL DRILL **31-22** **Checking the Brake Warning Light System in a Non-CAN-bus System**

1. Perform a bulb check and observe the brake warning light. If it is on, go to step 2. If it is off, check the fuse with a test light. If it is OK, check the warning lamp bulb with an ohmmeter.

2. Make sure the parking brake is released and turn the ignition key to the "run" position. The brake warning lamp should be off. If not, go to step 6.

3. If the warning lamp is off, apply the parking brake. The lamp should illuminate. If it does, check the operation of the other switches. If they work fine, there are no faults present in the system.

SKILL DRILL | 31-22 | Checking the Brake Warning Light System in a Non-CAN-bus System, continued

4 If the brake warning light is off when the parking brake is on, disconnect the wire from the parking brake switch and ground the wire. The brake warning light should illuminate. If it does, test the parking brake switch with a DVOM.

5 If the warning lamp does not illuminate with the parking brake wire grounded, suspect an open circuit between the parking brake wire and the warning lamp. Use a DVOM and wiring diagram to diagnose the fault.

6 If the light stayed on in step 2, apply and release the parking brake several times. If this turns it off, clean or adjust the parking brake mechanism or switch. If it is still on, then, one at a time, disconnect each of the switches that activate it: parking brake, low fluid level, pressure differential, and ignition. If disconnecting one of the switches turns the light off, then test that switch for misadjustment or a shorted condition. If the warning lamp is still on, suspect a short to ground in the wiring harness between the switches and the warning lamp bulb. Use a wiring diagram and DVOM to identify the location of the fault.

operation of the other switches. If they work fine, there are no faults present in the system. (**Photo 3**)

4 If the brake warning light is off when the parking brake is on, disconnect the wire from the parking brake switch and ground the wire. The brake warning light should illuminate. If it does, suspect the parking brake switch is faulty and test its operation with a DVOM. (**Photo 4**)

5 If the warning lamp does not illuminate with the parking brake wire grounded, suspect an open circuit between the parking brake wire and the warning lamp. Use a DVOM and wiring diagram to diagnose the problem. (**Photo 5**)

6 If the light stayed on in step 2, apply and release the parking brake several times. If this turns it off, clean or adjust the parking brake mechanism or switch. If it is still on, then, one at a time, disconnect each of the switches that activate it: parking brake, low fluid level, pressure differential, and ignition. If disconnecting one of the switches turns the light off, then test that switch for misadjustment or a shorted condition.

7 If the warning lamp is still on, suspect a short to ground in the wiring harness between the switches and the warning lamp bulb. Use a wiring diagram and DVOM to identify the location of the fault. (**Photo 6**)

Checking the Parking Brake and Indicator Light System

To check the parking brake and indicator light system operation, follow the steps in **SKILL DRILL 31-23**:

1. Count the number of clicks it takes to apply the parking brake and compare that to the manufacturer's specifications. If incorrect, follow the specified procedure to adjust it.

2. With the parking brake applied, turn the ignition switch to the "run" position. The red brake warning lamp should be illuminated.

3. Release the parking brake. The warning lamp should turn off. If it does, the parking brake warning light system is operating properly.

4. If the lamp does not turn off, disconnect the wire to the parking brake switch. If the light turns off, test the parking brake switch.

5. If it does not turn off, check the operation of the other warning lamp switches and circuit.

Inspecting and Maintaining Parking Brakes

To inspect and maintain parking brakes, follow the steps in **SKILL DRILL 31-24**:

1. Safely raise the vehicle slightly off the ground on a lift and place the transmission in neutral.

2. Count the number of clicks it takes to firmly apply the parking brake and compare that to specifications. If incorrect, follow the specified procedure to adjust it.

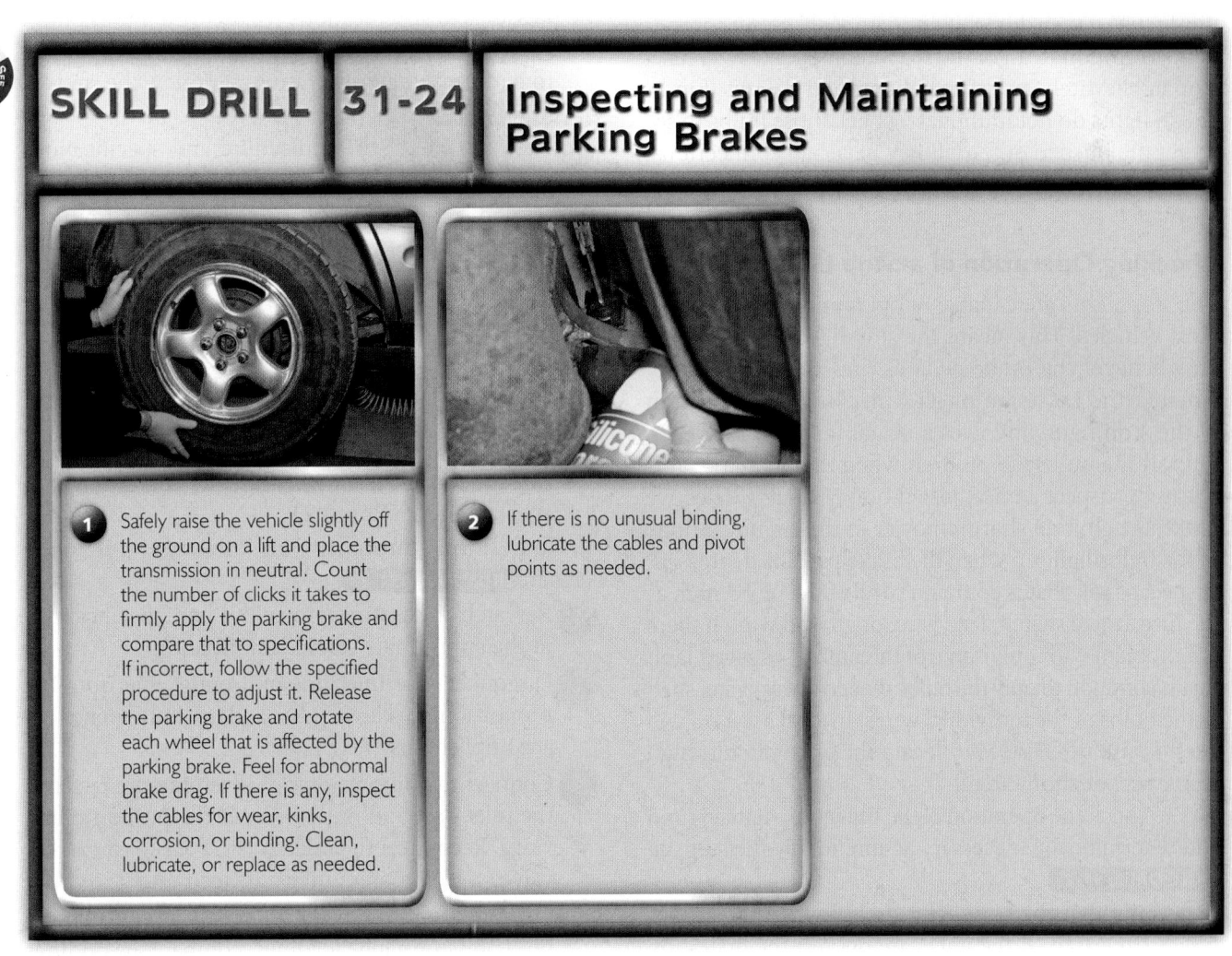

SKILL DRILL 31-24 Inspecting and Maintaining Parking Brakes

1. Safely raise the vehicle slightly off the ground on a lift and place the transmission in neutral. Count the number of clicks it takes to firmly apply the parking brake and compare that to specifications. If incorrect, follow the specified procedure to adjust it. Release the parking brake and rotate each wheel that is affected by the parking brake. Feel for abnormal brake drag. If there is any, inspect the cables for wear, kinks, corrosion, or binding. Clean, lubricate, or replace as needed.

2. If there is no unusual binding, lubricate the cables and pivot points as needed.

3 Release the parking brake and rotate each wheel that is affected by the parking brake. Feel for abnormal brake drag. If there is any, inspect the cables for wear, kinks, corrosion, or binding. Clean, lubricate, or replace as needed. **(Photo 1)**

4 If there is no unusual binding, lubricate the cables and pivot points as needed. **(Photo 2)**

Diagnosing Stop Light

The mechanical system (non-CAN-bus) circuit is simply a normally closed switch in series with two to six brake light bulbs connected in parallel with each other. This circuit is also protected by a fuse. Some vehicles use separate fuses for the center high mount stop lamp (CHMSL) and the side stop lights. The switch is turned on and off by the movement of the brake pedal. Diagnosis starts with operating the stop lights and observing their reaction, and comparing that to a wiring diagram to see how the manufacturer has wired the circuit. If they do not illuminate at all, check components common to all of the stop lights such as the fuse, stop light switch, and stop light ground circuit. If individual lights do not illuminate, check those bulbs to see if they are burned out, or if they have bad connections, terminals, or wires.

Checking Operation of a Stop Light System

The stop lights are capable of operating at all times on most vehicles. This means the stop lights should come on whenever the brake pedal is pressed, regardless of whether the key is on or off. Checking the operation of the stop lights involves a visual inspection of each bulb. If the bulbs are on even when the brake pedal is released, suspect a misadjusted brake pedal, a defective brake switch, or a short to power in the circuit. If none of the bulbs light up when the brake pedal is depressed, suspect a fault that is common to all of the bulbs such as the fuse, brake switch, feed wire, or ground wire. If there is a problem with only some of the bulbs, suspect a fault that is common to only the bulbs that do not operate, such as the bulbs or the individual wires. In any case, you will need to use the DVOM to locate the open circuit, high resistance, or short circuit.

To check the operation of the brake stop light system and determine any necessary action, follow the steps in **SKILL DRILL 31-25**:

1 Verify that the stop lights are off when the brakes are released. If the lights are on, test the operation of the brake pedal and brake switch.

2 Observe the stop lights when the brake pedal is applied. All lights including the CHMSL should be illuminated.

3 If some or all of the stop lamps do not illuminate, test them with a DVOM.

4 If the bulbs are OK, consult the wiring diagram to determine potential causes of the fault in the circuit.

5 Use the wiring diagram and a DVOM to identify the cause of the fault.

Diagnosing Hydraulic Concerns

Control valves do not normally give technicians trouble. They tend to operate rather dependably. But like any other mechanical component, they can fail. Understanding how they operate will give you a head start on diagnosing concerns associated with them. Generally, the best way to test them is to connect a pressure gauge set designed for the high pressures within a brake system to the output of the valve. Operating the brake system and comparing the pressures to specifications will tell you if the control valve is operating correctly.

To perform a metering valve test, follow the steps in **SKILL DRILL 31-26**:

1 Research the testing procedure and specifications in the appropriate service information.

2 Disconnect the inlet line and outlet line from the metering valve. Use a flare nut wrench to accomplish this. **(Photo 1)**

3 Connect the metering valve pressure tester to the inlet port and outlet port of the metering valve. Reconnect the inlet line to the metering valve, with the pressure gauge teed into it.

4 Operate the brake pedal and observe both pressure gauge readings; compare the findings to specifications. **(Photo 2)**

To perform a proportioning valve test, follow the steps in **SKILL DRILL 31-27**:

1 Research the testing procedure and specifications in the appropriate service information.

2 Disconnect the inlet line and outlet line from the proportioning valve. Use a flare nut wrench to accomplish this.

3 Connect the proportioning valve pressure tester to the inlet port and outlet port of the proportioning valve. Reconnect the inlet line to the proportioning valve, with the pressure gauge teed into it.

4 Operate the brake pedal as specified and observe both pressure gauge readings; compare the findings to specifications.

SKILL DRILL | 31-26 | Testing Metering Valve

1. Research the testing procedure and specifications in the appropriate service information. Disconnect the inlet line and outlet line from the metering valve.

2. Connect the metering valve pressure tester to the inlet port and outlet port of the metering valve. Reconnect the inlet line to the metering valve, with the pressure gauge teed into it. Operate the brake pedal and observe both pressure gauges; compare the findings to specifications.

SKILL DRILL | 31-28 | Testing Pressure Differential Valve

1. Research the testing procedure and specifications in the appropriate service information. Disconnect the electrical connector from the pressure differential valve and connect an ohmmeter between the terminal on the valve and the body of the valve. Have an assistant lightly apply the brake pedal and hold until the bleeder screw is closed.

2. Open the front bleeder screw on the driver's side of the vehicle and watch the ohmmeter reading. It should go to zero. Close the bleeder screw and move to the rear driver's side wheel. Again, with the assistant applying light pressure to the pedal, open the driver's side rear wheel bleeder screw slightly and watch the meter reading. It should go to OL and then back to zero as the valve moves to the "off" position and then to the "on" position.

To perform a pressure differential valve test, follow the steps in SKILL DRILL 31-28:

1. Research the testing procedure and specifications in the appropriate service information.

2. Disconnect the electrical connector from the pressure differential valve, and connect an ohmmeter between the terminal on the valve and the body of the valve.

3. Have an assistant lightly apply the brake pedal and hold until the bleeder screw is closed. **(Photo 1)**

4. Open the front bleeder screw on the driver's side of the vehicle and watch the ohmmeter reading. It should go to zero. If it does, the valve is capable of turning on the brake warning light. If it doesn't, the valve is faulty and needs to be replaced.

5. Close the bleeder screw and move to the rear driver's side wheel.

6. Again, with the assistant applying light pressure to the pedal, open the driver's side rear wheel bleeder screw slightly and watch the meter reading. It should go to OL and then back to zero as the valve moves to the "off" position and then to the "on" position. If it does, the valve is capable of turning on the brake warning light. If not, the valve is faulty and needs to be replaced. **(Photo 2)**

Wrap-up

Ready for Review

▶ The principle behind hydraulic brakes is Pascal's Law, which states that pressure applied to a fluid in one part of a closed system will be transmitted without loss to all other areas of the system.

▶ A substantial leak in the hydraulic braking system will prevent enough pressure from building to exert the necessary braking force.

▶ Engineers design brakes that have precise (but unequal from front to back) amounts of braking force at each wheel.

▶ The three variables related to pressure and force in hydraulic systems are: input force, working pressure, and output force.

▶ Main components of the hydraulic braking system are: brake pedal, brake fluid, and master cylinder.

▶ The brake pedal multiplies force from the driver's foot to the master cylinder.

▶ Brake fluid has a high boiling point, a low freezing point, and is hygroscopic (absorbs water).

▶ Brake fluids are graded by the Department of Transportation on: pH value, viscosity, resistance to oxidation, stability, and boiling point.

▶ Master cylinders convert force exerted from the brake pedal into hydraulic pressure to activate wheel brake units.

▶ Types of master cylinders are: single piston and tandem (required on modern cars).

▶ Single piston master cylinders use a primary cup to seal pressure in the cylinder and a secondary cup to prevent fluid loss.

▶ A single piston master cylinder traps brake fluid and forces it into the brake lines.

▶ Residual pressure valves are used on drum brake systems to maintain brake fluid pressure and prevent air entry when the brakes are off.

▶ Modern vehicles have tandem master cylinders to ensure braking ability in at least one circuit despite a leak.

▶ Differential pressure switches monitor loss of pressure between the hydraulic circuits.

▶ Braking units can be split front-to-rear, diagonally, or in an L shape.

▶ Diagonal and L-shaped braking splits retain 50% braking capability even if half the system fails.

▶ Quick take-up master cylinders work to compensate for the large running clearance maintained by low-drag brake calipers.

▶ It can be dangerous to add brake fluid without diagnosing the reason for a low fluid level.

▶ Always ask customers questions to gather diagnostic information; try a test drive to understand what the customer is experiencing.

▶ Always try to discern the root cause of a vehicular problem.

▶ Common tools that are used to repair hydraulic brake systems are: brake bleeder wrenches, vacuum brake bleeders, pressure brake bleeders, and valve gauge sets.

▶ Bleeding the brakes removes air form the hydraulic braking system.

▶ The three most common brake bleeding methods are: manual, pressure, and vacuum (gravity is also used).

▶ Flushing the brake fluid involves bleeding out the air and replacing the old brake fluid with new.

▶ Always select the proper grade of brake fluid for the vehicle you are working on.

▶ Determining if brake fluid should be flushed can be done by: time/mileage, DVOM-galvanic reaction test, boiling point test, or test strip.

▶ DVOM-galvanic reaction test, brake fluid testers, and brake fluid test strips can all be used to check for brake fluid contamination.

▶ Manual bleeding requires the least amount of tools and is best when a small amount of bleeding is needed.

▶ Pressure bleeding requires more equipment and is best when the hydraulic system needs a full flush.

▶ After bleeding, always check that bleeder screws are properly tightened with no leaks, refill master cylinder and reinstall reservoir cup, and properly dispose of brake fluid.

▶ Brake pedal inspection includes brake pedal height, free play, and travel.

▶ Free play is the clearance between the brake pedal linkage and master cylinder piston.

▶ Brake pedal travel is the distance from its rest position to its applied height.

▶ Check the master cylinder for leaks if: the brake fluid is low in the reservoir, the brake warning light is on, or the brake pedal reserve height is too low.

▶ Inspect the master cylinder for internal leaks only if the brake pedal sinks.

▶ Bench bleed the master cylinder prior to installing it to minimize time needed to bleed the hydraulic brake system.

▶ Master cylinder pushrod length should only be adjusted if: someone changed the adjustment setting, the brake pedal linkage has been repaired or adjusted, or the power booster is being replaced.

▶ Brake lines are made of double-walled steel and coated to help resist corrosion.

▶ Damaged brake lines should be replaced not repaired; always use the correct tubing bender to avoid kinks.

▶ The two types of brake line flares are inverted double and ISO.

▶ Brake hoses transmit the brake system hydraulic pressures to the wheel units and must be of the proper length to be effective.

▶ Pinching or kinking a brake hose can cause it to fail.

▶ Inspect brake hoses for: cracks, bulges, abrasion or wear, kinks, and internal breakdown.

▶ Hydraulic braking systems use proportioning valves, metering valves, pressure differential valves, or anti-lock hydraulic control units to modify hydraulic pressure.

▶ Proportioning valves reduce brake pressure to the rear wheels and are pressure-sensitive or load-sensitive.

▶ Load-sensitive proportioning valves adjust rear brake pressure according to the weight of the vehicle's load.

▶ Pressure-sensitive proportioning valves use a poppet piston to limit the rate of braking pressure increase to the rear brakes.

▶ Metering valves work to ensure rear brake pressure is applied before front brake pressure.

▶ The combination valve combines individually operating proportioning valves, metering valve and pressure differential valve in one unit and cannot be repaired.

▶ Brake warning lights alert drivers to: engagement of the parking brake, low brake fluid intake, and unequal pressure in the hydraulic brake system.

▶ Stop lights are mounted on the rear of a vehicle and alert other drivers that the vehicle is being braked.

▶ As of 1986, all vehicles must have a center high-mount stop lamp (CHMSL) to reduce incidence of rear-end collisions.

▶ Power brake units are either vacuum assist (most common) or hydraulic assist.

▶ Vacuum boosters have single or dual diaphragms to extract power from atmospheric pressure and transmit force to the master cylinder.

▶ A 12-inch vacuum booster is capable of generating enough psi to stop a vehicle weighing thousands of pounds.

▶ A vacuum booster works off of the difference between manifold vacuum and atmospheric pressure; a difference in these pressures creates more force on the master cylinder pistons.

▶ Inspect and test power brake systems whenever the customer complains that the brakes are dragging, the brake pedal is harder to push than normal, the pedal height has changed, or the engine operation changes more than a minimal amount when the brake pedal is applied.

Key Terms

aerate The tendency to create air bubbles in a fluid.

bleeding The process of removing air from a hydraulic braking system.

brake fluid Hydraulic fluid that transfers forces under pressure through the hydraulic lines to the wheel braking units.

brake hose A flexible section of the brake lines between the body and suspension to allow for steering and suspension movement.

brake lines Made of seamless, double-walled steel, and able to transmit over 1000 psi (6895 kPa) of hydraulic pressure through the hydraulic brake system.

CAN-bus circuit A two-wire communication network that transmits status and command signals between control modules in a vehicle.

compensating port Connects the brake fluid reservoir to the master cylinder bore when the piston is fully retracted, allowing for expansion and contraction of the brake fluid.

electrohydraulic braking (EHB) A hydraulic braking system that uses an electrically driven hydraulic pump to pressurize fluid for use in the master cylinder.

free play The amount of clearance between the brake pedal linkage and the master cylinder piston.

hygroscopic A substance that attracts and absorbs water (e.g., brake fluid).

inlet port Connects the reservoir with the space around the piston and between the piston cups in a brake master cylinder.

input force The force applied to the input piston, measured in either pounds or kilograms.

International Standards Organization (ISO) flare A method for joining brake lines, also called a bubble flare. Created by flaring the line slightly out and then back in, leaving the line bubbled near the end.

inverted double flare A method for joining brake lines that forms a secure, leak-proof connection.

load transfer Weight transfer from one set of wheels to the other set of wheels during braking, acceleration, or cornering.

manual bleeding A bleeding method where one person manually operates the brake pedal while the other person opens and closes the bleeder screws on the wheel brake units to allow the air and old brake fluid to be pushed out.

metering valve A valve used on vehicles equipped with older rear drum/front disc brakes to delay application of the front disc brakes until the rear drum brakes are applied. Located in line with the front disc brakes.

output force Force that equals the working pressure multiplied by the surface area of the output piston, expressed as pounds, newtons, or kilograms.

outlet port Links the cylinder to the brake lines.

Pascal's law The law of physics that states that pressure applied to a fluid in one part of a closed system will be transmitted equally to all other areas of the system.

poppet valve A valve that controls the flow of brake fluid at usually preset pressures.

pressure bleeding A bleeding method that uses clean brake fluid under pressure from an auxiliary tool or piece of equipment to force the air and old brake fluid from the hydraulic braking system.

pressure differential valve A valve that monitors any pressure difference between the two separate hydraulic brake circuits; it usually contains a switch to turn on the brake warning light when there is a pressure difference.

primary cup A seal that holds pressure in the master cylinder when force is applied to the piston.

primary piston A brake piston in the master cylinder moved directly by the pushrod or the power-booster; it generates hydraulic pressure to move the secondary piston.

proportioning valves Valves used mostly on older vehicles equipped with rear drum brakes to reduce rear wheel hydraulic brake pressure under hard braking or light loads. Located in line with the rear brakes.

quick take-up master cylinders Cylinders used on disc brake systems that are equipped with low-drag brake calipers to quickly move the brake pads into contact with the brake rotors.

quick take-up valve A valve used to release excess pressure from the larger piston in a quick take-up master cylinder once the brake pads have contacted the brake rotors.

recuperation Process by which brake fluid moves from the reservoir past the edges of the seal into the chamber in front of the piston. This prevents air from being drawn into the hydraulic system caused by low pressure when the brake pedal is released quickly.

residual pressure valve (residual check valve) In drum brake systems, a valve that maintains pressure in the wheel cylinders slightly above atmospheric pressure so that air does not enter the system through the seals in the wheel cylinders.

secondary cup A seal that prevents loss of fluid from the rear of each piston in the master cylinder.

secondary piston A piston that is moved by hydraulic pressure generated by the primary piston in the master cylinder.

single-piston master cylinder A master cylinder with a single piston that creates hydraulic pressure for all wheel units. If there is a leak in the system, there is a loss of pressure for all wheel units.

split diagonally A brake system in which the left front wheel is hydraulically paired with the right rear wheel and the right front wheel is paired with the left rear. This preserves 50% of the braking capability if one of the brake circuits begins to leak.

split front to rear A brake system in which the front brakes operate on one hydraulic circuit and the rear brakes from the other.

tandem master cylinder A master cylinder that has two pistons that operate separate braking circuits so that if a leak develops in one circuit, the other circuit can still operate.

vacuum bleeding Bleeding process that uses a vacuum bleeder to pull the air and old brake fluid from the system.

working pressure The pressure within a hydraulic system while the system is being operated.

ASE-Type Questions

1. Tech A says that hydraulic pressure is applied equally in all directions throughout a closed system. Tech B says that air in the hydraulic system will cause the brake pedal to be spongy. Who is correct?
   a. Tech A
   b. Tech B
   c. Both A and B
   d. Neither A nor B

2. Tech A says that a brake pedal that does not return all the way will cause the brake warning light on the instrument panel to stay on. Tech B says that a brake pedal that does not return will cause the brake lights to stay on. Who is correct?
   a. Tech A
   b. Tech B
   c. Both A and B
   d. Neither A nor B

3. Tech A says that brake fluid should periodically be checked for excessive moisture content. Tech B says that brake fluid should be replaced every 12,000 miles. Who is correct?
   a. Tech A
   b. Tech B
   c. Both A and B
   d. Neither A nor B

4. Tech A says that DOT 5 brake fluid should be used in all vehicles today because it is silicone based and will not absorb water. Tech B says that mixing DOT 4 and DOT 3 is not recommended because of different boiling points, but both are hydroscopic. Who is correct?
   a. Tech A
   b. Tech B
   c. Both A and B
   d. Neither A nor B

5. Tech A says that the secondary piston in a master cylinder is operated by hydraulic force. Tech B says that the brake pedal return spring returns the master cylinder pistons to their original position. Who is correct?
   a. Tech A
   b. Tech B
   c. Both A and B
   d. Neither A nor B

6. Tech A says that the low level brake fluid switch on a master cylinder will turn on the brake warning light when the system is low on fluid. Tech B says that the low level switch also monitors the condition of the fluid and will activate the warning light when the brake fluid needs to be replaced. Who is correct?
   a. Tech A
   b. Tech B
   c. Both A and B
   d. Neither A nor B

7. Tech A says that the metering valve controls pressure to the rear brakes. Tech B says that the proportioning valve controls pressure to the front brakes. Who is correct?
   a. Tech A
   b. Tech B
   c. Both A and B
   d. Neither A nor B

8. Tech A says that the vacuum booster uses vacuum and atmospheric pressure to multiply the driver's foot pressure applied to the master cylinder push rod. Tech B says that the vacuum booster increases the vacuum in the brake system. Who is correct?
   a. Tech A
   b. Tech B
   c. Both A and B
   d. Neither A nor B

9. Tech A says that bench bleeding a master cylinder will prevent having to bleed air from the brake lines during replacement. Tech B says that bench bleeding the master cylinder makes bleeding the brakes on the vehicle easier. Who is correct?
   a. Tech A
   b. Tech B
   c. Both A and B
   d. Neither A nor B

10. Tech A says that a faulty vacuum booster can affect engine operation. Tech B says that steel brake line can be replaced with a copper line, since it is easier to bend into shape. Who is correct?
    a. Tech A
    b. Tech B
    c. Both A and B
    d. Neither A nor B

CHAPTER 32

NATEF Tasks

Disc Brake System

Knowledge Objectives

After reading this chapter, you will be able to:
1. Describe the components of the disc brake system. (pp 1058–1060)
2. Describe how the components of the disc brake system work together during braking operations. (pp 1058–1059)
3. Describe the advantages and disadvantages of the disc brake system. (pp 1059–1060)
4. Describe the purpose of disc brake calipers. (pp 1060–1063)
5. Describe the components of disc brake calipers. (pp 1061–1063)
6. Describe the purpose of disc brake pads. (pp 1063–1067)
7. Describe the principle of the coefficient of friction and how it affects brake lining materials. (pp 1064–1067)
8. Describe the components that are employed to prevent noise in disc brakes. (pp 1066–1067)
9. Describe the types of wear indicators for disc brakes. (pp 1067–1068)
10. Describe the purpose of disc brake rotors. (pp 1068–1069)
11. Describe the types of disc brake rotors. (p 1069)
12. Describe how the parking brake system operates in a disc brake system. (pp 1070–1071)
13. Describe the types of parking brakes in a disc brake system. (pp 1070–1071)
14. Describe the process of diagnosing issues with a disc brake system. (pp 1071–1072)

Skills Objectives

After reading this chapter, you will be able to:
1. Remove and inspect the caliper. (pp 1072–1075)
2. Inspect caliper mountings, slides, and pins. (pp 1075–1076)
3. Inspect brake pads and wear indicators. (pp 1075–1077)
4. Check the brake pads. (p 1077)
5. Disassemble the caliper. (pp 1077–1078)
6. Reassemble the caliper. (pp 1078–1080)
7. Retract and readjust the piston on an integrated parking brake. (pp 1080–1081)
8. Inspect and measure the disc brake rotor. (pp 1082–1084)
9. Remove and reinstall the disc brake rotor. (pp 1084–1086)
10. Refinish the disc brake rotor while it is on the vehicle. (pp 1086–1088)
11. Refinish the disc brake rotor while it is off the vehicle. (pp 1087–1090)
12. Inspect and replace wheel studs. (pp 1091–1093)
13. Install a wheel, torque lug nuts, and make final checks and adjustments. (pp 1091–1095)

▶ Introduction

Disc (also spelled disk) brakes are so named because they create braking power by forcing flat friction pads against the sides of a rotating disc. This disc is also called a disc brake rotor, or rotor. The vehicle wheels are bolted to the disc **FIGURE 32-1**. The applied force is created in the caliper, which straddles the pads and rotor. Higher applied forces can be used in disc brakes than in drum brakes, because the design of the rotor is stronger than the design of the drum **FIGURE 32-2**. Since heat is generated on the outside surfaces of the rotor, it can be easily transferred to the atmosphere. Disc brakes are effective at creating substantial braking power using a fairly simple design that is relatively easy for technicians to service and repair.

> ▶ **TECHNICIAN TIP**
>
> The purpose of the disc brake system is to provide an effective means to slow the vehicle under a variety of conditions in an acceptable distance and manner. The better a braking system can do this, the more likely the vehicle will avoid an accident.

FIGURE 32-1 Disc brake operation.

FIGURE 32-2 Disc versus drum brakes.

▶ You are the Automotive Technician

A customer comes into the service department. She has been experiencing a pulsating brake pedal and high pitched sqealing during braking on her 2009 Town and Country minivan, which has 41,000 miles on the odometer. After reviewing the vehicle's service history on your computer, you notice the vehicle has never had any brake service. You advise the customer that you will need to complete a more thorough inspection to determine what is causing the issues. After completing a visual inspection of the brakes, and measurement of the rotor's thickness and parallelism, you see that the front brake linings have worn down to the wear indicators and the rotors are warped beyond specifications. You inform the customer of your findings and recommend that the vehicle needs new front brake pads installed, and the rotors refinished. You also recommend that the brake fluid be flushed, since the fluid is beyond the end of its two-year life.

1. What conditions can cause a rotor to become warped?
2. What conditions would require replacement of the rotors rather than just refinishing them?
3. What are the relatively common maximum specifications for rotor runout and thickness variation?

Purpose and Overview

Disc brakes operate on the same principle as all friction brakes. They generate stopping power by applying friction materials to moving surfaces, thus transforming the vehicle's kinetic energy into heat energy. This is accomplished by disc brake calipers using hydraulic pressure from the master cylinder to create a mechanical clamping action, forcing the brake pads onto the surface of the rotor, creating friction. As the vehicle's kinetic energy is transformed into heat energy, the vehicle's speed decreases.

 ## Disc Brake System

Modern passenger vehicles are almost always equipped with disc brakes on at least the front two wheels, and many manufacturers are using them on all four wheels. The primary components of the disc brakes are:

- Rotor
- Caliper
- Brake pads **FIGURE 32-3**

The **rotors** are the main rotating part of this brake system. They are durable and resist being damaged by the high temperatures that occur during braking. In high-performance vehicles, the rotors are made from composite materials, ceramics, or carbon fiber; otherwise, they are usually made of cast iron.

The **caliper** straddles the rotor and houses the disc brake pads and an activating piston(s). The calipers use hydraulic pressure from the master cylinder to apply the brake pads. They are usually bolted to the steering knuckle or, in the case of a nonsteering axle, to a suspension component. Calipers need to be inspected at the same time as the brake pads.

The **disc brake pads** are located inside the caliper or caliper mounting bracket. The pads clamp onto the rotor to slow or stop the vehicle. The disc brake pad consists of a friction material bonded or riveted to a steel backing plate. With this design, the pads will wear out over time and need to be replaced periodically.

Disc Brake Operation

Disc brakes can be used on all four wheels of a vehicle, or a combination of brake types can be used, with disc brakes on the front wheels and drum brakes on the rear. When the brake pedal is depressed, a **pushrod** transfers the force through a **brake booster** to a hydraulic master cylinder. The master cylinder converts the pedal force into hydraulic pressure, which is then transmitted via brake lines and hoses to one or more pistons at each brake caliper **FIGURE 32-4**. The pistons operate on friction pads

to provide a clamping force on a rotor that is attached to the wheel hub. This clamping action is designed to stop the rotation of the rotor and the wheel.

The rotors are free to rotate with the wheels due to wheel bearings and the hubs that contain them. The hub can be part of the brake rotor or a separate assembly that the rotor slips over and is bolted to by the lug

FIGURE 32-3 The disc brake system.

Master cylinder

Pedal

Secondary piston   Primary piston

FIGURE 32-4 The master cylinder converts the pedal force into hydraulic pressure, which is then transmitted via brake lines and hoses to one or more pistons at each brake caliper.

nuts **FIGURE 32-5**. On rear-wheel drive vehicles, the rotor is mounted onto the driving axle or hub and may be held in place by the wheel. On front-wheel drive vehicles, it can be mounted on the front hub and wheel bearing assembly.

The brake caliper assembly is normally bolted to the vehicle axle housing or suspension **FIGURE 32-6**. In most cases, the brake is positioned as close as possible to the wheel, but there are exceptions. Some high-performance cars with **independent rear suspension (IRS)** use inboard disc brakes on the rear wheels. The calipers are mounted on or next to the differential, which is directly mounted to the vehicle body. Manufacturers claim improved vehicle handling for this design because it reduces the vehicle's unsprung weight by taking the differential assembly and brakes from the suspension and mounting them to the body. Because the wheels and axles are now lighter, the vehicle's springs can do a better job of keeping the wheels on the ground, especially on uneven road surfaces.

Disc brake pads require much higher application pressures to operate than drum brake shoes because they are not self-energizing. This additional clamping pressure is created by increasing the diameter of the caliper pistons. Unfortunately, this means the brake pedal travel is lengthened to move the additional fluid being displaced by the larger caliper pistons. Building in more pushrod travel would require more room under the dash. Manufacturers have overcome this problem by equipping most disc brake systems with a power booster. Because of the high forces needed to apply a disc brake, using it as a parking brake is more challenging. Some manufacturers have chosen to design more complicated calipers, while others have built an auxiliary drum brake assembly into the center of the rear disc brake rotors to provide for parking brake operation. This is referred to as a top hat design.

FIGURE 32-5 The hub and hubless rotors.

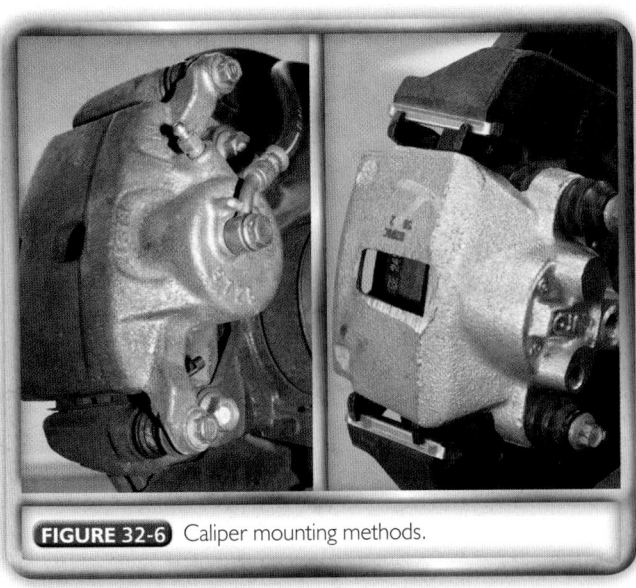

FIGURE 32-6 Caliper mounting methods.

Advantages and Disadvantages

Disc brakes have a number of advantages over drum brakes. They also have some disadvantages. In most cases, the advantages outweigh the disadvantages. One of the biggest advantages is that disc brakes can generate and transfer greater amounts of heat to the atmosphere; because most of the friction area of a rotor is exposed to air, cooling is far more rapid than for a drum brake. This faster cooling makes them better suited for high-performance driving or heavy-duty vehicles and reduces the likelihood of brake fade.

Also, because of their shape, rotors tend to scrape off water more effectively. After being driven through water, disc brakes operate at peak performance almost immediately. Further, due to their design, disc brakes are self-adjusting and do not need periodic maintenance or rely on a self-adjusting mechanism that is prone to sticking (see the Disc Brake Calipers section). Lastly, in most cases, disc brakes are also easier to service than drum brakes.

While disc brakes have a number of benefits over drum brakes, there are some disadvantages. Probably the most apparent disadvantage is that disc brakes are much more prone to noise. Their design tends to create squeals and squeaks, which can be very annoying. Many a technician has spent time servicing perfectly functional disc brakes due to excessive noise complaints. Another issue is that the rotors warp easier than in drum brake systems. Since the brake pads are pressing on each side of the rotor, thickness variations of as small as 0.0003" (0.0076 mm) can cause brake pedal pulsations, requiring resurfacing or replacement. The last disadvantage is that since disc brakes are not self-energizing, they need higher clamping forces, which requires a power booster. This also makes it harder to use them as effective parking brakes.

> ### ▶ TECHNICIAN TIP
>
> While there may appear to be more disadvantages to disc brakes versus drum brakes, the advantages are generally considered much more critical than the disadvantages. Thus, disc brakes are preferred over drum brakes in most applications.

▶ Disc Brake Calipers

In most applications, the disc brake caliper assembly is bolted to the vehicle axle housing, or **steering knuckle**, and clamps the brake pads onto the rotors to slow the vehicle. There are two main types of calipers: **fixed calipers** and **sliding or floating calipers** FIGURE 32-7 . Sliding or floating calipers are the most common type used in passenger vehicles because they are easier to build and are more compact. All calipers are fitted with a **bleeder screw** on the top of the piston bore to allow for the removal of air within the disc brake system as well as to help in performing routine brake fluid changes.

Fixed calipers are rigidly bolted in place and cannot move or slide. This makes their application of braking forces more precise than floating calipers. They commonly have one to four pistons on each side of the rotor FIGURE 32-8 . When the brakes are applied,

hydraulic pressure forces the pistons on both sides of the caliper inward, causing the brake pads to come in contact with the rotor FIGURE 32-9 . Once the pad-to-rotor clearance is taken up, the hydraulic pressure rises equally on each side of the caliper, applying both brake pads equally.

The sliding or floating caliper has brake pads located on each side of the rotor, but all of the pistons are only on one side, usually the inside of the rotor. Thus, the hydraulic force is generated on one side of the rotor, but the unique design applies equal braking force to both sides of the rotor. This distribution of force is possible because the caliper is mounted on pins, or slides, that allow it to move (float or slide) from side to side as necessary. This movement allows pistons on one side of the rotor to generate force on both sides of the rotor at the same time.

FIGURE 32-8 Fixed calipers with multiple pistons.

FIGURE 32-7 Fixed and sliding/floating calipers.

FIGURE 32-9 Fixed caliper being applied.

When the brakes are applied, hydraulic pressure forces the piston toward the rotor. This takes up any clearance between the brake pad and rotor and starts to push the pad into the rotor. Since the caliper is free to move on the pins or slides, it gets pushed away from the rotor, pulling the outer brake pad into contact with the outside of the rotor. Once all clearance is taken up on the outer brake pad, the clamping force will increase equally on both brake pads, applying the brakes **FIGURE 32-10**.

O-Rings

In disc brake calipers, the piston is sealed by a stationary square section sealing ring, also called a **square cut O-ring** **FIGURE 32-11**. This O-ring has a square cross-section and is fitted in a machined groove in the caliper. The O-ring is compressed between the piston and caliper housing, creating a positive seal to keep the high-pressure brake fluid from leaking out. It also prevents air from being drawn into the system when a low-pressure situation is created in the hydraulic system when the brake pedal is released quickly.

When the brakes are applied, the piston moves outward, slightly deforming the O-ring seal **FIGURE 32-12**. When the brakes are released, the elasticity or flexibility of the seal causes it to return to its original shape. This action of the sealing ring retracts the piston to provide a small running clearance between the rotor and pads. As the brake pads wear, the piston needs to move outward a bit farther than the sealing ring can stretch or flex. The sealing ring is designed to allow the piston to slide through it in this situation, taking up the extra clearance and making the disc brakes self-adjusting.

FIGURE 32-10 Sliding/floating caliper application.

> **TECHNICIAN TIP**
>
> Since the force generated by the O-ring to retract the piston is fairly small, any corrosion or buildup on the piston or bore will cause the piston to stick and not retract. This holds the brakes in the applied position, causing brake drag, overheated brakes, and poor fuel economy. Technicians can identify this situation by using an infrared temperature gun to measure the temperature of each brake rotor after test-driving the vehicle. The temperatures should be approximately the same on each side. If they are not, suspect a stuck or binding caliper.

O-ring groove
in caliper

FIGURE 32-11 O-rings. **A.** Square cut O-ring and O-ring cut to show square section. **B.** Square cut O-ring groove in caliper.

FIGURE 32-12 Square cut O-ring. **A.** Square cut O-ring during brake application. **B.** Square cut O-ring during brake release.

FIGURE 32-13 Low-drag caliper.

free of pitting or rust; therefore, steel pistons are chrome plated. This gives the surface a hard, wear-resistant, and corrosion-resistant finish. Chrome can still rust, but it is much more corrosion resistant than steel. Another way manufacturers have dealt with the corrosion issue is by making pistons out of a **phenolic resin**. Pool balls also are made from phenolic resin, which is very dense when it hardens and does not corrode or rust, making for a good sealing surface in brake systems. Although the phenolic pistons themselves do not corrode, the cast iron bore of the caliper does corrode and rust and can therefore cause a phenolic piston to seize in the bore **FIGURE 32-14**.

Some calipers, sometimes called **low-drag calipers**, are designed to maintain a larger brake pad-to-rotor clearance by retracting the pistons a little bit farther. This is accomplished by modifying the sealing groove in the caliper so the outside of the groove is slightly angled toward the rotor **FIGURE 32-13**. This position allows the seal to flex a bit farther upon brake application and then retract the piston a greater distance. These systems use a "quick take-up" or "fast fill" master cylinder to maintain adequate brake pedal reserve height.

The primary sealing surface is the outside diameter of the piston. It is critical that this surface be smooth and

FIGURE 32-14 Corroded caliper piston bore.

Phenolic pistons transfer heat slower than steel pistons **FIGURE 32-15**, which is a good thing because they transfer less heat from the brake pad to the brake fluid. This helps prevent boiling of the brake fluid in the caliper under heavy brake usage. Calipers with phenolic pistons are therefore less susceptible to brake failure from boiling brake fluid.

There is also a dust boot that seals the surfaces of the piston and caliper bore from outside dirt and moisture. This seal connects to both the piston and the caliper and must be expandable to allow the piston to move outward as the brake pads wear. It also must be free from cuts and holes; otherwise the piston and bore could corrode and cause the piston to bind in the bore, causing brake drag.

Caliper Lubrication

Floating calipers are mounted in place by **guide pins** and **bushings** **FIGURE 32-16**. The pins allow the caliper to move in and out as the brakes are operated and as the brake pads wear. Since the calipers move on the pins, the bushings must be lubricated with high-temperature, waterproof disc brake caliper grease when they are serviced. This will help prevent them from binding or sticking. Inspecting, cleaning, and lubricating the pins and pin bores, including any bushings and dust boots, are important steps in disc brake repair.

Sliding calipers have matching machined surfaces on the caliper and caliper mount that allow the caliper to slide in the mount **FIGURE 32-17**. The sliding mount holds the caliper in position and prevents it from rotating when the brakes are applied. The machined mounts allow the caliper to move side to side as necessary to operate the brakes or adjust for brake pad wear. The surfaces must be

FIGURE 32-16 Floating caliper guide pins.

FIGURE 32-17 Sliding caliper.

cleaned and lubricated with the same high-temperature, waterproof grease as the floating calipers when the calipers are serviced. Sliding calipers are held in place by a spring steel clip or shim that is bolted to the caliper mount.

▶ Disc Brake Pads and Friction Materials

Disc brake pads consist of friction material bonded or riveted onto a steel **backing plate** **FIGURE 32-18**. **Bonded linings** are more common on light-duty vehicles since they are less expensive to build and the bonding agent can fail under the very high temperatures of heavy-duty use. **Riveted linings** are used on heavier-duty or high-performance vehicles. Metal rivets provide a mechanical connection to hold the lining to the backing plate that is less susceptible to failure under high temperatures. Since the rivets actually pinch some of the lining between the rivet head and the backing plate, the linings must be changed sooner than bonded linings. Otherwise, the

FIGURE 32-15 Heat transfer. **A.** Phenolic piston (slow heat transfer). **B.** Steel piston (fast heat transfer).

FIGURE 32-18 Bonded and riveted brake pads.

FIGURE 32-19 Brake pad locating lugs.

FIGURE 32-20 Brake rotor wear.

rivet heads would contact the rotor and wear a groove in the face of the rotor. The backing plate has **lugs** that correctly position the pad in the caliper assembly and help the backing plate maintain the proper position to the rotor **FIGURE 32-19**. Disc brakes are usually designed so that the thickness of the pads can be checked easily once the wheel has been removed. Most disc brakes also are designed to allow the pads to be replaced with a minimum of disassembly.

Some pads have a groove cut into the friction surface. This groove helps ventilate gases that build up at the surface of the friction material under heavy brake application. It also can help modify the harmonic vibration quality of the friction material to reduce brake squeal. On some pads, the depth of this groove is set so that as the pad wears thinner, the remaining groove gets smaller; when it can no longer be seen, the pad should be replaced.

The composition of the friction material affects brake operation. Materials that provide good braking with low pedal pressures tend to lose efficiency when they get hot, thus increasing the stopping distance. They also tend to wear out quicker. Materials that maintain a stable friction coefficient over a wide temperature range generally require higher pedal pressures to provide efficient braking. They also tend to put added wear on the disc brake rotor, reducing its useful life **FIGURE 32-20**.

Brake Friction Materials

Friction is the force that acts to prevent two surfaces in contact from sliding against each other. The amount of friction between two surfaces is expressed as a ratio and is called the coefficient of friction. When friction occurs, the kinetic energy (motion) of the sliding surfaces is converted into thermal energy (heat). Some combinations of materials, such as a hockey puck on ice, have a very low coefficient of friction. There is very little friction between

them and therefore almost no sliding resistance. Rubber tires against a dry hard road surface have a high coefficient of friction, which means they tend to grip and resist sliding against each other.

Disc brake pads and drum brake linings are made from materials that have a moderate coefficient of friction **TABLE 32-1**. They also must be able to absorb and

TABLE 32-1: Brake Lining Coefficient of Friction (Sliding)	
Materials Involved	**Coefficient of Friction—Dry Sliding**
Rubber and concrete	.6–.85
Steel and cast iron	.23
Copper and cast iron	.29
Brass and cast iron	.3
Leather and oak	.52
Brake lining (FF rating)	.35–.45

Applied | Math

AM-17: Charts/Tables/Graphs: The technician can interpret charts, tables, and graphs to determine the manufacturer's specifications for a given system.
Algebra (9–12)
C3: Draw reasonable conclusions about a situation being modeled.
Representation
A2: Select, apply, and translate among mathematical representations to solve problems.
Technicians regularly apply math concepts to disc brake diagnosis and repair. For example, a technician will measure the amount of rotor thickness variation and runout if there is a brake pedal pulsation problem. Let's say the technician performed these measurements and came up with a thickness variation of 0.0025" (0.064 mm) and a runout of 0.0015" (0.038 mm) on the left front rotor. Next the technician looks up the manufacturer's specification chart and found that the maximum allowable thickness variation is 0.0005" (0.013 mm) and the maximum allowable runout is 0.003" (0.076 mm) for the vehicle being worked on. Using the information from the chart, the technician determines that the thickness variation is excessive by 0.002" (0.051 mm) (0.0025" [0.064 mm] − 0.0005" [0.013 mm] = 0.002" [0.051 mm]) and the runout is OK since it is under the maximum allowable specification. But even so, since the thickness variation is out of specifications, the rotor will need to be refinished or replaced to bring it back within specification.

disperse large amounts of heat without their braking performance being adversely affected. As the heat in brake pads and linings builds up, the coefficient of friction capability of the material—and consequently its stopping power—is reduced. This is called brake fade. Minimizing or overcoming fade is a major factor in the design of brakes and the development of brake friction materials.

Brake friction materials were historically made from asbestos compounds because of the excellent heat resistance of that material. Now that asbestos has been proven to be toxic, it is generally banned and is not normally used. Today, brakes are manufactured from a variety of different materials, including:

- Non-asbestos organic (NAO) materials—Organic materials such as Kevlar and carbon
- Low-metallic NAO materials—Small amounts of copper or steel and NOA materials
- Semimetallic materials—A higher quantity of steel, copper, and/or brass

Safety

Don't assume that a brake pad doesn't contain asbestos; it is still found in some applications.

- Ceramic materials—Ceramic fiber materials and possibly a small amount of copper

The choice of brake lining compound depends on the application. Lighter passenger vehicles generate less heat in the brakes than heavy or high-performance vehicles. Living in a very hilly region of the country, or where there is a lot of stop-and-go traffic, will put added demands on the brake pads. The optimum brake composition for any given vehicle or use is a combination of weighted qualities, including:

- Stopping power
- Heat absorption and dispersion
- Resistance to fade
- Recovery speed from fade
- Wear rate
- Performance when wet
- Operating noise
- Price

For instance, owners of small economy vehicles tend to value a longer pad life and minimal operating noise rather than resistance to fade in extreme conditions. Owners of high-performance cars, however, may consider fade resistance and stopping power at high speeds more important than noise levels or wear rate.

The Society of Automotive Engineers (SAE) has adopted letter codes to rate brake lining materials' coefficient of friction. The rating is written on the edge of the friction linings and is called the **edge code** **FIGURE 32-21**. The lower the letter, the less friction the material has, and the harder the brake pedal must be applied to achieve a given amount of stopping power. These code letters represent the following coefficients of friction:

- C: ≤ 0.15
- D: 0.15–0.25
- E: 0.25–0.35
- F: 0.35–0.45
- G: 0.45–0.55
- H: > 0.55
- Z: Unclassified

The lining is tested both cool and hot. The rating is a two letter designation such as "FF." The first letter is for the cool performance and the second letter is

FIGURE 32-21 Brake lining edge code.

FIGURE 32-22 Brake pad shims and guides.

for the hot performance. For example, FF has a cool coefficient of friction of 0.35–0.45 and the same coefficient of friction at the hot temperature. It also is very possible that the hot and cold ratings differ from each other. For example, if the rating is FE, the coefficient of friction reduces as the temperature of the lining heats up. Notice that the coefficient of friction range is quite wide for each letter designation. Linings with the same letter ratings may not have the same braking performance as each other. This means that an EE-rated lining from one manufacturer is likely to have different braking characteristics than an EE-rated lining from another manufacturer. Always use high-quality brake lining from reliable companies to help avoid brake issues.

Anti-Noise Measures

Disc brakes are more prone to annoying brake squealing than are drum brakes. Brake squealing is caused by vibrations set up between the brake pad and rotor. Manufacturers have addressed this problem in a number of ways:

1. Using softer linings with a higher coefficient of friction, which are less prone to noise than harder linings with a lower coefficient of friction
2. Adding **brake pad shims and guides** to the brake pads, which help cushion the brake pad and absorb some of the vibration **FIGURE 32-22**
3. Using springs to tightly hold the pads in place to minimize vibration **FIGURE 32-23**
4. Contouring and grooving the lining material in a way that minimizes vibration **FIGURE 32-24**

FIGURE 32-23 Example of brake pad retainers.

FIGURE 32-24 Brake lining grooves and contouring.

5. Incorporating **bendable tangs** on the brake pad backing plate that allow technicians to crimp the tangs so they are more firmly mounted in the caliper **FIGURE 32-25**

> **TECHNICIAN TIP**
>
> Some manufacturers claim that refinishing their rotors removes enough material from the rotor that it can cause the brakes to squeal due to less mass, which changes the harmonic vibration qualities of the rotor. They recommend replacing the rotors any time the rotors are worn enough to need resurfacing.

Technicians also can apply noise-reducing compounds to the brake pads. One is a type of high-temperature liquid rubber compound that is applied to the back of the brake pad. When it cures, it stays flexible and absorbs brake pad vibrations and helps reduce brake noise. Another compound is a specially designed liquid that is applied directly to the face of the lining material. This compound helps to modify the lining's coefficient of friction slightly, making it less likely that the lining will squeal. Make sure you apply the correct compound to the correct side of the brake pad.

> **Applied** | **Science**
>
> **AS-36: Sound: The technician can demonstrate an understanding of the role sound plays in identifying various problems in the vehicle.**
> Sound is a series of waves that travel through a gas, liquid, or solid and can often be heard by the human ear. Sound waves are created by vibrating objects, such as a guitar string. Moving objects that are in sliding contact with each other are highly likely to create sound. One example of this is fingernails dragging on a chalkboard. The fingernails vibrate on the surface of the chalkboard and create sound waves that are then heard by the ear.
> Technicians commonly use differences in sound to assist in diagnosing disc brake problems. For example, brake pads that are worn down to the metal backing plate make a deep grinding noise when the brakes are applied. Listening to hear which wheel or wheels the noise is coming from helps identify the source of the problem. In the same way, if the disc brakes are equipped with a scratcher style of brake warning system, the brakes will make a high-pitched screeching noise. Many times this noise will happen when the vehicle is being driven when the brakes are not applied. One way to help determine which side the noise is coming from is by driving the vehicle next to a concrete traffic wall or building. If the noise is on that side, it will get much louder than when not near the wall.

FIGURE 32-25 Brake pad bendable tangs.

▶ Wear Indicators

Some manufacturers provide a means of notifying the driver that the brake pad linings are worn to their minimum limit. This helps ensure that the brake linings do not wear down to the point that they cannot properly perform their job anymore. Excessively thin brake linings tend to heat up quicker than thicker linings, which can lead to premature brake fade. Not all manufacturers use a brake lining wear indicator. In those cases, it is especially important to inspect the brakes at regular intervals, usually during tire rotations or oil changes.

Types

Some manufacturers use a mechanically operated wear indicator to notify the driver that the brake pads are worn to their minimum limit. This is achieved by a spring steel **scratcher** mounted to the brake pad **FIGURE 32-26**. Part of the scratcher extends below the brake pad backing plate at the lining's minimum wear thickness. When the friction material wears down far enough, the scratcher contacts the surface of the rotor and makes a squealing noise similar to fingernails on a chalkboard. This distinctive noise means the brakes need service right away. When you replace the brake pads, make sure they come

> **TECHNICIAN TIP**
>
> In many cases, the scratchers will start to make noise when the brakes are not applied and stop making noise when the brakes are applied, as applying the brakes tends to dampen the vibrations.

FIGURE 32-26 The scratcher brake wear indicator.

equipped with new scratchers set to the correct depth so they can function the next time the pads wear down.

Some manufacturers use a warning lamp or warning message on the dash to alert the driver that the lining is worn to its minimum thickness. These systems have an electrical contact installed on the brake pad at the point of the lining's minimum wear thickness. When the pad wears to this minimum thickness, the contact touches the rotor as the brakes are applied, prompting a warning light or warning message that tells the driver the disc brake pads are due for replacement. These contacts can be manufactured into the pad or they can be clipped onto the pad. The contacts are normally replaced when the pads are replaced. Make sure that either the contacts come with the new pads or order them along with the pads.

Disc Brake Rotors

The brake disc or rotor is the main rotating component of the disc brake unit. The wheel is bolted to the rotor and they rotate together, leading some manufacturers to integrate the anti-lock brake system (ABS) tone wheel into the rotor. Since friction between the rotor and brake pads generates great amounts of heat, rotors must be able to withstand high temperatures. The pads are also forced onto the surface of the rotor with potentially thousands of pounds of force, so the rotor must be strong and have a durable surface. The rotors are usually made of cast iron. To reduce weight, some manufacturers use a two-part rotor with a cast iron disc and a stamped steel center hat. This style of rotor is called a composite rotor. Some heavy-duty and/or high-performance vehicles have rotors

made of reinforced carbon, carbon ceramic, or composite ceramic substances to reduce weight and withstand much higher temperatures.

Since the rotor surfaces are squeezed between two brake pads, any unevenness of the rotor surfaces will cause pulsation of the brakes as the thicker and thinner portions pass between the brake pads. The rotor surfaces must be parallel to each other to avoid this situation. Rotors can fail in two ways: parallelism, which is also called thickness variation, and lateral runout. **Parallelism** is the most critical condition. If the rotor's thickness varies by as little as 0.0003" (0.0076 mm), the rotor will tend to push the brake pads outward at any high spots. This tends to create more pressure on the brake pads and slows the vehicle down faster at that point. It also pushes up on the brake pedal as fluid is being forced back to the master cylinder. The result is a pulsation of the brake pedal and a surging of the vehicle while braking, which is usually more noticeable at lower braking speeds.

Lateral runout, also called warpage, is the side-to-side movement of the rotor surfaces as the rotor turns. A warped rotor can be within specifications for parallelism but out of specification for lateral runout. Lateral runout tends to move the caliper pistons in the same direction as each other, so brake fluid is not pushed back to the master cylinder. However, the caliper tends to be moved side to side. This movement can cause the steering wheel to shimmy as the warped rotor follows the brake pads, if the lateral runout is greater than about 0.003" (0.076 mm).

Also, runout causes the pads to rub on high spots of the rotor when the brakes are not being applied, causing uneven wear and/or the depositing of pad material on the rotor, which leads to thickness variation concerns.

> ### TECHNICIAN TIP
>
> Rotors can be warped by improperly torquing the lug nuts. Always use a properly calibrated torque wrench (or the proper torque stick if the shop policy allows) to torque the lug nuts to the manufacturer's specified torque.

For proper operation, rotors must maintain their shape and resist warpage under high heat and pressure conditions. Because of these requirements, they are usually made of cast iron. On motorcycles, rotors are often made of stainless steel for cosmetic reasons. Disc brakes also are equipped with a dust shield to help protect the rotor. Dust shields help keep dust, water, and other road debris away from the inside surface of the rotor. They also can help direct air flow to the rotor to assist with heat transfer to the atmosphere. Dust shields are commonly made of stamped sheet metal, but they also can be made of plastic. Dust shields can become damaged during brake repair so always inspect them for proper clearance before installing the wheel assembly.

Types of Rotors

Rotors can be solid or ventilated **FIGURE 32-27**. **Solid rotors** are less expensive and usually found on smaller vehicles. **Ventilated rotors** are used to improve heat transfer to the atmosphere. These passageways are designed to use centrifugal force to cause air to flow through the center of the rotor when it is rotating. Ventilated rotors are used on heavier vehicles or high-performance vehicles. Some ventilated rotors are directional, meaning they are designed to force air through the rotor in one direction only **FIGURE 32-28**. If the rotor is rotated in the wrong direction, it will not pump air properly and will overheat easier.

> ### TECHNICIAN TIP
>
> If you hear a loud scraping or grinding noise when you test-drive a vehicle after servicing the brakes, check to see if the dust shield is contacting one of the rotors. If so, it can make a lot of loud grinding noises. Since it is thin sheet metal, chances are good that it is bent. It can usually be bent back into shape easily.

Disc brake rotors with holes or slots machined into their surface dissipate heat quicker **FIGURE 32-29**. They also help to remove water quickly from the surface of the pad in wet driving conditions. Since the pads wipe across the holes or slots, the surface of the pad is prevented from becoming hard and glassy smooth from the friction and heat of use. However, this scraping action reduces the overall life of the brake pad, so these types of rotors are generally only used in high-performance or race vehicles.

Most disc brake rotors are stamped with the manufacturer's minimum thickness specification **FIGURE 32-30**. This minimum thickness ensures an adequate amount of thermal mass for stopping power **FIGURE 32-31**. When material is removed, there is not as much material to absorb heat and the rotor heats up faster. The excess heat can lead to brake fade sooner. Also, when the brake pads wear, if the thickness of the rotor were below this minimum, the piston could be pushed out beyond the edge of the sealing ring, which would cause the brakes to lose hydraulic pressure and fail. Make sure the rotors are always above the manufacturer's minimum thickness before putting them back in service.

FIGURE 3-27 Rotors. **A.** Standard solid rotors. **B.** Ventilated rotors.

FIGURE 32-28 Directional ventilated rotor.

FIGURE 32-29 Slotted and drilled rotor.

FIGURE 32-30 Rotor with minimum thickness stamped on it.

400° F   500° F

Rotor-Standard Thickness   Rotor-Below Minimum Thickness
(At end of moderate hill)   (At end of moderate hill)

FIGURE 32-31 Rotor thickness and heat capacity.

▶ Parking Brakes

Parking brakes are designed to hold the vehicle stationary when parked. Manufacturers are required to design the vehicle so the parking brake will hold the vehicle for a given amount of time on a specified grade in both directions. The parking brake must be separately activated from the service brakes, and the driver must be able to latch it into the applied position. Parking brakes can be foot operated or hand operated. Since disc brakes require higher applied forces to operate, they are a bit more difficult to use as parking brakes. However, manufacturers have overcome this challenge in a couple of ways.

Types of Parking Brakes

Currently most parking brakes are mechanically applied by use of a cable and ratcheting lever assembly. Parking brakes on disc brake units are primarily of two types: an integrated parking brake caliper and the top hat drum style. Alternatively, electric parking brakes are being

used on some vehicles. The electric motor can pull on a conventional parking brake cable, or the electric motor can be mounted on the caliper and directly drive the caliper piston to apply force to the brake pads.

Integrated Mechanical Parking Brake Calipers

The integrated parking brake mechanically forces the disc brake piston outward, forcing the brake pads to clamp the rotor when the parking brake is applied **FIGURE 32-32**. A lever on the back side of the caliper is pulled by the parking brake cable. The lever converts that motion to rotary motion on a shaft that enters the rear of the caliper cylinder. The shaft uses a seal to prevent fluid leakage from the bore. The shaft has a coarse thread machined into it, which threads into a nut assembly inside the caliper piston. As the shaft is turned by the parking brake lever, the nut causes the piston to be forced outward, applying the brakes. Releasing the parking brake cable allows a spring to unwind the shaft and release the pressure on the brake pads.

Top Hat Design Parking Brake

The top hat design gets it name from the shape of the rotor. The rotor has a deeper offset than normal, giving the appearance of a top hat. The offset portion allows room for a drum surface within the center of the rotor. Drum brake shoes are mechanically forced outward into contact with the inside of the brake drum, which locks the wheel. Releasing the parking brake allows the springs to retract the brake shoes from contact with the drums.

Electric Parking Brake

The electric parking brake uses an electric motor to apply the disc brake assemblies. The cable style uses an electric motor to pull standard parking brake cables, which apply standard integrated mechanical parking brake calipers. The electrically integrated caliper style

FIGURE 32-32 Integrated parking brake operation.

uses an electric motor mounted on the caliper to directly apply the brakes. Pushing a parking brake button on the dash causes the motor to either tension the cable or directly apply the parking brake. Electric parking brakes also can be integrated with the controller area network bus (CAN-bus) system to provide additional features beyond just holding the vehicle when it is parked. It can be used to automatically hold the vehicle while it is stopped on a hill to prevent it from rolling backward or forward. It also can be automatically released by the vehicle's **electronic control module (ECM)** when the throttle is applied for starting to move away from the stop. It also may work with the vehicle's proximity detector when backing up. If the system detects the vehicle getting too close to an object, the ECM can apply the electric parking brake to stop the vehicle and prevent it from striking the object.

▶ Diagnosis

Disc brake diagnosis usually starts with understanding the customer's concern. Communicating directly with the customer is the best way to do that, but the customer is not always available. An experienced service advisor will gather the required information, so you should read the service advisor's notes on the repair order carefully or speak with him or her directly. Once you understand the customer's concern, a test-drive is usually needed to verify the accuracy of the concern. This is a good opportunity to test the brakes under a variety of conditions. Replicating the customer concern is important in order to address the situation that the customer is experiencing.

During the test-drive, find a safe place to operate the brakes at a variety of speeds with a variety of brake pedal pressures, especially trying to mimic the conditions the customer described. It is may be necessary to go on a test drive with the customer driving, allowing him or her to operate the vehicle in the way that makes the problem evident and point out the particular situation he or she is experiencing. Also, it is good to have the customer along in case the problem does not occur, in which case he or she won't think you don't believe them or are ignoring the issue.

If there is a concern related to the anti-lock brake system (ABS) that requires a test drive, extreme caution is required so that an accident doesn't happen. Since ABS operates only during extreme braking or poor traction conditions, you run the risk of being rear-ended by a vehicle behind you or losing control of the vehicle if you apply the brakes hard enough to activate the ABS. So make sure the vehicle is being tested away from all other traffic. Remember that if the yellow ABS warning lamp is illuminated, the ABS system is deactivated, and you should not try to activate ABS on a test drive. If the yellow ABS lamp is off, the ABS system should be active and ready to activate. It is helpful when testing ABS to do so on a surface with limited traction, such as wet pavement or a dirt road. When you do apply the brakes firmly, ABS activation can typically be felt as pulsations in the brake pedal and possibly the steering wheel. The vehicle should brake quickly while maintaining steering control. In some cases, a "poor traction" lamp may illuminate, telling you that the ABS system had to activate. This warning lamp will usually turn off after several seconds. If the yellow ABS warning lamp illumines, it typically means that the vehicle's ECM has observed a fault in the ABS system and will need to be checked for DTCs.

Once the customer concern has been verified, you will hopefully have enough information to know how best to proceed. This could be as simple as performing a visual inspection of the brake fluid level and condition, removing the wheels to disassemble and inspect the brake units, looking up technical service bulletins, or reviewing the diagnostic troubleshooting chart for the particular symptom in the service information to determine the next step.

Suspension and steering system faults can appear to be brake system faults. An example of this is a pulling condition while braking. If the strut rod bushings on the suspension are worn, then braking the vehicle will cause the wheel to move rearward; at the same time, that will cause the steering angle to change, causing the wheel to point in a direction other than straight down the road, imitating a brake pull.

The braking system on a vehicle must be restored to its proper operation. Diagnosis of any problem must identify all issues that would prevent the brakes from operating normally. Lawyers and technicians have been known to say, "He who touched the brake system last, owns it!" What this means is that if there is a problem in the brake system and you inspected it or worked on it, you are very likely liable for anything that went wrong with it. Brake system failures are more likely to lead to vehicle accidents than failures of most systems. Any diagnosis and subsequent repairs need to be thorough and complete.

> ### ▶ TECHNICIAN TIP
>
> One way to help identify if a problem is coming from the front or rear brakes is to test-drive the vehicle in a safe place at a relatively low speed and lightly apply the parking brake. If the condition is still present, the problem is with the rear brakes, since the parking brakes are usually on the rear wheels. If the condition is not present, the problem is likely with the front brakes.

Tools

The tools that are used to diagnose and repair brake systems include:

- **Brake lining thickness gauges**—Used to measure the thickness of the brake lining

- **Brake wash station**—Used to clean drum and disc brake dust

- **Caliper piston pliers**—Used to grip caliper pistons when removing them

- **Disc brake rotor micrometer**—Used to measure the thickness and parallelism of a rotor

- **Dial indicator**—Used to measure the lateral runout (side to side) of the rotor

- **Parking brake cable pliers**—Used to install parking brake cables

- **Caliper piston retracting tool**—Used to retract caliper pistons with integrated parking brakes

- **C-clamp**—Used to push pistons back into the caliper bore on non-integrated parking brakes

- **Off-car brake lathe**—Used to machine drums and rotors that are off the vehicle

- **On-car brake lathe**—Used to machine rotors that are on the vehicle

- **Caliper dust boot seal driver set**—Consists of a driver and a variety of adapters used to install various sizes of dust boot seals **FIGURE 32-33**

Diagnosing Disc Brakes

To diagnose poor stopping, noise, vibration, pulling, grabbing, dragging, or pulsation concerns and determine any necessary actions, follow the steps outlined in the remainder of this chapter. While braking concerns are generally easier to diagnose than most of the other systems on the vehicle, the large variety of conditions listed makes it imperative that you have a good understanding of disc brake and hydraulic theory. It also helps to use all of your senses to assist you in identifying the location of the fault. As a reminder, **TABLE 32-2** lists some of the common faults to consider for each concern.

Verify the customer concern by operating the vehicle if safe to do so. Depending on the concern, it may be as simple as stepping on the brake pedal without moving the vehicle and feeling the pedal sink to the floor, or it could require a more detailed test-drive to observe the fault the customer is describing. Regardless of the condition, it is almost always good practice to research any technical service bulletins (TSBs) for the particular situation. If no related TSBs are found, research the service information to familiarize yourself with the

system and the manufacturer's diagnostic procedure for the condition. Perform any diagnostic tests to identify the cause of the condition. This could be a visual inspection or any other prescribed test, such as a power booster test. It could also involve a detailed testing sequence, such as testing the proportioning and metering valves. Once you have identified the cause of the fault, determine the action that will rectify the fault.

▶ Maintenance and Repair
Removing and Inspecting Calipers

Removing the caliper is necessary for replacing the brake pads on most vehicles. It also allows access for machining

TABLE 32-2: Common Brake Issues	
Concern	**Fault**
Poor stopping	• Power booster not operating properly • Internal master cylinder leak; air in the hydraulic system • Metering valve or proportioning valve blocking fluid flow • Improperly adjusted drum brakes • Improper friction lining material • Contaminated linings
Noise	• Friction lining material too hard • Lining worn down to metal • Worn caliper slides/guide pins • Component-specific noises
Vibration	• Improper friction lining material • Rotor surface finish not correct • Foreign object (mud, rocks, etc.) in rotor • Warped rotor • ABS operating
Pulling	• Plugged or restricted brake hose • Stuck caliper piston • Seized caliper guide pins • Contaminated lining • Lining worn down to metal • Air in the hydraulic system
Grabbing	• Contaminated lining • Stuck caliper piston • Internal master cylinder leak • Misadjusted drum brakes
Dragging	• Stuck caliper piston • Seized caliper guide pins • Misadjusted master cylinder pushrod length • Binding brake pedal • Plugged restricted brake line or hose
Pulsation	• Warped rotors • Rotor parallelism • ABS operation

FIGURE 32-33 Disc brake tools. **A.** Brake lining thickness gauges. **B.** Brake wash station. **C.** Caliper piston pliers. **D.** Disc brake rotor micrometer. **E.** Dial indicator. **F.** Parking brake cable tool. **G.** Caliper piston retracting tool. **H.** Off-car brake lathe. **I.** On-car brake lathe. **J.** Dust boot seal/bushing driver set.

of the rotors on the vehicle, removal of the rotors for replacement, or machining of the rotors off the vehicle. Further, it allows for a thorough inspection of the caliper, pads, and rotor to determine the cause of a brake concern. To remove the caliper assembly, inspect for leaks and damage to the caliper housing, and determine any necessary actions, follow the steps in **SKILL DRILL 32-1**:

1 Research the procedure for removing the caliper in the appropriate service information. Follow this procedure. The following steps are general in nature and should not be substituted for the manufacturer's specific procedure.

2 If the caliper is likely to be reinstalled on the vehicle or rebuilt and reinstalled, it is good practice to loosen the bleeder screws slightly and then retighten them. Doing so ensures that they are not seized in place and that they will be able to be loosened later when bleeding the system. Failure to do this now could waste a lot of time later trying to repair a bleeder screw when it breaks off. **(Photo 1)**

3 If the caliper is being rebuilt or a new caliper will be installed, it is good practice to flush the old brake fluid from the system at this time, so that old brake fluid will not have to be bled through the new or newly rebuilt caliper. Also, leave the master cylinder reservoir level low so that pushing the caliper pistons into their bores will not overflow the reservoir. **(Photo 2)**

4 To minimize the amount of brake fluid draining out of the brake lines or hoses when they are removed, you might want to use a brake pedal holding tool to slightly apply the brakes and block off the compensating ports in the master cylinder. Just remember that the brake lights will stay on if you don't pull the brake light fuse. **(Photo 3)**

5 Remove the brake line or hose from the caliper. Be careful not to lose the two brake hose copper (or aluminum) sealing rings, if equipped. **(Photo 4)**

6 Push the caliper pistons back into their bores slightly. Use of a small pry bar or C-clamp will usually force the piston back just far enough so that the caliper can be removed from the pads and rotor once the caliper is loose from its mount. **(Photo 5)**

7 Remove the caliper assembly from its mountings, following the service manual procedure. Be careful to avoid dislodging brake dust, which may contain asbestos. **(Photo 6)**

8 Inspect the caliper for leaks or damage, including the piston dust boot.

9 Determine any necessary actions. **(Photo 7)**

> **TECHNICIAN TIP**

Some technicians pinch off the flexible brake hoses with vice grip pliers. This should be avoided because it crimps the hose, potentially damaging it internally and/or externally.

SKILL DRILL | **32-1** | **Removing and Inspecting Calipers**

1. Research the procedure for removing the caliper in the appropriate service information. Loosen the bleeder screws slightly and then retighten them.

2. If the caliper is being rebuilt or a new caliper will be installed, it is good practice to flush the old brake fluid from the system at this time.

3. Use a brake pedal holding tool to slightly apply the brakes and block off the compensating ports in the master cylinder to avoid excess fluid leakage.

SKILL DRILL | 32-1 | **Removing and Inspecting Calipers, continued**

4. Remove the brake line or hose from the caliper. Be careful not to lose the sealing rings.

5. Push the caliper pistons back into their bores slightly. While many use a screwdriver as shown, a pry bar is a safer choice.

6. Remove the caliper assembly from its mountings.

7. Inspect the caliper for leaks or damage, including the piston dust boot. Determine any necessary actions.

Inspecting Caliper Mountings, Slides, and Pins

The caliper mountings and slides/pins are placed under heavy loads and forces. They also operate in harsh environments. It is common that they experience wear over time. They can also corrode and bind up. Clean caliper mountings and slides/pins thoroughly, and inspect them closely.

To clean and inspect caliper mountings and slides/pins for operation, wear, and damage and to determine any necessary actions, follow the steps in **SKILL DRILL 32-2**:

1. Clean the caliper mountings and slides/pins using equipment/procedures for dealing with asbestos/hazardous dust. Once the dust is taken care of, you

may need to use a brake cleaning solvent to clean the components further. (**Photo 1**)

2. Inspect the caliper mountings and slides/pins for signs of wear and damage. Also look for stripped threads on the pins or caliper.

3. Determine any necessary actions. (**Photo 2**)

Inspecting Brake Pads and Wear Indicators

The wear indicator system could be a scratcher type or a sensor type. It is also very possible that the vehicle does not incorporate any type of wear indicator system. Checking this system usually consists of verifying that the sensor or scratcher is not contacting or nearly contacting the brake rotor. Some manufacturers require that the sensor be grounded with a test lead and that the brake pad warning lamp or warning message come on.

To check the operation of the brake pad wear indicator system and determine any necessary actions, follow the steps in SKILL DRILL 32-3:

1 Research the service information to determine the type of wear indicator system utilized and the procedure to test it.

2 Check that it is not contacting or nearly contacting the rotor. It is also good practice to measure the brake pad lining thickness and compare it to

SKILL DRILL | **32-2** | **Inspecting Caliper Mountings, Slides, and Pins**

1 Clean the caliper mountings and slides/pins using equipment/procedures for dealing with asbestos/hazardous dust.

2 Inspect the caliper mountings and slides/pins for wear and damage. Determine any necessary actions.

SKILL DRILL | **32-3** | **Inspecting Brake Pads and Wear Indicators**

1 Determine the type of wear indicator system utilized. Check that it is not contacting or nearly contacting the rotor.

2 If the system is a sensor style, test the system to verify that the system is operational. Determine any necessary actions.

the manufacturer's minimum specifications. If the brake pads are near the end of their useful life, it would be good practice to inform the customer and recommend replacement of the pads. **(Photo 1)**

3 If the system is a sensor style, test the system to verify that the system is operational.

4 Determine any necessary actions. **(Photo 2)**

Checking Brake Pads

Removing the brake pads is the most thorough way to inspect the brake pads. During a routine maintenance inspection where there are no customer concerns regarding the brakes, a simple measurement of the lining thickness is usually adequate. But if there are customer concerns with the brakes, it may be necessary to remove the pads for a more detailed inspection. This could show cracks in the lining or other defects that wouldn't be otherwise seen from the outside. It also allows for a more thorough inspection of the retaining hardware. Also pay attention to the way the brake pads come off, as some pads have slight differences (such as locating nipples) that make it easy to install them incorrectly. To remove, inspect, and replace pads and retaining hardware and to determine any necessary actions, follow the steps in **SKILL DRILL 32-4**:

1 Remove the pads and retaining hardware. If necessary, clean the parts with the appropriate equipment or cleaner.

2 Inspect all pads, retaining hardware, and anti-noise shims for wear or damage. Problems could include cracked linings and worn or missing retaining hardware or shims. **(Photo 1)**

3 Measure the remaining brake pad thickness and compare to specifications. Inspect the pads to see if they are wearing evenly. If not, it could indicate a caliper or caliper mounting issue.

4 Determine any necessary actions. **(Photo 2)**

Disassembling Calipers

Calipers are disassembled and cleaned for a couple of reasons. The first is to diagnose a brake system concern related to one or more calipers. For example, if the vehicle has a brake pull, it could be caused by a sticking caliper piston. Disassembling the caliper will allow you to verify whether that is the case or not. They also need to be disassembled and cleaned if they are going to be rebuilt. Some shops rebuild the calipers themselves, but most shops just replace them with rebuilt calipers if necessary. Disc brake calipers are usually side specific, meaning they are designed to be installed on a particular side of the vehicle. Failure to install them on the correct side usually results in the bleeder screws being on the bottom of the caliper cylinder. This will prevent air from being bled from the caliper and result in a very spongy brake pedal.

> **TECHNICIAN TIP**
>
> Because you have the rotor exposed, skip ahead to the sections on inspecting and servicing rotors, and complete the tasks listed there. This will save you time and effort. Pick up here once you are done with the rotor.

SKILL DRILL | 32-4 | Checking Brake Pads

1 Remove the pads and retaining hardware. Inspect all pads, retaining hardware, and anti-noise shims for wear or damage.

2 Measure the remaining brake pad thickness and compare to specifications. Determine any necessary action(s).

To disassemble and clean the caliper assembly; inspect parts for wear, rust, scoring, and damage; and replace the seal, boot, and damaged or worn parts, follow the steps in **SKILL DRILL 32-5**:

1 Disassemble the caliper, following the service manual procedure. If this involves using compressed air to remove the piston, be very careful, as the piston can pop out with great force, enough to break finger bones or pinch fingers off. Always use an approved cushion between the caliper piston and caliper housing. Keep your fingers away from the area. (**Photo 1**)

2 Clean all of the caliper parts according to the service manual procedure. Make sure the sealing ring groove is completely clean. This can be performed by scraping the groove with a variety of pick tools, such as dental picks, and then wiping out the groove with a rag. (**Photo 2**)

3 Inspect each of the parts for damage, rust, and wear. Also check the caliper pin bores or bushings for wear or damage. (**Photo 3**)

4 Measure the caliper bore-to-piston clearance with a feeler gauge and compare to specifications, if available.

5 Determine any necessary actions. (**Photo 4**)

Reassembling Calipers

Reassembling the caliper requires patience and attention to detail. Ensure that the sealing ring groove is spotless and that the O-ring gets seated fully in the groove. Use

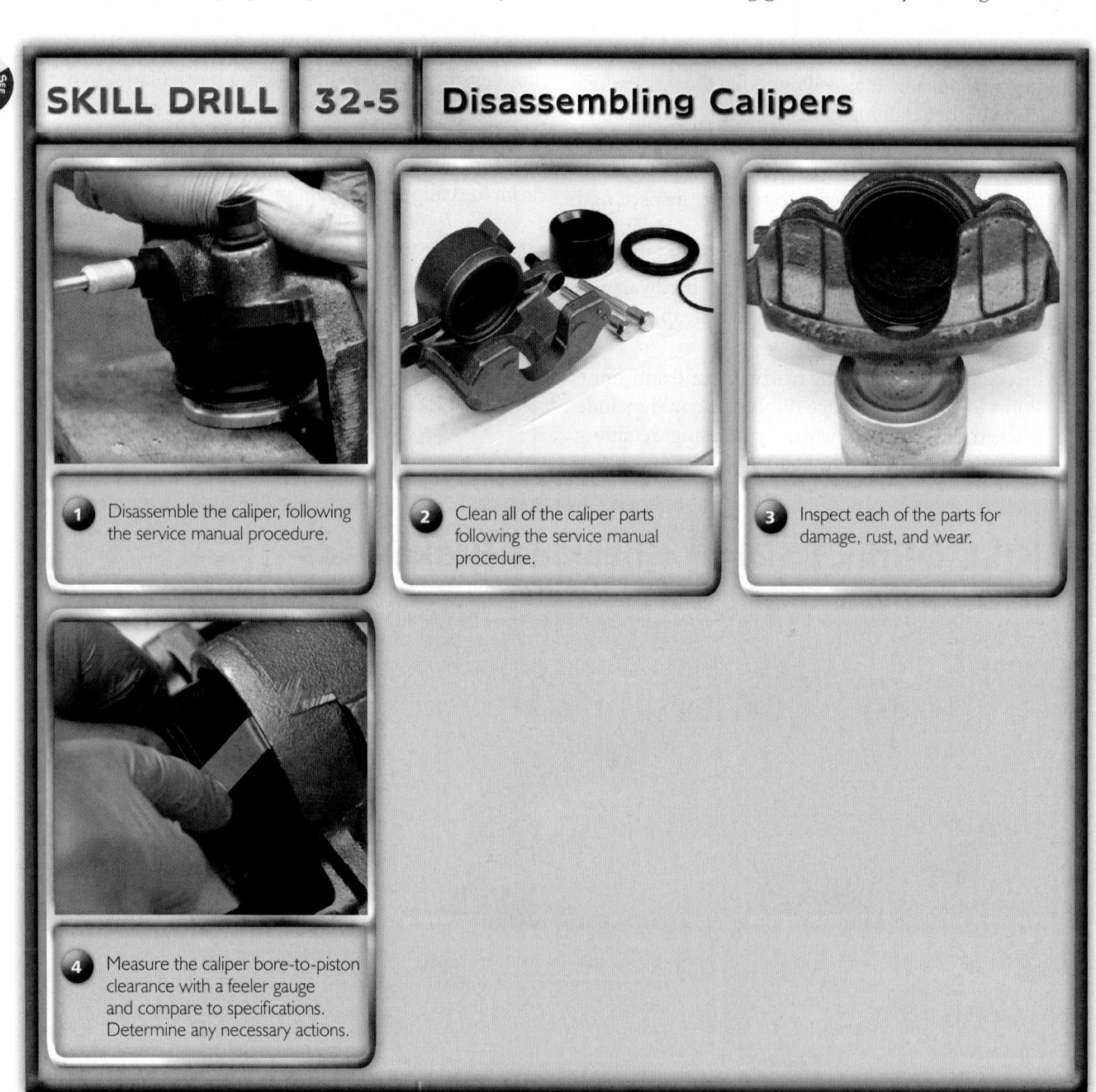

SKILL DRILL | **32-5** | **Disassembling Calipers**

1 Disassemble the caliper, following the service manual procedure.

2 Clean all of the caliper parts following the service manual procedure.

3 Inspect each of the parts for damage, rust, and wear.

4 Measure the caliper bore-to-piston clearance with a feeler gauge and compare to specifications. Determine any necessary actions.

clean brake fluid or approved caliper piston assembly lube on the piston and sealing ring prior to installing it. Also check the service manual to see when the piston dust boot needs to be installed. Some calipers require the dust boot to be installed in the caliper before installing the piston. In this case, a special technique using air pressure to "balloon" the dust boot is required so the piston can slip inside it. Ask your supervisor to demonstrate this technique.

To reassemble, lubricate, and reinstall the caliper, pads, and related hardware; seat pads; and inspect for leaks, follow the steps in **SKILL DRILL 32-6**:

1 Make sure the rotor has been properly installed on the hub/spindle and that the hub mating surface is free of rust or dirt. **(Photo 1)**

> **TECHNICIAN TIP**
>
> In some cases, the piston cannot be removed with compressed air due to the piston being seized in the bore. If this happens, reinstall the calipers on the vehicle without the pads, bleed the brakes, and use the brake pedal to force the stuck piston out of the caliper. You may have to block any nonseized pistons so they don't pop out; that way, just the seized piston gets pushed out.

2 Reassemble the caliper assembly, following the manufacturer's procedure. Lubricate the sealing

SKILL DRILL | 32-6 | Reassembling Calipers

1. Make sure the rotor has been properly installed on the hub/spindle and the hub surface is free of rust or dirt.

2. Reassemble the caliper assembly, following the manufacturer's procedure.

3. Assemble the pads, hardware, and caliper on the caliper mountings using the specified lubricant. Lubricate all moving parts.

4. Reinstall the brake line fittings using two new copper washers (if equipped).

5. Tighten the brake line fitting and caliper bolts to the proper torque. Bleed the brakes following the manufacturer's procedure.

6. Seat the pads by applying the brake pedal several times, not allowing the pedal to go all the way to the floor.

| SKILL DRILL | 32-6 | Reassembling Calipers, continued |

7 If the brake pedal is spongy, you will need to bleed the brakes of any remaining trapped air in the system.

8 Inspect the system for any brake fluid leaks, no matter how small.

ring, piston, and any other moving parts. Be careful to not pinch, twist, or cut the sealing ring and dust boot. **(Photo 2)**

3 Assemble the pads, hardware, and caliper on the caliper mountings using the specified lubricant. **(Photo 3)**

4 Reinstall the brake line fittings using two new copper washers (if equipped). Place one between the brake line fitting and the head of the banjo bolt and the other between the brake line fitting and the caliper. **(Photo 4)**

5 Tighten the brake line fitting and the caliper mounting bolt(s) to the proper torque.

6 Bleed the brakes following the manufacturer's procedure. See the brake bleeding skill drills in the Hydraulics and Power Brakes chapter for more information. **(Photo 5)**

7 Seat the pads by applying the brake pedal several times. It is a good idea to place your left foot under the brake pedal so that when applying the pedal with your right foot, the pedal does not push the master cylinder pistons farther into the master cylinder bore, which could dislodge sludge or cut the lips of the master cylinder primary seals. Applying the brake will force the brake caliper pistons to adjust to the proper clearance for proper

brake application. You may need to start the vehicle to enable the power booster to help you fully apply the brakes, especially if the vehicle is equipped with integrated parking brake calipers. **(Photo 6)**

8 If the brake pedal is spongy, you will need to bleed the brakes of any remaining trapped air in the system. **(Photo 7)**

9 If the brake pedal is firm and does not sink over time, there could still be a small leak that would cause a future brake failure. Inspect the system for any brake fluid leaks, no matter how small; if found, inform your supervisor/instructor. **(Photo 8)**

Retracting and Readjusting Pistons on an Integrated Parking Brake

Retracting the caliper piston on an integrated parking brake system is different than on a standard caliper. Since the integrated parking brake system uses a threaded shaft to force the piston outward from the caliper bore, it cannot just be retracted with a C-clamp. The piston will need to be screwed back in on the threaded shaft to retract it into the bore. This is accomplished by using a tool that mates to slots, grooves, or holes in the outer face of the piston. The tool is then turned by hand or wrench to screw the piston back into the bore. Be careful to not tear the piston dust boot during this operation.

To retract the caliper piston on an integrated parking brake system, follow the steps in **SKILL DRILL 32-7**:

1 Research the procedure for retracting the caliper piston on an integrated parking brake system in the appropriate service information, paying close attention to which direction the piston needs to be turned.

2 Select the proper adapter or tool to match the caliper piston. There are several types of tools that work. One is a multisided cube with a variety of projections of varying configurations on each side. This cube fits on the end of a ratchet. The ratchet and tool need to be held tightly against the piston so it does not slip. There are other more application-specific tools that use the caliper housing to keep the tool from slipping out of the holes in the piston. This style works the best if you have access to one. **(Photo 1)**

3 Install the tool and turn it in the direction that causes the piston to retract. **(Photo 2)**

4 Continue turning until the piston is lightly seated at the bottom of its bore. **(Photo 3)**

5 Make sure the dust boot is seated properly in its grooves. **(Photo 4)**

SKILL DRILL | 32-7 | Retracting and Readjusting Pistons on an Integrated Parking Brake

1 Research the procedure for retracting the caliper piston. Select the proper adapter or tool to match the caliper piston.

2 Install the tool and turn it in the direction that causes the piston to retract.

3 Continue turning until the piston is lightly seated at the bottom of its bore.

4 Make sure the dust boot is seated properly in its grooves.

Inspecting and Measuring Disc Brake Rotors

The rotor thickness, lateral runout, and thickness variation must be within specifications for the rotor to function properly. Rotors that are too thin cannot handle as much heat and will experience brake fade sooner than thicker rotors will. They also may cause the piston to be pushed out of the caliper bore far enough that the sealing ring no longer seals the piston. This would lead to a lack of braking action on at least half of the system.

Excessive thickness variation will cause brake pedal pulsation and the vehicle to have a surging feeling while coming to a stop. Excessive lateral runout tends to cause the steering wheel to shimmy. It also can cause an excessive thickness variation problem due to the high spot of the rotor continuously hitting the brake pad while driving down the road. This constant rubbing on the high spot of the rotor will wear it slightly, leading to excessive thickness variation across the face of the rotor.

To clean, inspect, and measure rotor thickness, lateral runout, and thickness variation and to determine any necessary action(s), follow the steps in **SKILL DRILL 32-8**:

1 Research the procedure and specifications for inspecting the rotor in the service information.

2 If you have not already done so, remove the caliper assembly, brake pads, and any hardware following the manufacturer's procedure.

3 Clean the rotor with approved asbestos removal equipment. **(Photo 1)**

4 Inspect the rotor for hard spots or hot spots, scoring, cracks, and damage. **(Photo 2)**

5 Measure the rotor thickness at the deepest groove or thinnest part of the rotor and compare to specifications. If it is under the allowed size, it will need to be replaced. If it needs to be machined and it is above the minimum thickness, check to see how badly it is scored. Remember that removing 0.015" (0.38 mm) on each side of the rotor results in the thickness being reduced by 0.030" (0.76 mm). Many rotors only start with 0.060" (1.52 mm) of machinable material when they are new. **(Photo 3)**

6 Measure the thickness of the rotor in a minimum of five to eight places around face of the rotor. Calculate the maximum thickness variation by subtracting the minimum thickness from the maximum thickness and compare it to specifications. **(Photo 4)**

SKILL DRILL | **32-8** | **Inspecting and Measuring Disc Brake Rotors**

1 Research the procedure and specifications for inspecting the rotor. If you have not already done so, remove the caliper assembly, brake pads, and any hardware. Clean the rotor with approved asbestos removal equipment.

2 Inspect the rotor for hard spots or hot spots, scoring, cracks, and damage.

3 Measure the rotor thickness at the deepest groove or thinnest part of the rotor and compare to specifications.

SKILL DRILL | 32-8 | Inspecting and Measuring Disc Brake Rotors, continued

4 Measure the thickness of the rotor in a minimum of five to eight places around the face of the rotor. Calculate the maximum thickness variation and compare to specifications.

5 Set up a dial indicator to measure lateral runout. Rotate the rotor and find the lowest spot on the rotor, then zero the dial indicator.

6 Slowly rotate the rotor to find the highest spot on the rotor. Read the dial indicator showing maximum runout.

7 Keep turning the rotor to make sure the dial indicator does not read below zero. If it does, rezero the dial caliper on the lowest spot. Keep turning the rotor to find the highest spot and reread the dial indicator. Compare all of your readings to the specifications and determine if the rotor is fit for service, is machinable, or needs to be replaced.

7 Set up a dial indicator to measure lateral runout. Rotate the rotor and find the lowest spot on the rotor, then zero the dial indicator. **(Photo 5)**

8 Slowly rotate the rotor to find the highest spot on the rotor. Read the dial indicator showing maximum runout. **(Photo 6)**

9 Keep turning the rotor to make sure the dial indicator does not read below zero. If it does, rezero the dial caliper on the lowest spot.

10 Keep turning the rotor to find the highest spot and reread the dial indicator.

11 Compare all of your readings to the specifications, and determine if the rotor is fit for service, is machinable, or needs to be replaced. **(Photo 7)**

Removing and Reinstalling Rotors

Removing the rotor is usually required when the rotor needs to be replaced because it is under the specified minimum thickness or would be after machining. It also would need to be removed to be refinished on an off-car brake lathe or to service the wheel bearings or axle shaft. Also, hubless rotors that are being machined with an on-car brake lathe need to be removed to clean off the rust and dirt accumulated between the rotor and the hub.

Rotors are designed to be mounted in one of two ways: hub style or hubless style. The hub style has the wheel bearing hub cast into the rotor. This style generally requires disassembly of the wheel bearing hub to remove the rotor from the vehicle. The hubless style uses a wheel bearing hub separate from the rotor, with the rotor held onto the hub by the wheel studs and lug nuts. Some hubs also use small screws to hold the rotor on the hub whenever the wheel is removed from the vehicle. Removing hubless rotors is generally easier than removing hub-style rotors, although some manufacturers design their rotors to unbolt from the rear side of the bearing hub. In these applications, the wheel bearing hub must be removed before the rotor can be removed from the hub.

To remove and reinstall the rotor, follow the steps in **SKILL DRILL 32-9**:

1 Research the procedure for removing and reinstalling the brake rotor in the appropriate service information.

2 If you have not already done so, remove the caliper assembly, brake pads, and any hardware, following the manufacturer's procedure.

3 If the caliper mount straddles the rotor, remove it according to the specified procedure. This is usually accomplished by removing bolts behind the rotor. **(Photo 1)**

4 **To remove the hubless-style rotor**, first mark the rotor for reinstallation in the correct position. A permanent marker, crayon, or center punch can be used to do this. **(Photo 2)**

5 If there are screws or speed nuts holding the rotor to the hub, remove them following the specified manufacturer procedure. **(Photo 3)**

6 Remove the rotor from the hub. **(Photo 4)**

7 **To remove the hub-style rotor**, remove the wheel bearing locking mechanism (cotter pin, lock nut, or peened washer). **(Photo 5)**

8 Remove the wheel bearing adjusting nut, thrust washer, and outer bearing. **(Photo 6)**

9 If the rear bearing must be removed for service or replacement of the rotor, use the following procedure to remove the inner bearing and grease seal.

SKILL DRILL | **32-9** | **Removing and Reinstalling Rotors**

1 Research the procedure for removing and reinstalling the brake rotor. If you have not already done so, remove the caliper assembly, brake pads, and any hardware. If the caliper mount straddles the rotor, remove it.

2 To remove the hubless-style rotor, mark the rotor for proper reinstallation.

3 If there are screws or speed nuts holding the rotor to the hub, remove them.

SKILL DRILL | **32-9** | **Removing and Reinstalling Rotors, continued**

4 Remove the rotor from the hub.

5 To remove the hub-style rotor, remove the wheel bearing locking mechanism.

6 Remove the wheel bearing adjusting nut, thrust washer, and outer bearing.

7 Follow the steps of the inner bearing and grease seal removal procedure if the rear bearing must be removed.

8 To reinstall a hubless-style rotor, clean all mounting surfaces on the hub and rotor and remove any burrs.

9 Slip the rotor over the wheel studs.

10 If the rotor uses small screws to hold the rotor to the hub, reinstall those and tighten to the proper torque.

11 Spin the rotor to ensure it spins true and does not contact any other components such as the dust shield.

12 To reinstall a hub-style rotor, see the wheel bearing service skill drills in the Wheel Bearing chapter. Be sure to properly lock the adjustment nut in place once adjustment is completed.

SKILL DRILL | 32-9 | Removing and Reinstalling Rotors, continued

13 Spin the rotor to ensure it spins true and does not contact any other components such as the dust shield.

- Reinstall the adjusting nut onto the spindle about five turns.
- Grasp the rotor on the top and bottom, and push it toward the center of the vehicle.
- Hold slight downward pressure as you firmly pull the rotor toward yourself. This should cause the adjusting nut to catch the wheel bearing and to pull it and the seal out of the rear of the hub.
- The grease seal will need to be replaced with a new one.
- Now would be a good time to perform any other rotor-related tasks such as inspecting and measuring a rotor, refinishing a rotor, and servicing wheel bearings. Perform those tasks and return here to reinstall the rotor.
- If a new rotor is being installed, make sure to clean off any anticorrosion coating it was shipped with. Follow the rotor manufacturer's procedure to remove this coating. **(Photo 7)**

10 **To reinstall a hubless-style rotor**, first clean all mounting surfaces on the hub and rotor and remove any burrs. **(Photo 8)**

11 Slip the rotor over the wheel studs. **(Photo 9)**

12 If the rotor uses small screws to hold the rotor to the hub, reinstall those and tighten to the proper torque. **(Photo 10)**

13 Finally, spin the rotor to ensure it spins true and does not contact any other components such as the dust shield. **(Photo 11)**

14 **To reinstall a hub-style rotor**, follow the wheel bearing service skill drills in the Wheel Bearings

chapter to pack, install, and adjust the wheel bearings.

15 Be sure to properly lock the adjustment nut in place once the adjustment is completed. **(Photo 12)**

16 Finally, spin the rotor to ensure it spins true and does not contact any other components such as the dust shield. **(Photo 13)**

Refinishing Rotors on Vehicle

Rotors need to be refinished when they have excessive runout, thickness variation, or grooving. A brake lathe refinishes the rotor surfaces by removing metal and truing the surfaces. If the grooving or surface defects are too great, the rotor may require the removal of too much metal to satisfactorily refinish the surfaces. The rotor thickness should always be remeasured once the refinishing is complete to ensure it is above the manufacturer's minimum thickness.

Rotors can be refinished while on the vehicle or off the vehicle. On-vehicle refinishing is preferred by most manufacturers (those who allow refinishing of their rotors) because it minimizes runout issues between the hub and rotor. Since the rotor is being machined as it is mounted on the vehicle, it is being refinished true to the hub and other brake components. This minimizes any lateral runout issues. To refinish a rotor while it is on the vehicle and to measure final rotor thickness, follow the steps on **SKILL DRILL 32-10**:

1 Research the brake lathe manufacturer's procedure for properly refinishing the rotor. Follow those guidelines completely.

2 If working on a hubless-style rotor, remove the rotor and clean any dirt, rust, and debris from the mating surfaces of the rotor and hub.

3 If working on a hub-style rotor, measure the wheel bearing end play. If excessive, adjust the bearings so there is no end play. Just remember to readjust them properly when the refinishing process is complete.

4 Mount the on-car brake lathe to the rotor. **(Photo 1)**

5 Perform the runout calibration on the brake lathe. Some brake lathes require manual compensation, while other machines can perform this as part of their features. Follow the lathe manufacturer's procedure. **(Photo 2)**

6 Adjust the cutting bits and cut off any lip at the edge of the rotor. **(Photo 3)**

7 Make sure the cutting bits will not contact the rotor face, and move the cutting head toward the inner diameter of the rotor face.

8 Set the cutting bits to the proper cutting depth for machining. This is usually between 0.004 and 0.015 of an inch. Too little removal tends to overheat the edge of the cutting bit. Too much can overload the lathe, as well as make the rotors much thinner. **(Photo 4)**

9 Install the anti-chatter device, if specified. This will help give an acceptable finish on the rotor surfaces. **(Photo 5)**

10 Engage the automatic feed and watch for proper machining action.

11 If necessary, repeat this step until all damaged surface areas have been removed on both sides of the rotor. **(Photo 6)**

12 If necessary, perform a finish cut on the rotor. Many newer machines use an elliptical motion to give a nondirectional finish, so a finish cut is not needed. **(Photo 7)**

13 Remeasure the rotor thickness to determine if the rotor is above minimum thickness specifications. **(Photo 8)**

14 If you had to adjust the wheel bearings in Step 3, readjust the bearings so they have the specified end play or preload.

Refinishing Rotors off Vehicle

Refinishing a rotor while it is off the vehicle is a bit different than on-vehicle refinishing. The major difference

SKILL DRILL 32-10 Refinishing Hubless Rotors on Vehicle

1 Research the brake lathe manufacturer's procedure for properly refinishing the rotor. Mount the on-car brake lathe to the rotor after cleaning the rust and dirt from between the rotor and hub or adjusting the wheel bearing so there is no end play.

2 Perform the runout calibration on the brake lathe.

3 Adjust the cutting bits and cut off any lip at the edge of the rotor.

SKILL DRILL | **32-10** | **Refinishing Hubless Rotors on Vehicle, continued**

4. Make sure the cutting bits will not contact the rotor face, and move the cutting head toward the inner diameter of the rotor face. Set the cutting bits to the proper cutting depth for machining.

5. Install the anti-chatter device, if specified.

6. Engage the automatic feed and watch for proper machining action. If necessary, repeat this step until all damaged surface areas have been removed on both sides of the rotor.

7. If necessary, perform a finish cut on the rotor.

8. Remeasure the rotor thickness to determine if the rotor is above minimum thickness specifications.

is in the setup. Hub-style and hubless-style rotors each require their own way of being mounted on the brake lathe. Most hub-style rotors use the **bearing races** to drive and center the rotor on the lathe spindle. Thus, bearing adapters of the proper size need to be selected and used (see the Wheel Bearings chapter). The spindle nut then clamps the rotor onto the spindle through these bearing adapters and races. Hubless rotors are centered using a spring-loaded centering cone to align the rotor's centering hole with the spindle. Clam shell clamps are then used on each side of the rotor to clamp it to the lathe spindle. Composite rotors use a special adapter which drives the rotor from the center hole and, at the same time, clamps it firmly between solid plates.

To refinish a rotor while it is off the vehicle and measure final rotor thickness, follow the steps in **SKILL DRILL 32-11**:

1. Research the brake lathe manufacturer's procedure for properly refinishing the rotor. Follow those guidelines completely.

2. Clean nicks, burrs, or debris from the mounting surfaces of the rotor including the centering hole, if used. Since the rotor is clamped to the lathe spindle, all of the surfaces on the rotor that contact the lathe components must be free of nicks, burrs, and rust; therefore, they must be cleaned prior to mounting the rotor on the lathe. This is especially true of a hubless-style rotor. (**Photo 1**)

3 Mount the rotor onto the lathe. Check that the rotor is running true on the lathe. (**Photo 2**)

4 Install the anti-chatter band or anti-chatter pucks on the rotor. (**Photo 3**)

5 Make sure the cutting bits will not contact the rotor face, and move the cutting head in about one-quarter the way from the outer diameter of the rotor face. Turn on the lathe. (**Photo 4**)

6 Set the cutting bits to the proper cutting depth for machining the ridge. (**Photo 5**)

7 By hand, move the cutting head outward toward the ridge. Slowly remove the ridge. (**Photo 6**)

8 Once the ridge is removed, run the cutting head all the way in to the inner face of the rotor. (**Photo 7**)

9 Set the cutting bits to the proper cutting depth for machining the rotor face. (**Photo 8**)

SKILL DRILL | 32-11 | Refinishing Rotors off Vehicle

1 Research the brake lathe manufacturer's procedure for properly refinishing the rotor. Clean nicks, burrs, or debris from the mounting surfaces of the rotor including the centering hole.

2 Mount the rotor. Check that the rotor is running true on the lathe.

3 Install the anti-chatter band or anti-chatter pucks on the rotor.

4 Position the cutting head about one-quarter the way in from the outer diameter of the rotor. Turn on the lathe.

5 Set the cutting bits to the proper cutting depth for machining the ridge.

6 By hand, move the cutting head outward toward the ridge. Slowly remove the ridge.

10 Engage the automatic feed on "fast" cut and watch for proper machining action. Some machines are called a "single-cut" or "single-pass" lathe and offer only one cutting speed.

11 If necessary, repeat the previous step until all damaged surface areas have been removed on both sides of the rotor. **(Photo 9)**

12 If necessary, perform a finish cut on the rotor. This is usually done on "slow" speed. **(Photo 10)**

13 Use sandpaper or a drill with a sanding pad to give the rotor faces a nondirectional finish. **(Photo 11)**

14 Remeasure the rotor thickness to determine if the rotor is above minimum thickness specifications. **(Photo 12)**

15 Wash the machined rotor in a hot soapy water solution or parts washing cabinet to remove any metal particles, and dry.

SKILL DRILL | **32-11** | **Refinishing Rotors off Vehicle, continued**

7 Once the ridge is removed, run the cutting head all the way in to the inner face of the rotor.

8 Set the cutting bits to the proper cutting depth for machining the rotor face.

9 Engage the automatic feed on "fast" cut and watch for proper machining action. Some single-cut machines only have one cutting speed. If necessary, repeat this step until all damaged surface areas have been removed on both sides of the rotor.

10 If necessary, perform a finish cut on the rotor. This is usually done on "slow" speed.

11 Use sandpaper or a drill with a sanding pad to give the rotor faces a nondirectional finish.

12 Remeasure the rotor thickness to determine if the rotor is above minimum thickness specifications.

Inspecting and Replacing Wheel Studs

Wheel studs need to be replaced when they have been damaged or broken off due to improper installation or normal wear and tear. Wheel studs can be damaged by being overtightened and stretched. Look for a necked-down or thinned-out section of the stud, which is most likely to happen within the threaded area of the stud. Stretched studs need to be replaced. Studs can also have their threads damaged by cross-threading or seizing of the lug nut on the stud. It is best to replace the stud and nut if this occurs. Lastly, wheel studs may even break off if they are overtightened beyond their stretch point. It is always a good idea to consider replacing all of the studs on a wheel (and maybe the ones on the other wheels also) if one stud is broken off, as it is likely that all of the others have been weakened.

Some vehicles are designed to allow for the removal and replacement of the wheel studs while the hub and wheel flange are still installed on the vehicle. The manufacturer may have provided a recessed spot in the steering knuckle where the studs have enough clearance to be removed; thus, the flange needs to be positioned in that particular position. Other vehicles do not have enough clearance on the back side for the stud to be removed; thus, the hub and flange must be removed from the vehicle.

There are two primary methods of replacing lug studs: the **drawing-in method** and the **hydraulic press method**. The drawing-in method uses the lug nut to draw in the wheel stud. It is accomplished by inserting the new stud into the wheel stud hole in the flange, installing enough heavy-duty washers over the stud to allow the lug nut to draw the wheel stud into the flange when tightened. The lug nut is placed flat side in, on the stud, and tightened. Make sure that as the stud is pulled in the lug nut does not run out of threads on the stud. If it does, remove the nut and add washers. Keep tightening the lug nut until the wheel stud bottoms out in the flange. Verify that the head of the stud is fully seated in the flange.

The hydraulic press method uses a press to force the wheel stud into the flange until it bottoms out. This method requires the hub and flange to be removed from the vehicle. Make sure the flange is positioned and supported properly on the press table. Sometimes it is best to use a short piece of pipe (a bit longer than the wheel stud) to support the flange while the stud is being pressed in. Once the stud is installed, verify that it is fully seated in the flange.

To inspect and replace wheel studs, follow the steps in **SKILL DRILL 32-12**:

1. Inspect the wheel studs and lug nuts for damage. Look for signs of stretched studs, cross-threaded lug nuts, and broken-off studs.

2. Determine if the stud can be removed with the flange on or off the vehicle. **(Photo 1)**

3. **To perform the drawing-in method**, first position the flange so the stud has clearance on the back side to be removed. **(Photo 2)**

4. Remove any damaged studs with a hammer. Be careful not to damage any of the surfaces on the flange and hub, including the wheel speed sensor and tone ring. **(Photo 3)**

5. Insert the stud in the hole in the flange and rotate it so that all of the flutes on the stud line up with the notches in the flange. **(Photo 4)**

6. Place enough heavy duty washers over the stud to prevent the lug nut from bottoming out on the threads. **(Photo 5)**

7. Place the lug nut onto the stud, flat side in. Tighten it until the stud bottoms out in the flange.

8. Inspect the threads on the stud and lug nut to make sure they did not get damaged. **(Photo 6)**

9. **To perform the hydraulic press method**, first remove the hub and wheel flange from the vehicle following the manufacturer's procedure. **(Photo 7)**

10. Use the press to push out any damaged lug studs. **(Photo 8)**

11. Insert the new lug stud into the wheel flange hole. Line up the flutes on the stud with the notches in the flange. **(Photo 9)**

12. Support the hub and flange so the press is pushing the stud straight into the flange. **(Photo 10)**

13. Push the stud in until it bottoms out in the flange. **(Photo 11)**

14. To complete the drawing-in method and the hydraulic press method, verify that each stud is fully seated in the flange. **(Photo 12)**

15. Reinstall the hub and flange on the vehicle if they were removed. **(Photo 13)**

Installing Wheels, Torquing Lug Nuts, and Making Final Checks

This step, while fairly simple, can result in problems if it is not done properly. Overtightening the lug nuts can cause the wheel studs to break either immediately, or worse, after the vehicle has been driven for a period of time. Overtightening also can cause warpage of the rotors, which results in the need to refinish or replace them. Undertightening can lead to loosening of the lug nuts and result in the wheel working its way off the vehicle. This can cause the driver to lose control of the vehicle and potentially result in an accident. Lug nuts should be tightened to the proper torque, in the specified sequence. All manufacturers specify the sequences for each of their vehicles. The torque pattern is usually in some form of a star or cross.

Be careful which way you install the lug nuts. Many wheels use a tapered hole that matches the tapered end of the lug nut and centers the wheel on the wheel flange. Other wheels use a flat surface that matches flat surfaces on the lug nuts. But no matter what, the lug nut surface *must* match the mating surface of the wheel. Always check that these surfaces match.

When installing lug nuts, the weight should be off the vehicle so that the wheel is off the ground or is barely touching the ground. The lug nuts should easily center the wheel on the hub. This is especially important on aluminum wheels that use a flat lug nut seating surface. The lug nuts can dig into the sides of the lug nut holes

SKILL DRILL 32-12 Inspecting and Replacing Wheel Studs

1 Inspect the wheel studs and lug nuts for damage. Look for signs of stretched studs, cross-threaded lug nuts, and broken-off studs. Determine if the stud can be removed with the flange on or off the vehicle.

2 To perform the drawing-in method, position the flange so the stud has clearance on the back side to be removed.

3 Remove any damaged studs with a hammer. Be careful not to damage any of the surfaces on the flange and hub, including the wheel speed sensor and tone ring.

4 Insert the stud in the hole in the flange and rotate it so that all of the flutes on the stud line up with the notches in the flange.

5 Place enough heavy-duty washers over the stud to prevent the lug nut from bottoming out on the threads.

6 Place the lug nut onto the stud, flat side in. Tighten it until the stud bottoms out in the flange. Inspect the threads on the stud and lug nut to make sure they did not get damaged.

SKILL DRILL | 32-12 | Inspecting and Replacing Wheel Studs, continued

7 To perform the hydraulic press method, remove the hub and wheel flange from the vehicle following the manufacturer's procedure.

8 Use the press to push out any damaged lug studs.

9 Insert the new lug stud into the wheel flange hole. Line up the flutes on the stud with the notches in the flange.

10 Support the hub and flange so the press is pushing the stud straight into the flange.

11 Push the stud in until it bottoms out in the flange.

12 To complete the drawing-in method and the hydraulic press method, verify that each stud is fully seated in the flange.

13 Reinstall the hub and flange on the vehicle if it was removed.

There is some controversy regarding the use of a lubricant or antiseize on wheel studs and lug nuts. Since the purpose of a lubricant or antiseize is to prevent the components from sticking, CDX errs on the side of not using those products, for fear of the lug nuts coming loose. Also, the torque given for the lug nuts is dry (no lubricant) so torquing them to specifications would lead to overtorquing. At the same time, in areas of the country prone to rust, it is understandable why some want to put a very light amount of antiseize only on the threads of the wheel stud, being careful not to get any on the contact seat of the wheel and lug nut. Doing so would prevent rust from building up on the threads. However, the lug nut torque would need to be reduced due to the lubricant. CDX prefers to install lug nuts dry and avoid this issue altogether. Many shops have their customers sign on the repair order that they will return and the wheel torque will be rechecked after 50 to 500 miles of driving to make sure the wheels have not loosened.

process of transferring pad material onto the rotor evenly, as well as cooking off the resins that are used to bind the friction material together in the pad. Burnishing results in long, quiet brake life, which results in satisfied customers.

For burnishing to happen properly, the rotor and pad material need to be heated slowly and evenly. This is done by making a specified number of stops from a specified speed, with the appropriate wait times between stops. In some cases, brake lining manufacturers want you to perform a series of stops at light to moderate brake application. Other manufacturers specify a series of moderate to heavy stops. Always check the manufacturer's procedure to burnish the brakes once the brake job is complete. This process will help avoid the dreaded disc brake squeal.

To install the wheel, torque lug nuts, and make final checks and adjustments, follow the steps in **SKILL DRILL 32-13**:

1. Start the lug nuts on the wheel studs. Make sure the lug nut surface matches the wheel hole. The lug nuts should be able to be turned by finger. **(Photo 1)**
2. Carefully run all of the lug nuts down so they are seated in the wheel. Make sure the wheel is centered on the hub. **(Photo 2)**
3. Lower the vehicle so the tires are partially on the ground to keep them from turning while tightening the lug nuts. **(Photo 3)**
4. Use a torque wrench to tighten each lug nut to the proper torque in the proper sequence. **(Photo 4)**

and cause the wheel to not center properly. Once the lug nuts are against the wheel, work the wheel onto the lug nut shafts. Then you can torque them down properly. Once the lug nuts are torqued properly and the brake system checked, it is time for a test drive to verify proper brake operation, and to burnish the new brake pads and rotor surfaces. Burnishing, also called bedding in, is the

SKILL DRILL   **32-13**   **Installing Wheels, Torquing Lug Nuts, and Making Final Checks**

1. Start the lug nuts on the wheel studs, being careful to match up the surfaces.

2. Carefully run all of the lug nuts down so they are seated in the wheel.

3. Lower the vehicle so the tires are partially on the ground to keep them from turning while tightening the lug nuts.

SKILL DRILL | 32-13 | Installing Wheels, Torquing Lug Nuts, and Making Final Checks, continued

4 Use a torque wrench to tighten each lug nut to the proper torque in the proper sequence.

5 Once all of the lug nuts have been torqued, go around them again, this time in a circular pattern to ensure that you did not miss any in the previous pattern.

6 If the vehicle was equipped with hubcaps and valve stem caps, reinstall them.

7 Check the brake fluid level in the master cylinder reservoir. Start the vehicle and check the brake pedal for proper feel and height. Check the parking brake for proper operation. Also inspect the system for any brake fluid leaks and loose or missing fasteners.

5 Once all of the lug nuts have been torqued, go around them again, this time in a circular pattern to ensure that you did not miss any in the previous pattern. (**Photo 5**)

6 If the vehicle was equipped with hubcaps and valve stem caps, reinstall them. (**Photo 6**)

7 Check the brake fluid level in the master cylinder reservoir.

8 Start the vehicle and check the brake pedal for proper feel and height. Check the parking brake for proper operation. Also inspect the system for any brake fluid leaks and loose or missing fasteners. (**Photo 7**)

Wrap-up

Ready for Review

- Disc brakes create braking power by forcing flat friction pads against the outer faces of a rotor.
- The vehicle's kinetic energy is transformed into heat energy by the disc brake components, which slow the vehicle when applied.
- Disc brake assemblies consist of a caliper, brake pads, and a rotor.
- Caliper pistons use hydraulic pressure to create a clamping force of the brake pads to the faces of the rotor.
- Disc brake pads require much higher application pressures to operate than drum brake shoes because they are not self-energizing.
- Advantages of disc brakes over drum brakes: more effective at transferring heat to the atmosphere, self-adjusting, resistant to water fade, and easier to service.
- Disadvantages of disc brakes compared to drum brakes: more prone to noise, more prone to pedal pulsations due to warpage, and more difficult to use as an emergency brake.
- Disc brake calipers come in two main styles: fixed and floating/sliding.

- In disc brake calipers, the piston is sealed by a square cut O-ring.
- Floating/sliding calipers require clean and lubricated pins, bushings, or guides for proper operation.
- Brake pad lining is either riveted or bonded to the pad backing plate.
- Brake pad lining is available in a variety of materials with varying amounts of coefficient of friction.
- Brake pads may use shims, spacers, guides, and bendable tangs to help minimize squealing.
- Brake pad wear indicators, if used, can be of the mechanical or electronic type.
- Rotors rotate with the wheels and are usually made of durable cast iron with friction surfaces that run true and parallel.
- Brake rotors can be solid or ventilated.
- Disc brake parking brakes can be of the integrated caliper style, top hat drum style, electric pull-cable style, and the integrated electric motor caliper style.
- Diagnosing brake faults requires good information from the customer, an adequate test-drive when possible, and a good understanding of brake theory.

Key Terms

backing plate A metal plate to which the brake lining is fixed.

bendable tangs Small tabs on the brake pad backing plate that are crimped on to the caliper, creating a secure fit and reducing noise.

bearing races Hardened metal surfaces that roller or ball bearings fit into when a bearing is properly assembled.

bleeder screw A screw that allows air and brake fluid to be bled out of a hydraulic brake system when it is loosened and seals the brake fluid in when it is tightened.

bonded linings Brake linings that are essentially glued to the brake pad backing plate; more common on light-duty vehicles.

brake booster A vacuum or hydraulically operated device that increases the driver's braking effort.

brake lining thickness gauge A tool used to measure the thickness of the brake lining.

brake pad shims and guides Small pieces of metal that cushion the brake pad and absorb some of the vibration, helping to cut down on unwanted noise.

brake wash station A piece of equipment designed to safely clean brake dust from drum and disc brake components.

bushing An insert with an inner bearing surface that is fitted into a hole in an object, allowing the object to rotate or slide on a pin or shaft.

caliper A hydraulic device that uses pressure from the master cylinder to apply the brake pads against the rotor.

caliper dust boot seal driver set A set of drivers used to install metal-backed caliper dust boot seals.

caliper piston pliers A tool used to grip caliper pistons while removing them.

caliper piston retracting tool A tool used to retract caliper pistons on integrated parking brake systems.

C-clamp A tool used to push pistons back into the caliper bore on non-integrated parking brakes.

dial indicator Tool used to measure the lateral runout of the rotor.

disc brake pads Brake pads that consist of a friction material bonded or riveted to a steel backing plate; designed to wear out over time.

disc brake rotor micrometer A specially designed micrometer used to measure the thickness of a rotor.

drawing-in method A method for replacing wheel studs that uses the lug nut to draw the wheel stud into the hub or flange.

edge code A code printed on the edge of a friction lining that describes its coefficient of friction.

electronic control module (ECM) A computer that receives signals from input sensors, compares that information with preloaded software, and sends an appropriate command signal to output devices; used to manage the anti-lock brake system (ABS).

fixed caliper A type of brake caliper bolted firmly to the steering knuckle or axle housing, having at least one piston on both sides of the rotor.

guide pins Pins that allow the caliper to move in and out as the brakes operate and as the brake pads wear.

hydraulic press method A method for replacing wheel studs that uses a press to force the wheel stud into the flange until it bottoms out.

independent rear suspension (IRS) A type of suspension system where each rear wheel is capable of moving independently of the other.

lateral runout Also called warpage, the side-to-side movement of the rotor surfaces as the rotor turns.

low-drag caliper A caliper designed to maintain a larger brake pad-to-rotor clearance by retracting the pistons farther than normal.

lug A flange that is shaped to assist with aligning objects on other objects.

off-car brake lathe A tool used to machine (refinish) drums and rotors after they have been removed from the vehicle.

on-car brake lathe A tool used to machine (refinish) rotors while they are still attached to the vehicle.

parallelism Also called thickness variation; both surfaces of the rotor should be perfectly parallel to each other so that brake pulsations do not occur.

parking brake cable pliers A tool used to install parking brake cables.

phenolic resin A material used to create some brake pistons that is very resistant to corrosion and heat transfer.

pushrod (braking system) A mechanism used to transmit force from the brake pedal to the master cylinder.

riveted linings Brake linings riveted to the brake pad backing plate with metal rivets and used on heavier-duty or high-performance vehicles.

rotor The main rotating part of a disc brake system.

scratcher A thin, spring steel wear indicator that is fixed to the backing plate of the brake pad; it emits a high-pitched squeal when the brakes are applied if the brake pads have become too thin.

sliding or floating caliper A type of brake caliper that only has piston(s) on the inboard side of the rotor. The caliper is free to slide or float, thus pulling the outboard brake pad into the rotor when braking force is applied.

solid rotor A type of brake rotor made of solid metal.

square cut O-ring An O-ring with a square cross-section that is used to seal the pistons in disc brake calipers.

steering knuckle A device that connects the front wheel to the suspension; pivots on the top and bottom, thus allowing the front wheels to turn.

ventilated rotor A type of brake rotor with passages between the rotor surfaces that are used to improve heat transfer to the atmosphere.

wheel studs Threaded fasteners that are pressed into the wheel hub flange and used to bolt the wheel onto the vehicle.

ASE-Type Questions

1. Tech A says that disc brakes operate on the principle of friction. Tech B says that disc brakes operate on the principle of regeneration. Who is correct?
   a. Tech A
   b. Tech B
   c. Both A and B
   d. Neither A nor B

2. Tech A says that some vehicles use fixed calipers. Tech B says that some vehicles use sliding/floating calipers. Who is correct?
   a. Tech A
   b. Tech B
   c. Both A and B
   d. Neither A nor B

3. Tech A says that disc brakes require higher application pressures than drum brakes. Tech B says that disc brakes are self-energizing. Who is correct?
   a. Tech A
   b. Tech B
   c. Both A and B
   d. Neither A nor B

4. Tech A says that fixed calipers use one or more pistons only on one side of the rotor. Tech B says that sliding/fixed calipers use one or more pistons on both sides of the rotor. Who is correct?
   a. Tech A
   b. Tech B
   c. Both A and B
   d. Neither A nor B

5. Tech A says that calipers use a round section O-ring to seal each piston. Tech B says that calipers use a square section O-ring to seal each piston. Who is correct?
   a. Tech A
   b. Tech B
   c. Both A and B
   d. Neither A nor B

6. Tech A says that pistons plated with chrome resist rust. Tech B says that pistons made of phenolic resin do not corrode and rust. Who is correct?
   a. Tech A
   b. Tech B
   c. Both A and B
   d. Neither A nor B

7. Tech A says that some vehicles are equipped with a spring-steel brake pad wear indicator that drags on the rotor when the lining thickness is low. Tech B says that some vehicles are equipped with an electric brake pad wear sensor that activates a warning on the dash. Who is correct?
   a. Tech A
   b. Tech B
   c. Both A and B
   d. Neither A nor B

8. Tech A says that rotors should be measured for thickness variation (parallelism). Tech B says that rotors should be measured for lateral runout. Who is correct?
   a. Tech A
   b. Tech B
   c. Both A and B
   d. Neither A nor B

9. Tech A says that rotors that are too thin cannot handle as much heat and will experience brake fade sooner. Tech B says that brake pedal pulsation is the result of air in the hydraulic system. Who is correct?
   a. Tech A
   b. Tech B
   c. Both A and B
   d. Neither A nor B

10. Tech A says that a micrometer is used to measure rotor thickness variation. Tech B says that a micrometer is used to measure rotor lateral runout. Who is correct?
    a. Tech A
    b. Tech B
    c. Both A and B
    d. Neither A nor B

CHAPTER 33

Drum Brake System

Knowledge Objectives

After reading this chapter, you will be able to:
1. List the components of the drum brake system. (pp 1102–1103)
2. Describe how the components of the drum brake system work together during the braking process. (pp 1103–1104)
3. Describe the principle of self-energization. (pp 1103–1104)
4. Define and describe servo action. (p 1104)
5. Describe the types of drum brake systems. (pp 1104–1105)
6. Describe the types of brake drums. (pp 1105–1106)
7. Describe the purpose of the backing plate and its components. (p 1106)
8. Describe the purpose of the wheel cylinder and its components. (pp 1106–1108)
9. Describe the types of wheel cylinders. (p 1108)
10. Describe the purpose of brake shoes and linings. (p 1108)
11. Describe the two processes of attaching lining to brake shoes. (p 1110)
12. Describe the common brake noises that indicate an issue with the drum brakes. (pp 1110–1111)
13. Describe the purpose of springs and hardware in the drum brake system. (p 1111)
14. Describe the types of springs used in drum brake systems. (p 1111)
15. Describe the types of self-adjusters used in drum brake systems. (pp 1111–1113)
16. Describe how the parking brake system operates in a drum brake system. (p 1113)
17. Describe the process of diagnosing issues with drum brakes. (p 1113)

Skills Objectives

After reading this chapter, you will be able to:
1. Remove, clean, inspect, and measure the brake drums. (pp 1114–1117)
2. Refinish a brake drum. (pp 1117–1119)
3. Disassemble and reassemble duo-servo brakes. (pp 1119–1122)
4. Disassemble and reassemble non-servo brakes. (pp 1122–1123)
5. Remove, inspect, and install wheel cylinders. (pp 1122–1124)
6. Pre-adjust brakes and install brake drums and wheel bearings. (pp 1123–1125)
7. Install wheel, torque lug nuts, and make final checks. (pp 1125–1126)

Introduction

Drum brakes get their name from the rotating drum-shaped component called a brake drum (or simply drum). The drums are bolted to the vehicle's axle hubs by the lug nuts. This means the wheels and drums rotate together. Friction lining on brake shoes is forced against the inside of the drums by hydraulic wheel cylinders, causing friction and absorbing the vehicle's kinetic energy. Since heat is created inside of the drums, the heat has to transfer through the drum material before it can be transferred to the atmosphere. Situations such as heavy loads or long downhill grades where the brakes are used heavily can lead to overheating of the lining, drums, or brake fluid, resulting in a loss of braking, called brake fade.

Most drum brakes require the removal of the drum to inspect the condition of the brake lining and inside drum surface. Drum brake design requires more parts and components, so service and repair can be a bit more complicated than for disc brakes. However, drum brakes are generally less expensive to manufacture and easier to adapt a parking brake to.

Drum Brake Systems

While many vehicles use disc brakes on all four wheels, drum brakes can be found on the rear wheels of vehicles with a combination of disc and drum brakes, and on all four wheels of older vehicles. Drum brakes can be designed to match the braking requirements of various vehicles. Heavier duty vehicles like pick-up trucks use larger diameter brake drums and shoes, as well as wider

brake shoes and drum surfaces. These factors allow the drum brakes to create, absorb, and transfer a greater amount of heat energy. The main components of the drum brake system are **FIGURE 33-1**:

- **Brake drum**: The brake drum fits over the brake linings and forms the braking surface for the brake linings. It is usually made from cast iron and machined so the inside surface rotates true.
- **Backing plate**: The backing plate is made from stamped steel and is bolted to the steering or suspension components. It supports the wheel cylinder(s), brake shoes, and hardware.
- **Wheel cylinder**: The wheel cylinder is attached to the backing plate. The wheel cylinder pistons

FIGURE 33-1 The main components of a drum brake system.

You are the Automotive Technician

You are working in San Francisco, CA, on your company's fleet vehicles, which are about 6 years old. Today you are performing a rear brake inspection on a light duty truck. The driver has indicated that the parking brake isn't able to completely hold the vehicle on some of the steepest hills he has to park on. You operate the parking brake and notice that it can be pushed all the way to the floor before it is completely tight. This means you will have to visually inspect the rear brake assemblies.

1. How is the parking brake similar to and different from the rear drum brakes?
2. What are the possible faults in the service brakes (drum brake style) that could cause the parking brake to be out of adjustment?
3. In what order should the drum brakes and parking brakes be adjusted?

push the brake shoes into contact with the brake drum to slow or stop the vehicle.

■ **Brake shoes**: The brake shoe consists of the steel shoe and the brake lining friction material. The brake shoes are held against the backing plate by hold-down springs and clips.

■ **Springs and clips**: Return springs retract the brake shoes when the brakes are released. Other springs work with the self-adjuster and with parking brake linkage operation.

■ **Automatic brake self-adjuster**: The automatic self-adjuster automatically adjusts the brakes to maintain a specified amount of running clearance between the shoes and drum. It operates in one of two ways—either when using the brakes while backing up or as part of applying the parking brake. It also makes periodic brake adjustment unnecessary.

■ **Parking brake mechanism**: The parking brake linkage mechanically operates the brake shoes (service brakes) to hold the vehicle stationary when the driver applies the parking brake.

Drum Brake Operation

Drum brakes were once common on all four wheels of a vehicle, but now they are usually found only on the rear wheels in disc–drum applications. In drum brake systems, when the brake pedal is depressed, a pushrod transfers the force to a hydraulic master cylinder. The master cylinder converts the brake pedal force into hydraulic pressure, which is then transmitted without loss via the brake lines and hoses to one or two wheel cylinders at each drum brake assembly. The pistons within each wheel cylinder are forced outward by the hydraulic pressure and apply force to the brake shoes, forcing them into each rotating drum **FIGURE 33-2**. Since the brake shoes are anchored to the backing plate, preventing them from rotating freely with the drum, the friction generated between the moving surfaces slows down the rotation of the drum and the wheel.

The drums are free to rotate with the wheels due to wheel bearings in the hub or on the axle. The hub can be part of the drum or a separate assembly that the drum slips over and is bolted to by the wheel and lug nuts. On most rear driving wheels, the drum slips over the axle flange and is held on by the wheel and lug nuts.

Each drum brake has two brake shoes with a friction material called a lining attached. These shoes expand against the inside surface of a brake drum and slow the wheel. The harder the linings are forced against the brake drum, the greater the braking force applied. They can be expanded mechanically or hydraulically. Drum brake systems need to be adjusted to allow for wear of the lining.

FIGURE 33-2 The pistons within each wheel cylinder are forced outward by the hydraulic pressure and apply force to the brake shoes, forcing them into each rotating drum.

> **TECHNICIAN TIP**
>
> Servicing the wheel bearings is a common part of a brake job if the vehicle has serviceable wheel bearings. If the vehicle uses non-serviceable bearings, the bearings should be checked during a brake job and replaced if they are worn out. See the Wheel Bearings chapter for more information on wheel bearings and service.

As the lining wears, the brake shoes must be pushed farther outward to contact the drum. This wearing causes only the top portion of the linings to contact the drum, reducing the surface area of the lining that can dissipate the created heat. Also, if they are not adjusted, the brake pedal reserve height will be too low to be safe.

Self-Energizing and Servo Action

Drum brakes are **self-energizing**. This means they can increase the force with which they are applied. When brake shoes come into contact with the moving drum, the friction tends to carry them in the direction the drum is rotating. Because the brake shoes are inside the drum and anchored at one end, this has a wedging effect on the brake shoe. This wedging effect assists the driver in applying the brakes, making it so the driver does not have to push so hard on the brake pedal. Brake shoes are designed in a leading or trailing manner. **Leading shoes** are installed so the direction they are applied is the same as the forward rotation of the drum. Leading shoes are self-energizing. **Trailing shoes** are installed so the direction they are applied is opposite of the forward rotation of the drum. Trailing shoes are not self-energizing. In fact, they tend to have reduced energization, meaning they are not nearly as efficient at developing braking force as leading shoes are.

<u>Servo action</u> as related to brakes means that one brake shoe, when activated, applies an increased activating force to the other brake shoe, in proportion to the initial activating force. This further enhances the self-energizing feature of some drum brakes. We will cover this topic in greater depth later in this chapter.

Types of Drum Brake Systems

There are three types of drum brake systems: twin leading shoe, leading/trailing shoe (also called single leading shoe), and duo-servo. Each type uses similar drum brake components but functions a bit differently. All three types are self-energizing in at least one direction. The first two types are non-servo brakes. The duo-servo drum brake system uses servo action in both directions. Each of the three types have pros and cons and designers use the type that best fits the vehicle application.

Twin Leading Shoe Drum Brake Systems

The <u>twin leading shoe drum brake system</u> is the least common type in modern automotive use. This system was once popular on front wheels because it is very efficient at braking in the forward direction. Since the vehicle travels much faster forward than it does in reverse, this matched the braking needs well. The large forward stopping power the twin leading shoe drum brake system generated also allowed the system to operate without a power brake booster.

Twin leading shoe drum brake systems use two single-piston wheel cylinders (also called single-acting wheel cylinders)—one near the top of the backing plate and one near the bottom. Each wheel cylinder activates one of the brake shoes. The brake shoes are anchored at the closed end of the opposite wheel cylinder. It is called a twin leading shoe drum brake system because both shoes are arranged in a leading shoe (self-energizing) configuration in the forward direction. This arrangement gives very good stopping power in the forward direction. When applied in the reverse direction, the braking force is much less, only about 30% as efficient. This type of drum brake system was usually accompanied by one of the other types of brakes on the rear wheels to be used as a parking brake. The twin leading shoe drum brake system is very well suited for motorcycles since they are driven mostly in the forward direction and rarely reverse.

Leading/Trailing Shoe Drum Brake Systems

The <u>leading/trailing shoe drum brake system</u> is very common on the rear wheels of front-wheel drive vehicles due to their equal braking forces in both the forward and reverse direction. This system uses a single wheel cylinder with two pistons (also called a double-acting wheel cylinder), usually mounted near the top of the backing plate **FIGURE 33-3**. Each piston operates one of the brake shoes. Each shoe is anchored at the bottom of the backing plate. This arrangement makes one shoe a leading shoe and the other a trailing shoe. In the forward direction, the front piston forces the front brake shoe into the drum, and it acts like a leading shoe. The rear piston pushes the rear brake shoe into contact with the drum, but it acts as a trailing shoe, so it does not create as much braking power.

When the brakes are applied when the car is reversing or facing uphill, the rear shoe becomes a leading shoe and the front shoe becomes a trailing shoe. The leading/trailing shoe drum brake system works equally well in both directions. It is also important to note that it does not provide maximum braking in either direction; it tends to produce a lesser but equal amount of force in both directions. This makes it ideal for the rear wheels of front-wheel drive vehicles since approximately 70–80% of the braking power needed under heavy braking occurs at the front wheels and only 20–30% at the rear wheels.

Duo-Servo Drum Brake Systems

<u>Duo-servo drum brake systems</u> get their name from using the servo action in both the forward and reverse direction. Like the leading/trailing system, the system uses a single wheel cylinder with two pistons (also called a double-acting wheel cylinder), usually mounted near the top of the backing plate **FIGURE 33-4**. The bottom of each brake shoe is not anchored to the backing plate but is connected by an adjustable, floating link. This configuration allows the bottom of the brake shoes to move in the direction of the drum. What keeps the shoes from just spinning around with the drum? There is an anchor pin

FIGURE 33-3 The leading/trailing shoe drum brake system.

FIGURE 33-4 A duo-servo drum brake system.

Labels in figure: Anchor · Wheel cylinder · Secondary shoe (toward rear of vehicle) · Primary shoe · Floating bottom link (star wheel)

at the top of the backing plate above the wheel cylinder that prevents each shoe from rotating past that point. The shoes can move away from the anchor pin, but they are stopped by it when they rotate toward it.

When the brakes are applied, the front piston overcomes the weaker front return spring tension to move the forward shoe into contact with the drum. When the shoe contacts the drum, the friction causes it to start to rotate with the drum. This puts a small force through the bottom connecting link and applies (servo action) the bottom of the rear shoe, pushing it into contact with the rotating drum. The top of that shoe is thus carried into the anchor pin at the top of the backing plate, causing both shoes to stop rotating. The brakes generate a small amount of force at this point.

As the driver applies more force to the brake pedal, the forward piston in the wheel cylinder pushes the front shoe harder into the rotating drum, which causes the front shoe to apply more force to the rear shoe. This forces the rear shoe harder into the drum as the anchor pin prevents it from rotating. Since hydraulic pressure is the same on both pistons in the wheel cylinder, the rear piston also tends to push the rear shoe outward into the drum, which helps apply it, although not in a completely complimentary direction.

Since the front shoe multiplies the force applying the rear shoe, the rear shoe does more of the braking work. If the linings were the same length front to rear, then the rear one would wear out much faster. This is why manufacturers put more lining on the rear shoe than on the front shoe. They might also use linings with different coefficients of friction for each of the shoes to get the desired braking load between the two shoes. It is important, therefore, to install the correct shoe in the correct position. Failure to do so will cause the brake linings to wear unevenly, as well as work improperly.

Brake Drums

Brake drums provide the rotating friction surface that the brake lining contacts. They are usually made from cast iron due to its ability to withstand high temperatures, absorb a lot of heat, and maintain its shape. To enhance the cooling of the brake drum, some manufacturers add cooling fins to the outside of the brake drum, while others make the brake drum out of aluminum **FIGURE 33-5**.

Brake drums are machined to a specific diameter from the manufacturer, which is called its standard diameter. Manufacturers specify the maximum allowable inside diameter a brake drum can be worn or machined to and usually stamp or cast that specification on the outside of the brake drum. This specification is commonly 0.060" (1.524 mm) over the standard diameter on many brake drums, but it can be as low as 0.030" (0.762 mm) over standard, or as high as 0.090" (2.286 mm) over standard on some passenger vehicles. Always check the manufacturer's specifications. Remember that taking 0.015" (0.381 mm) off of one side of the brake drum surface also removes 0.015" (0.381 mm) from the other side for a total of 0.030" (0.762 mm).

Brake drums that are heavily grooved or warped will likely need to be replaced. Even if they are not grooved, they need to be measured since they may have been refinished one or more times before, making them oversized. Never put an oversized brake drum back in service, because it does not have as much mass to absorb brake heat, and it also is not as strong as a drum that is within specifications.

Types of Brake Drums

Like rotors, brake drums can have an integrated hub called a hub-style drum or a separate hub called a hubless-style drum. Hubless drums are the most common in passenger

FIGURE 33-5 Brake drums. **A.** Without cooling fins. **B.** With cooling fins.

vehicles because of the high percentage of sealed wheel bearings being used. Since the wheel bearings in this case do not need to be packed with grease periodically, they do not need to be removed unless they wear out. Manufacturers design the brake drum to slip over the lug studs on the wheel flange and to be held on by the wheel and lug nuts. Hubless drums are less expensive to replace when they no longer meet the manufacturer's specifications.

Hub-style drums have a one-piece integrated hub/drum assembly. The wheel bearings are housed in the hub and are usually serviceable. If they are serviceable, then it is standard procedure to pack the wheel bearings with the specified grease and replace the grease seals during a brake job. More steps are required to remove hub-style drums from the vehicle than hubless drums, and they are more expensive to replace.

FIGURE 33-6 The backing plate.

Backing Plate

All of the brake unit components, except the brake drum, are mounted on a backing plate bolted to the vehicle axle housing or suspension. The backing plate is usually pressed into a very specific configuration from heavy-gauge steel **FIGURE 33-6**. It has a raised edge on its outer surface that fits into a groove or recess in the brake drum and helps keep out dust, dirt, and water spray. It also has holes stamped in it for the wheel cylinder, hold-down pins and the parking brake cable to pass through. Some vehicles have one or two openings in the backing plate to allow for manual adjustment of the brake shoes. These holes are plugged with rubber grommets that need to be reinstalled after adjusting the brakes.

Anchor Pins and Pad Surfaces for Shoes

One of the most important components of the backing plate is the **anchor pin** (or anchor block). The anchor pin must be able to take all of the braking force when the brakes are applied, so it must be strong and firmly attached to the backing plate **FIGURE 33-7**. The anchor pin may also hold the shoe guide, return springs, and self-adjuster cable on duo-servo–style brakes.

The inside surface of the backing plate has flat or raised brake shoe contact pads stamped into it. The brake shoes are held against the brake shoe contact pads by spring pressure and are free to move side to side. Over time, the brake shoes can wear a groove in the surface of the contact pad. During brake shoe replacement, these contact pads need to be cleaned and inspected. If there is no wear, then a very light coat of white lithium grease can be applied to the contact pads to lessen any wear during the life of the new brake shoes. If there is light wear, this can be cleaned up with a file or small handheld grinder.

FIGURE 33-7 Two style of anchor pins mount on backing plates.

If the grooves are too deep, the backing plate will need to be replaced.

Wheel Cylinders

The wheel cylinder is located inside the brake drum and is either bolted or firmly clipped to the backing plate **FIGURE 33-8**. It converts hydraulic pressure from the master cylinder into mechanical force that pushes the brake linings against the inside of the brake drum.

Wheel cylinders usually contain one cylinder housing, one or two pistons, a lip seal for each piston, a spring and expander set, a dust boot for each open end of the cylinder, a pushrod for each piston, and a bleeder screw. Wheel cylinder housings are usually made of cast iron or aluminum alloy, and they operate under extreme pressures and temperatures.

The **cylinder bore**, or inside diameter of the cylinder, is created by drawing a properly sized ball bearing through the bore **FIGURE 33-9**. This technique gives the surface a

FIGURE 33-8 The wheel cylinder mounted on the backing plate.

FIGURE 33-9 Wheel cylinder components.

hard, smooth finish. It is also why most manufacturers recommend replacing, rather than honing, the wheel cylinder if it has pits or corrosion. Cylinder bores on aluminum wheel cylinders are usually anodized to help resist corrosion. They also should not be honed, as this would remove the protective finish. Some cylinder bores are sleeved with stainless steel to be longer wearing and more resistant to corrosion.

No matter the type of material used, the cylinder and pistons are manufactured to a precise diameter. This provides the proper amount of clearance between them. It also maintains the proper tension of the piston seal to the cylinder bore, which helps hold pressure in and the air out. These are other reasons why honing the cylinder bore is frowned upon.

Contamination, particularly from water, lowers the boiling point of the brake fluid (which is hygroscopic) and may cause pitting and rusting of the inner surface of the wheel cylinder. Such damage can result in leakage of brake fluid from the cylinder or stuck pistons. The sealing surface in a wheel cylinder is the inside surface of the cylinder bore. This surface must be clean, smooth, and free of pitting. The wheel cylinder cups the seal against the surface of the cylinder bore and prevents the brake fluid from leaking out of the cylinder. Hydraulic pressure forces the lip of the seal into the surface of the cylinder bore even harder when the brakes are applied. The sealing cups are made of materials that are compatible with the type of brake fluid specified for the particular vehicle. Using the wrong seal compound in a brake system or mixing the wrong brake fluid in the brake system can cause seal damage and brake failure. Always verify that the brake fluid and components are compatible with each other.

Wheel cylinder pistons are usually made of anodized aluminum. They have a built-in mating surface for the pushrods to engage. Most pistons use a flat surface that supports the piston seal, but some pistons use a seal that fits within a machined groove at its inner end. Piston-to-cylinder clearance is critical for proper operation, so verify that the cylinder and piston are not worn beyond the specified clearance.

Wheel cylinders may be fitted with a spreader and a light expansion spring to keep the lips of the seal in contact with the cylinder bore during times of low pressure, such as during retraction and while at rest. This helps keep air from being drawn into the cylinder. A flexible dust boot fits over the open ends of the cylinder and allows for piston movement. At the same time, it helps keep brake dust and moisture away from the inside of the cylinder and piston.

Wheel cylinders are fitted with a bleeder screw to allow for bleeding of air and old brake fluid from the hydraulic brake system. The bleeder screw is a hollow screw. It has a taper on the end that mates with a matching tapered seat in the wheel cylinder. These tapered seats seal when the bleeder screw is closed. The bleeder screw has been cross-drilled into the center hole just above the taper. This way, when the bleeder screw is loosened slightly, the tapered seat opens and brake fluid enters the cross-drilled passage into the center hole and flows out the end of the bleeder screw. Tightening the bleeder screw closes off the tapered seat and holds pressure in the wheel cylinder. Bleeder screws have a small rubber dust cap that fits over the exposed end of the screw to keep water, dirt,

> ### ► TECHNICIAN TIP
>
> During a brake inspection, it is good practice to carefully peel back the dust boot from the wheel cylinder and see if there is any brake fluid behind the dust boot. If there is, the wheel cylinder is starting to leak and should be replaced.

and debris from entering the center hole and plugging it up or rusting it in place. Always remember to replace these caps when you finish bleeding the drum brakes.

Types of Wheel Cylinders

Wheel cylinders come in different configurations. They are either single acting or dual acting. Single-acting cylinders use a single piston, meaning that the force is generated in one direction only. Dual-acting cylinders use two pistons opposite of each other, meaning that the force acts in two different directions **FIGURE 33-10**. Most modern vehicles use double-acting wheel cylinders because they are simpler to design, install, and bleed. Dual-acting wheel cylinders use a common cylinder with a piston and lip seal in each end. There is usually a coil spring with expanders on each end, positioned between the lip seals. The expander helps to hold the seal lips against the cylinder bore when there is little or no hydraulic pressure.

Single-acting wheel cylinders are used on some non-servo drum brakes. Each wheel cylinder only has one piston, so the cylinder bore is closed off at the opposite end. There are two of these cylinders on each wheel assembly, one for each brake shoe. The wheel cylinder is very similar to the double-acting cylinder in that it is made of the same materials and has an aluminum piston, a lip seal, a spring and expander, a dust boot, a pushrod, and a bleeder screw.

FIGURE 33-10 Dual-acting wheel cylinder.

▶ TECHNICIAN TIP

One way to help identify if a problem is coming from the front or rear brakes is to test-drive the vehicle in a safe place at a relatively low speed and lightly apply the parking brake. If the condition is still present, the problem is with the rear brakes, since the parking brakes are usually on the rear wheels. If the condition is not present, the problem is likely with the front brakes.

▶ Brake Shoes and Linings

The drum brake system uses metal brake shoes that have holes, slots, and tabs for springs and hardware to attach to. The brake shoes also have friction material called linings attached to them. Linings can be riveted but are more often bonded to the brake shoes.

Brake Lining Materials

The composition of the lining material affects brake operation. Materials that provide good braking with low pedal pressures tend to lose efficiency when they get hot **FIGURE 33-11**. This means the stopping distance will be increased. They also tend to wear out more quickly. Materials that maintain a stable friction coefficient over a wide temperature range generally require higher pedal pressures to provide efficient braking. They also tend to put added wear on the brake drum friction surface, reducing its useful life. Drum brakes are usually designed so that the condition of the lining can only be checked once the drum has been removed.

Brake lining selection requires knowledge of the customer expectations and driving habits. For example, you will need to choose a different lining material for a vehicle that regularly carries heavy loads versus one that is road raced on a track on the weekends. Selecting lining that does not match the driver's needs will result in a lack of customer satisfaction and vehicle repair returns.

Safety

Brake friction materials were historically made from asbestos compounds because of the excellent heat resistance of that material. Asbestos compounds are now known to be toxic and are generally banned. Do not assume that a brake shoe does not contain asbestos, as it is still found in some applications. Brakes are now manufactured from a variety of different materials that may be non-asbestos organic (NAO), low-metallic NAO, semimetallic, and ceramic.

FIGURE 33-11 Brake lining coefficient of friction.

As the heat in brake pads and linings builds up, the coefficient of friction capability of the material—and consequently its stopping power—is reduced. This reduction is called brake fade. Minimizing or overcoming brake fade is a major factor in the design of brakes and the development of brake friction materials.

Primary and Secondary Brake Shoes

The terms primary and secondary refer to the brake shoes in a duo-servo brake system. The primary shoe goes toward the front of the vehicle, and the secondary shoe goes toward the rear of the vehicle FIGURE 33-12.

FIGURE 33-12 Primary and secondary brake shoes.

New technicians tend to make a couple of rookie mistakes when it comes to duo-servo brake installation. The first relates to the way the new brake shoes are packaged in their box. The manufacturer generally puts the brake shoes in the box in like pairs. What this means is that both primary shoes are in the bottom of the box and both secondary shoes are in the top of the box (or vise versa). When students remove the top two shoes to install them, and compare them to each other, they find that the shoes match (they shouldn't if they are for a duo-servo system). The students assume the matching shoes belong on the same side of the vehicle and install them accordingly FIGURE 33-13. They then do the same with the other two brake shoes (which also match each other) on the other side of the vehicle. So both primary shoes are now installed on one side of the vehicle, and both secondary shoes are installed on the other side.

The second mistake involves installing the shoes in the wrong position on the backing plate. When students install the brake shoes on the first assembly, they may look carefully at the assembly and determine (correctly) that the primary shoe goes on the forward side of the backing plate, which for the driver's side is the left side of the backing plate. They then determine that the secondary shoe goes on the right side of the backing plate. When they move to the passenger side of the vehicle, they believe they have already determined that the primary shoe goes on the left side of the backing plate just like the other side. Unfortunately, that is the *rear* side of the backing plate and the secondary shoe should be installed in that position. So, the vehicle has the brake shoes installed correctly on one side but incorrectly on the other side FIGURE 33-14. Watch for these mistakes as you perform brake inspections and service.

FIGURE 33-13 A common installation error: The primary shoes are on one side of the vehicle, and the secondary shoes are on the other.

FIGURE 33-14 Another common installation error: the primary and secondary shoes are swapped from side to side.

In most cases, the primary and secondary metal shoes are the same, but the linings installed on the brake shoes are of different length. Since the primary shoe applies the secondary shoe, the secondary shoe is responsible for doing most of the braking work. Therefore, the primary shoe lining is shorter in length, and the secondary shoe lining is longer. The primary lining may also have a different coefficient of friction than the secondary lining. New shoes are normally labeled with "pri" (for primary) or "sec" (for secondary) on the edge of the lining. Verify that you are installing the lining in the proper position.

Riveted and Bonded Friction Materials

Lining on brake shoes is much thinner than on disc brake pads due to the much greater surface area of the brake shoe lining. Drum brake shoes consist of friction material or lining bonded or riveted onto a steel shoe **FIGURE 33-15**. Bonded brake linings are more common on light-duty vehicles since they are less expensive to build. Also, lighter vehicles do not subject the brake linings to as much heat, so the bonding agent is not as likely to fail as it would on heavier vehicles. Bonded linings are glued under high pressure and temperature to ensure that the bonding is as strong as possible.

Riveted linings are used on heavier duty or high-performance vehicles. Metal rivets, usually made of copper or aluminum, provide a mechanical connection to hold the brake lining to the shoe. This means rivets are less susceptible to failure under high temperatures. However, since the rivets actually pinch some of the brake lining between the rivet head and the metal shoe, the brake linings cannot wear down as much before the rivets contact the drum. Riveted linings must be changed sooner than bonded linings to prevent the rivet heads

from contacting the drum and wearing a groove in the friction surface.

Coefficient of Friction Edge Coding

The Society of Automotive Engineers has adopted codes to rate brake lining materials' coefficient of friction. The rating is written on the edge of the friction linings and is called the edge code. The Disc Brake System chapter discusses these ratings in detail.

Drum Brake Noises

Drum brakes are not prone to squealing like disc brakes are, but that does not mean they never make noise. One of the most common sounds that drum brakes make is a groaning noise. It can be caused by excessive brake dust in the drum that causes the brakes shoes to skip and catch, which sounds like a groan. Removing the drum and cleaning the excess brake dust or replacing the brake shoes due to wear usually resolves this issue **FIGURE 33-16**.

Another noise that drum brakes can make is a grinding noise. If the friction lining wears all the way down to the metal shoe, the shoe and drum can make a metal-on-metal grinding noise. This noise can only be resolved by replacing the brake shoes and refinishing or replacing the drum. Keeping drum brakes from making unwanted noises is pretty simple—keep them clean and inspect the brake lining thickness periodically, replacing it when it gets to the specified minimum thickness.

The last common noise that drum brakes can make is a clicking noise. This can be caused by two situations. First, it could be that the brake shoes have worn grooves in the contact pads on the backing plate and are causing the clicking noise when the shoe moves into and out of the groove. Second, it could be that the brake drum's

FIGURE 33-15 The drum brake shoe and lining.

FIGURE 33-16 Brake dust.

surface finish cut is too rough and acts like the threads on a screw. When the lining contacts the surface of the drum, the lining follows the threaded finish of the drum and the linings thread themselves away from the backing plate. When the brakes are released, the hold-down springs snap the brake shoes back against the backing plate.

Springs and Hardware

Drum brakes use a variety of springs and hardware to control the action of the brake shoes **FIGURE 33-17**. Each type of brake uses its own arrangement of these components. Pay close attention to how they are installed before removing them. It is good practice to only disassemble and reassemble the brake components on one side of the vehicle at a time. That way you can refer to the other side if you forget how something came apart. Generally speaking, there are several categories of springs used in drum brakes: return, hold-down, and specialty.

Return Springs

<u>Return springs</u> retract the brake shoes when the driver releases the brake pedal. Each return spring either connects to one brake shoe and the backing plate anchor pin or directly to the other brake shoe. In both cases, they pull the brake shoes back into their rest position. Return springs can integrate one or more coil springs in the length of the spring or it can be a large U-shaped spring. Return springs are generally quite stiff, making them a challenge to install. Brake pliers can make installation easier. Even though return springs may look the same front to rear within a particular brake assembly, be aware that they can have different amounts of strength. On duo-servo brakes, the primary return spring is weaker than

the secondary return spring, so the primary shoe can be applied before the secondary shoe.

The coils on return springs should be tightly wound together, meaning that the coils should be touching each other, with no space between them. Any space indicates that the return spring has been stretched and needs to be replaced. Return springs are normally replaced in sets. If one spring needs to be replaced, they all should be replaced to avoid mismatched components. Also, due to the high temperatures and the large number of apply and return cycles that drum brake springs must endure, some manufacturers and shops recommend replacing the return springs and hardware during every brake job.

Hold-Down Springs

<u>Hold-down springs</u> do just what their name suggests—they hold the brake shoes against the backing plate. They can be coil springs in combination with a spring retainer and a pin, sometimes referred to as a brake nail, that extends through the backing plate, brake shoe, and center of the spring; or they can be coil springs lying on their side and connected to the pin beside them. They can also use U-shaped spring steel clips in combination with a pin that extends through the backing plate and brake shoe.

Specialty Springs

<u>Specialty springs</u> are used to return links and levers on the parking brake system or the self-adjuster mechanism. Specialty springs can be of all different shapes and sizes and can be used to push or pull components into proper position. Be sure to install each specialty spring in the correct position so that each of the brake systems works as intended. If in doubt, check the other wheel brake unit or the service information to see how it is assembled.

Self-Adjusters

Brake shoe lining wears over time and increases the clearance between the brake lining and drum. This increased clearance causes the wheel cylinder pistons to travel farther to move the brake shoes out to contact the surface of the drums. It also causes the brake pedal to travel farther before activating the brakes, reducing the reserve pedal height, which leaves the driver vulnerable if a hydraulic failure occurs. To safeguard against these dangers, all manufacturers have been required since 1968 to incorporate a self-adjusting mechanism into their drum brake systems that is capable of maintaining proper shoe-to-drum clearance.

FIGURE 33-17 Examples of brake springs and hardware.

Types of Self-Adjusters

The first type of self-adjuster is used on most duo-servo brakes. It has an adjustable threaded star wheel assembly holding the bottoms of the brake shoes apart. The link has three main parts: the threaded barrel, the nonthreaded barrel (and possible thrust washer), and the star wheel, which is threaded on one end and smooth on the other **FIGURE 33-18**. Both barrels have slots that fit to tabs on the brake shoes, preventing them from turning. The star wheel's threaded end screws into the threaded barrel. The smooth end of the star wheel fits into the nonthreaded barrel **FIGURE 33-19**. As the star wheel is turned, the thread causes the self-adjuster to lengthen. This takes up excess brake shoe clearance, as needed. The question is what turns the star wheel?

A movable self-adjuster link is held against the star wheel. The link is moved up and down by the action of applying the brakes while the vehicle is backing up. If the link moves far enough, it will catch another tooth of the

FIGURE 33-18 A self-adjuster on a duo-servo–style brake.

FIGURE 33-19 A star wheel assembly.

star wheel and the spring action will turn the star wheel one tooth, adjusting the brakes shoes outward just a bit. This process continues until the brake shoe clearance is taken up enough so that the self-adjuster link cannot move far enough to catch another tooth on the star wheel. As the brake linings wear, the clearance increases and the movement of the link increases to the point that it catches another tooth. This continues for the life of the brake lining.

The self-adjuster link is moved by a cable or rod, which is connected to the anchor pin at the top of the backing plate. The movement of the secondary brake shoe, when the brakes are applied while backing up, causes the self-adjuster link to be pulled by the cable or rod. The position of the link and cable or rod is critical to the operation of the self-adjuster assembly. The link should be level with the star wheel and close to its centerline. Also, the star wheel assembly is side specific, meaning that the threads on each star wheel are opposite of each other, so they turn in opposite directions.

A similar style of self-adjuster works off of the parking brake assembly. It is usually used on non-servo brakes. The star wheel linkage is threaded and is usually mounted between the brake shoes just below the wheel cylinder. There is a pivoting self-adjuster link attached to one brake shoe, and a spring pulls the lever down. As the parking brake is applied, the parking brake lever pushes the star wheel linkage toward the other shoe. The end of the linkage pivots the self-adjuster link upward against spring pressure. If it travels far enough, it will catch the next tooth. As the parking brake is released, the spring pulls the self-adjuster link down and rotates the star wheel one tooth. This expands the star wheel linkage and reduces the brake shoe clearance slightly. This process continues until the excess clearance of the brake shoe to the drum is taken up. The self-adjuster link will then be unable to catch another tooth until the clearance opens a bit more as the brake linings continue to wear.

Some manufacturers use a ratcheting-style self-adjuster. This type uses two toothed pieces held in contact with each other by spring pressure. They can slide over each other in one direction, but hold in the other direction. The two pieces allow excessive shoe-to-drum clearance to be taken up when the brake pedal is applied and then prevent the shoes from fully returning to their rest position when the brakes are released. As the service brakes are applied, the shoes move apart. If they travel far enough, the toothed pieces slide over each other until the shoes contact the drum. When the brakes are released, the components allow a small amount of inward brake shoe movement to occur, which creates the proper shoe-to-drum clearance. This style of self-adjuster generally can be adjusted in one brake pedal application, reducing the amount of time spent pre-adjusting the brake shoes when they are being replaced.

Parking Brake Systems

Drum parking brake systems mechanically apply the regular service brake shoes. Since drum brakes are self-energizing, it is easier to generate the force needed to apply them mechanically than it is to apply disc brakes. The parking brake cable attaches to the bottom of the parking brake actuating lever in the drum brake assembly. The other end of the lever is attached to the top end of one of the brake shoes with a pin or tang. A strut rod runs from near the top of the actuating lever to the other brake shoe **FIGURE 33-20**. When the cable is pulled, the lever pivots on the strut rod, pushing the top of the brake shoe rearward and the strut rod forward. Since the strut rod is connected to the other shoe, pulling the lever forces the brake shoes apart and into firm contact with the drum, holding the vehicle stationary. Releasing the cable allows the brake retracting springs to pull the brake shoes away from the drums.

FIGURE 33-20 A parking brake assembly for a drum brake.

Diagnosis
Diagnosing Drum Brakes

To diagnose issues with the drum brakes, verify the customer concern by operating the vehicle if it is safe to do so. Depending on the concern, it may be as simple as stepping on the brake pedal without moving the vehicle and feeling the brake pedal sink to the floor, or it could require a more detailed test-drive to observe the fault the customer is describing. Never test-drive the vehicle if the brake pedal goes to the floor. Depending on the condition, it is good practice to research any technical service bulletins (TSBs) for the particular situation. If no related TSBs are found, research the service information to familiarize yourself with the drum brake system and the manufacturer's diagnostic procedure for the condition. Perform any diagnostic tests to identify the cause of the condition. Diagnosis could involve a visual inspection or any other prescribed tests. It could also involve a detailed testing sequence. Once you have identified the root cause of the fault, determine the action that will rectify the fault.

Caring for the Customer

It is common to have more than one condition present in a brake system when you diagnose it, such as worn brake shoes, a leaky wheel cylinder, and a leaky seal in the master cylinder. It is good practice to perform a thorough inspection of the brake system whenever one condition is present to determine if any others are present at the same time. This prevents you from having to go back to the customer to get permission to perform the additional work after he or she has agreed to the initial repair, giving the customer cause to doubt your competence or integrity.

Maintenance and Repair

Tools

The tools used to diagnose and repair drum brake systems include **FIGURE 33-21**:

- Brake wash station—Used to clean drum and disc brake dust.

- **Brake spring pliers**—Used to remove and install return springs.

- **Hold-down spring tool**—Used to remove and install hold-down springs.

- **Drum brake micrometer**—Used to measure inside brake drum diameter.

- **Brake shoe adjustment gauge**—Used to pre-adjust brake shoes before installing the drum.

- **Brake spoon**—Used to adjust brake shoes when the drum is installed.

- **Wheel cylinder piston clamp**—Used to hold the pistons in the wheel cylinder while the brake shoes are removed.

- Off-car brake lathe—Used to machine drums and rotors that are off the vehicle.

- Parking brake cable pliers—Used to install parking brake cables on the parking brake lever.

- **Parking brake cable removal tool**—Used to remove the parking brake cable from the backing plate.

Removing, Cleaning, Inspecting, and Measuring Brake Drums

Brake drums need to be removed for a variety of reasons, such as inspecting the thickness of the brake linings, checking for wheel cylinder leaks, and packing wheel bearings. While removed, the brake drums should be inspected visually for any damage. They should also be measured with a drum micrometer to verify that they are smaller than the specified maximum diameter. If not, they need to be replaced.

Before removing the brake drum, you need to determine if it is a hub style, or hubless (slip-off) style. Most light-duty vehicles now use hubless drums. You can usually tell which style of brake drum you are working on by looking at the holes for the lug studs. If there is clearance between the stud and drum, it is likely a hubless brake drum. You can also look at the

clearance between the center hole of the brake drum and the hub. A hubless brake drum will have a parting line at the centering hole. A hub-style brake drum will appear to be one solid piece.

Because of the tight clearances between the hub and brake drum on a slip-off style brake drum, the surfaces can rust together. You may have to use a medium or large ball-peen hammer to hammer on the drum between the lug studs. Make sure you do not hit the lug studs because you will damage them. Some drums can be rusted on very solidly. If you are having difficulty breaking the drum loose, seek the assistance of your supervisor. A torch may be needed to heat up the drum to break the rust bond.

To remove, clean, inspect, and measure brake drums and determine any further actions, follow the steps in **SKILL DRILL 33-1**:

1. To perform this procedure on a hubless-style drum, first make matching marks on the drum and hub for reinstallation in the correct position. A permanent marker, crayon, or center punch can be used.

   - If there are screws or speed nuts holding the drum to the hub, remove them following the specified procedure. The speed nuts can be discarded and are not needed upon reassembly. The screws will be reused.

   - Remove the drum from the hub. **(Photo 1)**

2. To perform this procedure on a hub-style drum, remove the wheel bearing locking mechanism (cotter pin, lock nut, or peened washer).

   - Remove the wheel bearing adjusting nut, thrust washer, and outer bearing.

   - If the rear bearing needs to be removed for service or replacement of the drum, use the following procedure to remove the inner bearing and grease seal. **(Photo 2)**

   - Reinstall the adjusting nut onto the spindle about five turns.

   - Grasp the drum/hub assembly on the top and bottom and push it toward the center of the vehicle. Hold slight downward pressure as you firmly pull the drum/hub assembly toward yourself. This should cause the adjusting nut to catch the wheel bearing and pull it and the seal out of the rear of the hub. The grease seal will need to be replaced with a new one.

3. Once the drum is removed, clean, inspect, and measure it.

FIGURE 33-21 Drum brake tools. **A.** Brake wash station. **B.** Brake spring pliers. **C.** Hold-down spring tool. **D.** Drum brake micrometer. **E.** Brake shoe adjustment gauge. **F.** Brake spoon. **G.** Wheel cylinder piston clamp. **H.** Off-car brake lathe. **I.** Parking brake cable pliers. **J.** Parking brake cable removal tool.

4 Clean the drum with approved asbestos removal equipment. Refer to the equipment manufacturer's operation manual and follow all directions fully.

5 Inspect the drum for hard spots/hot spots, scoring, cracks, and damage. **(Photo 3)**

6 Measure the drum diameter at the deepest groove or most worn part of the drum and compare to specifications. If it is over the size limit, it will need to be replaced. If it needs to be machined and is below the maximum diameter, check to see how badly it is scored.

7 Find the smallest diameter of the drum and write down the reading.

8 Find the largest diameter of the drum and write down that reading.

9 Calculate the difference between the two readings, which is the out-of-round measurement, and compare it to specifications.

10 Determine any necessary actions. **(Photo 4)**

SKILL DRILL 33-1   Removing, Cleaning, Inspecting, and Measuring Brake Drums

1 To remove a hubless-style drum, first make matching marks on the drum and hub for reinstallation in the correct position.
- If there are screws or speed nuts holding the drum to the hub, remove them following the specified procedure. The speed nuts can be discarded and are not needed upon reassembly. The screws will be reused.
- Remove the drum from the hub.

2 To remove a hub-style drum, first remove the wheel bearing locking mechanism (cotter pin, lock nut, or peened washer).
- Remove the wheel bearing adjusting nut, thrust washer, and outer bearing.
- If the rear bearing needs to be removed for service, or replacement of the drum, remove the inner bearing and grease seal.

3 Reinstall the adjusting nut onto the spindle about five turns. Grasp the drum/hub assembly on the top and bottom and push it toward the center of the vehicle. Hold slight downward pressure as you firmly pull the drum/hub assembly toward yourself. This should cause the adjusting nut to catch the wheel bearing and pull it and the seal out of the rear of the hub. The grease seal will need to be replaced with a new one. Once the drum is removed, clean, inspect, and measure it. Clean the drum with approved asbestos removal equipment. Inspect the drum for hard spots/ hot spots, scoring, cracks, and damage.

SKILL DRILL | 33-1 | Removing, Cleaning, Inspecting, and Measuring Brake Drums, continued

4. Measure the drum diameter at the deepest groove or most worn part of the drum and compare to specifications. If it is over the size limit, it will need to be replaced. If it needs to be machined and is below the maximum diameter, check to see how badly it is scored. Find the smallest diameter of the drum and write down the reading. Find the largest diameter of the drum and write down that reading. Calculate the difference between the two readings, which is the out-of-round measurement, and compare it to specifications. Determine any necessary actions.

TECHNICIAN TIP

Once the brake drum is loose from the hub, it can sometimes be difficult to remove it from over the shoes due to wear on the drum friction surface. The wear leaves a lip on the outer edge of the brake drum that the brake shoes hit when the brake drum is being pulled off. This condition prevents the brake drum from being removed. If it occurs, you will need to manually back off the self-adjuster with a brake spoon so that the brake shoes are not expanded as far. Once the star wheel is backed off, the lip of the brake drum should slide over the brake shoes and you can clean, inspect, and measure it. Just remember that you will have to hold the self-adjuster link away from the star wheel so that the star wheel can be backed off.

Refinishing Brake Drums

Brake drums need to be refinished when they have excessive grooving or are out-of-round. They are refinished using a brake lathe. A **brake lathe** refinishes the drum friction surface by removing metal and making it perfectly round with the proper finish. If the grooving or surface defects are too great, the drum may require the removal of too much metal to satisfactorily refinish the surface. The drum diameter should always be remeasured once the refinishing is complete to ensure that it is under the manufacturer's maximum diameter. Never put a brake drum that is over the maximum size back in service, because it does not have the ability to absorb as much heat.

Hub-style and hubless-style drums are mounted on the brake lathe differently. Most hub-style drums use the bearing races to drive and center the drum on the lathe spindle. Bearing adapters of the proper size need to be selected and used. The spindle nut then clamps the drum onto the spindle through these bearing adapters and races.

Hubless drums can be mounted on the composite rotor adapter or centered using a spring-loaded centering cone to align the drum's centering hole with the spindle. Clam shell clamps are then used on each side of the drum to clamp it to the lathe spindle.

To refinish a brake drum and measure final drum diameter, follow **SKILL DRILL 33-2**:

1 Research the brake lathe manufacturer's procedure for properly refinishing the drum. Follow those guidelines.

2 Clean any nicks, burrs, or debris from the mounting surfaces of the drum including the centering hole, if used. Since the drum is clamped to the lathe spindle, all of the surfaces on the drum that contact the lathe components must be free of nicks, burrs,

SKILL DRILL   33-2   Refinishing Brake Drums

1 Research the brake lathe manufacturer's procedure for properly refinishing the drum. Clean any nicks, burrs, or debris from the mounting surfaces of the drum. Mount the drum on the brake lathe. Check to see that the drum is running true on the lathe.

2 Install the anti-chatter band on the drum.

3 Set the position of the cutting tool so that the brake drum is close to the brake lathe when the cutting bit is in the far corner of the drum. Make sure the cutting bits will not contact the face of the drum, and move the cutting head about 0.5" (12.7 mm) in from the outside of the drum. Turn on the brake lathe and set the depth of the cutting tool so it just touches the surface of the drum. Slowly remove the ridge.

4 Run the drum all the way in so the cutting bit is in the inner corner of the drum.

5 Set the cutting bit to the proper depth and lock it in place. Engage the automatic spindle feed and set it to the proper speed (if equipped), lock it in place, and watch for proper machining action. Repeat this step until the worn surface areas have been removed all the way around the surface of the drum. If the brake lathe is not a single-cut machine, perform a finish cut on the drum.

6 Move the drum well away from the cutting bit and use sandpaper to give the drum surface a non-directional finish. Remeasure the drum diameter and discard if above specifications.

and rust and cleaned prior to mounting the drum on the lathe. This is especially true of a hubless-style drum.

3. Mount the drum on the brake lathe. Visually check to see that the drum is running true on the lathe and is not wobbling. If it wobbles, turn off the lathe, dismount the drum, and recheck for burrs, debris, or any other condition that causes it to wobble. **(Photo 1)**

4. Install the anti-chatter band on the drum. It will prevent the drum from vibrating during the machining process, which would create a rough finish and dull the cutting bit. **(Photo 2)**

5. Set the position of the cutting tool so that the brake drum is close to the brake lathe when the cutting bit is in the far corner of the drum. This will allow you to cut the full width of the drum's surface and minimize vibration.

6. Make sure the cutting bits will not contact the face of the drum, and move the cutting head about 0.5" (12.7 mm) in from the outside of the drum.

7. Turn on the brake lathe and set the depth of the cutting tool so it just touches the surface of the drum. This gets it ready for machining the ridge on the outside edge of the braking surface.

8. Rotate the brake lathe's handwheel so that the drum moves outward and the cutting bit contacts the ridge. Keep turning slowly to remove the ridge. **(Photo 3)**

9. Once the ridge is removed, run the drum all the way in so the cutting bit is in the inner corner of the drum. **(Photo 4)**

10. Set the cutting bit to the proper depth for machining the surface of the drum and lock it in place.

11. Engage the automatic spindle feed and set it to the proper speed, lock it in place, and watch for proper machining action. Some single-cut machines only have one speed.

12. If necessary, repeat this step until the worn surface areas have been removed all the way around the surface of the drum.

13. If the brake lathe is not a single-cut machine, perform a finish cut on the drum. This cut is usually done on a slower spindle feed speed. **(Photo 5)**

14. Move the drum well away from the cutting bit and use sandpaper to give the drum surface a non-directional finish.

15. Remeasure the drum diameter to determine if the drum is above the maximum-diameter specifications; if so, discard the drum. **(Photo 6)**

Applied   Science

AS-37: Vibrations/Waves: The technician can demonstrate an understanding of the types and causes of vibrations caused by out-of-balance or excessively worn systems.

Sound is very important in diagnosing problems in a motor vehicle. Sound is a series of waves that travel through a gas, liquid, or solid, many of which can be heard by the human ear. For example, the solid rumble strips on the sides of the highway make a continuous noise or vibration when driven over by a motor vehicle.

Sound can help you to diagnose a worn wheel bearing that needs replacing. As a wheel bearing becomes worn, the case hardening on the bearing race begins to wear away due to constant friction between the bearing race and the bearing rollers. As the case hardening starts to wear, the bearing race develops low spots in the race. As the flat bearing rollers start to roll over the high and low spots in the bearing race, a noise will occur.

To diagnose the noise of a worn bearing in a motor vehicle, you can hoist the vehicle, spin the wheel, and listen for a noise. Or you can test-drive the vehicle and gently turn the steering wheel from side to side. As the vehicle moves from side to side, more weight is placed on each side of the bearing due to centrifugal force. You will hear a louder noise as you turn away from the side with the faulty bearing.

Removing, Cleaning, and Inspecting Brake Shoes and Hardware

Drum brakes need to be disassembled for a variety of reasons such as when the brake lining has worn beyond specifications, the wheel cylinders are faulty, the self-adjuster is stuck or damaged, or the axle seal has failed and leaked gear oil or wheel bearing grease onto the brake lining. Drum brakes are generally more complicated to change than disc brake pads, so care needs to be taken when working on them. There is usually a combination of springs, links, levers, guides, and retainers. It is easy to install these items incorrectly. It is good practice to carefully examine each brake assembly before disassembling to verify that it was assembled correctly previously.

Brake shoes and springs are always replaced in axle sets. If one rear brake assembly has linings contaminated with grease from a failed axle seal, the lining on both wheel brake units will need to be replaced. The same goes with springs. The other parts are left to the discretion of the technician and any shop policies.

Regarding star wheel assemblies, there is some controversy as to whether the threads should be lubricated. The argument on one side is that if you do not lubricate the threads, then they will be likely to rust and freeze up. The other side argues that any lubricant on the threads will attract brake dust and gum up the threads. There is some truth to both arguments. CDX would suggest using

a light coating of lubricant on the threads in areas where the star wheel is likely to come in contact with salt, mud, or water because rust and corrosion are a greater hazard than dust gumming up the threads. In areas where the assembly is unlikely to come in contact with those conditions, use no lubricant on the threads. But always follow the manufacturer's recommended procedure, if specified.

To remove, clean, inspect, and reassemble a duo-servo brake, follow the steps in **SKILL DRILL 33-3**:

1 In the appropriate service information, research and follow the procedure for disassembling the brake assembly. Manufacturers use many drum brake configurations, so the following steps are general in nature and should not be substituted for the manufacturer's procedure.

2 Clean the brake shoes, hardware, and backing plates using equipment and procedures for dealing with asbestos and/or dust. **(Photo 1)**

3 To disassemble a duo-servo brake, first remove the return springs, cable guide (if installed), and shoe guide. Set everything aside in the order it will go back on. Remove the parking brake strut and spring.

4 Remove the primary shoe hold-down spring, retainer, and pin.

> ▶ **TECHNICIAN TIP**
>
> Since it can be hard to remember where all of the parts fit inside of a drum brake assembly, it is good practice to disassemble only one side at a time, leaving the other side as a reference for when you reassemble the first side. Or, use a digital camera to take a couple of reference pictures before disassembly.

> ▶ **Caring for the Customer**
>
> If one wheel cylinder is leaking, how long until the other wheel cylinder starts leaking? And if it does leak, will it contaminate the new brake lining? Take into consideration the age and condition of the components when you inspect the system and give the customer your recommendation.

SKILL DRILL | **33-3** | **Removing, Cleaning, Inspecting, and Reassembling a Duo-Servo Brake**

Hub & Bearing has been removed for clarity

1 Research the procedure for disassembling the brake assembly. Clean brake shoes, hardware, and backing plates using equipment and procedures for dealing with asbestos/dust.

2 To disassemble a duo-servo brake, first remove the return springs, cable guide (if installed), and shoe guide. Remove the parking brake strut and spring. Remove the primary shoe hold-down spring, retainer, and pin. Remove the self-adjuster spring and star wheel assembly and primary shoe.

3 Remove the secondary hold-down spring, retainer, pin, and secondary shoe. Disassemble the parking brake lever from the brake shoe and hardware from the backing plate. Finally, clean and inspect all parts according to the manufacturer's procedure.

SKILL DRILL | 33-3 | Removing, Cleaning, Inspecting, and Reassembling a Duo-Servo Brake, continued

4 To reassemble a duo-servo brake, first reassemble the parking brake lever on the brake shoe and parking brake cable. Reassemble the star wheel assembly, lubricate the floating end, and set aside. Also lubricate the pads on the backing plate. Install both shoes to the backing plate with the hold-down spring assemblies. Install the shoe guide and self-adjuster cable over the anchor pin.

5 Install the cable guide and return spring in the secondary shoe. Also align the wheel cylinder pushrod in the shoe. Position the secondary shoe in place and use brake spring pliers to install the return spring over the anchor pin. Install the parking brake strut rod onto the secondary shoe, and pull the primary shoe engaged with the parking brake strut rod. Install the return spring in the primary shoe and use brake spring pliers to stretch the return spring over the anchor pin. Install the self-adjuster link, cable, and spring into position. Install the star wheel between the bottoms of the two shoes. Finally, check the fit of all springs, clips, and levers.

5 Remove the self-adjuster spring and star wheel assembly and primary shoe. **(Photo 2)**

6 Remove the secondary hold-down spring, retainer, pin, and secondary shoe.

7 Disassemble the parking brake lever from the brake shoe and hardware from the backing plate, being careful not to lose any parts and remembering how they go back together.

8 Finally, clean and inspect all parts according to the manufacturer's procedure. **(Photo 3)**

9 To reassemble a duo-servo brake, first reassemble the parking brake lever on the brake shoe and parking brake cable.

10 Reassemble the star wheel assembly, lubricate the floating end, and set aside. Also lubricate the contact pads on the backing plate.

11 Install both shoes to the backing plate with the hold-down spring assemblies.

12 Install the shoe guide and self-adjuster cable over the anchor pin. **(Photo 4)**

13 Install the cable guide and return spring in the secondary shoe. Also align the wheel cylinder pushrod in the shoe.

14 Position the secondary shoe in place and use brake spring pliers to install the return spring over the anchor pin.

15 Install the parking brake strut rod onto the secondary shoe, and pull the primary shoe engaged with the parking brake strut rod.

16 Install the return spring in the primary shoe and use brake spring pliers to stretch the return spring over the anchor pin.

17 Install the self-adjuster link, cable, and spring into position.

18 Install the star wheel between the bottoms of the two shoes.

19 Finally, check the fit of all springs, clips, and levers. (**Photo 5**)

To disassemble, clean, inspect, and reassemble a non-servo brake, follow the steps in **SKILL DRILL 33-4**:

1 In the appropriate service information, research and follow the procedure for disassembling the brake assembly. Manufacturers use many drum brake configurations, so the following steps are general in nature and should not be substituted for the manufacturer's procedure.

2 Clean the brake shoes, hardware, and backing plates using equipment and procedures for dealing with asbestos and/or dust.

3 To disassemble a non-servo brake, first remove the hold-down springs, retainers, and pins.

4 Spread the shoes apart and remove the parking brake strut and self-adjuster components. (**Photo 1**)

5 Remove the return springs.

6 Disassemble the parking brake lever from the brake shoe and hardware from the backing plate, being careful not to lose any parts and remembering how they go back together.

7 Clean and inspect all parts according to the manufacturer's procedure. (**Photo 2**)

8 To reassemble a non-servo brake, first assemble and lube the self-adjuster/parking brake strut assembly. Lube the backing plate pads.

9 Place one shoe on the backing plate and install the hold-down spring and pin.

10 Place the self-adjuster/parking brake strut on the installed brake shoe. (**Photo 3**)

11 Place the retracting springs on both shoes, and fit the loose shoe to the backing plate, being sure to line up the wheel cylinder pushrods, the self-adjuster, and the parking brake mechanism.

12 Install the hold-down spring and pin.

13 Finally, check the fit of all springs, clips, and levers. (**Photo 4**)

Removing, Inspecting, and Installing, Wheel Cylinders

If a wheel cylinder is leaking or binding, there is a good chance that the cylinder bore is corroded and pitted,

SKILL DRILL 33-4 Disassembling, Cleaning, Inspecting, and Reassembling a Non-Servo Brake

1 Research the procedure for disassembling the brake assembly. Clean brake shoes, hardware, and backing plates using equipment and procedures for dealing with asbestos/dust. To disassemble a non-servo brake disassembly, first remove the hold-down springs, retainers, and pins. Spread the shoes apart and remove the parking brake strut and self-adjuster components.

2 Remove the return springs. Disassemble the parking brake lever from the brake shoe and hardware from the backing plate. Finally, clean and inspect all parts.

3 To reassemble a non-servo assembly, first assemble and lube the self-adjuster/parking brake strut assembly. Lube the backing plate pads. Place one shoe on the backing plate and install the hold-down spring and pin. Place the self-adjuster/parking brake strut on the installed brake shoe.

SKILL DRILL | **33-4** | **Disassembling, Cleaning, Inspecting, and Reassembling a Non-Servo Brake, continued**

4. Place the retracting springs on both shoes, and fit the loose shoe to the backing plate, being sure to line up the wheel cylinder pushrods, the self-adjuster, and the parking brake mechanism. Install the hold-down spring and pin. Check the fit of all springs, clips, and levers.

requiring removal and replacement of the wheel cylinder. Wheel cylinders also need to be removed if the backing plate is being replaced. Very few shops rebuild wheel cylinders anymore. If you are reusing the wheel cylinder, make sure the bleeder screw can be opened. Because they are hollow, they break off easily, making bleeding virtually impossible.

To remove, inspect, and install wheel cylinders, follow the steps in **SKILL DRILL 33-5**:

1. Use a flare nut or line wrench to unscrew the brake line from the wheel cylinder.

2. Remove the wheel cylinder from the backing plate following the procedure in the service information. **(Photo 1)**

3. Peel back the dust boots and check for brake fluid behind them. If any is found, the piston seal is leaking and the wheel cylinder should be replaced. **(Photo 2)**

4. Disassemble the wheel cylinder and inspect each part for damage, wear, or missing components.

5. Determine any necessary actions. **(Photo 3)**

6. If the cylinder can be reused, rebuild it, preferably with new seals and dust boots. If not, replace it with a new wheel cylinder.

7. When reinstalling the wheel cylinder on the backing plate, it is best to first start the brake line three or four full turns using just your fingers. This will help prevent cross-threading the wheel cylinder and make it much easier to start the brake line. Otherwise, you risk ruining the wheel cylinder and brake line fitting.

8. Install and tighten any mounting screws. After that, tighten the brake line with a flare nut or line wrench. **(Photo 4)**

Pre-Adjusting Brakes and Installing Drums and Wheel Bearings

Pre-adjusting the brake shoes and parking brake is a routine step in a drum brake job. It saves time because it is faster to adjust the brakes with the drum off than it is when the drum is installed. The pre-adjustment sequence is important. Start by making sure the parking brake is fully released. Then look at the shoes to make sure the parking brake adjustment is not holding the brake shoes in the applied position. You can see this by verifying that the brake shoes are up against their stops on the top and bottom of each shoe. If they are not firmly against them, loosen the parking

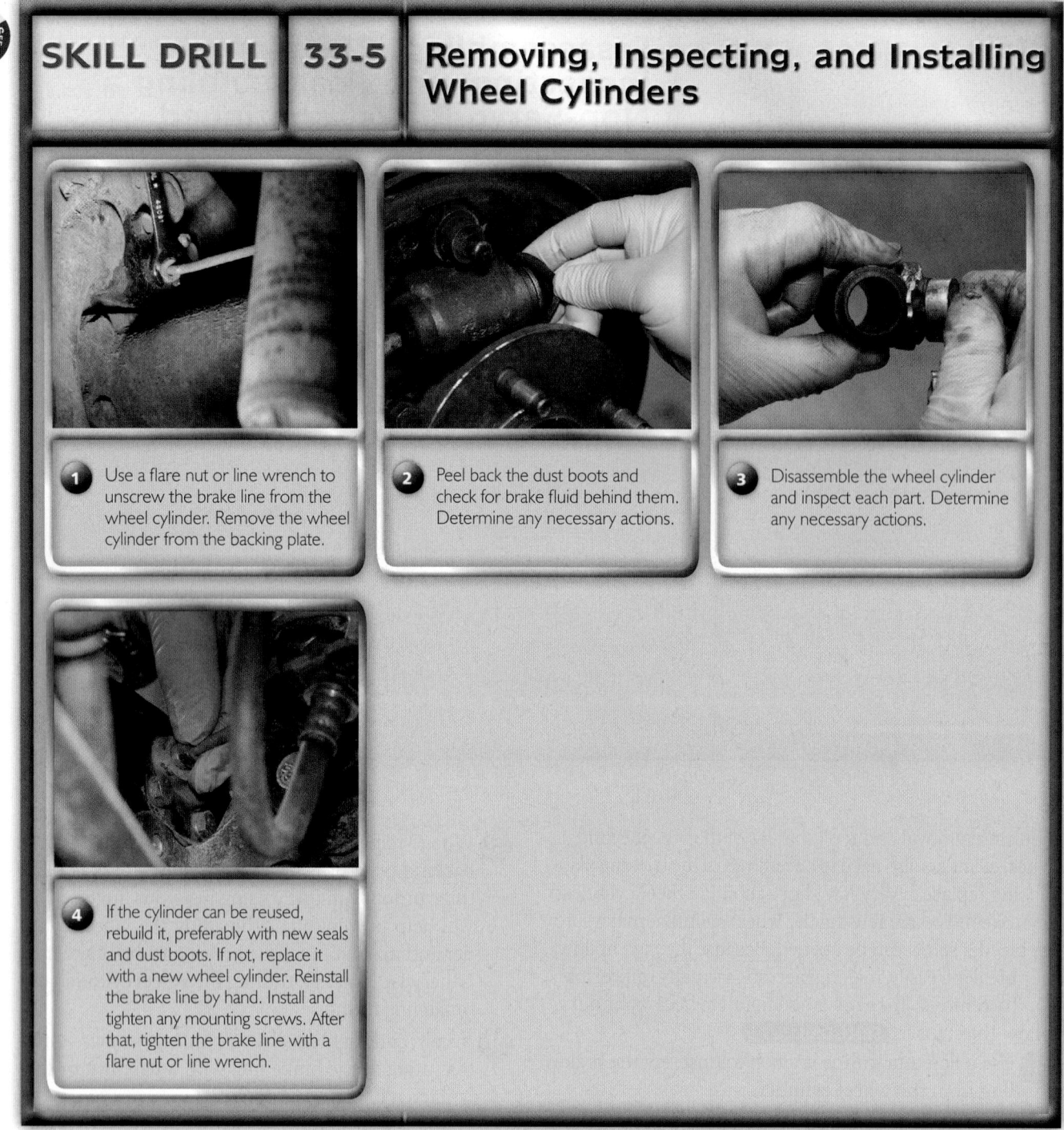

SKILL DRILL | 33-5 | Removing, Inspecting, and Installing Wheel Cylinders

1 Use a flare nut or line wrench to unscrew the brake line from the wheel cylinder. Remove the wheel cylinder from the backing plate.

2 Peel back the dust boots and check for brake fluid behind them. Determine any necessary actions.

3 Disassemble the wheel cylinder and inspect each part. Determine any necessary actions.

4 If the cylinder can be reused, rebuild it, preferably with new seals and dust boots. If not, replace it with a new wheel cylinder. Reinstall the brake line by hand. Install and tighten any mounting screws. After that, tighten the brake line with a flare nut or line wrench.

brake adjustment. Then adjust the service brakes. Once they are adjusted, adjust the parking brake.

To pre-adjust brake shoes and the parking brake and to install brake drums or drum/hub assemblies and wheel bearings, follow the steps in **SKILL DRILL 33-6**:

1 Make sure the brake shoes are centered on the backing plate. (**Photo 1**)

2 Using the brake pre-adjustment gauge, set the gauge to the drum diameter and lock it in place. (**Photo 2**)

3 Place the pre-adjustment gauge over the center of the brake shoes. (**Photo 3**)

4 Adjust the star wheel until the centers of the brake shoes just contact the pre-adjustment gauge. (**Photo 4**)

5 Temporarily install the brake drum to verify that the drum fits over the shoes without excessive drag. Adjust the shoes as necessary.

6 Pre-adjust the parking brake according to the manufacturer's procedure.

7 If the drum has serviceable wheel bearings, repack, install, adjust, and secure them following the manufacturer's procedure. See Skill Drills 1–5 in the Wheel Bearings chapter. (**Photo 5**)

SKILL DRILL | 33-6 | Pre-Adjusting Brakes and Installing Drums and Wheel Bearings

1. Make sure the brake shoes are centered on the backing plate.

2. Set the pre-adjustment gauge to the drum diameter and lock it in place.

3. Place the pre-adjustment gauge over the center of the brake shoes.

4. Adjust the star wheel until the centers of the brake shoes just contact the pre-adjustment gauge.

5. Test install the brake drum to verify the drum fits. Adjust the shoes as necessary. Pre-adjust the parking brake according to the manufacturer's procedure. If the drum has serviceable wheel bearings, repack, install, adjust, and secure them.

Installing Wheels, Torquing Lug Nuts, and Making Final Checks

This procedure, while fairly simple, can result in problems if it is not performed properly. Overtightening the lug nuts can cause the wheel studs to break either immediately or, worse, after the vehicle has been driven for a period of time. Undertightening can lead to loosening of the lug nuts and result in the wheel working its way off the vehicle. This can cause the driver to lose control of the vehicle and potentially result in an accident.

Lug nuts should be tightened to the proper torque, in the specified sequence. All manufacturers specify these

details for each of their vehicles. The torque pattern is usually either in some form of a star or cross. Be careful which way you install the lug nuts. Many wheels use a tapered hole that matches the tapered end of the lug nut and centers the wheel on the wheel flange. Other wheels use a flat surface that matches flat surfaces on the lug nuts. No matter what, the lug nut surface **must** match the mating surface of the wheel. Always check that these surfaces match.

When installing lug nuts, the weight should be off the vehicle. The lug nuts should easily center the wheel on the hub. Proper centering is especially important on aluminum wheels that use a flat lug nut sealing surface. The lug nuts can dig into the sides of the lug nut holes and cause the wheel to not center correctly. Once the lug nuts are up against the wheel, work the wheel up onto the lug nut shafts. Then you can torque them down properly.

There is some controversy regarding the use of a lubricant or antiseize on wheel studs and lug nuts. Since the purpose of a lubricant or antiseize is to prevent the components from sticking, the lug nuts may loosen up. The torque given for the lug nuts assumes that the lug stud is dry (no lubricant), so torquing them to specifications would lead to overtorquing. In areas of the country that are prone to rust, it is understandable why some want to put a very light amount of antiseize only on the threads of the wheel stud, being careful not to get any on the contact seat of the wheel and lug nut; doing so would prevent rust from building up on the threads. However, the lug nut torque would need to be reduced due to the lubricant. To avoid this issue, install the lug nuts dry.

To install the wheel, torque lug nuts, and make final checks and adjustments, follow the steps in **SKILL DRILL 33-7**:

1. Start the lug nuts on the wheel studs by hand. Make sure the lug nut surface matches the wheel hole. You should be able to turn the lug nuts by finger. (A few applications require you to install the hubcaps before installing the lug nuts, as the nuts hold the hubcap in place.)

2. Carefully run all of the lug nuts down so they are seated in the wheel. Make sure the wheel is centered on the hub.

3. Lower the vehicle so the tires are partially on the ground to hold them from turning while tightening the lug nuts.

4. Use a torque wrench to tighten each lug nut to the proper torque in the proper sequence.

5. Once all of the lug nuts have been torqued, go around them again, this time in a circular pattern to ensure that you did not miss any in the previous pattern. **(Photo 1)**

6. If the vehicle was equipped with hubcaps and valve stem caps, reinstall them. **(Photo 2)**

7. Check the brake fluid level in the master cylinder reservoir.

8. Start the vehicle and check the brake pedal for proper feel and height.

9. Check the parking brake for proper operation.

10. Inspect the system for any brake fluid leaks and loose or missing fasteners. **(Photo 3)**

SKILL DRILL 33-7 Installing Wheels, Torquing Lug Nuts, and Making Final Checks

1. Start the lug nuts on the wheel studs by hand. Carefully run all of the lug nuts down so they are seated in the wheel. Lower the vehicle so the tires are partially on the ground. Use a torque wrench to tighten each lug nut to the proper torque in the proper sequence. Once all of the lug nuts have been torqued, go around them again, this time in a circular pattern.

2. Reinstall hubcaps and valve stem caps.

3. Check the brake fluid level in the master cylinder reservoir. Start the vehicle and check the brake pedal for proper feel and height. Check the parking brake for proper operation. Inspect the system for any brake fluid leaks and loose or missing fasteners.

Wrap-up

Ready for Review

- The main components of the drum brake system are: brake drum, backing plate, wheel cylinder, brake shoes, springs and clips, automatic brake self-adjuster, and parking brake mechanism.
- Drum brakes are usually located on the rear wheels of disc-drum applications.
- Hydraulic pressure forces pistons to move the brake shoes into contact with the brake drums.
- Leading brake shoes are applied in the same direction as the brake drum's forward rotation and are self-energizing; trailing brake shoes are applied in the opposite direction of the brake drum's forward rotation and are not self-energizing.
- Drum brake systems can be: twin leading shoe (least common), leading/trailing shoe, and duo servo.
- Twin leading shoe brake systems are more efficient in forward braking than reverse braking.
- Leading/trailing shoe brake systems provide equal, but not maximum, braking in both directions.
- Duo-servo drum brake systems use servo action for the front brake shoes to multiply the force to the rear shoes, causing rear brake shoes to do more braking work.
- Brake drums are machined to the manufacturer's specified standard diameter and should be replaced once refinished beyond specifications.
- Brake drums styles are hub or hubless (most common in passenger vehicles).
- All brake unit components (except brake drum) are mounted to the backing plate.
- Brake shoe contact pads provide a smooth surface for the brake shoes to ride on.
- Wheel cylinders contain a housing, pistons, piston lip seals, spring and expander set, dust boots, push rods, and a bleeder screw.
- Wheel cylinders should be replaced rather than honed if corrosion or pitting occurs.
- Wheel cylinders are single acting (one piston, force generated in one direction) or dual acting (two pistons, force generated in two directions).
- Steel brake shoes have lining material bonded (or riveted) to them to create friction for braking.
- Duo-servo brake systems have primary brake shoes (front of vehicle, shorter shoe lining) and secondary brake shoes (rear of vehicle, longer shoe lining).
- Drum brakes may make the following noises: groaning (excess brake dust in the drum), grinding (worn friction lining), or clicking (grooves worn into backing plate contact pads or rough finish cut on the drum).
- Drum brakes use return, hold-down, and specialty springs.
- Drum brakes must have self-adjusters to maintain proper shoe-to-drum clearance.

Key Terms

anchor pin A component of the backing plate that takes all of the braking force from the brake shoes.

automatic brake self-adjuster A system on drum brakes that automatically adjusts the brakes to maintain a specified amount of running clearance between the shoes and drum.

backing plate A stamped steel plate, bolted to the steering or suspension, which supports the wheel cylinder, brake shoes, and other hardware.

brake drum A short, wide, hollow cylinder that is capped on one end and bolted to a vehicle's wheel; it has an inner friction surface that the brake shoe is forced against.

brake lathe A tool used to refinish the drum surface by removing a small amount of metal and returning it to a concentric, non-directional finish.

brake shoe A steel shoe and brake lining friction material that apply force to the brake drum during braking.

brake shoe adjustment gauge An adjustable tool used to pre-adjust the brake shoes to the diameter of the brake drum.

brake spoon A tool used to adjust the brake lining-to-drum clearance when the drum is installed on the vehicle.

brake spring pliers A tool used for removing and installing brake return springs.

cylinder bore The inside diameter of a cylinder.

drum brake micrometer A tool used for measuring the inside diameter of the brake drum.

duo-servo drum brake system A system that uses servo action in both the forward and reverse direction.

hold-down springs Springs that hold the brake shoes against the backing plate.

hold-down spring tool A tool used for removing and installing hold-down springs.

leading shoes Brake shoes that are installed so that they are applied in the same direction as the forward rotation of the drum and thus are self-energizing.

leading/trailing shoe drum brake system Type of brake shoe arrangement where one shoe is positioned in a leading manner and the other shoe in a trailing manner.

parking brake cable removal tool A tool used to compress the spring steel fingers of the parking brake cable so that the cable can be removed from the backing plate.

parking brake mechanism A mechanism that operates the brake shoes or pads to hold the vehicle stationary when the parking brake is applied.

return springs Springs that retract the brake shoes to their released position.

self-energizing The property of drum brakes that assists the driver in applying the brakes; when brake shoes come into contact with the moving drum, the friction tends to wedge the shoes against the drum, thus increasing the braking force.

servo action A drum brake design where one brake shoe, when activated, applies an increased activating force to the other brake shoe, in proportion to the initial activating force; further enhances the self-energizing feature of some drum brakes.

specialty springs Springs used to return links and levers on the parking brake system or the self-adjuster mechanism.

springs and clips Various devices that hold the brake shoes in place or return them to their proper place.

trailing shoes Brake shoes installed so that they are applied in the opposite direction to the forward rotation of the brake drum; not self-energizing and less efficient at developing braking force.

twin leading shoe drum brake system Brake shoe arrangement in which both brake shoes are self-energizing in the forward direction.

wheel cylinder A hydraulic cylinder with one or two pistons, seals, dust boots, and a bleeder screw that pushes the brake shoes into contact with the brake drum to slow or stop the vehicle.

wheel cylinder piston clamp A tool that prevents the pistons from being pushed out of the wheel cylinders while the brake shoes are being replaced.

ASE-Type Questions

1. Tech A says that parking brakes on drum brake vehicles use separate brake shoes for back up in an emergency. Tech B says that parking brakes on drum brake vehicles mechanically operate the standard drum brake shoes. Who is correct?
   a. Tech A
   b. Tech B
   c. Both A and B
   d. Neither A nor B

2. Tech A says that most brake drums are designed to be machined if minor surface issues are present. Tech B says that brake drums can be reused if they are machined over specifications, as long as the surface is smooth. Who is correct?
   a. Tech A
   b. Tech B
   c. Both A and B
   d. Neither A nor B

3. Tech A says that duo-servo brake shoes are only anchored on the top. Tech B says that typically duo-servo brake shoes adjust automatically during normal brake applications in a forward direction. Who is correct?
   a. Tech A
   b. Tech B
   c. Both A and B
   d. Neither A nor B

4. Tech A says that when inspecting brake shoes, if the shoes are unequally worn, this could be caused by a stuck wheel cylinder piston. Tech B says that the lining on the primary shoe is typically shorter in length and is installed toward the front of the vehicle. Who is correct?
   a. Tech A
   b. Tech B
   c. Both A and B
   d. Neither A nor B

5. Tech A says that it is almost impossible to install self-adjusters on the wrong side of the vehicle. Tech B says that grease seals can be reused. Who is correct?
   a. Tech A
   b. Tech B
   c. Both A and B
   d. Neither A nor B

6. Tech A says to use an air hose to clean the backing plate of dust and contamination. Tech B says to use a brake cleaning solution to clean the backing plate of dust and contamination. Who is correct?
   a. Tech A
   b. Tech B
   c. Both A and B
   d. Neither A nor B

7. Tech A says that riveted lining is usually for heavy duty or high performance vehicles. Tech B says that you need to identify each shoe individually to help ensure proper installation. Who is correct?
   a. Tech A
   b. Tech B
   c. Both A and B
   d. Neither A nor B

8. Tech A says that a grinding noise in drum brakes generally requires replacing the brake shoes and resurfacing or replacing the drums. Tech B says that a click noise in drum brakes requires replacing the brake shoes and resurfacing or replacing the drums. Who is correct?
   a. Tech A
   b. Tech B
   c. Both A and B
   d. Neither A nor B

9. Tech A says that brake shoe linings saturated with brake fluid from a leaky wheel cylinder can be cleaned with brake cleaner and reused as long as they aren't worn out. Tech B says that brake shoes should be replaced in axle sets. Who is correct?
   a. Tech A
   b. Tech B
   c. Both A and B
   d. Neither A nor B

10. Tech A says that when performing a brake job on the rear axle of an older vehicle, inspection finds brake fluid under the dust boot; this suggests wheel cylinder replacement on both rear wheels. Tech B says that when a drum brake return spring has failed, springs on both rear wheels need to be replaced. Who is correct?
    a. Tech A
    b. Tech B
    c. Both A and B
    d. Neither A nor B

CHAPTER 34

Knowledge Objectives

After reading this chapter, you will be able to:
1. Describe the components of a wheel bearing. (pp 1132–1133)
2. Describe the advantages and disadvantages of serviceable and sealed wheel bearings. (p 1133)
3. Describe the difference between friction and anti-friction bearings. (p 1133)
4. Describe advantages and disadvantages of ball and roller types of wheel bearings. (pp 1133–1135)
5. Describe how side load (thrust) impacts bearing selection. (pp 1134–1135)
6. Describe the purpose of double-row wheel bearings. (p 1135)
7. Describe a unitized wheel bearing hub. (p 1135)
8. Describe the purpose of grease seals. (pp 1135–1137)
9. Describe the different wheel bearing lubricant designations. (pp 1137–1138)
10. Describe wheel bearing end play and preload. (p 1139)
11. Describe the process of diagnosing wheel bearing concerns. (pp 1139–1140)

Wheel Bearings

Skills Objectives

After reading this chapter, you will be able to:
1. Remove, clean and inspect wheel bearings. (pp 1140–1142)
2. Pack wheel bearings by hand. (pp 1142–1143)
3. Pack wheel bearings using a bearing packer. (p 1143)
4. Install wheel bearings. (pp 1143–1144)
5. Install the locking mechanism on a wheel bearing. (pp 1144–1145)
6. Replace a wheel bearing and race. (pp 1145–1146)
7. Remove and reinstall a sealed wheel bearing using the unitized wheel bearing hub style. (pp 1146–1148)

▶ Introduction

Wheel bearings are a commonly overlooked component. All wheel bearings used to be the serviceable type, requiring periodic maintenance every 24,000–30,000 miles (38,624–48,280 km), consisting of disassembly, cleaning, inspecting, reassembly, and adjusting. With the introduction of sealed wheel bearings that do not need periodic service, many manufacturers switched to using them on most of their lighter duty vehicles. As a result, many technicians do not give the wheel bearings as much consideration as they once did. However, both types of wheel bearings can fail, and vehicles with serviceable wheel bearings still need maintenance, so it is important that you become familiar with wheel bearings.

In this chapter, you will learn about each wheel bearing component and the role wheel bearings play in helping to keep the vehicle safe. Because wheel bearings can require maintenance, you will learn how to accurately diagnose common issues and recommend the proper service or repair to the customer. You will also learn how to properly maintain and, if necessary, replace today's wheel bearings.

▶ Wheel Bearings Overview

<u>Wheel bearings</u> play a critical role in the vehicle by allowing the wheels to roll with a minimum of friction while still maintaining accurate wheel positioning under all driving conditions. Most wheel bearing assemblies include the following components: an <u>outer race</u>, an <u>inner</u> <u>race</u>, <u>roller bearings</u> or <u>ball bearings</u>, and a <u>bearing cage</u> to hold the rollers or balls in place **FIGURE 34-1**. The rollers or balls are made of hardened metal and roll between the two races. The races are also made of hardened metal and are carefully formed to match the contour of the rollers or balls, so all of the components roll easily against each other.

Each race either fits firmly within a housing or fits firmly on a shaft. In many situations, the races are an <u>interference fit</u> with the housing or shaft, which means they must be pressed into place with a high amount of force. In other words, the races are designed so that when they are installed, they should not rotate in or on their respective components. The rollers or balls are specifically designed

FIGURE 34-1 Components of a wheel bearing.

to provide the rolling function. Because the races, rollers, and balls are made of hardened metals, they are designed to resist wear and damage. However, overloading the vehicle can put the wheel bearings under a greater load than they are rated for, which can cause them to fail. In the same way, using improper or insufficient lubricant can cause them to fail. Wheel bearing failure is discussed in detail later in this chapter.

There are two categories of wheel bearings: **serviceable bearings** and **sealed bearings**. Serviceable bearings are designed so they can be disassembled and serviced, while sealed bearings are not. Serviceable bearings must be serviced periodically by disassembling, cleaning, inspecting, repacking them with the specified lubricant, reinstalling, and adjusting them. Sealed bearings are designed so they cannot be disassembled or adjusted. Sealed bearings are manufactured with the proper clearance and filled with the specified lubricant from the factory. They are designed to last the life of the vehicle, but bearings do wear out or fail occasionally and need to be replaced. We will discuss sealed bearing failure and replacement in detail later in the chapter.

> ### TECHNICIAN TIP
>
> Roller and ball bearing assemblies are called **anti-friction bearings** because the components are in rolling contact with one another and therefore have minimal friction. A sleeve-type bearing, or **bushing**, such as a clutch pilot bushing, is called a **friction bearing**, as the components are in sliding contact with one another. Anti-friction bearings run much more freely than friction bearings.

Wheel Bearing Types

Wheel bearings commonly are of the following types: cylindrical roller bearing, tapered roller bearing, ball bearing, double-row ball bearings, and double-row tapered roller bearings. Each one is designed for a particular application. For example, roller bearings support the load over a larger surface area so they can carry heavier loads than ball bearings. Manufacturers determine the type of wheel bearing they will use, based on the particular application and its requirements. You will need to be familiar with each type of wheel bearing to successfully service a variety of vehicles.

Cylindrical Roller Bearings

Cylindrical roller bearing assemblies use rollers that are cylindrical in shape, so that the races are parallel to each other with the rollers between them **FIGURE 34-2**.

This type of wheel bearing assembly is used in situations where the wheel bearing is not subject to side loads. It is common in rear axles of rear-wheel drive vehicles, where the rear axles are held from moving side to side by means other than the wheel bearings, such as a differential assembly that uses thrust bearings to prevent the axle from moving side to side. Since all side-to-side movement is controlled within the differential assembly, the cylindrical roller bearing assemblies solely support the vehicle's weight.

In many instances, cylindrical roller bearing assemblies use the surface of the axle as the inner bearing race. The cylindrical roller bearings ride directly on the axle shaft. In this situation, if the cylindrical roller bearing assembly fails, the axle shaft most likely will need to be replaced along with the bearing assembly. Some bearing manufacturers have designed replacement cylindrical roller bearing assemblies that ride farther out on the axle shaft than the original bearing, so the axle may not need to be replaced in this situation.

Cylindrical roller bearing assemblies are manufactured to have the proper running clearance between the rollers and races, so no adjustment of this type of wheel bearing is needed. However, they do require lubrication to cushion the rollers and races while operating. Lubrication also removes the heat generated between the rolling surfaces and transmits it to the housing and ultimately the atmosphere. This transfer of heat is usually accomplished by the **gear lube**, which is filled high enough in the differential housing to flow outward to the cylindrical roller bearings. The gear lube is retained in the housing by a **grease seal**, which is located in the outer end of the axle housing outside of the cylindrical roller bearing assembly. This arrangement allows the cylindrical roller bearing assembly to be lubricated while still retaining the

FIGURE 34-2 Cylindrical roller bearing assembly.

gear lube in the housing. At the same time, any dirt and contaminants are sealed out of the housing.

Tapered Roller Bearings

Tapered roller bearing assemblies are commonly used where heavier loads need to be supported and the wheel bearings are put under a side load (thrust) condition. Wheel bearing side load conditions occur when the vehicle is cornering. When the wheel is being turned, the vehicle wants to keep going straight. This causes the bottom of the outside wheel to be pushed inward and the bottom of the inside wheel outward, which puts them both under a side load condition. In this situation, cylindrical roller bearing assemblies would just allow the wheel to slide sideways on the axle, which means they cannot control the side load (thrust) condition. However, tapered roller bearing assemblies can.

With tapered roller bearing assemblies, the races and rollers are tapered in such a manner that all of the tapered angles meet together at a common point **FIGURE 34-3**. This design allows the tapered rollers to freely roll between the angled inner and outer races. The tapered rollers are contained in a bearing cage, which holds the tapered bearings to the inner race as a unit. The inner race is called the cone. The outer race is called the cup. The cone and cup make up a tapered roller bearing assembly.

Because the components are on an angle to the centerline of (and not parallel to) the axle shaft, they can control side movement (thrust) in one direction unlike a cylindrical roller bearing assembly. Tapered roller bearing assemblies are generally used in opposing pairs so they can control side movement (thrust) in both an inward and outward direction. When used in pairs, the individual

tapered roller bearing assemblies are generally referred to as inner (or inboard) and outer (or outboard) bearings. The inner bearing assembly is closer to the centerline of the wheel so it supports most of the vehicle weight. Because of this, the inner bearing assembly is typically larger than the outer bearing assembly.

Some manufacturers have designed double-row tapered roller bearing assemblies, which combine two opposing tapered roller bearing assemblies into one unit. This design provides excellent side thrust–carrying capacity and at the same time excellent load-carrying capacity. For more information, see the section Sealed Wheel Bearings.

Because tapered roller bearing assemblies use tapered components, the wheel bearing assembly must be adjusted to have the proper **running clearance** between the tapered rollers and races when the bearing assemblies are installed. The running clearance is the amount of space between components during operation. If the tapered roller bearing clearance is too tight, the components will bind and overheat due to increased pressure and because the rollers squeeze out too much grease, making the lubricating film too thin. If the tapered roller bearing is adjusted with too much clearance, excessive side-to-side and up-and-down movement will occur, which can cause the components to hammer against each other, damaging the surfaces of the tapered roller bearings and races.

Lubrication of serviceable tapered wheel bearing assemblies is usually accomplished in one of two ways—wheel bearing grease or gear lube. If wheel bearing grease is specified, the tapered wheel bearing will need to be packed with new grease before installing it, since the grease is very thick and does not flow unless it is heated up. Packing a bearing means that the spaces between the rollers and races are completely filled with grease. Packing is best performed with a bearing packing tool, but it can be successfully performed by hand; it just takes a bit longer. This grease, plus a small reserve amount, will provide lubrication for the tapered wheel bearing assembly as it is in service. For detailed information on this procedure, see the Wheel Bearing Maintenance section.

Some tapered wheel bearing assemblies are lubricated with gear lube from the axle housing just like the cylindrical bearing assemblies. They do not need to be packed since gear lube flows relatively easily and fills the spaces once the proper amount of gear lube is added to the axle housing. Keeping the gear lube at the proper level is critical for long life of a tapered wheel bearing assembly. If the gear lube gets too low, the tapered wheel bearing assemblies will be starved for lubrication, overheat, and become damaged. Some front axle housings on four-wheel drive vehicles use

Tapered roller bearings

FIGURE 34-3 With tapered roller bearings, the common axis of bearings and races provides minimal rolling resistance.

separate, sealed bearing chambers to hold a quantity of gear lube. In either type of system, grease seals help retain the gear lube in the system as well as seal out contaminants.

Ball Bearings

Deeply grooved ball bearing assemblies are used as wheel bearings on a lot of light-duty vehicles because they have a lower rolling resistance. The much smaller contact area between the balls and races prevents a ball bearing assembly from being used on larger vehicles, which experience higher loads. Ball bearing assemblies consist of an inner race, an outer race, ball bearings, and a ball bearing cage. The balls roll in deep channels in the races. Side loads are controlled by the balls rolling against the sides of the channels. Since there is much less surface area between the balls and the sides of the channels compared to the tapered roller bearing, ball bearing assemblies are limited in how much side load they can handle. At the same time, the small surface area allows them to roll freer than roller bearings, and they therefore help manufacturers decrease drag on a vehicle, which increases fuel efficiency. Ball bearing assemblies depend on lubricants similar to roller bearings; but in most cases, they are usually designed as a sealed bearing assembly. This means that the proper type and amount of lubrication is sealed inside the ball bearing assembly by the manufacturer and never needs routine maintenance or packing. But if ball bearings become worn or faulty, they must be replaced. This will be discussed further in Skill Drill 34-7: Remove and Reinstall Sealed Wheel Bearings Using the Unitized Wheel Bearing Hub Style.

Ball bearing assemblies also come in a **double-row ball bearing assembly** configuration **FIGURE 34-4**. The double-row configuration gives the ball bearing

assembly twice the surface contact area so it can control greater amounts of loads and side loads than a single-row bearing assembly. Virtually all wheel bearings using a ball bearing assembly are of the double-row ball bearing variety, and they are commonly used in automotive light vehicle applications.

The outer race is usually a one-piece unit, while the inner race is usually two separate pieces. The inner races are manufactured to create the correct running clearance when the double-row ball bearing assembly is torqued in place. In automotive wheel bearing applications, the double-row ball bearing assembly may come as a **unitized wheel bearing hub** with the bearing assembly installed in the hub and the wheel flange installed in the center of the bearing assembly **FIGURE 34-5**. In this way, the old ball bearing assembly can be unbolted, and a new one bolted in its place with minimal labor and no adjustments needed. This is virtually a zero maintenance system until it wears out, and then it is usually replaced as a unit.

> **TECHNICIAN TIP**
>
> Ball bearings roll easier than roller bearings since they have a smaller contact area; thus, they provide a small increase in vehicle efficiency.

Seals and Axle Seals

All wheel bearings rely on some sort of seal to keep the lubricant in and contaminants out. Some wheel bearings have the seal built right into the bearing assembly, such as the sealed bearings that will be covered in detail in the next section. Other wheel bearings rely on a completely

FIGURE 34-4 A double-row ball bearing assembly.

FIGURE 34-5 A unitized wheel bearing hub assembly.

separate grease seal. Wheel bearing grease seals seal against a rotating surface so that lubricants cannot leak from the bearing side of the seal past the shaft to the other side of the seal. They also prevent any dirt and contaminants from getting past the seal into the bearing. In some applications, the grease seal is a press-fit into the axle housing, which is stationary, and seals against the axle shaft, which is rotating. In other applications, the grease seal is press-fit into the wheel hub, which rotates, and seals against the spindle, which does not rotate.

Most axle seals consist of a stamped sheet metal case and flexible sealing lip with an internal **garter spring** **FIGURE 34-6**. The metal seal case is constructed to be a press-fit when installed in the housing. The outside surface of the metal case usually comes precoated with a thin layer of sealer compound to seal minor surface imperfections between the seal case and the housing. The sealing lip is carefully designed and precisely manufactured so that it will seal the specified lubricant. Many seals use a garter spring to help hold the lips of the seal in contact with the shaft it is sealing. The garter spring helps maintain an adequate seal if the parts are slightly out of alignment or if there is a small amount of runout or clearance between the seal and shaft.

Seals come in a variety of configurations, so it is critical to use the specified seal for the application you are servicing. The sealing lip can also be made from a variety of materials. Always purchase seals from a reputable manufacturer so you can be confident it will do its job and last a long time. When you install a seal, always remember to pre-lube the sealing lip with a small amount of oil or grease. This will prevent it from overheating during the initial use resulting in premature failure of the seal.

Sealed Wheel Bearings

Some vehicles use sealed wheel bearings. These bearing assemblies are designed and manufactured as completely sealed units. They can be single row or double row, depending on the vehicle application, and can be made up of ball, cylindrical roller, or tapered roller types of bearings. The bearing assemblies are prefilled with lubricant and have integrated grease seals built into them to contain the lubricant **FIGURE 34-7**. They also are manufactured with the proper running clearance, so they do not need to be adjusted. This saves the vehicle manufacturer money by decreasing the time it takes to install them during vehicle assembly. It also makes for a more reliable and consistent installation process since every unit comes preset at the proper clearance. This style of wheel bearing assembly is also beneficial to vehicle owners since it is designed to last the life of the vehicle during normal use and does not need periodic maintenance, which saves owners money.

Another application for sealed wheel bearings is unitized wheel bearing hubs. These usually include either a double-row ball bearing assembly or a double-row tapered roller bearing assembly installed in a housing that is bolted onto the knuckle or axle housing. In many cases,

FIGURE 34-6 Components of a typical seal.

FIGURE 34-7 Sealed bearing.

it also has the wheel flange pressed into the inner race of the wheel bearing. This unit can easily be unbolted from the suspension and replaced as a unit—bearing, hub, and flange. Unitized wheel bearing hubs also provide the benefits offered by the sealed wheel bearing, so manufacturers have embraced them for many of their vehicles. On some vehicles equipped with ABS brakes, the ABS sensor is integrated into the unitized wheel bearing assembly.

Wheel Bearing Arrangements for Rear Drive Axles

Rear drive axles come in three different designations: full floating, semi-floating, and ¾ floating. Each designation refers to how the axle and wheel are supported by the wheel bearings. It is also important for you to understand the differences so that you will be able to service each style properly. In a full floating axle arrangement, the axle only carries a twisting force. The weight of the vehicle is fully carried by a pair of tapered roller bearing assemblies, which ride between the hub and axle tube. The axle does not carry any of the vehicle load since the wheel is bolted directly to the bearing hub. The hub also controls side thrust. Full floating axles handle heavy loads better than the other styles, so they are used in heavy-duty applications such as one-ton pick-ups, trucks, and vans.

In a semi-floating axle, the wheel flange is part of the axle, which is supported by a single bearing assembly (usually a ball or cylindrical roller bearing style) near the flange end of the axle. The bearing assembly rides between the axle and the axle tube, so all of the weight is put on the axle flange, which transfers the weight to the wheel bearing assembly. In this case, the axle and bearing assembly each carry the full weight of the vehicle. The axle also provides the twisting force for the wheel. This arrangement is generally considered the lightest duty of the three types of axle designations.

In a ¾-floating axle design, there is a single bearing assembly (usually a ball or cylindrical roller bearing style) between the outside of the axle tube and the hub. The axle has a wheel flange that bolts to the hub and provides lateral support for the hub and wheel, while the bearing assembly supports the weight of the vehicle. The axle also provides the twisting force for the wheel. This arrangement is generally considered heavier duty than the semi-floating axle, but lighter duty than the full floating axle.

▶ Wheel Bearing Maintenance

While sealed wheel bearings are used on a higher percentage of vehicles and require no maintenance, serviceable wheel bearings do need periodic maintenance. Maintenance consists of disassembling, cleaning, inspecting, repacking, installing, and adjusting the bearings. This is commonly performed during brake shoe/pad replacement or at intervals specified by the vehicle manufacturer, usually around 24,000–30,000 miles (38,624–48,280 km). A normal part of servicing wheel bearings includes the replacement of the old grease seals with new ones along with the **cotter pin** (if used), which retains the wheel bearing adjusting nut. A cotter pin is a soft metal pin that can be bent into shape and is used to retain the bearing adjusting nut. Ensure that the correct replacement parts and grease are available before starting the job.

Lubrication

All wheel bearings require lubrication to extend their useful life. There are two common types of lubricants used—gear lube and bearing grease. Each application specifies one or the other. They cannot be substituted, due to the different housing and seal designs each lubricant demands. Gear lube is somewhat thicker than engine oil. Since gear lube flows much easier than grease, the bearing assembly runs in a housing partially filled with gear lube. The gear lube is thin enough to flow around and between the rollers, lubricating them and helping to prevent overheating of the wheel bearing assemblies.

In many rear-wheel drive vehicles, the wheel bearing assemblies are open to the axle housing, which is partially filled with gear lube that also lubricates the differential assembly. Maintenance of this system involves draining the old gear lube and refilling the system with the specified new gear lube. In most cases, this can be performed without disassembling the wheel bearings by removing a drain plug or bolt and filling the system through the **fill plug** FIGURE 34-8. A fill plug is usually threaded and can

FIGURE 34-8 Drain and fill points for rear axle assembly.

be removed to allow the level of a fluid to be checked and filled. Some manufacturers have chosen to use a rubber fill plug that snaps into the fill hole. The level of gear lube should normally be within 0.25" (6.35 mm) of the bottom of the fill plug hole.

> **TECHNICIAN TIP**
>
> If the level of gear lube is lower than it should be, suspect a leaking axle shaft grease seal. This can usually be verified by looking at the inside of each tire and the back side of the brake backing plate. If gear lube is present, the grease seal is leaking and needs to be replaced. Also check the wheel bearing to make sure it is not faulty; to do so, follow the bearing diagnosis procedure listed later in this chapter.

In order to properly perform maintenance on wheel bearings, you will need to understand the different characteristics of gear lube and bearing grease. This will help ensure that you select the proper lubricant for the task you are performing. Gear lube is classified by the Society of Automotive Engineers (SAE) according to its viscosity and by the American Petroleum Institute (API) according to its service grade. **Viscosity** refers the thickness of the gear lube; the higher the number, the thicker the gear lube. Vehicle manufacturers specify a certain viscosity of gear lube based on the climate the vehicle is operated in or the load it is carrying, so understanding viscosity is very important when servicing vehicles.

Standard viscosities for gear lube are 70W, 75W, 80W, 85W, 90, and 140. The W stands for "winter" or the gear lube's cold temperature viscosity. The non-W ratings are the viscosity of the gear lube at a predetermined hot temperature. Similar to engine oil, gear lube is available in multiviscosity configurations such as 75W–90, 80W–90, or 85–140. Unlike engine oil, the temperature for the W rating varies according to the standard being met. For example, 70W has a maximum allowable temperature for its viscosity of −67°F (−55°C), while 85W is −10°F (−23°C). The manufacturers have gone to great lengths to specify the proper gear lube for their vehicles. Make sure you follow their recommendations when choosing the gear lube for a particular vehicle.

Current ratings of the API service grade are GL-1, GL-4, and GL-5. Generally, the higher the number, the better the lubricant. GL-1 has minimal additives, which makes it unsuitable for modern applications, although it is still used in some heavy truck manual transmissions. GL-4 is intended for use with bevel-type gears

operating under moderate speeds and loads, such as in many manual transmissions. GL-5 has about twice as much extreme pressure additive as GL-4, so it is intended for most differentials that use hypoid-type gears operating under high-speed/low-speed, high-torque, and shock-load conditions. It can also be used in some manual transmissions. Always check the manufacturer's specifications to determine the proper gear lube for the application you are working on.

Most serviceable wheel bearings require **grease** as their lubricant. Grease is made of a base oil, plus a thickening agent, and specific additives to meet the requirements of the application. **Lithium soap** is a common thickening agent in automotive grease. Other greases use calcium or **molybdenum thickening agents**. Some add small amounts of copper and/or lead to enhance the grease's ability to withstand extreme pressures.

Automotive wheel bearing grease is a thickened lubricant, designated as a plastic solid. This means that while it is thick enough at room temperature to maintain its shape if left undisturbed, it is thin enough to be squeezed into and out of small spaces. Its consistency is similar to a glob of gel toothpaste.

The thickness of grease is graded by the **National Lubricating Grease Institute (NLGI)** TABLE 34-1.

Since it does not flow at room temperature, the grease needs to be packed into the spaces around the rollers when the wheel bearing assemblies are installed. This also needs to be done when the grease wears out and must be replaced. Packing a wheel bearing assembly can be done by hand or with a **bearing packer**, which is a tool that forces grease into the spaces between the bearing rollers. Packing a bearing assembly should be done only after thoroughly cleaning and inspecting the rollers and races for wear, damage, or corrosion. If any of these are present, the bearing assembly should be replaced.

TABLE 34-1: NLGI Rating System

NLGI Number	Consistency
00	Semifluid
0	Very soft
1	Semisoft
2	Soft—Common wheel bearing grease
3	Semifirm
4	Firm
5	Very firm

Courtesy of the National Lubricating Grease Institute

Adjustment

All wheel bearings need the proper **end play** or **preload** to operate correctly. End play, in the context of wheel bearings, refers to the amount of inward and outward movement of the hub due to the clearance within the bearing assembly. Preload refers to the absence of clearance in the bearing and the specified amount of pressure forcing the bearing components together. Sealed bearings and double-row bearing assemblies come from the manufacturer with the proper clearance machined into them. These wheel bearings are designed so that when the components are tightened together, the races butt up against each other in such a way that the proper clearance is maintained. For these wheel bearings, it is only critical that the retaining bolt or bolts are torqued to the proper specification. This is usually quite high and can typically exceed 200 foot pounds (ft-lb; 271.1 newton meters [Nm]). Be sure to check the manufacturer's torque specifications for the application you are working on.

On adjustable wheel bearings, the proper clearance must be set using the **adjusting nut**. In this case, the adjusting nut is only tightened lightly so that a small amount of clearance or preload is maintained between the rollers and races, depending on the manufacturer's specifications. The adjusting nut is then locked in place by a locking mechanism so that it cannot loosen. This is critical to prevent the wheel from falling off and causing injury. The most common locking mechanism uses a **keyed washer** (hardened), adjusting nut, **lock cage**, and cotter pin **FIGURE 34-9**. On four-wheel drive vehicles, the locking mechanism commonly includes a keyed washer (hardened), adjusting nut, **keyed lock washer** (or tang washer), and **lock nut** **FIGURE 34-10**. To learn more about the procedure for adjusting wheel bearings, see Skill Drill 34-1.

FIGURE 34-9 Typical cotter pin-style wheel bearing locking mechanism.

Lock washer Lock nut

Bearing adjusting nut

Lock nut socket and breaker bar

FIGURE 34-10 Typical lock nut-style wheel bearing locking mechanism.

▶ Diagnosis

Wheel bearings can be damaged from excessive loads such as overloading the vehicle, shock loads such as hitting a large pot hole, improper adjustment, or just plain wear over time. The wheel bearings must hold up under difficult circumstances, so suspect faulty bearings whenever an unusual rumbling, whirring, howling, or rough sound comes from the wheel areas when the vehicle is being driven. The noise usually can be heard once the vehicle gets up to 15–20 mph (24.1–32.2 kph) and gets louder as the vehicle speeds up.

Loose or worn wheel bearings can also cause the vehicle to wander, shimmy, or vibrate. For these concerns, it is best to lift the wheels off the ground and check the wheel bearings for looseness by grabbing the tire at the 6 o'clock and 12 o'clock positions and lightly wiggling it back and forth. Watch the inside of the wheel to see if the play is coming from the wheel bearings and not the ball joints. Then grab the wheel at the 3 o'clock and 9 o'clock positions and again lightly wiggle the wheel back and forth. Watch to see if the play is coming from the wheel bearings and not the tie rod ends. If there is play in the wheel bearings and the vehicle uses sealed bearings, they will need to be replaced. If the vehicle uses serviceable bearings, the maximum allowable play is approximately 0.010" (0.254 mm). If greater than that, they will need to be disassembled, cleaned, inspected, repacked, reinstalled, and readjusted if they are still in good condition.

One way to isolate a wheel bearing noise from a transmission noise is to drive the vehicle at the speed at which it is making the noise and then shift into a higher or lower transmission gear while maintaining the same speed. If the noise speeds up or slows down, then it is a transmission-related issue. If it stays relatively the same, accelerate, coast, and decelerate the vehicle. If the noise changes, suspect the differential or universal joints. If the noise stays relatively steady, it is most likely related to the wheel bearings.

To determine which side the bearing noise is coming from, you can sometimes drive the vehicle at the speed at which it is making the noise and then lightly rock the car side to side using the steering wheel. If the noise gets louder when the car is steered right, then it is usually the left side with the bad bearing, and vise versa. Only perform this test in a safe place such as an abandoned parking lot. Another challenge is distinguishing a wheel bearing noise or a tire noise. The best approach to this problem is to drive over different road surfaces such as asphalt and concrete. If the noise changes, it is likely a tire problem. If the noise does not change, it is likely to be a faulty wheel bearing.

If you cannot determine the source of the noise on a test-drive, you might be able to determine the source of the noise by placing the vehicle on a hoist and rotating the wheels. If the vehicle has a MacPherson strut suspension, raise and support the vehicle and spin the wheel by hand while holding on to the coil spring with the other hand, feeling for a vibration or roughness. The spring tends to magnify the wheel bearing roughness, which can be felt with some practice. If the suspect wheel is a drive wheel, have an assistant drive the vehicle in gear while on the hoist, and listen to the wheel bearings with a stethoscope. Since the vehicle is running on the hoist, this can be a hazardous situation and must only be performed under the close guidance of your supervisor.

Failure Analysis

Wheel bearings can be inspected and determinations made about why the wheel bearing failed. Getting to the source of the problem is important to ensure that the same thing does not happen to the new wheel bearings. Failure analysis starts with removing the faulty wheel bearing and cleaning it and the races thoroughly. Once they are clean, visually inspect the wheel bearing components and compare your findings to the wheel bearing manufacturer's failure analysis chart. This information should lead you to what caused the wheel bearing failure.

Once the cause of the wheel bearing failure has been determined, measures will need to be taken to ensure that the failure does not repeat itself. For example, if the bearing and race surfaces show signs of rust or corrosion, you will want to inspect and replace the grease seals along with replacing the wheel bearing assembly. Also, if the wheel bearing is so worn that there are metal shavings in the wheel hub and grease, a thorough clean-

ing of the wheel hub will be required so that all of the metal shavings are removed and will not ruin the new bearing assembly.

Some wheel bearing failures involve the races spinning in either the machined bore of the wheel hub or on the surface of the spindle/axle. This can lead to wear of the wheel hub or spindle/axle, which requires replacement of these components. Be sure to inspect the wheel hub and spindle/axle closely for any damage every time the wheel bearings are removed and serviced.

▶ Maintenance and Repair
Tools

Here is a list of common tools used to maintain and repair wheel bearings:

- Bearing packer
- Seal puller
- Wheel bearing race installer/seal installer set
- Wheel bearing lock nut sockets
- Cotter pin removal tool
- Dust cap pliers

Repacking and Adjusting Wheel Bearings

Serviceable wheel bearings should be serviced periodically according to the manufacturer's scheduled maintenance chart, whenever brake work is being performed, or if a faulty wheel bearing is suspected. When servicing wheel bearings, it is critical that the proper grease is used. Also avoid mixing different types of grease by thoroughly cleaning all old grease from the wheel bearings. Another option is to use a bearing packer, with the same kind of grease, to force the old grease out of the wheel bearings **FIGURE 34-11**. Make sure the grease in the bearing packer is not contaminated with dirt or debris and is correct for the vehicle being serviced.

When reinstalling wheel bearings, it is critical to follow the manufacturer's adjustment procedure. Always use new grease seals and cotter pins (if used). Doing so will prevent grease leaks and ensure that the adjusting nut does not back off, causing an unsafe driving situation.

To remove, clean, inspect, repack, and install wheel bearings, and to install the locking mechanism, follow the steps in Skill Drills 1–7. To remove, clean, and inspect the wheel bearings, follow the steps in **SKILL DRILL 34-1**:

1 Remove the wheel bearing dust cap with dust cap pliers or a narrow cold chisel and hammer. (**Photo 1**)

2 Remove the locking mechanism. The locking mechanism could incorporate one of the following: a cotter pin, a cotter pin and locking cage, a bent locking washer that needs to be straightened, or a lock nut that is tightened tightly against the adjusting nut to lock them both in place.

FIGURE 34-11 A bearing packer.

3 Remove the adjusting nut, keyed washer, and outer bearing.

4 Reinstall the adjusting nut approximately five turns back onto the spindle. (**Photo 2**)

5 Grasp the drum/rotor at the 1 o'clock and 7 o'clock positions or 11 o'clock and 5 o'clock positions. While holding downward pressure, quickly pull the drum/rotor toward you. The adjusting nut should catch the inner bearing race and pop the grease seal and bearing out of the hub, leaving them sitting on the spindle. Be careful to not smash your fingers on the spindle while pulling the drum/rotor toward you. (**Photo 3**)

6 Wipe any old grease off of the wheel bearings, races, and spindle with a rag and give them a quick visual inspection for damage. If there is any visible damage, consult the bearing diagnosis chart to identify any faults. (**Photo 4**)

7 If the wheel bearings appear to be in serviceable condition, completely clean the wheel bearings, races, and hub of all old grease and any contaminants.

SKILL DRILL | 34-1 | Removing, Cleaning, and Inspecting Wheel Bearings

1 Remove the wheel bearing dust cap with dust cap pliers or a narrow cold chisel and hammer.

2 Remove the locking mechanism. Remove the adjusting nut, keyed washer, and outer bearing. Reinstall the adjusting nut approximately five turns back onto the spindle.

3 Grasp the drum/rotor at the 1 o'clock and 7 o'clock positions or 11 o'clock and 5 o'clock positions. While holding downward pressure, quickly pull the drum/rotor toward you. The adjusting nut should catch the inner bearing race and pop the grease seal and bearing out of the hub, leaving them sitting on the spindle.

SKILL DRILL | 34-1 | Removing, Cleaning, and Inspecting Wheel Bearings, continued

4 Wipe any old grease off of the wheel bearings, races, and spindle with a rag and give them a quick visual inspection. Consult the bearing diagnosis chart to identify any faults.

5 If the wheel bearings are in serviceable condition, completely clean the wheel bearings, races, and hub. If using solvent to clean any of the components, make sure there is no solvent-contaminated grease left on the parts.

6 Give the parts a final inspection, and consult the bearing diagnosis chart if there are any signs of damage. Using the specified grease, pack both wheel bearings, being careful to keep dirt and debris out of the grease (see Skill Drills 34-2 and 34-3).

If using solvent to clean any of the components, make sure there is no solvent-contaminated grease left on the parts, because it will reduce the effectiveness of the lubricant. **(Photo 5)**

8 At this point, give them a final thorough inspection, and consult the bearing diagnosis chart to identify any faults. Using the specified grease, pack both wheel bearings, being careful to keep dirt and debris out of the grease. **(Photo 6)**

To pack grease by hand, follow the steps in SKILL DRILL 34-2:

1 Using a pair of latex or nitrile (nitro) gloves, place a small glob of grease in the palm of your nondominant hand.

2 Place the index finger of your other hand through the bearing center hole with the larger diameter facing down. **(Photo 1)**

3 Push the large diameter of the bearing down the edge of the grease into your palm. This should force grease into the space between the bearings and races.

4 Continue this process until grease comes out of the top of the bearing. **(Photo 2)**

5 Carefully turn the bearing as a unit to a new space, and keep forcing grease between the bearings. Do this until all of the spaces are full. **(Photo 3)**

6 Smear some grease around the outside of the bearing. Repeat this process on the other bearing. **(Photo 4)**

To pack grease with a bearing packer, follow the steps in SKILL DRILL 34-3:

1 Make sure the bearing packer has the proper grease and that it is uncontaminated.

2 Place the wheel bearing with the narrow side down.

3 Place the packer cone on the top of the wheel bearing.

4 Pack the wheel bearing following the packer's instructions.

5 Remove the wheel bearing. Wipe off any old grease.

6 Smear some new grease around the outside of the wheel bearing.

7 Repeat this process on the other wheel bearing.

8 Be careful not to set a packed wheel bearing down on a dirty surface.

SKILL DRILL | 34-2 | Packing Grease by Hand

1 Using a pair of latex or nitrile (nitro) gloves, place a small glob of grease in the palm of your nondominant hand. Place the index finger of your other hand through the bearing center hole with the larger diameter facing down.

2 Push the large diameter of the bearing down the edge of the grease into your palm. This should force grease into the space between the bearings and races. Continue this process until grease comes out of the top of the bearing.

3 Carefully turn the bearing as a unit to a new space, and keep forcing grease between the bearings. Do this until all of the spaces are full.

4 Smear some grease around the outside of the bearing. Repeat this process on the other bearing.

To install wheel bearings, follow the steps in **SKILL DRILL 34-4**:

1 Place a small amount of extra grease in the center of the hub. Do not fill it completely. Some technicians say to only smear a thin layer all the way around the inside of the hub to prevent the surface from rusting. Other technicians say to only place enough inside of the hub to bring it level with the bearing races. Either way, not very much grease is needed to keep the bearings lubricated, so go easy on the amount of grease you place in the hub.

2 Place the inner wheel bearing in its race, narrow side toward the race.

3 Install the new grease seal, being careful not to damage it. The use of a seal driver is best, but many seals can be installed with just a hammer if you are careful to keep it straight as it is being installed. Place a small amount of grease on the lip of the seal to provide it with initial lubrication. **(Photo 1)**

4 Without getting grease on the drum/rotor, carefully install it on the spindle, making sure the inner bearing fully seats against the spindle flange.

5 Install the outer bearing on the spindle and into the race. **(Photo 2)**

SKILL DRILL | 34-4 | Installing Wheel Bearings

1 Place a small amount of extra grease in the center of the hub. Do not fill it completely. Place the inner wheel bearing in its race, narrow side toward the race. Install the new grease seal, being careful not to damage it. Place a small amount of grease on the lip of the seal to provide it with initial lubrication.

2 Without getting grease on the drum/rotor, carefully install it on the spindle, making sure the inner bearing fully seats against the spindle flange. Install the outer bearing on the spindle and into the race.

3 Install the keyed washer and adjusting nut on the spindle and tighten until finger tight. Tighten the adjusting nut to the specified seating torque (usually about 20 ft-lb [27.1 Nm]) while turning the drum/rotor. This squeezes the excess grease out from between the wheel bearings and races while seating the bearings. Loosen the adjusting nut approximately one-sixth to one-quarter turn without turning the drum/rotor, and then tighten the adjusting nut to the specified preload torque. This is usually about 15–25 in.-lb (1.69–2.82 Nm).

6 Install the keyed washer and adjusting nut on the spindle and tighten until finger tight.

7 Tighten the adjusting nut to the specified seating torque (usually about 20 ft-lb [27.1 Nm]) while turning the drum/rotor. This squeezes the excess grease out from between the wheel bearings and races while seating the bearings. Note: Do NOT leave the bearing this tight, as it is too tight for operation of the vehicle. Make sure you perform the next step!

8 Loosen the adjusting nut approximately one-sixth to one-quarter turn without turning the drum/rotor, and then tighten the adjusting nut to the specified preload torque. This is usually about 15–25 in.-lb (1.69–2.82 Nm). Note: The unit is *inch* pounds, NOT foot pounds. Don't mistake the two! **(Photo 3)**

To install the locking mechanism, follow the steps in **SKILL DRILL 34-5**:

1 Install the locking mechanism.

2 **If it is a cotter pin**, insert the new cotter pin through the **castellated nut** or locking cage and spindle (the spindle may have more than one hole).

The short leg of the cotter pin should be against the castellated nut, and the long leg should be toward you. With the cotter pin fully engaged in the notch, bend the outer leg toward you and up over the end of the spindle. Cut it off just short of the spindle. Also cut the short leg off so it does not extend beyond the nut or cage. Make sure the cotter pin will not hit the inside of the dust cap. **(Photo 1)**

3 **If it is a bendable tang locking style**, then place the tang washer against the adjusting nut and thread the locking nut up against it. Torque the locking nut to the specified torque, and bend the appropriate tang out toward you against the flat side of the locking nut with a small pry bar to lock the adjustment in place. **(Photo 2)**

4 **If it is a locking nut style**, then tighten the lock nut to the specified torque. This is usually a substantial torque of 50 ft-lb (67.79 Nm) or more. **(Photo 3)**

5 Install the dust cap, being sure it is fully seated in the hub. Make sure the drum/rotor turns freely without binding or making any unusual noises. **(Photo 4)**

SKILL DRILL | 34-5 | Installing the Locking Mechanism

1. Install the locking mechanism. If it is a cotter pin, insert the new cotter pin through the castellated nut or locking cage and spindle. The short leg of the cotter pin should be against the castellated nut and the long leg should be toward you. With the cotter pin fully engaged in the notch, bend the outer leg toward you and up over the end of the spindle. Cut it off just short of the spindle. Also cut the short leg off so it does not extend beyond the nut or cage. Make sure the cotter pin will not hit the inside of the dust cap.

2. If it is a bendable tang locking style, then place the tang washer against the adjusting nut and thread the locking nut up against it. Torque the locking nut to the specified torque, and bend the appropriate tang out toward you against the flat side of the locking nut with a small pry bar to lock the adjustment in place.

3. If it is a locking nut style, then tighten the lock nut to the specified torque. This is usually a substantial torque of 50 ft-lb (67.79 Nm) or more.

4. Install the dust cap, being sure it is fully seated in the hub. Make sure the drum/rotor turns freely without binding or making any unusual noises.

TECHNICIAN TIP

Some technicians simulate the preload torque by placing a 12" crescent wrench on the nut and using the hanging weight of the crescent wrench when it is parallel to the ground. Do not let it drop into position; just lower the handle to where it stops turning the nut. This should be when the handle is approximately level. If not, reposition the crescent wrench on the nut and allow it to lower until it stops parallel.

Replacing Wheel Bearings and Races

Wheel bearings and races need to be replaced only when they are damaged. If one part of the wheel bearing is damaged, all parts must be replaced. So if the tapered roller bearings are damaged, both the bearing and the race of that bearing need to be replaced at the same time. On serviceable bearings, the inner race, roller bearings, and bearing cage are one unit, which generally slips off of the spindle. The outer race is usually press-fit into the hub and will need to be driven or pressed out and a new one press-fit back in. It is critical that the seat in the hub be spotlessly clean with no burrs or the bearing race will not seat properly and the bearing will fail prematurely.

To replace a wheel bearing and race, follow the steps in **SKILL DRILL 34-6**:

1. With the wheel bearings removed from the wheel hub, clean and inspect the bearings and races. If damaged, or directed by your supervisor, determine which race to remove.

2. Using a hydraulic press or a hammer and punch from the opposite side of the hub, carefully force the race from the hub. In either case, it is critical that the race be removed as straight as possible to prevent damaging the hub. **(Photo 1)**

3. Clean the inside diameter of the hub in a parts washer.

4. Remove any burrs with a fine file or Dremel™, and remove any debris from the seat.

5. Lightly lubricate the outside surface of the new race and set it thick side down in the hub. **(Photo 2)**

6. Using a hydraulic press or a hammer and bearing race installer, carefully drive the race until it is

fully seated in the hub. When using a hammer and punch, a sharp metallic sound should be produced when it is fully seated, compared to the dull thud as it is being driven into place.

7. Inspect the race to verify that it is fully seated. Also check for any damage caused by installation.

8. If everything is good, pack the new bearing and install it according to Skill Drills 34-2 through 34-5. **(Photo 3)**

Removing and Reinstalling Sealed Wheel Bearings

Sealed wheel bearings come in two configurations. The first is a replaceable sealed bearing only. On most front wheels, this wheel bearing is pressed between the hub and wheel flange and is the more difficult of the two to replace. The second configuration consists of a unitized wheel bearing hub including a sealed wheel bearing, a removable wheel bearing hub, and possibly the wheel flange. In most cases, this type can be unbolted from the suspension system and a new one bolted in its place, and it is ready to go.

SKILL DRILL | 34-6 | Replacing Wheel Bearings and Races

1. With the wheel bearings removed from the wheel hub, clean and inspect the bearing and race for damage. Determine which bearing and race need to be replaced. Using a hydraulic press or a hammer and punch from the opposite side of the hub, carefully force the race from the hub. Keep it as straight as possible while removing it.

2. Clean the inside diameter of the hub in a parts washer. Remove any burrs with a fine file or Dremel™, and remove any debris from the seat. Lightly lubricate the outside surface of the new race and set it thick side down in the hub.

3. Using a hydraulic press or a hammer and bearing race installer, carefully drive the race until it is fully seated in the hub. When using a hammer and punch, a distinct sharp metallic sound should be produced when it seats. Inspect the race to verify that it is fully seated. Also check for any damage caused by installation. If everything is good, pack the new bearing and install it according to Skill Drills 34-2 through 34-5.

The replaceable bearing style needs to be pressed apart with a hydraulic press or a special sealed bearing removal/installing tool. If using the hydraulic press method, the steering knuckle will need to be removed from the vehicle so it can be placed on the hydraulic press. If the special sealed bearing tool is used, most bearings can be removed while the steering knuckle is still installed on the vehicle, which can save the technician a fair amount of time. To remove and reinstall a sealed wheel bearing assembly using the unitized wheel bearing hub style, follow the steps in **SKILL DRILL 34-7**:

1. Loosen the axle hub nut, if equipped, while the tire is still on the ground. This nut could be tightened to 200 ft-lb (271.1 Nm) or more, so it is easier to break loose with the tire preventing the axle from spinning while loosening the nut. Some vehicles will require you to remove a locking mechanism such as a cotter pin to remove the axle nut.

2. Remove the wheel and brake assembly following the specified procedure. Also disconnect the ABS connector and/or sensor if mounted to the hub, so as not to damage the sensor, connector, or wiring. **(Photo 1)**

3. If the wheel you are working on is a drive wheel, remove the axle hub nut and tap the drive axle loose with a dead blow hammer. Be careful to not damage the threads on the end of the axle. **(Photo 2)**

4. Unbolt and remove the hub assembly from the steering knuckle, which is usually held on by approximately four bolts.

5. Clean the steering knuckle and check the hub seat for nicks, burrs, or other damage. **(Photo 3)**

6. Carefully compare the new hub to the old one, then fit the new hub assembly (over the axle shaft, if equipped) to the knuckle, making sure it is fully seated, and torque the mounting bolts to the specified torque.

7. Reassemble the brake assembly and ABS sensor, if removed, following the specified procedure, install the wheel, and torque the lug nuts. Be sure the correct ends of the lug nuts are facing the wheel.

8. Install the drive axle nut, if equipped. Use a new hub nut if called for by the manufacturer, and torque to specifications. **(Photo 4)**

SKILL DRILL 34-7 Removing and Reinstalling Sealed Wheel Bearings Using the Unitized Wheel Bearing Hub Style

1. Loosen the axle hub nut, if equipped, while the tire is still on the ground. Remove the wheel and brake assembly following the specified procedure. Also disconnect the ABS connector and/or sensor if mounted to the hub.

2. If the wheel you are working on is a drive wheel, remove the axle hub nut and tap the drive axle loose with a dead blow hammer.

3. Unbolt and remove the hub assembly from the steering knuckle. Clean the knuckle assembly and check the hub seat for nicks, burrs, or other damage.

SKILL DRILL | 34-7 | Removing and Reinstalling Sealed Wheel Bearings Using the Unitized Wheel Bearing Hub Style, continued

4. Carefully compare the new hub to the old one, then fit the new hub assembly (over the axle shaft, if equipped) to the knuckle, making sure it is fully seated in place, and torque the mounting bolts to the specified torque. Reassemble the brake assembly and ABS sensor following the specified procedure, install the wheel, and torque the lug nuts. Install the drive axle nut, if equipped. Use a new hub nut if called for by the manufacturer, and torque to specifications.

Wrap-up

Ready for Review

- Wheel bearings allow wheels to roll with minimum friction.
- Wheel bearing assemblies include: outer race, inner race, roller or ball bearings, and a bearing cage.
- Categories of wheel bearings are serviceable or sealed.
- Types of wheel bearings are: cylindrical roller bearing, tapered roller bearing, ball bearing, double-row ball bearing, and double-row tapered roller bearings.
- Cylindrical roller bearing assemblies have parallel races flanking the rollers and are most commonly used in rear axles of rear-wheel drive vehicles.
- Cylindrical roller bearing assemblies rely on lubrication to cushion the rollers and transfer heat to the atmosphere.
- Tapered roller-bearing assemblies have tapered rollers housed in a bearing cage, are used for heavier loads, are used in pairs, and control side movement.
- Tapered roller bearing assemblies must be adjusted for proper running clearance.
- Ball bearings are used in light-duty vehicles, are designed as a manufacturer-sealed bearing assembly, and should be replaced as a unit.

- Wheel bearings are sealed to keep out contaminants and contain the lubricant.
- Serviceable wheel bearings need periodic maintenance, including replacing old grease seals and the cotter pin.
- Wheel bearings are lubricated by gear lube or bearing grease.
- Gear lube is classified by viscosity (thickness) and service grade.
- Bearing grease is graded by thickness; it holds its shape at room temperature.
- For correct operation, wheel bearings must be adjusted for proper end play preload.
- Wheel bearing locking mechanisms include a keyed washer, adjusting nut, lock cage, and cotter pin.
- Damage to wheel bearings may be from: vehicle overload, shock loads, improper adjustment, or wear over time.
- Wheel bearing assembly diagnosis may include wiggling the tire (with vehicle lifted) by hand, by test-driving, or placing on a hoist and rotating the wheels.
- Determine the cause of wheel bearing failure so that the new bearings are not damaged for the same reason.

Key Terms

adjusting nut The nut used to adjust the end play or preload of a wheel bearing.

anti-friction bearing Wheel bearing assemblies that use surfaces that are in rolling contact with each other to greatly reduce friction compared to surfaces in sliding contact.

ball bearings The rolling components of a wheel bearing consisting of hardened balls that roll in matching grooves in the inner and outer races.

bearing cage The component in a wheel bearing that maintains the proper spacing between the roller bearings or ball bearings.

bearing packer A tool that forces grease into the spaces between the bearing rollers.

bushing A sleeve type bearing made of metal or plastic bearing material used to support a rotating shaft.

castellated nut An adjusting nut with slots cut into the top such that it resembles a castle; used with a cotter pin to prevent the nut from turning.

cotter pin A one-use soft metal pin that can be bent into shape and is used to retain bearing adjusting nuts.

cylindrical roller bearing assembly A type of wheel bearing with races and rollers that are cylindrical in shape and roll between inner and outer races, which are parallel to each other.

double-row ball bearing assembly A single ball bearing assembly using two rows of ball bearings riding in two channels in the races.

end play The in-and-out movement of the hub caused by clearance within the wheel bearing assembly.

fill plug Usually a threaded plug that can be removed to allow the level of a fluid to be checked and filled. This could also be a rubber snap fit plug.

friction bearing A bearing that uses sliding motion between components, such as a clutch pilot bearing.

garter spring A coiled spring that is fitted to the inside of the sealing lip of many seals, used to hold the lip in contact with the shaft.

gear lube A type of lubricant primarily used to lubricate transmission and differential gears but also used to lubricate some wheel bearings.

grease A lubricating liquid thickened to make it suitable for use with many wheel bearings.

grease seal A component that is designed to keep grease from leaking out and contaminants from leaking in.

inner race The inside component of a wheel bearing that has a smooth, hardened surface for rollers or balls to ride on.

interference fit A condition when two parts are held together by friction because the outside diameter of the inner component is slightly larger than the inside diameter of the outer component.

keyed lock washer The washer that fits between the adjusting nut and the lock nut; the face of the washer is drilled with a series of holes that mate to a short pin from the adjusting nut, locking it to the spindle. Also referred to as a tang washer.

keyed washer The washer that fits between the adjusting nut and the wheel bearing and that has the center hole keyed to fit a slot on the spindle or axle tube.

lithium soap A thickening agent for grease to give it the proper consistency.

lock cage The stamped sheet metal cap that fits over the bearing adjustment nut and is secured by a cotter pin going through it and the spindle/axle.

lock nut The nut that holds the adjusting nut from turning; usually tightened much tighter than the adjusting nut.

molybdenum thickening agent A compound used in some greases to give it the needed consistency.

National Lubricating Grease Institute (NLGI) An organization that grades the thickness of automotive and industrial grease.

outer race The outside component of a wheel bearing that has a smooth, hardened surface for rollers or balls to ride on.

preload A condition where the wheel bearing components are forced together under pressure and therefore have no end play.

roller bearings The rolling components of a wheel bearing consisting of hardened cylindrical or tapered rollers.

running clearance The amount of space between wheel bearing components while in operation.

sealed bearings Wheel bearings that are assembled by the manufacturer with the proper lubrication and sealed for life; cannot normally be disassembled.

serviceable bearings Wheel bearings that can be disassembled, cleaned, inspected, packed, reinstalled, and adjusted.

tapered roller bearing assembly A type of wheel bearing with races and rollers that are tapered in such a manner that all of the tapered angles meet at a common point, which allows them to roll freely and yet control thrust.

unitized wheel bearing hub An assembly consisting of the hub, wheel bearing(s), and possibly the wheel flange, which is preassembled and ready to be installed on a vehicle.

viscosity The measurement of the thickness of a liquid.

wheel bearing A component that allows the wheels to rotate freely while supporting the weight of the vehicle, made up of an inner race, outer race, rollers or balls, and a cage.

ASE-Type Questions

1. Tech A says that cylindrical roller bearings can carry more weight than similarly sized ball bearings. Tech B says that tapered roller bearings used in opposing pairs, control side thrust. Who is correct?
   a. Tech A
   b. Tech B
   c. Both A and B
   d. Neither A nor B

2. Tech A says that a tapered roller bearing assembly has less rolling resistance than a similarly sized ball bearing assembly. Tech B says that the bearing assembly in a unitized wheel bearing assembly can normally be disassembled, cleaned, and repacked. Who is correct?
   a. Tech A
   b. Tech B
   c. Both A and B
   d. Neither A nor B

3. Tech A says that over time a grease seal can wear a groove in the sealing surface of the axle or shaft. Tech B says that grease seals need to be replaced every time the bearing is removed. Who is correct?
   a. Tech A
   b. Tech B
   c. Both A and B
   d. Neither A nor B

4. Tech A says that in a full floating axle, the axle does not support the weight of the vehicle. Tech B says that when installing tapered wheel bearings, the final torque should be about 20 ft/lbs. Who is correct?
   a. Tech A
   b. Tech B
   c. Both A and B
   d. Neither A nor B

5. Tech A says that serviceable wheel bearings can be repacked by removing the dust cap, filling it with grease, and reinstalling it. Tech B says that the cotter pin must be replaced with a new one every time it is removed. Who is correct?
   a. Tech A
   b. Tech B
   c. Both A and B
   d. Neither A nor B

6. Tech A says that the grease level in the final drive is okay as long as you can touch the level with your finger. Tech B says that the grease level should normally be no more than ¼" below the threads on the fill plug hole. Who is correct?
   a. Tech A
   b. Tech B
   c. Both A and B
   d. Neither A nor B

7. Tech A says that wheel bearings need to be replaced as a set, bearing and race. Tech B says that the wheel bearings and races on both sides of the vehicle must be replaced if one side fails. Who is correct?
   a. Tech A
   b. Tech B
   c. Both A and B
   d. Neither A nor B

8. Tech A says that unitized hubs have a wheel nut with a higher installation torque than serviceable wheel bearings. Tech B says that unitized hubs have the proper bearing end play designed into the assembly once they are torqued properly. Who is correct?
   a. Tech A
   b. Tech B
   c. Both A and B
   d. Neither A nor B

9. Tech A says when installing a bearing race you should use a 3-lb hammer and a brass drift. Tech B says that when installing a bearing race you should use a 3-lb hammer and a ⅜" drive extension. Who is correct?
   a. Tech A
   b. Tech B
   c. Both A and B
   d. Neither A nor B

10. Tech A says that when a race is fully seated, a sharp metallic sound will be produced when installation is complete. Tech B says that to be sure a race is fully seated, the wheel bearing adjusting nut should be tightened to at least 100 ft-lbs of torque, which will finish seating it. Who is correct?
    a. Tech A
    b. Tech B
    c. Both A and B
    d. Neither A nor B

CHAPTER 35

> ## Knowledge Objectives

After reading this chapter, you will be able to:
1. Describe the safety advantages of EBC systems. (p 1154)
2. Describe the three most common EBC systems. (pp 1154–1155)
3. Describe understeer and oversteer conditions. (pp 1154–1155)

Electronic Brake Control

Knowledge Objectives, continued

4. Describe the basic principles of operation of anti-lock brake systems. (pp 1155–1164)
5. Describe the purpose, function, and types of ABS master cylinders. (pp 1158–1159)
6. Describe the purpose, function, and types of hydraulic control units. (pp 1159–1161)
7. Describe the difference between hydraulic control units with different numbers of channels. (pp 1160–1161)
8. Describe the purpose, function, and types of accumulators. (pp 1160–1161)
9. Describe the purpose, function, and types of wheel speed sensors. (pp 1161–1163)
10. Describe the purpose and function of the brake switch. (p 1163)
11. Describe the basic principles of operation of traction control. (pp 1164–1165)
12. Describe additional functions that can be built into basic EBC systems. (pp 1164–1165)
13. Describe the methods used by the traction control system to reduce engine torque. (p 1165)
14. Describe the purpose and function of the steering wheel position sensor. (pp 1165–1166)
15. Describe the purpose and function of the yaw sensor. (pp 1165–1166)
16. Describe the basic principles of operation of electronic stability control. (pp 1165–1167)
17. Describe the process of diagnosing EBC systems. (pp 1167–1172)

Skills Objectives

After reading this chapter, you will be able to:
1. Test variable reluctance sensors. (pp 1168–1169)
2. Test magneto-resistive sensors. (pp 1169–1170)
3. Bleed the EBC system hydraulic circuits. (pp 1171–1172)
4. Depressurize high-pressure components of EBC systems. (p 1172)
5. Remove and install EBC system electrical and hydraulic components. (p 1172)

▶ Introduction

<u>Electronic brake control (EBC) systems</u> have greatly increased the safety of vehicles over the years by integrating computer controls into the braking system. Standard hydraulic brake systems have limitations on how effectively they can stop a vehicle. The driver can only input braking force to the system through the brake pedal, which applies hydraulic pressure at predetermined ratios to the front and rear brakes. In a panic situation, the driver is unable to apply the exact amount of force to maintain the maximum amount of braking. Too little force and the vehicle does not stop as quickly. Too much force and the tires skid, making the vehicle's stopping distance longer. At the same time, if the front wheels skid, the driver will lose the ability to steer the vehicle. If the rear wheels skid, the car could spin out and possibly roll over.

Even if the driver could apply the perfect amount of braking force, there is no way to accommodate different amounts of traction at each wheel, such as when one or two wheels are on pavement and the other tires are on loose gravel. This situation can also lead to a loss of control of the vehicle.

In the quest for increased safety, manufacturers developed a series of EBC systems. The first-generation EBC system was the anti-lock brake system (ABS). The ABS system was designed to prevent wheels from locking up under braking conditions and shorten most panic stop distances. ABS systems also helped the driver maintain steering control of the vehicle. The Principles of Braking chapter covers this topic in detail.

▶ Basic Operation of Electronic Brake Control Systems

ABS systems use a computer that monitors the speed of each wheel as the brakes are applied. If one or more wheels begin to lock up, the computer sends electrical signals to <u>solenoid valves</u> that momentarily hold or release hydraulic pressure to that wheel until it speeds up and starts rolling again. Once that happens, the computer allows hydraulic pressure to be applied to that wheel again, slowing it down. This process is repeated very rapidly as the vehicle is brought to a stop. Because the tires remain in rolling contact with the road surface, the vehicle can be steered, allowing the driver to maintain directional control (steerability) of the vehicle and thereby decreasing the chances of a collision. These actions are completely dependent on the driver applying pressure to the brake pedal.

While the basic ABS system does a good job of managing the braking effort of the driver in a panic stop situation, it is limited to using the hydraulic pressure the driver exerts on the system. This means that the standard ABS system by itself cannot increase the hydraulic pressure in the ABS system; nor can it apply hydraulic pressure separate from the driver. As long as the driver is exerting firm pressure on the brake pedal, ABS can work to minimize the stopping distance and steerability of the vehicle.

The second enhancement to the EBC system was the <u>traction control system (TCS)</u>. With the addition of a high-pressure pump and a few <u>isolation valves</u> to

▶ You are the Automotive Technician

A long-time customer brings his 2007 Ford Explorer into the shop to get his brakes inspected. He claims that the brake pedal pulsates when he applies the brakes. You ask him if he has had any recent work done on the vehicle. He explains that he recently had new tires put on. He also explains that while leaving the parking lot, a car pulled out in front of him and he had to lock up the brakes to avoid hitting him. He was startled by heavy brake pulsations, which have gotten worse each time he uses the brakes. He is wondering if there is a problem with the anti-lock brakes.

1. Is there a problem with the ABS system? What will you say to the customer?
2. What do you suspect is causing the pedal pulsations, and how did it occur?
3. How would you diagnose a problem when the ABS warning lamp is illuminated?

the basic ABS system, manufacturers found that they could assist the driver in minimizing wheel slip while the vehicle is being accelerated. This is especially effective on slippery road surfaces such as gravel, snow, and ice. In most vehicles, the vehicle's traction is only as good as the traction on the tire with the least traction. So if one tire is on a patch of ice, the vehicle may not have enough traction to move, and will ultimately become stuck. The TCS system applies brake pressure to the slipping tire, which causes more of the engine's torque to be transmitted to the wheel or wheels with the most traction. If necessary, the TCS system can also request that the engine's power train control module reduce the power output of the engine to further enhance traction. These actions are automatic and do not require any input from the driver.

The next enhancement to the EBC system was the **electronic stability control (ESC) system**. ESC takes the ABS and TCS systems to the next level. By adding sensor information regarding the driver's directional intent (from the **steering wheel position sensor**) and sensor information regarding the vehicle's actual direction (from the **yaw sensor**), the EBC module (EBCM) can detect the start of an **understeer**, **oversteer**, or potential rollover condition. Understeer and oversteer are conditions that happen when a vehicle is traveling too fast for a particular corner. During understeer, the vehicle's front wheels are turned more sharply than the vehicle's path FIGURE 35-1. The front tires are actually sliding somewhat sideways

toward the outside of the corner. The greater the understeer, the more the tires slide. Understeer is also referred to as "push," as in "the vehicle is pushing in the corners."

Oversteer is just the opposite. It occurs when the vehicle is turning more sharply than the front wheels are being steered. This happens when the rear tires are sliding sideways toward the outside of the corner. Oversteer is also referred to as "loose," as in "the vehicle is getting loose in the corners." Most passenger vehicles are designed to have a bit of understeer because this condition is easier for a driver to recover from than an oversteer.

Using information provided by the sensors of the ESC system, plus the wheel speed sensors, the EBCM monitors the stability of the vehicle and can command individual brakes to be applied and request decreased engine torque as necessary. For example, if a vehicle is traveling too fast around a right-hand corner and the front wheels are starting to lose traction (understeer), the control system can apply the right rear brake to help pivot the vehicle around the right rear tire, assisting it to turn and at the same time slowing the vehicle slightly. If additional measures are needed, additional brakes can be applied and the engine torque reduced. The control system performs these functions automatically without any driver input other than steering the vehicle in the direction intended.

FIGURE 35-1 During understeer, the vehicle's front wheels are turned more sharply than the vehicle's path.

Caring for the Customer

It is important for customers to know that ABS, TCS, and ESC are not guarantees of avoiding an accident. These systems are designed to help drivers who are driving in a responsible manner to avoid an accident. Drivers can easily exceed the ability of these systems.

Anti-Lock Braking System Overview

The ABS system is designed to prevent wheels locking or skidding, no matter how hard the brakes are applied or how slippery the road surface, and to maintain steering control of the vehicle. The primary components of the ABS braking system are:

- ABS master cylinder: Creates hydraulic pressure for each of the two hydraulic brake circuits.
- EBCM or electronic control unit (ECU): An onboard computer that is programmed to monitor sensor data and send output control signals to

electronic solenoid valves, which modify brake pressure to individual wheel brake units.

- **Hydraulic control unit (HCU)** or modulator: Contains electric solenoid valves controlled by the EBCM to modify hydraulic pressure in each hydraulic circuit **FIGURE 35-2**. Most systems also contain an **accumulator** to store brake fluid under pressure.
- Power booster: Boosts driver brake pedal force on the master cylinder.
- **Wheel speed sensor**: A device that monitors wheel speed and sends that signal to the EBCM.
- **Brake switch**: An on/off switch that informs the EBCM of whether or not the driver is applying the brakes.

The EBCM may be located inside the vehicle, mounted near the HCU, or it could be integrated into the HCU. In many cases, it is a separate module from the power train control module and may be part of the vehicle's **body control module (BCM)**. The body control module is the computer that controls the electrical system in the body of the vehicle. The EBCM receives input signals from the ABS sensors, compares that data to information stored in its memory, decides what actions are necessary, and sends output commands to the HCU.

The HCU or modulator is connected in-line with the brake lines between the master cylinder and the wheel brake units. It houses electric solenoid valves that control the flow of brake fluid to each wheel. The HCU receives operating signals from the EBCM to control the brakes under ABS conditions.

The power booster and master cylinder assembly is mounted on the firewall. In most current applications, these components operate similarly to non-ABS power boosters and tandem master cylinders. Some manufacturers use a portless master cylinder to allow brake fluid to return to the master cylinder reservoir more easily than a master cylinder fitted with a compensating port. When the brakes are operating without ABS action, the brake pressure is controlled by the driver's foot pressure, which is assisted by the power booster. In other words, the ABS system only affects brake pressure when one or more wheels are starting to skid.

The wheel speed sensor consists of a toothed tone wheel (or tone ring) that rotates with the road wheels and a pick-up assembly that generates a speed signal. The wheel speed sensor is located near the wheel hub in many applications **FIGURE 35-3**. The wheel speed sensor sends an electrical signal that varies with the speed of the wheel to the EBCM. Wheel speed sensors can be **variable reluctance sensors** (magnetic induction), generating an analog AC sine wave signal **FIGURE 35-4**. Wheel speed sensors can also be of the magneto-resistive or

FIGURE 35-3 A wheel speed sensor and tone wheel.

FIGURE 35-2 A hydraulic control unit (HCU).

FIGURE 35-4 An oscilloscope pattern from a wheel speed sensor.

Hall effect type, generating a digital square wave signal. These signals can be used by the EBCM to determine the speed of each wheel. We will cover the operation of these sensors in much greater depth in the ABS Components section.

Anti-Lock Braking System Operation

Applying brakes too hard or on a slippery surface can cause the wheels to lock. When the wheels lock, steering control is lost and, in most cases, longer stopping distances result due to the reduced friction of the sliding tire. The ABS system prevents the wheels from locking or skidding, no matter how hard the brakes are applied or how slippery the road surface. Steering stays under control and the stopping distances are generally reduced.

When the ignition switch is turned on, the ABS controller illuminates the yellow ABS warning lamp and performs an automatic self-check of the system. If the system check passes, the controller will extinguish the warning lamp indicating to the driver that the ABS system is functional. Some ABS systems will perform an additional self-check once the vehicle is traveling greater than approximately 3–5 mph (4.8–8 kph). Failures in the ABS system will cause the controller to illuminate the ABS warning light in the instrument panel.

As the wheels start to turn, the wheel speed sensors generate small electrical signals and send them to the EBCM. When the brakes are applied, the wheels' rotational speed is reduced. As the speed changes, the signal sent to the EBCM changes in like manner. If the control unit detects that a wheel might be slowing too quickly and starting to lock, it sends an output signal to the appropriate solenoid valve in the HCU to modify the hydraulic pressure to the affected wheel brake unit.

Principles of ABS Braking

Braking force and the tendency of the wheels to lock up are affected by a combination of factors such as the friction of the road surface; the type, condition, and loading of each tire; and the difference between the vehicle speed and the speed of the wheels. It should be noted that maximum traction happens with approximately 10–20% tire slip. Thus, maximum braking traction occurs when the wheels are rotating 10–20% slower than the vehicle speed. In the same way, maximum traction during acceleration occurs when the wheels are rotating 10–20% faster than the vehicle speed. At the same time, traction falls off quickly above 20% wheel slip, which is why ABS is so effective. It allows just enough slip to keep the tires at close to their maximum traction. It does

so by rapidly modulating the hydraulic pressure in the vehicle's brake system.

During normal braking, as the rotational speed of each wheel falls equally, no ABS intervention is needed. In this condition, the EBCM does not energize the solenoid valves in the hydraulic unit. The master cylinder hydraulic pressure is applied to the wheel brake units, and the ABS is not involved. However, even though the ABS is passive during normal braking, the EBCM is constantly monitoring the speed of each wheel, looking for any wheel that begins to decelerate more rapidly than any of the other wheels.

If one wheel speed sensor signals more severe wheel deceleration—which means the wheel is beginning to slip—the EBCM sends current to the appropriate solenoid valve **FIGURE 35-5**. The first level of valve action isolates that brake circuit from the master cylinder. This stops the braking pressure at that wheel from rising and keeps it constant. If the wheel speed sensors indicate that the wheel is still decelerating too rapidly, the EBCM commands the appropriate solenoid valve to release braking pressure. The solenoid valve opens a passage from the brake circuit, releasing the hydraulic pressure to that brake unit. Brake fluid is released from the specific brake circuit back to the master cylinder. Pressure in the brake circuit is reduced so that the wheel is not being braked.

If the wheel speed sensors indicate that reducing the brake pressure is allowing the wheel to roll again, the EBCM stops sending current to the hydraulic unit and de-energizes the solenoid valves. This lets the hydraulic pressure increase so that the brake is again applied by the master cylinder pressure. This cycle repeats itself at up to 16 times per second. It is normal in an ABS system for

FIGURE 35-5 HCU solenoid valve arrangement.

the valves in the HCU to keep changing position as they modulate the brake pressure that is being applied. These changes in valve position normally cause rapid hydraulic pulsations, which can be felt by the driver through the brake pedal. The solenoid valves also make a fairly loud clicking noise as they cycle on and off.

ABS Components
ABS Master Cylinder

ABS master cylinders come in two major configurations: integral and nonintegral **FIGURE 35-6**. Integral ABS systems are mostly found on older vehicles. They combine the tandem master cylinder, HCU, and power booster in one unit. The power booster consists of a high-pressure electric pump and accumulator that operates the integrated master cylinder. Brake fluid passes from the master cylinder portion of the assembly to the HCU portion where pressures are modified by the computer-controlled solenoid valves.

Nonintegral ABS systems use a fairly standard tandem master cylinder and a typical vacuum or hydraulic power booster. The booster assists the driver in applying force to the master cylinder. The master cylinder sends fluid under pressure to the HCU, which is a separate assembly that is installed in-line with the brake lines between the master cylinder and the wheel brake units. If the pressure needs are modified, the computer-controlled solenoid valves in the HCU will carry out the commands.

Purpose and Operation of the ABS Master Cylinder

Nonintegral ABS master cylinders are usually identical to non-ABS master cylinders. They both use primary and secondary pistons in a common housing with a common bore. Some of these master cylinders utilize a portless ABS master cylinder design, which does not use a compensating port on the secondary circuit. Instead, the secondary piston incorporates a center valve **FIGURE 35-7** that controls the opening and closing of a supply port in the piston. At rest, the supply port is open and connects the reservoir with the front brake circuit. The primary piston still uses an inlet port and a compensating port; therefore, the portless design is only used on the secondary circuit.

When the brake is applied, the primary piston moves and closes its compensating port. Fluid pressure in the primary circuit rises. It acts with the primary piston spring to move the secondary piston forward, closing the center valve. Pressure builds in the secondary circuit. Pressure keeps building in both circuits and applies the brakes in both circuits.

FIGURE 35-6 Nonintegral and integral master cylinder assemblies.

FIGURE 35-7 Portless ABS master cylinder.

If braking conditions are such that the hydraulic modulator must return brake fluid to the master cylinder, then, for the front brake circuits, brake fluid is returned to the front section. This forces the secondary piston back against the force of the primary piston spring and the rear brake pressure. If enough brake fluid returns, the center valve opens and allows the brake fluid to return to the master cylinder reservoir. If brake fluid is returned from the rear brake circuit, the secondary and primary pistons tend to be forced apart, which generally moves the primary piston rearward. If it travels far enough, brake fluid will return to the reservoir through the compensating port.

The amount of brake fluid that returns to the master cylinder is determined by the degree of anti-lock braking control. With as many as 16 ABS control cycles per second, the rapid changes in hydraulic pressure cause brake fluid pulsations to be sent back to the master cylinder; these pulsations can be felt by the driver at the brake pedal.

Hydraulic Control Unit (HCU)

In a standard ABS system, the HCU houses electrically operated hydraulic control valves (solenoid valves) that control brake pressure to specific wheel brake circuits. Each separate hydraulic circuit within the HCU has one or two solenoid valves that provide three operating conditions: apply, hold, and release. During the apply mode, the solenoid valves allow brake fluid to freely flow through the HCU hydraulic control circuit to the specific brake circuit. In this case, the driver is in full control of the brakes through the master cylinder.

In the hold mode, a solenoid valve "isolates" the master cylinder from the brake circuit. This prevents brake pressure from building any further. The brake pressure to the wheel is held at that level until the solenoid valve is commanded to change its position. In the release mode, a solenoid valve "dumps" the brake circuit pressure to the wheel, allowing it to start rolling again. The solenoid valve opens a passage back to the accumulator where brake fluid is stored until it can be returned by an electric pump to the master cylinder reservoir.

The isolation valve and dump valve can be separate valves or they can be combined into a common assembly.

> **TECHNICIAN TIP**
>
> Many, but not all, HCUs are sealed units and cannot be serviced. If you are working on a vehicle with a sealed HCU and it is faulty, it will have to be replaced. This can be quite costly.

Either way, they open and close passageways. However, if they are separate valves, they use a separate **electric solenoid** to operate each valve. If the valve and electric solenoid are combined in a common assembly, then they have one electric solenoid that operates the valve in three positions—one position for apply, one for hold, and one for release.

Purpose and Operation of the HCU

The ABS control module (or EBCM) sends commands in the form of electrical signals to the HCU. The HCU executes the commands, using one or two solenoid valves for each hydraulic circuit, depending on the type of HCU. Since the control valves are situated between the master cylinder and the wheel brake units, they can allow, block, or release hydraulic pressure going to the brake units.

In a normal non-ABS braking scenario, brake pedal force is transmitted to the master cylinder, then through the non-energized open isolation valve to the brake unit at the wheel. When the signals from the wheel speed sensors show no tendency for the wheels to lock up, the EBCM does not send any control current to the solenoid valves. The solenoid valves are not energized and the hydraulic pressure from the master cylinder flows freely through the HCU to the brake units at each wheel.

When the control unit detects any lock-up tendency, it sends a command current to the isolation solenoid valve. This current causes the solenoid valve to close, isolating the brake circuit from the master cylinder. That holds the hydraulic pressure between the solenoid valve and the brake circuit constant—regardless of whether the master cylinder hydraulic pressure rises or falls.

If the wheel speed sensors signal that excessive wheel deceleration is continuing, the control module commands the dump valve to open. This reduces the braking pressure by opening a passage from the brake circuit to the accumulator. A pump in the HCU sends brake fluid back to the master cylinder, pushing one or both pistons rearward in the bore.

If the sensors indicate that the lower pressure has allowed the wheel to speed up, the EBCM de-energizes the solenoid valve(s), closing the dump valve and opening the isolation valve. The hydraulic pressure from the master cylinder is again allowed to apply the brakes, and the wheel is again slowed. This process continues until the vehicle comes to a stop or the driver lifts his or her foot from the brake pedal. In most standard ABS systems, the hydraulic pressure in the brake circuits can never rise above the master cylinder pressure.

Types of HCUs

There are a number of HCUs that vehicle manufacturers use, and they generally fall into a few categories. The first category relates to how many channels the system has. A **channel** generally means the number of electrical wheel sensor circuits and hydraulic circuits a system has **FIGURE 35-8**. A single-channel system uses one sensor circuit with the speed sensor typically located in the differential and one hydraulic control circuit to control both rear wheels.

A two-channel system is similar but uses two separate speed sensors and hydraulic control circuits, one for each rear wheel. The two hydraulic control circuits apply brake pressure separately to the rear wheels. A three-channel system is configured so that each front wheel has its own speed sensor and hydraulic control circuit, while the rear brakes use a single speed sensor with a single hydraulic control circuit. A four-channel system uses separate speed sensors and hydraulic control circuits for each of the four wheels.

Another difference among types of HCUs is the number of solenoid valves per hydraulic control circuit. Some HCU units use a single, three-position solenoid valve per circuit, while others use dual, two-position valves per hydraulic circuit. The first position of the single, three-position valve allows brake fluid to flow through the apply port, while blocking the release port. The second position blocks the apply port and the release port. The third position blocks the apply port and opens the release port. Thus, the single, three-position valve has all three conditions—apply, hold, and release.

The dual, two-position valve style of HCU uses one solenoid valve to open and close the apply port. This is commonly called the isolation valve. When this valve is not energized, the apply port is open. The second solenoid valve opens and closes the release port. When this valve is not energized, the release port is blocked. The EBCM operates each of these valves independently to

FIGURE 35-8 The four types of ABS channels. **A.** Single-channel system. **B.** Two-channel system. **C.** Three-channel system. **D.** Four-channel system.

obtain apply, hold, and release functions. Because there are twice as many solenoid valves and each valve needs its own electrical control circuit, the EBCM is more complicated and costly to build. Therefore, EBCMs are specifically designed to work with only the specified type of HCU, and EBCMs and HCUs cannot be randomly interchanged.

Another difference between HCUs is the type of accumulator used, low pressure or high pressure. **Low-pressure accumulators** hold brake fluid in a spring-loaded chamber when it is released by the dump valves during an EBC event. The hydraulic pressure remains fairly low since an electric pump returns the released brake fluid to the master cylinder when brake fluid in the accumulator reaches a certain point. When the electric pump turns on, the fluid returning to the master cylinder pushes the brake pedal toward the driver's foot, causing the brake pedal to rise. This can be confusing to drivers because it feels like someone is under the dash pushing the brake pedal back toward them.

High-pressure accumulators are used to store brake fluid under high pressure for one of two purposes: to be used as a power booster for applying the integrated master cylinder or to be used to independently apply the wheel brake units when the EBCM commands it. When used as a power booster, pressure in the accumulator is maintained by a high-pressure electric pump. The pump is activated by a pressure switch and relay when the hydraulic pressure falls below a certain point. When the pressure reaches the specified upper pressure limit, the pressure switch opens and deactivates the electric pump. The hydraulic pressure is then used to boost the driver's foot pressure on the master cylinder when the driver depresses the brake pedal. If the high-pressure pump fails for any reason, the accumulator holds enough brake fluid at high pressure to apply the brakes 10 to 20 times before the boost is used up. If that occurs, the brakes will still operate but will require much higher foot pressure.

The accumulator used to supply brake pressure to the HCU also uses a high-pressure pump, pressure switch, and relay to maintain an operating pressure of approximately 1200–2700 psi (8274–18,616 kPa), depending on the system **FIGURE 35-9**. The high-pressure pump pushes the brake fluid against a high-pressure nitrogen chamber, which holds pressure on the brake fluid. The hydraulic pressure is used to independently apply the brakes during a TCS or ESC event. If the high-pressure pump fails while driving and the hydraulic pressure falls below the

FIGURE 35-9 High-pressure accumulator.

Safety

Be careful to follow the manufacturer's procedures when working on EBC systems. High-pressure brake fluid stored in the accumulator is dangerous.

pump's specified "on" pressure, the EBCM will disable the ABS system and illuminate the yellow warning lamp alerting the driver to an ABS system fault.

Wheel Speed Sensors

Wheel speed sensors create electrical signals based on the rotational speed of each wheel they monitor. Wheel speed sensors do so by using principles of electromagnetism to generate an analog or digital electrical signal. This signal is read by the EBCM to determine the speed of each wheel, as well as the rate of deceleration of each wheel. This information is used to determine if a wheel is starting to lock up and skid.

A wheel sensor assembly consists of a toothed tone wheel (or tone ring) that rotates with the wheels and a stationary pick-up assembly attached to the hub or axle housing. The **pick-up assembly** and **tone wheel** do not touch each other; a small gap, called an **air gap**, must be maintained at the specified clearance. Since there is no mechanical connection, there is virtually no wear unless a foreign object gets between them. As each tooth of the tone wheel approaches the pick-up, a small voltage is created that pushes current flow in one direction inside the pick-up assembly. As each tooth leaves the pick-up assembly, voltage is generated that pushes current flow in the opposite direction. This process creates a full-cycle sine wave for each tooth on the tone wheel **FIGURE 35-10**. The faster the wheel is turned, the faster the sine wave rises and falls. The speed at which the sine wave rises and falls is referred to as frequency. Frequency is measured in hertz, where one hertz equals one full-cycle sine wave per second.

The height of the sine wave, called its amplitude, also tends to change with speed. At very slow vehicle speeds, when the vehicle is just creeping along, the amplitude of the sine wave is very low. As the speed increases, so does the amplitude, along with the frequency. This alternating current sine wave signal is sent to the ECU, which evaluates and compares it to other speed sensor signals to determine if a wheel is about to lock up.

Types of Wheel Speed Sensors

The three most common types of wheel speed sensors are the variable reluctance (magnetic induction style), **magneto-resistive**, and **Hall effect** styles. The variable reluctance type is simpler and usually less expensive for manufacturers to use. This style is sometimes called a passive system since it is self-contained and needs no outside power to function. Magnetic induction occurs when the teeth on the tone wheel pass the sensor, creating an analog AC voltage signal. The faster the tone wheel rotates, the faster the AC signal

frequency. This AC signal is sent to the ECU where it is processed and then compared to the AC signals from the other wheels.

Most variable reluctance wheel speed sensors are two-wire sensors, which complete the circuit back to the ECU. The variable reluctance sensor assembly consists of a coil of wire around a permanent magnet, with each end of the coil connected to one of the wheel speed sensor terminals, which connect directly into the EBCM. Since this type of sensor operates on principles of magnetism, the air gap between the toothed tone wheel and sensor is critical. If the air gap is too small, the parts could contact each other, damaging them. If the air gap is too large, the sensor output signal to the ECU could be too weak and trigger a code or cause the sensor to work intermittently.

One drawback to the variable reluctance sensor is that since it depends on the speed of movement of the tone wheel to create a signal, it does not function effectively below vehicle speeds of around 5 mph (8 kph). In other words, the amplitude of the sine wave it creates at slow speeds is not high enough for the EBCM to read it. This can prevent the ABS from functioning during the last part of a braking event. On a very slippery road surface such as ice, the lack of ABS functionality at that speed could lengthen the stopping distance significantly.

The magneto-resistive and Hall effect sensor systems are called active systems because they require an outside power source to operate. If the sensor loses power or ground, it cannot generate an output signal. The power wire originates from the EBCM and normally supplies the magneto-resistive or Hall effect sensor systems with a reference voltage of between 5 and 12 volts, depending on the manufacturer. This helps ensure that the sensor is not affected by changes in the vehicle's electrical system voltage. A signal wire transmits the output signal from the sensor to the EBCM. The magneto-resistive and Hall effect sensors can be a three-wire arrangement, with the third wire being a dedicated ground, or a two-wire arrangement with ground being provided by the chassis.

The magneto-resistive speed sensor and Hall effect wheel speed sensor types operate similar to all Hall effect sensors. A reference voltage and ground are supplied to the sensor assembly, where internal circuitry causes a small current to flow across the semiconductor bridge/Hall material. If the bridge/Hall material is exposed to a magnetic force, the magnetism forces the current to flow to one side of the bridge/Hall material. This produces a small difference in voltage across

FIGURE 35-10 Wheel speed sensor sine wave. **A.** Signal during low vehicle speed. **B.** Signal during moderate vehicle speed. **C.** Signal during high vehicle speed.

the sides of the bridge/Hall material **FIGURE 35-11**. This voltage is then amplified and processed into a digital "on" signal (circuit is pulled to ground) and sent to the EBCM. As the magnetic field is removed, the small signal voltage across the bridge/Hall material falls to 0V. The signal sent to the EBCM will be a digital "off" signal (reference voltage). As the magnetic field is alternately applied and removed, the sensor will send a digital square wave on/off signal corresponding to the changes in the magnetic field. Because the magnetic field does not have to be moving for the bridge/Hall effect voltage to be created, the sensor works all the way down to 0 mph (0 kph). This allows the ABS to continue functioning until virtually reaching a full stop.

FIGURE 35-11 Hall effect operation.

> ### TECHNICIAN TIP
>
> Testing wheel speed sensors is dependant on knowing which kind of sensor the vehicle uses. Do not assume all two-wire sensors are of the variable reluctance style. With the ignition switch set to the "run" position and the wheels stationary, use your digital volt-ohmmeter (DVOM) to properly back-probe both sensor wires for voltage. If neither wire has voltage, suspect a variable reluctance sensor. If one of the two wires has a reference voltage, you are likely dealing with a magneto-resistive or Hall effect sensor.

Brake Switch

In addition to activating the rear brake lights, the brake switch sends an electrical input signal to the EBCM telling it if the driver is applying the brakes or not. If the brakes are being applied, the EBCM will activate the appropriate solenoid valves if the wheel speed sensors signal that the wheels are starting to lock up. If the brake switch indicates that the brakes are not being applied and the wheel speed sensors are showing unequal speeds indicating a slippery road surface, the EBCM on some vehicles will illuminate a low traction warning lamp alerting the driver to the low traction condition.

The brake switch is a normally closed switch, meaning that if the switch is not affected by any outside force, electrical current will flow through it. The brake pedal pushes the brake switch open when the brakes are released. As soon as the driver steps on the brake pedal, the spring in the brake switch closes the contacts and sends electrical current (signal) to activate the brake lights. This electrical signal is also sent to the EBCM, signaling it that the driver is applying the brakes. In some systems, the brake switch is only used to signal the body control module, which then sends current to illuminate the brake lights.

More advanced EBC systems may use a brake pedal position sensor, which indicates how far and fast the brake pedal is being pushed. It sends a variable signal based on the application of the brakes, which the EBCM uses to determine brake pedal travel and speed. This gives the EBCM additional information about the type of braking that is being performed, which can be used to modify the ABS intervention.

ABS Electronic Brake Control Module (EBCM)

The EBCM is made up of electronic circuitry to process input signals, an electronic data processor, computer memory, and output drivers to control the output devices such as the electric solenoid valves. The EBCM is programmed from the manufacturer to make brake control decisions and send output commands to the controlled devices based on sensor input data, which are compared to the data maps in its memory. These maps are designed to account for all of the reasonable braking conditions that the vehicle could experience. The EBCM continuously monitors the sensor data for any indication that one or more wheels are about to lock up.

The EBCM receives signals from several sources **FIGURE 35-12**. A switch at the brake pedal provides a brake on/off condition or, on some vehicles, a brake pedal position signal. An input from the ignition switch signals that the driver has turned the ignition on. Some control units monitor the battery voltage and use the rise in charging system voltage to indicate that the engine is actually running. The **vehicle speed sensor** reports the speed of the vehicle. Each of these input signals is used by the EBCM to know if a wheel starts to lock while the driver is applying the brakes and which ABS actions are necessary to prevent a full skid condition.

Some ABS control modules have additional functionality designed into them. One example is electronic brake proportioning. This feature does away with the mechanical proportioning valve and duplicates that action electronically by using the ABS valves to reduce rear brake hydraulic pressure under moderate brake pedal application. The EBCM restricts pressure to the rear wheels based on how hard the brake pedal is being applied. In this case, the EBCM does not wait until a wheel sensor reports that one or both rear wheels are locking up; instead, it reduces rear brake pressure slightly before lock-up occurs. It does this during moderate and heavy braking because

of weight being transferred from the rear wheels to the front wheels, reducing the traction at the rear wheels.

The EBCM performs an automatic system self-check and warning lamp bulb check on the ABS system every time the key is turned to the "run" position. If the EBCM detects a fault, the ABS warning lamp will remain on and most, but not all, systems store the fault in the EBCM memory. The faults are stored as diagnostic trouble codes (DTCs) for retrieval by technicians when diagnosing ABS system faults.

Some ABS systems provide **blink codes**, also known as flash codes, through the ABS warning lamp when a specific terminal is grounded or two specific terminals are shorted together. If a code is stored in the EBCM memory, the EBCM will blink the ABS warning lamp in a manner that indicates a particular trouble code. For example, a code 12 would be one blink followed by a short pause, then two rapid blinks followed by a long pause. Each code is usually displayed three times before the next code is displayed. Once all codes have been displayed, the codes will start at the beginning again.

Other ABS systems require a scan tool that connects to the EBCM or power train control module data link connector to read the **fault codes**. Fault codes indicate which circuit is experiencing a fault, such as an open left front wheel speed sensor circuit. The fault codes also can indicate if there is a condition the EBCM determines is out of acceptable tolerances, such as wheel speeds that do not match within the specified tolerance. The cause could be as simple as having a tire of the wrong size installed on the vehicle or having properly sized tires not inflated to the same pressure. Technicians use service information to determine how to diagnose the problem and locate the cause of the fault.

FIGURE 35-12 EBCM circuit.

Caring for the Customer

It is important for the customer to know that the ABS system is disabled when the ABS yellow warning lamp is on. The brakes will work normally, but without ABS function.

Traction Control System (TCS) Overview

While a basic ABS system can prevent skidding by holding or releasing individual brake circuit pressure, it has no ability to apply the brakes apart from the driver-created hydraulic pressure. This system works fine as long as the tire slippage is a result of the driver applying the brakes. However, tires also slip because the engine torque accelerating them exceeds their traction with the road surface; in this scenario, they can slip, spin, or break loose, causing a loss of control of the vehicle. The TCS system was developed to prevent the drive wheels from slipping while the vehicle is being accelerated. It is active up to a manufacturer-specified speed. Above that speed, traction control is deactivated by the EBCM because further acceleration is unlikely to cause the wheels to lose traction.

To obtain traction control capabilities, manufacturers have added a few design features to the basic ABS system, one of which is a high-pressure electric pump that maintains high-pressure brake fluid in an accumulator. This pressure is used to activate brake units on the drive wheels independently of the driver. The sensors are the same as in the ABS system, but the ability to apply the individual drive wheel brakes is needed; thus, two to four extra solenoid valves, called **boost valves**, are added to the HCU **FIGURE 35-13**. These boost valves direct hydraulic pressure from the accumulator to the ABS solenoid valves so that individual wheel brake units can be applied independently. Additional programming is added to the EBCM to control the high-pressure pump and extra HCU valves and to decide when each of them needs to be activated.

Operation of the TCS

When the TCS is active, the EBCM monitors the speed of the individual drive and nondrive wheels along with the vehicle speed from the vehicle speed sensor. If the driven wheels are accelerating at different speeds from each other or the nondriven wheels, the EBCM can identify which wheel or wheels are slipping. It will then take action to

reduce the torque to the appropriate wheels by first applying the brake to any wheels that are slipping. It does this by activating the isolation valve to close off the supply port from the master cylinder. It then activates the boost valve to pressurize the brake circuit on the spinning wheel to slow it down. If that is not enough to prevent the slippage, the EBCM will request reduced power from the engine. This can be accomplished by reducing the throttle plate opening, by shutting down one or more fuel injectors, by reducing the engine timing, or by selecting a higher gear in the transmission. Once the wheel speeds return to proper parameters, the EBCM will return the TCS system to normal and continue to monitor the wheels for slippage.

Some TCS systems can be temporarily deactivated by a TCS function switch located on the dash or center console. If the driver deactivates TCS, the system will not intervene during wheel slip. Drivers will disable the TCS for a variety of reasons. They might be climbing a long hill on a rough gravel road, which would continuously activate traction control, overheating the brakes. Or they might want to show off by "roasting" the tires or experience driving without traction control such as on a racetrack. The TCS will automatically default back to "on" during the next ignition switch cycle. In most cases, if the TCS is deactivated, the ABS system will still be active.

TECHNICIAN TIP

Manufacturers use various strategies in their TCS systems, and not all of them apply the brakes as a first step. Some of them reduce engine power first. Even so, EBCMs today operate very fast, so there may only be a few milliseconds between each action.

▶ Electronic Stability Control (ESC) Overview

ABS does a good job of preventing wheels from locking up under hard braking or poor traction conditions and allows the driver to maintain directional control of the vehicle. TCS also does a good job of maintaining traction when the vehicle is driven in a relatively straight line. However, drivers can lose directional control of the vehicle while driving aggressively, taking emergency steering actions, or if there are sudden changes in the traction of the road surface while in a turn. These situations can cause the vehicle to understeer (push) or oversteer (fishtail). It can also cause vehicles with a high center of gravity, such as an SUV, to roll over. All of these situations can lead to serious accidents.

To Wheel Brake Assembly

From Master Cylinder

Solenoid Windings

Boost Pressure from High Pressure Accumulator

To Low Pressure Accumulator

Isolation Valve (Normally open)

Boost Valve (Normally closed)

Dump Valve (Normally closed)

FIGURE 35-13 An HCU with boost valves.

If any of these situations are imminent, the ESC system can independently activate individual wheel brake units as necessary to help keep the driver from losing control of the vehicle. ESC utilizes the ABS and TCS systems, but with a few enhancements to more actively interface with the vehicle's operation in maintaining directional stability while the vehicle is being steered. A US Insurance Institute for Highway Safety 2006 study estimated that if all vehicles were equipped with ESC, approximately 10,000 fatal accidents in the United States could be avoided each year. This finding led the Department of Transportation to require that all vehicles of less than 10,000 lb (4536 kg) gross vehicle weight, and manufactured after September 1, 2011, be equipped with an ESC system that meets their minimum specifications.

The ESC system integrates a yaw sensor, **steering angle sensor**, and sometimes a **roll-rate sensor** into the basic ABS and TCS systems. It also adds new programming parameters into the EBCM to monitor the vehicle's stability, as well as added output command capabilities to apply individual drive wheel and nondrive wheel brake units independent of the driver. The yaw sensor measures the amount of directional rotation of the vehicle on its vertical axis. In other words, it tells the EBCM the rate at which the vehicle is turning. The steering angle sensor tells the computer what the driver's directional intent is. If equipped, the roll-rate sensor tells the computer the rate of roll and the amount of roll that the vehicle is experiencing. The EBCM continuously monitors these signals and compares them to preprogrammed scenarios and decides which, if any, brake units need to be applied, and if engine torque needs to be reduced to keep the vehicle stable.

Safety

Most standard passenger vehicles are designed with a bias toward understeer. It is generally agreed that understeer is easier for the average driver to recover from. However, many performance vehicles are designed with a slight bias toward oversteer, which can be managed by an experienced driver while driving aggressively.

TECHNICIAN TIP

The yaw sensor operates similarly to a Wii or other video game controllers. Its internal circuitry senses movement and sends an output signal directly related to the movement it senses.

Operation of ESC

If the ESC system is activated, the ECBM monitors the yaw sensor signal, the steering angle sensor signal, and the roll-rate sensor signal, as well as the wheel speed sensor signals. If the vehicle is beginning to understeer, oversteer, or roll, the EBCM will detect it in the signal values. It will then apply up to three wheel brake units to help bring the vehicle back within proper stability parameters. If that does not stop the stability issue, the EBCM will request a reduction in engine power through the power train control module to help slow the vehicle further. On most vehicles, the EBCM will illuminate a warning lamp on the dash or sound a beeper signifying when the ESC system has detected the start of a skid and reacted to it. This way the driver will be informed that he or she is on the verge of losing control of the vehicle.

On most vehicles, the ESC system defaults to "on" so it is always active. Some vehicles have a switch on the dash or center console to temporarily deactivate the system. This can be useful when driving in mud or sand when traction is virtually nonexistent and the ESC system cannot function effectively. Even though some ESC systems can be turned off, they may still monitor the operation of the vehicle and reactivate the ESC system under certain situations, such as driving above a specified speed or if a spin is detected while the brakes are being applied.

Some ESC systems incorporate a switch that allows the driver to select one or more varying levels of assist from the ESC, such as "touring," "track," or "sport." This option allows the driver to experience differing levels of wheel slip by being able to push the vehicle closer to the edge of control than when ESC is fully activated, while still having the ESC system available as a backup, but with limited assistance. When driving on a racetrack, for example, the driver may want full control of the vehicle instead of being limited by the ESC system.

In the continuous search for new bells and whistles to impress customers and enhance safety, manufacturers have designed other features into ESC systems, such as:

- Hill assist: Holds the brake pressure until the throttle is depressed and the vehicle starts to move forward.
- All-wheel drive traction control: Applies brake pressure as needed to any of the four individual wheels that may be slipping to maintain power to the wheels with the most traction.
- Engine braking control: Increases the engine torque if the ESC system detects wheel slippage during deceleration.

Many ESC-equipped vehicles monitor signals from other sensors as well to help prevent a loss of control of the vehicle; these sensors include the throttle position sensor, vehicle speed sensor, and brake pedal position sensor. When diagnosing an ESC system fault, research the sensors monitored by the EBCM.

- Panic stop assist: Detects a driver's rapid throttle release and lightly applies the brakes to dry the rotors and prepare the brakes for a panic stop.
- Accident avoidance: Works in conjunction with adaptive cruise control to monitor objects in front of the vehicle. If the ESC system detects an imminent collision, it can apply the brakes or boost the brake pressure over driver pressure.
- Hill descent control: Works in conjunction with the ESC system to control the speed of the vehicle when going down loose, rough, or slippery slopes.
- Trailer sway control: Detects trailer sway and uses the ESC system to keep it under control.
- Optimized hydraulic braking: Monitors brake pressure in each brake circuit and increases it above boosted pressure if deemed necessary.

Diagnosis

The diagnosis of ABS, TCS, and ESC systems starts with a thorough understanding of the particular type of system you are working on. Refer to the service information to familiarize yourself with the manufacturer's description and operation of the system. In cases where the system warning lamp is illuminated, access the diagnostic trouble codes (DTCs) with a compatible scan tool or code retrieval key. Any DTCs can be diagnosed following the steps laid out in the service information pertaining to the specific DTCs indicated. In cases where the system warning lamp is not illuminated, indicating there are no faults stored in memory, you can sometimes follow the symptom charts listed in the service information. That and a good understanding of the system will help you diagnose the cause of EBC faults.

Tools

The tools used to diagnose and repair ABS, TCS, and ESC systems include FIGURE 35-14:

- **ABS code retrieval key**: A stamped sheet metal key used to access the ABS blink codes on earlier GM vehicles.

FIGURE 35-14 Tools used to diagnose electronic brake systems. **A.** A digital storage oscilloscope/diagnostic scan tool. **B.** A handheld diagnostic oscilloscope. **C.** A digital volt-ohmmeter.

- **Scan tool**: Handheld electronic tool used for accessing ABS codes and live data from the EBCM. Some have bidirectional abilities used to command certain outputs, such as activating a solenoid during a diagnostic routine or when bleeding the brakes. Also used to clear codes after repairs are completed.
- **Oscilloscope**: Handheld electronic tool used to see electrical signals such as wheel speed sensor patterns.

- DVOM: Handheld meter used to measure volts, ohms, and amps in electrical circuits.
- <u>ABS proportioning valve depressor</u>: Device that depresses the proportioning valve on some ABS systems while bleeding the brakes.
- <u>ABS pressure tester</u>: Device that allows the technician to test accumulator and HCU pressure issues.

Diagnosing All EBC Systems

If the yellow warning lamp is illuminated indicating there is a fault in the system, retrieve any DTCs following the procedure listed in the service information. If the yellow warning lamp is not illuminated and the brakes are not functioning properly on a vehicle with an EBC system, suspect a problem that is not monitored by the EBCM. This could be from a fault in the base brake system such as warped rotors, contaminated friction lining, or a seized caliper piston. Diagnose these problems like you would on a non-EBC system. It could also be a problem in the hydraulic system, including the HCU, such as a dump valve that is stuck partially open or an isolation valve that is stuck closed. Even systems that are monitored by the EBCM can cause operating concerns without the yellow warning lamp being illuminated. An example would be a wheel speed sensor that does not have the correct air gap. Using the manufacturer's diagnostic symptom charts and system diagrams and having a good understanding of brake, hydraulic, and system theory will help you diagnose the cause of the concern.

Most EBC-related faults set DTCs and store them in memory. A good starting point for diagnosis is retrieving any stored DTCs with a scan tool or code retrieval key. The service information will provide a testing procedure for each of the fault codes. Following the steps listed and using an understanding of brakes, electricity, and the circuit being tested will help lead you to the cause of the fault.

To diagnose EBC system electronic control(s) and components by retrieving DTCs, first connect the scan tool to the data link connector. Navigate to the code retrieval screen and record any DTCs. Research the diagnostic procedure for the stored DTCs in the service information. Follow the diagnostic chart to diagnose the cause of the fault. Once the fault has been corrected, clear the diagnostic code and verify that it does not reset. This may involve a test-drive.

Diagnosing Wheel Speed Sensors and Tone Wheels

Wheel speed sensors are a high-probability cause of illuminated EBC warning lamps and stored DTCs, since they are usually mounted where they are exposed to the elements and in harm's way. Testing them for electrical faults is a common step in EBC diagnosis. Measuring the output signal with digital storage oscilloscope (DSO) or a graphing multimeter (GMM) and comparing it to known good signals is the most conclusive method of testing the sensors.

Variable reluctance–type sensors (passive) create an analog AC sine wave. Magneto-resistive–type sensors (active) and Hall effect sensors (active) create a digital square wave signal. The sensor electrical circuits can be tested with a DVOM for opens, shorts, high resistance, and grounds.

The tone wheel can usually be visually inspected for any faults, such as broken or damaged teeth. Just make sure you inspect the teeth all the way around the tone wheel and not just in one section.

To test and diagnose EBC system speed sensors (digital and analog), tone wheel, and circuits, first read any diagnostic codes with a scan tool or other code retrieval method. Using the diagnostic codes, determine which wheel speed sensor or sensor circuit is at fault. Research the service information to determine what type of speed sensors the vehicle is equipped with and the specified testing procedure.

To test variable reluctance sensors, follow the steps in **SKILL DRILL 35-1**:

1. Disconnect the suspect sensor, measure its resistance, and compare the reading to the specifications.
2. If the resistance does not meet the manufacturer's specifications, replace the sensor. **(Photo 1)**
3. If it is within specifications, test the two-wire circuit back to the EBCM for opens, shorts, high resistance, and grounds. Repair as necessary. **(Photo 2)**
4. If the circuit is good, reconnect the speed sensor connector and attach a GMM or DSO to one of the sensor wires. **(Photo 3)**
5. Spin the tone wheel and observe the pattern. It should be a clean AC analog pattern of sufficient amplitude (voltage). **(Photo 4)**
6. If the pattern is not correct, inspect the tone wheel for damage and replace as necessary. **(Photo 5)**
7. If the tone wheel is good, replace the wheel speed sensor.
8. If the pattern looks OK, you may have to compare it to the other wheel speed sensor signals while driving the vehicle.
9. After repair, clear the diagnostic codes, if directed by the service information. **(Photo 6)**

SKILL DRILL | 35-1 | Testing Variable Reluctance Sensors

1. Disconnect the suspect sensor, measure its resistance, and compare the reading to the specifications. If the resistance does not meet the manufacturer's specifications, replace the sensor.

2. If it is within specifications, test the two-wire circuit back to the EBCM for opens, shorts, high resistance, and grounds. Repair as necessary.

3. If the circuit is good, reconnect the speed sensor connector and attach a GMM or DSO to one of the sensor wires.

4. Spin the tone wheel and observe the pattern. It should be a clean AC analog pattern of sufficient amplitude (voltage).

5. If the pattern is not correct, inspect the tone wheel for damage, and replace as necessary.

6. If the tone wheel is good, replace the wheel speed sensor. If the pattern looks OK, you may have to compare it to the other wheel speed sensor signals while driving the vehicle. After repair, clear the diagnostic codes, if directed by the service information.

To test magneto-resistive sensors, follow the steps in **SKILL DRILL 35-2**:

1. Make sure the ignition switch is in the "run" position, and measure the available voltage at the suspect sensor. Also check the ground for voltage drop. (**Photo 1**)

2. If the voltage does not meet the manufacturer's specifications, test the circuit for opens, shorts, high resistance, or grounds. Repair as necessary. (**Photo 2**)

3. If the voltage to the sensor is within the manufacturer's specifications, connect a GMM or DSO to the signal wire. (**Photo 3**)

4. With the key in the "run" position, spin the tone wheel and observe the pattern. It should be a clean

SKILL DRILL 35-2 Testing Magneto-Resistive Sensors

1. Make sure the ignition switch is in the "run" position, and measure the available voltage at the suspect sensor. Also check the ground for voltage drop.

2. If the voltage does not meet the manufacturer's specifications, test the circuit for opens, shorts, high resistance, or grounds. Repair as necessary.

3. If the voltage to the sensor is within the manufacturer's specifications, connect a GMM or DSO to the signal wire.

4. With the key in the "run" position, spin the tone wheel and observe the pattern. It should be a clean digital square wave signal of the appropriate height and shape. If the pattern is not correct, inspect the tone wheel for damage and replace as necessary. If the tone wheel is good, replace the wheel speed sensor. After repair, clear the codes, if directed by the service information.

digital square wave signal of the appropriate height and shape.

5. If the pattern is not correct, inspect the tone wheel for damage, and replace as necessary. If the tone wheel is good, replace the wheel speed sensor.

6. After repair, clear the codes, if directed by the service information. **(Photo 4)**

AS-85: Problem Solving: The technician can use computers, scan tools, and on-board data to diagnose problems.

Vehicles presenting with ABS warning lights illuminated are now almost an everyday occurrence in most workshops. The first step in the diagnostic process is to read the DTCs stored on the ABS module. The most common cause of ABS malfunctions is faults in wheel speed sensor circuits. Common causes of wheel speed sensor circuit faults include corroded or poorly tensioned connectors, mismatched tire rolling diameters, and physical sensor failures.

Possibly the most effective way to diagnose wheel speed sensor circuit faults is to utilize the live data function of your scan tool. Start in the shop, looking at the speed readings and making sure they are all equal before you even test-drive the car. An inconsistency indicates a fault. During the road test, look at the graphed data outputs from all of the sensors; they should all look consistent. A graph that differs from the others indicates a faulty circuit. Once you have identified the affected circuit, the next step is to test at the sensor with a graphing multimeter or an oscilloscope.

Diagnosing Braking Concerns Caused by Vehicle Modifications

The EBC systems are engineered so that all of the parts and the programming work together for the purpose of assisting the driver in maintaining control of the vehicle. If any of the original components get replaced with nonstandard parts, the EBC systems will not perform as designed, putting the occupants at risk. Examples of this could be as simple as installing a smaller spare tire on the vehicle due to the original (correctly sized) tire going flat. The smaller tire turns at a faster rotation than the original tire, confusing the EBC system; consequently, the yellow warning lamp illuminates and the EBC system is disabled. In the same way, installing larger tires with a greater circumference will cause the wheel speed sensors to report a slower wheel speed than the vehicle is actually traveling. Since the EBCM is not calibrated to match this parameter, the system cannot respond appropriately, and again a DTC will be reported and the EBC system shut down.

Changing curb height causes the vehicle's center of gravity to change. Taller vehicles tend to transfer weight more easily. In the case of braking, the weight is transferred to the front wheels, unloading the rear wheels. This makes the rear wheels more prone to lock up. In the case of cornering, the weight transfers to the

outside wheels, unloading the inside wheels. This makes the vehicle more susceptible to rollover. In both of these cases, the EBCM is not programmed to take into account the non-stock height of the vehicle. Therefore, the EBCM would not be able to properly anticipate the vehicle's actions in these scenarios.

Changing final drive ratios causes the same situation as changing tire size. The vehicle wheel speed sensors will report a different speed than the vehicle speed sensor, and the EBCM will set a code and disable the system. Also, mismatched final drive ratios on four-wheel drive vehicles can affect the EBC systems, as they can cause the wheels to rotate at slightly different speeds, front to rear.

In some cases, the EBCM can be reprogrammed with the new vehicle information, or an EBCM that does match the new parameters of the vehicle may be available for installation. In any case, technicians need to be aware of how these factors affect the EBC systems. They also need to know how to verify that the components match the information programmed into the EBCM.

Maintenance and Repair
Bleeding the EBC System

Bleeding the EBC system can be easy or difficult. If care is taken to never allow air to enter the hydraulic system, most EBC systems can be bled just like a non-EBC system. However, if air is allowed into the EBC system, it can become trapped in the HCU, requiring a scan tool to operate the solenoid valves to help bleed the air from the EBC system.

Many EBC systems also require that a detailed step-by-step process be followed to successfully purge the air. The best advice is to always make sure that air never enters the EBC system while bleeding the brakes. The easiest way to do so is to check the level of brake fluid in the master cylinder reservoir often while bleeding the brakes and to always add fluid well before it gets low enough to allow air to enter the master cylinder. Also, cap any open lines or components so the brake fluid does not drain out of the lines while the system is open. Remember that DOT 5, the silicone brake fluid, should never be used in an EBC system unless the manufacturer clearly specifies it, as it is prone to aeration in the HCU.

To bleed the EBC system's hydraulic circuits, follow the steps in **SKILL DRILL 35-3**:

1. Research the bleeding procedure in the service information. Follow the specified procedure precisely. The following steps are given as an example of one manufacturer's bleeding process.

2 Connect a pressure bleeder to the brake fluid reservoir, but do not pressurize it yet.

3 Install bleeder hoses over the bleeder screws at each wheel. Submerse the other end of each hose in a container partially filled with clean, specified brake fluid.

4 Connect the scan tool to the data link connector and access the ABS bleed function.

5 Apply the specified amount of pressure from the pressure bleeder.

6 Follow the instructions on the screen of the scan tool.

7 Once the scan tool indicates that the HCU is bled, it may direct you to bleed the brakes manually to remove any remaining air from the system.

8 Remove the pressure bleeder, top off the reservoir, and test the brake pedal feel.

Removing and Installing Electric and Hydraulic Components of the EBC System

Removing and installing electric and hydraulic components of the EBC system is normally only required when there is a fault within the HCU. Since many HCUs are non-serviceable, they will need to be replaced as a unit. This may require depressurizing the high-pressure accumulator on some of these units. If the HCU is serviceable and the faulty components are available, follow the manufacturer's service procedure to remove and install the faulty component. Failure to do so could damage the HCU and render it inoperable.

To remove and install EBC system electrical/electronic and hydraulic components, follow **SKILL DRILL 35-4**:

1 Research the manufacturer's procedure for removing and installing the component on the vehicle you are working on.

2 Follow all instructions carefully, and be sure to replace all components and tighten all fasteners according to specifications.

Depressurizing High-Pressure Brake Components

Depressurization of an EBC system's high-pressure components is needed on some systems when specific tasks are being performed such as during the removal or disassembly of certain EBC system components. Always check the service manual to determine if depressurization is needed.

In many vehicles, depressurization of the accumulator can be accomplished in one of the following ways:

- Verifying that the ignition switch is in the "off" position (to disable the electric pump) and depressing the brake pedal 30–50 times
- Pulling the ABS fuse or relay to prevent the electric pump from charging the system
- Using a scan tool to depressurize the system
- Following the manufacturer's specific timeout process, which depressurizes the system automatically

To depressurize high-pressure components of the EBC system, follow **SKILL DRILL 35-5**:

1 Research the procedure for depressurizing the accumulator in the service information. Be sure to carefully follow all instructions. The following steps are given as an example of one manufacturer's process.

2 Verify that the ignition switch is turned to the "off" position.

3 Remove the ABS fuse from the fuse box.

4 Apply the brakes firmly at least 40 times.

5 Apply the brakes and verify that there is no power assist. If there is, pump the brakes an additional 10 times and verify that there is no assist remaining. Do not work on the brake system if any power assist remains.

Wrap-up

Ready for Review

- Electronic brake control systems integrate computer controls to prevent wheel lock-up, shorten panic stop distances, help drivers maintain steering control, and improve vehicle stability.
- Basic anti-lock brake systems control hydraulic pressure hold and release via solenoid valves, but cannot function independently of the driver's applied brake pressure.
- Traction control systems minimize wheel slip by automatically applying brake pressure to a slipping wheel's brake unit and reducing engine output.
- Electronic stability control systems use steering wheel position sensors, yaw sensors, and wheel speed sensors to independently monitor vehicle stability and apply brakes as necessary.
- Primary components of an anti-lock braking system are: ABS master cylinder, electronic brake control module/electronic control unit, hydraulic control unit/modulator, power booster, wheel speed sensor, and brake switch.
- Braking force and wheel lock-up are affected by friction of road surface and type, condition, and loading of each tire.
- Maximum traction occurs with 10–20% tire slip.
- Wheel speed sensors signal the EBCM, which sends current to the solenoid valve, which then holds or releases hydraulic braking pressure.
- ABS master cylinders are integral (mainly in older vehicles) or nonintegral with the HCU.
- Solenoid valves provide three operating conditions: apply, hold, and release.
- The hydraulic control unit executes the commands of the ABS control module.
- Hydraulic control units differ by number of channels (one, two, three, or four), number of solenoid valves (single or dual), and type of accumulator (low or high pressure).
- Wheel speed sensors send electric signals to the EBCM to determine speed and rate of deceleration for each wheel.
- Wheel sensor assemblies are comprised of a toothed tone wheel and a pickup assembly, separated by an air gap.
- Types of wheel speed sensors are: variable reluctance, magneto-resistive, and Hall effect.
- The EBCM is comprised of electronic circuitry, electronic data processor, computer memory, and output drivers.
- The EBCM receives input signals from: the brake switch, ignition switch, vehicle speed sensor, wheel speed sensors, and sometimes the battery.
- The ESC system includes a yaw sensor (directional rotation), steering angle sensor (driver's directional intent), and roll-rate sensor (rate and amount of vehicle roll).
- Some TCS and ESC systems can be manually deactivated by the driver.
- EBCM systems can self-diagnose and store faults as diagnostic trouble codes (DTCs) for technicians to retrieve.

Key Terms

ABS code retrieval key A specially shaped metal key that is inserted into the data link connector to retrieve DTCs.

ABS pressure tester A high-pressure gauge designed to connect to the HCU and used to measure high hydraulic pressures in the system.

ABS proportioning valve depressor A tool used to hold the proportioning valve open on some ABS HCUs.

accumulator A storage container that holds pressurized brake fluid.

air gap The space or clearance between two components, such as the space between the tone wheel and the pick-up coil in a wheel speed sensor.

blink codes Codes used to communicate DTCs; they are given by the EBCM as a series of blinks illuminated by the ABS warning lamp.

body control module (BCM) The computer that controls the electrical system in the body of a vehicle, including power windows, door locks, heating and A/C systems, and in some cases the EBC system.

boost valve A valve located in the HCU that is controlled by the EBCM; it allows brake fluid under high pressure to flow into the HCU hydraulic circuits to apply the brakes when commanded.

brake switch The electrical switch that is activated by the brake pedal; it turns on the brake lights and signals the EBCM that the brakes are being applied.

channel The number of wheel speed sensor circuits and hydraulic circuits the EBCM monitors and controls.

common bore When a single cylinder is used for two pistons. A tandem master cylinder would be an example of two pistons in one bore.

electric solenoids An electrically operated valve, which in brake systems is used to control the flow of brake fluid in the hydraulic system.

electronic brake control (EBC) system A hydraulic brake system that has integrated electronic components for the purpose of closely controlling hydraulic pressure in the brake system.

electronic stability control (ESC) system A computer-controlled system added to ABS and TCS to assist the driver in maintaining vehicle stability while steering.

fault codes An alphanumeric code system used to identify potential problems in a vehicle system.

Hall effect An electrical effect where electrons tend to flow on one side of a special material when exposed to a magnetic field, causing a difference in voltage across the special material. When the magnetic fields is removed, the electrons flow normally and there is no difference of voltage across the special material. This effect can be used to determine the position or speed of an object.

high-pressure accumulator A storage container designed to contain high-pressure liquids such as brake fluid.

hydraulic control unit (HCU) An assembly that houses electrically operated solenoid valves used in electronic braking systems; also called a modulator.

integral ABS system A brake system in which the master cylinder, power booster, and HCU are all combined in a common unit.

isolation valve The valve in the HCU that either allows or blocks brake fluid that comes from the master cylinder from entering the HCU hydraulic circuit.

low-pressure accumulator A storage container for brake fluid coming from the release valves, which is under relatively low pressure.

magneto-resistive sensor A type of wheel speed sensor that uses an effect similar to a Hall effect sensor to create its signal.

nonintegral ABS systems A brake system in which the master cylinder, power booster, and HCU are all separate units.

oscilloscope A tool that shows graphically what is happening to voltage over a period of time; it is used to diagnose electrical faults.

oversteer A condition in which the rear wheels are slipping sideways toward the outside of the turn.

pick-up assembly A component with a wire coil wrapped around a ferrous metal core; it is used to generate an electrical signal when a magnetic field passes through it.

roll-rate sensor A sensor that measures the amount of roll around the vehicle's horizontal axis that a vehicle is experiencing.

scan tool A tool used to read codes, access live data, and communicate with the vehicle's computers.

solenoid valve An electrically operated valve that when used in brake systems is designed to control the flow of brake fluid in the hydraulic system.

steering angle sensor A sensor that measures the amount of turning a driver desires. This information is used by the ESC system to know the driver's directional intent.

steering wheel position sensor A sensor that signals to the EBCM both the position and speed of the steering wheel.

tone wheel The part of the wheel speed sensor that has ribs and valleys used to create an electrical signal inside of the pick-up assembly.

traction control system (TCS) A computer-controlled system added to ABS to help prevent loss of traction while the vehicle is accelerating.

understeer A condition in which the front wheels are turned further than the direction the vehicle is moving and the front tires are slipping sideways toward the outside of the turn.

variable reluctance sensor A type of wheel speed sensor that uses the principle of magnetic induction to create its signal.

vehicle speed sensor The component that creates an electrical signal based on the speed of the vehicle, which is sent to the EBCM.

wheel speed sensor A device that creates an analog or digital signal according to the speed of the wheel.

yaw sensor A sensor that measures the amount a vehicle is turning around its vertical axis. This information is used by the ESC system to know how much a vehicle is turning.

ASE-Type Questions

1. Tech A says that an anti-lock brake system (ABS) helps shorten the stopping distance during a panic stop. Tech B says that antilock brake systems work by increasing the hydraulic pressure in the brake system so the brakes can be applied harder. Who is correct?
   a. Tech A
   b. Tech B
   c. Both A and B
   d. Neither A nor B

2. Tech A says that traction control can reduce the power output of the engine to increase traction. Tech B says that electronic stability control increases the risk of rollover. Who is correct?
   a. Tech A
   b. Tech B
   c. Both A and B
   d. Neither A nor B

3. Tech A says that an electronic braking system has sensors that monitor wheel speed. Tech B says that under steer is generally easier to recover from than over steer. Who is correct?
   a. Tech A
   b. Tech B
   c. Both A and B
   d. Neither A nor B

4. Tech A says that ABS controls braking every time the brakes are used. Tech B says that during an ABS event, it is normal for the brake pedal to pulsate. Who is correct?
   a. Tech A
   b. Tech B
   c. Both A and B
   d. Neither A nor B

5. Tech A says that during anti-lock braking, brake fluid may be returned to the master cylinder. Tech B says that solenoid valves in the hydraulic control unit will isolate the master cylinder from the brake circuit when it is in the "hold" mode. Who is correct?
   a. Tech A
   b. Tech B
   c. Both A and B
   d. Neither A nor B

6. Tech A says that mismatched tires may cause the ABS system to register a fault code. Tech B says that a traction control system may automatically apply brake pressure to a wheel brake unit even if the vehicle is not being braked. Who is correct?
   a. Tech A
   b. Tech B
   c. Both A and B
   d. Neither A nor B

7. Tech A says that an ABS key-on system test checks for faults in the vehicle's base brake system. Tech B says that on most vehicles ABS DTCs are stored in memory for later retrieval. Who is correct?
   a. Tech A
   b. Tech B
   c. Both A and B
   d. Neither A nor B

8. Tech A says that a yaw sensor tells the computer the vehicle's actual direction. Tech B says that raising a vehicle's curb height has no effect on the electronic stability control system. Who is correct?
   a. Tech A
   b. Tech B
   c. Both A and B
   d. Neither A nor B

9. Tech A says that a scan tool may be required to bleed air from the ABS brake system. Tech B says that some vehicles have a high-pressure accumulator that may need to have the pressure bled off before hydraulic brake repairs are made. Who is correct?
   a. Tech A
   b. Tech B
   c. Both A and B
   d. Neither A nor B

10. Tech A says that some ABS wheel speed sensors create a square wave digital pattern. Tech B says that some wheel speed sensors create an AC sine wave pattern. Who is correct?
    a. Tech A
    b. Tech B
    c. Both A and B
    d. Neither A nor B

SECTION VII

Electric

CHAPTER 36

NATEF Tasks

Electrical/Electronic Systems
General Electrical System

			Page
■ Research applicable vehicle and service information, vehicle service history, service precautions, and technical service bulletins.	MLR AST MAST		1209
■ Replace electrical connectors and terminal ends.	MLR AST MAST		1217–1218
■ Perform solder repair of electrical wiring.	MLR AST MAST		1218–1220
■ Repair wiring harness (including CAN-bus systems).	AST MAST		1220

Knowledge Objectives

After reading this chapter, you will be able to:
1. Describe the basic principles of electricity and the units of voltage resistance and current flow. (pp 1180–1183)
2. Describe common electrical terms and their application. (pp 1180–1191)
3. Describe common semiconductors, how they work, and their use. (pp 1183–1184)
4. Identify the difference between AC and DC. (pp 1185–1187)
5. Identify common sources and effects of electricity. (pp 1191–1192)
6. Undertake basic Ohm's law calculations. (pp 1195–1198)
7. Describe series and parallel circuits. (pp 1198–1201)
8. Describe electrical and electronic components and their application. (pp 1201–1211)
9. Describe the characteristics of wires, cables, harnesses, and shielding, and explain their correct application. (pp 1211–1214)
10. Explain basic networking and multiplexing as it applies to vehicles. (p 1215)

Principles of Electrical Systems

Skills Objectives

After reading this chapter, you will be able to:
1. Strip wire insulation. (pp 1216–1217)
2. Install a solderless terminal. (pp 1217–1218)
3. Solder wires and connectors. (pp 1218–1220)
4. Repair a wiring harness (including CAN-bus systems). (p 1220)

Introduction

The application of electrical principles in the repair of modern vehicles has become increasingly important for vehicle technicians as the electrical and electronic complexity of vehicles has increased. As hydrocarbons become scarcer and more expensive, the increased use of sophisticated electrical and electronic systems in vehicles to improve efficiency and economy will continue into the future. This trend is supported by the increasing popularity of hybrid vehicles and the investment by manufacturers in future technology, such as electric vehicles and fuel cell technology. To work on the current and future vehicles, it is increasingly important for the technician to have a sound understanding of electrical terminology, the behavior of electricity, and electrical component and circuit theory. The technician also needs to be able to read wiring diagrams, measure electrical quantities in the shop, calculate electrical values, and understand the quantities used. Your success as a technician will depend on your ability to apply these electrical principles and understand how they relate to the operation of virtually every vehicle system.

Electrical Fundamentals

Understanding the behavior of electricity can be more difficult than understanding other concepts such as four-stroke engine theory or the operation of disc brakes. For all intents and purposes, electricity cannot be seen, so you will have to use your imagination and visualize what it is doing. At the same time, electricity is governed by the laws of physics, so learning how electricity behaves can be approached in a logical manner, as with any other science. By applying yourself, over time it will make more and more sense.

In this chapter, we will explore the various types of circuits and how electricity behaves within each type. We will also explore electrical components and see how they either use electricity to perform various types of work or control electricity so that it can be applied to various devices in an appropriate manner.

To get started, it is helpful to know that electricity is made up of tangible objects. Even if we cannot normally see these objects with our eyes, we can imagine them in our minds. In fact, it may be helpful to think of electricity as nothing more than the movement of specific particles from one point to another. Imagine a line of marbles rolling through a tube or drops of water through a pipe. The moving marbles or drops of water can perform work if they are directed against another object with force. In the same way, electricity can perform work if it is directed at objects that can extract energy from the moving particles, such as lights and electric motors. That is where some of electricity's magic comes in. The moving electrical particles carry a negative charge and are attracted to a positive charge or are repelled by a negative charge. These attractive and repelling forces are what cause the particles to move and perform work. As we continue, just remember that electricity is the movement of particles from one place to another. The fascinating way it does this will be explained next.

You are the Automotive Technician

The customer has complained that the fog lights no longer illuminate when turned on. Checking for a blown fuse is one of the first steps in diagnosing an electrical problem on any system in a car. The fuse box on the vehicle you are working on today is located on the passenger's side cabin. The inside cover of the fuse box identifies the location of the fog light fuse. You test it with a DVOM and find battery power on only one side of the fuse, which indicates that it is blown. You then disconnect the wiring harness connectors from both fog lights and measure the resistance at the harness connector, between the input wire and the frame of the vehicle. The ohmmeter reads 0.2 ohms indicating a short circuit to ground. You see that the vehicle has had a winch installed recently. As you visually inspect the area, you see a bundle of wires pinched between the winch bracket and the vehicle's frame. Loosening the winch bracket and removing the wires causes the ohmmeter to read an expected OL. To permanently solve the problem you will need to perform wire repairs on each of the damaged wires.

1. What caused the fuse to blow?
2. What other types of circuit protection devices do manufacturers use?
3. What is the process for repairing wires in a harness?

Basic Electricity

All questions about the nature of electricity lead to the composition of matter. All matter is made up of atoms **FIGURE 36-1**. Every atom has a nucleus, with at least one positively charged proton and, in most atoms, at least one neutron that has no charge. Moving around the nucleus are one or more negatively charged electrons. Electrons travel in different rings or shells around the nucleus. Each ring or shell can contain a specific maximum number of electrons. Any additional electrons must fit into the next higher ring or shell. With equal numbers of protons and electrons, the charges within an atom cancel each other out, leaving the atom with no overall charge. In this state, the electrons and protons are content to stay in the atom as they are.

An atom with more electrons than protons has an overall negative charge and is called a negative ion **FIGURE 36-2**. Ion simply means the atom has an imbalance of electrical charges due to the gain or loss of electrons. This negative ion is not balanced, so it is looking for a change. Since the electrons have the same negative charge, they repel one another, and the repelling force wants to push one of the electrons away from the atom.

A deficiency of electrons gives the atom an overall positive charge. This atom is called a positive ion. It is also not balanced and is looking for a change. In this case, it is exerting an attracting force on electrons to try to pull one into its atom from another atom. If a negative ion and positive ion are close enough, the negative charge of the negative ion exerts a repelling force on the extra electron, causing it to be pushed away from its atom; at the same time, the positive ion exerts an attracting force on the extra electron. These repelling and attracting forces cause the electron to be pushed and pulled from the negative atom to the positive atom, balancing both atoms out. The flow of electrons from atom to atom is called current flow and is the basic concept of electricity.

Not all atoms can give up or accept electrons easily. Materials that can do so easily are called conductors, while those that cannot do so easily are called insulators **FIGURE 36-3**. The explanation of what makes a good conductor or a good insulator is quite complex and is found in the theories of quantum mechanics, which address the arrangement and behavior of electrons around the nuclei of atoms. To simplify matters, it is safe to say that in some materials there are electrons, called **free electrons**, located on the outer ring, called the valence ring. These electrons are only loosely held by the nucleus and are free to move from one atom to another when an electrical potential (pressure) is applied. In fact, atoms with fewer electrons in the valence ring are the best **conductors**, one electron being the best conductive material. This is because the single electron by itself in the valence ring is held the most

loosely by the nucleus. Materials made up of atoms with one to three valence ring electrons are considered conductors. The more atoms that have free electrons a particular

FIGURE 36-1 Parts of an atom.

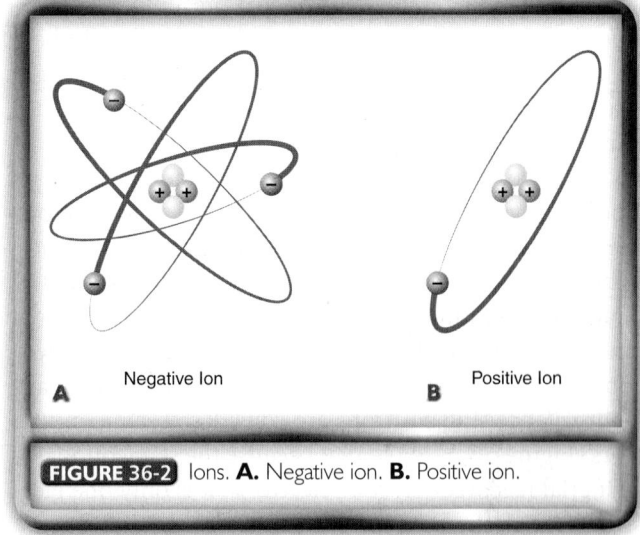

FIGURE 36-2 Ions. **A.** Negative ion. **B.** Positive ion.

FIGURE 36-3 **A.** Conductor. **B.** Insulator. **C.** Semiconductor.

material has, the better it can conduct electrons. Metals typically have lots of free electrons because of the atoms' structure and are therefore good conductors.

Every substance, even air, will conduct an electrical current if enough electrical pressure (voltage) is applied to it, but the word *conductor* normally is used for materials that allow current flow with little resistance. Most metals are good conductors. The most common conductor used in automobiles is copper. It is used in virtually all of the wiring that connects automotive components together. The more electrons a conductor must carry, the heavier the gauge or thickness the wire needs to be.

Materials that do not conduct electrons easily are called **insulators**. Most plastics are good insulators. The plastic covering on a wire is an example of this. The ceramic portion of a spark plug is also a good insulator. In insulators, electrons in the valence ring are bound much more tightly to the nucleus. A good insulator does not support current flow because it has no or very few free electrons, and the electrons it does have cannot move freely; therefore, an insulator prevents the movement of electrons when an electrical potential is applied. Insulators are made up of atoms that have five to eight valence ring electrons. The greater the number of valence ring electrons, the better the insulator (Figure 36-3).

Semiconductors are materials that conduct electricity more easily than insulators but not as well as conductors. Semiconductors such as silicon are crucial in electronics. They are used to make electronic components, such as transistors and microchips, that can switch the material from a conductor to an insulator and back again very quickly and without mechanical means. Atoms that have four valance ring electrons are considered semiconductors (Figure 36-3). Note that because the semiconductor material has precisely four electrons, it is only one electron away from becoming an insulator or a conductor. If an electron is added, it becomes an insulator; if an electron is removed, it becomes a conductor. Thus, the semiconductor material can be used as a switch to control whether electrons flow though the semiconductor material or are stopped by it. All we have to do is add or subtract electrons from the semiconductor material, which we will explore further in a later section.

Movement of Free Electrons

Free electrons are necessary for electrical current, but for the free electrons to move easily, they need two things—a complete pathway, or circuit, and a force that makes them move. The force from a battery can cause electrons to move. Like charges repel, so the negative electrons repel each other and are forced from the negative terminal of

the battery. Unlike charges attract, so the electrons are attracted toward the positive protons in the positive side of the battery. In this case, free electrons flow in one direction only. This is called direct current. Most, but not all, circuits in passenger vehicles operate on direct current. The larger the charge between the negative and the positive terminal, the more strongly the positive terminal attracts and the negative terminal repels the free electrons. This attraction/repelling acts as a force driving the electrons along. The greater the force, the stronger the electrical current. The force is called **electromotive force**, and it is also referred to as voltage. So you could say that voltage is the force that motivates electrons to move and is measured in volts.

> **TECHNICIAN TIP**
>
> Since electrical current is the flow of electrons, it is natural to say that the direction of current is the direction in which the free electrons move—from negative to positive—which is called the **electron theory**. However, before the discovery that they are negatively charged, it was thought the natural way for electrons to flow was from positive to negative, which is called the **conventional theory**. Most wiring diagrams are written from the conventional theory perspective, while electronic circuits are typically designed and operate on the electron theory perspective. Thus, both concepts are still in use. In fact, a third theory exists that closely mirrors the conventional theory, called the **hole theory**. It states that while negative electrons do move from negative to positive, holes move from positive to negative as electrons move from atom to atom; in this case, holes (current) flow from positive to negative, and are sometimes called "positive holes." What's most important to remember is that voltage causes current to flow through conductive paths (resistance). We will be using the conventional and hole theories when explaining the electrical concepts throughout this text unless otherwise noted.

Electrical Resistance

Also affecting the current flow in a circuit is **electrical resistance**, measured in **ohms**. All materials have resistance—even good conductors. There are four factors that determine the level of electrical resistance:

1. Type of material: This refers to how many free electrons a material has.
2. Length of the conductor: As length increases, so does resistance.

3. Diameter of the conductor: The larger the conductor, the greater the amount of current it can carry.
4. Temperature of the conductor: The higher the temperature, the harder it is for free electrons to pass through and the higher the electrical resistance.

While all materials have some resistance to current flow based on the number of free electrons the material has, a **resistor** is a component designed to extract energy from the current flow by forcing it through a restriction in the circuit. A typical resistor has a set resistance, usually marked or coded on its surface. Electrical resistance is somewhat like the electrical equivalent of friction in the mechanical world: It is the degree to which a material opposes, or resists, the passage of an electrical current. Good conductors have low resistance, while insulators have high resistance. Electrical energy lost through resistance is converted into heat.

Resistance is measured in ohms. Under most conditions, except temperature change, the resistance of an object is a constant and does not depend on the amount of the voltage or the amount of current passing through it. At the same time, **Ohm's law** tells us that if we increase current flow through a resistance, the voltage used by that resistance will increase. So in that sense, the resistance did not change, but the voltage drop did **FIGURE 36-4**. When diagnosing circuits, we usually use a voltmeter to look for excessive voltage drops that reduce the available voltage at the load. An ohmmeter would not normally work in this case, since it generally cannot read less than 0.1 ohms. This amount of resistance in a 10-amp circuit would cause a 1.0-volt drop, which is way beyond the allowable maximum voltage drop

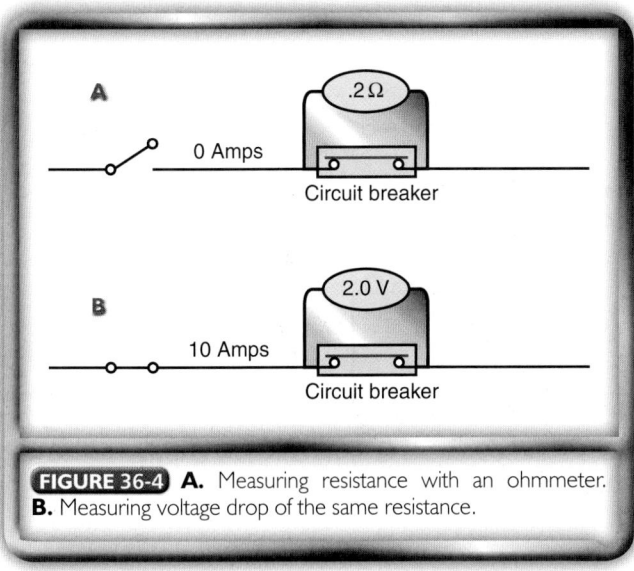

FIGURE 36-4 A. Measuring resistance with an ohmmeter. **B.** Measuring voltage drop of the same resistance.

for a wire, which will be discussed further in the Meter Usage and Circuit Diagnosis chapter. The relationships between current, voltage, and resistance are calculated using Ohm's law. This concept will be discussed in detail later in this chapter.

Semiconductors

The term electronics usually refers to devices in which *electrons* are conducted through a vacuum, gas, or **semiconductor**. Automotive applications such as electronic control units mostly use semiconductors such as diodes, transistors, and power transistors. A semiconductor's electrical resistance is higher than that of most conductors, but lower than that of most insulators. A semiconductor's conducting ability depends on two kinds of **charge carriers**:

- The first type of charge carrier is the negative electron. This kind of semiconductor contains an excess of free electrons. They can be made to flow and carry charge.
- The second type of charge carrier is the hole. Holes occur when an electron moves from its existing place to a new place, leaving a void where it was. Because the holes are positive, a voltage can make them move toward the negative pole. When connected in a circuit, both the electrons and the holes move, but in opposite directions.

The number of charge carriers, either an excess of electrons or deficiency of electrons (causing holes in a material), can be altered by **doping**, or adding very small quantities of impurities to a semiconductor material. A doped semiconductor always has an excess of one type of charge carrier. For example, electrons in excess make it an **N-type** semiconductor. N stands for negative. Holes in excess make it a **P-type** semiconductor. P stands for positive. Each of these materials responds to positive or negative current flow oppositely.

Semiconductor Operation

Most electronic components combine P-type and N-type semiconductors. The point where they join is called the **PN junction**. In this area, the **depletion layer** occurs, and some electrons and holes cancel each other out and few charge carriers are present. The depletion layer is very thin and acts like an insulator.

A **diode** is one P-type semiconductor material joined to one N-type semiconductor material with a single PN junction. If it is connected to a voltage source so that the P region is connected to a negative pole and the N region to a positive pole, then the negative pole attracts the holes, and the positive pole attracts the electrons. This enlarges the depletion layer and the insulated space. As a result, current cannot flow across the junction. Diodes are discussed further later on in the chapter.

Semiconductors are very versatile substances and are widely used to make various electronic components. Their conductivity can be manipulated and precisely controlled by doping with impurities to make transistors. They can also be designed to vary their conductance in magnetic fields to make Hall-effect devices and to vary their light to make photoelectric diodes and transistors. Semiconductor devices are replacing many other kinds of switching devices such as mechanical switches and relays. They are small, light, and use low operating voltages. They are reliable, require no maintenance, and are relatively easy to manufacture, but they are sensitive to heat and voltage spikes.

Semiconductor Materials

Many different materials have an atomic structure that can be used to make semiconductors. **Silicon** is the most widely used semiconductor material because it has a useful temperature range and is abundant, cheap, and easy to manufacture. **Germanium** was among the first semiconductor materials to be developed and is less widely used than silicon, but it is useful in very high-speed devices

when alloyed with silicon. High-speed semiconductors widely use **gallium-arsenide**; however, it is more expensive and more difficult to manufacture. **Silicon carbide** has been used to create blue **light-emitting diodes (LEDs)**, and it can withstand high operating temperatures.

Electrical Circuits

Electrical circuits are designed to perform electrical work in a controlled manner. They can be compared to a small city; the roads are like wires, the stoplights are like switches, and businesses are like electrical devices where work happens. And cars are like electrons that deliver the workers to the workplace. Electrical circuits can be very basic, consisting of a power supply, a fuse, a switch, a component that performs work, and wires connecting them all together **FIGURE 36-5**. The power source—for example, the battery—creates a potential difference across its terminals measured in volts. It pushes a flow of electrons (current flow), measured in amps, when the switch is in the closed position completing the path. The current flows through the fuse into the circuit wires to the lamp where the resistance of the lamp filament causes it to glow, producing light. The current continues to flow through the lamp filament and the return pathway through the wires back to the battery to complete the circuit. When the switch is moved to the open position, the current path is broken and current flow stops, turning the lamp filament off.

A circuit can be much more complex than the one just described. But even then, most circuits contain a power source, circuit protection device, control mechanism, load, and connecting wires. As you understand the principles of electricity and how it behaves, you will be able to understand more complicated circuits.

FIGURE 36-5 Simple circuit.

Volts, Amps, and Ohms

Volts, amps, and ohms are three basic units of electrical measurement. Voltage is the potential or electrical pressure difference between two points in an electrical circuit and is measured in **volts**. For example, the voltage of a typical car battery is 12 volts. This is the potential difference or electrical pressure between the positive and the negative battery terminal. It can be measured with a voltmeter or **multimeter** set to read voltage. Voltage can be measured by hooking a voltmeter across two parts of a circuit where you want to measure the difference in volts. It might be easier to understand if you think of voltage as the electrical force or pressure in a circuit or battery, just like the water pressure that exists in the bottom of a full tank of water or a home plumbing service.

The ampere, or **amp**, is the unit used to describe how much current or how many electrons are flowing at a given point in a given amount of time when work is being performed—for example, when a lamp is operating. An amp is a measure of the number of electrons flowing past a given point in 1 second. An amp is equal to 6.28 billion billion electrons past a given point in 1 second. Yes, billion billion is correct. To say it another way, think of a pile of 1 billion electrons. One amp would equal the number of elections in 6.28 billion of those piles travelling past a given point in a circuit in 1 second. That is impressive! No wonder we can't see them! And just to get you thinking, a starter motor may draw about 200 amps. Amperage, or current flow, can be thought of as a faucet being turned on and water flowing. Each drop of water is like an electron. Current flow is measured in amps by placing an **ammeter** into the circuit so that the current flows through the meter.

The ohm is the unit used to describe the amount of electrical resistance in a circuit or component. The higher the resistance, the less current (amps) that will flow in the circuit for any particular voltage. The lower the resistance, the higher the current that will flow in the circuit. Using the water analogy, if you kink a hose with the water running, less water will come out of the hose for a given pressure. If you kink the hose more, more resistance will be added and even less water will flow through the hose. Lessening the kink will lower the resistance and allow more water to flow. Resistance in a simple electrical circuit works the same way.

An ohmmeter is used to measure the amount of resistance in a component or circuit. The ohmmeter pushes a small amount of current through the part being tested, so an ohmmeter is usually used on a component or wire that has been disconnected from the rest of the circuit. The amount of resistance in the component changes the amount of current that the ohmmeter can push through the component. The more current that the ohmmeter can push through the component, the lower the resistance will read on the ohmmeter.

Direct Current and Alternating Current

Electrons need to flow in a circuit for work or action to be undertaken. For example, the action of a lamp glowing brightly is caused by the flow of electrons through the filament, heating it up and causing it to glow. There are two fundamental types of **current flow**: **direct current (DC)** and **alternating current (AC)** **FIGURE 36-6**. DC is produced by a battery. The battery maintains the same positive and negative **polarity**; therefore, the current

FIGURE 36-6 Waveforms. **A.** Direct current **B.** Alternating current.

flows in one direction only. The characteristics of DC are the fixed polarity of the applied voltage and the flow of charges in only one direction. It is possible to have varying DC; however, the charges always flow in the one direction and the applied voltage polarity remains the same.

AC is the type of current in your home electricity supply. It continuously changes its direction of current flow, and the alternating voltage repeatedly reverses or alternates its polarity. Thus, the current flow moves back and forth within a circuit. AC is produced in what is called a **sine wave**. It operates on a cycle, gradually building to a maximum current flow in one direction (positive value), then gradually reducing to zero, then gradually building to a maximum current flow in the other direction (negative value), and finally gradually reducing back to zero current. In most cases, this cycle can occur many times a second. For example, the AC flow in the house supply changes direction 60 times per second. **Hertz** is the measurement of frequency and indicates the number of cycles per second. So, since the AC supply in the home typically changes polarity 60 times a second, its frequency is 60 hertz, or 60 Hz. Hertz simply means "cycles per second."

Applied | Science

AS-58: AC/DC: The technician can explain the difference between direct and alternating current.
Direct current (DC) and alternating current (AC) are two forms of electricity that are produced differently and have different uses. DC electricity is the simpler form. It starts in one place and then flows in the same direction to its destination. AC electricity flows in one direction for a period of time, then changes direction over and over again continuously.

In modern automotive applications, AC electricity is generated by the alternator using electromagnets. The AC electricity is converted to DC, or rectified, by diodes in the alternator before being supplied to the vehicle's electrical systems or being stored in the battery.

AC is used in vehicles to a lesser extent than DC. Alternators use it to create current flow to charge the battery and run the electrical accessories. The AC is first transformed to DC before it leaves the alternator so it can be effectively put to use in the DC electrical system.

AC is used in the electric motors on most hybrid vehicles. Since those motors generally require high amounts of electrical power, and because AC is more efficient than DC, AC is more advantageous for that

Applied | Science

AS-53: Electricity: The technician can demonstrate an understanding of and explain the properties of electricity as they relate to lighting, engine management, and other electrical systems in the vehicle.
Most automotive electrical systems use 12-volt DC electricity supplied from the vehicle's battery to power items such as light bulbs, electric motors, and heater elements. Some circuits may use switching with varying degrees of resistance to control the output from the circuit's load; examples may include interior blower fan motors that run at varying speeds and the vehicle's fuel gauge, which uses a variable resistor to determine the position of the gauge.

Engine and power train management systems are also powered from the vehicle's 12-volt battery but use various other voltages to monitor operating parameters via sensors. Some sensors operate using a reference voltage, generally 5 volts, which is modified to determine operating parameters. Examples could be a digital crankshaft position/speed sensor or a digital mass airflow meter. The reference voltage is effectively switched "on" or "off" by the digital sensor, producing a square-wave output with a frequency that changes according to the engine speed or airflow rate.

Some sensors generate their own voltage; examples include zirconia oxygen sensors, analog crankshaft or camshaft position sensors, which generate AC voltage, and piezoelectric knock sensors. Voltages generated from these sensors are monitored by the electronic control unit (ECU) to determine engine operating parameters.

Some computer-controlled devices can simply be turned on and off. A cooling fan may be turned on when the coolant reaches a temperature of 219°F (104°C) for example and turned back off when the coolant temperature falls below 201°F (94°C) for example. Pulse-width modulation provides a means for a computer to control a device with variable operating parameters. Fuel injectors, for example, need to be open for differing amounts of time depending on the fueling requirements of the engine. An ECU can control injector opening time by sending a pulsed signal with shorter or longer duration.

TECHNICIAN TIP

While the United States has chosen 60 Hz for the electrical grid, many other countries use 220 volts at 50 Hz and have different-shaped plugs. If you travel to these countries, make sure to purchase the proper converter or transformer so your electrical devices will work and not be damaged.

application. The AC is created by a sophisticated electronic inverter.

Some manufacturers use sensors that create an AC signal that varies in frequency. This varying signal is sent to the vehicle's computer as an indication of changes within the system being monitored. The computer can use that signal to make adjustments based on its programmed software.

In general, electrical components are designed to work on either AC or DC, but not both. For example, a DC motor will not work on AC, and vice versa. Devices can

Applied | Math

AM-14: Mentally: The technician can determine the proper mathematical operation (addition, subtraction, multiplication, or division) and mentally arrive at the solution.
Determining the operating parameters of electrical circuits can require a selection of different mathematical operations. Some examples may include adding the resistance of individual components in a series circuit to determine the total resistance of the circuit, dividing the voltage by the resistance to determine the current flow in a parallel circuit, or multiplying the amperage of a circuit by its resistance to determine the voltage a device is using.

Applied | Math

AM-44: Formulas: Using formulas, the technician can predict the outcome(s) under different variations.
Ohm's law, a mathematical formula, can be applied to predict the outcome of changes made to electrical systems. Say we have a 12-volt automotive electrical circuit to drive a bulb in an interior light. A customer has complained that the interior light in his car is not bright enough and has requested that a higher wattage bulb be fitted. (Caution: We are only using this as an example. Additional wattage creates additional heat, which can cause the fuse to blow, or in an extreme case, a fire. It is recommended that you never modify a vehicle from the manufacturer's original condition.) The resistance of bulbs varies according to their wattage. Generally, the higher the wattage, the lower the resistance.

The original 5-watt bulb fitted to the vehicle had a resistance of 30 ohms. Through Ohm's law, we know that current flow equals voltage divided by resistance, or in this case 0.4 amps. The new 10-watt bulb to be fitted has half the resistance, 15 ohms. Current flow in the circuit is now calculated as 12 volts divided by 15 ohms, which is 0.8 amps, which provides twice the wattage.

Applied | Math

AM-46: Equivalent Form: The technician can write or rewrite an algebraic equation to solve for any unknown variables.
Ohm's law is commonly used to calculate the value of an unknown variable from known values in electrical circuits. The equation is commonly stated as voltage (V) equals current flow (A) multiplied by resistance (R), or $V = AR$. To calculate current flow or resistance, instead of voltage, the equation must be rewritten. To apply the rules of basic algebra, anything we do to one side of the equation we must also do to the other. To calculate current flow, we need the A by itself on one side of the equation, so we divide both sides by R to arrive at $A = V/R$. To calculate resistance, the R must stand alone, so we divide both sides of the equation by A to arrive at $R = V/A$. Ohm's law is commonly represented in a triangle or circle format, making the correct algebraic equation very simple to find.

be made to convert or change AC to DC and DC to AC. For example, a battery charger that has an input AC of 110 volts at 60 Hz power can change this to 14 volts DC through a transformer and rectifier to charge a battery. Devices are also available to change DC into AC, and are called **inverters**. For example, an inverter could have an input of 12 volts DC and convert that to 110 volts AC at 60 Hz. AC and DC power sources can be of any voltage and are not limited to the relatively low 12 volts DC found in the batteries on vehicles or the 110 volts AC found in the home power supply. For example, some hybrid vehicles use high-voltage DC invertors drawing 200 to 300 volts DC to power the 500-volt three-**phase** AC to power the main electric traction motors or accessory motors. Phase refers to the number of separate staggered **power windings** in the motor or alternator. Generally, three-phase motors or alternators produce more output than single-phase motors or alternators because they can maintain a much more even voltage compared to single-phase AC.

Power (Source or Feed) and Ground

Power and ground are terms to describe the beginning and end of a circuit. Power, source, and feed signify the supply side (beginning) of the circuit, where the electricity originates. Ground signifies the return side of the circuit **FIGURE 36-7**. In conventional theory, the supply side is the positive side of the circuit, and the return side is the negative side of the circuit, which we will be using throughout this text. In a vehicle, the positive battery post is considered the source. The power or feed side of a circuit refers to the wires and

FIGURE 36-7 Power and ground.

components that originate at the positive post of the battery and end at either a switch or a load, whichever occurs first.

<u>Ground</u> is a term used by technicians to indicate the portion of the circuit that returns current flow to the negative side of the battery. The ground side of the circuit starts at the negative post of the battery and ends at either a load or a switch, whichever occurs first. The term ground is also used to mean a direct connection with the negative side of the circuit, as in "the switch is grounded." Also, if you are told to ground something, that means it needs to be connected to the negative side of the circuit. Many vehicles connect the chassis and body to the negative battery terminal, which means most of the metal components on the vehicle are grounded. As a result, many manufacturers use the chassis as the return path to the negative battery terminal, as this cuts down on the amount of wire needed in the vehicle. At the same time, many computer circuits use dedicated ground wires from their sensors back to the computer so that the electrical signal is accurate and not affected by any stray electrical signals on the ground circuit.

Applied | Math

AM-48: Algebraic Expressions: The technician can use Ohm's law and the power law to determine circuit parameters that are out of tolerance.

The power law, or Watt's law, is a mathematical equation describing the relationship of voltage, current, and power in electrical circuits. Power may be defined as the amount of work done in a given period of time. Understanding this equation is useful in calculating characteristics within circuits. The power law is written as

Power (watts) = Voltage (volts) × Current (amps).

An unknown parameter can be calculated from any two known parameters. Like Ohm's law, the power law is commonly represented in a triangle diagram, as shown here:

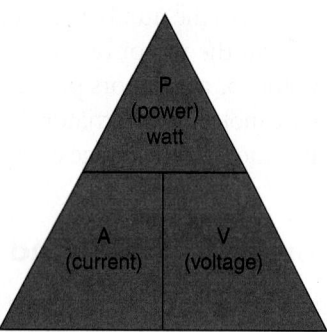

For example, we have an electrical circuit driving a power window motor in a passenger car. The vehicle operates on a 12-volt electrical system. The wattage of the window motor is 22 watts. To calculate the current flow in the circuit, we divide the power (or the motor's wattage) by the voltage, or P/V. In this case the amperage would be 22/12, or 1.8 amps.

Applied | Science

AS-60: Ground: The technician can demonstrate an understanding of the problems associated with having an electrical circuit inadequately grounded.

Ground problems can present some of the most challenging issues encountered in automotive diagnostics. Let's illustrate why ground points are so important on motor vehicles. In a simple circuit, we might have a battery, a fuse, and a load, all connected by wire. In automotive applications, manufacturers take advantage of the conductivity of metal car and truck bodies by connecting the ground side of electrical components to the vehicle's body or chassis. The negative side of the battery is also connected to the body, so instead of electrical current returning to ground via wiring, it is conducted through the body.

If we have a component with no ground connection, we have an open circuit and no current flow. Loose or dirty ground connections create a point of high resistance in the circuit, resulting in lower current flow and excessive voltage drop. This results in lamps illuminating dimly, electric motors not working or not working at full speed, and running problems in computer-controlled systems. In some circuits, issues may be encountered with electricity finding alternative paths to ground. You may sometimes see vehicles with brake lights flashing along with, or opposite to, turn signal lights. This is commonly caused by a poor ground in the taillight circuit.

Continuity, Open, Short, and High Resistance (Voltage Drop)

The terms *continuity, open, short,* and *high resistance* are often used to describe a circuit's or component's condition. For example, the wiring harness could be described as having a short or the connector as having an open circuit. **Continuity** is achieved when an electrical circuit has a continuous and uninterrupted electrical connection and is thereby capable of conducting current and working as designed. No continuity means there is a break in the circuit and current cannot flow past the break. It can be measured with a digital volt-ohmmeter (DVOM) in ohms between two points in a circuit. For example, if a technician suspects that a circuit has a break or bad connections in the wiring, the continuity could be measured between two points. A faulty circuit has high resistance or no continuity. A circuit with continuity has very low resistance. But be careful, checking the circuit for continuity cannot determine all electrical faults. If the continuity test determines that there is a break in the circuit, you can bank on that and track it down to determine the fault. However, if the continuity test determines that there is continuity, you still don't know for sure that the circuit is good. It is possible that while the circuit has continuity, it has excessive resistance that could affect the operation of the electrical device under normal current flow. Thus, continuity testing is limited in what it can indicate. It is a great test for determining whether a wire or component is open or whether two circuits are shorted together.

The term **open** describes a low-voltage circuit that does not have a complete circuit and therefore cannot conduct current. In other words, the circuit does not have continuity. For example, when a switch is turned off, the circuit is open and no current can flow. Open can also be used to describe a fault in a circuit. For example, if the fuse is open-circuited, which describes a blown fuse, no current will be able to flow. A multimeter or test lamp can be used to test for an open circuit. An open circuit has infinite resistance—so much resistance that it is not measurable.

The term **short**, in its purest definition, describes a circuit fault in which current takes a shorter path, resistance-wise, through an accidental or unintended route. The low-resistance fault causes abnormally high current flow in the circuit and may cause the circuit protection devices, such as fuses or circuit breakers, to open the circuit. An example of a pure short would be insulation on the windings within a relay coil that has worn through and is allowing current to bypass many of the windings **FIGURE 36-8**. In this case, resistance decreases, amperage increases, and the magnetic field created by the

winding becomes weaker, potentially causing the relay to not operate.

A pure short circuit is not the only type of short circuit. There are three additional types of short circuits that you need to understand. The first is a short to ground. In this case, the circuit has an unintended path directly to ground. For example, if the wire from the brake switch to the brake lights rubs through the wire insulation on a sharp edge of a body panel, the bare wire may make contact with the metal panel and cause a short to ground when the brake pedal is pressed **FIGURE 36-9**. A short to ground causes increased current flow and will typically blow the circuit fuse.

Another type of short is a short to power. In this case, the circuit has an unintended path directly to a power source. An example would be two wires in a harness that have melted together, one that supplies power

FIGURE 36-8 Short circuit.

FIGURE 36-9 Short to ground.

to the blower motor and one that feeds power from the brake light switch to the brake lights **FIGURE 36-10**. In this example, turning on the ignition switch would cause the brake lights to come on because power would be sent to the blower fuse and then, due to the short in the wiring, to the brake lights.

Unintended **high resistance** in a circuit causes a reduction in current flow in the circuit as well as a drop in voltage at the resistance. Both of these cause the intended circuit device to not operate effectively or at all. Unintended high resistance can also cause an overheating condition at the area of resistance, which can melt wire insulation or plastic **connectors**. This condition can be caused by a number of faults, including corroded or loose harness connectors, wire that is too thin for the circuit current flow, incorrectly connected terminals, and poorly soldered joints **FIGURE 36-11**.

Voltage drop is another name for high resistance, and voltage drop testing is the best way of finding high resistance in the feed side or ground side of the circuit. For a voltage drop to occur, two conditions must present: resistance and current flow. Thus, a voltage drop in a circuit indicates that there is resistance present and current is flowing, or trying to flow, through the resistance. If the high-resistance fault is excessive, it will reduce both the voltage and the current flow in the circuit, affecting its performance. For example, a voltage drop in the headlight circuit will cause the lights to be dim, reducing their performance. A high resistance in the main battery lead to the starter motor will cause the starter to crank the engine over slowly or not at all. The voltage drop can be measured in a circuit by placing a voltmeter across two different points in a circuit while the circuit is being operated. For example, to measure the voltage drop in the main positive battery lead to the starter motor, the

voltmeter's black lead would be placed on the positive battery lead and the red lead would be placed on the main battery lead of the starter motor, and the voltage would then be read on the meter while the engine is cranked **FIGURE 36-12**.

> **TECHNICIAN TIP**
>
> Since current flowing through a resistance causes heat, you can sometimes locate the high resistance in the circuit just by feeling the wires and connections. For example, if one of the battery posts is corroded between the post and the battery cable, a voltage drop will be present when the starter is engaged. If you operate the starter for several seconds and then feel each battery terminal, the one with excessive resistance will be warmer than the other terminal.

FIGURE 36-11 High-resistance fault.

FIGURE 36-10 Short to power.

FIGURE 36-12 Voltage drop testing the positive battery cable.

Sources of Electricity

Electricity is a unique source of energy. Not only can it be transformed into a variety of other kinds of energy, such as thermal energy, light energy, chemical energy, and mechanical energy, it can be created easily in a variety of ways. Think of other types of energy such as coal and oil. They are much harder to create, generally relying on natural processes over a long period of time. This section explores different ways that electricity can be produced.

A common and easily observable source of electricity is the static electricity produced in thunderstorms. Other ways that electricity can be produced include the movement of a conductor through a magnetic field, the application of pressure to a special type of crystal, the conversion of sunlight by solar cells, and chemical reactions. Regardless of the way it is produced, electricity is always the movement of electrons in a conducting circuit. Let's see how we can get those electrons moving so they can do work for us.

Electrostatic Energy

Static electricity can be induced by rubbing two insulators together. During this process, one material loses electrons to the other. The insulator losing electrons becomes positively charged. The other insulator gains electrons to become negatively charged.

When these two highly charged surfaces are brought close enough together, electrons leap across the gap causing a spark and canceling out the charge imbalance. This electron transfer can be experienced as an electric shock. It applies to any charged surfaces where the imbalance in charge is great enough to make the electrons leap the gap. The spark can be dangerous. Near fuel vapor at a gas station, it can even cause an explosion.

Safety

There have been many fires caused by the operator starting the refueling process, getting back into the vehicle to check on a child or put a credit card away, sliding back out across the seat of the vehicle (without touching the metal of the vehicle), and then grabbing the refueling nozzle, at which time a spark ignites the fumes escaping from the filling tank. Always touch the metal of the vehicle or fuel pump before touching the refueling nozzle. Also, fires have reportedly resulted from customers sliding their plastic gas cans out of the back of a plastic-lined pick-up bed, creating a spark when the nozzle touched the can or when the pour spout touched the gas tank.

Thermoelectric Energy

If two different metals are joined and heated, a small electrical current can be generated. For a temperature rise of around 392°F (200°C), the potential difference created is about 9 millivolts. The point that is heated is called a **hot junction**, and the whole system is called a **thermocouple**. In developing engine designs, manufacturers use thermocouples to measure the high temperatures of components, such as spark plugs and exhaust systems. Thermocouples are also used to measure exhaust gas temperature on race cars to determine the best air–fuel ratio so that the engine parts will not be overheated. Pilots in general aviation use thermocouples to measure the exhaust gas temperature to adjust the fuel mixture as the airplane changes altitude.

Electrochemical Energy

When two dissimilar metals are immersed in an acidic liquid called an **electrolyte**, the breakdown of chemicals into charged particles, called **ions**, results in a flow of electricity. The process is called **electrolysis**. This principle is applied in the standard lead-acid battery used in most vehicles, covered more thoroughly in the Batteries, Starting, and Charging Systems chapter.

Photovoltaic Energy

Solar cells convert sunlight directly into electricity and are used in a wide variety of applications to supply electricity. They are made of semiconducting materials similar to those used in computer chips. When sunlight is absorbed by these materials, the photons knock electrons loose from their atoms, causing the electrons to flow through the material to produce electricity. This process of converting light (photons) to electricity (voltage, which moves electrons) is called the **photovoltaic (PV) effect FIGURE 36-13**. When light energy strikes the surface of PV

FIGURE 36-13 Photovoltaic effect.

semiconductor materials, the materials emit electrons. These freed electrons can then be made to flow in a circuit where they are used to perform work. The principle is applied in some ignition systems and in vehicle speed sensors by creating signals used to time the ignition sparks or by telling the computer how fast the vehicle is moving. It is also used to sense the amount of daylight to operate automatic headlights and is used in heating, ventilation, and air-conditioning (HVAC) systems to determine the sun load on the vehicle. In addition, it is the principle of the solar cell.

> ### ► TECHNICIAN TIP
>
> The term photovoltaic comes from the Greek *photos*, meaning light, and the name of the Italian physicist Volta, after whom the volt (and consequently voltage) is named. Photovoltaic means literally "of light and electricity."

Piezoelectric Energy

When crystals of certain materials, such as quartz, are subjected to mechanical stress, an electrical potential is produced across the crystals **FIGURE 36-14**. The process is also reversible. A potential electrical difference across the crystal will physically distort the crystal. The best-known simple application of **piezoelectric** energy is the sparking lighters that ignite gas in grills, barbecues, or cooktops, but the piezoelectric principle is also used in automobiles in knock sensors and pressure sensors and in some electronic fuel injectors.

Electromagnetic Induction

Electromagnetic induction is the creation of an electrical voltage—or the potential difference—across a conductor within a changing magnetic field. When a conductor cuts across a magnetic field, current flows in the conductor. It flows one way when the conductor cuts the field in one direction, then reverses as it cuts the field in the opposite direction. Thus, it creates alternating current, or AC.

Moving a wire inside a magnetic field produces a current flow. Similarly, moving a magnet inside a stationary coil of wire produces the same effect. For example, to generate electricity, a magnet can be rotated inside an iron yoke with a coil of wire wound around the stem of the yoke to form a complete circuit with an ammeter, which indicates current flow **FIGURE 36-15**. As the magnet

> ### Applied | Science
>
> **AS-75: Electromagnetism: The technician can explain the relationship between current in a conductor and strength of the magnetic field.**
> Faraday's law of induction describes the ways that a voltage can be generated within a conductor moved through a magnetic field. Simply stated, whenever there is a change in the number of magnetic field lines passing through a conductor, whether the conductor is moved or changes occur in the magnetic field, a voltage is generated in the conductor. When the strength of the magnetic field is increased, there is an increase in the number of magnetic field lines. If we have a conductor moving through the magnetic field and the rate of movement remains constant, the increased intensity of the magnetic field will result in more magnetic field lines passing through the conductor, increasing the voltage generated.

FIGURE 36-14 Piezoelectric energy.

FIGURE 36-15 Electromagnetic induction using a magnet rotating inside an iron yoke and winding.

rotates, the ammeter deflects for current flow. For every half-revolution, current flow reverses. Increasing the speed of the magnet increases the amount of electrical energy produced. Electromagnetic induction is applied in alternators, ignition coils, and some sensors on the vehicle.

To have induction, you have to have three things: a winding, a magnet, and relative movement (i.e., movement of one past the other). The amount of induction is dependent upon the strength of the magnetic field, the number of windings, the speed of the movement, and the relative distance between the field and the winding.

▶ Effects of Electricity

Whenever electricity flows, it produces effects. For example, light, heat, chemical reactions, and magnetism are all effects of the flow of electricity. Sometimes those effects are the primary reason for the activity. For example, magnetic effects are used to generate electricity. At other times, the effects are just by-products of the activity. For example, current flowing in the conductors of a generator produces heat as a by-product and is wasted energy. No transformation of energy from one form to another is 100% efficient. There is always waste, which usually shows up as heat. For example, a typical incandescent light bulb creates light, but only about 10% of the electricity is converted to light. About 90% is wasted as heat.

Heating Effects

Heat is not always bad. Sometimes we need to create heat, such as in circuit breakers and heaters **FIGURE 36-16**. As current flows through motor vehicle circuits, most of the electrical energy is transformed into other kinds of

FIGURE 36-16 Heating effect of electricity.

energy. Headlights transform the energy into intense heat that then makes the bulb filaments glow white hot and produce light. The energy can also defog a window or can be used to provide circuit protection from excessive current flow.

Chemical Effects

Chemical effects of electricity depend on ions. Recall that ions are electrically charged atoms or groups of atoms. Atoms that gain electrons become negatively charged. Atoms that lose electrons become positively charged.

When two different metal plates are immersed in an electrolyte, one loses electrons and becomes positive. The other gains them and becomes negative. Negative ions in a solution are attracted to the positive **plate**, and positive ions to the negative plate, and a chemical reaction can occur.

In a lead-acid battery, the electrical and chemical differences between the sets of plates create a potential difference or voltage, which makes the current flow in a circuit. It flows in one direction only, so it is called direct current, or DC. As electrons move through the electrical circuits in the vehicle from one set of plates to the other, the same compounds form on the plates. If this happens for too long, there will be no potential difference between the plates and current stops flowing, leaving a discharged battery. Of course, a battery can be recharged, which reverses the process so that current is pushed backward through the battery, reversing the chemical reaction and restoring the potential difference between its sets of plates.

Light Effects

The production of light can also be an effect of electricity. An example of this is the LED. The LED is a semiconductor diode that creates light by emitting photons from its PN junction when a current flows through it **FIGURE 36-17**. At one time, LEDs were available only in the red, green, and yellow tints. More recently, they have become available in many different colors and have grown in light intensity. They are now replacing traditional bulbs as lighting sources and produce as much or more light with less heat loss, using much less energy. LEDs are also being used as headlights on some top-end cars, and it is likely that as LED technology improves and prices come down, they will be installed on more and more new vehicles.

Electromagnetic Effects

Electricity can also create magnetic effects, referred to as electromagnetism. An electromagnet creates magnetic forces that attract both ferrous metals and unlike magnetic

FIGURE 36-17 Light created by an LED.

Anode

Cathode

Battery

the magnetic fields, which strengthens the magnetic effect. The size of the electromagnet is determined by its application. A fuel injector will contain a small electromagnetic coil using very fine wire, whereas a starter motor will use heavier wire in larger coils.

Many components use electromagnetism to operate. If a component has an electrical connection and movement is created by or within the component, then that component will use an electromagnet. Devices such as relays, solenoids, and motors use electromagnets to create movement. Ignition coils and transformers use electromagnetic induction to raise or lower voltage outputs. These devices will be examined further later in the chapter.

Applied	Science

AS-63: Generators: The technician can explain how the movement of a conductor in a magnetic field will generate electricity.
When a conductor is moved through a magnetic field, an electrical current is generated within the conductor. This phenomenon is known as electromagnetic induction. Alternatively, the conductor can remain stationery while the magnetic field is moved in relation to it. The generation of a voltage depends directly on the movement of either the conductor or the magnetic field. Without movement there is no voltage generated.

Electromagnetic induction works by exposing the electrons within the conductor to a magnetic force acting perpendicular to both their motion and the magnetic field, which forces them to move through the conductor, creating a charge.

charges and that repel like magnetic charges. These forces can be used to create mechanical movement, such as in a relay or electric motor. In electrical systems, **magnetism** occurs when a current passes through a conductor and a magnetic field is created around it. If the wire is wound into a coil, the magnetic fields combine to create a stronger and denser magnetic field, with a north and a south pole, just like a permanent magnet. Turn the current flow off, and the magnetic field collapses and disappears. By turning current to the coil on and off, this magnetic effect can be turned into a mechanical movement, pulling a switch open or closed. This is the principle behind a **relay**.

Reverse the current flow through the coil, and the north and south poles reverse.

Therefore, by passing electrical current through a coil, a magnetic field is produced, and turning it off causes the magnetic field to collapse. This is the operational theory behind an **electromagnet**. Electromagnets are constructed by winding a conductor wire, many hundreds or thousands of times, around a soft iron or metal core and passing a current through the coil. The strength of the magnetic field produced is determined by the number of turns, or coils, and the value of the current flow through the conductor. The metal core uniformly aligns

Ohm's Law and Circuits

Ohm's law helps us to understand the relationship between volts, amps, and ohms. They always have to balance out. If they do not, you made a mistake. Ohm's law tells us that it takes 1 volt to push 1 amp through 1 ohm of resistance. That gives us the relationship among the three units. Volts and resistance are physical things. Volts are the surplus of electrons creating electrical pressure. Resistance is the physical restriction of the conductor. Amps are the amount of electrons moved. That means that amps are the result of both the volts and resistance. For example, if resistance doubles and voltage stays the same, current flow must be cut in half. To illustrate this relationship, consider the following: If you steadily push (voltage) a loaded wheelbarrow twice as far up a hill (ohms), you will only move half the amount of dirt in a given amount of time **FIGURE 36-18**. It is the same with the electrical circuit: If the pressure (volts) stays the same but the restriction (ohms) doubles, then the electrons (amps) will be reduced by half. Conversely, if the voltage is doubled and the resistance stays the same, then amperage will double.

If you understand the preceding, then you are well on your way to diagnosing electrical problems. Here is a question. If the amps in a circuit are lower than they should be, what are the two possible causes? First, the source voltage could be low. In that case, you would use a voltmeter to measure the source voltage at the battery. The second possibility is that the resistance in the circuit is too high. In that case, you would use a voltmeter to see if there is an excessive voltage drop on both sides of the circuit that would be caused by high resistance. If the voltage drop is within specifications, you would use an ohmmeter to measure the resistance of the load.

Most of the time when circuits fail it is because the current flow is too low or nonexistent. Yes, it is possible that the battery is dead or discharged, but more likely there is high resistance as a voltage drop either in the feed side or the ground side of the circuit. Or the electrical device has too much resistance or is open. Performing a voltage drop test on both sides of the circuit will quickly identify if there is an excessive voltage drop present. And a resistance check of the electrical device will indicate a high resistance or open condition in the component. Knowing the specifications that go along with these steps will enable you to repair more than half of the electrical problems on a vehicle.

Circuits are made up of components and interconnecting conductors, such as wires, arranged to manage and control the flow of electrons to perform specific electrical tasks. Understanding circuits and how to take electrical measurements is essential to perform electrical repair activities. Circuits come in two basic configurations: series circuits and parallel circuits. The two types can also be combined into what is called a series-parallel circuit. Understanding how electricity behaves within each of these circuits will help you know how the circuit operates and how to approach diagnosis. It will also allow you to apply Ohm's law correctly to each type of circuit. We will look at the types of circuits further after finishing our discussion of Ohm's law.

Ohm's Law and Ohm's Law Calculations

Because Ohm's law is a relationship between volts, amps, and ohms, and because they must always balance out, if we know any two of the values, then we can calculate the third. If resistance stays the same but voltage rises, then the greater force pushes more current through the circuit. If resistance stays the same but voltage decreases, then less current will flow through the circuit. That means that the total current flow of a circuit in amps always equals the voltage divided by the resistance.

In calculating Ohm's law, R stands for resistance, V for voltage, and A for current (A is for amps).* Depending on which value you wish to solve for, you will apply one of the following three formulas:

- $A = V/R$
- $V = A \times R$
- $R = V \div A$

Voltage can vary across different points in a circuit, but determining the current at any point can be found without an ammeter by using Ohm's law.

Using the Ohm's law circle will help you remember which math operation to use FIGURE 36-19. All you have

FIGURE 36-18 Current flow is the result of voltage and resistance.

* Note that some sources use E for voltage and I for current. Also, we intentially reversed the R and A in the Ohm's law circle to highlight the fact that Amps is ALWAYS the result (product) of Volts and Resistance. If the amps are not correct, it is because either the Volts or Resistance is wrong.

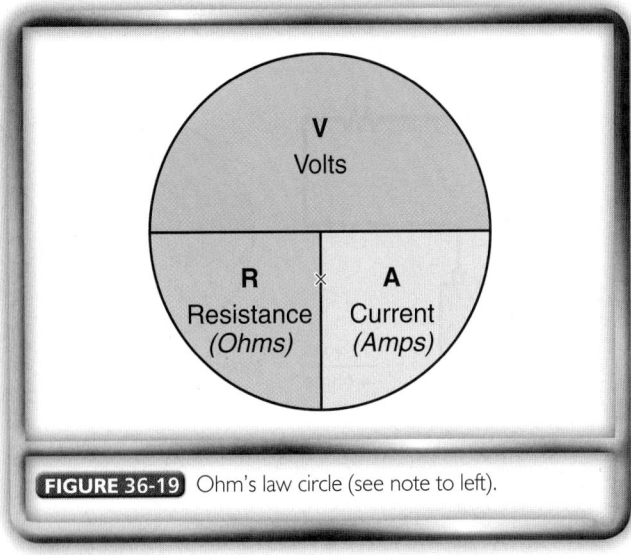

FIGURE 36-19 Ohm's law circle (see note to left).

to do is place your finger over the value you are looking for. If you place your finger on the top value (volts), then you would multiply amps by resistance. If you place your finger on one of the side values, then you would divide volts by the other value. This means two things. First, the values always have to balance. And second, as long as you know any two values, the third can be calculated. This is especially helpful when determining current flow, because instead of breaking into a circuit to measure current with a meter, if the voltage and resistance are known, Ohm's law may be used to calculate amps.

For example, battery voltage can be measured. Let's use 12 volts. The value of the resistor, 4 ohms, is on its casing. Current then equals voltage (12 volts) divided by resistance (4 ohms). We can quickly calculate that there are 3 amps of current flowing through every point in the circuit **FIGURE 36-20** .

Solving Ohm's Law

Using the rules of Ohm's law gives an accurate method of determining values in an electrical circuit. To assist with these problems, use the Ohm's law circle (Figure 36-21). If the value of V and R are known, then to find A, V is divided by R. Place your thumb over A and the circle tells you this formula. Similarly, if V and A are known, then R can be found by dividing V by A. If A and R, are known, then V is found by multiplying A by R.

In the circuit diagram in Figure 36-22, the value of the amperage is not known. The applied voltage is 12 volts (V) and the resistance is 4 ohms (Ω). To find the value of A, simply divide V by R, or 12 by 4. The value of A is 3 amps (A).

In the circuit diagram in **FIGURE 36-21** , the value of the applied voltage is not known but the amperage and resistance are. To find the value of V, multiply A by R, or 6 amps by 4 ohms. The answer is 24 volts.

In the circuit diagram in **FIGURE 36-22** , the value of the current flow is unknown. To find the value of A, divide

| **Applied** | **Science** |

AS-70: Ohm's Law: The technician can demonstrate an understanding of and explain the use of Ohm's law in verifying circuit parameters (resistance, voltage, amperage).
Ohm's law quantifies the relationship between amperage, voltage, and resistance in any given circuit. It provides a means to calculate any one of these parameters from the values of the other two. Ohm's law is easiest applied through the use of a circle diagram like the one shown here:

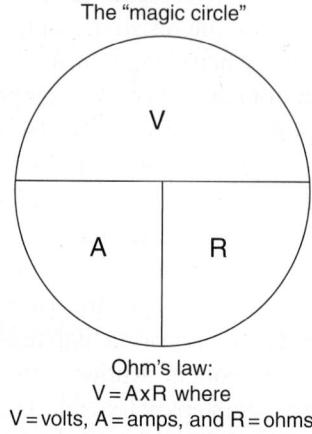

The "magic circle"

Ohm's law:
V = A x R where
V = volts, A = amps, and R = ohms

These diagrams are used by placing your finger over the parameter you are trying to calculate, then reading the remainder of the diagram to identify the calculation you need to perform. For example, if you need to work out the amperage flowing in the circuit, block off the A, and your calculation is V ÷ R, or voltage divided by resistance. For a 12-volt automotive circuit with 20 ohms of resistance, your calculation is 12 ÷ 20, to arrive at 0.6 amps.

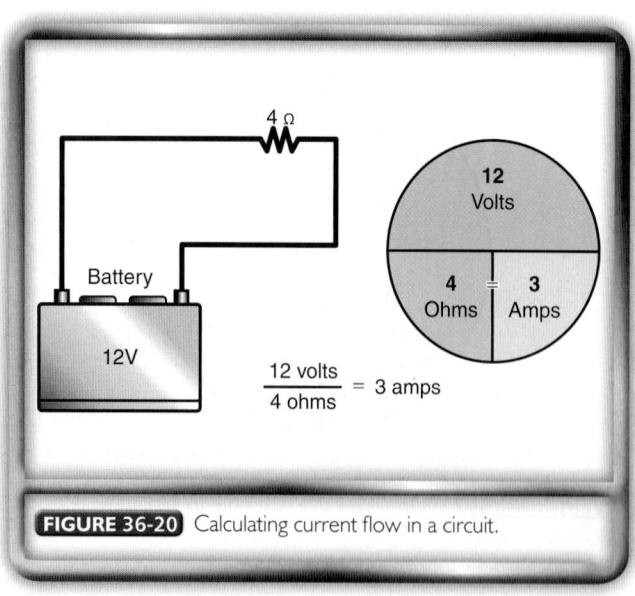

FIGURE 36-20 Calculating current flow in a circuit.

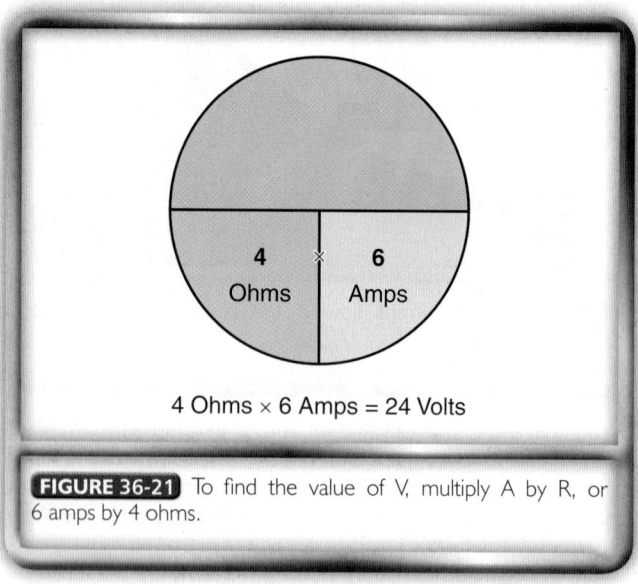

FIGURE 36-21 To find the value of V, multiply A by R, or 6 amps by 4 ohms.

V by R, or in this case, 12 volts divided by 3 ohms. The value of A is 4 amps.

$$\frac{12 \text{ volts}}{3 \text{ ohms}} = 4 \text{ amps}$$

FIGURE 36-22 To find the value of A, divide V by R, or in this case, 12 volts divided by 3 ohms.

Applied Science

AS-71: Resistance: The technician can demonstrate an understanding of the relationship of resistance to heat, voltage drop, and circuit parameters.

The electrical resistance of a component is the component's opposition to the flow of electrical current. Any resistance in a circuit creates a voltage drop across the resistive component, be it a resistor, a bulb, an electric motor, or merely a wire. The amount of voltage drop is proportional to the amount of resistance. Resistors work by dissipating energy in the form of heat; therefore, for a given amount of current flowing in a circuit, the higher the resistance of a component, the more heat it will produce.

Let's look at an example using a rear window defogger. The defogger elements form a resistor in the circuit. In this case, heat is produced by the resistor grid to defog the window. The resistance of each grid line creates a steady voltage drop across the length of the grid line. Current flowing through the grid line then creates heat. Broken grid lines cannot conduct current flow, so there is no voltage drop, nor heat generated in that grid line. Battery voltage (12 volts) is applied across the element when you switch on the defogger. If you were to measure the voltage at the center of one of the grid lines in the element, you should expect to see a voltage of approximately 6 volts. If the grid is burned open on the ground side, then the voltage would read about 12 volts, since there cannot be a voltage drop if there is no current flow. If the grid was burned open on the power side, the voltage would be near 0 volts because the current flow cannot get past the open circuit to the middle of the grid line. Moving the voltmeter toward the side with the break can pinpoint the exact location of the broken grid line so that repairs can be made.

Electrical Power and the Power Equation

Energy is the potential to do work. However, work is done only when the energy is released. A disconnected battery is not doing work, but it has the potential to do work and is therefore a source of energy. The difference in electron supply at the battery terminals creates electrical force and is sometimes called the potential difference. In the case of a standard charged automotive battery, it has a potential of approximately 12 volts. Tapping this potential means turning one form of energy, the battery's chemical energy, into another form of energy, electrical energy.

Turning one form of energy into another is called energy transformation. The amount of energy transformed is the amount of work done. When a person's legs turn the pedals of a bicycle, chemical energy (from oxygen and food) is being turned into mechanical energy. A motorcycle engine turns chemical energy into thermal energy, and then into mechanical energy. In each case, **work** is being done, but there is a difference with the motorcycle—it does the work more quickly, delivering more mechanical energy faster. That difference is called **power**. Power is the rate at which work is performed. It is also known as the rate of transforming energy. In an electrical circuit, power refers to the rate at which electrical energy is transformed into another kind of energy.

The unit of electrical power is the **watt**. One watt is produced when 1 volt causes 1 amp of current to flow. From this comes the power equation: P, the power in watts, equals V, the voltage in volts, multiplied by A, the current in amps. This calculation is applied similarly to Ohm's law and is typically represented as a triangle **FIGURE 36-23**.

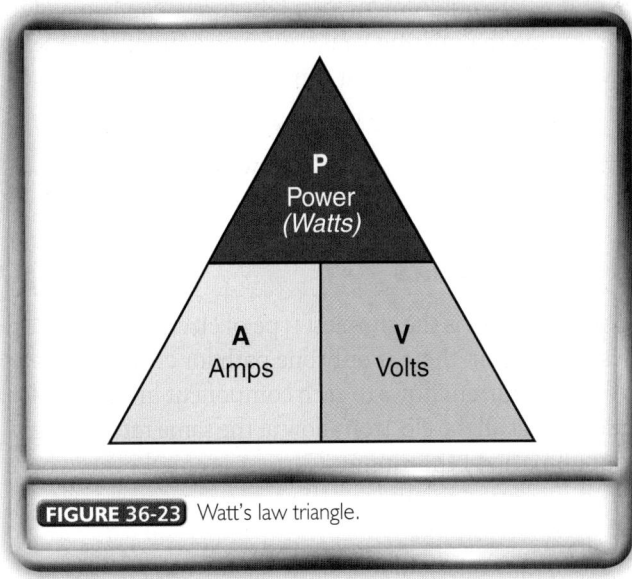

FIGURE 36-23 Watt's law triangle.

When current flows in a circuit with a resistor in it, the resistor becomes hotter as it converts electrical energy into heat energy. If this circuit is powered by a 12-volt battery with a current of 2 amps, using the power equation ($P = V \times A$) we can determine that the resistor is using 24 watts of power.

It is also possible to simplify and transpose the power equation. If power equals voltage times current, then:

- Voltage equals power divided by current: $V = P \div A$
- Current equals power divided by voltage: $A = P \div V$

Solving Power Equations

Electrical power is a measurement of the rate at which electricity is consumed or created. When used in relation to loads, it is a measure of electricity consumed. A light bulb uses a certain amount of electrical power, but the power used is not an indication of brightness; it is a measure of power consumption. When used in relation to generators, it is a measure of electrical power produced. One volt pushing 1 amp equals 1 watt of electrical power. To calculate power, the current flow in the circuit is multiplied by the voltage used. So,

$P = A \times V$, or Watts = Amps × Volts

This is demonstrated by the diagram in Figure 36-25. For reference purposes, 746 watts equal 1 horsepower.

If a 12-volt circuit with a single light has a current flow of 5 amps, then applying the formula will yield:

- $P = A \times V$
- $P = 5\,A \times 12\,V$
- $P = 60\,W$

The power consumed by the circuit is 60 watts, and the bulb will carry a rating of 60 watts. This rule can be applied to any circuit where the voltage and current flow are known. However, if the values of voltage or current flow are not known, then Ohm's law can be used to determine the missing value. As an example: $V = A \times R$. By expanding $P = A \times V$, it can be said that

$P = A \times (A \times R)$, or $P = A^2 \times R$.

Similarly, by applying $A = V \div R$, we have

$P = (V \div R) \times V$, or $P = V^2 \div R$.

Series Circuits

A series circuit is the simplest type of electrical circuit. In a series circuit, there is only one path for current to flow. All of the current flows to each component in turn. It also means that all the electrons flow at the same rate throughout all parts of the circuit. Current is equal everywhere within a series circuit.

In a series circuit, if there is more than one resistance in the circuit, those resistances are connected one after the other; thus the resistances add up. The total resistance in a series circuit is the sum of all of the individual resistances. For example, imagine a circuit with three resistors in series, each having 4 ohms of resistance, powered by a 12-volt battery. Total resistance of the three 4-ohm resistors is 12 ohms, since resistance adds up in a series circuit. According to Ohm's law, if 12 volts is applied to a circuit that has 12 ohms of resistance, the resulting current flow will be 1 amp.

However, the voltage at different points within the circuit changes, as the electromotive force, or pressure, drops from a potential difference of 12 volts as it leaves the battery to virtually no difference, no voltage at all, as it returns to the battery. At each point in the circuit where current flows through a resistance, a drop in voltage occurs, which is called a voltage drop. Voltage drops are good when they occur inside of an intended load. They are bad when they occur where they are not wanted.

In FIGURE 36-24, after the first resistor, voltage has dropped from 12 to 8 volts. After the second, it is down to 4 volts. After the third, it is 0 volts. The voltage drop across each resistor can be found by subtracting the voltage after a resistor from the voltage before it, or the difference can be measured. The voltmeter will read 4 volts in each case because that is the difference between the two points, the potential difference, or voltage.

Ohm's law can be used in series circuits to calculate voltage, resistance, and current. Any one of these can be calculated as long as the values of the other two are known.

The series circuit laws listed here provide a summary of how electricity behaves in a series circuit, which is

FIGURE 36-24 Voltage drop in a series circuit.

defined as a circuit with multiple loads but only one path for current to flow:

- Current flow stays the same in a series circuit. Current flow is the same in all parts of the circuit.
- Voltage drops as current goes through resistance(s) in series. The applied voltage is equal to the sum of the individual voltage drops (Kirchhoff's voltage law).
- Resistance adds up in series. Total circuit resistance is equal to the sum of the individual resistances; for example, $R_T = R_1 + R_2 + R_3$, and so on.

Parallel Circuits

In a series circuit, components are connected like links in a chain. If any link opens, current to all of the components is cut off. In a parallel circuit, all components are connected directly to the voltage supply **FIGURE 36-25**. If any connection or component fails in a parallel circuit, current continues to flow normally through the remaining circuits. This is one reason why parallel circuits are used in automotive applications, such as headlight and tail-light systems. If one lamp fails, current continues to flow through the other lamps in parallel. In a series circuit, all would go out, which could be disastrous.

Also, since all components connect directly to the battery terminals, the metal of the vehicle's chassis can become one of the conductors. One terminal of the battery and one terminal of each component can be connected anywhere on the body or chassis to complete the circuit. This is called a common, or ground, connection. It saves a lot of connecting wire.

While electricity always behaves according to the laws of physics, when it operates in a parallel circuit, there are some additional laws you need to know. The parallel circuit laws listed here should be applied when working with parallel circuits:

- The voltage across all branches of a parallel circuit are equal.
- The total current in a parallel circuit equals the sum of the current flowing in each branch of the circuit.
- The total resistance of a parallel circuit decreases as more branches are added. Total parallel circuit resistance will always be less than the lowest branch resistance.

Let's look at those laws a bit more closely. A feature of a properly working parallel circuit is that the voltage across each branch is the same as the other branches. No matter how many branches are added, or removed, as long as they are in parallel, the voltage across them will be the same as across each of the other branches, including the battery. Another feature of a parallel circuit is that the current flowing in each branch is determined by the resistance of that branch along with the voltage used by that branch.

In a parallel circuit where the resistors in each branch are the same, the current flowing in each branch is also the same. The sum of their individual currents is equal to the total current flowing in the entire parallel circuit. When the resistances are not equal, the current divides in accordance with the resistance of each branch, but the total current flow is still the sum of the currents flowing in each branch **FIGURE 36-26**.

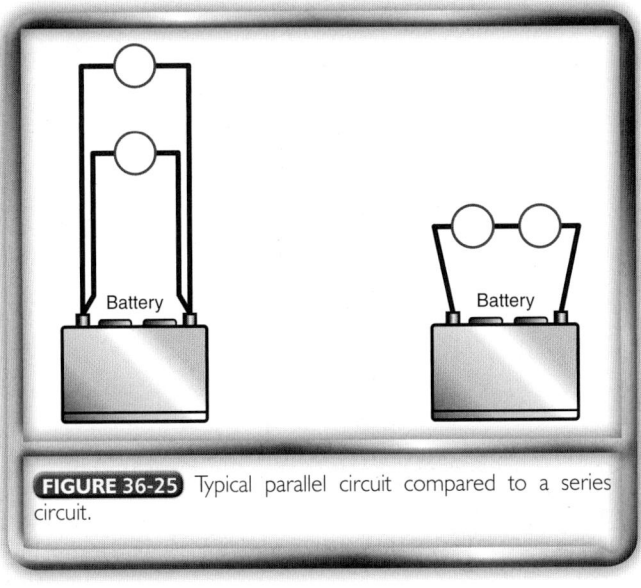

FIGURE 36-25 Typical parallel circuit compared to a series circuit.

FIGURE 36-26 Parallel circuit with unequal resistances.

Parallel Circuit Resistance

Resistance in a parallel circuit is not as easily calculated as it is in a series circuit, because as branches are added, another path for current to flow to ground is added. Adding extra paths reduces the circuit's total resistance to current flow. For example, if you have a 12-volt parallel circuit with three branches, each branch having a 12-ohm resistor that allows 1 amp of current flow, and you then add another parallel branch with a 12-ohm resistor to the circuit, the result will be the opposite of what might be expected. Current increases from 3 amps to 4 amps. This is because in a parallel circuit adding more branches provides more pathways, but decreases the overall circuit resistance; thus, current flow increases. This is like having a freeway with three lanes and bumper-to-bumper traffic. If you add a fourth lane, the resistance to flow decreases and cars can move more easily. Another visual example would be if you had a bucket full of water and the bucket had three holes in the bottom. If another hole were added, the total flow out of the bucket would speed up, which means the resistance to flow decreases. To calculate resistance, use the formula in **FIGURE 36-27** and substitute the value of each resistor in the place of R_1, R_2, etc.

Series-Parallel Circuits

When electrical components are wired together one after another so that there is only one path for current flow, they are said to be wired "in series." When they are wired together side by side, so there is more than one path for current to flow, they are said to be wired "in parallel." A **series-parallel circuit** is made of both a series circuit and a parallel circuit. The series circuit can be before or after the parallel portion of the circuit. Series-parallel circuits can be analyzed using the same electrical laws that apply to separate series or parallel circuits; you just have to apply the series laws to the series portion and the parallel laws to the parallel portion.

A circuit for dash lights is an example of a series-parallel circuit in an automotive application. In this situation, a variable resistor is connected in series with a number of dash lights, which are connected in parallel to each other. When the variable resistor is turned, the resistance changes. As the resistance increases, the voltage drop across the potentiometer increases and the current flow decreases. This lowers the voltage and current flow to the dash lights, making the dash lights dimmer. When the variable resistor is turned such that its resistance is lowered, the voltage drop across it is reduced and the current flow in the circuit increases, making the dash lights brighter. Since the dash lights are in parallel, they each receive the same amount of voltage, and the total circuit current flow is divided equally between them, making them equally bright as one another.

Kirchhoff's Current Law

Kirchhoff's current law describes a fundamental electrical principle and is used by technicians in understanding how all electrical circuits work. Many technicians would understand the principle behind the law without necessarily associating it with Kirchhoff. Simply stated, the law is that current entering any junction is equal to the sum of the current flowing out of the junction. For example, in a junction of three conductors, current is flowing in at 10 amps from conductor A and out by the other two conductors, B and C **FIGURE 36-28**. According to Kirchhoff's current law, the sum of the current in conductors B and C will equal the current flowing into the junction at conductor A, or 10 amps.

$$R_T = \cfrac{1}{\cfrac{1}{R1} + \cfrac{1}{R1} + \cfrac{1}{R1}}$$

2 resistors in parallel

$$R_T = \frac{R1 \times R2}{R1 + R2}$$

FIGURE 36-27 Calculating parallel resistance with uneven resistances.

10 Amps flowing

5 Amps

5 Amps

Battery

12V

FIGURE 36-28 Kirchhoff's current law: Current entering a junction is equal to the sum of the current flowing out of the junction.

Electrical Components

Electrical components such as switches, fuses, circuit breakers, resistors, capacitors, and relays are all used in a circuit to modify or manage the flow of current. Each component performs a specific task within the circuit and will be connected into its particular circuit. To ensure the components' correct operation, they will often have terminals numbered or marked with the connections and be referenced in wiring diagrams or schematics.

Some components are **polarity sensitive**. This means they must be connected into the circuit with the correct polarity to each lead. For example, some capacitors, and most semiconductor components, are polarity sensitive. Polarity-sensitive components have the polarity marked on at least one connection to ensure that the user connects them into the circuit correctly.

Switches

A **switch** is an electrical device used to turn the current on and off in a circuit. When turned off, switches open the circuit, stopping current flow; when turned on, they close the circuit, allowing current to flow. For example, switch off—light goes out; switch on—light comes on. There are many different types and configurations of switches, including toggle switches, push-button switches, and specialty switches for turn signal indicators and windshield wipers **FIGURE 36-29**. The most basic switches have only two terminals and are simply on or off.

More complex switches have many terminals and contacts inside them to switch a number of circuits at the same time. The **turn signal switch** is an example of a more complex switch. It has three positions: center for off, pushed in one direction for the left turn signals, pushed in the other direction for the right turn signals. **Circuit or schematic diagrams** show switches, their contacts, and the surrounding circuits so that the technician can identify how they operate in a circuit. The terminals on the switch are often numbered or lettered to indicate the correct way of connecting them into their circuits and to show the mating connectors in the wiring diagrams.

Fuses, Fusible Links, and Circuit Breakers

Fuses and **circuit breakers** are designed to protect electrical circuits by opening the circuit if the current flow is excessive. The most common kinds of circuit protection devices are fuses, fusible links, circuit breakers, and positive temperature coefficient (PTC) thermistor protection devices. Fuses and circuit breakers are rated in amps, and their ratings are usually marked on them. Fusible links are typically rated by their wire size.

Fuses are typically used in lighting and accessory circuits where current flow is usually moderate. Usually, a fuse contains a metal strip that is designed to overheat and melt when subjected to a specified excessive level of current flow, breaking the circuit and stopping the excessive current flow from potentially damaging the wiring harness and more valuable components. Fuses come in a variety of configurations, from cylindrical glass cartridge fuses to plastic blade fuses **FIGURE 36-30**. They also come in a variety of sizes and amp ratings. Fuses are typically housed in fuse boxes located around the vehicle, typically under the hood and/or dash.

A fusible link is made of a short length (usually 6" [15 cm] or less) of smaller diameter wire that has a lower melting point than standard wire and insulation

FIGURE 36-29 Typical automotive switches.

FIGURE 36-30 Various fuses.

that is fire resistant. Fusible links are typically placed near the battery to protect the wiring harness between the battery and any fuse boxes. In most cases, they are used to carry higher current flows than fuses, and typically feed power to one or more circuits **FIGURE 36-31**. Fusible links are fairly durable, and do not fail very often, unless there is a substantial short circuit in the system or the fusible link wire is abused by excessive flexing or pulling on it. Some newer vehicles use maxi-fuses, which are large blade-type fuses, instead of fusible links.

Circuit breakers are different from fuses and fusible links in two ways. First, they are not destroyed by excess current. And secondly, they can be reset, either automatically or manually. In a circuit breaker, a bimetallic strip heats up and bends, opening a set of contacts and breaking the circuit when current flow becomes excessive. In most types, as the strip cools, it resumes its original shape. The contacts then close, completing the circuit once more. These are called self-resetting circuit breakers. Manual breakers must be reset by hand, which could involve flipping a lever or inserting a small rod to reset the bimetal spring once it cools down.

PTC thermistors are also used as circuit protection devices. They have very low resistance at room temperature, but increase in resistance as the temperature increases. If too much current starts to flow through a PTC, the small voltage drop creates heat in the PTC. The increased heat produces increased resistance, which further increases the voltage drop. This cycle continues quickly until the PTC reaches its maximum resistance. This heightened resistance effectively shuts off most of the current flow to the protected device. PTCs generally reset once power is removed and they are allowed to cool. They are typically integrated into components such as power window motors and door locks.

Flasher Can/Control

The **flasher can** is the control mechanism for the turn signal lights on the vehicle. As the name suggests, it flashes or turns the turn signal lights on and off at a regular rate to indicate a change in the vehicle's direction. Flasher cans are mechanical devices, while flasher controls are generally electronic devices **FIGURE 36-32**. Both types perform the same job, but the electronic version is more reliable and consistent. Flasher cans operate like an automatically resetting circuit breaker, meaning they use a bimetallic strip to open and close the switch contacts. This opening and closing gives them a distinctive clicking sound that, along with the turn signal indicator lights on the dash, tells the driver when the turn signals are on so that they remember turn them off when needed. Electronic flasher controls control the on/off function electronically, which

FIGURE 36-31 A fusible link is typically placed near the battery and carries the current needed to power an individual circuit or a range of circuits.

FIGURE 36-32 Flasher control and flasher can.

means they can be designed to operate over a wider range of current flow, which makes them ideal for trailer towing. In many cases, the hazard lamps are also operated by a flasher can or flasher control.

Relays

Relays are switches that are turned on and off by a small electrical current. They are ideal for using a small current to control a larger current. An example would be the horn circuit. A small current can be turned on and off by the horn switch in the steering wheel, using a light-duty switch and wires. The small current is then used to activate the relay, which sends the larger current to the horn. Thus, larger wires are needed only up front where they can be shorter, and smaller wires can be used to run up the steering column. Most electrical components found in a motor vehicle are controlled by relays. ECUs use relays to control components such as fuel pumps, headlights, and the cooling fan. All of these circuits carry large electrical loads.

The relay is made up of an electromagnet, a set of switch contacts, terminals, and the case. The electromagnet is a winding of fine metal-insulated wire wrapped around an iron core. Each end of the winding is connected to one of the terminals. The contacts usually consist of three contacts—two fixed and one movable. The movable contact is fixed to a spring-loaded armature blade and is held against one of the fixed contacts, which is called the **normally closed (NC)** contact. When the relay coil is activated, the electromagnet pulls the movable armature blade contact away from the NC contact and against the **normally open (NO)** contact, sending power out to the controlled device. It also opens the NC contact points on that type of relay.

When the contact points are closed, current flows across the contact points and out to the electrical device to the rest of the circuit. As long as the small control current flows through the relay windings, the much larger current for the load will flow through the relay's contact points. A **solid-state relay** acts like a mechanical relay but does not have any moving parts. This means that electronic relays do not use mechanical switches, but instead use transistorized circuitry to turn the circuit on and off. They also do not make any sound, unless they were specifically designed with components to do that.

Automotive relay terminals use one of two standard labeling systems: 85, 86, 30, 87a, and 87 or 1, 2, 3, 4, 5 **FIGURE 36-33**.

- 85 or 1 = One end of the relay winding
- 86 or 2 = The other end of the relay winding
- 30 or 3 = Common—movable switch contact
- 87a or 4 = NC fixed contact to the common
- 87 or 5 = NO fixed contact to the common

When electromagnetic relays are de-energized, the collapse of the magnetic field induces a large voltage spike in the relay coil windings. If unchecked, this voltage can be transmitted back into the circuit where it can damage electronic components. Some relays deal with this danger by placing either a suppression diode or a resistor in parallel with the winding **FIGURE 36-34**. Doing so reduces the voltage spike by shunting the voltage spike from the output side of the coil back to the input side of the coil. This design prevents the voltage from spiking so high when the relay is de-energized. When replacing a relay that has spike protection, make sure to use a new relay that is specified for the application.

FIGURE 36-33 Relay schematic.

FIGURE 36-34 Spike-protected relays.

Solenoids

A **solenoid** is an electromechanical device that coverts electrical energy into mechanical linear (back-and-forth) movement. Solenoids can be used to pull or push. In a simple solenoid, insulated wire is wound many times around a hollow cylindrical form. A sliding mild steel core is made to fit inside the hollow form. When the winding is energized, the resulting magnetic field attracts the mild steel, drawing it into the form and producing linear motion. Solenoids can be very strong and produce a lot of mechanical energy. Solenoid design may incorporate return springs, multiple windings, electrical contacts, and mechanical connections.

Fuel injectors and starter motor solenoids are two of the many solenoid-type components used in a motor vehicle. The operation of a solenoid is similar to a relay, but where a relay uses a magnetic field to close an electrical circuit, a solenoid uses a magnetic field to create lateral movement and, in the case of a starter solenoid, to also close heavy electrical contacts. The metal core, used by the electromagnet to strengthen the magnetic field, is referred to as an **armature**. It is spring loaded so that it is positioned partially outside the electromagnetic coil and is free to move in and out. When the coil is energized, the magnetic field draws the armature into the center of the coil. If the armature is attached to a lever or plunger, it will be forced to move as well. Stopping current flow causes the electromagnet to de-energize and the spring pushes the armature out again.

Another device that uses a solenoid is a vehicle horn. When the armature is drawn in by the electromagnetic coil, it opens a set of electrical contacts so that current flow through the coil is stopped. This stoppage causes the armature to move out again, closing the contacts, drawing the armature back in. This process occurs at very high speeds. The vibration caused by the rapid movement is transferred to a diaphragm, and the familiar horn sound is produced.

Applied Science

AS-62: Short Circuit: The technician can demonstrate an understanding of the processes used to locate a short circuit in an electrical/electronic system.
Two types of short circuit can occur in electrical systems. In a short to ground, electrical current finds its way to ground before it was intended, usually due to compromised wiring insulation that allows wiring to touch the metal vehicle body. In a short to power, a circuit is exposed to voltage flowing in another circuit, generally also due to broken wiring insulation. The effect of either type of short will depend on the layout of the circuit and where the short occurs in relation to the load.

The most common indicator of a short circuit is a fuse blowing due to excessive current flow. Traditionally, diagnosing the location of the short has required being able to segment the circuit by disconnecting fuses, components, switches, or harness plugs and checking individual sections of the circuit for integrity. Electronic short-circuit finders are now available that send an electrical signal along the circuit. A receiver is run along the circuit until it stops receiving a signal, at which point the location of the short has been found.

Applied Science

AS-69: Fuse: The technician can explain the role of a fuse or fusible link as a protective device in an electrical or electronic circuit.
A fuse, or fusible link, is a form of overcurrent protection device. It consists of a conductive metal strip that melts when subjected to more than a specified level of current. When the fuse "blows," the circuit is broken and no current flows in the remainder of the circuit. Fuses are installed for two reasons: They can prevent excessive current flow from damaging more expensive components elsewhere in the circuit, and they can prevent overheating within wiring and components, which could potentially cause a fire.

Applied Science

AS-61: Parallel/Series Circuits: The technician can explain current flow and voltage in series and parallel circuits.
The terms "series" and "parallel" describe different ways in which components in a circuit can be connected. In a series circuit, all components are connected along a single path. Electricity can flow only one way, so the flow of electrons, or the current flow, within the circuit is the same at all points. The voltage in the system will change at different points due to voltage drops at various resistors. In a parallel circuit, components are connected so that the circuit divides into two or more paths before recombining. All components are connected to the same voltage supply, so the same voltage is applied to all components. Current flow in different branches of a parallel circuit changes depending on the resistance in each branch; therefore, different branches of the circuit may experience differing amperage if their resistance values are different.

▶ **LINK**
Refer to the Batteries, Starting, and Charging Systems chapter for a detailed description of the starter solenoid operation.

Motors

While solenoids use magnetic fields to create lateral movement, electric motors use magnetic fields to create rotary movement. Motors consist of two main components: the armature and the field. The armature contains electromagnetic coils. The field contains either electromagnets or permanent magnets. The interaction between the magnetic fields of the stationary field coils and the magnetic fields of the moveable armature coils causes the armature to rotate. Since the armature coils can be energized and create electromagnetic fields, those fields can be turned on and off so that they attract and repel the fields of the stationary magnetic fields. The design and orientation of the electromagnetic coils ensure that the armature continues to turn as it rotates through various positions. The armature is connected to the electrical supply by a set of carbon brushes that contact a **commutator**, which is a segmented component of the armature. The commutator and brushes act as switches to control the current flow through the windings of the armature **FIGURE 36-35**. The brushes allow the electrical connection to occur even when the armature is spinning.

> ▸ **LINK**
> Refer to the Batteries, Starting, and Charging Systems chapter for more information on motors.

Ignition Coils and Transformers

Ignition coils and transformers both operate under the principles of electromagnetic induction. They use electromagnetism to produce electricity, rather than mechanical movement. An ignition coil can be described as a **step-up transformer**. This is because the output can be 60 kilovolts (or more), which is higher than the input, nominally 12 volts.

Two sets of coil windings are used. One coil, referred to as a **primary winding**, is wound around a second, the **secondary winding**. The primary coil typically has 200 to 300 turns of light-gauge wire while the secondary has approximately 30,000 to 60,000 turns of very fine wire. When current is passed through the primary winding, the magnetic field builds surrounding both the windings. When the current is turned off, the magnetic field collapses with enough speed to induce high voltage in the primary winding (self induction) and very high voltage in the secondary winding (mutual induction) by the rapidly moving (collapsing) magnetic field. Voltage is induced into each of the thousands of windings of the secondary coil. This voltage is strong enough to overcome the infinite resistance of the spark plug gap and push current across the gap, causing a spark with enough heat to ignite the airfuel mixture in the cylinder.

The **transformer action** causes heat to be produced. In the past, the internal coils were immersed in cooling oil, allowing the heat to be conducted to the case. Modern ignition coils do not use oil. They are usually constructed using a heat-conducting hard resin and are cooled by their location on a heat sink or in a stream of air. The advent of computer controls has allowed the time that current flows through the primary windings to be minimized to reduce heat and electrical loads, while still providing enough spark to ignite the airfuel mixture

Step-down transformers operate under the same operating principles. The only difference is that the secondary coil has fewer turns than the primary, providing a lower induced output. These transformers are used on power poles to lower the voltage to your house or school and on low-voltage devices in your home that are plugged into your 110-volt outlets, such as cell phone chargers.

FIGURE 36-35 Simplified electric motor diagram.

> ▶ **TECHNICIAN TIP**
>
> You might expect a transformer to be a great way to boost the amount of electrical power that is transmitted, but it isn't. The amount of power after the transformation is relatively the same as before the transformation. For example, if we raise the voltage from 12 volts to 120 volts, the amperage will decrease from, say, 10 amps to 1 amp. Thus, the wattage stays the same:
>
> 12 volts × 10 amps = 120 watts
> 120 volts × 1 amp = 120 watts
>
> Also, remember that transformers are not 100% efficient, so some of the power is lost as heat.

Resistors

Resistors are electrical components that resist a current running through them. Putting a resistor in a circuit causes a drop in voltage across the resistor. It also reduces the amperage in the circuit. Resistors are commonly used to control the voltage and amperage that reaches various components. It is important to remember that each electrical component has its own resistance. Most high-wattage resistors that can carry large amperage contain a coil of high-resistance wire wound around a ceramic form to dissipate heat.

Fixed Resistors

<u>Fixed resistors</u> are generally cylinders with connecting metal leads projecting along the axis of the cylinder at each end. Most axial resistors are marked with a series of colored stripes to indicate their resistance and tolerance levels. Fixed resistors can be manufactured as very tiny devices without leads and can be built into integrated circuits with many other miniaturized components.

Variable Resistors

Resistors found on circuit boards are normally fixed in value. Some resistors found in the motor vehicle are variable. <u>Variable resistors</u> can have their value altered by movement of a slide or by temperature change. The three types of variable resistors are rheostats, potentiometers, and thermistors. Variable resistors can be linear, meaning their resistance value varies proportionally with movement or temperature change, or nonlinear, meaning the resistance change is not proportional with movement.

Rheostats

A <u>rheostat</u> is a mechanical variable resistor with two connections. It consists of a resistance wire wrapped in a loose coil connected to the supply at one end only. A moveable wiper is connected to the other circuit connection and is made to move over the wire manually **FIGURE 36-36**. When the wiper is close to the beginning of the coil, the total resistance value is very small. As the wiper is positioned closer to the end of the coil, the resistance value increases. Rheostats are commonly used in dash light dimmer circuits and some fuel gauge sender units. They alter the current flow and voltage in a circuit.

Potentiometers

<u>Potentiometers</u> are mechanical variable resistors with three connections, two fixed and one moveable. They act as voltage dividers and as such alter the voltage in a circuit. A resistance wire is wrapped between two fixed connections. One fixed connection is attached to the electrical supply, the other to a ground. The third moveable connection is moved across the coil by a wiper in a similar fashion to a rheostat. The variable voltage output is taken from this point. Throttle position sensors are potentiometers.

Thermistors

As mentioned earlier, thermistors are conductors in which resistance value is affected by temperature. There are two types: **negative temperature coefficient (NTC)** and **positive temperature coefficient (PTC)** **FIGURE 36-37**. NTC thermistors alter their resistance value inversely to temperature. As the temperature increases, resistance value decreases. PTC thermistors alter their resistance value proportionally to temperature. As temperature rises, so does the resistance value. NTC thermistors are the most

FIGURE 36-36 Mechanical variable resistors. **A.** Potentiometer. **B.** Rheostat.

FIGURE 36-37 Thermistors. **A.** NTC thermistor resistance. **B.** PTC thermistor resistance.

common and are used in circuits for ECU inputs. They are the sensing elements of devices such as coolant and air temperature sensors.

Resistor Ratings

Resistance is measured in ohms, represented by the Greek letter omega (Ω). Resistors are rated in ohms as well, to indicate how strongly they will oppose any current flowing through them. Because resistors work by converting some of the electrical energy passing through them into heat, they also have a power rating. Only the resistance value is marked. The resistor's power rating is determined by its size.

Regardless of their power rating, resistors are small, so identification by numbers is impractical. To identify their value, many resistors are marked with four or five colored bands. Each color represents a numeric resistance value. The color bands are set close to each other and read from left to right. The last band, or tolerance band, is spaced farther apart. **FIGURE 36-38** shows the resistor colors.

Capacitors

A **capacitor** can quickly store a small amount of electrical energy, at which point it is charged. There are two surfaces inside the capacitor, separated by insulating material. When the capacitor is charged, one surface is positively charged and the other is negatively charged.

When a circuit is closed between its terminals, the capacitor releases its charge. At this point, it is discharged.

A typical capacitor stores the charge on thin sheets of foil, with sheets of insulation between them. These are rolled together to form a protective canister. A capacitor's **capacitance** (C) is a measure of the amount of **charge** (Q) stored on each plate for a given potential difference or **voltage** (V) that appears between the plates. In general, as the capacitance and voltage rating of the capacitor increase, the physical size of the capacitor increases. Some DVOMs can measure the capacitance of a capacitor. That way they can be tested, if they are suspected of being faulty.

▶ Electronic Components

The term *electronic components* tends to be used for those components that have no moving parts, such as diodes, transistors, and integrated circuits. Each component has a particular function and when arranged in circuits interacts with other components to control electrical and electronic functions. Individual components may be mounted in a housing to operate as a sensor: for example, an engine temperature sensor. Or, many components can be arranged in circuits and mounted on circuit boards to perform various functions. Examples of this would be the many electronic components used in control units to manage virtually all of the systems on a vehicle, including ignition, fuel, and emission systems, as well as entertainment, lighting, safety, and security systems.

Diodes

A diode can be thought of as the electronic version of a one-way check valve. By restricting the direction of movement of charge carriers, it allows an electrical current to flow in one direction, but essentially blocks it in the opposite direction.

A diode is made up of semiconductor material, one half being P material and the other half being N material. Diodes have a single PN junction. If the diode is connected to a current source, with the P region connected to a negative pole and the N region to a positive pole, the holes will be attracted toward the negative pole and the electrons to the positive pole. This movement enlarges the depletion layer, which makes the insulated space larger, stopping current flow across the junction. Such diodes are referred to as *reverse biased*.

When the voltage source is reversed, lots of holes flow across the junction toward the negative pole, and electrons travel in the opposite direction toward the positive pole. The PN junction floods with charge carriers, the depletion layer disappears, and with it, the insulator

FIGURE 36-38 Resistor colors.

effect disappears. In this direction, the diode allows current to flow. Such diodes are referred to as *forward biased*.

Using conventional current flow, a diode lets a low-voltage current flow through it if current flows from its P side to its N side, but stops current flowing through it from its N side to its P side.

A **Zener diode** is designed to block current flow through it, but if the voltage is large enough, it can force current to flow through the diode. This is called **breakdown**. As breakdown voltage is reached, the Zener diode's resistance suddenly collapses. It lets a large current flow through it, without damage. Because Zener diodes respond to certain voltage changes similar to switches, they are used in voltage regulators.

LEDs, another type of diode, are available in a range of colors and are often used as indicator lights on electrical and electronic appliances. High-powered white LEDs are increasingly being used to replace traditional incandescent light bulbs; they emit light when they are connected in a forward direction **FIGURE 36-39**.

Transistors

A **transistor** is a semiconductor device used as a switch and to amplify currents. A transistor is a key component in almost any electronic device. There are two kinds: NPN and PNP. The **NPN transistor** has a P-type semiconductor between two N-type semiconductors. A **PNP transistor** has an N-type semiconductor between two P-types **FIGURE 36-40**.

Each of the three regions has a terminal. The center region is always called the base. The outer regions are the collector and the emitter. In the symbol for a transistor, the emitter is the terminal with the arrow. It always points toward the negative material.

FIGURE 36-40 Transistors. **A.** The NPN transistor has a P-type semiconductor between two N-type semiconductors. **B.** A PNP transistor has an N-type semiconductor between two P-type semiconductors.

In a circuit, transistors can act as an electronic switch. If an open control switch is connected to the base, the depletion layer at one PN junction will block current from flowing through the transistor and powering the load.

When the control switch is closed, a small current flows through the emitter–base PN junction. The base has only a limited number of charge carriers, so extra ones flow across the emitter–collector PN junction, letting current operate the load. The transistor then operates as a low-resistance conductor. Most transistors have about 0.5 volts of voltage drop across the emitter–collector junction while current is flowing. A small current through the base lets larger current flow across the emitter–collector junction. The transistor is then said to be turned on.

FIGURE 36-39 Diode symbols. **A.** Zener diode symbol. **B.** LED symbol.

Applied **Science**

AS-78: Magnetic Fields/Forces: The technician can explain the effect of magnetic fields on unshielded circuits in control modules.
Shielding is applied to electrical circuits to prevent unwanted electromagnetic induction, where errant voltages may be generated in unshielded circuits due to electromagnetic interference. Some systems within control modules, particularly sensor inputs, work with high-sensitivity and very low voltages. In these cases, even a small induced voltage, known as "noise," can have serious effects on the running of the vehicle or the functionality of safety systems. The control unit may effectively respond to the noise as if it is actually a signal from a sensor.

AS-79: Semiconductor Devices: The technician can demonstrate an understanding of the capability of semiconductor devices to rapidly modify engine operation parameters.

Semiconductor devices are the foundation of modern electronics, having replaced vacuum tubes in nearly all applications. Common semiconductor devices include transistors and many types of diodes. They are used in all types of electronic devices, from radios and televisions to mobile phones and computers, including those used in automotive applications.

Semiconductor devices have enabled the development of automotive engine management systems due to their small size, high resilience to shock and vibration, and high reliability. They can also operate at very high speed, which allows increasingly accurate control of an engine's running parameters. ECUs in modern vehicles may now run at sampling rates exceeding 1.5 million times per second.

AS-81: Photocells: The technician can demonstrate an understanding of the purpose of photocells.

An example of a photocell is a sun load sensor which is usually mounted on top of the dashboard. The sensor is a part of the heating, ventilation and air-conditioning (HVAC) system. Its purpose is to send a signal to the programmer based upon the amount of sunlight that is striking it. The signal information will cause the programmer to adjust the system output according to sensor output voltage.

AS-82: Photocells: The technician can demonstrate the measurement processes used to determine the output of photocells.

A technician is diagnosing an electrical concern with a vehicle's heating, ventilation, and air-conditioning (HAVC) system. Several steps have been taken in the initial testing of the system. At this point, the service information refers the technician to the testing of the sun load sensor which is a photovoltaic device. A digital multimeter will be used to measure the output of the photocell in DC volts in most cases. A scan tool can sometimes be utilized, if so this would be the preferred method. For the exact procedure, consult the manufacturer's service information.

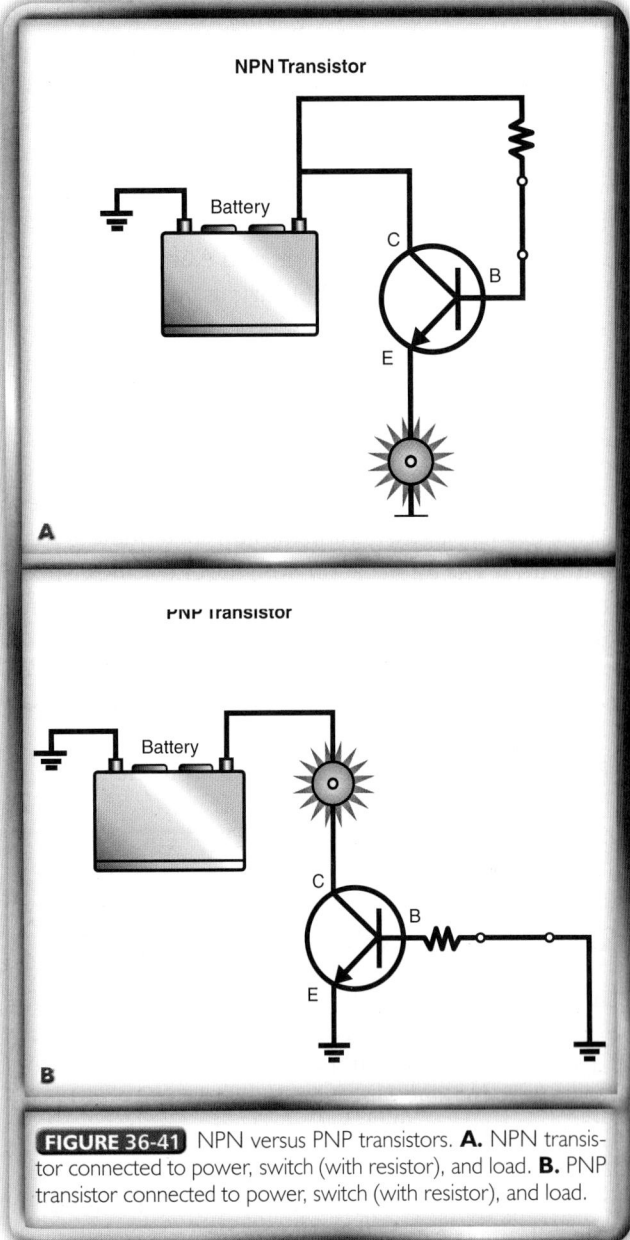

FIGURE 36-41 NPN versus PNP transistors. **A.** NPN transistor connected to power, switch (with resistor), and load. **B.** PNP transistor connected to power, switch (with resistor), and load.

One difference between PNP and NPN transistors is whether the base is activated by positive current flow or negative current flow **FIGURE 36-41**. In the case of an NPN transistor, positive current, through a resistor (to limit current flow to the base), is applied to the base. In a PNP transistor, a ground (through a resistor) is applied to the base. Transistors can be placed in the feed side of a circuit or on the ground side of a circuit.

Control Modules

A **control module** or unit is a generic term that identifies an electronic unit that controls one or more electrical systems in the vehicle. Vehicles may have many control units installed, each with a specific purpose. For example, there are engine, transmission, body and suspension, entertainment, anti-theft, and many other control units. Control modules monitor a number of inputs from sensors and circuits, process those data according to the information programmed into their memory, and send output commands to actuators and electrical devices, which control the operation of various components and systems on the vehicle. On modern vehicles, the control units share information on a data **bus**, which is a common set of wires that connect the modules together so that information or data can be shared across the network. For example, the transmission control unit needs to know road speed, as does the control unit that operates the dash instruments and the anti-lock brake system control unit. The information from the one vehicle speed sensor is shared across the data bus to all three control units.

> ▶ **LINK**
> Refer to the On-Board Diagnostics chapter for more information on control modules.

Microprocessors, Sensors, and Voltage-Generating Devices

<u>Microprocessors</u> or central processing units (CPUs) are programmable devices that are found in vehicle ECUs. They are computers that monitor information from inputs such as sensors and make decisions based on their program, then output signals to actuators and electrical devices on the vehicle. Microprocessors control and monitor most electrical systems on the modern vehicle. For example, there are microprocessor control units for the engine, transmission, suspension, brakes, steering, and main body control functions. Modern diagnostic equipment connects into the microprocessors on the vehicle via a data link connector to provide information on system performance to the technician. It is not unusual for the microprocessors on a vehicle to require programming updates. Updating is performed by reflashing or reprogramming the memory in the microprocessors with an update supplied by the manufacturer.

There are many different types of sensors installed into the modern vehicle, and they are used to provide information to the microprocessors on the vehicle. A sensor essentially converts a mechanical action into electrical signals that can be read by the microprocessors

in the control units. For example, the sensor installed near the crankshaft converts the rotary movement of the crankshaft into electrical signals that tell the microprocessor each time the crankshaft has rotated through a certain number of degrees and where it is in relation to top dead center of a cylinder, typically cylinder 1. The temperature sensor converts the temperature of the engine coolant into an electrical signal that can be read by a microprocessor.

> ▶ **LINK**
> Refer to the On-Board Diagnostics chapter for more information on sensors.

Delay Circuits

<u>Delay circuits</u> are added to vehicles to build in specific time delays in turning on or off electrical devices. For example, most modern vehicles have a time delay built into the interior lights on vehicles. After closing the door, the lamp will often stay on for a predetermined time before slowly turning off. The delay circuit can be constructed from electronic components or it can be programmed into an ECU that controls the circuit. Modern vehicles are increasingly using ECUs with programmed timers to perform time-delay functions.

Speed Control Circuits

<u>Speed control circuits</u> are used on the vehicle to control the speed of motors or accessories. A common use is the control of the fan speed in the vehicle's HVAC system and the electric radiator fans. Essentially, the speed control circuit manages the speed of a fan motor to control the amount of air movement through the system.

Most speed control systems use pulse-width modulation to control motor speed. Pulse width (or duty cycle) refers to the percentage of time a circuit is fully on, versus fully off. A pulse width of 50% means that the circuit is on 50% of the time and off 50% of the time **FIGURE 36-42**. This provides about 50% of the electrical power to the motor, which allows it to operate at about 50% power. Likewise, a 25% pulse width means that the electrical power is on 25% of the time. Since the pulse width is cycled on and off very fast (sometimes exceeding 10,000 cycles per second), power to the motor appears very smooth and the motor power is controlled very accurately. Like the time-delay circuit, speed control circuits are constructed from electronic components that can be in dedicated modules or integrated into the vehicle's power train control module that controls the circuit.

FIGURE 36-42 Pulse-width modulation. **A.** 25% duty cycle. **B.** 50% duty cycle. **C.** 75% duty cycle.

FIGURE 36-43 Wire. **A.** Standard wire (stripped). **B.** Ribbon cable (stripped).

Wires and Wiring Harnesses

Wires and wiring harnesses are the arteries of the vehicle's electrical system, and as such they need to be kept in good condition, free of any damage or corrosion. They carry the electrical power and signals through the vehicle to control virtually all of the systems on a vehicle. As technology in vehicles has increased, so, too, has the number of wires and cables installed on these vehicles. Although wireless communication is being used in some vehicle security, entertainment, and tire pressure monitoring systems, wires are still the dominant signal carriers in a vehicle. To help protect wires and keep them organized, they are bundled together in a wiring harness. A number of wiring harnesses are located throughout the vehicle.

Wires

Electrical wires are used to conduct current around the vehicle. Wire can also be referred to as cable, although cable typically refers to large-diameter wire. Automotive **wire** is commonly a multistranded copper core wrapped with seamless plastic insulation. Copper is typically used as it offers low electrical resistance and remains flexible even after years of use. The insulation is designed to protect the wire and prevent leakage of the current flow so that it can get to its intended destination. **Ribbon cable** is a series of wires that are formed side by side and joined along the wire insulation; they are flat like a ribbon **FIGURE 36-43**. Ribbon cable works well when several wires run from one component to another. The ribbon design groups them so they can be routed neatly and easily. Ribbon cable is often found inside computers and

other electronic components. It is used for connecting between printed circuits or between printed circuits and other components. Some wires, especially signal wires and communication wires, are shielded, which helps to prevent electromagnetic interference, also referred to as "noise."

Shielding

In certain locations within a vehicle and in environments where strong electromagnetic interference (EMI) is present, wiring harnesses are subject to a situation where unwanted electromagnetic induction occurs. This interference is referred to as electrical noise or EMI noise. To prevent noise, some vehicles use **shielded wiring harnesses**. The type of shielding used can be one of three forms: twisted pair, Mylar tape, and drain lines.

Twisted Pair

Twisted pair uses two wires delivering signals to a common component. The wires are uniformly twisted through the entire length of the harness and end at a terminating resistor. The twisted wires along with the terminating resistor have the effect of canceling any noise that occurs in the wires, reducing the loss of data in the transmitted signals. The controlled area network, or CAN, bus in a modern vehicle may use one or more twisted pairs to connect all the vehicle control units with common data line(s) to share information.

> ▶ **LINK**
> Refer to the On-Board Diagnostics chapter for more information on control with the CAN-bus.

Mylar Tape

Mylar tape is an electrically conductive material that is wrapped around a wiring harness inside the outer harness layer. Any noise that attempts to reach the wires inside the shield are absorbed by the Mylar, where it will be conducted to ground via a ground connection. The shielding is important to prevent electrical noise penetrating into the electrical wiring. If the harness is exposed, the Mylar will have to be rewrapped so that noise cannot penetrate into the harness.

Drain Lines

A drain line is a noninsulated wire that is wrapped within a wiring harness. The drain wire is connected to ground at the harness source end and conducts any noise to ground, negating the noise effect. If the drain wire is cut, it will be inoperative, so it is important that the wire not be cut or left disconnected.

Wire Sizes

Wire size is very important for the correct operation of electrical circuits. Selecting a wire gauge that is too small for an application will have an adverse effect on the operation of the circuit. This will cause voltage drop and poor performance, or, in extreme cases, the wire will get hot enough to melt the insulation. Selecting a wire gauge that is too large increases costs and weight and the size of wiring harnesses.

The resistance of a wire affects how much current it can carry. Even good conductors have a slight amount of resistance. The resistance of a wire is determined by its length, diameter, construction material, and temperature. The longer the wire and the smaller the diameter, the higher the resistance. The shorter the wire and the larger the diameter, the lower the resistance.

There are two scales used to measure the sizes of wires: the metric wire gauge and the American wire gauge (AWG) TABLE 36-1. The metric system measures the cross-sectional area of the conductor in square millimeters. The AWG system uses a rating number; the larger the rating number, the smaller the wire and the lower its current-carrying capability. Most countries use the metric scale. American manufacturers are split, with some using AWG and others using the metric scale.

To select the correct wire gauge for any given application, it is best to refer to a wire chart. Manufacturers and standards bodies use wire gauge charts to define how much current each wire gauge can carry safely and efficiently. A vehicle uses a variety of wire sizes depending on the requirements of each particular circuit.

The correct wire size for an application can be looked up on a wire size chart if you know the amperage of the

circuit and the length of the wire. But be careful of the chart you use, since many of them allow up to a 10% voltage drop over the length of the wire, which is way more than is allowed in most automotive circuits. For example, if a 12-volt circuit is designed for a maximum current flow of 10 amps and is approximately 20′ (6.1 meters) long, using the AWG table as a reference, you can determine that the correct wire gauge to use is 12 AWG TABLE 36-2.

TABLE 36-1: Metric Wire Size Comparison and American Wire Gauge (AWG)

Metric Wire Sizes	AWG Wire Sizes
0.22	24
0.35	22
0.5	20
0.8	18
1.0	16
2.0	14
3.0	12
5.0	10
8.0	8
13.0	6
19.0	4
32.0	2

TABLE 36-2: AWG Wire Sizes Based on Amperage and Wire Length*

Circuit Amps	Wire Length from Battery to Load						
	2 Feet	5 Feet	7.5 Feet	10 Feet	15 Feet	20 Feet	25 Feet
2	20	20	20	18	18	18	16
5	18	18	18	18	16	14	14
8	18	16	16	14	14	12	12
10	16	16	16	14	12	12	10
12	16	16	14	14	12	12	10
15	16	16	14	12	10	10	8
18	16	14	12	12	10	8	8
20	14	14	12	10	10	8	8
25	14	12	12	10	8	8	6
30	12	12	10	10	8	6	6

*Chart is based on a maximum 0.4-volt drop per wire size; shorter distances are less than a 0.4-volt drop.

There are two different methods of describing the conductor size within these standards. A wire may be described in metric size as 5.0, indicating it has a cross-sectional area of 5.0 millimeters squared (mm^2). It can also be expressed as 10/0.5, indicating there are 10 strands of wire, each with a cross-sectional area of 0.5 mm^2. The same system can be applied to the AWG rating.

Length Versus Resistance

Copper is used to conduct electrical current because of its low resistance value. However, it does offer some resistance, and as the length of the wire increases, so, too, does the resistance within the wire. To overcome the effect of resistance, the greater the length of the wire, the larger the cross-sectional area needs to be. Increasing the cross-sectional area overcomes the resistance and maintains the current-carrying capacity of the circuit. Refer to Table 36-2 for information on wire size and current-carrying capacity.

Terminals and Connectors

Terminals are installed to the ends of wires to provide low-resistance termination to wires. They allow electricity to be conducted from the end of one wire to the end of another wire. In many cases, they allow the wires to be disconnected and reconnected. They come in many different types and sizes to suit various wire sizes and termination requirements FIGURE 36-44. For example, there are push-on spade terminals, eye ring terminals to accommodate screws, butt connectors, and male and female terminals that are designed to be separated and reconnected. Most terminals are the crimp type, which require the use of special tools to crimp the terminal to the end of the wire. They can be insulated or noninsulated.

Some solder-type terminals, which require the use of a soldering iron and solder, are still in use and require the use of electric or gas soldering irons, flux, and solder to make the connection. When soldering wiring, always use a rosin or rosin-core solder; never use an acid-core solder, since acid can cause corrosion and high resistance over time.

Terminals can be installed as a single terminal on a wire or grouped together in a wiring harness with a connector housing, also called wiring harness connectors. Connector housings have male and female sides and are usually shaped so that they can be connected in only one way. They will often incorporate a locking mechanism so the plug cannot accidentally work loose. Many of these connectors are weatherproofed to keep moisture out. Special tools are usually needed to insert and remove the terminals from the connector housing.

Wiring Harnesses

Wiring harnesses, also known as wiring looms or cable harnesses, are used throughout the vehicle to group two or more wires together within a sheath of either insulating tape or tubing FIGURE 36-45. Often, harnesses on modern vehicles contain many wires, each terminating at crimped terminals inserted into connector or harness plugs. There are usually a number of harnesses within the vehicle interconnecting with various connector plugs, as required to form the wiring system of the vehicle. Wiring harnesses run around the engine bay, through the dash and interior cabin, and to the rear of the vehicle. They are attached to the vehicle with harness fasteners such as body clips or wire ties, and rubber sealing grommets are used when the harness passes through the metal bodywork.

FIGURE 36-44 Terminals and connectors are installed to the ends of wires to provide low-resistance termination to wires.

FIGURE 36-45 Typical wiring harness.

▶ Wiring Diagram Fundamentals

Wiring diagrams, also known as electrical schematics or electrical diagrams, use abstract graphical symbols to represent electrical circuits and their connection or relationship to other components in the system. They are essentially a map of all of the electrical components and their connections **FIGURE 36-46**. The wiring on modern vehicles is very complex, with many wires and components interconnected. A single wiring diagram of the whole vehicle would be very difficult to read. To make it easier, the wiring diagrams are split up into systems and subsystems to reduce the complexity on each page. For example, there is a wiring diagram for the starter system, a separate one for the charging system, and others for the engine, transmission, anti-lock brakes, headlights, taillights, and so on.

Wiring diagrams contain large amounts of information in the form of lines and symbols. The technician will need to decode this information by interpreting the symbols and connections and relating them to the actual components on the vehicle. To assist in understanding the wiring diagrams, manufacturers supply keys on the diagrams, which are lists of the component symbols and their names, wiring color codes, harness connectors, and pin numbers. Armed with all of this information, the technician can read the wiring diagram and identify circuits as they relate to the actual components and circuits on the vehicle.

Printed/Integrated Circuits

Printed circuits or circuit boards are insulated boards approximately $\frac{1}{16}$ (25 mm) thick that are designed to

hold electronic components such as microprocessors and their associated components. Conductive tracks on the surface of the printed circuits connect the leads of the electronic components to each other to form complex circuits. Printed circuit boards can be very complex

FIGURE 36-46 Typical wiring diagram.

> **▶ TECHNICIAN TIP**
>
> Modern vehicles have many electrical components, wiring connectors, and wires. To work on vehicles, you need an understanding of how all the components are assembled together and arranged in circuits. Electrical symbols and circuit diagrams are a way to provide this information in a logical way that represents the physical wiring harness and components attached to vehicles **FIGURE 36-47**. Every electrical device and component has a corresponding electrical symbol. Many of the symbols are standardized and used universally by manufacturers, although in some cases, variations may exist. Manufacturers' diagrams and manuals contain keys to identifying the various symbols used and their meaning.
>
> | Symbol | Name | Symbol | Name |
> | --- | --- | --- | --- |
> | | Coaxial cable | | Capacitor |
> | | Shielded wire | | Resistor |
> | | Junction point | | Potentiometer |
> | | Ground connection | | NPN Transistor |
> | | Chassis ground | | PNP Transistor |
> | | Connector | | Diode |
> | | Lamp | | Zener diode |
> | | Pushbutton indicating lamp, letters added within half circle denotes side of system in operation | | Tachometer |
> | N.O. N.C. | Element of any manually mechanical operated switch. Normally open or closed as indicated | | Motor |
> | N.O. N.C. | Contacts or any microswitch or relay, normally open or closed as indicated | | Battery |
> | | Circuit breaker | | Switch |
> | | Coil of a solenoid or relay | | Relay |
> | | Transformer | | |
> | | Fuse | | |
>
> **FIGURE 36-47** Every electrical device and component has a corresponding electrical symbol.

with many high-density integrated circuit components installed. Many boards have more than one layer of conductive tracks. They often have two layers and as many as 16 to accommodate the complex circuitry required to connect many integrated circuits.

Networking and Multiplexing

Even the most basic vehicles include many electronically controlled systems. If each electronic system had its own ECU, harness, and sensors, the weight of the added components would negate any efficiency the system provided. A vehicle's multiple electronic systems could require more than 1 mile, or 1.6 kilometers, of insulated wiring, consisting of around 1000 individual wires and many terminals.

One solution to the problem is the use of a system that integrates sensors into a common wiring harness by combining many of the individual systems, where possible, into a multiplexed serial communications network so that they can share information. An added advantage of such a system is that if there is less wire and fewer connections, there is less chance of poor connections causing faults.

One system is referred to as a **controlled area network bus (CAN-bus)**, and it uses two thin wires (called a twisted pair) to connect, or multiplex, many of the control units and their sensors to each other. The output devices are referred to as nodes.

The advantage of a multiplex network is that it enables a decreased number of dedicated wires for each function; therefore, there is a reduction in the number of wires in the wiring harness, reduced system cost and weight, and improved reliability, serviceability, and installation. In addition, common sensor data, such as vehicle speed and engine temperature, are available on the network, so data can be shared, thereby reducing the number of sensors.

Networking makes it more efficient to add or modify system functionality through the addition of control units and the use of software updates. These updates allow the manufacturer to provide fixes for issues that may crop up after vehicles have been delivered to customers and put into service. Other control units can be added to the system by simply connecting them to the network and the new controlled device. Software can then be updated if necessary to control the new device. A diagnostic scan tool can be connected to the CAN-bus circuit to both extract operational information and command controlled devices to operate, which assists greatly in diagnosis and fault finding.

Fiber Optics

Fiber optics are long, thin strands of very pure glass or plastic about the diameter of a human hair. They can be arranged in bundles and are then called **optical cables**. Light signals can be transmitted along the cable over very long distances. Light is transmitted along the cable, bouncing from wall to wall along the way as it is transmitted through the cable. It can do this because the inner wall of the optical fiber has a mirror finish. This means the light continues to travel along the cable even when it bends around corners.

Optical fiber can be used to transmit digital data for computers or simply to light up dash gauges in a vehicle. The optical fiber is especially suited to reliably transmitting a large amount of digital data. In vehicle, optical fiber cables could be used to replace existing copper data bus systems.

Optical fiber has several advantages over other available technology. It is less expensive and thinner, it can carry much more data than copper wires, it has less signal degradation over length, and it is less affected by interference. Unlike electrical signals, light in one fiber does not interfere with light in another fiber. Optical fiber is nonflammable, lightweight, and flexible. One disadvantage to optical fiber is that it requires more complex splicing procedures.

▶ Wire Maintenance and Repair

Wires are generally trouble free and long lasting. But they can be damaged. Generally speaking, any issues with wiring are more likely to be with the terminals than with the wires themselves. Terminals can corrode, lose their tension, or push back up inside the connector, leading to poor connections and voltage drops. If you suspect a problem with a wire, first inspect the ends. If no problems are found, look for mechanical damage to the wire or wiring harness itself. When a wire is damaged, it is usually due to one of several conditions. One possibility is that the wire has been physically broken, such as a wire that was not disconnected when removing a major component such as the engine or transmission. Another issue is when a wire gets pinched between components such as between the engine and the transaxle when replacing a clutch. The pinched wire can cause either a short circuit or an open circuit. Wires can also be misrouted so that they lay on a hot surface such as the exhaust manifold, which melts the insulation and causes the wires to short. In all of these cases, the problem can typically be spotted visually. One problem that may be harder to spot is if a circuit shorts out and melts one or more wires together within a harness. In this case, you may have to open up the wiring harness and inspect the wires. Next, we will cover how to repair wires, terminals, and connectors.

Stripping Wire Insulation

An insulating layer of plastic covers electrical wire used in automotive wiring harnesses. When electrical wire is joined to other wires or connected to a terminal, the insulation needs to be removed. Wire stripping tools come in various configurations, but they all perform the same task. The type of tool you use or purchase will depend on personal preference and the amount of electrical wire repairs you perform. A good pair of wire strippers removes the insulation without damaging the wire strands. Never use a knife or other type of sharp tool to cut away the insulation, as it often cuts away some of the strands of wire as well. This is known as ringing the wire, which effectively reduces the current-carrying capacity of the wire

To strip wire insulation, follow the steps in **SKILL DRILL 36-1**:

1. Choose the correct stripping tool for the wire you are stripping. **(Photo 1)**
2. Most wire strippers can remove the insulation from different gauges of wire, so select the hole in the stripper that is closest to the diameter of the wire to be stripped.
3. Place the wire in the hole and close the jaws firmly around it to cut the insulation. If you have selected

the right gauge, the tool will cut through the insulation but not through the copper core. Only remove as much insulation as is necessary to do the job. Insufficient bare wire may not achieve a good connection, and excessive may expose the wire to a potential short circuit with other circuits or to ground. Also, removing more than 0.5" (12.7 mm) of insulation at a time can stretch and damage the core. **(Photo 2)**

4. Some strippers automatically cut and remove the insulation. Others just make the cut and hold the wire tightly; you then need to pull firmly on the wire to remove the insulation and expose the copper core. To keep the strands together after the insulation is stripped away, give them a light twist. **(Photo 3)**

Installing a Solderless Terminal

Solderless terminals are used by the factory throughout the vehicle, primarily at connectors. If a wire itself needs to be repaired, it should be soldered back together instead of using solderless terminals to reconnect the wires. Solderless terminals are quick to install and effective at conducting electricity across joints that are designed to be disconnected. Solderless terminals require a clean, tight connection. It is important to make sure the wire and the connection are clean before attaching any terminals. You should use connections that match the size of the wire. Many solderless connectors are color coded for the size of wire they are designed to work with, such

SKILL DRILL **36-1** **Stripping Wire Insulation**

1. Choose the correct stripping tool.

2. Select the hole that matches the diameter of the wire to be stripped. Place the wire in the hole and close the jaws firmly around it to cut the insulation.

3. Remove the insulation. To keep the strands together, give them a light twist.

as yellow 12-10 AWG, blue 16-14 AWG, and red 22-18 AWG. Use the correct wire stripper to strip only as much insulation off as needed to allow the wire to fully engage the terminal. To keep the wires together after stripping them, give them a slight twist. Do not twist the wire too much; otherwise you risk a poor wire-to-terminal connection. Use the correct crimping tool for the connection. Using the wrong type of tool will cause the connection to have a poor grip on the wire.

To install a solderless terminal, follow the steps in **SKILL DRILL 36-2**:

1. Select the terminal for the wire and connector you are using. There are different types and sizes of wire terminals, but the procedure for installing all of them is the same. Make sure you have the correct size of terminal for the wire to be terminated and that the terminal has the correct volt/amp rating for the job it is to perform.

2. Remove an appropriate amount of the protective insulation from the wire with the proper stripping tool. **(Photo 1)**

3. You will get a better connection if you do not twist the strands together tightly before placing them through the terminal, as this gives the terminal more surface area to come in contact with the wires when crimped. However, it can be difficult to insert the wires into the terminal if they are loose strands. Twist them together just enough to help you insert them cleanly. Place the solderless terminal onto the wire. It is important that the stripped end of the

SKILL DRILL | 36-2 | Installing a Solderless Terminal

1. Make sure you have the correct size of terminal for the wire to be terminated and the terminal has the correct volt/amp rating. Remove an appropriate amount of the protective insulation from the wire.

2. Lightly twist the wire strands and place the terminal onto the wire.

3. Use a proper crimping tool for the terminal you are crimping. Do *not* use pliers, as they have a tendency to cut through the connection. Select the proper anvil.

4. Crimp the core section first. Use firm pressure so that a good electrical contact will be made, but not excessive force, as this can bend the pin or terminal.

5. If crimping an uninsulated terminal, lightly crimp the insulation tabs so that they hold the insulation firmly.

wire be flush with, or only slightly beyond, the crimping portion of the terminal. **(Photo 2)**

4 Use the proper crimping pliers for the terminal you are installing. Do *not* use standard pliers, as they have a tendency to cut through the connection, which can cause trouble during service. Select the proper anvil for the connector or terminal selected. **(Photo 3)**

5 Crimp the core section first. Use firm pressure so that a good electrical contact will be made, but not excessive force, as this can deform the pin or terminal. **(Photo 4)**

6 If crimping an uninsulated terminal, lightly crimp the insulation tabs so that they hold the insulation firmly. **(Photo 5)**

7 A note about alternative terminals: Some types of crimp terminals do not have an insulation component fixed to them. These come in two parts, and the insulator is supplied as a separate component. In these cases, always make sure the core of the wire to be crimped extends through the core tabs in the terminal.

Soldering Wires and Connectors

Solder used in automotive electrical applications is an alloy typically made up of 60% tin and 40% lead. Solder needs to change from a solid state into liquid easily and return to its solid state quickly. Solder is available as solid or flux cored. Solid solder requires an external flux to be applied in the soldering process. Flux is needed to prevent the metals from being joined due to oxidization when they are heated. Flux-cored solder has a bead of flux within the center of the solder. Flux in flux-cored solder can have either an acid base or a rosin base. Acid flux is designed to be used on nonelectrical metal joints such as radiators and must be removed after the soldering process so that the joint does not corrode. Rosin flux solder is used on electrical connections because it is much less likely to corrode the metals than acid flux. Acid flux and rosin flux also come in paste form that can be brushed onto the joint if using solid-core solder.

Solder is applied with a hot soldering iron. The soldering iron is heated electrically or by an external source such as a butane or oxyacetylene torch. The soldering iron tip absorbs heat that is then applied to the materials to be joined. Once they are hot enough, solder can be melted between the components. It solidifies as it cools, "gluing" the metal pieces together.

For a connection to be successful, the soldering iron needs to be clean and "tinned." Cleaning may be as simple as heating the tip and wiping it on a damp cloth. Or, with

▶ TECHNICIAN TIP

One mistake students make is trying to apply the solder directly to the tip of the soldering iron while the iron is heating up the wires. This does melt the solder, but it is likely that the wire is not hot enough for the solder to stick to it; instead the solder just globs on top of the wires, leading to what is called a cold joint. A cold joint has high resistance and the wires are likely to break loose from the solder. One sign that the solder joint is good is that you can clearly see the outline of the wires on the surface of the solder, all the way around the joint.

the soldering iron cold, you may need to use a file to remove oxidized metal and reshape it so it can effectively transfer heat to the wires. The tinning process assists in transferring heat to the wire, by leaving a small amount of liquid solder on the tip which increases the surface area where the tip contacts the wires. To tin the soldering iron, the tip is heated and a small amount of solder is applied to the tip. Excess solder is removed with a cloth rag. The soldering iron tip is heated and then applied to the wire so heat is transferred to the wire. The solder is then applied to the wire opposite the soldering iron. Once the wire is up to soldering temperature, it will melt the solder and pull the solder into the strands of wire producing a strong, effective joint. Do not apply too much heat to the wire or two things will happen. First, the solder will be drawn too far up the strands of wire making a very long, nonflexible joint that is subject to breaking. The second problem is that the insulation may overheat and melt.

To solder wires and connectors, follow the steps in **SKILL DRILL 36-3**:

1 When using a soldering iron, you must be careful not to burn yourself or any part of the vehicle you are working on. The tip of the soldering iron has to be hot enough to melt metal solder, so make sure it is in a safe position and not touching anything while it is heating up.

2 While the soldering iron is heating, remove an appropriate amount of the protective insulation from the wires. Always use a proper stripping tool that is in good condition. If you intend to seal the joint with a heat-shrink sleeve, cut a section of this tubular material long enough to overlap the wire insulation on both sides of the joint and slide it over the end of one of the wires before joining them. **(Photo 1)**

3 Twist the wires together to make a good mechanical connection between them. If there are impurities in the solder, and the wires are not directly touching each other, then although there may be a strong physical connection, there may not be a good electrical connection. It is also very important that the surfaces be very clean before soldering or there will be a poor connection. **(Photo 2)**

4 Tin the soldering iron tip, and use the soldering iron to gently heat up the wires while placing the solder opposite of the soldering iron. Allow the solder to be drawn into the joint, ensuring that just enough solder runs smoothly into the wires. **(Photo 3)**

SKILL DRILL | 36-3 | Soldering Wires and Connectors

1 Safely position the soldering iron while it is heating up. While the soldering iron is heating, remove an appropriate amount of the protective insulation from the wires with wire strippers.

2 Twist the wires together to make a good mechanical connection between them.

3 Tin the soldering iron tip and gently heat up the wires while placing the solder opposite of the soldering iron. Allow the solder to be drawn into the joint.

4 A good solder joint where the solder has been drawn in.

5 Once the electrical connection has been made and it has cooled enough for you to handle it, slide the insulator sleeve cover over the joint and use a heat gun to shrink the tubing around the joint.

6 To solder a wire to a terminal connector, it is best to crimp it in place as before and use the solder to "glue" the joint together. Place the heated iron onto the terminal to get it hot enough to melt the solder applied to the end of the crimped wire tabs. Some solder will be pulled between the terminal and the wire. Cover the terminal with heat-shrink tubing.

(5) Be careful not to use too much solder. Also, if you apply too much heat, you will melt the wire insulation. When you have finished soldering, clean any excess flux from the joint with a damp rag. **(Photo 4)**

(6) Once the electrical connection has been made and it has cooled enough for you to be able to handle it, slide the insulator sleeve over the joint. There are different types of sleeves. The most popular type is heat-shrink tubing, which shrinks when heat is applied to it with a heat gun. Another type contains a glue, which when heated with the heat gun melts into and seals the joint. If there is no heat-shrink tubing available, then it is possible to seal and protect the splice with electrical insulating tape. **(Photo 5)**

(7) To solder a wire to a terminal connector, it is best to crimp it in place as before and just use the solder to "glue" the joint together.

(8) Place the heated iron onto the terminal to get it hot enough to melt the solder applied to the end of the crimped wire tabs. Some solder will be pulled between the terminal and the wire. Be careful not to use too much solder. If you get the terminal too hot, the wire insulation will start to melt.

(9) Once the electrical connection has been made and it has cooled down enough for you to be able to handle it, you can place the heat-shrink tubing over the terminal, heat it up with a heat gun, and place the connection into service. **(Photo 6)**

Repairing a CAN-Bus Harness

Always check manufacturer information for the correct procedures when repairing wiring. For a repair on a CAN-bus system, extreme caution must be taken. The CAN-bus system carries high-speed data information and is susceptible to communication errors if the repair is not completed according to the manufacturer's recommendations. When measuring resistance or voltage on a CAN-bus, always use a digital multimeter and disconnect the negative battery terminal when measuring resistance.

CAN-bus wires are usually a twisted pair with terminating resistors to reduce noise and interferences. Use the correct-sized wires and terminals (if necessary) when making repairs. The challenge in repairing a twisted pair is that you need to perform the solder repair on wires that are twisted together. Simply put, trying to solder one wire back together when the other wire is very close to it is tough. Also, it is harder to use shrink tubing since the wires are twisted. It is possible to make these repairs; it just takes a bit of practice and patience. If both wires in the twisted pair need to be repaired, it is best to stagger the joints so that both joints are not side by side, which could lead to a short circuit. To prevent damage, ensure that all insulation is replaced and the harness is secured correctly. If using a soldering iron and solder to make repairs, use a rosin-core flux and clean the joint before insulating to finalize the repair. Heat-shrink tubing of the appropriate size ensures a sealed and insulated joint.

Wrap-up

Ready for Review

▶ Increasingly, vehicle technicians must have an understanding of the electrical principles involved in vehicle system operation.

▶ Atoms contain negatively charged electrons moving around a nucleus, in which there are positively charged protons and neutrons with no charge.

▶ Atoms with excess electrons have a negative charge and create a negative ion; those deficient in electrons have a positive charge and create a positive ion.

▶ Free electrons can move from one atom to another if an electrical potential is applied.

▶ Materials with many free electrons are good electrical conductors.

▶ Copper is the most common conductor.

▶ Insulators are materials that do not conduct current easily; an example is plastic.

▶ Semiconductor refers to a material that conducts electricity more easily than an insulator, but not as well as a conductor.

▶ Free electrons require a pathway or circuit, and a force to act upon them, such as a battery.

▶ Like charges repel, and unlike charges attract.

▶ The attraction of free electrons that creates a force is called voltage.

▶ The four factors that determine electrical resistance level are the type of material and the length, size, and temperature of the conductor.

▶ Electrical resistance refers to the degree to which a material opposes the passage of an electrical current.

▶ Resistance is measured in ohms and is constant in an object unless the temperature changes.

▶ A semiconductor's ability to conduct electricity depends on negative electrons and holes.

▶ The number of charge carriers in a semiconductor can be changed by adding small quantities of impurities (doping).

▶ The PN junction of a semiconductor is located at the depletion layer.

▶ Semiconductors can prevent or allow current flow, depending on connection to a current source.

▶ Semiconductor materials include silicon, germanium, gallium-arsenide, and silicon carbide.

▶ Electrical circuits contain a power supply, a current flow on/off switch, a functional component, a conductive pathway, and a protection device (e.g., a fuse).

▶ Voltage is the electrical pressure difference between two points in an electrical circuit.

▶ The ampere (amp) is the unit used to describe how much current is flowing at a given point within a circuit when the functional component is operational.

▶ The ohm is the unit used to describe electrical resistance in a circuit or component.

▶ Direct current (DC) flows in one direction only; alternating current (AC) continuously changes its direction of flow.

▶ Electrical components can work only on AC or DC, but not both.

▶ Circuits may be described in terms of continuity, open, short, and high resistance.

▶ Electrostatic energy occurs when two insulators are rubbed together, with one losing electrons to become positively charged and the other gaining electrons to become negatively charged.

▶ Thermoelectric energy is produced by joining and heating two different metals.

▶ Electrochemical energy is produced via electrolysis, which is the immersion of two dissimilar metals in a conducting liquid to break down chemicals into ions.

▶ Photovoltaic energy is produced via solar energy cells.

▶ Piezoelectric energy is produced when certain crystals are subjected to mechanical stress.

▶ Electromagnetic induction is created when a conductor cuts across a magnetic field.

▶ The effects of electricity include light (LED bulbs), heat (headlights), chemical reactions (lead-acid battery), and magnetism (electric motors).

▶ Electromagnets are used in relays, solenoids, and motors, while electromagnetic induction is used in ignition coils and transformers.

▶ Relays are used to control circuits that carry high current flow; they can be normally open (NO) or normally closed (NC).

▶ Solenoids operate similarly to a relay, but create lateral movement rather than closing a circuit.

▶ Electric motors rely on magnetic fields to create rotary movement.

- Ohm's law states that the total resistance of a circuit always equals the voltage divided by the amperage.
- The term "work" refers to transforming one form of energy into another.
- Power refers to the rate at which work is done, or the rate of transforming energy.
- The watt is the unit of power.
- Kirchhoff's current law states that electrical current entering any junction is equal to the sum of the current flowing out of the junction.
- In a series circuit, current can flow in only one path and all electrons flow at the same rate.
- Voltage drop refers to the pressure lost by driving the current through a resistor.
- The electrical properties of a series circuit are as follows: current flow is the same in all parts of the circuit; the applied voltage is equal to the sum of the individual voltage drops; and total circuit resistance is equal to the sum of the individual resistances.
- All components in a parallel circuit are directly connected to the voltage supply; hence the voltage across each component is equal to battery voltage.
- Parallel circuit laws are as follows: the voltage across all branches of a parallel circuit are the same; the total current equals the sum of the current flowing in each branch; the amount of current in each branch is inversely proportional to the resistance of the branch; and the total resistance of a parallel circuit can be calculated as $R_T = (R_1 \times R_2)$ divided by $(R_1 + R_2)$. Or $R_T = 1/ 1/R_1 + 1/R_2 + 1/R_3$.
- Series-parallel circuits contain both a series circuit and a parallel circuit.
- Electrical components must be correctly connected onto circuits and may have numbered or marked terminals to ensure proper connection.
- Circuit protection devices, which break the circuit during excessive current flow, are fuses, fusible links, and circuit breakers.
- Resistors are used to control voltage that reaches various components because they resist the current running through them.
- Resistor types include fixed, variable, thermistors, metal oxide varistors, and ballast resistors.
- Resistors are rated by both resistance value and power rating.
- Resistance value is indicated by colored bands, and tolerance is indicated by the number of identifying bands.
- Variable resistor types are rheostats, potentiometers, and thermistors.
- Thermistors are a type of conductor in which resistance value is affected by temperature.
- Capacitors are used to store electrical energy and are rated by capacitance, which is the amount of change stored in each plate for a given potential voltage between the plates.
- Diodes are used to restrict current flow to one direction only.
- Transistors (NPN and PNP types) are used as switches and to amplify currents.
- Control modules are designed to monitor multiple inputs from sensors and circuits and respond to those inputs.
- Delay circuits can turn on or off an electrical device after a specified time delay.
- Microprocessors are designed to monitor and control most electrical systems on a modern vehicle.
- Most vehicle wires are braided copper with plastic insulation, but other types are shielded wires and ribbon.
- Wire shielding to prevent noise (unwanted electromagnetic induction) can be twisted pair, Mylar tape, or drain lines.
- Proper operation of electrical circuits requires correct wire size.
- Length and diameter of a cable determine its resistance.
- Copper has low resistance value, although as the wire length increases, so does resistance within the wire; therefore, the cross-sectional area needs to increase to overcome resistance.
- Terminals and connectors are fitted to the ends of cables to provide low-resistance cable termination.
- Terminals can be push-on spade terminals, eye ring terminals, and solder-type terminals.
- Connectors can be permanent cable joiners, wiring harness connectors, or male or female connectors.
- Wiring harnesses are used to bind wires together within a sheath of insulating tape or tubing.
- Wiring diagrams are generally split up into systems and subsystems.
- Microprocessors and their assorted components are mounted on circuit boards with conductive tracks designed to connect electronic component leads with one another.
- Electronically controlled systems are integrated to a multiplexed serial communications network, such as a controlled area network bus (CAN-bus).
- Fiber-optic cables can transmit light signals over very long distances.

▶ Electrical measurement tools include the ammeter, voltmeter, ohmmeter, and digital multimeter.

Key Terms

alternating current (AC) A type of current flow that flows back and forth.

American wire gauge (AWG) A standard used to identify different wire sizes.

ammeter A device used to measure current flow.

amp An abbreviation for amperes, the unit for current measurement.

armature The rotating wire coils in motors and generators. It is also the moving part of a solenoid or relay, and the pole piece in a permanent magnet generator.

breakdown The loss of electrical insulation properties.

bus An electrical circuit for distributing electrical signals bidirectionally.

butt connector A crimp or solder joint that creates a permanent connection.

capacitance The ability of a capacitor to store an electrical charge.

capacitor A device that can quickly store a small amount of electrical energy, at which point it is charged.

charge In measuring capacitance, the amount of electrical energy present.

charge carrier A mobile particle that has a positive or negative electrical charge.

circuit or schematic diagram A pictorial representation or road map of the wiring and electrical components.

circuit breaker A device that trips and opens a circuit, preventing excessive current flow in a circuit. It is resettable to allow for reuse.

commutator A device made on armatures of electric generators and motors to control the direction of current flow in the armature windings.

conductor A material that allows electricity to flow through it easily. It is made up of atoms with one to three valance ring electrons.

connector The plastic housing on the end of a wiring harness that holds the wire terminals in place. It can also refer to a type of wire terminal that connects wires together or to a common point such as a bolt.

continuity A conductive path between two points.

control module A generic term that identifies an electronic unit that controls one or more electrical systems in the vehicle; also called a control unit.

controlled area network bus (CAN-bus) A wire data network found in vehicles to connect control modules so they can communicate quickly and easily.

conventional theory The theory that electrons flow from positive to negative.

current flow The flow of electrons, typically within a circuit or component.

delay circuit A combination of electrical and electronic components that provide a time delay for switching an electrical circuit.

depletion layer An area of neutral charge in semiconductors.

diode A two-lead electronic component that allows current flow in one direction only.

direct current (DC) Movement of current that flows in one direction only.

doping The introduction of impurities to pure semiconductor materials to provide N- and P-type semiconductors.

drain line A wire included in a harness with one end grounded to reduce interference or noise being induced into the harness.

electrical power A measurement of the rate at which electricity is consumed or created.

electrical resistance A material's property that slows down the flow of electrical current.

electrolysis A method of using electrical current to create a chemical reaction.

electrolyte A mixture of water and acid that contains free ions that make it electrically conductive.

electromagnet A conductor wound in a coil that produces a magnetic field when current flows through it.

electromagnetic induction The production of an electrical current in a conductor when it moves through a magnetic field or a magnetic field moves past it.

electromotive force An electrical pressure or voltage.

electron theory The theory that electrons, being negatively charged, repel other electrons and are attracted to positively charged objects; thus electrons flow from negative to positive.

energy The ability to do work.

eye ring terminal A type of crimp or solder terminal that has an enclosed eyelet to connect the terminal with a bolt or screw.

fiber optics Fine glass fibers through which light is transmitted.

fixed resistor A resistor that has a fixed value.

flasher can A mechanism that turns the vehicle's turn signal and hazard flasher bulbs on and off.

free electron An electron located on the outer ring, called the valence ring, that is only loosely held by the nucleus and that is free to move from one atom to another when an electrical potential (pressure) is applied.

fuse A safety device that self-destructs to prevent excessive current flowing in a circuit in the event of a fault.

gallium-arsenide A semiconductor used in high-frequency circuits.

germanium A type of semiconductor.

ground The return path for electrical current in a vehicle chassis, other metal of the vehicle, or dedicated wire.

hertz The unit for electrical frequency measurement.

high resistance The resistance of a component or circuit relative to a low resistance. It can also refer to a faulty circuit where a section or component has excess unwanted resistance.

hole theory The theory that as electrons flow from negative to positive, holes flow from positive to negative.

hot junction The heating point of a thermocouple.

insulator A material that has properties that prevent the easy flow of electricity. These materials are made up of atoms with five to eight electrons in the valance ring.

invertor A device that changes direct current into alternating current.

ion An atom that has fewer electrons than protons (positive) or that has more electrons than protons (negative).

Kirchhoff's current law An electrical law stating that the sum of the current flowing into a junction is the same as the current flowing out of the junction.

light-emitting diode (LED) A diode that emits light when current flows through it.

magnetism The force that attracts or repels magnetic charges; or the property of a material to respond to a magnetic field.

male and female terminal A crimp or solder terminal on which the male and female ends join to create a removable low-resistance connection.

microprocessor An electronic control unit that can process data and control one or more devices.

multimeter A test instrument used to measure volts, ohms, and amps. A digital multimeter may also be called a digital volt-ohmmeter (DVOM).

mylar tape Polyester film that may be metalized and incorporated into a wiring harness to provide electrical shielding.

negative temperature coefficient (NTC) A characteristic of materials whereby resistance decreases as temperature increases.

normally closed (NC) An electrical contact that is closed in the at-rest position.

normally open (NO) An electrical contact that is open in the at-rest position.

NPN transistor A transistor in which P-type material is sandwiched between two layers of N-type material.

N-type Semiconductor material with a small amount of extra electrons.

ohm The unit for measuring electrical resistance.

Ohm's law A law that defines the relationship between current, resistance, and voltage.

open A term used to describe a circuit that does not have a complete path for current to flow.

optical cable A cable that contains a number of optical fibers.

phase A term used to describe one set of windings from an alternator or alternating current electric motor.

photovoltaic (PV) effect The conversion of sunlight into electricity.

piezoelectric A type of electricity in which a material such as a quartz crystal produces voltage when mechanical pressure distorts it.

plate A flat thin square or rectangular sheet of material often used to describe the arrangement of positive and negative electrodes in batteries.

PN junction The junction between N- and P-type semiconductor materials.

PNP transistor A transistor in which N-type material is sandwiched between two layers of P-type material. This type of semiconductor material has holes, meaning it is missing electrons.

polarity The state of charge, positive or negative.

polarity sensitive A term used to describe a component that must be connected into a circuit with the correct polarity to its terminals.

positive temperature coefficient (PTC) A characteristic of materials whereby resistance increases as temperature increases.

potentiometer Also called a pot, a three-terminal resistive device with one terminal connected to the input of the resistor, one terminal connected to the output of the resistor, and the third terminal connected to a movable wiper arm that moves up and down the resistor.

power The rate at which work is done; electrical power is measured in watts.

power winding The current-carrying winding in an alternator or motor.

primary winding The coil of wire in the low voltage circuit that creates the magnetic field in a step-up transformer.

printed circuit The fine copper strip or track attached to an insulated board for mounting and connecting electronic components.

P-type Semiconductor material with holes where electrons are missing.

push-on spade terminal A disconnectable type of crimp or solder terminal used to terminate electrical wires.

relay An electromechanical switching device whereby the magnetism from a coil winding acts on a lever that switches a set of contacts.

resistor A component designed to have a fixed resistance.

rheostat An adjustable resistor that varies current flow through a circuit.

ribbon cable A type of flat harness in which cables are insulated from each other but joined together side by side.

secondary winding The coil of wire in which high voltage is induced in a step-up transformer.

semiconductor A material used to make microchips, transistors, and diodes.

series-parallel circuit A circuit that has both a series and a parallel circuit combined into one circuit.

shielded wiring harness A wiring harness that has shielding built into it to protect it from induced electrical interference.

short Also called a short circuit, the flow of current along an unintended route.

silicon A material commonly used to make semiconductors.

silicon carbide A type of material used to make semiconductors.

sine wave A mathematical function that describes a repetitive waveform such as an alternating current signal.

solder-type terminal A terminal that requires soldering to fasten the terminal to the cable or wire.

solenoid An electromagnet with a moving iron core that is used to cause mechanical motion.

solid-state relay A relay that performs the function of a mechanical relay but using only electronic components.

speed control circuit A circuit that controls the speed of a motor.

step-down transformer A transformer used to reduce the voltage, such as to allow a battery charger operated on 120 volts to charge a 12-volt battery.

step-up transformer A transformer used to increase the voltage from a lower input voltage to a higher output, such as an ignition coil.

switch An electrical device with contacts that turns current flow on and off.

terminal A means of providing a low-resistance connection/termination at the end of a wire.

thermistor A temperature-sensitive resistor. Its resistance varies substantially with temperature change.

thermocouple A temperature-sensing component that consists of two dissimilar metals that produce voltage proportional to temperature.

transformer action The transfer of electrical energy from one coil to another through induction in a transformer.

transistor A semiconductor device that allows a small current in the base lead to control a larger current through the emitter collector leads.

turn signal switch A switch that turns the left and right turn signal lights on and off.

twisted pair Two conductors that are twisted together to reduce electrical interference.

variable resistor A component that has a mechanism for varying resistance.

volt The unit used to measure potential difference or electrical pressure.

voltage The electrical pressure that causes current to flow in a circuit.

voltage drop The amount of potential difference between two points in a circuit.

watt The unit for measuring electrical power.

wire A conductor usually made of multistranded copper with an external insulated coating.

wiring diagram A schematic drawing and symbol representation of the wiring and components; also called electrical schematic.

wiring harness A collection of wires or cables insulated from each other but bound together.

wiring harness connector A plug that contains multiple terminals with male and female ends.

work The process by which one type of energy is transformed into another type of energy.

Zener diode A diode that forward biases when a certain voltage is reached.

ASE-Type Questions

1. Tech A says that if the specified fuse keeps blowing, it is generally OK to replace it with a larger fuse. Tech B says that a fusible link is one type of circuit protection device. Who is correct?
   a. Tech A
   b. Tech B
   c. Both A and B
   d. Neither A nor B

2. Tech A says that the movement of electrons in a circuit is called current flow. Tech B says that the movement of electrons in a circuit is measured in amps. Who is correct?
   a. Tech A
   b. Tech B
   c. Both A and B
   d. Neither A nor B

3. Tech A says that electromotive force is also known as voltage. Tech B says that when electrons flow in one direction only, this is DC. Who is correct?
   a. Tech A
   b. Tech B
   c. Both A and B
   d. Neither A nor B

4. Tech A says that 18 AWG wire is larger than 12 AWG wire. Tech B says that the larger the diameter of the conductor, the more electrical resistance it has. Who is correct?
   a. Tech A
   b. Tech B
   c. Both A and B
   d. Neither A nor B

5. Two technicians are discussing electron flow. Tech A says that in "conventional theory" current is believed to flow from positive to negative. Tech B says that in "electron theory" current is believed to flow from negative to positive. Who is correct?
   a. Tech A
   b. Tech B
   c. Both A and B
   d. Neither A nor B

6. Tech A says that hertz is the number of cycles per second. Tech B says that hertz is the amount of current flow produced by an alternator. Who is correct?
   a. Tech A
   b. Tech B
   c. Both A and B
   d. Neither A nor B

7. Two technicians are discussing a series circuit with four resistors of various resistances. Tech A says that current flow will be different in each resistor. Tech B says that current flow will be the same in each resistor. Who is correct?
   a. Tech A
   b. Tech B
   c. Both A and B
   d. Neither A nor B

8. Tech A says that a voltage drop is typically used to find excessive resistance in a circuit. Tech B says that high resistance creates heat at the point of resistance in the circuit. Who is correct?
   a. Tech A
   b. Tech B
   c. Both A and B
   d. Neither A nor B

9. Tech A says that in a series circuit with two resistors of 120 ohms each, the total circuit resistance is 240 ohms. Tech B says that in a parallel circuit with two resistors of 120 ohms each, the total circuit resistance is 240 ohms. Who is correct?
   a. Tech A
   b. Tech B
   c. Both A and B
   d. Neither A nor B

10. Tech A says that a relay is a one-way electrical check valve used in alternators to change AC into DC. Tech B says that a relay uses electromagnetism to open or close a switch. Who is correct?
   a. Tech A
   b. Tech B
   c. Both A and B
   d. Neither A nor B

CHAPTER 37

Meter Usage and Circuit Diagnosis

Knowledge Objectives

After reading this chapter, you will be able to:
1. Explain how to set up a digital volt-ohmmeter (DVOM). (pp 1230–1233)
2. Describe how to measure volts, ohms, and amps. (pp 1234–1235)
3. Understand the use of the DVOM in taking voltage measurements. (pp 1235–1243)
4. Understand the use of the DVOM in taking current measurements. (pp 1243–1248)
5. Understand the use of the DVOM in taking current and voltage measurements in a series circuit. (pp 1249–1257)
6. Understand the use of the DVOM in measuring volts, ohms, and amps in a parallel circuit. (pp 1258–1262)
7. Understand the use of the DVOM in measuring current and voltage in a series-parallel circuit. (pp 1262–1264)
8. Understand the use of the DVOM in measuring voltage and amperage in a circuit with a variable resistor. (p 1265)
9. Understand the use of the DVOM in measuring current and voltage in a circuit with a capacitor connected in series with a lamp. (pp 1266–1267)
10. Describe how to use an oscilloscope to check circuit waveforms. (pp 1267–1268)

Skills Objectives

After reading this chapter, you will be able to:
1. Check circuit waveforms. (pp 1267–1269)
2. Use Ohm's law to diagnose circuits. (pp 1269–1271)
3. Use wiring diagrams to diagnose electrical circuits. (pp 1271–1272)
4. Use a DVOM to measure voltage. (pp 1272–1273)
5. Check circuits with a test light. (pp 1273–1274)
6. Check circuits with fused jumper leads. (pp 1274–1275)
7. Locate opens, shorts, grounds, and high-resistance faults. (pp 1275–1276)
8. Inspect and test circuit protection devices. (p 1276)
9. Inspect and test switches, connectors, relays, solenoid solid-state devices, and wires. (p 1277)

▶ Introduction

Digital volt-ohmmeters (DVOMs) and oscilloscopes are electrical measuring tools frequently used to diagnose and repair electrical faults. Like many diagnostic tools, practice is required to understand how the DVOM and oscilloscope are used to take electrical measurements and connect them into electrical circuits to ensure correct readings are obtained. Once a reading is obtained, it needs to be interpreted and applied, in conjunction with knowledge of electrical theory, to diagnose the circuit being tested. This chapter provides an explanation of how to use and set up a DVOM for measuring voltage, amperage, and resistance.

This chapter also has a number of exercises that will expand your knowledge on using a DVOM, allowing you to practice taking readings and apply the results. It also relates the practical circuit examples and DVOM readings to Ohm's law calculations. Basic oscilloscope use and typical waveforms are also covered. Knowing how to properly use DVOMs and oscilloscopes along with interpreting and applying their readings will allow you to diagnose electrical faults, making you very valuable to your employer.

▶ Digital Volt-Ohmmeter

A **digital volt-ohmmeter (DVOM)** or digital multimeter (DMM) is a versatile and useful piece of test equipment **FIGURE 37-1**. It is called a digital meter because the meter gives a numerical reading on a digital display. An analog meter, by comparison, uses a needle that hovers over a series of scales, requiring the technician to determine the numerical value of the reading. Digital meters are easier to

read, which means that a technician is less likely to get the wrong reading. The DVOM tends to be the first test tool selected for electrical diagnosis and repairs. Basic DVOMs can measure alternating current (AC) and direct current (DC) voltage, AC and DC amperage, and resistance. Most modern DVOMs can also measure frequency and temperature and have a dedicated diode test capability.

DVOMs come in a variety of layouts and quality. You will want to get used to the meters in your shop so you will know their capabilities and how to use them. Most

FIGURE 37-1 A digital volt-ohmmeter (DVOM) is a versatile and useful piece of test equipment.

You are the Automotive Technician

Your supervisor requested that you train the shop apprentice on how to use a DVOM. You will be using the DVOM to teach the apprentice how to take simple measurements that will come in handy when doing vehicle inspections such as measuring battery and charging system voltage; testing a fuse to see if it is blown; and how to perform a voltage drop on a simple circuit. The apprentice explains what volts, ohms, and amps are, so you show him how to set up the meter for each of these tests. Once he is competent in setting up the meter, you show him how to take each type of reading. The following is the list of questions your supervisor has asked you to review with the new employee after the hands-on training:

1. What are the most common measurements taken by a DVOM, and how is the meter hooked up in the circuit for each one?
2. Describe the different ways that a voltage drop can be measured.
3. What two things are needed to have a voltage drop?

DVOMs of average quality are "fused," meaning that one or more "fast-blow" fuses are included inside the DVOM. If the amperage is too high, the fuse will blow, protecting the meter. If the meter is unfused, it will not be protected and could be damaged if used incorrectly when measuring amperage.

DVOMs and test leads also should have a CAT rating listed on the front. CAT is short for "category." Each level, or CAT, is designed to work safely on higher-powered electrical systems TABLE 37-1. CAT ratings were not designed initially for automotive meters since most vehicles use low voltage, but with more and more hybrid and electric vehicles on the road, which operate on very high voltages, CAT ratings are becoming important for automotive technicians. Hybrid vehicles typically require meters and test leads rated as CAT III or CAT IV. Another thing to keep in mind if you are working on high-voltage systems is that you need to wear a pair of certified and tested rubber-insulated gloves, most likely with leather protectors over top. Always use the proper CAT-rated meter and leads along with the proper personal protective equipment when working on high-voltage systems.

DVOM Use

DVOMs are used to take many different electrical measurements on electrical circuits and are one of the first tools used when conducting electrical repair or diagnosis work. As a voltmeter, the DVOM can measure electrical voltage within circuits; for example, the available voltage at a fuse, switch, or lamp. The DVOM can also measure resistance of a component, connector, or cable, such as the resistance of an ignition coil to check against specifications. DVOMs can also measure current flow in circuits, such as when the amount of current flow through a fuse needs to be checked against specifications. Clearly, a DVOM is a very versatile tool, explaining why it is the most commonly used electrical diagnosis tool. In the next several sections we will further explore DVOMs and how to use them.

DVOM Components

There are two main components of a DVOM, the main instrument body and the test leads that connect the DVOM to the circuit being tested. The DVOM main instrument body has a function switch to choose the type of electrical measurement to be taken, digital display to report the readings, and sockets to connect test leads. Test leads are used to connect the DVOM to or into the circuit being tested and come in pairs: one red, the other black. Basic leads have a probe on one end for making the connection with the electrical circuit being tested and a connector on the other end for plugging into the sockets of the DVOM. A wide variety of test leads and adapters are available to make it easier to use the DVOM; for example, alligator clips enable hands-free connection of the leads. Adapters such as temperature probes and inductive current clamps connect to the input sockets of the DVOM and convert temperature or current flow into a voltage that can be measured by the DVOM.

Ranges and Scales

DVOMs read very small quantities in the one-ten thousandths of a unit range up to very large quantities in the range of millions of units in the case of resistance measurements. It is not possible for DVOMs to effectively and accurately measure such ranges with only a single range or scale; they must have multiple ranges or scales. But before we can talk about those ranges, we need to understand that the DVOM screen can only display four or five digits. This means that symbols must be used to substitute for some of the digits. TABLE 37-2 shows the common symbols, their prefix, and the factor they represent. You will

TABLE 37-1: Meter CAT Ratings

Overvoltage Category	Short Description	Examples
CAT I	Electronics	Low-power electronic equipment such as copiers, etc.
CAT II	Single-phase plug-in tools and equipment	Portable tools, appliances, etc.
CAT III	Three-phase fixed equipment and single-phase commercial lighting	Equipment in fixed installations (this is the minimum rating required for hybrid vehicles)
CAT IV	Three-phase utility connection, any outdoor wires	Main power wires from the utility company; outside wire for lighting (this rating is for heavier-duty meters and leads for hybrid vehicles)

TABLE 37-2: DVOM Values

Factor	Prefix	Symbol
1,000,000	mega	M
1,000	kilo	k
1	No prefix	
0.001	milli	m
0.000001	micro	µ

have to place the appropriate electrical symbol, V, A, or Ω, behind the factor symbol based on what you are measuring. For example, 2168 mV would be the same as 2168 millivolts. It could also be called 2.168 volts, since there are 1000 millivolts in 1 volt. Either designation is correct. The challenge is taking the meter reading and making sense of it, which takes practice.

Once you understand the symbols and what value they represent, you are ready to decide which range to set the meter to. TABLE 37-3 lists a typical set of DVOM ranges; however, there is no single range or scale value used by DVOM manufacturers. The resolution indicates the accuracy of the count within any given range and is different for each range. To achieve the most accurate reading, always select the lowest range possible for the value being measured. For example, if you are measuring 12 volts, you should select the 60-V range, because 6 volts would be too low and 600 volts would be less accurate.

Most modern DVOMs have an automatic ranging capability while maintaining the ability to be used in a manually selected range, which means the user can determine the range. When used in the auto range, the DVOM selects the best range for the value being measured so that the technician does not have to be concerned with manually setting the range. But be careful! The meter does not give you flashing light warnings that it has changed ranges, so it is extremely easy to miss that. Many a technician has been led down the wrong diagnostic path by thinking the 12.6 on the meter was volts when in fact the meter had auto-ranged to millivolts; so instead of having full power, the battery being tested had almost *no* power. To prevent this mistake, many instructors require their students to use only manual ranging when using their meter.

TABLE 37-3: DVOM Ranges

Function	Range	Resolution
mV DC	0–600.0 mV	0.1 mV
V DC	0–6.000 V	0.001 V
	0–60.00 V	0.01 V
	0–600.0 V	0.1 V
	0–1000 V	1 V
Ohms	0–600.0 Ω	0.1 Ω
	0–6.000 kΩ	0.0001 kΩ
	0–60.00 kΩ	0.01 kΩ
	0–600.0 kΩ	0.0001 MΩ
	0–40.00 MΩ	0.01 MΩ

Min/Max and Hold Setting

Many DVOMs have special settings incorporated into their design to assist you in taking measurements of rapidly changing values or to freeze the display so that an individual reading is not lost. In the **min/max setting**, the DVOM will record in memory the maximum and minimum reading obtained during the time the DVOM is connected to a source to take a reading. The min/max setting is often used to measure vehicle battery voltage while the engine is cranking or the battery is charging. During cranking of the starter motor, current is at its highest, but for only a fraction of a second when the engine initially starts to crank. Cranking is also when the battery voltage is at its lowest. In min/max mode, a DVOM will capture the minimum and maximum battery voltage. A limitation in the use of the DVOM is the sample rate. The sample rate is the speed at which the DVOM can sample the voltage. The DVOM does not continuously sample the voltage; rather, it checks the voltage at regular intervals or at a sample rate. While this occurs quickly—for example, every 100 milliseconds—it does mean that if a transient voltage occurs between samples, it will not be recorded by the DVOM. Where quicker sample rates are required, other tools such as oscilloscopes can be used.

The **hold function** allows the display to be frozen. When the hold function is activated, the display will hold the value on the display until the function or DVOM is turned off. A variation of the hold function is the "auto hold" function found on some DVOMs. When activated, the auto hold function takes a measurement and freezes or holds the display until the function or DVOM is turned off. This function can be useful when taking measurements in difficult locations, such as underneath a dash where you may not be able to watch the meter display while making the meter connections.

Setting Up a DVOM

To set up a DVOM to take accurate measurements, you need to know if you will be measuring resistance, voltage, or current. You should also know the reading that you are expecting so you can be sure to set up the meter appropriately. If very high voltages are to be measured, it is important to make sure the DVOM and leads match the appropriate CAT rating for use at the voltages you will be testing. All of this information will determine the way in which you set up the DVOM, including the connections you need to make on the DVOM and the range you select. Resistance measurements should be undertaken with the circuit disconnected. If measuring the resistance of components, they should be removed from the circuit.

The following steps describe how to set up a DVOM:

1. Know what you are testing—volts, amps, or ohms.
2. Know the value you expect to be reading (specification).
3. Select leads and probes to suit the measuring task.
4. Connect the leads to the DVOM.
5. Use the function switch to select the type of measurement to be undertaken (e.g., resistance, volts, or amps; DC or AC).
6. Select the correct meter range if you are using a manual range meter.
7. Connect the leads to the circuit being tested.
8. Read the meter display.

Test Leads: Common and Probing

Many people incorrectly label the red lead as positive and the black lead as negative. However, if you look at your meter near the test lead terminals, you will not see a "+" or a "−" anywhere. What you will see is "A" (typically 10 A), "mA," "common," and "V/Ω." Common just means that the terminal is "common" to all of the functions of the meter. In other words, this lead does not need to be moved when different functions of the meter are typically accessed. On the other hand, the red lead does have to move, depending on what function of the meter is being used. That is why it is labeled with the V/Ω symbol, and not "+." If you find this distinction questionable, consider the following: When we measure various electrical signals at the same time on an oscilloscope, we need more than just the red lead. In fact, we typically use a yellow, a blue, and a green test lead. In all of these situations, the test lead (no matter the color) acts as a probe into the circuit. So rather than referring to the red lead as the positive lead, it is more accurate to refer to it as the probing lead for the DVOM. Then we can introduce probing leads of other colors when we use an oscilloscope.

The other important note is that the meter screen will always read what the probing lead is touching. For example, if the common lead is touching the battery's negative post and the probing lead is touching the positive post, the meter screen will display a "+" before the reading. That means that the probing lead is touching something more positive than the common lead. If we reverse the leads, the meter screen will display a "−" before the number, meaning that the probing lead is touching something more negative than the common lead. When you understand this concept, rather than jumping to the conclusion that "the meter leads are hooked up backward," you will be ready to start diagnosing all kinds of strange electrical problems, especially with ground issues and charging system issues.

Probing Techniques

A **probing technique** is the way in which the DVOM probes are connected into circuits. There are many different types of probes and probing techniques you can use, depending on the circuit being tested. Some examples are alligator clips, fine-pin probes, and insulation piercing clips **FIGURE 37-2**. Make sure you know the voltage limits of the probes you use, since high-voltage measurements require special probes that are designed for that purpose.

Never use excessive force when probing; doing so may bend or damage connectors and terminals. The standard probe leads that are supplied with a DVOM are basic straight metal probes useful for making quick measurements in circuits, but they do require the use of both hands to hold them in place. Leads with alligator clips, which come in various sizes, allow the DVOM leads to be clipped onto the circuit and held in place, freeing up your hands for other tasks. These clips are particularly useful for connecting to larger terminals, such as battery terminals.

Back-probing occurs when the probe is pushed in from the back of a connector to make a connection. To perform this task, very fine pins are used to reduce the possibility of damage. The pins are designed to slip into the back of connectors and provide contact without causing damage. Insulation piercing probes are also available but should be used with caution. They have sharp fine pins that pierce the insulation on conductors to create a connection. Remember to always reinsulate the hole that the probe makes to prevent any corrosion. Use liquid insulation or a similar product to reinsulate; do not use room temperature vulcanizing (RTV) silicone, which attracts moisture as it cures, potentially causing corrosion. Since it may result in damage to the insulation or conductor, this type of probe should be used only as a last resort.

FIGURE 37-2 There are many different leads and probing techniques you can use, depending on the circuit being tested.

Measuring Volts, Ohms, and Amps

The most common measurements taken with DVOMs are voltage, resistance, and current. To take voltage measurements, the probing lead (red) is connected to the volts/ohms, or V/Ω, terminal, and the common lead (black) is connected to the common, or COM, terminal of the DVOM. An appropriate range or auto range is selected on either AC or DC voltage, depending on the voltage to be measured. The probing lead is typically connected to the positive side of the circuit being tested, and the common lead to the negative side. Watch your screen. If the "+" or "−" is not what you were expecting, check the leads to verify they are connected the way you intended.

Applied	Math

AM-1: Whole Numbers: The technician can add whole numbers to determine measurement conformance with the manufacturer's specifications.
An alternator is being tested to determine if it meets manufacturer's specifications. If an alternator is damaged due to a blown diode or similar problem, it is usually out of specifications by a wide margin. For this type of alternator the output specification is 95 amperes. The technician tests the alternator that puts out 65 amps. The service material states a good alternator will provide an output that is within 15 amps of its rated value. The technician adds 15 amps to the original 65 amps which is a total of 80 amps. This is below the specifications of 95 amps for this type of alternator.

In this example, we are working with whole numbers. If a number has a negative sign, a decimal point, or a part that's a fraction, it is not considered a whole number.

Applied	Math

AM-2: Decimals: The technician can add decimal numbers to determine conformance with the manufacturer's specifications.
A starter has been rebuilt and the technician wants to check the pinion clearance. A feeler gauge will be used to determine this clearance. Manufacturer's specifications for this clearance are from 0.010" to 0.140", with 0.070" considered the midpoint. The technician's feeler gauge set only goes to 0.045", which fits too loosely in the gap. He places a 0.025" blade next to the 0.045" blade, which together, fits in the gap with just the right tension. The selected gauges are 0.025" plus 0.045" to equal a total of 0.070".

In this example, we are working with decimal numbers. Decimals are numbers that are expressed using a decimal point.

If you still get an unexpected reading, stop and analyze the situation. Ask yourself, what could cause the meter to read that way? Then brainstorm the options.

> **TECHNICIAN TIP**
>
> A technician recently posted an electrical problem on a technical forum. He said that he had hooked up a voltmeter with the black (common) lead on the negative battery terminal and the red (probing) lead on the vehicle engine ground with the engine running. The meter read a negative number. He asked the forum if he had the meter leads hooked up backward. He received several comments saying yes, he had hooked them up backward. However, those technicians were not correct. His probing lead was registering a reading that was more negative than the common lead. But what could be more negative than the negative post of the battery? When the engine is running, the alternator can be more negative than the negative battery post. So what his DVOM was trying to tell him was that there was a voltage drop between the negative battery post and the alternator frame. If he would have understood that the probing lead was not lying to him, that it was reporting exactly what it was touching compared to what the common lead was touching, then he could have started down the path to diagnosing what it indicated. In this case, he should have been looking for a dirty ground connection between the negative battery post and the engine block.

Most DVOMs can measure milliamps or 10 to 20 amps directly through the meter. The correct range needs to be selected, along with AC or DC. The red probe is connected to the A terminal, and the black lead is connected to the COM terminals. On some DVOMs, there may be a separate mA terminal that the red probe plugs into to measure milliamps. To measure current, the DVOM is connected in series with the circuit, with the probing lead closest to the positive terminal of the power supply or battery. Quality DVOMs typically have an internal fuse that will blow if excessive current flows through it. This fuse is designed to help prevent damage to the meter.

If larger amperage needs to be measured, then current clamps can be connected to the DVOM, and, depending on their range, they can measure high currents, such as starter motor current draw of 400 amps or more. Current clamps are available in a variety of current-measuring ranges. The current clamp fastens around the conductor and measures the strength of the magnetic field produced from current flowing through the conductor and outputs a voltage that the DVOM reads as voltage, which is directly related to the amount of current flowing in amps. When using current clamps, the DVOM is set to read volts. Current clamps also have the advantage that they clamp around the conductor, so the circuit does not need to be broken into to insert the DVOM in series as you would with standard probes on an ammeter.

To accurately measure the resistance of a component, you should remove or isolate the component from the circuit. Doing so removes the possibility of any parallel circuit resistance affecting the resistance measurement. If you need to measure resistance in a circuit, always make sure the power is disconnected. In order to read resistance, batteries inside the DVOM supply the circuit with power to take the measurement. If power is not removed from the circuit being tested, it disrupts the measurement and can provide a false reading or potentially damage the DVOM. To take resistance measurements, the red (probing) lead is connected to the V/Ω terminal, and the black (common) lead is connected to the COM terminal of the DVOM. You will need to select an appropriate range or auto range to measure resistance. The red probing lead is connected to one side of the component being tested, and the black common lead is connected to the other side.

TECHNICIAN TIP

DVOMs come in many forms. Always follow the specific manufacturer's instructions in the use of the DVOM or serious damage either to the DVOM and/or to the electrical circuit could result.

▶ Voltage Exercises

The following voltage exercises are designed to explain the use of the DVOM in taking DC voltage measurements. Examples are given to show the use of different ranges on the meter display and voltage drops in the series circuits across equal and unequal loads. It is important to understand that the sum of the series voltage drops equals the supply voltage as explained in Kirchhoff's voltage law.

Voltage Ranges

Typically, a DVOM has both an auto range and a manual range capability. The way in which you select auto range and manual range will vary depending on the DVOM. Different DVOMs have different range settings. For example, one DVOM's setting could be 6 V, 60 V, and 600 V, and another's 4 V, 40 V, and 400 V. **FIGURE 37-3**

shows a circuit with two resistors in a series with a 12-volt DC supply. Various DVOM ranges can be compared by measuring the voltage drops across each of the resistors. The DVOM has the following ranges: 600.0 mV, 6.000 V, 60.00 V, 600.0 V, and 1000 V. **TABLE 37-4** provides results of voltmeter readings and a DVOM's display to show how different ranges affect the way in which the DVOM readings are displayed.

FIGURE 37-3 Measuring volts in a circuit with two unequal resistors connected in series with a 12-volt DC supply.

TABLE 37-4: Example of the Effect of Different Ranges on DVOM Readings

Voltmeter	Range	Meter Display	Explanation
V_3	Auto range	8.00	Auto ranging selects the correct range for the voltage being read.
V_4	Auto range	4.000	
V_3	6 V	OL	OL means overload and indicates the voltage being read is higher than the maximum allowed for the range.

(continues)

TABLE 37-4: Example of the Effect of Different Ranges on DVOM Readings (continued)

Voltmeter	Range	Meter Display	Explanation
V_4	6 V	4.000	The 6-V range is the best range to most accurately measure 4 V. Note how it has three digits after the decimal point.
V_3	60 V	8.00	The 60-V range is the best range to most accurately measure 8 V.
V_4	60 V	4.00	Four volts can also be read on the 60-V range; however, when compared to the 6-V range, there are two digits rather than three after the decimal point. This reading will not be as accurate on this range.
V_3	600 V	8.0	On these ranges, the DVOM still reads but the measurements are not as accurate. To get the most accurate reading, a DVOM range should be selected that is slightly higher than the reading expected.
V_4	600 V	4.0	
V_3	1000 V	8	
V_4	1000 V	4	

Voltage Drop

Voltage drop is measured with a voltmeter and is the potential difference between two points in a circuit. The sum of all the voltage drops in a series circuit equals the supply voltage, while the voltage drop across all parallel circuit branches is the same. Voltage drop does occur in all parts of the circuit, but in a correctly working vehicle circuit, the vast majority of voltage drop is across the component or load we want to do work, such as the headlight bulb.

Unwanted voltage drop becomes a problem if it becomes excessive and occurs in parts of the circuit other than the load. For example, ideally the only resistance in the circuit would be the headlight bulb. If this were the case, then all of the battery voltage would be dropped (used up) across the headlight bulb. In practice, however, resistance exists in the cables and connec-

tors within the circuit. In a good circuit, the resistance of the cables, terminals or connectors, and switches is very low, causing small and insignificant amounts of voltage drop. A problem arises when excessive voltage drop occurs in the circuit cables, connectors, and switches, which reduces the efficiency of the circuit. Excessive voltage drop is a fault in the circuit and can cause problems; for example, it will result in yellow or dim headlights. To test for unwanted voltage drop of the conductors, switches, and connectors, measure the voltage across each of these parts of the circuit and add the voltage drops together. In a 12-volt system, the total unwanted voltage drop across each side of the whole circuit should not exceed 0.5 volts or 1.0 volt for a 24-volt circuit. And individual voltage drops across an individual wire, connection, or common switch should be less than 0.2 volts.

Applied   Math

AM-5: Decimals: The technician can subtract decimal numbers to determine conformance with the manufacturer's specifications.

A technician is performing a battery state of charge test using a hydrometer. This procedure can be used on automotive batteries that have removable individual filler caps. The tube of the hydrometer is inserted into one of the battery cells. The technician will gently draw electrolyte into the hydrometer. The float indicator will rise and float freely. The specific gravity can be obtained by reading the indicator at eye level. When doing this procedure, it is important to consider the hazards of battery electrolyte, which contains sulfuric acid. Eye protection and rubber gloves are needed for personal protection. After reading the hydrometer, the electrolyte is returned to the cell from which it was withdrawn. The same procedure will be repeated for the other five cells.

Manufacturer's specifications state that a fully charged battery should show a specific gravity of approximately 1.260 with electrolyte temperature at 80° Fahrenheit. The results of the readings of each cell will be compared to a chart that shows specific gravity as compared to state of charge. If the electrolyte temperature is above or below 80° Fahrenheit, corrections must be made by one of several methods. In this case, the technician consulted a temperature correction chart.

The technician observed that at 40° F, the correction factor would be to subtract 0.016 points. The reading for cell one was 1.240. To compensate for the huge temperature difference between 80° and 40° Fahrenheit, corrections are needed. In this example, we have 1.240 minus (-) 0.016 = 1.224 for the adjusted specific gravity of one of the battery cells. The next step would be to look at the readings for the other five cells of the battery.

Applied | **Math**

AM-3: Mentally: The technician can mentally add two or more numbers to determine conformance with the manufacturer's specifications.

AM-6: Mentally: The technician can mentally subtract decimal and whole numbers to arrive at a difference for comparison with the manufacturer's specifications.

In this scenario, a technician is using a DVOM to test the resistance of a coil pack for a V-6 engine. The ignition coil pack is suspected to be faulty due to a failed power balance test in which the cylinder was not properly contributing to the performance of the engine. Since coil designs are different, manufacturers' testing procedures vary. With the key off and the battery lead to the coil disconnected, the ohmmeter function of the DVOM will be used to check resistance. The technician will measure the resistance of the primary and secondary windings. In this case, the specifications for the primary windings are 0.3–1.0 ohms. Before taking this reading, the technician checks the resistance in the leads of his DVOM. This was determined to be 0.2 ohms of resistance and will be subtracted (mentally) from the primary resistance reading. Using service information, the technician places the leads of the DVOM in proper slots of the component and obtains a reading of 0.8 ohms. He mentally subtracts 0.2 ohms for the resistance in the meter leads for a corrected reading of 0.6 ohms. This is within specifications for the primary windings.

The next step is the readings for the secondary windings of the coil pack. The manufacturer's specifications are 8000 ohms–9000 ohms. The technician places the meter leads as shown in the service information and obtains a reading of 6,200 ohms. Mentally, the technician subtracts this and records the information on the repair order. The coil pack is 1,800 ohms below minimum specifications. The technician will install a known good component (coil pack) for a test to see how the engine performs.

To measure voltage drop, the DVOM needs to be used on the voltage range. To perform this measurement process, you will need to set the function switch to "auto range volts DC" on the DVOM (some technicians prefer to use manual range, so they will not be fooled by auto range), and connect the black lead to COM and the red (probing) lead to V/Ω. Voltage drop can be measured across components, connectors, or cables. The probing lead of the DVOM is normally connected to the point in the circuit where you want to know the voltage. For example, if you want to know what the voltage is at the positive post of the battery, then you would connect the red lead to the positive post of the battery and the black lead to the negative post of the battery. The voltmeter would then read the amount of voltage greater than is at the negative terminal.

If you are performing a voltage drop test, for example, on the feed side of the horn circuit, you could connect the black lead to the positive terminal of the battery and the red lead to the input wire of the horn (the wire connected to the horn). When you activate the horn, the voltmeter will read the amount of voltage drop in the feed side of the circuit. For example, it might be –4.2 volts. This means that the voltage is 4.2 volts less at the input of the horn (red lead) than it is at the positive battery post (black lead). In this case, the "–" means less than. So there are 4.2 volts less at the horn than at the positive battery post. Since the voltage drop is more than 0.5 volts, this is an excessive voltage drop in that portion of the circuit, and the voltmeter leads will need to be moved wire by wire closer together until the point of the voltage drop is located.

You could make the same measurement with the DVOM leads reversed. If you place the red lead on the positive battery post and the black lead on the input of the horn, the meter would then read 4.2 volts. In this case it shows positive. This is because the red lead is on the positive post of the battery, which is 4.2 volts higher than the horn input where the black lead is connected. As you can see, voltmeter leads can be hooked up in a couple of ways. Just remember that the meter always reads what the red lead is touching.

FIGURE 37-4 shows a series circuit of two resistors with a 12-volt battery and switch. In this example of

FIGURE 37-4 Measuring voltage in a circuit with two unequal resistors connected in series with a 12-volt battery and the switch open.

how to measure voltage drop, the voltage in various parts of the circuit will be measured with the switch in the open position. **TABLE 37-5** gives an explanation of the voltage measurements and validates the measurements with Ohm's law calculations with the switch in the open position.

FIGURE 37-5 shows a series circuit of two resistors with a 12-volt battery and switch. In this example of how to measure voltage drop, the voltage in various parts of the circuit will be measured with the switch in the closed position. **TABLE 37-6** gives an explanation of the voltage measurements and validates the measurements with Ohm's law calculations with the switch in the closed position.

Unwanted voltage drops in vehicle circuits can cause real problems and faults. For example, a corroded or bad chassis ground can cause a voltage drop that reduces the voltage and current available to components. **FIGURE 37-6** shows a simple circuit with a bulb connected via a switch across a 12-volt circuit. In this circuit, a corroded ground connection has caused a resistance that is dropping 2 volts across it. **TABLE 37-7** analyzes the voltage drops across the corroded ground connection and explains how it reduces the voltage across the bulb, which in turn will cause poor illumination.

FIGURE 37-5 Measuring voltage in a circuit with two unequal resistors connected in series, with a 12-volt battery and the switch closed.

TABLE 37-5: Explanation of Voltage Measurements in Figure 37-4

Measured Voltage	Explanation
$V_1 = 12$ V	V_1 is measuring the voltage directly across the supply battery, so the voltage reading will be the battery voltage.
$V_2 = 12$ V	With the switch in the open position, no current flows in the circuit. The probing lead is connected directly to the battery via the cable, while the black lead is connected to the negative battery terminal via the two series resistors. Because no current flows in the circuit, there is no voltage drop across the two resistors; therefore, the entire battery voltage drop is across the open circuit switch.
$V_3 = 0$ V	No current is flowing in the circuit; therefore, resistor R_1 has no voltage drop across it. This can be calculated using Ohm's law: Voltage Drop = Resistance × Current $= 4\,\Omega \times 0$ A $= 0$ V drop This would be the same as having a garden hose with a kink in it but with the water shut off at the house. The pressure would be the same on both sides of the kink in the hose, since there is no flow.
$V_4 = 0$ V	No current is flowing in the circuit; therefore, resistor R_2 has no voltage drop across it. This can be calculated using Ohm's law: Voltage Drop = Resistance × Current $= 2\,\Omega \times 0$ A $= 0$ V drop

TABLE 37-6: Explanation of Voltage Measurements in Figure 37-5

Measured Voltage	Explanation
$V_1 = 12\ V$	V_1 is measuring the voltage directly across the supply battery, so the voltage reading will be the battery voltage.
$V_2 = 0\ V$	With the switch in the closed position, current flows in the circuit. The switch contacts ideally will have no resistance when closed, so the voltage drop across the contacts will be 0 V. In actual circuit operation, there will always be a slight amount of resistance that will drop a slight amount of voltage in a good switch, but for our examples in this chapter, we will assume there is none.
$V_3 = 8\ V$	With the switch closed, current can flow in the circuit. The amount of voltage drop across R_1 will be 8 V. This can be calculated using Ohm's law: $\text{Voltage Drop} = \text{Resistance} \times \text{Current}$ $= 4\ \Omega \times 2\ A \text{ (see note below)}$ $= 8\ V\ \text{drop}$ Note: To calculate total circuit current, use this formula: $I_T = V_T \div R_T$ $= 12 \div 6\ \Omega$ $= 2\ A$
$V_4 = 4\ V$	With the switch closed, current can flow in the circuit. The amount of voltage drop across R_2 will be 4 V. This can be calculated using Ohm's law: $\text{Voltage Drop} = \text{Resistance} \times \text{Current}$ $= 2\ \Omega \times 2\ A$ $= 4\ V\ \text{drop}$

FIGURE 37-6 Measuring voltage in a simple circuit with a switch and one bulb, but with high resistance due to a corroded ground.

TABLE 37-7: Analysis of Voltage Drops in Figure 37-6

Measured Voltage	Explanation
$V_1 = 12\ V$	V_1 is measuring the voltage directly across the supply battery, so the voltage reading will be the battery voltage.
$V_2 = 0\ V$	With the switch in the closed position, current flows in the circuit. The switch contacts ideally will have no resistance when closed, so the voltage drop across the contact will be 0 V.
$V_3 = 10\ V$	With the switch closed, current can flow in the circuit. The amount of voltage drop across the bulb is 10 V, because 2 V is being dropped across the corroded ground connection.
$V_4 = 2\ V$	With the switch closed, current can flow in the circuit. The amount of voltage drop across the corroded ground connection is 2 V. This amount of voltage drop robs the

(continues)

TABLE 37-7: Analysis of Voltage Drops in Figure 37-6 (continued)

Measured Voltage	Explanation
	bulb of part of the source voltage and would cause the bulb to be very yellow and dim. The box around the resistor and ground indicates the resistance is within the ground connection. High resistance always robs voltage from the designed loads in the circuit and reduces amperage in the circuit.
$V_5 = 2$ V	V_5 is measuring the same voltage as V_4; the red and black leads of both DVOMs are connected to points with the same potential.

Note that an incandescent bulb filament is a heating element and its resistance varies greatly as the current going through it varies.

Applied   Math

AM-4: Whole Numbers: The technician can divide whole numbers to determine differences for comparison with the manufacturer's specifications.
AM-7: Whole Numbers: The technician can divide whole numbers to determine differences for comparison with the manufacturer's specifications.
Battery load testing is a procedure that uses a simulated starter current draw on a battery. The results of this test can be compared to manufacturer's specifications for the condition of the battery. There are a number of steps to complete regarding a battery load test using a carbon pile unit. One of the steps is to use one-half CCA rating to determine the load to be applied to the battery. CCA stands for cold cranking amps, which is one of the battery's primary ratings. In this example, we have a 770 CCA battery and the load to be applied will be one-half of that amount. To determine this, we can divide by two to give us the 385 CCA load to apply. Another way to describe this would be: 770 CCA/2 = 385 CCA (test load).
    In this example, we are dividing whole numbers. Division is the opposite of multiplication.

Applied   Math

AM-8: Decimals: The technician can divide decimal numbers to determine measurement conformance with the manufacturer's specifications.
In this scenario, a technician is installing a new starter on a Chevrolet automobile. This type of starter requires a

shim or series of shims between the starter mounting flange and the engine block.
    The manufacturer's specifications for this operation are 0.020 inch to 0.060 inch clearance between the pinion gear and flywheel. There is also a note of caution in the manufacturer's service information. The note of caution states: Failure to correct a clearance problem can lead to broken flywheel teeth or starter motor housings.
    The technician measured the clearance and found it to be 0.010 inch. He needs to install the starter with the proper number of shims to equal the mid-point of the specifications. This would equal 0.040 inch clearance, so he needs to increase the clearance by 0.030 inch to reach his goal. The service information states that each shim will increase the clearance approximately 0.005 inch.
    The technician is aware that he needs to divide 0.030 inch by 0.005 inch to determine the number of shims required to meet the mid-point of the specifications. We have 0.030 inch divided by 0.005, which equals six shims required. The technician installs six shims and measures the clearance at approximately 0.040, which is well within the specified range.

Voltage Drop Across Multiple Loads

To measure voltage drop, the DVOM is used on the voltage range. Select "auto range volts DC" on the DVOM, and connect the black lead to COM and the red lead to V/Ω. Voltage drop can be measured across components, connectors, or cables, but current has to be flowing to get an accurate measurement. Remember, the leads when checking voltage can be placed in either direction. Just remember which way you placed them so you understand what the reading means. We will show the red lead on the most positive side for purposes of the following diagrams.

    In **FIGURE 37-7**, the resistors in the series circuit each have the same value—3 ohms. **TABLE 37-8** lists the circuit voltages and provides an explanation for each.

Voltage Drop Across Unequal Loads

To measure voltage drop, the DVOM must be set on the voltage range. Select "auto range volts DC" on the DVOM, and connect the black lead to COM and the red lead to V/Ω. Voltage drop can be measured across components, connectors, or cables accurately *only* when current is flowing. Remember, the leads when checking voltage can be placed in either direction. Just remember which way you placed them so you understand what the reading means. We will show the red lead on the most positive side for purposes of the following diagrams.

FIGURE 37-7 Measuring voltage in a circuit with two equal resistance bulbs connected in series.

TABLE 37-8: Explanation of Circuit Voltages in Figure 37-7

Figure	Measured Voltage	Explanation
A	$V_1 = 12\,V$	V_1 is measuring the voltage directly across the supply battery, so the voltage reading will be the battery voltage regardless of the position of the switch.
B	$V_1 = 12\,V$	
A	$V_2 = 12\,V$	With the switch in the open position, no current flows in the circuit. The red DVOM lead is connected directly to the battery via the cable, while the black lead is connected to the negative battery terminal through the two series resistors. Because no current flows in the circuit, there is no voltage drop across the two resistors; therefore, the entire battery voltage drop is across the open circuit switch.
B	$V_2 = 0\,V$	The switch contacts ideally will have no resistance when closed, so the voltage drop across the contacts will be 0 V.
B	$V_3 = 6\,V$	With the switch closed, the amount of voltage drop across R_1 will be 6 V. This can be calculated using Ohm's law: Voltage Drop = Resistance × Current = 3 Ω × 2 A (see note below) = 6 V drop Note: To calculate total circuit current, use this formula: $I_T = V_T \div R_T$
B	$V_4 = 6\,V$	With the switch closed, the amount of voltage drop across R_2 will be 6 V. This can be calculated using Ohm's law: Voltage Drop = Resistance × Current = 3 Ω × 2 A = 6 V drop R_1 and R_2 are of the same resistance, so they will have the same voltage drop. Summing the voltage drops of R_1 and R_2 will equal the supply voltage: V_T = The sum of the voltage drops in a series circuit = VD R_1 + VD R_2 = 6 V + 6 V = 12 V

FIGURE 37-8 Measuring voltage in a circuit with two bulbs of unequal resistance connected in series.

TABLE 37-9: Explanation of Circuit Voltages in Figure 37-8

Figure	Measured Voltage	Explanation
A B	$V_1 = 12\ V$ $V_1 = 12\ V$	V_1 is measuring the voltage directly across the supply battery, so the voltage reading will be the battery voltage regardless of the position of the switch.
A	$V_2 = 12\ V$	With the switch in the open position, no current flows in the circuit. The red DVOM lead is connected directly to the battery via the cable, while the black lead is connected to the negative battery terminal via the two series resistors. Because no current flows in the circuit, there is no voltage drop across the two resistors; therefore, the entire battery voltage drop is across the open circuit switch.
B	$V_2 = 0\ V$	With the switch in the closed position, current flows in the circuit. The switch contacts ideally will have no resistance when closed, so the voltage drop across the contacts will be 0 V.
B	$V_3 = 8\ V$	With the switch closed, current can flow in the circuit. The amount of voltage drop across R_1 will be 8 V. This can be calculated using Ohm's law: Voltage Drop = Resistance × Current $\qquad$ = 4 Ω × 2 A (see note below) $\qquad$ = 8 V drop Note: To calculate total circuit current, use this formula: $\qquad I_T = V_T \div R_T$
B	$V_4 = 4\ V$	With the switch closed, current can flow in the circuit. The amount of voltage drop across R_2 will be 4 V. This can be calculated using Ohm's law: Voltage Drop = Resistance × Current $\qquad$ = 2 Ω × 2 A $\qquad$ = 4 V drop R_1 and R_2 are of different resistances, so each will have a voltage drop proportional to its resistance. In a series circuit, the higher resistance will have a greater proportion of the voltage drop. You will notice that R_1 has twice the amount of resistance that R_2 has; thus it takes twice the amount of voltage to push current through R_1 as it does through R_2. Summing the voltage drops of R_1 and R_2 will equal the supply voltage: V_T = The sum of the voltage drops in a series circuit $\qquad$ = VD R_1 + VD R_2 $\qquad$ = 8 V + 4 V $\qquad$ = 12 V

FIGURE 37-8 shows that the resistors in the series circuit have different values; R_1 is 4 ohms and R_2 is 2 ohms. **TABLE 37-9** lists the circuit voltages and provides an explanation for each.

▶ Current Exercises

In this section, the exercises are designed to explain the use of the DVOM when taking DC current measurements. Undertaking the exercises will improve your understanding of Ohm's law and current measurements. Examples are given to demonstrate measuring current and to show the magnetic fields produced around a conductor when current flows. It is important to understand that current is the same in all parts of a properly working series circuit. Always remember that an ammeter must be connected in series within the circuit. That means that the circuit must be broken in two and each end of the ammeter connected to one of the two broken ends. This method will ensure that all of the current flowing through the circuit flows through the ammeter.

In this exercise, voltage and current measurements will be taken. For voltage measurements, select "auto range volts DC" on the DVOM, and connect the red lead to V/Ω and the black lead to COM. For current measurements, select "auto range amps DC" on the DVOM. Connect the red lead to the A socket and the black lead to the COM socket. If using a manual-range DVOM, you will need to select an appropriate range.

FIGURE 37-9 shows a circuit with a single resistor with a 12-volt DC supply. The DVOM will be used to measure both voltage and current. **TABLE 37-10** provides an explanation of the DVOM readings and shows how they relate to Ohm's law.

Measuring Current

To conduct this exercise, the DVOM must be set to read "DC amps." The red lead will be connected to the A socket and the black lead connected to the COM socket. If using a manual-range DVOM, select an appropriate range. If unsure which range is appropriate, start with the largest range and work down.

FIGURE 37-10 shows a circuit with two resistors in series with a 12-volt DC supply. The DVOM can be connected in various parts of the circuit to measure the current flow. **TABLE 37-11** shows the results and an explanation of the ammeter readings in a series circuit.

TABLE 37-10: Explanation of DVOM Readings in Figure 37-9

Measurements	Explanation
$V_1 = 12\ V$	With the switch closed, current will flow through the resistor. The amount of voltage drop across R_1 will be 12 V—the full battery voltage. This can be calculated using Ohm's law: Voltage Drop = Resistance × Current 　　　　= 2 Ω × 6 A (see note below) 　　　　= 12 V drop Note: To calculate total circuit current, use this formula: $I_T = V_T \div R_T$ 　　= 12 ÷ 2 Ω 　　= 6 A
$A_1 = 6\ A$	With the switch closed, the current flow through the resistor will be 6 amps. Since there is only one resistor in the circuit, its current flow will be the same as total current flow for the circuit.

FIGURE 37-9 Measuring voltage and current flow in a circuit with a single resistor and a 12-volt DC supply.

FIGURE 37-10 Measuring amperage in a circuit with two resistors in series with a 12-volt DC supply.

TABLE 37-11: Explanation of DVOM Readings in Figure 37-10

Measured Current	Explanation
A_1 = 2 A	With the switch closed, the current will flow through the series circuit. The amount of current flow through R_1 will be 2 A, or 2000 milliamps (mA). This can be calculated using Ohm's law. As this is a series circuit, the current flow in the circuit will be the same in all parts of the circuit. To calculate the current flow in the series circuit: Current = Voltage ÷ Resistance = 12 V ÷ 6 Ω (see note below) = 2 A Note: To calculate the total circuit current, use this formula: $I_T = V_T ÷ R_T$
A_2 = 2 A	With the switch closed, the current flow will be the same in all parts of the series circuit; therefore, current flow on the ammeter will always be the same regardless of its position in the circuit. The same current flow will be read on A_1, A_2, and A_3.

Applied Math

AM-9: Mentally: The technician can mentally divide decimal and whole numbers to determine conformance with the manufacturer's specifications.
In this scenario, the technician is using a DVOM to measure cooling fan current flow in amps, and will determine circuit resistance in ohms using Ohm's law.

The first step is to locate proper service information for the vehicle that would cover the following items: fuse block diagram, cooling fan circuit diagram, and specifications or current flow for cooling fan motor. The cooling fan relay will then be removed. The DVOM will be set up to measure current by placing the red lead to the 10A connection on the meter. The black lead will be placed in the COM connection. In this testing procedure, the DVOM is connected in series with the red lead in socket 30 and the black lead in socket 87. With the cooling fan motor in operation, the technician observes a reading of 3 amps. The specifications for this vehicle call for a range of 2.3–4.6 amps to operate the cooling fan motor.

To determine the resistance of this circuit, we will use the formula, R = V/A. This is a form of Ohm's law (Voltage = Amps × Resistance); R = 12 volts/3 amps =

4 ohms of resistance. The technician was able to calculate this mentally using Ohm's law. In this example, whole numbers were used but a similar procedure would be used with decimals. For example, if the resistance was 3.5 volts, our formula would be R = 12 volts/3.5 amps = 3.42 ohms. For the decimal portion of this example, the technician may need a calculator, but mentally, the formula would be used.

Applied Math

AM-10: Whole Numbers: The technician can multiply whole numbers to determine differences for comparison with the manufacturer's specifications.
An automotive battery is composed of six individual cell compartments within a case. The individual cells are joined by cell connectors in series with one another. Each cell has an open circuit voltage of approximately 2.1 volts at 80° Fahrenheit. When fully charged, a 12-volt automotive battery has an actual open circuit voltage of 12.6 volts at 80°. For easy calculations with whole numbers, we have 2 volts × 6 = 12 volts, which is why we refer to it as a 12-volt battery.

A technician was in the process of checking valve springs for proper tension during the overhaul of a V-8 engine. The valve springs did not meet manufacturer's specifications and all new valve springs are needed. There are four valve springs per cylinder × eight cylinders. We have whole numbers to multiply, which can be written as 4 × 8=32. A quantity of 32 new valve springs is needed to complete the cylinder head work.

Current and Magnetic Fields

In this example, a relay controlled by a switch will be used to switch the current through a resistor. The compass is used to demonstrate that a magnetic field is produced around the relay winding when the current flows through it. To conduct this experiment, set the DVOM to measure "DC amps." Connect the red lead to the A socket and the black lead to the COM socket. If using a manual-range DVOM, select an appropriate range.

FIGURE 37-11 shows a circuit with a relay controlled by a switch and a single resistor with a 12-volt DC supply. The compass is used to show that when energized the relay winding produces a magnetic field. The DVOM will be used to measure current. **TABLE 37-12** shows the current flow through the circuit and provides an explanation of the circuit, current flow, and how Ohm's law calculations can be used.

FIGURE 37-11 Measuring amperage in a circuit with a relay controlled by a switch and a single resistor with a 12-volt DC supply.

TABLE 37-12: Explanation of DVOM Readings in Figure 37-11

Measured Current	Explanation
A_1 = 200 mA	When the switch is closed, the current will flow through the relay winding. The magnetic field generated by current flowing through the winding will cause the main relay contacts to close, which in turn will supply current to the resistor. The compass positioned near the winding will change its heading indicating the presence of a magnetic field from the winding. The amount of current through the relay winding is 200 mA. The resistance of the winding can also be calculated using Ohm's law if the current flow through the winding resistance is known: $$R = V \div I$$ $$= 12 \div 0.2\,A$$ $$= 60\,\Omega$$
A_2 = 6 A	With the switch closed, the relay contact will close and the current flow through the resistor will be 6 A. As there is only one resistor in the circuit, its current flow will be the same as total current flow for the circuit. To calculate the current flow in the resistor circuit, use this formula: $$Current = Voltage \div Resistance$$ $$= 12\,volts \div 2\,\Omega$$ $$= 6\,A$$

▶ Resistance Exercises

In this section, the exercises are designed to explain the use of the DVOM in measuring resistance. Resistance measurements are used to check components or circuits against the manufacturer's specifications; for example, the resistance of sensors. Examples are given to demonstrate measuring resistance and to describe how the resistance affects current flow. It is important to understand that current flow is inversely proportional to resistance. The higher the resistance, the less current that will flow. The reverse is also true: The lower the resistance, the higher the current flow.

Measuring Resistance

In this exercise, a resistance measurement will be taken. For resistance measurements, you need to select "auto range Ω" on the DVOM, and connect the red lead to V/Ω and the black lead to COM. If using a manual-range DVOM, select an appropriate range by starting at the highest range and working your way down. Resistance measurements should only be taken with power disconnected, and ideally, with the component disconnected from the circuit.

FIGURE 37-12 shows a circuit with a lamp in series with a resistor and a 12-volt DC supply. The DVOM will be used to measure resistance. **TABLE 37-13** shows the measurement that can be expected from the circuit.

FIGURE 37-12 Measuring resistance in a circuit with a lamp in series with a resistor and a 12-volt DC supply.

TABLE 37-13: Explanation of DVOM Readings in Figure 37-12

Measurement	Explanation
$R_1 = 100\,\Omega$	The switch should be open to measure resistance. If possible, one lead of the resistor should be disconnected from the circuit. The DVOM leads should be connected to the V/Ω and COM sockets. The DVOM switch should be placed in the Ω or resistance position. Reversing the DVOM connections will have no effect on the DVOM reading.

FIGURE 37-13 Measuring volts, amps, and ohm in a circuit with a 100 ohm resistor and a 12-volt DC supply.

Resistance Effects on Current— Exercise 1

In this exercise, resistance, voltage, and current measurements will be taken. For resistance and voltage measurements, select "auto range volts DC" on the DVOM, and connect the red lead to the V/Ω and the black lead to COM. Always make resistance measurements with the component disconnected from the circuit. For current measurements, select "auto range amps DC" on the DVOM. The red lead will be connected to the A socket and the black lead connected to the COM socket. If using a manual-range DVOM, select an appropriate range.

FIGURE 37-13 shows a circuit with a resistor and a 12-volt DC supply. The DVOM will be used to measure resistance, voltage, and current. **TABLE 37-14** shows the measurements that a DVOM would read in the circuit, explains the readings, and describes how Ohm's law is applied.

Resistance Effects on Current— Exercise 2

In this exercise, resistance, voltage, and current measurements will be taken. For resistance and voltage measurements, you will need to select "auto range volts DC" on the DVOM, and connect the red lead to V/Ω and the black lead to COM. Always make resistance measurements with the component disconnected from the circuit. For current measurements, select "auto range amps DC" on the DVOM. The red lead will be connected to the A socket and the black lead connected to

TABLE 37-14: Explanation of DVOM Readings in Figure 37-13

Measurements	Explanation
$R_1 = 100\,\Omega$	The switch should be open to measure resistance. If possible, one lead of the resistor should be disconnected from the circuit. Reversing the DVOM connections will have no effect on the DVOM reading. Resistance can be calculated if the voltage and current are known: Resistance = Voltage ÷ Current = 12 V ÷ 0.12 A = 100 Ω
$V_1 = 12\,V$	With the switch closed, $V_1 = 12$ V. This can also be calculated if the current flow and resistance are known: Voltage Drop = Resistance × Current = 100 Ω × 0.12 A = 12 V drop Note: In practice, fuses have a very low resistance and, therefore, will have a very small voltage drop.
$A_1 = 0.12\,A$	With the switch closed, $A_1 = 0.12$ A. To calculate the current flow: Current = Voltage ÷ Resistance = 12 V ÷ 100 Ω = 0.12 A

FIGURE 37-14 Measuring volts, amps, and ohm in a circuit with a 1,000 ohm resistor and a 12-volt DC supply.

FIGURE 37-15 Measuring volts, amps, and ohm in a circuit with a 100 Ω resistor and a 12-volt DC supply in series with an LED.

the COM socket. If using a manual-range DVOM, select an appropriate range.

FIGURE 37-14 shows a circuit with a resistor and a 12-volt DC supply. The DVOM will be used to measure resistance, voltage, and current. **TABLE 37-15** shows the measurements of the circuit by a DVOM, explains the measurement, and describes how Ohm's law is applied.

Resistance Effects on Current—Exercise 3

In this exercise, resistance, voltage, and current measurements will be taken. For resistance and voltage measurements, you will need to select "auto range volts DC" on the DVOM, and connect the red lead to V/Ω and the black lead to COM. Always make resistance measurements with the component disconnected from the circuit. For current measurements, select "auto range amps DC" on the DVOM. Connect the red lead to the A socket and the black lead to the COM socket. If using a manual-range DVOM, select an appropriate range.

FIGURE 37-15 shows a circuit with a resistor and a 12-volt DC supply in series with a light-emitting diode (LED). The DVOM will be used to measure resistance, voltage, and current through R_1, a 100-ohm resistor in Figure 37-15. **TABLE 37-16** provides the measurement taken of the circuit by a DVOM, explains the circuit and the measurements, and describes how Ohm's law is applied.

TABLE 37-15: Explanation of DVOM Readings in Figure 37-14

Measurements	Explanation
$R_1 = 1000\ \Omega$, or 1 kΩ	The switch should be open to measure resistance. If possible, one lead of the resistor should be disconnected from the circuit. Resistance can be calculated if the voltage and current are known: Resistance = Voltage ÷ Current = 12 V ÷ 0.012 A = 1000 Ω
$V_1 = 12\ V$	With the switch closed, $V_1 = 12\ V$. This can also be calculated if the current flow and resistance are known: Voltage Drop = Resistance × Current = 1000 Ω × 0.012 A = 12 V drop
$A_1 = 0.012\ A$	With the switch closed, $A_1 = 0.012\ A$. To calculate the current flow: Current = Voltage ÷ Resistance = 12 V ÷ 1000 Ω = 0.012 A

Resistance Effects on Current—Exercise 4

In this exercise, measurements for resistance, voltage, and current will be taken. For resistance and voltage

TABLE 37-16: Explanation of DVOM Readings in Figure 37-15

Measurements	Explanation
$R_1 = 100\ \Omega$	The switch should be open to measure resistance. If possible, one lead of the resistor should be disconnected from the circuit. Resistance can be calculated if the voltage and current are known: Resistance = Voltage ÷ Current = 0.202 V ÷ 0.00202 A = 100 Ω
$V_1 = 0.202\ V$	With the switch closed, $V_1 = 0.202$ V. This can also be calculated if the current flow and resistance are known: Voltage Drop = Resistance × Current = 100 Ω × 0.00202 A = 0.202 V drop
$A_1 = 2.02\ mA$	With the switch closed, $A_1 = 0.00202$ A, or 2.02 mA or 2020 μA. Note: The resistance of the LED cannot be measured, so its resistance is being ignored for this experiment. To calculate the current flow: Current = Voltage ÷ Resistance = 0.202 V ÷ 100 Ω = 0.00202 A

TABLE 37-17: Explanation of DVOM Readings in Figure 37-16

Measurements	Explanation
$R_1 = 10,000\ \Omega$, or 10 kΩ	The switch should be open to measure resistance. If possible, one lead of the resistor should be disconnected from the circuit. Note: The resistance of the LED cannot be measured, so its resistance is being ignored for this experiment. Resistance can be calculated if the voltage and current are known: Resistance = Voltage ÷ Current = 9.75 V ÷ 975 μA = 10 kΩ
$V_1 = 9.75\ V$	With the switch closed $V_1 = 9.75$ V. This can also be calculated if the current flow and resistance are known: Voltage Drop = Resistance × Current = 10 kΩ × 975 μA = 9.75 V drop
$A_1 = 975\ \mu A$	With the switch closed, $A_1 = 975$ μA. For a given voltage, circuit current decreases as resistance increases. To calculate the current flow through R_1: Current = Voltage ÷ Resistance = 9.75 V ÷ 10 kΩ = 975 μA

FIGURE 37-16 Measuring volts, amps, and ohms in a circuit with a 10 kΩ resistor and a 12-volt DC supply in series with an LED.

measurements, you will need to select "auto range volts DC" on the DVOM, and connect the red lead to V/Ω and the black lead to COM. Always make resistance measurements with the component disconnected from the circuit. For current measurements, select "auto range amps DC" on the DVOM. Connect the red lead to the A socket and the black lead to the COM socket. If using a manual-range DVOM, select an appropriate range.

FIGURE 37-16 shows a circuit with a resistor and a 12-volt DC supply in series with an LED. The DVOM will be used to measure resistance, voltage, and current through R_1, a 10 kΩ resistor. **TABLE 37-17** provides the measurement taken of the circuit by a DVOM, explains the circuit and the measurements, and describes how Ohm's law is applied.

Series Circuit Exercises

These series circuit exercises are designed to explain the use of the DVOM for current and voltage in a series circuit. Current and voltage measurements are often used to diagnose faults in electrical circuits. Examples are given to demonstrate the use of measuring voltage and current and to describe how current flows and how voltage drop and current are affected by resistance in a series circuit.

It is important to remember that current flow is the same in all parts of a good series circuit, and the sum of the voltage drops across individual resistors in a series circuit is equal to the supply voltage. The exercise also examines how the addition of resistors in a series circuit affects the current flow and voltage drops.

Series Circuit—Exercise 1

In this exercise, voltage measurements will be taken from the series circuit. To measure voltage drop, set the DVOM on the voltage range. Select "auto range volts DC" on the DVOM, and connect the black lead to COM and the red lead to V/Ω. You can measure voltage drop across components, connectors, or cables, but the current has to be flowing to get accurate measurements. Remember, the leads when checking voltage can be placed in either direction. Just remember which way you placed them so you understand what the reading means. We will show the red lead on the most positive side for purposes of the following diagrams.

FIGURE 37-17 shows a typical circuit with a battery supply, fuse, switch, and resistor. In figure A the switch is open, and in figure B the switch is closed. **TABLE 37-18** provides the measurements taken of the circuit by a DVOM, explains the circuit and the measurements, and describes how Ohm's law is applied.

Series Circuit—Exercise 2

In this exercise, voltage measurements will be taken from the series circuit. To measure voltage drop, the DVOM must be set on the voltage range. Select "auto range volts DC" on the DVOM, and connect the black lead to COM and the red lead to V/Ω. Voltage drop can be measured across components, connectors, or cables only when current is flowing. Remember, the leads when checking voltage can be placed in either direction. Just remember which way you placed them so you understand what the reading means. We will show the red lead on the most positive side for purposes of the following diagrams.

FIGURE 37-17 Measuring voltage in a typical circuit with a battery supply, fuse, switch, and resistor.

TABLE 37-18: Explanation of DVOM Readings in Figure 37-17

Figure	Measured Voltage	Explanation
A B	$V_1 = 12\,V$ $V_1 = 12\,V$	V_1 is measuring the voltage directly across the supply battery, so the voltage reading will be the battery voltage regardless of the position of the switch.
A	$V_2 = 0\,V$	With the switch in the open position, no current flows in the circuit. The red DVOM lead is connected directly to the battery via the cable, while the black lead is connected to the switch side of the fuse. Because the switch is open, there is no access to the negative side of the battery; therefore, the DVOM will read 0 V.

(continues)

TABLE 37-18: Explanation of DVOM Readings in Figure 37-17 *(continued)*

Figure	Measured Voltage	Explanation
B	$V_2 = 0\ V$	With the switch in the closed position, current flows in the circuit. Ideally, the fuse has no resistance, so the voltage drop across the fuse will be 0 V. Note: In practice, fuses will have a very low resistance and will therefore have a very small voltage drop.
A	$V_3 = 12\ V$	With the switch in the open position, no current flows in the circuit. The red DVOM lead is connected directly to the battery via the cable, while the black lead is connected to the negative battery terminal via the resistor. Because no current flows in the circuit, there is no voltage drop across the resistor; therefore, the entire battery voltage drop is across the open circuit switch.
B	$V_3 = 0\ V$	With the switch in the closed position, current flows in the circuit. The switch contacts ideally will have no resistance when closed, so the voltage drop across the contacts will be 0 V.
A	$V_4 = 0\ V$	With the switch in the open position, no current flows in the circuit. Because no current flows in the circuit, there is no voltage drop across the resistor. This can be calculated using Ohm's law: Voltage Drop = Resistance × Current = 10 Ω × 0 A = 0 V drop
B	$V_4 = 12\ V$	With the switch closed, current can flow in the circuit. The amount of voltage drop across R_1 will be 12 volts. This can be calculated using Ohm's law: Voltage Drop = Resistance × Current = 10 Ω × 1.2 A = 12 V drop
B	$V_T = 12\ V$	The sum of all the voltage drops in Figure 37-17B should add up to the supply voltage. This can be calculated using Ohm's law: V_T = VD Fuse + VD Switch + VD Resistor = 0 + 0 + 12 = 12 V

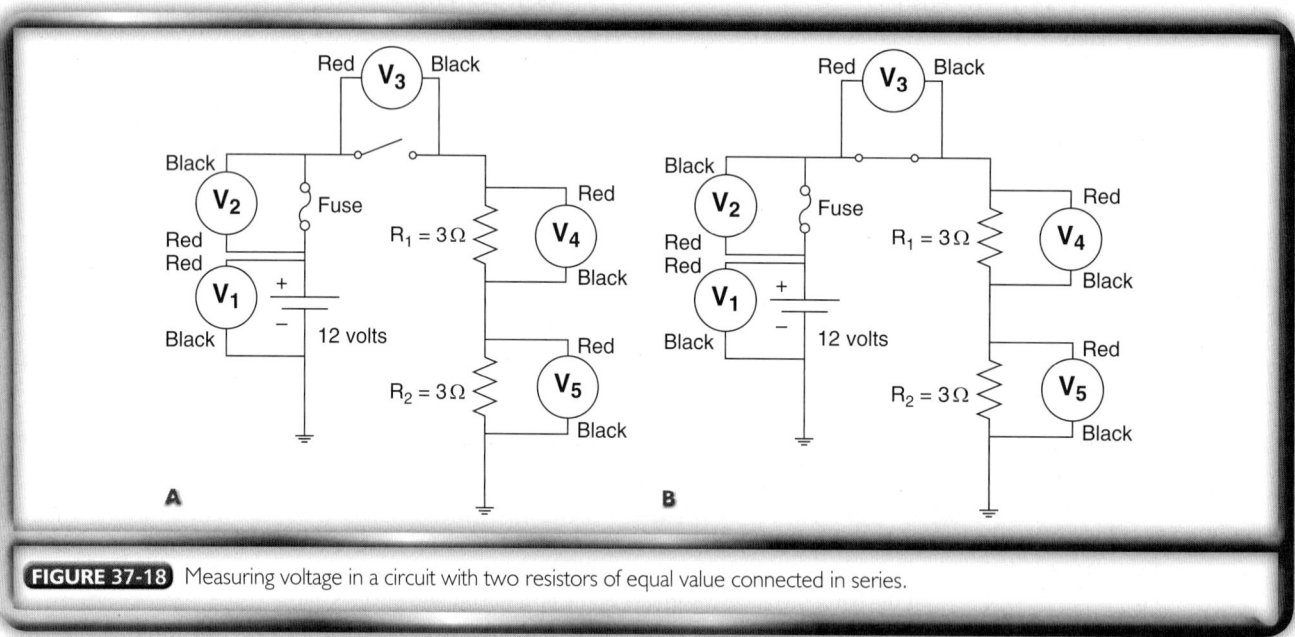

FIGURE 37-18 Measuring voltage in a circuit with two resistors of equal value connected in series.

FIGURE 37-18 shows two resistors of equal value connected in series. **TABLE 37-19** provides the measurements taken of the circuit by a DVOM, explains the circuit and the measurements, and describes how Ohm's law is applied.

Series Circuit—Exercise 3

In this exercise, voltage measurements will be taken from the series circuit. To measure voltage drop, the DVOM is used on the voltage range. Select "auto range volts DC" on the DVOM, and connect the black lead

TABLE 37-19: Explanation of DVOM Readings in Figure 37-18

Figure	Measured Voltage	Explanation
A B	$V_1 = 12$ V $V_1 = 12$ V	V_1 is measuring the voltage directly across the supply battery, so the voltage reading will be the battery voltage regardless of the position of the switch.
A	$V_2 = 0$ V	With the switch in the open position, no current flows in the circuit. The red DVOM lead is connected directly to the battery via the cable, while the black lead is connected to the switch side of the fuse. Because the switch is open, there is no access to the negative side of the battery; therefore, the DVOM will read 0 V.
B	$V_2 = 0$ V	With the switch in the closed position, current flows in the circuit. The fuse ideally has no resistance, so the voltage drop across the fuse will be 0 V.
A	$V_3 = 12$ V	With the switch in the open position, no current flows in the circuit. The red DVOM lead is connected directly to the battery via the cable, while the black lead is connected to the negative battery terminal via the series resistors. Because no current flows in the circuit, there is no voltage drop across the resistor; therefore, the entire battery voltage drop is across the open circuit switch.
B	$V_3 = 0$ V	With the switch in the closed position, current flows in the circuit. The switch contacts ideally will have no resistance when closed, so the voltage drop across the contacts will be 0 V.
A	$V_4 = 0$ V	With the switch in the open position, no current flows in the circuit. Because no current flows in the circuit, there is no voltage drop across the resistor. This can be calculated using Ohm's law: Voltage Drop = Resistance × Current $= 3\,\Omega \times 0$ A $= 0$ V drop
B	$V_4 = 6$ V	With the switch closed, current can flow in the circuit. The amount of voltage drop across R_1 will be 6 V. This can be calculated using Ohm's law: Voltage Drop = Resistance × Current $= 3\,\Omega \times 2$ A (see note below) $= 6$ V drop Note: To calculate total circuit current, use this formula: $I_T = V_T \div R_T$ $= 12 \div 6$ $= 2$ A
A	$V_5 = 0$ V	With the switch in the open position, no current flows in the circuit. Because no current flows in the circuit, there is no voltage drop across the resistor. This can be calculated using Ohm's law: Voltage Drop = Resistance × Current $= 3\,\Omega \times 0$ A $= 0$ V drop
B	$V_5 = 6$ V	With the switch closed, current can flow in the circuit. The amount of voltage drop across R_2 will be 6 volts. This can be calculated using Ohm's law: Voltage Drop = Resistance × Current $= 3\,\Omega \times 2$ A (see note below) $= 6$ V drop Note: To calculate total circuit current, use this formula: $I_T = V_T \div R_T$ $= 12 \div 6$ $= 2$ A
B	$V_T = 12$ V	The sum of all the voltage drops in Figure 37-18B should add up to the supply voltage. This can be calculated using Ohm's law: $V_T = $ VD Fuse + VD Switch + VD R_1 + VD R_2 $= 0 + 0 + 6 + 6$ $= 12$ V

to COM and the red lead to V/Ω. Voltage drop can be measured across components, connectors, or cables as long as current is flowing in the circuit. The red lead of the DVOM is normally connected to the positive side of the component.

FIGURE 37-19 shows two resistors in a series; this time each resistor is of a different value. **TABLE 37-20** provides the measurement taken of the circuit by a DVOM, explains the circuit and the measurements, and describes how Ohm's law is applied.

Series Circuit—Exercise 4

In this exercise, voltage measurements will be taken from the series circuit. To measure voltage drop, the DVOM must be set on the voltage range. Select "auto range volts DC" on the DVOM, and connect the black lead to COM and the red lead to V/Ω. Voltage drop can be measured across components, connectors, or cables as long as current is flowing in the circuit. The red lead of the DVOM is normally connected to the positive side of the component.

FIGURE 37-19 Measuring voltage in a circuit with two unequal resistors in series.

TABLE 37-20: Explanation of DVOM Readings in Figure 37-19

Figure	Measured Voltage	Explanation
A	$V_1 = 12 V$	V_1 is measuring the voltage directly across the supply battery, so the voltage reading will be the battery voltage regardless of the position of the switch.
B	$V_1 = 12 V$	
A	$V_2 = 0 V$	With the switch in the open position, no current flows in the circuit. The red DVOM lead is connected directly to the battery via the cable, while the black lead is connected to the switch side of the fuse. Because the switch is open, there is no access to the negative side of the battery; therefore, the DVOM will read 0 V.
B	$V_2 = 0 V$	With the switch in the closed position, current flows in the circuit. The fuse ideally has no resistance, so the voltage drop across the fuse will be 0 V.
A	$V_3 = 12 V$	With the switch in the open position, no current flows in the circuit. The red DVOM lead is connected directly to the battery via the cable, while the black lead is connected to the negative battery terminal via the series resistors. Because no current flows in the circuit, there is no voltage drop across the resistor; therefore, the entire battery voltage drop is across the open circuit switch.

Figure	Measured Voltage	Explanation
B	$V_3 = 0$ V	With the switch in the closed position, current flows in the circuit. The switch contacts ideally will have no resistance when closed, so the voltage drop across the contacts will be 0 V.
A	$V_4 = 0$ V	With the switch in the open position, no current flows in the circuit. Because no current flows in the circuit, there is no voltage drop across the resistor. This can be calculated using Ohm's law: Voltage Drop = Resistance × Current = 4 Ω × 0 A = 0 V drop
B	$V_4 = 4$ V	With the switch closed, current can flow in the circuit. The amount of voltage drop across R_2 will be 4 V. This can be calculated using Ohm's law: Voltage Drop = Resistance × Current = 4 Ω × I A (see note below) = 4 V drop Note: To calculate total circuit current, use this formula: $I_T = V_T \div R_T$ = 12 ÷ 12 = I A
A	$V_5 = 0$ V	With the switch in the open position, no current flows in the circuit. Because no current flows in the circuit, there is no voltage drop across the resistor. This can be calculated using Ohm's law: Voltage Drop = Resistance × Current = 8 Ω × 0 A = 0 V drop
B	$V_5 = 8$ V	With the switch closed, current can flow in the circuit. The amount of voltage drop across R_1 will be 8 V. This can be calculated using Ohm's law: Voltage Drop = Resistance × Current = 8 Ω × I A (see note below) = 8 V drop Note: To calculate total circuit current, use this formula: $I_T = V_T \div R_T$ = 12 ÷ 12 = I A
B	$V_T = 12$ V	The sum of all the voltage drops in Figure 37-19B should add up to the supply voltage. Also, note that the higher value series resistor has the higher voltage drop in the series circuit. This can be calculated using Ohm's law: V_T = VD Fuse + VD Switch + VD R_1 + VD R_2 = 0 + 0 + 4 + 8 = 12 V

FIGURE 37-20 shows diagrams of a circuit with two series resistors; R_1 is now an 8-ohm resistor, and R_2 is a 4-ohm resistor. In Figure 37-20A the switch is open, and in Figure 37-20B the switch is closed. **TABLE 37-21** provides the measurement taken of the circuit by a DVOM, explains the circuit and the measurements, and describes how Ohm's law is applied.

Series Circuit—Exercise 5

In this exercise, voltage measurements will be taken from the series circuit. To measure voltage drop, set the DVOM on the voltage range. Select "auto range volts DC" on the DVOM, and connect the black lead to COM and the red lead to V/Ω. Voltage drop can be measured across

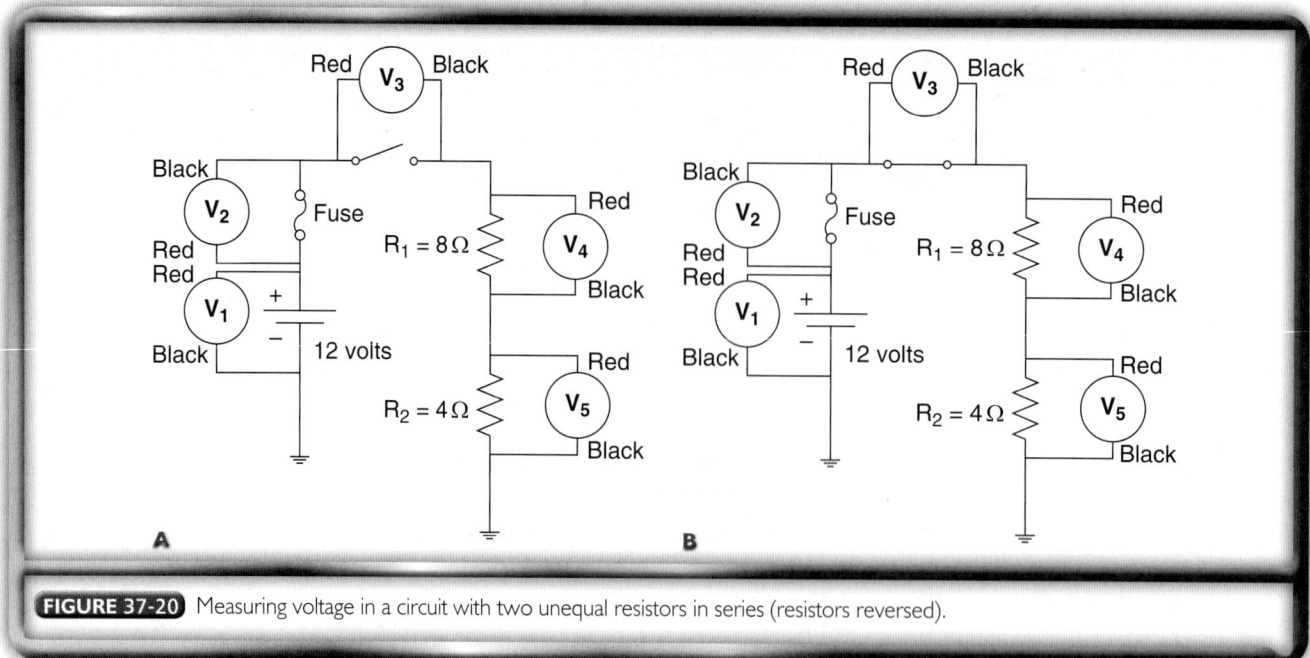

FIGURE 37-20 Measuring voltage in a circuit with two unequal resistors in series (resistors reversed).

TABLE 37-21: Explanation of DVOM Readings in Figure 37-20

Figure	Measured Voltage	Explanation
A	$V_1 = 12\,V$	V_1 is measuring the voltage directly across the supply battery, so the voltage reading will be the battery voltage, regardless of the position of the switch.
B	$V_1 = 12\,V$	
A	$V_2 = 0\,V$	With the switch in the open position, no current flows in the circuit. The red DVOM lead is connected directly to the battery via the cable, while the black lead is connected to the switch side of the fuse. Because the switch is open, there is no access to the negative side of the battery; therefore, the DVOM will read 0 V.
B	$V_2 = 0\,V$	With the switch in the closed position, current flows in the circuit. The fuse ideally has no resistance, so the voltage drop across the fuse will be 0 V.
A	$V_3 = 12\,V$	With the switch in the open position, no current flows in the circuit. The red DVOM lead is connected directly to the battery via the cable, while the black lead is connected to the negative battery terminal via the series resistors. Because no current flows in the circuit, there is no voltage drop across the resistor; therefore, the entire battery voltage drop is across the open circuit switch.
B	$V_3 = 0\,V$	With the switch in the closed position, current flows in the circuit. The switch contacts ideally will have no resistance when closed, so the voltage drop across the contacts will be 0 V.
A	$V_4 = 0\,V$	With the switch in the open position, no current flows in the circuit. Because no current flows in the circuit, there is no voltage drop across the resistor. This can be calculated using Ohm's law: Voltage Drop = Resistance × Current $= 8\,\Omega \times 0\,A$ $= 0\,V$ drop
B	$V_4 = 8\,V$	With the switch closed, current can flow in the circuit. The amount of voltage drop across R_1 will be 8 volts. This can be calculated using Ohm's law: Voltage Drop = Resistance × Current $= 8\,\Omega \times 1\,A$ (see note below) $= 8\,V$ drop Note: To calculate total circuit current, use this formula: $I_T = V_T \div R_T$ $= 12 \div 12$ $= 1\,A$

Figure	Measured Voltage	Explanation
A	$V_5 = 0\ V$	With the switch in the open position, no current flows in the circuit. Because no current flows in the circuit, there is no voltage drop across the resistor. This can be calculated using Ohm's law: $$\text{Voltage Drop} = \text{Resistance} \times \text{Current}$$ $$= 4\ \Omega \times 0\ A$$ $$= 0\ V\ \text{drop}$$
B	$V_5 = 4\ V$	With the switch closed, current can flow in the circuit. The amount of voltage drop across R_2 will be 4 V. This can be calculated using Ohm's law: $$\text{Voltage Drop} = \text{Resistance} \times \text{Current}$$ $$= 4\ \Omega \times 1\ A\ (\text{see note below})$$ $$= 4\ V\ \text{drop}$$ Note: To calculate total circuit current, use this formula: $$I_T = V_T \div R_T$$ $$= 12 \div 12$$ $$= 1\ A$$
B	$V_T = 12\ V$	The sum of all the voltage drops in Figure 37-20B should add up to the supply voltage. Also, note that the higher value series resistor has the higher voltage drop in the series circuit. This can be calculated using Ohm's law: $$V_T = \text{VD Fuse} + \text{VD Switch} + \text{VD } R_1 + \text{VD } R_2$$ $$= 0 + 0 + 8 + 4$$ $$= 12\ V$$

FIGURE 37-21 Voltage measurements in a series circuit with unequal resistances.

components, connectors, or cables as long as current is flowing in the circuit. The red lead of the DVOM is normally connected to the more positive side of the component.

FIGURE 37-21 shows diagrams of a series circuit with three unequal resistances. **TABLE 37-22** provides the voltage measurements taken of the circuit by a DVOM, explains the circuit and the measurements, and describes how Ohm's law is applied.

TABLE 37-22: Explanation of DVOM Readings in Figure 37-21

Figure	Measured Voltage	Explanation
A B	$V_1 = 12\,V$ $V_1 = 12\,V$	V_1 is measuring the voltage directly across the supply battery, so the voltage reading will be the battery voltage regardless of the position of the switch.
A	$V_2 = 0\,V$	With the switch in the open position, no current flows in the circuit. The red meter lead is connected directly to the battery via the cable, while the black lead is connected to the switch side of the fuse. Because the switch is open, there is no access to the negative side of the battery; therefore the meter will read 0 V.
B	$V_2 = 0\,V$	With the switch in the closed position, current flows in the circuit. The fuse ideally has no resistance, so the voltage drop across the fuse will be 0 V.
A	$V_3 = 12\,V$	With the switch in the open position, no current flows in the circuit. The red meter lead is connected directly to the battery via the cable, while the black lead is connected to the negative battery terminal via the series resistors. Because no current flows in the circuit, there is no voltage drop across the resistor; therefore, the entire battery voltage drop is across the open circuit switch.
B	$V_3 = 0\,V$	With the switch in the closed position, current flows in the circuit. The switch contacts ideally will have no resistance when closed so the voltage drop across the contacts will be 0 V.
A	$V_4 = 0\,V$	With the switch in the open position, no current flows in the circuit. Because no current flows in the circuit, there is no voltage drop across the resistor. This can be calculated using Ohm's law: $\text{Voltage Drop} = \text{Resistance} \times \text{Current}$ $= 5\,\Omega \times 0\,A$ $= 0\,V \text{ drop}$
B	$V_4 = 2\,V$	With the switch closed, current can flow in the circuit. The amount of voltage drop across R_1 will be 2.4 V. This can be calculated using Ohm's law: $\text{Voltage Drop} = \text{Resistance} \times \text{Current}$ $= 2\,\Omega \times 1\,A \text{ (see note below)}$ $= 2\,V \text{ drop}$ Note: To calculate total circuit current, use this formula: $I_T = V_T \div R_T$ $= 12 \div 12$ $= 1\,A$
A	$V_5 = 0\,V$	With the switch in the open position, no current flows in the circuit. Because no current flows in the circuit, there is no voltage drop across the resistor. This can be calculated using Ohm's law: $\text{Voltage Drop} = \text{Resistance} \times \text{Current}$ $= 5\,\Omega \times 0\,A$ $= 0\,V \text{ drop}$
B	$V_5 = 5\,V$	With the switch closed, current can flow in the circuit. The amount of voltage drop across R_2 will be 4.8 V. This can be calculated using Ohm's law: $\text{Voltage Drop} = \text{Resistance} \times \text{Current}$ $= 5\,\Omega \times 1\,A \text{ (see note below)}$ $= 5\,V \text{ drop}$ Note: To calculate total circuit current, use this formula: $I_T = V_T \div R_T$ $= 12 \div 12$ $= 1\,A$
A	$V_6 = 0\,V$	With the switch in the open position, no current flows in the circuit. Because no current flows in the circuit, there is no voltage drop across the resistor. This can be calculated using Ohm's law: $\text{Voltage Drop} = \text{Resistance} \times \text{Current}$ $= 5\,\Omega \times 0\,A$ $= 0\,V \text{ drop}$

Figure	Measured Voltage	Explanation
B	$V_6 = 5\,V$	With the switch closed, current can flow in the circuit. The amount of voltage drop across R_3 will be 4.8 V. This can be calculated using Ohm's law: $$\text{Voltage Drop} = \text{Resistance} \times \text{Current}$$ $$= 5\,\Omega \times 1\,A \text{ (see note below)}$$ $$= 5\,V \text{ drop}$$ Note: To calculate total circuit current, use this formula: $$I_T = V_T \div R_T$$ $$= 12 \div 12$$ $$= 1\,A$$
B	$V_T = 12\,V$	The sum of all the voltage drops in Figure 37-21B should add up to the supply voltage. This can be calculated using Ohm's law: $$V_T = \text{VD Fuse} + \text{VD Switch} + \text{VD } R_1 + \text{VD } R_2 + \text{VD } R_3$$ $$= 0 + 0 + 2 + 5 + 5$$ $$= 12\,V$$ Also, note that the higher value series resistor has the higher voltage drop in the series circuit. Resistors of the same value have the same voltage drop.

FIGURE 37-22 Current flow in a circuit with three unequal resistors in series.

Series Circuit—Exercise 6

To conduct this exercise, the DVOM must be set to read "DC amps." The red lead will be connected to the A socket and the black lead connected to the COM socket.

If using a manual-range DVOM, select an appropriate range.

FIGURE 37-22 shows a circuit with three resistors in series with a 12-volt DC supply. The DVOM can be connected in various parts of the circuit to measure the

TABLE 37-23: Explanation of DVOM Readings in Figure 37-22

Figure	Measured Current	Explanation
A	$A_1 = 0$ A	With the switch off, the current flow through A_1 will be 0 A.
B	$A_1 = 1$ A	With the switch closed, the current will flow through the series circuit. The amount of current flowing through the resistors will be proportional to the 50 Ω of total resistance and will be 0.24 A. This can be calculated using Ohm's law: Current = Voltage ÷ Resistance = 12 V ÷ 12 Ω (see note below) = 1 A Note: To calculate the total circuit current, use this formula: $I_T = V_T \div R_T$
B	$A_2 = 1$ A	With the switch closed, the current flow will be the same in all parts of the series circuit; therefore, current flow on the ammeter will always be the same, regardless of its position in the circuit. The same current flow will be read on A_1, A_2, A_3, A_4, and A_5.

current flow. In Figure 37-22A the switch is open, and in Figure 37-22B the switch is closed. **TABLE 37-23** provides the measurement taken of the circuit by a DVOM, explains the circuit and the measurements, and describes how Ohm's law is applied.

Parallel Circuit Exercises

In this section, the exercises are designed to explain the use of the DVOM in measuring volts, amps, and ohms in a parallel circuit. Parallel circuits are commonly used in the vehicle's electrical system, especially for lights. Understanding how they work and the relationship between voltage, amperage, and resistance in parallel circuits will help you to diagnose electrical faults. Examples are given to demonstrate how to measure volts, amps, and ohms and to show how current flows and voltage drops in a parallel circuit. It is important to remember the laws for a parallel circuit: resistance goes down when more parallel paths are added, current flow from individual legs add up in parallel, and voltage stays the same at all common parallel circuit inputs. The following exercises help to reinforce the understanding of these laws.

Parallel Circuits—Exercise 1

In this exercise, voltage measurements will be taken from the parallel circuit. To measure voltage drop, the DVOM must be set up to measure voltage. Select "auto range volts DC" on the DVOM, and connect the black lead to COM and the red lead to V/Ω. Voltage drop can be measured across components, connectors, or cables as long as current is flowing in the circuit. The red lead of the DVOM is normally connected to the positive side of the component. **FIGURE 37-23** shows three resistors connected in parallel across a 12-volt supply. **TABLE 37-24** provides the measurements taken of the circuit by a

FIGURE 37-23 Measuring voltage across three unequal resistors connected in parallel across a 12-volt supply.

DVOM, explains the circuit and the measurements, and describes how Ohm's law is applied.

Parallel Circuits—Exercise 2

To conduct this exercise, the DVOM must be set to read "DC amps." Connect the red lead to the A socket and the black lead to the COM socket. If using a manual-range DVOM, select an appropriate range.

FIGURE 37-24 shows a circuit with a single resistor and a 12-volt DC supply. The DVOM can be connected in various parts of the circuit to measure the current flow. **TABLE 37-25** provides the measurements taken of the circuit by a DVOM, explains the circuit and the measurements, and describes how Ohm's law is applied.

Parallel Circuits—Exercise 3

To conduct this exercise, the DVOM must be set to read DC amps. Connect the red lead to the A socket and the

TABLE 37-24: Explanation of DVOM Readings in Figure 37-23

Measured Voltage	Explanation
$V_1 = 12$ V	V_1 is measuring the voltage directly across the supply battery, so the voltage reading will be the battery voltage, regardless of the position of the switch.
$V_2 = 12$ V	With the switch closed, current can flow in the circuit. The amount of voltage drop across R_1 will be 12 V. The amount of current through R_1 can be calculated using Ohm's law: $$IR_1 = VR_1 \div R_1$$ $$= 12\text{ V} \div 12\ \Omega$$ $$= 1\text{ A}$$ If the current and resistance are known, then voltage drop can be calculated: $$VR_1 = IR_1 \times \text{Resistance } R_1$$ $$= 1\text{ A} \times 12\ \Omega$$ $$= 12\text{ V}$$
$V_3 = 12$ V	The amount of voltage drop across R_2 will be 12 V. The amount of current through R_2 can be calculated using Ohm's law: $$IR_2 = VR_2 \div R_2$$ $$= 12\text{ V} \div 6\ \Omega$$ $$= 2\text{ A}$$ If the current and resistance are known, then voltage drop can be calculated: $$VR_2 = IR_2 \times \text{Resistance } R_2$$ $$= 2\text{ A} \times 6\ \Omega$$ $$= 12\text{ V}$$
$V_4 = 12$ V	The amount of voltage drop across R_3 will be 12 V. The amount of current through R_2 can be calculated using Ohm's law: $$IR_3 = VR_3 \div R_3$$ $$= 12\text{ V} \div 2\ \Omega$$ $$= 6\text{ A}$$ If the current and resistance are known, then voltage drop can be calculated: $$VR_3 = IR_3 \times \text{Resistance } R_3$$ $$= 6\text{ A} \times 2\ \Omega$$ $$= 12\text{ V}$$

From the above, we can determine that the voltage drop across a parallel branch is the same for all components, regardless of their resistance. The total circuit current flow is equal to the sum of the individual branch currents.

FIGURE 37-24 Measuring amperage in a circuit with a single resistor and a 12-volt DC supply.

TABLE 37-25: Explanation of DVOM Readings in Figure 37-24

Measured Current	Explanation
$A_1 = 3$ A	With the switch closed, current will flow through the circuit. The amount of current flow through R_1 will be 3 A. As this is a series circuit, the current flow in the circuit will be the same in all parts of the circuit. This can be calculated using Ohm's law: $$\text{Current} = \text{Voltage} \div \text{Resistance}$$ $$= 12\text{ V} \div 4\ \Omega$$ $$= 3\text{ A}$$

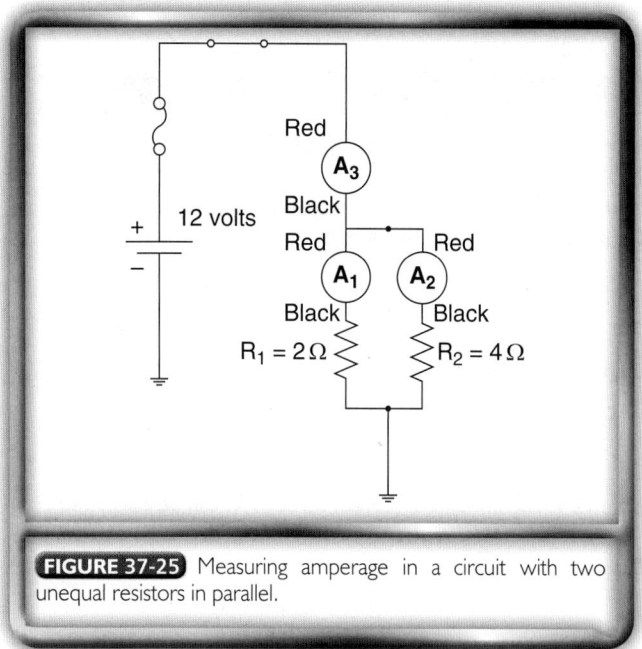

FIGURE 37-25 Measuring amperage in a circuit with two unequal resistors in parallel.

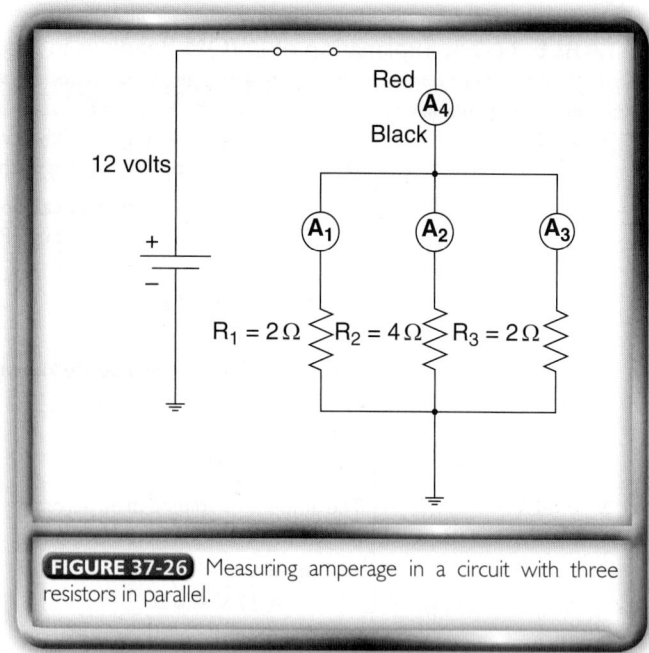

FIGURE 37-26 Measuring amperage in a circuit with three resistors in parallel.

TABLE 37-26: Explanation of DVOM Readings in Figure 37-25

Measured Current	Explanation
$A_3 = 9\,A$	With the switch closed, the current will flow through the circuit. Due to its position in the circuit, A_3 will measure total current flow or I_T and will be 9 A.
$A_1 = 6\,A$	A_1 is positioned so that it only measures the current flow through R_1, and its current flow will be 6 A.
$A_2 = 3\,A$	A_2 is positioned so that it only measures the current flow through R_2, and its current flow will be 3 A.

The current flows can be calculated using Ohm's law in two ways:

Calculate current flow through each resistor and add them together:	Calculate total resistance R_T and use it to then calculate I_T total current:
$IR_1 = VR_1 \div R_1$ $= 12\,V \div 2\,\Omega$ $= 6\,A$ $IR_2 = VR_2 \div R_2$ $= 12\,V \div 4\,\Omega$ $= 3\,A$ $I_T = IR_1 + IR_2$ $= 6 + 3$ $= 9\,A$	$R_T = \dfrac{1}{\dfrac{1}{R_1} + \dfrac{1}{R_2}}$ $R_T = \dfrac{1}{\dfrac{1}{2} + \dfrac{1}{4}}$ $R_T = 1.3333\,\Omega$ $I_T = V_T \div R_T$ $= 12\,V \div 1.3333\,\Omega$ $= 9.0002\,A$

Note: R_T is 1.3 recurring. It has been rounded to four decimal places; this gives the variance of 0.0002 in the I_T calculation. In practice, this small variation can be ignored.

black lead to the COM socket. If using a manual-range DVOM, select an appropriate range.

FIGURE 37-25 has two resistors in parallel. The additional resistor in parallel will cause an increase in circuit current flow and a decrease in total circuit resistance. **TABLE 37-26** provides the measurements taken of the circuit by a DVOM, explains the circuit and the measurements, and describes how Ohm's law is applied.

Parallel Circuits—Exercise 4

To conduct this exercise, the DVOM must be set to read DC amps. Connect the red lead to the A socket and the black lead to the COM socket. If using a manual-range DVOM, select an appropriate range.

FIGURE 37-26 has three resistors in parallel. With the additional resistors, the total circuit current will increase while the total circuit resistance will decrease. **TABLE 37-27** provides the measurements taken of the circuit by a DVOM, explains the circuit and the measurements, and describes how Ohm's law is applied.

Parallel Circuits—Exercise 5

To conduct this experiment, the DVOM must be set to read DC amps. Connect the red lead to the A socket and the black lead to the COM socket. If using a manual-range DVOM, select an appropriate range.

FIGURE 37-27 has four resistors in parallel. With the additional resistors, the total circuit current will increase while the total circuit resistance decreases even more.

FIGURE 37-27 Measuring amperage in a circuit with four resistors in parallel.

TABLE 37-27: Explanation of DVOM Readings in Figure 37-26

Measured Current	Explanation
$A_4 = 15$ A	With the switch closed, the current will flow through the circuit. Due to its position in the circuit, A_3 will measure total current flow or I_T and will be 15 A. The total current in the circuit increases as additional load or resistances are added in parallel.
$A_1 = 6$ A	A_1 is positioned so that it only measures the current flow through R_1, and its current flow will be 6 A.
$A_2 = 3$ A	A_2 is positioned so that it only measures the current flow through R_2, and its current flow will be 3 A.
$A_3 = 6$ A	A_3 is positioned so that it only measures the current flow through R_3, and its current flow will be 6 A.

The current flows can be calculated using Ohm's law in two ways:

Calculate current flow though each resistor and add them together:	Calculate total resistance R_T and use it to then calculate I_T total current:
$IR_1 = VR_1 \div R_1$ $\quad = 12\,V \div 2\,\Omega$ $\quad = 6$ A $IR_2 = VR_2 \div R_2$ $\quad = 12\,V \div 4\,\Omega$ $\quad = 3$ A $IR_3 = VR_3 \div R_3$ $\quad = 12\,V \div 2\,\Omega$ $\quad = 6$ A $I_T = IR_1 + IR_2 + IR_3$ $\quad = 6 + 3 + 6$ $\quad = 15$ A	$R_T = \dfrac{1}{\dfrac{1}{R_1} + \dfrac{1}{R_2} + \dfrac{1}{R_3}}$ $R_T = \dfrac{1}{\dfrac{1}{2} + \dfrac{1}{4} + \dfrac{1}{2}}$ $R_T = 0.8\,\Omega$ $I_T = V_T \div R_T$ $\quad = 12\,V \div 0.8\,\Omega$ $\quad = 15$ A

TABLE 37-28: Explanation of DVOM Readings in Figure 37-27

Measured Current	Explanation
$A_5 = 27$ A	With the switch closed, the current will flow through the circuit. The amount of current flow through A_5 will be 27 A. The total current in the circuit increases as additional load or resistances are added in parallel.
$A_1 = 6$ A	A_1 is positioned so that it only measures the current flow through R_1, and its current flow will be 6 A.
$A_2 = 3$ A	A_2 is positioned so that it only measures the current flow through R_2, and its current flow will be 3 A.
$A_3 = 6$ A	A_3 is positioned so that it only measures the current flow through R_3, and its current flow will be 6 A.
$A_4 = 12$ A	A_4 is positioned so that it only measures the current flow through R_4, and its current flow will be 12 A.

The current flows can be calculated using Ohm's law in two ways:

Calculate current flow though each resistor and add them together:	Calculate total resistance R_T and use it to then calculate I_T total current:
$IR_1 = VR_1 \div R_1$ $\quad = 12\,V \div 2\,\Omega$ $\quad = 6\,A$ $IR_2 = VR_2 \div R_2$ $\quad = 12\,V \div 4\,\Omega$ $\quad = 3\,A$ $IR_3 = VR_3 \div R_3$ $\quad = 12\,V \div 2\,\Omega$ $\quad = 6\,A$ $IR_4 = VR_4 \div R_4$ $\quad = 12\,V \div 1\,\Omega$ $\quad = 12\,A$ $I_T = IR_1 + IR_2 + IR_3 + IR_4$ $\quad = 6 + 3 + 6 + 12$ $\quad = 27\,A$	$R_T = \dfrac{1}{\dfrac{1}{R_1}+\dfrac{1}{R_2}+\dfrac{1}{R_3}+\dfrac{1}{R_4}}$ $R_T = \dfrac{1}{\dfrac{1}{2}+\dfrac{1}{4}+\dfrac{1}{2}+\dfrac{1}{1}}$ $R_T = 0.4444\,\Omega$ $I_T = V_T \div R_T$ $\quad = 12\,V \div 0.4444\,\Omega$ $\quad = 27.0027\,A$ Note: R_T is 0.4 recurring. It has been rounded to four decimal places; this gives the variance of 0.0027 in the I_T calculation. In practice, this small variation can be ignored.

TABLE 37-28 provides the measurements taken of the circuit by a DVOM, explains the circuit and the measurements, and describes how Ohm's law is applied.

Notice how the current in the circuit increases with each additional load. This is also what happens with a power strip; each time an additional item is plugged in, the current increases. Overloading the circuit may cause the protection device to trip or in extreme cases could cause a fire. Never overload an electrical circuit, whether on a vehicle or in the shop.

Applied   Math

AM-45: <, >, =, e.g.: The technician can interpret symbols to determine conformance with the manufacturer's specifications.

In this scenario, we will look at three of the most common symbols used in technical manuals.

<, > These symbols are lesser than: <, and greater than: >. An example of this would be describing the specification for the maximum limit for an A.C. voltage from an alternator (< .5 volts A.C).

= This symbol is a mathematical symbol used to indicate equality. An example would be the formula for Ohm's law which is $E = I \times R$

"e.g." means "for example." It comes from the Latin expression, *exempli gratia*, for the sake of an example. An example of this would be: The technician will use a precision measuring instrument (e.g., micrometer) to measure the part.

Applied   Math

AM-47: Specified Symbols: The technician can use conventional symbols (E for voltage, etc.) to solve problems using formulas such as Ohm's law, E=IR.

Voltage, current, and resistance have a specific relationship to each other. This concept forms the basis for electrical diagnosis.

George Ohm discovered that it takes one volt to push one amp through one ohm of resistance. Ohm's law is $E = I \times R$ or Voltage = Amps $\times$ Resistance. If you know two of the three values for an electrical circuit, you can find the missing one. To find resistance, the formula is volts divided by amps. To find voltage, the formula is amp multiplied by resistance. To find current, or amps, the formula is volts divided by resistance.

In this example, we have an electrical circuit that has a current flow of 2 amps being pushed by 12 volts. We want to find the resistance. Our formula will be R=V/A:

R = V/A

R= 12 volts/2 amps

R= 6 ohms, which is our circuit resistance.

Series-Parallel Circuit Exercise

In this section, the exercises are designed to explain the use of the DVOM in measuring current and voltage in a series-parallel circuit. Series-parallel circuits are found in vehicles, such as in dash light dimmer circuits, although they are not as common as parallel circuits. Typically, a series-parallel circuit occurs when unwanted resistance shows up in series with a parallel circuit. For example, if the brake light switch contacts become worn out, they can create a voltage drop in series with the brake lights, causing them all to be dimmer than they should be. Understanding how series-parallel circuits work and the relationships between current flow, voltage drops, and resistance will help you diagnose these types of electrical faults. Examples are given to demonstrate measuring voltage and current and to show how current flow and voltage drop are affected by resistance in a series-parallel circuit. It is important to understand that to analyze and calculate current flow and voltage drop, the total resistance of the circuit needs to be

considered. The voltage drop across the parallel branch will be the same for all resistances in the parallel branch, and the sum of the current flow in each branch is equal to the total parallel circuit current flow. These exercises also examine how the addition of resistors in series to a parallel circuit affects the circuit current flow and circuit resistance.

In this exercise, voltage and current measurements will be taken from the series-parallel circuit formed by resistors R_1, R_2, R_3, and R_4. See **FIGURE 37-28**. To measure voltage drop, the DVOM must be set on the voltage range. Select "auto range volts DC" on the DVOM, and connect the black lead to COM and the red lead to V/Ω. Voltage drop can be measured across components, connectors, or cables as long as current is flowing in the circuit. The red lead of the DVOM is normally connected to the positive side of the component. To measure current, the DVOM must be set to read DC amps. Connect the red lead to the A socket and the black lead to the COM socket. If using a manual-range DVOM, select an appropriate range. **TABLE 37-29** provides the measurements taken of the circuit by a DVOM,

FIGURE 37-28 A series-parallel circuit formed by resistors R_1, R_2, R_3, and R_4.

TABLE 37-29: Explanation of DVOM Readings in Figure 37-28

Figure	Measurement	Explanation
A	$V_1 = 0$ V	With the switch off, there will be no current flow in the circuit, and as V_1 is positioned after the switch, the voltmeter red lead has no circuit to the positive battery terminal.
B	$V_1 = 6.31$ V	With the switch closed, the current can flow in the circuit. The amount of voltage drop across R_1 will be 6.31 V. This can be calculated with Ohm's law, which will require a number of steps:

(continues)

TABLE 37-29: Explanation of DVOM Readings in Figure 37-28 *(continued)*

Figure	Measurement	Explanation
		1. Calculate total resistance R_T. To do so, first calculate the resistance of the parallel branch: $$R_{PB} = \frac{1}{\frac{1}{R_1}+\frac{1}{R_2}+\frac{1}{R_3}}$$ $$R_{PB} = 1\frac{1}{100}+\frac{1}{1000}+\frac{1}{10000}$$ $$R_{PB} = 90.0901\ \Omega$$ Next, sum the series resistor R_1 and the total resistance of the parallel branch R_{PB}: $$R_T = R_1 + R_{PB}$$ $$= 100 + 90.0901$$ $$= 190.0901\ \Omega$$ 2. Now that resistance total is known, the total circuit current can be calculated I_T: $$I_T = V_T \div R_T$$ $$= 12\ V \div 190.0901$$ $$= 0.0631\ A,\ or\ 63.1\ mA$$ 3. Voltage drop across R_1 can now be calculated using the total current flow I_T and the resistance of R_1 (see note). $$VD\ R_1 = I_T \times R_1$$ $$= 0.0631 \times 100$$ $$= 6.31\ V$$ Note: I_T is used because R_1 is in series with the parallel branches; therefore, current flow through R_1 will be the same as I_T
A	$V_2 = 0\ V$	With the switch off, there will be no current flow in the circuit, and as V_2 is positioned after the switch, the voltmeter red lead has no circuit to the positive battery terminal.
B	$V_2 = 5.6847\ V$	The amount of voltage drop across the parallel branches will be 5.6847 V. This can also be calculated with Ohm's law by using the figures calculated earlier in the experiment. Resistance of the parallel branches and I_T: $$R_{PB} = 90.0901\ \Omega$$ $$I_T = 0.0631\ A,\ or\ 63.1\ mA$$ $$VD\ Parallel\ Branch = I_T \times Resistance\ R_{PB}$$ $$= 0.0631\ A \times 90.0901\ \Omega$$ $$= 5.6847\ V$$
B	$A_1 = 0.0568\ A$	Current flow through R_2 on the left side of the parallel branches is 0.0568 A, or 56.8 mA. This can also be calculated with Ohm's law. To calculate current flow through R_2, the voltage drop across R_2 and its resistance are used: $$IR_2 = VDR_2 \div R_2$$ $$= 5.6847 \div 100$$ $$= 0.0568\ A,\ or\ 56.8\ mA$$
B	$A_2 = 0.0057\ A$	Current flow through R_3 on the left side of the parallel branch is 0.0057 A, or 5.7 mA. This can also be calculated with Ohm's law. To calculate current flow through R_2, the voltage drop across R_2 and its resistance are used: $$IR_2 = VDR_2 \div R_2$$ $$= 5.6847 \div 1000$$ $$= 0.0057\ A,\ or\ 5.7\ mA$$

Figure	Measurement	Explanation
B	$A_3 = 0.0006$ A	Current flow through R_3 on the left side of the parallel branches is 0.0006 A, or 0.6 mA. This can also be calculated with Ohm's law. To calculate current flow through R_2, the voltage drop across R_2 and its resistance are used: $$IR_2 = VDR_2 \div R_2$$ $$= 5.6847 \div 10,000$$ $$= 0.0006 \text{ A, or } 0.6 \text{ mA}$$
B		The series current in the circuit splits across the parallel branches of resistance. The amount of current through each part of the parallel branch is dependent on the resistance of each branch. The higher the resistance of the branch, the less current that flows through it. Adding the parallel branches' current equals the total current I_T: $$I_T = IR_2 + IR_3 + IR_4$$ $$= 0.0568 + 0.0057 + 0.0006$$ $$= 0.0631 \text{ A, or } 63.1 \text{ mA}$$

explains the circuit and the measurements, and describes how Ohm's law is applied. Please note that calculations have been rounded to four decimal places.

 ## Variable Resistors

In this section, the exercises are designed to explain the use of the DVOM in measuring voltage and amperage in a circuit with a variable resistor, as well as a potentiometer. Understanding the relationships between voltage, resistance, and current as the variable resistor is adjusted will help you diagnose electrical faults. Examples are given to demonstrate measuring voltage and current and to show how current flows and how voltage drop and current are affected by the position of the wiper of the potentiometer. It is important to understand that as the position of the wiper of the potentiometer is changed, so too is the voltage and current flow to a load connected to the potentiometer.

Applied Math

AM-12: Mentally: *The technician can mentally multiply numbers that include decimal numbers to determine conformance with the manufacturer's specifications.*
In this scenario, a technician is conducting a voltage drop test on the positive side of the starter circuit. As described in the text, a voltage drop occurs when current flows through a resistance. The higher the resistance, the higher the voltage drops. So we could say that a voltage drop test checks for excessive resistance in a

circuit. When testing for a voltage drop, always have the circuit operating. That way, the circuit will have current flowing so any voltage drops will be evident.
The technician begins by placing the DVOM selector on the 20V DC scale. He starts testing at the battery and checks step by step all the way to the starter motor using the direct method of voltage drop testing. The technician uses both test leads on the same side of the circuit. The tests include battery post to cable clamp, cable clamp to the end of the cable at the solenoid, and from the solenoid to the starter motor terminal. At each of the test points, an assistant cranked the engine over to load the circuit. Each of the three connection points had a reading of 0.30 volt. The technician mentally multiplied those decimal numbers to obtain a total of 0.90 volt (3 × 0.30 volt = 0.90 volt). This reading is in excess of the manufacturer's specifications of 0.5 volt. The technician will now clean each of the connection points and retest.

Variable Resistors Exercise

In this exercise, a variable resistor is used as a potentiometer, or voltage divider. For voltage measurements, you will need to select "auto range volts DC" on the DVOM and connect the red lead to V/Ω and the black lead to COM. For current measurements, select "auto range milliamps DC" on the DVOM. Connect the red lead to the A socket and the black lead to the COM socket. If using a manual-range DVOM, you will need to select an appropriate range.

FIGURE 37-29 shows circuits with a 250-Ω variable resistor in the circuit as a voltage divider with a 12-volt DC supply. In Figure 37-29A, the wiper of the variable resistor is set so that minimum voltage will occur at V_1. In Figure 37-29B, the variable resistor is set so that maximum voltage can occur at V_1. Only two states for the variable resistor are analyzed in this section, although the

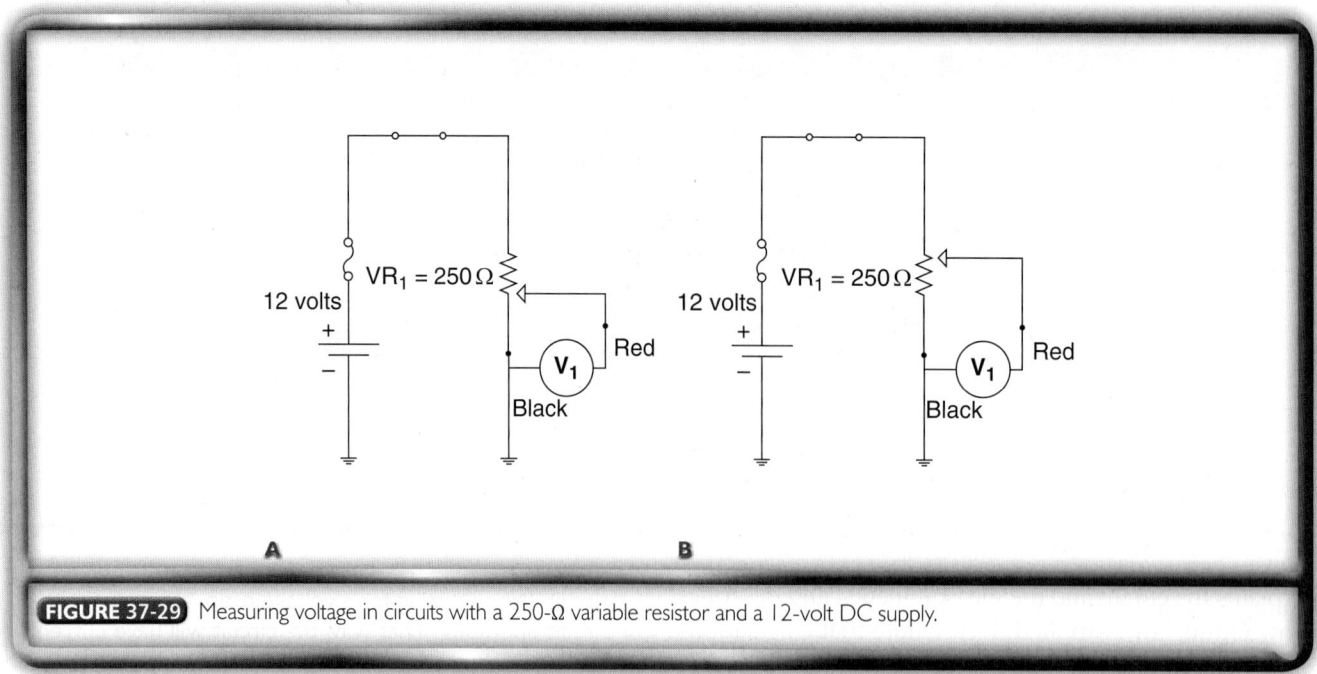

FIGURE 37-29 Measuring voltage in circuits with a 250-Ω variable resistor and a 12-volt DC supply.

TABLE 37-30: Explanation of DVOM Readings in Figure 37-29

Figure	Voltage Measurements	Explanation
A	V_1 = 0.005 V	With the switch in the closed position, current can flow in the circuit. The fixed resistor (250 Ω) between the two outer legs of the variable resistor will have a consistent current flow and voltage drop of 12 V. The variable wiper provides a varying voltage output depending on the wiper's position, which can be read on V_1. With the wiper in the position shown in Figure 37-29A, V_1 will read very close to ground potential because almost all of the voltage was dropped through the fixed resistor; hence, the reading of 0.005 V.
B	V_1 = 12 V	With the wiper in the position shown in Figure 37-29B, V_1 will read very close to supply potential; hence, the reading of 12 V.

variable resistor is continuously variable and the voltage at V_1 will vary depending on the position of the wiper. The DVOM will be used to measure voltage V_1, a voltage divider output from the variable resistor VR_1. **TABLE 37-30** provides the measurements taken of the circuit by a DVOM and explains the circuit and the measurements. When the wiper in Figure 37-29 is at the upper or lower limits, in practice there may be a small amount of the variable resistor left on the outer edges.

 Capacitors

In this section, the exercises are designed to explain the use of the DVOM in current and voltage in a circuit with a capacitor connected in series with a lamp. It will give you an understanding of how voltage and current change as the capacitor charges. Understanding how capacitors work in a circuit will help you to diagnose

electrical faults. Examples are given to demonstrate measuring voltage and current and to show how current flow and voltage drop change as a capacitor charges. It is important to understand that as the capacitor charges, the voltage drop across it increases and the current flow decreases.

Capacitors—Exercise 1

In this exercise, a capacitor is connected in series with a lamp. For voltage measurements, select "auto range volts DC" on the DVOM and connect the red lead to V/Ω and the black lead to COM. For current measurements, select "auto range milliamps DC" on the DVOM. Connect the red lead to the A socket and the black lead to the COM socket. If using a manual-range DVOM, select an appropriate range. **FIGURE 37-30** shows a capacitor connected in series with a lamp with a 12-volt DC supply. The DVOM will be used to measure voltage across the capacitor and lamp

FIGURE 37-30 Measuring voltage in a circuit with a capacitor connected in series with a lamp and a 12-volt DC supply.

TABLE 37-31: Explanation of DVOM Readings in Figure 37-30

Measurement	Explanation
V_1	The instant the switch is in the closed position, current can flow in the circuit as the capacitor is discharged. Current flow will initially be high and will gradually reduce as the capacitor charges As the lamp is in a series, the capacitor will light up brightly in the first instance. As the capacitor charges, the current will decrease and the lamp will become dim before going out as the capacitor fully charges and the current flow stops. V_1 will initially be very low and then increase as the capacitor charges.
V_2	V_2 will initially be high as high current through the lamp produces a high voltage drop. As the capacitor charges, the current flow reduces, as does the voltage drop across the lamp. When the capacitor is fully charged, V_2 will reduce to 0 V, and V_1 will be 12 V.
A_1	A_1 will initially be high. As the capacitor charges, it will reduce until it reaches 0 V once the capacitor is fully charged.

when the switch is turned on. TABLE 37-31 provides the measurements taken of the circuit by a DVOM and explains the circuit and the measurements.

Waveforms and Scope Testing

Oscilloscopes are commonly referred to as lab scopes, or just scopes, and are a very important test instrument for vehicle diagnostics. An oscilloscope provides a graph of voltage values over a time period, typically called a waveform, and displays them on a screen. An oscilloscope has a screen, a number of control knobs or buttons, and test sockets to connect the probing leads into the scope FIGURE 37-31. There are many manufacturers of oscilloscopes, and the design and specifications of each will vary based on the speed and voltage of waveforms to be measured. Oscilloscopes can be designed to do general electronic measurements or specifically designed for automotive work. Automotive oscilloscopes have special ranges and leads to perform specific automotive measurements; for example, high-voltage probes measure ignition waveforms.

Oscilloscopes may be analog, displaying waveforms as they occur, or digital. Digital storage oscilloscopes (DSOs) can display waveforms as they occur and store the waveform for later analysis. DSOs are increasingly popular for automotive use because stored waveforms can be compared with known good waveforms. Scopes may incorporate their own screen, usually an LCD display, or connect to a computer by a USB cable and use the computer screen.

Oscilloscopes have a very fast sampling rate, which means they can take many samples per second and display the results on the screen. For example, some DSOs can take a sample every millionth of a second or even faster. Fast sample rates allow the oscilloscope to capture signals that occur for a very short time. The oscilloscope's sampling speed is a huge advantage over a DVOM,

FIGURE 37-31 Typical oscilloscope.

which may take a sample every 200 thousandths of a second. The oscilloscope can also display the waveform, which provides much more diagnostic information than a numerical reading on a DVOM.

Scopes usually have two or more channels. Four channels are common and are used to display up to four different waveforms at the same time. Multiple channels allow the timing of various waveforms to be compared to each other. The timing and relationships of each waveform can be compared to each other and to the manufacturer's specifications.

Voltage is displayed on the vertical axis, and time is displayed on the horizontal axis, or from left to right across the screen. The technician selects the appropriate voltage and time ranges for each axis to capture the waveform on the screen. The pattern can then be read as voltage changes that happen over a period of time. The divisions on the sides and bottom of the screen allow for the measurement of each section of the waveform.

Applied | **Math**

AM-13: Add/Subtract/Divide/Multiply: The technician can estimate the results of basic arithmetic operations and can accurately round numbers up or down.

The following scenario will give us a review of the application of basic arithmetic operations related to starter current draw. An automobile with a V8 engine has the manufacturer's specifications for starter current draw at 180 amps. The specifications allow for a tolerance of plus or minus 10%. The technician must determine whether the starter circuit will fall within manufacturer's specifications.

Specifications are 180 amps but we have a tolerance of plus or minus 10%. Let's determine what those numbers will be in terms of amps. 180 × .90 will give us the minus 10% factor. 180 × .90 = 162 amps. Now, for the plus 10% factor. 180 × 1.10 = 198 will give us the plus 10% factor. Now we know that the specifications for starter draw are 162–198 amps with 180 amps considered the ideal current draw, which could be rounded off to 160 and 200.

When the starter current draw is measured, it reads 310 amps. Our specifications were 198 amps maximum. If we subtract 198 from 310, we have 112 amps over the specifications, indicating a faulty starter motor or partially seized engine.

To accurately round numbers up or down, here are some tips:

- You can round numbers to give a rough idea of an amount or quantity.
- 862 bolts in stock are closer to 900 than to 800, so you could round to 900.
- A population of 76,310 could be rounded to 76,000.

Checking Circuit Waveforms

Automotive oscilloscopes tend to come in a kit with specialized leads and probes for connection into automotive-specific circuits. For example, there are ignition, fuel injection, current probes, temperature, and pressure sensors. Correct setup of an oscilloscope is essential to accurately read circuit waveforms without damage to the circuit being tested, or to the oscilloscope. The two critical settings are the voltage and the time base. Similar to any meter, the voltage scale of the expected reading needs to be set. It can be set manually, or the oscilloscope may have an automatic range function. Time base is the amount of time being read per division on the screen. The scope screen is typically split horizontally with 10 divisions. Oscilloscopes can measure very fast signals, and it is not unusual to have time base ranges from 100 nanoseconds per division to 200 seconds per division.

Oscilloscopes are capable of reading voltages as low as 50 millivolts up to maximum voltages of 50 or 100 volts. Sometimes on vehicles, higher voltages need to be measured. For example, the primary voltage of an ignition coil requires a higher voltage reading. In these circumstances, **attenuators** can be fitted to the probe leads to reduce the maximum voltage to safe levels for the oscilloscope to measure. An attenuator is a device that reduces the amount of voltage passing through it. For example, a 20:1 attenuator divides the amount of voltage passing through it by a factor of 20. Thus, 20 volts input will appear as an output of 1 volt. Always connect the oscilloscope leads according to the manufacturer's specifications. The correct connection of ground leads is important to ensure minimal interference in the waveform. In most cases, the ground lead should be connected directly to the negative battery terminal.

To check circuit waveforms, follow the steps in **SKILL DRILL 37-1**:

1. Determine the circuit to be tested and the likely voltages and frequency of the waveform to be measured. Set the voltage level and time base on the oscilloscope to begin measurements. **(Photo 1)**
2. Connect the leads to the points in the circuit to be measured. **(Photo 2)**
3. Capture waveforms from the circuit being tested.
4. Analyze the waveform, comparing it to the manufacturer's specifications or known good waveforms. Determine any necessary actions. **(Photo 3)**

SKILL DRILL 37-1   Checking Circuit Waveforms

1. Determine the circuit to be tested and the likely voltages and frequency of the waveform to be measured. Set the voltage level and time base.

2. Connect the leads to the points in the circuit to be measured.

3. Capture waveforms from the circuit being tested. Analyze the waveform, comparing it to the manufacturer's specifications or known good waveforms.

Applied | Math

AM-41: Proportion/Congruence: The technician can distinguish the congruence of measurements with tolerances specified by the manufacturer.

The word *congruence* comes from the word *congruent*, which means to agree or correspond with. A definition is "equal in size and shape."

In this segment we will consider the throttle position sensor (TPS). The throttle position sensor sends vital throttle plate position information to the powertrain control module (PCM). A TPS is a potentiometer that is a three-wire variable resistor used to monitor movement. The movement is the throttle shaft rotation in degrees. The PCM sends a 5-volt reference signal to the TPS sensor. There is also a ground wire and a signal return wire to the PCM.

A TPS can be tested to some degree with a DVOM, but the best test instrument is the oscilloscope. With this instrument, the technician can watch the signal. It should sweep up and down smoothly with no drop outs or spikes. This is where the congruence comes in. The performance of the TPS signal should be in a congruent style. The slope of the graph should agree or correspond with tolerances specified by the manufacturer. If so, we have congruence of measurements to meet manufacturer's specifications.

▶ Electrical Circuit Testing

Electrical circuit testing begins with understanding circuit types and how electricity behaves within them. Add to that the ability to use meters and oscilloscopes to measure the values of voltage, amperage, and resistance, along with understanding how to read wiring diagrams so you will know how the circuits are constructed, and you will be well on your way to diagnosing electrical faults successfully. Those are the concepts we will be exploring in this section. Feel free to refer back to the previous circuits to help you remember how electricity behaves, as well as how meters are hooked up for specific measurements. Let's kick this off by seeing how Ohm's law can help us predict the behavior of electricity.

Using Ohm's Law to Diagnose Circuits

Ohm's law can be used in two ways to help in diagnosing electrical circuit faults. The first is by using it to perform the math to predict and verify measurements. The second way is by using the relationships it demonstrates to guide you through the diagnosis process.

When using Ohm's law in the first way, it is used to calculate electrical quantities in a circuit and is valuable in cross-checking actual measured results within the circuit. For example, if the resistance and voltage of a circuit are known, then the theoretical current can be calculated using Ohm's law. The calculated result can then be compared to the measured results from an ammeter to determine if the circuit is functioning correctly. Technicians will often do a quick calculation, sometimes just in their head, to obtain an approximate value of an electrical quantity before they take actual measurements. Doing so allows them to anticipate what they will be measuring and to set the measuring tool to the correct range.

Always remember that a calculation may only yield an approximate value; in actual circuits, variations or tolerances exist in components, causing differences between calculated values and actual measurements.

Using Ohm's law the second way helps you to understand the relationship between volts, amps, and ohms. For example, if voltage stays the same but resistance decreases, amperage must increase. In the case of a short circuit, the resistance decreases and the amperage increases, potentially blowing the fuse. In the opposite scenario, where resistance increases, current flow decreases. This is the case when a corroded or loose connection introduces excessive resistance to the circuit. It also results in less electrical power (volts and amps) to operate the intended load.

What does Ohm's law tell us to expect when the voltage changes? If voltage decreases and the resistance stays the same, then amperage will decrease. This results in less power being able to operate the load. If the voltage increases and the resistance stays the same, then amperage will increase. If amperage and voltage both increase, then the electrical power operating the load will also increase. This condition can shorten the life of, or even burn out, the load.

So, how do amperage changes affect volts and amps? That is a good question. But if you think about it, amperage is a result of, or product of, the voltage and resistance. Amperage cannot exist without both voltage and resistance—a means of pushing the amperage (voltage) and a path for the amperage to flow (resistance). If you ask yourself, what is the amperage doing in a circuit? the answer will always be, it is doing whatever the voltage and resistance allow it to do. If the amperage is low, then you know that one of two conditions is present—either the voltage is low or the resistance is high. If the amperage is high, then either the voltage is high or the resistance is low. Understanding this relationship between volts, amps, and ohms will help you know what test you need to perform next during diagnosis.

Since amperage is a product of voltage and resistance, it is a good idea to keep your eye on the amperage. What this means is that if you have a circuit fault, you can generally see what the amperage is doing; it is either high or low. If you truly cannot see what the current is doing, like in a solenoid, you will have to measure it. But in most cases, you can see it; the fuse blew because the current was too high, the lights are dim because the current is too low, etc. If current is low (most common scenario), then Ohm's law tells you that it is because either the voltage is low or the resistance is high. On the flip side, if your eye determines that the current is high, then either the voltage is high or the resistance is low.

For example, let's say that the left front headlight is dim. Your eye determines that the current in that circuit is low. Thus, either the voltage is low or the resistance is high. Now you just have to test for those two things. Use a voltmeter to measure the voltage at the battery. If low, determine why the battery voltage is low. If good, check the voltage across both sides of the headlight with the circuit on. It should be within 1.0 volt of the battery voltage. If not, then switch to looking for the high resistance. This is accomplished by first measuring the voltage drop on each side of the headlight. If there is an excessive voltage drop on one side, follow the circuit back toward the battery to identify the cause. If the voltages on both sides of the headlight are within specifications, the problem is most likely the headlight itself. You may be able to check the resistance of the headlight itself and compare it to a known good bulb. Or you may have to measure the current flow through the bulb and compare that to specifications, since its resistance increases greatly due to heat when it is illuminated.

If the current flow appears too high, then the circuit may have too much voltage or too little resistance. Measuring the battery voltage is an easy way to check for too much voltage. Using an ohmmeter to check the resistance of the load and comparing that to specifications will tell you if it is shorted. If it is not, then use the ohmmeter to check the wire harness for any short circuit conditions.

To use Ohm's law to diagnose circuits, follow the steps in **SKILL DRILL 37-2**:

1. Identify the circuit to be tested and determine the expected voltage, current, and resistance of the component or circuit. Using Ohm's law, calculate the expected voltage, current flow, or resistance of the circuit.

2. Set up the DVOM for a continuity or resistance check. Make sure there is no power connected to any circuit that you test for continuity. Next prepare the DVOM for testing just like you did for voltage by inserting the black probe into the COM terminal and the red probe into the V/Ω terminal.

3. Turn the rotary dial of the DVOM to the mode for measuring ohms, which also measures continuity. The digital display should now give you an "Out of Limits" reading indicating that there is not a continuous circuit connection between the two probes (some meters show "OL," and others place "1" on the left of the display). Touch the probe ends together. The display should now give a zero reading, or very close to zero, which indicates no resistance. This means there is a continuous circuit

through the probes. Some DVOMs also indicate continuity with an audible tone.

4. Check a fuse. One typical use of the test is to determine whether a fuse needs to be replaced. If the fuse has been overloaded and "blown," then it will no longer complete a circuit when a DVOM is used to test it. To check this, place the black probe on one end of the fuse and the red probe on the other. If the fuse is functioning correctly, then the reading will be zero, indicating a complete, or closed, circuit. If the fuse is open, then there will be no reading and no tone, indicating an incomplete, or open, circuit.

5. A continuity or resistance test is used to check for a broken circuit caused by a break in a cable or lead or caused by a component becoming disconnected. The same test can also confirm whether there is continuity between components that are not supposed to be connected, a condition known as a short circuit. This test can also be used to check circuits that are suspected to have a high resistance.

6. Compare the test results with the calculated results from step 1. Key things to note are any variations between the calculated and measured results. Determine whether the variations can be accounted for within the tolerances of the components or whether a fault exists.

> **TECHNICIAN TIP**

When using an ohmmeter to measure resistance or to check continuity with a DVOM, the circuit must be powered down to avoid a wrong reading. The best way to ensure this is by disconnecting the component from the circuit.

Using Wiring Diagrams to Diagnose Electrical Circuits

Vehicle wiring diagrams or schematics may be available as paper-based manuals, computer programs, or online resources. They are produced by manufacturers and some aftermarket publishing companies. Increasingly, repair information is accessed via the Internet using subscription services that are regularly updated. To use wiring diagrams, an understanding of the symbols, abbreviations, and connector coding used in the diagrams is required. These are usually found on the diagram or in information pages. See the chapter Lighting Systems for examples of some of the common symbols used.

Reading a wiring diagram is like reading a road map. There are a lot of interconnected circuits, wires, and components to decipher. Learning to read wiring diagrams takes a bit of time and experience, but knowing that circuits usually consist of a power source, a switch, a load, and a ground is a good start. Jorge Menchu of AESWave has been promoting a novel approach of using color crayons to help understand how a particular circuit in a wiring diagram operates. The following is a paraphrased version of that process.

Begin by printing out a copy of the wiring diagram for the circuit being diagnosed. Color all of the wires green that are directly connected to "ground". Color all of the wires red that are "hot" at all times. Color all of the wires orange that are "switched to power." Color all of the wires yellow that are "switched to ground." If there are any wires that reverse polarity, such as power window motor wires, mark those with side-by-side orange and yellow lines. Finally, color any variable wires, such as signal wires, blue.

Coloring the wires on the wiring diagram in this way does several things. First, it forces you to determine what each wire in the diagram does, which helps you get the total picture. Second, it helps to organize your thoughts so that you can understand how electricity flows through the circuit. Third, it helps to keep you from losing your place or forgetting what a particular wire does. And fourth, it can give you confidence that you have properly diagnosed the problem when you know why the circuit is not working properly and exactly where the problem is located **FIGURE 37-32**.

To use wiring diagrams to diagnose electrical circuits, follow the steps in **SKILL DRILL 37-3**:

1. Identify the correct wiring diagram for the vehicle and system circuit being repaired and print a copy.

FIGURE 37-32 Color coding of the wires helps to understand the circuit.

2 Color each wire (using the wiring diagram's color code key) on the wiring diagram for the circuit that requires diagnosis. Note components, wire coding, and harness connectors.

3 Determine circuit test points and their location on the wiring diagram. Find the same test point on the vehicle and perform the appropriate electrical test.

4 Depending on the results of the test, continue to use the wiring diagram to guide you in performing additional tests on the circuit until the fault has been located.

Using a DVOM to Measure Voltage

The electrical system is becoming increasingly complex on modern vehicles, and measuring voltages with a DVOM is a very common task when diagnosing electrical faults. For most measurements, set the DVOM to auto range for ease of use. Select DVOM leads and probe ends to match the task at hand; for example, if you need to take a measurement but require both hands to be free, use probe ends with alligator clips. Ensure that you do not exceed the maximum allowable voltage or current for the DVOM. If you are measuring high voltages, wear appropriate personal protective equipment, such as high-voltage safety gloves, long-sleeved shirts and pants, and protective eyewear, and remove any personal jewelry or items that may cause an accidental short circuit.

When using a voltmeter for measuring voltage, you have a couple of options. One is just a simple voltage test. This typically involves placing the common lead on a good ground and the red probing lead on the input side of an electrical component. Doing so will give you a reading of how much more voltage is at the probing lead than is at the common lead. But that only gives us an indication of voltage. It does not tell us how much voltage we started with or how much voltage did not make it through the circuit. Therefore, be careful when using this test to determine if the voltage is good.

A better test is a voltage drop test. A voltage drop occurs when current flows through a resistance. The higher the resistance, the higher the voltage drop. We could say that a voltage drop test measures for excessive resistance in a circuit. When testing for a voltage drop, always have the circuit turned on. That way, the circuit will have current flowing, thereby making voltage drops evident. Just to be clear, in a real circuit, no current flow means no voltage drop.

There are two ways to do a voltage drop test: the direct method and the indirect method **FIGURE 37-33**. The direct method uses both test leads on the same side of the circuit. It will directly read how much voltage is lost

FIGURE 37-33 Voltage drop testing—direct method.

between those two points. The indirect method leaves the black lead on the negative battery terminal (or other good ground) all the time. The probing lead is moved from one point (generally the positive battery terminal) to another point (generally the input of the load). The second reading is then subtracted from the first reading to give the amount of the voltage drop. As you can see, the first method requires no math, so it is less prone to errors.

So how do you place the leads in the circuit when performing a direct voltage drop test? Let's assume we are checking the positive side of the circuit for voltage drops. If we stick with the idea that the red lead is the probing lead, then it makes sense to place the black lead on the positive battery post and probe with the red lead. Let's pretend we are measuring the voltage drop on the positive side of the circuit feeding the low beam filament on the left headlight. With the headlights on low beam, the voltmeter reads –0.71 volts. Wait a minute, there is that negative reading again. Remember, we are measuring voltage drop, so it makes sense that the meter would read that the voltage is 0.71 volts *less than* (–) the voltage at the black lead. By the way, a 0.71-volt drop is beyond the 0.5-volt drop maximum allowed on one side of a circuit; thus, each part of the feed side of the circuit needs to be voltage drop tested to find the excessive voltage drop.

And how should the leads be placed when checking voltage drop on the ground side of the circuit? If we are looking to measure voltage drop, then we need to place the black lead on the output terminal of the headlight and the red lead on the negative battery terminal. Turn on the low beam headlights and measure the voltage drop. In this case, the meter reads –0.24 volts. Again, it is telling us that the voltage is dropping, this time 0.24 volts, on the return trip to the negative battery terminal.

To look at it another way, you could place the black lead on the negative battery terminal and the red lead on the output side of the headlight. Turn the headlight on and take the reading again. This time it measures 0.24 volts. Why isn't it negative this time? Good question. It is telling us that there are 0.24 volts more at the output of the headlight than at the negative post of the battery. In other words, the negative side of the circuit has 0.24 volts more at the start of the return path for current flow than it does at the end of the path, which is the negative battery terminal. Thus, we could hook up the meter either way; we just need to know which way we have it connected in the circuit and what reading we expect, whether it is negative or positive. Just don't get in the habit of ignoring the + and – signs. These signs are indicators that can help us know what is happening within a given circuit.

The other method of voltage drop testing is the indirect method. This method involves taking two voltage readings and subtracting them from each other to determine the voltage drop. This method is useful when working far away from the battery, where connecting one of the voltmeter leads to the battery is not possible, such as when checking lights at the rear of a vehicle. The indirect method involves first measuring the voltage at the battery with the electrical device turned on. This is the base reading. The second measurement is taken at the load that is being tested while the circuit is on. The leads are placed on the input to the load and the ground near the load. This will give the voltage that is available to the load. The last thing to do is subtract the voltage at the load from the battery voltage; any difference is the voltage drop in the system. Note, however, that the drop could be on the power side or the ground side of the circuit, so further testing must be performed if the voltage drop is excessive.

To use a DVOM to measure voltage, follow the steps in **SKILL DRILL 37-4**:

1. Prepare the DVOM for testing voltage by connecting the black lead to the COM terminal and the red lead to the V/Ω terminal. **(Photo 1)**

2. Turn the rotary dial until you have selected the mode for volts DC. The reading on the DVOM should now be at zero. Some DVOMs will automatically sense the correct voltage range when a voltage is detected. On other DVOMs you will need to set the voltage range before using the DVOM. **(Photo 2)**

3. Connect the black lead to the negative battery terminal and the red lead to the positive battery terminal. Interpret the results. If the battery is fully charged, the DVOM will give a reading that is 12.6 volts or more. If it is *not* fully charged, the reading will be less than 12.6 volts. **(Photo 3)**

Checking Circuits with a Test Light

Nonpowered test lamps are useful in determining if electrical power is present in a part of a circuit. But you should always first test the test light on a known good power and ground before using it to test a circuit. It is possible that the bulb in the test light is burned out. You want to know that before performing any tests. If the test light

SKILL DRILL | **37-4** | **Using a DVOM to Measure Voltage**

1. Prepare the DVOM for testing voltage by connecting the black lead to the COM terminal and the red lead to the Volt/Ohms (V/Ω) terminal.

2. Turn the rotary dial until you have selected the mode for volts DC. The reading on the DVOM should now be at zero.

3. Connect the black lead to the negative battery post and the red lead to the positive post. Measure the voltage and interpret the results.

illuminates, the two ends of the test light are touching both a power and a ground. If the light does not illuminate, the circuit is missing one or both of those elements or the test light is faulty. Test lights are great to grab to perform simple tests such as testing fuses. The test light lead can be quickly grounded and the probe end touched to each end of the suspect fuse. If both ends light, the fuse itself is good (but the fuse box terminal could be loose). If only one side of the fuse lights the test lamp, then the fuse is blown.

To avoid damaging the test light, make sure the circuit voltage you are testing does not exceed the test light's rating. Most test lights are rated for 6- or 12-volt systems, and using the light in a 24-volt system will usually blow the bulb. You should *not* use a test light to test SRS (supplemental restraint systems), as unintended deployment of the airbags could result, a very dangerous and costly mistake. Also, using a test light on a computer circuit designed for very small amounts of current flow can damage the circuit.

To check circuits with a test light, follow the steps in **SKILL DRILL 37-5**:

1 Connect the end of the light with the clip on it to the negative battery terminal. Touch the probe end of the test light to the positive battery terminal. The light should come on. (**Photo 1**)

2 Connect the clip to any known good ground close to the area to be tested. A typical known good ground is any unpainted metal surface on the vehicle that is directly attached to the battery ground return system. (**Photo 2**)

3 Locate the device to be tested and place the probe so that the test light circuit is parallel to it. If there is voltage present, the light will come on. (**Photo 3**)

Checking Circuits with Fused Jumper Leads

Jumper leads can be used in a number of ways to assist in checking circuits. They can be created by the technician or purchased in a range of sizes, lengths, and fittings, or connectors. They are used to extend connections to allow circuit readings or tests to be undertaken with a DVOM, an oscilloscope, current clamps on fuses, relays, and connector plugs on components. In some circumstances, jumper leads may provide an alternate current or ground source for components being tested. Regardless of their application, it is important that the circuit remain protected by a fuse of the correct size. To determine the correct size of fuse for any particular application, refer to the manufacturer's information.

To check circuits with fused jumper leads, follow the steps in **SKILL DRILL 37-6**:

1 Identify the circuit to be checked and determine the fuse rating for the circuit.

2 Select appropriate jumper leads with the correct fuse rating.

3 Install the jumper lead into the circuit. Perform any required circuit checks. Never use a jumper lead to jump across a load; doing so bypasses circuit resistance and will likely cause excessive current to flow in the circuit.

SKILL DRILL 37-5   Checking a Circuit with a Test Light

1 Connect the end of the light with the clip on it to the negative battery terminal. Touch the probe end of the test light to the positive battery terminal. The light should come on.

2 Connect the clip to a known good ground. A typical known good ground is any unpainted metal surface on the vehicle that is directly attached to the battery ground return system.

3 Place the probe on the terminal to be tested. If voltage is present, the light will come on.

Safety

Be very careful how you hook up any type of jumper leads, fused or unfused. If you hook them up to the wrong branch of a circuit, especially electronic circuitry, damage can be extensive. There is the old "magic smoke" saying: "Electrical and electronic components work off of the principle of magic smoke. Once the magic smoke is allowed to escape from the component, the component will never function again." Don't use jumper leads in a way that would let the "magic smoke" out of the circuit.

Applied Science

AS-77: Capacitance: The technician can demonstrate an understanding of the role of capacitance in timer circuits such as RC timers or a MAP sensor.
Sensors are the components of the system providing input to the computer making it possible for it to carry out its operations.

The MAP sensor, or manifold absolute pressure sensor, plays a big role in proper engine performance. There are several different types of MAP sensors. Some of the popular styles are the variable voltage MAP sensor, the variable-inductance MAP sensor, and the variable-capacitance MAP sensor. Here, we will focus on the variable-capacitance MAP sensor.

The variable-capacitance MAP sensor consists of two aluminum oxide plates in a chamber that is connected by tubing to the engine's intake manifold. This sensor is capable of generating an output signal in hertz proportional to the change in manifold pressure. This is the key point that the technician should understand. The electrical output signal to the computer is directly proportional to engine load as the manifold pressure changes. At engine idle, the vacuum is at approximately 17–21 in. Hg. at sea level. Under this condition, the MAP sensor hertz will be approximately 95. When the engine is at wide open throttle, the vacuum is almost zero inches of mercury, which is converted to a hertz reading of approximately 160. The MAP sensor sends the proportional signal to the computer as a result in changes in engine load. The computer responds by providing more or less fuel to the injectors as well as performing a number of other vital tasks.

Locating Opens, Shorts, Grounds, and High Resistance

DVOMs, test lamps, and simulated loads tend to be the tools used most often for locating opens, shorts, grounds, and high-resistance faults. Refer to the chapter Principles of Electrical Systems for more information on opens, shorts, grounds, and high resistance faults. An **open**
circuit is a break in the electrical circuit where either the power supply or ground circuit has been interrupted. Most open circuits can be located by probing along the circuit at various points testing for power and by checking for an effective ground at the ground point. A systematic check of the circuit is required by first performing a voltage drop check on each side of the affected circuit. An open circuit will cause a voltage drop equal to the source voltage. Once the voltage drop is isolated to one side of the circuit, voltage drop testing can continue on that side, working the leads closer together in steps. Also, use your understanding of electrical systems to consider the most likely places for the open circuit, such as a blown fuse or a faulty switch. And don't forget that the load could also be open. If the voltage drop test on each side of the circuit is within specifications, use an ohmmeter to check whether the load is open, if possible. Some loads such as diodes cannot be tested with a standard ohmmeter. In this case, follow the manufacturer's diagnostic procedure.

Shorts, or **short circuits**, can occur anywhere in the circuit and can be difficult to locate, especially if it is intermittent. A short is a circuit fault in which current travels along an accidental or unintended route and can be thought of as a shorter path for current to flow. The short may occur within the load, such as shorted relay windings, or it can be in the wiring, where a wire is shorted to ground or to supply voltage. A short will typically cause lower than normal circuit resistance. The low-resistance fault would cause an abnormally high current flow in the circuit and may cause the circuit protection devices, such as fuses or circuit breakers, to open the circuit. A short to supply voltage may cause the circuit to remain live even after the switch is turned off. For example, a short between a wire with power on all the time and a wire switched by the ignition switch would cause the circuit controlled by the ignition switch to remain on even after the switch is turned off. Just remember that shorts can be caused by faulty components or damaged wiring.

Shorts that happen within components, such as a relay coil, can usually best be tested by comparing the reading of an ohmmeter to specifications. Shorts that occur in wire harnesses are usually best tested by disconnecting each end of the affected harness and using an ohmmeter to test for unwanted continuity between various wires. A reading on the ohmmeter when connected to two separate wires indicates a short circuit between them. A true short between wires would be indicated by a very low ohm reading, typically around 1 ohm or less.

Grounds is a term often used in conjunction with shorts and is usually a reference to a short to ground. An initial test can be conducted by carrying out resistance checks or disconnecting the load. For example, if testing the blower motor, first disconnect the blower motor. If the short is still in place, then the wiring between the fuse or circuit breaker and the load must be at fault. To further narrow down the site of the short to ground, inspect the wiring harness, looking for obvious signs of damage. Another test can be conducted by connecting a test lamp or buzzer in place of a fuse. Current will flow through the test lamp or buzzer and find a ground through the short. Parts of the circuit can then be disconnected along the wiring harness to narrow down the location of the short. Specialized short circuit detection tools are also available. They work by sending a signal through the wiring harness where a short is suspected. A receiving device is then moved along the wire loom and will indicate when a short is located. This type of device can be very useful in situations where it is difficult to access the wiring, such as within large wire looms or under vehicle trim.

Short to power refers to a condition where power from one circuit leaks into another circuit. A short to power situation usually causes strange electrical issues. In some cases, one or more circuits will operate when they should not. Or in the case of sensor wires, the incorrect signals caused by the short to power can cause the computer to make very wrong decisions based on the faulty data. In this case, the engine, transmission, or other computer-controlled component can react strangely. Shorts to power are diagnosed first with a voltmeter to check for the unwanted voltage. Next, an ohmmeter is used to isolate the problem in the wire harness.

High resistance refers to a circuit where there is unintended resistance, which then causes the circuit to not perform properly. It can be caused by a number of faults, including corroded or loose harness connectors, incorrectly sized cable for the circuit current flow, incorrectly fitted terminals, and poorly soldered joints. The high resistance causes an unintended voltage drop in a circuit when the current flows. This drop reduces the amount of voltage that can be used by the load. The high-resistance fault will also reduce the current flow in the circuit. The reduction in voltage and current to the load reduces the amount of electrical power to load (Power = Voltage × Current), affecting its performance. Unwanted high resistance can best be located by conducting a voltage drop test in the power and ground circuits.

If the high resistance is within the load, such as a relay coil, then the resistance can be checked with an ohmmeter and compared to specifications. Some devices, such as a fuel injector or ignition coil, may need further testing using an oscilloscope. In this way, the waveform can be evaluated, which can indicate issues that an ohmmeter cannot identify as easily.

Inspecting and Testing Circuit Protection Devices

Protection devices are designed to prevent excessive current from flowing in the circuit. Protection devices like fuses and fusible links are sacrificial, meaning that if excessive current flows, they will blow or trip and have to be replaced. Circuit breakers can be reset. Once they trip, they either reset automatically or require a manual reset by pushing a button or moving a lever. Fuses, fusible links, and circuit breakers are available in various ratings, types, and sizes, and must always be replaced with the same rating and type.

In most vehicles, protection devices are situated in the power or feed side of the circuit. A blown or faulty fuse can be tested using a DVOM or test lamp. A good fuse will have virtually the same voltage on both sides. A blown fuse will typically have battery voltage on one side of the fuse and 0 volts on the other side. They can also sometimes be visually inspected. This may require the removal of the fuse from the fuse holder. The fusible element should be intact and, if measured by an ohmmeter, should have a very low resistance. The contacts on both the fuse and the fuse holder should be clean and free of corrosion and should fit snugly together.

> **TECHNICIAN TIP**
>
> It is fine to condemn fuses if they are obviously blown, but if they appear intact, do not rely on your eyes. Over time, fuses heat slightly and cool. This heating and cooling process can cause the fuse to become brittle and crack. The crack can be very fine, almost invisible, yet not conduct electricity, leading your diagnosis astray.

To inspect and test circuit protection devices, follow the steps in **SKILL DRILL 37-7**:

1. Identify the protection device to be inspected and tested.
2. Conduct a visual inspection.
3. Set up a DVOM to read volts or use a test lamp.
4. Energize the affected circuit, if necessary.
5. Test for voltage on both sides of the circuit protection device. Determine and perform any necessary actions.

Inspecting and Testing Switches, Connectors, Relays, Solenoid Solid-State Devices, and Wires

Inspection of electrical devices and wires usually starts with a visual inspection of the electrical circuit and is followed up with electrical testing. The visual inspection looks for breakage, corrosion, or deformity and includes examination of the insulation for any worn or melted spots. In the case of switches, solenoid contacts, and relay contacts, an electrical inspection is necessary. For example, all switches would require voltage drop testing to see if they operate properly without excessive resistance. Additionally, solenoid and relay contacts can wear out and produce excessive resistance, so performing a voltage drop test on them is a valid testing procedure. Some solenoids can be disassembled and visually inspected. In this case, the solenoid cap may be removed and the contacts visually inspected. Typically, if there is an excessive voltage drop across the contacts, the contacts will be pitted and burned. Measuring resistance also comes into play when a shorted relay or solenoid winding is suspected.

DVOMs and test lamps are used for most basic testing, with more specialized test equipment, such as oscilloscopes, being used if necessary. It is important to note that test lamps should not be used on electronic circuits due to their higher current draw, which could overpower the electronic components. Some tests, such as resistance tests, can be conducted on components in or out of the circuit. In-circuit tests are often preferred, as they usually provide the opportunity to test the component under load or during operational conditions. After in-circuit testing, components can be removed for individual testing, if required.

Manufacturers produce diagnostic flowcharts that guide the technician through a diagnostic sequence based on test results. In complex circuits, it is good practice to gather as much information as possible about the operation of the circuit and the customer concern. With that information, and the diagnostic flowchart, formulate a testing sequence for diagnosing the fault. Going through this process will help you to understand the problem and to identify possible causes, and a potential sequence of testing.

Wrap-up

Ready for Review

▸ The digital volt-ohmmeter (DVOM) or digital multimeter (DMM) is electrical measurement tool used to diagnose and repair electrical faults.

▸ To properly use a DVOM requires time and effort to learn the parts and how it works.

▸ The DVOM can measure volts, ohms, and amps in a circuit.

▸ An advanced DVOM can measure frequency, temperature, and has a dedicated diode test capability.

▸ A DVOM is the first tool used to take electrical measurements.

▸ The DVOM allows the technician to see the movement of electrical impulses that cannot be seen without some type of electrical test equipment.

▸ The DVOM can measure electrical volts within circuits.

▸ The DVOM can measure ohms, which is the resistance of a circuit.

▸ The DVOM can measure amps, which is the current flow of a circuit.

▸ The main parts of the DVOM is the main body and the two current leads.

▸ The main body has a function switch, a connection point for the leads, and a digital display to show values.

▸ The leads are black for negative and red for positive connections.

▸ There is a wide selection of leads for the DVOM to enhance the testing capabilities.

▸ Before you can use a DVOM, the technician needs to know the quantity of the measurement (volt, ohm, or amp).

▸ The DVOM can read a wide range of scales depending what position is selected.

▸ The DVOM can read from low to high values.

▸ The DVOM in auto range will select the best value for the range being measured.

▸ The min/max setting gives the technician the ability to measure circuits that are only on momentarily.

▸ The hold function freezes the value measured.

▸ There are many different ways to probe a circuit depending on the circuit being tested.

▸ The probes should never be forced as this could damage the circuit being tested and the probes being used.

▸ If the technician uses the back probe method, the holes probed need to be resealed to keep moisture out.

▸ The most common measurements taken with the DVOM are voltage, current, and resistance.

▸ Depending on measurements taken, the leads need to be in the correct location on the body of the DVOM.

▸ If the leads are connected in the wrong place on the DVOM, it could cause a fuse to blow.

▸ When voltage is measured, the leads are placed parallel to the circuit being measured.

▸ When current is measured, the leads are placed in series with the circuit being measured.

▸ When resistance is measured, the component should be isolated from the circuit so no power is present.

▸ The meter is very useful in finding opens, shorts, grounds, and high resistance.

Key Terms

attenuator A device that reduces the power of a signal without distorting its waveform.

digital volt-ohmmeter (DVOM) A test instrument with a digital display for measuring voltage, resistance, and current. Also called a digital multimeter (DMM).

grounds Fault conditions in a circuit where the circuit is unintentionally contacting a grounded component or wire. This may result in a short, in the case of a power wire, or it could cause a circuit to stay live in the case of a switched ground circuit.

high resistance A term that describes a circuit or components with more resistance than designed.

hold function A setting on a DVOM to store the present reading.

min/max setting A setting on a DVOM to display the maximum and minimum readings.

open circuit A circuit that has a break that prevents current from flowing.

oscilloscope A test instrument that graphs voltage over time and displays the results on a screen.

probing technique The way in which test probes are connected to a circuit.

short circuit A condition in which the current flows along an unintended route.

short to power A condition in which current flows from one circuit into another.

waveform A graphical plot of voltage over time that is displayed on an oscilloscope.

ASE-Type Questions

1. Tech A says that total resistance goes up as more parallel paths are added. Tech B says that total amperage goes up as more parallel paths are added. Who is correct?
   a. Tech A
   b. Tech B
   c. Both A and B
   d. Neither A nor B

2. Tech A says that when reading DC voltage on a meter, a "+" before the number means that there is a higher voltage at the red lead than the black lead. Tech B says that a "−" before the number means that there is a lower voltage at the red lead than the black lead. Who is correct?
   a. Tech A
   b. Tech B
   c. Both A and B
   d. Neither A nor B

3. Tech A says that to read amperage the meter needs to be hooked up in series in a circuit. Tech B says that to read amperage at a load, place one lead of the ammeter on the input side of the load and the other lead on the output. Who is correct?
   a. Tech A
   b. Tech B
   c. Both A and B
   d. Neither A nor B

4. Tech A says that when checking amperage on a battery, hook the red lead to positive and the black lead to ground. Tech B says that a resistance reading on a light bulb requires the DVOM to be hooked to each side of the bulb and the switch turned on. Who is correct?
   a. Tech A
   b. Tech B
   c. Both A and B
   d. Neither A nor B

5. Tech A says that when checking a voltage drop across an open switch, a measurement of 12 volts means the circuit is open. Tech B says that when checking voltage drop across an open switch, a measurement of 12 volts means the switch contacts are closed. Who is correct?
   a. Tech A
   b. Tech B
   c. Both A and B
   d. Neither A nor B

6. A customer complains of slow engine cranking. Tech A says that the starter is faulty and should be replaced. Tech B says that performing a voltage drop test on the high current side of the starter circuit is a valid test in this situation. Who is correct?
   a. Tech A
   b. Tech B
   c. Both A and B
   d. Neither A nor B

7. Tech A says that when resistance increases, current flow decreases. Tech B says that when voltage decreases, current increases. Who is correct?
   a. Tech A
   b. Tech B
   c. Both A and B
   d. Neither A nor B

8. Tech A says that an open circuit will typically cause higher current flow, which will blow the fuse. Tech B says that a short to ground can typically be found by checking voltage at different points in the circuit. Who is correct?
   a. Tech A
   b. Tech B
   c. Both A and B
   d. Neither A nor B

9. Tech A says that when a fuse has popped, it just needs to be replaced, since it performed its job. Tech B says that when a fuse has blown, the circuit needs to be diagnosed because the fuse was probably not the problem. Who is correct?
   a. Tech A
   b. Tech B
   c. Both A and B
   d. Neither A nor B

10. Two technicians are discussing scope testing. Tech A says that the vertical axis of the screen shows voltage. Tech B says that the horizontal axis shows time. Who is correct?
    a. Tech A
    b. Tech B
    c. Both A and B
    d. Neither A nor B

CHAPTER 38

NATEF Tasks

Batteries, Starting, and Charging Systems

NATEF Tasks, continued

- Inspect and test starter relays and solenoids; determine necessary action. **MLR** **AST** **MAST** 1315–1317

- Remove and install starter in a vehicle. **MLR** **AST** **MAST** 1317–1318

- Differentiate between electrical and engine mechanical problems that cause a slow-crank or no-crank condition. **MLR** **AST** **MAST** 1318–1319

Charging System

- Perform charging system output test; determine necessary action. **MLR** **AST** **MAST** 1327

- Perform charging circuit voltage drop tests; determine necessary action. **MLR** **AST** **MAST** 1327–1328

- Inspect, adjust, or replace generator (alternator) drive belts, check pulleys, and tensioners for wear; check pulley and belt alignment. **MLR** **AST** **MAST** 1328–1331

- Remove, inspect, and reinstall generator (alternator). **MLR** **AST** **MAST** 1329–1331

- Diagnose (troubleshoot) charging system for cause of undercharge, no-charge, or overcharge conditions. **AST** **MAST** 1331

Required Supplemental Tasks
Shop and Personal Safety

- Demonstrate awareness of the safety aspects of high voltage circuits (such as high intensity discharge (HID) lamps, ignition systems, injection systems, etc.). 1290–1292

- Demonstrate awareness of the safety aspects of supplemental restraint systems (SRS), electronic brake control systems, and hybrid vehicle high voltage circuits. 1311–1312

Knowledge Objectives

After reading this chapter, you will be able to:
1. Describe battery types, ratings and sizes, and construction. (pp 1282–1288)
2. Explain the operation of lead-acid batteries. (p 1285)
3. Explain the operation of the starting system and its components. (pp 1303–1312)
4. Explain the operation of the charging system and its components. (pp 1319–1326)

Skills Objectives

After reading this chapter, you will be able to:
1. Perform a battery state-of-charge test using a hydrometer, refractometer, or DVOM. (pp 1292–1293)
2. Test battery capacity. (pp 1293–1295)
3. Identify electronic modules, security systems, radios, and other accessories that require reinitialization or code entry following battery disconnect. (p 1295)
4. Maintain or restore electronic memory functions. (p 1295)
5. Inspect, clean, fill, or replace the battery, battery cables, clamps, connectors, and hold-downs. (pp 1296–1297)
6. Charge a battery. (pp 1298–1299)
7. Jump-start a vehicle. (pp 1299–1301)
8. Measure parasitic draw with a standard parasitic load test and a Chesney parasitic load test. (pp 1301–1303)
9. Test the starter draw and the starter circuit voltage drop. (pp 1312–1314)
10. Inspect and test the starter control circuit, relays, and solenoids. (pp 1315–1317)
11. Remove and install a starter in a vehicle. (pp 1317–1318)
12. Perform a charging system output test and a charging circuit voltage drop test. (pp 1327–1328)
13. Replace an alternator. (pp 1329–1331)

Introduction

The electrical system on modern vehicles is becoming increasingly complex with an increasing reliance on electrical power to assist in the management and control of not only the engine and emissions system, but also almost all aspects of the vehicle, including brakes and suspension, navigation, entertainment, information retrieval, and much more. Almost every system on modern vehicles relies on electrical and electronic components and theory, electronic control modules, and networking systems to connect everything together.

Fundamental to the automobile is the 12-volt storage battery, the engine starting system, and the electrical charging system. Once the engine is started, all of the vehicle's electrical systems rely on the charging system to provide sufficient power output and precise voltage control for the vehicle's on-board electrical and electronic circuits. Let's start with the battery, which provides the necessary standby (and reserve) power to get things started.

The Battery

As you learned in the Principles of Electrical Systems chapter, electricity is a very flexible and useful energy that can be used easily in a variety of ways. But one drawback to electricity is that it cannot be stored easily in its electrical form for later use. This means that electricity must be stored in another form of energy and reconverted to electricity when needed. This is where batteries enter the discussion.

Batteries were developed in the early 1800s, and since that time many varieties and designs have been developed. The battery is part of everyday life and is widely used in modern electrical and electronic devices. Batteries store electricity in chemical form, which is possible because electricity causes a chemical reaction within the battery. In other words, the electrical energy is transformed into chemical energy. The chemical reactions change the composition of the chemicals, which then are stored until the electrical energy is needed. When electricity is needed, the chemicals react with each other, transforming the chemical energy back into electrical energy.

A battery consists of two dissimilar metals, an insulator material separating the metals, and an **electrolyte**, which is an electrically conductive solution FIGURE 38-1. The strength of the battery depends on the materials used.

FIGURE 38-1 Components of a simple battery.

You are the Automotive Technician

A seven year old vehicle has just been towed into the shop with a no-crank condition. The driver of the vehicle informs you that it was acting strange; the wipers were running slow, the headlights were dim, and the battery light was on. He pulled off the highway and a few minutes later the engine died and wouldn't start. He thinks that the vehicle needs a new battery, but agrees to let you diagnose the problem. After writing up the repair order and looking up the service history, you inspect the vehicle visually. The shop apprentice has already partially charged the battery. You notice that the battery is the original one and the terminals are quite dirty. After using a battery terminal tool to clean the battery terminals, you test the battery with a conductance tester and find it has degraded from its original 650 CCAs to 185 CCAs. With a booster battery connected, the vehicle starts and runs normally. You test the alternator output and find its maximum output is about 15 amps, and the alternator ripple indicates faulty diodes or stator assembly. The last test you perform is a starter draw test. The specifications are 150–190 amps and it measures 165 amps.

1. Why did the vehicle act strange and die?
2. Which parts need to be replaced and why?
3. If the starter still wouldn't crank, nor make any noise, after the battery was replaced and the terminals cleaned, what would you test and why?

The traditional automotive battery type is the lead-acid battery. It is available in many different shapes, sizes, and designs to meet the requirements for various applications. For example, the battery used for starting a vehicle's engine is different from the marine deep cycle battery. Each requires different design characteristics for obviously different applications. Vehicle batteries are designed to provide high current draws for short periods of time, while deep cycle batteries supply smaller, continuous loads over longer periods of time. Although the size, case configuration, and design may change, the fundamental components and their operation remain the same.

Lead-Acid Flooded Cell and Gel Cell Batteries

The wet cell lead-acid battery is the main storage device in automotive use. It is called a flooded cell battery because the lead plates are immersed in a water–acid electrolyte solution. An automotive battery can supply very high discharge currents while maintaining a high voltage, which is useful when cold starting. It gives a high power output for its compact size, and it is rechargeable.

The standard 12-volt car battery consists of six cells connected in series. Each cell has a nominal 2.1 volts, for a total of 12.6 volts for a fully charged "12-volt" battery. Each cell contains two sets of electrodes (called plates), one set of lead (Pb) and the other set of lead dioxide (PbO_2), in an electrolyte solution of diluted sulfuric acid (H_2SO_4). As the battery discharges, the sulfuric acid is absorbed into the lead plates and both of the plates slowly turn into lead sulfate. At the same time, the strength of the electrolyte becomes less acidic as the acid is absorbed into the plates. Recharging the battery reverses this process.

In a conventional open wet cell battery, charging generates hydrogen and oxygen gas by separating them from the water in the electrolyte, creating a highly explosive mix. Overcharging or rapid charging causes some gas to escape from the battery; this is called **gassing**. The sulfuric acid contained in batteries is highly corrosive and can also be very harmful to metal, painted surfaces, and skin. Always wear protective clothing and use extra care when handling batteries.

In automotive storage batteries, the main storage device is the wet cell. The nominal 2.1 volts of each cell does not depend on the size of the cell; however, its current capacity does. The surface area of the plates in a cell determines the cell's current capacity. In a lead-acid battery, positively and negatively charged plates are assembled so that they are alternated. All of the positive plates are connected to each other in parallel, and all of the negative plates are connected to each other in parallel **FIGURE 38-2**. The more plates, the greater the current capacity of the cell. Since the plates are arranged alternately, they need to be close to each other but not touching. If they touch, an internal short circuit in the cell will occur, which is typically what has happened in a battery with a "dead" cell. The positive and negative plates have shorted together and therefore discharge that cell completely. Normally, the plates are kept from touching each other by separators, usually made of plastic.

The battery's six 2.1-volt cells are connected in series to form the battery, which gives the battery a nominal voltage of 12.6 volts. The cells are sealed from each other and filled with dilute sulfuric acid. The battery case is usually made of plastic or hard rubber. With the cells in series, one end of the battery is connected to the negative post and the other end is connected to the positive post **FIGURE 38-3**.

FIGURE 38-2 Typical plate arrangement in a wet cell battery.

FIGURE 38-3 Interconnections between all six cells in a battery showing the most negative and positive points of the battery.

Ratings and Sizing

Batteries have different ratings and sizing to fit the needs of a variety of vehicles. Ratings have to do with the electrical specifications of a battery, while sizing has to do with the physical attributes of the battery. Both are important when selecting or replacing a battery. Physical attributes of the automotive battery include the size of the battery case, the arrangement of the battery terminals (top or side mounted), and the size or type of battery terminal post (round-tapered posts or screw-on terminals).

Batteries sizes are designated by the Battery Council International (BCI) and given a group number. Individual groups are specified by dimension in length, width, and height. Note that a physically larger battery does not necessarily mean a higher electrical capacity, so always check the ratings in addition to the BCI group size. Other designations relate to the **battery terminal configuration**, which refers to the placing of the positive and negative terminals on the battery **FIGURE 38-4**. The position of the battery posts varies with each layout. Battery catalogs will specify the correct battery for each vehicle and terminal layouts. Different types of battery posts are also available for batteries, including lug terminals, side terminals, and standard posts **FIGURE 38-5**.

Battery Ratings

The **electrical capacity**, or the amount of charge a typical lead-acid battery can store, is determined primarily by the total surface area of the plates, but also to some extent by the thickness of the plates. The more plate surface area there is, the higher the electrical capacity of the battery. Automotive battery plates tend to be manufactured in a standard size, so a common method of increasing surface area is to increase the number of plates per cell.

FIGURE 38-4 Typical types of layouts that use a lettering system for identification purposes.

FIGURE 38-5 Battery posts. **A.** Side terminal. **B.** Standard post.

For example, a 12-volt 11-plate cell will have a higher capacity than a 12-volt 9-plate cell.

There are several methods used to rate automotive battery capacity. The three most common are **cold cranking amps (CCA)**, **cranking amps (CA)**, and **reserve capacity**. CCA measures the load in amps that a battery can deliver for 30 seconds while maintaining a voltage of 1.2 volts per cell (7.2 volts for a 12-volt battery) or higher at 0°F (–18°C). CA measures the same thing, but at a higher temperature—32°F (0°C). This can cause confusion since a 500-CCA battery has about 20% more capacity than a 500-CA battery, so it is important to keep the ratings straight. Reserve capacity is the time in minutes that a new fully charged battery at 80°F (27°C) will supply a constant load of 25 amps without its voltage dropping below 10.5 volts for a 12-volt battery. This rating approximates the amount of time that a vehicle can be driven before the battery dies, if the charging system fails completely. The CCA, CA, and reserve capacity are typically marked on automotive batteries, and technicians use these ratings when testing battery performance and when selecting batteries for particular vehicle applications.

Low-Maintenance and Maintenance-Free Batteries and Cells

There are many types of batteries, with variations of cell design available for vehicles. Some batteries are specifically designed for starting, some for extended-load marine usage, some for low-maintenance or maintenance-free applications. Low-maintenance batteries require little, if any, topping off of the water in the electrolyte. The plates and venting system are designed so that they do not normally gas and release water vapor to the atmosphere. Low-maintenance batteries still have removable caps so that electrolyte can be checked and topped off if necessary.

> **TECHNICIAN TIP**
>
> Since lead is relatively soft, when it is used in the lead plates of a battery it is prone to bending and stretching. Many years ago, antimony was added to the plates to strengthen them, but this caused the cells to gas off water, which caused the electrolyte level to fall over time, requiring periodic topping off. Calcium was added to one or both plates to reduce water usage.

Maintenance-free batteries are fully sealed and do not require the electrolyte to be topped off. In some cases they use a gel-type electrolyte instead of a liquid. **Absorbed glass mat** batteries have the electrolyte absorbed within a mat of fine glass fibers. The plates in this type of fully sealed battery can be made flat or wound in a cylindrical cell. Because the electrolyte in absorbed glass mat batteries is a gel, which does not spill, this type of battery is especially handy for rough handling or tipping. In fact, this type of battery can even be mounted on its side and still perform well. Thus the absorbed glass mat battery is especially suited for off-road and racing vehicles.

A sealed or low-maintenance battery typically has no removable cell covers, so you cannot adjust or test the fluid levels inside. However, some of these batteries do have a visual indicator (a single-cell hydrometer float) that provides information on the status of the charge and condition of one of the battery cells. Each manufacturer provides details of these visual indicators; refer to these when performing an inspection.

Battery Charging and Discharging Cycle

In a discharged lead-acid cell, the active material of both plates becomes lead sulfate, and the electrolyte becomes mostly water as the acid is absorbed into the plates. The result is a very weak sulfuric acid solution in the electrolyte. When being charged, the battery is connected to a direct current (DC) electrical supply with electrical pressure (voltage) higher than that of the battery's total cell voltage. The charging device acts like an electron pump, forcing electrons to move from the positive plates to the negative plates in the battery.

At the negative plates, sulfate is discharged, which changes the chemical composition of the plates back into

sponge lead and also creates a stronger solution of sulfuric acid in the electrolyte. At the same time, lead peroxide is formed at the positive plates, which helps to restore the cell's electrical potential or voltage.

The charging process increases the amount of acid in the electrolyte, making the electrolyte stronger. When further charging no longer makes the electrolyte stronger, charging is complete. Connecting a lead-acid battery to a load causes chemical changes as the battery discharges. At the positive plate, sulfate from the sulfuric acid in the electrolyte joins with lead to form lead sulfate, and oxygen from the plate joins the hydrogen from the electrolyte to form water. Lead sulfate also forms at the negative plate, as sponge lead forms with sulfate from the electrolyte **FIGURE 38-6**.

Overall, the percentage of acid in the electrolyte falls, and the percentage of water rises, reducing the strength of the electrolyte. As the cell discharges, the plates develop the same composition, which reduces the potential of the cell. Recharging the battery restores the difference between its sets of plates.

FIGURE 38-6 **A.** Charging cycle. **B.** Discharging cycle.

Battery Temperature Monitoring

Battery temperature plays an important role in the performance of a battery, and every battery has an ideal operating temperature range. In cold weather, battery performance drops dramatically due to a slowing of the chemical reaction process. At hotter temperatures, battery performance increases, but if the temperature increases too high, battery life may be compromised. Some vehicles monitor the battery temperature by placing a temperature probe in contact with the battery case. The power train control module (PCM) then controls the levels of current flow and voltage at which the battery is charged. Generally speaking, the colder the battery temperature, the higher the rate of charging; and the hotter the battery temperature, the slower the rate of charging. Smart chargers and battery management systems use the feedback from the temperature probe to manage the charge rate of a battery, ensuring the battery is at capacity and the temperature is within the optimal range, thereby promoting longer battery life.

Battery Operating Conditions

Batteries have a range of operating conditions under which the best possible performance and lifetime can be achieved. They should be kept clean, dry, and fully charged; have minimal vibration and the correct level of electrolyte; be kept at a moderate temperature (e.g., 77°F [25°C]); and be well secured. A battery's lifetime is shortened by the following conditions:

- Being fully discharged or having deep discharge cycles
- Remaining over- or undercharged
- Experiencing high discharge rates for extended periods
- Experiencing excessive vibration
- Being exposed to extremes of temperature
- Having dirt or moisture around the case
- Developing corrosion

Poor maintenance and operating conditions reduce the battery's operating life.

Rechargeable Cell Batteries

Batteries and cells continue to be developed to create more efficient, higher density batteries. Consumer electronic devices such as mobile phones and laptop computers have been driving the development of new battery technologies such as nickel-cadmium (Ni-Cd), nickel-metal hydride (Ni-MH), and lithium ion (Li-ion). All of these batteries are types of rechargeable cell batteries, as are lead-acid batteries. Nickel-cadmium batteries contain older technology and have been replaced by nickel-metal hydride batteries, as both have a nominal cell voltage of 1.2 volts. The nickel-metal hydride battery can have two to three times the energy density of a nickel-cadmium battery, which means that for the same size case, they can store two to three times the energy. This makes nickel-metal hydride batteries especially useful for drive motor applications such as in hybrid electric, plug-in hybrid, and battery electric vehicles. They also tend not to have the memory effect that plagued the nickel-cadmium batteries of the past. The memory effect required nickel-cadmium batteries to be fully discharged between charge cycles to ensure the maximum performance of the battery was maintained.

The lithium ion is a newer type of rechargeable cell and is now used in many consumer electronic devices, such as cell phones and laptop computers. Such applications paved the way for further breakthroughs in the use of lithium-ion batteries in hybrid-electric or battery-electric vehicles; these vehicles use what is known as the rechargeable energy storage system (RESS). A lithium-ion battery has one of the highest energy density ratios of common batteries in production today. This high energy density means the battery can store more energy than comparable batteries of other types. This is a real advantage for vehicle applications. They also have a low

> **TECHNICIAN TIP**
>
> Back in the day when many people worked on their own cars, a very handy do-it-yourselfer bought a top-shelf battery for his vehicle from the local parts store. After a couple of weeks, the customer brought the battery back saying it had a dead cell. The store employee checked it out and sure enough, it had a dead cell, so they gave him a new battery. A few weeks later, the customer returned with the same problem. The store employee apologized profusely and gave him another battery. Sure enough, the customer was back within the month with another bad battery. By this time, the owner figured something had to be going on, so he went to the customer's home to check it out. When he got there, he saw a beautiful 57 Chevy with a tilt front end. One quick look told him everything he needed to know. When the tilt front end was installed, the battery tray had to be removed. The customer found a nice new spot to mount the battery tray, bolting it right on the top of the upper control arm for the suspension. So every bump in the road bounced the battery and literally shook it to death. Needless to say, the customer ended up paying for a few ruined batteries.

self-discharge rate, which means they can sit on the shelf for long periods without discharging. They do have a shelf-life even if they are not used. For example, they typically last for up to 5 years from the date of manufacture, whether they are used or not.

The actual cell voltage depends on the final materials used to make the cell. The typical cell voltage for a lithium-ion battery is 3.6 volts. In contrast, cell voltage of a nickel-cadmium or nickel-metal hydride battery is 1.2 volts, and a typical lead-acid battery is 2.1 volts. Like all batteries, the lithium-ion cell has an anode, a cathode, and an electrolyte. When discharging, the lithium ions are removed from the anode and added into the cathode. When the cell is charging, the reverse occurs.

Lithium-ion batteries may suffer from **thermal runaway** and cell rupture if overheated or overcharged. In extreme cases, thermal runaway may result in an explosion. Extreme care should be taken when handling or charging lithium-ion batteries; always follow the manufacturer's recommendations. In hybrid or electric vehicle applications, many small dry cell battery-sized cells are connected in series and in parallel arrangements to form a battery pack that delivers the power requirements of the vehicle. Following safety precautions is extremely important because RESS battery packs develop voltages in excess of 200 volts.

Advantages of lithium-ion batteries include:

- High energy density: There is more power per pound.
- Low self-discharge: Self-discharge is typically less than half of that of nickel-cadmium.
- Low maintenance: No periodic discharge is required.
- No memory
- Low internal resistance: They are good for high current requirements.

Disadvantages of lithium-ion batteries include:

- Need for circuit protection to ensure current and voltage are within safe limits
- Limited shelf-life, even if not used
- Sensitivity to high temperatures
- Increased cost of manufacturing (however, these costs are being reduced as research improves the technology)
- Potential for damage if completely discharged

It should be noted that battery research is extremely intensive, driven by the search for evermore energy-dense renewable energy storage systems. As new developments find their way to market, expect to see even more variations of lithium-type batteries being used in hybrid electric and battery electric vehicles.

Applied Science

AS-54: Batteries: The technician can demonstrate an understanding of the electrochemical reactions that occur in wet cell and dry cell batteries.

A vehicle that has a no crank condition is towed into a dealership. The technician assigned to the job has completed his diagnosis of the problem and determined that the vehicle has a faulty battery. An apprentice technician working under his supervision also discovered that the hold down clamp on the battery was missing.

At break time, the apprentice asked the technician why he thought that the battery failed. The technician explained his thoughts by going back to the basics of battery construction and the electrochemical reactions that occur during various events. The battery case can be thought of as a container. Inside this container are six separate compartments or cells, which are the energy producing units. Each cell has a number of plates soaked in an electrolyte solution of about 64% water and 36% sulfuric acid. The plates are separated into the anode or negative side and the cathode or positive side.

As stated in our text, connecting a lead acid battery to a load causes chemical changes as the battery discharges. At the positive plate, sulfate from the electrolyte joins with lead to form lead sulfate, and oxygen from the plate joins the hydrogen from the electrolyte to form water. Lead sulfate also forms at the negative plate, as sponge lead forms with sulfate from the electrolyte. Overall, the percentage of acid in the electrolyte falls, and the percentage of water rises, which reduces the strength of the electrolyte. As the cell discharges, the plates develop the same composition, which reduces the potential of the cell. Recharging the battery again restores the difference between its sets of plates.

The technician explained his theory of the failure of the battery to the missing hold down clamp. With the battery not being securely fastened, plate material breaks off and drops down into the bottom of the battery case. This will eventually cause the plates to short out. He went on to explain that all batteries will eventually wear out but the excessive vibration shortened the life of the battery.

Battery Cables and Terminals

Battery cables and terminals are designed to carry high discharge currents that are required during cranking of the automotive engine. Battery cable terminals are usually made of lead or zinc-plated brass. There are a number of designs, the most common being a cone design that provides a large surface contact area with the ability to tighten the terminal onto the battery post using a nut and bolt. The tapered cone allows easy removal of the clamp when the bolt is loosened. The larger positive and smaller negative terminals are slightly different in size to ensure correct connection of the cables when installing or servicing the battery **FIGURE 38-7**.

FIGURE 38-7 Battery terminals.

Another type of battery terminal is the side terminal. It gets its name because the battery connection is on the side of the battery. The terminal is a flat circle with a center bolt that bolts the terminal tightly to the battery connection. Side terminal batteries seem to avoid some, but not all, of the oxidation issues of a top-post battery. One shortcoming of a side terminal battery is that it is harder to get a good connection when using jumper cables or a jumper box to jump-start the vehicle. One less common battery terminal is a flat terminal with a hole through the center. The post on the battery sticks up vertically with at least one side flat and a matching hole through the post. The battery terminal butts up against the flat post, and a bolt inserted through the battery post and terminal holds them firmly together.

> **TECHNICIAN TIP**
>
> Installing a battery into a vehicle backwards instantly destroys expensive on-board electronics, as some technicians and do-it-yourself vehicle owners have unfortunately discovered.

Battery cables are usually made of many fine strands of copper wire bound tightly together and insulated to make a cable with high current capacity. There are a number of cable sizes available to handle various current capacities. For example, a small-displacement spark-ignition engine requires far less current to crank than, for example, a high-compression diesel (compression-ignition) engine of the same displacement. Battery terminals are usually crimped or soldered onto the battery cables to ensure strong, low-resistance connections. Often, heat-shrink tubing with sealing adhesive is used over the joint to ensure it is kept clean and protected from corrosion. Battery cables should be protected from chafing or damage, and terminals should be kept clean and free of corrosion.

> **TECHNICIAN TIP**
>
> Corrosion from the battery can creep into and destroy a battery cable beneath the insulation and may not be visible. An engine cranking voltage drop test is the most reliable way to detect such high resistance caused by corrosion.

> **TECHNICIAN TIP**
>
> When buying battery cables or jumper cables, be careful to verify the wire size. Some wire manufacturers place very thick insulation over a small wire size, making the cable look bigger than it is. Remember, it is the size of the wire that determines current flow, not the size of the insulation.

> **Applied Science**
>
> **AS-55: Acids/Bases: The technician can identify the effects of the pH of a solution on various systems.**
> A technician has replaced a heater core in a vehicle, a task that required many hours of labor due to its location. The technician filled the cooling system with the type of antifreeze recommended by the manufacturer with a 50/50 mix of distilled water. After running the engine to check for leaks, the technician used a coolant test strip to verify the proper pH level of the coolant. The test strip indicated a pH level of 10, which is in the correct range of 9.8 to 10.2 pH. Any reading below 9.0 indicates that the coolant may cause damage to the water pump, radiator, heater core, or other components. This condition is known as electrolysis.
> An acid is a substance that produces hydrogen ions. A base is a substance that produces hydroxide ions. The pH scale is used to tell how acidic or base a substance is. A hand-held refractometer is a precision optical device used to measure the concentration or mix ratio of liquids. This instrument is more accurate than test strips for pH testing.
> In addition to pH testing of the cooling system, brake fluid can be also checked with test strips or a refractometer. The safe range for brake fluid ranges from 7.0 to 11.5 on the pH scale. Battery electrolyte can be tested with a hydrometer or a refractometer. When a battery is discharging, the specific gravity of the electrolyte is dropping. When a battery is being charged, the situation is reversed. Electric current is forced into the battery by the vehicle's alternator or a battery charger. The specific gravity of the battery goes up as a result.

Battery Condition

Batteries do not last forever. Over time and use, the plates start to lose effectiveness as lead paste falls off the plates and collects in the bottom of the battery case. This type of damage is especially likely to develop in a battery subjected to high vibration and shock, as when subjected to off-road travel. As plate material becomes deposited in the bottom of the battery case, it eventually shorts out the plates and renders that cell useless, which causes the battery to fail under load.

A battery may also become sulfated, meaning the surfaces of the plates harden, making it more difficult for the acid to be absorbed into the plate. As a result, the battery can no longer readily accept a charge or cannot adequately discharge under load. Leaving a battery on a slow charger overnight and then finding that it fails a load test in the morning is an indication of a sulfated battery. Sulfated batteries cannot create the necessary current flow and should be replaced and recycled.

Parasitic Draw

Parasitic draw refers to the current draw that occurs once the vehicle has been turned off and the systems have shut down. All modern vehicles have a certain minimum amount of parasitic current draw that is used by the vehicle's **keep alive memory (KAM)** circuits. KAM systems maintain memory functions and monitor systems. For example, the vehicle's theft-deterrent system is part of this parasitic current draw. Excessive parasitic draw will discharge the battery prematurely. Typically, when the ignition is switched off, the vehicle's engine stops and the vehicle systems begin to shut down, which is called "going to sleep" or "entering sleep mode." Vehicle systems will turn off at different rates and do not necessarily immediately turn off as soon as the ignition is off. For example, some vehicles may take up to a couple of hours before the last system goes to sleep and the parasitic draw reaches its minimum value. A low-amp clamp capable of measuring milliamps or an ammeter is the tool commonly used to measure parasitic draw from the battery. We will explore another option when we get to the parasitic draw skill drill (Skill Drill 38-9). Manufacturers will specify how much parasitic draw is acceptable and the waiting period required after the ignition is switched off before the measurement can be accurately taken.

Jump Starting

Jump starting of a vehicle requires the use of a slave battery along with high-current–capacity leads made with clamps on each end that can connect over the battery terminals.

The slave battery is connected in parallel from the slave (charged) battery to the host (discharged) battery to provide additional capacity to crank and start the vehicle. Jump starting should be performed with caution, as incorrect polarity or voltage spikes can cause damage to the sensitive electronic components installed on either of the vehicles. The safest way to deal with a discharged battery is to remove and charge it or replace it. If jump starting must be undertaken, make sure the slave battery is fully charged. Use jumper leads equipped with electrical spike protection. Spike-protected leads have a built-in device to prevent damaging electrical spikes from reaching electronic equipment. It is important to ensure that the leads are connected with the correct polarity to prevent damage to electronic components and to connect and disconnect leads in the correct sequence as explained in the skill drill on jump-starting a vehicle (Skill Drill 38-7).

Safety

Never allow a spark or flame around a battery, and never try to jump-start a frozen, faulty, or open-circuit battery; doing so could cause the battery to explode, causing injury.

Battery Service Precautions

When servicing batteries, always ensure that you have the right personal protective equipment (e.g., safety eyewear, gloves, and shop clothing). Never wear any conductive jewelry, such as neck chains, watches, or rings, when working on or near batteries as they may provide an accidental short-circuit path for high currents. If the battery is being, or has been recently, charged, ensure that the space around the battery is well ventilated. Avoid making any sparks, which may ignite the gassing hydrogen–air

Safety

The editor has been in the vicinity of two batteries when they blew up. One was from across the shop and sounded like a bomb going off. A student had been welding a van door when a spark from the welding ignited the hydrogen gases. Fortunately, the battery was on the opposite side of the door from where the student was working. The battery case was blown apart and acid was thrown 5 to 10 feet in all directions. Fortunately, no students were within that range. Always keep sparks away from batteries.

mixture. Never create a low-resistance connection or short across the battery terminals. Always remove the negative or ground terminal first when disconnecting battery cables, as doing so reduces the possibility of a wrench creating an accidental short to ground from the positive terminal to any grounded metal surface, which would cause a very large spark.

Battery Recycling

Batteries contain many environmentally damaging chemicals and metals. If they find their way into a landfill, the acid and metals can contaminate the soil and waterways. Correct disposal of batteries by recycling them is good for the environment, and the precious metals can be reclaimed for reuse. Many municipalities require battery recycling and levy a "core charge" on every new automotive battery sold. The core charge is refunded if an old battery is brought in and exchanged for the new one. This process helps prevent batteries from being discarded in the trash or left lying around. Check local laws and regulations to ensure that batteries are disposed of correctly.

Battery Maintenance

Batteries require regular maintenance consisting of inspection, cleaning, testing, and charging when discharged. Good times to check batteries are during oil changes and in the fall, prior to cold weather setting in, which makes the battery work harder.

Ensure the battery electrolyte level is correct by checking the markings on the case or by looking in each cell to ensure the plates are well covered. Make sure the exterior case is dry and free of dirt. Dirt on top of the battery can actually cause premature self-discharge of the battery as current "leaks" across the path of dirt or grime. This mixture can become conductive and drain the battery over time. To tell if the surface of the battery needs to be cleaned, use a digital volt-ohmmeter (DVOM) set to volts to measure the voltage on the surface of the top of the battery. You can do this by placing the black lead on the negative battery post and rubbing the red lead around the top of the battery, measuring the voltage present there. Any voltage over about 0.2 volts means the battery should be cleaned with a mixture of baking soda and water, but make sure not to get any of that mixture down inside of the battery, as it will tend to neutralize the electrolyte, ruining the battery.

Keeping the battery and terminals clean is one of the best maintenance tasks for the money. The lead in the battery posts and terminals oxidizes over time. Unfortunately, lead oxide is an insulator. Therefore, if the lead surfaces of the post and terminal oxidize, the insulator effect can cause the vehicle to not crank over, stranding the driver. Lead oxide can be identified by its dark gray or black color. The only effective way of removing it is with a special battery terminal scraper or wire brush, which will restore the lead to its shiny silver color. Once the battery terminal is reinstalled and tightened, the terminals should be coated with a battery oxidation inhibitor spray to help slow down the oxidation process.

Batteries sometimes need to be recharged when lights are left on (a parasitic drain) or when the vehicle has not been driven for several weeks or months. Knowing how to properly diagnose and recharge a battery is an important task that you will need to become proficient with. Performing a battery state-of-charge test with a hydrometer or refractometer is a good indicator of whether the battery needs to be charged or not. Another maintenance check of the battery is the conductance test, which indicates the capacity of the battery and how much life is left in the battery.

Applied   Science

AS-56: Density/Specific Gravity: The technician can explain the role of specific gravity in determining the condition of the system.

A technician is assigned to perform a battery state-of-charge (SOC) test on an automotive battery with removable filler caps. This procedure is a specific gravity test using a battery hydrometer.

The technician would normally use an electronic battery tester for a capacitance test, but due to technical difficulties, it has to be repaired. This type of test is used often on today's vehicles but sometimes other methods are used, such as the battery hydrometer.

When working with battery electrolyte, there are important safety precautions to take. Eye protection is a must and suitable gloves should be worn while working with batteries. Clothing can be damaged as well as the vehicle's paint by battery electrolyte, which is about 36% sulfuric acid.

Observing the safety precautions, the technician uses a hydrometer to draw some electrolyte from each cell and record the information on a sheet of paper. As stated in our text, a very low overall reading of 1.150 or below indicates a low state of charge. A high overall reading of about 1.280 indicates a high state of charge. The reading from each cell should be the same. If one or two cells are .050 different from the rest, it indicates there is something wrong with the battery. See temperature corrections chart to adjust for temperature variations that are above or below 70°F (21 degrees C) for the battery electrolyte temperature.

Safety

To ensure safety when working on batteries, take the following precautions:

- Make sure the hood is secured with a hood stay rod.
- Don the appropriate personal protection equipment before starting the job. Remember that batteries contain acid; if this acid is splashed in your eyes, it can blind you or seriously damage your eyes.
- Follow the manufacturer's personal safety instructions to prevent personal injury or damage to the vehicle you are working on.

Testing Battery State of Charge and Specific Gravity

While the capacitance test is the preferred test of battery condition, other tests may still be used. One of those tests is the state-of-charge test. State-of-charge testing tells us how charged or discharged a battery is, not how much capacity it has. The degree of the battery's charge is handy to know when testing starting and charging system issues, as well as just about any other electrical issue. Unfortunately, most batteries are of the low-maintenance or no-maintenance type and may not provide access to the electrolyte in the cells for state-of-charge testing. Older batteries with removable caps may be tested for sufficient state of charge by testing the electrolyte for acid content.

Recall that the acid level drops as the battery becomes discharged. One of the most accurate ways of testing the state of charge is to use a hydrometer or refractometer to measure the specific gravity of the electrolyte in each of the battery's cells. The higher the specific gravity, the higher the percentage of acid in the electrolyte, which corresponds to a high battery state of charge.

TECHNICIAN TIP

When performing a state-of-charge test, keep these tips in mind:

- When filling a battery that is not fully charged, never fill it to the top of the full line, as charging the battery will raise the electrolyte level.
- Small amounts of electrolyte in the hydrometer may leak out and damage the vehicle's paint or your clothing.
- Do not inadvertently remove electrolyte from one cell or add it to another cell when testing; doing so will cause incorrect readings.

TABLE 38-1: State of Charge as Indicated by Voltage Reading

Voltage	Percentage of Charge
12.6 or greater	100
12.4–12.6	75–100
12.2–12.4	50–75
12.0–12.2	25–50
11.7–12.0	> 0–25
0.0–11.7	0 (no charge)

The hydrometer's reading, unlike that of the refractometer, must be corrected for electrolyte temperature. Since the hydrometer draws electrolyte into it to raise a float, the electrolyte level must be at least slightly above the top of the plates. If it is not, then distilled water will need to be added and the battery fully charged.

A very quick indicator of battery state of charge is the open circuit voltage test. This test uses a DVOM to accurately measure the voltage of a battery that has been sitting with no charge for at least 10 minutes. The voltage reading can roughly indicate the battery state of charge. For example, 12.6 volts or above indicates a fully charged battery, 12.4 volts indicates a charge of approximately 75%, and 12.0 indicates a battery with almost no charge **TABLE 38-1**.

To perform a battery state-of-charge test, follow the steps in **SKILL DRILL 38-1**:

1. If the battery is not a sealed unit, it will have individual or combined removable caps on top. Remove them and look inside to check the level of the electrolyte. If the level is below the tops of the plates and their separators inside, add distilled water or water with a low mineral content until it covers them. Be careful not to overfill the cells; they could "boil" over when charging, which will need to happen before measuring the specific gravity.

2. Using a hydrometer designed for battery testing, draw some of the electrolyte into the tester and look at the float inside it. A scale indicates the battery's relative state of charge by measuring how high the float sits in relation to the fluid level. A very low overall reading (1.150 or below) indicates a low state of charge. A high overall reading (about 1.280) indicates a high state of charge. The reading from each cell should be the same. If one or two cells show a difference of 0.050 or more from the rest, there is something wrong with the battery. Be sure to consult temperature correction tables if the battery electrolyte temperature is not at, or about, 70°F (21°C). **(Photo 1)**

3 Using the refractometer, place one or two drops of electrolyte on the specimen window and lower the cover plate. Make sure the liquid completely covers the specimen window. If not, add another drop of electrolyte.

- Look into the eyepiece with the refractometer under a bright light.
- Read the scale for battery acid. The point where the dark area meets the light area is the reading. Compare the readings to the values given in Step 2. **(Photo 2)**

4 For open circuit voltage testing with a DVOM, perform the following actions: With the engine not running, select the volts DC position on your DVOM and attach the probes to the battery terminals (red to positive, black to negative). With all vehicle accessories switched off and the battery near 70°F (21°C), the voltage reading should be 12.6 volts if the battery is fully charged. This may be slightly lower at cooler temperatures. **(Photo 3)**

Testing Battery Conductance

When in doubt of how well a battery can meet demands placed upon it, it should be tested. The use of electronic battery testers has by and large replaced the need for hydrometer and other invasive types of battery testing. In fact, many manufacturers are now requiring the use of a conductance test instead of a high-amperage load test in order for warranty coverage to be considered **FIGURE 38-8**. Many of the testers have integrated printers, and for the battery to be warranted, a printout of the test result has to accompany the replaced battery.

The conductance tester sends low-frequency signals into the cells to determine the battery's ability to conduct

FIGURE 38-8 Conductance tester being used.

SKILL DRILL 38-1 **Testing the Battery's State of Charge**

1 Check and adjust the fluid level. Charge the battery if distilled water is added. Test the specific gravity of each of the cells by using a hydrometer designed for battery testing. Draw some of the electrolyte into the tester and read the scale.

2 To test the specific gravity with a refractometer, place a drop or two of electrolyte on the specimen window and lower the cover plate. Look into the eyepiece with the refractometer under a bright light. Read the scale for battery acid. The point where the dark area meets the light area is the reading.

3 To conduct an open circuit voltage test, select the volts DC position on your DVOM and attach the probes to the battery terminals (red to positive, black to negative). Compare the reading to Table 38-1.

current. The greater the ability to conduct current, the higher the CCA capacity of the battery. Since batteries deteriorate over time, their CCA capacity also deteriorates. The conductance tester is able to predict a battery's CCA capacity by measuring its conductance, which provides a near linear comparison between the two. Since conductance testing takes only a minute or two to complete, it is a good way to show customers the status of their battery and how that condition changes over time. If the conductance test shows that the battery no longer meets specifications, then customers will know that the battery is at the end of its useful life and must be replaced to avoid it failing and leaving them stranded.

Testing Battery Capacity

The load test has been used for years to test a battery's capacity and internal condition, but some manufacturers have been saying that their batteries should *not* be load tested, and instead should be conductance tested. They claim that load testing can damage the battery. Therefore, always check the service information before performing a load test.

As the name suggests, the load test subjects the battery to a high rate of discharge, and the voltage is then measured after a set time to see how well the battery creates that current flow. In other words, if the battery can maintain a high rate of discharge for a specified time and the voltage is still relatively high, then you know the battery is in good shape. Conversely, if the voltage falls off fairly quickly, the battery is not in very good condition. It is kind of like two people running a mile sprint. The one who does it in 5 minutes is likely in pretty good shape. The one who takes 20 minutes is likely in poor shape. It is similar with batteries. The faster the rate at which a battery can create current flow, the higher its voltage, indicating a higher capacity. Another way to think of a load test is that we are testing the battery's ability to produce the high starting current, while maintaining enough voltage to operate the ignition and electronic control systems.

You will remember that CCAs reflect the load in amps that a battery can deliver for 30 seconds while maintaining a voltage of 7.2 volts or higher at 0°F (−18°C). Since vehicle and battery manufacturers specify the CCA rating for every vehicle and battery, that rating is used to calculate the load placed on the battery when load testing. The battery can be either in or out of the vehicle but must be at, or near, a full state of charge for the test to be accurate. The electrolyte temperature should be approximately 70°F (21°C) for the most accurate results, because a cold battery cannot produce current flow as efficiently

and will show a false fail result. When load testing a battery, use the following testing parameters:

> Test load = half the CCA of the battery you are testing (verify it is sized correctly for the vehicle)
>
> Load test time = 15 seconds
>
> Results: Pass = 9.6 volts or higher; Fail = less than 9.6 volts

If the battery fails the load test, one further test is required before condemning the battery. The battery needs to be slow charged until it is fully charged (can take up to 20 hours), then repeat the load test. If it still fails, the battery is sulfated and needs to be replaced. If it passes, test the vehicle's charging system to see if it is charging the battery properly.

> ### ▶ TECHNICIAN TIP
>
> Technicians used to perform a 3-minute charge test on batteries if they failed the load test. But this test is being discouraged by battery and vehicle manufacturers due to its potential of damaging the battery or vehicle. Thus, we will not discuss this test method further.

To load test a battery, follow the steps in **SKILL DRILL 38-2**:

1. With the tester controls off and the load control turned to the off position, connect the tester leads to the battery. Observe the correct polarity and be sure the leads fully contact the battery terminals.

2. Place the inductive amps clamp around either the black or the red tester cables in the correct orientation. **(Photo 1)**

3. Verify that the temperature of the battery is within the testing parameters. Use an infrared temperature gun to determine the battery temperature by measuring the temperature of the side of the battery. If the tester you are using has an adjustment for temperature, set it to the actual temperature of the battery.

4. If you are using an automatic load tester, enter the battery's CCA and select "test" or "start." If you are using a manual load tester, calculate the test load, which is usually half of the CCA. If the battery starts to smoke or gas, replace the battery. Turn the control knob or press the start button. **(Photo 2)**

5. Maintain this load for 15 seconds while watching the voltmeter. At the end of the 15-second test load, read the voltmeter and immediately turn the

SKILL DRILL | 38-2 | Load Testing a Battery

$$\frac{700\ CCA}{2} = 350\ A$$
Testing Amperage

1. With the tester controls off and the load control turned to the off position, connect the tester leads to the battery. Place the inductive amps clamp around either the black or the red tester cables in the correct orientation.

2. Verify that the temperature of the battery is within the testing parameters. Use an infrared temperature gun to determine the temperature by measuring the temperature of the side of the battery. If you are using an automatic load tester, enter the battery's CCA and select "test" or "start." If you are using a manual load tester, calculate the test load, which is usually half of the CCA.

3. Maintain this load for 15 seconds while watching the voltmeter. Read the voltmeter and immediately turn the control knob off. At room temperature, the voltage should be 9.6 volts or higher at the end of the 15-second draw. If the battery is colder than room temperature, look up the compensated minimum voltage. Determine any necessary action.

control knob off. Typically, at room temperature, the voltage should have been 9.6 volts or higher at the end of the 15-second draw. If the battery is colder than room temperature, you may need to refer to a battery reference sheet to find the compensated minimum voltage. Using the results from the test, determine any necessary action. **(Photo 3)**

Identifying Modules that Lose Their Initialization During Battery Removal

Many electronic modules in vehicles, such as radio and driver-specific presets, require a small amount of power to maintain their KAM (memory). When the battery is disconnected from the vehicle, the memory of specific electronic systems is usually lost. For some systems this can be annoying. The PCM may lose its adaptive learning data, which means the vehicle will have to relearn this information during a period of driving that could take several days. For other systems, such as the security system, loss of memory may prevent the vehicle from being restarted or the radio from being used. At the very least, it may require the dealer or manufacturer to be contacted for vehicle-specific codes to reinitiate the vehicle systems.

Check the manufacturers' and owners' information to determine what systems will be affected by the power loss. You will need to identify any system that will require security or initialization codes to be reentered, and ensure the procedure and equipment are available to reinitialize systems or modules.

In some cases, it may be possible to use a 9-volt memory minder or memory saver to maintain the vehicle's memory while the vehicle battery is disconnected. This should supply enough power to maintain the memory for small jobs such as changing the battery—provided the vehicle doors or trunk are not opened, causing the interior lights to illuminate and essentially drain the 9-volt battery. Many technicians advocate using an external 12-volt DC power supply connected to the data link control with a suitable cable. If the cigarette lighter socket is always powered on, this too can be used for supplying power to the vehicle while the battery cables and connectors are being serviced. Just remember that providing power back into the circuit makes the system susceptible to short circuits by providing a ground to any of the powered wires or terminals.

To identify electronic modules, security systems, radios, and other accessories that require reinitialization or code entry following battery disconnect, follow the steps in **SKILL DRILL 38-3**:

1. In the appropriate service information or owner's manual, find the section that lists the information on the electronic modules, security systems, radios, and other accessories that require reinitialization or code entry. For example, the immobilizer, radio, engine, and transmission each have their own section.

2. From the service information, list the systems and modules that may require initialization.

To maintain or restore electronic memory functions, follow the steps in **SKILL DRILL 38-4**:

1. Identify which modules, if any, require reinitialization or code entry when the battery is disconnected following Skill Drill 38-3.

2. Identify the correct procedure and any needed tools, and verify that initialization codes are available.

3. If maintaining memory function, install a memory minder prior to the vehicle battery being disconnected.

4. If reinitializing the electronic systems, use the correct codes to reinitialize the modules if required.

Inspecting, Cleaning, Filling, and Replacing the Battery and Cables

As noted earlier, batteries last longer if they are properly maintained. In fact, one of the most common causes of vehicle no-starts is dirty/corroded battery cables. Inspecting, cleaning, and filling (if not maintenance free) are common tasks that should be performed every 6 months to 1 year on top-post batteries, and 1 to 2 years on side-post batteries.

Automotive batteries can look lighter than they really are. Always lift them with care, and get help if needed. When reconnecting the battery, be sure you do not connect the battery incorrectly (with reverse polarity); doing

so will send current in the reverse direction through the electrical system. The reverse current flow will likely damage some or all of the electronic control units (ECUs) throughout the vehicle. So what started out as a simple maintenance task becomes an expensive diagnosis and repair job that the shop has to perform at no charge to the customer.

To inspect, clean, fill, or replace the battery, battery cables, clamps, connectors, and hold-downs, follow the steps in **SKILL DRILL 38-5**:

1. Always remove the cable clamp from the negative terminal first. Then remove the positive terminal clamp. While they are disconnected, bend the cables back, or if necessary, tie them out of the way so that they cannot fall back and touch the battery terminals accidentally. **(Photo 1)**

2. Remove the battery hold-downs or other hardware securing the battery. Depending on the type of vehicle, you will need to unbolt, unscrew, or unclip the restraint and move it away from the battery. **(Photo 2)**

3. Keeping it upright, remove the battery from its tray and place it on a clean level work surface. Visually inspect the battery for damage, cracks, loose or leaking posts, etc. If found, the battery will need to be replaced. **(Photo 3)**

4. Measure the voltage on the top of the battery with a DVOM. Place the black lead on the negative post and move the red lead across the top of the battery until you find the highest reading. The higher the voltage reading, the larger the potential drain. **(Photo 4)**

5. Carefully clean the case of the battery and the battery tray either by washing them down with a mixture of baking soda and water, flushing them off with clean water, and drying them off with some paper towels, or by wiping them down with damp paper towels if the battery and tray are not very dirty. It is best to wear rubber gloves while doing this in case any corrosive electrolyte has leaked from the battery. Safely dispose of the paper towels. **(Photo 5)**

6. Clean the battery posts with a battery terminal tool. On lead posts and terminals, the preferred tool is a scraper style since it is designed to produce smooth surfaces that are more airtight when clamped together. Many technicians use the wire brush style of battery terminal tool, which leaves rougher surfaces that are more likely to corrode.

7. Clean the cable terminals with the same battery terminal tool. Examine the battery cables for fraying or corrosion. If the damage looks

SKILL DRILL | 38-5 | Inspecting, Cleaning, Filling, and Replacing the Battery and Cables

1 Remove the cable clamp from the negative terminal first. Then remove the positive terminal. Bend the cables back out of the way so that they cannot fall back and touch the battery terminals accidentally.

2 Remove the battery hold-downs or other hardware securing the battery.

3 Keeping it upright, remove the battery from its tray and place it on a clean work surface. Inspect the battery for damage.

4 Measure the voltage on the top of the battery with a DVOM. Place the black lead on the negative post and move the red lead across the top of the battery until you find the highest reading.

5 Carefully clean the battery case and the battery tray.

6 Clean the battery posts with a battery terminal tool. Clean the cable terminals with the same battery terminal tool. Examine the battery cables for fraying or corrosion.

7 Reinstall the cleaned and serviced battery. Replace the hold-downs and make sure the battery is securely held in positions. If installing a new battery, ensure that it meets the original manufacturer's specifications.

8 Reconnect the positive battery terminal and tighten it in place. Once the positive terminal is finished, reconnect the negative terminal and tighten it.

9 Coat the terminal connections with anti-corrosive paste or spray to keep oxygen from the terminal connections. Test that you have a good electrical connection by starting the vehicle.

extensive, the cables and clamps should be replaced. (**Photo 6**)

8 Reinstall the cleaned and serviced battery. Replace the hold-downs and make sure the battery is securely held in position. If a new battery needs to be installed, be sure to compare the outside dimensions as well as the type of terminals and their locations prior to installation. These MUST meet the original manufacturer's specifications. (**Photo 7**)

Applied   Science

AS-74: Activity of Metals: The technician can explain the conductivity problems in a circuit when connectors corrode due to electrochemical reactions.

A dealership technician has a do-it-yourself neighbor who enjoys working on vehicles in his driveway. The neighbor has questions from time to time for the professional technician. The do-it-yourselfer is restoring a fairly old vehicle in his spare time. He just purchased a new battery and a new starter, but the engine will not crank over. The technician demonstrated how to do a voltage drop test using a DVOM (digital volt-ohm meter). The problem was in a battery cable connection at the starter solenoid mounted on the fender well of the vehicle. When the cable end was removed from the solenoid, corrosion was found. After removing the corrosion from both surfaces and reattaching the cable, the engine cranked over properly. The do-it-yourself neighbor realized that he did not actually need a new battery and starter.

This is an example of a conductivity problem when connectors corrode due to electrochemical reactions. All metals on the vehicle can rust. Battery terminal corrosion is one of the main concerns regarding vehicle maintenance. The terminal corrosion can be removed with a wire brush but periodic maintenance will still be needed. External corrosion on battery terminals is very easily spotted but internal corrosion between the battery post and cable clamp will not be seen. It is necessary to take the connection apart and clean each surface with a battery terminal cleaning brush. Connections with corrosion problems will increase resistance at the battery terminals, which will reduce the voltage to the electrical system.

When working with automotive batteries, be sure to keep safety in mind. This includes wearing eye protection and suitable gloves. When disconnecting battery cables, there is a definite order to follow. As stated in our text, always remove the cable clamp from the negative terminal first. The negative terminal is marked with a minus sign. Then remove the positive terminal, the one with the plus sign. You will later replace them in reverse order, positive cable first, and then the negative cable. While they are disconnected, bend the cables back, or if necessary, tie them out of the way, so that they cannot fall back and touch the terminals accidentally.

---

9 Reconnect the positive battery terminal and tighten it in place. Once the positive terminal is finished, reconnect the negative terminal and tighten it. (**Photo 8**)

10 Coat the terminal connections with anti-corrosive paste or spray to keep oxygen from the terminal connections. Test that you have a good electrical connection by starting the vehicle. (**Photo 9**)

Charging the Battery

Vehicle batteries may become discharged and require charging particularly if the vehicle has been sitting idle without starting for more than a couple of weeks or if the charging system is faulty. Ideally a battery is fully charged before being tested for faults. Battery state of charge can be determined by a battery tester. If charging is needed, slow charging is less stressful on a battery than fast charging is. It can take more than 20 hours depending on the state of charge. Some manufacturers recommend removing the negative battery terminal while charging a battery to reduce risk to the vehicle's electronics. If the battery needs to be disconnected during charging, remember to verify if the vehicle's adaptive memory needs to be maintained. After charging the battery, it is good practice to clean the battery posts and cable terminals.

To charge a battery, follow the steps in **SKILL DRILL 38-6**:

1 Verify whether the battery needs to be disconnected during charging and, if so, whether the adaptive memory needs to be maintained. Visually inspect the battery to ensure there are no cracks or holes in the casing. Also make sure the battery has not been frozen and the sides of the battery case are not bulging outward.

2 Verify that the charger is unplugged from the wall and turned off. Connect the red lead from the charger to the positive battery terminal. Connect the black lead from the charger to the negative battery terminal. (**Photo 1**)

3 Turn the charger on to a slow, automatic charge. Check the charger amperage output to ensure the battery is charging correctly. A slow charger usually charges at a rate of less than 5 amperes. A fast charger charges at a much higher ampere rate, depending on the original battery state of charge, and should only be used under constant supervision. *Never exceed 15.6 volts* when charging a 12-volt battery. (**Photo 2**)

4 Once the battery is charged, turn the charger off. Disconnect the black lead from the negative battery terminal and the red lead from the positive battery terminal.

SKILL DRILL 38-6 | Charging a Battery

1 Verify whether the battery needs to be disconnected during charging and, if so, whether the adaptive memory needs to be maintained. Inspect the battery casing and ensure that the battery has not been frozen. Verify that the charger is unplugged and off. Connect the red lead to the positive terminal and the black lead to the negative terminal.

2 Turn the charger on to a slow, automatic charge.

3 Once the battery is charged, turn the charger off. Allow the battery to stand for at least 5 minutes before testing the battery. Using a capacitance tester, load tester, refractometer, or hydrometer, test the charged state of the battery.

5 Allow the battery to stand for at least 5 minutes before testing the battery. Using a capacitance tester, load tester, refractometer, or hydrometer, test the charged state of the battery. **(Photo 3)**

Applied Science

AS-72: Voltage: The technician can demonstrate an understanding of and explain system voltage generation, uses, and characteristics.

Voltage generation in the majority of modern automotive applications relies on an engine-driven alternator. Using the principle of electromagnetic induction, alternators generate alternating current (AC) electricity through the use of a moving magnet within a coil of wire. AC electricity needs to be converted to direct current (DC) before being used in automotive systems or stored in a battery. The AC electricity is "rectified," or converted to DC, by being passed through a bridge of diodes mounted in the alternator. Diodes are small solid-state devices that allow current flow in only one direction. The resulting DC electricity can be used to power various vehicle systems, including processing modules, electric motors, and lights, and can also be used to charge the vehicle's battery.

Generators, which produce DC electricity, were once commonly used in automotive applications but were replaced by alternators when small, inexpensive diodes became available. Alternators are more practical, simpler to produce, and less maintenance-intensive.

Applied Science

AS-64: Motors: The technician can demonstrate an understanding of the role of the generator/alternator in maintaining battery and system voltage.

A vehicle is in the shop for an illuminated battery light on the instrument panel. The repair order states that the customer had to jump-start the vehicle in order to drive it to the shop. An apprentice technician has been given the job of diagnosing this vehicle with the help of an experienced technician, if required. The apprentice starts by verifying the customer's concerns and finds the vehicle once again requires a jump start. When the engine starts, the battery light on the dash remains on. Checking under the hood, the apprentice finds what appears to be a new battery. Reading further on the repair order, the customer states that he replaced the battery two days ago. The apprentice connects his DVOM (digital volt-ohm meter) and obtains a reading of 10.2 volts. It is obvious to the apprentice that the alternator is not charging at all. The experienced technician performs a voltage drop test and agrees that a new or remanufactured alternator should be installed.

As stated in our text, the alternator converts mechanical energy into electrical energy by electro-magnetic induction. In a simple version, a bar magnet rotates in an iron yoke, which concentrates the magnetic field. A coil of wire is wound around the stem of the yoke. As the magnet turns, voltage is induced in the coil, producing a current flow. A typical charging voltage will be from 13.8 to 14.2 volts DC, which will keep the battery fully charged at 12.6 volts at 70°F (21 degrees C).

Jump-Starting the Vehicle

Before attempting to jump-start a vehicle, you need to make sure the battery is not frozen. You cannot jump-start a frozen battery. Before you disconnect the service battery from the discharged battery, it is good practice to place a load across the discharged battery, such as turning on the headlamps, to absorb any sudden rise in voltage that may occur as the alternator suddenly increases its output. There are many sensitive electronic devices in most modern vehicles that are very susceptible to voltage surges. One method of reducing the risk of damage to such devices is using jumper leads that have a built-in surge protector. Separate surge protector devices can also be used to reduce the possibility of such surges and voltage spikes.

An option that is less risky when jump-starting a vehicle is the use of a jump box. A jump box does not involve a charging system, which lessens the risk of voltage spikes. This device contains a relatively large battery and has short cables and spring-loaded clamps attached to it that can be connected directly to the dead battery. It may produce enough electrical energy to start the vehicle.

Another risk is overheating and damaging the vehicle's alternator. With all of the electrical draws on the vehicle, today's alternators work harder than ever. Adding the job of fully recharging the battery on top of the regular electrical loads can push an alternator into the danger zone. Because of the risk of damaging the electronics and alternator, many manufacturers (and tow companies) are now refusing to jump-start newer vehicles or authorize that practice. They now recommend either externally charging the battery or replacing the battery with a charged battery.

To jump-start a vehicle, follow the steps in **SKILL DRILL 38-7**:

1. Position the vehicle with the charged battery close to the vehicle with the discharged battery, but not touching. The vehicles should be positioned such that your jumper cables can comfortably reach from one battery to the other.
2. Connect the red or orange lead to the positive terminal of the discharged battery. **(Photo 1)**
3. Connect the other end of this red or orange lead to the positive terminal of the charged battery. **(Photo 2)**
4. Connect the black lead to the negative terminal of the charged battery. **(Photo 3)**
5. Connect the other end of the black lead to a paint-free ground on the engine block of the vehicle with the discharged battery, and as far away as possible from the battery. Do NOT connect the lead to the negative terminal of the discharged battery itself; this may cause a dangerous spark. Also, do not connect the black lead to the body or chassis, as the ground wire from the body back to the negative battery terminal is usually too small to carry the current needed for jump-starting the vehicle. **(Photo 4)**
6. Try to start the vehicle with the discharged battery. If the booster battery does not have enough charge to start the other vehicle at this point, start the engine in the booster vehicle and allow it to partially charge the dead battery for several minutes. Try again to start the vehicle with the discharged battery. Turn the headlights on to reduce the risk of a voltage spike damaging the electronic equipment.

SKILL DRILL 38-7 Jump-Starting a Vehicle

1. Position the vehicle with the charged battery close to the vehicle with the discharged battery, but not touching. Connect the red or orange lead to the positive terminal of the discharged battery.

2. Connect the other end of this red or orange lead to the positive terminal of the charged battery.

3. Connect the black lead to the negative terminal of the charged battery.

SKILL DRILL | 38-7 | Jump-Starting a Vehicle, continued

4 Connect the other end of the black lead to a paint-free ground on the engine block of the vehicle with the discharged battery.

5 Start the vehicle with the discharged battery. Turn the headlights on to prevent a possible voltage spike damaging the electronic equipment. Disconnect the jumper leads in the reverse order that you connected them. If the charging system is working correctly and the battery is in good condition, the battery will be recharged while the engine is running.

7 Disconnect the jumper leads in the reverse order that you connected them. Remove the negative lead from the good ground away from the battery. Then remove the negative lead from the booster battery. Next, remove the positive lead from the booster battery, and lastly, disconnect the other end from the battery in the vehicle you have just started. If the charging system is working correctly and the battery is in good condition, you may want to charge the battery while the engine is left running; however, this places a tremendous heat load on today's smaller sized high-output alternators. It would be better to drive a short distance to where it can be fully charged with a battery charger. **(Photo 5)**

Measuring Parasitic Draw

All modern vehicles have a small amount of current draw when the ignition is turned off. This charge is used to run some of the vehicle systems, such as the security system and radio memory. The vehicle computer systems also require a small amount of power to maintain the computer memory while the vehicle is off. The parasitic current draw should be a relatively small amount of current, since excessive draw will discharge the battery over a short amount of time.

Parasitic current draw does not necessarily immediately drop to its lowest level the instant the ignition is turned off. This usually occurs over a period of time as various systems go into hibernation or sleep mode, which can take up to a few hours. Consult the manufacturer's service information to determine the maximum allowable parasitic current draw and the time period, after the ignition is turned off, and the time it takes the modules to go to sleep.

Parasitic current draw can be measured in several ways, the most common being the process of using an ammeter capable of measuring milliamps and inserting it in series between the battery post and the battery terminal. The ammeter is usually put in series with the negative battery lead. If the vehicle is equipped with systems or modules that will require electronic memory to be maintained, follow the procedure for identifying modules that lose their initialization during battery removal and maintain or restore electronic memory functions. Note that the timers may reset during the process of disconnecting the battery terminal and connecting the ammeter in series, so you may have to wait for the timers to go back to sleep. If excessive parasitic draw is measured, disconnect fuses or systems one at a time while monitoring parasitic current draw to determine the systems causing excessive draw.

Disconnecting the battery can be avoided if a sensitive low-current (i.e., milliamps) clamp is available. The low-amp **current clamp** measures the magnetic field generated by a very small current flow through a wire or cable. Placing the low-amp current clamp around the negative battery cable will allow you to measure the parasitic draw. If excessive parasitic draw is measured, disconnect fuses or systems one at a time while monitoring parasitic current draw to determine the systems causing the excessive draw.

The last way to measure a parasitic draw is a bit controversial, but it is well worth trying out since it can save a lot of time and requires no special tools other than a DVOM. It is named the Chesney parasitic load test after its creator, Sean Chesney. Instead of using an ammeter to measure the draw, an ohmmeter is used. Before doing anything, set the ohmmeter to ohms (the lowest scale), touch the meter leads together, and read the screen. The reading is the resistance of the meter leads and is called the "delta" value, which is the meter's true zero when used with those leads. Typically an ohmmeter will read about 0.1 ohms when the leads are touched together. Remember this number for later. Some meters have a delta feature that recalibrates the ohmmeter to zero when the leads are placed together and the delta button is pushed. If your meter has this delta feature, you can use it so that you will not have to remember the delta reading.

Next, with the battery terminals still connected to the battery, place the black lead on the negative post of the battery and the red lead on an unpainted surface of the alternator housing. Read the ohmmeter and subtract the delta value from the reading. This reading corresponds to the relative parasitic draw on the system.

Through testing, Chesney found that a draw of about 35 milliamps equaled an ohm reading of about 0.3 ohms delta (above the delta value) on a DVOM with 10 megohms of impedance, and about 0.6 ohms delta on a DVOM with 20 megohms of impedance **FIGURE 38-9**. Anything above those readings indicates an excessive parasitic draw. You may be skeptical of this method, so go out and try it on any vehicle. Simulate a parasitic draw by opening the driver's door, which illuminates the dome light, and watch the ohmmeter. It went up, right? Close the door. As soon as the light went off, the ohmmeter reading went back down, right? If you use this test and find an excessive draw, you can pull fuses one at a time, watching for the ohmmeter reading to decrease. If it does not decrease after removing all of the fuses, suspect an unfused circuit such as the alternator diodes or the ignition circuit on some vehicles.

To measure parasitic draw with a standard parasitic load test, follow the steps in **SKILL DRILL 38-8**:

1. Research the parasitic draw specifications in the appropriate service information for the vehicle you are diagnosing. Typically this is between 0.035 amps and 0.050 amps (35–50 milliamps).

2. Connect the low-current clamp around (or insert the ammeter in series with) the negative battery cable and measure the parasitic draw. Compare the parasitic draw to specifications. **(Photo 1)**

3. Disconnect the circuit fuses one at a time to determine the cause of excessive parasitic current draw. Determine any necessary actions. **(Photo 2)**

SKILL DRILL 38-8 Measuring Parasitic Draw—Standard Test

1. Research the parasitic draw specifications in the service information. Connect the low-current clamp around the negative battery cable and measure the parasitic draw. Compare the parasitic draw to specifications.

2. Disconnect the circuit fuses one at a time to determine which circuit has the excessive parasitic current draw. Determine any necessary actions.

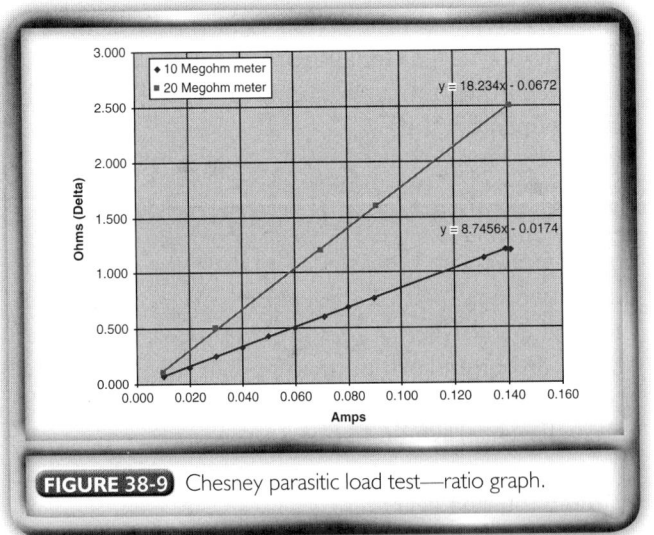

FIGURE 38-9 Chesney parasitic load test—ratio graph.

To measure parasitic draw with a Chesney parasitic load test, follow the steps in **SKILL DRILL 38-9**:

1. Set the DVOM to read ohms (lowest scale if available). Connect the leads together and read the meter screen. This is the meter's delta reading. **(Photo 1)**
2. Place the black meter lead on the negative battery post and the red lead on the alternator case. **(Photo 2)**
3. Read the meter and compare the reading to the Chesney parasitic load ratio graph (Figure 38-10). If there is excessive parasitic load, pull fuses one at a time to identify the faulty circuit. **(Photo 3)**

Engine Starting (Cranking) Systems

The starting system provides a method of rotating (cranking) the vehicle's internal combustion engine (ICE) to begin the combustion cycle. In early vehicles, this was done by the use of a hand-crank handle. Modern vehicles use an electric starter motor that draws its electrical power from the vehicle's battery. The starter is designed to work for short periods of time and must crank the engine at sufficient speed in order for it to start. Modern starting systems are very effective provided that they, and the battery, are well maintained.

The starting/cranking system consists of the battery, high- and low-amperage wires, a solenoid, a starter motor assembly ring gear, and the ignition switch. On PCM-activated starting systems, there is also the PCM, a relay, and all of the related sensors that feed information to the PCM. A control circuit determines when and if the cranking circuit will function.

The control circuit starts sometimes with a fuse, the ignition switch (or PCM circuitry), the starter relay, a safety switch, and/or a combination relay/starter solenoid. All vehicles equipped with an automatic transmission use a neutral safety switch or a similar device, and many vehicles equipped with a manual transmission have a clutch safety switch.

An on-board computer (PCM) and a security system may also determine if and when the starting system will function.

SKILL DRILL 38-9 Measuring Parasitic Draw—Chesney Parasitic Load Test

1. Set the DVOM to read ohms (lowest scale if available). Connect the leads together and read the meter screen. This is the meter's delta reading.
2. Place the black meter lead on the negative battery post and the red lead on the alternator case.
3. Read the meter and compare the reading to the Chesney parasitic load ratio graph. If there is excessive parasitic load, pull fuses one at a time to identify the faulty circuit.

During the cranking process, two actions occur. The pinion of the starter motor engages with the flywheel ring gear, and the starter motor then rotates to turn over, or crank, the engine. The starter motor is an electric motor mounted on the engine block or transmission. It is typically powered by the 12-volt storage battery, although some hybrid vehicles use the high-voltage battery to operate the starter motor. It is designed to have high turning effort (torque) at low speeds. The starter cables are the heaviest in the vehicle since they carry the high current needed by the starter motor. The starter motor causes the engine flywheel and crankshaft to rotate from a resting position and keeps them turning until the engine fires and runs on its own.

Starter Motor Principles

The starter motor converts electrical energy to mechanical energy for the purpose of cranking the engine over. There are three sections to the typical starter—the electric motor, the drive mechanism, and the solenoid. The starter motor is mounted on the transmission or cylinder block in a position to engage a ring gear around the outside edge of the engine flywheel, flex plate, or torque converter. Starting is usually accomplished by the operator activating a starter switch built into the ignition lock assembly, or a start button. A relatively small current flows through a neutral safety switch or clutch switch to a starter relay that controls a larger current to operate the starter solenoid, which is typically mounted atop the starter motor. The solenoid plunger moves the drive pinion gear into engagement with the ring gear and also closes a set of heavy-duty contacts. This allows a very large current to flow from the battery to the starter motor, rotating the armature and drive pinion gear, causing the crankshaft to rotate. When the engine starts and is able to run on its own, the operator usually releases the key and the solenoid spring withdraws the pinion gear from the ring gear and brings the armature

to a halt. On many modern vehicles, the PCM signals the relay to continue the cranking process once a crank signal is received from the operator until the vehicle starts or the starting operation times out.

Direct-Drive/Gear Reduction Styles

Starter motors can be designed to drive the ring gear in one of two ways: either direct-drive or gear reduction. In the direct-drive system, the starter drive is mounted directly on one end of the armature shaft. The starter drive transfers the rotating force of the armature directly to the engine flywheel **FIGURE 38-10**. In this arrangement, the only gear reduction is the reduction between the pinion gear and the ring gear.

Gear reduction starters use an extra gear between the armature and the starter drive mechanism. They have a reduction of about 4:1. The gear reduction allows the starter to spin at a higher speed with lower current **FIGURE 38-11**. It also enables the starter to be downsized yet create a higher torque output. Two types of gearing systems are normally used: spur gears or planetary gears. Spur gears require the armature to be offset via a gear housing that holds the starter drive. A gear reduction system using planetary gears does not require an offset housing; the planetary gears are housed in the drive-end housing in line with the starter drive.

Starter Motor Construction, Including the Brake Washer

A starter motor normally consists of the following components: field coils or large permanent magnets, an armature, a commutator, brushes, a drive pinion with an overrunning clutch, and a drive pinion engagement solenoid and shift fork **FIGURE 38-12**. The armature is the revolving component of the DC motor. The armature

FIGURE 38-10 Armature and starter drive from a direct-drive starter.

FIGURE 38-11 Gear reduction starter.

shaft is supported at each end by bushings or bearings pressed into end frames, which locate the armature

FIGURE 38-12 Exploded view of a starter motor.

FIGURE 38-13 Electrical schematic of the power flow. **A.** Permanent magnet starter. **B.** Series-wound starter.

centrally in the outer casing (i.e., the "barrel") of the motor and between the field coils or permanent magnets.

The commutator end frame carries copper-impregnated carbon brushes, which conduct current through the armature when it is being rotated in operation. The brushes are mounted in brush holders and are kept in contact with the commutator by tensioned spiral springs.

Half of the brushes are connected directly to the end frame and ground the armature windings via the engine block to the negative battery terminal. The other brushes are insulated from the end frame and connect to the positive battery terminal via the main starter solenoid input terminal. This connection is direct from the solenoid in the case of a permanent magnet starter, and is indirect via the electromagnetic field poles in a series-wound motor **FIGURE 38-13**.

Starter Magnet Types

Starter motors use two magnet types: electromagnetic and permanent magnet **FIGURE 38-14**. Electromagnetic fields are formed by current flow through heavy strip copper windings, wound around iron pole shoes, which are then fastened

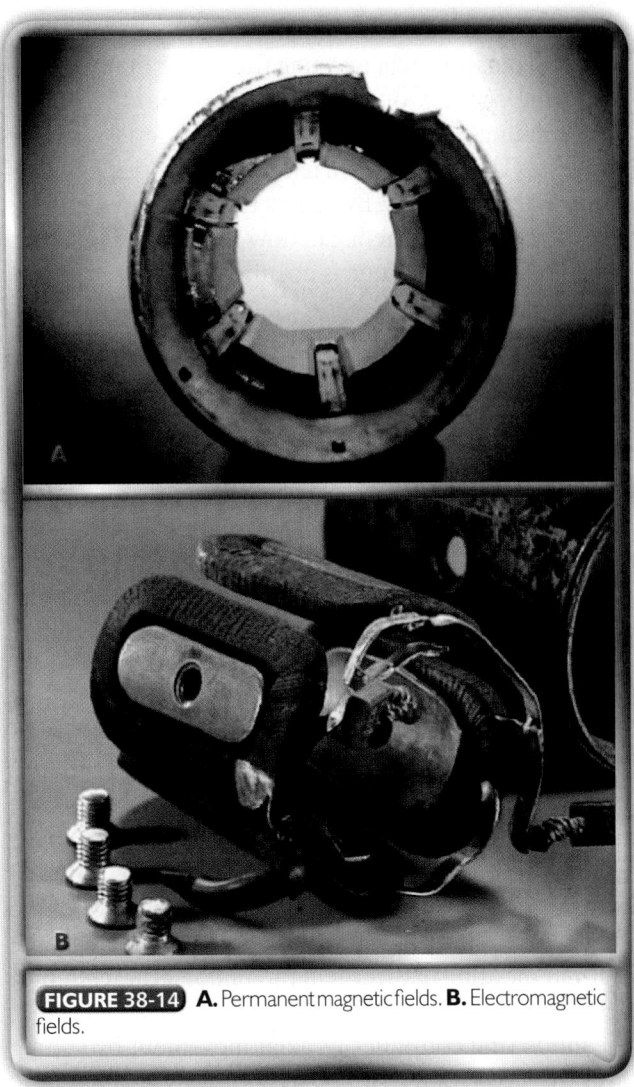

FIGURE 38-14 **A.** Permanent magnetic fields. **B.** Electromagnetic fields.

to the starter case/barrel. Permanent magnets are located similarly but do not need electricity and therefore occupy less space. The case is made of iron and serves to concentrate the magnetic field produced by the field magnets.

Starter motors with electromagnetic field windings for light vehicle applications are typically series-wound motors. Because the resistance of the field and armature windings is low, the current flow is high when the motor starts under load, and this generates a strong magnetic field that will produce high torque at low speeds. This high initial torque drops sharply as the motor speed increases because of the **counter-electromotive force (CEMF)** or voltage generated in the armature windings as the motor armature spins in the magnetic field. The CEMF increases with armature speed and opposes current flow. It reduces both current flow and torque output. The faster the motor turns, the less current it draws and the less torque it develops. For example, on a typical V6 engine with standard compression, the initial surge through the starter is usually over 500 amps, but as the armature starts to spin, the CEMF opposes the current flow, reducing it to around 120 amps (average) within about a second. This initial surge and subsequent drop of amperage can be observed on an oscilloscope when testing the starter motor.

Some series-wound motors have parallel-wired field windings, but they are still wired in series with the armature. These starters are referred to as series-parallel–wound starter motors. By connecting the field windings in this way, more current can flow in the circuit, and an overall increase in torque is obtained.

Starter Motor Engagement

Engagement is provided by operation of the ignition switch in the start position or when commanded by the PCM, which activates a starter-mounted solenoid whose plunger is engaged with the end of a pinion shift lever and operating fork. Solenoid operation moves the operating fork, causing the pinion to engage with the ring gear and also causing the plunger contacts to bridge with the main starter terminals. The fork is located in a guide ring on the pinion drive, which is coupled to the pinion gear via a roller-type overrunning clutch. It is designed to transmit drive in one direction only and freewheel in the opposite direction.

The pinion drive is mounted on a slight helix that is machined onto the armature shaft to form a very coarse thread. This arrangement allows the pinion drive to rotate slightly when it is moved toward the ring gear. This feature, together with a chamfer on the leading edge of the ring gear and pinion gear teeth, is designed to assist the teeth in meshing. However, if the pinion gear teeth butt against the ring gear teeth and engagement is prevented, the guide ring continues its axial movement by sliding over the sleeve of the drive and compressing a meshing

spring until the solenoid plunger contacts bridge the main terminals and the armature begins to turn.

Slight armature rotation and the force from the meshing spring push the pinion teeth into mesh with the ring gear. The meshing spring forces the pinion farther into the ring gear until the pinion contacts a stop ring on the armature shaft. This prevents further axial movement. The starter drive is locked to the shaft via the helix. The one-way clutch drives the pinion gear and transfers the armature rotation to the ring gear.

The pinion has only a small number of teeth compared to the ring gear, usually around 17:1, meaning the armature will rotate 17 times for each revolution of the flywheel. The gear reduction with this ratio also multiplies the torque from the starter motor 17 times, allowing a relatively small electric motor to turn the much larger ICE. If a gear reduction starter is used, then the torque is multiplied further, giving more cranking power from the same size starter motor.

As soon as the engine starts, it may easily run at 1000 revolutions per minute (rpm) or more. If still engaged, the engine would then turn the starter pinion gear about 17 times faster, or 17,000 rpm. Turning that fast would destroy the armature. At this instant, the freewheeling of the overrunning clutch prevents the armature from turning too fast should the driver not release the ignition key from the start position.

The pinion remains meshed as long as the engaging lever is held in the engaged position. Releasing the starter switch (or the PCM terminating the crank signal) allows the solenoid plunger return spring to disengage the pinion gear from the ring gear by returning the engaging lever, starter drive, and pinion gear to their original position.

Commutation and Brushes

When current flows in a conductor, an electromagnetic field is generated around it. If the conductor is placed so that it cuts across a stationary magnetic field, the conductor will be forced out of the stationary field. This occurs when the lines of force of the stationary field are distorted by the electromagnetic field around the conductor and try to return to a straight-line condition. Reversing the direction of current flow in the conductor will cause the conductor to move in the opposite direction. This is known as the motor effect and is greatest when the current-carrying conductor and the stationary magnetic field are at right angles to each other.

A conductor loop that can freely rotate within the magnetic field is the most efficient motor design. In this position, when current flows through the loop, the stationary magnetic field is distorted and the lines of force try to straighten. This forces one side of the loop up and the other side of the loop down, thus turning the loop

FIGURE 38-15. The turning motion is called the motor effect and causes the loop to rotate until it is at 90 degrees to the magnetic field. To continue rotation, the direction of current flow in the conductor must be reversed at this static neutral point. A commutator is used to continually reverse the current flow to maintain rotation of the loop **FIGURE 38-16**. For example, a commutator consists of two semicircular segments that are connected to the two ends of the loop and are insulated from each other. Carbon-impregnated brushes provide a sliding connection to the commutator to complete the circuit and allow current to flow through the loop.

Applied Science

AS-75: Electromagnetism: The technician can explain the relationship between current in a conductor and strength of the magnetic field.

Electromagnetism can be defined as the physical relationship between a magnet and electricity. Michael Faraday is best known for his discoveries of electromagnetism back in 1831. His biggest breakthrough was his invention of the electric motor.

Today's automotive electrical systems use a variety of electromagnetic devices to accomplish a wide range of tasks. We have both AC and DC electric motors/generators when you consider hybrid vehicles. Automotive starters and generators (alternators) operate on the electromagnetic principle. Electric fuel pumps, cooling fan motors, and windshield wiper motors all produce a turning force based on the principles of magnetic fields.

The basic concept of the electromagnetic principle is to place a rotating armature inside of field windings. The field windings are stationary insulated electrical wires formed into a circular pattern. A magnetic field is created when current flows through the field winding. The armature spins as a result of the magnetic field. An example of this would be a starter motor.

In the case of a charging system, we can see the relationship of the output of the generator (alternator) voltage by increasing the number of turns, or windings, in the stator. We could also increase the output voltage by the rotor's magnetic field being increased.

Rotation begins with both sides of the conductor loop cutting the stationary field. When the loop passes the point where the field is no longer being cut, the momentum of rotation carries the loop and the commutator segments over so that the brushes maintain current flow in the same direction in each side of the loop relative to the stationary field.

This process will maintain a consistent direction of rotation of the loop. In order to achieve a uniform motion and torque output, the number of loops must be increased. The additional loops smooth out the rotational forces.

A starter motor armature has a large number of conductor loops and therefore has many segments on the commutator **FIGURE 38-17**.

FIGURE 38-15 Simple single-loop motor and electromagnetic fields—with commutator and brushes.

FIGURE 38-16 Simple single-loop motor and electromagnetic fields at the switching point of the commutator.

FIGURE 38-17 Simple multiloop motor and electromagnetic fields—with commutator and brushes.

Solenoid Operation

The solenoid on the starter motor performs two main functions: It switches the high current flow required by the starter motor on and off, and it engages the starter drive with the ring gear. The solenoid is typically a cylindrical device mounted on the starter motor **FIGURE 38-18**. It is constructed with two electrical windings, a **pull-in winding** and a **hold-in winding**, which will be explained in a moment. One end of the solenoid has a moving soft iron plunger, which is connected to a lever that moves the starter drive. The other end has an insulated cap with electrical connections to the solenoid windings along with a set of high-current contacts and a movable copper disc that completes the cranking circuit when the solenoid plunger is drawn forward **FIGURE 38-19**. Once the cranking circuit is completed, current flows from the battery to the starter fields and armature.

The starter control circuit activates the solenoid winding to draw the plunger forward. The control circuit can be activated directly by the ignition switch on some vehicles or by the PCM on other vehicles. When the control circuit is activated, it supplies battery power to the two windings in the starter solenoid. One of these is a pull-in winding, which draws a higher current and creates a stronger magnetic field than the other winding—the hold-in winding. The inputs of both windings are connected to the S-terminal (control circuit) on the solenoid. Both windings are wound in the same direction in the solenoid housing. The output of the pull-in winding is connected to the main starter terminal leading to the field and armature windings, which provides ground to the pull-in winding until the solenoid contacts close. The output of the hold-in winding is connected to ground on the starter casing, which provides ground to the hold-in winding at all times.

When the starter is activated, current passes through both starter windings. The magnetic fields from both windings work together to attract the solenoid plunger toward the main starter terminals in the solenoid cap **FIGURE 38-20**. Plunger movement also operates the shift fork lever, thus engaging the drive pinion with the flywheel ring gear. The plunger contacts a switching pin, which transfers the motion through a contact spring, closing the main solenoid terminals. This allows a large current to flow from the battery through the starter motor windings, causing armature and pinion rotation, and rotation of the engine crankshaft. However, closing the contacts does another very important task; it shorts-to-power the output wire of the pull-in winding, resulting in two sequential actions. First, the short-to-power means that the pull-in winding has battery voltage applied to

FIGURE 38-18 The solenoid uses two electrical windings: a hold-in winding and a pull-in winding.

FIGURE 38-19 Solenoid starter contacts and starter drive linkage.

both the input and the output of the winding, stopping the current flow through the pull-in winding and stopping that magnetic field. But the hold-in winding still has power from the control circuit, so it continues to hold the plunger in place while the starter cranks. In fact, during engine cranking, the action of the helix on the rotating armature shaft causes the pinion gear to be held firmly in mesh with the flywheel ring gear. The hold-in winding is used only to ensure that the moving contact continues to bridge the main starter terminals **FIGURE 38-21**.

Once the engine starts, the control circuit is deactivated, and now is when the second action comes into play. The current stops flowing through the control circuit

to supply the input of the hold-in and pull-in windings, but the output of the pull-in winding is still activated through the bridged solenoid contacts, so current flows backwards through the pull-in winding and then forward through the hold-in winding **FIGURE 38-22**. Since the current flows in the two windings are opposite to each other, the two magnetic fields oppose each other and tend to cancel each other out, thereby allowing the plunger return spring to retract the plunger. This disconnects the power from the pull-in and hold-in windings as well as the starter motor, causing it to stop cranking the engine. As the return spring in the solenoid returns the plunger, it also retracts the pinion gear to its rest position.

Ford Starter with Moveable Pole Shoe

Some Ford vehicles use a separate starter relay in the engine compartment, instead of a solenoid, to control the high current for the starter motor. A spring-loaded pole shoe on the starter itself is magnetically pulled into position when current is supplied to the starter **FIGURE 38-23**. As the pole shoe moves into position, a shift fork attached to it engages the starter drive with the flywheel ring gear, thereby negating the need for a separate starter solenoid. Other functions of this type of starter are similar to those described previously.

Starter Control Circuit

The starter control circuit provides a means of operating the starter motor only within certain parameters, such as when the transmission is in park, the clutch is depressed, the brake pedal is applied, or the proper ignition switch is being used. These requirements help prevent accidentally

FIGURE 38-20 Both windings energized and solenoid plunger starting to move toward the cap.

FIGURE 38-21 The solenoid plunger bridging the contacts and causing the motor to turn and shorting to power the output of the pull-in winding.

FIGURE 38-22 Current flow through the windings when the ignition key is turned from the crank position.

FIGURE 38-23 Ford moveable pole shoe starter.

FIGURE 38-24 Basic starter control circuit. **A.** Neutral safety switch circuit. **B.** Clutch switch circuit.

starting the vehicle in gear **FIGURE 38-24**, which could cause an accident or injury, and also help prevent the vehicle from being stolen. For many years, manufacturers have placed switches in series with the starter solenoid windings, which prevents the starter from being activated unless each of the switches is closed. If the vehicle was equipped with an automatic transmission, then a neutral safety switch was incorporated into the shifter linkage so that the switch was only closed when the transmission was in park or neutral. If the vehicle was equipped with a standard transmission, then a clutch switch was installed such that it was closed by pressing the clutch pedal to the floor. Newer vehicles with their computer controls can monitor that information, and more, so that the starter will not activate until all of the required parameters are met. Once they are met, the PCM either activates a starter relay, which activates the starter solenoid, or the PCM activates the solenoid directly. With PCM-controlled starters, the starter control circuit becomes part of the vehicle theft-deterrent system, since the starter action can be disabled to prevent the vehicle from being started and stolen, as you will see in the next section.

Vehicle Immobilization Systems

There are many different names given to vehicle immo-bilization systems. Each manufacturer produces its own version, each with subtle differences. Vehicle immobilizers generally comprise a computer-managed security system that disables the vehicle starter and engine systems by using an electronic system to uniquely identify each vehicle key by a security code system. Some keys have a built-in elec-tronic circuit board used to store the code. This system makes it very difficult to start the vehicle with anything other than a correctly coded vehicle key. It also means that the key not only needs to be cut to fit the lock, but it must also be coded electronically to match the vehicle. Key cod-ing is usually done with a scan tool with the correct software and a pass-through device that enables the body control module (BCM) to be programmed from the Internet.

The key identification system has two states of opera-tion: mobilized and immobilized (or secure). When mobi-lized, the vehicle and engine components are allowed to operate normally. While in the immobilized or secure state, the key identification system is activated to protect the vehicle and prevent the engine from starting and/ or cranking. The system is set to immobilize when the engine is switched off and the key removed. Usually the system will incorporate a flashing warning lamp on the dash to identify that it is immobilized. To mobilize the system, the key needs to be inserted into the ignition switch and turned to the on position, or the operator has to be in possession of the electronic smart key, step on the brake pedal, and push the start button. The vehicle's security system will check to see if the key that is inserted has the correct code to enable the system. If the codes are recognized, the system will allow the engine to start.

Some General Motors vehicles have used a key with a built-in resistor. Only when the key with the correct value of resistance is inserted into the ignition switch will the immobilizer module enable the starter control circuit to operate.

Keyless Starting/Remote Starting

Immobilizer systems now use keyless starting. The vehicle has a start button on the dash and does not require the key to be inserted into an ignition switch. In this type of wireless system, the start button will start the vehicle only if the key is in the proximity of the vehicle—for example, in the driver's pocket—and if the driver is stepping on the brake pedal. The vehicle detects the key wirelessly and mobilizes the system so the engine can start if the button is pressed. A further variation of this is where the vehicle can be started remotely (for example, inside the house) by pressing a start button on the key fob instead of a button on the dash. This is handy in hot or cold climates when warming or cooling the vehicle is desired prior to entering the vehicle.

Starter Drives and the Ring Gear

The starter drive transmits the rotational drive from the starter armature to the engine via the ring gear that is mounted on the engine flywheel, flex plate, or torque converter. The starter drive is composed of a pinion gear, an internal spline that mates with the slightly curved external spline on the armature shaft, an overrunning clutch, and a return spring. The pinion gear is small in comparison to the ring gear, which means the starter turns many times faster than the engine ring gear. This also gives a large amount of mechanical advantage to the starter motor, allowing it to crank over the much larger ICE.

The overrunning clutch drives the pinion gear in one direction, while allowing it to freewheel in the opposite direction. The overrunning clutch uses roller bearings housed between an inner and an outer shell. The outer shell has tapered ramps built into it in which the roller bearings ride **FIGURE 38-25**. Springs push the rollers toward the tapered ends of the ramps. In the forward direction, the rollers roll slightly between the tapered ramps and are pinched between the inner and outer shells, thereby locking the assembly and driving the pinion gear. In the opposite direction (once the engine starts), the rollers roll up the inclined ramps against spring pressure, unlocking the rollers and allowing the pinion gear to freewheel.

FIGURE 38-25 Starter drive one-way clutch.

The overrunning clutch prevents the starter motor from being driven by the engine once the engine starts, which would spin the armature faster than it could handle. Without the overrunning clutch, the vehicle engine would overspeed the starter motor, causing significant damage.

When the starter solenoid is activated, the starter drive teeth engage the ring gear. The solenoid plunger is connected to the starter drive by a lever and pushes the starter drive into mesh with the ring gear. It also retracts the starter drive once the solenoid has been deactivated.

Starter Location Variation

Engine design usually dictates the location of the vehicle starter motor. Traditionally, most starter motors are mounted on one side of the engine so they can mesh with the ring gear. Starter motors can be difficult to see by just looking into the engine bay; they are often tucked up under exhaust manifolds or engine covers. On transverse engines, they are often mounted on the side closest to the firewall, which can make them difficult to locate. Starter motors are sometimes more easily accessed from underneath the vehicle. Often engine covers and components will need to be removed to gain access to difficult starter motor locations. On some engines, such as the General Motors Northstar engine, the starter motor is mounted at the top of the engine under the intake manifold. You may have to check the service information to locate the starter motor on some vehicles.

Hybrid Vehicle Starters

Hybrid vehicles use both an ICE and electric motors to power the vehicle's drive train, although some manufacturers have released (so-called) hybrid vehicles that are driven entirely by an ICE and use only an idle-stop feature. Most hybrid vehicles use a high-voltage electric motor for engine start-up, auxiliary power, and regenerative braking functions. Regardless of the hybrid configuration, the ICE still requires a method to crank it over. On most hybrid vehicles, this task is undertaken by the hybrid's main electric drive motor, which can spin the ICE at a much faster and smoother rate, causing it to start almost instantly. On some hybrids, a more conventional ICE starter is also provided to start the engine if the main high-voltage battery bank is discharged.

Starter Draw Testing

Testing starter motor current draw is a good indicator of overall starter motor performance. Manufacturers will specify the current draw for starter motors, and any tests must be performed with a fully charged and correct capacity battery for the vehicle. Starter motors can be tested in two ways: on vehicle or off vehicle. The on-vehicle test is usually called a starter draw test, while the off-vehicle test is called a no-load test. Manufacturers will provide specifications for one or both of the tests.

Ideally, the starter motor current draw should be tested under load, which is often easier to accomplish while the starter motor is mounted in the vehicle. Starter current draw is at its highest when the starter pinion gear first engages with the engine flywheel. As the starter motor and engine cranking speed increase, the current draw decreases and quickly stabilizes once the engine reaches full cranking speed. There is a variety of starter test equipment used to test starter draw. Each device will operate slightly differently, but all should have an inductive high-current ammeter to measure the cranking current flow and a voltmeter to measure the cranking voltage. The inductive ammeter is better to use than a standard ammeter because it does not require any battery cables to be removed; it is quickly clamped around the main starter cable. When conducting the test, the engine must be disabled so it will crank but not start. The current flow and voltage will be measured during cranking and compared to specifications.

To test the starter draw, follow the steps in **SKILL DRILL 38-10**:

1. Research the specifications for the starter draw test. Prepare the starter tester by setting it up to measure starter current. This may require setting it to "starter," "starter testing," or something similar.

2. Connect the red lead to the positive terminal of the battery and the black lead to the negative terminal of the battery. **(Photo 1)**

3. Connect the amps clamp around either the positive or the negative battery lead in the correct orientation. Make sure all of the appropriate wires are inside the clamp and the clamp is completely closed. **(Photo 2)**

4. Disable the engine from starting by one of the following methods:
   a. Clear flood mode: This mode is programmed by manufacturers on many electronic fuel injection vehicles. It can be activated by holding the throttle down to the floor before turning the key. If the engine starts, lift your foot off the throttle and try another method.
   b. Pull the fuel pump relay and run the engine until it dies.
   c. Disconnect the fuel injectors or ignition coils.
   d. Disconnect the spark plug wires. **(Photo 3)**

5. With the engine disabled, crank the engine and read the amps and volts as soon as the amps stabilize.

6. Compare the readings to specifications and determine any necessary actions. **(Photo 4)**

Testing Starter Circuit Voltage Drop

The electrical circuit of the starter motor consists of a high-current circuit and a control circuit. The high-current circuit consists of the battery, main battery cables to the starter motor solenoid, solenoid contacts, and heavy ground cables back to the battery from the engine and chassis. The control circuit activates the solenoid and can either be PCM controlled or non-PCM controlled. We will look at testing the control circuit voltage drop in the next section. Voltage drop can occur across both the high-current and control circuits; however, the high-current circuit is more susceptible to voltage drop due to the much larger amount of current flowing in the circuit. One thing to remember is that when testing the voltage drop on the high-current side, for the measurement to be meaningful, the starter must be activated by the solenoid. The starter does not necessarily have to turn, but the solenoid must at least click when the ignition switch is engaged. If the solenoid does not click, then you will need to test the control side of the starter circuit.

A voltmeter or DVOM is used to measure voltage drop across all parts of the circuit. A voltmeter with a minimum/maximum range setting is very useful when measuring voltage drop because it will record and hold the maximum voltage drop that occurs for a particular operation cycle.

> ▶ **LINK**
> Refer to the Meter Usage and Circuit Diagnosis chapter for more information on DVOMs.

Voltage drop is tested while the circuit is under load. The DVOM is connected in parallel across the component or part of the circuit that is to be tested for voltage

SKILL DRILL | 38-10 | Testing the Starter Draw

1. Research the specifications for the starter draw test. Prepare the starter tester by setting it up to measure starter current. Connect the red lead to the positive terminal of the battery and the black lead to the negative terminal of the battery.

2. Connect the amps clamp around either the positive or the negative battery lead in the correct orientation. Make sure all of the appropriate wires are inside the clamp and the clamp is completely closed.

3. Disable the engine from starting by one of the following methods:
   a. Clear flood mode: This mode is programmed by manufacturers on many electronic fuel injection vehicles. It can be activated by holding the throttle down to the floor before turning the key. If the engine starts, lift your foot off the throttle and try another method.
   b. Pull the fuel pump relay and run the engine until it dies.
   c. Disconnect the fuel injectors or ignition coils.
   d. Disconnect the spark plug wires.

4. With the engine disabled, crank the engine and read the amps and volts as soon as the amps stabilize. Compare the readings to specifications and determine any necessary actions.

drop. Usually the most efficient method is to test large sections of the circuit first and, if required, narrow down the test to individual components to identify precisely where excessive voltage drop is located. For example, you can connect the black probe to the ground side of the starter motor and the red probe to the negative battery terminal, operate the starter with the engine disabled, and record the voltage drop across the ground circuit while the starter motor is cranked. Manufacturers will specify the maximum allowable voltage drop, but a rule of thumb is no more than 0.5 volts (500 millivolts) for a 12-volt circuit.

The same test should also be performed on the positive side of the circuit. On most vehicles, the starter cable is connected to the input of the solenoid, while the output of the solenoid is connected to the input of the starter motor. Since the heavy contacts are located between the input and the output terminals of the solenoid, where possible, it is best to measure the voltage drop from the positive battery post to the starter motor input (not the solenoid input). That way you are measuring any voltage drop across the solenoid contacts, which are a high-probability failure point. Check the service information for safe methods of disabling the engine so it will not start.

To test starter circuit voltage drop, follow the steps in **SKILL DRILL 38-11**:

1 Set the DVOM to volts. Connect the black lead to the positive battery post and the red lead to the input of the starter (not the input of the solenoid unless that is the only accessible terminal). **(Photo 1)**

2 Crank the engine and read the maximum voltage drop for the positive side of the circuit. **(Photo 2)**

3 Connect the black lead to the negative battery post and the red lead to the starter housing. Crank the engine and read the voltage drop.

4 If the voltage drop is more than 0.5 volts on either side of the circuit, use the voltmeter and wiring diagram to isolate the voltage drop. Determine any necessary actions. **(Photo 3)**

> **TECHNICIAN TIP**
>
> A faulty battery will affect voltage drop tests, so always ensure that the battery is fully charged and in good condition before performing tests.

Inspecting and Testing the Starter Control Circuit

The starter control circuit activates the starter solenoid, which activates the starter motor. If there is a problem in the starter control circuit, the vehicle will likely not crank over at all, or maybe intermittently. The control circuit is made up of the battery, fusible link, ignition switch, neutral safety switch (automatic vehicles), clutch switch (manual vehicles) starter relay, and solenoid windings. If the starter is controlled by the PCM, then you must be

SKILL DRILL 38-11   Testing Starter Circuit Voltage Drop

1 Set the DVOM to volts. Connect the black lead to the positive battery post and the red lead to the input of the starter (not the input of the solenoid unless that is the only accessible terminal).

2 Crank the engine and read the maximum voltage drop for the positive side of the circuit.

3 Connect the black lead to the negative battery post and the red lead to the starter housing. Crank the engine and read the voltage drop. If the voltage drop is more than 0.5 volts on either side of the circuit, use the voltmeter and wiring diagram to isolate the voltage drop. Determine any necessary actions.

aware of all of the circuits, such as the immobilizer circuit and the PCM itself.

Before performing any tests, you should know and confirm the customer's concern. The manufacturer's wiring diagrams should be consulted to determine the circuit operation and to identify all components in the starter control circuit.

Once an understanding of the customer concern and circuit operation is obtained, it is time to test. Start by placing the DVOM's red lead on the starter input terminal and the black lead on the starter housing. Measure the voltage with the key in the crank position. At that point, assuming a fault in the control circuit is present, the voltage at the control circuit will be less than about 10.5 volts. If it is, you will need to perform voltage drop tests on the power side of the control circuit to determine which side(s) of the circuit the voltage drop is located on. If the voltage drop is less than 0.5 volts, then the voltage drop on the starter ground circuit should be measured with the voltmeter. If the voltage drop is excessive, perform individual voltage drops on the ground leg. If both the control circuit power and the ground circuit voltage are within specifications, the resistance of the solenoid pull-in and hold-in windings will need to be measured. If out of specifications, the solenoid or starter motor and solenoid will need to be replaced.

To inspect and test the starter control circuit, follow the steps in **SKILL DRILL 38-12**:

1. Use a DVOM to measure voltage between the solenoid control circuit terminal on the solenoid and the housing of the starter while the engine is cranking.

2. If the voltage is less than 10.5 volts, measure the voltage drop on the power side of the circuit.

3. If the voltage drop is less than 0.5 volts, measure the voltage drop on the ground side of the circuit.

4. If the voltage drop is higher than 0.5 volts on either side of the circuit, use the wiring diagram to guide you in isolating the voltage drop on that side of the circuit.

5. If the voltage drops are within specifications on both sides of the circuit, continue to the next test.

Inspecting and Testing Relays and Solenoids

The starting system typically contains solenoids and relays that activate the control circuit. The solenoid is mounted on the starter motor, while the starter circuit relay is usually in or near the main fuse box with other similar devices.

Before performing any tests, ensure that the vehicle battery is charged and in good condition. The manufacturer's wiring diagrams should be checked to determine the circuit operation, identification, and location of all components in the starter circuit.

Relays must be tested in two or three ways depending on the relay. The simplest test is to measure the resistance of the relay winding. If it is out of specifications, the relay will need to be replaced. If it is OK, the contacts will need to be tested for an excessive voltage drop. The best way to do this is by using an adapter that fits between the relay and the relay socket. This will allow the normal circuit current flow to flow through the contacts so that a voltage drop measurement can be taken. Any excessive voltage drop across the relay contacts will require the replacement of the relay. The last test is used only on relays with a suppression diode in parallel with the relay winding. Connect a reasonably fresh 9-volt battery across the relay winding terminals in one direction, and then switch polarity by turning the battery around. If the diode is good, the relay should click in one direction and not in the other. If it clicks in both directions, the diode is open. If it does not click in either direction, the relay winding is open or the diode is shorted.

Solenoids can be difficult to test on the vehicle due to poor access, and tests will usually be limited to voltage and voltage drop tests on the main contacts. For other tests, such as pull-in and hold-in winding tests, the starter motor will usually need to be removed. Care should be taken when testing relays and solenoids to ensure that cables are not shorted to ground and the engine is not accidentally cranked over.

The first test to perform is a voltage drop test across the solenoid contacts. Place the red lead on the solenoid B-positive input and the black lead on the solenoid B-positive output. The voltage drop should be less than 0.5 volts. If not, replace the starter assembly. Testing of the solenoid winding requires partial disassembly of the solenoid. Therefore, it is usually best to disconnect the control circuit connector from the solenoid and use a jumper wire to activate the solenoid. If the solenoid and starter operate, there is probably a fault in the vehicle's control circuit that needs further testing. If the solenoid or starter does not work (and the ground circuit is good), then the starter is likely faulty and will need to be replaced.

To inspect and test relays and solenoids, follow the steps in **SKILL DRILL 38-13**:

1. To test a relay, measure the resistance of the relay winding and compare to specifications. If out of specifications, replace the relay. (**Photo 1**)

2. Use a relay adapter to mount the relay on top of the relay socket so you can check the control

SKILL DRILL | 38-13 | Inspecting and Testing Relays and Solenoids

1 To test a relay, measure the resistance of the relay winding and compare to specifications. If out of specifications, replace the relay.

2 Use a relay adapter to mount the relay on top of the relay socket so you can check the control circuit wiring and perform voltage drop tests on the contacts. Activate the relay while measuring the voltage across the relay winding. If it is near battery voltage, the control circuit wiring is OK.

3 Measure the voltage across the contacts with the relay NOT activated. This should read near battery voltage if both sides of the switched circuit are OK. If not, perform voltage drop tests on each side of the switch circuit. Activate the relay while measuring the voltage drop across the contacts. If it is more than 0.5 volts, the relay will need to be replaced.

4 To test a starter solenoid, measure the voltage drop across the solenoid contact terminals with the key in the crank position. If more than 0.5 volts, replace the solenoid or starter assembly.

5 If the solenoid does NOT click with the key in the crank position, remove the electrical connection for the control circuit at the solenoid.

6 Use a jumper wire to apply battery voltage to the control circuit terminal on the solenoid and see if the solenoid clicks. Determine any necessary actions.

circuit wiring and perform voltage drop tests on the contacts.

3 Activate the relay while measuring the voltage across the relay winding. If it is near battery voltage, the control circuit wiring is OK. **(Photo 2)**

4 Measure the voltage across the contacts with the relay NOT activated. This should read near battery voltage if both sides of the switched circuit are OK.

If not, perform voltage drop tests on each side of the switch circuit.

5 Activate the relay while measuring the voltage drop across the contacts. If it is more than 0.5 volts, the relay will need to be replaced. **(Photo 3)**

6 To test a starter solenoid, measure the voltage drop across the solenoid contact terminals with the key in the crank position. If it is more than

0.5 volts, replace the solenoid or starter assembly. (**Photo 4**)

7 If the solenoid does NOT click with the key in the crank position, remove the electrical connection for the control circuit at the solenoid. (**Photo 5**)

8 Use a jumper wire to apply battery voltage to the control circuit terminal on the solenoid and see if the solenoid clicks. If it does, then there is likely a fault in the control circuit wiring. If the solenoid still does NOT click (and the ground circuit is good), then the solenoid windings or starter brushes are likely worn (sometimes tapping on the starter while the key is turned to the crank position will free up the brushes enough that the pull-in winding can operate). Determine any necessary actions. (**Photo 6**)

Removing and Installing a Starter

Starter motors are usually located close to the flywheel end of the engine. They can be in difficult-to-reach locations, and some engine components or covers may need to be removed to gain access. In most cases, the starter can be accessed more easily from underneath the vehicle. Always disconnect the negative battery lead before attempting to remove or install a starter motor, and be sure to use a memory minder if specified by the manufacturer.

To remove and install a starter in a vehicle, follow the steps in **SKILL DRILL 38-14**:

1 Disconnect the negative terminal of the battery after determining whether a memory minder is required. (**Photo 1**)

2 Remove any engine covers or components required to gain access to the starter.

3 Remove starter motor electrical connections, noting how the wires were routed. In some vehicles, the wires cannot be accessed until the starter is removed. (**Photo 2**)

4 Loosen the starter motor mounting bolts and remove them while holding the starter so it does not fall. The starter is quite heavy and can pinch fingers or break toes if it slips or falls. (**Photo 3**)

5 Remove the starter motor, being careful to catch any shims that might be between the starter and the block.

6 Reinstall the starter motor by reversing these steps, and verify its proper operation. (**Photo 4**)

Differentiating Between Electrical and Mechanical Problems

Failure to crank over properly, whether a slow-crank or a no-crank condition, can be caused by electrical or

SKILL DRILL | **38-14** | **Removing and Installing a Starter**

1 Disconnect the negative terminal of the battery after determining whether a memory minder is required.

2 Remove any engine covers or components required to gain access to the starter. Remove starter motor electrical connections, noting how the wires were routed. In some vehicles, the wires cannot be accessed until the starter is removed.

3 Loosen the starter motor mounting bolts and remove them while holding the starter so it does not fall.

SKILL DRILL   38-14   Removing and Installing a
Starter, continued

4 Remove the starter motor, being careful to catch any shims that might be between the starter and the block. Reinstall the starter motor by reversing these steps, and verify its proper operation.

mechanical problems. For example, slow cranking could result from an electrical fault such as high resistance in the solenoid contacts. This problem could be resolved by replacing the starter with a new or remanufactured unit. But the slow-crank condition could also be caused by a mechanical engine fault such as a spun main bearing that is causing a lot of drag on the crankshaft, preventing the starter from cranking it over at normal speed. In this case, the entire engine will need to be rebuilt. As you can imagine, telling customers that they need a new starter motor when in fact they need a new engine (costing 10–20 times as much money) will not make them very happy with you. It is important to be able to differentiate between the two types of faults so that a wrong diagnosis can be avoided and the problem fixed appropriately the first time.

Typical electrical problems that can cause starting system problems include loose, dirty, or corroded terminals and connectors, a discharged or faulty battery, a faulty starter motor, or a faulty control circuit. Mechanical problems that may cause starting system problems include seized pistons or bearings, hydrostatic lock from liquid in the cylinder(s) (e.g., a leaky fuel pressure regulator or water ingestion during off-road operation), incorrect ignition or valve timing, a seized alternator or other belt-driven device, and so on. Gathering as much customer and vehicle information as possible will assist in narrowing down the options of what is causing the fault.

The order in which various tests are undertaken is determined by the likelihood of a particular fault occurring given the facts you gather. For example, if the vehicle is in a parking lot, there is a better chance that the fault is an electrical fault in the starting system than if the vehicle is out in the woods, in the middle of a huge puddle of mud and water, which would tend to move the odds toward a hydrolocked or seized engine. You will also need to consider the ease of conducting a particular test or performing a visual inspection for determining the fault. For example, it is easier to perform a starter draw test than it is to pull the oil pan and inspect the main bearings. Always check for the most common and easiest faults first.

If possible, measure starter motor current draw; excessive draw may indicate a starter motor electrical fault or a mechanical engine fault. A slow crank accompanied with low draw typically points to high resistance in the main starter circuit or the starter itself. A slow crank accompanied by a high draw could be due to a fault in the starter or to engine mechanical fault. If a mechanical fault is suspected, check the oil and coolant for signs of contamination. If the coolant and oil are mixing, suspect a head gasket or cracked head/block issue. If the oil and coolant are not contaminated, turn the engine over by hand to see if it is tight compared to a similar known good engine. If it is harder to turn than it should be, remove the accessory drive belt, spin each of the accessories, and try to turn the engine over again. If still hard to turn over, you will have to go deeper in your visual inspection and start disassembling components based on the information you have gathered along the way. For example, if the crankshaft cannot be turned a complete revolution, remove the spark plugs and see if liquid is ejected out of one or more spark plug holes. If so, the engine was hydrolocked and you will need to determine the cause. If no liquids are ejected, then you will need to disassemble the engine further until you determine the cause of the mechanical resistance.

The important thing to remember is that slow-crank and no-crank conditions can be caused by both electrical and mechanical faults, so don't jump to conclusions. You need to identify the root cause of the fault so you can advise the customer on what is needed to repair the vehicle.

▶ Charging Systems

Compared to older vehicles, modern vehicles are increasingly dependent on electronic and electrical systems that require a constant and reliable supply of electrical power. Alternators (sometimes called AC generators, or just generators) supply the electrical energy required for modern vehicles. The terms generator and alternator are often used interchangeably to describe the electrical generating component. Strictly speaking, the DC generator has not been used on most vehicles since the 1960s. Thanks to solid state electronics and circuitry, alternators have taken over due to their superior operating characteristics, including:

- Greater wattage output at lower rpm
- Higher rpm
- Smaller physical size and weight for a given output
- Greater reliability and longer service life (brushes)

Both DC generators and alternators produce electricity by relative movement of conductors in a magnetic field, which induces an electrical potential or voltage within the conductors. The key difference between an alternator and a DC generator is which component rotates or moves to generate electricity. In the DC generator, the conductors that generate power rotate as part of the armature, which rotates within a magnetic field created by the stationary pole shoes. In the alternator, the magnetic field is created by the rotor, which rotates within the stationary stator windings to generate electricity there. In both cases, there is relative movement between the magnetic field and the conductors.

The charging system provides electrical energy for all of the electrical components on the vehicle. The main parts of the charging system include the battery, the alternator, the voltage regulator (which may be integrated into the alternator), a charge warning light, and wiring that completes the circuits.

The battery stores an electrical charge in chemical form, acts as an electrical dampening device for variations in voltage or voltage spikes, and provides the electrical energy for cranking the engine. Once the engine is running, the alternator—which is connected to the engine and driven by a drive belt—converts some of the mechanical energy of the engine into electrical energy to supply energy to all the electrical components of the vehicle. The alternator also charges the battery to replace the energy used to start the engine. The voltage regulator circuit maintains optimal battery state of charge by sensing and maintaining a required charging system output voltage.

Older vehicles have separate (discrete) regulators mounted on the firewall. The next generation of charging systems included regulators that were incorporated inside the alternator. More recently, the PCM is used to control the charging system more efficiently by controlling alternator output based on a number of parameters such as electrical load, engine load and rpm, alternator capability, battery temperature, fuel economy benefits, and more.

Alternator Principles

The alternator converts mechanical energy into electrical energy by electromagnetic induction. In a simplified version, a bar magnet rotates in an iron yoke, which concentrates the magnetic field. A coil of wire is wound around the stem of the yoke. As the magnet turns, voltage is induced in the coil, producing a current flow **FIGURE 38-26**. When the north pole is up and south is down, voltage is induced in the coil, producing current flow in one direction. As the magnet rotates, and the positions of the poles reverse, the polarity of the voltage

FIGURE 38-26 Electromagnetic induction.

reverses as well and, as a result, so does the direction of current flow. Current that changes direction in this way is called alternating current, or AC. In this example, the change in direction occurs once for every complete revolution of the magnet.

Alternating Current

The value of the <u>electromotive force (EMF)</u> or voltage potential induced by an AC generator depends on four factors. The first is the strength of the magnetic field. Increasing the strength of the magnetic field increases the value (voltage output) of the induced EMF. The second factor is the speed at which the magnet rotates. The third factor is the relative distance between the magnet and conductors, and the last factor is the number of turns of wire on the stationary coil.

A single-phase AC generator has only one stationary coil, which creates a single sine wave. In a typical automobile alternator, three or possibly four separate coils of wire, or phase windings, are common. The windings are arranged so that when the magnet is rotated, it generates a three-phase (or four-phase) output. The phases are equally spaced in time, and this results in a phase shift of, in the case of a three-phase AC generator, one phase every 120 degrees **FIGURE 38-27**.

Alternator Components

The alternator consists of a stationary winding assembly called the stator, a rotating electromagnet called the rotor with a slip ring, a brush assembly, a rectifier assembly, two end frames, and a cooling fan and drive pulley **FIGURE 38-28**. A voltage regulator monitors battery voltage and varies current flow through the rotor field circuit, thus controlling the strength of the magnetic field of the rotating magnet. Field current varies as required to perhaps 5 or more amps to keep up with the output demand of the electrical system of perhaps 120 or more amps for a typical automobile. The voltage regulator's job then is to control the output of the alternator so that the system voltage is maintained within specified limits.

Rectification

<u>Rectification</u> is a process of converting AC into the DC that is required by the battery and nearly all of the automobile systems. To change AC to DC, automotive alternators use a rectifier assembly consisting of diodes in a specific configuration. Remember that a diode allows current to flow in one direction but blocks the flow of current in the other direction. A so-called three-phase "bridge" rectifier has a minimum of six diodes (three

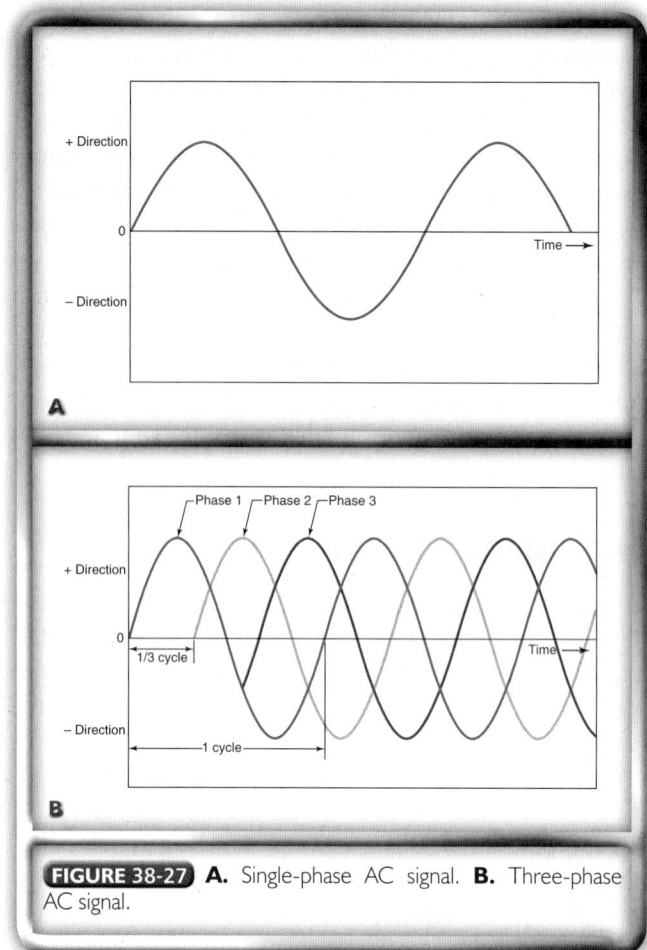

FIGURE 38-27 **A.** Single-phase AC signal. **B.** Three-phase AC signal.

FIGURE 38-28 The alternator.

positive and three negative) to rectify the AC output of the stator windings to DC output from the rectifier. A diode bridge gets its name from two diodes in series bridged with a wire. If one end of a stator winding is connected between the diodes on the bridge, then the current flows through the ground diode into the winding and out of the winding and through the positive diode. In a three-phase alternator, one side of each winding is connected to one of the bridges. Since the other end of each winding is connected to at least one other winding, a complete path from the negative diode through a stator winding(s) and the positive diode can be completed as needed.

As the rotor rotates, each time the magnetic field changes from north to south and south to north, the polarity of each phase winding reverses and, as a result, the current changes direction. No matter what direction the current is flowing in the stator windings, the diodes in the rectifier only allow current to flow into the rectifier and out of the rectifier in one direction (DC). So the diodes take the current flowing no matter what direction through the stator windings and use the current flow (even if it is reversed) to push electrons out of the rectifier's positive terminal. For example, as the rotor turns, it induces a voltage in a stator winding, which generates current flow in one direction. In this position, and with this polarity, the current path is as follows: output of winding A, positive diode A, alternator terminal B-positive, positive battery terminal, battery ground (B-negative), alternator ground, negative diode B, output of winding B, neutral or star point **FIGURE 38-29**.

When the rotor's magnet rotates further, windings B and C come under the influence of the magnetic field. The current path then is as follows: winding C, at star point, winding B, positive diode B, alternator terminal B-positive, positive battery terminal, battery ground,

alternator ground, negative diode C, output of winding C **FIGURE 38-30**. As the rotor moves through its various positions, individual phase currents change in magnitude and polarity, but the output current to the battery and the electrical circuits remains in one direction only. This is because the individual phase windings are set 120 degrees apart (three-phase system).

Thus, two things are happening. First, the three phases are split so that as the voltage in one phase is falling, the voltage in the next phase is still rising. As the second phase is falling, the third phase is rising. And as the third phase is falling, the first phase is rising again **FIGURE 38-31**.

FIGURE 38-30 Current flow through a single phase in the reverse direction.

FIGURE 38-29 Current flow through a single phase in the forward direction.

FIGURE 38-31 Three phases—not rectified.

Second, by redirecting the current so that it is flowing in the positive direction, the diodes effectively flip all of the current flow activity, from below the neutral point of the graph to the positive side, which smoothes out the power flow even further **FIGURE 38-32**.

The top of the waveform is called the alternator ripple. A ripple that is consistent across each winding indicates that the stator windings and diodes are each creating current flow and voltage consistently. Inconsistent ripple indicates a fault in either the diodes or the stator windings.

Study the illustrations carefully so that you understand the role the diode bridge plays in providing the relatively smooth DC output required by the automobile's systems.

Phase Winding Connections

Two methods of connection can be used for the stator or phase windings: wye and delta configuration. It all depends on how much alternator output is required. In the wye method of connection, one end of each phase winding is taken to a central point where the ends are connected together. This is known as the star or neutral point. The other end of each winding is connected in the bridge rectifier circuit between a positive and a negative diode. Each winding is then always part of a complete circuit, and when current is flowing, it is always flowing through two series windings at the same time.

In the delta method, the windings are connected in the shape of a triangle. Connections are then taken from each point of the triangle, straight to the bridge circuit. In this arrangement, only one winding sits between two legs of the rectifier.

Rotor Circuit

Current is provided to the rotor by means of the copper slip rings on the rotor and brushes. The rotor can be supplied with power in a variety of ways. On older vehicles, rotors on many vehicles were supplied power by means of three extra diodes, called a diode trio, and connected to the bridge rectifier circuit **FIGURE 38-33**. These extra diodes are known as field diodes or exciter diodes, and the alternator is said to be self-exciting. However, this self-excitation can only occur when the alternator is producing an output.

When the ignition is on, current flows from the positive battery terminal through the ignition switch and charge indicator lamp to the L terminal of the alternator **FIGURE 38-34**. The circuit is completed through the slip rings and rotor field winding, and through the voltage regulator, to ground on the vehicle frame.

FIGURE 38-33 Diode trio supplies power to the rotor in some alternators.

FIGURE 38-34 Current flow from the charge indicator lamp to start the alternator charging.

FIGURE 38-32 Three phases—rectified.

The small amount of current flowing in the circuit illuminates the indicator lamp and provides the initial excitation of the field winding. This slightly magnetizes the rotor iron claw pole shoes and produces a weak magnetic field to get the generation process started.

When the rotor is driven (turned by the pulley) from the engine crankshaft, the rotating magnetic field induces a voltage in the stator phase windings, which is then fed to the bridge rectifier to create DC. From there, DC goes to the B-positive alternator output terminal. Stator output is also fed to the exciter diodes so that DC current can flow to the field circuit, restricted only by the resistance of the field winding (and the regulator circuit). This strengthens the magnetic field, and the output voltage rises quickly.

The voltage regulator takes control of the field circuit to limit field current to maintain a preset regulated output voltage at the B-positive terminal voltage of

Applied Science

AS-73: Electrochemical Reactions: The technician can demonstrate an understanding of the ion transfer process that occurs in an automotive battery.

A vehicle is in the shop for routine maintenance and a general inspection is being performed. The technician observes that the battery appears to be old and finds a code on the battery indicating it was manufactured six years ago.

At lunch time, the technician discusses the topic of batteries with another technician. He has the opinion that an automotive battery should be replaced every five years to prevent possible starting problems. Jim does not agree as he believes there are too many variables to make this determination. This leads to a discussion of how a lead acid battery works.

As stated in our text, in a discharged lead-acid cell, the active material of both plates becomes lead sulfate, and the electrolyte becomes mostly water as the acid is absorbed into the plates. The result is a very weak sulfuric acid solution in the electrolyte. When being charged, the battery is connected to a DC electrical supply with electrical pressure (voltage) higher than that of the battery's total cell voltage. The charging device acts like an electron pump, forcing electrons to move from the positive plates to the negative plates in the battery.

At the negative plates, sulfate is discharged, which changes the chemical composition of the plates into sponge lead and also creates a stronger solution of sulfuric acid in the electrolyte. At the same time, lead peroxide is formed at the positive plates, which helps to restore the cell's electrical potential or voltage.

The charging process increases the amount of acid in the electrolyte, making the electrolyte stronger. When further charging no longer makes the electrolyte stronger, charging is complete.

approximately 14 volts. As the voltage on each side of the charge indicator lamp is now equal (between the lamp and the diode trio), there is no current flow through the lamp, and the lamp is turned off.

The alternator is now charging and since the output voltage at the B-positive alternator terminal is greater than that of the battery, current flows to the battery to begin the recharging process.

Voltage Regulation

The alternator's output is determined by the amount of current flowing through the rotor. The greater the current flow through the rotor, the stronger the magnetic field generated. The stronger the magnetic field, the stronger the alternator output. The voltage regulator monitors battery voltage and adjusts the current flow through the rotor appropriately.

When the engine is running and voltage output is low, the regulator allows more current to flow through the rotor field winding. This increased current flow strengthens the magnetic field, which raises the induced voltage in the stator windings, and alternator output then increases. As the output voltage increases to the maximum regulated voltage, the voltage regulator reduces the current flow through the rotor, reducing alternator output. Regulator switching takes place in milliseconds, so the voltage to the battery is fairly constant. This process occurs quickly enough to maintain consistent system voltage even as loads are switched on or off. Today's field circuits are electronically controlled by a pulse-width–modulated signal, for even smoother regulation and quicker control.

An A- or B-Type Regulating Circuit?

Switching of the field current may be done on the positive side of the rotor windings or on the ground side. In an A-type regulating circuit, alternator B-positive output is fed directly to the rotor; voltage regulation is done on the ground side of the field. In a B-type circuit, the voltage regulator is on the positive side of the field; the ground is constant. Knowing the difference is necessary in order to properly bypass a voltage regulator (full-fielding) when diagnosing some charging systems. For example, many alternators are designed with A-type circuits and a grounding tab on the regulator. The grounding tab provides a method of full-fielding the charging system with the engine running. The tab is grounded by placing a small metal rod or screw driver on the metal tab and then shorting it out by moving the side of the metal rod against the alternator frame. This grounds the A-type field causing full current to flow through the rotor, causing full alternator output. Caution: This procedure puts the charging system in an unregulated condition, which can cause the system voltage to increase high enough to damage electronic components. Only perform this test at idle, and for a few seconds. If the charging system is a B type, then battery power needs to be fed to the field. This is usually accomplished by using a test lead or jumper lead to supply power to the correct terminal. Make sure you do not mix up the types of charging systems or supply power or ground to the wrong place, as you can damage the electronic components.

High-Voltage Charging Systems

As the number of electrical components increases, vehicles require increasing amounts of available electricity. Vehicles have traditionally used 12-volt batteries and a 14-volt charging system, but to meet the increased demand from today's systems, such as electric drives, higher voltage batteries, and battery packs, an appropriately higher voltage electrical system is necessary.

The advantages of using higher voltage systems include increased power for systems and accessories, fewer concerns about voltage drop across the system, and the use of smaller diameter wires for a higher power draw, which reduces the overall weight of the vehicle.

If we apply Ohm's law, we can appreciate the differences between the voltage systems. For example, consider a vehicle with a conventional 14-volt system that has a charging current of 100 amps. Using Ohm's law (voltage × current = power), we can calculate that 14 volts times 100 amps equals 1400 watts. In a higher voltage system, less current is needed to deliver the same amount of power. By comparison, using Ohm's law again, but this time with a 42-volt system, we find that 1400 watts divided by 42 volts equals 33.3 amps. For the same amount of power (i.e., work), the current has been decreased by two-thirds. This means that for any given current flow, the cable diameter on a 42-volt system can be reduced in size and many relays and associated wiring could be eliminated.

Despite these virtues, 42-volt systems have not taken a very strong hold of the market yet. But as electrical demands in vehicles increase, and given the fact that reasonably sized, affordable, and reliable alternators above about 160 amps are more difficult to manufacture, the 42-volt charging system may yet be recognized as an option that can supply the needed power.

One method of creating higher amperage and voltage is the integrated starter alternator damper used by General Motors. It combines the vehicle starter motor and alternator into a single unit built into the flywheel, which sits between the engine and the transmission. In this case, it can function as a high-powered starter motor, which is especially useful in hybrid vehicles for stop/start systems. Once the engine is running, it functions as an alternator, charging the 12-volt battery and running all of the accessories. In some cases, it may also generate higher voltage to operate high-voltage accessories such as electric power steering and air-conditioning compressors. It can also be used for regenerative braking to recapture energy that would otherwise be lost.

Alternator Construction

Vehicle alternators are available in various output amperages to meet the demands of vehicle variations. It is not unusual for a typical modern light vehicle alternator to have an output of about 150 amps or more to ensure the electrical system is capable of powering the electrical systems. Regardless of the make or model, the fundamental construction and components of alternators are very similar. The main components of an alternator include the end frames, bearings, rotor, stator, brushes, cooling fan, regulator, and rectifier.

Rotor

The rotor is an electromagnet that rotates freely in the alternator. The rotor is supported on each end by ball bearings. It consists of a coil of insulated wire wound around an iron core and pressed onto a steel shaft. An iron pole piece is fastened on each side of the coil assembly so that the projections or claws (which are bent) interlace. The ends of the rotor coil winding are connected to insulated slip rings mounted on the shaft. The spring-loaded brushes maintain contact with the slip rings at all times so that current can flow into and out of the rotor winding.

When a current is passed through the slip rings and the coil winding, it establishes strong north and south poles at the ends of the iron core and the shaft. The projections then take on the same polarity as the end of the shaft on which they are mounted. This forms pairs of north and south poles that are alternately spaced around the rotor circumference. The rotor usually has 8 to 12 poles, which are tapered to reduce noise and create a smooth AC sine wave output as the rotor rotates. When the rotor is fully energized, the magnetic field requires a fair amount of mechanical energy to rotate the rotor inside of the stator. In fact, a high-current alternator can use more than 5 horsepower from the crankshaft to operate. Thus, any sizable electrical load will affect fuel economy. Also, a fan is either pressed or slipped onto the rotor shaft to assist in cooling the rotor and stator windings and rectifier assembly.

Stator

The stator consists of a cylindrical, laminated iron core, which carries the three (or four) phase windings in slots on the inside **FIGURE 38-35**. The windings are insulated from each other and also from the iron core. They form a large number of conductor loops, which are each subjected to the rotating magnetic fields. The stator is mounted between two end housings, and it holds the stator windings stationary so that the rotating magnetic fields can permeate the windings. The windings can be oriented in the wye or delta configuration. These can be identified as follows: The wye configuration has only one common connection for each of the three or four windings, typically consisting of three to five wires. The delta configuration typically has three separate connections, each consisting of two or three wires.

Alternator End Frames and Bearings

The alternator housings are typically constructed from aluminum with vents within the frames to provide for a large amount of airflow to assist in dissipating heat. The housings accept the bearing assemblies, which support the rotor at the drive and slip ring ends. A pulley that is driven by a belt is mounted at the drive end of the alternator. Some housings also accept some or all of the diodes, which are pressed into holes in the housing.

Slip Rings and Brush Assembly

Slip rings and brushes aid in making an electrical connection to the rotating rotor assembly **FIGURE 38-36**. The slip rings are normally copper bands, molded onto an insulating material, then pressed onto the steel shaft of the rotor. Each end of the rotor winding is connected to one of the copper bands, so that as the rotor rotates, the brushes maintain a constant connection with each end of the winding; the brushes carry the current from the stationary end frame to the moving rotor. Brushes are made of a combination of copper and carbon and are carried in brush holders mounted in the end frame of the alternator. They are spring loaded to maintain contact with the slip rings, and they wear out over time.

Rectifier Assembly

The diodes for rectification (converting AC to DC) are mounted on heat sinks to assist in dissipating the heat generated in the diodes. Each diode drops approximately 0.7 volts and thus tends to run hot. The diodes must be properly cooled to avoid premature failure. Three or more diodes are mounted on each heat sink. One heat sink has the positive diodes while the other has the negative diodes **FIGURE 38-37**. The positive diode heat sink is insulated from the frame and is connected through the output

FIGURE 38-36 Slip rings and brushes aid in making an electrical connection through a rotating assembly.

FIGURE 38-35 The stator consists of a cylindrical, laminated iron core, which carries the three-phase windings in slots on the inside.

FIGURE 38-37 Positive and negative diode schematic, including diode trio.

terminal to the positive battery terminal. The negative diode heat sink is connected to the frame, which allows the return circuit, via the negative battery terminal, to be completed. Some alternators use a diode trio assembly to supply power to the field windings once the alternator is charging. Each of these diodes is connected to one end of a stator winding.

Alternator Cooling Fan and Pulley

The alternator's cooling fan is a powerful centrifugal type of fan **FIGURE 38-38**. It is mounted on the rotor shaft and may be an integral part of the drive pulley or part of the rotor. It is essential to maintain a cooling stream of air over the diodes and stator. Due to the short length of the rotor, the cooling air needs to be spiraled in. This creates a long cooling path for the air and helps maintain component temperatures within the manufacturer's specifications. To achieve this spiraling effect, the cooling fins on the plate have different openings—small and large. To get the maximum cooling effect, the alternator fan must be driven in the correct direction. Refer to the manufacturer's specifications to determine the correct direction if removing and replacing the fan.

Voltage Regulator

The voltage regulator in modern vehicles is a solid state electronic device. It may be installed inside the alternator or, for older vehicles, mounted on the fender well as a separate component. Modern vehicles control the alternator output voltage from within the PCM or BCM. The internal regulator as a whole is a replacement part and is not usually serviceable. The regulator's electronic circuit senses the battery voltage and switches the rotor circuit on and off rapidly in order to maintain a constant voltage output up to the alternator's maximum output current.

FIGURE 38-38 Alternator fan and pulley.

More recent developments have seen the alternator regulator function built into the main PCM of the vehicle. The control principle is the same: Output voltage is controlled by switching the rotor's field circuit on and off. However, the PCM makes voltage adjustments based on a larger number of inputs, such as engine and ambient temperature, battery temperature, engine cranking, engine load, desired regeneration during deceleration, and electrical load. In most cases, an alternator that is PCM controlled also uses an internal regulator. The PCM works in conjunction with the regulator to control the output of the alternator. In some cases, the PCM communicates the desired charge rate to the regulator, and the regulator adjusts the current flow through the rotor appropriately. The regulator then reports the alternator load and any faults to the PCM. If any faults develop, the PCM will store one or more pertinent codes and will illuminate the malfunction indicator light on the instrument cluster.

Charging System Output Test

Vehicle charging systems are voltage regulated, which means that the alternator will try to maintain a set voltage across the electrical systems. As electrical load current increases in the vehicle systems, voltage starts to drop. The voltage regulator senses this voltage drop and increases the current output of the alternator, which in turn increases system voltage to try to maintain the correct voltage in the system. The testing of an alternator output initially involves the testing of the system's regulated voltage using a voltmeter. Regulated voltage is the voltage at which the regulator is allowing the alternator to create only a small charge due to the battery being relatively charged, as evidenced by the greatly reduced current output. Regulated voltage should be between the manufacturer's specified minimum and maximum regulated voltage. If it is incorrect, verify that there are no voltage drops on the alternator and regulator. If no voltage drops are found, the regulator is likely faulty and will need to be replaced.

Once the regulated voltage is confirmed, it is time to check the charging system output. This is done by using an external electrical load such as a carbon pile to reduce the battery voltage, thereby tricking the regulator into full-fielding the alternator, making it produce maximum amperage output. This output is read using an inductive ammeter and should then be compared to the manufacturer's rated output specifications. An alternator that puts out within 10% of its rated output is OK. Less than that indicates a faulty regulator, faulty alternator, or excessive voltage drop(s) on the alternator output or ground circuits.

TECHNICIAN TIP

Back in the day of DC generators, it was acceptable to test the charging system by removing one of the battery terminals from the battery post. If the engine kept running, the charging system was working. If the engine died, the charging system was not working. On alternator-equipped vehicles, doing this test is very risky, since any voltage spike caused from disconnecting the battery terminal can destroy any of the electronics in the vehicle. Thus, this test is no longer valid on virtually all vehicles on the road today.

To perform a charging system output test, follow the steps in **SKILL DRILL 38-15**:

1. Connect a charging system tester to the battery with the red lead to the positive post, the black lead to the negative post, and the amps clamp around the alternator output wire.

2. Start the engine, turn off all accessories, and measure the regulated voltage at around 1500 rpm. The regulated voltage is the highest voltage the system achieves once the battery is relatively charged, as evidenced by the ammeter reading less than about 15–20 amps when the amps clamp is around the alternator output cable. Typical regulated voltage specifications are wider than they used to be due to the ability of the PCM to adjust the output voltage for a wide range of conditions. Thus, typical readings could be about 13.2–15.5 volts on newer vehicles and 13.5–14.5 volts on older vehicles. Always check the specifications.

3. Operate the engine at about 1500 rpm and either manually or automatically load down the battery just enough to obtain the maximum amperage output without pulling battery voltage below 12.0 volts. This reading should be compared against the alternator's rated output. Normally, readings more than 10% out of specifications indicate a problem.

Testing Charging System Circuit Voltage Drop

An excessive voltage drop in the charging system output and ground circuit tends to cause one of two problems: (1) The battery is not be fully charged because although the alternator is creating the specified voltage, the voltage drop is reducing the amount of voltage to the battery, or (2) the battery is fully charged, but the alternator is working at a higher voltage to do so,

potentially overheating it. Which of the two issues is occurring depends on where the voltage is sensed. If it is sensed at the alternator, then the battery will generally be undercharged. If the voltage is sensed at the battery, then the alternator will work at the higher voltage. Knowing the system will help you diagnose voltage drop issues in the output and ground circuits of the charging system.

The external alternator output circuit components consist of the wires and fuse or fusible link between the positive battery post and the alternator output terminal, and the ground wire back to the battery from the engine and chassis. Voltage drop may occur anywhere in the output current circuit and ground circuit but is especially common at the terminals and connectors due to the high charging system current flowing through them. Even a small amount of resistance can cause significant voltage drop when conducting these higher levels of current flow.

As with testing for voltage drop at the starter circuit, a voltmeter or DVOM is used to measure voltage drop across all parts of the circuit. A voltmeter with a minimum/maximum range setting is very useful when measuring voltage drop, as it will record and hold the maximum voltage drop that occurs for a particular operation cycle. Voltage drop tests are only valid when the circuit is under load, because voltage drops can only occur when current is flowing. The greater the flow, the greater the voltage drop, if resistance is present. Therefore, when testing for voltage drop, always perform the test when the circuit is being operated.

To measure for voltage drop, the DVOM is connected in parallel across the component, cable, or connection that is to be tested. Usually it is most efficient to first measure the voltage drop on both the entire positive side and the entire negative side of the circuit, and if required, narrow down the test to individual components to identify precisely where excessive voltage drop is located (individual voltage drops in a simple circuit add up). For example, you can connect the black probe to the output side of the alternator and the red probe to the positive post of the battery. Then, operate the charging system under a heavy load by turning on as many electrical items as possible or by using a load tester to load down the battery. Record the voltage drop across the output side of the circuit while the alternator is fully charging. Then perform the same test on the ground side of the circuit from the negative battery terminal to the frame of the alternator. Manufacturers will typically specify the maximum allowable voltage drop, but a rule of thumb is no more than 0.5 volts (500 millivolts) for each side of a 12-volt circuit.

To perform a charging circuit voltage drop test, follow the steps in **SKILL DRILL 38-16**:

1. Set the DVOM up to measure voltage, and select min/max if available. Connect the red probe of the DVOM to the output terminal of the alternator and the black probe to the positive post of the battery. The red probe goes on the positive battery post because, in this case, the alternator output terminal is higher voltage than the positive battery terminal. For the meter to read correctly, the leads need to be connected as listed. **(Photo 1)**

2. Start the engine and turn on as many electrical loads as possible or use an external load bank to load the battery. Read the maximum voltage drop for the output circuit. **(Photo 2)**

3. Move the leads to measure the voltage drop on the ground circuit by placing the black probe on the alternator case and the red probe on the negative terminal of the battery. With the engine running and the circuit still loaded, read the maximum voltage drop for the ground circuit.

4. If the measurements are excessive, check each part of the circuit for excessive voltage drops by slowly bringing the probes closer together on each section of the circuit. Determine any necessary actions. **(Photo 3)**

Replacing an Alternator

Alternators need to be replaced whenever they are electrically or mechanically faulty. Electrical faults include no-charge, undercharge, or overcharge conditions. Mechanical faults include worn and noisy bearings, or other internal or external mechanical damage. When replacing an alternator, there are some precautions, the first being that battery voltage is always present at the output terminal of the alternator. This means that if the battery terminal is not removed from the battery and a wrench is placed on the output terminal of the alternator, a very large spark could occur if the wrench touches something metal. So always disconnect at least one battery terminal prior to removing the alternator. Also, check the manufacturer's information regarding maintaining the adaptive memory, if necessary.

The alternator must not be operated with the battery disconnected or with the terminals at the back of the alternator disconnected. Even though most vehicle

SKILL DRILL 38-16 Testing Charging Circuit Voltage Drop

1. Set the DVOM up to measure voltage, and select min/max if available. Connect the red probe of the DVOM to the output terminal of the alternator and the black probe on the positive post of the battery.

2. Start the engine and turn on as many electrical loads as possible or use an external load bank to load the battery. Read the maximum voltage drop for the output circuit.

3. Move the leads to measure the voltage drop on the ground circuit by placing the black probe on the alternator case and the red probe on the negative terminal of the battery. Read the maximum voltage drop for the ground circuit. If the measurements are excessive, check each part of the circuit for voltage drop by slowly bringing the probes closer together on each section of the circuit. Determine any necessary actions.

electrical systems are described as being 12 volt, they typically operate at between 13.8 to 14.5 volts. If the system is not operating in this range, the drive belt may have become loose, or excessive voltage drops in the charging or voltage-sensing circuit may be the cause. If all of these components check out, the alternator, external voltage regulator, internal regulator, or even the built-in voltage-regulating circuit in the ECM/BCM may be faulty. Make sure you have identified the cause of the fault before removing the alternator.

To replace an alternator, follow the steps in **SKILL DRILL 38-17**:

1. Install fender covers on the vehicle. Research any adaptive memory or reinitialization issues in the service information, or use a memory minder to maintain the memories of any modules. Remove the negative battery terminal from the post. Store the terminal so that it cannot come in contact with the battery post while you are working on the vehicle. **(Photo 1)**

2. Loosen the drive belt and remove it from the alternator pulley. Check the condition of the belt to see if it is still serviceable. **(Photo 2)**

3. Locate the electrical connections at the rear of the alternator and note their positions. Loosen any securing fasteners or covers, and remove terminals one at a time. In some cases, the electrical terminals are encased in a plug. When removing electrical wires and connections, make sure you reinstall the securing fastener to its thread so it does not get lost. On some applications, you will have to remove the

alternator mounting bolts to move the alternator some to gain access to the connections. **(Photo 3)**

4. Loosen the securing fasteners that hold the alternator to its mounting bracket(s), making sure the alternator is supported. Next, remove the fasteners completely and then remove the alternator from the engine bay. Some mountings have spacers that might fall out as the bolts are removed. Note the position of the spacers before removal. **(Photo 4)**

5. Reinstall the alternator. Situate the alternator in the mounting bracket(s) and, while still supporting the alternator, loosely start the securing fasteners that hold the alternator to its mounting bracket(s). **(Photo 5)**

6. Reinstall the electrical wires to their correct terminals, referring to the manufacturer's information to check that the connections are correct. Once all of the wires are installed, check the security of any fastening devices. **(Photo 6)**

7. Install the drive belt over the alternator drive pulley. If necessary, use a belt tension gauge to adjust the belt to the correct tension. To prevent damage in service, the belt should not be under- or over-tightened. **(Photo 7)**

8. Reattach the negative battery terminal to the negative post of the battery. Make sure the fastener is tight. Replace any battery terminal covers. **(Photo 8)**

9. Turn or activate the ignition to the on position, and make sure the charge light on the vehicle dash panel illuminates. Start the engine and determine

SKILL DRILL | 38-17 | Replacing an Alternator

1. Install fender covers. Verify any memory issues and remove the negative terminal of the battery.

2. Loosen the drive belt and remove it from the alternator pulley. Check the condition of the belt to see if it is still serviceable.

3. Locate the electrical connections at the rear of the alternator and note their positions. Loosen any securing fasteners or covers, and remove terminals one at a time.

SKILL DRILL | 38-17 | Replacing an Alternator, continued

4 Loosen the securing fasteners that hold the alternator to its mounting bracket(s), making sure the alternator is supported. Remove the alternator.

5 Reinstall the alternator. Situate the alternator in the mounting bracket(s) and, while still supporting the alternator, loosely start the securing fasteners that hold the alternator to its mounting bracket(s).

6 Reinstall the electrical wires to their correct terminals, referring to the manufacturer's information. Check the security of any fastening devices.

7 Install the drive belt over the alternator drive pulley and, using the correct tools, adjust the belt to the correct tension.

8 Reattach to the negative post of the battery. Make sure the fastener is tight and replace any battery terminal covers.

9 Turn the ignition to the on position and make sure the charge light on the instrument panel illuminates. Start the engine see if the charge light goes off. Measure the regulated voltage and maximum alternator amperage output. Remove the fender covers and return any tools used to their correct place.

if the charge light goes off. With a charging system tester, measure the regulated voltage and maximum alternator amperage output, as in Skill Drill 38-16, and compare to specifications.

10 Remove the fender covers and return any tools used to their correct place. **(Photo 9)**

Diagnosing Undercharge and Overcharge

Undercharging and overcharging are both bad for a vehicle. Undercharging leads to electrical systems that do not function fully, and the battery may not fully charge, leading to an early death due to sulfation. Overcharging can lead to short life of bulbs and other electrical devices, while at the same time overcharging the battery, which can increase gassing and loss of water from the electrolyte. Maintaining a proper charge is critical to long life and proper operation of the electrical system.

The voltage regulator maintains a constant voltage output from the alternator up to the maximum output current. Always check the manufacturer's specifications for alternator regulated voltages; more and more manufacturers are using PCM-controlled charging systems, which means the voltages can have a wider range than non-PCM-controlled systems.

As a rule of thumb, for a typical non-PCM-controlled 12-volt charging system, the regulated alternator output voltage should be between 13.8 and 14.5 volts. If the voltage measured is outside of the manufacturer's specifications, further testing will need to be performed to determine the cause.

For this task, we will assume that the charging system is charging (not a no-charge condition) and that it is either not charging fully or is overcharging. If the system is overcharging, it can almost always be tracked to either a faulty voltage regulator or a faulty regulator ground, both of which can cause the alternator to overcharge.

An undercharge condition has many more potential causes, such as a loose drive belt, voltage drop in the charging system wiring, faulty regulator, worn brushes in the alternator, high resistance in the rotor, open or shorted diodes, open or shorted stator windings, or even a shorted cell on a battery. Always check for the easiest and most common faults first. For example, check that the drive belts are not slipping, particularly under load. Also verify that the battery does not have a shorted cell and that its capacity is adequate.

If nothing obvious can be found wrong, then you will need to dig deeper. One way to do this is to use an oscilloscope to check the alternator ripple. The ripple will indicate faulty stator windings or diodes, meaning the alternator needs to be replaced. If the ripple is OK and the voltage output is low, then testing for voltage drops on the output and ground circuit is a good step. If voltage drops are found, then they will need to be repaired and the system retested. If there are no voltage drops, then the fault is likely to be located inside of the alternator, such as a faulty regulator, worn brushes, or a faulty rotor, which would also require replacement of the alternator.

Wrap-up

Ready for Review

- The primary components of the battery are the case, cover, vent caps, plates, separators, electrolyte, and terminals.
- Batteries operate by storing electrical energy in chemical form.
- The discharge of electrolytes produces battery current.
- The standard automotive battery has 2.1 volts per cell, with six cells holding 12.6 volts on a fully charged battery.
- Batteries are classified into groups, and only certain groups and layouts will fit certain vehicle applications.
- Batteries are rated by electrical capacity, cold cranking amps, and amp hour ratings.
- There are two chemicals that make the battery a safety hazard: hydrogen gas and sulfuric acid.
- The absorbed-glass mat battery is good for rough handling and can be mounted on its side compared to the electrolyte battery.
- Battery temperature plays a critical part in battery life. When a battery is cold, it takes more power to start the vehicle; when a battery is to hot, its life is diminished significantly.
- Lithium-ion batteries are the future and are especially being used in hybrids. However, they have not replaced the conventional battery in most applications.
- There are two ways to connect the battery to the vehicle: the top-post design and the side-post design.
- Batteries must be kept free of corrosion, as corrosion is the fastest way to destroy a battery and cable.
- If a vehicle seems to have a dead battery after sitting, the battery needs to be checked for parasitic draw.
- Jump-starting a vehicle is one of the simplest automotive tasks to perform, but done incorrectly, it can cause battery and possible vehicle damage. Always ensure the proper polarity when connecting the dead and good batteries together.
- When servicing a battery, always wear the proper personal protective equipment.
- Battery maintenance requires inspecting, cleaning, testing, and charging. Always follow all applicable technical data when performing battery maintenance.
- Batteries need to be recycled once their life cycle is used up. They contain hazardous materials that cannot be put in a landfill.
- The best way to test a battery's capacity and internal condition is through a battery load test.
- The starting system provides a method of rotating (cranking) the vehicle's internal combustion engine (ICE) to begin the combustion cycle.
- The starting system consists of a battery, cables, a solenoid, a starter motor, a ring gear, and an ignition switch.
- The starter motor converts electrical energy to mechanical energy.
- Some starters operate through gear reduction, giving the same amount of torque at less size and weight.
- A starter motor is basically an electromagnet.
- The starter motor pinion must mesh with the engine ring gear to turn the engine over and allow the vehicle to start.
- Once the engine starts running on its own, the starter must disengage from the ring rear to avoid damaging the starter or the ring gear.
- The solenoid on the starter motor performs two main functions: It switches the high current flow required by the starter motor, and it engages the starter drive with the ring gear.
- Vehicle immobilizers generally comprise a computer-managed security system that disables the start and engine systems by using an electronic system to uniquely identify each vehicle key by a security code system.
- Hybrid vehicles use both an ICE and electric motors to power the vehicle's drive train.
- Testing starter motor current draw is a good indicator of overall starter motor performance.
- Compared to older vehicles, newer vehicles put a higher demand on the charging system, as many systems are required not only to operate the vehicle but also to operate an array of entertainment systems.
- The DC generator has not been used on vehicles since the 1960s.
- The AC generator, or alternator, is used on today's vehicles both to recharge the vehicle battery and to run numerous other electrical accessories on the vehicle.

▶ The alternator converts mechanical energy into electrical energy.

▶ The alternator changes AC to DC by using a rectifier with diodes to allow electrical current to flow in one direction only.

▶ The alternator has a regulator, either built in or external, to keep the alternator from overcharging the battery.

▶ The more amps the alternator can produce, the more accessories the vehicle electrical system can handle.

▶ The first item that should be checked if an alternator is not charging according to the manufacturer's specifications is the belt tension and condition.

Key Terms

<u>absorbed glass mat</u> A type of lead-acid battery.

<u>battery terminal configuration</u> The placement of positive and negative battery terminals.

<u>cold cranking amps (CCA)</u> A standard for rating the ability of a vehicle battery to supply high current under cold operating conditions.

<u>counter-electromotive force (CEMF)</u> Voltage created in the field windings as the motor rotates, which opposes battery voltage and limits motor speed.

<u>cranking amps (CA)</u> A standard similar to CCA, but that measures the battery's function at a higher temperature—32°F (0°C)

<u>current clamp</u> A device that clamps around a conductor to measure current flow. It is often used in conjunction with a DVOM.

<u>electrical capacity</u> The ability of a circuit or component to carry electrical loads.

<u>electrolyte</u> The liquid in lead-acid battery cells. It is a mixture of about 67% water and 33% sulfuric acid.

<u>gassing</u> The escape of gas from the battery.

<u>hold-in winding</u> A low-current winding found in starter solenoids that holds the plunger in the activated position.

<u>keep alive memory (KAM)</u> A certain minimum amount of parasitic current draw that is used by the vehicle's circuits to maintain memory functions and monitor systems.

<u>parasitic draw</u> Unwanted drain on the vehicle battery when the vehicle is off.

<u>pull-in winding</u> A high-current winding found in starter solenoids that pulls the solenoid plunger into the activated position.

<u>rectification</u> A process of converting AC into DC required by the battery and nearly all of the automobile systems.

<u>reserve capacity</u> A standard used to specify the time in minutes that a battery will supply a load of 25 amps at 80°F (27°C) without its voltage dropping below 10.5 volts.

<u>thermal runaway</u> A cycle during battery charging in which heating lowers resistance, which in turn increases current flow, which in turn further increases heat created. During this cycle, dangerous gases may build up, creating the potential for an explosion or damage through excessive current flow.

ASE-Type Questions

1. Tech A says that a battery stores electrical energy in chemical form. Tech B says that a battery creates direct current. Who is correct?
   a. Tech A
   b. Tech B
   c. Both A and B
   d. Neither A nor B

2. Tech A says that a 12-volt battery has six cells. Tech B says that the more plates a cell in a battery has, the more voltage it creates. Who is correct?
   a. Tech A
   b. Tech B
   c. Both A and B
   d. Neither A nor B

3. Tech A says that a parasitic draw is measured in volts. Tech B says that pulling fuses one at a time can help locate a parasitic draw. Who is correct?
   a. Tech A
   b. Tech B
   c. Both A and B
   d. Neither A nor B

4. Tech A says that when disconnecting the battery, the negative terminal should be disconnected first. Tech B says that baking soda and water will remove oxidation from battery terminals. Who is correct?
   a. Tech A
   b. Tech B
   c. Both A and B
   d. Neither A nor B

5. Tech A says that checking the specific gravity will indicate the battery's cold cranking amps. Tech B says that a battery load test should be performed when the battery is heavily discharged. Who is correct?
   a. Tech A
   b. Tech B
   c. Both A and B
   d. Neither A nor B

6. Tech A says that some starters use gear reduction to improve efficiency. Tech B says that a starter converts electrical energy to mechanical energy. Who is correct?
   a. Tech A
   b. Tech B
   c. Both A and B
   d. Neither A nor B

7. Tech A says that the pull-in winding is short-circuited when the solenoid is fully engaged. Tech B says that the starter drive has a built-in one-way clutch. Who is correct?
   a. Tech A
   b. Tech B
   c. Both A and B
   d. Neither A nor B

8. Tech A says that a voltage drop of 0.8 volts on the starter ground circuit is within specifications. Tech B says that high starter draw current could be caused by a spun main bearing in the engine. Who is correct?
   a. Tech A
   b. Tech B
   c. Both A and B
   d. Neither A nor B

9. Tech A says that the first item to check if an engine does not crank is the voltage to the S-terminal on the starter. Tech B says that the first item to check if an engine does not crank is battery voltage. Who is correct?
   a. Tech A
   b. Tech B
   c. Both A and B
   d. Neither A nor B

10. Tech A says that the voltage regulator controls the strength of the rotor's magnetic field. Tech B says that the voltage regulator is installed between the output terminal of the alternator and the positive terminal of the battery. Who is correct?
    a. Tech A
    b. Tech B
    c. Both A and B
    d. Neither A nor B

CHAPTER 39

NATEF Tasks

Lighting Systems

Knowledge Objectives

After reading this chapter, you will be able to:
1. Describe different types of lighting found on a vehicle and the function of each type. (pp 1338–1352)
2. Explain the operation and benefits of various lighting systems. (pp 1342–1352)

Skills Objectives

After reading this chapter, you will be able to:
1. Check lighting and peripheral systems. (p 1356)
2. Check and change an exterior light bulb. (pp 1356–1357)
3. Check and change a headlight bulb. (pp 1356–1358)
4. Aim headlights. (pp 1358–1359)
5. Check digital instrument circuits. (p 1360)
6. Check warning device operation. (p 1360)

Introduction

Well-designed vehicle lighting systems enhance vehicle safety by increasing the driver's visibility while operating the vehicle and by clearly signaling the driver's intent to those around the vehicle. Lighting systems are also used inside the vehicle to indicate messages to the driver and provide convenience to any occupants. Manufacturers continue to improve and develop their lighting systems as new technology becomes available. Modern lighting system features include the increased use of light-emitting diode (LED) and xenon lighting, electronic body control units to manage lighting, and high-intensity discharge (HID) lamps, which are much brighter than the traditional sealed-beam or halogen units. Many vehicles also have systems that warn you if lamps are not working properly.

Lighting Systems

Lighting systems improve visibility at night and make a vehicle visible to other road users. A lighting switch activates taillights, park lights, and headlights to allow the driver to see ahead and be seen from the side and rear. A beam selector switch allows the driver to change the beams from high to low, or vice versa, as required. Brake lights operate when the brake pedal is depressed or when a vehicle control module is automatically applying the brakes. Red or amber turn signals alert other drivers of a change in direction and are mounted so they can be seen from the front, the rear, and sometimes the sides of the automobile. The emergency flasher system operates both front and rear turn signals at the same time as a warning to others. Other circuits operate courtesy, or convenience, lights, back-up (reverse) lights, fog lights, and fault indicators.

Types of Lamps

Modern vehicles use many different kinds and sizes of lamps, also known in some places as light bulbs or light globes. There are several lamp types available, including standard incandescent lamps, halogen lamps, vacuum tube fluorescent (VTF) lighting, HID xenon gas systems, LEDs, and more. Conventional incandescent lamps are being replaced in many applications by these other more efficient types of lights.

Incandescent and Halogen

Incandescent lamps consist of one or more filaments that heat up to approximately 5000°F (2760°C) and glow white hot **FIGURE 39-1**. The filament material does not burn because most of the oxygen in the bulb has been replaced by inert gases that stop combustion from occurring. The power in watts consumed is often marked on the lamp; wattage (work performed) is found by multiplying the voltage used by the lamp by the current flowing through it. The higher the wattage, the more light that can be created when compared to a similar type of bulb. Incandescent bulbs are inefficient, converting only about 10% of the electricity to visible light.

Halogen lamps are another type of incandescent lamp, but they are filled with a halogen gas such as

---

You are the Automotive Technician

A customer brings his 2010 Dodge Avenger into the auto dealership for a 60,000 mile service checkup. You take the vehicle back to the service bay. Part of the 60,000 mile service is to check the lighting and peripheral systems. Your coworker operates each of the lights while you check the front lights and then the rear lights. You notice that the center high mount stop light (CHMSL) on the trunk lid is not functioning, but the brake lights are working normally. The customer agrees to allow you to diagnose it. After referring to the manufacturer's information and wiring diagrams, you see that the CHMSL is on the same fuse as the brake lights, so that does not need to be investigated further. You see also that the brake switch feeds both the CHMSL and brake lights, so that does not need to be investigated further. Based on your reading of the wiring diagram, you determine that the problem is between the brake switch and CHMSL, between the CHMSL and the ground, or the CHMSL bulbs or unit are faulty. You test the power and ground at the CHMSL terminals with the brake pedal applied. You find 12.2 volts available. Since the CHMSL is a sealed LED-style assembly, you know it will need to be replaced. The customer approves the repair, and you install the new CHMSL and test the vehicle again. Your coworker verifies that the light is working properly. You review the work and invoice with the customer, thank him for his business, and set him up in the automated email system to send a reminder to schedule his next maintenance visit.

1. Why didn't you have to check the fuse or brake switch?
2. What did the 12.2 volt reading at the CHMSL terminals tell you?
3. How do wiring diagrams save time?

FIGURE 39-1 Incandescent bulb with single filament.

FIGURE 39-2 Halogen bulb.

bromine or iodine FIGURE 39-2 . These lamps have a much longer life and are generally brighter and produce more light per unit of power consumed. However, they become very hot in use. They are manufactured from highly heat-resistant materials, and the bulbs must be handled carefully because they are sensitive and can be damaged even by finger oil residue left by fingerprints.

Vacuum Tube Fluorescent

Vacuum tube fluorescent (VTF), also called vacuum fluorescent display (VFD), is used for instrumentation displays on vehicle instrument panel clusters. This type of lighting emits a very bright light with high contrast and can display in various colors. Usually VTF displays are of bar graphs, seven-segment numerals, multisegment alphanumeric characters, or a dot-matrix pattern. VTF displays include different kinds of alphanumeric characters and symbols to alert drivers of various conditions.

High-Intensity Discharge

High-intensity discharge (HID) headlamps produce light with an electric arc rather than a glowing filament FIGURE 39-3 . The high intensity of the arc comes from metallic salts that are vaporized within an arc chamber. HIDs produce more light for a given level of power consumption than ordinary tungsten or halogen bulbs. Automotive HID lamps are commonly called "xenon headlamps," though they are actually metal halide lamps that contain xenon gas. The light from HID headlamps exhibits a distinct bluish tint as compared with the yellow-white color of tungsten-filament headlamps.

HID headlamp bulbs do not run on low-voltage direct current; they require a **ballast** with an internal or an external igniter that is either integrated into the bulb

FIGURE 39-3 HID headlamp assembly.

or included as a separate unit or part of the ballast. The ballast increases the voltage substantially and controls the current to the bulb.

HID headlamps produce between 2800 and 3500 lumens from between 35 and 38 watts, while halogen filament headlamp bulbs produce between 700 and 2100 lumens from between 40 and 72 watts at 12.8 volts. The advantage of using HID headlight systems is that they offer substantially greater luminance than halogen bulbs (about 3000 lumens versus 1400 lumens for comparable halogen bulbs). If the higher-output HID light source is used in a well-engineered headlamp optic, the driver gets more usable light. Studies indicate that drivers react faster and more accurately to roadway obstacles when using good HID headlamps than when using halogen headlamps; therefore, good HID headlamps contribute to driving safety.

The contrary argument is that HID headlamps can impact negatively the vision of oncoming traffic due to their high intensity and the "flashing" effect caused by the rapid transition between low and high illumination in the field of illumination. This potential distraction increases the risk of a head-on collision between a vehicle using HID headlamps and a blinded oncoming driver. Scientific studies of headlamp glare from HID systems has shown that for any given intensity level, the light from HID headlamps is 40% more glaring than the light from tungsten-halogen headlamps.

Some countries mandate that HID headlamps may only be installed on vehicles (except motorcycles) with lens-cleaning systems (to reduce glare) and automatic self-leveling systems (which prevent dazzling oncoming traffic). These systems are usually absent on vehicles not originally equipped with HID lamps, so if a halogen headlamp is retrofitted with an HID bulb, light distribution with illegal levels of glare will be produced.

Another disadvantage of HID headlamps is that they are significantly more costly to produce, install, purchase, and repair. However, some of this cost is offset by the longer lifespan of the HID burner relative to halogen bulbs.

Light-Emitting Diode

Light-emitting diodes (LEDs) have been used for some time in various automotive applications, such as warning indicators and alphanumeric displays. More recent developments in LED technology have seen the production of a wider range of colors and LEDs that are brighter than previous types. It is now possible to get LEDs that emit bright red, green, blue, yellow, and clear or white light. This has made it possible to use LEDs for many new applications, such as more general lighting applications. For example, LEDs are now often used for stop lights, turn signals, and interior lighting on vehicles **FIGURE 39-4**.

One of the advantages of LEDs is that they turn on instantly. This is particularly useful in brake lights, as they can reduce the braking light response time by two-tenths of a second. This translates to an extra 16' (4.9 meters) of stopping distance for vehicles traveling at highway speeds. LEDs also have better visibility in inclement weather, operate at cooler temperatures, consume less energy, are much smaller, and can last up to 100 times longer, reducing the cost of servicing. LEDs can be specifically designed for LED lighting and also as LED replacement bulbs for more traditional bulb holders.

For automotive applications, a number of LEDs are grouped together to provide the amount of light required for the application. Additionally, LED light lenses are specifically designed with light-focusing prisms and lenses to focus the light generated by the LEDs. A typical LED has a voltage drop of 1.2 to 3.5 volts across it,

FIGURE 39-4 LED lights.

depending upon the color, when it is forward biased and emitting light.

When used in automotive lighting, many LEDs are required to give off a specified amount of light. To do so they are usually connected in groups called series strings. A number of series strings are then connected in parallel until enough LEDs are connected to give off the required amount of light.

LEDs work best when the voltage to them and the current flow through them remains constant at a preset level. There are two main ways to achieve this; the first is via a resistor. The second and more preferred way is through the use of a voltage regulation circuit.

Some LED lights are multivoltage, which means they can work on both 12- and 24-volt systems. These lights are normally used in aftermarket products, which can be installed in a wide range of vehicles.

Lamp/Light Bulb Information

All lamps or light bulbs have letters and numbers stamped on them that typically indicate their part number and often the operating voltage and power consumed. For instance, in a bulb marked 12V/21W, the filament will consume 21 watts of power when 12 volts is applied across the filament. While the wattage is not necessarily an indication of light output, it can be generally assumed that the higher the wattage, the greater the light output.

Lamps and light bulbs come in a variety of configurations to fit the various applications within a vehicle. One designation is how many filaments the bulb has **FIGURE 39-5**. Single-filament bulbs are common for use as courtesy lights, dash lights, and warning lights. Dual-filament bulbs have two filaments of different wattage; one filament emits a small amount of light, and the

FIGURE 39-5 Dual-filament bulb.

FIGURE 39-6 Bayonet-style bulbs.

FIGURE 39-7 Wedge-style bulbs.

FIGURE 39-8 Festoon-style bulbs.

second filament emits more light. These bulbs work well as a combination taillight and brake light. Headlights can also be dual-filament bulbs. In some cases, the low beam filament is lower wattage than the high beam filament, but not always. In a headlight, the filaments are positioned to give a different profile of light. Low beams emit light closer to the vehicle and angled slightly toward the side of the road, while high beams tend to focus farther down the road and straight ahead.

Another feature that differs among lights is the type of base on the lamp—in other words, what type of socket it is retained in. Bayonet-style bulbs have been around for a long time. They get their name from the two retaining pins on the side of the base **FIGURE 39-6**. The pins follow slots in the side socket and at the bottom, and the slots turn sideways into a small pocket. The pins are retained in the pocket by the spring-loaded base in the bottom of the socket, which pushes the bulb upward. This design resists vibration very well. Removal of the bulb requires carefully pushing in on the bulb and rotating the bulb slightly counterclockwise and pulling it out. One or two electrical contacts are built into the bottom of the bulb's base. If the bulb is a dual-filament bulb with two contacts on the base, then the pins will be unequal height so that the contacts will be registered properly with the contacts in the socket.

Many newer bulbs use a wedge base either made from the glass bulb itself or with a built-in plastic base **FIGURE 39-7**. The bulbs are pushed straight into the socket, and tension from the socket retains the bulb. The electrical contact on the glass-based bulbs is made by wires extending from the base of the bulb and bent over opposite sides of the wedge.

Dome lights use festoon lights, which have a base on each end of a cylindrical light bulb **FIGURE 39-8**. Each end of the filament is connected to one of the bases. Generally, the bases fit in spring steel contacts, which hold the light bulb securely in place.

Types and Styles of Lighting Systems

There are many different styles and types of lights. Each style and type is designed to perform specific roles. For example, warning lamps, turn indicators, stop lights, taillights, courtesy lamps, and headlamps all perform different roles. Lamp locations, color, and brightness are governed by regulations to ensure consistency and safety in the application of lighting on vehicles. Lighting regulations should always be consulted before modifying or adding to any of the vehicle lighting systems. Well-maintained lighting systems improve road safety for all drivers.

Courtesy Lights

Courtesy lights or lamps are used to provide ambient lighting in the cabin. They are usually low-intensity or low-wattage bulbs and can be overhead, in the doors, glove compartment, and the trunk. Door and latch switches control the various lamps for the trunk and glove compartment. Courtesy lights are usually controlled by the vehicle body computer with inputs from the ignition and door switches either in the handle, latch, or door pillar. Courtesy lights may be designed with timing circuits that allow for the cabin lamps to stay on for a short period after all the doors are shut or the vehicle is locked.

Warning Lights

Warning lamps are usually part of the instrument cluster and are controlled by electronic control units in the vehicle on a modern vehicle. Warning lamps provide the vehicle operator with information regarding the operation of the main vehicle systems, such as the vehicle battery charge level, oil pressure level, and airbag system status **FIGURE 39-9**. When the ignition initially comes on, the warning lamps usually light up as part of a self-test to show that they are in working order. Once the engine starts, the warning lamps should extinguish and not come on again while the engine is running, unless there is a system fault. Some vehicles have warning lights that self-test while the vehicle is being cranked. This function is performed by the "proofing circuit" in the ignition switch, which grounds certain warning lights when turned to the "crank" position.

FIGURE 39-9 Warning lamp.

Park/Tail/Marker/License Lights

Park, tail, and marker lights are all low-intensity or low-wattage bulbs used to mark the outline or width of the vehicle. Park and tail lamps tend to be installed close to the corners of the vehicle. Park lamps are placed to the front of the vehicle, or in some cases they are incorporated in the headlight assembly and are white or yellow in color. Tail lamps are red and usually installed in a cluster assembly with the stops lamps at the rear of the vehicle.

License plate lamps produce a white light and are designed to illuminate the lettering on the license plate at night without the white light itself being seen from the rear. The bulbs are connected in parallel to each other so that the failure of one filament will not cause a total circuit failure. A license plate illumination lamp or lamps are usually connected in parallel to the taillights and operate whenever the taillights are on.

Taillights are usually incorporated in a cluster assembly at the rear of the vehicle. Government regulations control the height of the lamps and their brightness.

Park lights are located at the front of the vehicle and are used at night when the vehicle is parked on the side of the road and are also on anytime the headlights are on. They use low-wattage bulbs and may have a lens or diffuser that makes the emitted light widespread. In some cases, park lights are incorporated in the headlight assembly. Park lights operate when the light switch is moved to the park light position. For safety reasons, park lights and taillights continue to operate when the light switch is moved to the headlight position. The bulbs are connected in parallel with each other.

On computer-controlled lighting systems, the park lights and taillights are BCM controlled. The lights are supplied with power and ground through a networked light controller. The controller is connected to a network/bus system (discussed later in this chapter) by the twisted pair of communication wires. The park light switch is hardwired to a module. When the park light switch is activated, the module sends a park light request out on the network where the appropriate controllers pick up the message and supply power or ground to the appropriate light bulb filaments to illuminate the park lights.

Marker lights are used to mark the sides of some vehicles are often located down the sides of the vehicle or trailer. They can be located on the front and rear fenders. On newer vehicles, they are sometimes placed on side-view mirrors, or between the front and the rear doors on large SUVs or pick-ups **FIGURE 39-10**. Red marker lamps face toward the rear, and yellow lamps face toward the front of the vehicle. These lights are designed to work when the park lights or headlights are selected and sometimes operate as turn signals so a driver can warn others of his or her intent to switch lanes or turn a corner.

Government regulations control the positioning of lights, including the height of the lamps' beam and their brightness. The park, tail, marker, and license plate lamps operate when the headlight switch is in both the park and the headlight-on positions. The bulbs are connected in parallel to each other so that the failure of one filament will not cause a total circuit failure. Tail and park lamps may use separate fuses, so if one circuit fails the other will continue to operate.

Brake Lights and CHMSL

Brake lights, which may also be called stop lights, are red lights mounted to the rear of the vehicle. They are usually incorporated in the taillight cluster. Many vehicles by law now have a higher additional third brake light mounted on top of the trunk lid or on the rear window. This light is called a center high mount stop light (CHMSL), or "chimsul" **FIGURE 39-11**. The brake lights are activated whenever the driver operates the foot brake to slow or to stop the vehicle or when a control module automatically applies the brakes. The lighting circuit consists of the battery, fusible links and fuses, a brake light switch, brake light bulbs, wiring to connect the components, and the ground circuit to return current from the light to the battery. It may also include a BCM to command the lights on when the proper inputs are present.

On older vehicle models, when the operator of the vehicle depresses the brake pedal, a switch mounted on the pedal support closes. This allows the electrical current to flow from the battery through the fuse, through the switch, to the brake lamp and to return to the battery by the ground circuit. When the driver releases the pedal, it returns to the rest position and opens the brake switch. The flow of electrical current stops and the brake lamps

FIGURE 39-10 Marker lights on an SUV.

FIGURE 39-11 Center high mount stop light.

are extinguished. Today, computer-controlled brake lights are activated by the body control module (BCM) when the computer sees an input from the brake pedal switch.

Applied Science

AS-33: Refraction: The technician can demonstrate an understanding of refraction as it occurs in systems that employ fiber optics.

A vehicle is in the shop for repairs to the lighting system. The repair order cites as the customer concern that the illumination for the console-mounted shifter indicator is not working. The driver is unable to determine which gear is selected for the automatic transmission at night.

Ethan is the apprentice technician at the dealership who was given the assignment of solving this concern. The first step is to verify the customer concern by covering the windows of the vehicle to simulate night conditions. Ethan looks up the manufacturer's information on a shop computer. Expecting to find an illustration showing the location of a bulb for illumination, he finds the procedure for removal of the illumination control. He then begins the disassembly procedure to get to the components involved. Rather than a conventional light socket and bulb, Ethan finds a fiber-optic lighting assembly that provides illumination for the shifter indicator.

Fiber optics components have been used by Mercedes-Benz, BMW, Daimler, Audi, Porsche, Volvo, and Cadillac. Some of the applications include dashboard lights, interior lights, taillights, and entertainment and information systems.

Refraction is defined as the change in direction of light due to a change in speed as it passes from one medium to another. A reference for the path of light is described in respect to the normal path of light. If light enters a new medium and is slowed down, it bends to the normal path. If it speeds up, it bends away from the normal path.

Aftermarket lighting accessories that are available today include fiber-optic taillights with reverse lights for certain vehicles. These lights are advertised to be considerably brighter than stock units and to light up faster and run cooler. Due to the use of fiber rather than light bulbs, fiber-optic lights are said to be vibration-proof.

Back-up Lights

The back-up lights, also called reverse lights, are white lights mounted at the rear of a vehicle. They provide the driver with vision behind the vehicle at night and also alert other drivers to the fact that the vehicle is in reverse. The lighting circuit consists of the battery, fuses and fusible links, the ignition switch, the back-up light (reverse) switch or a combined transmission back-up light/neutral safety switch on the transmission, back-up lamps, wiring to connect the components, and the ground circuit to allow current to return to the battery through the vehicle chassis.

When the ignition is on, and the vehicle is placed in reverse gear, the current flows from the battery, through the ignition switch, and through the closed reverse lamp or transmission position switch on the transmission. Electrical current then flows out of the closed switch to the back-up lamps and returns to the battery by the vehicle chassis ground circuit. Modern vehicles use network/bus systems and the BCM to command the back-up lights to come on.

Back-up lights are the only white lights on the rear of the vehicle. Since they operate only in reverse, other drivers can tell that the driver is backing up. This is why it is illegal to have broken tail/brake/turn signal lenses in the rear of the vehicle since white light would be visible, confusing other drivers.

Turn Signal Lights

Turn signal indicators are located on the extreme corners of the vehicle. They are usually amber in the front and can be either red or amber in the rear. A column-mounted switch, operated by the driver, commands a pulsing current to the indicator lights on one side of the vehicle or the other. These pulsing lights warn other road users of the driver's intended change of direction.

Once activated, they continue until the switch is cancelled either by the operator or by a cancelling mechanism in the switch. The cancelling mechanism operates to return the switch to its central or "off" position after a turn has been completed and the steering wheel is returned to the straight-ahead position. The circuit consists of the battery, fusible links and fuses, the ignition switch, the flasher unit, a three-position switch used as the direction indicator switch, the lights at the front and rear of the vehicle, indicator lights mounted in the instrument cluster to indicate to the driver which way the switch has been operated, wiring to connect all of the components, and the ground circuit to return the electrical current to the battery.

If the indicator switch is turned to indicate a right-hand turn, current from the battery typically flows through the fusible link to the ignition switch, where it is directed through a fuse to the flasher unit. The flasher unit uses a timing circuit to pulse the current flowing out of the flasher unit 60 to 120 times per minute. This pulsing current is directed through the indicator switch to the right-hand indicator lights at the front and rear of the vehicle, causing the lamps to flash on and off. An indicator light on the instrument cluster also blinks in sync with the turn signals. The operation of the flasher unit also produces a clicking sound to audibly inform the driver that the indicators are in operation.

When the turn signal switch is returned to the off position, no current flows through the flasher unit, so the timer circuit is switched off. When the turn signal switch is turned in the opposite direction, it directs the pulsing current to the left-hand lights at the front and rear of the vehicle as well as the left-hand indicator light on the instrument cluster. Older vehicles used a thermo-mechanical flasher unit that relied on heat from the current flow to cause the flasher unit to work. It is very important to use bulbs of the proper wattage on all types of flasher units, as the speed of the flash may be incorrect if incorrect bulbs are used.

These indicators can also be computer controlled. The BCM commands the appropriate turn indicators to come on as it sees an input from the turn signal switch, and flashes it at the proper rate. The computer turns off the turn signals when a steering angle sensor signals the steering wheel is being centered. It can also cancel the turn indicators if the vehicle is driven for a programmed amount of time or distance without the steering wheel being turned. Often a chime will alert the driver if the turn indicator has been left on for too long. On many computer-controlled turn signals, the turn signals will not work at all when the computer senses the wrong amperage flow.

Turn Signal Lights—Domestic and Import Systems

All turn signal lamps flash, but there are variations in layout and design. This is most noticeable when comparing some domestic and imported vehicles. Imported vehicles tend to have separate amber-colored turn signal lamps on both the front and the rear of the vehicle. Some domestic vehicles use the rear brake lamps as turn signals by flashing the brake lamp on one side to indicate the turn. Wiring schematics should always be checked because the dual function of the brake lamps means the wiring for brake lamps on vehicles with this feature is different than those where the brake lamps perform only during braking **FIGURE 39-12**. In such cases,

FIGURE 39-12 Typical wiring diagram showing domestic-type turn signals.

current for the brake lights must flow first from the brake switch and then through the turn signal switch, and on to the individual brake lights. This design tends to make the study of the current path more complicated, since there are two inputs—one for the turn signals and one for the brake lights. So the turn signal switch is much more complicated on a domestic-style turn signal switch than an import-style switch.

Hazard Warning Lights

All modern vehicles are equipped with hazard warning lights. This circuit is similar to the turn indicator lights except that it simultaneously causes a pulsing in all exterior indicator lights and both indicator lights on the instrument panel. Hazard lights can warn other road users that a hazardous condition exists or that the vehicle is standing or parked in a dangerous position on the side of the road. The hazards also use a flasher unit that can be a separate unit or the same as that used for the turn signals. The BCM may control the hazard lights when it sees an input from the hazard switch or an input from the restraints control module indicating a vehicle crash.

Daytime Running Lights

Daytime running lights (DRLs) are an additional safety feature designed on vehicles to improve the vehicle's visibility to other drivers in all weather conditions. They are existing lights that turn on when the vehicle is running and turn off when the engine stops. The lamps on the front are the headlights, which are typically operated at about a 60% power level, providing light without excessively decreasing bulb life or using full electrical power. The lamps used on the rear in DRL systems are the taillights.

DRLs are mandatory on modern vehicles licensed in Canada and some other countries. In the United States, DRLs are permitted but not required. Their use is somewhat controversial. First, if they are too bright, they can cause daytime glare. Second, they tend to mask the visibility of turn signals, making it harder for other drivers to determine a vehicle's intent. Overall, they have not been proved to reduce accidents or increase safety. They also require energy to operate, which reduces fuel economy and increases carbon dioxide emissions.

Headlights

Headlights are built into the front of a vehicle to illuminate the road ahead of the vehicle when driving at night or in other conditions of reduced visibility. In headlights, most vehicles require two beams to provide for a high beam and low beam operation. The beams are created by separate filaments, included either in one light bulb or in separate bulbs. These filaments must be positioned correctly in relation to the highly polished reflector. This is called focusing and is carried out when designing the light assembly and lens for the vehicle. The high beam filament is positioned at the focal point of the reflector to project the maximum amount of light forward and parallel to the reflector axis **FIGURE 39-13**. This light is then shaped by the lens, which is made up of many small glass or plastic prisms fused together. These prisms bend the light horizontally and vertically to achieve the desired light pattern for road illumination.

The low beam filament is often placed above and slightly to one side of the high beam filament. Mounting the low beam filament in this position produces a beam of light that is projected downward and toward the curb side **FIGURE 39-14**. With this arrangement, the high beam filament produces the most concentrated light output, while the low beam filament gives a downward and dispersed beam that is less likely to blind oncoming drivers.

Headlight Design

Generally speaking, the headlight circuit consists of the battery, the fusible link or maxi-fuse, headlight fuses, the headlight switch, the headlight relay(s), the beam selector switch, headlights, the high beam indicator light, wiring of a suitable size to carry the electrical current through the circuit, and the ground circuit. Modern vehicles use the BCM to manage headlight functions.

On older, noncomputer-controlled systems, when the headlights are switched on, current is supplied from the battery and proceeds through the fusible link or maxi-fuse,

FIGURE 39-13 High and low beam filament position in relation to the reflector.

FIGURE 39-14 Low beam filament position in relation to the reflector.

FIGURE 39-15 Replaceable halogen bulb.

headlight fuse(s), headlight switch, and dimmer switch, reaching either the low or the high beams. In more recent, noncomputer-controlled systems, some vehicles use relays to control the current through the low or high beam circuits. In this configuration, the beam selector switch either powers or grounds the relay windings in each of the relays, depending on the position of the beam selector switch. Activating the beam selector switch in the low beam position creates a magnetic field inside the low beam relay that closes the relay contacts, which allows electrical current to flow to the low beams. Activating the beam selector switch in the high beam position creates a magnetic field inside the high beam relay that closes the relay contacts, turning on the high beams.

The beam selector switch is a single-pole, double-throw switch, meaning it has one movable pole but makes contact in two positions. In the high beam position, the current is switched to the high beam circuit. In the low beam position, the current is switched to the low beam circuit. The beam selector switch can be set to switch a common power input to two outputs, or it can switch a common ground input to two outputs.

As with other advanced-technology on-board systems, modern vehicles use a network/bus system to manage these and other headlight and dimmer functions. On many vehicles, the headlight switch and dimmer switch are just inputs to a control module that sends a headlight "on" or "off" request over the network. The appropriate light controller processes the request and actually commands the lights on or off, sometimes with the help of relays—especially for high beams.

A sealed-beam headlight has a highly polished aluminized glass reflector that is fused to the optically

designed lens. It is a completely sealed unit that has the filaments accurately positioned in relation to the reflector. Most older vehicles used two dual-filament 7" (178-mm) round lamps; for a time, four single-filament 5.25" (133-mm) round lamps were used. Other older vehicles used two large dual-filament 7.875" (200-mm) rectangular lamps, or four smaller rectangular single-filament lamps. Regardless of size, when a filament fails in a sealed-beam light, the whole sealed unit must be replaced.

A semi-sealed beam headlight uses a replaceable bulb with a prefocus collar. The collar locates the bulb in the headlight and also controls the correct positioning of the filaments to the reflector and lens **FIGURE 39-15**. Some replaceable headlight bulbs have a partial shield below the low beam filament. This shield prevents light from the filament from striking the lower part of the reflector, which would be reflected higher than the midpoint of the lamp. The shield provides the primary shape of the low beam. The final shaping of the beam is carried out by small cylindrical prisms in the headlight lens. This provides a low beam that is asymmetrical. The asymmetrical lens pattern causes light to be thrown upward at a 15-degree angle on the curb side to better illuminate objects, persons, or animals close to the road.

Types of Headlights

Headlight systems have traditionally used reflector-type lighting systems. In a reflector headlight, the light from the bulb is reflected forward by a specially shaped reflector. An alternative is a projection-type headlight system. This type of headlight often has a smaller front lens; however, it produces a high-intensity forward beam. It uses a lens system to project the light forward, rather than the traditional reflector system **FIGURE 39-16**. A projector-style light can use a standard incandescent bulb, or more commonly, an HID light.

HID lights use light from an electric arc rather than heating up a filament until it glows **FIGURE 39-17**. High voltage is applied to tungsten electrodes. Xenon gas inside the bulb is then ionized and creates an electrical path between the electrodes, which lowers the resistance of the gap. As the temperature rises, metallic salts are vaporized and provide a stable arc, emitting much light. To initially jump the gap, a ballast and igniter raise the vehicle's low-voltage direct current (DC) to as much as

FIGURE 39-16 Projector bulb assembly.

FIGURE 39-17 HID headlight assembly.

25,000 volts alternating current (AC). Once the light reaches full operation, voltage is maintained between approximately 40 and 85 volts AC, depending on the system. HID lights give off a brighter and bluer light than halogen bulbs with less electrical energy, so they help fuel efficiency slightly. They last two to four times as long as a halogen bulb but are quite a bit more expensive. Also, they take up more room in the engine compartment.

Some vehicles use LED lights as headlights. They are not currently as bright as HID lights but are at least as bright as halogen lights. LED lights are known for low power consumption, but for LEDs to create enough light to function as headlights, they must consume almost as much energy as HID lights. Still, LED technology continues to improve. One drawback of current LED headlights is that high temperatures degrade or damage them. Thus, heat sinks and cooling measures are needed, which add complexity, cost, and space.

Night vision is another relatively new technology that enhances a driver's visual perception in dark or poor weather conditions. There are two types of night vision systems: active and passive. Active systems use an infrared light generator that projects infrared light in front of and to the side of the roadway ahead. A special camera picks up the reflected infrared radiation. The image is then displayed either on the windshield using a heads-up display or on an LCD screen on the dash or navigation system.

Passive night vision systems use a heat-sensing camera (thermal imaging) to pick up thermal radiation emitted by objects. This system does not have an infrared light source on the vehicle. The captured thermal image is then displayed either on a heads-up display or on an LCD screen. One benefit of the thermal system is that it can be programmed to recognize pedestrians and animals and can then either place an outline around them on the display or flash a warning symbol.

Driving Lights

Driving lights are used to supplement vehicle headlight systems. The driving lights are installed on the front of the vehicle and provide higher intensity illumination over longer distances than standard headlight systems **FIGURE 39-18**. Vehicle design rules and regulations specify the limitations in relation to the positioning and lens configuration of driving lights. It is essential that the local regulations are adhered to when mounting or adjusting driving lights.

There are many types of driving lights available. They come in different sizes, shapes, lens pattern, and bulb wattage. In some instances, a single driving light can be installed to suit particular applications, but lights are normally installed in pairs.

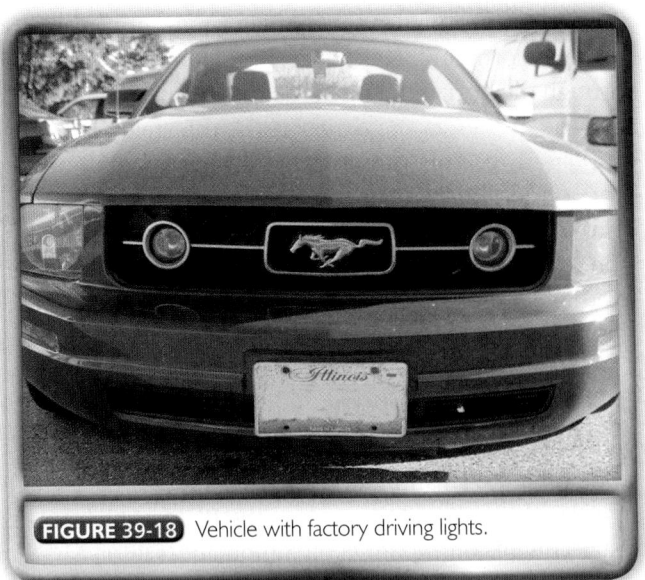

FIGURE 39-18 Vehicle with factory driving lights.

Most driving lights use quartz halogen bulbs in the 55- to 120-watt range. The quality of the reflector is extremely important in driving lights to get optimum performance. Driving lights are wired so that they operate only when the high beam is operating. This safety feature ensures that driving lights turn off when the headlights are switched from high to low beam, thus ensuring that oncoming traffic is not blinded by excessive light. While many performance vehicles come equipped with driving lights, they can be added to almost any vehicle. If they are, a relay and circuit breaker should always be used for circuit protection reasons.

Fog Lights

Fog lights are used with other vehicle lighting in poor weather such as thick fog, driving rain, or blowing snow. Because fog is made up of water droplets suspended in the air, it can reflect headlights back into the driver's eyes at night. In such conditions, fog lights can help drivers see farther ahead and illuminate the road's edges at reasonable speeds. They are used with park lights and low beam headlights but not with high beams.

Most older fog lights have yellow-colored reflectors, although more recently, white fog lights have become more widely used because yellow lenses reduce fog light brilliance by about 30%. Fog lights typically use quartz halogen bulbs and are available in different shapes and sizes. Fog lights are usually mounted lower than headlights and tend to be aimed straight forward and low FIGURE 39-19 . Fog light lenses have a sharp cutoff pattern so that most of the light projected remains below the driver's eye level.

Fog lights are typically wired with a relay and circuit breaker. The method of connection of fog lights will depend on local regulations. They may be wired to work only with park lights and to turn off when headlights are used or to work when high beams are used. The BCM normally controls the function of the fog lights if they are installed as original equipment.

Cornering Lights

To improve visibility during night driving, some vehicle manufacturers provide cornering lights FIGURE 39-20 . Cornering lights are white lights usually installed into the bumper or fender and are designed to provide side lighting when the vehicle is turning corners. The additional lighting provided by cornering lights helps the driver to

FIGURE 39-19 Vehicle with factory fog lights.

FIGURE 39-20 Cornering lights.

see the curb and any obstacles that may not be illuminated by the headlights. Cornering lights turn on only when the headlights and turn signal switches are on, and turn off automatically when the turn signal cancels. Even though they come on with the turn signals, their light is steady; that is, they don't blink.

Smart Lighting

Different lighting technologies can be mounted individually, or together, to form comprehensive adaptive lighting systems, otherwise known as smart lighting. Automatic headlight leveling systems ensure that the headlights are always correctly aligned, regardless of the load the vehicle is carrying. When a vehicle is loaded, the suspension settles, changing the angle of the headlights to the road. The resulting angle can cause glare into oncoming traffic. Auto-leveling headlights use a sensor to monitor the angle of the vehicle to the road **FIGURE 39-21**. This information is then used to automatically adjust the headlights. They adjust up or down so the headlights always stay correctly adjusted. In this system, the load sensors provide information to a control module that operates servomotors installed on the headlights, causing the headlights to tilt up and down.

Another function of adaptive headlights is the ability to adjust the length of the headlight beam based on the distance of oncoming traffic. In this system, a dash-mounted camera can determine the distance of oncoming traffic and relay that information to the BCM, which then continuously adjusts the length of the headlight beam. Some manufacturers add the ability to shade or block light within the beam based on the position of oncoming traffic. Either shields are moved to block light from specific areas or, in the case of LED lights, specific LEDs are switched off to provide the shaded area. In either case, maximum illumination is maintained without blinding oncoming drivers.

Some types of headlights can improve forward lighting while cornering. This type of headlight swivels slightly through the horizontal plane, so that the headlight turns into the corner as the driver turns the steering wheel **FIGURE 39-22**. This provides better illumination of the road as the vehicle turns through the corner. In this system, sensors from the steering wheel provide information to a BCM that causes servomotors installed on the headlights to operate, causing the lights to swivel in the desired direction.

BCM Lighting Systems

When driving at dusk, the ambient light can fade slowly. In some vehicles, an ambient light sensor determines when light levels are low. It is read by the BCM, which turns the headlights on, when set on "automatic" **FIGURE 39-23**.

Automatic "dimming" headlights use a light sensor located at the front of the vehicle or on the dash to detect

FIGURE 39-22 Headlights that shine around a corner.

FIGURE 39-21 Auto-leveling headlights.

FIGURE 39-23 Automatic headlight system.

light from oncoming vehicles. If the headlights are on, low beam is selected automatically. This prevents oncoming traffic from being dazzled by the vehicle's high beam. If the light sensor is not signaling that a vehicle is approaching within the defined range, the BCM will select high beams. As a vehicle approaches, the light sensor will signal the BCM, which will select the low beams again. Most vehicles have an adjustable knob that will set the sensitivity of the light sensor. Making it less sensitive will cause the BCM to switch to low beam when the approaching vehicle is closer in range. More sensitivity will cause the BCM to select low beams when the vehicle is farther away.

A delayed "off" feature allows the headlights to be left on after the engine has stopped and the doors are closed or locked. This feature allows the driver to safely see his or her way from the vehicle. The headlights automatically turn off after a period of time. On some vehicles, the BCM will turn the headlights off if the headlights are left on after the ignition is off and the driver's door is left opened. On other vehicles, headlight warning alarms sound if the headlights are left on after the engine has been turned off and a door is opened. This feature reduces the risk of the headlights draining the battery. Many vehicles have an adjuster or can be programmed to tailor the length of this delay time up to a few minutes.

On some vehicles, the BCM, in concert with a lamp-out module, illuminates a warning light in the instrument panel cluster when an exterior light bulb such as a stop, tail, or turn signal light has failed. To detect this malfunction, the lamp-out module compares current flowing through these circuits to values stored in the computer's memory. If the current flowing is outside the set parameters, the warning light will illuminate. Besides providing the correct amount of light, this is another reason to always use bulbs of the proper wattage.

The BCM can be programmed to command the interior lighting to remain on after the doors have been closed for a set period of time, to allow the occupants to locate a seat belt or insert the ignition key. It can also turn on the interior lighting when the ignition is turned off to allow the occupants to locate door handles and other items.

Networking and Multiplexing

Even the most basic modern vehicles include many electronically controlled systems. If each electronic system had its own ECU, harness, and sensors, the weight of the added components would negate some of the efficiency it provides and would add cost to the vehicle. A vehicle's multiple electronic systems could require miles of insulated wiring, splices, and terminals.

One solution to reduce the amount of wiring required is the use of a system that integrates sensors into a common wiring harness, called a **bus**. The bus combines all the individual systems wherever possible into a **multiplexed** serial communications network. An added advantage of such a system is that with less wire and fewer connections, there is less chance of dirty connections causing faults. Of course, if a network fails, it can shut down the entire network and with it the controlled devices. Also, troubleshooting a networked system requires more training and more tools than a simple digital volt-ohmmeter (DVOM).

With networking, a single (or multiple) network consisting of one or more twisted pairs of wires, with terminating resistors at the end of each pair, carries digital information throughout the entire vehicle. In many cases, there is a medium- or low-speed bus for nonsafety systems and a high-speed bus for systems such as anti-lock brakes, supplemental restraint systems, and many of the engine controls. All components "listen" to the signals carried on the network and respond when requested to do so. All networked data/information is shared throughout the vehicle. Such a system is often referred to as a **controlled area network bus (CAN-bus)** **FIGURE 39-24**. The thin twisted pair of wires connects all the on-board control modules to each other. Thus, the power train control module (PCM), BCM, electronic brake control module, transmission control module, and many others are networked together and communicate, much like "party lines" on old-fashioned telephone systems. Output devices that respond to commands on the network are referred to as nodes. All nodes hear all data on the network, but only respond when called upon to perform some action or diagnostic function.

The advantage of a multiplex network is that it enables a decreased number of dedicated wires for each function, and therefore a reduction in the number of wires in the wiring harness. This network also reduces system weight and improves reliability, serviceability, and installation.

FIGURE 39-24 Typical CAN-bus diagram.

Sensor data multiplexed on the network are prioritized. For example, such information as vehicle speed and engine temperature data is shared on the network for other systems such as the instrument panel cluster to access and use for their purposes. This design helps to reduce the number of sensors needed. Some information being shared takes priority over other. For example, a message related to a loss of engine oil pressure would take precedence over a lamp outage message. In such a case, the vehicle operator must be immediately alerted to the urgent fault.

Networking of data also allows greater vehicle content flexibility because functions can be added or modified through software changes. Other control units, such as those related to trailer towing, can be added as required to the system by simply connecting them into the network and updating the software to integrate it into the network. You can think of this process as being similar to adding a printer to your home computer system; plug it in, configure it, and start using it.

A diagnostic scan tool is connected to the CAN-bus network to both monitor and extract operational information to assist in diagnosis and fault finding. Factory scan tools and other so-called bidirectional scanners are used to command engine and vehicle components to operate in order to confirm their correct function.

▶ Lighting Circuits

Each lighting circuit has particular operating characteristics based on its purpose and the system design. Knowing how a circuit is designed to operate and how it interacts with other related circuits will help you to better know how to go about diagnosing the system. A typical lighting circuit may be made up of the battery, fuses or circuit breakers, switches, relays, lamps, and wiring to connect the components. Manufacturers design the circuits to operate in specific ways and then create schematics or wiring diagrams, which are a diagrammatic layout of the entire circuit to assist in the repair and maintenance of lighting circuits. Learning how to read wiring diagrams takes time and practice. Understanding circuit design, operation, and wiring diagram information can then be used to diagnose circuit faults.

Lighting System Wiring Diagrams

The layouts of electrical circuits and their components are shown as diagrams made up of symbols and connecting lines. Being able to read a wiring diagram is probably the most important skill when trying to trace and correct a fault in an electrical system.

Not all wiring diagrams use the same symbols or the same numbering system. It is helpful to refer to the manufacturer's service information for specific details on how to read a particular wiring diagram.

The illustrations below show some of the common symbols and what they represent.

1. **FIGURE 39-25** shows the battery and fuse symbols.
2. **FIGURE 39-26** shows the ground and connector symbols.
3. **FIGURE 39-27** shows the switch symbols.
4. **FIGURE 39-28** shows the resistors, coils and relay symbols.
5. **FIGURE 39-29** shows the semiconductor symbols.
6. **FIGURE 39-30** shows the capacitor and device symbols.
7. **FIGURE 39-31** shows the motors, generators, and solenoid symbols.
8. **FIGURE 39-32** shows the gauges and warning device symbols.

FIGURE 39-25 Battery and fuse symbols.

FIGURE 39-26 Ground and connector symbols.

FIGURE 39-27 Switch symbols.

FIGURE 39-30 Capacitor and device symbols.

FIGURE 39-28 Resistors, coils, and relay symbols.

FIGURE 39-31 Motors, generators, and solenoid symbols.

FIGURE 39-29 Semiconductor symbols.

FIGURE 39-32 Gauges and warning device symbols.

HID Safety Precautions

HID lamps produce a very bright white light. Manufacturers use various designs of HID lamps. Regardless of the design, they generally require a high-voltage spark of up to 25,000 volts to start and a high operating voltage (e.g., 40–85 volts AC) to maintain light. To generate the voltages required to operate, a transformer and electronic circuitry called a ballast are used to supply electrical components.

Several safety precautions should be taken when working on HID systems. There is a risk of electrocution, burns, or shock from the high voltages generated by the HID system. If diagnosing the HID system, be very careful when working on the system when it is live. You should wear safety glasses, high-voltage safety gloves, and safety boots, and you should ensure that the vehicle, engine compartment, and ground under the vehicle are dry. Do not touch the ballast while it is operating; it will often be generating a lot of heat. Persons with active electronic implants, such as heart pacemakers, should not work on HID headlamps. If changing out the bulb, make sure the headlights are turned off. The manufacturer may specify that the battery be disconnected when replacing the bulb. If so, follow the manufacturer's instructions.

There is also a risk of injury caused by exposure to ultraviolet light produced by the HID lamp if the lamp is operated outside of its housing. Once ignited, the pressure inside an HID bulb can build up to a very high pressure (around 220 pounds per square inch, 1517 kilopascals) due to the high operating temperature (about 1500°F [816°C]). This pressure creates a potential explosion hazard, so do not attempt to power an HID bulb outside of the headlamp assembly to test it or operate it near flammable gases or liquids. Also, the bulb must be maintained in a horizontal position when it is on; otherwise it may overheat and fail. HID headlamps use various heavy metals in their construction; therefore, it is important to always dispose of the bulbs in an environmentally friendly way. Avoid breaking bulbs, as there is also a risk of poisoning caused by inhalation or skin contact of heavy metal vapors and toxic salts.

Checking Lighting and Peripheral Systems

When checking lighting and peripheral systems, be sure to work in a systematic manner to avoid missing a faulty bulb or other component. A vehicle may have warning lights that will activate only if that circuit is in use. You may need to turn that circuit on to see the warning light. If you are unsure of where these are, ask your supervisor.

To check lighting and peripheral systems, follow the steps in **SKILL DRILL 39-1**:

1. In a darkened area, turn on or activate the ignition. The dash warning lights should be displayed. Start the engine. If any warning light stays on after the engine is started, it could indicate a problem in one of the vehicle's safety or mechanical systems. If you are unsure about what any of the warning lights mean, consult the owner's manual.

2. Make sure the vehicle's horn is working. If the horn is not working, locate it under the hood with the help of manufacturer's information. Check the wiring to make sure there is a good contact. If necessary, use a wiring diagram and DVOM to isolate the fault.

3. Have someone stand behind the vehicle to report any problems. Turn the ignition to run. Switch on the park lights, taillights, marker lights, and license plate lights. Do the same for left and right turn indicator lights. Depress the brake pedal to make sure the brake lights work and have the proper intensity. Also, place the transmission in reverse and check the back-up lights.

4. With someone in front of the vehicle, make sure the high and low headlight beams, park lights, turn signals, driving lights, fog lights, and cornering lights are all working properly.

5. With the interior light switch in the correct position, open the driver's side door to make sure the interior lights work.

6. If any of these lights do not operate, you may need to replace a bulb, or diagnose the fault.

Checking and Changing an Exterior Light Bulb

Light bulbs have a limited life span and burn out occasionally. Inspecting the lighting system's operation periodically, such as during oil changes, will help identify any light bulb issues. If none of the bulbs in a particular circuit is working, there may be a bigger electrical problem to resolve, requiring diagnosis. Many tail, brake, and signal light bulbs have more than one filament inside them. These bulbs normally have offset pins to ensure proper orientation of the electrical contacts in the socket.

Be sure to look carefully at the bulb you are replacing to make sure you do not try to force the bulb in the wrong way. Also, make sure you don't replace a dual-filament bulb with a single-filament bulb since that can short both lighting circuits together, causing the lights to work very strangely. Some bulbs have a colored glass envelope that enables them to be used with a clear lens. If you replace a bulb of this type, make sure you replace it with one of the same color.

To check and change an exterior light bulb, follow the steps in **SKILL DRILL 39-2**:

1. Determine the method used to secure the lamp unit or lens cover and remove the cover or lamp unit to expose the bulb. If no screws are found on the lens cover, it may be necessary to remove the entire assembly to access the bulb or there may be access from behind.

2. If the bulb is pin mounted, gently grip the bulb and push it inward. Turn the bulb slightly counterclockwise and pull it out of the bulb holder. **(Photo 1)**

3. Inspect the bulb holder to make sure there is no corrosion. If there is, clean it with a bulb socket wire brush or emery cloth. **(Photo 2)**

4. Insert the new bulb into the bulb holder, depress it fully, turn it slightly clockwise and release it.

5. Make sure the bulb is secure, and test its operation by switching it on and off. Replace the cover or unit, and test it again. **(Photo 3)**

Checking and Changing a Headlight Bulb

There are many types of headlight bulbs available. Always make sure you replace a bulb with one of exactly the same type. Sealed-beam units require that the whole light be replaced when one filament has failed. If the reflector in the sealed-beam light shows signs of degradation, it also indicates that you must change the unit. If both lights operate but are not bright when switched on, start the engine to see if this solves the problem; the battery may be in a poor state of charge. When replacing a halogen bulb, avoid touching it with your fingers, which can leave a residue from your fingers on the outer surface. This residue can cause the bulb to crack or shatter and burn

Safety

The glass in a light bulb is thin, and if it breaks, it is extremely sharp. Since bayonet-style lights need to be pushed in to be released, and they can become corroded in place, and it may take a lot of force to push them in. Placed under such high pressure, the glass can break and severely cut the skin and even the tendons in fingers. If a bulb does not come out easily, stop, use a folded rag, and try to remove it again. If it shatters, the rag will help to protect your fingers.

SKILL DRILL 39-2   Checking and Changing an Exterior Light Bulb

1. Remove the cover to expose the bulb. If the bulb is pin mounted, gently grip the bulb and push it inward. Turn the bulb slightly counterclockwise and remove it from the bulb holder.

2. Inspect the bulb holder to make sure there is no corrosion. If there is, clean it with a bulb socket wire brush or emery cloth.

3. Insert the new bulb into the bulb holder, depress it fully, turn it slightly clockwise, and release it. Test it by switching it on and off. Then replace the cover, and test it again.

out after a short time of operation. If you inadvertently touch the bulb, clean it with alcohol and a lint-free cloth. Do not use gasoline or paraffin to clean the bulb.

To check and change a headlight bulb, follow the steps in **SKILL DRILL 39-3**:

1. Assessing headlight operation is always more accurately carried out in a dim environment. Switch the vehicle headlights on at low beam, then switch to high beam. Check that the high beam indicator on the instrument panel is operating. Note the change in the intensity of the lights. If one of the lights does not operate, that headlight will need to be diagnosed and potentially replaced.

2. Determine the type of lamp installed on the vehicle and obtain a replacement. Many vehicles today are equipped with halogen headlights. These are twice as powerful as older sealed-beam units and need to be handled carefully. Always follow the manufacturer's handling instructions.

3. Unplug the electrical connector at the back of the lamp unit. On most vehicles, it is not necessary to remove the lamp unit from the vehicle. If equipped, unscrew the bulb-retaining ring or twist the bulb from its housing. (**Photo 1**)

4. Remove the old bulb and replace it with the new one. Handle the new bulb only by its base or, if supplied, by the card cover. It is very important that you never touch the surface of the bulb with your fingers, as this will cause it to burn out very quickly. (**Photo 2**)

5. Replace the unit and the retaining ring or bulb assembly, and then plug in the connector. Switch on the lights again to confirm that they are both operating correctly. (**Photo 3**)

> ### TECHNICIAN TIP
>
> A customer with sealed-beam headlights once complained of poor headlight performance. When the technician turned on the lights, they both worked but didn't seem to create much light. As the technician opened the hood to investigate further, he noticed something strange. The headlights were shining light out the back of the lights, illuminating the engine compartment. He inspected the lights and found that the metallic reflector in the sealed beams had pretty much all flaked away, allowing most of the light to exit the rear of the bulb, instead of being reflected forward. Replacing the sealed-beam headlights with new ones fixed the customer's concern.

Aiming Headlights

Although the principle of aiming headlights is the same in the majority of cases, the legal rules can differ from region to region. Be sure to check the requirements for

SKILL DRILL | **39-3** | **Checking and Changing a Headlight Bulb**

1. Test the vehicle headlights. Obtain the replacement lamp for the vehicle. Unplug the electrical connector at the back of the lamp unit.

2. Remove the old bulb and replace it with the new one. Handle the new bulb only by its base or, if supplied, by the card cover.

3. Replace the unit and the retaining ring or bulb assembly, and then plug in the connector. Switch on the lights again to confirm that they are both operating correctly.

your location. If you are unsure of what these are, ask your supervisor. Some manufacturers may suggest that the headlights be aimed on high beam, others on low beam, and in cases of separate high and low beams, both beams may need to be aimed independently. The manufacturer may also suggest that a load be placed in the vehicle, to simulate the ride height of the vehicle when it is travelling down the road. Headlights are typically aligned both vertically and horizontally so that as much of the road is illuminated as possible, without blinding oncoming traffic. Some vehicles have headlights that adjust automatically; do not try to adjust those unless you are diagnosing a fault in the system.

When aiming or aligning headlights, there are a couple of possible methods to utilize. The first, while no longer commonly used, involves an on-vehicle headlight aligner. This method was used extensively on sealed-beam headlights. The aligners are calibrated to the floor at the point where the front and rear wheels contact the concrete. Then the aligners are installed on the headlights with a built-in suction cup, which holds them in place. The aligners use a set of mirrors that can be calibrated to local regulations so that the headlights can be aligned properly.

With the introduction of aerodynamic headlights using removable halogen bulbs, off-vehicle headlight aligners became more popular. These aligners sit in front of the vehicle after being calibrated for the floor slope and orientation with the vehicle. With the headlights on, adjustments can be made by following the instructions on the aligner. Refer to the manufacturer's information for specific information regarding headlight aiming.

To aim headlights, follow the steps in **SKILL DRILL 39-4**:

1. Make sure the tires are inflated properly, the wheels point straight ahead, and there is no extra weight in the vehicle.
2. Move the vehicle into the correct position in relation to the headlamp aligner unit following the equipment manufacturer's instructions.
3. Calibrate the aligner to any floor slope and for the vehicle being aligned. If this is not performed accurately, the headlights will not be aimed correctly. **(Photo 1)**
4. On the types of aligners that require the headlights to be on during alignment, turn the headlights on to a low beam setting. The center of the illuminating beams should be in the lower right quadrants of the chart or wall markings or as specified by the manufacturer. **(Photo 2)**
5. The high beam should be centered, falling on the intersections of the horizontal and vertical marks or as specified by the manufacturer.

SKILL DRILL | 39-4 | Aiming Headlights

1. Make sure the tires are inflated properly, the wheels point straight ahead, and there is no extra weight in the vehicle. Position the vehicle correctly in relation to the headlamp aligner unit following the equipment manufacturer's instructions. Calibrate the aligner for any floor slope and for the vehicle being tested.

2. On the types of aligners that require the headlights to be on during alignment, turn the headlights on to a low beam setting. The center of the illuminating beams should be in the lower right quadrants of the chart or wall markings or as specified by the manufacturer.

3. The high beam should be centered, falling on the intersections of the horizontal and vertical marks or as specified by the manufacturer. If necessary, turn the adjustment screws on the headlight so the lights point to the correct places or bubbles on the levels are centered, depending on the type of aligner equipment you are using.

6 If necessary, locate the adjustment screws on the headlight and turn them so the lights point to the correct places, or bubbles on the levels are centered, depending upon which type of aligner equipment you are using. Diagnose the cause of brighter-than-normal, intermittent, dim, or no-light operation to determine necessary action. **(Photo 3)**

Headlight Brightness

Headlight brightness is critical to safe driving. Too dim, and the road ahead will not be adequately illuminated. Too bright, and the life of the headlight will be shortened, making it prone to early burnout. In most cases, the headlights are more likely to be too dim than too bright. Bulbs that are too bright indicate that either the charging system voltage is too high and needs to be measured with a DVOM or someone may have replaced the headlights with an aftermarket set, which may be illegal. Checking bulb numbers will verify this condition.

If the headlights are too dim, there can be several causes. The most common one is high resistance in the light circuit. This can be checked by measuring the voltage drop on both the power side of the bulb and the ground side. The voltage drop should be less than 0.5 volts on each side. If an excessive voltage drop is indicated, use a wiring diagram to research the circuit. Once you know how it is wired, use the DVOM to isolate the voltage drop by using the meter to measure each segment of the circuit. When the high resistance is located, perform the needed repair, whether that is a wire repair or a connector, switch, or relay replacement. If the voltage drop is less than 0.5 volts on each side, suspect the light bulb is wearing out. One way to verify this is with a light intensity meter. This meter can measure the amount of light energy the lamp is producing, so you can compare that to specifications. If the light is being supplied with the specified voltage, but it is not creating enough light, the bulb will need to be replaced.

Checking Digital Instrument Circuits

Instrument systems on modern vehicles are controlled by electronic circuits and sensors. Electronic control modules receive information from various sensors and send digital signals to various instruments to display the information. The data from sensors and instruments are sent and received on the CAN-bus vehicle network.

A diagnostic scan tool connected to the vehicle will greatly assist in diagnosing digital instruments. Use the scan tool to check fault codes and vehicle PIDs to check if sensors and instruments are operating correctly. A DVOM

and oscilloscope can also be used to check sensor outputs and confirm correct operation. Research the diagnostic procedures and sensor outputs in the manufacturer's information. Always disconnect sensors before conducting resistance checks. Automotive test lamps should not be used on digital circuits because they draw too much current and can overload the circuit. Be careful not to accidentally short wires or terminals to ground or power, as doing so may damage the circuits.

You should always inspect sensors, connectors, and wires for corrosion or damage. Connector plugs and pins should be tight with straight pins that have good connectivity. If back-probing wires or connectors is required, ensure that the pins are not damaged. If wire insulation is pierced, make sure it is reinsulated with tape or liquid insulation. Do not use room-temperature vulcanizing (RTV) silicone, as it can create absorb moisture as it cures, which may promote corrosion.

To check digital instrument circuits, follow the steps in **SKILL DRILL 39-5**:

1 Identify the digital circuit to be tested. Research the correct test procedure from the manufacturer's information.

2 Check fault codes and circuit PIDs using a scan tool.

3 Inspect the sensor, wires, and connectors.

4 Test the sensor with a DVOM or oscilloscope to determine correct output.

5 If the sensor tests OK, check the wiring harness for continuity back to the instrument panel, and determine necessary action.

Checking Warning Device Operation

Warning devices are installed on the vehicle to provide the driver with information about critical vehicle operating and safety systems, including the battery, supplemental restraint system (SRS), anti-lock brake system (ABS), park brake, oil pressure, and engine temperature. In some cases, the systems use sensors to relay information to the warning device, such as low oil pressure. In this case, the oil pressure may need to be measured with an external oil pressure gauge. If the oil pressure is OK, then the oil pressure switch may be faulty and will need to be replaced. In other circuits, such as the ABS system, the PCM may send a signal through each wheel speed sensor to measure its continuity. In this case, you will need to measure the resistance of the sensor or the continuity of the wiring harness.

The warning devices may be controlled by an electronic control unit (ECU). SRS systems are very dangerous; for example, they control the deployment of airbags by using pyrotechnical charges. Check the manufacturer's procedures and properly disable the SRS system before working on it. Check vehicle faults codes and PIDs for possible faults. A DVOM or oscilloscope may be used to check signal voltages from sensors used on the vehicle warning devices.

To check warning device operation, follow the steps in **SKILL DRILL 39-6**:

1 Identify the circuit to be tested. Research the correct test procedure from the manufacturer's information.

2 Check fault codes and circuit PIDs using a scan tool. Inspect the sensors, wires, and connectors.

3 Test the affected circuit and any sensors with a DVOM or oscilloscope to determine the correct output.

4 If sensors or devices test OK, check the individual circuits for continuity.

5 Identify the circuit to be tested. Research the correct test procedure from the manufacturer's information.

Wrap-up

Ready for Review

▶ Incandescent lamps consist of one or more filaments, which heat up until they glow.

▶ Halogen lamps have a much longer life and are generally brighter and produce more light per unit of power consumed, but they become very hot during use.

▶ High-intensity discharge (HID) headlamps produce light with an electric arc rather than a glowing filament.

▶ Light-emitting diodes (LEDs) have been used for some time in various automotive applications, such as warning indicators and alphanumeric displays.

▶ One of the advantages of LEDs is that they turn on instantly.

▶ All lamps or light bulbs have letters and numbers stamped on them that indicate the power consumed by bulb operation at the nominal operating voltage.

▶ Lighting regulations should always be consulted before modifying or adding to any of the vehicle lighting systems.

▶ Park, tail, and marker lamps are all low-intensity or low-wattage lamps used to mark the outline or width of the vehicle.

▶ Brake lights, which may also be called stop lights, are red lights mounted to the rear of the vehicle.

▶ Reverse lights, also called back-up lights, are the bright white lights on the back of the vehicle that allow the operator to see behind the vehicle when backing up.

▶ Hazard lights can warn other road users that a hazardous condition exists or that the vehicle is standing or parked in a dangerous position on the side of the road; they normally use the same bulbs as the turn signal indicators.

▶ The dim or low beam is usually set to the outside of the front, and the high beams are closer to the front center of the vehicle.

▶ The driving lights are installed on the front of the vehicle and provide higher intensity illumination over longer distances than standard headlight systems.

▶ Different lighting technologies can be mounted individually, or together, to form comprehensive adaptive lighting systems, otherwise known as smart lighting.

▶ Auto-leveling headlights use a sensor to monitor the angle of the vehicle to the road.

▶ In some vehicles, an ambient light sensor determines when light levels are low; this then allows the body control computer to turn the exterior lights on.

▶ Networking, CAN-bus, or multiplexing light systems eliminate the amount of wire required for the lighting system and are controlled through a main computer.

▶ Warning lamps provide the vehicle operator with information regarding the operation of the main vehicle systems, such as the vehicle battery charge, oil pressure level, and airbag system status.

▶ A typical lighting circuit is made up of the battery, fuses or circuit breakers, switches, lamps, and wiring to connect the electrical circuit.

▶ For motor vehicles and trailers, two red tail lamps operate when the headlight switch is in the park position and the headlight position.

- Daytime running lights (DRLs) automatically operate when the vehicle is running and turn off when the engine stops.
- The layouts of electrical circuits and their components are shown as diagrams made up of symbols and connecting lines.
- Being able to read and interpret electrical circuit layouts can cut a technician's troubleshooting time in half; this is a skill all technicians need to learn.
- When checking lighting and peripheral systems, be sure to work in a systematic manner or you could miss a faulty bulb or other component.

- If all of the bulbs on one fuse do not work, check the fuse.
- When replacing a bulb, always ensure there is no corrosion in the bulb socket, as this will shorten the life of the new bulb and add resistance in the circuit.
- Always make sure you replace a bulb with one of exactly the same type.
- It is critical that headlights be aimed correctly so as not to impair an oncoming vehicle and to allow correct visibility for the driver.

Key Terms

<u>ballast</u> A device that increases lighting voltage substantially and controls the current to the bulb.

<u>bus</u> A system of networking circuits in which various on-board modules are connected to one another, allowing the exchange of information between them.

<u>controlled area network bus (CAN-bus)</u> The data network used to connect various electronic systems on vehicles to share data.

<u>halogen lamp</u> A type of bulb that produces a bright white light.

<u>high-intensity discharge (HID)</u> A type of lighting that produces light with an electric arc rather than a glowing filament.

<u>incandescent lamp</u> The traditional bulb that uses a heated filament to produce light.

<u>light-emitting diode (LED)</u> A type of lighting various automotive applications, such as warning indicators and alphanumeric displays.

<u>multiplex</u> The carrying of multiple signals on one wiring circuit. Digital signals are multiplexed on a dedicated CAN-bus or similar network. Also referred to by the abbreviation MUX.

<u>vacuum tube fluorescent (VTF)</u> A type of lighting used for instrumentation displays on vehicle instrument panel clusters. This type of lighting emits a very bright light with high contrast and can display in various colors. Also called vacuum fluorescent display (VFD).

ASE-Type Questions

1. Tech A says that a voltage drop on the ground side of a bulb won't affect its brightness because the electricity has already been used up. Tech B says that a voltage drop is one way to determine if there is unwanted resistance in a circuit. Who is correct?
   a. Tech A
   b. Tech B
   c. Both A and B
   d. Neither A nor B

2. Tech A says that incandescent bulbs resist vibration well. Tech B says that HID headlamps require up to approximately 25,000 volts to start. Who is correct?
   a. Tech A
   b. Tech B
   c. Both A and B
   d. Neither A nor B

3. Tech A says that many automotive light bulbs have more than one filament inside. Tech B says that some lights use a filament made of quartz. Who is correct?
   a. Tech A
   b. Tech B
   c. Both A and B
   d. Neither A nor B

4. Tech A says that LED brake lights illuminate faster than incandescent bulbs. Tech B says that LED brake lights have more visibility and last longer. Who is correct?
   a. Tech A
   b. Tech B
   c. Both A and B
   d. Neither A nor B

5. Tech A says that if the brake light switch is open, neither brake light will illuminate. Tech B says that the back-up lights are connected in parallel with the tail lights. Who is correct?
   a. Tech A
   b. Tech B
   c. Both A and B
   d. Neither A nor B

6. Tech A says that some brake lights get power from the brake switch through the turn signal switch. Tech B says many turn signals use amber lights. Who is correct?
   a. Tech A
   b. Tech B
   c. Both A and B
   d. Neither A nor B

7. Tech A says that daytime running light systems illuminate the tail lights to enhance visibility. Tech B says that the CHMSL is illuminated when the tail lights are activated. Who is correct?
   a. Tech A
   b. Tech B
   c. Both A and B
   d. Neither A nor B

8. Tech A says that some turn signals are flashed by a flasher can. Tech B says that some turn signals are flashed by the BCM. Who is correct?
   a. Tech A
   b. Tech B
   c. Both A and B
   d. Neither A nor B

9. Tech A says that mutiplexed lights are controlled by an electronic control module. Tech B says that some headlights can adjust side to side when the vehicle is cornering. Who is correct?
   a. Tech A
   b. Tech B
   c. Both A and B
   d. Neither A nor B

10. Tech A says that if a bulb is dim when operated, the circuit likely has a short to ground. Tech B says that if a bulb is dim, you should perform a voltage drop test on the power and ground side of the bulb. Who is correct?
   a. Tech A
   b. Tech B
   c. Both A and B
   d. Neither A nor B

CHAPTER 40

Body Electrical System

Knowledge Objectives

After reading this chapter, you will be able to:
1. Explain the principles of operation of the CAN-bus system. (pp 1367–1368)
2. Describe the different network configurations of the CAN-bus system. (p 1368)
3. Explain the purpose of the different electric motor types—brush, brushless, permanent magnet, and stepper. (p 1373)
4. Describe the operation of the horn system. (p 1379)
5. Describe the operation of the power door locks. (p 1382)
6. Describe the operation of the wiper system. (p 1384)
7. Describe the operation of the heated seat and mirrors. (pp 1386–1387)
8. Describe the operation of the cruise control system. (pp 1388–1390)
9. Describe the purpose and operation of the supplemental restraint system (SRS). (pp 1390–1391)
10. Describe the operation of the entertainment system. (pp 1395–1396)
11. Describe the operation of the anti-theft system. (pp 1398–1400)

Skills Objectives

After reading this chapter, you will be able to:
1. Check for module communication (including CAN-bus systems) errors using a scan tool. (pp 1369–1371)
2. Perform software transfers, software updates, or flash reprogramming on electronic modules. (pp 1371–1372)
3. Test the electric motor. (pp 1378–1379)
4. Diagnose the horn system. (pp 1379–1382)
5. Remove the door panel. (pp 1383–1384)
6. Test the washer system. (pp 1384–1386)

Introduction

Electrical systems on modern vehicles are becoming increasingly complex with the addition of a range of electronic and accessory systems, such as global positioning systems, entertainment systems, security systems, electric seats, and heated glass. Many of these systems are controlled by body computer systems. Increasingly, the electrical and electronic assemblies are interconnected through vehicle data networks that require sophisticated diagnostic techniques. The shop technician requires an in-depth knowledge of these systems, including how they work and interconnect through the vehicle network. Diagnostics requires the use of sophisticated diagnostic tools that connect to the vehicle computer systems to examine system and sensor functions and data.

CAN-bus System

The terms **controller area network (CAN)** and **bus** are used together (often as "CAN-bus") to describe the data-sharing network in vehicles. The many sensors and electronic control modules can share information across a common network using the CAN-bus protocol to communicate efficiently and effectively. CAN-bus is a broad protocol developed by Bosch to share data and information across a network. In electrical and electronic systems, a bus is a means of connecting many electrical or electronic components for either data or power sharing. There are several signal protocols that have been developed for use with second-generation on-board diagnostics (OBDII), including SAE J1850 PWM, SAE J1850 VPM, ISO 9141-2, ISO 14230 KW, and ISO 15765 CAN-bus (C&B).

Within the CAN-bus system design, there are several different network layouts or designs, and there may be a gateway or hub controller, but no single dominant electronic control module; each receives the same data and simply chooses the data it needs to work effectively. It is a robust system, and many modules can send and receive data without corruption or interference. The CAN-bus system continues to develop and, although standards are in place, manufacturers may use different terminology to describe their particular systems. As CAN-bus has developed, so too have the network speeds. CAN-bus A is a low-speed network, CAN-bus B is a medium-speed network, and CAN-bus C is a high-speed network. Higher-speed networks are used for critical data such as supplemental restraint systems, anti-lock brake systems, and engine controls. Lower-speed networks are used for lesser priority data such as data related to entertainment systems. CAN-bus systems will continue to evolve and new standards will be developed; however, the fundamental operating principles are likely to remain the same. And since CAN-bus-compliant diagnostic systems have been required on all vehicles sold in the United States since 2008, it is even more important that you be familiar with them.

Principles of Operation

The CAN-bus system uses digital data, called binary data, which have only two states: 0 or 1. All the data can be coded in binary form using a series of 0s and 1s. Each 0 or 1 is called a bit of information, and a group of eight bits is called a byte. The 0s and 1s are represented on the data bus as low and high voltages **FIGURE 40-1**. Each module on the data bus sees all data, so along with the

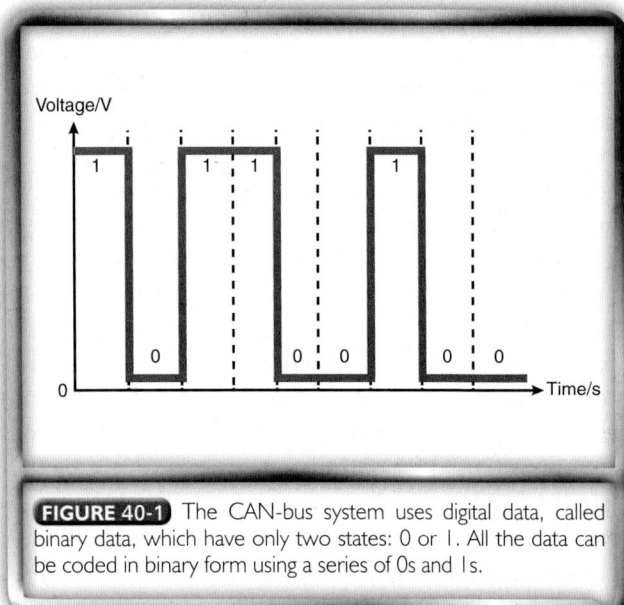

FIGURE 40-1 The CAN-bus system uses digital data, called binary data, which have only two states: 0 or 1. All the data can be coded in binary form using a series of 0s and 1s.

FIGURE 40-2 Typical CAN-bus-H and CAN-bus-L signal.

actual data, other information like message headers is required to identify sender and recipient modules along with message priority, wake-up commands, and state of health messages. These details are all coded in binary form and sent along the data bus. The data are grouped into blocks of data, each with a beginning and an end, and each module is capable of reading the binary data, interpreting the required data, and sending its own messages along the data bus.

Some networks transmit and receive signals over a single wire, but most have dual wires and are commonly called "CAN-bus high (H)" and "CAN-bus low (L)," with the same message sent on both lines **FIGURE 40-2**. This system provides redundancy in the case of a fault or interference on a single line. The signal on each CAN-bus line is a differential signal, meaning they are a mirror image, or opposite polarity, of each other. The actual voltages used on the data lines to represent a 0 or 1 will vary with each manufacturer.

Configurations and Terminal Resistors

The network configurations, or how the network connects to each module, will vary with each manufacturer. Some use a simple series configuration; others use variations of series networks and parallel network connections with descriptive names, such as looped series, star parallel, or bussed parallel **FIGURE 40-3**. Regardless of how the network is physically connected, the CAN-bus-H and CAN-bus-L system will have terminating resistors connected to the data lines to form a loop through the resistors. The value of resistors can vary by manufacturer, but high-speed CAN-bus systems tend to use dual 120-ohm

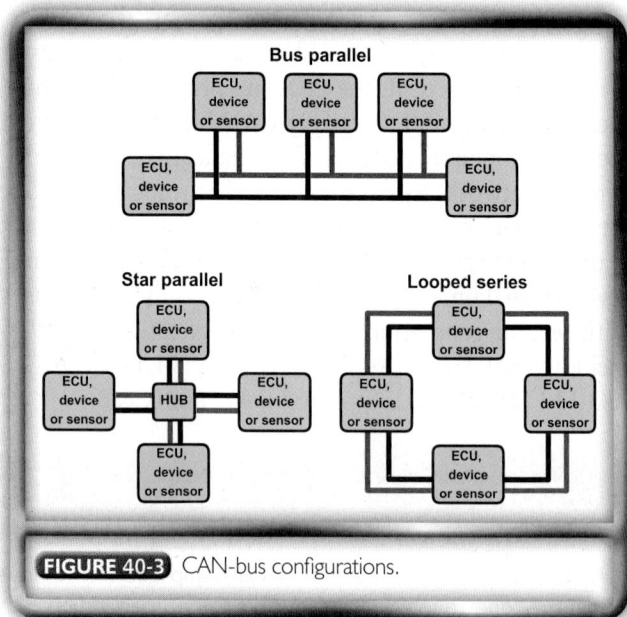

FIGURE 40-3 CAN-bus configurations.

resistors, giving a total of 60 ohms per pair since they are connected in parallel, but typically at opposite ends of the bus **FIGURE 40-4**.

The resistors can be connected externally in the wiring harness or connectors but are usually integrated internally into modules. The data lines are also twisted together with a specific twist rotation per length. This twisting, in combination with the terminating resistors, reduces the amount of interference on the data lines. The CAN-bus system has a **data link connector (DLC)** that provides a connection into the data network. The DLC is also used to connect scan tools into the network. It can also be used to conduct voltage and waveform tests on the CAN-bus.

FIGURE 40-4 A network diagram with terminating resistors.

Testing the CAN-bus System

When there is an issue with the CAN-bus system, a diagnostic trouble code (DTC) with a "U" designation will typically be set indicating the nature of the fault. Testing of the CAN-bus system requires a combination of diagnostic tools, including scan tools, digital volt-ohmmeter (DVOM), digital storage oscilloscope (DSO), and DLC breakout boxes. The scan tool connects to the DLC and provides access to the DTCs, and depending on the functionality of the scan tool, it may provide access to the data stream. The scan tool can be used to identify any fault codes that may have been logged by the vehicle's systems. Fault codes may provide good information on what particular part of the system or type of fault needs to be diagnosed. The DVOM can be used to measure CAN-bus data line resistances, system voltages, and grounds to ensure basic circuit integrity.

A DLC breakout box is a tool that connects to the DLC and provides easy access to the terminals in the DLC socket to connect DVOMs and DSOs. Some breakout boxes also provide a visual indication of pin voltages with colored LEDs on the sockets. A capable dual-channel DSO can display the high- and low-voltage data signals present on the CAN-bus and display them on the screen. The CAN-bus-H and CAN-bus-L data signals can be compared because they should be the mirror image of each other. The signal can also be examined for any interference on the data line that may cause faults or loss of data. Some DSOs are capable of decoding the CAN-bus data to provide a more accurate comparison of the high and low signals.

Depending on the nature of the fault, it may be necessary to disconnect various modules within the CAN-bus. Disconnecting modules that are equipped with the terminating resistors during diagnosis or testing may affect the communications on the network due to increased interference. Always refer to the manufacturer's information for test and repair procedures.

TECHNICIAN TIP

Knowing the configuration of the network can help you diagnose it. For example, you will use a scan tool to look at the active modules on the network; if any are missing, knowing the sequence of the control modules can lead you to the area of concern. Checking for continuity of CAN-H or CAN-L between the last active module and the first missing module will show you if the CAN wire is open. Also, knowing where the terminating resistors are located in the circuit will allow you to measure the resistance between CAN-H and CAN-L. If the resistance is 60 ohms, both terminating resistors and the CAN lines between them are not open. Resistance of 120 ohms indicates an open line or resistor in one side of the circuit. Using the diagrams and schematics will help you pinpoint faults in the system.

Using a Scan Tool

Many different types and brands of scan tools are available, and the vehicle and system coverage varies with each scan tool. Some scan tools require hardware keys to be inserted for each different type of vehicle; others may have provisions for vehicle manufacturer and model to be selected using software. Always ensure that you understand how to connect and set up the specific scan tool for the vehicle you are working on.

Using the scan tool may require the vehicle's ignition system to be on for an extended period of time without the engine running. The electrical load may be such that the vehicle's battery will discharge; a battery support unit may need to be connected to ensure the vehicle's battery does not discharge. Battery support units are high-current output power supplies with a steady voltage supply used to support the battery when the engine is not running. Do not use a standard battery charger to perform this role, as many do not have a steady direct current (DC) voltage supply and they may cause interference on the CAN-bus-H and -L circuits or damage components.

Checking for Module Communication Errors Using a Scan Tool

Modern vehicles will have multiple modules to control the various vehicle systems. The number of modules and the purpose of each will vary among manufacturers

AS-66: Electricity/Measurement: The technician can demonstrate an understanding of the correct procedure to measure the electrical parameters of voltage, current, and resistance.

A vehicle is in the shop for multiple interior electrical problems. The systems affected are the power seats, power windows, power door locks, and interior lighting. This problem was initially intermittent, but at this point the affected systems are not functioning.

The technician assigned to this repair has a good knowledge of troubleshooting automotive electrical circuits with a DVOM. He often helps other technicians who are in need of assistance on electrical concerns. In order to explain voltage, current, and resistance, the technician likes to use an analogy of a water hose. The water pressure available signifies voltage, the flow of water through the hose is the current measured in amps, and a kink or crimp in the hose is like the resistance in the electrical circuit. Resistance in a water hose application can be wanted or unwanted according to the purpose. When watering small plants, we want more resistance in the hose to reduce the amount of water flow. In the electrical system, there are times when we want increased resistance to reduce voltage, such as for low-speed windshield wiper operation.

In repairing the vehicle, the technician will do a voltage drop test to determine if there is a bad ground causing the multiple circuit problems. He is using a long jumper wire along with his DVOM to accomplish the test. The technician attaches a long jumper lead to the negative battery post, which connects to the COM or black test lead of the DVOM. The DVOM is set to read DC volts, and the red lead is used to check the ground side of the components in question. This test will be performed with each separate component under load, such as when attempting to operate a window. A good ground should have a reading of 0.10 volt or less. The technician finds a very high reading for each of the affected circuits and determines that the problem is in a corroded multiple ground connection point. Using the manufacturer's service information, the technician finds the

four ground connections secured by a single bolt behind the driver's side kick panel. Each ground connector is cleaned on both sides with emery cloth. The frame location is cleaned also and the bolt securely tightened. The DVOM reading is now 0.07 volt, and all circuits are working properly.

AS-67: Ammeter/Voltmeter: The technician can demonstrate an understanding of how to correctly measure electrical current and voltage in a circuit.

The digital volt-ohmmeter (DVOM) is the testing and measuring device used by most technicians working on today's vehicles. While separate ammeters are available for measuring current in amperes, and separate voltmeters are available for measuring voltage in a circuit, for the purposes of this article, we will consider the DVOM as being the meter of choice.

To measure electrical current with the DVOM, it is helpful to know that current is the volume of electrons flowing in a circuit. Amps and milliamps are a measure of the volume of electrons. To measure current below 10 amps, place the meter in series with the load. If the current is expected to be above 10 amps, an inductive pickup must be used. Turn off the power to the circuit and determine where the test leads should be attached. Put the black test lead into the COM input jack. Plug the red test lead into the 10 amps or 300 milliamps position and select DC amps. Connect the test probe's tips to the circuit across the break so current will flow through the meter in series. Turn on the circuit and view the reading on the meter.

To measure voltage with a DVOM, it is helpful to know that voltage is the electrical pressure that causes electricity to flow. Voltage is the difference in electrical potential between the "hot" side of the battery and the "ground" side. To make a voltage measurement, the meter leads must be connected across the load or component being measured. When testing an automotive battery, you must wear safety glasses. Place the red lead on the positive post of the battery. Place the black lead on the negative post of the battery. A fully charged automotive battery should be approximately 12.66 volts at 70°F (21°C).

and even vehicle models. Modules communicate using the CAN-bus on the vehicle. If there are communication errors on the network, some or all of the modules will not be able to operate. Also, one or more U codes will be set, indicating a fault in the communication network. If the network is active or partially active, a scan tool may be able to help you diagnose the fault.

One of the best things you can do is connect to the CAN-bus DLC and compare your findings to the service information. Typically, if a device is not showing as present, you will need to physically locate that module and first check it for power and ground. If those are correct, then use the scan tool to command the module to operate the device

and check the communication wire to see if it is receiving the signal. Or you can use a DVOM to measure the resistance of the network signal wire. If the power and ground are sufficient, and if the signal wire(s) are communicating the proper signal and the module is not responding, chances are that the module is faulty and needs to be replaced.

To check for module communication (including CAN-bus systems) errors using a scan tool, follow the steps in **SKILL DRILL 40-1**:

1. Research the correct procedure for module communications from the manufacturer's information.
2. Locate the DLC and connect the scan tool.

SKILL DRILL | 40-1 | Checking for Module Communication Errors Using a Scan Tool

1. After researching the correct procedure in the manufacturer's information, locate the DLC and connect the scan tool. Power on the scan tool and turn the ignition on. Establish scan tool communications with the vehicle.

2. Check fault codes using the scan tool, and follow the diagnostic procedure in the service information. Check to see if any modules are inactive, or not listed as active, that should be.

3. Command the module to take the appropriate action and observe the response. If you do not receive the proper response, refer to the service information for the diagnostic procedure.

3 Power on the scan tool, and turn the ignition on.

4 Establish scan tool communications with the vehicle. **(Photo 1)**

5 Check fault codes using the scan tool, and follow the diagnostic procedure in the service information.

6 Check to see if any modules are inactive, or not listed as active, that should be. **(Photo 2)**

7 Command the module to take the appropriate action and observe the response. If you do not receive the proper response, refer to the service information for the diagnostic procedure. **(Photo 3)**

Performing Software Transfers, Updates, or Flash Reprogramming on Electronic Modules

Diagnosing and repairing vehicles may require software transfers, software updates, or flash reprogramming of the vehicle's electronic modules with the manufacturer's latest update. Manufacturers do periodically update the software for vehicle modules to enhance vehicle operation. Flash reprogramming tools are available and connect to the vehicle's DLC to update vehicle software, and manufacturers make updates available over the Internet, usually through a subscription service.

Using the flash program tool may require the vehicle's ignition system to be on for an extended period of time without the engine running. The electrical load may be such that the vehicle battery will discharge, which may cause a fault in the reprogramming. A battery support unit needs to be connected to ensure that the vehicle's battery does not discharge. Battery support units are high-current output power supplies with a steady voltage supply used to support the battery when the engine is not running. Do not use a standard battery charger to perform this role, as many do not have a steady DC voltage supply and they may cause interference or damage components resulting in damage to the vehicle. Never shut the key off or lose power during the middle of a flash, as module damage can occur.

To perform software transfers, software updates, or flash reprogramming on electronic modules, follow the steps in **SKILL DRILL 40-2**:

1 Research the correct procedure for module software transfers, software updates, or flash reprogramming from the manufacturer's information. Obtain the latest vehicle software program updates from the manufacturer.

2 Load the updates into the flash programmer.

3 Connect a battery support unit to the vehicle. **(Photo 1)**

4 Locate the DLC and connect the flash program tool.

5 Power on the flash program tool, and turn the ignition on. **(Photo 2)**

| SKILL DRILL | 40-2 | Performing Software Transfers, Software Updates, or Flash Reprogramming on Modules |

1. Obtain the latest vehicle software program updates from the manufacturer, and load the updates into the flash programmer. Connect a battery support unit to the vehicle.

2. Locate the DLC. Connect and power on the flash program tool. Turn the ignition on.

3. Establish flash program tool communication with the vehicle.

4. Identify the vehicle modules to be updated, and use the flash program tool to perform software transfers, software updates, or flash reprogramming.

5. Disconnect the flash programmer and check the vehicle's functionality.

6. Establish flash program tool communication with the vehicle. (**Photo 3**)

7. Identify the vehicle modules to be updated.

8. Use the flash program tool to perform software transfers, software updates, or flash reprogramming. (**Photo 4**)

9. Disconnect the flash programmer. Check the vehicle's functionality and reinstate the vehicle. (**Photo 5**)

Electric Accessory Motors

Electric motors rotate as a result of the interaction of magnetic fields; that is, magnetic poles repel each other, and opposite poles attract. Two magnetic fields are required for motor action: one in the casing and the other in the rotating armature. The magnetic field in the casing can be generated by permanent magnets or many windings of fine copper wire wound in loops called field coils. The armature's magnetic field is generated in loops of wire that form the armature windings. Motor action occurs through the interaction of the magnetic fields of the field coils and the armature, which causes a rotational force to act on the armature, creating the turning motion **FIGURE 40-5**. From there, the rotary motion can be used to drive a variety of devices. Many times, the speed of the motor must be geared down so that more torque can be obtained, such as with windshield wipers and many actuators. Most of the time, the gears are located inside the motor housing, so if one or more gears go bad (e.g., stripped teeth), then the motor may still spin but

FIGURE 40-5 Typical brush-type motor.

the output gear or lever will not move as designed. Thus, listening for motor rotation can help you diagnose the problem. For example, if the windshield wipers do not move when activated, yet you can hear the motor running, you know that the electrical circuitry is working but the movement isn't getting from the motor to the wipers. This example could be an internal gear problem in the motor, or it could be a problem with the wiper linkage. But at least you will have a good head start on diagnosing the fault.

Motor Types—Brush, Brushless, Permanent Magnet, and Stepper Type

Electric motors are designed to perform specific functions. They all work on the same fundamental principle of the interaction of magnetic fields; however, their construction varies. One of the most common types of DC electric motors is the **permanent magnet type**. In this type of motor, the magnetic field in the casing is produced by permanent magnets, while the armature has an electromagnetic field generated by passing electrical current through loops or windings to produce the motor action. Power is supplied to the armature loops by brushes riding on the commutator, which continually changes the current flow in the armature loops as it rotates. This changes the polarity of the magnetic field in the armature, producing the motor action effect as the armature magnetic field interacts with the permanent magnets in the casing.

A **brushless DC motor**, as the name suggests, does not have any brushes and is sometimes called an "electronically commutated motor." In this type of motor, an electronic control module replaces the brushes and commutator. A brushless motor has permanent magnets rotating around a fixed armature or stator. Having a fixed stator eliminates the need to have brushes. The current flow

still needs to be continually alternated in the stationary stator to produce motor action, and this is achieved by an electronic control module. A brushless DC motor has several advantages over brush motors, including improved efficiency and reliability. In addition, brushless motors create less electrical interference because there are no sparks created by brushes making and breaking contact on the commutator.

A **stepper motor** is a type of brushless motor with a key difference: It is designed to rotate in fixed steps through a set number of degrees. The stepper motor is controlled by an electronic microcontroller and has a number of wound coils, each controlled independently by the controller. Each time the controller energizes a coil for a short period of time, the motor armature turns a set number of degrees and stops **FIGURE 40-6**. For example, if a motor were to turn 20 degrees for each step, it would require a minimum of 18 pairs of coils—one coil for each 20 degrees of rotation (totaling 360 degrees). Energizing each coil in rapid succession creates rotational movement. Stepper motors can also be used to rotate a short distance and then stop or go in the reverse direction for a set number of degrees by controlling each coil individually through the microcontroller. Stepper motors are increasingly used in vehicles; for example, the electronic throttle body uses a stepper motor to open and close the throttle plate one step at a time, as directed by the power train control module (PCM).

FIGURE 40-6 Typical stepper motor.

Blower Motor and Circuits

The **blower motor** in a vehicle is usually the permanent magnet type and moves air over the air-conditioning evaporator and heater core. The blower motor circuit incorporates a speed control for the motor. Speed can be controlled by using a number of resistors connected in series and a switch to select between combinations of resistors or a more complex electronic speed control module. The blower motor circuit consists of the power supply, fuse, on/off switch, speed control, relay, and the motor itself **FIGURE 40-7**. In vehicles equipped with air conditioning, the blower motor control circuit is incorporated into the control circuits for the air-conditioning system.

Cooling Fans and Circuits

Electric cooling fans for the radiator are increasingly common, particularly for transversely mounted engines and as supplementary cooling fans for vehicles equipped with air conditioning. Cooling fans in modern vehicles are usually switched by relays, which are controlled by an electronic control unit based on information from the coolant temperature sensor. Control units can be quite complex and can incorporate variable speed and on/off control. The control circuits are designed to ensure that the operating temperature of the engine is kept as close as possible to the temperature at which the engine operates most efficiently.

The basic electric cooling fan circuit contains the battery or power supply, fuse, relay, fan control circuits, and fans **FIGURE 40-8**. The actual circuit and its complexity will vary by manufacturer and vehicle model. The circuit diagram or schematic for the fan system should be examined before attempting any diagnosis.

FIGURE 40-7 A blower motor circuit.

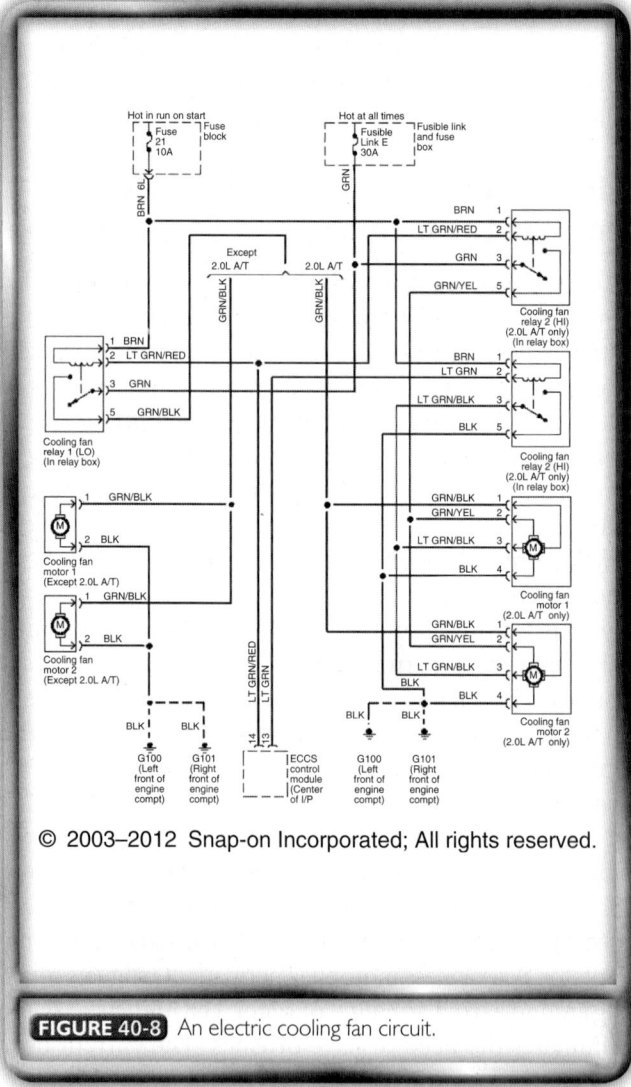

FIGURE 40-8 An electric cooling fan circuit.

Power Mirrors

Power mirrors use permanent magnet electric motors to control the up-and-down, in-and-out movement of the passenger and driver side mirrors. Most mechanisms use two motors for each mirror, one each for up-and-down and in-and-out movements **FIGURE 40-9**. The motors are reversible so that they can provide the movements in either direction. The control circuit turns the motors on and off, controls direction of rotation, and provides dynamic braking. Reversal of the motors is achieved by reversing current flow through the armature. The mechanical arrangements for connection of the motors to the mirrors will vary by manufacturer and vehicle model.

Dynamic braking is critical in this application because it ensures that the motor stops quickly without overrun, thus ensuring that the mirror stops quickly when the power is removed by the driver operating the switch. Dynamic braking is achieved by ensuring that the same potential is applied to both brushes at the time the switch is turned off. The circuit in shows a basic control circuit

> **TECHNICIAN TIP**
>
> On many modern vehicles, the mirrors are operated by a body computer so that when the vehicle is put into reverse, one or both of the mirrors rotate down so the driver can see the ground/curb. Also, many luxury vehicles have driver presets and allow different drivers to set preferences such as seat position, tilt/telescoping of the steering wheel, radio station, pedal position, and mirror position. These presets are tied to the individual key each driver uses. Also, many mirrors incorporate directional indicators that flash when the turn signals or hazards are on. All of these features are more easily integrated into the vehicle due to the CAN-bus system.

that reverses the motor and provides dynamic braking. The typical power mirror circuit includes the battery supply, fuse or circuit breaker, control switches, relays, and motors. The control switches usually incorporate a switch to select between passenger and driver side mirrors and a joystick-type switch with east, west, north, and south positions to control the up-and-down, in-and-out movements.

Power Windows

Electric windows use permanent magnet motors located in each of the passenger doors and sometimes in a rear door to control the up-and-down movement of vehicle windows. The motors are reversible to provide the movement in either direction. The control circuit turns the motors on and off, controls direction of rotation, and provides dynamic braking. Reversal of the motors is achieved by reversing current flow through the armature. A switch on each door controls the direction of travel, and a master switch panel to control all windows is usually located on the driver's side front door. If equipped, a lockout switch in the master switch panel disables the switches for the other window switches.

The mechanical arrangements for connecting the motors to the windows will vary by manufacturer and vehicle model. They will usually comprise a window regulator made up of gears and scissor-acting levers or a cable and lever system **FIGURE 40-10**.

Modern vehicles will often have more sophisticated electric window control systems to improve safety and usability. They include one-touch up and down, where a single full push on the control switch in either direction enables the window to go all the way up or down without the need to hold the switch. The control system monitors current flow and can reverse the window winding if it senses excessive resistance such as would occur if an arm were caught or trapped in the window.

FIGURE 40-9 A basic power mirror showing the position of both motors.

FIGURE 40-10 The mechanical components for a window regulator system.

The electric window system includes the battery supply, fuses or circuit breakers, switches at each door and the master panel in the driver's side door, relays, and the DC motor **FIGURE 40-11** .

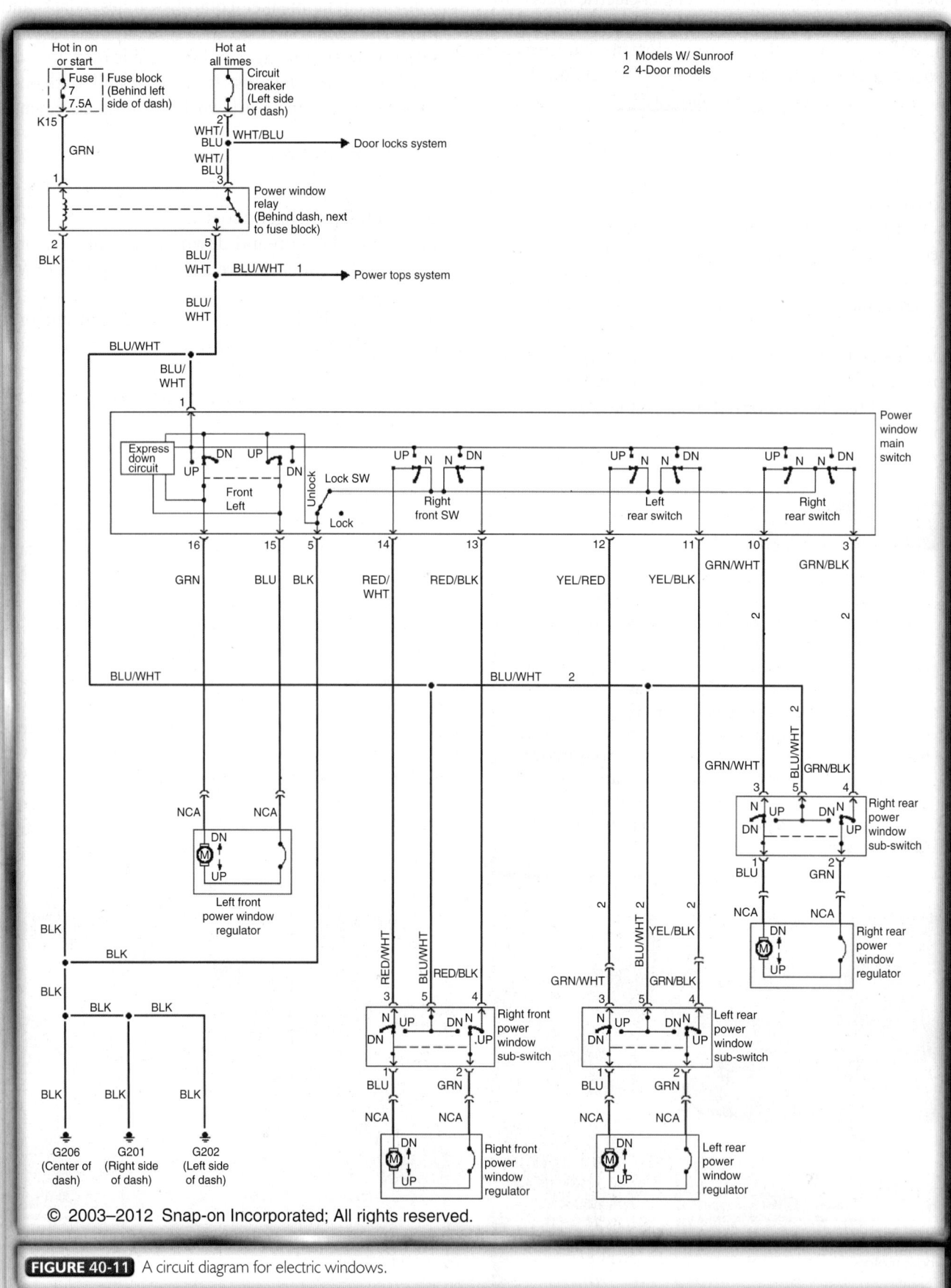

FIGURE 40-11 A circuit diagram for electric windows.

On some one-touch systems, if power is lost, the window controller will have to be re-initialized for it to learn where full up is before the one-touch function will work.

Power Seats

Electric or powered seats are becoming standard equipment on modern vehicles. They have a number of electric motors to provide adjustment to the relative position of the seat front to rear, seat height, tilt of the seat base, and often, lumbar support. There can be four or more electric motors, which are DC-permanent magnet types and are reversible to provide the movements in either direction. The control circuit turns the motors on and off, controls direction of rotation, and provides dynamic braking. Reversal of the motors is achieved by reversing current flow through the armature. The mechanical arrangements for connection of the motors to the seat mechanisms will vary by manufacturer and vehicle model. More sophisticated electric seat systems are controlled by an electronic control unit and can "remember" seat and mirror positions for each driver. The electrical system includes the battery supply, fuses or circuit breakers, switches, relays, electronic control unit, if equipped, and DC motors **FIGURE 40-12**. In most systems, the switches control relays, which in turn control the motors.

FIGURE 40-12 A circuit diagram for electric seats.

Electric Height Adjustment of Control Pedals

Electric pedal height adjustment allows the repositioning of the brake and accelerator pedals in and out from the firewall. This provides the driver with additional ergonomic comfort by allowing him or her to more effectively position the driving controls in relation to seat and steering position. The movement of the pedals is achieved by a reversible motor driven screw **FIGURE 40-13**. Operating the switch activates the drive motor, which in turn rotates an adjustment screw, moving the pedals in toward the firewall or out toward the driver. The accelerator pedal and brake pedal move together and the same distance so the pedal relationship to each other is maintained. The circuit consists of the fuse or circuit breaker, an adjustment switch, and the reversible motor. Additionally, the system is likely to be controlled by an electronic control unit and may incorporate memory functions and additional safety features, such as inhibitor circuits, that prevent it from operating when the vehicle is in reverse or cruise control is enabled.

Testing Electric Motors

Electric motors wear out and fail, but they can also be affected by faulty gears and levers or electrical circuits and control devices. Knowing how to test them and their circuits is important. DVOMs and automotive test lights will be used to measure voltages and test fuses, relays, switches, and power and ground connection. The DC motors may be located in doors or in locations that require the removal of vehicle trim components. Permanent magnets within DC motors are brittle and may be damaged if the outer casing is struck with a hammer or other hard object. This activity will require you to work with motors, gears, and mechanical levers, which may create a crush injury hazard; keep fingers away from mechanisms. Always wear the correct protective eyewear and clothing, use the appropriate safety equipment, and apply fender covers, seat protectors, and floor mat protectors.

To test the electric motor, follow the steps in **SKILL DRILL 40-3**:

FIGURE 40-13 Adjustable pedal assembly.

SKILL DRILL | 40-3 | Testing the Electric Motor

1. Research circuit operation and circuit diagrams for the motor-driven accessory requiring repair from the manufacturer's information. Measure and record the voltage at the battery.

2. Use a DVOM to measure the power and ground at the motor while it is being operated. If the voltage reading is more than 1.0 volt lower than battery voltage, perform voltage drop tests on each side of the circuit to determine which side has the fault.

3. Once the faulty side has been identified, measure the voltage drop on each section of the circuit to locate the high resistance. If the total power and ground voltage to the motor was within 1.0 volt of battery voltage, there is a fault in the motor. Determine any necessary actions.

Research circuit operation and circuit diagrams for the motor-driven accessory requiring repair from the manufacturer's service information.

2 Measure and record the voltage at the battery. **(Photo 1)**

3 Use a DVOM to measure the power and ground at the motor while it is being operated. If the voltage reading is more than 1.0 volt lower than battery voltage, perform voltage drop tests on each side of the circuit to determine which side has the fault. **(Photo 2)**

4 Once the faulty side has been identified, measure the voltage drop on each section of the circuit to locate the high resistance.

5 If the total power and ground voltage to the motor was within 1.0 volt of battery voltage, there is a fault in the motor, which will require further diagnosis, if there is a control circuit built into it, or replacement. Determine any necessary actions. **(Photo 3)**

▶ Horn Systems

The vehicle horn is a sound making safety device to warn others of a vehicle's presence. Legislation requires vehicles to have a working horn and in most cases also prescribes the sound level required to be made by the horn. Single horns may be installed but often they will be installed in pairs, one each of a high and low note to produce a harmonious sound and to give redundancy if one horn fails.

Horn, Relay, Switch, and Clock Spring

The sound of a horn is produced by the vibration of a metal diaphragm, which is operated by an electromagnet switched by a set of contacts. The diaphragm is connected to an armature that moves inside an electromagnet. When the electromagnet is on, the diaphragm is pulled by the armature toward the electromagnet; as this occurs, a trip ring opens the contacts, allowing the diaphragm to spring back to its original position. This cycle happens many times a second, producing sound through the rapid vibration of the diaphragm.

The horn switch is usually mounted in the steering wheel and requires a method to maintain an electrical connection to the circuit as the steering wheel rotates. On vehicles with a driver's side airbag, the clock spring performs this function. The clock spring is also used to carry the electrical signals for the driver airbag circuit and may be used for sound system or cruise control circuits if they are built into the steering wheel. The clock spring is a rotating device with flexible ribbon cable and rotates as the steering wheel rotates **FIGURE 40-14**. It is designed to

FIGURE 40-14 A clock spring.

> **TECHNICIAN TIP**
>
> Vehicles without a driver's side airbag usually use a slip ring and brush assembly in place of a clock spring to transmit the electricity across the rotating steering wheel connection.

turn two or three times in each direction from the center point and cannot rotate endlessly in a single direction. It must be adjusted when it is installed to match the position of the steering wheel to avoid it reaching the end of its travel in any single direction.

The horn circuit is made up of the battery power supply, a fuse or circuit breaker, a relay, the horn switch, and the clock spring. The horn switch is usually a grounding circuit. The switch grounds the relay winding, which in turn supplies power through the relay contacts to operate the horn **FIGURE 40-15**. The horns on many newer vehicles can be operated by pressing the panic button on a fob. They may chirp when locking or unlocking and honk when a breach of security has happened. In most cases, these horns are operated by a body computer when the correct inputs arrive.

Testing the Horn System

The horn circuit can fail in many ways. Any of the components in the circuit can go bad, as can the wiring. Using a DVOM to measure voltages and test voltage drops on fuses, relays, switches, and power and ground connection will tell you how to proceed when testing the circuit. The horn switch is usually mounted within the steering wheel and is usually connected through the steering column by a clock spring. The clock spring must be correctly centered when it is installed to ensure it has enough travel

FIGURE 40-15 A typical horn circuit.

getting to the horn, check the voltage drop on the ground side. If the voltage drop is fine, the horn is bad. In this case, tap the horn while it is energized. It is possible the contacts inside the horn are dirty or rusty, and tapping on the horn may free them up. If so, you will know that the rest of the circuit is operational. You will probably want to replace the horn since it is likely to go bad again soon.

If the horn does not have power when activated, it is good to go to the horn relay to perform the next tests. At the relay, you have access to each of the legs in the circuit—power from the horn fuse, the output terminal to the horn, power from the fuse feeding the winding, and the horn switch terminal. Using the DVOM and a jumper lead, you can check each of these legs. Remove the relay and using the DVOM, check for power from each fuse. If present, use the jumper lead from the horn fuse input to the horn output (at the relay connector) and see if the horn honks. If it does not honk, check the wiring between the relay and the horn. If it does honk, use a DVOM to check the continuity of the horn switch leg with the horn switch depressed. There should be continuity between the horn switch terminal on the relay and ground. If there is, then the relay is faulty.

To diagnose the horn system, follow the steps in **SKILL DRILL 40-4**:

1. Confirm that the horn does not operate. Research circuit operation and circuit diagrams for the horn from the manufacturer's service information.

in each direction. The horn switch usually grounds the horn relay winding, which in turn sends power to the horn.

When testing the horn, it may be easiest to first test to see if power is getting to the horn when the horn is activated since it is not uncommon for horns to go bad, especially if they are rarely used or are overused. If power is

SKILL DRILL | 40-4 | Testing the Horn System

1. Confirm that the horn does not operate. Research circuit operation and circuit diagrams for the horn from the service information. Check for power and ground at horn when the horn switch is operated. If power and ground are present, the horn is faulty and needs to be replaced.

2. If there is no power to the horn, remove the relay and check for battery voltage at terminal 30 (or 3). If battery voltage is not present, check the horn fuse and the rest of the feed circuit.

3. If battery voltage is present, jump terminal 30 (or 3) to terminal 87 (or 5). The horn should honk. If it doesn't, check for an open wire between terminal 87 and the horn with a DVOM.

SKILL DRILL | 40-4 | Testing the Horn System, continued

4. If the horn now honks, check that either terminal 85 or 86 has battery voltage. If one does, then the other should be the horn switch leg.

5. Connect a DVOM between the switch leg terminal and ground. Operate the horn switch; resistance should decrease to less than an ohm. If it doesn't, search out the high resistance or open circuit back to the horn switch. Suspect either the clock spring or the horn switch itself.

6. If the switch leg is good, measure the resistance between terminals 85 and 86 on the horn relay itself. The resistance should be between about 40 and 100 ohms. If not, replace the relay.

7. If the resistance is good, either measure the voltage drop across the switch contacts of the relay (30 and 87) or substitute a known good relay.

2. Check for power and ground at the horn when the horn switch is operated. If power and ground are present, the horn is faulty and needs to be replaced. **(Photo 1)**

3. If there is no power to the horn, remove the relay and check for battery voltage at terminal 30 (or 3). If battery voltage is not present, check the horn fuse and the rest of the feed circuit. **(Photo 2)**

4. If battery voltage is present, jump terminal 30 (or 3) to terminal 87 (or 5). The horn should honk. If it does not, check for an open wire between terminal 87 and the horn with a DVOM. **(Photo 3)**

5. If the horn now honks, check that either terminal 85 or 86 has battery voltage. If one does, then the other should be the horn switch leg. **(Photo 4)**

6. Connect a DVOM between the switch leg terminal and ground. Operate the horn switch; the resistance should decrease to less than an ohm. If it does not, search out the high resistance or open circuit back to the horn switch. Suspect either the clock spring or the horn switch itself. **(Photo 5)**

7. If the switch leg is good, measure the resistance between terminals 85 and 86 on the horn relay itself. The resistance should be between about 40 and 100 ohms. If not, replace the relay. **(Photo 6)**

If the resistance is good, either measure the voltage drop across the switch contacts of the relay (30 and 87) or substitute a known good relay. **(Photo 7)**

▶ Power Door Locks

Power or electric door locks are a common option in modern vehicles and are installed in each door. They are often integrated with the vehicle's security system and remote locking systems and are called central locking systems. Many vehicles also have trunk locks incorporated into the vehicle's electric locking system. The driver's side door is usually a master door lock, which means that when it is locked or unlocked with the key (or the remote fob) the other locks follow suit.

Power door locks use an electrical actuator to move the mechanical door lock mechanism. There are two main types of actuators: a DC motor actuator and a solenoid type. The DC reversible permanent magnet motor type is enclosed in a single casing with a number of gears for speed reduction that connect to a rack-and-pinion gear set for conversion of the rotational motion into linear motion to operate the lock. A centrifugal clutch built into the motor main gear allows the door locks to be operated manually.

The solenoid-type actuator has a permanent magnet with a north and south pole mounted on a moving plunger and a stationary coil wound around the outside. It can move in both directions. The magnetic fields of the permanent magnet on the plunger react with the magnetic fields of the coils producing linear movement of the plunger. The plunger's direction of movement can be reversed by controlling the direction of current flow in the coil. The connecting rod of the plunger is connected to the door locking mechanism. The electric door lock circuit consists of the power supply, fuses or circuit breakers, the actuator (motor or solenoid), relays, switches, and cabling. Relays are typically used to switch the motors or solenoids.

Electric Lock and Keyless Entry Systems

Keyless entry systems and the engine immobilizer or security systems are separate systems, although they are usually linked so that the security system is enabled or disabled as the vehicle is locked and unlocked. Keyless entry is also known as remote key locking, and additional features such as alarms and warning devices may be incorporated into the system. The system is usually controlled by a wireless fob with various buttons or a wireless proximity fob, which operates provided it is near the vehicle and is used to lock and unlock the vehicle.

On CAN-bus systems, many vehicles are programmed to lock the vehicle when it is put into gear (automatic transmission) or when it reaches a certain miles per hour (mph) and unlock when put back into park. Most of these systems can be programmed by the driver to enable or disable this feature. Some vehicles have stepped unlocking, which allows one push of the remote fob to unlock the driver's door only and two pushes to unlock all doors. This feature can be programmed on some vehicles as well.

Types of Systems

Manufacturers continue to develop various systems for controlling electric vehicle locks; each has its own subtle differences. Despite the differences, the systems tend to fall into two common types: **remote keyless entry (RKE)** and **passive keyless entry (PKE)**. The RKE system uses a fob transmitter that is usually attached to the key or key ring. The fob has a number of buttons or keys for remotely locking and unlocking the doors or trunk. The PKE system uses a fob transmitter but does not require any action by the user. The vehicle senses if the fob is within range of the vehicle and automatically unlocks the door when the person touches the handle, without the need to press any buttons.

Principles of Operation

The RKE system consists of a fob transmitter and a receiver inside the vehicle. When a key or button is pressed, the fob transmits a coded signal that is received by the vehicle's receiver, provided it is within range. The **body electronic module (BEM)** recognizes the key's code and activates the vehicle's electric door locks.

The PKE system consists of an electronic key that is carried on the person's body. Once the electronic key is in close proximity to the vehicle, communication is established between the vehicle's system and the key. If the key is authenticated, the vehicle unlocks the door when the door handle is touched, without the need for any buttons or keys to be pressed. The same authentication system can be used to control the vehicle's start system, security system, and engine immobilizer.

Testing Electric Locks

Door lock systems can fail for a variety of reasons, from a dead battery in the remote fob to worn-out door lock switches and actuators. If the system is a CAN-bus system, the network or control module could be faulty. When starting a diagnosis on the electric lock system, it is good to verify what works and what doesn't. For example, if the system works from the lock button on the driver's door but not on the passenger door, you will probably want to focus on the passenger door switch.

Once you have an idea of how the circuit is operating, it is a good idea to consult the system's wiring diagram so you can understand how the circuit is supposed to work. Then you can build your diagnostic strategy. At that point, it is probably time to break out the DVOM, automotive test light, scan tool, and lab scope to help trace how electricity is flowing, and not flowing, in the circuit. You will be looking for opens, shorts, high resistance, and improper signals in the electrical circuit and for mechanical faults in the motors, solenoids, and linkage.

Removing the Door Panel

Removing door panels requires the removal of the arm rest, door lever, window crank, and any switch panels mounted on the door. In most cases, the door panel itself will be attached to the door using clips, so they will have to be pried out of their holes. Some manufacturers use a few screws to provide extra security. To pry the door panel from the door, it is best to use a nonmetallic door panel tool to prevent damage to the door or paint finishes. Special tools may be required to release the clip that holds the manual window handles in place, if equipped. Preserve the inner lining for reuse by carefully removing it from the door frame. Carefully examine the door lining for screws and fastenings that may need to be removed before attempting to pry off the door panel.

To remove the door panel, follow the steps in **SKILL DRILL 40-5**:

1. Research the process for removing and reinstalling the door panel from the manufacturer's service

SKILL DRILL | **40-5** | **Removing the Door Panel**

1. Research removal and reinstallation of the door panel from the manufacturer's service information. Remove fixtures such as the arm rest.

2. Remove the switch panel.

3. Remove the cables, and carefully pry the panel from the frame.

4. Remove the inner liner from the frame, preserving it for reuse.

5. Reinstall the door panel using the reverse procedure while ensuring all electrical connections are reinstalled.

information. Remove fixtures such as the arm rest. **(Photo 1)**

2 Remove the switch panel. **(Photo 2)**

3 Remove the cables.

4 Carefully pry the panel clips from the frame. **(Photo 3)**

5 Remove the inner liner from the frame, preserving it for reuse. **(Photo 4)**

6 Reinstall the door panel using the reverse procedure while ensuring that all electrical connections are reinstalled. **(Photo 5)**

► Wiper/Washer System

The wiper and washer system is an important vehicle safety system. The wipers ensure that the driver has a clear line of sight through the windshield by removing any excess moisture from the glass. The wipers usually have a number of speeds and intermittent operation for varying rainfall conditions. The washers provide a cleaning spray that, when used in conjunction with the wipers, helps to clean road grime from the windshield. Some vehicles use a wiper and washer for the rear glass, and even some headlights as well.

Wiper and Delay Circuits

The wiper motor will usually have a high and low speed and a time delay or intermittent operation. Intermittent operation will be controlled by a timer circuit, which may be a discrete electronic timer or controlled by the vehicle body computer. Incorporated into the circuit and activated by the motor gear is a parking switch to ensure that the motor stops when the wiper blades are in the park position. The DC motor is dynamically braked to make sure the motor stops instantly without overrun in the park position. To provide high and low speed, the wiper motor is equipped with three brushes. Two brushes are placed 180 degrees apart, as they are in a standard motor, while the additional or third brush is located off-center. When current is switched from the low-speed brush to the high-speed brush, it provides higher rotational speed of the armature due to the different interaction of the magnetic fields.

The wiper circuit consists of the battery, a fuse or circuit breaker, the ignition switch, the wiper switch, an intermittent timer and/or body computer, and the motor assembly with park switch **FIGURE 40-16**. The park switch is built inside the motor and gearbox housing and switches a power feed to the low-speed brush when the

wiper switch is in the off position and the wiper blades are in the park position. This dynamically brakes the motor because power is now applied across both brushes in the motor, bringing the motor to a quick stop. Intermittent operation is achieved by pulsing the low-speed circuit with a temporary power, causing the motor to move off the park position. With the power pulse removed, the motor continues on a single wipe of the windshield through the park switch until it again reaches the park position.

Wiper circuits can also be ground-switched circuits. For example, the ignition switch provides a power feed to the motor through a fuse or circuit breaker, and the wiper switch, depending on the switch position, switches the high- or low-speed brush to ground. Some vehicles use a rain sensor mounted in or near the windshield, which will signal the body computer to operate the wipers accordingly.

Testing the Washer System

The windshield and back window washer systems are made up of the washer bottle to hold the washer fluid, a DC electric pump, nozzles to spray the glass, and tubing to carry the washer fluid from the pump to the nozzles. The DC motor on the pump is a permanent magnet motor and has power supplied to one brush from the ignition circuit and the other brush grounded by the switch. The switch for the washer is usually located on the same switch assembly as the wipers. Operating the washer switch will usually also operate the wipers for at least one cycle; however, some systems allow for multiple wipe cycles before parking the wiper blades.

Both the electrical circuit and the pump discharge circuit will need to be tested for correct operation. The electrical circuit consists of the power supply, fuse, switch, and DC pump motor and can be tested with a test lamp or DVOM. The pump or washer fluid discharge circuit is made up of the pump, the washer fluid supply or tank, the tubes that carry the washer fluid to the washer nozzles, and the nozzles. You may find that blowing air through the discharge circuit and nozzles cleans out any debris that may be plugging the pump. Just be careful that you don't overpressurize the system and cause an inaccessible hose to be blown off of a fitting. Also, ensure adequate washer fluid in the tank before conducting any tests.

To test the washer system, follow the steps in **SKILL DRILL 40-6**:

1 Check for the correct solution level in tanks, and listen for washer pump operation. **(Photo 1)**

FIGURE 40-16 A wiper circuit diagram.

2 If an electrical fault is indicated by no washer motor sound, check for battery voltage and ground at the pump, when it is activated. (**Photo 2**)

3 If the power or ground circuit is faulty, perform voltage drop tests on the faulty side, until the fault is located. (**Photo 3**)

4 If the power and ground circuits are good, then measure the resistance of the pump motor and compare to specifications. (**Photo 4**)

5 If the pump spins when activated, but does not pump washer fluid, check the hoses and nozzles

for obstructions. Blow out with compressed air if necessary. (**Photo 5**)

Testing the Wiper System

The windshield wipers can fail in a number of ways. First, they may completely not work, such as when a fuse or motor is bad. Second, they may work on only some speeds, such as when the switch or one of the brushes in the motor is faulty. Third, they may not work on the intermittent speed, such as when the delay module is faulty. Fourth, they may not park, as when

SKILL DRILL 40-6   Testing the Washer System

1. Check for the correct solution level in tanks, and listen for washer pump operation.

2. If an electrical fault is indicated by lack of a washer motor sound, check for battery voltage and ground at the pump, when it is activated.

3. If the power or ground circuit is faulty, perform voltage drop tests on the faulty side, until the fault is located.

4. If the power and ground circuits are good, measure the resistance of the pump motor and compare to specifications.

5. If the pump spins when activated but does not pump washer fluid, check the hoses and nozzles for obstructions. Blow out with compressed air if necessary.

the park contacts in the motor are faulty or the wiper switch is bad. Each of these faults can be diagnosed by using a DVOM and referring to the wiring diagram to locate the fault. Another fault with wiper systems is that the linkage wears out, which can prevent one or both of the wiper arms from operating. To diagnose this, you will want to inspect the linkage for loose or disconnected joints.

This activity will require you to work with motors, gears, and mechanical levers, which may create a crush injury hazard; keep fingers away from mechanisms.

Always wear the correct protective eyewear and clothing, use the appropriate safety equipment, and apply fender covers, seat protectors, and floor mat protectors.

▶ Heated Glass, Mirrors, and Seats

Temperature differentials between the air temperature and glass surfaces in vehicles can cause moisture to condense on the glass surfaces or fog up. Heating the glass is an effective way to reduce the moisture buildup and

FIGURE 40-17 A heated window grid.

FIGURE 40-18 Heated seat.

improve visibility. Both the rear window and vehicle mirrors can be heated to reduce moisture condensation. Most vehicle manufacturers use an electric heater element attached to the glass to provide a heat source **FIGURE 40-17**. Mirrors have heater elements attached to the rear of the glass in a zigzag pattern to provide coverage across the mirror surface. The rear cabin window has a fine element heating foil attached to the inside of the glass. The element is made fine enough that it does not impair driver vision but creates sufficient heat to ensure that the window remains free of condensed moisture. The heated glass circuit has a power supply, a fuse, a switch, and usually a relay to switch the high current draws of the heating elements.

Heated seats provide additional passenger comfort, particularly in cold climates. Seats are heated with an electric element made inside the seat base and sometimes the seat back **FIGURE 40-18**. The element is controlled by a dash switch and relay. The circuit usually has a relay connected to a thermostat to ensure that the seat does not become overheated. Some systems may also have temperature controls with high and low settings to further provide passenger comfort.

Low- and High-Voltage Systems

Heated glass and seats tend to draw a substantial amount of electrical current, which adds to the ever-increasing electrical current needed to meet the demands of the electrical systems. To meet these demands, manufacturers must consider the overall design and effectiveness of the electrical system. One approach is to continue increasing the current output of the standard 12V systems. Another

approach being explored is to increase the system voltage to higher voltage outputs. High-voltage systems have a number of advantages over low-voltage systems, including less susceptibility to voltage drop and reduced current for the same wattage output (see Watt's law), which enables the use of smaller diameter conductors for the same wattage output.

Testing Heated Accessories

DVOMs and automotive test lights will be used to measure voltages and test fuses, relays, switches, and power and ground connections. Methodically work through the circuit, testing voltage and current against the manufacturer's specifications. An infrared thermometer may be useful in determining the effectiveness of heating elements. The heating elements will draw high circuit current. Always ensure that power is disconnected before connecting ammeters, and ensure that the test instrument is capable of measuring the expected current draw. The heat generated by the heating elements may cause injury, so always test the surface temperature before touching. Always wear the correct protective eyewear and clothing, use the appropriate safety equipment, and apply fender covers, seat protectors, and floor mat protectors.

Cruise Control Systems

Cruise control systems provide a convenience for the driver and are increasingly installed as a standard accessory on vehicles. Cruise control allows the driver to set a cruise speed for the vehicle, which it then memorizes and maintains without throttle input from the driver. For safety reasons, the cruise control has a minimum speed that must be met before it can be set and is deactivated when the driver touches the brake pedal or, in the case of manual transmissions, the clutch pedal. Driver controls built in to the steering wheel or column turn the system on and off, allow the speed to be set, and provide deceleration and acceleration controls.

Types of Systems

Cruise control systems can be installed as an aftermarket device or can be original equipment installed by the manufacturer. Manufacturer-equipped systems enable better integration of the cruise control into the overall vehicle systems and may be linked to stability control systems such as traction control. One of two basic types of main actuators will be fitted to the throttle body: electric or vacuum operated **FIGURE 40-19**. The electric actuator is a reversible DC motor that is geared and connected to the throttle plate through a mechanical connection such as a cable. The vacuum-operated system uses a vacuum to operate a vacuum servo, which is connected to the throttle plate by a cable.

Principles of Operation

The basic cruise control system works by comparing actual vehicle speed to a programmed target speed. The driver programs a set target speed and the cruise control system's PCM attempts to accelerate or decelerate the vehicle to maintain the target speed by commanding a throttle actuator to control the throttle valve. Cruise control components can be spilt into two main groups: driver controls and system components. Driver controls include the on/off switch, dash indicator lamp, and control switches, such as set, coast, resume, and accelerate. System components include the electronic control unit, speed sensor, clutch switch (for manual transmissions) or transmission range switch (for automatic transmissions), brake pedal switch, and throttle actuator **FIGURE 40-20**.

Electronic Throttle Control

Where a vehicle is equipped with electronic throttle control, the cruise control is integrated into the engine control system and does not require an additional throttle actuator. Electronic throttle control systems have no physical connection between the accelerator

FIGURE 40-19 Cruise control. **A.** Electric. **B.** Vacuum.

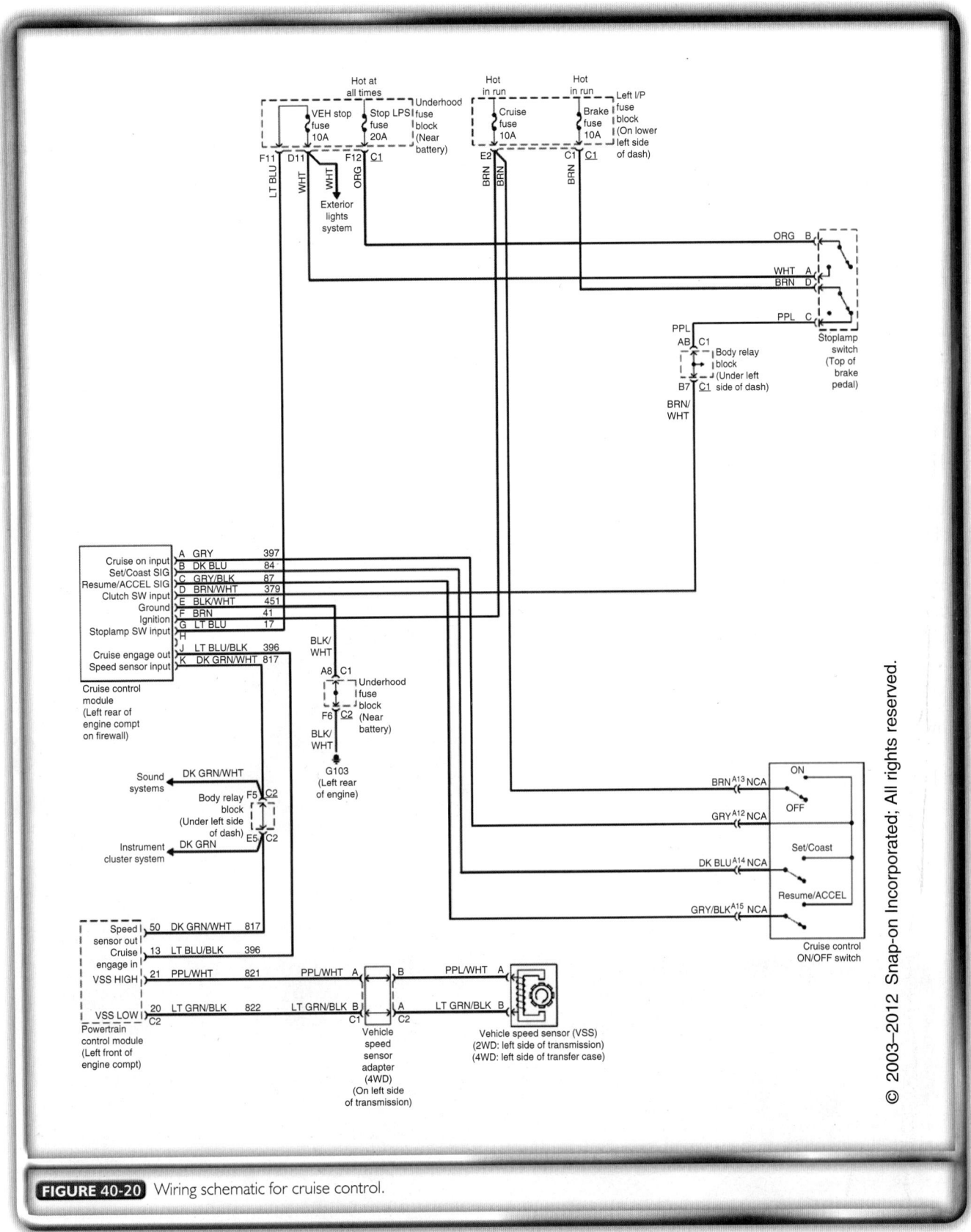

FIGURE 40-20 Wiring schematic for cruise control.

pedal and the throttle. Instead the accelerator pedal has an electrical sensor built into it that is monitored by

the PCM. The PCM controls the position of the throttle based on the position of the accelerator pedal by sending signals to a stepper motor connected to the throttle body **FIGURE 40-21**. A stepper motor is a special type of electric motor that is designed to move by a fixed number of degrees in either direction. The PCM adjusts the stepper motor in fine increments to control the throttle valve opening based on the position of the accelerator pedal.

Active Cruise Control

Active or dynamic cruise control systems adapt to the driving environment by sensing and adjusting vehicle speed based on changing conditions. For example, they can maintain the desired speed where possible while keeping a safe distance from the vehicle in front. The systems also incorporate driver warnings for potential collision or the requirement for driver intervention. The advantage of these systems is that the driver does not constantly have to adjust the cruise control in heavier traffic conditions where traffic speed may be variable. Active cruise control requires additional sensors such as radar or laser systems to sense the speed of the vehicle in front and steering angle sensors to determine vehicle direction. Some active cruise control systems also incorporate brake control. These systems, in addition to controlling the throttle, can apply the brakes if necessary.

Testing the Cruise Control System

How you test the cruise control system really depends on the type of system. For a vacuum-operated system, you will need to check the vacuum hoses and controls in addition to the electric controls. For a fully electronic throttle system, you will need to use a scan tool and DVOM to diagnose the system. Either way, the manufacturer's service information will guide you through the appropriate test sequences and procedures.

FIGURE 40-21 Electronic throttle control.

Supplemental Restraint Systems

The <u>supplemental restraint system (SRS)</u> is used to describe passenger safety devices installed on vehicles such as airbags and seat belt pre-tensioners **FIGURE 40-22**. Manufacturers continue to develop and improve airbag technology to make vehicles safer. When first introduced, a single airbag was usually installed on the driver's side. Now, it is not unusual for modern vehicles to have six airbags, along with side-impact protection known as side curtains.

Purpose and Operation of the SRS

Vehicle safety systems are designed to protect occupants during accidents and can be classified as primary (passive) systems and secondary (active) systems. Primary

FIGURE 40-22 **A.** Airbag. **B.** Seat belt pre-tensioner.

systems are ready to operate in any accident. They include bumper bars, body panels, seat belts, crumple zones, and collapsible steering columns. A secondary system has to be activated to work and is only necessary in severe accidents. The two most popular types of secondary systems are SRS airbags and seat belt pre-tensioners.

Seat belts secure and restrain the occupant within the seat and vehicle cabin, and in minor collisions perform their task well. In a more severe impact, inertia causes the occupant to move further and with greater force. This increases the possibility of injury caused by the restraining force exerted by the seat belt or from the occupant striking interior equipment. In these situations, airbags provide additional protection for the occupants.

If a vehicle is equipped with an airbag, it deploys during a severe collision, offering a greater degree of protection from injury. Airbags provide cushioning against the effects of inertia. The bag deploys toward the occupant's approaching body, inflated rapidly by pressurized nitrogen gas. Typically, inflation takes no longer than three hundredths (0.03) of a second. The airbag is not a nice

soft pillow, but a strong counterforce to react against the inertia of the occupants. It is not designed to be comfortable; it is designed to minimize injury. Immediately after absorbing the momentum, the airbag deflates, having done its job.

Airbags and Pre-tensioners

Airbags are usually described as the SRS, but in some countries, wearing seat belts is not mandatory. In this case, airbags become the primary restraint mechanism, and they need to trigger at lower speeds and be larger in volume. There are a number of different types of airbags. Their size and location is determined by the type of protection they offer FIGURE 40-23.

The most common location for an airbag is in the center of the steering wheel. Here, it protects the driver from frontal impacts. Airbags are also commonly installed on the passenger side of dashes for the same reason. Side-impact airbags are located in the sides of front seats to protect the occupants from side impacts. Curtain side airbags

FIGURE 40-23 A. Driver's side airbag. B. Passenger's side airbag. C. Side airbag. D. Knee airbag.

are located in the side edge of roof linings to protect the occupant's head from side impacts. The airbag assembly consists of a nylon bag, <u>squib</u>, igniter, gas generator, and airbag triggering mechanism **FIGURE 40-24**.

There are two types of airbag triggering mechanisms: electrical and mechanical. Most airbags are triggered electrically, with a small electrical current delivered from a remote SRS control unit. Mechanically activated systems use inertia to move a triggering pin. Regardless of the type of triggering mechanism, the airbag deploys due to simultaneous explosions occurring within the squib, the igniter, and the gas generator. These three parts are located in a metal housing attached to the back of the airbag assembly.

When the control unit determines that the airbag should be deployed, the electrical current triggers the squib. The heat generated causes the igniter to burn, which in turn explodes the gas generator. The high-pressure nitrogen gas is produced and the airbag rapidly inflates. When the airbag assembly is mounted, it sits behind a pad, which may have a fracture line cast into the inner face. When the airbag deploys, the force of the generated gas causes the cover pad to rupture, allowing the bag to fully inflate.

Safety

Airbags, when they deploy, inflate toward the occupant at more than 100 mph (160 kph). Because of this force and speed, they have been known to break wrists and even cause death when not used properly. Always keep the seat positioned so you are at approximately arm's length from the steering wheel; that is, the steering wheel should be at least 10" to 12" (25 to 50 cm) from your chest. Also make sure your hands are in the 9 o'clock and 3 o'clock positions. The old 10 and 2 position can lead to your hands being thrown back toward you or outward (remember that 100+ mph), both of which can injure you.

Mechanically deployed airbags do not have any electrical circuitry. The squib is ignited with a firing pin. Under severe deceleration, inertia causes a steel ball to release a firing pin into the squib. Once the squib has been triggered, the deployment process is identical to electrically triggered airbags. The airbag is fully inflated within three hundredths (0.03) of a second, cushioning the head and upper chest of the occupant as it moves forward.

The airbag is made from nylon and is folded into the front face of the assembly. Older airbags were coated in cornflower, which acts as a lubricant for the fabric during deployment. Newer ones use either more slippery fabric or silicone to allow the airbag to inflate without binding. Relatively large holes are usually located in the rear face of the airbag to allow the nitrogen gas to escape. This deflates the airbag and provides a slightly cushioned surface, rather than a hard one, to help protect the occupant.

A new type of airbag was recently released called a pedestrian airbag. It is located under the rear edge of the hood. When a collision with a pedestrian is imminent, the hood retracts slightly and the airbag inflates to cover a portion of the windshield **FIGURE 40-25**. This system can protect pedestrians from direct impact with the windshield.

Seat Belt Pre-tensioners

Seat belt pre-tensioners are used to tighten the seat belt in a severe frontal accident. Both mechanical and electronic control systems are available. The most common type relies on an explosive charge that is detonated electronically by a sensor within the seat belt tensioning mechanism **FIGURE 40-26**. This explosion moves a piston that pulls on a steel cable causing the belt to tighten by approximately 4" (100 mm). The design allows for the belt to tension before the occupant has moved forward in the seat.

FIGURE 40-24 Parts of an airbag assembly.

FIGURE 40-25 Pedestrian airbag.

FIGURE 40-26 Seat belt pre-tensioner.

FIGURE 40-27 Typical crash sensors.

FIGURE 40-28 Safing sensor is typically located in the SRS control unit.

Mechanical systems rely on inertia to move a sensing mass. This releases a spring to pull on a cable, thus tightening the belt. Once the pre-tensioner has triggered, a ratchet prevents the seat belt from loosening. When the seat belt is removed from the buckle, it cannot be reinserted, and the assembly will need to be replaced.

Rip stitching is used on seat belts in conjunction with an airbag and seat belt pre-tensioners. During a collision, the pre-tensioners initially pull the seat belt tight; however, the stitching gradually tears, allowing the occupant to move forward into the airbag at a controlled rate.

For safety reasons, these belts must be replaced once they have had their stitching ripped. Manufacturers generally fit warning labels within the fold to indicate the belt is to be replaced when the label is revealed. Ripping the stitching exposes the warning label.

Sensors, Control Module, and Circuitry

Crash sensors can be installed in various positions throughout the vehicle. Their location depends upon the direction of deceleration they are designed to detect. Some manufacturers place the sensors within the PCM. Others are located behind the front bumper, headlights, and dash **FIGURE 40-27**.

Side-impact sensors are located in the doorsills or B-pillar. They inform the SRS control unit of a side impact and whether to deploy the left or right side airbags. When the sensors indicate that a predetermined deceleration rate has been exceeded and it is from the appropriate direction, the SRS control unit deploys the relevant airbags.

If the collision is from the front, the driver and passenger airbags will deploy. If the collision is from the side, the sensor determines whether the seat-mounted airbag or the curtain airbags for one side of the vehicle will deploy. With more refined designs, the passenger airbag deploys only if there is an occupant in the seat. Deployment can also depend on the weight of the occupant and whether the passenger airbag switch, if equipped, is turned on.

To prevent incorrect and unnecessary deployment, systems include a safing sensor mounted within the SRS control unit **FIGURE 40-28**. The SRS control unit will only pass current through the squib if both the safing sensor and a crash sensor indicate simultaneously that a predetermined deceleration rate has been exceeded.

Capacitors within the SRS control unit are used to store electricity and act as a backup power supply if the vehicle has its battery destroyed or disconnected in an accident. The capacitors supply the electricity required to keep the SRS system operational for a short time. If a fault is detected in the system, the SRS warning light is illuminated and stays on.

Some seat-mounted side-impact airbags also operate without electricity. When the side of a vehicle is crushed inward, a detonator mounted on the lower outside edge of the seat is activated. Pyrotechnic tubes connect the detonator to the airbags, which in turn ignite the squib. Many vehicles use two-stage side-impact bags. This design provides protection to an occupant's upper torso over a more extended time.

Smart Airbag Technology

Manufacturers continue to improve the safety devices installed on vehicles, including airbags. Smart airbag technology is the use of intelligence in the control of airbag deployment in the event of an accident rather than deployment with maximum force. The improvements include the use of information regarding the severity of the accident, seat position, and weight of the occupant as inputs for controlling airbag deployment. Airbags in systems with smart technology are capable of varying the size and force of the airbag as needed. These adjustments can be performed in one of several ways: diverting some of the gas from the airbag inflation system into the dash, using a dual-chamber airbag, or using a dual-stage airbag that has two charges that can be used individually or together. It is now possible for the control systems to deploy the airbags with a more appropriate amount of force, customizing the protection to the occupant.

Diagnosing the SRS

Working on the SRS can be very dangerous. Consult the manufacturer's service information for the vehicle you are working on, and ensure all safety precautions are followed. Accidental deployment of the airbag system could happen if you inadvertently probe the wrong wire. Many manufacturers use yellow wiring to denote wiring for the airbag system, but don't assume all do. Always be aware of the system/circuit you are working on. And make sure you properly disable any SRS devices as directed by the service information.

Whenever the SRS light is steadily illuminated on the instrument panel, one or more codes related to the fault is likely stored in the computer's memory. Retrieving the codes will give you a very good idea of where in the system the fault is located. Using the manufacturer's service information to further diagnose the fault will be required to safely and accurately locate the cause of the fault.

> ▶ **LINK**
> Refer to the Servicing the Steering System chapter for detailed steps on disabling the SRS.

Safety

While an airbag is powerful enough to counteract the weight of a moving body during an accident, it doesn't take much electricity to ignite one. In fact, a fresh 9-volt battery will provide more than enough electrical energy to set it off. In the same way, an ordinary test lamp connected to 12 volts can ignite the airbag if the wrong wire is probed. Always be careful when working around SRS systems.

Proximity Sensors

To allow for safer parking, proximity sensors can be mounted in the front or rear bumpers **FIGURE 40-29**. These color-matched sensors emit ultrasonic sound waves that the human ear cannot detect. These piezoelectric sensors are used to transmit and receive coded sound waves. The control unit determines the distance between the sensor and an obstacle by measuring the time taken for the sound wave to leave and return to the sensor. Normally four sensors are used to allow for full coverage across the width of the vehicle. Proximity to obstacles can be indicated by separate audible and visual alarms, or by integrating warning sounds with the vehicle's audio system. If a trailer is attached to a coupling, the rear sensors are disabled automatically when the harness plug is inserted. Front sensors can be disabled manually in stop-start or stop-and-go traffic.

FIGURE 40-29 Proximity sensor.

FIGURE 40-30 Back-up camera and display.

FIGURE 40-31 Modern entertainment system.

Safety

Just because an airbag has been deployed doesn't mean it is safe. Dual-stage airbags may be designed with two ballistic charges, and only one of them may have been deployed. Airbags must have all charges deployed before disposal. But only do so according to the manufacturer's service information.

A system related to proximity sensors involves back-up cameras and displays FIGURE 40-30. This system uses a camera mounted at the rear of the vehicle that is activated when the vehicle is put in reverse. The camera's image is then displayed either on the rearview mirror or on the entertainment system's LCD panel, showing the driver what is behind the vehicle. This feature greatly reduces the risk of backing over a child or something that was left behind the vehicle such as a bicycle.

 Entertainment System

Entertainment systems in vehicles are becoming more refined and complex as the technology becomes more accessible and affordable. The basic system incorporates a radio, CD player, MP3 player or iPod control, and multiple speakers with faders, bass control, and treble control. Increasingly, vehicles are being equipped with touch-screen LCD displays, DVD players for passengers, and satellite entertainment systems FIGURE 40-31. Vehicles also often have integrated Bluetooth for cell phone connection and hands-free communication.

Types of Systems

Entertainment systems can range from quite basic to expensive audio visual systems that are highly integrated. The basic system will contain a head unit for control of the radio and CD player along with inputs for MP3 players. More complex systems will incorporate satellite entertainment, DVD players for passengers, game consoles, multiple LCD screens, amplifiers, and complex speaker systems with bass drivers. The head unit in the dash is the main control unit for controlling the subsystems installed on the vehicle. It is also quite common on modern vehicles for the navigation system to be built into the entertainment system and share the head unit LCD screen and controls.

Principles of Operation

Modern vehicles integrate audio, video, and communication systems into a network. This allows for a high-quality, compact, and ergonomic system that combines entertainment features with simple operation. Controls are centralized with hardware, such as CD stackers and DVD players located remotely.

Communication between components requires a combination of hard wiring and data buses. With data buses being used, audio messages can be broadcast over the audio system that relate to other vehicle systems. For example, a voice message can say "the park brake is on" or "left rear tire is underinflated." This system allows for features such as the interruption or replacement of audio entertainment when there is an incoming phone call, or simply muting the audio to allow a hands-free phone conversation.

Audio control functions are usually located on the central control pod or on the component's head unit. Vehicles can integrate the common audio controls on the steering wheel, and some respond to verbal commands from the driver to allow for safer driving.

The music played on a system usually comes from one of several sources: magnetically on a cassette tape, optically on a CD or DVD, by radio frequency from radio stations or satellites, or from other portable devices. The information is decoded or processed by the control unit and outputted to speakers located throughout the vehicle.

Another function provided by the body control unit is that of speed-dependent volume. The control unit has an input from the vehicle speed sensor that allows it to gradually increase the audio system's volume proportionally with road speed. As speed increases, and with it engine and road noise, the audio volume increases. As speed decreases, the audio volume decreases.

Viewing screens for onboard TV, DVD, and games can be located in the dash; however, if the screen is viewable by the driver, it must be disabled when the vehicle is in motion. This may be done automatically in some vehicles. Other mounting points are from the roof or integrated into the rear of seat headrests. Control units can be hardwired or wireless using an infrared remote control.

Diagnosing the Entertainment System

The entertainment system is comprised of many different functions built into one system. So testing will need to be guided by the manufacturer's service information for the fault that is present. Problems can range from poor radio reception to failure of the global positioning system (GPS). Always verify the concern by checking what is and is not working properly. If there is a radio reception issue, check the radio by selecting a station that you know comes in well in your location. Check for good power and ground connections to the entertainment system components by checking the circuits under load. A lab scope may be useful to detect any unwanted ripple or noise in the power circuit. Ensure that power connections are clean and tight. If interference is suspected, attempt to isolate the cause by turning off electrical items until interference is reduced. Check the antenna for corrosion-free connections and faults; try a substitute antenna to confirm performance. Also check all vehicle grounds.

Satellite Communication

Thousands of satellites, serving a variety of purposes, are continually in orbit high above the earth. The use of satellite technology in vehicle systems provides an ever-increasing array of options for vehicle manufacturers. It is an area of automotive technology that increases the flexibility and power of many onboard systems. Satellite technology is used in navigation, vehicle tracking, vehicle theft recovery, communication, and Internet access. A GPS is used to determine the exact location of a vehicle on the earth's surface **FIGURE 40-32**. The GPS forms a critical part of vehicle tracking systems; however, many other components are required to keep track of the vehicle.

Most vehicle tracking systems can work very accurately for short periods of time without satellites once their initial position has been determined. Onboard sensors such as vehicle speed and steering wheel position sensors can be used to keep track of the almost exact vehicle location.

Triangulation/Trilateration

The GPS relies on a group of at least 24 satellites (and as many as 32) orbiting approximately 12,600 miles (20,200 km) above the earth. The vehicle is equipped with a receiving antenna and computer system. The GPS receiver on the vehicle has to locate four or more of these satellites, determine the distance to each, and use this information to establish its own location. This operation is based on a mathematical principle called **trilateration**. Trilateration in three-dimensional space is quite complex. For ease of understanding, the term generally used in the automotive industry to describe how the GPS positioning system operates is **triangulation**, which is the process of finding the position of an unknown point based on forming a triangle with two known points.

FIGURE 40-32 GPS mapping system.

For simplicity, the dimensions used to determine these points are commonly known as latitude, longitude, and elevation. If a group of three satellites are used to form a triangle, 12,600 miles (20,200 km) above the earth, the shape and size of this triangle establishes the position of each satellite relative to the others. Correspondingly, any fixed point on the surface of the earth will triangulate with the satellites **FIGURE 40-33**. The number of fixed points is infinite. What the GPS does to calculate position is form many triangles with different pairs of satellites. Each satellite has an atomic clock onboard and regularly transmits a unique radio frequency (RF) signal simultaneously with all other global positioning satellites. The RF signals travel out across space in all directions.

The speed at which an RF signal travels in space is approximately 186,000 miles per second (300,000 km/sec), the speed of light in a vacuum. Each of these transmitted signals will reach the GPS antenna of the vehicle. The time taken for the RF signal to travel from each satellite and arrive at the vehicle is dependent on the distance each satellite is from the vehicle. The greater the distance, the greater the time taken. The vehicle's onboard GPS system needs to know three things to determine the location of the vehicle:

1. The time it takes for the signal to travel from the satellites to the vehicle
2. The position of each satellite
3. The accurate time

Given these facts, enough information is available to form a three-dimensional figure of a pyramid. The base of the pyramid is formed by the location of the satellites, and the apex of the pyramid is the location of the vehicle on the earth, a point derived from triangulation of the known points of the base.

The GPS equipment knows that all of the apexes (the position of the GPS) of each triangle must be in the same lateral position. Adding more satellites makes this more accurate because it gives the GPS more triangles to work with. Satellites are positioned so that every location of the earth's surface has access to at least four satellites 24 hours a day.

Satellites rely on the use of solar energy for their operating power and to maintain position. As the earth and moon move through their orbits, varying gravitational forces are placed on the satellites. The system allows for accurate positioning, ensuring that the satellites do not move from their correct location.

Inaccuracies caused by weather conditions do occur as the RF signal moves into the earth's atmosphere and travels through air. The density of air varies, and traveling through denser air slows the RF signal. Inaccuracies also occur when RF signals are reflected off objects such as large buildings. Solar radiation can also cause inaccuracies.

Satellite Navigation

Once trilateration has been determined, mapping software stored in memory can be used to generate an overlay map and data for the driver on a display screen **FIGURE 40-34**. As the vehicle moves, the GPS continues to provide the necessary information to allow for plotting of position on the map. Various maps are available to cover the different continents.

Accurate and reliable navigation is possible even when satellite signals become unavailable. This is achieved by using electronic sensors to monitor vehicle variables such as pitch, roll, yaw, road speed, steering angle, acceleration, and deceleration. By using the information from these sensors, the navigation system is not continually and totally reliant on satellites.

FIGURE 40-33 GPS positioning systems operate on triangulation, the process of finding the position of an unknown point based on forming triangles with known points.

FIGURE 40-34 GPS mapping screen.

During normal operation, the computer program compares vehicle position data derived from the satellites and onboard sensor information to ensure high levels of accuracy. In addition, ground-based stations may be used in suitable locations as an absolute reference point.

Satellite navigation features may include multiple languages and a choice of voice gender. With destination and journey plotting, the most suitable route is provided, and deviation from the recommended route causes the system to provide an alternate route. It may also include directional information provided with a combination of screen icons, maps, and audible instructions; a self-learning route memory function; congestion avoidance, which can warn of the latest traffic bottlenecks and suggest alternative routes; various monitor color display settings; infrared remote control; trip computer; speed-dependent setting; and telephone mute for sound systems.

Telematics

Automotive **telematics** is a satellite-based system that combines two-way communication and information technology within the vehicle. The vehicle is equipped with a satellite transceiver enabling data to be sent to and from the vehicle **FIGURE 40-35**.

This system allows for vehicle tracking and security features, monitoring of onboard systems, messaging, delivery of travel information, entertainment functions, and use of safety and fleet management systems that monitor information such as location, distance traveled, speed, stops, and fuel usage.

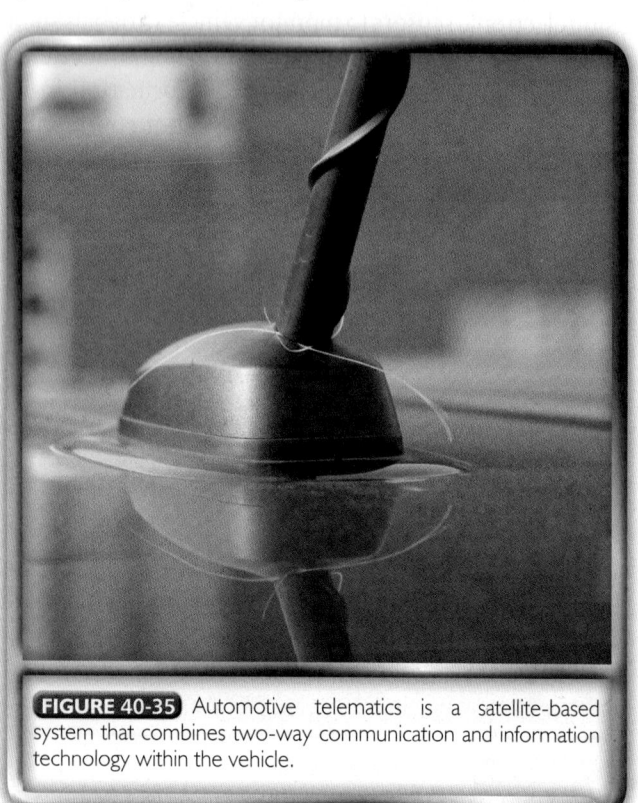

FIGURE 40-35 Automotive telematics is a satellite-based system that combines two-way communication and information technology within the vehicle.

A vehicle manufacturer may offer telematics as a service to its customers. The benefits of this can include the location and immobilization of a stolen or lost vehicle, notification to emergency services after SRS deployment, engine shutdown and door unlocking in the event of a severe accident, roadside assistance, and remote diagnosis.

▶ Anti-theft Systems

Modern vehicle anti-theft systems are devices or methods used to prevent the unauthorized use of the vehicle or its component parts and incorporate a number of technologies to discourage the theft of vehicles. Manufacturers continue to develop cost-effective means to reduce the risk of vehicle theft through a combination of physical and electronic protections. They also try to discourage theft by removing any incentive by making component parts worthless through tagging or marking.

Types of Systems

Theft-deterrent systems aim to prevent the vehicle being entered, started, or driven. The actuators used to achieve this are the electric door locks and windows, the starter motor relay, engine management systems, transmission shift solenoids, and an audible alarm.

In an effort to reduce theft, some vehicle manufacturers equip sophisticated theft-deterrent systems to their vehicles. Theft-deterrent systems can be divided into four categories:

- Component identification
- Vehicle locking (including keyless entry and remote starting)
- Engine and transmission immobilization
- Audible and visible alarms

Component Identification

Component identification, or visible identification of major components, can be a deterrent for theft. Some manufacturers etch the vehicle identification number (VIN) onto labels that are attached to various components on the vehicle, such as fenders, doors, the hood and trunk, and major mechanical components such as the engine and transmission. Etching the VIN onto all windows with a small sand blaster is unobtrusive and makes the vehicle less attractive to steal. If the vehicle is resold or used for parts, the monetary value is reduced.

Microdots are small plastic particles that can have either the VIN or a unique number printed on them **FIGURE 40-36**. They are practically invisible to the naked eye but can be seen by using an ultraviolet light and a magnifying glass. They are mixed with an adhesive and sprayed onto the underside of the vehicle into the wheel wells and engine bay. A small transfer affixed to

FIGURE 40-36 Microdot component identification.

the vehicle displays that such a system has been used, making the vehicle less attractive to a thief.

Vehicle Locking

Door lock systems have come a long way. Initially, all locks were operated manually. A key was inserted in the door lock, and when turned, it would unlock only that door. The remaining doors needed to be unlocked manually, via the lock knob or lever. Releasing the key would return it to the same position it was in when inserted so it could be removed. When central locking was introduced, the lock mechanism on the driver's door had a microswitch that, when turned, activated electric solenoids on the remaining doors and trunk and unlocked or locked them. Further enhancement allowed manufacturers to introduce a security system that automatically locked the doors once the vehicle had reached a preset speed. This feature is mandatory in some countries.

Dead locking adds a further level of security. If the key is turned a quarter turn and removed, a second microswitch activates small electric motors in each door lock mechanism, mechanically locking them.

In keyless systems, remote control keys and key fobs transmit a coded signal that is received by the vehicle's theft-deterrent module. If the code meets preset criteria, the module closes a switch that enables either the driver's door or all doors to be locked and unlocked as required. Pressing the

button a second time when locking some vehicles activates the dead lock actuators and deadlocks the vehicle.

For the remote key and computer to exchange information, wireless communication is needed. High-frequency electromagnetic fields (i.e., RF signals) are used. This system relies on the same basic technology as cell phones, TV, and radio, but at much lower power.

The remote fob can have one button for locking and unlocking; two buttons, where one locks and the other unlocks; three buttons, where the third button activates the trunk or tailgate; four buttons, where the fourth activates a panic alarm; or five buttons, where the fifth remotely starts the vehicle. Some vehicles actively transmit a radio code looking for a specific key. As the driver approaches the vehicle, the vehicle locates the key and the theft-deterrent module prepares to unlock the vehicle. On some vehicles, when the driver leaves the vehicle and the key is out of range, the theft-deterrent module locks the vehicle.

When keyless entry is used, personalization of systems is possible. They can be programmed to recognize different keys, with each driver having his or her own specific key. This allows for different settings to be made that are unique to each driver. When a specific key is identified, the theft-deterrent module communicates with the body control unit. Specific settings are remembered from that key, so the seat, steering wheel, and mirror position automatically adjust to the driver as well as climate control settings for cabin temperature and system modes. Entertainment system settings such as radio station presets, volume and audio settings, and transmission shift point preferences can all change to the driver's individual preferences. This system also allows for a valet key, or even a "teen driver" key to be used, limiting engine power, vehicle speed, and maximum radio volume, as well as preventing other vehicle settings from being changed.

Engine and Transmission Immobilization

Immobilization occurs when the theft-deterrent system prevents the vehicle's engine from starting or the transmission from operating without the properly authorized key. Audible and visible alarms may be activated when the locking or immobilization systems are tampered with. The immobilization system is enabled when the lock button is pressed on the remote key, when the doors are locked manually with the door key, or when a period of time has elapsed, typically 15 seconds, after the engine has stopped. The immobilization system is disabled by pressing the unlock button on the remote fob.

The key fob and theft-deterrent computers have to be capable of transmitting and receiving coded information. Operational characteristics vary greatly among manufacturers, and because it is a theft-deterrent system, details are a closely kept secret.

Most systems use a coded system known as "rolling codes." The coded data transmitted and received between the key fob and the theft-deterrent computer randomly change. Thus, the code used to lock and immobilize a vehicle is different from the one used to unlock and mobilize a vehicle. Manufacturers who use this system have seen a dramatic reduction in theft, noticeably from joy riders. The code is transmitted as a digital number, typically containing 16 digits, giving the possibility of billions of different code numbers. When the lock button is pressed, the control unit and key preset the agreed code, which will be used to unlock the vehicle and deactivate the theft deterrent.

Pressing any button on the remote fob transmits an RF signal, even if the vehicle cannot read it, and changes the rolling code unit from that exchanged between the control module and the fob. The system allows an error factor of 25 steps either side of the agreed code for deactivation before the fob transmits a "false code," which causes the control module to disregard the key.

Alarms

Vehicles may also be equipped with alarm systems designed to sound high-decibel sirens or horns if an intruder attempts to break into or move a vehicle. Such systems can be independent of other vehicle systems, although on modern vehicles they are often integrated into the vehicle security system. The alarm system is typically wirelessly armed when the vehicle is locked and disarmed when it is unlocked. Often the system provides an audible chirp when armed and disarmed so the vehicle driver knows the alarm status. A basic alarm system is triggered by the door switches, which also turn on the interior lights while more complex systems may incorporate more complex sensors, such as ultrasonic movement sensors. If triggered, the alarm will usually sound for 30 seconds or so before resetting and sounding again if the trigger is still present.

A higher level of anti-theft involves monitoring the vehicle for unauthorized opening of the doors, hood, trunk, and fuel filler door, and for activity that is occurring in the vehicle that should not be. The computer that controls the system monitors input signals from various devices. Switches are located at each door, the hood and trunk openings, and the fuel filler door. Vibration sensors detect any unusual vehicle movement such as lifting, jacking, or towing. Ultrasonic sensors detect any movement inside the cabin. Voltage monitoring sensors check for operation of the starter motor, ignition system, or fuel pump. Any of these conditions will cause the alarm to be activated.

Diagnosing the Anti-theft System

The anti-theft system is likely to be controlled by the vehicle's BEM and may include immobilizer systems. Modern vehicle keys are coded to the BEM, and replacement keys need to be programmed for the vehicle. Systems may require security codes to be entered for initialization if the vehicle battery is disconnected, so always verify that you have the codes before disconnecting the vehicle's battery. Vehicle anti-theft systems may be connected to sirens, horns, and lights.

Since the anti-theft system is computer controlled and has self-diagnostics built into it, using a scan tool to retrieve any codes from the system will be a good place to start your diagnosis. Once you have the codes, you can follow the service information to diagnose the specific components or circuits related to the fault. Also, with the scan tool you will most likely be able to command actions to happen such as locking the doors. If the system is a CAN-bus system, you will also likely be able to observe the confirmation signals on the data bus. The service information will guide you through the process of checking the individual circuits or devices.

| Applied | Science |

AS-68: Electrical: The technician can use precision electrical test equipment to measure current, voltage, and resistance.

A vehicle that was traded in at the dealership is being checked to determine if it can qualify as a certified pre-owned vehicle. The checklist for this certification includes over 120 items to be inspected. Some of the electrical tests can be performed by using a DVOM. This testing will include measuring current in amps, voltage in DC volts, and resistance in ohms. The DVOM is capable of performing these tests; however, some shops may have electrical test equipment that would work more efficiently than the DVOM for specific tests.

The measure of current in amps will be the alternator output in amps. For this test, an auxiliary item called an amp clamp will be used. This is due to the very high amperage output by many alternators. The amp clamp will be placed around all of the wires near the positive battery post. It is best to follow the specific instructions given by the vehicle manufacturer and the test equipment or DVOM manufacturer. Alternator outputs of over 100 amps are not unusual.

The charging system voltage can be checked with a DVOM set to the DC 20 volts position. Place the red lead on the positive battery post and the black lead on the negative battery post. Eye protection is a must when working with batteries. The charging system voltage usually ranges from 13.8 to 14.8 volts DC.

An example of a resistance measurement would be the testing of an electronic ignition coil pack. Set the DVOM to the ohms position. With the engine off, place the meter leads on the primary coil terminals. If you do not have an auto-ranging meter, try the lowest ohms setting. All coil packs should have close to the same resistance values. The manufacturer's service information will provide exact specifications and further testing instructions.

Wrap-up

Ready for Review

▶ Electrical systems on modern vehicles are becoming increasingly complex with the addition of a range of electronic and accessory systems, such as global positioning systems, entertainment systems, security systems, electric seats, and heated glass. Many of these systems are controlled by body computer systems.

▶ The controller area network (CAN-bus) and the bus system are used together in vehicle terminology (often called "CAN-bus") to describe the data-sharing network in vehicles. The many sensors and engine control units or modules can share information across a common network using the CAN-bus protocol to communicate efficiently and effectively with low data loss.

▶ Diagnosing and repairing vehicles may require software transfers, software updates, or flash reprogramming of the vehicle's electronic modules with the manufacturer's latest update.

▶ Electric cooling fans for the radiator are increasingly common, particularly for transversely mounted engines and as supplementary cooling fans for vehicles equipped with air conditioning.

▶ Power mirrors use permanent magnet electric motors to control the up-and-down, in-and-out movement of the passenger's and driver's side mirrors.

▶ Electric windows use permanent magnet motors located in each of the passenger doors and sometimes in a rear door to control the up-and-down movement of vehicle windows.

▶ The sound of a horn is produced by the vibration of a metal diaphragm, which is operated by an electromagnet switched by a set of contacts.

▶ Technicians today need to know how to service all the accessories behind the door panels. This is a critical skill that must be mastered without damaging the accessory, wiring, or door panel.

▶ The wiper and washer system is an important vehicle safety system. The wipers ensure that the driver has a clear line of sight through the windshield by removing any excess moisture from the glass.

▶ In the basic cruise control system, the driver programs a set target speed and the cruise control system's electronic control unit attempts to accelerate or decelerate the vehicle to maintain the target speed by commanding a throttle actuator to control the throttle butterfly.

▶ Active or dynamic cruise control systems adapt to the driving environment by sensing and adjusting vehicle speed based on changing conditions.

▶ Vehicle safety systems are designed to protect occupants during accidents; they can be classified as primary, or passive, systems and secondary, or active, systems.

▶ Seat belt pre-tensioners are used to tighten the seat belt in a severe frontal accident; both mechanical and electronic control systems are available.

▶ Crash sensors can be installed in various positions throughout the vehicle. Their location depends upon the direction of deceleration they are designed to detect.

▶ The global positioning system (GPS) relies on a group of at least 24 satellites orbiting approximately 12,600 miles (20,200 km) above the earth.

▶ Automotive telematics is a satellite-based system that combines two-way communication and information technology within the vehicle.

Key Terms

blower motor An electric motor, usually the permanent magnet type, that moves air over the air-conditioning evaporator and heater core.

body electronic module (BEM) An electronic control module for body electrical systems.

brushless DC motor An electric motor that does not have any brushes and is sometimes called an "electronically commutated motor." In this type of motor, an electronic control module replaces the brushes and commutator.

bus The data transport system for electronic control modules.

controller area network (CAN) The network that connects the vehicle's electronic control modules.

data link connector (DLC) The port to which a scan tool can be connected.

passive keyless entry (PKE) An active system that senses the proximity of a fob and locks or unlocks the vehicle.

permanent magnet electric motor An electric motor in which the magnetic field in the casing is produced by permanent magnets, while the armature has an electromagnetic field generated by passing electrical current through loops or windings, thereby producing the motor action.

remote keyless entry (RKE) A system that remotely unlocks and locks the vehicle without the use of a traditional key.

squib The component inside the airbag inflator that triggers the airbag deployment.

stepper motor A type of brushless motor with a key difference: It is designed to rotate in fixed steps through a set number of degrees.

supplemental restraint system (SRS) A passenger safety system, such as airbags and seat belt pretensioners.

telematics Satellite-based, two-way communication with the vehicle's electronic systems.

triangulation A method of locating an object using mathematics based on forming a triangle with two known points.

trilateration A method of locating points by the measurement of distances using geometry.

ASE-Type Questions

1. Tech A says that CAN A is a low-speed data network. Tech B says that CAN C is a high-speed network. Who is correct?
a. Tech A
b. Tech B
c. Both A and B
d. Neither A nor B

2. Tech A says that CAN C uses two 120-ohm resistors with a total circuit resistance of 60 ohms. Tech B says that CAN C uses two 120-ohm resistors with a total circuit resistance of 240 ohms. Who is correct?
a. Tech A
b. Tech B
c. Both A and B
d. Neither A nor B

3. Tech A says that a twisted pair of wires in a wire loom makes it easier to route wires to their destination. Tech B says that the twisted pair of wires transmit signals of opposite polarity on the two lines. Who is correct?
a. Tech A
b. Tech B
c. Both A and B
d. Neither A nor B

4. Tech A says that during troubleshooting, you should never disconnect an electronic control unit or module that is powered up. Tech B says that when flashing an electronic control unit or module, make sure no power loss or disconnect occurs, as the electronic control unit or module may be damaged. Who is correct?
a. Tech A
b. Tech B
c. Both A and B
d. Neither A nor B

5. Tech A says that stepper motors are used as blower motors to achieve various speeds controlled by the driver. Tech B says that stepper motors are used where precise movement must occur, such as in electronic throttle controls. Who is correct?
a. Tech A
b. Tech B
c. Both A and B
d. Neither A nor B

6. Tech A says that microdots are used as a theft deterrent in some vehicles. Tech B says that microdot is the name given to a single datum transmitted over a CAN-bus. Who is correct?
a. Tech A
b. Tech B
c. Both A and B
d. Neither A nor B

7. Tech A says that the clock spring is a device used in the steering wheel to transmit signals across the rotating electrical connection. Tech B says that the clock spring must be wound correctly during installation, as it only allows turning both ways a certain number of rotations. Who is correct?
a. Tech A
b. Tech B
c. Both A and B
d. Neither A nor B

8. Tech A says that most SRS systems use a safing sensor to reduce the possibility of accidental deployment of the airbags. Tech B says that airbags are designed to act like a nice soft pillow in an accident. Who is correct?
a. Tech A
b. Tech B
c. Both A and B
d. Neither A nor B

9. Tech A says that if airbags have been deployed, the affected seat belts and pre-tensioners need replaced. Tech B says that there are relatively large holes in the rear of an airbag that allow it to quickly deflate after deployment. Who is correct?
a. Tech A
b. Tech B
c. Both A and B
d. Neither A nor B

10. Tech A says that in some vehicles, airbag deployment can be based on the speed of the impact and the weight of the driver. Tech B says that the SRS seat belt pre-tensioners tighten the seat belt when you connect the seat belt. Who is correct?
a. Tech A
b. Tech B
c. Both A and B
d. Neither A nor B

SECTION VIII

Heating and Air Conditioning

CHAPTER 41

NATEF Tasks

There are no NATEF tasks for this chapter.

Knowledge Objectives

After reading this chapter, you will be able to:
1. Explain the licensure requirements for working on an air-conditioning system. (pp 1409–1410)
2. Explain the principles of the heating, ventilation, and air-conditioning (HVAC) system. (pp 1410–1414)
3. Explain the three methods of heat transfer. (pp 1411–1412)
4. Describe heat energy and how it is measured. (p 1412)
5. Explain the four main components in an air-conditioning system. (pp 1414–1415)
6. Describe air-conditioning components and operation. (pp 1414–1427)
7. Describe the three types of refrigerants. (pp 1415–1416)
8. Explain the three main types of refrigerant oil and the refrigerant they can be used with. (pp 1416–1417)
9. Explain the operation of each type of compressor. (pp 1417–1419)
10. Explain how a fixed orifice tube air-conditioning system operates. (pp 1429–1430)
11. Explain the difference between an accumulator and a receiver/filter/drier. (pp 1430, 1432)
12. Explain how a thermal expansion valve air-conditioning system operates. (pp 1430–1433)
13. Describe heating system components and operation. (pp 1433–1437)

Principles of Heating and Air-Conditioning Systems

▶ Introduction

This chapter will explain the processes involved in regulating the temperature inside the passenger compartment of a vehicle. The quality and temperature of the surrounding air strongly influence a driver's performance and concentration. Within a passenger vehicle, the heating, ventilation, and air-conditioning (HVAC) system is designed to maintain a comfortable temperature in the vehicle cabin and also provide fresh, filtered, quality air on a constant basis. Depending on the outside temperature and the desired cabin temperature, the supplied air is either heated, cooled, or both.

The HVAC system of most passenger vehicles uses the heat created by normal engine operation to raise the temperature in the passenger compartment. Refrigerant is used to cool the air in the passenger compartment. To ensure that the air brought into the vehicle is free from dust and debris, many vehicles pass the air through a cabin air filter that removes foreign particles. Without proper maintenance, the HVAC system can break down, resulting in an unpleasant ride for the passengers, particularly during the summer and winter months. Accordingly, it is critical that the automotive technician be familiar with the components of the HVAC system and understand how each component works so that the system can be maintained and serviced when necessary.

▶ History of Automotive Heating and Cooling

There is some debate about the origins of systems for heating the passenger compartment of vehicles. What has been confirmed is the use of gas lamps in the early 1900s for heat. Passengers would bring a small gas lamp into the compartment for heat, but it was not connected to the vehicle in any way. Around 1917–1920, some vehicles transferred exhaust gas through pipes into the compartment to provide heat. The first use of air heated from normal engine operation to warm the passenger compartment dates from the late 1920s. These vehicles had rudimentary blowers that simply funneled air from around the engine into the cabin. By the 1930s, the first true heating systems using engine coolant, similar to what is still used today, were developed.

Automotive air conditioning has a long history, beginning with a discovery by Michael Faraday. In 1820, Faraday discovered how to create cool air by passing air over an evaporating coil of compressed ammonia. Although this was a great advance in comfort, ammonia is a caustic agent and hazardous to humans, causing skin burns, lung damage, and possibly asphyxiation. In 1902, Willis Carrier invented and patented the first electric air conditioner. A great advance was made in 1928 when a research division of General Motors produced **chlorofluorocarbons (CFCs)**, a chemical compound containing chlorine, fluorine, and carbon. CFCs made it possible for

▶ You are the Automotive Technician

A customer brings his vehicle to the auto shop for a routine maintenance check. He will be driving his vehicle from New York to Florida this fall and won't be returning until the following spring. He is worried how his vehicle's HVAC system will perform during his long trip and during his stay in Florida. He isn't familiar with auto shops in Florida, so he wants you to inspect the system and suggest any repairs it may need.

1. What are the two types of automotive air-conditioning systems?
2. Refrigerants are another important part of the HVAC system. Why is identifying refrigerants becoming an important part of repairing air-conditioning systems?
3. What license is required for technicians to work with refrigerants?

air-conditioning systems to be used by consumers with no apparent harm, unlike the ammonia systems.

In 1939, Packard introduced the first automotive air-conditioning system as an add-on luxury unit **FIGURE 41-1**. The add-on was offered for $274, which in today's money would be more than $4000. Automotive air conditioning is now standard on most production vehicles because of customer demand as well as the increased fuel economy that comes from increased aerodynamic efficiency. Having the windows rolled up while driving at moderate and high speeds reduces wind drag and increases aerodynamic efficiency in most vehicles.

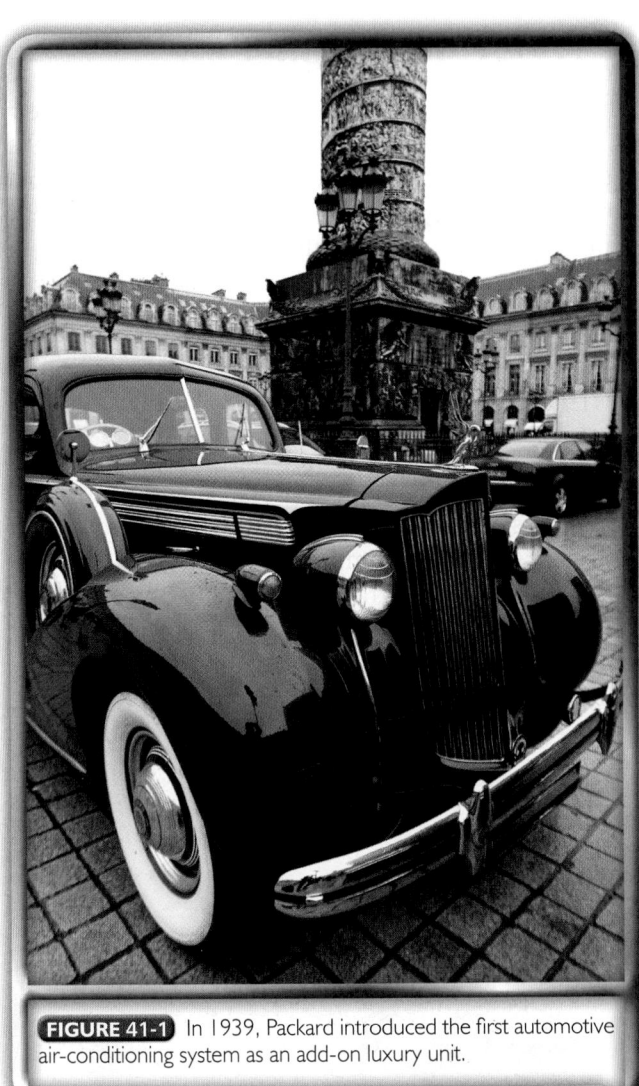

FIGURE 41-1 In 1939, Packard introduced the first automotive air-conditioning system as an add-on luxury unit.

> **TECHNICIAN TIP**
>
> Almost all manufacturers rely on the air conditioner's ability to remove moisture from the air to meet the defrost time standard set by the U.S. Department of Transportation.

HVAC Legislation

Automotive air conditioning is federally regulated by the <u>Environmental Protection Agency (EPA)</u>. Section 609 of the <u>Clean Air Act (CAA)</u>—the federal law that regulates air emissions from stationary and mobile sources—contains all of the motor vehicle air-conditioning (MVAC) requirements and laws. Among other things, this law authorizes the EPA to establish National Ambient Air Quality Standards (NAAQS) to protect public health and public welfare and to regulate emissions of hazardous air pollutants.

This act sets the standards for shops that do air-conditioning work. It mandates that each shop maintain a current government-issued license and stipulates what certifications are required for technicians doing MVAC procedures. It also outlines the specific refrigerants that can be safely used for each application and how refrigerants must be stored and reclaimed, even citing the specific approved equipment technicians may use.

Licensure

Automotive air-conditioning service and repair technicians need to have a special license **FIGURE 41-2**. The license is granted after passing the 609 test, which is a self-study course that can be found online through companies such as Automotive Service Excellence (ASE), Mobile Air Conditioning Society (MACS), and Mainstream Engineering. Passing the test results in a lifelong license. Since the license never expires, the technician is responsible for keeping up to date with all new regulations and technology. The 609 license also allows the technician to purchase a few select refrigerants, such as R-12 and R-134a (refrigerants are identified with a letter R, followed by a series of numbers that indicate their chemical composition). The 609 license does not mean

THIS CERTIFICATE HEREBY CONFIRMS

Henry Ford

has successfully completed
the ASE Refrigerant Recovery & Recycling
Review and Certification Program
This day of April 10, 1998

111-11-1111 MVAC
Certification Number

Ronald H. Weiner
President, ASE

FIGURE 41-2 EPA 609 license.

that the technician knows how to repair the automotive air-conditioning systems, but that the technician knows the laws and will comply with all regulations.

Applied | Science

AS-29: Expansion/Contraction: The technician is able to demonstrate an understanding of the expansion and contraction of system parts as a result of heat generated during the use of the system.
When matter is heated, it expands, or becomes larger in size. Conversely, when cooled, it contracts, or becomes smaller (assuming the change in temperature does not cause the matter to change state). Thermal expansion (or TX) valves, found in many air-conditioning systems, operate via these principles. The function of a TX valve is to regulate to flow of liquid refrigerant from the evaporator back to the compressor, thereby also regulating the temperature of refrigerant.

The valve is actuated against spring pressure by a temperature-sensing bulb, filled with a similar gas to the refrigerant used in the air-conditioning system. As the refrigerant temperature at the evaporator outlet increases, the pressure in the bulb increases due to expansion of the gas and causes the TX valve to open. When the evaporator outlet temperature drops, the pressure in the bulb decreases as the gas contracts and allows spring pressure to close the valve.

Applied | Science

AS-84: Relative Humidity: The technician can demonstrate an understanding of and discuss relative humidity in terms of its effect on automotive heating and air-conditioning systems.
Relative humidity is essentially a measure of how moist the air is, or in more detail, the amount of water vapor in the air expressed as a percentage of the amount that the air can "hold" at a given temperature. The warmer air is, the more moisture it is able to hold.

In a car air-conditioning system, warm air is forced through a cold (below dew point) evaporator core. This condenses the water vapor in the air into its liquid form and drains it away, much like the way water condenses on the outside of a cold soda can. Thus, water vapor in the incoming air is removed and the relative humidity in the vehicle's cabin is lowered. On humid days, the system removes more water vapor from the air, and you may notice larger than usual amounts of water draining from the evaporator onto the ground underneath the vehicle.

While you may expect heating the incoming air to have the opposite effect, in reality this is not the case. Cool air is passed through a hot heater core (generally heated by coolant from the engine's cooling system), which also has a drying effect, lowering the relative humidity in the cabin.

▶ HVAC Principles

The function of air conditioning in the HVAC system is to reduce the temperature and humidity inside the passenger compartment to a level that ensures passenger comfort **FIGURE 41-3**. The HVAC system achieves this by removing excess heat from the passenger compartment through a series of thermal and chemical transformations. In other words, heat is removed from the passenger compartment and transferred by the air-conditioning system to the outside air.

The HVAC system is governed by the principles of physics just like all of the other systems on a vehicle. Understanding the physics will help you to know when a system is operating properly and when it needs to be serviced. One of the simplest concepts concerns heat transfer: Heat always transfers from hot objects to cold objects. Another concept concerns density: Liquids are denser than gases. Thus liquids tend to be pulled to the bottom by gravity, and gases tend to float to the top.

FIGURE 41-3 The HVAC system reduces the temperature inside the passenger compartment by removing excess heat through a series of thermal and chemical transformations.

Another simple concept is the relationship between temperature and pressure: When pressure is raised on a gas, its temperature also rises; when pressure is lowered, so does its temperature. These and other principles will be explored in greater depth in the following sections.

Cold and Hot

The conditions "cold" and "hot" are more of a feeling than a science. Cold is simply a relative term for the absence of heat, or it can be regarded as a condition that exists after heat has been removed. Heat energy is in all matter, from gases (oxygen), to liquids (water), to solids (metal). One might think that 32°F (0°C) is cold, but more heat energy is present than at −19°F (−28°C). Heat energy cannot be created or destroyed; it can only be transferred from one object to another. Heat always travels from a warmer object to a cooler object.

Consider this age-old question: Does ice cause your hand to be cold, or does your hand warm up the ice? The answer is that your hand is warming up the ice and the extreme transfer of heat energy makes your hand feel cold. The warming of the ice is known as **heat transfer**. Heat transfer can take place by one of three methods: conduction, convection, or radiation. The HVAC system relies on all three types of heat transfer. **Conduction** is the process of transferring heat through matter by the movement of heat energy through solids from one particle to another. For example, if you hold a lighter up to a steel pipe, the heat from the flame will travel through the steel, eventually heating the entire pipe.

Heat transfer by **convection** is the circulatory movement that occurs in a gas or fluid with areas of differing temperatures due to the variation of the density and the action of gravity. Consider a container of water being heated on a stove. If you put a drop of food coloring in one part of the water and start to heat the water, you can readily see the circulation of the water within the container. As the water heats up, it expands and becomes lighter than the surrounding water. This causes a column of water to rise to the top; the cooler water then falls to the bottom. Thus, a cycle occurs of warmer water rising to the top, pushing cooler water to the bottom. The convection currents have the same effect of a small pump pushing the water around in a set pathway.

Radiation is the transfer of heat through the emission of energy in the form of invisible waves **FIGURE 41-4**. The sun radiates energy to the earth over the vast miles of outer space; the electromagnetic radiation readily travels through the vacuum of space. When this energy

is absorbed, it becomes converted to heat—that is, the heat you feel as the sun touches your body on a warm day. Of course, the direction in which the radiation travels can be changed or redirected, as when a sheet of shiny aluminum foil reflects the sun's rays and bounces the energy in another direction.

The cooling cycle begins in the passenger compartment with the radiation of heat from the rays of the sun penetrating through the windows. The interior air heats up and the driver turns on the air-conditioning function of the HVAC system. Convection currents from the heated air in the passenger compartment flow over an

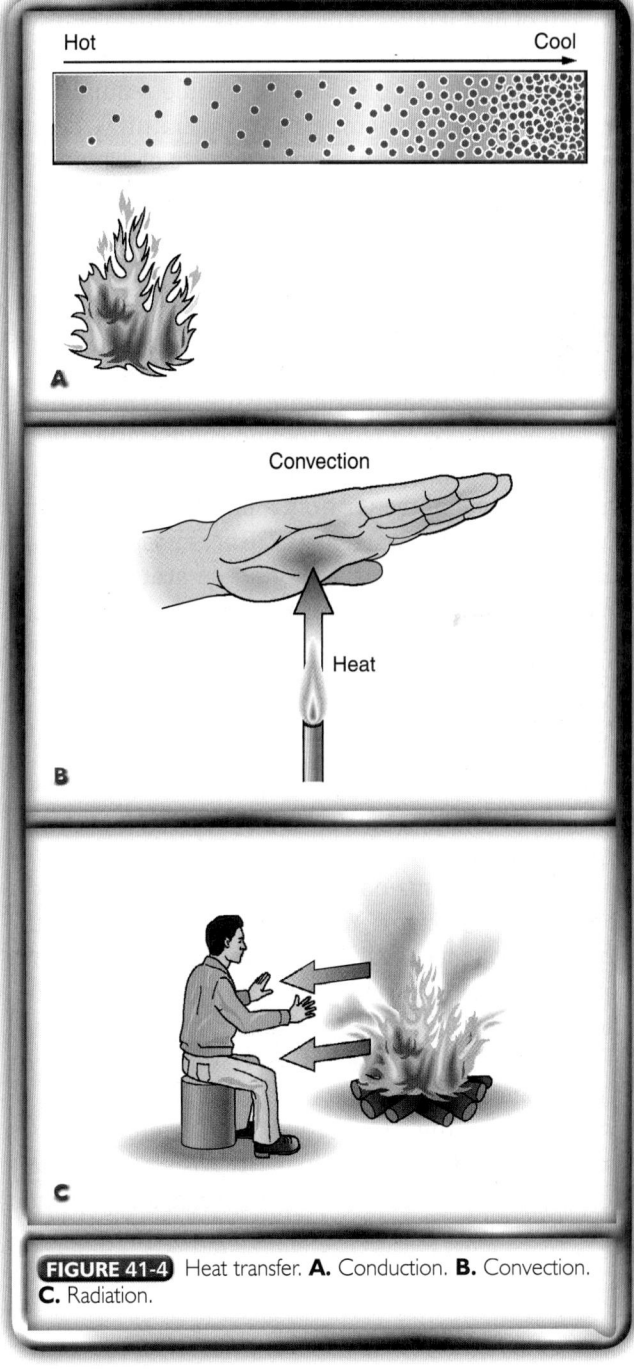

FIGURE 41-4 Heat transfer. **A.** Conduction. **B.** Convection. **C.** Radiation.

evaporator core of refrigerant, causing a conduction of heat through the metal coils of the evaporator. The metal coils of the evaporator then transfer the heat by conduction to the refrigerant, causing convection currents to transfer heat through the refrigerant. The refrigerant is then circulated by the compressor and carried to the condenser where conduction and convection dissipate the heat to the surrounding air and ultimately to the atmosphere.

Heat Energy

Heat energy is measured in **British thermal units (Btu)**. The Btu is a measurement of heat quantity and is a standard unit of measurement of heat energy. It describes the amount of heat it takes to move temperature up or down in degrees. One pound of water at **atmospheric pressure** and at a temperature of 32°F (0°C) would require 1 Btu of energy added to increase the temperature 1 degree Fahrenheit. A change in the temperature of 1 pound of water from 32°F (the freezing point of water) to 212°F (100°C) (the boiling point of water) would require 180 Btu of heat energy.

Water cannot get any hotter than 212°F at atmospheric pressure. The temperature will not rise because the molecules have reached their maximum speed of movement at atmospheric pressure. Temperature is increased only by moving the molecules faster. If the water is exposed to any more energy, it will start to change its state of matter from a liquid to a gas: steam. Turning a pound of water at 212°F at atmospheric pressure into steam requires 970 Btu. The heat required to change the water at its maximum temperature from a liquid to a gas is called **latent heat of evaporation**. This latent heat is called "hidden heat" because it cannot be felt or measured with a thermometer. Heat that can be felt and measured with a thermometer is called sensible heat. The amount of heat given up by steam to turn back into a liquid is the same 970 Btu and is called **latent heat of condensation**.

Taking the same pound of water from a liquid to a solid is called freezing. You must remove heat from the liquid to make ice. At 32°F, the molecules in the water cannot move any slower without changing state. At 32°F, the **latent heat of freezing** begins. It takes the removal of 140 Btu from 1 pound of 32°F water to change its state into ice.

The changing of state in liquids, referred to as vaporizing and condensing, is the basis of air conditioning. It takes more heat to evaporate a liquid than to freeze a liquid. This is why air conditioning uses the process of evaporating a liquid to absorb a large amount of heat energy. By evaporating liquids, the air conditioner can remove the heat from the cabin air, which contains the heat to cause the vaporization, thereby making the occupant feel cool. It is the same principle by which sweat cools human beings. Heat is absorbed by the evaporating sweat droplets on the skin, thereby removing heat from the body and cooling it. Similarly, by evaporating liquids, the air conditioner can remove large amounts of heat from the air and make the occupant feel cooler.

Refrigerant Principles

Manipulating nature's law of **vaporization** and **condensation** of liquids and gases is how the air conditioner forces ambient passenger compartment air to become cool and less humid for the driver and passengers of the vehicle. For the cycle of vaporization and condensation to occur, the air conditioner needs a fluid that vaporizes and condenses at the correct temperature and pressure. It also must be able to change its state in the continuous cycle of vaporization and condensation without breaking down. The fluid used for these purposes is **refrigerant**. The refrigerant in the air-conditioning system must have a boiling point well below freezing to manipulate its boiling and condensing points by changing pressure. The super low boiling point of most refrigerants allows the system to control the vaporization and condensation point of the refrigerant at normal ambient temperatures. A commonly used refrigerant is R-134a, a hydrofluorocarbon that contains none of the ozone-depleting chlorine found in old refrigerants.

With the use of refrigerants, maintaining vaporization and condensing points at normal ambient temperatures is simply done by raising or reducing the pressure of the refrigerant. At atmospheric pressure, R-134a boils at about −15°F (−26°C), so in most normal conditions it is in its gaseous state. By adding a small amount of pressure to the refrigerant, the boiling point of the refrigerant will rise. Indeed, a low pressure (approximately 15 pounds per square inch [psi], or 103 kilopascals [kPa]) in a refrigerant can force the boiling point of the refrigerant to be just above freezing (32°F [0°C]). Likewise, to allow the R-134a to condense back into a liquid, its boiling point can be increased well above the ambient temperature by further increasing its pressure. Forcing the refrigerant's boiling point so that it is well above ambient temperatures allows it to be cooled by ambient air so that it will condense back

AS-23: Phases/States: The technician can explain in detail the three states of matter.

Solids, liquids, and gases are the three most common states of matter on earth. The distinction between them is based on characteristics relating to the shape and volume of the piece of matter in question.

Solid matter retains a fixed volume and shape. There are many examples of solid matter used in motor vehicles, from the cast iron, steel, and aluminum used to build engines, to the fabric and plastic materials used in interiors. Liquid matter retains a fixed volume but the shape adapts to the shape of the container they are held within. Again, there are many liquids used in motor vehicles. In the case of gases, the matter does not retain a fixed volume, but expands to fill whatever volume is available. Air-conditioning refrigerant is an interesting example of a compound that takes the form of both a liquid and a gas in different sections of the air-conditioning system.

AS-28: Conduction/Convection: The technician is able to explain the concept of heat transfer in terms of conduction, radiation, and convection in automotive systems.

Heat can be transferred via three methods; conduction, convection, and radiation. Put simply, conduction is the transfer of heat through solid matter, convection is the transfer of heat through liquid or gas relying on the movement of currents, and radiation is the transfer of heat energy through space by means of electromagnetic waves.

All three of these methods of transfer come into play when trying to keep the inside of your car cool. The heat you feel in the cabin originates from the sun. The sun's heat travels by radiation, and you feel it coming through the glass windows into the vehicle cabin. Heat is transferred through the cabin via convection, with the hot glass panels heating the air inside and causing it to move in currents. When turned on, the air-conditioning system moves the hot air through the cold evaporator core. The heat is moved to the evaporator core via convection and dissipated through the metal evaporator core by conduction.

into a liquid within the condenser and stay a liquid all the way to the restriction.

With the refrigerant boiling below the temperature of the air in the passenger compartment, the air condi-

tioner will forcefully remove the heat from the passenger compartment's air by using the heat from the air in the passenger compartment to boil the refrigerant. R-134a under low pressure (15–25 psi [103–172 kPa]) boils at about 32°F (0°C). Warm air from the passenger compartment is circulated from the passenger cabin across the evaporator containing R-134a, causing it to boil. As R-134a boils, it absorbs that heat and pulls it along with the moving R-134a away from the evaporator. The process continually repeats as the fan circulates the air, and the operating air-conditioning system continually circulates refrigerant, resulting in a continual supply of cool air to the cabin. The air returning to the passenger compartment will feel cool to the driver and passengers because the heat was removed from the air when the heat was used to boil the refrigerant. The heat from the air is absorbed by the refrigerant, changing the state of the refrigerant from liquid to gas, while at the same time cooling the air.

If the temperature of the refrigerant falls below the freezing point of water during this process, the air conditioner must shut off. The air passing over the evaporating refrigerant is full of moisture, so the extreme heat removal will cause any moisture in the air to condense on the cold surface of the evaporator. The water vapor in the air could freeze on the outside of the evaporator and block the airflow that is needed to cause the refrigerant to vaporize. The air must keep flowing over the evaporator, renewing the heat source to keep the refrigerant evaporating (boiling) efficiently without freezing.

Differential Gas Pressure

Every vehicle's air conditioner has a low side (approximately 20–40 psi [138–276 kPa] depending on outside temperature) and a high side (approximately 170–230 psi [1172–1586 kPa]). The low side is designed to allow easy transformation of the refrigerant from a liquid to a gas. The high side enables the transfer of heat out of the refrigerant to the atmosphere so it changes back from a gas to liquid.

Starting at the compressor, a low-pressure gas is compressed into a high-pressure gas and is pumped into the condenser located in the front of the vehicle radiator. The gaseous refrigerant is cooled by the air passing through the condenser and leaves the condenser as a high-pressure liquid. The high pressure is required to enable the change from gas to liquid. From there, the liquid travels through a small orifice (restriction) that reduces the pressure (a fixed orifice tube or thermal expansion valve). After the restriction, the low side of the system begins. The low-pressure liquid leaves the metering device and travels to the evaporator, which is usually located under the dash. As the low-pressure liquid travels through the evaporator, a fan blows the warm to hot cabin air across the fins, adding heat to the refrigerant until it boils. As it boils, it absorbs heat from the air and the refrigerant is transformed back into a gas. The gaseous refrigerant then travels back to the compressor to start the cycle over.

▶ Air-Conditioning Components and Operation

Each HVAC system uses refrigerant and four major components. Each component has a specific job and purpose. The components are the compressor, condenser, restriction, and evaporator **FIGURE 41-5**. The air-conditioning cycle starts with the **compressor**. The compressor changes a low-pressure refrigerant gas to a high-pressure gas. The compressor also provides the needed refrigerant movement in the system. Without the movement of refrigerant, the system could not exchange the heat from the condenser and the evaporator. Moving refrigerant also allows for the pressure drop to occur in the restriction. Without movement, the restriction could not drop the pressure. Refrigerant enters the compressor as a low-pressure gas from the evaporator. The compressor's function is to increase the

pressure of the gaseous refrigerant and then push it into the condenser.

Forcing a gas to become a liquid is achieved through condensing. So the next component after the compressor in the air-conditioning system is the **condenser**. Hot high-pressure gas enters the condenser from the compressor. The gas flows through a series of coils in the condenser and ambient air passes over the outside of the finned coils. The engine's radiator fan and/or dedicated condenser fans move ambient air across the condenser coils and fins. The cooler outside air removes the heat from the hot high-pressure gas and the gas begins to condense into a liquid. Emerging from the outlet of the condenser is a relatively hot, high-pressure liquid. The condenser transforms gas to liquid on the high side of the system.

The air conditioner is a **closed loop system**, meaning that nothing else enters or exits the system; the refrigerant just continues to cycle through the system, changing pressure and state to complete the task of cooling the cabin. Before the liquid can be evaporated back into a gas for the compressor, the pressure needs to be dropped so the boiling point can be lowered below the passenger compartment air temperature, thus allowing vaporization to remove the heat from the passenger compartment air. Dropping pressure occurs by flowing a liquid through a **restriction**.

The restriction lowers the pressure using the Bernoulli principle. Daniel Bernoulli stated that if the flow of a fluid remains constant, the energies of the fluid remain constant; changing one of the two energies (up or down) affects the other energy oppositely. The two energies in fluid are velocity and pressure. These energies react opposite to each other. When velocity increases, the pressure must drop if the flow remains constant. The restriction causes a significant increase in refrigerant velocity because the compressor is constantly moving fluid in the closed loop system.

The fluid flowing through the restriction is a liquid. Liquids are considered incompressible (Pascal's law). Forcing a noncompressible fluid through a small orifice causes the velocity in the restriction to rise. If the velocity of the liquid rises, the pressure of the liquid must drop according to the Bernoulli principle. Raising the velocity and dropping the pressure is how the restriction transforms the high-pressure liquid refrigerant to a low-pressure liquid refrigerant. The reduced pressure reduces the boiling point of the refrigerant and turns the refrigerant into a low-pressure liquid ready for the evaporator to vaporize the liquid into a gas.

FIGURE 41-5 The components of an air-conditioning unit.

The next component in the air-conditioning system is the <u>evaporator</u>. The evaporator transforms low-pressure liquid to a low-pressure gas. The transformation from liquid to gas begins when the air from the passenger compartment passes over the evaporator coils and fins. The pressure on the refrigerant is held between 20 and 40 psi (138 and 276 kPa); the pressure on the low side of the system reduces the refrigerant's boiling point to a bit over 33°F (1°C). The liquid refrigerant absorbs heat from any source available as it boils. This heat comes from the air flowing through the evaporator core.

The vaporization of the refrigerant is forced to happen just above the freezing point of water so that the evaporator core will not freeze. Any heat source will amplify the boiling process. By moving air across the evaporator coils, the convection currents pass over the evaporator coils, causing conduction of heat to the refrigerant through the tubes of the evaporator. The conduction of heat through the coils then provides the needed energy to boil (evaporate) the liquid refrigerant to a gas. It also strips the air of much of its heat energy and moisture, making the air flowing from the duct cool and crisp.

Refrigerant

Proper air-conditioning operation requires that all of the components, including the refrigerant, work efficiently. Without proper refrigerant levels, or if any one component is not functioning properly, the air conditioner will not cool the passenger compartment effectively. Each component requires that the refrigerant level be correct and that the previous component deliver the refrigerant to it in the correct state. The evaporator requires a low-pressure liquid; the compressor requires a low-pressure gas; the condenser requires a high-pressure gas; and the restriction requires a high-pressure liquid.

Types of Refrigerant

<u>Dichlorodifluoromethane (R-12)</u>, a member of the CFC family of gases, was the first common refrigerant to be used in an automotive air conditioner. The first part of the word refers to chlorine, a primary component of CFCs that is banned by the U.S. government in refrigerants because of its detrimental effects on the atmosphere. It is nonflammable, nontoxic, and stable at all temperatures; does not react with aluminum, steel, or copper; and is soluble in mineral oils. It has a boiling point of −21.8°F (−29.9°C). In the early 1990s, R-12 was

found to be one of the leading causes of the depletion of the ozone layer and was outlawed for new vehicle installation. Although you will not find R-12 in today's production vehicles, you may still have customers with older cars using R-12.

<u>Tetrafluoroethane (R-134a)</u> was the replacement for R-12. It is a hydrofluorocarbon, or HFC. Although R-134a has a boiling point of −15.3°F (−26.3°C), which is nearly the same as R-12's boiling point, R-134a can only be substituted for R-12 (retrofitted) by following a specific procedure. The common refrigerant R-134a uses a polyalkalene glycol (PAG) oil to lubricate the air-conditioning components, and R-12, the less common refrigerant, uses mineral oil. One reason it is so important to always use the correct refrigerant is that PAG oil mixed with mineral oil creates a hazardous gas that can corrode the air-conditioning system. The mixture is also considered a contaminant and must be handled as hazardous waste. To help prevent the wrong lubricant or refrigerant being installed during servicing, the service ports on air-conditioning systems have been changed so that the service equipment for an R-12 system cannot be connected to an R-134a system. Common PAG oils are PAG 46, PAG 100, PAG 133, and PAG 150.

> ▶ **LINK**
> Refer to the Heating and Air-Conditioning Systems and Servicing chapter for more information on R-134a.

R-134a is nonflammable and is accepted by the automotive world to be safe for automotive air conditioners. R-134a, which is a liquid, boils well below normal room temperatures and, in vaporizing, will absorb tremendous amounts of heat without increasing its own

> **TECHNICIAN TIP**
>
> Identifying refrigerants has become an important part of repairing air-conditioning systems. The accidental mixing of refrigerants or the mixing of different types of refrigerant oil could cause damage to the system and the machines that service air conditioners. Before reclaiming a system, you need to identify the type of refrigerant in the vehicle to prevent the accidental contamination of the refrigerant in your recovering machine.

temperature. Unfortunately, recent discoveries show that R-134a is a major contributor to greenhouse gases, so it is being phased out. Tetrafluoropropene (HFO-1234yf) is the preferred replacement.

HFO-1234yf is the latest refrigerant for mobile air-conditioning systems. It has a greatly reduced global warming potential (GWP) of 4, compared to a GWP of 1430 for R-134a refrigerant. Its atmospheric lifetime is only 11 days, compared to 13 years for R-134a. It is slightly flammable, but the safety risk has been determined to be significantly less than the risk associated with gasoline. Also, HFO-1234yf is more costly to produce than R-134a, so that will impact customers as their systems need servicing. HFO-1234yf uses a PAG-type oil with different additives on belt-driven compressors and polyolester (POE) oil for electrically driven compressors. HFO-1234yf uses service ports that are different than those used with R-12 or R-134a, so contamination issues can be avoided **FIGURE 41-6**.

Refrigerant Oils

The oil used in refrigeration systems must be compatible with the refrigerant used. The old refrigerant R-12 used mineral oil. R-134a uses a PAG oil and POE oil is recommended for use with HFO-1234yf **FIGURE 41-7**. The oil is necessary to keep moving parts in the compressor lubricated and is used on the gaskets and seals to protect and help seal. It must be able to move throughout the system without foaming and be compatible with the

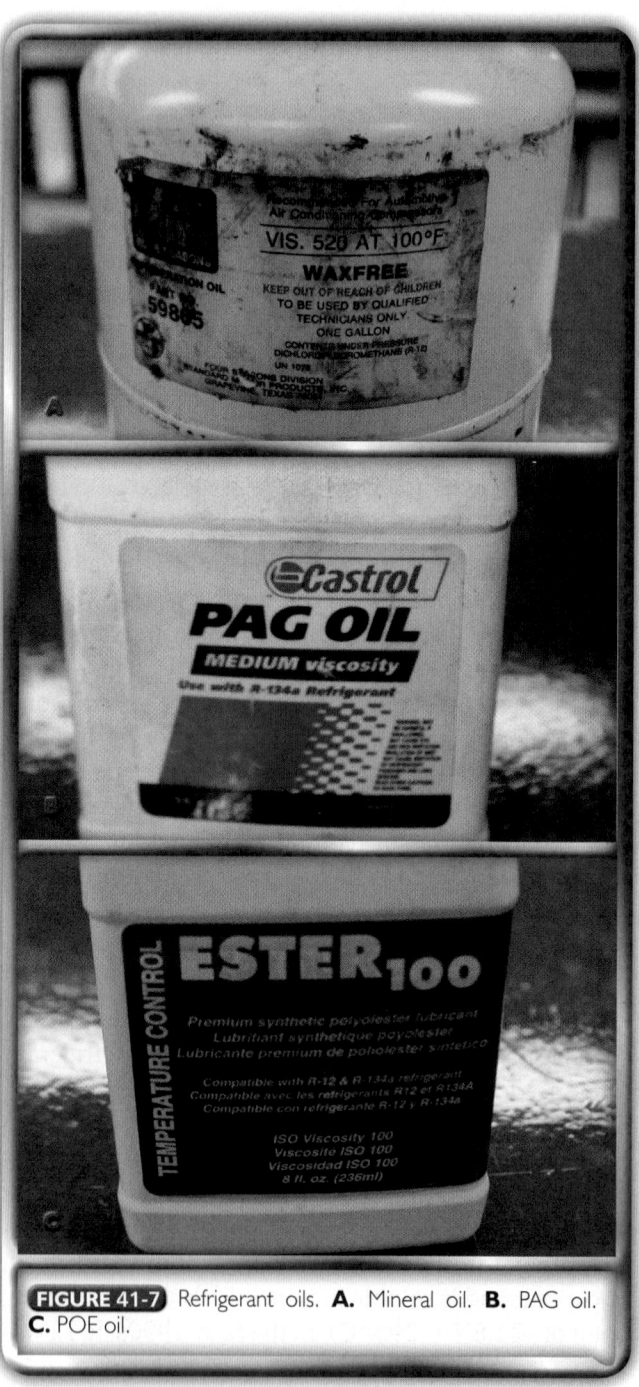

FIGURE 41-7 Refrigerant oils. **A.** Mineral oil. **B.** PAG oil. **C.** POE oil.

FIGURE 41-6 Service ports. **A.** R-12. **B.** R-134a.

refrigerant and the pressure changes taking place. The oil is picked up and carried throughout the system in the refrigerant, so some oil will be found in all the major air-conditioning system components (compressor, evaporator, receiver dryer or accumulator, and condenser). The oil in the compressor is just as important as oil in an engine. Without it, the compressor will overheat and destroy itself.

Mineral oil is clear to light yellow, and PAG oil is usually a light blue color. As the oil picks up dirt or becomes contaminated, it will turn brown or black, depending on the level of contamination.

POE oil can sometimes be used with R-134a. It can also be recommended when retrofitting R-134a in R-12 systems since POE oils are not as reactive to small traces of mineral oil residue. Both POE and PAG oils absorb moisture, so be sure to cap the oil bottle whenever you are not pouring it.

Compressor

The compressor is a vital component of the air-conditioning system. It changes the refrigerant from a low-pressure gas to a high-pressure gas so the boiling point of the refrigerant is brought above ambient temperature. The compressor also provides the pressure needed to move the refrigerant through the entire air-conditioning system. Without the movement of refrigerant, the air conditioner could not exchange heat from the condenser or the evaporator. The pressure from the compressor also keeps the refrigerant moving through the tight restriction of the metering device. There are three general types of compressors: piston, scroll, and rotary vane. Although there may be differences in components, the purpose is the same.

The **axial piston compressor** is one of the most common types of compressor **FIGURE 41-8**. Cylinders are placed around the drive shaft and parallel to its axis. Each cylinder has a pair of single-ended pistons facing apart, allowing a separate pumping chamber at each end of the cylinder. Each pumping chamber has a set of suction and discharge reed valves. The suction reed valves are connected to the inlet port of the compressor by machined passageways. The discharge valves are connected to the discharge port and also by machined passageways. A swash plate is attached to the drive plate at an angle and is positioned between the two rows of opposing pistons. Rotation of the drive shaft causes the outer edge of the swash plate to constantly change its linear position, which moves the pistons back and forth in their respective cylinders.

FIGURE 41-8 An axial piston compressor.

The pistons are connected to the outer edge of the **swash plate** by swiveling ball joints. The action of the swash plate and ball joints continually moves the pistons back and forth in the cylinder. As the volume above a piston increases, refrigerant is drawn into the cylinder through the **suction reed valves**. When the volume above a piston reduces, the refrigerant is forced out of the cylinder through the **discharge reed valves**.

Compressor Operation

The compressor circulates refrigerant through the air-conditioning system by taking low-pressure gas from the evaporator and moving the gas to the high-pressure side of the system. When the piston is drawn away from the compressor head, the pumping chamber volume increases and the **inlet reed valve** allows low-pressure refrigerant to enter the pumping chamber. As the piston moves down to the bottom of the chamber, the cavity fills with as much vaporized refrigerant as the chamber can hold at low side pressures. After the piston reaches the bottom of its stroke, it begins to move up toward the head of the compressor. The low side reed valve is forced shut due to the pressure increase as the piston begins to move up in the bore of the cylinder. As the chamber size becomes smaller, the pressure of the refrigerant begins to rise until the high side reed valve opens. The high side reed valve is pushed off its seat because the pressure of the refrigerant in the chamber becomes slightly higher than the pressure in the high side of the system. Compression of the refrigerant also raises its temperature, and hot high-pressure gas is created in the compressor chamber **FIGURE 41-9**.

Temperature on the high side of the system will rise 10 to 15 times that of the low side due to the increase in pressure on the refrigerant. The hot high-pressure gas is then forced out of the pumping chamber into a hose connected to the compressor.

Sanden Wobble Plate Compressor

The **Sanden wobble plate compressor** can be found on many different vehicle types. Sanden is one of the major compressor manufacturers, but it is not the only company to manufacture a wobble plate style. The choice of a wobble plate compressor, Sanden's or any other manufacturer's version, is up to the vehicle's designer.

The wobble plate compressor works in much the same way as the axial piston compressor except that it has only a single row of pistons instead of two opposing rows of pistons. Each cylinder has one suction valve (reed valve) and one discharge valve (reed valve). Pistons moving away from the suction valve create a low-pressure area, which draws refrigerant through the suction valve into the cylinder from the low-pressure side of the system.

As each piston moves toward the discharge valve, refrigerant is pumped out of the cylinder through the discharge valve into the high side of the system.

The Sanden wobble plate compressor is comprised of many moving parts. The wobble plate is connected to the drive shaft of the compressor and is fixed on an angle. As the wobble plate rotates, the cam rotor is forced to move the connecting rods, which are connected between the cam rotor and the pistons in the compressor. The linear movement of the connecting rod moves the piston in a reciprocating motion (back-and-forth motion). Each piston has a suction reed valve and a discharge reed valve that allow refrigerant to enter and exit from each chamber.

Rotary Vane Compressor

Rotary vane compressors are used as air-conditioning compressors as well as transmission oil pumps and power steering pumps **FIGURE 41-10**. Each one works on the same principles. A cylindrical vane cartridge is connected to the drive shaft and rotates within a cylinder. The vane cartridge typically has three or four machined slots that carry spring-loaded sliding vanes. The vanes are free to move in their slots so that each vane rides up against the sides of the cylinder. The vane cartridge is offset in the cylinder so that the vanes create an expanding volume in half of the cylinder and a decreasing volume in the other half of the cylinder. Rotation of the vane cartridge causes the vanes to move in and out of their slots as the vanes move from the suction side of the cylinder to the discharge side of the cylinder. As the volume increases between the vanes, refrigerant is drawn into the cylinder. And as the volume decreases between the vanes, refrigerant is discharged from the cylinder. This style of pump does not need valves to prevent backflow, as the flow is continuous as long as the compressor is turning. As with any compressor, it

FIGURE 41-9 Compressor operation.

FIGURE 41-10 Rotary vane compressors.

depends on the vehicle's designers to determine which compressor is to be used.

Sanden Scroll-Type Compressor

The <u>Sanden scroll-type compressor</u> uses two interwoven scrolls **FIGURE 41-11**. One scroll is fixed and the other oscillates. The oscillating scroll is connected to the drive shaft, which is rotated by the compressor clutch. As the oscillating scroll is rotated around the stationary scroll, the low-pressure gas is drawn into the low side of the compressor pump. The oscillating scroll forces the gas to compress and flow to the center of the scroll. The outlet port is in the center of the scrolls. The gas is then forced from the outlet port to the high side of the system. **FIGURE 41-11** Sanden scroll-type air-conditioning compressor.

Variable Displacement Compressor

Many manufacturers are now using variable displacement air-conditioning compressors on their vehicles. Variable displacement means that the compressor can change the amount of refrigerant it moves from near 0% up to 100%. This variability allows some compressors to even do away with the compressor clutch, making it driven all of the time. Most variable compressors are of the axial piston or wobble plate style. Variable displacement is accomplished by changing the angle on the swash plate or wobble plate, which lengthens or shortens the stroke of the pistons. The swash plate or wobble plate angle can be adjusted by internal refrigerant pressures pushing against a spring to maintain proper discharge pressure. Commonly in newer vehicles, the angle of the plate is controlled electronically, making for very accurate control of compressor discharge.

Air-Conditioning Compressor Clutch

The <u>air-conditioning compressor clutch</u> is an electromagnetic device that uses a metal plate with no friction material and spring steel to engage and disengage the compressor to the <u>drive pulley</u> **FIGURE 41-12**. The clutch on a compressor works like the clutch on a manual transmission, except on a manual transmission the action is mechanically operated and on a compressor it is electrical. Regardless, the outcome is the same. When the clutch is disengaged (not connected), the pulley attached via a belt to the crankshaft can spin freely. When the clutch is engaged or connected, it forces the internal drive shaft in the compressor to spin and move the pistons, scroll, or rotor. The clutch assembly uses metal-to-metal friction that allows the components to grab each other when engaged. An electric clutch coil controls the clamping action by engaging and disengaging the clutch assembly. When electricity flows through a wire, a magnetic field is created. By winding the wire into a coil, the field is magnified. More windings equal more magnetism. When electricity is applied to the clutch windings, a magnetic field pulls the metal clutch assembly into the spinning pulley and engages the compressor.

The resistance value of the coils determines the amount of electrical current flow through the wire. The lower the resistance value, the more current that can flow. For electromagnets to work there must be relatively low resistance so that enough current can flow through the windings. Resistance is measured in ohms. The <u>clutch electrical winding</u> typically has a resistance value of 3–5 ohms on a 12-volt DC air-conditioning compressor. When a switch or transistor turns on (or off) the electricity to the clutch electrical winding, a magnetic field energizes (or collapses). When the magnetic field is energized, the metal spring-loaded clutch plate is forced to engage the drive pulley being driven by the engine. This engagement drives the compressor and causes refrigerant to move through the air-conditioning system.

FIGURE 41-11 Sanden scroll-type air-conditioning compressor and clutch.

FIGURE 41-12 A compressor clutch.

Though the air-conditioning compressor clutch is not serviced separately in most air-conditioning repair shops, checking its clearance is important when installing a new compressor. If the gap is too large, the magnet will not be strong enough to pull it in. If the gap is too small, the clutch plate may rub against the pulley when it is not engaged and overheat the clutch plate surfaces resulting in part failure. The air-conditioning compressor clutch clearance can vary from manufacturer to manufacturer. As a rule of thumb, air-conditioning compressor clutch clearance should be between 0.015" and 0.025" (between 0.38 and 0.64 mm), but always check the manufacturer's service information.

Compressor Clutch Components

The components of the compressor clutch begin with the pulley portion, which rides on a bearing located on the compressor body. The bearing of the pulley is replaceable and is usually retained by a snap ring. Refer to service information before trying to make a repair. The windings of the clutch coil are mounted behind the pulley. The clutch coil is a replaceable part in many compressors. The clutch portion consists of a flexible piece of steel that moves when the magnetic field is created and provides a friction coupling with the pulley of the compressor. The clutch portion is attached to the compressor shaft. The compressor shaft is what moves the pistons, rotor, or scroll in the compressor to pressurize the refrigerant. The clutch on most compressors has a shim located under it to allow the technician to adjust the correct amount of space between the two parts of the clutch (the clutch and the pulley). If this adjustment is not correct, one of two things may result: The clutch will slip and burn up the friction surface (resulting eventually in no compressor operation), or the compressor will not be able to turn off. Be sure to check your service information when replacing a clutch on an air-conditioning compressor.

Muffler

The air-conditioning system can use mufflers to dampen pulsations and noise from the compressor. The muffler is constructed of a hollow cylinder with baffling **FIGURE 41-13**. As the gaseous refrigerant enters or exits the compressor, the rotating of the different cylinders in the compressor causes a pulsation of gas that can surge in the air-conditioning system and cause unwanted harmonics. The muffler absorbs the pressure pulsations by allowing the gaseous refrigerant in the system to expand into a larger chamber. The pulsations are also dampened by using a baffle system, which forces the refrigerant to slow down in the muffler and prevents the pulsations from affecting the rest of the air-conditioning system.

Condenser

The condenser is normally positioned in front of the radiator where it is exposed to maximum **ram airflow** when the vehicle is in motion **FIGURE 41-14**. Ram airflow refers to the airflow created in front of a moving vehicle; as the vehicle moves forward, air is forced through the condenser by the force of the vehicle's speed. The airflow is assisted by the engine cooling fan or by one or more auxiliary electric fans, which create airflow when the vehicle is stationary or at lower speeds. The condenser is usually made as a continuous aluminum or copper tube meshed with a compact series of fins surrounding it. It is a one-piece unit with no serviceable parts. The fins are small metal protrusions that increase the surface area available to maximize the amount of heat transferred from the refrigerant to the outside air.

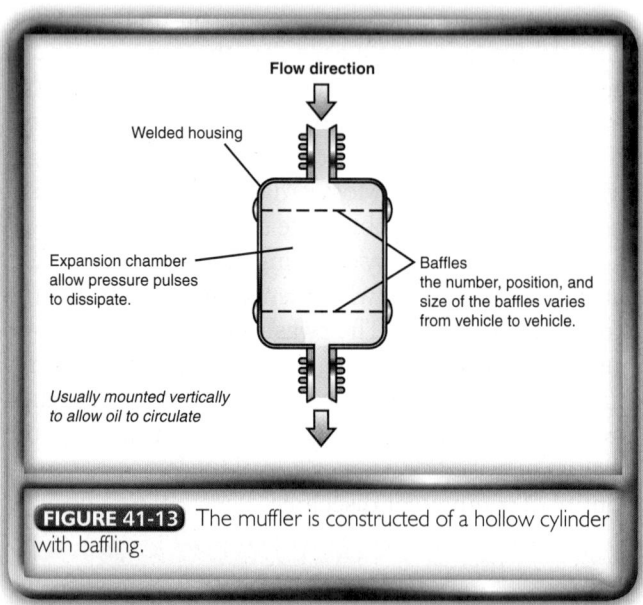

FIGURE 41-13 The muffler is constructed of a hollow cylinder with baffling.

FIGURE 41-14 A condenser.

Applied Science

AS-17: Pressure: The technician can measure pressures in hydraulic or pneumatic systems and compare them to the manufacturer's specifications.

A crucial step in diagnosing air-conditioning system failures is the measurement of the refrigerant pressures. Pressures are measured in two separate places in the system: High-side pressure is measured on the discharge side of the compressor, low-side pressure is measured on the suction side of the compressor. Manufacturer service manuals will outline system pressure specifications and the operating requirements to measure them. Some potential scenarios illustrating problems may include:

- If pressure readings are low on both sides of the system, the most common cause is a leak, or leaks, in the system allowing the loss of refrigerant. This is the most common form of air-conditioning system failure.
- If the pressure readings are the same on both sides of the system, the likelihood is that the compressor is not working.
- If the high side pressure is extremely high or the low pressure side is showing vacuum, suspect an internal blockage in the system.

Condenser Operation

The condenser transforms the hot high-pressure gaseous refrigerant on the high side of the system back into a high-pressure liquid. As it passes through the condenser, the airflow across the fins cools the refrigerant, transforming it back into a liquid.

The gaseous refrigerant in the condenser is at a higher temperature than the outside air flowing across the condenser coils. Putting the refrigerant under pressure raises the boiling point because it now takes more vapor pressure (created by heat) to overcome the pressure in the system. The greater the pressure, the higher the boiling point. The air crossing the condenser is now cooler than the boiling point of the refrigerant. The cool air absorbs the heat of the refrigerant, changing the refrigerant back into a liquid.

The refrigerant is able to condense because the pressure of the compressor increased the boiling point of the refrigerant; thus, the ambient air flowing across the condenser causes the refrigerant to condense into a liquid. Just so you understand the difference, relatively cool air from the passenger cab causes the refrigerant to boil, while relatively warm ambient air causes the refrigerant to condense. The only means by which this can happen is the manipulation of the boiling point (pressures) in the system. In other words, because of the pressure drop on the refrigerant, cool cabin air causes the refrigerant to boil. And once the pressure is raised,

relatively warm ambient air will cause the refrigerant to condense. Manipulating the pressure on the refrigerant lowers or raises the temperature at which the refrigerant boils and condenses.

Condensers are made in one of two designs: serpentine and parallel flow **FIGURE 41-15**. Serpentine condensers are constructed from a single tube. The tube snakes back and forth across the condenser. All the refrigerant flows along the same path throughout the single tube. This design causes the refrigerant to take a long path from the inlet to the outlet, giving a lot of time for the refrigerant to transfer its heat to the atmosphere. However, less refrigerant can flow through the single tube, so its efficiency is not high.

Parallel flow condensers are constructed with multiple tubes in parallel with each other and flow refrigerant more like a radiator for engine coolant. Parallel flow condensers allow more surface area to be exposed to the refrigerant. When the area of exposure is increased, a faster and more efficient condensing of the refrigerant occurs. By using a parallel flow condenser, the efficiency of the air-conditioning system can be increased by up to 25%. This allows the air-conditioning system to be more compact, lightweight, and fuel efficient.

FIGURE 41-15 Condensers. **A.** Serpentine condenser. **B.** Parallel flow condenser.

The choice of condenser is up to the vehicle's designers and engineers. They are, for the most part, interchangeable, though the parallel flow condenser is usually used on bigger vehicles that need the higher efficiency or on small vehicles when space is an issue.

Condenser Fan

The condenser fan is designed to pull or push air from in front of the vehicle through the condenser to remove heat and reduce the high side pressure **FIGURE 41-16**. In older models, the condenser fan ran off of the belt drive on the front of the engine and was mechanically spun by the speed of the pulley. These systems have been almost completely replaced by newer, higher efficiency, more controllable electric fans. The electric fans are controlled by relays, which turn on and off the fans as conditions dictate. Turning on the air-conditioning system on many vehicles commands the fan to run. High side pressure switches or transducers input their signals to the HVAC module and can cause the fan(s) to operate. Many systems can vary the speed and number of fans that operate.

Restriction

There are two common types of restrictions: the fixed orifice tube and the thermal expansion valve **FIGURE 41-17**. A fixed orifice tube restriction is a device with a metered hole in it and a metal or plastic screen to keep out any debris. It allows only a specific amount of liquid refrigerant through at a time. This restriction causes the pressure to drop at that point. No matter what the cabin and evaporator temperatures are, the fixed orifice tube restriction will allow only the specified amount of refrigerant through.

The thermal expansion valve has a sensing device on the outlet side of the evaporator that senses changes in temperature. It also has a valve that can vary the amount of opening to allow more or less liquid refrigerant through. By sensing the temperature coming out of the evaporator, the system can adjust for heat in the cabin. A hot cabin causes the entire refrigerant to boil and creates a high pressure, and the valve will open more to adapt. A cooler cabin generates an incomplete change of state (not all the refrigerant boils), and the valve will close to assure that only refrigerant gas is leaving the evaporator. Additionally, as the cabin temperature is cooled by the air conditioner, the valve can vary its output and change the amount of refrigerant passing through and improve the boiling process.

Restriction Operation

The restriction changes the velocity and pressure of the refrigerant. The refrigerant needs pressure in order to be moved through the tight fit of the restriction. The refrigerant going through the restriction essentially "uses up" its own pressure to do this, so when it emerges on the other side of the restriction, it is at a lower pressure **FIGURE 41-18**. Lowering the pressure of the refrigerant will also lower the boiling point of the refrigerant. The vaporizing point of the refrigerant has to be below the

FIGURE 41-17 Restrictions. **A.** Fixed orifice tube. **B.** Thermal expansion valve.

FIGURE 41-16 Condenser fans.

passenger compartment air temperature but slightly above freezing for the evaporator to function properly.

The restriction lowers the pressure using the Bernoulli principle. As discussed earlier, Bernoulli stated that if the flow of a fluid remains constant, the energies of the fluid remain constant; changing one of the two energies (up or down) of fluid affects the other energy oppositely. Simply stated, a liquid in a confined area will create equal pressure throughout the area when pressure is applied. To illustrate this principle, consider a quick experiment: Take a plastic bottle and poke very small holes in it. Fill it with water and watch how slowly the water drains out. Now refill it and put air pressure to the top and watch how quickly and uniformly the water comes out of the holes.

In an air-conditioning system, the refrigerant flowing through the restriction is a liquid. A primary rule in automotive theory is that a liquid cannot be compressed; this is Pascal's law. Liquids are used to transmit pressure especially for this reason. Brake fluid is a great example. If the brake system is working correctly and is full of fluid with no air, the pressure created as the brake pedal pushes on the fluid creates equal pressure throughout. If air is introduced, the pedal travels farther because bits of air can be compressed. Another practical example is when a person steps into a completely full bathtub and the tub overflows. Even the mass of the heaviest person cannot stop the tub from overflowing because the water cannot be compressed. Forcing a noncompressible fluid through a small orifice causes the velocity in the restriction to rise. If the velocity of the liquid rises, the pressure of the liquid must drop according to the Bernoulli principle. The lower-pressure liquid exiting the restriction is in exactly the correct state and pressure for the evaporator. Raising the velocity and dropping the pressure is how the restric-

tion transforms the high-pressure liquid refrigerant to a low-pressure liquid refrigerant.

Evaporator

The evaporator does not really have components. It is a one-piece unit with no serviceable parts. Like the condenser, it has fins to increase the surface area of the unit and small tubes through which refrigerant flows. It also has an inlet and an outlet pipe through which it connects to the rest of the system. It looks similar to a heater core. The evaporator is usually mounted in the passenger compartment and is positioned so that air from the passenger compartment can be passed across its external surface **FIGURE 41-19**. It is normally constructed of copper or aluminum tubes with fins attached to increase the surface area. The greater the surface area, the more heat transfer from convection (air) to conduction (evaporator tubes) to convection (refrigerant). More fins will increase the surface area of the evaporator and allow a greater area for the air to transfer the energy to the evaporator tubes. This will maximize the rate of heat removal from the air.

Evaporator Operation

The evaporator transforms liquid to a gas in the air conditioner. The job of the evaporator is to take a low-pressure liquid and transform it to a low-pressure gas. The transformation from liquid to gas begins when the air from the passenger compartment passes over the evaporator tubes and fins. The pressure on the refrigerant is typically held between 20 and 40 psi (138–276 kPa); the pressure on the low side of the system reduces the refrigerant's boiling point. Because of the low boiling point, the warm air inside the cabin is absorbed by the

FIGURE 41-18 Pressure drop and speed increase through a restriction.

FIGURE 41-19 An evaporator.

evaporating refrigerant, transforming it from liquid to gas. This heat comes from the air flowing over the evaporator.

The vaporization of the refrigerant is forced to happen at a specific temperature because of the manipulation of the pressure on a liquid that normally boils at negative temperatures. Any heat source will amplify the boiling process. By moving air across the evaporator tubes, the convection currents pass over the evaporator tubes, causing conduction of heat transfer to the refrigerant through the tubes of the evaporator. The conduction of heat through the tubes then provides the needed energy to evaporate the liquid refrigerant to a gas.

The process of transferring heat from the air to the coils then to the refrigerant is the air-conditioning process. After the entire exchange of heat from the air to the refrigerant, the by-product is what makes the driver and passengers feel cool. The air passing over the evaporator coils is stripped of its energy. Moisture and available heat are removed. The air flowing from the air ducts is crisp, cool, and low in moisture. Without airflow across the evaporator coils, the energy could not be removed from the air and the vehicle occupants would not feel the cool air flowing from the ducting.

Dual Evaporator System

Some vehicles, such as conversion vans, minivans, and SUVs, use a dual evaporator system composed of two different units to cool the vehicle. One unit is placed at the front of the vehicle and the other at the rear. This provides passengers in the rear their own airflow, so they don't have to depend on airflow from the front vents. The front unit is typically placed under the dash like normal, and a rear unit is placed on either side of the back passenger compartment to hide the unit. The lines for the rear unit run from the front, as it shares the compressor and condenser with the front unit. In many cases, a solenoid valve is used to allow refrigerant to flow or not to flow to the rear evaporator. If the rear air-conditioning unit is selected by depressing the switch, current will flow through the solenoid valve opening it up so that refrigerant can flow through the rear evaporator. When the rear unit is turned off, the solenoid valve closes. These rear units also have their own blower motor and, in many cases, their own controls.

Hoses, Pipes, and Lines

The terms *pipe* and *line* are used to describe the same metal tubes. The air-conditioning system and the cooling system do not share any hoses or pipes. The two systems are separated from each other, although many of the hoses and pipes used for air conditioning and heating run to

the same locations and may even look similar. Hoses and pipes are used to carry the refrigerant, both liquid and gas, from component to component. Metal pipes are used for their strength, particularly where no give or movement is necessary. Hoses are used around components that move, such as the compressor, which moves as the engine rocks on its rubber mounts **FIGURE 41-20**. If pipes were used in such applications, they would eventually break from the stress of the movement. However, hoses are not as strong as pipes and tend to be porous.

The hoses and pipes in an air-conditioning system must be capable of withstanding the high pressures and temperatures found inside the system and must be able to flex and withstand the vibrations and movement of the engine. Air-conditioning hoses must meet SAE (Society of Automotive Engineers) standard J2064. SAE J2064 states that all air-conditioning hoses must be a **barrier-type hose**. Barrier-type hose is constructed with a nylon inner core to prevent moisture **ingression** (movement into the system) and permeation of refrigerant from the air-conditioning system. In particular, R-134a has a smaller molecular structure that can pass through smaller holes than R-12 could, so barrier-type hoses are required to keep the R-134a within the closed air-conditioning system. In other words, it must prevent moisture for entering the air-conditioning system through the hose material, and it must prevent refrigerant from leaking through the hose material. Nylon is effective at preventing both of these occurrences.

The hose connections are secured to the hose using special unions known as crimps that must be carefully assembled to avoid leaks **FIGURE 41-21**. Special crimping tools or machines are needed to correctly crimp a metal pipe to a hose. Most R-134a crimps are a bubble type, named for how they appear when done properly. The

FIGURE 41-20 Flexible hoses allow for small amounts of engine movement and vibration during operation.

FIGURE 41-21 Hose connections.

metal pipe is slid into the hose and the crimp is applied over the hose to squeeze it tightly against the pipe. Typically, shops purchase these assemblies already made, as the equipment to do it is expensive and the process must be precisely done by skilled technicians.

Pipes are rigid tubes of aluminum or steel often found connecting components that are fixed to the body of the vehicle. Due to the dense makeup of metal pipes, they are less prone to develop leaks. All pipes must have properly formed bends and must be secured to the vehicle body to prevent fatigue cracks or holes made by abrasion.

Hose Size

Air-conditioning hoses are sized by the size of the tube they are designed to fit over. This means that the inside diameter of the hose is smaller than the fitting, allowing a press fit between the hose and fitting. Standard air-conditioning hose is designed to fit over 5/16", 3/8", 1/2", and 5/8" fittings and tubes. The dash system is used by the hydraulic industry, but the automotive industry has applied a number system. This system refers to a hose by how many 16ths of an inch the fitting is that the hose fits over. So a 5/16" hose is referred to as a #5; a 3/8" (6/16ths) hose as a #6; a 1/2" (8/16ths) hose as a #8; and a 5/8" (10/16ths) hose as a #10.

> **TECHNICIAN TIP**
>
> The **double crimping** of the hose to fitting ends will cause leaks. Double crimping occurs when the technician overcrimps the fitting in the hose press in an attempt to get a better seal. The best practice for hose crimping is to use the proper dies and hose/fittings for the job.

> **TECHNICIAN TIP**
>
> Even though the air-conditioning hoses are built to withstand high pressures and temperatures, they can develop leaks, especially around the fittings or anywhere the hose is repeatedly flexed or chafed. Inspecting hoses and fittings is a critical task during air-conditioning service.

O-Rings

<u>O-rings</u> are an essential part of the air-conditioning system **FIGURE 41-22**. O-rings are rubber circles that come in many sizes and types of rubber depending on what they are being used to seal. They are placed on the male end of a fitting. The male end fits into the female end, and the O-ring seals between the inside of the female fitting and the outside of the male fitting to keep refrigerant from leaking around the connection. Most R-134a systems use three O-rings in the male pipe to create a good seal. All O-rings must be lubricated with the proper refrigerant oil when installing.

FIGURE 41-22 O-rings. **A.** R-12–compatible O-rings (nitrile butadiene rubber [NBR]). **B.** R-134a–compatible O-rings (hydrogenated nitrile butadiene rubber [H-NBR]).

Automotive air-conditioning O-rings are made from special materials. Older air-conditioning systems used a **nitrile butadiene rubber (NBR)** compound for the O-rings. This material is not as flexible as pure rubber, but is designed to be compatible with the chemicals in R-12 and mineral oils.

O-rings are also made out of **hydrogenated nitrile butadiene rubber (H-NBR)**. H-NBR was designed to be compatible with the chemical structure of R-134a and PAG oils. The change was required by the federal government in 1992. Like NBR, it is not as flexible as pure rubber. Unlike NBR O-rings, H-NBR O-rings are compatible with R-134a.

Pressure Switches

High pressures and low pressures can cause severe damage to air-conditioning system components. **High-pressure switches** are mounted in the high-pressure side of the air-conditioning system and have their switch contacts in series with the air-conditioning compressor clutch circuit. If the pressure exceeds the switch setting, the switch will open a circuit in the air-conditioning compressor clutch and the compressor will stop circulating refrigerant. On some electronic HVAC systems, the high-pressure switch or transducer sends a signal to the HVAC module and the module reduces the output of a variable displacement compressor and/or turns off the compressor clutch by turning off the clutch relay.

Low-pressure switches are mounted in the low-pressure side of the air-conditioning system and are also connected in series with the air-conditioning compressor clutch. Low pressures can occur in air-conditioning systems when the refrigerant has escaped. With little or no refrigerant flowing, lubricating oil flow is also reduced, which can damage the compressor. Low pressure causes the contacts in the low-pressure switch to open and break the electrical supply to the air-conditioning compressor clutch, stopping its operation. Like high-pressure switches or transducers on some electronic HVAC systems, the low pressures can be input to the module to turn the system off. When this happens, most systems are programmed to output a diagnostic trouble code (DTC) to the module, which can be accessed with the proper scan tool.

System Wiring

Early air-conditioning systems did not have much in the way of electrical systems. A power and ground wire to the compressor to engage the clutch was necessary, and many of the wires had to pass through a low- and/or high-pressure switch placed in the appropriate line on the system. If the pressure got too low or too high, the switch would open and no electricity could flow to the clutch. These were safety devices to keep the system from destroying itself. On many systems, the low-pressure switch would open and close often, causing the clutch to cycle on and off. This was used as a control device to keep the pressures where they needed to be. The high-pressure switch was also used to control the condenser fan. The other wiring necessary was for the blower motor in the vehicle. The blower controlled the speed of the air blowing from the vents and was controlled by a switch on the dash and a resistor block designed to control fan speed. Many of the new systems have a lot more wiring to accomplish these and other tasks with relays that are controlled by computers.

Schrader Valves

Schrader valves are used on many systems both to hold pressure and to allow a gauge or piece of equipment to be attached to the system. For example, the air in the tires is held in, measured, and inflated at the tire's Schrader valve. Schrader valves are placed on both the low and the high side of an air-conditioning system to allow an entry point for checking pressures. Schrader valves are placed in the ports and designed to accept either the low or high side of the hose from the air-conditioning servicing equipment. When the gauge fittings are inserted, they push down the Schrader valve to allow pressure to be released into the gauge hoses. When the gauge fittings are removed, spring pressure pushes the Schrader valve closed to stop the release of refrigerant **FIGURE 41-23**. Some Schrader valves are removable with the use of a Schrader valve tool. Once the system pressure has been released, the tool is used to unscrew the Schrader valve and check the O-ring and replace the component, if necessary. Sometimes the valve is not replaceable and the whole line containing the Schrader valve must be replaced.

Driers

Driers, called desiccants, are placed in the receiver dryer or the accumulator **FIGURE 41-24**. The desiccant is held

FIGURE 41-24 Air-conditioning system desiccant bag.

FIGURE 41-23 Air-conditioning Schrader valve.

> **TECHNICIAN TIP**
>
> The most common refrigerant desiccants are **XH-7** and **XH-9**. They are crystalline alkali metal alumina-silicate in beaded form. Both are used in R-134a units, but XH-7 is designed for pure R-134a while XH-9 is designed for systems that may not be pure. American-made vehicles use XH-7 because the R-134a is regulated, but many imports do not have the same regulations and may use XH-9.

in a bag and serves as a drying agent to absorb any excess moisture in the system. The desiccant can become oversaturated if a system is left open and large amounts of moist air enter. If the system has been open for a period of time, then the receiver dryer or accumulator will need to be replaced.

Sight Glass

The sight glass was an important inspection device on R-12 systems. The site glass was a glass portal that allowed you to look into the air-conditioning system and see the liquid refrigerant flow. If there were bubbles in the liquid, then the system was low. If no bubbles were seen, then the system was either full or empty (since an empty system would not have any liquid for bubbles to be suspended in). The site glass is still on some systems but should not be used with R-134a. Due to the chemical makeup of R-134a, some small bubbles will always be present. In fact, the appearance of no bubbles in R-134a indicates that the system is overfilled. Because R-12 is no longer used on new vehicles, the site glass is no longer considered a valid test.

> **TECHNICIAN TIP**
>
> Service port caps are used to cap off the service ports for two reasons: (1) to keep dirt and contaminants from collecting in the service port and (2) to provide a secondary seal for the Schrader valve to prevent the loss of refrigerant from the valve. They should always be tightened properly. Also, some repair facilities use tamper-proof caps that cannot be removed without destroying the strap that holds the cap in place. These caps are used to prevent someone from tampering with the air-conditioning system; typically any warranty becomes void if they are broken. So be aware of this if you encounter tamper-proof service caps.

Types of Automotive Air-Conditioning Systems

There are two definitive system types: <u>fixed orifice tube system</u> and <u>thermal expansion valve (TXV) system</u> **FIGURE 41-25**. The difference is that the TXV is adjustable based on the temperature of the outlet pipe from the evaporator, whereas the fixed orifice tube provides a nonadjustable passage for the refrigerant to pass through. Each type of air-conditioning system contains one subcomponent that is vital to the operation and efficiency of the air-conditioning unit. The type of restriction being used will determine which subcomponent is required. Fixed orifice tube systems use an **accumulator** to ensure that a pure gas is delivered to the compressor, and TXV systems use a receiver filter drier to ensure that a pure liquid is delivered to the restriction.

The fixed orifice tube system has the accumulator on the low side line between the evaporator and the compressor. Since this system cannot adapt to temperature changes in the cabin, it is likely that during cooler weather or as the cabin temperature decreases the refrig-

erant in the evaporator will not fully boil. This means that some liquid refrigerant will still be present as it heads for the compressor. Since liquid cannot be compressed, its presence in the compressor may cause damage from trying to compress a noncompressible substance. The accumulator's job is to prevent liquid from getting into the compressor and causing damage. Liquid and gaseous refrigerant are both able to enter the accumulator. In the accumulator, the liquid falls to the bottom because it is heavier, and the gas rises to the top. The outlet of the accumulator only draws from the top; therefore, it only allows gaseous refrigerant to reach the compressor. The liquid in the bottom is heated by the gas passing through it and heat from the engine compartment, and it boils and rises to be used as a gas.

The TXV system has a receiver dryer in the high side line between the condenser and the TXV. This system can adapt to the temperature changes in the evaporator, so unlike the fixed orifice system, it does not need the safety device for the compressor. The receiver dryer also lets in liquid and gaseous refrigerant, but it actually draws the liquid from the bottom on the outlet side. The receiver stores the accumulated liquid refrigerant in case of a sudden change of temperature in the cabin. If the cabin is cool because the air conditioning has been on for a while and the customer opens a window or door, hot air rushes in, raising the outlet temperature of the evaporator and causing the TXV to rapidly open. This rapid opening stimulates a rush of the extra liquid refrigerant from the receiver to the evaporator to keep it from drawing a vacuum and becoming inefficient.

FIGURE 41-25 Types of automotive air-conditioning systems. **A.** Fixed orifice tube system. **B.** Thermal expansion valve system.

Applied | **Science**

AS-19: Fahrenheit/Centigrade: The technician measures system temperatures and converts them to degrees Fahrenheit or degrees Centigrade as required. A common HVAC-related concern is air-conditioning systems failing to cool effectively. Prior to carrying out any diagnosis, technicians must determine whether or not the system is operating properly. This is determined by measuring the output temperature at the center vents in the vehicle's dash.

Once the vent temperature has been measured, it should be compared to manufacturer's specifications to determine if the system is operating effectively. Measuring instruments are available reading in either degrees Centigrade or degrees Fahrenheit. The unit of measurement in which specifications are published may vary according to the manufacturer. It may be necessary to convert the measured temperatures from degrees Centigrade to degrees Fahrenheit, or vice-versa, to determine if the reading meets specifications.

Fixed Orifice Tube Air-Conditioning System

The fixed orifice tube air-conditioning system is a common type of air-conditioning system in the automotive world. The components that make this system unique are the fixed orifice tube, pressure cycling switch, and accumulator. The fixed orifice tube is a metering device that forces high-pressure liquid into low-pressure liquid. The orifice, or hole, is designed to allow a specific amount of refrigerant through at a designated speed. The pressure cycling switch is normally used in conjunction with the fixed orifice tube. It is installed on the low-pressure line or the accumulator to turn the air-conditioning clutch on and off at certain pressures. The accumulator is placed between the evaporator and the compressor to collect any liquid refrigerant and prevent it from entering the compressor. The accumulator also houses the desiccant.

The fixed orifice tube air-conditioning system is less efficient than the TXV system, since the amount of refrigerant that flows through the restriction cannot be controlled directly. The orifice tube metering orifice is fixed, meaning it is nothing more than a nonadjustable hole. Since it is fixed, it cannot vary the amount of refrigerant flow. It also cannot compensate for engine rpm changes like the TXV system, so refrigerant flows through it continuously while the compressor is running. The only thing that changes the flow is the pressure difference between the high side and the low side. Since the hole of the fixed orifice tube is very small, refrigerant can only pass through it slowly. As the pressure on each side of the tube starts to equalize, meaning the high-pressure side is not too much higher than the low-pressure side, it becomes harder to move the refrigerant through the hole. Once the two pressures are equal, the flow of refrigerant stops.

Fixed Orifice Tube

The fixed orifice tube is constructed from a plastic outer shell and a bronze, small, fixed-diameter tube with a mesh screen before and after the fixed orifice **FIGURE 41-26**. The color of the plastic tube is used to identify the diameter of the orifice. For example, one manufacturer uses blue tubes that have an orifice of 0.067" (1.7 mm), red tubes with an orifice of 0.062" (1.6 mm), orange tubes with an orifice of 0.057" (1.4 mm), green tubes with an orifice of 0.052" (1.3 mm), and brown tubes with an orifice of 0.047" (1.2 mm). The different sizes of the orifices are for different flow rates for larger and smaller systems.

The fixed orifice tube is placed in the air-conditioning system between the condenser and the evaporator, near the inlet of the evaporator. There is a directional arrow on the fixed orifice tubes to let the technician know the proper way the fixed orifice tube needs to be installed.

FIGURE 41-26 The fixed orifice tube is constructed from a plastic outer shell and a bronze, small, fixed-diameter tube with a mesh screen before and after the fixed orifice.

When installing the fixed orifice tube, make sure to lube the O-rings on the fixed orifice tube with refrigerant oil, and use the proper orifice tube installation tool. Failure to use caution will lead to breakage of the fixed orifice tube or damage to the O-rings.

Because the fixed orifice tube has no moving parts, flooding the evaporator with liquid is a common occurrence. This happens when the rpm of the engine changes rapidly. Liquid from the evaporator could potentially enter the compressor and cause a seized compressor, which would permanently damage it. This is why fixed orifice tube systems need either a pressure cycling switch and an accumulator or a variable displacement compressor and an accumulator.

> ### ▶ TECHNICIAN TIP
>
> When removing the fixed orifice tube, note the color of the fixed orifice tube and compare it to specifications. Replace the fixed orifice tube with the proper color of tube, which is usually the color you removed. If a different color is accidently installed, the system will not work properly.

Low-pressure Cycling Switch

The <u>low-pressure cycling switch</u> is typically mounted on the accumulator in a fixed orifice tube system. The low-pressure cycling switch also acts as a low-pressure safety switch for the air-conditioning system. If the air-conditioning system loses all refrigerant, the switch will turn off the compressor clutch and possibly save the compressor from failure due to no refrigerant and oil.

The low-pressure cycling switch is a normally open contact switch that uses system pressure to cycle the compressor on and off during normal operation. The air-conditioning pressure switch is normally open and does not allow electricity to go to the compressor clutch or clutch relay unless low side pressure is between approximately 20 and 46 psi (between 138 and 317 kPa). Below approximately 20 psi, the switch opens. As refrigerant pressure drops on the low side due to the compressor pulling refrigerant from the low side, the low-pressure cycling switch will remain closed until the pressure on the low side of the air-conditioning system falls below about 20 psi. Once the pressure falls below 20 psi, the low-pressure cycling switch opens and the compressor stops pulling refrigerant from the low side. The low-pressure cycling switch will remain open until the pressure rises on the low side of the air-conditioning system to around 46 psi again. These systems are often referred to as cycling clutch orifice tube (CCOT) systems.

Accumulator

The accumulator is located between the outlet of the evaporator and the inlet of the compressor **FIGURE 41-27**. It has no serviceable parts, though desiccant is located inside the accumulator. The outlet tube of the accumulator is U-shaped. The gaseous refrigerant rises to the top and is able to exit via the outlet tube. Any liquid refrigerant falls to the bottom of the accumulator and is heated and converted into a gas as hotter gases pass through the accumulator. This system prevents liquid refrigerant from exiting the accumulator. The job of the accumulator is to make sure that liquid refrigerant does not enter the compressor. However, some accumulators have a small hole in the bottom of the U-shaped outlet tube so that a small, measured amount of oil can be drawn into the compressor for lubrication purposes.

Since the fixed orifice tube system does not have moving parts in the restriction to slow or stop the refrigerant flow, the system may flood the evaporator, potentially allowing liquid to enter the compressor. This liquid refrigerant could cause the compressor to seize. This potential problem is why the accumulator is placed between the evaporator and the compressor. The accumulator has no moving parts. It does have desiccant pouches inside to help dry the refrigerant of any moisture.

> **TECHNICIAN TIP**
>
> The outside of the accumulator can frost over when the vehicle comes to a complete stop because the refrigerant that flooded the evaporator is caught by the accumulator and is boiling off and cooling down, condensing any moisture on the outside of the accumulator. This moisture freezes on the outside of the accumulator, then melts and forms a puddle under the vehicle when it stops, similar to the puddle from the evaporator drain. This puddle can look like the vehicle has a coolant leak, but it is just water that condensed on the accumulator and is nothing to worry about.

Thermal Expansion Valve Air-Conditioning System

In a TXV air-conditioning system, the components necessary for system operation are the condenser, the evaporator, the compressor, the receiver drier, the TXV, connecting pipes and hoses, a thermostat switch, blower fans, and pressure switches. The TXV is located at the entry to the evaporator and provides a throttling or restricting function to control the quantity of refrigerant entering the evaporator. The TXV controls flow through the use of a passage that can open or close using pressure on a diaphragm. A temperature sensing bulb normally containing refrigerant is attached to the diaphragm via a metal tube. The bulb is attached to the outlet side of the evaporator. The temperature changes in the outlet side cause the refrigerant to expand and contract. As it does so, it adds or removes pressure on the diaphragm to allow it to open and close the valve. As the refrigerant boils completely in the evaporator, it raises the temperature of the outlet pipe. The higher temperature in the pipe raises the pressure in the bulb, which pushes on the diaphragm to open the valve. As the air cools in the

FIGURE 41-27 Accumulator.

passenger compartment, not all the refrigerant passing through the evaporator turns to gas, which means the temperature coming out is cooler, thus lowering the bulb pressure and in turn closing the valve.

The TXV air-conditioning system is charged with refrigerant and a quantity of lubricating oil that circulates with the refrigerant at all times. When the air-conditioning system is switched on, an electromagnetic clutch is energized on the compressor drive plate and the compressor is driven by the engine crankshaft. Vaporized refrigerant is drawn from the low-pressure side of the system by the intake side of the compressor. It is discharged from the compressor as a high-pressure, high-temperature vapor (compressing the refrigerant raises its temperature) and flows to the condenser where it is cooled by the air flowing across the condenser coils and fins. The high pressure and the reduction in heat cause the refrigerant vapor to condense and turn into a liquid, which flows to the receiver drier. The liquid refrigerant must pass through the filter and **desiccant** to reach the pickup tube, where the refrigerant can flow on to the TXV. Desiccant is a chemical compound that can absorb moisture and help keep the air-conditioning system dry.

Thermal Expansion Valve

At the TXV, the amount of liquid refrigerant flow is determined by the action of a spring-loaded valve, which is controlled by different pressures on each side of a connecting diaphragm **FIGURE 41-28**. The pressure in chamber A is determined by a temperature-sensing bulb that

Valve   Pressure spring

Diaghragm

Equalizing circuit

Liquid/vapor

Capillary tube

Temperature sensing bulb   Air fins

Vapor

IN   **OUT**
Liquid refrigerant   Refrigerant vapor

FIGURE 41-28 Thermal expansion valve.

is taped to the evaporator outlet and insulated from air temperatures. The sensing bulb is filled with refrigerant and is connected to chamber A by a capillary tube. The temperature at the evaporator outlet determines the pressure in the bulb. Higher temperatures will give higher pressures, which will tend to open the TXV wider and allow more refrigerant to flow through. Lower temperatures will give lower pressures, which will tend to close the TXV and reduce the flow of refrigerant.

The pressure in chamber B is determined by the refrigerant pressure in the evaporator and by the force supplied from the valve spring—often called a **superheat spring**. The superheat spring is designed to ensure that the temperature of the refrigerant leaving the evaporator is between 5°F and 20°F higher than the boiling point of the refrigerant at the current operating pressure. This difference in temperature is called superheat, and it ensures that all liquid refrigerant that enters the evaporator is vaporized before it leaves.

When the compressor switches on, the suction from the compressor removes refrigerant vapor from the evaporator and lowers its pressure. This reduces the pressure in chamber B and allows the pressure in chamber A to move the TXV away from its seat, by the action of the diaphragm. High-pressure liquid flows through the orifice and enters the evaporator as a low-pressure liquid. The temperature of the refrigerant leaving the evaporator is interpreted by the internal or external sensing bulb attached to the outlet of the evaporator. If the temperature is low, the refrigerant in the sensing bulb will contract and pressure in chamber A of the TXV will reduce. The diaphragm moves and the TXV moves toward the valve seat to reduce the quantity of refrigerant entering the evaporator. If the temperature is high, the refrigerant in the sensing bulb expands and exerts more pressure in chamber A, causing the valve to move away from its seat and allowing more refrigerant to enter the evaporator.

The amount of refrigerant flowing depends on the quantity of heat to be removed from the air passing over the evaporator fins. More heat means that more refrigerant is required to remove it. Less heat means that less refrigerant is required. A number of control devices are fitted into the system to ensure maximum efficiency, and these operate as described in the section on the fixed orifice system.

The TXV is a self-adjusting restriction. It can be internally or externally compensated. Older TXVs had a long tube with the sensing ball at the end of the tube. The sensing ball was an external unit to the actual TXV body, so it was externally compensated. Most of the new units are known as TXV blocks, or H blocks because of how they look FIGURE 41-29. These units are all encompassed within the block. Both the inlet and the outlet pipe run through the block; thus it is internally compensated since the sensing ball is inside the block. The TXV uses refrigerant trapped in a chamber to control the restriction's opening. If the evaporator starts to flood, the temperature leaving the evaporator drops and the refrigerant trapped in the TXV chamber contracts, closing the restriction and not allowing any more system refrigerant to enter the evaporator. By shutting off the TXV, the evaporator cannot be flooded and there is no need for an accumulator in this system. The refrigerant will begin to back up in the system; the receiver drier will act as extra storage for the air-conditioning system while the TXV closes.

The TXV is constructed of cadmium-plated steel or of aluminum. Three types are commonly used: the internally equalized valve, the externally equalized valve, and the H block valve. Each of these valves has the same job—to open and close the port. The **internally equalized valve** uses pressure from the inlet pipe to overcome the pressure created from the outlet pipe's heat. Lower heat on the outlet pipe creates lower pressure, and the pressure from the inlet pipe is able to overcome it and move the valve. The **externally equalized valve** uses the sensing bulb on the outlet side to overcome spring pressure to open the valve. The **H block valve** uses the outlet side like the external valve, but both the inlet and the outlet pipe go through the block, so the sensing bulb is built into the block.

Thermal Switch Cycling

The **thermal cycle switch** is a normally closed, temperature-controlled switch that controls the

FIGURE 41-29 TXV block.

compressor clutch. It is located and installed in the fins of the evaporator inside the evaporator housing. The thermal cycle switch is opened and closed by the pressure of the gaseous refrigerant contained in the capillary tube as it expands and contracts with temperature. As the evaporator cools off, the gas contracts in the capillary tube. When the gas in the tube contracts enough, the pressure diaphragm retracts and the thermal cycle switch opens, shutting the compressor clutch off. As the evaporator warms due to no refrigerant movement, the gas in the capillary tube expands and the switch closes again, causing the compressor clutch to reengage.

> ### TECHNICIAN TIP
>
> When removing the thermal cycle switch, mark the depth of the old one before removal. This will allow you to install the new one to the same depth.

Receiver Filter Drier

The **receiver filter drier (RFD)**, often just called a receiver drier, is located between the condenser outlet and the TXV inlet FIGURE 41-30. The RFD has several functions, all of which are important for the operation of the TXV system. The name of the component—receiver, filter, drier—explains what the component does. The main job of the RFD is to ensure that pure liquid refrigerant is being delivered to the expansion valve located close to the evaporator on the inlet side. The delivery of the pure liquid is accomplished by means of the siphon tube on the outlet port of the RFD. The siphon tube extends to the bottom of the RFD, allowing it to siphon pure liquid only. The liquid that flows from the outlet of the condenser is under high pressure. This high-pressure liquid can include some vapor bubbles, which stay in the top of the RFD, where they condense into liquid.

The next job of the RFD is to act as a surge tank for refrigerant when the TXV closes due to low temperatures and pressures in the evaporator. When the restriction closes, refrigerant backs up in the air-conditioning system because the compressor is still running and the temperature in the evaporator is not cool enough for the thermal cycle switch to turn off the compressor. The RFD acts as a storage container during these times.

The RFD is constructed with a mesh and cloth filter media. The **filter media** (the desiccant in a cloth bag) passes the refrigerant through the filter so no debris can enter the TXV and damage the valve. The RFD also uses a desiccant in the RFD to help remove any moisture that might be present in the refrigerant.

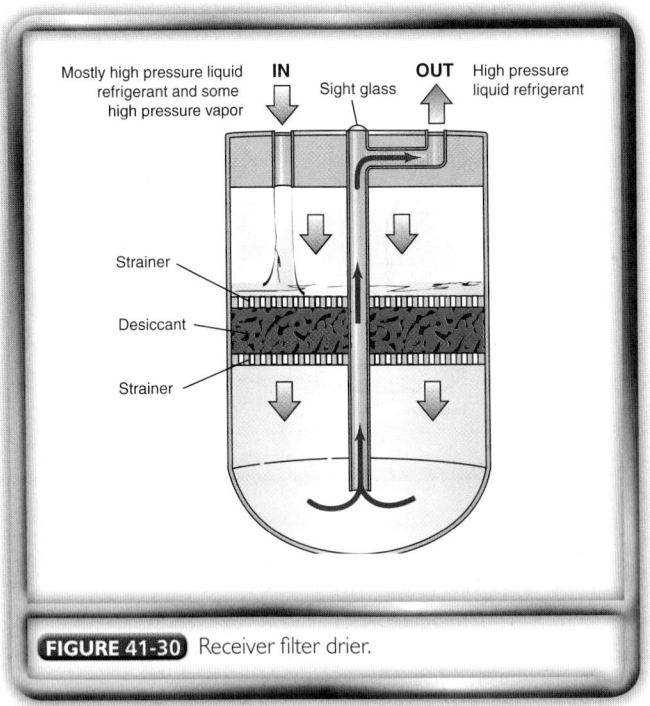

Mostly high pressure liquid refrigerant and some high pressure vapor

IN Sight glass OUT High pressure liquid refrigerant

Strainer

Desiccant

Strainer

FIGURE 41-30 Receiver filter drier.

TECHNICIAN TIP

It is important not to overcharge the air-conditioning system, because the storage capacity of the RFD will be lost and pressure will tend to rise very quickly in the high side. Overcharging refers to adding more refrigerant to the system than is specified by the manufacturer, such as adding 32 ounces of refrigerant into a system designed to hold a maximum of 28 ounces. With refrigerant capacity being reduced by manufacturers (some systems hold less than 16 ounces when properly filled), the systems cannot tolerate improper charge amounts as well as older vehicles.

Heating System Components and Operation

Many of the components used to warm the passenger cabin of a vehicle also function in removing heat from the engine. The key shared components are the radiator, thermostat, water pump, and upper and lower radiator hoses. As the engine heats up from the process of burning fuel to create power, the coolant in the engine is also heated, reaching temperatures of 180–205°F (82–96°C) under normal conditions and 235°F (113°C) or more in hot climates or under heavy vehicle loads. The heat from the hot coolant opens the thermostat and the water pump

pushes the coolant into the radiator, which is located in front of the engine. Airflow from the vehicle moving and/or the cooling fans passes over the radiator and the heat is transferred to the air, warming the air and reducing the temperature of the coolant. The coolant is then cycled back through the engine to restart the process. Heated coolant is also pumped to a heater core where the blower causes air to flow through the heater core and is warmed. The heated air is directed into the passenger compartment.

Just as the pressure inside of the air-conditioning system is manipulated to control the boiling point of the refrigerant, the cooling system is kept under pressure to prevent the coolant from boiling at the normal boiling point of water, which is 212°F (100°C). The cap holds the pressure at approximately 8–20 psi (55–138 kPa) depending on what the manufacturer designed the system to be safely pressurized to. Raising the pressure 1 psi (7 kPa) raises the boiling point of water approximately 3°F, so water in a cooling system with a 15-psi (103-kPa) radiator cap will not boil until 45°F above 212°F, or 257°F (125°C). And if the water is mixed with anti-freeze, the boiling point will be even higher.

Applied Math

AM-40: Proportion: The technician can solve problems that determine the proportion of variables of a solution and determine if that proportion is within the manufacturer's specifications.

Engine coolant is composed of a mixture of antifreeze, commonly ethylene glycol or propylene glycol, and water. Different operating temperature ranges may require different ratios of antifreeze to water to ensure adequate cooling system performance. A common mixture ratio is 50% antifreeze to 50% water, but other ratios may be specified by antifreeze manufacturers for extreme temperature ranges.

Coolant concentration can be checked with an antifreeze hydrometer, which indicates the proportion of antifreeze in the system. Coolant concentration should be checked during vehicle servicing. Topping up cooling systems with water is a common practice, but the proportion of antifreeze in the system is reduced. If measurement indicates that the proportion of antifreeze in the system is low, some coolant must be drained from the system, which can then be refilled with antifreeze to the correct proportion. Too much antifreeze in the system can cause poor cooling, if this occurs some coolant must be drained from the system and the system refilled with water to the correct proportion.

Safety

In the same way that liquid refrigerant boils when its pressure is lowered, so too does coolant. If an engine is overheating, never remove the radiator pressure cap. If you do, and the coolant is above 212°F (100°C), then the coolant will instantly turn into steam and shoot out of the radiator like a geyser, potentially burning you badly. Let all engines cool before opening the radiator pressure cap.

Heater Core

In the heating system, two hoses run from the engine to a heater core (small radiator). The heater core is located inside the cabin in the plastic box with the air-conditioning evaporator. As air is moved through the fins of the heater core, hot air is removed and sent out of the vents to heat the passenger cabin. The heater core is made from tubes that have thin metal fins connected to them, which increase the surface area tremendously. Since the tubes are also made of relatively thin metal, they can corrode from the inside and develop pinhole leaks from old acidic anti-freeze. Changing a heater core can be a time-consuming and costly job in many of today's vehicles, so regular cooling system maintenance can pay off for a customer.

Heater Control Valve and/or Blend Door

To adjust the amount of heat delivered to the cabin, some heating systems use a control valve on the inlet of the heater core to control the flow of hot coolant through the heater core. The valve can be mechanically operated by a cable, vacuum operated by a vacuum diaphragm, or electrically operated by an electric motor. Other vehicles use a blend door to control how much airflow goes through the heater core based on the driver's request using the temperature settings on the dash. Blend doors can be operated mechanically, by vacuum, or by electric motors. Most vehicles either use a heater control valve or a blend door to control the amount of heat delivered to the passenger compartment **FIGURE 41-31**.

Heating and Ventilation

To improve driver and passenger safety, a supply of fresh air is necessary to maintain comfort and reduce fatigue. Fresh air is drawn from outside usually through air ducts at the base of the windshield and directed to the passenger compartment. The air is then delivered through a system of ducts and air doors, which are positioned to direct air to particular points inside the passenger compartment.

FIGURE 41-31 Most vehicles either use a heater control valve or blend door to control the amount of heat delivered to the passenger compartment. **A.** Typical heater control valve. **B.** Typical blend door.

Vehicle Heating and Ventilation Components

Some of the heat generated by the burning fuel in the engine is removed by the cooling system. The hot coolant is pumped through a heater core usually located in the vehicle cabin. As cool air blows across the heater core, the air is heated by the warm coolant. The coolant is then pumped back through the engine to pick up heat from the engine and the cycle continues. In the dash is a control system for the blower fan speed. The blower fan blows the warm or cool air out of the ducts. The control system also has a temperature control that either opens a blend door that determines how much air blows across the heater core or around it, or controls a heater control valve that varies the amount of hot water being pumped through the heater core. In most vehicles, all air flows through the evaporator on its way to the heater core.

If cold air is desired, then the air-conditioning system is activated to cool the evaporator. If the cool or cold setting is selected, then either the blend door will divert the air around the heater core or the heater control valve will prevent coolant from flowing through it. If warm or hot air is desired, then the air conditioner will be off and either the blend door will divert the air through the heater core or the heater control valve will allow hot coolant to flow through the heater core. If defrost is desired, then both the air conditioner and the heater will operate. The air first goes through the evaporator, and most of the moisture is pulled from the air. Then the air is directed through the heater core where it is heated. This causes hot, dry air to be blown onto the windshield, which defrosts it quickly.

Another control regulates location of airflow. There are several doors designed to direct the air to the feet (floor ducts), head (vent ducts), windshield (defrosting ducts), or a combination of locations, such as the feet and windshield. This control also has a vent setting that allows fresh air in, then directs it to the vents. Vehicles with air conditioning can have a recirculation switch or lever, or they can have a "max" or "maximum" setting. This setting closes the door to the outside air to allow the air-conditioning system to work with only the air already present in the cabin. Using only the air within the cabin produces better cooling because the air-conditioning system will be cooling air that has already been through the air-conditioning system rather than hot, muggy air from outside the vehicle. Recirculation can also be used on some vehicles to help keep the moisture out when using the defroster.

Vehicle Heating and Ventilation Operation

Air doors can be controlled by cables, **vacuum servos**, or **electric servos**. Servos are devices designed to do work. They are hooked to the ventilation doors and open and close them according to the request from the control assembly. Vacuum servos use a vacuum control at the control head. Vacuum is supplied by the engine and run into the control head with a small hose called a vacuum hose (it is normally black). The control head can route this vacuum to the correct servo by turning the dial on the control head. Each setting has a different-colored hose coming out and going to a separate servo or, in some cases, to a dual servo that can move in two directions. Traditionally, these systems have doors that can be only opened or closed, because they either have vacuum pulling on a diaphragm or they do not. Newer vehicles have electric servos. They are the same as the old, mechanical servos except instead of vacuum, they use electric motors to open and close the doors. These can be adapted to only partially open a door. Most of these systems are computer controlled so the system knows when a door opens and when it does not and can set trouble codes if a door malfunctions. In this way, the servos can direct air to the vent ducts, floor ducts, windshield ducts, and rear passenger compartment ducts.

A fan, usually driven by an electric motor, is used to assist the air to flow through the radiator and condenser when demands are high or when vehicle speeds are low. When vehicle speeds are low, there may not be enough airflow to cool the coolant and the refrigerant. In these conditions, the fan comes on to pull the air through the radiator and the condenser to keep the vehicle from overheating and also to allow the refrigerant to condense. Some vehicles have two or more fans, typically one for the radiator and one or more for the condenser. They frequently are positioned side by side and attached to the radiator, just as in applications with one fan. Each fan has different controls regulating when they come on or turn off. Most vehicles with electric fans will turn on at least one fan when the air conditioning is on to aid in the cooling of the refrigerant.

The heating system of most passenger vehicles uses hot engine coolant flowing through a **heater core**, which

---

Applied | **Science**

AS-9: Scientific Methods: The technician develops a theory relative to the cause of the problem based on the information provided, then tests the hypothesis to determine the solution.

A vehicle is presented to the workshop with an air conditioning problem. The customer is concerned that all air from the ventilation system is being directed to the windshield and that turning the direction control to either the face or feet positions has no effect.

The vehicle in question uses a vacuum-operated system to control blend-door positions in the HVAC system. The technician forms a theory that the system may have a vacuum leak, based on the fact that, in the event of no vacuum, the system defaults to defroster operation to ensure the driver retains visibility and is able to safely operate the vehicle.

The technician first confirms that the HVAC vacuum line is connected to the engine's intake manifold then forms a hypothesis that the vacuum leak is occurring within the HVAC system located inside the vehicle's cabin. He is able to confirm this hypothesis by connecting a vacuum pump to the HVAC line in the engine bay and confirming that the system does not hold vacuum. Individual components and sections of vacuum line in the cabin are then individually tested to ensure they hold vacuum. A common failure in this scenario is an internal vacuum leak in the direction control assembly.

is usually mounted under the dash **FIGURE 41-32**. The heater core is connected to the engine's cooling system by flexible rubber hoses, which allow for movement and a reduction in the level of engine noise and vibration transmitted into the passenger compartment. The heater core is a small radiator consisting of **tubes**, **fins**, and **tanks**. The tubes are the metal pipes running side to side or up and down that the coolant travels through. Fins are small, flat metal pieces placed between the tubes to help transfer heat from the coolant to the air. The fins are in direct contact with the hot pipes and absorb the heat. The heat is then absorbed by the air flowing through the fins, warming the air, which is then blown back into the passenger cabin. Metal or plastic tanks line the sides of the tubes, connecting them together and assisting with coolant flow. The coolant flow is created by the engine water pump directing the coolant through the heater core and then back to the engine. In some applications, a heater control valve is located in one of the heater coolant hoses to adjust the quantity of coolant flowing through the heater core.

The coolant enters the heater core from the warm engine, and the air that is passed over the heater core from the passenger compartment cools the coolant in the heater core. The transfer of heat from the hot coolant to the air passing over the heater core is what causes the temperature to rise in the air duct. The air that has been heated by the heater core is warm but still moist because the heat from the heater core cannot condense the moisture out of the air. This condition of warm moist air does not have an adverse effect on the passengers in most cases.

Defroster

When the air conditioner is allowed to operate during the defrost cycle, the air is dried from the moisture removal occurring as air passes over the evaporator before passing over the heater core. The result of air passing over both cores is dry and heated air. The dry hot air from the defrost duct hits the windshield, and the moisture from the glass is quickly drawn into the air. The defrost time of passenger vehicles has decreased considerably because of the air conditioner being switched on during the defrost cycle.

Blower Motors

Blower motors are electric motors that determine the rate of air flow out of the vents. Attached to the spinning shaft of the motor is what is called the "squirrel cage," a plastic cage with fins to pull or push air **FIGURE 41-33**. The speed is controlled by the driver (except in electronically controlled systems) through the fan switch and a series of resistors to limit the fan speed. Blower motors can be positioned either before the evaporator and heater core or after in the HVAC system. When placed after, they pull the air through the evaporator and heater core in the box. Placing the blower before pushes air through the evaporator and heater core in the box.

Blower Motor Resistor Packs/Speed Controls

The resistor pack or resistor block is the most common blower motor control. It uses resistors in series to regulate the speed of the fan **FIGURE 41-34**. The more resistance there is in the circuit, the less current available to spin the fan. The lowest speed (speed 1) passes the current through several resistors. The highest speed uses no resistors so the motor has full current flow. The amount of resistors in a pack depends on the number of different speed settings.

FIGURE 41-32 The heating system.

FIGURE 41-33 Blower motor and squirrel cage fan.

FIGURE 41-34 Blower motor resistor and switch schematic.

FIGURE 41-35 Cabin filters. **A.** Clean. **B.** Dirty.

On vehicles with electronic air-conditioning systems or automatic systems where the customer just sets a desired temperature, the fan is controlled by a variable resistor called a rheostat that allows the computer to change fan speed infinitely by varying resistance such as a light dimmer in a house. Other systems use **pulse width modulation** to control fan speed. Normally this is done by controlling "on" time compared to "off" time on the ground side of the circuit. The longer the on time, the faster the fan will spin.

Cabin Air Filters

Many manufacturers have added cabin air filters to the inlet side of the heating/air-conditioning box where fresh air enters the cabin. This filter is designed to catch dust and outside contaminates so they do not get blown into the cabin. Many are paper just like the air filter for the engine and as such should be checked regularly and replaced when they begin to clog or they will cause the system to be inefficient due to poor airflow **FIGURE 41-35**. Some manufacturers are using activated charcoal cabin filters, which help trap odors and airborne pollutants such as carbon monoxide and oxides of nitrogen. Cabin air filters usually should be replaced once a year or between 12,000 and 15,000 miles.

▶ HVAC Developments

With the advent of electric and hybrid passenger cars, the HVAC system continues to evolve. The heater core in your car may soon be a thing of the past; reversing the refrigerant flow through the air-conditioning system would turn your evaporator core into a condenser and provide ample heat for the passenger compartment. This is the same principle that heat pumps operate on. They can reverse the flow of refrigerant, which turns them from a heater to an air conditioner.

Another development is electric compressors, which are already taking the place of less-efficient belt-driven compressors. The amount of energy loss from the drive belt and electric clutch is too high for hybrid and electric vehicles that need to conserve all the power possible. As passenger cars evolve, so must the air-conditioning system; greater efficiency and less power consumption will be the drivers of new air-conditioning systems.

Wrap-up

Ready for Review

▶ The heating, ventilation, and air conditioning (HVAC) system maintains a comfortable temperature inside a vehicle and uses an air filter to provide fresh, filtered air.

▶ The vehicle heating system and automotive air conditioning system were developed in the 1930s.

▶ The Environmental Protection Agency regulates automotive air conditioning via Section 609 of the Clean Air Act.

▶ Automotive HVAC technicians must obtain a license to verify that they are familiar with federal rules and regulations.

▶ HVAC systems use heat transfer to ensure temperature comfort inside a vehicle.

▶ Heat transfer can take place via conduction, convection, or radiation.

▶ A vehicle's air conditioner transforms the refrigerant from a liquid to a gas and back to liquid.

▶ Heat energy (the amount of heat needed to move a temperature up or down by degrees) is measured in British thermal units (BTUs).

▶ The temperature at which a liquid changes to gas is called latent heat of evaporation; likewise, the temperature at which a liquid forms a solid (ice) is called latent heat of freezing.

▶ Vehicle air conditioners use a refrigerant for the vaporization and condensation process.

▶ HVAC systems have four major components: evaporator, compressor, condenser, and the restriction.

▶ The compressor is designed to increase the pressure of the refrigerant (in gas form) and push it into the condenser.

▶ A vehicle's air conditioner is a closed loop system.

▶ The condenser is designed to move gas through a series of coils and cool it into a liquid.

▶ The restriction works to transform high pressure liquids into low pressure liquids.

▶ The evaporator vaporizes liquid into gas as it removes heat energy from the passenger compartment.

▶ Each HVAC system component requires the refrigerant to be delivered in the proper state and at the correct level.

▶ Components of a compressor include: pulley, clutch, axial plate, piston, reed valves, and body.

▶ One of the most common types of compressor is an axial piston compressor.

▶ Refrigerant moves through the air conditioning system because of the high pressure and volume of gas leaving the compressor.

▶ The condenser uses ram air flow and the engine cooling fan to cool the refrigerant.

▶ A restriction can be a fixed orifice tube or a thermostatic expansion valve.

▶ The velocity and pressure of the refrigerant changes when it moves through the restriction.

▶ Bernoulli's principle states that the speed/flow of a liquid changes in opposition to the liquid's pressure (when one increases, the other decreases).

▶ Pascal's law states that liquid cannot be compressed.

▶ The evaporator is a one-piece unit of copper or aluminum tubes, with no serviceable parts.

▶ Automotive air conditioners can be fixed orifice tube systems or thermal expansion valve (TXV) systems.

▶ Fixed orifice tube systems use an accumulator to prevent liquid from entering the compressor.

▶ TXV systems use a receiver filter dryer to draw in and store liquid refrigerant.

▶ Air doors are controlled by cables, vacuum servos, or electric servos.

▶ Vehicle heating systems rely on a hot engine coolant flowing through a heater core—a small radiator comprising tubes, fins, and tanks.

Key Terms

accumulator The air-conditioning component used on fixed orifice systems to protect the compressor by storing liquid refrigerant so it does not reach the compressor.

air-conditioning compressor clutch The device which connects and disconnects the drive pulley to the compressor shaft and operated by electro-magnetism.

atmospheric pressure The pressure of the air surrounding everything caused by gravity and the weight of air. The higher from sea level, the lower the atmospheric pressure.

axial piston compressor A design of compressor that uses an angled plate (swash plate) to create the piston movement.

barrier-type hose A rubber hose made with a nylon bladder inside to contain substances with small molecular structures, such as R-134a.

British thermal unit (Btu) A measure of heat energy. It takes 1 Btu to raise the temperature of 1 pound of water 1°F.

chlorofluorocarbon (CFC) A manufactured compound designed to be used as a refrigerant. It is now illegal due to the high chlorine content.

Clean Air Act (CAA) A policy signed into law in 1990 that sets standards for air pollution to eliminate ozone-depleting elements.

closed loop system A totally self-contained system with no materials entering or exiting.

clutch electrical winding An electromagnetic control device that creates a magnetic field that pulls in the clutch to make contact with the pulley.

compressor A belt- or electrically driven device designed to increase refrigerant pressure and cause refrigerant to travel through the air-conditioning system.

condensation The changing of a gas into a liquid through cooling.

condenser The air-conditioning component located in the front of the vehicle designed to allow high-pressure refrigerant to change states from gas to liquid.

conduction The process of transferring heat through matter by the movement of heat energy through solids from one particle to another.

convection The process of transferring heat by the circulatory movement that occurs in a gas or fluid as areas of differing temperatures exchange places due to variations in density and the action of gravity.

desiccant A drying agent used in air-conditioning systems to absorb moisture.

dichlorodifluoromethane (R-12) An inert, colorless gas that can be used as a refrigerant. It is stored in white containers.

discharge reed valve A flat, spring-loaded valve used as a check valve on the discharge side of a compressor.

double crimping Overcrimping or recrimping a fitting to keep it from leaking. It normally results in a bigger leak and is not recommended.

drive pulley The disc shaped device which is driven by the accessory drive belt and used to power the compressor.

electric servo An air-conditioning door actuator controlled by electricity.

Environmental Protection Agency (EPA) A government agency concerned with air quality and pollution issues related to the environment.

evaporator The air-conditioning component normally located in the passenger compartment designed to allow low-pressure refrigerant liquid to change states to a gas.

externally equalized valve A style of TXV where the external valve uses the sensing bulb on the outlet side to overcome spring pressure to open the valve.

filter media A screen designed to keep debris from the TXV that is normally located in the receiver dryer.

fin A small, flat piece of metal placed between the tubes to help with the transfer of heat from the coolant to the air, refrigerant to air, or air to refrigerant. The metal heats up due to contact with the hot pipes in the case of a radiator or heater core and from hot air in the case of an evaporator.

fixed orifice tube system A system with a fixed orifice tube that uses an accumulator between the evaporator and the compressor.

H block valve A style of TXV that has an outlet side like the external valve; however, both the inlet and the outlet pipe go through the block, so the sensing bulb is built into the block.

heat transfer The flow of heat from a hotter part to a cooler part; it can occur in solids, liquids, or gases.

heater core A heat-exchanging device that transfers heat converted by the fuel burning in the engine to the passenger compartment.

high-pressure switch A switch designed to open at a predetermined high pressure to protect the compressor; it is normally located on the high side line near the compressor.

hydrogenated nitrile butadiene rubber (H-NBR) A man-made rubber with the same characteristics as NBR but with better resistance to heat.

ingression The passing of foreign bodies, such as moist warm air, through the air-conditioning lines or fittings.

inlet reed valve A flat spring-loaded valve that allows gaseous refrigerant to enter the compressor.

internally equalized valve A style of TXV where the internally equalized valve uses pressure from the inlet pipe to overcome the pressure created from the outlet pipe heat. Lower heat on the outlet pipe creates lower pressure, and the pressure from the inlet pipe is able to overcome it and move the valve.

latent heat of condensation The amount of heat removal necessary to change the state from a gas to a liquid without changing the actual gauge temperature.

latent heat of evaporation The amount of heat required to change the state from a liquid to a gas without raising the actual gauge temperature.

latent heat of freezing The amount of heat removal required to change the state from a liquid to a solid without changing the actual gauge temperature.

low-pressure cycling switch A device installed on the low-pressure line or the accumulator to turn the air-conditioning clutch on and off at specified pressures.

low-pressure switch A device used in nonvariable air-conditioning compressors. It cycles the air-conditioning clutch in response to changes in low side pressure.

nitrile butadiene rubber (NBR) A man-made rubber that is more resistant to oils and acids than natural rubber; it is compatible with R-12.

O-ring A small donut shaped rubber ring used to seal connections between air-conditioning components.

parallel flow condenser A condenser with multiple parallel tubes flowing from one side tank to the other.

pulse width modulation A digital on/off electrical signal used as a variable control for devices such as solenoids.

radiation The transfer of heat through the emission of energy in the form of invisible waves.

ram airflow The flow of air created by a vehicle moving down the road.

receiver filter drier (RFD) The air-conditioning component used on TXV systems to filter and store liquid refrigerant to supply liquid refrigerant to the TXV. It is located between the condenser and the TXV.

refrigerant The name given to a chemical compound designed to meet the needs of the refrigeration system.

restriction A blockage that partially stops or slows the flow of a material such as refrigerant.

rotary vane compressor A compressor design that spins with vanes attached that extend to create the air-conditioning pressure required to run the system.

Sanden scroll-type compressor A compressor design that uses two spiral forms, one spinning and one stationary, to create the pressure needed to drive the air-conditioning system.

Sanden wobble plate compressor A compressor design that utilizes an offset shaft connected to the crankshaft to create the reciprocating motion of the pistons.

serpentine condenser A condenser with one tube snaking back and forth.

suction reed valve A flat, spring-loaded valve used as a check valve on the suction side of a compressor.

superheat spring A spring used as part of the control in the TXV to ensure refrigerant leaving the evaporator is boiled completely or superheated.

swash plate Another name for an axial plate.

tanks Metal or plastic pieces that line the pipes used to connect the tubes together to allow the coolant to continue to flow.

tetrafluoroethane (R-134a) An inert colorless gas that can be used as a refrigerant. It is stored in light blue containers.

thermal cycle switch A normally closed switch located in the fins of the evaporator that controls the air-conditioning compressor clutch. It is opened and closed by the temperature changes in the evaporator.

thermal expansion valve (TXV) system A system with a valve designed to sense evaporator outlet temperature and vary the inlet orifice size accordingly.

tubes Metal pipes running side to side or up and down that the coolant or refrigerant travels through.

vacuum servo An air-conditioning door actuator controlled by a vacuum.

vaporization The changing of a liquid to a gas through boiling.

XH-7 A form of desiccant used with pure R-134a.

XH-9 A form of desiccant used when the refrigerant may not be pure, such as with some imports.

ASE-Type Questions

1. Tech A says that one advantage of an air conditioner is that the system removes water from the air. Tech B says that air conditioners are needed to remove moisture from the inside of the windshield to meet the mandated defrost time. Who is correct?
   a. Tech A
   b. Tech B
   c. Both A and B
   d. Neither A nor B

2. Tech A says that the EPA regulates automotive air-conditioning systems. Tech B says that EPA tests air-conditioning systems every 5 years. Who is correct?
   a. Tech A
   b. Tech B
   c. Both A and B
   d. Neither A nor B

3. Tech A says that an accumulator creates the pressure needed for the air-conditioning system to operate. Tech B says that the high side refers to refrigerant entering the compressor. Who is correct?
   a. Tech A
   b. Tech B
   c. Both A and B
   d. Neither A nor B

4. Tech A says that heat is removed from the passenger compartment by the heater core. Tech B says that heat in the cab is removed through by the refrigerant and is released to the outside air at the condenser. Who is correct?
   a. Tech A
   b. Tech B
   c. Both A and B
   d. Neither A nor B

5. Tech A says that conduction is when heat transfers through solids. Tech B says that radiation is when heat travels through space. Who is correct?
   a. Tech A
   b. Tech B
   c. Both A and B
   d. Neither A nor B

6. Tech A says that the air-conditioning compressor creates high-pressure liquid. Tech B says that the metering device creates a physical change in refrigerant from a liquid to a gas. Who is correct?
   a. Tech A
   b. Tech B
   c. Both A and B
   d. Neither A nor B

7. Tech A says that when an air-conditioning system freezes up, the refrigerant freezes and stops the cooling process. Tech B says that when an air-conditioning unit freezes up, the evaporator coils are covered with frozen water molecules that stop airflow across the coils, thus preventing cooling. Who is correct?
   a. Tech A
   b. Tech B
   c. Both A and B
   d. Neither A nor B

8. Tech A says that the evaporator is on the high side of the system. Tech B says that the condenser transfers heat to the atmosphere. Who is correct?
   a. Tech A
   b. Tech B
   c. Both A and B
   d. Neither A nor B

9. Tech A says that R-134a replaced R-12 as an approved refrigerant. Tech B says that HFO-1234yf refrigerant is flammable. Who is correct?
   a. Tech A
   b. Tech B
   c. Both A and B
   d. Neither A nor B

10. Tech A says that the engine thermostat controls the available coolant temperature for the heater system. Tech B says that the heater core can have engine coolant or refrigerant flowing through it depending on whether heat or cool is commanded. Who is correct?
    a. Tech A
    b. Tech B
    c. Both A and B
    d. Neither A nor B

CHAPTER 42

NATEF Tasks

Heating and Air-Conditioning Systems and Service

NATEF Tasks, continued

- Inspect, test, and/or replace A/C compressor clutch components and/or assembly; check compressor clutch air gap and adjust as needed. — **AST** **MAST** 1466–1468

- Remove, inspect, and reinstall A/C compressor and mountings; determine required oil quantity. — **AST** **MAST** 1468–1470

- Remove and inspect A/C system mufflers, hoses, lines, fittings, O-rings, seals, and service valves; perform necessary action. — **AST** **MAST** 1470–1471

- Remove, inspect, and reinstall receiver/drier or accumulator/drier; determine required oil quantity. — **AST** **MAST** 1471–1473

- Remove, inspect, and install expansion valve or orifice (expansion) tube. — **AST** **MAST** 1474–1475

Operating Systems and Related Controls

- Identify the source of A/C system odors. — **MLR** **AST** **MAST** 1452

Refrigerant Recovery, Recycling, and Handling

- Perform correct use and maintenance of refrigerant handling equipment according to equipment manufacturer's standards. — **AST** **MAST** 1456, 1461, 1463–1464

- Identify and recover A/C system refrigerant. — **AST** **MAST** 1456–1457, 1461–1463

- Recycle, label, and store refrigerant. — **AST** **MAST** 1463–1464

- Evacuate and charge A/C system; add refrigerant oil as required. — **AST** **MAST** 1476–1480

Knowledge Objectives

After reading this chapter, you will be able to:
1. Describe the principles of the air-conditioning service process. (pp 1445–1446)
2. Discuss air conditioner capacity and why it is important to determine the proper charge. (pp 1447–1448)
3. Explain the process of performance testing the air-conditioning system. (pp 1449–1450)
4. Explain the purpose and methods of leak testing. (pp 1457–1461)

Skills Objectives

After reading this chapter, you will be able to:
1. Performance-test the air-conditioning system. (p 1450)
2. Inspect the evaporator housing water drain. (p 1451)
3. Eliminate air-conditioning system odors. (p 1452)
4. Identify refrigerant type. (pp 1456–1457)
5. Test for leaks using a sniffer device. (pp 1458–1459)
6. Perform a dye test to find a leak. (p 1459)
7. Perform nitrogen testing to find a leak. (pp 1460–1461)
8. Perform the reclaim process. (pp 1461–1463)
9. Recycle refrigerant. (pp 1463–1464)
10. Inspect the condition of removed refrigerant oil. (p 1464)
11. Determine the need for an additional air-conditioning system filter, and perform necessary action. (p 1465)
12. Inspect, test, and replace the compressor clutch. (pp 1466–1468)
13. Remove, inspect, and reinstall the compressor. (pp 1468–1470)
14. Remove and inspect air-conditioning mufflers, hoses, lines, and fittings. (pp 1470–1471)
15. Remove, inspect, and reinstall the condenser. (pp 1471–1472)
16. Remove, inspect, and install the receiver/drier or accumulator. (pp 1471–1473)
17. Remove, inspect, and install a thermal expansion valve. (pp 1472–1474)
18. Remove, inspect, and install an orifice tube. (pp 1474–1475)
19. Use a vacuum gauge to evacuate an air-conditioning system. (pp 1476–1477)
20. Use a micron gauge to evacuate an air-conditioning system. (pp 1476–1478)
21. Add oil to the air-conditioning system. (pp 1479–1480)
22. Charge an air-conditioning system. (p 1480)
23. Change the vacuum pump oil in an air-conditioning machine. (pp 1481–1482)

Introduction

Having an HVAC system that operates correctly is important to most people, especially in climates where there are temperature extremes, both hot and cold. For this reason, HVAC system diagnosis and repair can be very rewarding, both professionally and financially. Servicing HVAC systems starts with having a good understanding of the theory of operation and components of an HVAC system, which is laid out in the Principles of Heating and Air Conditioning Systems chapter. Once you understand those concepts, it is time to learn about the processes and tools used in the diagnosis and repair of the system. That is the purpose of this chapter. Pay close attention to the details; they will help you learn not only how to service the system, but also how to avoid problems that could damage the components.

The HVAC system is generally a very reliable system. When it does present a problem, it usually results in poor performance, and the customer concern is poor cooling or no cooling. When that is the case, the technician will usually start with a performance test, which tests the function of the system. By performing this test, the technician verifies that there is a problem and will likely understand what is wrong, and what the next steps need to be. As you learn about each of the testing and service procedures, keep in mind the basics you learned in the Principles of Heating and Air Conditioning Systems chapter and ask yourself how they apply to the task at hand. Doing so will help ensure that you properly perform the basic service and repair procedures necessary to maintain a properly functioning HVAC system.

The Air-Conditioning Service Process

The air-conditioning system is a complex system with many principles involved in making the unit function properly. Successful diagnosis and repair of the air-conditioning system requires a general step-by-step process. The following is an overview of that process on a typical vehicle brought in for an air-conditioning repair. Remember, technicians must be EPA 609 certified to handle refrigerants.

1. Carrying out a *performance test* of the air-conditioning system is the first step in the diagnostic process. **Performance testing** is the term used to describe the standard air-conditioning testing process. You need to look at all of the components and compare how the air-conditioning unit is functioning versus how it is designed to function. Typically, it consists of turning on the air conditioner to its maximum setting with the windows closed and raising the engine revolutions per minute (rpm) to 1200–2000. The vent temperature in the cabin is checked and compared to the temperature and humidity specifications on the manufacturer's temperature chart.

2. After the performance test is complete, the next step is *diagnosing any faults* that are causing the system to operate incorrectly. This could be as simple as a slipping belt, any of the components not working properly, or a leak in the system. The next step depends on the diagnosis.

▶ You are the Automotive Technician

A new customer stops by the shop with his 8-year-old vehicle and requests that the air-conditioning system be serviced. His concern is that it isn't performing the way it should and isn't cool enough. He says that the AC has worked well up until now and hasn't needed any work. He is wondering if it just needs some extra refrigerant?

You explain that if it is low on refrigerant, then topping it off would make it work better. But that will only last for a short amount of time, and then he will be back in this same situation. Also, it could end up damaging the system if the oil leaks out, or moisture gets in. You suggest that he allow you to diagnose the problem, which will tell him why it isn't working properly, and then he will have an opportunity to approve the repair costs. The standard diagnostic fee includes performance testing the vehicle, leak testing the system, up to two pounds of refrigerant, and diagnosis of any faults. He agrees to allow you to diagnose the vehicle.

1. What is involved in performance testing the AC system?
2. What are some possible causes of the AC system not providing enough cooling?
3. How would you determine whether the system is low on refrigerant?
4. How would you perform a leak check on a system that is empty due to a relatively large leak?

3. If the diagnosis determines that a component of the air-conditioning system is not working properly, then leak testing is not needed and you will go straight to reclaiming refrigerant. If the diagnosis is that the refrigerant is low, you will need to perform a leak test next. The electronic leak detector (sometimes called a sniffer) and dye leak tester need the air-conditioning system to be relatively full of refrigerant, while nitrogen testing requires an empty air-conditioning system. If nitrogen testing is the leak test method to be performed, proceed to the reclaim step.

4. *Leak testing* is the next step. If the system is charged, then electronic leak detectors or fluorescent dye testing are good methods. If the refrigerant has leaked out of the system, then nitrogen testing is a good method of leak testing. Use the three-step method listed later in this chapter to determine whether there is a leak, and take the appropriate action. Do not forget to vent the nitrogen to the atmosphere.

5. *Reclaiming* the air-conditioning system before any repair or nitrogen testing is required by the Environmental Protection Agency (EPA), section 609 of the Clean Air Act. Reclaiming involves first checking the system to see if there has been any sealant added to it. The second step is identifying the refrigerant and removing all of it using an approved machine, then measuring and recording the amount of refrigerant and oil that was removed from the system. If the oil removed is greater than 1 ounce (30 milliliters [mL]), then the air-conditioning system should be flushed and the base oil amount should be installed. Compare the amount of reclaimed refrigerant to the under-the-hood sticker and determine whether the air-conditioning system may have been under- or overcharged. If undercharged, suspect a leak and leak check with nitrogen.

6. *Repair* the air-conditioning problem. Now that the air-conditioning system has been diagnosed and tested, the system fault can be repaired. Take the appropriate action and precautions that the repair requires. At this point, the air-conditioning system can be flushed and the base oil installed if needed. If less than 1 ounce (30 mL) of base oil needs to be added to the system, this step will wait until after the evacuation is complete. Finish the repair and continue to the evacuation.

7. *Evacuation* of the air-conditioning system is the next step after all repairs are made. Evacuation is the process of creating a low pressure or vacuum in the air-conditioning system using a vacuum pump and gauges. Water boils and turns into a gas at normal ambient temperatures when placed in a vacuum, so this process can remove any moisture that entered the system. This process usually requires a strong vacuum for a minimum of 15 minutes for removal of all the moisture. Follow the proper procedure for the evacuation with a mechanical gauge or using a more accurate micron gauge. After the evacuation is complete, the oil for the air-conditioning system can be added. After the oil is added to the air-conditioning system, the vehicle is ready for the charging process.

8. *Charging* the air-conditioning system to the proper refrigerant level is an important process of the air-conditioning repair. When adding refrigerant to the system, be sure that you add the correct amount. After the refrigerant has been charged into the air-conditioning system, rotate the compressor shaft by hand to push out any liquid that may have entered the compressor during the charge process.

9. *Post-testing* of the air-conditioning system is recommended to catch any masked problems that did not appear when the original problem was diagnosed. It is a repeat of the performance test to ensure that all moisture is removed and a recheck of the pressure gauges to be sure the high- and low-side pressures are as specified. All readings should be checked against a diagnostic chart. If you used an electronic leak detector or dye leak testing method, it is a good idea to confirm that there are no leaks. If the vehicle passes the post-test and the air-conditioning system is in good functioning order, then you are ready to contact the customer.

Determining Refrigerant Type

The only way to determine the type of refrigerant in a system is with the aid of a refrigerant identifier **FIGURE 42-1**. This easy-to-use device connects to the low-side air-conditioning fitting and takes a reading of the refrigerant. It will give a readout such as 100% R-134a, or if the system is contaminated, you may see a reading such as 60% R-134a 40% R-12. As long as the refrigerant is pure, it can be recycled using a reclaiming machine and reused. If it is contaminated by the wrong refrigerant or the wrong oil, then it is considered a hazardous waste and must be put in a separate unit and disposed of according to state law. The air-conditioning sticker under the hood lists the type of refrigerant and how much should be in the system.

Acid Tests

The acid test is used to check refrigerant for acidic contaminants and water intrusion. This is a critical part of vehicle HVAC maintenance because acids are capable of destroying the metal lines and compressor; however, it is often overlooked in shops. There are many different makes of acid test kits available from many different companies, though all are composed of either a test strip dipped into the refrigerant **FIGURE 42-2** or a tube for collecting a sample and then adding a testing chemical. The refrigerant changes the strip color or turns color in the sample tube, which is then compared to a color chart supplied by the manufacturer to determine if any acid is present. Be sure to read the test manufacturer's instructions; some tests must be performed with the compressor off the vehicle while others require the refrigerant to be drained before testing. There are tests available that can be installed on the service port where it collects a small amount of the refrigerant.

FIGURE 42-1 Refrigerant identifier.

FIGURE 42-2 Typical acid test strip being used.

Air Conditioner Capacity

The proper <u>charge</u> (amount of refrigerant) of the air-conditioning system is important because if the amount of refrigerant is too low or too high, the resulting change in system operating pressure will change the boiling point of the refrigerant, making it unable to effectively remove heat in the evaporator. The air-conditioning system has safety features built into it. For example, the low-pressure safety switch turns the compressor off if the pressure drops too low due to a low charge of refrigerant, and the high-pressure safety switch turns the compressor off if the pressure gets too high due to an overcharge. Since the system pressures vary greatly during operation, the switches are designed to allow operation within a wide window. Thus, they should not be used as indicators of a proper charge.

The proper charge for the air conditioner can be found under the hood on the air-conditioning identification sticker **FIGURE 42-3**. The sticker should detail the oil capacity, charge amount, and type of refrigerant. The type of refrigerant must remain the same because cross-contamination will create a hazardous substance.

There are different ways to measure the refrigerant to be added. Some systems give you the charge amount in kilograms, pounds, pounds with ounces, and straight ounces. The machine that you use to charge the system will determine the type of measurement you will need or need to convert to. If the sticker is not under the hood of the vehicle, you will need to turn to service information or industry literature. Charging a vehicle without knowing the correct amount of refrigerant is playing a guessing game and is likely to lead to a poor-performing system and customer dissatisfaction.

FIGURE 42-3 An air-conditioning identification sticker.

State of Charge

<u>State of charge</u> in the air-conditioning system refers to the amount of refrigerant in the system compared to how much should be in the system. It is best tested by removing all the refrigerant from the air-conditioning system, comparing that amount to the manufacturer's specifications, then recharging the system with the proper amount of refrigerant, as specified by the service information. If the air conditioner cannot be discharged for any reason and the state of charge needs to be determined, then you need to start your diagnosis by performance testing the air-conditioning system on the vehicle (see the Diagnosis section). But the best way to make sure the air-conditioning system is properly charged is to remove all refrigerant from the system and reinstall the proper amount of refrigerant.

Undercharge

An undercharged air-conditioning system contains less refrigerant than the system calls for. For example, if the system is designed to hold 16 ounces of refrigerant but only 8 ounces are removed during the system evacuation, then the state of charge is half of what it should be. This air-conditioning system would be referred to as undercharged. Systems become undercharged for two primary reasons: (1) There is a leak in the system, or (2) someone working on the vehicle previously did not properly charge the system. Either way, you should plan on leak testing the system to verify that there is not a leak. The following two sections will discuss how each type of system responds to an undercharged condition.

Orifice Tube System

In a typical orifice tube system, an undercharge of refrigerant will cause a rapid cycle time (rapid turning on and off) of the air-conditioning clutch. The rapid cycle of the air-conditioning clutch is caused by the low-pressure cycle switch. This switch, located on the low-pressure line or in the accumulator housing, is designed to turn off at a predetermined pressure, such as 20 pounds per square inch (psi, or 138 kilopascals [kPa]). This prevents the air conditioner from running when there is not enough refrigerant with oil in it passing through the compressor to keep it lubricated, which can cause it to fail. In an undercharged system, it is most likely running fairly close to the predetermined turn-off pressure all the time. When the compressor turns on in this scenario, it draws refrigerant from the low side, creating lower pressure. As a result, the clutch will cycle frequently. The air from the ducts will feel warm to the hand instead of cold, and the air-conditioning gauge readings will be lower than normal.

Thermal Expansion Valve System

The thermal expansion valve (TXV) system is more sensitive to a low charge than the orifice tube system. This is because the TXV low-pressure safety switch is located on the high side of the system. In the TXV system, there is not a pressure switch located on the low side of the system. If the charge is below normal but not completely drained, the air-conditioning system can run below atmospheric pressure (vacuum) on the low side of the air-conditioning system because there is nothing to shut the compressor off. If the air-conditioning system is running below atmospheric pressure, any leak on the low side will allow air and moisture into the system. This may occur due to a blockage in the system or when the system is undercharged. If air and moisture contaminate the air-conditioning system, acid will be created in the oil, corroding the components from the inside out. The air duct will feel slightly cool and the air-conditioning gauges on both the high and the low side will read below normal.

Overcharge

<u>Overcharging</u> the air-conditioning system will affect the orifice tube and TXV systems in the same manner. Both the low- and the high-side gauges will be running higher than normal. The air in the ducts will feel slightly cool, and the **air-conditioning compressor clutch** will run for a few seconds, then turn off for a long period of time. This behavior is caused by the system pressure having to return to normal levels for the clutch to engage again.

Diagnosis

The most common air-conditioning complaint that brings vehicles into the shop is simply that the air conditioner is not performing. Usually the root cause is leaks in the system. Other issues that could cause the same complaint are compressor failure, debris causing system blockages on the high or low side, or system blockages caused by moisture freezing in the system. These problems occur far less often than leaks, but do happen. Normally, a check of the gauge pressures will indicate what is going on. When both gauges read low pressure, the system may be low on refrigerant. If the gauges read low pressure on the high side, high pressure on the low side, or about equal pressures, it usually means that the compressor is not working. If the low side reads as a vacuum, there is a blockage in the low side of the system that is not allowing refrigerant to pass. Extremely high-pressure readings on the high side indicate that there is a blockage on the high side or an airflow restriction across the condenser.

On occasion, the problem of not blowing cold air is not the air-conditioning system at all; rather, the blend door or heater control valve is not closing adequately to keep air or hot coolant from passing through the heater core. This can be identified by checking pressures and determining that the air-conditioning system is performing correctly and moving on to the next logical cause, a heater that is not turning off.

Another driver complaint is unusual smells when running the air conditioner. The air-conditioning box has a drain tube that allows removal of water collected from the moist air as it condenses on the cold evaporator and drips into the box. If the drain is not working correctly, has been knocked off, or is plugged, then the water will provide a breeding ground for bacteria and the smell will be distributed throughout the cabin. This problem is fixed by clearing the drain, spraying the system with a disinfectant and allowing it to sit, then running the system on high to blow everything out with all the doors open.

When diagnosing air-conditioning systems, you need to look at all of the factors involved. Always refer to service information, precautions, history, and service bulletins.

Applied Science

AS-26: Temperature: The technician can define heat and determine its affect in vehicle components by taking temperature readings.

Heat may be defined as a form of energy that flows between two pieces of matter due to a difference in their temperature. Essentially, it is the condition of something being hot. A complaint that sometimes occurs is that a car's air-conditioning system blows hot air from the vents instead of cooling.

A check of the vent temperature with a thermometer will quickly confirm the complaint. There are two potential scenarios here:

- If the vent temperature is not as cold as it should be, but is below ambient temperature, then you would need to proceed with diagnosis of the air conditioning system.
- If the vent temperature is above ambient temperature, then you should first suspect the heater system.

Automotive heater systems, on water-cooled vehicles, function by allowing hot engine coolant to flow through a heater core, placed in the ventilation air stream inside the cabin. A heater valve is fitted to control the flow of coolant through the heater core. The faults described above are most often caused by a faulty heater valve allowing coolant to flow through the heater core while the heater is turned off.

> ### TECHNICIAN TIP
>
> If the duct temperature is warmer than the ambient temperature, then the heater control valve is stuck on or the blend door is not positioned properly. Use hose pinch pliers to shut off the flow to the heater core and then retest the air-conditioning system.

Some of the variable factors in air conditioning are the weather, air moisture content, temperature, overall condition of the vehicle, and type of vehicle. Obviously the temperature is important, as the hotter or colder the outside air, the harder it is to heat or cool it. Moisture in the air, through either humidity or precipitation, can stick to the fins of the evaporator and freeze. Since the evaporator is used in air conditioning and defrost to dry the air, a frozen evaporator can affect both the heating and the cooling systems. If a vehicle is running badly, the air conditioning may be turned off to try to correct the issue by the power train control module (PCM). Slipping belts will cause the compressor to spin slowly or not at all. Any leaks in passenger doors or windows will cause outside air to enter, which will have to be conditioned. The size and color of the vehicle make a difference. Big vehicles have more space, and the materials in the vehicle hold heat or cold; therefore, it takes longer to condition the air. A black vehicle will absorb heat and can be very difficult to cool on a hot sunny day. A cloudy day will decrease the heat load on the vehicle, increasing the air-conditioning system's efficiency and possibly giving the impression that the system is cooling fine.

> ### TECHNICIAN TIP
>
> The one rule for diagnosis of an air-conditioning system is "when in doubt, suck it out." This means if you cannot find the problem while diagnosing, remove all refrigerant and start over from a base charge. Starting with a known base charge will remove any question if the refrigerant is too low or too high or if there is any moisture causing a problem in the system.

Performance Testing

The pretest and inspection of the air-conditioning system are the first step in the diagnostic process. *Performance testing* is the term used to describe the standard air-conditioning testing process. You need to look at all of the components and compare how the air-conditioning unit is functioning versus how it is designed to function. When testing the air-conditioning system, make sure to have all of the controls at the maximum settings. The heater fan needs to be on the highest speed. The heater control knob should be on the coldest setting. The airflow should be set to the dash vents. An external fan needs to be supplying air to the condenser to simulate driving conditions.

The engine's rpm should be at 1200, which is the ideal and average rpm for the majority of air-conditioning systems on vehicles. Before testing the air-conditioning system, let the system stabilize for a few minutes to allow the refrigerant to equalize and the temperatures to reach the proper level.

To performance test an air-conditioning system, follow the steps in **SKILL DRILL 42-1**:

1. Start the vehicle. Place a fan in front of the vehicle to simulate the airflow that occurs when driving. **(Photo 1)**

2. Close all windows and turn the air conditioner to its maximum setting. **(Photo 2)**

3. Raise the engine rpm to 1200–2000.

4. Check the vent temperature in the cabin using a thermometer. Compare the temperature recorded to the diagnostic chart in the manufacturer's service information. **(Photo 3)**

> ### TECHNICIAN TIP
>
> Performance testing of the air-conditioning system must be done before and after the repair. Doing so will help ensure that you identify any faults before starting the repairs, as well as verify that the faults are completely repaired.

Abnormal Noises

The compressor is the most common source of abnormal noises arising from the air conditioner. If the compressor fails internally, it may make a knocking noise. Restrictions are another cause of odd noises. Restrictions rattle the air-conditioning pipes, especially if the restriction comes and goes. While performance testing the system, abnormal noises can occur while the air-conditioning system is operating. Listen for noises that may occur when the compressor clutch is engaged. If the noise disappears when the compressor clutch disengages, then the noise is from the air-conditioning system. Be sure to listen for noises under the hood as well as in the vehicle's passenger compartment. Turn off and on the compressor clutch and move the controls on the dash, listening to determine whether the noises appear and disappear.

SKILL DRILL | 42-1 | Performance Testing an Air-Conditioning System

1. Turn on the vehicle. Place a fan in front of the vehicle to simulate the airflow that occurs when driving.

2. Close all windows. Turn the air conditioner to its maximum setting.

3. Raise the engine rpm to 1200–2000. Check the vent temperature in the cabin using a thermometer. Compare the temperature recorded to the diagnostic chart in the manufacturer's service manual.

Applied | Math

AM-33: Temperature: The technician can use standard and metric temperature measurement instruments to measure system temperature and determine conformance to metric specifications.

The most common air conditioning concern encountered in the workshop environment is the air-conditioning system failing to effectively cool the cabin of the vehicle. Technicians need to determine whether the system is operating effectively before proceeding with diagnosis. This is determined by measuring the vent temperature as the air enters the vehicle cabin.

This test involves a thermometer being inserted into the air vents and the temperature being measured with the air-conditioning controls being set to cold and the fan set to its highest speed (the remainder of this test procedure is outlined in the performance testing section of the text).

Once the vent temperature is measured, it must be compared to the manufacturer's specifications to determine if the system is operating effectively. If specifications are published in metric units, either a metric thermometer should be used or readings must be converted from Fahrenheit to Centigrade to determine if the measured temperature conforms to specifications.

TECHNICIAN TIP

As a general rule, the duct temperature should be no greater than 17°F above the evaporator temperature. The optimum vent temperature is from 38°F to 48°F. The air-conditioning clutch cycle should not allow the duct temperature to have greater than a 5° swing from high to low while staying within the range of 38°F to 48°F. If the swing is out of the 5° range, the thermal switch or the pressure cycle switch may need to be replaced, if equipped.

Inspecting the Condenser for Airflow Restrictions

The condenser is normally inspected when high-side pressures are too high and the system is not cooling well. Road debris, leaves, and animal fur and feathers are common culprits, but anything that sits in front of the condenser can cause this issue. This inspection should also be performed with any air-conditioning tune-up or inspection, such as those offered by many shops before summer. Use a flashlight on the back of the condenser. Look in from the outside of the vehicle for the light coming through the

TECHNICIAN TIP

There are factory adjustments on both the thermal cycle switch and the pressure cycle switch. The adjustments are for achieving optimum performance at the factory. Trying to adjust either of the switches because of an incorrect temperature swing may mask the faulty switch for a short time. If these switches are incorrectly functioning, replacement is the proper and recommended procedure for the repair.

condenser. Move the light across the entire condenser. If the light is not showing, the condenser needs to be cleaned.

When cleaning the condenser for debris, shop air or a water hose may be used to remove the debris, but be careful to not fold over the fins. If the shop air and a water hose do not remove the restriction, the condenser must be removed and professionally cleaned.

Inspecting the Evaporator Housing Water Drain

As the air-conditioning system is running, the evaporator will sweat water throughout the day. The water collected needs to be drained from the evaporator housing. A drain hose is connected to the evaporator housing and exits through the vehicle's firewall. Checking that the drain is not plugged is a common diagnostic procedure.

To inspect the evaporator housing water drain, follow the steps in **SKILL DRILL 42-2**:

1. Determine that the drain tube is clogged by allowing the air-conditioning system to run while observing the drain tube for water drops. In the case of a plugged drain, no water or very few drops are found.

2. Carefully use low-pressure shop air and an air nozzle to blow air into the drain tube. Note that water will come out of the drain tube when the clog is removed and will result in a large discharge of malodorous water; stand back.

3. When the water has completely drained, the task has been performed. Advise the customer to periodically check for a water puddle under the vehicle; if one is not present, the clog may have reoccurred, and removal of the air box may be necessary to open the air box and clean out any remaining debris.

Eliminating Air-Conditioning System Odors

Air-conditioning systems are prone to unpleasant odors. Since warm, moist air is passed through the cold evaporator, most of the moisture condenses on the surface of the evaporator and drips to the bottom of the air box. This moisture then sits in the air box and ducts where it is dark—an ideal place for mold and bacteria to grow. The mold and bacteria produce odors that are directed at the passengers when the fan is turned on. The ducts also provide an appealing space that mice and other small animals use for building their nests. The nests themselves can give off odors, and sometimes one or more rodents die, giving off a very foul odor.

Identifying and eliminating the cause of the odor usually makes customers very appreciative. If you find that an odor is stronger in one position than in the others, the smell is likely coming from that duct. If the odor is in all positions, the problem is likely in the heater/evaporator housing. Keep testing until you can pinpoint the source of the odor. Check for odors as you try each of the following: selecting "fresh" air and turning the fan on high, selecting the dash vent, selecting each vent setting, turning the heater on high, and turning the air conditioner on.

If the drain tube becomes clogged with leaves or debris over time, the water will not be able to drain; it will stagnate and begin growing bacteria, creating an unpleasant odor. The solution to this concern is to unclog the drain tube. If odors continue to be a problem and the drain tube is open, the use of an anti-odor kit may be necessary. These kits require gaining access to the evaporator, either by complete removal of the evaporator, removal of the fan, or removal of the resistor pack, or by drilling a small hole into the air box. When access is gained to the evaporator, a spray chemical cleaner is used on the evaporator fins and allowed to dry. A follow-up chemical coating is then applied, which keeps bacteria from growing on the fins of the evaporator. If a hole was drilled into the air box according to the directions of the kit, a repair kit is usually included to repair the hole. Sometimes this will be a very strong piece of adhesive tape or a plug that will attach to the hole. Drilling a hole into the air box is not the preferred method and can result in air leaks and noise. Follow the directions of the kit to ensure a quality repair.

To eliminate air-conditioning system odors in the case of a clogged drain, follow the steps in **SKILL DRILL 42-3**:

1. Verify that the drain is not plugged. Open all of the doors on the vehicle to allow it to air out a bit.
2. Turn the blower fan on medium speed.
3. Operate the system in all zones and see if the smell is stronger in one position than the others. If so, inspect that portion of the system. If the smell is

equally strong in all positions, inspect the heater/evaporator housing. If the odor is caused by mold or bacteria buildup, use an anti-odor kit to clean and kill any buildup.

Cabin Air Filter

Many vehicles now include a cabin air filter in the HVAC system to filter the air before it enters the system. The filter is housed in the air box and can be accessed from one of a variety of positions, depending on the vehicle. The access may be from under the hood near the firewall, under the windshield, or behind the glove box. It is usually fairly easy to remove and replace once you find the access cover. This filter should be inspected during every service and replaced according to the manufacturer's specified interval, typically once a year or every 12,000 to 15,000 miles (19,000 to 24,000 kilometers [km]). When inspecting the cabin air filter, use the same guidelines as for an engine air filter. Hold it up to a light and look at it to see if the light shines through or if it is blocked from being dirty. Also check it for any cracks, tears, or deformities that would cause it to be ineffective.

Air-Conditioning System Conditions

Within the air-conditioning system are protective devices designed to shut down air-conditioning operations to prevent further damage. These protection devices are generally thermal units, fuses, or circuit breakers. Generally, if one of these devices is triggered, the cause is overcurrent, meaning the current flow has become elevated. Too much current flow can melt wires and parts. Overcurrents result from shorts in the wires or electrical components, such as the air-conditioning clutch coil. A short to ground on any of these gives a direct path for electricity or current to flow past the device it is supposed to operate and instead pass to the ground side of the battery. Once an overcurrent is detected, repairs should be performed based on the specific cause of the overcurrent. Each part and vehicle will have its own special procedure.

Pressure switches, whether high or low, will have a cutoff pressure to protect the air-conditioning system. A high-pressure switch located on the high-side line may have a cutoff pressure of 400 psi (2758 kPa). At that pressure, the switch opens because the pressure is high enough to cause the **hoses** and **lines** to rupture. A low-pressure switch with a cutoff of 15 psi (103 kPa) will open because not enough refrigerant, which carries the lubricating oil, will be able to get to the compressor, and the internal moving parts may fail or overheat.

Computer-controlled air-conditioning systems have the same fail-safes as regular systems, but when the pressure switches sense a problem, they send that information to the PCM, which will determine if the system should be shut down until repaired. The PCM may also shut down the air conditioning if there is a charging problem or an overheating issue and the PCM determines that the extra load on the engine created by the air conditioning needs to be shut down until the other problem is resolved.

If an electrical issue occurs, the problem must be tracked using a digital volt-ohmmeter (DVOM), which is the electrical diagnostic tool used to check voltage, current flow, and resistance of circuits. Once located, the component will need to be replaced or the wire repaired and the fuse replaced.

Low pressure normally requires refilling the air-conditioning system and finding and repairing the leak. The other issues require diagnosing and repairing the issue that caused the computer to shut off the air conditioning, then clearing the codes in the PCM so it will reset and turn the air conditioning back on. These problems are found using a scan tool to pull the codes, then diagnosing the code using a diagnostic manual.

In each of these situations, the technician must refer to the vehicle's service information and follow the steps appropriate for the vehicle type and air-conditioning model.

▶ Maintenance and Repair

Tools

To maintain and repair air-conditioning systems, you will need the following tools:

- *Sealant detector*: Sealant detectors detect the presence of sealant in the air-conditioning system. Allowing sealant to be drawn into a refrigerant identifier or **air-conditioning machine** can ruin them **FIGURE 42-4A** .
- **Refrigerant identifiers**: Refrigerant identifiers hook to the low-side fitting of the air-conditioning system to determine whether the refrigerant is pure or whether it is contaminated with another refrigerant or air. Identifying refrigerant can save the costly procedure of flushing out your reclaim/recycle machine and save you from having to dispose of contaminated refrigerant **FIGURE 42-4B** .
- **Reclaim/recycle machine**: If the air-conditioning machine is used for any air-conditioning work on a customer's vehicle, it is required to meet the EPA requirements. This machine hooks up to the air-conditioning service ports on the vehicle and can check pressures, but also has a storage tank to hold refrigerant **FIGURE 42-4C** . It also has a vacuum pump to evacuate air-conditioning systems. Refrigerant must be recovered or sucked

into the machine before repairs are done to the air-conditioning system. Once the repairs are done, the air-conditioning system must be evacuated or vacuumed out to create a low pressure to remove moisture. Once this is done, the machine normally can refill the vehicle's air-conditioning system either from the recycled tank, which contains refrigerant removed from vehicles, sent through a filter, then stored in the tank, or from the virgin tank, which contains new refrigerant. Most shops will draw from the recycle tank until it is too low to charge a vehicle, and then use the virgin tank.

FIGURE 42-4 **A.** Sealant detector. **B.** Refrigerant identifiers. **C.** Reclaim/recycle machine.

■ **Pressure gauge set**: A reliable pressure gauge set is one of the most important air-conditioning tools to obtain. Pressure gauge sets come in both mechanical and digital styles and are used to diagnose and service air-conditioning systems. Both types of gauge sets have a low-side and a high-side pressure gauge connected to a common manifold that can be used for manual servicing of the air-conditioning system. The hoses connect to each gauge and are connected to the manifold by valves and passageways in the manifold **FIGURE 42-5**. The two knobs on the front of the manifold connect the high and low hoses to the service port on the manifold. When using the gauge set, make sure both service knobs are in the closed position before connecting them to a system. The hoses on the gauge set are connected to the gauge directly; opening the service valves only connects the passageways from the hoses to the service port. On a digital gauge set, you will need to calibrate each gauge to zero so the pressures will read accurately. Follow the instructions in the operator's manual for the procedure on calibrating the gauge to zero.

Both the high-pressure and the low-pressure gauges need to be non-liquid filled if they are mechanical gauges. Oil-filled gauges do not allow the needle to move fast enough for you to see **pressure transients**, which are fluctuations observed as the gauges bounce between pressures rather than holding at one position or moving smoothly up and down the gauge. Being able to see the needle oscillations will provide valuable information when performing certain diagnostic scenarios. For example, a compressor with one bad piston will cause the high-side pressure to bounce when that piston is trying to push

refrigerant. Another example is when water is in the system and freezes a line. When it starts to thaw, the affected side's gauge will bounce as the pressure changes from the temporary blockage. Gauge sets are also built into most R/R/R machines (Recover, Recycle, evacuate, leak test, and Recharge).

■ **Anemometer**: The air coming out of the vent needs to have enough flow to keep fresh air passing over the evaporator. Without air, the refrigerant will not boil. For the air-conditioning system to function properly, the velocity needs to be at a minimum of 800 feet per minute (fpm). The most accurate way to test the velocity is to use an anemometer **FIGURE 42-6A**. Anemometers measure the velocity of the air in fpm.
■ **Retrofit kit**: This aftermarket kit has the fittings and oil to change an R-12 unit over to R-134a **FIGURE 42-6B**.
■ **PT chart**: A PT chart, which stands for pressure-temperature chart, is used to determine what the high- and low-side pressures should be at a given outside temperature and humidity in a properly functioning system **FIGURE 42-6C**.
■ **Vacuum pump**: Vacuum pumps are rated in the total volume of air that can be removed every minute. They are used to create low pressure or vacuum in the system. The volume is measured in cubic feet per minute (CFM). The most common pumps are the 5-CFM and 6-CFM models, although some new air-conditioning machines have a 7-CFM pump.
■ *Electronic leak detector*: Sometimes called a "sniffer," this device is used to locate small refrigerant leaks by electronically reacting to refrigerant gas **FIGURE 42-6D**.
■ *Dye leak detector*: This solution is used to detect refrigeration leaks **FIGURE 42-6E**.
■ **Oiler**: This device is used to add oil to the air-conditioning system.
■ **Vacuum gauge**: This gauge is designed to read negative pressure or vacuum **FIGURE 42-6F**.
■ **Micron gauge**: This electronic device is designed to measure vacuum precisely **FIGURE 42-6G**.
■ *Line wrenches*: Line wrenches are box-end wrenches or wrenches designed to go all the way around the

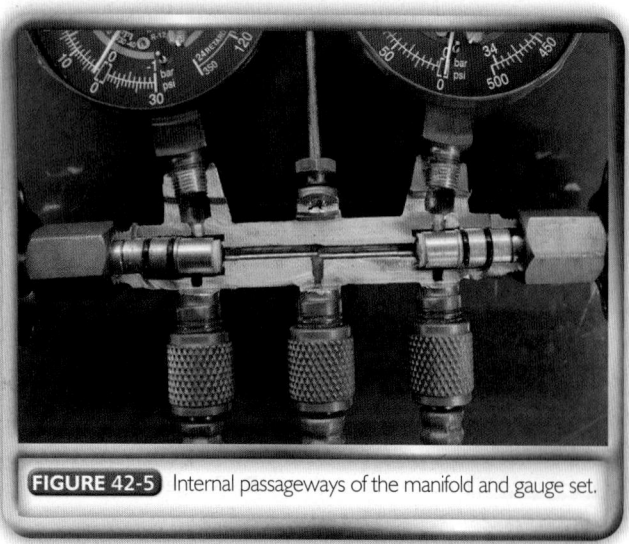

FIGURE 42-5 Internal passageways of the manifold and gauge set.

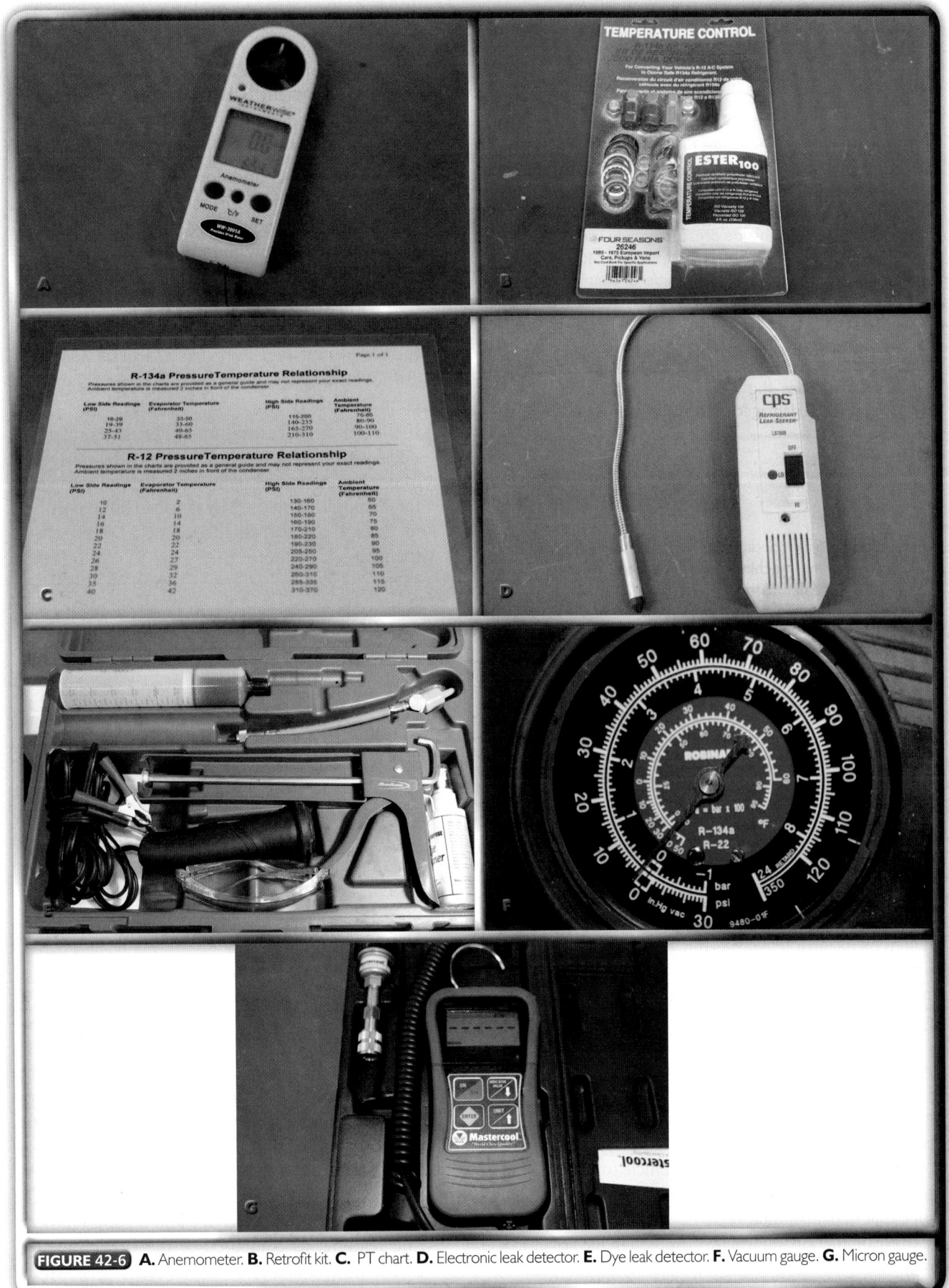

FIGURE 42-6 **A.** Anemometer. **B.** Retrofit kit. **C.** PT chart. **D.** Electronic leak detector. **E.** Dye leak detector. **F.** Vacuum gauge. **G.** Micron gauge.

The low-pressure gauge is unique in that it displays both pressure and vacuum. It has a maximum pressure of about 120 psi (827 kPa) and a low pressure of 30" Hg (vacuum measured in inches of mercury, or 102 kPa). The low-pressure gauge needs to display vacuum readings for diagnostic purposes and to ensure that the proper vacuum levels are achieved when evacuating the system. The high-side pressure gauge usually has a maximum pressure of about 500 psi (3447 kPa). Most systems will run with the high-side pressure around 120 psi (827 kPa); but if the condenser fan is not functioning, the pressure could rise as high as 400 psi (2758 kPa). This is why you need such a large pressure range on the high-side gauge. Otherwise, if the system pressure exceeds the maximum gauge reading, the gauge could be damaged, or it could even explode.

Modifying the air-conditioning machine or repairing the air-conditioning machine should be performed by an authorized dealer to maintain its certification, not by the air-conditioning technician.

nut or bolt with a slot cut out of the box part to allow the technician to slide the wrench over the tube or hose.

Identifying the Refrigerant Type

Refrigerant should be tested to determine its type any time the refrigerant will be recovered. If the refrigerant in the vehicle is contaminated and put in the recovery bottle of the air-conditioning machine, the whole bottle in the machine is contaminated and should be treated as hazardous waste. If it is not caught while in the machine, it will contaminate every vehicle that has air-conditioning refrigerant installed from that machine's recovery bottle.

Another condition that needs to be identified is whether sealer has been added to the vehicle's air-conditioning system. Many small cans of refrigerant come with sealant inside. Sealer can ruin refrigerant identifiers and air-conditioning machines. While not a lot of vehicles have sealer in them, all it takes is one vehicle to contaminate and damage your air-conditioning equipment. Most experts agree that sealant should *never* be used. If there is a leak, fix the leak! Identifying whether the system has sealer in it should be the first step in the refrigerant-identifying process.

To identify the refrigerant type, follow the steps in **SKILL DRILL 42-4**:

1. Use a sealant identifier to check whether there is any sealant in the system. If there is, notify your supervisor.
2. Turn on the refrigerant identifier and allow the machine to warm up. (**Photo 1**)
3. Locate the high- and low-side pressure service ports. Connect the refrigerant identifier to the low side of the air-conditioning system and open the service valve. Follow the prompts on the refrigerant identifier, and record the refrigerant type and amount of air, if any. (**Photo 2**)
4. Ensure that the under-the-hood sticker matches the refrigerant types on the refrigerant identifier. Turn off the service valve and disconnect the refrigerant identifier.
5. If the refrigerant does not match the under-the-hood sticker, reclaim the contaminated refrigerant into a contaminated tank and label the refrigerant for disposal. If the refrigerant is 100% pure and matches the under-the-hood sticker, continue to the next step. (**Photo 3**)
6. Select the proper pressure gauge set for the refrigerant type in the vehicle. After selecting the pressure gauge set, make sure the service valves on the gauges are in the off or shut position. (**Photo 4**)
7. Connect the service chuck of the pressure gauge to the air-conditioning system.
8. Open the valves and watch the high- and low-pressure gauges. Record the pressure. If the high- and low-side gauges are the same pressure and you could not identify the refrigerant, then use the PT chart to determine whether there are noncondensable gases (air) in the air-conditioning system. (**Photo 5**)
9. Measure the ambient temperature 6" to 8" [15 to 20 cm] in front of the condenser) and the pressure on the pressure gauge set.
10. Compare the pressure to the PT chart for that type of refrigerant. If the pressure on the gauge is higher than the PT chart, the air-conditioning system has noncondensable gases. If the pressure on the gauge is lower than the PT chart, the air-conditioning system is low on refrigerant and a leak should be suspected. If the reading matches another refrigerant on the chart, then the refrigerant needs to be identified before recycling. A good reading (one in the normal ranges) on the gauge and a good temperature reading, as compared to the PT chart, indicate that there are no noncondensable gases in the

SKILL DRILL 42-4 Identifying the Refrigerant Type

1 Turn on the refrigerant identifier and allow the machine to warm up.

2 Connect the refrigerant identifier to the low side of the air-conditioning system and open the service valve. Follow the prompts on the refrigerant identifier, and record the refrigerant type and amount of air, if any.

3 Turn off the valve and disconnect the refrigerant identifier. If the refrigerant does not match the under-the-hood sticker, reclaim the contaminated refrigerant into a contaminated tank and label the refrigerant for disposal. If the refrigerant is 100% pure and matches the under-the-hood sticker, continue to the next step.

4 After selecting the pressure gauge set, make sure the service valves on the gauges are in the off or shut position.

5 Connect the service chuck of the pressure gauge to the air-conditioning system. Open the valves, watch the high- and low-pressure gauges, and record the pressure. If the high- and low-side gauges are the same pressure and you could not identify the refrigerant, use the PT chart to determine whether there are noncondensable gases in the air-conditioning system.

6 Measure the ambient temperature (6" to 8" [15 to 20 cm] in front of the condenser) and the pressure on the pressure gauge set. Compare the pressure to the PT chart for that type of refrigerant.

system. The air-conditioning system could still be below the charge amount recommended, but it is not completely out of refrigerant. (Photo 6)

Leak Testing

The air-conditioning system is a sealed system that must not leak; however, leaks do occur and are a common reason that the air-conditioning system is not working properly. Leak testing should be performed on every air-conditioning system that is low on refrigerant or has just been repaired. Leak testing can be done by several methods: sniffer testing, dye testing, and nitrogen testing.

The sniffer and dye leak tests require that the air-conditioning system be full of refrigerant, while nitrogen testing requires an empty air-conditioning system. If a nitrogen test is the method being used, first reclaim the air-conditioning system.

Electronic Sniffer Testing

Types of **electronic sniffers** include **ultrasonic**, **heated diode**, and **corona-suppression**. Ultrasonic sniffers are supersensitive microphones that can pick up the hiss of a leak that is too small to be heard by human ears. Heated diode sniffers use electricity to determine if there is a leak. R-134a passing by the diode is broken down, thereby creating an electrical current charge; the internal mechanics of the diode use this charge to determine how much refrigerant has passed. The diode beeps or chirps at increasing rates as the rate of refrigerant increases. The heated diodes are considered the best sniffers for R-134a. Corona-suppression sniffers function in much the same way as the heated diode, except that any particle passing through the device, including dust, will set it off. With corona-suppression, refrigerant gas is used as an insulator to slow current between electrodes. Each of these electronic sniffers requires that the air-conditioning system have a charge of refrigerant for the leak detector to detect a leak.

The sniffer needs to be moved slowly and evenly around the components and lines. You determine where the leak is by watching the sniffer lights and listening to the sniffer sounds. Starting with the sensitivity on a high setting and turning down the sensitivity as the alarms and lights get louder and brighter will help you pinpoint the problem. Moving with a steady hand and taking your time is critical to using this device.

When using the sniffer, be sure there is no wind or draft on the vehicle. A draft or air movement over the vehicle could cause the refrigerant to not enter the sniffer or could mask the noise of the leak, preventing the sniffer from hearing the leak.

To test for leaks using a sniffer device, follow the steps in **SKILL DRILL 42-5**:

1. Make sure the air-conditioning system has refrigerant by installing a pressure gauge set and checking the readings against the PT chart.

2. Select a fairly sensitive setting for the sniffer. Slowly move the wand around and under all of the air-conditioning lines and components. If a leak is detected, turn the sensitivity down and pinpoint the exact location of the leak. Once the leak is located, move the wand tip from the leak to outside the vehicle. This allows the sniffer to "breathe" clean air, cleaning out its sensors and stopping the alarm. (**Photo 1**)

3. Reclaim the refrigerant and repair the leak. (**Photo 2**)

4. Always recheck for a leak after the system is properly recharged. (**Photo 3**)

SKILL DRILL | **42-5** | **Testing for Leaks Using a Sniffer**

1. Make sure the air-conditioning system has refrigerant. Slowly move the wand of the leak detector around and under all the air conditioning lines and components. If a leak is detected, turn the sensitivity down to pinpoint the exact location of the leak.

2. Reclaim the refrigerant and repair the leak.

3. Always recheck for a leak after the system has been properly recharged.

Dye Testing

Using ultraviolet (UV) light and refrigerant dye is a common way to test for leaks in an air-conditioning system. Some vehicle manufacturers add dye during the manufacturing process. When using dye for the first time on an air-conditioning system, the dye needs to be injected as a concentrate into the system. Most machines have a special port for injecting the dye. Injecting concentrated dye into the low side of the air-conditioning system should be done with the vehicle off. When installing dye for the first time, the air-conditioning system needs to be operated so that the dye is distributed throughout all parts of the air-conditioning system.

If the vehicle already has dye installed, or after the vehicle has been test-driven after a new dye injection, locating the leak requires using a UV light. When using a UV light, make sure all safety precautions are followed, including wearing UV safety glasses. Finding leaks with a UV light is easier in the dark; installing a cover over the hood of a vehicle will help you to find the leak.

To perform a dye test to find a leak, follow the steps in **SKILL DRILL 42-6**:

1 Check system pressure to be sure there is enough refrigerant to turn on the compressor. Turn on the compressor. If the compressor does not come on, add refrigerant in small increments until the compressor runs. **(Photo 1)**

2 Add the dye through the low-pressure port using a dye injection system. Run the air-conditioning system to circulate the dye. The system may have to run for several minutes or even several days, depending on the size of the leak. If the leak cannot be located, allow the customer to drive the vehicle for a few days to a week and return the vehicle for inspection. **(Photo 2)**

3 Using a black light, follow the lines, hoses, components, and compressor seal, looking for the orange or green glow of the dye, which indicates a leak. If a leak is not found in the lines or hoses, it may be in the evaporator; the blower motor resistor may need to be removed to see into the air-conditioning box.

4 Recover the refrigerant in the system, repair the leak, evacuate and recharge the refrigerant, and recheck for leaks. **(Photo 3)**

Nitrogen Testing

Nitrogen testing has been used in the home and transport refrigeration repair industry for a long time, but it is not

SKILL DRILL | 42-6 | Testing for Leaks Using Dye

1 Turn on the compressor. If the compressor does not come on, add refrigerant in small increments until the compressor runs.

2 Add the dye through the low-pressure port using a dye injection system. Run the air-conditioning system to circulate the dye. The system may have to run for several minutes or even several days, depending on the size of the leak.

3 Using a black light, follow the lines, hoses, and components, looking for the orange or green glow of the dye, which indicates a leak. If a leak is not found in the lines or hoses, the blower motor resistor may need to be removed to see into the air-conditioning box. Repair the leak.

as common in the automotive industry. It works great for testing discharged systems or for prechecking for a leak after repairs have been made and before recharging the system. Nitrogen testing requires a nitrogen tank, pressure regulator, adapters, and a **microleak detector** solution like Refrigeration Technology's BIG BLU. Soapy water is not recommended due to corrosive properties and the inability to show microleaks. This is why a microleak detector solution is recommended. The nitrogen is used to simulate working conditions of the air-conditioning system and will provide enough force to make high-pressure leaks leak.

To perform nitrogen testing to find a leak, follow the steps in **SKILL DRILL 42-7**:

1. The air-conditioning system needs to be reclaimed of all refrigerant. See Skill Drill 42-8 to perform this skill.

2. Attach the nitrogen hose of the nitrogen bottle to the low- or high-side service port on the vehicle. Once the quick coupler on the nitrogen hose has been connected and the Schrader valve depressed, start the nitrogen leak test procedure.

3. Turn the regulator on the nitrogen tank to 100 psi (689 kPa). As the pressure in the system rises, look and listen for any leaks. If a leak is located, stop the process and repair the problem.

4. Turn the regulator on the nitrogen tank to 200 psi (1379 kPa). When 200 psi is reached, look for bulging hoses and listen for noises.

5. Turn the regulator on the nitrogen tank to 300 psi (2068 kPa). Once 300 psi is reached, let the system maintain that pressure for 1 minute. Do not exceed 350 psi (2413 kPa); doing so could cause the high-pressure relief valve to vent.

6. After 1 minute, start to spray the leak solution on all of the fittings, hoses, and air-conditioning system components. After spraying the leak solution on the air-conditioning system, it may take upwards of 20 minutes for a leak to present itself.

7. After the nitrogen test is finished, release the nitrogen to the atmosphere. Repair the leak.

Safety

When nitrogen testing, safety glasses, gloves, and a face shield are required. Weak components or hoses may burst under nitrogen testing conditions.

Safety

Dry nitrogen is the only gas to be used in the air-conditioning system for leak detecting and removing traces of flushing chemicals from the system. Using any other propellant may cause harm and damage. Dry nitrogen is an inert gas and will not explode or ignite like other gases such as compressed air and oxygen.

Reclaiming and Recovering the Air-Conditioning System

Any time the air-conditioning system needs to be opened up, the refrigerant must be removed so that refrigerant will not be released into the atmosphere. Removing refrigerant is called **reclaiming** or **recovering**. The reclaiming process uses the air-conditioning machine to remove refrigerant from the system. It is also a good method of measuring the existing refrigerant charge in a vehicle, which will verify whether the system was undercharged, overcharged, or properly charged. The air-conditioning machine can measure the amount of refrigerant recovered from the vehicle. Comparing the amount removed to the specified capacity will allow you to determine the charge status. Another reason to recover refrigerant from a vehicle is to remove any noncondensable gases that are mixed in with the refrigerant.

Applied   Science

AS-20: Liquids/Solids: The technician can measure the volume of a liquid in a system and compare it to the manufacturer's specifications.

Repairing refrigerant leaks in air-conditioning systems is a common workshop activity. Apart from repairing the cause of the leak, it is also important to know that air-conditioning compressors require internal lubrication, thus it is important to ensure that systems are refilled with the correct volume of oil when completing leak repairs.

When working on leak repairs, refrigerant recovery is a necessary step before disconnecting any part of the system. During recovery, any oil removed from the system in held in a graduated container by the recovery machine to enable the volume of oil removed from the system to be measured. Oil removed from the system must be replaced with the same amount of new oil (if one ounce or less) to ensure adequate compressor lubrication. If the oil removed from the system is found to be contaminated, the system will need to be fully flushed and refilled with the amount of oil specified by the manufacturer.

TECHNICIAN TIP

The amount of refrigerant removed will give insight into the condition of the vehicle's air-conditioning system. Compare the weight removed to the under-the-hood sticker amount. If the amount recovered is less than the sticker indicates, there is likely a leak in the system. If there is more than the sticker indicates, then someone else has likely worked on the system, so you will want to give it a good inspection. If it had the correct amount of refrigerant, then the system most likely has no leaks.

To perform the reclaim process, follow the steps in SKILL DRILL 42-8:

1 Identify the refrigerant using the refrigerant identifier, and verify that there is no sealer in the system.

2 Start the reclaim process by hooking up the air-conditioning machine to the low- and high-side service ports. **(Photo 1)**

3 Open the valves and turn on the air-conditioning machine. Select the reclaim mode and follow the prompts on the screen. **(Photo 2)**

4 When the refrigerant has been removed, record the amount of refrigerant removed and compare it to the sticker on the vehicle. **(Photo 3)**

5 The air-conditioning machine will drain any excess oil that might have been reclaimed. The refrigerant oil that is drained should be minimal or nonexistent. Record the amount of oil that is discharged, and install the same amount if the total oil removed is less than 1 ounce (30 mL). If the oil drain discharges more than 1 ounce, the air-conditioning system will need to be flushed using a flush machine, removing all of the oil from the system.

6 After the old oil is flushed, reinstall the proper amount of new oil to the system. **(Photo 4)**

Recycling, Labeling, and Storing Refrigerant

In certain situations, the air-conditioning machine may become full of refrigerant. This will prevent you from recovering any more air-conditioning systems. Removing the refrigerant and storing the refrigerant in an approved container will allow the air-conditioning machine to continue to be used. The refrigerant tank cannot be the virgin disposable tank that the new refrigerant came in. The new virgin refrigerant tanks are a one-use-only tank and have a one-way check valve in the valve stem to prevent refilling of the tank.

SKILL DRILL | 42-8 | Reclaiming and Recovering the Air-Conditioning System

1 Identify the refrigerant using the refrigerant identifier, and verify that there is no sealer in the system. Start the reclaim process by hooking up the air-conditioning machine to the low- and high-side service ports.

2 Open the valves and turn on the air-conditioning machine. Select the reclaim mode and follow the prompts on the screen.

3 When the refrigerant has been removed, record the amount and compare it to the sticker on the vehicle.

SKILL DRILL | 42-8 | Reclaiming and Recovering the Air-Conditioning System, continued

4. The refrigerant oil that was drained should be minimal or nonexistent. Record the amount of oil that is discharged. Install the same amount if the total oil removed is less than 1 ounce (30 mL). If the oil drain discharges more than 1 ounce, flush the air-conditioning system using a flush machine, removing all of the oil from the system. After the old oil is flushed, reinstall the proper amount of new oil to the system.

To recycle refrigerant, follow the steps in **SKILL DRILL 42-9**:

1. Obtain a DOT-approved refrigerant container. There are several sizes, from 15-lb to 500-lb (7- to 227-kg) tanks. The recommended size for most repair shops is a 60-lb (27-kg) container.

2. Connect the air-conditioning machine's hoses to the tank with the appropriate adapters in an air-conditioning retrofit kit. Use the high- or low-side adapters from the retrofit kit to connect the quick chuck fittings to the 1/4" SAE fittings on the tank.

3. Open the tank valves. Open the quick chuck Schrader depressors on the quick chucks. At this point, you are ready to charge the tank just as you would charge a vehicle.

4. Use the keypad on the air-conditioning machine and select the "charge" mode. Determine the amount of refrigerant you want to transfer, and enter that weight into the display.

5. Begin to charge the refrigerant tank. Do not fill the tank to more than 60% of the total gross capacity of the tank. The total gross capacity is written on the tank, and the technician must mathematically determine what 60% of it is.

6. After the tank is filled with refrigerant, label the tank with the type and the weight of refrigerant. By labeling the tank with the type and weight, the next technician can determine the type and whether there is enough free space to charge any more refrigerant into the tank.

7. Close the tank valves and disconnect the hoses from the tank.

8. Store the refrigerant in a cool, dry place where the sunlight cannot directly hit the tank.

> ### TECHNICIAN TIP
>
> Recycling refrigerant is one of the processes the air-conditioning machine can perform. After reclaiming the refrigerant, most air-conditioning machines automatically recycle the refrigerant. The filter system in the machine will return the refrigerant to a level of purity accepted by the EPA.

Inspecting the Condition of Removed Refrigerant Oil

After the reclaim process, the air-conditioning machine will deposit any oil removed during the reclaim into a graduated container on the machine. By measuring the amount of oil removed, the technician will know exactly how much oil needs to be put back into the system. Only new oil should be installed.

To inspect the condition of removed refrigerant oil, follow the steps in **SKILL DRILL 42-10**:

1. Look at the old oil and check its condition. If the oil is black or acid test strips indicate the presence of contaminants, the air-conditioning system needs to be flushed of all the contaminated oil. **(Photo 1)**

2. Check the under-the-hood sticker for the proper system oil and the amount. Flush the air-conditioning system if necessary. **(Photo 2)**

Now that the air-conditioning system has been diagnosed and tested, the system fault can be repaired. Take the appropriate action and precautions that the repair requires. At this point, the air-conditioning system can be flushed and the base oil installed if needed. If less than 1 ounce (30 mL) of base oil needs to be added to the system, this step will wait until after the evacuation is complete. Finish the repair and continue to the evacuation.

Air-Conditioning System Flush

The air-conditioning system should be flushed if the compressor comes apart or if the desiccant bag breaks open. In both of these situations, the loose parts or desiccant pellets will start to move through the system, causing blockages. Another reason to flush the air-conditioning system is contaminated oil. A special flush machine is used to flush the air-conditioning system. However, not all of the components are designed to be flushed, such as the compressor, orifice tube or TXV, accumulator, and receiver filter drier. Be sure to check the manufacturer's service information to verify which components can safely be flushed. After the system has been reclaimed, remove the hoses from the air-conditioning machine and hook up the flush machine. Several different types of machines are available, but normally a cleaning agent is poured into the machine, then an air hose is plugged into the machine. A valve on the machine releases the cleaning agent through

SKILL DRILL | **42-10** | **Inspecting the Condition of Removed Refrigerant Oil**

1. Look at the old oil and check its condition. If the oil is black or acid test strips indicate the presence of contaminants, the air-conditioning system needs to be flushed of all the contaminated oil.

2. Check the under-the-hood sticker for the proper system oil and the amount. Flush the air-conditioning system if necessary.

AIR CONDITIONER

PRODUCT OF MITSUBISHI HEAVY INDUSTRIES, LTD

SAE-J639
CHARGE HFC-134a 21.5oz (0.61kg)
LUBRICANT SUN PAG 56
CAUTION: SYSTEM TO BE SERVICED BY QUALIFIED PERSONNEL

the system, pushed by the shop's air pressure. Another valve is used to push air through the system to remove the cleaning agent. Some shops prefer to use nitrogen to blow any residual cleaning agent from the system, as it contains no moisture, unlike air. The system is now ready to have oil added and the system recharged. Follow the instructions provided with the flushing machine carefully.

Additional Air-Conditioning Filters

While thoroughly flushing a system usually removes all debris and contaminants, it is possible that small particles can be wedged or trapped in place. Installing an additional filter provides an extra level of protection for the compressor and expansion valve or orifice tube. Additional filters are designed to catch a small amount of debris that may still be in the system, not to substitute for an adequate flush. Additional filters are generally placed in the liquid line after the condenser, but before the restriction. Any straight section of tubing between these two points can be used. The proper amount of tubing is cut out of the system so that the filter can be installed in the line. Always follow the filter manufacturer's directions when cutting the air-conditioning lines and installing the filter.

To determine the need for an additional air-conditioning system filter and to perform the necessary actions, follow the steps in **SKILL DRILL 42-11**:

1. If the air-conditioning compressor failed or if there is other debris in the system, an additional air-conditioning filter is recommended. Obtain the correct filter for the application you are repairing and locate the best position to install the additional filter.
2. Cut the lines using a tubing cutter and carefully deburr the ends of the tubing and clean out any shavings.
3. Install the filter, seals, and nuts in the proper order and orientation.
4. Tighten the nuts to the specified torque.
5. Evacuate and charge the system, then check for leaks.

Inspecting and Replacing a Drive Belt

Inspecting the drive belt of the compressor is an important part of air-conditioning maintenance and repair. If the belt is worn, the engine cannot drive the compressor properly. On hot days, the refrigerant pressures are high and the compressor needs an effective drive belt to prevent slipping and causing excessive heat buildup around the clutch. The air-conditioning system requires that the compressor move the refrigerant at the correct velocity for the cooling of the passenger compartment to be at its peak efficiency. The drive belt is the first link in

the system and needs to be in good condition and proper tension to ensure efficient air conditioning.

> ▶ **LINK**
> Refer to the Cooling Systems chapter to see the skill drill for inspection and replacement of a drive belt.

Inspecting, Testing, and Replacing the Compressor Clutch

Testing of the clutch assembly should occur when the air-conditioning pressure is high enough to turn on the clutch, but the clutch is not coming on or is not staying on. Typically, this component is checked using a DVOM. The technician needs to determine whether the clutch coil is receiving full power and ground. If it is, but still will not turn on, then the clutch coil should be checked for high resistance. If the resistance is too high according to the service information, it needs to be replaced. This number is usually 3–5 ohms. If full power and ground are not present, then wiring and switches need to be inspected and tested according to the wiring diagram.

The air gap is the space between the clutch assembly and the air-conditioning pulley. This gap needs to be checked to be sure it is correct according to specifications in the service information. If the gap is too small, the clutch will drag on the pulley, creating heat and ruining the clutch. If the gap is too large, the coil will not be able to create a strong enough magnetic pull to pull the clutch in and hold it against the pulley, or it will pull it in but will not be able to hold it in place when the engine's rpm are raised. A voltage drop in the electrical circuit that energizes the clutch coil may also prevent the compressor clutch from engaging. If it does engage, it will not be able to grip tightly enough and will begin to slip, creating heat and scoring the clutch surface.

An air-conditioning compressor pulley or bearing may need service when noise is detected from the bearing as the engine is running. The pulley spins at all times when the engine is running and the bearing may fail and make noise. If the bearing has failed, then the pulley will have to be removed. When replacing the compressor clutch, the pulley will need to be removed as well.

> **TECHNICIAN TIP**
>
> A brown dust on the air-conditioning compressor clutch indicates that there is slippage that could be caused by low voltage and current to the compressor clutch circuit. Slippage could also be caused by the clutch clearance being set too large.

To inspect, test, and replace the compressor clutch, follow the steps in **SKILL DRILL 42-12**:

1. Inspect the air gap of the clutch. With the clutch disengaged, use feeler gauges to measure the air gap between the **drive pulley** and the clutch drive plate. The air gap should be within the manufacturer's specifications. If the air gap is too small, inspect the clutch surfaces; if they are still in good condition, skip to step 4 to remove the clutch and add shims to bring the clearance back into specifications. **(Photo 1)**

SKILL DRILL 42-12 Inspecting, Testing, and Replacing the Compressor Clutch

1. Inspect the air gap of the clutch. With the clutch disengaged, use feeler gauges to measure the air gap between the drive pulley and the clutch drive plate. If the air gap is too small, follow the manufacturer's procedure to adjust the air gap.

2. If the air gap is too large, check to see whether the pulley bearing is worn, causing the pulley to wobble and make contact with the clutch.

3. To check the condition of the electrical circuit, perform an amperage test to the compressor clutch. Measure the vehicle's voltage and clutch resistance (12-volt clutch resistance typically should be 3–5 ohms). Measure the amperage and compare the readings to the calculation. If the readings are in specification, adjust the clutch air gap. If the amperage is out of specification, diagnose the electrical system and replace the clutch.

4. Remove the clutch plate center bolt or nut. If the compressor uses shims, be careful to remove these for later use.

5. Using the appropriate puller, remove the clutch plate.

6. Remove the pulley snap ring, and slide the pulley and bearing off the compressor.

SKILL DRILL | **42-12** | **Inspecting, Testing, and Replacing the Compressor Clutch, continued**

7. Remove the snap ring from the compressor clutch coil, and pull from compressor.

8. Reinstall the components in reverse order. When reinstalling the clutch plate, be sure to adjust the air gap (typical air gap will be 0.012" to 0.025" [0.03 to 0.06 mm]). Check specifications in your service information for the correct air gap.

9. Torque the center bolt or nut to specifications.

2. If the air gap is too large, check to see if the pulley bearing is worn, causing the pulley to wobble and make contact with the clutch, which will wear out the clutch material quickly. The system should also be checked electrically using a DVOM to ensure that the clutch coil is not being energized or partially energized when it should not be. (Typically, this situation is caused by a rewiring of the system following an improper diagnosis.) Too large of an air gap is most likely caused by excessive wear of the clutch and usually requires replacement. **(Photo 2)**

3. The electrical portion of the clutch needs to be tested if there is excessive wear. To check the condition of the electrical circuit, perform an amperage test to the compressor clutch. The amperage test is necessary to determine if any further electrical testing is required. To start the amperage test, the vehicle's voltage and clutch resistance need to be measured (12-volt clutch resistance typically should be 3–5 ohms). Using Ohm's law, divide voltage by resistance to determine the amount of amperage that should be flowing in the electric clutch circuit. Measure the amperage and compare the readings to the calculation. The amperage must be within 5% of the calculation. If the readings are within specification, the clutch air gap can be adjusted. If the amperage is out of specification, the electrical system needs to be diagnosed and the clutch replaced. **(Photo 3)**

4. Remove the clutch plate center bolt or nut. If the compressor uses shims, be careful to remove these for later use. **(Photo 4)**

5. Using the appropriate puller, remove the clutch plate. **(Photo 5)**

6. Remove the pulley snap ring, and slide the pulley and bearing off the compressor. **(Photo 6)**

7. Remove the snap ring from the compressor clutch coil, and pull it from the compressor. **(Photo 7)**

8. Reinstall the components in reverse order. When reinstalling the clutch plate, be sure to adjust the air gap (typical air gap will be 0.012" to 0.025" [0.3 to 0.6 mm]). Check specifications in your service information for the correct air gap. **(Photo 8)**

9. Torque the center bolt or nut to specifications. **(Photo 9)**

Removing, Inspecting, and Reinstalling the Compressor

The compressor needs to be inspected any time there is a compressor failure or leaks are suspected.

To remove, inspect, and reinstall the compressor, follow the steps in **SKILL DRILL 42-13**:

1. Check for sealant and identify the refrigerant. Reclaim the refrigerant, making note of the amount removed. Compare this amount to the factory specifications.

2. Remove the belt using a serpentine belt tool or the proper wrench. Remove tension from the tensioner and slide the belt off, noting routing for reinstallation. **(Photo 1)**

3. Remove the hoses from the air-conditioning system. Cap the lines with the appropriate plugs or tape. **(Photo 2)**

4. Unplug the compressor clutch. **(Photo 3)**

5. Remove the mounting bolts following the manufacturer's specifications. **(Photo 4)**

6. Pour oil from the compressor into a graduated cylinder, and check the oil for acid using acid test strips.

SKILL DRILL | **42-13** | **Removing, Inspecting, and Reinstalling the Compressor**

1. Reclaim the refrigerant, making note of the amount removed. Compare this amount to the factory specifications. Remove the belt using a serpentine belt tool or the proper wrench. Remove tension from the tensioner and slide the belt off, noting routing for reinstallation.

2. Remove the hoses from the air-conditioning system. Cap the lines.

3. Unplug the compressor clutch.

4. Remove the mounting bolts following the manufacturer's specifications. Pour oil from the compressor into a graduated cylinder, and check the oil for acid using acid test strips.

5. Check the resistance of the clutch coil, and check the pulley for wobble that may be caused by a faulty bearing. Check the plugs for corrosion. Check the tag on the new compressor for oil.

6. Install the new compressor; tighten the mounting hardware to specifications.

| SKILL DRILL | 42-13 | **Removing, Inspecting, and Reinstalling the Compressor, continued** |

7 Install the air-conditioning lines with new sealing rings.

8 Plug in the compressor clutch, and install the drive belt. Proceed to the evacuation procedure.

---

7 Check the resistance of the clutch coil, and check the pulley for wobble that may be caused by a faulty bearing. Check the plugs for corrosion.

8 Check the tag on the new compressor for oil; the tag will state whether the new compressor is wet (contains oil) or dry (no oil). If it is dry, read the instruction information for the correct amount and type of oil to add. **(Photo 5)**

9 Install the new compressor; tighten the mounting hardware to specifications. **(Photo 6)**

10 Install the air-conditioning lines with new sealing rings. **(Photo 7)**

11 Plug in the compressor clutch, and install the drive belt. Proceed to the evacuation procedure. **(Photo 8)**

Removing and Inspecting Air-Conditioning Mufflers, Hoses, Lines, and Fittings

The removal of hoses and lines is done for replacement purposes or to access another component. Some lines have male and female threaded ends that bolt together, while others use retainer springs to snap them together. If the hoses are bolted together, line wrenches are used. If they use a spring lock, there is a spring lock release tool that comes in different sizes for different-sized lines. The spring lock tool goes between the fittings and spreads the spring so that the lines can be pulled apart. Any time lines are loosened, the **O-rings** in the fittings must be replaced or there is potential for leaks.

To remove and inspect air-conditioning **mufflers**, hoses, lines, and fittings, follow the steps in **SKILL DRILL 42-14**:

1 After performing a reclaim, begin to remove and inspect the muffler, hoses, lines, and fittings. When inspecting mufflers, shake the muffler and listen for any noise. If the muffler sounds like it contains loose debris, it is faulty and needs to be replaced. **(Photo 1)**

2 Inspect each hose to ensure that it is limber and pliable, not stiff and brittle. **(Photo 2)**

3 The air-conditioning fittings need to be clocked so there is no rubbing with other components. *Clocking* means noting the routing of the hose so it can be reinstalled correctly. The hoses and lines must be kept away from heat sources in the engine that could melt them and moving parts that could wear a hole in them.

4 O-rings are lubricated and installed to prevent refrigerant leaks at fitting points. When installing O-rings, be sure to remove the old O-rings and install new ones each time the fitting is removed and replaced. O-rings are usually deformed during hose removal, so new ones of the correct size and type must be used when reinstalling the hoses. There are special O-rings designed to work with air-conditioning oils and the different types of refrigerant. Be sure to read the product information manual before installing to ensure that the O-ring is compatible with your system. **(Photo 3)**

SKILL DRILL | 42-14 | Removing and Inspecting Air-Conditioning Mufflers, Hoses, Lines, and Fittings

1 After performing a reclaim, remove and inspect the muffler, hoses, lines, and fittings. Shake the muffler and listen for noise. If the muffler sounds like it contains loose debris, it is faulty and needs to be replaced.

2 Inspect each hose to ensure that it is limber and pliable, not stiff and brittle.

3 Clock all hoses, fittings, and components so they are not rubbing against other components. Replace, lubricate, and install O-rings to prevent refrigerant leaks at fitting points.

Removing, Inspecting, and Reinstalling the Condenser

The condenser may be removed to access the radiator or if replacing the condenser because it is plugged, damaged, or leaks. Since the condenser sits in the front of the vehicle, it is damaged quite often in wrecks or by debris flying off the road. It may also have to be removed on some vans for engine removal. Same basic hand tools are necessary as well as wrenches or spring clip removal tools. The process for removing the condenser varies by vehicle type, make, and model. Refer to the service information for specific steps. Also refer to the service information to determine how much oil is needed.

To remove, inspect, and reinstall a condenser, follow the steps in **SKILL DRILL 42-15**:

1 After reclaiming the air-conditioning system, remove all necessary components to access the condenser. This may include removing the grill, radiator, fans, and coverings. Refer to the manufacturer's specific procedures on component removal. **(Photo 1)**

2 Remove the inlet and outlet lines on the condenser. **(Photo 2)**

3 Remove the hold-down bolts for the condenser. **(Photo 3)**

4 Install the new condenser. Fasten the condenser with the mounting hardware. **(Photo 4)**

5 Install new O-rings on the air-conditioning lines. **(Photo 5)**

6 Install the inlet and outlet lines.

7 Replace all of the components in reverse order from removal. Evacuate the air-conditioning system if all other air-conditioning repairs are complete. **(Photo 6)**

Removing, Inspecting, and Installing the Receiver/Drier or Accumulator

The receiver/drier or **accumulator** needs to be removed and inspected whenever there are leaks or the desiccant is failing to dry the refrigerant. Desiccant failures arise when the system is left open for long periods of time and the desiccant absorbs too much moisture. It can also occur if the desiccant bag ruptures and desiccant has entered the rest of the system or if the compressor has come apart internally. The process for removing the receiver/drier or accumulator differs greatly from

SKILL DRILL 42-15 Removing, Inspecting, and Reinstalling the Condenser

1. After reclaiming the air-conditioning system, remove all necessary components to access the condenser. Refer to the manufacturer's specific procedures on component removal.

2. Remove the inlet and outlet lines on the condenser.

3. Remove the hold-down bolts for the condenser.

4. Install the new condenser. Fasten the condenser with the mounting hardware.

5. Install new O-rings on the air-conditioning lines.

6. Install the inlet and outlet lines. Replace all of the components in reverse order from removal. Evacuate the air-conditioning system if all other air-conditioning repairs are complete.

vehicle to vehicle. Refer to the service information of the vehicle for the specific procedure. Also refer to the service information to determine the amount of oil needed.

To remove, inspect, and install the receiver/drier or accumulator/drier, follow the steps in **SKILL DRILL 42-16**:

1. After reclaiming the air-conditioning system, remove the inlet and outlet lines from the receiver/drier or the accumulator. **(Photo 1)**

2. Remove the mounting clamps from the receiver/drier or accumulator. Remove the receiver/drier or accumulator. **(Photo 2)**

3. Lubricate and install new O-rings on both the inlet and the outlet lines. **(Photo 3)**

4. Install the new receiver/drier or accumulator and tighten the clamps. **(Photo 4)**

5. Install the inlet and outlet lines. Proceed to the evacuation if all other repairs were made. **(Photo 5)**

Removing, Inspecting, and Installing a TXV

A TXV would be removed for inspection if the diagnostic process led to the TXV being stuck open or closed,

SKILL DRILL | 42-16 | Removing, Inspecting, and Installing the Receiver/Drier or Accumulator

1. After reclaiming the air-conditioning system, remove the inlet and outlet lines from the receiver/drier or the accumulator.

2. Remove the mounting clamps from the receiver/drier or accumulator; remove the receiver/drier or accumulator.

3. Lubricate and install new O-rings on both the inlet and the outlet lines.

4. Install the new receiver/drier or accumulator and tighten the clamps. Install the inlet and outlet lines.

5. Proceed to the evacuation if all other repairs were made.

which would be determined by gauge pressures and air-conditioning performance. If stuck open, the high-side pressures would be low and the low-side pressures would be high. If stuck closed, the high-side pressures would be high and the low-side pressures would be low and could even go into a vacuum.

When working with the expansion valve, caution must be used in all aspects of the removal and installation of the valve. Typically, the TXV is mounted on the front of the evaporator. When removing and installing the inlet and outlet lines to the evaporator, a line wrench must be used so the nuts or bolts are not damaged or rounded off. A second wrench is used to hold the other end of the line so you do not twist it and break it off. One nut will be on the line; the other nut will be on the TXV. Twist the nut on the line and hold the nut on the TXV so as not to deform or break the TXV. A backup

wrench on the expansion valve must be used also. The lines from the evaporator are aluminum, and the fittings are typically brass, so the use of an open-ended wrench will distort the brass and cause the fitting to leak. The exact procedure for removing, inspecting, and installing a TXV varies widely from vehicle to vehicle and by TXV manufacturer. Refer to the service information for the precise process.

To remove, inspect, and install a TXV, follow the steps in **SKILL DRILL 42-17**:

1. After reclaiming the air-conditioning system, use a wrench to loosen the bolt holding the liquid and suction line block to the expansion valve. **(Photo 1)**

2. Remove the center stud going through the expansion valve. Gently remove the lines from the expansion valve. **(Photo 2)**

SKILL DRILL | 42-17 | Removing, Inspecting, and Installing a TXV

1 After reclaiming the air-conditioning system, use a wrench to loosen the bolt holding the liquid and suction line block to the expansion valve.

2 Remove the center stud going through the expansion valve. Gently remove the lines from the expansion valve.

3 Remove the bolts holding the expansion valve to the evaporator inlet.

4 Install new gaskets or O-rings onto the new expansion valve and the suction and liquid lines.

5 Install the new expansion valve and torque the bolts to specification.

6 Install a new mounting stud. Reinstall the lines to the expansion valve and tighten retaining nut. Evacuate the system if all other repairs were made.

3 Remove the bolts holding the expansion valve to the evaporator inlet. **(Photo 3)**

4 Install new gaskets or O-rings onto the new expansion valve and the suction and liquid lines. **(Photo 4)**

5 Install the new expansion valve and torque the bolts to specification. **(Photo 5)**

6 Install a new mounting stud. Reinstall the lines to the expansion valve and tighten retaining nut. Evacuate the system if all other repairs were made. **(Photo 6)**

Removing, Inspecting, and Installing an Orifice Tube

The orifice tube needs to be replaced when the same gauge readings as a blocked TXV are observed, as it can block up with debris in the system. It should also be replaced if the compressor comes apart because it can catch debris from the compressor and become clogged. The process for removing, inspecting, and installing an orifice tube varies from model to model and vehicle to vehicle. Refer to the service information for the precise procedure.

SKILL DRILL | **42-18** | Removing, Inspecting, and Installing an Orifice Tube

1. Locate the orifice tube and determine whether it is serviceable. After locating the serviceable orifice tube, remove the line where the orifice tube is housed.

2. Using small needle-nose pliers or the orifice tube removal tool, pull out the old orifice tube from the housing. Note the color of the old orifice tube.

3. Select the new orifice tube, making sure to replace with the properly colored tube. Lubricate the orifice tube O-rings, and install the new one with the direction arrow pointing in the direction of refrigerant flow.

4. Lubricate and install new O-rings on the line, and reinstall the line. Proceed to the evacuation if all other repairs were made.

To remove, inspect, and install an orifice tube, follow the steps in **SKILL DRILL 42-18**:

1. After reclaiming the air-conditioning system, locate the orifice tube and inspect the lines to see if it is serviceable. If the orifice is not serviceable, the entire line must be changed with a new one from the factory (there are aftermarket kits for making the orifice tube serviceable on nonserviceable vehicles).

2. After locating the serviceable orifice tube, remove the line where the orifice tube is housed. **(Photo 1)**

3. Using small needle-nose pliers or the orifice tube removal tool, pull out the old orifice tube from the housing. Note the color of the old orifice tube and compare it with the service information. **(Photo 2)**

4. Select the new orifice tube, making sure to replace the old one with the properly colored tube.

5. Lubricate the orifice tube O-rings, and install the new one with the direction arrow pointing in the direction of refrigerant flow. **(Photo 3)**

6. Lubricate and install new O-rings on the line, and reinstall the line. Proceed to the evacuation if all other repairs were made. **(Photo 4)**

Removing, Inspecting, and Reinstalling the Evaporator

Removal of the evaporator is typically done only if it is being replaced. Often, the entire dash assembly must be removed before the evaporator box can be accessed;

therefore, many basic hand tools are required. Once the dash is removed, the air-conditioning evaporator box is unbolted from the vehicle, and then the case can be split open by removing more screws to access the evaporator. The lines in and out of the evaporator must be removed before the box can be removed, and this is just like the other lines. The procedure for removing the evaporator varies greatly, as it is situated differently in each type of vehicle make and model. In fact, some late-model Chevy Camaros require that the windshield be removed to provide access to remove the air box. This procedure may even require a new windshield to be installed. Refer to the service information for the particular vehicle for specific instructions. To remove, inspect, and reinstall the evaporator, you will need to follow the manufacturer's service information.

Evacuating the Air-Conditioning System

After all repairs are made, the air-conditioning system needs to be evacuated to remove all of the moisture from the air introduced into the lines from opening up the air-conditioning system. Evacuating the air-conditioning system requires either air-conditioning gauges and a vacuum pump or an air-conditioning machine. Either way, the process is the same. To remove moisture from the air-conditioning system, the pressure in the lines needs to be lowered with a vacuum pump. This pressure drop will lower the boiling point of the water in the air-conditioning system. When the system at sea level reaches a vacuum of 29.5" Hg (100 kPa), the boiling point will be lowered to 60°F (16°C). Since the boiling point is now lower than ambient air temperature, the moisture in the air-conditioning system's lines and components will boil. The vapor will be evacuated out of the air-conditioning system through the vacuum pump.

Evacuating the Air-Conditioning System Using a Vacuum Gauge

If an air-conditioning machine is unavailable, the air-conditioning system can be evacuated using air-conditioning gauges and a vacuum pump. The processes are essentially the same. When evacuating the air-conditioning system, the vacuum gauge readings need to be timed and watched. Whether a vacuum gauge or a micron gauge is being used, the time that it takes to achieve the boiling point pressure from a boiling point chart needs to be timed. The time it takes for the vacuum pump to pull down the air-conditioning system's pressure is important because there could still be small leaks that were not found during the leak test. These leaks will cause the time it takes

to reach the boiling point to be longer than it should be.

When timing the vacuum gauge readings, you can use the timer on the air-conditioning machine. The time it should take to achieve the boiling point pressure at the ambient temperature with a 5-CFM pump or greater is 5 minutes. If the vacuum pump cannot pull the pressure in the air-conditioning system to the boiling point pressure in 5 minutes or less, the air-conditioning system has leaks that need to be found.

If using a mechanical vacuum gauge, once the air-conditioning system reaches the boiling point pressure, the vacuum pump needs to be left on the air-conditioning system for an additional 10 minutes to fully evacuate the air-conditioning system. You will notice that the default time for most air-conditioning machines is 15 minutes, which allows for the air-conditioning system to reach the boiling point and for the additional 10 minutes for the moisture to be removed.

To use a vacuum gauge to evacuate an air-conditioning system, follow the steps in **SKILL DRILL 42-19**:

1. Hook up the high and the low side to the air-conditioning gauges. (**Photo 1**)
2. Open the high- and low-side valves on the gauges. (**Photo 2**)
3. Hook the pump to the center hose (normally a yellow hose), and turn on the pump. (**Photo 3**)
4. After 20 minutes, turn off the pump and close the valves. (**Photo 4**)
5. Note the vacuum readings. The vacuum should be around 28" Hg or 29" Hg (95 or 98 kPa). Watch the gauges for 5 minutes to be sure the vacuum holds. If the vacuum drops off, there is a leak in the air-conditioning system. (**Photo 5**)

Evacuating the Air-Conditioning System Using a Micron Gauge

The micron gauge is used in conjunction with the mechanical pressure gauge on your air-conditioning machine. They are able to measure vacuum very precisely. Where a vacuum gauge will have markings at 29" then 30" of vacuum, the micron gauge can measure accurately between 29" and 30" to determine exactly how well the system is being evacuated. Many vacuum pumps are measured in microns; the fewer microns it can go down to, the better. If you have two pumps and one can draw down to 500 microns and the other down to 25 microns, the second pump will do a better job of evacuating the system. Some air-conditioning machines will have a micron gauge built in. With the micron gauge, the pressure is measured in microns, or one-thousandths of 1 millimeter. To put it in perspective, in 1 inch, there are 25,400 microns. So, 0 microns equals a perfect

SKILL DRILL | 42-19 | Using a Vacuum Gauge to Evacuate an Air-Conditioning System

1. Hook up the high and the low side to the air-conditioning gauges.

2. Open the high- and low-side valves on the gauges.

3. Hook the pump to the center hose (normally a yellow hose), and turn on the pump.

VACUUM COMPLETE
ANY KEY EXITS
KOOLKARE

LOW   HIGH

4. After 20 minutes, turn off the pump and close the valves.

5. Note the vacuum readings. The vacuum should be around 28" Hg or 29" Hg (95 or 98 kPa). Watch the gauges for 5 minutes to be sure the vacuum holds. If the vacuum drops off, there is a leak in the air-conditioning system.

vacuum (roughly 30" Hg), and 25,400 microns equals approximately 29" Hg. This super-fine measurement of vacuum allows you to read accurately enough to ensure that all of the moisture has been removed from the air-conditioning system.

When the micron gauge reaches 29" Hg, you still have 25,400 microns of mercury to obtain a perfect vacuum. A mechanical gauge is not accurate enough to see such small pressure movements. If using a micron gauge, watch until it hits 1000 microns or less. A reading of 1000 microns or less tells you that all the moisture is gone. The micron gauge should reach the boiling point of pressure within 5 minutes of turning on the pump. If it does not, then there is still a leak in the system.

To use a micron gauge to evacuate an air-conditioning system, follow the steps in **SKILL DRILL 42-20**:

1. Refer to the boiling point chart for the boiling point pressure in microns. Connect the gauge set and vacuum pump. **(Photo 1)**

2. Turn the vacuum pump on to begin the evacuation process. Evacuate for a minimum of 15 minutes. Time the pressure gauge reading. **(Photo 2)**

3. The pressure gauge should reach the boiling point pressure from the boiling point chart within 5 minutes. **(Photo 3)**

4. If the pressure gauge hits the pressure within 5 minutes, continue to allow the machine to evacuate the air-conditioning system until the micron gauge

SKILL DRILL | 42-20 | Using a Micron Gauge to Evacuate an Air-Conditioning System

1. Refer to the boiling point chart for the boiling point pressure in microns. Connect the gauge set and vacuum pump.

2. Turn the vacuum pump on to begin the evacuation process. Evacuate for a minimum of 15 minutes. Time the pressure gauge reading.

3. The pressure gauge should reach the boiling point pressure from the boiling point chart within 5 minutes.

4. If the pressure gauge hits the pressure within 5 minutes, continue to allow the machine to evacuate the air-conditioning system until the micron gauge reaches 1000 microns. When the micron gauge reaches 1000 microns, the air-conditioning system is moisture free.

reaches 1000 microns. When the micron gauge reaches 1000 microns, the air-conditioning system is moisture free. **(Photo 4)**

TECHNICIAN TIP

If the micron does not hit 1000 microns within the total vacuum time, then spin the clutch of the compressor and watch the pressure gauge. If the pressure rises, the clutch seal is faulty.

Determining Recommended Oil and Capacity

As previously discussed, the refrigerant R-12 used a mineral oil, while R-134a uses a polyalkylene glycol (PAG) oil. PAG oil is available in many different viscosities. Each individual air-conditioning system will have a capacity of a specific oil. Often, if you replace just one component, the capacity chart will list how much oil should be replaced for that particular component. Unless the entire system is replaced, some oil will remain in the system. Read the manufacturer's service information for specific instructions.

Adding the Proper Oil Amount

Oil should be put back into the air-conditioning system after the evacuation cycle and while pressure is lower than atmospheric pressure in the air-conditioning system. The oiler uses atmospheric pressure to push oil into the air-conditioning system. The air-conditioning system is still at a vacuum state. Since pressure in a vacuum is less than pressure outside, the oil is easily pulled in by the low pressure or vacuum. What actually happens is that the pressures try to equalize. If you have oil in the hose that is allowing outside pressure into the vacuum or lower pressure, the higher pressure pushes the oil in as it tries to equalize pressures. Most air-conditioning machines have a port that a special graduated cylinder screws into. When the port is opened with the cylinder attached, the pressure equalization forces the oil in. You should replace the amount of oil that was removed during the reclaim process if it was less than 1 ounce (30 mL). If the oil removed during the reclaim process was more than 1 ounce, the air-conditioning system needs to be flushed, and a base charge of oil needs to be established.

To add oil to the air-conditioning system, follow the steps in **SKILL DRILL 42-21**:

1. Evacuate the air-conditioning system and watch the vacuum gauge to be sure it does not bleed up, which would indicate that there is a leak.

2. If no leaks appear after 5 minutes, it is okay to add the recommended amount of oil. Open the oiling valve as recommended in the service information. **(Photo 1)**

3. Shut off the valve when the proper amount of oil has been added. **(Photo 2)**

4. Recharge the air-conditioning system with the amount of refrigerant noted on the under-the-hood air-conditioning sticker or in the service information (see Skill Drill 42-22).

SKILL DRILL 42-21 Adding Oil to the Air-Conditioning System

1. Evacuate the air-conditioning system and watch the vacuum gauge to ensure that it does not bleed up. If no leaks appear after 5 minutes, install the oil. Open the oiling valve as recommended by the air-conditioning machine information.

2. Shut off the valve when the proper amount of oil has been added. Recharge the air-conditioning system with the amount of refrigerant noted on the under-the-hood air-conditioning sticker or in the service information (see Skill Drill 42-22).

Charging the Air-Conditioning System

Charging a system is performed after the air-conditioning system has been evacuated and any oil is replaced. The only tool needed is the air-conditioning machine, with the correct type and amount of refrigerant in it. Charge the air-conditioning system to the proper factory level by reading the under-the-hood sticker or obtaining the amount from the manufacturer.

To charge an air-conditioning system, follow the steps in **SKILL DRILL 42-22** :

1. Hook the air-conditioning machine to the high- and low-side service ports. Open the valves. **(Photo 1)**

2. Because it varies by machine, follow the instructions display on the air-conditioning machine for charging. On the display, enter the amount of refrigerant to be charged and select "start" to begin charging the air-conditioning system.

3. If charging on the high side only, when the charging begins, watch the low-side pressure gauge. If the low-side gauge does not reach zero before 10 seconds, the TXV or orifice tube is bad. Filling from the high side would cause the refrigerant to pass through the TXV or the fixed orifice tube. If it is plugged, the system would have to be recovered again and the component replaced. If the machine fills from the low side or both sides, this test is invalid. **(Photo 2)**

4. If the pressure reaches a positive pressure number too rapidly, the reed valves in the compressor are likely bad. The pressure should rise on the low-side gauge slowly and smoothly. Refrigerant is passing quickly through the compressor because of a broken valve. This test is valid only on machines charging from the high side only. The compressor in this situation would need to be replaced. Allow the machine to finish charging the refrigerant, and follow any prompts on the screen. Finally, performance test the system and check for leaks if any fittings have been opened. **(Photo 3)**

Refrigerant Equipment Maintenance

Regular maintenance prompts may appear as you use the air-conditioning machine. If they do, then follow the instructions on the screen. When the air-conditioning machine alerts you that it needs service, you should contact the local service department for the machine.

SKILL DRILL | **42-22** | **Charging the Air-Conditioning System**

1. Hook the air-conditioning machine to the high- and low-side service ports. Open the valves.

2. Follow the instructions display on the air-conditioning machine for charging. On the display, enter the amount of refrigerant to be charged and select "start" to begin charging the air-conditioning system.

3. If charging on the high side only, watch the low-side pressure gauge. The pressure should rise on the low-side gauge slowly and smoothly. Allow the machine to finish charging the refrigerant, and follow any prompts on the screen. Performance test the system and check for leaks if any fittings have been opened.

Vacuum pump oil is one of the regular maintenance items that you will be prompted to change after approximately each 10 hours of vacuum use. Vacuum pump oil can be changed by the shop technician. Failure to change the oil will result in increased pump wear, as well as causing the pump to not be able to draw as deep of a vacuum. Changing the pump oil regularly will extend the life of the pump and make it reach maximum vacuum quicker. You will need a drain pan for the old oil and new vacuum pump oil for the pump.

To change the vacuum pump oil in an air-conditioning machine, follow the steps in **SKILL DRILL 42-23**:

1. When it is time to change the vacuum pump oil, the machine will warm up the oil so it is easier to drain. In most machines, the vacuum pump is behind a cover inside of the air-conditioning machine, which must be removed before use. Remove the drain plug, and drain the oil into the drain pan. The drain plug is near the bottom of the housing. **(Photo 1)**

2. Refer to the air-conditioning machine user manual to find out what type and how much oil to install. Remove the fill plug, install the drain plug, and tighten. The fill plug will be near the top, but not normally all the way on the top. Use a funnel to add the new oil. **(Photo 2)**

3. Turn on the pump and check that oil is halfway up the sight glass (if the pump has a sight glass). If the level is below half, then add a small amount of oil to bring it to the halfway mark. If it is over half, then drain some oil. **(Photo 3)**

4. Reinstall the fill plug and check for leaks. **(Photo 3)**

SKILL DRILL 42-23 Performing Refrigerant Equipment Maintenance

1. Remove the drain plug and drain the oil.

2. Remove the fill plug, install the drain plug, and tighten. Use a funnel to add the new oil.

3. Turn on the pump and check for leaks. Check that the oil level is halfway up the sight glass. If under the halfway mark, add oil. If over, drain some oil Recheck. Reinstall the fill plug and check for leaks.

Inspecting and Testing the Heater Control Valves

The heater control valves should be tested if the customer complains of no heat or poor air conditioning. The heater control valve, if equipped, regulates coolant flow to the heater core for heat and limits flow for air conditioning. Some are vacuum controlled and some are cable controlled. Cable-controlled models must be checked to ensure that the cable is free and working. Vacuum-controlled models should be checked to ensure that the vacuum is supplied to the valve at the right time and that the valve will hold vacuum. If there is a problem with cable or vacuum operation, then the control head in the dash will probably have to be removed, inspected, and repaired. If the cable or vacuum is working, then the operation of the valve should be checked. Have someone move the temperature lever from hot to cold while watching the valve. If the cable or vacuum servo is moving the control arm on the valve, then the valve is probably okay and the problem is elsewhere in the system, although the valve could be plugged or slipping on the shaft. Therefore, you may have to remove it from the heater hose and visually inspect that the valve opens and closes.

Removing, Inspecting, and Reinstalling the Heater Core

Heater cores are usually removed only because leaks are present. Leaks from the heater core can result in coolant misting out of the vents or coolant dripping onto the passenger-side carpet, or both. Because this process is complex and different on nearly every model of vehicle, you will need to follow the steps in the vehicle manufacturer's service information. One thing to remember is that the heater core inlet and outlet tubes are made of thin metal and soldered into thin metal tanks. Twisting the heater hoses to get them off will almost always result in ripping the heater core tubes out of the tanks. Carefully use a hose slitter or knife to slit the hose lengthwise over the heater core tubes, and then peel the hoses off of the tubes. The procedure for removing the heater core varies greatly, since it is situated differently in each type of vehicle make and model. Refer to the service information for the particular vehicle for specific instructions. To remove, inspect, and reinstall the heater core, you will need to follow the manufacturer's service information.

Wrap-up

Ready for Review

- Technicians must be EPA 609 certified to handle refrigerants.
- Performance testing of the air-conditioning system is one of the first steps in diagnosis.
- A performance test involves external cooling for the condenser, running the engine between 1200–2000 RPMs, placing the air-conditioning on max cold, the fan on high, and measuring the duct temperature, and then comparing the duct temperature to a system performance chart from the manufacturer.
- Servicing the air-conditioning system involves performance testing the system, diagnosing any issues, leak testing, identifying the refrigerant, reclaiming the refrigerant, performing any repairs, evacuating the system, recharging, retesting for leaks, and performance testing.
- Identifying refrigerant helps avoid mixing refrigerants, which cannot be reused and must be stored separately.
- Acid is formed inside an air-conditioning system when water is present.
- Acid test strips can be used to test for the presence of acid.
- An undercharged air-conditioning system contains less refrigerant than the system calls for.
- The one rule for diagnosis of an air-conditioning system is "when in doubt, suck it out."
- The compressor is the most common source of abnormal noises arising from the air conditioner.
- If the high-side pressures are too high and the system is not cooling well, check the air flow through the condenser.
- Clearing the drain hose can clear up odors. If this does not work, an anti-odor kit may be required.
- Confirm the refrigerant in the system by using a refrigerant identifier.
- The air distribution system is designed to circulate air through the heating and cooling system, then into the passenger cabin.
- Refrigerant must be tested for acidic contaminants and water intrusion.
- Charge refers to the amount of refrigerant in the air-conditioning system.
- The TXV system is more sensitive to low charge (low refrigerant level) than the fixed orifice tube system.
- Components of a heating system include: radiator, thermostat, water pump, upper and lower radiator hoses, heater core, and heater control valve.
- Steps to the diagnosis and repair of air-conditioning systems are pretest and inspection, leak test, reclaiming refrigerant, problem repair, evacuation, charging, and post-testing.
- The two most common air-conditioning customer complaints are: the system is not working or the system has an unusual smell.
- Problems with air-conditioning system performance may be due to system leaks, compressor failure, or system blockages due to debris or frozen moisture.
- Variable factors, such as weather, air moisture content, temperature, condition and type of vehicle, and color and size of vehicle, all affect air-conditioning system functioning.
- Air-conditioning performance testing should be done before and after a repair.
- Air-conditioning system inspection should include possible condenser airflow restrictions, evaporator housing water drain, air filter, hoses and belts, coolant pressure, radiator cap vacuum and pressure, cooling fan, fan clutch, fan shroud, air dams, and heater control valves.
- Air-conditioning systems are equipped with protective devices designed to shut down the system if the pressure becomes elevated.
- Tools needed to maintain and repair air-conditioning systems include: sealant detector, reclaim/recycle machine, refrigerant identifiers, pressure gauge sets, air-conditioning machine, anemometer, retro fit kit, pressure-temperature chart, vacuum pump, electronic leak detector, dye leak detector, oiler, vacuum gauge, micron gauge, and line wrench.
- Methods of leak testing are sniffer testing, dye testing, and nitrogen testing.
- Refrigerant leaks can be detected by sniffers via ultra-sonic, heated diode, or corona-suppression.
- Any time the air-conditioning system is opened, the refrigerant must be recovered (reclaimed).
- The air-conditioning system should be flushed if the compressor comes apart, the desiccant bag breaks open, or the oil is contaminated.
- Use caution when removing and installing a TXV to avoid creating leaks.
- Following a repair, the air-conditioning system should be evacuated via an air-conditioning machine or air-conditioning gauges and a vacuum pump.

Key Terms

accumulator A device placed between the evaporator and the compressor to collect liquid refrigerant and prevent it from entering the compressor.

air-conditioning compressor clutch An engagement device connected to the compressor crankshaft to engage the crankshaft with a belt-driven pulley.

air-conditioning machine A machine designed to recover, recycle, evacuate, leak test, and recharge (R/R/R) the air-conditioning system.

anemometer A device that measures airflow in feet per minute (fpm).

charge The amount of refrigerant present in the system or the process of installing refrigerant in the system.

corona-suppression An electronic sniffer used for detecting refrigerant leaks.

drive pulley Any belt-driven pulley used to power an accessory such as power steering or the air-conditioning compressor.

heated diode A sniffer that uses electricity to determine if there is a refrigerant leak; considered the best sniffer for R-134a.

hoses Flexible lines used to direct liquids or gases.

lines Term used interchangeably with pipes or tubes.

microleak detector A solution used to detect refrigeration leaks.

micron gauge A device designed to measure vacuum very precisely.

muffler A device to quiet the pipes of the air-conditioning system with baffles placed inside to deaden the sound of refrigerant moving.

oiler A device used to add oil to the air-conditioning system.

O-ring Rubber-type rings available in different sizes used to seal pipe fittings.

overcharging Overfilling of the air-conditioning system; may result in poor cooling or mechanical failure of the system.

performance testing The process of recreating a driving situation to check air-conditioning performance and vent temperature.

pressure gauge set A set of calibrated gauges for high and low pressure that can show pressure and vacuum readings for use with air-conditioning systems.

pressure transients Minor fluctuations on the gauges that may indicate a problem.

PT chart A pressure-temperature chart that shows the relationship between air-conditioning pressures and evaporator temperature.

reclaim/recycle machine An air-conditioning machine designed to remove and recycle refrigerant for reuse.

reclaiming The process of removing refrigerant from the air-conditioning system by using an air-conditioning machine; also called recovering.

recovering See *reclaiming*.

refrigerant identifiers Devices used to check for impurities in the air-conditioning system.

retrofit kit An aftermarket kit that has the fittings and oil to change an R-12 unit over to an R-134a unit.

sniffer An electronic device used to determine the source of leaks.

state of charge The amount of refrigerant in a system compared to how much should be in it.

ultrasonic A method of leak detection that uses a sensitive microphone to hear small refrigerant leaks by amplifying the hissing noise.

vacuum gauge A gauge designed to read negative pressure or vacuum.

vacuum pump A pump used to evacuate the air-conditioning system and put it into a deep vacuum or low pressure to remove moisture.

ASE-Type Questions

1. Tech A states that the wider the gap on an air-conditioning clutch, the greater the ohm reading when checking the windings. Tech B states that the air-conditioning clutch is electromagnetically operated. Who is correct?
   a. Tech A
   b. Tech B
   c. Both A and B
   d. Neither A nor B

2. Tech A states that an air-conditioning performance test usually requires that an auxiliary condenser fan be used during the test. Tech B states that a performance test will show if the air-conditioning system is contaminated with sealer. Who is correct?
   a. Tech A
   b. Tech B
   c. Both A and B
   d. Neither A nor B

3. Tech A states that refrigerant in a vehicle should be identified before recovering the refrigerant. Tech B states that refrigerant doesn't need to be identified if you are only topping up a system with refrigerant. Who is correct?
   a. Tech A
   b. Tech B
   c. Both A and B
   d. Neither A nor B

4. Tech A states that when evacuating an air-conditioning system, the vacuum should be maintained for approximately 10 minutes after the system reaches the boiling point pressure of water. Tech B states that the primary purpose of evacuating an air-conditioning system is to remove any moisture from the system. Who is correct?
   a. Tech A
   b. Tech B
   c. Both A and B
   d. Neither A nor B

5. Tech A states that the system should be flushed if the compressor came apart. Tech B states that the system should be flushed if the oil is contaminated. Who is correct?
   a. Tech A
   b. Tech B
   c. Both A and B
   d. Neither A nor B

6. Tech A states that when using pressurized nitrogen to locate a leak, an electronic sniffer should be used. Tech B states that electronic sniffers are used when the system has at least a minimal refrigerant charge. Who is correct?
   a. Tech A
   b. Tech B
   c. Both A and B
   d. Neither A nor B

7. Tech A states that microns are a much more accurate unit of measuring vacuum than inches of mercury (Hg). Tech B states that microns are a much more accurate measure of time than seconds. Who is correct?
   a. Tech A
   b. Tech B
   c. Both A and B
   d. Neither A nor B

8. Tech A states that to determine how much Freon is needed in a system, you must refer to identifying labels on the vehicle or the service manual. Tech B states that to determine the amount of Freon needed, you just charge the system until the pressures look correct. Who is correct?
   a. Tech A
   b. Tech B
   c. Both A and B
   d. Neither A nor B

9. Tech A states that when removing any part of an air-conditioning system, the oil should be drained from it and measured so that the same amount can be reinstalled. Tech B states that oil should only be in the compressor, and if any oil is found in any other components, it means that the receiver drier is faulty. Who is correct?
   a. Tech A
   b. Tech B
   c. Both A and B
   d. Neither A nor B

10. Tech A states that if moisture enters the air-conditioning system, acid will be created. Tech B states that evacuating an air-conditioning system will boil moisture, which will be removed from the system as a gas. Who is correct?
   a. Tech A
   b. Tech B
   c. Both A and B
   d. Neither A nor B

CHAPTER 43

NATEF Tasks

Heating and Air Conditioning
Refrigeration System Component

Page

- Identify hybrid vehicle air-conditioning system electrical circuits, service and safety precautions. **MLR** **AST** **MAST** 1498–1499

General

- Using a scan tool, observe and record related heating, ventilation, and air-conditioning (HVAC) data and trouble codes. **AST** **MAST** 1500–1503

Operating Systems and Related Controls

- Check operation of automatic or semiautomatic heating, ventilation, and air-conditioning (HVAC) control systems; determine necessary action. **AST** **MAST** 1501–1502

- Inspect and test A/C heater-blower, motors, resistors, switches, relays, wiring, and protection devices; perform necessary action. **AST** **MAST** 1504–1506

- Diagnose air-conditioning compressor clutch control systems; determine necessary action. **AST** **MAST** 1505–1507

- Diagnose malfunctions in the vacuum, mechanical, and electrical components and controls of the HVAC system; determine necessary action. **AST** **MAST** 1507–1508

- Inspect and test A/C-heater control panel assembly; determine necessary action. **AST** **MAST** 1508–1509

- Inspect and test A/C-heater control cables, motors, and linkages; perform necessary action. **AST** **MAST** 1509

- Inspect A/C-heater ducts, doors, hoses, cabin filters, and outlets; perform necessary action. **AST** **MAST** 1510–1511

Heating, Ventilation, and Engine Cooling Systems

- Diagnose temperature control problems in the heater/ventilation system; determine necessary action. **MAST** 1511–1512

Electronic Climate Control

Knowledge Objectives

After reading this chapter, you will be able to:
1. Describe the three different forms of climate control systems: manual, semiautomatic, and automatic. (pp 1486–1488)
2. Describe the components of the climate control system. (p 1488)
3. Explain the function of the electronic control unit (ECU) of an HVAC system and how its various sensors control the vehicle's climate. (pp 1488–1492)
4. Explain the different types of HVAC control panels and their features. (pp 1492–1494)
5. Describe the components of the air-conditioning compressor clutch. (pp 1494–1495)
6. Describe the function of the blower motor and blower speed control. (pp 1495–1496)
7. Explain the principles of a hybrid air-conditioning system and how it operates. (pp 1498–1499)

Skills Objectives

After reading this chapter, you will be able to:
1. Check the operation of an automatic or semiautomatic HVAC control system. (pp 1501–1502)
2. Use a scan tool to diagnose air-conditioning systems. (p 1502)
3. Inspect and test the electric cooling fan. (pp 1502–1504)
4. Inspect and test the blower motor. (pp 1504–1506)
5. Test the air-conditioning compressor clutch control system. (pp 1506–1507)
6. Inspect and test the HVAC control panel assembly. (pp 1507–1509)
7. Inspect and test the HVAC control cables. (p 1509)
8. Inspect the air-conditioning system heater ducts, doors, and cabin filters. (pp 1509–1511)
9. Diagnose temperature control problems in the HVAC system. (p 1512)

Introduction

Electronic climate control systems provide the driver and passengers with a means of automatically moderating the environment inside the vehicle. This chapter will offer insight into the operation of these systems and their components. The chapter will also include diagnostic information on determining faults in the climate control system and information on testing the various components. An electronic heating ventilation and air-conditioning system is more technically challenging to diagnose than a mechanical air-conditioning system, and when not functional, many customers will turn to a highly qualified technician to repair it quickly and accurately.

Climate Control Overview

Climate control systems in modern vehicles come in three different forms: **manual**, **semiautomatic**, and **automatic**. Manual control systems allow the operator to control the direction of airflow, the blower motor speed (to control airflow speed), and the temperature of the outlets. The manual system gives the operator full control of the climate control system and does not use a computer or **electronic control unit (ECU)**. Semiautomatic control systems also allow the operator to select the direction of airflow, the blower motor speed, and the temperature. However, the ECU then controls when the air-conditioning compressor turns on and off

and the amount of heat that is discharged. The ECU controls heat by one of two methods—a blend door in the air box or a heater control valve in one of the heater hose lines. In a blend door system, the airflow goes through the evaporator and then a blend door moves to direct all of the airflow either across the heater core for maximum heat or around the heater core for cold. The blend door can move any amount between these positions to "blend" the cold and hot air **FIGURE 43-1**. The heater valve uses a heater control valve, which controls how much coolant flows through the heater core (it regulates the coolant flow to the heater core) **FIGURE 43-2**.

ECUs automatically maintain the operator-selected climate (temperature) preference within the passenger cabin. The climate control system manages the three subsystems—heating, ventilation, and air conditioning—and uses each subsystem to match the climate to the settings selected. If the operator selects auto control and 78°F (26°C), the ECU will check all inputs to determine the temperature outside the vehicle and inside the vehicle. When the temperatures are determined, the ECU will move the doors in the air box to keep the temperature at the requested value. The ECU may have to turn on or off the air-conditioning compressor to reach the temperature requested.

The climate control system also controls the speed of the blower fan, speeding it up to effect a quick change in climate when the passenger cabin temperature is substantially different from the climate control system setting. Once the climate approaches the desired setting, the fan

You are the Automotive Technician

A woman comes into the shop complaining that her air conditioning isn't cool enough to maintain the temperature she desires in her 2010 Honda Pilot. When she turns her A/C on, it is cool at first, but turns to warm air blowing from the vents after 5 minutes. You perform a system performance test and find that when the vehicle is started up cold, the A/C ducts deliver cool air according to the manufacturer's temperature chart. But over time, the ducted air temperature starts to warm up even though the A/C temperature is at its minimum setting. After about 5 minutes, the ducted air temperature has warmed up to the point that it is warmer than the outside air temperature. You use a pair of hose clamping pliers and clamp off one of the flexible heater hoses. With the engine and A/C still operating, the ducted air temperature starts to fall and after just a couple of minutes, returns to the specified temperature. You now know that this is a heater control problem and not an A/C control problem.

1. During a performance test, when is it normal for the ducted air temperature to be warmer than outside air?
2. Why did you clamp off the flexible heater hose?
3. What caused the ducted air temperature to fall back to its normal temperature?

FIGURE 43-1 Blend door.

FIGURE 43-2 Heater control valve.

FIGURE 43-3 Actuators. **A.** Electric actuator. **B.** Vacuum actuator.

speed will gradually reduce to maintain the selected temperature.

Climate control requires the use of electronic sensors to determine the heat (sun) load on the vehicle, ambient air temperature, cabin air temperature, evaporator temperature, engine coolant temperature, position of various doors, and desired temperature setting. The ECU of an HVAC system needs all these inputs so that it can make the correct adjustments to the air distribution system. Achieving the requested temperature is the mission of the ECU, and the inputs allow a good "feel" to ensure it is reaching its target. The sensors provide the ECU with a sense or feel for temperature inside and outside the vehicle, as well as tell how much heat from the sun is coming through the windshield. By being

able to "feel" conditions, the ECU can make correct adjustments to temperature to meet the demands of the operator. The ECU gathers information from the sensors and sends commands to control fan speed, heater core coolant flow, air-conditioning clutch activation, compressor displacement, blend doors, and fresh air/recirculation doors.

Actuators are used to carry out some of the ECU commands and operate doors in the air box to control the temperature of the air and direct it to the selected zone—windshield, floor, vent, or bilevel. Actuators come in two styles: electrically operated and vacuum operated FIGURE 43-3. The actuators are connected to the air doors by links or levers and position the doors to obtain the proper airflow through the system.

Climate Control Components

The climate control system involves many components. Each component fits into one of three categories **FIGURE 43-4**. The first category is the ECU, which is the brains of the system. The second category is the HVAC sensors, also called inputs, which provide information to the control unit. The last category is comprised of the HVAC-controlled devices, which cause components such as the actuators and the blower motor to function. We will look at each of the components in more detail and see how they work together to control the climate within the passenger compartment.

The Electronic Control Unit of an HVAC System

An ECU works with sensors and actuators to control the climate inside the vehicle. It controls the HVAC system. The ECU gathers information from sensors that detect changes in ambient temperature, cabin temperature, coolant temperature, and solar radiation. The ECU evaluates signals from the sensors to determine the necessary operating conditions to meet the desired climate. It then controls actuators to move dampers and valves that control the volume, temperature, and direction of the cool air delivered by the air-conditioning system.

The ECU contains a micro-computer. The starting point of any control module is the **printed circuitry**. Resistors, capacitors, transistors, and integrated circuits are soldered onto the circuit board to create the control module or computer. The circuitry is mounted inside a metal or plastic housing to protect it from damage.

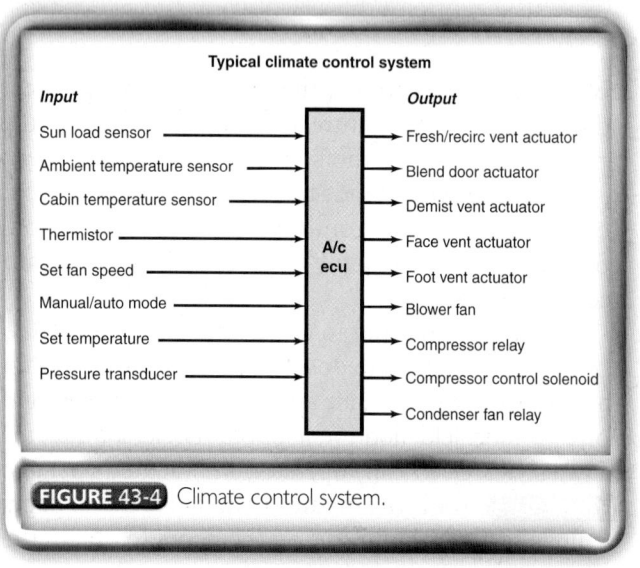

Typical climate control system

Input		Output
Sun load sensor		Fresh/recirc vent actuator
Ambient temperature sensor		Blend door actuator
Cabin temperature sensor		Demist vent actuator
Thermistor	A/c ecu	Face vent actuator
Set fan speed		Foot vent actuator
Manual/auto mode		Blower fan
Set temperature		Compressor relay
Pressure transducer		Compressor control solenoid
		Condenser fan relay

FIGURE 43-4 Climate control system.

The control module or ECU must be programmed after it is constructed. The programming loaded into the ECU contains all the data to make the system operate properly. One such piece of data programmed is the data map used to determine the voltage versus temperature that is received from interior and exterior temperature sensors. In some automatic climate control systems, the control panel and ECU are one piece and are not located separately.

The ECU receives signals in the form of **voltages** from each of the sensors. There are two kinds of temperature sensors, also called thermistors because their resistance value changes significantly as temperature changes. One is called a **negative temperature coefficient (NTC) thermistor** since its resistance goes down as it is heated, opposite of most materials. The other is the positive temperature coefficient (PTC) thermistor. Its resistance goes up as it is heated. Be sure to consult the service information to verify the type of thermistors used in the vehicle you are working with. Most manufacturers use the NTC type, which increases resistance as the temperature goes down. For example, as the temperature sensor is exposed to colder temperatures, the resistance will increase, causing the signal voltage to decrease. The ECU compares the **signal voltage values** from the temperature sensors with values stored in its memory, programmed in when the module is installed into the vehicle. If a difference in voltage values occurs, the ECU determines the action needed to ensure that the temperature requested by the operator is matched. The ECU may need to change the position of the actuators or increase or decrease blower motor fan speed.

Some actuators will provide a **feedback signal** to the ECU in the form of a voltage signal. The voltage signal is used by the ECU to determine what position the actuators are in and whether they are moving. The feedback sensor is a potentiometer, which is a variable resistor that changes resistance values as the position of the wiper contact changes. The actuator's potentiometer works in the same way as the throttle position sensor. As the position of the door changes, the actuator's potentiometer signals its position to the ECU. Refer to the description and operation section of the service information to find out how the vehicle's particular actuator operates.

The ECU also controls the speed of the interior ventilation fan (blower motor fan). On some vehicles, the ECU provides a pulse-width–modulated signal to control the motor's speed, and works by repeatedly turning on and off the current flow to the component. The longer the percent of time the current is turned on, the faster the fan runs **FIGURE 43-5**. The speed of the interior ventilation

FIGURE 43-5 Pulse-width–modulated on the ground side of circuit.

FIGURE 43-6 Thermistors. **A.** NTC thermistor resistance. **B.** PTC thermistor resistance.

fan is infinitely variable between a stopped condition and the fan's maximum speed. This design provides a continuously variable speed capability and therefore an infinite number of speeds, which allows the fan to operate at a more appropriate speed. A typical resistor pack blower motor, in contrast, has only four speeds. With only four speeds, it is more likely that any single speed is a bit too fast or a bit too slow.

Automatic Climate Control Sensors

As just discussed, the ECU of an HVAC system needs to know the temperature of the ambient air, the cabin air temperature, the temperature of the air-conditioning evaporator, the temperature of the coolant circulating through the heater core, and whether the vehicle is in bright sunlight. All this information allows the ECU to "feel" its surroundings (interior and exterior temperatures, for example) and to determine from its programming where to position air box doors, how fast to run the blower fan, and whether to turn the air-conditioning compressor on or off. In most instances the temperature sensors used in the climate control air-conditioning system are thermistors **FIGURE 43-6**. Although they may vary in appearance, their general operating characteristics are the same; as temperature changes, so does the resistance. Negative temperature coefficient (NTC) thermistors are usually used in automotive applications **FIGURE 43-7**.

When connected into a circuit, the temperature sensor changes the voltage signal at the ECU. The ECU reads the sensor voltage, interprets it into a temperature, and compares this reading with information stored in its memory. The ECU continuously monitors the signals

FIGURE 43-7 A negative temperature coefficient (NTC) thermistor.

from all of the sensors so it can make any adjustments as necessary. As an example of the need for the ECU to adjust as necessary, suppose the operator were to leave the air-conditioning controls set to auto with the desired temperature set to 70°F (21°C) while the vehicle is sitting in a garage that is air conditioned to 75°F (24°C). The driver then starts the vehicle and backs it out into the full sun where it is 98°F (37°C). The ECU will register the sun load sensor, which detects large amounts of sun, and the exterior sensor, which detects 98°F (37°C). With this information, the air-conditioning compressor will be commanded on for longer periods to cycle cold refrigerant into the evaporator, the blend door will move to full cold, and fan speed will ramp up.

Ambient Air Temperature Sensor

The <u>ambient air temperature sensor</u> measures the temperature of the outside air **FIGURE 43-8**. It is usually located in front of the air-conditioning condenser where the forward motion of the vehicle and the action of the condenser fans force air over the sensor. The ambient air temperature sensor is a thermistor. The ECU sends a 5-volt reference signal to the thermistor, and the signal is returned to the ECU as a voltage from somewhere near 0.5 up to 4.5 volts. The ECU has an internal voltmeter that looks at the voltage across an internal resistor. If there is no return path back to the ECU, then the voltage stays high (is not pulled down across the resistor). If there is a return path to the ECU, then the voltage across the internal resistor will be low, since the voltage is pulled down. If the outside air is cold, the resistance of the ambient air temperature sensor will be high and the voltage at the ECU will also be high. If the outside air temperature is hot, the ambient air temperature sensor resistance will be low and the voltage at the ECU will be low. If the outside air temperature is low, the ECU will not have to run the compressor as much or move the blend door to as cold a position. The ECU will not allow the air-conditioning compressor to turn on if the ambient air temperature is below a set temperature, typically around 40°F (4°C). The ambient air temperature sensor is also used as an input for the driver display of the outside temperature.

Cabin Air Temperature Sensor

The <u>cabin air temperature sensor</u> may be mounted in a tube-type device called an <u>aspirator</u> **FIGURE 43-9**. The aspirator is a tube that directs airflow to the in-vehicle temperature sensor. One end of the aspirator tube is open to cabin air and the other is connected to the interior fan. The interior fan creates a flow of air through the aspirator that is directed to the cabin air temperature sensor. The cabin air temperature sensor is a thermistor. A 5-volt reference is sent to the thermistor (cabin air temperature sensor) and is varied depending on the temperature. The cabin air temperature sensor is a valuable input to the ECU to ensure that the temperature is meeting the operator-requested temperature.

Engine Coolant Temperature Sensor

The <u>engine coolant temperature sensor</u> signals to the ECU the temperature of the coolant flowing in the heater core. Some climate control systems have a separate engine coolant temperature sensor, usually located near the engine coolant temperature sensor. The engine coolant temperature sensor is a thermistor and works the same as an exterior or interior temperature sensor.

Applied | Math

AM-32: Fahrenheit/Centigrade: The technician can identify whether a temperature measurement must be made using a measuring device that measures in degrees Centigrade, or degrees Fahrenheit.
Reading in degrees Centigrade or degrees Fahrenheit is largely dependent on the system of measurement used in the publication of specifications for the system.

Ideally, if system specifications are published in metric measurements, an instrument measuring in degrees Centigrade should be used. If standard measurements are used in specifications, an instrument measuring in degrees Fahrenheit would be a better choice. If the appropriate measuring instrument is not available, it is possible to convert Centigrade readings to Fahrenheit, and vice-versa for the purpose of comparing measured readings to specifications. Water freezes at 0° and boils at 100° in the Celsius or Centigrade scale. Water freezes at 32° and boils at 212° in the Fahrenheit scale.

FIGURE 43-8 An ambient air temperature sensor.

FIGURE 43-9 A cabin air temperature sensor in an aspirator tube.

The signal from the engine coolant temperature sensor is used in conjunction with the signals from the ambient air sensor, the sun load sensor, and the cabin air temperature sensor to control heater and fan operation. For example, suppose the ECU registers the following readings: coolant temperature 60.8°F (16°C), ambient air temperature 32°F (0°C), sun load –0, and cabin air temperature 32°F (0°C). The heater valve will open fully, the blend door will move to maximum airflow across the heater core, and the fan speed will be slow and steady. As the engine and the passenger cabin warm up, the ECU will monitor that on the various sensors and will take the appropriate action on the doors, valves, and fan.

Sun Load Sensor

The **sun load, or solar, sensor** is located on the dash panel where it is exposed to light entering through the windshield of the vehicle **FIGURE 43-10**. As sunlight increases, the passengers get the sensation that it is hotter than it really is inside the passenger compartment. The ECU uses the sun load sensor to increase the fan speed and adjust the blend door. The sun load sensor is a **photodiode**. The photodiode works by varying resistance as sunlight brightness changes. These sensors use a 5-volt reference signal and a signal wire. As sunlight becomes brighter, resistance increases and lowers the voltage signal back to the ECU, similar to how a thermistor works. The ECU has a table programmed into the memory that is able to compare the voltage signal to a sun load amount. Photodiodes are used in many other household electronics, including your TV. The photodiode picks up the remote signal when you control the volume or the channel.

When connected to the ECU, a change in light intensity is registered as a change in voltage. The ECU uses this information to gauge the amount of solar heat load the vehicle is experiencing and adjusts the amount of cooling or heating needed.

Air-Conditioning Pressure Sensor

The **air-conditioning pressure sensor** (transducer) is a three-wire sensor that monitors the **air-conditioning system pressure** **FIGURE 43-11**. Typically, air-conditioning systems will use two pressure sensors to monitor refrigerant pressure—a high-side pressure sensor and a low-side pressure sensor. Both of these sensors "measure" pressure in pounds per square inch or pascals.

The air-conditioning system must have enough refrigerant pressure to ensure that refrigerant oil can be circulated through the air-conditioning compressor. If refrigerant pressure is too low, the air-conditioning compressor will not turn on, which is a precaution designed into the system to keep the compressor from being damaged. The pressure will get too low in the event

FIGURE 43-10 A sun load sensor.

FIGURE 43-11 A three-wire air-conditioning pressure sensor.

that there is a leak in the system, or improper refrigerant flow. The low-pressure sensor is located on the low-pressure side of the air-conditioning system.

The high-pressure sensor is located on the high-pressure side of the air-conditioning system. The high-pressure sensor is designed to keep pressures from going too high and causing the pressure relief valve in the compressor to release refrigerant to the air. The relief valve is a safety device built into the compressor by manufacturers to ensure that pressures cannot get too high in the system and rupture a line. The ECU of the HVAC system can turn on the condenser cooling fan, which is sometimes the same fan used to pull air through the radiator, to reduce the temperature of the refrigerant, which in turn reduces pressure.

Either the low-pressure sensor or the high-pressure sensor can send a **variable voltage signal** to the ECU based on the pressure in the system. The air-conditioning pressure sensor's voltage will vary with pressure from about 0.5 to 4.5 volts; this information is again compared to programmed information in memory to determine the pressure in the system and the correct action.

Applied | **Science**

AS-80: Mechanical Transducers: The technician can demonstrate an understanding of the role mechanical transducers play in sending an electrical control signal to modify the system's operation.

Transducers are electronic devices which convert one form of energy to another. Position sensors are a form of transducer employed in many automotive systems. They indicate the position of components by converting kinetic (motion) energy into electrical energy.

Climate control systems use various doors to control the direction and temperature of airflow into the cabin. These are commonly known as "blend doors". In order for the climate control ECU to effectively manage the operation of the system and achieve the cabin conditions desired by the driver, it must be able to monitor the position of the blend doors. This is accomplished by blend door actuators being fitted with transducers which feed information back to the ECU regarding door positions.

Evaporator Temperature Sensor

The **evaporator temperature sensor** is located in the airstream where the air leaves the evaporator and signals to the ECU the temperature of the air **FIGURE 43-12**. It is usually a two-wire, NTC-type thermistor. The evaporator temperature sensor works in the same manner as the exterior and interior temperature sensors, lowering resistance as the temperature goes up. Information programmed within the ECU recognizes the changes in resistance and translates that into a temperature reading. The evaporator temperature sensor is used to ensure that the evaporator does not get too cold. The evaporator gets moisture on it due to the warmer moist air moving to the colder surface temperature of the tubes and fins of the evaporator. The moisture is attracted to the evaporator, as it is the coldest part exposed to the warm air inside the vehicle, which also contains moisture. If the evaporator temperature drops too low, the moisture will freeze on the evaporator and block airflow through the fins. If this happens, cold air will stop flowing to the passenger compartment. When the air conditioner is turned off for a while to let the evaporator warm, the ice will melt and airflow will be cold and normal when the air conditioner is turned back on. The evaporator temperature sensor will ensure that the evaporator does not get too cold by either reducing the compressor on time or shortening the stroke of a variable displacement compressor to reduce the amount of refrigerant flowing in the system. Of course, if it uses

FIGURE 43-12 An evaporator temperature sensor.

a thermal expansion valve, then the ability to modify refrigerant flow will also help keep the evaporator from freezing.

HVAC Control Panel

One other input to the ECU of the HVAC system comes from the HVAC control panel. The operator can tell the ECU where to deliver air and at what temperature, using switches that produce an **on/off–type signal**. The ECU will receive either a 12-volt signal or 0 volts. For example, pushing the windshield defrost button sends an "on–12 volt" signal to the ECU. Pushing the floor button cancels the defrost button. The defrost button now sends an "off–0 volt" signal to the control unit. At the same time, the floor button sends an "on–12 volt" signal to the ECU for the floor vent.

The ECU also receives instructions from the operator regarding the desired cabin temperature via the control panel. The desired temperature selection is used to tell the ECU what temperature the operator wishes the inside of the vehicle to be. The ECU then adjusts the position of valves and doors to achieve the desired temperature and direction of airflow.

Control Panel Types

The control panel buttons, knobs, and dials vary from vehicle to vehicle and from system to system, depending on whether the system is manual, semiautomatic, or fully automatic. There are also dual-zone and rear climate control panels.

If the system is a manual control panel, there will be a rotary or linear switch for fan speed, a rotary or linear switch for modes (floor, defrost, vent, or vent and floor), and a rotary or linear switch for temperature. On some models, an air-conditioning button will be on the panel, as well as a recirculation button.

On a semiautomatic system, the control panel has a rotary temperature switch, a rotary fan switch, a rotary mode switch, a recirculation button, and possibly an economy button that will limit the air-conditioning compressor operation in an attempt to improve fuel mileage. This system uses an ECU to determine when to run the compressor and the amount of heat to match the desired temperature selected by the operator. The missing control is the air-conditioning button, since the ECU controls operation based on its input sensors.

The fully automatic system control panel has a fan rotary switch, a temperature selection switch or rotary switch, and mode switches. There is an economy button and an auto button to place the system in automatic mode. The operator can select manual control of this system, so all buttons previously discussed with the manual control panel are present on the automatic panel as well. The control panel has a digital display to show the temperature selected **FIGURE 43-13**.

The dual-zone temperature control panel is designed to allow the driver and passenger to control temperature delivered to their side of the vehicle and has resulted in a more pleasant passenger compartment for each individual. The control panel for this design contains the same buttons used in other systems but has two temperature control switches. With dual controls, the air box must have two blend doors and two blend door actuators to allow for separate temperature control.

The last system available is the rear climate control panel. The control panel at the front of the vehicle has a rear button in addition to all the other buttons and switches covered. When the rear button is selected, the rear panel controls located at the back of the vehicle are activated. The driver can turn off control of the panel at the rear by pressing this button on the front panel. With the rear air control panel selected on the front panel, the rear passengers can typically select temperature, fan speed, and mode **FIGURE 43-14**.

Control Panel Components

The control panel assembly could be a mechanical system that operates via cables, such as the **heater control cables**, vacuum valves, or electrical switches. It could also be an automatic system that is operated

FIGURE 43-13 Control panels. **A.** Manual. **B.** Automatic.

FIGURE 43-14 Rear climate control. **A.** Front control panel with switch to activate the rear air-conditioning. **B.** Rear control panel.

electronically. Cable systems tend to be found only on older vehicles. The cables bind up over time and do not work properly, so most manufacturers have moved away from control cables. The components of the control panel vary according to the type of system used. Electric control panels contain electric switches that connect to the system wires. Most of the switches located on a modern control panel are inputs to the ECU.

Vacuum systems contain vacuum switches or valves that direct source vacuum from a vacuum canister connected to engine vacuum to different vacuum servos **FIGURE 43-15**.

The vacuum canister is installed on the vacuum system to ensure that vacuum is present for the control panel to use even when the engine is at wide open throttle (vacuum goes away under wide open throttle). Thus, the canister provides a reserve of vacuum so the controls can continue to operate. The vacuum switches or valves connect vacuum hoses together at the panel. For example, when the operator wants air to come out at the floor, he or she selects the floor mode and the switch or valve will connect the source vacuum line to the floor vacuum servo, which moves the mode door to the floor position.

HVAC-Controlled Devices

The controlled devices carry out the commands of the operator. If more airflow is commanded, the operator will move a switch, dial, or lever indicating the desired outcome. That information will be transmitted as a signal that will cause the fan to speed up. The same goes for the preferred location of ducted air. If the operator selects vent, then the signal will be transmitted to the appropriate actuator and cause an air door to open or close. Each of the controlled devices causes an action to be carried

out in the HVAC system. We will look at those devices one at a time.

Relays

Several different relays can be used in an HVAC system to control electric components such as the **air-conditioning compressor clutch** and condenser fan **FIGURE 43-16**. Relays control a relatively large current flow in one part of a circuit by a much smaller current flow. Some of these relays are controlled by the ECU of the HVAC system, which sends the smaller current flow signal to the relay when it wants to turn on the particular device that the relay operates. The small current in the relay creates a strong magnetic field in the relay windings, which pulls a set of higher current contacts together. The contacts send battery power to the fan or compressor clutch, which is then energized and operates. When the ECU determines that the device no longer needs to operate, it stops the signal to the relay, which stops the current flow in the windings and turns off the magnetic field. The spring in the relay now pulls the contacts apart, stopping the current flow to the controlled device and turning it off.

The ECU can control either the power side of the relay winding, which would then usually have the ground side connected directly to ground, or the ground side of the relay winding, which means that the power side of the winding is most likely connected to power through a fused circuit from the ignition switch. Relay windings are normally equipped with a mechanism to reduce voltage spikes, which are induced in the windings when the relay is deactivated. The voltage suppression can take the form of either a diode or a resistor wired in parallel with the winding. In this way, a path for the voltage spike is provided through the diode or resistor back to the other side of the winding. Voltage spikes can travel back through the circuit and damage electronic

FIGURE 43-15 Vacuum canister connected to engine vacuum.

FIGURE 43-16 Relay-activated compressor clutch electrical diagram.

devices, so always be sure to use relays with the proper voltage suppression for the vehicle you are repairing.

FIGURE 43-17 Blower motor.

Blower Motor

One of the controlled devices used in the climate control system is the blower motor. The **blower motor** is the means of moving air into and through the passenger cabin. The blower motor is an electric motor that is attached to a circular fan sometimes referred to by technicians as a squirrel cage fan. The blower motor runs at different speeds to provide the operator with the desired amount of airflow. One way of changing the speed is through the use of a blower motor resistor pack. A blower motor resistor pack is a set of different resistors. As a resistance increases, voltage drops (Ohm's law) and will make the motor spin at a slower pace. The resistors are selected through the fan speed switch. As you select the next speed, you are adding another resistor in series with the blower motor **FIGURE 43-17**.

Blower Motor Speed Control

The blower motor supplies the airflow to move air around the inside of the passenger cabin. It usually is located in the ventilation system before the air-conditioning evaporator and draws air from either the passenger cabin or outside the vehicle.

In a manual air conditioner, the fan control switch connects **resistors in series** with the blower motor to control its speed **FIGURE 43-18**. The fan switch directs current to certain resistors, which reduce the voltage and current to change fan speed. The higher the resistance connected in line with the blower motor, the slower the blower motor will operate. Reducing the resistance increases the blower motor operating speed, since less resistance increases the voltage and current to the motor. Think of a flashlight as the batteries die. The bulb gets dimmer since voltage is lower, but if we insert new batteries, the bulb gets brighter because the higher voltage can push more amperage or current through the bulb.

FIGURE 43-18 Blower motor schematic.

A motor will run slower if the voltage is lower and faster if the voltage is higher.

Changing the resistance to the blower motor is accomplished by using the fan control switch to select which resistor(s) the current will pass through. Each time we change the switch position, we change the resistance of the circuit and change the voltage. When we select full speed, the resistors are bypassed and full voltage is applied to the motor. Most manual air-conditioning systems use three resistors to give four operator-selectable speeds of the blower motor. This system works the same as described previously by selecting one resistor to put into the circuit based on the switch position. As we want the motor to spin slower, we increase the resistance to the motor (decreasing the voltage and amperage). In the three-resistor pack, we have three speeds that result from resistance added to the circuit. We also have full voltage, which is the fourth speed; this is a circuit with all resistance removed from the circuit except the motor. Resistors can be used on either the positive (B+) side or the negative (B–) side of the motor, depending upon the manufacturer's preference.

When current flows through a resistance, heat is generated. Since the blower motor draws quite a bit of current flow when it is operating, the blower motor resistors generate quite a bit of heat. To help prevent them from overheating, they are usually made of fairly heavy metal, wound in a loose series of coils and placed in the blower airstream. So while the blower motor is operating, airflow from the fan is blown across the resistor coils to help prevent them from overheating.

> ### TECHNICIAN TIP
>
> Some resistor blocks incorporate one or more thermal fuses to protect the circuit if the blower resistors overheat. Since the thermal fuses and resistors are in the blower motor airstream, airflow helps to keep them from overheating. If the cabin air filter becomes clogged or the blower motor becomes bound up, airflow will be reduced and the thermal fuse can overheat and blow. If a thermal fuse, or even a regular blower motor fuse blows, check for poor blower motor current flow, binding of the fan, and a restricted cabin air filter.

On some vehicles, the highest fan (blower motor) speed may be powered directly from a dedicated fan relay. This design enables full-speed blower motor operation. The fan control switch is connected to a relay. The fan control switch gives 12 volts to the control coil of the relay. Ground is usually constant by a wire connected straight to ground. When the coil gets 12 volts, a magnetic field is produced and the contacts in the relay close.

The relay applies full battery voltage to the blower motor fan to give high speed. The reason a relay is used is so the fan switch does not have to handle the full blower motor amperage flowing through it. It takes very little amperage to make the magnetic field, but it takes a lot of amperage to run the blower motor at full speed, and this high amperage would damage the fan control switch **FIGURE 43-19**. In some vehicles, the relay can be used to supply a full ground (B–) to the ground side of the motor instead of the power side (B+).

In automatic climate control systems, the speed of the blower motor can be controlled electronically by the ECU of the HVAC system. The ECU controls the speed by pulsing voltage to the fan. This system is called pulse width modulation. The longer the voltage is on, the faster the fan runs. A shorter pulse width signal produces a lower fan speed. The ECU can produce a progressively variable fan speed between zero and maximum speed by varying the pulse width. Recall that the blower motor resistor design gives us four total fan speeds. By pulsing voltage longer or shorter, we are able to create an infinite numbers of speeds. The ECU controls the speed of the blower motor automatically depending on the difference between the interior cabin temperature and the operator-selected temperature. When the difference in temperature is large, the blower motor speed is high to increase air circulation through the cabin. As the difference in temperature decreases, the blower motor speed decreases.

Air Box and Air Doors

The blower motor is attached to the air box. The air box is a plastic housing that holds other components of the climate control system, such as the heater core and the evaporator. The air box also includes the doors that direct airflow to different discharge areas within the passenger compartment such as the vents, floor, or

FIGURE 43-19 Blower motor high speed may be controlled by a relay.

windshield defroster. There are several doors that control airflow and air temperature. The blend door directs air through or around the heater core to deliver hot or cold air into the passenger cabin. The mode door changes the location of air delivery to floor, defrost, or vent. The recirculation door is designed to work with the maximum air-conditioning button or switch and will shut airflow off from outside the vehicle and instead recirculate air from inside the passenger compartment back through the evaporator. By moving this air through the evaporator again and again, the temperature inside the vehicle can be reduced more quickly **FIGURE 43-20**. The blower motor and resistor pack are bolted into the air box as well. The reason the resistor pack is bolted into the air box is to ensure that the resistor pack does not get too hot; air from the squirrel cage fan needs to flow over the resistors.

Vacuum-Style Servo Motors

Actuators are mechanical devices that create rotary or linear movement. They are sometimes called servos, or servo motors. Actuators move the air box doors to control temperature and position of the airflow from the air distribution system. Actuators can be electric or vacuum powered. Electric actuators come in two styles—geared motor and solenoid. Geared motor actuators are used in HVAC systems, while solenoid actuators are used in systems such as door locks and fuel door latches.

The **vacuum servo** differs from the electric actuator in that it is a sealed container with a spring and diaphragm inside. The vacuum servo uses vacuum on a diaphragm to pull a link or lever that is connected to the air box door **FIGURE 43-21**. The diaphragm is connected to one of the air box doors by means of a rod or linkage. When vacuum is released, the spring will push the diaphragm back to its starting position. Vacuum is applied to the actuator

through the control head and will only be present or removed when movement is needed.

Vacuum servos can be controlled electrically by using a solenoid to control the vacuum source **FIGURE 43-22**. The use of a solenoid allows electrical control of a vacuum source. Solenoids are operated by providing power and ground. The ECU of the HVAC system usually controls the ground side. When ground is supplied to the solenoid by the ECU, the solenoid activates and vacuum is applied through the solenoid valve to the vacuum servo. To release the vacuum servo, the ECU turns the ground off to the solenoid and allows the vacuum to bleed off, which makes the door return to the original position.

Electric Servo Motors

Movement of air box doors can also be achieved by using <u>electric servo motors</u>, also referred to as actuators. Electric actuators respond to output signals from the

FIGURE 43-21 Vacuum servo construction.

FIGURE 43-20 The recirculation door is designed to shut airflow off from outside the vehicle and instead recirculate air from inside the passenger compartment back through the evaporator.

FIGURE 43-22 Vacuum solenoid diagram.

ECU of the HVAC system. The electric actuator performs the same job as the vacuum servo, moving the air box doors. Electric actuators use an electric motor and gears to create either rotary or linear motion, which is used to operate the air doors. The electric actuator may incorporate <u>limit switches</u> to stop current to the electric actuator when the maximum travel of the door has been reached **FIGURE 43-23**. This stoppage prevents the electric actuator from burning out. Other actuators use stepper motors that can be controlled by the ECU precisely one step at a time. This design gives precise movement to the door, and the ECU can monitor the position of the door by knowing how many steps opened or closed it, as commanded by the actuator.

Some electric servo motors also use a <u>potentiometer</u> to signal to the ECU the position of the blend door and, if it is moving, the direction in which it is traveling. The potentiometer is a variable resistor that will vary resistance with movement. The potentiometer functions as a position sensor and is used as a throttle position sensor on the engine. The potentiometer is a three-wire sensor that has a 5-volt reference voltage, a signal wire that provides feedback to the ECU (in this case), and a ground **FIGURE 43-24**. When the voltage from the actuator sensor matches the programmed information in the memory of the ECU, the door is in the correct position desired and the actuator's electric motor will stop moving. For maximum cooling effect, the blend door is moved to stop airflow through the heater core; in this position, the voltage signal back to the ECU is at its lowest value. As the blend door is moved to allow airflow through the heater core, the voltage at the signal wire progressively increases until at the maximum heat position, where the voltage signal is at its highest. The ECU is thus aware of the blend door position, movement, and direction of travel.

FIGURE 43-23 Scan tool data from an actuator that sends feedback to the ECU.

FIGURE 43-24 Electric actuator with potentiometer. The potentiometer is a three-wire sensor that has a 5-volt reference voltage, a feedback wire that signals back to the ECU (in this case), and a ground.

Hybrid Air-Conditioning System Principles

The air-conditioning system in hybrid vehicles is almost always a climate-controlled HVAC system. This is because there are additional demands put on the HVAC system by the hybrid vehicle. One demand is the need to provide cooling, either directly or indirectly, to the high-voltage battery to prevent it from being overheated. As such, the ECU of the HVAC system must be able to take control of the air-conditioning system and operate as needed to keep the battery at the proper temperature. To accomplish this, the ECU monitors the battery temperature with a temperature sensor.

Another difference in some hybrid vehicles is the ability for the driver to remotely activate the HVAC system to cool the vehicle before entering it. The driver can operate a button on the key fob from inside his or her home or office to activate the HVAC system and begin cooling the passenger compartment. This system requires a higher level of system control.

For the most part, the components in the HVAC system of a hybrid vehicle are the same as in the systems discussed previously, but there are differences. The compressor in the hybrid air-conditioning system may be driven by the internal combustion engine (ICE) through a standard belt and <u>electromagnetic clutch arrangement</u>, just like a standard air-conditioning compressor clutch arrangement. Most hybrids now use a high-voltage electric motor, which directly drives the compressor **FIGURE 43-25**. This style does not have a belt driving it. If the compressor has orange, high-voltage wires connected to it, then the compressor uses a high-voltage electric motor for driving

The voltage in high-voltage compressor systems is very dangerous. Only technicians certified to work on high-voltage systems should attempt diagnosis and repair on these systems. Voltages can run up to 500 volts. This voltage can be lethal and requires the use of leak-tested, insulated electrical Class 0 1000-volt gloves (and protective covers). It also requires a Cat III–certified digital volt-ohmmeter (DVOM), which is rated to withstand 1000 volts. Also, never attempt to pierce the insulation on high-voltage wires; doing so can cause severe injury or death as well as major damage to the electrical circuit.

FIGURE 43-25 Electrically driven air-conditioning compressor.

FIGURE 43-26 Dual-drive air-conditioning compressor.

the air-conditioning compressor. In this case, the electric air-conditioning compressor motor can be turned on and off as needed by the ECU without the ICE operating. It can also vary the compressor speed based on the amount of cooling needed. This system greatly improves efficiency and reduces emissions.

Some hybrids use **dual-drive air-conditioning compressors** **FIGURE 43-26**. These compressors can be belt driven by the ICE or by a high-voltage motor. The belt may drive a larger-capacity scroll, while the electric motor drives a smaller-capacity scroll. These systems can usually be identified by orange high-voltage cables and a belt-driven clutch. This type of system allows the larger compressor scroll to be driven by the ICE whenever it is running. The electric motor drives the smaller scroll when the engine is off and the vehicle is being powered by the storage batteries or when extra cooling is needed while the ICE is operating. The benefit of this type of system is that the air conditioner continues to operate as needed when the ICE shuts off (such as at a stoplight) to keep the occupants comfortable. When the ICE starts, it will power the compressor instead of pulling power from the high-voltage battery pack. The lower amount of power pulled from the battery pack allows it to recharge more quickly, resulting in better economy.

TECHNICIAN TIP

The compressors in most hybrid vehicles require special oil in their air-conditioning system. Always check the manufacturer's recommendation for HVAC oil, and do not mix with the wrong oil.

Diagnosis

Many new vehicles are designed with HVAC systems that have built-in self-diagnostics. In these systems, the ECU is programmed to recognize signals or situations that are out of specifications and display a diagnostic trouble code (DTC). You can use this information to help determine the cause of the system fault.

At the same time, you will need to use your understanding of the system's theory of operation and apply that to the way the system is operating. It is always good practice to perform a system performance test and run the system through all of its operating parameters, noting any deviations from the manufacturer's specified operation. Using any DTC information, along with any system operational issues, will allow you to research and follow the manufacturer's troubleshooting chart and locate the cause of the fault. The more you practice this process, the better you will become at it.

Tools

Several tools are necessary for the service and repair of the HVAC system. Proper training on the use of these tools is required to ensure that you do not hurt yourself, damage the vehicle, or damage the tool itself.

- Infrared thermometer: This tool ensures that the vehicle is reaching full operating temperature. The infrared thermometer allows temperature testing without actually opening the cooling system while hot. Opening a hot cooling system is very dangerous and can result in serious burns to the technician's face, body, and hands if the temperature is close to or above boiling. Use extreme caution when working with the cooling system.

- Digital volt-ohmmeter (DVOM): A DVOM is absolutely necessary when working with electronics. It has a very high internal resistance, which keeps the meter from pulling too much current from the electronic parts being tested. An older-style analog meter could cause too much current flow during testing and damage components. The DVOM is used to test for correct voltages at electrical components in the HVAC system and to test wiring for high resistance. Back probes are necessary to test electrical components while they are operating **FIGURE 43-27**.

- Fused jumper wire: The wire should be fused so that if hooked up incorrectly it is more likely to blow the fuse than to damage the vehicle's wiring. This tool is used to jump suspected bad switches or relays for testing purposes. However, just because it is less likely to damage wires, does not mean it will not damage electronics. It will. Always verify that you are hooking it up correctly.

FIGURE 43-27 A DVOM with a set of back probes is necessary to test electrical components while they are operating.

- A scan tool: This tool is necessary for checking DTCs in the ECU of the HVAC system and for performing bidirectional controls of electrical loads. Some vehicles have diagnostics built in to the control panel, and in those cases the use of a scan tool will only be necessary for bidirectional control of the electrical loads, such as for the cooling fan, blower motor, or electric actuators.

Applied | Science

AS-100: Flow Rate: The technician can demonstrate an understanding of how variances in flow rate in airflow sensors and cooling systems can affect engine performance.

Airflow has a fundamental effect on cooling system performance as a steady flow of cool air though the radiator core is essential to remove heat from the system. Radiator fans are fitted to provide additional airflow through the radiator at times when airflow is insufficient. In late model vehicles, radiator fans are controlled by the ECU in response to coolant temperature sensor readings.

When a vehicle is stationery or moving slowly airflow is generally insufficient to keep the engine cool. In response to high coolant temperatures the ECU will operate the fan. This occurs in cycles with the fan turned on when a high specified coolant temperature is reached, then turned off when the system temperature returns to a lower specified value. When the vehicle is moving quickly airflow increases, so little or no fan operation may be required.

Safety

Never jump across the load (the electrical part of the circuit doing the work), such as the cooling fan or electric actuator. Doing so will remove the load from the circuit and create a direct short to ground.

Common Issues

Before working on the HVAC system, be sure to check technical service bulletins matching your vehicle for any issues similar to the customer concern. A common issue a technician might encounter with the automatic HVAC system is the failure of electric actuators. Electric actuators have small plastic gears inside that can strip out if the mode doors get jammed or develop drag when turning. Before installing the new actuator, be sure to test the door operation by turning the door by hand and noting the drag on the door. If you are unsure, compare the drag to another door that is easily accessible.

If the vehicle uses vacuum servos to control the mode doors and blend door, failure in the vacuum hose(s) can result in failed operation. Refer to the vacuum chart for the HVAC system you are working on to properly diagnose the concern. Vacuum leaks can be found by using a handheld vacuum pump on one end of the vacuum hose and plugging the other end or by using a smoke machine to blow smoke into the vacuum lines. A visual inspection looking for wisps of smoke leaking out of hoses or vacuum servos will help to determine the exact location of the leak. Vacuum servos will fail at times, and they are best tested by use of a handheld vacuum pump. Using a handheld vacuum pump, pull a vacuum on the servo and watch for movement. If no movement is noted, ensure that the door to which the servo is connected is not binding. If the door is not binding, does the servo hold vacuum? If not, replace the leaky servo. If movement is noted, does the servo hold vacuum? If not, replace the leaky servo.

Sensor failure is possible and typically will result in a DTC being stored in the ECU. Refer to the manufacturer's service information on details for accessing DTCs on the system you are servicing. Refer to the description of any system you are unfamiliar with to ensure that you understand how the system works. You cannot fix something if you are unsure whether it is broken.

Checking Operation of Automatic or Semiautomatic HVAC Control Systems

Checking the operation of the automatic or semiautomatic HVAC system is really just a performance check for the system. It is required when a customer complains of an HVAC issue. This check will allow you to verify that there is an issue and to determine the extent of the issue. One of the first steps is to research the system's operation in the service information, which will give you a good idea of how to perform a thorough testing. Some vehicles require auxiliary airflow provided by an external condenser fan, while others will specify the parameters that need to be met for the results to be accurate. The service information will also likely provide you with temperature charts to which you can compare your results. Always follow the manufacturer's testing procedure.

To check the operation of automatic or semiautomatic HVAC control systems, follow the steps in **SKILL DRILL 43-1**:

1. Research the testing procedure in the service information. Start the engine and allow the system to normalize.

2. Operate all of the controls and verify the operation of each setting, including the fan speeds,

SKILL DRILL 43-1 Checking the Operation of Automatic or Semiautomatic HVAC Control Systems

1. Research the testing procedure. Start the engine and allow the system to normalize. Operate all of the controls and verify the operation of each setting, including fan speeds, air-conditioning and heater on/off control, airflow modes (defrost, vents, floor), temperature control, and any other features.

2. Measure the duct temperature. Compare this temperature to specifications and confirm that it matches the temperature settings.

air-conditioning and heater on/off control, airflow modes (defrost, vents, floor), temperature control, and any other features of the system. **(Photo 1)**

3 Measure the duct air temperature. Compare this temperature to specifications and confirm that it matches the temperature settings. **(Photo 2)**

Using a Scan Tool to Observe and Record HVAC-Related Data and Codes

Scan tools are used to pull codes from a particular computer. Not all HVAC systems use computer controls, so it is important to check the engine computer for issues relating to how the vehicle runs that could affect HVAC performance. If the HVAC system is computer controlled, this check should be done before a performance test, as some codes will cause the computer to shut off the HVAC system to protect it. Codes are letters and numbers that can be looked up in a diagnostic chart to see what kind of problem the computer encountered. There are many different types of scan tools available on the market, each with its own specific procedure for use. The technician must read and follow the instructions provided with the particular scan tool being used.

To use a scan tool to diagnose HVAC systems, follow the steps in **SKILL DRILL 43-2**:

1 Hook up the scanner. Any vehicle manufactured since 1996 must be OBD-II compliant. One of the

requirements is that the scanner plug be identical and located within a certain distance from the steering wheel. The scanner is plugged into this plug to access information. Older vehicles had a plug, but each manufacturer had a different type of plug and location for it. Scanners have a cable with the OBD-II plug or a plug that would accept several different adapters to fit different vehicles that were built before 1996. **(Photo 1)**

2 Write down all of the air-conditioning codes. For example, a Ford vehicle may have a code 24 or 25, which relates to blend door issues. Each make and model of vehicle and air-conditioning system will have their own unique codes. Check any freeze-frame data and write that down. **(Photo 2)**

3 Look at the scan data, such as the various system temperatures and pressures, and identify any abnormal readings. When repairs are completed, follow the service information for the vehicle and clear the codes. **(Photo 3)**

Inspecting and Testing the Electric Cooling Fan

Inspecting and testing the electric cooling fan will be necessary for several customer concerns. The concerns for testing the cooling fan can vary from overheating of the vehicle's engine to an air-conditioning system that does not get cold enough. The tools

SKILL DRILL 43-2 Using a Scan Tool to Observe and Record HVAC-Related Data and Codes

1. Connect the scanner to the diagnostic connector.
2. Write down all of the air-conditioning codes. Check any freeze-frame data and write that down.
3. Look at the scan data, such as the system temperatures and pressures, and identify any abnormal readings. When repairs are completed, clear the trouble codes.

required for testing the cooling fan include a scan tool, a DVOM, a fused jumper wire, back probes, and service information. It is critical that you have a thorough understanding of how the system works before attempting a repair.

To inspect and test the electric cooling fan, follow the steps in **SKILL DRILL 43-3**:

1. Verify the customer concern by turning on the HVAC system and observing the cooling fan. If the cooling fan does not come on when the system is turned on, install the scan tool and find the bidirectional controls for the cooling fan; then turn the cooling fan on. **(Photo 1)**

2. If the cooling fan still does not run when commanded, find the coolant fan relay, remove the relay, and find the two connections that provide power to the cooling fan (this is the switch side of the fan relay). **(Photo 2)**

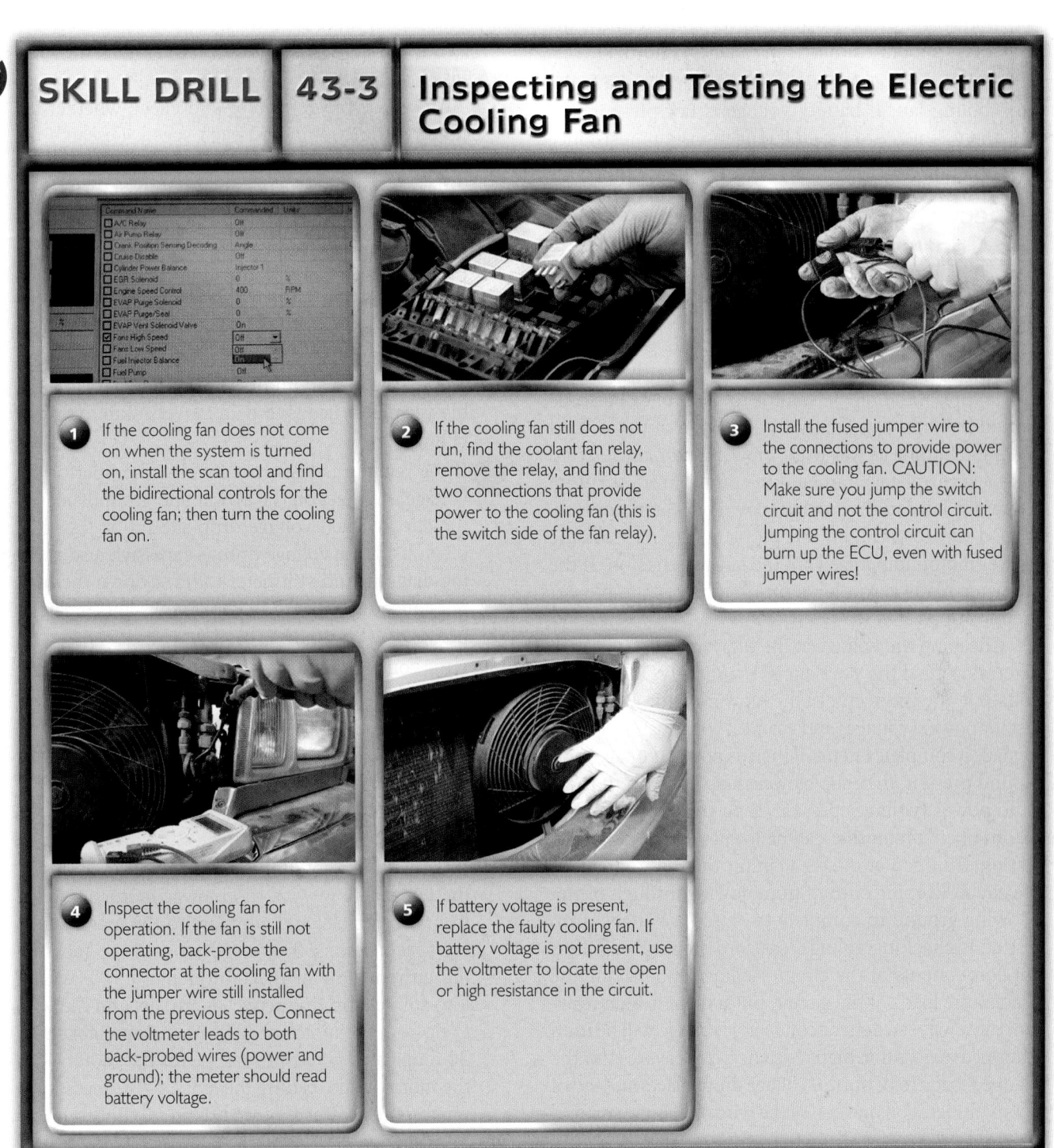

SKILL DRILL | 43-3 | Inspecting and Testing the Electric Cooling Fan

1. If the cooling fan does not come on when the system is turned on, install the scan tool and find the bidirectional controls for the cooling fan; then turn the cooling fan on.

2. If the cooling fan still does not run, find the coolant fan relay, remove the relay, and find the two connections that provide power to the cooling fan (this is the switch side of the fan relay).

3. Install the fused jumper wire to the connections to provide power to the cooling fan. CAUTION: Make sure you jump the switch circuit and not the control circuit. Jumping the control circuit can burn up the ECU, even with fused jumper wires!

4. Inspect the cooling fan for operation. If the fan is still not operating, back-probe the connector at the cooling fan with the jumper wire still installed from the previous step. Connect the voltmeter leads to both back-probed wires (power and ground); the meter should read battery voltage.

5. If battery voltage is present, replace the faulty cooling fan. If battery voltage is not present, use the voltmeter to locate the open or high resistance in the circuit.

3 Install the fused jumper wire to the connections; this will provide power to the cooling fan. CAUTION: Make sure you jump the switch circuit and not the control circuit. Jumping the control circuit can burn up the ECU, even with fused jumper wires! **(Photo 3)**

4 Inspect the cooling fan for operation. If the fan is still not operating, back-probe the connector at the cooling fan with the jumper wire still installed from the previous step. Connect the voltmeter leads to both back-probed wires (power and ground); the meter should read battery voltage. **(Photo 4)**

5 If the meter reads battery voltage, replace the faulty cooling fan. If battery voltage is not present, use the voltmeter to locate the open or high resistance in the circuit. **(Photo 5)**

Inspecting and Testing Blower Motors and Control Circuits

Blower motors and control circuits (typically, a rotary switch and a resistor pack) are usually not complicated. Basic electrical testing with a DVOM and a good wiring diagram will usually isolate the problem fairly quickly. The failure of the blower motor to operate can also be caused by an object falling through one of the defrost vents and finding its way to the blower motor fan, referred to as a squirrel cage fan, and keeping it from turning. A jammed fan could result in a blown blower motor fuse. A good way to check for this problem is to measure the blower motor amperage with the fan switched on. If the ammeter reads zero, the control circuit or the blower motor is open.

Checking the voltage at the blower motor will help determine what the problem is. Using a DVOM, test for voltage at the connector of the blower motor. Be sure to test for power (voltage) and ground; you must have both to make a complete circuit. If there is power (voltage) and ground present, then the blower motor is open. If there is no power (voltage) present, then the control circuit has an open circuit that can be located by voltage drop testing. An open circuit is a circuit that has a break in the circuit keeping current from flowing through or not allowing ground to complete the circuit. Voltage drop testing is checking voltage loss across a wire or different components of the circuit. Voltage should only be used in the loads of the circuit, but if there is high resistance in a wire, switch, or connector, voltage will be used (dropped) across that high resistance and leave less for the planned load. To perform a voltage drop, place one lead of your voltmeter on one end of the wire or component and

the other lead on the other end. With the circuit operating, read the voltage drop. More than 0.2 volts means you have high resistance in that wire, switch, or connector.

If you are using an ammeter, note if it reads near or higher than specifications. If so, the fan will need to be removed and checked for foreign objects (jamming the fan), binding of the fan motor shaft, or a shorted motor. A shorted motor means the windings of wire inside the fan have shorted together and reduced the resistance of the motor. Low resistance will create excessive current flow and slower motor speed.

To inspect and test a blower motor, follow the steps in **SKILL DRILL 43-4** :

1 Turn on the blower motor and check whether the motor is functioning on each speed. Research the diagnostic procedure in the appropriate service information to test the control circuit of the blower motor. **(Photo 1)**

2 Use a DVOM to test for power and ground by back-probing the wires at the connector of the blower motor. Turn the ignition switch to "run" and the fan switch to the speed that does not operate, and read the meter. If the meter reads more than about 3 volts, the fan should be operating. If it isn't, the blower motor needs to be removed, skip to step 4. **(Photo 2)**

3 If the reading is less than 3 volts, then perform a voltage drop test on the power and ground sides of the circuit. Each voltage drop should be less than 0.5 volts. If the voltage drop is excessive, use a wiring diagram and voltmeter to track down the high resistance or opening in the circuit, and repair as necessary. **(Photo 3)**

4 If the control circuit tests good but the fan is making unusual noises or is not operating correctly, remove the blower motor by disconnecting the electrical connector and removing any bolts, nuts, or clips retaining the blower motor to the air box. **(Photo 4)**

5 Inspect the fan blades and fins for foreign objects or binding. **(Photo 5)**

6 If the fan is in good operating condition, measure the current flow with the blower motor removed from the vehicle, and compare to the manufacturer's specifications. There are two ways to measure the current flow of the blower motor: (1) with a low-amp clamp (inductive clamp) around the wire to or from the motor or (2) with an ammeter set to 20 amps and wired in series with the motor. Run the motor while reading the amperage. If necessary, replace the blower motor and retest. **(Photo 6)**

SKILL DRILL | 43-4 | Inspecting and Testing a Blower Motor

1 Turn on the blower motor and check whether the motor is functioning on each speed. Research the testing procedures for the condition found.

2 Use a DVOM to test for power and ground by back-probing the wires at the connector of the blower motor. Turn the ignition switch to "run" and the fan switch to the speed that does not operate, and read the meter. If the meter reads more than about 3 volts, the fan should be operating. If it isn't, the blower motor needs to be removed. (see photo 4).

3 If the reading is less than 3 volts, then perform a voltage drop test on the power and ground sides of the circuit. If the voltage drop is excessive, use a wiring diagram and voltmeter to track down the high resistance or opening in the circuit, and repair as necessary.

4 If the control circuit tests good but the fan is making unusual noises or is not operating correctly, remove the blower motor by disconnecting the electrical connector and removing any bolts, nuts, or clips retaining the blower motor to the air box.

5 Inspect the fan blades and fins for foreign objects or binding.

6 If the fan is in good operating condition, measure the current flow with the blower motor removed from the vehicle, either (1) with a low-amp clamp (inductive clamp) around the wire to or from the motor or (2) with an ammeter set to 20 amps and wired in series with the motor. Run the motor while reading the amperage. If necessary, replace the blower motor and retest.

Testing Air-Conditioning Compressor Clutch Control Systems

The air-conditioning compressor clutch control system needs to be checked whenever the clutch does not engage or slips; you will notice that the center of the compressor pulley (the front portion of the pulley) is not turning or is clicking on and off. This can be caused by a bad clutch coil, an electrical fault in the control circuit, a clutch air gap that is too big, or a low refrigerant level, which causes the pressure to be too low to activate the pressure switch. A DVOM and a wiring diagram will be needed to locate any control circuit faults.

To test the air-conditioning compressor clutch control system, follow the steps in **SKILL DRILL 43-5**:

1. Research the testing procedure and specifications in the appropriate service information. Unplug the compressor clutch electrical two-wire connector located at the front of the air-conditioning compressor. Check the resistance of the clutch windings. If the resistance does not match the manufacturer's specifications, replace the clutch coil. **(Photo 1)**

2. Check supply voltage and ground to the compressor clutch connector. Place the red lead on the positive side of the clutch connector, and place the black lead on the negative side of the clutch connector. Ensure that the air-conditioning compressor is turned on. Near-full battery voltage should be displayed on your meter. **(Photo 2)**

3. Perform a voltage drop test of power and ground. Connect the red lead of your voltmeter to the positive terminal of the clutch coil connector. Connect the black lead to the battery positive. Ensure that the air-conditioning clutch is turned on with the control panel. Look for a drop or loss of voltage on the positive side of no more than 0.4 volts. If more than 0.4 volts is found, the power side has high resistance in it and you will

---

SKILL DRILL | **43-5** | **Testing Air-Conditioning Compressor Clutch Control Systems**

1. Research the testing procedure and specifications in the appropriate service information. Unplug the compressor clutch electrical two-wire connector located at the front of the air-conditioning compressor. Check the resistance of the clutch windings. If the resistance does not match the manufacturer's specifications, replace the clutch coil.

2. Check supply voltage and ground to the compressor clutch connector. Place the red lead on the positive side of the clutch connector, and place the black lead on the negative side of the clutch connector. Ensure that the air-conditioning compressor is turned on. Your meter should display near battery voltage.

3. Perform a voltage drop test of power and ground. Connect the red lead of your voltmeter to the positive terminal of the clutch coil connector. Connect the black lead to battery positive. Ensure that the air-conditioning clutch is turned on with the control panel. Look for a drop or loss of voltage on the positive wire of no more than 0.4 volts. If more than 0.4 volts is found, the power wire has high resistance in it. Repeat the step for the ground side by connecting the red lead to the negative terminal and the black lead to the battery negative.

need to narrow down the source of the voltage drop. Repeat the step for the ground side by connecting the red lead to the negative terminal clutch connector and the black lead to the battery negative. **(Photo 3)**

Diagnosing Malfunctions in the HVAC Controls

Diagnosis of ECU systems can be complicated because the system components are interrelated. For example, the blend door may be in a position that is causing the duct air temperature to be too hot. This could be caused by a temperature sensor that is reporting the wrong temperature to the ECU, which is commanding the blend door to be in the position it is in. Or maybe the blend door is being held in position by an object that fell into the defrost vents. Or maybe the electric actuator is worn out and cannot respond to the signal it receives from the ECU. Another cause could be that the ECU is damaged and sending an incorrect signal to the blend door actuator. You will need to research the manufacturer's diagnostic procedures and follow the procedure relating to the symptoms present. Be sure to check technical service bulletins as a beginning step for the concern you have.

Many new vehicles are designed with HVAC systems that have built-in self-diagnostics. This means that the ECU is programmed to recognize signals or situations that are out of specifications and to display a DTC. You can use this information to help determine the cause of the system fault. On some systems, you will need to hold down the auto button while pressing the temperature increase button or other sequence of button presses. Refer to the specific service information, since this is not standard among vehicles. This process will enter the control panel into diagnostic mode. You will be able to display any trouble codes on the screen of the control panel. If the vehicle is set up for scan tool diagnosis, you will be able to pull the code(s) with the scan tool.

For example, suppose a particular model of Honda comes into the shop and you are assigned to work on it. The customer complaint is that the rear climate control panel is inoperative and blank (no display). When service information is checked, you notice that body DTCs may be set by faults in the HVAC system. When you pull up DTCs with the scan tool, you find a code for a loss of communication with the rear panel. Following the troubleshooting chart, you perform circuit tests and find a poor connection in the communication wire connector. Repairing the connector and retesting reveals that you have corrected the concern.

Diagnosing Malfunctions in the Electrical Controls of HVAC Systems

Malfunctions in the electrical controls can come in many forms. Be sure to follow the manufacturer's service information on every issue. The use of electrical wiring diagrams is necessary for successful testing. Common issues include failure of electrical components such as actuators, switches, connectors, wiring, or grounds. Pin fit issues in connectors have become one of the more common faults in electrical systems. Terminals in connectors are the small metal devices made to mate to each other to carry the voltage signals and current through to the mating wire. If the terminal pins and sockets fit loosely with each other, the component may be inoperative or may operate intermittently. Wiggling the testing connectors of the affected circuit is a good way to find pin fit issues.

Diagnosing Malfunctions in the Vacuum and Mechanical Components and Controls of the HVAC System

Common failures in the vacuum system include vacuum leaks. Refer to the manufacturer's service information to diagnose this system properly. You will need a vacuum chart to show operation of the vacuum controls for the HVAC system. To test for a leaking vacuum line, you will need to gain access to the vacuum connections of the vacuum line suspected. Connect one end of a handheld vacuum pump while the other end is plugged. If vacuum is able to be held on the hose, it is not leaking and the problem lies beyond the line. Vacuum servos can fail by not pulling completely or not at all. Apply vacuum to the servo to see if it is functioning correctly.

Vacuum controls can also be tested with the vacuum pump. Hook up to the port shown in the vacuum chart and make sure vacuum comes out of the corresponding vacuum port that the chart shows. A blockage, or leak, in the valve or switch will keep the vacuum from passing through, and replacement of the vacuum control will be necessary.

Inspecting and Testing the HVAC Control Panel Assembly

The control panel assembly usually needs to be inspected and tested only when the HVAC system does not deliver the selected temperature or placement of the air. This task depends on the type of system you are working on and the manufacturer's diagnostic procedure. There are several types of control panels, including manual, semiautomatic, automatic, dual-temperature control, and rear air-conditioning systems. Be sure to refer to the appropriate service information. The next Skill Drill is conducted with a manual system equipped with a blend door and electric actuators.

To inspect and test the HVAC control panel assembly, follow the steps in **SKILL DRILL 43-6**:

1 First, research the operation and diagnostic procedure for the control panel assembly. Then start by operating all of the heater and air-conditioning controls. Note any faults. If equipped, remove clips and bolts holding hush panels under the dash. Removal of additional panels may be needed to gain visual access to the actuators. (**Photo 1**)

2 Move the temperature control switch from maximum to minimum. (**Photo 2**)

3 Observe the blend door linkage for movement. If no movement is detected, test the actuator system according to service information. If movement is present, remove the actuator by undoing

SKILL DRILL | **43-6** | **Inspecting and Testing the HVAC Control Panel Assembly**

1 After researching the operation and diagnostic procedure for the control panel assembly, start by operating all of the heater and air-conditioning controls. Note any faults. Remove clips and bolts holding hush panels under the dash.

2 Move the temperature control switch from maximum to minimum.

3 Observe the blend door linkage for movement. If no movement is detected, test the actuator system according to service information. If movement is present, remove the actuator by undoing the retainers securing it to the air box.

4 Move the blend door by hand and check whether it is broken at the shaft or is binding. If the blend door is broken, the entire air box must be removed. Refer to service information for removal and repair.

5 Move each control and watch the appropriate doors for proper movement.

the retainers securing it to the air box, typically a couple of screws. (**Photo 3**)

4 Move the blend door by hand and check whether it is broken at the shaft or is binding. If the blend door is broken, the entire air box must be removed. Refer to service information for removal and repair. (**Photo 4**)

5 Move each control and watch the appropriate doors for proper movement. (**Photo 5**)

> **TECHNICIAN TIP**
>
> Check the linkages at the ends of the cables to make sure they are operating the doors and valves properly.

Inspecting and Testing HVAC Control Cables

Inspecting and testing system control cables and linkages usually will be needed only when the air conditioner or heater is not delivering the proper temperature of air or is delivering airflow to a different mode than selected. This will happen when a cable is binding, is broken, or has popped off its linkage at the door or control head. The HVAC control panel will need to be visually inspected and tested, requiring you to gain access to the cables and linkages. Access is different for each vehicle, so research the procedure in the appropriate service information.

To inspect and test the HVAC control cables, follow the steps in **SKILL DRILL 43-7**:

1 Research the operation and diagnostic procedure for the control panel assembly. Move the control panel switch or levers, and observe the doors on the air box for movement. (**Photo 1**)

2 If movement is not noted, inspect for a broken cable or a cable that has popped off of the control lever or door. (**Photo 2**)

3 If a cable has popped off, reinstall it with the proper retainer—usually a push clip—and retest the cable system. (**Photo 3**)

Inspecting the HVAC System: Heater Ducts, Doors, and Cabin Filters

Because the HVAC system ducts and doors direct airflow to specific areas within the passenger cabin, it is important that they function as shown on the control panel; for instance, if you select floor mode, air should come

SKILL DRILL 43-7 Inspecting and Testing the HVAC Control Cables

1 Begin by researching the operation and diagnostic procedure for the control panel assembly. Move the control panel switch or levers, and observe the doors on the air box for movement.

2 If movement is not noted, inspect for a cable that is broken or has popped off of the control lever or door.

3 If a cable has popped off, reinstall it with the proper retainer and retest the cable system.

out at the floor. Inspecting the HVAC system ducts is accomplished by operating the system in all positions and verifying that it is being controlled appropriately. If not, each position on the HVAC control panel will indicate the air door or duct that is affected.

This inspection of the ducts and doors offers a good opportunity to inspect any cabin filters to see if they need to be replaced. In systems where the cabin air filter is in the fresh air intake, you can use an anemometer to check the difference in the speed of the vent airflow with the system in recirculation mode compared to fresh air mode. Any difference indicates a filter restriction. In systems where the cabin air filter filters recirculated air as well, you will need to remove the cabin air filter and hold it up to a light to determine if it needs to be replaced.

To inspect the heater ducts, doors, and cabin filters, follow the steps in **SKILL DRILL 43-8** :

1 Start the vehicle and turn the fan switch to the maximum setting. **(Photo 1)**

2 Turn the mode selector through all the positions and make sure the air is distributed through the appropriate vents. Turn the mode selector to dash vents and recirculate. **(Photo 2)**

3 Take an average airflow measurement from all vents (800 fpm minimum average). If no flow-meter is available, test the amount of airflow with your hand or a piece of paper and compare to a similar vehicle. **(Photo 3)**

4 Move the fresh air/recirculate control to the fresh air position and retest the airflow to see if the cabin filter is plugged. Make sure at least one window or door is open to avoid restricting airflow. The air-flow should not drop. **(Photo 4)**

5 If the cabin air filter filters all air in the system, remove the cabin air filter and hold it up to a light to see if it is plugged. Replace it if it is restricted or damaged. **(Photo 5)**

Diagnosing Temperature Control Problems in the HVAC System

To diagnose temperature control problems, the technician must fully understand how temperature change is controlled in the HVAC system being serviced. Refer to the description and operation in the service information. The need to diagnose temperature control problems will arise when the customer is not able to get the vehicle

SKILL DRILL | **43-8** | **Inspecting the Heater Ducts, Doors, and Cabin Filters**

1 Start the vehicle and turn the fan switch to the maximum setting.

2 Turn the mode selector through all the positions and make sure the air is distributed through the appropriate vents. Turn the mode selector to dash vents and recirculate.

3 Take an average airflow measurement from all vents (800 fpm minimum average). If no flowmeter is available, test the amount of airflow with your hand or a piece of paper and compare to a similar vehicle.

SKILL DRILL | 43-8 | Inspecting the Heater Ducts, Doors, and Cabin Filters, continued

4 Move the fresh air/recirculate control to the fresh air position and retest the airflow to see if the cabin filter is plugged. Make sure at least one window or door is open to avoid restricting airflow. The airflow should not drop.

5 If the cabin air filter filters all air in the system, remove the cabin air filter and hold it up to a light to see if it is plugged. Replace it if it is restricted or damaged.

cold enough or hot enough inside the passenger cabin. The cause of such a customer concern can be as simple as a thermostat issue or as complex as an electrical or electronics issue. To diagnose this type of complaint, refer to the manufacturer's service information for troubleshooting charts. The tools required for this job vary greatly depending on the cause of the concern and the type of HVAC control system you are working with. The next Skill Drill will assume use of an automatic HVAC control system with an ECU. The tools required are a scan tool appropriate for the vehicle, a DVOM, back probes (small pins to test for voltage at the back side of the connector), an infrared thermometer, and service information.

To diagnose temperature control problems in the HVAC system, follow the steps in **SKILL DRILL 43-9**:

1 Research the operation and diagnostic procedure for the control panel assembly. Verify the customer concern.

2 Check for full operating temperature of the engine by pointing an infrared thermometer at the thermostat housing. If the temperature is not hot enough, the thermostat is NOT sealing the coolant

in the engine and will likely need to be replaced. (**Photo 1**)

3 Test for codes with the scan tool. If a code is set, follow the troubleshooting chart for the code pulled. If no code is set, follow the symptom-based troubleshooting chart. (**Photo 2**)

4 If a code is set for the electric actuator for the blend door, pull up bidirectional controls in the scan tool and command the blend door to operate while visually inspecting the movement of the actuator. It may be necessary to remove the actuator to see movement. (**Photo 3**)

5 If movement is found at the actuator, inspect for a broken or binding door by turning the door by hand. If no movement is found at the actuator, perform the test for voltage (power and ground) at the actuator while commanding it. (**Photo 4**)

6 If no power and ground are found, back-probe the wires for the actuator at the connector of the ECU voltage (power and ground) while commanding the actuator. If no power and ground are coming from the ECU, the ECU will need to be replaced. (**Photo 5**)

SKILL DRILL 43-9 Diagnosing Temperature Control Problems in the HVAC System

1 Research the operation and diagnostic procedure for the control panel assembly and verify the customer concern. Check for full operating temperature of the engine by pointing an infrared thermometer at the thermostat housing. If the temperature is not hot enough, the thermostat is likely will need to be replaced.

2 Test for codes with the scan tool. If a code is set, follow the troubleshooting chart for the code pulled. If no code is set, follow the symptom-based troubleshooting chart.

3 If a code is found for the electric actuator for the blend door, pull up bidirectional controls in the scan tool and command the blend door to operate while visually inspecting the movement of the actuator.

4 If movement is found at the actuator, inspect for a broken or binding door by turning the door by hand. If no movement is found at the actuator, perform the test for voltage (power and ground) at the actuator while commanding it.

5 If no power and ground are found, back-probe the wires for the actuator at the connector of the ECU voltage (power and ground) while commanding the actuator. If no power and ground are coming from the ECU, the ECU will need to be replaced.

Wrap-up

Ready for Review

- Climate control systems can be manual, semiautomatic, or automatic.
- Manual climate control systems give the driver full control over blower motor speed, temperature of outlets, and direction of airflow.
- Semiautomatic control systems use an A/C ECU to turn on or off the A/C compressor, while the driver controls temperature request, blower motor speed, and airflow position.
- In automatic control systems the driver selects a temperature and the A/C ECU manages the subsystems necessary to achieve that temperature (heat, A/C, and air distribution).
- The A/C ECU requires input from electronic sensors to determine: vehicle heat load; desired temperature setting; and the temperature of ambient air, cabin air, evaporator, and engine coolant.
- An electric actuator or a vacuum servo may be used to move air box doors.
- Components of a climate control system include: blower motor, air box, heater core, evaporator, actuator, and control head.
- The blower motor is attached to a circular fan and provides the desired amount of airflow to the vehicle cabin.
- The doors that control airflow include: blend door, mode door, and recirculation door.
- A potentiometer is a three-wire sensor that signals the position of the blend door to the A/C ECU.
- A negative temperature coefficient thermistor (temperature sensor) gains resistance as the temperature drops, while a positive temperature coefficient thermistor loses resistance with lowered temperatures.
- Actuator feedback signals may be in the form of voltage signals.
- A pulse width modulation refers to a pulsing current flow that controls a blower motor's speed and provides an infinite number of speeds.
- The sun load (or solar) sensor is a photo diode that reads light entering the windshield of the vehicle.
- The air conditioning pressure sensor monitors refrigerant pressure.
- The evaporator temperatures sensor ensures that the evaporator maintains the correct temperature by controlling compressor cycling.
- Control panels vary according to car type and A/C ECU system. Panels may have rotary switches, recirculation buttons, auto mode, or digital temperature display, and systems may offer dual temperature control or rear-climate control.
- Control panel assemblies may be mechanical or automatic. Mechanical systems may operate cables, vacuum valves, or electrical switches.
- The blower motor speed is determined by resistors connected to the fan control switch that feed voltage to the motor.
- In some vehicles the highest blower motor speed receives a full 12 volts from a dedicated fan relay.
- The A/C compressor is turned on/off by the A/C compressor cultch.
- Components of a compressor clutch include the pulley, clutch coil, compressor shaft, and a shim.
- Hybrid cars may use a standard A/C compressor clutch arrangement or may use a dual-drive A/C compressor.
- Common HVAC system issues are: electric actuator failure, vacuum hose failure, and sensor failure.
- Vehicles with HVAC systems equipped with self-diagnostics will provide a diagnostic trouble code that can help determine the cause of system failure.
- Use manufacturers' troubleshooting charts when diagnosing HVAC controls malfunctions.
- Electrical malfunctions in HVAC systems may be due to failure of actuators, switches, connectors, wiring, grounds, or may be due to pin fit issues.
- Consider using an infrared thermometer to check coolant temperature without removing the radiator cap.
- Inspect and test blower motors for foreign objects, shorted motor, or binding of the fan motor shaft.
- Possible causes of the compressor clutch control system not working are: bad clutch coil, electrical fault in control circuits, large clutch air gap, or low refrigerant level.
- Inspect and test the heater control panel assembly and control cables if the system is not delivering proper air temperature.
- Air conditioning systems can grow mold and bacteria from trapped condensed moisture, which can then give off an unpleasant odor, necessitating use of an anti-odor kit.
- Tools needed for inspection, maintenance, and repair of an HVAC system include: infrared thermometer, digital volt ohm meter (DVOM), back probes, fused jumper wire, and a scan tool.

Key Terms

actuator A device that moves the air doors of the air box. It is controlled by input from the climate control panel.

air-conditioning compressor clutch The mechanical coupler that is electromagnetically engaged and provides a way of uncoupling the compressor from the accessory drive belt.

air-conditioning pressure sensor A sensor that gives an input signal of refrigerant pressure in the air-conditioning system to the ECU.

air-conditioning system pressure The refrigerant pressure contained within the air-conditioning system.

ambient air temperature sensor A thermistor that is used to measure the air temperature outside the vehicle.

aspirator A tube that is used to direct airflow across the cabin air temperature sensor.

automatic climate control system A system that automatically adjusts the heating or cooling to meet a specified temperature demanded by the passengers.

blower motor The electric motor and fan that move air through the passenger compartment.

cabin air temperature sensor A thermistor that measures air temperature inside the vehicle.

climate control system A system that provides the heating and cooling of air inside the passenger compartment for passenger comfort.

dual-drive air-conditioning compressor An air compressor drive used on some hybrid vehicles. The compressor can be driven by the accessory belt or by an electric motor.

electric servo motor Also referred to as an electric actuator, a motor that provides movement to operate the air doors in an air box to control air temperature and air movement.

electromagnetic clutch arrangement An arrangement used in hybrid air-conditioning systems to drive the compressor. The air-conditioning clutch is an electromagnetic clutch that works by creating a strong magnetic field that pulls the clutch into mesh with the pulley on the air compressor.

electronic control unit (ECU) When referring to the HVAC system, the electronic module that makes the "decisions" of the climate control system settings based on input sensors and the module programming.

engine coolant temperature sensor A thermistor that measures the temperature of the engine coolant.

evaporator temperature sensor A thermistor that reads the temperature of the evaporator, used to ensure that the evaporator does not freeze.

feedback signal A voltage signal sent back to an electronic control unit. The feedback signal is how the control module is able to interpret temperature or other information from its sensors.

heater control cables Cables that control the air doors in an air box as part of the air distribution system.

limit switches Switches that turn off power flow to an electric motor when a particular limit is reached.

manual climate control system A climate control system fully controlled by the operator.

negative temperature coefficient (NTC) thermistor A thermistor that gains resistance as temperature goes down and loses resistance as temperature goes up.

on/off–type signal A signal that is either a 12-volt signal or zero volts. Typically, switches provide on/off signals. Some systems use a 5-volt reference signal instead of a 12-volt signal.

photodiode An electronic component that creates a varying voltage or current output based on the amount of light striking it.

potentiometer A sensor that acts as a variable resistor when a wiper arm moves across its resistive material.

printed circuitry Circuitry that forms the framework for electronic module construction. A printed circuit board holds electronic components that are soldered into place.

resistor in series A resistor added to the circuit before or after the load to drop voltage to the load.

semiautomatic climate control system A system that provides automatic function of the heater or cooling only, leaving fan speed and mode selection to the operator.

signal voltage value Measured voltage in a signal return circuit that is compared to a specified voltage value published by the manufacturer.

sun load (solar) sensor A photodiode that varies voltage based on light. It is used to determine the radiant heat coming from the sun into the passenger cabin and gives an input signal of sunlight load to the ECU.

thermistor A temperature-controlled variable resistor. As temperature changes, so does resistance.

vacuum servo A vacuum-controlled device that moves the air doors of the air box. It is controlled by the vacuum that comes from the vacuum-type climate control panel.

variable voltage signal A signal that changes based on what the sensor is reading; for example, as temperature varies, so does the voltage signal to the ECU.

voltage The pressure aspect of electricity, measured to show the potential of a circuit to do work.

ASE-Type Questions

1. Tech A says that a temperature blend air door controls how much air bypasses the heater care. Tech B says that the regulation blend air door controls fresh air. Who is correct?
   a. Tech A
   b. Tech B
   c. Both A and B
   d. Neither A nor B

2. Tech A says that in a temperature blend air system, the air conditioner runs continuously. Tech B says that in a blend air system, there is always heated coolant in the heater core. Who is correct?
   a. Tech A
   b. Tech B
   c. Both A and B
   d. Neither A nor B

3. Tech A says that air flow in the vents is controlled by adding or removing a second or third motor to increase or decrease air flow. Tech B says that blower motor speed is controlled by controlling current to make the blower motor run faster or slower. Who is correct?
   a. Tech A
   b. Tech B
   c. Both A and B
   d. Neither A nor B

4. Tech A says that "fresh air" setting pulls air from the cabin. Tech B says that when it is hot outside, the "recirculate" setting will cool the cabin better. Who is correct?
   a. Tech A
   b. Tech B
   c. Both A and B
   d. Neither A nor B

5. Tech A says that when an electric actuator fails, replace it with new. Tech B says that when an electric or vacuum actuator fails, always verify the door moves freely and there are no vacuum leaks. Who is correct?
   a. Tech A
   b. Tech B
   c. Both A and B
   d. Neither A nor B

6. Blend air systems use actuators to move doors to mix air flow. Tech A says that actuators are positioned by an A/C ECU, by checking air flow with sensors. Tech B says that actuators are positioned by an A/C ECU and the actuator has a potentiometer to tell the A/C ECU the position of the door. Who is correct?
   a. Tech A
   b. Tech B
   c. Both A and B
   d. Neither A nor B

7. Tech A says some newer vehicles use pulse width modulation to control blower motor speeds which leads to smooth changes in speeds. Tech B says that the evaporator temperature sensor is used to control cab temperature in the passenger compartment. Who is correct?
   a. Tech A
   b. Tech B
   c. Both A and B
   d. Neither A nor B

8. Tech A says that the A/C high pressure switch controls the condenser cooling fan. Tech B says that the A/C ECU controls the condenser cooling fan. Who is correct?
   a. Tech A
   b. Tech B
   c. Both A and B
   d. Neither A nor B

9. Tech A says that the air gap between the clutch and the compressor directly relates to how much voltage is required to engage the clutch. Tech B says that if system voltage is low or the gap between the A/C clutch and compressor is too large, the clutch will not engage. Who is correct?
   a. Tech A
   b. Tech B
   c. Both A and B
   d. Neither A nor B

10. Tech A says that when troubleshooting an automatic temperature controlled A/C or heating problem one of the first steps should be to check codes for any related faults. Tech B says that active codes make troubleshooting more effective. Who is correct?
    a. Tech A
    b. Tech B
    c. Both A and B
    d. Neither A nor B

SECTION IX

Engine Performance

CHAPTER 44

NATEF Tasks

Engine Repair
General   Page

- Remove and replace timing belt; verify correct camshaft timing.   **MLR** **AST** **MAST**   1539–1541

Engine Performance
General Engine Diagnosis

- Research applicable vehicle and service information, vehicle service history, service precautions, and technical service bulletins.   **MLR** **AST** **MAST**   1520–1547

- Identify and interpret engine performance concerns; determine necessary action.   **AST** **MAST**   1522–1527

- Verify correct camshaft timing.   **AST** **MAST**   1534–1536

Knowledge Objectives

After reading this chapter, you will be able to:
1. Explain the difference between external combustion engines and internal combustion engines. (pp 1520–1521)
2. Explain the relationships between pressure, temperature, and volume. (pp 1522–1524)
3. Explain force, work, and power. (pp 1524–1525)
4. Describe reciprocating and rotary motion. (pp 1527, 1546–1547)
5. Explain the five events common to all internal combustion engines. (pp 1527–1528)
6. Describe the functions of the cylinder head. (p 1534)
7. Describe the difference between a cam-in-block engine and an overhead cam (OHC) engine. (p 1535)
8. Describe how the camshaft works. (pp 1535–1536)
9. Describe how the valve train and timing function. (pp 1538–1540)
10. Describe intake and exhaust manifold. (pp 1542–1543)
11. Describe the basic principles of operation and components of the two-stroke spark-ignition engine. (pp 1543–1544)
12. Explain the differences between two- and four-stroke engines. (p 1544)
13. Describe how the crankshaft turns the reciprocating motion of the piston into rotary motion. (pp 1545–1546)
14. Explain the basic principles of operation and components of the rotary spark-ignition engine. (pp 1545–1546)

Motive Power Types—Spark-Ignition (SI) Engines

Skills Objectives

There are no skills objectives for this chapter.

Introduction

The internal combustion engine is an irreplaceable part of modern society. We rely on it to haul food and water, deliver passengers to their destinations, and even save lives. Over time the internal combustion engine has seen many changes; however, the basics have remained similar. In this chapter, we will cover the types of spark-ignition engines that are available, identify the components that make up the engine, and describe how these components operate together.

Principles of Thermodynamic Internal Combustion Engines

Thermodynamics is generally defined as the branch of physical science that deals with heat and its relation to other forms of energy such as mechanical energy. In this chapter, we will discuss how heat energy is used in the internal combustion engine to produce power and make work happen.

In automotive applications, the useful effect is to move a vehicle down the road as well as provide motive (moving) power for all of the onboard systems. Engines used for motive power may be classified as external combustion or internal combustion engines. External combustion means that the fuel is being burned outside of the engine, while internal combustion means the fuel is burned inside of the engine. Two examples of the external combustion engine are the steam engine and the Stirling engine **FIGURE 44-1**.

FIGURE 44-1 External combustion engines **A.** Steam engine. **B.** Stirling engine.

At one time, external combustion engines, such as steam engines, were used to power almost all equipment. Steam engines are the best example of external engines powering equipment such as farm tractors, railroad trains, automobiles, boats and ships, and more. Even a steam-powered airplane was produced, although it never became popular.

In a steam engine, steam is created in an external boiler (external combustion) and used to push a piston back and forth in a cylinder. Most steam engines applied steam alternately to each side of the piston, so the piston was powered in both directions. One problem with steam engines is that they take a relatively long time to generate steam pressure, so you could not just hop in a steam-powered car and take off. The boilers also presented an explosion hazard if they generated too much pressure or if the boiler weakened due to rust.

The Stirling engine is also an external combustion engine. It holds promise as an alternative source of power but has not become popular for transportation since its output cannot be easily varied. Solar-powered Stirling engines are gaining popularity as home power sources because they are environmentally friendly. Since solar energy is used to provide the heat for the engine, there are no by-products of combustion to worry about. Stirling engines can run almost silently and therefore can be used near people without disturbing them.

The **internal combustion engine** has almost completely replaced the external combustion engine and has been around for well over a century. It is still the favored mode of power for the transportation industry, whether for on-road applications (cars, trucks, buses, etc.) or for non-road applications (tractors, trains, ships, etc.). This chapter focuses on spark-ignition internal combustion engines, since they are the most widely used engines in modern automobiles.

> ▶ **LINK**
> Refer to the Alternative Fuel Systems chapter for more information on hybrid vehicles, flex-fuel vehicles, "pure" battery-electric vehicles (BEVs), fuel cell vehicles (FCVs), and other alternative-fueled vehicles.

Gasoline (spark ignition) and diesel (compression ignition) engines are prime examples of internal combustion engines. Fuel is burned *inside* the internal combustion engine. According to Charles's law, when a gas is heated, it expands. Since fuel contains energy in chemical form, when it is burned in a sealed combus-

tion chamber, it creates high pressure that pushes on a moveable piston. The moving piston produces power to do work.

The internal combustion engine (ICE) can be classified in two ways: as a reciprocating piston engine or as a rotary engine. The gasoline **piston engine** uses a crankshaft to convert the reciprocating movement of the pistons in their cylinder bores into rotary motion at the crankshaft. The piston engine may be of the **two-stroke** or **four-stroke** design. The **rotary engine** uses a rotating motion rather than reciprocating motion. It uses ports rather than valves to control intake and exhaust flow. Both the piston and the rotary engine will be described in greater detail later in this chapter.

Piston engines are either **spark ignition (SI) engines** or **compression-ignition (CI) engines**. In SI engines, liquid fuels such as gasoline, ethanol, methanol, or butenol are compressed and ignited by an electrical spark, which jumps across the air gap of a spark plug in the combustion chamber. Timing of combustion is totally reliant on when the spark jumps across the electrodes of the spark plug **FIGURE 44-2**. In diesel engines, air in the sealed combustion chamber is compressed so tightly that it becomes hot enough to ignite the fuel as soon as it is injected into the combustion chamber. Timing of the combustion process is reliant on when the fuel is injected; therefore, CI engines do not use spark plugs **FIGURE 44-3**.

> ▶ **LINK**
> Refer to the Compression-Ignition Engine chapter for a more complete description of diesel engines.

FIGURE 44-2 Combustion in a spark-ignition (SI) engine.

FIGURE 44-3 Combustion in a compression-ignition (CI) engine.

FIGURE 44-4 Pressure changes temperature. **A.** As pressure goes up, temperature goes up. **B.** As pressure goes down, temperature goes down.

► Principles of Engine Operation

Engines operate according to the unchanging laws of physics and thermodynamics. Understanding the physics and science involved with an engine will help you to diagnose engine problems. For example, knowing that pressure rises when the volume of a sealed container is reduced will help you to understand the need for sealing the chamber for maximum power.

Realize, too, that when molecules are tightly packed together, they produce far more expansion pressure during combustion than when they are not. Valves and ports in the engine's cylinder head(s) provide a means of sealing the combustion chamber. If the valves leak, the pressure in the cylinder will not rise as it should during the compression stroke of the piston. If there is too little pressure squeezing the air/fuel mixture together in the cylinder, the mixture will not get packed tightly enough, and less engine power will be developed when it is ignited.

A good example of the importance of compression would be the burning of black powder in open air; it will produce fire and smoke but no explosion. If the same powder is wrapped tightly, it becomes a fire cracker (or even a stick of dynamite)—exploding the wrapping and producing the bang. More power is produced when air and fuel are compressed into a tightly packed space.

Pressure and Temperature

Recall that according to Charles's law, in a sealed chamber, the pressure and temperature of a gas are directly related to each other. As pressure rises, so does temperature; as pressure decreases, so does temperature. For example, think of a portable propane bottle used when boiling water on a camp stove. The bottle has a fixed amount of gas inside of it. As the propane is used, the metal propane bottle gets ice cold and frosts over due to the pressure being released.

In contrast, think of a cylinder with a moveable plunger at one end **FIGURE 44-4**. This plunger seals tightly in the cylinder so that no air can escape past the plunger. Installed on the other end of the cylinder are a pressure gauge and a thermometer. As we push the plunger in, the air pressure rises in the sealed cylinder as the air molecules are squeezed together. As the air molecules are squeezed together more tightly, the pressure and the temperature rise as a result of friction between the air molecules as they bounce off each other with greater force. The air in the cylinder heats up as this happens, so we see not only the pressure rise on the pressure gauge but also the temperature rise on the thermometer. The same amount of heat is in the cylinder as when uncompressed, but when it is compressed, the heat is concentrated; thus, the temperature rises.

A diesel engine uses this principle to ignite the fuel injected into an engine cylinder. The air is compressed so tightly that it becomes hot enough to ignite the fuel when it arrives; this is why diesel engines are called compression-ignition engines. Again using our plunger in a cylinder example, what happens when the plunger is pulled outward? Pulling out the plunger reduces gas pressure and gives the molecules more room to move; they

FIGURE 44-5 Temperature changes pressure. **A.** As temperature goes up, pressure goes up. **B.** As temperature goes down, pressure goes down.

1. Compressing the air/fuel mixture raises its heat energy level.

2. Igniting the fuel increases the heat and pressure even higher.

3. The high combustion temperature causes high cylinder pressures which force the piston down the cylinder.

Compressed air/fuel mixture

Piston travel direction

Burning air/fuel mixture

Piston travel direction

FIGURE 44-6 Burning a compressed gas increases temperature, producing more pressure and increased force.

affect each other less and temperature decreases. Thus, a drop in pressure produces a lower temperature because even though the same amount of heat is contained in the cylinder, the heat is more spread out.

Looking at a related scenario, what happens to pressure when the gas *temperature* changes? When a gas is heated, its molecules start to move more quickly and want more space. Heating a gas in a sealed container will increase the pressure in the container (thermal expansion) **FIGURE 44-5**. Cooling a gas has the opposite effect. As the molecules slow down, they demand less space. As a result of cooling a gas in a sealed container, the pressure will drop.

Temperature and Energy

The temperature of a gas is one measure of how much energy it has. The more energy a gas has, the more work it can do. The heating of gas particles makes them move faster, which produces more pressure. This pressure exerts more force on the container in which the gas is located, which is how an ICE functions. Pressure is first raised through compression and then through combustion of the air/fuel mixture. Burning the air/fuel mixture increases the heat temperature inside the container tremendously, which creates the necessary pressure to produce work. The more energy the air/fuel mixture has, the more force it exerts on the piston and the more work the piston can do **FIGURE 44-6**. This principle takes place during the power stroke and pushes the piston down the sealed container.

Latent (stored) heat energy exists in various kinds of fuels; it is released to do work when the fuel is ignited and burned. Types of fuels that contain latent heat energy include liquid fuels such as gasoline, diesel, and ethanol; gaseous fuels such as natural gas, propane, and hydrogen; and solid fuels such as gunpowder, wood, and coal. Latent heat energy is often measured and expressed as British thermal units, abbreviated Btu.

One Btu equals the heat required to raise the temperature of 1 pound (lb) of water by 1°F. Gasoline has a comparatively high Btu per gallon rating of around 14,000 Btu. Diesel fuel is even more energy dense, however, at around 25,000 Btu per gallon. Coal has a much lower Btu rating, which is one reason why both the home heating and the transportation (rail) industries have moved from coal to petroleum (i.e., home heating oil and diesel fuel) for better energy efficiency (transport and storage of a liquid fuel is also lots easier).

Pressure and Volume

Pressure and volume are inversely related; as one rises, the other falls. A cylinder with a pressure gauge and movable piston is a good example. It contains air, and as the piston is pushed in, the inside air is forced into a smaller volume. At the same time, the pressure gauge shows an increase in pressure. It is this increase in pressure that allows the pump to do its work. When the piston is pulled out, the volume occupied by the gas grows larger, and the pressure drops. A larger volume will have less gas pressure, and when the volume is reduced, the gas pressure will rise. Keep in mind that larger pressures are desirable to increase the amount of work done in an engine **FIGURE 44-7**.

Force, Work, and Power

Effort to produce a push or pull action is referred to as **force**. A compressed spring applies force to cause, or resist, movement. A tensioned lifting cable applies force to cause lifting movement. Force is measured in pounds, kilograms, or newtons. When force causes movement, **work** is done **FIGURE 44-8**.

For example, when the compressed spring or the tensioned lifting cable causes movement, work is performed. Without movement, work cannot be performed even if force is applied. *Work is equal to distance moved times force applied.* If the lifting cable of a hoist lifts a 250-lb engine 4' in the air, the amount of work done is equal to 4' times 250 lb, or 1000 foot-pounds of work. Work is measured in foot-pounds (ft-lb), watts, or joules. Work can only be accomplished when something is moved.

> ## ▶ TECHNICIAN TIP
>
> Holding a heavy starter motor in place while trying to get the bolts started is not technically work; it is force. Although it seems like you are working hard, your arm muscles twitching as you stand under the vehicle and hold the part in place, you are not performing work in the true physics sense. It takes movement, along with force, to qualify as work. So lifting the starter from the ground to its position on the engine is work, but holding it there is not work. Understanding the difference between these two terms will give you a good foundation for understanding power.

The rate or speed at which work is performed is called **power** **FIGURE 44-9**. The more power that can be produced, the more work can be performed in a given amount of time. Power is measured in ft-lb per second or ft-lb per minute. If an electric motor can lift a 600-lb weight 20' in 10 seconds, power used would be equal to

20 (feet) × 600 (lb) ÷ 10 (seconds) =   1200 ft-lb per second.

One horsepower equals 550 ft-lb per second, or 33,000 ft-lb per minute. So 1200 ft-lb per second equals 2.18 horsepower. The watt or kilowatt (1000 watts) is the metric unit of measurement for power, where 746 watts equals 1 horsepower. So the electric motor in the example would be developing 2.18 (horsepower) times 746 (watts), which equals 1627 watts, or 1.627 kilowatts, of power.

Work = distance moved × force applied
= 4 ft × 150 lb
= 600 ft-lb

4 feet

150 pounds

FIGURE 44-8 Work.

FIGURE 44-7 Volume affects pressure.

Power = (distance moved × force applied) / time
= (4 ft × 150 lb) / 2 seconds
= 300 ft-lb / second
= 0.54 HP

4 feet in 2 seconds

150 pounds

1 Horsepower (HP) = 550 ft-lb per second

FIGURE 44-9 Formula for power.

Power and Torque

<u>Torque</u> is described as a twisting force. Movement does not have to occur to have torque. Torque is applied before or during movement. When a twist cap on a water bottle is removed, maximum torque is applied just before the cap starts to turn. When the same cap is tightened, maximum torque is applied once the cap starts to get tight. The concept of "twisting force" should always come to mind when the term torque is used. When a piston is pushed down a cylinder during the power stroke, it applies force to a connecting rod linking the piston and crankshaft, causing the crankshaft to rotate. The rotational force applied to the crankshaft is called torque.

The unit of measurement for torque in the imperial system is ft-lb; in the metric system it is newton meters. If a force of 100 lb is applied to the end of a 1' long wrench (lever) attached to a bolt, the resulting torque applied to the wrench will be 100 ft-lb.

The measurement of engine power is calculated from the amount of torque at the crankshaft and the speed at which it is turning in rpm. The formula for engine horsepower is:

$$\text{Horsepower} = \text{rpm} \times \text{ft-lb} \div 5252.$$

For example, if an engine creates 500 ft-lb of torque at 4000 rpm, then the amount of horsepower is:

$$500 \times 4000 \div 5252, \text{ or } 380 \text{ horsepower at } 4000 \text{ rpm.}$$

Because horsepower would change with rpm, it is necessary to express not only the power value but to include the engine speed, in rpm, at which it occurs. Power can also be measured in kilowatts. A kilowatt (1,000 watts) is equivalent to 1000 newtons per meter per second.

The formula for computing an engine's horsepower might seem confusing since we said earlier that 1 horsepower equals 33,000 ft-lb per minute; yet we divide the product of torque × rpm by 5252. Why do we use 5252 instead of 33,000? The reason is a bit complicated, having to do with the definition of ft-lb. When relating to *work*, ft-lb means force times distance moved. That works well in a lifting situation but not so well in a twisting (torque) situation. In a *torque* situation, ft-lb means a twisting force applied to a shaft—that is, applied force times lever distance of the applied force. Thus, it is possible for torque to result in no movement, only an applied force. And we label that force in ft-lb even though for work or power to happen, movement must take place.

To calculate the twisting power of a shaft, we need a way to add *distance moved* and *time* to the equation so that power can be represented; we can't just say that 33,000 ft-lb = 1 horsepower when talking about torque. That is why rpm is included in the formula. Because rpm refers to a certain number of revolutions per minute, it includes both time and distance. But how much distance is 1 rpm? The answer relates to radians. A radian describes how many radius distances there are in the circumference of a circle <u>FIGURE 44-10</u>. Since there are 3.14 diameters in the circumference of a circle, there are twice as many, or 6.28, radius distances (radians) in the circumference of any circle. The larger the circle, the longer the radians, but still only 6.28 of them fit within the total circumference. And that is where we get our distance. Since torque relates to an equivalent amount of force a certain distance from the rotational center (radius), and there are 6.28 radians in the circumference of a circle, every revolution equals a distance of 6.28 radians.

To convert torque ft-lb to work ft-lb, there has to be movement. We can either multiply the rpm by 6.28 and use the 33,000 (ft-lb per horsepower) factor, or divide the 33,000 ft-lb by 6.28 (distance around a circle in radians) and come up with a new factor, which is 5252, that we can use with the original "torque × rpm" numbers for calculating engine horsepower. To keep the numbers more manageable, most people go with the 5252 factor. Thus, if we multiply the ft-lb of torque × rpm and divide that number by 5252, we will have calculated the engine's horsepower at that particular rpm.

Torque Versus Horsepower

As torque is a twisting or turning force, <u>horsepower</u> is the rate (in time and distance) at which that force (torque) is produced. Torque alone does not mean work has been accomplished. It takes movement and time to accomplish a given amount of work in a given amount of time (horsepower). At the same time, for an engine to produce torque, it has to be running. So the rotation of

FIGURE 44-10 Radians in the circumference of a circle.

the crankshaft (torque × distance) in a running engine means that work and power are occurring since torque × rpm gives us power **FIGURE 44-11**. Also, an engine will put out varying amounts of torque and power as it is operating. Thus, if it is producing torque, it is producing power. Factors that affect an engine's torque output include engine **volumetric efficiency** (the rate of air intake and exhaust) at various crankshaft speeds and internal component friction (**parasitic losses**). In a naturally aspirated engine (nonpressurized intake system), torque peaks at the rpm where the engine's cylinders fill the most with air. Torque starts to drop as engine speed increases past peak torque rpm.

Actually, in a naturally aspirated (naturally breathing, nonpressurized) engine, air never completely fills the combustion chamber while the engine is running. Peak engine torque rpm occurs at the peak volumetric efficiency (somewhere around 85% in an unmodified engine). Peak torque usually occurs at some low- to mid-rpm engine speed, depending on bore and stroke of the engine, as well as intake and exhaust port size and valve timing.

Since engine rpm tends to rise faster than torque falls off (above peak volumetric efficiency), an engine's maximum horsepower occurs at a higher rpm than the peak torque rpm. At some point in the rpm range, the torque on the crankshaft drops so low that the crankshaft can no longer do additional work and the horsepower actually starts to decrease. Remember, it is horsepower that does the work, but torque makes it happen. Engine torque (and therefore horsepower) increases can be achieved through any engine modifications that improve volumetric efficiency **FIGURE 44-12**. In fact, a turbocharger or supercharger will increase an engine's volumetric efficiency well

above 100%. For example, a 1.6-liter Volkswagen diesel engine when turbocharged to its rated 11 lb of boost would be theoretically equivalent, horsepower-wise, to a naturally aspirated 2.8-liter engine.

FIGURE 44-11 An automotive chassis dynamometer measures output of the engine at the wheels of the vehicle.

FIGURE 44-12 The relationship between torque and horsepower.

AS-50: Work: The technician can explain the relationship between torque and horsepower.

Two technicians are discussing the relationship between torque and horsepower during their break time at work. Al believes that torque is the turning force at the engine's crankshaft. Bob says that horsepower is the rate at which force is produced. Both technicians are correct as they discuss the unique relationship of torque and horsepower. One cannot exist without the other.

When we compare a race car to a bulldozer, we can see two different applications of torque and horsepower. A bulldozer has lots of torque but the engine may be operating at 2,000 RPM. A race car may be operating at 8,000 RPM with a lower amount of torque. Low-speed torque is needed in some situations and high-rpm horsepower is needed in others. (Additional information on the relationship between torque and horsepower is described in this chapter.)

Engine Load Factor

Load factor or power range is typically used in regard to diesel engines and describes how long an engine can produce its maximum power output. An engine that is quite powerful may not be designed to produce its maximum power over long periods. A gasoline engine in a car may give good acceleration in short bursts, but it can overheat and/or fail if operated at maximum speed and power for too long. In contrast, due to its robust construction, a heavy-duty diesel engine in a large truck is designed to operate near or at its maximum speed and load for long periods without damage.

One way to describe the load factor of an engine is to give its power as an average over a certain period. This is stated as a percentage and is called load factor. An engine required to operate at maximum power over 10 hours is said to have a load factor of 100%. Using that as a standard, most car engines typically only operate at about 20% to 30%, as evidenced by the drive cycle of a typical automobile. A **drive cycle** is the operating range of an engine from start-up until shutdown when finished performing its job. A typical vehicle will accelerate, decelerate, and idle many times during a typical daily drive. It will never be run at 100% load for an entire drive cycle; in fact, it may never reach 100%.

▶ Four-Stroke Spark-Ignition Engines

The SI engine used in today's vehicles operates on the four-stroke cycle principle: It takes four strokes of the piston to complete one cycle. When the piston in a cylinder is at the position farthest away from the crankshaft, it is at **top dead center (TDC)**. When the piston in the cylinder is at a position closest to the crankshaft, it is said to be at **bottom dead center (BDC)**. When the piston moves from TDC to BDC or from BDC to TDC, one **stroke** has occurred **FIGURE 44-13**. Two or more strokes are called **reciprocating motion**, meaning an up-and-down motion within the cylinder. Piston engines are therefore referred to as reciprocating engines.

Piston engines can be simple, single-piston engines such as those on lawn mowers, or they can be much more complicated, multipiston engines, such as those in automobiles, trucks, and heavy equipment. Multicylinder engines come in various cylinder arrangements. Some automotive engines have cylinders arranged in a line (in-line engine), with pistons one behind each other. Some automobile engines are flat, with opposed cylinders lying horizontally. This style of engine is called a boxer engine. Other automobile engines have cylinders at an angle (a V-type engine), with the pistons forming a V configuration.

Basic Four-Stroke Operation

In a single four-stroke cycle, only one stroke out of four delivers new energy to turn the crankshaft. The four strokes must include the five key events common to all ICEs: intake, compression, ignition, power, and exhaust **FIGURE 44-14**. The **intake stroke** starts with the exhaust valve closed, the intake valve(s) opening, and the piston moving from TDC to BDC. As the piston moves down, the volume above the top of the piston increases. This

FIGURE 44-13 Piston movement from TDC to BDC or from BDC to TDC is one stroke.

1. Intake
2. Compression
3. Power
4. Exhaust

Ignition occuring
(BTDC of
compression
stroke)

FIGURE 44-14 The basic four-stroke cycle.

makes pressure inside the cylinder lower than the pressure outside the cylinder. Higher outside air pressure forces the air (usually with fuel) into the cylinder. As the piston reaches BDC, the intake valve(s) closes, and the intake stroke ends.

The **compression stroke** starts near BDC when the intake valve(s) closes. The piston moves from BDC to TDC. As the piston moves up, the air–fuel mixture is compressed into a smaller and smaller volume. Compression of air caused by the moving piston causes the air/fuel charge temperature to rise, making ignition easier and the combustion (burning of fuel) more complete and efficient.

As the piston reaches TDC of the compression stroke, the next event occurs: **ignition**. The air/fuel mixture is ignited and burns rapidly, at up to about 4500°F (2482°C). The heat of combustion causes burning gases to expand greatly (thermal expansion), which creates very high pressure in the combustion chamber. This pressure is also applied to the top of the piston, which is free to move down the cylinder. The **power stroke** occurs as this extreme force moves the piston from TDC to BDC with both valves remaining closed. The exhaust valve(s) starts to open near BDC.

At the end of the power stroke, the **exhaust stroke** occurs as the piston moves from BDC to TDC and pushes the burned gases out of the cylinder through the open exhaust valve(s). When the piston nears TDC, the exhaust valve(s) starts to close and the intake valve(s) starts to open, and the four-stroke cycle starts over from the beginning. Note that the crankshaft has completed two full rotations during the four-stroke cycle. Thus, four complete strokes make one complete cycle.

Applied Science

AS-99: Rotational: The technician can explain how rotational motion can be converted to linear motion and why balance is important in rotating systems.
When working in an automotive repair facility, it is important that the technician understand basic engine operation. The text has explained much regarding each component of the engine block assembly and cylinder head. The technician should know that reciprocating motion is an up and down motion such as the pistons in a cylinder. The crankshaft converts this linear motion into rotational motion.

It is also important to know that the camshaft lobe converts rotary motion into linear motion. As described in the text, the lobe is the raised portion on a camshaft used to lift the lifter and open the valve. Opening the valve requires linear motion on overhead cam engines as well as cam in block engines. The text describes a cam as an egg-shaped piece (lobe) mounted on the camshaft. The egg shape of the cam lobe is designed to lift the valve open, hold it open, and let it close. This is the operation that converts rotating motion into linear motion.

Balance is extremely important in a rotating system for a number of reasons. In order to have a smooth running engine, balance is necessary. In order to have long engine life and dependability, balance is also necessary. On the crankshaft, we have a vibration damper or harmonic balancer as described in the text. This important component is carefully engineered to meet the needs of a specific engine regarding proper balance.

Engine Measurement—Size

ICEs are designated by the amount of space (volume) their pistons displace as they move from TDC to BDC, which is called **engine displacement**. So, a 5.4-liter V8 engine has 8 cylinders that displace a total volume of 5.4 liters. Displacement can be listed in cubic centimeters, liters, or cubic inches. To find an engine's displacement, you need to know the bore, stroke, and number of cylinders for a particular engine.

The diameter of the engine cylinder is the **cylinder bore**. The bore is measured across the cylinder, parallel with the **block deck**, which is the machined surface of the block farthest from the crankshaft. Automotive cylinder bores can vary in size from less than 3" to more than 4".

The distance the piston travels from TDC to BDC, or from BDC to TDC, is called the **piston stroke**. Piston stroke is determined by the offset portion of the crankshaft called the **throw**. The crankshaft will be described in greater detail later in this chapter. Piston stroke also varies from less than 3" to more than 4". Generally speaking, the longer the stroke, the greater the engine torque produced. A shorter stroke enables the engine to run at higher rpm to create greater horsepower. Engine specifications typically list the bore size first and the stroke length second (bore vs. stroke).

The volume that a piston displaces from BDC to TDC is **piston displacement**. Increasing the diameter of the bore or increasing the length of the stroke will produce a larger piston displacement. The formula for calculating piston displacement is **FIGURE 44-15** :

cylinder bore squared × 0.785 × the piston stroke.

This formula works for calculating both the standard displacement in cubic inches, or the metric displacement in cubic centimeters (ccs) or liters.

For example, a 5.4-liter (329-cubic inch) V8 truck engine has a 3.55" bore, a 4.16" stroke, and 8 cylinders. Using the formula for displacement:

3.55 × 3.55 (bore²) = 12.6025 × 0.785 (constant)
= 9.893 × 4.16 (stroke) = 41.155-cubic inch piston displacement.

Once you know the piston displacement, the next step to finding engine displacement is to multiply piston displacement times the number of cylinders in the engine **FIGURE 44-16**. Continuing from the previous example:

41.155-cubic inch piston displacement × 8 (number of cylinders) = 329.24-cubic inch engine displacement.

The displacement of an engine (also called engine size) can be altered by changing cylinder bore (diameter), piston stroke (length), or the number of cylinders.

> ### TECHNICIAN TIP
>
> An engine with the same size bore and stroke is referred to as a square engine. An engine with a larger bore than stroke is called an oversquare engine (short-stroke engine). An engine with a bore smaller than the stroke is called an undersquare engine (long-stroke engine). Oversquare engines tend to make their power at higher rpm, while undersquare engines tend to make their power at lower rpm.

Compression ratio compares cylinder volumes with the piston at BDC and at TDC **FIGURE 44-17**. Maximum cylinder volume will be at BDC, and minimum cylinder volume will be at TDC. The ratio is given as two numbers. A compression ratio listed as 8:1 (8 to 1) means that the maximum cylinder volume is eight times larger than the minimum cylinder volume. Compression ratio is affected by changing the size and shape of the top of the piston, changing the size of the combustion chamber, or altering valve timing. The higher the compression ratio, the higher the compression pressures within the combustion

Bore = 3.550"

Displacement = (bore² × (π / 4)) × stroke
= (3.550" × 3.550" × 0.785) × 4.160
= 9.893 square inches × 4.160
= 41.155 cubic inches

Stroke = 4.160"

FIGURE 44-15 Piston displacement.

Engine displacement = (bore² × (π / 4)) × stroke × number of cylinders
= (3.550" × 3.550" × 0.785) × 4.160" × 4
= 9.893 square inches × 4.160" × 4
= 164.62 cubic inches

Bore = 3.550"

Stroke = 4.160"

FIGURE 44-16 Engine displacement.

Compression ratio 9:1

TDC

BDC

FIGURE 44-17 The compression ratio of an engine is found by taking the volume of the cylinder at BDC and comparing it to the volume at TDC. In this example, a 9:1 compression ratio is found.

chamber and therefore the higher the thermal expansion during combustion, making the engine more fuel efficient. But too high of a compression ratio can cause the air–fuel mixture to be ignited by the high compression temperature before the correct time, which is when the spark occurs. This early ignition can cause damage to the engine bearings and piston; therefore, manufacturers design their engines with an optimum compression ratio.

Atkinson and Miller Cycle Engines

The **Miller cycle** engine and the **Atkinson cycle** engine are both variations on the traditional four-stroke SI engine. These engines operate more efficiently but produce lower power outputs for the same displacement. In a conventional four-stroke cycle, the compression and the power (expansion) strokes are the same length. Increasing engine efficiency by increasing the stroke and raising the expansion ratio also raises the compression ratio. There is a limit to how high the compression ratio can be because raising it too much results in high enough temperatures to ignite the air–fuel mixture prematurely, before the ignition spark occurs. The Miller and the Atkinson cycles overcome this by using valve timing variations to make the effective compression stroke shorter than the expansion stroke. The effective compression stroke is shortened by delaying the closing of the intake valve at the beginning of the compression stroke. This shortens the distance that the piston has to compress the air–fuel mixture. The combustion chamber is slightly smaller so that the engine will still have a normal compression ratio. Thus, the compression pressure at ignition is still typically the same as that of a conventional four-stroke engine. The effective expansion stroke is lengthened by delaying the opening of the exhaust valve until closer to BDC, so more of the pressure created by the expansion of the burning gases can act on the piston longer, applying pressure to the crankshaft for a longer time and increasing efficiency.

Because some of the intake gases are pushed back from the cylinder into the intake manifold, Miller and Atkinson engines can use a larger throttle opening for a given amount of power. This design results in lower manifold vacuum, reduced pumping (parasitic drag) losses, and increased fuel efficiency. The Miller cycle engine adds an engine-driven supercharger to increase volumetric efficiency and boost power output when required. When the engine is operating at low load and speed, the supercharger is not needed. A clutch disengages the drive so there is no unnecessary drag on the engine. When extra power is required, the clutch is engaged and the supercharger boosts the amount of air drawn into the engine, supercharging the cylinder.

The Atkinson cycle engine is efficient within a specific operating range (the so-called engine "sweet spot" of peak torque rpm), typically between 2000 and 4500 rpm, but its overall power output and torque are lower than a conventional ICE. This type of engine is less useful as a primary power source, but it is ideal in applications such as a series-parallel hybrid vehicle where it can work in tandem with a battery-driven electric motor as well as charge the high-voltage battery.

Also, the lower maximum operating rpm allows engine components to be of lighter construction and weight as compared to a conventional ICE. Lighter and smaller components reduce friction and increase engine efficiency. In addition, the crankshaft is mounted slightly off-center from the cylinder bores. This position reduces the thrust load on the piston, thereby reducing power loss due to friction.

Scavenging

Scavenging is the process of using a column of moving air to create a low-pressure area behind it to assist in removing any remaining burned gases from the combustion chamber and replacing these gases with a new charge. As the exhaust stroke ends and the intake stroke begins, both valves are open for a short time. The time that both valves are open is called **valve overlap**. As the exhaust gases leave the combustion chamber, the flow tends to continue, creating a low pressure behind it that helps to draw the intake air and fuel charge in. At the same time, the flow of the air and fuel charge being pushed (by atmospheric pressure) into the combustion chamber also helps to push the remaining exhaust gases out. The flow effect during this valve overlap is called scavenging. Valve overlap has a desirable effect during high power/high rpm demand as more air and fuel are able to be pulled into the engine; however, during engine idling, valve overlap produces a rougher idle as exhaust gases are moving slowly and tend to be drawn back into the intake manifold, diluting the incoming air. The rpm at which the most efficient scavenging occurs contributes to peak volumetric efficiency and engine peak torque. Better exhaust scavenging and induction system (intake) breathing work together to improve volumetric efficiency. This is achieved by smoothing intake and exhaust passages, using tuned intake and exhaust runners (to maximize ram effect and scavenging), and using a low back-pressure exhaust.

▶ Components of the Spark-Ignition Engine

The SI engine is the most widely used engine to power passenger vehicles in the United States. It is the vehicle's main power plant, providing power to drive the vehicle down the road and operate the many accessories that drivers have come to expect, such as power steering, air conditioning, entertainment systems, and other features. SI engines have evolved over their 125-year life, but the fundamental principles are still the same: an air/fuel mixture is brought into the cylinder, it is compressed to increase its energy, it is ignited by a high-voltage spark, the mixture burns rapidly causing the thermal expansion needed to push the piston down, and the exhaust gases are pushed out of the cylinder. Modern materials, machining processes, and lubricants have made these engines longer-lasting, more powerful, and more environmentally friendly than ever.

Manufacturers have made incredible gains in the manufacturing of engines and engine components. Many of these gains are due to new technologies that have found their way into the automotive field. Engine blocks and cylinder heads are commonly manufactured from lightweight aluminum, valve covers and intake manifolds are being made of durable plastic materials, pistons are made of newer aluminum alloys, and in some cases connecting rods are manufactured from powdered metals.

The engine can be divided into a couple of main assemblies: the bottom end and the top end. The engine's so-called "bottom end" is the crankcase where the crankshaft, bearings, and connecting rod "big ends" reside. They also make up what is called the rotating assembly. The so-called "top end" is where the cylinder heads and combustion chambers reside. The engine block contains the pistons and connecting rods, crankshaft, and flywheel; if of the cam-in-block configuration, it also contains the camshaft. The cylinder head(s) contains the overhead valves and valve train; if of the cam-in-head configuration (overhead cam), it also contains the camshaft. Each of these assemblies and components will be explored further.

Short Block and Long Block

If a rebuilt engine is needed, an engine subassembly may be purchased. A short block replacement includes the engine block from below the head gasket to above the oil pan. A cam-in-block engine also includes the camshaft and timing gears. An overhead-cam short block does not include the camshaft or timing gears. A long block replacement engine includes the short block, plus the cylinder head(s), new or reconditioned valve train, camshaft and timing chain, and/or gears (or timing belt) **FIGURE 44-18**. A long block engine replacement still requires swapping parts from the original engine to the long block, including the intake and exhaust manifolds, fuel injection system, the starter, alternator, power steering pump, and air-conditioning compressor.

Cylinder Block, Crankshaft, and Flywheel

The cylinder block is the single largest part of the engine. The block can be made of cast iron or aluminum, which is much lighter. The block casting includes the cylinder bore openings, also known as cylinders, which are machined into the block to allow for the fitting of pistons **FIGURE 44-19**. The block deck is the top of the block and is machined flat. The cylinder head bolts to the block deck. Passages for the flow of coolant and lubrication are machined or cast into the block. Holes machined into the bottom of the block called main bearing bores have removable main caps and are used to hold the crankshaft in place. Each cap is held in place with two or more bolts. Reinforcements for strength and attachment points for related parts are also machined into the block. The lowest portion of the block is called the crankcase because it houses the crankshaft.

The oil pan completes the crankcase. On most modern engines, the main bearing caps are now a part of the engine girdle, also called a bed plate. The use of a girdle provides an even stronger design as all main bearing caps are connected and reinforce each other.

The crankshaft can be made of cast iron or forged steel, or can be machined out of a solid piece of steel. The crankshaft converts the reciprocating motion of the

FIGURE 44-18 The engine contains many parts that work together to power the vehicle.

pistons into rotary motion at the crankshaft. The rotary motion is transferred to the engine flywheel and transmission to ultimately (in a conventional vehicle) drive the wheels. The crankshaft is machined for main bearing support and for the connecting rods **FIGURE 44-20**. The crankshaft is supported by Babbitt-lined main bearing inserts, which fit in the main bearing saddles of the block. End movement of the crankshaft is limited by a thrust bearing at one end of the main bearings.

The crankshaft has main journals that are machined and polished to fit into the block's main bearings. Offset from the crankshaft centerline are the rod journals, also called throws. They are essentially the levers of the crankshaft. The longer the throw of the crankshaft, the longer the stroke of the piston and the more torque that can be produced from the engine. The rod journals are also machined and polished. As the crankshaft turns, the rod journals' "big ends" circle around the centerline of the crankshaft. To prevent vibration, counterweights are formed on the crankshaft. The counterweights balance the weight of the piston assembly, connecting rods, and rod journals. At the front of the crankshaft is a "snout" that provides a mount for a vibration damper (harmonic

balancer) and drive gears, sprockets, or pulleys. The back of the crankshaft has a flange where the flywheel is connected by bolts or studs. A **flywheel** is a weighted assembly that stores kinetic energy from each power stroke and helps keep the crankshaft turning through nonpower strokes. Vehicles with manual transmissions have a clutch assembly attached to the flywheel. Vehicles with automatic transmissions use a flex plate and torque converter assembly. The effect on the crankshaft is the same with either assembly—that of storing energy and keeping the crankshaft rotating smoothly.

Connecting Rod and Piston

A connecting rod is made of cast iron or steel in most engines, although some race cars and exotic sports cars use aluminum or titanium connecting rods to make the engine rev quicker and higher, producing more power. The connecting rod connects the piston to the crankshaft and transfers piston movement and combustion pressure to the crankshaft rod journals. The piston end (small end) of the connecting rod follows the reciprocal movement of the piston, pivoting on a piston pin or "wrist pin" attachment. The wrist pin attaches the piston to the connecting rod and fits into a one-piece bushing in the small end of the rod. The other end (large end) of the connecting rod attaches to the crankshaft throw or rod journal through the use of a removable rod cap that bolts to the end of the connecting rod body. The connecting rod and cap are machined to allow the fit of the connecting rod bearing.

The connecting rod causes piston movement during the intake, compression, and exhaust strokes, which are nonpower strokes. The connecting rod needs to be strong for its size to prevent twisting or bending under

FIGURE 44-20 The basic parts of the crankshaft.

The valve head is disc shaped, and the top of the valve head faces the combustion chamber. A machined surface on the back of the valve head is the **valve face** FIGURE 44-29. The valve face seals on a hardened valve seat in the cylinder head. Located between the valve head and the valve face is a flat surface on the outer edge of the valve head called the **valve margin**. The margin helps to prevent the valve head from melting under the heat and pressure of combustion. A shaft attached to the valve head is the **valve stem**. The stem operates in a **valve guide** in the cylinder head. The valve stem and guide work together to maintain valve alignment as the valve slides open and closed. The opposite end of the stem has grooves machined into its end to receive locking pieces, sometimes referred to as valve **keepers**, that retain a valve spring retainer and spring on the valve. Keepers hold the retainer, preventing it from coming loose while under tension from the valve spring, and preventing the parts from coming loose under normal use. Engines may have two to five valves per cylinder.

Intake and Exhaust Valves

Intake and exhaust valves, in conjunction with the camshaft(s), are the controlling mechanism of the ICE. If the valves do not open and seal at the proper times, combustion will be irregular, weak, or nonexistent. The valves are an incredibly important part of the four-stroke ICE. The intake valve tends to run much cooler than the exhaust since it is always passing cool air and fuel past it when it lifts off its seat. The exhaust valve, in contrast, runs very hot since when it lifts off its seat it is surrounded by extremely hot exhaust gases. Because the exhaust valve runs hotter than the intake valve, some manufacturers use sodium-filled valves, which transfer heat away from the head of the valve more quickly. The valve face may also be coated in a material called Stellite, which is a mixture of chromium and cobalt that can hold up to higher heat. The problem with getting the exhaust valve too hot is that it can either melt or it will deform the sealing surface of the face as it slams closed. The need for new, stronger materials will persist as engines are pushed for maximum power and minimum fuel consumption.

Valve Arrangement

Valves may be arranged in one of two methods: the L-head arrangement and the overhead valve, or I-head, arrangement FIGURE 44-30. L-head engines have not been used in automobiles for many years due to inefficiency and exhaust emissions. You will find them on automobile engines up through the early 1950s and on older lawn and garden equipment engines. The L-head engine's valves are located in the block beside the piston. The "flathead Ford" is a well-known V8 engine that used this L-head style of valve arrangement until 1954. Many other vehicles until that time used flathead engines as well. The term flathead is appropriate, as the head is very thin, acting essentially as a cap to the cylinders. It does not have to be very thick due to the valves being in the block and not in the head.

In the I-head arrangement, the valves are placed in the cylinder head above the piston. This design allows for a better porting arrangement for air to flow smoothly into and out of the engine for better power and improved fuel economy. Today, the I-head is the design found on all automotive engines.

Mechanical and Hydraulic Valve Train

The valve train is the combination of parts that work together to open and close the valves of the engine.

FIGURE 44-29 The parts of a valve.

FIGURE 44-30 In the L-head valve arrangement, valves are placed beside the piston in the engine block, whereas in the I-head, valves are in the head.

The valve train operates off of the camshaft, and the part that rides against the cam lobe is the **valve lifter**. The lifter transfers motion from the cam lobe to a pushrod, or may directly act on the valve and spring, depending on if the cam is in the engine block or on the cylinder head. The valve lifter works as a mechanical spacer, providing a hardened bearing surface that slides across the cam lobe. If the lifter is a mechanically solid piece, it is said to be a mechanical lifter, and therefore the engine is said to have a mechanical valve train. If the lifter has a hydraulic plunger in its center, it is a hydraulic lifter, and the engine is said to have a hydraulic valve train. The hydraulic plunger allows for the expansion and contraction of components during engine warm-up and cool down.

With a hydraulic valve train, valve adjustment is made by the hydraulic lifter, which takes up any clearance automatically. If a mechanical valve train is used, valve adjustments will be necessary at periodic intervals to ensure proper clearance is maintained as parts in the valve train wear.

Roller Rockers and Lifters

Roller-equipped rocker arms are used on many new engines because they reduce friction and increase engine efficiency. They may also be used to replace the cast or stamped steel rocker arms that have been used for many years as part of a standard valve train **FIGURE 44-31**.

A typical rocker arm has a **fulcrum**, a half-round bearing, or a shaft that the rocker moves on as a bearing surface. One end of the rocker touches the top of the valve stem, and the metal slides across the valve as it pushes the valve open and then lets it close. The other end of the rocker arm connects with the pushrod. The rocker's sliding motion across the valve stem and center pivot results in friction, and friction creates loss of power and wear. To remedy this, needle bearings and a roller may be added to the end of the rocker where it contacts the valve stem, and needle bearings are added to the pivot point where the fulcrum is. This system greatly reduces friction and results in a more powerful and reliable valve train.

Rocker arms are designed to increase the amount of lift designed into the cam lobe because they work off-center as a lever. A typical rocker arm has the center pivot closer to the pushrod end. This design causes the valve end of the rocker arm to move more than the pushrod end. Many rocker arms have a 1.5:1 lift ratio, which means that the valve moves 1.5 times farther than the pushrod. High-performance rockers have even higher ratios, such as a 1.6:1 or 1.7:1. These rockers increase the lift of the valve even more than a standard rocker arm.

The other friction loss point in the valve train is at the lifter as it rides upon the cam lobe. To reduce this friction loss, rollers with needle bearings are added to the base of the lifter on some engines. The lifter now rolls on the cam lobe profile rather than sliding on it. This modification further reduces friction in the valve train, resulting in more power delivered to the engine flywheel, and less wasted as heat. The use of rollers on the lifters also allows the use of more aggressive cam lift profiles. Such profiles would rapidly wear an ordinary flat lifter and cam lobe. This difference between cam profiles used with flat tappets versus roller lifters means camshafts and tappets should never be interchanged. Also, the roller lifter must be held in position so that it does not turn in the lifter bore and scrape on and wear the cam lobe. To prevent this, a retainer keeps the lifter from turning sideways.

Valve Clearance

Valve clearance is the amount of slack between the rocker arm or cam follower and the valve stem, or the cam and the lifter if it is a bucket-style OHC engine **FIGURE 44-32**. If valve clearance is too large, the valves will tick and make enough noise to irritate the operator and increase wear of the valve train. If valve clearance is too small, the valve can be held open longer than it should be. As the cylinder head and valve train parts heat, they expand, so adequate clearance is needed to allow for this expansion. Insufficient valve clearance could result in burned valves. Some valves are adjustable through the use of adjusting screws, nuts, or metal shims. Other valves are nonadjustable and the rocker arm simply bolts to the head, or the valve lifter is a preset dimension before it is installed under the camshaft if it is a bucket setup. Bucket lifters contain solid metal discs (shims) of different thicknesses. These shims are used to preset the proper valve clearance during cylinder head assembly or during a major tune-up.

FIGURE 44-31 This roller rocker with a roller lifter compared to the standard rocker and flat lifter.

Valve Timing

Valve timing is critical to the proper operation of the ICE. Many performance gains can be made by simply changing valve timing, but it all depends on what range of rpm (i.e., maximum power) is desired. Valve timing is a mechanical setting, and once set, it cannot be changed without physically changing the timing components in some way **FIGURE 44-33**.

FIGURE 44-32 Valve adjustments. **A.** Rocker arm screw and locknut. **B.** Rocker arm center bolt.

FIGURE 44-33 Valve timing marks.

For standard-performance engines, the technician will set timing components to marks the factory has made on the engine. The camshaft is driven by a chain, gears, or a toothed timing belt. The timing chain is typically designed to last the life of the engine, whereas the timing belt is a required maintenance part that must be changed on a regular scheduled maintenance plan. In some vehicles, not doing so results in damage to the engine if the belt breaks. It is critical that the technician take care when reinstalling the belt or chain to ensure that the timing marks are lined up correctly. The intake and exhaust valves must open at the correct point in the rotation of the crankshaft so that the pistons will be in the correct position and not strike the valves.

Theoretical Four-Stroke Cycle Engine Valve Timing

When the piston is sitting at TDC and preparing to go down, the intake valve opens and air is drawn in with fuel (unless direct injected). The intake valve closes at BDC and the air/fuel is compressed as the piston moves back up to TDC where ignition happens. Once fuel is ignited, the piston is driven back down to BDC where the exhaust valve opens, and the piston moves back to TDC pushing the exhaust out of the cylinder.

In reality, the valves open and close sooner or later than in this description. Because of inertia and other forces, the valves need enough open time to allow gases to flow in and out of the engine. If the valves opened and closed as described in the preceding paragraph, the valves would have 180 degrees of cam duration (TDC to BDC, and BDC to TDC). Although this would be fine for very low-rpm engines, it would not work for high-rpm engines. Thus, we begin the intake stroke by opening the intake valve as the piston is still moving up and the exhaust valve is still slightly open, but closing **FIGURE 44-34**.

FIGURE 44-34 The intake valve starts to open while the piston is still moving up on the exhaust stroke. The exhaust valve is closing, but not closed until the piston starts moving back down.

As air flows into the cylinder, it gains velocity, which creates a column of air that has inertia and keeps the airflow moving, or racing, into the cylinder. If we keep the intake valve open after BDC, air continues to rush in because of the inertia of the airflow. This is called column inertia; as a column of air flows into the combustion chamber, it creates inertia, which keeps air flowing until its inertial energy is spent. This principle of airflow allows the intake valve to be left open even when the piston is starting back up in the cylinder. The inertia causes air molecules to pack together more tightly, especially at higher engine rpm, thus creating a ram-air effect.

As the cam allows the valve spring to close the intake valve, the piston continues moving toward TDC and squeezes the air and fuel into a small package. Sometime near TDC, the spark plug ignites the fuel and air. Doing so early allows enough time for the air/fuel mixture to be ignited and burn, which produces power. Air/fuel has a fairly constant burn time, so as engine rpm increases, the spark will have to occur earlier (in degrees) **before top dead center (BTDC)** to make sure maximum pressure is developed shortly **after top dead center (ATDC)**. (Note: This concept is covered in greater detail in the Engine Performance section.)

As air/fuel burns, it heats and expands the air, which pushes the piston down. As the piston moves down, the exhaust valve begins to open shortly before the piston reaches BDC. This timing allows the pressure in the cylinder to escape before the piston starts moving back up. More importantly, it allows time to open the exhaust valve far enough so that at higher rpm there is enough time to effectively evacuate the cylinder. When the piston travels back toward TDC, the intake valve begins to open slightly before TDC. The exhaust valve is still open past TDC, with exhaust gases rushing out; this helps provide the scavenging effect discussed earlier. The exhaust valve will hang open on some engines a small amount after the piston begins to move down on the intake stroke in order to allow maximum scavenging effect. All airflow that happens in the engine, whether in or out, is helped by the column inertia effect.

Consider again the definition of valve overlap described earlier. In the real world, even standard camshaft grinds (valve timing) include some degree of valve overlap at BDC and TDC. Yet in traditional engine designs, camshaft design and valve timing are a compromise for street engine use. Racing engines are designed with greater valve lift, longer valve duration (valve open time in degrees of camshaft rotation), and increased valve overlap to maximize the effect of fuel and air inertia encountered at higher rpm.

At cranking speeds, there is not much column inertia, so having the valve open for a long time would reduce engine intake vacuum and make the engine difficult to start because the intake air would move back out past the intake valve as the piston travels up on the compression stroke. With no column inertia to speak of, leaving the intake valve hanging open during the initial portion of the compression stroke will lower engine compression.

The other problem that can result with large overlap is that at cranking speeds the intake will be opening during the exhaust stroke, allowing exhaust gases still burning to work their way out the intake valve and create a backfire in the intake manifold (not a desirable effect). When the engine starts and the speed of airflow increases, column inertia starts to increase, reducing the problems experienced while cranking.

The timing of the valve train is basically controlled by the physical shape of the cam lobes. We can move the entire cam forward or backward in relation to the crankshaft position to make the events happen sooner or later in the piston stroke. Advancing or retarding cam timing should not be confused with ignition timing, however, which is when the spark occurs. Cam timing can be controlled in fixed valve timing engines by installing different gears and a chain or belt.

Aftermarket performance companies manufacture cam gears that can be advanced or retarded manually to gain additional power at the desired rpm. Advancing cam timing closes the intake valve sooner, giving more cranking compression, again because of low column inertia. This results in more torque and power in the low rpm range. If we retard cam timing, then the intake valve closes later and gives us more torque and power at a higher rpm range. Since the column inertia is greater at high rpm, more air can be pushed into the engine if the valve is held open later in the four-stroke cycle. Cam duration (valve open time) is built into the cam lobe profile and cannot normally be changed. Duration determines how long the valves remain open and closed. By advancing or retarding the cam opening or closing time, we can affect how long the valves stay open or closed; that is, the point at which they open and close in the cycle can be designed for a distinct engine purpose (peak torque rpm range). Serious valve overlap is typically not used on turbocharged or supercharged engines, as air forced into the engine by the turbo or supercharger would be forced out of the exhaust during overlap.

Variable Valve Timing

We can see from the previous section that the ability to control the advance and retard of the cam timing is a huge benefit to engine performance. Retarded timing provides greater engine efficiency when large amounts of air are flowing into the engine at higher rpm. Advanced timing is useful when the engine needs high torque during lower engine rpm operations. In past applications, an engine designer would have to decide which valve timing best served the operating range of the engine and then design the camshaft for that purpose.

For optimum engine performance in a vehicle used both for commuting and for rallying or racing, what if an electronic module could manage optimum valve timing for such widely differing engine demands? Well, today's automobiles do almost that by using electronically controlled, hydraulically assisted variable valve timing while the engine is operating. Twin camshafts are advanced or retarded through the use of cam phasers or actuators. The **phaser** typically takes the place of the standard cam gear or pulley and uses oil pressure from the engine oil pump to move (some advance, some retard) the camshafts when commanded by the **power train control module (PCM)**. One type of actuator or phaser uses a twisted gear arrangement and a return spring. When oil pressure pushes against the gear mechanism, the cam rotates and advances. When oil pressure is released, the return spring brings the cam back to the fully retarded position. At rest, these types of actuators may be either fully retarded or fully advanced.

The other type of actuator used is the **vane-type phaser**. This phaser uses vanes similar to what is used in a vane-type oil pump to move the camshaft. Oil pressure moves into the phaser and pushes on one side of the vane to advance the cam timing. When oil pressure is switched to the other side of the vane, the camshaft is retarded. Cam timing is adjusted according to what the PCM desires based on its input sensors. If oil pressure is held constant, the cam phaser will likewise hold cam timing constant. The cam phaser uses a mechanical stop to limit maximum valve timing advance or retard.

Cam phasers can be used on any camshaft arrangement, such as cam-in-block or OHC engines. If the cam is a single cam with exhaust and intake lobes, then both intake and exhaust will be affected by rotating the camshaft to the advanced or retarded position. In a DOHC engine, some engine designers use a phaser on the exhaust camshaft only. The phaser used with this type of engine is not intended for increased engine power, but rather for better exhaust gas recirculation. If the exhaust valve is held open later in the exhaust stroke, then it will also hang open later into the intake stroke, which can result in exhaust gases being pulled back into the engine. The exhaust gases pulled back into the engine dilute the incoming air–fuel mixture with an inert gas to help reduce oxides of nitrogen emissions.

Because **inert gas** does not react chemically, it cools the combustion chamber to reduce oxides of nitrogen or NOx.

▶ **LINK**
Refer to the Emission Control chapter for more information on NOx.

Controlling NOx in this way allows for the elimination of the exhaust gas recirculation (EGR) valve on some vehicles. In other DOHC engines, the phaser can be installed only on the intake camshaft for greater engine power, or it can be installed on both the intake and the exhaust camshafts. The newest cam phaser in use relies on an electric motor–driven phaser to vary the cam timing; this type of phaser is more accurate, since it does not rely on the oil being a consistent viscosity or squeaky clean.

Variable cam timing is controlled by the PCM. There are several inputs used to ensure that the ECM is able to control the timing accurately. These inputs are the same inputs used by the PCM to control fuel delivery and ignition system timing. The PCM also must know oil temperature to ensure that the oil viscosity is not too thick or thin. Based on input from an oil temperature sensor, the PCM will either allow or disable variable valve timing; the viscosity of the oil must be correct for accurate valve timing. The PCM must know the amount of engine load to determine the need for an advance or retard of cam timing. To calculate engine load, the PCM primarily uses the following inputs:

- Mass airflow sensor or manifold absolute pressure sensor
- Throttle position sensor
- Intake air temperature sensor
- Engine coolant temperature sensor
- Crankshaft position sensor

The PCM relies on feedback to ensure that the cams are rotating as commanded; the cam position sensor (CMP) is used for this function. The output of the PCM is delivered to the cam timing solenoid. The cam solenoid allows oil pressure to move into the cam phaser. The solenoid is turned on and off with a **pulse-width modulation (PWM)** signal. PWM is the variable rapid (in milliseconds) time-based on/off switching of a DC signal. The longer the solenoid device is turned off, the less it opens; the longer it is turned on, the more it opens. In this way, the solenoid can regulate the amount, and direction, of oil flow to the cam phaser to alter camshaft/valve timing.

▶ TECHNICIAN TIP

PWM is used to control outputs such as fuel injectors, shift solenoids, torque converter clutches, and even interior vehicle lighting.

Valve Train Drives

The valve train is driven by the camshaft, which in turn is driven by a chain or belt (depending on the engine design) driven by the crankshaft **FIGURE 44-35**. In older engine designs, the camshaft was driven by a gear-to-gear arrangement like that found in small lawnmower engines. The trouble with a gear-to-gear design is that it tends to be a bit noisy compared to a chain or belt and the camshaft needs to be relatively close to the crankshaft. In any four-cycle engine design, the camshaft must rotate at half of crankshaft speed. This may be accomplished by using a camshaft gear or pulley that has twice the number of teeth as the crankshaft gear. The ratio of the crank to cam gear is 2:1; thus it takes two turns of the crankshaft to turn the camshaft one turn.

The timing chain drive is louder than a belt, but the belt will not last as long as the timing chain and if exposed to fluids or dirt will wear out more quickly. The timing chain must have a constant supply of engine oil to lubricate the chain to keep it from wearing out quickly. Timing gears rarely jump time, but if the timing chain or belt breaks, serious engine damage could result, depending on if it is a freewheeling engine or an interference engine. A freewheeling engine will not be damaged, but in an interference engine, the valves will be tap-dancing on the piston crowns, bending the valves, with the valves possibly punching holes in the pistons.

The **freewheeling engine** has enough clearance between the pistons and the valves so that in the event the timing belt breaks any valve that is hanging all the way open will not contact the piston, thus preventing engine damage. A broken timing belt will be an inconvenience to the customer. The engine dies and will not restart; the good news is that no mechanical engine damage occurs. By contrast, the **interference engine** has minimal clearance between the valves and pistons during normal operation. When the timing belt breaks, the pistons keep moving and hit the remaining open valves. A broken timing belt on an interference engine means a huge repair expense and in some cases the entire engine will need to be replaced. The manufacturer's service information will normally tell you if the engine is an interference engine.

The timing chain camshaft drive used in a cam-in-block engine is very different from that used in the OHC engine. The pushrod engine typically uses a chain behind a timing chain cover located on the front of the engine. This type of timing chain is fairly short since the camshaft is close to the crankshaft. Some pushrod engines use a timing chain tensioner to ensure that the correct timing chain tension is maintained; however, most designs do not use a tensioner. The timing chain tensioner applies pressure against the chain; as the chain wears and gets longer, the tensioner takes up play in the chain. As the timing chain stretches, cam timing may become retarded. Slack of the chain affects the positioning of the cam gear in relation to the crank gear. Retarded cam timing in this case can create undesirable engine performance problems.

The OHC engine requires a longer timing chain or belt, and in this design one or more tensioners are required. The timing chain in an OHC engine typically has hard plastic-type guides for the chain to slide on and assist the tensioner(s) with correct tracking and tension of the timing chain. The OHC timing chain must run in oil to ensure that the chain is lubricated. Without oil the chain would wear out rapidly.

A belt system uses a toothed or cogged belt to turn toothed or cogged pulleys on the camshaft. The belt is a scheduled maintenance replacement item and needs to be replaced at the mileage or time recommended by the manufacturer (e.g., 60,000 miles [100,000 kilometers] or 5 years, whichever occurs first).

Intake Manifold

The intake manifold is part of the air intake (induction) system of the engine package. It sits between the throttle body and the cylinder head(s). On a V-type engine, it

FIGURE 44-35 Cam drives. **A.** Belt-driven OHC. **B.** Chain-driven OHC.

usually is located between the cylinder heads. For an inline engine, it bolts to the side of the head. Intake manifolds deliver air (air with fuel on carbureted or throttle body–injected engines) to the cylinder head.

Intake manifold designs have seen many changes since the first engines. Once rectangular and boxy in shape, they are now sleek. The materials from which they are made has also changed. Intake manifolds were first manufactured in cast iron, and later in lightweight aluminum. Now, most manufacturers are using even lighter thermoplastic materials for intake manifolds. Lighter engines usually equate to better fuel economy, so manufacturers are always looking for new lighter materials to make their vehicles more fuel efficient. How smooth the inside of the intake manifold is, its inside diameter, and its length all affect how an intake manifold will contribute to engine performance. Some sportier vehicles use variable-length "tuned" intake runners, which switch between a shorter or longer path for the air to flow, depending on engine rpm. Intake manifold design can greatly affect engine performance; this topic is discussed further in the Induction and Exhaust chapter.

Exhaust Manifold

The exhaust manifold is the output side of the engine's breathing apparatus. With a crossflow head, the exhaust manifold bolts to the cylinder head across from the intake manifold and is designed to carry exhaust gases out of the engine and deliver them to the exhaust system. As with intake manifolds, exhaust manifold design can have a great impact on the performance of the engine due to scavenging. So-called "tuned headers," for example, direct exhaust gases from each individual cylinder using equal-length tubes (runners) to scavenge (extract) the exhaust from neighboring cylinders.

> ▶ **LINK**
> Refer to the Induction and Exhaust chapter for more information about the exhaust system.

 ## Two-Stroke Spark-Ignition Engines

Two-stroke engines are notable in their ability to produce a large power to weight ratio. The power capabilities of this engine come from the fact that every other stroke (TDC to BDC) is a power stroke. However, there are drawbacks to this engine design—namely that it is a high-emissions engine. Almost all car manufacturers have moved away from two-stroke production.

Basic Two-Stroke Cycle Engine Principles

The two-stroke SI engine is different from the four-stroke SI engine. In a two-stroke engine, the inlet and exhaust ports are opened and closed by the movement of the piston; there are no poppet valves like those used in the four-stroke cycle engine. The two-stroke engine is still an ICE and shares the five events common to all SI engines. What is different is the method of air induction and scavenging used:

- *Intake* occurs in two parts. First, the air–fuel mixture is drawn into the crankcase as the piston moves up. It is then transferred from the crankcase to above the piston when the piston moves down.
- During *compression*, the mixture is forced into a small volume as the piston moves up.
- During *ignition*, the spark from the spark plug ignites the mixture and it burns.
- During the *power stroke*, energy released by combustion generates the force that pushes the piston down and turns the crankshaft.
- During *exhaust*, leftover gases are expelled from the cylinder when the piston is near BDC.

As in all ICEs, expanding gases drive the piston down and turn the crankshaft and flywheel, which pushes the piston back up to TDC in the cylinder.

With the two-stroke cycle engine, the crankshaft makes one revolution (two strokes) for every complete cycle. In one revolution of the crankshaft, two piston strokes occur: one down and one up. Each downward stroke of the piston is a power stroke and turns the crankshaft.

The two-stroke cycle engine differs from the four-stroke cycle engine because the upward piston movement creates suction in the crankcase to pull the air–fuel mixture into it as the piston moves from BDC to TDC. The air and fuel sit in the crankcase until the piston begins to move down, which then creates a small pressure in the crankcase, referred to as crankcase compression. As the piston moves downward with the power stroke, it uncovers a transfer port and the fuel and air rush into the cylinder from the crankcase.

The piston begins moving up toward TDC, creating another draw of air and fuel into the crankcase. The air and fuel above the piston get squeezed in the combustion chamber and the spark plug ignites the mixture. As the piston moves down, it also uncovers the exhaust port, and exhaust gases exit the exhaust system. As the piston moves farther down, it uncovers the transfer port again, and crankcase compression pushes the air and fuel into the cylinder once again.

To summarize, with upward movement of the piston, compression of the air–fuel mixture is happening in the cylinder above the piston, and intake of new air and fuel is happening in the crankcase below the piston. When the piston moves down, power is being applied to the crankshaft, exhaust is happening, and crankcase compression is building to push air and fuel through the transfer port into the cylinder. The placement of the ports makes all these processes possible and eliminates the use of valves to let fuel and air in and exhaust out.

Two-Stroke Intake System

The intake system of a two-stroke engine is called a piston port system because the piston acts as a valve to cover and uncover the ports, allowing flow into and out of the cylinder. But because the crankcase alternates between vacuum and pressure as the piston goes up and down, there needs to be a valve between the crankcase and the carburetor. Manufacturers use either a reed valve or a rotary valve for this purpose.

A **reed valve** is a small flexible metal plate that covers the inlet port **FIGURE 44-36**. The reed valve is made of spring metal and can be attached to the crankcase or to the inlet port. The reed valve acts like a one-way check valve and opens and closes automatically, according to changes in pressure in the crankcase. For performance applications, such as in off-road motorcycle racing, a different reed valve may be used to change the performance characteristics of the engine.

Some two-stroke intake systems use a rotary valve. The crankcase has a port open to the carburetor, and a rotary valve that covers and uncovers that port. The rotary valve is mounted on the crankshaft. As the crankshaft turns, the rotary valve rotates with it, opening and closing the inlet port as it does so. This ensures that pressure does not push backward into the carburetor as the piston pressurizes the crankcase.

FIGURE 44-36 Two-stroke reed valve operation.

Four- and Two-Stroke Engine Differences

In a two-stroke gasoline engine, lubrication is usually performed by mixing oil with the gasoline. The oil lubricates the moving parts within the engine but also burns in the combustion chamber. This oil causes smoke to be emitted from the exhaust, which is one reason two-stroke engines have been dropped for automotive use. The exhaust emissions are beyond today's emissions regulation cutoff points.

Two-stroke engines do have some attractive benefits. The first is their lightweight, compact, and powerful package. These features make them ideal for handheld equipment such as weed cutters and chain saws. They can be run in any position since there is no worry of oil leaking out of the sump or fuel out of the carburetor. They are also simple, using fewer parts, so they are easier and less expensive to build. Pressurized oil and oil passages are not needed for the crankshaft and connecting rod bearings in two-stroke engines. Most two-stroke engines use roller bearings on the crankcase, which are splash lubricated by the oil mixed in with the gas as it churns in the crankcase. Many two-stroke engines are air cooled, thus eliminating the water-based cooling system of the four-stroke engine. There is no oil pan with an oil pump or oil in it, nor a radiator with coolant in it. The two-stroke engine does not use any of the valve train components used by four-stroke engines, so even more weight is shed from the engine package. These are some of the benefits of the two stroke engine.

Again, the downfall to the two-stroke engine design is the pollution released from the engine due to burning oil in the fuel and the amount of unburned fuel exhausted from the engine due to scavenging of the exhaust. It is estimated that 25% of the incoming oil and fuel leaves the exhaust unburned in a typical two-stroke engine. The oil and fuel represent hydrocarbons released to the atmosphere, and wasted energy. The four-stroke engine releases fewer hydrocarbons since it controls inlet and outlet flow better. The release of less pollution makes the four-stroke engine the choice for most manufacturers trying to meet pollution requirements of the Environmental Protection Agency. While companies continue to produce two-stroke engines and have found ways to make them pollute less, much research is still needed to improve this engine design.

▶ Rotary Combustion Spark-Ignition Engine

As we have seen from the two-stroke engine, the fewer parts that are used, the better the power production and the smaller the engine can be. The rotary engine fits into the same category of using fewer parts to produce power. The rotary combustion (RC) engine has found its way into automobiles, planes, helicopters, boats, motorcycles, lawn mowers, and other applications. Displacement has varied from tiny air-cooled models to much larger liquid-cooled, multirotor units.

The rotary engine is also called the "Wankle" engine because it was improved upon by Felix Wankle for automotive use in the 1940s. The RC engine was commercially released in 1964 in the NSU Wankel Spider and in 1967 with a two-rotor engine in the NSU RO80. Under license from NSU, Mazda successfully used the rotary engine in several vehicles from the late 1960s all the way through the RX series. The engines were a redefining period for engine development, but were never really a success for a number of other companies.

Basic Principles of the Rotary Engine

The rotary engine (aka, Wankle engine) is not as common as the four-stroke or two-stroke cycle engines, but its basic principle is well accepted. The rotary engine layout is vastly different from that of a reciprocating engine. The piston engine is called a reciprocating engine because the pistons move back and forth over the same path. This reciprocating motion is converted to rotary motion at the crankshaft.

By contrast, a rotary engine does not use a piston that reciprocates; rather, it has a rotor that—you guessed it—rotates. The rotary engine does not need to convert inefficient reciprocating motion to rotary motion since the rotor functions as the piston in the engine. In the reciprocating engine, the piston assembly must stop at BDC and move back up to TDC, then back down to BDC, and so on, many times a second. The stopping and starting of the piston assembly puts tremendous pressure on the connecting rod and rod bolts. Due to inertia, the piston tries to move out of the top of the cylinder bore and through the bottom of the oil pan. The rotary engine does not have to stop–start its "piston" as it rotates. The rotor is roughly triangular in shape and turns inside of a housing. The housing works on a geometric principle called an epitrochoid curve. An **epitrochoid curve** is the circular movement around the perimeter of another circle. The rotor moves in a unique pattern to ensure that the rotor ends follow the oblong shape of the housing **FIGURE 44-37**.

Because the rotor spins, rather than moving up and down, engine operation is relatively smooth and vibration free. Each rotor and housing is akin to that of a three-cylinder two-stroke engine because of the rotor's three-sided shape. The rotor has three working chambers; thus, for each rotation of the rotor, we get three power pulses. Low-end torque is improved to the point that (while not recommended) a four-speed transmission rotary vehicle can be driven and accelerated from a standstill in fourth gear without excessive lugging. Rotary engines can be

made with one, two, or even three or more rotor housings stacked side to side.

Let's look at the basic principles of a rotary engine. While it appears different, the rotary engine is still an ICE. Recall the five events common to all ICEs: intake, compression, ignition, power, and exhaust.

The rotary engine's intake cycle occurs when one face of the rotor passes the intake port and draws the air/fuel mixture into the working chamber through the inlet port **FIGURE 44-38**. The turning rotor then carries it around to

FIGURE 44-37 Cutaway of a rotary engine.

FIGURE 44-38 Operation of a rotary engine.

the spark plugs. Along the way, the volume of the working chamber decreases and compresses the mixture. The mixture is ignited and combustion occurs. Expanding gases produce a power pulse, driving the rotor farther around. When the exhaust port is uncovered, exhaust occurs as the rotor sweeps burned gases out of the housing. Each face of the rotor is a separate working chamber, so three combustion events occur for each single revolution of the rotor.

Basic Components of the Rotary Engine

The rotor is mounted in an oval-shaped housing. The housing is made of aluminum alloy, but the curved interior surface has hard chromium plating. This surface has to put up with the wear and tear of the rotor seals sliding against it as it turns in the housing. Cooling passages machined into the housing allow coolant to flow around the outside surface of the housing to cool the engine.

There are usually two spark plugs fixed to the housing that enable combustion to occur; these are referred to as leading and trailing spark plugs. The combustion chamber design is a long trough, which can contribute to incomplete combustion due to the large surface area of the chamber and the distance the flame travels in the combustion chamber. Designers found that by installing a leading and trailing plug a more efficient combustion process could be produced. The rotor housing also has an intake port to let air and fuel into the combustion chamber and an exhaust port to expel burned gases.

The rotor has three apexes, or points, which have seals to seal between the rotor and the rotor housing. These seals work like piston rings in a reciprocating piston engine. Side and corner seals create a seal between the rotor and the side housing to prevent combustion gases from leaking around the rotor at the apex seals. The rotor also has oil seals on the side of the rotor that keep oil from inside the rotor from finding its way into the combustion chamber.

The combustion chamber of the rotary engine is formed by hollows in the flanks of the rotor. These hollows are sometimes called bathtubs. Front and rear housings, or side housings, are bolted to each side of the rotor housing. If it is a two-rotor engine, there is an intermediate housing between the two rotors. An internal gear in each rotor meshes with a corresponding stationary gear in the front and rear housings.

When combustion occurs, the meshing of the teeth forces the rotor to walk around the stationary gear. The teeth being in mesh combines with an eccentric shaft to make the rotor follow the curved surface of the housing,

and it gives the rotor planetary motion. The rotor is attached to the eccentric shaft at points called rotor journals. This eccentric shaft is like a crankshaft in a piston engine but with the journals off-center. Because the rotor is off-center, the force applied to the shaft is off-center too. The whole shaft is supported by main journals, so the final output is smooth rotary motion.

Engine Power Pulses

A single-rotor rotary engine will produce three power pulses per rotor rotation or one power pulse per eccentric shaft rotation. In a four-stroke engine, there is one power pulse per cylinder for every two crankshaft revolutions, and in a two-stroke engine, there is one power pulse per cylinder for each crankshaft revolution. Because of the ratio of the gears in the housings and rotor, the eccentric shaft makes one revolution for each power phase. That is the same as three eccentric shaft revolutions for each rotation of the rotor. So the eccentric shaft turns at three times the speed of the rotor. A standard rotary engine typically has two rotors, offset from each other, in separate chambers, so it ends up with two power pulses per revolution of the eccentric shaft.

Renesis Rotary Engine

Due to emission and fuel economy requirements, Mazda updated the standard rotary engine to the Renesis engine. The operating cycle of the Renesis rotary engine is the same as a conventional, or Wankel, rotary engine, but with some design changes that improve fuel economy under load and compliance with current emission regulations. There is a low-output version of this engine for use with automatic transmissions and a high-output version for use with manual transmissions. The low-output Renesis engine has two intake ports, primary and secondary. The ports were enlarged and moved to the side of the housing. In this position, they can open sooner, improving power and torque, extending engine efficiency over a wider range of engine speeds, and reducing port overlap, which resulted in unburned fuel exiting the exhaust port.

The intake manifold has primary, secondary, and auxiliary ducts. The primary duct has no control valve; the secondary and auxiliary ducts are controlled by butterfly valves. At low engine speeds, air flows into the engine through the primary intake ducts only, keeping the air velocity in the manifold high, which provides better air–fuel mixing. At medium engine speeds, and when engine load is high enough, the secondary intake ducts are opened by butterfly valves, reducing restriction and increasing airflow and torque. Intake manifolds on reciprocating piston engines now use a similar system called intake manifold runner control. The rotary engine opens an extra air duct on the air cleaner at high engine speeds, allowing more air to be drawn into the engine.

The high-output engine has three intake ports—primary, secondary, and auxiliary. At engine speeds above 6000 rpm, the auxiliary duct opens, allowing the engine to draw air in through all six ports (three intake ports per rotor), further increasing engine breathing. A butterfly valve located between each housing's main intake duct is used at speeds above 7000 rpm to shorten the effective length of the intake tubes so that pressure pulses force more air into the engine.

Low-output engines have two fuel injectors per rotor: primary and secondary. The primary fuel injectors operate at all times; the secondary injectors operate at engine speeds over 3700 rpm and when the engine load demands more fuel. The high-output engine has additional primary injectors, named "primary 2," which only operate at very high speed and load conditions. The exhaust ports in a Renesis engine have also been enlarged and moved to the side of the combustion chamber housing. In this location, the exhaust ports open later than in a conventional rotary engine, and the rotor has been machined to delay the closing point. These changes deliver a longer expansion stroke and increase thermal efficiency.

Wrap-up

Ready for Review

- Most modern vehicles use internal combustion engines.
- Internal combustion engines are typically either piston (spark ignition, using reciprocating motion of pistons) or rotary (spark ignition, using planetary motion).
- Piston engines can be spark ignition (passenger vehicles; uses a spark plug) or compression ignition (diesel vehicles; no spark plug).
- Pressure and temperature have a direct relationship in that when pressure rises so does temperature, and vice versa.
- Internal combustion engines work by heating a gas, which increases pressure (thermal expansion), creating force to push the piston down the cylinder.
- Pressure and volume have an inverse relationship: when one increases, the other decreases.
- Force (effort) tends to cause movement, which creates work; the speed at which this happens is known as power.
- Work = distance moved × force applied.
- Power = distance × force / time in minutes.
- Engine power is measured by the amount of torque (turning effort) applied to the crankshaft, times the RPM at which it is turning divided by 5252.
- Torque and power produced by an engine are called engine output.
- Horsepower refers to the speed at which torque is produced.
- Load factor refers to the period of time a vehicle can operate at maximum speed and power.
- Piston stroke refers to the distance traveled from top dead center (TDC) to bottom dead center (BDC) (or BDC to TDC).
- Internal combustion engines have either a two-stroke or four-stroke cycle.
- In a four-stroke cycle, five events must occur: intake, compression, ignition, power, and exhaust.
- The compression ratio of an engine is based on cylinder volume at BDC compared to cylinder volume at TDC, and can be affected by changes in piston stroke, piston head shape, head gasket thickness, and combustion chamber size.
- Piston displacement (the volume of movement from BDC to TCD) is calculated as: bore squared × 3.14 × stroke / 4.
- Engine displacement is calculated as piston displacement × number of engine cylinders.

- Two variations on the typical four-stroke spark ignition engine are the Miller cycle engine and the Atkinson cycle engine, both of which use valve timing variations to create unequal compression and expansion strokes.
- The Miller cycle engine has an engine-driven compressor that functions at high load and speed to boost power output.
- The Atkinson cycle engine is ideal for hybrid vehicles, as it has a lower power output and torque than conventional engines.
- Valve overlap refers to the short time that both intake and exhaust valves are open, allowing more air and fuel into the engine during high power high rpm.
- Major components of an internal combustion engine include: cylinder block, crankshaft, flywheel, connecting rod and piston, intake manifold, oil pan, oil pump, exhaust manifold, cylinder head, valve train, and engine camshaft.
- The cylinder block, the largest engine component, includes cylinder bores, coolant and lubrication passages, and the crankcase.
- The function of the crankshaft is to convert the piston's reciprocating motion into rotary (turning) motion.
- The flywheel stores energy from each piston's power stroke to smooth out the power strokes.
- The connecting rod connects the piston to the crankshaft and causes piston movement (via the crankshaft) during non-power strokes.
- Components that make up and support the piston are: piston head, piston rings (compression and oil control), ring grooves, ring lands, piston skirt, pin hole, and pin boss.
- Compression and combustion gases can leak past piston rings and enter the crankcase; this is known as blowby.
- The purpose of an intake manifold is to deliver air or air and fuel to the cylinder head.
- Oil for the engine lubrication system is stored in the oil pan.
- The camshaft opens the valves and allows them to close at the right time, which ensures correct engine operation.
- Parts of the camshaft lobe include: base circle, nose, cam lobe centerline, and cam lobe ramps.
- Engineers designing camshaft lobes must consider the issues of lift and duration, as well as the cam centerline and separation.

▸ Parts of an intake valve include: head, face, margin, and stem.

▸ The intake valve is typically larger and tends to run cooler than the exhaust valve.

▸ Exhaust valves are typically smaller, allow exhaust to exit the cylinder, and tends to be run hotter than intake valves.

▸ Modern automotive engines have valves arranged in the cylinder head above the piston, known as an I head arrangement.

▸ The valve lifter can be hydraulic or mechanical and transfers motion from the cam lobe to the valve train or directly to the valve.

▸ Roller rocker arms act as levers to increase the camshaft's lift of the valve.

▸ Valve clearance must be accurate, so as not to create noise (meaning clearance is too high) or a loss of compression past the valve (clearance is too low).

▸ Timing of when valves open and close is vital to proper engine function; timing belts will need periodic replacement and must be aligned with engine timing marks.

▸ Valve timing can be modified during engine design by advancing or retarding cam timing, which gives the effect of more torque and power at a lower rpm or higher rpm range, respectively.

▸ Variable valve timing allows cam timing to be adjusted during engine operation.

▸ Cam actuators can be a twisted gear arrangement or a vane-type phaser.

▸ The engine control module (ECM) controls variable cam timing using the following inputs: mass airflow sensor or manifold absolute pressure sensor, throttle position sensor, intake air temperature sensor, engine coolant temperature sensor, and crankshaft position sensor.

▸ Using a pulse width modulation signal, the cam solenoid regulates amount and direction of oil flow to the cam phaser.

▸ Engine design—freewheeling or interference—determines the amount of damage that will result if the timing belt breaks.

▸ Two-stroke engines use the piston to open and close intake and exhaust ports allowing air-fuel to enter the cylinder.

▸ All events of an internal combustion engine are accomplished by a two-stroke engine within one up and one down stroke of the piston.

▸ Two-stroke engines use either a reed valve or rotary valve to allow air and fuel into the crankcase.

▸ Two-stroke engines eliminate the camshaft and valve train, making them lighter than four-stroke engines.

▸ Four-stroke engines release fewer hydrocarbons into the atmosphere and are more likely to meet EPA regulations.

▸ Rotary, or Wankel, engines use a rotor in place of a piston and move it in an epitrochoid curve to create a nearly vibration-free engine operation.

▸ Rotary engines have two spark plugs—leading and trailing—per rotor to enable complete combustion.

▸ The rotor moves along the curved surface of its housing and pushes on an eccentric shaft to produce power.

▸ A rotary engine cycle has four phases: intake, compression, power, and exhaust.

▸ Each of the three faces of the rotor act as a combustion chamber, and have a power pulse every revolution of the rotor.

▸ The Renesis rotary engine is designed with improved fuel economy via modified intake and exhaust ports.

▸ A Renesis engine can be low output (for automatic transmissions) or high output (for manual transmissions).

Key Terms

after top dead center (ATDC) The position of the piston once it has moved beyond top dead center.

alloy The mixture of materials to make a substance that has properties different from the original materials. Aluminum alloy has silica added to make it perform better than pure aluminum.

Atkinson cycle An engine cycle that uses a longer effective exhaust stroke than intake stroke to reduce exhaust emissions. This type of engine is widely used in hybrid-electric vehicles.

base circle The rounded bottom part of the camshaft (off the lobe) where the valves remain closed or at rest.

before top dead center (BTDC) The position of the piston when it has not yet reached top dead center.

block deck The "top" of the engine block and cylinder bore where the cylinder head is bolted on.

blowby gas The result of combustion gases leaking past the compression rings and getting into the crankcase.

bottom dead center (BDC) The position of the piston at the end of its stroke when it is closest to the crankshaft.

cam The egg-shaped lobe machined to a shaft used to cause opening and closing of the valves of a four-stroke cycle engine.

cam-in-block engine An engine in which the camshaft is located in the engine block rather than on the cylinder head.

cam lobe centerline The location of the cam lobe in relation to top dead center of the engine in degrees.

cam lobe ramp The rise of the lobe from the base circle to the top of the lobe, which is where the valve starts to lift, on the side opposite of where it starts to close.

cam lobe separation The number of degrees between the centerline of the intake lobe and the centerline of the exhaust lobe; this with cam duration determines the amount of valve overlap.

camshaft The part of the engine that activates the valve train by using lobes riding against lifters.

coil bind A result of excessive valve lift. When the coils of the spring touch each other, the spring breaks, flattening the cam lobe and bending the pushrod.

column inertia The principle that as a column of air flows, it creates inertia, which keeps air flowing until its inertia energy is spent; sometimes referred to as a "ram effect" when using tuned intake or exhaust systems.

compression-ignition (CI) engine An internal combustion engine that uses the heat of compression to ignite the compressed air-fuel mixture.

compression ratio (CR) The volume of the cylinder with the piston at bottom dead center as compared to the volume of the cylinder at top dead center, given in a ratio such as 9:1 CR.

compression stroke The stroke of the piston during which air and fuel is being compressed into a small area prior to ignition.

cylinder bore The hole in the engine block that the piston fits into.

drive cycle The operating range of an engine from start-up until shutdown when finished performing its job.

dual overhead cam (DOHC) A design that, in a V-engine, includes four cams; also called a twin cam engine.

duration The amount of time the valve stays open, given in degrees of rotation of the crankshaft.

engine displacement The size of the engine given in cubic inches, cubic centimeters, and liters. It is found by multiplying the piston displacement by the number of cylinders the engine has. Sometimes called "swept volume."

epitrochoid curve The circular movement around the perimeter of another circle. This is the movement that the rotary engine uses to ensure that the rotor stays in contact with the housing.

exhaust stroke The stroke of piston during which the exhaust valve is open and the piston is moving from bottom dead center to top dead center to push exhaust gas out of the cylinder.

external combustion engine An engine that runs on heat applied externally to the cylinder. For example: the steam engine.

flathead engine An L-head engine with valves in the block.

flywheel The heavy, circular flat plate that keeps the engine rotating when power is not produced, such as on the exhaust, intake, and compression strokes.

force The effort to produce a push or pull action.

four-stroke engine An engine that uses four strokes—intake, compression, power, and exhaust—to complete its cycle.

freewheeling engine An engine that has enough clearance between the piston and the valves so that in the event the timing belt or chain breaks, the valves that are hanging all the way open will not contact the piston, thus preventing engine damage.

fulcrum A half-round bearing that the rocker moves on as a bearing surface.

horsepower An amount of work performed in a given time.

ignition The lighting of the fuel and air mixture in the combustion chamber.

inert gas A gas that will not react chemically.

intake stroke The stroke of the piston from top dead center to bottom dead center during which the intake valve is open and air is pulled into the cylinder.

interference engine An engine that has minimum clearance between the valves and the pistons during normal operation; in the event that the timing belt or chain breaks, the open valves will be contacted by the piston and bend the valves, possibly breaking the piston.

internal combustion engine An engine that burns a fuel internally and creates movement due to thermal expansion of gases.

keepers Locking devices that keep the valve retained by the valve spring seat.

lift The amount the valve will open. The more the valve lifts off its seat, the more air can get into and out of the engine.

lobe The raised portion on a camshaft; used to lift the lifter and open the valve.

Miller cycle An engine cycle that uses a longer exhaust stroke than intake stroke through delayed closing of the intake valve. This engine uses a supercharger to pressurize air into the cylinder when needed.

overhead cam (OHC) engine An I-head engine with the camshaft located on top of the cylinder head rather than in the block.

parasitic loss A loss of engine efficiency caused by internal friction, inefficient breathing, etc.

phaser A device that is able to shift camshaft timing while the camshaft is turning. This device takes the place of the standard timing belt pulley or timing chain gear.

piston clearance The clearance between the piston and the cylinder wall that allows for lubricating oil to reduce friction.

piston displacement The volume of air that is moved by the piston from bottom dead center to top dead center.

piston engine An engine that uses pistons that move when expanding gases from combustion press against them.

piston pin boss The reinforced area of the piston where the piston wrist pin attaches the piston to the connecting rod.

piston skirt The area below the ring groove area of the piston that prevents the piston from cocking and becoming jammed in the cylinder bore.

piston stroke The up or down motion the piston makes from one limiting position to the other.

power The rate or speed at which work is done.

power stroke The stroke during which combustion is pushing the piston from top dead center to bottom dead center in the cylinder. This stroke is where power is produced.

power train control module (PCM) The electronic "brain" controlling the engine and related systems. The PCM handles more tasks than the former ECM (engine control module) used on earlier emission-controlled vehicles.

pulse width modulation (PWM) The rapid yet variable on-time signal used to smoothly actuate output devices like solenoids, lights, etc.

pushrod A tubular rod that stands between the tappet and the rocker arm in an overhead valve engine; the pushrod transfers cam motion to the rocker arm.

reciprocating motion An up-and-down motion within the cylinder.

reed valve A small flexible metal plate that covers the inlet port of a two-stroke engine and opens and closes to let air and fuel into the crankcase.

ring lands The metal between the ring grooves that supports the rings as the piston moves.

rocker arm The fulcrum that transfers pushrod endwise motion to the valve stem.

rotary engine A nonreciprocating engine with a rotor and housing instead of pistons.

scavenging The process of removing burned gases from the cylinder through the use of moving airflow pulling or extracting the gases out.

spark ignition (SI) engine An engine that relies on an electrical spark to ignite the air and fuel mixture.

stroke The movement of an object in a straight line. The piston sees four strokes during one combustion cycle in a four-stroke cycle engine, meaning it moves up and down twice each during a cycle.

tappet Another name for a valve lifter. Tappets may be flat or have rollers to ride on the cam lobes.

throw The offset area of the crankshaft where the connecting rod bolts on.

top dead center (TDC) The position of the piston when it is farthest from the crankshaft.

torque The amount of twisting force applied in a turning application, usually measured in foot-pounds.

two-stroke engine An engine that uses only two strokes to complete its running cycle.

valve face A machined surface on the back of the valve head; this area seals onto the valve seat in the cylinder head.

valve guide An insert in the cylinder head through which the valve stem passes and moves.

valve lifter A device that transfers motion from the cam lobe to a pushrod or directly acts on the valve and spring, depending on if the cam is in the engine block or the cylinder head; sometimes called a tappet.

valve margin The flat surface on the outer edge of the valve head between the valve head and the valve face.

valve overlap The time, usually expressed in degrees of crankshaft rotation, during which both the intake valve and the exhaust valve are open at the same time.

valve stem The shaft that is attached to the valve head and provides the sliding surface for the valve in its guide as it opens and closes.

vane-type phaser A cam phaser that uses vanes inside to allow oil pressure to push against and change cam timing as it is turning.

volumetric efficiency A ratio, given as a percentage, of the amount of air actually inducted at a given engine speed at full throttle compared to the internal engine displacement. For a normally aspirated engine (without supercharging or turbocharging), an engine's volumetric efficiency may peak at around 85%. Peak engine torque is developed at peak volumetric efficiency.

work The result of force creating movement.

ASE-Type Questions

1. Tech A says that engines using compression ignition control timing by regulating when fuel is injected into the cylinder. Tech B says that engines using spark ignition control timing by regulating when fuel is injected into the cylinder. Who is correct?
   a. Tech A
   b. Tech B
   c. Both A and B
   d. Neither A nor B

2. Tech A says that horsepower is a measurement of the amount of work being performed. Tech B says that horsepower can be calculated by multiplying torque by rpm and dividing by 5252. Who is correct?
   a. Tech A
   b. Tech B
   c. Both A and B
   d. Neither A nor B

3. Tech A says that in a four-stroke engine, the piston is at TDC four times to complete the cycle. Tech B says that the air/fuel mixture is ignited once every two strokes. Who is correct?
   a. Tech A
   b. Tech B
   c. Both A and B
   d. Neither A nor B

4. Tech A says that spark ignition typically occurs before TDC. Tech B says that spark ignition typically occurs after TDC. Who is correct?
   a. Tech A
   b. Tech B
   c. Both A and B
   d. Neither A nor B

5. Tech A says that valve overlap occurs between the exhaust stroke and the intake stroke. Tech B says that valve overlap occurs to assist in scavenging the cylinder. Who is correct?
   a. Tech A
   b. Tech B
   c. Both A and B
   d. Neither A nor B

6. Tech A says that compression ratio is the comparison of the volume above the piston at BDC to the volume above the piston at TDC. Tech B says that scavenging of the exhaust gases occurs once the exhaust valve closes. Who is correct?
   a. Tech A
   b. Tech B
   c. Both A and B
   d. Neither A nor B

7. Tech A says that the weight of the flywheel smooths out the engine's power pulses. Tech B says that the flex plate and torque converter perform the same function as the flywheel. Who is correct?
   a. Tech A
   b. Tech B
   c. Both A and B
   d. Neither A nor B

8. Tech A says that an interference engine is designed so that the pistons can hit the valves if the timing belt breaks. Tech B says that the shape of the cam lobe determines how long and far the valves are held open. Who is correct?
   a. Tech A
   b. Tech B
   c. Both A and B
   d. Neither A nor B

9. Tech A says that blowby gases occur when compression and combustion gases leak past the piston rings. Tech B says that a rotary engine uses reed valves to control air flow into the cylinder on intake. Who is correct?
   a. Tech A
   b. Tech B
   c. Both A and B
   d. Neither A nor B

10. Tech A says that the principle of thermal expansion is what pushes the piston down the cylinder on the power stroke. Tech B says that the piston is pulled down the cylinder on the intake stroke. Who is correct?
    a. Tech A
    b. Tech B
    c. Both A and B
    d. Neither A nor B

CHAPTER 45

NATEF Tasks

Engine Repair
Lubrication and Cooling Systems

				Page
■ Perform oil and filter change.	MLR	AST	MAST	1574–1581
■ Perform oil pressure tests; determine necessary action.		AST	MAST	1582–1583
■ Inspect, test, and replace oil temperature and pressure switches and sensors.		AST	MAST	1586–1587

Knowledge Objectives

After reading this chapter, you will be able to:
1. Describe the components of lubricating oil. (p 1556)
2. Describe the functions of lubricating oil. (p 1557)
3. Describe the types of common additives added to lubricating oil. (p 1558)
4. Describe the three types of oil. (pp 1561–1562)
5. Identify the components of the lubrication system. (pp 1562–1570)
6. Describe the operation of the lubrication system. (pp 1570–1572)
7. Describe the types of lubrication systems and how they operate. (pp 1570–1572)

Engine Lubrication

Skills Objectives

After reading this chapter, you will be able to:
1. Check the engine oil. (pp 1572–1574)
2. Drain the engine oil. (pp 1574–1576)
3. Replace a spin-on filter. (pp 1577–1578)
4. Replace a cartridge filter (replaceable element). (pp 1578–1579)
5. Refill the engine oil. (pp 1579–1581)
6. Test the oil pressure. (pp 1582–1583)
7. Inspect the oil sensors. (pp 1584–1585)
8. Inspect the engine assembly for fuel, oil, coolant, and other leaks. (pp 1585–1586)
9. Inspect, test, and replace the oil temperature and pressure switches. (pp 1586–1587)

Introduction

Machinery, like our automobiles, relies on lubrication to keep the moving parts from wearing out quickly. Lubricating oil is processed from crude oil in a refinery with gasoline and diesel, along with many other beneficial and useful products. Oil is much more than simply crude oil dumped into our engine's crankcase; it is heavily processed to remove impurities, and many additives are put into the processed oil by scientists in a lab to enhance its lubricating qualities.

Each moving part in the engine needs lubricating oil. The system that moves the oil through the engine is called the lubrication system. This chapter will cover the theory of lubrication systems and the methods and specialized tools involved to ensure that you can properly diagnose and correct common problems associated with this system.

▶ Oil

Oil originates from the ground as **crude oil** FIGURE 45-1. Crude oil varies in color from a dirty yellow to dark brown to black. It can be thin like gasoline or a thick oil- or tarlike substance. Crude oil is pumped from the ground and processed into many products such as fuel for use in diesel and gasoline vehicles. Crude oil is also broken down into other products, which are used in plastics manufacturing as well as in kerosene, aviation fuel, asphalt, cosmetics, pharmaceuticals, and many other products. Many of the products refined from crude oil are used in the transportation industry. For example, **lubricating oil** is distilled from the crude oil and used as a base stock. Additives are added to the base stock to make the lubricating oil useful in engines. Other additives, such as thickening agents, are added to the base stocks and used as lubricating grease in bearings. The additives that are added to the base stock perform a variety of tasks such as keeping acids from forming, cutting down on oxidation, and maintaining the correct viscosity over a broader temperature range.

FIGURE 45-1 Crude oil straight from the ground.

▶ You are the Automotive Technician

A customer brings his 5-year-old vehicle into your shop for an oil and filter change. The vehicle is right at the recommended 7,500 mile interval. He said he has noticed some oil spots on his garage floor, and the oil level was a bit below the "add" mark this morning when he checked it. He is concerned that he has an oil leak, and he would like to know why the oil pressure light on the dash didn't indicate that his oil level was low. You pull the vehicle onto the hoist. The oil light comes on when the key is turned to "run" and goes off once the engine starts, proving that the oil pressure warning light circuit is working. With the engine running, you find a that a drop of oil forms every so often on the end of the oil pressure switch, indicating it is leaking and needs to be replaced. None of the engine seals and gaskets show any signs of leakage.

1. What are the functions that oil performs inside an engine?
2. Why didn't the oil pressure light indicate that the oil was below the "add" line?
3. How often should the oil and filter be changed?

Functions of Lubricating Oil

Lubricating oil performs five main functions: lubricates, cushions, cools, cleans, and seals. Lubrication involves reducing friction, protecting against corrosion, and preventing metal-to-metal contact between the moving surfaces. Friction occurs between all surfaces that come into contact with each other. When moving surfaces come together, friction tends to slow them down. Friction can be useful, as in a brake system. In the moving parts of engines, friction is a bad thing and will lead to serious damage. Friction can make metal parts so hot they melt and fuse together. When this happens, an engine is said to have seized.

Lubrication reduces unwanted friction and reduces wear on moving parts. Clearances, such as those between the crankshaft journal and crankshaft bearing, fill with lubricating oil so that engine parts move or float on layers of oil instead of directly on each other **FIGURE 45-2**. By reducing friction, less power is needed to move these components and more of the engine's power can be used to turn the crankshaft instead of wasted as heat; the result is increased power to move the vehicle and better fuel economy.

How long an engine lasts depends mostly on how well it is lubricated, especially at the points of

Layer of oil →

FIGURE 45-2 Clearances fill with lubricating oil so that engine parts move or float on layers of oil instead of directly on each other.

extreme loading, or high-wear areas, such as between the cam lobe and cam follower. At the same time, the connecting rod and crankshaft bearings take large amounts of stress as the piston tries to drive through the crankshaft each time the cylinder fires. A power stroke can put as much as 2 tons of force on the main bearings. The lubricating oil between the surfaces helps to cushion these shock loads, similar to the way a shock absorber absorbs a bump in the road.

Lubricating oil also helps cool an engine. The lubricating oil collects heat from the engine's components and then returns to the sump, where it cools. The heat from the lubricating oil is picked up by the air moving over the oil sump. Many heavy-duty and high-performance vehicles have cooling fins on their oil pan or even a separate oil cooler to help the oil do its job of cooling critical engine components.

Lubricating oil also works as a cleaning agent. There are additives in the lubricating oil that allow it to collect particles of metal and carbon and carry them back to the oil sump. Larger pieces fall to the bottom of the oil sump, while smaller pieces are suspended in the oil and are removed when the oil moves through the oil filter. When oil is changed, most of the particles are removed with the oil filter and old oil.

The last function of oil is that it seals. It plays a key role in sealing the piston rings to the cylinder walls. Without a small film of oil between the rings and cylinder walls, blow-by gases would be much higher, resulting in diluted oil, lower compression, lower power, and lower fuel economy.

Corrosion Protection

Acids build up in the engine due to the accumulation of combustion by-products and moisture. Blow-by gases contain chemicals that are trapped in the oil. The chemicals react and form acids. When the engine is turned off, it begins to cool. The cooling process creates moisture that then condenses into droplets that fall into the oil and form acids. The acids attack the internal components causing unnecessary damage. The oil contains anticorrosion additives that coat the engine surfaces, helping to protect them from the effects of the acid.

Viscosity

For oil to do all of the work that is expected of it, it must have special properties. Its viscosity is crucial. **Viscosity** is a measure of how easily a liquid flows. Low-viscosity liquid is thin and flows easily. High-viscosity liquid is thick and flows slowly. Lubricating oil must be thin enough to circulate easily between moving parts, but not so thin that it will be squeezed out easily. If it is too viscous, it moves too slowly to protect the moving parts, especially in a cold engine. As engine machining and metal technology have become more advanced, the clearances between lubricated parts have decreased. As a result, engine manufacturers have specified thinner oils for their engines so that oil can flow into the smaller clearances. The thinner oil also flows more easily, which increases fuel economy.

Applied | **Science**

AS-25 Inhibitors: The technician can explain the need for additives in automobile lubricants.
Automotive lubricants are composed of base stock plus an additive package. In addition to engine oil, additives are used in lubricants for manual and automatic transmissions, as well as differentials.

Oil additives are a very necessary part of modern lubricants. The improvements in modern automotive lubricants are one of the factors that enable vehicles to last longer than ever before. Oil additives consist of chemical compounds that have many beneficial functions.

Detergents are additives that help keep the oil clean. Corrosion (or rust) inhibiting additives work to prevent oxidation of engine parts. According to Wikipedia, a corrosion inhibitor is a chemical compound that, when added to a liquid or gas, decreases the corrosion rates of a material, typically a metal or an alloy.

Oil Additives

Special chemicals called additives are added to the base oil by the oil companies. Different combinations of these additives allow the oil to do different jobs in an engine. A description of common additives follows:

- **Extreme-pressure additives** coat parts with a protective layer so that the oil resists being forced out under heavy load.
- **Oxidation inhibitors** stop very hot oil from combining with oxygen in the air to produce a sticky tarlike material, which coats parts and clogs the oil **galleries** and drain-back passages. Oil galleries are the passageways that carry oil through the engine. They are either cast or drilled into the engine block and head(s).
- **Corrosion inhibitors** help stop acids from forming that cause corrosion, especially on bearing surfaces. Corrosion due to acid etches into bearing surfaces and causes premature wear of the bearings.

- **Antifoaming agents** reduce the effect of oil churning in the crankcase and minimize foaming. Foaming allows air bubbles to form in the engine oil, reducing the lubrication quality of oil and contributing to breakdown of the oil due to oxidation. Since air is compressible, oil with foam reduces the ability of the oil to keep the moving parts separated, causing more wear and friction. The antifoaming additives keep these conditions from occurring.
- **Detergents** reduce carbon deposits on parts such as piston rings and valves.
- **Dispersants** collect particles that can block the system, separate them from each other, and keep them moving. They will be removed when the oil is changed.
- **Pour point depressants** keep oil from forming wax particles under cold temperature operation. When wax crystals form, they result in the **gelling** of the oil and keep oil from flowing during cold start-up conditions. Gelling is the thickening of oil to a point that it will not flow through the engine; it becomes close to a solid in extreme cold temperatures.
- Base stock derived from crude oil will not retain its viscosity if the temperature gets cold enough, so viscosity improvers are added to the stock. A **viscosity index improver** is an additive that helps to reduce the change in viscosity as the temperature of the oil changes. Viscosity index improvers also keep the engine oil from becoming too thin during hot operation.

> **TECHNICIAN TIP**
>
> Before multiviscosity oils, it was a normal practice for engines to need one grade of lubricating oil for summer and another for winter.

Oil Rating Standards

There are several certifying bodies for engine oil, each with its own standards. The three most common are the American Petroleum Institute (API), the American Society of Automotive Engineers (SAE), and the International Lubricant Standardization and Approval Committee (ILSAC). However, there are three others that technicians must be aware of: the Japanese Automotive Standards Organization (JASO), the Association des Constructeurs

Européens d'Automobiles (ACEA), also called the European Automobile Manufacturers Association, and the vehicle manufacturers' (OEM) own standards. Let's look at them one at a time.

American Petroleum Institute (API)

The API sets minimum performance standards for lubricants including engine oils. The API has a two-part classification: service class and service standard. The API service class has two general classifications: S for spark ignition engines and C for compression ignition engines, also referred to as "commercial." Engine oil that meets the API standards may display the API Service Symbol, which is also known as the API "donut." This protocol is important to understand because oil rated S only cannot be used in compression ignition engines unless they also carry the C rating and vice versa. Be careful that the wrong oil is not used in a particular engine.

The API service standard (SA) was used in engines up to 1930, which means pure mineral oil without any additives. As engine manufacturers improved engine technology—or as government regulations changed, such as requiring reduced amounts of phosphorus—engine oil with new qualities was required, and the API would introduce a new rating level. The API SN level was added in October 2010 for 2011 gasoline vehicles. API CJ-4 was added in 2010 to meet four-stroke diesel engine requirements.

The API symbol is the donut symbol located on the back of the oil bottle **FIGURE 45-3**. In the top half of the symbol is the service class—S or C—and the service standard that the oil meets. The center part carries the SAE viscosity rating for the oil. The API symbol may also carry an energy saving designation if it is a fuel-saving oil. Be sure to use oil that has a correct API rating and also an energy-conserving designation in all North American vehicles.

FIGURE 45-3 The API donut shows the API service class and service standard, the viscosity, the ILSAC performance rating, and the energy-conserving designation.

Society of Automotive Engineers (SAE)

Engine oil producers must also meet the SAE viscosity rating for each particular oil. Engine oil with an SAE number of 50 has a higher viscosity, or is thicker, than an SAE 20 oil. Oils with low viscosity ratings, such as SAE 0W, 5W, and 10W (the "W" stands for winter viscosity), are tested at a low temperature—around 0°F (−17.8°C). These ratings indicate how the oil will flow when started cold in cold climate conditions. Oils with high viscosity ratings, such as SAE 20, 30, 40, and 50, are tested at a high temperature—around 210°F (98.9°C). These ratings indicate how the oil will flow when the engine is being used under loaded conditions in hotter conditions.

Modern oils are blends of oils that combine these properties. The oils are blended with viscosity index improvers to form multigrade, or multiviscosity, oils. They provide better lubrication over a wider range of climatic conditions than monograde oils. These oils are classified by a two-part designation, such as SAE 0W-20. In this example, when the oil was tested at 0°F (−17.8°C), it met the specifications for a viscosity of 0W weight oil, and when the same oil was tested at 210°F (98.9°C), it met the viscosity specifications for 20 weight oil. Multiviscosity oils flow easily during cold engine start-up but do not thin out as much as the engine and oil come up to operating temperature. These properties allow the oil to get to the components quicker during start-up while maintaining its ability to cushion components when it is hot. While multiviscosity oils extend the operating temperature range of the engine, always refer to the vehicle's service information to determine the correct oil viscosity to use for the climate the engine will be operated in.

> ### ▶ TECHNICIAN TIP
>
> In most cases, higher rated engine oils are backward compatible. This means you can use SM oil in a vehicle that requires SL. But there is one exception that some technicians have found. SN-rated oil has very low levels of phosphorus and zinc, which aids in flat tappet camshaft lubrication. So if you are working on an older engine that uses flat tappets, you probably do not want to use SN-rated oil, but SM instead.

Applied Science

Viscosity is the measurement of a liquid's resistance to flow. This concept is often best understood by example. Imagine you have a small funnel that you fill with honey. You will find that the funnel drains quite slowly. If you filled the funnel with water, it would drain almost instantly. The difference is because honey has a higher viscosity than water.

Late-model engines are assembled with tighter clearances between moving parts to maximize efficiency and minimize mechanical noise. High-viscosity oil, as used in older vehicles, will not move quickly enough to protect crucial parts in late-model engines, especially on a cold start. Low-viscosity oils, used in older engines, will flow too rapidly past components with large clearances and will provide insufficient lubrication and insufficient oil pressure. The result in both cases is excessive mechanical noise and premature failure with continued operation.

International Lubricant Standardization and Approval Committee (ILSAC)

ILSAC works in conjunction with the API in creating new specifications for gasoline engine oil. However, ILSAC requires that the oil provide increased fuel economy over a base lubricant. These oils should reduce vehicle owners' fuel costs a small amount compared to an oil that does not meet the ILSAC standard. Like the API standard, ILSAC issues sequentially higher rating levels each time the standards are changed. ILSAC GF-5 replaced GF-4 and became the standard in September 2011. Engine oils that meet the GF-4 and GF-5 standard can display the API starburst symbol, which the API created to verify that the oil meets the highest ILSAC standard.

Association des Constructeurs Européens d'Automobiles (ACEA)

The ACEA classifications formulated for engine oils used in European vehicles are much more stringent than the API and ILSAC standards. Some of the characteristics the ACEA-rated oil must score high on are soot thickening, water, sludge, piston deposits, oxidative thickening, fuel economy, and after-treatment compatibility. While some of these may be tested by the API and ILSAC, the standards are set high to achieve ACEA certification ratings. This means that the engine oil provides additional protection or characteristics that API- or ILSAC-rated oils may not match. If you are servicing a European vehicle, it is advised that you do not go by any API recommendations;

instead, make sure the oil meets the recommended ACEA rating specified by the manufacturer or the manufacturer's own specification rating.

Japanese Automotive Standards Organization (JASO)

The JASO standards set the classification for motorcycle engines, both two-stroke and four-stroke, as well as Japanese automotive diesel engines. For four-cycle motorcycle engines, the JASO T 903:2011 came into effect in October 2011 and designates different ratings for wet clutch (MA) and dry clutch (MB). For two-stroke motorcycles, JASO M 34:2003 came into effect in October 2003. And for automotive diesel engines, JASO M355:2008 came into effect in August 2008.

OEM-Specific Standards

As engine manufacturers continued to design new features or longer drain intervals into their engines, faster than some of the oil rating organizations could (or would) change their standards, engine manufacturers came up with their own standards. These standards are specific to individual manufacturers or even individual engines of a particular manufacturer. A few examples follow: Oil meeting Volkswagon's VW 506.00 standard are suitable for use on diesel engines (not with single injector pump) with an extended service interval of up to 31,000 miles or 2 years. Oil meeting General Motor's dexos1™ is specified for use in all 2011 GM vehicles except those equipped with Duramax diesel engines and is backward compatible in all older GM vehicles. Its viscosity is SAE 5W-30 and meets the ACEA A3/B3 standard. It has a service interval of up to 18,600 miles. Oil meeting BMW's Longlife-04 standard is approved for fully synthetic long-life oil and is usually required for BMWs equipped with a diesel particulate filter.

As you can see, it is important to understand the oil requirements for the vehicle you are working on and only use the specified oil. Using the wrong oil can result in severe damage to the engine. Furthermore, using the wrong oil can void the customer's warranty, leaving the customer, or your shop, responsible for repairs. Long gone are the days of grabbing five bottles of any 10W-30 oil off the shelf and putting it into any car that rolls through the door.

> **TECHNICIAN TIP**
>
> Be sure to check the owner's manual or service manual of the vehicle to ensure that you are using the correct oil rating and viscosity for the engine. Do not use just any oil that is sitting on the parts shelf.

American Petroleum Institute Classifications

The API classifies oils into five groups:

1. Group 1 oils are produced by simple distillation of crude oil, which separates the components of the oil by their boiling point, and by the use of solvents to extract sulfur, nitrogen, and oxygen compounds. This method was the only commercial refinement process until the early 1970s, and the bulk of commercial oil products on the market are still produced by this process, such as conventional engine oils.

2. Group 2 and group 3 oils are refined with hydrogen at much higher temperatures and pressures, in a process known as **hydro-cracking**. This process results in a base mineral oil with many of the higher performance characteristics of synthetic oils.

3. The more heavily hydro-cracked group 3 oils have a very high viscosity index (above 120) and many, but not all, of the higher performance characteristics of a full polyalphaolefin (PAO) synthetic oil. Although not fully synthetic, these oils can be sold as synthetic oil in North America.

4. Group 4 oils are all of the full synthetic PAO group (most common true synthetic).

5. Group 5 includes all other types of synthetic oil.

> ### TECHNICIAN TIP
>
> Over time, lubricating oil breaks down by reacting with dissolved atmospheric oxygen. In most refineries, impurities are removed by using solvent. **Hydrogenating** is a newer process that is more effective at removing impurities. Hydrogenation is the use of hydrogen during refining to assist with removing impurities. By hydrogenating the oil, and with the use of oxidation-inhibiting additives, this deterioration rate can be slowed by more than a hundredfold. Hydrogenating also reduces the presence of aromatic hydrocarbons, thereby giving more effective oxidation inhibitor action, minimizing sludge and varnish deposits, and generally avoiding other related machinery problems.

Types of Oil

There are three types of oils sold by oil manufacturers: conventional, synthetic, and synthetic blend. **Conventional oil** is processed from petroleum and uses additives to help the oil work properly in today's high-tech engines. **Synthetic oil** can be man-made or highly processed petroleum. Synthetic oil has fewer impurities since it either is made in a lab, rather than pumped from the ground, or, if it is pumped from the ground, is more highly refined and processed. Synthetic blends are used because they are cheaper to purchase and give the benefit of half synthetic. Manufacturers publish the required oil for each vehicle in the owner's manual.

Conventional Oil

Conventional oil is processed from crude oil pumped from the ground **FIGURE 45-4**. The crude oil contains many impurities that are removed during the refining process. One of the impurities found in all crude oil is wax. This wax is removed during refining and is used for candle wax; it also serves as an additive in some food and candy. Wax is not a good thing in oil since it creates a thickening effect when it gets cold, becoming too thick to flow through the engine. Crude is broken down into mineral oil, which is then combined with additives to enhance the lubricating qualities. Without the additives, conventional oil would not work well. It would foam

FIGURE 45-4 Conventional oil is processed from crude oil pumped from the ground.

easily, break down quickly, and corrode the engine parts after being in the engine for a short time.

Synthetic Oil

There are two main categories of synthetic lubricating oils: type 3, which is not a true synthetic, and type 4 (PAO), which is a true synthetic. Both types of synthetics are more costly to manufacture, since the base stocks are more highly refined or are developed in a lab, and are therefore more costly to the customer. Synthetic lubricants have a number of advantages over conventional oils. They offer better protection against engine wear and can operate at the higher temperatures needed by performance engines. Synthetic oils have better low temperature viscosity, which allows the oil to be circulated through the engine more quickly during low temperature engine start-ups. Synthetics have fewer wax impurities that coagulate at low temperatures, they are chemically more stable, and they are generally thinner so they allow for closer tolerances in engine components without loss of lubrication. Modern high-performance engines run much tighter tolerances, so the need for a thinner oil that is able to hold up under higher temperatures is desirable. Some synthetics also last considerably longer, extending oil change intervals to 20,000 miles (30,000 kilometers [km]) or more, which benefits the environment by reducing the used oil stream and reducing the need for finding new sources of oil.

True synthetic oils are based on man-made hydrocarbons, commonly **polyalphaolefin (PAO)** oil, which is a man-made oil base stock—meaning it is not refined from crude oil. Synthetic oils were developed in Germany during World War II due to the lack of crude oil. Synthetic oil was used primarily in jet engines due to the high heat demands of these engines. Normal conventional oil would create heavy carbon deposits on bearings due to the extreme heat, which led to failures. Amsoil was the first synthetic to be approved by the API in 1972. Many companies now offer synthetic oils. Very few synthetic oils on the market are full PAO oils. Many of the oils allowed to be labeled as synthetic are in fact blends of processed **mineral oil** (highly refined base stock refined from crude oil) and PAO, or even just highly refined base stock, that possess lubrication qualities similar to PAOs.

Synthetic Blends

Synthetic blends give some of the benefit of the full synthetic with the cost effectiveness of conventional oil. These oils are a mix of conventional high-quality oil and full synthetic oil. They need to be changed sooner than a full synthetic but less frequently than conventional oil. The more pure the base stock is after the refinement process, the longer the oil will last in the engine. Some

manufacturers are now recommending synthetic blend oil over conventional oil due to the better protection and performance of these types of oils. Because it is half synthetic, half conventional, the full benefit of the thinner, higher performance pure synthetic is diluted, but in turn the conventional half is improved by adding oil that has no impurities. If the vehicle will be used hard, such as for hauling or towing, synthetic blends will perform better than conventional oil because of the ability of the synthetic oil to stand up to the higher heat and heavier load placed on the engine.

> ### ▶ TECHNICIAN TIP
>
> Be sure to use at least the minimum recommended oil by the manufacturer. Manufacturers of engines spend a lot of money and time designing engines that are efficient and long lasting. Always follow the manufacturer's recommendations.

▶ Lubrication Systems

The **lubrication system** is a series of engine components that work together to keep the moving parts inside an engine lubricated **FIGURE 45-5**. Proper lubrication ensures that the engine runs cooler, produces maximum power, and gets maximum fuel efficiency. Lubrication also ensures that the engine will last for a long time. The lubrication system has many components that work together to deliver the oil to the correct locations in the engine. A typical lubrication system consists of an **oil sump**, an oil pump strainer (also called a pickup

FIGURE 45-5 The lubrication system.

tube), an **oil pump**, a pressure regulator, **oil galleries**, an oil filter, and a low pressure warning system.

The oil is stored in the oil sump. Oil is drawn through the oil pump strainer from the oil sump by an oil pump. The oil travels from the oil pump to the oil filter, which removes particles of dirt from the oil. Oil moves from the filter to the oil galleries. Oil galleries are small passages in the cylinder block and head(s) that direct oil to the moving parts. Oil that has been pumped to the crankshaft main bearings travels through oil-ways to the connecting rods. Oil may also be splashed from the connecting rods onto the cylinder walls, and the circulation of the oil assists with the cooling of the internal parts.

Oil Pan

The **oil pan** is located at the bottom of the engine **FIGURE 45-6**. On a wet sump lubricating system, the oil pan holds the entire volume of the oil required to lubricate the engine. The lowest point of the oil pan is the oil sump. This is where the **oil pump strainer** is located. The deep point in the oil pan ensures that there should never be a shortage of oil for the oil pump to pick up if the correct amount of oil is in the engine. The oil pan is sealed to the engine with silicone or an oil pan gasket. The sump is equipped with a drain plug that allows the oil to be drained from the engine during oil changes **FIGURE 45-7**.

Oil Sump

There are two types of oil sump systems—the wet sump system and the dry sump system. In a wet sump lubrication system, the oil is kept in the oil sump ready for continuous use. A wet sump system is used on most production vehicles because of its low cost. Typically, a dry sump system is used in high-performance applications

FIGURE 45-7 A drain plug allows oil to be drained during oil changes.

where ground clearance or extra capacity is needed. A dry sump system uses a shallower oil pan than the typical wet sump deep oil pan, which allows the engine to sit lower in the engine compartment.

In a wet sump system, the oil sump is part of the oil pan that is bolted to the bottom of the engine and forms the lower portion of the crankcase. It is a reservoir or storage container for the engine lubricating oil, and a collector for oil returning from the engine lubricating system. The oil sump is formed from stamped sheet metal or cast aluminum and is shaped to ensure that oil will return to its deepest section. The oil pickup tube and strainer are located in this deep section to ensure they stay submerged in oil and to prevent air from being drawn into the oil pump. The oil sump's large external surface area helps heat transfer from the oil to the outside air. In some designs, the oil sump is an aluminum alloy casting with fins and ribs to assist in this heat transfer.

In a dry sump system, the oil is not stored under the engine in an oil pan. The oil collection pan is part of the dry sump system that is used on some cars and motorcycles. It replaces the oil sump in the wet sump system, but it is much shallower. It collects the oil after it has circulated through the engine and directs it to the pickup strainer on the scavenge pump. The scavenge pump pulls oil from the sump and moves it to the oil reservoir located outside the engine. A pressure pump pulls engine oil from the oil tank, or reservoir, and delivers it to the engine under pressure. Since no oil is stored in the engine in this system, a dipstick that is normally used to check oil levels in the sump is not needed. The oil tank that the oil is stored in will require either a dipstick or a sight glass so that the oil level can be checked.

Some high-performance vehicles have a **windage tray**, which is a pan located close to the crankshaft, fitted

FIGURE 45-6 The oil pan.

to prevent churning of the oil by the rotation of the crankshaft **FIGURE 45-8**. The windage tray can be made from stamped sheet metal or a one-way mesh screen that allows oil to flow down through the mesh, but not the other way. This design helps keep oil away from the rotating crank as much as possible. **Baffles** are flat pieces of steel placed around the oil pump pickup in the oil pan to prevent oil from surging away from the pickup during cornering, braking, and accelerating. Baffles are commonly used on vehicles that experience strong g-forces, such as rally cars, stock cars, and drag-racing cars.

Pickup Tube

Between the oil sump and oil pump is a **pickup tube** with a flat cup and a wire mesh strainer immersed in the oil. The pickup tube pulls oil from the oil sump by suction of the oil pump and atmospheric pressure. A strainer on the pickup

FIGURE 45-8 A windage tray.

tube stops large particles of debris from entering the oil pump and damaging it. The pickup tube leads to the inlet of the oil pump, on the low-pressure side of the oil pump. The pickup tube fits tightly into the oil pump and is usually bolted in place by a bracket to ensure that it does not fall out due to vibration. If the pickup tube were to fall out, the engine would not receive oil, since the pump would not reach down into the sump from which oil is drawn.

Oil Pump

Oil pumps move oil from one side of the pump to the other. Most oil pumps are of the positive displacement type. This means that they move a given amount of oil from the inlet to the outlet each revolution. The faster the pump turns, the more oil that is pumped. Oil pressure is determined by two factors: (1) the size of the leaks in the system, which in the case of an engine means the amount of clearance between the bearings and the journals and the diameter of any spurt holes, and (2) the amount of oil flowing in the system. As you can imagine, an engine has a fairly consistent set of leaks. When the engine is new, the leaks are fairly small. When the engine has acquired many miles, the leaks are larger. This is why engine oil pressure falls over the life of the engine. In fact, low oil pressure can mean one of three things (other than a bad oil pressure gauge). Either the oil leaks inside the engine have gotten excessive (e.g., worn bearings), the oil pump is worn out and not creating as much flow as it needs to, or the oil is thinner than it should be (e.g., saturated with gasoline from a leaky fuel injector), which causes it to drain from the leaks faster than it should.

Oil pumps may be driven from the camshaft or the crankshaft. In a **rotor-type oil pump**, an inner rotor drives an outer one; as they turn, the volume between them increases **FIGURE 45-9A**. The larger volume created

FIGURE 45-9 **A.** Rotor-type oil pump. **B.** Crescent pump. **C.** Geared oil pump.

between the rotors lowers the pressure at the pump inlet, creating a vacuum. Outside atmospheric pressure, which is higher, forces oil into the pump, and the oil fills the spaces between the **rotor lobes**. As the lobes of the inner rotor move into the spaces in the outer rotor, oil is squeezed out through the outlet. In other words, oil is drawn into the spaces between the lobes on the inlet side and travels around with the lobes. The oil cannot get back to the inlet side because the lobes come together, and it is therefore forced out of the pump outlet.

The **crescent pump** uses a similar principle **FIGURE 45-9B**. It is usually mounted on the front of the cylinder block and straddles the front of the crankshaft. The inner gear is then driven by the crankshaft directly. An external toothed gear meshes with the inner one. Some gear teeth are meshed but others are separated by the crescent-shaped part of the pump housing. The increasing volume between gear teeth causes pressure to fall, creating a vacuum, and atmospheric pressure pushes oil into the pump. Oil is then carried around between the gears and crescent before being discharged to the outlet port.

In a **geared oil pump**, the driving gear meshes with a second gear **FIGURE 45-9C**. As both gears turn, their teeth separate, creating a low-pressure area. Higher atmospheric pressure outside forces the oil up into the inlet, which fills the spaces between the gear teeth. As the gears rotate, they carry oil around the chamber. As the teeth mesh again, oil is forced from the outlet into the oil gallery and toward the oil filter where it is filtered of any particles.

Oil Pressure Relief Valve

A normal oil pump is capable of delivering more oil than an engine needs. Extra volume provides a safety measure to ensure the engine is never starved for oil. As the oil pump rotates, and engine speed increases, the volume of oil delivered also increases. The fixed clearances between the moving parts of the engine slow the escaping of oil back to the oil sump, and pressure builds up in the lubrication system. An **oil pressure relief valve** stops excess pressure from developing. It is like a controlled leak, releasing just enough oil back to the oil sump to regulate the pressure in the whole system. The oil pressure relief valve contains a spring that is calibrated to a specific pressure. When the pressure is reached, the oil pressure relief valve slides open just enough to bleed sufficient oil back to the pan to maintain the preset maximum relief pressure. If the engine speed and oil flow increase, the pressure relief valve will open farther and allow more oil to escape back to the sump. If the engine speed and oil flow decrease, the pressure relief valve will close an appropriate amount.

Applied Math

AM-29: Volume: The technician can use various measurement techniques to determine the volume as applicable.
Two technicians are examining an engine oil pan as it is being cleaned. It is a standard automotive pan from a V6 engine and has a rectangular shape. Randy says that the volume of the pan could be calculated by multiplying the area of the base times the height. Tom agrees with this and adds that in the U.S. system of measurement the result would be in cubic inches which can be converted into quarts.

At break time, they decide to measure the pan and calculate its volume in quarts. The pan measures 6 inches wide, 9 inches long, and 5.35 inches deep. The area of the base is 6 × 9, which is 54 square inches. Next, they multiply times the height of 5.35 inches for 288.9 square inches. This is approximately 5 quarts (considering one quart is equal to 57.750 cubic inches).

To calculate the example in metric units the process would be very similar except that we would be using metric units. Centimeters would be used for the linear units to determine the base × height. There would be cubic centimeters to convert to liters.

TECHNICIAN TIP

So what is the difference between a high-pressure oil pump and a high-volume oil pump? A high-pressure pump has a stiffer pressure relief spring, which allows the pump to create higher oil pressure. A high-volume pump has greater volume between the rotor or gear teeth, usually accomplished by making both the rotor/gear and the oil pump housing deeper. This design causes more oil to be drawn into the pump during each revolution, and therefore more oil is forced out of the pump each revolution. Generally speaking, a high-volume pump is more beneficial; because it can pump more oil, the pressure will not fall as quickly as the engine experiences wear and tear.

Oil Filters

There are two basic oil-filtering systems: full-flow and bypass **FIGURE 45-10**. The most common, **full-flow filters**, are designed to filter all of the oil before delivering it to the engine. The location of the filter right after the oil pump ensures that all of the oil is filtered before it is sent to the lubricated components. The bypass filtering system is more common on diesel engines and is used in

FIGURE 45-10 **A.** Full-flow filtering system. **B.** Bypass filtering system.

FIGURE 45-11 Pleated oil filter paper.

conjunction with a full-flow filtering system. The **bypass filter** is discussed later in this section.

Oil filters use a pleated filter paper for the filtering medium **FIGURE 45-11**. Oil flows through the paper and as it does so, it filters out particles in the oil. Most full-flow oil filters will catch particles down to 30 microns. A micron is 0.000039" (0.001 mm)—a very small particle. A human

hair's thickness can be as small as 50 microns, for example. As the oil filter catches these fine particles, the paper filter element will begin to clog, making it harder for the oil to flow through. As the engine is initially started cold for a few seconds, or if the filter becomes clogged, the bypass valve will open to let unfiltered oil flow to the lubricated components. The manufacturers believe it is better to have unfiltered oil flow to components than no oil at all. To prevent excessive engine wear, it is critical to change the oil filter at the manufacturer's recommended interval.

There are two common types of oil filters: spin-on and cartridge **FIGURE 45-12**. The spin-on type is the most common. It uses a one-piece filter assembly with a crimped housing and threaded base. The pleated paper filter element is formed into the inside of the crimped housing. This kind of filter spins off with the use of an oil filter wrench and tightens by hand force only. A square-cut rubber O-ring fits into a groove in the base of the filter and seals the base of the filter to the engine block. A new

FIGURE 45-12 **A.** Spin-on filter and O-ring. **B.** Cartridge paper filter, housing, and bolt.

O-ring comes with the filter, so it gets replaced with the filter. Be aware, though, that the old O-ring may stick to the filter adapter on the engine block. If you do not notice this and leave the old O-ring on along with the new O-ring, the old one will not be able to stay in place because it is not in any groove. As a result, it will get pushed out of place when the engine is started and most, if not all, of the engine oil will be pumped out onto the ground. Always check for the old O-ring when removing the oil filter.

The cartridge style of oil filter uses a separate reuseable metal or plastic housing and a replaceable filter cartridge. It is typically held together in one of two ways: threaded center bolt or screw-on housing. If it uses a center bolt, it will have a sealing washer between the bolt and the housing to prevent oil from leaking out. There is also a seal that fits either between the cylindrical housing and the filter adapter on the block or between the cylindrical housing and the end cap, depending on the design. Cartridge filters must be disassembled, the housing cleaned, and the paper filter element and any O-rings or seals replaced with new ones.

Applied Math

AM-30: Volume: The technician can determine if the existing volume is within the manufacturer's recommended tolerance.
A technician was instructed to change the engine oil and filter on a late model automobile. In addition to this, he was also to change the automatic transmission fluid and filter. The technician has access to manufacturer's service information, which he consulted before starting the tasks. The service information stated that 5.5 quarts of oil would be needed for an engine oil change with filter replacement. Concerning the automatic transmission fluid and filter change, the manual stated 9.5 quarts are needed for this service.

The technician begins working by draining the engine oil and filter. As he puts the new oil into the engine, the technician counts the number of quart containers. He discovers that after the engine was started, to fill the oil filter and shut off, it takes a total of 5.5 quarts to bring the oil level to the exact full mark on the dipstick. By this method, the technician was able to determine that the existing volume is within the manufacturer's tolerance.

At this point, the technician goes on to the transmission fluid and filter change. He drains the fluid and changes the filter. As before, the technician counts the number of quart containers necessary for filling the system properly. He pours in one quart at a time, in order to take an accurate count. The technician observes that it takes 9.5 quarts to fill the system to the full line on the dipstick, with the engine running in park. By this method, the technician is able to verify that the existing volume is within the manufacturer's tolerance.

Most oil filters on diesel engines are larger than those on similar gasoline engines, and some diesel engines have two oil filters. Diesel engines produce more carbon particles than gasoline engines, so the oil filter can have a full-flow element to trap larger impurities and a bypass element to collect sludge and carbon soot. In a bypass system, the bypass element filters only some of the oil from the oil pump by tapping an oil line into the oil gallery. It collects finer particles than a full-flow filter. After this oil is filtered, it is returned to the oil sump. If the bypass filter were to clog and stop oil flow, the flow of oil lubricating the engine components would not be affected.

TECHNICIAN TIP

Magnets are also used as a type of filter. They attract ferrous metal particles and hold them in place until they can be cleaned off. Some manufacturers use magnetic drain plugs, which then need to be inspected and cleaned off as part of an oil change. Others place a magnet to the inside or outside of the oil pan. Although this style cannot readily be cleaned, it does hold the magnetic particles in place so they cannot travel freely.

Spurt Holes and Galleries

Pistons, rings, and pins are lubricated by oil thrown onto the cylinder walls from the connecting rod bearings. Some connecting rods have **oil spurt holes** that are positioned to receive oil from similar holes in the crankshaft **FIGURE 45-13**. Oil can then spurt out at the point in the engine cycle when the largest area of cylinder wall is

FIGURE 45-13 Some connecting rods have oil spurt holes, which are positioned to receive oil from similar holes in the crankshaft.

exposed. This oil sprays from the connecting rod holes and lubricates the cylinder walls and piston wrist pin, and may help cool the underside of the piston.

Oil is fed to the cylinder head through oil galleries and on to the camshaft bearings and valve train. When oil reaches the top of the cylinder head and lubricates the valve train, it has completed its pressurized journey. The oil drains back to the oil sump through oil drain-back holes located in the cylinder head and engine block.

> **▶ TECHNICIAN TIP**
>
> In many cases, the ends of the oil galleries are plugged with a threaded pipe plug or a small soft plug. During an engine rebuild, these plugs are normally removed and the galleries cleaned with stiff wire brushes. It is very important to make sure the plugs have been reinstalled with a sealer and tightened properly so that they do not leak. Many a technician has started up a newly rebuilt engine and had oil pour out of the bell housing, all because one or more of the oil gallery plugs were missing.

Oil Indicators

A lubrication system failure can be catastrophic to the engine. Because of the damage that would happen if the lubrication system failed, a warning system is installed to let the driver know the system has failed. If oil pressure falls too low, a pressure sensor threaded into a gallery can activate a low oil pressure warning light, register pressure on a gauge, or turn on a low oil pressure warning message **FIGURE 45-14**. The pressure sensor is also commonly called a sending unit since it sends a signal to the light, gauge, or message center in the dash. If the sending unit is designed as part of a warning lamp system, it is made up of a spring-loaded diaphragm and a set of switch contacts and is commonly called a pressure switch. Oil pressure is on the engine side of the diaphragm and a spring is on the other. With the engine off and the ignition switch in the run position, the oil pressure is zero, so the spring holds the diaphragm toward the engine and the switch contacts are closed (i.e., making contact with each other). This causes current to flow from the warning lamp in the dash through the closed switch contacts in the sending unit to ground, which turns on the warning light. When the engine is started, oil pressure increases above spring pressure and the diaphragm is pushed away from the engine, opening the switch contacts and turning off the warning light. In some vehicles, the sending unit sends the electrical signal to the BCM, which is programmed to turn the light on below a certain pressure. This is how the system should work when everything is working

FIGURE 45-14 If oil pressure falls too low, a pressure sensor in a gallery can **(A)** activate a warning light, **(B)** register on a gauge, or **(C)** turn on a warning message.

normally. If the oil pressure drops below spring pressure while the engine is running, the light will come on, warning the driver of the low oil pressure condition.

If the sending unit is part of an oil pressure gauge system, it usually uses a variable resistor within the sending unit. The variable resistor is moved by the oil pressure moving the diaphragm against the spring pressure. As the pressure increases, the diaphragm is forced against spring pressure and changing the resistance of the variable resistor. This changes the amount of current flowing through the oil pressure gauge and causes it to read higher. If the engine oil pressure drops, then the spring pushes the diaphragm toward the engine, again changing the resistance of the variable resistor and the current flowing through the oil pressure gauge, decreasing the pressure reading on the gauge. Some factory-installed oil pressure gauges include a warning light to warn the driver of low oil pressure. In many instances, a driver may not notice that the oil pressure gauge reading has dropped and will keep driving the vehicle, leading to engine damage. But the warning light is designed to catch the driver's attention so that he or she can stop the vehicle and investigate the cause of the low oil pressure.

If the sending unit is part of a driver information system, then the sending unit could be of the switch type or the variable resistance type. It usually also would include a sensor for low oil level monitoring and maybe even an oil temperature monitor. You will need to investigate various manufacturers' driver information systems to familiarize yourself with the different systems and strategies each manufacturer uses.

Oil Coolers

Engines that operate under severe conditions may use an **oil cooler** to cool the oil in the engine. There are two types of oil coolers: oil-to-water coolers and oil-to-air coolers. In some engines, an oil-to-water oil cooler and the oil filter are on the same mounting on the cylinder block. The oil cooler acts as a heat exchanger and works by transferring heat from the oil to the coolant from the cooling system. Coolant circulates through tubes in the cooler, and oil fed from the lubrication system surrounds the tubes. As the coolant circulates, heat is removed from the oil. In the oil-to-air design, the oil cooler is mounted in the airstream at the front of the vehicle **FIGURE 45-15**. This type of oil cooler uses the flow of air passing across its fins to cool the oil circulating through it and works the same as a radiator. Most vehicles equipped with a tow package will have one of these two types of oil coolers. High-performance vehicles that will be operated at high speeds and/or temperatures can also have an oil cooler installed from the factory or as an aftermarket accessory.

Oil Analysis

Oil will suspend particles as the engine wears. Analysis of the engine oil is a useful way to see what parts are wearing in the engine. The military as well as many companies use oil analysis to ensure that the engine oil is changed at the appropriate interval. A small tube is slipped down the oil dipstick tube all the way to the oil pan sump. A vacuum device is hooked to this tube to pull a sample of oil from the pan to a collection container. This sample is labeled with the vehicle information and sent to a lab. The lab thoroughly analyzes the oil and reports the findings back to the shop. The report lists physical properties such

FIGURE 45-15 An oiler cooler system.

as viscosity, condensed water, fuel dilution, anti-freeze, acids, metal content, and oil additives. Each of these attributes can be used to determine the condition of the oil as well as the engine. When oil analysis is performed for a particular engine on a regular basis, issues can usually be addressed before they become catastrophic. Oil analysis is typically used in heavy vehicle applications that may use 3 or more gallons (11.4 or more liters) of engine oil. Some race teams will analyze the engine oil to ensure that the engine is not being damaged.

As a technician, a simple test to check for excessive engine wear is to take a white paper towel and wipe the oil from the dipstick on it. Hold the towel to the light and move it back and forth to see if light reflects from metal. If metal is in the oil, there is substantial wear happening inside the engine.

Oil Monitoring Systems

Oil monitoring systems are used to inform the driver when the oil needs to be changed. There are several types of **oil monitoring systems**. Some oil systems are simply timers that keep track of mileage and will activate a warning light to notify the driver when it is time to change the engine oil. Other systems are very sophisticated, analyzing the conductivity of the oil through a sensor in the oil pan and monitoring changes that indicate it is time to change the oil. Depending upon the feedback from the sensor, the monitoring system computer will activate the change oil light or message to warn the driver that it is time to change the oil.

Another monitoring system, called an oil-life monitor, calculates the expected life of the oil and displays it to the driver. The computer receives inputs from several sensors that take into account the number of start-ups, mileage, driving habits/conditions, temperature, length of run time, and other data to calculate the remaining life of the oil, which is displayed as a percentage. When the oil is freshly changed and the oil-life monitor is reset, it will say the oil life is 100%. As the oil life wears out, the monitor will read closer to 0% oil life, informing the driver of the need to change the oil. Since it monitors the conditions

the oil is operating under, the life of the oil can change drastically depending on the conditions. For example, if the vehicle were only driven in moderate temperatures for long distances, the oil would be good thousands of miles longer than a vehicle driven in stop-and-go traffic and with long periods of idling. Each vehicle equipped with an oil monitoring system has a specific reset procedure to turn the light or message off after an oil change.

▶ Types of Lubrication Methods

Pressure System

Modern vehicle engines use a **pressure, or force-feed, lubrication system** where the oil is forced throughout the engine under pressure **FIGURE 45-16**. In gasoline engines, oil will not flow up into the engine by itself so the oil pump collects it through a pickup tube and strainer and forces it through an oil filter, then into passageways, called galleries, in the engine block. The galleries allow oil to be fed to the crankshaft bearings first, then through holes drilled in the crankshaft to the connecting rods. The oil also moves from the galleries onto the camshaft bearings and the valve mechanism. After circulating through the engine, the oil falls back to the oil sump to cool. This design is called a wet sump lubrication system.

Some engines use a dry sump lubrication system. It uses all of the parts that make up a wet sump system and it lubricates the engine in the same way. It differs from the wet sump system in the way the oil is collected and stored. In a dry sump system, the oil falls to the bottom of

FIGURE 45-16 A pressure, or force-feed, lubrication system.

> **TECHNICIAN TIP**
>
> As a technician, you will have to be able to find the procedure to turn the light off and reset the oil monitoring system. Refer to the service manual or owner's manual for resetting procedures. The reset procedures range from something as simple as pushing a button, to having to go through a set of steps, to having to use a dedicated tool.

the engine into an oil collection pan. A <u>scavenge pump</u> then pumps it to an oil tank where it is stored until the normal oil pump collects it and pumps it through the filter and engine in the normal way. Because there is no oil storage sump under the engine, the engine can be mounted much lower than in a wet sump system, which allows the vehicle to have a much lower center of gravity. The oil tank can be positioned away from the engine where it can get best cooling and the amount of oil in the system can be much greater than in the wet sump system since space is less of an issue.

Diesel engines are lubricated in much the same way as gasoline engines, but there are a few differences. Diesel engines typically operate at the top end of their power range, so their internal operating temperatures are usually higher than those in similar gasoline engines. Thus, the parts in diesel engines are usually more stressed. Since diesel fuel is ignited by the heat of compression, the compression pressures (and compression ratio) are much higher than in gasoline engines. Diesel fuel has more British thermal units (BTUs) of heat energy than gasoline, so it produces more heat when it is ignited, placing more stress on the engine's moving parts. Because of stress from the higher compression and combustion pressures/temperatures, parts have to be much heavier, and with heavier parts, oil must be able to handle higher shear forces. As a result, diesel oils need a different range of properties and are classified differently, usually with a C rating in the API system. It is also common for many diesel engines to use an oil-to-water cooler to cool the oil in the engine. The cooler and oil filter are usually on the same mounting on the cylinder block.

FIGURE 45-17 A splash lubrication method.

lubrication for lubricating the cylinder walls, pistons, wrist pin, valve guides, and sometimes the timing chain. The oil that is splashed around usually comes from moving parts that are pressure-fed; as the oil leaks out of those parts as designed, it is thrown around and provides splash lubrication to the needed components.

Most small four-stroke gasoline engines use only splash lubrication to lubricate all of the parts on the engine including the crankshaft bearing, camshaft, and lifters. On horizontal-crankshaft engines, a <u>dipper</u> on the bottom of the connecting rod scoops up oil from the crankcase for the bearings. The dipper is also able to splash oil up to the valve mechanism. Alternatively, an <u>oil slinger</u> can be driven by the crankshaft or camshaft. A slinger is a device that runs half-submerged in the engine oil. The oil is slung from the slinger upward by centrifugal force to lubricate moving parts. A similar system is used in most small vertical-crankshaft engines. Oil is also splashed up to the valve mechanism from the centrifugal force of the slinger spinning at engine speed.

Two-Stroke Engine Premix Fuel Systems

Most two-stroke gasoline engines use a specified gasoline–oil mixture for lubrication. Two-stroke oil is different than engine oil, and the two cannot be substituted for each other. They must be used according to the manufacturer's specifications. For many small two-

---

Applied	Science

AS-92: Friction: The technician can explain the need for lubrication to minimize friction.
Oil is a good lubricant in an engine because it has a low coefficient of friction. It creates a protective layer between two metal components, which both have a high coefficient of friction. The high coefficient of friction produces heat, causing the metal to expand, potentially creating engine wear and damage. Oil keeps the two metal components from rubbing against each other, thus preventing damage.

Splash Lubrication

Not all lubricated engine components are lubricated by the pressure-fed system. Some are lubricated by the <u>splash lubrication</u> method **FIGURE 45-17**. In this method, the oil is thrown around and gets into spaces that need lubrication. Automotive and diesel engines use splash stroke engines, the oil and fuel are premixed according to the engine manufacturer's specification. For example, an engine may require a 40:1 mixture, which is 40 parts gasoline to 1 part oil. The mixture of air, oil, and fuel passes through a sealed crankcase on its way to the combustion chamber. The crankcase thus becomes part of the fuel intake system and cannot be used as an oil sump. As the air, fuel, and oil enter the crankcase, the fuel evaporates, leaving behind enough oil to keep parts coated and lubricated. The crankshaft and connecting rod bearings in two-stroke engines typically are ball and roller types. Because the components of this kind of bearing only roll over each other, they require a minimum of lubrication.

Two-Stroke Engine Oil Injection Systems

Some two-stroke gasoline engines use an oil injection system. This system does not require that the oil and gasoline be mixed manually. An engine-driven oil pump takes oil from a tank and pumps a measured amount directly into the engine where it will mix with the fuel and lubricate the internal engine parts **FIGURE 45-18**. The oil pump is designed to deliver the correct amount of oil for the engine speed and the throttle setting. However, since only a small amount of oil is needed, the orifice that the oil is sprayed out of is very tiny. It is easily plugged by any debris that is allowed to fall into the oil tank when it is filled.

> ### ► TECHNICIAN TIP
>
> When fueling a two-stroke engine, it is easy to forget that the gasoline must be mixed with oil. If you forget and put only gasoline in it, you will ruin it very quickly. To make matters worse, a new engine cannot tolerate this fueling error as well as an older engine. There are therefore quite a few worn out two-cycle engines sitting around, retired long before their time.

► Maintenance and Repair

Tools

The tools for lubrication repair include **FIGURE 45-19**:

- A variety of oil filter wrenches to remove the oil filter
- A set of wrenches and a socket set to remove the oil drain plug and any engine covers
- A mirror and a quality light for leak testing
- A special socket to remove many of the oil pressure switches or sensors
- A digital volt-ohmmeter (DVOM) to test wiring and sensors of the oil warning light or gauge

FIGURE 45-18 An oil injection system in a two-stroke engine.

FIGURE 45-19 Tools for lubrication repair. **A.** Oil filter wrench. **B.** Coolant pressure tester. **C.** Set of wrenches. **D.** Light. **E.** Mirror. **F.** DVOM.

Checking the Engine Oil

Checking the engine oil level regularly is necessary and should be performed during every fuel fill-up or every other fuel fill-up, depending on the age and condition of the vehicle. There is a danger of damaging the engine if the engine oil drops too low in the oil sump. The oil level can be low either because there is an oil leak or because the engine is consuming oil by burning it. Burning engine oil could be due to worn piston rings, worn valve guides, or a malfunction with the positive crankcase ventilation (PCV) system. Checking oil level should also be part of any pretrip check or part of a predelivery inspection on a new car at the dealership. Predelivery inspections are performed on new vehicles before delivering to the purchaser and help to ensure that the vehicle is being delivered in the condition the manufacturer specifies and without any known faults or defects that would reflect negatively on the customer satisfaction index for the manufacturer or dealer.

Always make sure the vehicle is on a level surface and the engine is off before taking a reading. If you do not, you will get inaccurate readings. Also wipe the dipstick off and reinsert it fully before removing it and reading it. When reading it, hold the dipstick horizontal so the oil will not run down the stick. Typically, the amount of oil needed to raise the oil level from the bottom of the "safe" mark on the dipstick to the "full" mark is about a quart. This amount may vary, so always check the service manual to determine the correct quantity. Always install the recommended amount and type of oil given in the service manual. Although fresh oil is translucent and oil that needs to be replaced often looks black and dirty, it is usually difficult to assess the condition of engine oil simply by its color. Oil loses its clean, fresh look very quickly but may still have a lot of life left in it.

The best guide to knowing when to change the oil is the vehicle's oil-life monitor, if equipped. It will tell you the percentage of oil-life remaining before a change is needed. If the vehicle is not equipped with an oil-life monitor, check the oil change sticker on the windshield or ask the owner for oil change records to determine if the oil needs to be changed. This can ensure that the oil is not changed too often, which would be an unnecessary expense for the customer. Our job as technicians is to provide high-quality work only when it is truly needed by the customer. Part of being a professional is letting customers know when they do and when they do *not* need a service performed. Informing the customer of what needs to be done and what does not, along with an explanation, helps to build trust with the customer and often results in the customer returning to your shop for future repairs.

If the oil on the dipstick is not blackish in color but looks milky gray, it is possible that there is water (or coolant) being mixed into the oil. This could indicate a serious problem somewhere inside the engine, such as a leaking head gasket or a cracked head, and you should report this to your supervisor immediately. Engine operating conditions can also influence the oil's condition. For instance, continuously stopping and starting the engine with very short operating cycles can cause condensation to build up inside the engine. An extreme case of this will cause very rapid oil deterioration and will require frequent oil changes. The oil of a vehicle that is running too rich or that has a leaking fuel injector will smell like fuel and will be very thin. These problems can ruin an engine quickly, as oil will not adequately lubricate the moving surfaces in the engine. If you had to add oil to the engine, do not forget to reinstall the filler cap after topping off the oil.

To check the engine oil, follow the steps in **SKILL DRILL 45-1**:

1. Locate the dipstick located on the side or front of the engine block. It is usually very easy to find, with a distinctively shaped or brightly colored handle.

2. With the engine off, remove the dipstick, catching any drops of oil on a rag, and wipe it clean. Observe the markings on the lower end of the stick, which indicate the "full" and "add" marks or specify the "safe" zone. **(Photo 1)**

3. Replace the dipstick and push it back down into the sump as far as it will go. Remove it again, and hold it level while checking the level indicated on the bottom of the stick. If the level is near or below the "add" mark, then you will need to determine if the engine just needs topped off to the full level with fresh oil or replaced with new oil and oil filter. **(Photo 2)**

4. Check the oil for any conditions such as unusual color or texture. Report these to your supervisor. Check the oil monitoring system, oil sticker, or service record to determine if the oil needs changed. (Some oil monitoring systems show the percentage of life left in the oil.) **(Photo 3)**

5. If additional oil is needed, estimate the amount by checking the service manual guide to the dipstick markings. Unscrew the oil filler cap at the top of the engine, and using a funnel to avoid spillage, turn the oil bottle so the spout is on the high side of the bottle and gently pour the oil into the engine. Recheck the oil level. **(Photo 4)**

6. Replace the oil filler cap, and check the dipstick again to make sure the oil level is still correct. **(Photo 5)**

Safety

If the engine has been running, be careful not to burn your hand or arm on the exhaust manifold or any other hot part of the engine when reaching for the dipstick. Remember, the dipstick and the oil on it will also be hot. Dripping oil from the dipstick will smoke or burn if it falls on any hot engine surfaces.

▶ TECHNICIAN TIP

Make sure the hood is secure with a hood prop rod, if necessary. Always make sure you wear the appropriate personal protection equipment before starting the job. It is very easy to think that nothing can happen on a basic job like checking the oil level.

SKILL DRILL | 45-1 | Checking the Engine Oil

1 Locate the dipstick. With the engine off, remove the dipstick, catching any drops of oil on a rag, and wipe it clean. Observe the markings on the lower end of the stick, which indicate the "full" and "add" marks or specify the "safe" zone.

2 Replace the dipstick and push it back down into the sump as far as it will go. Remove it again, and hold it level while checking the level indicated on the bottom of the stick. If the level is near or below the "add" mark, then you will need to determine if the engine just needs topped up to the full level with fresh oil or replaced with new oil and oil filter.

3 Check the oil for any conditions such as unusual color or texture. Report these to your supervisor. Check the oil monitoring system, oil sticker, or service record to determine if the oil needs changed. (Some oil monitoring systems show the percentage of life left in the oil.)

4 If additional oil is needed, estimate the amount by checking the service manual guide to the dipstick markings. Unscrew the filler cap at the top of the engine, and using a funnel to avoid spillage, turn the oil bottle so the spout is on the high side of the bottle and gently pour the oil into the engine. Recheck the oil level.

5 Replace the oil filler cap, and check the dipstick again to make sure the oil level is now correct.

Draining the Engine Oil

Draining the engine oil is a necessary task any time the oil and filter are to be changed or whenever the oil pan needs to be removed for service work. Draining the engine oil for an oil change is necessary after a certain time or mileage interval to remove the dirt and particulates that are suspended in the oil. As the engine wears, the very small pieces of metal will get suspended in the oil. Removing the old contaminated oil helps to make the engine last longer. Always follow the manufacturer's oil change interval, and remember

When removing the drain plug, be sure to use the proper-sized wrench or socket. Always inspect the drain plug gasket for damage before reusing; some manufacturers require the use of a new drain plug gasket each time the drain plug is removed. Always look up and torque the drain plug to proper specifications, as overtightening could damage the threads of the plug and oil pan, and undertightening could cause an oil leak or the plug to vibrate loose and fall out, resulting in the loss of all the engine oil.

that normal use and severe use have different oil change intervals.

When draining the oil, several precautions are necessary. First, the engine oil is normally changed after the engine is fully warmed up. This helps to stir up any contaminants, making them easier to flush out with the draining of the oil. However, that means that the oil can be 200–300°F (93–149°C), so use disposable gloves and don't burn yourself.

Second, make sure you locate the correct drain plug—or in some cases, the correct *two* drain plugs. Some vehicles have a drain plug on the transmission/transaxle that can be mistaken for the oil drain plug. If in doubt, look it up or ask your supervisor to point it out.

Third, many drain plugs are either angled off of the bottom radius of the oil pan or almost sideways at the bottom side of the pan. This means when the drain plug is removed, hot oil will want to spray sideways. Always make sure you take into consideration what path the oil will take. Oil can shoot out pretty far. The lower the drain pan is compared to the drain plug, the harder it will be to judge the distance the oil will spray.

Fourth, the drain plug gasket can be of the integrated silicone, long-life style that rarely needs to be replaced. The gasket can also be a one-time-use gasket made of plastic, aluminum, or fiber. This type of gasket should be replaced during every oil change since it is crushed to conform to any irregularities of the pan and drain plug. Because it is crushed, it will not conform as easily the next time it is tightened. This means that someone may think it needs to be tightened excessively to prevent seepage. Overtightening can strip the threads on the oil pan, especially if it is made of aluminum, or can strip the threads on the drain plug itself. Replace a non-silicone drain plug gasket every time it is removed.

To drain the engine oil, follow the steps in **SKILL DRILL 45-2**:

1. Before you begin, clean up any oil spills, obtain the oil drain container (and make sure it has enough room for the oil to be drained), have enough new oil of the correct type to refill the engine later, have the correct oil filter, and ensure that the engine oil is up to operating temperature before starting the oil change. **(Photo 1)**

2. Identify the location of the oil drain plug, which is low on the oil pan. Some vehicles have two drain plugs, draining separate sump areas. If the drain plug is leaking, damaged, or does not look right, inform your supervisor. To minimize the possibility of damage to the head of the bolt, you will need a box wrench or socket to remove and replace the drain bolt. Be very careful that you do not remove the transmission drain plug by mistake. **(Photo 2)**

3. Position the drain pan so it will catch the oil. Remove and inspect the drain plug and gasket. Replace the gasket if it is the replaceable type. If the threads are damaged, then the bolt may need to be replaced. Look for solid metal particles stuck to the bolt and report these to your supervisor. They may indicate an undiagnosed problem with the engine. **(Photo 3)**

4. Allow the oil to drain while you are dealing with the drain plug gasket and oil filter (see Skill Drill 45-3). **(Photo 4)**

5. Screw in the drain plug all the way by hand and then tighten it to the torque specified by the manufacturer. You will find this information in the vehicle service information. Wipe any drips from the underside of the engine. **(Photo 5)**

6. Safely dispose of the drained oil according to all local regulations. **(Photo 6)**

Refer the customer to the owner's manual to determine when the oil should be changed. That could be based on a mileage interval, time interval, or oil-life monitor. You may also need to verify whether the vehicle is operated under normal or severe conditions. Severe conditions may include driving in low temperatures, stop-and-go driving, dusty conditions, short trips, towing, etc. Intervals for severe driving conditions are sooner than normal driving intervals.

SKILL DRILL 45-2   Draining the Engine Oil

1 Before you begin, clean up any oil spills, obtain the oil drain container (and make sure it has enough room for the oil to be drained), have enough new oil of the correct type to refill the engine, have the correct oil filter, and ensure that the engine oil is up to operating temperature before starting the oil change.

2 Identify the location of the oil drain plug. Some vehicles have two drain plugs, draining separate sump areas. If the drain plug is leaking, damaged, or does not look right, inform your supervisor. Use a box wrench or socket to remove and replace the drain bolt. Be careful that you do not remove the transmission drain plug by mistake.

3 Position the drain pan so it will catch the oil. Remove and inspect the drain plug and gasket; replace as necessary.

4 Allow the oil to drain while you are dealing with the drain plug, gasket, and oil filter (see Skill Drill 45-3).

5 Screw in the drain plug all the way by hand and then tighten it to the torque specified by the manufacturer. Wipe any drips from the underside of the engine.

6 Safely dispose of the drained oil according to all local regulations.

Replacing Oil Filters

Oil filters are designed to filter out particles that find their way into the oil. The filter will catch particles that result from carbon from the combustion process that leaks past piston rings or small metal flakes that result from normal engine wear. The engine oil will suspend some of the particles while the heavier particles will fall to the bottom of the oil pan. The oil filter is designed to catch the particles and let the oil flow through. It is critical to change the oil filter at the manufacturer's recommended mileage to help ensure that it does not become clogged.

When changing a spin-on oil filter, be careful of a few things. First, an oil filter wrench is only used to remove an oil filter. It is never used to install an oil filter. Installation must be performed by hand.

Second, the O-ring that seals the spin-on oil filter to the block tends to stick on the engine block when the filter is being removed. This can lead to double-gasketing, which occurs when the new O-ring in the new filter is installed over the old O-ring. Since the groove in the filter is only deep enough to hold the new O-ring, the old one is not held in place. Once the engine is started, the oil pressure pushes it out of place and oil is pumped very quickly out of the engine and onto the floor. This not only makes a huge mess and wastes good oil, but if you don't realize it has happened, the engine could be damaged in only a minute or two of running. Always check that the old O-ring was removed with the filter. If it was not, reach up and peel it off of the filter mounting.

Third, when installing the spin-on oil filter, smear a bit of oil on the surface of the O-ring. Doing so lubricates it so that it will spin with the oil filter as it is being tightened. Failure to lube the O-ring can cause it to bind and roll out of the oil filter groove when the filter is being tightened.

Last, when installing the spin-on oil filter, it can be hard to see how it is going on the threaded filter adapter. If you get it cross-threaded, it will leak just like a double-gasketed O-ring. Plus you are likely to damage the threads on the adapter, making it harder to install the filter in the future. To prevent this problem, always start the filter by turning it with your fingers. Once you suspect it is started, stop and try to lift the filter off of the adapter. If it comes off, it has not started. Try to start it by finger again; then try to lift it off. If it does not lift off, then it has started onto the threads. Now count the turns that the filter spins on. It should go on at least five full turns before the gasket contacts the filter mounting surface if it is not cross-threaded. You can then tighten it by

hand the appropriate amount as specified by the filter manufacturer, typically about three-quarters to one turn.

Manufacturers are returning to using cartridge filters more and more because it is easier to properly dispose of the oil. It also reduces the amount of waste generated from used spin-on filters. When changing a cartridge filter, be aware of the following situations. First, the only parts that get replaced are the paper filter cartridge and the O-rings or seals. All of the other parts are reused, so do not damage them or throw them away during disassembly.

Second, some cartridge filters are near the bottom of the engine, while others are on top. Use the service information to help you locate the filter. If the filter is on the top of the engine, there is a good chance that you will need to prefill the cartridge before installing the filter end cap. Again, check the service information for the vehicle you are working on.

Third, be careful with tightening a cartridge filter, as it is easy to crack or damage the housing—especially if it is plastic. Always follow the manufacturer's torque procedure.

Last, since the filter housing is being reused, it is important that it is clean before being reinstalled. You may need to wash it out in a clean solvent tank. Just be sure that you also remove any solvent residue before reinstalling it.

To replace a spin-on filter, follow the steps in **SKILL DRILL 45-3**:

1. Before removing an oil filter, refer to the service information for the vehicle and identify the type of filter required. Make sure a suitable replacement filter is available.

SKILL DRILL | 45-3 | Replacing a Spin-on Filter

1. Check for new filter availability. Locate the filter being changed. It will usually be located on the side of the engine block or at an angle underneath the engine. Select the proper oil filter wrench.

2. Position a drain pan to catch any oil that will leak from the filter.

3. Remove the filter. Clean the seating area on the engine so that its surface and the surface of the new filter can seal properly. Make sure the O-ring from the removed filter is not still stuck to the filter mounting surface.

SKILL DRILL | 45-3 | Replacing a Spin-on Filter, continued

4 Confirm you have the correct replacement filter. Smear a little oil on the surface of the new O-ring.

5 Screw in the filter until the filter just starts and ensure that it cannot be pulled off. Then turn the filter by hand until the filter lightly contacts the base. Be careful not to cross-thread the oil filter.

2 The filter will usually be located on the side of the engine block or at an angle underneath the engine but can be separate from the engine. Select the proper oil filter wrench. **(Photo 1)**

3 Position a drain pan to catch any oil that will leak from the filter and remove the filter. **(Photo 2)**

4 Clean the sealing area on the engine so that its surface and the surface of the new filter can seal properly. Make sure the O-ring from the removed filter is not still stuck to the filter mounting surface. **(Photo 3)**

5 Confirm you have the correct replacement filter.

6 Smear a little oil on the surface of the new O-ring. This will help to make a tight seal, but it will also prevent the gasket from binding and distorting while it is being tightened. **(Photo 4)**

7 Screw in the filter until it just starts and verify it cannot be pulled off. Then turn the filter by hand at least 5 turns until the filter lightly contacts the base. **(Photo 5)**

8 To help judge how far to turn the filter to tighten it, mark the outside of the filter with a marker or a dab of oil (but remember to wipe the oil off when you have finished). Do not overtighten the filter. Typically, three-quarters to a full turn is adequate torque for a seal that will not leak, but make sure to follow the tightening instructions for the filter,

which are on the filter and/or the box it came in. Be careful not to cross-thread the oil filter on the threaded adapter fitting.

To replace a cartridge filter (replaceable element), follow the steps in **SKILL DRILL 45-4**:

1 Before removing a cartridge-style oil filter, refer to the service information for the vehicle and identify the type of filter required. Make sure a suitable replacement filter is available.

2 The filter may be located on the side of the engine block, at an angle underneath the engine, or on the top of the engine. If the filter is located in a plastic end cap housing, be sure to use the special tool that the service information calls for. The housing can be damaged if the correct tool is not used. **(Photo 1)**

3 Position a drain pan to catch any oil that will leak from the filter. Unscrew the filter cartridge retaining bolt or oil filter cap, and remove the cartridge filter and housing or end cap. **(Photo 2)**

4 Remove the filter and clean the housing or end cap as necessary, and replace any O-rings or gaskets on the assembly. **(Photo 3)**

5 Smear a little oil on the surface of any new O-rings. This will help them slide back together without rolling or cutting an O-ring. Install the new filter cartridge into its housing. **(Photo 4)**

SKILL DRILL | 45-4 | Replacing a Cartridge Filter (Replaceable Element)

1 Before removing a cartridge-style oil filter, make sure a suitable replacement filter is available. The filter may be located on the side of the engine block, at an angle underneath the engine, or on the top of the engine. If the filter is located in a plastic end cap housing, be sure to use the special tool that the service information calls for.

2 Position a drain pan to catch any oil that will leak from the filter. Unscrew the filter cartridge retaining bolt or oil filter cap, and remove the cartridge filter and housing or end cap.

3 Remove the filter and clean the housing or end cap as necessary, and replace any O-rings or gaskets on the assembly.

4 Smear a little oil on the surface of any new O-rings. Install the new filter cartridge back into its housing.

5 If the cartridge is on the top of the engine, the service information may direct you to pour a specified amount of oil into the filter cavity before the end cap is installed. Screw the cartridge bolt or end cap back in place and tighten to the specified torque. Be careful not to cross-thread the oil filter bolt or end cap.

6 If the cartridge is on the top of the engine, the service information may direct you to pour a specified amount of oil into the filter cavity before the end cap is installed. Screw the cartridge bolt or end cap back in place and tighten to the specified torque. Be careful not to cross-thread the oil filter bolt or end cap. **(Photo 5)**

Refilling Engine Oil

Refilling an engine's oil supply is necessary when performing an oil and filter change. It may also be necessary to refill the engine oil after a lubrication system part has been replaced, if the oil was drained. Always add the recommended amount of oil and grade of oil listed in the service information. After adding the required amount of oil, be sure to start the engine to build oil pressure and fill the oil filter, and then shut the engine off to check for leaks and the level on the dipstick. Fill the oil to the max line and no farther.

To refill the engine oil, follow the steps in **SKILL DRILL 45-5**:

1 Using the service information, research the correct grade and the quantity of oil you will need to fill

the engine. Turn the container of oil so that the spout is on the high side of the bottle. Pour the oil into the funnel carefully so that no oil is spilled onto the outside of the engine, and pour slowly enough to avoid the risk of blowback or overflow. Fill the engine only to the level indicated on the engine dipstick, not until the oil is coming out the top of the filler hole. Replace the filler cap. **(Photo 1)**

SKILL DRILL 45-5 | Refilling the Engine Oil

1 Using the service information, research the correct grade and the quantity of oil you will need to fill the engine. Turn the container of oil so that the spout is on the high side of the bottle. Pour the oil into the funnel carefully so that no oil is spilled onto the outside of the engine, and pour slowly enough to avoid the risk of blowback or overflow. Fill the engine only to the level indicated on the engine dipstick. Replace the filler cap.

2 Start the engine and check the oil pressure indicator on the dash. If the oil pressure is inadequate, stop. Do not continue to run the engine.

3 If the oil pressure is good, turn the engine off and check underneath the vehicle to make sure no oil is leaking from the oil filter or drain plug.

4 With a level vehicle, check the oil level again with the dipstick. It may be necessary to top off the engine by adding a small quantity of oil to compensate for the amount absorbed by the new filter. Do not overfill.

5 Refer to the owner's manual or the service information, and install a static sticker.

6 Reset the maintenance reminder system to remind the owner when the next oil change is due.

2 Start the engine and check the oil pressure indicator on the dash. If the oil pressure is inadequate, stop. Do not continue to run the engine. **(Photo 2)**

3 If the oil pressure is good, turn the engine off and check underneath the vehicle to make sure no oil is leaking from the oil filter or the drain plug. **(Photo 3)**

4 With the vehicle level, check the oil level again with the dipstick. It may be necessary to top off the engine by adding a small quantity of oil to compensate for the amount absorbed by the new filter. Do not overfill. **(Photo 4)**

5 Refer to the owner's manual or the service information, and install a static sticker. **(Photo 5)**

6 Reset the maintenance reminder system to remind the owner when the next oil change is due. **(Photo 6)**

▶ Diagnosis

Common Issues

Some of the common issues in lubrication systems found in the repair shop tend to stem from the same common variable—the customer. Changing the engine oil at the recommended time is the most important maintenance item the customer can have performed. Failure to change oil results in sludge formation, which clogs the oil passageways and keeps oil from lubricating critical parts. When bearings fail to get enough lubricant, they begin to wear and then will seize, resulting in the need for a new or rebuilt engine. An engine replacement is a vastly more expensive alternative to the relatively inexpensive oil change the customer did not want to pay for or did not have time for. As technicians, we need to educate customers on the importance of maintaining their vehicles.

Another common issue is oil leaks. You will need to be able to diagnose where that puddle of oil on the customer's garage floor is coming from. Oil will run down the engine from valve covers or the camshaft seals and may appear to be coming from a lower point. Remember to look over the engine closely and check all mating surfaces. Oil leaking from seals of rotating parts will typically sling oil in a circle; for example, a crankshaft seal will sling oil around the front of the engine in a circular pattern.

Another common area to look for leaks is on the oil pressure sending unit. The sending unit uses a diaphragm, which can develop a hole over time. When this happens, oil will typically leak out of the body either at the crimp or at the terminal end while the engine is running. If you watch it while it is running, you will usually see it drip. Just be aware that if the sending unit is at a downward angle, then oil from another location can possibly run down to it and then drip off of it. So always look above the sending unit. If there is little to no oil above it, the sending unit is bad.

Noises are another lubrication issue found in the repair shop. Low oil pressure can result in valve lifters not pumping up, creating valve train noise. The use of an oil pressure gauge will show if the noise is related to low oil pressure or if it is a result of worn parts with improper running clearances. Low oil pressure can be caused by a low oil level or too thin of oil in the crankcase. It could also be caused by worn bearings or oil pump. Oil can be low for a couple reasons: It may have leaked away or it may have burnt off. An engine can leak its lubricating oil from seals or gaskets that are intended to seal the oil in. Burning the engine oil can be caused by worn piston rings or by worn valve guides that let oil into the combustion chamber or by an improperly operating PCV system. Some engines even use an automatic cut-out that turns off the engine if oil pressure falls too low.

Too little oil in the engine is a problem, but so is too much oil. The crankshaft can whip it into foam and cause leaks by flooding the seals. Another problem with excessive oil is the **drag** produced when the crankshaft hits the oil in the oil pan and tries to stop the crankshaft from turning. This condition will cause a loss of power and result in more fuel consumption. Additionally, the foaming caused by the crankshaft hitting the oil will result in the oil pump starving the engine of precious lubricating oil. Air in the oil will cause problems, since the pump will send this air to the moving parts and cause damage.

> **▶ TECHNICIAN TIP**
>
> Remember that oil will sometimes blow upward when the vehicle is driving down the highway or blow back under the vehicle, so always try to imagine how oil is being thrown around. The use of fluorescent dye may be necessary if a leak is covering more than one area of the engine. It may also be necessary to pressure wash the undercarriage and retest for a large leak.

> **▶ TECHNICIAN TIP**
>
> In the case of finding a leak, always remember that you need to find the root cause of the problem. Gaskets and seals are only designed to withstand a certain amount of pressure before they leak. If the engine has excessive blow-by or the PCV system is not working properly, pressure can build up in the crankcase causing oil to leak past gaskets and seals. A quick way to check for crankcase pressure is to start the engine and then remove the crankcase fresh air intake tube or hose from the engine and cover the engine side of it. If a vacuum develops, the crankcase is not pressurizing. If pressure develops, further diagnosis of the PCV system and piston rings is necessary.

Tools

The tools used for diagnosis of the lubrication system include:

- An oil pressure gauge, with various size adapters that screw into the pressurized oil passage, is used to measure the engine's oil pressure.
- A mechanic's stethoscope is used to pinpoint noises from the engine. The stethoscope will allow you to verify where the noise is coming from, such as the valve train or the timing belt. Stethoscopes can also be electronic versions with headphones, which tend to be more sensitive.
- A DVOM is used to test the electrical circuits of oil pressure sensors and gauges.
- Fluorescent dye and a black light are useful tools to find oil leaks. Fluorescent dye specially made for engine oil is added to the crankcase. The engine is run to circulate the oil and then a black light is used to pinpoint the location of the leak.
- Oil pressure sending unit sockets are useful tools for removing and installing oil pressure sending units.
- A resistance substitution box is used to diagnose gauge problems by substituting precise resistances in the gauge circuit and comparing the gauge reading to the specifications.

Testing the Oil Pressure

Oil pressure testing will need to be performed whenever low oil pressure is suspected and the oil level is within the "safe" range. If the oil pressure gauge in the dash of the vehicle shows low, you will need to verify that it is correct with a manual test gauge. If the test gauge indicates a different pressure from the vehicle's gauge, you will need to test the gauge according to the manufacturer's procedure.

(If an engine is noisy, it may be necessary to check oil pressure to verify that the engine is repairable. An engine that has been operated for long periods of time with no or low oil pressure will have extensive damage and in almost all cases will require complete engine replacement or overhaul. So if the noise is accompanied by low oil pressure, the low oil pressure will need to be diagnosed first. If the noise is accompanied by normal oil pressure, then further diagnosis of the noise is warranted.)

You will need a quality oil pressure gauge of the correct pressure reading and correct threaded adapters. The oil pressure gauge will usually be installed where the oil pressure sensor (sometimes called an oil pressure sending unit or oil pressure switch) is located. Remove the oil pressure sensor and install the oil pressure gauge in its place. If oil pressure is lower than specifications, refer to service information for additional information. There may be excessive clearance in the engine bearings (which causes oil to bleed off and pressures to decline), and/or the oil pump may be worn. If the oil pressure is higher than specifications, suspect a sticking oil pressure regulator. Be sure to follow service information to troubleshoot this condition.

To perform oil pressure testing, follow the steps in **SKILL DRILL 45-6**:

1. Locate the oil pressure sensor by using the component locator in your service information. It is often located near the oil filter. **(Photo 1)**

SKILL DRILL | 45-6 | Testing the Oil Pressure

1. Locate the oil pressure sensor by using the component locator in the service information.

2. Place an oil drain pan under the engine to catch any oil when you remove the oil pressure sensor.

3. Disconnect the wire harness connector, and remove the oil pressure sensor from the engine using the recommended tool in the service information.

SKILL DRILL | **45-6** | **Testing the Oil Pressure, continued**

4. Match the adapter thread to the thread on the pressure sensor to ensure that the correct adapter will be screwed into the engine.

5. Carefully thread the adapter into the engine, ensuring that you do not cross-thread the adapter.

6. Connect the oil pressure gauge, then start and completely warm up the engine. Compare the readings to the specifications in the service information.

7. Remove the manual pressure gauge and adaptor. Using a thread sealant, reinstall the oil sending unit and torque to specifications.

8. Install the wire harness connector and start the engine. Inspect for oil leaks and proper pressure gauge operation.

2. Place an oil drain pan under the engine to catch any oil when you remove the oil pressure sensor. **(Photo 2)**

3. Disconnect the wire harness connector, and remove the oil pressure sensor from the engine using the recommended tool in the service information. **(Photo 3)**

4. Match the adapter thread to the thread on the sending unit to ensure that the correct adapter will be screwed into the engine. **(Photo 4)**

5. Carefully thread the adapter into the engine, ensuring that you do not cross-thread the adapter. **(Photo 5)**

6. Connect the oil pressure gauge, then start and completely warm up the engine.

7. Compare the readings to the specifications in the service information. Your specifications may be at two different engine speeds; if so, you will need to check at both speeds. **(Photo 6)**

8. Remove the manual pressure gauge and adaptor. Using a thread sealant, reinstall the oil sending unit and torque to specifications. **(Photo 7)**

9. Install the wiring and start the engine. Inspect for oil leaks and proper pressure gauge operation. **(Photo 8)**

Safety

The lubrication system contains pressures up to approximately 80 psi (552 kPa), which will shoot oil a good distance. Be sure to wear safety glasses, and be careful if the engine oil is hot, as it could cause burns.

Inspecting Oil Sensors

Oil sensors feed oil pressure information back to the gauge or warning light to issue the operator a warning if oil pressure goes too low. Many oil sensors are typically variable resistors that change resistance based on pressure changes. The variable resistance causes the gauge to read differing amounts, depending on the variable resistance. Others have a fixed resistance in line with a spring-loaded switch. When oil pressure is above the spring pressure, the switch closes and the gauge indicates a midpoint reading. When oil pressure is below the spring pressure, the switch opens and the gauge reading falls toward the low pressure side. Testing oil pressure sensors usually involves substituting the specified resistance in place of the sensor and observing the reaction of the oil pressure gauge. Be sure to follow service information to diagnose the sensor you are working with. Use care with hot engines, as serious burns can result.

To inspect the oil sensors, follow the steps in **SKILL DRILL 45-7**:

1. Locate the oil sensor by using service information.

2. Read and understand the description and operation of the sensor system for the vehicle you are working on. Typically the oil pressure sensor will have three wires (one for voltage, one for ground, and one for the signal return). Disconnect the connector to the sensor. **(Photo 1)**

3. Find the voltage feed wire color by using the wiring diagram for the vehicle and use a variable resistor to connect between the voltage feed wire and the signal return wire. Be sure to locate the correct

SKILL DRILL | 45-7 | Inspecting Oil Sensors

1. Locate the oil sensor by using the service information. Typically the oil pressure sensor will have three wires. Disconnect the connector wire to the sensor.

2. Find the voltage feed wire color by using the wiring diagram for the vehicle and use a variable resistor to connect between the voltage feed wire and the signal return wire.

3. Change the resistance of the variable resistance while monitoring the oil pressure gauge in the dash. The gauge will move as specified as resistance changes if the gauge and wiring are good.

4. Replace the oil sensor if the gauge responds correctly. If the gauge does not respond, then inspect the wiring and gauge.

wires by using the wiring diagram and connector end view. **(Photo 2)**

4 Change the resistance of the variable resistance while monitoring the oil pressure gauge in the dash. The gauge will move as specified as resistance changes if the gauge and wiring are good. **(Photo 3)**

5 Replace the oil sensor if the gauge responds correctly. If the gauge does not respond correctly, then inspect the wiring and gauge. Depending upon the year of the vehicle, an output command for the oil pressure gauge or light might be possible with a scan tool. **(Photo 4)**

Inspecting the Engine Assembly for Fuel, Oil, Coolant, and Other Leaks

Fluid leaks are a common problem that you will repair. Fluids are sealed in the various components on the vehicle, and with time seals and gaskets will begin to leak. When the vehicle begins to leak any of these fluids, customers will usually notice a puddle in their driveway or on their garage floor. The other thing customers may notice is the smell of oil or other fluids burning on the hot engine, or they may see smoke if the fluid is leaking on the exhaust pipes. When looking for the source of leaks, the color, smell, and feel of the fluid can help identify which type of fluid is leaking. Knowing the color of each of the fluids in the vehicle will help you know where to focus your inspection. Remember that gravity pulls leaking fluids down, so always look toward the highest spot that is wet, unless it is a pressure leak that is spraying or a leak onto a rotating part, such as the harmonic balancer, which would throw the fluid outward.

To inspect an engine assembly for fuel, oil, coolant, and other leaks, follow the steps in **SKILL DRILL 45-8**:

1 Raise the vehicle on a lift following the lift point diagrams located in the service information. Verify the customer complaint of a leak by identifying which fluid is leaking. No repair can be made without first verifying what is leaking.

2 Pinpoint the location of the leak. The use of fluorescent dye may be necessary to pinpoint the exact location of the leak. Fluorescent dye will glow when a black light shines on it. If an oil leak is present, you may have to start the engine and look for leaks while it is running, but be extra cautious around moving and hot parts. **(Photo 1)**

3 If a coolant leak is present, it may be necessary to place a pressure tester on the coolant system and pressurize the system. Some leaks will not show up until the vehicle is warm and the cooling system

SKILL DRILL **45-8** **Inspecting the Engine Assembly for Fuel, Oil, Coolant, and Other Leaks**

1 Raise the vehicle on a lift. Verify the customer complaint of a leak by identifying which fluid is leaking. Pinpoint the location of the leak using fluorescent dye if necessary. If an oil leak is present, you may have to start the engine and look for leaks while it is running, but be very careful around moving and hot parts.

2 If a coolant leak is present, you may need to place a pressure tester on the coolant system to pressurize the system. Use a mirror and flashlight if necessary to look behind the engine or between components.

3 Repair the leak following the manufacturer's specifications.

is under pressure. Others may only leak when the engine is cold, but that is unusual. It may be necessary to use a mirror and flashlight to look behind or between components. **(Photo 2)**

4 Repair the leak following the manufacturer's specifications. **(Photo 3)**

Safety

> Fluids leaking onto a hot exhaust component can result in a fire. Point out any leaks found to your supervisor, and be sure to note them on the repair order. The leak poses a fire hazard, so the owner needs to be notified. Fuel leaks always pose an extreme danger; they should be fixed immediately.

Inspecting, Testing, and Replacing Oil Temperature and Pressure Switches

The oil temperature sensor or the oil pressure sensor or switches need to be inspected when there is an issue with a gauge or warning light. The driver of the vehicle may notice that the gauge or light does not operate correctly. It is your job to diagnose the gauge or light system. It may be that the gauge or light is operating as designed and operator education is necessary. For the times when the gauges or lights are not operating as designed, following the manufacturer's troubleshooting procedure will assist you in proper diagnosis. The steps listed in Skill Drill 45-9 are a guide and should not take the place of the manufacturer's specifications. The diagnostics may reveal that a sensor or switch needs to be replaced. Remember, some oil will run from the hole that the sensor is threaded into, so use a container or rag to catch any residual fluid.

To inspect, test, and replace the oil temperature and pressure switches, follow the steps in **SKILL DRILL 45-9**:

1 Locate the oil pressure switch or sensor. Use the manufacturer's service information to locate the component.

2 Disconnect the connector to the switch or sensor. If it is a sensor, determine which wire is the feedback to the gauge or warning light. Use a wiring diagram to ensure that the correct wire is identified. You may need to use a connector end view to double-check that the correct wire is found. Refer to the manufacturer's service information. **(Photo 1)**

3 Use a nonpowered test light to ground the feedback wire to see if the gauge or light responds. Providing you have the correct setup and the right wire, the gauge should move one direction or the warning light should glow. **(Photo 2)**

4 If the gauge or light does not respond, then use an ohmmeter to test the wiring coming back to the gauge or light for an open or high resistance. If the

SKILL DRILL | 45-9 | Inspecting, Testing, and Replacing Oil Temperature and Pressure Switches

1 Locate the oil pressure switch or sensor. Disconnect the connector to the switch or sensor. If it is a sensor, determine which wire is the feedback to the gauge or warning light. You may need to use a connector end view to ensure that the correct wire is found.

2 Use a nonpowered test light to ground the feedback wire to see if the gauge or light responds. The gauge should move one direction or the warning light should glow.

3 If the gauge or light does not respond, then use an ohmmeter to test the wiring coming back to the gauge or light for an open or high resistance. If the gauge or light does respond, then the sensor or switch is bad.

SKILL DRILL | 45-9 | Inspecting, Testing, and Replacing Oil Temperature and Pressure Switches, continued

4 Replace the oil pressure sensor or switch. Use the proper socket to remove the sensor or switch. If the new sensor does not come with thread sealant, use thread sealant on the threads, then install and torque the new sensor to the manufacturer's specifications. Double-check the oil level after replacement, as the oil level may have dropped.

gauge or light does respond, then the sensor or switch is bad. **(Photo 3)**

5 Replace the oil pressure sensor or switch. Use the proper socket to remove the sensor or switch. If the new sensor does not come with thread sealant, use thread sealant on the threads, then install and torque the new sensor to the manufacturer's specifications. Remember to double-check the oil level after replacement, as the oil level may have dropped. **(Photo 4)**

Wrap-up

Ready for Review

▸ Lubrication oil is distilled from crude oil and has additives to prevent acid formation, reduce oxidation, and maintain correct viscosity.

▸ Functions of oil include reduces friction, cushions, cleans, cools, and seals.

▸ Viscosity refers to how easily a liquid flows.

▸ Oil additives include: extreme pressure additives, oxidation inhibitors, corrosion inhibitors, anti-foaming agents, detergents, dispersants, pour point depressants, and viscosity index improvers.

▸ Engine oil also works to suppress engine noise and protect against corrosion.

▸ The three types of oils are: conventional, synthetic, and synthetic blend.

▸ Conventional oil is refined from crude oil and requires additives to function effectively.

▸ Synthetic oil is developed in a lab, is longer lasting, operates at higher temperatures, protects better against engine wear, and is more costly to manufacture.

▸ Synthetic blends combine conventional and synthetic oils.

▸ The American Petroleum Institute classifies oil into groups 1–5.

▸ Components of a lubrication system include: oil pan, oil sump, pick-up tube, oil pump, oil pressure relief valve, oil filter, spurt holes, and gallery.

▸ Oil sump systems can be wet sump or dry sump.

▸ Types of oil pumps are: rotor type, crescent pump, and geared oil pump.

▸ The two most basic oil filtering systems are full-flow filters (most common) and bypass filters.

▸ Vehicles are equipped with oil indicators, oil monitoring systems, and some with an oil cooler.

▸ Types of lubrication systems are: splash, pressure (or force feed), two-stroke engine premix, or two-stroke engine oil injection.

▸ Common lubrication system issues are infrequent oil changes, oil leaks, and valve train noise due to low oil pressure.

▸ Tools used to diagnose the lubrication system include: oil pressure gauge, mechanic's stethoscope, digital volt ohm meter, and fluorescent dye.

▸ Diagnosis of the lubrication system may include: oil analysis; checking engine oil; oil pressure testing; inspecting oil sensors; and inspecting the engine assembly for fuel, oil, coolant, and other leaks.

▸ Always check a vehicle's service manual when changing engine oil to determine the correct quantity.

▸ If the vehicle's oil pressure gauge reads low, verify this with a test gauge.

▸ Lubrication repair tools include: oil filter wrench, wrenches and socket set, mirror, good quality light, digital volt ohm meter, and a special socket for removing oil pressure switches or sensors.

▸ Maintenance and repair procedures include: draining the engine oil; replacing the oil filter; refilling engine oil; and inspecting, testing, and replacing oil pressure and temperature switches.

Key Terms

antifoaming agents Oil additives that keep oil from foaming as it moves through the engine.

baffles Metal plates that are welded into the oil sump. These plates help to keep the oil at the oil pickup screen when the vehicle is cornering, braking, or accelerating hard. Oil will move during these conditions, and the baffles will help to keep it from moving away from the pickup.

bypass filter An oil filter system that only filters some of the oil.

conventional oil Oil that is processed from crude oil; about 20% of oil is additives.

corrosion inhibitors Oil additives that keep acid from forming in the oil.

crescent pump An oil pump that uses a crescent-shaped part to separate the oil pump gears from each other, allowing oil to be moved from one side of the pump to the other.

crude oil Material pulled from the earth, originating from organic compounds broken down over time and formed into petroleum. This material is processed in a refinery to break down into various hydrocarbon substances such as diesel, gasoline, and mineral oil, among others.

detergents Oil additives that help to keep carbon from sticking to engine components.

dipper A type of splash lubricating system used in small engines. It works like a spoon scooping up oil and throwing it upward onto the crankshaft and other wear surfaces.

dispersants Oil additives that keep contaminants held in suspension in the oil, to be removed by the filter or when the oil is changed.

drag The slowing down of the crankshaft when it strikes the oil in the crankcase.

extreme loading Large pressure placed on two bearing surfaces. Extreme loading will try to press oil from between bearing surfaces.

extreme-pressure additive An oil additive that ensures that a protective coating is given to moving engine parts and that keeps oil from being forced out under extreme pressure. Helps oil to cushion components.

full-flow filter An oil filter installed on production cars. This oil filter cleans all oil coming from the oil pump on its way to the lubricated components.

galleries Passageways drilled or cast into the engine block or head(s), which carry pressurized lubricating oil to various moving parts in the engine, such as the camshaft bearings.

geared oil pump An oil pump that has two gears running side by side together to move oil from one side of the pump gears to the other.

gelling A thickening effect of oil in cold weather. This is not a desirable trait for lubricating oil, as it will not flow when it is gelling. Wax content in base stock mineral oil makes gelling worse.

hydro-cracking A process in which group 2 and group 3 oils are refined with hydrogen at much higher temperatures and pressures. This process results in a base mineral oil with many of the higher performance characteristics of synthetic oils.

hydrogenating A process used during refining of crude oil. Hydrogen is added to crude oil to create a chemical reaction to take out impurities such as sulfur.

lubricating oil Processed crude oil with additives to help it perform well in the engine.

lubrication system A system of parts that work together to deliver lubricating oil to the various moving parts of the engine.

mineral oil Base stock processed from crude oil in a refinery, used as the base material of all conventional oil.

oil cooler A device that takes heat away from engine oil by passing it near either engine coolant or outside air. Cooling the engine oil helps to keep it from overheating and breaking down.

oil galleries Oil passages that are drilled into the engine block and cylinder head(s). These passageways carry oil from the oil pump to critical moving parts.

oil monitoring system A system that alerts the driver when it is time to change engine oil. These systems will need to be reset for the customer after an oil change is performed.

oil pan The metal pan that covers the bottom of the engine, contains oil sump where engine oil is held.

oil pressure relief valve A valve usually located in the oil pump that limits the oil pressure. When oil pressure is reached, excessive pressure is bled back to the sump.

oil pump A device that pumps lubricating oil through the engine.

oil pump strainer A screen located on the oil pump pickup that keeps debris from being picked up by the oil pump.

oil slinger A device used on small engines, located on the crankshaft or driven by the camshaft. It works to fling oil up onto moving engine parts.

oil spurt holes Holes drilled into the connecting rod that spray oil up onto the cylinder walls and the piston wrist pins.

oil sump The lower part of the oil pan that holds lubricating oil for the engine. The oil pickup screen sits in this low point.

oxidation inhibitor An oil additive that helps keep hot oil from combining with oxygen to produce sludge or tar.

pickup tube A tube connected to the oil pump that acts like a straw for the oil pump to pull oil from the sump of the oil pan.

polyalphaolefin (PAO) A man-made base stock (synthetic) used in place of mineral oil. Oil molecules are more consistent in size and no impurities are found in this oil since it is made in a lab.

pour point depressants Oil additives that keep wax crystals from forming and causing the oil to gel during cold operation.

pressure, or force-feed, lubrication system A lubrication system that has a pump to pressurize the lubricating oil and push it through the engine to moving parts.

rotor lobes Lobes or rounded edges on rotors that squeeze oil and create pressure.

rotor-type oil pump An oil pump that uses rounded gears to squeeze oil through.

scavenge pump A pump used with a dry sump oiling system to pull oil from the dry sump pan and move it to an oil tank outside the engine.

splash lubrication A lubrication system that relies on oil being splashed onto moving parts by rotating engine parts striking the oil. These systems are typically used in small engines.

synthetic blend A blend of conventional engine oil and pure synthetic oil.

synthetic oil Synthetic oil that, in its pure form, uses man-made base stocks and is not derived from crude oil. This oil lasts longer and performs better than normal oil. The base stock additives are similar to those in conventional oils.

viscosity The ability of a liquid to flow.

viscosity index improver An oil additive that resists a change in viscosity over a range of temperatures.

windage tray A plate that bolts onto the bottom of the engine between the crankshaft and the oil pan, helping to keep the crankshaft from contacting the engine oil.

ASE-Type Questions

1. Tech A says that one function of oil is to clean. Tech B says that one function of oil is to cushion. Who is correct?
   a. Tech A
   b. Tech B
   c. Both A and B
   d. Neither A nor B

2. Two techs are discussing 5W20 oil. Tech A says the W stands for "weight". Tech B says the W stands for "Winter." Who is correct?
   a. Tech A
   b. Tech B
   c. Both A and B
   d. Neither A nor B

3. Tech A says that the higher the viscosity number, the thicker the oil. Tech B says that most modern vehicles use single weight oil. Who is correct?
   a. Tech A
   b. Tech B
   c. Both A and B
   d. Neither A nor B

4. Tech A says that spin-on oil filters need RTV gasket sealer to seal the gasket. Tech B says that some oil filters use a replaceable paper filter cartridge. Who is correct?
   a. Tech A
   b. Tech B
   c. Both A and B
   d. Neither A nor B

5. Tech A says that the oil pressure will typically be low if the oil level is at the "add" line on the dipstick. Tech B says that a cracked pickup tube could cause low oil pressure. Who is correct?
   a. Tech A
   b. Tech B
   c. Both A and B
   d. Neither A nor B

6. Tech A says that most oil pumps are of the positive displacement style. Tech B says that oil pumps are designed to deliver more oil than is needed for an engine. Who is correct?
   a. Tech A
   b. Tech B
   c. Both A and B
   d. Neither A nor B

7. Tech A says that it takes about 1 pint of oil to raise the oil level from "add" to "full." Tech B says that it takes about 1 quart to raise it that much. Who is correct?
   a. Tech A
   b. Tech B
   c. Both A and B
   d. Neither A nor B

8. Tech A says that oil pressure is reduced when bearing clearances increase. Tech B says that oil pressure is regulated by the pressure relief valve. Who is correct?
   a. Tech A
   b. Tech B
   c. Both A and B
   d. Neither A nor B

9. Tech A says that a full-flow oil filter filters all of the oil going to the bearings. Tech B says that a bypass filter bypasses the pump, so that any particles in the oil won't damage the pump. Who is correct?
   a. Tech A
   b. Tech B
   c. Both A and B
   d. Neither A nor B

10. Tech A says that if the oil pressure reads low, the oil pressure sending unit should be replaced. Tech B says that if the oil pressure is low, the oil pressure should be measured using a separate pressure tester. Who is correct?
    a. Tech A
    b. Tech B
    c. Both A and B
    d. Neither A nor B

CHAPTER 46

Engine Cooling

Knowledge Objectives

After reading this chapter, you will be able to:
1. Explain the principles and methods of heat transfer. (pp 1594–1595)
2. Explain the basic principles of the cooling system. (pp 1595–1596)
3. Discuss boiling point and pressure, electrolysis, and centrifugal force. (pp 1597–1598)
4. Describe how the cooling system functions. (pp 1599–1600)
5. Describe the components of the cooling system. (pp 1601–1602)

Skills Objectives

After reading this chapter, you will be able to:
1. Test the cooling system pressure and verify the engine operating temperature. (pp 1616–1617)
2. Inspect and test the cooling fan. (pp 1617–1619)
3. Test the heater control valve. (pp 1619–1620)
4. Use a hydrometer to test the freeze point of the coolant. (pp 1620–1621)
5. Use a refractometer to test the freeze point of the coolant. (pp 1620–1621)
6. Inspect and adjust an engine drive belt. (pp 1625–1626)
7. Check and replace a coolant hose. (pp 1628–1629)
8. Remove and replace a thermostat and a radiator. (pp 1629–1634)
9. Remove, inspect, and reinstall a heater core. (p 1634)

▶ Introduction

Cooling systems play a critical role in the life span of the engine. Typically, a great deal of focus is placed on engine lubrication and the maintenance of the engine's lubrication system, but little focus is placed on the engine's cooling system. Yet, because the Department of Transportation has stated that cooling system failure is the leading cause of mechanical breakdowns on the highway, it deserves our attention. The cooling system can have a huge effect on the lubrication system and can also affect engine emissions and fuel economy, thus making its role a significant one.

This chapter will explain the importance of modern cooling system maintenance. We will cover coolant, what it is made of, how it works, and what will happen if the cooling system is not maintained. The chapter will also discuss all the components of the cooling system and how each contributes to the function of the cooling of the engine.

▶ Cooling Fundamentals

Heat is thermal energy. It cannot be destroyed; it can only be transferred. It always moves from areas of higher temperature to areas of lower temperature. This principle is applied to the transfer of heat energy from engine parts to ambient air using the coolant as a medium to carry it. To control this heat transfer, it is necessary to understand how heat behaves. Heat travels in three ways:

1. From one solid to another, by a process called <u>conduction</u>.
2. Through liquids and gases by a process called <u>convection</u>, whereby heat follows paths called convection currents.
3. Through space, by <u>radiation</u> (**FIGURE 46-1**).

Heat Transfer

The internal combustion engine relies on the heat of combustion to produce torque to move the vehicle and

FIGURE 46-1 Conduction is the movement of heat energy through solids, convection is the movement of heat through liquids or gases, and radiation is the movement of heat through space.

▶ You are the Automotive Technician

A customer brings his 2009 Honda Accord into your dealership complaining about the coolant boiling over on hot days. The engine gauge gets higher than normal, but never to the red zone, when steam comes out from under the hood. You ask some clarifying questions and he gives these answers; it happens most during stop and go traffic on his way home from work, which is at the hot time of the day. He isn't sure if the electric cooling fan is coming on or not since he is focused on traffic. He says that the quick lube shop takes care of his fluids, so he doesn't know if it is using coolant or not. He agrees to let you diagnose it, so you take it back to the shop and verify that the coolant level is near the full mark. You then take a minute to plan your steps for diagnosis.

1. What are the possible causes for coolant that boils over below the red zone?
2. How can engine operating temperature be verified?
3. What two factors determine the boiling point of coolant?
4. What are some of the most likely causes of coolant that boils over when in the red zone?

AS-27: Heat: The technician can demonstrate an understanding of the effect of heat on automotive systems.

The heat created by burning fuel in the internal combustion engine causes rapid expansions of pressure, which drives the pistons (see the Motive Power Types—Spark-Ignition (SI) Engines chapter). Some of the heat from the combustion process must be dissipated so that it does not overheat or melt engine parts. This is the job of the engine cooling system. The cooling system helps the engine to quickly come up to its specified operating temperature and to maintain that temperature in spite of ambient weather conditions or engine load. If the engine is not allowed to warm up properly, other systems will not operate properly. For example, the engine coolant temperature will greatly affect the engine air–fuel mixture (fuel trim) and thus fuel economy and emissions. Operation of the evaporative emission system and other systems is also affected by engine temperature, so it is important that the cooling system be maintained to operate correctly.

AS-30: Fusion/Vaporization: The technician can demonstrate an understanding of how heat causes a change in the state of matter.

Vaporization and fusion are two ways in which the application of heat can cause matter to change states. Vaporization refers to the transitional phase from liquid to vapor, while fusion refers to the transitional phase from solid to liquid. Both concepts have applications in the shop.

Pressurized cooling systems in motor vehicles are designed to prevent vaporization, in this case from boiling. Water boils at 212°F (100°C) at atmospheric pressure at sea level. When coolant in the cooling system is pressurized, its boiling point is raised, allowing the system to continue to cool the engine at temperatures over 212°F (100°C). Vaporization must be avoided because, unlike liquids, vapors do not effectively remove heat from engine components. Most cooling systems have pressure limits of 14 to 15 pounds per square inch (psi, or 97 to 103 kilopascals [kPa]), effectively raising the boiling point of the coolant by approximately 45°F (25°C).

In contrast, water turns from a liquid to a solid (freezes) at 32°F (0°C). When water freezes, it expands approximately 10%. Pressure from ice is strong enough to break cast iron, which would cause leaks in the cooling system, causing extensive damage to the engine. Anti-freeze is used to lower the freezing point of water to prevent freezing of the water and anti-freeze mixture, called coolant.

FIGURE 46-2 Heat loss in a gasoline engine.

power accessories. Unfortunately, much of the heat produced during combustion is not used productively and must be removed to avoid overheating of the engine. No matter how efficiently fuel burning occurs, and no matter the size of the engine, the heat energy generated never completely transforms into kinetic energy **FIGURE 46-2**. Some heat energy remains unused for powering the vehicle and is typically wasted in three ways: (1) About 33% is wasted by being dumped straight out of the exhaust to the atmosphere (some of this wasted energy can be recovered by a turbocharger); (2) about 33% is wasted by the cooling system, which prevents overheating of the engine components; and (3) about 5% is wasted by internal friction and from radiating off of hot engine components straight to the atmosphere. This leaves only about 25% to 30% of the original energy that is used for powering the vehicle and its accessories. However, turbocharged vehicles recover some of the energy lost from the exhaust, bringing engine efficiency up to near 35%.

Principles of Engine Cooling

From the second law of thermodynamics, we know that heat always moves from hot to cold. These principles are put to use in the automotive cooling system to keep everything working properly. The automotive cooling system provides a means of transferring heat from the hot parts of the engine to ambient air. This can be accomplished through a group of parts working together to circulate coolant throughout a sealed system to carry heat away from those engine parts. Heat can then be released to outside air or to air entering the passenger compartment for comfort purposes.

Manufacturers use various cooling system configurations, but the basic concept is to transfer excessive heat from hotter to cooler environments or materials. Regardless of the parts used by the manufacturer, the job is the same. You might be thinking that if some engine cooling is good, then more must be better. But that is not the case. Engines have an ideal operating temperature somewhere around 200°F (93°C), give or take 20°F (11°C), depending on the vintage of the vehicle. The purpose of the cooling system is to allow the engine to warm up to its optimum temperature as quickly as possible, and then transfer any excess heat energy to the atmosphere, thereby maintaining that ideal temperature.

Most automotive engines are liquid-cooled, although some manufacturers have used air-cooled engines. A liquid-cooled system uses **coolant**, a fluid that contains special anti-freezing and anti-corrosion chemicals mixed with water. In general terms, a water pump causes coolant to flow through passages in the engine, picking up heat along the way, and then through a cooler radiator where it gives up that heat. The radiator accepts hot coolant from the engine and lowers its temperature. As air moves over and through the radiator, the heat energy is transferred from the coolant to the ambient air. The lower-temperature coolant is returned to the engine to absorb more heat energy and continue the cycle.

The circulation of the coolant is controlled by the thermostat. It opens and closes coolant flow from the engine to the radiator. When the engine is cold, coolant circulates through the engine (and heater core) only. Once the engine warms up, the thermostat opens and allows coolant from the engine to flow through the radiator.

Some newer vehicles use a coolant heat storage system (CHSS). This system uses a vacuum-insulated container, similar to a Thermos bottle. The storage container holds an amount of hot coolant and maintains the temperature for up to three days when the engine is shut down. When the vehicle is started the next time, a small electric water pump preheats the engine by circulating this hot coolant through the engine, which greatly reduces hydrocarbon exhaust emissions during start-up and warm-up.

Air cooling is common on smaller internal combustion engines. Most engines use cooling fins. Their design makes the exposed surface area as large as possible, which allows more heat energy to radiate away and be carried off in convection currents in the air. Many small engines also use a fan to direct air through and over the cooling fins, which increases the cooling capacity. Air-cooled engines have fallen out of favor in passenger vehicles because they are harder to maintain at a stable temperature, thereby increasing emissions output of the engine **FIGURE 46-3**.

FIGURE 46-3 A cylinder from an air cooled Volkswagen engine. Note the cooling fins around the cylinder.

Vehicle Coolant

Coolant is a mixture of water and anti-freeze, which is used to remove heat from the engine. If an engine did not have the heat removed from it, it would fail very quickly. Coolant absorbs the heat from the engine by convection. Since coolant contacts the hot metal directly, it is a very effective heat sink. The coolant is important for three reasons: (1) It prevents an engine from overheating while in use, (2) it keeps the engine from freezing while not in use in cold climates, and (3) it prevents corrosion of the parts in the cooling system.

Water alone is by far the best coolant there is, since it can absorb a larger amount of heat than most other liquids. But water has some drawbacks. It freezes if its temperature drops below 32°F (0°C) (the temperature at which water becomes a solid). As water freezes, it expands into a solid. If it expands in the coolant passages inside the engine, these passages—typically made of cast aluminum or cast iron—will not flex to allow expansion and will break. This renders the engine inoperative and unrepairable in most cases.

Another thing to realize about using water alone as a coolant is that water is corrosive and causes metal to rust. Think about a piece of unpainted metal that is lying outside in the rain. Rust and corrosion build up quickly on that metal simply because of the reaction (oxidation) of the metal, water, and oxygen. Anti-freeze prevents corrosion and rusting through anti-corrosion additives (called corrosion inhibitors) mixed into the solution. Another important note on water is that water contains minerals and will potentially lead to excessive deposits even when added to anti-freeze. Because of this, most manufacturers recommend using distilled water for cooling systems.

Anti-freeze is mixed with water to lower the freezing point of water and reduce the chances of cracking the engine block, cylinder heads, and other cooling system components. Anti-freeze is made from one of two base chemicals—ethylene glycol or propylene glycol—plus a mixture of additives to protect against corrosion and foaming. Ethylene and propylene glycol may achieve a maximum very low freezing point of –70°F (–57°C) when mixed with the appropriate amount of water. **Ethylene glycol** is a chemical that resists freezing but is very toxic to humans and animals. **Propylene glycol** is another chemical that resists freezing but is not toxic and is used in nontoxic anti-freezes. Either of these anti-freezes will actually freeze around 0°F (–18°C) if not mixed with water, so water is a necessary part of coolant. The freezing point of coolant will vary depending upon how much water is added to the anti-freeze **FIGURE 46-4**. Because anti-freeze does not absorb heat as effectively as water, it should not be mixed at a ratio higher than 65% anti-freeze and 35% water. Using a higher proportion of anti-freeze will actually reduce the cooling quality of the mixture and raise the operating temperature of the engine.

The best coolant is a 50/50 balance of water and anti-freeze, making it an ideal coolant for both hot and cold climates and providing adequate corrosion protection. Also, when anti-freeze is added at a 50% mixture, the boiling point increases from 212°F (100°C) to around 228°F (109°C). As you can see, this is an extremely beneficial characteristic of anti-freeze as manufacturers continue to build engines that are more powerful, create more heat, and operate at higher temperatures.

Anti-freeze can be purchased as straight anti-freeze (100%) or as a 50/50 premix with water. Straight anti-freeze that you buy from the dealer or parts store consists of three parts: glycol (around 96%), corrosion inhibitors and additives (around 2–3%), and water (around 2%).

FIGURE 46-4 Freezing point of anti-freeze and water solution.

Glycol, as discussed previously, keeps the freezing point low and the boiling point high. Corrosion inhibitors and additives prevent corrosion and erosion, resist foaming, ensure coolant is compatible with cooling system component materials and hard water, resist sedimentation, and balance the acid to alkaline content of the anti-freeze. Water is added to blend the inhibitors with the glycol.

Anti-freeze is an amazing chemical that performs a monumental task in the operation of our vehicles. It works so well that it is often overlooked for maintenance by the customer. However, because the additives wear out and become less effective over time, coolant does need to be changed at recommended intervals. Doing so reduces the possibility of engine damage and failure over time. Likewise, lubrication enhancers, which keep the water pump and seals functioning properly, wear out and need to be replaced.

Boiling Point and Pressure

The **boiling point** of a liquid is the temperature at which it begins to change from a liquid to a gas. Water at sea level atmospheric pressure 14.7 psi (101.4 kPa or 1 atmosphere [atm]) boils at 212°F (100°C). Atmospheric pressure becomes lower as elevation is increased. Because atmospheric pressure is lower at higher elevations (such as in the mountains), the boiling temperature of a liquid in an unsealed system is lower. Think of it as *lower pressure = lower boiling point*. Conversely, raising the pressure has the opposite effect; it raises the boiling point of a liquid. Stated another way, a liquid in a vacuum has a lower boiling point than when that same liquid is at atmospheric pressure. A liquid under pressure higher than atmospheric pressure has a higher boiling point than when that liquid is at atmospheric pressure. Thus, the boiling point of a liquid varies depending upon the surrounding environmental pressure. For a given pressure, different liquids boil at different temperatures.

This principle is used to enable water in the engine's cooling system to remain a liquid at temperatures well above the normal boiling point of 212°F (100°C). The pressurized coolant in the cooling system boils at a

Safety

Because the pressurized coolant in the cooling system boils at a higher temperature than when the radiator pressure cap is removed, you should NEVER remove a radiator pressure cap on a hot engine. If the coolant is above 212°F (110°C), all of the coolant will turn to steam as soon as the pressure is released, pushing superheated steam out the radiator, potentially scalding you.

higher temperature than when the radiator pressure cap is removed (or if the system has a leak).

Over the years, manufacturers intentionally have raised the operating temperature of their engines for more efficient combustion and reduced emissions. A pressurized cooling system can handle the extra heat without boiling over. Pressurizing the cooling system can mean that the cooling system can be downsized (for less weight and space requirement) and still cool the engine effectively. Also, with a higher temperature differential between the cooling system's operating temperature and the outside ambient air, the radiator is more effective at radiating excess heat from the coolant. In today's vehicles, most automotive cooling systems are pressurized at 13–17 psi (89.6–117.2 kPa). However, some factory radiator caps are rated as high as 24 psi (165.5 kPa), and high-performance systems can go as high as 34 psi (234.4 kPa).

> ## TECHNICIAN TIP
>
> The term "psig" is another way of saying the pressure that is read on a normal American pressure gauge. The "g" stands for gauge. So gauge pressure is the amount of pressure measured above 1 atm (atmospheric pressure). A compound pressure gauge typically reads both above and below atmospheric pressure. It measures psig above zero, and inches of vacuum (or mm of mercury) below zero.
>
> In contrast, the term "psia" means *absolute pressure*, which does not include atmospheric pressure. In other words, a psia gauge would read 14.7 psig at sea level. If you want to know the absolute pressure (in psia), just add gauge pressure (psig) to atmospheric pressure (usually considered 14.7 psi at sea level).

Electrolysis

Electrolysis is the process of pulling chemicals (materials) apart by using electricity or by creating electricity through the use of chemicals and dissimilar metals. Electrolysis is used in manufacturing to create some metals, gases, and chemicals. You may have performed electrolysis in a science class by passing electrical current through water to break the hydrogen out of the water. Electrolysis is what takes place in the automotive battery. Two dissimilar metals are submerged in an acid solution, resulting in the reaction that is called electricity. Another common experiment in science class is the potato battery, made from two different types of metal stuck into the potato and used to power a digital clock or a light bulb.

Electrolysis can occur in places where it is not desired and can have undesirable effects. For instance, in automotive cooling systems, electrolysis is possible when the coolant breaks down and becomes more acidic.

Many types of metal are used in the engine, such as cast iron, aluminum, copper, and brass. Introducing an acid solution into a mix of metals will produce electricity. When this electricity is produced, the movement of the electrons will begin to erode away the metal in the system. Eventually, pinholes will be created in the thinner, softer cooling system components (typically, the heater core or aluminum cylinder head). To combat electrolysis, the customer needs to have regular scheduled maintenance of the coolant performed, including flushing out of the old coolant and replacing it with new coolant. Electricity can also appear in the cooling system due to faulty grounds on accessories or even the starter motor circuit. Electricity is known to follow the path of least resistance and will be partially carried through the coolant where it can erode metals, if that path is easier than its intended path. We will discuss how to test for electrolysis later in this chapter and will revisit bad grounds at that point.

Centrifugal Force

Centrifugal force is a force pulling outward on a rotating body. For example, if you were to take a tennis ball and tie it to a string and swing it around you, centrifugal force would pull the tennis ball outward making the string taut. Another example of centrifugal force occurs when a vehicle turns a curve. Centrifugal force resists the turning of the vehicle and tries to keep the vehicle moving in a straight line, creating a sliding condition if centrifugal force is great enough. Centrifugal force can be useful in some cases, such as in the water pump. When coolant enters the center of the water pump and the internal rotor spins, centrifugal force moves the liquid outward toward the outlet **FIGURE 46-5**. Centrifugal force pushes the coolant into the engine block and head passageways that surround the cylinders. The coolant then travels through the radiator to be cooled.

FIGURE 46-5 When coolant enters the center of this pump and the internal rotor spins, centrifugal force moves the liquid outward.

Applied Science

AS-101: Proportion Mixtures: The technician can correctly mix fluids using proportions.

As discussed earlier, engine coolant is composed of water and anti-freeze. The normally recommended mixture of these two liquids is 50/50—50% water and 50% anti-freeze—which provides freeze protection to about –34°F (–37°C). Automotive cooling system capacity typically is given in quarts or liters, with smaller vehicles requiring perhaps 5 quarts (or liters) and larger SUVs with air conditioning requiring up to 20 or more quarts (or liters).

If a vehicle's specifications call for a total of 16 quarts of coolant, then a 50/50 mixture would consist of 8 quarts of anti-freeze mixed with 8 quarts of distilled water. A 10-quart system would require 5 quarts of each, and so forth. The challenge in ensuring a 50/50 mix is the unknown mixture that remains in the cooling system, since not all of the coolant will drain out. If the system has been flushed with clean water and drained, then to end up with a 50/50 mix, the technician would first add the entire 50% of anti-freeze and then top off the rest with clean water, leaving a 50/50 mix. If the coolant was flushed out with a 50/50 mix, then the technician can premix coolant and top the cooling system off with that. After topping off the cooling system, be sure to run the engine to circulate the coolant and then check the mixture's freeze point with a hydrometer or refractometer.

Coolant can now be purchased premixed for convenience, but you will be paying for 50% water, plus the cost of shipping it, so it is less expensive to mix your own coolant.

FIGURE 46-6 Coolant moves through the engine and then to the radiator to transfer heat to the air.

Cooling Systems

Almost all modern vehicles have engine cooling systems that use a liquid coolant to transfer heat energy from parts of the internal combustion engine to outside air. (Note: Other cooling systems, such as those used for turbocharger intercoolers/aftercoolers or hybrid high-voltage battery packs, may use air-to-air systems to cool the engine's intake air or high-voltage battery). In the engine's liquid-cooled system, coolant is forced to flow around and through parts of the engine to pick up excess heat and carry it through flexible hoses to the radiator. Engine heat is transferred from hotter components to cooler ones. The cooling fan forces air over the fins of the radiator, as necessary, to assist the transfer of heat energy from the coolant to the ambient air **FIGURE 46-6**. The coolant also flows through coolant hoses to the heater core, which is located in the air box in the passenger compartment and provides heat for the passengers when needed. **Cooling hoses** (i.e., radiator hoses and heater hoses) are flexible rubber tubes that connect stationary components of the cooling system, such as the heater core and radiator, to the

engine, which is allowed to move on its flexible mounts. Engine movement in its flexible rubber mounts would cause nonflexible coolant hoses to break over time.

Air Cooling

Air engine cooling is common on smaller internal combustion engines and was used in the past on some automobiles like the early Volkswagen Beetle and Porsches. Air cooling of an automobile was not ideal from an emissions standpoint; nor did it always provide sufficient cabin heat for the passenger compartment. All automobiles are now water cooled, although small engines can still be found in older automobiles that are air cooled. Air cooling uses heat-dissipating fins on the engine cylinders and heads to allow the movement of air to absorb heat and carry it away from the engine through special ducting. Since the air does the work of keeping the engine cool, an air-cooled system is very simple and light compared to a water-cooled one. This is one of several reasons why most small aircraft engines are air cooled. A major drawback to air cooling is that the engine has to be exposed to the airstream for best cooling. Many motorcycles were air cooled, but as the engines became more powerful, a more effective cooling system became necessary. Most motorcycle engines produced today are water cooled.

Air-cooled engines in automobiles usually are not exposed to the air; rather, the engine is housed in an enclosed engine bay. Still, for a vehicle moving at highway speed, airflow over the engine may be high enough to prevent overheating. At lower speeds or during idling, heat may build up and overheat the engine. One way to remove excess heat from the engine is to use a fan, along with shrouds and ducts, to direct air over or even between

FIGURE 46-7 An air-cooled motorcycle engine uses fins to cool the engine and works by convection as air moves through the fins.

Air-cooled engine

the cylinders. An engine that uses these components is called a "forced draft" air-cooled engine. Some air-cooled engines are "open draft" air-cooled, which require the engine to be moving through the air to have sufficient airflow **FIGURE 46-7**.

Liquid Cooling

In modern vehicles, radiators are low and wide to allow the hood to sit lower to the ground for aerodynamics. Because of this design, modern vehicles use a water pump that pulls coolant from the radiator and forces it through passages, called **water jackets**, in the engine block and cylinder head. Coolant absorbs heat by conduction from the engine and becomes hotter. The heated coolant then moves to the radiator for cooling; air flowing over and through the radiator causes heat to be absorbed from the coolant by the air.

All engines operate best when they are at their full operating temperature, commonly referred to as the operating temperature. Most engine wear and high exhaust emissions occur during the warm-up period. Ideally, we want the engine to get to operating temperature as quickly as possible, but not overheat. In order to accomplish this, a thermostat is used to regulate the coolant temperature. The thermostat initially blocks coolant flow to the radiator, keeping coolant circulating in the engine where it heats up quickly and does not pull heat from the warming engine. Once operating temperature is reached, the thermostat starts to open and allows coolant to flow to the radiator to remove excessive heat. The thermostat does not normally open completely, but adjusts between its fully closed or fully open position continually to maintain an optimum engine operating temperature, regardless of engine load.

Coolant Flow—Normal and Reverse Flow

In a water-cooled cooling system with normal flow, the flow of coolant starts at the water pump. Cold coolant is moved through the engine and starts to warm up as the engine begins to run. The coolant travels up through the engine assisted by the water pump. The pump relies on centrifugal force of the impeller (rotor) to force coolant through the cooling passageways of the engine. The coolant flows around the cylinders where combustion is taking place and picks up excess heat. Heat transfers from around the cylinders to the coolant as it moves past them. It then moves upward through the cylinder head, where it passes over the top of the combustion chamber in the head and flows around the valve guides, all the while picking up more heat as it passes those hotter surfaces.

From the head it will move to the thermostat, which works like a trapdoor: If it is closed, the coolant will continue to circulate within the engine, flowing through a bypass hose or passage to move back down to the water pump, which was the starting point of its journey again. The thermostat is meanwhile sensing the coolant's temperature, and at a specified temperature it begins to open. As the thermostat opens, the coolant begins to flow through the radiator hose and to the radiator. Coolant enters the radiator's inlet tank and then the radiator core, where it flows through small tubes that have heat-dissipating fins on the outside. The tubes act like fins on an air-cooled engine to transfer the coolant's heat to the outside air. As it cools, coolant moves to the cool side of the radiator to begin its journey back to the engine through the other radiator hose. The coolant's return flow to the engine is aided by the suction created by the water pump impeller.

One problem with this normal-flow system was discovered on race cars, which develop more heat than a standard automobile. Because race car engines run hotter, and cylinder heads in general run hotter than engine blocks, the heads would get too hot and fail. The hottest part of any engine is the cylinder head, since this is where the combustion chamber is located. High cylinder head temperatures tend to increase chances of detonation and failure of head gaskets. As a cylinder head heats more than the cylinder block, it will expand further and slide across the head gasket more. When the head does this many times, the gasket is more likely to fail.

In the normal-flow cooling system, coolant goes through the engine block first and then moves to the hottest part—the cylinder head. As a result, the cylinder head operates at a hotter temperature than the cylinder block. Engineers found that if they changed the flow design, they could keep the cylinder head and block closer to the same temperature by pushing coolant through the head first, thus making the head, valves, and head gaskets last longer. Therefore, in some reverse-flow cooling systems, coolant flows to the cylinder heads first and then through the engine block.

In the typical reverse-flow design, coolant starts from the radiator and flows through the radiator outlet hose to the thermostat and then to the water pump. The thermostat is located on the inlet side of the engine to help regulate cold coolant more closely and to help reduce temperature shock to engine components. Coolant moves to the cylinder head first, where it can do the most cooling, then moves through the block and back to the radiator through the other radiator hose. Since the flow through the radiator is the same, it is simply the flow through the engine that has changed. This design differs only in the way coolant flows, head to block; all the components are generally the same. In other reverse-flow designs, coolant may flow from the thermostat in the lower radiator hose to the bottom of the radiator then up to the top of the radiator and back to the cylinder heads, through the block, through the thermostat, and on to the lower radiator.

One problem with the reverse-flow design was easily fixed: As coolant moved through the hottest part of the engine, steam tended to form and get stuck at the head cooling passages, since this is the highest part of the engine. Since the engine will overheat if gas pockets get stuck in the water passageways, the solution was to drill holes in the head for steam to escape and to run a tube from the head back to a **surge tank**, where the steam turns back into coolant and is recycled through the system. The surge tank will be discussed in greater detail later in the chapter.

Rotary Engine Cooling System

The cooling system of the rotary engine is not much different from the piston engine's cooling system. The engine itself is extremely different since it does not use pistons but instead uses a triangular part called a rotor that moves with combustion and turns the crankshaft. The cooling system uses a standard radiator, thermostat, and radiator hoses. Water flows from the radiator to the water pump then into the **rotor housing**, which is essentially the engine block of the rotary engine; this is where the rotor moves. The rotor housing has passageways (water jackets) cast and machined into it, which go around the rotor housing and allow heat to be pulled from around the rotor where combustion is taking place. After coolant moves through the water jackets, it finds its way to the thermostat where it returns to the radiator.

▶ Cooling System Components

The primary components of a vehicle cooling system are:

- *Radiator*: The radiator is usually made of copper, brass, or aluminum tubes with copper, brass, aluminum, or plastic tanks on the sides or top for coolant to collect in. Air is drawn over the radiator to transfer heat energy to ambient air. The fins on the tubes of the radiator give more surface area for **heat dissipation**—the spreading of heat over a large area to ease heat transfer.
- *Thermostat*: The thermostat regulates coolant flow to the radiator. It opens at a predetermined temperature to allow coolant flow to the radiator for cooling. It also enables the engine to reach operating temperature more quickly for reduced emissions and wear.
- *Recovery system*: The recovery system uses an **overflow tank** to catch any coolant that is released from the radiator cap when the coolant heats up. It works like a catch can.
- *Surge tank*: This pressurized tank is piped into the cooling system. Coolant constantly moves through it. It is used when the radiator is not the highest part of the cooling system. Remember, air collects at the highest point in the cooling system.
- *Water pump*: This pump is used to force coolant throughout the cooling system in order to transfer heat energy. The water pump is typically driven off the engine timing belt or accessory belt. On some engines, it is driven by the camshaft timing chain.
- *Cooling fan*: This fan forces air through the radiator for heat transfer. Cooling fans can be

driven by a belt or by an electric motor. The fan can be controlled by viscous fluid or thermostatic sensors, switches, and relays.

- *Radiator hoses*: These hoses are used to connect the radiator to the water pump and engine. They are usually made of formed, nylon-reinforced rubber. Some radiator hoses use coiled wire inside them to prevent hose collapse as the cooling system temperature fluctuates.
- *Heater hoses*: These hoses connect the water pump and engine to the heater core. They carry heated coolant to the heater core to be used to heat the passenger compartment.
- *Drive belts*: These belts provide power to drive the water pump and other accessories on the front of the engine. Three types are used: V-belts, serpentine (also called multi-groove) belts, and toothed belts.
- *Temperature indicators*: Temperature indicators provide information to the operator about engine temperature. The temperature gauge indicates engine temperature continuously. A temperature warning indicator comes on only when the engine is overheating to warn the operator that engine damage will occur if the vehicle is driven much farther.
- *Water jackets*: Water jackets are passages surrounding the cylinders and head on the engine where coolant can flow to pick up excess heat. They are sealed by replaceable core plugs.
- *Heater core*: The heater core is a small radiator used to provide heat to the passenger compartment from the hot coolant passing through it. The amount of heat can be controlled by a heater control valve.
- *Coolant*: Coolant is the liquid used to prevent freezing, overheating, and corrosion of the engine.
- *Auxiliary coolers*: Auxiliary coolers are used to cool automatic transmission fluid, power steering fluid, EGR gasses, and compressed intake air. Each of these coolers transmits heat to either the cooling system or directly to the atmosphere. Because there is such a wide variety of auxiliary coolers, refer to the manufacturer's service information for how to properly inspect the auxiliary cooler for leaks and proper operation.

Radiator

The **radiator** is located in a convenient position under the hood of the vehicle where maximum airflow can pass through it. Its actual location under the hood depends on the engine configuration, the available space, and the

shape or line of the hood itself. The radiator consists of top and bottom tanks or side tanks and a core. The radiator core allows the coolant to pass through it in either a vertical or a horizontal cross-flow direction. In addition, the radiator core serves as a good conductor of heat away from the engine.

The materials used in the radiator must be good heat conductors, such as brass, copper, or aluminum. Brass or copper is often used for tanks when combined with a brass or copper core. Modern vehicles often use plastic tanks combined with an aluminum core. This design saves weight and cost while still providing good heat transfer.

The core consists of a number of cooling tubes that carry coolant between the two tanks. The tubes can be in a horizontal (cross-flow) design or a vertical (down-flow) design **FIGURE 46-8**. In a **down-flow radiator**, the cooling tubes run top to bottom, with the tanks on the top and bottom. In a **cross-flow radiator**, the cooling tubes are arranged horizontally, with one tank on each side. Because of this arrangement, the same amount of cooling area can be achieved without the need for a very tall radiator; instead, it will be wide and short. This design feature allows the hood profile to be lower to allow for better aerodynamics, which improves fuel economy and safety by increasing the driver's vision in front of the vehicle. The function of both types of radiator configurations is the same, which is to cool the coolant before it reenters the engine.

In both the cross-flow and the down-flow design, the core is built of the same components. Although having only cooling tubes exposed to airflow would cool the coolant somewhat, radiators are designed with heat-dissipating

FIGURE 46-8 Cross-flow radiators have cooling tubes mounted horizontally, whereas down-flow radiators have tubes mounted vertically, requiring a taller hood profile.

fins to allow more surface area to dissipate heat, which is then released to the air. Coolant touches tube walls, and fins touch the tubes, so heat is removed from the coolant by conduction into the cooling fins, then by convection at the surface of the fins. Air rushing by the fins carries the heat away. Liquid coolant emerges cooler at the outlet of the radiator, since the coolant was able to give up much of its heat to the atmosphere.

Radiator Shrouding

In the interest of fuel economy (less drag coefficient), vehicle hood lines have become more streamlined and engine compartments smaller and more crowded. These changes in turn make it more difficult for ram air to flow through the radiator and around the engine. Airflow is therefore greatly reliant on shrouding above, behind, and below the radiator to direct ram air to

FIGURE 46-9 Radiator shrouding.

the radiator and from it **FIGURE 46-9**. Shrouds are also used around the radiator fan to help draw air through the entire radiator core and not just in front of the fan blades. Also, the fan shroud prevents air from simply circulating around the tips of the fan blades, instead of being drawn through the radiator. If the shrouding is removed and not replaced, such as after service has been performed, the engine will not be cooled as efficiently as it should be and will likely overheat, especially on hot days.

Radiator Pressure Cap

If coolant boils, it can be as damaging to an engine as having it freeze. Boiling coolant changes the coolant from a liquid into a gas in the engine water jackets. No liquid is left in contact with the cylinder walls or head, causing heat transfer to stop or slow to the point of overheating. Without cooling, the pistons will seize as temperatures soar with each combustion cycle, and engine meltdown can take place.

One way to prevent coolant from boiling is to use a radiator pressure cap. As coolant temperature rises, the coolant expands and pressure in the cooling system rises. The increased pressure raises the boiling point of the coolant. Engine temperature keeps rising, and the coolant expands further. Pressure builds against a spring-loaded valve in the radiator cap until, at a preset pressure, the valve opens and releases a small amount of coolant. When this valve opens, the coolant leaves the radiator through the overflow tube to the overflow container **FIGURE 46-10**. In past designs, the overflow tube would drop the coolant onto the ground, which was an environmental hazard. By releasing coolant into a coolant overflow container, the coolant can be pulled back into the system once it cools.

FIGURE 46-10 **A.** Pressure valve being forced open. **B.** Vacuum valve being pulled open.

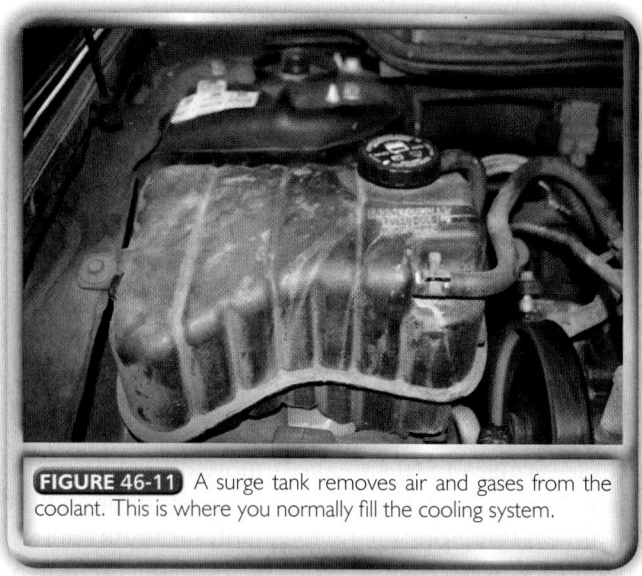

FIGURE 46-11 A surge tank removes air and gases from the coolant. This is where you normally fill the cooling system.

Coolant loses temperature in the radiator when the engine is off. When coolant cools, it contracts, and with this contraction, it creates a vacuum (low pressure) in the radiator. A vacuum valve is located in the radiator cap that will open and allow coolant to be pulled back into the radiator from the overflow container. Because of this design, no coolant is lost as with the older systems that dropped coolant onto the ground. The vacuum valve in the cap also stops low pressure from developing in the radiator and causing collapsed radiator hoses as a result of atmospheric pressure on the outside of the hose crushing the hose against the vacuum in the system.

Surge Tank

Some vehicles are equipped with a surge tank. The surge tank has coolant constantly running through it and is located higher than the top of the radiator. If the radiator sits lower than any other part in the cooling system, then gas will collect in whatever component is highest. On some vehicles this may be the heater core. To solve this problem, engineers have installed a surge tank and placed it so it is the highest component in the system. Thus, any gas in the system will make its way to this tank, ensuring that only liquid coolant circulates through the system. The surge tank has at least one line in and one line out. It is usually made of hardened plastic, which allows for a visual checking of the fluid level through the plastic. This tank is usually where the cooling system is filled or topped off with coolant. In many vehicles with a surge tank, the pressure cap is mounted on the surge tank instead of the radiator **FIGURE 46-11** .

Recovery System

A coolant recovery system maintains coolant in the system at all times. The recovery system consists of an overflow bottle, a sealed radiator pressure cap, and a small hose connecting the bottle to the radiator neck **FIGURE 46-12** . As engine temperatures rise, the coolant expands.

FIGURE 46-12 A coolant recovery system.

Pressure builds against a valve in the radiator cap until, at a preset pressure, the valve opens. Hot coolant flows out of the radiator, through the connecting hose, and into an overflow bottle. As the engine cools, coolant contracts and pressure in the cooling system drops below atmospheric pressure. Atmospheric pressure in the overflow bottle opens the vacuum valve in the radiator cap, and overflow coolant flows back into the radiator. Like water, air contains oxygen, which reacts with metals to form corrosion. With use of a recovery system, no coolant is lost and excess air is kept out of the system.

Thermostat and Housing

The **thermostat** is located under the thermostat housing. The thermostat regulates the flow of coolant, allowing coolant to flow from the engine to the radiator when the engine is running at its operating temperature. The thermostat prevents coolant from flowing to the radiator when the engine is cold to allow the engine to warm up more rapidly to reduce engine wear and emissions.

The thermostat is a spring-loaded valve that is controlled by a wax pellet located inside the valve **FIGURE 46-13**. As the temperature of the coolant rises, the wax pellet will melt and expand, forcing the spring-loaded valve open at a preset temperature. As the valve opens, coolant is allowed to flow through it. The thermostat works like a door to control movement of coolant. When the engine is cold, the door is closed; when hot, the door opens. Some dashboard temperature gauges show a slight swing of engine temperatures as the thermostat cycles slightly toward open or closed.

Some engines are designed such that the coolant bypass passage is directly under the thermostat. In those situations, the thermostat may have a flat disc attached to the bottom of it, which moves along with the thermostat. When the thermostat fully opens, the flat disc blocks off the bypass passage so that all coolant must flow through the radiator. Yet, when the thermostat partially closes, the bypass passage will be partially open. This helps give more effective cooling when the thermostat is fully open.

Most thermostats have a small hole on one side of the thermostat valve that allows any air in the system to move past the closed thermostat when the valve is closed. This is especially helpful when the cooling system has been drained and is being filled. The hole will usually contain a little pin called a jiggle valve or jiggle pin to help break the surface tension of the coolant and allow any air to flow slowly through the hole. Air trapped in the cooling system is thus able to slowly find its way to the uppermost part of the cooling system where it can be bled. When installing the thermostat, the jiggle valve

should be in the uppermost position so that as much air as possible can be bled from the system.

The thermostat and housing are normally located on the outlet side of the coolant flow from the engine. However, on some engines they are located on the inlet side of the engine. The thermostat is identified by being located in the housing connected to the inlet radiator hose. The reason for installing the thermostat on the inlet side is to better control the amount of cold water that rushes into the engine, which can create a temperature shock to the engine.

Some vehicles include a manual bleed valve on the thermostat housing or within a high part of the cooling system. After the vehicle cooling system has been serviced and refilled, the technician should carefully open the bleed valve to vent any trapped air to the atmosphere. It is good practice to bleed the system again once the engine has warmed up.

Water Pump

The water pump is usually belt driven from a pulley on the front of the crankshaft. The engine drives the water pump using an accessory V-belt or the timing belt. Some newer vehicles use an electrically driven water pump. Internally, the water pump has fanlike blades on an impeller or rotor, which is turned by a shaft connected to the pulley. The shaft rides on a heavy-duty double-row ball bearing for long life and to withstand belt tension. The shaft is sealed where it enters the pump chamber. Most water pumps have a small weep hole that sits between the seal and the bearing and vents any coolant that leaks past the seal to be drained to the outside of the engine **FIGURE 46-14**. Checking this hole for signs of coolant

FIGURE 46-13 The thermostat has a moving valve that is controlled by a wax pellet. When the wax is cool, the valve stays closed; as temperature increases, the wax melts and forces the valve open.

FIGURE 46-14 Cutaway view of water pump and weep hole.

leakage is part of the process of inspecting the engine for leaks.

The water pump is usually located at the front of the engine block; a hose typically connects it to the output of the radiator where the relatively cool coolant emerges. Coolant enters the center of the pump. As the impeller rotates, it catches the coolant and flings it outward with centrifugal force. This type of water pump is called a centrifugal pump, meaning that it creates movement of the coolant due to centrifugal force, but does not cause much buildup of pressure. Coolant is driven through the outlet into the water jackets of the engine block and to the cylinder heads. Coolant can be directed to critical hot spots, such as around the exhaust ports in the cylinder head, to stop localized overheating. The cylinder head gasket has holes of various sizes to help determine how much coolant should flow to these and other locations of the head. If the head gasket is not properly installed, cylinder head damage may result from localized overheating.

Replacing a water pump is a fairly common task that used to be performed mostly as a result of noise or leak issues on accessory-belt driven water pumps **FIGURE 46-15**. But now with many water pumps being driven by timing belts, it is common to replace the water pump along with the timing belt at the belt's recommended replacement schedule **FIGURE 46-16**. When changing this type of pump, the timing belt will need to be removed, so following the manufacturer's procedure will be necessary to prevent damage to the valves and pistons. Once the drive belt is removed from either style of water pump, the removal of the pump involves the unbolting of the pump, carefully prying it off of the mating surface, cleaning the mounting surface, and re-bolting it back in place with the appropriate gasket or O-ring.

Cooling Fan

Cooling fans are used to provide airflow through the radiator core for engine cooling. This is most needed during slow driving or stop-and-go driving. There are two main categories of cooling fans: engine driven and electric. Engine-driven cooling fans may be located on the water pump shaft or in a few cases may be attached directly to the engine crankshaft. Most vehicles today use one or more electrically driven engine cooling fans, which are mounted directly to the radiator. On a fan that is driven by the engine, engine horsepower is directly needed to drive the fan, requiring extra fuel even when the fan is not needed. Such fans are also noisy and dangerous to work around.

It takes a fair amount of energy to turn a fan, which ultimately comes from the crankshaft, consuming energy that could be used to drive the vehicle down the road. Yet, the fan is not needed during cold engine operation.

It is also not needed when the vehicle is traveling above about 35 mph (56 kph) and the airflow is strong enough to cool the radiator without using the fan. For years, vehicle manufacturers have sought ways to reduce the energy the fan uses. One type of fan design (called a flex fan) uses flexible steel or plastic blades that straighten out and lessen their **pitch** as engine speed increases. This design increases fuel economy and reduces noise

Another type of engine-driven fan uses a **viscous coupler** to connect the water pump pulley to the cooling fan. The viscous coupler is called a fan clutch since it can engage and disengage the fan from the pulley. The fan clutch typically uses two discs that have closely fitted interwoven rings and grooves. When viscous silicone oil is allowed to fill the small spaces between the rings and the grooves, it transmits torque from one disc to the other, and is used to transmit torque across the two halves of the hub. A bimetallic spring on the front moves as air

FIGURE 46-15 Replacing a water pump.

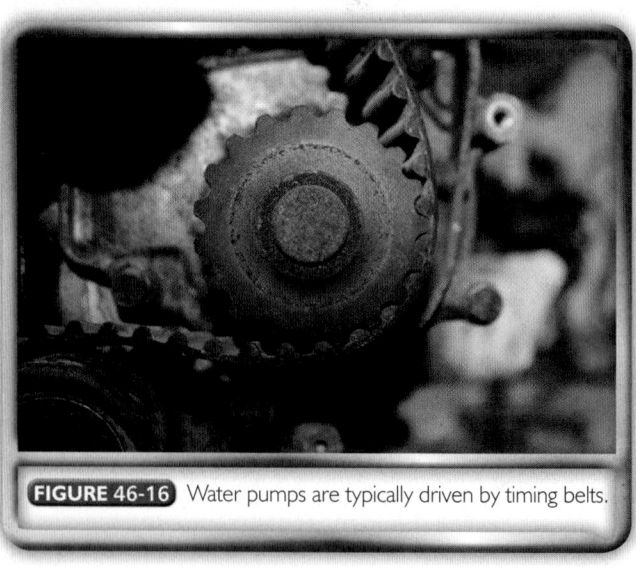

FIGURE 46-16 Water pumps are typically driven by timing belts.

temperature from the radiator changes. This spring is attached to a valve that turns and allows more silicone oil to flow into the coupler, thereby transmitting more of the pulley's speed to the fan to move more air. As air temperature decreases from air flowing through the radiator, the bimetallic spring turns the valve and the silicone oil moves out of the coupler back to the reservoir located in the clutch body. This causes the fan to slow and move less air. This type of fan is driven at all times by the accessory belt. The benefit of using a viscous clutch is to increase fuel economy by being able to cycle on and off.

A variation of the clutch fan is the solenoid-controlled fan clutch, which operates in the same manner as the thermostatic fan clutch. The clutch uses oil to control the speed of the fan in relation to engine speed (allows slip to slow fan down) and temperature of the air moving across the radiator. The only difference in the operation is that the bimetallic spring is removed and an electric solenoid is installed on the front of the clutch. This solenoid is controlled by the power train control module (PCM), based on engine coolant temperature. As temperature increases, more oil is allowed to flow to the viscous coupler and fan speed increases. As temperature decreases, oil is directed back to the reservoir in the body of the clutch and fan speed decreases. On this type of fan, a feedback sensor provides actual fan speed or rpm information back to the PCM.

As fan designs evolved to increase efficiency, and as more vehicles moved to front-wheel drive, which turns the front of the engine away from the radiator, the electric fan was introduced. Now it is by far the most common and simple type of cooling fan. It can be turned on and off easily whenever it is needed, and it can operate at full speed even though the engine is idling. This versatility makes it very efficient. It only runs when the engine is above the ideal operating temperature. In addition, since it can run at full speed independent of the engine, it can move plenty of air to cool the engine effectively.

Electric fans use an electric motor to turn an attached fan. In most cases, the fan blades are made of plastic, making them safer than metal blades. The blades can be designed to either push or pull air through the radiator, so mounting options are increased. The electric fan is controlled by one of two methods: A control module, such as the PCM, is used to energize a fan relay to turn the fan on and off, or a thermo-control switch is used. The PCM knows the temperature of the engine by means of the coolant temperature sensor. The PCM can then supply either power or ground to the fan relay, energizing the relay and fan.

The **thermo-control switch** is a temperature-sensitive switch that is mounted into the radiator or into a coolant passage on the engine. When engine temperature gets hot enough (say, 215°F [102°C]), the thermo-control switch will close and either send power directly to the fan or cause a relay to be activated, which turns on the fan. Once the engine coolant temperature cools back down, the switch opens and the fan stops.

Thermo-control switches often operate on the bimetallic strip principle. These consist of two different metals or alloys laminated back to back. As different metals and alloys heat and cool, they expand and contract at different rates. That means that if two different metals are joined, and then heated, the greater expansion of one will force the whole strip to flex into a curved shape. As the strip changes shape, it can be designed to complete an electric circuit by closing a switch, which turns the fan on.

With an electric fan, the electricity to run it comes from the alternator, which comes from the engine, which comes from the gasoline fuel. Because an electric fan typically needs to operate only part of the time, fuel is saved whenever it is off. Some manufacturers use multiple fans and control them separately, while others use multispeed fans to provide only enough fan operation to keep the coolant at the proper temperature.

Another type of cooling fan is the hydraulically operated fan. In many cases, it uses power steering fluid from the power steering pump to power the fan **FIGURE 46-17**. Because the power steering pump can create substantial power, hydraulically driven fans can be used to draw a large amount of air through the radiator. They are sometimes used on vehicles with heavy trailer towing capacities, as well as ordinary vehicles. The system consists of the power steering pump, a fluid control device, the hydraulic fan motor, and high-pressure connecting hoses. The fan is typically controlled by a pulse-width–modulated solenoid valve. The solenoid controls how

FIGURE 46-17 Hydraulically operated cooling fan.

much hydraulic fluid is directed to the fan motor. That way the PCM can vary the signal to the solenoid valve, which controls the amount of hydraulic fluid to the fan motor, which determines how fast it spins. One benefit of the hydraulically controlled fan is that it can be operated at near full speed and force even at idle, similar to an electric fan. Yet it can tap into more engine power than the electric fan, so it can be more heavy duty.

Radiator Hoses

On most vehicles there are two radiator hoses: the upper hose and the lower hose, also called the inlet hose and the outlet hose. <u>Radiator hoses</u> are rubber hoses that are subject to high pressure; they are therefore reinforced with a layer of fabric, typically nylon, to give them strength and prevent them from ballooning, and yet still be flexible. They are often molded into a special shape to suit the particular make and model of vehicle. Some radiator hoses, especially lower hoses, have a spiral wire inside to keep the hose from collapsing during heavy acceleration when the water pump is drawing a lot of water from the radiator. The reason radiator hoses need to be flexible is that engines are mounted on flexible engine mounts to reduce noise and vibration. Since the radiator is mounted to the vehicle body, which does not move with the engine, the hoses must be able to move.

The top radiator hose is typically attached to the thermostat housing, which allows the heated coolant to enter the inlet side of the radiator. The bottom or lower radiator hose is connected between the outlet of the radiator and the inlet of the water pump. The radiator hoses are held in position by clamps. These can be spring clamps, wire wound clamps, or worm drive clamps. Radiator hoses deteriorate over time and use. They can also be damaged by oil or fuel leaking on them. Thus, they need to be inspected and changed periodically. Many vehicle manufacturers recommend radiator and heater hose replacement approximately every 4 to 5 years or 48,000 to 60,000 miles (77,000 to 97,000 km). When servicing hoses, be sure to reinstall the clamps correctly or the seal between the hose and the component will leak. Every component has a raised ridge built into it. The hose clamp has to clamp on the inside of this ridge, but not on top of it. If the hose clamp is on top of the ridge, the hose is likely to pop off once the cooling system becomes pressurized **FIGURE 46-18**.

Heater Hoses

The heater hoses carry a smaller volume of coolant than do the radiator hoses. Some heater coolant hoses have special shapes and must be ordered specially for the

FIGURE 46-18 **A.** Proper installation of radiator hose clamp. **B.** Improper installation.

vehicle being serviced. Other heater hoses are straight and can be replaced by heater hose that is supplied on a roll. The construction of the heater hose is the same as the radiator hose, with a reinforcing material embedded into it.

There are two hoses for the heater core: one inlet hose and one outlet hose. The heater hose directs hot coolant to the heater core to provide heat to the inside of the passenger compartment. Some vehicles will use a coolant control valve in line with the heater core hose. The **coolant control valve** controls the flow of hot coolant to the heater core as requested by the driver. The fittings on the valve, like other fittings in the cooling system, usually have a raised ridge to aid in sealing and keeping the hose from blowing off. The heater hoses are sealed and retained by the use of a hose clamp. As with radiator hoses, be sure to install hose clamps correctly. All hoses are subject to hot coolant and high underhood temperatures, and they will deteriorate and fail over time. Some coolant hoses are made of silicone, which is designed to withstand heat better and last longer than the standard rubber hose. Be sure to inspect hoses whenever you are servicing the customer's vehicle.

FIGURE 46-19 The cooling system may have multiple flexible coolant hoses, as seen in this cooling system schematic.

Coolant Hoses

There are additional coolant hoses that carry hot coolant through the cooling system, which are often ignored when checking hoses **FIGURE 46-19**. As part of a maintenance inspection, the technician will inspect the upper and lower radiator hoses along with the heater hoses, but may forget about these other hoses, which can fail if neglected. It is critical that these hoses be checked. Any break in the system will dump the coolant and cause the engine to quickly overheat.

One of the additional hoses is the bypass hose. The bypass hose is typically located on the water pump and connects to the intake manifold on many V-configured engines, such as a V6 or V8. This hose allows the water pump to circulate the water in the engine when the thermostat is closed. This hose is made of the same materials as the radiator hoses and heater hoses. Another coolant hose that may be used is a throttle body coolant line. This hose runs from the intake up to the throttle body to keep the throttle body from freezing during cold outside temperatures when there is high moisture content in the air. The cold wet air being pulled through the throttle plate may create ice, restrict airflow, and cause the throttle to stick. Running coolant through the throttle body eliminates this problem. There are many possible configurations of additional cooling system hoses, such as to remote oil coolers, turbochargers, or even some alternators. In a compressed natural gas vehicle, coolant hoses are routed to the CNG pressure regulator under the vehicle to keep the regulator warm. A similar setup may be used for the engine's idle air control motor and more. The point is to be sure to inspect all of the coolant hoses used on the vehicle.

Drive Belts

Typically, the water pump is turned by a belt that is driven by the crankshaft. This belt may be part of the accessory drive belt system found on the front of the engine. If the belt is located on the front of the engine, it may be tensioned by a separate tensioner or by simply moving a component such as the alternator on slotted bolt holes. Some engines use the camshaft timing belt or chain as the drive for the water pump.

There are four types of drive belts **FIGURE 46-20**:

- *V-type:* A V-type belt has a wedge-shaped interior and sits inside a corresponding groove in the pulley. The sides of the V-belt wedge in the sides of the pulley.
- *Serpentine:* A serpentine-type belt, also called a multigroove V-belt, has a flat profile with a number of small V-shaped grooves running lengthwise along the inside of the belt. These grooves are the exact reverse of the grooves in the outer edge of the pulleys; they increase the contact surface area, as well as prevent the belt from slipping off the pulley as it rotates. The serpentine belt is used to drive multiple accessories and to save underhood space forward of the engine. It winds its way around the crankshaft pulley, water pump, alternator, air-conditioning compressor, and tensioner. Most serpentine belts use a spring-loaded tensioner to maintain proper tightness of the belt and prevent it from slipping.
- *Stretch belt:* A stretch belt looks like an ordinary serpentine belt but is found on vehicles without a tensioner. It is made of a special material that allows it to stretch just enough to be installed over the pulleys, but then shrink back to its original

FIGURE 46-20 Belts. **A.** V-belt. **B.** Serpentine belt. **C.** Stretch belt. **D.** Timing belt.

size, which is shorter than the distance around the pulleys. This stretchiness keeps the belt properly tensioned. Stretch belts require special tools to install and are usually cut off when being removed.

- *Toothed belt:* The toothed belt has teeth on the inside that are perpendicular to the belt and fit inside the teeth of a gear. Timing belts are always toothed belts to keep the camshaft running exactly half the speed of the crankshaft. To save on labor cost, these belts are generally replaced whenever a water pump replacement is required. And the water pump is generally replaced whenever the timing belt is changed.

The technician must be careful when replacing drive belts to avoid tensioning them too much, or too little. If excessive tension is placed on the belt, the water pump bearing can be overloaded, get hot, and fail due to excessive working load. Follow the manufacturer's service information for correct tensioning.

Tensioners

Tensioners are used to keep the drive belt tight around the pulleys to ensure the least amount of slippage without causing damage to component bearings. Tensioners can be either manual or automatic. Manual tensioners come in a wide variety of configurations. One type uses a pulley that is adjusted by turning a tensioning bolt. When the bolt is tightened, the pulley moves against the belt with increased tension; if the bolt is rotated the other direction, tension decreases. The tensioner is locked in place by tightening the nut on the front of the pulley.

A spring-loaded automatic tensioner is typically used with serpentine accessory belts **FIGURE 46-21**. This type of tensioner is very simple to operate and adjusts itself, so there is no chance of getting it too tight. However, be sure to note the routing of the serpentine belt when servicing it; there are many pulleys to route around, and it can become confusing if you do not have a routing picture. Automatic tensioners can wear out and cause belt slippage or become noisy. Also, a seized front engine drive component such as a tensioner can cause a no-crank, or slow crank, engine condition that mimics a seized engine. Simply loosening or removing the belt may help to diagnose the problem.

If the water pump is driven by the timing belt, one of two types of tensioners may be used. One type is the spring-loaded tensioner, in which a spring sets the tension and a bolt locks the tensioner into position. The other type is the oil-actuated tensioner. The oil-actuated tensioner uses oil pressure from the engine to provide additional tension on the belt. Regardless of the style of tensioner, belt tension can be checked with a belt tension

FIGURE 46-21 A spring-loaded automatic tensioner is typically used with serpentine accessory belts.

tool and compared to specifications, which are typically published in the service information.

Temperature Indicators

Temperature indicators can come in two forms: a temperature gauge or a temperature light located in the instrument cluster **FIGURE 46-22**. The two forms are sometimes used in conjunction. Overheating can heavily damage an engine, so a warning indicator is necessary. A temperature warning light is a good indicator of an overheating condition, but it cannot indicate a condition where the engine stays below operating temperature, which causes excess engine wear, increased emission output, and decreased fuel economy. A temperature gauge indicates to the driver whether the temperature is normal, below normal, or above normal. But drivers can forget to monitor it, which means that the engine could overheat without the driver noticing. Thus, a warning light in addition to a temperature gauge gives the best of both worlds.

Temperature gauges and warning lights both operate from a signal sent from a coolant temperature sensor located on the engine in a coolant passage. When engine coolant gets hotter than it should, the sensor causes the warning light or message to turn on to alert the driver that the engine is overheating. The temperature gauge also uses a sensor, which is designed to continuously indicate the temperature of the engine. The sensor for either type of warning device sits in engine coolant so that an accurate reading is always given—that is, as long as there is no air in the cooling system.

There may also be a low coolant indicator that shows when engine coolant level is low. This system works by having a low level sensor in the surge tank or overflow

FIGURE 46-22 **A.** Temperature gauge. **B.** Temperature warning lamp.

bottle that turns on a warning light in the instrument cluster if the coolant level falls below an acceptable level. If the low coolant indicator illuminates, there is a good chance that the cooling system has a leak that will need to be found.

Water Jackets

Coolant passages such as water jackets are cast into the block and heads during the manufacturing process. They are designed to allow coolant to circulate around the tops and sides of the cylinders and are critical for the transfer of excess heat energy. It is crucial to the efficiency of heat transfer to keep the coolant passages free of scaling and buildup that can restrict heat transfer and coolant flow by ensuring proper cooling system maintenance. As part of proper maintenance, the technician must drain, flush, and refill the cooling system according to the recommended maintenance intervals. (Also see earlier reference to head gasket design.)

Core Plugs

Core plugs are also known as soft plugs or expansion plugs. These aluminum, brass, or steel plugs are designed

to seal the openings left from the casting process where the casting sand was removed **FIGURE 46-23**. Under some conditions, the core plugs might pop out if the engine coolant is allowed to freeze—that is, if the proper mixture of anti-freeze was not used. Because water expands when it freezes, the block or heads can crack internally or externally near the coolant passages. Sometimes the core plug will be pushed out and the coolant will leak out before the block cracks; however, that is not what they are designed for, so do not rely on soft plugs to protect the engine from freezing. Also, core plugs can rust out and start leaking coolant, so do not forget to inspect them when trying to locate a coolant leak.

Heater Core

The heater core is simply a small radiator that is mounted inside the heater box in the passenger compartment. As air is blown past the fins of the core, heat energy is radiated to the air and used to heat the passenger compartment for comfort. The heater core connects to the engine's cooling system and is supplied with hot water by circulation of the water pump. Typically, hot water enters the bottom of the radiator and exits the top; thus, the hot water flows from the bottom to the top of the heater core so more heat can be pulled from the coolant. Heater cores are typically constructed of aluminum, brass, or copper.

Heater Control Valve

If used, the heater control valve is mounted in one of the heater hoses that supply coolant to the heater core. This valve controls the flow of coolant to the heater core to control the temperature of the air desired by the operator. The climate control panel, which is adjusted by the operator, controls this valve. This feature is discussed further in the Electronic Climate Control chapter.

FIGURE 46-23 Core plugs are designed to seal the openings left from the casting process of the block and heads.

Air Doors and Actuators

The heater box consists of many air doors, which are plastic or metal flaps that seal off parts of the air box to control airflow **FIGURE 46-24**. The air doors are moved by one of three methods: cable, vacuum actuator, or electric actuator, called a stepper motor. The **actuator** is a device that is electrically or vacuum controlled and is used to physically move doors within the heater box to control airflow. This system is discussed in detail in the Electronic Climate Control chapter.

The layout and function of the doors depend on the design of the system. Most systems flow air through the evaporator at all times, while air can be diverted around the heater core when heat is not wanted. Also, for best defrost operation, the air is directed first over the evaporator to remove any moisture from the air. Then it is directed over the heater core to warm it up. This process results in dry, warm air to defog or defrost the windshield.

Coolant Types

As mentioned earlier, water-cooled engines must be protected from freezing, boiling, and corrosion. Water absorbs a larger amount of heat than most other liquids. But it freezes at a relatively high temperature, and it is corrosive. Mixing anti-freeze with water provides an adequate coolant solution by lowering the freezing point of water, raising the boiling point of water a bit, and providing anti-corrosive properties.

There are several types of coolants available for use in the liquid-cooled automobile engine. The recommended coolant depends on the original equipment manufacturer's (OEM) recommendation. It may be influenced by the metallurgy of the engine parts and the length of time or

A typical air box

FIGURE 46-24 Typical heater box and air doors.

mileage that the manufacturer has determined between scheduled services.

It is important to note that brands and types of coolant (anti-freeze) will differ from one manufacturer to another. Some believe coolant can be identified according to its color, which may be anything from green or purple to yellow/gold, orange, blue, or pink. OEM cooling system designs and coolant recommendations have changed in recent years, so the color of coolant is no longer a reliable way to identify a particular type of anti-freeze. Mixing types of anti-freeze can cause a reaction that turns the chemicals in anti-freeze to sludge that plugs up the passages in the system, including the radiator and heater core. Always read the container label and follow OEM coolant recommendations.

Most coolant types start with a base of ethylene glycol and add specific corrosion inhibitors, lubricants, and other additives, which all determine the type of coolant it is. Each coolant will have antifoaming and antiscale additives. Maintaining the proper coolant acid/alkaline pH balance is also critical (which will also determine when to perform coolant replacement).

Ethylene glycol is a toxic chemical that works very well as an anti-freeze. Ethylene glycol mixes well with water and has a low viscosity, allowing it to circulate easily through the cooling system. Propylene glycol performs essentially the same as ethylene glycol except it is not as toxic. In fact, propylene glycol anti-freeze is sold as a non-toxic coolant. The types of ethylene glycol or propylene glycol anti-freeze/coolants available, based on the categories of corrosion inhibitors used in them, are as follows:

- Inorganic acid technology (IAT)
- Organic acid technology (OAT)
- Hybrid organic acid technology (HOAT)
- Poly organic acid technology (POAT)

The first category of coolant, IAT, is an early designed chemical formula that became available in the 1930s and was green in color. This coolant is still in use today. It contains phosphate and silicate as corrosion additives. Phosphate protects iron and steel parts, while silicate keeps aluminum from corroding. IAT coolant needs to be changed every 2 years or 24,000 miles (39,000 km), since the additives break down.

The second category, OAT, is a longer-lasting coolant. Called extended-life coolant, it is designed to be changed at 5 years or 150,000 miles (241,000 km), a giant increase in the change interval from IAT coolant. OAT coolant was introduced in North America around 1994 and was intended for certain vehicles of that year and newer. One example of OAT is Dex-Cool, the orange coolant used by GM. The anti-corrosion additives in OAT coolant do not break down as quickly, which explains the longer service time. The primary additives in OAT coolant are organic acids, such as sebacate. These coolants do not use the additives used in IAT coolants.

The third category, HOAT, is a coolant that contains a mixture of inorganic and organic additives. This type of coolant can use silicate and organic acid; it is the best of both worlds of coolants. Some manufacturers found that without silicate, problems arose if the system was not properly serviced, such as oxidation of the coolant, leading to breakdown of the corrosion inhibitors and, ultimately, failure of engine parts and gaskets. Other tests indicate that silicates cause premature water pump failures. Less silicate is present in HOAT coolant than in IAT coolants, so this coolant is still considered extended life and will need to be changed at 5 years or 150,000 miles (241,000 km). An example of this type of coolant is the yellow coolant used by Ford.

The fourth category, POAT, is a relatively new coolant that contains a proprietary blend of corrosion inhibitors. It is a very long-life coolant, providing up to 7 years or 250,000 miles (402,000 km) of protection. It is claimed that it is compatible with most other types of coolant, but check the manufacturer's current service information.

Within the OAT or HOAT classifications, manufacturers may specify different corrosion additives and colored dyes. It is important that you service the vehicle with the coolant that is called for by the manufacturer. In most cases, you should never mix two or more types of coolants and/or refill with a type other than that originally used in a vehicle. Doing so will likely compromise the cooling system's service life and cause premature failure of the system.

▶ Diagnosis

The cooling system is an often overlooked part of the automobile. It does its job very effectively and is rarely thought of, until problems arise. The lack of periodic service of the cooling system according to OEM maintenance schedules is the leading reason that cooling systems fail. Properly performed cooling system maintenance will ensure that the cooling system continues to perform as designed.

Common failures of the cooling system can require repairs ranging from simple to complex. An example of a failure that would require a simple repair is a radiator hose clamp that has not been installed properly and that is creating a leak. The customer notices the leak and brings the vehicle in for service. An example of a more complex repair is a vehicle that needs a new head and block

because a severe pH imbalance in the cooling system has heavily corroded the internal metal. Corrosion can build up to the point that normal cooling system operation cannot be restored without replacing multiple parts, including the engine itself, due to corrosion pitting of the engine block or cylinder head, leading to an internal coolant leak. Corrosion can also coat and/or block coolant passages and lead to an engine that runs hotter than normal or overheats.

Another common customer complaint is that the heater does not produce heat when turned on. This issue can result from a group of problems that will have to be diagnosed by the technician, but often the culprit is a stuck-open thermostat that will not let the engine come up to operating temperatures. If the thermostat fails, it can fail in either the open position or the closed position. If it sticks closed, the result will be an overheating condition since coolant cannot get to the radiator to be cooled. If it sticks open, the engine will not warm up fully, leading to excessive engine wear, higher emissions, and reduced fuel economy.

Overheating conditions can have several causes, such as low coolant level due to a leak, a stuck-closed thermostat, a faulty radiator cap, clogged radiator tubes or fins, an inoperative cooling fan, a water pump impeller that is eroded or slipping on the shaft, or a blown head gasket, to name a few. Understanding how the cooling system works, as well as the manufacturer's test procedures, is necessary to successfully diagnose and repair the vehicle.

When diagnosing a cooling system problem, you need to use all of your senses to help determine what is wrong. Your sense of touch can allow you to feel for hot and cold parts in the system. For example, if the engine is overheating, but the upper radiator hose is cold, that could indicate a thermostat that is stuck closed. Your sense of smell could pick up the scent of anti-freeze leaking into the passenger compartment from a leaky heater core. Your sense of hearing can tell you that the accessory belt is loose and the water pump is slipping. And your sense of sight could see the telltale stream of coolant leaking out of the water pump weep hole or a rusted-through soft plug. It is advisable not to use your sense of taste when diagnosing cooling system issues.

If the problem cannot be determined by your senses alone, you may have to resort to tools or equipment to help you locate the issue. A cooling system pressure tester will allow you to pressurize the cooling system and radiator cap and check for any visible leaks. Starting the engine and using an exhaust analyzer to sniff the vapors coming out of the neck of the radiator can indicate if there is a small leak from one of the combustion chambers, which is leaking combustion gases into the cooling system. Using a cylinder leakage tester and pressurizing each cylinder can help locate which cylinder has the combustion leak, due to either a blown head gasket or a cracked head. If the leak is a small external leak and the source cannot be located easily, you may need to use a fluorescent dye and black light to help make it stand out better.

An infrared temperature gun is a useful tool that can be used to measure the operating temperature of the engine to verify that the engine really is overheating or not. Or it can be used to check the radiator for cold spots, which would indicate blockage within the core of the radiator. A scan tool can be a quick way to monitor the operating temperature, verify any cooling system diagnostic trouble codes (DTCs), or command the electric fan to come on. As you can see, understanding how cooling systems operate along with observing what is happening, and having a few tools available, can take you a long way toward diagnosing customers' cooling system concerns.

Tools

A properly trained and experienced technician will use special tools for diagnosing and servicing the engine cooling system. These tools include **FIGURE 46-25**:

- *Coolant system pressure tester:* Used to apply pressure to the cooling system to diagnose leakage complaints. Under pressure, coolant may leak internally to the combustion chamber, intake or exhaust system, or the engine lubrication system. It can also leak externally to the outside of the engine.
- *Hydrometer:* Used to test coolant mixture and freeze protection by testing the specific gravity of the coolant. You must use a hydrometer specifically designed for the anti-freeze you are testing.
- *Refractometer:* Used to test coolant mixture and freeze protection by testing the fluid's ability to bend light. This tester can be used with any type of anti-freeze.
- *Coolant pH test strips:* Used to test the acid-to-alkalinity balance of the coolant.
- *Coolant dye kit:* Used to aid leak detection by adding dye to coolant and using an ultraviolet light source (black light) to trace to the source of the leak; the dye glows fluorescent when a black light is shined on it.
- *Infrared temperature sensor:* A noncontact thermometer used to check actual temperatures and variations of temperature throughout the cooling system to help pinpoint faulty parts and system blockages.
- *Thermometer:* Used to check the temperature of air exiting the heating ducts.
- *Voltmeter:* Used to check for electrical problems such as cooling fan and temperature gauge issues.
- *Belt tension gauge:* Used to check belt tension.
- *Serpentine belt wear gauge:* Used to check if the serpentine belt grooves are worn past their specifications.
- *Radiator clamp pliers:* Used to safely remove spring-type radiator clamps.
- *Borescope:* Used for examining internal passages for evidence of a coolant leak.
- *Scan tool:* Used to activate the cooling fan through bidirectional controls for testing; to monitor cooling sensor operation and to command air door actuators when testing low heat complaints; and to read DTCs related to cooling system operation.
- *Cooling system flush machine:* Used to flush coolant backward through the system with cleaners

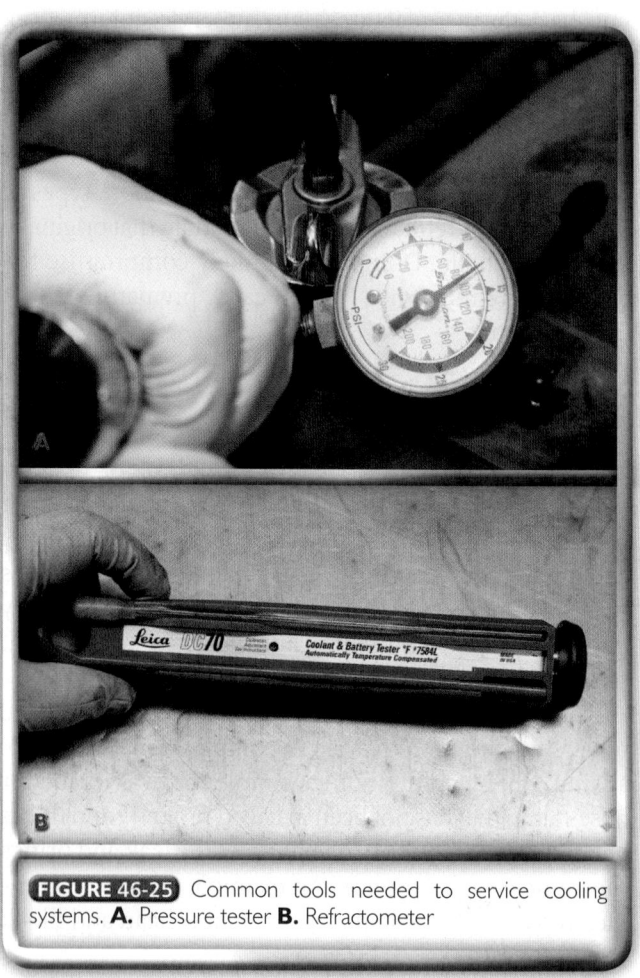

FIGURE 46-25 Common tools needed to service cooling systems. **A.** Pressure tester **B.** Refractometer

that remove corrosion buildup and old coolant. Most of these machines have their own pump so the vehicle does not have to run to perform the flush.

- *Exhaust gas analyzer:* Used to detect exhaust gases that are finding their way into the cooling system due to a leaking head gasket or damaged head or block. Be careful not to allow liquid coolant to be picked up by the analyzer probe.

Visual Inspection

Many times a visual inspection of the cooling system will give you a good indication of any issues. Check the level of the coolant in the overflow bottle and radiator. At the same time, check the condition of the coolant to see if it is cloudy or contaminated. Also check the belt condition and for the proper tension, and check hoses for any leaks or wear. If the sweet aroma of coolant is detected when the engine is first started, check for leaking coolant at the heater box drain, which would indicate a possible cracked or rotted leaking heater core. Check the engine exhaust for white smoke. A head gasket failure or a cracked head or valve seat may cause coolant to leak into the exhaust manifold and be seen as white smoke, especially when combustion pressures are high when accelerating. Also start the engine with the radiator cap off and look for bubbles from combustion in the radiator. Bubbles would indicate a leak in the combustion chamber, likely at the head gasket. Disassembly and inspection would need to occur to verify that it is the head gasket and not a cracked head or block.

Safety

When working around the cooling system, care must be taken particularly if the engine is at operating temperature, as the coolant may be hot enough to scald. Always allow the system to cool before removing the radiator or pressure cap, and use extreme caution when removing the radiator cap. If you must remove the radiator cap from a hot system, wear protective gloves and eyewear and place a cloth fender cover or other large rag on top of the radiator cap before releasing it slowly, to the first (safety) point, to prevent the pressure inside from erupting.

Testing the Cooling System for Leaks

Pressure testing the cooling system for leaks is usually an effective way to locate leaks since it causes coolant to leak out much more quickly, making leaks easier to locate.

But before you pressurize the system, make sure it is topped off with coolant or water. Otherwise, the leak could be above the coolant level and only leak air, which is much harder to observe. Topping off leads to quicker pressurization because it removes air, which is compressible. Also, if the system is full of liquid, the pressure reading on the gauge will fall faster if there is a leak.

The pressure tester puts pressure on the cooling system, and with pressure applied, leaks generally show up easily, as identified by coolant coming from the source. The use of a droplight and a mirror may be necessary to see behind the engine or in tight areas. Don't forget to check the heater core in the passenger compartment. If the pressure gauge is losing pressure, ensure that the tester is installed correctly; if it still loses pressure, ensure that the tool is working properly. Once the tool is verified and you cannot find an external leak, you will know that the cooling system may be leaking internally into the engine. Check engine oil for evidence of coolant. It will have a milky appearance on the dipstick. If coolant is not leaking into the oil, it could be leaking into the cylinder. Remove the spark plugs and look for coolant being burned in the cylinders, as evidenced by a color-stained spark plug insulator. A combustion chamber experiencing a coolant leak will appear to be steam cleaned. A borescope can be used to inspect the cylinders through the spark plug holes.

Normally the engine should be off when carrying out any visual inspection of the system or when you connect test equipment such as the pressure tester. However, it is possible that the leak only occurs when the engine is running, such as around the water pump seal, making it necessary to run the engine while testing. If you do have to run the engine after the tester has been installed and pressurized, make sure to watch the pressure gauge and release excess pressure as the engine heats up. When the engine is running, make sure you keep well away from any rotating or hot parts.

Also remember to pressure test the radiator cap, since a leak at the cap will prevent the cooling system from building pressure. Low pressure on the coolant leads to a lower boiling point, which can cause coolant to boil at normal operating temperatures. Many a technician has been fooled into thinking that the vehicle had a serious overheating problem after changing the thermostat, water pump, and so on, when all it needed was a radiator cap.

A pressure tester is normally used to test the cooling system for both internal and external leaks. Most pressure testers are hand operated and come with a number of adapters to fit a variety of cooling systems. Adapters are used to connect the tester to the radiator, surge tank, or radiator cap.

To test the cooling system pressure, follow the steps in **SKILL DRILL 46-1**:

1 Before pressure testing the system, inspect it for any obvious signs of leaks. These may show up as puddles under the vehicle or on the engine. Check for obvious leaks at the radiator core, radiator tanks, coolant and heater hoses, water pump seal and weep hole, heater box drain, and all accessible engine core plugs. Also inspect the cooling fan, drive belt, and radiator cap and seals.

2 The operating pressure should be indicated on the outside of the radiator cap. Refer to the service information or vehicle owner's manual to check that the pressure cap installed has the correct pressure rating. Attach the radiator cap to the tester with an adapter, and pump up the pressure. The pressure should hold just below the relief pressure setting. If the cap will not hold or cannot reach pressure, or if it does not vent at that pressure, then replace it with a new cap of the correct type and pressure rating. (**Photo 1**)

3 Before pressure testing the integrity of the cooling system, top off the coolant level. Attach the cooling system tester to the radiator. Pump up the system pressure to slightly above the specified radiator cap pressure. (**Photo 2**)

4 Observe the pressure reading over a few minutes. During this time, inspect the entire cooling system for any signs of leakage. If the pressure drops, and there is no visible external leak, then the leak is probably internal. If there are any visible leaks, or the pressure drops, discuss the test results with your supervisor. (**Photo 3**)

> ### ▶ TECHNICIAN TIP
>
> If you need to replace a pressure cap, use only a cap with the correct recommended pressure. If a cap with a lower pressure rating is installed, it will lower the boiling point of the coolant. Alternatively, a higher rated cap will increase the boiling point and could result in a hose, radiator, or heater core bursting if pressures get too high.

Verifying Engine Operating Temperature

Technicians need to verify engine operating temperature whenever the customer complains about an overheating issue, an underheating issue such as inadequate heat from the heater, or poor fuel economy. Verifying the operating temperature involves using an

SKILL DRILL | 46-1 | Testing the Cooling System Pressure

1 Inspect for leaks. Verify specified cooling system pressure, install the radiator cap on the pressure tester, and pressurize the cap to the correct pressure. It should hold pressure at approximately the rated pressure and vent at slightly above the rated pressure.

2 Top off the radiator with coolant or water, and install the tester. Pressurize the system to the specified cap pressure.

3 Watch the pressure reading for a drop while performing a visual check for any leaks. Check heater hoses, soft plugs, and any heater cores; determine necessary action.

infrared noncontact temperature gun to check whether the on-vehicle temperature indicators, such as the temperature gauge and coolant temperature sensor, are operating accurately. The temperature gun, as described earlier, measures the amount of heat energy (temperature) of an object. Just realize that some objects do not conduct heat as well as others; if you can point the temperature gun at a metal component, it will produce a more accurate reading. If pointed toward the engine's thermostat housing (or next to it), with the engine fully warmed up, a close approximation of the engine's operating temperature can be measured and compared to the specifications. Note that a vehicle with an electric fan will usually have two listed temperatures—one temperature at which the fan should turn on and another temperature at which it should turn off. Anywhere between those temperatures is the operating temperature in this situation. If the operating temperature is correct, verify that the vehicle's temperature gauge is reading accurately. Also, use a scan tool and compare the reading from the coolant temperature sensor to the temperature gun reading to verify that the PCM is receiving the correct temperature signal.

To verify the engine operating temperature, follow the steps in **SKILL DRILL 46-2**:

1. If the vehicle is in for an overheating concern, verify that the coolant level is correct before starting the engine. If the coolant is low, check for the presence of a leak before measuring the operating temperature. Start the engine and allow it to reach full operational temperature, monitoring the temperature along the way in case it starts to overheat.

2. Using an infrared temperature gun, test the temperature of the engine near the location of the thermostat or coolant temperature sensor. Compare to specifications.

3. Using a scan tool, retrieve the engine coolant temperature sensor temperature reading.

4. Be aware that there will be some temperature difference because the temperature sensor is sitting in the coolant and the temperature gun is measuring the surface temperature near the sensor.

5. Compare the results from the temperature gun, the coolant temperature sensor, and the vehicle's temperature gauge; this gives you a good idea of the engine's operating temperature.

Inspecting and Testing the Cooling Fan

The cooling fan is a critical part in the cooling system. When coolant moves through the engine, it picks up heat. Even if the coolant is picking up the heat from the engine and moving it to the radiator, air still has to move across the radiator to remove the heat from the coolant. The cooling fan must operate to pull air across the radiator at times when airflow is low, such as when sitting in traffic. If the cooling fan stops working and the vehicle sits in traffic, engine heat will continue to build, possibly until the coolant's boiling point is reached. If reached, the pressure relief valve in the radiator cap will vent, releasing steam from the radiator and producing a hissing sound. The customer may note that a temperature warning light has come on and/or the temperature gauge has moved to its full hot position. If the engine is operated in this condition, it will be damaged. It is possible to even create damage to the automatic transmission if the engine gets too hot since the transmission fluid is typically cooled through the cooler located in the radiator.

When testing the fan, start by determining what type of fan the vehicle is equipped with—mechanical fan, clutch fan, electric fan, or hydraulic fan. Mechanical fans are the easiest to inspect, typically requiring only a visual inspection. Check the condition and tension of the drive belt, the condition of the pulley, and the condition of the fan blades themselves. Especially look for cracks in any metal fan blades, since they can cause the blade to be ripped off and thrown with deadly force. It is also possible that someone previously installed the fan blades backward, which lowers the effectiveness of the fan.

A clutch fan is inspected in the same way as the mechanical fan, but the clutch also needs to be tested. First, with the engine off, the bearings in the fan clutch can be tested by trying to move the blades frontward and backward, and then rotating them to see if there is any play in the bearings in any direction. To test the operation of the fan clutch, some manufacturers specify placing cardboard in front of the radiator to block most of it. The engine is then started with the vehicle in the shop, while monitoring the engine temperature and watching/listening to see if the fan clutch engages at the proper engine temperature. If it does not, it most likely will need to be replaced, although some fan clutches can be refilled with silicone oil.

Electric fans are quite reliable. If they do cause trouble, it is usually because they don't come on when they are supposed to. Since electric fans are electrically operated, diagnosing them is quite different than diagnosing mechanical fans. Be aware that some electric fans can come on automatically, even when the key is off, so be careful when working around them. In fact, you should unplug the fan's electrical connector before physically inspecting the fan assembly. Just be sure to reconnect it when you are finished. Once the fan is disconnected, check that the fan is free to turn and does not catch or bind on any of the shrouding. If it is free to rotate, then the electrical system and the fan motor itself will need to be tested.

To inspect and test the cooling fan, follow the steps in **SKILL DRILL 46-3**:

1 Refer to manufacturer's service information for proper operation of the cooling fan. For this example, we will be using an electric cooling fan on a 1996 or newer vehicle.

2 Install a scan tool to the data link connector, often located under the dash, and establish communication with the vehicle.

3 Find the bidirectional controls of the scan tool and command the cooling fan on.

4 If the cooling fan comes on and runs, check for intermittent operation by wiggling connectors and wiring to the cooling fan. If the fan stops intermittently when wiggling connectors, check for improper pin fit in the connector. You may have to replace the connector to repair this concern. If the fan continues to operate during wiggle test, move to the next step. **(Photo 1)**

5 Pull up cooling temperature sensor data on the scan tool. Point an infrared temperature gun at the

SKILL DRILL | 46-3 | Inspecting and Testing the Cooling Fan

1 Install the scan tool. Find the bidirectional controls and command the fan on. Verify fan operation.

2 Use a temperature gun to measure the operating temperature and compare its reading to the coolant temperature displayed on the scan tool. If substantially different, diagnose the issue and determine necessary actions.

3 If the fan does not operate, wiggle test the fan wires.

5 If it still does not work, measure the voltage drop to the input terminal of the fan. If substantially less than battery voltage is present, use a wiring diagram of the fan circuit to diagnose the cause.

5 If voltage is present to the input terminal, measure the voltage drop on the ground side of the fan.

6 If the voltage drop is acceptable on the ground side, measure the continuity of the fan motor with an ohmmeter. If out of specs, replace the fan motor.

thermostat housing to verify that engine operation temperature is nearly the same as that displayed on the scan tool. If the temperature is off excessively, then testing of the coolant temperature sensor and wiring will have to be performed. **(Photo 2)**

6 If the fan does not operate, wiggle test the fan wires. If it still does not work, measure the voltage drop to the input terminal of the fan. If there is no voltage, then using a wiring diagram of the fan circuit, diagnose the cause. **(Photo 3)**

7 If voltage is present at the input terminal, check the voltage drop on the ground side of the fan circuit. **(Photo 4)**

8 If the ground is good, check the continuity of the fan motor with an ohmmeter. If out of specs, replace the fan motor. **(Photo 5)**

Inspecting and Testing Heater Control Valves

Heater control valves control the flow of coolant to the heater core so that the operator can control heater output. If this valve becomes stuck open, the operator will not be able to turn down the heat or the air conditioning will not be as cold as before. If the valve sticks shut, the customer will complain of no heat in the vehicle. The problem can be with the valve or the control system. The valve can get plugged up with contaminants in the coolant, or the lever can slip on the shaft that turns the valve. If it is cable operated, the cable can slip, or even corrode in place. If it is vacuum operated, the diaphragm can get a hole in it, the vacuum hose can leak or fall off, or the vacuum controller can quit working. If it is electrically operated, the motor can seize or the circuit can go bad. Heater control valves can also leak coolant, so they need to be inspected for leaks. In fact, one of the first indicators of low coolant in a vehicle is that the heater stops blowing hot air, or blows hot air intermittently. Always verify that the coolant is full before spending too much time tracking down any kind of heater issues.

To test the heater control valve, follow the steps of the **SKILL DRILL 46-4**:

1 Verify that the coolant level is full. Bring the engine up to operating temperature by running the engine for the appropriate amount of time.

2 Locate the heater control valve in line with the heater hose running to the heater core. **(Photo 1)**

3 Have an assistant turn the temperature selector to hot and observe if the control valve lever is moving and the vent temperature is becoming hot. **(Photo 2)**

4 Have an assistant turn the temperature selector to cold and observe if the control valve lever is moving and the vent temperature is becoming cold. If the lever is not moving, determine if it is actuated by vacuum, cable, or electricity. Follow service information to diagnosis. One helpful tip is that both heater hoses will be hot if coolant is flowing through the heater core. One will be hot and the other cooler if it is not running through the heater

SKILL DRILL 46-4 Inspecting and Testing Heater Control Valves

1 Verify that the cooling system is topped off, and bring the engine to full operating temperature. Locate the heater control valve.

2 Move the temperature control to hot and measure the vent temperature. It should be hot.

3 Move the temperature control to cold and measure the vent temperature. It should be cool.

core. This could be due to a heater control valve that is stuck closed or a plugged-up heater core. Determine necessary action. (**Photo 3**)

▶ Maintenance and Repair
Preventive Maintenance Schedules

Preventive maintenance of the cooling system is critical for long life and reliability of the engine. Failure to perform required maintenance will result in cooling system failure, which can lead to breakdowns and major engine damage. Manufacturers publish the required maintenance for the vehicle in the owner's manual and in the service information. The maintenance schedule lists which services are due at a particular mileage or date. With standard IAT coolant, a maintenance schedule will say "every 2 years or 24,000 miles, whichever comes first." Belts and hoses have similar inspection and maintenance requirements. These service intervals are critical to follow, so always check the maintenance schedule for the vehicle you are working on.

EPA Guidelines

As discussed in the coolant section of this chapter, ethylene glycol anti-freeze, the most common anti-freeze, is highly toxic to humans and animals. Because of this, the Environmental Protection Agency (EPA) has strict regulations for the handling and disposal of vehicle coolant. Coolant should never be dumped into a storm drain or down a shop floor drain. Coolant is a poison and should only be poured into an approved container and either be recycled in house or removed by a licensed recycler.

Care must be taken when a spill occurs when servicing a vehicle; it should be cleaned up promptly according to EPA regulations. Taking a little extra time to place a catch pan under the component being removed can prevent a spill and save time in the long run. Also, coolant should never be mixed with oil or other liquids; separate catch pans should always be used and marked accordingly.

Measuring Freeze Protection

The use of a hydrometer or refractometer is necessary when testing the freeze protection of the coolant in the cooling system. The customer may request this service as part of a winterization package performed by the shop. Any time coolant is replaced in the cooling system, the freeze point should be verified.

The hydrometer is a tool that measures the specific gravity of a liquid. When coolant is drawn into the hydrometer, a float will rise at a certain level depending upon the density of the coolant. Anti-freeze has a higher specific gravity than water, so the higher the float rises in the liquid, the greater the percentage of anti-freeze in the mix. One drawback to hydrometers is that they are typically anti-freeze specific. That means you will need one for ethylene glycol and one for propylene glycol, as the specific gravities of the two chemicals are different. Another drawback is that as the temperature of the coolant goes up, the specific gravity goes down. Some hydrometers have a built-in thermometer and a chart, allowing you to compensate for the temperature of the coolant.

A refractometer can also tell the proportions of anti-freeze and water in the coolant mix (or the level of freeze protection) by measuring a liquid's specific gravity. It works by allowing light to shine through the fluid. The light bends in accordance with the particular liquid's specific gravity. The bending of the light displays on a scale inside the tool, indicating the specific gravity of the fluid. One nice thing about a refractometer is that it has a scale for both types of anti-freeze and reads the freeze point accurately.

To use a hydrometer to test the freeze point of the coolant, follow the steps in **SKILL DRILL 46-5**:

1. Remove the pressure cap. Be sure the cooling system is cool before removing the cap.
2. Determine the type of anti-freeze and verify that the hydrometer is designed to be used with it.
3. Place the hydrometer tube into the coolant and squeeze the ball on top of the tool. (**Photo 1**)
4. Release the ball to draw in a sample of coolant. Make sure the level of coolant drawn in is above the minimum line. (**Photo 2**)
5. Read the scale on the tool to verify the freeze protection of the coolant.
6. Return the coolant sample to the radiator or surge tank. (**Photo 3**)

To use a refractometer to test the freeze point of the coolant, follow the steps in **SKILL DRILL 46-6**:

1. Remove the pressure cap. Be sure the cooling system is cool before removing it. (**Photo 1**)
2. Determine the type of anti-freeze and verify that the refractometer is designed to be used with it.
3. Place a few drops of coolant on the sample plate on the top of the tool. (**Photo 2**)
4. Hold the refractometer roughly level under a light, look through the viewfinder, and read the scale to verify the freeze protection of the coolant.
5. Return the coolant sample to the radiator or surge tank. (**Photo 3**)

SKILL DRILL | **46-5** | **Using a Hydrometer to Test the Freeze Point of the Coolant**

1. Remove the pressure cap. Place the hydrometer tube in the coolant and squeeze the ball on top.

2. Release the ball to pull a coolant sample into the hydrometer. Verify it is above the minimum level in the tester.

3. Read the scale on the tool to verify the freeze protection of the coolant. Return coolant sample to the radiator or surge tank.

SKILL DRILL | **46-6** | **Using a Refractometer to Test the Freeze Point of the Coolant**

1. Remove the pressure cap. Be sure the cooling system is cool first.

2. Determine the type of anti-freeze and verify that the refractometer is designed to be used with it. Place a few drops of coolant on the sample plate on the top of the tool.

3. Hold the refractometer roughly level under a light, look through the viewfinder, and read the scale to verify the freeze protection of the coolant. Return the coolant sample to the radiator or surge tank.

Testing the Coolant pH

pH testing is performed whenever cooling system maintenance service is requested, or if there is reason to suspect the coolant has outlived its useful life. It can be accomplished with test strips that turn color based on the level of acidity in the coolant, or electronic testers that measure the pH of the coolant directly can be used. pH testing of coolant is a great way to determine if the corrosion inhibitors are still working in the anti-freeze. As corrosion inhibitors break down over time, the solution of water and anti-freeze will become more acidic. As the acid level builds, so will corrosion and electrolysis in the cooling system. If the coolant is left in this acidic condition, it will create permanent erosion to component surfaces that may require replacement of affected components.

To test the coolant pH, follow the steps in **SKILL DRILL 46-7**:

1. Ensure that the coolant is relatively cool before removing the radiator cap.

2. If using a pH test strip kit, read the instructions to know how long to dip the strip in the coolant, and how long to wait to compare the color of the test pad to the chart. Also, some strips have a second test pad on the strip that indicates the percentage of anti-freeze in the coolant, so verify the time for that also.

3. Dip litmus paper into the coolant and wait the amount of time directed by the instructions. Compare the color of the litmus paper to the color scale on the kit.

4. If using an electronic pH tester, turn on the tester and immerse it in the coolant. Read the meter. Some cooling system experts suggest performing a coolant flush if the pH level is below 8.5.

Testing for Electrolysis

As the search for greater fuel efficiency continues and lighter-weight nonconductive materials find their way into our engines and vehicles, problems have arisen that result in the need for new training of technicians. Electrolysis, described earlier in this chapter, is the reaction of different metals to an acid solution to produce electricity. It can result in negative effects on the cooling system. In this case, electrolysis can erode metals from the inside of the cooling system, leading to damage.

Electrolysis can also be due to faulty grounds in the electrical system. If a circuit has a faulty ground, the current will try to find its way back to the battery in whatever way it can. And that can include sending some of the current flow through the coolant. For example, if the engine ground is dirty and has an excessive voltage drop, then when the engine is cranked over, some of the current could flow through the coolant to another ground. Current flowing through the coolant can erode metal surfaces in the cooling system. In this case, the coolant is not at fault, and flushing will have little to no effect on the condition. Repairing the failed ground is the solution in this case. To verify that electricity is finding its way into the cooling system, voltage can be measured when various electrical loads are operated to see if there is any stray voltage in the coolant. If voltages

are over 0.3 volts when the load or loads are activated, then you will have to perform electrical diagnosis of the circuit being tested.

To perform electrolysis testing for a suspected coolant problem, follow the steps in **SKILL DRILL 46-8**:

1. Connect the black lead of the voltmeter to a good engine ground.

2. Hold the red lead of the voltmeter in the coolant in the radiator.

3. Observe the voltage reading. If it is greater than 0.3 volts (300 millivolts), flush the cooling system, refill, and retest. If less than 0.3 volts, there is no problem found. Determine necessary action.

Checking and Adjusting Coolant

Checking and adjusting coolant implies two separate tasks. First, is the level at the full mark? Second, is the level of freeze protection appropriate for the climate the vehicle is operated in? Checking coolant level should be part of every oil change so that any leaks can be identified before they become more serious. You may also need to check or adjust coolant level if the customer's low coolant indicator comes on. There are usually two correct level marks on the reservoir because the coolant in the system expands and contracts according to changes in its temperature. The coolant level should not be below the lower mark when the vehicle is cold. It should be near the upper mark when the coolant is hot. If the coolant is indeed low, testing for a coolant leak will be necessary.

Verification of coolant condition can be performed by a checking its pH level with a test strip or electronic tester. Its freeze protection level can be tested with a coolant hydrometer or refractometer. If either of these tests shows that the coolant does not meet specifications, it will need to be flushed and replaced.

To check and adjust coolant, follow the steps in **SKILL DRILL 46-9**:

1. Most modern vehicles have a coolant system that uses a transparent recovery or surge tank as a coolant reservoir. Check the level of coolant in this reservoir; if the engine is hot, the level should be visible near the upper mark. If the engine is cold, it should be at or above the lower mark.

2. Before adding new coolant, check the specific gravity of the coolant in the system with a coolant hydrometer or refractometer. Draw some coolant up into the hydrometer, or place a couple of drops onto the sample plate, and read the freeze

protection level on the gauge. These tools will indicate the freezing point of the coolant mixture in the system, so you can tell if it has the right proportions of anti-freeze and water.

3 Check the service information for the recommended type and mixture of coolant that will produce an appropriate level of protection for the conditions where the vehicle will be used. Use a funnel to add enough coolant to bring the level up to the appropriate mark. Replace the coolant reservoir cap. If the level was low, find the cause of the loss.

Draining and Refilling Coolant

Draining and refilling coolant will be necessary if the customer requests a preventive maintenance service to flush the cooling system. Another reason you may need to perform this task is if corrosion is discovered in the system or if the coolant was contaminated by an incorrect fluid being added to the radiator, such as mistakenly adding power steering fluid to the coolant reservoir. Any time you have to replace a part of the cooling system, you will have to drain and refill the coolant. The discovery of electrolysis in the radiator will also require flushing the cooling system.

Your shop may have a coolant flushing machine, which will change the steps of the following skill drill. If you are using a flushing machine, follow the directions for the machine you are using.

To drain and refill coolant, follow the steps in **SKILL DRILL 46-10**:

1 Locate the cooling system drain plug or valve on the bottom tank of the radiator, if equipped. Place a clean catch pan large enough to contain all the coolant underneath the drain valve.

2 Carefully remove the pressure cap. This will allow air into the cooling system so that it can drain quickly and completely. Open the drain valve so that the coolant can drain into the pan below. When all the coolant has drained out, close the drain valve. **(Photo 1)**

3 Carefully remove the block drain plugs and allow the coolant to drain into the catch pan. **(Photo 2)**

4 Check the shop service information for the capacity of the system and the recommended type and mixture of coolant for the operating conditions of the vehicle. Measure the recommended amount of coolant. Using a funnel, pour it in through the top of the radiator or surge tank and squeeze the upper hose to help push out any excess air.

5 Start the engine and verify the proper level. Air can be trapped in the cooling system, so leave the radiator cap off to allow it to escape, and run the engine until the thermostat opens to allow the coolant to circulate and get rid of trapped air. Fill the radiator, then replace the radiator cap and again bring the engine up to operating temperature. Check the

SKILL DRILL | 46-10 | Draining and Refilling Coolant

1 Locate the radiator drain plug, if equipped, and place a catch pan marked for coolant underneath the drain valve. Drain the radiator into the catch pan.

2 Remove the block drain plugs and allow the coolant to drain into the pan.

3 Refill the cooling system with the proper coolant mix after closing the drain plugs. Start the engine and verify the proper level. Dispose of coolant in an approved way.

coolant level in the reservoir and top it off to the high or hot engine mark.

6. Dispose of waste. Anti-freeze is toxic, so dispose of the waste coolant carefully and in an environmentally recommended way. **(Photo 3)**

Flushing the Coolant

Coolant flushing is necessary either as a preventive maintenance service performed by most shops or because the coolant is worn out or contaminated. It will be necessary if the corrosion inhibitors in the coolant are found to be worn out or if some type of contamination is found. Flushing of the coolant is performed in one of two ways: manually or with a flushing machine. Most shops have a coolant flushing machine; if you are using this machine, follow the directions on the machine since they are all different. In this example, we will perform the manual flush.

To flush the coolant, follow the steps in **SKILL DRILL 46-11**:

1. Locate the radiator drain plug, if equipped, and place a coolant catch pan under the drain plug. Be sure you know which direction to turn it to open. Some drain plugs are quarter-turn valves and are plastic. If turned too far, these drain plugs will break off. These drain plugs cannot always be found as a replacement part, and replacement of the entire radiator may be necessary.

2. Drain the coolant into the catch pan. Loosen and remove the pressure cap so coolant can flow out more freely. **(Photo 1)**

3. Remove drain plugs located on the engine block, if equipped. Be sure to check the service manual for the location of these plugs. Allow the coolant to drain from the block. **(Photo 2)**

SKILL DRILL | 46-11 | Flushing the Coolant

1. Locate the radiator drain plug, if installed. Drain the coolant into the catch pan.

2. Remove any engine drain plugs in the block and allow the block to drain into the catch pan.

3. Remove the surge tank or overflow tank and clean thoroughly with hot water.

4. Reinstall the tank and all drain plugs, and refill the radiator with clean water. Start the engine and allow it to warm fully.

5. Drain water from the radiator and engine block. Replace all drain plugs.

6. Refill the radiator with a 50/50 mix of anti-freeze and water. Bleed any air from the system using a vacuum bleeding system or by running the engine with the cap off and keeping the system full.

4. Remove the overflow or surge tank, drain coolant into the catch pan, and using hot water, clean the container until all deposits are removed. **(Photo 3)**

5. Reinstall the tank and all drain plugs.

6. Refill the radiator with clean water and start the engine. **(Photo 4)**

7. Allow the engine to reach full operating temperature. The water will cycle through the engine and wash out any remaining coolant and debris. A cooling system flush additive may be used by some shops.

8. Drain water from cooling system, remembering to remove any drain plugs in the engine to remove water from the engine block.

9. Replace all drain plugs in the cooling system. **(Photo 5)**

10. Refill the cooling system with a 50/50 mix of the required anti-freeze and distilled water. Refer to the manufacturer's service information for the correct anti-freeze to use in the vehicle you are servicing. Distilled water is recommended since it has no minerals in it, which would result in deposits in the cooling system. If the vehicle has heavy deposits in the cooling system, the cleaning process may need to be repeated several times to remove all the deposits. If the cooling system has been contaminated with some type of oil, a soapy solution will have to be used to remove the oil residue. This cleaning may need to be repeated until all traces of oil are removed.

11. Unless vacuum filling the cooling system, make sure to run the engine with the radiator cap removed until the thermostat opens to remove all trapped air. Then top off the radiator and fill the overflow tank to the full mark. **(Photo 6)**

Inspecting and Adjusting an Engine Drive Belt

Inspecting the engine drive belt should be part of any maintenance inspection. Never try to inspect belts with the engine running. Adjusting the drive belt may be necessary if the vehicle is not equipped with an automatic tensioner. Drive belts will stretch over time with use and may require adjustment. When adjusting belts, if they are too loose, they will squeal or chirp and slip. If the belt is too tight, it will put extra force against the bearings on the accessories being turned, which can cause them to wear out prematurely. Conditions to look for on a drive belt include:

- *Cracks:* Cracks in a belt used to indicate that immediate replacement was needed. With today's belts, many manufacturers tolerate a certain number of cracks per inch. Check the manufacturer's specifications before recommending a belt be replaced.

- *Oil contamination:* A belt that has been soaked in oil will not grip properly on the pulleys and will slip. If the oil contamination is severe enough for this to happen, diagnose and repair the cause of the oil contamination and replace the belt.

- *Glazing:* Glazing is shininess on the surface of the belt, which comes in contact with the pulley. If the belt is worn, the glazing could be caused by the belt "bottoming out" in the pulley, and it should be replaced. If it is not old and worn, glazing could simply indicate that the belt is not tight enough. Tightening the belt may be all that is necessary, depending on how bad the glazing is.

- *Tears:* Torn or split belts are unserviceable and should be replaced immediately.

- *Bottoming out:* When V-type or serpentine-type belts become very worn, the bottom of the V-shape may contact the bottom of the groove in the pulley, preventing the sides of the belt from making good contact and wedging with the sides of the pulley groove. This reduced friction causes slippage. A belt worn enough to bottom out should be replaced. V-belts can be inspected for the depth of the belt in the pulley visually. A serpentine belt can be checked with a plastic wear gauge. If the plastic tool is even with the top of the belt ribs, or lower, the belt needs to be replaced.

- *Pulley wear:* Always inspect the pulley when inspecting the belt.

To inspect and adjust an engine drive belt, follow the steps in **SKILL DRILL 46-12**:

1. On a V-belt, twist the belt so that you can see the underside of the V shape. Look for signs of wear and damage. You may need a flashlight to see clearly. An excessively cracked or glazed belt or a torn belt will need to be replaced. **(Photo 1)**

2. Serpentine belts should be checked using a serpentine belt wear gauge. **(Photo 2)**

3. Check the belt tension by attaching the tension gauge to the longest belt span. Compare your reading to the specifications in the vehicle service information.

4. On manually adjusted belts, select the correct wrench or socket to loosen the adjustment locking fastener. This is usually on the alternator mounting or on a separate idler pulley. **(Photo 3)**

5. The slotted style is adjusted by prying. Pry between a solid part of the adjustable component (not the center or rear housing) and a strong part of the

SKILL DRILL | **46-12** | **Inspecting and Adjusting an Engine Drive Belt**

1. If a V-belt, twist the belt so that you can see the underside of the V shape.

2. If a serpentine belt, check the ribs with a serpentine belt gauge.

3. Check the belt tension by attaching the belt tension gauge to the belt and measure the tension. On manually adjusted belts, loosen the locking fastener.

4. For the slotted style, use a pry bar and carefully pry the adjustable component until the belt tension is adjusted. Tighten the locking fastener.

5. On the style that uses a tensioning screw, tighten the tensioning screw until the belt is properly tensioned. Tighten the locking fastener.

6. Check belt tension with the belt tension gauge. Start the engine and verify proper operation.

engine, and pull in the direction that will apply tension to the belt. Tighten the locking fastener. (**Photo 4**)

6. On a style that uses a tensioning screw, loosen the locking fastener and tighten the tensioning screw until the belt is properly tensioned. Tighten the locking fastener. (**Photo 5**)

7. Check the tension again with the gauge; if necessary, loosen the fastener and adjust the belt again until it is at the correct tension for the vehicle.

8. Start the engine and observe the belt to make sure it is properly seated and operating correctly. Stop the engine and recheck the tension. (**Photo 6**)

> **TECHNICIAN TIP**
>
> ***Manual belt tension versus automatic belt tension:*** Many vehicles require the technician to manually adjust the tension on the belt. Other vehicles have an automatic spring tensioning system. There are several different types of tension gauges, so follow the operating instructions for the tool. If you do not have a tension gauge, you can estimate the tension by pushing the belt inward with your thumb. If it is correctly tensioned, you should be able to deflect the belt only about half an inch for each foot of belt span between pulleys.

Replacing an Engine Drive Belt

Replacement of an engine drive belt may be necessary when the belt is cracked, glazed, separating, and getting ready to fail. Verifying that the pulley system is not damaged will be the first step if noise is a problem. Perform a pulley alignment check as part of inspecting the drive belt system if noise is a concern or if belts are being thrown off. Checking pulley alignment is done with a straightedge across the face of the pulleys or with a special laser that fits in the grooves of the pulley. If it is a serpentine belt system, the pulley edges should be within 1/16" (1.6 mm) of alignment with each other.

Another reason to replace belts would be if the customer requests belt replacement as part of the vehicle's preventive maintenance.

To replace a standard engine drive belt, follow the steps in **SKILL DRILL 46-13**:

1. On a manually adjusted belt, locate the locking fastener and loosen it. It is usually on the alternator mounting or on a separate pulley. Move the adjusting mechanism in far enough to allow you to remove the belt. (**Photo 1**)

2. On an automatic belt tension system, rotate the tensioning device back so that you can remove the belt. This is done with a breaker bar when a square opening is provided in the adjuster or with a special automatic adjuster tool for all others. (**Photo 2**)

3. Look for cracks and other forms of damage in the belt. Inspect the pulleys for sideways movement, which indicates worn bearings, and spin

SKILL DRILL 46-13   Replacing an Engine Drive Belt

1. On a manually adjusted belt, locate and loosen the adjustment locking fastener. Loosen the belt and remove it.

2. On an automatically adjusted belt, locate the spring-loaded idler pulley, install an adjuster tool, and pry the tensioner back. Remove the belt.

3. Inspect the belts and pulleys for wear and damage. Check all drive pulleys for alignment with a straightedge or laser.

4. Select the correct replacement belt. Install the V-belt or serpentine belt, if equipped. Make sure the belt is properly routed around the pulleys and fully seated in each pulley.

5. Correctly tension the new belt. Start the engine and verify proper operation. Stop the engine and recheck the tension.

the pulleys by hand to check that the bearings are rotating freely, without noise.

4 Check the pulleys for alignment with a straight-edge or pulley laser tool. Also check the tensioner alignment. **(Photo 3)**

5 Obtain the correct size and type of replacement belt specified in the service information, and compare it with the belt you have just removed. They should be very similar, although the old belt may have stretched and worn in use.

6 On a V-belt, install the new belt, making sure it is properly seated in the V-shape groove in the pulley.

7 If the belt is a serpentine type, make sure it is the correct width and squarely aligned in the pulley grooves. If it is not correctly aligned, the belt will be damaged and may be thrown off the pulleys. **(Photo 4)**

8 Correctly tension the new belt. To do so, use the proper tools, and then check the belt with a tension gauge. With automatic tension systems, gently allow the automatic tensioner to apply the tension to the belt.

9 Start the engine, and observe the belt to make sure it is properly seated and operating correctly. Stop the engine and recheck the tension. **(Photo 5)**

Checking and Replacing a Coolant Hose

Checking and replacing coolant hoses is a very important job of the technician. If the hose is deteriorating, it will eventually burst and coolant will be pumped out of the engine, resulting in overheating. Coolant hoses should be checked anytime the vehicle is in the shop for a maintenance inspection. If you find one defective radiator hose, the chances are that the other hose(s) may be deteriorating in the same way and will soon need to be replaced. For this reason, most technicians will generally replace both radiator hoses at once as a sensible precaution. Do not forget that there may be many hoses in the cooling system and you will need to inspect all of them to ensure proper function of the cooling system. You may need to use a flashlight to inspect the coolant hoses so that you can clearly see if the surface is starting to crack. Radiator hose problems include:

- *Swollen hose:* This hose has lost its elasticity and is swelling under pressure. It may soon rupture; typically you will see a bubble protruding from the side of this hose. Replace this hose immediately.
- *Hardened hose:* This hose has become brittle and will break and leak. Verify hardening by squeezing the hose and comparing it to a known good hose.

- *Cracked hose:* This hose has cracked and will soon start to leak. Verify cracking by a visual inspection.
- *Soft hose:* This hose has become very weak and is in danger of ballooning or bursting. Verify softening by squeezing the hose and comparing it to a known good hose.

> **TECHNICIAN TIP**
>
> "You can't diagnose bad if you don't know good." This saying is very appropriate when checking radiator hoses. It is a good idea to check the feel of radiator and heater hoses on a variety of new vehicles to become familiar with what new hoses feel like. Then it will be easy to identify the bad ones.

Hose clamps come in several forms and will require different tools to properly remove or replace. These clamps secure the hose to the component it is connected to. Be sure to follow proper installation instructions to prevent future leaks from this seal. Types of clamps include:

- *Gear or worm clamp:* Adjust with a screwdriver or nut driver.
- *Banded or screw clamp:* Adjust with a screwdriver.
- *Wire clamp:* This spring clamp is not adjustable. It is fitted and removed with special hose clamp pliers, which have grooved jaws.

Clamps are not expensive, so it is good practice to fit new ones at the same time as new hoses. Even if not corroded, the old clamps may have become distorted when being removed from an unserviceable hose. The time and money associated with replacing clamps are very small when thinking of the results of your customer losing a hose and becoming stranded.

To check and replace a coolant hose, follow the steps in **SKILL DRILL 46-14**:

1 Locate both the hoses that carry coolant between the radiator and the engine. One is at the inlet and the other is at the outlet of the radiator. Squeeze each hose. It should feel pliable and springy. If it feels very soft and weak or very hard and brittle, it will need to be replaced. Look for signs of swelling or cracking, particularly near the hose clamps. Check that the clamps are holding the hoses firmly in position and are not damaged or corroded.

2 Drain the coolant from the system before removing either of the hoses. Remove the clamp using the appropriate tool. If the hose is stuck and will not pull off easily, be careful to not damage the radiator fitting by using too much force. It is better

SKILL DRILL | **46-14** | **Checking and Replacing a Coolant Hose**

1. Inspect the hoses by squeezing them, and visually inspect the clamps. Remove the hose clamp. Carefully pull or cut the hose off the fittings.

2. Verify that the replacement hose is correct. Cut to length if necessary. Reinstall the new hose all the way into position. Install new clamps.

3. Refill coolant, verify correct level, and pressure check for leaks.

to cut the hose in several places so that you can peel it away from the radiator fitting. Clean the hose fittings thoroughly on both the engine and the radiator with fine sandpaper or emery cloth so that a good seal is made with the new hose. **(Photo 1)**

3. Obtain new hoses and compare them with the removed hoses to make sure they are the same length and diameter. If the hose is a molded type, the new one must also have the same preformed curve. Note that some hoses must be cut to length. Use the original hose as a guide.

4. Place new loosened clamps over the hose ends and then slide the hose fully into position on the engine and radiator fittings. Position the clamps about ¼" (6 mm) from the end of the hose. Be careful not to overtighten and damage the hoses, but it is important that they do not fall off once the pressure in the cooling system increases. Spring clamps will apply the proper tightness if the clamp is installed correctly and the clamp is not damaged. **(Photo 2)**

5. Refill the cooling system, pressure check the system, and then run the engine for a few minutes. Check the hose connections to make sure there are no leaks. When the engine is at its normal operating temperature, check the tightness of the clamps again, as the clamps and hoses will

both expand at different rates as they heat up. **(Photo 3)**

Safety

Never try to assess the serviceability of a coolant hose while the engine is hot. Let it cool so that you can handle the hoses comfortably and safely. Always ensure the engine is turned off before attempting to check the coolant hoses, and always wear the appropriate personal protection equipment before starting the job. It is easy to hurt yourself, even when the most exhaustive protection measures are taken.

Removing and Replacing a Thermostat

It will be necessary to remove and replace a thermostat in the event that the thermostat is found to be faulty, creating either an overheating concern or an underheating concern. You may want to suggest to the customer a thermostat replacement during a cooling system flush or water pump replacement as a precautionary maintenance step. Before starting a repair or service task on the cooling system, allow sufficient time for the system to cool adequately before opening the pressurized system.

Drain at least 50% of the coolant in the system to avoid spills. Once the thermostat has been removed, clean any old gasket material and corrosion that has built up on both sealing surfaces where the thermostat seats. Properly position the thermostat air bleed valve (if equipped). Always install a new gasket and/or O-ring seal when installing the thermostat. Make sure the thermostat is fully seated in the groove and stays there before installing the housing. In most cases, if the thermostat falls out of its recessed groove, one of the thermostat housing ears will break off when the bolts are tightened, and the thermostat itself is likely to be damaged. Tighten the housing bolts to the correct torque. Use the manufacturer's procedure to properly bleed all air from the cooling system.

To remove and replace a thermostat, follow the steps in **SKILL DRILL 46-15**:

1 Drain the coolant from the cooling system using an approved catch container.

2 Unbolt the thermostat housing from the engine. Be very careful not to damage the housing, as it is generally made from aluminum or a similar fragile material. Remove the thermostat. **(Photo 1)**

3 Inspect the mating surfaces. Inspect the thermostat housing and remove any gasket material from the mating surface of the housing. Inspect the other mating surface and remove any gasket material from its surface. Also be sure the recessed grove is clean and free from any debris. **(Photo 2)**

4 Inspect the new thermostat to ensure that the part number and temperature rating are correct.

5 Install the new thermostat, ensuring that the air bleed hole is in the correct position (toward the top, vertically). Check that the thermostat is fully seated in its groove. **(Photo 3)**

SKILL DRILL 46-15 Removing and Replacing a Thermostat

1 Drain the coolant from the cooling system using an approved catch container. Remove the thermostat.

2 Inspect the thermostat housing and clean any gasket material from the mating surfaces. Clean and inspect the thermostat groove.

3 Install the new thermostat with the bleed valve in the correct position.

4 Install the gasket or O-ring and thermostat housing.

5 Torque to housing specifications.

6 Refill the cooling system to the proper level.

6 Fit the correct type of gasket or O-ring for the vehicle you are working on. (**Photo 4**)

7 Carefully install the thermostat housing to the engine and torque it into place. (**Photo 5**)

8 Refill the cooling system with coolant. Run the engine to circulate the coolant and remove any air trapped in the system. Check that the temperature indicator gauge shows that the coolant temperature is in the normal operational range. Top off the radiator or reservoir with coolant if necessary. (**Photo 6**)

Inspecting and Testing Fans, Fan Clutch, Fan Shroud, and Air Dams

The need to inspect and test fans and fan shrouds will arise when the customer complains of overheating. Air dams are located under the vehicle and are designed to direct airflow into the radiator as the vehicle is moving down the road. If the air dam is damaged or missing, the engine temperature may be higher than originally designed while driving on the highway. If the vehicle only overheats while stopped, it could be an issue with the fan shroud, which directs airflow through the radiator. The shroud is what surrounds the cooling fan and allows a maximum amount of air to be moved by the cooling fan. If the shroud is missing, air will be pulled from around the fan blades rather than pulling air through the radiator. A visual inspection of these components will verify whether they are in proper position and operating as designed.

A mechanical or electric fan can fail, which will also result in air not being pulled through the radiator. A quick test to verify that air is moving through the radiator is to hold a piece of paper in front of the radiator and see if suction pulls the paper in. If it does not, then air is not being pulled through the radiator. Follow the service manual information on diagnosing the fan equipped on your vehicle.

To inspect the shroud/air dam and test the electric cooling fan, follow the steps in **SKILL DRILL 46-16**:

1 Visually inspect all shrouds, ducts, and air dams around the radiator and fan for damaged or missing pieces.

2 If equipped with a fan clutch, rotate the fan and check it for looseness, play, or binding. If bad, replace the fan clutch. (**Photo 1**)

3 If the fan clutch feels free, place cardboard in front of most of the radiator. Start the engine and monitor the engine temperature with a temperature gun. Verify that it cycles on at the proper temperature. If not, replace the fan clutch. (**Photo 2**)

SKILL DRILL 46-16 Inspecting the Fan Shroud/Air Dam and Testing the Electric Cooling Fan

1 Visually inspect all shrouds, ducts, and air dams around the radiator and fan for damaged or missing pieces. If equipped with a fan clutch, rotate the fan and check it for looseness, play, or binding. If bad, replace the fan clutch.

2 If the fan clutch feels free, place cardboard or a fender cover in front of most of the radiator. Start the engine, monitor the engine temperature with a temperature gun, and verify that the fan cycles on at the proper temperature. If not, replace the fan clutch.

3 If equipped with an electric fan, connect a scan tool to the data link connector under the dash. Locate the bidirectional command menu and command the cooling fan on. This will activate the relay and should send power to the fan.

| **SKILL DRILL** | **46-16** | **Inspecting the Fan Shroud/Air Dam and Testing the Electric Cooling Fan, continued** |

4 Verify that the fan is turning. Verify that air is flowing across the radiator by seeing if a piece of paper will be pulled into the front of the radiator. If the fan is not operating, locate the cooling fan relay, remove the relay, and check for the presence of power and ground at the appropriate terminals in the relay block. Two terminals should have battery positive voltage, and two terminals should have battery negative voltage.

5 If all terminals read properly, test the relay winding for continuity. If out of specifications, replace the relay.

6 If OK, install a relay socket tester and reinstall the relay into the relay box, then activate the electric fan. Measure the voltage drop on each leg of the circuit and the relay contacts themselves. Trace the path that indicated a problem, and locate the voltage drop or defective component. Determine the necessary actions based on your findings.

4 If equipped with an electric fan, connect a scan tool to the data link connector under the dash.

5 Locate the bidirectional command menu and command the cooling fan on. This will activate the relay and should send power to the fan. **(Photo 3)**

6 Verify that the fan runs by visually inspecting that the fan is turning.

7 Verify that air is flowing across the radiator. Use a piece of paper to ensure airflow is strong enough to pull the paper to the radiator.

8 If the fan is not operating, locate the cooling fan relay, remove the relay, and check for the presence of power and ground at the appropriate terminals in the relay block. Two terminals should have battery positive voltage, and two terminals should have battery negative voltage. **(Photo 4)**

9 If all terminals read properly, test the relay winding for continuity. If out of specifications, replace the relay. **(Photo 5)**

10 If OK, install a relay socket tester and reinstall the relay into the relay box, then activate the electric fan. Measure the voltage drop on each leg of the circuit and the relay contacts themselves.

11 Trace the path that indicated a problem, and locate the voltage drop or defective component. Determine the necessary actions based on your findings. **(Photo 6)**

Removing and Replacing a Radiator

A radiator may need to be replaced due to an overheating condition traced to partially plugged radiator tubes. If this is found to be the case, the radiator will need to be removed and can be sent out to a radiator shop for cleaning. A good flush of the entire cooling system will be necessary as further clogging will be likely, especially in the heater core.

Another reason to remove the radiator is for leaks traced to the radiator through the use of the coolant pressure tester or coolant dye and an ultraviolet light. Some radiators can be repaired by a radiator shop, but a cost analysis must be performed to see if doing so is more cost effective for the customer than buying a new radiator.

When replacing the radiator, make sure the coolant catch tray is large enough to catch any spills and has the capacity to hold all the system coolant. If you are replacing the coolant, dispose of the old coolant properly in accordance with environmental and legislative requirements. If reusing the old fluid, keep it stored in a covered and uncontaminated container. Most situations will require replacement of the coolant. If, for example, the vehicle just had new coolant installed, you may want to catch and reuse the coolant.

Inspect the cooling system hoses and clamps. Replace them if worn or damaged. When removing the hose from the radiator fitting, do *not* twist it; doing so can damage the fitting or even rip it out of the radiator. If it does not easily release, carefully work a tool between the hose and the fitting, breaking it loose all the way around. If the hoses are to be replaced, you can carefully slit them with a knife or hose-cutting tool and peel them off the fitting, which is less likely to damage the fitting.

When replacing hoses, reinstall them all the way onto the fittings. Make sure the clamps are installed just beyond the flared or barbed segment, not on top of it. Placing a clamp on top of the flare or barb will likely result in the hose being blown off the fitting. Many vehicles have automatic transmission cooler lines attached to the radiator. Remember to disconnect these lines when removing the radiator, and always reinstall them before refilling the system with coolant. Remember when you disconnect these lines that transmission fluid will leak out. Do not mix coolant and oil! Using a separate catch container will ensure that coolant and oil are not mixed.

Refill the system with the correct coolant at the proper anti-freeze/water ratio. It is advisable to pressure test the system to check for leaks upon completion of the job. Start the engine, warm it up until the thermostat has opened, and check for proper operation of the cabin heater. Check for proper coolant level after it cools sufficiently.

To remove and replace a radiator, follow the steps in **SKILL DRILL 46-17**:

1. Place a catch pan below the radiator and remove the drain plug, if equipped. Drain the coolant from the system. Replace the drain plug and dispose of the drained coolant in an environmentally approved manner. **(Photo 1)**

2. Carefully remove any hoses and tubes that are attached to the radiator, being careful not to damage the radiator fittings.

3. Unscrew any shrouds or covers from the radiator.

4. Remove the bolts or screws that hold the radiator in position in the engine bay, and lift the radiator from its location. **(Photo 2)**

SKILL DRILL | 46-17 | Removing and Replacing a Radiator

1. Place a catch pan below the radiator and remove the drain plug. Drain the coolant from the system. Replace the drain plug and dispose of the drained coolant.

2. Unscrew any shrouds or covers from the radiator. Remove the bolts or screws that hold the radiator in position in the engine bay, and lift the radiator from its location.

3. Inspect the radiator, then place it into position and replace the securing bolts or screws. Refit the shrouds or covers. Rotate the fan and belts by hand to check that the covers do not restrict movement. Attach the coolant hoses to the radiator. Refill the system and verify the correct level.

5 Visually inspect the radiator to ensure that it is suitable for reinstallation in the vehicle. If the radiator fins are blocked by debris, carefully clean the fins with a dry brush or garden hose. If the radiator is damaged, advise your supervisor so a decision can be made about whether to repair it or replace it.

6 Place the radiator into position and replace the securing bolts or screws. Reinstall the shrouds or covers. Rotate the fan and belts by hand to check that the covers do not restrict movement. Attach the hoses and tubes to the radiator.

7 Refill the system with new coolant of the correct type. Run the engine to circulate the coolant and remove any air trapped in the system. Check that the temperature indicator gauge shows that the coolant temperature is in the normal operational range. Top off the radiator or reservoir with coolant, if necessary. **(Photo 3)**

Removing, Inspecting, and Reinstalling the Heater Core

Removal of a heater core may become necessary if the customer notices a puddle of coolant on the carpet in the vehicle, usually on the passenger side. Typically, the heater core will leak, fill the air box, and drip onto the floor inside the vehicle. The other concern the customer may have is the smell of coolant inside the vehicle, or the complaint of a film on the inside of the windshield, which upon inspection is coolant that is being discharged with the air when the customer uses the defroster. The removal of a heater core is not an easy task, as sometimes it may be necessary to pull the entire dash from the vehicle. It is highly recommended to take pictures of the process as you go, to make reassembly easier. Follow the manufacturer's service information to perform this task. The procedure in the following skill drill is generic and may be substantially different than on the vehicle you are working on.

To remove, inspect, and reinstall the heater core, follow the steps in **SKILL DRILL 46-18**:

1 Find service information on the removal and replacement of the heater core for the vehicle you are working on. Determine if the air-conditioning refrigerant needs to be recovered.

2 Drain the coolant from the radiator.

3 If the air-conditioning evaporator needs to be removed, recover the air-conditioning refrigerant.

4 Remove necessary dash panels and covers, making sure to collect screws in a magnetic tray or plastic bag. Mark screws to remind you where they

were removed from. This becomes more critical the longer the vehicle is apart; it can be hard to remember after a couple weeks have gone by.

5 Remove heater core hoses (and remove air-conditioning lines to the evaporator, if necessary).

6 Locate all bolts securing the air box to the bulkhead of the vehicle and remove, if necessary.

7 Pull the air box from the vehicle, if necessary.

8 Remove the bolts holding the air box halves together, and separate the halves.

9 Remove the heater core.

10 Now is a good time to clean the air box of any debris or gunk in the bottom around the drain; doing so could prevent a vehicle from coming back at a later date for an air-conditioning odor complaint. Inspect all air box doors to ensure there are no cracks or dry-rotting rubber or foam. If found, the doors will need to be replaced.

11 Install the new heater core and reverse the steps to reinstall the air box. Properly refill the cooling system and recharge the air-conditioning system.

Applied | **Science**

AS-48: Centrifugal/Centripetal: The technician can explain the relationship of centrifugal/centripetal force to the functioning or a failure of a rotating system.

An automotive instructor is presenting a class on the vehicle's cooling system. He has an assortment of new and used water pumps to serve as training devices. The instructor begins by stating that the water pump operates on the principle of centrifugal force. As our text indicates, *centrifugal* force is a force pulling outward on a rotating body. *Centripetal* force is just the opposite. Wikipedia states that *centrifugal* is from a Latin word meaning, "to flee the center." *Centripetal* is from a word meaning, "to seek the center." These are forces which are opposite in direction.

The impeller is the rotating portion of the water pump which is equipped with fins to direct the coolant outward, based on the principle of centrifugal force. The correct flow rate is based upon the design of the water pump's impeller.

During class, new and used water pumps are inspected to find out the condition of the impeller. Erosion damage is visible on several of the used pumps in the area of the impeller fins. Erosion is a physical wearing away of the metal caused by contaminants in the coolant. These contaminants include dirt, grit or sediment circulating in the coolant. The instructor stresses proper cooling system maintenance to prevent premature failure of the water pump and other system components.

Wrap-up

Ready for Review

- Most cooling systems rely on coolant, a special mix of chemicals (anti-freeze) and water.
- Coolant absorbs heat from the engine, is cooled in the radiator, and flows back to the engine to absorb more heat.
- Heat travels in one of three ways: conduction, convection, or radiation.
- Coolant works to keep an engine from overheating and from freezing.
- Coolant must contain anti-freeze to prevent the water content from freezing and to reduce corrosion.
- Anti-freeze contains either ethylene glycol (toxic) or propylene glycol (nontoxic).
- The combination of water and anti-freeze lowers the freezing point and raises the boiling point of both components.
- Manufacturers can create more efficient combustion by raising the engine's operating temperature, creating more pressure, and causing coolant to boil at a higher temperature.
- Radiator caps maintain a specified pressure throughout the cooling system, generally 13–17 psi (89.6–117.2 kPa).
- Changing coolant regularly prevents acid buildup and electrolysis.
- The stationary parts of the cooling system (heater core and radiator) are connected to the engine via radiator and cooling hoses.
- Modern vehicles have replaced the thermo-siphon process for moving coolant through the engine with a water pump that forces coolant through the system.
- An engine thermostat regulates coolant circulation, keeping it in the engine until the engine reaches operating temperature.
- Engineers have developed a reverse-flow cooling system in which coolant is first pushed through the cylinder head, thereby better equalizing temperature between the block and head, which extends the life of the head gasket.
- Engines with the reverse-flow cooling system must have a surge tank to capture steam and reconvert it to coolant.
- Rotary engines use similar cooling systems to piston engines, with a radiator, thermostat, radiator hoses, and water jackets.
- The radiator's function is to allow coolant to pass through it and to conduct heat away from the engine.
- Cooling tubes in the radiator core run in a vertical (down-flow) or horizontal (cross-flow) design.
- Radiator pressure caps contain a spring-loaded valve to allow excess coolant to pass into the overflow container, and a vacuum valve to allow coolant to be pulled from the overflow container back into the radiator when it is needed.
- A surge tank is situated as the highest component so that it collects any air present in the system and allows for easy air removal.
- In a recovery system, coolant flows into an overflow container and then back into the radiator so that no coolant is lost.
- The thermostat's valve is controlled by a wax pellet that melts and expands and forces the valve open against spring pressure.
- Thermostats installed on the inlet side of the engine better control the amount of cold water flowing into the engine.
- The water pump uses centrifugal force to drive coolant into the water jackets.
- A fan clutch is driven by an accessory belt and uses a viscous fluid to control speed changes of the fan, determined by air temperature from the radiator.
- A solenoid-controlled fan clutch replaces the bimetallic spring with an electric solenoid controlled by the power train control module.
- Radiator hoses must be correctly clamped to the radiator assembly or a leak will develop.
- Some heater hoses contain a coolant control valve to regulate coolant flow when the air conditioner is turned on.
- The three types of drive belts for the water pump are V-belts, serpentine belts, and toothed belts.
- To ensure minimal slippage, drive belts are tightened around the pulley by tensioners.
- Either a temperature gauge or a temperature light can function as a coolant temperature indicator.
- Coolant passages are critical to the transfer of heat energy so coolant must be serviced regularly to prevent the passages from becoming clogged.
- The heater box contains air doors and actuators that work to control passenger compartment airflow.
- IAT coolant is the standard green coolant used in many vehicles and must be changed every 2 years or 24,000 miles (39,000 km).
- OAT coolant is an extended-life coolant that should be changed every 5 years or 150,000 miles (241,000 km).

- HOAT coolant (yellow) combines inorganic and organic additives and is also an extended-life coolant.
- POAT coolant, the newest type, is a very long-life coolant that should be changed every 7 years or 250,000 miles (402,000 km).
- Cooling systems need regular maintenance to ensure engine longevity.
- Common cooling system diagnostic concerns include coolant leaks, thermostat that is stuck closed or open, faulty water pump, inoperative cooling fan, or failed head gasket.
- Test pH concentration of the coolant to ensure the anti-freeze acid inhibitors are working correctly.
- Measure the voltage of the coolant to determine if electrolysis is occurring due to acidic coolant or faulty grounds.
- Always follow EPA regulations for handling and disposing of coolant.
- Coolant condition and level should be checked regularly; coolant should be at the correct level mark (upper or lower) according to engine temperature.
- When removing and replacing a radiator, be sure to properly catch, handle, and dispose of or replace the coolant.
- Do not attempt to remove or replace the thermostat until the engine has cooled for at least 30 minutes.
- Potential engine drive belt problems can be belts that are cracked, oil soaked, glazed, torn, or bottomed out.
- Coolant freeze point can be verified by a hydrometer or refractometer, both of which indicate the specific gravity of the fluid, revealing the ratio of anti-freeze to water.
- Removing and reinstalling the heater core can be challenging; taking pictures as you go is highly recommended for ease of reassembly.

Key Terms

actuator A device that is electrically or vacuum controlled and is used to physically move doors within the heater box to control airflow.

boiling point The temperature at which a substance begins to change from a liquid to a gas.

centrifugal force A force pulling outward on a rotating body.

conduction Movement of heat energy through solids.

convection Movement of heat energy through gases or liquids.

coolant A fluid that contains anti-freeze mixed with water.

coolant control valve A valve that blocks off coolant flow to keep hot water from entering the heater core when less heat is requested by the operator.

cooling hoses Flexible hoses that connect the stationary components of the cooling system, such as heater core and radiator, to the engine, which is mounted on flexible mounts.

cross-flow radiator A radiator that uses cooling tubes that run horizontal with tanks on each end. This design allows lower hood profile for better vehicle aerodynamics.

down-flow radiator A radiator that uses cooling tubes that run vertical. This design requires a higher hood profile.

electrolysis The process of pulling metals apart by using electricity or by creating electricity through the use of chemicals and dissimilar metals.

ethylene glycol A chemical used as anti-freeze that provides the lower freezing point of coolant and raises the boiling point. It is a toxic anti-freeze.

heat dissipation The spreading of heat over a large area to increase heat transfer.

overflow tank A tank used to catch any coolant that is released from the radiator cap (works like a catch can).

pitch The angle of a fan blade. A steeper pitch draws more air, while a shallower pitch draws less air.

propylene-glycol A chemical used as anti-freeze. It is labeled as a nontoxic anti-freeze.

radiation The movement of energy through space such as the movement of energy from the sun to the earth.

radiator A device that takes hot coolant and cools it by passing heat energy to the surrounding air.

radiator hoses Rubber hoses that connect the radiator to the engine. Because they are subject to pressure, they are reinforced with a layer of fabric, typically nylon.

rotor housing The engine block of the rotary engine. The rotor moves within it.

surge tank A sealed tank that captures coolant coming from the head that has turned to steam and changes the steam back to coolant to be reused by the cooling system.

thermo-control switch A temperature-sensitive switch that is mounted into the radiator or into a coolant passage on the engine to control electric fan operation.

thermostat Located under the thermostat housing, the thermostat regulates the flow of coolant, allowing coolant to flow from the engine to the radiator when the engine is running at its operating temperature.

viscous coupler Called a fan clutch, a hub that connects the water pump drive to the cooling fan using a temperature-sensitive viscous fluid to cause the fan to turn faster as the temperature of the air pulled through the radiator increases.

water jackets The passages in the engine block and cylinder head that surround the cylinders, valves, and ports.

ASE-Type Questions

1. Tech A says that the cooling system is designed to keep the engine as cool as possible. Tech B says that the heater core can remove heat from the cooling system. Who is correct?
   a. Tech A
   b. Tech B
   c. Both A and B
   d. Neither A nor B

2. Tech A says that the thermostat is open until the engine warms up, and then it closes. Tech B says that a faulty radiator cap can be the cause of boiling coolant. Who is correct?
   a. Tech A
   b. Tech B
   c. Both A and B
   d. Neither A nor B

3. Tech A says that when pure anti-freeze is used in the cooling system, the protection level is –70°F. Tech B says that Tech B says that pure antifreeze will cool the engine better than water. Who is correct?
   a. Tech A
   b. Tech B
   c. Both A and B
   d. Neither A nor B

4. Tech A says that some drive belts are a stretch fit design. Tech B says that the thermostat may have a bleed valve that should be accurately positioned when the thermostat is replaced. Who is correct?
   a. Tech A
   b. Tech B
   c. Both A and B
   d. Neither A nor B

5. Tech A says that the design of a surge tank system helps to purge air from the cooling system. Tech B says that overflow tanks are pressurized. Who is correct?
   a. Tech A
   b. Tech B
   c. Both A and B
   d. Neither A nor B

6. Tech A says that when you find coolant hoses collapsed, the radiator pressure cap has failed. Tech B says that overflow tanks are reservoirs designed to hold coolant and allow flow back to the radiator. Who is correct?
   a. Tech A
   b. Tech B
   c. Both A and B
   d. Neither A nor B

7. Tech A says that electric cooling fans are used to cause a large airflow over the radiator at high vehicle speeds. Tech B says that electric cooling fans are used to cause a large airflow over the radiator at low vehicle speeds. Who is correct?
   a. Tech A
   b. Tech B
   c. Both A and B
   d. Neither A nor B

8. Tech A says that there are a number of coolant types that each has its own life span. Tech B says that mixing of coolants is generally ok, since all coolants use the same chemical base. Who is correct?
   a. Tech A
   b. Tech B
   c. Both A and B
   d. Neither A nor B

9. Tech A says that coolant leaking out of the water pump weep hole is normal. Tech B says that a refractometer measures the specific gravity of a liquid. Who is correct?
   a. Tech A
   b. Tech B
   c. Both A and B
   d. Neither A nor B

10. Tech A says that a cooling system pressure tester can be used to find leaks in the cooling system. Tech B says that the cooling system pressure tester can be used to test the pressure at which the radiator cap vents. Who is correct?
    a. Tech A
    b. Tech B
    c. Both A and B
    d. Neither A nor B

CHAPTER 47

NATEF Tasks

Engine Performance
Ignition System

Page

- Diagnose (troubleshoot) ignition system–related problems such as not starting, hard starting, engine misfire, poor drivability, spark knock, power loss, poor mileage, and emissions concerns; determine necessary action. **AST** **MAST** 1661

- Inspect and test crankshaft and camshaft position sensor(s); determine necessary action. **AST** **MAST** 1666–1668

- Inspect, test, and/or replace ignition control module and power train/engine control module; reprogram as necessary. **AST** **MAST** 1668

- Remove and replace spark plugs; inspect secondary ignition components for wear and damage. **MLR** **AST** **MAST** 1669–1671

Computerized Engine Controls

- Access and use service information to perform step-by-step diagnosis. **AST** **MAST** 1669

Knowledge Objectives

After reading this chapter, you will be able to:
1. Explain the basic principles of a modern ignition system. (pp 1640–1645)
2. Describe the functions of the major components in an ignition system. (pp 1645–1649)
3. Describe the various types of ignition systems. (pp 1650–1660)
4. Explain the process involved in diagnosing ignition system issues. (p 1661)
5. Safely perform the NATEF tasks related to ignition systems. (pp 1661–1671)
6. List the steps involved in maintaining and repairing ignition system components. (pp 1662–1671)

Ignition Systems Overview

Skills Objectives

After reading this chapter, you will be able to:

1. Perform a spark test. (pp 1661–1662)
2. Inspect the primary and secondary circuits. (pp 1662–1663)
3. Test the ignition coil. (pp 1663–1664)
4. Test a pickup coil. (pp 1664–1665)
5. Test a spark plug wire. (pp 1665–1666)
6. Inspect a distributor cap and rotor. (pp 1666–1667)
7. Test the crankshaft and camshaft position sensors. (pp 1666–1668)
8. Test an ignition module. (p 1668)
9. Replace the spark plugs and spark plug wires. (pp 1669–1671)

▶ Introduction

The air–fuel mixture inside each cylinder must be ignited for it to release its energy and create pressure to force the piston down the cylinder on the power stroke. Gasoline engines use the heat of a **high-voltage spark** to ignite the mixture. The purpose of the ignition system is to create the high-voltage spark and deliver it at the right time to each cylinder.

The ignition system consists of a primary (low-voltage) circuit and a secondary (high-voltage) circuit. The primary circuit connects and disconnects the ignition coil, which changes the low voltage of the vehicle battery into the high voltage needed to create the spark that is sent across the spark plug electrodes. The secondary circuit distributes the high voltage from the coil, or coils, to the spark plug at each cylinder. Although there are several types of ignition systems, the common components include the spark plugs, the ignition coil, and a device for triggering the ignition coil.

For an engine to run smoothly and efficiently, the high-voltage spark must cross the spark plug electrode as the piston approaches top dead center of the **compression stroke**. The ignition system must also be able to advance or retard the timing of the spark, based on engine conditions such as load, speed, and driver input. This chapter explains the principles and operation of modern ignition systems and covers the basics of diagnosis, maintenance, and repair.

▶ Ignition Principles

When the driver turns the key to the start position (or presses the electronic start button), an electrical connection is made between the vehicle battery and the primary winding of the ignition coil. As the engine is cranked, a switching circuit turns the primary ignition coil circuit on and off. The coil's function is to amplify the battery's low voltage and high current into very high voltage and low current. This high voltage is delivered from the ignition coil to each cylinder, where the spark plugs are installed **FIGURE 47-1**. As the high

FIGURE 47-1 An ignition system circuit.

▶ You are the Automotive Technician

Today a customer visits your shop for a scheduled 60,000 mile service on her 2009 vehicle. The service information says to replace the spark plugs and inspect the secondary ignition system, consisting of the ignition coils and spark plug boots. When you twist the spark plug boots to pull them off of the plugs, several of the boots tear, requiring replacement. After the boots are off, you use compressed air (while wearing safety glasses) to blow out any debris from around the spark plugs. You remove the plugs one at a time and inspect them. The deposits are light and show that they are burning correctly—not too hot nor too cold. The gaps are worn as expected. You inspect the ignition coils. The terminals and insulation look good, and you will be replacing all of the boots.

1. How would you prevent the boots from sticking to the spark plugs the next time?
2. How would you test to see if the ignition system was working on a vehicle that cranked but didn't start?
3. If this customer drove only short trips of a mile or two, would you recommend a spark plug with a hotter heat range or colder heat range? If so, why?

AS-76: Coil: The technician can explain how a coil can increase the battery voltage needed to fire a spark plug.

An ignition coil is a step-up transformer, increasing the vehicle's battery voltage to a high voltage necessary to fire the spark plugs and ignite the air–fuel mixture in the cylinders. Coils operate via the concept of electromagnetic induction, which dictates that a moving magnetic field (or a change in a stationery magnetic field in the case of an ignition coil) can induce a current in a wire exposed to the field.

The internal makeup of a coil is basically an iron core with two windings of wire, both wound around the core. The secondary winding is wound with considerably more turns than the primary, typically at a ratio of about 100:1.

In operation, battery voltage is applied to the primary winding, creating a magnetic field. This process is called saturation. The secondary winding is exposed to this field. To create a spark, the primary circuit is interrupted, or turned off, by a power train control module, ignition module, or breaker points. This interruption causes the magnetic field to collapse and a high voltage to be induced into the secondary winding. The increase in voltage is provided by the difference in the number of turns between the windings. Current in the secondary winding is directed to the spark plugs.

voltage pushes current across the spark plug electrodes, the air–fuel mixture is ignited, causing very high pressure, which in turn pushes the piston down on the power stroke.

The ignition system has undergone changes in technology over the decades to meet requirements for dependability, reduced maintenance expectations, and increasingly strict emission standards. The original system was the **contact breaker point ignition system**—a mechanical system with a switch, called **contact breaker points**, that was opened and closed as the engine was running **FIGURE 47-2**. The points turned the primary ignition circuit on and off, which created a spark that was distributed to each spark plug in the firing order.

The first advancement was the replacement of the mechanical switch with an electronic switching device **FIGURE 47-3**. This device lacked moving components, meaning minimal wear on the switching device and very little, if any, maintenance. The device was called an **electronic ignition system—distributor type**, since it still used a distributor to dispense the spark to the various cylinders.

The next advancement was eliminating the distributor by using dedicated ignition coils—one coil for each pair of cylinders. This was called a **waste spark ignition system** **FIGURE 47-4**. A four-cylinder engine would have two ignition coils, a six-cylinder engine would have three coils, and so on. Eliminating the distributor meant doing away with the last mechanical component of the ignition system, which again resulted in increased reliability and reduced maintenance issues.

FIGURE 47-2 Contact breaker point ignition system.

FIGURE 47-3 Electronic ignition system—distributor type.

FIGURE 47-4 A waste spark ignition system.

FIGURE 47-5 A coil-on-plug ignition system.

The latest development has been to give each cylinder its own ignition coil. This is called a **direct ignition system** or **coil-on-plug** ignition system **FIGURE 47-5**. This system puts the ignition coil directly on top of the spark plug, thus eliminating the spark plug wires, which are subject to damage and wear.

Primary and Secondary Circuits

The ignition system uses an **induction coil** to convert relatively low-voltage and high-current flow into very high-voltage and very low-current flow. The low-voltage side is called the **primary circuit**, and the high-voltage side is called the **secondary circuit**. The battery supplies the low-voltage and high-current flow to power the primary circuit. The induction coil steps up the low voltage in the primary circuit to the high voltage in the secondary circuit. A problem in the primary circuit will affect the secondary circuit, so technicians need a complete understanding of both circuits when diagnosing faults relating to the ignition system **TABLE 47-1**.

Faraday's Law

Most automotive ignition systems use ignition coils that operate on the principles of an induction coil. Automotive induction coils step up the nominal battery voltage of 12 volts to the voltage needed to bridge the gap across the spark plug electrodes, which can be up to 100,000 volts. These induction coils operate according to Faraday's law.

Faraday's law states that relative movement between a conductor and a magnetic field allows four ways by which voltage can be induced in a conductor:

1. Moving a magnet so that the magnetic lines of force cut across a conductor, as in an alternator.

TABLE 47-1: Primary and Secondary Circuit Components

Contact Breaker System	
Primary Circuit Components	**Secondary Circuit Components**
Battery	Ignition coil—secondary winding
Ignition switch	Coil wire
Ballast resistor	Distributor cap
Ignition coil—primary winding	Rotor
Capacitor	Spark plug wires
Contact breaker points	Spark plugs
Electronic Ignition—Distributor-Style System	
Primary Circuit Components	**Secondary Circuit Components**
Battery	Ignition coil—secondary winding
Ignition switch	Coil wire
Ignition coil—primary winding	Distributor cap
Ignition module	Rotor
Triggering device	Spark plug wires
	Spark plugs
Electronic Ignition—Distributorless-Style System	
Primary Circuit Components	**Secondary Circuit Components**
Battery	Ignition coils—secondary windings
Ignition switch	Spark plug wires
Ignition coils—primary windings	Spark plugs
Ignition module	
Triggering device	
Direct Ignition System	
Primary Circuit Components	**Secondary Circuit Components**
Battery	Ignition coils—secondary windings
Ignition switch	Spark plugs
Ignition coils—primary windings	
Ignition module	
Triggering device	

2. Moving a conductor so that it cuts across the stationary magnetic field, as in a generator.

3. Starting, stopping, or changing the rate of current flow in a conductor. This causes the conductor

to induce an electromagnetic field into itself and occurs in the primary windings of an ignition coil. This process is called self-induction.

4. Starting, stopping, or changing the rate of current flow in a conductor that is positioned close to a second conductor. This is called mutual induction. It is used to induce high voltage in the secondary winding of the ignition coil.

When any of these methods are used to induce voltage in a conductor, the value of that voltage depends on the density, or strength, of the magnetic field. The stronger the field, the greater the induced voltage. It is also influenced by the number of turns of the coil. The more turns, the greater the induced voltage. The speed at which the lines of force are cut also affects the voltage induced. The greater the speed, the greater the induced voltage. In the induction coil, the secondary winding has many thousands of turns of fine enameled copper wire. The primary winding, with a few hundred turns of relatively heavy wire, is positioned close to the secondary winding. A soft iron core is positioned centrally to concentrate the magnetic field. Current flow through the primary winding establishes a magnetic field around the windings. The higher the current flow, the stronger the field.

Sudden interruption of the primary current effectively disconnects the battery from the coil and current flow ceases. As a result, there is no externally applied voltage source to dictate the voltage value across the ends of the primary winding. The magnetic field collapses into the iron core, returning its stored energy to the coil by cutting across the coil's primary and secondary windings. This produces a self-induced voltage in the primary winding and a mutually induced voltage in the secondary winding.

The maximum value of the secondary voltage is partly determined by the ratio of the number of turns in the secondary winding to the number of turns in the primary winding (in this case, approximately 100 to 1) and by the value of the self-induced voltage in the primary winding (in this case, 300 volts). If this coil is 100% efficient, the maximum voltage available from the secondary winding would be 300 volts multiplied by 100, or 30,000 volts.

Since the value of the self-induced voltage in the primary winding is also influenced by the rate of collapse of the magnetic field, which is determined by the rate of change of the current flow through the coil, it is essential that the primary current be switched off as quickly as possible. All ignition systems make provisions to ensure that this occurs. This subject will be covered in greater detail later in this chapter.

Required Voltage Versus Available Voltage

Understanding the terms "required voltage" and "available voltage" will help you diagnose ignition systems. **Required voltage** is the amount of voltage required to initially get current to jump the spark plug gap. When the voltage reaches the point where current is flowing in the secondary circuit, the required voltage drops to a much lower level, just sufficient enough to sustain current flow and the spark. This gives the air–fuel mixture the opportunity to ignite during the duration of the spark.

The other factor is available voltage. **Available voltage** is the maximum amount of voltage available to try to push current to jump the spark plug gap if the gap were infinite. In other words, available voltage is the maximum amount of voltage that the ignition coil can put out. It is very important that the available voltage is always higher than the required voltage **FIGURE 47-6**. If the available voltage falls below required voltage, or if required voltage is ever higher than the available voltage, there will not be enough voltage to push current across the gap and create a spark. Since the spark between the spark plug electrodes is required to ignite the air–fuel mixture, higher required voltage or lower available voltage will prevent the spark from occurring, which causes the cylinder to not fire, which is called a misfire.

As a vehicle is driven over time, generally the required voltage will increase while the available voltage decreases. The required voltage usually increases primarily because

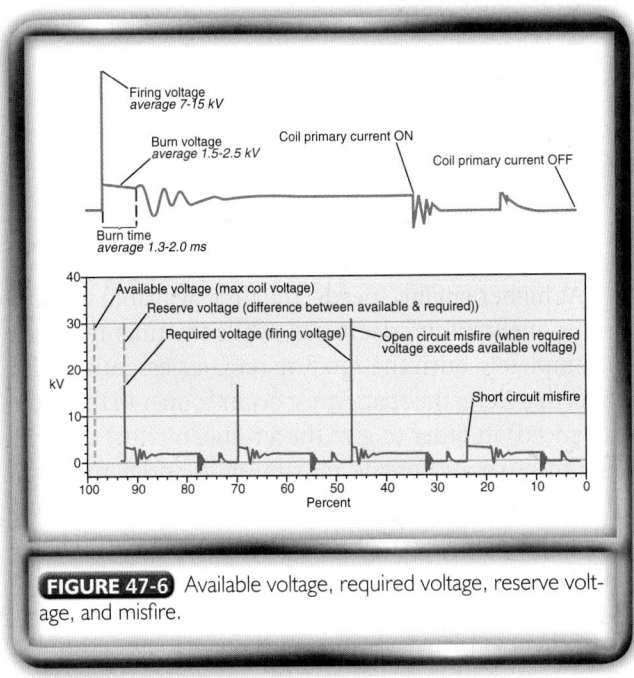

FIGURE 47-6 Available voltage, required voltage, reserve voltage, and misfire.

of the growing gap of the spark plug as it wears over time. However, it can also increase due to any open circuits in the secondary side of the circuit, such as a broken rotor tip or an open spark plug wire. Manufacturers design their ignition systems to have an amount of reserve voltage above the required voltage so that misfire is prevented. But if the vehicle's ignition system is not maintained, this reserve voltage is reduced and the engine is prone to misfire, especially when accelerating or climbing a hill. Inspecting all of the components and replacing any that are worn will restore the available voltage to what it should be and reduce the required voltage to within specifications. This will restore the ignition system to its proper operation.

> ### ►TECHNICIAN TIP
>
> Required voltage is increased by spark plug gaps that are too wide or worn, compression pressures that are higher than normal, or lean mixtures. Available voltage is affected by faults in the primary or secondary circuits such as shorted coil windings or high resistance in the primary circuit.

Spark Timing

The timing of the spark is critical to the smooth and efficient operation of the engine. For any given engine speed and load, the correct **spark timing** varies according to a number of factors, including:

- Air–fuel ratio
- Detected knock
- Engine speed
- Engine load
- Engine temperature
- Air temperature
- Transmission gear selected
- Throttle position

At higher engine speeds, the time available to burn the air–fuel mixture decreases, while the time required to completely burn the mixture remains essentially the same; therefore, the spark must occur sooner in the cycle (advanced) in order to give the air–fuel mixture enough time to burn and create maximum cylinder pressure soon after top dead center. As the throttle is opened and the engine load increases, the spark does not need to be advanced as much, because there is more pressure in the cylinders and the engine is not spinning very fast; thus, there is plenty of time for the air–fuel mixture to

burn. However, as the engine's revolutions per minute (rpm) continue to increase, especially under a light load, the timing must be advanced significantly. If the timing is advanced too far, then the engine begins to knock. If it is equipped with a knock sensor located on the engine block, the sensor sends a signal to the **power train control module (PCM)**. The PCM may also be called an **engine control module (ECM)** or an **electronic control unit (ECU)**. The PCM then retards the timing to decrease or eliminate the knock. At lower engine temperatures, the fuel does not atomize as quickly and requires the spark to be advanced.

In early vehicles that use a distributor, base spark timing is set at idle speeds by positioning the distributor body in relation to its rotating cam. The timing is almost always indexed to the **number one cylinder**, and the contact breaker points are operated in turn by each cam lobe to provide the same timing point for succeeding cylinders in the firing order. This initial setting, which in most, but not all, cases occurs before top dead center, allows time for maximum pressure in the cylinder to develop, just as the piston is descending on the power stroke.

Today's vehicles use electronically triggered ignition systems. The timing is engineered into the design of the engine and is not adjustable. The timing components are fixed in position within the distributor (if used) or on the engine block and crankshaft or flywheel **FIGURE 47-7**. The initial timing specification is programmed into the PCM software.

As engine speed increases, there is increasingly less time for the air–fuel mixture to be ignited and for this maximum pressure to develop; therefore, the ignition point must be advanced. That is, it must start earlier in

FIGURE 47-7 A crankshaft position sensor.

relation to the piston's position during the compression stroke. This adjustment must occur automatically in relation to engine speed and engine load.

Older vehicles with nonelectronically controlled spark timing and early electronic ignition systems use mechanical means to adjust spark timing according to engine rpm and load. To advance the timing in response to rpm, a centrifugal type of **advance mechanism** is used, called a mechanical advance. This device is located either above or below the distributor base plate and rotates with the distributor shaft. As engine speed rises, the flyweights on the advance mechanism are thrown outward by centrifugal force. Since the distributor cam is able to pivot on the distributor shaft a limited number of degrees, the weights act against their springs and move the distributor cam forward, advancing the timing.

The load-sensitive advance mechanism, called the **vacuum advance unit**, is operated by **intake manifold vacuum** via a port on the **throttle body** (**FIGURE 47-8**). It acts to adjust the timing based on engine vacuum, which changes as engine load changes. The port is connected by a vacuum line to a sealed chamber on one side of a spring-loaded diaphragm. A mechanical link on the other side connects the diaphragm to the **distributor base plate**, also called the **breaker plate**. The distributor base plate is a moveable metal plate located in the distributor, beneath the distributor cap on which the contact breaker points are mounted. As vacuum is applied, the diaphragm moves against the spring to rotate the base plate, and since the base plate carries the contact breaker points, the contacts meet the distributor cam earlier in rotation, advancing the spark.

FIGURE 47-8 A vacuum advance mechanism.

Today's vehicles all use the PCM to control spark timing. Various sensors, such as the throttle position sensor, mass airflow sensor, rpm signal, and many other engine sensors, send input to the PCM. The ideal spark timing for all engine conditions is programmed into the PCM using software. The PCM then calculates the timing and controls the ignition coils either directly or through a driver located on the coil.

Standard Components of an Ignition System

Most ignition systems include a battery, ignition switch, ignition coil(s), high-tension leads (also called spark plug wires), and spark plugs. The battery is the same one used to start the vehicle and provide electrical power to all electrical loads when the engine is not running. The ignition switch is used to connect the ignition system to the battery during operation and disconnect it from the battery to turn the engine off. The ignition coil is needed to amplify the battery voltage into very high voltage.

The high-tension leads connect the coil to the distributor cap center terminal and the distributor cap side terminals to the terminals on the top of the spark plugs. On distributorless and coil-on-plug systems, the high-tension lead connects directly from the coil to the spark plug. Coil-on-plug systems have no high-tension leads at all. The spark plugs are threaded into the top of each cylinder and provide a place for the spark to jump within the combustion chamber.

Battery

An automotive battery is a chemical-electrical device that provides voltage to all electrical loads while the engine is not running, and when the loads exceed the output of the alternator. The **battery** supplies the electrical energy to the ignition circuit during start-up. Most modern vehicles use a 12-volt lead acid rechargeable battery located in the engine compartment, in the trunk, or under the rear seats. Once the engine is started, the alternator provides power for all electrical loads by charging the battery.

Ignition Switch

The **ignition switch** has more functions than simply starting and stopping the engine. It provides a way to disconnect most electrical accessories from the battery with an ignition key. The common position of an ignition switch include:

- Lock and off: The key can only be removed from the lock position. When this occurs, all nonessential electrical circuits are disabled and the steering column lock is enabled. If equipped, the engine immobilizer and theft-deterrent system are normally activated at this time. Many modern vehicles also include an off ignition point. Turning the key from the lock to the off position unlocks the steering column, but it does not enable any electrical systems or disable the engine immobilizer or theft-deterrent system.

- Accessory: This position allows power to be supplied to the vehicle entertainment system, the blower fan, and in some vehicles the wipers, electric windows, and sunroof. The features enabled by the accessory position are mainly for passenger convenience. Prolonged use of any of them without the engine running will drain the battery.

- On/run: When the switch is turned to the on position, most warning lamps on the instrument panel should illuminate. This is to test the operation of the lamps. On vehicles that are not equipped with engine immobilizers, this position also activates the accessories and ignition system. Vehicles that are equipped with engine immobilizers do not normally activate these systems until the key is turned to the start position.

- Start/crank: The start position activates the starter motor relay and/or solenoid, which enables the engine to crank and start the engine. Vehicles without engine immobilizers can start immediately, as the required electrical systems will have already been activated when the key was turned to the on position. In vehicles equipped with engine immobilizers, a number of the essential electrical systems are not normally enabled until the key is turned to the start position. When this occurs, communication between various control units determines whether to allow the engine to start or not. Starting is achieved by deactivating the immobilizer and activating the ignition, fuel, and charging systems. There may be a slight delay while this communication is occurring.

The key itself can consist of two parts. The first is a mechanical type that works in the key barrel and turns to unlock the steering column and switch through the various stages of off, accessories, on, and start. Many modern vehicles now come equipped with an immobilizer system that disables the ignition, fuel, and starter systems unless a transponder device with the correct code is within close range of a receiver in the vehicle. The immobilizer system uses a randomly selected **rolling code**—a constantly changing, numeric code that is communicated with the engine immobilizer and security system by a radio frequency signal. The frequency transmitter is usually located in the key assembly itself

and is usually powered by magnetic induction through a winding around the key barrel. The receiver is often also found in the steering column, near the key barrel. If the correct code is not recognized, or if someone attempts to start the vehicle by some other means, the system will remain armed and prevent the vehicle from starting. In some vehicles, the starting system may be disabled in place of, or in addition to, the fuel and ignition systems.

In many automatic transmission vehicles, the ignition switch also has a transmission shift interlock device connected to it. In these vehicles, the gear selector must be moved into the park position before the key can be removed from the lock position. In the same way, the transmission shift lever cannot be moved out of park until the key has been turned to the on/run position and the brake pedal has been depressed.

Ignition Coil

Ignition coils are basically **step-up transformers**. Ignition coils are electrical devices that amplify the low voltage available from the vehicle's battery to the very high voltage needed for the current to jump the electrodes of the spark plugs, thereby causing spark **FIGURE 47-9**. There are two sets of windings in an ignition coil: the **primary winding** and the **secondary winding**.

When battery voltage pushes current through the primary windings of an ignition coil, a magnetic field is created. When the primary circuit is opened, the collapsing magnetic field induces a voltage of more than 20,000 volts in the secondary winding. This voltage pushes current through the secondary circuit to the electrodes of the spark plugs, creating the needed spark for the power strokes.

FIGURE 47-9 Cutaway of a basic ignition coil.

A standard ignition coil has a rod-shaped laminated iron core, which is located centrally by an insulator at its base. The secondary winding, with 15,000 to 30,000 turns of very thin **enameled copper wire**, is wound around the core and is insulated from the core by layers of treated insulated paper. The primary winding, with a few hundred turns of much heavier copper wire, is wound on the outside of the secondary. A shield of soft iron surrounds the outer windings, and the complete assembly is inserted into a one-piece steel or aluminum container or encased in an epoxy housing. On older coils, the container is then filled with special oil, which provides good electrical insulation and permits rapid heat dissipation. Epoxy-encased coils are cooled by the surrounding air.

The coil has two terminals, positive and negative, for external connection to the primary circuit. The ends of the primary winding are connected internally to each of these terminals. Provisions are also made externally for a heavy insulated center terminal to connect the high-tension coil leads.

One end of the secondary winding is connected to this center terminal, and the other end is connected either to one end of the primary winding or in some applications to a separate ground. On waste spark systems, each end of the secondary winding is attached to a spark plug with a spark plug wire (two plugs per coil). Coil-on-plug and coil-near-plug systems usually have one end of the secondary winding grounded and the other end connected to the high-tension terminal of the spark plug.

High-Tension Leads

High-tension leads, also known as HT leads or spark plug wires, connect the secondary ignition components together, such as the coil to the distributor cap and the distributor cap to the spark plugs. High voltage from the ignition coil pushes current to the distributor cap and on to the spark plugs along these leads and jumps across the spark plug gap, creating the hot spark needed for combustion. The high-tension leads conduct the high output voltage generated in the secondary ignition circuit when each ignition pulse occurs. They link the **high-tension terminal(s)** of the ignition coil, the distributor cap, and spark plugs.

With the higher voltages that today's electronic ignition systems have to endure because of the increased spark plug gaps and leaner air–fuel mixtures, the insulation material on the high-tension leads is now much thicker than in earlier models. The core of the high-tension lead is typically made of carbon-impregnated linen or fiberglass **FIGURE 47-10**. It has a specific resistance, or opposition, to current flow that helps reduce the radio frequency interference emitted from the high-tension leads. A crimped terminal at each end provides for connection of the components.

Coil Wire

If a distributor is used, typically a coil wire is used to transmit the high voltage from the ignition coil to the center terminal of the distributor cap. On systems where the coil is mounted inside the distributor, there is no coil wire. The high voltage is transmitted through a terminal in the distributor cap. On systems that do not use a distributor, there is no coil wire. Instead, the high-tension leads connect the terminals of coil packs directly to the terminals of the spark plugs.

Braided glass
Ferrite or EPDM core
Silicone insulation layer
High dielectric strength insulator
Variable pitch coil
Glass fiber core

FIGURE 47-10 The parts of a high-tension lead.

Spark Plug

The **spark plug** consists of a plated metal shell with a ceramic insulator and an electrode extending through the center of the insulator. Threads on the metal shell allow it to be screwed into the cylinder head. A short side electrode is attached to one side and bent toward the center electrode. The electrodes are made from a special alloy wire with a manufacturer-recommended gap between them. The spark bridges this gap to ignite the air–fuel mixture in the combustion chamber. When the spark jumps from one electrode to the other (usually from the center electrode to the side electrode), it ignites the air–fuel mixture inside the cylinders.

Most modern spark plugs are made of a ceramic heat insulator, partially covered by a steel shell that threads into the cylinder head at the top of the combustion chamber **FIGURE 47-11**. All spark plugs include at least one side electrode and may have as many as four side electrodes. Spark plugs either use a taper design or a washer type of gasket to form a seal between the spark plug and the cylinder head. Modern spark plugs also include an internal resistor to suppress voltage spikes when the spark plug is energized. The reduced voltage spikes prevent radio frequency interference.

Spark plugs are identified by three different features:

- Thread size or diameter
- Reach or length of the thread
- Heat range or operating temperature

FIGURE 47-11 Spark plug.

Spark Plug Components

The metal case of a spark plug removes heat from the insulator and passes it on to the cylinder head. It also provides structural strength to cope with the torque force applied when tightening the plug into place. The case also acts as the ground for the current passing through the electrodes.

The insulator covering the center electrode is usually made from an aluminum oxide ceramic with a high tolerance to heat and electrical voltage. The ribbing design, the exact composition of the insulator material, and the length of the insulator can all partly determine the heat range of the plug. For example, a spark plug with a shorter path for heat to flow from the center of the spark plug to the coolant flowing through the cylinder head has a cooler heat range. A spark plug with a longer path for heat to flow has a hotter heat range.

The spark plug seals the combustion chamber when installed, and the seals make sure it is kept airtight. The seal can be a hollow metal washer, which at the correct torque setting is partially crushed between the flat surface of the head and the plug just above the threads. Or the seal can be provided by a carefully machined taper on the spark plug body that mates with a matching machined taper in the spark plug hole in the cylinder head.

A terminal at the outer end of the spark plug connects it electrically to the ignition system. Most ignition leads clip on the spark plug. In a few applications, they may be held in place by a threaded nut. The side electrode runs very hot and is usually made of nickel steel or another high-temperature metal and welded to the side of the metal spark plug case. Some spark plug designs have multiple side electrodes that create the gap between the side of the center electrode and the side electrode.

The <u>center electrode</u> is the hottest part of the spark plug. Generally it takes less voltage for a spark to jump from a hot surface to a cooler surface, so many older ignition systems were designed to jump from the center electrode to the side electrode. However, with today's high-energy ignition systems, this is no longer a factor. The electrons stream from the sharp edges of the electrodes, and as these edges erode and become less sharp, it becomes more difficult for the electrons to jump the air gap, causing an increase in the required voltage. It used to be necessary to maintain spark plugs by sandblasting built-up deposits from the internal surfaces and filing the electrodes sharp again, but as low-erosion materials such as platinum and iridium have become available, this is not necessary. Spark plugs now usually last a lot longer (up to 100,000 miles [160,000 km]) and are replaced rather than refurbished. Be careful when installing plugs on some waste spark systems, which use polarity sensitive spark plugs that have platinum only on one electrode and therefore need to be installed in the correct spark plug hole. Manufacturer's service information will provide this information.

> ### TECHNICIAN TIP
>
> The same spark plug can sometimes be used in different engines with different gap settings; therefore, the gap should be checked with an accurate spark plug gauge and, if necessary, adjusted according to the specifications in the service information when the spark plug is first installed. The gap is critical to engine performance. A narrow gap may give a spark too weak to ignite the air–fuel mixture effectively. A gap too wide may fail to produce any spark at all. Either way, the wrong gap will reduce engine power and fuel efficiency and will increase emissions. One exception to the gapping rule is iridium spark plugs. The gap should not be adjusted, as the iridium is brittle and can snap off. Verify that their gap meets specifications. If the gap is wrong, they will have to be replaced.

Spark Plug Size

Spark plug size refers to the diameter of the threads of the spark plug. Nearly all of today's light-duty vehicles use either a 14-millimeter (mm) or an 18-mm spark plug, although some manufacturers use 16-mm "high-thread" spark plugs or even 12-mm long-reach spark plugs. Most manufacturers have been switching toward smaller plugs to allow for larger or more valves in the cylinder head. Both the Society of Automotive Engineers (SAE) and the International Organization for Standardization (ISO)

have a set of standards that cover length, hex size, thread diameter, and thread pitch.

Spark Plug Reach

<u>Spark plug reach</u> is the distance from the seat of the spark plug to the end of the spark plug threads. The purpose of spark plug reach is to ensure that the spark plug electrodes are in the most efficient position for combustion within the cylinder. If the reach is too long, the piston may strike the spark plug while moving up. If the reach is too short, the spark may occur inside of the threaded spark plug hole, resulting in a misfire. Some spark plugs are only threaded on the bottom half or in the case of "high thread" plugs, the top half of their reach. Always install the specified spark plug for the engine you are working on.

Heat Range

Spark plugs should operate between average temperatures of 746°F and 1460°F, or 400°C and 800°C. This is referred to as the <u>heat range</u>. The operating temperature of a spark plug refers to the temperature at the sparking tip of the spark plug inside a running engine. The temperature that a spark plug will reach depends on the distance the heat must travel from the insulator on the firing end to reach the outer shell of the plug and enter the cylinder head and the water jacket. If the heat path is long, the spark plug will retain more heat and therefore will run at a higher temperature than one with a short heat path. If the tip is too hot, pre-ignition can occur.

If it is too cold, deposits may form on the insulator, causing spark energy loss. Hot-rated spark plugs are better insulators, keeping more of the engine heat in the tip of the spark plug. A cold-rated plug conducts more of the heat out of the spark plug tip. The heat range of a spark plug is affected by a wide range of characteristics, including its design profile and the types of material used in its manufacture, as well as the operating conditions of the engine.

> ### TECHNICIAN TIP
>
> Spark plug cooling is affected by spark plug torque. Since almost all of the heat from the spark plug must be transferred through the threads of the spark plug to the cylinder head, properly torquing the spark plugs will keep the threads in contact with the head, allowing heat to transfer more quickly. This allows the plug to operate at its designed temperature, instead of overheating and causing pre-ignition.

► Types of Ignition Systems

Several types of ignition systems have been used over the years. Contact breaker point ignition systems were used on earlier vehicles and relied on mechanical devices to create the spark. On later vehicles, the mechanical contact breaker was eliminated, and an electronic means of connecting and disconnecting the primary circuit was used. Modern vehicles no longer use a distributor and send the high voltage from the coil packs or individual coils directly to the spark plugs.

The main difference among these systems is in the way the primary circuits are controlled to produce the secondary spark. The primary circuit is switched on and off, thus creating and then collapsing the primary magnetic field. This switching can be done with breaker points in older vehicles or by electronic switches in modern vehicles.

Contact Breaker Point Ignition Systems

Contact breaker point ignition systems were used on early-model vehicles, providing a mechanical means of quickly connecting and disconnecting the primary side of the ignition coil to ground. The contact breaker is a mechanically operated electrical switch that is fixed to the distributor base plate and opened and closed by the distributor cam with the rotation of the engine. This process builds up and collapses the magnetic field in the ignition coil in order to create a high-voltage output of the ignition coil.

Located in the distributor, the contact points are opened by **cam lobes**, or protrusions on the otherwise round distributor shaft, and closed by a spring. The number of lobes is equal to the number of cylinders, so that the contact breaker points open the circuit and activate the ignition coil at the end of each compression stroke for each cylinder. In order for the spark plugs to fire at the correct moment, the distributor must be installed in the right position. Most manufacturers specify that the ignition **rotor** be located under the distributor cap terminal of the number one cylinder with the piston of the number one cylinder at top dead center of the compression stroke.

Contact breaker point ignition systems provide a simple means of establishing and interrupting the current flowing in the primary ignition circuit. A basic system consists of:

- The battery: Provides a source of energy.
- The ignition switch: Provides the driver control over system operation.

- An ignition coil: Provides step-up transformer action.
- Contact breaker points: Opened and closed by lobes on the distributor cam as the engine rotates to make and break the primary circuit at the correct time in the ignition cycle **FIGURE 47-12**.
- A capacitor: Assists in the rapid collapse of the ignition coil's magnetic field. Any voltage surge across the contacts will charge the capacitor, rather than cause damaging arcing. The condenser is typically mounted on the breaker plate or on the side of the distributor.
- A distributor: Rotates at half the speed of the crankshaft to house the contact breaker points and distribute the high voltage from the ignition coil and spark plugs, thus igniting the air–fuel mixture in each cylinder in the correct firing order.
- Connecting wires and leads suitable for conducting the current flowing in the ignition system, at the appropriate voltage level.

Opening and closing the contact breaker switches the primary current off and on. When the contacts begin to separate, the primary current tends to flow on, producing an arc across the contacts. The capacitor absorbs this surge of **inductive current** by providing a very short-term, alternative path, in parallel with the opening contacts. The capacitor charges to the peak value of the primary winding voltage. By the time this has occurred, the gap between the contacts is too wide for a spark to discharge between them. This abrupt interruption of the primary circuit assists in the rapid collapse of the magnetic field and, hence, an increase in the value of the voltage induced in the primary and secondary windings.

As soon as the secondary voltage reaches a value great enough to bridge the gap across the spark plug, the voltage in the primary circuit falls to a value below that of the charged capacitor. The capacitor then discharges

FIGURE 47-12 Contact breaker point operation.

back through the primary circuit. The spark at the spark plug needs to last for about a minimum of 1 millisecond (0.001 second) to provide enough heat to light the air–fuel mixture. The time the current is flowing across the electrodes is called the spark duration. Extra-long spark duration causes excessive wear on the spark plug electrodes.

The **condenser** is made up of two plates constructed from narrow strips of aluminum foil that are insulated from each other by a special waxed paper, called a dielectric. The plates and insulating paper are rolled up tightly together and sealed in a metal can by crimping the end over onto a gasket. A spring in the base forces the plates and insulation against the gasket to keep out moisture. One plate is connected to the capacitor case and, through its retaining screw, to ground. The other plate is connected to the external connecting lead. When the capacitor is fitted, any voltage surge across the contacts will charge the capacitor, rather than cause damaging sparking. The condenser is typically mounted to either the inside or the outside of the distributor.

> **TECHNICIAN TIP**
>
> The condenser is a critical component of the primary circuit in point-type ignition systems. Without it, the points arc as they are opened. This arcing causes a slow stopping of the primary current flow, which causes a slow collapsing of the magnetic field in the ignition coil, which in turn causes low voltage output of the secondary windings. If you have weak spark output on a point-type ignition system, do not be like a former student and overlook the very simple and inexpensive condenser. This student ended up replacing the spark plugs, spark plug wires, cap, rotor, points, ignition coil, and carburetor before he asked for help. The wise old technician, after listening to his story, pulled out a used condenser and connected it to the negative side of the coil and ground with a couple of test leads and asked the student to try starting the engine. The student was amazed when it started right up and ran like new.

> **TECHNICIAN TIP**
>
> The secondary spark occurs when the points open, not when they close. It is the rapid collapse of the magnetic field that induces the high voltage in the secondary windings. Knowing that the spark occurs just as the points open helps a technician static-time an engine after an engine rebuild or when the distributor has been removed.

Dwell Angle

With the primary circuit being switched on and off repeatedly, each ignition coil has to be designed for a particular application so that it operates efficiently. For a four-stroke, four-cylinder engine running at 2000 rpm, 4000 sparks must be supplied every minute. The time available to make and break the primary circuit each time is very short. As engine speed rises, the time available is even shorter; therefore, it is important to ensure that the length of time the current flows through the primary winding is sufficient to create the necessary magnetic field.

The condition in which the magnetic field is completely built is called coil saturation. In contact breaker systems, it is during this brief time that the contacts are closed and the primary current is flowing. For example, once the eccentric cam lobe on the distributor shaft spins past the rubbing block on the contact breaker points, a spring closes the contacts and allows battery voltage to push current through the completed primary circuit, building the magnetic field in the ignition coil primary windings. Current flows through the primary windings until the next eccentric cam pushes one contact point away from the other. The amount of time, in **degrees of distributor rotation**, that the contacts are closed is called the **dwell angle**.

The setting of the contact breaker gap influences this closed period. Once it has been set, the dwell angle remains fixed regardless of engine speed. A large gap gives a small dwell angle, since the eccentric cam only contacts the contact breaker for a short time during the distributor shaft's rotation. A small gap gives a large dwell angle, because the eccentric cam is closer to the contact breaker and keeps it open longer. The manufacturer's recommended

> **TECHNICIAN TIP**
>
> As the rubbing block wears, the point gap decreases and the dwell increases. Setting the dwell to the lower end of the specifications will allow the dwell to stay within specifications longer. The downside is that the wider point gap will also give a shorter dwell time, which reduces the saturation time for the coil, reducing its available voltage at very high engine rpm. This could cause intermittent misfire, which is sometimes referred to as "shooting the ducks" on the racetrack. Also, for every degree the dwell increases as the rubbing block wears, the timing retards one degree, reducing fuel mileage and power and increasing emissions. As a result, engines need "tuned up" every 10,000 to 15,000 miles (16,000 to 24,000 km) to install a new set of points and condenser, set the dwell angle, and adjust the ignition timing.

gap provides the specified dwell angle for each application, assuming there is no wear on the distributor cam. The dwell angle should be adjusted to specifications, and then the point gap should be checked for cam lobe wear. The proper gap ensures there is sufficient spacing between the wide-open contacts to prevent arcing.

Ballast Resistor

A **ballast resistor** limits the amount of current flowing in an electrical circuit **FIGURE 47-13**. The most common automotive use for a ballast resistor is to reduce the voltage and current to the ignition coil by being inserted in series in the primary circuit between the ignition switch and the positive terminal of the ignition coil. It is usually located near the ignition coil where it can dissipate its heat into the air.

When the ignition key is turned to the start position and the starter begins to crank the engine, a heavy load is placed on the battery. This load will cause the battery voltage to drop. Ignition systems must be designed to fire the air–fuel mixture on this reduced voltage. Yet, when the engine is running, ignition systems must be able to run on approximately 14 volts, since the charging system is charging the battery. The ballast resistor is key to providing the correct voltage to the ignition system. When the voltage is low because the engine is cranking over, a resistor bypass circuit bypasses the resistor, giving full cranking voltage to the coil. When the ignition switch is turned back to the run position, the resistor bypass circuit is disabled so current has to flow through the resistor, dropping its voltage from 14 volts to approximately 7 volts. More modern solid-state electronic ignition systems do not need a ballast resistor because they have been designed to handle a wider range of voltages.

Distributors

The **distributor's** main function is to distribute the spark to the spark plugs in the correct sequence and at the correct time in the engine cycle **FIGURE 47-14**. It includes a distributor cap, rotor, switching device, and a shaft with cam lobes for operating the switching device. The switching device is used to connect and disconnect the primary circuit. The distributor also houses the vacuum and mechanical (centrifugal) timing advance mechanisms on older engines. These are used to advance the timing of the spark under certain driving conditions.

The **distributor cap** covers the end of the distributor to protect the components inside. It also provides a connection point between the rotor and the spark plug leads. The rotor is a high-voltage rotating switch that transfers the secondary voltage from the center terminal of the distributor to the side terminals. The distributor distributes the high-voltage pulses to the individual spark plug wires in the correct sequence and at the correct instant in the engine cycle. In some applications, the ignition coil is mounted inside of the distributor; the cap covers the coil and provides an electrical path from the coil's output terminal to the center of the rotor. In other applications, the ignition coil is bolted to the top of the distributor cap on the outside and covered with a plastic shield. In this instance, the center of the coil sits right above the rotor, and a hole drilled in the cap allows a spring-loaded button to transfer the current pushed by the high voltage directly to the center of the rotor.

FIGURE 47-13 A ballast resistor in an ignition circuit.

FIGURE 47-14 Distributor.

An insulated **rotor arm** with a brass or steel electrode is keyed to the shaft directly above the cam and rotates within a molded insulated distributor cap held by clips or screws on the distributor housing. The distributor cap has the same number of connecting terminals for the spark plug wires as there are spark plugs, and a central terminal is connected to the high-tension lead from the ignition coil. An internal spring-loaded carbon brush conducts each high-voltage pulse from the central terminal to the center of the rotor electrode as it turns.

The high-voltage spark is timed to occur when the rotor electrode is aligned with a fixed electrode inside the distributor cap. The high voltage bridges the small gap between the electrodes, driving current through the ignition terminal for that cylinder and bridging the gap at the spark plug.

As the rotor turns inside the distributor cap, the high-voltage electrical surges take place successively for each cylinder according to the firing order. This is accomplished by arranging the high-tension leads, according to their place in the firing order, on the distributor cap. For example, an in-line four-cylinder engine typically has a firing order of 1-3-4-2. If the distributor shaft were designed to spin clockwise, the high-tension leads would be arranged on the cap with cylinder 3 positioned 90 degrees clockwise from cylinder 1. The lead for cylinder 4 would be 90 degrees clockwise from cylinder 3, and the lead for cylinder 2 would be 90 degrees clockwise from cylinder 4.

Centrifugal Advance Units

The **centrifugal advance mechanism** (also called mechanical advance) controls ignition timing in relation to engine speed. It is located within the distributor and can be above or below the contact points' base plate. It operates on the distributor shaft. The distributor shaft has two sections that turn on the same axis. The lower shaft is driven by the camshaft, and the upper shaft controls the opening time of contact points. Both shafts are joined by the centrifugal advance mechanism. Its function is to turn the upper shaft forward within limits in relation to the lower shaft, proportional to engine speed.

The lower shaft has two flyweights attached, each pivoted at opposite ends and controlled by a spring. As the shaft is turned, they are thrown outward by the effect of centrifugal force. The faster the shaft turns, the more they move outward. Slowing the shaft speed reduces the amount of centrifugal force, and spring force pulls them back in.

A slot in each weight is keyed to the upper shaft, and as the weights move outward, they turn the upper shaft

in relation to the lower shaft. This movement has the effect of advancing the opening of the contact points in relation to engine speed. The relationship between speed and advance is determined by how heavy the weights are and by the tension of the springs. The maximum advance is determined by limiting the movement of the weights with slots and pins or bushings.

Vacuum Advance Units

The vacuum advance mechanism controls **ignition advance** in relation to engine load. At light load, an engine is more efficient when the timing is advanced slightly. Under heavy load, the timing must be retarded slightly to avoid "pinging" or spark knock. Its function is to improve fuel economy and, in doing so, reduce exhaust emissions. Vacuum is routed from the carburetor to a spring-loaded diaphragm housing attached to the distributor. The diaphragm is attached to a pull rod that, when operating, acts on the distributor base plate, turning it opposite to the direction of distributor shaft rotation. The movement results in the contact points' opening time being advanced during light engine loads and retarded during heavy engine loads.

Manufacturers designed their vacuum advance to operate on one of three types of vacuum: ported, manifold, or venturi **FIGURE 47-15**. On older vehicles, ported vacuum is the most common. It is obtained through a small slit in the throttle bore located just above the throttle plate. This slot has no vacuum at idle, creating no vacuum advance at idle. As the throttle is opened, the vacuum to the slit increases, causing some vacuum advance, which

FIGURE 47-15 Vacuum sources: ported, manifold, and venturi.

tapers off at wide-open throttle. Manifold vacuum is obtained through a small hole in the throttle bore just below the throttle plate. It provides strong vacuum at idle and less vacuum as the throttle is opened. Venturi vacuum is obtained from a port that is connected to the smallest diameter of the venturi. This system has no vacuum at idle, but as airflow increases through the venturi, the vacuum increases. The vacuum in each of these systems acts on the vacuum diaphragm causing the timing to advance as vacuum increases, or retard as vacuum decreases. Since the vacuum responds differently in each type of vacuum, the manufacturer would specify the base timing and the advance curve profile for the engine.

Engine Spark Timing

Engine manufacturers include timing marks on their engines so that the technician can check and adjust the engine timing if some conditions have changed. There are two types of timing on gasoline engines: valve timing and ignition timing. Valve timing refers to the position of the valves in relation to the piston stroke. During the four-stroke cycle, the valves must open and close at the proper times. Engine manufacturers place marks on the gears, sprockets, or pulleys and the corresponding surfaces of the block and head to allow the valve timing to be properly set whenever the valve timing components are being replaced.

The ignition timing refers to the point at which the spark plug "fires" near the end of the compression stroke. On older vehicles with distributors, the base timing can be adjusted by rotating the position of the distributor housing in relation to the engine. On newer engines, the timing is not adjustable since the computer controls it based on all of the sensor information.

> **▷ TECHNICIAN TIP**
>
> Some newer engines still use a distributor for distributing the high-voltage spark, but they use a crankshaft position sensor to control the timing of the spark. Turning the distributor on this application interferes with the rotor to cap alignment. It does not actually change the timing. So just because it has a distributor does not mean that adjusting it will change the spark timing.

Electronic Ignition Systems

In **electronic ignition systems**, the contact breaker points are eliminated and the primary circuit is switched or triggered electronically with a power transistor located in the ignition module. In general, an electronic ignition system will have a stationary component and a component that spins with the distributor shaft, which is driven by the camshaft. When the spinning component and the stationary component interact as designed, a signal is sent to the ignition module where the transistor switches the primary circuit on and off, creating and collapsing the magnetic field in the coil primary winding. This is typically accomplished through the use of an inductive pickup, a **Hall-effect switch**, or an **optical sensor**. Many of the components, such as the battery, ignition switch, spark plugs, and wiring, in an electronic ignition system are essentially the same as those in a contact breaker point ignition system. The following sections describe only those components of an electronic ignition system that are not part of a contact breaker point ignition system.

Components of Distributor-Type Systems

Early electronic ignition systems included an ignition module and a triggering device coupled with a standard distributor. The triggering device can be a magnetic pulse generator, also known as a pickup coil, a Hall-effect switch, or an optical sensor. The triggering device sends signals to the ignition module to open and close the primary circuit. This causes a magnetic field to build up and collapse in the primary winding in the same way that the point ignition system does. The collapsing magnetic field in the primary circuit induces a voltage into the secondary windings of the ignition coil, producing the high voltage needed for sparking. This high voltage pushes current to the spark plugs, where the current jumps across the spark plug electrodes, creating the heat to ignite the air–fuel mixture.

Ignition Modules

Ignition modules are used in virtually every type of ignition system except the contact breaker point system. In its simplest form, it uses the information from the triggering device to turn the primary circuit on and off. As technology progressed, processing power was added to the module so that the dwell time could be modified. Thus, the dwell time could be shortened during low engine rpm and lengthened as rpm increased. This flexibility helps to prevent overheating of the ignition coil and transistor during low speed while still maintaining adequate time for coil saturation during all engine speeds. Further refinement saw current-limiting circuitry added to the ignition module, which allowed for the use of low-impedance ignition coils. After that, manufacturers started to use their PCMs to work along with the ignition module. The module typically provided for base timing while the engine was being started and then switched over and allowed the PCM to control ignition timing through the ignition module once the engine was running. In early electronic-ignition vehicles, the ignition module was typically located in one of three places: in the distributor, on the distributor, or away from the distributor on the firewall, inner fender, or air cleaner housing. On many waste spark systems, the ignition module is located either under the ignition coils or within the coil assemblies. On newer vehicles, the ignition module functions are completely controlled by the PCM, in many cases eliminating the need for an external ignition module.

Induction-Type Systems

Induction-type systems are electronic systems that use a magnetic pulse generator, also called a variable reluctor sensor (VR sensor), to generate an AC signal. They come in a variety of configurations, but all of them have a **stator** (also called a pickup coil) mounted on the distributor body and a rotor unit (also called a **reluctor** or trigger wheel) attached to the distributor shaft **FIGURE 47-16**. The reluctor has one tooth for each cylinder. As it spins, the teeth interact with the stator to trigger the ignition module. The stator may have only one projection with a stationary coil of fine enameled wire wound around it, or it may have a circular permanent magnet with a number of projections or teeth corresponding to the number of engine cylinders, and a stationary coil of fine enameled copper wire wound on a plastic reel and positioned inside or around the magnet. As the reluctor rotates, the teeth on the reluctor approach and leave the stator teeth, changing the air gap between them. As this occurs, the strength of the magnetic field changes, increasing as the teeth approach, reaching a maximum when they are in alignment and decreasing as they move away.

A **stationary winding** is an extended length of wire wrapped into a circle. As the stationary winding is influenced by the magnetic field, a voltage is induced across the ends of the winding each time the magnetic field changes. If the winding forms part of a complete circuit, the voltage will cause a current to flow. As the teeth approach, the strength of the magnetic field increases, inducing a voltage and current flow in the winding. The polarity of the voltage is said to be positive as it produces a current flow in a certain direction. When the teeth are in alignment, the magnetic field is at its strongest, but at that point, it is not changing. Voltage and current now fall to zero.

As the teeth move away, the strength of the magnetic field changes again, once more inducing voltage and causing current to flow in the winding. This time, current flow is in the opposite direction, and the polarity is now said to be negative. Since polarity changes every time the teeth approach and leave the stator teeth, the voltage produced is an alternating current voltage, and current flow is also alternating **FIGURE 47-17**.

After the positive pulse is received, a **dwell control section** of the ignition module determines when the primary circuit will be switched on and for how long current will flow in the primary winding. The dwell period can be varied according to engine speed, improving coil efficiency. At low engine speeds, the dwell period is short when measured in degrees, but when measured in time, it is enough to fully saturate the coil. As engine speed increases, the dwell period increases, which helps to maintain an adequate amount of time for coil saturation.

Ignition coils employed with electronic systems are referred to as **low-inductance coils** because their primary winding resistance and number of turns are low. Current flow is much higher than with contact breaker point systems and reaches its optimum level sooner. A current-limiting device within the control circuit limits maximum current flow to a safe value.

FIGURE 47-16 Types of inductive ignition pickup coils.

FIGURE 47-17 Typical ignition pickup coil scope pattern.

Ignition advance, according to engine speed and load, may be provided by centrifugal and vacuum advance mechanisms or through the ignition module or PCM on newer vehicles.

The induction winding is connected to the ignition module and forms part of an **internal module control circuit** FIGURE 47-18 . This section of the ignition module is responsible for receiving the trigger signal. With the ignition switched on and the engine stationary, battery voltage is applied to the coil's positive terminal. However, there is no current flow through the primary winding as the switching transistor is in the off state. Battery voltage, therefore, can also be read at the coil's negative terminal.

With engine rotation, the reluctor teeth on the distributor shaft approach the stator teeth or pickup coil and a voltage of positive polarity is induced in the winding. This voltage signals the control circuit to turn the primary current on, and a voltage is applied to the base/emitter of the **switching transistor**. The switching transistor acts as a relay. When activated, it allows current to flow through the ignition coil primary winding and through the collector/emitter of the switching transistor to ground. The magnetic field is built up in the ignition coil. Further rotation of the reluctor causes the teeth to align with the stator teeth or pickup coil and then move away.

Simply stated, the primary winding in the ignition coil is continuously turned on and off as the reluctor teeth spin past the stator. This causes the secondary windings in the ignition coil to generate a high voltage that is used to create a spark at the end of the compression stroke of each cylinder.

Hall-Effect Sensors and Operation

Another type of electronic ignition system is the Hall-effect type. In Hall-effect systems, a Hall-effect generator, also called a Hall-effect sensor or switch, can be located inside the distributor to signal an ECU to turn the primary circuit on and off. Hall-effect generators operate by using a potential difference, or voltage, created when a current-carrying conductor is exposed to a magnetic field. If a magnetic field is applied at right angles to the direction of current flow in a conductor, the lines of magnetic force permeate the conductor and the electrons flowing in the conductor are deflected to one side of the conductor. This deflection creates a potential difference or voltage across the conductor. The stronger the magnetic field, the higher the voltage. This dynamic is called the Hall-effect voltage, and if the magnetic field is alternately shielded and exposed, it can be used to trigger a switching device. Hall devices are made of semiconductor material, which can quickly respond when shielded from or exposed to a magnetic field.

In a distributor, the Hall-effect generator and its **integrated circuit** are located on one leg of a U-shaped assembly, mounted on the distributor base plate FIGURE 47-19 . An integrated circuit is a semiconductor chip that contains miniature versions of various electrical components within one housing. A permanent magnet is located on the other leg, and an air gap is formed between them. An **interrupter ring**, which has the same number of blades and windows as engine cylinders, is rotated by the distributor shaft, moving the blades through the air gap. The purpose of an interrupter ring is to systematically block and expose the magnetic

FIGURE 47-18 Schematic of an electronic ignition system that uses an induction-type triggering component.

FIGURE 47-19 Hall-effect setup in a distributor.

field. The ring is shaped like a very shallow cup with slits, or windows, cut into it at evenly spaced intervals. It is made of a ferrous metal.

When a window is aligned with the assembly, the magnetic field is at its strongest, and its lines of magnetic force permeate the Hall generator material. The Hall generator material creates a voltage that is used to switch the primary circuit to ground. When the interrupter ring rotates so that the blade aligns with the assembly, the magnetic field is shielded from the generator, and the Hall material does not create a signal voltage; thus, the primary circuit is not switched to ground. With continuous rotation, the blades repeatedly move in and out of the air gap, and the signal voltage turns on and off repeatedly. This can be used to control the operation of the ignition coil primary circuit.

Optical-Type Sensors

Another type of electronic ignition system uses a light-emitting diode (LED) and a phototransistor to create an optical sensor **FIGURE 47-20**. The optical sensors located inside the distributor can be used to sense the position of the crankshaft and send an appropriate voltage signal to the ignition module or PCM. A signal rotor plate is attached to the distributor shaft. Although various designs are used, a typical rotor plate has 360 slits at 1-degree intervals on its outer edge. Inboard of these slits are four slits on a four-cylinder engine, six slits on a six-cylinder engine, and so on. One slit is larger than the others to identify the position of the number one cylinder to the PCM.

As the rotor plate turns, it passes between an LED above the rotor plate and a phototransistor below the plate. When provided with a suitable voltage, LEDs transmit a fine beam of light. Phototransistors receive this light and use it to make a voltage output signal. When a slit is in alignment, the light beam passes through it and a signal is transmitted to the control unit. When the slit is out of alignment, the light beam is interrupted and the signal falls to zero.

The control unit uses the signals it receives at every 1 degree to gauge engine rpm and **crank angle position** in 1-degree increments. It uses the signals from the inner slits to gauge the piston position, with the signature slit identifying the number one piston. The signals from both sets of diodes are converted to on/off pulses in the sensor's internal circuitry.

After computing data from the various input sensors against the optimum settings for each operating condition recorded in its memory, the control unit determines ignition timing. It then switches the primary circuit on and off by controlling the operation of a power transistor often mounted close to the ignition coil. The power transistor has its emitter connected to ground. The collector is connected to the coil's negative terminal, and the base is connected to the control module. A voltage applied from the module sends a small current through the base/emitter portion of the transistor to switch it on. Current can then flow from the ignition switch, through the coil primary winding and the collector/emitter, to complete the primary circuit.

Once the appropriate dwell period has elapsed, the module switches off the voltage applied to the base of the transistor, and the transistor switches off the primary circuit. The high secondary voltage then pushes current to the center of the rotor arm and to the appropriate cylinder. This cycle is repeated for each cylinder in turn.

FIGURE 47-20 Optical sensor ignition system.

> ### TECHNICIAN TIP
>
> The optical sensor is very precise due to the small slits that the light passes through. However, because they are so small, they can easily become blocked by dirt, debris, or even oil. Make sure the slits in the rotor plate stay clean when working around it.

Components of Distributorless-Type Systems

In **distributorless ignition systems**, also known as electronic ignition systems, the distributor is eliminated and replaced by multiple ignition coils. In waste spark systems, there is one ignition coil for each pair of companion cylinders. For direct ignition systems, there is one ignition coil for each cylinder. Signals from a <u>crankshaft position sensor</u> and, if equipped, a <u>camshaft position sensor</u> are used by the PCM to control the on/off signal to the primary windings of the coils. Both of these sensors are either Hall-effect or induction-type sensors to let the PCM know the positions of the crankshaft and the camshaft. Not all manufacturers use a camshaft position sensor, as the PCM only needs to know when the number one cylinder is at top dead center to give the proper spark timing on waste spark systems.

With waste spark systems, each spark plug is fired by a high-voltage impulse from an ignition coil shared with a companion cylinder. The distributorless systems that have a dedicated coil for each spark plug are referred to as coil-on-plug or coil-over-plug systems. The main advantage of the distributorless ignition system is the elimination of all the mechanical parts included in a distributor assembly such as bushings, bearings, the breaker plate assembly, and advance mechanisms. Also, the distributorless ignition system has eliminated maintenance items such as a distributor cap, rotor, contact points, and condenser.

Crank and Cam Sensors

Crankshaft and camshaft position sensors are used in distributorless ignition systems to calculate engine speed and determine engine position. The crankshaft position sensor can be mounted at the front, middle, or back of the engine and functions like a pulse generator in a distributor. The reluctor or trigger wheel is mounted to the flywheel, the crankshaft, or the crankshaft pulley. The camshaft position sensor monitors the position of the camshaft to let the PCM know which cylinder is approaching its power stroke. The two sensors work together to control the firing of the spark plugs, including advance and retard functions. They are also used for fuel injector control. These sensors provide more accurate readings than contact breaker points, since there are fewer mechanical parts to wear, which affects accuracy.

As an example, in one system the identification of each pair of cylinders and a signal for their triggering is provided by a dual crank sensor fixed to the engine timing cover. This contains two Hall-effect switches sharing a central magnet that forms two air gaps between them. Two <u>concentric interrupter rings</u>, which look like one shallow cup placed inside a larger shallow cup with a number of blades and windows on their outer edges, are mounted on the rear of the crankshaft balancer and rotate through the air gaps **FIGURE 47-21**. The voltage signals provided allow the ignition module to identify which pair of companion cylinders must be provided with ignition.

FIGURE 47-21 The interrupter rings on a six-cylinder engine's crankshaft pulley.

Waste Spark Ignition System

In a waste spark system for a six-cylinder engine, three ignition coils, each with their own primary and secondary windings, can be combined to form one coil pack or can be three separate coils. Each ignition coil serves two cylinders, with each end of the secondary winding attached by a high-tension lead to a spark plug. These two plugs are on companion cylinders—that is, cylinders where the pistons reach top dead center at the same time. The cylinder on the compression stroke is said to be the <u>event cylinder</u>, because it is the one getting ready to produce power, and the cylinder on the exhaust stroke is the <u>waste cylinder</u>, since the spark has no effect on engine operation.

When the high voltage is induced in the secondary winding, the secondary circuit is completed by current flowing through the high-tension lead to the center electrode on one spark plug, bridging the gap and creating a spark in that cylinder, traveling through the cylinder head, bridging the spark plug gap in the companion cylinder, and flowing back through that high-tension lead to its starting point at the ignition coil. The cylinder on the compression stroke with its charge of fuel and air is "fired" by its spark, driving the piston down on the power stroke, while the spark at the plug of the cylinder on exhaust simply serves to complete the circuit, and is "wasted."

When the crankshaft rotates through one revolution, the roles are reversed, and the waste cylinder becomes the event cylinder. Firing of both spark plugs again takes place, and this cylinder now drives its piston down on the power stroke. This same process occurs on each pair of companion cylinders as they approach the top dead center position. The primary circuit in each coil must therefore trigger at the correct time in each crankshaft revolution. Timing is controlled by the PCM based on all of the engine sensor input.

Direct Ignition System

Most current production gasoline engines use a single ignition coil for each cylinder. These ignition systems are similar to waste spark ignition systems but use one ignition coil for each cylinder rather than shared coils or a coil pack. In these systems, the coils can be all separate coils with spark plug boots or can be placed in an insulated cassette with each coil attached to a spark plug boot and connected directly to its spark plug **FIGURE 47-22**. This design eliminates the necessity for high-tension leads and reduces the possibility of current not making it to the spark plug.

The same sensor inputs previously discussed allow the PCM to determine ignition firing order and to set ignition timing according to operating conditions. Some manufacturers use the term direct ignition to identify their waste spark systems. Other manufacturers refer to their coil-on-plug ignition systems as direct ignition systems.

Distributorless Ignition System Timing

The spark timing for distributorless ignition systems is controlled by the PCM. The PCM decides the best time to

FIGURE 47-22 A direct ignition coil and boot.

fire the spark plugs. It makes this decision based on information received from sensors, such as the **mass airflow sensor**, which measures the airflow into the engine; the **manifold absolute pressure (MAP) sensor**, which determines the actual pressure in the intake manifold; the **throttle position sensor (TPS)**, which indicates how much the throttle plate is open; the **cam** and **crank angle sensors**; and the coolant temperature sensor. Once the PCM has evaluated all the sensor information, it decides when to fire the spark plugs based on its stored programming. To do this, the PCM switches the power transistors that control the primary current for each coil. Some systems use a knock sensor, which generates a small voltage signal when the engine is pinging. When the PCM senses this knock sensor signal, it is programmed to retard the ignition timing a few degrees. If the pinging continues, the timing is further retarded in steps until the pinging stops or the timing reaches its minimum limit. If the pinging stops, the PCM advances the timing 1 or 2 degrees and monitors the knock sensor again. If no pinging is detected, the PCM continues to advance the timing a small amount in steps until it detects pinging again or the timing reaches its maximum limit. This process is continuously applied so that the ignition timing is maintained near the most efficient point for fuel economy and emissions.

Another technique some manufacturers use in detecting detonation or pinging, as well as misfires, is called an "ion sense" or "compression sense" system. This type of system uses additional circuitry in the ignition module or PCM that monitors the amount of voltage it takes to ionize the space between each spark plug's electrodes. As pressure increases, so does the amount of voltage it takes to ionize the gap. Thus, the monitoring circuitry can tell when the air–fuel mixture has been ignited prior to the spark jumping the gap. It can also tell when the cylinder pressure does not rise in the cylinder and registers that as a misfire. In the case of detonation or pinging, the PCM will likely retard the timing to try to reduce the pinging. In the case of a misfire, the PCM will

> ### TECHNICIAN TIP
>
> A knock sensor is not very good at distinguishing between pinging and mechanical noise such as the knocking from a loose air-conditioning bracket. A loose vibrating bracket may mimic the frequency of engine knock, and the knock sensor will generate the signal voltage equal to engine knock. This error will cause the vehicle to lack power and will reduce fuel economy. Ion sense only looks at cylinder pressure, so it is less likely to be fooled.

set the proper diagnostic trouble code (DTC) when the enabling criteria have been met for that code.

 ## Diagnosis

A healthy ignition system is critical to the proper operation of an engine. Faulty or worn ignition parts may contribute to hard starting, no starting, lack of power, rough running, and other drivability problems. If a vehicle runs poorly or will not start, a thorough visual inspection of the ignition system should be performed. Prior to testing an ignition system, the service information and specifications must be obtained. It is also important to look for any technical service bulletins (TSBs) that may apply.

If the vehicle is not equipped with an OBDII system, it is good to inspect the spark to see if there is enough to jump the gap inside the combustion chamber. It takes a much higher voltage to create a spark that will jump the gap of the spark plug when it is under the compression forces inside the cylinder. Just because a spark can be made to jump the gap of a spark plug when it is removed from an engine does not mean it will do so in the engine. Use a spark tester to verify that the spark is able to jump a 3/8" to 1/2" (9.5 to 12.7 mm) gap. If it can jump that gap outside the engine, it is strong enough to jump across the spark plug gap inside the engine. Just be sure to inspect the spark plug to make sure it is not contaminated (fouled) and that the ceramic center is not broken and falling down, concealing the gap between the electrodes.

If the vehicle is equipped with an OBDII system, then the PCM will monitor the engine for misfires on each cylinder as well as individual ignition coil operation. Therefore, scanning the PCM for any related DTCs will help you locate any areas of concern for further diagnosis. The DTCs can be looked up in the service information to find the diagnostic procedure.

Tools and Test Equipment

Several general and specialty tools are required to properly diagnose and service an ignition system. A special spark plug socket is needed to remove and reinstall the spark plugs. These sockets are deeper than regular sockets, come primarily in three sizes (9/16", 5/8", and 13/16"), and have a rubber insert. The rubber insert makes removal and installation easier because it is designed with a small hole in the center to support the ceramic top of the spark plug. This insert allows the spark plug socket to grip the spark plug when installing it in a deep well. It also holds the spark plug centrally within the socket, preventing the spark plug from being cocked sideways inside the socket, which can break the ceramic insulator.

A spark plug gapping tool is used to measure and adjust the spark plug gap before installation. A high-tension insulated wire puller makes it easier to remove stuck high-tension wires from spark plugs. Spark testers are used to test the condition of spark plugs and to see whether there is adequate spark getting to the spark plug. On a coil-on-plug system, a special coil-on-plug tester is used to check the coils for output.

A digital volt-ohmmeter (DVOM) is frequently required to test for power, ground, and continuity within the ignition primary circuit and continuity in secondary circuits. A test light is used to test for power and grounds within the primary circuit. It is a light spliced into a wire and used as an indicator of the presence of voltage. It has a spring-loaded clip on one end and a probe on the other. In more difficult ignition system diagnosis, an **oscilloscope** or lab scope is used to observe the electrical patterns created by the triggering devices and ignition coil.

Scope Pattern Fundamentals

One of the primary tools for evaluating the condition of the ignition system is the oscilloscope or lab scope. These tools display voltage in relation to time on a screen. Voltage is displayed on the vertical axis, while time is displayed on the horizontal. For example, if the voltage output to cylinder number one is 2000 volts and that voltage is on for 3 milliseconds (0.003 second), the vertical axis will reveal the voltage and the horizontal axis will show the lapsed time while the voltage is on. The oscilloscope can be used to test both the primary and the secondary circuits, as they tend to mirror each other. While the oscilloscope historically has been most frequently used to test the condition of the secondary side of the circuit, with the advent of coil-on-plug systems where the secondary portion of the circuit is not accessible, the lab scope is now being used on the primary side of the circuit **FIGURE 47-23**.

FIGURE 47-23 Typical lab scope primary coil-on-plug pattern.

When testing the secondary side of the circuit, the oscilloscope can display several scope patterns. A __parade pattern__ shows all the cylinders firing in sequence **FIGURE 47-24**. It shows how much voltage is required to fire each spark plug and displays those voltages for every spark plug on the screen. If the voltage to one of the cylinders is too high, too low, or nonexistent, it can quickly be identified by viewing the "parade."

When viewing the parade pattern, the tall lines indicate the voltage required to ionize the spark plug gap. This is called the __firing line__. A high firing line on just one cylinder indicates high resistance in that spark plug circuit, typically from a wide gap in the secondary side of the circuit. This may be due to an open or disconnected spark plug wire or a spark plug gap that is too wide. A low firing line indicates low resistance, a short in the circuit, or low compression. Low resistance can be caused by a shorted spark plug wire or a fouled spark plug. On ignition systems that use a distributor, if the coil wire or rotor has a large gap, then all of the firing lines will be high.

Many oscilloscopes have the ability to stack each spark plug's ignition pattern vertically, which is called __raster__. Raster allows a technician to compare each __spark line__ to each other which tells how much voltage it takes to keep the spark burning and for how long. Raster is also helpful for viewing the timing of each event to the other cylinders, such as the firing line. If everything is good, all of the firing lines should be straight above one another. If there is wear on the timing chain or the distributor shaft is bent, then the firing lines will have an S shape to them. The greater the S, the bigger the problem, since the firing line occurs when ignition occurs in the combustion chamber. Therefore, any difference in firing line alignment means that the cylinders are not firing at the same time in the cycle as each other. In this case, cylinder 1 may be properly timed, but all of the other cylinders may be in an advanced or retarded condition.

Diagnosing Ignition System Issues

Concerns relating to the ignition system typically involve drivability. They may be nonstarting, hard starting, lack of power, misfiring, or any concern related to how smooth or responsive an engine is. After verifying the concern and any related concerns, perform a visual inspection with the engine off and again with the engine running. Look for loose connections, broken or corroded terminals, and maintenance items that appear to need replacement. Also, check for the high-tension leads to see if they are resting on hot engine parts or arcing. If an engine is running rough or lacks power, use a scan tool to check for misfire data or any DTCs. If it is not an OBDII vehicle, remove and inspect the spark plugs.

The condition of the spark plugs, when viewed on the electrodes side, can give a good indication of major engine problems. For example, if the electrodes are covered in oil, there may be worn valve seals or oil-control piston rings. If the electrodes are covered with black carbon, the engine may be running rich. Inspect the rotor and the inside of the distributor cap for cracks and carbon tracks. Replace any parts that are worn, cracked, or broken. A spark test should be performed to see if there is an adequate spark at the spark plug while the engine is being cranked, and always refer to the manufacturer's recommended procedure once you have completed a visual inspection and performed a spark test. Test-drive the vehicle once the repair is completed.

FIGURE 47-24 Typical parade scope pattern.

Safety

While the secondary voltage is very high (up to 100,000V), the current flow is very low. Because the current flow is so low, an ignition system shock is unlikely to kill you directly (unless you have a pacemaker), but it could hurt you. If you get shocked by the high voltage, it will hurt, and you will likely jerk away from it. This can cause you to get tangled up in the fan belts, or ram your head into the hood safety latch, which could seriously injure you. Always respect secondary ignition systems and work around them carefully.

Spark Testing

A spark test should be performed when an engine will not start, has one or more cylinders misfiring, or has other drivability problems, such as a lack of power, or stalling. A spark tester can look like a regular spark plug, but it has a large alligator clip attached to its side, or it can be an adjustable tester that allows you to adjust the gap. If the spark jumps across the specified gap of the spark tester, then the spark is high enough to jump across the spark plug gap in the combustion chamber.

To perform a spark test, follow the steps in **SKILL DRILL 47-1**:

1. Remove the high-tension lead or coil from the end of the spark plug. **(Photo 1)**

2. Connect a spark tester to the boot of the coil or high-tension lead, and attach the clamp to a good ground. **(Photo 2)**

3. Crank the engine and watch for a spark across the tester electrodes. A properly functioning ignition system will produce a blue spark.

4. If there is no spark present, test the spark plug wire or coil, distributor cap, and rotor on that plug. If there is still no spark at any of the cylinders, continue on to the next skill drill. **(Photo 3)**

Inspecting the Ignition Primary and Secondary Circuits

The primary and secondary wiring should be checked for cuts, abrasions, and signs of arcing. The primary wires are the two to four smaller wires attached to the ignition coil(s), and the secondary wires are the larger wires leading from the coil pack to the spark plugs or from the distributor cap to the spark plugs, depending on the type of ignition system. Loose or corroded wires can also cause an ignition system to perform poorly.

To inspect the primary and secondary circuits, follow the steps in **SKILL DRILL 47-2**:

1. To see whether there is any spark coming out of the ignition coil, remove the coil secondary wire from either the distributor cap or the spark plug and install a spark tester that has been set to the proper test gap (usually ⅜" to ½" [9.5 to 12.7 mm]). Crank the engine and check for a spark at the spark tester. **(Photo 1)**

2. If the ignition coil does not produce a spark, check the primary circuit for power and switching.

3. To test for power, switch the ignition on and connect the red lead of the multimeter to the positive terminal of the coil and the black lead to ground. A typical reading is 10 to 12 volts. If using a test light, the light should illuminate brightly. **(Photo 2)**

4. Place the red meter lead or test light on the negative side of the coil and the black lead on a good ground. Crank the engine and look for the meter

SKILL DRILL | 47-1 | Performing a Spark Test

1. Remove the high-tension lead or coil from the end of the spark plug.

2. Connect a spark tester to the boot of the coil or high-tension lead, and attach the clamp to a good ground.

3. Crank the engine and watch for a spark across the tester electrodes. A properly functioning ignition system will produce a blue spark. If there is no spark present, test the spark plug wire or coil, distributor cap, and rotor on that plug. If there is still no spark present, continue on to the next skill drill.

SKILL DRILL | 47-2 | Inspecting the Primary and Secondary Circuits

1. Remove the secondary wire from the center terminal of the distributor cap, install a spark tester, and crank the engine to see if there is any spark coming out of the ignition coil.

2. Use a test light or connect the red lead of a multimeter to the positive terminal at the coil and the black lead to a good ground with the key switched on. A typical reading is 10 to 12 volts. If using a test light, the light should illuminate brightly.

3. Place the red meter lead (or the test light probe) on the negative side of the coil and the black lead on a good ground. Crank the engine. The test light or meter should rapidly switch on and off, indicating the coil is being triggered.

to <u>oscillate</u> or the test light to flash rapidly, indicating the coil is being switched on and off. (**Photo 3**)

5. If there is power present and the coil is being switched, proceed with checking the coil. If there is no power to the positive side and/or no switching at the negative side, the ignition coil or primary wiring may be defective.

Testing the Ignition Coil

Whether an engine uses a single ignition coil, an <u>ignition coil pack</u>, or one coil for each cylinder, it is critical that the ignition coil or ignition coils are operating properly. A faulty ignition coil may cause hesitation under acceleration or may prevent an engine from starting. Ignition coils can fail in a few ways. The primary and secondary windings may be open or shorted. A DVOM is used to measure the resistance of the primary and secondary windings and compared to factory specifications. Another way ignition coils can fail is breakdown of the insulating material. This can happen if the secondary terminal of the coil becomes carbon tracked and allows voltage to push current to ground; or if there is an internal breakdown of the insulation, the voltage can push current to the primary circuit or ground. Finding breakdowns in coil insulation requires the coil to be activated and the available voltage to be measured on an oscilloscope and compared to specifications. If there is a weak spark or no spark during the spark test and the spark plug wires and primary circuit have been tested and are found to be satisfactory, the ignition coil may be faulty.

To test the ignition coil, follow the steps in **SKILL DRILL 47-3**:

1. Obtain the recommended testing procedure for the particular vehicle you are testing. Inspect and test ignition primary and secondary windings of the ignition coil(s). All the coil terminals should be clean, secure, and free of corrosion. (**Photo 1**)

2. To test the primary side, disconnect the primary and secondary wires, and connect an ohmmeter to the coil's positive and negative terminals. A typical reading is less than 5 ohms. (**Photo 2**)

3. To test the secondary windings, place one ohmmeter lead to the secondary tower terminal and the other to one of the primary terminals or the coil secondary ground, if equipped. In general, the readings should be between 5000 and 15,000 ohms. If the readings are not within the manufacturer's specifications, replace the ignition coil. (**Photo 3**)

SKILL DRILL | 47-3 | Testing the Ignition Coil

1 Inspect and test ignition primary and secondary windings of the ignition coil(s). All the coil terminals should be clean, secure, and free of corrosion.

2 To test the resistance of the primary windings, place the ohmmeter leads on each of the two primary winding terminals. If the reading is not within specifications, the coil is faulty and must be replaced.

3 To test the secondary windings, place one ohmmeter lead on the secondary tower terminal and the other to one of the primary terminals, or the coil secondary ground, if equipped. If the reading is not within specifications, the coil is faulty and must be replaced.

4 If the coil readings are OK, perform a spark test as in Skill Drill 47-1 to verify that the coil can produce a spark which will jump at least ½" (13 mm).

4 If the coil readings are OK, perform a spark test as in Skill Drill 47–1 to verify that the coil can produce a spark which will jump at least ½" (13 mm). **(Photo 4)**

Diagnosing the Pickup Assembly

A pickup assembly is typically tested when a vehicle will not start because of a lack of spark. You need to know which style of pickup assembly the vehicle is equipped with: magnetic, Hall effect, or optical. There should be an on/off signal being generated at the ignition coil's negative terminal. If there is not, the pickup assembly should be tested.

To perform a test of the magnetic pickup assembly, follow the steps in **SKILL DRILL 47-4**:

1 Obtain the factory service procedures and specifications from the appropriate service information (see Skill Drill 47-9).

2 Disconnect the electrical connector from the pickup coil. **(Photo 1)**

SKILL DRILL | 47-4 | Testing a Pickup Coil

1. Disconnect the electrical connector from the pickup coil.

2. Measure the resistance between the two terminals of the pickup coil by placing the leads of an ohmmeter to each terminal of the pickup coil. If the reading is not within specifications, the pickup coil is faulty and should be replaced. If the reading is within specifications, wiggle the pickup coil wires while watching the ohmmeter reading. It should not change.

3. Connect a lab scope to the pickup coil windings. Crank the engine over and observe the AC pattern.

3. Measure the resistance between the two terminals of the pickup coil by placing the leads of an ohmmeter to each terminal of the pickup coil. If the reading is within specifications, wiggle the pickup coil wires inside and outside of the distributor while watching the ohmmeter to see if there is any change in the resistance caused by a broken or partially broken wire. **(Photo 2)**

4. Connect a lab scope to the pickup coil windings. Crank the engine over and observe the air-conditioning pattern. If the reading or pattern is not within specifications, the pickup coil is faulty and should be replaced. **(Photo 3)**

Testing the Spark Plug Wire

A faulty spark plug wire may cause a misfire, high exhaust emissions, poor fuel economy, and/or a lack of power. Over time, spark plug wires become brittle and frayed and tend to have higher resistance; they can internally burn in two, causing an open. An open spark plug wire can cause the engine to run poorly or may cause the cylinders with the faulty wires to misfire. Misfires can cause catastrophic damage to the catalytic converters on the vehicle, so misfires are serious issues if left undiagnosed and not repaired.

If the vehicle has an intermittent misfire and is equipped with spark plug wires, you can use a spray bottle with plain water to mist the wires while the engine is running. Or you can use a grounded test lead and run it along the wires with the engine running. If the spark plug wires have a weak spot in the insulation, you should be able to see and hear the spark jumping to another wire, the test lead, or conductive engine part. If the vehicle is equipped with a coil-on-plug system, or if the spark plug wires fit down inside of a recessed well, then you can use insulated pliers to carefully lift the coil or plug wire boot off the spark plug while the engine is running and see if the spark is jumping through a hole or crack in the boot to the side of the spark plug well or the grounded test lead.

To test a spark plug wire, follow the steps in **SKILL DRILL 47-5**:

1. Disconnect the spark plug wire at both ends by grasping the boots on the ends and twisting while pulling the wire off. This can be done by hand or with a spark plug wire puller. Inspect each wire for cracks, brittleness, or burnt spots. **(Photo 1)**

2. Place one lead of the ohmmeter on each end of the spark plug wire.

SKILL DRILL | 47-5 | Testing a Spark Plug Wire

1 Disconnect the spark plug wire at both ends by grasping the boots on the ends and twisting while pulling the wire off. Inspect each wire for cracks, brittleness, or burnt spots.

2 Place one lead of the ohmmeter on each end of the spark plug wire. Flex the wire while reading the ohmmeter.

3 Replace the spark plug wires, start the engine, and lightly mist water on the spark plug wires or run a grounded test lead along each wire. If the readings are not within specifications or if the wires arc, replace the spark plug wires, making sure to route them in their factory positions to prevent damage.

3 Flex the wire while measuring to detect a broken conductor within the wire. A good wire will have a maximum of 3000 to 7000 ohms of resistance per foot of wire. (**Photo 2**)

4 Start the engine and lightly mist water on the spark plug wires or run a grounded test lead along each wire. If the readings are not within specifications or if the wires arc, replace the spark plug wires, making sure to route them to their factory routing locations and spacing. (**Photo 3**)

Inspecting the Distributor Cap and Rotor

A defective distributor cap or rotor can also prevent a spark plug from firing or cause a weak spark. If an engine has a misfire or exhibits a lack of power, poor fuel economy, or high emissions, the distributor cap and rotor should be inspected. Distributor caps and rotors become carbon tracked over time. This means that the high voltage ionizes the surface of the plastic parts and eventually can create a path to ground or to another spark plug terminal. This carbon track will allow electricity to flow along that path instead of firing the proper spark plug. Carbon tracks look like small hairline cracks but can become much more noticeable over time. A faulty distributor cap or rotor may also cause an engine to run rough, backfire, or not start at all.

To inspect a distributor cap and rotor, follow the steps in **SKILL DRILL 47-6**:

1 Remove the distributor cap from the top of the distributor by unscrewing it or removing the clips. (**Photo 1**)

2 Check for cracks, carbon tracks, and burned terminals. Also check the center terminal for wear. (**Photo 2**)

3 The rotor should be checked for burned contacts and cracks in the plastic housing. If the rotor is held in place by a retaining screw, make sure it is tight. (**Photo 3**)

Testing Crankshaft and Camshaft Position Sensors

A defective crankshaft or camshaft position sensor will typically prevent an engine from starting. In some cases, it will cause the engine to die intermittently. If an engine cranks but will not start, the crankshaft and camshaft positions should be tested after performing a spark test. Note that some crankshaft position sensors are adjustable and will not function properly if they are out of adjustment. If a DTC indicates a problem with the crankshaft or camshaft position sensor, do not assume that the sensor is faulty. Test the entire circuit, including the wiring, according to the manufacturer's procedures. The crankshaft and camshaft position sensor can be tested with a lab scope or digital multimeter.

SKILL DRILL | **47-6** | **Inspecting a Distributor Cap and Rotor**

1. Remove the distributor cap from the top of the distributor by unscrewing it or removing the clips.

2. Check for cracks, carbon tracks, and burned terminals, and also check the center terminal for wear.

3. Check the rotor for burned contacts and cracks in the plastic housing. If the rotor is held in place by a retaining screw, make sure it is tight.

SKILL DRILL | **47-7** | **Testing the Crankshaft and Camshaft Position Sensors**

1. Remove the connector from the sensor by removing any lock clips that may be present, and pull the connector off.

2. If it is an inductive-type sensor, use an ohmmeter to read the resistance, and compare the readings to the specifications. Replace the sensor if its resistance is too high or too low, indicating that it is defective.

3. If the sensor is a Hall-effect or optical sensor, or the previous reading is normal, use a lab scope to observe the sensor signal and compare to a known good pattern. If faulty, replace the sensor.

To test the crankshaft and camshaft position sensors, follow the steps in **SKILL DRILL 47-7**:

1. Obtain the manufacturer's test procedures and specifications (see Skill Drill 47-9).

2. Remove the connector from the sensor by removing any lock clips that may be present, and pull the connector off. **(Photo 1)**

3 If it is an inductive-type sensor, use an ohmmeter to read resistance. Place one lead on each terminal of the sensor being tested and compare the readings to the specifications. **(Photo 2)**

4 If the sensor's resistance is too high or too low, it is defective and should be replaced. If the sensor is a Hall-effect or optical sensor, or the previous reading is normal, then a lab scope should be used to observe the signal from the sensor and compared to a known good pattern. If faulty, replace the sensor. **(Photo 3)**

Testing the Ignition Module

On modern engines, the spark at the spark plugs is controlled by the ignition module and/or the PCM. If either of these parts is defective, the engine will not start or will run erratically. Some modules are grounded through their mounting hardware, so it is important that the module is clean and fastened securely. The ignition module may be mounted to the side or inside of the distributor. Or it may be mounted under the ignition coils with the coils bolted to it. Many manufacturers recommend that heat-conductive silicone grease be applied to the bottom of the ignition module prior to installation. Both the ignition module and the PCM are sealed units and cannot be serviced. If they are defective, they must be replaced.

To test an ignition module, follow the steps in **SKILL DRILL 47-8**:

1 Obtain the manufacturer's test procedures and specifications (see Skill Drill 47-9).

2 Test all the input wires leading to the ignition module for proper voltage and ground signals. **(Photo 1)**

3 Check for proper output signals from the ignition module with the key set to run and while cranking according to the manufacturer's specifications.

4 If the specified inputs are present but the ignition module will not produce the proper output signals, the ignition module is faulty and should be replaced. **(Photo 2)**

5 With a multimeter set to read volts, check the voltage drop between the ignition module and ground on the engine. If the voltage drop is more than 0.1 volt, check for corrosion or rust between the ignition module and the surface it is mounted to. Clean the corrosion or rust and reinstall the ignition module. **(Photo 3)**

SKILL DRILL | 47-8 | Testing an Ignition Module

1 Test all the input wires leading to the ignition module for proper voltage and ground signals.

2 Check for proper output signals from the ignition module with the key set to run and while cranking according to the manufacturer's specifications. If the specified inputs are present but the ignition module will not produce the proper output signals, the ignition module should be replaced.

3 Check the voltage drop between the ignition module and ground on the engine with a multimeter set to read volts. If the voltage drop is more than 0.1 volt, check for corrosion or rust between the ignition module and the surface it is mounted to. Clean the corrosion or rust and reinstall the ignition module.

TECHNICIAN TIP

The electronic circuits inside of an ignition module are more prone to failure when hot. Some cars and light trucks die but then start right up once towed to the repair shop. This makes it difficult for the technician to diagnose. If a vehicle dies but will restart after it cools down, the ignition module may be at fault. This intermittent condition can quickly be tested by placing a few ice cubes on the ignition module. If the vehicle starts while the vehicle is still hot with the ice cubes on the ignition module, then use a heat gun to carefully warm the module back up. If the engine dies, the ignition module is faulty and should be replaced.

Finding Vehicle Specifications

Each component of the electronic ignition system has a specification for voltage or resistance values, as determined by the manufacturer. This information is normally accessed in an online format, from either a subscription service or the manufacturer-supplied service information system. The technician needs to access this information in order to make accurate tests and diagnoses. The basic steps are outlined in SKILL DRILL 47-9:

1. Obtain the website address for the service information system used by your repair shop. There may be a user name and password for the business as a whole or each technician may have individual login information.
2. If not using an online service, obtain the service manual for the vehicle you are servicing.
3. Using the year, make, and model of the vehicle, locate the section that covers the ignition system. This section is usually located within the "Engine Performance" or "Engine Electrical" section; it may also be within the "Engine Controls" section.
4. Locate and record the specifications for the pickup sensors, spark plug wires, ignition coil (primary and secondary windings), or any other related component. The specifications will be in ohms or volts, or sometimes in frequency (Hz).
5. Print out or write down the specifications for use at the vehicle while you are testing.

▶ Removing and Replacing Secondary Ignition Components

As the vehicle ages, the components of the secondary ignition system will wear. Periodic replacement of the spark plugs and high-tension leads (spark plug wires)

or coil boots is required to maintain vehicle performance and to meet emission standards. The main components to be replaced on today's vehicles are the spark plugs and the high-tension leads (if equipped) and coil-on-plug coil boots on some applications. High tailpipe emissions, hard starting, or misfiring under load may indicate a need for service of these ignition components.

Servicing the Spark Plug

According to most maintenance schedules, the spark plugs should be replaced every 30,000 to 50,000 miles (50,000 to 80,000 km). Some newer vehicles use high-performance spark plugs that are made with platinum, iridium, or gold palladium and do not require replacement until the engine reaches 100,000 miles (160,000 km). When service is needed, avoid attaching the spark plug wires to the wrong cylinder by replacing the spark plugs one at a time. Note that some manufacturers recommend that the spark plugs only be replaced on a cold engine to avoid damaging the threads in the cylinder head. Check the service procedure before attempting to replace the spark plugs on a hot engine. Some manufacturers have very specific procedures for removing their spark plugs, and the procedure should be followed exactly or broken-off plugs can occur. Even when following exact procedures, some applications still result in broken-off spark plugs, and the proper tools and procedures will need to be followed for replacement.

It is quicker to set the spark plug gap on all of the new spark plugs at one time. Although most spark plugs come pre-gapped, they should be checked to make sure they were not damaged during shipping. Some spark plugs, such as those made with iridium, are not to be adjusted; if the gap is off, they are to be replaced, as they break very easily.

To replace the spark plugs, follow the steps in SKILL DRILL 47-10:

1. Check the electrode gap of each spark plug. To check the gap of a spark plug, find the correct-sized gauge on the gapping tool and attempt to place it between the center and the side electrode. (Photo 1)
2. If the gap of the spark plug is correct, there will be a slight drag between the gapping tool gauge and the spark plug electrodes as the gauge is installed and removed. If the gap is too big, the outer electrode should be bent down slightly until it is correct. If the gap is set too small, bend the outer electrode away from the center electrode until the gapping tool fits snuggly between the two electrodes.

SKILL DRILL | 47-10 | Replacing the Spark Plugs

1 Check the electrode gap of each spark plug by finding the correct-sized gauge on the gapping tool and attempt to place it between the center and the side electrode.

2 To gain access to a spark plug, first remove the spark plug wire by gripping its boot by hand or with a high-tension wire puller and gently pulling it off of the spark plug.

3 Clean out the spark plug pocket with compressed air.

4 Remove the spark plug, using the correct-sized spark plug socket.

5 If the new plugs are equipped with a gasket, ensure they are installed properly. Install the spark plugs by hand to avoid cross-threading. Use a torque wrench to properly tighten the spark plug.

6 Once the spark plug is installed, reinstall the spark plug wire by pushing it on to the terminal of the spark plug until it snaps into place.

---

3 To gain access to a spark plug, first remove the spark plug wire by gripping its boot by hand or with a high-tension wire puller and twist it to help break it loose. Gently pull it off of the spark plug. **(Photo 2)**

4 Inspect the spark plug pocket area for debris or dirt; blow out the debris if necessary so that it does not fall into the cylinder when the plug is removed. **(Photo 3)**

5 Using the correct-sized spark plug socket, remove the spark plug. **(Photo 4)**

6 If the new spark plug uses a sealing gasket, make sure the gasket is in place. To avoid cross-threading,

the spark plugs should initially be installed and run down by hand. A torque wrench should then be used to properly tighten the spark plug. **(Photo 5)**

7 Once the spark plug is installed, the spark plug wire should be reinstalled by pushing it on to the terminal of the spark plug until it snaps into place. **(Photo 6)**

Replacing the Spark Plug Wires

The spark plug wires, high-tension leads, or COP boots should be replaced periodically. There is not usually a recommended replacement interval stated in the owner's maintenance schedules for spark plug wires. Many shops recommend replacement at about the 100,000-mile (160,000-km) range. When replacing a set of plug wires, replacing one spark plug wire at a time will help prevent you from getting the wires and cylinders mixed up. It is also good to lay out the wires shortest to longest so that you can match up the wires if they are not numbered. Some spark plug boots are designed to use a high-temperature dielectric grease to prevent the boots from sticking to the spark plug porcelain. In some cases, you will need to burp any trapped air from the spark plug wire boots with a small dull screwdriver so that the air does not push the boots back off.

To replace the spark plug wires, follow the steps in **SKILL DRILL 47-11**:

1. Remove one end of the wire (or boot) from the distributor cap, coil pack, or COP coil.
2. Remove the other end from the spark plug with a high-tension wire puller by twisting the boot on the spark plug while gently pulling it off. **(Photo 1)**
3. If dielectric grease is specified for the spark plug boots, use a cotton swab to spread a small amount around the inside of the boot. **(Photo 2)**
4. Install the new spark plug wire by pushing one end onto the spark plug and the other onto the distributor cap, coil pack, or COP coil. The spark plug wires should be routed the way they were from the factory with the proper spacers to prevent damage. **(Photo 3)**

SKILL DRILL | 47-11 | Replacing the Spark Plug Wires

1. Remove one end of the wire (or boot) from the distributor cap, coil pack, or COP coil. Remove the other end from the spark plug with a high-tension wire puller by twisting the boot on the spark plug while gently pulling it off.

2. If dielectric grease is specified for the spark plug boots, use a cotton swab to spread a small amount around the inside of the boot.

3. Install the new spark plug wire by pushing one end onto the spark plug and the other onto the distributor cap, coil pack, or COP coil. The spark plug wires should be routed in their factory positions to prevent damage.

Wrap-up

Ready for Review

- Ignition systems have a primary (low-voltage) circuit to connect and disconnect the ignition coil and a secondary (high-voltage) circuit to send voltage from the battery to the spark plug.
- Common components of an ignition system are the spark plugs, high tension leads ignition coil, and ignition-coil triggering device.
- Principles of an ignition system involve a circuit activating the ignition coil, which converts the battery's low voltage to high voltage. The voltage then travels to the spark plug in each cylinder, igniting the air–fuel mixture and creating enough pressure to push down the pistons.
- The original contact breaker ignition system was replaced with an electronic ignition system of the distributor type.
- Modern systems are direct ignition systems (or coil-on-plug), which have a dedicated coil for each cylinder.
- The amount of available voltage should always be higher than the amount of required voltage.
- As ignition components age and become worn, required voltage increases and available voltage decreases.
- Spark timing is affected by any of these factors: air–fuel ratio, detected knock, engine speed, engine load, engine temperature, and throttle position.
- Spark timing must be correct in order to give the air–fuel mixture enough time to burn.
- Modern vehicles have electronically programmed spark timing via the PCM; older vehicles mechanically advance or retard the spark timing.
- Common points on an ignition switch are the lock and off functions and the accessory, on/run, and start/crank positions.
- Automatic transmission vehicles may employ a transmission shift interlock device to ensure that the gear selector is in park before key removal can occur.
- Standard ignition coils contain primary and secondary windings around a rod-shaped laminated iron core.
- The main difference among types of ignition systems is the method used to control the primary circuit to produce the secondary spark.
- In the primary circuit, a magnetic field develops that is interrupted by the ignition triggering device, thus collapsing the field and returning stored energy to ignition coil terminals.
- Because the secondary winding has approximately 100 times as many turns as the primary winding, it can produce 100 times greater voltage.
- Basic contact breaker point ignition systems are comprised of the battery, ignition switch, ignition coil, contact breaker points, capacitor, distributor, and appropriate voltage-connecting wires and leads.
- The purpose of the distributor is to transfer the spark to the spark plugs with the correct sequence and timing.
- The distributor cap provides rotor and spark plug lead connection.
- The distributor controls ignition timing in relation to speed via a centrifugal advance mechanism and ignition timing in relation to vehicle load via a vacuum advance mechanism.
- Vehicles regulate voltage to the ignition system via a ballast resistor, which is inserted in the primary circuit and lowers the voltage.
- Spark plugs all have at least one, and up to four, side electrodes, as well as an internal resistor to suppress voltage spikes and prevent radio frequency interference.
- Spark plugs are identified by thread size or diameter, reach or length of thread, and heat range or operating temperature.
- Spark plug components include the metal case, insulator, terminal, side electrode, and center electrode.
- To work effectively, spark plugs must have proper reach (distance from sealing area to end of spark plug threads) and proper heat range (operating temperature, generally 746°F to 1,460°F [400°C to 800°C]).
- High-tension leads carry a high-voltage spark from the ignition coil to the distributor cap and on to the spark plugs.
- Engine timing can refer to valve timing or ignition timing.
- How long the contacts are closed and current is flowing in a contact breaker system is determined by the dwell angle.
- Electronic ignition systems electronically trigger the primary circuit (rather than using a contact breaker).
- The triggering device of an electronic ignition system can be a magnetic pulse generator (pickup coil) or a Hall-effect switch.

- Ignition modules process information from various sensors and then interrupt the signal to the primary winding of the ignition coil.
- Induction-type systems use a magnetic pulse generator with a stator and a reluctor attached to the distributor body and shaft, respectively.
- Induction-type systems produce an alternating current voltage.
- The internal module control circuit receives the trigger signal.
- The reluctor teeth spin past the stator, turning on and off the primary winding and causing the secondary windings to generate a high-voltage spark at the end of each cylinder's compression stroke.
- Hall-effect systems use a potential difference, or voltage, which is used as a switch device.
- In a Hall-effect system, the magnetic field is alternately blocked and exposed by an interrupter ring.
- Some ignition systems use a phototransistor to receive light from an LED and transform it into a voltage output signal.
- In distributorless ignition systems, the distributor is eliminated so crankshaft and camshaft position sensors help determine when to send a signal to the coil's primary windings by monitoring which cylinder is approaching its power stroke.
- In a six-cylinder, waste spark engine, each set of two cylinders is paired with an ignition coil. The cylinders alternate between an event cylinder and a waste cylinder.
- The PCM controls spark timing for distributorless ignition systems via information from the following sensors: mass airflow sensor, manifold absolute pressure sensor, throttle position sensor, cam and crank angle sensors, engine speed sensor, knock sensor and coolant temperature sensor.
- Special tools and equipment for ignition system diagnostics include the spark plug socket, spark plug gapping tool, high-tension wire puller, spark tester, test light, a digital multimeter, scan tool and an oscilloscope.
- Oscilloscopes test the condition of the secondary circuit and can show if voltage to any of the cylinders is too high, too low, or nonexistent.
- The first step in diagnosing ignition system issues is to conduct a visual inspection to look for loose connections, broken or corroded terminals, or any components that need replacing.
- Inspect the primary and secondary circuit wiring for cuts, abrasions, and signs of arcing.
- Test the ignition coil for primary and secondary winding resistance.
- If the vehicle will not start, performing a spark test is a good step.
- Test to ensure that the spark plug wire, distributor cap and rotor, crankshaft and camshaft position sensors, and ignition modules are in proper working order.
- Always follow manufacturer-recommended procedure for diagnosing each ignition system component.
- Spark plugs and spark plug wires will wear over time and require replacement; check the manufacturer's recommendations for replacement schedules.

Key Terms

advance mechanism A device used to trigger an earlier spark based on engine conditions.

available voltage The maximum amount of voltage that the induction coil secondary is capable of putting out.

ballast resistor Used to limit the amount of current flowing in the ignition primary circuit.

battery An electrochemical device used to supply voltage to a vehicle's electrical systems.

breaker plate The movable plate which the breaker points are mounted on and which pivots as the vacuum advance pulls on it.

cam angle sensor A sensor that measures cam angle position.

cam lobes Raised areas or protrusions on an otherwise round shaft.

camshaft position sensor A sensor mounted near the camshaft and used to send camshaft and valve position information to the PCM.

center electrode The electrode located in the center of a spark plug. It is the hottest part of the spark plug.

centrifugal advance mechanism An ignition timing device, located above or beneath the distributor base plate, that rotates with the distributor cam and is used to advance the spark. As engine speed rises, the flyweights on the advance mechanism are thrown outward by centrifugal force. Since the distributor cam is able to pivot on the distributor shaft, the weights act against their springs and move the distributor cam forward.

coil-on-plug A type of ignition system used on late-model vehicles that uses one coil placed above each spark plug.

compression stroke The stroke in the four-stroke cycle in which the air–fuel mixture is compressed.

concentric interrupter rings Two interrupter rings that have the same center.

condenser (capacitor) A self-contained unit that is connected electrically in parallel with the contact breaker points and used to assist the rapid collapse of the magnetic field in the coil by preventing the contact breaker points from arcing. Also used on some coils to reduce radio frequency interference.

contact breaker point ignition system A type of ignition system that uses a mechanical means of turning the primary circuit on and off.

contact breaker points A mechanically operated electrical switch that is fixed to the distributor base plate and opened and closed by the distributor cam

with the rotation of the engine. The contacts normally form a self-contained unit, fixed to the base plate by a retaining screw engaged in a slot in the fixed contact.

crank angle position The position of the crankshaft, measured in degrees.

crank angle sensor A sensor that measures crank angle position.

cranking Rotating the engine by turning the ignition key to the start position.

crankshaft position sensor A sensor mounted near the crankshaft and used to send engine speed and position signals to the PCM.

degrees of distributor rotation A measure of the amount that the distributor rotates, where one complete circle is equal to 360 degrees.

direct ignition system May refer to a waste spark ignition or a coil-on-plug ignition system, in which the coils are directly attached to the spark plugs.

distributor The part of an ignition system that distributes the spark to the spark plugs in the correct sequence and at the correct time. It includes a distributor cap, rotor, shaft, and usually a switching device.

distributor base plate A round metal plate near the top of the distributor that is attached to a distributor housing; also called a breaker plate.

distributor cap The top portion of a distributor, used to make a connection between the spinning rotor and the high-tension leads.

distributorless ignition system An ignition system that does not include a distributor. It uses signals from the crankshaft position sensor and the camshaft position sensor sent to the PCM to determine when to send a signal to the ignition module.

dwell angle The amount of time that the primary circuit is energized, measured in degrees of distributor rotation.

dwell control section Part of the ignition control circuit that determines when the primary circuit will be switched on and for how long current will flow in the primary winding. The dwell period can be varied according to engine speed, improving coil efficiency.

electronic control unit (ECU) A computer that controls the ignition and fuel control and emissions control systems on an engine; also called the engine control module (ECM) or power train control module (PCM).

electronic ignition system—distributor type An ignition system that uses a distributor but replaces the contact points with an electronic triggering device.

electronic ignition system An ignition system that uses a nonmechanical (electronic) method of triggering the ignition coil's primary circuit.

enameled copper wire Wire that uses a thin layer of enamel as insulating material. The thinness of the insulation allows the wire to be closely wound in a coil, creating a dense magnetic field when current flows through it.

engine control module (ECM) A computer that controls the ignition and fuel control and emissions control systems on an engine; also the electronic control unit (ECU) or power train control module (PCM).

event cylinder The cylinder that uses the spark to ignite the air–fuel mixture on a waste spark ignition system.

firing line The tall lines on a parade pattern that indicate the voltage required to initially jump the spark plug gap.

Hall-effect switch The portion of an electronic ignition system used to trigger the ignition system. Hall-effect switches operate by using a potential difference, or voltage, created when a current-carrying conductor is exposed to a magnetic field. If a magnetic field is applied at right angles to the direction of current flow in a conductor, the lines of magnetic force permeate the conductor, and the electrons flowing in the conductor are deflected to one side. This deflection creates a potential difference across the conductor. The stronger the magnetic field, the higher the voltage.

heat range The rating of a spark plug's operating temperature.

high-tension leads The heavy insulated wires used to connect the distributor cap terminals to the spark plugs, and the ignition coil to the distributor cap, or on waste spark systems, the coils to the spark plugs.

high-tension terminals The terminals on the coils and distributor cap that the high-tension leads are connected to.

high-voltage spark The electrical arc that takes place between the center and the side electrode of a spark plug.

ignition advance The means of causing the spark to occur earlier within the compression stroke for better performance and fuel economy during changing engine conditions.

ignition coil A device used to amplify an input voltage into the much higher voltage needed to jump the electrodes of a spark plug.

ignition coil pack A group of two or more ignition coils housed in one assembly.

ignition module An electronic component that electronically controls the ignition coil or coils.

ignition switch A switch operated by a key or start/stop button and used to turn on or off a vehicle's electrical and ignition system.

induced voltage The creation of voltage in a conductor by movement of a magnetic field that is near that conductor.

induction coil An electrical transformer that uses magnetic fields to produce high-voltage pulses from low-voltage direct current.

induction-type system A type of ignition system that uses a magnetic pulse generator to trigger the spark.

inductive current The current that has been created across a conductor by moving it through a magnetic field.

intake manifold vacuum Pressure that is less than atmospheric pressure that develops in the intake manifold of a running engine equipped with a throttle plate. It is a measure of the vacuum in the intake manifold.

integrated circuit A semiconductor chip that contains miniature versions of various electrical components within one housing.

internal module control circuit A section of the ignition module responsible for receiving the trigger signal.

interrupter ring A ferrous metal ring, shaped like a very shallow cup with slits or windows cut into it at evenly spaced intervals. The ring has the same number of blades and windows as engine cylinders and is rotated by the engine moving the blades through an air gap. The purpose of an interrupter ring is to systematically block, and expose, the magnetic field in a Hall-effect sensor in order to turn the primary ignition circuit on and off.

low-inductance coils Ignition coils designed with low primary winding resistance and a low number of turns. Current flow on these coils is much higher than with contact breaker point systems and reaches its optimum level sooner.

manifold absolute pressure sensor A sensor that is used to measure vacuum or pressure in the intake manifold.

mass airflow sensor PCM input that measures the mass of the air entering the engine.

number one cylinder Typically the cylinder located farthest forward on the engine. It is the first cylinder in the firing order.

optical sensor A sensor that generates a voltage when excited by a beam of light.

oscillate To cycle above and below a given value.

oscilloscope A tool that shows graphically what is happening to voltage over a period of time; it is used to diagnose electrical faults.

parade pattern The display of all the cylinders firing in sequence on an oscilloscope.

power train control module (PCM) A computer that controls the ignition and fuel control and emissions control systems on an engine; also called the electronic control unit (ECU) or engine control module (ECM).

primary circuit The low-voltage circuit that turns the coil on and off.

primary winding The low-voltage coiled copper wiring found in an ignition coil.

raster The scope pattern where all of the ignition firing sequences are stacked vertically on top of each other.

reluctor A rotating, toothed wheel that changes the reluctance of a material to conduct magnetic lines of force.

required voltage The amount of voltage needed to push current across the electrodes of a spark plug located in the combustion chamber.

rolling code A constantly changing, randomly selected numeric code that is communicated with the engine immobilizer and security system.

rotor A high-voltage rotating switch that transfers voltage from the distributor cap's center terminal to the outer terminals.

rotor arm The portion of the rotor that extends toward, but not touching, the outer distributor cap terminals.

secondary circuit The part of an ignition system that operates on higher voltage and delivers the necessary high voltage to the spark plugs.

secondary winding The high-voltage copper wiring found in an ignition coil.

spark line The horizontal line immediately after the firing line on an ignition pattern. It shows how much voltage and the length of time the spark is burning.

spark plug A device that provides a gap for the high-voltage spark to occur in each cylinder.

spark plug reach The length of the spark plug from the seat to the end of the threads.

spark timing The point at which a spark occurs at the spark plug relative to the position of the piston.

stationary winding An extended length of wire wrapped into a circle. These windings are fixed as opposed to some types, which are meant to spin.

stator Portion of an electronic ignition system that is mounted to the base of the distributor. It has a circular permanent magnet with a number of projections or teeth corresponding to the number of engine cylinders, and a stationary coil of fine enameled copper wire wound on a plastic reel and positioned inside the magnet.

step-up transformer An electrical device containing many turns of wire, used to amplify low voltage into high voltage.

switching transistor An electronic device used to control the flow of current through the ignition coil primary winding.

throttle body The housing on an intake manifold that is used to control the amount of filtered air that enters the cylinders.

throttle position sensor A sensor that measures how far the throttle valve is opened.

vacuum advance unit A mechanism that controls ignition timing advance in relation to engine load and causes the spark at the spark plug to occur sooner based on engine conditions. Its function is to improve fuel economy and, in doing so, reduce exhaust emissions.

waste cylinder The cylinder in a waste spark ignition system that receives a spark near the top of its exhaust stroke.

waste spark system An ignition system in which each ignition coil serves two cylinders, with each end of the secondary winding attached by a high-tension lead to a spark plug. The spark is used to ignite the air–fuel mixture in one cylinder and has no effect on the other cylinder.

ASE-Type Questions

1. Tech A says that contact breaker points are a mechanical switch that opens and closes once for every ignition spark that is created. Tech B says that contact breaker points send high voltage directly from the points to the spark plugs. Who is correct?
   a. Tech A
   b. Tech B
   c. Both A and B
   d. Neither A nor B

2. Tech A says that as engines gain miles, the spark plug gap increases, which raises the ignition system's available voltage. Tech B says that misfire occurs when required voltage is higher than available voltage. Who is correct?
   a. Tech A
   b. Tech B
   c. Both A and B
   d. Neither A nor B

3. Tech A says that as engine RPM increases, spark timing generally increases. Tech B says that as engine load increases, spark timing generally decreases. Who is correct?
   a. Tech A
   b. Tech B
   c. Both A and B
   d. Neither A nor B

4. Tech A says that a Hall-Effect switch uses light to turn a circuit on and off. Tech B says that waste spark systems don't need distributors. Who is correct?
   a. Tech A
   b. Tech B
   c. Both A and B
   d. Neither A nor B

5. Tech A says that coil-on-plug ignition systems use one coil to fire two cylinders. Tech B says that you should twist spark plug boots before removing them. Who is correct?
   a. Tech A
   b. Tech B
   c. Both A and B
   d. Neither A nor B

6. Tech A says that the ignition system will maintain spark at the spark plug for approximately 23 degrees of crankshaft rotation. Tech B says that the duration of spark in the spark plug only lasts 2 to 3 degrees of crankshaft rotation. Who is correct?
   a. Tech A
   b. Tech B
   c. Both A and B
   d. Neither A nor B

7. Tech A says that the positive side of the coil primary circuit is switched. Tech B says that the negative side of the coil primary circuit is switched. Who is correct?
   a. Tech A
   b. Tech B
   c. Both A and B
   d. Neither A nor B

8. Tech A says that the advantage of distributorless ignition systems is no moving parts to maintain. Tech B says that the coil primary winding can best be tested with a voltmeter. Who is correct?
   a. Tech A
   b. Tech B
   c. Both A and B
   d. Neither A nor B

9. Tech A says that an inductive pick-up coil can be tested for shorts and grounds with an ohmmeter. Tech B says that an inductive pick-up coil pattern can be tested with a labscope. Who is correct?
   a. Tech A
   b. Tech B
   c. Both A and B
   d. Neither A nor B

10. Tech A says that on a secondary ignition pattern, the firing line shows how much voltage it take to jump the spark plug gap. Tech B says that The firing line tells how long the spark lasted. Who is correct?
    a. Tech A
    b. Tech B
    c. Both A and B
    d. Neither A nor B

CHAPTER 48

NATEF Tasks

Engine Performance
Fuel, Air Induction, and Exhaust Systems

Page

- Diagnose (troubleshoot) hot or cold no-starting, hard starting, poor drivability, incorrect idle speed, poor idle, flooding, hesitation, surging, engine misfire, power loss, stalling, poor mileage, dieseling, and emission problems; determine necessary action. **MAST** 1683–1722

- Replace fuel filter(s). **MLR** **AST** **MAST** 1714–1717

- Inspect and test fuel pumps and pump control systems for pressure, regulation, and volume; determine necessary action. **AST** **MAST** 1717–1719

- Check fuel for contaminants; determine necessary action. **AST** **MAST** 1719–1721

- Inspect and test fuel injectors. **AST** **MAST** 1721–1722

Knowledge Objectives

After reading this chapter, you will be able to:
1. Explain the principles of the gasoline fuel system. (pp 1681–1682)
2. Describe the characteristics of gasoline fuel. (pp 1682–1683)
3. Explain stoichiometric ratio and how it applies to engine fuel. (p 1684)
4. Describe the mechanical operation of a carburetor. (pp 1686–1692)
5. Discuss the components of the fuel supply system. (pp 1692–1697)
6. Describe the differences between single-point and multipoint injection systems. (pp 1697–1698)
7. Explain the principles and components of the EFI fuel supply system. (pp 1697–1703)
8. Describe the components that create efficient combustion. (pp 1701–1702)
9. List the various sensors of the EFI system. (pp 1704–1711)
10. Explain the causes of engine knock. (p 1710)

Gasoline Fuel Systems

Introduction

Today's gasoline <u>fuel systems</u> must meter a precise amount of fuel into the engine under a wide range of operating conditions. The most important job of the fuel system is optimizing engine performance while keeping fuel consumption and emissions to a minimum. Although carburetors were commonly used on vehicles up until about 30 years ago, they didn't perform these jobs adequately **FIGURE 48-1**. Their limitations prompted the development of fuel injection, starting with mechanically operated systems that typically sprayed a continuous flow of fuel through fuel injectors at each individual intake port in the intake manifold. These systems were sometimes referred to as "bug sprayers" since they put out a continuous fine mist. The amount of fuel sprayed was controlled mechanically by an airflow-operated fuel distributor. The more air that entered the engine, the more fuel that was sprayed.

Mechanical fuel injection still could not meet the increasingly stringent emissions standards, so electronic fuel injection (EFI) was introduced. In this way, fuel delivery could be controlled electronically, allowing continuous adjustments to the air–fuel ratio. Most early EFI systems used throttle body injection (TBI), wherein one or two injectors were mounted in a throttle body. These systems looked like a simplified carburetor.

As technology progressed, multipoint fuel injection (MPFI or just PFI) became more prevalent, involving one injector installed in the intake manifold near the intake port of each cylinder. This design allowed more equal distribution of fuel among the cylinders, which improved fuel economy and reduced emissions further. But even that wasn't the end of the line for new innovations. Gasoline direct injection (GDI) places the fuel injectors in the cylinder head where they can spray fuel directly into the combustion chamber. This technology allows manufacturers to operate the engine on much leaner mixtures than has otherwise been possible during certain engine operating conditions.

To make EFI of any type function correctly, an electronic control unit (ECU), also called a power train control module (PCM), is needed to determine the proper quantity of fuel to be delivered. For the PCM to make the proper determination, information from a variety of electronic sensors is needed. It is the wide variety of information that allows the fuel injection system to operate so precisely and efficiently. As a technician, it is critical to have a deep understanding of how these systems and components operate. This understanding will give you a head start on properly inspecting, diagnosing, and repairing fuel system faults for your customers, and thus keeping their vehicles operating at peak efficiency and performance.

You are the Automotive Technician

A new customer brings her late model vehicle into your shop complaining that it hasn't been "running right" for the last few weeks. She took it to another shop where the technician said it needed a tune-up and changed the spark plugs, oxygen sensors, fuel filter, and air filter. It improved, but then started getting worse. At first the MIL came on intermittently, but now is on most of the time. The vehicle seems to be low on power, as well, and yesterday, it didn't start. When it started today, she thought she should bring it in. You explain that you will need to diagnose the problem. She authorizes the diagnostic charge. You scan the PCM and find a P0171 (system too lean bank 1), and a P0174 (system too lean bank 2). Since the oxygen sensors are new and look like they are OEM replacements, you decide to perform a fuel pump pressure and volume test. You will also perform an alcohol content test on a small sample of the fuel after the volume test.

1. Why do you suspect a fuel pump problem in this situation?
2. If the fuel pump passes the pressure test, should you perform the volume test? Why or why not?
3. How could too much alcohol in the gasoline cause the engine to run too lean?

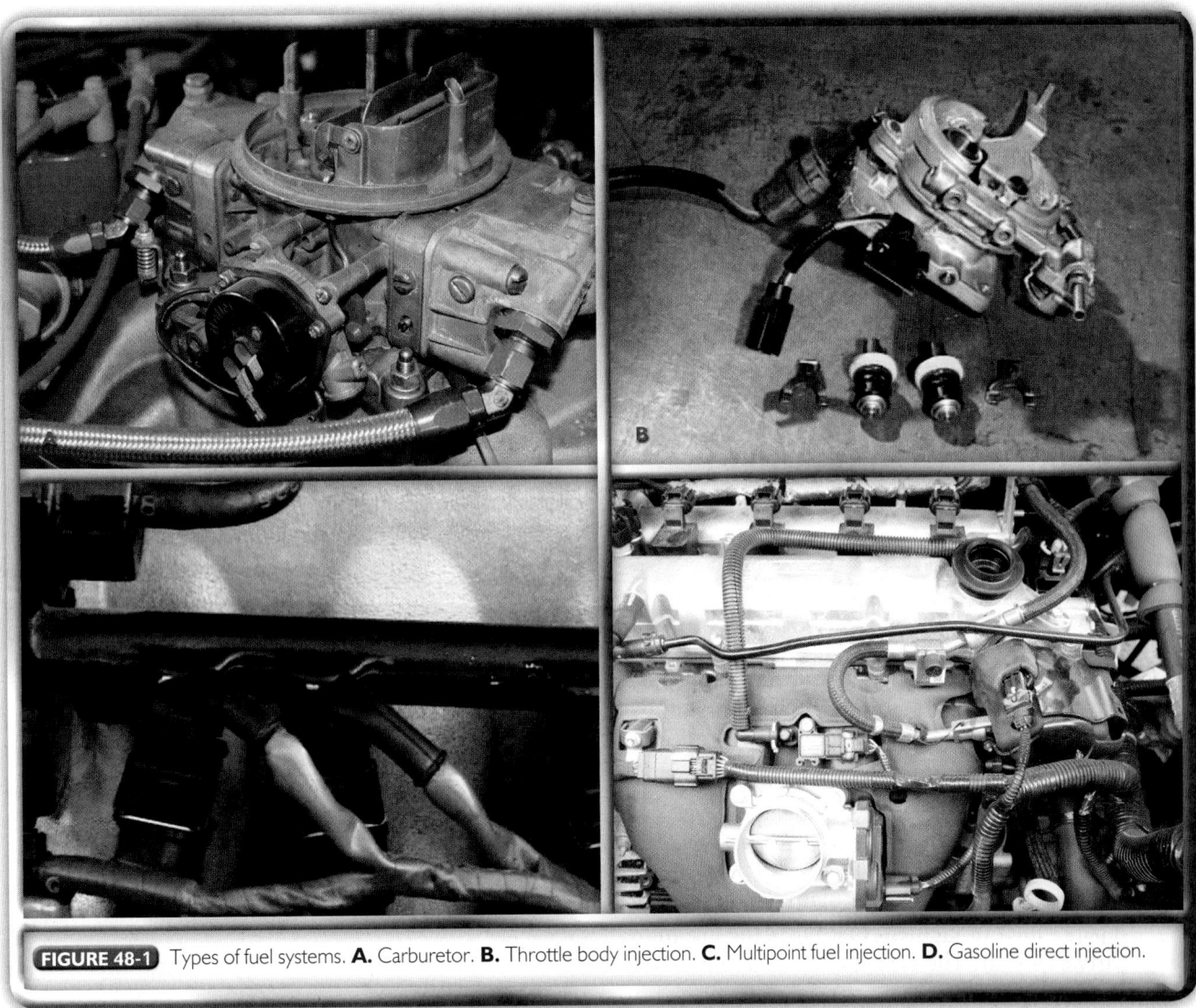

FIGURE 48-1 Types of fuel systems. **A.** Carburetor. **B.** Throttle body injection. **C.** Multipoint fuel injection. **D.** Gasoline direct injection.

Gasoline Fuel System Principles

The purpose of a fuel system is to provide the ideal air–fuel mixture for the operating conditions of the internal combustion engine. Liquid fuel will not burn. Fuel needs to be vaporized, turning from a liquid to a gas. It then needs to be mixed with the proper amount of air. It takes time and temperature for fuel to vaporize fully. The smaller the liquid droplets, the faster they can be vaporized. The process of making the droplets small is called atomization. A fuel system needs to atomize the fuel as small as possible so that it can be vaporized before it is ignited.

As explained in the introduction, older cars and trucks used a carburetor to atomize the fuel and mix it with air. Modern gasoline-powered vehicles use EFI systems, which atomize the fuel into much smaller particles, giving superior efficiency and performance over carburetors.

One of the reasons that carburetors cannot atomize fuel as efficiently as fuel injection systems is because the principles of operation are different. Pressure differential is central to all fuel systems. The greater the differential, the easier it is to atomize the fuel. A carburetor works off of pressures below atmospheric pressure (vacuum), which involves a relatively low pressure differential. Fuel injection, in contrast, works off of pressures above atmospheric pressure, which generally involves a much higher pressure differential **FIGURE 48-2**. With a very small pressure difference, as in a carburetor, fuel passages must be much larger. This means the fuel entering the airstream in a carburetor is in much larger droplets than fuel that is sprayed out of a very small hole at high pressure in a fuel injection system.

Modern fuel injection systems have three subsystems:

- **Fuel supply system**: This system provides pressurized, filtered gasoline to the fuel injectors or carburetor (in older vehicles). The fuel supply

FIGURE 48-2 The main difference between carburetion and fuel injection is that carburetion works off of pressures below atmospheric pressure (vacuum), and fuel injection works off of pressures above atmospheric pressure.

system draws in gasoline from the gas tank (fuel cell) and delivers it under pressure to a fuel metering device. Today's vehicles typically use an in-tank electric fuel pump. Older vehicles used a mechanical fuel pump that was typically mounted on the engine and driven by the camshaft.

■ **Air supply system**: The air supply system, also called the induction system, provides clean filtered air for combustion in the engine. An air filter is a paper filter or **element** that filters the incoming dirty/dusty air. The element is usually housed in a plastic or metal air cleaner housing located in the engine compartment. Engineers have made numerous configurations to prevent water and dirt intrusion. In addition, air intake sounds have been carefully analyzed, and intake systems have been engineered to give the optimum vehicle performance while providing smooth and quiet operation.

■ **Fuel metering system**: This system constantly meters and adjusts the amount of fuel that the engine is burning. The most common type of EFI fuel metering is multipoint fuel injection. Although specific systems vary, many of the systems have similar parts. For example, most vehicles with multipoint fuel injection systems have sensors, fuel injectors, and a PCM.

▶ Gasoline Fuel

Gasoline fuel is derived from crude oil. Crude oil is taken out of the ground as a liquid mixture of highly flammable compounds of hydrogen and carbon, called hydrocarbons, together with impurities. It is then processed into

many fuel and lubricant products at an oil refinery through the fractional distillation process in which the crude oil is heated in the base of a tower and allowed to condense at different temperatures (levels) of the tower. More volatile compounds rise to the top of the tower, while less volatile compounds stay low in the tower **FIGURE 48-3**.

Gasoline is very volatile, mixing easily with air to form gas or vapor. The more effectively liquid gasoline is changed into vapor, the more efficiently it burns in the engine. Thus, high volatility is desirable. However, gasoline vapor allowed to mix with air in the open is highly explosive; therefore, it can be very dangerous, and gasoline must be handled with care. High volatility also can create excessive hydrocarbon emissions, which, if vented to the atmosphere, contribute to air pollution and smog. If liquid gasoline is heated, it is even more volatile. If it vaporizes in the fuel pump, bubbles of vapor can block the flow of fuel and stop the engine. This situation is called **vapor lock**.

A typical gasoline is mainly a mixture of paraffins, naphthenes, aromatics, and olefins, together with some other organic compounds and contaminants such as sulfur. Some of these contaminants can cause corrosion, so they must be removed. Tight regulations in some countries limit the allowed proportion of aromatics, olefins, and sulfur in gasoline. Gasoline in its raw processed form is not suitable for use in vehicle engines; it must be enhanced with different additives such as detergents, octane boost-

FIGURE 48-3 In processing gasoline from crude oil, more volatile compounds rise to the top of the tower, while less volatile compounds stay low in the tower.

ers, and oxygenates such as ethanol. Detergents help to keep the fuel system clean, especially the fuel injector nozzles and intake valves. Octane boosters make it harder to ignite the gasoline, and oxygenates add oxygen to the fuel, which helps reduce carbon monoxide pollutants by slightly leaning out the air–fuel mixture.

When a mixture of gasoline (petrol) and air is compressed inside an engine cylinder, it heats up. If the compression of the engine is high enough, and if the fuel is able to ignite easily enough, the air–fuel mixture may spontaneously ignite before the spark plug is fired at the optimum ignition moment. This is called pre-ignition, better known as **knocking**.

Gasoline fuel can be modified during processing by including additives so that it is less prone to spontaneously ignite. This ignition characteristic is known as its **octane rating**. The less easily the fuel ignites, the higher the octane rating. Higher compression engines are more susceptible to engine knock, so they require fuels with a higher octane rating—that is, fuels that ignite less readily.

A gasoline's octane rating is measured by the producer. There are two different methods used to measure the octane rating of a fuel—the Research Octane Number (RON) and the Motor Octane Number (MON). Depending on the composition of the fuel, the MON of a modern gasoline will be about 8 to 10 points lower than the RON; however, there is no direct link between RON and MON. Both are measurements of a fuel's resistance to knock, but the MON is a better measure of how the fuel behaves when under load.

In most countries, including the whole of Europe and much of the rest of the world, the RON rating is the one that is usually displayed on the pump at filling stations. In the United States and Canada, and some other countries, the displayed fuel rating is an average of the RON and the MON rating: (RON + MON)/2. Consequently, whatever the rating may be called at the pump, the rating number for identical fuels will on average be about 4 to 5 points higher in Europe than they will appear to be in the United States.

There is a popular belief that fuels with higher octane ratings will improve performance in vehicles that are designed to run on fuels with lower octane ratings. This is largely a myth, although some premium fuels do have higher energy ratings. Higher-powered engines usually have a higher compression ratio, so they generally require more expensive higher-octane fuels to prevent pre-ignition and detonation. Higher octane does not in itself mean higher energy output, so a fuel designed for a high-compression engine will not necessarily deliver any more power in a lower compression engine. Engines perform best when used with the fuel that has the engine manufacturer's recommended octane rating.

Octane can be boosted with additives. Prior to the introduction of catalytic converters, tetraethyl lead was added to boost octane. Lead was also used to lubricate valve faces and seats, which slowed down wear. But lead also would coat the catalytic converter and oxygen sensor, rendering them inoperable. So leaded fuel was phased out for general vehicle use, and unleaded fuel took its place. So-called "unleaded gasoline" may contain small amounts of lead, but maximum levels are tightly controlled. Octane is now boosted with additives of ethanol, aromatic hydrocarbons, and ethers.

▶ Controlling Fuel Burn

For gasoline to burn properly, it must be mixed with the right amount of air. For a gasoline engine, the air–fuel ratio by mass is about 14.7 to 1. By volume, it is about 11,000 to 1—not much gasoline, but lots of air. A lean air–fuel mixture has more air in proportion to the amount of fuel. A slightly lean mixture gives good fuel economy and low exhaust emissions—suitable for cruising conditions. A mixture that is too lean can make an engine run rough and overheat. A rich air–fuel mixture has less air in proportion to the amount of fuel. A slightly rich mixture can produce more power at lower temperatures, but the extra fuel it uses steps up fuel consumption and greatly increases emissions. A mixture that is too rich fouls spark plugs and causes incomplete burning, and that reduces power.

Combustion

In normal combustion, the spark plug ignites the mixture, and a small ball of flame forms around the tip of the plug **FIGURE 48-4**. The piston finishes compressing the

FIGURE 48-4 In normal combustion, the spark plug ignites the mixture, and a small ball of flame forms around the tip of the plug.

mixture. The flame spreads faster and moves evenly to halfway through the mixture, and the piston reaches top dead center. The flame picks up more speed, then shoots out to consume the rest of the mixture. Combustion ends with the piston a short way down the cylinder. Ideally, this would completely burn all of the fuel that entered the cylinder, extracting the maximum thermal energy from the gasoline.

Detonation/Pre-ignition

Detonation is a violent collision of flame fronts in the cylinder, caused by uncontrolled combustion. It occurs after the spark plug has fired. The sudden rise in pressure can cause the remainder of the mixture to ignite spontaneously creating a second flame front that collides with the first front, making a knocking sound **FIGURE 48-5**. Sustained detonations can raise temperatures enough to cause pre-ignition, also called auto-ignition. Pre-ignition occurs before normal combustion, when something in the combustion chamber heats up enough to ignite the mixture before the spark plug fires. A mixture may also ignite simply because it is unstable under the higher heat and pressure. Detonation and pre-ignition can cause severe damage and must be avoided. Many engine management systems use knock sensors to detect detonation, and the PCM retards ignition timing to certain limits to try to stop it. Knock sensors are discussed in greater detail later in the chapter.

An engine that keeps running after it is switched off is said to be running-on or **dieseling**. That's because, as in a diesel engine, the fuel is igniting just from heat with no spark from the plug. This situation may even cause an engine to run backwards for a brief time when it comes to a stop. Dieseling can be caused by a high idling speed, an overheated engine, too many carbon deposits in the chamber, or use of a gasoline with an octane rating that is too low. On carburetors, it can be prevented by a special valve in the carburetor idle circuit that cuts off fuel when the ignition is turned off, or a solenoid can be used to return the **throttle** to a below-idle position. Fuel-injected vehicles do not experience dieseling unless there is a leaking injector when the ignition is turned off and the PCM shuts off the injector(s).

Stoichiometric Ratio

The term **stoichiometric ratio** describes the chemically correct air–fuel ratio necessary to achieve complete combustion of the fuel and air. In other words, it is when all of the oxygen completely combines with the fuel, leaving no molecules of either remaining. All of the oxygen and fuel have been chemically combined through complete combustion. It is represented by the Greek letter lambda (λ). For gasoline fuel, the stoichiometric air–fuel ratio is 14.7 parts air to 1 part fuel by mass, not volume. By volume, that equals 11,000 gallons or liters of air to every 1 gallon or liter of fuel—a ratio of 11,000:1. So if the air–fuel mixture is at the stoichiometric air–fuel ratio of 14.7 to 1, then the lambda value is 1 (λ = 1).

If an air–fuel mixture has a higher figure, say a lambda value of 1.05, there is more air in proportion to the fuel than 14.7 to 1; in fact, it is about 15.5:1, and the mixture is slightly lean. A mixture with a lower lambda value, say 0.95, has proportionately less air than fuel, approximately 14.0:1, and the mixture is slightly rich.

The exhaust gas oxygen sensor (often written as "O_2" sensor) is also called the lambda sensor, since it can be used to indicate the amount of oxygen in the exhaust so that the PCM can maintain a lambda that oscillates just above and below 1. The upstream oxygen sensor is usually installed in the exhaust manifold, where it measures the percentage of oxygen in the exhaust gases. A high percentage of oxygen may mean too little fuel is entering the engine, the mixture is too lean, and lambda is greater than 1. The sensor delivers this information to the PCM, which adjusts the mixture accordingly. Similarly, a low percentage of oxygen may indicate too much fuel is entering the engine, the mixture is too rich, and lambda is less than 1. Different fuels have a different stoichiometric ratio. For instance, methanol's air–fuel ratio is 6.4:1, and ethanol's is 9:1, again measured by mass not volume.

FIGURE 48-5 Pre-ignition occurs before normal ignition. Detonation occurs after normal ignition.

Internal Combustion Requirements

There are three key components of internal combustion:

1. Air: Air is an oxygen-rich combustible gas.
2. Fuel: In this chapter, the fuel referred to is gasoline.
3. Pressure/vacuum differential: Pressure or vacuum is used to force the first two components into the combustion chamber, where they are compressed and ignited.

Air

Air is one of the essential components of the internal combustion engine. The components of air are a mixture of gases and small particles, which vary in composition. There are four primary components of the earth's atmosphere: nitrogen, oxygen, argon, and carbon dioxide **FIGURE 48-6**.

The density of air is its mass per unit volume. Thus, a volume of air at high density has a higher mass than the same volume at low density. And if there is a larger mass of air, it will contain proportionally more oxygen. The density of air in the atmosphere changes at different temperatures and altitudes. That means the air that enters an engine at different locations could have very different amounts of oxygen. The amount of oxygen in air directly affects how well it supports combustion, so it can be important in determining an air–fuel ratio for an engine.

Fuel

As described throughout this chapter, gasoline is the fuel for the process of internal combustion. Derived from crude oil (petroleum), gasoline can be a powerful form of energy when mixed with air and pressurized.

Pressure

Pressure and negative pressure, or **vacuum**, are terms used daily in the automotive industry. Manufacturers recommend a pressure to which tires need to be inflated. And manifold vacuum is used to operate a power brake booster. Gases exert pressure on all bodies they make contact with. This applies also to the air in the earth's atmosphere. Air has mass, and as a result it exerts pressure, called atmospheric pressure, not only on the earth's surface, but also on all objects on the earth's surface.

Atmospheric pressure varies with altitude. At sea level, it is calculated as 14.7 pounds per square inch (psi), or 101 kilopascals (kPa). But if this is so, why does a pressure gauge read zero when it is not in use? This is because the gauge indicates only pressure above atmospheric pressure. This reading is called gauge pressure **FIGURE 48-7**. If you needed to know absolute pressure, an absolute pressure gauge would be required, and it would read 14.7 psi at sea level. Absolute pressure equals gauge pressure plus atmospheric pressure. Readings on an oil pressure gauge, or a tire gauge, should really have 14.7 psi added to them (at seal level) for true pressure. It is normal practice, however, for the gauge reading alone to be taken as the accepted value since atmospheric pressure is present at sea level.

If pressure being measured is below atmospheric pressure, a pressure gauge with its zero reading is of no value. Therefore, for pressures below atmospheric pressure, as in manifold vacuum, a vacuum gauge is normally used.

In a gasoline engine, the position of the throttle plate controls the volume of air, or air–fuel mixture, entering

FIGURE 48-6 There are four primary components of the earth's atmosphere: nitrogen, oxygen, argon, and carbon dioxide.

FIGURE 48-7 Absolute pressure versus gauge pressure.

the manifold. At <u>idle</u> speed, the pistons draw air away from the manifold at a faster rate than it can pass the throttle plate into the manifold, creating a high vacuum, or low pressure. At wide-open throttle, depending on load, the vacuum is much less, and pressure in the manifold rises closer to atmospheric pressure **FIGURE 48-8**.

A vacuum gauge can be calibrated in inches of mercury in a scale reading from 0" to 30", or if using millimeters of mercury, the scale reads from 0 to 760 mm. The scale is derived from the fact that atmospheric pressure at sea level supports a column of mercury 30" (760 mm) high. This glass tube, closed at one end, is filled with mercury, then inverted in a bowl of mercury. The space above the mercury is a vacuum, and atmospheric pressure on the exposed surface of the mercury supports the column. As noted, atmospheric pressure supports a 30" (760-mm) column of mercury at sea level, but at higher altitude, its height falls, which indicates that atmospheric pressure at that altitude is less. Thus, this scale can be used to indicate the degree of vacuum, or depression, that exists below atmospheric pressure. At idle speeds, a vacuum gauge connected to the intake manifold will indicate a reading of approximately 15" to 21" (308 to 530 mm) of mercury, depending on altitude.

Some engine management systems signal changes in atmospheric pressure by using a barometric pressure sensor in the PCM. This is because, above sea level, air pressure is reduced; to maintain the correct air–fuel ratio, a vehicle must reduce the amount of fuel delivered to the engine.

The Carburetor

The purpose of any fuel supply system is to deliver fuel to the engine in a form in which it can mix with air to form a combustible mixture. The fuel must be finely atomized to mix with the air.

Initially, manufacturers used carburetors and mechanical fuel pumps on their vehicles to deliver fuel to the engine. The carburetor system is a supply-and-demand fuel delivery system. The carburetor was usually fed gasoline by an engine-driven mechanical fuel pump. Traditionally, fuel pumps for a carburetor-type fuel system were a diaphragm-type pump mounted to the engine block and driven directly by the camshaft. Whenever the engine was running, the pump would draw fuel from the tank and deliver it to the carburetor with a low amount of fuel pressure. This delivery of fuel was then held up at the carburetor's float bowl, which was kept at bay by a needle and seat **FIGURE 48-9**. The pressure in the fuel line was low; thus delivery into the carburetor occured when the float lowered enough to allow fuel to pass by the needle through the seat. Once the bowl was full again, the needle was closed off against the seat. In actual operation at a steady speed, the float dropped just enough to allow the same amount of fuel in that was being drawn out.

Carburetors, when tuned properly, delivered fuel effectively. However, if not properly maintained over time, they would cause drivability and emissions problems. As electronics came into play in the automotive industry, carburetors were eventually phased out, with manufacturers

FIGURE 48-8 Engine vacuum. **A.** At idle. **B.** Partial throttle.

FIGURE 48-9 Float bowl and float system.

opting for more effective, efficient, and reliable **electronic fuel injection (EFI)** systems.

The EFI system can be either a circulation system or a returnless system. In a circulation system, fuel is drawn from the tank by a fuel pump and delivered to solenoid-operated injection valves, called **injectors**. Fuel pressure at the injector(s) is maintained by a fuel pressure regulator, and excess fuel flows back to the tank through a return line. On most returnless systems, the pressure is controlled by the speed of the pump, and the pump only delivers the amount of fuel being injected.

The fuel filter is directional. It is fitted between the pump and the injectors to stop contaminants reaching other parts of the system. It can be mounted externally on the chassis frame or on the fuel pump assembly in the fuel tank.

We are covering carburetion lightly so that you will have some background on how these systems operate in case you ever have to work on one. But more importantly, understanding the mechanical operation of a carburetor can help you to understand the operation of a fuel injection system. If you have no interest in carburetors, skip this section and move on to the fuel injection section.

The carburetor supplies the engine with the correct air–fuel mixture for all conditions of operation.

- It atomizes the fuel and mixes it with air.
- It controls the delivery of this correct mixture to the intake system.

Carburetors come in different designs **FIGURE 48-10**. Most carburetors are of the downdraft design, but there are also side-draft carburetors and updraft carburetors. These terms refer to the direction air flows through the

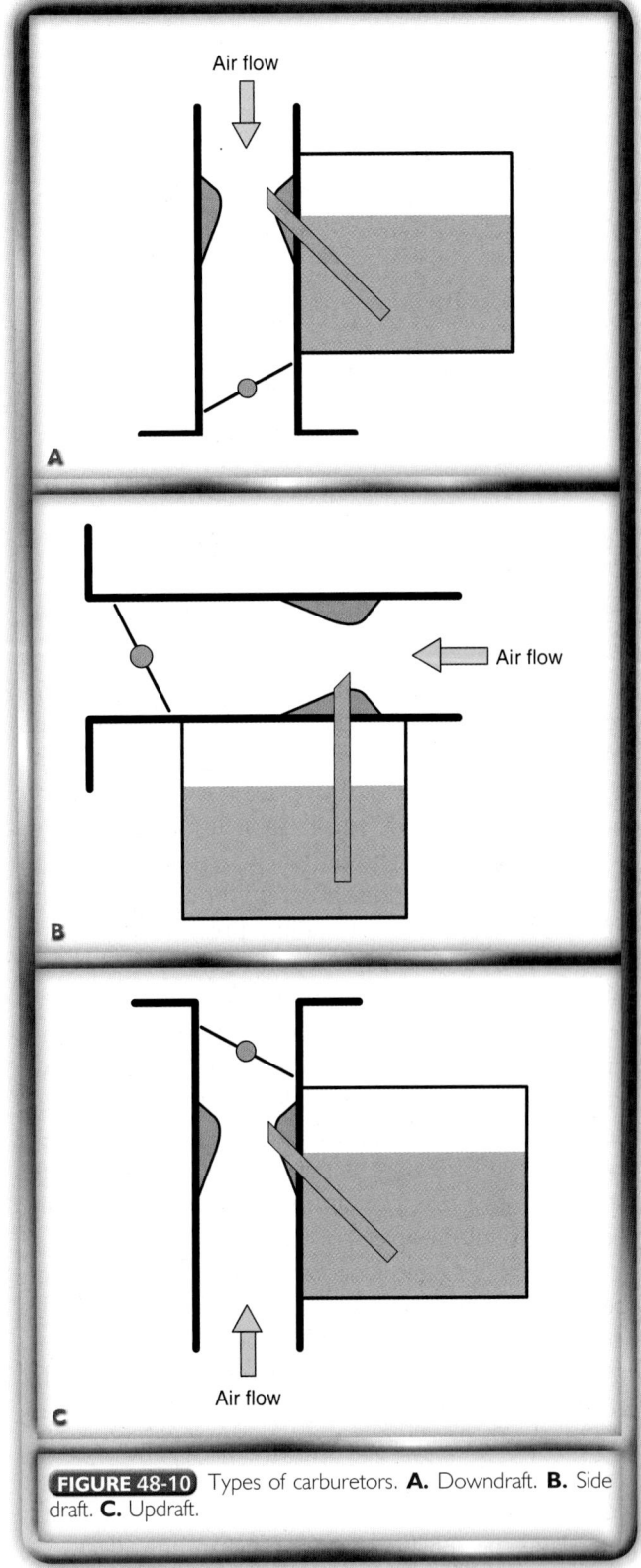

FIGURE 48-10 Types of carburetors. **A.** Downdraft. **B.** Side draft. **C.** Updraft.

carburetor. Each type has a float bowl where a float and a needle valve control the fuel level. The air horn and **venturi** are located in the top of the barrel of the carburetor. A throttle valve controls airflow through the venturi and is linked to the throttle pedal.

Atmospheric pressure
Booster venturi
Low pressure area
Main venturi

FIGURE 48-11 As air is drawn through the venturi, its speed increases and its pressure drops, creating a low-pressure area.

As the piston moves through its intake stroke, it creates a low-pressure area, and as a result, air from the atmosphere flows through the venturi **FIGURE 48-11**. The venturi is narrower than the rest of the barrel, and it is shaped to make the air speed up as it passes through. A similar effect occurs around the wings of aircraft. The shape of the wing section speeds up the airflow over the top of the wing and creates a low-pressure area there, lower than the atmospheric pressure below. The result is an upward force that provides lift for the aircraft.

The shape of the venturi is designed to apply the same principle, known as the Bernoulli effect. It creates a low-pressure area where the end of the nozzle protrudes into the airflow. Atmospheric pressure in the float bowl is then greater than the pressure on the end of the nozzle, forcing fuel from the nozzle. The fuel mixes with the passing air, breaking up into droplets, or atomizing.

Depressing the accelerator increases air speed through the carburetor, thus lowering air pressure at the nozzle. Pressure on the fuel in the float bowl stays constant, so more fuel is forced into the venturi to mix with the increased air. This keeps the air–fuel ratio roughly constant for a range of throttle openings. The throttle valve also controls flow of mixture into the engine. Opening it lets more mixture be delivered, which increases engine power and speed. Closing it has the opposite effect.

Carburetor Operation

The carburetor is a mechanical device that delivers the correct mixture of air and fuel to each of the cylinders for combustion during the power stroke. It is bolted to the intake manifold. While the engine is running, the intake stroke

of each piston creates a low-pressure area (vacuum) in the intake manifold. The vacuum created in a mechanically sound gasoline engine at sea level is between 18" and 21" (457 and 533 mm) of mercury. With atmospheric pressure at sea level being 14.7 psi (101 kPa), a moderate pressure differential results. That differential in pressure allows the clean filtered air to enter the carburetor. This pressure is used to meter out the correct amount of fuel over varying and constantly changing condition requirements. Ideally, the carburetor precisely governs the air–fuel mixture.

Carburetor Circuits

The basic carburetor components are housed inside a metal casting called the carburetor body. This carburetor body serves as the mounting point for the various essential carburetor system components, which are grouped together to create carburetor circuits. Each of the carburetor circuits is designed to provide a certain function to the carburetor. The six circuits are the float, idle, main metering, power, accelerator pump, and choke.

Float Circuit

The <u>float chamber</u> holds a quantity of ready-to-use fuel at atmospheric pressure. Its supply is refilled by a float-driven valve; as the level drops, the float drops too and opens an inlet, which allows the fuel pump to deliver more fuel to the float chamber. The float rises with the replenished fuel level, closing off the inlet. To allow atmospheric pressure to act on the fuel, the float bowl is open to either the atmosphere (unbalanced carburetor), the air horn above the venturi (balanced carburetor), or the <u>charcoal canister</u> (evaporative emission carburetor) **FIGURE 48-12**. If the float level is too low, more airflow through the venturi will be required to pull out the fuel, leaning out the air–fuel ratio. Consequently, too high of a float level will cause the mixture to be too rich. Float adjustment is important when rebuilding a carburetor. Flooding a carburetor also produces rich mixtures. Flooding can be caused by a worn needle and seat, or by dirt trapped between the needle and seat that causes the level in the float bowl to rise and fuel to dribble from the nozzle, resulting in little or no venturi action.

Idle and Off-Idle Circuits

When the throttle valve is closed or nearly closed, the manifold vacuum created behind the throttle is sufficient to pull a small amount of fuel and air through small openings located after the butterfly valve **FIGURE 48-13**. This design is called the idle circuit, and it enables the engine to keep running when there is not enough air speed through the venturi to create a vacuum. As the throttle valve opens slightly, the manifold vacuum is reduced, so

FIGURE 48-12 Float bowl, float, and needle and seat.

FIGURE 48-14 A main metering jet in the float bowl meters fuel passing into the discharge nozzle.

FIGURE 48-13 Idle and off-idle circuit.

additional small openings are revealed to compensate for this. This design is the "off-idle" circuit.

Main Metering Circuit

The main metering circuit comes into action above fast idle, as airflow through the venturi increases. A main **metering jet** in the float bowl meters fuel passing into the discharge nozzle **FIGURE 48-14**. How much fuel leaves the nozzle depends on the pressure difference created by the airflow through the venturi. As the throttle opens, and airflow increases and speeds up, more and more fuel is drawn from the discharge nozzle. However, the mass of air does not increase in proportion with the speed, and as a result, high speeds can produce a mixture that is too

rich. To correct this, more air can be added. This is called compensation by air correction.

As the throttle opens and engine speed increases, the level in the jet well falls, exposing air bleed holes in the discharge tube. Air can now mix with the fuel and prevent the mixture from becoming too rich. As the throttle opens farther, the fuel level falls too, exposing more airholes. More air bleeds in to maintain the correct mixture. Main metering fuel flow can typically be adjusted by replacing the removable jets with jets having larger or smaller orifices.

Power Circuit

The size of the main jet is selected to provide the best mixture for economy under cruising conditions. When the throttle is open wide for maximum power, a richer mixture is required. The extra fuel is provided by a power valve, with a vacuum piston and rod opening it as it is needed. At low speeds, intake manifold vacuum is transferred through a passage to the vacuum piston. This holds the piston up and keeps the power valve closed. With the throttle valve fully open for full engine power, the vacuum in the intake manifold falls. A spring pushes down the vacuum piston and rod to open the power valve. Additional fuel flows through the power valve to enter the fuel well and add to the fuel from the main jet. This provides the extra fuel needed to enrich the mixture for full power. Some carburetors use metering rods instead of a vacuum piston. The metering rods are pulled down into the main jets at idle and cruise to restrict the fuel flow. When manifold vacuum drops under heavy load, springs push the metering rod(s) up, increasing the opening size of the main jet(s). Other carburetors use a diaphragm-type power valve that opens an additional passage when vacuum drops under load.

Accelerator Pump Circuit

Extra fuel is also needed for accelerating. Suddenly opening the throttle increases the airflow, but fuel cannot flow from the discharge nozzle quickly enough to match it. An extra squirt of fuel is needed, which is where the **accelerator pump circuit** comes into play. Depressing the pedal compresses a duration spring that exerts a force on the plunger of a small plunger pump **FIGURE 48-15**. This pressurizes fuel below the plunger and closes off the inlet valve. Fuel flows past a check valve and enters the airstream from a discharge nozzle above the venturi. The duration spring extends the time for delivering the fuel. Releasing the pedal lets the linkage move the plunger upward. The check valve closes and the inlet valve opens to let fuel refill the pump chamber from the float bowl, priming it for the next shot of fuel. Thus, whenever the throttle is opened, the **accelerator pump** discharges a small amount of fuel into the throat of the carburetor. So constantly working the throttle pedal when driving down the road wastes fuel.

The Choke

Fuel ignites less readily when cold, and if the engine is also cold, then some fuel vapor can condense out of the air–fuel mixture onto the intake manifold and cylinder walls. This loss of air makes the combustible mixture leaner. To compensate for this, a valve known as the **choke** restricts the flow of air at the entrance to the air horn, lowering the pressure at the venturi and off-idle circuits even though the throttle valve has been opened. In this way, fuel is sucked into the incoming air through all the fuel circuits—idle, off-idle, and main—at the same time.

The choke can be controlled manually by a cable that operates the valve. However, most are controlled automatically so that the valve is closed when the engine is cold and opens progressively as the engine warms up **FIGURE 48-16**. When the engine is warm, the fuel drawn into the manifold vaporizes readily, and the engine can be started without the aid of a choke. The choke should operate as briefly as possible. Overusing it produces rich mixtures that cause exhaust pollution and increase fuel consumption. Some later-model carburetors that used a cable-operated choke also used a spring-loaded choke release that turned the choke off after a set time.

Carburetor Barrels

Carburetors can have one, two, three, or four barrels. Extra barrels improve performance, particularly at high speeds, letting more air and fuel enter the cylinders than with a single barrel. However, a carburetor that is too large will reduce engine power because not enough airflow can be maintained through the venturi to draw the fuel out properly. Two-barrel carburetors have two outlets to the intake manifold and come in two basic designs. One has a common float chamber, with each barrel having a complete set of all other circuits and the throttles having the ability to open simultaneously. The float chamber may be straddled by two connected floats that almost surround the air passage. This design leaves the float chamber unaffected by cornering, climbing, accelerating, or braking.

In the other basic design, called a progressive carburetor, throttles open in two stages **FIGURE 48-17**. This design combines the two barrels to act as a single carburetor. The two stages combine good low-speed operation of a single-barrel design with the extra airflow of two barrels.

One of the two barrels of the carburetor has all the circuits needed to supply mixtures for the whole range

FIGURE 48-15 Accelerator pump circuit.

FIGURE 48-16 The choke.

of operation. It is called the primary side. The other barrel, the secondary side, supplies extra mixture, but only at high speed or full throttle. It normally has a main metering system and a nonadjustable idling system. The primary side has a choke for cold starting. When the engine is being started, the throttle on the secondary side is already closed, so a choke is not needed. From idle to medium speeds, only the primary throttle is open. When engine speed rises to where additional breathing capacity is needed, the secondary throttle opens to admit more air–fuel mixture. By the time the primary throttle is wide open, so is the secondary throttle. The opening of the throttles can be controlled mechanically or by a vacuum unit that is connected by a pull rod to a lever on the secondary shaft. When air flows past ports in the venturis, it produces low-pressure areas. A hose transmits this low pressure to a diaphragm chamber. This low pressure acts on the diaphragm and opens the secondary throttle.

Large-capacity V8 engines may use a four-barrel carburetor of two-stage design—effectively two, two-stage carburetors combined, with each side supplying four of the eight cylinders. A central molded plastic fuel bowl and suspended metering system can be incorporated into the design. The result is lowered fuel temperatures with more precise fuel metering and closer control over air–fuel ratios.

Computer-Controlled Carburetors

A **computer-controlled carburetor** normally uses an electronically controlled solenoid valve called a mixture control solenoid to respond to the PCM commands **FIGURE 48-18**. This type of carburetor system uses various sensors in the exhaust and engine to monitor operating conditions. In turn, these sensors send that information to the PCM. According to the sensor data, the PCM then calculates rich or lean fuel conditions and adjusts the air–fuel mixture accordingly. The computer constantly sends commands to the mixture-control solenoid to open and close air and fuel passages in the carburetor.

Mechanical Fuel Pump

Fuel pumps on carbureted systems can be electric or mechanical. The mechanical fuel pump for the carburetor system is usually mounted on the cylinder head or the engine block. It has a flexible diaphragm, which is a flexible piece of neoprene rubber separating two chambers **FIGURE 48-19**. This diaphragm is operated by an eccentric on the camshaft. The eccentric rotates, making the rocker arm move. This movement is transferred to the diaphragm, pulling it down. As a result, fuel is drawn into the pumping chamber on the other side of the diaphragm. The diaphragm spring moves the diaphragm up, forcing

FIGURE 48-17 A progressive carburetor.

FIGURE 48-18 A computer-controlled carburetor normally uses an electronically controlled solenoid valve.

FIGURE 48-19 The mechanical fuel pump has a flexible diaphragm—a flexible piece of neoprene rubber separating two chambers.

fuel from the pumping chamber, out of the pump and into the carburetor.

When the engine needs more fuel, the diaphragm moves through a long stroke to pump a lot of fuel. When less fuel is needed, pressure builds up in the fuel line to the carburetor and in the pumping chamber. The diaphragm spring cannot push the diaphragm so far, and the pumping stroke is reduced. Some pumps also have a return line to send excess fuel back to the tank. As the fuel circulates, it cools the fuel pump and lines, reducing the chance of vapor locks.

Electric Fuel Pump

Carburetor systems can also use electric fuel pumps. Most of these pumps are located outside the tank, though some are inside the tank. One widely used pump is the diaphragm type **FIGURE 48-20**. It has an electrical section and a mechanical section. When the ignition is switched on, current magnetizes the solenoid. The magnetic field energizes an armature, which pulls down the diaphragm. This creates a low-pressure area that draws fuel into the pump.

Pulling down the diaphragm breaks the circuit and stops the current, causing the solenoid to no longer be an electromagnet. The armature is released, and the diaphragm spring forces up the diaphragm, which forces fuel out of the pump and to the carburetor. This action continues, delivering fuel each time.

When the engine needs less fuel, pressure builds up in the fuel lines to the carburetor and reduces how much fuel is delivered. Some carburetor-equipped vehicles with electric pumps have a safety switch that prevents the pump from continuing to run if the engine stops.

► Electronic Fuel Injection Fuel Supply Components

The fuel supply system consists of several components that all play integral roles in delivering gasoline to the fuel injection system, including the following:

- Fuel tank
- Fuel filler neck
- Gas cap
- Evaporative emission control system (EVAP)
- Fuel pump relay
- Fuel pump
- Fuel tank sending unit
- Fuel filter
- Fuel lines
- Fuel rail
- Fuel pressure regulator
- Fuel injector(s)

Fuel Tank

The fuel tank (or gas tank, as it is sometimes called) is the primary reservoir of the on-board fuel supply. The typical fuel tank of modern vehicles consists of a gas cap, filler neck, fuel, fuel pump, and **gauge sending unit** **FIGURE 48-21**. Its primary function is to safely hold an adequate supply of gasoline for prolonged engine operation.

Where the tank is mounted depends on where the engine is and on space and styling. Safety demands that it be positioned well away from heated components and outside the passenger compartment. Tanks are made either of tinned sheet steel that has been pressed into shape or of nonmetallic materials. Aluminum or steel is used on commercial vehicles. The metal tank is usually

FIGURE 48-20 Diaphragm-type electric fuel pump.

FIGURE 48-21 The typical fuel tank of modern vehicles consists of a gas cap, filler neck, fuel, fuel pump, and gauge sending unit.

in two parts, joined by a continuous weld around the flanges where the parts fit together. Baffles make the tanks more rigid. They also prevent the surging and sloshing of fuel and ensure that fuel is available at the pickup tube.

Because fuel expands and contracts as temperature rises and falls, fuel tanks are vented to let them breathe. Modern emission controls prevent tanks from being vented directly to the atmosphere. They must use evaporative control systems. Vapor from the fuel tank is vented through a charcoal canister where fuel vapors are stored until they are burned in the engine. A vapor or vent line with a check valve connects the space above the liquid fuel with the canister. This valve opens above a specified pressure and lets through vapor but not liquid.

Liquid fuel closes the check valve and blocks the line, which stops it from reaching the charcoal. Some systems have a small container, called a liquid–vapor separator, above the fuel tank. It also prevents liquid fuel from reaching the charcoal.

Fuel Filler Neck

The fuel filler is where fuel enters the tank. The **fuel filler neck** is a pipe that extends above the fuel tank **FIGURE 48-22**. On older unleaded gasoline vehicles with catalytic converters, the filler neck was designed to prevent leaded fuel being added. Its diameter is smaller than those on leaded vehicles, and a trapdoor inside the filler can be opened only by the nozzle of the unleaded gasoline spout. The location of the filler neck depends on the design of the vehicle and location of the tank. The filler neck can incorporate the use of a blowback ball valve to prevent fuel from leaking from the vehicle during fill-ups and to deter gas theft.

FIGURE 48-22 The fuel filler neck.

Gas Cap

Modern vehicles are required by the Environmental Protection Agency (EPA) to have a nonvented gas cap. This nonvented cap prevents fuel vapors from being directly vented to the atmosphere, which wastes gasoline and contributes to air pollution. To help ensure that the cap is tightened properly, many of these caps use a ratchet system. Drivers tighten the cap until it ratchets. Newer Ford vehicles are using an Easy Fuel capless system **FIGURE 48-23**. There is no gas cap to remove when

FIGURE 48-23 Gas caps. **A.** Standard gas cap. **B.** New capless system.

refueling the vehicle. When the properly sized nozzle is placed on the top of the cap, latches release that open the valve and allow the nozzle to be fully inserted. This cap also reduces the amount of gasoline vapors that escape to the atmosphere when compared to a standard cap.

> **TECHNICIAN TIP**
>
> A loose or leaky gas cap can cause the malfunction indicator lamp (MIL) to illuminate on the dash when the evaporative emission system monitor runs and the leak is detected. Always check the tightness of the cap if an evaporative emission system leak code is present. If the cap is tight, you may want to test the cap for leaks on a cap tester before digging into the evaporative emission system to locate the leak.

Fuel Pump Relay

Fuel pumps can draw a considerable amount of current while they run. To carry that high current load, modern vehicles use a **fuel pump relay**. The relay is an electro-magnetically operated switch that basically activates the fuel pump when the ignition is turned on for priming the fuel system, when the engine is cranked, and when the engine is running. As low-amperage current is passed through the winding in the relay, a magnetic field is created that pulls the contacts together, controlling the larger current flow going to the fuel pump. The current operating the fuel pump relay winding is typically controlled by the PCM. In most cases, the PCM grounds the winding when it wants the fuel pump to operate.

Fuel Pump

Most fuel-injected vehicles use one or two electrical pumps to supply the fuel system with pressurized fuel. The pump either is mounted on the frame or, more likely, is located inside the fuel tank. If located in the tank, the pump is of the submersible type. Electric fuel pumps can be of the low-pressure type or the high-pressure type, depending on the fuel system used on the vehicle.

The fuel pump is electrically operated and electronically controlled. It is driven by a permanent-magnet electric motor, a sealed unit integral with the pump **FIGURE 48-24**. Fuel flows through the pump and around the electric motor when it is running. There is never an ignitable mixture (of air and fuel); only fuel is inside the pump housing, so there is virtually no danger of explosion. The pump is designed to deliver more fuel than the maximum requirement of the engine, so pressure in

FIGURE 48-24 The fuel pump is driven by a permanent-magnet electric motor, a sealed unit integral with the pump.

the fuel system is maintained at all times. Either a fuel pressure regulator maintains fuel pressure between the pump and the injectors or the speed of the pump is varied to maintain the correct pressure. Electric fuel pumps use various types of pump chambers, one of which is the roller cell. In this style, rollers float in channels in an offset rotor. As the rotor turns, the rollers are thrown outward, drawing fuel in as the space between the rollers expands, and forcing fuel out as the space decreases. Other types are the peripheral type and the side channel pump.

Fuel Tank Sending Unit

For obvious reasons, it is important for the driver to know how much fuel the vehicle has in the tank. The primary job of the **sending unit** is to send constant electrical signals to the gas gauge located in the driver information center or to the BCM, which then controls the gas gauge. The sending unit is a variable resistor that is attached to a float mechanism **FIGURE 48-25**. As the fuel level changes, so does the resistance and in turn the amount of current sent to the fuel gauge. This current directly indicates an accurate amount of fuel in the tank. On today's EFI vehicles, the sending unit is incorporated with the fuel pump and, in some cases, a replaceable or nonreplaceable fuel filter. The entire assembly has three jobs: pick up fuel from the bottom of the tank by way of the fuel pump, strain (filter/clean) the fuel and pressurize it, and, of course, report the level of fuel in the tank at the driver information center. These systems are meant to last at least the life of the warranty.

FIGURE 48-25 The sending unit is a variable resistor that is attached to a float mechanism.

FIGURE 48-26 Fuel and evaporative emission lines.

Filter Sock

Fuel contamination can be extremely detrimental to the fuel supply system as well as the engine itself. To this end, a **filter sock** is the first line of defense and is incorporated into the end of the fuel pickup tube. The sock typically consists of a fine mesh, which prevents most small particles from being drawn into the fuel pump and sent through the rest of the fuel system.

Fuel Lines

Fuel lines are usually made of metal tubing or synthetic materials. A fuel supply line carries fuel from the tank to the engine. A return line may also be provided to allow excess fuel to return to the tank. Returning the excess fuel helps prevent the formation of vapor that can occur in the fuel supply during hot conditions. Other lines that run along with the fuel lines include evaporative emission system lines, which connect between the fuel tank, charcoal canister, and intake manifold **FIGURE 48-26**. These lines can be damaged by rust or foreign objects or even by lifting a vehicle improperly with a jack or hoist.

Fuel Filter

The **fuel filter** typically consists of a pleated paper filter housed in a sealed container. Its primary function is to prevent contaminants from reaching the injectors. The paper filter can also prevent small amounts of water from getting past it since the paper absorbs the water, causing the fibers in the filter to swell and preventing any liquid from getting past it. Most fuel filters are directional, meaning

they must be installed in the proper direction. Usually an arrow on the filter indicates the direction of flow.

Fuel Rail

A **fuel rail** is a special manifold designed to provide a reservoir of pressurized fuel for the fuel injectors. The gasoline is fed from the fuel tank by way of the fuel lines. The fuel, under pressure of course, is supplied by the fuel pump. The fuel rail can also serve as a mounting place for the fuel pressure regulator. The couplings where the fuel lines meet the fuel rail are usually sealed by flared ends, quick-connect high-pressure O-rings, or banjo fittings **FIGURE 48-27**. These methods ensure a sealed, leak-proof joint between the parts. Many, but not all, fuel rails provide a means for connecting a fuel pressure tester to the rail. This design, called a Schrader valve, uses a one-way valve to hold pressure in the system while the pressure tester is connected and disconnected to the fuel rail. Schrader valves usually are covered by a screw-on cap with a seal inside to prevent leaks in the event the Schrader valve goes bad.

Fuel Pressure Regulator

Fuel pressure must be regulated in some manner. On port fuel-injected engines, the fuel pressure needs to be maintained above manifold pressure. Since manifold pressure changes with engine load, fuel pressure also needs to change with it. Some vehicles use a pressure regulator on the fuel rail, some are in the fuel tank, and others control fuel pressure by controlling the speed of the fuel pump. A **fuel pressure regulator** mounted on the fuel rail

FIGURE 48-27 Types of fuel line connections. **A.** Flare. **B.** Quick couplings. **C.** Banjo fitting.

FIGURE 48-28 A fuel pressure regulator mounted on the fuel rail incorporates a diaphragm-operated valve.

opens and closes the valve, which vents pressure back to the fuel tank through a return line. Fuel pressure builds against the diaphragm, and once it hits the preset pressure, the valve will open slightly and bleed off pressure. This action reduces the pressure on the diaphragm closing the valve. With the valve closed, the pressure rises again, until the valve once again opens.

This process is repeated over and over to maintain the pressure in a fuel system. However, this system does not adjust the pressure when the engine load is increased. The spring-loaded vacuum chamber is connected by a manifold vacuum line to the intake manifold. The vacuum pulls against spring pressure to modify the pressure at which the valve opens to allow fuel to return to the fuel tank. As the driver accelerates, the manifold vacuum diminishes. That, in turn, allows more spring pressure to push on the diaphragm, which then requires more fuel pressure to open the valve, providing higher fuel

incorporates a diaphragm-operated valve **FIGURE 48-28**. On one side of the valve is a pressure spring and engine vacuum. On the other side of the diaphragm is fuel pressure from the fuel pump. Movement of the diaphragm pressure in the fuel rail to maintain a consistent pressure drop across the injectors.

Fuel Injector

The modern fuel injector is simply a spring-loaded, electric-solenoid spray nozzle **FIGURE 48-29**. It incorporates a filter screen in the inlet and is usually sealed with O-rings to the fuel rail and intake manifold. The nozzle can be of several types, such as rotating disc style, pintle style, and ball-valve style. Each type has its own pros and cons. Its job is to spray the proper amount of gasoline in the proper pattern either into the intake ports, directly into the combustion chamber, or into a prechamber in response to signals from the PCM. It is positioned between the fuel rail and the intake manifold, or in the case of a GDI fuel system, between the fuel rail and the combustion chamber.

As you know, fuel is pressurized and waiting in the fuel rail. When the PCM sends an electric signal to the fuel injector, the injector opens for a specified time and then the current is stopped and an internal spring returns the injector to the closed position, where it waits for the next "on" command. This happens repeatedly hundreds of times per minute at each fuel injector. The fuel injectors are designed and built to very exacting tolerances, giving them a high degree of fuel delivery precision and a long service life.

The response time to lift the injector needle to the fully open position is about 1 millisecond. If battery voltage is low, this response time takes longer and the engine receives less fuel. The PCM can compensate for this delay in opening time by extending the pulse width of the injector(s).

Electronic Fuel Injection Principles

EFI systems employ electronically controlled injectors to spray the fuel into either the intake system or the cylinder directly. The following discussion covers the basic EFI systems you will encounter as an automotive technician and then describes specifically how these systems operate.

Types of EFI Systems

There are three basic EFI systems: throttle body injection, also called single-point injection; multipoint fuel injection; and gasoline direct injection, or simply direct injection **FIGURE 48-30**. The specific characteristics of each of these designs will be explained further, but they all operate on similar principles: Fuel is supplied to the injectors at the specified pressure, the PCM sends an electric signal to each injector to cause it to open for a certain amount of time (pulse width), and fuel is injected into the intake manifold or combustion chamber.

Throttle Body Injection Systems

<u>Throttle body injection (TBI)</u>, also known as single-point injection or central-point injection, is a system with one or two fuel injectors located centrally on the intake manifold, right above the throttle plates. Fuel is sprayed into the top center of the throttle body and then atomized with the incoming filtered air. This air–fuel mixture is then delivered to each of the engine's cylinders evenly. TBI is a simpler system, requiring only one or two injectors, meaning the PCM can be of a simpler, less powerful design. And since the fuel is sprayed above the throttle plates, it

FIGURE 48-29 The modern fuel injector is a spring-loaded, electric-solenoid spray nozzle.

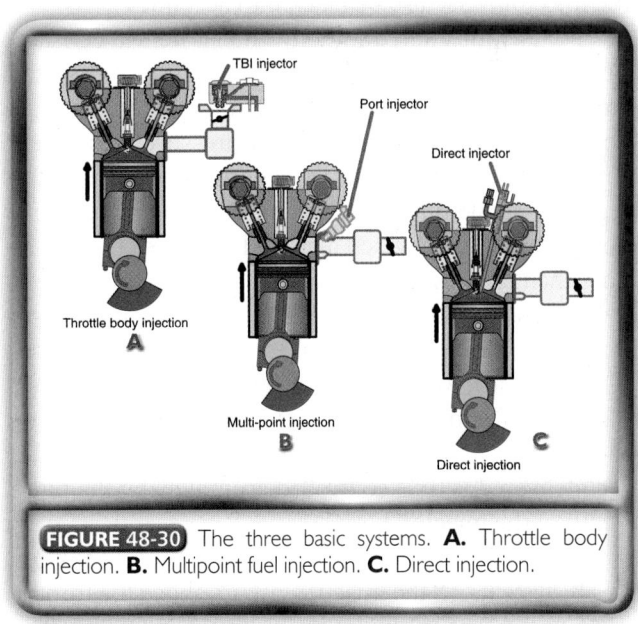

FIGURE 48-30 The three basic systems. **A.** Throttle body injection. **B.** Multipoint fuel injection. **C.** Direct injection.

is at atmospheric pressure, so the pressure drop across the injector is always the same. Thus, fuel pressure does not need to change with throttle opening or engine load.

In TBI systems, the central injector is normally triggered on every ignition pulse. However, if there are two injectors, alternate triggering may be used. At idling speeds, the frequency may be less to provide finer control. TBI is the predecessor to modern-day multipoint (or multiport) fuel injection.

Multipoint Fuel Injection Systems

In **multipoint fuel injection (MPFI)** systems, a fuel injector is used for each cylinder. The injector is located in the intake manifold near each intake valve and sprays fuel toward the valve. Each injector is connected to the fuel rail, which supplies the injector with fuel under pressure. Each injector also has an electrical connector that provides it with power and ground. Most electronic fuel injectors are supplied with constant battery voltage when the ignition key is in the run or crank position. The PCM then switches the negative side of the injector circuit to ground to turn it on. When the PCM switches the negative side of the circuit off, the spring in the injector closes the injector, and fuel stops spraying.

On return-style MPFI systems, a fuel pressure regulator inlet is connected to the fuel rail, and an outlet lets fuel return to the tank. A control diaphragm and pressure spring determine the exposed opening of the outlet and the amount of fuel that can return. Thus, the strength of the pressure spring determines fuel pressure in the fuel rail and keeps it at a fixed value. However, the pressure in the intake manifold varies considerably with changes in engine speed and with load, so the pressure drop across the injector must also be taken into account.

For any injection duration, if fuel is held at constant pressure, then as manifold pressure varies, so does the amount of fuel delivered. That means fuel pressure must be held constant above manifold pressure. This pressure is held by sealing the spring housing of the pressure regulator and letting it sense manifold pressure via a connecting hose. Then, when manifold pressure changes, so does the fuel pressure.

When manifold pressure is low (high vacuum), as it is at idling, fuel pressure is low. As manifold pressure rises (low vacuum), toward open throttle, fuel pressure rises. Since the injectors are all subjected to the same pressure, they all inject an equal amount of fuel. The quantity of fuel delivered is thus controlled accurately by the pulse width of the injector.

Note that manifold pressure sensing is not required in TBI systems, as the injection occurs above the throttle plate, at atmospheric pressure; thus fuel pressure is deter-

mined by the force of the regulator spring acting on the diaphragm. The injectors are sealed into the manifold by O-rings that prevent air entering at that point. The O-rings, together with plastic caps on the injector nozzles, also act as a barrier to heat being transferred to the injector body.

For a short time after an engine is switched off, the engine temperature keeps rising, which can produce vapor in the fuel lines. A check valve in the pump maintains the fuel pressure in the system after engine shut down, preventing the fuel from boiling (vaporizing) as it absorbs heat from the engine (heat soak) **FIGURE 48-31**. This pressure will diminish in about 20 to 30 minutes, but it ensures effective hot-starting capability of the engine.

When the engine is running, the circulation of fuel ensures that cool fuel is delivered at all times and that vapor formation in the lines is prevented. The pump control circuit normally allows the pump to operate for only a few seconds when the ignition is switched on; this is for priming the system. The pump control circuit allows the pump to operate during cranking and when the engine is running above a specified minimum revolutions per minute (rpm).

Gasoline Direct Injection Systems

With the pressures to reduce emissions and increase fuel economy, as well as gain an advantage over the competition and offset the escalating price of crude oil, manufacturers have looked to new technologies in fuel injection. Just as TBI replaced carburetion, **gasoline direct injection (GDI)** is the natural successor to **indirect fuel injection**. While indirect fuel injection atomizes fuel at or near the intake valve, GDI systems take their design cues from

FIGURE 48-31 For a short time after an engine is switched off, the engine temperature keeps rising, which can produce vapor in the fuel lines.

diesel technology by spraying the fuel directly into the cylinder **FIGURE 48-32**. Because of this direct injection, engines can run on extremely lean fuel mixtures—much leaner than stoichiometric (14.7 parts air to 1 part fuel). Their fuel mixtures can be as lean as 65 to 1!

The fuel injector of each cylinder is located in the cylinder head. Fuel is directly sprayed into the combustion chamber as an atomized mist at the precise time it is needed, depending on the operating conditions of the engine. The reason this type of engine can run so lean is because the injector can place the fuel in a localized spot surrounding the spark plug. This is called a stratified charge because the fuel is mixed with air in just a small area, not thoroughly dispersed among the entire amount of air in the combustion chamber.

So far GDI engines still use spark plugs. Use of spark plugs provides the computer with more choices as to when the fuel gets injected. For example, during heavy load conditions, a slightly rich mixture is injected during the intake stroke. This gives more time for the larger amount of fuel to mix more fully with the air, creating maximum power and reduced spark knock. During moderate engine loads, just enough fuel is injected during the intake stroke to create a stoichiometric air–fuel ratio, to again fully mix with the air. This results in good power and a very clean burn. Under light load or cruise conditions, if the fuel pump is designed to deliver the high pressures needed to overcome the compression pressures, the fuel is injected as described earlier, during the latter stages of the compression stroke, and is placed near the spark plug. This small amount of air and fuel is surrounded by a larger amount of air, which helps insulate the cylinder walls from the heat of combustion. This design reduces heat loss in the combustion chamber and increases fuel economy.

GDI fuel systems can be of either a low-pressure variety (only inject during the intake stroke or early in the compression stroke) or a high-pressure variety (can inject during the intake stroke, the compression stroke, and potentially the power stroke).

Operation of EFI Systems

As mentioned previously, the three EFI systems—TBI, MPFI, and GDI—all share certain operative principles. To properly diagnose and service these systems, the technician must understand such processes as the injection of fuel, delivery of air, and management of combustion.

Returnless Fuel Injection Systems

New vehicles have been using **returnless fuel injection systems** for the past 10 years or so. Manufacturers turned to using returnless fuel systems to reduce evaporative emissions. On a return-type system, the fuel returning to the tank is hot from engine heat. Hot fuel will readily vaporize and make the evaporative system work harder, requiring additional fuel vapor storage capacity. Since no hot fuel is returned to the tank in a returnless system, the fuel in the tank stays relatively cool, thus minimizing vaporization.

There are two types of returnless systems. One uses a pressure regulator in the fuel tank (mechanical), and the other controls the speed of the fuel pump to modify pressure (electronic). The in-tank regulator uses a spring-loaded pressure regulator similar to the type mounted to the fuel rail, except it does not change with manifold pressure and therefore does not use a vacuum hose. Excess fuel pressure is simply vented into the tank.

On the electronically controlled system, the PCM sends a square wave (digital) signal, which controls the speed of the fuel pump. The faster it turns, the higher the pressure and flow. The lower it turns, the lower the pressure and flow. The PCM monitors the fuel pressure through a fuel pressure sensor mounted on the fuel rail and controls the fuel pump based on engine speed, load, and other factors.

Simultaneous Fuel Injection

In MPFI, the injectors can be triggered in various ways. The simplest way is to trigger them at the same time or in groups. This is called simultaneous injection or grouped injection, and the injectors operate twice per cycle—once each crankshaft revolution, each time delivering half the fuel for the cycle. In a six-cylinder engine, the injectors are triggered on every third ignition pulse. The actual operating time of the injectors depends very much on battery voltage.

FIGURE 48-32 Injection systems. **A.** Direct injection system. **B.** Indirect injection system.

Sequential Fuel Injection

Sequential injection means injection occurs in the sequence of the firing order. The injectors follow the firing order of the engine. Each injector opens only once in each cycle, to deliver the fuel needed. Because each injector is controlled separately, the PCM needs to have individual drivers to turn each injector on and off. This system requires more computing power to manage each injector circuit. It also requires more wires back to the PCM, since each injector requires its own circuit. Since each injector fires only once per cycle, the timing of the injection pulse is important, and, therefore, the position of the number 1 cylinder and the camshaft must be known. This also adds to the complexity of the system over a TBI or simultaneous-injection system. Added load placed on the engine during idle can be compensated for by increasing the passageway of an idle speed control device or by opening the throttle plate slightly on drive-by-wire systems. Doing so lets more air bypass the throttle plate. This air has been measured by the airflow meter, so extra fuel is metered to maintain the same air–fuel ratio. The extra mixture thus delivered increases engine torque and maintains idle speed.

Air Supply

In MPFI systems, the air required for the combustion of the fuel is led from the air filter, through the throttle valve, and into the common manifold, or plenum chamber. From here, individual intake runners, or pipes, branch off to each cylinder. Ideally, all of these runners are of equal length **FIGURE 48-33**. The design of the intake system determines how large an air mass can be drawn into a

FIGURE 48-33 Individual intake runners branch off to each cylinder.

cylinder at any given engine rpm. This is where the most advantage can be taken of EFI, since it can achieve uniform distribution of the air delivered to the cylinders.

With unobstructed passages to each cylinder, the cylinder fills with air as efficiently as possible. The breathing of the engine, or its volumetric efficiency, is improved. The more air crammed into the cylinder, the denser the air–fuel mixture when ignition occurs. This increases the pressure on the piston as well as engine power output.

The temperature of the air influences how dense the air–fuel mixture will be. Cold air is denser than hot air, so it has a greater mass in any given volume. Thus, to ensure the entry of cool air, on most intake systems, the air entry to the intake is located away from engine heat. Since the manifold carries air only, it does not need to be heated by coolant. Filtered air arrives at the intake port as cool and dense as possible, ready for mixing with the fuel from the injector.

> ▶ **LINK:**
> Refer to the *Induction and Exhaust* chapter for more information on intake manifolds.

Air Measurement

The amount of air entering the engine must be measured or calculated so that the amount of fuel injected into it forms a mixture to suit the engine operating conditions at that time. The volume of air can be determined in two ways—speed density calculation or direct measurement.

The volume of air entering the engine varies according to the engine speed and the load, so if calculations are used, they are based primarily on the engine rpm, as measured by the crankshaft position sensor, and the engine load, as measured by the manifold absolute pressure sensor. Then using the intake air temperature, throttle position, and coolant temperature, the airflow can be calculated using preprogrammed fuel maps. The oxygen sensor is then used to provide feedback as to the richness or leanness of the fuel that has been injected.

A mass airflow (MAF) sensor directly measures the mass of filtered air entering the engine. It can be mounted on, or near, the air filter casing. All air entering the intake flows through the MAF sensor, then through a sealed, flexible hose or duct to the throttle body. It then enters the engine. Older systems used a vane-type airflow meter. These meters have a spring-loaded vane, or flap, that deflects according to how much air enters. The electrical signal to the PCM varies with this deflection, as contacts attached to the vane move across a potentiometer. The intake system must be airtight, with no leaks downstream of the meter; otherwise inaccurate signals will be sent to the PCM. Any air that leaks into the system without going through the airflow meter is called false air, or unmetered air. Since air bypasses the airflow meter, it tends to lean out the mixture because the PCM is not accounting for the extra air.

The Karman vortex airflow sensor measures airflow disruptions. There are three types of vortex sensors, all of which use an air regulator to first smooth out or reduce any turbulence in the air flow entering the sensor; a triangular vortex column then disrupts a portion of the air flow creating vortices or whirlpools in the air flow **FIGURE 48-34**. These "whirlpools" are then measured by one of three different methods:

1. Optical type—The air vortices cause a mirror to oscillate and interrupt an infrared signal.
2. Ultrasonic type—The whirlpools disrupt an ultrasonic beam that is transmitted through the air stream.
3. Pressure type—The pressure waves caused by the vortex column are measured by what is essentially a pressure sensor, similar to a MAP sensor. This is now the most common type.

Regardless of the method used to measure the whirlpools, all of these sensor types produce a 5-volt digital signal with a frequency that is proportional to the airflow through the sensor.

Fuel Shutoff Mode

With the emphasis that vehicle manufacturers place on safety, today's vehicles typically incorporate some sort of **fuel shutoff mode**. In the event of the vehicle suffering a collision or rollover accident, the vehicle will shut off the electric fuel pump in an effort to avoid possible fire and/or leakage. The vehicle uses various **accelerometers** to monitor key indicators of an accident requiring fuel shutoff. For safety purposes, most vehicles with a fuel shutoff system have a specific reset procedure that must be followed to restart the vehicle that has been in an accident **FIGURE 48-35**.

Efficient Combustion

For efficient operation of the catalytic converter, the mixture ratio must be maintained close to the stoichiometric ratio—14.7 parts air to 1 part fuel (or leaner during certain operating parameters). Efficiency of combustion can be monitored by measuring the percentage of oxygen in the exhaust gas. A high percentage may mean the mixture entering the cylinder is too lean.

The oxygen sensor in the exhaust manifold, or in the engine pipe, tells the PCM how much oxygen is in the exhaust gas. The PCM then varies injector opening time to achieve a correct mixture ratio. Feedback also allows

fuel settings to change as components age. This is called adaptive learning. The PCM memorizes its fuel settings for different operating conditions and stores them for future use. If a fault occurs in a component or part of a system, a fault code will be stored in memory and can be retrieved by connecting a scan tool to the data link connector. Information on the fault can then be analyzed.

Although most injectors operate at the nominal battery voltage of 12 volts, many sensors have a reference voltage of 5 volts. This adjustment is made by a voltage regulator in the control unit. It gives more accurate signaling, as fluctuations due to changes in battery voltage do not occur.

During engine operation, there are three main **pollutants** created: nitrogen oxides, carbon monoxide, and hydrocarbons. These three pollutants enter the catalytic

FIGURE 48-34 A triangular, vortex-generating rod disturbs the airflow and causes whirlpools of air to form in the body of the sensor.

FIGURE 48-35 The inertia switch.

FIGURE 48-36 The stoichiometric point.

FIGURE 48-37 Closed loop means the control unit is using feedback from the oxygen sensor to alter the injection setting.

converter. How efficiently they are converted depends on the composition of the exhaust gases, and that depends on the air–fuel mixture sent into the cylinder for combustion. The more ideal the mixture, the less pollutants produced.

If the air–fuel ratio supplied to the engine is too rich, then the nitrogen oxides are converted efficiently, but the carbon monoxide and the hydrocarbons are not. If the air–fuel mixture supplied to the engine is too lean, the opposite occurs: Carbon monoxide and hydrocarbons in the exhaust gas are converted efficiently, but the nitrogen oxides are not.

Highly efficient conversions of all three pollutants occur only in a narrow range of air–fuel ratios. This range, the stoichiometric point, occurs around the ideal air–fuel ratio of 14.7 to 1 **FIGURE 48-36**.

If the mixture ratio falls outside this range, the efficiency of conversion of either the nitrogen oxides or the hydrocarbons and carbon monoxide will rapidly decrease. Because of this strict requirement, vehicles with a three-way catalytic converter have a feedback system, called looping. The PCM monitors the air–fuel ratio by using an oxygen sensor, also known as a lambda sensor. This sensor obtains information about the composition of exhaust gases. It is located in the exhaust manifold and is connected to the PCM.

Closed loop can mean the control unit receives feedback from the oxygen sensor and acts on it to alter the injection setting **FIGURE 48-37**. Open loop can mean there is feedback to the control unit, but it is ignored, and the fuel settings are then determined from the programmed memory. Alternatively, open loop can mean there is no feedback to the control unit. In that case, too, fuel settings

are determined from the programmed memory. During cold starting, this sensor is at too low of a temperature to provide an output voltage to the control unit, so it operates in open loop. The same applies until the sensor warms up. The control unit is in open loop. It is only when the oxygen sensor reaches its operating temperature that a voltage corresponding to the air–fuel ratio is sent to the control unit. During normal operation, open loop may also occur during idle or under maximum power. It can also occur if there is a fault that causes the air–fuel ratio to be excessively rich for long periods. Similarly, it can occur if there is a fault that makes the ratio too lean for long periods.

When the oxygen sensor reaches its operating temperature, around 600°F (315°C), it sends an output voltage to the control unit to signal whether the mixture is richer or leaner than a lambda value of 1.00—that is, the air–fuel ratio of 14.7 to 1. When the mixture deviates from this point, the output voltage changes sharply above or below its switching point (approximately 0.45 volts) **FIGURE 48-38**.

The voltage of the signal from the oxygen sensor changes sharply when the air–fuel mixture changes from lean to rich. If the control unit sees the voltage as high, then the quantity of fuel injected is reduced. Similarly, if the mixture changes from rich to lean and the voltage is low, more fuel is injected to enrich the mixture.

The control unit then adjusts the pulse width of the injector accordingly to ensure the most efficient operation of the catalytic converter. During engine operation, this adjusting is continuous, and almost instantaneous, trying to maintain an air–fuel ratio for lambda equal to 1.

FIGURE 48-38 When the mixture deviates from the stoichiometric point, the output voltage changes sharply above or below its switching point of approximately 0.45 volts.

FIGURE 48-39 Fuel pump circuit.

Short- and Long-Term Fuel Trim

The computer is programmed with the expected injector pulse-width for nearly all operating conditions, but circumstances such as engine and fuel system wear, or differences in fuel, cause the mixture to be slightly off the expected value. The oxygen sensor is the computer's window into the exhaust stream, and is used to validate the accuracy of the computer's pulse width signal. If the mixture is slightly lean, the O_2 sensor will indicate that, and the PCM will richen up the mixture slightly. If the O_2 indicates a rich condition, the PCM will lean it out. This richening and leaning is called short term fuel trim (STFT). The PCM watches the average of the richening and leaning over short periods of time (less than a second) and calculates the percentage changed from the expected value and displays it as a positive (adding fuel) or negative (subtracting fuel) percentage. The PCM aims to keep the STFT at its midpoint, so that it can respond to any needed changes. If it sees the STFT start to creep away from the midpoint, the PCM will increase or decrease its base pulse-width setting, which will bring the STFT back to center. It will then record that base adjustment as a long term fuel trim (LTFT) percentage; again, either positive or negative.

STFT and LTFT are useful when diagnosing drivability concerns. If you see the LTFT more than single digits positive, it means the PCM thinks the vehicle is running too lean and is substantially richening the mixture up. This could be due to a vacuum leak, or it could be a weak O_2 sensor that can't produce as high of a reading as it did when it was new. If the LTFT is more than single digits negative, it means the PCM thinks it is running too rich, and is leaning it out. This could be caused by a leaky fuel injector or stuck open purge valve.

Fuel Pump Relay

Most fuel pumps are operated by a fuel pump relay. The relay controls power to the fuel pump. Typically the relay is controlled by the PCM **FIGURE 48-39**. Unlike a mechanical pump that would quit pumping if the vehicle were involved in an accident that resulted in the engine dying, an electric fuel pump will continue running as long as electricity is flowing to it. For safety's sake, the PCM will shut down the fuel pump relay if it does not see indications from the crankshaft position sensor that the engine is running above about 350 rpm. This way, the fuel pump is likely to be shut down in the event of an accident. The PCM can also operate the fuel pump for a few seconds if the ignition switch is turned on to prime the system or while the vehicle is being cranked.

Some vehicles use an inertia switch to turn the fuel pump off in the event of an accident. The inertia switch is held closed by a spring-loaded trigger. A loose weight is free to move within the area of the trigger. If the vehicle experiences enough of a shock in any direction, the weight will dislodge the trigger, opening the switch.

▶ Electronic Fuel Injection Sensors

Early fuel injection systems were mechanically timed. Although considered advanced technology for the era, those systems were soon phased out by modern-day EFI. The current EFI systems are constantly adjusting for various conditions and requirements to produce high levels of power at an acceptable and efficient rate. Many sensors are required to properly make the necessary adjustments

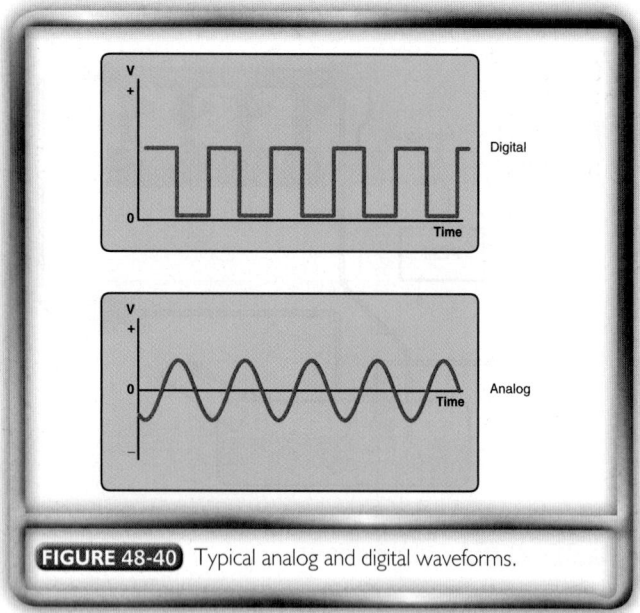

FIGURE 48-40 Typical analog and digital waveforms.

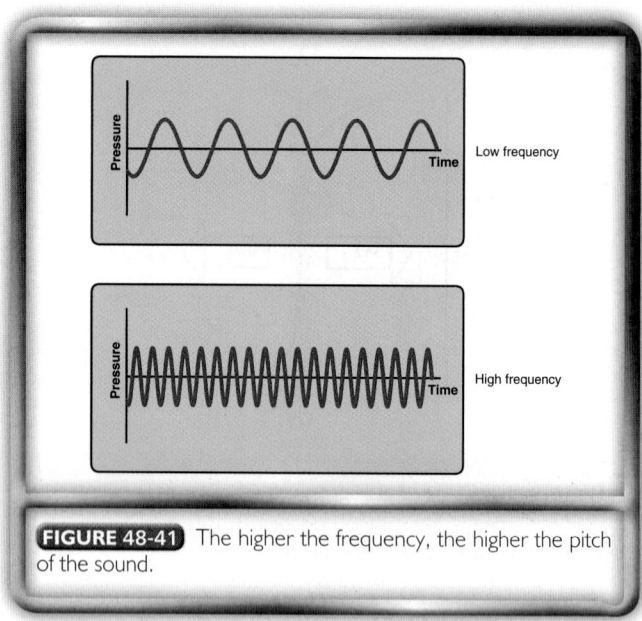

FIGURE 48-41 The higher the frequency, the higher the pitch of the sound.

for today's fuel emission requirements. But before we discuss each sensor, we need to explore the various types of electrical signals.

Digital Versus Analog Signals

Analog produces a signal that is smooth and gradually changing in strength, whereas a digital signal is a direct on/off with no in-between transition. Although a reliable system, analog signals lack the true reaction timing of the new age of digital signals. The advent of digital technology has given rise to higher powered processors that allow better control and monitoring of the systems on the vehicle, including the fuel injection system **FIGURE 48-40**.

Frequency

Sound travels through the air by producing pressure waves—areas of high pressure and areas of low pressure. The rate at which these waves reach our ears is called **frequency**. It is measured in cycles per second, where a cycle is the distance between waves, or wavelength. The higher the frequency, the higher the pitch of the sound **FIGURE 48-41**.

The range of human hearing is approximately 20 cycles per second to 20,000 cycles per second. An engine produces sounds across a wide range of frequencies. The mufflers and resonators in the engine exhaust system reduce these sounds to an acceptable level.

Potentiometer

A **potentiometer** is a mechanically variable resistor that, in EFI applications, is normally a film type. It can be linear or circular in construction and has three electrical connecting points. Two are at the ends of the resistor, and a third is attached to a center sliding contact, arranged to move across the resistor. A reference voltage is applied to the resistor so that a steady current flows through it. As the center sliding contact moves across the resistor, it measures the voltage at the point it is in contact with and provides a reference voltage for that position.

In automotive applications, the circular form is commonly used as a throttle position sensor, with the center contact attached to the throttle plate. The throttle plate position can then be monitored by the control unit.

Thermistors

A resistor that changes its resistance with the changes in temperature is called a **thermistor** **FIGURE 48-42**. Thermistors are used in various temperature-related controls on modern vehicles. Coolant temperature sensors, fuel temperature sensors, and ambient temperature sensors are just a few types. For example, the cabin temperature sensor's internal resistance may decrease when the cabin temperature increases. This resistance change causes a change in a voltage signal that could be used by the HVAC system to increase the air-conditioning airflow or to lower the vent temperature by moving the blend door. As a result, the system can maintain a driver-selected temperature.

EFI Sensors

The sensors used in an EFI system include:

- Crankshaft position sensor (CKP sensor)
- Ignition pickup
- Camshaft position sensor (CMP sensor)

FIGURE 48-42 A thermistor.

FIGURE 48-43 An inductive-type sensor and toothed wheel.

- Throttle position sensor (TPS)
- Engine coolant temperature sensor (ECT sensor or CTS) and intake air temperature sensor (IAT sensor)
- Oxygen sensor (before and after catalytic converts) (O_2 sensor or HO_2S)
- Manifold absolute pressure sensor (MAP sensor)
- Barometric pressure sensor (BARO sensor)
- Air-conditioning compressor clutch signal
- Knock sensor
- Vehicle speed sensor (VSS)
- Inertia sensors
- Fuel pressure sensors

Crankshaft Position Sensor

Crank angle sensing sends information on the speed and position of the crankshaft to the PCM for the control of ignition timing and injection sequencing. The control unit can then trigger the ignition and injection to suit virtually all operating conditions. The **crankshaft position (CKP) sensor** may be mounted externally on the crankcase housing or it may be inside the housing of the ignition distributor. There are different kinds of CKP sensors.

Inductive-type sensors sense the movement of the ring gear teeth on the flywheel, or a toothed disc on the crank pulley **FIGURE 48-43**. These sensors do not make physical contact. The sensor is mounted on the crankcase housing. It consists of a stator, with a central permanent magnet, and a soft iron core surrounded by an induction winding. The housing around all of these components is insulated from them.

The stator is positioned so that it has a very small clearance, or air gap, between the end of the soft iron core and the flywheel teeth. As the flywheel rotates, the teeth approach and leave the stator, and the air gap changes. As this occurs, the strength of the magnetic field changes. The winding is part of a complete circuit, so changing the magnetic field produces an alternating voltage and current.

As the tooth approaches the stator, the strength of the magnetic field increases. This induces a voltage, and current flow, in the winding. The polarity of the voltage is said to be positive, as it produces a current flow in a certain direction. When the tooth aligns with the stator, the magnetic field is at its strongest, but at that point, it is not changing. Voltage and current flow fall to zero.

As the tooth moves away from the stator, the strength of the magnetic field changes again, and once again voltage and current flow are induced in the winding. This time, current flow is in the opposite direction, and the polarity of the voltage is now said to be negative.

Since polarity changes every time a tooth approaches and leaves the stator, the voltage produced is an alternating current (AC) voltage, and the current flow in the winding is AC.

The toothed disc functions similarly. As the tooth approaches the stator, the magnetic field changes. It reaches a maximum when the tooth aligns with the stator, then changes again, decreasing as the tooth moves away. An alternating voltage is produced. It is the frequency of this alternating voltage that is used by the control unit to calculate engine rpm.

Crankshaft position is detected by a separate sensor, also an inductive type. It sends a signal to the control unit when a pin or bore passes, and generates one pulse per revolution. It signals the control unit that the number 1 piston is, for example, 80 degrees before top dead center. Ignition timing is then decided according to the operating conditions and is triggered to occur a certain number of degrees from that point. When only one sensor is used, the pulse inductor is shaped to provide information on both crankshaft speed and position. A disc attached to the crankshaft pulley has a number of equally spaced ribs around its circumference, but two ribs are omitted. The frequency of the pulse from each rib gives engine speed in rpm, but on each revolution, the pulse alters as the gap from the two missing ribs passes the sensor. This again gives the position of the number 1 piston.

A Hall-effect CKP sensor measures engine speed, represented in rpm of the crankshaft. The sensor is in very close proximity to a metal disc that is typically attached to the crankshaft or camshaft. Around the circumference of the disc there are evenly spaced teeth or cogs (square, even serrations) **FIGURE 48-44**. The sensor is stationary and usually located in the engine block, with an O-ring to seal in engine oil. It contains a magnetic coil, which reacts with the magnetic field as each cog passes by the tip of the sensor. When the crankshaft spins, induction current is set up around the magnetic coil. The cog edge of the crankshaft obstructs the sensor's magnetic field, creating a signal. This is what gives the PCM a measurement of the engine rpm.

Ignition Pickup-Style Position Sensor

The ignition pickup is primarily a Ford design. Known as PIP, which stands for profile ignition pickup, it is a Hall-effect vane switch that provides crankshaft position data to the Ford ECC-IV processor. These data allow the Ford ECC-IV system to make adjustments to the fuel injection according to the driver's requirements.

Camshaft Position Sensor

The camshaft position (CMP) sensor (or cam sensor) sends constant data to the computer to let it know which cylinder is on its power stroke as well as the position of the camshaft and valve. It does this by constantly reading a magnetic point on the camshaft or on the distributor housing **FIGURE 48-45**. The CMP sensor works in conjunction with a knock sensor and the computer to keep the ignition timing adjusted for all load conditions, thus reducing pinging and knocking.

Throttle Position Sensor

The throttle position sensor (TPS) gathers information on throttle position to allow the control unit to make adjustments according to operating conditions. It is located on the throttle body and operated by rotation of the throttle shaft. A potentiometer-type sensor monitors throttle position over its full range. One end has a 5-volt reference voltage from the control unit **FIGURE 48-46**. The other is connected to the control unit ground. A third wire runs from a sliding contact in the TPS sensor to the input circuits of the control unit. The sensor works like a variable resistor. As the angle of the throttle valve changes, so does the voltage signal along the third wire.

At closed throttle, the reading is usually below 1 volt. As the throttle valve opens, the voltage signal rises. At wide-open throttle, it is about 4.5 volts. This ongoing monitoring of throttle position provides accurate data for the control unit, allowing control over a wider range of operating conditions.

FIGURE 48-44 A Hall-effect CKP sensor measures engine speed, represented in rpm of the crankshaft.

FIGURE 48-45 The camshaft position (CMP) sensor sends data to the computer to let it know which cylinder is on its power stroke as well as the position of the camshaft and valve.

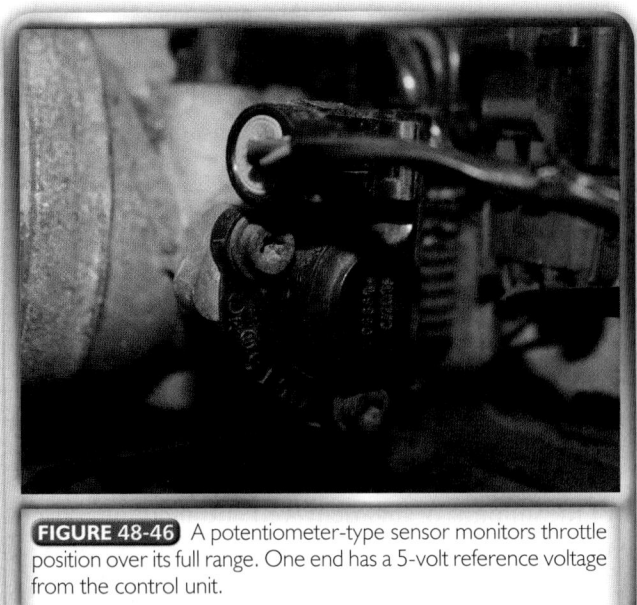

FIGURE 48-46 A potentiometer-type sensor monitors throttle position over its full range. One end has a 5-volt reference voltage from the control unit.

FIGURE 48-47 The coolant temperature sensor (CTS) is immersed in coolant in the cylinder head, block, or intake manifold.

FIGURE 48-48 Intake air temperature (IAT) sensor.

Engine Temperature Sensors

To maintain the air–fuel ratio within an optimum range, the control unit must take account of coolant temperature and air temperature. Extra fuel is needed when the engine is cold, and when the air is colder, and therefore denser.

The **coolant temperature sensor (CTS)** is immersed in coolant in the cylinder head, block, or intake manifold. It consists of a hollow threaded pin that has a resistor sealed inside it **FIGURE 48-47**. This resistor is made of a thermistor semiconductor material whose electrical resistance falls as temperature rises. The signal from the CTS is used by the PCM to control the mixture of the engine throughout its operating temperature.

Enrichment occurs during engine cranking, then slowly reduces as the engine warms up. This design ensures a smooth-running engine as soon as it is started. The control unit continually monitors coolant temperature during engine operation. Some manufacturers use a cylinder head temperature sensor instead of a CTS to signal engine temperature. It screws into the metal casting of the cylinder head to sense head temperature.

Air temperature is one factor that changes the density of air, so air temperature needs to be monitored by the PCM to better judge how much fuel needs to be injected. An air temperature sensor does just that. If the air temperature sensor is installed in the airflow sensor, it is positioned in the airstream and is called an **intake air temperature (IAT) sensor** **FIGURE 48-48**. When it is installed in the intake manifold, it is located in one of the intake runners and is called a manifold air temperature (MAT) sensor. In both cases, it relays information on air temperature and, therefore, the density of the air.

The control unit can then vary the injector pulse width accordingly.

Oxygen Sensor

An **oxygen sensor (before and after catalytic converter)** is positioned in the exhaust pipe and provides the engine management PCM with an electrical signal that relates to the amount of oxygen in the exhaust gas. The PCM uses this and other information to determine the correct amount of fuel to be injected into the engine.

Originally, automotive oxygen sensors were stoichiometric sensors. Although still in use today, they indicate only if the air–fuel ratio is rich (deficient oxygen) or lean (excess oxygen). They do not indicate how rich or how lean. Their output signal changes almost vertically on either side of an air–fuel ratio of stoichiometric, 14.7:1. It is the "Nernst cell" inside the sensor that produces this signal voltage. The Nernst cell operates by comparing the amount of oxygen in the exhaust gas to oxygen levels in the outside air **FIGURE 48-49**. To operate, this cell needs to be hot, approximately 600°F (315°C) or more. Exhaust gas can heat the sensor; however, when an internal heater is added, the sensor becomes operational more quickly and is called a heated oxygen sensor (HO_2S). This is most relevant when the sensor is positioned in cooler parts of the exhaust system away from the exhaust manifold.

As emission standards become tighter for both gasoline and diesel engines, a more precise signal is required. In these systems, the broad-band oxygen sensor (or wideband oxygen sensor) informs the PCM of a range of air–fuel ratios from 9:1 to atmospheric air. These systems are ideal for optimum emissions for vehicle gasoline or diesel engines, particularly where the incoming air is unthrottled and not restricted by a throttle butterfly lean-running GDI engine.

The wide-band oxygen sensor is far more sophisticated in operation than the earlier sensors, but it does include some similar parts. The Nernst cell is still used; however, the exhaust gas oxygen levels are referenced to a sealed chamber of air within the sensor and not outside air. These sensors have an electrical heating element that heats the sensor quickly from a cold start, typically in less than 10 seconds. This is a shorter time than that taken by the older sensors. This faster heating is achieved because the sensors have far less material within the sensing element.

Current through the heater is controlled by the PCM, allowing the correct operating temperature to be continuously maintained. A minute chamber within the sensor has access to the exhaust gas. It is this chamber that the Nernst cell samples exhaust gas from. This sensor uses a solid state pump to add or remove oxygen from the exhaust gas chamber **FIGURE 48-50**.

The computer controls the current flowing through the pump so that the Nernst cell output is at stoichiometric. Current flowing in one direction through the pump adds oxygen, while current in the opposite direction removes oxygen. The value and direction of current required to do this represents the level of oxygen in the exhaust gas. Reading this current allows the PCM to control the amount of fuel delivered and maintain correct emission levels.

Since 1996, nearly all manufacturers install an oxygen sensor before and after the catalytic converter to test for correct operation. For a catalytic converter to change exhaust gases correctly, it needs to be capable of storing and releasing oxygen from the catalyst. When this happens, the amount of oxygen entering the converter will differ from that leaving. The PCM uses these two signals along with response time to determine if the catalytic converter is functioning. If a malfunction is detected for a predetermined period, the MIL will be illuminated. Many manufacturers also use the rear oxygen sensor to fine-tune the fuel trim.

Manifold Absolute Pressure Sensor

Changes in engine speed and load cause changes in intake manifold pressure. A **manifold absolute pressure (MAP) sensor** measures these pressure changes and

FIGURE 48-49 Oxygen sensors, when at temperature, create an electrical signal based on the difference in oxygen in the exhaust stream compared to ambient air.

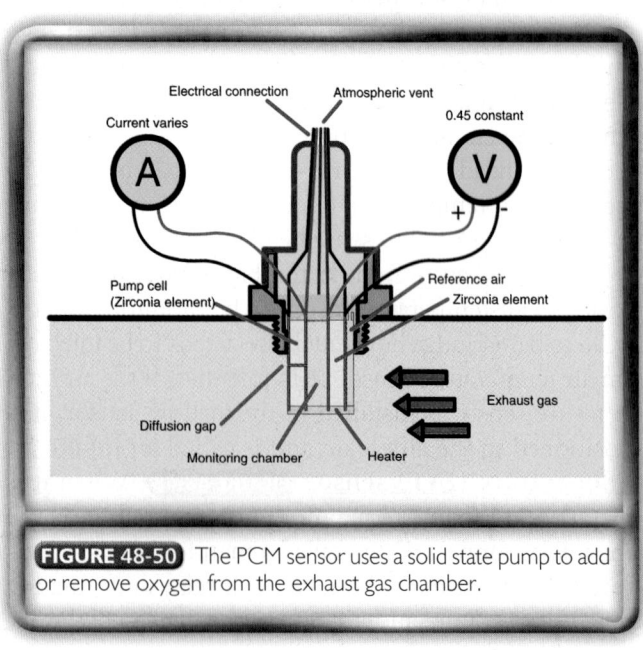

FIGURE 48-50 The PCM sensor uses a solid state pump to add or remove oxygen from the exhaust gas chamber.

converts them into an electrical signal. The signal may be an output voltage or a frequency. By monitoring output signals, the PCM senses manifold pressure and uses this information to calculate the basic fuel requirement. The MAP sensor can use a piezoelectric crystal. If there is a change in the pressure exerted on this crystal, the resistance changes. This alters its output signal. Some manufacturers also use the MAP sensor to monitor changes in manifold pressure when determining if the **exhaust gas recirculation (EGR) valve** opened or not.

The sensor is connected to the intake manifold by a small-diameter, flexible tube or is screwed directly into the manifold. The control unit typically sends a 5-volt reference signal to the sensor. As manifold pressure changes, so does the electrical resistance of the sensor, which in turn produces a change in the output voltage **FIGURE 48-51**. During idling, manifold pressure is low (high vacuum), which produces a comparatively low MAP output. With wide-open throttle, manifold pressure is higher, closer to atmospheric pressure (low vacuum), and voltage output is higher. Another type of MAP sensor that has been used by some manufacturers is one that sends a varying frequency to the PCM. As the sensor measures low manifold pressure, it sends a frequency signal. Frequency can be read on a digital volt-ohmmeter that has a frequency function.

Barometric Pressure Sensor

A **barometric pressure (BARO) sensor** measures barometric pressure, which helps to calibrate the fuel injection system. The barometric pressures at sea level and in Denver, Colorado, which is called the mile-high city because of its high altitude, are extremely different. The vehicle must function properly at both locations or anywhere in between. The BARO sensor works in conjunction with the MAP sensor to provide constant pressure difference information to the PCM. This information is critical for proper air–fuel mixture as well as ignition timing.

Older BARO sensors were typically mounted on the firewall or along the fender in the engine bay. Most late-model vehicles use the MAP sensor to take a barometric pressure reading before the vehicle is started, and the sensor is usually mounted on the intake manifold.

FIGURE 48-51 As manifold pressure changes, so does the electrical resistance of the sensor, which in turn produces a change in the output voltage.

Applied | Science

AS-10: Standard/Metric: The technician can convert measurements taken in the standard or metric system to specifications stated in either system.

An apprentice technician has been assigned to replace an intake manifold and fuel rail on a vehicle. An experienced technician is working with the apprentice on certain key points. Using the manufacturer's service information, the two technicians locate and discuss the proper torque specifications, which are given in both standard and metric units. The experienced technician explains that if only one specification is given, there are conversion factors available to determine the other torque value.

The common English term foot-pound (ft-lb) is sometimes interchangeably used with the preferred SAE term pound-foot (lb-ft). To convert 1 lb-ft to the metric unit of newton meters (Nm), we multiply the lb-ft value by 1.355 Nm. For example, 10 lb-ft = 13.55 Nm. To convert 1 Nm to lb-ft, we multiply the Nm value by 0.737 lb-ft. For example, 10 Nm = 7.37 lb-ft.

In addition to using these conversion factors, conversion tables are available. A number of interactive calculators are available online to convert various units from standard to metric and metric to standard.

Air-Conditioning Compressor Clutch Signal

When the air conditioning is turned on, it creates a load on the engine. This load, in turn, drags the engine down, especially during engine idle conditions on smaller engines. In vehicles equipped with the circuitry to do so, the clutch electrical circuit signals the PCM that the air conditioning has been turned on and that there will therefore be greater load on the engine. To counteract this load, the PCM sends a command to the engine idle speed controller to open slightly to maintain an acceptable engine rpm. This ultimately gives the driver smooth and quiet engine operation during idle with the air conditioning on.

AS-83: Barometric Pressure: The technician can demonstrate an understanding of the relationship of barometric pressure to engine performance.
Atmospheric pressure is a measure of the pressure exerted by the weight of the atmosphere. This is also called barometric pressure because barometers are used to measure it. The term barometer comes from the Greek words for weight and measure. A mercury barometer compares atmospheric pressure to a column of mercury and measures the results in inches or millimeters of mercury.

A barometric pressure (BARO) sensor measures barometric pressure and is crucial to most fuel injections systems. The barometric pressure varies by geographic elevation. The vehicle must function flawlessly in any given location. Accurate pressure readings are critical for proper air–fuel mixture as well as ignition timing.

The principle of the operation of barometric sensors is based upon the flexing of a silicon chip. The output voltage signal varies based upon the amount that the chip flexes due to barometric pressure. The PCM uses this information along with other data to determine the proper adjustments that should be made to the fuel system as well as other systems.

Knock Sensor

Engine knock occurs in the combustion chamber when there is an unwanted spike in pressure caused by pre-ignition or detonation. This unwanted and damaging event can be caused in different ways. Some vehicles are equipped with a **knock sensor**, the function of which is to monitor the noise that is created by the pressure spike. This noise, or "knock," can be created by an excessive load on the engine, ignition timing that is too advanced, or overheating of the engine. The PCM can adjust the ignition timing to help reduce the knocking, except in the case of engine overheating. In addition, adjustments to the ignition timing and fuel delivery can be made if the vehicle begins to overheat. The following is a brief description of what occurs during excessive engine load and during engine overheating:

- **Excessive load on the engine**
  1. Ignition starts.
  2. The expanding gases create a pressure wave designed to push the piston down.
  3. The forces opposing piston movement are too high.
  4. The piston accelerates slowly and maintains a small volume above the piston.
  5. The unburnt mixture is compressed by the advancing pressure wave.

  6. This fuel self-ignites due to an increase in temperature and creates its own flame front.
  7. The two advancing flame fronts create a huge spike in pressure, creating engine knock.
  8. This knock has enough energy to badly damage pistons, rings, spark plugs, and rod bearings.

- **Overheated engine—faulty thermostat**
  1. Ignition starts.
  2. The expanding gases create a pressure wave designed to push the piston down.
  3. The temperature of the unburnt fuel is too high due to the overheated engine.
  4. The unburnt mixture is compressed by the advancing pressure wave.
  5. This fuel self-ignites due to an increase in pressure/temperature and creates its own flame front.
  6. The two advancing flame fronts create a huge spike in pressure, creating engine knock.

One way of overcoming engine knock is to allow the fuel to be ignited later in the compression stroke. Doing so requires having less ignition advance. If the fuel is ignited later, then the pressures above the piston will be less during the early stages of the power stroke, eliminating engine knock.

> **TECHNICIAN TIP**
>
> Another way of preventing engine knock is to use fuel with a higher octane rating. This makes the fuel harder to ignite and slower to burn, both of which reduce engine knock.

The function of the knock sensor is to produce an electrical signal that the PCM can use to determine if knock has occurred. If knock is occurring, the PCM will retard the timing a few degrees and listen to detect whether the knock is still present. If so, the PCM will continue to retard the timing in steps, within its limits, until knock is eliminated. If knock is not occurring, the PCM will advance the timing a degree or two and listen for knock. The timing is kept at the optimum point for the driving conditions.

The sensor is screwed into the engine block, where it is influenced by all engine vibrations **FIGURE 48-52**. Using a piezoelectric crystal, the sensor produces a signal voltage proportional to the vibrations applied to it. The PCM interprets the strength, frequency, and timing of the signal to determine if knock has occurred. While knock sensor technology has improved, it cannot always

FIGURE 48-52 The sensor is screwed into the engine block, where it is influenced by all engine vibrations.

FIGURE 48-53 Fuel pressure sensor mounted on the fuel rail.

know the difference between engine knock and a loose air-conditioning compressor bracket that rattles when it is on. In this situation, the rattling air-conditioning compressor bracket causes a noise that the knock sensor picks up as engine knock. But since the "knock" in this case does not go away as the timing is retarded, the PCM gradually reduces ignition advance until it reaches its limits, causing low power, poor fuel economy, and possible engine overheating. Monitoring the knock sensor signal and amount of timing retard on a scan tool will help you identify this issue.

V-configured engines often have two knock sensors installed, known as twin knock sensors. This design allows the PCM to have control over knock on separate banks.

Vehicle Speed Sensor

The vehicle speed sensor (VSS) is a detection device that sends the vehicle speed information (i.e., how fast the vehicle is traveling) to the ECM. The VSS is sometimes located in the instrument cluster; however, most manufacturers mount these sensors on the transmission or transfer case.

Inertia Sensors

In a system that uses inertia sensors, the fuel pump will only operate when the safety circuit containing the inertia sensor is complete. In this circuit, there is a fuel cutoff switch that uses a mechanical device to break the circuit if the vehicle is involved in a serious enough accident. This inertia sensor consists of a steel ball held in a funnel-shaped container by a magnet.

If the vehicle is subjected to impact shock or if it tilts rapidly, the steel ball breaks free from the magnet's restraining force and rolls up the side of its container, pushing against the circuit-breaking switch, which shuts off the power to the fuel pump (or pumps if there is more than one). Once activated, the circuit remains in an open position until it is reset.

Fuel Pressure Sensor

Most vehicles now use a fuel pressure sensor mounted on the fuel rail **FIGURE 48-53**. This sensor allows the PCM to monitor the fuel pressure in the fuel rail so that it can control the speed of the fuel pump to maintain the correct pressure in the system.

Switches

While at idle, engine speed can be adversely affected by fairly minor changes in load. Loads from transmissions, power steering pumps, and air-conditioning compressors are examples. For optimum engine control, it is necessary for the PCM to be informed of these loads before the engine speed drops. Switches are used to inform the PCM when the power steering pump pressure is high, automatic transmission drive gear is selected, and the air-conditioning compressor is engaged. The result is excellent PCM control of idle speed as loads vary on the engine.

Misfire Monitoring

Engine **misfire** is a condition that can cause catalytic converters to overheat in a very short time. In normal operation, catalytic converters get very hot just dealing with a small amount of combustible gases. When a steady misfire occurs due to an ignition problem, the full volume of air and fuel from the misfiring cylinder is burned in the catalyst. This can turn the catalytic converter red hot and even cause it to melt down. Detecting misfire is important to prevent this. In fact, if the PCM detects a steady misfire, it will cause the MIL to blink (not just come on steady), warning that there is a catalyst-damaging fault in the system. Manufacturers incorporate misfire monitoring into vehicles after 1996 to address this risk.

AM-15: Mean/Median/Mode: The technician can calculate the average (mean) of several measurements to determine any variance from the manufacturer's specifications.

A new vehicle was purchased that was advertised to have a fuel economy rating of 24 mpg for city driving and 30 mpg for highway driving. The owner of the vehicle decided to calculate the average (mean) of several trips to see if the advertised ratings were correct. The plan was to check both city and highway driving separately using several tests for each category.

The city mileage test consisted of three separate fill-ups, with miles recorded from the odometer. The first fill-up required 14.1 gallons of fuel for 330 miles of driving, equaling 23.4 mpg. The second fill-up required 13.6 gallons of fuel for 338 miles, equaling 24.9 mpg. The third fill-up required 12.9 gallons for 286 miles, equaling 22.2 mpg. To calculate the average (mean), we will add 23.4 mpg + 24.8 mpg + 22.2 mpg and divide by 3. The result is 23.5 mpg for city driving, which is very close to the advertised 24 mpg.

The highway driving test consisted of two fill-ups on a road trip. The first fill-up required 9.5 gallons for 260 miles, equaling 27.4 mpg. The second fill-up required 10.1 gallons for 305 miles, equaling 30.2 mpg. To determine the mean, we add 27.4 mpg + 30.2 mpg and divide by 2. The result is 28.8 mpg, which is slightly less than the advertised 30 mpg for highway driving.

AM-18: Standard/Metric: The technician can measure/ test with tools designed for standard or metric measurements, and then convert the measurement to the system used by the manufacturer for specifications and tolerances.

A vehicle is in the shop for engine performance concerns. The vehicle has been running badly for about 2 weeks according to the repair order information. The symptoms are lack of power and engine stalling at times. Performing an underhood visual inspection, the technician does not find anything unusual. A scan tool check indicates there are trouble codes available.

The technician decides to check the fuel pressure, which is a quick and easy test. As he looks in his toolbox for the gauge, he remembers that he loaned his pressure gauge to someone and it has not been returned. The technician has one other fuel pressure gauge that is calibrated only in the metric unit bar. He connects this pressure gauge to the Schrader valve and starts the engine. With the engine running at idle, the gauge shows a reading of 3 bars. The technician uses the conversion

factor of 1 bar = 14.503 psi multiplied by 3 to obtain the result of 43.5 psi. The manufacturer's service information states that the vehicle should have 44 psi plus or minus 3 psi. This information confirms that the fuel pressure is acceptable, and the technician will now conduct a fuel volume test.

As an engine rotates through the four-stroke cycle, the speed of the crankshaft varies. This is due to the change in forces placed on the piston and crankshaft primarily during the compression and power strokes. These changes are predictable when the engine is operating. By using a high-definition (many teeth) CKP sensor/reluctor, the PCM can be programmed to monitor the speed of the crankshaft and look for the slowing down and speeding up for each power pulse. Misfire monitoring software identifies unacceptable changes in crankshaft speed indicating that a power pulse did not occur due to a misfire. The PCM can tell if just one cylinder is misfiring or if it is a random misfire. This information allows the PCM to store a cylinder-specific misfire code or a random misfire code. If the misfire is random and above a certain threshold, the PCM will likely illuminate a steady MIL. If one or more cylinders misfire above the point where the catalyst would be damaged, the MIL will be commanded to flash.

Output Signals

Output signals are what the computer sends to motors and actuators to do work. Remember, sensors send information; actuators, motors, and solenoids do the work. When a specific criterion is met or the driver gives a certain command, an output signal is sent to the corresponding "worker" (solenoid/actuator/motor). For example, suppose the driver presses the brake pedal and puts the vehicle in drive, then releases the brake to begin forward motion. At the appropriate point, the VSS indicates a predetermined speed criterion, which in turn signals the computer to send an output signal to activate the power locks on the doors.

Relays

A relay is often used as an actuator when the computer controls a high-current load. The computer controls the relay ground circuit. When a high-current job is requested or commanded, the computer simply completes the ground circuit and the relay coil field pulls the mechanical contacts closed, allowing the high current levels to flow to the appropriate load.

Ignition Control

To get the most effective and efficient use out of a gasoline engine, the ignition of the air–fuel mixture must be precise and powerful. As its name implies, the sole responsibility of the **ignition control module (ICM)** is to control the ignition, without flaw, hopefully for the life of the vehicle. The ICM receives signals, or inputs, from the CMP sensor, the CKP sensor, and the PCM. These inputs are then correlated to an exact firing moment for each spark plug at each cylinder at extremely high voltages. In addition, the timing of this high-voltage spark can be varied because of varying conditions or engine load. Locations of the ICM depend on the manufacturer's design choice and space; however, the ICM will usually be mounted on or around the ignition coils on a direct injection system, or on/in the distributor (if equipped).

Idle Speed Control Devices

The solenoid-type air control valve acts on signals from the control unit to bypass a measured airflow around the throttle plate **FIGURE 48-54**. The position of the valve depends on how much current the control unit applies to the solenoid. Maximum current flow opens the valve fully to give maximum airflow. This is generally the assumed position for starting; thereafter, the taper valve is positioned by pulsing the solenoid winding circuit at a predetermined frequency.

The amount of valve opening, and therefore the amount of airflow, depends on the *on* time of the pulse. A long *on* pulse with a short *off* pulse will produce a high average voltage, and therefore a large opening of the valve. A short *on* pulse with a long *off* pulse will produce a low average voltage, and therefore a small valve opening and an increase in airflow. This *on* and *off* time is called the duty cycle, and it is generally expressed as a percentage. A variation in pulse width, at the set frequency, is called pulse-width modulation.

In the stepper motor type of idle control, the tapered pintle is positioned using a screw and nut assembly **FIGURE 48-55**. The nut is part of a centrally located, permanent magnet armature. It engages with the screw on the pintle. Rotating the armature extends or retracts the pintle, which closes or opens the air passage. Rotation occurs by switching current flow in two coils. The pintle turns in forward or reverse steps, numbered from zero, with the bypass air passage fully closed, up to 255 for maximum airflow. This large number of steps allows the pintle position to be finely controlled.

When the idle speed is controlled by the position of the throttle plate, a direct current motor may be used

FIGURE 48-54 The solenoid-type air control valve acts on signals from the control unit to bypass a measured airflow around the throttle plate.

FIGURE 48-55 In the stepper motor type of idle control, the tapered pintle is positioned using a screw and nut assembly.

as a variable throttle stop. The controlling circuit can let current flow through the motor in either direction, to extend or retract the linear actuator.

Solenoid valves can also be used to bypass a predetermined amount of air around the throttle plate. These may come into operation for specific load compensation—for example, when the air-conditioning compressor is engaged. They open a passageway of fixed dimension and do not vary the opening.

Electronically Controlled Throttle

Commonly referred to as drive-by-wire or throttle-by-wire, an **electronically controlled throttle** is the replacement device for the long-standing standard of a throttle cable **FIGURE 48-56**. This system uses a pedal position sensor to calculate desired throttle position

FIGURE 48-56 An electronically controlled throttle is the replacement device for the long-standing standard of a throttle cable.

of the driver and the command is sent to the PCM. If the conditions are right, the PCM in turn sends a command to a throttle servomotor to open or close the throttle butterflies. The computer can regulate cruise consistency, acceleration, and deceleration to improve fuel economy, reduce emissions, and prevent sudden changes in speed that could affect the life of the drive train components.

Some late-model high-end vehicles may have a throttle response choice between "touring" and "sport." Touring has a small and conservative throttle response, thus increasing fuel economy, whereas in a sport setting, fuel economy takes a backseat to performance.

▶ Maintenance and Repair

Replacing a Fuel Filter

Fuel filters are a maintenance item and need to be replaced according to the manufacturer's specified replacement schedule, or anytime restricted flow is encountered. Fuel filters can be located in a variety of places depending on the vehicle. Common locations are under the vehicle in the fuel line, under the hood in the engine compartment, and inside the fuel tank as part of the fuel pump assembly. Since fuel pressure is maintained in all electric fuel pump systems, even when the engine is not running, it is important to bleed the pressure off before opening the system so that fuel does not spray everywhere. There are several ways to relieve the static pressure in the fuel system before removing the fuel lines. One way is to remove the fuel pump relay or the fuel pump fuse and run the engine until it dies. Another method is to connect a fuel pump gauge that has a bleed valve to the fuel rail test point, and bleed the excess pressure from the system into a gas can.

No matter how you bleed the static pressure in the fuel system, vent the pressure in the gas tank by removing the gas cap. Doing so will reduce the amount of gas that dribbles out of the lines when removing the filter. Always refer to the service information for the specific procedure for removing and replacing the fuel filter for the vehicle you are working on.

Some vehicles use metal or plastic lines that bolt onto the filter, using either a flared fitting or a banjo bolt. For either type, you will need to use the double wrench method to unbolt the line; otherwise you may twist or kink the metal or plastic line. The double wrench method uses two wrenches, one on the filter nut and the other on the flare nut or banjo bolt. Use the wrench on the filter nut to prevent the filter from twisting while applying force to the other wrench. Often you can place the wrench handles so they are at a slight angle to each other and squeeze them together to break the fittings loose.

Many newer vehicles use quick couplers to retain the fuel lines on the fuel filter. These couplers make it very quick and easy for the factory to install the filter since the fuel filter lines only have to be pushed into or onto the filter inlet and outlet. The quick coupler may use a plastic clip or a coiled spring to retain the line on the filter. Only use the proper release tool when removing the line; otherwise you can damage the fitting or line. Also, most quick coupler systems use O-rings to seal the fuel line to the filter. Make sure the O-rings are in good shape or replace them with new ones.

If the fuel lines connecting the fuel tank to the filter are flexible hoses rather than metal lines, check their condition to determine whether it is necessary to replace the hoses and clamps when you replace the filter. Some replacement filters come with these items; when they are supplied, you should always use them. If they are not supplied, but you need to replace them anyway, obtain a sufficient length of the proper type of new fuel line and suitable clamps. There are different types of clamps for flexible fuel lines, including spring type, worm type, or rolled edge. You will need to use the appropriate tool when installing new clamps on the hoses.

Some manufacturers have been installing the fuel filter in the fuel tank along with the fuel pump assembly. The only way to get to the pump and filter is through the top of the fuel tank. Sometimes manufacturers provide a removable access cover under the backseat that will allow you to get to the top of the tank. Other times the tank will need to be removed to gain access. Once the covers are removed, the fuel pump assembly can be carefully removed and the filter replaced.

Gasoline fuel vapor is explosive and highly flammable. Be careful not to spill any fuel onto a hot engine component where it could evaporate, ignite, and start a fire. Also take care not to cause any sparks while you are changing a fuel filter. Collect the gasoline waste in a metal container and dispose of it in an environmentally prescribed way. Always wear the appropriate personal protection equipment before starting the job.

To replace a fuel filter, follow the steps in **SKILL DRILL 48-1**:

1. Refer to the service information to identify the location and type of fuel filter and the correct procedure for removing and replacing it. If the engine is equipped with an electric fuel pump, release the pressure according to the service information. **(Photo 1)**

2. Obtain the correct replacement filter and components. Loosen the bracket holding the filter in

SKILL DRILL 48-1   Replacing a Fuel Filter

1. Refer to the service information to identify the location and type of fuel filter and the correct procedure for removing and replacing it. If the engine is equipped with an electric fuel pump, release the pressure according to the service information.

2. Obtain the correct replacement filter and components. Loosen the bracket holding the filter in place, if equipped. Follow the steps below according to the type of filter you are replacing.

For a flared fitting type of filter:
3. Disconnect the fuel line on the engine side of the filter using the double wrench method. If necessary, drain any excess fuel into a fuel-proof container.

4. Disconnect the fuel line on the inlet end of the fuel filter and remove it from the lines.

5. Reinstall the filter, making sure you have the filter facing in the right direction, with the flow indicator arrow pointing toward the engine. Tighten the fittings on both ends using the double wrench method.

For a quick disconnect filter:
6. Using the correct tool, release the quick disconnect connectors from the outlet end of the filter, catching any leaking fuel in a fuel-proof container.

SKILL DRILL | 48-1 | Replacing a Fuel Filter, continued

7 Release the quick disconnect connectors from the inlet end of the filter, and remove the filter from the lines.

8 Reinstall the filter, with the flow indicator arrow pointing toward the engine, and fully engage the lines, making sure they are secure.

9 Wipe any residual fuel off with a clean shop rag, and write the date and mileage on the filter. Remember to replace the fuel pump fuse, if removed.

10 Turn the key to the on position for 5 seconds, but *do not start the engine*, and then turn it back to off. Repeat the process two more times, checking the filter connections for leaks. If no leaks are found, start the vehicle, letting it run for 2 to 3 minutes before shutting it off. Recheck the filter connections for leaks.

place, if equipped. Follow the steps according to the type of filter you are replacing. **(Photo 2)**

For a flared fitting type of filter:

3 Disconnect the fuel line on the engine side of the filter using the double wrench method. If necessary, drain any excess fuel into a fuel-proof container. **(Photo 3)**

4 Disconnect the fuel line on the inlet end of the fuel filter and remove it from the lines. **(Photo 4)**

5 Reinstall the filter, making sure you have the filter facing in the right direction, with the flow indicator arrow pointing toward the engine. Tighten the fittings on both ends using the double wrench method. **(Photo 5)**

For a quick disconnect filter:

6 Using the correct tool, release the quick disconnect connectors from the outlet end of the filter, catching any leaking fuel in a fuel-proof container. **(Photo 6)**

7 Release the quick disconnect connectors from the inlet end of the filter, and remove the filter from the lines. **(Photo 7)**

8 Reinstall the filter, with the flow indicator arrow pointing toward the engine, and fully engage the lines, making sure they are secure. **(Photo 8)**

9 Wipe any residual fuel off with a clean shop rag.

10 Using a permanent marker, write the date and mileage clearly on the filter to indicate when the filter was last serviced. This is a good practice to help ensure the proper maintenance/service intervals. Remember to replace the fuel pump fuse, if removed. **(Photo 9)**

11 Turn the key to the on position for 5 seconds, but *do not start the engine*, and then turn it back to the off position. Repeat the process two more times, checking the filter connections for leaks. This process primes the filter that was void of fuel when you installed it.

12 If no leaks are found, start the vehicle. The engine may falter at first but will quickly recover. This is normal until the proper fuel pressure is achieved and the remaining air is bled out after a minute or so. Let the vehicle run for 2 to 3 minutes before shutting it off.

13 Recheck the filter connections for leaks. **(Photo 10)**

Inspecting and Testing Fuel Pumps

Fuel pumps need to be tested if a vehicle experiences low engine power or if the vehicle will not start due to a fuel-related issue. Some shops will test a fuel pump's performance, looking to see if it is nearing a failure. There are several ways to test a fuel pump: pressure/volume test, lab scope inductive current flow test, and scan tool data stream test. Each will be described in this section.

The pressure/volume test measures the fuel pressure being delivered to the fuel rail along with the volume of the fuel pump. Many, but not all, fuel-injected engines provide a test port that a fuel pressure tester can connect to. Once connected, the pressure can be measured with either just the key on or with the engine running. Manufacturers will give pressure specifications to compare the pressure readings with. If the pressure is low, and the system uses a return line from the pressure regulator on the fuel rail, you may need to pinch off the return line to see if the pressure goes up due to a faulty pressure regulator. If the pressure is within specifications, turn the engine off, but watch the pressure gauge. It should stay steady. If it drops, there is a leak in the system, either at the pressure regulator or at the check valve in the fuel pump.

The pressure may be within specifications and hold pressure when the engine is off, but the fuel pump volume may be low. Specifications are given in volume per amount of time, such as 1 pint in 30 seconds or 28 lb per hour, which will usually need to be converted to volume per amount of time. The volume is measured with the engine idling. Most EFI fuel pressure gauges have a valve that will allow fuel to be taken from the rail without killing the engine and then caught in a calibrated container. If the fuel flow is low, check to see if the fuel filter is plugged and restricting the flow. If the filter is OK, you may need to remove the fuel pump from the fuel tank and inspect the fuel sock at the bottom of the fuel pump to see if it is plugged. If all of the filters are not restricted but the pump volume is low, the pump will need to be replaced.

Some technicians like to use their lab scope to display the trace for the fuel pump's current flow. As each pair of segments of the fuel pump's commutator aligns with the brushes, current flows through the connected windings in the armature. If there is high resistance or a bad connection in one of the commutator segments or armature windings, the current flow will decrease. Since each pair of segments is connected to a different set of windings, the current flow can change for each set, if the resistance is different from each other. This will be evident on the lab scope by current pulses of different height in a repeating pattern.

Another technique to identify a fuel delivery fault is to use a scan tool and a test-drive. If possible, set the scan tool to record rpm, VSS, front oxygen sensors, short-term fuel trim, and long-term fuel trim, and then go on a test-drive. In a safe place and manner, briefly drive the vehicle under heavy load and at higher rpm. After returning to the shop, look at the recording; if you see a lean oxygen signal with a large increase in fuel trim, a fuel delivery problem is indicated. This problem could be as simple as a restricted fuel filter or something more severe such as a faulty pump or plugged fuel injectors.

To inspect and test fuel pumps, follow the steps in **SKILL DRILL 48-2** :

1 First research the specifications/procedures for testing the fuel pump in the appropriate service information. Install a fuel pump gauge on the fuel rail test port. **(Photo 1)**

2 Turn the key to the run position and measure the pressure. If none, test the fuel pump's electrical circuit. **(Photo 2)**

3 Start the engine, measure the pressure, and compare to specifications. If fuel pressure is low, you may want to momentarily pinch off the return line, if equipped, which deadheads the pump. If the pressure was low before pinching off the return line

SKILL DRILL | 48-2 | Inspecting and Testing Fuel Pumps

1 After researching the procedure for testing the fuel pump in the service information, install a fuel pump gauge on the fuel rail test port.

2 Turn the key to the run position and measure the pressure. If none, test the fuel pump's electrical circuit.

3 Start the engine, measure the pressure, and compare to specifications. With the engine running and the end of the fuel line from the fuel pressure gauge in a 1-quart plastic bottle, open the valve on the gauge and stop the fuel flow after 15 seconds.

4 Measure the amount of fuel delivered in that time, and compare to specifications.

5 If the pressure test or volume test was less than specified, you can use a lab scope and low-amps clamp to graph the current flow going to the fuel pump. Remove the fuel pump fuse and connect a jumper lead between the terminals in the fuse box. Place the amps clamp around the jumper lead.

6 Start the engine, look at the lab scope pattern, and compare the pattern to the service information.

and rises after pinching it off, the pressure regulator is faulty. If the pressure does not rise, either the fuel filter is restricted or the pump is likely to be faulty.

4 With the engine running and the end of the fuel line from the fuel pressure gauge in a 1-quart plastic bottle, open the valve on the gauge and stop the fuel flow after 15 seconds. **(Photo 3)**

5 Measure the amount of fuel delivered in that time, and compare to specifications. **(Photo 4)**

6 If the pressure test or volume test was less than specified, you may want to use a lab scope and low-amps clamp to graph the current flow going to the fuel pump. Remove the fuel pump fuse and connect a jumper lead between the terminals in the

SKILL DRILL | 48-2 | Inspecting and Testing Fuel Pumps, continued

Fuel Trim Data

Long Term FT Bank 2	1 %
Fuel Trim Cell	17
Short Term FT Avg. Bn1	30 %
Short Term FT Avg. Bn2	30 %
Long Term FT Avg. Bn1	0 %
Long Term FT Avg. Bn2	1 %
Loop Status	Closed Loop
HO2S Bank 1 Sensor 1	25 mV
HO2S Bank 1 Sensor 2	20 mV
	12 / 38

HO2S Bank 1 Sensor 2

Select Item | DTC | Quick Snapshot | More

7 Record rpm, VSS, front oxygen sensors, short-term fuel trim, and long-term fuel trim under heavy load and at higher rpm. After returning to the shop, look at your recording; if you see a lean oxygen signal with a large increase in fuel trim, the vehicle has a fuel delivery problem.

fuse box. Place the amps clamp around the jumper lead. **(Photo 5)**

7 Start the engine and look at the lab scope pattern. If it is a return-type fuel system, the current flow should rise and fall equally for each segment of the fuel pump commutator. Any low-current segments indicate a damaged commutator or armature. If it is a returnless system, check the service information to compare the pattern. **(Photo 6)**

8 On some vehicles, you can verify a fuel delivery problem by using a scan tool and recording data on a test-drive. Record rpm, VSS, front oxygen sensors, short-term fuel trim, and long-term fuel trim under heavy load and at higher rpm. After returning to the shop, look at your recording; if you see a lean oxygen signal with a large increase in fuel trim, the vehicle has a fuel delivery problem. **(Photo 7)**

Checking Fuel for Contaminants and Quality

It is easy to forget that fuel by itself can cause drivability issues if it becomes contaminated or old, or even if it is the wrong fuel for the vehicle. In fact, with more people owning diesel passenger vehicles and light trucks, you may encounter vehicles filled with the wrong fuel, such as a diesel car filled with gasoline, or vice versa. Also, higher blends of gasoline and alcohol make it easy to fill up a standard gasoline vehicle with E-85, which is 85% alcohol and 15% gasoline. A flex fuel vehicle will operate correctly on that blend, but a non–flex fuel vehicle will not. Anytime a vehicle is not running properly and other common causes have not identified the issue, you will want to check the fuel for contaminants and quality.

Short of sending fuel out to be tested by a lab, there are some simpler tests that can be done. All require getting a sample from the fuel supply, which is best taken from the fuel rail or where the gas enters the carburetor. That way you will be testing the fuel that the engine is running on. You will want to collect a cup or two of fuel in a clear container, preferably not glass, which can break easily. Allow the fuel to settle and look at it. Is it the right color? Is it cloudy? Does it have a separation line due to being contaminated with water? Does it smell right? If any of those conditions are not correct, you will need to drain the fuel system, flush it out, and replace the fuel filters. If the fuel passes the visual inspection, it is time to perform an alcohol content test. For this test, you will use a tall 100-mL graduated cylinder. A mixture of 10 mL of clean water and 90 mL of gasoline are carefully agitated for 30 seconds. The mixture is allowed to settle for a minute or two. Any alcohol in the fuel will absorb the water, raising the level above the original 10 mL. Each mL above 10 equals the percentage of alcohol in the gasoline. Most vehicles can tolerate 10% alcohol without causing any drivability issues. And flex fuel vehicles can typically operate on 85% alcohol.

To check fuel for contaminants and quality, follow the steps in **SKILL DRILL 48-3**:

1. Collect a quantity of fuel from the vehicle's fuel rail in a clear plastic container.

2. Allow the mixture to settle and check for contaminants, cloudiness, or improper odor. **(Photo 1)**

SKILL DRILL | **48-3** | **Checking Fuel for Contaminants and Quality**

1. Collect a quantity of fuel from the vehicle's fuel rail in a clear plastic fuel container. Let it settle and check for contaminants, cloudiness, or improper odor.

2. Pour 10 mL of water into the 100 mL graduated test tube.

3. Add 90 mL of gasoline, bringing the total volume to 100 mL.

4. Cap the test tube tightly. Slowly agitate the fuel–water mixture for 30 seconds. If there is any alcohol in the fuel, this motion will allow the water to be absorbed by the alcohol.

5. Allow the mixture to settle. Observe the level of the water in the bottom of the test tube. Anything higher than the initial 10 mL is the amount of alcohol in the fuel. List your observations and determine any necessary actions.

6. Carefully pour off the fuel in the test tube back into the fuel container. Make sure no water leaves the test tube. Properly dispose of the remaining water–fuel mixture.

3 Pour 10 mL of water into the 100-mL graduated test tube. (**Photo 2**)

4 Add 90 mL of gasoline, bringing the total volume to 100 mL. The water will settle to the bottom of the tube. (**Photo 3**)

5 Cap the test tube tightly with a rubber cork or other appropriate device.

6 Slowly and carefully agitate the fuel–water mixture for 30 seconds to bring the water into contact with the fuel. If there is any alcohol in the fuel, this motion will allow the water to be absorbed by the alcohol. (**Photo 4**)

7 Allow the mixture to settle for a minute or two. Observe the level of the water in the bottom of the test tube. Anything higher than the initial 10 mL is the amount of alcohol in the fuel. List your observations and determine any necessary actions. Note that most fuel sold in the United States has a 10% mixture of alcohol in it. (**Photo 5**)

8 Carefully pour off the fuel in the test tube back into the fuel container. Make sure no water leaves the test tube. Properly dispose of the remaining water–fuel mixture. (**Photo 6**)

Inspecting and Testing Fuel Injectors

Fuel injectors can fail electrically or mechanically. They can also become plugged or deposits can build up on the nozzle, affecting the spray pattern of the injector. If the injector fails completely, it will cause the cylinder to misfire. If the injectors have a poor spray pattern due to deposits, the engine may experience general roughness or random misfires that are not isolated to one or two cylinders. Before specifically testing an injector, it should be identified as causing a drivability issue. In other words, the ignition system, compression, vacuum leaks, and other engine mechanical faults can cause one or more cylinders to not work correctly, just like a fuel injector problem. Use all of your diagnostic skills and tools to narrow the fault down to the injectors. For example, you may need to retrieve the codes, read the data stream, or access mode 6 data to help you narrow down the area of the fault. If you suspect a fuel injector is causing the fault, you can quickly measure the resistance of the injector winding and compare it to specifications. Any improper resistance will require replacement of the injector.

If the injector resistance and on/off signal are good, you can perform an injector pressure drop test to see if the injector is restricted with deposits. This test uses a fuel pressure gauge and injector pulsing tool. The fuel pressure gauge is connected to the test port in the fuel rail, and the pulsing tool is connected to the battery and the suspect injector. The pulse tool pulses the injector a certain number of times, for a certain amount of time. The idea is that you will pressurize the fuel rail by turning the key to the on position and charging the fuel rail. Then start the pulse tool, which will pulse the injector the set amount of times. Read the pressure on the fuel pressure gauge, and compare this reading to the pressure reading after doing the same test on another injector. If the flow is the same between the two injectors, the pressure at the end of each test should be within a few psi of each other. If not, the one with the higher pressure at the end of the test is not allowing as much fuel to flow as the other, which could indicate deposit buildup on the nozzle or a restricted filter screen on the injector.

To inspect and test fuel injectors, first research the fuel injector testing procedure and specifications for the vehicle in the appropriate service information. Inspect the fuel injectors for leaks and damage, then follow the service information to test the fuel injectors. If the information does not provide a method for testing the injectors, follow the steps in **SKILL DRILL 48-4**:

1 Measure the resistance of each suspect fuel injector, and compare to specifications. If the resistance is not in specifications, replace the injector. (**Photo 1**)

2 Install the fuel pressure gauge on the fuel rail.

3 Connect the injector pulsing tool to one fuel injector, according to the tool maker's instructions, and set it for the appropriate number and time of pulses. (**Photo 2**)

4 Pressurize the fuel rail by turning on the ignition switch for a few seconds. Then turn the ignition switch off. Record the fuel pressure. (**Photo 3**)

5 Activate the injector pulsing tool for the appropriate amount of time. Watch the pressure gauge and record the pressure after the injector has been pulsed. (**Photo 4**)

6 Repeat this test on each fuel injector, remembering to pressurize the fuel rail each time before activating the injector pulsing tool. Record the pressure readings before and after each test.

7 Compare all readings to specifications and to each other. Determine any necessary actions. (**Photo 5**)

SKILL DRILL | 48-4 | Inspecting and Testing Fuel Injectors

1 Measure the resistance of the suspect fuel injector, and compare to specifications. If the resistance is not in specifications, replace the injector.

2 Install the fuel pressure gauge on the fuel rail. Connect the injector pulsing tool to one fuel injector, according to the tool maker's instructions, and set it for the appropriate number and time of pulses.

3 Pressurize the fuel rail by turning on the ignition switch for a few seconds. Then turn the ignition switch off. Record the fuel pressure.

4 Activate the injector pulsing tool for the appropriate amount of time. Watch the pressure gauge and record the pressure after the injector has been pulsed.

5 Repeat this test on each fuel injector, pressurizing the fuel rail each time before activating the injector pulsing tool. Record the pressure readings before and after each test. Compare all readings to specifications and to each other. Determine any necessary actions.

Wrap-up

Ready for Review

▸ The most important job of the fuel system is optimizing engine performance while keeping fuel consumption and emissions to a minimum.

▸ As a technician you must be able to properly inspect, diagnose, and repair fuel system components for your customers, thus keeping their vehicles running at optimum efficiency and performance.

▸ Modern fuel injection has three subsystems: fuel supply, air supply, and fuel metering.

▸ Vapor lock occurs when vapor forms in the fuel line; the bubbles of vapor block the flow of fuel at the pump and stop the engine.

▸ Engines perform best when used with the fuel that has the engine manufacturer's recommended octane rating.

▸ Combustion is the burning of the air–fuel mixture.

▸ Detonation is when the entire mixture explodes instead of burning smoothly across the combustion chamber.

▸ Gasoline must be burnt in a controlled manner or it will burn either too fast or too slow.

▸ The term stoichiometric ratio describes the chemically correct air–fuel ratio necessary to achieve complete combustion of the fuel and oxygen in the air.

▸ Air is one of the essential components of the internal combustion engine.

▸ Fuel pumps can be electrical or mechanical. The most common today are electrical and are installed in the fuel tanks.

▸ Most of today's vehicles use electronic fuel injection (EFI), which is better for fuel economy and emission controls.

▸ The typical fuel tank (or gas tank, as it is sometimes called) of modern vehicles consists of a gas cap, filler neck, fuel, fuel pump, and gauge sending unit. The tank's primary function is to hold an adequate supply of fuel.

▸ Modern vehicles are required by the Environmental Protection Agency (EPA) to have a nonvented gas cap. This nonvented cap prevents the dangerous fuel vapors from being directly vented to the atmosphere.

▸ There are three types of electronic fuel injection—throttle body injection (TBI), port fuel injection (PFI), and gas direct injection (GDI).

▸ Airflow and volume are critical in ensuring the engine has the correct ratio of air to fuel.

▸ All electronic fuel systems use sensors and other devices to tell the PCM how much fuel is needed for a given engine operating condition.

▸ The crankshaft position (CKP) sensor uses information on the speed and position of the crankshaft to control ignition timing and injection sequencing.

▸ The camshaft position (CMP) sensor sends constant data to the computer to let it know which cylinder is on its power stroke as well as the position of the camshaft and valve.

▸ The throttle position sensor (TPS) gathers information on throttle positions to allow the control unit to make adjustments according to operating conditions.

▸ Engine coolant temperature maintains the air–fuel ratio within an optimum range. The control unit must take account of coolant temperature and air temperature.

▸ Manifold absolute pressure (MAP) measures changes in engine speed and load and converts the findings into an electrical signal to control engine operations.

▸ The vehicle speed sensor (VSS) is a detection device that sends the vehicle speed information (i.e., how fast the vehicle is traveling) to the electronic control module.

▸ If the fuel system is maintained, it will give many years of dependable service to the vehicle's owner.

▸ Always refer to the manufacturer's technical data for the latest service information on the specific vehicle that is being serviced or repaired.

Key Terms

accelerator pump A small pump usually located inside the carburetor that sprays an extra amount of fuel into the carburetor air horn during acceleration.

accelerator pump circuit The carburetor circuit involved with heavy acceleration, directly connected to the accelerator pump. Also used to prime the engine during cold starting.

accelerometer An electronic instrument that measures the amount of acceleration in a specific direction.

air supply system Equipment in a motor vehicle that delivers air to the engine.

barometric pressure (BARO) sensor A sensor that measures atmospheric pressure.

camshaft position (CMP) sensor A detection device that signals to the PCM the rotational position of the camshaft.

charcoal canister A device used to trap the fuel vapors. The fuel vapors adhere to the charcoal, until the engine is started, and engine vacuum can be used to draw (purge) the vapors into the engine so that they can be burned along with the air–fuel mixture.

choke A device that provides a rich air–fuel mixture until the engine warms up by restricting the flow of air at the entrance to the carburetor, before the venturi.

computer-controlled carburetor A carburetor that changes and sets air–fuel ratio based on commands from a PCM that uses memory and input from sensors.

coolant temperature sensor (CTS) A thermistor usually screwed into a cylinder head water jacket. Usually the CTS is a negative temperature coefficient thermistor, or a resistor whose resistance varies, with temperature varying a voltage signal to the PCM.

crankshaft position (CKP) sensor A sensor similar to a Hall-effect switch that is used to monitor crankshaft position and speed.

detonation The condition in which the remaining fuel charge fires or burns too rapidly after the initial combustion of the air–fuel mixture. It is audible through the combustion chamber walls as a knocking noise.

dieseling A condition in which the engine continues to run after the ignition key is turned off. Also referred to as run-on.

electronically controlled throttle A system that uses electronic, instead of mechanical, signals to control the throttle. Sometimes called drive-by-wire.

electronic fuel injection (EFI) An injection system in which fuel delivery is controlled electronically, allowing continuous adjustments to the air–fuel ratio.

element The replaceable portion of a filter, such as an air filter element or oil filter element.

exhaust gas recirculation (EGR) valve A valve that allows a controlled amount of exhaust gas into the intake manifold during a certain period of engine operation. Used to lower nitrogen oxide exhaust emissions.

filter sock The first line of defense in the fuel supply system. The sock typically consists of a fine mesh, which prevents most small particles from being drawn into the fuel pump and sent through the rest of the fuel system.

float chamber A chamber that holds a quantity of fuel at atmospheric pressure ready for use.

frequency The rate of change in direction, oscillation, or cycles in a given time.

fuel filler neck The upper end of the fuel filler tube leading down to the fuel tank, which accepts the fuel hose nozzle at the gas station pump.

fuel filter A device that removes impurities (dirt and water) from the fuel before they reach the carburetor or injection system. Filters may be made of metal or plastic screen, paper, or gauze.

fuel metering system Equipment in a motor vehicle that delivers the proper amount of fuel to each cylinder.

fuel pressure regulator A system that controls the pressure of fuel entering the injectors.

fuel pump A mechanically or electrically driven vacuum device used to draw fuel from the tank and force it into the fuel system.

fuel pump relay A relay to turn on or off the high-amperage circuit of the fuel pump.

fuel rail Tubing that connects several injectors to the main fuel line.

fuel shutoff mode A safety precaution by which fuel is shut off when certain conditions are met during a vehicle crash.

fuel supply system Equipment in a motor vehicle that delivers fuel to the engine.

fuel system Equipment in a motor vehicle that delivers fuel to the engine.

gasoline A volatile, flammable liquid mixture of hydrocarbons, obtained from crude oil and used as fuel for internal combustion engines.

gasoline direct injection (GDI) A fuel injection system in which fuel is sprayed directly into the combustion chamber.

gauge sending unit A device used for transmitting a signal to control a fuel gauge.

idle The speed at which an engine runs without any throttle applied.

ignition control module (ICM) A general control unit of some electronic ignition systems, usually with current and dwell angle control, driver and output stage, and in some cases, electronic spark timing functions.

indirect fuel injection Any fuel injection that is not sprayed directly into the combustion chamber.

inductive-type sensor A sensor mounted on the crankcase housing that is used to sense the movement of the ring gear teeth on the flywheel, or a toothed disc on the crank pulley.

injector A valve that is controlled by a solenoid or spring pressure to inject fuel into the engine.

intake air temperature (IAT) sensor A sensor that measures the temperature of the incoming air through the air filtration system.

knocking A noise heard when the air–fuel mixture spontaneously ignites before the spark plug is fired at the optimum ignition moment.

knock sensor An engine sensor that detects pre-ignition, detonation, and knocking.

manifold absolute pressure (MAP) sensor A detection device that measures absolute air pressure in the intake manifold.

metering jet A calibrated orifice in a carburetor for fuel to flow through. Often it is replaceable for performance or economy desires.

misfire Failure of one or more cylinders to fire or complete combustion.

multipoint fuel injection (MPFI) An injection system in which fuel is injected into the intake ports just upstream of each cylinder's intake valve, rather than at a central point within an intake manifold. Also called multiport injection.

<u>octane rating</u> A standard measure of the performance of a motor or aviation fuel. The higher the octane number, the more heat the fuel can withstand before self-igniting.

<u>output signal</u> The voltage sent to solenoids and motors by the PCM to do work.

<u>oxygen sensor (before and after catalytic convertor)</u> An exhaust sensor used to measure the amount of oxygen in the exhaust gases produced by the engine PCM, used to determine fuel mixture and spark timing.

<u>pollutant</u> A potential threat to human health or the environment resulting from excessive amounts of chemicals and waste.

<u>potentiometer</u> A variable resistor that can be used to adjust voltage in a circuit.

<u>pressure</u> The force per unit area applied to the surface of an object.

<u>relay</u> A magnetically operated switch used to make or break current flow in a circuit.

<u>returnless fuel injection system</u> A type of injection system in which no hot fuel is returned to the tank, thus keeping the fuel in the tank relatively cool and minimizing vaporization.

<u>sending unit</u> The component in the fuel supply system responsible for sending constant electrical signals to the gas gauge located in the driver information center.

<u>stoichiometric ratio</u> The optimum ratio of air to fuel for combustion—14.7 parts air to 1 part fuel by weight.

<u>thermistor</u> A device that changes its resistance in relation to heat.

<u>throttle</u> A device used to produce acceleration by controlling the air–fuel mixture.

<u>throttle body injection (TBI)</u> A fuel injection system that uses one or more fuel injectors mounted above or in the throttle body itself. Also called single-point injection.

<u>throttle position sensor (TPS)</u> A potentiometer that sends an analog signal to the electronic control unit that corresponds to the position of the throttle valve.

<u>vacuum</u> A pressure in an enclosed area that is lower than atmospheric pressure.

<u>vapor lock</u> A situation in which vapor forms in the fuel line, and the bubbles of vapor block the flow of fuel and stop the engine.

<u>venturi</u> A restriction (narrowed area) in the air horn.

ASE-Type Questions

1. Tech A says that most electric fuel pumps are now mounted inside of the fuel tank. Tech B says that fuel flows through the center of the electric pump and is used to cool the pump. Who is correct?
   a. Tech A
   b. Tech B
   c. Both A and B
   d. Neither A nor B

2. Tech A says that the stoichiometric ratio is 14.7 gallons of air to 1 gallon of fuel. Tech B says it is 14.7 lbs of air to 1 lb of fuel. Who is correct?
   a. Tech A
   b. Tech B
   c. Both A and B
   d. Neither A nor B

3. Tech A says that some throttle plates are not mechanically connected to the gas pedal, but are operated by an electric motor. Tech B says that too much alcohol in gasoline can cause the engine to not run properly. Who is correct?
   a. Tech A
   b. Tech B
   c. Both A and B
   d. Neither A nor B

4. Tech A says that high octane fuel is harder to ignite than lower octane. Tech B says that using high octane fuel in an engine designed for lower octane will produce better fuel economy and power. Who is correct?
   a. Tech A
   b. Tech B
   c. Both A and B
   d. Neither A nor B

5. Tech A says that dieseling in a car today indicates a possible leaking injector. Tech B says that a tripped inertia switch means that there is a possible short in the fuel pump circuit. Who is correct?
   a. Tech A
   b. Tech B
   c. Both A and B
   d. Neither A nor B

6. Tech A says that a lambda greater than 1 means the engine is running rich. Tech B says that the amount of oxygen in the exhaust indicates how rich or lean the mixture is. Who is correct?
   a. Tech A
   b. Tech B
   c. Both A and B
   d. Neither A nor B

7. Tech A says that gauge pressure indicates pressure above atmospheric pressure. Tech B says that atmospheric pressure increases as elevation increases. Who is correct?
   a. Tech A
   b. Tech B
   c. Both A and B
   d. Neither A nor B

8. Tech A says that fuel pressure is regulated by a fuel pressure regulator on some vehicles. Tech B says that fuel pressure is regulated by controlling the speed of the fuel pump on some vehicles. Who is correct?
   a. Tech A
   b. Tech B
   c. Both A and B
   d. Neither A nor B

9. Tech A says that measuring the alcohol content in gasoline involves using water. Tech B says that as long as the fuel pressure is correct, you don't have to worry about fuel pump volume. Who is correct?
   a. Tech A
   b. Tech B
   c. Both A and B
   d. Neither A nor B

10. Tech A says that low battery voltage will require a longer injector pulse width time. Tech B says that engine temperature will affect the injector pulse width time. Who is correct?
    a. Tech A
    b. Tech B
    c. Both A and B
    d. Neither A nor B

CHAPTER 49

NATEF Tasks

Engine Performance
General Engine Diagnosis

		Page
■ Diagnose engine mechanical, electrical, electronic, fuel, and ignition concerns; determine necessary action.	**AST** **MAST**	1735

Computerized Engine Controls

		Page
■ Describe the importance of running all OBDII monitors for repair verification.	**MLR** **AST** **MAST**	1731–1735
■ Retrieve and record diagnostic trouble codes, OBD monitor status, and freeze-frame data; clear codes when applicable.	**MLR** **AST** **MAST**	1735–1736
■ Diagnose the cause of emissions or driveability concerns using stored or active diagnostic trouble codes; obtain, graph, and interpret scan tool data.	**MAST**	1736–1737, 1739
■ Diagnose emissions or drivability concerns without use of stored diagnostic trouble codes; determine necessary action.	**MAST**	1737
■ Inspect and test computerized engine control system sensors, powertrain/engine control module (PCM/ECM), actuators, and circuits using a graphing multimeter (GMM)/digital storage oscilloscope (DSO); determine necessary action.	**MAST**	1737–1738
■ Diagnose drivability and emission problems resulting from malfunctions of interrelated systems (cruise control, security alarms, suspension controls, traction controls, A/C, automatic transmissions, non-OEM–installed accessories, or similar systems); determine necessary action.	**MAST**	1738
■ Perform active tests of actuators using a scan tool; determine necessary action.	**AST** **MAST**	1739

On-Board Diagnostics

NATEF Tasks, continued

Emission Control Systems

- Interpret diagnostic trouble codes (DTCs) and scan tool data related to the emission control systems; determine necessary action. **AST** **MAST** 1739

Knowledge Objectives

After reading this chapter, you will be able to:
1. Explain what volatile organic compounds (VOCs) are and how they relate to vehicle emissions. (p 1730)
2. List some of the pollutants emitted by vehicles. (p 1730)
3. Explain the origins and purpose of OBDI and OBDII systems; explain the importance of monitoring on-board systems and reporting vehicle emission–related faults. (p 1731)
4. Describe the role of controller area networks (CANs). (p 1732)
5. Explain the purpose and function of DTCs. (pp 1732–1733)
6. Describe how scan tools work and what is involved in using them. (pp 1734–1735)
7. Explain the purpose and function of control modules such as the power train control module (PCM), the body control module (BCM), and the transmission control module (TCM). (pp 1733–1734, 1737–1738)

Skills Objectives

After reading this chapter, you will be able to:
1. Retrieve and record DTCs, OBD monitor status, and freeze-frame data; clear codes when applicable. (pp 1735–1736)
2. Diagnose the cause of drivability or emission concerns when there are stored or active DTCs present, and obtain, graph, and interpret scan tool data. (pp 1736–1737)
3. Inspect and test computerized engine control system sensors, the PCM, actuators, and circuits using a graphing multimeter or digital storage oscilloscope. (pp 1737–1738)
4. Diagnose drivability and emission problems resulting from malfunctions of interrelated systems. (p 1738)
5. Test actuators using a scan tool. (p 1739)
6. Interpret DTCs and scan tool data related to the emission control systems. (p 1739)

Introduction

The automobile we drive today has certainly evolved significantly—even over the last few years. Yet despite all the innovations, <u>emissions</u> from automobiles can still harm the environment, as well as our health, and therefore need to be monitored and kept in check.

In the United States, Congress has passed federal emission regulations, starting with the <u>Clean Air Act</u> in 1963. This basic research program was expanded in 1967 to help curb emissions from automobiles. Major amendments to the law, requiring regulatory controls for air pollution, were enacted in 1970, 1977, and 1990.

In some parts of the country (usually urban areas) where noncompliance with clean air laws exists, auto technicians know that vehicle emission testing and repair remedies are a big part of day-to-day business. Today, when a vehicle's <u>malfunction indicator lamp (MIL)</u>—formerly called a "check engine light"—is illuminated it means the vehicle is not complying with clean air regulations; in the interest of public health, keeping cars running clean is a mandate. Low tailpipe emissions also mean a vehicle is running efficiently, which helps to conserve energy.

 Pollutants

Vehicles emit evaporative emissions, known as <u>volatile organic compounds (VOCs)</u>, to the atmosphere. VOCs may be fuel or oil vapors emitted from the fuel tank, fuel lines, engine crankcase, or elsewhere. In earlier vehicles, engine draft tubes spewed VOCs from the crankcase onto the road, as evidenced by dark center-of-lane deposits on uphill stretches of our highways. Likewise, hot summer days once meant the smell of gasoline fumes around filling stations and parked cars—but not today!

Vehicles can also emit harmful emissions from the tailpipe. These pollutants include:

- <u>Carbon monoxide (CO)</u>
- <u>Hydrocarbons (HCs)</u>, or VOCs
- <u>Particulate matter (PM)</u>
- <u>Carbon dioxide (CO_2)</u>
- <u>Sulfur dioxide (SO_2)</u>
- <u>Oxides of nitrogen</u>—nitric oxide (NO) and nitrogen dioxide (NO_2)

Oxides of nitrogen and hydrocarbons react together to create ground-level ozone, which is considered a health hazard. Ground-level ozone especially affects children, the elderly, and those with respiratory problems. On "ozone alert days," such people are advised to stay indoors, and the operation of VOC-spewing lawn and garden equipment is discouraged. Some of the preceding gases also contribute to the greenhouse effect.

All of these pollutants to one degree or another are monitored and controlled by efficient on-board systems using state-of-the-art electronics. Computers run vehicle systems through self-tests at engine start-up and continue to do so once underway. If anything is out of the ordinary, the driver is alerted, a snapshot of operating conditions is saved for technicians to examine later, and, if needed, alternate operating strategies are initiated to protect the vehicle and the environment.

You are the Automotive Technician

Jim, a new customer, brings his vehicle into your shop for an illuminated malfunction indicator lamp (MIL). He says it has been on for about a week and wants to know if you have one of "those computers" that will tell you what is wrong with his vehicle. You tell him, as you chuckle, that you wish there was a tool you could buy that would do that, but you do have several scan tools and the training to know how to use them. With that and some good technical service information, you can diagnose what is causing the MIL to be on, so it can be fixed right the first time. Jim says that makes sense, as one of his co-workers had a similar problem and the shop he went to told him that the vehicle needed a particular part, but that part didn't fix the problem. The co-worker ended up buying several parts over a couple of visits and the MIL always came back on. Jim agrees to let you diagnose the problem.

1. What does the MIL being illuminated indicate?
2. What is "freeze frame" data? And how can it help you diagnose the problem?
3. What do monitors that report "passed" and "failed" indicate?

There have been many strategies implemented to clean up vehicle emissions, and in more recent years, closed-loop electronic systems have assumed the major responsibility. The following is an abbreviated timeline of the many strategies devised for curtailing light-duty vehicle emissions in the United States since the 1960s:

1961—First positive crankcase ventilation (PCV) systems required in California

1964—Sealed crankcase systems replace crankcase "draft tubes"

1968—Controls for crankcase VOCs, tailpipe CO, and hydrocarbons (PCV, AIR, etc.)

1969—Commencement of limiting oxides of nitrogen emissions by retarding ignition and valve timing

1971—Introduction of evaporative emission (EVAP) control systems (charcoal canisters)

1973—Exhaust gas recirculation (EGR) systems used to control oxides of nitrogen

1975—Unleaded gasoline phase in

1975—Oxidizing catalytic converters introduced

1981—Closed-loop systems and three-way catalysts introduced; first-generation on-board diagnostics (OBDI) enacted nationwide (OBDI started with California vehicles)

1996—Second-generation on-board diagnostics (OBDII) enacted nationwide

1998—Commencement of vehicle refueling emission controls

2003—Widespread adoption of controller area network (CAN) communication systems (originated in 1998 with Robert Bosch–equipped vehicles like Volkswagens)

Let's look further into what these on-board diagnostic (OBD) systems do and what features are available to help technicians diagnose and repair vehicle system **faults**.

▶ On-Board Diagnostic Systems

OBD systems are a great resource to help the technician work more efficiently and remove some of the guesswork involved in diagnosing problems in today's sophisticated vehicles. These systems use powerful on-board computers in harmony with sophisticated diagnostic equipment to pinpoint problems in vehicle systems and components. Various on-board computers (sometimes referred to as **modules**) inform the vehicle operator when a fault occurs and assist technicians in identifying and repairing malfunctioning circuits or components.

In the United States, two different types of OBD systems have been used. The first generation of on-board diagnostic (**OBDI**) systems operated under manufacturer standards, starting with California vehicles and becoming nationwide in 1981. The second generation of on-board diagnostic (**OBDII**) systems operate under standards set by the Society of Automotive Engineers (SAE) to conform with US Environmental Protection Agency (EPA) regulations. Some manufacturers started using OBDII with a few of their models in 1994 and 1995 to become familiar with the systems, but for the 1996 model year, OBDII was standardized and initiated nationwide.

Where OBDI monitored mainly for parts and wiring malfunctions, OBDII is an enhanced diagnostic system that identifies faults in anything that may affect the vehicle's emission system. OBDII tests vehicle operating systems for faults affecting vehicle drivability and those that may affect vehicle safety and emission efficiency. OBDII constantly monitors and manages some of the electronics that control the vehicle's emission systems, which in turn enables much tighter standards to be enforced, with cutoff points far lower than those previously possible.

Both OBDI and OBDII systems provide a certain degree of commonality in that all vehicle manufacturers must adhere to certain standards regarding nomenclature (names of parts) and fault description codes. This means that any so-called "generic" OBDII faults and background data can be accessed and read by **aftermarket** as well as original equipment manufacturer (OEM) test equipment.

Both OEM and aftermarket OBDII scan tools serve to access OBD information via the **data link connector (DLC)**. The DLC enables the scanner to access data stored in the vehicle's various computers **FIGURE 49-1**. The DLC itself is a 16-pin connector with a common (SAE J1962) size and shape. Regardless of vehicle make and model, its

FIGURE 49-1 The data link connector (DLC) enables the scanner to access data stored in the vehicle's various computers.

location is now fairly standardized as being within 2' of the steering wheel below the driver's side instrument panel.

OBD Terminology

The automotive technician needs to know and understand the "lingo" used in the diagnosis and repair of automobiles in the service bay. Before the SAE published the appropriate "recommended practices," OEMs used nonstandardized nomenclature. The SAE has helped to standardize automotive terms used by engineers and technicians alike. A complete listing of OBDI and OBDII terms is available from the SAE (**SAE J1930**).

CAN-Bus

Standard copper wiring bundles on vehicles have become a major weight and cost issue due to the increased interconnectivity required between on-board computers and components. To simplify wiring, **controller area networks (CANs)** have become commonplace in today's vehicles. A CAN is a localized (on-board) vehicle network that enables computers and components to send and receive signals across a shielded twisted pair of wires. The wires are shielded by being twisted around one another and carrying balanced (+ and −) signals to reduce the likelihood of radio frequency interference into the network. The shielded pair of wires forms a common loop around the vehicle to connect components and handle encoded messages between components. Thus, the various computers/modules can network, or "talk," to one another. For example, a throttle position sensor or coolant temperature sensor may provide valued information to a number of other on-board modules to serve their respective needs.

The CAN-bus is constantly monitored by the OBDII system. Additionally, for diagnostic purposes, data can be accessed by the technician using the appropriate scan tool to either read data or command certain actuator functions to operate and be tested **FIGURE 49-2**.

Diagnostic Trouble Codes

Diagnostic trouble codes (DTCs) indicate the component or circuit in which a fault has been detected. **Codes** are "set" (stored) in one or more of the vehicle's on-board computers once a fault is detected. A fault is generated when values being monitored determine the emissions would be 1.5 times the EPA Federal Test Procedure (FTP). For example, a short or open in the engine's coolant temperature circuit will cause the fuel system to run rich, increasing the emissions so a DTC will be set. Also, if two sensors send conflicting data, a fault is recorded and the MIL is illuminated. Some DTCs set due to implausibility and conditions that are

FIGURE 49-2 Data can be accessed by using the appropriate scan tool to either read data or command actuator functions to operate.

out of parameters, but it is not always a case of a failed component or wiring. Understanding how the affected system operates is very important when troubleshooting the OBDII system. If you don't know how it works, how can you fix it? Locating, reading, and understanding the strategy used by the manufacturer to generate the DTC is of utmost importance.

Emission-related DTCs are the same (generic) across all vehicle makes and models, as are the SAE-recommended names used to describe components and systems. Any number of on-board computer modules may communicate with one another using standardized digital "languages." Nonmanufacturer-specific codes—those that are in any way emission related—are now the same from one vehicle to the next. Refer to **SAE J2012** for more information on interpreting generic DTCs. Refer to OEM service manuals for interpreting OEM-specific (nongeneric) system codes.

If a vehicle system reports that a fault exists, the MIL located in the instrument cluster will likely illuminate **FIGURE 49-3**. Sometimes it takes two consecutive drive cycles, or "trips," to illuminate the MIL. The MIL alerts the driver that there is a problem. Even a loose gas cap will trigger a DTC and illuminate the MIL under certain conditions. Catalytic converter input and output are monitored and compared. If the converter's efficiency is out of range, the MIL will illuminate and a DTC will set.

If the catalytic converter is at risk, such as from overfueling or a continuous misfire, the MIL will flash, thus telling the driver to stop the vehicle immediately to avoid serious damage to the converter. Once a malfunction occurs, the MIL will remain on until the system returns to normal or the fault is seen as repaired; alternately, the code may be cleared from memory by the technician using a scan tool. OBD systems store DTCs in the computer's so-called keep alive memory (KAM). The codes remain in memory until power is disconnected for older vehicles; for newer vehicles, DTCs are saved even if the vehicle's battery is disconnected. DTC information remains stored in the respective control module's long-term memory regardless of whether a "hard" (continuous) or an intermittent fault has set the code.

A DTC may be generated by any of the numerous computer modules on board. It serves not only to inform the driver of a fault, but also to enable the automotive technician to determine where the fault has occurred. DTCs are used in conjunction with diagnostic flowcharts found in the manufacturer's service information to assist technicians in determining the likely cause of a failure.

Both OBDI and OBDII systems monitor engine sensors, fuel delivery components, and emission control devices that, if faulty, will cause problems. Simpler OBDI systems are normally limited to the detection of an open or short in a sensor or wiring. But OBDII systems monitor all emission-related components and circuits for opens, shorts, abnormal operation, and more.

OBDII codes use a series of letters and numbers grouped together to identify which system, component, or circuit is at fault. The first character of the code is a letter that identifies whether the fault is located within the power train (P), body (B), chassis controller (C), or communication system (U). The next four characters are numbers, starting with 0 or 1. A 0 indicates a generic OBDII code; a 1 indicates an OEM code. The next three numbers identify the system and component related to the fault. Refer to DTC charts (on the Internet or in service literature) for a complete listing of the hundreds of possible codes. The list grows constantly as on-board systems become even more sophisticated and unique, as with hybrid-electric vehicles.

Freeze-Frame Data

Since OBDII came about in 1996, technicians have had the ability to access **freeze-frame** snapshots that are automatically recorded in the vehicle's **power train control module (PCM)** when a vehicle fault occurs. If a more serious fault supersedes another previously less-serious recorded fault, freeze-frame data are updated. Difficult-to-find intermittent faults can thus be diagnosed by carefully reviewing data stored just before, during, and after the fault occurred. During a test-drive, such recorded data give the technician a valuable "instant replay" of what happened and when. For example, if the vehicle experienced a misfire while crossing a rough set of railroad tracks but at no other time. Modern **scan tools** can retrieve freeze-frame data and display them (via a graphing scan tool) for analysis after the fact **FIGURE 49-4**.

System Monitors

OBDII standards dictate that a vehicle's computer (PCM) must monitor emission systems with two priorities in mind. The first is the **continuous monitoring** of systems and components that could contribute to major emission failures. Possible faults include engine misfiring and an incorrect air/fuel mixture, which are monitored on a continuous basis by the PCM. Lower-priority faults

FIGURE 49-3 The malfunction indicator lamp (MIL).

FIGURE 49-4 A scan tool can retrieve and display freeze-frame data.

are monitored on a **noncontinuous** basis. In such cases, systems are checked only once during each engine **warm-up cycle**, or even less often, depending on certain circumstances such as ambient temperatures or fuel level.

Each time the engine is started, the PCM checks that components such as the oxygen sensor, catalytic converter, and other engine systems are functioning correctly. If a fault is detected, the MIL is illuminated, indicating that the vehicle needs attention.

If the condition is intermittent and the faulty system once again operates normally, the MIL will turn off after the vehicle has operated through three warm-up cycles, but the DTC will remain logged in the PCM's memory as a **history code** for a set period. If the fault does not reoccur within 40 drive cycles, the code will automatically be erased.

Drive Cycles

A **drive cycle** is essentially considered to include the following events: A vehicle starts, warms up, is accelerated, cruises, slows down, accelerates once more, decelerates, stops, and cools down. The EPA has established "drive cycles" for emission testing of various kinds of vehicles, and the light-duty vehicle (240-second) drive cycle is the basis for how OBDII **monitors** (tests) are run. A complete driving cycle should include diagnostics on all systems and be completed in under 15 minutes; however, sometimes certain monitors cannot be run during a drive cycle if qualifying conditions for running that particular monitor are not met. For example, an evaporative emission (EVAP) monitor will not run if the fuel tank is nearly full or nearly empty. In some cases, particular monitors cannot run until after others have been run and passed. EVAP monitoring will also not run if the engine coolant temperature monitor has not passed. State-run emission inspection stations in the Unites States will sometimes allow a vehicle to pass an emission inspection, even if one or two monitors have not run and passed.

Scan Tools

Essentially, a **scan tool** ("scanner") is a device able to electronically communicate with and extract data from the vehicle's one or more on-board computers. On-board computer modules include the PCM, **electronic brake control module (EBCM)**, **body control module (BCM)**, **transmission control module (TCM)**, and perhaps numerous others. Simple scan tools from the 80s could read and erase fault codes and little more. But as on-board systems became more complex, so too did professional-grade scan tools used in the service bay. Today, these scanners are sold to consumers.

Applied | **Science**

AS-18: Time: The technician uses direct and indirect methods to measure time and compare the results to the manufacturer's specifications.
A technician is troubleshooting a vehicle that has an intermittent problem with hesitation on acceleration. The technician has started his evaluation by conducting a visual inspection. After this, he uses a scan tool to check for codes but does not find any. He checks fuel pressure and volume, and both are within the manufacturer's specifications. The technician checks for service bulletins for this symptom but has not found any leads in this area.

Another technician suggests confirming that the injector pulse width meets the manufacturer's specifications, since he has a similar vehicle that had problems in this area. The technician checks the service manual and finds that the injector pulse width should be 2.5 to 2.7 milliseconds at engine idle. The manual also gives other pulse-width specifications for other engine speeds. Using a scan tool, the technician is able to verify that the pulse width is within the manufacturer's specifications at all published engine speeds. The scan tool data is on a direct-time basis as real-time engine data is being used.

Pulse width is the amount of time measured in milliseconds that a fuel injector delivers fuel to the cylinder. The injector pulse width depends on the input signals supplied to the PCM from its various engine sensors. The pulse width expands on acceleration and contracts under lighter loads.

Cost and complexity increase commensurate with the bells and whistles desired in a scanner. Automotive technicians today are finding that they must use faster and more accurate diagnostic instruments, such as graphing scan tools, to see hidden faults in component or system waveforms. Scanners are now used to monitor engine compression, vacuum, internal engine anomalies, and so forth. Called **bidirectional scanners**, they are used to cause various components and systems to operate for test purposes. Scanners are used along with digital storage oscilloscopes, portable five-gas **emission analyzers**, and other diagnostic equipment for much more effective time-saving diagnostic routines.

The scan tool is not a "magic bullet," however. A fault code found does not necessarily point directly to the problem. For example, a *P0171 Fuel System Too Lean* code could be caused by a defective oxygen sensor, but it could also be caused by an underreporting mass airflow sensor, a vacuum leak, use of the wrong fuel, and so on., so further testing is often required.

Training and experience play a major role in effectively using these modern information-gathering tools.

Understanding the principles of combustion theory, internal combustion engine operation, and emissions are essential ingredients for success. Something that is often forgotten in this electronic age is that engines, transmissions, and braking systems are still, by nature, mechanical devices. Electronics can control and monitor them, but they cannot overcome large physical defects. For instance, low compression due to a burned valve may go undiagnosed if a code is not set. After the scanner is used to read any codes, but before any electronic troubleshooting begins, a thorough visual examination of the mechanical parts of the system involved should be performed. Simple faults like a cracked or loose vacuum hose, or even a loose gas cap, may easily be found and corrected—whether a code is set or not.

Indeed, the field is demanding. It requires extensive training and also a sizeable investment. Opportunities abound for the technician who understands the theory and masters the use of the scanner to quickly and efficiently analyze, diagnose, and solve problems on today's advanced vehicle engine systems.

▶ Diagnosis and Testing

Diagnosing Engine Concerns

Modern vehicle engine systems are complex systems that have developed to provide performance and efficient use of fuel while ensuring that exhaust emissions meet strict environmental regulations. To achieve these demands, engineers have improved the performance of mechanical components and used computer control of the electrical, ignition, and fuel systems to ensure the highest possible efficiency while reducing exhaust emissions. Each of these systems must be working together, each interacting with the other correctly to ensure optimal engine operation. A fault in one system will affect the performance of other systems. For example, a plugged injector may cause a cylinder misfire, reducing engine power and also affecting the secondary ignition voltages. Diagnosis of the engine requires that you understand each of these systems, how they operate, and how their performance affects other systems and components.

To diagnose correctly, test for the cause of the customer's concern to verify the fault. Determine what faults may cause the symptoms and conduct mechanical, electrical, ignition, and fuel system checks to correctly identify the location and types of faults. It is also possible that a vehicle may have multiple faults; for example, a plugged injector may have been caused by poor-quality fuel.

Test equipment will need to be used to diagnose engine faults. This equipment may include OBD scanners, digital storage oscilloscopes, compression gauges, digital volt-ohmmeters (DVOMs), fuel system pressure gauges, and flowmeters. You will need to interpret the test results, compare the results to the manufacturer's specifications, and then apply the test results in a diagnostic pathway.

Retrieving and Recording DTCs, OBD Monitor Status, and Freeze-Frame Data

Modern vehicles are required to meet strict environmental emission regulations over the life of their operation. In order to meet these standards, vehicles are equipped with sophisticated electronic control units and sensors to monitor and adjust the engine fuel and the ignition and emission systems and to provide diagnostic capability to meet the required standards. Retrieving and recording DTCs, monitor status, and freeze-frame data are integral steps in diagnosing faults within vehicle systems. The technician must be able to do so anytime a vehicle sets a DTC or fails emission monitors.

Every vehicle sold is required to meet a drive cycle, which is designed to simulate actual driving conditions. The OBDII system constantly tests and analyzes each system's performance over the drive cycle. This is achieved through a set of PCM programs called monitors, which test each system's operation. The monitor will set a pass or fail based on each system test. The electronic systems will also record and store data for diagnostic purposes. The PCM will set and store DTCs if a fault is detected. Freeze-frame data are also stored, which provide a snapshot of particular PIDs before, during, and after the time of the fault being detected. Never delete or reset the diagnostic data until all testing has been completed. Ensure that any codes or data are recorded and safely stored.

To retrieve and record DTCs, OBD monitor status, and freeze-frame data, follow the steps in **SKILL DRILL 49-1**:

1. Select the scan tool to provide the best coverage for the type and make of vehicle.
2. Locate the DLC and connect the scan tool. **(Photo 1)**
3. Power on the scan tool, and turn the ignition on.
4. Establish scan tool communications with the vehicle. **(Photo 2)**
5. Retrieve and record the DTCs. **(Photo 3)**
6. Retrieve and record OBD monitor status. **(Photo 4)**
7. Retrieve and record freeze-frame data applicable to DTCs and monitors. **(Photo 5)**
8. Power off the scan tool, turn the ignition off, and disconnect the scan tool. **(Photo 6)**

SKILL DRILL   49-1   Retrieving and Recording DTCs, OBD Monitor Status, and Freeze-Frame Data

1. Select the scan tool to provide the best coverage for the type and make of vehicle. Locate the DLC and connect the scan tool.

2. Power on the scan tool, and turn the ignition on. Establish scan tool communications with the vehicle.

3. Retrieve and record the DTCs.

4. Retrieve and record OBD monitor status.

5. Retrieve and record freeze-frame data applicable to DTCs and monitors.

6. Power off the scan tool, turn the ignition off, and disconnect the scan tool.

Diagnosing the Cause of Drivability or Emission Concerns with DTCs

DTCs will often set when there is a fault within vehicle systems such as with drivability or emission concerns. When DTCs are set, the MIL will illuminate on the dash, indicating a fault. The DTCs are a good place to commence the diagnostic process. The technician should retrieve all codes and record them electronically or print them out. Diagnosis will require an analysis of the code's meaning and the system it relates to. The manufacturer's information or aftermarket code lists will be required to determine the meaning of each code.

Codes will indicate that a system is not functioning correctly. It is not unusual for multiple codes to be set.

Some codes may relate to the cause of the problem, and some may be set as an effect of the system not functioning correctly.

To diagnose drivability or emission concerns when there are stored or active DTCs present, and to obtain and interpret scan tool data, follow the steps in **SKILL DRILL 49-2**:

1. Locate the DLC and connect the scan tool.

2. Power on the scan tool, and turn the ignition on.

3. Establish scan tool communications with the vehicle.

4. Retrieve and record DTCs.

5. Look up DTC definitions in code books or the manufacturer's information.

6 Interpret results with reference to the manufacturer's information.

7 Diagnose drivability or emission concerns, and identify and recommend a course of action for repair.

8 Power off the scan tool, turn ignition off, and disconnect the scan tool.

Diagnosing Drivability or Emission Concerns Without DTCs

A vehicle may fail an emission test or a customer may complain about a drivability issue even though DTCs have not been set. Just because a DTC has not been set does not mean the vehicle is running perfectly. The ODBII system is designed to set fault codes if the vehicle exceeds the limits programmed within the system to meet the EPA Federal Test Procedure. Pass and fail points are different for every vehicle and are integrated within the system's operation, which is designed to compensate and keep emissions in check even in the event of a fault.

The PCM can make adjustments to ensure engine emissions continue to meet the standard. The PCM adjustments may have an effect on the vehicle's drivability, but because requirements are still met, no DTC is set. For example, an engine misfire may not set a DTC because the intermittent nature of the misfire is not enough to set a DTC and the PCM compensates by shutting down the injector in the misfiring cylinder, thereby ensuring that emissions remain within the standard. Additionally, in some cases, codes are not set if a PCM is faulty or a system fault is such that it prevents a code from being set.

To diagnose a vehicle when DTCs have not been set, you will need to rely on diagnostic procedures using test equipment such as scan tools to read system parameters, digital oscilloscopes, DVOMs, smoke machines, pressure gauges, and flowmeters. The technician needs to collect as much information as possible and analyze the result to narrow down the cause of the fault.

To diagnose drivability or emission concerns that do not involve stored or active DTCs, first gather information on the complaint from the customer. Verify the complaint and identify the symptoms. After referencing the manufacturer's information, use the correct diagnostic test equipment to conduct tests; then interpret the results and diagnose the drivability or emission concerns. Recommend a course of action for repair.

Testing Computerized Engine Control System Sensors, the PCM, Actuators, and Circuits

Graphing multimeters and digital storage oscilloscopes are used to make precise electrical measurements over time and display the results on a graph as a waveform. Given the complex systems found on vehicles today, these tools are essential in checking electrical and electronic signals to and from sensors and PCMs **FIGURE 49-5**. Typical graphing multimeters and digital storage oscilloscopes can store the results of captures as data on the instrument and in many cases also on a computer that can connect to the tool.

A graphing multimeter or a digital storage oscilloscope is used to verify signals going to and from electrical and electronic components. To use these tools, you will need to know how to hook the test equipment into the electrical circuit, set the test instrument to read accurately, and interpret the results of the capture. There are many different types of leads and adapters available for graphing multimeters and digital storage oscilloscopes, such as current probes, high-voltage probes, and pressure sensors. You will need to know when and where to use each lead and adapter to ensure accurate readings are taken.

To inspect and test computerized engine control system sensors, the PCM, actuators, and circuits using a graphing multimeter, follow the steps in **SKILL DRILL 49-3**:

1 Reference the manufacturer's information as necessary. Determine the circuit to be tested and the likely voltages and frequency of the waveform to be measured.

FIGURE 49-5 An oscilloscope being used to check electrical and electronic signals to and from a sensor.

SKILL DRILL | **49-3** | **Testing Engine Control System Sensors, the PCM, Actuators, and Circuits**

1. Determine the circuit to be tested and the likely voltages and frequency of the waveform to be measured. Set up the graphing multimeter or oscilloscope, setting the voltage level and time base to commence measurements.

2. Connect the leads to the points to be measured.

3. Capture the waveforms from the circuit under test. Analyze the waveform, comparing it to the manufacturer's specifications or known good waveforms. Determine the necessary actions.

2. Set up the graphing multimeter or oscilloscope, setting the voltage level and time base to commence measurements. **(Photo 1)**

3. Connect the leads to the points to be measured. **(Photo 2)**

4. Capture the waveforms from the circuit under test.

5. Analyze the waveform, comparing it to the manufacturer's specifications or known good waveforms. Determine the necessary actions. **(Photo 3)**

Diagnosing Drivability and Emission Problems Resulting from Malfunctions of Interrelated Systems

This task is performed when systems other than the engine management system cause problems with emissions or drivability. Drivability and emission problems can be caused by interrelated systems, such as automatic transmissions, cruise control, security systems, suspension control, air conditioning, and other non-OEM–installed accessories. Each of the systems, aside from the non-OEM accessories in most vehicles, is controlled by a system computer and has electronic diagnostic capability and associated fault codes. The technician needs to understand how each system works

and interacts with other systems. This way he or she can understand the cause and effect of faults and their impacts on other systems.

DTCs and customer information are the best place to start gathering information and planning a diagnostic pathway based on suspected systems and components. Non-OEM–installed accessories can make diagnosing difficult due to a lack of information and knowledge about the products, their installation, and how they work. Ensure that as much information as possible is gathered from the customer before commencing work.

To diagnose drivability and emission problems resulting from malfunctions of interrelated systems, follow the steps in **SKILL DRILL 49-4**:

1. Verify the customer complaint and identify the symptoms.
2. Plan diagnostic tests on interrelated systems with reference to the manufacturer's information.
3. Use diagnostic test equipment to conduct tests.
4. Interpret results with reference to the manufacturer's information.
5. Diagnose drivability and emission problems resulting from malfunctions of interrelated systems, and recommend a course of action for repair.

Testing Actuators

Actuators are devices such as solenoids, fuel injectors, and stepper motors. They are used to convert electrical signals into mechanical movement. A typical vehicle has many actuators that are controlled by the vehicle's computer systems to manage such functions as fuel injection, throttle position, and emission valves. Actuators will need to be tested for correct operation when faults occur in vehicle systems.

The test process will usually entail checking for correct signals to the actuator to verify that correct operation is possible and checking the mechanical and electrical operation of the actuator to ensure it is capable of working under operating conditions. Testing actuators may involve the use of test equipment such as DVOMs, digital storage oscilloscopes, and pressure gauges, and may require other tools such as jumper leads and power supplies. Many actuators operate on voltages supplied by the system computer and may operate at voltages other than battery voltage—for example, 5 volts. Always check the manufacturer's information for correct voltages, and always isolate an actuator from its control circuit before applying any external voltage or power supply to test its operation. Never jump battery or power supply voltages to an actuator while it is connected to its control circuit; doing so may result in damage to the system computer.

To test actuators, follow the steps in **SKILL DRILL 49-5**:

1. Reference the manufacturer's information, as necessary. Determine the actuators to be tested and the required operating parameters required for correct operation.

2. Select the appropriate test equipment.

3. Conduct actuator tests on and off the vehicle as required.

4. Analyze the test results against the manufacturer's specifications, and make recommendations as required.

Interpreting DTCs and Scan Tool Data Related to the Emission Control Systems

DTCs and scan tool data must be interpreted by the technician when there is a drivability or emission problem. Scan tools are an important test instrument for modern vehicles, as they allow access to the OBD and data systems. Scan tools fall into two main categories—aftermarket and OEM. OEM scanners are specific to a particular manufacturer's line of vehicles and will often provide additional functionality that aftermarket scanners cannot provide. Aftermarket scanners, in contrast, will usually work on multiple manufacturers' products, but not necessarily with the same degree of functionality as an OEM scan tool.

The scan tool is connected via the diagnostic plug, which allows access to stored fault codes and data that the vehicle computer systems have stored in regard to vehicle performance. Never erase data or fault codes before they have been accurately recorded. The manufacturer's information or code books will need to be referenced to identify fault codes and the systems they relate to.

To interpret DTCs and scan tool data related to the emission control system, follow the steps in **SKILL DRILL 49-6**:

1. Locate the DLC and connect the scan tool.

2. Power on the scan tool, and turn the ignition on.

3. Establish scan tool communications with the vehicle.

4. Retrieve and record the DTCs.

5. Look up the DTCs' definitions in code books or in the manufacturer's information.

6. Interpret the results, referencing the manufacturer's information.

7. Power off the scan tool, turn the ignition off, and disconnect the scan tool.

Wrap-up

Ready for Review

▸ Second-generation on-board diagnostics (OBDII) started in late 1995 and became standard in 1996. All vehicles use the same generic adapter for a generic scan tool to connect to the vehicles computer.

▸ Since California's emission laws of the 1960s, the standards for emissions have gotten more stringent, requiring many changes to subsequent vehicles.

▸ OBD systems help the technician work more efficiently and help take the guesswork out of diagnosing problems on today's sophisticated vehicles.

▸ OBD systems are a great resource, using powerful on-board computers in harmony with sophisticated diagnostic equipment to pinpoint problems in vehicle systems and components.

▸ Both OEM and aftermarket OBDII scan tools serve to access OBD information via the data link connector (DLC).

▸ The Society of Automotive Engineers (SAE) has standardized the terminology of parts and systems nomenclature (J1930) and across-the-board identification of generic DTCs (J2012).

▸ Diagnostic trouble codes (DTCs) are usually set after the vehicle has had two drive cycles with the same malfunction.

▸ Codes on OBD systems are categorized as power train (P), body (B), chassis controller (C), and communications system (U).

▸ Freeze-frame data are the best way for a technician to determine the conditions under which a concern happens which then helps determine the cause of the DTC.

▸ Scan tools, a lab scope, and a digital volt-ohmmeter (DVOM) are a technician's best tools when it comes to troubleshooting an OBD code.

▸ Always refer to the manufacturer's service information and follow the diagnostic flowcharts to ensure that the vehicle malfunction is identified and repaired correctly.

▸ Always use wiring diagrams when diagnosing any electric/electronic circuits in the OBD system, and do not forget about the grounds.

Key Terms

aftermarket That segment of the trade that supplies parts, services, and repair for vehicles outside of the original equipment manufacturer (OEM) or the dealer network.

bidirectional scanners Scanners used to monitor engine compression, vacuum, internal engine anomalies, and so forth by causing various components and systems to operate for test purposes.

body control module (BCM) An electronic unit that monitors and regulates electronic devices in the vehicle.

carbon dioxide (CO$_2$) A vehicle emission that is considered a primary greenhouse gas, though not toxic and not yet regulated.

carbon monoxide (CO) A vehicle emission produced by partially burned fuel that is colorless, odorless, and highly toxic and that causes asphyxiation when inhaled.

Clean Air Act Federal legislation enacted in the United States to reduce pollution, in part from automobiles.

code Another name for a fault code; *see* DTC.

continuous monitoring A term that describes OBDII monitors that run continuously throughout the drive cycle.

controller area network (CAN) A localized (on-board) vehicle network that enables computers and components to send and receive signals across a shielded twisted pair of wires.

data link connector (DLC) A device that enables a scan tool to access data stored in the vehicle's various computers.

diagnostic trouble code (DTC) A computer-driven on-board report regarding component or system faults following the running of monitors.

drive cycle A series of prescribed automobile operating conditions during which emissions testing is performed.

electronic brake control module (EBCM) The module that controls and monitors the anti-lock braking system.

emissions Tailpipe and volatile organic compound pollutants emitted by the automobile.

emission analyzer A service bay or lab device used for detecting/measuring vehicle emissions.

fault *See* diagnostic trouble code (DTC).

freeze-frame A feature of OBDII that records events before, during, and after a fault occurs.

history code A fault code that has occurred but is not current and is saved in the PCM's memory for 40 drive cycles.

hydrocarbon (HC) A microscopic unburned fuel particle that contributes to photochemical smog and helps form ground-level ozone.

malfunction indicator lamp (MIL) An indicator located in the instrument cluster that illuminates when the power train control module (PCM) detects a fault in one of the vehicle systems. Formerly called a check engine or service engine soon light.

module An electronic computer or circuit board that controls specific functions.

monitor An OBDII test run to ensure that a specific component or system is working properly.

noncontinuous monitor A monitor that runs only once per drive cycle.

OBDI The first generation of on-board diagnostic systems that originated for California vehicles.

OBDII The second generation of on-board diagnostic systems, which have been in effect for all US vehicles since 1996.

oxides of nitrogen A vehicle emission that contributes to ground-level ozone. Oxides of nitrogen are produced when nitrogen and oxygen react during combustion, given sufficient temperatures and pressures. Forms include nitrogen oxide and nitrogen dioxide.

particulate matter (PM) Unseen microscopic particles of carbon consisting of soot (especially prominent with diesel exhaust). PM clogs the lungs and is carcinogenic.

power train control module (PCM) The module that controls and monitors the engine ignition, fuel, and emission system functions.

SAE J1930 An SAE standard for across-the-board standardization of parts and systems nomenclature.

SAE J2012 An SAE standard for across-the-board identification of generic DTCs.

scan tool A plug-in electronic device for extracting and interpreting fault codes (DTCs) in the automobile, plus much more.

sulfur dioxide (SO$_2$) A pollutant resulting from sulfur in motor fuel and contributing to acid rain.

transmission control module (TCM) An electronic computer that controls transmission function; it may include adaptive learning capabilities for driver preferences.

volatile organic compound (VOC) The hydrocarbons in petroleum products that contribute to combustion.

warm-up cycle One drive cycle, during which the vehicle starts out cold, warms up, and then cools down after the driving cycle.

ASE-Type Questions

1. Tech A says that on OBDII vehicles, it is a good idea to clear the codes before diagnosis, and see if they reset. Tech B says that the DTC will tell you what part needs to be changed. Who is correct?
   a. Tech A
   b. Tech B
   c. Both A and B
   d. Neither A nor B

2. Tech A says that OBDI and OBDII use different DLC connectors. Tech B says that OBDII standardizes the designations for diagnostic trouble codes (DTCs). Who is correct?
   a. Tech A
   b. Tech B
   c. Both A and B
   d. Neither A nor B

3. Tech A says that monitors are designed to test if emission systems are working properly. Tech B says that monitors are designed to store sensor data about a fault if a DTC is set. Who is correct?
   a. Tech A
   b. Tech B
   c. Both A and B
   d. Neither A nor B

4. Tech A says that control modules communicate back and forth today using a CAN, which is a bundle of many individual wires, specially designed for fast communication speed. Tech B says that OBDII mandates that a DTC must be set if the emissions are more than 1.5 times the EPA FTP. Who is correct?
   a. Tech A
   b. Tech B
   c. Both A and B
   d. Neither A nor B

5. Tech A says that OBDII will allow a technician to hook up a generic scan tool to read DTCs and clear DTCs. Tech B says that when the MIL is on, the vehicle should not be driven. Who is correct?
   a. Tech A
   b. Tech B
   c. Both A and B
   d. Neither A nor B

6. Tech A says that something as simple as a loose gas tank fill cap will turn on the MIL. Tech B says that every digit of a DTC has identifying characteristics. Who is correct?
   a. Tech A
   b. Tech B
   c. Both A and B
   d. Neither A nor B

7. Tech A says that a "P" in the DTC stands for a powertrain code. Tech B says a "U" stands for an undetermined code. Who is correct?
   a. Tech A
   b. Tech B
   c. Both A and B
   d. Neither A nor B

8. Tech A says that on OBDII systems, the KAM stores DTCs forever. Tech B says that on OBDII systems, the KAM is erased when the battery is disconnected. Who is correct?
   a. Tech A
   b. Tech B
   c. Both A and B
   d. Neither A nor B

9. Tech A says that the MIL can turn off if the fault doesn't reappear in a certain number of tests. Tech B says that when an MIL is activated, the PCM stores the DTC until a predetermined number of drive cycles have been performed or cleared by a scan tool. Who is correct?
   a. Tech A
   b. Tech B
   c. Both A and B
   d. Neither A nor B

10. Tech A says some mechanical engine problems can cause OBDII DTCs to be set. Tech B says that OBDII codes only monitor the emission control system components. Who is correct?
    a. Tech A
    b. Tech B
    c. Both A and B
    d. Neither A nor B

CHAPTER 50

NATEF Tasks

Engine Performance
Fuel, Air Induction, and Exhaust Systems

		Page
■ Inspect throttle body, air induction system, intake manifold, and gaskets for vacuum leaks and/or unmetered air.	**AST** **MAST**	1764–1765
■ Verify idle control operation.	**AST** **MAST**	1766–1767
■ Inspect integrity of the exhaust manifold, exhaust pipes, muffler(s), catalytic converter(s), resonator(s), tailpipe(s), and heat shield(s); determine necessary action.	**MLR** **AST** **MAST**	1766–1767
■ Perform exhaust system back-pressure test; determine necessary action.	**AST** **MAST**	1767–1768

Knowledge Objectives

After reading this chapter, you will be able to:
1. Explain the basic principles of the intake system and its components. (pp 1746–1749)
2. Describe the functions of the exhaust system and its components. (pp 1758–1764)
3. Safely perform the NATEF tasks related to air induction and exhaust systems. (pp 1764–1768)
4. List the steps involved in inspecting, diagnosing, maintaining, and repairing the air induction and exhaust system's components. (pp 1764–1768)

Induction and Exhaust

Skills Objectives

After reading this chapter, you will be able to:

1. Inspect the throttle body, air induction system, intake manifold, and gaskets for vacuum leaks and/or unmetered air. (pp 1764–1765)
2. Verify idle control operation. (p 1766)
3. Inspect the integrity of the exhaust manifold, exhaust pipes, muffler(s), catalytic converter(s), resonator(s), tailpipe(s), and heat shield(s). (pp 1766–1767)
4. Perform exhaust system back-pressure test. (pp 1767–1768)
5. Test the operation of turbocharger/supercharger systems. (p 1768)

▶ Introduction

The intake and exhaust systems are critical parts of the internal combustion engine. The intake system ensures that clean, dry air is supplied to the engine, which is then mixed with fuel and burned in the combustion chamber, creating the thermal expansion that pushes the pistons down the cylinder. Clean, dry air is essential for proper combustion and a long-lasting engine, since dirt would get between the close-moving parts and cause premature wear of the engine. In fact, it takes only a tablespoon or two of dirt entering the engine through the intake system to ruin an engine. The intake system must provide a sealed passageway to the combustion chambers to ensure that no contaminants leak into the system and that no air is allowed to bypass the airflow sensor, which could create a drivability problem. The intake system also controls the amount of air entering the engine, by use of a throttle plate, which is how engine revolutions per minute (rpm) and power are controlled.

The exhaust system provides a path for the burned exhaust gases to safely exit the engine and travel out the rear of the vehicle. It also provides a method of reducing the noise from the power pulses and includes components that help reduce the harmful emissions in the exhaust stream. Getting rid of exhaust gases is just as important as getting air into the engine. If exhaust gases cannot leave the engine easily, then air will not be able to enter the engine easily. An efficient, free-flowing exhaust system will assist the engine in creating maximum power with minimal emissions. In this chapter, we will explore the operation, diagnosis, and testing of the components in both the intake and the exhaust systems.

▶ The Intake System

The intake system is primarily designed to control the flow of air delivered to the combustion chamber. In most fuel-injected and carbureted engines, fuel is mixed in the intake system so air and fuel are being delivered together. In diesel and gasoline direct-injection engines, fuel is injected directly into the combustion chamber where it is mixed with air; thus, only air (plus any positive crankcase ventilation and evaporative emissions) flows through the intake system. For any fuel to burn efficiently, no matter where it is injected, it must be vaporized and fully mixed with the proper amount of air. Vaporization starts when the fuel system atomizes the fuel by breaking it up into very small particles by spraying it into the charge of air. These small particles make it much easier to vaporize the fuel. Heat and low pressure also may be used to vaporize the atomized fuel.

Intake System Components

The primary components of the automotive intake system are the intake manifold, the throttle body, and the air induction system. The intake manifold is bolted to the cylinder head. Its construction and design depend on the engine for which it is created. The intake manifold directs airflow into each cylinder **FIGURE 50-1**, and when restricted by the throttle plate, it provides a source of vacuum for systems such as the power brake system.

FIGURE 50-1 The intake manifold.

The intake manifold creates a mounting place for a throttle body assembly. In throttle body injection, one or two fuel injectors, which are mounted in the top of the throttle body, spray fuel down into the intake manifold. In a port fuel-injected engine, a throttle body is bolted to the opening of the intake manifold and the injectors are mounted in the intake manifold near the intake valves FIGURE 50-2. The throttle body controls airflow with a butterfly valve or valves, also called throttle valves. The throttle valves are opened and closed either by a throttle cable or, if the engine uses an electronic throttle control, by an electric motor that opens and closes the throttle plates. Attached to the throttle body is a throttle position sensor, which provides throttle position information to the engine computer. The throttle body also includes vacuum ports for the operation of vacuum-controlled devices such as evaporative emission systems and the power brake booster.

The air induction system consists of the following components: an air cleaner and housing, solid and flexible-duct tubing, connectors, and sometimes a mass airflow sensor. The air induction system draws in ambient air through a filter from the environment, or a turbocharger or supercharger can push air through the induction system FIGURE 50-3. The inlet opening of the induction system may be located in various positions under the hood depending on the available space for the automotive engineer to work with.

Air Cleaner

The air cleaner filters the incoming air. In past designs, the air cleaner housing was made of stamped metal and housed a round air filter. Most air cleaners are now made of plastic and can vary in shape from square to round. The air cleaner element or filter may be manufactured from pleated paper or from oil-impregnated cloth or felt; in much older vehicles, it was manufactured in an oil bath

FIGURE 50-2 A. Throttle body injection. B. Port fuel injection.

FIGURE 50-3 The air induction system directs air from the inlet through an air filtration device and on to the intake manifold.

configuration. Another function of the air cleaner is to muffle the noise of the intake pulses and the incoming air, which travels at high speeds. The air cleaner can also act as a flame arrester. If a gasoline engine backfires, the air cleaner can contain the flame within the intake manifold or carburetor. The location of the air cleaner depends on the available space and the hood design.

A lot of air passes through the intake system into the engine. In a gasoline engine, the air–fuel mixture, by weight, is about 15 parts air to 1 part fuel. By volume, that's 10,000 times more air than fuel. When an engine consumes 10 gallons of gas, the air filter will have filtered 100,000 gallons of air. The air–fuel mixture enters the engine, so the air needs to be clean. Any abrasives that enter the engine can quickly cause wear and damage.

> ### ▶ TECHNICIAN TIP
>
> One way to tell if a pleated paper air filter needs to be changed is by holding it up to a light and seeing how much light passes through it. Just because it is a bit dirty on the outside doesn't mean it needs to be replaced. In fact, a lightly plugged filter prevents particles from going through the filter better than a brand new filter. But if it is too plugged, it will restrict airflow to the engine. If you can see a lot of light through it, it is reusable. If it restricts the light very much, it should be replaced.

An air cleaner on a multipoint electronic fuel-injected engine usually has a different shape from that on a carbureted engine, but it serves the same purpose. In many vehicles, the air cleaner is mounted where it can obtain cool, clean air. The air from the air cleaner is then carried to the throttle body by a long, flexible duct. Inside the air cleaner, a filter element filters the air and reduces noise. Many electronically fuel-injected systems have an airflow sensor after the air cleaner element, which accurately measures all air entering the engine and adjusts the air–fuel mixture accordingly; it is essential that there be no air leaks after the airflow sensor, as leaks will upset the air–fuel mixture. It is interesting to note that a **mass airflow (MAF) sensor** can measure air entering the engine down to tenths of a gram per second.

On most heavy-duty diesel engines and a few gasoline engines, the air cleaner assembly uses an air filter indicator to tell the operator whether the filter needs to be cleaned or replaced **FIGURE 50-4**. The indicator typically has a red band that will show if the filter is restricted. Some indicators lock in place, even when the engine is stopped, while others indicate filter condition only when the engine is running. The indicator is mounted between the air cleaner and the engine. When the air filter creates enough of a restriction, the vacuum produced in the intake tube causes the indicator to display the warning.

These indicators are a quick way to determine whether the air filter needs to be serviced. Some heavy-duty air cleaners also incorporate a cyclone-type precleaner, which is mounted directly onto the air cleaner unit **FIGURE 50-5**. The cyclone system uses angled vanes that give the incoming air a swirling motion. Centrifugal force throws the heavier dirt particles outward, and they collect in a bowl at the bottom of the cleaner where they can be removed manually. An efficient cyclone precleaner can remove up to 90% of particles before they reach the main filter element, greatly extending its life.

One type of air cleaner system is the long-life filtration system that is currently used on the Ford Focus. This air cleaner assembly is a nonserviceable unit that is designed to last 150,000 miles (240,000 km) or more. It is made to also capture any hydrocarbons being released from the throttle body and then allow them to be pulled back into the engine as air flows across the filter. The filter

FIGURE 50-4 Air cleaner with filter service indicator.

FIGURE 50-5 Cyclone-type precleaner.

element is made of specially designed foam. This filter can be serviced only by replacement of the entire assembly.

Ducting

Ducting can be made of hardened plastic with flexible rubber couplings to absorb engine movement. It may have a MAF sensor in line and be retained with worm-style clamps to seal the duct to the sensor. The ducting is what connects the ridged air cleaner to the throttle body of the intake manifold. Some ducting also includes air dampening, sometimes referred to as a Helmholtz resonator. A **Helmholtz resonator** is a container that is sealed and specially shaped to cancel noise created by pressure waves. The pressure wave bounces off the walls of the resonator and collides with the incoming waves, canceling the noise. On the vehicle, the resonator is a tube that is connected to the air ducting and is simply a sealed chamber that is open where it is connected to the air duct **FIGURE 50-6**. The pressure waves created when the engine pulls air into the air duct produce a loud suction sound that can be unpleasant to the owner. Use of the resonator minimizes the noise produced in the air intake system.

FIGURE 50-6 The air duct on some vehicles contains a resonator to cancel air noise as air flows through the intake.

Applied | Science

AS-38: Amplification: The technician can explain to a customer how sound can be amplified in a vehicle due to resonant cavities and other physical characteristics of the vehicle.

The noise level of a vehicle plays an important role in the overall satisfaction rating by the owner. A quiet vehicle is expected by the majority of vehicle owners. Some vehicle owners prefer the sound of a high-performance vehicle, and the noise level is not as much of a concern. Air intake and exhaust systems can be manufactured and modified for a variety of different sounds.

Back in 1863, physicist Herman Von Helmholtz did many studies regarding air-dampening devices. He discovered a resonator that uses the principle of sound waves colliding, resulting in the concept of canceling noise. The resonator can be used in the exhaust system to assist the muffler in further reducing noise. The resonator can also be used in the induction system. The benefit is the ability to muffle airflow noise. The Helmholtz resonator is basically a simple device consisting of a cavity with one or more short narrow tubes. For each application, the device must be precisely tuned. Concerning the air induction system, the resonator is installed between the air filter and the engine inlet. The design of the Helmholtz resonator creates a sound frequency that cancels out some of the engine noise. On some vehicles, there is a vacuum-activated valve that disables the effects of the resonator at certain rpm.

Applied | Science

AS-39: Carriers/Insulators: The technician can demonstrate an understanding of how sound generated in one place can be carried to other parts of the body or engine through metal and materials.

Sound travels through steel approximately 17 times faster than through the air. This is because the molecules in steel are closer together. Sound is produced when an object vibrates. Vibrations can pass from molecule to molecule quickly in materials such as steel.

When a vehicle has a bad wheel bearing that is producing a rumbling sound, it is often difficult to tell which of the four wheels the noise is coming from. In this case, you might try driving the vehicle alongside a building or a concrete block wall. Sound waves travel in all directions from their source. Some of them will strike the wall, and the noise will be reflected back toward the vehicle. A greater proportion of the sound waves will strike the wall when it is near the side of the vehicle with the faulty wheel bearing, meaning more sound waves will be reflected toward the vehicle. Thus, if the noise is louder when the passenger side is near the wall, the technician will know the faulty bearing is on the passenger side.

A mechanic's stethoscope can also be used to locate sounds on vehicles. The tip of the metal probe can be used to trace the sound to the source of the problem. There are now electronic devices that can be used to locate sounds on vehicles.

Diesel Induction Systems

The two main components of the four-stroke intake system are the air cleaner and the intake manifold. In a diesel engine, fuel is delivered directly to the combustion chamber. The intake system carries air only and typically does not have a throttle body. Diesels do not need a throttle plate to control engine rpm, since fuel delivery is what controls engine rpm. Most newer-model diesels equipped with an exhaust gas recirculation (EGR) valve use a throttle plate. The throttle plate on a diesel engine is designed to close off airflow to the engine to more easily introduce exhaust gases into the intake manifold, thus lowering cylinder temperatures and reducing oxides of nitrogen. The throttle plate can also be used in some diesel engines to govern the engine speed by simply closing down the amount of air that can be pulled into the engine.

To get more power on some diesel engines, one or more turbochargers or a supercharger is used to pressurize the air. Diesel engines may have more than one air cleaner, as needed for dealing with severe working conditions. The air cleaner is usually mounted away from the engine to obtain cleaner, cooler air.

Intake Manifolds

The intake manifold is usually a cast-iron, aluminum, or plastic part with several tubular branches. In a carbureted engine, the intake manifold directs the air–fuel mixture into the engine. The cross-sectional area of each tube needs to be kept small to maintain the high air speeds that improve vaporization. At the same time, intake manifold tube size should not be too small, since that restricts the airflow to the engine at higher speeds.

Intake Materials

Intake manifolds were originally made from cast iron, and later from light alloy metal castings. In modern vehicles, the intake manifold is made from special heat-resistant polymers and plastics **FIGURE 50-7**. Manifolds using this type of construction lighten manifold weight by up to 50% and contribute to higher fuel efficiency. These intake manifolds are normally molded from a glass fiber–reinforced grade of crystalline polymer that consists of a blend of syndiotactic polystyrene and polyamide. The polyamide nylon–based materials provide a good solution for these components because of their mechanical properties and their ease of processing during their manufacture. This type of material is ideally suited for replacing metal in under-the-hood applications because of its strength, stiffness, and chemical resistance under high-temperature operating conditions. In addition, intake manifolds made from polyamide nylon have improved the environmental performance of vehicles because of their light weight, which translates to improved fuel economy. The plastic can also be recycled, similar to cast iron and aluminum. The use of plastic has enabled more efficient airflow into the engine due to smoother surfaces of the manifold and

FIGURE 50-7 Plastic intake manifold.

has allowed for easier shaping of the manifold, creating better airflow characteristics.

Application of Intake Manifolds

The intake manifold has several tubular branches and carries air and/or air–fuel mixture from the air cleaner to the cylinder head. In carbureted engines and in throttle body injection systems, the intake manifold directs the air–fuel mixture into the engine. On many engines, the intake manifold has a mounting for the throttle body and a flange that bolts it onto the cylinder head. The cross-sectional area of each tube needs to be kept small to maintain the high air speeds that improve speed and turbulence. Yet, it cannot be too small, since that would restrict the airflow to the engine at higher engine speeds.

Cylinder heads that have intake and exhaust manifolds on opposite sides of the engine are known as cross-flow heads. That means the intake manifold is on one side and the exhaust manifold is on the other **FIGURE 50-8**. This design tends to produce more power because the flow of air moves more easily across the head rather than coming in and then turning back out the same side. Most modern engines are set up with a cross-flow cylinder head. The cross-flow head contains individual branches or ports to carry air and fuel into the combustion chamber. In past designs, two cylinders could share an intake port, but this design did not allow for free flow and was replaced with individual ports to allow for more power.

Variable Intake Systems

The air intake manifold for an electronic fuel injection multipoint engine normally has long branches of equal length. The long branches increase the pulsing effect of the airflow at lower engine rpm and help charge the cylinders.

FIGURE 50-8 Cross-flow head.

FIGURE 50-9 Changing intake manifold runner length allows power to be produced at more than one rpm range.

The more air drawn into the cylinder, the denser the air/fuel mixture is when the intake valve closes. The increased density of the air/fuel mixture determines how much pressure develops in the cylinder during combustion and the amount of force on the piston to turn the crankshaft.

The characteristic torque curve of a naturally aspirated engine depends mainly on how the engine's mean pressure changes across the rpm operating range. The design of the intake system largely determines the mass of air that can be drawn into a cylinder at a given engine speed; thus, the intake system largely determines the engine's torque curve. In general, a long intake manifold produces high torque at lower engine rpm because of the increased amount of time between the air pulses due to the inertia of the long column of air. The increased time between the pulses matches the longer time between lower rpm. Higher torque is obtained at higher engine rpm with a shorter intake manifold because of the shorter amount of time between the pulses due to the inertia of a shorter column of air. This ram air effect allows for more total airflow at and near the tuned rpm.

Manifolds that respond to changes in engine load and speed by changing their effective length in two or three stages are called variable inertia, or intake charging systems **FIGURE 50-9**. The primary section is long and narrow for the low range of rpm. The secondary section is shorter and wider for the high range of rpm. This combination maintains a high-speed airflow in the system. The three-stage manifold extends the torque curve even more, so that the torque curves overlap each other as advantageously as possible.

The different manifold stages are controlled by valves that are computer controlled by the engine management system to open at a specified engine speed and extend the torque output. The system is called intake manifold runner control (IMRC). Specific intake runner stages can be opened or closed off so that air is forced to run through the other set of runners. The runners are closed off by a butterfly-type valve that is moved by a stepper motor or vacuum actuator. The stepper motor or supply of vacuum is controlled by the engine control module.

Intake Air Heating

Heating of the intake manifold is required in a carbureted or throttle body–injected engine to provide greater vaporization of the fuel and to ensure that fuel does not collect on the cold walls, creating a lean mixture. Port fuel-injected or gasoline direct-injected intake manifolds do not normally need to be heated, since the manifold does not carry fuel. Also, the MAF sensor and intake air temperature sensor monitor the mass and temperature of the air entering the engine and send signals to the PCM so it can trigger the injectors to spray the proper amount of fuel to mix with the air.

There are several methods that manufacturers have used to heat intake manifolds, including hot engine coolant, hot exhaust gases, and electric heaters. Flowing hot engine coolant from the cooling system through passageways in the intake manifold heats the manifold **FIGURE 50-10**. However, it takes a while for the coolant to become hot, so this is not the fastest way to heat the intake manifold. Coolant continuously circulates through the manifold, even when the engine is fully warmed up.

Exhaust gases can also be directed through passageways in the intake manifold on V-type engines during engine warm-up. The hot exhaust gases are hot immediately and therefore heat the manifold up more quickly than coolant does. A heat riser valve at the end

FIGURE 50-10 Using hot engine coolant to heat the manifold.

This method was called an early fuel evaporation (EFE) system **FIGURE 50-12**. An enormous amount of heat passes through the exhaust manifold and is used to heat the incoming air. The heated air then enters the air cleaner and proceeds through the throttle body and intake manifold while it mixes with the fuel.

Once an engine is hot, the incoming air can become too hot, so the amount of hot air entering the engine needs to be controlled. On vehicles with emission controls, air cleaners use a thermostatic valve to control how much hot air enters the air cleaner. These systems are called heated air cleaners (HAC) and heated air systems (HAS). When the engine is started, only heated air is used. As engine temperature rises, the valve opens and

FIGURE 50-11 An electric heater.

of the exhaust manifold blocks most of the exhaust gases from exiting through the exhaust pipe. A passageway in the cylinder head directs the exhaust gases through a passageway in the cylinder head, through a chamber in the bottom of the intake manifold, out the passageway in the other cylinder head, and to the exhaust pipe on the other side of the engine. Once the engine is warm, the heat riser opens the valve in the exhaust, and exhaust gases can flow normally out of the exhaust pipe. If the heat riser valve sticks closed, the engine will run hotter than normal and will likely be low on power.

Electric heaters have also been used to preheat the air. A preheat grid is typically placed between the intake manifold and the throttle body **FIGURE 50-11**. During cold engine operation, current flows through the heating grid, warming the air passing through it. Once the engine reaches a certain temperature, the current flow to the grid is turned off and the engine operates normally. If the heater stays on too long, the heater grid can melt down, dropping particles down the intake manifold, which can damage the engine.

Another method of helping the fuel to vaporize in the intake manifold on carbureted and throttle body–injected engines is to warm the incoming air by passing it through a shroud around the exhaust manifold.

FIGURE 50-12 The heated air intake system, found on carbureted and throttle body injection systems, is used to ensure that fuel does not collect on the cold intake manifold.

blends cold ambient air with the hot air. This ensures that the temperature of the air supplied to the engine stays fairly constant. This valve can be a simple thermostatic (mechanical) type. Another way to control the amount of hot air is to use a vacuum control unit and a control valve mounted inside the air cleaner unit. The vacuum control unit has a diaphragm attached to the control valve. When a cold engine starts, vacuum from the intake manifold moves the diaphragm. It opens the valve and hot air flows into the air cleaner while closing the ambient air intake. A heat-sensitive valve in the air cleaner responds to changes in air temperature. Below a certain level, it opens, letting hot air flow into the air cleaner. As the temperature rises, it slowly closes, reducing the flow of hot air and blending in cooler air. When carburetors and the throttle body injection units were no longer installed in vehicles, heated intake air was no longer needed.

With a multipoint injection setup, the intake manifolds carry air only, so heating of the intake manifold is not needed. Also, the cross-sectional area of the tubes can be larger. Because more air can flow, the engine will produce more power. Fuel is injected directly into the intake ports of the cylinder head. The other possible fuel delivery method is the gasoline direct-injection system, which directs fuel straight into the combustion chamber. This system uses an intake similar to the multipoint injection setup, flowing air only through the intake. The fuel-injected engine manifold has a **plenum chamber** that provides a reservoir of air and helps prevent interference with the flow of air between individual branches. The plenum chamber is a large portion of the intake manifold after the throttle plate and before the intake runner tubes **FIGURE 50-13**.

Volumetric Efficiency

Volumetric efficiency compares the volume of air entering a cylinder during intake to the internal volume of the cylinder when the piston is at bottom dead center. It is usually expressed as a percentage. In a stock naturally aspirated engine, one without forced induction, volumetric efficiency can almost never be 100%. This is because of the resistance to the airflow that occurs at the throttle body, manifold, and intake valve **FIGURE 50-14**. However, some highly modified engines can exceed 100% due to the valve overlap being matched to the intake and exhaust manifold sizes and lengths, which maximize the ram air effect at the tuned rpm.

To understand volumetric efficiency, you must have a good understanding of the physics of airflow. Air likes to move in a straight manner and is affected by bends in the tubing that is used in the intake. Sharp bends force the air to move to the opposite side of the tube and force the air to pile up, slowing the airflow. Air also works like a bearing surface: Air near the surface of the manifold slows as friction of the tube wall resists its motion, while air in the center of the airstream tends to speed up as it moves over top of the slower air. All of these factors slow the airflow and reduce volumetric efficiency.

With forced induction, the incoming air is compressed by some sort of pump or compressor. Because of this greater pressure, a greater volume and mass of air is forced into the cylinder during the intake stroke, which takes the volumetric efficiency to well above 100%, increasing the engine's power output proportionately.

FIGURE 50-13 The port fuel injection manifold has a large open area, called the plenum chamber, and tubes that deliver air individually to each cylinder called intake runner tubes.

FIGURE 50-14 Volumetric efficiency of a normally aspirated engine.

Back-Pressure

Back-pressure in an exhaust system refers to a buildup of pressure in the system that interferes with the outward flow of exhaust gases. This area of high pressure acts as a kind of wall to stop gas flow. It can be caused by a blockage in a muffler or a similar restriction. One common cause of excessive back-pressure is a catalytic converter that has melted down and created a restriction in the exhaust stream. Catalytic converters become hotter as the combustible mixture is increased, such as from a misfire. The catalyst in the converter will melt if it gets hot enough and essentially block off the entrance to the small passageways. Back-pressure typically should be no more than 2.5 pounds per square inch (psi), or 17.2 kilopascals (kPa). If it is greater, it can create performance issues, as it will cause exhaust to back up into the combustion chamber, minimizing the amount of fresh air (combustible mixture) flowing into the engine. This reduces volumetric efficiency and engine power output.

Forced Induction

One way to improve engine output is to increase the amount of the air–fuel mixture that is burned in the cylinder (increasing volumetric efficiency). Volumetric efficiency can be boosted the most by what is called **forced induction**. Forced induction increases air pressure in the intake manifold above atmospheric pressure. Thus, an engine using forced induction can have a volumetric efficiency well above 100% **FIGURE 50-15**.

FIGURE 50-15 Volumetric efficiency of a forced induction engine.

One way to achieve forced induction is by using a turbocharger. A turbocharger uses energy that is normally wasted through the exhaust. Exhaust gases enter a turbine and make it spin. The turbine is connected to one end of a shaft, and a compressor is connected to the other. The more exhaust gases the engine produces, the faster the turbocharger spins and the more air is compressed and forced into the engine. Another way to achieve forced induction is to use a supercharger. A supercharger is turned by the crankshaft, compresses the air, and forces it into the engine. The faster the engine turns, the more air is moved by the supercharger.

Supercharger Systems

Power is produced when a mixture of air and fuel is burned inside an engine cylinder. If more air is forced into the cylinder, then more fuel can be burned and more power produced with each power stroke. A **supercharger** compresses the air in the intake system to above atmospheric pressure, which increases the density of the air entering the engine. Naturally aspirated engines operate with uncompressed air at atmospheric pressure, 14.7 psi (101 kPa). But a supercharger boosts that pressure another 6 psi (41.4 kPa) or higher.

In a supercharged system, there is a greater air mass flow rate—that is, a higher density and speed of airflow. Air pressure is increased by the compressor on the way into the engine and more fuel is added, which creates more pressure and power. The increased pressure causes the exhaust gases to exit much more rapidly, making the timing and exhaust sizing less important. Also, any residual gases will have less of an effect on the airflow entering the combustion chamber, since the supercharger boosts the manifold pressure substantially.

Although some of the extra power produced must be used to drive the supercharger, the net result is more total power from the crankshaft. The supercharger may include a **bypass valve** system that allows the supercharger to "idle" when "high power" is not required, releasing the pressure back to the supercharger inlet and allowing the engine to run without boost. The bypass valve can be mounted remotely or directly onto the intake port **FIGURE 50-16**. It allows air to move back past the compressor portion of the supercharger, keeping boost pressure low.

Several types of superchargers are manufactured for use on vehicles. The oldest version is the roots-style supercharger, which uses lobes to move air. This type of the supercharger does not compress air at the lobes, but rather pushes air around the sides of the housing and into the intake. It uses the stacking of the air against the intake valves to build boost pressure as the lobes come together and prevent air from leaking back between them. Another

FIGURE 50-16 The supercharger compresses air to feed to the intake and is run by the engine crankshaft.

FIGURE 50-17 The turbocharger compresses air to feed to the intake and is run by exhaust gases.

version of the supercharger is the twin screw type. The twin screw supercharger compresses air between the screws and forces it into the intake. This compressor design is very efficient but very expensive. Many after-market high-performance superchargers are centrifugal. This supercharger shaft is turned by a drive belt from the crankshaft and spins a compressor wheel, similar to what is used in the turbocharger. The supercharger shaft is connected by a set of gears to create a higher speed of the compressor. Since compressing air heats the air up, a heat exchanger can be located between it and the intake manifold. The heat exchanger is like a radiator that the air flows through to cool it before entering the engine.

Turbocharger Systems

A **turbocharger** is a forced induction system that uses wasted kinetic energy from the exhaust gases to increase the intake pressure. Like superchargers, turbochargers increase the amount of air that flows into the engine, but they have a negative effect on the flow of air out of the engine. This means that for maximum power output, valves, cam timing, and exhaust system design are more important in turbocharged systems than in supercharged systems.

The turbocharger uses exhaust gases to turn a turbine fan. A shaft connects the turbine to a centrifugal compressor **FIGURE 50-17**. The compressor compresses the air and forces it under pressure into the intake manifold. Since the turbine is turned by exhaust gases, it runs at very high temperatures. It, along with the compressor, can rotate at well over 100,000 rpm. The turbocharger needs a good supply of clean oil to lubricate the bearings and carry excess heat away from the turbocharger. Some engines also supply coolant to the turbocharger body to improve cooling.

FIGURE 50-18 The turbocharger wastegate actuator controls the amount of boost pressure going to the intake manifold.

Higher engine speeds mean increased exhaust gas volume, and that makes the turbocharger spin faster and force more air into the cylinders, which can damage the engine if allowed to get too high. When pressure increases in an engine, so does cylinder temperature. As the temperature increases, the possibility of detonation also increases, since the gasoline will ignite before the piston reaches the proper position in the cylinder. To control this risk of detonation, a device called a **wastegate** is installed on the exhaust inlet of the turbocharger. When air pressure in the intake manifold reaches a preset level, the wastegate automatically directs the exhaust gases so they bypass the turbine **FIGURE 50-18**. The wastegate can also be computer controlled to reduce intake air pressure in the case of detonation or knocking.

On a mechanically operated wastegate, the spring pressure in the diaphragm controls the pressure at which the wastegate valve opens. The wastegate actuator is a spring-loaded pressure diaphragm that moves when air pushes against it. The air moves into the chamber of the wastegate actuator and presses on the diaphragm, overcoming the spring force. This causes the control linkage to push the wastegate open, allowing exhaust gases to bypass the turbine wheel, which reduces the boost pressure. This process happens over again, and as pressure drops, the wastegate closes and allows exhaust to flow to the turbine wheel again. The wastegate actuator gets pressure from a line connected to the intake manifold. The wastegate can be computer controlled by a boost solenoid that delays the intake pressure from reaching the wastegate actuator. The computer receives information from the manifold absolute pressure sensor, which tells how much pressure is in the intake manifold.

A pressure relief valve may also be installed so that if the wastegate should fail, it can prevent an abnormal rise in manifold pressure. This relief valve is also known as a **blow-off valve**. A blow-off valve works against spring pressure, and as boost pressure rises above a predetermined amount, the pressure will push the valve against the spring pressure and open it, allowing excess pressure to "blow off" into the atmosphere.

The blow-off valve may also vent the pressure to the air cleaner box to reduce the turbocharger pressure release noise. The blow-off valve is located in the air intake tubing connected to the intake manifold. It is also used to ensure that when the throttle is abruptly shut, pressure does not rise excessively between the throttle body and the turbocharger compressor wheel **FIGURE 50-19**.

If pressure rises excessively, **compressor surge** will occur. Compressor surge is when manifold pressure rises above normal and works against the spinning exhaust turbine wheel, slowing it considerably. The pressure wave can then flow backward out of the compressor, creating a fluttering noise and continued pressure waves. Compressor surge, which is recognizable by a rapid fluttering sound, can be damaging to the compressor wheel, since the backing up pressure wave forces the wheel to slow.

Applied	Science

AS-40: Decibels/Intensity: The technician can demonstrate an understanding of how sound intensity can be measured.

The degree of loudness is measured in units called decibels (dB). The average human can hear sounds between 0 and 120 dB. One-time exposure to noises above 120 dB, or sustained exposure above 85 dB, can damage the ears. Decibels can be measured with a sound pressure level meter. These meters are available in analog and digital styles.

As a baseline, the decibel level of some common sounds are as follows:

- Conversational speech at a distance of 3 feet: 60 dB
- A diesel truck engine at a distance of 30 feet: 90 dB
- A chain saw at a distance of 3 feet: 110 dB
- A jet aircraft at takeoff at a distance of 150 feet: 150 dB

Technicians should be concerned about the decibel rating of sounds in the workplace as well as the exposure time. The length of time that a person is exposed to the sound is a very important factor. For example, the CDC recommends that a person should be exposed to a sound pressure level of 100 dB for no more than 15 minutes. Ear protection should be worn to protect your hearing based on the decibel rating and exposure time.

Since the turbocharger uses the energy of the exhaust gases, there is a short delay between when a driver opens the throttle and when maximum power is available. This delay is called turbo lag, and on larger engines, it can be quite noticeable if the turbocharger is not sized correctly. Because a turbocharger recycles heat energy that would otherwise be lost, a turbocharged engine can increase an engine's efficiency and fuel economy—as long as the vehicle is being driven conservatively. However, even though a turbocharger may seem to be offering additional energy for nothing, it can introduce problems of its own. The extra heat and power it generates can put an extra load on the engine's cooling and lubrication systems. This is why most turbocharged vehicles have shorter service intervals for oil changes than nonturbocharged vehicles.

As the air passes through the turbocharger, it heats up. Hot air is less dense than cool air, so it tries to expand

FIGURE 50-19 The blow-off valve is a spring-loaded valve that releases excessive pressure in the air intake tube going to the intake manifold.

again, and some of the benefits of compressing it are lost. To stop this expansion and improve efficiency, some engines use an intercooler to cool the compressed air. It fits between the turbocharger and the engine. It typically uses outside air to cool the compressed air, but on some applications, it may use the engine's cooling system to cool the compressed air.

When the turbocharger housing is large, boost pressure is higher at high speed, but lag is worse for a given exhaust flow. When the housing is small, boost pressure is high at lower speeds, but a restriction occurs in the exhaust system at high rpm. To combat turbo lag and avoid creating a restriction, several designs have been made. The first is the twin scroll turbocharger, which uses two passageways into the turbine housing from the exhaust manifold. The one passageway is controlled by a flap that can be closed to accelerate the exhaust flow, making the turbocharger operate at a higher boost at low engine speeds.

Another way to improve the turbo lag issue is to use twin turbochargers. Many manufacturers use two small turbochargers (one on each bank of the engine) that can spin up more quickly, thereby creating boost sooner. The turbo lag is decreased as boost is created at a lower engine speed, and yet additional boost is created at a higher speed since there are two turbochargers to deal with the total exhaust flow.

The final way to create boost pressure without lag is to use a variable-geometry turbocharger. The variable-geometry turbocharger uses a set of movable vanes or fingers that change the flow of exhaust gases through the turbine housing. Under low exhaust speed, the fingers are positioned so that the exhaust gases spin the turbine faster, creating boost. Under high rpm, the speed of the exhaust gases is very high; therefore, the fingers are moved so they do not overspeed the turbine while also not restricting the exhaust flow and creating backup of exhaust, which would lower power. This type of turbocharger offers the best of both worlds. Currently it is used on Ford's Powerstroke series of diesels.

Another new development in turbocharger technology is used on the BMW engine. The engine design uses reverse flow cylinder heads. The center of the V-type engine, which normally was for intake, is now for the exhaust passages. Exhaust leaves the head and moves into the twin turbochargers, one per engine bank. The intake manifold is now on the outside of the head. The different positioning of the turbochargers keeps exhaust temperatures high and produces more turbine speed, which increases the efficiency of the turbocharger. The catalytic converter also gets up to temperature faster, reducing emissions.

Applied Science

AS-41: Frequency/Hertz: The technician can explain how frequency of a sound can be used to identify normal and abnormal operating systems.
A vehicle is making a high-pitched whining sound upon acceleration. The sound seemed very abnormal to the owner of the vehicle, and it is now in the shop for diagnosis and repair. The technician test-drives the vehicle to verify the concern.

In a short distance, the technician verifies the high-pitched whining sound. The technician uses a mechanic's stethoscope to discover that the abnormal sound is coming from the alternator. Further diagnostic testing reveals that the alternator has a bad diode that is causing the whining sound. The recommendation to the customer is to replace the alternator.

Concerning the properties of sound, frequency is the number of waves produced in a given time. The frequency of sound waves determines the audible pitch, either high or low. Hertz is the unit used to measure the frequency of sound waves or pitch.

AS-42: Hearing: The technician can demonstrate an understanding of the role of listening for unusual sounds as part of a troubleshooting process.
A vehicle has been towed to a dealership with a no-start condition. A technician has been assigned to determine the cause of the problem. To assure that the cranking voltage will be sufficient, the technician connects a booster pack to the battery. While an assistant attempts to start the vehicle, the technician listens to the cranking rhythm of the engine. The engine has a very uneven cranking rhythm, which indicates uneven compression between cylinders. Using diagnostic equipment, the technician verifies that the engine has very low compression on several cylinders and has a broken timing belt. When the timing belt broke, many of the engine's valves were bent, resulting in the low compression.

Listening for unusual sounds can be an essential part of a troubleshooting process. It is helpful to use other methods as well to verify the diagnosis.

Intercoolers

A turbocharger or supercharger is used to increase the volume of air in the engine cylinder by compressing the air above atmospheric pressure. However, when air is compressed, it heats up, which causes the volume of the gas to increase, which lowers the air density. Hot air under pressure in a cylinder contains fewer oxygen molecules than cooler air at the same pressure in the same volume.

The purpose of an intercooler is to reduce the intake air temperature up to a few hundred degrees Fahrenheit before it enters the intake manifold. Decreasing air temperature increases the density of the pressurized

FIGURE 50-20 The intercooler cools compressed air to bring the temperature down before it is pushed into the intake.

FIGURE 50-21 The exhaust system prevents harmful exhaust gases from entering the passenger compartment, reduces the noise of combustion, removes exhaust gases from the engine, and reduces harmful emissions in the exhaust stream.

air and improves engine efficiency. The intercooler is most efficient when the turbocharger's boost pressure is near its maximum, typically above 15 psi, or 100 kPa. Most intercoolers operate on an air-to-air principle, by feeding compressed air from the turbocharger through the intercooler and then into the intake manifold. The intercooler works like a radiator. Inside it, the air passes through small tubes with thin fins attached. The heated compressed air flowing through the intercooler heats up the fins and the tubes, and as the vehicle moves forward, the cool outside air flowing across the fins pulls heat away from the tubes and fins. This heat transfer occurs constantly during engine operation. Some larger engine applications have a liquid-operated intercooler **FIGURE 50-20**. In this system, the air is fed through small tubes in a heat exchanger, and the vehicle coolant absorbs the heat and transfers it to the engine cooling system.

► The Exhaust System

The exhaust system is made up of several components that work together to perform four main functions: remove exhaust gases from the engine, quiet the exhaust noise, ensure that poisonous exhaust gases do not enter the passenger compartment, and reduce harmful emissions in the exhaust stream **FIGURE 50-21**. Exhaust flow is described as follows: Burned gases exit the cylinder through the exhaust port and pass into the exhaust manifold. The first pipe is usually called the engine pipe or down pipe. The down pipe is connected to the outlet of the manifold, which carries the exhaust gases to the catalytic converter. Catalytic converters were introduced in vehicles in the mid-1970s and were designed to reduce

exhaust emissions. The exhaust exits the converter and continues on through an intermediate pipe to the muffler, which reduces exhaust noise. Exhaust gases are then either passed through a resonator or simply discharged to the atmosphere through a tailpipe, usually at the rear, to the side or above the vehicle.

During engine operation, each time an exhaust valve opens, a pulse of hot exhaust gases is forced into the exhaust manifold. These hot gases produce a lot of noise, some of it at very high frequency. Even while quieting the exhaust noise, the exhaust system can be designed to enhance engine operation and efficiency. In fact, a well-designed system can improve drivability and performance.

Exhaust System Components

Exhaust Manifold

The exhaust manifold is bolted to the engine's cylinder head. It also usually provides a mounting place near its outlet for the oxygen sensor, since it is advantageous to position the sensor as close to the cylinders as possible. This position will help it warm up faster during a cold start. The exhaust manifold can be of a one-piece or a two-piece construction. It is usually made from either cast iron or stainless steel. Due to the extreme temperatures generated at the exhaust manifold, heat shields can be installed to protect other vehicle components from heat damage.

On many current vehicles, the exhaust manifold is often replaced with a header. The **header** is an exhaust manifold made of mandrel-formed steel tubes that are of equal lengths and join at a common collector. **Mandrel forming** is the use of a special pipe-bending tool to ensure that piping bends in a smooth arc and will not collapse, which would create a partial restriction. The equal length of the pipes ensures that the exhaust pulses create a more equal airflow out of each cylinder. Exhaust manifolds can be restricting, forcing the pistons to work harder to push the exhaust gases out. A header is freer flowing, allowing gases to leave the engine quickly **FIGURE 50-22**.

The headers also provide a **scavenging** effect to help remove exhaust gases from the cylinders. The outgoing pulse from one cylinder is timed to arrive at the junction at exactly the right time to help draw out the pulse from another cylinder. This setup is called tuned exhaust, and the lengths of the header tubes determine the rpm range they are tuned to. Tuned exhaust is widely used on high-performance vehicles and race cars. Performance gains can be realized by ensuring that exhaust gases flow freely, so that the engine can pull air in and push exhaust out efficiently. When a Formula One car is produced, extreme attention is given to exhaust tuning to ensure that the exhaust will flow correctly, resulting in the maximum power for the engine.

Engine Pipe

The engine pipe, or down pipe, is attached to the exhaust manifold and connects to the catalytic converter. The engine pipe is usually made of a nickel chromium material, which resists rust and corrosion to ensure it is long lasting. Some exhaust down pipes may also use stainless steel to ensure long life. The engine pipe may be attached to the exhaust manifold by spring-loaded bolts that allow the exhaust to move slightly as the engine moves in its mounts. Some engine pipes also have flexible connectors that allow flexing of the engine pipe as the engine moves in its mounts **FIGURE 50-23**.

Flexible Connections

There may be a flexible connection between the engine pipe and an intermediate pipe. The flexible connector is used close to the gap. Its main functions are to allow engine movement and to reduce vibration without passing it along the exhaust—especially in front-wheel drive vehicles **FIGURE 50-24**. The flexible connector also helps with the alignment of the pipes as the engine moves under load.

Catalytic Converter

A catalytic converter is used to convert unacceptable exhaust pollutants, such as carbon monoxide, hydrocarbons, and oxides of nitrogen into less dangerous substances. Three-way converters convert oxides of nitrogen back into nitrogen and oxygen, and the

FIGURE 50-23 The engine pipe connects the exhaust manifold to the catalytic converter and may contain a flexible connector.

FIGURE 50-22 An exhaust manifold is typically made of cast iron, and a header is made of steel tubing of equal length.

FIGURE 50-24 The flexible connector is used to allow the pipe to flex as the engine moves.

hydrocarbons and carbon monoxide to water and carbon dioxide. Older two-way catalytic converters converted hydrocarbons and carbon monoxide to water and carbon dioxide, but were not able to convert the oxides of nitrogen. A catalytic converter fits in line with the exhaust system. It is located close to the exhaust manifold so that it can reach its operating temperature as soon as possible **FIGURE 50-25**. Some manufacturers install a catalytic converter in the base of the exhaust manifold and another one downstream before the muffler.

Catalytic converters can become contaminated by lead and silicone. Leaded fuel must not be used in an engine with a catalytic converter, because lead will coat the catalyst and prevent it from doing its job. Some types of silicone sealer will also coat the catalyst. Once coated, the converter will most likely need to be replaced.

The catalytic converter operates by beginning and then maintaining a chemical reaction in the exhaust gases. It usually creates heat as it is converting the harmful gases to less harmful ones, so it can get extremely hot. Because of this, it has a heat shield to prevent heat from radiating to bodywork and other parts. The catalytic converter is covered in greater detail in the Emission Control chapter.

Exhaust Brackets

The exhaust components are supported along the length of the vehicle by brackets suspended from the underbody. The supports are usually rubber mounted and help isolate the vibrations of the exhaust from the main body of the vehicle. Rubber is preferred because of its natural dampening effect **FIGURE 50-26**.

FIGURE 50-25 The catalytic converter is located after the engine pipe and before the muffler. It changes harmful gases into nonharmful gases to be released to the atmosphere.

FIGURE 50-26 The exhaust is supported by rubber mounts that ensure that vibration is not felt by the driver.

Intermediate Pipe

The intermediate pipe connects the catalytic converter to the muffler. This pipe can be made to fit inside of the pipe of the catalytic converter and may be sealed with an exhaust clamp. The pipe may also have flanges on the ends that bolt to a flange on the catalytic converter and will have a gasket between the bolted flanges to seal the exhaust in.

The Muffler System

The function of a vehicle's muffler is to minimize the sounds coming from the exhaust system. These sounds originate from the combustion process within the engine. Exhaust noise becomes an issue as vehicle systems become generally quieter and as the number of vehicles on our roads increases.

To understand the operation of modern exhaust noise reduction systems, it is helpful to understand what sound is. We sense sound with our eardrum, located within the ear. The eardrum is made to move by variations in air pressure. Variations in air pressure can be created when a force is placed upon an object. An example is clapping your hands. As the two hands collide, they push the air surrounding them away. The moving air creates a wave of air pressure, or a sound wave. This sound wave moves your eardrum, which is interpreted as sound by your brain.

The engine produces noise, since each combustion process is a rapid burning of air and fuel—a controlled explosion. These explosions create a great deal of noise if they are not absorbed or canceled. *Noise absorption* refers to putting a sound material around a perforated pipe that the exhaust gases flow through. This is similar to placing noise-absorbing materials inside the walls of a house to make the rooms quieter. *Noise cancellation* is a system

Applied Science

AS-43: Noise/Acoustics: The technician can demonstrate an understanding of why the acoustics of the vehicle affect specific noises.

The acoustics of a vehicle is related to the behavior of sound waves in an enclosed space. Noise can enter the passenger compartment from a number of sources. The road noise when driving is one source of noise. Engine noise, tire noise, wind noise, and the noise of other vehicles are other sources. Dampening material around the vehicle cabin is a very good method of noise reduction.

Current automotive technology includes improvements in acoustic materials around the passenger compartment. Insulation is placed in trunk panels, rear wheel wells, doors, and the roof, as well as under the carpet. All of this insulation reduces unwanted environmental noise.

Today's vehicles differ widely in the way they are manufactured as related to noise and acoustic factors. On some vehicles, to reduce weight and be more price competitive, insulation and dampening materials have been reduced. In comparison, luxury vehicles may have more than 100 pounds of sound-deadening material placed carefully in the most needed areas to ensure a quiet environment.

Technicians should understand that noises may not be the same in all vehicles due to variations in manufacturing. The acoustics of a particular vehicle may differ widely as compared to another. On one type of vehicle, it may be typical for the driver to report a squealing sound from under the hood before a water pump failed. On another, the engine covers and multiple layers of dampening material between the engine and the passenger compartment may have a different effect on the driver hearing abnormal engine sounds.

AS-44: Overtones/Harmonics: The technician can explain that the presence of overtones may indicate changes in vibration in systems.

A technician in a luxury car dealership has replaced a number of water pumps on a certain model of a popular vehicle. The published labor rate for this water pump replacement is 11.2 hours. This greatly exceeds the average water pump replacement labor rate by three or four times.

The technician has observed that the water pump on this particular vehicle tends to have a slightly noisy bearing before it fails. As a preventive measure, the technician uses a stethoscope to listen to the sound of the water pump bearing when vehicles of this model are in for basic service. The pump sounds are checked with the stethoscope at idle, at 1000 rpm, and again at 1500 rpm. Over the years, the technician has developed the listening skills with his stethoscope to evaluate the condition of the water pump bearing on this particular vehicle model. When an abnormal condition exists during the stethoscope evaluation, the technician is aware of the situation and can detect the presence of an overtone, which is a higher tone above the average tone. This condition may indicate the first sign of a bearing with excessive vibration. The technician will make a record of his findings on the repair order to alert the owner of this concern. It would be better for the owner to schedule this service rather than having a water pump failure on a long trip.

that prevents the sound waves from leaving the exhaust system by canceling them out inside the muffler. These systems create gas pressures that are equal in force but opposite in direction to the noise source. These generated pressures are known as anti-noise. Any remaining sound is referred to as residual noise.

The muffler is designed to quiet the noises of combustion without restricting exhaust flow to the point of adversely affecting performance. The goal is to produce a vehicle that is smooth and quiet as well as powerful. A muffler may use a dissipative technique, which is sound absorption, or a noise-canceling technique, or both. Exhaust noise can be reduced by various means, including baffles and chambers, variable-flow exhaust, and electronic mufflers.

TECHNICIAN TIP

Pedestrians are faced with the opposite problem when dealing with hybrid and electric vehicles—the vehicles are too quiet. It is easy for pedestrians who are visually or hearing impaired, or who just aren't paying close attention, to walk out in front of one of these vehicles while it is operating on electric power. Federal guidelines are being written to address this issue.

Baffles and Chambers

The dissipative type muffler uses a perforated tube or baffle that is wrapped in fiberglass material, and this will absorb the noise of combustion as gases flow past. The baffle then gets welded or bolted into the exhaust pipe. Typically, aftermarket motorcycle mufflers have removable baffles to allow the owner to rewrap the fiberglass insulation or to remove it if a louder exhaust note is wanted.

The noise-canceling technique uses a large chamber that the exhaust pipe enters. The exhaust flows into the large chamber, and the exhaust gases bounce off of the chamber's wall. The exhaust gases bounce back toward the incoming gases, and the pressure waves collide, canceling the noise. The exhaust gases then flow out the opposite pipe to the tailpipe. There are several variations to the design of the noise-canceling muffler, which are intended to produce less back-pressure **FIGURE 50-27**.

Variable-Flow Exhaust

A moveable valve built within the exhaust system is used to change the path for exhaust to flow as well as the amount of exhaust back-pressure. This system is used on many high-end performance vehicles to ensure they meet noise restrictions. The system operates in two stages. In the first stage, when the engine rpm and throttle position are low, the exhaust takes a longer route through two or more mufflers/resonators. This design provides a longer path through silencers before the exhaust is expelled. It also provides a small amount of back-pressure, which further lowers the exhaust noise as well as the hydrocarbon emissions during valve overlap at low rpm. When the throttle is opened and engine speed increases, the second stage is activated. A valve opens and allows the exhaust to bypass some of the silencers in the system, making the exhaust path more free-flowing. The valve can be operated by:

- Exhaust gas pressure
- Vacuum diaphragm
- Electronic actuator

Adding a variable-flow exhaust to the baffle or chamber system reduces emission noise. This is because the system can partially respond to changes in engine speed and load. A version of this system is typically found on high-end exotics such as Ferrari, Aston Martin, or Lamborghini.

Electronic Mufflers

Any restriction to exhaust flow in the exhaust system creates back-pressure. Although some back-pressure can be beneficial, excessive back-pressure reduces volumetric efficiency. This in turn reduces engine efficiency. Electronic mufflers are designed to produce anti-noise without restricting exhaust flow. This computer-controlled system uses a microphone to detect the sound waves produced within the exhaust system. A computer-driven loudspeaker is operated to generate equal but opposite sound waves to cancel the exhaust noises. This use of opposing sound waves is sometimes called anti-noise. The anti-noise is applied to the exhaust stream in an electronic muffler. The result is a virtually silent exhaust without generating additional and unwanted back-pressure across all engine operating conditions. This system increases fuel economy and reduces exhaust emissions. The electronic muffler is a research part at the moment and has never been released on a production vehicle.

> ## TECHNICIAN TIP
>
> Some vehicles use the audio system to cancel noise inside the passenger compartment in order to combat engine noise. This is done in two ways. The first is to use the entertainment system to actively cancel engine and road noise. The second way is to use a speed-sensitive entertainment system that adjusts the volume of the entertainment system according to vehicle speed: low volume at low speed and higher volume at higher speed. This helps overcome objectionable noise.

Resonator

Some manufacturers use a resonator in the exhaust system. It is located between the muffler and the exhaust outlet. Its function is to reduce any resonance levels that the muffler could not adequately suppress **FIGURE 50-28**. Some manufacturers may use more than one resonator to quiet the combustion noises even further. Some resonators work on the Helmholtz principle—namely that air blown across a tube connected to a rounded container will create a vibration, and noise is produced, similar to

FIGURE 50-27 The muffler is one of two types of designs, either the dissipative type or the noise-canceling type.

FIGURE 50-28 The resonator is an assistant to the muffler to ensure engine noises are canceled adequately.

air blown across a bottle. This principle is then used to cancel noise by bouncing waves off of each other, reducing their intensity, which lowers the exhaust noise.

Applied Science

AS-45: Pitch/Frequency: The technician can explain the relationship of pitch to frequency.
Heinrich Hertz, a German physicist, was the first to prove the existence of electromagnetic waves. He did so by engineering a radio wave transmitter. In honor of his work, the unit for measuring frequency, hertz, is named after him. Because it is named after a person, its abbreviation (Hz) begins with a capital letter.

Frequency is the number of sound waves produced in a given time. The frequency of a sound wave determines its pitch, described in terms of how "high" or "low" the sound is. Humans can perceive sound waves ranging from 20 Hz (lowest pitch) to 20,000 Hz (highest pitch).

The concept of sound is based on the principle that a sound wave begins with a vibrating object. The frequency of a sound wave, or Hz, can be expressed as 1 Hz = 1 vibration/second. A diesel-powered generator used for backup electrical purposes is a 60-Hz unit, which is standard for the industry.

AS-46: Resonance: The technician can demonstrate an understanding of what happens when an object resonates.
In physics, resonance refers to the amplitude at which an object vibrates at a given frequency. There are a number of different types of resonance, including mechanical resonance. When a large group of soldiers are marching across a bridge, they are told to break step in order to avoid damaging the bridge's structure. If the soldiers' footsteps were to fall simultaneously, extreme vibrations could result, which the bridge might not be able to withstand.

In automotive applications, a vehicle with a tire that is out of balance vibrates when traveling at a certain speed. Resonance issues are often experienced in exhaust systems that have been modified and can produce a droning noise from vibration. Vehicle manufacturers in some cases have found it necessary to add mass (weight) to the various exhaust components to change the resonance frequency.

Tailpipe

The tailpipe takes the exhaust gases away from the vehicle. Its exit point must not allow any of the exhaust gases to enter the vehicle. The tailpipe is connected to the muffler and is held by flexible exhaust mounts. It is made of a non-corrosive and rust-resistant material to ensure long life.

Exhaust Gaskets

Exhaust components are sometimes bolted together. If they are, they may need to have a gasket to seal them. Exhaust gaskets can be found between the engine cylinder head and the exhaust manifold, the engine pipe and the catalytic converter, and possibly the catalytic converter and the muffler. The exhaust is extremely hot, so the gaskets must withstand the temperatures without burning **FIGURE 50-29**. Exhaust gaskets can be multilayered high-temperature alloys that are formed with graphite or mica to provide a good seal as exhaust components move with expansion and contraction. Donut gaskets are another type of exhaust gasket. They use spiral wound steel and filler material, which is shaped into a round design, that, when installed in ball-shaped pipe, provides seal while allowing the pipes to be joined even if they are slightly out of line. Some of these gaskets also allow for slight movement of the engine.

Ceramic Coatings

High-performance developments are being continuously incorporated into on-road vehicles as efficiency gains are sought. One technology that is now becoming commonplace is the use of metallic ceramic coatings. The most common applications for ceramic coatings are on the exhaust system, intake manifolds, and exhaust headers. When ceramic thermal barrier coatings are applied to exhaust manifolds or headers, they provide two advantages. First, they protect the headers from rust and corrosion, and second, they reduce heat loss, which can be translated into higher engine output. If the exhaust headers are internally coated, the hot exhaust gases travel at a higher velocity with less turbulence due to the smoother surface inside the system.

Internally, applying ceramic coating to the cylinder head's combustion chamber and exhaust ports has the effect of creating a thermal barrier from the hot gases to the cylinder head itself. This allows more of the thermal energy to be converted to mechanical energy, increasing an engine's efficiency. It also protects the base metal

FIGURE 50-29 Exhaust gaskets come in many forms and are used in the extreme temperature of the exhaust system.

from excess heat. The primary benefits of using metallic ceramic coatings are:

- A metallic ceramic coating, when applied to metal surfaces, protects against rust and corrosion and extends component life.
- As a thermal barrier, a ceramic coating enhances engine performance and significantly reduces engine compartment and component temperature.
- A ceramic coating will not chip, crack, or peel, and it can survive bending and thermal shock.
- A ceramic coating is highly resistant to corrosives.
- A ceramic coating can survive base metal temperatures up to 2000°F or 1100°C.
- A ceramic coating can come in a range of surface finishes and colors to suit a particular application.
- A ceramic coating is easily cleaned.

 ## Diagnosis and Testing

Inspecting the Throttle Body and the Induction System

The throttle body and the induction system ensure that the engine gets airflow into the cylinders. The throttle body allows control of engine rpm. If the induction system gaskets leak, engine performance problems will result. Some vehicles use a MAF sensor to send airflow information to the PCM. The PCM uses this information to accurately deliver fuel. If air leaks are present in the induction system downstream of the MAF sensor, then the sensor will not be able to measure the air coming into the engine. This additional air is sometimes referred to as "false air." As a result, the PCM will not deliver enough fuel based on the MAF signal and the engine will tend to run lean.

There are several ways to test for air leaks, including using a substitute fuel to artificially enrich the mixture at the point of the leak, using a smoke machine to fill the intake system and show any external leaks, and using an electronic stethoscope (or piece of heater hose) to listen for and pinpoint the leak. The use of a substitute fuel such as acetylene, propane, or carburetor cleaner is a quick and accurate method, but you risk catching the engine on fire. The technician carefully directs a small amount of fuel toward any suspected leaking components **FIGURE 50-30**. If an intake gasket is leaking, the vacuum will pull the gas into the intake manifold and the engine rpm will increase, or smooth out. If the engine has an idle control system, the rpm may not change much, except slightly when you uncover the leak and when you pull the fuel away. You may need to disable the system, or hold the throttle open just enough that the control system is not controlling the idle. You may also be able to use a scan tool to watch oxygen, short-term fuel trim, and injector

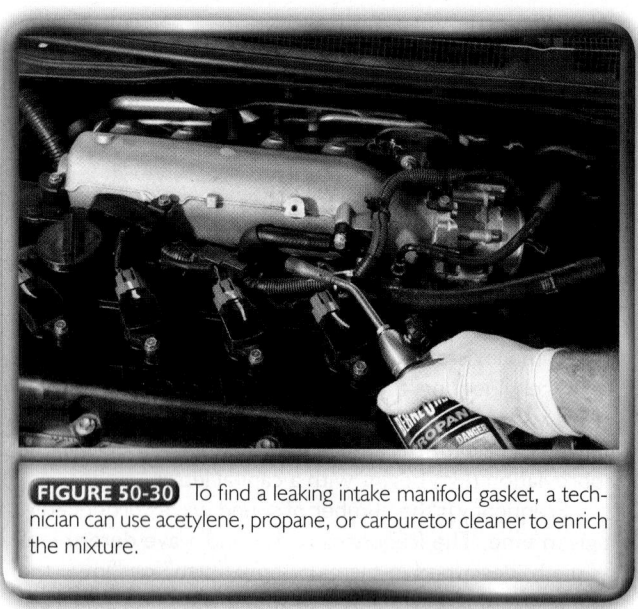

FIGURE 50-30 To find a leaking intake manifold gasket, a technician can use acetylene, propane, or carburetor cleaner to enrich the mixture.

pulse-width readings while applying and removing the acetylene or propane.

Leaks can also happen in the duct work, hoses, and diaphragms that are connected to the intake manifold, creating a false air condition. While the acetylene and propane may still find the leak, a smoke machine is invaluable. The smoke machine pushes smoke at low pressure out of the hose and into the intake manifold. The smoke machine can then be used to fill the entire intake system with smoke. If there are any leaks, the smoke will leak from inside the system to the outside. So anywhere the smoke is leaking from is an air leak. A high-intensity light can be used to make the smoke more visible.

Safety

Be careful using carburetor cleaner, or any flammable liquid, on a hot engine. Carburetor cleaner is a flammable material.

To inspect the throttle body, air induction system, and intake manifold for leaks, follow the steps in **SKILL DRILL 50-1**:

1. Start the engine and let the idle stabilize.
2. *Acetylene or a propane testing approach:* Place the hose near the suspected leak area. **(Photo 1)**
3. Open the fuel valve to slowly release the acetylene or propane. **(Photo 2)**
4. On vehicles without an idle control system, observe the rpm and smoothness of the engine. If the engine speed increases or smoothes out, then a vacuum leak is present. Determine any necessary repairs.
5. On vehicles with an idle control system, connect a scan tool and select data stream. Observe the

SKILL DRILL | 50-1 | Inspecting the Throttle Body, Air Induction System, and Intake Manifold

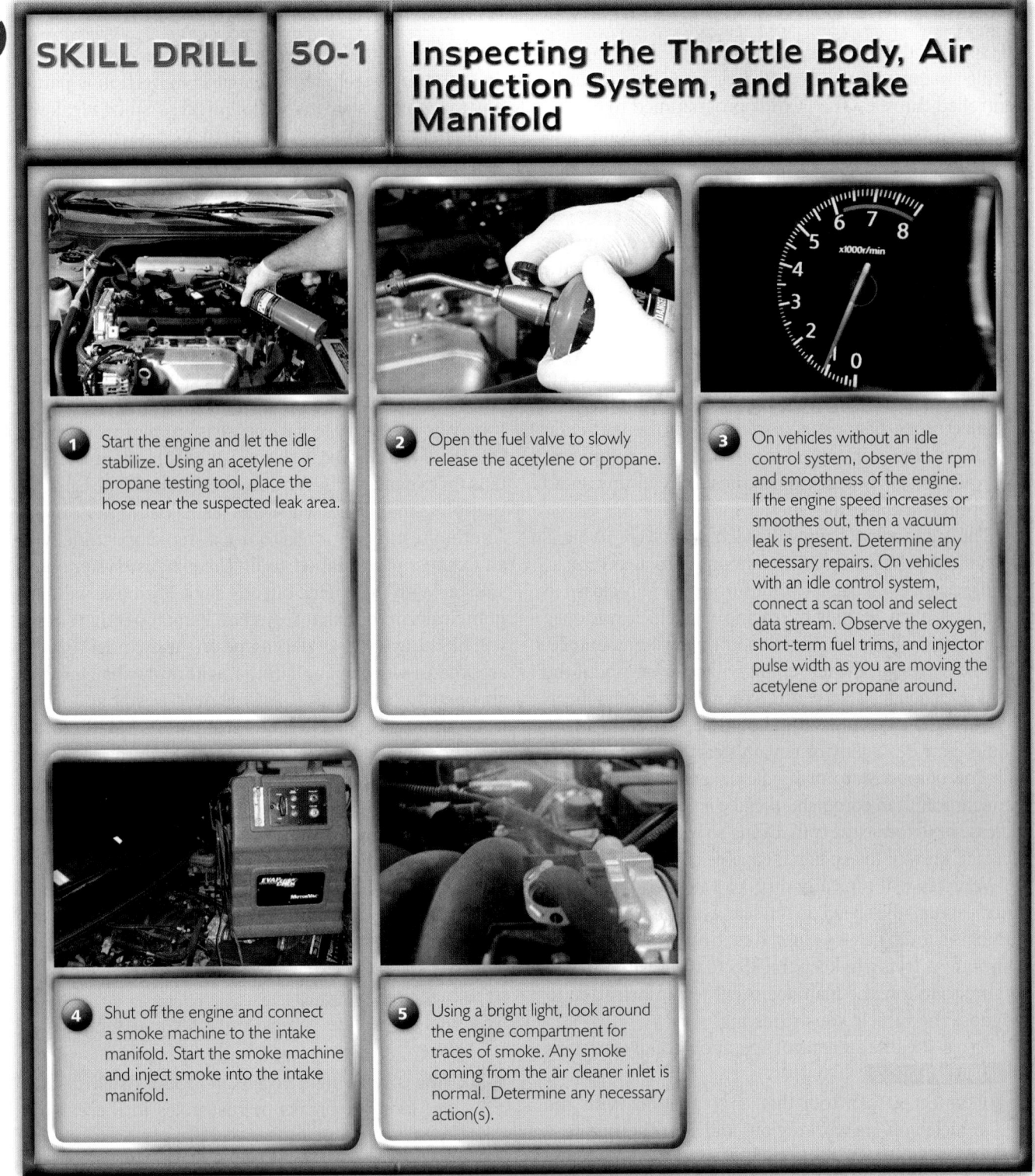

1 Start the engine and let the idle stabilize. Using an acetylene or propane testing tool, place the hose near the suspected leak area.

2 Open the fuel valve to slowly release the acetylene or propane.

3 On vehicles without an idle control system, observe the rpm and smoothness of the engine. If the engine speed increases or smoothes out, then a vacuum leak is present. Determine any necessary repairs. On vehicles with an idle control system, connect a scan tool and select data stream. Observe the oxygen, short-term fuel trims, and injector pulse width as you are moving the acetylene or propane around.

4 Shut off the engine and connect a smoke machine to the intake manifold. Start the smoke machine and inject smoke into the intake manifold.

5 Using a bright light, look around the engine compartment for traces of smoke. Any smoke coming from the air cleaner inlet is normal. Determine any necessary action(s).

oxygen, short-term fuel trims, and injector pulse width as you are moving the acetylene or propane around. (**Photo 3**)

6 *Smoke machine testing approach:* Shut off the engine and connect the smoke machine to the intake manifold.

7 Start the smoke machine and inject smoke into the intake manifold. (**Photo 4**)

8 Using a bright light, look around the engine compartment for traces of smoke. Any smoke coming from the air cleaner inlet is normal. Determine any necessary actions. (**Photo 5**)

Checking Idle Control Operation

Idle speed of the engine is controlled by the PCM through an idle air control motor or valve or by an electronically controlled throttle. The PCM is programmed to control idle speed based on the different operating conditions sensed by the input sensors. Inputs include rpm, the engine coolant temperature, the power steering pressure switch, and the air-conditioning switch. For example, when the PCM sees that the air conditioner is on, the idle control is moved to allow more air to bypass the throttle plate, or the throttle plate is opened more and the rpm will increase slightly or remain at its present rate.

The engine speed can surge if engine sensor inputs are out of range or if a vacuum leak is present. There are several reasons for an idle surge. Be sure to follow the manufacturer's diagnostic procedures for the particular vehicle you are working on for an idle system concern. The idle control system can also result in an unwanted low or high idle speed.

The scan tool will allow the technician to see what is happening with the idle control. In one particular vehicle, the idle control will display counts from 0 at fully closed to 140 at fully open. Starting the engine on a vehicle without a vacuum leak will result in the idle count showing around 20. If a leak is present, the idle count will be lower, and if the leak is bad enough, it can read 0. When the air conditioner is then turned on, the idle count should step up, and the rpm should increase slightly or remain steady. Most scan tools will allow output control of the idle air control, which means the technician can command the idle air control system to increase or decrease the rpm. Doing so will allow the technician to know if the system is capable of working or not.

Vehicles will typically display a desired idle speed and an actual idle speed on the scan tool data. These two numbers should be very close to each other, as the engine computer is trying to keep the idle to the desired speed. Be sure to follow the manufacturer's test information to diagnose the vehicle you are testing.

To test the idle air control operation, follow the steps in **SKILL DRILL 50-2**:

1. Connect a scan tool that is compatible with the vehicle you are working on, and start the engine.
2. Compare the desired idle speed to the actual idle speed. The speeds should be very close to each other.
3. Locate the output commands function in the scan tool.
4. Command a step-up of the idle speed and verify that it does so smoothly. Complete the same process for stepping down the idle speed. If the system is not operating correctly, follow the steps in the service information to diagnose the fault. Determine necessary actions.

Inspecting the Exhaust System

Inspection of the exhaust system is a necessary task as an automotive technician. Exhaust inspection is part of any mandatory state inspection process, since a leak will result in possible injury or death to the passengers due to carbon monoxide poisoning. Also, most municipalities have noise ordinances limiting the amount of noise an exhaust can emit. Special care should be taken to ensure that the exhaust system is not leaking. Exhaust leaks will create a black carbon marking.

A quick test for exhaust leaks is to use a rag to block off the exhaust flow from the tailpipe; if the exhaust system is not leaking, pressure will build and force the rag out of the pipe. If there are leaks in the exhaust, then hissing will be heard from the exhaust system through the leaks. It may be necessary to have an assistant perform this test (block off the tailpipe with a rag) while the technician listens for exhaust leaks. A mechanic's stethoscope can help pinpoint small leaks while this test is being performed. Another testing option is to use a smoke machine with an exhaust pipe adapter to fill the exhaust system with smoke. With the engine off, any signs of smoke will pinpoint leaks in the exhaust system. Remember that smoke will fill the cylinder of the engine on the cylinder that has an exhaust valve open. If both intake and exhaust valves are open due to overlap, then you may see smoke coming from the air cleaner assembly. This is considered normal and should not be confused as a leak from the exhaust.

The exhaust pipes can rust out over time. The water and corrosive chemicals in the exhaust stream corrode the pipe. A good way to test the integrity of the pipe is to use a large pair of adjustable pliers to squeeze the pipe. If it is springy or crushes easily, the pipe needs to be replaced. Make sure you check any low spots in the system along with bends in the pipe, as these are weak spots.

To inspect the exhaust system for leaks, follow the steps in **SKILL DRILL 50-3**:

1. Safely raise the vehicle on a lift and secure it in place.
2. Using a drop light to ensure good visual inspection, look for breaks or rust holes in the exhaust system.
3. Be sure to look at the exhaust manifolds for evidence of leaks. Exhaust leaks usually produce black carbon markings where the leaks are located. (**Photo 1**)
4. Have a helper hold a rag against the exhaust pipe(s) while the engine is idle to increase the pressure in the system. Listen and feel for any leaks. (**Photo 2**)
5. Use large adjustable pliers to test the integrity of the pipes by moderately squeezing the pipes. Any softness or brittleness indicates the pipe needs to be replaced. Determine necessary repairs. (**Photo 3**)

SKILL DRILL 50-3 Inspecting the Exhaust System for Leaks

1 Raise the vehicle on a lift and secure it in place. Use a drop light to inspect for leaks or rust holes in the exhaust system. Check the exhaust manifolds for evidence of exhaust leaks.

2 Have a helper hold a rag against the exhaust pipe(s) while the engine is idling to increase the pressure in the system. Listen and feel for any leaks.

3 Use large adjustable pliers to test the integrity of the pipes by moderately squeezing the pipes. Determine necessary repairs.

Performing an Exhaust Back-Pressure Test

An exhaust system back-pressure test is used to determine if there is a restriction that will create low power. A technician can use one of two methods to test for back-pressure. One method is to use a vacuum gauge connected to the intake manifold vacuum and raise the engine rpm to 2000 rpm for 2 minutes. If the vacuum gauge falls as the engine is held at 2000 rpm, then suspect a restricted exhaust system. The exhaust will begin to pile up at the restriction in the exhaust system, backing up all the way into the combustion chamber, and the intake stroke will not be able to pull in as much air, since the exhaust cannot fully escape. This backup will result in an engine that has low power or may even stall.

The technician may need to remove parts of the exhaust system to locate the restriction. Typically the technician will disconnect the connection between the catalytic converter and the muffler to eliminate the muffler and will retest. If the back-pressure is still present, then the converter will be disconnected and inspected. If the converter is clogged or restricted, the root cause of the converter failure will need to be diagnosed, such as an overly rich-running engine or a cylinder misfire, which can cause it to overheat and melt down.

The other method of testing the exhaust system for back-pressure is to use a pressure gauge installed into the exhaust stream to see how much exhaust pressure is backing up in the system. This can be done by removing an oxygen sensor near the exhaust manifold and screwing the back-pressure gauge into the hole. Another possible test point is the EGR passageway. After installing the back-pressure gauge, the engine is started and accelerated to about 2000 rpm, and the pressure is compared to specifications. Refer to the service information for the maximum amount of acceptable pressure in the exhaust system.

To perform an exhaust back-pressure test with a pressure gauge, follow the steps in **SKILL DRILL 50-4**:

1 Remove the oxygen sensor using a special oxygen sensor socket or wrench.

2 Thread the adapter into the oxygen sensor hole and connect a low-pressure gauge. **(Photo 1)**

3 Start the engine and observe any exhaust back-pressure. Exhaust back-pressure should be no more than 1.5 psi (10.3 kPa) at idle, as a rule of thumb, and no more than 3 psi (20.7 kPa) at 2000 rpm.

4 Increase the engine rpm to 2000 rpm and observe the pressure. Determine any necessary actions. **(Photo 2)**

5 Inspect the oxygen sensor gasket, put anti-seize on the sensor threads, and torque to the proper specifications. **(Photo 3)**

Performing a Turbocharger/Supercharger System Operation Test

Performing a turbocharger/supercharger test is a task that should be performed only by certified technicians

SKILL DRILL | **50-4** | **Testing the Exhaust System for Back-Pressure**

1. Remove the oxygen sensor. Install an adapter to the oxygen sensor hole and connect a low-pressure gauge.

2. Start the engine and observe any exhaust back-pressure, which should be no more than 1.5 psi (10.3 kPa) at idle and no more than 3 psi (20.7 kPa) at 2000 rpm. Increase the engine rpm to 2000 rpm and observe the pressure. Determine any necessary actions.

3. Inspect the oxygen sensor gasket, put anti-seize on the sensor threads, and torque to the proper specifications.

or under the oversight of the instructor. Testing the boost pressures that the system can produce requires operating the vehicle at wide-open throttle for a short time, making this an extremely risky test. Refer to the manufacturer's service information for specific turbocharger/supercharger diagnostic testing process for the vehicle you are working on.

The processes are similar when testing either the turbocharger or the supercharger for proper function. You will need a vacuum gauge that can measure low pressures (use a gauge that will read about 20% more than specifications). Both the supercharger and the turbocharger will put out a maximum pressure, but that pressure can be reached safely only while the engine is being loaded down by driving on the road, or better yet a chassis dynamometer. Connect the vacuum gauge to the intake vacuum port, and route it out the hood and through the passenger door window, or tape it to the outside of the windshield away from the windshield wipers, facing in **FIGURE 50-31**. Drive the vehicle in a safe place and manner. Observe the gauge for results. If no pressure is noted, check that the wastegate on the turbocharger is not sticking or that a pressure line is not disconnected. If the supercharger is not building pressure, check that the bypass valve is not sticking, a pressure line is not disconnected, or an electrical connection is not disconnected. If no faults are found, follow the service information procedure for further diagnostic steps.

FIGURE 50-31 Connect a vacuum/pressure gauge to the engine intake manifold and route it under the hood and through the passenger window, or tape it securely to the windshield.

To perform an operation test of a turbocharger/supercharger system, follow the steps in **SKILL DRILL 50-5**:

1. Connect a vacuum/pressure gauge to the engine intake manifold and route it under the hood and through the passenger window, or tape it securely to the windshield.

2. Drive the vehicle in a safe place and in a safe manner.

3. Observe the pressure rise and compare it to the manufacturer's specifications. Determine any necessary actions.

Wrap-up

Ready for Review

- The intake system ensures that clean, dry air is delivered to the engine to be mixed with fuel.
- Clean air is essential to a long-lasting engine.
- The intake system ensures that air and fuel are delivered to the engine efficiently.
- The primary components of the intake system are the intake manifold, the throttle body, and the air induction system.
- There are two types of intake manifolds: wet and dry.
- The air induction system consists of the following components: an air cleaner and housing, solid and flexible-duct tubing, and connectors.
- Ducting can be made of plastic for movement and connects the air cleaner to the intake manifold.
- The intake manifold provides a path for fuel and air to travel to the engine combustion chambers.
- Volumetric efficiency compares the volume of air entering a cylinder during intake to the internal swept volume of the cylinder when the piston is at bottom dead center.
- Back-pressure typically should never get higher than 3 psi (20.7 kPa). If it is greater, it can create poor performance issues, as it will cause exhaust to back up into the combustion chamber, minimizing the fresh airflow into the engine.
- Forced induction increases air pressure in the intake manifold above atmospheric pressure.
- A supercharger compresses the air intake to above atmospheric pressure, which increases the intake air density to the engine.
- A turbocharger is a forced induction system that uses wasted kinetic energy from the exhaust gases to increase the intake pressure.
- When using a turbocharger, exhaust gases turn the turbine, which in turn pulls in fresh air at a higher rate than normally aspirated engines.
- When air is compressed, it heats up; to keep the heating process to a minimum, an intercooler is used to cool the air prior to being injected into the engine.
- The exhaust system involves many components that work together to remove the by-products of combustion from the engine.

- The primary components of the exhaust system are the exhaust manifold, engine pipe (sometimes called the down pipe), catalytic converter, intermediate pipe, muffler, tailpipe, and exhaust brackets.
- The exhaust manifold provides a path for exhaust gases to escape the engine. In a high-performance engine, headers are tuned for better engine breathing.
- The flexible connector allows movement between the engine and the rest of the exhaust system and keeps the pipes aligned under a load.
- A catalytic converter is used to convert unacceptable exhaust pollutants, such as carbon monoxide, certain hydrocarbons, and oxides of nitrogen, into less dangerous substances.
- There may be one or two heated oxygen sensors after the catalytic converter.
- The rubber exhaust brackets support the system and allow movement and dampening action in the exhaust system.
- The function of a vehicle's muffler is to minimize the sounds coming from the exhaust system.
- The baffles in the exhaust system help to muffle the noises that the engine makes during normal operation.
- The tailpipe prevents the harmful exhaust fumes from entering the passenger compartment.
- Gaskets are used throughout the exhaust system to make a tight, leak-free system.
- The throttle body and the induction system ensure that the engine gets airflow into the cylinders and must be inspected for proper operation.
- Refer to applicable manufacturer's information when inspecting the induction system or the exhaust system.
- An exhaust back-pressure test will reveal whether there is a blockage in the exhaust system that will affect engine performance or drivability.

Key Terms

blow-off valve A valve that allows the release of excessive boost pressure from the turbocharger when the throttle plate is quickly closed.

bypass valve The pressure control valve of the supercharger. When the bypass valve opens, it lets air move around the supercharger compressor section, reducing the boost pressure.

compressor surge The backup of air against the throttle plate as it is closed. The turbocharger is still spinning, pressurizing air, when the throttle plate is closed. Air will stack up, creating a rapid slowing of the turbocharger compressor wheel. This can damage the compressor wheel.

forced induction The pressurization of airflow going into the cylinder through the use of a turbocharger or supercharger.

header A specially tuned exhaust manifold typically made of exhaust pipes. These pipes are usually made equal length to ensure equal flow between cylinders.

Helmholtz resonator A device that uses the principle of noise cancellation through the collision of sound waves. When necessary, the resonator is used in addition to the muffler to cancel additional sounds. This resonator may also be used on the induction system to muffle noise of airflow through the induction system. It is named after physicist Hermann Von Helmholtz.

mandrel forming The special bending of pipe to ensure the pipe does not collapse. The use of a pipe bender with mandrels allows for very tight bends without creating kinks or reducing the size of the pipe.

mass airflow (MAF) sensor The PCM input sensor that tells the computer the amount of air coming into the engine. The MAF sensor allows the correct calculated amount of fuel delivery to the engine. It is usually located in the ducting of the air cleaner system.

plenum chamber A large portion of the intake manifold after the throttle plate and before the intake runner tubes. The plenum provides a reservoir of air and helps prevent interference with the flow of air between individual branches.

scavenging The process of exhaust flow pulling fresh air into the cylinder as it creates a low-pressure area in the cylinder as it moves out of the cylinder.

supercharger A device that pressurizes airflow into the engine, working similar to a turbocharger. The supercharger is driven by the crankshaft through a belt or gears and does require power from the engine.

turbocharger A device that pressurizes airflow into the engine. The turbocharger works similar to a supercharger, but is driven by the exhaust gases.

wastegate A pressure regulator device that allows control of the pressure produced by the turbocharger. The wastegate moves to allow exhaust gases to bypass the turbine wheel of the turbocharger and flow down the exhaust pipe.

ASE-Type Questions

1. Tech A says that coolant circulates through some intake manifolds to help warm them up. Tech B says that some intake manifolds use an electric heater grid to warm up the intake air. Who is correct?
   a. Tech A
   b. Tech B
   c. Both A and B
   d. Neither A nor B

2. Tech A says that in some gas engines, the intake manifold runner length can be changed. Tech B says that some intake systems use resonators to quiet intake noise. Who is correct?
   a. Tech A
   b. Tech B
   c. Both A and B
   d. Neither A nor B

3. Tech A says that diesel engine rpm is controlled by a throttle plate. Tech B says that in a diesel engine, air and fuel are mixed in the plenum. Who is correct?
   a. Tech A
   b. Tech B
   c. Both A and B
   d. Neither A nor B

4. Tech A says that scavenging creates a low pressure in the cylinder by means of the exhaust gases flowing through the exhaust pipe. Tech B says that back pressure in the exhaust system increases the scavenging effect. Who is correct?
   a. Tech A
   b. Tech B
   c. Both A and B
   d. Neither A nor B

5. Tech A says that shorter intake manifolds produce higher torque at lower rpm. Tech B says that longer intake manifolds produce higher torque at high engine speeds. Who is correct?
   a. Tech A
   b. Tech B
   c. Both A and B
   d. Neither A nor B

6. Tech A says that air becomes heated as a supercharger compresses it. Tech B says that a turbocharger pulls the exhaust gases out of the engine, thereby increasing the scavenging effect. Who is correct?
   a. Tech A
   b. Tech B
   c. Both A and B
   d. Neither A nor B

7. Tech A says that a wastegate designed to direct waste gases to the intake manifold. Tech B says that a blow-off valve vents excess boost pressure from the turbocharger when the throttle is closed quickly. Who is correct?
   a. Tech A
   b. Tech B
   c. Both A and B
   d. Neither A nor B

8. Tech A says that most engines with a turbocharger have turbo lag. Tech B says that a variable-geometry turbocharger will overcome most turbo lag. Who is correct?
   a. Tech A
   b. Tech B
   c. Both A and B
   d. Neither A nor B

9. Tech A says that a catalytic converter operates best at cold temperatures. Tech B says that the catalytic converter is typically located after the muffler. Who is correct?
   a. Tech A
   b. Tech B
   c. Both A and B
   d. Neither A nor B

10. Tech A says that small vacuum leaks can be found with a vacuum gauge. Tech B says that the catalytic converter is typically located after the muffler. Who is correct?
    a. Tech A
    b. Tech B
    c. Both A and B
    d. Neither A nor B

CHAPTER 51

NATEF Tasks

Engine Performance
General Engine Diagnosis

Page

- Diagnose abnormal exhaust color, odor, and sound; determine necessary action. **AST** **MAST** 1798–1799

Emission Control Systems

- Diagnose emissions and drivability concerns caused by the evaporative emission control system; determine necessary action. **MAST** 1798–1799

- Diagnose oil leaks, emissions, and drivability concerns caused by the PCV system; determine necessary action. **AST** **MAST** 1799

- Diagnose emissions and drivability concerns caused by the EGR system; determine necessary action. **AST** **MAST** 1799–1800

- Diagnose emissions and drivability concerns caused by the secondary air injection and catalytic converter systems; determine necessary action. **MAST** 1800

- Inspect and test catalytic converter efficiency. **AST** **MAST** 1802–1803

- Inspect, test, and service positive crankcase ventilation (PCV) filter/breather cap, valve, tubes, orifices, and hoses; determine necessary action. **MLR** **AST** **MAST** 1803–1805

- Inspect, test, service, and replace components of the exhaust gas recirculation (EGR) system, including tubing, exhaust passages, vacuum/pressure controls, filters, and hoses; determine necessary action. **AST** **MAST** 1805

- Inspect and test electrical/electronic sensors, controls, and wiring of the EGR system; determine necessary action. **MAST** 1805

- Inspect and test electrical/electronically operated components and circuits of air injection systems; determine necessary action. **AST** **MAST** 1806

- Inspect and test components and hoses of the evaporative emission control system; determine necessary action. **MAST** 1806–1807

Emission Control

Knowledge Objectives

After reading this chapter, you will be able to:
1. Explain the composition of air in the atmosphere. (pp 1774–1775)
2. Describe the types of exhaust emissions released from the internal combustion engine. (pp 1776–1781)
3. Discuss how emissions can be reduced. (pp 1781–1785)
4. Define the term stoichiometric ratio. (p 1782)
5. List the types of emission control devices used. (pp 1785–1800)
6. Explain the process of emission testing an internal combustion engine. (pp 1800–1801)
7. Explain what is involved in the testing of individual emission control devices. (pp 1800–1807)

Skills Objectives

After reading this chapter, you will be able to:
1. Use a five-gas analyzer. (pp 1801–1802)
2. Test a catalytic converter for efficiency. (pp 1802–1803)
3. Inspect and service the PCV system. (pp 1803–1805)
4. Inspect and service the EGR system and sensors. (p 1805)
5. Inspect and service the secondary air injection system. (p 1806)
6. Inspect and test electrical components of secondary air injection systems. (p 1806)
7. Inspect and service the hoses of the evaporative emission system. (pp 1806–1807)

Introduction

Emissions are the release of substances into the atmosphere. They can occur naturally, from forest fires, volcanoes, and the decomposition of natural materials. Emissions can also be man-made, such as from vehicles and industrial sites. In automotive applications, most **emissions** are the by-product of combustion and are emitted from the exhaust system. Not all emissions from combustion are considered hazardous. Those emissions from the automobile that are hazardous can be managed by carefully designing the engine, accurately controlling the air to fuel ratio, or converting them to nonharmful or less harmful gases through the use of add-on emission control devices. Today's vehicle technology has reduced the harmful emissions a vehicle produces to almost zero. This chapter will detail the methods and control devices designed to either reduce those harmful emission gases or convert them into less harmful or nonharmful elements.

Composition of Air

The air we breathe is composed mainly of two gases: nitrogen and oxygen. Nitrogen by far makes up the largest percentage of air (78%). It is an inert gas, which means it does not react easily with other compounds. Oxygen (21%) is the second most abundant element in air. It is a highly reactive gas, which means it combines readily with almost all other elements. In many cases, oxygen reacts through the process of combustion, which is also called oxidation. These two gases account for approximately 99%

of the content of air. That leaves 1% for all of the other elements found in air, including carbon dioxide and argon.

The level of oxygen in the atmosphere is critical to humans. The gases in our atmosphere provide a balanced environment for plant, animal, and human life. Humans breathe in oxygen and exhale carbon dioxide; trees and plants take in carbon dioxide and give back oxygen. This process is part of the oxygen cycle **FIGURE 51-1**. There is also a nitrogen cycle, in which nitrogen from our atmosphere is converted to usable food for plants by bacteria in the ground. There is also a carbon cycle. Carbon fuels are burned and produce carbon dioxide in

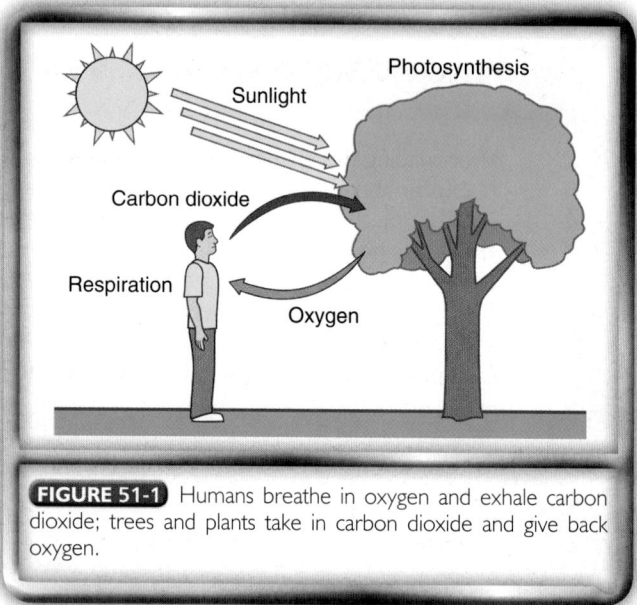

FIGURE 51-1 Humans breathe in oxygen and exhale carbon dioxide; trees and plants take in carbon dioxide and give back oxygen.

You are the Automotive Technician

A customer brings her car into your shop with the malfunction indicator lamp (MIL) illuminated. You explain to the customer that the light comes on to alert her that there is a problem with the vehicle that needs to be checked and diagnosed, and because some issues can cause further damage if left unchecked, she did the right thing by bringing it in. She authorizes you to perform the diagnosis. You first plug in the scan tool and pull the active diagnostic trouble codes (DTCs). There are several: P0133—O2 sensor circuit slow response B1S1; P0401—EGR flow insufficient detected; P0420—Catalyst efficiency below threshold—Bank 1. You know that a slow-responding oxygen sensor can affect the catalytic converter, so you start by diagnosing that DTC, and then diagnose the other two DTCs.

1. How can a slow-responding O2 sensor affect the catalytic converter?
2. Under what conditions should the EGR system operate?
3. What are at least two ways the catalytic converter can be tested?

TABLE 51-1: Percentages of Gases Contained in the Atmosphere

Gas	Percentage
Nitrogen (N_2)	78.08
Oxygen (O_2)	20.95
Water (H_2O)	0 to 4, variable
Argon (Ar)	.93
Carbon dioxide (CO_2)	.0360, variable
Neon (Ne)	.0018
Helium (He)	.0005
Methane (CH_4)	.00017, variable
Hydrogen (H_2)	.00005
Oxides of nitrogen (NO_x)	.00003, variable
Ozone (O_3)	.000004

the air, which is then converted to carbon and oxygen by plants. The carbon is used to grow the plant while oxygen is given back to the air.

While nitrogen and oxygen make up 99% of the air, the other 1% contains a variety of gases **TABLE 51-1**. Some of these gases can be useful in different ways. As a technician, while welding, you may have to use carbon dioxide, argon, or helium to keep oxygen away from the weld. These gases are used because if oxygen is allowed to come in contact with the molten metal of the weld, oxidation will occur and the weld will be weak and could fail. Neon is a gas, drawn from the atmosphere, that produces light when exposed to electricity and is used as an accent light in some show cars.

Sources of Emissions

The term *emission*, when used in automotive circles, normally refers to the pollution produced by a light vehicle during operation or while sitting stationary. All fuels, with the exception of pure hydrogen, produce pollution. **Emission control systems** are designed to limit the pollution caused by the storing and burning of various fuels. Emissions from current gasoline-fueled motor vehicles usually come from three sources: the fuel system, the crankcase, and the tailpipe.

The fuel tank allows liquid fuel to evaporate into a gas. If not controlled, those vapors can escape into the atmosphere and are called evaporative emissions. When gasoline or other hydrocarbon fuel is burned in the combustion chamber along with the oxygen and nitrogen from the air, emissions are created. Some of the emissions are pollutants and are released from the exhaust system

in the form of gases. These emissions are called tailpipe emissions. Some of the combustion gases leak past the compression rings and cylinder walls and find their way into the crankcase. These blow-by gases create pressure in the crankcase and if not controlled are vented into the atmosphere and are called crankcase emissions.

In a **compression-ignition engine** (diesel engine), emissions are created in the combustion chamber the same way as they are in spark-ignition engines and escape to the atmosphere through the exhaust and the crankcase breather. Diesel fuel does not evaporate as easily as gasoline, so evaporative emissions are not a major concern on vehicles powered by diesel fuel.

Regulated Emissions

Manufacturers are required by law and the Environmental Protection Agency (EPA) to control the emissions produced by their vehicles. The EPA requires every manufactured power train to pass a federal emission test before it can be sold in the United States. This test is called the Federal Test Procedure (FTP) and is designed to determine the emission output of that particular vehicle as classified by year, make, model, and drive train. The test uses a dynamometer that will duplicate the normal driving pattern of the typical commuter, known as the FTP drive cycle. As the vehicle is operated according to the FTP drive cycle, the emission output is monitored in grams per mile (g/mi). For the vehicle to pass, the emissions must stay under the limits for that type of vehicle. Other countries have other agencies that regulate emissions, but any vehicle entering the United States must pass the US FTP test.

Not only must the vehicles pass the test before they can be sold, they must be capable of detecting an emission failure over their life, as they are being operated. As of 1996, all vehicles must meet the **on-board diagnostics II (OBDII)** standard. OBDII is an automotive self-diagnostic system mandated by the EPA that requires a warning light to alert the driver of an emission system fault. The EPA requires that when a vehicle's emissions deviate from the FTP limit by 1.5 times, the warning light (malfunction indicator lamp [MIL]) must turn on and one or more specific diagnostic trouble codes (DTCs) be set in memory.

If the vehicle begins to run rich—for example, due to a leaking fuel injector—and the emission output exceeds 1.5 times the FTP limit, the engine management system must be able to detect the rich condition. The engine control module (ECM) will then turn the MIL on to warn the driver that the vehicle has a fault and requires service. The OBDII system was developed purely with the intent of keeping vehicles emission-compliant and warning drivers if they are not.

Regulated air pollutants can be divided into two groups: gases and particulates. The primary pollutant gases from vehicles include hydrocarbons, carbon monoxide, oxides of nitrogen, and sulfur dioxide. These pollutants can have a damaging effect on people, the atmosphere, and the natural environment. Particulates, often referred to as **particulate matter**, are tiny particles of solid or liquid suspended in the air. Particulate matter is graded in a size range from 10 nanometers to 100 micrometers in diameter. Particulates of less than 10 micrometers are dangerous to humans because they can easily become airborne and reach the lungs. Smaller particles also tend to stay airborne longer than larger particles, which settle more quickly.

Many countries have recognized the global effects that the continual release of pollutants into the earth's atmosphere can have. These countries have developed emissions laws or follow an international protocol on emission control standards. Vehicle manufacturers are required to comply with these laws to ensure that the emissions from the vehicles they produce meet the emission control standards.

Manufacturers design emission control systems for their vehicles, which monitor and control emissions so that they do not exceed the emission control limits. A **limit value** is the maximum amount of emissions that a vehicle is permitted to emit. Limit values are assigned to different classifications of vehicles. Passenger and light vehicle limit values are normally given in grams per mile in the United States and grams per kilometer in Europe. These regulations have become progressively more stringent as government regulations become tougher in an effort to further reduce vehicle emissions.

In the quest to meet the tougher emission control standards, many manufacturers are turning to hybrid technologies, which couple two power sources together (electric and gas). Hybrid vehicles have reduced emission output and meet tougher fuel economy standards. Alternative fuels, such as compressed natural gas (CNG) and propane, are also being used more frequently in the attempt to fur-

ther reduce pollutions. Ever-stricter emission control is at the forefront of vehicle design and construction.

Types of Emissions

Internal combustion engines produce several emission gases as part of the conversion process of turning fuel (chemical energy) into mechanical energy. There are three categories of emission gases: nonharmful, harmful, and debatable. The nonharmful gases are water (H_2O), nitrogen (N_2), and oxygen (O_2). The harmful gases are carbon monoxide (CO), oxides of nitrogen (NO_x), and sulfur dioxide (SO_2). The debatable gas is carbon dioxide (CO_2). Each of these gases will be explained in the following sections.

Water

Water is a natural by-product of complete combustion and is not harmful to the environment or our air quality. Water is formed by the engine when two hydrogen molecules from the fuel are drawn into the combustion chamber and are combined with one oxygen molecule **FIGURE 51-2**. Water is emitted as a result of complete combustion of hydrogen and oxygen. We could say that water is a by-product of completely burned hydrogen fuel. In fact, burning 1 gallon of gasoline in an engine creates about 1 gallon of water. Thus, water is formed in all internal combustion engines and is discharged along with all normal combustion gases through the exhaust system.

> **TECHNICIAN TIP**
>
> In a gasoline engine, about 1 gallon of water is created for every 1 gallon of gasoline burned. This water usually leaves the exhaust system as superheated steam since it is produced under very high combustion temperatures. If the exhaust pipe is cool because the engine was not running very long, the steam can condense into water and drip out of the tailpipe. Water also mixes with any sulfur dioxide in the exhaust and creates sulfuric acid. This water and sulfuric acid can sit in low spots in the exhaust system and rust or corrode any steel and iron components. Many manufacturers use exhaust system pipes and mufflers made of stainless steel, which resists rust and corrosion.

> **TECHNICIAN TIP**
>
> Historically, the regulated emissions have been hydrocarbons, carbon monoxide, oxides of nitrogen, and particulate matter. In recent years, carbon dioxide has been added to the list of emissions that are being regulated. Not all scientists agree with this regulation since carbon dioxide is necessary for plant life and is given off in human respiration.

Carbon Dioxide

Carbon dioxide is a by-product of complete combustion, along with water. When complete combustion of air and fuel occurs, one carbon molecule combines with two

FIGURE 51-2 Water is formed by the engine when two hydrogen molecules from the fuel are drawn into the combustion chamber and are combined with one oxygen molecule.

FIGURE 51-3 Complete combustion of air and fuel occurs when one carbon molecule combines with two oxygen molecules to form one carbon dioxide molecule.

oxygen molecules to form one carbon dioxide molecule **FIGURE 51-3**. So we could say that carbon dioxide is completely burned carbon fuel. Carbon dioxide is not normally considered a poisonous gas; in fact, humans exhale it as our bodies use the oxygen we breathe in, and plants use the carbon from carbon dioxide for growth while releasing the oxygen back into the atmosphere. However, some scientists consider carbon dioxide a serious contributor to global warming, and the EPA has labeled it as a pollutant. Thus, manufacturers are now finding ways to reduce it. Carbon dioxide is believed to act as a blanket, trapping heat and thereby raising the temperature of the earth's atmosphere. Since motor vehicles are a major source of carbon dioxide, governments are seeking ways to regulate them with the goal of reducing the total amount of carbon dioxide released into the atmosphere.

Carbon dioxide is also formed inside of catalytic converters. The catalytic converter completes the combustion process by adding another oxygen molecule to the carbon monoxide (CO) to convert it to carbon dioxide (CO_2). In addition, carbon dioxide is produced by diesel, liquid petroleum gas (LPG), propane, CNG, or any other carbon-based fuel used in a vehicle with an internal combustion engine.

Hydrocarbons

Gasoline, diesel, LPG, and natural gas are all hydrocarbon compounds. **Hydrocarbons** are created when raw fuel evaporates into the atmosphere or when it does not burn at all in the combustion chamber and is exhausted

out the tailpipe. In other words, hydrocarbon emissions are unburned fuel that escapes to the atmosphere.

Gasoline needs to evaporate easily so that it can mix with air to burn properly in an internal combustion engine. But this property also means it evaporates easily into the atmosphere at ordinary temperatures and pressures. For example, when a vehicle is being refueled, hydrocarbon vapors can escape from the filler neck into the atmosphere. When the vehicle is left in the sun, the temperature of the fuel increases, and fuel can evaporate from the tank.

> **TECHNICIAN TIP**
>
> Hydrocarbon emissions react with oxides of nitrogen (NO_x) in the presence of sunlight to produce **photochemical smog**, a brown haze that hangs in the sky, typically seen over large cities. Smog is a major health issue to humans because it affects lung tissue. Hydrocarbons are a major component of photochemical smog.

Carbon Monoxide

Carbon monoxide is a colorless, odorless, tasteless, flammable, and highly toxic gas. It is a product of the incomplete combustion of carbon and oxygen. The incomplete combustion can result from either too much fuel (carbon) or not enough air (oxygen). In these conditions, the carbon can only attach itself to one oxygen molecule, creating carbon monoxide **FIGURE 51-4**. We could say that carbon monoxide is partially burned fuel. Other causes of high carbon monoxide emissions are improper ignition timing, low combustion temperature, or low compression of the engine. Carbon monoxide emissions have been reduced in modern vehicles as a result of better engine design, better fuel management, and the use of catalytic converters in the exhaust system.

Most engine fuels, except pure hydrogen, are carbon-based. Unless the combustion process is perfect and complete, any internal combustion engine operating on a carbon-based fuel will tend to produce some carbon monoxide emissions. This is especially true when the combustion temperature is low, such as during a cold start, when there is not enough oxygen present to completely burn the fuel, or when there is insufficient time in the combustion chamber for complete combustion.

FIGURE 51-4 The incomplete combustion that creates carbon monoxide can result from either too much fuel (carbon) or not enough air (oxygen), causing the carbon to be able to attach only to one oxygen molecule.

Applied | Science

AS-24: Chemical Reactions: The technician can demonstrate an understanding of the chemical reactions that occur in the automotive engine that are related to the combustion of fuels and the operation of the catalytic converter.

An automotive teacher asks a student to use a hacksaw to cut apart a failed catalytic converter for evaluation purposes. When the converter is cut into two pieces, it is evident that the converter had melted down. The students find six large pieces of material that resemble rocks. The ceramic catalyst was damaged because of a super-heated condition that resulted from unburned fuel entering the converter. This teaching aid provides an introduction to the catalytic converter and how it works and relates to the combustion of fuels in an automotive engine.

The stoichiometric ratio is the ratio of air to fuel at which all of the oxygen in the air and all of the fuel are completely burned. This is the ratio of 14.7 parts of air to 1 part of fuel. Maintaining close control of the air–fuel ratio allows an engine to run cleaner than ever. In many cases, precise control of the air–fuel ratio has made the job of hydrocarbon (HC) and carbon monoxide (CO) related emission control devices much easier, since they are dealing with much smaller volumes of the pollutants. Catalytic converters use a base structure of ceramic material coated with precious metals to react with and break up or combine gases in the exhaust system. The catalytic converter cleans up the pollutants left over from combustion, and tailpipe emissions are reduced.

In the case of the failed converter that was cut apart for evaluation, the engine had a misfiring cylinder as a result of a faulty spark plug. The check engine light that was illuminated on the dash was ignored by the vehicle owner for about one month, resulting in the failure of the converter. The unburned fuel from the misfiring cylinder was ignited in the converter, causing overheating of the ceramic monolith.

Toxicity

Carbon monoxide is an extremely poisonous gas. Since you cannot see it or smell it, it is very dangerous. Inhaling carbon monoxide in a confined space can be lethal. Because it is known to come from the exhaust system, it is important not to allow any engine to run inside a workshop without venting the exhaust gases directly to the open air outside.

Victims of **carbon monoxide poisoning** can sometimes look healthy and pink-cheeked. This is because concentrations of carbon monoxide in the bloodstream give the blood a brighter red color than normal. Carbon monoxide binds much more easily than oxygen with hemoglobin, which is the blood component that carries life-giving oxygen around the body. As the hemoglobin becomes saturated with carbon monoxide, it becomes unable to carry oxygen. When the brain is starved of oxygen, the victim becomes unconscious, resulting in brain damage or death. Early signs of carbon monoxide poisoning include headaches, nausea, weakness, and irritability.

Since carbon monoxide is absorbed so easily by red blood cells, the following agencies set limits for the permissible exposure limit (PEL) for the workplace:

- OSHA PEL is 50 parts per million (ppm) for an 8-hour shift.
- The National Institute for Occupational Safety and Health (NIOSH) PEL is 35 ppm for an 8-hour shift with a ceiling of 200 ppm for any length of time.
- The American Conference of Governmental Industrial Hygienists (ACGIH) PEL is 25 ppm for an 8-hour shift and a 40-hour workweek.

Exposure levels of 400 ppm may be fatal in as little as 3 hours, and 6400 ppm may be fatal in as little as

30 minutes. As you can see, it doesn't take much carbon monoxide in the air to be hazardous. To further help you understand the smallness of the PELs, consider that 1% carbon monoxide equals 10,000 ppm of carbon monoxide. Vehicles with an emission-related problem can run perfectly well and still easily have carbon monoxide tailpipe readings between 3% and 5%, which equates to 30,000–50,000 ppm—more than 1000 times the allowable PELs given in the preceding list.

Safety

Be sure when working in a shop environment with a vehicle running that you provide adequate ventilation by using an exhaust extraction device (fan system and exhaust hoses designed to draw exhaust gases from the vehicle's exhaust pipe and push them outside of the shop). Small amounts of carbon monoxide can kill if proper ventilation is not provided.

First Aid

First aid for victims of carbon monoxide poisoning starts with recognizing the signs of exposure: shortness of breath, nausea, headache, dizziness, or lightheadedness. Awareness will allow you to make the decision to remove the other person, or yourself, before severe poisoning occurs. If the victim of carbon monoxide poisoning is unresponsive or demonstrates severe symptoms, call for qualified help and then assess the environment to determine if you can safely remove the person from further exposure. If you are trained, you may need to perform CPR. If available, give first aid oxygen as well. Continue to treat the victim until medical help arrives.

Oxides of Nitrogen

Air that is drawn from the atmosphere into an engine contains almost 80% nitrogen, which is normally considered to be an inert gas. Under the high temperature and pressure of combustion, nitrogen may combine with oxygen to produce **oxides of nitrogen** FIGURE 51-5. Since nitrogen is inert, it is typically produced in large amounts only when combustion temperatures of around 2500°F (1400°C) and above occur. A lean mixture will result in higher oxides of nitrogen because lean mixtures burn faster than rich mixtures, resulting in an excessive combustion temperature. The increase of available oxygen can oxidize the nitrogen at those high temperatures.

Oxides of nitrogen are claimed to be major contributors to photochemical smog, along with hydrocarbons and sunlight. For example, the brown-looking cloud that often hangs over large cities is photochemical smog. Oxides of nitrogen irritate the eyes, nose, and throat.

In extreme cases, such as regular exposure to high concentrations, coughing and lung damage can occur.

Sulfur Dioxide

Gasoline and diesel fuels contain sulfur as part of their chemical makeup. When sulfur burns in the combustion chamber, one sulfur molecule combines with two oxygen molecules, creating sulfur dioxide. Sulfur dioxide mixes with water vapor formed during the combustion process and produces sulfuric acid FIGURE 51-6. This corrosive compound is emitted into the atmosphere through the exhaust. Sulfuric acid is a major environmental pollutant, coming back to earth in contaminated rainwater, called acid rain. This acid rain has been responsible for degrading vast areas of arable land. As a result, the reduction or

FIGURE 51-5 Under the high temperature and pressure of combustion, nitrogen may combine with oxygen to produce oxides of nitrogen.

FIGURE 51-6 Sulfur dioxide mixes with water vapor formed during the combustion process and produces sulfuric acid.

removal of sulfur from motor fuels has become a major part of most countries' vehicle emission control programs.

High sulfur levels in fuel, when combined with water vapor, can also cause corrosive wear on valve guides and cylinder liners, which can lead to premature engine failure. Using proper lubricants and draining oil at the correct intervals help combat this effect and reduce the degree of corrosive damage. Many manufacturers have been using stainless steel in their exhaust pipes and mufflers to help resist corrosion caused by sulfur in these components.

Sulfur reduces catalyst efficiency in modern vehicles, and vehicles operating with higher sulfur gasoline have higher emissions than vehicles operating on lower sulfur gasoline. There is evidence that in some instances, sulfur in gasoline may also degrade the performance of oxygen sensors, which may contribute to higher tailpipe emissions.

Although regulations have reduced the permissible levels of sulfur in fuel, there are some side effects from using low-sulfur diesel fuel. The refining process used to reduce the sulfur level can reduce the natural lubricating properties of the diesel fuel, which is essential for the lubrication and operation of fuel system components such as fuel pumps and injectors. These components either need to be manufactured with higher quality materials or special lubricants need to be used to provide the required level of protection.

To reduce the sulfur content, oil companies change the overall chemical composition of the fuel, which can affect fuel pump seals, engine seals, and O-rings, some of which react to changes in fuel composition by swelling or shrinking. This problem can be fixed by performing regular maintenance of the fuel system and by replacing the seals with ones made of materials that are less susceptible to swelling or shrinking.

Particulates

Particulates are small particles of solid matter that are suspended in the air. Particulates from modern engines are usually small particles of carbon **FIGURE 51-7**. In spark-ignition engines, particulates are caused by incomplete combustion of rich air–fuel mixtures. In this case, the hydrogen burns away from the hydrocarbon molecule, leaving the carbon by itself. In compression-ignition engines, particulates are caused by either too rich of a mixture or a poorly mixed air–fuel mixture. This produces very rich areas in the combustion chamber, even though the overall mixture could be very lean. Newer compression-ignition engines use a particulate filter to catch and hold the particulates in the exhaust stream. In some systems, the particulate filter can be regenerated

FIGURE 51-7 Particulates from modern engines are usually small particles of carbon.

periodically by burning off the carbon particles. The ECM controls the regeneration process automatically, or a technician can command regeneration with a scan tool connected to the ECM.

Smog

Smog is produced in the atmosphere when unburned hydrocarbons and oxides of nitrogen react chemically with sunlight. Smog appears reddish brown on the horizon and can be seen over major cities. Smog is also known as ground-level ozone. Ozone blocks harmful ultraviolet light from the sun in the upper atmosphere; however, in the lower atmosphere, it creates irritation of the lungs and is believed to contribute to asthma.

▶ Controlling Emissions

Manufacturers are relatively free to determine how they will meet the standards, as long as they do meet the standards. They design systems and processes that will effectively and cost efficiently meet the standards. There are a couple of strategies that manufacturers use. The first is to design the engine in such a way as to reduce emissions as much as possible, such as building turbulence-enhancing strategies and precisely controlling valve and spark timing. The second strategy is to closely control the air–fuel mixture under all driving conditions, thereby minimizing emission output. The third strategy is to warm up the engine as quickly as possible, as well as operate it at higher temperatures than older engines. The final strategy is to integrate precombustion and post-combustion add-on devices that are designed to further reduce emission output.

Combustion

Since most emissions are by-products of combustion, accurately controlling combustion within the cylinders can minimize emission output. For fuel to burn efficiently, it needs to be fully evaporated and completely mixed with the right proportion of air. This is pretty easy to do in the controlled environment of a laboratory, but doing so repeatedly at a high rate of speed in very short periods of time under a huge variety of conditions is much more difficult. These are the conditions we are dealing with inside automotive combustion chambers. Thus, maintaining low emission output is a challenge and requires all of the engine's systems and components to be working properly for combustion to occur efficiently. In fact, a good general test that will tell you the overall condition of the engine and its control systems is an emission test. If the vehicle passes the emission test with clean results, that is a good indication that all of the engine systems and the engine itself are operating well.

Combustion Chamber Design

Combustion chamber design can affect the combustion process, which also affects the level of emissions. In the combustion chamber where surface temperatures are low, the combustion flame can be **quenched** **FIGURE 51-8**. The flame temperature drops so low in these areas that the flame goes out, or is quenched. Fuel left unburned in these zones is then exhausted as hydrocarbon and carbon monoxide emissions.

If the spark plug is positioned near the center of the combustion chamber so that the **flame front** travels evenly through the combustion chamber, combustion is more complete. The flame front is the rapid burning of the air–fuel mixture that moves outward from the spark plug across the cylinder. The flame front can be extinguished in cold areas of the cylinder, such as near the corner of the head and cylinder wall. Proper placement of the spark plug can help to minimize this effect.

The designs of intake ports and cylinder heads can aid in swirling mixtures as they travel to the combustion chamber. Swirling of the air and fuel helps to create a proper mixture of air and fuel vapors. If fuel does not stay in the air when being drawn into the combustion chamber, the mixture can fluctuate excessively and create drivability problems and excessive emissions, showing us how important proper movement of air is in the engine.

Gas flow rate affects the ability of air to hold fuel. Fast-moving air tends to hold fuel better than slow-moving air, which allows fuel to fall out of the airstream **FIGURE 51-9**. Fast-moving air more easily causes swirling of the air and fuel. Gas flow rate can be increased by the use of smaller intake ports. This design works well at keeping good airflow at low engine revolutions per minute (rpm). But at high rpm, it can restrict the airflow

FIGURE 51-8 Quench areas in a combustion chamber.

FIGURE 51-9 Gas flow rate affects the ability of air to hold fuel. Fast-moving air tends to hold fuel better than slow-moving air, which allows fuel to fall out of the airstream.

too much and reduce engine power. Some manufacturers overcome this problem by using two or more intake valves in each cylinder. With both valves open at high rpm, the overall size of the intake port opening is then increased and the gas flow rate increases. The more air that can flow into an engine, the more efficient that engine, and with better efficiency comes less emissions.

Changing valve timing also alters the combustion process. Reducing the valve overlap reduces the **scavenging effect**, which is when the exhaust gases moving out of the combustion chamber create a low-pressure area in the exhaust manifold, helping to pull air and fuel into the cylinder. If the valve overlap is excessive, unburned air and fuel can be pulled out of the exhaust valve, which will increase hydrocarbon emissions.

Stoichiometric Ratio

The **stoichiometric ratio**, also referred to as **lambda**, is the ratio of air to fuel at which all of the oxygen in the air and all of the fuel are completely burned. As you can imagine, complete combustion reduces hydrocarbons and carbon monoxide. The typical stoichiometric ratio for gasoline is 14.7:1 (14.7 parts air to 1 part gasoline by weight or mass). This ratio equates to a lambda reading of 1.0. Each fuel has its own stoichiometric ratio **TABLE 51-2**. As the air–fuel ratio moves away from the stoichiometric point, the hydrocarbons and carbon monoxide emissions increase. Maintaining close control of the air–fuel ratio allows an engine to run cleaner than ever. In many cases, precise control of the air–fuel ratio has made the job of hydrocarbon and carbon monoxide emission control devices much easier since they are dealing with much smaller volumes of the pollutants.

A rich condition means more fuel is introduced than the engine can completely burn. This is anything lower (richer) than 14.7:1 or less than 1.0 lambda. When this condition occurs, hydrocarbons can only partially burn because of the lack of oxygen. This rich condition creates large amounts of carbon monoxide. If excessively rich, some of the hydrocarbons will not burn at all, leaving hydrocarbons to pass through the engine unburned. Elevated amounts of carbon monoxide in the exhaust are a good indicator that the engine is running rich.

A lean condition means more air is introduced than the engine can completely burn. This is anything above (leaner than) 14.7:1 or greater than 1.0 lambda. When this condition occurs, not all of the hydrocarbons burn because the flame cannot reach some of the hydrocarbon molecules due to the excessive amount of oxygen and nitrogen molecules. Thus, the hydrocarbon molecules are pushed out of the exhaust pipe unburned. Elevated hydrocarbon readings (with low carbon monoxide readings) are a good indicator of a lean condition.

Carbon dioxide is a good indicator of whether the fuel is burning completely. For example, high readings of 12% to 15% of carbon dioxide in the exhaust indicate proper combustion efficiency. A smaller percentage of carbon dioxide in the exhaust indicates that combustion is not complete, indicating a rich or lean mixture, ignition problems, lowered compression, or exhaust system leak.

> ### TECHNICIAN TIP
>
> Carbon dioxide is a gas that manufacturers are trying to reduce. It is believed to contribute to global warming, and laws are underway that will require manufacturers to reduce its creation. Some of the ways that carbon dioxide can be reduced is by making vehicles smaller, lighter, and more aerodynamic; using smaller, more fuel-efficient engines; and using technology to shut down the engine when the vehicle is decelerating or stopped at a stop light.

Controlling Air–Fuel Ratios

Precise control of the air–fuel ratio is one of the main strategies for minimizing a vehicle's emission output. Keeping the air–fuel ratio close to the stoichiometric point produces minimal hydrocarbon and carbon monoxide emissions. Electronic fuel injection and engine management systems can adjust the air–fuel mixture within certain limits as parts wear and thereby maintain proper control of the air–fuel ratio over a broad range of conditions. These systems closely control the air–fuel ratio entering each cylinder and ensure the ignition timing matches operating conditions. Sensors around the engine

TABLE 51-2: Stoichiometric Ratios for Various Fuel Types

Fuel Types	Stoichiometric Ratio
Gasoline	14.7
No. 2 Diesel	14.7
Methanol	6.45
Ethanol	9.00
Propane	15.7
Compressed Natural Gas	17.2
Hydrogen	34.3

Source: Department of Energy website. Stoichiometric ratio is the ratio of air to fuel, expressed 14.7:1.

send information about airflow, coolant temperature, throttle position, engine speed, and other inputs to the ECM. The ECM uses this information to set fuel and ignition settings, which change as sensor data change. The ECM has a programmed memory that works like a reference chart. The manufacturer's engineers program the ECM to constantly adjust the fuel and spark depending on the values received from the sensors. For example, as airflow rises, the fuel increases proportionately.

Fuel delivery is controlled by the fuel injector. The typical fuel injector is simply an electric solenoid. When electrical current flows in the fuel injector winding, a magnetic field is produced (electromagnet), causing the fuel injector to open and allow fuel to flow through it into the intake manifold. The ECM (or power train control module [PCM]) opens the fuel injector for a longer or shorter period of time, creating more or less fuel delivery. The longer the fuel is delivered, the richer the mixture, and vice versa.

> ### TECHNICIAN TIP
>
> The pulse width of the fuel injector is a piece of data that can be read on a scan tool or lab scope to assist the technician in testing fuel delivery. The pulse width is the amount of time the fuel injector is turned on and fuel is sprayed into the intake manifold. It is measured in milliseconds. The longer the pulse width, the more fuel is delivered to the engine.

Changes in operating conditions can change mixture conditions. For instance, if an engine is being driven at moderate speed and the throttle is suddenly closed, any fuel condensed on the intake manifold walls or intake port of the cylinder head will be drawn into the cylinders. A smaller amount of air moves into the combustion chamber with the throttle plates closed, so turbulence tends to be poor, which can lead to incomplete combustion and the release of unburned gases into the exhaust.

To reduce this effect, the ECM detects that the throttle is being closed through the use of the throttle position sensor (TPS) and will reduce the fuel spray by reducing the on time of the injectors. If the engine is being used to slow the vehicle, the injectors can be completely shut off to save fuel and reduce pollution. This is called fuel cutoff mode. Newer engines with electronic throttle control can move the throttle plate independent of driver input. This feature allows the computer to control the throttle opening as well as the fuel injection pulse width to create a proper mixture during all driving conditions.

Closed Loop

Closed loop is an operating condition in what is called a feedback system. A feedback system uses an ECM (computer), which gathers information, makes decisions, and sends output commands to its controlled devices. The ECM collects sensor information on the system it is monitoring. This sensor information is in the form of electrical signals. It is brought into the computer through wires and is called "input" information. The ECM then processes the sensor information along with what it has in its programmed memory maps and creates output commands based on that information. The ECM sends its output commands through wires to the controlled devices, where they carry out those commands. The input sensors monitor the new reaction and report that information back to the ECM where it can be evaluated. The process then repeats itself. The operating condition in which a feedback system is controlling the outputs based on sensor feedback is called closed loop operation. The condition in which the feedback system is ignoring the feedback sensor information is called open loop operation. Engines operate in open loop when they are first started until they reach a specified operating temperature. They return to open loop status under varying conditions, depending on the manufacturer, such as cool down of the oxygen sensors, extended idling, and in some cases, wide-open throttle (WOT).

The feedback system can be very simple or very sophisticated. For example, a vehicle has a cruise control unit to help it maintain a set speed. When the vehicle speed sensor indicates that the vehicle speed falls below the set speed, the computer sends an output signal that causes the throttle plate to open slightly and increase the amount of air and fuel reaching the engine, thereby increasing the speed. A cruise control system can operate in closed loop based on its ability to receive and act on feedback sensor information. A feedback system in the fuel system can monitor the amount of oxygen in exhaust gases so that the ECM can maintain a constantly toggling air–fuel ratio just slightly above and below the stoichiometric point for ideal emission control operation.

The feedback system uses an oxygen sensor to detect rich and lean conditions in the exhaust stream. The oxygen sensor determines rich and lean by gauging the amount of oxygen in the exhaust gases. This indicates how well combustion is being completed, which in turn indicates the air–fuel mixture entering the engine. A voltage signal is relayed back to the ECM from this sensor to indicate whether the mixture is too rich or lean. More oxygen indicates a lean mixture; less indicates a rich mixture.

Based on the signal of the oxygen sensor, the ECM will change the pulse width signal to the fuel injectors to keep the air–fuel ratio toggling just above and below the stoichiometric point. The control module is programmed to not enter closed loop operation until the engine reaches a certain operating temperature since the oxygen sensor will not function properly until it reaches its minimum operating temperature. Today's engines have heated oxygen sensors that reduce warm-up time for closed loop operation to under 1 minute.

During open loop operation, the ECM ignores the oxygen sensor signal and operates based on a **programmed fuel delivery map**. A programmed fuel delivery map is a programmed chart that the manufacturer's engineers create to determine the approximate amount of fuel to deliver based on multiple sensors' input. Sensors include the manifold absolute pressure (MAP) sensor, the mass airflow (MAF) sensor, the crank sensor (which enables the ECM to calculate rpm), the throttle position sensor (TPS), the coolant temperature sensor (CTS), and the intake air temperature (IAT) sensor. The fuel map is programmed into the ECU memory and is automatically referenced to calculate fuel delivery.

The ECM then adjusts the amount of fuel being injected into the engine to toggle the air–fuel ratio very close to the chemically correct composition for complete combustion.

Precombustion/Postcombustion Treatment

The pollution emitted from the internal combustion engine can be reduced by taking actions both prior to combustion and after combustion. Precombustion treatment focuses on assuring that combustion happens in a controlled and complete manner that minimizes postcombustion pollutant gases. There are two primary precombustion emission control systems: the heated air intake system and the exhaust gas recirculation system. The heated air intake system was used on throttle body–injected (and carbureted) engines. It was designed to keep the air entering the engine at a constant temperature of approximately 100–110°F (38–43°C) to help vaporize the fuel in the intake manifold. The better vaporized the fuel, the more likely it could be distributed evenly within the air, and the cleaner the combustion gases. This system will be discussed further in the Emission Control Systems section.

Most port fuel injection systems do not need a heated air intake system because the fuel is sprayed into the intake manifold right next to the intake valve. The injector sprays a fine mist of fuel, which is easier to vaporize. Plus it does not have to sit or travel along a cold intake manifold where it can condense out of the air. Most new vehicles monitor the intake air temperature and use that to determine the mass of the air entering the engine and therefore know exactly how much fuel to inject.

The second precombustion emission control system is the exhaust gas recirculation system. This system recirculates some of the inert exhaust gases back into the intake manifold when combustion temperatures are high enough to create oxides of nitrogen. The inert gases help lower peak combustion temperatures below the threshold at which oxides of nitrogen are created. Exhaust gas recirculation systems will be covered in greater depth in the following Emission Control Systems section.

Postcombustion emission control systems deal with the remaining pollutants that are left over from the combustion process. There are two primary postcombustion systems: the secondary air injection system and the catalyst system. The secondary air injection system helps to complete the burning of hot hydrocarbons and carbon monoxide in the exhaust system by adding oxygen to the exhaust stream. The oxygen in the air reacts with the hydrocarbons and carbon monoxide and converts them to carbon dioxide and water.

The catalyst system reduces oxides of nitrogen back into nitrogen and oxygen and oxidizes hydrocarbons and carbon monoxide. Both of these systems help reduce tailpipe emissions to near zero if the engine and all of the systems are operating as designed. Both of these systems are covered in greater depth in the following section.

Emission Control Systems

Emission control systems have been created by manufacturers to minimize the amount of pollution released into the atmosphere from a vehicle and its internal combustion engine. Before the days of emission control systems, vehicles and engines produced very large amounts of pollutants, as evidenced by the number of smog days in many big cities. Even though there are now many more vehicles and many more miles driven, the number of pollution days in a year has been reduced substantially and continues to decline in most areas.

One of the earliest control devices was the positive crankcase ventilation (PCV) system. The system was first used around 1961 and later became a mandatory emissions device. PCV systems stop the release of hydrocarbons from the crankcase of the engine to the atmosphere. Another control device is the evaporative control system, known as the EVAP system. This system was used beginning around 1972 and later became a mandatory emission system. It is used to stop the release of hydrocarbons from the fuel tank to the atmosphere.

Exhaust gas recirculation (EGR) systems began to appear on the automobile around 1972 and became a mandatory part of emission controls. These systems control the release of oxides of nitrogen to the atmosphere by controlling the temperature of the combustion process. The use of a system called secondary air injection began in the late 1960s to limit hydrocarbon release from the engine during cold engine operation. The system injects air into the exhaust stream to mix with the hydrocarbons and aid in the conversion process as the exhaust exits the combustion chambers. Catalytic converters found their way onto the automobile around 1973. Catalytic convertors are used to reduce remaining pollutants in the exhaust stream before they leave the tailpipe. As catalytic converters were introduced, leaded gas was phased out. Lead in the gas would contaminate (coat) the catalyst in the convertor and render it inoperative.

Catalytic Converters

Catalytic converters are a primary emission control device. They perform a final cleanup of the tailpipe emissions on a properly running engine equipped with functioning emission control systems. Catalytic converters are not designed to handle the emission output of a poorly running engine or one with faulty emission control systems. Catalytic converters create heat as they convert harmful gases into less harmful gases. Forcing converters to deal with more gases than they are designed to handle can cause them to overheat. In some cases, they may even melt down internally, which ruins them.

Catalytic converters use a base structure of ceramic material coated with precious metals to react with and break up or combine gases in the exhaust system **FIGURE 51-10**. The term catalyst refers to a material that causes a chemical reaction without itself being consumed or changed in the reaction. Specific precious metals have the ability to act as a catalyst that can convert harmful exhaust gases to nonharmful or less harmful gases. Catalytic converters come in two types: oxidizing and reduction. Each type is used to react with particular gases.

The reduction catalyst contains a platinum and rhodium coating, which helps to reduce the oxides of nitrogen molecules into their base compounds. When a nitric oxide or nitrogen dioxide molecule comes into contact with the catalyst coating, the coating strips the

nitrogen atom out of the molecule and retains it. This frees up the one or two oxygen atoms in the molecule, which combine in pairs to form molecules of oxygen. The nitrogen atoms bond with other nitrogen atoms that are retained in the catalyst and form molecules of nitrogen; thus, two molecules of nitric oxide become one molecule of nitrogen and one molecule of oxygen, or two molecules of nitrogen dioxide become one molecule of nitrogen and two molecules of oxygen **FIGURE 51-11**.

The second type of catalyst is the oxidizing catalyst. It oxidizes any unburned hydrocarbons and carbon monoxide as they travel over the platinum and palladium coating. This aids the reaction of the carbon monoxide and hydrocarbons with any remaining oxygen in the

FIGURE 51-10 Catalytic converters use a base structure of ceramic material coated with precious metals to react with and break up or combine gases in the exhaust system.

FIGURE 51-11 The nitrogen atoms bond with other nitrogen atoms that are retained in the catalyst and form molecules of nitrogen.

exhaust gas **FIGURE 51-12**. Each carbon monoxide (CO) molecule combines with an oxygen (O) molecule to make one less-harmful carbon dioxide (CO_2) molecule. And two hydrogen (H) atoms combine with one oxygen (O) molecule to form one nonharmful water (H_2O) molecule.

Catalytic converters are referred to as either two-way or three-way catalytic converters. The **two-way catalytic converter** was the first type of catalytic converter designed. The two-way catalytic converter is an oxidizing catalyst and is named because it converts two gases, hydrocarbons and carbon monoxide, to carbon dioxide and water. The early two-way catalytic converters used a bed of catalytic pellets (pellet-style converter) that the exhaust passed through. More recent versions of the two-way (and three-way) catalytic converters are designed with a honeycomb catalytic element. The honeycomb structure provides long narrow passageways for the exhaust gases to flow through, which ultimately helps the gases to come in contact with the catalyst materials on the sides of the honeycomb walls. This contact between the gases and the catalyst promote oxidation of the hydrocarbons and carbon monoxide once the catalyst reaches its operating temperature.

Safety

> Catalytic converters must be above approximately 500°F (260°C) to begin conversion. Typically, they operate at 900–1600°F (482–871°C). Catalytic converters can cause serious burns, so use gloves and heat protection sleeves when working around a hot catalytic converter.

$$-2CO + O_2 \longrightarrow 2CO_2$$
$$-2C_2H_6 + 7O_2 \longrightarrow 4CO_2 + 6HO_2$$

Platinum and Palladium coating (exact composition varies between manufacturers)

Ceramic or Metal substrate

CO + HC + O₂

FIGURE 51-12 The oxidizing catalyst oxidizes any unburned hydrocarbons and carbon monoxide as they travel over the platinum and palladium coating.

Modern vehicles operating on petroleum-based fuels are fitted with three-way catalytic converters. **Three-way catalytic converters** contain both a reduction catalyst and an oxidizing catalyst. The term three-way is in relation to the three regulated emissions the three-way catalytic converter is designed to convert: carbon monoxide, hydrocarbons, and oxides of nitrogen. The reduction catalyst is in front and converts the oxides of nitrogen, nitric oxide, and nitrogen dioxide back into harmless nitrogen and oxygen molecules. The oxidizing catalyst then uses the oxygen from the reduction catalyst to oxidize the hydrocarbons and carbon monoxide into water and carbon dioxide.

Because of strict emission requirements, vehicles with three-way catalytic converters require a feedback system on the fuel system. The ECM monitors the oxygen content in the exhaust stream by using an exhaust gas oxygen (EGO) sensor, also known as a lambda sensor, mounted in the exhaust manifold. This sensor tells the engine computer how much oxygen is in the exhaust. The computer uses this information to control the pulse width of the fuel injectors.

The ECU can increase or decrease the amount of oxygen in the exhaust by adjusting the air–fuel ratio. The ECU ensures that the air–fuel ratio cycles at close to the stoichiometric point in normal driving conditions. This ensures that there is always sufficient oxygen in the exhaust system to allow the oxidization catalyst to deal with unburned hydrocarbons and carbon monoxide.

> **TECHNICIAN TIP**
>
> Each style of catalytic converter is designed for a specific vehicle; one size does not fit all. A converter intended for the treatment of a four-cylinder engine will not be efficient on an eight-cylinder engine. Be sure to install the correct catalytic converter in the correct vehicle. Always check the manufacturer's specifications before making a repair. Be careful with aftermarket catalytic converters, which may not use as much catalyst agent (precious metals) as the emission system requires.

AS-89: Catalytic Converter: The technician can explain the principles by which a catalytic converter modifies emission gases at the atomic level to provide a lower level of HC, CO, and NO_x in the final exhaust.
One of the greatest emission devices to be installed on vehicles is the catalytic converter. This component will last for the life of the vehicle if given proper care. Proper care for the converter would include maintaining the engine according to the manufacturer's service information. If the engine is operating normally, the converter won't have to work hard to accomplish its task. Catalytic converters are designed to provide control of hydrocarbons (HC), carbon monoxide (CO), and oxides of nitrogen (NO_x). Emissions are passed through the converters catalytic inlaid materials. Catalytic converter's may contain materials such as rhodium, palladium, platinum, or cerium. All of these special materials are considered to be precious metals. The reduction catalyst is in front and converts the oxides of nitrogen, nitric oxide, and nitrogen dioxide back into harmless nitrogen and oxygen molecules. The oxidizing catalyst then uses the oxygen from the reduction catalyst to oxidize the hydrocarbons and carbon monoxide into water and carbon dioxide.

A catalytic converter can be checked with an infrared noncontact thermometer. The outlet temperature should be 30 to 100 degrees higher than the inlet temperature at 2,500 rpm. There are several other tests that can be performed to verify that the catalytic converter is working properly. The manufacturer's service information should be consulted for more details.

FIGURE 51-13 Any vehicle produced after 1996 monitors catalyst efficiency by using two oxygen sensors.

Crankcase Emission Control

While the engine is running, some gases from the combustion chamber leak past the piston rings and the cylinder walls, down into the crankcase. This leakage is called **blow-by**. To prevent pressure buildup during operation, the crankcase must be ventilated. Unburned fuel (hydrocarbons) and water from condensation also find their way into the crankcase and sump. When the engine reaches its full operating temperature, the water and fuel in the crankcase evaporate. In older vehicles, crankcase vapors were vented directly to the atmosphere through a **breather tube** or road-draft tube. It was shaped so that air flowing past it while the vehicle was being driven helped draw the vapors from the crankcase. This resulted in blow-by gases being vented directly to the atmosphere.

Modern vehicles are required to direct crankcase blow-by gases and vapors back into the intake manifold where they can be returned to the combustion chamber to be burned. A common method of directing gases and vapors back to the intake is through the emission control system called the **positive crankcase ventilation (PCV)** system **FIGURE 51-14**. The PCV system regulates the flow of blow-by gases between the crankcase and the intake manifold.

Types of PCV Systems

There are three main types of PCV systems: **variable orifice**, **fixed orifice**, and **separator** type. All three types do the same job—ventilate blow-by gases back to the intake manifold to be burned in the combustion chamber.

In a variable-orifice type of system, a replaceable, spring-loaded **PCV valve** regulates gas flow. The position of the PCV valve is controlled by the pressure in the manifold. With the engine off, the spring holds the PCV valve in

Catalyst Monitoring

Any vehicle produced after 1996 monitors catalyst efficiency by using two oxygen sensors **FIGURE 51-13**. One oxygen sensor is in front of the catalytic converter, as in the past, and indicates the amount of oxygen in the exhaust stream as it leaves the cylinders. The reading from this sensor normally toggles rich and lean as the ECM is controlling the air–fuel ratio. The second oxygen sensor is located after the catalytic converter and measures the oxygen in the exhaust stream after it leaves the catalytic converter. Since the converter uses oxygen to oxidize the hydrocarbons and carbon monoxide, the oxygen content is normally lower after the converter and results in a higher and steadier oxygen sensor voltage. The catalyst monitor tracks both oxygen sensor readings to ensure that the gases are being effectively converted by the catalytic converter. As the catalytic converter fails, the rear sensor tends to track the oscillations of the front oxygen sensor. The ECM monitors these two oxygen sensor signals and will turn on the MIL and set a DTC once the catalyst efficiency degrades to a predetermined point.

the closed position, and air cannot enter the inlet manifold. This allows the engine to start. At idle, intake manifold pressure draws the PCV valve to the other end of the PCV valve's housing, where it allows only a small, measured amount of gases and air past the PCV valve. At wider throttle openings, the PCV valve plunger position allows maximum flow through the PCV valve's housing, which gives maximum crankcase ventilation and tends to match the higher amount of blow-by gases under that condition.

The PCV system is designed to remove more air than just blow-by gases, so there should almost always be more ventilation capacity than the amount of blow-by. The additional air that the system removes comes from a fresh air intake hose or tube, usually attached to the air cleaner assembly. The fresh air intake hose directs filtered air to one side or end of the crankcase. This intake point is usually as far as possible from the PCV valve to ensure that as much of the blow-by gases are pulled from the crankcase as possible, giving good ventilation.

The PCV system has two main purposes, to remove blow-by gases from the crankcase in a manner that is not harmful to the environment and to prevent a buildup of pressure in the crankcase. Modern PCV systems are of the closed (sealed) type. This means both ends of the PCV system are connected to the intake system. The PCV valve is connected directly to the intake manifold below the throttle plate, while the fresh air hose is connected to the air intake above the throttle plate. Having a closed system means any gases that cannot be handled through the vacuum side of the system are directed back through the fresh air connection to the air cleaner assembly, where they are drawn into the intake airstream, and burned in the combustion chamber.

The fixed-orifice type of PCV system usually involves a screw-in fitting with a small hole drilled in it. The hole creates a predetermined vacuum leak that draws a predetermined amount of crankcase vapors from the crankcase. Engineers have factored the vacuum leak into the engine management system to ensure the correct air–fuel mixture. The fixed orifice is typically mounted on or in the intake manifold.

The separator type of PCV system involves a valve that is hooked to the pressure side of the crankcase, an oil return line at the bottom of the valve, and a suction line on the other side. Oil that is mixed with blow-by gases enters the separator, and the heavy oil tends to fall out of the mixture to the bottom of the valve and return to the crankcase. The separator type is used on turbocharged applications since turbocharged systems pressurize the intake system and would close off a standard PCV valve.

Common PCV Failures

PCV failures can occur and potentially create drivability problems for the customer. The most common problem is when the PCV system has a vacuum leak. The hose connecting the PCV valve to the intake manifold can crack and create a vacuum leak. Vacuum leaks tend to cause a lean air–fuel mixture and create a rough idle, which is most noticeable while the vehicle is stopped at a stop light.

PCV systems can also become clogged. Over time, especially if the vehicle's oil changes are neglected, the PCV valve or hose can plug up with sludge. If this happens, the PCV system cannot ventilate the crankcase and blow-by gases will contaminate the oil further, which creates more sludge throughout the engine. Another common failure from a clogged PCV valve or hose is oil being pushed up into the housing. If oil is found in the air filter housing, the PCV system is either being overwhelmed by the blow-by gases (the piston rings are worn out), or the suction side of the PCV system is clogged/restricted. This causes the pressure to build up in the crankcase, which then forces oil mist up the fresh air hose to the air cleaner housing. In this case, check that there is strong vacuum present at the PCV valve when the engine is idling and that the valve is not restricted. Also test the crankcase pressure using a blow-by gauge.

Repeat engine oil leaks may be the result of excessive pressure in the crankcase. If this pressure cannot be removed, it will continue to build and eventually either push oil past the seals or in some cases even push oil seals and gaskets out of position, causing an oil leak. In the event of multiple gasket or seal failures or repeat failures, be sure to check that the PCV system is operating correctly by testing for the proper PCV system flow.

▶ Exhaust Gas Recirculation System

The **exhaust gas recirculation (EGR) system** was designed by automotive engineers in the 1970s to control the emission of oxides of nitrogen. Nitrogen is oxidized in large amounts once combustion temperatures reach approximately 2500°F (1371°C) **FIGURE 51-15**. This temperature is reached when the vehicle is under moderate to heavy loads and the air–fuel ratio is at stoichiometric or leaner. EGR systems were designed to operate during those times. As with all vehicle technology, EGR systems have evolved over time, and some newer engines use variable valve timing to draw some exhaust gases back into the cylinder through the exhaust valve, which is held open a little longer than typical.

Purpose and Operation

An **EGR valve** connects the exhaust port, or manifold, and the intake manifold **FIGURE 51-16**. If engine operating conditions are likely to produce oxides of nitrogen, the

FIGURE 51-15 The exhaust gas recirculation (EGR) system was designed by automotive engineers in the 1970s to control the emission of oxides of nitrogen. Nitrogen is oxidized in large amounts once combustion temperatures reach approximately 2500°F (1371°C).

FIGURE 51-16 Typical computer-controlled EGR system.

EGR valve opens, letting some burned exhaust gases pass from the exhaust into the intake system. During combustion, an amount of fresh air–fuel mixture is displaced by inert exhaust gases that do three things. First, they make it so there is not quite as much burnable mixture, which helps keep the temperature from rising as high as it otherwise would. Second, since they are inert and mix thoroughly with the rest of the air–fuel mixture, they cause the mixture to burn a bit slower, and therefore cooler, as the flame front must travel farther to burn around the inert molecules. Third, the inert gases absorb some of the heat of the burning gases. These three situations lower the peak combustion temperature, thus reducing the formation of the oxides of nitrogen.

The EGR valve can open only under the conditions that create oxides of nitrogen. Since oxides of nitrogen are not created in a cold engine, the EGR valve is unable to open until after the engine achieves its normal operating temperature. Another situation where the combustion temperatures are low is when the vehicle is at or near idle. The EGR valve does not operate at idle because there is only a small amount of air–fuel mixture being burned, so the combustion temperature is well below 2500°F (1371°C). There is one condition when oxides of nitrogen are being created in large amounts and the EGR valve does not operate: when the vehicle is operated at WOT. In this condition, the EGR system is shut off so that full engine power is available for emergency needs such as avoiding an accident. But most passenger vehicles do not operate very often or for very long at WOT, so the overall amount of oxides of nitrogen created is not substantial.

Some manufacturers have been able to accomplish the same reduction in oxides of nitrogen by using variable valve timing on their engines instead of the traditional EGR system. In situations where oxides of nitrogen can be created, the ECM retards the exhaust camshaft so that the exhaust valves are held open during the first part of the intake **stroke**. As the piston moves down slightly, the lower cylinder pressure pulls some of the exhaust gases back into the combustion chamber. These exhaust gases are used to dilute the air–fuel mixture with inert gases just like an external EGR system does. In this case, the ECM controls how long the exhaust valve remains open, which then affects the amount of exhaust gases that are retained in the cylinder. This is sometimes referred to as an internal EGR system, and the beauty is that it uses only the variable valve timing components, which are used for other fuel economy and drivability reasons. So there are fewer components to install and go bad.

Types of EGR Valves

There are two main types of EGR valves that can be found on current automobiles: the vacuum diaphragm type and the electrically operated type. Each of these types comes in a variety of styles. For vacuum diaphragm types, the EGR valve is available in three styles: the single-diaphragm valve, the negative back pressure valve, and the positive back pressure valve. The single-diaphragm EGR valve has a single, spring-loaded diaphragm that seals off the vacuum chamber **FIGURE 51-17**. The diaphragm is connected to and operates a **pintle**, which is a tapered valve that seals in a tapered seat and allows exhaust gas to flow into the intake manifold when it is open. When vacuum is applied to the chamber, the diaphragm moves against spring pressure and opens the valve. Spring pressure closes the valve when vacuum is released.

The **negative back pressure EGR valve** uses two diaphragms to operate **FIGURE 51-18**. The main diaphragm is connected to the pintle valve and is spring loaded just like the single-diaphragm valve. The second

diaphragm is connected through a hole in the pintle shaft to the exhaust side of the EGR valve. The second diaphragm opens and closes a bleed hole in the main diaphragm. A small spring holds this bleed valve in the closed position, allowing the main chamber to be operated by vacuum. Once the EGR valve opens, the pressure in the exhaust system keeps the bleed valve closed as long as there is not a vacuum in the exhaust system. If a vacuum occurs, then the bleed valve opens, which releases the vacuum in the main chamber and allows the main spring to close the EGR valve. This system ensures that the EGR valve is open only when the engine is under a load, as evidenced by the positive back pressure. It is helpful to remember that a negative back pressure EGR valve is released whenever there is negative exhaust pressure. This valve can be tested with a simple vacuum pump

> **TECHNICIAN TIP**
>
> In the combustion chamber, higher combustion temperatures tend to create more power. But high temperatures also create very high amounts of oxides of nitrogen. One way to overcome this is by understanding the difference between high peak-combustion temperature and high average-combustion temperature. High peak temperatures last for a very small time. While they produce a sharp spike in pressure, it does not last long and tends to give a hammer blow to the piston, which is not very effective in pushing it down the cylinder. The high average-combustion temperature maintains high average pressure, which is good for a longer, smoother push of the piston. It produces good power while minimizing the creation of oxides of nitrogen.

FIGURE 51-17 Single-diaphragm EGR valve.

FIGURE 51-18 Negative back pressure EGR valve.

to ensure that the valve and diaphragm will lift, hold, and close properly. In many cases, a negative back pressure EGR valve can be identified by the "N" at the end of the part number.

The **positive back pressure EGR valve** is very similar to the negative back pressure EGR valve. However, the small spring holds the bleed valve open until positive exhaust pressure acts on the second diaphragm and closes the bleed valve **FIGURE 51-19**. Once the bleed valve is closed, vacuum can operate on the main diaphragm to open the EGR pintle. If exhaust pressure falls, the bleed valve will open and bleed off the vacuum in the main diaphragm chamber, and the main spring will close the EGR pintle. Without exhaust gas pressure, the spring-loaded valve will not close and seal off the diaphragm chamber so that intake vacuum cannot pull on the main diaphragm and lift the pintle. Operation of any of these diaphragm types of EGR valves can be controlled through the use of a temperature-controlled vacuum valve or a computer-controlled actuator (EGR solenoid). In many cases, a positive back pressure EGR valve can be identified by the "P" at the end of the part number.

Electrically operated EGR valves are commonly used on vehicles today because they can be controlled much more accurately. There are two common types of electric EGR valves: pulse-width-modulated solenoid type and the **stepper motor EGR valve** type **FIGURE 51-20**. The pulse-width-modulated style uses a spring-loaded valve that is opened by an electric solenoid and closed by the spring. The ECM sends a pulse-width-modulated signal that varies the solenoid on/off times. The longer the pulse width, the higher the duty cycle of the solenoid and the farther the valve is held open. This design allows for reasonably good control of EGR flow.

The stepper motor EGR valve controls EGR flow much more precisely. The valve is moved in and out by means of a threaded rod that is turned in steps by the electric motor. The ECM sends signals to the stepper motor, which can open or close the valve one step at a time. Since the ECM also knows the engine temperature, throttle position, vehicle speed, and engine load, it can operate the valve only when EGR flow is needed and precisely control how much is allowed to flow. Most ECM-controlled EGR systems incorporate a feedback loop to ensure that the valve is working properly and EGR gases are flowing in the system. If the ECM detects a fault, it will set a DTC and illuminate the MIL.

Vacuum Controls in the EGR System

Older vehicles used vacuum controls solely to operate the EGR system **FIGURE 51-21**. In many cases, the throttle body had a vacuum port for the EGR system that was

FIGURE 51-19 Positive back pressure EGR valve.

FIGURE 51-20 Pulse-width-modulated EGR valve and stepper motor EGR valve.

FIGURE 51-21 Typical EGR vacuum control system.

positioned a little bit above the throttle plate. That way there would not be any vacuum to the port at idle or WOT. But when the throttle was partially open, the port would receive manifold vacuum to send to the EGR valve. Many vacuum-controlled EGR systems also used a temperature-sensitive vacuum valve that prevented vacuum from reaching the EGR valve until the engine reached operating temperature. This design prevented the EGR from operating when the engine was cold. Manifold pressure reaches the EGR valve when the engine is warm and when the EGR port is influenced by the position of the throttle. This is generally at moderate throttle openings, when a lean mixture could increase creation of oxides of nitrogen.

Electronic Controls in the EGR System

With the introduction of an ECM on automobiles, the control of the emission systems became much more efficient and accurate. The ECM controls the timing of when, how far, and how long the EGR valve opens, making it much more efficient than the **thermo control (temperature-controlled valve)** in vacuum-controlled EGR systems. The EGR valve is now controlled either indirectly by an **actuator**, which regulates the amount of intake manifold vacuum that is applied to the EGR diaphragm chamber, or directly through an electric solenoid or electric motor. Most electronically controlled EGR systems also include some type of feedback monitoring to allow the ECM to monitor the valve's operation. If the system fails, a diagnostic code is set, and the MIL is turned on to notify the driver of a problem.

With the invention of a stepper motor EGR valve, even more precise control of the EGR is possible. The EGR valve has a motor that is capable of moving in small steps to vary the opening of the pintle. This system is controlled by the ECM, which sends signals to the stepper motor to advance or retract one step at a time. It also incorporates a feedback system. This system eliminates the diaphragm and vacuum lines from the EGR system, which are common failure points of the system.

Computer Monitoring Strategies

With the introduction of OBDII, monitoring of the EGR system was made mandatory by the EPA, and each manufacturer became responsible for ensuring its system runs a self-test to verify it is operating correctly. The test is called an **EGR system monitor**. The ECM will run a test of the system to ensure that it is working properly. Preprogrammed conditions must be met prior to the monitor running; for example, the engine temperature, throttle position, and vehicle

speed all must be within certain parameters. Also, other system monitor tests, such as the catalyst efficiency monitor or oxygen sensor monitor, may need to have passed prior to the running of the EGR system monitor test.

Manufacturers have slightly different monitoring strategies for the EGR system. But once the parameters for running the monitor are met, all of the manufacturers have the ECM command the EGR valve to open and then watch for a sensor to report an expected change. This expected change could be an increased temperature of the EGR flow while the EGR valve is open as measured by a temperature sensor in the EGR passageway **FIGURE 51-22**. Or, it could be a certain amount of pressure drop in the intake manifold as measured by the MAP sensor when the EGR valve opens. Or, it could be the reduction in exhaust oxygen as measured by the oxygen sensor while the EGR valve is open. Another system uses a differential pressure sensor to measure the pressure drop of exhaust gases flowing through a restriction in the EGR passageway. Regardless of the type of monitoring, if the ECM sees a result that is outside of its expected readings, it will illuminate the MIL, set a DTC, and store freeze-frame data in the ECM memory.

> ### ▶ TECHNICIAN TIP
>
> It is important to know that the results of monitor tests are erased when DTCs are cleared. Since it can take days, weeks, or in some cases months for the monitors to run, it may be prudent to leave any DTCs in memory and let the ECM turn off the MIL once you have completed the repairs on the vehicle.

FIGURE 51-22 EGR temperature monitoring system.

Common EGR Failures

If the vehicle is using a <u>diaphragm-style EGR valve</u> (either the positive back pressure or negative back pressure type), the diaphragm could develop a leak, a vacuum line could crack or break, or a temperature control valve could stick open or closed. The EGR exhaust passageway could also clog from a buildup of carbon, which would block exhaust gases from entering the intake, and combustion temperatures would continue to climb. If the EGR system uses an actuator or solenoid to control vacuum, the actuator or solenoid could develop an electrical or mechanical fault, resulting in little to no vacuum to the EGR valve or full vacuum at all times. Stepper motor EGR valves can fail electrically or mechanically. In either case, the pintle will not operate correctly, creating idle or drivability problems.

▶ Evaporative Emission Control

The <u>evaporative emission (EVAP) system</u> is designed to ensure that hydrocarbons are not released into the atmosphere when fuel in the fuel tank begins to vaporize and build pressure. The EVAP system uses a charcoal canister and a series of hoses and valves to capture the hydrocarbon vapors that would normally be lost from the fuel tank and then deliver them to the intake manifold to be burned in the engine's combustion chambers **FIGURE 51-23**. The EVAP system stores the fuel vapors in the charcoal canister until the ECM determines they can be burned in the engine without affecting the drivability of the vehicle. Once the ECM determines that the conditions are right for burning off of the vapors, it will control the amount of vapors being released to the engine. The EVAP system also incorporates a monitoring system to ensure that there are no leaks in the fuel storage system, as well as verify that the vapors are being delivered, as designed, to be burned.

Fuel Storage

Before 1971, vehicles vented the fuel tank through the filler cap into the atmosphere. As fuel in the tank vaporized, vaporous hydrocarbons would escape from the filler cap and the carburetor. This is a waste of perfectly good fuel as well as a pollutant of the air we breathe. Nonvented filler caps were designed to help prevent the release of these vapors. But the system needs to accommodate changes in fuel tank level. Today, a <u>vacuum relief valve</u> somewhere in the system allows air to enter the fuel tank to relieve the low pressure as the fuel is drawn out of the tank or when the fuel contracts as the temperature drops. The vacuum relief valve also stops the fuel tank from collapsing in these situations.

The fuel cap may also incorporate a <u>pressure relief valve</u>. If the fuel tank's internal pressure exceeds the set value of the relief valve, the pressure relief valve releases a small amount of pressure to prevent the fuel tank from rupturing. Some modern caps have no valves at all and are completely sealed to stop the entry of air and water into the fuel tank and to stop the release of fuel vapor. Modern tanks also contain an <u>expansion volume</u>, which is an air chamber that allows for the expansion of liquid fuel on hot days. It can be either directly built into the top of the fuel tank or included as a separate chamber connected to the fuel tank by tubing.

A liquid–vapor separator may be connected to the fuel tank by a number of tubes. This separator allows a space for liquid fuel to separate from the vapors and return to the fuel tank **FIGURE 51-24**. This separation ensures that the liquid fuel does not get pushed into the charcoal

FIGURE 51-23 EVAP system.

FIGURE 51-24 Liquid vapor separator.

canister and ruin it. A **vapor line** is connected to the vapor space in the fuel tank or the liquid vapor separator and carries fuel vapors from the fuel tank to a storage container called a charcoal canister. This vapor line can incorporate a check valve, which is a valve with a steel or plastic ball in it. The check ball moves into the passageway to block fuel if the valve is turned on its side. If the vehicle is tilted too far from the horizontal and rolls over, the check valve stops liquid fuel from leaking and creating a fire hazard; thus, it is sometimes called a rollover valve.

Charcoal Storage

A charcoal canister is a canister filled with **activated charcoal** **FIGURE 51-25**. "Activated" means the charcoal is highly porous with a very large surface area that can absorb and store large quantities of fuel vapor. The charcoal canister is connected to the fuel tank vapor line, and the charcoal absorbs excess fuel vapor from the fuel tank, primarily when the engine is not running. In some earlier carbureted engine designs, the canister also has a vapor line connected to the **carburetor float bowl** to absorb any fuel vapors from it.

The charcoal canister is designed to store the fuel vapors for a limited time before it must be purged. **Purging** is the process of drawing fresh air up through the activated charcoal for the purpose of pulling the fuel vapors from the charcoal and burning them in the engine. Purging is designed to normally occur when the engine is above a minimum temperature and has run for a specified time. This system prevents the engine's air–fuel ratio from being thrown rich or lean by the flow of purged gases while the engine is warming up. Purging is an important process, as it prepares the canister to absorb fuel vapors the next time the vehicle is not running. Since all air that enters the engine must be filtered, most charcoal canisters have an air filter installed on the air intake.

Capturing evaporated fuel vapors is a critical part of reducing one of the major sources of hydrocarbon emissions. The rates of evaporation are not the same for all fuels. Evaporation is higher with gasoline than diesel, because gasoline is more volatile. Volatility is the ability of a fuel to evaporate more or less easily. If a fuel is more volatile, it is able to evaporate quickly and easily. Volatility is important for cold weather operation but causes excess vapor in warmer weather. For this reason, gasoline fuels are rated for winter or summer use, as the winter fuel must be more volatile due to the cooler atmospheric air temperature. Thus, a problem arises when a vehicle has a winter blend of gasoline in the tank and an unexpectedly hot spring day happens. The charcoal canister can then become overwhelmed with more vapor than it can handle and allow some of the vapor to escape past the canister to the atmosphere. Manufacturers size charcoal canisters to a particular amount of fuel tank capacity and fuel volatility. In fact, some vehicles with large fuel tanks require the use of two or more charcoal canisters to provide enough fuel vapor capacity for the vehicle.

Vacuum Controls in the EVAP System

Older vehicles use vacuum to control the opening and closing of the canister **purge valve**, which is spring-loaded in the closed position. Vacuum applied to the purge valve opens it so the canister can be purged. The vacuum signal to the purge valve is controlled by a thermal vacuum valve, which allows vacuum to pass through it to the purge valve only when the engine is above the specified operating temperature. The vacuum is provided by a ported vacuum tap just above the throttle plate, so vacuum is provided only when the vehicle is at cruise. At WOT the vacuum in the manifold falls to zero; thus, the canister cannot purge at WOT in the same way the EGR system cannot operate at WOT.

With the advent of early ECMs, manufacturers used an electrically operated **purge solenoid** to turn on and off the control vacuum to the purge valve **FIGURE 51-26**. In this way manifold vacuum can be controlled by the purge solenoid when the ECM sees that the engine is above the specified operating temperature and throttle opening. The ECM then sends an electrical signal to the purge solenoid, which opens its vacuum valve and allows manifold vacuum to open the purge valve and start purging the canister.

Electronic Controls in the EVAP System

Most recent EVAP systems are electronically controlled to allow for more precise purge control. The ECM takes into account engine temperature, rpm, throttle position, and calculated load to decide when and at what rate the vapors can be purged. The ECM then commands the purge valve to open and allow the manifold vacuum to

To intake manifold (via purge valve)

To/From fuel tank

Pressure relief valve

Vacuum relief valve

Activated charcoal

Foam filters

Atmospheric vent

FIGURE 51-25 Charcoal canister.

FIGURE 51-26 Electrically operated vacuum purge system.

purge vapor from the charcoal canister. The electronically controlled EVAP system also allows the use of a feedback system to monitor the efficiency of the system and turn on the MIL if a fault is found.

The purge valve can be opened by an integrated solenoid or stepper motor. If it is a solenoid style, it can be either an on/off solenoid or a pulse-width-modulated solenoid, depending on the vehicle. If it is a stepper motor style, then the ECM can progressively open and close the purge valve one step at a time.

The EVAP system also incorporates a **vent solenoid**. The vent solenoid activates a valve that allows fresh air to enter the canister during purge. The vent solenoid can also close off the vent valve, which prevents fresh air from entering the canister. This feature is used as part of the EVAP monitoring strategy and will be discussed in the next section.

Computer Monitoring Strategies in the EVAP System

The EVAP system monitoring is a bit different from the other emission control monitors. EVAP monitoring is required not only to detect faults that prevent proper purging of the canister but also to detect any leaks greater than 0.020" (0.51 mm) in the system. Manufacturers are free to design their own monitoring systems as long as the system can accurately detect the minimum specified fault. Because manufacturers have the ability to design their own systems, there is a wide variety of strategies and components used by the manufacturers. We will explore some of the more common strategies in this section.

In some cases, manufacturers use dedicated sensors such as a **purge switch**, which is located in the purge line and senses the flow of gases or the pressure drop caused by the flow of gases that are being purged **FIGURE 51-27**. The purge switch then signals the ECM that purge is actually happening. Other EVAP monitoring strategies

use the oxygen sensors to measure the decrease in exhaust oxygen content when the EVAP system is being purged. Another method is to accurately calculate the amount of fuel vapor in the purged gases by using the fuel trim correction data during purge.

Newer EVAP systems monitor purge operation by reading a **fuel tank pressure sensor**. The ECM system closes the vent solenoid, which seals off the EVAP system from outside air. The purge valve is opened to allow manifold vacuum to pull a vacuum on the system. If the purge system is operating correctly, the fuel tank pressure sensor will report an increase in vacuum that is within the specified pressure and time factors for the conditions currently present in that vehicle **FIGURE 51-28**. If the system passes the purge test, the ECM commands the purge valve to close, thus sealing off the EVAP system

FIGURE 51-27 Purge switch.

FIGURE 51-28 If the purge system is operating correctly, the fuel tank pressure sensor will report an increase in vacuum that is within the specified pressure and time factors for the conditions currently present in that vehicle.

from manifold vacuum. Since the vent solenoid is still closed, the EVAP system is completely sealed. The ECM monitors the fuel tank pressure sensor for a set time and looks for any loss of vacuum. If noted, the ECM will set a DTC based on the calculated size of the leak. The ECM is required to detect leaks as small as 0.020" (0.51 mm) (small leak). Larger leaks will set a separate DTC.

Common EVAP System Failures

EVAP systems are somewhat prone to failures. One weak area of the EVAP system is the gas cap. Since it is removed and reinstalled often, it is possible that it might not get tightened all the way. It should be tightened until it clicks to ensure there is no leak. Leakage could also result from a damaged gasket or seal. Gas cap leaks are detected by the monitor. A code is then set and the MIL turned on.

Another common EVAP fault relates to the rubber and plastic vacuum lines that run between the components of the EVAP system. These hoses carry the vapor from the fuel tank all the way to the intake manifold. A small hole or crack in the line will allow vapors to escape to the atmosphere. This hole will be detected by the EVAP monitor. A DTC will then be set, and the check engine light will come on. Many vehicles use a plastic fuel tank, which can crack and leak, resulting in an EVAP systems failure. Sometimes, the use of a smoke machine may be necessary to find the leak in the system.

Other failure areas for the EVAP system are the vent and purge solenoids. If the valve fails electrically, it may not open or close when commanded by the ECM. The valves can also fail mechanically and stick open or closed. The vent solenoid may also get plugged with mud or debris. These types of failures will typically result in a DTC being set and the MIL turning on.

▶ Secondary Air Injection

Secondary air injection is less common now than it was in previous years. There are several reasons for this. The first reason is improved engine design, which causes the engine to warm up much quicker and therefore emit fewer emissions. Improved engine design also enhances turbulence and mixing of the air and fuel, which has the effect of reducing the emissions. The second reason that engines run much cleaner is due to the much more accurate fuel delivery to the combustion chamber. And the last reason is due to the use of highly efficient three-way catalytic converters. In fact, many new vehicles are able to meet the tightened emission regulations even without the secondary air injection system. Of those vehicles that are equipped with a secondary air injection system, many only operate during engine warm-up to burn off

the increased hydrocarbons and carbon monoxide as well as help heat up the catalytic converter quicker.

When older carbureted and throttle body–injected engines were started up cold, they needed a richer mixture to operate due to the cold intake manifold surfaces, which condensed fuel out of the air and created a lean condition. This rich mixture resulted in the excessive release of hydrocarbons and carbon monoxide from the tailpipe until the engine warmed up. To reduce hydrocarbons and carbon monoxide, the secondary air injection system was added. It injected air (oxygen) into the hot exhaust gases as they left the combustion chamber. The extra oxygen caused the hot hydrocarbons and carbon monoxide to burn, converting them into water and carbon dioxide. The burning of the hydrocarbons and carbon monoxide also added extra heat to the exhaust stream, which helped warm up the catalytic converter more quickly, making it operational sooner. Once the catalytic converter heated up, the air (oxygen) was switched from upstream (near the exhaust valves) to downstream, where it entered the oxidizing catalyst in the converter. The extra oxygen was used to help oxidize any remaining hydrocarbons and carbon monoxide in the converter.

Secondary air injection systems use three valves to control airflow in the system. The **air switching valve** is used to switch air from upstream to downstream once the engine reaches the specified temperature. The **air diverter valve** diverts the injection air from the exhaust stream to the air cleaner assembly whenever additional air in the exhaust stream could cause backfiring in the exhaust, such as during deceleration or WOT. The last type of valve used in the system is a check valve **FIGURE 51-29**. It prevents hot exhaust gases from traveling backward through the hoses and valves to the air pump, which

FIGURE 51-29 Air diverter valve and check valve.

would overheat and ruin the hoses, valves, and pump in short order.

Early secondary air injection systems used a thermal vacuum switch in the vacuum line to control the switching valve. When the engine was cold, the thermal vacuum switch allowed vacuum to the switching valve, which moved the switching valve to the upstream position. Once the specified engine temperature was reached, the thermal vacuum switch would block the vacuum from reaching the switching valve and a spring moved the switching valve to the downstream position. In later designs, the air switching valve and diverter valve were operated by an electrical actuator controlled by the ECM for more precise control of the air injection system.

Secondary Air Injection Types

There are two main types of air injection systems: aspirated and pumped **FIGURE 51-30**. Aspirated systems use an aspirator valve to help facilitate the moving of air in the system instead of an air pump. Aspirated systems are also known as pulse air systems. The pumped type of system uses an air pump to move the air and may be belt driven by the engine or electrically driven by an electric

FIGURE 51-30 There are a two main types of air injection systems: aspirated **(A)** and pumped **(B)**.

motor. Any of these systems do the same job of ensuring that the exhaust stream receives oxygen at the correct locations and time.

The **pulse air system** uses the pulsations of the exhaust gas to open and close a **reed valve** (also called an aspirator valve), which is a flat metal valve that flexes when pressure is applied against it **FIGURE 51-31**. The reed valve admits air into the exhaust manifold in short bursts, but prevents air from moving back through the reed valve. Air drawn from the air filter enters the exhaust manifold through the reed valve. The pulse air injection is suited for engines with four cylinders or less because their exhaust pulsations are further apart and more pronounced, creating more efficient pulling of air into the exhaust stream.

Systems that use an **air pump** are installed on engines with more than four cylinders and supply a steady volume of air to the system. The air pump is commonly a mechanical vane-style pump that moves the air at low pressures, in some cases as low as 2 pounds per square inch (psi), or 13.8 kilopascals (kPa). If the air pump is belt driven, it can be driven by a V-belt or a serpentine belt.

Some systems have air pumps that are operated by an electric motor only when needed. The air pump is turned on and off by the ECM based on the needs of the emission system. The electrically driven air pump type is the most recent of the secondary air injection systems.

Common Air Injection System Failures

Secondary air injection system failures on older systems were numerous and more common because more mechanical parts were involved. The air pump itself had bearings that could fail and cause a pump and accessory belt failure. The switching and diverter valves could stick and direct air to the wrong place. Vacuum hoses and

FIGURE 51-31 Pulse air injection system.

valves would crack and break, creating a vacuum leak and failure of the entire secondary air injection system. The air distribution hoses to the exhaust manifold required the use of a check valve, which kept exhaust from flowing backward and destroying the switching and diverter valve, hoses and tubing, and air pump.

With the introduction of the ECM, electric controls replaced some of the vacuum-operated parts, which helped reduce the amount of failures. Common failures now include connector terminal pin fit issues that create open circuits or high resistance and other common electrical circuit faults.

Heated Air Intake Systems

Fuel must be in a vapor form for it to burn. Liquid fuel will not burn. So the challenge is to get liquid fuel to fully vaporize by the time it needs to be ignited, not much sooner and not later. Intake manifolds carry the fuel. Fuel tends to condense on the inside surface of the cold manifold. One method of minimizing this problem is use of a **heated air intake system**. This system collects hot air from around the exhaust manifold and mixes it with outside air entering the air cleaner assembly **FIGURE 51-32**. The system maintains a specified air temperature of air entering the engine. This simple system uses a temperature-sensitive valve inside the air cleaner. It operates a flap that blends the hot air with cool air, so that the intake manifold receives air at about 100–110°F (38–43°C), regardless of the outside air temperature. Maintenance of this consistent temperature assists in the proper **vaporization** of the fuel, particularly when the engine is cold.

FIGURE 51-32 Heated air intake systems use the air around hot exhaust manifolds to blend with outside air to supply warm air at a predetermined temperature.

Vaporization is also assisted in some engines, such as in the Toyota Prius, by circulating stored hot liquid coolant through passages in the intake manifold and cylinder head, thereby preheating them right before the engine is started. Another past method of preheating fuel and air mixtures before entering the combustion chamber was to use a hot wire mesh under the throttle body to assist in heating air to promote the vaporization of the fuel. Fuel will not mix easily in cold air temperatures, so the use of a heating grid assures a more combustible fuel mixture.

▶ Diagnosis

With emission control systems, often the first indication of any trouble is an illuminated MIL on the dash. In many cases, the vehicle may not exhibit any drivability issues. If the vehicle is equipped with an OBDII system, then using any stored DTCs will help isolate the fault. Diagnosis of emission control systems often starts with a good scan tool to access any DTCs. Once you have a DTC, service information, and any related technical service bulletins, you will have the information to determine the steps to locate the cause of the fault. If the vehicle's ECM has bidirectional capability, it may be helpful to operate suspect components and observe the results. For example, if there is a DTC regarding the canister vent solenoid, you might want to command it to close and then check to see if it indeed did close, both electrically and mechanically.

If there are no DTCs present, then having a good understanding of the types of emission control systems the vehicle is equipped with is a good place to start. This can best be found by researching the "description and operation" of the systems in the service information. Use that information plus any "symptom diagnosis" procedures to start diagnosing the system. Also, understanding the following information will help you track down the cause of the fault.

Diagnosing EVAP System–Related Concerns

EVAP system faults may or may not create drivability issues. If the EVAP system continues to purge at idle, a rough idle could be created. If the vapor line between the charcoal canister and the fuel tank is ruptured, there is likely to be no drivability issues, but the MIL will most likely be illuminated. Because the federal regulations require the OBDII system to monitor each of the emission control systems and turn on the MIL when the emission output is 1.5 times the FTP, emission control system faults normally are accompanied by an illuminated MIL. All vehicles built from 1996 up have enhanced evaporative systems. These systems can detect purge flow and leakage in the evaporative system.

To diagnose EVAP-related concerns, a good understanding of how the system operates is required. Use a scan tool to pull any diagnostic codes. The freeze-frame data stored can give a good indication of the conditions that set the code. Most manufacturers will have the technician record the freeze-frame data in order to recreate the operating conditions at the time of the fault. If diagnostic codes are present, follow the manufacturer's diagnostic trouble chart. If there are no diagnostic codes, use the scan tool to view the live sensor and actuator data for the EVAP system sensors and actuators. Compare the data displayed with the service information data. If necessary, command the actuators on one at a time and watch how the sensor data respond. The data, along with an understanding of the system, will likely lead you to the fault.

Diagnosing Abnormal Exhaust

To diagnose abnormal exhaust color, you have to understand what each color represents. Exhaust with a bluish tint represents oil that is being burned in the combustion chamber. This condition typically means the piston oil control rings are worn, there is excessive valve stem-to-guide clearance, or the valve seals are worn. Black exhaust represents an overly rich air–fuel mixture. This condition could be caused by a significant number of faults, such as a leaking or sticking fuel injector, a leaky vacuum diaphragm on the fuel pressure regulator, an open coolant temperature sensor circuit, or a MAP sensor reading incorrectly. All of these conditions would supply more fuel than needed, causing the engine to run rich and possibly emit black smoke. White exhaust represents water or coolant burning in the combustion chamber. This condition could be caused by a number of faults, such as a blown head gasket, a leaky intake manifold gasket, or a crack in the head or block that is allowing anti-freeze to leak into the combustion chamber.

To diagnose an abnormal exhaust, gain as much of an understanding of the customer concern relating to exhaust as possible. Understanding the customer's complaint is the first stage of the repair process. Does the customer have additional information to give you, such as whether the issue happens when the engine is cold or hot? Verify the customer concern by starting the engine and attempt to duplicate the conditions that the customer described. Research the possible causes of the concern in the appropriate service information or technical service bulletins. Perform any specified tests to verify the cause of the customer's concern.

Diagnosing PCV-related Concerns

A PCV system is used to remove blow-by gases from the crankcase in an environmentally friendly manner. If blow-by gases are not removed from the crankcase, pressure can build up and cause oil seals and gaskets to leak oil. Replacement of seals or gaskets might temporarily fix the problem until excessive pressure pushes the seal or gasket out of place again. Proper testing of the PCV valve system is critical to get to the root cause of the concern and avoid repeat failures.

To diagnose PCV-related concerns, first locate the PCV valve. Refer to the service information for location of the PCV valve and hoses. If the PCV valve is located in the valve cover, remove the PCV valve from the cover and ensure that a strong vacuum is coming through the valve with the engine running. This ensures the PCV valve and hose are clear. Reinstall the PCV valve into the valve cover and remove the breather tube from the air cleaner assembly. With the engine still running, check that vacuum builds up in the breather tube (and crankcase), indicating that the breather tube is clear and there is not excessive blow-by gases. Inspect all hoses for softening, brittleness, cracks, kinks, and holes. Cracks in hoses can result in vacuum leaks, which can create a poor idle situation. Inspect the PCV valve and ensure it has the correct part number for the vehicle. If the incorrect part is found, or the valve is sludged up or sticky, replace it with a new PCV valve.

> ### TECHNICIAN TIP
>
> Many vehicles have individual EGR passageways for individual intake manifold runners. If some of the passageways become clogged, too much EGR gases will go to the remaining open passageways when the EGR valve opens, causing an engine misfire. If the engine experiences rough engine operation when the EGR valve is open, suspect this condition.

Diagnosing EGR-related Concerns

EGR valves will typically cause two types of drivability concerns. One will be a rough idle concern, and the other will be a preignition or detonation concern known as **pinging**. Pinging can be referred to as the sound of marbles being shaken in a glass jar and is damaging to the engine if it is allowed to continue. Engines will ping under moderate and heavy loads such as climbing a hill or pulling a heavy load. If the EGR valve is stuck in a closed position or if passageways are clogged, pinging can result, along with excessive oxides of nitrogen emissions. If the

EGR valve is stuck in an open position, the engine will idle excessively rough and may stall at stops.

To diagnose EGR-related concerns, first gather the customer concern and as many specific details as possible. Consult the service information and research the "description and operation" of the EGR system for the vehicle you are working on. With either a scan tool or a vacuum pump (depending on the system; refer to the service information on testing), operate the EGR valve with the vehicle running. Idle should become rough, and the engine may eventually stall as the EGR valve is opened and exhaust gas flows into the intake manifold. If there is no difference, or very little difference, in the idle speed and quality, suspect plugged-up EGR passageways, or a faulty EGR valve. If the idle was substantially affected, perform testing of the control system to ensure that a signal is getting to the EGR valve. Verify that either a vacuum or an electrical signal is getting to the EGR valve when the engine is running at about 2000 rpm. If a signal is not getting to the EGR valve, inspect the remainder of the control circuit to identify the fault. With the information that you have collected, determine any necessary actions.

Diagnosing Concerns Related to the Secondary Air Injection System

The secondary air injection system consists of several components: an air pump, either belt driven or, on some newer models, electronic; distribution tubes and hoses; check valves that prevent exhaust flow back into the air pump; and air management valves or solenoids to direct the airflow. The air pump reduces hydrocarbons and carbon monoxide by pumping air into the exhaust stream and assisting the catalytic converter in converting the hydrocarbons and carbon monoxide to water and carbon dioxide. If air is not injected into the exhaust manifold when the engine is cold, the hydrocarbons and carbon monoxide emissions will be excessive. If the air is injected into the exhaust manifold at all times, the oxygen sensor will pick up on the excessive oxygen and tell the ECM a lean condition is present. The ECM will then richen up the fuel mixture, creating more emissions, poor gas mileage, and possibly a drivability issue. Check valves can burn out and separate, or the diaphragm may fail, creating an audible exhaust leak or exhaust flow back into the air management valves and possibly the air pump itself, damaging their plastic components.

To diagnose concerns related to the secondary air injection system, first check for diagnostic codes in the ECM with a scan tool. Pull any trouble codes and consult the service information. View the oxygen sensor readings on a scan tool. If the oxygen sensor readings indicate a lean condition, verify that the oxygen

sensor is functioning properly, and refer to the service information on further testing. Verify that air is not being injected to the wrong location or at the wrong time. You may have to pinch off the rubber supply hose from the pump. If the oxygen sensor now responds correctly, suspect an air injection system fault.

▶ Maintenance and Repair
Emission Testing

You must have a thorough understanding of emission control systems in order to test and repair an emission failure. Some states require emission testing to ensure that all emission control devices are working properly and that proper combustion is taking place. This could be as simple as verifying that there are no DTCs set in memory and that certain monitors have run. Or it could require a tailpipe emission test. There are several tools that can be used to ensure that emission systems are working properly. One of these tools is the **five-gas analyzer** **FIGURE 51-33**. This tool uses sensors to measure the level of gases in the exhaust stream. The technician compares the analyzer readings to the manufacturer's acceptable

> **TECHNICIAN TIP**
>
> The emissions standard chart is used to ensure that a vehicle passes the required emissions laws for the state. The chart may be labeled in percentage (%), parts per million (ppm), or grams per mile (g/mi). The EPA provides emissions standards for federal and California emissions, although individual states or municipalities may have their own standards.

FIGURE 51-33 Five-gas analyzer.

TABLE 51-3: Typical Emission Test Readings

	Hydrocarbon	Carbon Monoxide	Oxygen	Carbon Dioxide	Oxides of Nitrogen
With Converter	< 100 ppm	< 0.5%	0% to 2%	12% to 15%	< 100 ppm, idle

Note: This chart will not relate to all vehicles; refer to your state's specifications.
Source: Information from Arizona state emissions site.

levels for that particular vehicle. The manufacturer's specifications may be located in the software of the gas analyzer you are using, or your state emission inspection agency may provide the specifications for each vehicle. Some states require the use of the five-gas analyzer with a dynamometer; others require only a five-gas idle test or a combination of an idle and a 2000-rpm test.

A rule of thumb for emission testing is found in **TABLE 51-3**. This chart is for engines at idle and is typical of what a five-gas analyzer will display. Be sure to refer to your vehicle's specifications if performing an emission test for your state, as each power train option will create differing emissions.

Vehicles produced after 1996 use the OBDII requirements. This system contains additional sensors and testing strategies that have led some states to do away with mandatory five-gas dynamometer testing and instead perform an **on-board diagnostic (OBD)** system test to ensure that all tests (or monitors) have been run and passed by the engine's computer, and that there are no DTCs in memory. If an OBD test fails, a related diagnosis code may be set that alerts technicians to the fault. If all tests pass, an **idling five-gas test** may be performed. In an idling five-gas test, a five-gas analyzer takes a sample of gases from the exhaust pipe.

Setting Up a Gas Analyzer

A gas analyzer is a useful tool to determine problems with a vehicle by analyzing the tailpipe gases. If combustion is not working as designed or an emission control device is malfunctioning, excessive emissions will be released. Some states make this analysis a mandatory test conducted periodically (every one or two years) to certify that the vehicle is not excessively polluting the air.

When setting up an analyzer, there are several details to be aware of. The first is that all emission analyzers require a certain amount of time to warm up. Up to about 10 minutes is required on some machines. Any readings before the analyzer is fully warmed up will not be valid. Next, the sample hose is flexible, typically made out of rubber or hard plastic, with a metal flexible sniffer probe on the end. The hose and probe are susceptible to cracking. Cracks would allow ambient air to leak into the sample exhaust stream, diluting it and leading to

an incorrect reading. The hose and tube should be leak checked before every test, or at least once per day. Leak testing can normally be performed by plugging the holes in the metal sniffer tube and watching for the low flow indicator to illuminate on the analyzer. If it does illuminate, there are no substantial leaks in the sample hose and sniffer. If it does not illuminate, there is a leak that will need to be found and repaired.

The analyzer will also need to be zeroed before it can be used. On some analyzers, this step is done automatically; on others, it is manually performed. Just make sure you follow the instructions and zero the analyzer properly. Also, the analyzer should be checked with calibration gases, typically monthly. This process uses calibration gases of specific concentrations to run through the analyzer so that its accuracy can be checked. If the analyzer is operating correctly, it will display the proper readings for the particular calibration gas.

Preparing a five-gas analyzer to obtain exhaust readings requires several steps before the actual exhaust gas reading is obtained. To prepare a five-gas analyzer to obtain exhaust readings, follow the steps in **SKILL DRILL 51-1**:

1. Research the local emission limits for the vehicle you are analyzing. If there are no local requirements for the vehicle, follow federal or state requirements. When the standards are found for the vehicle, write down acceptable levels for idle and, if required, cruise readings.

2. Leak test the analyzer hose and probe by closing off the holes in the end of the probe and watching for the "low flow" indicator to illuminate. **(Photo 1)**

3. Calibrate the analyzer, including leak testing, if applicable. Follow the analyzer operation manual on proper calibration or required warm-up period to ensure accurate readings. The vehicle will also have to be up to operating temperature to ensure closed loop operation and proper catalyst temperature.

4. Insert the exhaust analyzer probe in the vehicle's exhaust pipe at least 18" (46 cm). The proper placement of the probe ensures that the readings are not being diluted with outside air. **(Photo 2)**

5. Allow the vehicle to idle and record the emission readings. At this point, your state procedure may require a higher engine speed (rpm) reading as

SKILL DRILL | **51-1** | **Using a Five-Gas Analyzer**

1. Research the local emission limits for this vehicle in the applicable manual or online sources. Warm up both the vehicle and the exhaust gas analyzer. Leak test the analyzer hose and probe.

2. Calibrate the analyzer, if applicable. Insert the exhaust analyzer probe in the vehicle's exhaust pipe at least 18" (46 cm).

3. Allow the vehicle to idle and record the emission readings. Compare your readings to the specifications and determine any necessary action(s).

well. The idle test results should be at or below the published acceptable emissions limits.

6. Compare your readings to the specifications and determine any necessary actions. The publications will give you acceptable levels for the make, model, and engine size of the vehicle you are working with. Comparing these specifications to the actual readings will determine if the vehicle passes the emission test or not. (**Photo 3**)

Catalytic Converter Testing

A catalytic converter can fail for a number of common reasons, including contamination, overheating, physical damage, or just old age. Contamination happens when the catalyst becomes coated by a substance such as lead from leaded fuel, silicone from improper sealants, or carbon from excessively rich conditions or repeated short driving trips. The contaminant prevents the exhaust gases from interacting with the catalyst, so the gases cannot be converted properly, if at all. Lead and silicone contamination cannot generally be cleaned from the catalyst, so the converter must be replaced in this case. Carbon-contaminated catalyst can sometimes be restored first by correcting any conditions that caused the engine to run rich, and second by driving the vehicle for an extended time at freeway speeds under a moderate load. This process will heat up the converter and possibly burn the carbon contaminants from the catalyst, restoring its function.

Overheating the catalyst can cause the catalyst material to burn off of the substrate, rendering it inoperative. Overheating can also melt the substrate, which can block

the passageways and restrict exhaust gas flow, reducing the engine's power and efficiency. Overheated catalysts cannot be restored and must be replaced.

Physical damage can happen due to an object such as a large rock striking the converter or from thermal shocks, which can happen if the hot converter is immersed in cold water, such as a deep pothole. The substrate, being made of a ceramic material, is quite brittle and can break reasonably easily. Physical damage can usually be found by first visually examining the converter shell for dents indicating abuse. Also, lightly tapping on the converter shell will cause any broken pieces of substrate to rattle around inside, indicating a broken catalyst. Physically damaged converters must be replaced. Also, if the catalyst is broken, it is possible that the broken pieces may be plugging up the rear of the converter or even the muffler. Check for this problem if the catalyst is broken.

Catalysts that are damaged due to contamination, overheating, or old age can be tested to see if they are still functioning. Testing the catalytic converter should be performed according to the manufacturer's service information. If no procedure is outlined in the service information, then it may be necessary to use one of the following tests.

If the vehicle is OBDII compliant, you can either use a scan tool that can access mode 6 and look at the test results for each of the catalyst monitors, or you can use a lab scope to compare the upstream and downstream oxygen sensor patterns to determine whether the catalyst is working efficiently. When using mode 6, you will need to research the specific codes that the manufacturer uses to identify each catalyst monitor, as well as the coding for the actual results. Once you know what you are looking at, you will be able to determine how well each catalyst is performing. For example, if the upper limit for the catalyst monitor in mode 6 is 20, and mode 6 shows it at a 3, you will know that the catalyst is working very well. If the monitor reading is 25, you will know that the convertor is not working well. Just make sure the rest of the ignition, fuel, and emission systems are working well before condemning a catalytic converter. Of course, this is true no matter how you test the converter.

Some manufacturers use mode 6 to display how many counts the catalyst monitor has detected oxygen sensor activity outside of the specified parameters indicating a faulty converter. Be sure to research the manufacturer's information when using mode 6 for diagnosis.

When using a lab scope connected to both the pre-cat O_2 sensor (short for pre-catalytic converter oxygen sensor) and the post-cat O_2 sensor, be sure the catalytic converter is up to operating temperature. If the catalyst is working properly, the downstream oxygen sensor will be relatively stable, while the upstream sensor will be constantly toggling between rich and lean. If the catalyst is not working properly, the upstream sensor will be toggling (indicating a properly operating fuel system), while the downstream sensor will also be toggling, similar to the upstream sensor.

A good test to use on a non-OBDII vehicle is called the **intrusive test**. When performing the intrusive test, a hole is drilled in the exhaust pipe in front of the converter so that an emission analyzer hose can be inserted into the exhaust stream entering the converter. That reading is then compared to a reading taken after the converter at the end of the tailpipe. If the catalyst is working properly, a general rule of thumb is that hydrocarbons, carbon monoxide, and oxides of nitrogen will be reduced by around 90%, assuming the engine is operating as designed. The upstream reading indicates if the engine is operating correctly by giving readings that are consistent with a stoichiometric ratio. The downstream reading indicates if the converter is operating correctly if the harmful emissions are being reduced by approximately 90%. Once the test is complete, the drilled hole is plugged with a stainless steel rivet.

> ## ▶ TECHNICIAN TIP
>
> Since the catalytic converter creates heat as it is operating, it was once thought that you could measure the temperature from the inlet side of the converter and compare that to the temperature at the outlet of the converter. If the converter was working properly, then there would be a 50–100°F increase of temperature at the outlet of the converter. But with fuel systems that run much tighter fuel ratios, that is no longer the case. Thus, this test is no longer considered to be valid on newer vehicles.

To test a catalytic converter for efficiency (lab scope method), follow the steps in **SKILL DRILL 51-2** :

1. First, ensure the vehicle is fully warm by performing a road test. After the road test, install a scan tool with graphing capability, and highlight the pre-cat O_2 sensor (the sensor in front of the converter labeled sensor 1) and the post-cat O_2 sensor (the sensor after the converter, which detects if the gases are converted, labeled sensor 2).

2. The cat O_2 sensors should be labeled, for example, HO_2B1S1 (for heated oxygen sensor, bank one, sensor one) and HO_2B1S2 (for heated oxygen sensor, bank one, sensor two). If the engine is a four-cylinder in-line engine, there is only one bank. Raise engine rpm to 2000 and watch the oxygen sensor readings.

3. Set the scan tool so it will graph both sensor readings. The front oxygen sensor will toggle from rich to lean, and the rear sensor (behind the converter) will tend to run at a steady midpoint reading because the converter is using much of the oxygen converting the hydrocarbons and carbon monoxide. If the rear oxygen sensor pattern tracks the front sensor, the catalytic converter is not functioning and will need to be replaced.

4. If the front sensor is not toggling properly, the engine or fuel system is not operating properly, and you will need to diagnose that condition further. You need to keep in mind the symptom-to-system-to-component-to-cause diagnostic process used by most manufacturers. If the catalytic converter failed, determine the cause of the failure. Replacement of the converter may mask the symptoms but only for a short time, and then they will show up again.

Inspecting and Servicing the PCV System

The PCV system draws crankcase gases out of the crankcase and burns them in the engine to reduce crankcase emissions. It is an important system that needs to be serviced on a regular maintenance interval determined by the manufacturer and published in its service information. A PCV valve test should be performed as part of a thorough tune-up service. Failure of the PCV system can result in drivability issues or repeat oil seal failures, creating oil leaks on the engine. Repeat oil seal or gasket failures are noted by checking vehicle service history and noting multiple replacements of a specific seal or gasket.

To test the PCV system, follow the steps in **SKILL DRILL 51-3** :

1. Locate the PCV valve. It is usually located in or near the valve cover or in the intake manifold.

SKILL DRILL | 51-3 | Inspecting and Servicing the PCV System

1. Locate the PCV valve. With the engine idling, remove the PCV valve and check for the presence of a strong vacuum.

2. Remove the hose and check that it is still pliable and not clogged with sludge deposits.

3. Remove the PCV valve and inspect it for deposits. If it is restricted, is sludged up, or sticks, replace it with a new one of the same type.

4. Reinstall the PCV valve into the valve cover, and remove the breather hose from the air cleaner assembly.

5. With the engine idling, block off the breather hose and feel for vacuum building up in the breather hose and crankcase, indicating that the PCV system can handle the amount of blow-by gases.

If you cannot identify it quickly, check with the service information. Be sure to look up the replacement interval while in the service information.

2. With the engine idling, remove the PCV valve from the valve cover, leaving the hose in place. When putting your finger over the opening of the PCV valve, you should feel strong vacuum. If not, the hose or valve may be restricted. **(Photo 1)**

3. Check that the hose is still pliable (but not squishy) and not clogged with sludge deposits. If the hose is

squishy, brittle, or plugged, or has buildup, then it should be replaced. **(Photo 2)**

4. Remove the PCV valve and inspect it for deposits. If it is restricted, is sludged up, or sticks, then replace it with a new one of the same type. If it is a fixed-orifice type, check that the orifice is clear. Clean it with a suitable solvent, if necessary. **(Photo 3)**

5. Reinstall the PCV valve into the valve cover, and remove the breather hose from the air cleaner assembly. **(Photo 4)**

6 With the engine idling, block off the breather hose and feel for vacuum building up in the breather hose and crankcase, indicating that the PCV system can handle the amount of blow-by gases. **(Photo 5)**

Inspecting and Servicing the EGR System

The EGR system is intended to reduce the amount of oxides of nitrogen that are formed during combustion. The introduction of exhaust gases reduces the combustion temperature, which in turn lowers oxides of nitrogen. EGR systems normally are not active on engines when cold, at idle, or at WOT. To inspect and service the EGR system, start by researching the description and operation in the service information. Then perform an output test on the EGR valve. With either a scan tool or a vacuum pump (depending on the system; refer to the service information on testing), operate the EGR valve with the vehicle running. Idle should become rough, and the engine may eventually stall as the EGR valve is opened and exhaust gas flows into the intake manifold. If the idle becomes rough, the EGR valve is capable of operating and the passageways are relatively clear. If there is no change in the engine idle speed when the EGR valve is activated, perform testing of the control system to ensure that a signal is getting to the EGR valve. This could be a vacuum signal or an electrical signal, depending on the type of EGR control system. If a signal is getting to the EGR valve, inspect the valve itself for faults and the EGR passageways to ensure they are not clogged.

With the information you have collected, determine the necessary actions. Remember that the EGR valve will be hot to the touch if the engine is warm. Because there are many types of EGR sensors, one description cannot adequately cover this procedure; therefore, the following steps are generic.

To test the EGR system, follow the steps in **SKILL DRILL 51-4**:

1 Determine the type of EGR valve the vehicle is equipped with and the test procedure needed. Assuming you are working with a digital EGR valve, follow the procedures in the service information.

2 Attach a scan tool to the data link connector (DLC) and retrieve any codes related to the EGR system. If diagnostic codes are present, follow the trouble chart in the service information for further diagnosis.

3 Follow the manufacturer's troubleshooting chart. If the troubleshooting chart tells you to inspect passageways, it may be necessary to remove the EGR valve to inspect.

4 Based on the diagnostic chart, determine the path to follow to repair the vehicle.

5 Verify the repair. Drive the vehicle to ensure that the repair was performed properly before releasing the vehicle to the customer.

Inspecting and Servicing the EGR Sensors

The method of inspecting EGR sensors depends on the type of sensor system used by the manufacturer. Some systems use sensors to monitor the position of the pintle and calculate EGR flow. Some use a temperature probe on the downstream side of the EGR valve and watch for the temperature rise when the EGR gases are flowing. Some use the MAP sensor to watch for the pressure change in the intake manifold when the EGR valve is commanded on. Many systems used on Ford Motor Company vehicles use a pressure sensor (called a Delta Pressure Feedback EGR [DPFE]) to monitor the pressure difference across a restriction in the EGR tube. When EGR gases flow across the restriction, a pressure difference occurs, which causes the sensor to change its signal, indicating EGR flow.

To diagnose EGR sensor–related concerns, first consult the service information and research the proper operation of the EGR system on the vehicle. You also need to verify that the EGR valve is operating. Follow the steps in the previous skill drill to test the EGR system's operation.

EGR sensors give feedback to the ECM that the EGR valve is flowing exhaust gas. If gas is not found to be flowing, the MIL will be turned on and a diagnostic code set. Further diagnosis using the service information will be needed. Because there are many types of EGR sensors, one description cannot adequately cover this procedure; therefore, the following steps are generic.

To test the EGR sensors, follow the steps in **SKILL DRILL 51-5**:

1 Research the procedure for testing the electrical sensors and wiring of the EGR sensor system in the service information.

2 Attach a scan tool to the DLC and retrieve any codes related to the EGR sensor. If diagnostic codes are present, follow the trouble chart in the service information for further diagnosis.

3 Follow the service information procedure for testing the EGR sensor and wiring. Testing will involve the use of a digital volt-ohmmeter (DVOM) and basic electrical testing. It may also require a scan tool to activate the EGR valve for testing purposes. Follow the service information for testing.

4 After following service procedures, determine any necessary actions.

Inspecting and Servicing the Secondary Air Injection System

The secondary air injection system is not as common as it once was due to the more accurate fuel systems, heated oxygen sensors, and faster warm-up. Always verify that the vehicle you are working on has a secondary air injection system. Testing the secondary air injection system starts with checking for any related DTCs. If any are present, then refer to the service information, which will provide detailed testing procedures. If no DTCs are present, then you will want to verify that the system is operating according to design; if not, you will have a better idea of where the problem is located.

To verify that the system is operating correctly, check to see where air is being directed during cold start-up and again when the engine warms up. Many times you can squeeze the air injection hoses and feel the pulsations of air flowing through it. By feeling each of the hoses, you can determine where and when air is being directed. Because the types of air injection systems are so great, one description cannot adequately cover this procedure; therefore, the following steps are generic.

To inspect the secondary air injection system, follow the steps in **SKILL DRILL 51-6** :

1. Check for any stored DTCs related to the secondary air injection system with a scan tool. If any are found, research the service information for proper procedures for diagnosing the codes. Ensure you have a proper understanding of the system's operation before attempting to repair the system.

2. Check the system's operation. Air should be directed toward the exhaust manifold during engine warm-up and to the converter once warm.

3. Determine necessary actions. If the air pump is locked or any mechanical components are seized, replace with new parts and retest the system.

Inspecting and Testing Electrical Components of Secondary Air Injection Systems

The air injection electrical system controls the operation of the air valves and, in some cases, the electric air pump. If the electrical system fails, a check engine light should illuminate and a diagnostic code will set. Start by retrieving any related DTCs. Follow the service information to diagnose the operation of the secondary air electrical system. Because the types of air injection electrical systems are so great, one description cannot adequately cover this procedure; therefore, the following steps are generic.

To test the electrical system of the secondary air injection system, retrieve any related DTCs and research the service information for the diagnostic procedures for a secondary air injection electrical concern. Be sure you understand the operation of the secondary air injection system. Follow the service information to diagnose any secondary air injection system faults, and replace or repair the faulty component.

Inspecting and Servicing the Hoses of the EVAP System

The hoses of the EVAP system carry the hydrocarbon vapors from the fuel tank to the charcoal canister and then to the engine to be burned. Valves and solenoids are used to control the flow of vapors into and out of the charcoal canister, as well as direct them into the engine depending on operating conditions. If a leak exists in the EVAP system (including the gas cap) or hoses, hydrocarbons can be released into the atmosphere. An EVAP system code will be set by the ECM if a leak is detected. If the leak is large, the PCM will set a P0455 (gross leak) DTC. If the leak is small, the PCM will set a P0456 (small leak) DTC. Other codes could indicate low purge flow or a fault in one of the sensors, valves, or solenoids. The service information will guide you through the proper diagnosis, depending on the DTC. However, a visual inspection of the hoses and components may give you a clue as to the cause of the fault.

To inspect the hoses and components of the EVAP system, follow the steps in **SKILL DRILL 51-7** :

1. Use a scan tool and check for codes related to the EVAP system. If a nonleak code is found, follow the diagnostic procedures for that code.

2. If the diagnostic code indicates a leak, connect an EVAP tester to the EVAP test port. (**Photo 1**)

3. Use the EVAP system leak detector to determine if the system is in fact leaking and, if so, how big the leak is. (**Photo 2**)

4. Use an approved smoke machine to help locate the leak. If smoke is detected, look in the area of the smoke to identify the cause of the leak. If no smoke is detected, the system could be leaking internally through a stuck-open purge valve or a leaky vent valve.

5. Repair according to the manufacturer's procedure. (**Photo 3**)

SKILL DRILL | 51-7 | Inspecting and Servicing the Hoses of the EVAP System

1. Use a scan tool and check for codes related to the EVAP system. If a code is found, follow the diagnostic procedures for that code. If the diagnostic code indicates a leak, connect an EVAP tester to the EVAP test port.

2. Use the EVAP system leak detector to determine if the system is in fact leaking and, if so, the size of the leak.

3. Use a smoke machine to help locate the leak. If smoke is detected, look in the area of the smoke to identify the cause of the leak. If no smoke is detected, the system could be leaking internally through a stuck-open purge valve or a leaky vent valve. Repair according to the manufacturer's procedure.

Wrap-up

Ready for Review

▶ In automotive applications, most emissions are the by-product of combustion and are emitted from the exhaust system.

▶ Not all emissions from combustion are considered hazardous.

▶ The term "emission", when used in automotive circles, normally refers to the pollution produced by a light vehicle during operation or while sitting stationary.

▶ The fuel tank allows liquid fuel to evaporate into a gas; if not controlled, those vapors can escape into the atmosphere and are called evaporative emissions.

▶ In a compression-ignition diesel engine, emissions are created in the combustion chamber the same way as in spark ignition engines and escape to the atmosphere through the exhaust and the crankcase breather.

▶ Manufacturers are required by law and the Environmental Protection Agency (EPA) to control the emissions produced by their vehicles.

▶ The federal test procedure (FTP) requires all manufacturers to pass a federal emission test before vehicles can be sold in the United States.

▶ Not only must the vehicles pass the test before they can be sold, but also they must be capable of detecting an emission failure over the life of the vehicle, as they are being operated.

▶ As of 1996, all new vehicles most meet the OBDII standard, meaning all vehicles must have the same self diagnostic connectors.

▶ The EPA requires that when a vehicle's emissions deviate from the FTP limit by 1.5 times, the warning light (malfunction indicator lamp) must turn on and one or more specific diagnostic trouble codes (DTC) set in memory.

▶ The OBDII system was developed purely with the intent of keeping vehicles emission compliant and warning drivers if they aren't.

▶ Regulated air pollutants can be divided into two groups: gases and particulates.

▶ Many countries follow an international protocol on emissions requiring vehicle manufacturers to comply with these laws.

▶ Historically, the regulated emissions have been hydrocarbons, carbon monoxide, oxides of nitrogen, and particulate matter. In recent years, carbon dioxide has been added to the list of emissions that are being regulated.

▶ There are three categories of emission gasses: non-harmful, harmful, and debatable.

Key Terms

activated charcoal Charcoal that will absorb large amounts of vapor, used in charcoal canisters to store and release fuel vapors.

actuator A mechanical part, usually controlled by electricity allowing a module to control something mechanical.

air diverter valve A valve that changes secondary air-flow from the exhaust stream to the air cleaner or vice versa.

air pump A device used to pump air to the exhaust stream to ensure the converter has enough oxygen to perform gas conversions.

air switching valve The valve used to switch secondary air from near the exhaust valve (upstream) to the catalytic converter (downstream) for the purpose of oxidizing hydrocarbons and carbon monoxide.

blow-by Pressure that leaks past the compression rings during compression and combustion.

breather tube A tube used in the PCV system to allow fresh air into the engine crankcase.

carbon dioxide A by-product of complete combustion, carbon dioxide is a chemical compound made up of two oxygen molecules bonded to a single carbon molecule.

carbon monoxide A poisonous gas released during combustion of rich air–fuel mixtures.

carbon monoxide poisoning Exposure to higher than tolerable levels of carbon monoxide, resulting in headaches, fatigue, or loss of consciousness, eventually resulting in death.

carburetor float bowl The part of the carburetor that holds fuel to be burned in the engine; the bowl is at a constant level of fuel to ensure adequate fuel is present during driving.

closed loop The operational status of the engine control system in which the oxygen sensor is providing feedback of rich or lean exhaust conditions and the control unit is varying fuel delivery based on that information.

compression-ignition engine An engine that uses the heat of compression to ignite the air–fuel mixture; also known as a diesel engine.

diaphragm-style EGR valve An EGR valve that is operated by a diaphragm that moves when vacuum is applied to it, opening a passageway for exhaust to flow.

EGR system monitor A control module diagnostic test that is run to ensure that the EGR valve and passageways are operating properly.

EGR valve A valve that connects the exhaust port, or manifold, and the intake manifold. If engine operating conditions are likely to produce oxides of nitrogen, the EGR valve opens, letting some burned exhaust gases pass from the exhaust into the intake system.

emission A gas that is released to the atmosphere; usually refers to a harmful gas.

emission control system A system of devices that are designed to control or reduce harmful gases released to the atmosphere.

evaporative emission (EVAP) system A system used to capture vapors or gases from an evaporating liquid.

exhaust gas recirculation (EGR) system A system that recirculates a portion of burned gases back into the combustion chamber to displace air and fuel and cool combustion temperatures.

expansion volume An engineered space that allows for growth of the volume of a liquid as it heats and expands.

feedback system A system that uses feedback to adjust what it is doing. Typically, a module gives a command and waits to see if the command was followed by use of a sensor.

five-gas analyzer A tool that uses sensors to measure the level of gases in the exhaust stream.

fixed-orifice PCV system A system in which a hole of a predetermined size is used as a means of pulling crankcase vapors into the intake manifold to be burned.

flame front The rapid burning of the air–fuel mixture that moves outward from the spark plug across the cylinder.

fuel tank pressure sensor A sensitive pressure sensor mounted in the fuel tank or EVAP system used to monitor the system for leaks.

heated air intake system A system that uses hot air from around the exhaust manifold to warm the air going into the intake manifold.

hydrocarbon A molecule made up of hydrogen and carbon. It is considered a harmful vehicle emission.

idling five-gas test A five-gas analysis test conducted during vehicle idling.

intrusive test A test in which a gas analyzer hose is placed into the exhaust stream before and after the catalytic converter; it may require drilling an access hole in the exhaust pipe in front of the converter.

lambda The ratio of air to fuel at which all of the oxygen in the air and all of the fuel are completely burned; See also *stoichiometric ratio*.

limit value The maximum amount of emissions that a vehicle is permitted to emit. Values are assigned to different classifications of vehicles.

negative back pressure EGR valve A dual-diaphragm EGR valve that uses vacuum in the exhaust manifold to operate a control diaphragm that opens and closes a vent in the main diaphragm chamber.

on-board diagnostic (OBD) The first generation of a self-diagnostic system built into the vehicle computer system that provided a means of warning the driver when the computer detected a problem in the system. This system allowed the technician to retrieve codes to assist in diagnosis of the vehicle.

on-board diagnostic II (OBDII) This generation of self-diagnostic systems mandated standardized diagnostic trouble codes and a data link connector. It also mandated monitoring of certain emission systems, such as the catalytic converter, oxygen sensor, EGR, and evaporative emissions.

oxides of nitrogen Gas created when nitrogen is combined with oxygen under the high temperature and pressure of combustion.

particulate matter Particles that are heavier than air that are released during combustion. It is the black smoke that is commonly emitted from a diesel engine.

PCV valve A valve that controls the amount of crankcase ventilation flow that is allowed and varies with changes in manifold pressure.

photochemical smog A brown haze that hangs in the sky, typically seen over large cities. Smog is a major health issue to humans because it affects lung tissue.

pinging A preignition or detonation concern that is damaging to the engine if it is allowed to continue. It is described as the sound of marbles being shaken in a glass jar.

pintle A tapered valve that sits in a tapered seat to seal a passageway for air or fuel.

positive back pressure EGR valve A dual-diaphragm EGR valve that uses pressure in the exhaust system to act on the control diaphragm, which closes a bleed valve in the main diaphragm, allowing the EGR valve to open only when there is positive exhaust pressure.

positive crankcase ventilation (PCV) system A system that draws blow-by gases from the crankcase into the intake to be burned.

pressure relief valve A valve that is designed to release pressure if it gets above a calibrated pressure; used in a gas cap as a safety device to release excessive pressure if pressure gets too high.

programmed fuel delivery map A chart programmed into the vehicle's computer that is referenced as the vehicle is running. Sensor input data are compared to the delivery map to calculate the desired output signal.

pulse air system The use of normal exhaust engine pulses to draw air into the exhaust stream.

purge solenoid A control device that lets fuel vapors move from the charcoal canister to the engine. The solenoid is controlled by the engine control module.

purge switch A device used to show the computer when purge is occurring. It is used as a feedback device to allow the computer to determine whether flow is happening.

purge valve A valve used to control the flow of evaporative emissions from the charcoal canister to the intake manifold.

purging The process of pulling stored fuel vapors from the charcoal canister and moving them into the engine to be burned.

quenched The state in a combustion chamber in which the flame cannot burn due to cold surfaces or poor distribution of the fuel mixture.

reed valve A flexible valve made from spring steel that flexes to open or close, usually due to pressure changes.

scavenging effect A condition caused by moving columns of air, which create a low-pressure area behind them, resulting in a pulling force that is used to pull the remaining burned gases from the combustion chamber. Valve timing affects the amount of scavenging effect an engine has.

separator PCV system A PCV system that uses a device that uses gravity to allow oil to fall to the bottom of the valve and be returned to the crankcase; the valve prevents liquid from traveling to the intake manifold.

stepper motor EGR valve An EGR valve that uses an electrically controlled motor to open the pintle in steps to let exhaust gases flow into the intake manifold.

stoichiometric ratio The exact ratio between air and fuel, at which both are burned completely. See also *lambda*.

stroke The movement of the piston in the engine from top dead center to bottom dead center, or vice versa. There are four strokes: intake, compression, power, and exhaust.

thermo control (temperature-controlled valve) A mechanical device that moves with temperature. It is typically used to control the flow of vacuum when the engine is either hot or cold.

three-way catalytic converter A converter that changes hydrocarbons, carbon monoxide, and oxides of nitrogen into harmless elements.

two-way catalytic converter A converter that changes only hydrocarbons and carbon monoxide into harmless elements.

vacuum-relief valve A mechanical valve used on the gas cap that prevents a low-pressure condition from occurring. It also ensures that the fuel tank will not collapse due to fuel usage or contraction of fuel on cooldown.

vaporization The ability of a liquid to evaporate.

vapor line A rubber or plastic line that carries vapors from the fuel tank to the charcoal canister.

variable-orifice PVC system A system in which a replaceable, spring-loaded PCV valve regulates gas flow. The position of the PCV valve is controlled by the pressure in the manifold.

vent solenoid A solenoid that allows fresh air to enter the evaporative system during a purge event. Also used for an evaporative system monitoring test.

ASE-Type Questions

1. Tech A says that the purge valve is part of the evaporative emission system. Tech B says that OBDII systems must illuminate the MIL when the emissions exceed 1.5 times the FTP. Who is correct?
   a. Tech A
   b. Tech B
   c. Both A and B
   d. Neither A nor B

2. Tech A says that carbon monoxide is partially burned fuel. Tech B says that oxides of nitrogen are unburned fuel. Who is correct?
   a. Tech A
   b. Tech B
   c. Both A and B
   d. Neither A nor B

3. Tech A says that hydrocarbons are a result of complete combustion. Tech B says that a catalytic converter creates a chemical reaction, changing carbon monoxide and hydrocarbons to water and carbon dioxide. Who is correct?
   a. Tech A
   b. Tech B
   c. Both A and B
   d. Neither A nor B

4. Tech A says that allowing hot exhaust gases into the engine through the EGR valve helps to warm up the engine during warm-up. Tech B says that rich fuel mixtures will create low amounts of carbon monoxide. Who is correct?
   a. Tech A
   b. Tech B
   c. Both A and B
   d. Neither A nor B

5. Tech A says that burning gasoline in an engine creates water as a by-product of combustion. Tech B says that variable valve timing can be used to reduce oxides of nitrogen, eliminating the need for an EGR valve on some engines. Who is correct?
   a. Tech A
   b. Tech B
   c. Both A and B
   d. Neither A nor B

6. Tech A says that the PCV system recirculates exhaust gases into the intake manifold. Tech B says that the PCV system recirculates blow-by gases into the intake manifold. Who is correct?
   a. Tech A
   b. Tech B
   c. Both A and B
   d. Neither A nor B

7. Tech A says that a closed loop system means the ECM is receiving feedback and adjusting the fuel injector on time as needed. Tech B says that lean means there is not enough air in the air–fuel mixture. Who is correct?
   a. Tech A
   b. Tech B
   c. Both A and B
   d. Neither A nor B

8. Tech A says that the EVAP system stores escaping hydrocarbons until the engine can burn them. Tech B says that catalytic converters were designed for regular leaded gas. Who is correct?
   a. Tech A
   b. Tech B
   c. Both A and B
   d. Neither A nor B

9. Tech A says that the EGR valve is open fully at idle so that the engine will not die. Tech B says that oxides of nitrogen are created in large amounts when the combustion temperature is above 2500°F (1400°C). Who is correct?
   a. Tech A
   b. Tech B
   c. Both A and B
   d. Neither A nor B

10. Tech A says that black exhaust indicates a very rich-running engine. Tech B says that white exhaust can indicate coolant in the exhaust. Who is correct?
    a. Tech A
    b. Tech B
    c. Both A and B
    d. Neither A nor B

CHAPTER 52

Knowledge Objectives

After reading this chapter, you will be able to:
1. Define what is meant by "alternative fuel." (p 1814)
2. Name at least five liquid alternative fuels to gasoline and petrodiesel fuel. (p 1814)
3. List five types of alternative fuel vehicles. (p 1814)
4. List five reasons for using alternative fuels instead of petroleum for transportation. (pp 1814–1815)
5. Describe the differences between a dedicated, bi-fuel, and a dual-fuel vehicle fuel system. (pp 1816–1819)
6. Define synthetic fuel and list three types. (p 1819)
7. List the major components used in a compressed natural gas (CNG) fuel system. (pp 1821–1822)
8. Describe what is done when performing a CNG vehicle inspection. (p 1822)
9. Describe some of the feedstocks used for biodiesel. (p 1822)
10. List the pros and cons for each of the alternative fuels, including British thermal rating (Btu) and octane rating, tailpipe emissions, safety issues, and availability. (pp 1822–1827)
11. List some of the feedstocks used for producing ethanol. (p 1824)
12. Describe some of the feedstocks used for methanol. (p 1824)
13. Describe the three basic hybrid drive configurations. (p 1830)

Alternative Fuel Systems

Skills Objectives

There are no skills objectives in this chapter.

Introduction

The use of alternative fuels in the internal combustion engine is nothing new. Back between 1890 and 1896, Henry Ford designed one of his first vehicles—the Quadricycle—to run on ethanol derived from local farm crop waste (Ford's Model T also ran on ethanol). Most of the earliest automobiles and trucks operated either on electricity or by using external combustion steam engines fueled with paraffin or internal combustion engines running on "town gas" produced from coal. But for a number of reasons (both political and practical), once discovered, petroleum replaced almost all other options for motor fuel used in light-duty road vehicles. Petroleum-based fuels have dominated the transportation sector for the last century. Presented with a long-standing record of gasoline use, some people question the logic of switching back to alternative fuels for powering our road vehicles.

Alternative Fuels

What are "alternative fuels," alternative fuel vehicles (AFVs), and alternative energy sources? An **alternative fuel** is essentially anything other than a petroleum-based motor fuel (gasoline or diesel fuel) that is used to propel a motorized vehicle. Alternative fuels may be liquid or gas (or electric) and contain a variety of latent heat energy for use in the internal combustion engine. An alternative fuel vehicle, then, is a vehicle powered by something other than petroleum. One example is an electric vehicle, which is fueled by electricity generated in a variety of ways (more on this later). Here is a list of some of the recognized alternative fuel vehicles currently produced:

- Flexible-fuel vehicles (FFVs)
- Dedicated and bi-fuel compressed natural gas vehicles (CNGVs)
- Liquefied natural gas vehicles
- Liquid petroleum gas (LPG, also called propane) vehicles
- Hydrogen-powered internal combustion engine (ICE) vehicles
- Battery electric vehicles (BEVs)
- Hybrid electric vehicles (HEVs)
- Hydrogen fuel cell (electric) vehicles (FCVs)

Some of the alternative fuels include:

- Ethanol (alcohol)
- Methanol (alcohol)
- Biodiesel
- Methane: compressed natural gas (CNG) and liquefied natural gas (LNG)
- Liquefied petroleum gas (LPG, also called propane) from methane
- Synthetic fuels
- Electricity (not a fuel, per se, but an energy source)

What has prompted the renewed interest in alternative fuels? Reasons for making the switch from time-proven petroleum to "alternatives" are widely debated and include the following:

- Enhancing energy security by using domestically sourced fuels/energy
- Reducing the export of funds to overseas oil producers

You are the Automotive Technician

A Toyota Prius hybrid, which is a high-voltage vehicle, is brought into the shop for a regular 120,000-mile service, requiring replacement of the spark plugs and other maintenance items. You know that you need to follow the latest safety precautions when servicing a high-voltage vehicle. First, you do some research on the Toyota website and locate the service information for this make and model. Next, you create a service plan to prepare the workspace for safety and determine which tools are needed and which technicians are trained to perform the work.

1. Why is it important to read the Toyota service information for the hybrid vehicle prior to servicing?
2. Why is it necessary to inform or work with someone else while you are servicing a high-voltage vehicle?
3. What is the standard equipment needed to work on high-voltage vehicles?
4. Why must the main high-voltage battery pack be disconnected before servicing a high-voltage vehicle?

- Reducing pollution from vehicle emissions
- Stimulating and bolstering the national and local economies (agri-business)

Boiled down, alternative fuels advance the "3E" causes of:

- Energy security
- Environmental concerns
- Economy

Let's look at each of these in more detail.

Energy Security

National security is a key issue in the United States, especially after the 9/11 terrorist attacks. For years, the United States has been importing oil from other countries. Oil importation for transportation has been as high as 70%. President George W. Bush said in his 2006 State of the Union Address that "Americans are addicted to oil." Foreign petroleum stakeholders have large petroleum energy reserves, some of whom are waging war against the United States. In an attempt to shift the playing field after the oil embargo of the 1970s, the United States Congress took action. In 1992, Congress passed the **Energy Policy Act (EPAct92)**, the intent of which was to advance, through mandates, the use of vehicles capable of using alternatives to gasoline and diesel. EPAct92 considered the previously listed vehicles (and fuels) as legitimate AFVs. In 1996, EPAct was amended to include synthetically derived fuels such as coal-to-gas liquids (derived from the Fischer-Tropsch method), bio-based fuels, and more.

Unfortunately, EPAct92 failed to account for the fact that an alternative fuel **infrastructure** did not, for the most part, exist in the United States. As a result, while federal, municipal, and private fleets were mandated to include AFVs as a certain percentage of their new vehicle purchases, alternative fuels, such as ethanol and methanol, were not widely available for use in these flexible-fueled vehicles (meaning they can use either alcohol or gasoline as their prime fuel). The Renewable Fuels Standard and other legislation helped to promote a greater availability of alternative fuels for on-road and off-road vehicles (agricultural, railroads, etc.) and for marine and aviation applications. Today the US military is a driving force in the move toward alternative fuels.

In considering the need to develop alternative fuel sources, another important point is that petroleum is not considered a renewable resource, meaning there is a finite amount of it. According to peak oil advocates, once supplies of quality petroleum become hard enough to extract from proven easily accessible reserves, the cost will become prohibitive. As sweet light crude oil becomes scarce, the cost of extracting deeper reserves rises, making crude oil more expensive. With developing countries like India and China seeing an increased number of automobiles on their roads, the worldwide demand for oil has caused sharp rises in the price of crude oil. Oil has become a valuable "black gold" commodity on the world market, making energy a strategic resource.

Environmental Concerns

Consider the pollution created by drilling for oil, refining it, and transporting the end products to the local filling station for purchase. Once burned in the internal combustion engine, the resulting tailpipe emissions must be tightly regulated. "Well-to-wheels" emissions are now being studied and regulated, to some degree or another, in most countries of the world. Greenhouse gas emissions are a huge worldwide concern. Global climate change is widely discussed, and pollutants are heavily regulated by many countries. Photochemical smog has created health issues for the young as well as for the elderly. Automobiles burning gasoline or petrodiesel fuel create the pollutants responsible for harm to humans and the environment, so transitioning to cleaner alternative energy and fuel choices can help reduce (mitigate) the effects of pollution. Later in the chapter, we will explore the various pollutants associated with petroleum burned in automobile engines and why alternative choices make sense.

Economic Concerns

To offset the unfavorable balance of US dollars sent overseas for petroleum, "home grown" bio-based fuels are being used. Congress has passed legislation requiring the use of alternatives to gasoline, and some states require that ethanol be blended at the pump with gasoline to help their farm economies. Nationwide, gasoline is widely blended with 10% ethanol (mostly corn-based ethanol), yet it still does not meet targets of nonpetroleum usage. Congressional targets for alternative fuel usage are difficult to reach because producers have hit the "blend wall," meaning ethanol supplies now outweigh market demand. The Environmental Protection Agency (EPA) has approved the use of 15% ethanol for 2001 and newer vehicles, and this should help both ethanol suppliers and the environment. Corn prices per bushel have risen from around $2 to $3 per bushel to more than $7 per bushel due to increased demand for fuel and for export overseas. The co-products of ethanol production, such as dried distiller grains, are sold as feed for livestock.

Other alternatives likewise are helping local economies to prosper. Soybeans and other US-grown feedstocks intended for use as biodiesel are finding their way to

Midwestern US markets. Some states mandate the use of 10% or more blends to encourage and assure local economies of a market for their products.

 ## Vehicle Emissions and Standards

As clean as they are by today's standards, left unchecked, internal combustion engines (ICEs) and fuel systems emit pollutants both from without and from within the tailpipe. The pollutants regulated by EPA emission standards are:

- <u>Carbon monoxide (CO)</u>: This product of partially burned fuel displaces oxygen in the bloodstream and causes asphyxiation.
- <u>Hydrocarbons (HC)</u>: These volatile organic compounds (VOCs) of unburned fuel contribute to photochemical smog.
- <u>Carbon dioxide (CO_2)</u>: Although harmless in small amounts, too much carbon dioxide is a serious atmospheric concern. It is considered a greenhouse gas.
- <u>Nitrogen oxides (NO_x)</u>: The various compounds of nitrogen contribute to the creation of smog in the presence of sunlight.
- <u>Particulate matter (PM)</u>: Mainly produced by diesel engines, PM is literally fine soot (measured in microns, or millionths of an inch). PM becomes trapped in the lungs and causes health issues. At one time PM-10 (10 microns large) was thought to be harmless; today even PM-2.5 is considered dangerous.

Emission Standards

<u>Emission standards</u> are set by various countries, states, and even localities. Standards affect cutoff points for the amount of pollutants that vehicles may release into the environment. Different countries focus on different pollutants depending on what environmental issues they are dealing with, but globally, most nations' emission standards have progressively tightened to the point that tailpipe exhaust is sometimes cleaner than what goes into the engine's intake system.

In the United States, the <u>Environmental Protection Agency (EPA)</u> controls federally mandated emission standards, mostly following the lead of California's clean air regulations. Some states, like California, have enacted more stringent emission standards than those of the EPA. The California Air Resources Board (CARB) is a department within California's EPA. California is the only state that is permitted to have such a regulatory agency, since it is the only state that had one before the passage of the federal Clean Air Act. Other states are permitted to

follow CARB standards, or use the federal ones, but not set their own.

We will not go into the actual cutoff points for each of the pollutants, vehicles, and locations or discuss when they became effective; the regulations are far too complex to list here. In general, however, regardless of where clean air regulations are regulated and enforced, pollution cutoff points have become progressively more stringent over time.

Low-Emission Vehicle Program Emission Standards

California used unique terms to describe vehicle compliance with their clean air regulations, and window stickers seen on vehicles reflected their compliance with California's clean air limits. For example, from 1994 to 1999, California's regulations were stricter than the US national "tier" regulations. The <u>Low Emission Vehicle (LEV) standard</u> included six major emission categories, each with several targets depending on vehicle weight and cargo capacity. Vehicles with a test weight up to 14,000 lb (6350 kg) were covered by these regulations. The major emission categories were:

- TLEV: Transitional Low Emission Vehicle
- LEV: Low Emission Vehicle
- ULEV: Ultra-Low Emission Vehicle
- SULEV: Super-Ultra Low Emission Vehicle
- ZEV: Zero-Emission Vehicle

The last category is largely restricted to electric vehicles and hydrogen vehicles, although such vehicles are usually partly reliant on grid-supplied power, which is derived from coal, oil, natural gas, hydro (water), or nuclear sources.

 ## Types of Alternative Fuels

Alternative fuels are used as a way of either reducing the operating cost of vehicles or reducing pollution from vehicle emissions, or both. Some alternative fuels such as alcohol can be mixed with traditional gasoline and used as a fuel additive to reduce the total amount of gasoline used. For example, some vehicles are designed to operate on two different fuels blended together in various mixture amounts by percentage. These are called <u>flexible-fuel vehicles (FFVs)</u>. Ethanol FFVs, for example, are designed to operate on 100% standard gasoline or up to 85% alcohol and 15% gasoline (called <u>E85</u>). Other fuels such as <u>compressed natural gas (CNG)</u> may replace the use of liquid fuel altogether. Such vehicles require a different fuel system. For example, a dedicated CNG vehicle uses only natural gas; a gasoline vehicle converted for both CNG fuel delivery as well as gasoline is called a bi-fuel vehicle. Let's look at the various alternative fuel and clean fuel vehicles in greater detail.

Liquefied Petroleum Gas

Liquefied petroleum gas (LPG), also called propane, is a liquid under pressure but boils into a gas at atmospheric pressure. LPG is a by-product of the process of refining crude oil or natural gas. It is odorless and colorless and has been used for many years to power specially modified gasoline engine vehicles. It is the third most common fuel used worldwide, and it is nontoxic and nonpoisonous, with a very small flammability range. LPG is heavier than air and is the least carbon-emitting hydrocarbon fuel available. It emits far fewer harmful emissions than gasoline because its gaseous state and less complex chemical makeup (C_3H_8) make it easier to burn completely. LPG can be used in a wide range of spark-ignition engines as an alternative to gasoline. It is generally cheaper than gasoline; therefore, it is popular for light-duty vehicles, medium-duty trucks, and shuttle vans used in high-mileage fleet applications like taxis and delivery vehicles, where the cost of vehicle modification can be recouped over time more easily through lower fuel costs. Propane is also domestically produced and provides nearly the same power, torque, and towing capacity as gasoline-powered vehicles.

LPG is stored at normal temperatures under moderate pressure (several hundred pounds) as a liquid and is therefore very energy dense for on-board storage. When the pressure is released to atmospheric, propane expands to 270 times its liquid volume and is burnt as a dry gaseous vapor. A fuel pressure regulator is fitted in the system to reduce storage tank pressure. Many engines use a gaseous vapor (fumigation) system, but newer vehicles are using liquid propane injection. A filter is fitted to the system to remove any particles that may be present in the propane. When propane is injected into the engine's intake manifold behind the intake valve, it becomes a clean vapor. For so-called fumigation systems, a special air–fuel mixer is installed at the engine's throttle body to ensure the correct amounts of LPG and air are mixed together to achieve the correct **stoichiometric ratio** (air–fuel mixture) for clean combustion.

Today's light- and medium-duty LPG-powered vehicles are fitted with LPG fuel control processors, which are on-board computers that control the sequential operation of fuel injectors. Many vehicle manufacturers, including Ford, GM, Toyota, and Mitsubishi, offer factory-fitted or tier 1 supplier-approved fumigation or liquid fuel-injected LPG systems. LPG fuel systems may also be installed by aftermarket conversion companies. The EPA mandates that any vehicle converted from gasoline to an alternative fuel must be as clean or cleaner than was the original gasoline system.

One drawback to LPG vehicles is the size of the fuel tank required. For this reason, most LPG conversions are payload-type vehicles that can accommodate placement of the on-board propane fuel tank. Still, the LPG fuel tank is far less costly than the cylinders used for CNG.

Applied | Science

AS-21: Fractional Distillation: The technician can explain the ignition characteristics of fuels resulting from varying levels of fractional distillation (i.e., fuels with differing chemical makeups).

The type of oil that comes from the ground is known as crude oil. It is a thin to thick, smelly liquid containing a mixture of hydrocarbons. The crude oil is not ready to be used until a separation process is completed. This separation process is known as fractional distillation and is accomplished by using the difference in boiling points.

A distillation tower is a tall steel tower. The crude oil is heated in a furnace before entering the tower. The tower acts as a huge heat exchanger. It works by becoming progressively cooler as the crude oil goes up the tower. This difference in the temperature separates the different fractions from each other. The hydrocarbon gases condense back into liquids as a result of the temperature decrease.

Motor oil is separated at approximately 626°F (330°C), diesel fuel is separated at approximately 482°F (250°C), and gasoline is separated at approximately 122°F to 158°F (50°C to 70°C). These products are separated into the basic categories of fuels or lubricants. Additives improve the products in a number of ways. For example, many types of gasoline have detergents designed to keep fuel systems clean.

Natural Gas

Natural gas (sometimes referred to simply as NG) is a fossil fuel often found in offshore gas fields or trapped in coal beds, aquifers, or petroleum domes. Natural gas is primarily methane, but may also include ethane, propane, butane, and other gases such as carbon dioxide, nitrogen, and helium. It requires no processing other than the filtering of physical impurities, water, sulfur, and the other gases mentioned previously. Almost all foreign gases other than the methane are removed during processing prior to its use as an automotive fuel. Since methane has no odor, an **odorant** called **mercaptan** is added so that leaks may be detected by humans. Methane is the cheapest and most efficient of all fuels when properly burned, but it requires a large amount of air for combustion. It is one of the most popular forms of alternative fuels for use in vehicles because of its availability, relatively low cost, and low emissions. Methane has a low carbon content, and its simple chemistry (CH_4) offers much cleaner exhaust (lower tailpipe emissions) compared to gasoline.

Methane has an octane number of 125 RON. This gives it a very high resistance to pre-ignition and to knock (abnormal detonation). Thus, gas engines can use a higher compression ratio—as high as 12:1, compared to a traditional gasoline/petroleum engine ratio ranging from 7.5:1 to 10:1. The higher compression ratio results in an increased power output and a greater fuel economy compared to gasoline. It also means natural gas engines have better thermal efficiencies than conventional engines.

Natural gas spark-ignition (SI) engines work on the same basic principles as gasoline-powered SI engines. The fuel is mixed with air and drawn into the cylinder of a four-stroke engine. The air–fuel mixture is ignited by a spark from a spark plug to generate the energy to move the piston and turn the crankshaft. The major changes between conventional SI engines and natural gas engines are in the fuel supply system and the method of mixing and induction of the air–fuel mixture. The difficulties of storing and distributing natural gas have inhibited the more widespread use of it as a fuel for vehicles. The benefits of natural gas can be more easily justified in high-use vehicles, so natural gas in both compressed and liquefied forms is more frequently used by buses, trucks, and taxis. Such vehicles also have a greater storage space for the natural gas fuel tanks.

Compressed Natural Gas

Compressed natural gas vehicles (CNGVs) use methane compressed for storage and use in light-duty passenger vehicles, delivery trucks, and buses. CNGVs carry natural gas typically compressed up to 3600 pounds per square inch (psi), or 25,000 kilopascals (kPa), and stored in heavy-duty cylinders of various types. The cylinders themselves are quite safe, being rated at four times the storage pressure of the fuel system. A fuel pressure regulator reduces natural gas storage pressure to around 100 psi (700 kPa) if fuel injected, and a second stage reduces it to near atmospheric pressure for a fumigation system. A filter is used to trap water or compressor oil "carryover" in the gaseous fuel. Natural gas is used in both bi-fuel (gas or gasoline is used) and dedicated (CNG only) SI engine vehicles. It is also used in dual-fuel **compression-ignition (CI) engines**.

What looks like exhaust smoke when a natural gas engine starts up is actually steam caused by the different ratio of hydrogen to carbon in the fuel. This results in a higher ratio of water to carbon dioxide in the exhaust, and water vapor is visible until the exhaust system heats up. In a CNGV, the exhaust is frequently more visible because it is more humid. This steam is not a result of soot, oil blow-by, or unburned hydrocarbons.

Under normal operating conditions, oil consumption should be about the same for natural gas engines as they are for traditional gasoline engines, although modern CNG engines require synthetic oils to control higher internal operating temperatures. However, the lubricating oil will generally be cleaner because there is less soot formed in combustion and unburned hydrocarbons cannot contaminate the lubrication oil. The same properties apply to LPG engines.

One drawback of CNGVs is their heavy cylinders and limited range, unless multiple cylinders are used. In that case, a lot of room is needed either under or over the vehicle (bus), or in the valuable payload space inside or outside (e.g., in the pick-up truck bed). Another drawback is the incremental cost of the CNG fuel system.

Liquefied Natural Gas

Liquefied natural gas (LNG) is used in heavy-duty long-haul trucks, heavy-duty refuse and delivery vehicles, buses, and so forth. LNG is almost pure methane and has a gasoline per gallon equivalent much closer to gasoline than CNG—a prime consideration for achieving reasonable vehicle range. For the LNG to become a more compact and easily stored liquid, it has to be cooled to an extremely low cryogenic temperature of –263.2°F (–164°C). The liquid remains very cold at all times or else it will boil off and greatly expand into a gaseous fuel.

LNG tanks are constructed with two walls of material separated by a layer of insulating material that is placed under a vacuum that enhances the long-term cooling of the fuel—as long as several weeks **FIGURE 52-1**.

FIGURE 52-1 LNG fuel tank.

A **float-type fuel gauge** is placed in the tank and raises or lowers in a tube for fuel level calculation. All LNG containers must be mounted within the normal extremities of the vehicle and in the correct orientation so that the internal baffles to limit fuel sloshing can be effective when the vehicle is in motion and so the correct evaporation space can be maintained. LNG systems usually circulate engine coolant through the final regulator to maintain the natural gas at a constant pressure and temperature before it is used. This feature is a very important requirement with LNG due to the extremely low temperature at which the gas is stored in its tank.

When refueling LNG tanks, a vapor return pipe prevents accidental overfilling and ensures that there is sufficient vapor space above the liquid in the tank. Excess liquid pumped in will discharge out again through this vapor return connection. As for the LNG infrastructure, the expense of compressor stations, LNG storage tanks, and LNG on-board fuel systems limits widespread acceptance of LNG in vehicles. Exceptions are the vehicles traveling so-called clean corridors. These are specifically designed and equipped US interstate highways with compressor stations and LNG refill locations strategically located to accommodate long-haul trucks. Long-haul global transit of methane is most economically done with LNG ocean-going ships, but establishing a land-based LNG refueling infrastructure comes at a price in terms of the extensive equipment required plus the energy used for compressing methane gas to cryogenic temperatures.

Manufactured Gases

Manufactured gases are derived from other forms of fuel such as wood or coal. These gases generally contain carbon monoxide, so are usually poisonous as well as flammable. **Producer gas** is a generic term that refers to a number of manufactured gases such as wood gas, town gas, and syngas. **Wood gas** is a hydrogen and methane gas created by a process of thermal gasification of wood or some other biomass. This gas was used to power ICEs and vehicles fitted with on-board gasifiers or trailer gasifiers, which produced the gas from other feedstocks while the vehicle was in transit. **Town gas** used for lighting and other uses was used for ICE vehicles during the very early days before petroleum became the fuel of choice (thanks to its energy density—Btu per gallon). Town gas, or coal gas, is mostly methane and is made by either the carbonization or the gasification of coal. Originally, this gas was a by-product of turning bituminous coal into the cleaner coke fuel. It is still extensively used for heating and cooking and for some industrial tasks, but it is not usually used to power automobiles.

Syngas, or synthetic gas, consists mainly of varying combinations of hydrogen and carbon monoxide, and it can be produced in a number of different ways, including the Fischer-Tropsch method for the gasification of coal. Syngas can be an intermediate step leading to a catalyzed chemical process to convert the gas to liquid (GTL) hydrocarbons, which can then be used as a synthetic lubricant or as a fuel. **Water gas** is mostly hydrogen and carbon monoxide, and it is created by passing steam over red-hot coke.

Bi-fuel engines and vehicles are capable of running on either gasoline or natural gas, though some engine modifications are required for them to run efficiently. Only one fuel is used at a time, but they may be switched seamlessly while underway. Bi-fuel vehicle engines tend to be limited by the lower compression ratio needed to accommodate gasoline.

Dual-fuel–powered vehicles run literally on two fuels at the same time. For example, in the dual-fuel diesel system, both diesel fuel and natural gas are injected directly into the combustion chamber, almost at the same time. Clean air is drawn into the cylinder from the manifold, and during the compression stroke, a small amount of diesel fuel is "pilot injected" into the combustion chamber. The diesel fuel starts ignition, and the combined fuel mixture burns as it would in an engine fueled with 100% diesel fuel. By using natural gas fuel this way, engine knock is no longer a problem and the compression ratios for the engine do not need to be altered. In the dual-fuel engine, the liquid fuel is typically injected from a center-located pintle in a dual-fuel injector. Once combustion is initiated, liquid injection is immediately followed by a main spray of gaseous CNG from holes surrounding the liquid fuel pintle. Injectors may be drop-in configured to convert a conventional diesel engine to dual fuel for fuel savings and to lower emissions. In other applications, natural gas is injected through a second injector into the combustion chamber.

▶ Diesel to Compressed Natural Gas Conversions

Some fleets use diesel engines converted to run on natural gas alone instead of diesel fuel by converting the CI engine to an SI engine. This is usually done by replacing the diesel injector in the engine's cylinder head with a spark plug and premixing the gaseous fuel with the intake air. The existing diesel fuel injection system is replaced with a high-tension SI system, and the natural gas fuel is mixed with air with port injectors, or with a carburetor-type spray ring or fumigation rail before the throttle body in the intake system. Compression ratios for SI engines need to be significantly lower than for diesel engines, so a spacer is usually fitted between the block and the head on the engine. This design reduces the compression ratio to around the necessary 12:1, but it also reduces the thermal efficiency of the engine, decreasing torque, particularly at low speed, which is a common advantage of CI engines.

In a dedicated natural gas conversion, the diesel injectors are replaced with spark plugs and the natural gas fuel is premixed with air before intake occurs. This is a relatively inexpensive conversion, and it allows the fleet to use cheaper, cleaner natural gas fuel.

With a dual-fuel CI system, the diesel injectors remain in place and the engine can still run on 100% diesel fuel if necessary. Natural gas is mixed with air in the inlet manifold, and the amount of diesel fuel injected is correspondingly reduced. Only a relatively small proportion of diesel fuel is necessary for ignition of the whole fuel mixture to occur through engine compression. Combustion in this way is actually more effective than with SI because the diesel fuel injector nozzle spray jets create a number of ignition sources, not just one. This allows for a more complete and rapid combustion.

Natural gas can account for up to 98% of the fuel content, as long as the remaining percentage is injected diesel fuel, although the higher the proportion of natural gas fuel in the mix, the greater the tendency of the engine to knock.

► Gaseous Fuel Storage Systems

LPG Fuel Storage Tanks

Because of the insulation used for LNG fuel storage, these systems are more complicated to design and much more costly to manufacture. Although the weight by mass of LNG fuel is about half that of diesel fuel, an LNG fuel tank is substantially heavier and bulkier.

There are two types of LPG storage container: **portable universal cylinders** and **permanently mounted tanks** **FIGURE 52-2**. Portable cylinders can be removed from a vehicle and taken to a refueling site to be filled. These are useful for off-road vehicles or remote sites where the vehicle itself cannot easily be taken to a filling station. When not installed on a vehicle, these containers must be stored in a secure outdoor area. They are called universal cylinders because they can be used in a vertical or horizontal position.

When a vehicle is capable of traveling to a refueling site, the tank should be permanently mounted to the vehicle. Permanently installed tanks must be placed in their correct orientation, and they usually carry marks to indicate the top of the tank. LPG containers must be

FIGURE 52-2 LPG fuel tanks. **A.** Portable. **B.** Permanent.

mounted within the extremities of the vehicle. The tanks used in automobiles (such as taxis) are usually found in the trunk of the passenger vehicle. In the case of pick-up trucks, the tank sits in or under the bed of the truck. LPG tanks are normally made of a heavy-gauge steel, as are the fuel lines and pressure safety valves used to supply the fuel to the vehicle system.

The normal working pressure of a tank varies depending on ambient temperatures and the quantity of fuel in the tank, but common operating pressures are normally within the range of 102 to 170 psi (700 to 1200 kPa). LPG tanks are constructed to withstand much higher pressures of approximately 1000 psi (7000 kPa). This is necessary because LPG expands when its temperature rises.

To make sure the fuel has room to expand, the tank is never filled to capacity. LPG tanks are fitted with a special refueling port and an overfill protection device—an **automatic fuel limiter**—which ensures that the tank cannot be filled past the safe fill limit of 80%. This design allows for fuel expansion on a hot sunny day, and tanks are generally painted white to reflect sunlight. LPG tanks are also equipped with pressure relief valves that can release propane vapors to the atmosphere to prevent the tank from rupturing under abnormally high-pressure conditions. A fuel lock-off lets fuel flow when the engine is running but shuts off the fuel supply as soon as the ignition is turned off or if the engine stops running, such as from a collision.

> **TECHNICIAN TIP**
>
> The basic LPG servicing procedures are limited to visual inspection and leak testing. Since LPG is heavier than air, an electronic leak detector is moved slowly below fittings to detect any leakage. Soap and water or leak detection spray may also be used for leak testing. The tank must be evacuated and purged before disassembling any of the fittings, and no welding is permitted on the container.

CNG Fuel Storage Cylinders and Systems

CNG is compressed and stored at very high pressures (3000 to 3600 psi [20,700 to 24,800 kPa]). The volume of space required for CNG storage tanks is almost twice that required for LNG tanks for delivering the equivalent mileage range.

Both fuel storage (depot) and vehicle storage tanks must be extremely robust due to the high pressures required for storing compressed gas. CNG cylinders come in four types (types 1 through 4), ranging from heaviest to lightest **FIGURE 52-3**. Type 1 cylinders are made of steel; type 2 are made of aluminum; type 3 are made of a combination of metal and an approved composite material; and type 4 (the lightest in weight) are made totally of a carbon composite material wound around a dense rubber core. Cylinders must be permanently marked "CNG" by the manufacturer. Pressurized containers for CNG use have a rated service pressure of not less than 3600 psi at 70°F (24,800 kPa at 21.1°C). They are tested under extreme conditions and must hold pressure to four times their rated service pressure.

Vehicle CNG fuel storage systems consist of one or more cylinders. Each is shock mounted in place using clamps that enable pressurized cylinders to expand when filled while still holding them firmly in place. The straps enable the vehicle chassis to deform as intended in a high-speed collision without deforming the CNG storage tank.

Each cylinder is fitted with a thermal- and/or pressure-activated pressure relief device (PRD), which releases gas in

FIGURE 52-3 CNG fuel tanks.

the vent of overpressurization. Each cylinder is equipped with either a manual safety shutoff valve or a solenoid lock-off device connecting to a power source. If more than one cylinder is used, a seamless steel tubing manifold connects the cylinders. If the cylinders are located under the vehicle, a shield protects the safety valve/lock-off and PRD. If cylinders could be exposed to sunlight, they are protected from ultraviolet damage by a cover.

Because CNG is a gas, not a liquid, it does not matter whether the container is standing up or lying down;

however, all CNG containers must be mounted within the extremities of the vehicle, for their protection. CNG cylinders may be found in the trunk of a passenger vehicle, inside a van or SUV, or underneath the vehicle in the rear or between the frame rails. In some applications, such as urban transit passenger buses, as many as eight or more CNG cylinders are mounted on the roof and are encased in a special fiberglass enclosure **FIGURE 52-4**. There are height restrictions for such applications to avoid serious damage to the cylinders caused by overhead hazards such as low bridges. Similarly, cylinders must be a minimum distance from the road with the vehicle fully loaded.

If the CNG tank is mounted within 8" (200 mm) of a heat source such as the exhaust pipe or muffler, then an effective heat shield must be mounted between the tank and the heat source without touching either. There must also be an insulator such as nylon or neoprene between the tank and its mounting bracket to protect it from movement wear and corrosion.

Note: For the latest CNGV installation and inspection specifications, refer to **National Fire Protection Association (NFPA)** standards published in their **NFPA-52** document.

FIGURE 52-4 CNG fuel tanks mounted on the roof of a bus.

Service procedures are normally limited to a so-called basic visual inspection for damage and rust, and leak testing. Leaks can be detected with an approved electronic methane leak detector or an approved leak test solution, which is sprayed over the tank, valve, PRD, lines, etc. Soap and water may also be used, but not ammonia. Bubbles in the solution indicate a leak. Since methane is lighter than air, testing is done above the fittings rather than below (as with propane). If a cylinder is suspected to have a problem, the vehicle should be immediately taken out of service, the cylinder defueled and removed from the vehicle, and a detailed cylinder inspection performed by a trained and certified tank inspector.

> **TECHNICIAN TIP**
>
> LNG tanks may be serviced only by specially trained and certified specialists.

▶ Biofuels

Biofuels are fuels derived from biological sources, such as corn, sugarcane, soybeans, and algae. Biofuels help to reduce consumption of petroleum fuels, which provides the previously stated benefits. In transportation, biofuels generally come in two major categories: biodiesel and bio-alcohol. Biodiesel is used in CI engines either as a blend with traditional petrodiesel or by itself. Bio-alcohol is used primarily as a blend with gasoline. Biofuel production has continued to increase over the years, although it still contributes only a small percentage of total energy use.

Biodiesel

Biodiesel is renewable fuel made by chemically combining natural oils from soybeans, cottonseeds, canola, animal fats, algae, jatropha seeds, or even recycled cooking oil with an alcohol such as methanol or ethanol, and a catalyst like lye. Depending on the fuel base stock, biodiesel fuels can be more expensive than diesel made of petroleum products (petrodiesel), but biodiesel burns with less particulate and with no **sulfur** or **aldehydes**, thus producing less harmful and irritating emissions.

The improved **lubricity** and zero sulfur content of biodiesel result in longer maintenance intervals, longer engine and fuel system life, and lower emissions. Biodiesel fuel is compatible with petrodiesel and may be used completely in place of petrodiesel, or in most applications may be blended with petrodiesel. A typical blend would be 20% biodiesel with 80% petrodiesel fuel **FIGURE 52-5**. Biodiesel tends to clean petrodiesel residues from the fuel

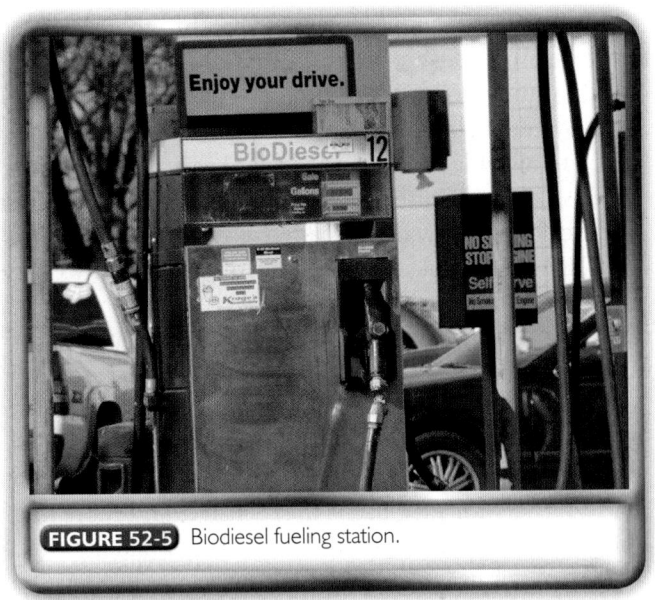

FIGURE 52-5 Biodiesel fueling station.

system, so fuel filters may require frequent servicing for the first few tank fills.

Biodiesel Use

Biodiesel, depending on the feedstock and process used, is a light yellow to dark gold liquid, with a **viscosity** very similar to petrodiesel fuel. Commercial blends of biodiesel and petrodiesel are designated with the letter "B" followed by the volumetric percentage of biodiesel in the blend: **B20 fuel**, the blend most commonly available, contains 20% biodiesel and 80% petrodiesel. **B100 fuel** is pure biodiesel (called "neat" diesel). Commercially produced biofuels must meet ASTM standards. Commercially processed biodiesel-blended fuels can run in any diesel engine designed for petroleum-based diesel fuels. Some diesel engines can run on **straight vegetable oil (SVO)** or on **waste vegetable oil (WVO)**, but only if it has been properly treated to remove the glycerin, which could otherwise gunk up injectors and engine parts like piston rings.

SVO is a pure form of vegetable oil or canola, peanut oil, soybean oil, and corn oil. WVO oil is filtered oil usually from restaurants but may be a combination of many restaurants. The filtered oil is sent to a processing plant where it is generally mixed with clean pure soybean oil for biofuel processing. The by-product of using this oil is the waste, which becomes greater when large parts of animal fats are present. The cleanest used restaurant oil comes from the frying of non-animal products. The risk of using restaurant oil is a batch that exceeds the heat range of the oil, generally over the 600°F (316°C), where the oils start breaking down structurally. This oil is unusable for the biofuel process.

Biodiesel may be more expensive to produce than petrodiesel, depending in part on governmental taxes and subsidies. Biodiesel blends tend to perform better than today's low-sulfur petrodiesel. Just a 1% blend of biodiesel adds lubricity lost yet needed to protect injectors from wear. Biodiesel burns cleaner with less smoke and may have a unique odor (like french fries!).

Biodiesel fuel has some drawbacks. It may make the engine harder to start in winter temperatures. High feedstock and production costs tend to limit wholesale commercial implementation, but the US military is committed to the use of alternatives such as biodiesel for defense purposes. Large-scale production demand will inevitably bring down the cost.

As with petrodiesel fuel, contamination with moisture can corrode components such as pumps and injectors, as well as encourage the growth of microbes. Biodiesel fuel can also degrade natural rubber gaskets and hoses. Today's vehicles use synthetics such as Viton to avoid such problems. Even older diesel vehicles can tolerate a blend of B5, and some original equipment manufacturers (OEMs) accept B20 or higher blend usage with no warranty concerns.

Biodiesel Characteristics

Biodiesel is both biodegradable and nontoxic. It produces significantly fewer emissions than petroleum-based diesel fuel. Tests have shown that the use of soybean biodiesel fuel (B100) in urban transit buses reduces net carbon dioxide emissions by over 75%. B100 (neat) biofuel contains about 11% oxygen, which improves combustion, reducing most exhaust pollutants. Drivers also note that the exhaust from biodiesel is less irritating than exhaust from petrodiesel-powered engines.

One of the most important characteristics of any diesel fuel is its ability to auto-ignite. The cetane number (a rating of how easily diesel fuel may be ignited) for biodiesel ranges from 46 to 57 for soybean oil, with an average of around 50. This means that biodiesel fuel ignites more quickly than petrodiesel, which normally has a cetane rating of 40 to 52.

Biodiesel is a better solvent than petrodiesel, so it helps clean the fuel system as it flows through it, and it can break down and flush out residue deposits in vehicles that have been running on petrodiesel. As some ocean-going fishing vessel captains have discovered, it is important to clean the fuel system and bring extra filters along when changing over to biodiesel fuel; the solvent action of biodiesel will quickly clog up fuel filters by flushing out accumulated deposits in older and dirty fuel systems.

Although it has some performance advantages, biodiesel does have some disadvantages, with biodiesel fuels made from yellow grease, or recycled cooking oil, performing worse than soy-based biodiesel. At lower temperatures, biodiesel fuel normally clouds and forms wax crystals, which can clog fuel lines and filters in a vehicle's fuel system. To combat this natural formation of restricting crystals, manufacturers add fuel line and filter heaters to the fuel systems. The **cloud point** is the temperature at which diesel fuel starts to appear cloudy, indicating that wax crystals have begun to form **FIGURE 52-6**. At even lower temperatures, fuel develops a waxy gel that cannot be pumped, thus starving the engine of fuel. The **pour point** is the temperature below which diesel fuel will not flow at all. The cloud point and the pour point temperatures for biodiesel are both higher than those for petrodiesel, so some operators report that it does not perform as well at low temperatures.

The energy efficiency of a vehicle is the percentage of the fuel's energy delivered as engine output. The energy content per unit of volume measure (Btu per gallon) of biodiesel is somewhat lower than that of petrodiesel, so biodiesel may be less economical to use. Fuel efficiency is usually expressed as miles traveled per gallon (mpg) of fuel, or kilometers per liter (km/L) of fuel. Vehicles running on higher blends of biodiesel may be less fuel efficient.

Ethanol

First-generation biofuels like **ethanol** are usually derived from an organic process—for example, the fermentation of sugars that come from plants such as corn, cane sugar, sugar beet, or grains. Second-generation **bio-ethanol** is derived from a variety of cellulose-based plants such as switchgrass. Third-generation biofuels like ethanol are algae based—that is, produced by/from algae. Algae-based ethanol production is the most promising in terms of yield per acre/hectare.

Bio-ethanol is a renewable resource and is also known as grain alcohol. Ethanol is heavier than air and

FIGURE 52-6 Diesel cloud point.

is **hygroscopic**, which means it readily absorbs water vapor from the atmosphere. Ethanol is a high-octane fuel (around 100 RON/MON/2 octane [see the Gasoline Fuel Systems chapter]), depending on various factors. It is a renewable fuel intended for SI engines. It is used in FFVs in the United States in a blend of up to 85% ethanol to 15% gasoline, called E85. Some countries use 100% ethanol instead of gasoline, which would be E100.

Ethanol is primarily used to reduce the negative emission effects of gasoline and as a gasoline oxygenate to replace harmful methyl tertiary-butyl ether. This mixture may be harmful to gasoline/petrol-fueled vehicles without the proper FFV seals and elastomers. Equipping an OEM vehicle for FFV use is inexpensive, and more and more OEMs are doing so in the interest of making their vehicle offerings "green." Vehicle computers calculate the percentage of ethanol blend by a variety of methods and alter injection quantity and spark timing to achieve the desired stoichiometric ratio of fuel and air and the resulting low emissions possible with ethanol.

Ethanol separates and evaporates quickly from water, which makes it less polluting to streams and waterways in the event of a spill. Compared to gasoline, ethanol burns particulate-free and releases fewer toxic emissions than gasoline/petrol. Its luminosity (visibility when it burns) is hard to detect in sunlight, thus making it somewhat dangerous in the event of a vehicle fire. It does release carbon dioxide during the combustion process, but again, less than the equivalent amount of gasoline/petrol. Ethanol holds even greater promise for reducing petroleum usage and providing greater engine power when engines are optimized (through valve timing or stroke variation) for use of higher octane ethanol, as compared to gasoline. When used in plug-in hybrid FFVs, such vehicles are said to achieve a gasoline per gallon equivalent as high as 500 mpg.

Methanol

Methanol is produced from wood products, natural gas, acetylene, or other organic materials (plant/animal wastes or garbage). It is highly poisonous and dangerous to the environment. It has a lower energy density than ethanol, and its **burn rate** (measured in feet per second) is not as high as that of gasoline fuel. Methanol is heavier than air and is hygroscopic. However, it has lower evaporative emissions than petrol/gasoline, as well as fewer toxic hydrocarbon emissions.

Methanol is sometimes referred to as wood alcohol because it is possible to produce it by fermenting biomass. **Biomass** is a renewable energy source, plant, or animal material used as a source of fuel. **Fuel methanol** is normally sold as a blend of 85% methanol and 15% unleaded premium gasoline/petrol, known as M85.

Methanol cannot be used in conventional vehicles without significant modifications. **M85 vehicles** are FFVs that can run on any mixture of methanol and gasoline/petrol, though the limit of methanol in the mixture is 85% in the United States. A **fuel composition sensor** tells the engine computer what percentage of methanol is in the fuel, and it adjusts the injection quantity ignition timing accordingly. This means that the FFV can run on conventional gasoline/petrol if methanol is not available; two separate fuel systems are not necessary.

Biobutenol

Biobutenol is produced in a similar fashion to ethanol, but butenol has characteristics similar enough to gasoline that it can be transported through the existing petroleum (pipeline) distribution infrastructure. Butanol has several advantages over ethanol, such as higher energy content, lower water absorption, and better blending ability. It can be used in conventional combustion engines without modification. Like ethanol, it can be produced through fermentation or by petrochemical methods. Butenol is not widely used but holds great promise as an alternative fuel for SI ICE-powered vehicles.

In summary, liquid fuels like biodiesel, ethanol, methanol, and butenol are perhaps the most transparent alternative fuels. With some limitations (petroleum pipelines are off-limits to some of these fuels), they are the least distinguishable from gasoline/petrol in how they are transported, refueled, and used. The fuel system of a car or truck needs only slight modifications in order to run on E85 or M85.

▶ Alternative Fuel Developments

While most alternative fuel technologies were developed many decades ago, many of them require expensive materials or manufacturing processes to mass produce them affordably. Developments and advancements are constantly being made in alternative fuel technologies. In this section, we will explore fuel cell technology, which is still in its infancy; battery electric vehicle and plug-in battery vehicle technologies, which are gaining traction with manufacturers; and hybrid vehicles, which have become much more common on the road.

Fuel Cells

Fuel cell technology has been used for many years in the space industry. Recent improvements in the technology and the need to seek alternative fuel technologies for the automotive industry have seen a number of manufacturers develop fuel cell technology for use in automobiles. In a vehicle powered by a fuel cell, the electric motor is powered by electricity generated by the fuel cell.

A **fuel cell** is an **electro-chemical device** that combines hydrogen and oxygen to produce water and in the process it produces electricity and heat. Fuel cells operate without combustion so they are virtually pollution free. Another electro-chemical device that you are already familiar with is a battery. In a battery, all the chemicals are stored inside, and it converts those chemicals into electricity. This means the battery eventually becomes discharged until it is recharged. In a fuel cell, the chemicals oxygen and hydrogen constantly flow through the fuel cell, like fuel through an engine, so it continues to produce electricity as long as oxygen and hydrogen are available.

There are four basic elements to a fuel cell, the **anode**, the **cathode**, the **electrolyte**, and the **catalyst** **FIGURE 52-7**. Pressurized hydrogen flows into the fuel cell anode. The platinum coating on the anode helps to separate the gas into protons (hydrogen ions) and electrons. The electrolyte in the center allows only the protons to pass through to the cathode side of the fuel cell. The electrons cannot pass through this electrolyte and therefore flow through an external circuit in the form of electrical current. At the same time, oxygen flows into the fuel cell cathode where another platinum coating helps the oxygen, protons, and electrons combine to produce pure water and heat.

A fuel cell only produces a voltage of about 0.7 volts. To get the required voltage for automotive applications, a fuel cell stack is created. The number of fuel cells in the stack determines the total voltage, and the surface area of the fuel cells determines the total current.

Hydrogen gas

Oxidant (Oxygen)

Excess hydrogen

Excess oxidant & water

Anode (Platinum catalyst)

Cathode

Polymer electrolyte membrane

FIGURE 52-7 Components of a fuel cell.

Fuel cells use hydrogen and oxygen to produce electricity. The oxygen can come from the air; however, hydrogen is not readily available. Hydrogen is difficult to store and distribute. To address this problem in automotive applications, an additional device called a **reformer** is used to separate hydrogen from other fuels, such as gasoline.

The fuel reforming process can be performed on a small scale on an as-needed basis immediately before its introduction into the fuel cell. One example would be for a fuel cell–powered vehicle to have a gasoline tank on board that would use the existing infrastructure of gasoline delivery. An on-board fuel processor would reform the gasoline into a hydrogen-rich stream that would be fed directly to the fuel cell.

At the present time, it is not practical to perform separation of other products of the reforming process from the hydrogen at this small scale. So to make fuel cells practical for automotive applications, vehicle manufacturers are developing better fuel cell systems and technology to improve the efficiency of the system while using readily obtainable fuels.

Hydrogen Fuel Cells

Hydrogen is the simplest and most plentiful element in the universe. It is a colorless, odorless, and tasteless gas. Hydrogen is the lightest element, yet it has the highest energy content per unit weight/mass of all energy-based fuels—three times the energy of gasoline/petrol.

Hydrogen can be extracted from virtually any hydrogen compound and is the ultimate clean energy carrier. It is safe to extract from a variety of sources, and hydrogen's energy can be harnessed in many pollution-free ways. Hydrogen can be burned directly as a fuel in an ICE instead of gasoline. It varies depending on the source of hydrogen, but total carbon dioxide emissions using hydrogen in the ICE vehicle can be less than half those of a conventional gasoline vehicle. Such vehicles are a slightly modified version of the traditional gasoline-powered engine.

Alternatively, hydrogen can be used to create electrical power in fuel cells to create power for electric motors, which in turn can power a vehicle. A fuel cell consists of two electrodes sandwiched around an electrolyte. Oxygen passes over one electrode and hydrogen over the other to generate electricity, water, and heat.

A fuel cell operates in some ways like a battery, but unlike a battery, it does not run down or require recharging. It will produce electrical energy and heat as long as hydrogen fuel and oxygen are supplied. While a battery is a closed electrical storage system with plates (electrodes) that react and change their chemical configuration as

that battery is charged or discharged, fuel cells are very different. A fuel cell's electrodes are relatively stable, but catalytic, and the fuel cell consumes hydrogen as a reactant that must be continuously replenished. Hydrogen is fed into the anode of the fuel cell. Oxygen (i.e., air) enters the fuel cell through the cathode. The hydrogen atom passes a catalyst, which causes the hydrogen to split into a proton and an electron. The protons pass through the electrolyte to the cathode, but the electrons must take a different path through a circuit that converts them to electrical current. In a **fuel cell (electric) vehicle (FCV)**, the current is used to charge a traction battery or to power electrical devices before they return to the cathode. The hydrogen electrons and protons then recombine with oxygen to become water molecules. Water is the "exhaust" from the fuel cell.

Besides the lack of harmful emissions, one of the main advantages of using hydrogen fuel cells as a generator of energy for traction batteries is their reliability. Fuel cells are compact and lightweight and have no moving parts, and they do not involve any of the explosive combustion processes necessary with conventional fuels.

Fuel Cell Vehicles

Gasoline-powered vehicles waste a lot of thermal energy. Fuel is used to heat and expand air to drive pistons and the crankshaft, with exhaust gases containing pollutants emitted to the atmosphere. Heat energy that has not been fully used by the expansion process is wasted through radiation and from the exhaust. FCVs, however, are cleaner and more efficient. The conversion of fuel to electricity is a direct electrochemical process with more energy extracted from the fuel source. And because the vehicle has fewer components in the drive system, such as pistons and camshafts, frictional losses and reliability issues associated with these components are eliminated.

Concept cars using hydrogen fuel cells have been in existence for many years, but FCVs have in the past struggled to produce electricity in sufficient quantity (kilowatts) at an acceptable cost. However, the first production line vehicle with a dedicated hydrogen fuel cell platform was made available for public sale in 2008. The Honda FCX Clarity has an effective driving range of approximately 280 miles (450 km) on one tank of hydrogen gas **FIGURE 52-8**. This is the equivalent to an EPA-certified 74 mpg (30 km/L). Other OEMs have since produced pre-production FCVs that are now being tested for reliability the world over. The downfall for FCVs occurs if the water in the fuel cell is allowed to freeze. If the water turns to ice, the expanding ice will ruin the fuel cell stack consisting of many electrodes.

FIGURE 52-8 Honda FCX Clarity.

A typical FCV will have a fuel cell stack, an air compressor to make sure enough air is being fed into the fuel cell, a radiator with circulating coolant, a hydrogen recirculating system to optimize efficiency, hydrogen storage tanks, a battery, and an electric motor. Either a lithium-ion battery or a supercapacitor may be used to provide supplemental power for the vehicle and to store energy generated during braking.

The hydrogen used comes from other fuel sources, such as from natural gas or by electrolyzing (electrically separating) water (H_2O) into its hydrogen and oxygen elements. While energy-intensive, even taking this part of the fuel production process into account, FCVs significantly reduce the amount of carbon dioxide emissions. Some companies use solar energy to electrolyze sea water, thus producing hydrogen in a truly sustainable fashion.

Systems used for transporting and storing CNG are somewhat similar to those needed for hydrogen. Because of its molecular structure (H_2)—the smallest of all elements—hydrogen tends to easily leak through ordinary storage media. It also tends to crystallize metal. Thus, one of the limitations in the more widespread use of hydrogen fuel cells in vehicles has been the relatively small number of available hydrogen refueling outlets. One way this may be overcome is by installing a domestic hydrogen generator as a standard element in a home heating system. This generator could be powered by the conventional domestic supply of natural gas, so your vehicle could be economically **slow-fill** refueled overnight in your own garage, rather than at a commercial filling station.

Fuel Cell Systems

Fuel cell power generating systems have separate hydrogen gas fuel and air intake ports, and an outlet for the waste water produced by the fuel cell process. Electrical current is generated by the fuel cell and is recovered through the anode and the cathode plates in the stack. Anti-freeze is circulated through the system as a coolant.

The electro-chemical reaction that creates electrical power takes place within individual fuel cells. The fuel cell system consists of many fuel cells arranged in a "stack." Together, they output enough electrical energy to drive a vehicle's electric motor. Each cell consists of a **membrane electrode assembly** sandwiched between **plates**. Tiny flow channels in the plates diffuse the hydrogen and oxygen gases onto the surface of the membrane, where a catalytic reaction occurs to split off hydrogen electrons to produce electricity **FIGURE 52-9**. The two gases then combine to form water, which is the only exhaust.

The reaction also generates significant heat, which must be removed. Coolant is circulated from a radiator between the fuel cells or through the plates without making direct contact with the membrane.

The individual fuel cells are combined in series into a stack so that the whole module will deliver a required output power. For example, suppose a stack produces 20 kilowatts of power **FIGURE 52-10**. Four such stacks combined will produce 80 kilowatts, enough to fully power an average vehicle. Smaller fuel cell stacks can be used as a range extender—an auxiliary power source used in combination with a battery. Some fuel cells are used to power smaller vehicles or as auxiliary generators for trucks and refrigeration units during overnight layovers or extended idle periods.

Battery Electric Vehicle Technology

Battery electric vehicle (BEV) principles were used more than a century ago, before the advent of gasoline-

FIGURE 52-9 Fuel cell creating electricity.

FIGURE 52-10 Fuel cells in a stack.

powered internal combustion vehicles. With modern-day improvements in vehicle systems and battery technology, electric vehicles are returning to the marketplace. Because more than 75% of daily commuters drive no more than 40 miles (about 65 km) a day, electric vehicles are becoming viable, as they can now deliver that range without needing to consume any gasoline or diesel fuel at all, and therefore, produce no emissions.

BEVs first enjoyed a brief resurgence during the late 1990s in the United States with a number of OEMs offering them for lease. These included GM's EV!, Toyota's RAV4 EV, Ford's Electric Ranger pick-up, and Nissan's Altra station wagon/crossover vehicle, to name a few. These vehicles were preproduction or limited production test vehicles mainly for California commuters, police or postal fleets, and other limited-range applications. The limitations included the lack of a recharging infrastructure and lack of a single charge port configuration; various conductive hookups were used along with the innovative inductive "paddle." The vehicles also suffered from disappointing range issues. Where lead-acid batteries offered a limited range-to-weight ratio, the nickel metal hydride batteries proved expensive and at the time somewhat unreliable. Thus, most BEVs of that period were recalled by the OEMs and crushed. But, the knowledge and technology gains from those electric vehicles propelled a new generation of HEVs and BEVs forward to the marketplace. As a result of improved development in battery technology and propulsion system management algorithms, many manufacturers are now entering the BEV market.

Electric Motors

Vehicles that include electric drive motors have many advantages over traditional vehicles. Lower noise and gas emissions are among the major benefits. Other benefits include fewer moving parts, fewer maintenance requirements, good low-speed torque output, and increased reliability.

Many applications of the alternating current (AC) and direct current (DC) electric motor are in use today. Different vehicle manufacturers apply these varying operating systems to fill chassis demands.

In vehicles designed for highway use, drive motor systems are computer controlled. The computer controls the direction, frequency, order, and amplitude of current flowing through the motor(s). The magnetic field produced by this current reacts with permanent magnets in the motor, causing the motor's rotor to rotate. Smaller non-road (golf cart style) or low-speed neighborhood electric road vehicles (NEVs) may use DC motors and relays to control the drive system. However, it is important to note that the AC systems used in on-road vehicles operate on dangerously high voltages, some as high as 500 to 650 volts.

The electric motor is connected to road wheels typically via planetary gears. A few vehicles use so-called wheel motors, which are built into the wheel hub to save valuable cargo-carrying space normally displaced by the drive system.

During deceleration or vehicle braking, the electric motor connected to the drive line serves as a generator to create energy normally lost as heat from friction created by braking. This energy, captured as high current during regenerative braking, is routed back into the battery for storage. The electric motor in some power trains is also used as a generator to provide partial recharging of batteries when the vehicle is coasting. This energy must be strictly controlled by the battery pack controller or serious damage to the battery system will result.

The most popular types of electric motors used are brushless, multiphase, synchronous, and permanent magnet motors.

- **Brushless**: Brushes and commutators are not used.
- **Multiphase**: The stator contains more than one winding, usually three.
- Synchronous: The speed of the rotor is synchronized to the frequency of current flowing through the **stator windings**. This design maintains excellent power and efficiency characteristics even at low speeds.
- **Permanent magnet**: The rotor is made from very powerful rare earth permanent magnet alloys—typically, neodymium-iron-boron or samarium-cobalt.

BEVs and Sustainable Energy Sources

When coupled with sustainable or renewable energy sources, the BEV can truly serve as an emissions-free vehicle. Sustainable energy may be provided by unlimited sources of supply. These sources include:

- Solar panels and reflectors (to drive steam turbines)
- Wind generators
- Tidal and wave-power generators
- Geothermal sources

These sources and others offer limitless energy sustainability, without the use of fossil fuels like petroleum or coal. The BEV itself normally uses only one power source—the battery. The battery powers traction motors to propel the vehicle. The vehicle is returned to a charging station to maintain the energy **FIGURE 52-11**. Alternatively, the batteries may be quickly swapped at a "refueling" station. With a BEV, the average distance is limited to the storage capacity of the battery and the efficiency of its motor. Most BEVs can travel about 80 to 100 miles (129 to 161 km) on a single charge, with some exceptions. Coda Automotive reportedly uses a lithium-iron phosphate battery pack and AC electric motor with

134 horsepower in their BEV. This plug-in electric sedan will travel 90 to 125 miles (145 to 201 km) on less than $4 of electricity. The Tesla Roadster is reportedly the first production automobile to use lithium-ion battery cells and the first production BEV (all-electric) to travel more than 200 miles (322 km) per charge. With such promising battery and vehicle technology, BEV range will likely extend to more than 300 miles (483 km) in the not-too-distant future.

The Chevy Volt is known as an extended-range electric vehicle. It uses a lithium-ion battery that can be recharged from a domestic electrical power outlet (110 or 220 volts AC). This vehicle, however, is not a pure electric vehicle but a form of hybrid vehicle, as it also has a small gasoline/petrol-powered engine that drives a generator to provide electric power, should the vehicle travel beyond its battery-only range.

Electric vehicles for road use today use AC motors. The DC motors used in electric concept cars were originally carryovers from the electric forklift industry. DC installations tend to be simpler and less expensive than an AC system. AC installations allow the use of a three-phase AC motor. A typical automotive AC drive motor would run at 240 volts with a 300-volt battery pack.

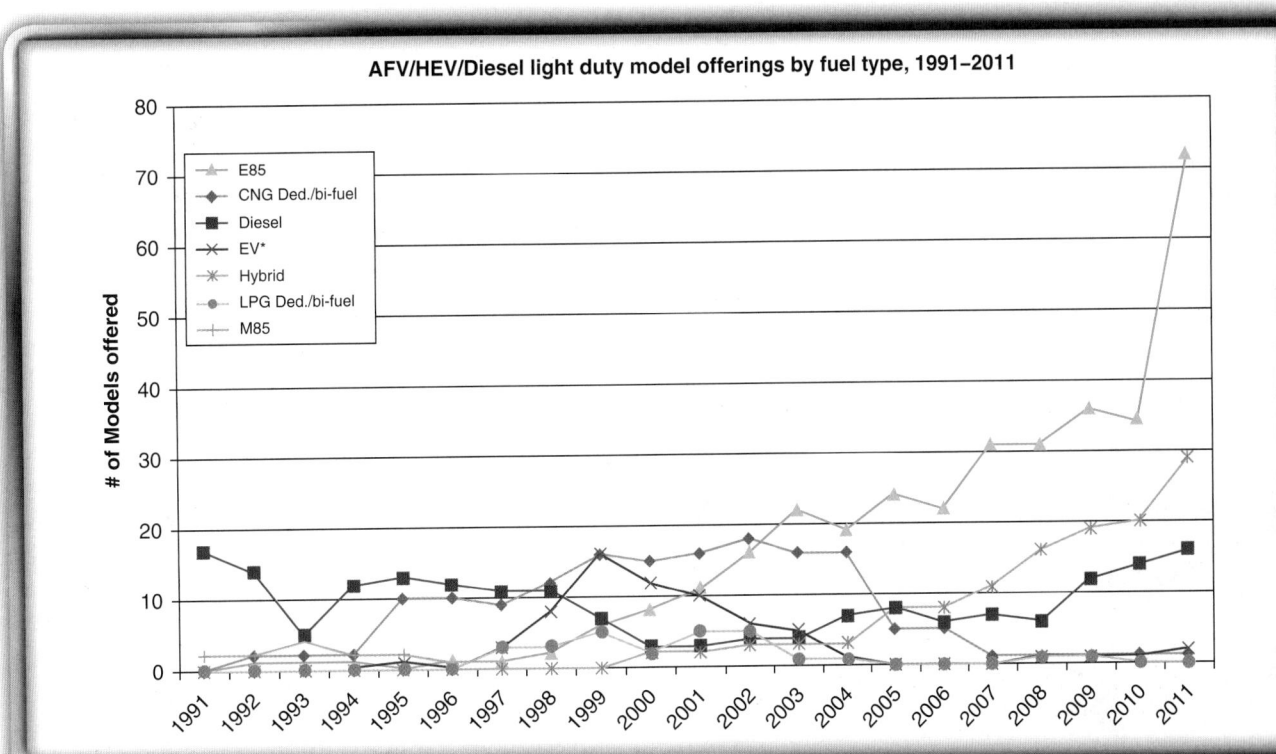

FIGURE 52-11 Notice that starting from 1999, close to 3 million hybrids rank second highest among AFVs in the United States. These numbers will continue to climb in the coming years. Note also that as of 2011 there are more than 7 million E85 (85% ethanol) FFVs on US roads. Most owners of these FFVs are unaware that they can handle alcohol fuel.

AC motors and controllers often incorporate a "regen" feature like that used with many commercial hybrid vehicle applications. This means that during braking, the motor functions as a generator to deliver otherwise lost kinetic energy into power to recharge the batteries.

Hybrid Electric Vehicles

If you consider diesel-electric submarines or diesel-electric locomotives, you will realize that the hybrid drive concept is anything but new **FIGURE 52-12**. Light- and medium-duty hybrids now come in a variety of configurations. Power from the ICE (running on natural gas, diesel, propane, or gasoline) combines with auxiliary backup or primary power from electric batteries, ultra- or supercapacitors, hydraulic-pneumatic accumulators, or even flywheels operating at super-high revolutions per minute (rpm). Other power options, such as microturbines, are used in nonroad special-purpose hybrids. US light-duty hybrids are almost exclusively gasoline-electric.

Hybrid electric vehicles (HEVs) use a combination of electric power and an ICE. They combine the different advantages of ICEs and electric motors to provide a vehicle that operates more efficiently. Usually, the engine drives a generator to provide the electricity, which is stored in batteries that then drive an electric motor. The engine may also drive the wheels directly. Hybrid vehicles are designed to drive like conventionally powered vehicles, while producing significantly lower emissions and increased fuel economy.

In conventional vehicles that have only an ICE, the engine must be large enough and powerful enough to produce momentary torque sufficient for rapid acceleration at low speeds or from a stationary position. Such an engine is larger than necessary for highway cruising, which requires far less power. The parasitic losses of the larger engine take their toll on fuel economy. A vehicle that has only an electric motor has its own complications. It must carry a large volume of heavy batteries to give it sufficient range to be useful, and these must be recharged or replaced when discharged.

While electric motors produce their maximum torque at stall speed, a gasoline engine is more efficient at higher rpm. Combining a small but efficient gasoline engine that is designed to operate at its optimum peak torque rpm with an electric motor that can double as a generator to recapture braking energy is both effective and efficient.

Hybrid Drive Configurations

There are three basic kinds of hybrid drive configurations:

- **Series hybrid**: The gasoline engine is used only to drive a generator and charge a battery, which produces power to drive an electric motor. The electric motor then drives the wheels of the vehicle. The gasoline engine is really only a battery charger inside an electric vehicle.
- **Parallel hybrid**: The engine always drives the wheels and keeps the batteries charged. The electric motor acts like a large starter motor, helping the engine to crank over when more power is needed, particularly when starting from rest or when accelerating rapidly. This allows the engine to be smaller and lighter and more fuel efficient than if it were the sole source of power in the vehicle.
- **Series-parallel hybrid**: This design allows both the engine and the motor to drive the vehicle, or either one by itself, under the control of an on-board computer that determines the optimum combination of power delivered to the wheels at any time. The engine can shut down completely when the batteries are charged. When needed, the gasoline engine fires up again to assist in driving the wheels or to recharge the battery. The engine can be optimized for efficiency within a narrow rpm range, and the overall combination of both power sources takes up little more room than a conventional all-purpose gasoline engine, and yet can deliver lower emissions and much greater fuel economy. This design is used by the Toyota Prius and Ford Escape.

FIGURE 52-12 Ford Focus–Electric being charged.

Almost all hybrids (except the Chevy Volt) transfer motive power to the wheels in either the parallel or the series-parallel drive configuration.

A variety of transmissions, clutches, and other features are used depending on the desired amount of performance (or alternatively, fuel economy) and the selling price. Some hybrids come with manual or automatic (up to eight speeds) planetary gear set transmissions; others come with continuously variable transmissions (some with sporty "paddle" type shifters). High-voltage controls vary also, along with the types of batteries and capacities, type of battery cooling, and so on. There may be one, two, or more high-voltage **electric machines** (drive motors/generators) used. These may be three-phase AC permanent magnet or inductive motors. Usually, the ICE provides power when the vehicle is traveling at higher speeds, and the electric motor is used when slowing to a halt and at lower speeds. The parallel hybrid arrangement is best suited to vehicles that travel greater distances between stops, such as more traditional passenger vehicles and delivery trucks.

Hybrid Vehicle Efficiency

HEVs are able to offset ICE efficiency by using smaller volumetric engine size and by running the ICE at the optimal torque and speed. Efficiency is also achieved through regenerative braking and by using displacement-on-demand cylinder deactivation, power-on-demand, and idle stop. **Regenerative braking** occurs when the drive motor(s) act as generators to recharge the traction batteries during deceleration or when braking. This feature reportedly saves around 10–15% on fuel consumption. **Displacement-on-demand** deactivates cylinders when operating under cruise or coasting conditions to save fuel. The **power-on-demand** feature temporarily shuts off the ICE when it is not needed, such as when idling or coasting. Drive may also be provided instead only by the electric motor, without burning fuel, thus saving energy and reducing emissions. **Idle stop** turns off the ICE when the vehicle is at a standstill. Expect all of these features to be more widely used as newer vehicles hit the market. Other fuel-saving features include variable valve timing, Atkinson cycle (five-cycle) or Miller cycle (five-cycle with low rpm boost) engines, and similarly interesting innovations.

> ▶ **LINK**
> Refer to the Motive Power Types chapter for more on these engines.

Hybrid vehicle types are classified by body style and by the degree of performance and luxury they offer. But technically speaking, they are also classified by how far they can be driven on batteries alone. For example, a "full hybrid" can cruise a limited distance without the engine running. A "partial hybrid" runs on ICE power at all times except when stopped. The vast majority, perhaps 90% of US registered HEVs, are full hybrids using drive systems with one or more planetary gear sets licensed from, or similar to, Toyota's Hybrid Synergy Drive design. A number of other OEMs are using the GM-originated Two-Mode hybrid drive system.

Hybrid System Components

The ICE in a hybrid vehicle is designed to operate only within its most efficient operating range, typically somewhere between 2000 and 4500 rpm, where engine peak **volumetric efficiency** and peak torque are developed. Its construction has lighter internal components than would otherwise be required, resulting in an efficient engine with low frictional qualities. It may also incorporate other fuel-efficient technologies such as engine cylinders that can be selectively shut down, multi-runner intake manifolds, and throttleless intake manifolds.

A powerful permanent magnet brushless motor/ generator is mounted adjacent to the engine **FIGURE 52-13**. It draws power from the battery to drive the vehicle in situations involving low load and speed, and it assists the engine to provide more power during acceleration. During deceleration and braking, it functions as a generator, reclaiming kinetic energy by converting it to electrical energy and storing it in the battery.

Often, a power splitting assembly is mounted between the ICE (engine) and the electric motor **FIGURE 52-14**.

FIGURE 52-13 Main traction motor.

FIGURE 52-14 Power splitting transmission.

FIGURE 52-15 A battery pack installed in a Toyota Prius.

FIGURE 52-16 Flywheel-mounted motor/generator.

This device functions as a **continuously variable transmission (CVT)** and transaxle assembly. The CVT does not "shift" from one gear to another in the usual sense; rather, it continuously varies the amounts of speed and torque from the engine and the motor to the wheels, selecting the best (most efficient) engine and motor rpm balance for any given driving condition.

Batteries have transitioned from lead-acid in early electric vehicles to sealed nickel–metal hydride 200- to 300-volt battery packs to sealed lithium-ion battery packs, which provide higher power output and are lighter than other battery types **FIGURE 52-15**. Their output may be inverted and raised to 650 volts by the power inverter to power the electric drive motors (also called electric machines, because they also generate electricity during overrun situations, such as when coasting). Hybrid battery packs are generally made up of a lot of small individual battery cells that are connected in series. They are monitored and managed by a control unit that controls the rate of charge and monitors their temperature.

A small permanent magnet brushless motor/generator replaces the engine flywheel **FIGURE 52-16**. It functions as the engine's starter motor and battery charger. It also provides additional power for the larger main motor/generator. A motor control unit controls the delivery of electrical current to and from the battery and the electric motors. It has its own cooling system to control its operating temperature. It also contains an AC to DC converter used to charge the battery, and a DC to AC power **inverter** to change direct current from the battery into alternating current to power the electric motors.

Hybrid Vehicle Operation

When the vehicle is moving from a stationary position, and when traveling at low to moderate speeds, the main electric motor/generator drives the vehicle. At these speeds, the ICE is less efficient and is normally used only to charge the battery.

During normal driving, the ICE starts and drives the generator and the power splitter/divider. Power from the generator is used to drive the electric motor. The motor control unit controls the **power divider/splitter** so that the drive remains at its most efficient. When accelerating and when using power from the ICE, the control unit draws power from the battery and directs it to the electric motor/generator, providing more power to the wheels than the ICE could supply on its own.

During deceleration and braking, the ICE is turned off. Inertia from the wheels drives the electric motor/generator, using the current produced to charge the battery. Normally this energy would be wasted as heat, but in the hybrid, it is recovered and reused. The **retarding effect** (vehicle slowing) caused by this system provides the same deceleration as normal engine braking would. Gentle application of the brake pedal does not apply the brakes. The braking effect is achieved by using the electric motor/generator, which converts the vehicle's inertial momentum into electrical energy to charge the battery.

When the vehicle is stationary and the brakes are applied, the ICE is stopped and power is not applied to the electric motor/generator. No fuel is burned and no emissions are produced. Releasing the brakes applies power to the electric motor. Moving the accelerator pedal activates the electric motor and, if required, the ICE to drive the vehicle.

Types of Hybrids and Electric Vehicles

There are various kinds of electric and hybrid vehicles on the market today. They may be classified by body style, but how is the *degree* of hybridization described? There seems to be some confusion. HEVs may be classified by the type of drive configuration used—such as planetary gear sets, multiple electric machines, and continuously variable transmissions. Other descriptions are thrown around with abandon. The following are some widely used descriptions you should be familiar with, but don't be surprised if other designations (often created for marketing appeal) are used for these hybrid vehicles.

Battery Electric Vehicles

BEVs need recharging when batteries are low. In the past, lead-acid or nickel-metal hydride batteries were typically used. Now lithium-ion and other types of batteries are used for greater range. Early BEVs include GM's EV-1, Ford's EV Ranger, Toyota's RAV-4 EV, and Nissan's Altra. Most of these early electric vehicles have been reclaimed and scrapped by the OEMs. Now, a whole new generation of electric vehicles is becoming available, such as the Nissan Leaf **FIGURE 52-17**. Watch for more BEVs to be released soon.

Hybrid Electric Vehicles

HEVs have two power sources, typically a gasoline ICE and high-voltage batteries working in both series and parallel. HEVs are not typically electric grid rechargeable, although some have been converted to plug-in HEVs (see the next section) for more than 100 mpg (43 km/L). HEV types include micro, partial, and full hybrid vehicles.

FIGURE 52-17 Nissan Leaf.

- Micro-hybrids include GM's Silverado and Sierra with start/stop features.
- Partial hybrids include Honda's Civic and Insight, in which the engine (ICE) does not shut off while the vehicle is underway.
- Full hybrids include the Toyota Prius models, the Ford Escape hybrid, and the Mercury Mariner hybrid. These and many others (perhaps 90%) of the market are considered full hybrids, as they can be driven short distances and at low speeds using only the (high-voltage) batteries.

Plug-in Hybrid Electric Vehicles

Many manufacturers are entering the **plug-in hybrid electric vehicle (PHEV)** market. A PHEV is different in that only one power source, the battery, is used to propel the vehicle for a certain distance, limited by the storage capacity of the battery and the efficiency of the motor. A PHEV-20, for example, is designed to go 20 miles (32 km) before the batteries need charging and the ICE is needed; a PHEV-40 can go 40 miles (64 km), etc. The ICE may also start up for added power before the batteries need a recharge. Ford, Toyota, and other light duty vehicle OEMs have PHEVs on test. PHEV automobiles achieve great fuel economy with some getting more than 100 mpg (43 km/L). Medium-duty vehicles from Mercedes-Benz and others offer PHEVs for commercial use. International Truck and Engine sells a PHEV school bus. Combined with FFV capability, PHEVs offer a good gasoline per gallon equivalent.

Extended-Range Electric Vehicles

Extended-range electric vehicles (EREVs) are plug-ins that have a relatively small auxiliary ICE to drive a generator for charging the batteries. The Chevy Volt is a series EREV.

Fuel Cell (Electric) Vehicles

FCVs are considered hybrid vehicles because they have two power sources. The sources typically are a hydrogen fuel cell "stack" and a storage device from which electric power is drawn. Regenerative braking electrical energy may be stored in the vehicle's high-voltage battery pack, or as with Honda's early FCX and others, in ultra- or supercapacitors, which can more quickly be charged or provide acceleration power as needed.

▶ Hybrid Vehicle Service

Before attempting to perform service operations on any hybrid vehicle, read the manufacturer's service information for the vehicle you are about to service. The service manual will instruct you in how to properly follow all safety procedures. The most important rule to remember is, never work on a high-voltage vehicle without first notifying someone who is trained in dealing with high-voltage electrocution. You need a responsible person in your work environment to check on you as you work around high voltage.

The matter of servicing hybrids safely is to be taken seriously. Always follow the manufacturer's safety and service procedures to keep out of trouble. There are many safety features built into hybrid vehicles to prevent accidental shock, but once you decide to venture into high-voltage areas, be prepared to spend some money on safety equipment. This is no time to pinch pennies! Some of the standard equipment for servicing HEV systems includes:

- OEM or equivalent scan tools
- A high-quality (three-phase CAT III or CAT IV) digital volt-ohmmeter (DVOM) with appropriate high-voltage leads
- Insulated gloves rated for 5000 volts and certified to 1000 volts (Class 0)
- Safety cones and safety tape (to mark off service areas) and other such items
- A retrieval hook in case someone becomes disabled from electrical shock

If you decide to service electric and hybrid vehicles, get the proper training on the high-voltage areas as well as a full understanding of how they operate. Stay alert and continually practice situational awareness.

Besides the high voltage dangers of a hybrid or electric vehicle, there are other precautions you need to be aware of. One of the first is that the vehicle should be completely powered down before working on it, since the ICE can start at any time it deems necessary. The vehicle should be in park, with the parking brake applied, and the power button powered down. The keyless fob, if equipped, should be more than 15' (4.6 m) from the vehicle.

Identifying and Disabling the High-Voltage System

There are plenty of opportunities to service HEVs without venturing into the high-voltage areas of the vehicle, such as changing oil. Just because you are not working on the main traction motor doesn't mean that you won't come into contact with other high voltage circuits. In many hybrid and electric vehicles, high voltage is used to operate a variety of accessories, such as power steering and air-conditioning, so you need to be aware that high voltage wires can be located nearly anywhere in the vehicle. These high voltage wires are recognized by orange (usually) convolute or wiring **FIGURE 52-18**. Some vehicles have used other colors, such as blue, to designate high-voltage wiring. Avoid working on these high-voltage areas of a hybrid vehicle without first having the proper training, service information, and experienced help on hand. The main high-voltage battery pack must be disconnected before service is performed on or around the high-voltage components. Every manufacturer has a different way of disconnecting high-voltage batteries from the main electrical system, but it usually involves a service plug that is removed from near the battery or a battery module switch that is turned to the off position, both of which will disconnect the battery from the high voltage system.

FIGURE 52-18 High-voltage wiring.

Before you disable the high voltage system, make sure you are wearing the appropriate PPE. Locate the high voltage battery disconnect (service plug) **FIGURE 52-19**. Release the lock, release the lever, and remove the service plug. Store it in a safe place where it cannot be reinserted accidentally. Wait for the specified time for the residual electricity to bleed off. Locate the high voltage access panel. Remove the bolts that secure the cover **FIGURE 52-20**. Then remove the cover, and, using the correctly rated meter, measure that there is no voltage at the specified terminals **FIGURE 52-21**.

Hybrid ICE Service Precautions

Hybrid vehicle ICEs require maintenance and service like other ICEs, such as changing the oil and filter and replacing belts (on those equipped with accessory drive belts). The last thing you want is to be electrocuted or have the engine start up while you are working on it. All hybrids are designed to operate uniquely; therefore, there are precautions specific to each vehicle model. Don't assume that the safety precautions for an older model are the same for a newer model, and vice versa. The first precaution is to make sure you have been trained to work on the particular hybrid or electric vehicle. If you are not properly trained to work on that particular hybrid vehicle, you should not work on it. Before starting any diagnostic, maintenance, or repair work, always check the service information for the specific safety or procedural requirements that the manufacturer has specified. Also, know how to power down the high-voltage system, and remember that it takes 5 to 15 minutes for the electrical charge to bleed off.

Hybrid Auxiliary (12v) Battery Service

On most hybrid vehicles, the 12-volt auxiliary battery is used to power up the vehicles computers and run virtually all of the accessories. Because it powers up the computers it is critical to starting the vehicle, even though it is generally not used to crank the engine over; that is typically done by one of the traction motors and high voltage battery. This means that the 12v battery in a hybrid vehicle is generally smaller than in a standard vehicle, making the battery is more susceptible to parasitic current draws, since they don't have as much current capacity. It is also located separately from the traction batteries; typically either under the hood, or in the trunk. In most cases, the 12v battery is charged from an inverter built into the hybrid electronic controller, instead of a separate alternator **FIGURE 52-22**.

FIGURE 52-19 Locate the high voltage battery disconnect (service plug).

FIGURE 52-20 Locate the high voltage access panel and remove the bolts that secure the cover.

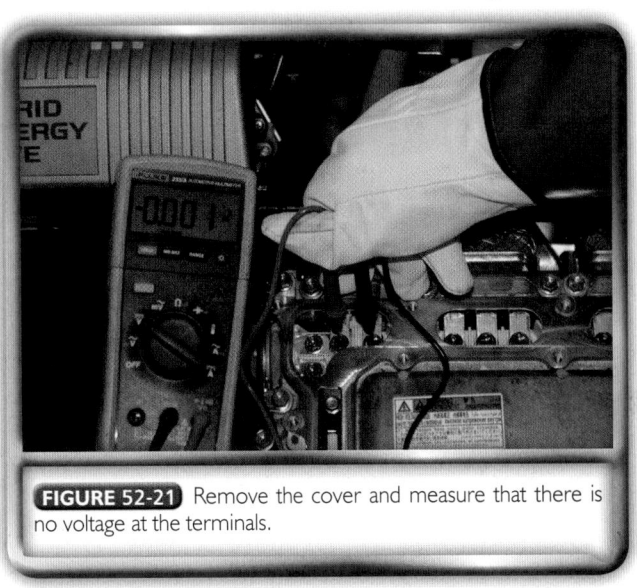

FIGURE 52-21 Remove the cover and measure that there is no voltage at the terminals.

FIGURE 52-22 A 12v Prius battery installed.

In most hybrids, the 12v battery is of the absorbed glass mat (AGM) construction. This battery is sensitive to overcharging, which can damage it, so a special battery charger is required whenever charging is needed. Some manufacturers recommend removing the 12v battery from the vehicle while it is charging to prevent any damage to the vehicle's electrical system. But this can erase the computer and entertainment memories, as well as activate the anti-theft system, so always follow the manufacturer's procedure when disconnecting a battery. Also, most manufacturers prohibit hybrid vehicles from being used to jump start another vehicle, due to the reduced size of the auxiliary battery, and the potential damage to the hybrid electrical system. The 12v battery can be tested in a similar manner to a lead-acid flooded cell battery, with either a load tester or a conductance tester, as described in the Batteries, Starting, and Charging Systems chapter. Again, it is preferable to remove the battery from the vehicle during testing.

Wrap-up

Ready for Review

- An alternative fuel is any fuel that powers a vehicle that is not petroleum-based motor oil.
- Alternative fuels are not new; they have been around since the 1890s.
- Alternative fuels have to meet the California Air Resources Board (CARB) standards to be certified.
- The push for alternative fuels is driven by the need for enhanced security, environmental concern, and economic factors.
- Alternative fuel is regulated by many different acts, starting in 1992.
- The Environmental Protection Agency (EPA) is the driving force behind alternative energy.
- There are many different standards for low-emission vehicles, beginning in the early 1980s and growing progressively stringent into 2012.
- Alternative vehicles are designed to reduce emissions and be more economical to operate.
- Compressed natural gas (CNG) and liquefied natural gas (LNG) were first introduced in the 1980s, but due to lack of refilling stations, they did not sell well to the consumer.
- The process to use either CNG or LNG requires the vehicle engine to be able to run on flexible fuels.
- CNG and LPG must be stored in special cylinders that will withstand pressures and damage.
- CNG and LPG containers are fitted with special pressure relief systems to release pressure as required.
- CNG and LNG must be protected from a heat source. In some designs, special heat shields are installed around the exhaust system to protect the container from excess heat.
- Leaks can be identified by using a special explosion meter that will find methane gas leaks.
- Biofuels are made by chemically combining natural oils from soybeans, cottonseeds, canola, animal fats, algae, jatropha seeds, or even recycled cooking oil with an alcohol such as methanol or ethanol, and a catalyst such as lye.
- There are different qualities of biodiesel fuels, and they should not be confused with the fuel made from old vegetable oil.
- The one main disadvantage to biodiesel is that starting in cold weather may require longer cranking of the engine.
- The military is the driving force in the use of alternative fuels like biodiesel.
- Biodiesel produces less emission than similar diesel fuels.
- Biodiesel has higher water content than traditional diesel fuels.
- Just like with typical diesel fuel, the centane number of biodiesel must be correct for overall engine performance, typically around 46–57; the higher the better.
- Ethanol is being used mainly to lower fuel emissions in vehicles and is made from three products: sugars, grains, and algae.
- Methanol or wood alcohol is being used in E85 vehicles, which means 85% of the fuel mixture is methanol.
- The advantage to methanol is the lower output of emissions.
- The main disadvantage with methanol is that it cannot be burned in conventional vehicles without major engine modifications.
- Biobutenol is similar to ethanol, but butenol has characteristics similar enough to gasoline that it can be transported through the existing petroleum (pipeline) distribution infrastructure.
- Biobutenol shows promise but is in the early stages of development.
- Fuel cell technology has been used a number of years by NASA; given the current need for alternative fuels, it has pushed for another look at this technology by several manufacturers.
- Fuel cells are complex systems that require oxygen and hydrogen to produce water to operate a vehicle.
- Fuel cells have zero pollutants; they exhaust only water.
- There are four elements to a fuel cell: the anode, cathode, electrolyte, and catalyst.
- Fuel cells do not produce enough energy by themselves; to achieve the required power they must be stacked.
- The electric motor shows great promise because it has fewer moving parts, less maintenance requirements, good low-speed torque output, and increased reliability.
- The computer gives the electric motor new life and has some advantages; the biggest disadvantage is the electric motor must have a battery to run it.

▶ Hydrogen fuel cells are simple and have three times the energy of gasoline. Fuel cell vehicles, however, are more efficient and cleaner.

▶ Battery electric vehicles (BEVs) are making a comeback with the addition of computer technology and lithium batteries.

▶ The Chevy Volt was supposed to be the first BEV, but it is really a hybrid, since it has a gasoline engine to recharge the battery.

▶ Hybrids have been used since World War II.

▶ The locomotives on the railroad tracks today are diesel electric; the engine charges the batteries and the locomotive runs on the batteries.

▶ Many city buses are diesel electric, which demonstrates that hybrid technology is not new; it is being redefined, with the new vehicles using computers to control operations.

▶ The engine in hybrids can be much smaller, as its main purpose is to recharge the hybrid's battery. The hybrid gets most of its power from the battery running the electrical drives.

▶ When you think of hybrids, think of electrical circuitry. There are series, parallel, and series parallel designs.

▶ On series hybrids, the engine runs only to supply the electric motor or charge the batteries.

▶ On parallel hybrids, the engine runs to charge the battery and directly assist propelling the vehicle.

▶ On series-parallel hybrids, the engine runs to charge the battery, operate the electric motor, and assist with propelling the vehicle all at the same time.

▶ Hybrids offset the power lost by internal combustion engines (ICEs) in several ways. One of the most efficient is the regenerative braking system.

▶ There are numerous hybrids, from plug-in to extended-range. They all work basically the same way: They allow the vehicle to be propelled by the electrical power. Thus, they are more fuel efficient.

▶ The hybrid normally starts out on electrical power, and as the need changes, the engine will come on to assist or recharge the batteries, depending on the design.

▶ The ICE is turned off during deceleration and braking.

▶ The ICE needs to start and run at higher rpm for peak efficiency.

▶ Hybrids can be dangerous. Always refer to the appropriate repair information.

▶ In hybrids, it is usually the orange wires that indicate high voltage. Other colors may be used, so check the manufacturer's information. Always wear special gloves to remove the access plugs to disable hybrids.

▶ Anytime service is performed, the technician needs to ensure that the hybrid is not in the ready mode and that everything is off.

Key Terms

aldehyde A pollutant/irritant in diesel fuel.

alternative fuel A nonpetroleum-based motor fuel.

anode A positively charged electrode or plate.

automatic fuel limiter A special refueling port and an overfill protection device fitted on LPG tanks, which ensure that the tank cannot be filled past the safe fill limit of 80%.

B20 fuel A fuel that is 20% biodiesel blended with 80% petrodiesel.

B100 fuel A fuel that is 100% biodiesel ("neat").

battery electric vehicle (BEV) A vehicle powered by battery only.

bi-fuel Two fuels used in a vehicle one at a time, such as compressed natural gas or gasoline.

biodiesel Renewable fuel made from organic feedstocks.

bio-ethanol A renewable fuel derived from a variety of cellulose-based plants.

biomass Organic matter used for fuel.

brushless An electric motor without brushes.

burn rate The rate of flame spread for liquid or gaseous fuel.

carbon dioxide (CO_2) A greenhouse gas emitted from the tailpipe.

carbon monoxide (CO) Partially burned fuel emitted from the tailpipe.

catalyst A device that changes chemical composition without self-destruction.

cathode A negatively charged electrode or plate.

cloud point The temperature at which wax (paraffin) in diesel fuel starts to solidify.

compressed natural gas (CNG) Methane compressed for on-board storage in cylinders.

compressed natural gas vehicle (CNGV) A vehicle that uses methane stored in high-pressure cylinders.

compression-ignition (CI) engine A diesel engine.

continuously variable transmission (CT) A transmission without individual gears or gear ratios.

displacement-on-demand A feature that allows cylinders to be taken off-line when not needed, such as at vehicle cruise.

dual-fuel system A system that allows an engine to burn two fuels at one time.

E85 A fuel with 85% ethanol and 15% gasoline blend.

electric machine Another name for a traction motor with regenerative capability.

electro-chemical device A device such as a battery or fuel cell that uses two forms of energy.

electrolyte The solution in a battery, such as sulfuric acid and water used in a lead-acid battery.

emission standards Cutoff points set by governmental agencies to limit tailpipe emissions.

Energy Policy Act (EPAct92) Regulations enacted in 1992 by the US Congress to promote the use of alternative fuel vehicles and fuels.

Environmental Protection Agency (EPA) In the United States, the agency that controls federally mandated emission standards.

ethanol Alcohol-based motor fuel made from starches and sugars.

flexible-fuel vehicle (FFV) A vehicle than can operate on two different fuels blended together in various mixture amounts by percentage.

float-type fuel gauge A system for determining the level of liquid fuel in a tank using a float and potentiometer.

fuel cell An electro-chemical device that uses hydrogen and oxygen to create electricity.

fuel cell (electric) vehicle (FCV) A vehicle that converts fuel to electricity in a direct electrochemical process, with more energy extracted from the fuel source than in traditional internal combustion engines.

fuel composition sensor A device that measures the percentage of alcohol in gasoline.

fuel methanol A toxic alcohol fuel.

hybrid electric vehicle (HEV) A vehicle that uses two power sources for propulsion, one of which is electricity.

hydrocarbon (HC) Unburned fuel emitted from the tailpipe.

hygroscopic The ability of a substance to attract and hold water molecules.

idle stop A feature that turns off the internal combustion engine when the vehicle is at a standstill.

infrastructure The system for supplying fuel for transportation use; includes ships, pipelines, trucks, etc.

inverter A device that converts direct current to alternating current.

liquefied natural gas (LNG) A cryogenic liquid produced from gaseous methane.

liquefied petroleum gas (LPG) Gaseous fuel at atmospheric pressure; commonly referred to as propane.

Low-Emission Vehicle (LEV) standard A program initiated in California to improve vehicle emission standards.

lubricity The ability to lubricate moving parts.

M85 vehicle A flexible-fuel vehicle, meaning any mixture of methanol and gasoline/petrol in the fuel tank can be used by the engine.

membrane electrode assembly The individual voltage-producing component in a fuel cell stack.

mercaptan An agent that smells like sulfur that is added to liquefied petroleum or natural gas to aid in detecting leaks.

methanol A motor fuel made from wood alcohol.

multiphase An electric motor that operates through more than one phase.

natural gas Methane; often referred to simply as NG.

National Fire Protection Association (NFPA) The agency that publishes standards for liquefied petroleum and compressed natural gas vehicles.

NFPA-52 A document from the NFPA that sets standards for compressed natural gas refueling stations and compressed natural gas vehicle fuel systems.

nitrogen oxides (NO$_x$) The various compounds of nitrogen that contributed to a smog-forming pollutant emitted from the tailpipe.

odorant An agent (mercaptan) that smells like sulfur that is added to liquefied petroleum or natural gas to aid in detecting leaks.

parallel hybrid A hybrid vehicle driven simultaneously by an internal combustion engine and an electric machine.

particulate matter (PM) Cancer-causing unburned soot from the tailpipe.

permanent magnet A material with natural or man-made constant magnetic properties.

permanently mounted tank A compressed natural gas or propane cylinder not designed to be portable.

plates The parts of a battery or fuel cell that contain materials that enable electrons to flow into or out of them.

plug-in hybrid electric vehicle (PHEV) A hybrid electric vehicle in which only one power source, the battery, is used to propel the vehicle for a certain distance, limited by the storage capacity of the battery and the efficiency of the motor.

portable universal cylinder A liquefied petroleum gas tank that can be moved or transported.

pour point The temperature at which diesel fuel is not gelled.

power divider/splitter A device that receives power from an internal combustion engine and electric machine to power a hybrid electric vehicle.

power-on-demand A feature that shuts down the engine when not needed to save fuel.

producer gas A generic term that refers to a number of manufactured gases such as wood gas, town gas, and syngas.

reformer An on-board device that extracts hydrogen from another source material.

regenerative braking A feature that allows drive motors to act as generators to recharge the traction batteries during deceleration or when braking.

retarding effect The result of retarding (slowing) the vehicle.

series hybrid A hybrid electric vehicle powered by an internal combustion engine, but driven by battery.

series-parallel hybrid A hybrid electric vehicle that uses the internal combustion engine and/or the battery pack for propulsion.

slow-fill The method of filling a compressed natural gas vehicle (such as overnight) so the cylinders are completely filled.

stator winding A winding in an alternator that creates the current output, or a winding in a motor that creates the needed magnetism for the motor to rotate.

stoichiometric ratio The air–fuel ratio for complete burning and lowest pollution; the stoichiometric ratio for a gasoline engine is 14.7 to 1 by weight.

straight vegetable oil (SVO) Biodiesel made from plants such as soybeans, jatropha, palms, etc.

sulfur A regulated by-product of petroleum-based (especially diesel) fuel.

syngas A man-made motor fuel.

town gas Locally available gas used to power early internal combustion engines.

viscosity The ability of a liquid to be poured.

volumetric efficiency A measure of how well an internal combustion engine can breathe at a given rpm at wide-open throttle.

waste vegetable oil (WVO) Used cooking grease or oil used for producing biodiesel fuel.

water gas A gas made from hydrogen and water.

wood gas A gas made by the carbonization or gasification of coal.

ASE-Type Questions

1. Tech A says that fuel cells only emit CO_2 to the atmosphere. Tech B says that fuel cells run on water. Who is correct?
   a. Tech A
   b. Tech B
   c. Both A and B
   d. Neither A nor B

2. Tech A says that ethanol-blended gas at 10% is a nationwide standard. Tech B says that 15% ethanol-blended gas has been approved for 2001 vehicles and newer. Who is correct?
   a. Tech A
   b. Tech B
   c. Both A and B
   d. Neither A nor B

3. Tech A says that high voltage wires in hybrid and electric vehicles are usually a special color. Tech B says that special high voltage shoes should be worn when working on high voltage vehicles. Who is correct?
   a. Tech A
   b. Tech B
   c. Both A and B
   d. Neither A nor B

4. Tech A says that E85 vehicles are designed to use 85% ethanol efficiently. Tech B says that hydrogen cars are not zero-emission vehicles. Who is correct?
   a. Tech A
   b. Tech B
   c. Both A and B
   d. Neither A nor B

5. Tech A says that LPG-fueled engines are low on horsepower and torque, but cost efficient. Tech B says that LPG-fueled vehicles are advantageous to a fleet as they can be fueled just about anywhere. Who is correct?
   a. Tech A
   b. Tech B
   c. Both A and B
   d. Neither A nor B

6. Tech A says that CNG fuel tanks hold 3600 psi (24,800 kPa). Tech B says that CNG engines emit white smoke, which is humidity. Who is correct?
   a. Tech A
   b. Tech B
   c. Both A and B
   d. Neither A nor B

7. Tech A says that LNG fuel is stored at approximately −263.2°F (−164°C). Tech B says that LNG fueling stations are the most common of all the alternative fuels. Who is correct?
   a. Tech A
   b. Tech B
   c. Both A and B
   d. Neither A nor B

8. Tech A says that dual-fuel–powered vehicles inject two fuels at the same time. Tech B says that bi-fuel engines inject two fuels at the same time. Who is correct?
   a. Tech A
   b. Tech B
   c. Both A and B
   d. Neither A nor B

9. Tech A says that when converting a CI diesel engine to an SI engine, you must lower the compression ratio in each cylinder. Tech B says that a diesel engine converted to use CNG and diesel fuel has a more complete and rapid combustion. Who is correct?
   a. Tech A
   b. Tech B
   c. Both A and B
   d. Neither A nor B

10. Tech A says that biodiesel mixed with diesel fuel will not reduce emissions. Tech B says that a 1% or more blend of biodiesel will extend the life of injectors. Who is correct?
    a. Tech A
    b. Tech B
    c. Both A and B
    d. Neither A nor B

Diesel Engines

CHAPTER 53

NATEF Tasks

There are no NATEF tasks for this chapter.

Knowledge Objectives

After reading this chapter, you will be able to:

1. Describe the principles of operation of four-stroke and two-stoke diesel engines. (pp 1847–1851)
2. Explain the four-stroke and two-stroke cycles of a diesel engine. (pp 1847–1851)
3. Explain the operation of a direct and indirect injection fuel delivery system. (pp 1848–1849)
4. Define the term "scavenging" as applied to a diesel engine. (p 1851)
5. Describe the three phases of combustion. (p 1851)
6. Describe the components of the diesel fuel system. (pp 1851–1858)
7. Explain the purpose of coolant and lubrication passages in the cylinder head. (p 1852)
8. Describe cylinder-head valve operation and components. (pp 1853–1854)
9. Describe diesel crankshaft design and structure. (pp 1855–1856)
10. Describe diesel engine piston design and structure. (pp 1857–1858)

Compression-Ignition Engines

Skills Objectives

There are no skills objectives for this chapter.

Introduction

The compression-ignition engine is a fuel-efficient engine that usually runs on diesel fuel, but can be easily adapted to alternative fuels such as vegetable-based biodiesel or synthetic fuels. As fuel efficient and powerful as these engines are, they have a reputation for being slow and noisy and for emitting smoke. Fortunately, today's compression-ignition diesel engines use computer controls with advanced engineering and design techniques to all but eliminate the basis for such a reputation. In fact, the modern diesel engine is quiet, efficient, and powerful, with drastically reduced emissions.

Market Forces and Technology

The oil embargo of the 1970s awakened Americans to the need for greater fuel economy, and manufacturers responded with a new breed of diesel cars, ranging from Volkswagen's 55-mpg diesel-fueled car, the Rabbit, to Lincoln's BMW-powered five-cylinder luxury sedan. But once gasoline again became plentiful, US motorists tired of the hassles of preglowing, ignition "rattle," foul exhaust, and soot on their driveways. Well-known engine failures and underperformance hastened the demise of the American love affair with diesel cars, and sales plummeted.

Despite their shortcomings, diesels of all types have remained a staple in the world's means of getting work done. Globally, drivers opt for the fuel economy of diesels to offset high motor fuel prices. But the stage was set for today's popularity for light-duty diesels in the United States around 1997. Tightening tailpipe emission standards resulted in advances in on-board clean diesel technology, and the robust economy of the time helped move the technology forward as well.

Emissions Advantage

According to the Diesel Technology Forum, new on-road diesel engine particulate matter ("soot") emissions have been reduced by 83% and oxides of nitrogen by 63% since 1988. Reportedly, the emission reductions achieved from 1990 through 1994 alone were massive. Emissions of hydrocarbons, carbon monoxide, and carbon dioxide, already inherently low with diesel engines, have also improved. At this point, continued clean air gains hinge on the availability of cleaner low-sulfur petro-diesel fuel, or the use of synthetic and biodiesel fuels. Cleaner fuels have been mandated by the US federal government's Environmental Protection Agency (EPA). Emission regulations for nonautomotive diesel equipment have likewise been enacted.

Public Perceptions

Until recent years, the medium and heavy on-road diesel market had not been as plagued with the jaundiced perceptions or federal regulations as have light diesel vehicles. Yet over time, the original equipment manufacturers (OEMs) have been converting their existing engine platforms from the use of in-line injection systems to **common rail**, with improved emissions and little required in the way of engine redesign and tooling. Today's diesel trucks in the United States are compliant with

You are the Automotive Technician

As an intern at an express delivery company, you have the opportunity to maintain some of the light duty diesel vehicles in the company's fleet. Because you are learning about diesel engines, your mentor tells you that diesel engines have significantly improved over the years. They offer improved efficiency and reduced emissions, and they are quieter than ever. As you are performing the scheduled maintenance on one of the vehicles, you ask your mentor the following questions:

1. If diesels don't have spark plugs, how do they run?
2. What is the difference between direct injection and indirect injection?
3. How does a two-stroke diesel engine operate?
4. What are the three phases of combustion?

on-board diagnostics, second generation (OBDII), with electronic systems managing the engine and power train. Some incorporate automatic start/stop of engines of parked vehicles (based on engine and cab/coach temperature and battery voltage) to lower diesel tailpipe emissions.

Along with the era of clean diesel technology came changing perceptions of diesels by US light vehicle drivers, and for good reasons. Volkswagen's 1.9 TDI (Turbo-Diesel Direct Injection) hallmarked direct injection and EDC in a diesel passenger vehicle. Reportedly, Volkswagen's four-cylinder TDI diesel engine produced 25 more horsepower than did the 1978 Oldsmobile V8 diesel, but is exactly *one-third the size*. Other OEMs have joined the race: Diesel two-wheel drive and four-wheel drive pick-ups and SUVs have become popular alternatives to gasoline-powered cars. Joining the traditional farm and construction light diesel vehicle markets are commuters, outdoors enthusiasts, sports fans, and the like, seeking greater fuel economy or hauling, towing, and off-road power in their diesel vehicles. The Chevy Duramax, Ford Powerstroke, and Dodge/Cummins 24-valve turbo-diesel packages offer popular "premium diesel" options to suit buyers' wants and needs and continue to sell like hotcakes.

In the service sector, diesel injection service dealers have taken note of the market trend. Where once reluctant to do on-vehicle repairs, preferring instead "over-the-counter" servicing of injectors, pumps, governors, and turbos, progressive service dealers now offer drive-through diesel vehicle service and repair. As always, there is a need for qualified diesel technicians, and programs exist for becoming certified. As a related skill set, diesel fuel injection service technicians use increasingly sophisticated test equipment that is more precise and more expensive. Aftermarket fuel system calibration is increasingly expected to equal the highly precise calibration standards of OEM equipment suppliers.

Compression-Ignition Engine Fundamentals

The compression-ignition engine is similar in operation to a spark-ignited gasoline engine, but with some specific differences. The gasoline engine power stroke begins as ignition occurs when the spark plug fires. With the compression-ignition engine, ignition occurs when fuel is injected in the very hot combustion chamber. The process begins with the air temperature inside the combustion chamber being raised by compression until it is hot enough to ignite the fuel. Then, at the proper time, fuel is injected and ignition immediately occurs. With a gasoline engine, usually the fuel is drawn into the combustion chamber with air on the intake stroke,

compression raises the combustion temperature to a point below ignition temperature, and then at the proper time, the spark plug fires and ignition occurs FIGURE 53-1. In the diesel engine, a spark plug is not needed for ignition, because the very hot air ignites the fuel when it is injected into the combustion chamber.

Four-Stroke Diesel Engines

The term four-stroke cycle means the piston must move up and down in four sequential strokes for every complete cycle of operation. The four-stroke cycle consists of (1) the **intake stroke** (piston moves down), (2) the **compression stroke** (piston moves up), (3) the **power stroke** (piston moves down), and (4) the **exhaust stroke** (piston moves up) FIGURE 53-2. Incidentally, for the piston to move up

FIGURE 53-1 Fuel igniting as a result of the spark plug firing.

FIGURE 53-2 A diesel engine with a four-stroke cycle.

and down in four sequential strokes, the crankshaft must rotate two complete revolutions. **Ignition** is another important event that occurs during the four-stroke cycle. Ignition occurs when fuel is injected, near the end of the compression stroke, into the very hot compressed air in the cylinder. The fuel is ignited by heat generated from compression. Therefore, just like in a spark ignition engine, there are five important events that must occur during engine operation.

Let's explore further how each of the four strokes in the four-stroke diesel engine cycle works. The intake stroke occurs when the piston moves from top dead center (TDC) to bottom dead center (BDC) with the intake valve(s) open; air is drawn into the cylinder. Then, the compression stroke occurs when the piston moves up with the intake valve(s) closed, and highly compresses the air trapped in the cylinder. Fuel is injected into the cylinder and ignited by the heat of the compressed air. Next, the power stroke occurs when, after ignition, the piston again moves from top to bottom. You may recall that when air is heated, it expands. The expansion of air (increase of pressure) is caused by the burning of the fuel during the power stroke. The increased pressure drives the piston toward BDC. Finally, the exhaust stroke occurs when the piston moves up, with the exhaust valve(s) open, exhausting the burned exhaust gases through the exhaust system. Remember, the four-stroke cycle requires two complete revolutions of the crankshaft **FIGURE 53-3** .

Volumetric Efficiency

Modern engines are designed for both smooth and efficient airflow into the engine and exhaust flow from the engine, with as little restriction as possible. The better this is performed, the greater the degree of an engine's **volumetric efficiency (VE)**. VE refers to the amount of fresh air taken into the cylinder on the intake stroke (or intake port opening) at a given revolutions per minute (rpm) in relation to the space in the cylinder (displacement) that exists at engine standstill. VE is expressed as a percentage. Normally, aspirated engines will have less than 100% VE due to (a variety of) breathing limitations, but a supercharged or turbocharged engine may enjoy a greater than 100% degree of VE.

Direct/Indirect Injection

A variety of fuel delivery systems for diesel engines have been used over the years, with each design operating on different principles. However, to meet strict emission control regulations, older fuel injection systems have given way to electronically controlled fuel systems operating on similar principles. Likewise, engine layout uses both **direct** and **indirect fuel injection** designs **FIGURE 53-4** .

Direct Injection

Direct injection means the fuel is injected directly into the combustion chamber. The advantage of this design is that it produces more power and is a simpler design than indirect injection. The disadvantages typically result

FIGURE 53-3 The four-stroke cycle. **A.** Intake. **B.** Compression. **C.** Power. **D.** Exhaust.

in more engine noise, harder starting, and higher emissions. Nonetheless, with electronic engine controls, direct injection is gaining popularity in the small diesel market.

With this design, the cylinder head usually has a flat surface, and the combustion chamber is formed in the piston crown **FIGURE 53-5**. At TDC there is very little clearance between the cylinder head and the top of the piston. In fact, in many designs if you were to remove the cylinder head gasket and replace the head on the block, you would not be able to turn the engine over because there would not be enough clearance between the two surfaces without the thickness of the head gasket present.

Modern fuel systems use electronically controlled high-pressure fuel systems that make quiet and smoke-free direct injection possible, and desirable. Through electronic controls, the fuel mixture can be infinitely controlled, producing maximum power with very low emissions.

> **TECHNICIAN TIP**
>
> Electronic controls have opened the door for consumers to increase the performance of their vehicles. So-called computer **power chips** are programmable performance chips marketed to increase horsepower and mileage of electronically controlled diesel engines. The use of such modifications can cause premature engine and drive line wear or even destruction of the engine; furthermore, use of such devices may void the vehicle's OEM warranty.

Indirect Injection

Indirect injection is another method of injecting fuel. It has been used for years with light-duty diesel vehicles as a means of reducing the characteristic "diesel clatter" caused by the ignition of fuel (discussed in the next section). With indirect injection, fuel is sprayed into a robust and very hot antichamber in the cylinder head, often called a **prechamber** **FIGURE 53-6**. The advantages of indirect injection are easier starting, a quieter running engine, and better emission control.

Prechambers have various and complex designs. Often, prechambers are designed to control the ignition and flame front to develop maximum heat energy transfer and complete burning of the fuel with a minimum shock wave. Along with the use of prechambers, various methods of controlling the rate of fuel injection have been used to quiet the ignition of fuel in light-duty (passenger vehicle) diesel engines. These include throttling-type nozzles (injector tips) with variable spray patterns and variable rates of injection, along with various prechamber and piston designs.

FIGURE 53-4 **A.** Direct injection. **B.** Indirect injection.

FIGURE 53-5 A direct injection cylinder.

FIGURE 53-6 Indirect injection is another method of injecting fuel into the combustion chamber.

Two-Stroke Diesel Engines

Most diesel (compression-ignition) engines use the four-stroke cycle. However, many applications, both on-road and off-road, have benefitted from the use of the two-stroke cycle diesel engine. The two-stroke engine performs all of the events of a four-stroke engine, but they are accomplished with two strokes of the piston and one revolution of the crankshaft **FIGURE 53-7**. Remember, the five events common to all internal combustion engines are intake, compression, ignition, power, and exhaust. The challenge is to accomplish all five of these events in half the time it takes to complete the same operations in a four-stroke engine.

The two-stroke diesel engine cycle works as follows: As the fuel mixture ignites, the piston is driven downward under the pressure of the power stroke. Before the piston reaches BDC, the exhaust valve(s) opens and begins exhausting burned gases. Next, as the piston continues downward, the intake ports, located at the bottom of the cylinder, are uncovered. As the intake ports are uncovered, air is forced into the cylinder by an engine-driven blower pushing the exhaust out and, at the same time, filling the cylinder with fresh intake air. As the piston starts moving upward, it covers the intake ports, and the compression stroke begins. As the piston approaches TDC, fuel is injected into the highly compressed air in the cylinder and the ignition process begins near TDC. As with the four-stroke cycle compression-ignition engine, the fuel is ignited by the heat of compression. The burning fuel mixture rapidly expands, developing maximum force on the piston at about 10 degrees after TDC, and pushes the piston down. This is the power stroke **FIGURE 53-8**. The cycle repeats as long as the engine is running. In these applications, the intake air blower is driven by the crankshaft. Turbochargers are also used at times to improve VE.

FIGURE 53-7 A two-stroke cycle diesel engine.

Exhaust and intake   Compression stroke   Power stroke

FIGURE 53-8 The two-stroke cycle.

Diesel Scavenging

<u>Scavenging</u> is particularly important in two-stroke diesel engines and ensures the efficient removal of hot exhaust gases from the cylinder and the refilling of it with fresh air. Without effective scavenging, diesel engines lose VE. The more air ingested into a cylinder, the more efficient and powerful the engine will be.

The scavenging process in a two-stroke diesel engine begins with an air pump or blower providing clean incoming air pressured slightly above that of outgoing exhaust gases. The blower delivers air to the air box surrounding the cylinder. When the piston uncovers the inlet ports, air enters the cylinder. This fills the cylinder with fresh air and helps blow out exhaust gases.

► The Three Phases of Combustion

Once fuel is injected into the cylinder, it goes through three phases during the ignition and heat energy transfer process. The three phrases are (1) <u>ignition delay/lag period</u>, (2) <u>flame spread</u>, and (3) <u>direct burning</u> **FIGURE 53-9**.

The ignition delay/lag period is the time it takes for the fuel to ignite after it is injected into the engine. Once the fuel ignites, there is a sudden pressure rise in the cylinder from the expansion of hot gases. "Diesel clatter" is caused by ignition lag, which occurs between the start of injection and the start of ignition. A small amount of fuel builds up in the combustion chamber before it ignites, and when it does, the rapid ignition of accumulated fuel causes a shock wave that resonates the combustion chamber. Interestingly, it is important to understand that the ignition delay period is directly affected by the <u>cetane number</u> of the fuel.

► Compression-Ignition Engine Components

Diesel engine components are exposed to higher operating temperatures, pressures, and forces than gasoline engines of similar displacement. Because of the higher compression ratios encountered, diesel engine parts are usually heavier and built more ruggedly than parts for comparable gasoline engines. Thus, diesel engines typically outlast gasoline engines. Many diesel engine blocks have removable cylinder sleeves or liners, which means that when rebuilding the engine, the liners can be replaced to bring the engine cylinders back to their original condition and size.

Engine Upper/Lower End

When looking at an engine assembly as a whole, the components can be viewed as two major parts: the engine block and the cylinder head. The cylinder head, normally located on top of the block, contains the valves and the valve-operating mechanisms. The block contains the pistons, sleeves, crankshaft and rods. The camshaft is often located in the block, but may be located in the cylinder head. Also, with some engine designs, two or even four camshafts may be used. The engine block and cylinder head are bolted together, along with their components, to make one unit.

Cylinder Block

The cylinder block provides the framework, strength, and structure needed for the compression ignition engine **FIGURE 53-10**. Also, it houses the crankshaft, connecting rods, pistons, camshaft, lifters, bearings, and timing gears. Additional components can be included in the block or attached to the block. These components include

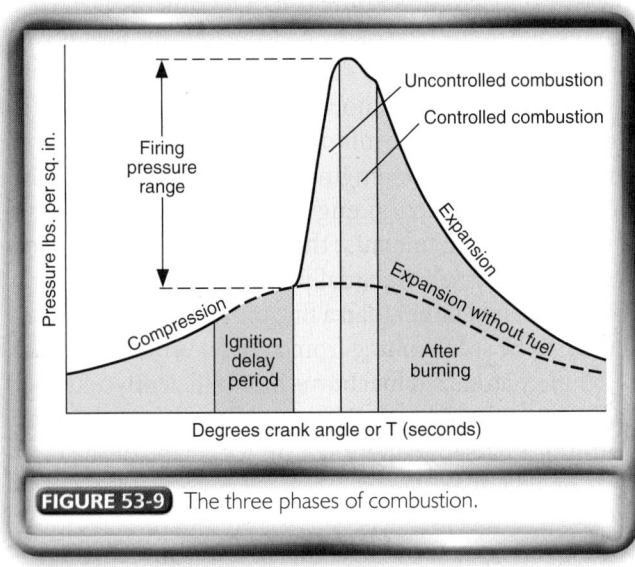
FIGURE 53-9 The three phases of combustion.

FIGURE 53-10 Engine block.

the fuel injection pump, air-conditioning compressor, vacuum pump, and auxiliary drives for components such as an air compressor to supply air brakes on heavy-duty vehicles.

Diesel blocks are usually made of cast iron. The "bottom end" of the diesel engine block is of heavier construction than comparable gasoline engine blocks due to the additional stress of higher torque developed with the diesel's longer stroke. To add strength and rigidity, the skirt of the block usually extends below the centerline of the crankshaft. The block is machined so that all of these major components are in perfect alignment with each other. The centerline of the crankshaft is the alignment point from which all other components are aligned. For example, the cylinder bores are aligned perpendicular to the crankshaft within critical alignment tolerances with the crankshaft centerline. Machined into the block are the cylinder bores.

As mentioned earlier, often the cylinder bores have removable sleeves, also called liners. The major advantage of removable liners is that they can be replaced during an engine repair or overhaul. The ability to replace all of the engine wear surfaces is one reason that diesel engines are able to be kept in use much longer than gasoline engines. The cylinder head attaches to the block at the cylinder bore opening and seals the cylinders.

Cylinder Head

Cylinder heads are cast of metal or alloy. They house the valves, injectors, and glow plugs, if used. Most cylinder heads in diesel engines are cast iron. Depending on the engine design, single or multiple heads may be used, even for an in-line engine. Using multiple cylinder heads avoids the necessity of using one large casting, which, apart from being heavy, is more likely to distort. The cylinder head contains the valves and valve operating components. These components include rocker arms or a rocker shaft, which are used to open and close the valves. Some engine designs also have the camshaft located in the cylinder head, making it an overhead cam engine.

Diesel Engine Passages

For the purpose of cooling and lubrication, diesel engines have passages cast or machined into the cylinder head and block. The cooling passages are generally cast during the manufacturing process **FIGURE 53-11**. They are formed by sand placed into the casting molds, which is removed after the casting process. After the sand is removed, the holes provided are plugged with welsh plugs, which are also called freeze plugs, core

FIGURE 53-11 The cooling passages are generally cast into the head during the manufacturing process.

plugs, sand plugs, and soft plugs. The term "freeze plugs" is a misnomer because their purpose is not to protect the block from freezing at all, but simply to provide a way of removing the sand after the casting process is complete. Oil passages, or oil galleries as they are often called, may be cast or machined into the block. They are used to distribute lubricating oil to the proper places in the block.

The combustion chamber may be formed into the piston crown in a variety of shapes and sizes. Diesel combustion chambers are different from those in gasoline engines, mainly because of the reduced area above the piston at TDC for higher compression and the way that compression ignition occurs. In a carbureted or port-injected gasoline engine, fuel already mixed with air enters the cylinder, and a spark plug ignites it. That is why gasoline engines are called spark-ignition engines. In a diesel engine, only air enters the combustion chamber during the intake stroke. The air is then highly compressed, and its temperature rises. Once fuel is injected, it ignites due to the heat of the compressed air. That is why diesel engines are called compression-ignition engines.

Fuel injectors are mounted in the cylinder head so that they reach either into the precombustion chamber (in indirect injection engines) or into the main chamber (in direct injection engines). The fuel is atomized and injected as a fine mist that is easily and completely ignited and burned. A partially clogged injector may spray a stream of fuel rather than a fine mist, thus causing black smoke to be seen coming from a diesel vehicle's tailpipe.

Finely atomized fuel burns more efficiently and completely than liquid fuel. Different injector (nozzle) spray patterns are used, depending on the shape of the combustion chamber.

Diesel Valves and Components

<u>Intake valves</u> and <u>exhaust valves</u> are used in an engine to provide a means for air to enter and exhaust gases to exit the cylinder. The much higher operating pressures and temperatures in the diesel engines put more stress on diesel valves, which are usually larger than those in gasoline engines. The intake valve provides a passage for air to enter the cylinder, so it runs cooler than an exhaust valve, which releases all of the hot gases after combustion. Often, exhaust valves are equipped with rotators that lessen the likelihood of hot spots developing on the valve and valve seat surfaces. Additionally, some exhaust valves are sodium filled to enhance dissipation of the heat caused by the combustion process.

In the diesel engine, the valves are usually parallel to the centerline of the engine. Small four-stroke engines usually have two valves per cylinder—one intake or inlet valve and one exhaust valve. The intake valve is usually larger than the exhaust valve, since atmospheric pressure is usually the force pushing air into the cylinder **FIGURE 53-12**. The exhaust valve is smaller because the exhaust is forced out by the movement of the piston. The more air that enters the cylinder, the more fuel can be mixed with it. With more fuel, the engine is able to produce more power, within reason. Intake and exhaust valves are precisely timed to open and close at the proper time during the engine's cycle of operation. Today's engines even use variable valve timing for optimum efficiency and low emissions under various operating conditions.

In the typical two-stroke diesel engine, air enters into the cylinder through inlet ports. The air entering the cylinders is pressurized by a blower or compressor. Therefore, there is no need for intake valves. However, the hot exhaust gases from combustion exit through two or possibly four exhaust valves per cylinder.

Valves are held in place by valve keepers located on the valve stem. The keepers seat into the valve retainer. The retainer is located on top of the valve spring and is supported by the cylinder head **FIGURE 53-13**. The valve guide is located in the cylinder head and guides the valve through its opening and closing movement. A rocker arm pivots, with one end making contact with the valve stem, compressing and releasing the valve spring so that the valve opens and closes **FIGURE 53-14**.

FIGURE 53-13 An assembled valve, keepers, retainer, and valve spring.

FIGURE 53-12 Diesel valve.

FIGURE 53-14 Rocker arm assembly.

In many diesels, overhead valves are driven by a system of pushrods. The components used to operate the valves include the following:

- **Camshaft**: A shaft with lobes that operates the valve mechanisms, controlling valve opening time and duration. It can be used to drive fuel injection pumps and mechanical fuel pumps.
- **Lifters**: Cylindrical components that ride on the rotating camshaft lobes to convert lobe movement to reciprocating movement of the valves through a linkage system.
- **Pushrods**: Long, thin cylindrical shafts that provide a linkage between the lifters and the rocker arms to control valve opening and closing.
- **Rocker arms**: Levers that transmit movement by the linkage system from the camshaft lobes to operate the valves.
- **Valves**: Devices that allow air to enter and exhaust gases to exit the cylinder.

Let's look at how the valves operate with the pushrod system. The camshaft is mounted in the engine block parallel to the crankshaft and is driven by the crankshaft through **timing gears**. As the camshaft rotates, the cam lobes push against valve lifters, which push a pushrod, which is linked between a rocker arm. The pushrod causes the rocker to pivot, forcing the valve down and opening the valve. The compressed valve spring tension returns the valve to its seat.

Some small high-speed diesel engines use one or more camshafts located in the cylinder head. These are called overhead cam engines. With this design, the camshaft is usually driven by the crankshaft through a timing chain, or a toothed belt. Overhead cam engines are usually found in light-duty passenger vehicles.

The camshaft keeps the valves operating in the correct timing sequence; the valves must operate when the piston is in the absolutely correct position.

Crankshaft/Camshaft Relationship

The timing between the pistons and valves is critical in both the two-stroke and the four-stroke engine. The intake and exhaust valves must open and close at the right point in the engine cycle or the engine will self-destruct when the valves make contact with the pistons.

As discussed previously, in a four-stroke engine, the crankshaft makes two complete revolutions per cycle. During the two revolutions of the crankshaft, the valves open and close once; therefore, because the valves are operated only once by the camshaft, the camshaft must complete only one revolution for each four-stroke cycle. Because the camshaft must rotate at half the crankshaft's speed, a method of timing these two shafts is required. Correct timing can be achieved by gears, chain and sprockets, or a toothed belt and sprockets (timing gears). The number of teeth on the crankshaft drive gear or sprocket must be one-half the number of teeth on the driven camshaft gear or sprocket, creating a 2:1 ratio.

To understand how this system works, it is important to understand the relationship between gears when one is driving and the other is driven. For example, take two gears with matching teeth, one with 40 teeth and the other, the driving gear, with 20. The larger cam gear or sprocket (the gear with twice as many teeth) rotates at half the speed of the smaller (crankshaft) gear. That is, the gear with fewer teeth rotates faster.

When timing chains or timing belts are used with sprockets, the number of cogs on the driving crankshaft sprocket is matched to the driven sprocket to accomplish the desired rotational speed and timing. Directly meshed crank and cam gears rotate in opposite directions; when chains or belts are used, the camshaft turns in the same direction as the crankshaft. Everything must happen at the right time as the crankshaft and camshaft turn. The camshaft actuates the rocker arms to open and close the valves as required.

If a timing chain or belt is worn, valve timing can be thrown off, which affects engine power and emissions. In the worst case, a chain or belt may break, resulting in engine destruction.

Camshaft Drives

As mentioned previously, camshafts can be driven by the crankshaft through different drive methods, such as gears, a chain, or a toothed timing belt **FIGURE 53-15**. The strongest and most reliable method of driving the camshaft is through gears; however, gears must mesh together, which makes the design and placement of these parts more complicated. Furthermore, gears tend to be noisy. A more convenient design is the use of a timing chain. Timing chains allow for more flexibility in the placement and design of engine parts. Gears and chains have to be lubricated, properly tensioned, and sealed inside the engine. Smaller displacement diesel engines may use a timing belt. Timing belts offer the greatest flexibility for engine design and camshaft placement. They can be unsealed outside the engine because they are not lubricated, and they are very quiet. However, they are the least reliable option. Where timing gears and chains seldom fail, timing belt replacement is highly recommended

FIGURE 53-15 **A.** Timing gears. **B.** Timing chain and sprockets.

FIGURE 53-16 A typical diesel crankshaft.

> **TECHNICIAN TIP**
>
> When installing a timing belt on a diesel engine, make sure to have the proper tools and to follow the manufacturer's procedures to the letter. If the timing belt is installed improperly, engine damage is likely to occur.

at specified intervals, which are based on duration of use or mileage.

Diesel Crankshaft

The **crankshaft** is the largest moving part in the engine. It converts the reciprocating (up-and-down or back-and-forth) movement of the pistons into rotating movement that transmits power through the transmission and final drive unit of the vehicle. Diesel crankshafts are usually manufactured from forged alloy steel. The forging could include exotic metals like nickel, chromium, manganese, and molybdenum. The crankshaft looks similar whether used on two-stroke or four-stroke diesel engines **FIGURE 53-16**.

The shape may appear unusual at first. The crankshaft is manufactured with bearing journals that are centered through the shaft. These journals, called **main bearing journals**, support the crankshaft in the engine block. Additionally, there are connecting **rod bearing journals** that are offset from the centerline of the shaft on so-called throws. In operation, the throws work like bicycle pedals. As the piston is forced down under power, it pushes down on the rod journal and crankshaft throw through the connecting rod.

A major challenge in the design and manufacture of crankshafts is balancing the uneven forces developed in the engine by the power strokes and the offset pressures applied to the crankshaft. Manufacturers design counterweights on the crankshaft to balance and offset forces applied by the pistons. Crankshaft counterweights keep the rotating components in balance and help the crankshaft to turn as smoothly as possible. A good way to understand this is to envision the action of a toy top. A top, when evenly balanced, spins smoothly. Adding a weight unbalances it. It can be made to spin properly again by adding an identical weight on the other side; the first weight is balanced by the second weight acting as a counterweight.

Crankshaft bearings are critical to the proper operation of a rotating crankshaft. Crankshafts use **main bearings** and connecting **rod bearings** **FIGURE 53-17**. The main bearings support the crankshaft in the block and provide a lubrication surface for the main bearing journals. The connecting rod bearings support the connecting rods as the crankshaft turns because of forces

FIGURE 53-17 Rod and main bearings.

FIGURE 53-18 A connecting rod with rod bearings installed.

FIGURE 53-19 Two types of thrust bearings. **A.** Main bearing with the thrust bearing surface manufactured as part of the main bearing. **B.** Thrust bearing made separately from the main bearing.

Applied | Math

AM-41: Proportion/Congruence: The technician can solve problems that determine the proportion of variables of a solution and determine if that proportion is within the manufacturer's specifications.
When two quantities are proportional, a change in one quantity corresponds to a predictable change in the other quantity.

An example of this would be an accelerator pedal position sensor (APP) on a diesel powered truck. The APP consists of two potentiometers that sense the position of the accelerator pedal. A reference voltage is supplied to each potentiometer by the electronic control module (ECM). As the accelerator pedal is depressed, the angle changes and the APP sends a proportional signal voltage to the ECM. With the throttle depressed 0%, the APP1 sensor voltage is 1.5 volts. With the throttle depressed 5%, the voltage signal is 1.65 volts. 10% equals 1.80 volts, 15% equals 1.95 volts, and so forth. The proportion is the same throughout the full travel range of the accelerator pedal. The greater % depressed is equal to a greater sensor voltage signal sent to the ECM. The second potentiometer (APP2) is a backup for safety purposes. It works on the same proportional basis but on a separate circuit to supply additional information to the ECM.

transmitted through the connecting rods **FIGURE 53-18**. They also provide a lubrication surface for the connecting rod journals.

The crankshaft also needs to be located to stop lateral (endwise) movement. This movement is stopped by using flanges, commonly called **thrust bearings**. Thrust bearings are made as part of, or separate from, one of the crankshaft's main bearings **FIGURE 53-19**. They are usually located at the balance point of the crankshaft. Often, the thrust bearing is located at the rear main bearing position of the crankshaft.

▶ The Flywheel

On the rear of the crankshaft of both the four-stroke and the two-stroke diesel engine is a heavy flywheel **FIGURE 53-20**. The flywheel stores torsional (torque)

FIGURE 53-20 A diesel engine flywheel.

energy from the power stroke and gives it back to the crankshaft to help it keep turning between power strokes. In a four-stroke engine, only one stroke in four delivers power. In a single cylinder engine, the energy from this one power stroke must turn the crankshaft through the three remaining strokes. Without a flywheel, the crankshaft would slow down and stop. With multiple cylinder engines, lower-mass flywheels may be used.

Dual-Mass Flywheels

Some engines use a **dual-mass flywheel (DMF)**. The DMF eliminates excessive transmission gear rattle, reduces gear change/shift effort, and increases fuel economy.

There are two basic types of DMFs. The first is made up of a primary and a secondary flywheel with a series of torsion springs and cushions. There is a friction ring located between the inner and the outer flywheels that allows the inner and outer flywheels to slip. This feature is designed to alleviate any damage to the transmission when torque loads exceed the vehicle rating of the transmission. The friction ring is the weak spot in the system and can wear out if excessive engine torque loads are applied through it. The system also has a center support bearing that carries the load between the inner and the outer flywheels and is fitted with damper springs to absorb shocks.

The second type of DMF incorporates planetary gearing. It is designed for engines with stronger vibrations in the lower rpm range. In addition to greater driving and shifting comfort, the planetary DMF provides the benefit of lower fuel consumption because the idling rpm is lower.

DMFs are fitted to light-duty diesel trucks with standard manual transmissions and to higher performance luxury vehicles to dampen vibration in the drive train. This reduction in vibrations also allows vehicles to be operated for longer periods without long-term damage. Transmissions in light-duty diesel-powered trucks have a heightened sensitivity to fluctuating torsional inputs. This results in a strong torsional resonance or vibration that occurs during operation of the vehicle within normal driving ranges.

The function of the DMFs is to isolate torsion crankshaft spikes created by diesel engines with high compression ratios. By eliminating the torsion spikes, the system eliminates any potential damage to the transmission gear teeth. If the DMF were not used, the torsional frequencies could damage the transmission.

The DMF construction relocates the damper from the driven disc to the engine flywheel. This repositioning dampens engine torsional vibrations more than is possible with standard clutch disc dampening technology.

DMFs are designed to provide maximum isolation of the frequency below the engine's operating rpm, usually between 200 and 400 rpm. They are also most effective during engine start-up and shutdown.

Diesel Engine Pistons

As hard to imagine as it may seem, at 3000 rpm the pistons in high-speed diesel engines change direction 100 times per second. Imagine the extremes of heat and pressure! To withstand such stress, modern pistons are made of aluminum alloys. Most diesel pistons are forged, which makes them stronger than cast pistons. Their shapes and designs vary based on their application.

Many factors determine the design and shape of a piston. The top of the piston is part of the combustion chamber; therefore, the shape must match the fuel injection pattern to achieve the most efficient atomization of the air–fuel mixture. Piston shape is designed to develop maximum heat energy transfer and the most complete combustion possible. With today's strict emission control standards, piston shape and design are highly engineered.

Diesel engines using direct injection have an almost flat surface on the cylinder head, and almost all of the combustion chamber is shaped in the crown of the piston **FIGURE 53-21**. Engines with indirect injection usually have pistons with flatter piston heads and may include valve pockets—small indentations to provide valve clearance when at TDC.

FIGURE 53-21 A piston with the combustion chamber formed in the top of the piston.

FIGURE 53-22 A piston with compression rings and an oil control ring.

When the piston is fitted, there must not be too much clearance. It has to seal in the high pressures and temperatures generated by combustion. Sealing is accomplished by piston rings held in grooves in the side of the piston **FIGURE 53-22**. There are typically three ring grooves. The top two grooves are called compression rings. The lower ring is an oil control ring, which scrapes excess oil off the lower cylinder walls. The oil control ring has three parts: the upper and lower scraper rings and an expander.

Wrap-up

Ready for Review

- The five events common to all internal combustion engines are intake, compression, ignition, power, and exhaust.
- A four-stroke cycle engine completes the intake, compression, power, and exhaust strokes in two revolutions of the crankshaft.
- A two-stroke cycle engine completes the intake, compression, power, and exhaust strokes in one revolution of the crankshaft.
- The diesel fuel system consists of a lift pump, a fuel filter and water separator, a fuel injection pump, and high-pressure lines and nozzle holder assemblies.
- Today's engines use high-pressure common rail injection systems to meet rigid emission standards.
- Three phases of combustion are ignition delay period, flame spread, and direct burning.
- Diesel engine components are exposed to higher operating temperatures, pressures, and forces than gasoline engine components.
- Both four-stroke and two-stroke diesel engines have passages cast in the head to carry oil for lubrication and water for cooling.
- Direct and indirect fuel injection systems are two basic designs of fuel delivery control.
- Fuel injected directly into the combustion chamber is called direct injection.
- Fuel injected into a separate chamber in the cylinder head is called indirect injection.
- Intake and exhaust valves are used in an engine to provide a means for fresh air to enter and exhaust gases to exit the cylinder.
- Scavenging is the removal of hot exhaust gases from the cylinder and the refilling of it with fresh air.
- The crankshaft converts the reciprocating movement of the pistons into rotating movement that transmits power through the transmission and final drive unit of the vehicle.

Key Terms

camshaft A shaft with lobes that operates the valve mechanisms controlling valve opening time and duration. Also, it can be used to drive fuel injection pumps and mechanical fuel pumps.

cetane number A rating of the ignition quality of diesel fuel.

common rail A type of injection system using a common fuel manifold from which individual injectors are fed high-pressure fuel.

compression stroke The stroke in an engine cycle when the piston moves up with the valves closed, compressing the air trapped in the cylinder.

crankshaft A shaft that converts reciprocating power strokes into rotating movement.

direct burning The phase of combustion after ignition when the rest of the fuel is injected into the combustion chamber and there is a more gradual pressure change in the cylinder.

direct fuel injection A fuel injection system in which the fuel is injected directly into the combustion chamber.

dual-mass flywheel (DMF) A type of flywheel that eliminates excessive transmission gear rattle, reduces gear change/shift effort, and increases fuel economy.

exhaust stroke The stroke in an engine cycle when the piston moves up, with the exhaust valve(s) open, exhausting the burned exhaust gases out through the exhaust system.

exhaust valve A valve used in an engine to provide a means for exhaust gases to exit the cylinder.

flame spread The phase of combustion in which there is a sharp pressure rise in the combustion chamber because of the sudden combustion of the fuel.

ignition The burning of the fuel mixture ignited by the heat of compression.

ignition delay/lag period The time it takes for the fuel to ignite after the fuel is injected into the engine.

indirect fuel injection A fuel injection system in which the fuel is injected into a separate chamber in the cylinder head, often called a prechamber.

intake stroke The stroke in an engine cycle when the piston moves from top dead center (TDC) to bottom dead center (BDC).

intake valve A valve used in an engine to provide a means for air to enter the cylinder.

lifter A cylindrical component that rides on the camshaft lobe to transmit lobe movement to the valves through a linkage system.

main bearing A bearing that supports the crankshaft in the block and provides a lubrication surface for the main journals.

main bearing journal A bearing surface that supports the crankshaft in the engine block.

power chip An aftermarket performance programmable chip marketed to increase horsepower and mileage of electronically controlled diesel engines.

power stroke The stroke in an engine cycle after ignition, when the piston again moves from top to bottom under the power.

prechamber A separate combustion area designed into a diesel cylinder head.

pushrod A long, thin cylindrical shaft that provides a linkage between the lifters and the rocker arms to control valve opening and closing.

rocker arm A lever that transmits movement by the linkage system from the camshaft lobes to operate the valves.

rod bearing A plain bearing that supports the connecting rods and transmits power from the piston to the crankshaft journal to turn the crankshaft. It also provides a lubrication surface for the connecting rods.

rod bearing journal A bearing surface that is offset from the centerline of the crankshaft.

scavenging The removal of hot exhaust gases from the cylinder and the refilling of it with fresh air.

thrust bearing A bearing that controls the lateral, or endwise, movement of a crankshaft.

timing gear A gear that synchronizes the timed events of rotational engine components like camshafts and fuel injection pumps.

valve A means for air to enter and exhaust gases to exit the cylinder.

volumetric efficiency (VE) The amount of air taken into the cylinder on the intake stroke, or intake port, opening in relation to the space in the cylinder.

ASE-Type Questions

1. Tech A says that the valves seal combustion pressure in the combustion chamber. Tech B says that the correct order of events to accomplish one cycle of operation is intake, compression, ignition, power, and exhaust. Who is correct?
   a. Tech A only
   b. Tech B only
   c. Both A and B
   d. Neither A nor B

2. Tech A says that it takes one revolution of the crankshaft to complete one four-stroke cycle. Tech B says that it takes two revolutions of the crankshaft to complete one two-stroke cycle. Who is correct?
   a. Tech A only
   b. Tech B only
   c. Both A and B
   d. Neither A nor B

3. How many revolutions does the camshaft make in one four-stroke cycle?
   a. ½
   b. 1
   c. 2
   d. 3

4. Tech A says that the three phases of combustion are ignition delay, flame spread, and direct burning. Tech B says that the cetane rating refers to the compression ratio of a diesel engine. Who is correct?
   a. Tech A only
   b. Tech B only
   c. Both A and B
   d. Neither A nor B

5. Tech A says that diesel direct injection sprays fuel directly into the combustion chamber. Tech B says that diesel indirect injection sprays fuel into the intake manifold. Who is correct?
   a. Tech A only
   b. Tech B only
   c. Both A and B
   d. Neither A nor B

6. Tech A says that a two-stroke engine must have intake valves to operate. Tech B says that a two-stroke engine could have four exhaust valves and no intake valves. Who is correct?
   a. Tech A only
   b. Tech B only
   c. Both A and B
   d. Neither A nor B

7. Tech A says that proper scavenging contributes to volumetric efficiency of the engine. Tech B says that a blower increases volumetric efficiency of the engine. Who is correct?
   a. Tech A only
   b. Tech B only
   c. Both A and B
   d. Neither A nor B

8. All of these describe the diesel process EXCEPT:
   a. heat of compression.
   b. spark plug.
   c. glow plug.
   d. direct or indirect ingnition.

9. Tech A says that the crankshaft converts rotating motion into reciprocating motion. Tech B says that the crankshaft lateral movement is controlled by a thrust bearing. Who is correct?
   a. Tech A only
   b. Tech B only
   c. Both A and B
   d. Neither A nor B

10. Tech A says that diesel engine pistons are normally made of aluminum alloys. Tech B says they are often made of machined stainless steel. Who is correct?
    a. Tech A only
    b. Tech B only
    c. Both A and B
    d. Neither A nor B

CHAPTER 54

▶ NATEF Tasks

There are no NATEF tasks for this chapter.

Knowledge Objectives

After reading this chapter, you will be able to:

1. Explain why high-pressure components are necessary in a diesel engine. (pp 1865–1866)
2. Describe technological methods used to develop quiet diesel engines. (p 1868)
3. Explain why clean diesel technology is important in the development of modern diesel engines. (pp 1868–1869)
4. Describe the role of the fuel injection pump and governor. (pp 1869–1870, 1878–1879)
5. Explain how combustion chamber configuration affects diesel engine emissions. (pp 1870–1871)
6. Explain how volumetric efficiency is increased through turbocharging. (p 1871)
7. Explain biodiesel use, advantages, and disadvantages. (pp 1871–1872)
8. Define the characteristics of biodiesel fuel. (pp 1872–1873)
9. Describe the construction and purpose of diesel fuel tanks and lines. (p 1873)
10. Describe the construction and purpose of diesel fuel filters. (pp 1873–1874)
11. Describe the construction and operation of lift pumps. (pp 1874–1875)
12. Describe the construction and operation of in-line fuel injection pumps. (pp 1876–1878)
13. Explain the operation of mechanical and pneumatic governors. (pp 1878–1879)
14. Describe the construction and operation of distributor-type diesel fuel injection pumps. (p 1879)
15. Explain the operation of diesel engine glow plugs. (pp 1880–1881)
16. Describe basic diesel electronic fuel control systems. (p 1882)
17. Describe the construction and operation of common rail injection systems. (pp 1882–1883)
18. Describe the construction and operation of the hydraulically actuated electronically controlled unit injection (HEUI) diesel injection system. (p 1883)

Diesel Fuel Systems

Skills Objectives

There are no skills objectives for this chapter.

Introduction

Diesel engine fuel injection systems have many different designs. Some technicians think there are only one or two methods of delivering fuel to the diesel engine. In fact, there are several diesel fuel injection system designs, such as the unit injector, plunger pump, distributor pump, and common rail fuel injection systems, to name only a few. Historically, manufacturers like Detroit Diesel, Cummins, and Mack have had completely different fuel injection systems. Considering the various designs mentioned, today's diesel engines extensively use electronic fuel controls with increased fuel delivery pressures designed to meet today's strict emission control standards.

Because of their durability and fuel efficiency, diesel engine passenger vehicles have been growing in popularity, particularly in Europe, where diesel vehicles outsold petrol/gasoline vehicles for the first time in 2006, and where the trend toward diesel is still growing. Diesel engines are more robust in construction because they operate with much higher compression ratios—high enough to make the compressed air in the cylinder hot enough to spontaneously ignite the fuel when it is introduced into the combustion chamber. Once the fuel is injected, ignition lag creates the familiar diesel knock, a loud clattering sound that has generally been tolerated by drivers of heavy goods vehicles, but is less acceptable to the discerning owners of more luxurious passenger vehicles. This lag time is called the **ignition delay period**, which is the time it takes for the fuel to ignite after being injected into the engine.

Diesel Fuel System Operation

Although there are different compression-ignition (CI) fuel injection systems in use today, they are all related in their basic operation. The fuel injection systems must use a quality fuel having the correct characteristics for proper operation.

All fuel injection systems must have a fuel storage and supply system that delivers clean filtered fuel to high-pressure components. The high-pressure components must inject the fuel at a pressure high enough to overcome the compression developed in a CI engine.

Diesel Fuel Injection

A diesel engine high-pressure fuel injection system operates by injecting fuel into the cylinder at precisely the right time with the exact amount of fuel needed. The amount of fuel injected is varied to suit the load on the engine and to control engine speed.

With a normally aspirated diesel engine, the intake manifold is unrestricted for a full flow of air. Unlike most gasoline engines where an air/fuel mixture is drawn into the cylinder on the intake stroke, only air is drawn into the cylinder of diesel engines.

In a basic diesel fuel system, a fuel tank holds the diesel fuel **FIGURE 54-1**. The fuel is transferred to the injection system from the fuel tank by a **lift pump**. The lift pump is also called a transfer pump or a supply pump. Its job is to keep the injection pump full of fuel. A sedimenter, or separator, removes any water and large particles in the

You are the Automotive Technician

A customer comes into the Mercedes-Benz dealership with his diesel ML350. He explains that he is having difficulty starting his vehicle in cold weather. He informs you of the cetane rating in the fuel he has been using, and you determine that the low rating might be contributing to his problem. You advise him that you will need to complete a more thorough inspection to determine what needs to be repaired. You ask him to wait in the customer lounge during the inspection and you tell him you will keep him informed. After using several different time-measured tools and techniques, you determine that the system's timing is not in conformance with the manufacturer's specifications. You return to the lounge and tell the customer that your recommendation is retiming the system to the manufacturer's specifications for a more consistent start-up in cold weather.

1. What is the difference between a low and high cetane number?
2. Why are water traps or separators important in diesel fuel systems?
3. What are three types of lift pumps that are common on light-duty diesel cars and trucks?
4. What are some of the benefits with the latest "clean diesels"?

FIGURE 54-1 A basic fuel injection system.

forces than gasoline engines of similar size. Also, diesel engine parts are usually heavier and built more ruggedly than those of similar output gasoline engines. The high compression ratio heats the air in the combustion chamber to a temperature high enough to ignite the fuel when it is injected. These high injection pressures are needed to overcome the compression and combustion pressures in the combustion chamber and break up the fuel into atomized particles.

As previously described, because of these high pressures, the injector pump and the injector are made from highly polished, accurately sized components in order to limit loss of pressure in the system.

The injector pump can be an in-line type **FIGURE 54-2**, or it can be a rotary type **FIGURE 54-3**. Both types are driven by the engine. During operation,

fuel. Additionally, a fuel filter removes minute particles that are measured in microns to ensure that contamination and damage of system components does not occur.

An injection pump delivers fuel under very high pressure to the injectors through injector pipes. It must send the correct amount of fuel, and it must send it at the correct time in the engine cycle. An injector, at each cylinder, sprays fuel into each combustion chamber. Leak-off pipes, also called fuel return lines, return excess fuel used for lubrication and cooling from the injection pump and injectors back to the tank. They also help to remove air from the system. A **governor** controls engine speed, and a control lever on the governor is connected to the accelerator pedal.

The basic diesel fuel injection system is divided into two sections: the low-pressure side, or supply side, and the high-pressure side, or delivery side. The low-pressure side cleans the fuel and delivers it to the high-pressure side where the fuel is pressurized and delivered to the fuel injectors. The high-pressure side of the fuel injection system must raise the pressure of the fuel high enough to open an injector. This allows the fuel to be injected into the combustion chamber at the correct time.

Dirt and water can damage the diesel fuel injection system, which operates with very close tolerances and highly polished components; therefore, a very efficient filtration system is required to ensure all traces of dirt and water are removed. The polished finish is achieved by lapping two components together to form a matched set. Matched components must not be interchanged after lapping is completed.

High-Pressure Components

Light automotive diesel engine components are exposed to much higher operating temperatures, pressures, and

FIGURE 54-2 A typical in-line fuel injection pump.

FIGURE 54-3 A Bosch VE distributor fuel injection pump.

the quantity of air taken in on the intake stroke is not determined by the driver's control of the throttle. However, the driver does control how much fuel is delivered to the engine.

A characteristic of all diesel engines is that at a fixed fuel setting, the amount of fuel delivered to the engine will increase as engine speed and pump speed increase. This is called the **rising characteristic** of the fuel injection system, and unless it is controlled, overspeeding of the engine will result. To achieve this control, all diesel engines use a governor to manage how much fuel is delivered from the injection pump, to the injectors, and into the engine.

Governors can be operated mechanically, pneumatically, hydraulically, or electronically. They can also be used in combination with one another. Usually, today's governors are electronically controlled.

Diesel engines need assistance to make cold starting easier. Most diesel fuel injection systems inject extra fuel when starting to ensure sufficient fuel will vaporize and burn in the combustion chamber. To make cold starting easier, some engines use preheaters, also called glow plugs. They heat only the air; it is important to understand that they do not ignite the fuel during the combustion process, but simply heat the intake air so that during compression the air in the cylinder is preheated to a point where normal ignition/combustion can take place during the engine cycle.

Diesel Fuel and Cetane Rating

Like gasoline, diesel is a compound of hydrogen and carbon extracted from crude oil. There are different grades of diesel fuel for diesel engines. What is commonly sold in a service station is highly refined and is suitable for use in high-speed diesel engines, including those in light automotive use. Additionally, diesel fuel has a rating called the cetane number.

The cetane number is a rating of a diesel fuel that expresses ignition quality and defines how easily the fuel will ignite when it is injected into the cylinder. The lower a fuel's cetane number, the longer it takes to reach ignition point. Using a fuel with a cetane number that is too low will increase the amount of diesel knock in an engine. A higher cetane number means the fuel is more prone to self-ignition. Better self-igniting properties of the fuel result in a shorter ignition delay period, which produces better control of the fuel combustion process. A shorter delay period results in easier starting, quieter engine operation, and lower emissions due to complete combustion of the fuel mixture in the cylinder.

It is interesting that when comparing the diesel fuel cetane number to the gasoline octane number, the self-igniting properties are opposite. That is, the higher the octane rating, the less self-igniting the fuel. Where the diesel fuel ignites from the heat of compression after fuel injection, ignition in a gasoline engine occurs when a spark is introduced to the air/fuel mixture; therefore, it is harmful for a gasoline fuel mixture to self-ignite. In fact, the term we use for self-ignition of a gasoline mixture is uncontrolled combustion, or pre-ignition.

Once fuel is ignited, a sharp pressure rise occurs in the combustion chamber due to the sudden rate of combustion of the fuel. This phase is called flame spread. The greater the rate of pressure increase, the greater the combustion "knock." Combustion knock is the result of sudden and intense pressure changes within the cylinder.

As the rest of the fuel is injected into the combustion chamber, there is a more gradual pressure change in the cylinder. This is called the direct burning phase of combustion. It occurs when the engine is operated at full load. As a final note, as the piston continues to move down during the power stroke, fuel particles left in the cylinder are burned and assist the downward movement of the piston.

When diesel fuel is injected into the cylinder, it does not ignite instantly. It takes time for the heat of the compressed air in the cylinder to heat the fuel sufficiently for it to ignite. This period of time from the start of injection to the start of combustion is called the ignition delay period. During this delay period, fuel continues to be injected into the cylinder.

When the fuel is heated sufficiently, it erupts into flame and burns. Combustion occurs. The sudden pressure rise sends a shock wave through the combustion chamber that can be heard outside the engine. This sound is called diesel knock.

Diesel knock can also be caused by poor atomization of the fuel, which can take too long to reach combustion temperature. However, the knock referred to here is the result of uncontrolled combustion. This type of combustion means the fuel ignites when it wants to, not at the proper time for complete controlled combustion and heat energy transfer, as designed by the engine manufacturer. Uncontrolled combustion is damaging to the engine **FIGURE 54-4**.

Another important factor relating to diesel fuel is low-temperature operation. During low temperatures, the fuel becomes thicker. If the temperature is too low, paraffins in the fuel begin to solidify and form waxes. These waxes can block filters, causing fuel starvation and low power output. To help prevent this, filters are fitted close to the engine, and sometimes heaters are used. The term used for the beginning of fuel gelling or "change of state" of the fuel is "cloud point" or "waxing."

Diesel fuel also acts as a lubricant for the fuel system components. Clearances between the components of a fuel injection system are extremely close. In fact, they can be in the hundred-thousandth of an inch range (0.00001")—so close, that if you were to hold the plunger of a pumping element in your hand, you would not be able to reinstall it until it cooled because of the expansion from the heat of your hand. Therefore, filtration is

FIGURE 54-4 Uncontrolled combustion is damaging to the engine.

critical for a diesel fuel system. Usually, a primary and a secondary fuel filter are used to keep the fuel free of water and abrasive particles.

Diesel Fuel Characteristics

The main factors that affect the performance of diesel fuel are the cetane rating of the fuel, the fuel's viscosity, its cloud point, and the extent to which the fuel is contaminated. As mentioned earlier, the cetane number, or rating, expresses ignition quality of diesel fuel and is a comparative measure of the speed with which diesel fuel ignites under compression. The higher the number, the faster the fuel ignites. If the fuel does not burn rapidly after the piston has reached top dead center then it may not burn completely during the power stroke, in which case it will not deliver the maximum possible power, and unburned fuel may then escape into the atmosphere as black exhaust smoke.

Diesel fuel should have a minimum cetane number of 40 for direct injection diesel engines and 35 for indirect injection diesel engines **FIGURE 54-5**. Fuels with lower cetane ratings contribute to harder starting, ignition delay, power loss, and decreased fuel economy. Cetane improver additives can improve ignition and reduce white smoke during cold weather start-ups.

Diesel fuel's **viscosity value** measures its resistance to flow. Diesel fuel with viscosity that is either too high or too low can cause serious damage to the engine's injection system. As discussed earlier, the clearances between the fuel injection components are very close. It is so close that improper fuel viscosity will cause a lack of lubrication. As a result, the injection components can be ruined.

The **cloud point** is the temperature at which fuel turns cloudy. When the fuel temperature drops to the fuel's cloud point, paraffin waxes that occur naturally in diesel fuel crystallize and cling together, making the fuel appear cloudy. This is known as "waxing" and, if not

Description	#1 Diesel	#2 Diesel
Flash point °F min	100	125
Viscosity at 104°F	1.3 - 2.4	1.9 - 4.1
Cetane number min	50	50
Cetane index min	45	45
Distillation temp 95% max	550 F	640 F
Sulfur content % max	0.05	0.05

FIGURE 54-5 A cetane number, or rating chart.

prevented, can clog filters and stop fuel flow to the engine. Clouding can be combated by using fuels with a lower cloud point, providing heat to the tanks, or including a cloud point improver to the fuel. This improver separates the clinging wax particles so they can pass through the fuel filters. Some oil companies produce special winter-grade fuels for cold weather operation.

Diesel fuel is vulnerable to contamination, particularly from water in the tank and from various types of sediment. As the fuel is fed into the system from the bottom of the tank, it is easy for contaminants to enter the system with the fuel. As the fuel in the tank is used, air from the atmosphere enters the tank. Water condenses on the walls of the tank and runs down into the fuel.

The water is heavier than the fuel and usually ends up in the bottom of the tank along with sediment such as rust, or scale, or weld slag. Water in the fuel can cause injector seizures and engine failure. It also accelerates component wear. Water traps or separators are very important in diesel fuel systems. Dirt and other debris can clog fuel filters and form deposits, resulting in reduced power and excessive fuel system wear.

Engine Knock

The annoying rattle of older diesel engine designs has largely been subdued by a combination of engineering and fuel improvements. This has been accomplished through advanced injector design with better spray patterns, and injection timing control **FIGURE 54-6**. Also, improved compression temperatures and increased fuel cetane values have significantly lowered the noise levels of modern diesel engines. Additionally, fast computer processors allow precise electronic control of injection so that the combustion process can be smoothed to allow the up-and-down transitions of the pistons to occur without the traditional diesel clatter.

In a modern quiet diesel engine, fuel injection timing and delivery are electronically controlled through **pulse-width modulation**, which is the time that the fuel injectors are turned off and on to inject a precise amount of fuel **FIGURE 54-7**. **Duty cycle** is another term that can be used for pulse-width modulation. Here is how it works: The injectors are first pulsed with a small lean pilot injection to start the ignition process with less noise, quickly followed by a main injection of fuel to develop engine torque and complete the power stroke, finishing with an additional pulse to assist with after-burning pollutants in the converter. The result of all the combined refinements is dramatically smoothed idle revolutions per minute (rpm) and roughness, far less combustion noise, no smoke, less odor and emissions, and improved fuel consumption.

FIGURE 54-6 Fuel injector spray patterns.

FIGURE 54-7 An injector pattern from a 6.0L Ford Power-stroke.

Diesel Emissions

Clean diesel emissions are extremely important to our planet; therefore, we need to be able to understand the effects of diesel emissions. The result of complete combustion is water (H_2O) and **carbon dioxide** (CO_2). Both of these are natural parts of our environment, although some scientists believe that CO_2 in high concentrations acts as a greenhouse gas. At this time, the only way to reduce CO_2 emissions on diesel engines is to reduce the amount of fuel burned. This can be accomplished by making engines and vehicles more fuel efficient, or by driving them less.

The most deadly pollutant is **carbon monoxide**. Carbon monoxide is a result of partially burned diesel fuel and is a serious health hazard to humans because it can reduce oxygen delivery to organs and cause death.

Two additional exhaust emission pollutants we are concerned with actually mix with sunlight to form ozone (smog) and acid rain. They are **hydrocarbons** and **nitrogen oxides**. Hydrocarbons, or unburned fuel, are the result of incomplete combustion. Nitrogen oxides are the result of high temperature combustion.

Diesel-powered vehicles are increasing in popularity at a rapid rate around the globe. One of the main reasons for this rise in popularity is the emergence of **electronic diesel control (EDC)**. This system uses a processing unit (computer) in conjunction with input and output devices to accurately control fuel delivery in modern diesel engines **FIGURE 54-8**.

EDC has enabled cleaner, more complete combustion with lower emissions, greater economy and power, and lower noise levels not previously achievable with either direct or indirect combustion chambers. In modern diesel engines, soot emissions, properly called **particulate matter**, have been reduced by up to 83%. Nitrogen oxide emissions resulting from the heat of combustion have been reduced by 63% since 1988. Moreover, hydrocarbon, carbon monoxide, and carbon dioxide emissions, already inherently low with diesel engines, have improved—with the trend set to continue.

Since 2007, all highway diesel engines have been required to have a **diesel particulate filter (DPF)** **FIGURE 54-9**. Its job is to convert particulate matter, or soot, into ash. Soot can best be described as unburned particles left over from the combustion process. Ash is what is left after the soot has been incinerated. The conversion is accomplished through a catalytic process in the DPF. Often, it takes additional fuel with a spark or high temperatures to complete the process. After time,

the ash builds up in the DPF and needs to be removed. This service interval is typically 150,000 miles (240,000 kilometers [km]) for an on-road vehicle.

Another clean diesel technology is called **selective catalytic reduction**. It is an active emission control system that injects a liquid **reductant**, or reducing agent, through a special catalyst into the exhaust stream of a diesel engine. The reductant, or reducing, agent is **urea**, which is a chemical reactant specifically designed for use in selective catalytic reduction systems to reduce nitrogen oxides. In the industry, urea is called **diesel exhaust fluid (DEF)**. It causes a chemical reaction that converts nitrogen oxides into nitrogen, water, and very small amounts of carbon dioxide, which is exhausted through the tailpipe.

"Clean diesels" have the ability to completely and efficiently burn fuel within the engine. Additional benefits include quieter engines with a higher horsepower to weight ratio. The primary enhancements include improved fuel delivery systems, improved configuration of combustion chambers, and turbocharging.

Fuel Delivery Systems

For many years, diesel engines have been controlled by mechanical governors through intricately designed linkages, levers, and springs. The mechanical governors are phenomenal in their smoothness of operation and accuracy. When studying these old governors, one cannot help but marvel at the genius it took to design and build them. However, with the new strict emission regulations established to protect the environment, the old reliable friends have to go.

FIGURE 54-8 The electronic diesel control (EDC) has a processing unit and input and output devices.

FIGURE 54-9 A diesel particulate filter (DPF).

Modern diesel engines need to make fuel adjustments in milliseconds, mid-revolution of the crankshaft. Therefore, the industry must now turn to electronics for fuel control. Nearly all diesels today are manufactured with EDC. Examples of today's fuel injection control system are the common rail system and the hydraulically actuated electronically controlled unit injectors, which will be discussed later in this chapter.

Fuel injection is now done under much higher pressures for complete atomization of fuel sprayed directly into the superheated air of the combustion chamber. Furthermore, electronic control means varying rates of fuel delivery per cylinder and degree of crankshaft movement. Additionally, it must be done under varying speed and load conditions for quieter and smoother performance. EDC can also compensate for extremes in temperature by injecting the precise amount of fuel to match ambient temperatures.

Safety

Modern high-pressure fuel injection systems can easily spray fuel into your body. Always wear eye protection and do not search for a fuel leak by placing your hand on a fuel injection line.

New combustion chamber design methods also aid fuel delivery to make engines cleaner and quieter. As an example, one method to reduce ignition clatter at idle is the use of a smaller pilot spray to initiate the combustion cycle, with greater amounts of fuel following ignition. Delivery tapers off near the completion of the combustion cycle for complete burn and low emissions. This and other innovative designs are possible through research, and are important to improve efficiency and meet new emission standards for diesel engines.

Combustion Chamber Configuration

The shape and depth of the combustion chamber and piston, the number and placement of valves, the design of intake ports (designed for greater swirl), and the placement of the injectors all play a role in clean diesel design and reduction of particulate matter and nitrogen oxides. Also important to clean diesel combustion chamber configuration are the two methods of supplying pressurized fuel: direct and indirect fuel injection. Remember that indirect injection means the fuel is injected into a separate chamber in the cylinder head, often called a prechamber **FIGURE 54-10**, and direct injection means the

fuel is injected directly into the combustion chamber **FIGURE 54-11**.

Older diesel engines typically used the direct injection system. Since it injected the fuel directly into the cylinder, it was a simple and powerful design. Unfortunately, it produced excessive smoke and high exhaust emissions. A better design was the indirect injection system that used a separate chamber, or combustion area, to better control emissions and the noise level of the engine. Often called a prechamber or precombustion chamber engine, the separate combustion chamber also provided a convenient location for glow plug installation to assist starting the engine in cold temperatures. However, with

FIGURE 54-10 With indirect injection, fuel is injected into a separate combustion chamber.

FIGURE 54-11 With direct injection, the fuel is injected directly into the combustion chamber.

the coming of very strict emission control standards, there has been a shift back to the direct fuel injection system with electronic controls. Additionally, the latest electronically controlled fuel injection systems operate at very high injection pressures, in the range of 18,000 to 24,000 pounds per square inch (psi), or 124,000 to 165,000 kilopascals (kPa). Electronically controlling this high pressure to an infinite degree makes today's clean diesel engine technology possible.

Turbocharging

Turbocharging increases volumetric efficiency (VE) and reduces nitrogen oxides. As a result, more power can be derived from smaller displacement engines with greater fuel economy. It is important to remember that VE is the amount of air taken into the cylinder on the intake stroke, or intake port, opening in relation to the space in the cylinder. Turbochargers act as compressors and pump more air into the cylinder; therefore, through increased airflow, the flow pattern, or swirl, is also improved, combustion efficiency improves, and the engine emissions are lowered. Intake air intercoolers enhance the benefits of the turbocharger by lowering air temperatures entering the combustion chamber **FIGURE 54-12**. Cooler air is denser,

FIGURE 54-12 An engine equipped with a turbocharger and intake air intercooler.

which means more can enter the combustion chamber by volume. Since the intercooler lowers combustion air temperature, it lowers nitrogen oxide emissions.

Other Improvements

Thanks to electronics and higher voltage systems, other improvements include "instant-hot" glow plugs, variable valve timing, exhaust gas recirculation cooling, electronic variable geometry and electronically assisted turbocharger nozzle and waste gate management, and electric water and power steering pumps. Additionally, improvements have been made in air-conditioning compressors, drive-by-wire, brake-by-wire, and collision avoidance. Also, **on-board diagnostic (OBD) and OBDII** systems are now commonly used to monitor the entire power train and enable satellite connectivity. Other refinements include various types of exhaust aftertreatment (catalysts) for lowering nitrogen oxides and particulate traps for reducing particulate matter.

The second generation of OBD systems (OBDII) is now standard for all vehicles. It is the industry standard for onboard diagnostics that monitors engine and related component operation. OBDII has been mandated since 1996. However, on-board technology can't produce all the necessary improvements alone. Today's much lower sulfur content in diesel fuel will help.

Nontraditional fuel delivery methods are also helping to lower emissions. For example, dual-fuel diesels make use of direct-replacement high-pressure injectors or use electronically controlled port-type gaseous injectors. Aftermarket accessories and electronic "chips" are being advertised for improving performance within clean air limits for the popular clean-technology diesel engines. Other nontraditional methods are being rapidly developed in the industry. When purchasing and installing aftermarket components, always be sure they comply with, and are approved by, the manufacturer. Keep in mind that the manufacturer's warranty may be voided by installation of unapproved aftermarket products.

▶ Biodiesel Fuel

Biodiesel is a light-yellow to dark-yellow liquid, with a viscosity similar to standard diesel fuel. It is a non petroleum-based processed fuel derived from vegetable oils, principally soybeans but also rapeseed (canola), which can be used in diesel vehicles. Yellow grease, which is primarily recycled cooking oil from restaurants, can also be used as a diesel fuel. Vegetable oil as a base for fuel oil in diesel engines has been around for many years; however, commercial production of biodiesel did not begin until the 1990s. Some modified diesel engines can run on straight vegetable oil (SVO) or on waste vegetable oil (WVO).

Commercial blends of biodiesel and petroleum diesel are designated with the letter "B" followed by the volumetric percentage of biodiesel in the blend. The blend most commonly available is B20; it contains 20% biodiesel and 80% petroleum diesel. B100 is pure biodiesel. Commercially processed biodiesel blended fuels can run in any diesel engine designed for petroleum-based diesel fuels.

Biodiesel is generally more expensive to produce than petroleum diesel. However, in some countries, such as Germany, biodiesel can be cheaper to buy than regular diesel fuel because of taxes and subsidies. Biodiesel blends actually tend to perform better than petroleum diesel. Unfortunately, high production costs and limited availability of raw materials continue to limit wholesale commercial implementation.

Biodiesel fuel has some drawbacks. It can make the engine harder to start and produce less power and more smoke than standard diesel fuel. It is hygroscopic, meaning that although it is oil-based and does not readily mix with water, it attracts water from the atmosphere. Contamination with moisture can corrode components such as pumps and injectors, as well as encourage the growth of microbes in the vegetable fuel. Biodiesel fuel can also degrade natural rubber gaskets and hoses. This is not a major problem as most components are now made of synthetic rubber, which is not affected.

Biodiesel Characteristics

Biodiesel is both biodegradable and nontoxic, and has significantly fewer emissions than petroleum-based diesel fuel. Tests have shown that the use of soybean B100 biodiesel fuel in urban transit buses reduces net carbon dioxide emissions by more than 75%. B100 fuel contains about 11% oxygen, which improves combustion, reducing most exhaust pollutants. Biodiesel users also note that the exhaust smells better than the exhaust from engines burning conventional diesel.

One of the most important characteristics of any diesel fuel is its ability to auto-ignite. The cetane number for biodiesel ranges from 46 to 57 for soybean oil, with an average of around 50. This means biodiesel fuel ignites more quickly than petroleum diesel, which normally has a cetane rating ranging from 40 to 52. As a result of the increased ignition quality, diesel engines run more quietly, smoothly, and cleanly than engines with standard diesel fuel.

Lubricity is a measure of a fuel's lubricating properties. Fuel injectors and some types of fuel pumps rely on the fuel itself for lubrication. Sulfur is an important lubricating component of petroleum diesel fuel, but ultralow-sulfur petroleum diesel is limited to containing a maximum of 15 parts per million of sulfur by weight. The addition of a very low proportion of biodiesel, even a 1% or 2% volumetric blend with low-sulfur petroleum diesel, substantially improves the fuel's lubricity.

Biodiesel is a better solvent than petroleum diesel, so it helps to clean the fuel system. However, it can break down and flush out residue deposits in vehicles that have been running on standard petroleum diesel fuel. As a result, it is important to clean the lines before changing over to biodiesel fuel. If this is not done, the solvent action of the fuel will quickly clog fuel filters by flushing out accumulated deposits in older and dirty fuel systems. Additionally, it would be wise to change the fuel filters more often until you are sure the fuel system is completely clean.

Although it has some performance advantages, biodiesel does have some disadvantages. Biodiesel fuels made from yellow grease, or recycled cooking oil, perform worse than soybean-based biodiesel. It is important to understand that recycled waste cooking oils are inherently an unknown product, whereas biodiesel products that are refined professionally have been tested to meet **American Petroleum Institute (API)** standards. The API sets the standards for all American petroleum products, including natural gas and biodiesel fuels.

As previously mentioned, at low temperatures, diesel fuel forms wax crystals, which can clog fuel lines and filters in a vehicle's fuel system. The cloud point is the temperature at which a fuel starts to appear cloudy, indicating that wax crystals have begun to form. At even lower temperatures, diesel fuel becomes a gel that cannot be pumped at all. The **pour point** is the temperature below which the fuel will not flow. The cloud point and the pour point temperatures for biodiesel are both higher than those for petroleum diesel, so it performs less well at low temperatures.

The energy efficiency of a vehicle is the percentage of the fuel's energy delivered as engine output. The energy content per unit of volume measure of biodiesel is around 11% lower than that of petroleum diesel, so biodiesel is less economical to use. Energy efficiency is usually expressed as miles traveled per gallon of fuel, or kilometers per liter of fuel; therefore, vehicles running on biodiesel are likely to achieve fewer distance units per volume units of fuel. This is calculated by multiplying the lower efficiency factor of biodiesel (11%) by the proportion of biodiesel in the fuel. In B20 fuel, the biodiesel component is 11% less efficient, but it only makes up 20% of the total fuel; thus, 11% times 20% equals 2.2% fewer miles or kilometers traveled.

Although more expensive to produce than petroleum diesel, biodiesel is becoming more and more common in many countries as an alternative to regular diesel fuels. Certainly, the biodiesel blends are already well established in the industry. At the very least, biodiesel fuels reduce our dependence on fossil fuels and support our local economy. These and the other advantages discussed indicate that biodiesel fuel is here to stay.

▶ Diesel Fuel System Components

The diesel fuel supply components are critical to the proper operation of a diesel fuel injection system. They must supply the high-pressure injection components with extremely clean fuel, in sufficient amounts for proper operation under varying load and environmental conditions. Not only that, the system is so sensitive that if air is drawn into the supply of fuel, the engine will stop running. Filtration is important enough that two fuel filters are normally used in a two-step process to ensure the cleanliness of the fuel.

Diesel Tanks and Lines

The fuel tank stores fuel in a convenient location, away from the engine. It is commonly made of steel or aluminum. **Baffles** are plates usually installed vertically in the fuel tank to control sloshing of the fuel. They also ensure that the pickup tube is always submerged in fuel, thereby stopping air from entering the system. The inside of the tank can be treated to prevent rust. Galvanizing must never be used, because diesel fuel reacts with zinc to produce powdery flakes that can block fuel filters.

Usually, in light commercial diesel engines, two fuel lines are used. One supplies, or transfers, the fuel from the tank to the filters, and then to the fuel injection pump.

The other is the return line. It carries excess fuel back to the tank. The fuel return line is used for lubricating and cooling the injectors and the injector pump. It is also used for bleeding air from the filters. The return line pressure is low; therefore, it is often made from a synthetic rubber hose material.

The fuel supply lines are usually made of seamless steel tubing, coated with tin to prevent rust. Sometimes cadmium is used instead of tin. Fuel lines must be large enough to provide enough fuel flow for maximum power. They are supported under the vehicle by nylon insulators in brackets. Sections of reinforced synthetic rubber hoses allow for movement, and vibration of components. The reinforcement is needed because the fuel line is subject to variations in pressure, which usually run between 20 and 30 psi (138 to 207 kPa), to supply the injection pump with fuel.

High-pressure fuel injector lines connect the fuel injection pump to the injectors. Pressures in injector lines can reach up to 29,000 psi (200,000 kPa) on some engines. They are made of cold-drawn, annealed, seamless steel tubing. The bore of the pipe is kept to the smallest diameter possible, and all of the pipes are the same length. If pipes of different lengths were used, it would affect injection timing. It is important to understand that high-pressure lines should never be bent because doing so will cause them to flake internally, which can ruin the fuel injector.

Diesel Fuel Filters

Diesel fuel filters are very important to the operation of a diesel engine. Because of the close tolerances of the injection system components, the fuel system must be kept exceptionally clean. The system is kept so clean that diesel fuel filters are rated in microns. A **micron** is 0.000039" (0.001 mm). Currently, some manufacturers specify final fuel filtration down to 3 to 5 microns. To put that in perspective, the diameter of a human hair is typically about 40 to 120 microns.

Typically, a diesel engine fuel injection system has two fuel filters. A primary filter, located between the fuel tank and the supply pump, filters particles to 30 to 50 microns. A secondary fuel filter, located between the supply pump and the high-pressure fuel injection pumping element, filters particles to 10 to 12 microns. As mentioned, some secondary filters are specified to remove particles down to 3 to 5 microns.

Additionally, diesel fuel filters must remove water from the fuel system. This is accomplished with water separators or traps, sometimes called sedimenters **FIGURE 54-13**. They can be separate units or combined with an impregnated paper element filter. Separate units pass the incoming fuel over an inverted funnel. At the edge of the funnel, the fuel changes direction very quickly. Water and dirt are heavier than fuel, so they are trapped, away from the funnel edge. With gravity, they settle at the base of the trap. The lower housing is usually clear for easy inspection, and it can include a drain plug so sediment can be drained daily.

The most common type of filter material in light diesel vehicles is resin-impregnated paper, pleated to offer a large surface area for the fuel. These filters are considered the most efficient. A fuel filter with the resin-impregnated paper element can be combined with a water separator. When this combined unit is used, the method of fuel flow is determined by the manufacturer. With some filters, fuel flows from outside to inside. In others, it flows from the base to the top, or from top to bottom.

Some of the filters use paper elements, with the fuel flow options the same as previously described. In another method, fuel first passes through the paper element to trap abrasive particles. Any water in the fuel is usually in the form of small droplets, which are forced through the paper element. Once through the filter, the small droplets combine into larger droplets and form a sediment layer in the base of the filter. The bowl may be transparent and may contain a drain plug.

Other filter types pass fuel into the separator or sedimenter first and force the larger particles out of suspension by a change in direction. The fuel is then forced through a filtering medium, ready for use. This filter usually contains a disposable element. Often, the base has a drain plug for daily draining of the water from the filter.

Additionally, a water level switch can activate a light on the dash to warn the operator that the chamber may need draining. The switch has a float that is lighter than water but heavier than fuel. In the float is a magnet. As the float rises with the water level in the fuel, the magnet closes a reed switch, which turns on a warning light in the instrument cluster. The operator can then remove the drain plug to drain the water.

Lift Pump

The lift pump is a low-pressure pump that supplies fuel to the injection pump, or unit injectors. Often called a transfer or supply pump, the lift pump transfers fuel from the tank to the fuel injection system. In modern vehicles, the tank is mounted below the engine, and the fuel has to be lifted to the level of the engine. Three types of lift pumps are common on light-duty diesel cars and trucks: diaphragm, plunger, and vane.

Diaphragm Lift Pump

The diaphragm lift pump can be mounted on the engine or on the injection pump **FIGURE 54-14**. It is fitted with inlet and outlet valves, and an eccentric on a camshaft acts on a two-piece rocker arm connected to a diaphragm. Rotating the eccentric causes the rocker arm to pivot on its pin and pull the diaphragm down. This compresses the diaphragm return spring and increases the volume in the pumping chamber above the diaphragm.

Atmospheric pressure at the fuel tank forces fuel along the fuel line to open the inlet valve. Fuel flows into the pumping chamber. The eccentric keeps rotating, and the rocker arm is released. The spring exerts force on the diaphragm to pressurize the fuel in the chamber.

FIGURE 54-13 A fuel filter combined with a water separator.

FIGURE 54-14 A mounted diaphragm-type lift pump.

This pressure closes the inlet valve and opens the outlet valve, letting fuel be delivered to the injection system.

If the system does not need all of the fuel delivered, the pressure in the outlet fuel line rises to the same level as in the pumping chamber. This pressure holds down the diaphragm and keeps the diaphragm return spring compressed. As a result, the split linkage in the rocker arm allows the lever to maintain contact with the eccentric, without acting on the diaphragm pull rod; therefore, pumping ceases until the pressure drops and pumping action needs to resume.

Plunger Lift Pump

A second type of lift pump in light vehicle applications is the plunger pump. It is mounted on the in-line injection pump and is driven by a cam inside the in-line injection pump housing. Internally, a spring-loaded cam follower converts the rotary motion of the camshaft into reciprocating motion. The reciprocating motion is transferred to a spring-loaded plunger, fitted with close tolerance in a cylindrical bore. It has two spring-loaded check valves, which are called the inlet valve and the outlet valve **FIGURE 54-15**.

As the engine drives the injection pump, the lobe of the camshaft pushes the cam follower into the plunger pump. The cam follower acts directly on the plunger, pushing it toward the end of the cylinder bore. Fuel is displaced from one side of the plunger, through the outlet check valve, to the other side of the plunger. When the cam follower retracts, spring force on the plunger moves the plunger out of the cylindrical bore. Fuel from the fuel tank enters behind the plunger through the inlet check valve. Fuel in front of the plunger is displaced out of the pump to the fuel injection system.

Vane Lift Pump

A vane lift pump is used in distributor-type injection pumps. Also known as a transfer pump, it is mounted on the input shaft and pumps fuel whenever the distributor pump is driven by the engine **FIGURE 54-16**. It consists of a rotor, mounted off-center in a pump housing. Slots are machined into the rotor to carry vanes.

As the rotor rotates, the vanes can move into, and out of, the slots. The vanes seal on the edges of the rotor slots and the pump housing. Trapped fuel is carried around by the action of the rotor until the leading vane uncovers the outlet port. Since the rotor is offset, as it continues to turn, the volume between the vanes reduces, and fuel is squeezed out of the pump. A pressure relief valve controls the pump's operating pressure.

Priming Pump

Some diesel engines in light vehicle applications have a priming lever, plunger, or diaphragm button on the lift pump. Separating the priming pump for the removal of air from the fuel system is called bleeding, or priming. Air can enter the system during filter replacement or when a fuel line is disconnected. Without a priming pump, the engine would require excessive cranking, which could damage the starter motor and/or discharge the battery.

The diaphragm lift pump often has a lever that acts on the diaphragm rocker arm. Moving the priming lever moves the diaphragm down. Releasing the lever allows the diaphragm return spring to force the diaphragm up. The action of the diaphragm and valves during bleeding is the same for normal operation of the pump.

Since distributor-type injection pump systems use an internal vane pump, their fuel supply system incorporates

FIGURE 54-15 A plunger-type lift pump.

FIGURE 54-16 A vane lift pump in a distributor-type injection pump.

a diaphragm-type priming pump, usually located on top of the fuel filter. The diaphragm is connected to an actuating button **FIGURE 54-17** and is held in its uppermost position by a diaphragm spring. Reed valves connect the priming pump housing to the filter. Pressing down on the actuating button reduces the volume in the pumping chamber, which forces fuel into the filter element. Releasing the button lets the spring lift the diaphragm, which increases the volume in the pumping chamber. Air pressure in the fuel tank then forces fuel into the pumping chamber.

A plunger-type priming pump is often used with plunger lift pumps, which are mounted on in-line fuel injection pumps. It can also be mounted on top of fuel filter housings for distributor-type injector pump systems. The plunger priming pump consists of a plunger and a barrel assembly, mounted on the side of the plunger pump or filter housing. This plunger priming pump uses the valves of the plunger lift pump to direct fuel flow.

Plunger pumps mounted on the top of filter housings contain inlet and outlet check valves. Pulling the primer plunger increases chamber volume, which decreases the pressure in the chamber below atmospheric pressure. Fuel in the tank is forced along the fuel lines, through the inlet check valve, and into the pumping chamber.

> ▶ **TECHNICIAN TIP**
>
> When the plunger-type priming pump is not in use, the hand knob must be screwed closed. This stops fuel from leaking out past the plunger. It also prevents air from leaking into the priming plunger barrel.

FIGURE 54-17 Diaphragm-type priming pump installed on a filter housing.

Pushing the plunger into the barrel decreases the volume in the chamber, which forces fuel out through the outlet check valve.

In-Line Injection Pump

Some diesel engines use in-line fuel injection pumps to meter and pressurize the fuel **FIGURE 54-18**. The basic principle is for a plunger to act on a column of fuel to lift an injector needle off its seat. A pumping element and delivery valve for each cylinder are located inside the pump **FIGURE 54-19**.

FIGURE 54-18 An in-line fuel injection pump.

FIGURE 54-19 Fuel injection pumping element.

The element has a barrel, with a mated plunger inside. Their accurate fit and highly polished finish ensure minimal fuel leakage past them without requiring additional seals. The barrel usually has two holes, or ports, called the inlet, or fill, port and the spill port. The ports are located in the injection pump fuel gallery. The gallery contains filtered fuel from the low-pressure supply system.

At the top of the barrel are a delivery valve, a delivery valve holder, and the high-pressure steel pipe to carry fuel to each cylinder **FIGURE 54-20**. When the fuel pressure rises, the delivery valve is lifted off its seat. When the plunger covers the fill and spill ports, fuel is pressurized and flows to the injector. When injection ceases, the pressure below the delivery valve drops to gallery, or supply, pressure.

To meter the fuel, the upper end of the plunger has a vertical groove, extending from its top to an annular groove. The top edge of this annular groove is cut in a helix shape, also called the control edge **FIGURE 54-21**. Rotating the plunger controls the duration of the stroke for which the spill port is covered. This is called the **effective stroke**. It determines how much fuel is delivered to the injector **FIGURE 54-22**.

A short effective stroke means a small amount of fuel is injected. A longer effective stroke lets more fuel be delivered. To stop the engine, the vertical groove on the plunger is aligned with the spill port. This alignment stops pressure in the barrel from rising because the fuel can pass through the groove and exit through the spill port.

The plunger is rotated by a control sleeve, a rack, and a pinion. Moving the rack rotates the pinion, the control sleeve, and then the plunger. The rack's movement is controlled by the governor.

The stroke of the plunger is accomplished by a camshaft, cam follower, and spring, which move the plunger in a reciprocating motion. When the plunger is below the ports, fuel from the gallery enters the barrel above the plunger, thus ensuring that the barrel is full of fuel. As the camshaft rotates, the plunger is pushed past the ports, which traps and pressurizes the fuel.

Moving the plunger farther raises the pressure of the fuel. The increased pressure forces the fuel out past the delivery valve, along the fuel line to the injector. Fuel flows to the injector until the control edge of the helix uncovers the spill port. The pressurized fuel above the plunger then moves down the vertical groove, to the annular groove, and into the spill port.

The delivery valve prevents fuel from leaking from the pipe back into the element. It reduces pressure in the fuel line to ensure there is no dribbling by the injector. This pressure reduction is accomplished by a relief plunger and a conical face, which is held against its matching seat

FIGURE 54-20 A delivery valve, delivery valve spring, and delivery valve holder at the top of a plunger barrel.

FIGURE 54-21 A pumping plunger with a helical control edge.

FIGURE 54-22 The effective stroke is the duration of the plunger movement after the spill port is covered.

by the delivery valve spring. The relief plunger on the valve is a close fit inside the bore of the delivery valve seat.

The delivery valve operates as follows: Fuel pressure above the delivery valve forces the valve toward its seat bore, sealing the area above and below the delivery valve. Further movement of the delivery valve toward its seat increases the volume in the injector pipe and reduces the pressure therein. This drop in pressure causes the injector needle to snap shut, helping to prevent fuel dribble from the injector. The conical face of the delivery valve then contacts the seat, further sealing the plunger from the injector pipe.

Mechanical or Pneumatic Governors

Governors on in-line pumps are usually mechanical or pneumatic. The primary job of the governor is to maintain a set engine speed regardless of load. Maintaining the speed is accomplished by balancing governor spring tension with fly weight position. For example, increased governor spring tension increases fuel delivery and engine speed; increased engine speed causes the fly weights to move outward from centrifugal force, reducing fuel delivery and engine speed.

A mechanical governor uses rotating fly weights to control movement of the fuel control rack against a spring. Removing the load from the engine lets its speed rise. Centrifugal force pushes out the weights, which push a sleeve against the spring. The force from the spring tries to push the rack to the maximum fuel position. The force on the sleeve from the fly weights acts against the spring to try to push the rack to the minimum fuel position **FIGURE 54-23**.

For any governor position, the fuel control rack determines the volume of fuel delivered, and therefore engine speed. During idling, the governor prevents the

engine from stalling. It also stops it from overspeeding. Thus, mechanical governors in automotive use are called idling and maximum speed governors, because idling speed and maximum speed are all they control. They can also be called limiting speed governors. For other throttle positions, the operator determines the rack position by moving the position of the floating link, which increases or decreases governor spring tension.

A pneumatic governor takes advantage of a principle called the **venturi effect** to control fuel delivery **FIGURE 54-24**. When air flows through a constricted section of pipe, there is a reduction in pressure. To be clear, when we talk about a pressure lower than atmospheric pressure, we are talking about vacuum. Therefore, vacuum increases as airflow increases through the constriction.

The pneumatic governor has a manifold-mounted venturi unit, linked by tubing to a sealed diaphragm assembly on the in-line injection pump housing. This venturi unit has a main venturi and an auxiliary one. A throttle butterfly in the intake manifold controls airflow through the venturi and into the engine.

Here is how it works: When the engine is not running, the diaphragm spring pushes the diaphragm and fuel control rack toward the full-fuel position. With the engine running at idle, the throttle butterfly is almost closing the intake, and air flows through the auxiliary venturi at high velocity. The high airflow produces low pressure, which is transferred through the connecting hose to the sealed chamber on the spring side of the diaphragm. Atmospheric pressure on the pump side now forces the diaphragm and rack toward the no-fuel position. This reduces the effective pump stroke and the amount of fuel injected.

Depressing the accelerator allows more air to enter the engine but decreases the air velocity through the auxiliary venturi. Pressure in the sealed chamber rises and

FIGURE 54-23 A typical mechanical governor.

FIGURE 54-24 The pneumatic governor takes advantage of the venturi effect to control fuel delivery.

allows the spring to move the diaphragm, and control rack, against atmospheric pressure to increase the fuel delivered. The diaphragm position at any given time is determined by the air velocity through the auxiliary venturi, in accordance with engine speed and load. This provides a rack setting that allows the correct quantity of fuel to be injected to match the operating condition.

Distributor-Type Injection Pump

The distributor-type pump uses a vane-type transfer pump to fill the single pumping element. This transfer raises fuel pressure to injection pressure. A distribution system then distributes fuel to each cylinder in the firing order of the engine. The most common type in light automotive use is the Bosch VE pump.

Driven from the engine, a drive shaft rotates a plunger and a cam disc. Cams on the face of the disc have as many lobes as cylinders in the engine. A plunger spring holds the cam disc against rollers that rotate on their shafts. The lobes move the plunger to-and-fro in its barrel, making it rotate and reciprocate at the same time **FIGURE 54-25**.

Its rotation operates the fuel inlet port to the pumping chamber and at the same time distributes pressurized fuel to the correct injector. The reciprocating motion pressurizes the fuel in the pumping chamber. The plunger's pumping action forces fuel through a delivery valve to the injector. The plunger has a central passage, a connecting passage to the distributing slit, and a cross-drilling to a control sleeve. As the plunger rotates, each intake slit aligns with the intake port, and the distributing slit with the distributing port.

As the plunger rotates, the intake slit moves away from the intake port. At the same time, the plunger is acted on by the cams, causing it to move axially along the barrel, pressurizing the fuel in the pumping chamber. The

distributing slit now uncovers the distribution port, and the pressurized fuel passes through the delivery valve to the injector. Further rotation of the plunger closes off the distribution port and opens the intake port. At the same time, the plunger spring moves the plunger back along the barrel for the next pumping stroke.

For intake, fuel from the feed pump reaches the open intake port in the barrel. The intake slit aligns with the intake port, and fuel fills the pumping chamber and passages in the plunger. For injection, the plunger rotates to close off the intake port and moves along the barrel to pressurize fuel in the pumping chamber. The distributing slit aligns with the distribution port, where the pressurized fuel forces the delivery valve off its seat and reaches the injector. In this phase, a cutoff port in the plunger is covered by the control sleeve.

To end fuel delivery, the plunger's cutoff port moves out of the control sleeve and lets pressurized fuel spill back into the pump housing. This relieves pressure in the pumping chamber, the delivery valve closes, and injection ceases.

Metering the fuel is controlled by the effective stroke of the control sleeve, and the effective stroke is determined by the action of the governor sliding the control sleeve along the plunger. Sliding it one way opens the cutoff port earlier and reduces effective stroke. Sliding it the other way delays its opening and increases effective stroke. The governor changes the position of the control sleeve to vary the quantity of fuel delivered, according to throttle position and load. When the ignition is switched off, an electrical solenoid closes off the intake port and stops fuel delivery.

Diesel Injectors

The injector assembly has several main parts **FIGURE 54-26**. The nozzle assembly is made up of a needle and body.

FIGURE 54-25 The internal components of a Bosch VE distributor fuel injection pump.

FIGURE 54-26 A fuel injector nozzle assembly—needle and body, pressure spring, and nozzle body.

A pressure spring and spindle hold the needle on the seat in the nozzle body. A nozzle holder, sometimes called the injector body, may allow for mounting of the injector on the engine and for some method of adjusting the spring force applied to the needle valve. A cover keeps out dirt and water.

The injection pump delivers fuel to the injector. The fuel passes through a drilling in the nozzle body to a chamber above where the needle valve seats in the nozzle assembly. As fuel pressure in the injector gallery rises, it acts on the tapered shoulder of the needle valve, increasing the pressure until it overcomes the force from the spring and lifts the needle valve from its seat. The highly pressurized fuel enters the engine at a high velocity in an atomized spray.

As soon as delivery from the pump stops, pressure under the needle's tapered shoulder drops, and the spring force pushes the needle down on the seat, cutting off the fuel supply to the engine. Some of the fuel is allowed to leak between the nozzle needle and the body to cool and lubricate the injector. This fuel is collected by the return, or leak-off line, and delivered to the fuel tank for later use. Since the return line is a low-pressure fuel line, it is a good place to check for the presence of a good fuel supply, or air in the system.

There are two main types of injector nozzle: hole and pintle **FIGURE 54-27**. Hole-type nozzles are commonly used in direct injection engines. They can be single hole or multi-hole, and they operate at very high pressures, up to 3000 psi (20,700 kPa). They give a hard spray, which is necessary to penetrate the highly compressed air. The fuel has a high velocity and good atomization, which are desirable characteristics in open combustion chamber engines.

In pintle-type nozzles, a pin, or pintle, protrudes through a spray hole. The shape of the pintle determines the shape of the spray and the atomization of the spray pattern. Pintle nozzles open at lower pressures than hole-type nozzles. They are used in indirect injection engines, where the fuel has a comparatively short distance to travel and the air is not as compressed as in the main chamber.

Glow Plugs

A glow plug is a heating element that assists in raising the temperature in the combustion chamber, which makes the engine easier to start in cold weather. The glow plugs are only used for cold, initial starting of the engine. They are needed because a diesel engine is a CI engine, which means the engine starts solely from the heat of compression.

If the engine is cold and the ambient temperature of the air intake to the diesel engine is too low, much of

FIGURE 54-27 **A.** Hole-type injector nozzle. **B.** Pintle-type injector nozzle.

the heat generated by the initial rotations of the engine will be conducted away into the engine block and other components, and into the environment. If that happens, the air–fuel mixture temperature in the cylinder may not be raised sufficiently by engine compression for ignition to occur. Glow plugs preheat the incoming air so that ignition can occur more easily. This assists a cold engine to start more reliably. Once the engine is running, the glow plugs are no longer required

A glow plug consists of a heating element and a resistor-type heating element attached to the end of a plug that penetrates the combustion chamber or precombustion chamber. When the glow plug is activated, current flows through the resistor causing it to heat up, which then raises the temperature of the incoming air. The glow plugs are activated by turning the key on before cranking of a typical modern diesel engine for somewhere between 10 and 20 seconds prior to the engine firing. Older and less efficient diesel engines, or worn engines, may require much longer preheating times to start the engine.

There are a variety of methods for altering the timing and style of the electronic fuel injection process in modern automotive diesel engines to ensure reliable

FIGURE 54-28 Heated air intake grid.

cold starting. Even though glow plugs are fitted, they are rarely used for more than a few seconds. Glow plug resistor elements, also called filaments, must be made of materials that are resistant both to heat and to oxidation. Examples of such materials are platinum and iridium.

Some diesel engines use a heated air intake grid rather than glow plugs. The grid heater is usually placed in the intake manifold **FIGURE 54-28**. This component is activated prior to starting the engine, and the heated grid raises the temperature of the incoming air similar to the glow plug.

Safety

When starting an engine with glow plugs or a heated air intake grid, do not use starting fluid or an explosion could occur. Be sure to follow starting instructions given in the manufacturer's service information.

Applied | Math

AM-34: Time: The technician can use different time measurement tools and techniques to determine if the system's timed or sequenced operating parameters conform with the manufacturer's specifications.

A medium-duty diesel-powered truck is in the shop with fuel injection pump problems. The owner had not maintained the fuel system properly and water entered the injection pump, causing its failure. A diesel technician is assigned to install a replacement fuel injection pump along with new fuel filters. The engine is a mechanically injected diesel and the fuel pump can be turned slightly right or left due to a mounting flange, which is slotted.

The technician carefully installs the pump and aligns the timing marks as accurately as possible at 2 degrees

before top dead center (TDC). After starting the engine and checking for leaks, the technician asks his supervisor to listen to the sound of the engine. The supervisor and technician both agree that a diesel timing light is needed to assure that the timing is correct.

A diesel timing light differs from the timing light that is used on gasoline engines. There are no spark plugs on a diesel engine, so a spark-triggered light can't be used. The diesel timing light uses a photoelectric sensor that installs in the glow plug opening to have access to the combustion area. In addition to this, an inductive sensor is placed very close to the harmonic balancer to process a signal from a mark on the balancer.

The timing light evaluates readings from these two sensors to determine a timing result. This method is much more accurate than merely aligning the timing marks that are found on the injector pump mounting flange. If a timing light is not used, the engine timing could be too far advanced or retarded. This could result in excessive emissions being produced or engine power output could be reduced.

Cummins and Detroit Diesel Injection

Unit injectors have been available for many years in heavy commercial diesel engines. These include the Cummins Pressure Time system and the Detroit Diesel system. Diesel fuel injectors are all very similar in construction. However, with this system, the high fuel injection pressure is developed in the injector rather than from a separate pump. For both systems, actuation is a result of an extra lobe on the engine camshaft for each cylinder. This extra lobe actuates the injector at the appropriate point in the engine cycle. Each cylinder has an injector that is fed by a common fuel rail and return line.

In the Cummins Pressure Time system, the fuel pressure in the fuel lines is very high, and the cam lobe has a low point that allows the injector needle to be lifted by the fuel pressure and enter the cylinder at a given time, which is determined by the cam lobe on the camshaft. The amount of fuel that is injected at any particular time is controlled by adjusting the fuel pressure in the system.

In the Detroit Diesel system, each injector is like an individual plunger pump and fuel injector in one assembly. The injection cam on the camshaft has a high point on it and rapidly increases the fuel pressure in the unit injector, forcing the fuel down into the nozzle, which then lifts the needle and allows the fuel into the cylinder. The amount of fuel that is injected is controlled by a small control rack in the unit injector, which is connected to the throttle system via a common rod that links all the unit injectors together.

▶ Diesel Electronic Control

In the past, diesel engines earned a reputation for being loud and dirty. Moreover, light-duty diesels in automotive applications were considered slow, loud, and dirty. Highly reliable electronic fuel control systems have made today's diesel engines fast, quiet, and clean. In fact, today's diesel engines are more efficient than ever. Basically, an electronically controlled fuel system that consists of a computer receives information from various input devices, makes decisions, and directs the action of output devices. That is, it controls the exact amount of fuel injected into the combustion chamber. The computer or electronic control unit (ECU) is capable of making fuel metering decisions in microseconds. Another name that is used for the computer is **power train control module (PCM)**. Other names and acronyms are also used depending on the manufacturer and the function of the computer.

Input devices include sensors and switches that provide the information necessary for the computer to make accurate fuel control decisions. Examples of input devices are throttle position, ambient temperature, engine coolant temperature, rpm, vehicle speed, and transmission gear. Other inputs monitored include crankshaft position, brake and clutch operation, battery voltage, cruise control request, and temperatures of oil, fuel, and exhaust. Additionally, intake air, oil, and fuel pressures are monitored. These devices can be variable resistors, switches, or transducers. They may range from very simple to complex electrical and electronic circuits.

The most obvious output device is the fuel injector, which is often operated by an attached solenoid. Other output devices could include the glow plugs, cooling fan, idle control, air conditioner, and warning devices. Often, output devices are electric motors and solenoids. Additionally, the computer monitors the fuel and emissions for OBDII and sets diagnostic codes when necessary.

Diesel Electronic Control Systems

Increasingly stringent emission standards have made better control of the diesel combustion process necessary. Electronically controlled diesel systems give very precise control of the fuel injection and combustion process. Electronic controls have delivered other benefits besides a reduction in fuel consumption and emissions. These benefits include an increase in power and torque and improved engine responsiveness. Other benefits include a reduction in engine noise and diesel knock and improved and expanded diagnostic capabilities through the use of scan tools.

Diesel electronic control systems monitor and control many variables. Engine speed is one variable controlled to maintain a smooth functional idle and to limit the maximum engine speed, power, and torque to keep the engine output within safe limits. Another variable controlled is the fuel injector operation, including the timing, rate, and volume of fuel injected. Additionally, exhaust gas emissions are analyzed to determine combustion efficiency and pollutant levels.

An electronic communications network, called the data bus, allows exchange of data between computers. It is necessary for efficient operation and fault diagnosis. Modern diesel vehicles often operate with several computers, or processing units. These computers are used for different functions of vehicle operation. They can include computers specifically used to control the engine, transmission, and body systems.

These computers require extremely prompt communication with each other and function within a hierarchy of operation. For example, when you consider vehicle stability control, anti-lock braking, airbag deployment, and engine operation, which computer data are most import, and in what order? How fast is the information needed? You can see why a computer data bus network is important to manage communication between the vehicle's computers.

Common Rail Diesel Injection System

One of the most popular diesel fuel injection systems used today is the **common rail system (CRS)** **FIGURE 54-29**. This system delivers a precisely controlled quantity of atomized fuel, which leads to better fuel economy, a reduction in exhaust emissions, and a significant decrease in engine noise during operation. In the CRS, a pump, separate from the injectors, develops the high pressure

FIGURE 54-29 A common rail system (CRS).

needed for fuel injection. This high-pressure fuel is directed to an accumulator, or rail, that is used to create a common reservoir of fuel, which is also separate from the fuel injectors. This fuel is under a consistent controlled pressure.

The high-pressure pump increases the fuel pressure in the accumulator to 23,200 psi (160,000 kPa). The pressure is set by the PCM, which is independent of the engine speed and quantity of fuel being injected into any of the cylinders. The fuel is then transferred through rigid pipes to the fuel injectors. There, the correct amount of fuel is injected into the combustion chambers.

The injectors used in a CRS are triggered externally by the EDC unit. The EDC controls the engine injection parameters, including the pressure in the fuel rail and the timing and duration of injection. It does this by monitoring the input devices discussed earlier in the chapter. The EDC can make fuel delivery decisions and adjustments in fractions of a second, producing a cleaner, quieter, and more efficient engine. Diesel fuel injectors used in CRS injection operate differently from conventional fuel injectors used in the jerk, or plunger, pump system. With that system, the plungers are controlled by the camshaft position and speed. With the CRS, injectors are controlled by a magnetic solenoid on the injector. Hydraulic force from the pressure in the system is used to open and close the injector. However, the solenoid controls the available pressure and is triggered by the EDC unit.

Some injectors use piezo crystal wafers to actuate the injectors. These crystals expand rapidly when connected to an electric field. In a piezo in-line injector, the actuator is built into the injector body very close to the jet needle and uses no mechanical parts to switch injector needles. The EDC unit precisely meters the amount of fuel injected and improves atomization of the fuel by controlling the injector pulsations. This system results in quieter, more fuel-efficient engines, cleaner operation, and more power output.

Safety

When working around running engines, be alert for unguarded rotating and moving engine components in case someone failed to reinstall a protective guard or device.

HEUI Fuel Injection System

Another popular fuel injection system is the **hydraulically actuated electronically controlled unit injector (HEUI)** system **FIGURE 54-30**. This diesel fuel injection system operates by drawing fuel from the tank using a

FIGURE 54-30 A hydraulically actuated electronically controlled unit injector (HEUI) fuel injection system.

tandem high- and low-pressure fuel pump. The pump circulates fuel via the low side of the pump at low pressure through a combination of fuel filter, water separator, and heater bowl. Then, fuel flows back through the high side of the pump at high pressure into the fuel galleries, located in the cylinder head, and through to the injector units.

Safety

When working on modern diesel engines with high-pressure fuel systems, be sure you have the correct manufacturer's service information for the engine. On some models, residual pressure may exist in the fuel lines even though the engine is not running.

The injectors are controlled by a PCM. The PCM controls the duration of fuel injection pulses based on a range of input variables discussed earlier in the chapter. Once the injector solenoid has been activated, oil from a high-pressure oil pump hydraulically actuates the injectors. In other words, the injectors are operated by hydraulic pressure instead of a cam and mechanical linkage.

By varying the oil pressure, injection can be controlled independently of the engine speed, or crankshaft and camshaft position. A solenoid-actuated valve controls the high-pressure oil flow, which is applied to the top of an intensifier piston in the injector. This can increase injection pressures to 18,000 to 24,000 psi (124,000 to 165,000 kPa). The area of the head of the intensifier piston is approximately seven times the area of its plunger. As a result, a 7:1 pressure increase on the fuel beneath the plunger can be achieved.

Wrap-up

Ready for Review

- Examples of diesel fuel injection system designs are unit injector, plunger pump, distributor pump, and common rail fuel injection.
- A high-pressure fuel injection system injects fuel into the cylinder at precisely the right time with the exact amount of fuel needed.
- High injection pressures are needed to overcome the compression and combustion pressures in the combustion chamber.
- The cetane number or rating of a diesel fuel expresses ignition quality and defines how easily the fuel will ignite when it is injected into the cylinder.
- Factors that affect the performance of diesel fuel are the cetane rating, viscosity, cloud point, and contamination.
- Quiet diesel technology has been accomplished through advanced injector design with better spray patterns and injection timing control.
- Clean diesel technology, through electronic diesel control (EDC), has produced cleaner, more complete combustion with lower emissions, greater economy, more power, and lower noise levels.
- EDC can vary the rate of fuel delivery per cylinder and degree of crankshaft movement.
- The shape and depth of the combustion chamber plays an important role in the reduction of particulate matter and nitrogen oxides.
- Turbocharging increases volumetric efficiency (VE).
- On-board diagnostics, second generation (OBDII), systems are the industry standard for on-board diagnostics that monitor engine and related component operation.
- Biodiesel is a non petroleum-based processed fuel derived from vegetable oils.
- Biodiesel is both biodegradable and nontoxic, and has significantly fewer emissions than petroleum-based diesel fuel.

- Diesel fuel tanks should be kept full to prevent water condensing on tank surfaces and contaminating the fuel.
- Diesel fuel filters are rated in microns; a micron is 0.000039" (0.001 mm).
- The lift pump is a low-pressure pump that transfers fuel from the tank to the fuel injection system.
- There are three types of lift pumps on light-duty diesel cars and trucks: diaphragm, plunger, and vane.
- A priming pump is a separate pump used for removal of air from the fuel system.
- An in-line fuel injection pump has a pumping element and delivery valve for each cylinder inside the pump.
- The primary job of the governor is to maintain a set engine speed regardless of load.
- The most common type of distributor pump in light automotive use is the Bosch VE pump.
- A diesel fuel injector delivers highly pressurized fuel in an atomized spray to the combustion chamber.
- Glow plugs preheat the incoming air so that ignition can occur more easily.
- Cummins and Detroit Diesel engine unit injector fuel delivery systems develop high fuel injection pressure in the injector rather than from a separate pump.
- Highly reliable electronic fuel control systems have made diesel engines fast, quiet, and clean.
- The common rail system (CRS) uses a separate high-pressure pump to increase the fuel pressure in the accumulator (rail) to 23,200 psi (160,000 kPa).
- The hydraulically actuated electronically controlled unit injector (HEUI) diesel injection system operates the injectors by hydraulic pressure instead of a cam and mechanical linkage.

Key Terms

American Petroleum Institute (API) The organization responsible for setting the standards for all American petroleum products including natural gas and biodiesel fuels.

baffle A plate installed vertically in the fuel tank to control sloshing of the fuel.

carbon dioxide An exhaust emission that causes changes to the atmosphere; also called greenhouse gas.

carbon monoxide An exhaust emission that poses a serious health hazard to humans and can reduce oxygen delivery to organs.

cloud point The temperature at which fuel starts to appear cloudy.

common rail system (CRS) A diesel fuel injection system that uses a pump to develop high-pressure fuel directed to an accumulator or rail.

diesel exhaust fluid (DEF) A urea chemical reactant specifically designed for use in selective catalytic reduction systems to reduce nitrogen oxides.

diesel particulate filter (DPF) A filter that converts particulate matter, or soot, into ash.

duty cycle Another term for pulse-width modulation.

effective stroke The duration of plunger stroke with the spill port covered, which determines the amount of fuel injected.

electronic diesel control (EDC) A computer or electronic control unit that controls diesel fuel injection systems.

governor A device that controls how much fuel is delivered to the injector.

hydraulically actuated electronically controlled unit injector (HEUI) A diesel fuel injection system that operates by drawing fuel from the tank using a tandem high- and low-pressure fuel pump.

hydrocarbon An exhaust emission that mixes with nitrogen oxides and sunlight to form ozone (smog) and acid rain. Hydrocarbons result from incomplete combustion.

ignition delay period The time it takes for the fuel to ignite after the fuel is injected into the engine.

lift pump A pump that transfers fuel from the fuel tank to the fuel injection system; also called a transfer pump or supply pump.

micron A unit of measurement equal to 0.000039" (0.001 mm).

nitrogen oxide An exhaust emission that results from high-temperature combustion. Nitrogen oxides mix with hydrocarbons and sunlight to form ozone (smog) and acid rain.

on-board diagnostics (OBD) and OBDII The industry standards for on-board diagnostics that monitor engine and related component operation. OBDII was mandated for 1996 model year for cars and light-duty trucks.

particulate matter Particles that are heavier than air that are released during combustion; informally called soot.

pour point The temperature below which the fuel will not flow.

power train control module (PCM) A computer or electronic control unit that controls engine and related vehicle systems.

pulse-width modulation The time that the fuel injectors are turned off and on to inject a precise amount of fuel.

reductant A reducing agent.

rising characteristic A characteristic at a fixed fuel setting where the amount of fuel delivered to the engine will increase as engine speed and pump speed increase.

selective catalytic reduction An active emission control system that injects a liquid reductant, or reducing agent, through a special catalyst into the exhaust stream of a diesel engine.

urea A chemical reactant specifically designed for use in selective catalytic reduction systems to reduce nitrogen oxides. Also called diesel exhaust fluid.

venturi effect The reduction in pressure that results when a fluid or air flows through a constricted section of pipe.

viscosity value A measurement of resistance to diesel fuel flow.

ASE-Type Questions

1. Tech A says that a lift pump is another name for an in-line fuel injection pump. Tech B says that a lift pump injects fuel into the cylinder precisely at the right time with the exact amount of fuel needed. Who is correct?
   a. Tech A only
   b. Tech B only
   c. Both A and B
   d. Neither A nor B

2. Tech A says that high injection pressures are needed to overcome the compression and combustion pressures in the combustion chamber. Tech B says that high injection pressures are needed to heat the combustion chamber so that the fuel will ignite. Who is correct?
   a. Tech A only
   b. Tech B only
   c. Both A and B
   d. Neither A nor B

3. Tech A says that the cetane number expresses the moisture content of diesel fuel. Tech B says that the cetane rating expresses the ignition quality of diesel fuel. Who is correct?
   a. Tech A only
   b. Tech B only
   c. Both A and B
   d. Neither A nor B

4. Tech A says that "viscosity value" is a measure of a fuel's resistance to flow. Tech B says that "cloud point" is the temperature at which fuel turns cloudy. Who is correct?
   a. Tech A only
   b. Tech B only
   c. Both A and B
   d. Neither A nor B

5. Tech A says that the ignition delay period is the time it takes for the fuel to ignite after the fuel is injected into the engine. Tech B says that "lag time" is the time it takes for the fuel to ignite after the fuel is injected into the engine. Who is correct?
   a. Tech A only
   b. Tech B only
   c. Both A and B
   d. Neither A nor B

6. Tech A says that pulse-width modulation refers to the time that the fuel injectors are turned off and on. Tech B says that duty cycle is another term for pulse-width modulation. Who is correct?
   a. Tech A only
   b. Tech B only
   c. Both A and B
   d. Neither A nor B

7. Tech A says that nitrogen oxide emissions result from low-temperature combustion and are a serious health hazard to humans. Tech B says that carbon monoxide is the result of high-temperature combustion. Who is correct?
   a. Tech A only
   b. Tech B only
   c. Both A and B
   d. Neither A nor B

8. Tech A says that diesel exhaust fluid (DEF) is the liquid observed at the tailpipe during cold engine starts. Tech B says that a diesel particulate filter (DPF) is used to convert particulate matter, or soot, into ash. Who is correct?
   a. Tech A only
   b. Tech B only
   c. Both A and B
   d. Neither A nor B

9. Tech A says that an electronic communications network called the data bus allows exchange of data between computers. Tech B says that an electronic communications network called the data bus is necessary for efficient operation and fault diagnosis. Who is correct?
   a. Tech A only
   b. Tech B only
   c. Both A and B
   d. Neither A nor B

10. Tech A says that the final filtration of diesel fuel should remove particles down to between 50 and 75 microns. Tech B says that the final filtration of some modern diesel fuel injection systems can be 3 to 5 microns. Who is correct?
    a. Tech A only
    b. Tech B only
    c. Both A and B
    d. Neither A nor B

APPENDIX A
2013 NATEF Automobile Accreditation Task List Correlation Guide

Task List	MAST	AST	MLR	Chapter
Engine Repair				
General: Engine Diagnosis; Removal and Reinstallation (R & R)				
Complete work order to include customer information, vehicle identifying information, customer concern, related service history, cause, and correction.	P-1	P-1	NA	10
Research applicable vehicle and service information, vehicle service history, service precautions, and technical service bulletins.	P-1	P-1	P-1	10
Verify operation of the instrument panel engine warning indicators.	P-1	P-1	P-1	8
Inspect engine assembly for fuel, oil, coolant, and other leaks; determine necessary action.	P-1	P-1	P-1	10
Install engine covers using gaskets, seals, and sealers as required.	P-1	P-1	P-1	15
Remove and replace timing belt; verify correct camshaft timing.	P-1	P-1	P-1	44
Perform common fastener and thread repair, to include: remove broken bolt, restore internal and external threads, and repair internal threads with thread insert.	P-1	P-1	P-1	6
Inspect, remove, and replace engine mounts.	P-2	P-2	NA	11
Identify hybrid vehicle internal combustion engine service precautions.	P-3	P-3	P-3	52
Remove and reinstall engine in an OBDII or newer vehicle; reconnect all attaching components and restore the vehicle to running condition.	P-3	P-3	NA	11
Cylinder Head and Valve Train Diagnosis and Repair				
Remove cylinder head; inspect gasket condition; install cylinder head and gasket; tighten according to manufacturer's specifications and procedures.	P-1	P-1	NA	12
Clean and visually inspect a cylinder head for cracks; check gasket surface areas for warpage and surface finish; check passage condition.	P-1	P-1	NA	12
Inspect pushrods, rocker arms, rocker arm pivots and shafts for wear, bending, cracks, looseness, and blocked oil passages (orifices); determine necessary action.	P-2	P-2	NA	12
Adjust valves (mechanical or hydraulic lifters).	P-1	P-1	P-1	15
Inspect and replace camshaft and drive belt/chain; includes checking drive gear wear and backlash, end play, sprocket and chain wear, overhead cam drive sprocket(s), drive belt(s), belt tension, tensioners, camshaft reluctor ring/tone-wheel, and valve timing components; verify correct camshaft timing.	P-1	P-1	NA	15
Establish camshaft position sensor indexing.	P-3	NA	NA	12
Inspect valve springs for squareness and free height comparison; determine necessary action.	P-3	NA	NA	12
Replace valve stem seals on an assembled engine; inspect valve spring retainers, locks/keepers, and valve lock/keeper grooves; determine necessary action.	P-3	NA	NA	15
Inspect valve guides for wear; check valve stem-to-guide clearance; determine necessary action.	P-3	NA	NA	12
Inspect valves and valve seats; determine necessary action.	P-3	NA	NA	12

Task List	MAST	AST	MLR	Chapter
Check valve spring assembled height and valve stem height; determine necessary action.	P-3	NA	NA	14
Inspect valve lifters; determine necessary action.	P-2	NA	NA	12
Inspect and/or measure camshaft for runout, journal wear, and lobe wear.	P-2	NA	NA	12
Inspect camshaft bearing surface for wear, damage, out-of-round, and alignment; determine necessary action.	P-3	NA	NA	12
Engine Block Assembly Diagnosis and Repair				
Remove, inspect, or replace crankshaft vibration damper (harmonic balancer).	P-2	P-2	NA	13
Disassemble engine block; clean and prepare components for inspection and reassembly.	P-1	NA	NA	13
Inspect engine block for visible cracks, passage condition, core and gallery plug condition, and surface warpage; determine necessary action.	P-2	NA	NA	13
Inspect and measure cylinder walls/sleeves for damage, wear, and ridges; determine necessary action.	P-2	NA	NA	13
Deglaze and clean cylinder walls.	P-2	NA	NA	13
Inspect and measure camshaft bearings for wear, damage, out-of-round, and alignment; determine necessary action.	P-3	NA	NA	12
Inspect crankshaft for straightness, journal damage, keyway damage, thrust flange and sealing surface condition, and visual surface cracks; check oil passage condition; measure end play and journal wear; check crankshaft position sensor reluctor ring (where applicable); determine necessary action.	P-1	NA	NA	13
Inspect main and connecting rod bearings for damage and wear; determine necessary action.	P-2	NA	NA	13
Identify piston and bearing wear patterns that indicate connecting rod alignment and main bearing bore problems; determine necessary action.	P-3	NA	NA	13
Inspect and measure piston skirts and ring lands; determine necessary action.	P-2	NA	NA	13
Determine piston-to-bore clearance.	P-2	NA	NA	15
Inspect, measure, and install piston rings.	P-2	NA	NA	15
Inspect auxiliary shaft(s) (balance, intermediate, idler, counterbalance or silencer); inspect shaft(s) and support bearings for damage and wear; determine necessary action; reinstall and time.	P-2	NA	NA	13
Assemble engine block.	P-1	NA	NA	15
Lubrication and Cooling Systems Diagnosis and Repair				
Perform cooling system pressure and dye tests to identify leaks; check coolant condition and level; inspect and test radiator, pressure cap, coolant recovery tank, and heater core; determine necessary action.	P-1	P-1	P-1	46
Identify causes of engine overheating.	P-1	P-1	NA	46
Inspect, replace, and adjust drive belts, tensioners, and pulleys; check pulley and belt alignment.	P-1	P-1	P-1	46
Inspect and test coolant; drain and recover coolant; flush and refill cooling system with recommended coolant; bleed air as required.	P-1	P-1	P-1	46
Inspect, remove, and replace water pump.	P-2	P-2	NA	46
Remove and replace radiator.	P-2	P-2	NA	46
Remove, inspect, and replace thermostat and gasket/seal.	P-1	P-1	P-1	46
Inspect and test fan(s) (electrical or mechanical), fan clutch, fan shroud, and air dams.	P-1	P-1	NA	46

(continued)

Task List	MAST	AST	MLR	Chapter
Perform oil pressure tests; determine necessary action.	P-1	P-1	NA	45
Perform engine oil and filter change.	P-1	P-1	P-1	45
Inspect auxiliary coolers; determine necessary action.	P-3	P-3	NA	46
Inspect, test, and replace oil temperature and pressure switches and sensors.	P-2	P-2	NA	45
Inspect oil pump gears or rotors, housing, pressure relief devices, and pump drive; perform necessary action.	P-2	NA	NA	20
Automatic Transmission and Transaxle				
General: Transmission and Transaxle Diagnosis				
Identify and interpret transmission/transaxle concern, differentiate between engine performance and transmission/transaxle concerns; determine necessary action.	P-1	P-1	NA	20
Research applicable vehicle and service information fluid type, vehicle service history, service precautions, and technical service bulletins.	P-1	P-1	P-1	16
Diagnose fluid loss and condition concerns; determine necessary action.	P-1	P-1	NA	20
Check fluid level in a transmission or a transaxle equipped with a dip-stick.	P-1	P-1	P-1	20
Check fluid level in a transmission or a transaxle not equipped with a dip-stick.	P-1	P-1	P-1	20
Perform pressure tests (including transmissions/transaxles equipped with electronic pressure control); determine necessary action.	P-1	NA	NA	20
Diagnose noise and vibration concerns; determine necessary action.	P-2	NA	NA	20
Perform stall test; determine necessary action.	P-3	P-3	NA	20
Perform lock-up converter system tests; determine necessary action.	P-3	P-3	NA	20
Diagnose transmission/transaxle gear reduction/multiplication concerns using driving, driven, and held member (power flow) principles.	P-1	P-1	NA	17
Diagnose electronic transmission/transaxle control systems using appropriate test equipment and service information.	P-1	NA	NA	20
Diagnose pressure concerns in a transmission using hydraulic principles (Pascal's Law).	P-2	P-2	NA	20
Check transmission fluid condition; check for leaks.	NA	NA	P-2	20
In-Vehicle Transmission/Transaxle Maintenance and Repair				
Inspect, adjust, and replace external manual valve shift linkage, transmission range sensor/switch, and park/neutral position switch.	P-2	P-2	P-2	20
Inspect for leakage; replace external seals, gaskets, and bushings.	P-2	P-2	NA	20
Inspect, test, adjust, repair, or replace electrical/electronic components and circuits including computers, solenoids, sensors, relays, terminals, connectors, switches, and harnesses.	P-1	P-1	NA	20
Drain and replace fluid and filter(s).	P-1	P-1	P-1	20
Inspect, replace, and align powertrain mounts.	P-2	P-2	P-2	20
Inspect for leakage at external seals, gaskets, and bushings.	NA	NA	P-2	20
Off-Vehicle Transmission and Transaxle Repair				
Remove and reinstall transmission/transaxle and torque converter; inspect engine core plugs, rear crankshaft seal, dowel pins, dowel pin holes, and mating surfaces.	P-1	P-1	NA	20
Inspect, leak test, and flush or replace transmission/transaxle oil cooler, lines, and fittings.	P-1	P-1	NA	20
Inspect converter flex (drive) plate, converter attaching bolts, converter pilot, converter pump drive surfaces, converter end play, and crankshaft pilot bore.	P-2	P-2	NA	20

Task List	MAST	AST	MLR	Chapter
Describe the operational characteristics of a continuously variable transmission (CVT).	P-3	P-3	P-3	21
Describe the operational characteristics of a hybrid vehicle drive train.	P-3	P-3	P-3	21
Disassemble, clean, and inspect transmission/transaxle.	P-2	NA	NA	20
Inspect, measure, clean, and replace valve body (includes surfaces, bores, springs, valves, sleeves, retainers, brackets, checkvalves/balls, screens, spacers, and gaskets).	P-2	NA	NA	20
Inspect servo and accumulator bores, pistons, seals, pins, springs, and retainers; determine necessary action.	P-2	NA	NA	20
Assemble transmission/transaxle.	P-2	NA	NA	29
Inspect, measure, and reseal oil pump assembly and components.	P-2	NA	NA	20
Measure transmission/transaxle end play or preload; determine necessary action.	P-1	NA	NA	20
Inspect, measure, and replace thrust washers and bearings.	P-2	NA	NA	20
Inspect oil delivery circuits, including seal rings, ring grooves, and sealing surface areas, feed pipes, orifices, and check valves/balls.	P-2	NA	NA	20
Inspect bushings; determine necessary action.	P-2	NA	NA	20
Inspect and measure planetary gear assembly components; determine necessary action.	P-2	NA	NA	20
Inspect case bores, passages, bushings, vents, and mating surfaces; determine necessary action.	P-2	NA	NA	20
Diagnose and inspect transaxle drive, link chains, sprockets, gears, bearings, and bushings; perform necessary action.	P-2	NA	NA	20
Inspect, measure, repair, adjust or replace transaxle final drive components.	P-2	NA	NA	20
Inspect clutch drum, piston, check-balls, springs, retainers, seals, and friction and pressure plates, bands and drums; determine necessary action.	P-2	NA	NA	20
Measure clutch pack clearance; determine necessary action.	P-1	NA	NA	20
Air test operation of clutch and servo assemblies.	P-1	NA	NA	20
Inspect roller and sprag clutch, races, rollers, sprags, springs, cages, retainers; determine necessary action.	P-2	NA	NA	20
Manual Drive Train and Axles				
General: Drive Train Diagnosis				
Identify and interpret drive train concerns; determine necessary action.	P-1	P-1	NA	24
Research applicable vehicle and service information, fluid type, vehicle service history, service precautions, and technical service bulletins.	P-1	P-1	P-1	24
Check fluid condition; check for leaks; determine necessary action.	P-1	P-1	NA	24
Drain and refill manual transmission/transaxle and final drive unit.	P-1	P-1	P-1	24
Check fluid condition; check for leaks.	NA	NA	P-1	24
Clutch Diagnosis and Repair				
Diagnose clutch noise, binding, slippage, pulsation, and chatter; determine necessary action.	P-1	P-1	NA	23
Inspect clutch pedal linkage, cables, automatic adjuster mechanisms, brackets, bushings, pivots, and springs; perform necessary action.	P-1	P-1	NA	23
Inspect and replace clutch pressure plate assembly, clutch disc, release (throw-out) bearing and linkage, and pilot bearing/bushing (as applicable).	P-1	P-1	NA	23

(continued)

Task List	MAST	AST	MLR	Chapter
Bleed clutch hydraulic system.	P-1	P-1	NA	23
Check and adjust clutch master cylinder fluid level; check for leaks.	P-1	P-1	P-1	31
Inspect flywheel and ring gear for wear and cracks; determine necessary action.	P-1	P-1	NA	23
Measure flywheel runout and crankshaft end play; determine necessary action.	P-2	P-2	NA	23
Check for system leaks.	NA	NA	P-1	31
Transmission/Transaxle Diagnosis and Repair				
Inspect, adjust, and reinstall shift linkages, brackets, bushings, cables, pivots, and levers.	P-2	P-2	NA	25
Describe the operational characteristics of an electronically-controlled manual transmission/transaxle.	P-3	P-3	P-3	24
Diagnose noise concerns through the application of transmission/transaxle powerflow principles.	P-2	NA	NA	24
Diagnose hard shifting and jumping out of gear concerns; determine necessary action.	P-2	NA	NA	24
Diagnose transaxle final drive assembly noise and vibration concerns; determine necessary action.	P-3	NA	NA	24
Disassemble, inspect, clean, and reassemble internal transmission/transaxle components.	P-3	NA	NA	20
Drive Shaft and Half Shaft, Universal and Constant-Velocity (CV) Joint Diagnosis and Repair				
Diagnose constant-velocity (CV) joint noise and vibration concerns; determine necessary action.	P-1	P-1	NA	26
Diagnose universal joint noise and vibration concerns; perform necessary action.	P-2	P-2	NA	26
Inspect, remove, and replace front wheel drive (FWD) bearings, hubs, and seals.	P-1	P-1	P-2	26
Inspect, service, and replace shafts, yokes, boots, and universal/CV joints.	P-1	P-1	P-2	26
Check shaft balance and phasing; measure shaft runout; measure and adjust driveline angles.	P-2	P-2	NA	26
Drive Axle Diagnosis and Repair				
Ring and Pinion Gears and Differential Case Assembly				
Clean and inspect differential housing; check for leaks; inspect housing vent.	P-2	P-2	P-2	26
Check and adjust differential housing fluid level.	P-1	P-1	P-1	26
Drain and refill differential housing.	P-1	P-1	P-1	26
Diagnose noise and vibration concerns; determine necessary action.	P-2	NA	NA	26
Inspect and replace companion flange and pinion seal; measure companion flange runout.	P-2	P-2	NA	26
Inspect ring gear and measure runout; determine necessary action.	P-3	NA	NA	26
Remove, inspect, and reinstall drive pinion and ring gear, spacers, sleeves, and bearings.	P-3	NA	NA	26
Measure and adjust drive pinion depth.	P-3	NA	NA	26
Measure and adjust drive pinion bearing preload.	P-3	NA	NA	26
Measure and adjust side bearing preload and ring and pinion gear total backlash and backlash variation on a differential carrier assembly (threaded cup or shim types).	P-3	NA	NA	26

Task List	MAST	AST	MLR	Chapter
Check ring and pinion tooth contact patterns; perform necessary action.	P-3	NA	NA	26
Disassemble, inspect, measure, and adjust or replace differential pinion gears (spiders), shaft, side gears, side bearings, thrust washers, and case.	P-3	NA	NA	26
Reassemble and reinstall differential case assembly; measure runout; determine necessary action.	P-3	NA	NA	26
Limited Slip Differential				
Diagnose noise, slippage, and chatter concerns; determine necessary action.	P-3	NA	NA	26
Measure rotating torque; determine necessary action.	P-3	NA	NA	26
Drive Axles				
Inspect and replace drive axle wheel studs.	P-1	P-1	P-2	26, 32
Remove and replace drive axle shafts.	P-1	P-1	NA	26
Inspect and replace drive axle shaft seals, bearings, and retainers.	P-2	P-2	NA	26
Measure drive axle flange runout and shaft end play; determine necessary action.	P-2	P-2	NA	26
Diagnose drive axle shafts, bearings, and seals for noise, vibration, and fluid leakage concerns; determine necessary action.	P-2	NA	NA	26
Four-wheel Drive/All-wheel Drive Component Diagnosis and Repair				
Inspect, adjust, and repair shifting controls (mechanical, electrical, and vacuum), bushings, mounts, levers, and brackets.	P-3	P-3	NA	26
Inspect front-wheel bearings and locking hubs; perform necessary action(s).	P-3	P-3	NA	26
Check for leaks at drive assembly seals; check vents; check lube level.	P-3	P-3	P-2	26
Identify concerns related to variations in tire circumference and/or final drive ratios.	P-3	P-3	NA	26
Diagnose noise, vibration, and unusual steering concerns; determine necessary action.	P-3	NA	NA	26
Diagnose, test, adjust, and replace electrical/electronic components of four-wheel drive systems.	P-3	NA	NA	26
Inspect front-wheel bearings and locking hubs; perform necessary action(s).	NA	NA	P-3	26
Disassemble, service, and reassemble transfer case and components.	P-3	NA	NA	26
Suspension and Steering				
General: Suspension and Steering Systems				
Research applicable vehicle and service information, vehicle service history, service precautions, and technical service bulletins.	P-1	P-1	P-1	27
Identify and interpret suspension and steering system concerns; determine necessary action.	P-1	NA	NA	27
Steering Systems Diagnosis and Repair				
Disable and enable supplemental restraint system (SRS).	P-1	P-1	P-1	28
Remove and replace steering wheel; center/time supplemental restraint system (SRS) coil (clock spring).	P-1	P-1	NA	28
Diagnose steering column noises, looseness, and binding concerns (including tilt mechanisms); determine necessary action.	P-2	P-2	NA	28
Diagnose power steering gear (non-rack and pinion) binding, uneven turning effort, looseness, hard steering, and noise concerns; determine necessary action.	P-2	P-2	NA	28

(continued)

Task List	MAST	AST	MLR	Chapter
Diagnose power steering gear (rack and pinion) binding, uneven turning effort, looseness, hard steering, and noise concerns; determine necessary action.	P-2	P-2	NA	28
Inspect steering shaft universal-joint(s), flexible coupling(s), collapsible column, lock cylinder mechanism, and steering wheel; perform necessary action.	P-2	P-2	NA	28
Remove and replace rack and pinion steering gear; inspect mounting bushings and brackets.	P-2	P-2	NA	28
Inspect rack and pinion steering gear inner tie rod ends (sockets) and bellows boots.	P-2	P-2	P-1	28
Determine proper power steering fluid type; inspect fluid level and condition.	P-1	P-1	P-1	28
Flush, fill, and bleed power steering system.	P-2	P-2	P-2	28
Inspect for power steering fluid leakage; determine necessary action.	P-1	P-1	P-1	28
Remove, inspect, replace, and adjust power steering pump drive belt.	P-1	P-1	P-1	28
Remove and reinstall power steering pump.	P-2	P-2	NA	28
Remove and reinstall press fit power steering pump pulley; check pulley and belt alignment.	P-2	P-2	NA	28
Inspect and replace power steering hoses and fittings.	P-2	P-2	P-2	28
Replace power steering pump filter(s).	P-1	P-1	P-2	28
Inspect and replace pitman arm, relay (centerlink/intermediate) rod, idler arm and mountings, and steering linkage damper.	P-2	P-2	NA	28
Inspect, replace, and adjust tie rod ends (sockets), tie rod sleeves, and clamps.	P-1	P-1	NA	28
Test and diagnose components of electronically-controlled steering systems using a scan tool; determine necessary action.	P-3	NA	NA	28
Identify hybrid vehicle power steering system electrical circuits and safety precautions.	P-2	P-2	P-2	28
Suspension Systems Diagnosis and Repair				
Diagnose short and long arm suspension system noises, body sway, and uneven ride height concerns; determine necessary action.	P-1	P-1	NA	29
Diagnose strut suspension system noises, body sway, and uneven ride height concerns; determine necessary action.	P-1	P-1	NA	29
Inspect, remove and install upper and lower control arms, bushings, shafts, and rebound bumpers.	P-3	P-3	NA	29
Inspect, remove and install strut rods and bushings.	P-3	P-3	NA	29
Inspect, remove and install upper and/or lower ball joints (with or without wear indicators).	P-2	P-2	NA	29
Inspect, remove and install steering knuckle assemblies.	P-3	P-3	NA	29
Inspect, remove and install short and long arm suspension system coil springs and spring insulators.	P-3	P-3	NA	29
Inspect, remove, and install torsion bars and mounts.	P-3	P-3	NA	29
Inspect, remove and install front stabilizer bar (sway bar) bushings, brackets, and links.	P-3	P-3	NA	29
Inspect, remove and install strut cartridge or assembly, strut coil spring, insulators (silencers), and upper strut bearing mount.	P-3	P-3	NA	29
Inspect, remove and install track bar, strut rods/radius arms, and related mounts and bushings.	P-3	P-3	NA	29
Inspect rear suspension system leaf spring(s), spring insulators (silencers), shackles, brackets, bushings, center pins/bolts, and mounts.	P-1	P-1	P-1	29
Inspect electric power-assisted steering.	P-3	P-3	P-3	28

Task List	MAST	AST	MLR	Chapter
Related Suspension and Steering Service				
Inspect, remove, and replace shock absorbers; inspect mounts and bushings.	P-1	P-1	P-1	29
Remove, inspect, and service or replace front and rear wheel bearings.	P-1	P-1	NA	34
Describe the function of the power steering pressure switch.	P-3	P-3	P-3	28
Wheel Alignment Diagnosis, Adjustment, and Repair				
Diagnose vehicle wander, drift, pull, hard steering, bump steer, memory steer, torque steer, and steering return concerns; determine necessary action.	P-1	P-1	NA	29
Perform prealignment inspection and measure vehicle ride height; perform necessary action.	P-1	P-1	P-1	29
Prepare vehicle for wheel alignment on alignment machine; perform four-wheel alignment by checking and adjusting front and rear wheel caster, camber and toe as required; center steering wheel.	P-1	P-1	NA	29
Check toe-out-on-turns (turning radius); determine necessary action.	P-2	P-2	NA	29
Check SAI (steering axis inclination) and included angle; determine necessary action.	P-2	P-2	NA	29
Check rear wheel thrust angle; determine necessary action.	P-1	P-1	NA	29
Check for front wheel setback; determine necessary action.	P-2	P-2	NA	29
Check front and/or rear cradle (subframe) alignment; determine necessary action.	P-3	P-3	NA	29
Reset steering angle sensor	P-2	P-2	NA	29
Wheels and Tires Diagnosis and Repair				
Inspect tire condition; identify tire wear patterns; check for correct tire size and application (load and speed ratings) and adjust air pressure; determine necessary action.	P-1	P-1	P-1	27
Diagnose wheel/tire vibration, shimmy, and noise; determine necessary action.	P-2	P-2	NA	27
Rotate tires according to manufacturer's recommendations.	P-1	P-1	P-1	27
Measure wheel, tire, axle flange, and hub runout; determine necessary action.	P-2	P-2	NA	27
Diagnose tire pull problems; determine necessary action.	P-2	P-2	NA	27
Dismount, inspect, and remount tire on wheel; balance wheel and tire assembly (static and dynamic).	P-1	P-1	P-1	27
Dismount, inspect, and remount tire on wheel equipped with tire pressure monitoring system sensor.	P-2	P-2	P-2	27
Inspect tire and wheel assembly for air loss; perform necessary action.	P-1	P-1	P-1	27
Repair tire using internal patch.	P-1	P-1	P-1	27
Identify and test tire pressure monitoring system (indirect and direct) for operation; calibrate system; verify operation of instrument panel lamps.	P-2	P-2	P-2	27
Demonstrate knowledge of steps required to remove and replace sensors in a tire pressure monitoring system.	P-1	P-1	P-2	27
Related Suspension and Steering Service				
Inspect pitman arm, relay (centerlink/intermediate) rod, idler arm and mountings, and steering linkage damper.	NA	NA	P-1	28
Inspect tie rod ends (sockets), tie rid sleeves, and clamps.	NA	NA	P-1	28
Inspect upper and lower control arms, bushings, and shafts.	NA	NA	P-1	29
Inspect and replace rebound and jounce bumpers.	NA	NA	P-1	29

(continued)

Task List	MAST	AST	MLR	Chapter
Inspect track bar, strut rods/radius arms, and related mounts and bushings.	NA	NA	P-1	29
Inspect upper and lower ball joints (with or without wear indicators).	NA	NA	P-1	29
Inspect suspension system coil springs and spring insulators (silencers).	NA	NA	P-1	29
Inspect suspension system torsion bars and mounts.	NA	NA	P-1	29
Inspect and replace front stabilizer bar (sway bar) bushings, brackets, and links.	NA	NA	P-1	29
Inspect strut cartridge or assembly.	NA	NA	P-1	29
Inspect front strut bearing and mount.	NA	NA	P-1	29
Inspect rear suspension system lateral links/arms (track bars), control (trailing) arms.	NA	NA	P-1	29
Brakes				
General: Brake Systems Diagnosis				
Identify and interpret brake system concerns; determine necessary action.	P-1	P-1	NA	32
Research applicable vehicle and service information, vehicle service history, service precautions, and technical service bulletins.	P-1	P-1	P-1	30, 32
Describe procedure for performing a road test to check brake system operation; including an anti-lock brake system (ABS).	P-1	P-1	P-1	32
Hydraulic System Diagnosis and Repair				
Diagnose pressure concerns in the brake system using hydraulic principles (Pascal's Law).	P-1	P-1	NA	31
Measure brake pedal height, travel, and free play (as applicable); determine necessary action.	P-1	P-1	P-1	31
Check master cylinder for internal/external leaks and proper operation; determine necessary action.	P-1	P-1	NA	31
Remove, bench bleed, and reinstall master cylinder.	P-1	P-1	NA	31
Diagnose poor stopping, pulling or dragging concerns caused by malfunctions in the hydraulic system; determine necessary action.	P-3	P-3	NA	32
Inspect brake lines, flexible hoses, and fittings for leaks, dents, kinks, rust, cracks, bulging, wear, loose fittings and supports; determine necessary action.	P-1	P-1	P-1	31
Replace brake lines, hoses, fittings, and supports.	P-2	P-2	NA	31
Fabricate brake lines using proper material and flaring procedures (double flare and ISO types).	P-2	P-2	NA	31
Select, handle, store, and fill brake fluids to proper level.	P-1	P-1	P-1	31
Inspect, test, and/or replace components of brake warning light system.	P-3	P-3	NA	31
Identify components of brake warning light system.	P-2	P-2	P-3	31
Bleed and/or flush brake system.	P-1	P-1	P-1	31
Test brake fluid for contamination.	P-1	P-1	P-1	31
Check master cylinder for external leaks and proper operation.	NA	NA	P-1	31
Drum Brake Diagnosis and Repair				
Diagnose poor stopping, noise, vibration, pulling, grabbing, dragging or pedal pulsation concerns; determine necessary action.	P-1	P-1	NA	33
Remove, clean, inspect, and measure brake drum diameter; determine necessary action.	P-1	P-1	P-1	33
Refinish brake drum and measure final drum diameter; compare with specifications.	P-1	P-1	P-1	33
Remove, clean, and inspect brake shoes, springs, pins, clips, levers, adjusters/self-adjusters, other related brake hardware, and backing support plates; lubricate and reassemble.	P-1	P-1	P-1	33

Task List	MAST	AST	MLR	Chapter
Inspect wheel cylinders for leaks and proper operation; remove and replace as needed.	P-2	P-2	P-2	33
Pre-adjust brake shoes and parking brake; install brake drums or drum/hub assemblies and wheel bearings; perform final checks and adjustments.	P-2	P-2	P-2	33
Install wheel and torque lug nuts.	P-1	P-1	P-1	32, 33
Disc Brake Diagnosis and Repair				
Diagnose poor stopping, noise, vibration, pulling, grabbing, dragging, or pulsation concerns; determine necessary action.	P-1	P-1	NA	32
Remove and clean caliper assembly; inspect for leaks and damage/wear to caliper housing; determine necessary action.	P-1	P-1	P-1	32
Clean and inspect caliper mounting and slides/pins for proper operation, wear, and damage; determine necessary action.	P-1	P-1	P-1	32
Remove, inspect, and replace pads and retaining hardware; determine necessary action.	P-1	P-1	P-1	32
Lubricate and reinstall caliper, pads, and related hardware; seat pads and inspect for leaks.	P-1	P-1	P-1	32
Clean and inspect rotor; measure rotor thickness, thickness variation, and lateral runout; determine necessary action.	P-1	P-1	P-1	32
Remove and reinstall rotor.	P-1	P-1	P-1	32
Refinish rotor on vehicle; measure final rotor thickness and compare with specifications.	P-1	P-1	P-1	32
Refinish rotor off vehicle; measure final rotor thickness and compare with specifications.	P-1	P-1	P-1	32
Retract and re-adjust caliper piston on an integrated parking brake system.	P-3	P-3	P-3	32
Check brake pad wear indicator; determine necessary action.	P-2	P-2	P-2	32
Describe importance of operating vehicle to burnish/break-in replacement brake pads according to manufacturer's recommendations.	P-1	P-1	P-1	32
Power-Assist Units Diagnosis and Repair				
Check brake pedal travel with, and without, engine running to verify proper power booster operation.	P-2	P-2	P-2	31
Check vacuum supply (manifold or auxiliary pump) to vacuum-type power booster.	P-1	P-1	P-1	31
Inspect vacuum-type power booster unit for leaks; inspect the check-valve for proper operation; determine necessary action.	P-1	P-1	NA	31
Inspect and test hydraulically-assisted power brake system for leaks and proper operation; determine necessary action.	P-3	P-3	NA	31
Measure and adjust master cylinder pushrod length.	P-3	P-3	NA	31
Miscellaneous (Wheel Bearings, Parking Brakes, Electrical, etc.) Diagnosis and Repair				
Diagnose wheel bearing noises, wheel shimmy, and vibration concerns; determine necessary action.	P-3	P-3	NA	34
Remove, clean, inspect, repack, and install wheel bearings; replace seals; install hub and adjust bearings.	P-1	P-1	P-1	34
Check parking brake cables and components for wear, binding, and corrosion; clean, lubricate, adjust or replace as needed.	P-2	P-2	P-2	31
Check parking brake operation and parking brake indicator light system operation; determine necessary action.	P-1	P-1	P-1	31
Check operation of brake stop light system.	P-1	P-1	P-1	31
Replace wheel bearing and race.	P-2	P-2	P-2	34

(continued)

Task List	MAST	AST	MLR	Chapter
Remove and reinstall sealed wheel bearing assembly.	P-2	P-2	NA	34
Inspect and replace wheel studs.	P-1	P-1	P-1	32
Electronic Brake, Traction and Stability Control Systems Diagnosis and Repair				
Identify and inspect electronic brake control system components; determine necessary action.	P-1	P-1	NA	35
Identify traction control/vehicle stability control system components.	P-3	P-3	P-3	35
Describe the operation of a regenerative braking system.	P-3	P-3	P-3	30
Diagnose poor stopping, wheel lock-up, abnormal pedal feel, unwanted application, and noise concerns associated with the electronic brake control system; determine necessary action.	P-2	NA	NA	35
Diagnose electronic brake control system electronic control(s) and components by retrieving diagnostic trouble codes, and/or using recommended test equipment; determine necessary action.	P-2	NA	NA	35
Depressurize high-pressure components of an electronic brake control system.	P-3	NA	NA	35
Bleed the electronic brake control system hydraulic circuits.	P-1	NA	NA	35
Test, diagnose, and service electronic brake control system speed sensors (digital and analog), toothed ring (tone wheel), and circuits using a graphing multimeter (GMM)/digital storage oscilloscope (DSO) (includes output signal, resistance, shorts to voltage/ground, and frequency data).	P-3	NA	NA	35
Diagnose electronic brake control system braking concerns caused by vehicle modifications (tire size, curb height, final drive ratio, etc.).	P-3	NA	NA	35
Electrical/Electronic Systems				
General: Electrical System Diagnosis				
Research applicable vehicle and service information, vehicle service history, service precautions, and technical service bulletins.	P-1	P-1	P-1	36
Demonstrate knowledge of electrical/electronic series, parallel, and series-parallel circuits using principles of electricity (Ohm's Law).	P-1	P-1	P-1	37
Demonstrate proper use of a digital multimeter (DMM) when measuring source voltage, voltage drop (including grounds), current flow and resistance.	P-1	P-1	P-1	37
Demonstrate knowledge of the causes and effects from shorts, grounds, opens, and resistance problems in electrical/electronic circuits.	P-1	P-1	P-2	37
Check operation of electrical circuits with a test light.	P-1	P-1	P-2	37
Check operation of electrical circuits with fused jumper wires.	P-1	P-1	P-2	37
Use wiring diagrams during the diagnosis (troubleshooting) of electrical/electronic circuit problems.	P-1	P-1	NA	37
Diagnose the cause(s) of excessive key-off battery drain (parasitic draw); determine necessary action.	P-1	P-1	NA	38
Inspect and test fusible links, circuit breakers, and fuses; determine necessary action.	P-1	P-1	P-1	37
Inspect and test switches, connectors, relays, solenoid solid state devices, and wires of electrical/electronic circuits; determine necessary action.	P-1	P-1	NA	37
Replace electrical connectors and terminal ends.	P-1	P-1	P-1	36
Repair CAN/BUS wiring harness.	P-3	P-3	NA	36
Perform solder repair of electrical wiring.	P-1	P-1	P-1	36
Check electrical/electronic circuit waveforms; interpret readings and determine needed repairs.	P-2	NA	NA	37
Repair wiring harness (including CAN/BUS systems).	P-1	NA	NA	36

Task List	MAST	AST	MLR	Chapter
Use wiring diagrams to trace electrical/electronic circuits.	NA	NA	P-1	37
Measure key-off battery drain (parasitic draw).	NA	NA	P-1	38
Battery Diagnosis and Service				
Perform battery state-of-charge test; determine necessary action.	P-1	P-1	P-1	38
Confirm proper battery capacity for vehicle application; perform battery capacity test; determine necessary action.	P-1	P-1	P-1	38
Maintain or restore electronic memory functions.	P-1	P-1	P-1	38
Inspect and clean battery; fill battery cells; check battery cables, connectors, clamps, and hold-downs.	P-1	P-1	P-1	38
Perform slow/fast battery charge according to manufacturer's recommendations.	P-1	P-1	P-1	38
Jump-start vehicle using jumper cables and a booster battery or an auxiliary power supply.	P-1	P-1	P-1	38
Identify high-voltage circuits of electric or hybrid electric vehicle and related safety precautions.	P-3	P-3	P-3	52
Identify electronic modules, security systems, radios, and other accessories that require reinitialization or code entry after reconnecting vehicle battery.	P-1	P-1	P-1	38
Identify hybrid vehicle auxiliary (12v) battery service, repair, and test procedures.	P-3	P-3	P-3	52
Starting System Diagnosis and Repair				
Perform starter current draw tests; determine necessary action.	P-1	P-1	P-1	38
Perform starter circuit voltage drop tests; determine necessary action.	P-1	P-1	P-1	38
Inspect and test starter relays and solenoids; determine necessary action.	P-2	P-2	P-2	38
Remove and install starter in a vehicle.	P-1	P-1	P-1	38
Inspect and test switches, connectors, and wires of starter control circuits; determine necessary action.	P-2	P-2	P-2	38
Differentiate between electrical and engine mechanical problems that cause a slow-crank or a no-crank condition.	P-2	P-2	NA	38
Charging System Diagnosis and Repair				
Perform charging system output test; determine necessary action.	P-1	P-1	P-1	38
Diagnose (troubleshoot) charging system for causes of undercharge, no-charge, or overcharge conditions.	P-1	P-1	NA	38
Inspect, adjust, or replace generator (alternator) drive belts; check pulleys and tensioners for wear; check pulley and belt alignment.	P-1	P-1	P-1	38
Remove, inspect, and re-install generator (alternator).	P-1	P-1	P-2	38
Perform charging circuit voltage drop tests; determine necessary action.	P-1	P-1	P-1	38
Lighting Systems Diagnosis and Repair				
Diagnose (troubleshoot) the causes of brighter-than-normal, intermittent, dim, or no light operation; determine necessary action.	P-1	P-1	NA	39
Inspect interior and exterior lamps and sockets including headlights and auxiliary lights (fog lights/driving lights); replace as needed.	P-1	P-1	P-1	39
Aim headlights.	P-2	P-2	P-2	39
Identify system voltage and safety precautions associated with high-intensity discharge headlights.	P-2	P-2	P-2	39
Gauges, Warning Devices, and Driver Information Systems Diagnosis and Repair				
Inspect and test gauges and gauge sending units for causes of abnormal gauge readings; determine necessary action.	P-2	P-2	NA	39
Diagnose (troubleshoot) the causes of incorrect operation of warning devices and other driver information systems; determine necessary action.	P-2	P-2	NA	39

Task List	MAST	AST	MLR	Chapter
Horn and Wiper/Washer Diagnosis and Repair				
Diagnose (troubleshoot) causes of incorrect horn operation; perform necessary action.	P-1	P-1	NA	40
Diagnose (troubleshoot) causes of incorrect wiper operation; diagnose wiper speed control and park problems; perform necessary action.	P-2	P-2	NA	40
Diagnose (troubleshoot) windshield washer problems; perform necessary action.	P-2	P-2	NA	40
Accessories Diagnosis and Repair				
Diagnose (troubleshoot) incorrect operation of motor-driven accessory circuits; determine necessary action.	P-2	P-2	NA	40
Diagnose (troubleshoot) incorrect electric lock operation (including remote keyless entry); determine necessary action.	P-2	P-2	NA	40
Diagnose (troubleshoot) incorrect operation of cruise control systems; determine necessary action.	P-3	P-3	NA	40
Diagnose (troubleshoot) supplemental restraint system (SRS) problems; determine necessary action.	P-2	P-2	NA	40
Disable and enable an airbag system for vehicle service; verify indicator lamp operation.	P-1	P-1	P-1	40
Remove and reinstall door panel.	P-1	P-1	P-1	40
Check for module communication errors (including CAN/BUS systems) using a scan tool.	P-2	P-2	NA	40
Describe the operation of keyless entry/remote-start systems.	P-3	P-3	P-3	40
Verify operation of instrument panel gauges and warning/indicator lights; reset maintenance indicators.	P-1	P-1	P-1	40
Verify windshield wiper and washer operation, replace wiper blades.	P-1	P-1	P-1	40
Diagnose (troubleshoot) radio static and weak, intermittent, or no radio reception; determine necessary action.	P-3	NA	NA	40
Diagnose (troubleshoot) body electronic system circuits using a scan tool; determine necessary action.	P-3	NA	NA	40
Diagnose the cause(s) of false, intermittent, or no operation of anti-theft systems.	P-3	NA	NA	40
Describe the process for software transfers, software updates, or flash reprogramming on electronic modules.	P-3	NA	NA	40
Perform software transfers, software updates, or flash reprogramming on electronic modules.	P-3	NA	NA	40
Heating and Air Conditioning				
General: A/C System Diagnosis and Repair				
Identify and interpret heating and air conditioning problems; determine necessary action.	P-1	P-1	NA	42
Research applicable vehicle and service information, vehicle service history, service precautions, and technical service bulletins.	P-1	P-1	P-1	42
Performance test A/C system; identify problems.	P-1	P-1	NA	42
Identify abnormal operating noises in the A/C system; determine necessary action.	P-2	P-2	NA	42
Identify refrigerant type; select and connect proper gauge set; record temperature and pressure readings.	P-1	P-1	NA	42
Leak test A/C system; determine necessary action.	P-1	P-1	NA	42
Inspect condition of refrigerant oil removed from A/C system; determine necessary action.	P-2	P-2	NA	42
Determine recommended oil and oil capacity for system application.	P-1	P-1	NA	42
Using a scan tool, observe and record related HVAC data and trouble codes.	P-3	P-3	NA	43

Task List	MAST	AST	MLR	Chapter
Refrigeration System Component Diagnosis and Repair				
Inspect and replace A/C compressor drive belts, pulleys, and tensioners; determine necessary action.	P-1	P-1	P-1	42
Inspect, test, service or replace A/C compressor clutch components and/or assembly; check compressor clutch air gap; adjust as needed.	P-2	P-2	NA	42
Remove, inspect, and reinstall A/C compressor and mountings; determine recommended oil quantity.	P-2	P-2	NA	42
Identify hybrid vehicle A/C system electrical circuits and service/safety precautions.	P-2	P-2	P-2	43
Determine need for an additional A/C system filter; perform necessary action.	P-3	P-3	NA	42
Remove and inspect A/C system mufflers, hoses, lines, fittings, O-rings, seals, and service valves; perform necessary action.	P-2	P-2	NA	42
Inspect A/C condenser for airflow restrictions; perform necessary action.	P-1	P-1	P-1	42
Remove, inspect, and reinstall receiver/drier or accumulator/drier; determine recommended oil quantity.	P-2	P-2	NA	42
Remove, inspect, and install expansion valve or orifice (expansion) tube.	P-1	P-1	NA	42
Inspect evaporator housing water drain; perform necessary action.	P-1	P-1	NA	42
Determine procedure to remove and reinstall evaporator; determine required oil quantity.	P-2	P-2	NA	42
Remove, inspect, and reinstall condenser; determine required oil quantity.	P-2	NA	NA	42
Diagnose A/C system conditions that cause the protection devices (pressure, thermal, and PCM) to interrupt system operation; determine necessary action.	P-2	NA	NA	42
Heating, Ventilation, and Engine Cooling Systems Diagnosis and Repair				
Inspect engine cooling and heater systems hoses; perform necessary action.	P-1	P-1	P-1	46
Inspect and test heater control valve(s); perform necessary action.	P-2	P-2	NA	46
Determine procedure to remove, inspect, and reinstall heater core.	P-2	P-2	NA	42
Diagnose temperature control problems in the heater/ventilation system; determine PCM to interrupt system operation; determine necessary action.	P-2	NA	NA	43
Operating Systems and Related Controls Diagnosis and Repair				
Inspect and test A/C-heater blower motors, resistors, switches, relays, wiring, and protection devices; perform necessary action.	P-1	P-1	NA	43
Diagnose A/C compressor clutch control systems; determine necessary action.	P-2	P-2	NA	43
Diagnose malfunctions in the vacuum, mechanical, and electrical components and controls of the heating, ventilation, and A/C (HVAC) system; determine necessary action.	P-2	P-2	NA	43
Inspect and test A/C-heater control panel assembly; determine necessary action.	P-3	P-3	NA	43
Inspect and test A/C-heater control cables, motors, and linkages; perform necessary action.	P-3	P-3	NA	43
Inspect A/C-heater ducts, doors, hoses, cabin filters, and outlets; perform necessary action.	P-1	P-1	P-1	43
Identify the source of A/C system odors.	P-2	P-2	P-2	42
Check operation of automatic or semi-automatic heating, ventilation, and air-conditioning (HVAC) control systems; determine necessary action.	P-2	P-2	NA	43

(continued)

Task List	MAST	AST	MLR	Chapter
Refrigerant Recovery, Recycling, and Handling				
Perform correct use and maintenance of refrigerant handling equipment according to equipment manufacturer's standards.	P-1	P-1	NA	42
Identify and recover A/C system refrigerant.	P-1	P-1	NA	42
Recycle, label, and store refrigerant.	P-1	P-1	NA	42
Evacuate and charge A/C system; add refrigerant oil as required.	P-1	P-1	NA	42
Engine Performance				
General: Engine Diagnosis				
Identify and interpret engine performance concerns; determine necessary action.	P-1	P-1	NA	44
Research applicable vehicle and service information, vehicle service history, service precautions, and technical service bulletins.	P-1	P-1	P-1	44
Diagnose abnormal engine noises or vibration concerns; determine necessary action.	P-3	P-3	NA	10
Diagnose the cause of excessive oil consumption, coolant consumption, unusual exhaust color, odor, and sound; determine necessary action.	P-2	NA	NA	51
Diagnose abnormal exhaust color, odor, and sound; determine necessary action.	P-2	P-2	NA	51
Perform engine absolute (vacuum/boost) manifold pressure tests; determine necessary action.	P-1	P-1	P-1	10
Perform cylinder power balance test; determine necessary action.	P-2	P-2	P-2	10
Perform cylinder cranking and running compression tests; determine necessary action.	P-1	P-1	P-1	10
Perform cylinder leakage test; determine necessary action.	P-1	P-1	P-1	10
Diagnose engine mechanical, electrical, electronic, fuel, and ignition concerns; determine necessary action.	P-2	P-2	NA	49
Verify engine operating temperature; determine necessary action.	P-1	P-1	NA	46
Verify correct camshaft timing.	P-1	P-1	NA	44
Verify engine operating temperature.	NA	NA	P-1	46
Computerized Engine Controls Diagnosis and Repair				
Retrieve and record diagnostic trouble codes, OBD monitor status, and freeze frame data; clear codes when applicable.	P-1	P-1	P-1	49
Access and use service information to perform step-by-step (troubleshooting) diagnosis.	P-1	P-1	NA	47
Perform active tests of actuators using a scan tool; determine necessary action.	P-2	P-2	NA	49
Describe the importance of running all OBDII monitors for repair verification.	P-1	P-1	P-1	49
Diagnose the causes of emissions or driveability concerns with stored or active diagnostic trouble codes; obtain, graph, and interpret scan tool data.	P-1	NA	NA	49
Diagnose emissions or driveability concerns without stored diagnostic trouble codes; determine necessary action.	P-1	NA	NA	49
Inspect and test computerized engine control system sensors, powertrain/engine control module (PCM/ECM), actuators, and circuits using a graphing multimeter (GMM)/digital storage oscilloscope (DSO); perform necessary action.	P-2	NA	NA	49
Diagnose driveability and emissions problems resulting from malfunctions of interrelated systems (cruise control, security alarms, suspension controls, traction controls, A/C, automatic transmissions, non-OEM installed accessories, or similar systems); determine necessary action.	P-3	NA	NA	49

Task List	MAST	AST	MLR	Chapter
Ignition System Diagnosis and Repair				
Diagnose (troubleshoot) ignition system related problems such as no-starting, hard starting, engine misfire, poor driveability, spark knock, power loss, poor mileage, and emissions concerns; determine necessary action.	P-2	P-2	NA	47
Inspect and test crankshaft and camshaft position sensor(s); perform necessary action.	P-1	P-1	NA	47
Inspect, test, and/or replace ignition control module, powertrain/ engine control module; reprogram as necessary.	P-3	P-3	NA	47
Remove and replace spark plugs; inspect secondary ignition components for wear and damage.	P-1	P-1	P-1	47
Fuel, Air Induction, and Exhaust Systems Diagnosis and Repair				
Diagnose (troubleshoot) hot or cold no-starting, hard starting, poor driveability, incorrect idle speed, poor idle, flooding, hesitation, surging, engine misfire, power loss, stalling, poor mileage, dieseling, and emissions problems; determine necessary action.	P-2	NA	NA	48
Check fuel for contaminants; determine necessary action.	P-2	P-2	NA	48
Inspect and test fuel pumps and pump control systems for pressure, regulation, and volume; perform necessary action.	P-1	P-1	NA	48
Replace fuel filter(s).	P-1	P-1	P-1	48
Inspect, service, or replace air filters, filter housings, and intake duct work.	P-1	P-1	P-1	8
Inspect throttle body, air induction system, intake manifold and gaskets for vacuum leaks and/or unmetered air.	P-2	P-2	NA	50
Inspect and test fuel injectors.	P-2	P-2	NA	48
Verify idle control operation.	P-1	P-1	NA	40
Inspect integrity of the exhaust manifold, exhaust pipes, muffler(s), catalytic converter(s), resonator(s), tail pipe(s), and heat shields; determine necessary action.	P-1	P-1	P-1	50
Inspect condition of exhaust system hangers, brackets, clamps, and heat shields; repair or replace as needed.	P-1	P-1	P-1	8
Perform exhaust system back-pressure test; determine necessary action.	P-2	P-2	NA	50
Check and refill diesel exhaust fluid (DEF).	P-3	P-3	P-3	8
Test the operation of turbocharger/supercharger systems; determine necessary action.	P-3	NA	NA	50
Emissions Control Systems Diagnosis and Repair				
Diagnose oil leaks, emissions, and driveability concerns caused by the positive crankcase ventilation (PCV) system; determine necessary action.	P-3	P-3	NA	51
Inspect, test, and service positive crankcase ventilation (PCV) filter/ breather cap, valve, tubes, orifices, and hoses; perform necessary action.	P-2	P-2	P-2	51
Diagnose emissions and driveability concerns caused by the exhaust gas recirculation (EGR) system; determine necessary action.	P-3	P-3	NA	51
Diagnose emissions and driveability concerns caused by the secondary air injection and catalytic converter systems; determine necessary action.	P-2	NA	NA	51
Diagnose emissions and driveability concerns caused by the evaporative emissions control system; determine necessary action.	P-2	NA	NA	51
Inspect and test electrical/electronic sensors, controls, and wiring of exhaust gas recirculation (EGR) systems; perform necessary action.	P-2	NA	NA	51

(continued)

Task List	MAST	AST	MLR	Chapter
Inspect, test, service, and replace components of the EGR system including tubing, exhaust passages, vacuum/pressure controls, filters, and hoses; perform necessary action.	P-2	P-2	NA	51
Inspect and test electrical/electronically-operated components and circuits of air injection systems; perform necessary action.	P-3	P-3	NA	51
Inspect and test catalytic converter efficiency.	P-2	P-2	NA	51
Inspect and test components and hoses of the evaporative emissions control system; perform necessary action.	P-1	P-1	NA	51
Interpret diagnostic trouble codes (DTCs) and scan tool data related to the emissions control systems; determine necessary action.	P-3	P-3	NA	49
Required Supplemental Tasks				
Shop and Personal Safety				
Identify general shop safety rules and procedures.				3
Utilize safe procedures for handling of tools and equipment.				6
Identify and use proper placement of floor jacks and jack stands.				7
Identify and use proper procedures for safe lift operation.				7
Utilize proper ventilation procedures for working within the lab/shop area.				4
Identify marked safety areas.				3
Identify the location and the types of fire extinguishers and other fire safety equipment; demonstrate knowledge of the procedures for using fire extinguishers and other fire safety equipment.				3
Identify the location and use of eye wash stations.				3
Identify the location of the posted evacuation routes.				3
Comply with the required use of safety glasses, ear protection, gloves, and shoes during lab/shop activities.				4
Identify and wear appropriate clothing for lab/shop activities.				4
Secure hair and jewelry for lab/shop activities.				4
Demonstrate awareness of the safety aspects of supplemental restraint systems (SRS), electronic brake control systems, and hybrid vehicle high voltage circuits.				38, 39
Demonstrate awareness of the safety aspects of high voltage circuits (such as high intensity discharge (HID) lamps, ignition systems, injection systems, etc.).				38, 39
Locate and demonstrate knowledge of material safety data sheets (MSDS).				3
Tools and Equipment				
Identify tools and their usage in automotive applications.				6
Identify standard and metric designation.				6
Demonstrate safe handling and use of appropriate tools.				6
Demonstrate proper cleaning, storage, and maintenance of tools and equipment.				6
Demonstrate proper use of precision measuring tools (i.e. micrometer, dial-indicator, dial-caliper).				6
Preparing Vehicle for Service				
Identify information needed and the service requested on a repair order.				5
Identify purpose and demonstrate proper use of fender covers, mats.				7
Demonstrate use of the three C's (concern, cause, and correction).				5

Task List	MAST	AST	MLR	Chapter
Review vehicle service history.				5
Complete work order to include customer information, vehicle identifying information, customer concern, related service history, cause, and correction.				5
Preparing Vehicle for Customer				
Ensure vehicle is prepared to return to customer per school/company policy (floor mats, steering wheel cover, etc.).				7

APPENDIX B
NATEF Integrated Applied Academic Skills Correlation Guide

Applied Math	Chapter	Applied Science	Chapter	Applied Communication	Chapter
AM-1	37	AS-1	4	AC-1	9
AM-2	37	AS-2	3	AC-2	9
AM-3	37	AS-3	3	AC-3	9
AM-4	37	AS-4	3	AC-4	9
AM-5	37	AS-5	3	AC-5	9
AM-6	37	AS-6	10	AC-6	9
AM-7	37	AS-7	5	AC-7	9
AM-8	37	AS-8	5	AC-8	9
AM-9	37	AS-9	41	AC-9	9
AM-10	37	AS-10	48	AC-10	9
AM-11	14	AS-11	5	AC-11	9
AM-12	37	AS-12	30	AC-12	9
AM-13	37	AS-13	12	AC-13	9
AM-14	36	AS-14	12	AC-14	9
AM-15	48	AS-15	29	AC-15	9
AM-16	10	AS-16	14	AC-16	9
AM-17	32	AS-17	41	AC-17	9
AM-18	48	AS-18	49	AC-18	9
AM-19	13	AS-19	41	AC-19	9
AM-20	13	AS-20	42	AC-20	9
AM-21	29	AS-21	52	AC-21	9
AM-22	29	AS-22	54	AC-22	9
AM-23	25	AS-23	41	AC-23	5
AM-24	29	AS-24	51	AC-24	9
AM-25	29	AS-25	45	AC-25	9
AM-26	29	AS-26	42	AC-26	9
AM-27	27	AS-27	46	AC-27	9
AM-28	27	AS-28	41	AC-28	9
AM-29	45	AS-29	41	AC-29	9
AM-30	45	AS-30	46	AC-30	9
AM-31	13	AS-31	46	AC-31	9
AM-32	43	AS-32	46	AC-32	9
AM-33	42	AS-33	39	AC-33	9
AM-34	54	AS-34	10	AC-34	9
AM-35	24	AS-35	10	AC-35	9
AM-36	8	AS-36	32	AC-36	9
AM-37	13	AS-37	33		
AM-38	14	AS-38	50		
AM-39	14	AS-39	50		
AM-40	41	AS-40	50		
AM-41	53	AS-41	50		
AM-42	26	AS-42	50		
AM-43	16	AS-43	50		
AM-44	36	AS-44	50		
AM-45	37	AS-45	50		
AM-46	36	AS-46	50		
AM-47	37	AS-47	27		

Applied Math	Chapter	Applied Science	Chapter
AM-48	36	AS-48	46
AM-49	23	AS-49	17
AM-50	8	AS-50	44
AM-51	29	AS-51	30
AM-52	28	AS-52	29
AM-53	20	AS-53	36
		AS-54	38
		AS-55	38
		AS-56	38
		AS-57	36
		AS-58	36
		AS-59	40
		AS-60	36
		AS-61	36
		AS-62	36
		AS-63	36
		AS-64	38
		AS-65	47
		AS-66	40
		AS-67	40
		AS-68	40
		AS-69	36
		AS-70	36
		AS-71	36
		AS-72	38
		AS-73	38
		AS-74	38
		AS-75	38
		AS-76	47
		AS-77	37
		AS-78	36
		AS-79	36
		AS-80	43
		AS-81	36
		AS-82	36
		AS-83	48
		AS-84	41
		AS-85	35
		AS-86	17
		AS-87	31
		AS-88	29
		AS-89	51
		AS-90	30
		AS-91	30
		AS-92	45
		AS-93	12
		AS-94	18
		AS-95	15
		AS-96	31
		AS-97	44
		AS-98	21
		AS-99	44
		AS-100	43
		AS-101	46
		AS-102	15
		AS-103	45

GLOSSARY

abrasive discs (cutting wheels) Abrasive wheels or flat discs fitted to bench, pedestal, and portable grinders.

ABS code retrieval key A specially shaped metal key that is inserted into the data link connector to retrieve DTCs.

ABS pressure tester A high-pressure gauge designed to connect to the HCU and used to measure high hydraulic pressures in the system.

ABS proportioning valve depressor A tool used to hold the proportioning valve open on some ABS HCUs.

absorbed glass mat A type of lead-acid battery.

acceleration An increase in a vehicle's speed.

accelerator pedal The foot-operated pedal used by the driver to increase and decrease the amount of power the engine develops.

accelerator pump circuit The carburetor circuit involved with heavy acceleration, directly connected to the accelerator pump. Also used to prime the engine during cold starting.

accelerator pump A small pump usually located inside the carburetor that sprays an extra amount of fuel into the carburetor air horn during acceleration.

accelerometer An electronic instrument that measures the amount of acceleration in a specific direction.

accessory drive pulley A round circular metal disc attached to the front of the engine crankshaft with a rubber/fiber belt that helps operate automotive accessories.

accumulator (heating and cooling system) A device placed between the evaporator and the compressor to collect liquid refrigerant and prevent it from entering the compressor.

accumulator (manual transmission) A device used to reduce the speed of clutch or band application to help prevent harsh shifting.

accumulator (brakes) A storage container that holds pressurized brake fluid.

Ackermann angle The angle the steering arms make with the steering axis, projected toward the center of the rear axle.

Ackermann principle The geometric alignment of linkages in a vehicle's steering such that the wheels on the inside of a turn are able to move in a different circle radius than the wheels on the outside.

activated charcoal Charcoal that will absorb large amounts of vapor, used in charcoal canisters to store and release fuel vapors.

active control A system of providing constant feedback from sensors in the vehicle to the control unit.

actuating The act of making something move or work.

actuator (heating and cooling system) A device that is electrically or vacuum controlled and is used to physically move doors within the heater box to control airflow.

actuator (general) A mechanical part, usually controlled by electricity allowing a module to control something mechanical.

adaptive air suspension A suspension system that uses rubber bags or bladders filled with air to support the weight of the vehicle.

adjustable bushing A brace or nylon part that pushes against the rack to adjust the mesh of the rack teeth to the pinion teeth.

adjusting nut The nut used to adjust the end play or preload of a wheel bearing.

adjustment sleeve A component that connects the tie-rods together and to the center link on some applications, providing the adjustment point for toe-in or toe-out, depending on the manufacturer's specifications.

advance mechanism A device used to trigger an earlier spark based on engine conditions.

aerate The tendency to create air bubbles in a fluid.

after top dead center (ATDC) The position of the piston once it has moved beyond top dead center.

aftermarket That segment of the trade that supplies parts, services, and repair for vehicles outside of the original equipment manufacturer (OEM) or the dealer network.

air checking The use of compressed air to check clutch and servo operation on transmissions during and after assembly.

air diverter valve A valve that changes secondary airflow from the exhaust stream to the air cleaner or vice versa.

air drier A device fitted to compressed air lines to remove moisture.

air drill A compressed air–powered drill.

air gap The space or clearance between two components, such as the space between the tone wheel and the pick-up coil in a wheel speed sensor.

air hammer A tool powered by compressed air with various hammer, cutting, punching, or chisel attachments. Also called an air chisel.

air impact wrench An impact tool powered by compressed air designed to undo tight fasteners.

air nozzle A compressed air device that emits a fine stream of compressed air for drying or cleaning parts.

air pump A device used to pump air to the exhaust stream to ensure the converter has enough oxygen to perform gas conversions.

air ratchet A ratchet tool for use with sockets powered by compressed air.

air spring A part that provides the springing action or auxiliary spring. It is typically used in air suspension systems or heavy truck applications.

air supply system Equipment in a motor vehicle that delivers air to the engine.

air switching valve The valve used to switch secondary air from near the exhaust valve (upstream) to the catalytic converter (downstream) for the purpose of oxidizing hydrocarbons and carbon monoxide.

air-conditioning compressor clutch The mechanical coupler that is electromagnetically engaged and provides a way of uncoupling the compressor from the accessory drive belt.

air-conditioning machine A machine designed to recover, recycle, evacuate, leak test, and recharge (R/R/R) the air-conditioning system.

air-conditioning pressure sensor A sensor that gives an input signal of refrigerant pressure in the air—conditioning system to the ECU.

air-conditioning system pressure The refrigerant pressure contained within the air-conditioning system.

air-operated braking system A braking system that uses compressed air operating on large-diameter diaphragms to provide force to the braking assembly; also called air brakes.

aldehyde A pollutant/irritant in diesel fuel.

Allen wrench A type of hexagonal drive mechanism for fasteners.

alloy The mixture of materials to make a substance that has properties different from the original materials. Aluminum alloy has silica added to make it perform better than pure aluminum.

all-wheel drive (AWD) A drive train arrangement in which all of the wheels drive the vehicle.

alternating current (AC) A type of current flow that flows back and forth.

alternative fuel A nonpetroleum-based motor fuel.

aluminum rod A lightweight, strong, either cast or forged metal shaft that connects the piston assembly to the crankshaft assembly.

ambient air temperature sensor A thermistor that is used to measure the air temperature outside the vehicle.

American Petroleum Institute (API) The organization responsible for setting the standards for all American petroleum products including natural gas and biodiesel fuels.

American wire gauge (AWG) A standard used to identify different wire sizes.

ammeter A device used to measure current flow.

amp An abbreviation for amperes, the unit for current measurement.

anchor pin A component of the backing plate that takes all of the braking force from the brake shoes.

anemometer A device that measures airflow in feet per minute (fpm).

angle grinder A portable grinder for grinding or cutting metal.

anisotropic An object that has unequal physical properties, along its various axes. Used in head gaskets to pull heat laterally from the edge surrounding the combustion chamber to the water jacket.

anode A positively charged electrode or plate.

antibinding The release of something when it gets stuck.

antifoaming agents Oil additives that keep oil from foaming as it moves through the engine.

anti-friction bearing Wheel bearing assemblies that use surfaces that are in rolling contact with each other to greatly reduce friction compared to surfaces in sliding contact.

anti-lock brake system (ABS) A safety measure for the braking system that uses a computer to monitor the speed of each wheel and control the hydraulic pressure to each wheel to prevent wheel lock-up.

applied force Pressure placed on something.

arc joint pliers Pliers with parallel slip jaws that can increase in size. Also called Channellocks.

arm The primary load-bearing element of a vehicle's suspension system, commonly known as control arm. Can also mean the steering arm, which applies the driver's turning effort to the steering knuckle.

armature The rotating wire coils in motors and generators. It is also the moving part of a solenoid or relay, and the pole piece in a permanent magnet generator.

asbestos A mineral with needle-like fibers that can become embedded in lung tissue and cause cancer.

aspect ratio The ratio of sidewall height to section width of a tire.

aspirator A tube that is used to direct airflow across the cabin air temperature sensor.

asymmetric tread pattern A tread pattern that differs on each side and, therefore, is usually directional.

Atkinson cycle An engine cycle that uses a longer effective exhaust stroke than intake stroke to reduce exhaust emissions. This type of engine is widely used in hybrid-electric vehicles.

atmospheric pressure The pressure of the air surrounding everything caused by gravity and the weight of air. The higher from sea level, the lower the atmospheric pressure.

attenuator A device that reduces the power of a signal without distorting its waveform.

automatic brake self-adjuster A system on drum brakes that automatically adjusts the brakes to maintain a specified amount of running clearance between the shoes and drum.

automatic climate control system A system that automatically adjusts the heating or cooling to meet a specified temperature demanded by the passengers.

automatic fuel limiter A special refueling port and an overfill protection device fitted on LPG tanks, which ensure that the tank cannot be filled past the safe fill limit of 80%.

automatic load-adjustable shock absorber Typically, an air shock absorber used in an automatic load-sensing system that adjusts ride height (ground clearance) automatically such as when additional weight is added to the vehicle.

automatic oiler A device fitted to compressed air systems to oil air tools.

automatic ride control actuator An electric stepper motor mounted on top of the shock that changes orifice size inside the shock.

Automotive Service Excellence (ASE) An independent, nonprofit organization dedicated to the improvement of vehicle repair through the testing and certification of automotive professionals.

Automotive Youth Educational Systems (AYES) An independent, nonprofit organization that is a partnership between automotive manufacturers, their dealerships, and affiliated secondary automotive programs.

available voltage The maximum amount of voltage that the induction coil secondary is capable of putting out.

aviation snips A scissor-like tool for cutting sheet metal.

axial load The load applied in line with a shaft. It can be controlled with thrust bearings.

axial piston compressor A design of compressor that uses an angled plate (swash plate) to create the piston movement.

axle The shaft of the suspension system to which the tires and wheels are attached; used to transmit driving torque to the wheels.

B100 fuel A fuel that is 100% biodiesel ("neat").

B20 fuel A fuel that is 20% biodiesel blended with 80% petrodiesel.

back clearance The area or space behind the piston rings when the rings are in the piston ring grooves.

backing plate (disc brakes) A metal plate to which the brake lining is fixed.

backing plate A stamped steel plate, bolted to the steering or suspension, which supports the wheel cylinder, brake shoes, and other hardware.

backlash clearance The amount of movement between the pinion teeth versus the ring teeth.

baffle A plate installed vertically in the fuel tank to control sloshing of the fuel.

baffles Metal plates that are welded into the oil sump. These plates help to keep the oil at the oil pickup screen when the vehicle is cornering, braking, or accelerating hard. Oil will move during these conditions, and the baffles will help to keep it from moving away from the pickup.

balance shaft A metal shaft attached and located inside the engine cylinder block assembly to counteract crankshaft vibrations.

ball bearings The rolling components of a wheel bearing consisting of hardened balls that roll in matching grooves in the inner and outer races.

ball hone An assembly of metal rods, with abrasive stones attached, that is inserted into the cylinder and spun to break the glazing off the cylinder walls and make a new crosshatched pattern.

ball joint A swivel connection mounted in the outer end of the front control arm. These swivels are typically constructed with a ball and socket to allow pivoting.

ballast resistor Used to limit the amount of current flowing in the ignition primary circuit.

ball-peen (engineer's) hammer A hammer that has a head that is rounded on one end and flat on the other; designed to work with metal items.

ball-return guide A special passage or metal tube through which the balls move in recirculating ball steering boxes.

ballast A device that increases lighting voltage substantially and controls the current to the bulb.

band brake A braking system that uses a metal band lined with friction material to clamp around the outside of a wheel or drum.

band A metal band with friction material bonded to one side. The band is contracted around a drum to stop the drum from spinning.

bar A metric unit of measure for pressure.

barometric pressure (BARO) sensor A sensor that measures atmospheric pressure.

barrier cream A cream that looks and feels like a moisturizing cream but has a specific formula to provide extra protection from chemicals and oils.

barrier-type hose A rubber hose made with a nylon bladder inside to contain substances with small molecular structures, such as R-134a.

base circle The rounded bottom part of the camshaft (off the lobe) where the valves remain closed or at rest.

battery charger A device that charges a battery, reversing the discharge process.

battery electric vehicle (BEV) A vehicle powered by battery only.

battery terminal configuration The placement of positive and negative battery terminals.

battery An electrochemical device used to supply voltage to a vehicle's electrical systems.

baulk-ring synchromesh unit A synchronizer used in all current transmissions. It uses a blocking ring. Also called a blocker ring synchromesh unit.

bead seat The part of the wheel that the tire seals against.

beam axle A suspension system in which one set of wheels is connected laterally by a single beam or shaft.

beam-type axle A rear-wheel drive axle assembly that has a solid tube incorporating the differential gears.

bearing cage The component in a wheel bearing that maintains the proper spacing between the roller bearings or ball bearings.

bearing crush The force created to seat the bearing by the extra bearing material when the ends of the bearing inserts touch each other and are forced against each other.

bearing inserts Components made out of soft metal materials that are replaceable and come in pairs; also called half-shell bearings.

bearing packer A tool that forces grease into the spaces between the bearing rollers.

bearing races Hardened metal surfaces that roller or ball bearings fit into when a bearing is properly assembled.

bedding-in The process of a valve wearing into the valve seat and creating a positive seal around the whole diameter.

before top dead center (BTDC) The position of the piston when it has not yet reached top dead center.

belt alternator starter (BAS) A type of hybrid drive system that uses a belt-driven alternator/ starter that operates on 42 volts.

belt routing label A label that lists a diagram of the serpentine belt routing for the engine accessories.

bench grinder (pedestal grinder) A grinder that is fixed to a bench or pedestal.

bench vice A device that securely holds material in jaws while it is being worked on.

bendable tangs Small tabs on the brake pad backing plate that are crimped on to the caliper, creating a secure fit and reducing noise.

bias-ply A tire constructed in a latticed, crisscrossing structure, with alternate plies crossing over each other and laid with the cord angles in opposite directions.

bidirectional control The ability to command different solenoids and actuators "on" and "off" to check their operation.

bidirectional scanners Scanners used to monitor engine compression, vacuum, internal engine anomalies, and so forth by causing various components and systems to operate for test purposes.

bi-fuel Two fuels used in a vehicle one at a time, such as compressed natural gas or gasoline.

billet The roughly shaped steel piece that has been cast or forged but has not undergone its final machining.

bimetal Aluminum, tin, and silicon alloy metals placed together with steel to form one piece of material and used for bearing materials.

biodiesel Renewable fuel made from organic feedstocks.

bio-ethanol A renewable fuel derived from a variety of cellulose-based plants.

biomass Organic matter used for fuel.

bleeder screw A screw that allows air and brake fluid to be bled out of a hydraulic brake system when it is loosened and seals the brake fluid in when it is tightened.

bleeding The process of removing air from a hydraulic braking system.

blind rivet A rivet that can be installed from its insertion side.

blink codes Codes used to communicate DTCs; they are given by the EBCM as a series of blinks illuminated by the ABS warning lamp.

block deck The "top" of the engine block and cylinder bore where the cylinder head is bolted on.

blocking ring A synchronizer part that increases or decreases a gear's speed to match shaft speed so that the synchronizer sleeve can lock the gear to the shaft. Also called baulk ring.

blow-by Pressure that leaks past the compression rings during compression and combustion.

blow-off valve A valve that allows the release of excessive boost pressure from the turbocharger when the throttle plate is quickly closed.

blowby gas The result of combustion gases leaking past the compression rings and getting into the crankcase.

blower motor An electric motor, usually the permanent magnet type, that moves air over the air-conditioning evaporator and heater core.

bob weights Weights used during the balancing process that are used to mimic the exact weight of the piston and connecting rod weights for that particular rod bearing journal.

body control module (BCM) The computer that controls the electrical system in the body of a vehicle, including power windows, door locks, heating and A/C systems, and in some cases the EBC system.

body electronic module (BEM) An electronic control module for body electrical systems.

boiling point The temperature at which a substance begins to change from a liquid to a gas.

bolt A type of threaded fastener with a thread on one end and a hexagonal head on the other.

bolt cutters Strong cutters available in different sizes, designed to cut through non-hardened bolts and other small-stock material.

bonded linings Brake linings that are essentially glued to the brake pad backing plate; more common on light-duty vehicles.

boost valve A valve located in the HCU that is controlled by the EBCM; it allows brake fluid under high pressure to flow into the HCU hydraulic circuits to apply the brakes when commanded.

bore A tool used to make a hole in or through an object.

bored out An object that has been bored.

boring bar A long bar used to position and align a single-point tool, such as an engine cylinder block boring machine, for boring operations.

bottom dead center (BDC) The position of the piston at the end of its stroke when it is closest to the crankshaft.

bottoming tap A thread-cutting tap designed to cut threads to the bottom of a blind hole.

box-end wrench A wrench or spanner with a closed or ring end to grip bolts and nuts.

brake assist (BA) An enhanced safety system built in to some ABS systems that anticipates a panic stop and applies maximum braking force to slow the vehicle as quickly as possible.

brake booster A vacuum or hydraulically operated device that increases the driver's braking effort.

brake drum A short, wide, hollow cylinder that is capped on one end and bolted to a vehicle's wheel; it has an inner friction surface that the brake shoe is forced against.

brake fade The reduction in stopping power caused by a change in the brake system such as overheating, water, or overheated brake fluid.

brake fluid Hydraulic fluid that transfers forces under pressure through the hydraulic lines to the wheel braking units.

brake hose A flexible section of the brake lines between the body and suspension to allow for steering and suspension movement.

brake lathe A tool used to refinish the drum surface by removing a small amount of metal and returning it to a concentric, non-directional finish.

brake lines Made of seamless, double-walled steel, and able to transmit over 1000 psi (6895 kPa) of hydraulic pressure through the hydraulic brake system.

brake lining thickness gauge A tool used to measure the thickness of the brake lining.

brake pad shims and guides Small pieces of metal that cushion the brake pad and absorb some of the vibration, helping to cut down on unwanted noise.

brake pedal emulator A brake pedal assembly used in electronically controlled braking systems to send the driver's braking intention to the computer; it mimics the feel of a standard brake pedal.

brake shoe A steel shoe and brake lining friction material that apply force to the brake drum during braking.

brake shoe adjustment gauge An adjustable tool used to pre-adjust the brake shoes to the diameter of the brake drum.

brake spoon A tool used to adjust the brake lining-to-drum clearance when the drum is installed on the vehicle.

brake spring pliers A tool used for removing and installing brake return springs.

brake switch The electrical switch that is activated by the brake pedal; it turns on the brake lights and signals the EBCM that the brakes are being applied.

brake technician A technician who specializes in working on vehicle brake systems.

brake wash station A piece of equipment designed to safely clean brake dust from drum and disc brake components.

brake-by-wire system A braking system that uses no mechanical connection between the brake pedal and each brake unit. The system uses electrically actuated motors to apply brake force.

brakes A system made up of hydraulic and mechanical components designed to slow or stop a vehicle.

braking torque The torque acting to twist the axle housing around its center during braking.

breakdown The loss of electrical insulation properties.

breaker plate The movable plate which the breaker points are mounted on and which pivots as the vacuum advance pulls on it.

breather tube A tube used in the PCV system to allow fresh air into the engine crankcase.

brinelling Damage done to the surface of a bearing caused by excessive load, which exceeds the limit of the bearing material, typically from shock loads.

British thermal unit (Btu) A measure of heat energy. It takes 1 Btu to raise the temperature of 1 pound of water 1°F.

broach-style surfacer A tool used in resurfacing the engine block.

brushless An electric motor without brushes.

brushless DC motor An electric motor that does not have any brushes and is sometimes called an "electronically commutated motor." In this type of motor, an electronic control module replaces the brushes and commutator.

bucket-style lifter A bucket-shaped lifter assembly that sits on top of the valves and is operated directly by the camshaft. It can be hydraulic or mechanical.

bump steer The undesired condition produced when hitting a bump where the vehicle darts to one side as the steering linkage is pushed or pulled as a result of the travel of the suspension.

burn rate The rate of flame spread for liquid or gaseous fuel.

bus A system of networking circuits in which various on-board modules are connected to one another, allowing the exchange of information between them.

bushing An insert with an inner bearing surface that is fitted into a hole in an object, allowing the object to rotate or slide on a pin or shaft.

butt connector A crimp or solder joint that creates a permanent connection.

bypass filter An oil filter system that only filters some of the oil.

bypass valve The pressure control valve of the supercharger. When the bypass valve opens, it lets air move around the supercharger compressor section, reducing the boost pressure.

C-clamp A clamp shaped like the letter C; it comes in various sizes and can clamp various items.

cabin air temperature sensor A thermistor that measures air temperature inside the vehicle.

caliper A hydraulic device that uses pressure from the master cylinder to apply the brake pads against the rotor.

caliper dust boot seal driver set A set of drivers used to install metal-backed caliper dust boot seals.

caliper piston pliers A tool used to grip caliper pistons while removing them.

caliper piston retracting tool A tool used to retract caliper pistons on integrated parking brake systems.

cam The egg-shaped lobe machined to a shaft used to cause opening and closing of the valves of a four-stroke cycle engine.

cam angle sensor A sensor that measures cam angle position.

cam lobe centerline The location of the cam lobe in relation to top dead center of the engine in degrees.

cam lobe ramp The rise of the lobe from the base circle to the top of the lobe, which is where the valve starts to lift, on the side opposite of where it starts to close.

cam lobe separation The number of degrees between the centerline of the intake lobe and the centerline of the exhaust lobe; this with cam duration determines the amount of valve overlap.

cam lobes Raised areas or protrusions on an otherwise round shaft.

camber The side-to-side vertical tilt of the wheel. It is viewed from the front of the vehicle and measured in degrees. Negative camber is when the top of the tire is closer to the center of the vehicle than the bottom of the tire.

cam-in-block engine An engine in which the camshaft is located in the engine block rather than on the cylinder head.

camshaft A shaft with lobes that operates the valve mechanisms controlling valve opening time and duration. Also, it can be used to drive fuel injection pumps and mechanical fuel pumps.

camshaft follower A slider or roller placed in direct contact with the lobes of the OHC camshaft that pushes on the tip of the valve to open it.

camshaft lobe The eccentric "egg-shaped" portion of the camshaft that pushes on the valve lifter or camshaft follower.

camshaft position (CMP) sensor A sensor mounted near the camshaft and used to send camshaft and valve position information to the PCM.

CAN-bus circuit A two-wire communication network that transmits status and command signals between control modules in a vehicle.

canted valves A valve arrangement in the cylinder head where the valves are at an angle to the cylinder bore. Canting the valves can make for a straighter path for air to flow into and out of the intake and exhaust ports.

capacitance The ability of a capacitor to store an electrical charge.

capacitor A device that can quickly store a small amount of electrical energy, at which point it is charged.

carbon dioxide (CO_2) A vehicle emission that is considered a primary greenhouse gas, though not toxic and not yet regulated.

carbon monoxide (CO) A vehicle emission produced by partially burned fuel that is colorless, odorless, and highly toxic and that causes asphyxiation when inhaled.

carbon monoxide poisoning Exposure to higher than tolerable levels of carbon monoxide, resulting in headaches, fatigue, or loss of consciousness, eventually resulting in death.

carburetor float bowl The part of the carburetor that holds fuel to be burned in the engine; the bowl is at a constant level of fuel to ensure adequate fuel is present during driving.

carrier The part of the throw-out bearing assembly that holds the bearing.

casing plies A network of cords that give the tire shape and strength; also known as casing cords.

cast rod A connecting rod that is created by the metal casting process.

castellated nut An adjusting nut with slots cut into the top such that it resembles a castle; used with a cotter pin to prevent the nut from turning.

caster The angle formed through the wheel pivot points when viewed from the side in comparison to a vertical line through the wheel.

casting line A by-product of the metal casting process that forms a line found on parts that are cast in metal.

catalyst A device that changes chemical composition without self-destruction.

cathode A negatively charged electrode or plate.

center bolt A fastener or bolt found in the middle of the harmonic balancer or cam sprocket that attaches it to the crankshaft or the camshaft.

center electrode The electrode located in the center of a spark plug. It is the hottest part of the spark plug.

center punch Less sharp than a prick punch, the center punch makes a bigger indentation that centers a drill bit at the point where a hole is required to be drilled.

centerline The imaginary line drawn down the exact center of the vehicle from front to back.

centrifugal advance mechanism An ignition timing device, located above or beneath the distributor base plate, that rotates with the distributor cam and is used to advance the spark. As engine speed rises, the flyweights on the advance mechanism are thrown outward by centrifugal force. Since the distributor cam is able to pivot on the distributor shaft, the weights act against their springs and move the distributor cam forward.

centrifugal force A force pulling outward on a rotating body.

centrifugal switch A switch that is only activated when centrifugal forces are placed on a vehicle.

cetane number A rating of the ignition quality of diesel fuel.

chamfer A rounded or angled edge located on the blocking ring, with ridges machined into it to help grab the cone surface of the gear.

chamfering The process of cutting into the top of the oil passage hole with a specialized chamfering tool or regular drill bit to make the top of the oil hole more like a 45-degree angle, to keep the edge from digging into the bearing the way a 90-degree edge would.

channel The number of wheel speed sensor circuits and hydraulic circuits the EBCM monitors and controls.

charcoal canister A device used to trap the fuel vapors. The fuel vapors adhere to the charcoal, until the engine is started, and engine vacuum can be used to draw (purge) the vapors into the engine so that they can be burned along with the air–fuel mixture.

charge (electrical) In measuring capacitance, the amount of electrical energy present.

charge (heating and cooling system) The amount of refrigerant present in the system or the process of installing refrigerant in the system.

charge carrier A mobile particle that has a positive or negative electrical charge.

chassis dynamometer A machine with rollers that allows a vehicle to attain road speed and load while sitting still in the shop.

chassis technician A technician who specializes in working on vehicle suspension and steering systems.

chassis The main support frame in a vehicle. It includes the running gear, such as suspension, the engine, and the drive train.

check valve Also known as a shuttle valve, a valve that allows the flow of hydraulic oil in one direction only. It is typically used to allow oil to escape quickly from an application device when shifting gears.

chlorofluorocarbon (CFC) A manufactured compound designed to be used as a refrigerant. It is now illegal due to the high chlorine content.

choke A device that provides a rich air–fuel mixture until the engine warms up by restricting the flow of air at the entrance to the carburetor, before the venturi.

circuit breaker A device that trips and opens a circuit, preventing excessive current flow in a circuit. It is resettable to allow for reuse.

circuit or schematic diagram A pictorial representation or road map of the wiring and electrical components.

Clean Air Act (CAA) A policy signed into law in 1990 that sets standards for air pollution to eliminate ozone-depleting elements.

cleaning gun A device with a nozzle controlled by a trigger fitted to the outlet of pressure cleaners.

climate control system A system that provides the heating and cooling of air inside the passenger compartment for passenger comfort.

clock spring A special rotary electrical connector located between the steering wheel and the steering column that maintains a constant electrical connection with the wiring system while the vehicle's steering wheel is being turned.

closed loop The operational status of the engine control system in which the oxygen sensor is providing feedback of rich or lean exhaust conditions and the control unit is varying fuel delivery based on that information.

closed loop system A totally self-contained system with no materials entering or exiting.

cloud point The temperature at which wax (paraffin) in diesel fuel starts to solidify.

clutch binding A condition in which the clutch disc is dragging, leading to grinding gears during gear shifts and possibly clutch chatter.

clutch chatter A condition in which the clutch shudders when the clutch pedal is released and the vehicle starts to move forward.

clutch disc The center component of the clutch assembly, with friction material riveted on each side. Also called a clutch plate or friction disc.

clutch electrical winding An electromagnetic control device that creates a magnetic field that pulls in the clutch to make contact with the pulley.

clutch fork The part of the clutch linkage that operates the throw-out bearing.

clutch pedal The foot-operated pedal used by the driver to engage and disengage the clutch.

clutch safety switch An electrical switch that is operated by the clutch pedal and keeps the starter motor from cranking the engine over until the clutch is fully depressed.

clutch system A mechanically operated assembly that connects and disconnects the engine from the transmission.

coarse (UNC) Used to describe thread pitch; stands for Unified National Coarse.

code Another name for a fault code; *see* DTC.

coefficient of friction A value assigned to materials to describe the amount of friction when two objects slide against each other.

coil bind A result of excessive valve lift. When the coils of the spring touch each other, the spring breaks, flattening the cam lobe and bending the pushrod.

coil spring pressure plate A type of pressure plate that uses coil springs to provide the clamping force.

coil spring Spring steel wire that is heated and wound into a coil that is used to support the weight of a vehicle.

coil-on-plug A type of ignition system used on late-model vehicles that uses one coil placed above each spark plug.

cold chisel The most common type of chisel, used to cut cold metals. The cutting end is tempered and hardened so that it is harder than the metals that need to be cut.

cold cranking amps (CCA) A standard for rating the ability of a vehicle battery to supply high current under cold operating conditions.

collet A cone-shaped tool that encloses and grips a rod or shaft when inserted into the sleeve of a lathe or other machine.

column inertia The principle that as a column of air flows, it creates inertia, which keeps air flowing until its inertia energy is spent; sometimes referred to as a "ram effect" when using tuned intake or exhaust systems.

combination pliers A type of pliers for cutting, gripping, and bending.

combination wrench A type of wrench that has an open end on one end and a box-end wrench on the other.

combustion chamber The area of an engine in which the air/fuel mixture is burnt. It consists of the bottom of the cylinder head and the top of the piston.

combustion pressure The force exerted by the expanding gases during the burning process. It is what causes the internal combustion engine to operate.

common bore When a single cylinder is used for two pistons. A tandem master cylinder would be an example of two pistons in one bore.

common rail system (CRS) A diesel fuel injection system that uses a pump to develop high-pressure fuel directed to an accumulator or rail.

common rail A type of injection system using a common fuel manifold from which individual injectors are fed high-pressure fuel.

commutator A device made on armatures of electric generators and motors to control the direction of current flow in the armature windings.

companion flange A splined flange that transmits power from the drive shaft to the pinion gear.

compensating port Connects the brake fluid reservoir to the master cylinder bore when the piston is fully retracted, allowing for expansion and contraction of the brake fluid.

compliance bushing A rubber bushing with a voided section molded in it that allows component movement under torque application. It is typically used in control arms on front-wheel drive vehicles to minimize torque steer issues.

complicated fracture A fracture in which the bone has penetrated a vital organ.

compound planetary gear set Two or more simple planetary gear sets connected together.

compressed air equipment Tool or machinery that operates on compressed air.

compressed natural gas (CNG) Methane compressed for on-board storage in cylinders.

compressed natural gas vehicle (CNGV) A vehicle that uses methane stored in high-pressure cylinders.

compression ratio (CR) The volume of the cylinder with the piston at bottom dead center as compared to the volume of the cylinder at top dead center, given in a ratio such as 9:1 CR.

compression ring A metal ring found inside the grooves on the side of the engine piston.

compression ring groove A square groove found on the outside of the piston skirt in which the piston ring fits.

compression stroke The stroke of the piston during which air and fuel is being compressed into a small area prior to ignition.

compression tester A device used to measure the amount of compression pressure a cylinder can generate.

compression-ignition engine An engine that uses the heat of compression to ignite the air–fuel mixture; also known as a diesel engine.

compressor A belt or electrically driven device designed to increase refrigerant pressure and cause refrigerant to travel through the air-conditioning system.

compressor surge The backup of air against the throttle plate as it is closed. The turbocharger is still spinning, pressurizing air, when the throttle plate is closed. Air will stack up, creating a rapid slowing of the turbocharger compressor wheel. This can damage the compressor wheel.

computer-controlled carburetor A carburetor that changes and sets air–fuel ratio based on commands from a PCM that uses memory and input from sensors.

concentric interrupter rings Two interrupter rings that have the same center.

concentricity (valve) A term used to describe a valve seat where the valve seat and valve stem share a common center. In this design, the valve can seal against the seat no matter how it is rotated.

concentricity (hole) The roundness of a hole. If the hole is not round it can also be referred to as out of round.

condensation The changing of a gas into a liquid through cooling.

condenser The air-conditioning component located in the front of the vehicle designed to allow high-pressure refrigerant to change states from gas to liquid.

condenser (capacitor) A self-contained unit that is connected electrically in parallel with the contact breaker points and used to assist the rapid collapse of the magnetic field in the coil by preventing the contact breaker points from arcing. Also used on some coils to reduce radio frequency interference.

conduction The process of transferring heat through matter by the movement of heat energy through solids from one particle to another.

conductor A material that allows electricity to flow through it easily. It is made up of atoms with one to three valance ring electrons.

connecting rod A cast or forged metal rod that connects the engine pistons to the engine crankshaft.

connector The plastic housing on the end of a wiring harness that holds the wire terminals in place. It can also refer to a type of wire terminal that connects wires together or to a common point such as a bolt.

conservation of energy A physical law that states that energy cannot be created or destroyed.

constant mesh A term used to describe two or more parts, such as gears, that are in constant contact with each other.

constant velocity (CV) joints Joints commonly used in front-wheel drive vehicles to allow flexibility of the axle while turning.

contact breaker point ignition system A type of ignition system that uses a mechanical means of turning the primary circuit on and off.

contact breaker points A mechanically operated electrical switch that is fixed to the distributor base plate and opened and closed by the distributor cam with the rotation of the engine. The contacts normally form a self-contained unit, fixed to the base plate by a retaining screw engaged in a slot in the fixed contact.

continuity A conductive path between two points.

continuous monitoring A term that describes OBDII monitors that run continuously throughout the drive cycle.

continuously variable transmission (CT) A transmission without individual gears or gear ratios.

continuously variable transmission (CVT) A type of transmission that has no fixed gears, as in a conventional transmission, but rather can adjust gear ratios infinitely within the design of the transmission.

control arm The primary load-bearing element of a vehicle's suspension system, commonly referred to as an A-arm or wishbone. These arms may be used as an upper and lower pivot point for the wheel assembly. They attach to the chassis with rubber bushings that allow up-and-down movement of the tire and wheel assembly.

control module A generic term that identifies an electronic unit that controls one or more electrical systems in the vehicle; also called a control unit.

control unit Any device that controls another object such as a computer.

controlled area network bus (CAN-bus) A wire data network found in vehicles to connect control modules so they can communicate quickly and easily.

controller area network (CAN) A localized (on-board) vehicle network that enables computers and components to send and receive signals across a shielded twisted pair of wires.

convection The process of transferring heat by the circulatory movement that occurs in a gas or fluid as areas of differing temperatures exchange places due to variations in density and the action of gravity.

conventional oil Oil that is processed from crude oil; about 20% of oil is additives.

conventional theory The theory that electrons flow from positive to negative.

convertible A vehicle that converts from having an enclosed top to having an open top by a roof that can be removed, retracted, or folded away.

coolant When anti-freeze concentrate is mixed with water, the resulting mixture is called engine coolant. Most manufacturers recommend a 50/50 mixture.

coolant control valve A valve that blocks off coolant flow to keep hot water from entering the heater core when less heat is requested by the operator.

coolant label A label that lists the type of coolant installed in the cooling system.

coolant temperature sensor (CTS) A thermistor usually screwed into a cylinder head water jacket. Usually the CTS is a negative temperature coefficient thermistor, or a resistor whose resistance varies, with temperature varying a voltage signal to the PCM.

cooler flow test The placement of a specialty measuring device into the transmission cooler line to measure fluid flow to the cooler. Low cooler flow can be a sign of other issues with the pump and lubrication system.

cooling hoses Flexible hoses that connect the stationary components of the cooling system, such as heater core and radiator, to the engine, which is mounted on flexible mounts.

core plug A metal cap for the holes that are used to remove core sand used during the casting process.

cored solder Solder that is in the form of a hollow wire. The center is filled with flux, which is used as a cleaning agent while the solder is being applied to the metal surfaces.

cornering force (suspension system) The force applied to an axle that shifts the axle in relation to the position of the body when turning.

cornering force (wheels) The force between the tread and the road surface as a vehicle turns.

corona-suppression An electronic sniffer used for detecting refrigerant leaks.

corrosion inhibitors Oil additives that keep acid from forming in the oil.

cotter pin A one-use soft metal pin that can be bent into shape and is used to retain bearing adjusting nuts.

coupe A two-door vehicle that has seating for two people and may have a small rear seat.

crank angle position The position of the crankshaft, measured in degrees.

crank angle sensor A sensor that measures crank angle position.

crank core The rough, unfinished crankshaft assembly that has just left the foundry or forging area.

crankcase The bottom area of the engine cylinder block where the crankshaft is located.

cranking amps (CA) A standard similar to CCA, but that measures the battery's function at a higher temperature—32°F (0°C)

cranking Rotating the engine by turning the ignition key to the start position.

crankshaft A part mounted in the lower side of the engine block that has offset journals that rotate to change the up-and-down motion of the pistons into rotary motion at the crankshaft.

crankshaft end play The amount of forward and rearward movement of the crankshaft in the main bearings. Crankshaft end play is controlled by the engine main bearing thrust bearing.

crankshaft journals Smooth, curved, machined areas where other parts fit to the crankshaft.

crankshaft position (CKP) sensor A sensor used by the PCM to monitor engine speed. It can be one of three types of sensors—Hall effect, magnetic pickup, or optical.

crescent pump An oil pump that uses a crescent-shaped part to separate the oil pump gears from each other, allowing oil to be moved from one side of the pump to the other.

crimp The bent shape of the oil ring expander that allows it to provide outward force on the oil rings.

cross-arm A description for an arm that is set at right angles or 90 degrees to another component.

cross-cut chisel A type of chisel for metal work that cleans out or cuts key ways.

cross-flow radiator A radiator that uses cooling tubes that run horizontal with tanks on each end. This design allows lower hood profile for better vehicle aerodynamics.

crosshatch A pattern of lines placed at angles to each other, appearing as a series of Xs across a surface.

crude oil Material pulled from the earth, originating from organic compounds broken down over time and formed into petroleum. This material is processed in a refinery to break down into various hydrocarbon substances such as diesel, gasoline, and mineral oil, among others.

crush sleeve A collapsible spacer between the bearings that provides a means of maintaining a preset torque on the pinion nut.

cubic boron nitride (CBN) cutter An engine block resurfacing tool used on cast iron parts.

current clamp A device that clamps around a conductor to measure current flow. It is often used in conjunction with a DVOM.

current flow The flow of electrons, typically within a circuit or component.

curved file A type of file that has a curved surface for filing holes.

CV joint CV is an abbreviation for constant velocity, a type of universal joint used on the drive axles or half-shafts of a vehicle. Usually refers to front-wheel drive vehicles.

cylinder bore The hole in the engine block that the piston fits into.

cylinder head The part of the engine that is bolted to the engine block and caps off the top of the combustion chamber.

cylinder leakage tester A device that pumps air into the cylinder and measures the percentage of air that is leaking out of the cylinder.

cylindrical roller bearing assembly A type of wheel bearing with races and rollers that are cylindrical in shape and roll between inner and outer races, which are parallel to each other.

data link connector (DLC) The connector through which the scan tool communicates to the vehicle's computers; it will display the readings from the various sensors and can retrieve trouble codes, freeze-frame data, and system monitor data.

dead axle An axle that does not have the capability to drive the vehicle. It is usually found on the rear of front-wheel drive vehicles.

dead blow hammer A type of hammer that has a cushioned head to reduce the amount of head bounce.

deceleration A decrease in a vehicle's speed.

deck The surface area at the top of the engine block against which the cylinder head seals.

deep dish wheel A wheel with negative offset, which gives the outside of the wheel a deep dish appearance. Deep dish refers to the side of the wheel that is farthest from the drop center.

deflecting force A force that moves an object in a different direction or into a different shape.

degree wheel A disc with 360 one-degree markings near its outer edge; it bolts to the front of the crankshaft and is used to check valve and cam timing.

degrees of distributor rotation A measure of the amount that the distributor rotates, where one complete circle is equal to 360 degrees.

delay circuit A combination of electrical and electronic components that provide a time delay for switching an electrical circuit.

depletion layer An area of neutral charge in semiconductors.

depth filter A hydraulic filter that has thick filter media to trap dirt and other particles of various sizes as they pass through the filter.

depth micrometer A measuring device that accurately measures the depth of a hole.

desiccant A drying agent used in air-conditioning systems to absorb moisture.

detent mechanism The mechanism that holds or helps hold the shift rail into position to ensure that the gear does not pop out when selected and to let the driver feel when a shift is completed.

detent valve See *kickdown valve*.

detergents Oil additives that help to keep carbon from sticking to engine components.

detonation The condition in which the remaining fuel charge fires or burns too rapidly after the initial combustion of the air–fuel mixture. It is audible through the combustion chamber walls as a knocking noise.

diagnostic trouble code (DTC) A code set by the computer indicating system or component malfunction.

diagonal cutting pliers Cutting pliers for small wire or cable.

dial bore gauge An accurate measuring device for inside bores, usually made with a dial indicator attached to it.

dial indicator An accurate measuring device where measurements are read from a dial and needle.

diaphragm pressure plate A slightly conical, spring steel plate used to provide the clamping force for the clutch assembly.

diaphragm-style EGR valve An EGR valve that is operated by a diaphragm that moves when vacuum is applied to it, opening a passageway for exhaust to flow.

dichlorodifluoromethane (R-12) An inert, colorless gas that can be used as a refrigerant. It is stored in white containers.

die stock A handle for securely holding dies to cut threads.

diesel exhaust fluid (DEF) A mixture of urea and water that is injected into the exhaust system of a late-model diesel-powered vehicle to reduce exhaust nitrogen oxide emissions.

diesel exhaust fluid (DEF) A urea chemical reactant specifically designed for use in selective catalytic reduction systems to reduce nitrogen oxides.

diesel particulate filter (DPF) A filter that converts particulate matter, or soot, into ash.

dieseling A condition in which the engine continues to run after the ignition key is turned off. Also referred to as run-on.

differential gear set The arrangement of gears between two axles that allows each axle to spin at its own speed when the vehicle is going around a corner.

differential gears Gears situated in the final drive assembly that are meshed together and with both axles, allowing the wheels to rotate at different speeds when turning a corner.

digital volt-ohmmeter (DVOM) A test instrument with a digital display for measuring voltage, resistance, and current. Also called a digital multimeter (DMM).

diode A two-lead electronic component that allows current flow in one direction only.

dipper A type of splash lubricating system used in small engines. It works like a spoon scooping up oil and throwing it upward onto the crankshaft and other wear surfaces.

direct burning The phase of combustion after ignition when the rest of the fuel is injected into the combustion chamber and there is a more gradual pressure change in the cylinder.

direct current (DC) Movement of current that flows in one direction only.

direct drive A condition in which the engine and transmission output are turning at the same rate of speed.

direct fuel injection A fuel injection system in which the fuel is injected directly into the combustion chamber.

direct ignition system May refer to a waste spark ignition or a coil-on-plug ignition system, in which the coils are directly attached to the spark plugs.

direct TPMS A type of automated tire pressure monitoring system that measures tire pressure and possibly temperature via a sensor installed inside each wheel.

direct-acting telescopic shock absorber A shock absorber designed to reduce spring oscillations.

directional and asymmetric tread pattern A tread pattern that is both directional and asymmetric, which means the tire is designed to rotate in only one direction and has one side that must face outward to ensure that the tire performs as designed under operating conditions.

directional tread pattern A tread pattern designed to pump water out from under the tire; each tire must be placed in a particular spot on the vehicle.

disc brakes A type of brake system that forces stationary brake pads against the outside of a rotating brake rotor.

disc brake pads Brake pads that consist of a friction material bonded or riveted to a steel backing plate; designed to wear out over time.

disc brake rotor micrometer A specially designed micrometer used to measure the thickness of a rotor.

discharge reed valve A flat, spring-loaded valve used as a check valve on the discharge side of a compressor.

dislocation The displacement of a joint from its normal position; it is caused by an external force stretching the ligaments beyond their elastic limit.

dispersants Oil additives that keep contaminants held in suspension in the oil, to be removed by the filter or when the oil is changed.

displacement-on-demand A feature that allows cylinders to be taken off-line when not needed, such as at vehicle cruise.

distributor base plate A round metal plate near the top of the distributor that is attached to a distributor housing; also called a breaker plate.

distributor cap The top portion of a distributor, used to make a connection between the spinning rotor and the high-tension leads.

distributor The part of an ignition system that distributes the spark to the spark plugs in the correct sequence and at the correct time. It includes a distributor cap, rotor, shaft, and usually a switching device.

distributorless ignition system An ignition system that does not include a distributor. It uses signals from the crankshaft position sensor and the camshaft position sensor sent to the PCM to determine when to send a signal to the ignition module.

doping The introduction of impurities to pure semiconductor materials to provide N- and P-type semiconductors.

double Cardan joint A type of joint that uses two Cardan joints housed in a short carrier and that reduces the change in velocity of a single Cardan joint by using the second joint to cancel out the changes in velocity of the first joint.

double crimping Overcrimping or recrimping a fitting to keep it from leaking. It normally results in a bigger leak and is not recommended.

double flare A seal that is made at the end of metal tubing or pipe.

double-clutching A technique used to shift gears when a nonsynchronized transmission is used. The driver must push the clutch in multiple times to change gears.

double-insulated Tools or appliances that are designed in such a way that no single failure can result in a dangerous voltage coming into contact with the outer casing of the device.

double-row ball bearing assembly A single ball bearing assembly using two rows of ball bearings riding in two channels in the races.

down-flow radiator A radiator that uses cooling tubes that run vertical. This design requires a higher hood profile.

drag The slowing down of the crankshaft when it strikes the oil in the crankcase.

drag link A steel or iron rod that transfers movement of the pitman arm to a relay lever.

drain line A wire included in a harness with one end grounded to reduce interference or noise being induced into the harness.

drawing-in method A method for replacing wheel studs that uses the lug nut to draw the wheel stud into the hub or flange.

drift punch A type of punch used to start pushing roll pins to prevent them from spreading.

drill chuck A device for securely gripping drill bits in a drill.

drill press A device that incorporates a fixed drill with multiple speeds and an adjustable worktable. It can be free-standing or fixed to a bench.

drill vice A tool with jaws that can be attached to a drill press table for holding material that is to be drilled.

drivability technician A technician who diagnoses and identifies mechanical and electrical faults that affect vehicle performance and emissions.

drive axle assembly The components that make up the drive axle including the axles, final drive assembly, bearings, and axle housing.

drive axle An axle that provides power to a wheel.

drive cycle The operating range of an engine from start-up until shutdown when finished performing its job.

drive line angularity The relationship of the driveshaft to the component that the driveshaft attaches, measured in degrees of angle.

drive pulley Any belt-driven pulley used to power an accessory such as power steering or the air-conditioning compressor.

drive shaft The hollow tube with flexible joints on each end that transmits power from the transmission to the final drive unit.

drive train A term used to identify the engine, transmission/transaxle, differential, axles, and wheels.

driveline vibrations Rotational fluctuations caused by out-of-balance, misaligned, worn, or bent driveline components.

driven center plate The friction disc that is held firmly against the flywheel by a pressure plate and transfers power from the flywheel to the transmission input shaft.

driving thrust The force transferred from the tire contact patch through the axle housing and front half of the spring to the fixed shackle point that pushes the vehicle along the road.

drop center A wheel design with part of the center section of the wheel a smaller diameter than the rest. It is used for mounting and demounting the tire.

drum brake micrometer A tool used for measuring the inside diameter of the brake drum.

drum brakes A type of brake system that forces brake shoes against the inside of a brake drum.

drum-style parking brake A mechanically operated drum brake that can be set while the vehicle is not moving to serve as a parking brake.

dry flanged sleeve A metal cylinder with a flange embedded into the block pressed into an engine cylinder to give it a new wear surface. The flanged sleeve is held in by the cylinder head.

dry sleeve A metal cylinder that is pressed into an engine cylinder block that does not come in direct contact with coolant. It is held in place with an interference fit.

dual overhead cam (DOHC) engine An engine design that is like the overhead cam engine but with two camshafts used per cylinder head; one operates the intake valves and the other operates the exhaust valves.

dual-clutch transmission A type of automatically shifting manual transmission in which two separate input shafts are connected to their own clutch. Shifting of the gears alternates between the two input shafts.

dual-drive air-conditioning compressor An air compressor drive used on some hybrid vehicles. The compressor can be driven by the accessory belt or by an electric motor.

dual-fuel system A system that allows an engine to burn two fuels at one time.

dual-mass flywheel (DMF) A type of flywheel that eliminates excessive transmission gear rattle, reduces gear change/shift effort, and increases fuel economy.

duo-servo drum brake system A system that uses servo action in both the forward and reverse direction.

duration The amount of time the valve stays open, given in degrees of rotation of the crankshaft.

duty cycle Another term for pulse-width modulation.

dwell angle The amount of time that the primary circuit is energized, measured in degrees of distributor rotation.

dwell control section Part of the ignition control circuit that determines when the primary circuit will be switched on and for how long current will flow in the primary winding. The dwell period can be varied according to engine speed, improving coil efficiency.

dynamic imbalance A tire imbalance that causes the wheel assembly to turn inward and outward with each half revolution.

E85 A fuel with 85% ethanol and 15% gasoline blend.

ear protection Protective gear worn when the sound levels exceed 85 decibels, when working around operating machinery for any period of time, or when the equipment you are using produces loud noise.

edge code A code printed on the edge of a friction lining that describes its coefficient of friction.

effective stroke The duration of plunger stroke with the spill port covered, which determines the amount of fuel injected.

EGR system monitor A control module diagnostic test that is run to ensure that the EGR valve and passageways are operating properly.

EGR valve A valve that connects the exhaust port, or manifold, and the intake manifold. If engine operating conditions are likely to produce oxides of nitrogen, the EGR valve opens, letting some burned exhaust gases pass from the exhaust into the intake system.

EH2 rim The specialized rim design that is used with some run-flat tires.

elasticity The amount of stretch or give a material has.

electric braking system A braking system used to provide braking to trailers; the drum brakes are electrically activated in the trailer when the driver applies the brakes on the towing vehicle.

electric machine Another name for a traction motor with regenerative capability.

electric power steering system (EPS) A steering system that uses an electric motor and sensors to provide feedback to the vehicle's computer systems to decrease steering effort.

electric servo An air-conditioning door actuator controlled by electricity.

electric servo motor Also referred to as an electric actuator, a motor that provides movement to operate the air doors in an air box to control air temperature and air movement.

electric solenoids An electrically operated valve, which in brake systems is used to control the flow of brake fluid in the hydraulic system.

electrical capacity The ability of a circuit or component to carry electrical loads.

electrical power A measurement of the rate at which electricity is consumed or created.

electrical resistance A material's property that slows down the flow of electrical current.

electrical technician A technician who diagnoses, replaces, maintains, identifies fault with, and repairs electrical wiring and computer-based equipment in vehicles.

electrically assisted steering (EAS) A power-assist system that uses an electric motor to replace the hydraulic pump to decrease steering effort.

electrically powered hydraulic steering (EPHS) A steering system that uses an electric motor to produce hydraulic assist for steering.

electro-chemical device A device such as a battery or fuel cell that uses two forms of energy.

electrohydraulic braking (EHB) A hydraulic braking system that uses an electrically driven hydraulic pump to pressurize fluid for use in the master cylinder.

electrolysis The process of pulling metals apart by using electricity or by creating electricity through the use of chemicals and dissimilar metals.

electrolyte A mixture of water and acid that contains free ions that make it electrically conductive.

electrolyte (batteries) The liquid in lead-acid battery cells. It is a mixture of about 67% water and 33% sulfuric acid.

electromagnet A conductor wound in a coil that produces a magnetic field when current flows through it.

electromagnetic clutch arrangement An arrangement used in hybrid air-conditioning systems to drive the compressor. The air-conditioning clutch is an electromagnetic clutch that works by creating a strong magnetic field that pulls the clutch into mesh with the pulley on the air compressor.

electromagnetic induction The production of an electrical current in a conductor when it moves through a magnetic field or a magnetic field moves past it.

electromotive force An electrical pressure or voltage.

electron theory The theory that electrons, being negatively charged, repel other electrons and are attracted to positively charged objects; thus electrons flow from negative to positive.

electronic brake control (EBC) system A hydraulic brake system that has integrated electronic components for the purpose of closely controlling hydraulic pressure in the brake system.

electronic brake control module (EBCM) The module that controls and monitors the anti-lock braking system.

electronic continuously variable transmission (ECVT) A type of hybrid transmission that often uses two electric motors in combination with an ICE.

The two electric motors and the ICE transfer power through a planetary gear set, allowing an infinite amount of gear ratios.

electronic control module (ECM) A computer that receives signals from input sensors, compares that information with preloaded software, and sends an appropriate command signal to output devices; used to manage the anti-lock brake system (ABS).

electronic control unit (ECU) A computer that controls the ignition and fuel control and emissions control systems on an engine; also called the engine control module (ECM) or power train control module (PCM).

electronic control unit (ECU) (heating and cooling system) When referring to the HVAC system, the electronic module that makes the "decisions" of the climate control system settings based on input sensors and the module programming.

electronic diesel control (EDC) A computer or electronic control unit that controls diesel fuel injection systems.

electronic fuel injection (EFI) An injection system in which fuel delivery is controlled electronically, allowing continuous adjustments to the air–fuel ratio.

electronic ignition system An ignition system that uses a nonmechanical (electronic) method of triggering the ignition coil's primary circuit.

electronic ignition system—distributor type An ignition system that uses a distributor but replaces the contact points with an electronic triggering device.

electronic pressure control (EPC) solenoid A pulse width–modulated solenoid used to control transmission line pressure in an automatic transmission.

electronic reverse lockout An electronic solenoid used to prevent accidental engagement into reverse gear while the vehicle is moving forward.

electronic stability control (ESC) system A computer-controlled system added to ABS and TCS to assist the driver in maintaining vehicle stability while steering.

electronically controlled throttle A system that uses electronic, instead of mechanical, signals to control the throttle. Sometimes called drive-by-wire.

element The replaceable portion of a filter, such as an air filter element or oil filter element.

emission analyzer A service bay or lab device used for detecting/measuring vehicle emissions.

emission control system A system of devices that are designed to control or reduce harmful gases released to the atmosphere.

emission standards Cutoff points set by governmental agencies to limit tailpipe emissions.

emission A gas that is released to the atmosphere; usually refers to a harmful gas.

enameled copper wire Wire that uses a thin layer of enamel as insulating material. The thinness of the insulation allows the wire to be closely wound in a coil, creating a dense magnetic field when current flows through it.

end play (transmission) Referring to the input or output shaft, fore-and-aft movement in the transmission.

end play (wheels) The in-and-out movement of the hub caused by clearance within the wheel bearing assembly.

end play (manual transmission) Unwanted lateral movements of the worm shaft.

Energy Policy Act (EPAct92) Regulations enacted in 1992 by the US Congress to promote the use of alternative fuel vehicles and fuels.

energy The ability to do work.

engine balancer An expansive bench unit complete with computer controls, a lathe and drill press for machining metal for the balancing procedure, and all necessary adapters for most applications of crankshaft assemblies.

engine bearing A specially designed metal piece that supports circular moving parts.

engine block deck The portion of the engine cylinder block on which the head gasket lies on and to which the cylinder head is bolted.

engine block dowel pinhole The hole where the engine cylinder block dowel pins are fixed.

engine configuration The way engine cylinders are arranged—for example, V, flat, or in-line.

engine control module (ECM) A computer that controls the ignition and fuel control and emissions control systems on an engine; also the electronic control unit (ECU) or power train control module (PCM).

engine coolant temperature (ECT) sensor A sensor that changes resistance based upon coolant temperature; also known as a thermistor.

engine coolant temperature sensor A thermistor that measures the temperature of the engine coolant.

engine displacement The size of the engine given in cubic inches, cubic centimeters, and liters. It is found by multiplying the piston displacement by the number of cylinders the engine has. Sometimes called "swept volume."

engine hoist A small crane used to lift engines.

engine-driven hydraulic pump A power steering pump driven by a belt or gear off of the crankshaft.

Environmental Protection Agency (EPA) Federal government agency that deals with issues related to environmental safety.

epitrochoid curve The circular movement around the perimeter of another circle. This is the movement that the rotary engine uses to ensure that the rotor stays in contact with the housing.

ethanol Alcohol-based motor fuel made from starches and sugars.

ethylene glycol A chemical used as anti-freeze that provides the lower freezing point of coolant and raises the boiling point. It is a toxic anti-freeze.

evaporative emission (EVAP) system A system used to capture vapors or gases from an evaporating liquid.

evaporator temperature sensor A thermistor that reads the temperature of the evaporator, used to ensure that the evaporator does not freeze.

evaporator The air-conditioning component normally located in the passenger compartment designed to allow low-pressure refrigerant liquid to change states to a gas.

event cylinder The cylinder that uses the spark to ignite the air–fuel mixture on a waste spark ignition system.

exhaust brake A brake system that restricts the flow of exhaust gases through the engine by closing a butterfly valve located in the exhaust manifold. Restricting the exhaust flow causes the engine speed to slow down, slowing the vehicle.

exhaust gas recirculation (EGR) system A system that recirculates a portion of burned gases back into the combustion chamber to displace air and fuel and cool combustion temperatures.

exhaust gas recirculation (EGR) valve A valve that allows a controlled amount of exhaust gas into the intake manifold during a certain period of engine operation. Used to lower nitrogen oxide exhaust emissions.

exhaust stroke The stroke in an engine cycle when the piston moves up, with the exhaust valve(s) open, exhausting the burned exhaust gases out through the exhaust system.

exhaust valve The valve through which exhaust gases are forced out of the combustion chamber.

expander The part of an oil control ring that holds the ring against the cylinder wall.

expansion volume An engineered space that allows for growth of the volume of a liquid as it heats and expands.

Extended Mobility Technology (EMT) Tires with thick sidewalls that allow the tire to be driven on even when it has no air pressure.

extension housing A component of the automatic transmission housing that covers the output shaft of the transmission. The extension housing also supports the end of the driveshaft and may hold components such as the vehicle speed sensor, speedometer drive assembly, and governor assembly.

external bleeding The loss of blood from an external wound; blood can be seen escaping.

external combustion engine An engine that runs on heat applied externally to the cylinder. For example: the steam engine.

external drive shaft A shaft used to transfer power from the transmission to the live axle.

externally equalized valve A style of TXV where the external valve uses the sensing bulb on the outlet side to overcome spring pressure to open the valve.

extreme loading Large pressure placed on two bearing surfaces. Extreme loading will try to press oil from between bearing surfaces.

extreme-pressure additive An oil additive that ensures that a protective coating is given to moving engine parts and that keeps oil from being forced out under extreme pressure. Helps oil to cushion components.

eye ring terminal A type of crimp or solder terminal that has an enclosed eyelet to connect the terminal with a bolt or screw.

fast chargers A type of battery charger that charges batteries quickly.

fasteners Devices that securely hold items together, such as screws, cotter pins, rivets, and bolts.

fault codes An alphanumeric code system used to identify potential problems in a vehicle system.

fault *See* diagnostic trouble code (DTC).

feedback signal A voltage signal sent back to an electronic control unit. The feedback signal is how the control module is able to interpret temperature or other information from its sensors.

feedback system A system that uses feedback to adjust what it is doing. Typically, a module gives a command and waits to see if the command was followed by use of a sensor.

feeler gauge A thin blade device for measuring space between two objects.

ferrous metals Metals that have an iron compound in their makeup or that are magnetic.

fiber optics Fine glass fibers through which light is transmitted.

fill plug Usually a threaded plug that can be removed to allow the level of a fluid to be checked and filled. This could also be a rubber snap fit plug.

fillet area The area of the crankshaft that meets up with the rod bearing journal or main bearing journal.

fillet The radius portion of an inside corner that reduces stress at the corner.

filter media A screen designed to keep debris from the TXV that is normally located in the receiver dryer.

filter sock The first line of defense in the fuel supply system. The sock typically consists of a fine mesh, which prevents most small particles from being drawn into the fuel pump and sent through the rest of the fuel system.

fin A small, flat piece of metal placed between the tubes to help with the transfer of heat from the coolant to the air, refrigerant to air, or air to refrigerant. The metal heats up due to contact with the hot pipes in the case of a radiator or heater core and from hot air in the case of an evaporator.

final drive assembly An assembly used to power the drive wheels and allow the wheels to rotate at different speeds as the vehicle turns.

final drive A component that provides a final gear reduction and allows for the difference in speed of each wheel when cornering.

fine (UNF) Used to describe thread pitch; it stands for Unified National Fine.

finished rivet A rivet after the completion of the riveting process.

fire rings Steel rings integrated into the cylinder head gasket nearest the combustion chambers that provide extra sealing to seal in the high combustion pressures.

firing line The tall lines on a parade pattern that indicate the voltage required to initially jump the spark plug gap.

first aid The immediate care given to an injured or suddenly ill person.

first-degree burns Burns that show reddening of the skin and damage to the outer layer of skin only.

five-gas analyzer A tool that uses sensors to measure the level of gases in the exhaust stream.

fixed caliper A type of brake caliper bolted firmly to the steering knuckle or axle housing, having at least one piston on both sides of the rotor.

fixed orifice tube system A system with a fixed orifice tube that uses an accumulator between the evaporator and the compressor.

fixed resistor A resistor that has a fixed value.

fixed-orifice PCV system A system in which a hole of a predetermined size is used as a means of pulling crankcase vapors into the intake manifold to be burned.

fixed-type joint A joint that does not slide to allow for shaft lengthening or shortening; it simply allows for angle changes as the suspension moves.

flame front The front edge of the burning air/fuel mixture in the combustion chamber.

flame front The rapid burning of the air–fuel mixture that moves outward from the spark plug across the cylinder.

flame propagation The movement of the flame through the combustion chamber during the combustion process.

flame spread The phase of combustion in which there is a sharp pressure rise in the combustion chamber because of the sudden combustion of the fuel.

flare nut wrench A type of box-end wrench that has a slot in the box section to allow the wrench to slip through a tube or pipe. Also called a flare tubing wrench.

flashback arrestor A spring-loaded valve installed on oxyacetylene torches as a safety device to prevent flame from entering the torch hoses.

flasher can A mechanism that turns the vehicle's turn signal and hazard flasher bulbs on and off.

flat blade screwdriver A type of screwdriver that fits a straight slot in screws.

flat seat with washer A type of lug nut that is flat where it bolts to the wheel and has a washer affixed that allows it to turn independent of the hex part of the lug nut.

flat seat without washer A type of lug nut that is flat where it bolts to the wheel.

flat tappet A camshaft specifically designed to push on flat bottom lifters (nonroller types). It typically has a higher rolling resistance than the roller-style camshafts.

flathead engine An L-head engine with valves in the block.

flat-nosed pliers Pliers that are flat and square at the end of the nose.

flex hone A machine tool with abrasive stones that is used to refinish the inside of the cylinder walls.

flex plate A metal part attached to the rear of the crankshaft that connects to the torque converter in a vehicle with an automatic transmission.

flexible-fuel vehicle (FFV) A vehicle than can operate on two different fuels blended together in various mixture amounts by percentage.

float chamber A chamber that holds a quantity of fuel at atmospheric pressure ready for use.

floating pin A round metal pin that has a very small clearance but is free to float in the piston and connecting rod.

float-type fuel gauge A system for determining the level of liquid fuel in a tank using a float and potentiometer.

flow-control valve A valve used in power steering pumps to control the amount of flow out of the power steering pump.

fluid coupler A type of hydraulic coupling used on vintage vehicles to connect and transfer power from the engine to the transmission.

fluid dissipater A silicone fluid component that allows the mass of a fluid type harmonic balancer to rotate at a more constant speed than the crankshaft to help even out the torsional vibrations of the crankshaft.

flux A liquid or paste that protects a soldering or welding joint from oxidization.

flywheel ring gear Large, round, externally toothed gear that is usually press-fitt to the outer diameter of the flywheel and used along with the starter to crank the engine over.

flywheel The heavy, circular flat plate that keeps the engine rotating when power is not produced, such as on the exhaust, intake, and compression strokes.

force The effort to produce a push or pull action.

forced induction The pressurization of airflow going into the cylinder through the use of a turbocharger or supercharger.

forces capability map data Data preprogrammed into the electronic control unit's memory by the manufacturer and used to determine how much power assistance is needed based on input from the vehicle's speed sensor and steering sensor.

forcing screw The center screw on a gear, bearing, or pulley puller. Also called a jacking screw.

forged connecting rod A strong metal connecting rod hammered into shape by large presses used to connect the piston to the crankshaft.

four-post hoist A type of hoist that the vehicle is driven onto that uses two long, narrow platforms to lift the vehicle.

four-stroke engine An engine that uses four strokes—intake, compression, power, and exhaust—to complete its cycle.

four-wheel drive (4WD) A drive train layout in which the engine drive has either two wheels or four wheels depending on which mode is selected by the driver.

four-wheel steering system A steering system in which the front wheels are controlled normally and the rear wheels use a computer and electric motors to turn the rear linkage.

fracture split A method used on powdered metal connecting rods where the big end of the connecting rod is broken in half and can be identified by a ragged finish of the big end's parting surfaces.

free electron An electron located on the outer ring, called the valence ring, that is only loosely held by the nucleus and that is free to move from one atom to another when an electrical potential (pressure) is applied.

free play The amount of movement between two mating parts.

freewheeling engine An engine that has enough clearance between the piston and the valves so that in the event the timing belt or chain breaks, the valves that are hanging all the way open will not contact the piston, thus preventing engine damage.

freeze-frame A feature of OBDII that records events before, during, and after a fault occurs.

frequency The rate of change in direction, oscillation, or cycles in a given time.

friction The resistance created by surfaces in contact. Kinetic friction is resistance to motion when one surface moves over another. Static friction is resistance to motion between two surfaces that are not moving.

friction bearing A bearing that uses sliding motion between components, such as a clutch pilot bearing.

friction facing The material riveted to each side of the clutch disc that mates to the flywheel and pressure plate. Used to provide friction and a wear surface for the clutch assembly.

front bearing retainer The housing that bolts the input shaft bearing in place on the front of the transmission.

front hydraulic pump A hydraulic pump used to supply lubrication oil and hydraulic pressure to the different components inside the automatic transmission.

front-wheel drive (FWD) A drive train layout in which the engine drives the front wheels.

fuel cell An electro-chemical device that uses hydrogen and oxygen to create electricity.

fuel cell (electric) vehicle (FCV) A vehicle that converts fuel to electricity in a direct electrochemical process, with more energy extracted from the fuel source than in traditional internal combustion engines.

fuel composition sensor A device that measures the percentage of alcohol in gasoline.

fuel filler neck The upper end of the fuel filler tube leading down to the fuel tank, which accepts the fuel hose nozzle at the gas station pump.

fuel filter A device that removes impurities (dirt and water) from the fuel before they reach the carburetor or injection system. Filters may be made of metal or plastic screen, paper, or gauze.

fuel metering system Equipment in a motor vehicle that delivers the proper amount of fuel to each cylinder.

fuel methanol A toxic alcohol fuel.

fuel pressure regulator A system that controls the pressure of fuel entering the injectors.

fuel pump A mechanically or electrically driven vacuum device used to draw fuel from the tank and force it into the fuel system.

fuel pump relay A relay to turn on or off the high-amperage circuit of the fuel pump.

fuel rail Tubing that connects several injectors to the main fuel line.

fuel shutoff mode A safety precaution by which fuel is shut off when certain conditions are met during a vehicle crash.

fuel supply system Equipment in a motor vehicle that delivers fuel to the engine.

fuel system Equipment in a motor vehicle that delivers fuel to the engine.

fuel tank pressure sensor A sensitive pressure sensor mounted in the fuel tank or EVAP system used to monitor the system for leaks.

fulcrum The point around which a lever rotates and that supports the lever and the load.

fulcrum ring A steel ring that is used as a pivot point for the diaphragm spring in the pressure plate.

full floating axle An axle that does not support any weight; if removed, the vehicle will still roll on its wheels.

full frame construction Construction of the frame using a heavy steel channel iron or boxed steel. The frame runs from the front of the vehicle to the rear as one solid piece, and the body of the vehicle attaches to this part by bolts and rubber body mounts.

full-flow filter An oil filter installed on production cars. This oil filter cleans all oil coming from the oil pump on its way to the lubricated components.

fuse A safety device that self-destructs to prevent excessive current flowing in a circuit in the event of a fault.

galleries Passageways drilled or cast into the engine block or head(s), which carry pressurized lubricating oil to various moving parts in the engine, such as the camshaft bearings.

gallium-arsenide A semiconductor used in high-frequency circuits.

garter spring A coiled spring that is fitted to the inside of the sealing lip of many seals, used to hold the lip in contact with the shaft.

garter spring lip seal A seal that has a spring to maintain pressure on the seal's surface to prevent leakage.

gas direct injection (GDI) cylinder head A cylinder head designed to accept a gasoline injector directly in the combustion chamber instead of in the intake manifold.

gas welding goggles Protective gear designed for gas welding; they provide protection against foreign particles entering the eye and are tinted to reduce the glare of the welding flame.

gasket A rubber, cork, or paper spacer that goes between two parts to seal the gap between the parts.

gasket scraper A broad sharp flat blade to assist in removing gaskets and glue.

gasoline A volatile, flammable liquid mixture of hydrocarbons, obtained from crude oil and used as fuel for internal combustion engines.

gasoline direct injection (GDI) A fuel injection system in which fuel is sprayed directly into the combustion chamber.

gassing The escape of gas from the battery.

gauge sending unit A device used for transmitting a signal to control a fuel gauge.

gear A relatively round, rotating part with internal or external teeth that are designed to mesh with another gear for the purpose of transmitting torque.

gear lube A type of lubricant primarily used to lubricate transmission and differential gears but also used to lubricate some wheel bearings.

gear pullers A tool with two or more legs and a cross bar with a center forcing screw to remove gears.

gear pump A type of front pump used on some vehicles that uses two rotating gears to force fluid out of the pump.

gear ratio The ratio of the number of turns that a drive gear must complete to turn the driven gear one turn. Typically this is a calculation of the driven gear to the drive gear. Ratios are listed, for example, as 2:1 or 4.3:1.

gear reduction The use of a small gear to drive a large gear. The result is in an increase in torque but a decrease in speed.

gear set Two or more gears that are in mesh with each other.

gear shift lever The lever that the driver uses to shift the transmission.

gear synchronizer An assembly in the transmission that is used to bring two unequally spinning shafts or gears to the same speed when upshifting or downshifting.

geared oil pump An oil pump that has two gears running side by side together to move oil from one side of the pump gears to the other.

gelling A thickening effect of oil in cold weather. This is not a desirable trait for lubricating oil, as it will not flow when it is gelling. Wax content in base stock mineral oil makes gelling worse.

germanium A type of semiconductor.

girdle A metal device connected to the bottom of the engine cylinder block to create strength for the main bearing caps.

governor pressure The pressure created by the governor, which is used to make the shift valves upshift and is proportional to vehicle speed.

governor A device that controls how much fuel is delivered to the injector.

gradient resistance Resistance encountered when a vehicle travels up a hill, requiring torque to be applied to overcome it.

gravity pouring The casting process used for creating metal parts.

grease A lubricating liquid thickened to make it suitable for use with many wheel bearings.

grease seal A component that is designed to keep grease from leaking out and contaminants from leaking in.

grinding wheels and discs Abrasive wheels or flat discs fitted to bench, pedestal, and portable grinders.

ground The return path for electrical current in a vehicle chassis, other metal of the vehicle, or dedicated wire.

grounds Fault conditions in a circuit where the circuit is unintentionally contacting a grounded component or wire. This may result in a short, in the case of a power wire, or it could cause a circuit to stay live in the case of a switched ground circuit.

guide pins Pins that allow the caliper to move in and out as the brakes operate and as the brake pads wear.

H block valve A style of TXV that has an outlet side like the external valve; however, both the inlet and the outlet pipe go through the block, so the sensing bulb is built into the block.

half-shaft An axle that has CV joints on each end and that fits between the transaxle and wheel. Typically, one is used on each side of a vehicle.

Hall-effect An electrical effect where electrons tend to flow on one side of a special material when exposed to a magnetic field, causing a difference in voltage across the special material. When the magnetic field is removed, the electrons flow normally and there is no difference of voltage across the special material. This effect can be used to determine the position or speed of an object.

Hall-effect switch The portion of an electronic ignition system used to trigger the ignition system. Hall-effect switches operate by using a potential difference, or voltage, created when a current-carrying conductor is exposed to a magnetic field. If a magnetic field is applied at right angles to the direction of current flow in a conductor, the lines of magnetic force permeate the conductor, and the electrons flowing in the conductor are deflected to one side. This deflection creates a potential difference across the conductor. The stronger the magnetic field, the higher the voltage.

halogen lamp A type of bulb that produces a bright white light.

hard rubber mallet A special-purpose tool with a head made of hard rubber; often used for moving things into place where it is important not to damage the item being moved.

hard shifting A shifting problem in which the shifter will not move smoothly into the desired gear, requiring excessive force by the driver to set it into gear.

hardened seat A valve seat that has undergone a heat-treating process to become more robust and capable of withstanding the severe demands of today's vehicles and drivers.

harmonic balancer A round metal disc connected to the front of the crankshaft that smoothes out torsional vibrations created by the crankshaft.

hatchback A vehicle that has a shared passenger and cargo area; it typically is available in three- and five-door arrangements.

hazard Anything that could hurt you or someone else.

hazardous environment A place where hazards exist.

hazardous material Any material that poses an unreasonable risk of damage or injury to persons, property, or the environment if it is not properly controlled during handling, storage, manufacture, processing, packaging, use and disposal, or transportation.

head gasket A thin piece of material, often a multilayered, bimetallic sheet used to seal the cylinder head assembly to the engine block.

header A specially tuned exhaust manifold typically made of exhaust pipes. These pipes are usually made equal length to ensure equal flow between cylinders.

headgear Protective gear that includes items like hairnets, caps, or hard hats.

heat buildup A dangerous condition that occurs when the glove can no longer absorb or reflect heat and heat is transferred to the inside of the glove.

heat dissipation The spreading of heat over a large area to increase heat transfer.

heat fade Brake fade caused by the buildup of heat in braking surfaces, which get so hot they cannot create any additional heat, leading to a loss of friction.

heat range The rating of a spark plug's operating temperature.

heat transfer The flow of heat from a hotter part to a cooler part; it can occur in solids, liquids, or gases.

heated air intake system A system that uses hot air from around the exhaust manifold to warm the air going into the intake manifold.

heated diode A sniffer that uses electricity to determine if there is a refrigerant leak; considered the best sniffer for R-134a.

heater control cables Cables that control the air doors in an air box as part of the air distribution system.

heater core A heat-exchanging device that transfers heat converted by the fuel burning in the engine to the passenger compartment.

heavy line technician A technician who undertakes major engine, transmission, and differential overhaul and repair.

helical gears Gears that have teeth set on an angle to the gear face; they operate more quietly than spur gears.

helical-cut gear A type of gear in which the teeth are cut in a spiral down the axis of the gear.

helical-geared limited slip differential A type of differential that responds very quickly to changes in traction and that does not bind from friction in turns or lose its effectiveness since there are no clutches.

helix The curve created by a smooth spiral and used in the angle of gear teeth and coil springs.

Helmholtz resonator A device that uses the principle of noise cancellation through the collision of sound waves. When necessary, the resonator is used in addition to the muffler to cancel additional sounds. This resonator may also be used on the induction system to muffle noise of airflow through the induction system. It is named after physicist Hermann Von Helmholtz.

hemispherical cylinder head A combustion chamber that is hemispherical in shape with the valves in a crossflow arrangement and the spark plug near the center of the cylinder head directly over the top of the piston.

hertz The unit for electrical frequency measurement.

high resistance A term that describes a circuit or components with more resistance than designed.

high resistance The resistance of a component or circuit relative to a low resistance. It can also refer to a faulty circuit where a section or component has excess unwanted resistance.

high-intensity discharge (HID) A type of lighting that produces light with an electric arc rather than a glowing filament.

high-pressure accumulator A storage container designed to contain high-pressure liquids such as brake fluid.

high-pressure switch A switch designed to open at a predetermined high pressure to protect the compressor; it is normally located on the high side line near the compressor.

high-tension leads The heavy insulated wires used to connect the distributor cap terminals to the spark plugs, and the ignition coil to the distributor cap, or on waste spark systems, the coils to the spark plugs.

high-tension terminals The terminals on the coils and distributor cap that the high-tension leads are connected to.

high-voltage spark The electrical arc that takes place between the center and the side electrode of a spark plug.

history code A fault code that has occurred but is not current and is saved in the PCM's memory for 40 drive cycles.

hold function A setting on a DVOM to store the present reading.

hold-down spring tool A tool used for removing and installing hold-down springs.

hold-down springs Springs that hold the brake shoes against the backing plate.

hold-in winding A low-current winding found in starter solenoids that holds the plunger in the activated position.

hole theory The theory that as electrons flow from negative to positive, holes flow from positive to negative.

hollow punch A punch with a center hollow for cutting circles in thin materials such as gaskets.

honing The smoothing-out process of the cylinder walls performed after the boring process. This is the final step in refinishing the cylinder; it creates the proper crosshatched pattern necessary for the piston rings to seal and seat into to give the combustion chamber the proper seal.

Hooke's joint A joint that consists of a steel cross with four hardened bearing journals, mounted on needle rollers in hardened caps, which locate the cross in the eyes of the yokes. The cross swivels in the yokes as the drive is transferred across the joint.

horizontally opposed engine An engine with two banks of cylinders, 180 degrees apart, on opposite sides of the crankshaft. It is also called a flat engine or a boxer engine.

horsepower An amount of work performed in a given time.

hoses Flexible lines used to direct liquids or gases.

hot junction The heating point of a thermocouple.

hybrid drive system A drive system that uses two or more propulsion systems such as electric motors and an ICE.

hybrid electric vehicle (HEV) A vehicle that uses two power sources for propulsion, one of which is electricity.

hydraulic actuator A hydraulically controlled cylinder that engages or disengages the clutch pedal.

hydraulic control unit (HCU) An assembly that houses electrically operated solenoid valves used in electronic braking systems; also called a modulator.

hydraulic fade Brake fade caused by boiling brake fluid.

hydraulic jack A type of vehicle jack that uses oil under pressure to lift vehicles.

hydraulic press method A method for replacing wheel studs that uses a press to force the wheel stud into the flange until it bottoms out.

hydraulic pressure test The use of a hydraulic pressure gauge to measure the amount of hydraulic pressure produced in each gear range.

hydraulic valve lifter A small mechanical cylinder with a hydraulically operated internal piston used to automatically take up the slack (valve clearance) in the valve train.

hydraulically actuated electronically controlled unit injector (HEUI) A diesel fuel injection system that operates by drawing fuel from the tank using a tandem high- and low-pressure fuel pump.

hydrocarbon (HC) An exhaust emission that mixes with nitrogen oxides and sunlight to form ozone (smog) and acid rain. Hydrocarbons result from incomplete combustion.

hydro-cracking A process in which group 2 and group 3 oils are refined with hydrogen at much higher temperatures and pressures. This process results in a base mineral oil with many of the higher performance characteristics of synthetic oils.

hydrodynamic seal Oil seal flutes or swirls that are part of the oil seal and that create a pumping action to return oil to the transmission as the shaft rotates, enabling lubrication.

hydrogenated nitrile butadiene rubber (H-NBR) A man-made rubber with the same characteristics as NBR but with better resistance to heat.

hydrogenating A process used during refining of crude oil. Hydrogen is added to crude oil to create a chemical reaction to take out impurities such as sulfur.

hydrometer A tool that measures the specific gravity of a liquid.

hygroscopic A property of a substance or liquid that causes it to absorb moisture (water), as a sponge absorbs water. Brake fluid will absorb water out of the air; thus it is hygroscopic.

hypereutectic piston An aluminum piston that is cast with a 16% to 19% silicon content and that has minimal expansion rates.

hypoid bevel gear A special design of spiral bevel gear, with the centerline of the pinion below the centerline of the ring gear.

hypoid gear A type of helical gear used to change the direction of motion 90 degrees. The axis of the input gear does not line up on the centerline of the output gear

idle The speed at which an engine runs without any throttle applied.

idle stop A feature that turns off the internal combustion engine when the vehicle is at a standstill.

idler gear A gear used in between two gears to change the direction of the rotation of the driveshaft or drive axles in the transmission.

idling A condition in which a gear is spinning but not moving.

idling five-gas test A five-gas analysis test conducted during vehicle idling.

ignition The lighting of the fuel and air mixture in the combustion chamber.

ignition advance The means of causing the spark to occur earlier within the compression stroke for better performance and fuel economy during changing engine conditions.

ignition coil A device used to amplify an input voltage into the much higher voltage needed to jump the electrodes of a spark plug.

ignition coil pack A group of two or more ignition coils housed in one assembly.

ignition control module (ICM) A general control unit of some electronic ignition systems, usually with current and dwell angle control, driver and output stage, and in some cases, electronic spark timing functions.

ignition delay/lag period The time it takes for the fuel to ignite after the fuel is injected into the engine.

ignition module An electronic component that electronically controls the ignition coil or coils.

ignition switch A switch operated by a key or start/stop button and used to turn on or off a vehicle's electrical and ignition system.

impact driver A tool that is struck with a hammer to provide an impact turning force to remove tight fasteners.

incandescent lamp The traditional bulb that uses a heated filament to produce light.

included angle The angle of camber added or subtracted to the SAI angle. This is the angle of the pivot points in relation to the camber angle of the wheel. Also referred to as the diagnostic angle.

independent rear axle A type of rear suspension system that allows each wheel on the axle to move independently of the other.

independent rear suspension (IRS) A type of suspension system where each rear wheel is capable of moving independently of the other.

independent suspension A system for allowing the up-and-down movement of one tire without affecting the other tire on that axle.

independent suspension drive axle A type of suspension that allows each wheel on a drive axle to move independently of the other.

indirect fuel injection A fuel injection system in which the fuel is injected into a separate chamber in the cylinder head, often called a prechamber.

indirect TPMS A type of automated tire pressure monitoring system that uses the anti-lock braking system of a vehicle to measure the difference in the rotational speed of the four wheels to determine tire pressure.

induced voltage The creation of voltage in a conductor by movement of a magnetic field that is near that conductor.

induction coil An electrical transformer that uses magnetic fields to produce high-voltage pulses from low-voltage direct current.

induction hardening A process for hardening metal by touching it to a device that raises the temperature of the part with heat or magnets and then suddenly cooling it in water, oil, or another chemical.

induction-type system A type of ignition system that uses a magnetic pulse generator to trigger the spark.

inductive current The current that has been created across a conductor by moving it through a magnetic field.

inductive-type sensor A sensor mounted on the crankcase housing that is used to sense the movement of the ring gear teeth on the flywheel, or a toothed disc on the crank pulley.

inert gas A gas that will not react chemically.

inertia The resistance to a change in motion.

infrastructure The system for supplying fuel for transportation use; includes ships, pipelines, trucks, etc.

ingression The passing of foreign bodies, such as moist warm air, through the air-conditioning lines or fittings.

injector A valve that is controlled by a solenoid or spring pressure to inject fuel into the engine.

inlet port Connects the reservoir with the space around the piston and between the piston cups in a brake master cylinder.

inlet reed valve A flat spring-loaded valve that allows gaseous refrigerant to enter the compressor.

in-line engine An engine in which the cylinders are arranged side by side in a single row.

inner race The inside component of a wheel bearing that has a smooth, hardened surface for rollers or balls to ride on.

inner tie-rod or socket The inner tie-rod is attached to the end of the rack and allows for suspension movement and slight changes in steering angles.

input force The force applied to the input piston, measured in either pounds or kilograms.

input shaft speed sensor A sensor inside the transmission that measures the rpm of the input shaft. Also called a turbine shaft sensor.

inside micrometer A micrometer designed to measure internal diameters.

insulator A material that has properties that prevent the easy flow of electricity. These materials are made up of atoms with five to eight electrons in the valance ring.

intake air temperature (IAT) sensor A sensor that measures the temperature of the incoming air through the air filtration system.

intake manifold vacuum The measure of the pressure that is less than atmospheric pressure that develops in the intake manifold of a running engine equipped with a throttle plate.

intake port The port through which the air or air/fuel mixture travels from the throttle body area to the combustion chamber.

intake stroke The stroke in an engine cycle when the piston moves from top dead center (TDC) to bottom dead center (BDC).

intake valve The valve through which air and fuel enter the combustion chamber.

integral ABS system A brake system in which the master cylinder, power booster, and HCU are all combined in a common unit.

integral valve guide A valve guide machined into the cylinder head during cylinder head construction.

integrated circuit A semiconductor chip that contains miniature versions of various electrical components within one housing.

integrated motor assist (IMA) A Honda hybrid drive system that uses a moderate-sized electric motor installed between the engine and the transmission.

interference angle The built-in differences in the angles between the valve seat and the valve face for the purpose of providing quick wearing-in of the surfaces; there usually must be between ½ and 1 degree of difference.

interference engine An engine that has minimum clearance between the valves and the pistons during normal operation; in the event that the timing belt or chain breaks, the open valves will be contacted by the piston and bend the valves, possibly breaking the piston.

interference fit A condition when two parts are held together by friction because the outside diameter of the inner component is slightly larger than the inside diameter of the outer component.

interlock mechanism A mechanical device that prevents engagement of two different gears at the same time.

intermediate shaft A steel rod positioned at an angle from the steering column to the steering gear that functions in transferring movement from one to the other.

intermediate tap One of a series of taps designed to cut an internal thread. Also called a plug tap.

internal bleeding The loss of blood into the body cavity from a wound; there is no obvious sign of blood.

internal combustion engine An engine that burns a fuel internally and creates movement due to thermal expansion of gases.

internal module control circuit A section of the ignition module responsible for receiving the trigger signal.

internally equalized valve A style of TXV where the internally equalized valve uses pressure from the inlet pipe to overcome the pressure created from the outlet pipe heat. Lower heat on the outlet pipe creates lower pressure, and the pressure from the inlet pipe is able to overcome it and move the valve.

International Standards Organization (ISO) flare A method for joining brake lines, also called a bubble flare. Created by flaring the line slightly out and then back in, leaving the line bubbled near the end.

interrupter ring A ferrous metal ring, shaped like a very shallow cup with slits or windows cut into it at evenly spaced intervals. The ring has the same number of blades and windows as engine cylinders and is rotated by the engine moving the blades through an air gap. The purpose of an interrupter ring is to systematically block, and expose, the magnetic field in a Hall-effect sensor in order to turn the primary ignition circuit on and off.

intrusive test A test in which a gas analyzer hose is placed into the exhaust stream before and after the catalytic converter; it may require drilling an access hole in the exhaust pipe in front of the converter.

inverted double flare A method for joining brake lines that forms a secure, leak-proof connection.

inverter A device that converts direct current to alternating current.

invertor A device that changes direct current into alternating current.

ion An atom that has fewer electrons than protons (positive) or that has more electrons than protons (negative).

isolation valve The valve in the HCU that either allows or blocks brake fluid that comes from the master cylinder from entering the HCU hydraulic circuit.

jack stands Metal stands with adjustable height to hold a vehicle once it has been jacked up.

jake brake A brake system that consists of an extra exhaust valve on a diesel engine, which releases compressed gases from the combustion chamber at the top of the compression stroke; also called a compression brake.

journal saddle A semicircular cut located at the bottom of the engine block that is used to support the engine crankshaft.

keep alive memory (KAM) A certain minimum amount of parasitic current draw that is used by the vehicle's circuits to maintain memory functions and monitor systems.

keeper groove A groove machined into the top of the valve stem near the tip of the valve that is used to "lock in" the valve keepers to help retain the valve spring onto the valve assembly.

keepers Locking devices that keep the valve retained by the valve spring seat.

keyed lock washer The washer that fits between the adjusting nut and the lock nut; the face of the washer is drilled with a series of holes that mate to a short pin from the adjusting nut, locking it to the spindle. Also referred to as a tang washer.

keyed washer The washer that fits between the adjusting nut and the wheel bearing and that has the center hole keyed to fit a slot on the spindle or axle tube.

kickdown valve A type of spool valve that is connected to the throttle on the vehicle. The valve is used to force a downshift when the throttle is opened all the way, assuming the governor pressure is below a specified point. Kickdown valves are also called detent valves.

kinetic energy The energy of an object in motion; it increases by the square of the speed.

Kirchhoff's current law An electrical law stating that the sum of the current flowing into a junction is the same as the current flowing out of the junction.

knock sensor An engine sensor that detects pre-ignition, detonation, and knocking.

knocking A noise heard when the air–fuel mixture spontaneously ignites before the spark plug is fired at the optimum ignition moment.

knuckle The part that contains the wheel hub or spindle and attaches to the suspension components.

knurled A process in which a drill bit with a spiral groove is threaded through or run through the valve guide to create raised ridges on either side of the groove, effectively shrinking the size of the valve guide.

labor guide A guide that provides information to make estimates for repairs.

lambda The ratio of air to fuel at which all of the oxygen in the air and all of the fuel are completely burned; See also *stoichiometric ratio*.

latent heat of condensation The amount of heat removal necessary to change the state from a gas to a liquid without changing the actual gauge temperature.

latent heat of evaporation The amount of heat required to change the state from a liquid to a gas without changing the actual gauge temperature.

latent heat of freezing The amount of heat removal required to change the state from a liquid to a solid without changing the actual gauge temperature.

lateral runout Also called warpage, the side-to-side movement of the rotor surfaces as the rotor turns.

leading shoes Brake shoes that are installed so that they are applied in the same direction as the forward rotation of the drum and thus are self-energizing.

leading/trailing shoe drum brake system Type of brake shoe arrangement where one shoe is positioned in a leading manner and the other shoe in a trailing manner.

leaf spring A spring made of one or more flat, tempered steel springs bracketed together that is used in the suspension system to support the weight of the vehicle.

lemon law buyback A consumer protection law used in some states to identify a new vehicle that has undergone several unsuccessful attempts to repair the same fault.

lever A tool that allows the user to move a large load over a small distance at one end by applying a small force over a greater distance from the other end.

L-head A type of four-stroke internal combustion engine having both intake and exhaust valves located in one side of the engine block, which are operated by lifters actuated by a single camshaft. It is sometimes called a flat head because there are no valves in the head.

lift The amount the valve will open. The more the valve lifts off its seat, the more air can get into and out of the engine.

lift pump A pump that transfers fuel from the fuel tank to the fuel injection system; also called a transfer pump or supply pump.

lifter A cylindrical component that rides on the camshaft lobe to transmit lobe movement to the valves through a linkage system.

light line technician A technician who diagnoses and replaces the mechanical and electrical components of motor vehicles.

light-emitting diode (LED) A diode that emits light when current flows through it.

limit switches Switches that turn off power flow to an electric motor when a particular limit is reached.

limit value The maximum amount of emissions that a vehicle is permitted to emit. Values are assigned to different classifications of vehicles.

limited slip differential assembly A differential assembly that uses a clutch assembly or gear assembly to allow a limited amount of slip between the two axles. It is used to increase drive wheel traction in slippery conditions.

limp-in mode A transmission operating mode in which limited computer controls are needed to operate for the purpose of getting the vehicle to a shop.

line bored/line honed A process for correcting a mainline that is out of line.

line pressure A hydraulic pressure that is used to apply bands and clutches, and is regulated by the pressure regulator valve.

line pressure sensor A variable resistor sensor used to monitor line pressure. It sends a signal back to the PCM where it can be translated into a psi reading.

linear motion Movement in a straight line.

lines Term used interchangeably with pipes or tubes.

lip-type dynamic oil seal A seal with a precisely shaped dynamic rubber lip that is held in contact with a moving shaft by a garter spring. An example would be a valve seal or camshaft seal.

liquefied natural gas (LNG) A cryogenic liquid produced from gaseous methane.

liquefied petroleum gas (LPG) Gaseous fuel at atmospheric pressure; commonly referred to as propane.

lithium soap A thickening agent for grease to give it the proper consistency.

live axle An axle that is powered and can move the vehicle. It is usually found on the rear of rear-wheel drive vehicles.

load transfer Weight transfer from one set of wheels to the other set of wheels during braking, acceleration, or cornering.

lobe The raised portion on a camshaft; used to lift the lifter and open the valve.

lock cage The stamped sheet metal cap that fits over the bearing adjustment nut and is secured by a cotter pin going through it and the spindle/axle.

lock nut The nut that holds the adjusting nut from turning; usually tightened much tighter than the adjusting nut.

locking hub four-wheel drive front axle hubs that are manually locked or unlocked by turning the knob on the hub.

locking pliers A type of plier where the jaws can be set and locked into position.

lockout solenoid The cam and lock pin operated by an electronic solenoid that keeps the reverse gear in lockout until it is selected.

lockout/tagout A safety tag system to ensure that faulty equipment or equipment in the middle of repair is not used.

long block An engine assembly that includes the short block and adds the valve train cylinder heads, timing cover, oil pan, and, in some cases, manifolds.

longitudinal The orientation of the engine in which the front of the engine is facing the front of the vehicle. It is most commonly found in rear-wheel drive vehicles.

lost foam A metal casting process that uses a foaming process to create the pattern of the part being cast in metal.

low-drag caliper A caliper designed to maintain a larger brake pad-to-rotor clearance by retracting the pistons farther than normal.

Low-Emission Vehicle (LEV) standard A program initiated in California to improve vehicle emission standards.

low-inductance coils Ignition coils designed with low primary winding resistance and a low number of turns. Current flow on these coils is much higher than with contact breaker point systems and reaches its optimum level sooner.

low-pressure accumulator A storage container for brake fluid coming from the release valves, which is under relatively low pressure.

low-pressure cycling switch A device installed on the low-pressure line or the accumulator to turn the air-conditioning clutch on and off at specified pressures.

low-pressure switch A device used in nonvariable air-conditioning compressors. It cycles the air-conditioning clutch in response to changes in low side pressure.

lube technician A technician who carries out scheduled maintenance activities on a range of mechanical and related vehicle components.

lubricating oil Processed crude oil with additives to help it perform well in the engine.

lubrication system A system of parts that work together to deliver lubricating oil to the various moving parts of the engine.

lubricity The ability to lubricate moving parts.

lug nuts Nuts that secure the wheel onto the wheel studs.

lug wrench A tool designed to remove wheel lugs nuts that is commonly shaped like a cross.

lug A flange that is shaped to assist with aligning objects on other objects.

M85 vehicle A flexible-fuel vehicle, meaning any mixture of methanol and gasoline/petrol in the fuel tank can be used by the engine.

MacPherson strut A strut used on an independent suspension where the spring and shock are joined together. Used on most front-wheel drive vehicles.

magnafluxing An electromagnetic process used to locate cracks in ferrous engine blocks and cylinder heads and other ferrous metal parts.

magnetic pickup tools An extending shaft, often flexible, with a magnet fitted to the end for picking up metal objects.

magnetism The force that attracts or repels magnetic charges; or the property of a material to respond to a magnetic field.

magneto-resistive sensor A type of wheel speed sensor that uses an effect similar to a Hall effect sensor to create its signal.

magneto-rheological fluid A fluid that has the unique characteristic of changing viscosity when exposed to a magnetic field.

main bearing A bearing that supports the crankshaft in the block and provides a lubrication surface for the main journals.

main bearing caps Sturdy caps placed over the main journals of the crankshaft assembly and fastened with either two or four bolts.

main bearing journal A bearing surface that supports the crankshaft in the engine block.

main cap girdle A metal attachment that strengthens and connects all the main bearing caps together. It can be integral from the main bearing caps, or separate.

main journal The smooth machined area of the crankshaft assembly that allows the crankshaft to rotate within the main bearings.

mainline The imaginary centerline down the engine cylinder block.

mains The specific round smooth journals of the crankshaft that rotate in main bearings.

male and female terminal A crimp or solder terminal on which the male and female ends join to create a removable low-resistance connection.

malfunction indicator lamp (MIL) An indicator located in the instrument cluster that illuminates when the power train control module (PCM) detects a fault in one of the vehicle systems. Formerly called a check engine or service engine soon light.

Mallory metal A tungsten alloy of copper and nickel that is used as a metal substitute added to the crankshaft counterweight for balancing purposes.

mandrel The shaft of a pop rivet.

mandrel forming The special bending of pipe to ensure the pipe does not collapse. The use of a pipe bender with mandrels allows for very tight bends without creating kinks or reducing the size of the pipe.

mandrel head The head of the pop rivet that connects to the shaft and causes the rivet body to flare.

manifold absolute pressure (MAP) sensor A vacuum sensor that is attached to the intake manifold by a passageway or vacuum hose. The sensor measures engine intake manifold pressure to determine engine load and sends a corresponding signal to the PCM.

manual adjustable-rate shock absorber A shock absorber that allows manual adjustment of the dampening rate.

manual bleeding A bleeding method where one person manually operates the brake pedal while the other person opens and closes the bleeder screws on the wheel brake units to allow the air and old brake fluid to be pushed out.

manual climate control system A climate control system fully controlled by the operator.

manual lever position (MLP) switch A switch that is used by the PCM to tell which gear range the driver has selected with the shift lever.

manually adjustable-air spring A rubber air bag placed inside coil springs to increase the spring's load-carrying ability. It is filled manually through a valve similar to a tire valve stem.

mass airflow (MAF) sensor A sensor located in the air intake system that is used to measure the mass of the air flowing into the engine.

master cylinder Converts the brake pedal force into hydraulic pressure, which is then transmitted via brake lines and hoses to one or more pistons at each wheel brake unit.

match mounting The process of matching up the tire's highest point with the rim's lowest point for the purpose of reducing the tire's radial runout.

material safety data sheet (MSDS) A sheet that provides information about handling, use, and storage of a material that may be hazardous.

measuring tape A thin measuring blade that rolls up and is contained in a spring-loaded dispenser.

mechanical advantage The process of using a device to get more output force than the amount of input force, with the trade-off being that the input distance is proportionately longer than the output distance.

mechanical disadvantage When the load distance on a lever is greater than the effort distance, which means the effort required to move the load is greater than the load itself.

mechanical fingers Spring-loaded fingers at the end of a flexible shaft that pick up items in tight spaces.

mechanical jack A type of vehicle jack that uses mechanical leverage to lift a vehicle.

mechanical pressure control regulator valve A spool valve and spring assembly that are used to control the amount of line pressure in a transmission.

membrane electrode assembly The individual voltage-producing component in a fuel cell stack.

memory saver (memory minder) Battery backup device for vehicle computer systems.

mercaptan An agent that smells like sulfur that is added to liquefied petroleum or natural gas to aid in detecting leaks.

meshed pinion A pinion when it is mated with the rack.

metallurgical bonding A process of sintering metals until they are fused together as one metal.

metering jet A calibrated orifice in a carburetor for fuel to flow through. Often it is replaceable for performance or economy desires.

metering valve A valve used on vehicles equipped with older rear drum/front disc brakes to delay application of the front disc brakes until the rear drum brakes are applied. Located in line with the front disc brakes.

methanol A motor fuel made from wood alcohol.

microleak detector A solution used to detect refrigeration leaks.

micrometer An accurate measuring device for internal and external dimensions. Commonly abbreviated mic.

micron A unit of measurement equal to 0.000039" (0.001 mm).

micron gauge A device designed to measure vacuum very precisely.

microprocessor An electronic control unit that can process data and control one or more devices.

Miller cycle An engine cycle that uses a longer exhaust stroke than intake stroke through delayed closing of the intake valve. This engine uses a supercharger to pressurize air into the cylinder when needed.

min/max setting A setting on a DVOM to display the maximum and minimum readings.

mineral oil Base stock processed from crude oil in a refinery, used as the base material of all conventional oil.

minivan A lighter-duty van used for carrying six to eight occupants or light cargo.

misfire Failure of one or more cylinders to fire or complete combustion.

modulator pressure A pressure created by the vacuum modulator that is proportional to engine load. Modulator pressure is used to delay transmission upshifting based upon engine load. It may also be used to raise line pressure to more firmly apply bands and clutches under higher engine loads.

module An electronic computer or circuit board that controls specific functions.

moly The abbreviation for the lubricant called molybdenum disulfide.

molybdenum thickening agent A compound used in some greases to give it the needed consistency.

monitor An OBDII test run to ensure that a specific component or system is working properly.

Morse taper A tapered mounting shaft for drill bits and chucks in larger drills and lathes.

Morse-style chain A heavy-duty chain constructed of many links and held together with pins. It is used in some transaxles and transfer cases to transmit torque from one component to another.

muffler A device to quiet the pipes of the air-conditioning system with baffles placed inside to deaden the sound of refrigerant moving.

multidisc clutch A type of holding device used by an automatic transmission to stop the movement of one component of a planetary gear set. It uses several thin friction discs and thin steel plates that are squeezed together when hydraulic pressure is applied to a piston in the clutch.

multilayer steel (MLS) head gasket A gasket composed of multiple layers of steel and coated with a rubberlike substance that adheres to metal surfaces. They are typically used between the cylinder head and the cylinder block.

multimeter A test instrument used to measure volts, ohms, and amps. A digital multimeter may also be called a digital volt-ohmmeter (DVOM).

multiphase An electric motor that operates through more than one phase.

multiplate clutch A clutch assembly that is comprised of two or more clutch plates and used to increase the torque-carrying capacity of the clutch.

multiplex The carrying of multiple signals on one wiring circuit. Digital signals are multiplexed on a dedicated CAN-bus or similar network. Also referred to by the abbreviation MUX.

multipoint fuel injection (MPFI) An injection system in which fuel is injected into the intake ports just upstream of each cylinder's intake valve, rather than at a central point within an intake manifold. Also called multiport injection.

mylar tape Polyester film that may be metalized and incorporated into a wiring harness to provide electrical shielding.

National Automotive Technicians Education Foundation (NATEF) An accrediting body for secondary and post-secondary automotive training programs; an independent, nonprofit organization under the umbrella of the ASE.

National Fire Protection Association (NFPA) The agency that publishes standards for liquefied petroleum and compressed natural gas vehicles.

National Lubricating Grease Institute (NLGI) An organization that grades the thickness of automotive and industrial grease.

natural gas Methane; often referred to simply as NG.

needle roller bearing Typically a small-diameter pin rolling bearing that can be held in a cage or placed into the inside diameter of a hole.

needle-nosed pliers Pliers with long tapered jaws for gripping small items and getting into tight spaces.

negative back pressure EGR valve A dual-diaphragm EGR valve that uses vacuum in the exhaust manifold to operate a control diaphragm that opens and closes a vent in the main diaphragm chamber.

negative camber Tilt of the top of the tire toward the centerline of the vehicle.

negative caster Forward tilt of the wheel pivot points from the vertical line.

negative offset A condition in which the plane of the hub mounting surface is positioned toward the brake side or back of the wheel centerline.

negative scrub radius A condition in which the point of center contact between the road surface and the tire and the point where the steering axis centerline contacts the road surface intersect above the road surface.

negative temperature coefficient (NTC) A characteristic of materials whereby resistance decreases as temperature increases.

negative temperature coefficient (NTC) thermistor A thermistor that gains resistance as temperature goes down and loses resistance as temperature goes up.

neutral steer A condition in which both the front and the rear tires of a vehicle are experiencing the same slip angle.

Newton's first law of motion A physical law that states that "an object will stay at rest or uniform speed unless it is acted upon by an outside force."

NFPA-52 A document from the NFPA that sets standards for compressed natural gas refueling stations and compressed natural gas vehicle fuel systems.

nippers (pincer pliers) Pliers designed to cut protruding items level with the surface.

nitriding A metal surfacing process that uses nitrogen ammonia gas to create a very thin, highly hardened surface.

nitridization process The nitriding metal surfacing process in which nitrogen ammonia gas is used inside a furnace and heated up and then cooled.

nitrile butadiene rubber (NBR) A man-made rubber that is more resistant to oils and acids than natural rubber; it is compatible with R-12.

nitrogen oxides (NOx) The various compounds of nitrogen that contributed to a smog-forming pollutant emitted from the tailpipe.

noise, vibration, and harshness (NVH) test A test to measure for any audible noises, vibrations, and harsh operation. It can be completed by the technician with or without the aid of an NVH tester. The tester is used to pinpoint the exact frequencies of the noise and vibrations.

noncontinuous monitor A monitor that runs only once per drive cycle.

nondirectional tread pattern A tread pattern that is nonspecific, allowing the tire to be placed on any wheel of a vehicle.

nonintegral ABS systems A brake system in which the master cylinder, power booster, and HCU are all separate units.

non-integral valve guide Also called a replaceable valve guide, a valve guide that is pressed into the cylinder head after the head has been constructed. These guides can be removed and replaced.

normally closed (NC) An electrical contact that is closed in the at-rest position.

normally open (NO) An electrical contact that is open in the at-rest position.

NPN transistor A transistor in which P-type material is sandwiched between two layers of N-type material.

N-type Semiconductor material with a small amount of extra electrons.

number one cylinder Typically the cylinder located farthest forward on the engine. It is the first cylinder in the firing order.

nut A fastener with a hexagonal head and internal threads for screwing on bolts.

Occupational Safety and Health Administration (OSHA) Government agency created to provide national leadership in occupational safety and health.

octane rating A standard measure of the performance of a motor or aviation fuel. The higher the octane number, the more heat the fuel can withstand before self-igniting.

odorant An agent (mercaptan) that smells like sulfur that is added to liquefied petroleum or natural gas to aid in detecting leaks.

off-car brake lathe A tool used to machine (refinish) drums and rotors after they have been removed from the vehicle.

offset area An area on the crankshaft that is offset from the crankshaft centerline and that becomes a counterweight.

offset screwdriver A screwdriver with a 90-degree bend in the shaft for working in tight spaces.

offset vice A vice that allows long objects to be gripped vertically.

ohm The unit for measuring electrical resistance.

Ohm's law A law that defines the relationship between current, resistance, and voltage.

oil control ring The widest of the metal rings on the piston head assembly that controls oil flow to and from the cylinder walls.

oil cooler A device that takes heat away from engine oil by passing it near either engine coolant or outside air. Cooling the engine oil helps to keep it from overheating and breaking down.

oil filter wrench A specialized wrench that allows extra leverage to remove an oil filter when it is tight.

oil monitoring system A system that alerts the driver when it is time to change engine oil. These systems will need to be reset for the customer after an oil change is performed.

oil pan The metal pan that covers the bottom of the engine, contains oil sump where engine oil is held.

oil pressure relief valve A valve usually located in the oil pump that limits the oil pressure. When oil pressure is reached, excessive pressure is bled back to the sump.

oil pump A device that pumps lubricating oil through the engine.

oil pump strainer A screen located on the oil pump pickup that keeps debris from being picked up by the oil pump.

oil ring groove A metal groove cut into the piston head assembly designed to hold the oil control ring, which lubricates the cylinder wall and pistons.

oil seal Any seal used to seal oil in and dirt, moisture, and debris out.

oil slinger A device that rides partially in the transmission fluid; as it spins, it flings oil to lubricate the internal workings of the transmission.

oil spurt holes Holes drilled into the connecting rod that spray oil up onto the cylinder walls and the piston wrist pins.

oil sump The lower part of the oil pan that holds lubricating oil for the engine. The oil pickup screen sits in this low point.

oiler A device used to add oil to the air-conditioning system.

oil galleries Oil passages that are drilled into the engine block and cylinder head(s). These passageways carry oil from the oil pump to critical moving parts.

on/off–type signal A signal that is either a 12-volt signal or zero volts. Typically, switches provide on/off signals. Some systems use a 5-volt reference signal instead of a 12-volt signal.

on-board diagnostic (OBD) The first generation of a self-diagnostic system built into the vehicle computer system that provided a means of warning the driver when the computer detected a problem in the system. This system allowed the technician to retrieve codes to assist in diagnosis of the vehicle.

on-board diagnostic II (OBDII) This generation of self-diagnostic systems mandated standardized diagnostic trouble codes and a data link connector. It also mandated monitoring of certain emission systems, such as the catalytic converter, oxygen sensor, EGR, and evaporative emissions.

on-car brake lathe A tool used to machine (refinish) rotors while they are still attached to the vehicle.

one-way clutch A type of holding device used by an automatic transmission to stop the movement of one component of a planetary gear set. It allows free spinning in one direction but will lock up when the part attempts to spin in the opposite direction.

open circuit A circuit that has a break that prevents current from flowing.

open differential assembly A differential assembly that allows both axles to turn at their own speed when turning a corner, but is dependent on the traction of the tires to deliver torque to the ground. If one wheel has no traction, all of the engine's torque will be used at that wheel, causing it to simply spin.

open fracture A fracture in which the bone is protruding through the skin or there is severe bleeding.

open A term used to describe a circuit that does not have a complete path for current to flow.

open-end wrench A wrench with open jaws to allow side entry to a nut or bolt.

optical cable A cable that contains a number of optical fibers.

optical sensor A sensor that generates a voltage when excited by a beam of light.

orifice A precisely sized hole used to reduce the speed and pressure of hydraulic oil flowing to a clutch or band.

O-ring Rubber-type rings available in different sizes used to seal pipe fittings.

O-ring seal A seal that is a complete circle. If a cutaway is done, it will also be a complete circle. These seals are usually set into a groove that is machined into the housing or part that does not move and is intended to be sealed.

O-ring valve stem seal A seal used where the valve spring retainer attaches to the valve stem to seal the juncture and prevent excessive oil from leaking into the valve stem.

oscillate To cycle above and below a given value.

oscillation The fluctuation of an object between two states. With regard to suspension springs, it refers to the uncontrolled compression and decompression of the spring following overshoot.

oscilloscope A tool that shows graphically what is happening to voltage over a period of time; it is used to diagnose electrical faults.

outer race The outside component of a wheel bearing that has a smooth, hardened surface for rollers or balls to ride on.

outer tie-rod The tie-rod attached between the tie-rod and the steering arm. It transfers the movement of the rack, pivoting as the rack is extended or retracted when the vehicle is negotiating turns.

outlet port Links the cylinder to the brake lines.

output force Force that equals the working pressure multiplied by the surface area of the output piston, expressed as pounds, newtons, or kilograms.

output signal The voltage sent to solenoids and motors by the PCM to do work.

outside micrometer A precision measuring instrument meant to measure the outside of components. It is usually accurate to 0.0001" (0.0025 mm).

overcharging Overfilling of the air-conditioning system; may result in poor cooling or mechanical failure of the system.

overdrive Any gear ratio that results in a torque reduction with a speed increase. Overdrive is used on vehicles to reduce the engine speed when traveling at highway speed in order to save fuel.

overflow tank A tank used to catch any coolant that is released from the radiator cap (works like a catch can).

overhauling The process of refurbishing the transmission to like-new condition.

overhead cam (OHC) engine An I-head engine with the camshaft located on top of the cylinder head rather than in the block.

overhead valve (OHV) engine An engine in which the valves are positioned in the cylinder head assembly, directly over the top of the piston.

overshoot The amount a spring extends (springs back) past its original length following compression.

oversteer A condition in which a vehicle's front slip angles are larger than the rear slip angles. This vehicle is said to be "pushing" in the corners.

owner's manual An informational guide supplied by the manufacturer; it contains basic vehicle operating information.

oxidation inhibitor An oil additive that helps keep hot oil from combining with oxygen to produce sludge or tar.

oxides of nitrogen A vehicle emission that contributes to ground-level ozone. Oxides of nitrogen are produced when nitrogen and oxygen react during combustion, given sufficient temperatures and pressures. Forms include nitrogen oxide and nitrogen dioxide.

oxyacetylene torch A gas welding system that combines oxygen and acetylene.

oxygen sensor (before and after catalytic convertor) An exhaust sensor used to measure the amount of oxygen in the exhaust gases produced by the engine PCM, used to determine fuel mixture and spark timing.

P-type Semiconductor material with holes where electrons are missing.

paddle A shifting mechanism or electronic control usually attached to the steering wheel.

pan inspection The process of removing the transmission pan to check for clutch material, metal, and other debris or contaminants.

panhard rod A metal rod used to hold the dead axle and keep it from moving from side to side through corners. It is mounted on the body or frame of the vehicle and the axle. Also referred to as a track bar.

parade pattern The display of all the cylinders firing in sequence on an oscilloscope.

parallax error A visual error caused by viewing measurement markers at an incorrect angle.

parallel flow condenser A condenser with multiple parallel tubes flowing from one side tank to the other.

parallel hybrid A hybrid vehicle driven simultaneously by an internal combustion engine and an electric machine.

parallel hybrid drive train A type of hybrid transmission in which power can flow from either a gasoline engine or an electric motor and any combination of the two.

parallelism Also called thickness variation; both surfaces of the rotor should be perfectly parallel to each other so that brake pulsations do not occur.

parallelogram steering system A non–rack-and-pinion system that uses a series of parts consisting of the pitman arm, idler arm, center link, and tie-rod assemblies that relays movement from the steering gearbox to the wheel assembly.

parasitic draw Unwanted drain on the vehicle battery when the vehicle is off.

parasitic loss A loss of engine efficiency caused by internal friction, inefficient breathing, etc.

parking brake A brake system used for holding the vehicle when it is stationary.

parking brake cable A mechanism used to transmit force from the parking brake actuating lever to the brake unit.

parking brake cable pliers A tool used to install parking brake cables.

parking brake cable removal tool A tool used to compress the spring steel fingers of the parking brake cable so that the cable can be removed from the backing plate.

parking brake mechanism A mechanism that operates the brake shoes or pads to hold the vehicle stationary when the parking brake is applied.

particulate matter (PM) Unseen microscopic particles of carbon consisting of soot (especially prominent with diesel exhaust). PM clogs the lungs and is carcinogenic.

parts program A computer software program for identifying and ordering replacement vehicle parts.

parts specialist The person who serves customers at the parts counters.

Pascal's law The law of physics that states that pressure applied to a fluid in one part of a closed system will be transmitted equally to all other areas of the system.

passive keyless entry (PKE) An active system that senses the proximity of a fob and locks or unlocks the vehicle.

PCV valve A valve that controls the amount of crankcase ventilation flow that is allowed and varies with changes in manifold pressure.

peening A term used to describe the action of flattening a rivet through a hammering action.

performance testing The process of recreating a driving situation to check air-conditioning performance and vent temperature.

permanent magnet A material with natural or man-made constant magnetic properties.

permanent magnet electric motor An electric motor in which the magnetic field in the casing is produced by permanent magnets, while the armature has an electromagnetic field generated by passing electrical current through loops or windings, thereby producing the motor action.

permanently mounted tank A compressed natural gas or propane cylinder not designed to be portable.

personal protective equipment (PPE) Safety equipment designed to protect the technician, such as safety boots, gloves, clothing, protective eyewear, and hearing protection.

phase A term used to describe one set of windings from an alternator or alternating current electric motor.

phaser A device that is able to shift camshaft timing while the camshaft is turning. This device takes the place of the standard timing belt pulley or timing chain gear.

phenolic resin A material used to create some brake pistons that is very resistant to corrosion and heat transfer.

Phillips head screwdriver A type of screwdriver that fits a head shaped like a cross in screws.

photochemical smog A brown haze that hangs in the sky, typically seen over large cities. Smog is a major health issue to humans because it affects lung tissue.

photodiode An electronic component that creates a varying voltage or current output based on the amount of light striking it.

photovoltaic (PV) effect The conversion of sunlight into electricity.

pick-up A vehicle that carries cargo; it has stronger chassis components and suspension than a sedan.

pick-up assembly A component with a wire coil wrapped around a ferrous metal core; it is used to generate an electrical signal when a magnetic field passes through it.

pickup tube A tube connected to the oil pump that acts like a straw for the oil pump to pull oil from the sump of the oil pan.

piezoelectric A type of electricity in which a material such as a quartz crystal produces voltage when mechanical pressure distorts it.

pilot bearing The bearing or bushing that supports the front of the transmission input shaft.

pin punch A type of punch in various sizes with a straight or parallel shaft.

pinging A preignition or detonation concern that is damaging to the engine if it is allowed to continue. It is described as the sound of marbles being shaken in a glass jar.

pinion shaft On a drive axle using a ring-and-pinion gear assembly, the input component that drives the ring gear.

pinions The small gears in a planetary gear set that revolve around the sun gear, also known as planetary gears.

pintle A tapered valve that sits in a tapered seat to seal a passageway for air or fuel.

pip mark A small indent or dimple on the piston ring that indicates which side of the ring is installed upward. It is also used on some timing sprockets.

pipe wrench A wrench that grips pipes and can exert a lot of force to turn them. Because the handle pivots slightly, the more pressure put on the handle to turn the wrench, the more the grip tightens.

piston The round metal plug found inside the engine cylinder that moves up and down inside the cylinder.

piston assembly All of the parts of the piston including the piston, piston rings, and piston pin.

piston clearance The clearance between the piston and the cylinder wall that allows for lubricating oil to reduce friction.

piston displacement The volume of air that is moved by the piston from bottom dead center to top dead center.

piston engine An internal combustion engine that uses cylindrical pistons moving back and forth in a cylinder to extract mechanical energy from chemical energy.

piston pin (wrist pin) A round circular metal manufactured part that attaches the piston assembly to the connecting rod assembly.

piston pin boss The reinforced area of the piston where the piston wrist pin attaches the piston to the connecting rod.

piston ring A metal ring that is placed in a square groove around a piston for sealing purposes.

piston ring groove A square-cut groove located on the piston designed to hold a metal piston ring.

piston skirt The area below the ring groove area of the piston that prevents the piston from cocking and becoming jammed in the cylinder bore.

piston slap An engine noise caused by excessive clear-ance between the piston skirt area and the cylinder wall.

piston stroke The distance the piston travels through the engine cylinder from top dead center to bottom dead center.

pitch circle diameter (PCD) The diameter of the imaginary circle drawn through the center of the wheel bolt holes.

pitch (brakes) Movement of a vehicle around its y-axis (the imaginary line across the center of the vehicle from left to right) that causes the vehicle to lower or rise on the front end during quick braking or acceleration.

pitch (bolts) On a helix, the distance moved in one full revolution of the cylinder.

pitch The angle of a fan blade. A steeper pitch draws more air, while a shallower pitch draws less air.

planet carrier The device that holds the planet gears in place, keeping them equally spaced.

planetary gears The small gears in a planetary gear set that revolve around the sun gear; also known as pinion gears.

plasma cutter A tool that uses electricity and compressed gas to produce a stream of high-temperature gas to cut metal.

Plastigauge® The trademarked name for a plastic gauging material used to check the clearances between two surfaces.

plate A flat thin square or rectangular sheet of material often used to describe the arrangement of positive and negative electrodes in batteries.

plenum chamber A large portion of the intake manifold after the throttle plate and before the intake runner tubes. The plenum provides a reservoir of air and helps prevent interference with the flow of air between individual branches.

pliers A hand tool with gripping jaws.

plug-in hybrid electric vehicle (PHEV) A hybrid electric vehicle in which only one power source, the battery, is used to propel the vehicle for a certain distance, limited by the storage capacity of the battery and the efficiency of the motor.

plunge-type joint The inner joint on the half shaft that allows for changes in shaft length.

ply rating A rating system that denotes the number of belt layers or plies that make up the tire carcass. In radial tires, ply rating denotes the relative strength of the plies, not the actual number of plies.

PN junction The junction between N- and P-type semiconductor materials.

pneumatic jack A type of vehicle jack that uses compressed gas or air to lift a vehicle.

PNP transistor A transistor in which N-type material is sandwiched between two layers of P-type material. This type of semiconductor material has holes, meaning it is missing electrons.

pocket bearing A roller in the rear of the input shaft that supports the front of the main shaft.

polarity The state of charge, positive or negative.

polarity sensitive A term used to describe a component that must be connected into a circuit with the correct polarity to its terminals.

policy A guiding principle that sets the shop direction.

pollutant A potential threat to human health or the environment resulting from excessive amounts of chemicals and waste.

polyalphaolefin (PAO) A man-made base stock (synthetic) used in place of mineral oil. Oil molecules are more consistent in size and no impurities are found in this oil since it is made in a lab.

polycrystalline diamond (PCD) cutter An engine block resurfacing tool used on aluminum parts.

pop rivet gun A hand tool for installing pop rivets.

poppet (mushroom) valve A cam-operated, spring-loaded mushroom-type valve used to control intake into, and exhaust out of, the combustion chamber.

poppet valve A valve that controls the flow of brake fluid at usually preset pressures.

portable universal cylinder A liquefied petroleum gas tank that can be moved or transported.

positive back pressure EGR valve A dual-diaphragm EGR valve that uses pressure in the exhaust system to act on the control diaphragm, which closes a bleed valve in the main diaphragm, allowing the EGR valve to open only when there is positive exhaust pressure.

positive camber Tilt of the top of the tire out from the centerline of the vehicle.

positive caster Backward tilt of the wheel pivot points from the vertical line.

positive crankcase ventilation (PCV) system A system that draws blow-by gases from the crankcase into the intake to be burned.

positive offset A condition in which the plane of the hub mounting surface is positioned toward the outside or front of the wheel centerline.

positive scrub radius A condition in which the point of center contact between the road surface and the tire and the point where the steering axis centerline contacts the road surface intersect below the road surface.

positive temperature coefficient (PTC) A characteristic of materials whereby resistance increases as temperature increases.

positive valve stem seal A valve seal located at the top of the valve guide that is a more positive seal than an umbrella or O-ring seal.

potentiometer A variable resistor that can be used to adjust voltage in a circuit.

pour point The temperature below which the fuel will not flow.

pour point depressants Oil additives that keep wax crystals from forming and causing the oil to gel during cold operation.

powdered metal rod A connecting rod manufactured through the process of heat, compression, and forging of powdered metals into a connecting rod.

power The rate at which work is done; electrical power is measured in watts.

power assist unit The electric motor in electric power assist steering systems.

power chip An aftermarket performance programmable chip marketed to increase horsepower and mileage of electronically controlled diesel engines.

power divider/splitter A device that receives power from an internal combustion engine and electric machine to power a hybrid electric vehicle.

power flow The path that power takes from the beginning of an assembly to the end. In a transmission, power flow changes as different gears are selected by the driver.

power section A chamber in the rack where pressurized fluid acts upon pistons that assist in steering.

power steering An option on a vehicle that allows movement of the steering wheel with decreased driver effort.

power steering pump A small hydraulic pump that provides assistance to the driver when turning the steering wheel.

power stroke The stroke during which combustion is pushing the piston from top dead center to bottom dead center in the cylinder. This stroke is where power is produced.

power take-off (PTO) A device attached to the transmission that is gear driven and can be used to run accessories such as winches and towing equipment. It can also refer to the gears that send power to the rear axle in a predominantly front wheel drive vehicle.

power tools Tools powered by electricity or compressed air.

power train control module (PCM) The electronic "brain" controlling the engine and related systems. The PCM handles more tasks than the former ECM (engine control module) used on earlier emission-controlled vehicles.

power train mount A rubber or metal bracket used to secure the engine and transmission into the vehicle. Some vehicles use hydraulic or electrohydraulic power train mounts.

power unit A belt or gear-driven pump that produces hydraulic pressure for use in the steering box or rack.

power winding The current-carrying winding in an alternator or motor.

power-on-demand A feature that shuts down the engine when not needed to save fuel.

power-splitting transmission (PST) A type of hybrid transmission that splits the power flow going to the wheels from one or more electric motors and an internal combustion engine.

prechamber A separate combustion area designed into a diesel cylinder head.

preload The level of pressure placed on bearings that ensures the bearings will be held together.

press-fit pin A description of how a piston pin is placed inside a connecting rod by pressing the pin into the connecting rod.

pressure The force per unit area applied to the surface of an object.

pressure bleeding A bleeding method that uses clean brake fluid under pressure from an auxiliary tool or piece of equipment to force the air and old brake fluid from the hydraulic braking system.

pressure differential valve A valve that monitors any pressure difference between the two separate hydraulic brake circuits; it usually contains a switch to turn on the brake warning light when there is a pressure difference.

pressure gauge set A set of calibrated gauges for high and low pressure that can show pressure and vacuum readings for use with air-conditioning systems.

pressure plate The assembly that applies and removes the clamping force on the clutch disc.

pressure relief valve A valve that is designed to release pressure if it gets above a calibrated pressure; used in a gas cap as a safety device to release excessive pressure if pressure gets too high.

pressure testing A process for checking the aluminum cylinder heads for cracks using air pressure.

pressure transducer A device used to measure engine vacuum and display it graphically on a lab scope.

pressure transients Minor fluctuations on the gauges that may indicate a problem.

pressure washer/cleaner A cleaning machine that boosts low-pressure tap water to a high-pressure output.

pressure, or force-feed, lubrication system A lubrication system that has a pump to pressurize the lubricating oil and push it through the engine to moving parts.

prick punch A pinch with a sharp point for accurately marking a point on metal.

primary circuit The low-voltage circuit that turns the coil on and off.

primary cup A seal that holds pressure in the master cylinder when force is applied to the piston.

primary piston A brake piston in the master cylinder moved directly by the pushrod or the power-booster; it generates hydraulic pressure to move the secondary piston.

primary winding The coil of wire in the low voltage circuit that creates the magnetic field in a step-up transformer.

printed circuitry Circuitry that forms the framework for electronic module construction. A printed circuit board holds electronic components that are soldered into place.

probing technique The way in which test probes are connected to a circuit.

procedure A list of the steps required to get the same result each time a task or activity is performed.

producer gas A generic term that refers to a number of manufactured gases such as wood gas, town gas, and syngas.

programmed fuel delivery map A chart programmed into the vehicle's computer that is referenced as the vehicle is running. Sensor input data are compared to the delivery map to calculate the desired output signal.

progressive rate of deflection The change in deflection rate that occurs as the weight of the vehicle changes. The greater the weight, the lower the rate of deflection due to increased resistance.

proportioning valves Valves used mostly on older vehicles equipped with rear drum brakes to reduce rear wheel hydraulic brake pressure under hard braking or light loads. Located in line with the rear brakes.

propylene-glycol A chemical used as anti-freeze. It is labeled as a nontoxic anti-freeze.

pry bar A high-strength carbon steel rod with off-sets for levering and prying.

PT chart A pressure-temperature chart that shows the relationship between air-conditioning pressures and evaporator temperature.

pull-in winding A high-current winding found in starter solenoids that pulls the solenoid plunger into the activated position.

pullers A generic term to describe hand tools that mechanically assist the removal of bearings, gears, pulleys, and other parts.

pulse air system The use of normal exhaust engine pulses to draw air into the exhaust stream.

pulse width modulation (PWM) A digital on/off electrical signal used as a variable control for devices such as solenoids.

pulse-width modulation (combustion) The time that the fuel injectors are turned off and on to inject a precise amount of fuel.

punches A generic term to describe a high-strength carbon steel shaft with a blunt point for driving. Center and prick punches are exceptions and have a sharp point for marking or making an indentation.

purge solenoid A control device that lets fuel vapors move from the charcoal canister to the engine. The solenoid is controlled by the engine control module.

purge switch A device used to show the computer when purge is occurring. It is used as a feedback device to allow the computer to determine whether flow is happening.

purge valve A valve used to control the flow of evaporative emissions from the charcoal canister to the intake manifold.

purging The process of pulling stored fuel vapors from the charcoal canister and moving them into the engine to be burned.

push-on spade terminal A disconnectable type of crimp or solder terminal used to terminate electrical wires.

pushrod A long, thin cylindrical shaft that provides a linkage between the lifters and the rocker arms to control valve opening and closing.

pushrod (braking system) A mechanism used to transmit force from the brake pedal to the master cylinder.

push-type clutch A typical clutch system used in modern vehicles where the clutch fork pushes the release bearing forward to release the friction facing from the pressure plate.

quadrant ratchet The device used in some cable-operated clutches to provide self-adjustment as the clutch disc wears. Some quadrant ratchets adjust if you lift up on the clutch pedal.

quench or squish area The narrow area between the top of the piston at top dead center and the cylinder head. It derives its name from the squishing of the air/fuel mixture into a small "charge."

quenched The state in a combustion chamber in which the flame cannot burn due to cold surfaces or poor distribution of the fuel mixture.

quick take-up master cylinders Cylinders used on disc brake systems that are equipped with low-drag brake calipers to quickly move the brake pads into contact with the brake rotors.

quick take-up valve A valve used to release excess pressure from the larger piston in a quick take-up master cylinder once the brake pads have contacted the brake rotors.

rack A steel rod driven by the pinion with tie-rods on each end or tie-rods connected to the center of the rack.

rack housing The outer shell of the rack-and-pinion steering system that is mounted to the chassis.

rack-and-pinion steering system A steering system composed of a steering wheel, a main shaft, universal joints, and an intermediate shaft. When the steering wheel is turned, movement is transferred by the main shaft and intermediate shaft to the pinion.

radial load The load that is perpendicular to a shaft, usually controlled by bearings or bushings.

radial tire A tire with two or more layers of casing plies and cord loops running radially from bead to bead.

radiation The transfer of heat through the emission of energy in the form of invisible waves.

radiator A device that takes hot coolant and cools it by passing heat energy to the surrounding air.

radiator hoses Rubber hoses that connect the radiator to the engine. Because they are subject to pressure, they are reinforced with a layer of fabric, typically nylon.

radius A straight line extending from the center of a circle to its edge or from the center of a sphere to its surface.

ram airflow The flow of air created by a vehicle moving down the road.

raster The scope pattern where all of the ignition firing sequences are stacked vertically on top of each other.

ratchet A generic term to describe a handle for sockets that allows the user to select direction of rotation. It can turn sockets in restricted areas without the user having to remove the socket from the fastener.

ratcheting box-end wrench A wrench with an inner piece that is able to rotate within the outer housing, allowing it to be repositioned without being removed.

ratcheting screwdriver A screwdriver with a selectable ratchet mechanism built into the handle that allows the screwdriver tip to ratchet as it is being used.

rattle gun A term used describe an air impact wrench based on the noise it makes.

Ravigneaux gear set A type of compound planetary gear set that uses two different sun gears and two different-diameter planets while only using one ring gear.

reaction force A force that acts in the opposite direction to another force.

rear-wheel drive (RWD) A drive train layout in which the engine drives the rear wheels.

rebound clip A metal strap that is warped around the leaf spring to prevent excessive flexing of the main leaf during rebound.

receiver filter drier (RFD) The air-conditioning component used on TXV systems to filter and store liquid refrigerant to supply liquid refrigerant to the TXV. It is located between the condenser and the TXV.

reciprocating motion An up-and-down motion within the cylinder.

reciprocating weight The amount of weight that is moving up and down. It is everything from the middle of the connecting rod upward, including the piston, wrist pin, and rings.

reciprocation The back-and-forth movement of the piston assembly inside the cylinder.

recirculating ball steering box A steering box that has worm gear inside a block with a threaded hole in it and gear teeth cut into its outside that engage the sector shaft to move the pitman arm; generally used on trucks and heavy vehicles.

reclaim/recycle machine An air-conditioning machine designed to remove and recycle refrigerant for reuse.

reclaiming The process of removing refrigerant from the air-conditioning system by using an air-conditioning machine; also called recovering.

recovering See *reclaiming*.

rectification A process of converting AC into DC required by the battery and nearly all of the automobile systems.

recuperation Process by which brake fluid moves from the reservoir past the edges of the seal into the chamber in front of the piston. This prevents air from being drawn into the hydraulic system caused by low pressure when the brake pedal is released quickly.

reductant A reducing agent.

reduction ratio The ratio between the turn of the steering wheel and the turn of the wheel, both measured in degrees.

reed switch A type of speed sensor that uses a magnetic field to open and close a movable set of contacts. It is used with a rotating magnet to measure rpm of a shaft and send the signal to the PCM.

reed valve A flexible valve made from spring steel that flexes to open or close, usually due to pressure changes.

reformer An on-board device that extracts hydrogen from another source material.

refrigerant The name given to a chemical compound designed to meet the needs of the refrigeration system.

refrigerant identifiers Devices used to check for impurities in the air-conditioning system.

refrigerant label A label that lists the type and total capacity of refrigerant that is installed in the A/C system.

regenerative braking Technology used in vehicles that allows the vehicle to recapture and store part of the vehicle's kinetic energy in a reusable form when braking. Primarily used in hybrid and electric vehicles.

relay An electromechanical switching device whereby the magnetism from a coil winding acts on a lever that switches a set of contacts.

relay lever A steel rod that transfers movement from the drag link to an idler arm.

release mechanisms Components that operate the clutch. Usually included are the throw-out bearing and the clutch fork. Some manufacturers include the operating system.

reluctor A rotating, toothed wheel that changes the reluctance of a material to conduct magnetic lines of force.

remote keyless entry (RKE) A system that remotely unlocks and locks the vehicle without the use of a traditional key.

repair order A form used by shops to collect information regarding a vehicle coming in for repair, also referred to as a work order.

required voltage The amount of voltage needed to push current across the electrodes of a spark plug located in the combustion chamber.

reserve capacity A standard used to specify the time in minutes that a battery will supply a load of 25 amps at 80°F (27°C) without its voltage dropping below 10.5 volts.

residual pressure valve (residual check valve) In drum brake systems, a valve that maintains pressure in the wheel cylinders slightly above atmospheric pressure so that air does not enter the system through the seals in the wheel cylinders.

resistor A component designed to have a fixed resistance.

resistor in series A resistor added to the circuit before or after the load to drop voltage to the load.

respirator Protective gear used to protect the wearer from inhaling harmful dusts or gases. Respirators range from single-use disposable masks to types that have replaceable cartridges. The correct types of cartridge must be used for the type of contaminant encountered.

restriction A blockage that partially stops or slows the flow of a material such as refrigerant.

retarding effect The result of retarding (slowing) the vehicle.

retrofit kit An aftermarket kit that has the fittings and oil to change an R-12 unit over to an R-134a unit.

return springs Springs that retract the brake shoes to their released position.

returnless fuel injection system A type of injection system in which no hot fuel is returned to the tank, thus keeping the fuel in the tank relatively cool and minimizing vaporization.

reverse boost valve A component of the pressure regulator valve that increases line pressure when the vehicle is in reverse.

reverse shift fork A shift fork used to engage the reverse gear.

rheostat An adjustable resistor that varies current flow through a circuit.

rib A design feature created in the metal casting/forging process that places extra metal area on a part for strength and durability, yet keeps the weight of the engine block low.

ribbon cable A type of flat harness in which cables are insulated from each other but joined together side by side.

ridge reamer A tool used to remove the metal lip on top of the cylinder walls caused by engine wear.

rigid non drive axle suspension A type of dead axle suspension system that is non-independent and uses a beam or solid axle.

rigid spring hanger The rigid part typically welded to the body or frame of the vehicle to which the front of the leaf spring is attached.

rigid-axle coil-spring suspension A dead axle that uses a coil spring.

rim The outer circular lip of the metal on which the inside edge of the tire is mounted.

rim flanges The outside edge of the wheel that helps keep the tire from popping off the wheel.

rim width The distance across the rim from one rim flange to the other.

ring gap The distance between the ends of the piston rings when the rings are seated against the inside of the engine cylinder.

ring gear The outer gear of a planetary gear set. The ring gear wraps around the outside of the planetary gears.

ring lands The metal between the ring grooves that supports the rings as the piston moves.

ring tension The built-in force created inside the piston rings due to the fact that the piston rings are made bigger than the cylinder walls to generate a scraping action against the cylinder walls.

rising characteristic A characteristic at a fixed fuel setting where the amount of fuel delivered to the engine will increase as engine speed and pump speed increase.

riveted linings Brake linings riveted to the brake pad backing plate with metal rivets and used on heavier-duty or high-performance vehicles.

rocker arm A lever that actuates a valve by pivoting near the center and pushing on the tip of the valve to open it.

rod A straight piece of steel used to transfer motion within the vehicle's suspension system. It typically has treads cut on one or both ends.

rod beam The area of connecting rod between the big and small ends.

rod bearing A bearing insert located in the big end of the connecting rod.

rod bearing journal A bearing surface that is offset from the centerline of the crankshaft.

rod cap The very bottom part of the connecting rod that retains the rod bearing inserts.

rod journal Also called the crankshaft rod throw, an area machined to a very smooth finish that contains an oil hole to provide oil to lubricate the surfaces of the crankshaft and rod bearing inserts.

roll Movement of a vehicle around its x-axis (the imaginary line down the center of the vehicle from front to back). It is commonly referred to as body roll or lean; when cornering, the body will try to move to the outside of the corner against the suspension.

roll bar Another type of pry bar, with one end used for prying and the other end for aligning larger holes, such as engine motor mounts.

roller bearing A long cylindrical roller held in position by a cage.

rolling code A constantly changing, randomly selected numeric code that is communicated with the engine immobilizer and security system.

rolling resistance Resistance that is present from tires contacting the road and wind resistance against the vehicle while rolling down the highway.

roll-rate sensor A sensor that measures the amount of roll around the vehicle's horizontal axis that a vehicle is experiencing.

room temperature vulcanizing (RTV) silicone A silicone adhesive that sets up or "vulcanizes" at room temperature.

rosin A type of liquid or paste (flux) used to prevent oxidization that is in solid form contained within the solder.

rotary engine An engine that uses a triangular rotor turning in a housing instead of conventional pistons.

rotary flow A type of fluid flow in a torque converter in which fluid flows around the centerline of the torque converter in a circle.

rotary vane compressor A compressor design that spins with vanes attached that extend to create the air-conditioning pressure required to run the system.

rotating assembly The assembly of the crankshaft, connecting rod, and piston that are found inside the engine cylinder block.

rotating weight The amount of weight that is moving in a circular motion, including everything from the center of the connecting rod down to the connecting rod cap and all components of the crankshaft.

rotational force The force created by the rotating wheel when the brakes are applied; it causes the brake components to twist the brake support and ultimately the vehicle in the direction of wheel rotation.

rotational speed The speed at which an object rotates, measured in revolutions per minute (rpm).

rotor (brakes) The main rotating part of a disc brake system.

rotor (engine) A high-voltage rotating switch that transfers voltage from the distributor cap's center terminal to the outer terminals.

rotor arm The portion of the rotor that extends toward, but not touching, the outer distributor cap terminals.

rotor housing The engine block of the rotary engine. The rotor moves within it.

rotor lobes Lobes or rounded edges on rotors that squeeze oil and create pressure.

rotor pump A type of front pump found in automatic transmissions. The rotor pump has two different-sized rotors that mesh together to force fluid out of the pump.

rotor-type oil pump An oil pump that uses rounded gears to squeeze oil through.

rubber bellows Rubber pieces positioned on each end of the rack to protect the inner joints from dirt and contaminants and retain the grease lubricant inside the rack-and-pinion housing.

rubber-bonded bushing A bushing that has a steel outer housing and inner sleeve with rubber inside; also known as a metalastic bushing.

run-flat technology A tire design that allows the vehicle to keep moving under driver control following a puncture or rapid loss of pressure.

running clearance The amount of space between wheel bearing components while in operation.

Rzeppa joint A type of fixed constant velocity joint that has an inner race, six steel ball bearings, a bearing cage, and an outer race.

SAE J1930 An SAE standard for across-the-board standardization of parts and systems nomenclature.

SAE J2012 An SAE standard for across-the-board identification of generic DTCs.

safe working load (SWL) The maximum safe lifting load for lifting equipment.

safety-type drop-center rim A rim designed with a slight hump at the inside edge of the bead ledges to hold the tire beads in place during a flat tire.

salvage title Also called a branded title; a record that a vehicle has been severely damaged or deemed a total loss by an insurance company.

sand or bead blasters A cleaning system that uses high-pressure fine particles of glass bead or sand.

Sanden scroll-type compressor A compressor design that uses two spiral forms, one spinning and one stationary, to create the pressure needed to drive the air-conditioning system.

Sanden wobble plate compressor A compressor design that utilizes an offset shaft connected to the crankshaft to create the reciprocating motion of the pistons.

sander/polisher A power tool with a rotating disc or head to which polishing or sanding discs can be attached.

scan tool A plug-in electronic device for extracting and interpreting fault codes (DTCs) in the automobile, plus much more.

scavenge pump A pump used with a dry sump oiling system to pull oil from the dry sump pan and move it to an oil tank outside the engine.

scavenging The process of removing burned gases from the cylinder through the use of moving airflow pulling or extracting the gases out.

scavenging effect A condition caused by moving columns of air, which create a low-pressure area behind them, resulting in a pulling force that is used to pull the remaining burned gases from the combustion chamber. Valve timing affects the amount of scavenging effect an engine has.

Schrader valve A one-way valve used in a valve stem.

scratcher A thin, spring steel wear indicator that is fixed to the backing plate of the brake pad; it emits a high-pitched squeal when the brakes are applied if the brake pads have become too thin.

screw extractor A tool for removing broken screws or bolts.

scrub brakes A brake system that uses leverage to force a friction block against one or more wheels.

scrub radius The distance between two imaginary points on the road surface—the point of center contact between the road surface and the tire, and the intersecting point where the steering axis centerline and the tire centerline contact the road surface.

sealed bearings Wheel bearings that are assembled by the manufacturer with the proper lubrication and sealed for life; cannot normally be disassembled.

secondary circuit The part of an ignition system that operates on higher voltage and delivers the necessary high voltage to the spark plugs.

secondary cup A seal that prevents loss of fluid from the rear of each piston in the master cylinder.

secondary piston A piston that is moved by hydraulic pressure generated by the primary piston in the master cylinder.

secondary winding The high-voltage copper wiring found in an ignition coil.

second-degree burns Burns that involve blistering and damage to the outer layer of skin.

second-order vibration Vibration that occurs at twice the engine rpm.

sedan A vehicle configuration that has an enclosed body, with a maximum of four doors to allow access to the passenger compartment.

selective catalytic reduction An active emission control system that injects a liquid reductant, or reducing agent, through a special catalyst into the exhaust stream of a diesel engine.

selective thickness shim A shim of a prescribed thickness that is used to control shaft clearances in a transmission.

selector gate The U-shaped cutaway in shift shafts that the shifter lever fits into.

selector shift rail A rod that is attached to the shift fork. These rails move when the shifter lever is moved against them.

self-energizing The property of drum brakes that assists the driver in applying the brakes; when brake shoes come into contact with the moving drum, the friction tends to wedge the shoes against the drum, thus increasing the braking force.

self-leveling A vehicle with automatic load-adjustable shock absorbers.

self-sealing tire A tire constructed with a flexible and malleable lining inside the tire around the inner tubeless membrane. The lining can seal small tread-area punctures instantly and permanently.

semiautomatic climate control system A system that provides automatic function of the heater or cooling only, leaving fan speed and mode selection to the operator.

semiconductor A material used to make microchips, transistors, and diodes.

semi-floating axle An axle that carries the weight of the vehicle; if removed, there is no way to connect the wheel to the vehicle.

sending unit The component in the fuel supply system responsible for sending constant electrical signals to the gas gauge located in the driver information center.

separator PCV system A PCV system that uses a device that uses gravity to allow oil to fall to the bottom of the valve and be returned to the crankcase; the valve prevents liquid from traveling to the intake manifold.

separator plate Sometimes called a spacer plate, a thin sheet metal plate installed between the valve body and the transmission case. Orifices can be installed in the separator plate, and check valves can work with holes in the plate.

series hybrid A hybrid electric vehicle powered by an internal combustion engine, but driven by battery.

series hybrid drive train A type of hybrid transmission in which power flows from the engine through an electric motor. The electric motor supplements the power from the engine to the wheels.

series-parallel circuit A circuit that has both a series and a parallel circuit combined into one circuit.

series-parallel hybrid A hybrid electric vehicle that uses the internal combustion engine and/or the battery pack for propulsion.

series-parallel hybrid drive train A type of hybrid drive train that can function as both a series hybrid and parallel hybrid. That means the gasoline engine can turn a generator that can be used to power an electric motor. The gasoline engine can also drive the vehicle directly through the transmission. And the electric motor can work in parallel with the gasoline engine to drive the vehicle.

serpentine condenser A condenser with one tube snaking back and forth.

service brake A brake system that is operated while the vehicle is moving to slow or stop the vehicle.

service campaign and recall A corrective measure conducted by manufacturers when a safety issue is discovered with a particular vehicle.

service consultant/advisor A service worker who works with both customers and technicians; the first point of contact for customers seeking vehicle repairs.

service history A complete list of all the servicing and repairs that have been performed on a vehicle.

service manager The shop supervisor who is responsible for the management of the service department.

serviceable bearings Wheel bearings that can be disassembled, cleaned, inspected, packed, reinstalled, and adjusted.

servo A hydraulic device consisting of a piston inside a cylinder that is used to apply a band. The servo also has a spring that releases the servo when it is no longer needed.

servo action A drum brake design where one brake shoe, when activated, applies an increased activating force to the other brake shoe, in proportion to the initial activating force; further enhances the self-energizing feature of some drum brakes.

setback The distance one wheel is set back from the wheel on the opposite side of the axle.

shaft The long, narrow component that carries one or more gears or has gears machined into it.

shielded wiring harness A wiring harness that has shielding built into it to protect it from induced electrical interference.

shift fork A mechanism that moves the synchronizer sleeve to lock the gear to the main shaft.

shift solenoid An electromechanical device used to control oil flow to bands and clutches in an automatic transmission to help shift the transmission.

shift valve A type of spool valve that has multiple fluid inputs and a spring; it is used to direct hydraulic pressure to a clutch or band needed for a shift.

shock Inadequate tissue oxygenation resulting from serious injury or illness.

shock absorber A device on a vehicle designed to absorb bumps and jolts caused from driving on irregular surfaces and to dampen body movement.

shop foreman The supervisor in a shop who oversees the work of technicians and staff and communicates with customers and external suppliers.

shop or service manual Manufacturer's or aftermarket information on the repair and service of vehicles.

short Also called a short circuit, the flow of current along an unintended route.

short block An engine assembly that includes the engine block, camshaft, timing set, pistons, rods, and crankshaft installed.

short circuit A condition in which the current flows along an unintended route.

short to power A condition in which current flows from one circuit into another.

short-/long-arm (SLA) suspension A type of control arm suspension system that uses a short control arm on the top and a long control arm on the bottom. This design ensures correct alignment angles when moving through bumps.

shroud A steel or plastic cover placed over the shock rod.

side force The pressure on the wheel that pushes it toward the outside or inside of the rim as the vehicle makes a turn.

side gear A gear that is splined to the axle shaft and meshes with the spider gears and allows the axles to rotate at their own speeds when cornering and turning.

side rail The thin portion of the oil control ring that is used to scrape oil off of the cylinder walls.

signal voltage value Measured voltage in a signal return circuit that is compared to a specified voltage value published by the manufacturer.

silicon A material commonly used to make semiconductors.

silicon carbide A type of material used to make semiconductors.

simple fracture A fracture that involves no open wound or internal or external bleeding.

Simpson gear set A type of gear set with two planetary gear sets that share a common sun gear.

sine wave A mathematical function that describes a repetitive waveform such as an alternating current signal.

single flare A sealing system made on the end of metal tubing.

single-piston master cylinder A master cylinder with a single piston that creates hydraulic pressure for all wheel units. If there is a leak in the system, there is a loss of pressure for all wheel units.

single-plate clutch A clutch assembly that uses only one plate to transfer torque from the engine to the transmission. This is the most common type of light vehicle clutch.

single-post hoist A type of vehicle hoist that uses a single central platform to lift a vehicle.

sintering The process of using pressure and heat to bond metal particles.

sintering process A metal hardening process in which the metal is fused together without melting.

slave cylinder The component in a hydraulically operated clutch that converts hydraulic pressure to mechanical movement at the clutch fork.

sledge hammer A heavy hammer, usually with two flat faces, that provides a strong blow.

sliding or floating caliper A type of brake caliper that only has piston(s) on the inboard side of the rotor. The caliper is free to slide or float, thus pulling the outboard brake pad into the rotor when braking force is applied.

sliding spline driveshaft A two-piece driveshaft that is joined in the middle with splines. The driveshaft can slide on itself to increase or decrease in length.

sliding T-handle A handle fitted at 90 degrees to the main body that can be slid from side to side.

slip angle A tire's sideways distortion that makes the vehicle follow a path at an angle to the direction the road wheel is pointing.

slip yoke Part of a two-piece driveshaft that is splined and allows for a change in length of the shaft as the suspension compresses and rebounds.

slippage A condition in which two surfaces in firm contact with each other slide.

slow charger A battery charger that charges at low current.

slow-fill The method of filling a compressed natural gas vehicle (such as overnight) so the cylinders are completely filled.

smart charger A battery charger with microprocessor-controlled charging rates and times.

snap ring The spring-steel C-shaped ring that is fitted in a groove and holds gears, bearings, and shafts in place.

snap ring pliers A pair of pliers for installing and removing snap rings or circlips.

sniffer An electronic device used to determine the source of leaks.

socket An enclosed metal tube commonly with 6 or 12 points to remove and install bolts and nuts.

soft plug A thin-walled, metal, cup-shaped disc designed to be pressed into a machined passageway in the block for the purpose of plugging it.

solder A mixture of lead and tin with a low melting point for connecting wires.

soldering irons A heating tool to heat solder and wires to produce a low-resistance joint.

solder-type terminal A terminal that requires soldering to fasten the terminal to the cable or wire.

solenoid An electromagnet with a moving iron core that is used to cause mechanical motion.

solenoid valve An electrically operated valve that when used in brake systems is designed to control the flow of brake fluid in the hydraulic system.

solid axle A single piece of steel that provides a simple means of mounting the hub and wheel units. Also called beam axle or straight axle.

solid rear axle A type of axle that has a one-piece axle housing, so that the action of hitting a bump with one wheel affects the other wheel.

solid rotor A type of brake rotor made of solid metal.

solid valve lifter A non-hydraulic valve lifter.

solid-state relay A relay that performs the function of a mechanical relay but using only electronic components.

solvent tank A tank containing solvents to clean vehicle parts.

spark ignition (SI) engine An engine that relies on an electrical spark to ignite the air and fuel mixture.

spark line The horizontal line immediately after the firing line on an ignition pattern. It shows how much voltage and the length of time the spark is burning.

spark plug A device that provides a gap for the high-voltage spark to occur in each cylinder.

spark plug reach The length of the spark plug from the seat to the end of the threads.

spark timing The point at which a spark occurs at the spark plug relative to the position of the piston.

specialty springs Springs used to return links and levers on the parking brake system or the self-adjuster mechanism.

speed brace A U-shaped socket wrench that allows high-speed operation. Also called a speeder handle.

speed control circuit A circuit that controls the speed of a motor.

speed sensor A sensor responsible for measuring the speed of the vehicle that is read by the speedometer.

speedy sleeve An aftermarket repair kit that consists of a thin metal sleeve that fits tightly over the seal surface of the axle, providing a new, undamaged surface for the seal to ride against.

splash lubrication A lubrication system that relies on oil being splashed onto moving parts by rotating engine parts striking the oil. These systems are typically used in small engines.

spline A ridge or tooth on a driveshaft that meshes with grooves in a mating piece and transfers torque to it, maintaining the angular correspondence between them.

splined Typically, a shaft and gear that have parallel grooves machined in them so they mate with each other and lock together rotationally.

splined section A flat key made into a shaft to accommodate changes in shaft length due to movement in wheel camber with suspension action.

splined torsional dampening center hub The center portion of a clutch disc that splines to the input shaft. It also incorporates a spring-loaded damper that absorbs engine pulsations for a smoother ride.

split ball gauge A measuring device used to accurately measure small holes.

split diagonally A brake system in which the left front wheel is hydraulically paired with the right rear wheel and the right front wheel is paired with the left rear. This preserves 50% of the braking capability if one of the brake circuits begins to leak.

split front to rear A brake system in which the front brakes operate on one hydraulic circuit and the rear brakes from the other.

spool valve A type of valve commonly used in automatic transmissions that resembles the spool that thread or fishing line comes on.

sport utility vehicle (SUV) A passenger vehicle built on a light-truck chassis; it is usually equipped with four-wheel drive and capable of hauling heavier loads than typical passenger vehicles.

sprain An injury in which a joint is forced beyond its natural movement limit.

spray wash cabinet A cleaning cabinet that sprays cleaning solution under pressure to clean vehicle parts.

spring A resilient steel part that stores energy when compressed and releases energy when released to its original state; available as a leaf spring, coil spring, or torsion bar.

spring eyes Rolled ends of some springs used to mount springs to the chassis.

spring pressure Pressure exerted by a metal coil usually measured in pounds.

spring shackle bushing A bushing that is positioned in the shackle that the leaf spring mounts to. Bushings allow the spring shackle to move as the leaf spring dimensions change over bumps.

spring-loaded key A part of the synchronizer that helps hold the synchronizer collar in position.

spring-loaded rack guide yoke A spring-containing part that pushes on the back side of the rack to help reduce the play between the rack and the pinion while still allowing for relative movement.

springs and clips Various devices that hold the brake shoes in place or return them to their proper place.

spur gear A type of gear in which the teeth of the gear are cut in a straight line down the axis of the gear.

square cut O-ring An O-ring with a square cross—section that is used to seal the pistons in disc brake calipers.

square file A type of file with a square cross section.

square thread A thread type with square shoulders used to translate rotational to lateral movement.

squib The component inside the airbag inflator that triggers the airbag deployment.

staged governor A governor in which the assembly uses two valves: a primary valve and a secondary valve.

stall Often referred to as stall speed, the maximum rpm difference between the turbine and the impeller in the torque converter.

stall test A test that involves raising the engine rpm to wide-open throttle while the brake is firmly applied and the transmission is in gear. The test is used to check torque convertor and transmission operation on some vehicles.

standard torque converter A hydraulic coupling device consisting of an impeller, turbine, stator, and housing; located between the engine and the transmission.

starter teeth Machined teeth located on the ring gear for meshing with the starter drive teeth located in the starter motor.

state of charge The amount of refrigerant in a system compared to how much should be in it.

static imbalance A tire imbalance resulting from a heavy spot on a tire; it will vibrate vertically with the heavy area slapping the road surface with each turn of the wheel.

static toe A setting designed to compensate for slight wear in steering components that may cause the wheels to turn outward or inward while the vehicle is in motion.

station wagon A vehicle configuration with four doors with a roof line that continues into the rear cargo area and a rear door for access.

stationary winding An extended length of wire wrapped into a circle. These windings are fixed as opposed to some types, which are meant to spin.

stator Portion of an electronic ignition system that is mounted to the base of the distributor. It has a circular permanent magnet with a number of projections or teeth corresponding to the number of engine cylinders, and a stationary coil of fine enameled copper wire wound on a plastic reel and positioned inside the magnet.

stator winding A winding in an alternator that creates the current output, or a winding in a motor that creates the needed magnetism for the motor to rotate.

steel hammer A hammer with a head made of hardened steel.

steel rule An accurate measuring ruler made of steel.

steel-disc–type rim A plain steel wheel that is typically covered by a hubcap.

steering angle sensor A sensor that measures the amount of turning a driver desires. This information is used by the ESC system to know the driver's directional intent.

steering arm An arm that extends from the steering knuckle. The tie-rods connect to these arms in order to steer the wheels.

steering axis inclination (SAI) The angle formed by an imaginary line running through the upper and lower steering pivots relative to vertical as viewed from the front.

steering box A device that converts the rotary motion of the steering wheel to the linear motion needed to steer the vehicle.

steering column A column affixed between the steering wheel and the steering box, usually made to collapse during a crash.

steering damper A device used to prevent shocks from irregular roads from being transmitted through the steering linkage and back to the steering wheel.

steering knuckle A device that connects the front wheel to the suspension; pivots on the top and bottom, thus allowing the front wheels to turn.

steering linkage Steel rods that connect the steering box to the steering arms on the steering knuckle.

steering sensor A sensor that can read both torque and rotation from the steering wheel.

steering system A term used to describe all of the components and parts involved in steering a vehicle.

steering wheel position sensor A sensor that signals to the EBCM both the position and speed of the steering wheel.

step-down transformer A transformer used to reduce the voltage, such as to allow a battery charger operated on 120 volts to charge a 12-volt battery.

stepper motor A type of brushless motor with a key difference: It is designed to rotate in fixed steps through a set number of degrees.

stepper motor EGR valve An EGR valve that uses an electrically controlled motor to open the pintle in steps to let exhaust gases flow into the intake manifold.

step-up transformer A transformer used to increase the voltage from a lower input voltage to a higher output, such as an ignition coil.

stoichiometric ratio The exact ratio between air and fuel, at which both are burned completely. See also *lambda*.

stop A rubber part used to control the movement of control arms (suspension arms).

straight edge A measuring device generally made of steel to check how flat a surface is.

straight grinder A powered grinder with the wheel set at 90 degrees to the shaft.

straight vegetable oil (SVO) Biodiesel made from plants such as soybeans, jatropha, palms, etc.

strain An injury caused by the overstretching of muscles and tendons.

stroke The movement of the piston in the engine from top dead center to bottom dead center, or vice versa. There are four strokes: intake, compression, power, and exhaust.

strut A shock absorber used on a MacPherson strut–type suspension.

stub axle An axle used for one wheel.

stub-axle carrier The body of the stub-axle knuckle.

stud A type of threaded fastener with a thread cut on each end rather than having a bolt head on one end.

subframe A mount attached to the vehicle that is used to support the engine and transaxle assembly.

suction reed valve A flat, spring-loaded valve used as a check valve on the suction side of a compressor.

sulfur A regulated by-product of petroleum-based (especially diesel) fuel.

sulfur dioxide (SO2) A pollutant resulting from sulfur in motor fuel and contributing to acid rain.

sulphuric acid A type of acid that when mixed with pure water forms the basis of battery acid or electrolyte.

sun gear The center gear of a planetary gear set around which the other gears rotate.

sun load (solar) sensor A photodiode that varies voltage based on light. It is used to determine the radiant heat coming from the sun into the passenger cabin and gives an input signal of sunlight load to the ECU.

supercharger A device that pressurizes airflow into the engine, working similar to a turbocharger. The supercharger is driven by the crankshaft through a belt or gears and does require power from the engine.

superheat spring A spring used as part of the control in the TXV to ensure refrigerant leaving the evaporator is boiled completely or superheated.

supplemental restraint system (SRS) A passenger safety system, such as airbags and seat belt pretensioners.

supporting statement A statement that urges the speaker to elaborate on a particular topic.

surface filter A filter that is a simple screen mechanism to catch dirt and other particles in the hydraulic oil as it passes through.

surface roughness average (Ra) A measurement used to classify how rough a particular mating surface is at the microscopic level.

surge protector An electrical protection device for preventing electrical surges.

surge tank A sealed tank that captures coolant coming from the head that has turned to steam and changes the steam back to coolant to be reused by the cooling system.

suspension action Movement of the chassis up and down.

suspension strut A shock absorber designed to reduce spring oscillations.

suspension system A system within a vehicle designed to isolate the vehicle body from road bumps and vibrations.

swash plate Another name for an axial plate.

sway bar A part used in vehicles as a stabilizer, or antiroll bar. It is connected to the chassis in the center, and each end is connected to one side of the suspension system. It is typically installed on the front, and sometimes the rear suspension.

swinging shackle A shackle connected to the rear of the multileaf spring that allows the leaf spring to move downward when a load is placed on the rear of the vehicle.

switch An electrical device with contacts that turns current flow on and off.

switching transistor An electronic device used to control the flow of current through the ignition coil primary winding.

symmetric tread pattern A tread pattern with the same tread pattern on both sides of the tire; typically nondirectional.

synchromesh transmission A modern transmission that uses gear synchronizers to match the speeds of gears and shafts during upshifts and downshifts.

synchronizer An assembly that allows for the selection of gears without grinding by matching the speed of the two assemblies.

synchronizer sleeve The sleeve that slides to lock the selected gear to the main shaft. The synchronizer sleeve is part of the synchronizer assembly.

syngas A man-made motor fuel.

synthetic blend A blend of conventional engine oil and pure synthetic oil.

synthetic oil Synthetic oil that, in its pure form, uses man-made base stocks and is not derived from crude oil. This oil lasts longer and performs better than normal oil. The base stock additives are similar to those in conventional oils.

tandem master cylinder A master cylinder that has two pistons that operate separate braking circuits so that if a leak develops in one circuit, the other circuit can still operate.

tang A part of the bearing insert that helps to lock the bearing insert into the bearing saddles and caps.

tanks Metal or plastic pieces that line the pipes used to connect the tubes together to allow the coolant to continue to flow.

tap A term used to generically describe an internal thread-cutting tool.

tap handle A tool designed to securely hold taps for cutting internal threads.

taper An object that is smaller in diameter at one end.

taper tap A tap with a tapper; it is usually the first of three taps used when cutting internal threads.

tapered roller bearing assembly A type of wheel bearing with races and rollers that are tapered in such a manner that all of the tapered angles meet at a common point, which allows them to roll freely and yet control thrust.

tapered seat A type of lug nut with a tapered end toward the rim that helps center the wheel on the wheel studs.

tappet Another name for a valve lifter. Tappets may be flat or have rollers to ride on the cam lobes.

technical service bulletin (TSB) Information issued by manufacturers to alert technicians of unexpected problems or changes to repair procedures.

telematics Satellite-based, two-way communication with the vehicle's electronic systems.

telescoping gauge A gauge that expands and locks to the internal diameter of bores; a caliper or outside micrometer is used to measure its size.

temperature grade A standardized grading system that indicates the extent to which heat is generated or dissipated by a tire.

tensile strength A measure of how strong a material is as it is being pulled apart.

terminal A means of providing a low-resistance connection/termination at the end of a wire.

test certificate A certificate issued when lifting equipment has been checked and deemed safe.

tetrafluoroethane (R-134a) An inert colorless gas that can be used as a refrigerant. It is stored in light blue containers.

thermal cycle switch A normally closed switch located in the fins of the evaporator that controls the air-conditioning compressor clutch. It is opened and closed by the temperature changes in the evaporator.

thermal expansion valve (TXV) system A system with a valve designed to sense evaporator outlet temperature and vary the inlet orifice size accordingly.

thermal runaway A cycle during battery charging in which heating lowers resistance, which in turn increases current flow, which in turn further increases heat created. During this cycle, dangerous gases may build up, creating the potential for an explosion or damage through excessive current flow.

thermistor A temperature-controlled variable resistor. As temperature changes, so does resistance.

thermo-control (temperature-controlled valve) A mechanical device that moves with temperature. It is typically used to control the flow of vacuum when the engine is either hot or cold.

thermo-control switch A temperature-sensitive switch that is mounted into the radiator or into a coolant passage on the engine to control electric fan operation.

thermocouple A temperature-sensing component that consists of two dissimilar metals that produce voltage proportional to temperature.

thermostat Located under the thermostat housing, the thermostat regulates the flow of coolant, allowing coolant to flow from the engine to the radiator when the engine is running at its operating temperature.

third-degree burns Burns that involve white or blackened areas and damage to all skin layers and underlying structures and tissues.

thixotropy The ability of a semisolid grease to flow when agitated or stressed.

thread file A type of file that cleans clogged or distorted threads on bolts and studs.

thread pitch The coarseness or fineness of a thread as measured by either the threads per inch or the distance from the peak of one thread to the next. Metric fasteners are measured in millimeters.

thread repair A generic term to describe a number of processes that can be used to repair threads.

three-angle grind A process of grinding the valve openings on the cylinder head so that air can pass through them more smoothly and quickly.

three-quarter floating axle An axle on which there is only one wheel bearing which bears the weight of the vehicle, but the axle prevents the wheel from tipping inward or outward.

three-way catalytic converter A converter that changes hydrocarbons, carbon monoxide, and oxides of nitrogen into harmless elements.

threshold limit value (TLV) The maximum allowable concentration of a given material in the surrounding air.

throttle A device used to produce acceleration by controlling the air/fuel mixture.

throttle body The housing on an intake manifold that is used to control the amount of filtered air that enters the cylinders.

throttle body injection (TBI) A fuel injection system that uses one or more fuel injectors mounted above or in the throttle body itself. Also called single-point injection.

throttle position sensor (TPS) A potentiometer that sends an analog signal to the electronic control unit that corresponds to the position of the throttle valve.

throttle position sensor A sensor that measures how far the throttle valve is opened.

throttle valve A type of spool valve that is connected to the throttle on a vehicle. The throttle valve creates a pressure proportional to throttle opening and is used to delay upshifting based on throttle opening.

throttle valve pressure The pressure created by the throttle valve that is proportional to throttle opening.

throw The part of the crankshaft that is offset for the connecting rods to mate with; also called connecting rod journal.

throw-out bearing The part of the clutch release mechanism that imparts clutch pedal force to the rotating pressure plate levers.

thrust angle The angle formed between the centerline of the rear axle in comparison to the centerline of the vehicle.

thrust bearing A main bearing insert that either has integrated flanges or separate flanges that provide bearing surfaces that prevent forward or lateral movement of the crankshaft assembly.

thrust bearing Also called a Torrington bearing, a small roller bearing assembly with the rollers laid flat axially around the centerline of the bearing. The bearing is used to control forward and backward movement of a part in an automatic transmission.

thrust line The imaginary line drawn through the center of the rear axle.

thrust washers Flat, washer-shaped bearings that provide a wear surface between two rotating components that are loaded axially.

thrust-type angular-contact ball bearing A type of bearing that uses a deep groove in the bearing races where the ball bearings ride; this design is for thrust conditions.

tie-rod A steering component that transfers linear motion from the steering box to the steering arms at the front wheels.

tie-rod assembly The part that fits between the rack and the steering arms and transfers the movement of the rack.

timing chain A steel chain connecting the crankshaft assembly to the camshaft assembly.

timing gear A gear that synchronizes the timed events of rotational engine components like camshafts and fuel injection pumps.

tin snips Cutting device for sheet metal, works in a similar fashion to scissors.

tire inflation pressure The level of air in the tire that provides it with load-carrying capacity and affects overall vehicle performance.

tire placard A metal, vinyl, or paper tag permanently affixed to a vehicle that indicates the appropriate tire size and inflation pressure for the vehicle.

tire pressure gauge A gauge used to measure the air pressure within a tire.

tire pressure monitoring system (TPMS) An automatic sensor system in most modern vehicles that alerts drivers of tire pressure problems.

tire valve The valve through which air is inserted into a tire to inflate it.

title history A detailed account of a vehicle's past.

toe-in When the front of the wheels, as seen from above, are closer together than the rear of the wheels.

toe-out on turns The difference in turning angle of the inside tire in comparison to the outside tire. This angle difference allows the tires to roll through the corner rather than the inside tire dragging. Also referred to as Ackermann angle.

toe-out When the rear of the wheels, as seen from above, are closer together than the front of the wheels.

toe-setting Setting of the toe-in or toe-out of the tires to the centerline of the vehicle.

tone wheel The part of the wheel speed sensor that has ribs and valleys used to create an electrical signal inside of the pick-up assembly.

top dead center (TDC) The position of the piston in the cylinder farthest from the crankshaft.

top hat parking brake A drum brake that is located inside a disc brake rotor in order to act as a parking brake.

toroidal CVT A type of CVT that uses moveable rollers in contact with input and output drive discs. The rollers transfer power from one drive disc to the other. Their position determines the effective gear ratio.

torque The amount of twisting force applied in a turning application, usually measured in foot-pounds.

torque angle A method of tightening bolts or nuts based on angles of rotation.

torque assist Use of an electric motor to supplement the engine's torque whenever additional torque is needed, allowing for a smaller ICE to be used.

torque converter A device that is turned by the crankshaft and transmits torque to the input shaft of an automatic transmission.

torque converter clutch (TCC) A hydraulically operated clutch located inside the torque converter that applies at predetermined conditions and stops torque converter slippage.

torque multiplication The increase of torque.

torque plate A 2" (51 mm) thick plate that is bolted where the cylinder head is fastened on the engine block.

torque sensor A device used to measure the load on the steering wheel.

torque smoothing A process that uses an electric motor to smooth out engine power pulses when an ICE is operating at low rpm or when the vehicle is using fuel management techniques such as cylinder deactivation.

torque specifications Supplied by manufacturers and describes the amount of twisting force allowable for a fastener or a specification showing the twisting force from an engine crankshaft.

torque steer A condition in which the vehicle pulls to one side during hard acceleration.

torque wrench A tool used to measure the rotational or twisting force applied to fasteners.

torque-to-yield A tightening procedure in which a bolt is designed to be slightly elastic when tightened; the elastic bolt retains an even pressure on the head gasket.

torque-to-yield (TTY) bolts Bolts that are tightened using the torque-to-yield method.

torsion bar A bar made of a steel alloy that is fixed rigidly to the chassis at one end and the suspension control arm at the other to support the weight of a vehicle.

torsion bar A spring-loaded piece of steel connected to the pinion gear at its bottom end and the input shaft at its top. Also, a torsion bar is a type of spring that some vehicles use to hold up a corner of the vehicle.

torsional load A force that is applied by clamping one end of an object to another object that is then twisted.

torsional vibrations The speeding up and slowing down of a shaft, which happen at a relatively high frequency. Crankshafts have torsional vibrations due to the power pulses of the pistons.

town gas Locally available gas used to power early internal combustion engines.

toxic dust Any dust that may contain fine particles that could be harmful to humans or the environment.

traction control system (TCS) A computer-controlled system added to ABS to help prevent loss of traction while the vehicle is accelerating.

traction grade A standardized grading system that indicates how well a tire will maintain contact with the road surface when wet.

trailing arm suspension A type of suspension system that uses upper and lower control arms.

trailing shoes Brake shoes installed so that they are applied in the opposite direction to the forward rotation of the brake drum; not self-energizing and less efficient at developing braking force.

transaxle A type of transmission typically used in front-wheel drive vehicles in which the transmission also includes the differential and final drive gear.

transfer case A component that is bolted to the back of the transmission and connects the front and rear axles via the driveshafts.

transformer action The transfer of electrical energy from one coil to another through induction in a transformer.

transistor A semiconductor device that allows a small current in the base lead to control a larger current through the emitter collector leads.

transmission An assembly that houses a variety of gear sets that allow the vehicle to be driven at a wider range of speeds and terrain conditions than would be possible without a transmission.

transmission control module (TCM) An electronic computer that controls transmission function; it may include adaptive learning capabilities for driver preferences.

transmission input shaft The shaft that brings engine torque into the transmission.

transmission oil temperature (TOT) sensor A type of variable resistor used inside the transmission to monitor oil temperature.

transmission specialist A technician who diagnoses, overhauls, and repairs transmissions.

transmission-mounted parking brake A drum brake that is mounted on the drive shaft just after the transmission to serve as a parking brake.

transverse The orientation of the engine in which the front of the engine is facing the side of the vehicle.

tread wear grade The number imprinted on the sidewall of a tire by the manufacturer as required by the National Highway Traffic Safety Administration (NHTSA) that indicates the tread life of a tire's tread.

triangular file A type of file with three sides so it can get into internal corners.

triangulation A method of locating an object using mathematics based on forming a triangle with two known points.

trilateration A method of locating points by the measurement of distances using geometry.

trim height The amount of ground clearance a vehicle has, measured from a point on the body or frame depending on the manufacturer. Also known as ride height.

trimetal The use of three different types of metals to build up a bearing insert to give it long-lasting wear characteristics.

truck A large heavy vehicle for carrying cargo.

tube flaring tool A tool that makes a sealing flare on the end of metal tubing.

tubes Metal pipes running side to side or up and down that the coolant or refrigerant travels through.

tubing cutter A hand tool for cutting pipe or tubing squarely.

tulip/tripod joint A constant velocity joint that has three equally spaced fingers shaped like a star. This configuration allows in-and-out movement of the shaft while allowing flexing.

turbocharger A device that pressurizes airflow into the engine. The turbocharger works similar to a supercharger, but is driven by the exhaust gases.

turn signal switch A switch that turns the left and right turn signal lights on and off.

turning radius A measure of how small a circle the vehicle can turn around when the steering wheel is turned to the limit.

twin leading shoe drum brake system Brake shoe arrangement in which both brake shoes are self-energizing in the forward direction.

twist drill A hardened steel drill bit for making holes in metals, plastics, and wood.

twisted pair Two conductors that are twisted together to reduce electrical interference.

two-mode hybrid A type of hybrid drive system in which there are two distinct modes of operation. In one mode, the electric motor can propel the vehicle and be used for regenerative braking; in the second mode, the electric motors can be used to assist the engine while the engine uses fuel management techniques such as cylinder deactivation.

two-post hoist A type of vehicle hoist that uses two parts (one on each side of vehicle) and four arms to lift the vehicle.

two-stroke engine An engine that uses only two strokes to complete its running cycle.

two-way catalytic converter A converter that changes only hydrocarbons and carbon monoxide into harmless elements.

ultrasonic A method of leak detection that uses a sensitive microphone to hear small refrigerant leaks by amplifying the hissing noise.

umbrella-style valve stem seal A seal that surrounds the top of the valve stem to prevent excessive oil from leaking into the valve stem.

understeer A condition in which a vehicle's front wheels turn sharper than the vehicle's direction when the vehicle is steered around a corner. This vehicle is said to be "loose" in the corners.

unibody construction A construction style that uses the body sheet metal as the frame of the vehicle. Typically this type of construction uses small frame sections called subframes.

unibody design A vehicle design that does not use a rigid frame to support the body. The body panels are designed to provide the strength for the vehicle.

uniform pitch A spring whose pitch (the distance from the center of one coil to the center of the adjacent coil) is the same distance throughout.

Uniform Tire Quality Grading (UTQG) A standardized grading system established by the National Highway Traffic Safety Administration (NHTSA) designed to provide tire buyers with a comparative measure of a tire's tread life, traction, and temperature characteristics.

unitized wheel bearing hub An assembly consisting of the hub, wheel bearing(s), and possibly the wheel flange, which is preassembled and ready to be installed on a vehicle.

universal joint (u-joint) A cross-shaped joint with bearings on each leg where one set of parallel legs is connected to the end of one shaft and the other set of parallel legs is connected to the end of a second shaft. This arrangement allows the shafts to operate at shallow angles to each other.

unsprung mass Any part of the steering and suspension system that is not supported by springs. A large amount of unsprung weight will cause the tire to hop off the ground when hitting bumps, as the weight will overcome dampening of the shock absorbers.

unsprung weight *See* unsprung mass.

urea A chemical reactant specifically designed for use in selective catalytic reduction systems to reduce nitrogen oxides. Also called diesel exhaust fluid.

US Department of Transportation (DOT) A federal agency that regulates transportation safety in the United States, including vehicles' wheels and tires. The DOT requires a code—a series of letters and numbers—to be stamped into the sidewall of every tire made for public use in the United States. These codes contain information such as the date of manufacture and the plant where the tire was manufactured.

V blocks Metal blocks with a V-shaped cutout for holding shafts while working on them. Also referred to as vee blocks.

V engine A term used to describe an engine configuration that uses a single bank of cylinders staggered at a shallow 15-degree V.

vacuum A pressure in an enclosed area that is lower than atmospheric pressure.

vacuum advance unit A mechanism that controls ignition timing advance in relation to engine load and causes the spark at the spark plug to occur sooner based on engine conditions. Its function is to improve fuel economy and, in doing so, reduce exhaust emissions.

vacuum bleeding Bleeding process that uses a vacuum bleeder to pull the air and old brake fluid from the system.

vacuum gauge A device used to measure the amount of vacuum an engine can generate during various operating conditions.

vacuum modulator A device on a hydraulically controlled transmission that converts engine manifold vacuum into an engine load signal called modulator pressure.

vacuum pump A pump used to evacuate the air-conditioning system and put it into a deep vacuum or low pressure to remove moisture.

vacuum servo A vacuum-controlled device that moves the air doors of the air box. It is controlled by the vacuum that comes from the vacuum-type climate control panel.

vacuum tube fluorescent (VTF) A type of lighting used for instrumentation displays on vehicle instrument panel clusters. This type of lighting emits a very bright light with high contrast and can display in various colors. Also called vacuum fluorescent display (VFD).

vacuum-relief valve A mechanical valve used on the gas cap that prevents a low-pressure condition from occurring. It also ensures that the fuel tank will not collapse due to fuel usage or contraction of fuel on cooldown.

validating statement A statement that shows common interest in the topic being discussed.

valve A device used to control the flow of air and fuel into the combustion chamber and exhaust gases out of the combustion chamber.

valve body An aluminum or cast iron housing inside the transmission that houses the majority of the valves that control transmission operation.

valve core The one-way spring-loaded valve that screws into the valve stem that allows air to be pumped into a tire and prevents it from flowing out.

valve cover gasket A gasket used to seal the valve cover (also called a rocker arm cover or cylinder head cover) to the cylinder head assembly.

valve face A machined surface on the back of the valve head; this area seals onto the valve seat in the cylinder head.

valve float A condition that occurs when the valves are moving so fast that the spring tension is not great enough to fully seat the valves as designed.

valve guide An insert in the cylinder head through which the valve stem passes and moves.

valve head The portion of the valve that is exposed to the combustion chamber and contains the valve face and margin.

valve keeper A device used to keep the valve spring retainers attached to the valve while in the cylinder head.

valve lifter A device that transfers motion from the cam lobe to a pushrod or directly acts on the valve and spring, depending on if the cam is in the engine block or the cylinder head; sometimes called a tappet.

valve margin The flat surface on the outer edge of the valve head between the valve head and the valve face.

valve overlap The time, usually expressed in degrees of crankshaft rotation, during which both the intake valve and the exhaust valve are open at the same time.

valve seat An integral part of the head, or circular metal rings that are pressed into the cylinder head, that makes up the mating surface where the valve face sits when it is closed.

valve spring A metal coil spring that returns valves to their fully closed positions after being opened.

valve spring retainer A washer-shaped piece of metal positioned near the top of the valve stem that holds the top of the valve spring to keep pressure on the valve while in the cylinder head.

valve stem The shaft that is attached to the valve head and provides the sliding surface for the valve in its guide as it opens and closes.

valve stem (tire) A rubber or steel piece that attaches the tire valve to the rim.

valve stem cap A cap that fits tightly onto the valve stem to prevent debris from clogging it and acts as a secondary seal.

valve tip The end of the valve stem against which the rocker arm, cam follower, or hydraulic bucket-style lifter directly presses to open the valve.

valve train A system encompassing all of the parts used in the opening and closing of the valves.

vane pump A type of front pump in an automatic transmission that uses small vanes placed radially around a center hub. The vanes may be forced out against the housing of the pump by centrifugal force. The volume between the vanes varies as the pump turns, resulting in fluid being forced out of the pump.

vane-type phaser A cam phaser that uses vanes inside to allow oil pressure to push against and change cam timing as it is turning.

vapor line A rubber or plastic line that carries vapors from the fuel tank to the charcoal canister.

vapor lock A situation in which vapor forms in the fuel line, and the bubbles of vapor block the flow of fuel and stop the engine.

vaporization The changing of a liquid to a gas through boiling.

variable displacement vane pump A type of front pump that uses a vane-style pump that can pivot so that its displacement can be varied.

variable reluctance sensor A type of wheel speed sensor that uses the principle of magnetic induction to create its signal.

variable resistor A component that has a mechanism for varying resistance.

variable voltage signal A signal that changes based on what the sensor is reading; for example, as temperature varies, so does the voltage signal to the ECU.

variable-diameter pulley (VDP) A type of CVT that uses two pulleys with moveable sheaves, allowing the effective diameter of the pulleys to change, resulting in variable gear ratios.

variable-orifice PVC system A system in which a replaceable, spring-loaded PCV valve regulates gas flow. The position of the PCV valve is controlled by the pressure in the manifold.

vehicle emission control information (VECI) label A label used by technicians to identify engine and emission control information for the vehicle.

vehicle hoist A type of vehicle lifting tool designed to lift the entire vehicle.

vehicle identification number (VIN) A unique serial number that is assigned to each vehicle produced.

vehicle inspection pit A trench permanently fitted into the floor of the shop to allow easy work access to the vehicle's underside.

vehicle jack A tool for lifting a vehicle.

vehicle safety certification (VSC) label A label certifying that the vehicle meets the Federal Motor Vehicle Safety, Bumper, and Theft Prevention Standards in effect at the time of manufacture.

vehicle speed sensor (VSS) A sensor used by the PCM to measure vehicle speed. It is often located in the transmission extension housing.

vent solenoid A solenoid that allows fresh air to enter the evaporative system during a purge event. Also used for an evaporative system monitoring test.

ventilated rotor A type of brake rotor with passages between the rotor surfaces that are used to improve heat transfer to the atmosphere.

venturi A restriction (narrowed area) in the air horn.

venturi effect The reduction in pressure that results when a fluid or air flows through a constricted section of pipe.

vernier calipers An accurate measuring device for internal, external, and depth measurements that incorporates fixed and adjustable jaws.

viscosity The measurement of the thickness of a liquid.

viscosity index improver An oil additive that resists a change in viscosity over a range of temperatures.

viscosity value A measurement of resistance to diesel fuel flow.

viscous coupler Called a fan clutch, a hub that connects the water pump drive to the cooling fan using a temperature-sensitive viscous fluid to cause the fan to turn faster as the temperature of the air pulled through the radiator increases.

viscous coupling An silicone clutch assembly used in all-wheel drive differentials to provide a slight amount of differential action for control of axle rotational speeds.

volatile organic compound (VOC) The hydrocarbons in petroleum products that contribute to combustion.

volt The unit used to measure potential difference or electrical pressure.

voltage drop The amount of potential difference between two points in a circuit.

voltage The pressure aspect of electricity, measured to show the potential of a circuit to do work.

volumetric efficiency (VE) A ratio, given as a percentage, of the amount of air actually inducted at a given engine speed at full throttle compared to the internal engine displacement. For a normally aspirated engine (without supercharging or turbo-charging), an engine's volumetric efficiency may peak at around 85%. Peak engine torque is developed at peak volumetric efficiency.

vortex flow State in which the fluid in the torque converter is traveling between the turbine, stator, and impeller.

W engine A term used to describe an engine configuration consisting of two VR cylinder banks in a deep V arrangement.

wad punch A type of punch that is hollow for cutting circular shapes in soft materials such as gaskets.

warding file A type of thin, flat file with a tapered end.

warm-up cycle One drive cycle, during which the vehicle starts out cold, warms up, and then cools down after the driving cycle.

warpage A change in the shape of a surface due to distortion or wear.

waste cylinder The cylinder in a waste spark ignition system that receives a spark near the top of its exhaust stroke.

waste spark system An ignition system in which each ignition coil serves two cylinders, with each end of the secondary winding attached by a high-tension lead to a spark plug. The spark is used to ignite the air–fuel mixture in one cylinder and has no effect on the other cylinder.

waste vegetable oil (WVO) Used cooking grease or oil used for producing biodiesel fuel.

wastegate A pressure regulator device that allows control of the pressure produced by the turbo-charger. The wastegate moves to allow exhaust gases to bypass the turbine wheel of the turbo-charger and flow down the exhaust pipe.

water fade Brake fade caused by water-soaked brake linings.

water gas A gas made from hydrogen and water.

water jacket A passageway for coolant to flow inside the engine block that is formed when the block is cast.

watt The unit for measuring electrical power.

Watt's linkage Another name for a rigid-axle coil-spring suspension that uses two bars similar to a panhard rod and a pivot point on the axle to keep the axle from moving in turns.

waveform A graphical plot of voltage over time that is displayed on an oscilloscope.

web A reinforced area of a metal part formed during the casting process to create strength and durability.

wedge combustion chamber A combustion chamber design where the valves are often directly lined up beside each other in a row and positioned at an angle over the pistons, forming a wedge-shaped combustion chamber.

weight matching The process of matching the tire's lightest point with the rim's heaviest point (generally at the valve stem) for the purpose of reducing the tire's radial imbalance.

weight transfer Weight moving from one set of wheels to the other set of wheels during braking, acceleration, or cornering.

Welch plug A soft, round, metal disc pressed into the engine block to plug a water jacket or oil passageway.

welding helmet Protective gear designed for arc welding; it provides protection against foreign particles entering the eye, and the lens is tinted to reduce the glare of the welding arc.

wet sleeve A replaceable steel cylinder installed into the block that provides a wear surface for the piston and rings. It is in direct contact with coolant on its outside surface.

wheel alignment The practice of aligning the wheels of the vehicle to the centerline of the vehicle and to each other. It ensures that the vehicle will handle correctly and gives best tire wear.

wheel assembly A term used to encompass all components of the wheel and tire.

wheel bearing A component that allows the wheels to rotate freely while supporting the weight of the vehicle, made up of an inner race, outer race, rollers or balls, and a cage.

wheel center The part of the wheel containing the holes for the lug studs.

wheel cylinder A hydraulic cylinder with one or two pistons, seals, dust boots, and a bleeder screw that pushes the brake shoes into contact with the brake drum to slow or stop the vehicle.

wheel cylinder piston clamp A tool that prevents the pistons from being pushed out of the wheel cylinders while the brake shoes are being replaced.

wheel retaining nuts Lug nuts used to hold the wheel on the hub.

wheel rim The part on which the tire is mounted. Also called a "wheel" or "rim."

wheel speed sensor A device that creates an analog or digital signal according to the speed of the wheel.

wheel studs Threaded fasteners that are pressed into the wheel hub flange and used to bolt the wheel onto the vehicle.

windage tray A plate that bolts onto the bottom of the engine between the crankshaft and the oil pan, helping to keep the crankshaft from contacting the engine oil.

wire A conductor usually made of multistranded copper with an external insulated coating.

wire feed welder A welding machine that automatically feeds the filler wire by operating a trigger mechanism on a welding gun.

wiring diagram A schematic drawing and symbol representation of the wiring and components; also called electrical schematic.

wiring harness A collection of wires or cables insulated from each other but bound together.

wiring harness connector A plug that contains multiple terminals with male and female ends.

wishbone control arm Another term for an A-arm.

wood gas A gas made by the carbonization or gasification of coal.

Woodruff key A half-round, rectangular key that is placed into a half-round, rectangular opening in the nose of the crankshaft or other round shafts found on the engine.

work The process by which one type of energy is transformed into another type of energy.

working pressure The pressure within a hydraulic system while the system is being operated.

worm A gear with a helical, threaded shaft that is attached to the steering column and meshes with a worm wheel that transfers motion from the steering wheel to the steering linkage.

worm gear steering A robust steering system frequently used on heavier vehicles that uses a worm to turn a meshed worm wheel to provide gear reduction, making steering easier for the driver.

worm shaft The protrusion of the worm gear that serves as the point of attachment to the steering column.

wrap leaf A spring containing spring eyes.

wrenches A generic term to describe tools that tighten and loosen fasteners with hexagonal heads.

XH-7 A form of desiccant used with pure R-134a.

XH-9 A form of desiccant used when the refrigerant may not be pure, such as with some imports.

yaw Movement of a vehicle around its z-axis (vertical axis) felt when the vehicle deviates from its straight path, as when skidding sideways and the rear comes around.

yaw sensor A sensor that measures the amount a vehicle is turning around its vertical axis. This information is used by the ESC system to know how much a vehicle is turning.

yield point The point at which a bolt is stretched so hard that it will not return to its original length when loosened; it is measured in pounds per square inch of bolt cross section.

Zener diode A diode that forward biases when a certain voltage is reached.

zero camber A tire with no tilt or zero camber angle.

zero offset A condition in which the plane of the hub mounting surface is even with the centerline of the wheel.

zero scrub radius A condition in which the point of center contact between the road surface and the tire and the point where the steering axis centerline contacts the road surface intersect at the road surface.

Zyglo™ A crack detection method used on engine blocks and cylinder heads that uses magnetism and a fluorescent light to find cracks in ferrous metal.

INDEX

Vapor line, 1794
Vapor lock, 1682
Vaporization, 1415, 1595, 1751, 1798
Vapors, 199, 1693
Variable displacement compressor, 1418
Variable displacement vane pump, 465,
 485, 487
Variable intake systems, 1750–1751
Variable orifice PCV system, 1787–1788
Variable reluctance wheel speed sensors, 1156, 1162, 1163,
 1168–1169
Variable resistors, 1206, 1265–1266, 1568
Variable voltage signal, 1491–1492
Variable-diameter pulley (VDP), 600–601
Variable-flow exhaust, 1762
Variable-geometry turbocharger, 1757
Variable-ratio gear, 846
Vehicle damage, 190–193
Vehicle Emission Control Information (VECI) label, 92
Vehicle identification number (VIN), 90–92, 1398
Vehicle immobilization systems, 1310–1311
Vehicle information, 245
Vehicle inspection pits, 199, 207–208
Vehicle jack. *See* Jacks and jack stands
Vehicle lock anti-theft, 1399
Vehicle operation, 22–24
Vehicle protection
 against corrosives and greases, 192
 from jacks and jack stands, 195–197
 from lifting equipment, 194–195
 against mechanical damage, 192
 when moving and road testing vehicles,
 192–193
Vehicle Safety Certification (VSC) label, 92
Vehicle speed sensor (VSS), 517–518, 675, 1164,
 1167, 1711
Vehicle wander, 930
Vehicle weight, braking and, 980
Vent solenoid, 1795
Ventilated rotors, 1069
Ventilation, 43, 70, 1779
Ventilation components, 1434–1436
Venturi effect, 1687–1688, 1878
Venturi vacuum advance, 1653–1654
Verbal feedback, 242
Vernier caliper, 104, 136–138
Vernier micrometers, 132, 134
Vibration
 balance shaft, 360
 diagnosing, 278
 in the drive train, 743–746
 harmonic balancer and, 358
 second-order, 360
 transaxle, 681
 wheel assembly runout and, 825
 wheel balance and, 798, 801
 wheel bearing damage and, 1139

Vice grips, 115–116
Viscosity, 1560
 of biodiesel, 1823
 of brake fluids, 1004
 diesel fuel, 1867
 of gear lube, 1138
Viscosity index improver, 1558
Viscosity modifiers, 463
Viscous coupling, 30, 742
Visual inspection
 automatic transmission diagnosis and, 543
 before beginning engine testing, 262
 for diagnosis, 1072
 for maintenance, 223–224
 tires, 801, 823
Volatility, 1794
Volkswagon, 1560, 1847
Volmeter, 1312
Voltage
 exercises in using DVOM and, 1235–1243
 Faraday's law and, 1642–1643
 looking for drops in, 1183
 measuring with DVOM, 1234–1235, 1272–1273
 in Ohm's law, 1194–1195
 overview of, 1182
 parallel circuits, 1199
 regulation of, 1323–1324
 required and available, 1643–1644
 in a series circuit, 1198
 setting up with oscilloscope, 1268
Voltage, battery, 173, 174, 176
Voltage drop, 1190, 1198
 blower motor, 1504–1505
 exercises in using DVOM and, 1235–1243
 to locate high resistance, 1276
 to locate open circuits, 1275
 measuring with DVOM, 1272–1273
 testing, 1327–1328
 testing starter circuit and, 1312–1314
Voltage regulator, 1326
Voltage spikes, 1494–1495, 1648
Voltmeter, 1183, 1185, 1614
Volts, 1185
Volumetric efficiency, 1753
Volumetric efficiency (VE), 1848, 1871
Vortex flow, 458
Vortex sensors, 1701
VR engine configuration, 25, 26–27
V-type belt, 219
V-type belt, 1609
Vulcanized rubber, 315
Vulcanizing (RTV) oxygen-safe silicone, 316, 432,433, 672

W

W engine configuration, 25, 27
W12 cylinders, 25
Wad punch, 120